D1677717

Frieder Stadtfeld:
Fachwörterbuch für Tourismus, Hotellerie und Gastronomie
Band 1: Deutsch – Englisch

Prof. Dr. Frieder Stadtfeld

Fachwörterbuch für Tourismus, Hotellerie und Gastronomie

Band 1

Deutsch – Englisch

FBV Medien-Verlags GmbH

Die Deutsche Bibliothek – CIP-Einheitsaufnahme

Stadtfeld, Frieder:
Fachwörterbuch für Tourismus, Hotellerie und Gastronomie / Frieder Stadtfeld. – Limburgerhof : FBV-Medien-Verl.-GmbH.
NE: HST

Bd. 1. Deutsch–Englisch. – 1993
ISBN 3-929469-03-0

Als Warenzeichen geschützte Wörter werden in diesem Wörterbuch in der Regel durch das Zeichen ® kenntlich gemacht. Fehlt ein solcher Hinweis, so begründet dies nicht die Annahme, daß eine Ware oder ein Warenzeichen frei ist und von jedem benutzt werden darf.

2. Auflage 1993
© FBV Medien-Verlags GmbH, D-67117 Limburgerhof, 1993
Alle Rechte vorbehalten. Nachdruck, auch auszugsweise,
nur mit Genehmigung des Verlags.
Layout und Druckvorlage: Jürgen Herber
Druck: Druck Partner Rübelmann, Hemsbach
Printed in Germany

ISBN 3-929469-03-0

Vorwort

Bedanken möchte ich mich bei allen Personen, die zu der Erstellung dieses Wörterbuchs einen Beitrag leisteten.

Das Wörterbuch basiert auf einem EDV-Programm, dessen Autor, Dr. Peter Schmitt, jede denkbare Hilfe gab.

Für praktische Ratschläge hinsichtlich des Wortmaterials gebührt den folgenden Kollegen ein besonderer Dank:

Professor L. A. Kreck, Washington State University;

Chris Cooper PhD und John Westlake, University of Surrey;

Frau Catherine Lacken, ehemals Lehrkraft an der Fachhochschule Rheinland-Pfalz;

Ray Garnett, Ealing College (jetzt Thames Valley University), London.

Die Bibliotheken dieser Universitäten boten eine Fülle von Material, das während eines von der Fachhochschule Rheinland-Pfalz gewährten Praxissemesters genutzt wurde.

Besonderer Dank gebührt auch den folgenden Personen aus der Hotel- und Tourismusindustrie: Hans Gemmer, Kurt Berndt, Jon Beecroft und Erwin Verhoog.

Gavin Konstam las Probeausdrucke. Abschließende Korrekturen wurden durch meine Frau und durch meinen Sohn gemacht, die von Brian Hunt und Maria Hunt unterstützt wurden.

Jürgen Herber erstellte mit seinen typographischen Kenntnissen die druckfertige Vorlage.

Preface

I would like to thank all persons who made a contribution to the compilation of this dictionary.

The basis of the dictionary is a software programme, whose author Dr. Peter Schmitt gave every possible help.

Special thanks are due to the following colleagues for practical suggestions concerning the terminology:

Professor L. A. Kreck, Washington State University;

Chris Cooper PhD, and John Westlake, University of Surrey;

Mrs. Catherine Lacken, former lecturer at the Fachhochschule Rheinland-Pfalz;

Ray Garnett, Ealing College (now Thames Valley University), London.

The libraries of these universities provided a wealth of material which was used during a sabbatical term granted by the Fachhochschule Rheinland-Pfalz.

Furthermore, special thanks are due to the following hotel and tourism experts: Hans Gemmer, Kurt Berndt, Jon Beecroft, and Erwin Verhoog.

Gavin Konstam read draft printouts. Final corrections were made by my wife and by my son, who were assisted by Brian Hunt and Maria Hunt.

Jürgen Herber used his desktop publishing skills to produce the fair copy.

Frieder Stadtfeld

30. September 1994 30 September 1994

Abkürzungen und Stilangaben   Abbreviations and Style Labels

abbr	Abkürzung	abbreviation
adj	Adjektiv	adjective
adv	Adverb	adverb
advert	Werbung	advertising
AE	amerikanisches Englisch	American English
arch	archaisch	archaic
archit	Architektur	architecture
attr	attributiv	attributive
BAY	bayrisch	Bavarian
BE	britisches Englisch	British English
CAN	kanadisch	Canadian
coll	umgangssprachlich	colloquial
derog	abwertend	derogatory
dial	dialektal	dialectal
etc.	et cetera	et cetera
etw	etwas	something
euph	euphemistisch	euphemistic
f	Femininum	feminine
fam	familiär	familiar
figur	figürlich, bildlich	figurative
form	formell	formal
fpl	Femininum und Plural	feminine and plural
FR	französisch	French
GR	griechisch	Greek
gastr	gastronomisch	gastronomic
hist	historisch	historical
humor	humoristisch	humorous
inform	informell	informal
iron	ironisch	ironic
ITAL	italienisch	Italian
jm	jemand, jemandem	someone, to someone
jn	jemanden	someone
js	jemandes	someone's
jur	juristisch	jurisdiction
LAT	lateinisch	Latin
lit	literarisch	literary
m	Maskulinum	masculine
med	Medizin	medicine
MEX	mexikanisch	Mexican
mil	militärisch	military
mpl	Maskulinum und Plural	masculine and plural
n	Neutrum	neuter
npl	Neutrum und Plural	neuter and plural

obs	obsolet, veraltet	obsolete
ökon	Ökonomie	economics
ÖST	österreichisch	Austrian
pl	Plural	plural
pl=sg	Plural als Singular	plural as singular
poet	poetisch	poetic
PORT	portugiesisch	Portuguese
prd	prädikativ	predicative
pron	Pronomen	pronoun
prp	Präposition	preposition
®	Warenzeichen	trademark
rare	rar, selten	rare
SCHW	Schweizerdeutsch	Swiss German
scient	wissenschaftlich	scientific
SCOT	schottisch	Scottish
sg	Singular	singular
sl	Slang	slang
s.o.	jemand	someone
SPAN	spanisch	Spanish
s.th.	etwas	something
tabu	tabu	taboo
vulg	vulgär	vulgar

abändern etw
 (geringfügig)
 ♦ alter s.th.
abbauen etw
 (Ausstellung etc.)
 ♦ dismantle s.th.
Abbauzeit, f
 (bei Ausstellungen etc)
 ♦ dismantling time
abbestellen
 → stornieren
ab dem 1. Mai für zwei Nächte
 ♦ from 1 May for two nights
ab dem 6. Juni
 ♦ from 6 June onward(s)
 ♦ from 6 June on
 ♦ from 6 June
ab Donnerstag
 ♦ from Thursday onward(s)
 ♦ from Thursday on
 ♦ from Thursday
abdunkelbar adj
 → verdunkelbar
abdunkelbarer Raum m
 → verdunkelbarer Raum
abdunkeln etw
 → verdunkeln etw
Abend, m
 ♦ evening
Abendanzug, m
 ♦ dinner clothes pl
Abendaufwartung, f
 (durch Zimmermädchen)
 ♦ evening turndown service
Abendbar f
 ♦ evening bar
 ♦ bar open in the evening
Abend bei einem Glas Wein verbringen
 ♦ while away the evening over a glass of wine
Abendbesuch, m
 ♦ evening visit
 ♦ visit in the evening
Abendbrigade, f
 ♦ evening brigade
Abendbrot n
 → Abendessen
Abendbüfett, n (Dinner)
 ♦ buffet dinner
 ♦ dinner buffet AE
Abendbüfett, n (Supper)
 ♦ buffet supper
 ♦ supper buffet AE
Abenddienst, m
 Abendservice m
 ♦ evening service
Abendempfang, m
 (Veranstaltung)
 ♦ evening reception

Abendempfang geben
 ♦ give an evening reception
Abendessen auslassen (Dinner)
 ♦ skip dinner
Abendessen auslassen (Supper)
 ♦ skip supper
Abendessen bestellen (Dinner)
 ♦ order dinner
Abendessen bestellen (Supper)
 ♦ order supper
Abendessen einnehmen (Dinner)
 ♦ take dinner
 ♦ have dinner
Abendessen einnehmen (generell)
 ♦ have an evening meal
 ♦ take an evening meal
Abendessen einnehmen (Supper)
 ♦ take supper
 ♦ have supper
Abendessengutschein, m (Dinner)
 ♦ dinner voucher
Abendessengutschein, m (Supper)
 ♦ supper voucher
Abendessen im Hotel, n
 ♦ dinner at the hotel
 ♦ dinner in the hotel
Abendessen im Hotel einnehmen (Dinner)
 ♦ have dinner at the hotel
 ♦ have dinner in the hotel
Abendessen ist fertig (Dinner)
 ♦ dinner is ready
 ♦ dinner is served
Abendessen ist fertig (Supper)
 ♦ supper is ready
 ♦ supper is served
Abendessen kochen
 ♦ cook dinner
Abendessen mit Tanz, n (Dinner)
 Tanzdiner n
 ♦ dinner dance
Abendessen mit Tanz, n (Supper)
 Tanzsouper n
 ♦ supper dance
Abendessen servieren (Dinner)
 ♦ serve dinner
Abendessen servieren jm (Dinner)
 ♦ serve dinner to s.o.
 ♦ serve s.o. dinner
Abendessen servieren jm (Supper)
 ♦ serve supper to s.o.
 ♦ serve s.o. supper
Abendessen servieren (Supper)
 ♦ serve supper
Abendessenumsatz, m (Dinner)
 ♦ dinner sales pl
 ♦ dinner turnover

Abendessenumsatz, m (Supper)
 ♦ supper sales pl
 ♦ supper turnover
Abendessenzeit, f (Dinner)
 (Zeitpunkt)
 ♦ dinnertime AE
 ♦ dinner-time BE
Abendessenzeit, f (Dinner)
 (Zeitraum)
 ♦ dinner period
Abendessenzeit, f (Supper)
 (Zeitpunkt)
 ♦ suppertime AE
 ♦ supper-time BE
Abendessenzeit, f (Supper)
 (Zeitraum)
 ♦ supper period
Abendessen zubereiten (Supper)
 ♦ prepare supper
Abendessenzuschlag m (Dinner)
 (Preis)
 ♦ dinner supplement
 ♦ supplement for dinner
Abendfähre, f
 ♦ evening ferry
Abendflug, m
 ♦ evening flight
abendfüllendes Programm, n
 ♦ full-length program AE
 ♦ full-length programme BE
Abendgast m
 (Essen)
 Gast zum Abendessen m
 ♦ dinner customer
 ♦ dinner guest
Abendgedeck, n (Dinner)
 Abendkuvert n
 Abendcouvert n
 ♦ dinner cover
 ♦ cover laid for dinner
 ♦ cover set for dinner
Abendgedeck, n (Supper)
 Abendkuvert n
 Abendcouvert n
 Nachtgedeck n
 ♦ supper cover
 ♦ cover laid for supper
 ♦ cover set for supper
Abendgericht, n (Dinner)
 ♦ dinner dish
Abendgericht, n (Supper)
 ♦ supper dish
Abendgesellschaft, f (Soiree)
 → Soiree
Abendgesellschaft geben für jn (Dinner)
 ♦ give a dinner party for s.o.
Abendgesellschaft geben für jn (Supper)
 ♦ give a supper party for s.o.

Abendgesellschaft geben (Supper)

Abendgesellschaft geben (Supper)
- give a supper party

Abendgetränk, n
- evening drink
- evening beverage

Abendhausdame f
Abendgouvernante f
- evening housekeeper

Abendimbiß, m
- evening snack

Abendkarte, f (Dinner)
Abendspeisekarte f
- dinner menu

Abendkarte, f (generell)
Abendspeisekarte f
- evening menu

Abendkarte, f (Supper)
Abendspeisekarte f
- supper menu

Abendkleid, n
(kleines Abendkleid)
- dinner dress

Abendkleidung erforderlich
- Evening dress required
- Black tie required

Abendkleidung erwünscht
- Evening dress requested
- Black tie requested

Abendkonzert, n
- evening recital
- evening concert

abendlicher Theaterbesuch m
- evening visit to the theater *AE*
- evening visit to the theatre *BE*

Abendmannschaft, f
(Personal)
- evening crew
- evening team

Abendmenüwahl f
- choice of evening menu

Abendprogramm n
- evening program *AE*
- evening programme *BE*

Abendrestaurant n
- evening restaurant

Abendschicht, f
- evening shift

Abends geschlossen
- Closed evenings
- Closed in the evening

Abendsitzung, f
- evening session

Abendspaziergang, m
- evening walk
- walk in the evening

Abendspezialität, f
- evening specialty *AE*
- evening speciality *BE*

abends spielt ein Trio zum Tanz auf
- in the evenings a trio plays for dancing

Abendunterhaltung f
- evening entertainment

Abendunterhaltungsprogramm, n
- evening entertainment program *AE*
- evening entertainment programme *BE*

Abend verbringen im intimen Kreis
- spend the evening with close friends

Abendvorführung, f
Abendshow f
- evening show

Abendvorstellung f
(Theater)
- evening performance

Abend war sehr lustig
- evening was great fun

Abendzeitung, f
- evening newspaper
- evening paper

Abendzimmermädchen n
- evening chambermaid
- evening maid
- evening maid service

Abenteuerkreuzfahrt, f
- adventure cruise

Abenteuerpark, m
- adventure park

Abenteuerspielplatz, m
- adventure playground

abfahren (Person)
→ abreisen

Abfahrt, f (generell)
→ Abreise

Abfahrten aller Schwierigkeitsgrade, f pl
(Ski)
- runs of all degrees of difficulty *pl*

Abfahrten verschiedener Schwierigkeitsgrade, f pl
(Ski)
- runs of various degrees of difficulty *pl*

Abfahrtsbahnhof, m
- departure station
- station of departure

Abfahrtsbahnsteig, m
- departure platform
- platform of departure

Abfahrtshang, m (Ski)
→ Skihang

Abfahrtsort, m (Stadt)
- place of departure

Abfahrtsstelle, f (Punkt)
Abfahrtspunkt, m
- departure point
- point of departure

Abfahrtstag, m (generell)
- day of departure
- departure day

Abfahrtszeit, f
- departure time
- time of departure

Abfahrtszeiten sind in Ortszeit angegeben
- departures are shown in local time

abfertigen etw
- handle s.th.
- deal with s.th.
- process s.th. *AE*

Abfertigung, f (bes. Personen)
- service
- dealing with s.o.

Abfertigungsgebühr, f
- handling charge
- handling fee

Abflug, m (technisch)
→ Start

Abflughafen, m
Abreiseflughafen m
- departure airport
- airport of departure

Abflugsteuer, f
- departure tax

Abflugsteuer erheben
- levy a departure tax

Abfluß, m
- drain

Abfluß ist verstopft
- drain is blocked

Abfüllanlage, f
(für Getränke)
- bottling plant

Abgabe, f
Taxe, f
- tax

Abgabe einziehen
Taxe einziehen
- collect a tax

Abgabe erheben
Taxe erheben
- raise a tax
- charge a tax

abgelegenes Restaurant, n
- remote restaurant
- out-of-the-way restaurant

abgenutztes Laken, n
- worn-out sheet

abgenutzte Wäsche f
- worn-out linen

abgeschiedene Lage, f
- secluded location
- secluded position
- secluded situation
- secluded setting

Abgeschiedenheit, f
- seclusion

abgestandenes Bier, n
- stale beer

abgetrenntes Kinderschwimmbecken n
- separate children's pool

abgewohnt, adj
→ verwohnt

abhalten etw
(Veranstaltung)
- hold s.th.

abhalten etw jährlich
- hold s.th. annually

Abhaltung von etw, f
- holding of s.th.

abhängen von der Größe der Gruppe
- depend on the size of the group
- depend on the size of the party

abhängen von der Saison
- depend on the season

abhauen, ohne die Rechnung zu bezahlen *sl*
- skip off without paying the bill *coll*

abholbereit sein
- be ready for collection

abholen etw
- pick s.th. up
- collect s.th.
- go and collect s.th.
- go and get s.th.
- fetch s.th.

abholen jn an der Haustür
- collect s.o. at the front door
- pick s.o. up at the front door

abholen jn (generell)
- collect s.o.
- call for s.o.
- fetch s.o.

abholen jn kostenlos
- collect s.o. free of charge
- pick s.o. up free of charge
- fetch s.o. free of charge

abholen jn (mit dem Auto)
- **pick s.o. up**
- meet s.o.

abholen jn vom Bahnhof
- **collect s.o. from the station**
- meet s.o. at the station
- pick s.o. up at the station
- fetch s.o. from the station

abholen jn vom Flughafen
- **meet s.o. at the airport**
- collect s.o. from the airport
- pick s.o. up at the airport
- fetch s.o. from the airport

abholen jn vom Hauptbahnhof
- **meet s.o. at the main railway station** AE
- meet s.o. at the main railway station BE
- collect s.o. from the main railway station AE
- collect s.o. from the main railway station BE
- pick s.o. up at the main railway station AE

abholen jn vom Hotel
- **collect s.o. from the hotel**
- pick s.o. up at the hotel
- meet s.o. at the hotel
- fetch s.o. from the hotel

abholen jn von
- **pick s.o. up at**
- collect s.o. from
- meet s.o. at
- fetch s.o. from

abholen jn von zu Hause
- **collect s.o. from his (her) home**
- pick s.o. up at his (her) home
- meet s.o. at his (her) home
- fetch s.o. from his (her) home

abholen jn zum Abendessen
- **pick s.o. up for dinner**

Abholstelle, f
- **pick-up point**

Abholung bei Ankunft, f
- **collection on arrival**

Abholungsdienst, m
- → Abholdienst

Abholung vom Bahnhof, f
- **collection from the station**

Abholzeit, f
- **pick-up time**

ab kommender Woche
- **starting next week**
- from next week

Ablauf des Mietverhältnisses, m
- **expiration of tenancy**

Ablauf des Pachtvertrags, m
- **expiration of the lease**

Abmeldeformalität, f (Check-out)
- **check-out formality**

Abmeldekarte, f
- **check-out card**

Abmeldesystem, n (Check-out)
- **check-out system**

Abmeldung, f (Check-out)
- **check out**
- checking out

Abneigung haben gegen etw
- **have no stomach for s.th.**

Abnutzung f
(durch Gebrauch)
Verschleiß m
- **wear and tear**

abrahmen
- **skim**

abraten von etw
- **advise against s.th.**

Abräumer, m
(im Restaurant)
Débarrasseur, m FR
- **clearer**
- clearing waiter
- débarrasseur FR
- busboy

abrechnen etw
- **settle accounts**
- balance accounts
- clear accounts

Abrechungscoupon, m
- **audit coupon**

Abreise, f (Check-out)
- **check-out**
- checking out

Abreise, f (Gast) sl
abreisender Gast, m
- **departure**
- departing guest

Abreise, f (generell)
Abfahrt, f
- **departure**
- setting out
- setting off
- starting
- going (away)

Abreisebenachrichtigung, f
(Rezeption)
Abreisemitteilung, f
- **departure(s) notification**
- notification of a departure
- notification of departures

Abreisebenachrichtigungsformular n
- **departure notification form**

abreisebereit, adj
abfahrtbereit, adj
- **ready to leave, adj**
- ready to depart, adj

abreisebereit sein
abfahrtbereit sein
bereit sein zur Abreise
- **be ready to leave**
- be ready to depart
- be ready for departure

Abreise beschleunigen
Abfahrt beschleunigen
Abflug beschleunigen
- **hasten one's departure**
- hasten s.o.'s departure

Abreisebuch n
- **departure book**

Abreisedatum, n
- → Abfahrtsdatum

Abreisedatum angeben
Abreisetermin angeben
- **state the date of departure**
- indicate the date of departure

Abreiseeinrichtung, f
Abfahrtseinrichtung, f
Abflugeinrichtung, f
- **departure facility**

Abreise erfolgt am Dienstag
Abfahrt erfolgt am Dienstag
Abflug erfolgt am Dienstag
- **departure will be on Tuesday**

Abreise erfolgt um 17 Uhr
Abfahrt erfolgt um 17 Uhr
Abflug erfolgt um 17 Uhr
- **departure is at 5 p.m.**
- departure is at 17 hours

Abreise festsetzen (auf den 8. November)
Abfahrt festsetzen (auf den 8. November)
Abflug festsetzen (auf den 8. November)
- **fix one's departure (for 8 November)**
- fix s.o.'s departure (for 8 November)

Abreiseflughafen, m
- **airport of departure**
- departure airport

Abreiseformalität, f
Ausreiseformalität, f
- **departure formality**

Abreisehafen, m
Abfahrtshafen, m
- **port of departure**
- departure port

Abreise hat sich verzögert
Abfahrt hat sich verzögert
Abflug hat sich verzögert
- **departure has been delayed**

Abreise hinausschieben
Abfahrt hinausschieben
Abflug hinausschieben
- **defer one's departure**
- defer s.o.'s departure
- postpone one's departure
- postpone s.o.'s departure
- put off one's departure

Abreise hinausschieben bis auf weiteres
Abfahrt hinausschieben bis auf weiteres
Abflug hinausschieben bis auf weiteres
- **defer one's departure until further notice**
- defer s.o.'s departure until further notice

Abreise hinausschieben um eine Woche
Abfahrt hinausschieben um eine Woche
Abflug hinausschieben um eine Woche
- **defer one's departure for one week**
- defer s.o.'s departure for one week

Abreise in letzter Minute, f
Abreise in letzter Sekunde, f
Abfahrt in letzter Minute, f
Abflug in letzter Minute, m
- **last-minute departure**

Abreise ist für 11 Uhr festgesetzt
Abfahrt ist für 11 Uhr festgesetzt
Abflug ist für 11 Uhr festgesetzt
- **departure is scheduled for 11 o'clock**

Abreise ist unerwartet
- **departure is unexpected**

Abreiseland, n
Abfahrtsland, n
Abflugland, n
- **country of departure**

Abreiseliste, f
- **departure(s) list**
- list of departures

Abreiseliste erstellen
Liste der abreisenden Gäste erstellen
- **compile a departures list**
- compile a departure list

Abreiseliste korrigieren
- **amend the departure(s) list**

Abreise mitteilen jm
- **inform s.o. of one's departure**
- inform s.o. of s.o.'s departure

Abreisemonat, m
Abfahrtsmonat, m
Abflugmonat, m
- **departure month**
- month of departure

Abreise nach London

Abreise nach London, f
 Abfahrt nach London, f
 ♦ departure for London
Abreise nach X, f
 Abfahrt nach X, f
 ♦ departure for X
abreisen am nächsten Morgen
 abfahren am nächsten Morgen
 ♦ leave the next morning
 ♦ depart the next morning
 ♦ leave the following morning
 ♦ depart the following morning
abreisen am Samstag
 abfahren am Sonnabend
 ♦ leave on Saturday
 ♦ depart on Saturday
abreisen (auschecken)
 → auschecken
abreisen binnen einer Stunde
 abfahren in einer Stunde
 ♦ leave within one hour
 ♦ depart within one hour
 ♦ leave within one's hour notice
 ♦ depart within one's hour notice
abreisen bis spätestens Mittwoch
 abfahren bis spätestens Mittwoch
 abfliegen bis spätestens Mittwoch
 ♦ leave by Wednesday at the latest
 ♦ depart by Wednesday at the latest
abreisend, adj
 abfahrend, adj
 abfliegend, adj
 ♦ departing, adj
Abreisender, m
 Abfahrender, m
 Abfliegender, m
 ♦ person departing
abreisender Gast, m
 abfahrender Gast, m
 abfliegender Gast, m
 Abgang, m sl
 ♦ departing guest
abreisen früh morgens
 abreisen früh am Morgen
 früh morgens abfahren
 früh morgens abfliegen
 ♦ leave early in the morning
 ♦ depart early in the morning
abreisen gegen 11 Uhr vormittags
 abfahren gegen 11 Uhr vormittags
 abfliegen gegen 11 Uhr vormittags
 ♦ leave at approximately 11 a.m.
 ♦ depart at approximately 11 a.m.
 ♦ leave at about 11 hours *mil*
 ♦ depart at about 11 hours *mil*
abreisen (generell)
 abreisen
 wegfahren
 ♦ leave
 ♦ depart
 ♦ go away
 ♦ go off
abreisen in einen Urlaub in Spanien
 abfahren in einen Urlaub in Spanien
 ♦ leave for a vacation in Spain *AE*
 ♦ leave for a holiday in Spain *BE*
abreisen mit dem Auto
 ♦ depart by car
abreisen mit dem Boot
 abreisen mit dem Schiff
 ♦ depart by boat

abreisen mit dem Bus (nach X)
 ♦ depart by bus (for X)
 ♦ depart by coach (for X) *BE*
abreisen mit dem Flugzeug
 ♦ depart by air
abreisen mit dem Schiff
 ♦ depart by ship
 ♦ depart by boat
abreisen mit dem Zug
 ♦ depart by train
 ♦ leave by train
abreisen mit dem Zug von X
 ♦ leave on the train from X
abreisen mit Flug 123
 abfliegen mit Flug 123
 ♦ depart on flight 123
 ♦ leave on flight 123
abreisen mit Kind und Kegel coll
 ♦ leave, bag and baggage *coll*
abreisen mit Verspätung
 → abfahren mit Verspätung
abreisen müssen
 ♦ have to leave
abreisen nach dem Abendessen
 abfahren nach dem Abendessen
 ♦ leave after dinner
 ♦ depart after dinner
abreisen nach Hause
 abfahren nach Hause
 ♦ leave for home
 ♦ depart for home
abreisen nach Schottland
 ♦ leave for Scotland
abreisen nach X
 ♦ leave for X
 ♦ set out for X
 ♦ start for X
 ♦ depart for X
abreisen ohne die Adresse zu hinterlassen
 ♦ depart without leaving one's address
abreisen ohne zu zahlen
 ♦ leave without paying
 ♦ depart without paying
abreisen um 11 Uhr vormittags
 abfahren um 11 Uhr vormittags
 ♦ leave at 11 a.m.
 ♦ depart at 11 a.m.
 ♦ leave at 11 hours *mil*
 ♦ depart at 11 hours *mil*
abreisen von A nach B
 abfahren von A nach B
 ♦ depart from A for B
 ♦ leave A for B
abreisen von Bahnsteig 4
 abfahren von Bahnsteig 4
 ♦ leave from platform 4
abreisen von einem Hotel
 ♦ depart from a hotel
 ♦ leave a hotel
 ♦ check out of a hotel
abreisen von X
 ♦ leave X
 ♦ depart from X
 ♦ start from X
abreisen von X mit dem Bus
 abfahren von X mit dem Bus
 ♦ leave X by bus *AE*
 ♦ depart from X by bus *AE*
 ♦ leave X by coach *BE*
 ♦ depart from X by coach *BE*

abreisen von X nach Z über Y
 abfahren von X nach Z über Y
 abfliegen von X nach Z über Y
 ♦ leave from X for Z via Y
 ♦ depart from X for Z via Y
abreisen wollen
 ♦ want to leave
 ♦ want to depart
Abreiseort, m (Punkt)
 Abfahrtsort, m
 Abflugsort, m
 ♦ point of departure
 ♦ departure point
Abreiseort, m (Stadt)
 Abfahrtsort, m
 Abflugsort, m
 ♦ departure place
 ♦ place of departure
Abreise stornieren
 Abreise absagen
 Abflug stornieren
 Abflug absagen
 ♦ cancel a departure
Abreisestunde f
 Abfahrtsstunde f
 ♦ departure hour
 ♦ hour of departure
Abreisetag, m
 ♦ departure day
 ♦ day of departure
Abreisetermin, m
 Abreisedatum, n
 Abflugtermin, m
 Abflugdatum, n
 ♦ date of departure
 ♦ departure date
Abreise verschieben
 Abreise hinausschieben
 ♦ postpone one's departure
 ♦ postpone s.o.'s departure
 ♦ defer one's departure
 ♦ defer s.o.'s departure
 ♦ put off one's departure
Abreise verschieben auf (den) 7. März
 ♦ postpone one's departure to 7 March
 ♦ postpone s.o.'s departure to 7 March
Abreise verschieben auf später
 Abreise verschieben auf einen späteren Termin
 ♦ postpone one's departure to a later date
 ♦ postpone one's departure until later
 ♦ postpone s.o.'s departure to a later date
 ♦ postpone s.o.'s departure until later
Abreise verschieben wegen einer Erkrankung
 ♦ postpone one's departure owing to illness
 ♦ postpone s.o.'s departure owing to illness
 ♦ postpone one's departure because of illness
 ♦ postpone s.o.'s departure because of illness
Abreise verschieben wegen etw
 Abreise verschieben aufgrund von etw
 ♦ postpone one's departure owing to s.th.
 ♦ postpone one's departure because of s.th.
Abreiseverspätung, f
 Abflugverspätung, f
 ♦ delay of departure
Abreise verzögern
 ♦ delay one's departure
 ♦ delay s.o.'s departure
Abreise von einem Hotel, f
 ♦ departure from a hotel
Abreise von X, f
 Abfahrt von X, f

Abflug von X, m
♦ departure from X
Abreise vorbereiten
sich auf die Abreise vorbereiten
sich zur Abfahrt rüsten *form*
♦ **prepare for departure**
Abreisevorbereitung, f
Abfahrtsvorbereitung, f
♦ **preparation for departure**
Abreisevorgang, m
♦ **departure procedure**
Abreise vorverlegen
♦ **bring forward one's departure**
♦ bring forward s.o.'s departure
♦ advance one's departure
♦ advance s.o.'s departure
Abreise vorverlegen auf 9 Uhr vormittags
♦ **advance one's departure to 9 hours**
♦ advance one's departure to 9 o'clock a.m.
Abreise vorverlegen auf Donnerstag
♦ **advance one's departure to Thursday**
Abreise vorverlegen um eine Woche
♦ **advance one's departure by one week**
Abreise vorverlegen von Freitag auf Montag
♦ **advance one's departure from Friday to Monday**
Abreisewoche, f
Abfahrtswoche, f
Abflugwoche, f
♦ **departure week**
♦ week of departure
Abreisezeit, f (Check-out)
Zeitpunkt der Abmeldung, m
Zeitpunkt der Abreise, m
Abmeldezeit, f
♦ **time of checking out**
♦ check-out time
Abreisezeit, f (generell)
Abfahrtszeit f
♦ **departure time**
♦ time of departure
Abreisezeit angeben
♦ **state the time of departure**
♦ indicate the time of departure
Abreisezeitpunkt, m (Check-out)
Zeitpunkt der Abmeldung, m
Zeitpunkt der Abreise, m
♦ **check-out time**
♦ time of checking out
Abreisezeit verlängern bis 15 Uhr (Hotel)
♦ **extend check-out time to 3 p.m.**
Abreisezeit verlängern (Check-out)
Check-out-Zeit verlängern
♦ **extend the check-out time**
Abreisezimmer, n
(Gegensatz zu 'Bleibezimmer')
♦ **room of a departing guest**
Abreise zum festgesetzten Termin, f
Abreise am festgesetzten Termin f
♦ **departure on the appointed date**
Abreise zur festgesetzten Zeit, f
Abfahrt zur festgesetzten Zeit, f
Abflug zur festgesetzten Zeit, m
♦ **departure at the appointed time**
Abreißkarte, f
(für Bestellungen)
♦ **tear-off card**
abrufen etw (auf dem Computer)
♦ **call up s.th. (on the computer)**
♦ retrieve s.th. (on the computer)

abrunden etw mit etw
(z.B. Mahl)
♦ **round off s.th. with s.th.**
Abruzzen, die, pl
♦ **Abruzzi, the, pl**
absacken
stark zurückgehen
♦ **slump**
Absage, f
→ Stornierung
Absagebrief, m
♦ **letter of cancellation**
♦ letter of cancelation *AE*
♦ letter cancelling s.th.
♦ letter canceling s.th. *AE*
Absage einer Konferenz, f
Konferenzabsage, f
♦ **cancellation of a conference**
♦ cancelation of a conference *AE*
Absage eines Besuchs, f
♦ **cancellation of a visit**
♦ cancelation of a visit *AE*
Absagefrist, f
→ Stornierungsfrist
absagen
→ stornieren
absagen jm
♦ **put s.o. off**
Absageschreiben, n
♦ **letter cancelling s.th.**
♦ letter canceling s.th. *AE*
♦ letter of cancellation
♦ letter of cancelation *AE*
Absatzkosten, pl
♦ **sales costs** *pl*
ABS-Bremse, f
♦ **ABS brake**
♦ anti-lock brake
abschieben jn zu jm
(z.B. unwillkommene Gäste)
♦ **palm s.o. off on s.o.**
Abschied, m (Abreise)
♦ **leaving**
♦ departure
Abschied, m (generell)
Abschiednehmen, n
♦ **parting**
♦ leave-taking
♦ farewell
Abschied feiern (als Gastgeber)
♦ **give a farewell party**
Abschied nehmen
♦ **say good-bye** *AE*
♦ say good-by *AE*
♦ say goodbye *BE*
Abschiednehmen, n
♦ **leave-taking**
♦ parting
Abschied nehmen auf französisch
sich empfehlen auf französisch
sich auf französisch verabschieden
♦ **filer à l'anglaise** *FR*
♦ take French leave
Abschied nehmen von etw
sich verabschieden von etw
♦ **take leave of s.th.**
Abschiedsabend, m
♦ **farewell evening**
Abschiedsbankett, n
Abschiedsfestessen, n
♦ **farewell banquet**

Abschiedscocktail, m
♦ **farewell cocktail**
Abschiedsessen, n (abends)
Abschiedsdiner, n
♦ **farewell dinner**
Abschiedsessen, n (Bankett)
→ Abschiedsbankett
Abschiedsessen, n (mittags)
Abschiedsmittagessen, n
♦ **farewell lunch**
♦ farewell luncheon
Abschiedsessen n (generell)
♦ **farewell meal**
Abschiedsfeier, f
→ Abschiedsfest
Abschiedsfeier, f
Abschiedszeremonie, f
♦ **farewell ceremony**
Abschiedsfest mit Essen, n
♦ **farewell dinner party**
Abschiedsfest schmeißen für jn *coll*
♦ **throw a farewell party for s.o.** *coll*
Abschiedsfete, f
Abschiedsfeier, f
♦ **farewell fete** *AE*
♦ farewell fête *BE*
♦ farewell party
Abschiedsgeschenk, n
Abschiedspräsent, n
♦ **farewell gift**
♦ farewell present
♦ leaving present
♦ leaving gift
Abschiedskonzert n
♦ **farewell concert**
Abschiedsmenü n
♦ **farewell menu**
Abschiedsparty f
♦ **farewell party**
Abschiedspräsent, n
→ Abschiedsgeschenk
Abschiedsrede, f
♦ **farewell speech**
Abschiedstanz m
♦ **farewell dance**
Abschiedsumarmung, f
♦ **farewell hug**
Abschiedsworte, n pl
♦ **words of farewell** *pl*
Abschlagszahlung, f
→ Teilzahlung, Anzahlung
Abschleppdienst, m
→ Pannenhilfe
Abschleppwagen, m
♦ **breakdown truck** *AE*
♦ breakdown lorry *BE*
♦ breakdown van *BE*
abschließend, adj
♦ **final, adj**
abschließende Plenarsitzung, f
Abschlußplenarsitzung, f
♦ **final plenary session**
abschließender Gang, m
(Mahlzeit)
Schlußgang, m
Abschlußgang, m
♦ **final course**
abschließendes Abendessen, n
abschließendes Diner, n
♦ **final dinner**

abschließendes Frühstück

abschließendes Frühstück, n
 ♦ final breakfast
abschließendes Mittagessen, n
 ♦ final luncheon
 ♦ final lunch
abschließendes Nachtessen, n
 ♦ final supper
abschließende Vorkehrungen, f pl
 Schlußvorkehrungen, f pl
 ♦ final arrangements pl
abschließende Vorkehrungen treffen
 Schlußvorkehrungen treffen
 ♦ make the final arrangements
Abschluß, m
 Ende, n
 ♦ completion
Abschlußabend, m
 Schlußabend, m
 ♦ final evening
 ♦ final night
Abschlußball, m (Saisonende)
 ♦ end-of-season ball
Abschlußbankett, n
 abschließendes Bankett n
 ♦ closing banquet
Abschluß des Kurses, m
 Abschluß des Lehrgangs, m
 ♦ completion of the course
Abschlußdiner, n
 Abschlußessen, n
 ♦ closing dinner
Abschluß eines Aufnahmevertrags, m
 ♦ conclusion of a reception contract
Abschluß eines Gastaufnahmevertrags, m
 ♦ conclusion of a guest reception contract
Abschlußfeier, f (generell)
 Schlußfeier, f
 Abschlußzeremonie, f
 ♦ closing ceremony
Abschlußfeier, f (Schule, Hochschule)
 ♦ graduation ceremony
Abschlußkonzert, n
 ♦ closing concert
Abschlußkonzert der Saison, n
 ♦ final concert of the season
Abschlußmittagessen, n
 ♦ closing luncheon
 ♦ closing lunch
Abschlußmorgen, m
 Abschlußvormittag, m
 ♦ final morning
Abschlußnacht, f
 ♦ final night
Abschlußrechnung, f (Faktur)
 → Endrechnung
Abschlußrechnung, f (generell)
 Schlußrechnung, f
 Endrechnung, f
 ♦ final account
 ♦ final bill
Abschlußrechnung, f (Restaurant/Lokal)
 → Endrechnung
Abschlußrede, f
 ♦ closing speech
Abschlußreise, f
 letzte Reise, f
 abschließende Reise, f
 ♦ final journey
Abschlußsitzung, f
 Abschlußrunde, f

 ♦ final session
 ♦ final meeting
Abschlußsitzung, f
 Schlußsitzung, f
 abschließende Sitzung, f
 ♦ closing session
Abschlußtag, m
 ♦ final day
Abschlußturnier, n
 Schlußturnier, n
 abschließendes Turnier, n
 ♦ final tournament
Abschlußveranstaltung, f
 abschließende Veranstaltung, f
 Schlußveranstaltung, f
 ♦ final event
 ♦ final function
Abschlußzahlung, f
 Schlußzahlung f
 Endzahlung f
 ♦ final payment
Abschlußzeremonie, f
 → Abschlußfeier
abschmecken etw (überprüfen)
 ♦ taste s.th.
abschmecken etw (würzen)
 würzen etw
 ♦ flavor s.th. AE
 ♦ flavour s.th. BE
 ♦ season s.th.
abschneiden etw
 (Brot, Fleisch etc)
 ♦ slice s.th. off
Abschnitt der Reise, m
 Reiseabschnitt, m
 ♦ section of the journey
 ♦ section of the tour
 ♦ section of the trip
abschrecken jn
 ♦ deter s.o.
 ♦ put s.o. off
abschreiben etw
 ♦ depreciate s.th.
 ♦ write s.th. off
abschreiben etw teilweise ökon
 ♦ write down s.th. ökon
Abschreibung, f (Wertminderung)
 ♦ depreciation
Abschreibung auf Betriebsanlagen, f
 ♦ depreciation on plant
Abschreibung auf das Anlagevermögen, f
 ♦ depreciation on fixed assets
Abschreibung auf die Betriebs- und Geschäfts-
 ausstattung, f
 ♦ depreciation on office furniture and
 equipment
Abschreibung auf etw
 ♦ depreciation on s.th.
Abschreibung auf Maschinen, f
 ♦ depreciation on machinery
Abschreibung auf Mobiliar, f
 ♦ depreciation on furniture
Abschreibung der Ausstattung, f
 ♦ depreciation of equipment
Abschreibung der Einrichtungsgegenstände, f
 Abschreibung des Mobiliars, f
 ♦ depreciation of furniture
Abschreibung der Gebäude, f
 Abschreibung eines Gebäudes, f
 ♦ depreciation of buildings
 depreciation of a building

Abschreibung für Investitionen, f
 ♦ depreciation for capital expenditure
Abschreibung für Wertminderung, f
 ♦ depreciation for wear and tear
 ♦ allowance for wear and tear
 ♦ wear and tear
abschreibungsfähige Kosten, pl
 ♦ service cost
Abschreibungskosten, pl
 → Abschreibung
Abschreibung von etw, f
 ♦ depreciation of s.th.
Abseilen, n
 ♦ abseiling
abseilen sich
 ♦ abseil
Abseillehrer, m
 ♦ abseil instructor
abseits der Touristenpfade
 ♦ off the beaten tourist tracks
 ♦ off the tourist track
 ♦ away from the tourist routes
abseits liegen von der Straße
 ♦ be off the road
abseits vom Trubel
 ♦ away from the bustle
abservieren
 abtragen
 abräumen
 ♦ clear away (the dishes)
 ♦ take away the dishes
 ♦ carry away the dishes
 ♦ remove the dishes
absetzen etw von der Speisekarte
 ♦ take s.th. off the menu
absetzen etw von einem Programm
 streichen etw von einem Programm
 ♦ take s.th. off a program AE
 ♦ take s.th. off a programme BE
absetzen jn (bei dem Bahnhof)
 ♦ put s.o. off (near the station)
 ♦ drop s.o. off (near the station)
absichern sich gegen eine Stornierung
 ♦ safeguard against (a) cancellation
 ♦ safeguard against (a) cancelation AE
absichtliche Überbuchung, f
 bewußte Überbuchung, f
 ♦ intentional overbooking
Absinth, m
 ♦ absinthe
 ♦ absinth
absolute Privatheit, f
 absolute Ruhe, f
 ♦ complete privacy
absolut unabhängig sein
 ♦ be absolutely free
Absolvent einer Hotelschule m
 ♦ graduate of a hotel school
Absprache, f
 → Vereinbarung
abspülen (Geschirr)
 ♦ wash the dishes
 ♦ do the dishes
 ♦ wash up BE
Abspülküche, f
 → Spülküche
abstauben etw
 ♦ dust s.th.
Abstecher, m (Ausflug)
 ♦ side trip AE

- trip
- excursion

Abstecher, m (Umweg)
- detour

Abstecher machen nach X (Ausflug)
- make a side trip to X *AE*
- go on a side trip to X *AE*
- make a trip to X
- go on a trip to X

Abstecher machen nach X (Umweg)
- make a detour to X

Abstecher unternehmen nach X (Ausflug)
- take a side trip to X

Abstecher wert sein (Ausflug)
- be (well) worth a side trip *AE*
- be (well) worth a trip

Abstecher wert sein (Umweg)
- be (well) worth a detour

Absteige, f (Penne)
- doss-house *BE*
- flophouse *AE*

Absteige, f (Stundenhotel)
Stundenhotel, n
- cheap hotel
- short-time hotel
- sleazy hotel

absteigen
(Pferd, Fahrrad)
- dismount

absteigen in einem Hotel (zum Übernachten)
Station machen in einem Hotel (zum Übernachten)
- put up at a hotel (for the night)
- stop at a hotel (for the night)

Absteigequartier, n
→ Absteige

abstellen etw
(z.B. Strom, Gas)
- cut off s.th.

abstellen etw in der Garage
- garage s.th.

Abstellgebühr, f (Auto)
→ Parkgebühr

Abstellraum, m
→ Lagerraum

abstempeln etw
→ stempeln etw

Abstimmung, f
(bei Konferenzen etc.)
- vote counting

Abstimmungsanlage, f
(bei Konferenzen etc.)
Abstimmanlage, f
- voting system
- vote counting system

Abstinenzler, m
Nichttrinker, m
Alkoholgegner, m
- abstainer
- teetotaller *BE*
- teetotaler *AE*
- total abstainer
- TT

Absturz, m
(Flugzeug)
- crash

abstürzen
(Flugzeug)
- crash

abstürzen auf etw
abstürzen in etw
- crash into s.th.

abstürzen ins Meer
- crash into the sea

Abt, m
- abbot

abtakeln
- unrig

Abtakelung, f
- unrigging

Abtei, f
- abbey

Abtei gründen
- found an abbey

Abteikirche, f
- abbey church

Abteil, n
(Zug)
Coupé, n *obs*
- compartment

Abteil dritter Klasse, n
Abteil in der dritten Klasse, n
Dritte-Klasse-Abteil, n
- third-class compartment

Abteil erster Klasse, n
→ Erste-Klasse-Abteil

Abteilungskoch, m
Abteilskoch, m
Partiekoch, m
- section cook

Abteilungskoch für Braten, m
→ Rotisseur

Abteilungskoch für Fische, m
→ Poissonnier

Abteilungskoch für kalte Küche, m
→ Gardemanger

Abteilungskoch für Soßen, m
→ Saucier

Abteilungskoch für Suppen, m
→ Potagier

Abteilungskoch für Vorspeisen, m
→ Hors d'oeuvrier

Abteilungskoch für Zwischenspeisen, m
→ Entremetier

Abteilungsleiter, m
Leiter einer Abteilung, m
- departmental manager
- department head
- head of (a) department *BE*

Abteilungsleitung f
- departmental management
- management of a department
- head of (a) department

Abteilungspersonal, n
- department staff
- department personnel

Abteilung von einer Abreise informieren
- inform a department of a departure

Abteilung von einer Ankunft informieren
- inform a department of an arrival

Abteil zweiter Klasse, n
→ Zweite-Klasse-Abteil

Abteiruine, f
- ruined abbey
- abbey ruins *pl*

abtelefonieren jm
- telephone s.o. not to come
- telephone s.o. canceling s.th. *AE*
- telephone s.o. cancelling s.th. *BE*
- put s.o. off by phone

abtelegrafieren jm
- send s.o. a telegram not to come
- send s.o. a telegram canceling s.th. *AE*
- send s.o. a telegram cancelling s.th. *BE*
- wire s.o. not to come

Äbtissin, f
- abbess

abtragen (Geschirr)
- remove the dishes
- take away the dishes
- carry away the dishes
- clear away the dishes

abtragen (Tisch)
- clear (away) the table

Abtropfbrett, n *gastr*
- draining board *gastr*

Abtropfgestell, n (für Teller)
- plate rack *AE*
- plate-rack *BE*

ab und zu sich einen genehmigen *coll*
ab und zu etwas trinken
- take a drop now and then *coll*

Abwärtstrend, m
Rückgang, m
- downswing
- downturn

abwaschen etw
waschen etw
- wash s.th.

abwaschen (Geschirr)
- do the washing-up *BE*
- do the dishes
- wash the dishes
- wash up *BE*

Abwäscher, m
→ Spüler

Abwaschküche f
→ Abspülküche

Abwaschlappen, m
→ Spültuch

Abwaschmädchen, n
→ Spülmädchen

Abwaschraum, m
→ Spülraum

Abwaschwasser, n
→ Spülwasser

Abwasser, n
- waste water
- sewage

Abwasseranlage, f
- sewage system

Abwasserkanal, m
(von Gebäuden)
- mains drainage

Abwasserkläranlage, f
- sewage treatment plant

Abwasserleitung, f
- sewer

Abwasserreinigung, f
Abwasserklärung, f
- sewage treatment

abwasserverschmutzter Strand, m
- sewage-polluted beach

Abwasserverschmutzung, f
- sewage pollution

Abwechslung, f
- change

Abwechslung brauchen
- need a change

Abwechslung haben
- have a change

abwechslungsreich, adj
- varied, adj
- full of variety, adj

abwechslungsreiche Diät

abwechslungsreiche Diät, f
♦ varied diet
abwechslungsreiche Gerichte, n pl
♦ varied dishes pl
abwechslungsreiche Kost, f
♦ rich variety of dishes
♦ varied cooking
♦ varied cuisine
♦ varied diet
abwechslungsreiche Kost bieten
♦ offer a rich variety of dishes
abwechslungsreiche Küche, f (Speisen)
♦ varied cuisine
♦ varied cooking
abwechslungsreiche Küche bieten
♦ offer a varied cuisine
abwechslungsreiche Landschaft f
♦ varied scenery
♦ varied countryside
♦ varied landscape
abwechslungsreiches Essen, n
♦ varied food
abwechslungsreiches Land, n
♦ varied country
abwechslungsreiche Speisekarte, f
♦ varied menu
abwechslungsreiche Speisekarte anbieten
♦ offer a varied menu
abwechslungsreiche Speisekarte bieten
♦ provide a varied menu
abwechslungsreiches Programm n
♦ varied program AE
♦ varied programme BE
abwechslungsreiche Strecke, f
abwechslungsreiche Route, f
♦ varied route
abwechslungsreiche Unterhaltung, f
vielseitige Unterhaltung, f
♦ varied entertainment
Abwechslung suchen
Veränderung suchen
Wechsel suchen
♦ seek change
Abwechslung zum Stadtleben, f
♦ change from city life
abweichen vom Kurs
♦ go off course
abweichen von der Route
♦ deviate from the route
Abweichung, f
Abweichen, n
♦ deviation
abweisen jn
(Gast wegschicken)
♦ turn s.o. away
♦ send s.o. away
Abwertung, f
♦ devaluation
Abwicklung, f
Bearbeitung, f
♦ processing (s.th.)
♦ handling (s.th.)
♦ dealing (with s.th.)
Abzeichen, n
Ansteckbnadel, f
♦ badge
abzeichnen lassen etw (Rechnung)
signieren lassen etw
♦ have s.th. signed
abzeichnen (Rechnung)
→ unterzeichnen

abziehen etw vom Preis
♦ deduct s.th. from the price
♦ deduct s.th. from the rate
abziehen etw von der Rückerstattung
einbehalten etw von der Rückerstattung
♦ deduct s.th. from the refund
abziehen etw von etw (Summe)
verrechnen etw mit etw
♦ deduct s.th. from s.th.
abzweigen
(Straße)
♦ branch
Abzweigung nehmen
♦ take a turning
Académie Culinaire de France, f FR
♦ Académie Culinaire de France FR
Achenpaß, m
♦ Achen Pass, the
Achensee, m
(Eigenname)
♦ Achen Lake, the
achtbettig, adj
♦ eight-bedded, adj
♦ eight-bed, adj
achtbettiges Zimmer, n
♦ eight-bedded room
Achtbettzelt, n
♦ eight-berth tent
Achtbettzimmer, n
♦ eight-bed room
♦ eight-bedded room
achteckig, adj
♦ octagonal, adj
achteckiger Teller, m
♦ octagonal plate
achteckiger Tisch, m
♦ octagonal table
achte Etage, f
→ achtes Stockwerk
achten auf die Linie
♦ watch one's figure
Achterbahn, f
(auf dem Jahrmarkt)
Berg- und Talbahn, f
♦ roller coaster
♦ coaster
♦ switchback BE
Achterbahnfahrt, f
Berg- und Talbahnfahrt, f
♦ roller coaster ride
♦ coaster ride AE
♦ switchback ride BE
Achterdeck, n
♦ quarterdeck
♦ afterdeck
Achterdeckkabine, f
♦ quarterdeck cabin
achter Gang, m (Menü)
♦ eighth course
achtes Stockwerk, n
achte Etage, f
achtes Geschoß, n
♦ ninth floor AE
♦ ninth story AE
♦ eighth floor BE
♦ eighth storey BE
achtgängig, adj (Essen)
♦ eight-course, adj
consisting of eight courses

achtgängiges Diner, n
achtgängiges Abendessen, n
♦ eight-course dinner
achtgängiges Essen, n
♦ eight-course meal
achtgängiges Menü, n
♦ eight-course menu
achtgängiges Mittagessen, n
♦ eight-course luncheon
♦ eight-course lunch
achtgeschossig, adj
→ achtstöckig
achtmonatige Seereise, f
♦ eight-month voyage
achtsitzig, adj
♦ eight-seater, adj
achtstöckig, adj attr (Gebäude)
♦ eight-floor, adj attr
♦ eight-story, adj attr AE
♦ eight-storey, adj attr BE
achtstöckig, adj prd (Gebäude)
♦ eight-storied, adj prd AE
♦ eight-storeyed, adj prd BE
achtstöckiges Hotel, n
♦ eight-floor hotel
♦ eight-story hotel AE
♦ eight-storey hotel BE
achtstöckig sein (Gebäude)
achtgeschossig sein
♦ be eight-storied AE
♦ be eight-storeyed BE
achtstündiger Marsch, m
♦ eight hours' march
achtstündige Verspätung, f
♦ eight-hour delay
Achttagepaß, m
♦ eight-day pass
Achttagereise, f
→ achttägige Reise
achttägig, adj
♦ eight-day, adj
♦ eight days', adj
♦ of eight days duration
♦ lasting eight days
achttägige Reise, f
Achttagereise, f
♦ eight-day tour
Achtung Stufe!
(Hinweisschild)
♦ Mind the step!
achtwöchig, adj
♦ eight-week, adj
♦ lasting eight weeks
♦ of eight weeks' duration
♦ eight weeks', adj
achtwöchige Reise, f
♦ eight-week journey
♦ eight-week tour
♦ eight-week trip
achtwöchige Tournee, f
♦ eight-week tour
Achtzehn-Loch-Golfplatz m
18-Loch-Golfplatz m
♦ eighteen-hole golf course
♦ 18-hole golf course
Achtzehn-Loch-Meisterschaftsgolfplatz, m
18-Loch-Meisterschaftsgolfplatz, m
♦ eighteen-hole championship golf course
♦ 18-hole championship golf course

Achtzehn-Loch-Puttinggrün, n
- eighteen-hole putting green *AE*
- eighteen-hole putting-green *BE*

achtzehnte Etage, f
→ achtzehntes Stockwerk

achtzehntes Geschoß, n
→ achtzehntes Stockwerk

achtzehntes Stockwerk, n
achtzehnte Etage, f
achtzehntes Geschoß, n
- nineteenth floor *AE*
- nineteenth story *AE*
- eighteenth floor *BE*
- eighteenth storey *BE*

achtzigste Etage, f
→ achtzigstes Stockwerk

achtzigstes Geschoß, n
→ achtzigstes Stockwerk

achtzigstes Stockwerk, n
achtzigste Etage, f
achtzigstes Geschoß, n
- eighty-first floor *AE*
- eighty-first story *AE*
- eightieth floor *BE*
- eightieth storey *BE*

achtzimmerig, adj
- eight-roomed, adj
- eight-room, adj

Acht-Zimmer-Villa, f
- eight-room villa

ADAC Empfohlen
(Hinweisschild)
- ADAC Commended

Adapter, m
→ Zwischenstecker

Ad-hoc-Besuch, m
- ad hoc visit

Ad-hoc-Charterverkehr, m
- ad hoc charter traffic

Ad-hoc-Tour, f
- ad hoc tour

Adlige, f
- noblewoman

Adliger, m
- nobleman

à DM 123
- at DM 123 each
- at DM 123 a piece

Adreßbuch, n
Adressenbuch n
- address book

Adresse, f
Anschrift, f
- address

Adresse angeben jm
seine Adresse geben jm
- give s.o. one's address
- give s.o. s.o.'s address

Adresse hinterlassen
- leave one's address

Adresse im Heimatland, f
- address in (one's) home country

Adressenänderung, f
- change of address

Adressenarchiv, n
- address files *pl*

Adressenbuch, n
→ Adreßbuch

Adressenliste, f
Anschriftenliste, f
Adressenverzeichnis, n

- address list
- list of addresses
- mailing list

Adresse überprüfen
Adresse prüfen
- check an address

Adressiermaschine, f
- addressing machine

adressierter Umschlag, m
- addressed envelope

Adreßkartei, f
- address index
- index of addresses

adrett, adj
- neat, adj

adrettes Zimmer, n
- neat room

adrett möbliert, adj
- neatly furnished, adj

adrett möbliertes Zimmer, n
- neatly furnished room

Adria, f
- Adriatic, the

Adriaferienort, m
Adriaurlaubsort, m
- Adriatic resort

Adriaküste, f
- Adriatic coast

Adriatische Meer, das, n
- Adriatic Sea, the

Advent, m
Adventszeit, f
- Advent

Adventsbasar, m
- Advent basar
- Advent bazaar

Adventsfeier, f
- Advent celebration

Adventsparty, f
Adventsfeier, f
- Advent party

Aerobic, n
- aerobics *pl*

Aerobickurs, m
Aerobicklasse, f
- aerobics class
- aerobic class

Aerobicräume, m pl
- aerobics suite

Aerobicstudio, n
- aerobics studio

Affinitätsgruppe f
- affinity group

Afghane, m
- Afghan
- Afghanistani

Afghanin, f
- Afghan girl
- Afghan woman
- Afghan
- Afghanistani

afghanisch, adj
- Afghan, adj

Afghanistan
- Afghanistan

Afrika
- Africa

Afrikaner, m
- African

Afrikanerin, f
- African girl

- African woman
- African

afrikanisch, adj
- African, adj

Afrikareise, f (in Afrika)
Afrikarundreise, f
- tour of Africa
- African tour

Afrikareise, f (nach Afrika)
Reise nach Afrika, f
- tour to Africa
- journey to Africa
- trip to Africa

Afrikaspezialist, m
- Africa specialist

Afrikatourismus, m
- African tourism
- tourism to Africa

Afrikatourist, m
- African tourist
- tourist to Africa

Afrikatournee, f
- African tour

Afrikaworkshop, m
- Africa workshop
- African workshop

AG, f
Aktiengesellschaft, f
- plc *BE*
- PLC *BE*
- public limited company *BE*

Ägäis, die, f
- Aegean, the

Ägäische Meer, das, n
- Aegean Sea, the

Ägäischen Inseln, die, f pl
- Aegean Islands, the *pl*

Ägäisküste, f
- Aegean coast

Agenda, n pl
→ Tagesordnung

Agent, m
Mittler, m
Vermittler, m
- agent

Agentur, f
- agency

Agenturbestellung, f
→ Agenturbuchung

Agentur betreiben
- run an agency
- operate an agency

Agenturbuchung f
- agency booking

Agenturfiliale, f
Agenturstelle, f
- agency outlet

Agenturgebühr, f
Vermittlungsgebühr, f
- agency fee

Agenturgutschein, m
(z.B. von Reisebüro)
- agency voucher

Agenturleiter, m
- agency manager

Agenturnetz, n
- agency network

Agenturreservierung, f
- agency reservation

Agenturstempel, m
- agent's stamp

Agenturumsatz

Agenturumsatz, m
 ♦ agency sales *pl*
 ♦ agency turnover
Agenturvereinbarung, f
 Agenturvertrag m
 ♦ agency agreement
Agenturvertrag, m
 ♦ agency contract
Agrarmesse, f
 → Landwirtschaftsmesse
Agrarreise, f
 ♦ agricultural tour
Ägypten
 ♦ Egypt
Ägypter, m
 ♦ Egyptian
Ägypterin, f
 ♦ Egyptian girl
 ♦ Egyptian
ägyptisch, adj
 ♦ Egyptian, adj
ägyptische Art, adv *gastr*
 nach ägyptischer Art, adv *gastr*
 ♦ Egyptian style, adv *gastr*
Ahornsirup, m
 ♦ maple syrup
Ahr, f
 ♦ Ahr River
 ♦ River Ahr
 ♦ Ahr
Ahrtal, n
 ♦ Ahr valley
Ahrwein, m
 ♦ Ahr wine
Aide-cuisinier, m/f *FR*
 Beikoch, m
 Beiköchin, f
 ♦ aide-cuisinier *FR*
 ♦ assistant cook
Aide de cuisine, m/f *FR*
 Küchenhilfe, f
 ♦ aide de cuisine *FR*
 ♦ kitchen helper *AE*
 ♦ kitchen hand
 ♦ kitchen help
Aide de réception, m/f *FR*
 Empfangsgehilfe, m
 Empfangsgehilfin, f
 ♦ aide de réception *FR*
 ♦ junior receptionist
 ♦ trainee receptionist
Aide de salle, m/f *FR*
 ♦ aide de salle *FR*
Aide d'étage, m/f *FR*
 ♦ aide d'étage *FR*
Aide directrice, f *FR*
 Direktionsassistentin, f
 ♦ aide directrice *FR*
 ♦ assistant manager
Aide du patron, m/f *FR*
 ♦ aide du patron *FR*
Airbus, m
 ♦ airbus
Airlinegutschein, m
 Gutschein einer Fluggesellschaft m
 ♦ airline voucher
Airliner, m *coll*
 (Mitarbeiter einer Fluggesellschaft)
 ♦ airliner
Airline Tour Order, f
 ATO

 ♦ airline tour order
 ♦ ATO
akklimatisieren sich (an etw)
 ♦ acclimatise (oneself to s.th.)
 ♦ acclimatize (oneself to s.th.)
Akklimatisierung, f
 ♦ acclimatisation
 ♦ acclimatization
Aknebehandlung, f
 ♦ acne treatment
Akrobat, m
 ♦ acrobat
Akropolis, f
 ♦ Acropolis, the
Aktentasche, f
 Aktenmappe f
 ♦ briefcase
Aktiengesellschaft, f
 AG, f
 ♦ joint-stock corporation *AE*
 ♦ joint-stock company
 ♦ public limited company *BE*
 ♦ plc *BE*
 ♦ PLC *BE*
Aktionärsversammlung, f
 Generalversammlung, f
 ♦ stockholders' meeting *AE*
 ♦ shareholders' meeting *BE*
Aktionsferien, pl
 Aktionsurlaub, m
 ♦ action holiday *BE*
 ♦ action vacation *AE*
aktionsgeladener Urlaub, m
 aktionsgeladene Ferien, pl
 ♦ action-packed vacation *AE*
 ♦ action-packed holiday *BE*
Aktionsplan, m
 ♦ action plan
Aktionsprogramm, n
 ♦ action program *AE*
 ♦ action programme *BE*
Aktionstag, m
 ♦ action day
Aktionsurlaub, m
 Aktionsferien, pl
 ♦ action vacation *AE*
 ♦ action holiday *BE*
Aktionsurlaubszentrum, n
 Aktionsferienzentrum, n
 ♦ action holiday centre *BE*
 ♦ action vacation center *AE*
Aktionswoche, f
 ♦ action week
Aktionswochenende, n
 ♦ action weekend
 ♦ action-packed weekend
Aktiva, pl
 (Bilanz)
 ♦ assets *pl*
Aktiva und Passiva, pl
 ♦ assets and liabilities *pl*
Aktiven, m/f pl
 ♦ active, the *pl*
 ♦ energetic, the *pl*
aktiver Besucher, m
 ♦ energetic visitor
 ♦ active visitor
aktiver Urlaub, m
 ♦ active vacation *AE*
 ♦ active holiday *BE*

aktiver Vulkan, m
 ♦ active volcano
Aktivfreizeit, f
 → Aktivurlaub
Aktivkurzurlaub, m
 ♦ activity break
Aktivprogramm, n
 ♦ activity program *AE*
 ♦ activities program *AE*
 ♦ activity programme *BE*
 ♦ activities programme *BE*
Aktivurlaub, m
 Aktivferien, pl
 ♦ activity vacation *AE*
 ♦ activity holiday *BE*
Aktivurlauber, m
 Aktivferiengast, m
 aktiver Urlauber, m
 aktiver Feriengast, m
 ♦ active vacationer *AE*
 ♦ active holidaymaker *BE*
Aktivwoche, f
 ♦ activity week
Aktivwochenende, n
 ♦ activity weekend
aktueller Kurs, m
 ♦ current rate
aktueller Preis, m
 gerade geltender Preis, m
 Tagespreis, m
 ♦ current price
 ♦ current rate
aktuelles Programm, n
 laufendes Programm n
 ♦ current program *AE*
 ♦ current programme *BE*
aktuelles Saisonangebot, n
 ♦ offer for (the) current season
Akupunktur, f
 ♦ acupuncture
Akustik f
 ♦ acoustics *pl*
akute Bettenknappheit f
 ♦ acute shortage of beds
akuter Bettenmangel, m (Knappheit)
 → akute Bettenknappheit
akuter Bettenmangel, m (völliges Fehlen)
 ♦ acute lack of beds
akuter Unterkunftsmangel, m (Knappheit)
 ♦ acute shortage of accommodations *AE*
 ♦ acute shortage of accommodation *BE*
akuter Unterkunftsmangel, m (völliges Fehlen)
 ♦ acute lack of accommodations *AE*
 ♦ acute lack of accommodation *BE*
Alabasterbildnis, n
 Alabasterfigur, f
 ♦ alabaster effigy
à la carte, adv
 nach der Karte, adv
 ♦ a la carte, adv *AE*
 ♦ à la carte, adv *BE*
A-la-carte-Abendessen, n (Dinner)
 A-la-carte-Diner, n
 ♦ à-la-carte dinner
 ♦ a-la-carte dinner *AE*
A-la-carte-Abendessen, n (Supper)
 A-la-carte-Nachtessen, n *SCHW*
 ♦ à-la-carte supper
 ♦ a-la-carte supper *AE*

A-la-carte-Angebot, n
- à-la-carte offer
- a-la-carte offer *AE*

A-la-carte-Auswahl, f
- à-la-carte selection
- a-la-carte selection *AE*

à la carte auswählen
- à la carte wählen
- select à la carte *Be*
- choose à la carte *BE*
- select a la carte *AE*
- choose a la carte *AE*

A-la-carte-Bedienung, f
A-la-carte-Service, m
- à-la-carte service
- a-la-carte service *AE*

à la carte bestellen
nach der Karte bestellen
- order a la carte *AE*
- order à la carte *BE*
- order from the menu

A-la-carte-Bestellung, f
- à-la-carte order
- order à la carte
- ordering à la carte
- a-la-carte order *AE*
- order a la carte *AE*

A-la-carte-Betrieb, m
- à-la-carte establishment
- à-la-carte operation
- a-la-carte establishment *AE*
- a-la-carte operation *AE*

à la carte essen
→ essen à la carte

A-la-carte-Frühstück, n
- à-la-carte breakfast
- a-la-carte breakfast *AE*

A-la-carte-Gast, m
- à-la-carte guest
- a-la-carte guest *AE*

A-la-carte-Gericht, n
- à-la-carte dish
- a-la-carte dish *AE*

A-la-carte-Geschäft, n
- à-la-carte business
- a-la-carte business *AE*

A-la-carte-Gutschein, m
- à-la-carte voucher
- a-la-carte voucher *AE*

A-la-carte-Karte, f
→ A-la-carte-Speisekarte

A-la-carte-Küche, f (Raum)
- à-la-carte kitchen
- a-la-carte kitchen *AE*

A-la-carte-Küche, f (Speisen)
- à-la-carte cuisine
- à-la-carte cooking
- a-la-carte cuisine *AE*
- a-la-carte cooking *AE*

A-la-carte-Kunde, m
- à-la-carte customer
- a-la-carte customer *AE*

A-la-carte-Kundin f
→ A-la-carte-Kunde m

A-la-carte-Mahlzeit, f
- à-la-carte meal
- a-la-carte meal *AE*

A-la-carte-Menü, n
- à-la-carte menu
- a-la-carte menu *AE*

A-la-carte-Mittagessen, n
- à-la-carte luncheon
- à-la-carte lunch
- a-la-carte luncheon *AE*
- a-la-carte lunch *AE*

A-la-carte-Nachtessen, n
→ A-la-carte-Abendessen

A-la-carte-Rechnung, f
- à-la-carte bill
- a-la-carte check *AE*

A-la-carte-Restaurant, n
- à-la-carte restaurant
- a-la-carte restaurant *AE*

A-la-carte-Service, m
→ A-la-carte-Bedienung

A-la-carte-Speise f
→ A-la-carte-Gericht

A-la-carte-Speisekarte, f
Große Speisekarte, f
Große Karte, f
- à-la-carte menu
- a-la-carte menu *AE*

à la carte speisen
nach der Karte speisen
- dine à la carte *AE*
- dine à la carte *BE*

A-la-carte-Spezialität, f
- a-la-carte specialty *AE*
- à-la-carte speciality *BE*

à la minute, adv
auf Bestellung zubereitet, adv
- à la minute, adv
- to order, adv
- cooked to order, adv

Alarmanlage, f
→ Einbruchwarnanlage

Alaska
- Alaska

Alaskakreuzfahrt, f
- Alaska cruise

Albaner, m
- Albanian

Albanerin, f
- Albanian girl
- Albanian woman
- Albanian

Albanien
- Albania

albanisch, adj
- Albanian, adj

Albergo, m *ITAL*
- albergo *ITAL*

Aldeburgher Festspiele, die, n pl
- Aldeburgh Festival, the

al dente, adv *ITAL*
- al dente, adv *ITAL*

Ale, n
(obergäriges Bier in GB)
- ale

Alemanne, m
- Alemannian

Alemannen, die, pl
- Alemanni, the *pl*

alemannisch, adj
- Alemannic, adj
- Alemannian, adj

alemannische Spezialität, f *gast*
- Alemannian speciality *gast*
- Alemannian specialty *AE gast*
- Alemannic speciality *gast*
- Alemannic specialty *AE gast*

Aletschgletscher, m
- Aletsch Glacier, the

Aleuten, pl
- Aleutian Islands, the *pl*

Algarve, f
- Algarve, the

Alge, f
Tang, m
Algen, f pl
- alga
- algae *pl*

Algenbad, n
- algae bath

Algenwickel, m
- algae wrap

Algerien
- Algeria

Algerier, m
- Algerian

Algerierin, f
- Algerian girl
- Algerian woman
- Algerian

algerisch, adj
- Algerian, adj

alias, adv
- alias, adv
- also known as, adv
- aka, adv *inform*

Alkohol, m
- alcohol
- liquor

alkoholarm, adj
- low-alcohol, adj
- low in alcohol

alkoholarmes Bier n
- low-alcohol beer

alkoholarmes Getränk, n
- low-alcohol drink
- low-alcohol beverage

Alkoholausschankzeiten, f pl
→ Schankzeit, Ausschankzeit

Alkohol ausschenken (an jn)
- serve alcohol (to s.o.)

Alkoholessig, m
- spirit vinegar

alkoholfrei, adj
- alcohol-free, adj
- nonalcoholic, adj *BE*
- non-alcoholic, adj

alkoholfreies Bier, n
- nonalcoholic beer *AE*
- non-alcoholic beer *BE*

alkoholfreies Getränk, n
- alcohol-free beverage
- soft drink

Alkoholgegner, m
Abstinenzler, m
- teetotaler *AE*
- teetotaller *BE*
- abstainer
- total abstainer
- TT

Alkoholgehalt, m
(von Getränken)
- proof
- alcohol content *AE*
- alcoholic content

Alkoholika, pl
→ alkoholische Getränke

Alkoholiker

Alkoholiker, m
  Trunksüchtiger, m
  ♦ alcoholic
  ♦ drunkard
alkoholisch, adj
  ♦ alcoholic, adj
alkoholische Getränke ausschenken
  ♦ serve alcoholic drinks
  ♦ serve alcoholic beverages
alkoholischer Getränkebestand, m
  alkoholischer Getränkevorrat, m
  Vorrat an alkoholischen Getränken, m
  Spirituosenvorrat, m
  Spirituosenbestand, m
  ♦ liquor stock
alkoholisches Getränk, n
  ♦ alcoholic beverage
  ♦ alcoholic drink
  ♦ liquor jur
Alkoholismus, m
  ♦ alcoholism
Alkoholismus bekämpfen
  ♦ fight alcoholism
Alkoholkonsum, m
  Alkoholverbrauch, m
  ♦ consumption of alcohol
  ♦ alcohol consumption
Alkoholkonsument, m
  ♦ alcohol consumer
Alkoholmißbrauch, m
  ♦ alcohol abuse
Alkoholproblem, n
  ♦ drink problem
Alkoholproblem haben
  ♦ have a drink problem
alkoholreich, adj
  ♦ high-alcohol, adj
  ♦ high in alcohol
Alkoholschmuggler, m
  ♦ rum-runner AE
  ♦ bootlegger
Alkoholsteuer, f
  ♦ alcoholic beverage tax
  ♦ liquor excise AE
Alkohol trinken
  ♦ drink alcohol
Alkoholverbot, n
  ♦ ban on alcohol
  ♦ prohibition
Alkoholverbrauch, m
  Alkoholkonsum, m
  ♦ alcohol consumption
  ♦ consumption of alcohol
Alkoholvergiftung, f
  ♦ alcohol poisoning
Alkoven, m
  ♦ alcove
Alkovenbett, n
  ♦ alcove bed
Alkovenzimmer, n
  ♦ alcove room
allabendlich, adv
  ♦ every evening, adv
  ♦ every night, adv
Alle Appartements werden einmal wöchentlich gereinigt
  ♦ All apartments are cleaned once a week
Alle Betten sind belegt
  ♦ All beds are occupied
Allee, f
  ♦ tree-lined road
  ♦ tree-lined street
  ♦ (tree-lined) avenue
  ♦ tree-lined boulevard
Alle Einzelheiten sind in dem Prospekt aufgeführt
  ♦ All details are outlined in the brochure
Alle früheren Tarife sind ungültig
  ♦ All previous tariffs are void
Alle Gäste erhalten ein Begrüßungsgetränk und ein Abschiedsessen (Dinner)
  ♦ All guests will have a welcome drink and
  ♦ a farewell dinner
Alle Gerichte werden auf Bestellung zubereitet
  ♦ All dishes are cooked to order
Alle Hotelzimmer sind ausgebucht
  Alle Hotelzimmer sind belegt
  ♦ All hotel rooms are booked (up)
Alleinbenutzung, f
  Einzelbelegung, f
  ♦ sole use (of a room)
  ♦ single occupancy
Alleinbenutzung eines Zimmers, f
  Einzelbelegung eines Zimmers, f
  ♦ single occupancy of a room
  ♦ sole use of a room
Alleinbenutzungszuschlag m
  ♦ single-occupancy supplement
  ♦ supplement for single occupancy
allein essen
  ♦ eat by oneself
alleiniger Besitz, m
  ♦ single ownership
alleiniger Mieter, m
  → Alleinmieter
Alleinkoch, m
  Alleinköchin f
  ♦ general cook
  ♦ sole cook
  ♦ only cook
Alleinmieter, m
  alleiniger Mieter m
  ♦ sole tenant
  ♦ single tenant
Alleinnutzer eines Zimmers, m
  alleiniger Nutzer eines Zimmers, m
  ♦ sole occupant of a room
Alleinnutzung, f
  → Alleinbenutzung
allein oder in Gruppen reisen
  ♦ travel alone or in groups
Alleinpacht, f
  ♦ exclusive leasehold
  ♦ exclusive lease
Alleinpatissier, m
  ♦ general pastry-cook
  ♦ sole pastry-cook
  ♦ only pastry-cook
Alleinportier, m
  ♦ general porter
  ♦ sole porter
  ♦ only porter
allein reisen
  ♦ travel alone
alleinreisend, adj
  ♦ unaccompanied, adj
  ♦ traveling on one's own, adj AE
  ♦ travelling on one's own, adj BE
  ♦ traveling alone, adj AE
  ♦ travelling alone, adj BE
alleinreisende Frau, f
  ♦ unaccompanied lady
  ♦ unaccompanied woman
  ♦ woman travelling alone BE
  ♦ woman traveling alone AE
Alleinreisender, m
  → Einzelreisender, Individualreisender
alleinreisender Minderjähriger, m
  Minderjähriger ohne Begleitung, m
  ♦ UM
  ♦ unaccompanied minor
alleinreisendes Kind n
  ♦ unaccompanied child
  ♦ child traveling alone AE
  ♦ child travelling alone BE
allein sein
  ♦ be on one's own
allein sein wollen
  ♦ want to be on one's own
allein skilaufen
  allein skifahren
  ♦ ski on one's own
alleinstehend, adj (Gebäude)
  ♦ detached, adj
alleinstehend, adj (Person)
  → ledig, unverheiratet
Alleinstehender, m
  Alleinstehende f
  ♦ single
  ♦ single man
  ♦ single woman
alleinstehendes Haus, n
  → freistehendes Haus
Alleinunterhalter, m
  ♦ general entertainer
  ♦ solo entertainer
Alleinunterhaltung, f
  ♦ one-man show
allein Urlaub machen
  ♦ vacation alone AE
  ♦ holiday alone BE
Alleinvermittler, m
  alleiniger Vermittler, m
  ♦ sole booking agent
  ♦ only booking agent
Alleinvertreter, m
  ♦ sole agent
Alleinvertretung, f
  ♦ sole agency
Alleinvertretungsvereinbarung, f
  ♦ sole agency agreement
Alleinwanderung, f
  ♦ solo hike
Alle Leistungen inbegriffen
  ♦ All services included
Alle Mahlzeiten werden gemäß Verzehr berechnet
  ♦ All meals are charged as taken
Alle Nebenkosten sind inbegriffen
  ♦ All extras are included
allen Komfort genießen
  ♦ enjoy all the comforts
  ♦ enjoy all the amenities
Alle Preise inklusive Bedienung und Mehrwertsteuer
  Alle Preise inkl. Bedienung und Mwst.
  ♦ All prices include service and value added tax
  ♦ All prices include service and VAT
Alle Preise ohne Mehrwertsteuer
  ♦ All prices exlusive of value added tax
  ♦ All rates exclusive of value added tax
Alle Preise sind in $
  ♦ All prices in $
  ♦ All rates in $

alle Puppen tanzen lassen
   die Puppen tanzen lassen
   ♦ have a fling
   ♦ live it up
Allerbeste an Komfort und Service bieten, das
   ♦ offer the ultimate in comfort and service
Allerbeste an Luxus und Qualität bieten, das
   ♦ provide the ultimate in quality and luxury
alle Rekorde brechen
   ♦ break all records
Allergie, f
   ♦ allergy
Allergie haben
   ♦ have an allergy
Allerweltshotel, n *derog*
   ♦ run-of-the-mill hotel *derog*
Allerweltskost, f *derog*
   ♦ run-of-the-mill fare *derog*
Allerweltsrestaurant, n *derog*
   ♦ run-of-the-mill restaurant *derog*
alles aufessen
   ♦ eat it all up
Alles aussteigen!
   ♦ All out!
Alle Schlafzimmer mit eigenen Sanitäreinrichtungen
   ♦ All bedrooms have private facilities
Alles einsteigen!
   ♦ All aboard!
alles Eßbare, n
   ♦ everything eatable
alles Gute wünschen jm
   ♦ wish s.o. all the best
alles inbegriffen
   ♦ everything included
   ♦ all included
   ♦ all-in *BE coll*
Alle sind herzlich zur Teilnahme eingeladen
   ♦ All are cordially invited to participate
Alles-Inklusiv-Arrangement, n
   Alles-Inklusiv-Vereinbarung, f
   ♦ all-inclusive arrangement
   ♦ all-in arrangement
Alles-Inklusiv-Aufenthalt, m
   ♦ all-inclusive stay
Alles-Inklusiv-Cluburlaub, m
   Alles-Inklusiv-Clubferien, pl
   ♦ all-inclusive club vacation *AE*
   ♦ all-inclusive club holiday *BE*
Alles-Inklusiv-Gebühr f
   ♦ all-inclusive fee
   ♦ all-inclusive charge
Alles-Inklusiv-Hotelarrangement n
   Alles-Inklusiv-Hotelvereinbarung f
   ♦ all-inclusive hotel arrangement
Alles-Inklusiv-Kreuzfahrt, f
   ♦ all-inclusive cruise
Alles-Inklusiv-Menü, n
   ♦ all-inclusive menu
Alles-Inklusiv-Preis, m
   ♦ all-inclusive price
   ♦ all-inclusive rate
Alles-Inklusiv-Urlaubsort, m
   Alles-Inklusiv-Ferienort, m
   ♦ all-inclusive resort
alles ist 1 a *coll*
   ♦ everything is A 1 *coll*
   ♦ everything is first class
alles ist in Butter *coll*
   alles ist in schönster Ordnung
   ♦ everything is in apple-pie order *coll*

alles Nötige veranlassen
   ♦ make all necessary arrangements
Alle Stornierungswünsche müssen in schriftlicher
   Form vorgenommen werden
   ♦ All cancellation requests must be made in writing
   ♦ All cancelation requests must be made in writing *AE*
alles tun für js Komfort
   ♦ do everything for s.o.'s comfort
Alles umsteigen!
   ♦ All change!
Alle Zimmer haben (eine) Dusche
   ♦ All rooms have showers
Alle Zimmer haben ein eigenes Bad
   ♦ All rooms have private baths
Alle Zimmer haben Landblick
   ♦ All rooms have land view
Alle Zimmer haben Meerblick
   Alle Zimmer haben Meeresblick
   ♦ All rooms have sea view
Alle Zimmer können als Einzelzimmer vermietet werden
   ♦ All rooms can be rented as single rooms *AE*
   ♦ All rooms can be let as single rooms *BE*
Alle Zimmer liegen nach Norden
   ♦ All rooms face north
Alle Zimmer liegen nach Osten
   ♦ All rooms face east
Alle Zimmer liegen nach Süden
   ♦ All rooms face south
Alle Zimmer liegen nach Westen
   ♦ All rooms face west
alle Zimmer liegen zum Garten
   ♦ All rooms face the garden
alle Zimmer liegen zum Meer
   ♦ All rooms face the sea
Alle Zimmer liegen zum Park
   ♦ All rooms face the park
Alle Zimmer mit Aussicht
   ♦ All rooms have a view
Alle Zimmer mit Bad oder Dusche
   ♦ All rooms with bath or shower
Alle Zimmer mit Balkon
   ♦ All rooms with balcony
Alle Zimmer mit Land- oder Meerblick
   Alle Zimmer mit Land- oder Meeresblick
   ♦ All rooms have land- or seaviews *AE*
   ♦ All rooms have land- or sea views *BE*
Alle Zimmer mit Privatbad, Radio, Farbfernseher und Telefon
   ♦ All rooms with private bath, radio, color TV and telephone *AE*
   ♦ All rooms with private bath, radio, colour TV and telephone *BE*
Alle Zimmer mit Wechselsprechanlage und Radio
   ♦ All rooms with intercom and radio
Alle Zimmer sind bis 28. August ausgebucht
   ♦ All rooms are booked (up) until 28 August
Alle Zimmer sind gleich
   ♦ All rooms are identical
Alle Zimmer sind schallisoliert
   ♦ All rooms are sound-insulated
Alle Zimmer sind verschieden
   ♦ All rooms are different
Allgäu, n
   (Region)
   ♦ Allgäu, the
   ♦ Algäu, the

Allgäuer Alpen, die, pl
   (Region)
   ♦ Allgäu Alps, the *pl*
   ♦ Algäu Alps, the *pl*
Allgäuer Berge, die, m pl
   ♦ Allgäu mountains, the *pl*
   ♦ Algäu mountains, the *pl*
Allgäuregion, f
   ♦ Allgäu region
   ♦ Algäu region
allgemeine Ausgaben, f pl
   allgemeine Aufwendungen, f pl
   ♦ general expenses *pl*
allgemeine Geschäftsbedingungen, f pl
   AGB, f pl
   ♦ terms of trade *pl*
   ♦ terms of business *pl*
   ♦ standard-form contract conditions *pl*
allgemeine Öffentlichkeit, f
   ♦ general public, the
allgemeiner Aufwand, m
   ♦ general expenditure
allgemeine Reisebedingungen, f pl
   ♦ general travel conditions *pl*
Allgemeinraum, m
   → öffentlich zugänglicher Raum
Alltagshetze, f
   Hetze des Alltags, f
   ♦ hurry of daily life, the
Alltagstrott, m
   ♦ daily grind
Alltagstrott entkommen
   ♦ escape the daily grind
Allwetterattraktion, f
   ♦ all-weather attraction
Allwetterbad, n
   Allwetterbecken, n
   ♦ all-weather pool
Allwetterbetrieb, m
   ♦ all-weather operation
   ♦ all-weather establishment
Allwettereinrichtung, f
   ♦ all-weather facility
Allwetterschwimmbad, n
   Allwetterschwimmbecken, n
   Allwetterbad, n
   ♦ all-weather swimming pool *AE*
   ♦ all-weather swimming-pool *BE*
   ♦ all-weather pool
Allwetterspielfeld, n
   ♦ all-weather pitch
Allwettertennisplatz, m
   ♦ all-weather tennis court
Allzweckhalle, f
   Allzwecksaal, m
   ♦ all-purpose hall
Allzweckraum, m
   Allzweckzimmer, n
   ♦ all-purpose room
Almhütte, f
   ♦ Alpine hut
Alpen, die, pl
   ♦ Alps, the, *pl*
Alpenausflug, m
   Ausflug in die Alpen, m
   ♦ Alpine excursion
   ♦ excursion to the Alps
Alpenbach, m
   ♦ Alpine stream

Alpenblick

Alpenblick, m
- Alpine view
- view of the Alps

Alpendorf n
- Alpine village

Alpenerholungsort, m
Alpenferienort, m
Alpenort, m
- Alpine resort

Alpengebiet, n (groß)
Alpenregion, f
- Alpine region

Alpengebiet, n (klein)
- Alpine area

Alpengipfel, m
- Alpine summit

Alpenglühen, n
- Alpine glow

Alpenheilbad, n
- Alpine health resort

Alpenhotel n
- Alpine hotel

Alpenkurort, m
- Alpine spa

Alpenlandschaft, f
- Alpine scenery
- Alpine landscape

Alpenpark, m
- Alpine park

Alpenpaß, m
- Alpine pass

Alpenpflanze, f
- Alpine plant

Alpenrepublik, f
- Alpine republic

Alpenroute, f
Alpenstrecke, f
- Alpine route

Alpenstadt, f (Großstadt)
- Alpine city

Alpenstadt, f (kleine Stadt)
- Alpine town

Alpenstock, m
- alpenstock

Alpenstraße, f (Eigenname)
- Alpine Road, the

Alpenstraße, f (generell)
- Alpine road

Alpental, n
- Alpine valley

Alpentourismus, m
Alpenfremdenverkehr m
- Alpine tourism
- tourism to the Alps

Alpentourist, m
- Alpine tourist
- tourist to the Alps

Alpen überqueren
- cross the Alps

Alpenüberquerung, f
- crossing of the Alps

Alpenverein, m
- Alpine Club, the

Alpenvorland, n
- foothills of the Alps pl

Alpenwelt, f
- Alpine world

Alpenwiese, f
Alpenmatte, f
- Alpine meadow

alphabetische Gästekartei f
- alphabetical guest index
- guests' alphabetical index

alphabetische Gästeliste f
alphabetisches Gästeverzeichnis n
- alphabetical guest list

alphabetische Kartei f
- alphabetical index

alphabetische Reihenfolge, f
- alphabetical order

Alphorn, n
- Alpine horn

Alpinismus, m
- alpinism

Alpinist, m
- alpinist
- mountaineer

Alpinklettern, n
Alpinklettersport, m
- Alpine climbing

Alpinschule, f
- Alpine ski and mountaineering school

Alpinski, m
Alpinskilauf, m
Ski Alpin, m
- Alpine skiing
- downhill skiing

Alpinskifahrer, m
Alpinskiläufer, m
- Alpine skier
- downhill skier

Alpinskipiste, f
- Alpine ski run
- Alpine ski piste

Alpinskischule, f
- Alpine ski school
- down-hill ski school

Alptraum, m
- nightmare

Alpträume haben
- have nightmares

als Leihgabe
- as a loan

als schlechtes Omen nehmen etw
- take s.th. as a bad omen

Alstersee, m
(in Hamburg)
- Alster Lake, (the)

Altaigebirge, n
- Altai Mountains, the pl

Altar, m
- altar

Altarbild, n
Altargemälde, n
- altarpiece

Altargemälde, n
- altar painting

Altarraum, m
- chancel

Altartisch, m
- altar table

Altbier, n
(obergäriges Bier)
Alt, n
- Altbier
- ale

alteingeführt, adj
alteingesessen, adj
- old-established, adj
- well-established, adj

alteingeführtes Hotel n
- old-established hotel

alteingeführtes Restaurant, n
- old-established restaurant

alteingesessen, adj
→ alteingeführt

alte Jungfer, f
- old maid

Altenheim n
Altersheim n
- old people's home
- old folk's home coll
- home for the elderly

Altennachmittag, m
→ Seniorennachmittag

Altentagesstätte, f
- senior day care center AE
- geriatric day-care center AE
- geriatric day-care centre BE

alter Baumbestand, m
- mature trees pl

ältere Leute, pl
- elderly people pl
- older people pl

Alte Residenz, f (Eigenname)
- Old Residence, the

alter Garten, m
- mature garden

Alternativangebot, n
Ersatzangebot, n
anderweitiges Angebot, n
Ausweichangebot, n
- alternative offer BE
- alternate offer AE

Alternativbehandlung, f med
alternative Behandlung, f med
- alternate treatment AE med
- alternative treatment BE med

alternative Formen des Tourismus, f pl
- alternate forms of tourism AE pl
- alternative forms of tourism BE pl

alternativer Tourismus, m
alternativer Fremdenverkehr, m
- alternate tourism AE
- alternative tourism BE

alternativer Tourist, m
- alternate tourist AE
- alternative tourist BE

alternativer Urlaub, m
→ Alternativurlaub

Alternativkosten, pl
Opportunitätskosten, pl
- opportunity cost
- opportunity costs pl

Alternativprogramm, n
Ersatzprogramm, n
anderweitiges Programm, n
- alternative programme BE
- alternate program AE

Alternativreisen, n
Alternativreiseverkehr, m
- alternate travel AE
- alternative travel BE

Alternativreisender, m
- alternate traveler AE
- alternative traveller BE

Alternativurlaub m
alternativer Urlaub, m
Alternativferien, pl
- alternative Ferien, pl

♦ alternative holiday BE
♦ alternate vacation AE
Altersbeschränkung, f
  Altersbegrenzung, f
  ♦ age restriction
Altersgrenze, f
  ♦ age limit
Altersgruppe, f
  ♦ age group
  ♦ age bracket
Altersheim, n
  Altenheim, n
  ♦ home for the aged
  ♦ old people's home
Altersprofil, n
  ♦ age profile
Altersruhesitz, m
  Ruhesitz (im Alter), m
  ♦ retirement home
Alterssegment, n
  ♦ age segment
  ♦ age group
Altersstruktur, f
  ♦ age structure
Alterswohnung, f
  Seniorenwohnung, f
  ♦ retirement flat BE
  ♦ retirement apartment AE
alter Trakt, m
  alter Flügel, m
  ♦ old wing
altertümliche Möbel, n pl
  ♦ old-world furniture sg
alter Wein, m
  ♦ old wine
altes Gebäude, n
  ♦ old building
  ♦ ancient building
alte Siedlung, f
  ♦ ancient settlement
Altes Rathaus, n (Eigenname)
  ♦ Old Town Hall, the
ältestes erhaltenes Gebäude, n
  ♦ oldest building that survives
ältestes Hotel in Schottland, n
  ♦ oldest hotel in Scotland
alte und doch junge Stadt, f
  ♦ old and yet young town
Alte Welt, die, f
  ♦ Old World, the
altmodisch, adj
  ♦ old-fashioned, adj
altmodische Gastlichkeit, f
  ♦ old-fashioned hospitality
altmodische Möbel, n pl
  ♦ old-fashioned furniture sg
altmodischer Komfort, m
  ♦ old-fashioned comfort
altmodischer Service, m
  ♦ old-fashioned service
altmodisches Hotel, n
  ♦ old-fashioned hotel
Altmühltal, n
  ♦ Altmühl valley, the
Altrhein, m
  ♦ Old Rhine, the
Altstadt f
  ♦ Old Town, the
  ♦ old part of the town
  ♦ old part of the city

Altstadtfest, n
  ♦ Old Town festival
Aluminiumfolie, f
  ♦ aluminium foil BE
  ♦ aluminum foil AE
am 22. September
  ♦ on 22 September
am 22. September um 20 Uhr
  ♦ on 22 September at 8 p.m.
  ♦ on 22 September at 22 hours
am Abend
  ♦ in the evening
am Abend des 8. November
  ♦ on the evening of 8 November
Am Abend spielt die Hauskapelle zum Tanz auf
  ♦ In the evening, there is dancing to the resident
  ♦ band
am Anfang der Reise
  am Reiseanfang
  ♦ at the start of the journey
  ♦ at the start of the trip
  ♦ at the start of the tour
Amateur, m
  ♦ amateur
Amateurorchester, n
  ♦ amateur orchestra
Amateursportveranstaltung, f
  ♦ amateur sports event
  ♦ amateur sport event
  ♦ amateur sporting event
Amateurverein, m
  Amateurclub, m
  ♦ amateur club
Amateurwettbewerb, m
  ♦ amateur competition
Amateurwettkampf, m
  ♦ amateur contest
am Aufenthaltsbeginn
  ♦ at the beginning of the stay
am Aufenthaltsende
  ♦ at the end of the stay
Amazonas, m
  ♦ Amazon River, the
  ♦ River Amazon, the
  ♦ Amazon, the
am Beginn der Reise
  am Reisebeginn
  zu Beginn der Reise
  zu Reisebeginn
  ♦ at the beginning of the journey
  ♦ at the beginning of the tour
  ♦ at the beginning of the trip
am Beginn der Reisen
  ♦ at the start of one's travels
  ♦ at the beginning of one's travels
am besten besucht, adj
  ♦ best attended, adj
am besten besuchte Veranstaltung, f
  ♦ best attended event
  ♦ best attended function
am besten erhalten, adj
  ♦ best preserved, adj
am besten erhaltenes Schloß, n
  ♦ best preserved castle
am Bett
  ♦ at the bedside
Ambiente, n
  ♦ ambience
  ♦ ambiance

Ambiente abgeben für etw
  ♦ supply the ambience for s.th.
  ♦ supply the ambiance for s.th.
Ambiente eines Hotels, n
  ♦ ambience of a hotel
  ♦ ambiance of a hotel
Ambiente genießen von etw
  ♦ enjoy the ambience of s.th.
  ♦ enjoy the ambiance of s.th.
Ambiente ist freundlich
  ♦ ambience is friendly
  ♦ ambiance is friendly
Ambiente schaffen (für etw)
  ♦ create an ambience (for s.th.)
  ♦ create an ambiance (for s.th.)
am Dienstag
  ♦ on Tuesday
am Donnerstag
  ♦ on Thursday
am Dorfende
  ♦ at the end of the village
am Dorfrand
  ♦ at the edge of the village
  ♦ on the outskirts of the village
  ♦ on the edge of the village AE
am Ende der Fahrt
  am Fahrtende
  ♦ at the end of the trip
American Bar f
  ♦ American bar
American breakfast, n
  → amerikanisches Frühstück
American Plan, m
  Zimmer mit Vollpension, n
  AP, m
  ♦ American Plan
  ♦ AP
  ♦ full-board terms pl
Amerika
  ♦ America
Amerikabesucher, m
  ♦ visitor to America
Amerikaner, m
  ♦ American
Amerikanerin, f
  ♦ American girl
  ♦ American woman
  ♦ American
amerikanisch, adj
  ♦ American, adj
amerikanische Art, adv gastr
  nach amerikanischer Art, adv gastr
  ♦ American style, adv gastr
Amerikanischer Abend, m
  ♦ American Evening
Amerikanischer Hotel- und Motelverband, m
  ♦ American Hotel and Motel Association
Amerikanischer Reisebüroverband, m
  ♦ American Society of Travel Agents
  ♦ ASTA
amerikanischer Service, m
  Service à l'américaine, m FR
  ♦ American service
  ♦ service à l'américaine FR
amerikanisches Frühstück, n
  (mit Eierspeisen, Speck, Toast)
  ♦ American breakfast
Amerikaprospekt, m
  ♦ America brochure
Amerikareise, f (in Amerika)
  Amerikarundreise, f

Amerikareise

Amerikareise
- tour of America
- American tour

Amerikareise, f (nach Amerika)
Reise nach Amerika, f
- tour to America
- journey to America
- trip to America

Amerikareisen, n
Amerikareiseverkehr, m
- travel to America

Amerikatournee, f
- American tour
- tour of America

am Eröffnungstag
- on the opening day

am Fluß entlang
entlang des Flusses
- along the riverside

am Freitag
- on Friday

am frühen Abend
- early in the evening
- in the early evening

am frühen Morgen
am frühen Vormittag
- early in the morning
- in the early morning

am frühen Nachmittag
- in the early afternoon

am frühen Vormittag
→ am frühen Morgen

am Frühstückstisch
- at the breakfast table

am Fuß von etw
(Berg)
- at the foot of s.th.

am häufigsten besuchte Stadt, f
- most frequently visited town

am häufigsten konsumiertes Getränk, n
- most frequently consumed drink
- most frequently consumed beverage

am Hungertuch nagen
nichts zu essen haben
- be on short commons *idiom*
- dine with Duke Humphrey *idiom*

am Kamin sitzen
am Feuer sitzen
- sit by the fireside

am linken Ufer (Fluß)
auf dem linken Ufer (Fluß)
- on the left bank

am Meer, adv
an der See, adv
- by the sea, adv

am meisten bereist, adj
am meisten gereist, adj
am meisten befahren, adj
- most travelled, adj
- most traveled, adj *AE*

am Mittag
mittags, adv
- at noon

am Mittelmeer
- in the Mediterranean

am Mittwoch
- on Wednesday

am Montag
- on Monday

am Morgen, adv
am Vormittag, adv
- in the morning, adv

am Nachmittag
- in the afternoon

am Ort angebautes Gemüse, n
- locally grown vegetable

Amortisation, f (Anlageabschreibung)
- amortisation
- amortization
- depreciation
- writing-off

Amortisation, f (Schulden)
Tilgung, f
Amortisierung, f
- amortisation
- amortization
- liquidation *BE*
- amortizement *BE*

amortisieren etw (abschreiben)
→ abschreiben

Amortisierung, f
→ Amortisation

amouröser Besuch, m
- amorous visit

Amphitheater, n
- amphitheater *AE*
- amphitheatre *BE*

am Rand der Wüste
am Wüstenrand
- at the edge of the desert
- on the edge of the desert *AE*

am rechten Ufer (Fluß)
auf dem rechten Ufer (Fluß)
- on the right bank

am Samstag
am Sonnabend
- on Saturday

am Sonnabend
→ am Samstag

am Sonntag
- on Sunday

am späten Nachmittag
- in the late afternoon

am späten Vormittag, adv
am späten Morgen, adv
spät morgens, adv
- late in the morning, adv

am Stadtrand (Großstadt)
- on the outskirts of a city
- at the edge of a city
- on the edge of a city *AE*

am Stadtrand (kleine Stadt)
- on the outskirts of a town
- at the edge of a town
- on the edge of a town *AE*

am Stand (Messe)
- at the stand
- on the stand

am stärksten befahrene Strecke, f
- most heavily travelled route
- most heavily traveled route *AE*

am Strand
auf dem Strand
- on the beach

am Strand liegen
auf dem Strand liegen
- lie on the beach

am Strandrand
- on the edge of the beach

am Tisch servieren
- serve at table

am Tisch sitzen (beim Essen)
- sit at table

am Tisch sitzen (generell)
- sit at the table

Amtliche Prüfungsnummer, f
(Wein)
A.P. Nummer, f
- certification number

amtlicher Führer m
(Buch)
- official guide

amtlicher Zimmernachweis, m
amtliche Zimmervermittlung f
- official accommodation service
- official booking agency

Amtrak-Zug, m
- Amtrak train *AE*

Amtstelefon, n
- post office telephone
- G.P.O. telephone *BE*

Amtstelefonanschluß, m
- post office telephone connection
- G.P.O. telephone connection *BE*

Amt zur Förderung des Tourismus, n
Verband zur Förderung des Fremdenverkehrs, m
- tourism promotion board

am Ufer der Themse
- on the bank of the Thames

am Ufer (Fluß)
- on the bank

am Ufer (Meer, Binnensee)
- on the shore

amulante Behandlung, f
- ambulant treatment

amüsanter Gast, m
unterhaltsamer Gast m
- entertaining guest

Amuse-gueule, m FR
Appetithappen m
Appetithäppchen n
- amuse-gueule *FR*
- appetizer
- appetiser

Amüsement, n
→ Vergnügung

amüsieren sich
sich vergnügen
- amuse oneself
- enjoy oneself
- have a good time
- have fun

amüsieren sich riesig
- enjoy oneself hugely

Amüsierviertel n
- pleasure quarter

am Verhandlungstisch
- at the negotiating table
- at the bargaining table

am Verhandlungstisch Platz nehmen
- sit down at the negotiating table
- sit down at the bargaining table

am Vormittag
→ am Morgen

am Waldrand
- on the edge of a wood
- at the edge of a wood
- on the edge of a forest
- at the edge of a forest

am wenigsten besucht, adj
- least visited, adj

am wenigsten besuchter Ort, m
- least visited place

am wenigsten besuchtes Gebiet, n
 ◆ least visited area
 ◆ least visited region
am Wochenende
 ◆ on the weekend *AE*
 ◆ at the weekend *BE*
am Zusammenfluß von X und Y
 ◆ at the confluence of X and Y
Analyse der Umsatzzusammensetzung, f
 ◆ sales mix analysis
 ◆ analysis of the sales mix
Ananas, f
 ◆ pineapple
Ananasbowle, f
 ◆ pineapple cup
 ◆ pineapple bowl
Ananaschutney, n
 ◆ pineapple chutney
Ananascoupe, f
 ◆ pineapple coupe
Ananaseiskrem, f
 Ananaseis, n
 ◆ pineapple ice cream *AE*
 ◆ pineapple ice-cream *BE*
 ◆ pineapple ice
Ananasflambé, n
 flambierte Ananas, f
 ◆ pineapple flambé
 ◆ flamed pineapple
Ananasgelee, n
 ◆ pineapple jelly
Ananaskaltschale, f
 ◆ cold pineapple soup
Ananaskompott, n
 ◆ stewed pineapples *pl*
 ◆ pineapple compôte *BE*
 ◆ pineapple compote *AE*
Ananaskonfitüre, f
 ◆ pineapple jam
Ananasmilchmixgetränk, n
 ◆ pineapple milk shake
Ananaspudding, m
 ◆ pineapple pudding
Ananasring, m
 ◆ pineapple ring
Ananassaft, m
 ◆ pineapple juice
Ananassalat, m
 ◆ pineapple salad
Ananasscheibe, f
 ◆ pineapple slice
 ◆ slice of pineapple
Ananasschiffchen, n
 ◆ pineapple barquette
Ananassorbet, n
 ◆ pineapple sorbet
Ananassoufflé, n
 Ananasauflauf, m
 ◆ pineapple soufflé *BE*
 ◆ pineapple souffle *AE*
Ananastorte, f
 ◆ pineapple tart
Ananaswürfel, m
 ◆ pineapple cube
Anatole, m
 Anatolier, m
 ◆ Anatolian
Anatolien
 ◆ Anatolia
anatolisch, adj
 ◆ Anatolian, adj

Anbau, m (Erweiterungsgebäude)
 Erweiterungsgebäude, n
 Erweiterungsbau, m
 ◆ extension
anbieten etw. auf der Speisekarte
 ◆ offer s.th. on the menu
anbieten etw zu demselben Preis
 ◆ offer s.th. at the same price
 ◆ offer s.th. at the same rate
anbieten etw zum Komfort seiner Gäste
 ◆ offer s.th. for the comfort of one's guests
anbieten jm etw
 offerieren jm etw
 ◆ offer s.o. s.th.
 ◆ offer s.th. to s.o.
anbieten jm seine Dienste
 ◆ offer s.o. one's services
 ◆ offer one's services to s.o.
Anbieter, m
 ◆ supplier
 ◆ provider
Anbieter und Käufer, m
 ◆ supplier and purchaser
Anbieter von Fremdenverkehrsleistungen, m
 Anbieter von touristischen Leistungen, m
 touristischer Leistungsanbieter, m
 ◆ provider of tourist services
Anbindung, f
 Anschluß, m
 ◆ access
an Bord
 ◆ on board
an Bord des Schiffes
 an Bord eines Schiffes
 ◆ on board the ship
 ◆ on board a ship
 ◆ on board
an Bord eines Flugzeuges gehen
 ◆ board a plane
an Bord eines Schiffes gehen
 an Bord gehen
 ◆ board a ship
an Bord gehen
 ◆ embark
 ◆ board
an Bord gehen in X
 ◆ embark at X
 ◆ embark in X
an Bord gehen von etw
 etw besteigen
 ◆ board s.th.
an Bord von etw, adv
 ◆ aboard s.th., adv
Andalusien
 ◆ Andalusia
Andalusier, m
 ◆ Andalusian
Andalusierin, f
 ◆ Andalusian girl
 ◆ Andalusian woman
 ◆ Andalusian
andalusisch, adj
 ◆ Andalusian, adj
andalusische Art, adv *gastr*
 nach andalusischer Art, adv *gastr*
 ◆ Andalusian style, adv *gastr*
an dem gewünschten Termin
 ◆ on the requested date
 ◆ for the requested date
an dem (von Ihnen) genannten Termin
 an dem (von Ihnen) genannten Datum

 ◆ on the date mentioned (by you)
 ◆ on the date in question
Anden, die, pl
 ◆ Andes, the *pl*
Andendorf, n
 ◆ Andean village
an den gewünschten Tagen
 an den gewünschten Terminen
 ◆ on the dates required
 ◆ on the desired dates
 ◆ on the dates in question
an den gewünschten Terminen
 ◆ on the desired dates
Andenken, n
 Souvenir, n
 ◆ souvenir
Andenken an etw, n
 ◆ souvenir of s.th.
Andenkenboutique f
 Souvenirboutique f
 ◆ souvenir boutique
Andenkengeschäft n
 Andenkenladen m
 Souvenirgeschäft n
 Souvenirladen m
 ◆ souvenir store *AE*
 ◆ souvenir shop *BE*
Andenkenjäger, m
 Souvenirjäger, m
 ◆ souvenir hunter
Andenken kaufen
 ◆ buy a souvenir
Andenken sammeln
 ◆ collect souvenirs
Andenkensammler, m
 ◆ collector of souvenirs
Andenkenstand, m
 Souvenirstand, m
 ◆ souvenir stand
 ◆ souvenir stall *BE*
Andenken suchen
 Souvenir suchen
 ◆ look for a souvenir
 ◆ seek a souvenir
Andenluft, f
 ◆ Andean air
Andenstadt, f
 ◆ Andean town
an den Tisch gerufen werden
 zu Tisch gerufen werden
 ◆ be called to the table
an den Tisch rufen jn
 zu Tisch rufen jn
 ◆ call s.o. to the table
Anden überqueren
 ◆ cross the Andes
an den Wochenenden
 ◆ on weekends *AE*
 ◆ at weekends *BE*
an der Bar sitzen
 ◆ sit at the bar
andere Kultur erleben
 ◆ experience another culture
Andere Länder, andere Sitten
 ◆ Other countries, other customs
anderen Konferenzort wählen
 ◆ choose a different conference venue
andere Welt betreten
 ◆ enter another world
an der Grenze (zu Frankreich)
 ◆ on the border (with France)

an der Küste

an der Küste
 ♦ on the coast
an der Nordsee
 ♦ on the North Sea
an der Ostsee
 ♦ on the Baltic Sea
 ♦ on the Baltic
an der Riviera
 ♦ on the Riviera
an der See
 am Meer
 ♦ at the seaside
 ♦ by the seaside
an der Seeseite
 an der Meerseite
 ♦ on the seafront AE
 ♦ on the sea front BE
an der Straße von A nach B
 ♦ on the road from A to B
Änderung, f (geringfügig)
 ♦ alteration
 ♦ modification
Änderung, f (umfassend)
 ♦ change
Änderung der Nachfrage, f
 → Nachfrageänderung
Änderung des Abreisetermins, f
 ♦ change of departure
Änderung des Abreisetermins hat eine Gebühr von DM 123 zur Folge
 ♦ change of departure will incur a charge of DM 123
Änderung im Freizeitverhalten, f
 ♦ change in leisure patterns
Änderung in letzter Minute, f
 Änderung in letzter Sekunde, f
 ♦ last-minute change
Änderungserklärung f
 (Buchung)
Änderungsgebühr, f
 ♦ alteration charge
 ♦ alteration fee
 ♦ amendment fee
 ♦ amendment charge
Änderungswunsch, m
 (z.B. bei Buchung)
 ♦ alteration request
 ♦ request for alteration
Änderungswunsch wird als Stornierung behandelt
 ♦ alteration request is treated as a cancellation
 ♦ alteration request is treated as a cancelation AE
Änderung vorbehalten
 (Preis etc.)
 ♦ Subject to alteration
Änderung vornehmen bei etw
 Änderung vornehmen an etw
 ♦ make a change to s.th.
Änderung vornehmen (geringfügig)
 ♦ make an alteration
 ♦ modify s.th.
anderweitige Hotelunterkunft, f
 anderweitige Hotelunterbringung, f
 Ersatzhotelunterkunft, f
 Ersatzhotelunterbringung, f
 ♦ alternative hotel accommodation BE
 ♦ alternate hotel accommodation AE
anderweitiges Bett, n
 Ersatzbett, n
 Ausweichbett, n
 ♦ alternative bed BE

 ♦ alternate bed AE
 ♦ spare bed
anderweitiges Zimmer n
 → Ersatzzimmer
anderweitige Unterkunft, f
 → Ausweichunterkunft
anderweitige Unterkunft anbieten
 ♦ offer alternate accommodation AE
 ♦ offer alternative accommodation BE
an die frische Luft gehen
 ♦ go out into the fresh air
 ♦ go out into the open air
an die frische Luft setzen jn coll
 hinauswerfen jn coll
 ♦ chuck s.o. out coll
 ♦ throw s.o. out
an die See reisen
 ♦ travel to the seaside
 ♦ go to the seaside
An diesem Tisch haben vier Leute Platz
 ♦ This table seats four
an die Tür gehen
 ♦ answer the door
Andorra
 ♦ Andorra
Andorraner, m
 ♦ Andorran
Andorranerin, f
 ♦ Andorran girl
 ♦ Andorran woman
 ♦ Andorran
andorranisch, adj
 ♦ Andorran, adj
Andrang, m
 Zustrom, m
Andrang, m
 Ansturm, m
 ♦ influx
 ♦ stream
 ♦ throng
anerkannt, adj
 genehmigt, adj
 ♦ approved, adj
anerkannte Grundsätze der Hotelführung, f pl
 ♦ established principles of hotel operation pl
anerkannte Kreditkarte, f
 ♦ recognised credit card
 ♦ recognized credit card
anerkannte Piste, f (Ski)
 ♦ recognised ski run
 ♦ recognized ski run
anerkannter Kurort, m
 ♦ recognised spa
 ♦ recognized spa
anerkannter Reisemittler, m
 ♦ recognised travel agent
 ♦ recognized travel agent
anerkannte Segelschule, f
 genehmigte Segelschule, f
 ♦ approved sailing school
anerkanntes Heilbad, n
 ♦ recognised health resort
 ♦ recognized health resort
anerkanntes Hotel, n
 ♦ recognised hotel
 ♦ recognized hotel
Anerkanntes Hotel (Plakette)
 ♦ Approved Hotel (plaque)
anerkanntes Reisebüro, n
 ♦ recognised travel agency
 ♦ recognized travel agency

Anfahrt, f
 → Anreise
Anfang der Reise, m
 Beginn der Reise, m
 ♦ commencement of the tour form
 ♦ commencement of the journey form
 ♦ commencement of the trip form
 ♦ beginning of the tour
 ♦ start of the tour
anfangen zu trinken
 zum Trinker werden
 ♦ take to drink
Anfänger, m
 ♦ beginner
 ♦ novice
Anfängerbecken, n
 (Schwimmbad)
 ♦ learners' pool
 ♦ learner's pool
Anfängerhang, m
 (Ski)
 → Anfängerhügel
Anfängerhügel, m
 (Ski)
 Anfängerhang m
 ♦ beginners' slope
 ♦ nursery slope
Anfängerkurs, m
 Anfängerlehrgang, m
 Kurs für Anfänger, m
 Lehrgang für Anfänger, m
 ♦ beginners' course
 ♦ course for beginners
 ♦ beginners' class
Anfängerlift m
 (Ski)
 ♦ nursery lift
Anfänger ohne Vorkenntnisse, m
 ♦ complete beginner
Anfängerunterricht, m
 ♦ beginners' instruction
 ♦ beginners' lessons pl
Anfang Juli
 ♦ beginning of July
 ♦ at the beginning of July
Anfangsbarmaid, f
 ♦ junior barmaid
Anfangsbarman, m
 ♦ junior barman
Anfangsberatung, f
 Eingangsberatung, f
 erste Beratung, f
 ♦ initial consultation
Anfangsbestand m
 (Lager)
 Eröffnungsbestand m
 ♦ opening stock
Anfangs-Chef de réception, m
 ♦ junior chef de réception
Anfangs-Chef de service, m
 ♦ junior chef de service
 ♦ junior service manager
Anfangscommis, m
 ♦ junior commis
Anfangsconcierge, m/f
 ♦ junior concierge
Anfangsdatum, n
 Anfangstermin, m
 ♦ beginning date
 ♦ starting date
 ♦ commencement date form

Anfangseconomatgouvernante, f SCHW
→ Anfangslagerverwalterin
Anfangsgouvernante, f SCHW
♦ junior housekeeper
Anfangsinventar, n
anfängliches Inventar n
♦ opening inventory
♦ beginning inventory
♦ initial inventory
♦ opening stock
Anfangskellner, m
♦ junior waiter
Anfangsküchenchef, m
♦ junior chef
Anfangslagerverwalterin, f
♦ junior storekeeper
Anfangsoberkellner, m
♦ junior headwaiter
Anfangsrezeptionist, m
→ Empfangssekretär
Anfangssaaltochter, f SCHW
Anfangskellnerin, f
♦ junior waitress
Anfangssekretär, m
♦ junior secretary
Anfangstermin, m
Anfangsdatum, n
♦ starting date
♦ beginning date
♦ commencement date form
Anfangstermin des Urlaubs, m
Anfangsdatum des Urlaubs, n
♦ starting date of the vacation AE
♦ starting date of the holiday BE
♦ commencement date of the vacation AE
an Fest- und Feiertagen
♦ on high days and holidays
anfliegen einen Ort
(Linienflug)
♦ have a service to a place
Anflug, m
♦ approach
anfordern etw bei jm (schriftlich)
(Prospekt etc.)
anfordern etw von jm
♦ write to s.o. for s.th.
anfordern etw bei jm (telefonisch)
(Prospekt etc.)
anfordern etw von jm
♦ telephone s.o. for s.th.
♦ phone s.o. for s.th
♦ call s.o. for s.th.
Anforderung, f
Bedürfnis, n
♦ requirement
Anforderungen angeben
♦ state one's requirements
Anforderungen entsprechen von jm
♦ cater for s.o.'s requirements
Anforderungen erfüllen
Bedürfnisse erfüllen
♦ meet the requirements
Anforderungen nicht genügen
♦ not fulfill the requirements AE
♦ not fulfil the requirements BE
Anforderungskarte, f
♦ request card
Anfrage, f (Antrag)
→ Antrag

Anfrage, f (Informationswunsch)
♦ inquiry
♦ enquiry
Anfrage beantworten
♦ answer an inquiry
♦ answer an enquiry
♦ reply to an inquiry
♦ reply to an enquiry
Anfrage bearbeiten
♦ deal with an inquiry
♦ deal with an enquiry
♦ handle an inquiry
♦ handle an enquiry
♦ process an inquiry
Anfragecoupon m
♦ inquiry coupon
♦ enquiry coupon
Anfrage erhalten (von jm)
♦ receive an inquiry (from s.o.)
♦ receive an enquiry (from s.o.)
Anfragen an Herrn X
♦ Inquiries to Mr X
♦ Enquiries to Mr X
Anfragen bitte an Herrn X
♦ Inquiries please to Mr X
♦ Enquiries please to Mr X
Anfragen erbeten unter Nummer 123
(Zeitungsannonce)
♦ Inquiries requested under box 123
♦ Enquiries requested under box 123
Anfragen sind zu richten an Herrn X
♦ Inquiries should be directed to Mr X
♦ Enquiries should be directed to Mr X
Anfrage richten an jn
♦ direct an inquiry to s.o.
♦ direct an enquiry to s.o.
♦ address an inquiry to s.o.
♦ address an enquiry to s.o.
Anfrage wegen etw
Anfrage bezüglich etw
♦ inquiry about s.th.
♦ enquiry about s.th.
Angabe im Hotelprospekt, f
♦ information (given) in the hotel brochure
angebautes Zimmer n
♦ extension room
angebliches Dienstreisen, n
♦ junketing AE
Angebot, n (Gegensatz zu Nachfrage)
♦ supply
Angebot, n (Offerte)
Offerte, f
♦ offer
Angebot, n (Palette)
→ Palette
Angebot an Bieren, n (Palette)
♦ range of beers
Angebot an Hotelbetten, n (Gegensatz zu Nachfrage)
Hotelbettenangebot, n
♦ supply of hotel beds
Angebot an Hotelunterkünften, n (Gegensatz zu Nachfrage)
♦ supply of hotel accommodations AE
♦ supply of hotel accommodation BE
Angebot an Hotelunterkünften, n (Palette)
♦ range of hotel accommodations AE
♦ range of hotel accommodation BE

Angebot an Hotelzimmern, n(Gegensatz zu Nachfrage)
Hotelzimmerangebot, n
♦ supply of hotel rooms
Angebot an Speisemöglichkeiten, n (Palette)
♦ range of dining possibilities
♦ range of dining facilities
Angebot an Touristenattraktionen vergrößern
♦ expand the range of tourist attractions
Angebot an Unterkünften, n(Gegensatz zu Nachfrage)
Unterkunftsangebot, n
♦ supply of accommodations AE
♦ supply of accommodation BE
♦ accommodation supply
Angebot buchen
♦ book an offer
angeboten, adj
♦ offered, adj
♦ provided, adj
♦ on offer
Angebot endet am 31. August
Offerte endet am 31. August
♦ offer closes on 31 August
angebotenen Service verbessern
♦ improve the service offered
angebotener Service, m
♦ service offered
♦ offered service
Angebot gilt von Sonntag bis Mittwoch
♦ offer is valid from Sunday to Wednesday
Angebot in letzter Minute, n
♦ last-minute offer
Angebot ist gültig bis 1. September
Angebot gilt bis 1. September
♦ offer is valid until 1 September
Angebot nutzen
♦ take advantage of an offer
Angebot sagt jm zu
♦ offer appeals to s.o.
Angebot solange Vorrat reicht
♦ offer subject to availability
Angebotspalette, f
angebotene Leistungspalette, f
♦ range of services offered
♦ range of services
Angebotsseite, f
Anbieterseite, f
♦ supply side
Angebotsspektrum, n
→ Angebotspalette
Angebot übersteigt die Nachfrage
♦ supply exceeds demand
Angebot und Nachfrage
Angebot (n) und Nachfrage (f)
♦ supply and demand
Angebot von Unterkünften, n (Palette)
→ Unterkunftsangebot
Angebot von Zimmernächten, n
♦ supply of room-nights
Angebot zurückziehen
♦ withdraw an offer
angebrannt, adj
♦ burnt, adj
angebranntes Fleisch, n
♦ burnt meat
angebrannt riechen
♦ smell burnt
angebrannt schmecken
♦ taste burnt

angefallene Kosten   20

angefallene Kosten, pl
  ♦ costs incurred pl
  ♦ cost incurred
Angegebene Preise sind Nettopreise
  ♦ Prices quoted are net
  ♦ Rates quoted are net
angegebener Preis, m
  ♦ quoted price
  ♦ quoted rate
angegebene Zimmerkapazität, f
  ♦ stated room capacity
angegliedert, adj
  ♦ affiliated, adj
angegliedertes Hotel, n
  (einer Gruppe angegliedert)
  ♦ affiliated hotel
angehende Führungskraft, f
  ♦ management trainee
angehender Hallenportier, m
  ♦ trainee hall porter
angehender Manager, m
  ♦ trainee manager
Angelausflug, m
  ♦ angling excursion
angelernt, adj
  ♦ trained on the job, adj
  ♦ semi-skilled, adj
angelernte Kraft, f
  angelernter Arbeiter m
  ♦ semi-skilled worker
angelernter Koch, m
  ♦ semi-skilled cook
Angelexpedition, f
  Fischfangexpedition, f
  ♦ fishing expedition
Angelfreund, m
  Angelbegeisterter, m
  ♦ angling enthusiast
  ♦ fishing enthusiast
Angelgelegenheit, f
  ♦ opportunity for angling
  ♦ angling opportunity
  ♦ opportunity for fishing
  ♦ fishing opportunity
Angelgerät, n
  Angelzeug, n
  ♦ angling gear
  ♦ fishing gear
Angelkarte, f
  Angelschein, m
  ♦ angling permit
  ♦ angling license
  ♦ angling licence
  ♦ angler's license
  ♦ angler's licence
Angelkurzurlaub, m
  ♦ angling break
  ♦ fishing break
Angeln, n
  Angelsport, m
  ♦ angling
  ♦ fishing
Angelort, m
  ♦ angling resort
Angelpunkt des Reisens (zwischen A und B), m
  Drehscheibe der Reisen (zwischen A und B), f
  ♦ fulcrum of travel (between A and B)
Angelsachse, m
  ♦ Anglo-Saxon
angelsächsisch, adj
  ♦ Anglo-Saxon, adj

Angelsaison f
  ♦ angling season
Angelschein, m
  Angelerlaubis, m
  ♦ angler's license
  ♦ angler's licence
  ♦ angling permit
  ♦ angling license
  ♦ angling licence
Angelsee, m
  Fischsee, m
  ♦ fishing lake
Angelsport, m
  → Angeln
Angelsportler, m
  → Angler
Angeltageskarte, f
  ♦ one-day angling permit
Angelurlaub, m
  Angelferien, pl
  ♦ angling vacation AE
  ♦ angling holiday BE
Angelverein, m
  Anglerverein, m
  ♦ angling club
Angelwettbewerb, m
  → Wettangeln
Angelwoche, f
  ♦ angling week
  ♦ one week's angling
Angelwochenende, n
  ♦ angling weekend
Angelzentrum, n
  ♦ angling center AE
  ♦ angling centre BE
angemeldet, adj
  registriert, adj
  ♦ registered, adj
angemeldete Personenzahl, f
  (Gäste)
  ♦ number of registered guests
Angemeldeter, m (Kurs)
  ♦ enrollee AE
angemeldeter Gast, m
  ♦ registered guest
angemeldeter Platz, m
  (Camping)
  ♦ registered site
angemeldetes Hotel n
  (bei Behörden)
  ♦ registered hotel
angemeldet sein für eine Pauschalreise
  ♦ be booked on a package tour
  ♦ be booked on an inclusive tour
angemeldet sein in einem Hotel
  ♦ be booked into a hotel
angemessen ausgebildetes Personal, n
  ♦ adequately trained personnel
  ♦ adequately trained staff
angemessene Entschädigung, f
  ♦ adequate compensation
  ♦ adequate damages pl
angemessene Miete f
  ♦ fair rent
angemessene Parkfläche, f
  ♦ adequate parking area
  ♦ adequate parking space
angemessen möbliert, adj
  ausreichend möbliert, adj
  ♦ adequately furnished, adj

angemessen möbliertes Zimmer n
  ♦ adequately furnished room
angenehm, adj
  ♦ pleasant, adj
angenehme Atmosphäre, f
  schöne Atmosphäre f
  ♦ pleasant atmosphere
angenehme Atmosphäre schaffen
  ♦ create a pleasant atmosphere
angenehme Gesellschaft, f
  (Personen)
  ♦ enjoyable company
Angenehme Nachtruhe!
  → Schlafen Sie gut!
angenehmen Aufenthalt garantieren
  ♦ guarantee a pleasant stay
angenehmen Aufenthalt jm wünschen
  ♦ wish s.o. a pleasant stay
  ♦ hope that s.o. will have a pleasant stay
angenehmen und behaglichen Aufenthalt jm wünschen
  ♦ wish s.o. a pleasant and comfortable stay
angenehmen Urlaub bereiten jm
  angenehme Ferien jm bereiten
  ♦ provide a pleasant vacation for s.o. AE
  ♦ provide a pleasant holiday for s.o. BE
angenehmer Aufenthalt, m
  schöner Aufenthalt, m
  ♦ pleasant stay
  ♦ enjoyable stay
angenehme Reise haben
  ♦ have a pleasant journey
angenehmer Urlaub, m
  angenehme Ferien, pl
  ♦ pleasant vacation AE
  ♦ pleasant holiday BE
angenehmes Klima, n
  ♦ pleasant climate
angenehmes Leben haben
  ♦ live comfortably
Angenehmes mit dem Nützlichen verbinden
  ♦ combine business with pleasure
angenehmes Zimmer, n
  ♦ pleasant room
angenehme Umgebung, f
  ♦ pleasant surroundings pl
angenehm möbliert, adj
  ♦ pleasantly furnished, adj
angenehm überrascht, adj
  ♦ pleasantly surprised, adj
angenehm überrascht sein
  ♦ be pleasantly surprised
angenommener Name, m
  ♦ assumed name
  ♦ fictitious name
angerichtet, adj gastr
  ♦ dressed, adj gastr
angerichtet in einem Korb
  ♦ dressed in a basket
angeschlossene Ausstellung, f
  ♦ associated exhibition
angeschlossenes Hotel n
  (Gruppe angeschlossen)
  ♦ associate hotel
angeschlossen sein an ein Buchungssystem
  ♦ be affiliated to a booking system
angesprochene Zielgruppe, f
  ♦ addressed target group
Angestellter, m jur
  Angestellte, f jur
  ♦ employee

angestochen, adv (Bier)
vom Faß, adv
Bier vom Faß, n
• on tap, adv
• beer on tap
angestrebt, adj
anvisiert, adj
• targeted, adj
• target, adj
angetrunken, adj
• slightly drunk, adj
• slightly intoxicated, adj
• tipsy, adj *coll*
angewandte Reisegeographie, f
• applied travel geography
angewiesen sein auf Hotels
• be dependent on hotels
Angler, m
Angelsportler, m
• angler
Anglerparadies n
• angler's paradise
• fisherman's paradise
Angola
• Angola
Angolaner, m
• Angolan
Angolanerin, f
• Angolan girl
• Angolan woman
• Angolan
angolanisch, adj
• Angolan, adj
Angostura (Getränk)
• Angostura
• Angostura Bitters
Angostura (Rinde)
• angostura
angrenzen an etw
• adjoin s.th.
• be adjacent to s.th.
• border on s.th.
angrenzend, adj
nebeneinander liegend, adj
• adjacent, adj
• adjoining, adj
• neigboring, adj *AE*
• neighbouring, adj *BE*
angrenzend (an etw), adj
• adjacent (to s.th.), adj
angrenzender Stand, m
• adjacent stand
angrenzende Stadt, f
• adjacent town
angrenzende Straße, f
• adjacent street
• adjacent road
angrenzendes Zimmer, n
Nachbarzimmer, n
Nebenzimmer, n
• adjoining room
Angriff gegen Touristen, m
• attack on tourists
Angst haben vor dem Fliegen
Flugangst haben
• be afraid of flying
Angst vor dem Fliegen, f
Flugangst, f
• plane phobia
• fear of flying
• pterophobia *scient*

Angusrindfleisch, n
• Angus beef
anhalten, um etw zu trinken
• stop for a drink
anhalten bei einem Restaurant zum Mittagessen
• stop at a restaurant for lunch
anhalten in X
(Zug)
• call at X
anhalten unterwegs für das Mittagessen
• stop en route for lunch
anhalten zu einem Picknick
• stop for a picnic
anhalten zu einer kurzen Rast
• stop for a short rest
• stop for a brief rest
anhalten zu einer Rast
• stop for a rest
Anhalter, m
Anhalterin, f
Tramper, m
Tramperin, f
• hitchhiker *AE*
• hitch-hiker *BE*
Anhängeblatt, n
(Speisekarte, Reklame)
• tip-on
Anhänger, m (Fahrzeug)
• trailer
Anhängerfahrpreis, m
• trailer fare
Anhängerkupplung, f
(z.B. für Wohnwagen)
• tow-bar
Anhöhe, f
• promontory
Animateur, m
• social director
• entertainments officer
• animateur *FR*
• guest host
Animation, f
• activities to amuse and entertain guests
• entertainment
Animationsangebot n
• amusement and entertainment offered
• range of amusement and entertainment offered
Animationsgruppe, f
• social programme group *BE*
Animationspersonal, n
• social staff
• social personnel
Animationsprogramm, n
• program to amuse and entertain guests *AE*
• programme to amuse and entertain guests *BE*
Animierdame, f
Animiermädchen n
• nightclub hostess *AE*
• night-club hostess *BE*
• B-girl *AE sl*
• sitter *sl*
animieren jn zum Trinken
• incite s.o. to drink
Animierkneipe, f
• dive with hostesses *sl*
• dive with B-girls *AE sl*
Animierlokal, n
• bar with hostesses *AE*
• bar with B-girls *AE sl*
• pub with hostesses *BE*

Anis, m
• aniseed
Anisette, f
Anislikör, m
• anisette
an jedem Dienstag
• every Tuesday
an jedem zweiten Tag, adv
→ jeden zweiten Tag
Anker lichten
auslaufen
• weigh anchor
Ankerlichten, n
• unmooring
Anker werfen
• cast anchor
• drop anchor
Ankleidebereich m
• dressing area
Ankleidenische, f
Ankleidealkoven, m
• dressing alcove
ankleiden sich
• dress
• get dressed
• put on one's clothes
ankleiden sich zum Abendessen
• dress for dinner
Ankleideraum, m
→ Ankleidezimmer
Ankleidespiegel m
• dressing mirror
Ankleidezimmer, n
Ankleideraum, m
• dressing room
• dressing-room *BE*
anklopfen
an die Tür klopfen
• knock on the door
ankommen als erster
• arrive first
• be the first to arrive
ankommen als letzter
• arrive last
• be the last to arrive
ankommen am Bahnhof
• arrive at the station
ankommen am Mittag
(12 Uhr)
• arrive at noon
ankommen am Montag
• arrive on Monday
ankommen an dem Ziel
ankommen an dem Zielort
• arrive at the destination
ankommen (Anklang finden)
Anklang finden (bei jm)
• catch on (with s.o.) *coll*
• be well received (by s.o.)
ankommen an Ort und Stelle
ankommen an seinem Ziel
• arrive at one's destination
ankommen auf dem Flughafen
ankommen am Flughafen
• arrive at the airport
ankommen auf dem Frankfurter Flughafen
• arrive at Frankfurt Airport
ankommen auf dem Landweg
• arrive by land

ankommen auf dem Luftweg
   anreisen auf dem Luftweg
   ♦ arrive by air
ankommen auf dem Seeweg
   ♦ arrive by sea
ankommen auf dem Straßenweg
   ♦ arrive by road
ankommen auf einem Flughafen
   ♦ arrive at an airport
ankommen bis (spätestens) 18 Uhr
   ♦ arrive by 18 hours (at the latest)
   ♦ arrive by 6 o'clock p.m. (at the latest)
ankommen bis (spätestens) Freitag
   ♦ arrive by Friday (at the latest)
ankommen bis zur angegebenen Zeit
   ♦ arrive by the time stated
ankommend, adj (Flug)
   ♦ incoming, adj
ankommend, adj (generell)
   ♦ arriving, adj
ankommender Flug, m
   ankommendes Flugzeug, n
   ♦ incoming flight
ankommender Gast, m
   Arrivée, f *SCHW*
   ♦ arriving guest
   ♦ arrival
ankommender Verkehr, m (Flug)
   ♦ incoming traffic
ankommen frühestens um 15 Uhr
   ♦ arrive at 3 p.m. at the earliest
   ♦ arrive at 15 hours at the earliest *mil*
ankommen gegen 17 Uhr
   ankommen gegen 5 Uhr nachmittags
   ♦ arrive at approximately 5 p.m.
   ♦ arrive at approximately 17 hours *mil*
   ♦ arrive at about 5 p.m.
   ♦ arrive at about 17 hours *mil*
ankommen im Hotel
   ankommen in dem Hotel
   ♦ arrive at the hotel
ankommen in einem Land
   ♦ arrive in a country
ankommen in Scharen
   ♦ arrive in droves
ankommen in X am Dienstag, den 7. März um 17 Uhr
   ♦ arrive at X on Tuesday, 7 March at 5 p.m.
   ♦ arrive in X on Tuesday, 7 March at 5 p.m.
ankommen in X (Großstadt)
   ♦ arrive in X
ankommen in X (kleiner Ort)
   ♦ arrive at X
ankommen in X spät in der Nacht
   ♦ arrive at X late at night
   ♦ arrive in X late at night
ankommen mit dem 3-Uhr-Zug
   ♦ arrive on the 3 o'clock train
   ♦ arrive with the 3 o'clock train
ankommen mit dem Auto
   ankommen mit dem Pkw
   anreisen mit dem Auto
   anreisen mit dem Pkw
   ♦ arrive by car
ankommen mit dem Boot
   ankommen mit dem Schiff
   anreisen mit dem Boot
   anreisen mit dem Schiff
   ♦ arrive by boat
ankommen mit dem Bus in X
   ♦ arrive by bus at X

   ♦ arrive by bus in X
   ♦ arrive by coach at X *BE*
   ♦ arrive by coach in X *BE*
ankommen mit dem Bus von X
   ankommen mit dem Bus aus X
   ♦ arrive on the bus from X
   ♦ arrive on the coach from X *BE*
ankommen mit dem Dampfer
   ♦ arrive by steamer
ankommen mit dem eigenen Hubschrauber
   ♦ arrive in one's own helicopter
ankommen mit dem Flugzeug
   anreisen mit dem Flugzeug
   ♦ arrive by plane
   ♦ arrive by air
ankommen mit dem Hubschrauber
   ♦ arrive by helicopter
ankommen mit dem Intercity-Zug
   ♦ arrive on the Intercity train
ankommen mit dem Schiff
   ♦ arrive by ship
   ♦ arrive by boat
ankommen mit dem Schiff von X
   ankommen mit dem Schiff aus X
   ♦ arrive on the ship from X
   ♦ arrive on the boat from X
ankommen mit dem Schnellzug von X
   ankommen mit dem Schnellzug aus X
   ♦ arrive on the express train from X
ankommen mit dem Taxi
   ♦ arrive by taxi
ankommen mit dem Zug
   ♦ arrive by train
ankommen mit der Bahn
   ♦ arrive by rail
ankommen mit der Fähre
   ♦ arrive by ferry
ankommen mit der Fähre von X
   ankommen mit der Fähre aus X
   ♦ arrive on the ferry from X
ankommen mit einem Charterflug
   ♦ arrive on a charter flight
ankommen mit Flug LH 427 aus X
   ♦ arrive on flight LH 427 from X
ankommen mit Verspätung
   eintreffen mit Verspätung
   verspätet ankommen
   verspätet eintreffen
   ♦ arrive late
ankommen mit wenig Gepäck
   ♦ arrive with little baggage *AE*
   ♦ arrive with little luggage *BE*
ankommen nach der angegebenen Zeit
   ♦ arrive after the time stated
ankommen ohne Gepäck
   ♦ arrive without (one's) baggage *AE*
   ♦ arrive without (one's) luggage *BE*
ankommen (Person)
   eintreffen
   ♦ arrive
   ♦ show up *sl*
   ♦ check in
   ♦ get in
ankommen pünktlich
   → pünktlich ankommen
ankommen um 10 Uhr vormittags
   ♦ arrive at 10 a.m.
   ♦ arrive at 10 in the morning
   ♦ arrive at 10 hours *mil*
ankommen um 16 Uhr
   ♦ arrive at 4 p.m.

   ♦ arrive at 4 in the afternoon
   ♦ arrive at 16 hours *mil*
ankommen um 2 Uhr
   ♦ arrive at 2 o'clock
ankommen um 8.30 Uhr
   ♦ arrive at 8.30
ankommen (Verkehrsmittel)
   ♦ arrive
   ♦ get in
   ♦ get into
ankommen von X
   ankommen aus X
   anreisen aus X
   ♦ arrive from X
ankommen zu einem Besuch von X
   ♦ arrive on a visit to X
ankommen zu einer ungünstigen Zeit
   ankommen zur unpassenden Zeit
   ♦ arrive at an inconvenient time
ankommen zur angegebenen Zeit
   ♦ arrive at the time stated
ankommen zur verabredeten Zeit
   ♦ arrive at the appointed time
ankommen zwischen 17 und 18 Uhr
   ♦ arrive between 5 and 6 p.m.
   ♦ arrive between 17 and 18 hours *mil*
Ankömmling, m
   → Neuankunft
ankreuzen etw
   (auf Formular)
   ♦ tick s.th.
Ankunft
   (Hinweisschild)
   ♦ Arrivals
Ankunft, f (Check-in)
   Anmeldung f
   ♦ check-in
   ♦ checking in
Ankunft, f (generell)
   ♦ arrival
Ankunft, f (Person)
   ankommende Person, f
   Arrivée, f *SCHW*
   ♦ arriving person
   ♦ arrival
Ankunft am 3. Juli zur gleichen Zeit
   ♦ arriving on 3 July at the same time
   ♦ arrival on 3 July at the same time
Ankunft avisieren jm
   avisieren jn
   ♦ notify s.o. of s.o.'s arrival
   ♦ inform s.o. of s.o.'s arrival
   ♦ advise s.o. of s.o.'s arrival
Ankunft bestätigen
   ♦ confirm one's arrival
   ♦ confirm s.o.'s arrival
Ankunft des Tourismus, f
   ♦ advent of tourism
Ankunft erfolgt am Mittwoch
   ♦ arrival will be on Wednesday
Ankunft erwarten von jm
   js Ankunft erwarten
   ♦ await s.o.'s arrival
   ♦ await the arrival of s.o.
Ankünfte und Abreisen festhalten
   ♦ register the arrivals and departures
Ankünfte und Abreisen vermerken
   ♦ record the arrivals and departures
Ankünftezahl, f
   → Ankunftszahl

Ankunft feiern mit etw
 ◆ celebrate the arrival with s.th.
Ankunft frühestens Donnerstagnachmittag
 ◆ arrival on Thursday afternoon at the earliest
 ◆ arriving on Thursday afternoon at the earliest
Ankunft hat sich verzögert
 ◆ arrival has been delayed
Ankunft heute nacht
 ◆ arriving tonight
 ◆ arrival tonight
Ankunft hinausschieben
 ◆ defer one's arrival
 ◆ postpone one's arrival
Ankunft im Hotel, f
 ◆ arrival at the hotel
Ankunft in letzter Minute, f
 Ankunft in letzter Sekunde f
 ◆ last-minute arrival
Ankunft in X, f (Großstadt)
 ◆ arrival in X
Ankunft in X, f (kleiner Ort)
 ◆ arrival at X
Ankunft ist für Freitag festgelegt
 Ankunft ist für Freitag vorgesehen
 ◆ arrival is scheduled for Friday
Ankunft melden von jm
 ◆ announce s.o.'s arrival
Ankunft mit der Bahn, f
 Anreise mit der Bahn, f
 ◆ arrival by rail
Ankunft mitteilen jm
 Ankunft avisieren jm
 avisieren jn
 ◆ inform s.o. of one's arrival
 ◆ advise s.o. of s.o.'s arrival
 ◆ notify s.o. of s.o.'s arrival
Ankunft morgen früh (Telex)
 ◆ arriving early tomorrow
 ◆ arrival early tomorrow
Ankunft nicht vor 21 Uhr (Telex)
 ◆ arriving not before 9 p.m.
 ◆ arriving not before 21 hours *mil*
 ◆ arrival not before 21 hours *mil*
 ◆ arrival not before 9 p.m.
Ankunft nicht vor Freitag
 ◆ arriving not before Friday
 ◆ arrival not before Friday
Ankunftsbahnsteig, m
 ◆ arrival platform
 ◆ platform of arrival
Ankunftsbenachrichtigung f
 (Rezeption)
 Ankunftsmitteilung f
 ◆ arrival(s) notification
 ◆ notification of arrivals
Ankunftsbenachrichtigungsformular n
 (Rezeption)
 ◆ arrival notification form
Ankunftsbuch n
 ◆ arrival(s) book
 ◆ book of arrivals
Ankunftsdatum, n
 Ankunftstermin, m
 Anreisedatum, n
 Anreisetermin, m
 ◆ date of arrival
 ◆ arrival date
Ankunftsdatum angeben
 ◆ give the date of arrival
 ◆ give the arrival date

 ◆ state the date of arrival
 ◆ state the arrival date
Ankunftsdatum beachten
 ◆ note the arrival date
 ◆ note the date of arrival
Ankunftseinrichtung, f
 ◆ arrival facility
Ankunftsflughafen, m
 Landeflughafen, m
 ◆ airport of arrival
 ◆ arrival airport
Ankunftsformalität, f
 ◆ arrival formality
Ankunftsgebäude, n
 ◆ arrivals building
Ankunftshafen, m
 ◆ port of arrival
 ◆ arrival port
Ankunftshalle, f (Flughafen)
 ◆ arrival hall *AE*
 ◆ arrival lounge *BE*
Ankunftsliste, f
 Liste der ankommenden Gäste, f
 Anreiseliste, f
 Liste der anreisenden Gäste, f
 ◆ arrivals list
 ◆ arrival list
 ◆ list of arrivals
Ankunftsliste durchsehen
 ◆ look through the arrivals list
 ◆ look through the arrival list
Ankunftsliste erstellen
 ◆ compile the arrival(s) list
Ankunftsliste vorbereiten
 ◆ prepare the arrival(s) list
Ankunftsmonat m
 ◆ arrival month
 ◆ month of arrival
Ankunftsnacht f
 ◆ arrival night
 ◆ night of arrival
Ankunftsort, m (Punkt)
 ◆ arrival point
 ◆ point of arrival
Ankunftsort m (Stadt)
 ◆ place of arrival
Ankunftsritual, n
 ◆ ritual of arrival
Ankunftsstelle, f (Punkt)
 ◆ point of arrival
 ◆ arrival point
Ankunftsstunde f
 ◆ arrival hour
 ◆ hour of arrival
Ankunftstafel, f
 (Bahnhof etc.)
 ◆ arrival board
Ankunftstag, m
 Anreisetag, m
 ◆ day of arrival
 ◆ arrival day
Ankunftstermin, m
 Ankunftsdatum, n
 ◆ arrivale date
 ◆ date of arrival
Ankunftstermin ändern
 Ankunftsdatum ändern
 ◆ change one's arrival date
Ankunfts- und Abfahrtstafel, f
 ◆ arrival and departure board

Ankunfts- und Abflugtafel, f
 ◆ arrival and departure board
Ankunfts- und Abreiseliste f
 → Mouvementliste
Ankunftsvorgang, m
 ◆ arrival procedure
Ankunftswoche f
 ◆ arrival week
 ◆ week of arrival
Ankunftszahl, f
 → Zahl der Ankünfte
Ankunftszeit, f (Check-in)
 Belegungszeitpunkt, m
 ◆ time of checking in
 ◆ check-in time
Ankunftszeit, f (generell)
 ◆ arrival time
 ◆ time of arrival
Ankunftszeit ändern
 ◆ change one's arrival time
Ankunftszeitpunkt, m (Check-in)
 → Eintreffenszeit
Ankunft verschieben
 ◆ postpone one's arrival
Ankunft verschieben auf Freitag
 ◆ postpone one's arrival to Friday
Ankunft verschieben um weitere zwei Wochen
 ◆ postpone one's arrival for another two weeks
Ankunft verschieben um zwei Tage
 ◆ postpone one's arrival for two days
Ankunft von jm, f
 ◆ arrival of s.o.
Ankunft voraussichtlich um 20 Uhr
 ◆ arrival at approximately 20 hours
 ◆ arriving at about 20 hours
 ◆ arrival at approximately 8 p.m.
 ◆ arriving at about 8 p.m.
Ankunft vorverlegen
 ◆ bring forward one's arrival
 ◆ advance one's arrival
 ◆ bring forward s.o.'s arrival
 ◆ advance s.o.'s arrival
Ankunft zum festgesetzten Termin, f
 → termingerechte Ankunft
Ankunft zur festgesetzten Zeit, f
 ◆ arrival at the appointed time
Anlage, f (Brief)
 ◆ enclosure
Anlage, f (Einrichtung)
 → Einrichtung
Anlage, f (Gebäude)
 ◆ complex
Anlage, f (Plan)
 Anordnung, f
 Entwurf, m
 Grundriß, m
 ◆ layout
Anlage, f (System)
 System, n
 ◆ system
Anlageabschreibung, f
 Abschreibung des Anlagevermögens, f
 ◆ depreciation of fixed assets
 ◆ capital allowance
Anlage betreiben
 Komplex betreiben
 ◆ operate a complex
Anlage der Stadt, f
 Stadtanlage, f
 ◆ layout of the town

Anlage eröffnen 24

Anlage eröffnen
   Komplex eröffnen
   ♦ open a complex
Anlagevermögen, n
   ♦ fixed assets *pl*
   ♦ tangible assets *pl*
   ♦ capital assets *pl*
Anlageverzinsung, f
   Ertrag des investierten Kapitals, m
   ♦ return on investment
an Land, adv
   ♦ ashore, adv
an Land gehen
   ♦ go ashore
an Land kommen
   ♦ come ashore
Anlaß begehen mit großer Feierlichkeit
   ♦ celebrate an occasion with great ceremony
Anlaß feiern
   Anlaß begehen
   ♦ celebrate an occasion
anlaufen etw
   (Schiff)
   ♦ call at s.th.
Anlaufhafen, m
   ♦ port of call
Anlaufkosten, pl
   ♦ startup costs *pl*
   startup cost
   ♦ initial costs *pl*
   ♦ initial cost
Anlegemöglichkeit, f
   ♦ mooring facility
anlegen mit einer Jacht in X
   mit einer Yacht anlegen in X
   ♦ moor a yacht at X
Anlegeplatz, m
   (für Wasserfahrzeuge)
   Anlegestelle, f
   ♦ mooring
   ♦ mooring space
   ♦ mooring place
Anlegesteg, m
   (für Wasserfahrzeuge)
   Anlegestelle, f
   ♦ landing stage
   ♦ jetty
Anlegestelle, f
   ♦ mooring point
anlernen jn
   ♦ train s.o. (on the job)
an meinem ersten Aufenthaltstag
   ♦ on the first day of my stay
Anmeldebedingungen, f pl (Kurs)
   ♦ conditions of enrolment *pl*
   ♦ conditions of enrollment *AE pl*
   ♦ enrolment conditions *pl*
   ♦ enrollment conditions *AE pl*
Anmeldebereich, m
   ♦ registration area
Anmeldebescheinigung, f (Kurs)
   ♦ certificate of enrolment
   ♦ certificate of enrollment
Anmeldebescheinigung zusenden jm (Kurs)
   ♦ send a certificate of enrolment to s.o.
   ♦ send a certificate of enrollment to s.o. *AE*
Anmeldebogen m
   Meldebogen m
   ♦ registration sheet

Anmeldecoupon, m (Buchung)
   Buchungscoupon m
   ♦ booking coupon
Anmeldedatum, n (generell)
   ♦ registration date
   ♦ date of registration
Anmeldedatum, n (Kurs)
   ♦ date of enrolment
   ♦ date of enrollment *AE*
Anmeldeerklärung f
   ♦ registration statement
Anmeldeformalität, f (Check-in)
   ♦ check-in formality
Anmeldeformular, n (Buchung)
   → Buchungsformular
Anmeldeformular, n (generell)
   Anmeldungsformular, n
   Meldezettel, m
   ♦ registration form
Anmeldeformular, n (Kurs)
   ♦ enrolment form
   ♦ enrollment form *AE*
Anmeldefrist, f
   Anmeldungsfrist, f
   Anmeldeschluß, m
   ♦ registration deadline
   ♦ deadline for registration
Anmeldegebühr, f (Buchung)
   Buchungsgebühr, f
   ♦ booking fee
   ♦ booking charge
Anmeldegebühr, f (generell)
   Anmeldungsgebühr, f
   Meldegebühr, f
   ♦ registration charge
   ♦ registration fee
Anmeldegebühr, f (Kurs)
   ♦ enrolment charge
   ♦ enrolment fee
   ♦ enrollment charge *AE*
   ♦ enrollment fee *AE*
Anmeldekarte, f (Kurs)
   ♦ enrolment card
   ♦ enrollment card *AE*
Anmeldeliste, f
   Meldeliste, f
   ♦ registration list
anmelden jn
   registrieren jn
   ♦ register s.o.
anmelden sich am Empfangsschalter
   anmelden sich am Rezeptionsschalter
   ♦ register at the front desk *AE*
   ♦ register at the reception desk
   ♦ check in
anmelden sich auf einem Platz (Camping)
   ♦ register at a site
anmelden sich bei der Polizei
   polizeilich anmelden sich
   ♦ register with the police
anmelden sich bei einer Konferenz
   ♦ register at a conference
anmelden sich einzeln
   ♦ register individually
anmelden sich für etw (generell)
   anmelden sich zu etw
   ♦ register for s.th.
anmelden sich für etw (Kurs)
   → einschreiben sich für etw
anmelden sich (generell)
   ♦ register

anmelden sich in einem Hotel
   eintragen sich in das Fremdenbuch
   ♦ register with a hotel
   ♦ register at a hotel
anmelden sich zu einem Flug
   einchecken zu einem Flug
   ♦ check in for a flight
anmelden sich zu einem Kongreß
   ♦ register for a convention
   ♦ register for a congress
anmelden sich zu einem Kurs
   ♦ enrol in course
   ♦ enroll in a course *AE*
   ♦ enrol in a class
   ♦ enroll in a class *AE*
   ♦ register for a course
anmelden sich zu einem Lehrgang
   anmelden sich zu einem Kurs
   ♦ sign up for a course
anmelden sich zu einem Seminar
   ♦ register for a seminar
anmelden sich zu einer Konferenz
   ♦ register for a conference
anmelden sich zu einer Messe
   ♦ register for a fair
anmelden sich zu einer Reise
   ♦ sign up for a tour
anmelden sich zu einer Tagung
   ♦ register for a meeting
Anmeldepflicht, f
   Anmeldezwang, m
   Meldepflicht, f
   Meldezwang, m
   ♦ compulsory registration
   ♦ obligatory registration
   ♦ obligation to register
anmeldepflichtig, adj
   → meldepflichtig
Anmelder, m
   Buchender, m
   Bucher, m
   Besteller, m
   ♦ person making a booking
   ♦ person booking s.th.
   ♦ person booking in
   ♦ booker
Anmeldeschalter, m (Abfertigung)
   → Abfertigungsschalter
Anmeldeschalter, m (generell)
   Anmeldungsschalter, m
   ♦ registration counter
   ♦ registration desk
Anmeldeschluß, m (generell)
   ♦ closing date for registrations
   ♦ deadline for registrations
   ♦ final registration date
Anmeldestelle, f
   ♦ registration point
   ♦ check-in point
Anmeldetermin m
   ♦ registration date
Anmeldetisch, m
   (z.B. bei Konferenz)
   Anmeldungstisch, m
   ♦ registration table
Anmeldeverfahren, n (Kurs)
   ♦ enrolment procedure
   ♦ enrollment procedure *AE*
Anmeldevorgang, m
   Anmeldeverfahren, n

- ◆ check-in procedure
- ◆ check-in process

Anmeldezeitraum, m (generell)
- ◆ period of registration

Anmeldezwang m
- → Anmeldepflicht

Anmeldung, f (Buchung)
- → Buchung

Anmeldung, f (Check-in)
- ◆ checking in
- ◆ check-in

Anmeldung, f (generell)
- Einschreibung, f
- Registrierung, f
- ◆ registration

Anmeldung, f (Kurs)
- ◆ enrolment
- ◆ enrollment AE

Anmeldung, f (Rezeption)
- → Rezeption

Anmeldung an Ort und Stelle, f
- ◆ on-site registration

Anmeldung bearbeiten (generell)
- ◆ process a registration
- ◆ deal with a registration
- ◆ handle a registration

Anmeldung bei der Polizei, f
- polizeiliche Meldung f
- ◆ registration with the police

Anmeldung der Gäste, f
- ◆ check-in of guests
- ◆ checking in guests

Anmeldung erhalten (generell)
- ◆ receive a registration

Anmeldung faxen an jn
- ◆ fax one's registration to s.o.
- ◆ telefax one's registration to s.o.

Anmeldung findet von 8.00 bis 12.00 Uhr statt
- ◆ registration takes place from 8 to 12 o'clock

Anmeldung für ein Seminar, f
- ◆ registration for a seminar

Anmeldungsannahme f
- → s. Buchungsannahme

Anmeldungsart, f (Buchung)
- Buchungsart, f
- ◆ type of booking
- ◆ booking type

Anmeldungsart, f (generell)
- ◆ registration type
- ◆ type of registration

Anmeldungsformalitäten, f pl (generell)
- Meldeformalitäten, f pl
- ◆ registration formalities pl

Anmeldungsformular ausfüllen
- Anmeldeformular ausfüllen
- ◆ complete a registration form
- ◆ fill out a registration form AE
- ◆ fill in a registration form BE

Anmeldungsformular zurücksenden an jn
- Anmeldeformular einsenden an jn
- ◆ return a registration form to s.o.

Anmeldungsgebühr, f
- → Anmeldegebühr

Anmeldungskosten, pl
- Anmeldekosten, pl
- ◆ registration costs pl
- ◆ registration cost
- ◆ cost of registration

Anmeldungsschalter, m (Konferenz etc)
- ◆ registration desk

Anmeldung stornieren
- Anmeldung rückgängig machen
- ◆ cancel a registration

Anmeldungsvorgang, m
- Meldevorgang, m
- Anmeldungsprozedur, f
- ◆ registration procedure
- ◆ registration process

Anmeldungswunsch, m (Kurs)
- ◆ enrolment request
- ◆ enrollment request AE

Anmeldungszeit, f
- Anmeldezeit f
- ◆ registration time

Anmeldung zu etw, f (generell)
- ◆ registration for s.th.

Anmerkung, f
- ◆ note

anmieten etw
- ◆ rent s.th.
- ◆ hire s.th. BE

Anmietung, f (kurz, meist Mobilien)
- Mieten, n
- Miete, f
- ◆ hiring BE
- ◆ renting AE
- ◆ rental

Anmietung, f (lang, meist Immobilien)
- Mieten, n
- Miete, f
- ◆ renting

Anmietung einer Halle, f
- Hallenanmietung, f
- Anmietung eines Saals, f
- Saalanmietung, f
- ◆ renting (of) a hall
- ◆ hiring (of) a hall BE
- ◆ hall rental AE
- ◆ hall hire BE

Anmietung eines Boots, f
- ◆ renting (of) a boat
- ◆ rental of a boat AE
- ◆ hire of a boat BE
- ◆ hiring a boat BE

Anmietung eines Privathauses, f
- ◆ renting (of) a private house

Anmietung eines Raumes, f
- Raumanmietung, f
- ◆ renting (of) a room AE
- ◆ hiring (of) a room BE
- ◆ hire of a room BE

Anmietung eines Saals, f
- Saalanmietung f
- Anmietung einer Halle, f
- Hallenanmietung, f
- ◆ renting (of) a large room
- ◆ renting (of) a hall
- ◆ hall rental AE
- ◆ hall hire BE

Anmietung von Geräten, f
- ◆ rental of equipment AE
- ◆ renting equipment AE
- ◆ hiring (of) equipment BE

anmutiger Service, m
- eleganter Service, m
- ◆ gracious service

anmutige Umgebung, f
- elegante Umgebung, f
- ◆ gracious surroundings pl

Annahme einer Zimmerreservierung f
- ◆ acceptance of a room reservation

Annahmeerklärung, f
- ◆ notice of acceptance

Annahmefrist, f (Zeitraum)
- ◆ period of acceptance

Annahmezeit, f
- (Zeit, bis zu der Gast eintreffen muß)
- → Bereithaltezeit

annehmbares Preisniveau, n
- ◆ acceptable price level
- ◆ acceptable rate level

Annehmlichkeit, f
- ◆ amenity
- ◆ convenience

Annehmlichkeiten des Lebens, f pl
- ◆ amenities of life pl
- ◆ comforts of life pl
- ◆ sweets of life pl

Annehmlichkeiten für Kinder, f pl
- ◆ amenities for children pl

Annehmlichkeiten nutzen
- ◆ use the amenities
- ◆ make use of the amenities

Annehmlichkeit im Freien, f
- ◆ outdoor amenity

Annehmlichkeit im Haus, f
- Annehmlichkeit im Innern, f
- ◆ indoor amenity

Annonce, f (Werbung)
- → Anzeige

Annonceur, m (Küche)
- Ansager, m
- ◆ announcer
- ◆ annonceur FR

Annonceuse, f (Küche)
- ◆ female announcer
- ◆ annonceuse FR

annoncieren etw
- ◆ announce s.th.

annullieren (etw)
- stornieren (etw)
- absagen (etw)
- zurücktreten (von etw)
- ◆ cancel (s.th.)

annulliert, adj
- → storniert

annullierter Flug, m
- ◆ cancelled flight
- ◆ canceled flight AE

Annullierung, f
- Stornierung, f
- ◆ annulment
- ◆ cancellation
- ◆ cancelation AE

Annullierungsbedingungen, f pl
- → Stornierungsbedingungen

Annullierungsdatum, n
- → Stornierungsdatum

Annullierungsgebühr, f
- → Stornierungsgebühr

Annullierungsgebühr erheben
- → Stornierungsgebühr erheben

Annullierungstermin, m
- → Stornierungstermin

Annullierungswunsch, m
- → Stornierungswunsch

Anorak, m
- ◆ anorak

Anordnung der Möbel in einem Zimmer, f
- ◆ disposition of furniture in a room

Anordnung der Stühle und Tische, f
- ◆ arrangement of the chairs and tables

an Ort und Stelle

an Ort und Stelle, adv
- ◆ on the spot, adv
- ◆ on the premises, adv *jur*
- ◆ in situ, adj *LAT jur*

an Ort und Stelle verzehren etw
an Ort und Stelle konsumieren etw
- ◆ consume s.th. on the premises *jur*

an Ostern
zu Ostern
- ◆ at Easter

anpassen sich an eine andere Kultur
- ◆ adjust to a different culture

Anpassung des Angebots an die Nachfrage, f
- ◆ adjustment of supply to demand

an Pfingsten
zu Pfingsten
- ◆ at Whitsun

Anreise
(Kapitelüberschrift)
- ◆ How to Get There
- ◆ How to Get to (X)
- ◆ Getting There

Anreise, f
- ◆ journey to one's destination
- ◆ journey
- ◆ outward journey
- ◆ approach
- ◆ travelling to X

Anreiseart, f
- ◆ form of travel

Anreisedatum, n
- → Ankunftsdatum

Anreiseliste, f
Liste der anreisenden Gäste, f
Ankunftsliste, f
Liste der ankommenden Gäste, f
- ◆ list of arrivals
- ◆ arrival(s) list

Anreisemöglichkeit, f
- ◆ possibility of traveling (to a destination) *AE*
- ◆ possibility of travelling (to a destination) *BE*
- ◆ how to get to (a destination)

Anreisemonat m
- → Ankunftsmonat

anreisen
- ◆ travel to one's destination
- ◆ travel

Anreise nach England, f
- ◆ travel to England

anreisen aus der ganzen Welt
- ◆ travel from around the globe

anreisen aus X
- ◆ travel from X
- ◆ come from X

anreisen mit dem Auto
- → ankommen mit dem Auto

anreisen mit dem Bus
- ◆ arrive by bus
- ◆ arrive by coach *BE*

anreisen mit dem Flugzeug
- → ankommen mit dem Flugzeug

Anreiseroute, f
- → Reiseroute

Anreise selbst organisieren
- → Reise selbst organisieren

Anreisetag, m
- ◆ day of the journey
- ◆ day of arrival
- ◆ arrival day

Anreisetermin, m
- → Ankunftstermin

Anreisewoche f
- → Ankunftswoche

Anreiz bieten
- ◆ provide an incentive

Anreiz geben
- ◆ give an incentive

Anrichte, f (Raum)
- → Anrichteraum

Anrichte, f (Tisch)
Anrichtetisch, m
- ◆ dresser

Anrichtebereich, m
- ◆ servery area *BE*

anrichten etw (Speisen)
- ◆ dress s.th.
- ◆ prepare s.th.

anrichten etw (Speisen auftragen)
auftragen etw
auftischen etw
- ◆ dish up s.th.
- ◆ serve s.th.

Anrichteraum, m
Anrichte, f
- ◆ servery room *BE*
- ◆ service room
- ◆ pantry

Anrichteweise, f
- ◆ service form
- ◆ form of service

anrüchiges Hotel, n
Hotel mit schlechtem Ruf n
- ◆ hotel of ill repute

Anrufbeantworter, m
Telefonanrufbeantworter, m
- ◆ answerphone *AE*
- ◆ telephone answering machine
- ◆ answering machine
- ◆ Ansaphone *BE*
- ◆ telephone answerer *AE coll*

Anrufbeantwortung, f (Service)
- ◆ answerphone service
- ◆ Ansaphone service *BE*

anrufen jn
telefonieren mit jm
- ◆ phone s.o.
- ◆ telephone s.o.
- ◆ call s.o.
- ◆ give s.o. a ring *BE*

anrufen jn direkt
- ◆ call s.o. direct

anrufen vom Zimmer aus
- ◆ telephone from one's room
- ◆ phone from one's room

Anrufer, m (Telefon)
Anrufender, m
- ◆ caller

Ansage machen (generell)
ansagen
- ◆ announce

ansagen sich als Gast
- ◆ announce one's visit

Ansager, m (Conférencier)
Conférencier, m
- ◆ compère *BE*
- ◆ compere *AE*

Ansager, m (Festlichkeit)
- ◆ MC
- ◆ master of ceremonies
- ◆ emcee *coll*

Ansager, m (Küche)
- → Annonceur

Ansager, m (Veranstaltungen)
- ◆ announcer

Anschaffungskosten, pl (anläßlich des Erwerbs)
- ◆ acquisition costs *pl*
- ◆ cost of acquisition

Anschaffungskosten, pl (generell)
- ◆ initial cost
- ◆ original cost
- ◆ prime cost
- ◆ initial outlay

Anschaffungspreis, m
- ◆ original price
- ◆ acquisition price
- ◆ purchase price
- ◆ cost price

Anschlagtafel, f
Schwarzes Brett, n
- ◆ bulletin board *AE*
- ◆ notice-board *BE*

anschließend an die Vorstellung
nach der Aufführung
- ◆ after the performance
- ◆ following the performance
- ◆ subsequent to the performance

anschließen sich einer Gruppe
- ◆ join a group

Anschlußaufenthalt, m (generell)
- → Verlängerungsaufenthalt

Anschlußaufenthalt, m (nach Konferenz)
- ◆ post-conference stay

Anschlußbuchung, f (generell)
Zusatzbuchung, f
Nachbuchung, f
- ◆ follow-up booking
- ◆ additional booking

Anschlußbuchung, f (nach Konferenz)
- ◆ post-conference booking

Anschlußbuchung, f (nach Kongreß)
- ◆ post-convention booking

Anschlußbuchung, f (Zug)
- ◆ booking (of) a seat in a connecting train

Anschlußbus, m
- ◆ connecting bus
- ◆ connecting coach *BE*

Anschlußflug, m
- ◆ connecting flight

Anschlußflughafen, m
- ◆ connecting airport

Anschluß haben an die Autobahn
Anbindung haben an die Autobahn
- ◆ have access to the highway *AE*
- ◆ have access to the motorway *BE*

Anschluß haben (Passagier)
- ◆ make a connection

Anschlußhotel, n (nach Konferenz)
- ◆ post-conference hotel

Anschluß in X, m (Passagier)
- ◆ connection in X
- ◆ connection at X

Anschlußprogramm, n (Ergänzung)
- → Beiprogramm

Anschlußprogramm, n (nach Konferenz)
- ◆ post-conference program *AE*
- ◆ post-conference programme *BE*

Anschlußprogramm, n (nach Kongreß)
- → Kongreßanschlußprogramm

Anschlußrechnung, f
- ◆ continuation bill
- ◆ follow *sl*

Anschlußreise, f
- ◆ add-on trip

26

Anstieg der Gästezahl

Anschlußstelle, f
  (Telefon, Strom)
  ♦ plug-in point
Anschluß suchen (Freunde suchen)
  Freunde suchen
  ♦ try to make friends
Anschluß suchen (Gesellschaft suchen)
  ♦ seek company
Anschlußverkehr, m
  Anschluß, m
  ♦ connecting service
Anschluß verpassen
  Anschluß versäumen
  ♦ miss a connection
  ♦ miss the connection
Anschlußzug, m
  ♦ connecting train
  ♦ connection
  ♦ connexion *BE*
anschnellen lassen etw auf etw
  hochschnellen lassen etw auf etw
  ♦ boost s.th. to s.th.
Anschriftenliste, f
  Adressenliste, f
  Adressenverzeichnis, n
  ♦ mailing list
  ♦ address list
  ♦ list of addresses
ansetzen etw für den 08. November
  → terminieren etw für den 08. November
Ansichtskarte, f
  ♦ picture postcard
Ansichtskartenstadt, f
  ♦ picture-postcard town
an Silvester, adv
  zu Silvester, adv
  an Sylvester, adv
  zu Sylvester, adv
  ♦ on New Year's Eve, adv
ans Meer fahren
  ♦ go to the seaside
An Sonn- und Feiertagen Geschlossen
  ♦ Closed on Sundays and Bank Holidays *BE*
  ♦ Closed on Sundays and Public Holidays
an Spitzenbesuchstagen
  ♦ on peak visiting days
an Spitzentagen
  ♦ on peak days
  ♦ on the busiest days
Ansprache, f
  ♦ speech
  ♦ address
Ansprache halten
  Festansprache halten
  ♦ deliver an address
Ansprache mit programmatischem Inhalt, f
  ♦ keynote address
ansprechend, adj
  angenehm, adj
  ♦ agreeable, adj
  ♦ appealing, adj
  ♦ congenial, adj
ansprechende Atmosphäre, f
  sympathische Atmosphäre, f
  ♦ congenial atmosphere
ansprechende Bar, f
  sympathische Bar, f
  ♦ congenial bar
ansprechender Wein, m
  ♦ pleasant wine

ansprechendes Abendessen, n (Dinner)
  ♦ agreeable dinner
ansprechendes Abendessen, n (Supper)
  ♦ agreeable supper
ansprechendes Gasthaus, n
  ♦ appealing bar *AE*
  ♦ appealing pub *BE*
ansprechendes Mittagessen, n
  ♦ agreeable lunch
  ♦ agreeable luncheon
ansprechendes Zimmer, n
  ♦ agreeable room
ansprechende Umgebung, f
  sympathische Umgebung, f
  ♦ congenial surroundings *pl*
ansprechen jn (Werbung, Angebot)
  ♦ appeal to s.o.
Anspruch auf Entschädigung, m
  → Schadensersatzanspruch
Ansprüchen eines anspruchsvollen Gästekreises gerecht werden
  ♦ cater for the needs of a discerning clientele
Ansprüche stellen an etw
  ♦ make demands on s.th.
Anspruch haben an jn
  ♦ have a claim on s.o.
Anspruch haben auf eine Provision
  ♦ have a claim to commission
Anspruch haben auf etw
  ♦ have a claim to s.th.
Anspruch haben auf Schadensersatz
  ♦ be entitled to compensation
  ♦ be entitled to damages
anspruchslos, adj (einfach)
  einfach, adj
  schlicht, adj
  ♦ plain, adj
  ♦ simple, adj
anspruchslos, adj (genügsam)
  genügsam, adj
  bescheiden, adj
  ♦ modest, adj
  ♦ unpretentious, adj
  ♦ unassuming, adj
anspruchsloser Esser, m
  ♦ modest eater
anspruchsloser Gast, m
  ♦ easily satisfied guest
  ♦ guest who can be satisfied easily
anspruchsloses Programm, n
  ♦ lowbrow program *AE*
  ♦ lowbrow programme *BE*
anspruchslos leben
  (z.B. im Freien während einer Fahrt)
  primitiv leben
  ♦ rough it *coll*
  ♦ live rough
anspruchsvoll, adj
  ♦ demanding, adj
  ♦ discerning, adj
  ♦ discriminating, adj
  ♦ hard to satisfy (to please)
  ♦ fastidious, adj
anspruchsvolle Abfahrt, f
  (Ski)
  ♦ demanding run
anspruchsvolle Kundschaft, m
  ♦ demanding clientele
  ♦ discerning clientele
anspruchsvoller Gast, m
  ♦ discerning guest

  ♦ demanding guest
  ♦ discriminating guest
anspruchsvoller Gästekreis, m
  ♦ discerning clientele
  ♦ demanding clientele
anspruchsvoller Gaumen, m
  ♦ discriminate palate
anspruchvollsten Gast zufriedenstellen
  ♦ satisfy the most demanding guest
  ♦ satisfy the most discerning guest
anständiges Essen, n (generell)
  ♦ decent food
anständiges Essen, n (Mahlzeit) *coll*
  (reichlich und gut)
  ♦ square meal *coll*
  ♦ decent meal
anständiges Frühstück, n
  ♦ decent breakfast
anständiges Hotel, n
  ehrbares Hotel, n
  ♦ decent hotel
  ♦ reputable hotel
anständiges Trinkgeld n
  ♦ decent tip
Anstandsbesuch, m
  Höflichkeitsbesuch, m
  ♦ courtesy call
  ♦ courtesy visit
Anstandsdame spielen bei jm
  ♦ chaperone s.o.
  ♦ act as a chaperone
anstandshalber begleiten jn zu etw
  als Anstandsdame begleiten jn zu etw
  ♦ chaperone s.o. to s.th.
Ansteckblume, f
  Ansteckstrauß, m
  Anstecksträußchen, n
  ♦ boutonniere *AE*
  ♦ boutonnière *BE*
ansteckende Krankheit, f
  ♦ contagious disease
anstehen bei der Paßkontrolle
  ♦ line up for passport control
anstehen für eine Karte
  ♦ queue for a ticket
  ♦ line up for a ticket
anstehen für etw
  ♦ line up for s.th.
  ♦ queue for s.th.
anstehen zum Frühstück
  Schlange stehen zum Frühstück
  ♦ queue up for breakfast *BE*
  ♦ line up for breakfast
Anstieg der Ankünfte, m
  ♦ increase in arrivals
  ♦ rise in arrivals
Anstieg der Besucherzahlen, m
  ♦ increase in visitor numbers
Anstieg der Buchungen, m
  Buchungsanstieg, m
  ♦ climb in bookings
  ♦ rise in bookings
  ♦ increase in bookings
Anstieg der Buchungszahl, m
  ♦ rise in the number of bookings
  ♦ increase in the number of bookings
Anstieg der Gästezahl, m
  ♦ rise in the number of guests
  ♦ increase in the number of guests

Anstieg der Gesamtgästezahl

Anstieg der Gesamtgästezahl, m
- ♦ increase in the total number of guests
- ♦ rise in the total number of guests

Anstieg der Gesamtkundenzahl, m
- ♦ increase in client total
- ♦ rise in client total

Anstieg der Übernachtungszahlen, m
- Zuwachs der Übernachtungszahlen, m
- Übernachtungsanstieg, m
- Übernachtungszuwachs, m
- ♦ rise in the number of nights spent
- ♦ increase in the number of nights spent

anstoßen auf die Braut
- ♦ drink to the bride

anstoßen auf etw
- trinken auf etw
- ♦ toast (to) s.th.
- ♦ drink to s.th.

anstoßen auf jn
- trinken auf jn
- ♦ toast (to) s.o.
- ♦ drink to s.o.

anstoßen auf js Gesundheit
- trinken auf js Gesundheit
- ♦ toast s.o.'s health
- ♦ drink to s.o.'s health

anstrahlen etw
- → illuminieren etw

Anstrahlung, f
- → Illumination

anstrengende Fahrt, f
- ♦ strenuous trip
- ♦ hard trip

anstrengende Reise, f
- ♦ strenuous journey
- ♦ strenuous tour
- ♦ strenuous trip
- ♦ arduous journey
- ♦ arduous tour

anstrengender Spaziergang, m
- ♦ strenuous walk

anstrengender Urlaub, m
- anstrengende Ferien, pl
- ♦ strenuous vacation AE
- ♦ strenuous holiday BE

anstrengende Veranstaltung, f
- ♦ strenuous event
- ♦ strenuous function

anstrengende Wanderung, f
- ♦ strenuous ramble
- ♦ strenuous hike

ans Ufer schwimmen
- ♦ swim to the shore

Antarktis, f
- ♦ Antarctica
- ♦ Antarctic, the

Antarktiskreuzfahrt, f
- Kreuzfahrt in die Antarktis, f
- ♦ Antarctica cruise
- ♦ cruise to Antarctica
- ♦ cruise to the Antarctic

Anteil am Urlaubsmarkt, m
- Urlaubsmarktanteil, m
- Anteil am Ferienmarkt, m
- Ferienmarktanteil, m
- ♦ share of the vacation market AE
- ♦ share of the holiday market BE

Anteil der ausländischen Besucher, m
- ♦ proportion of foreign visitors
- ♦ proportion of visitors from overseas

anthropologisches Museum, n
- ♦ anthropological museum

Antigua
- ♦ Antigua

antik, adj
- ♦ antique, adj

antike Möbel, n pl
- ♦ antique furniture sg

antikes Spielzeug, n
- ♦ antique toys pl

antike Stadt Ephesos, f
- ♦ ancient town of Ephesos

Antillen, die, pl
- ♦ Antilles, the pl

Antipasto, m ITAL
- Vorspeise, f
- ♦ antipasto ITAL
- ♦ hors d'oeuvre

antiquiert, adj
- ♦ antiquated, adj

antiquierte Möbel, n pl
- ♦ antiquated furniture sg

Antiquitätengeschäft, n
- Antiquitätenladen, m
- ♦ antiques store AE
- ♦ antique shop BE
- ♦ antiques shop BE

Antiquitätenhändler, m
- ♦ antique dealer

Antiquitätenjäger, m
- ♦ antique hunter

Antiquitätenmarkt, m
- ♦ antiques market
- ♦ antique market

Antiquitätenmesse, f
- ♦ antiques fair

Antiquitätensammler, m
- ♦ antiques collector
- ♦ collector of antiques

Antiquitätensammlung, f
- ♦ collection of antiquities
- ♦ antiquity collection

Antrag, m (Gesuch)
- ♦ application

Antrag auf Erteilung eines Visums, m
- Visumantrag, m
- ♦ application for a visa
- ♦ visa application

Antragsformular, n (generell)
- ♦ application form

Antragsformular, n (Versicherung)
- ♦ claim form

Antragsgebühr, f
- ♦ application fee
- ♦ application charge

Antrag stellen auf etw
- ♦ make an application for s.th.
- ♦ apply for s.th.

Antragsteller, m
- → Bewerber

Antritt einer Reise, m
- Reiseantritt, m
- Reisebeginn, m
- ♦ setting out on a journey
- ♦ beginning of a journey
- ♦ starting on a journey
- ♦ commencement of the journey form
- ♦ departure

Antrunk, m
- ♦ first drink

Antrunk haben
- als erster trinken
- ♦ have the first drink
- ♦ take the first drink
- ♦ drink first

antworten auf etw
- → beantworten etw

antworten jm
- ♦ answer s.o.
- ♦ reply to s.o.
- ♦ give s.o. an answer

Antwort erwarten
- Antwort gern entgegensehen
- ♦ await a reply
- ♦ await an answer
- ♦ look forward to s.o's reply
- ♦ look forward to an answer

Antwort gern entgegensehen
- Antwort erwarten
- ♦ look forward to a reply
- ♦ look forward to an answer
- ♦ await a reply
- ♦ await an answer

Antwort gern entgegensehen von jm
- ♦ look forward to s.o.'s reply
- ♦ look forward to s.o.'s answer

Antwortkarte, f
- Rückantwortkarte, f
- Rückkarte, f
- ♦ reply card
- ♦ answer card
- ♦ response card AE

Antwortkarte ausfüllen
- ♦ fill out a reply card AE
- ♦ complete a reply card
- ♦ fill in a reply card BE

Antwortkarte beilegen
- ♦ enclose a reply card

Antwortkarte zurücksenden
- ♦ return a reply card
- ♦ send back a reply card

Antwortschein, m
- Rückantwortschein, m
- ♦ reply coupon

Antwortschreiben, n
- Antwortbrief, m
- schriftliche Antwort, f
- ♦ written answer
- ♦ written reply
- ♦ answer
- ♦ reply
- ♦ letter sent in reply to s.th.

An- und Abreise zu jeder Tageszeit
- ♦ arrival and departure at any time of the day

Anwalt für Grundstücksübertragungen, m
- ♦ conveyancer BE

Anwaltsgebühren, f pl
- → Rechtsanwaltsgebühren

an Weihnachten
- an Weihnacht
- ♦ at Christmas
- ♦ at Xmas

Anwender, m
- → Benutzer

Anwendung, f
- ♦ application

Anwesen, n
- Lokal, n
- ♦ premises pl

anwesend sein
  präsent sein
  ♦ be present
anwesend sein bei einer Feier
  einer Feier beiwohnen
  ♦ be present at a celebration
anwesend sein bei etw
  beiwohnen etw
  ♦ be present at s.th.
Anwesenheit, f
  Teilnahme, f
  ♦ presence
  ♦ attendance
Anwesenheitsliste, f (bei Veranstaltungen)
  Präsenzliste f
  ♦ attendance list
  ♦ list of attendants
  ♦ list of persons present
  ♦ record of attendance
Anwesen zu vermieten
  (Hinweisschild)
  ♦ Property for rent AE
  ♦ Property to let BE
an Wochentagen, adv
  wochentags, adv
  ♦ on weekdays, adv
  ♦ during the week, adv
Anzahl der Nächte f
  → Zahl der Übernachtungen
Anzahl der Personen, f
  → Personenzahl
Anzahl der Übernachtungen, f
  → Zahl der Übernachtungen
anzahlen etw a conto
  ♦ pay s.th. on account
anzahlen etw als Kaution
  ♦ pay s.th. as a deposit
anzahlen etw als Ratenzahlung
  ♦ make a down payment
Anzahlung, f (a conto)
  Akontozahlung, f
  ♦ payment on account
Anzahlung, f (Ratenkauf)
  ♦ down payment
  ♦ installment AE
  ♦ instalment BE
Anzahlung, f (Sicherheit)
  ♦ deposit
Anzahlung abziehen von der Gesamtrechnung
  Anzahlung verrechnen mit der Gesamtrechnung
  ♦ deduct a deposit from the total bill
  ♦ deduct a deposit from the total check AE
Anzahlung entrichten an ein Hotel
  Anzahlung an ein Hotel machen
  ♦ make a deposit to a hotel AE
  ♦ pay a deposit to a hotel BE
Anzahlung erbitten (Sicherheit)
  Kaution verlangen
  Kaution erbitten
  ♦ ask for a deposit
Anzahlung erhalten (Sicherheit)
  ♦ receive a deposit
Anzahlung fordern (Sicherheit)
  Anzahlung verlangen
  ♦ demand a deposit
  ♦ require a deposit
Anzahlung ist bei der Buchung zu entrichten
  ♦ deposit is payable at the time of booking
Anzahlung ist nicht erforderlich
  ♦ deposit is not required

Anzahlung ist nicht rückerstattbar
  Anzahlung ist nicht erstattbar
  ♦ deposit is not returnable
Anzahlung ist verloren
  ♦ deposit is forfeit
  ♦ deposit is forfeited
  ♦ deposit is lost
Anzahlung leisten (von DM 500)
  ♦ make a deposit (of DM 500) AE
  ♦ pay a deposit (of DM 500) BE
  ♦ deposit (DM 500)
Anzahlung machen
  Anzahlung leisten
  ♦ pay a deposit BE
  ♦ make a deposit AE
Anzahlung nicht erforderlich
  ♦ No deposit required
Anzahlungsbetrag m
  ♦ amount of deposit
Anzahlung schicken
  ♦ send a deposit
Anzahlungseingang, m
  ♦ receipt of a deposit
Anzahlungserstattung, f
  Erstattung der Anzahlung, f
  ♦ refund of the deposit
  ♦ deposit refund
Anzahlungshauptbuch, n
  ♦ deposit ledger
Anzahlungsquittung, f
  ♦ deposit receipt
Anzahlungsquittung ausstellen
  ♦ issue a deposit receipt
Anzahlungsquittungsbuch, n
  ♦ deposit receipt book
Anzahlungsquittungsbuch führen
  ♦ keep a deposit receipt book
Anzahlungsüberweisung, f
  ♦ transfer of (a) deposit
  ♦ transferring a deposit AE
  ♦ transferring a deposit BE
Anzahlung überweisen
  ♦ transfer a deposit
Anzahlung verbuchen
  Anzahlung vermerken
  ♦ record a deposit
Anzahlung verbuchen im Anzahlungshauptbuch
  ♦ enter a deposit in the deposit ledger
Anzahlung verfällt
  ♦ deposit will be forfeit
  ♦ deposit is forfeit
Anzahlung verlangen (von jm)
  Kaution fordern (von jm)
  ♦ require a deposit (from s.o.)
  ♦ request a deposit (from s.o.)
Anzahlung verlieren
  Anzahlung einbüßen
  ♦ forfeit a deposit
Anzahlung von 50 % erforderlich bei der Buchung
  ♦ deposit of 50 % required on booking
Anzahlung von DM 123 ist zu leisten vor dem ...
  ♦ deposit of DM 123 is payable before ...
  ♦ deposit of DM 123 is payable prior to ...
Anzahlung wünschen
  Anzahlung verlangen
  Kaution wünschen
  Kaution fordern
  ♦ request a deposit
  ♦ require a deposit

Anzahlung zurückbehalten
  Anzahlung einbehalten
  ♦ retain a deposit
Anzahlung zurückerstatten (an jn)
  ♦ refund a deposit (to s.o.)
Anzeige, f (Werbung)
  Annonce, f
  Inserat, n
  ♦ advertisement
  ♦ ad BE coll
  ♦ advert BE coll
anzeigen jn bei der Polizei
  ♦ lodge information with the police against s.o.
Anzeigenkampagne, f
  → Werbekampagne
Anzeigenkampagne starten
  Werbekampagne starten
  ♦ launch an advertising campaign
Anzeigetafel, f
  ♦ display board
  ♦ wall screen
Anzumeldender, m
  ♦ person subject to registration
anzünden etw
  (z.B. Zigarette)
  ♦ light s.th.
AP, m
  American Plan, m
  Zimmer mit Vollpension, n
  ♦ AP
  ♦ American Plan
  ♦ full-board terms pl
à part, adv FR
  getrennt, adv
  einzeln, adv
  ♦ à part, adv FR
Aparthotel n
  ♦ apart hotel
A-part-Service, m
  (Restaurant)
  Einzelservice, m
  ♦ à-part service
  ♦ a-part service AE
Aperitif, m
  ♦ aperitif
  ♦ pre-dinner drink
  ♦ pre-lunch drink
Aperitifbar, f
  ♦ aperitif bar
Aperitif bestellen
  ♦ order an aperitif
Aperitifbestellung, f
  ♦ aperitif order
  ♦ ordering an aperitif
  ♦ ordering aperitifs
Aperitifcocktail, m
  Cocktail vor dem Essen, m
  ♦ before-dinner cocktail
Aperitif einnehmen
  ♦ take an aperitif
Aperitifempfang, m
  ♦ aperitif reception
Aperitif genießen
  Aperitif zusprechen
  ♦ enjoy an aperitif
Aperitif servieren
  ♦ serve an aperitif
Aperitif vorschlagen
  ♦ suggest an aperitif

Aperitifwein

Aperitifwein, m
♦ aperitif wine
♦ appetizer wine
Apéro, m FR
Aperitif, m
♦ apéro FR
♦ aperitif
APEX-Tarif, m
Super-Flieg-und-Spar-Tarif, m
♦ APEX tariff
♦ advance purchase excursion tariff
Apfel, m
♦ apple
Apfelauflauf, m
♦ apple soufflé
♦ apple souffle AE
Apfelbaum, m
♦ apple tree
Apfelbeignets, m pl
♦ apple fritters pl
Apfelcharlotte, f
♦ apple charlotte
Apfeleiskrem, f
Apfeleis, n
♦ apple ice cream AE
♦ apple ice-cream BE
♦ apple ice
Apfel entkernen
♦ core an apple
Apfelfüllung, f
♦ apple stuffing
♦ apple filling
Apfelgegend, f
♦ apple country
Apfelgelee, n
♦ apple jelly
Apfel im Schlafrock, m
♦ apple dumpling
♦ apple baked in crust
Apfelkaltschale, f
♦ cold apple soup
Apfelkompott, n
♦ stewed apples pl
♦ apple compôte BE
♦ apple compote AE
Apfelkonfitüre, f
♦ apple jam
Apfelkuchen, m
♦ apple cake
Apfelkuchen, m (gedeckt)
♦ apple pie
Apfel-Merrettichsoße, f
Apfel-Krensoße, f ÖST
♦ horseradish sauce with apples
Apfelmilchmixgetränk, n
♦ apple milk shake
Apfelmost m (alkoholisch)
♦ apple cider
♦ cider
♦ hard cider AE
Apfelmost m (ohne Alkohol)
→ Apfelsaft
Apfelmus, n
Apfelpüree, n
♦ apple purée
♦ apple puree AE
Apfelpfannkuchen, m
♦ apple pancake
Apfelpudding, m
♦ apple pudding

Apfelpunsch, m
♦ apple punch
Apfelpüree, n
→ Apfelmus
Apfelsaft m
♦ apple juice
Apfelsaison, f
Apfelzeit, f
♦ apple season
Apfelsalat, m
♦ apple salad
Apfelschale, f
♦ apple skin
Apfel schälen
♦ peel an apple
Apfelscheibe, f
♦ apple slice
♦ slice of apple
Apfelschnaps, m
♦ applejack AE
Apfelschnitte, f
Apfelkruste, f
♦ apple crust
Apfelsine, f
→ Orange
Apfelsorbet, n
♦ apple sorbet
Apfelsoße, f
♦ apple sauce
Apfelstrudel, m
♦ apple strudel
Apfelsuppe, f
♦ apple soup
Apfeltasche, f
♦ apple turnover
Apfeltorte, f
♦ apple tart
Apfelwein, m
♦ apple wine
Apfelweinschenke, f
♦ apple-wine tavern
à point, adv FR
halb durchgebraten, adj
♦ à point, adv FR
♦ medium-done, adj
♦ rare, adj AE
♦ lightly done, adj BE
♦ just done, adj BE
Apotheke, f (Arznei)
♦ pharmacy AE
♦ drugstore AE
♦ chemist's shop BE
♦ chemist's BE coll
Apotheke, f (Nepp) sl
♦ expensive place
♦ expensive shop
Apothekenmuseum, n
♦ pharmaceutical museum
Apothekennotdienst, m
♦ emergency pharmacist service
App.
Appartement n
♦ apt.
♦ apartment
Appalachen, die, pl
♦ Appalachians, the pl
Appalachen-Wanderweg, m
♦ Appalachian Trail, the
Appartement, n
App.

♦ apartment
♦ apt.
Appartementanlage, f
Appartementkomplex m
♦ apartment complex
Appartementanlage betreiben
♦ operate an apartment complex
Appartementart f
Appartementtyp m
♦ apartment type
♦ type of apartment
Appartementbereich, (abstrakt)
Appartementsektor, m
♦ apartment sector
Appartementbereich, m (konkret)
♦ apartment area
Appartementbeschreibung f
♦ apartment description
♦ description of an apartment
Appartement besichtigen
♦ view an apartment
♦ look at an apartment
Appartementbesitzer m
♦ apartment owner
♦ owner of an apartment
Appartement besteht aus drei Zimmern
♦ apartment consists of three rooms
Appartementbett n
♦ apartment bed
♦ bed in an apartment
Appartement bietet vier Personen Unterkunft
Appartement bietet vier Personen Platz
♦ apartment sleeps four persons
♦ apartment accommodates four persons
Appartement buchen
♦ book an apartment
Appartementdorf, n
♦ apartment village
Appartementeinnahmen, f pl
♦ apartment takings pl
♦ apartments takings pl
Appartementfläche, f
♦ apartment area
Appartement frei haben
♦ have an apartment free
♦ have an apartment vacant
♦ have a vacancy
Appartement für fünf Personen, n
♦ apartment for five persons
♦ apartment sleeping five persons
Appartement für Selbstversorger, n
→ Selbstverpflegungsappartement
Appartementgast, m
♦ apartment guest
Appartementgröße, f
♦ apartment size
♦ size of the apartment
Appartement haben
♦ have an apartment
Appartementhaus, n
→ Mietshaus
Appartementhotel n
♦ apartment hotel
Appartement im obersten Stockwerk, n
♦ top-floor apartment
Appartement in einer früheren Stallung, n
♦ mews apartment
Appartementinhaber, m
Appartementbewohner, m
♦ occupant of an apartment

Appartement in regelmäßigen Abständen reinigen
 ♦ clean an apartment at regular intervals
Appartement in Zeiteigentum, n
 → Timeshare-Appartement
Appartement ist bezugsfähig
 ♦ apartment is ready for occupation
Appartement ist bezugsfertig
 ♦ apartment is ready to move in(to)
Appartement ist eigengenutzt
 ♦ apartment is owner-occupied
Appartement ist leer
 (ohne Möbel oder unbewohnt)
 ♦ apartment is empty
Appartement jeden zweiten Tag reinigen
 ♦ clean an apartment every other day
Appartement kann bis zu sechs Personen aufnehmen
 ♦ apartment can accommodate up to six persons
Appartement kann samstags besichtigt werden
 ♦ apartment can be viewed on Saturdays
Appartementküche, f
 ♦ apartment kitchen
Appartement läßt sich gut vermieten
 ♦ apartment rents well *AE*
 ♦ apartment lets well *BE*
Appartement liegt im obersten Stockwerk
 ♦ apartment is situated on the top floor
Appartementmiete, f
 ♦ apartment rent
 ♦ apartment charge
Appartement mieten
 ♦ rent an apartment
Appartement mitbenutzen
 Appartement teilen mit jm
 ♦ share an apartment
 ♦ share an apartment with s.o.
Appartement mit drei Schlafzimmern, n
 ♦ three-bedroom apartment
 ♦ apartment with three bedrooms
Appartement mit einem Schlafzimmer, n
 ♦ one-bedroom apartment
 ♦ apartment with one bedroom
Appartement mit Hotelservice, n
 ♦ apartment with hotel service
Appartement mit Kochgelegenheit, n
 ♦ efficiency apartment *AE*
 ♦ efficiency *AE*
 ♦ housekeeping apartment
 ♦ apartment with cooking facility
Appartement mit Kochnische, n
 ♦ apartment with kitchenette
Appartement mit Küche, n
 ♦ apartment with kitchen
Appartement mit Küchenbenutzung, n
 ♦ apartment with use of the kitchen
 ♦ apartment with kitchen privileges
Appartement mit Service, n
 Appartement mit Bedienung, n
 ♦ service apartment
 ♦ serviced apartment
Appartement mit vier Schlafzimmern, n
 ♦ four-bedroom apartment
 ♦ apartment with four bedrooms
Appartement mit Vollservice, n
 ♦ fully serviced apartment
Appartement mit zwei Schlafzimmern, n
 ♦ two-bedroom apartment
 ♦ apartment with two bedrooms

Appartement nebenan, n
 ♦ apartment next door
 ♦ next-door apartment
Appartement ohne Hotelservice, n
 ♦ apartment without hotel service
Appartement ohne Trennwände, n
 ♦ open-plan apartment
Appartement ohne Verpflegung, n
 ♦ apartment only
Appartementpersonal n
 ♦ apartment staff
 ♦ apartment personnel
Appartementpreis, m
 ♦ apartment price
 ♦ apartment rate
Appartementreinigung f
 ♦ apartment cleaning
 ♦ cleaning of an apartment
Appartementschlüssel, m
 ♦ apartment key
Appartements in ausgesuchten Lagen
 ♦ apartments in choice locations
Appartement steht leer
 (ist unbewohnt)
 ♦ apartment is vacant
Appartement steht von Mai bis Juli zur Verfügung
 ♦ apartment is available from May to July
Appartement steht zum Verkauf
 ♦ apartment is for sale
Appartement täglich reinigen
 ♦ clean an apartment daily
Appartement teilen mit jm
 ♦ share an apartment with s.o.
Appartement überprüfen
 ♦ check an apartment
 ♦ inspect an apartment
Appartementunterbringung, f
 → Appartementunterkunft
Appartementunterkunft, f
 Appartementunterbringung, f
 ♦ apartment accommodation
Appartementurlaub, m
 Appartementferien, pl
 ♦ apartment vacation *AE*
 ♦ apartment holiday *BE*
Appartement vermieten
 ♦ rent (out) an apartment *AE*
 ♦ let an apartment *BE*
Appartement wird einmal pro Woche gereinigt
 ♦ apartment is cleaned once a week
Appartement wöchentlich reinigen
 ♦ clean an apartment weekly
Appartementzimmer n
 ♦ apartment room
Appartement zu vermieten
 (Hinweisschild)
 ♦ Apartment to let *BE*
 ♦ Apartment for rent *AE*
Appenzeller Käse, m
 ♦ Appenzell cheese
Appetit, m
 Eßlust, f
 ♦ appetite
Appetit anregen
 Appetit reizen
 ♦ stimulate the appetite
 ♦ whet the appetite
 ♦ sharpen the appetite
appetitanregend, adj (Arznei)
 ♦ stimulating the appetite, adj

appetitanregend, adj (Speise)
 → appetitlich
appetitanregendes Essen, n
 appetitliches Essen, n
 ♦ appetising food
 ♦ appetizing food
appetitanregendes Mittagessen, n
 ♦ appetising lunch
 ♦ appetising luncheon
Appetit anregen mit etw
 ♦ stimulate one's appetite with s.th.
 ♦ whet one's appetite with s.th.
 ♦ sharpen one's appetite with s.th.
Appetitanreger, m (pikant)
 (Speise oder Getränk)
 Appetithäppchen, n
 ♦ appetizer
 ♦ appetiser
Appetitanregung f
 ♦ stimulation of appetite
Appetit auf etw, m
 ♦ appetite for s.th.
Appetit bekommen
 ♦ pick up an appetite
 ♦ work up an appetite
Appetitbissen, m
 → Appetithappen
Appetitbrötchen, n
 ♦ savory sandwich *AE*
 ♦ savoury sandwich *BE*
 ♦ savory roll *AE*
 ♦ savoury roll *BE*
Appetit finden an etw
 (oft verneint)
 ♦ relish s.th.
Appetit haben
 ♦ feel peckish
Appetit haben (auf etw)
 ♦ have an appetite (for s.th.)
 ♦ be hungry (for s.th.)
 ♦ feel like having s.th.
Appetithappen, m
 Appetithäppchen n
 Amuse-gueule m *FR*
 ♦ savory *AE*
 ♦ savoury *BE*
 ♦ canapé *FR*
 ♦ amuse-gueule *FR*
 ♦ titbit
Appetit ist mir vergangen, der
 ♦ I have lost my appetite
 ♦ I've lost my appetite
Appetit kommt beim Essen, der
 ♦ Appetite comes with eating
appetitlich, adj
 lecker, adj
 appetitanregend, adj
 appetitreizend, adj
 ♦ appetising, adj
 ♦ appetizing, adj
 ♦ delicious, adj
 ♦ savory, adj *AE*
 ♦ savoury, adj *BE*
appetitliches Gericht, n
 appetitanregendes Gericht, n
 ♦ appetising dish
 ♦ appetizing dish
appetitlich präsentiert, adj
 ♦ presented appetizingly, adj
 ♦ presented appetisingly, adj

Appetitlosigkeit

Appetitlosigkeit, f
- loss of appetite
- lack of appetite
- anorexia *scient*

Appetit machen auf etw
- whet one's appetite for s.th.

appetitmachend, adj
→ appetitanregend

Appetit machen jm
- give an appetite to s.o.
- give s.o. an appetite

Appetitmacher, m
→ Appetitanreger

Appetitmangel, m
- lack of appetite
- loss of appetite

Appetit nehmen jm
- take away s.o.'s appetite

Appetit stillen
- satisfy one's appetite

Appetit verderben
- spoil one's appetite
- spoil s.o.'s appetite

Appetit vergehen
- take away one's appetite
- spoil one's appetite

Appetit verlieren
- lose one's appetite

Appetitzügler, m
Appetithemmer, m
- appetite suppressant

applaudieren jm
- applaud s.o.

Apple Toddy, m
Apfelgrog, m
- apple toddy

Apprenti, m *FR*
(in Restaurant)
Lehrling, m
Pikkolo, m *ITAL*
- apprenti *FR*
- apprentice
- piccolo *ITAL*

Après-Ski, n
- après-ski
- apres-ski *AE*
- after-ski

Après-Ski-Bar, f
- après-ski bar
- apres-ski bar *AE*

Après-Ski-Beschäftigung, f
- après-ski activity
- apres-ski activity *AE*

Après-Ski-Drink, m
→ Après-Ski-Getränk

Après-Ski-Getränk, n
- après-ski drink
- après-ski beverage
- apres-ski drink *AE*
- apres-ski beverage *AE*

Après-Ski-Kleidung, f
- après-ski clothes *pl*
- après-ski clothing
- apres-ski clothes *AE pl*
- apres-ski clothing *AE*
- après-ski outfit *BE*

Après-Ski-Leben, n
- après-ski life
- apres-ski life *AE*

Après-Ski-Nachtleben, n
- après-ski nightlife
- apres-ski nightlife *AE*

Après-Ski-Programm, n
- après-ski program *AE*
- après-ski programme *BE*

Après-Ski-Spaß, m
- après-ski fun

Après-Ski-Szene, f
- après-ski scene

Après-Ski-Treffpunkt, m
- après-ski meeting place
- apres-ski meeting place *AE*

Après-Ski-Unterhaltung, f
- après-ski entertainment
- apres-ski entertainment *AE*

Après-Ski-Veranstaltung, f
- après-ski event
- après-ski function
- après-ski activity
- apres-ski event *AE*
- apres-ski function *AE*

Aprikose, f
Marille, f *ÖST*
- apricot

Aprikosenauflauf, m
Aprikosensoufflé, n
- apricot soufflé
- apricot souffle *AE*

Aprikosenbaum, m
- apricot tree

Aprikosenbeignets, m pl
- apricot fritters *pl*

Aprikosenbowle, f
- apricot cup
- apricot bowl

Aprikosenchutney, n
- apricot chutney

Aprikosencreme, f
- apricot cream

Aprikoseneis, n
- apricot ice cream *AE*
- apricot ice-cream *BE*

Aprikoseneisbombe, f
- apricot ice-bomb

Aprikosenfüllung, f
- apricot stuffing

Aprikosenkaltschale, f
- cold apricot soup

Aprikosenknödel, m
- apricot dumpling

Aprikosenkompott, n
- stewed apricots *pl*
- apricot compôte *BE*
- apricot compote *AE*

Aprikosenkonfitüre, f
- apricot jam

Aprikosenkuchen, m
- apricot cake

Aprikosenlikör, m
- apricot brandy

Aprikosenmilchmixgetränk, n
- apricot milk shake

Aprikosenparfait, n
- apricot parfait

Aprikosenpudding, m
- apricot pudding

Aprikosensaft, m
- apricot juice

Aprikosenschnitte, f
Aprikosenkruste, f
- apricot crust

Aprikosensorbet, n
- apricot sorbet

Aprikosensoße, f
- apricot sauce

Aprikosentorte, f
- apricot tart

April, m
- April

Aprilauslastung, f
Auslastung im April, f
- April load factor
- load factor in April

Aprilbelegung, f
Aprilauslastung, f
- April occupancy
- occupancy in April

Aprilfeier, f
- April celebration

Apriltagung, f
Apriltreffen, n
- April meeting

Aprilurlaub, m
- April vacation *AE*
- April holiday *BE*

Aprilwoche, f
- April week

Apsis, f
Apsiden, f pl
- apse
- apses *pl*

Apulien
- Apulia

apulisch, adj
- Apulian, adj

Aquaplaning, n *(Fahrzeug)*
- aquaplaning

Aquarellmalerei, f
- watercolor painting *AE*
- watercolour painting *BE*

Aquarium
- aquarium

Äquator, m
- equator

Äquatorialguinea
- Equatorial Guinea

Äquatortaufe, f
- crossing-the-line ceremony

Äquator überqueren
- cross the line
- cross the equator

Araber, m
- Arab

Arabien
- Araby

arabisch, adj
- Arab, adj

Arabische Halbinsel, f
- Arabian Peninsula, the

arabische Nächte, pl
- Arabian nights *pl*

arabischer Kaffee, m
- Arabian coffee

arabische Welt, f
- Arab world, the

Arabische Wüste, f
- Arabian Desert, the

Aralsee, m
- Lake Aral

Aran-Inseln, f pl
- Aran islands, the *pl*

arbeiten
- work

arbeiten als Barmann
- bartend *AE*
- work as a barman

arbeiten als Koch in einem Hotel
- be employed as a cook in a hotel

arbeiten als Reiseleiter
- work as a tour guide

arbeiten als Teilzeitkraft
- work on a part-time basis

arbeiten als Vollzeitkraft
- work on a full-time basis

arbeiten an seinem Image
- work on one's image

arbeiten im Empfang
- work in reception
- work at reception

arbeiten im Empfangsbüro
im Empfangsbüro arbeiten
- work in the reception office

arbeiten in einem Hotel
in einem Hotel arbeiten
- have a job in a hotel
- work in a hotel

arbeiten mit einem Gutscheinsystem
- operate a voucher system

arbeiten mit einer Auslastung von 80 %
- operate at an 80 % occupancy

arbeiten mit Gewinn
mit Gewinn arbeiten
- operate at a profit

arbeiten mit Gutscheinen
mit Gutscheinen arbeiten
- operate with vouchers

arbeiten mit optimaler Auslastung
- operate at optimum occupancy

arbeiten mit Verlust
mit Verlust arbeiten
- operate at a loss

arbeiten mit voller Auslastung
mit voller Belegung arbeiten
- operate at full occupancy

arbeiten ohne Pause
- work without a break
- work nonstop *AE*
- work non-stop *BE*

arbeiten rund um die Uhr
rund um die Uhr arbeiten
- work around the clock
- work round the clock

arbeiten wie ein Pferd
- work like a horse

Arbeiterfreizeitclub, m
Arbeiterverein, m
- working men's club

Arbeiterkneipe, f
- working men's bar *AE*
- working men's pub *BE*

Arbeitnehmer im Gastgewerbe, m
gastgewerblicher Arbeitnehmer, m
- employee in the hotel and catering trade *BE*
- employee in the hospitality industry *AE*

Arbeitnehmervergünstigungen, f pl
- employee benefits *pl*

Arbeitsbedingungen, f pl
- working conditions *pl*

Arbeitsbereich, m
(z.B. in Suite)

- work area *AE*
- working area *BE*

Arbeitsbesuch, m
- working visit

Arbeitserlaubnis, f
Arbeitsgenehmigung, f
- labor permit *AE*
- labour permit *BE*
- work permit

Arbeitsessen, n (Dinner)
- working dinner
- business dinner

Arbeitsessen, n (Lunch)
→ Arbeitsmittagessen

Arbeitsfrühstück, n
- working breakfast

Arbeitsgenehmigung, f
Arbeitserlaubnis, f
Beschäftigungserlaubnis, f
- work permit
- labor permit *AE*
- labour permit *BE*

Arbeitsgenehmigung erhalten
Arbeitserlaubis erhalten
- receive a work permit

Arbeitsgenehmigung für Ausländer, f jur
- alien's work permit *AE jur*
- alien's labour permit *BE jur*

Arbeitsgruppe, f
- work group
- working group
- working party
- study group

Arbeitsgruppensitzung f
- session of a working group

Arbeitsgruppe unter dem Vorsitz von jm
- working group chaired by s.o.
- working party chaired by s.o.

Arbeitsgruppe zu etw, f
- working group dealing with s.th.
- working party dealing with s.th.

arbeitsintensiv, adj
- labor-intensive, adj *AE*
- labour-intensive, adj *BE*

arbeitsintensive Dienstleistung, f
- labor-intensive service *AE*
- labour-intensive service *BE*

Arbeitskräfteangebot, n
- supply of labor *AE*
- supply of labour *BE*

Arbeitskraft einstellen
- hire an employee
- engage an employee

Arbeitskräftemangel m (Knappheit)
- shortage of labor *AE*
- shortage of labour *BE*
- labor shortage *AE*
- labour shortage *BE*

Arbeitskräfteüberschuß, m
- surplus of labor *AE*
- surplus of labour *BE*

Arbeitsleben, n
- working life

Arbeitslohn, m
Bezahlung, f
- pay
- wages *pl*

Arbeitslöhne, m pl
(Bilanz)
- labor cost *AE*
- labour cost *BE*

Arbeitsmarkt, m
- labor market *AE*
- labour market *BE*

Arbeitsmittagessen, n
Arbeitsessen, n
- working luncheon
- working lunch

Arbeitsplatz im Tourismus, m
Arbeitsstelle im Fremdenverkehr, f
touristischer Arbeitsplatz, m
- job in tourism

Arbeitspreis pro Stunde, m
- labor rate per hour *AE*
- labour rate per hour *BE*

Arbeitsraum, m
- work room

Arbeits-Schlafzimmer, n
- study-bedroom

Arbeitsseminar, n
- working seminar

Arbeitssitzung, f
- work session *AE*
- working session *BE*

arbeitssparend, adj
- labor-saving, adj *AE*
- labour-saving, adj *BE*

arbeitsstellengebundene Unterkunft, f
- tied accommodation

arbeitsstellengebundene Cottage, f
- tied cottage

Arbeitsstunde, f
- workhour *AE*
- working hour *BE*

Arbeitstag, m
Werktag, m
- workday
- working day

Arbeitstagung, f (Konferenz)
Arbeitstreffen, n
- working conference
- work conference

Arbeitstagung, f (Treffen)
Arbeitstreffen, n
- working meeting
- business meeting
- work meeting

Arbeitsurlaub, m
- working vacation *AE*
- working holiday *BE*

Arbeitsurlaubsmarkt, m
- working vacation market *AE*
- working holiday market *BE*

Arbeitsverhalten, n
(Gegensatz zu Freizeitverhalten)
- work pattern

Arbeitsvertrag, m
- service contract
- contract of service

Arbeitswoche, f
- workweek *AE*
- working week *BE*

Arbeitszeit, f
- working time
- workhours *AE pl*
- working hours *BE pl*

Arbeitszimmer n
- study

Arboretum, n
- arboretum

Archäologe

Archäologe, m
- ◆ archaeologist
- ◆ archeologist

Archäologie, f
- ◆ archaeology
- ◆ archeology

archäologisch, adj
- ◆ archaeological, adj
- ◆ archeological, adj

archäologische Entdeckung, f
- ◆ archaeological discovery
- ◆ archeological discovery

archäologische Fundstücke, n pl
- ◆ archaeological remains pl
- ◆ archeological remains pl

archäologische Reise, f
Archäologiereise, f
- ◆ archaeological tour
- ◆ archeological-tour

archäologischer Fund, m pl
Ausgrabungsfund, m
- ◆ archaeological find
- ◆ archeological find

archäologischer Ort, m
- ◆ archaeological site
- ◆ archeological site

archäologisches Ausstellungsstück, n
- ◆ archaeological exhibit
- ◆ archeological exhibit

Archäologisches Museum, n
- ◆ Archaeological Museum
- ◆ Archeological Museum

Arche Noah, f
- ◆ Noah's Ark

Architekt, m
- ◆ architect

architektonisch, adj
- ◆ architectural, adj

architektonisches Merkmal, n
- ◆ architectural feature

architektonisch interessant, adj
- ◆ architecturally interesting, adj

Architektur, f
Baukunst, f
- ◆ architecture

Architekturbüro, n
- ◆ architect's office

Architekturdenkmal, n
- ◆ architectural monument

Architekturerbe, n
- ◆ architectural heritage

Architekturzentrum, n
- ◆ architectural center AE
- ◆ architectural centre BE

Ardennen, die, pl
- ◆ Ardennes, the, pl

Ardennerschinken, m
- ◆ Ardennes ham

Ardennerwald, m
(Region)
- ◆ Forest of Ardennes, the

Arena, f
- ◆ arena

Arenabestuhlung f
- ◆ arena-style seating
- ◆ arena seating

Arenaform f
(Bestuhlung)
- ◆ arena style

Argentinien
- ◆ Argentina
- ◆ Argentine, the

Aristokrat, m
- ◆ aristocrat

aristokratisch, adj
- ◆ aristocratic, adj

aristokratisches Hotel, n
- ◆ aristocratic hotel

Arkade, f
- ◆ arcade

Arkadenstraße, f
- ◆ arcaded street

Arktis, f
- ◆ Arctic, the

arktisch, adj
- ◆ arctic, adj

Arktisexpedition, f
- ◆ Arctic expedition
- ◆ expedition to the Arctic

Arlberg, m
- ◆ Arlberg, the

Arlbergpaß, m
- ◆ Arlberg Pass, the

Arlbergpaßstraße, f
- ◆ Arlberg Pass Road, the

Arlbergtunnel, m
- ◆ Arlberg Tunnel, the

Armagnac, m
- ◆ Armagnac

Armatur, f
- ◆ fittings pl

Armbehandlung, f
- ◆ arm treatment

Armbrust, f
- ◆ crossbow

Armbrustschießwettbewerb, m
Armbrustschießwettkampf, m
- ◆ crossbow shooting competition
- ◆ crossbow shooting contest

Arme des Morpheus, m pl
(Schlaf)
- ◆ arms of Morpheus pl

Ärmelkanal, m
- ◆ Channel, the

Ärmelkanalhafen, m
- ◆ Channel port

Ärmelkanalüberfahrt, f
- ◆ Channel crossing

Ärmelkanal überqueren
- ◆ cross the Channel

Ärmelkanalverbindung, f
- ◆ Channel link

Armenien
- ◆ Armenia

Armenier, m
- ◆ Armenian

Armenierin, f
- ◆ Armenian girl
- ◆ Armenian woman
- ◆ Armenian

armenisch, adj
- ◆ Armenian, adj

Armenküche, f
Suppenküche, f
- ◆ food bank AE
- ◆ soup kitchen AE
- ◆ soup-kitchen BE

Armenviertel, n
- ◆ poor quarter

arm essen jn
- ◆ eat s.o. out of house and home

Armpackung, f med
- ◆ arm wrap med

armselige Behausung, f
- ◆ humble dwelling

armselige Bude, f
- ◆ hovel

Armstütze, f
- ◆ armrest

Aroma, n
- ◆ aroma

Aroma genießen von etw
- ◆ savor the aroma of s.th. AE
- ◆ savour the aroma of s.th. BE

Aromamassage, f
- ◆ aroma massage

Aromaölbad, n med
- ◆ aroma oil bath med

Aromatherapeut, m
- ◆ aromatherapist

Aromatherapiegesichtsbehandlung, f
- ◆ aromatherapy facial treatment
- ◆ aromatherapy facial

Aromatherapieheilmassage, f
- ◆ aromatherapy remedial massage

Aromatherapiemassage, f
- ◆ aromatherapy massage

Aromatherapiepraxis, f
Aromatherapieräume, m pl
- ◆ aromatherapy suite

Aromatherapieprogramm, n
- ◆ aromatherapy program AE
- ◆ aromatherapy programme BE

aromatisch, adj
- ◆ aromatic, adj

aromatischer Geschmack, m
- ◆ aromatic flavor AE
- ◆ aromatic flavour BE

aromatisches Getränk, n
- ◆ aromatic drink
- ◆ aromatic beverage

Arrak, m
- ◆ arrack
- ◆ arrak

Arrangement, n (eines Musikstücks)
- ◆ arrangement

Arrangement, n (generell)
Vereinbarung, f
Vermittlung, f
Absprache, f
- ◆ arrangement

Arrangement, n (Pauschale)
→ Pauschalarrangement

Arrangement anbieten jm (generell)
- ◆ offer an arrangement to s.o.

Arrangement ändern (geringfügig)
- ◆ alter an arrangement
- ◆ alter the arrangement
- ◆ alter one's arrangement

Arrangement ändern (umfassend)
- ◆ change an arrangement
- ◆ change the arrangement
- ◆ change one's arrangement

Arrangement bestätigen
Vereinbarung bestätigen
- ◆ confirm an arrangement

Arrangement buchen (generell)
Arrangement bestellen
- ◆ book an arrangement

34

Arrangement buchen (Pauschale)
♦ book a package deal
Arrangement für Selbstfahrer, n
♦ self-drive arrangement
Arrangement im Büfettstil, n
♦ buffet-style arrangement
Arrangementpreis, m
(z.B. bei Pauschalarrangement)
♦ package deal price
♦ package deal rate
Arrangement wählen (generell)
Arrangement auswählen
♦ choose an arrangement
♦ select an arrangement
Arrangement zusammenstellen
♦ put together an arrangement
Arrangeur, m
(bes. von Musikstücken)
♦ arranger
arrangieren etw für jn
besorgen etw für jn
vermitteln etw jm
♦ arrange s.th. for s.o.
♦ make the necessary arrangements for s.o.
Arrivée, f SCHW
→ Ankunft, ankommender Gast
Art der Bezahlung, f
→ Zahlungsart
Art des Arrangements, f
♦ type of arrangement
Art des Reisens, f
Art des Reiseverkehrs, f
♦ kind of travel
Arthritis, f
♦ arthritis
Arthritis behandeln
♦ treat arthritis
arthritische Beschwerden, f pl
♦ arthritic disorders pl
Artischocke, f
♦ artichoke
Artischockenboden, m
♦ artichoke bottom
Artischockencremesuppe, f
♦ artichoke cream soup
Artischockenherz, n
♦ artichoke heart
Artischockenpastete, f
♦ artichoke pie
♦ artichoke pâté
Artischockensalat, m
♦ artichoke salad
Artischockensoufflé, n
Artischockenauflauf, m
♦ artichoke soufflé BE
♦ artichocke souffle AE
Artischockensuppe, f
♦ artichoke soup
Art Luxushotel, f
♦ deluxe type of hotel AE
♦ luxury type of hotel
Art von Hotel, f
♦ kind of hotel
Arundeler Festspiele, n pl
♦ Arundel Festival, the
Arzneimitteltherapie, f
Medikamententherapie, f
♦ drug therapy
Arzt, m
♦ doctor
♦ physician

Ärztekonferenz, f
Ärztetagung, f
♦ medical conference
Ärztekongreß, m
medizinischer Kongreß m
Medizinerkongreß m coll
♦ medical convention
♦ medical congress
Ärzteseminar, n
♦ medical seminar
Ärztetagung, f
♦ medical meeting
♦ medical conference
♦ conference of physicians
Arzthonorar, n
♦ medical fee
Arztkosten, pl
♦ medical expenses pl
ärztliche Beratung, f
♦ medical consultation
♦ medical advice
ärztliche Betreuung, f
♦ medical care
♦ medical service
ärztliche Diät, f
♦ medical diet
ärztliche Hilfe, f
♦ medical help
ärztlicher Berater, m
♦ medical adviser
ärztlicher Rat, m
♦ medical advice
ärztliche Therapie, f
♦ medical therapy
ärztliche Überwachung, f
♦ medical supervision
ärztliche Untersuchung, f
♦ medical examination
ärztlich überwacht, adj
♦ medically supervised, adj
ärztlich überwachtes Gesundheitsprogramm, n
♦ medically supervised health program AE
♦ medically supervised health programme BE
ärztlich verordnet, adj
♦ medically prescribed, adj
Arztpraxis, f
♦ doctor's office AE
♦ doctor's practice BE
Arztservice m
Arztdienst m
♦ medical service
♦ doctor available
Arztsuite, f
(in Hotel)
♦ doctor's suite
♦ medical suite
Äsche, f
♦ grayling
Aschenbahn, f
♦ cinder track
Aschenbecher, m
♦ ashtray
Aschenbecher austauschen
Aschenbecher wechseln
♦ change ashtrays
Aschenbecher leeren
♦ empty an ashtray
Aschenbecher mitgehen lassen coll
Aschenbecher klauen
♦ pinch an ashtray sl

Aschenbecher säubern
♦ clean an ashtray
Ascheneimer, m
♦ ash can AE
Aschermittwoch, m
♦ Ash Wednesday
Aserbeidschan
Aserbaidschan
♦ Azerbaijan
Aserbeidschaner, m
Aserbaidschaner, m
♦ Azerbaijani
aserbeidschanisch, adj
aserbaidschanisch, adj
♦ Azerbaijan, adj
Asiate, m
♦ Asian
Asiatin, f
♦ Asian girl
♦ Asian woman
♦ Asian
asiatisch, adj
♦ Asian, adj
asiatisch-pazifischer Raum, m
asiatisch-pazifische Region, f
♦ Asia-Pacific region, the
Asien
♦ Asia
Asienfahrt, f
♦ Asian trip
♦ Asian ride
Asienreise, f (in Asien)
Asienrundreise, f
♦ tour of Asia
♦ tour through Asia
♦ Asian tour
Asienreise, f (nach Asien)
Reise nach Asien, f
♦ tour to Asia
♦ journey to Asia
♦ trip to Asia
Asientournee, f
♦ Asian tour
Asowsche Meer, das, n
♦ Sea of Azov, the
asphaltiert, adj
♦ asphalted, adj
asphaltierter Bereich, m
asphaltierte Fläche, f
♦ asphalted area
Asphaltstraße, f
♦ tarmac road
♦ tarmac street
Asphalttennisplatz, m
♦ tarmac tennis court
Aspik, m/n
Sülze, f
♦ aspic
♦ jelly
Assistent, m
♦ assistant
Assistent der Geschäftsleitung, m
♦ assistant manager
♦ assistant to the manager
Assistent des Bankettleiters m
♦ assistant banquet manager
♦ assistant banqueting manager BE
Assistent des Catering Managers, m
♦ assistant catering manager

Assistent des geschäftsführenden Direktors

Assistent des geschäftsführenden Direktors, m
 ♦ assistant managing director
 ♦ assistant to the managing director
Assistent des Küchenchefs, m
 ♦ assistant chef
 ♦ assistant head chef
 ♦ chef's assistant
Assistent des Marketingleiters, m
 ♦ assistant marketing manager
Assistent des Nachtmanagers, m
 ♦ assistant night manager
Assistent des Restaurantleiters, m
 ♦ assistant restaurant manager
 ♦ assistant to the restaurant manager
Assistent des Verkaufsleiters, m
 ♦ assistant sales manager
Assistent des Wirtschaftsdirektors, m
 Assistent des F&B-Managers, m
 ♦ assistant food and beverage manager
 ♦ assistant f&b manager
Assistentin der Ersten Hausdame, f
 Assistentin der Generalgouvernante, f SCHW
 ♦ assistant executive housekeeper AE
 ♦ assistant to the executive housekeeper AE
 ♦ assistant head housekeeper BE
 ♦ assistant to the head housekeeper BE
Assistentin der Hausdame, f
 Hausdamenassistentin, f
 ♦ assistant to the housekeeper
 ♦ assistant housekeeper
Assistentin der Wäschebeschließerin, f
 ♦ assistant linen keeper
Asthma, n
 ♦ asthma
Asthmatherapie, f
 ♦ asthma therapy
Asthmatiker, m
 ♦ asthmatic
asthmatisch, adj
 ♦ asthmatic, adj
astrologische Uhr, f
 ♦ astrological clock
Astronaut, m
 ♦ astronaut
astronomische Uhr, f
 ♦ astronomical clock
astronomisch hohe Rechnung, f
 ♦ astronomical bill
Asyl, n (Heim)
 ♦ asylum
 ♦ home
Asyl, n (politisch)
 ♦ asylum
Asyl, n (Zufluchtsort)
 ♦ asylum
 ♦ place of refuge
 ♦ refuge
 ♦ sanctuary
Asylantrag, m
 Antrag auf Asyl, m
 ♦ application for asylum
 ♦ asylum application
Asyl beantragen
 ♦ apply for asylum
Asylbewerber, m
 ♦ asylum applicant
Asyl erhalten
 ♦ receive asylum
 ♦ be granted asylum
Asyl für Obdachlose n
 → Obdachlosenasyl

Asyl jm gewähren
 ♦ grant s.o. asylum
Asylrecht n
 ♦ right of asylum
Asyl suchen
 ♦ seek asylum
Asylsuchender, m
 ♦ asylum-seeker
 ♦ person seeking asylum
Atelier, n
 ♦ atelier
 ♦ studio
atemberaubend, adj
 ♦ breathtaking, adj
atemberaubende Blicke bieten auf etw
 atemberaubende Ausblicke bieten auf etw
 atemberaubende Aussichten bieten auf etw
 ♦ provide breathtaking views of s.th.
atemberaubende Landschaft, f
 ♦ breathtaking scenery
 ♦ breathtaking landscape
 ♦ breathtaking countryside
atemberaubender Blick, m
 atemberaubender Ausblick m
 atemberaubende Aussicht f
 ♦ breathtaking view
atemberaubende Rundsicht, f
 atemberaubende Panoramaaussicht, f
 atemberaubender Panoramablick, m
 ♦ breathtaking panoramic view
Athener, m
 ♦ Athenian
athenisch, adj
 ♦ Athenian, adj
ätherisches Öl, n
 ♦ essential oil
Äthiopien
 ♦ Ethiopia
Äthiopier, m
 ♦ Ethiopian
Äthiopierin, f
 ♦ Ethiopian girl
 ♦ Ethiopian woman
 ♦ Ethiopian
äthiopisch, adj
 ♦ Ethiopian, adj
Athlet, m
 ♦ athlete
Athos-Halbinsel, f
 ♦ Mount Athos peninsula, the
Atlantik, m
 ♦ Atlantic, the
 ♦ Atlantic Ocean, the
Atlantikblick, m
 Blick auf den Atlantik, m
 ♦ Atlantic view
 ♦ view of the Atlantic
Atlantikküste, f
 ♦ Atlantic coast, the
Atlantikküste besuchen
 ♦ visit the Atlantic coast
Atlantikstrand, m
 ♦ Atlantic beach
Atlantik überqueren
 ♦ cross the Atlantic
Atlantiküberquerung, f
 Überquerung des Atlantiks, f
 ♦ Atlantic crossing
 ♦ crossing the Atlantic
Atlantikufer, n
 ♦ Atlantic shore

Atlantische Ozean, der, m
 ♦ Atlantic Ocean, the
Atlas, m
 ♦ atlas
Atlasgebirge, n
 ♦ Atlas Mountains, the pl
Atmosphäre, f
 (Stimmung)
 ♦ atmosphere
Atmosphäre, in der man entspannen kann
 ♦ atmosphere in which one can relax
 ♦ atmosphere in which one can unwind
Atmosphäre ausstrahlen
 ♦ exude an atmosphere
 ♦ breathe an atmosphere
Atmosphäre beleben
 ♦ liven up the atmosphere
Atmosphäre besitzen von etw
 ♦ have an atmosphere of s.th.
Atmosphäre bewahren von etw
 ♦ retain the atmosphere of s.th.
Atmosphäre bieten von etw
 ♦ offer an atmosphere of s.th.
 ♦ provide an atmosphere of s.th.
Atmosphäre der Entspannung, f
 ♦ atmosphere of relaxation
Atmosphäre der guten alten Zeit, f
 ♦ old-world atmosphere
 ♦ olde-worlde atmosphere humor
Atmosphäre eines Hotels genießen
 ♦ enjoy the atmosphere of a hotel
Atmosphäre einfangen
 ♦ capture the atmosphere
Atmosphäre erhalten von etw
 ♦ preserve the atmosphere of s.th.
 ♦ keep the atmosphere of s.th.
Atmosphäre erzeugen
 ♦ generate an atmosphere
Atmosphäre genießen
 ♦ enjoy an atmosphere
Atmosphäre haben
 ♦ have an atmosphere
Atmosphäre in dem Hotel ist angenehm
 ♦ atmosphere at the hotel is pleasant
Atmosphäre in dem Hotel ist entspannt
 ♦ atmosphere at the hotel is relaxed
Atmosphäre in dem Hotel ist sehr angenehm
 ♦ atmosphere at the hotel is very pleasant
Atmosphäre ist gemütlich
 ♦ atmosphere is cosy
 ♦ atmosphere is cozy AE
 ♦ atmosphere is comfortable
Atmosphäre schaffen
 ♦ create an atmosphere
Atmosphäre spüren
 Atmosphäre fühlen
 ♦ feel the atmosphere
Atmosphäre verleihen etw
 ♦ give s.th. an atmosphere
 ♦ lend s.th. an atmosphere
Atmosphäre verlieren
 ♦ lose its atmosphere
Atmosphäre von Komfort, f
 ♦ atmosphere of comfort
Ätna, m
 ♦ Mount Etna
ATO
 Airline Tour Order, f
 ♦ ATO
 ♦ airline tour order

Atoll, n
♦ atoll
Atrium, n
♦ atrium
Atriumgalerie, f
♦ atrium gallery
Atriumgebäude, n
♦ atrium building
Atriumhalle, f
Atriumlobby f
♦ atrium lobby
Atriumhotel, n
♦ atrium hotel
Attersee, m
♦ Atter Lake, (the)
Attraktion, f
♦ attraction
attraktiv, adj
♦ attractive, adj
attraktiv angelegtes Gelände, n
♦ attractively laid-out grounds pl
attraktive Lage, f
♦ attractive location
♦ attractive situation
♦ attractive position
attraktiver Preis, m
♦ attractive price
♦ attractive rate
attraktiv gelegen, adj
♦ attractively situated, adj
♦ attractively positioned, adj
♦ attractively located, adj
attraktiv möbliert, adj
♦ attractively furnished, adj
attraktiv möbliertes Zimmer, n
♦ attractively furnished room
Aubergine, f
Eierfrucht, f
♦ aubergine
♦ egg-plant
Auberginesalat, m
♦ aubergine salad
Audienz bei dem Papst, f
♦ audience with the pope
Audienz bei der Königin, f
♦ audience with the Queen
Audienz bei jm, f
♦ audience with s.o.
Audienz bekommen bei jm
♦ get an audience with s.o.
Audienz sichern sich bei jm
♦ secure an audience with s.o.
Audiovisionstechniker, m
♦ audio-visual technician
audiovisuell, adj
♦ audio-visual, adj
♦ AV
audiovisuelle Anforderungen, f pl
♦ audio-visual requirements pl
audiovisuelle Anlagen, f pl
♦ audio-visual facilities pl
♦ AV facilities pl
audiovisuelle Ausrüstung, f
audiovisuelle Ausstattung, f
♦ audio-visual equipment
♦ AV equipment
audiovisuelle Präsentation, f
♦ audio-visual presentation
♦ AV presentation

audiovisuelles Hilfsmittel, n
♦ audio-visual aid
♦ AV aid
audiovisuelles Material, n
♦ audio-visual material
♦ AV material
audiovisuelles Programm, n
♦ audio-visual program AE
♦ AV program AE
♦ audio-visual programme BE
♦ AV programme BE
audiovisuelle Vorführung, f
Audiovisionschau, f
♦ audio-visual show
♦ AV show
Auditoriumbestuhlung, f
♦ auditorium-style seating
♦ auditorium seating
auf Anfrage
♦ on application
♦ on request
auf Ausstellung gehen
♦ go on exhibition
aufbauen etw (Ausstellung etc.)
machen etw
♦ mount s.th.
Aufbaumannschaft, f (Ausstellung)
♦ mounting team
Aufbautag, m (Ausstellung)
♦ build-up day
Aufbauzeit, f (Ausstellung)
♦ build-up time AE
♦ setting-up time BE
auf besondere Einladung
♦ by special invitation
auf Bestellung, adv
♦ to order, adv
auf Bestellung zubereitet
♦ prepared to order
♦ cooked to order
auf Besuch kommen (zu jm)
zu Besuch kommen (zu jm)
♦ come on a visit (to s.o.)
♦ come to see s.o.
auf Besuch sein bei jm
Besuch machen bei jm
♦ be on a visit to s.o.
aufbewahren etw
♦ keep s.th.
♦ retain s.th.
Aufbewahrungsmöglichkeit, f
→ Lagereinrichtung
Aufbewahrungsschein, m (Gepäck)
→ Gepäckschein
aufblasbare Matratze, f
♦ inflatable mattress
aufbleiben die ganze Nacht
♦ stay up all night
aufbleiben (nicht schlafengehen)
♦ stay up
aufbleiben und warten auf jn
♦ wait up for s.o.
aufbrechen
♦ start off
♦ set off
aufbrechen bei Sonnenuntergang
♦ set off at sundown
aufbrechen in den Urlaub
starten in den Urlaub
in die Ferien aufbrechen

♦ set off on vacation AE
♦ set off on holiday BE
aufbrechen nach dem Abendessen
♦ set out after dinner
♦ set off after dinner
♦ start after dinner
♦ depart after dinner
aufbrechen nach Italien
♦ set off for Italy
aufbrechen nach X
♦ set out for X
♦ set off for X
♦ start (out) for X
♦ start (off) for X
♦ depart for X
aufbrechen von A nach B
♦ set off from A to B
aufbrechen zu der Reise in das Winterquartier
♦ set out for the journey to the winter quarters
aufbrechen zu der Reise nach X
♦ set out for the journey to X
aufbrechen zu einem Ganztagsausflug
♦ set off on a full-day excursion
aufbrechen zu einer Asienreise
♦ set off on a tour of Asia
aufbrechen zu einer Campingfahrt
♦ set off for a camping trip
aufbrechen zu einer Expedition
♦ set out on an expedition
aufbrechen zu einer Fahrt
♦ set out for a trip
aufbrechen zu einer langen Wanderung
♦ set out on a long walk
♦ set off for a long walk
aufbrechen zu einer Reise
♦ set out on a tour
♦ set out on a journey
♦ set out on a trip
♦ set off on a tour
♦ embark on a tour
aufbrechen zu einer Seereise um die Welt
♦ set sail for a voyage around the world
aufbrechen zu etw
aufbrechen nach etw
♦ set off for s.th.
aufbrechen zu Fuß
♦ set off on foot
aufbrechen zum Gipfel
aufbrechen zu dem Berggipfel
♦ set off for the peak
♦ set off for the mountain peak
auf das Bett legen sich
♦ lie down on the bed
auf das Land fahren
aufs Land fahren
♦ go to the country
♦ get out into to the countryside
auf dem Balkan
♦ in the Balkans
auf dem Bettrand sitzen
♦ sit on the edge of the bed
auf dem Bett sitzen
♦ sit on the bed
auf dem Grundstück
♦ on the premises
auf dem Höhepunkt der Saison
auf dem Saisonhöhepunkt
♦ at the height of the season
auf dem Höhepunkt der Urlaubszeit
auf dem Höhepunkt der Ferienzeit

auf dem Hotelgebiet 38

◆ at the height of the vacation season *AE*
◆ at the height of the holiday season *BE*
auf dem Hotelgebiet
auf dem Hotelsektor
◆ in the hotel field
auf dem Land wohnen (dauernd)
◆ live in the country
auf dem Land wohnen (vorübergehend)
◆ stay in the country
auf dem Luftweg
◆ by air
auf dem Programm stehen
◆ be on the program *AE*
◆ be on the programme *BE*
◆ feature on the program *AE*
◆ feature on the programme *BE*
auf dem Rückweg sein
◆ be on the way back
◆ be on one's way back
auf dem Saisonhöhepunkt
→ auf dem Höhepunkt der Saison
auf demselben Platz stehen
(Gebäude)
◆ stand on the same site
auf demselben Stockwerk
auf demselben Geschoß
auf derselben Etage
◆ on the same floor
auf dem Weg nach Frankreich
◆ en route to France
◆ on the way to France
auf dem Weg nach X
unterwegs nach X
◆ on the way to X
◆ en route to X
◆ en route for X
auf dem Weg sein nach X
◆ be off to X
◆ be on the way to X
auf dem Weg von A nach C über B
◆ on the way from A to C via B
auf dem Weg von Madrid nach Rom
◆ en route from Madrid to Rome
auf dem Weg von X
◆ on the way from X
auf dem Weg zurück nach X
◆ on the way back to X
auf dem Weingut abgefüllt, adj
Gutsabfüllung, f
◆ estate-bottled, adj
auf dem Weingut abgefüllter Wein, m
◆ estate-bottled wine
auf dem Zimmer essen
◆ eat in one's room
◆ have a meal in one's room
auf dem Zimmer sein
◆ be in one's room
auf den Namen von XYZ
(z.B. Rechnung)
◆ in the name of XYZ
auf den Strich gehen
◆ walk the streets
auf den Weg machen sich
◆ set off
auf der Basis von etw
◆ on the basis of s.th.
auf der Durchreise durch X
◆ on one's way through X
◆ while passing through X
auf der Durchreise sein
auf der Durchfahrt sein

◆ be passing through (a place)
◆ pass through
auf der Etage
◆ on the floor
◆ on the floors
auf der Fahrt
◆ on the trip
auf der Heimreise befindlich
(bes. Schiff)
auf der Heimreise
◆ homeward bound
auf der Heimreise befindlich, adj
◆ homebound, adj
auf der Hinreise befindlich
(bes. Schiff)
auf der Hinreise
◆ outward bound
auf der Hochzeitsreise sein
auf Hochzeitsreise sein
◆ honeymoon
auf der Konferenz
bei der Konferenz
◆ at the conference
auf der Krim
◆ in the Crimea
◆ in Crimea
auf der Messe
◆ at the fair
auf der Reise
◆ on the journey
◆ on the trip
◆ during the journey
◆ during the trip
◆ on (the) tour
auf der Reise von A nach B
◆ on the journey from A to B
◆ on its journey from A to B
auf der Rückfahrt
◆ on the return trip
◆ on the way back
auf der Speisekarte haben etw
◆ have s.th. on the menu
auf der Speisekarte sein
auf der Speisekarte stehen
◆ be on the menu
auf der Suche nach etw
◆ in search of s.th.
auf der Terrasse
◆ on the terrace
◆ on the patio
auf der Terrasse sitzen
◆ sit on the terrace
auf der Toilette sein
◆ be in the toilet
auf der Veranda sitzen
◆ sit on the veranda
◆ sit on the verandah
auf der Warteliste stehen
◆ be on the waiting list *AE*
◆ be on the wait list *AE*
◆ be on the waiting-list *BE*
◆ stand-by
auf Diät
◆ on a diet
auf Diät gesetzt werden
auf Diät gesetzt sein
◆ be put on a diet
auf Diät setzen jn
◆ put s.o. on a diet

auf die Beine stellen etw *fam*
etw organisieren
◆ lay on s.th. *fam*
auf die billige Tour etw machen *coll*
◆ do s.th. on the cheap *BE coll*
auf die Bühne bringen etw
◆ put s.th. on the stage
◆ stage s.th.
auf (die) Hochzeitsreise gehen
◆ go on honeymoon
auf die Jagd gehen
◆ go hunting
◆ go shooting
auf die Pauke hauen
die Puppen tanzen lassen
◆ paint the town red
auf die Rechnung setzen etw
◆ charge s.th. to the account
◆ put s.th. on the bill
auf die Schwarze Liste setzen jn
◆ blacklist s.o.
◆ put s.o. on the blacklist
auf die Speisekarte setzen etw
◆ put s.th. on the menu
aufdonnern etw
◆ tart s.th. up
aufdonnern sich
◆ doll up
auf eigenen Füßen stehen
allein weiterkommen
◆ paddle one's own canoe
auf eigenen Wunsch
◆ at one's own request
aufeinanderfolgende Nächte, f pl
◆ consecutive nights *pl*
aufeinanderfolgende Tage, m pl
◆ consecutive days *pl*
auf eine Expedition gehen
◆ go on an expedition
auf eine Fahrt gehen
Fahrt machen
◆ go on a trip
◆ go for a ride
auf einem Lehrgang sein
bei einem Kurs sein
◆ be on a course
auf einem oberen Stockwerk
auf einem oberen Geschoß
auf einer oberen Etage
◆ on one of the upper floors
auf einem unteren Stockwerk
auf einem unteren Geschoß
auf einer unteren Etage
◆ on one of the lower floors
auf einen Ausflug gehen
◆ go on an outing
◆ go on an excursion
auf eine Reise gehen
verreisen
◆ go on a tour
◆ go on a journey
◆ go on a trip
auf einer Expedition
◆ on an expedition
auf einer Expedition sein
Expedition machen
◆ be on an expedition
auf einer Fahrt
◆ on a trip

auf einer Fahrt sein
Fahrt machen
♦ be on a trip
auf einer Kreuzfahrt
♦ on a cruise
auf einer Kreuzfahrt sein
♦ be on a cruise
auf einer langen Reise
♦ on a long journey
♦ on a long tour
♦ on a long trip
auf einer Party
→ bei einer Party
auf einer Pauschalreise sein
eine Pauschalreise machen
♦ be on a package tour
auf einer Pilgerfahrt sein
auf einer Wallfahrt sein
Pilgerfahrt machen
Wallfahrt machen
♦ be on a pilgrimage
auf einer Reise
♦ on a tour
♦ on a journey
♦ on a trip
auf einer Reise sein
Reise machen
♦ be on a tour
♦ be on a journey
♦ be on a trip
auf einer Wanderung sein
Wanderung machen
♦ be on a hike
♦ be on a walk
auf einer Weltreise
♦ on a world tour
auf einer 'à-la-carte'-Basis
♦ on an 'à-la-carte'-basis
auf eine Wanderung gehen
wandern
♦ go on a ramble
♦ go on a hike
auf eine Weltreise gehen
♦ go on a world trip
♦ go on a world tour
auf eine Zechtour gehen
→ Zechtour machen
auf Einladung
♦ by invitation
auf Einladung von jm
♦ at the invitation of s.o.
auf Empfehlung von jm
auf js Empfehlung
♦ on recommendation of s.o.
♦ on s.o.'s recommendation
Aufenthalt, m (Verkehrsmittel)
♦ stop
♦ halt
Aufenthalt, m (Verweilen)
♦ stay
Aufenthalt abbrechen
♦ cut short a stay
♦ curtail a stay
♦ break off a stay
Aufenthalt abkürzen
Aufenthalt verkürzen
♦ curtail a stay
♦ cut short a stay
♦ shorten a stay

Aufenthalt absagen
Aufenthalt stornieren
♦ cancel a stay
Aufenthalt als zahlender Gast, m
♦ stay as a paying guest
Aufenthalt angenehm und schön machen
♦ make a stay comfortable and enjoyable
Aufenthalt außer Haus, m
♦ stay away from home
Aufenthalter, m SCHW
♦ nonpermanent resident AE
♦ non-permanent resident BE
Aufenthalt genießen
♦ enjoy one's stay
Aufenthalt gestalten
Aufenthalt planen
♦ plan a stay
♦ plan one's stay
♦ organise a stay
♦ organise one's stay
Aufenthalt haben
(Person, bei einer Reise)
♦ stay over
♦ lay over AE
Aufenthalt im Ausland, m
→ Auslandsaufenthalt
Aufenthalt in der Wochenmitte, m
♦ midweek stay
Aufenthalt in einem Hotel, m
→ Hotelaufenthalt
Aufenthalt jm zur Qual machen
♦ make s.o.'s stay an ordeal
Aufenthalt mit drei Übernachtungen, m
♦ three-night stay
♦ three nights' stay
Aufenthalt mit zwei Übernachtungen, m
♦ two nights' stay
♦ two-night stay
Aufenthalt plötzlich beenden
Aufenthalt unerwartet beenden
♦ cut short a stay
Aufenthaltsbedingungen, f pl
♦ conditions of (a) stay pl
Aufenthaltsbeginn, m
♦ beginning of stay
♦ beginning of one's stay
♦ beginning of s.o.'s stay
♦ commencement of stay form
♦ commencement of one's stay form
Aufenthaltsbeginn verschieben
♦ postpone the beginning of one's stay
Aufenthaltsbeschränkung, f
♦ limitation of (the period of) stay
♦ limitation of (the period of) residence
Aufenthaltsbewilligung, f
→ Aufenthaltserlaubnis
Aufenthaltsdauer, f
Aufenthaltslänge, f
Verweildauer, f
♦ duration of stay
♦ duration of one's stay
♦ length of stay
Aufenthaltsdauerbeschränkung, f
♦ length of stay restriction
♦ restriction of the length of stay
Aufenthaltsdauer kürzen von zehn auf fünf Tage
Aufenthaltsdauer abkürzen von zehn auf fünf Tage
Aufenthaltsdauer verkürzen von zehn auf fünf Tage
♦ cut the length of stay from ten to five days

Aufenthaltsdauerverlängerung, f
♦ length of stay extension
♦ extension of the length of stay
Aufenthaltsende, n
♦ end of stay
♦ end of one's stay
♦ end of s.o.'s stay
Aufenthaltserlaubnis, f
Aufenthaltsgenehmigung f
♦ residence permit
♦ permit of residence
Aufenthaltsgebühr, f
→ Ferienortabgabe
Aufenthaltsgenehmigung, f (kurzzeitig)
♦ visitors' permit
Aufenthaltsgenehmigung, f (langzeitig)
→ Aufenthaltserlaubnis
Aufenthaltsgenehmigung, f (USA)
♦ green card AE
Aufenthaltsgenehmigung erhalten
Aufenthaltserlaubnis erhalten
♦ receive a residence permit
Aufenthaltsgenehmigung für Ausländer, f jur
♦ alien's residence permit jur
Aufenthaltsgestaltung, f
Aufenthaltsplanung, f
♦ planning (of) a stay
♦ planning (of) one's stay
Aufenthaltsgutschein, m
(für Unterkunft und Verpflegung)
♦ board and lodging voucher
Aufenthaltsjahr, n
♦ year of stay
♦ year of one's stay
♦ year of s.o.'s stay
Aufenthaltskosten, pl
♦ cost of board and lodging
♦ cost of one's stay
♦ cost of s.o.'s stay
Aufenthaltslänge, f
Aufenthaltsdauer, f
♦ length of stay
♦ duration of stay
♦ duration of one's stay
Aufenthaltsmonat, m
♦ month of stay
♦ month of one's stay
♦ month of s.o.'s stay
Aufenthaltsnacht, f
♦ night of stay
♦ night of one's stay
♦ night of s.o.'s stay
Aufenthalt so angenehm wie möglich machen
Aufenthalt so angenehm wie möglich gestalten
♦ make a stay as pleasant as possible
♦ make a stay as enjoyable as possible
♦ make a stay as comfortable as possible
Aufenthaltsort, m
Wohnort m
♦ dwelling place
Aufenthaltsperiode, f
→ Aufenthaltszeit
Aufenthaltspreis, f
Aufenthaltskosten, pl
♦ cost of one's stay
♦ cost of s.o.'s stay
♦ cost of board and lodging
Aufenthaltsraum, m (Heim)
Gemeinschaftsraum, m
♦ common room
♦ recreation room

Aufenthaltsraum

Aufenthaltsraum, m (Hotel)
Gemeinschaftsraum, m
♦ public room
♦ lounge
Aufenthaltsraum, m (in Heim)
Freizeitraum, m
Spielraum, m
♦ recreation room
Aufenthaltsraum, m (Ruheraum)
→ Ruheraum
Aufenthaltsraum eines Gasthofs, m
♦ common room of an inn
Aufenthaltsraum mit Farbfernsehen, m (Hotel)
♦ lounge with color T.V. *AE*
♦ lounge with colour T.V. *BE*
Aufenthaltsraum mit Fernsehen, m (Hotel)
♦ lounge with T.V.
Aufenthaltstag, m
♦ day of stay
♦ day of one's stay
♦ day of s.o.'s stay
Aufenthaltstaxe f
(Steuer)
♦ local tax
♦ visitors' tax
♦ tourist tax
Aufenthaltsurlaub, m
♦ centred holiday *AE*
Aufenthaltsverkürzung, f
Aufenthaltsabkürzung f
♦ curtailment of a stay
♦ cutting short a stay
Aufenthaltsverlängerung, f
♦ extension of (one's) stay
♦ extending one's stay
♦ prolongation of (one's) stay
♦ prolonging one's stay
♦ lengthening one's stay
Aufenthaltswoche, f
♦ week of stay
♦ week of one's stay
♦ week of s.o.'s stay
Aufenthaltszeit, f
♦ time of stay
♦ period of stay
Aufenthaltszeitraum, m
♦ period of stay
Aufenthaltszimmer für Dozenten, n
(in Hochschule)
♦ senior common room
Aufenthaltszimmer für Studenten, n
(in Hochschule)
♦ junior common room
Aufenthalt übersteigt drei Wochen
Aufenthalt überschreitet drei Wochen
♦ stay exceeds three weeks
Aufenthalt verkürzen um einen Tag
♦ cut short one's stay by one day
♦ cut one's stay by one day
♦ curtail one's stay by one day
Aufenthalt verlängern
♦ extend one's stay
♦ prolong one's stay
Aufenthalt verlängern auf drei Wochen
♦ extend one's stay to three weeks
Aufenthalt verlängern um eine Woche
♦ extend one's stay by one week
Aufenthalt verlängern um zwei Nächte
♦ extend one's stay by two nights
Aufenthalt verschieben
♦ postpone a stay

Aufenthalt verschieben bis auf weiteres
♦ postpone a stay until further notice
Aufenthalt verschieben um 6 Monate
♦ postpone a stay for 6 months
Aufenthalt verschieben wegen einer plötzlichen Erkrankung
♦ postpone a stay owing to sudden illness
Aufenthalt verschieben wegen unvorhersehbarer Umstände
♦ postpone a stay due to unforeseen circumstances
Aufenthalt von drei Nächten, m
♦ three nights' stay
♦ stay of three nights
Aufenthalt von drei Tagen, m
♦ stay of three days
♦ three days' stay
Aufenthalt von einer Nacht, m
♦ stay of one night
♦ one-night stay
Aufenthalt von zwei Wochen, m
♦ stay of two weeks
♦ two-week stay
Aufenthalt vorzeitig abbrechen
♦ break off one's stay prematurely
♦ curtail one's stay
Aufenthalt während der Woche, m
♦ stay during the week
Aufenthalt zu einem angenehmen Erlebnis machen
♦ make a stay a pleasant experience
aufessen (etw)
♦ eat up (s.th.)
♦ finish s.th.
auffahren auf etw
♦ run into the rear of s.th.
♦ crash into s.th.
Auffahrt, f (Zufahrt)
(am Haus)
Zufahrt, f
♦ driveway *AE*
♦ drive
Auffahrt zum Hotel, f
→ Hotelauffahrt
auffordern jn zum Tanz
♦ ask s.o. for a dance
Auffrischungskurs, m
Auffrischungslehrgang, m
Wiederholungskurs, m
Wiederholungslehrgang, m
♦ refresher course
aufführen etw auf der Speisekarte
♦ list s.th. on the menu
Aufführung im Freien, f
Freilichtaufführung, f
♦ open-air performance
auffüllen etw
(Glas etc.)
♦ top up s.th.
♦ refill s.th.
Auffüllung, f
Wiederauffüllung, f
Ergänzung, f
♦ replenishment
Auffüllung der Vorräte, f
Wiederauffüllung der Vorräte f
Ergänzung der Vorräte f
♦ replenishment of supplies
aufgedonnertes Hotel, n
♦ tawdry hotel

aufgegebene Route, f
aufgegebene Strecke, f
♦ abandoned route
aufgegebenes Gepäck, n
♦ checked(-in) baggage *AE*
♦ left luggage *BE*
aufgehobenes Visum, n
♦ cancelled visa
♦ canceled visa *AE*
aufgelaufen, adj
♦ accrued, adj
aufgelaufene Kosten, pl
♦ accrued charges *pl*
aufgelaufener Mietzins, m
Mietrückstand, m
♦ accrued rent
aufgelaufene Zinsen, m pl
♦ accrued interest *sg*
aufgeräumt, adj (Zimmer)
♦ tidy, adj
aufgeräumtes Zimmer, n
ordentliches Zimmer, n
♦ tidy room
auf Geschäftsreise sein
auf einer Geschäftsreise sein
Geschäftsreise machen
♦ be on a business trip
aufgetakelt, adj
betakelt, adj
♦ rigged, adj
aufgetaut, adj (generell) *gastr*
♦ thawed, adj *gastr*
aufgetaut, adj (Tiefkühlkost) *gastr*
♦ defrosted, adj *gastr*
aufgewärmt, adj
♦ warmed-over, adj *AE*
♦ warmed-up, adj *BE*
aufgewärmtes Gericht, n
♦ warmed-over dish *AE*
♦ warmed-up dish *BE*
auf gewerblicher Basis
auf kommerzieller Basis
♦ on a commercial basis
aufgrund höherer Gewalt
♦ due to force majeure
♦ due to act of God
auf halbem Weg, adv
♦ halfway, adv *AE*
♦ half-way, adv *BE*
auf halbem Weg gelegen zwischen A und B
♦ situated halfway between A and B *AE*
♦ located halfway between A and B *AE*
♦ positioned halfway between A and B *AE*
♦ situated half-way between A and B *BE*
♦ located half-way between A and B *BE*
auf Halbpensionsbasis
♦ on a half-board basis
♦ on a demipension basis *AE*
♦ on a half-pension basis *AE*
aufhalten sich in einem Hotelzimmer
♦ stay in a hotel room
aufhalten sich in X
♦ stay at X
♦ stay in X
Aufhebung des Pachtverhältnisses, f
♦ cancellation of the lease
♦ cancelation of the lease *AE*
Auf Ihr Spezielles!
(Trinkspruch)
♦ Your special good health!

Auf Ihr Wohl!
(Trinkspruch)
- To your health!
- Your health!
- Cheers!

auf js Kosten
auf Kosten von jm
- at s.o.'s expense
- at the expense of s.o.

auf js Wohl trinken
- toast s.o.
- drink a toast to s.o.

Aufkleber, m
- sticker

Aufkommensland, n
Entsenderland, n
Herkunftsland, n
- generating country

Aufkommensmarkt, m
Entsendermarkt, m
Herkunftsmarkt, m
- generating market

auf Konzessionsbasis
- on a concession basis

auf Kosten des Hauses
auf Kosten des Wirts
- on the house

auf Kosten von jm
auf js Kosten
- at the expense of s.o.
- at s.o.'s expense

aufkündigen etw
→ kündigen etw

auf Lager, adv
- on stock, adv
- in stock, adv
- in hand, adv
- on hand, adv

auf Lager halten etw
- have s.th. in stock
- keep s.th. in stock
- keep s.th. in store
- stock s.th.

auflauern jm
abfangen jn
ausrauben jn
überfallen jn
- waylay s.o.

Auflauf, m gastr
→ Soufflé

Auflaufform, f
- oven dish

auflisten etw in alphabetischer Reihenfolge
aufführen etw in alphabetischer Reihenfolge
- list s.th. in alphabetical order

auflisten etw in einem Katalog
aufführen etw in einem Katalog
- list s.th. in a catalogue
- list s.th. in a catalog AE

aufmachen sich auf eine Reise
sich auf eine Reise begeben
- embark on a journey

aufmachen sich nach X
- start for X
- set out for X
- make for X
- take one's way to X

auf meine Kosten
- at my cost

auf meinen Namen
(z.B. Rechnung)
- in my name

aufmerksam, adj
- attentive, adj

aufmerksame Bedienung, f
- attentive waiter
- attentive waitress
- attentive service

aufmerksamer Service, m
aufmerksame Bedienung, f
- attentive service

aufmerksames Personal, n
- attentive staff
- attentive personnel

auf Mietbasis
- on a rental basis
- on a hire basis BE

aufmöbeln etw coll
- revamp s.th.

Aufnahme, f (Technik)
- recording

Aufnahmeeinrichtung, f (Technik)
- recording facility

Aufnahmefranchisegebühr, f
- initial franchise fee

Aufnahmegebiet, n
aufnehmendes Gebiet, n
Empfängergebiet, n
- receiving area
- reception area

Aufnahmegebühr, f
- initial fee

Aufnahme in einen Katalog, f
- inclusion in a catalogue
- inclusion in a catalog AE

Aufnahme in einen Prospekt, f
- inclusion in a brochure

Aufnahmekapazität, f
(eines Gebiets oder eines Transportmittels)
Beförderungskapazität, f
- carrying capacity

Aufnahmeland, n
aufnehmendes Land, n
Empfängerland, n
- receiving country
- host country

Aufnahmeprüfung, f
(Kurs)
- entrance examination

Aufnahmeprüfung machen
(Kurs)
- sit an entrance examination

Aufnahmevertrag, m
Gastaufnahmevertrag, m
- reception contract
- guest reception contract

Aufnahmevertrag abschließen
- conclude a reception contract

Aufnahmevertrag unterzeichnen
Aufnahmevertrag unterschreiben
- sign a reception contract

Aufnahme von Nahrung und Getränken, f
- intake of food and drink

aufnehmen (beherbergen)
unterbringen
Platz bieten
- accommodate

aufnehmen etw in das Programm
in das Programm aufnehmen etw

- include s.th. in the program AE
- include s.th. in the programme BE

aufnehmen etw in einen Prospekt
- include s.th. in a brochure

aufnehmen etw in seinen Reiseverlauf
aufnehmen etw in seine Reisestrecke
- include s.th. in one's itinerary

aufnehmen ins Hotel jn
→ einchecken jn

aufnehmen jn bei sich (als Mieter)
- take s.o. in

aufnehmen jn bei sich (langfristig)
jm ein Heim geben
- give s.o. a home

aufnehmen jn freundlich
- receive s.o. in a friendly manner

aufnehmen jn gastlich
- receive s.o. as a guest
- receive s.o. hospitably

aufnehmen jn vorübergehend
unterbringen jn vorübergehend
- accommodate s.o. (temporarily)
- put s.o. up

auf nüchternen Magen
auf leeren Magen
- on an empty stomach

auf Pacht
- by lease
- on lease

auf Pachtbasis
- on a lease basis

auf Pauschalbasis
- on a flat-rate basis
- on a lump-sum basis

Aufpreis, m
- surcharge
- extra charge
- additional charge

Aufpreis berechnen
→ Aufpreis erheben

Aufpreis erheben (bei allen Touristen)
Aufpreis fordern (von allen Touristen)
- levy a surcharge (on all tourists)
- impose a surcharge (on all tourists)

Aufpreis fordern
Aufpreis verlangen
Aufpreis erheben
- require a surcharge
- request a surcharge
- demand a surcharge
- levy a surcharge

Aufpreis für Garage
- Garage extra

Aufpreis haben
- carry a supplement

Aufpreis ist auf 10 % des Grundpreises begrenzt
- surcharge is limited to 10 % of the basic price

Aufpreis wird nicht spezifiziert
- surcharge is not itemized

Aufpreis zahlen
- pay a surcharge

auf Provisionsbasis
- on a commission basis
- on commission

aufräumen etw
- tidy s.th.

aufrechnen etw gegen etw
- offset s.th. against s.th. AE
- set s.th. off against s.th. BE

auf Reisen gehen

auf Reisen gehen
- ◆ go traveling *AE*
- ◆ go travelling *BE*

auf Reisen sein
unterwegs sein
- ◆ be traveling *AE*
- ◆ be travelling *BE*

aufrichtigen Dank zum Ausdruck bringen jm
- ◆ express sincere appreciation to s.o.

aufrücken
(Sitzplatz)
- ◆ move up

Aufruf zum Essen m
- ◆ dinner call

auf Safari gehen
- ◆ go on safari

Aufschlag, m
→ Zuschlag, Aufpreis

aufschlagen etw auf einen Preis
- ◆ add s.th. to a price
- ◆ add s.th. to a rate

aufschlüsseln etw
(Statistik)
- ◆ break down s.th.
- ◆ classify s.th.
- ◆ give a breakdown of s.th.

Aufschlüsselung, f
(Statistik)
- ◆ breakdown
- ◆ classification

Aufschlüsselung der Auslastungsquoten, f
- ◆ breakdown of (the) load factor rates

Aufschlüsselung der Belegungsquoten, f
Aufschlüsselung der Auslastungsquoten, f
- ◆ breakdown of the occupancy rates

Aufschlüsselung nach Abteilungen, f
- ◆ breakdown by departments

auf schmale Kost gesetzt sein
- ◆ be put on short commons *coll*
- ◆ be kept on short commons *coll*

auf Schusters Rappen
→ per pedes

auf Schusters Rappen reisen *humor*
(zu Fuß)
- ◆ pad it
- ◆ hoof it

Aufschwung in der Wirtschaft, m
- ◆ upturn in the economy

auf See
- ◆ at sea

auf seinem Zimmer bleiben
in seinem Zimmer bleiben
- ◆ stay in one's room

aufsein (nicht schlafen)
- ◆ be up

aufs Geratewohl
- ◆ on the off chance

Aufsicht, f
Kontrolle, f
Leitung, f
- ◆ supervision
- ◆ control
- ◆ inspection

Aufsicht haben über etw
→ beaufsichtigen etw

Aufsicht haben über jn
beaufsichtigen jn
- ◆ supervise s.o.

Aufsichtsperson, f
Aufsichtskraft, f
- ◆ supervisor
- ◆ attendant

Aufsichtspersonal, n
- ◆ supervisory staff
- ◆ supervisory personnel

aufs Klo gehen *coll*
- ◆ go to the loo *BE coll*
- ◆ go to the john *AE coll*

aufs Ohr legen sich *fam*
- ◆ turn in *fam*

aufs Örtchen gehen *coll*
aufs Klo gehen *coll*
- ◆ go to the john *AE coll*
- ◆ go to the loo *BE coll*
- ◆ spend a penny *BE coll*
- ◆ powder one's nose *BE coll*

aufspielen für jn
(Musik)
- ◆ play for s.o.

aufspielen (Musik)
- ◆ play
- ◆ strike up music

aufspielen zum Tanz
- ◆ play dance-music
- ◆ provide music for dancing
- ◆ play for dancing
- ◆ play music for dancing

aufspielen zur Unterhaltung
- ◆ play for entertainment

aufstehen (aus dem Bett)
- ◆ get up
- ◆ get out of bed
- ◆ rise

aufstehen (generell)
sich erheben
- ◆ rise

aufstehen mit den Hühnern *coll*
- ◆ rise with the lark

aufstehen vom Tisch
vom Tisch aufstehen
- ◆ leave the table
- ◆ get up from the table

Aufstieg, m
Aufstieg zum Gipfel, m
- ◆ uphill climb
- ◆ climb to the summit

Aufstiegschance, f
- ◆ career opportunity

Aufstieg zur Spitze wird mit einer herrlichen Aussicht belohnt
- ◆ climb to the top is rewarded with a magnificent view

Aufstrich, m *gastr*
- ◆ spread *gastr*

auf Stundenbasis
- ◆ on an hourly basis

auftakeln (schiff)
- ◆ rig up

Auftakt, m
→ Beginn

auftauen etw (generell) *gastr*
- ◆ thaw s.th. *gastr*

auftauen etw (Tiefkühlkost) *gastr*
- ◆ defrost s.th. *gastr*

auf Teilpensionsbasis
- ◆ on a partial board basis
- ◆ on a part board basis

auftischen etw
(auch übertragen, Ausreden etc.)
- ◆ serve s.th. up

auftischen etw jm
servieren etw jm
- ◆ serve s.th. to s.o.
- ◆ serve s.o. s.th.

auftischen lassen etw
→ bestellen etw

auf Touren kommen
in Fahrt kommen
- ◆ pick speed

auf Tour gehen
auf Reise gehen
- ◆ go on tour

auf Tournee, adv
auf Tour, adv
auf Reise, adv
- ◆ on tour, adv

auf Tournee gehen
- ◆ go on tour

auf Tournee sein
auf Tour sein
- ◆ be on tour

auf Tournee sein in Italien
- ◆ be on tour in Italy

auftragen etw
(Speise)
- ◆ serve s.th. (up)
- ◆ dish up s.th.

Auftraggeber, m *jur*
(eines Agenten, Bevollmächtigten)
- ◆ principal *jur*

Auftraggeber und Bevollmächtigter, m
- ◆ principal and agent

auftreten als Gastgeber
als Gastgeber fungieren
- ◆ act as the host
- ◆ act as host

auftreten als Gastgeberin
als Gastgeberin fungieren
- ◆ act as the hostess
- ◆ act as hostess

auftreten als Veranstalter
als Veranstalter fungieren
- ◆ act as the organiser of a function
- ◆ be the organiser of a function

auftreten als Vermittler
als Vermittler fungieren
- ◆ act as agent

auftreten in etw
- ◆ perform in s.th.
- ◆ appear on s.th.

Auftritt absagen
Vorstellung absagen
- ◆ cancel a performance

auf unbestimmte Zeit
- ◆ for an indefinite time
- ◆ indefinitely

auf und ab gehen in seinem Zimmer
- ◆ pace up and down one's room

auf und davon
- ◆ up and away

auf unsere Kosten
- ◆ at our expense

auf unserer Reise
- ◆ on our journey
- ◆ on our trip
- ◆ on our tour

auf Unterkunftssuche sein
- ◆ be on the look-out for accommodation *BE*

auf Urlaub, adv (Ferien)
im Urlaub, adv
in Ferien, adv

- ♦ on holiday, adv BE
- ♦ on vacation, adv AE

auf Urlaub (Arbeitnehmer)
- ♦ on leave

auf Urlaub (Beamter)
- ♦ on furlough

auf Urlaub gehen
- → in Urlaub gehen

auf Urlaub (Militär)
- ♦ on pass

auf Urlaub sein (Arbeitnehmer)
- ♦ be out on leave

auf Urlaub sein (Ferien)
- im Urlaub sein
- in Ferien sein
- ♦ be away on holiday BE
- ♦ be on holiday BE
- ♦ be (away) on vacation AE

auf Verlangen
- ♦ on demand

auf vielfachen Wunsch
- ♦ by popular request

auf Vollpensionsbasis
- ♦ on a full-board basis
- ♦ on a full-pension basis AE

auf Vorjahresniveau
- ♦ at the previous year's level

aufwachen
- ♦ wake up
- ♦ awaken

aufwachen in der Nacht
- ♦ wake up in the night

Aufwand, m (generell)
- ♦ expenditure
- ♦ expense
- ♦ cost

Aufwand, m (Gewinn- und Verlustrechnung)
- ♦ expense AE
- ♦ expenditure BE

Aufwandart, f
- ♦ type of expenditure
- ♦ expenditure type

auf Wanderschaft gehen
- ♦ take to the road

auf Wanderschaft sein
- ♦ be on one's travels

Aufwand für etw, m
- ♦ expense for s.th. AE
- ♦ expense on s.th. BE
- ♦ expenditure on s.th. BE
- ♦ expenditure for s.th. AE

Aufwand pro verfügbares Zimmer, m
- Aufwand pro vermietbares Zimmer m
- ♦ expense per available room AE
- ♦ expenditure per available room BE

Aufwand pro Zimmer, m
- ♦ expense per room AE
- ♦ expenditure per room BE

Aufwand pro Zimmer pro Tag, m
- ♦ expense per room per day AE
- ♦ expenditure per room per day BE

Aufwandseite, f
- (Gewinn- und Verlustrechnung)
- ♦ expense side AE
- ♦ expenditure side BE

Aufwandskategorie, f
- ♦ expenditure category
- ♦ expense category AE

Aufwandsposten, m
- Aufwandsposition f

- ♦ expense item AE
- ♦ expenditure item BE

aufwärmbare Speise, f
- ♦ reheatable food

aufwärmen etw (Speise)
- ♦ warm s.th. over AE
- ♦ warm s.th. up BE
- ♦ reheat s.th.

aufwärmen sich
- wärmen sich
- ♦ warm oneself

aufwarten bei Tisch
- ♦ wait on table AE
- ♦ wait at table BE

aufwarten einem Gast
- ♦ wait on a guest
- ♦ serve a guest

aufwarten jm (bedienen)
- ♦ wait on s.o.
- ♦ serve s.o.
- ♦ attend on s.o.

Aufwartungsdienst, m
- (Betten werden aufgedeckt)
- Aufwartungsservice, m
- ♦ turn-down service
- ♦ maid service

aufwecken jn
- wecken jn
- ♦ wake s.o. up

Auf welchen Namen, bitte?
- ♦ In whose name, please?

aufwendig eingerichtet, adj
- ♦ sumptuously appointed, adj

aufwendig eingerichtetes Zimmer, n
- ♦ sumptuously appointed room

aufwendig möbliert, adj
- → aufwendig eingerichtet

aufwendig möbliertes Zimmer, n
- ♦ sumptuously furnished room

Aufwendungen unter Kontrolle halten
- ♦ control expenses

Aufwendung zuordnen etw
- ♦ allocate an expense to s.th.

Aufwendung zuordnen jm
- ♦ allocate an expense to s.o.

Auf Wiedersehen!
- ♦ Good-bye! AE
- ♦ Good-by! AE
- ♦ Goodbye! BE
- ♦ Bye! coll
- ♦ By! AE coll

auf Wohnungssuche gehen
- ♦ go house-hunting

auf Wunsch
- ♦ on request
- ♦ if requested
- ♦ if required

auf Wunsch von jm
- auf js Wunsch
- ♦ at s.o.'s request
- ♦ at the request of s.o.

auf Zehenspitzen
- auf leisen Sohlen
- ♦ on tiptoe

aufzeichnen etw
- aufnehmen etw
- ♦ record s.th.

auf Zimmersuche sein
- ♦ be on the room hunt
- ♦ be on the look-out for digs BE coll

auf Zimmertemperatur
- ♦ at room temperature

Aufzug, m
- → Fahrstuhl

Aufzug benutzen
- ♦ use an elevator AE
- ♦ use a lift BE

Aufzugbenutzer, m
- → Fahrstuhlbenutzer

Aufzugbenutzung, f
- Fahrstuhlbenutzung, f
- ♦ use of the elevator AE
- ♦ using an elevator AE
- ♦ use of the lift BE
- ♦ using a lift BE

Aufzugboy, m
- → Liftboy

Aufzugführer, m
- Aufzugsführer, m
- Fahrstuhlführer, m
- ♦ elevator attendant AE
- ♦ lift attendant BE

Aufzuggebühr, f
- Liftgebühr, f
- ♦ elevator fee AE
- ♦ litf fee BE

Aufzugsanlage, f
- Liftanlage, f
- ♦ lift system BE
- ♦ elevator system AE

Aufzugsführer, m
- → Fahrstuhlführer

Aufzugsschacht m
- ♦ elevator shaft AE
- ♦ lift shaft BE

Auge erfreuen
- ♦ delight the eye
- ♦ please the eye

Augenbehandlung, f
- ♦ eye treatment

Augenbrauentönung, f
- Augenbrauenfärbung, f
- ♦ eyebrow tinting

Augenkontakt, m
- ♦ eye contact

Augen offenhalten
- ♦ keep one's eyes open

Augen sind größer als der Magen
- ♦ eyes are bigger than one's stomach

Augenweide, f
- Augenschmaus, m
- ♦ feast for the eyes
- ♦ sight for sore eyes coll

Auge und den Gaumen erfreuen
- das Auge und den Gaumen erfreuen
- ♦ delight both the eye and the palate

August, m
- (Monat)
- ♦ August

Augustauslastung, f
- Auslastung im August, f
- ♦ August load factor
- ♦ load factor in August

Augustbelegung, f
- Augustauslastung, f
- ♦ August occupancy
- ♦ occupancy in August

Augustfeier, f
- ♦ August celebration

Augustinerkirche, f
- ♦ Augustinian church

Augustinerkloster

Augustinerkloster, n (Frauen)
♦ Augustinian convent
Augustinerkloster, n (Männer)
♦ Augustinian monastery
Augustinermönch, m
♦ Augustinian monk
Augustinernonne, f
♦ Augustinian nun
Augustinerorden, m
♦ Augustinian order
Augustinerpriorei, f
♦ Augustinian priory
Augustloch, n
Augustflaute, f
♦ August trough
Augusttagung, f
Augusttreffen, n
♦ August meeting
Augusturlaub, m
♦ August vacation AE
♦ August holiday BE
Augustwoche, f
♦ August week
Auktion, f
→ Versteigerung
Aula, f
(Hochschule, Schule)
♦ auditorium AE
♦ assembly hall BE
Aula der Universität, f
♦ assembly hall of the university
au naturel, adv FR
(Speise oder Getränk)
♦ au naturel, adv FR
♦ cooked plain
aus aller Welt
aus der ganzen Welt
♦ from around the world
♦ from all over the world
aus Anlaß der Jahrhundertfeier
♦ in celebration of the centenary
aus Anlaß seines 50. Geburtstags
♦ on the occasion of his 50th birthday
aus Anlaß von etw
♦ on the occasion of s.th.
Ausbau des Tourismus, m
→ Tourismusentwicklung
ausbauen (Anlage)
♦ develop
ausbauen (Gebäude)
Gebäude erweitern
♦ enlarge
♦ expand
♦ extend
ausbeinen etw
♦ bone s.th.
ausbilden jn
schulen jn
♦ train s.o.
ausbilden jn als Koch
jn zum Koch ausbilden
♦ train s.o. to be a cook
ausbilden lassen sich als Empfangsherr
♦ train for receptionist
ausbilden lassen sich zum Koch
♦ train as cook
Ausbildung, f (Schulung)
♦ training
Ausbildung als Koch machen
Ausbildung zum Koch absolvieren
♦ be trained as a cook

Ausbildung am Arbeitsplatz, f
♦ on-the-job training
♦ training on the job
Ausbildung erhalten
♦ receive training
Ausbildung im eigenen Betrieb, f
♦ in-house training
Ausbildungsbetrieb m
♦ firm which takes trainees
♦ hotel which takes trainees
Ausbildungsdirektor, m
♦ training director
Ausbildungserfordernis, n
♦ training requirement
Ausbildungsgaststätte, f
Lehrgaststätte, f
♦ training public house BE
♦ training bar AE
Ausbildungshotel, n
Übungshotel, n
Trainingshotel, n
♦ training hotel
Ausbildungskreuzfahrt, f
♦ training cruise
Ausbildungskurs, m
Ausbildungslehrgang, m
Schulungskurs, m
♦ training course
Ausbildungsleiter, m
♦ training manager
Ausbildungsplan m
♦ training plan
Ausbildungsplatz, m
♦ training place
Ausbildungsplatz erhalten bei jm
♦ obtain a training place with s.o.
Ausbildungsprogramm, n
Schulungsprogramm, n
Trainingsprogramm, n (Sport)
♦ training program AE
♦ training programme BE
Ausbildungsprogramm für die Ausbilder, n
♦ train-the-trainer program AE
♦ train-the-trainer programme BE
Ausbildungsschiff, n
♦ training ship
♦ training vessel
Ausbildungszeit, f
♦ training period
Ausbildungszentrum, n
♦ education center AE
♦ education centre BE
ausbleiben (Gäste)
wegbleiben
fortbleiben
♦ fail to come
♦ stay away
Ausblicke in alle Richtungen, m pl
Ausichten in alle Richtungen, m pl
♦ views in all directions pl
Ausblick m
→ Blick
Ausbruch einer Lebensmittelvergiftung, m
♦ outbreak of food poisoning
auschecken
abreisen
abfahren
♦ check out
Auschecken, n
→ Abmeldung

auschecken jn
♦ check out s.o.
aus dem Bett steigen
aufstehen
♦ get out of bed
aus dem Bett werfen jn
♦ drag s.o. out of bed
aus dem Haus jagen jn
♦ drive s.o. out of the house
♦ turn s.o. out of the house
aus dem Haus stehlen sich
♦ steal out of the house
aus der ganzen Welt
aus aller Herren Länder
aus aller Welt
♦ from all over the world
aus der Normannenzeit
aus normannischer Zeit
♦ from Norman times
aus der Quarantäne entlassen sein
♦ be out of quarantine
ausdrückliche Zustimmung, f
♦ express consent
aus elisabethanischer Zeit
♦ dating from Elizabethan times
auserlesen, adj
ausgezeichnet, adj
♦ excellent, adj
♦ selected, adj
♦ select, adj
♦ exquisite, adj
auserlesene Weine, m pl
♦ excellent wines pl
Ausfahrt, f (Autobahn)
♦ exit
ausfallen (Veranstaltung)
♦ not take place
ausfegen etw
(Unterkunft)
fegen etw
♦ sweep s.th.
ausfliegen
→ Ausflug machen
Ausflug, m (generell)
♦ excursion
♦ trip
♦ outing
♦ jaunt
Ausflug, m (ins Freie, oft mit Picknick)
♦ outing
Ausflug absagen
Ausflug stornieren
♦ cancel the excursion
♦ cancel the outing
Ausflug am Ort, m
Ausflug in die Umgebung, f
♦ local excursion
Ausflug an das Meer, m
♦ excursion to the seaside
♦ trip to the seaside
♦ outing to the seaside
Ausflug arrangieren
♦ arrange an excursion
♦ arrange a trip
♦ arrange an outing
Ausflug auf einem Fluß, m
♦ excursion on a river
Ausflug buchen
♦ book an excursion
Ausflug durchführen
♦ run an excursion

Ausflug improvisieren
♦ improvise an excursion
♦ improvise a trip
♦ improvise an outing
Ausflug in die Berge, m
Ausflug in das Gebirge, m
♦ excursion to the mountains
Ausflug in die Umgebung, m
♦ excursion to the surrounding area
Ausflug in die Vergangenheit, m (generell)
♦ excursion into the past
Ausflug in die Vergangenheit, m (persönlich)
♦ excursion down memory lane
Ausflug leiten
♦ conduct an excursion
Ausflügler, m
(max. 24 Stunden von zu Hause weg)
Ausflüglerin, f
♦ excursionist
♦ day-tripper
♦ tripper
Ausflug machen
♦ go on an excursion
♦ make an excursion
♦ go on a trip
♦ make a trip
♦ go on an outing
Ausflug machen in die Berge
Ausflug in das Gebirge machen
♦ make an excursion to the mountains
♦ go on an excursion to the mountains
Ausflug mit dem Auto, m
♦ excursion by car
♦ trip by car
Ausflug mit Führung, m
→ geführter Ausflug
Ausflug nach X, m
♦ excursion to X
♦ outing to X
♦ trip to X
Ausflugsangebot, n (Gegensatz zu Nachfrage)
♦ excursions available *pl*
♦ excursions offered *pl*
♦ excursions on offer *pl*
Ausflugsangebot, n (Palette)
♦ range of excursions
Ausflugsarrangement, n
♦ excursion arrangement
Ausflugsautobus, m (historisch)
♦ charabanc *BE hist*
♦ char-à-banc *BE hist*
♦ char-à-bancs *BE hist*
♦ char à bancs *FR*
Ausflugsboot, n
♦ excursion boat
Ausflugsbus, m
♦ excursion bus
♦ excursion coach *BE*
Ausflugscafé, n
♦ cafe (catering) for excursionists *AE*
♦ cafe (catering) for day trippers *AE*
♦ café (catering) for excursionists *BE*
♦ café (catering) for day-trippers *BE*
Ausflugsdampfer, m
♦ excursion steamer
Ausflugsdauer, f
♦ duration of an excursion
Ausflugseinrichtungen, f pl
♦ facilities for excursions *pl*
Ausflugsfahrpreis, m
♦ excursion fare

Ausflugsführer, m
♦ excursion guide
Ausflugsgasthof, m
♦ inn (catering) for excursionists
♦ inn (catering) for day-trippers
Ausflugsgaststätte, f
♦ bar (catering) for excursionists *AE*
♦ pub (catering) for excursionists *BE*
♦ restaurant (catering) for excursionists
Ausflugsgebiet, n
♦ excursion area
♦ area for excursions
♦ touring area
Ausflugskarte, f
♦ excursion ticket
Ausflugslokal, n
♦ place for excursions
Ausflugsmöglichkeit, f
♦ excursion possibility
♦ possibility of making an excursion
Ausflugsmöglichkeiten, f pl
Tourenmöglichkeiten, f pl
♦ opportunities for excursions *pl*
Ausflugsort, m
Besichtigungsort, m
♦ place of interest
♦ place to visit
Ausflugsortbesuch, m
♦ visit to a place of interest
Ausflugsort besuchen
♦ visit a place of interest
Ausflugsprogramm n
♦ excursion program *AE*
♦ excursion programme *BE*
Ausflugsraddampfer, m
♦ excursion paddle steamer
Ausflugsrestaurant, n
♦ restaurant (catering) for excursionists
♦ restaurant (catering) for day-trippers
♦ roadhouse
Ausflugsschiff, n
♦ excursion ship
♦ excursion boat
♦ excursion vessel
Ausflugstag, m
♦ excursion day
Ausflugstourismus, m
♦ excursion tourism
Ausflugstourist, m
♦ excursion tourist
Ausflugsveranstalter, m
♦ excursion operator
Ausflugsverkehr, m (Wochenende)
→ Wochenendverkehr
Ausflugsziel, n (bestimmtes)
♦ destination of an excursion
♦ destination of a trip
♦ destination of an outing
♦ excursion destination
Ausflugsziel, n (generell)
→ Ausflugsort
Ausflug unternehmen
♦ take an outing
♦ take a trip
Ausflug unternehmen nach X
♦ take an outing to X
♦ take a trip to X
Ausflug veranstalten
Ausflug organisieren
♦ organise an excursion
♦ organize an excursion

Ausflug verpassen
Ausflug versäumen
♦ miss an excursion
Ausflug zu Fuß, m
♦ excursion on foot
♦ outing on foot
Ausflug zusammenstellen
♦ put together an excursion
ausführen etw (durchführen)
durchführen etw
♦ carry out s.th.
ausführen etw (zollfrei)
♦ take s.th. out (duty free)
ausführen jn
ausgehen mit jm
♦ take s.o. out
♦ go out with s.o.
ausführen jn zum Abendessen
♦ take s.o. out to dinner
♦ take s.o. out for dinner
ausführliche Informationen, f pl
♦ detailed information *sg*
♦ full information *sg*
Ausführlicher Prospekt auf Wunsch
♦ Detailed brochure on request
♦ Detailed brochure upon request
ausführliches Informationsmaterial anfordern
♦ write for detailed information
♦ telephone for detailed information
♦ phone for detailed information
ausführliches Informationspaket, n
♦ comprehensive information folder
♦ comprehensive information pack
ausführliches Informationspaket beilegen (Brief)
♦ enclose a comprehensive information folder
♦ enclose a comprehensive information pack
ausführliches Informationspaket jm senden
♦ send a comprehensive information folder to s.o.
♦ send a comprehensive information pack to s.o.
Ausfuhr von Devisen, f
Devisenausfuhr, f
♦ export of foreign currency
♦ export of foreign currencies
ausgabefreudig, adj
♦ free-spending, adj
Ausgabe für etw, f
♦ expense on s.th. *BE*
♦ expense for s.th. *AE*
Ausgaben durch ausländische Besucher, f pl
♦ expenditure by foreign visitors
♦ expenditure by overseas visitors
Ausgaben für Freizeit und Erholung, f pl
Freizeit- und Erholungsausgaben, f pl
♦ recreation spending
Ausgabenkategorie, f
♦ expense category
Ausgabenorgie, f
♦ orgy of spending
Ausgabe pro Besuch, f
♦ expenditure per visit
Ausgabe pro Tag, f
♦ expenditure per day
♦ daily expenditure
Ausgabestelle, f
(für Karten etc)
Ausgabebüro, n
♦ issuing office
Ausgabetermin, m
→ Ausstellungsdatum

Ausgabeverhalten

Ausgabeverhalten, n (Einstellung)
 ♦ spending attitude
Ausgabeverhalten, n (Muster)
 ♦ expenditure pattern
 ♦ expense pattern
Ausgang, m (Gebäude)
 ♦ way out
 ♦ exit
Ausgangsland, n
 Herkunftsland, n
 Ursprungsland, n
 ♦ origin country
 ♦ country of origin
Ausgangspreis, m
 ♦ starting price
 ♦ starting rate
Ausgangspunkt, m (einer Reise)
 ♦ point of origin
Ausgangspunkt, m (Punkt)
 ♦ starting point
 ♦ base
Ausgangspunkt, m (Stadt)
 ♦ starting place
Ausgangspunkt, m (Unternehmen, Reise)
 ♦ jumping-off place BE
 ♦ jumping-off point BE
Ausgangspunkt der Tour, m
 Ausgangspunkt der Reise, m
 ♦ starting point of the tour
Ausgangspunkt einer Wanderung, m
 ♦ starting point of a walk
 ♦ starting point of a hike
Ausgangspunkt für eine Expedition, m
 ♦ starting point for an expedition
Ausgangspunkt für Reisen, m
 Ausgangspunkt für Touren, m
 ♦ touring base
Ausgangssperre, f
 → Sperrstunde
Ausgangssperre beginnt um 22 Uhr
 ♦ curfew starts at 10 p.m.
ausgebeint, adj
 ♦ boned, adj
ausgeben einen coll
 einen ausgeben coll
 Runde schmeißen coll
 ♦ stand a round of drinks
 ♦ stand a round
ausgeben sich als (Künstler)
 ♦ pass oneself as (an artist)
 ♦ palm oneself off as (an artist)
ausgebildeter Führer, m
 ♦ trained guide
ausgebildeter Hotelier, m
 ♦ trained hotelier
ausgebildetes Personal, n
 → Fachpersonal
ausgebucht, adj
 ♦ fully booked, adj
 ♦ booked to capacity, adj
 ♦ booked up, adj
ausgebucht ab dem 15. April
 ♦ fully booked from 15 April onward(s)
 ♦ booked up from 15 April onward(s)
ausgebucht bis 10. Juli
 ♦ fully booked until 10 July
 ♦ booked up until 10 July
ausgebucht bis auf weiteres
 ♦ fully booked until further notice
 ♦ booked up until further notice

ausgebucht sein
 vollbelegt sein
 ♦ be fully booked
 ♦ be booked to capacity
ausgebucht von Mai bis September
 ♦ fully booked from May until September
 ♦ booked up from May until September
ausgebucht zur Zeit
 ♦ fully booked at present
 ♦ booked up at present
ausgedehnte Reise, f
 ♦ extensive tour
ausgedehnter Spaziergang, m
 langer Spaziergang, m
 ♦ long walk
aus Gefälligkeit, adv
 aus Höflichkeit, adv
 ♦ by courtesy, adv
aus Gefälligkeit wohnen bei jm (dauernd)
 ♦ live with s.o. by courtesy
ausgefüllte Antwortkarte, f
 ♦ completed reply card
ausgefülltes Buchungsformular, n
 ausgefülltes Bestellformular n
 ♦ completed booking form
ausgeglichene Ernährung, f
 ♦ balanced nutrition
ausgeglichene Kost, f
 ♦ balanced diet
ausgeglichene Kost essen
 ♦ eat a balanced diet
ausgeglichene Mahlzeit, f
 ausgeglichenes Essen, n
 ♦ balanced meal
ausgegraben, adj
 ♦ excavated, adj
ausgegrabene römische Villa, f
 ♦ excavated Roman villa
ausgegrabene Siedlung, f
 ♦ excavated settlement
ausgehen
 ♦ go out
ausgehen, um etw zu essen
 ♦ go out for a meal
ausgehen, um etw zu trinken
 ♦ go out for a drink
ausgehen mit jm
 (zum Essen etc)
 ausführen jn
 ♦ go out with s.o.
 ♦ take s.o. out
ausgehen zum Essen
 außer Haus essen
 ♦ dine out
 ♦ eat out
ausgehen zum Mittagessen
 ♦ go out for lunch
ausgehungert sein
 ♦ be starving
 ♦ be starved
ausgelassene Mahlzeit, f
 nicht eingenommene Mahlzeit f
 ♦ skipped meal
 ♦ meal not taken
ausgelassene Veranstaltung, f
 laute Veranstaltung, f
 Spektakel, n
 ♦ boisterous function
ausgelastet, adj
 voll ausgelastet, adj
 ♦ fully utilized, adj

 ♦ fully utilised, adj
 ♦ operating at full capacity, adj
 ♦ occupied, adj
ausgelastet sein zu 30 %
 ♦ have a 30 % load factor
 ♦ have a load factor of 30 %
ausgelegter Fußboden, m
 (mit Teppich)
 ausgelegter Boden m
 ♦ carpeted floor
ausgelernter Koch, m
 ♦ fully trained cook
ausgereifter Käse, m
 ♦ mature cheese
ausgereifter Wein, m
 ♦ mature wine
ausgeruht, adj
 erholt, adj
 ♦ well-rested, adj
 ♦ rested, adj
 ♦ relaxed, adj
ausgeruht ankommen
 ♦ arrive rested
ausgeruht und frisch ankommen
 ♦ arrive fresh and relaxed
ausgerüstet sein mit etw
 ♦ be fitted with s.th.
 ♦ be equipped with s.th.
ausgeschildert, adj
 beschildert, adj
 ♦ signposted, adj
ausgeschilderter Wanderweg, m
 ♦ signposted hiking path
 ♦ signposted hiking trail
 ♦ signposted walking trail
 ♦ signposted footpath BE
ausgeschilderter Weg, m
 ausgeschilderter Pfad, m
 ♦ signposted path
 ♦ signposted trail
ausgeschildert sein
 ♦ be signposted
ausgeschlafen sein
 ausgeschlafen haben
 ♦ have had enough sleep
 ♦ get slept out AE
 ♦ be slept out AE
ausgeschlossen sein bei einem Besuch
 ♦ be excluded from a visit
ausgesonderte Wäsche, f
 ♦ discarded linen
ausgestattet, adj
 ausgerüstet, adj
 ♦ equipped, adj
ausgestellt, adj (Gegenstand)
 ♦ on display, adv
 ♦ on show, adv
 ♦ on view, adv
ausgestellt, adj (Karte)
 ♦ issued, adj
ausgestellt sein
 ♦ be on display
 ♦ be on show
 ♦ be on view
ausgestellt unter einem Dach
 ♦ on display under one roof
 ♦ on show under one roof
 ♦ on view under one roof
ausgestopfter Vogel, m
 ♦ stuffed bird

ausgesuchte Lage, f
♦ choice location
aus gesundheitlichen Gründen
♦ for reasons of health
aus Gesundheitsgründen
♦ for health reasons
ausgewählter Standort, m
♦ selected location
ausgewähltes Gericht, n
♦ selected dish
ausgewähltes Hotel, n
♦ selected hotel
ausgewählte Umgebung, f
gepflegte Umgebung, f
exklusive Umgebung, f
♦ select surroundings pl
ausgezeichnete Auswahl an Gerichten, f
♦ excellent choice of dishes
ausgezeichnete Bade- und Schwimmöglichkeiten anbieten
♦ offer excellent facilities for bathing and swimming
ausgezeichnete Küche, f (generell)
→ exzellente Küche
ausgezeichnete Küche probieren (Speisen)
♦ sample the excellent cuisine
♦ sample the excellent cooking
ausgezeichnete Lage, f
♦ excellent situation
♦ excellent position
♦ excellent location
♦ excellent setting
ausgezeichneten Rahmen bieten für etw
♦ offer an excellent setting for s.th.
♦ provide an excellent setting for s.th.
ausgezeichneten Service bieten
♦ offer excellent service
ausgezeichnet erhalten, adj
♦ excellently preserved, adj
ausgezeichnet erhalten sein
♦ be excellently preserved
ausgezeichneter Jahrgang, m
(Wein)
♦ excellent vintage
ausgezeichneter Service, m
♦ excellent service
ausgezeichnetes Essen, n
ausgezeichnete Mahlzeit, f
♦ excellent meal
ausgezeichnetes Essen servieren
♦ serve excellent meals
ausgezeichnete Skibedingungen bieten
♦ offer excellent skiing
ausgezeichnet möbliertes Zimmer, n
♦ excellently furnished room
ausgiebig reisen
♦ travel extensively
ausgraben etw
♦ excavate s.th.
Ausgräber, m
♦ excavator
Ausgrabung, f
♦ excavation
Ausgrabungen besichtigen
♦ visit the excavations
Ausgrabungsmuseum, n
♦ museum of excavations
Ausgrabungsort, m
Ausgrabungsstätte, f
Ausgrabungsstelle, f
♦ excavation site

aushandeln etw neu
neu aushandeln etw
♦ renegotiate s.th.
aushändigen etw an jn
♦ hand out s.th. to s.o.
♦ issue s.th. to s.o.
Aushändigung, f
♦ issue
♦ issuing
Aushändigung des Schlüssels, f
♦ issue of the key
♦ issuing the key
Aushandlung eines Vertrags, f
♦ negotiation of a contract
aushängen etw
auslegen etw
ausstellen etw
zeigen etw
♦ display s.th.
aushelfen jm
♦ help s.o. out
Aushilfe, f (Person)
Aushilfskraft, f
♦ temporary helper AE
♦ temporary help
♦ stopgap coll
Aushilfe am Samstag, f
♦ Saturday person
♦ Saturday man
♦ Saturday boy
♦ Saturday girl
Aushilfe beschäftigen
♦ employ s.o. on a casual basis
♦ employ s.o. as a temporary help
Aushilfe gesucht
(Hinweisschild)
♦ Help wanted
Aushilfe suchen
♦ look for s.o. to help out
Aushilfsangestellter, m
Aushilfsangestellte f
♦ temporary employee
♦ casual employee
Aushilfsbedienungspersonal, n
♦ casual waiting staff
♦ casual waiting personnel
Aushilfsbeschäftigung, f
♦ temporary employment
Aushilfsempfangsherr m
Aushilfsrezeptionist m
♦ relief receptionist
Aushilfskellner, m
Hilfskellner, m
♦ temporary waiter
♦ relief waiter
♦ extra waiter
Aushilfskellnerin, f
Hilfskellnerin, f
♦ extra waitress
♦ relief waitress
♦ temporary waitress
Aushilfskoch, m
♦ extra cook
♦ relief cook
♦ temporary cook
Aushilfskraft, f (bes. für Büroarbeiten)
♦ temporary clerk
♦ temp BE coll
Aushilfskraft, f (generell)
♦ temp BE coll

♦ temporary worker
♦ help
Aushilfskräfte, f pl
♦ casual labor AE
♦ casual labour BE
Aushilfskräfte engagieren
Aushilfskräfte einstellen
♦ engage casual labor AE
♦ hire casual labour BE
Aushilfspersonal, n
Hilfspersonal, n
♦ casual staff
♦ casual personnel
♦ temporary staff
♦ temporary personnel
♦ extra staff
Aushilfsserviererin, f
→ Aushilfskellnerin, f
Aushilfsserviertochter, f SCHW
→ Aushilfskellnerin
Aushilfsstelle, f
Aushilfsjob, m
♦ casual job
aushilfsweise, adv
(Personal)
♦ on a casual basis, adv
♦ temporarily, adv
aushilfsweise arbeiten
♦ work on a casual basis
♦ help s.o. out
aushilfsweise beschäftigtes Personal, n
→ Aushilfspersonal
aushilfsweise beschäftigt sein
♦ have a casual job
aushöhlen etw gastr
♦ scoop s.th. gastr
aus keltischer Zeit
♦ from Celtic times
Ausklang, m
Ende n
♦ end
♦ finish
♦ conclusion
♦ finale
Ausklang eines Festes, m
♦ end of a party
♦ end of a festivity
ausklingen (Fest)
♦ come to an end
♦ end
auskommen ohne etw
♦ manage without s.th.
♦ do without s.th.
auskommen ohne Heizung
♦ manage without heating
aus Kostengründen
♦ on grounds of cost
Auskunft, f (Büro)
→ Auskunftsstelle
Auskunft, f (Information)
→ Information
Auskünfte einholen über etw
♦ make inquiries about s.th.
♦ make enquiries about s.th.
Auskünfte geben
Anfragen beantworten
♦ answer inquiries
♦ answer enquiries
Auskunft erteilen
Auskünfte erteilen
♦ give information

Auskunft erteilen mündlich

Auskunft erteilen mündlich
 ♦ give information verbally
Auskünfte und Preise auf Anfrage
 ♦ **Information and prices on request**
 ♦ Information and rates on request
Auskunft geben jm über etw
 Auskunft erteilen jm über etw
 ♦ **give s.o. information about s.th.**
 ♦ give s.o. information on s.th.
Auskunftsabteilung, f
 Informationsabteilung, f
 ♦ **inquiry department**
 ♦ enquiry department
 ♦ information department
Auskunftsbüro, n
 → Auskunftsstelle
Auskunftsbürokraft, f
 ♦ **inquiry office clerk**
 ♦ enquiry office clerk
Auskunftsdienst m
 → Informationsservice
Auskunftsschalter, m
 Informationsschalter, m
 ♦ **inquiry desk**
 ♦ enquiry desk
 ♦ inquiries desk
 ♦ enquiries desk
Auskunftsstelle, f
 Auskunftsbüro n
 ♦ **inquiry office**
 ♦ enquiry office
Auskunftsstellenpersonal, n
 ♦ **inquiry office staff**
 ♦ enquiry office personnel
Auskunftszentrale, f
 Informationszentrale, f
 ♦ **inquiry center** AE
 ♦ enquiry center AE
 ♦ inquiry centre BE
 ♦ enquiry centre BE
auskurieren etw
 ♦ **cure s.th. completely**
ausladen etw
 entladen etw
 ♦ **unload s.th.**
ausladen jn (Gast)
 Einladung zurückziehen
 ♦ **cancel an invitation**
 ♦ ask s.o. not to come
Ausladung, f (eines Gasts)
 ♦ **cancellation of an invitation**
 ♦ cancelation of an invitation AE
Auslage, f
 (vom Hotel etc. bis zur Begleichung vorgestreckt)
 Auslage für einen Gast, f
 ♦ **disbursement**
 ♦ visitor's paid out
 ♦ VPO
Ausland, n
 ♦ **foreign country**
 ♦ foreign countries pl
 ♦ overseas country
Ausländer, m
 ♦ **foreigner**
 ♦ person from abroad
 ♦ alien jur
Ausländeranteil, m
 ♦ **number of foreign visitors**
 ♦ number of overseas visitors
 ♦ proportion of foreign visitors
 ♦ proportion of overseas visitors

Ausländerbettnacht, f
 (durch ausländische Touristen)
 ♦ **foreign tourist bed-night**
ausländerfeindlich, adj
 xenophob, adj
 ♦ **hostile to foreigners, adj**
 ♦ xenophobic, adj
Ausländerübernachtung, f (generell)
 ♦ **foreign visitor staying overnight**
Ausländerübernachtung, f (Statistik)
 Zahl der Ausländerübernachtungen, f
 ♦ **number of nights spent by foreign visitors**
ausländisch, adj
 ♦ **foreign, adj**
 ♦ from abroad
ausländische Destination, f
 Auslandsdestination, f
 ausländischer Zielort, m
 Auslandszielort, m
 Auslandsreiseziel, n
 ♦ **foreign destination**
ausländische Küche, f
 ♦ **foreign cuisine**
 ♦ foreign cooking
ausländischer Aussteller, m
 ♦ **foreign exhibitor**
 ♦ foreign exhibiter AE
ausländischer Besucher, m
 Besucher aus dem Ausland, m
 ♦ **visitor from abroad**
 ♦ foreign visitor
ausländischer Gast, m
 → Auslandsgast
ausländischer Reisender, m
 ♦ **foreign traveller**
 ♦ foreign traveler AE
ausländischer Staatsgast, m
 ♦ **foreign state guest**
 ♦ foreign official guest
ausländischer Student, m
 ♦ **foreign student**
ausländisches Essen, n
 fremdländisches Essen, n
 ♦ **foreign food**
ausländische Spezialität, f
 ♦ **foreign speciality**
 ♦ foreign specialty AE
ausländische Tourismusnachfrage, f
 ♦ **foreign tourist demand**
Auslandsankünfte, f pl
 Ankünfte aus dem Ausland, f pl
 ♦ **foreign arrivals** pl
Auslandsaufenthalt, m
 Aufenthalt im Ausland m
 ♦ **stay abroad**
Auslandsbesuch, m
 Besuch im Ausland, m
 ♦ **visit abroad**
Auslandsbesucher, m
 ausländischer Gast, m
 Besucher aus dem Ausland, m
 ♦ **foreign visitor**
 ♦ foreign guest
 ♦ visitor from abroad
 ♦ guest from abroad
Auslandsbesucherübernachtung, f
 (Statistik)
 Übernachtung eines ausländischen Besuchers, f
 ♦ **foreign visitor night**

Auslandsbettnacht, f
 (Statistik)
 ♦ **foreign bed-night**
Auslandsbüro, n
 ♦ **office abroad**
Auslandserfahrung, f
 ♦ **experience gained abroad**
Auslandsfahrt, f
 Fahrt ins Ausland, f
 ♦ **trip abroad**
Auslandsferien, pl
 Auslandsurlaub, m
 ♦ **foreign holiday** BE
 ♦ holiday abroad BE
 ♦ foreign vacation AE
 ♦ vacation abroad AE
Auslandsflug, m
 ♦ **international flight**
Auslandsflug, m (in das Ausland)
 ♦ **outbound flight**
Auslandsfremdenverkehrsausgaben, f pl
 Ausgaben der ausländischen Touristen, f pl
 ♦ **foreign tourist expenditure**
Auslandsgast, m
 ausländischer Gast m
 Gast aus dem Ausland, m
 ♦ **foreign guest**
 ♦ foreign visitor
 ♦ guest from abroad
 ♦ visitor from abroad
Auslandshotel, n
 ausländisches Hotel, n
 Hotel im Ausland, n
 ♦ **foreign hotel**
 ♦ hotel abroad
Auslandskreuzfahrt, f
 ♦ **cruise abroad**
Auslandsmarketing, n
 ♦ **foreign marketing**
Auslandsmarkt, m
 ausländischer Markt, m
 ♦ **foreign market**
Auslandsmesse, f
 ausländische Messe, f
 ♦ **foreign fair**
 ♦ foreign trade fair
Auslandsnachfrage, f
 ausländische Nachfrage, f
 ♦ **foreign demand**
 ♦ demand abroad
Auslandspauschalreise, f
 ♦ **foreign inclusive tour**
 ♦ foreign package tour
Auslandspauschalurlaub, m
 Auslandspauschalferien, pl
 ♦ **foreign package vacation** AE
 ♦ foreign package holiday BE
Auslandsreise, f
 ♦ **tour abroad**
 ♦ trip abroad
 ♦ journey abroad
Auslandsreiseintensität, f
 ♦ **foreign travel intensity**
Auslandsreise machen
 ♦ **make a journey abroad**
 ♦ make a trip abroad
 ♦ travel abroad
Auslandsreisemarkt, m
 ausländischer Reisemarkt, m
 ♦ **foreign travel market**

Auslandsreisen, n
　Auslandsreiseverkehr, m
　♦ foreign travel
　♦ traveling abroad *AE*
　♦ travelling abroad *BE*
　♦ travel abroad
Auslandsreisender, m
　♦ tourist traveling abroad *AE*
　♦ tourist travelling abroad *BE*
Auslandsreise unternehmen
　Reise ins Ausland unternehmen
　♦ take a journey abroad
　♦ take a trip abroad
　♦ take a tour abroad
Auslandsreiseverkehr, m (in das Ausland)
　Auslandsreisen, n
　♦ outbound travel
Auslandsreiseziel, n
　♦ foreign travel destination
　♦ foreign destination
Auslandsrepräsentant, m
　Auslandsvertreter, m
　♦ foreign representative
　♦ representative abroad
Auslandstelefongespräch, n
　♦ foreign telephone call
　♦ foreign phone call
Auslandstourismus, m
　Tourismus aus dem Ausland, m
　♦ foreign tourism
　♦ tourism from abroad
Auslandstourist, m (aus dem Ausland)
　ausländischer Tourist, m
　Tourist aus dem Ausland, m
　♦ foreign tourist
　♦ tourist from abroad
Auslandstourist, m (im Ausland)
　→ Auslandsreisender
Auslandstourist, m (in das Ausland)
　♦ outbound tourist
Auslandstournee, f
　♦ tour abroad
Auslandstournee machen
　♦ make a tour abroad
　♦ tour foreign countries
Auslandsunfall, m
　Unfall im Ausland, m
　♦ accident abroad
Auslandsurlaub, m
　Auslandsferien, pl
　♦ vacation abroad *AE*
　♦ foreign vacation *AE*
　♦ holiday abroad *BE*
　♦ foreign holiday *BE*
Auslandsurlauber, m
　ausländischer Urlauber m
　♦ foreign vacationer *AE*
　♦ vacationer from abroad *AE*
　♦ foreign holidaymaker *BE*
　♦ holidaymaker from abroad *BE*
Auslandsurlaub machen
　♦ take a vacation abroad *AE*
　♦ take a foreign vacation *AE*
　♦ take a holiday abroad *BE*
　♦ take a foreign holiday *BE*
Auslandsveranstaltung, f
　♦ foreign event
　♦ event abroad
　♦ foreign function
　♦ function abroad

Auslandsverkehr, m (in das Ausland)
　Verkehr ins Ausland, m
　♦ outbound traffic
auslasten etw
　♦ use s.th. to capacity
　♦ utilize s.th. to capacity
　♦ utilise s.th. to capacity
Auslastung, f (Transport)
　♦ load factor
Auslastung, f (Unterkunft)
　→ Belegung
Auslastung beläuft sich auf 60 %
　♦ load factor amounts to 60 %
Auslastung berechnen
　♦ calculate the load factor
Auslastung beträgt 70 %
　♦ load factor is 70 %
Auslastung bleibt unter 70 %
　♦ load factor remains under 70 %
Auslastung erhöhen
　♦ raise the load factor
Auslastung erreichen von 90%
　90%ige Auslastung erreichen
　♦ achieve a load factor of 90%
　♦ achieve a 90% load factor
Auslastung erreicht eine Höhe von 55 %
　♦ load factor reaches a level of 55 %
Auslastung erreicht im Durchschnitt 40 %
　♦ load factor averages 40 %
Auslastung erzielen von 80 %
　♦ experience 80 % load factor
Auslastung fällt auf 40 %
　♦ load factor decreases to 40 %
　♦ load factor drops to 40 %
　♦ load factor falls to 40 %
Auslastung fällt um 4 %
　♦ load factor decreases by 4 %
　♦ load factor drops by 4 %
　♦ load factor falls by 4 %
Auslastung fällt unter 40 %
　♦ load factor falls below 40 %
　♦ load factor drops below 40 %
Auslastung fiel von 60 % auf 55 %
　♦ load factor dropped from 60 % to 55 %
　♦ load factor decreased from 60 % to 55 %
　♦ load factor fell from 60 % to 55 %
Auslastung haben
　♦ have an load factor
　♦ enjoy a load factor
Auslastung halten
　Auslastungsniveau halten
　♦ maintain the load factor
Auslastung im Januar, f
　Januarauslastung, f
　♦ load factor in January
　♦ January load factor
Auslastung in der Wochenmitte, f
　♦ midweek load factor
Auslastung in Prozent, f
　prozentuale Auslastung, f
　Auslastungsquote in Prozent, f
　♦ percentage load factor
Auslastung ist befriedigend
　→ Auslastung ist zufriedenstellend
Auslastung ist gleichmäßig
　♦ load factor is even
Auslastung ist rückläufig
　♦ load factor is decreasing
Auslastung ist steigend
　♦ load factor is increasing

Auslastung ist überdurchschnittlich
　♦ load factor is above average
　♦ load factor is higher than average
Auslastung ist ungleichmäßig
　♦ load factor is uneven
Auslastung ist unterdurchschnittlich
　♦ load factor is below average
　♦ load factor is lower than average
Auslastung ist zufriedenstellend
　Auslastung ist befriedigend
　♦ load factor is satisfactory
Auslastung läßt (viel) zu wünschen übrig
　♦ load factor leaves much to be desired
　♦ load factor leaves a lot to be desired
Auslastung liegt bei 50 %
　♦ load factor is approximately 50 %
　♦ load factor is about 50 %
Auslastung liegt unter dem Durchschnitt
　→ Auslastung ist unterdurchschnittlich
Auslastung melden von 80 %
　♦ report a load factor of 80 %
Auslastung nähert sich 70 %
　♦ load factor approaches 70 %
Auslastung optimieren
　♦ maximise the load factor
　♦ maximize the load factor
Auslastung prognostizieren
　Auslastung vorhersagen
　♦ forecast the load factor
Auslastung pro Jahr, f
　♦ load factor per year
Auslastung pro Monat, f
　♦ load factor per month
Auslastung pro Tag, f
　♦ load factor per day
Auslastung pro Woche, f
　♦ load factor per week
Auslastungsabfall, m
　Auslastungsrückgang, m
　Auslastungsverminderung, f
　♦ fall in the load factor
　♦ decrease in the load factor
　♦ drop in the load factor
auslastungsabhängig, adj
　♦ depending on the load factor, adj
Auslastungsänderung, f
　♦ load-factor change
　♦ change in (the) load factor
Auslastungsberechnung, f
　♦ calculation of the load factor
　♦ calculating the load factor
Auslastung schätzen
　♦ estimate the load factor
Auslastungsdaten, pl
　♦ load factor data
Auslastungseinbruch, m
　♦ slump in the load factor
Auslastungsergebnis, n
　♦ load factor achieved
Auslastungsgewinnschwelle, f
　♦ break-even load factor
Auslastungsgrad, m
　→ Auslastungsniveau
Auslastungsgrad von 80% erzielen
　♦ achieve an 80% load factor
Auslastung sinkt
　Auslastung geht zurück
　Auslastung fällt
　Auslastung nimmt ab
　♦ load factor drops
　♦ load factor decreases

Auslastungskontrolle

- load factor falls
- load factor diminishes

Auslastungskontrolle, f
- load factor control
- control of (the) load factor

Auslastungskrise, f
- load factor crisis

Auslastungskrise stoppen
- halt the load factor crisis

Auslastungskurve, f
- load factor graph

Auslastungslücke, f
- load factor gap

Auslastungsmuster, n
  Auslastungsschema, n
  Belegungsmuster, n
- load factor pattern
- pattern of the load factor

Auslastungsniveau, n
  Auslastungsgrad, m
- load factor level

Auslastungsniveau übersteigt 90 %
- load factor exceeds 90 %

Auslastungsproblem, n
- load factor problem

Auslastungsproblem haben
- have a load factor problem

Auslastungsprognose, f
  Auslastungsvorhersage, f
- load factor forecast

Auslastungsquote, f
  Auslastungsrate, f
- load factor rate

Auslastungsquote in Prozent, f
  → Auslastung in Prozent

Auslastungsquoten aufschlüsseln
- give a breakdown of the load factor rates

Auslastungsrate, f
  → Auslastungsquote

Auslastungsrate anheben
- raise the load factor rate

Auslastungsrate steigern auf 80%
- increase the load factor rate to 80%

Auslastungsrisiko, n
- load factor risk

Auslastungsrisiko tragen
- bear the load factor risk

Auslastungsrückgang, m
- decrease in the load factor
- drop in the load factor
- fall in the load factor

Auslastungsschätzung, f
- estimate of the load factor
- estimating the load factor

Auslastungsschema, n
  Auslastungsmuster, n
- pattern of the load factor
- load factor pattern

Auslastungsschwankung, f
- fluctuation in the load factor
- variation in the load factor

Auslastungsstand halten
- maintain the load factor level
- maintain the load factor

Auslastungsstatistik, f
- load factor statistics *pl*

Auslastungsstatistik erstellen
- compile load factor statistics

Auslastungssteigerung, f
  Auslastungserhöhung, f

- increase in the load factor
- rise in the load factor

Auslastungssteigerung um 5 % von 60 auf 65 %
- increase in the load factor by 5 % from 60 to 65 %

Auslastungssteigerung von 10 %, f
- increase in the load factor by 10 %
- 10 % increase in the load factor

Auslastungstabelle, f
- load factor table

Auslastung steigt
  Auslastung nimmt zu
  Auslastung erhöht sich
- load factor increases
- load factor grows
- load factor rises

Auslastungstendenz, f
  → Auslastungstrend

Auslastungstrend, m
  Auslastungstendenz, f
- load factor trend

Auslastungsüberblick, m
  Auslastungsübersicht, f
- load factor survey

Auslastungsverhältnis, n
- load factor ratio

Auslastungsverringerung, f
  Auslastungssenkung, f
- reduction of the load factor

Auslastungsvorhersage, f
  Auslastungsprognose, f
- forecast of the load factor
- load factor forecast
- forecasting the load factor

Auslastungszahl, f
- load factor figure

Auslastungszeitraum, m
- load factor period

Auslastungsziel, n
  angestrebte Auslastung, f
- targeted load factor

Auslastung übersteigt 50 %
- load factor exceeds 50 %

Auslastung übersteigt eine bestimmte Zahl
- load factor exceeds a certain figure

Auslastung verbessern
- increase the load factor
- improve the load factor
- raise occupancy

Auslastung verbessern
  Auslastungsrate verbessern
  Auslastungsquote verbessern
- improve the load factor

Auslastung von 30 % durch Stammgäste erzielen
- derive 30 % of the load factor from regular guests

Auslastung von 70 % haben
- have a load factor of 70 %

Auslastung von 80 % überschreiten
- exceed 80 % load factor
- surpass 80 % load factor

Auslastung von 90 % verzeichnen
- record a 90% load factor
- record a load factor of 90 %

Ausläufer, m (Gebirge)
  → Vorgebirge

Auslegerboot, n
- outrigger

Auslegerbrücke, f
- cantilever bridge

Auslegerkanu, n
- outrigger canoe

ausleihen etw an jn
  ausleihen jm etw
- lend s.th. to s.o.
- lend s.o. s.th.

ausleihen etw (geben)
- lend s.th.

ausleihen etw (nehmen)
  leihen etw
  borgen etw
- borrow s.th.

ausleihen gegen Gebühr (geben)
- hire out s.th.
- rent (out) s.th.

ausleihen gegen Gebühr (nehmen)
- hire s.th.
- rent s.th.

Auslese, f (Wein)
- choice wine
- superior wine

Ausleuchtung, f
  → Beleuchtung

Auslieferung, f (Person)
- extradition

Auslieferungsvertrag, m
  Auslieferungsvertrag (mit einem Land), m
- extradition treaty
- extradition treaty (with a country)

Auslieferungsvertrag haben mit Deutschland
- have an extradition treaty with Germany

auslogieren jn
  → ausquartieren jn

ausmachen etw
- account for s.th.

Ausnahmepreis m
  ausnahmsweiser Preis m
- exceptional rate
- exceptional price

aus nah und fern
- from near and far

ausnehmen etw *gastr*
  Innereien entfernen aus etw
- gut s.th. *gastr*

ausnehmen jn *coll*
  neppen jn
  bescheißen jn *vulg*
  übervorteilen jn
- rip s.o. off *sl*
- overcharge s.o.

auspacken (etw)
- unpack (s.th.)

auspassieren
  sich abmelden in einem Hotel
- check out
- check out of a hotel

auspennen (sich) *coll*
- sleep one's fill

aus persönlichen Gründen
- for personal reasons

aus Preisgründen
- for reasons of price
- for price reasons

auspressen etw
- squeeze s.th.

ausprobieren etw
- try s.th.

ausquartieren jn (generell)
- lodge s.o. elsewhere
- dislodge s.o.
- move s.o. out

ausquartieren jn (Militär)
♦ billet out s.o.
ausquartieren jn (zwangsweise)
♦ turn s.o. out
Ausquartierung, f
♦ dislodgment
♦ dislodgement
♦ change of lodgings
♦ lodging elsewhere
ausquetschen etw
→ auspressen etw
ausrauben etw
ausplündern etw
♦ ransack s.th.
ausreichend, adj
♦ sufficient, adj
♦ adequate, adj
♦ enough, adj
ausreichende Parkmöglichkeiten, f pl
genügende Parkgelegenheiten, f pl
ausreichender Parkplatz, m
♦ adequate parking facilities pl
ausreichender Parkraum, m
ausreichender Parkplatz m
♦ adequate parking space
ausreichende Sanitäreinrichtungen, f pl
♦ sufficient sanitary facilities pl
ausreichende Unterkunft, f
angemessene Unterkunft, f
angemessene Unterbringung, f
♦ adequate accommodation
Ausreise (aus einem Land), f
Abreise (aus einem Land), f
♦ departure (from a country)
♦ leaving (a country)
Ausreisebeschränkung, f
♦ exit restriction
♦ restricted exit
Ausreiseerlaubnis, f
Ausreisegenehmigung, f
♦ exit permission
♦ exit permit
♦ permission to leave
Ausreiseformular, n
♦ departure form
Ausreisegebühr, f
♦ exit fee
♦ departure fee
Ausreisegenehmigung, f
Ausreiseerlaubnis, f
♦ exit permit
♦ exit permission
♦ permission to leave
ausreisen
Land verlassen
♦ leave a country
♦ depart from a country
♦ leave
ausreisen nach einem Land
ausreisen in ein Land
♦ leave for a country
♦ depart for a country
Ausreisepapier, n
Ausreisedokument, n
♦ exit document
Ausreisesichtvermerk, m
→ Ausreisevisum
Ausreisesperre, f
→ Ausreiseverbot
Ausreisestatistik, f
♦ departure statistics pl

Ausreisesteuer, f
♦ departure tax
Ausreisetermin, m
Ausreisedatum, n
♦ departure date
Ausreiseverbot, n
Ausreisesperre, f
♦ ban on leaving the country
Ausreisevisum, n
Ausreisesichtvermerk, m
♦ exit visa
Ausreisevisum ausstellen
♦ issue an exit visa
Ausreisevisum beantragen
♦ apply for an exit visa
Ausreisezeit, f
Ausreisezeitpunkt, m
♦ time of exit
Ausreißer, m
(Person)
♦ runaway
ausrichten etw (als Gastgeber)
Gastgeber sein bei etw
♦ host s.th.
Ausrichter, m (Gastgeber)
→ Gastgeber
Ausrichter, m (Veranstalter)
Organisator, m
♦ oganising body
♦ organizing body
♦ organiser
♦ organizer
Ausrichter einer Ausstellung, m
♦ exhibit organiser AE
♦ organizer of an exhibition
♦ exhibition organiser
♦ exhibition organizer
Ausrichter einer Tagung, m
→ Tagungsausrichter
Ausrichter einer Veranstaltung, m
♦ organiser of a function
♦ organizer of an event
Ausrichter eines Balls, m
♦ organiser of a ball
♦ organizer of a ball
Ausrichtung, f (Veranstaltung)
♦ organisation
♦ organization
♦ arrangement
Ausrichtung eines Festivals, f
♦ organisation of a festival
♦ organization of a festival
Ausritt, m
→ Ritt
Ausruf, m
Ausrufenlassen n
♦ paging
Ausrufanlage, f
→ Rufanlage
ausrufen jn
(Gast ausrufen)
♦ page s.o.
ausrufen lassen jn
♦ have s.o. paged
Ausrufer, m (Küche)
Aboyeur, m *FR*
Ansager, m
♦ caller
♦ aboyeur *FR*
♦ announcer

ausruhen (sich)
♦ rest
♦ take a rest
♦ have a rest
ausruhen (sich) auf der Terrasse
♦ relax on the terrace
ausruhen sich auf seinen Lorbeeren
♦ rest on one's laurels
ausruhen (sich) ein wenig
♦ rest (oneself) a bit
ausruhen sich nach einer Reise
erholen sich nach einer Reise
♦ rest after a journey
♦ rest after a trip
♦ rest after a tour
Ausrüstung, f
Ausstattung, f
♦ equipment
Ausrüstung kann geliehen werden
♦ equipment can be borrowed
Ausrüstung kann gemietet werden
♦ equipment is available for rent *AE*
♦ equipment is available for hire *BE*
Ausrüstungsverleih, m
→ Geräteverleih
Ausschank, m (Aktivität)
(Getränke)
♦ serving s.th.
♦ selling s.th.
♦ service
Ausschank, m (Gaststätte)
→ Gaststätte
Ausschank, m (Getränkeverkauf)
→ Getränkeverkauf
Ausschank, m (Tresen)
♦ counter
♦ bar
Ausschank alkoholischer Getränke, m
♦ sale of alcoholic liquor
♦ selling alcoholic liquor
♦ serving (of) alocoholic beverages
Ausschankautomat, m
Getränkeautomat, m
♦ automatic beverage dispenser
♦ automatic drinks dispenser
Ausschankgenehmigung, f
→ Schankkonzession
Ausschank von alkoholischen Getränken, m
♦ sale of alcoholic beverages
♦ selling alcoholic beverages
♦ service of alcoholic beverages
♦ serving alcoholic beverages
Ausschank von Getränken, m
→ Getränkeausschank
Ausschankzeit, f
Schankzeit, f
Ausschankstunden, f pl
Schankstunden, f pl
♦ licensing hours *pl*
♦ licencing hours *pl*
♦ licensed hours *pl*
♦ licenced hours *pl*
Ausschau nach einer Unterkunft, f
♦ lookout for accommodation
Ausschau nach etw, f
♦ lookout for s.th.
ausschenken etw (generell)
♦ serve (out) s.th.
ausschenken etw (Getränk)
einschenken etw

ausschenken etw (verkaufen)

♦ pour out s.th.
♦ serve s.th.
ausschenken etw (verkaufen)
♦ sell s.th.
ausschenken jm etw
einschenken jm etw
♦ pour s.o. s.th.
Ausschiffung, f
♦ disembarkation
Ausschiffungsgebühr, f
♦ disembarkation charge
♦ disembarkation fee
Ausschiffungshafen, m
♦ disembarkation port
♦ port of disembarkation
Ausschiffungskarte, f
♦ disembarkation card
Ausschiffungsstelle, f
Ausschiffungspunkt, m
♦ disembarkation point
♦ point of disembarkation
ausschildern etw
♦ signpost s.th.
Ausschilderung, f
♦ signposting
Ausschilderung des Wohnwagenplatzes, f
♦ signposting of the trailer site *AE*
♦ signposting of the caravan site *BE*
ausschlafen etw
(z.B. Rausch)
♦ sleep s.th. off
ausschlafen (sich)
♦ have a long sleep
♦ have a good sleep
♦ sleep long (enough)
♦ sleep one's fill
♦ stay in bed
ausschlafen sich gründlich
♦ have a real good night's rest *AE*
♦ enjoy a really good night's rest *BE*
Ausschlußfrist, f
♦ closing date
Ausschlußfrist für Bewerbungen, f
♦ closing date for applications
Ausschlußklausel, f
♦ exclusion clause
Ausschuß, m
Komitee, n
♦ committee
Ausschuß für Fremdenverkehr, m
Ausschuß für Tourismus, m
♦ committee for tourism
Ausschußraum, m
♦ committee room
Ausschußsitzung, f
Komiteesitzung, f
♦ committee meeting
Ausschuß vorsitzen
einem Ausschuß vorsitzen
♦ chair a committee
Ausschuß zusammenrufen
Ausschuß einberufen
♦ convene a committee
Außenabort, m
♦ outhouse *AE*
Außenbecken, n
(Schwimmbad)
♦ outdoor pool
♦ exterior pool
Außenbereichskosten, pl
(bei Hotelbau)

Außenanlagenkosten, pl
♦ soft costs *pl*
Außenbezirk, m
(einer Stadt)
♦ outskirts *pl*
Außendoppelzimmer, n
nach außen gelegenes Doppelzimmer, n
♦ outside double room
Außendusche, f
Dusche im Freien, f
♦ open-air shower
Außeneinzelzimmer, n
nach außen gelegenes Einzelzimmer, n
♦ outside single room
Außenfahrstuhl, m
♦ outside elevator *AE*
♦ outside lift *BE*
Außenflur, m
♦ exterior corridor
Außengrenze, f
♦ external frontier
♦ external border
Außenhafen, m
♦ outer harbor *AE*
♦ outer harbour *BE*
Außenjacuzzi, m
♦ outdoor jacuzzi
Außenjoggingpfad, m
♦ outdoor jogging track
♦ outdoor jogging trail
Außenkabine, f
♦ outside cabin
Außenmarketing, n
♦ external marketing
Außenmaße, n pl
♦ outside measurements *pl*
Außenmauer, f
♦ exterior wall
♦ outside wall
Außenmöbel, n pl
♦ outdoor furniture *pl*
Außenplatz, m (Tennis)
♦ outdoor court
Außenpool, m
→ Außenbecken
Außenprivatsalon, m (Schiff)
nach außen gelegener Privatsalon, m
♦ outside state-room *AE*
♦ outside stateroom *BE*
Außenreparaturen, f pl
♦ outside repairs *pl*
Außenrestaurant, n
Restaurant im Freien, n
♦ outdoor restaurant
♦ open-air restaurant
Außenschwimmbad, n
Außenschwimmbecken, n
♦ exterior swimming-pool *AE*
♦ exterior swimming-pool *BE*
Außenschwimmbecken, n
→ Außenschwimmbad
Außenseiter, m
♦ outsider
Außensitzplatz, m
Außensitz, m
Außenplatz, m
nach außen gelegener Sitzplatz, m
♦ outside seat
Außensuite, f
(Schiff)
♦ outside suite

Außentennisplatz, m
Tennisfreiplatz, m
♦ outdoor tennis court
Außenterrasse, f
♦ outdoor terrace
Außentisch, m
♦ outside table
Außentreppe, f
♦ outside staircase
♦ exterior staircase
Außenwand, f
♦ outside wall
♦ exterior wall
Außenzimmer, n
Zimmer zur Außenseite n
nach außen gelegenes Zimmer n
♦ outside room
♦ outward room
Außer Betrieb
(Hinweisschild)
Defekt
♦ Out of order
♦ OOO
Äußere Mongolei, die, f
♦ Outer Mongolia
Äußeren Hebriden, die, pl
♦ Outer Hebrides, the *pl*
Äußeres, n
(eines Gebäudes)
♦ exterior
außer Gebrauch kommen
♦ fall into disuse
außergewöhnliche Lage, f
außergewöhnlicher Standort, m
♦ exceptional location
außergewöhnlicher Luxus, m
♦ exceptional luxury
außergewöhnlicher Service, m
♦ exceptional service
♦ outstanding service
außergewöhnlicher Wein, m
♦ exceptional wine
außergewöhnliche Umstände, m pl
♦ unusual cirumstances *pl*
außerhalb der Essenszeiten
♦ outside mealtimes
außerhalb der Messezeit, adv
♦ outside the trade-fair season, adv
♦ outside the fair season, adv
außerhalb der Saison, adv
♦ off season, adv
♦ out of season, adv
außerhalb der Schankzeit
(für alkoholische Getränke)
♦ outside licensing hours
♦ outside licensed hours
außerhalb der Servicezeit
♦ outside the hours of service
außerhalb der Stadtgrenze, adv (Großstadt)
♦ outside the city boundary
außerhalb der Stadtgrenze, adv (kleine Stadt)
♦ outside the town boundary
außerhalb des Campus wohnen
♦ live off the campus
außerhalb des Hotels
♦ outside the hotel
außer Haus essen
♦ eat away from home
♦ eat out

außer Haus schlafen
 ♦ sleep away from home
 ♦ sleep out
Außer-Haus-Verpflegung, f
 → Fremdverpflegung
außer Haus wohnen
 außerhalb des Hauses wohnen
 außerhalb wohnen
 ♦ live out
außer Hörweite
 ♦ out of earshot
außerplanmäßig, adj
 nicht programmgemäß, adj
 ♦ unscheduled, adj
 ♦ special, adj
außerplanmäßiger Flug, m
 ♦ unscheduled flight
außer Saison, adv
 außerhalb der Saison, adv
 ♦ out of season, adv
 ♦ off season, adv
Außersaisonzeit, f
 ♦ out-of-season period
äußerst diskret sein
 ♦ be extremely discreet
aus Sicherheitsgründen
 ♦ for reasons of safety
Aussicht, f
 Ausblick m
 Blick m
 ♦ view
 ♦ outlook
Aussicht haben hinüber zu etw
 Blick haben hinüber zu etw
 Ausblick haben hinüber zu etw
 ♦ have a view towards s.th.
 ♦ have a view to s.th.
Aussicht ist atemberaubend
 ♦ view is breathtaking
Aussichtsdeck, n
 ♦ observation deck
Aussichtsetage, f
 ♦ observation floor
Aussichtsfahrstuhl, m
 ♦ panoramic elevator AE
 ♦ panoramic lift BE
Aussichtsfenster, n
 Panoramafenster, n
 ♦ picture window
 ♦ panoramic window
 ♦ view window
Aussichtsplattform f
 ♦ observation platform
Aussichtsplatz, m
 ♦ lookout place
Aussichtspunkt, m
 ♦ lookout (point)
 ♦ observation point
 ♦ vantage point
 ♦ panoramic viewpoint
 ♦ viewpoint
Aussichtsrestaurant n
 ♦ panoramic restaurant
Aussichtsterrasse, f
 Panoramaterrasse, f
 ♦ panoramic terrace
 ♦ panoramic patio
Aussichtsturm, m
 ♦ observation tower
 ♦ viewing tower

 ♦ lookout (tower) AE
 ♦ look-out tower BE
Aussichtstürmchen, n
 Aussichtspunkt, m
 ♦ gazebo
Aussichtszimmer, n
 Aussichtsraum, m
 ♦ observation room
Aussicht versperren
 → Blick versperren
aussondern etw
 (z.B. Wäsche)
 ♦ discard s.th.
ausspannen
 sich entspannen
 ♦ unwind coll
 ♦ lay off AE
 ♦ take a rest
 ♦ get a break
 ♦ relax
ausspannen auf der Terrasse
 ♦ relax on the patio
 ♦ relax on the terrace
aussperren sich
 ♦ lock oneself out
ausstatten etw mit Möbeln
 ♦ equip s.th. with furniture
 ♦ furnish s.th.
Ausstattung, f (bes. Geräte)
 → Ausrüstung
Ausstattung, f (Bühne)
 Bühnenausstattung, f
 ♦ set
 ♦ stage set
Ausstattung, f (Einrichtung, Mobiliar)
 ♦ appointments pl
 ♦ furnishings pl
Ausstattungskosten, pl
 ♦ equipment costs pl
 ♦ equipment cost
Ausstattungsniveau, n
 ♦ level of equipment
 ♦ equipment level
Ausstechform, f gastr
 ♦ pastry cutter gastr
ausstehende Forderungen, f pl
 ♦ accounts receivable pl
ausstehende Miete, f
 ♦ rent receivable
aussteigen aus dem Auto
 ♦ get out of the car
aussteigen aus dem Bus
 ♦ get off the bus
 ♦ get off the coach BE
 ♦ alight from the bus form
 ♦ alight from the coach BE form
aussteigen aus dem Flugzeug
 ♦ get off the plane
 ♦ alight from the plane form
aussteigen aus dem Zug
 ♦ get off the train
 ♦ alight from the train form
aussteigen aus einem Fahrstuhl
 aussteigen aus einem Aufzug
 aussteigen aus einem Lift
 ♦ leave the elevator AE
 ♦ get out of the elevator AE
 ♦ leave the lift BE
 ♦ get out of the lift BE
aussteigen (aus Verkehrsmittel)
 ♦ get off

 ♦ get out
 ♦ get out of (s.th.)
 ♦ alight (from s.th.) form
 ♦ disembark (from s.th.)
aussteigen bei der nächsten Haltestelle
 ♦ get off at the next stop
aussteigen bei der nächsten Station
 ♦ get out at the next station
ausstellbar, adj (Messe)
 ♦ exhibitable, adj
ausstellen etw auf einer Messe
 ♦ exhibit s.th. at a fair
ausstellen etw (Dokument)
 ♦ make out s.th.
 ♦ issue s.th.
ausstellen (etw) im Ausland
 ♦ exhibit (s.th.) overseas
ausstellen etw (Messe)
 ♦ exhibit s.th.
 ♦ show s.th.
ausstellen etw öffentlich
 ♦ exhibit s.th. to the public
ausstellen (Messe)
 ♦ exhibit
Aussteller, m (Lizenz)
 ♦ grantor
Aussteller, m (Messe)
 ♦ exhibitor
 ♦ exhibiter AE
 ♦ exhibiting company
 ♦ exhibiting firm
Ausstellerbeirat, m
 ♦ exhibitors' advisory board
Aussteller einer Konzession, m
 ♦ grantor of a license
 ♦ grantor of a licence
Ausstellerfirma, f
 ♦ exhibiting firm
 ♦ exhibiting company
Ausstellerprofil, n
 ♦ exhibitor profile
Ausstellerumfrage, f
 ♦ survey of exhibitors
Ausstellerunterstützung, f
 ♦ exhibitor support
Ausstellerverzeichnis, n
 ♦ list of exhibitors
 ♦ list of exhibiters AE
Ausstellerwerbung, f
 Werbung durch die Aussteller, f
 ♦ exhibitor advertising
 ♦ exhibitors' advertising
Ausstellerzahl, f
 ♦ number of exhibitors
 ♦ exhibitor number
 ♦ number of exhibiters AE
Ausstellerzufahrt, f
 ♦ exhibitor access
 ♦ exhibiter access AE
Ausstellung, f (Fahrkarte etc)
 ♦ issuance AE
 ♦ issue
 ♦ issuing
Ausstellung, f (Messe)
 ♦ exhibition
 ♦ exhibit AE
 ♦ show
 ♦ exposition
 ♦ expo

Ausstellung abbauen

Ausstellung abbauen
♦ dismantle an exhibition
♦ dismantle an exhibit *AE*
Ausstellung abhalten
♦ hold an exhibition
♦ hold an exhibit *AE*
Ausstellung absagen
  Ausstellung streichen
♦ cancel an exhibition
♦ cancel an exhibit *AE*
Ausstellung arrangieren
♦ arrange an exhibition
♦ arrange an exhibit *AE*
Ausstellung aufbauen
♦ set up an exhibition
♦ set up an exhibit *AE*
♦ install an exhibition
♦ mount an exhibition
♦ mount an exhibit *AE*
Ausstellung ausrichten (als Gastgeber)
♦ host an exhibition
♦ host an exhibit *AE*
♦ host a show
Ausstellung befaßt sich mit etw
♦ exhibition deals with s.th.
♦ exhibit deals with s.th. *AE*
Ausstellung beherbergen
♦ house an exhibition
♦ house an exhibit *AE*
Ausstellung besuchen
♦ visit an exhibition
♦ visit an exhibit *AE*
♦ visit a show
Ausstellung dokumentiert etw
♦ exhibition documents s.th.
Ausstellung durchführen
♦ implement an exhibition
♦ implement an exhibit *AE*
Ausstellung einer Fahrkarte, f
  Fahrkartenausstellung, f
♦ issue of a ticket
♦ issuance of a ticket *AE*
♦ issuing a ticket
Ausstellung erklärt etw
♦ exhibition explains s.th.
♦ exhibit explains s.th. *AE*
♦ show explains s.th.
Ausstellung eröffnen
♦ open an exhibition
♦ open an exhibit *AE*
Ausstellung eröffnen mit einem Vortrag
♦ open an exhibition with a lecture
Ausstellung findet statt
♦ exhibition is being held
♦ exhibit is being held *AE*
Ausstellung für etw, f
♦ exhibition for s.th.
♦ exhibit for s.th. *AE*
Ausstellung geht bis (zum) 20. Mai
♦ exhibition is on until 20 May
♦ exhibit is on until 20 May *AE*
♦ exhibition runs until 20 May
♦ exhibit runs until 20 May *AE*
Ausstellung geht später auf Tournee
♦ exhibition will be touring later
♦ exhibit will be touring later *AE*
Ausstellung gestalten
  Ausstellung entwerfen
♦ design an exhibition
♦ design an exhibit *AE*

Ausstellung gibt einen Überblick über die Geschichte von etw
♦ exhibition traces the history of s.th.
♦ exhibit traces the history of s.th. *AE*
Ausstellung hat ihre Pforten geöffnet
♦ exhibition has opened its doors
♦ exhibit has opened its doors *AE*
Ausstellung hat ihre Pforten geschlossen
♦ exhibition has closed its doors
♦ exhibit has closed its doors *AE*
Ausstellung illustriert etw
♦ exhibition illustrates s.th.
♦ exhibit illustrates s.th. *AE*
Ausstellung im Freien, f
  Freiluftausstellung, f
♦ open-air exhibition
♦ open-air exhibit *AE*
Ausstellung ist nur für das Fachpublikum
♦ exhibition is only for the trade
♦ exhibit is only for the trade *AE*
Ausstellung ist untergebracht in etw
♦ exhibition is housed in s.th.
♦ exhibit is housed in s.th. *AE*
Ausstellung koordinieren
♦ coordinate an exhibition
Ausstellung leiten
♦ run an exhibition
♦ run an exhibit *AE*
Ausstellung machen
  Ausstellung aufbauen
♦ mount an exhibition
♦ mount an exhibit *AE*
♦ make an exhibition
♦ make an exhibit *AE*
♦ mount a display
Ausstellung mit dem Titel "ABC"
♦ exhibition entitled "ABC"
♦ exhibit entitled "ABC" *AE*
Ausstellung öffnet am 7. März
♦ exhibition opens on 7 March
♦ exhibit opens on 7 March *AE*
Ausstellung öffnet um 9 Uhr und schließt um 18 Uhr
♦ exhibition opens at 9 a.m. and closes at 6 p.m.
♦ exhibit opens at 9 a.m. and closes at 6 p.m. *AE*
Ausstellung organisieren
  Ausstellung veranstalten
♦ organise an exhibit *AE*
♦ organize an exhibition
♦ organise an exhibition
Ausstellung planen
♦ plan an exhibition
♦ plan an exhibit *AE*
Ausstellung portraitiert etw
  Ausstellung zeigt etw
♦ exhibition portrays s.th.
♦ exhibit portrays s.th. *AE*
Ausstellung präsentiert etw
♦ exhibition features s.th.
♦ exhibit features s.th. *AE*
Ausstellung präsentiert etw
♦ exhibition presents s.th.
♦ exhibit presents s.th. *AE*
Ausstellungsaktivität, f
♦ exhibition activity
♦ exhibit activity *AE*
Ausstellungsanforderung, f
♦ exhibition requirement
♦ exhibit requirement *AE*

Ausstellungsausschuß, m
  Ausstellungskomitee, n
♦ exhibition committee
Ausstellungsausstatter, m
♦ exhibition contractor
♦ exhibit contractor *AE*
Ausstellungsbedürfnis, n
♦ exhibition need
♦ exhibit need *AE*
Ausstellungsbeginn, m
♦ beginning of an exhibition
♦ beginning of an exhibit *AE*
♦ beginning of a show
Ausstellungsberater, m
♦ exhibition consultant
♦ exhibit consultant *AE*
Ausstellungsbereich, m
♦ exhibition area
♦ exhibit area *AE*
Ausstellungsbesuch, m
  Besuch einer Ausstellung, m
♦ exhibition visit
♦ visit to an exhibition
♦ visit to an exhibit *AE*
Ausstellungsbesucher m
♦ exhibition visitor
♦ visitor to an exhibition
♦ show visitor
♦ visitor to a (boat etc.) show
Ausstellungsbuchung, f
♦ exhibition booking
♦ booking an exhibition
Ausstellungsbude, f
  Ausstellungsstand, m
♦ exhibition booth
♦ exhibit booth *AE*
Ausstellungsdatum, n (Dokument)
  Ausgabetermin, m
♦ date of issue
Ausstellungsdatum, n (Exposition)
  Ausstellungstermin, m
♦ date of the exhibition
♦ exhibition date
Ausstellungsdauer, f
♦ duration of the exhibition
♦ duration of the exhibit *AE*
Ausstellungsdestination, f
  Ausstellungsziel, n
  Ausstellungszielort, m
♦ exhibition destination
♦ exhibit destination *AE*
Ausstellungsdienst, m
  Ausstellungsservice, m
♦ exhibition service
♦ exhibit service *AE*
Ausstellungsdirektor, m
  Ausstellungsleiter, m
♦ exhibition director
♦ exhibition manager
Ausstellungsdrucksache, f
♦ exhibition print
♦ exhibit print *AE*
Ausstellung sehen
♦ see an exhibition
♦ see an exhibit *AE*
Ausstellungseinheit, f
  Ausstellungsgruppe, f
♦ exhibition unit
Ausstellungseinrichtung, f
♦ exhibition facility
♦ exhibit facility *AE*

54

Ausstellungsende, n
- end of an exhibition
- end of an exhibit *AE*
- end of a show

Ausstellungserfahrung, f
- exhibition experience
- exhibit experience *AE*

Ausstellungseröffnung, f
Eröffnung einer Ausstellung, f
- opening of an exhibition
- opening of an exhibit *AE*
- opening of a show

Ausstellungsetage, f
- exhibition floor
- exhibit floor *AE*

Ausstellungsfläche, f (generell)
- display area
- display space

Ausstellungsfläche, f (Messe)
- exhibition space
- exhibition area
- exhibit area *AE*
- exhibit space *AE*

Ausstellungsfläche erweitern
- extend the exhibition area
- extend the exhibition space
- extend the exhibit area *AE*
- extend the exhibit space *AE*

Ausstellungsfläche mieten
Ausstellungsfläche anmieten
- rent exhibition space
- rent exhibit space *AE*
- hire exhibition space *BE*

Ausstellungsfläche reservieren
- reserve exhibition space
- reserve exhibit space *AE*

Ausstellungsfläche vergrößern
- expand the exhibition area
- expand the exhibition space
- expand the exhibit area *AE*
- expand the exhibit space *AE*

Ausstellungsfläche vermieten an jn
- rent exhibition space to s.o. *AE*
- rent exhibit space to s.o. *AE*
- hire out exhibition space to s.o. *BE*
- let exhibition space to s.o. *BE*

Ausstellungsfläche verringern
Ausstellungsfläche verkleinern
- reduce the exhibition area
- reduce the exhibition space
- reduce the exhibit area *AE*
- reduce the exhibit space *AE*

Ausstellungsfläche von 1.000 qm, f
- exhibition area of 1,000 sq.m.
- exhibit area of 1,000 sq.m. *AE*

Ausstellungsfotograf, m
- exhibition photographer
- exhibit photographer *AE*

Ausstellungsführer, m
- exhibition guide
- exhibit guide *AE*
- exhibitions guide
- guide to the exhibition
- guide to the exhibit *AE*

Ausstellungsgalerie, f
- exhibition gallery
- exhibit gallery *AE*

Ausstellungsgebäude, n
- exhibition building
- exhibit building *AE*
- exposition building

Ausstellungsgelände, n
- exhibition ground
- exhibition grounds *AE pl as sg*
- exhibition site

Ausstellungsgeschäft, n
- exhibition business
- exhibit business *AE*

Ausstellungsgesellschaft, f
- exhibition corporation *AE*
- exhibition company *BE*

Ausstellungsgestalter, m
- exhibition designer
- exhibit designer *AE*

Ausstellungsgestaltung, f
- exhibition design
- exhibit design *AE*
- designing an exhibition
- designing an exhibit

Ausstellungsgewerbe, n
- exhibition trade

Ausstellungsgröße, f
- exhibition size
- size of the exhibition

Ausstellungsgrundriß, m
- exhibition layout
- exhibit layout *AE*

Ausstellungsgut, n
Ausstellungsgüter, n pl
- exhibited article
- exhibited articles *pl*
- goods exhibited *pl*

Ausstellungshalle, f
- exhibition hall
- exhibit hall *AE*

Ausstellungshallenbesitzer, m
- exhibition hall owner

Ausstellungsindustrie, f
- exhibition industry

Ausstellungsjahr, n (Fahrkarte etc)
Ausgabejahr, n
- year of issue
- year of issuance *AE*

Ausstellungskalender, m
- exhibition calendar

Ausstellungskapazität, f
- exhibition capacity
- exhibit capacity *AE*

Ausstellungskatalog, m
- exhibition catalogue
- exhibition catalog *AE*
- exhibit catalog *AE*

Ausstellungskomplex, m
- exhibition complex
- exhibit complex *AE*

Ausstellungskonzept, n
- exhibition concept
- exhibit concept *AE*

Ausstellungskunde, m
- exhibition client

Ausstellungsleiter, m
- exhibition manager
- exhibit manager *AE*
- exhibition director

Ausstellungsleitung, f
- exhibition management
- exhibition board
- exhibit management *AE*

Ausstellungslokal, n
- exhibition premises *pl*

Ausstellungsmarkt, m
- exhibition market

Ausstellungsmaterial, n
- exhibition material
- exhibit material *AE*

Ausstellungsmiete, f
- exhibition rent *AE*
- exhibition hire *BE*

Ausstellungsmonat, m (Fahrkarte etc)
- month of issue
- month of issuance *AE*

Ausstellungsobjekt, n
→ Ausstellungsstück

Ausstellungsordnung, f
- exhibition regulations *pl*

Ausstellungsorganisation, f
- exhibition organisation
- organisation of an exhibition
- organising an exhibition

Ausstellungsorganisator, m
- organiser of an exhibition
- exhibition organiser
- organizer of an exhibition
- exhibition organizer
- exhibit organiser *AE*

Ausstellungsort, m (Fahrkarte etc)
Ausstellungsplatz, m
- place of issue
- place of issuance *AE*

Ausstellungsort, m (Schau)
- exhibition venue
- place where an exhibition is held
- exhibition site

Ausstellungspavillon, m
- exhibition pavilion
- exhibit pavilion *AE*

Ausstellungspersonal, n
- exhibition staff
- exhibition personnel
- exhibit staff *AE*
- exhibit personnel *AE*

Ausstellungsplatz, m
(Gelände)
- exhibition site

Ausstellung sponsern
- sponsor an exhibition
- sponsor an exhibit *AE*

Ausstellungsprogramm, n
- exhibition program *AE*
- exhibition programme *BE*

Ausstellungsprojekt, n
- exhibition project
- exhibit project *AE*

Ausstellungsrabatt, m
- exhibition discount

Ausstellungsraum, m
- exhibition room
- exhibit room *AE*
- showroom

Ausstellungsräumlichkeiten, f pl
- exhibition facilities *pl*
- exhibit facilities *AE pl*

Ausstellungsreihe, f
- series of exhibitions
- series of exhibits *AE*

Ausstellungssaal, m
- exhibit hall *AE*
- large exhibition room
- exhibition hall
- large exhibit room *AE*

Ausstellungssaison, f
- exhibition season
- exhibit season *AE*

Ausstellungssalon

Ausstellungssalon, m
  Ausstellungslounge, f
  ♦ exhibition lounge
  ♦ exhibit lounge *AE*
Ausstellungsservice, m
  → Ausstellungsdienst
Ausstellungssicherheit, f
  ♦ exhibition security
  ♦ exhibit security
Ausstellungsspezialist, m
  ♦ exhibition specialist
  ♦ exhibit specialist *AE*
Ausstellungsstadt, f (Großstadt)
  ♦ exhibition city
Ausstellungsstadt, f (kleine Stadt)
  ♦ exhibition town
Ausstellungsstand, m (bei einer Ausstellung)
  ♦ exhibition stand
  ♦ exhibit stand *AE*
  ♦ stand at an exhibition
  ♦ stand in an exhibition
  ♦ exhibit booth *AE*
Ausstellungsstand, m (generell)
  ♦ display stand
Ausstellungsstandausstatter, m
  ♦ exhibition stand contractor
  ♦ exhibit stand contractor *AE*
Ausstellungsstil, m
  ♦ exhibition style
Ausstellungsstück, n
  Exponat n
  ♦ exhibit
  ♦ object shown at an exhibition
  ♦ item on display
Ausstellungsstück leihen
  Ausstellungsstück verleihen
  ♦ lend an exhibit
  ♦ loan an exhibit *AE*; *BE form*
Ausstellungsstück zeigen
  ♦ display an exhibit
Ausstellungssystem, n
  ♦ exhibition system
  ♦ display system
Ausstellungstag, m (Fahrkarte etc)
  ♦ day of issue
  ♦ day of issuance *AE*
Ausstellungstechnik, f
  ♦ exhibition technique
  ♦ display technique
Ausstellungsteilnehmer, m
  ♦ exhibition delegate
  ♦ exhibit delegate *AE*
Ausstellungstermin, m
  Ausstellungsdatum, n
  ♦ exhibition date
  ♦ date of the exhibition
Ausstellungstourismus, m
  ♦ exhibition tourism
Ausstellungstourist, m
  ♦ exhibition tourist
Ausstellungstyp, m
  ♦ exhibition type
  ♦ exhibit type *AE*
  ♦ type of exhibition
  ♦ type of exhibit *AE*
Ausstellungsunternehmer, m
  → Ausstellungsaussteller
Ausstellungsveranstalter, m
  ♦ exhibition organiser
  ♦ organiser of an exhibition

♦ exhibit organiser *AE*
♦ organiser of an exhibit *AE*
Ausstellungsverkehr, m
  ♦ exhibition traffic
Ausstellungsverleih, m
  ♦ exhibition hire *BE*
  ♦ exhibition rental *AE*
Ausstellungsverleihfirma, f
  ♦ exhibition hire company
  ♦ exhibition rental company *AE*
  ♦ exhibit rental company *AE*
Ausstellungsvertrag, m
  ♦ exhibition contract
  ♦ exhibit contract *AE*
Ausstellungsvitrine, f
  → Vitrine
Ausstellungswand, f
  feste Stellwand, f
  ♦ display wall
Ausstellungswesen, n
  → Ausstellungsgewerbe
Ausstellungswoche, f (Fahrkarte etc)
  ♦ week of issue
  ♦ week of issuance *AE*
Ausstellungszelt, n
  ♦ exhibition tent
  ♦ exhibit tent *AE*
Ausstellungszentrum n
  ♦ exhibition center *AE*
  ♦ exhibit center *AE*
  ♦ exhibition centre *BE*
Ausstellungszone, f
  ♦ exhibition zone
  ♦ exhibit zone *AE*
Ausstellung über etw, f
  Ausstellung zu etw., f
  ♦ exhibition about s.th.
  ♦ exhibition on s.th.
  ♦ exhibit about s.th. *AE*
  ♦ exhibit on s.th. *AE*
Ausstellung veranstalten
  Ausstellung organisieren
  ♦ put on an exhibition
  ♦ put on an exhibit *AE*
  ♦ organise an exhibition
  ♦ organize an exhibit *AE*
Ausstellung verschieben
  ♦ postpone an exhibition
  ♦ postpone an exhibit *AE*
Ausstellung von etw, f
  ♦ exhibition of s.th.
  ♦ exhibit of s.th. *AE*
Ausstellung von (Herrn Peters)
  ♦ exhibition arranged by (Mr Peters)
  ♦ exhibit arranged by (Mr Peters) *AE*
Ausstellung von Kunstwerken, f
  ♦ exhibition of works of art
  ♦ exhibit of works of art *AE*
Ausstellung von Zeichnungen, f
  ♦ exhibition of drawings
  ♦ drawings exhibition
Ausstellung widmen jm
  ♦ dedicate the exhibition to s.o.
  ♦ dedicate the exhibit to s.o. *AE*
Ausstellung wird gezeigt
  ♦ exhibition is on show
  ♦ exhibit is on show *AE*
Ausstellung wird zur Zeit gezeigt in X
  ♦ exhibition is currently showing at X
  ♦ exhibition is currently showing in X

Ausstellung zeigen
  ♦ display an exhibition
  ♦ display an exhibit *AE*
Ausstellung zeigt etw
  ♦ exhibition shows s.th.
Ausstellung zeitgenössischer Kunst, f
  ♦ exhibition of contemporary art
Ausstellung zieht viel Aufmerksamkeit auf sich
  ♦ exhibition attracts much attention
  ♦ show attracts much attention
  ♦ exhibit attracts much attention *AE*
Ausstellung zu der Geschichte der Stadt, f
  ♦ exhibition on the history of the town
  ♦ exhibit on the history of the town
Ausstellung zu etw, f
  ♦ exhibition on s.th.
  ♦ exhibit on s.th. *AE*
Ausstellung zusammenstellen
  ♦ put together an exhibition
  ♦ put together an exhibit *AE*
Ausstiegsstelle, f
  (Bus)
  ♦ set-down point
ausstreichen etw
  → streichen etw
aussuchen etw
  auswählen etw
  wählen etw
  ♦ choose s.th.
  ♦ select s.th.
Austausch, m
  ♦ exchange
Austauschbesuch, m
  ♦ exchange visit
Austauschbesucher, m
  ♦ exchange visitor
Austauschfahrt, f
  ♦ exchange trip
Austauschfahrt durchführen
  ♦ run an exchange trip
Austauschorganisation, f
  ♦ exchange organisation
  ♦ exchange organization
Austauschpartner, m
  ♦ exchange partner
Austausch vermitteln
  Austausch arrangieren
  ♦ arrange an exchange
Austausch von Geschenken, m
  ♦ exchange of gifts
austeilen etw (aus etw)
  ausschöpfen etw (aus etw)
  ♦ ladle s.th. (out of s.th.)
austeilen etw (in Portionen)
  ♦ portion s.th. out
austeilen etw (Speisen)
  ♦ dish out s.th.
Auster, f
  ♦ oyster
Austernauflauf, m
  → Austernsoufflé
Austernbüfett, n
  ♦ oyster bar
Austerncanapé, n
  ♦ oyster canapé
  ♦ oyster canape *AE*
Austerncocktail, m
  ♦ oyster cocktail
Austernfisch, m
  → Katfisch

Austerngabel, f
♦ oyster fork
Austernhaus, n
♦ oyster house
Austernmesser, n
♦ oyster knife
Austernpastetchen, n
♦ oyster patty
Austernpastete, f
♦ oyster pie
♦ oyster pâté
Austernpilz, m
♦ oyster mushroom
Austern probieren
♦ sample oysters
Austernrestaurant, n
♦ oyster restaurant
♦ oyster bay
♦ restaurant serving oysters
♦ oyster bar
Austernsaison, f
Austernzeit f
♦ oyster season
Austernsalat, m
♦ oyster salad
Austernschiffchen, n
♦ oyster barquette
Austernsoße, f
♦ oyster sauce
Austernsoufflé, n
Austernauflauf, m
♦ oyster soufflé
♦ oyster souffle AE
Austernsuppe, f
♦ oyster soup
Austernzange, f
♦ oyster tongs pl
Austragungsort, m
♦ venue
Austragungsort für etw, m
♦ venue for s.th.
Austragungsort nutzen
♦ use a venue
Austragungsort verlegen von A nach B
♦ change the venue from A to B
Australien
♦ Australia
Australienreise, f (in Australien)
♦ Australian tour
♦ tour of Australia
Australienreise, f (nach Australien)
Reise nach Australien, f
♦ tour to Australia
♦ journey to Australia
♦ trip to Australia
Australientournee, f
♦ Australian tour
Australier, m
♦ Australian
♦ Aussie coll
Australierin, f
♦ Australian girl
♦ Australian woman
♦ Australian
australisch, adj
♦ Australian, adj
australischer Dollar, m
♦ Australian dollar
austrinken etw bis auf den letzten Tropfen
♦ drink s.th. to the last drop

austrinken etw bis zur Neige
austrinken etw bis auf den Boden
♦ drink s.th. to the dregs
austrinken etw (Getränk)
♦ drink up s.th.
♦ finish s.th.
♦ finish off s.th.
austrinken (Getränk)
♦ drink up
austrinken (Glas)
♦ empty
♦ finish
Austrinkzeit, f
(kurze Zeit nach Beginn der Sperrstunde)
Schonzeit, f
♦ drinking-up time BE
aus Übersee, adv
von Übersee, adv
♦ from overseas, adv
aus Übersee kommen
♦ come from overseas
ausverkauft, adj
♦ sold out, adj
♦ packed, adj
ausverkaufte Schau, f
♦ sellout show AE
♦ sell-out show BE
ausverkauftes Haus, n (Theater)
♦ packed house
ausverkauftes Konzert, n
♦ sellout concert AE
♦ sell-out concert BE
ausverkaufte Veranstaltung, f
♦ sellout AE
♦ sell-out BE
ausverkauft sein
♦ be sold out
♦ be fully booked
aus vielen Lebensbereichen
♦ from many walks of life
Auswahl, f
♦ choice
♦ selection
Auswahl an Appartements, f
♦ selection of apartments
Auswahl an Bieren, f
♦ choice of beers
♦ selection of beers
Auswahl an Eßlokalen, f
♦ choice of eating places
♦ selection of eating places
Auswahl an Getränken, f
Auswahl von Getränken, f
♦ selection of beverages
♦ selection of drinks
Auswahl an Käse, f
♦ choice of cheeses
♦ selection of cheeses
Auswahl an Salaten, f
♦ selection of salads
♦ choice of salads
Auswahl an Speisen ist riesengroß
♦ choice of food is vast
Auswahl an Speisen und Getränken, f
♦ choice of food and drinks
♦ selection of food and drinks
Auswahl an Weinen, f
♦ choice of wines
♦ selection of wines

Auswahl an Wohnungen, f
♦ selection of flats BE
♦ selection of apartments AE
Auswahl eines Hotels, f
♦ selection of a hotel
♦ choice of a hotel
♦ selecting a hotel
♦ choosing a hotel
Auswahl eines Konferenzortes, f
♦ selection of a conference venue
♦ choice of a conference venue
♦ selecting a conference venue
♦ choosing a conference venue
auswählen als Konferenzort
♦ select as a conference venue
♦ choose as a conference venue
auswählen etw
♦ select s.th.
♦ choose s.th.
♦ pick s.th.
auswählen etw aus mehreren Optionen
♦ choose s.th. from several options
♦ select s.th. from several options
Auswahl kalter Gerichte, f
♦ choice of cold dishes
Auswahlmenü, n
→ Wahlmenü
Auswahl von Gerichten, f
Auswahl an Gerichten f
♦ selection of dishes
♦ choice of dishes
auswandern nach X
♦ emigrate to X
Ausweichbett, n
→ Ersatzbett, anderweitiges Bett
Ausweichhotel, n
Ersatzhotel, n
anderweitiges Hotel, n
♦ alternativee hotel BE
♦ alternate hotel AE
♦ substitute hotel
Ausweichparkplatz, m (für mehrere Autos)
Ersatzparkplatz, m
♦ alternative car park BE
♦ over-flow car park BE
♦ alternate parking lot AE
Ausweichstraße, f
♦ alternative road BE
♦ alternate road AE
Ausweichtermin, m
→ Ersatztermin
Ausweichunterkunft, f
Ersatzunterkunft, f
anderweitige Unterkunft, f
anderweitige Unterbringung, f
♦ alternative accommodation BE
♦ alternate accommodation AE
Ausweichzimmer n
→ Reservezimmer
ausweisen etw (als etw)
♦ designate s.th. (as s.th.)
ausweisen jn (aus einem Land)
♦ expel s.o. (from a country)
♦ deport s.o. (from a country)
Ausweisung, f
♦ expulsion
♦ deportation
♦ eviction jur
Auswirkung auf die Auslastung haben
♦ have an effect on the load factor

Auswirkung auf die Belegung haben 58

Auswirkung auf die Belegung haben
  Auswirkung auf die Auslastung haben
  ♦ **have an effect on occupancy**
Auszeichnung, f
  Preis, m
  ♦ **award**
Auszeichnung gewinnen (für etw)
  Preis gewinnen (für etw)
  prämiiert werden (für etw)
  prämiert werden (für etw)
  ♦ **win an award (for s.th.)**
  ♦ **win a prize (for s.th.)**
Auszeichnungsempfänger, m
  Preisempfänger, m
  ♦ **award recipient**
  ♦ **recipient of the award**
Auszeichnung vergeben an jn
  ♦ **present an award to s.o.**
aus Zeitmangel
  ♦ **for lack of time**
aus Zeitmangel mußten wir improvisieren
  ♦ **for lack of time we had to improvise**
ausziehbar, adj
  (Möbel)
  ♦ **pull-out, adj**
ausziehbare Couch f
  Ausziehcouch f
  ♦ **pull-out couch**
ausziehbare Doppelcouch f
  ♦ **double pull-out couch**
  ♦ **double couch bed**
ausziehbare Doppelliege f
  ♦ **double pull-out divan**
ausziehbare Liege, f
  Ausziehliege f
  ♦ **pull-out divan**
ausziehbarer Tisch, m
  Ausziehtisch, m
  ♦ **pull-out table**
  ♦ **extension table**
  ♦ **sliding table**
ausziehbares Bett n
  Ausziehbett n
  ♦ **pull-out bed**
ausziehbares Doppelbett, n
  ♦ **double pull-out bed**
Ausziehbett n
  → ausziehbares Bett
Ausziehcouch f
  → ausziehbare Couch
ausziehen aus einem Zimmer
  ♦ **move out of a room**
ausziehen aus einer Wohnung
  ♦ **move out of an apartment** *AE*
  ♦ **move out of a flat** *BE*
ausziehen aus etw (Unterkunft)
  frei machen etw
  ♦ **move out of s.th.**
  ♦ **vacate s.th.**
ausziehen (aus Unterkunft)
  wegziehen
  ♦ **move out**
  ♦ **quit**
Ausziehliege, f
  → ausziehbare Liege
Ausziehtisch, m
  ausziehbarer Tisch, m
  ♦ **extension table**
  ♦ **pull-out table**
  ♦ **sliding table**

Auszubildender, m
  Azubi, m *coll*
  Lehrling, m *obs*
  ♦ **apprentice**
  ♦ **trainee**
Auszug, m (aus Unterkunft)
  ♦ **move**
  ♦ **moving (out)**
  ♦ **removal**
aus zwingenden Gründen
  ♦ **for compelling reasons**
Auto, n
  Wagen, m
  Pkw, m
  PKW, m
  ♦ **car**
  ♦ **automobile** *AE*
  ♦ **auto** *AE*
  ♦ **motor-car** *BE*
Auto abholen
  ♦ **collect a car**
  ♦ **pick up a car**
Auto abstellen
  → Auto parken
Autoabstellfläche, f
  Pkw-Parkfläche, f
  ♦ **car parking area**
  ♦ **car parking space**
Autoabstellgebühr, f
  Autoparkgebühr, f
  Pkw-Parkgebühr, f
  Pkw-Abstellgebühr, f
  ♦ **car parking charge**
  ♦ **car parking fee**
Autoabstellplatz, m
  → Parkplatz
Autoatlas, m
  ♦ **motoring atlas**
Auto auf dem hoteleigenen Parkplatz abstellen
  Auto auf dem hoteleigenen Parkplatz parken
  Wagen auf dem hoteleigenen Parkplatz abstellen
  Wagen auf dem hoteleigenen Parkplatz parken
  ♦ **park a car in the hotel's private parking lot** *AE*
  ♦ **park a car in the hotel's private car park** *BE*
Auto auf einem Parkplatz abstellen
  Auto auf einem Parkplatz parken
  ♦ **leave a car in a parking lot** *AE*
  ♦ **park a car in a parking lot** *AE*
  ♦ **leave a car in a car park** *BE*
  ♦ **park a car in a car park** *BE*
Autoaufzug, m
  Autolift m
  ♦ **automobile elevator** *AE*
  ♦ **auto elevator** *AE*
  ♦ **car lift** *BE*
Autoausflug, m
  Ausflug mit dem Auto, m
  ♦ **car excursion**
  ♦ **car trip**
  ♦ **excursion by car**
  ♦ **trip by car**
Autoausstellung, f
  Automobilausstellung, f
  ♦ **automobile show** *AE*
  ♦ **motor show** *BE*
  ♦ **car show**
Autobahn, f (gebührenfrei)
  gebührenfreie Autobahn, f
  ♦ **freeway** *AE*
  ♦ **toll-free motorway** *BE*

Autobahn, f (gebührenpflichtig)
  Mautautobahn, f
  ♦ **turnpike** *AE*
  ♦ **toll motorway** *BE*
Autobahn, f (generell)
  ♦ **highway** *AE*
  ♦ **motorway** *BE*
Autobahnauffahrt, f
  Autobahneinfahrt, f
  ♦ **highway entrance** *AE*
  ♦ **freeway entrance** *AE*
  ♦ **motorway access** *BE*
  ♦ **superhighway entrance** *AE*
Autobahnausfahrt f
  ♦ **highway exit** *AE*
  ♦ **motorway exit** *BE*
Autobahn benutzen
  ♦ **use the highway** *AE*
  ♦ **use the motorway** *BE*
Autobahnbenutzer, m
  ♦ **highway user** *AE*
  ♦ **motorway user** *BE*
Autobahn bringt uns nach X
  ♦ **highway brings us to X** *AE*
  ♦ **motorway brings us to X** *BE*
Autobahneinfahrt, f
  → Autobahnauffahrt
Autobahngebühr, f
  Autobahnmaut f
  ♦ **turnpike toll** *AE*
  ♦ **motorway toll** *BE*
  ♦ **toll**
  ♦ **highway toll** *AE*
Autobahnhotel n
  ♦ **highway hotel** *AE*
  ♦ **motorway hotel** *BE*
Autobahnkreuz, n
  Autobahnknoten, m *ÖST*
  ♦ **highway intersection** *AE*
  ♦ **motorway intersection** *BE*
Autobahnmaut, f
  Autobahngebühr, f
  ♦ **highway toll** *AE*
  ♦ **motorway toll** *BE*
  ♦ **turnpike toll** *AE*
Autobahnmotel, n
  ♦ **highway motel** *AE*
  ♦ **motorway motel** *BE*
Autobahn nehmen (nach X)
  ♦ **take the highway (to X)** *AE*
  ♦ **take the motorway (to X)** *BE*
Autobahnnetz, n
  ♦ **highway network** *AE*
  ♦ **highway system** *AE*
  ♦ **motorway network** *BE*
  ♦ **motorway system** *BE*
Autobahnpolizei, f
  ♦ **highway police** *AE*
  ♦ **motorway police** *BE*
Autobahnraststätte, f (Anlage)
  ♦ **highway service area** *AE*
  ♦ **motorway service area** *BE*
Autobahnraststätte, f (Lokal)
  ♦ **highway restaurant** *AE*
  ♦ **motorway restaurant** *BE*
Autobahnreise, f
  ♦ **highway journey** *AE*
  ♦ **motorway journey** *BE*
Autobahnreisen, n
  Autobahnreiseverkehr, m

- highway travel AE
- motorway travel BE

Autobahnreisender, m
- highway traveler AE
- motorway traveller BE

Autobahnverbindung, f
- highway connection AE
- highway link AE
- motorway connection BE
- motorway link BE

Autobahnverstopfung, f
Autobahnstau, m
- highway congestion AE
- motorway congestion BE

Autobeförderung, f
Autotransport, m
- car transportation AE
- car transport BE

Auto bereitstellen
Auto stellen
- provide a car

Autobesitz, m
- car ownership

Auto besitzen
- own a car

Autobesitzer, m
- car owner

Auto besteigen
- board a car

Autobestellung, f
Autobuchung, f
- car booking
- booking a car

Auto bietet vier Personen Platz
- car has room for four
- car has seats for four

Autobox, f
verschließbare Garage, f
- lock-up coll
- lock-up garage

Autobus, m
- motorbus
- motorcoach BE
- coach BE
- bus

Autobusunternehmen, n
→ Busunternehmen

Autocamper, m
- car camper
- auto camper AE

Autocamping, n
- car camping
- auto camping AE

Autocampingplatz, m
- motor camp AE

Autocar m SCHW
→ Bus

Autocarreisender m SCHW
→ Busreisender

Autodeck, n
(auf Schiff)
- car deck

Autodieb, m
- car thief

Autodiebstahl, m
- car theft

Autodroschke, f
- motor cab

Auto durchsuchen
- search a car

Auto einstellen in eine Garage
- put a car in a garage
- garage a car

Auto entführen
- hijack a car

Autofährdienst, m
Autofährverbindung, f
- car ferry service

Autofähre, f
- car ferry

Auto fahren
mit dem Auto fahren
- drive a car
- drive
- motor

Autofahren, n
- driving

Autofährenführer, m
(Information)
- car ferry guide

Autofahrer, m (generell)
- motorist
- driver

Autofahrer, m (Lenker)
- car driver
- driver

Autofahrerhof, m obs
Motel, n
- tourist court obs
- tourist cabin AE obs

Autofahrerhotel, n
Kraftfahrerhotel, n
Autohotel, n
- motor hotel BE

Autofährhafen, m
- car ferry port

Autofährstrecke, f
- car ferry route

Autofahrt, f
- car trip
- drive/trip (by car)
- automobile trip AE
- car ride
- motoring trip

Autofahrt machen
- go for a drive

Autofenster, n
- car window

autofrei, adj
- car-free, adj

autofreier Sonntag, m
- car-free Sunday

autofreie Zone, f
- car-free zone

Autogramm, n
- autograph

Autogramm geben
Autogramme geben
- sign autographs

Autogrammjäger, m
- autograph hunter
- autograph seeker

Autogrammsammler, m
- autograph collector

Autogrammstunde, f
- autograph session

Auto haben im Urlaub
- have a car on vacation AE
- have a car on holiday BE

Autohotel, n
→ Motor Hotel

Autoimbiß, m
- drive-in snack bar AE

Autoimbißlokal, n
- drive-in snack place

Autokarte, f
- car card

Autokino n
- drive-in movie theater AE
- drive-in movie AE
- drive-in cinema BE
- drive-in

Auto leasen
- lease a car

Autolift, m
→ Autoaufzug

Automarke, f
- car make

Automat, m (Restaurant)
→ Automatenrestaurant

Automat, m (Verkaufsgerät)
Warenautomat, m
- vending machine AE
- slot machine BE

Automatenbüfett, n
→ Automatenrestaurant

Automatenrestaurant, n
Automatenbüfett n
- automat AE
- slot-machine restaurant BE
- vending restaurant AE

Automatenspiele, n pl
- automatic games pl

Automatenspieler, m
- fruit machine gambler
- slot-machine gambler
- slot-machine player AE
- slot player AE

Automatenumsatz, m
(aus Verkaufsautomaten)
- vending sales AE pl
- vending turnover AE
- slot-machine sales BE pl
- slot-machine turnover BE

Automatenverkauf, m
- automatic vending
- vending

Automatenverpflegung, f
(Verpflegung aus Verkaufsautomaten)
- vending foodservice AE
- slot-machine catering BE

Automatik, f (Auto)
- automatic transmission

automatische Anrufbeantwortung f
→ Anrufbeantwortung

automatische Bowlingbahn, f
- automatic bowling alley

automatische Brandmeldeanlage, f
- automatic fire detection system

automatischer Anrufbeantworter, m
- automatic telephone answering machine
- automatic answering machine
- responder AE

automatischer Aufzug, m (Lift)
automatischer Lift, m
automatischer Fahrstuhl, m
- automatic elevator AE
- self-operating elevator AE
- automatic lift BE
- self-operating lift BE

automatischer Feuermelder, m
- automatic fire alarm *AE*
- automatic fire-alarm *BE*

automatischer Warnruf, m
- automatic alarm call

automatischer Weckdienst, m
- automatic early-call service
- automatic wake-up service
- automatic call service

automatische Stornierung, f
automatische Annullierung, f
automatischer Rücktritt, m
- automatic cancellation
- automatic cancelation *AE*

automatisiertes Buchungssystem, n
- automated booking system

automatisiertes Reservierungssystem, n
- automated reservation system
- automated reservations system

Automechaniker, m
- auto mechanic *AE*
- car mechanic *BE*

Automiete, f
- car hire *BE*
- car rental *AE*

Auto mieten
- rent a car *AE*
- hire a car *BE*

Automietvertrag unterschreiben
Automietvertrag unterzeichnen
- sign a car-rental contract *AE*
- sign a car-hire contract *BE*

Autominute, f
- one-minute drive (by car)
- minute's drive (by car)
- one minute by car

Autominute entfernt sein von X
- be a minute's drive (distant) from X

Auto mit Vorderradantrieb, n
- front-wheel drive car

Automobil, n
Kraftwagen, m
Kraftfahrzeug, n
Kfz, n
- automobile *AE*
- auto *AE*
- car

Automobilausstellung, f
Autoausstellung, f
- motor show *BE*
- automobile show *AE*
- car show

Automobilclub, m
Automobilklub, m
- automobile club

Automobilmuseum, n
- motor museum
- car museum

Automobilorganisation, f
- automobile organisation
- automobile organization

Automobilverband, m
- Automobile Association, the
- AA

Automuseum, n
- car museum
- motor museum

Autoomnibus, m
- motor omnibus

Autopannendienst, m
Autopannenservice, m
- car breakdown service

Auto parken
Auto abstellen
Wagen parken
Wagen abstellen
- park a car

Autopauschale, f
- motoring package

Autopflege, f
Wagenpflege f
- car service

Autopicknick, n
(nach Festen auf Parkplatz)
- tailgating *AE*

Auto probefahren
- test-drive a car

Autoradio, n
- car radio

Autorallye, f
Autosternfahrt, f
- car rally
- motor rally
- rally

Autoreifen, m
- car tire
- car tyre *BE*

Autoreise, f
Pkw-Reise, f
Autotour, f
- car journey
- car tour
- car trip
- motor tour

Autoreise mit Chauffeur, f
- chauffeur-driven car tour

Autoreisen, m
Autoreiseverkehr, m
- car travel
- travel by car

Autoreisender, m
Automobilist, m *form*
Autofahrer, m
- motoring tourist
- motorist
- tourist traveling by car *AE*
- tourist travelling by car *BE*

Autoreisezug, m
Autozug, m
- car sleeper train
- autotrain *AE*
- Motorail train *BE*

Autoreisezugdienst, m
Autoreisezugverkehr, m
- autotrain service *AE*
- car sleeper train service
- Motorail service *BE*

Autoreisezugverbindung, f
Autozugverbindung, f
- autotrain link *AE*
- autotrain connection *AE*
- Motorail link *BE*
- Motorail connection *BE*

Autorennen, n
- car race

Autorennsport, m
- car racing
- motor racing

Autorennstrecke, f
- car racing circuit
- motor racing track

Autoreparaturwerkstatt, f
Autowerkstatt, f
- car repair shop
- garage

Auto reservieren
Auto reservieren lassen
Wagen reservieren (lassen)
- reserve a car

Autorestaurant, n
Drive-in-Restaurant, n
- drive-in restaurant
- drive-in
- drive-through restaurant *AE*
- drive-thru restaurant *AE*
- drive-thru *AE coll*

autorisiertes Hotel n
- authorised hotel

Autoroute, f
Autostrecke, f
- car route
- motoring route

Autorundreise, f
- circular motor tour

Autosafaripark, m
- drive-through safari park
- drive-thru safari park *coll*

Autoschlange, f
- queue of cars
- car queue

Autoservice, m
→ Autopflege

Autostellplatz, m
- car parking space

Autostellplatz buchen
- book a car parking space

Autostellplatz reservieren
- reserve a car parking space

Autosteuer, f
Pkw-Steuer, f
- car tax

Autostopp, m
→ Trampen

Autostraße, f
- motor road

Autostunde, f
- one-hour drive (by car)
- hour's drive (by car)
- one hour by car
- hour's car ride

Autostunde entfernt sein von X
- be an hour's drive (distant) from X
- be within an hour's car ride of X

Autotelefon, n
- carphone

Autotourismus, m
- motoring
- touring by car

Autotourist, m
- tourist traveling by car *AE*
- tourist travelling by car *BE*
- motoring tourist

Autotransfer, m
(mit dem Auto)
- car transfer
- transfer by car

Autotür, f
- car door

Autotyp, m
♦ car type
♦ type of car
Autoüberfahrt, f
♦ car crossing
Auto überschlug sich
♦ car overturned
Autounfall, m
♦ car accident
♦ car crash
♦ automobile accident *AE*
♦ auto accident *AE*
Autourlaub, m
(*Urlaub mit Benutzung des Autos*)
♦ car vacation *AE*
♦ motoring vacation *AE*
♦ car holiday *BE*
♦ motoring holiday *BE*
Autourlauber, m
♦ vacation motorist *AE*
♦ motoring vacationer *AE*
♦ holiday motorist *BE*
♦ motoring holidaymaker *BE*
Autoverkehr, m
Kfz-Verkehr, m
♦ car traffic
♦ motor traffic
♦ automobile traffic *AE*
♦ auto traffic *AE*
Autoverkehr verringern
♦ reduce car traffic
Autoverleih, m
Autovermietung, f
♦ car hire *BE*
♦ car rental *AE*
♦ auto rental *AE*
Auto vermieten
Wagen vermieten
♦ rent (out) a car
♦ hire out a car *BE*
Autovermieter, m
♦ car lessor *jur*
Autovermietung, f
Autoverleih, m
♦ car rental *AE*
♦ auto rental *AE*
♦ car hire *BE*
Autovermietungsschalter, m
→ Mietwagenschalter
Autoversicherung, f
♦ car insurance
♦ motor insurance
Autovorführung, f
♦ car demonstration
Autovorstellung, f
(*Ausstellung*)
♦ car launch
Autowanderer, m
♦ driver-hiker *AE*
♦ motor tourist *BE*
Autowanderung, f
♦ walk for the motorist
Autowaschanlage, f
♦ car wash
Autowaschdienst, m
Autowaschservice
♦ car-wash service
Autowaschservice, m
→ Autowaschdienst
Autowerkstatt, f
→ Autoreparaturwerkstatt

Auto wird abgeschleppt (durch die Polizei)
♦ car will be towed away (by the police)
♦ car is towed away (by the police)
Autozug, m
Autoreisezug, m
♦ Motorail train *BE*
♦ autotrain *AE*
Autozugdienst, m
Autoreisezugdienst, m
♦ Motorail service *BE*
♦ autotrain service *AE*
Autozugendstation, f
Endstation des Autoreisezugs, f
♦ Motorail terminus *BE*
♦ autotrain terminus *AE*
Autozugfahrkarte, f
Autozugkarte, f
♦ Motorail ticket *BE*
♦ autotrain ticket *AE*
Autozugreise, f
Fahrt mit dem Autoreisezug, f
♦ Motorail journey *BE*
♦ autotrain journey *AE*
♦ autotrain ride *AE*
Auto zuhause lassen
♦ leave one's car at home
Auto zurückbringen
♦ return a car
♦ bring a car back
Autozuschlag, m
♦ car supplement
Average Cover, m
(*Restaurantumsatz geteilt durch Gesamtgästezahl*)
♦ average cover
avisieren jm etw
♦ advise s.o. of s.th.
avisieren jm jn
♦ advise s.o. of s.o.'s arrival
♦ inform s.o. of s.o.'s arrival
♦ notify s.o. of s.o.'s arrival
Avisierung, f
→ Benachrichtigung
Avocato, m
Avocatobirne, f
Avocado, f
Avocadobirne, f
♦ avocado
Avocatococktail, m
Avocadococktail, m
♦ avocado cocktail
Avocatosalat, m
Avocadosalat, m
♦ avocado salad
Avocatosuppe, f
Avocadosuppe, f
♦ avocado soup
Azoren, die, pl
♦ Azores, the *pl*
Azteke, m
♦ aztec
Aztekenreich, n
♦ Aztec Empire, the
aztekisch, adj
♦ Aztec, adj
♦ Aztecan, adj

B

b.
  bei
  ◆ nr.
  ◆ near
Babies willkommen
  ◆ Babies welcome
Baby, n
  Säugling, m
  ◆ baby
Babyaufsicht, f (Person)
  ◆ baby patroller
Babybad, n
  Babybadewanne, f
  ◆ baby bath
Baby beaufsichtigen
  ◆ mind a baby
Babybeaufsichtigung, f
  ◆ baby minding
  minding a baby
Babybeaufsichtigung gegen Entgelt
  ◆ Baby-minding at a charge
Babybett, n (generell)
  ◆ baby bed
  ◆ baby's bed
Babybett, n (mit hohen Seiten)
  ◆ baby's crib AE
  ◆ crib AE
  ◆ baby's cot BE
  ◆ cot BE
Babybettchen, n
  Babybett, n
  ◆ cot BE
  ◆ baby's cot BE
  ◆ crib AE
  ◆ baby's crib AE
Babybetten sind erhältlich für Kleinkinder
  ◆ cribs are available for infants AE
  ◆ cots are available for infants BE
babyfreundlich, adj
  ◆ baby-friendly, adj
  ◆ suitable for babies, adj
Babyhorchanlage, f
  Babywachanlage f
  ◆ baby-listening system
  ◆ baby-listening device
  ◆ baby-listening set
Babykontrolldienst, m
  Babyaufsicht, f
  ◆ baby patrol service
Babynahrung, f
  Säuglingsnahrung, f
  ◆ baby food
Babyphone, n
  ◆ baby phone
Babyraum, m
  ◆ baby room
Babysitter, m
  ◆ babysitter

Babysitter auf Wunsch
  ◆ babysitter on request
Babysitter benötigen
  ◆ require a babysitter
Babysitterdienst, m
  Babysitterservice m
  Babysitter m
  ◆ babysitting service
Babysitterservice m
  → Babysitterdienst
Babysitter vermitteln
  Babysitter arrangieren
  ◆ arrange a babysitting service
  ◆ arrange for a babysitter
Babytragetasche, f
  ◆ carry cot BE
Babyüberwachung, f
  Babywachdienst, m
  ◆ baby-listening service
  ◆ baby-listening
Babyüberwachungsgerät, n
  ◆ baby-listening device
Babywickeleinrichtung, f
  → Wickeleinrichtung
Babywickelraum, m
  ◆ baby changing room
Babywickeltisch, m
  ◆ baby changing table
Babywindel, f
  → Windel
Bacardi, m regist
  ◆ Bacardi regist
Bacchus
  ◆ Bacchus
Bacchuswein, m
  Bacchus, m
  ◆ Bacchus wine
  ◆ Bacchus
Bach, m
  ◆ brook
Bachchor, m
  ◆ Bach choir
Bachforelle, f
  ◆ brook trout
Back, f
  Vorderdeck, n
  ◆ forecastle
  ◆ fo'c's'le BE
  ◆ foredeck
Backblech, n
  ◆ baking tray
  ◆ baking tin
Backbordseite, f
  Backbord, n
  ◆ port side
  ◆ port
Backbuch, n
  ◆ baking book

backen (etw)
  ◆ bake (s.th.)
Bäcker, m
  ◆ baker
Bäckerei, f (Aktivität)
  Backen, n
  ◆ baking
Bäckerei, f (Gewerbe)
  ◆ baker's trade
Bäckerei, f (Laden)
  ◆ baker's shop
  ◆ baker's
  ◆ bakery
Bäckereikette, f
  ◆ bakery chain
Bäckerfest, n
  ◆ bakers' festival
Bäckergeselle, m
  ◆ journeyman baker
Bäckerinart, adv gastr
  nach Bäckerinart, adv gastr
  ◆ baker's style, adv gastr
Bäckerladen, m
  → Bäckerei
Bäckerlehrling, m
  ◆ apprentice baker
  ◆ trainee baker
Bäckermeister, m
  ◆ master baker
backfertig, adj
  → ofenfertig
Backfett, n
  (für Kuchen)
  ◆ shortening
Backfisch, m (Bratfisch)
  → Bratfisch
Backfisch, m (Teenager)
  → Teenager
Backform, f
  ◆ baking tin BE
  ◆ cake pan AE
Backgammon, n
  ◆ backgammon
Backgammonbrett, n
  ◆ backgammon board
Backgammon spielen
  ◆ play backgammon
Backhaus, n
  ◆ bakehouse
Backofen, m
  Ofen, m
  ◆ oven
Back Office, n
  (Buchhaltung etc)
  ◆ back office
Back-Office-Betrieb, m
  ◆ back-office operation

Back-Office-System, n
♦ back-office system
Back-of-the-House-Manager, m
♦ back-of-the-house manager
♦ back-of-house manager
Backpacker, m
→ Rucksacktourist
Backpapier, n
Butterbrotpapier, n
♦ greaseproof paper
Backpulver, n
♦ baking powder
Backrezept, n
♦ baking recipe
Backschüssel, f
Rührschüssel, f
♦ baking dish
Backsgast, m
Buggast, m
♦ forecastle man
Backstein, m
♦ brick
Backsteingebäude, n
♦ brick building
Backsteingotik, f
♦ brick Gothic
Backsteinkirche, f
♦ brick church
♦ brick-built church
Backteig, m (flüssig)
Rührteig, m
♦ batter
Backteig, m (generell)
♦ dough
Backwaren, f pl
♦ bread, cakes and pastries
Bad, n (generell)
♦ bath
Bad, n (im Freien)
♦ bathe
Bad, n (Kurort)
→ Kurort
Bad benutzen
♦ use a bath
♦ use the bath
Badbenutzung, f
♦ use of the bath
♦ using the bath
Badbesuch, m (Schwimmbad)
♦ visit to the pool
Badeanlage, f
Badekomplex, m
♦ bathing complex
Badeanstalt, f
♦ baths pl
Badeanzug, m
(bes. für Frauen)
♦ bathing suit
♦ bathing dress BE
Badearzt, m
→ Kurarzt
Badeaufenthalt, m
♦ bathing stay
Badeausflug, m
♦ bathing excursion
♦ bathing trip
Badeausflügler, m
♦ bathing excursionist
Badebecken, n
→ Schwimmbecken

Badebetrieb, m
♦ bathing establishment
♦ bathing operation
Badebucht f
♦ bathing cove
Badedestination, f
Badeziel, n
♦ bathing destination
Badeeinrichtung, f
Bademöglichkeit, f
♦ bathing facility
Badeerlebnis, n
Badeerfahrung, f
♦ bathing experience
Badeferien, pl (generell)
Badeurlaub, m
♦ bathing holidays BE pl
♦ bathing holiday BE
♦ bathing vacation
Badeferien, pl (Strandferien)
→ Strandferien
Badegast, m (Heilbad)
♦ visitor to a spa
♦ visitor to a health resort
♦ spa visitor
Badegast, m (Meer)
♦ visitor to a seaside resort
Badegast, m (Schwimmbad)
→ Badender, Schwimmer
Badegelegenheit, f (Möglichkeit)
♦ opportunity for bathing
♦ opportunity for swimming
Badegelegenheit, f (Platz)
♦ place to swim
Badehalle, f
→ Hallenbad
Badehaus, n
Badhaus, n
♦ bath house
Badehosen, f pl
(bes. für Männer)
♦ swimming trunks pl
♦ swim trunks AE pl
♦ bathing trunks pl
Badehotel n
♦ bathing hotel
Badehütte, f
♦ bathing hut
♦ cabana AE
Bad einlaufen lassen jm
♦ run s.o. a bath
Badeinsel, f (Insel)
♦ island suitable for a beach vacation AE
♦ island suitable for a beach holiday BE
Badeinsel, f (Ponton)
♦ pontoon (on the lake)
Badekabine, f
♦ bathing cabin
♦ bathing box
♦ cabana
Badekappe, f
♦ bathing cap
Badekarren, m hist
♦ bathing machine hist
Badekleidung, f
♦ bathing attire
♦ bathwear
Badekur, f
♦ cure at a spa
♦ spa cure

Badekur machen
♦ take a cure at a spa
♦ take a spa cure
Badelido, m
Lido, m
Badestrand, m
♦ bathing lido
♦ lido
Bademeister, m (Strand)
Rettungsschwimmer, m
♦ lifeguard AE
♦ life-guard BE
Bademöglichkeit, f
→ Badeeinrichtung
Baden
(Region)
♦ Baden
Baden, n
Badesport, m
♦ bathing
Badender, m
Badegast, m
Schwimmer, m
♦ bather
♦ swimmer
baden gehen
♦ go bathing
♦ go swimming
♦ go for a swim
baden (im Freien)
♦ bathe
♦ have a swim
♦ have a bathe BE
baden im Meer
♦ bathe in the sea
baden in der Sonne
sonnenbaden
sich sonnen
♦ bask in the sun
♦ bathe in the sun
♦ sunbathe
baden (in Wanne)
♦ have a bath
♦ take a bath
Badenixe, f
♦ bathing beauty
♦ bathing belle
baden jn
♦ bathe s.o.
Baden-Württemberg
(Region)
♦ Baden-Wuerttemberg
Badeort, m (generell)
♦ bathing resort
Badeort, m (Meer)
→ Seebad
Badeparadies n
♦ bather's paradise
♦ swimmer's paradise
Badeplatz, m
Platz zum Baden, m
♦ bathing place
Bäderkur, f
→ balneologische Behandlung
Bädertourismus, m
→ balneologischer Tourismus
Bädertourist, m
→ balneologischer Tourist
Bäderwesen, n
→ Balneologie

Bahnabreise

Badesaison, f (Heilbad)
♦ season at a spa
♦ season at a health resort
Badesaison, f (Schwimmen)
♦ bathing season
Badesalz, n
♦ bath salts pl
Badesee, m
♦ bathing lake
 lake suitable for bathing
Badestadt, f
→ Badeort
Badesteg, m
♦ jetty
Badestrand m
♦ bathing beach
Badetourismus, m (Meer)
♦ seaside tourism
♦ beach tourism
Badetourist, m (Meer)
♦ seaside tourist
♦ beach tourist
Badetradition, f
zweitausendjährige Badetradition, f
♦ bathing tradition
♦ two thousand years of bathing tradition
Badetuch, n
Badehandtuch n
♦ bath towel
Badetuchwechsel, m
♦ change of the bath towel
♦ changing the bath towel
Badetuch wechseln
♦ change the bath towel
Badeufer, n
(am Meer)
→ Strand
Badeurlaub, m (generell)
Badeferien, pl
♦ bathing vacation AE
♦ bathing holidays BE pl
♦ bathing holiday BE
Badeurlaub, m (Strandurlaub)
→ Strandurlaub
Badeurlauber, m
Badeferiengast, m
♦ bathing vacationer AE
♦ bathing holidaymaker BE
Badeverbot, n
♦ bathing ban
♦ ban on bathing
Badevergnügen, n
Badespaß, m
♦ bathing fun
Badewanne, f
♦ bathtub
♦ tub
Badewannenstöpsel, m
Badewannenverschluß m
♦ bath tub plug
♦ bath plug
Badewärter, m
→ Schwimmeister
Badewasser, n (Badewanne)
♦ bath water
♦ bath
Badewasser, n (generell)
♦ bathing water
Badewasserqualität, f
♦ bathing water quality

Badezelt, n
♦ bathing tent
Badezentrum, n
♦ bathing center AE
♦ bathing centre BE
Badezeug, n
♦ bathing things pl
Badezielort, m
Badeziel, n
Strandzielort, m
Strandziel, n
♦ beach destination
Badezimmer, n
Bad, n
B
♦ bathroom
♦ bath
♦ bthrm.
Badezimmerarmaturen, f pl
♦ bathroom fittings pl
Badezimmer benutzen
Bad benutzen
♦ use a bathroom
♦ use a bath
Badezimmerbenutzung, f
Badbenutzung, f
♦ use of the bathroom
♦ use of the bath
Badezimmerboden, m
Badboden, m
♦ bathroom floor
♦ bath floor
Badezimmerdusche, f
♦ bathroom shower
Badezimmer gemeinsam benutzen mit jm
Badezimmer teilen mit jm
♦ share a bathroom with s.o.
Badezimmergröße, f
♦ bathroom size
Badezimmerhocker, m
Badezimmerschemel m
♦ bathroom stool
Badezimmer instandhalten
♦ service a bathroom
Badezimmer ist frei
Bad ist frei
♦ bathroom is free
♦ bath is free
Badezimmer ist überschwemmt
♦ bathroom is flooded
Badezimmer liegt auf der anderen Flurseite
♦ bathroom is across the corridor
Badezimmer mit Beschlag belegen
♦ monopolise a bathroom
♦ monopolize a bathroom
Badezimmer mit Dusche/WC, n
♦ bathroom with shower/WC
Badezimmer mit Jacuzzi, n
♦ bathroom with jacuzzi
Badezimmer mit separater Dusche und Wanne, n
♦ bathroom with separate shower and tub
Badezimmermöbel, n pl
Badezimmermobiliar, n
♦ bathroom furniture sg
Badezimmerschrank, m
♦ bathroom cabinet
Badezimmerspiegel, m
Badspiegel, m
♦ bathroom mirror
♦ bath mirror

Badezimmer ständig mit Beschlag belegen
♦ hog the bathroom
Badezimmertelefon, n
♦ bathroom telephone
♦ bathroom phone
Badezimmertür, f
♦ bathroom door
Badezimmerwaage, f
♦ bathroom scales pl
Badezimmerwäsche, f
Badwäsche, f
Bäderwäsche, f
♦ bathroom linen
Badezimmerzuschlag, m
♦ bathroom supplement
♦ supplement for private bathroom
Badhaus, n
→ Badehaus
Badhotel, n
(in Badeort oder Kurort)
♦ health-resort hotel
♦ spa hotel
badisch, adj
♦ Baden, adj
Badische Bäderstraße, f
♦ Baden Spa Road, the
badischer Wein, m
♦ Baden wine
badisches Dorf, n
♦ Baden village
badische Spezialität, f
♦ Baden speciality
♦ Baden specialty AE
Badische Weinstraße, f
♦ Baden Wine Road, the
Badminton, n
♦ badminton
Badmintonball, m
♦ shuttlecock
♦ shuttle
Badmintonplatz, m
♦ badminton court
Badminton spielen
♦ play badminton
Bad nehmen
baden
♦ take a bath
♦ have a bath
Baedeker, m
♦ baedeker
Bagatelldiebstahl, m
kleiner Diebstahl, m
♦ petty theft
Baggage, f
→ Gepäck
Baggersee, m
♦ flooded gravel pit
♦ gravel pit used as bathing lake
♦ excavation pool
♦ excavation pond
Baguette, f FR
♦ French loaf
♦ baguette FR
♦ French bread
Bahama-Inseln, f pl
♦ Bahama Islands, the pl
Bahamas, die, pl
♦ Bahamas, the pl
Bahnabreise, f
Abreise mit der Bahn, f

Bahnanbindung

- ♦ rail departure
- ♦ departure by rail

Bahnanbindung, f
- ♦ rail access

Bahnankunft, f
- Ankunft mit der Bahn, f
- ♦ rail arrival
- ♦ arrival by rail

Bahnanreise
(Kapitelüberschrift)
- ♦ How to Get There by Rail

Bahnanreise, f
- ♦ travel by rail

Bahnausflug, m
- ♦ rail excursion
- ♦ rail trip

Bahnbegeisterter, m
- Eisenbahnbegeisterter, m
- ♦ rail enthusiast
- ♦ railroad enthusiast AE
- ♦ railway enthusiast BE

Bahnbenutzer, m
- ♦ rail user

Bahnbrücke, f
- ♦ rail bridge

Bahncard, f
- ♦ rail card

Bahndeck, n
(Zugfähre)
- ♦ rail deck

Bahnerfahrung, f
- Bahnerlebnis, n
- ♦ rail experience

Bahnfähre, f
- ♦ rail ferry

Bahnfahrer, m
- Bahnfahrgast, m
- ♦ rail passenger

Bahnfahrkarte, f
- Bahnfahrschein, m
- ♦ rail ticket

Bahnfahrkartenpreis, m
- ♦ rail ticket price

Bahnfahrplan, m
- ♦ rail schedule AE
- ♦ rail timetable BE

Bahnfahrpreis, m
- ♦ rail fare

Bahnfahrt, f
- ♦ rail trip
- ♦ rail journey
- ♦ rail ride

Bahnfan, m
- Bahnfreak, m
- ♦ rail buff

Bahnferien, pl
- Bahnurlaub, m
- ♦ rail holiday BE
- ♦ rail vacation AE

Bahngesellschaft, f
- ♦ rail company

Bahngleis, n
- ♦ rail track

Bahnhof, m
- ♦ railway station BE
- ♦ railroad station AE
- ♦ station

Bahnhofabholung, f
- ♦ collecting s.o. from the station
- ♦ fetching s.o. from the station
- ♦ collection from the station

- ♦ transportation from the station AE
- ♦ transport from the station BE

Bahnhofsbahnsteig, m
- Bahnsteig, m
- ♦ station platform
- ♦ platform

Bahnhofsbuffet, n
- → Bahnhofsgaststätte

Bahnhofsgaststätte, f
- Bahnhofsrestaurant, n
- Bahnhofsbuffet, n
- ♦ station restaurant

Bahnhofshalle, f
- ♦ station concourse
- ♦ concourse

Bahnhofshotel n
- ♦ station hotel

Bahnhofsmission, f
- ♦ Travellers' Aid Society
- ♦ Travellers' Aid Office

Bahnhofsnähe, f
- ♦ proximity to the station
- ♦ closeness to the station

Bahnhofsrestaurant, n
- → Bahnhofsgaststätte

Bahnhofsschild, n
- ♦ railroad station sign AE
- ♦ railway station sign BE

Bahnhofstransfer, m
- ♦ station transfer
- ♦ transfer to the station
- ♦ transfer from the station

Bahnhofsvorsteher, m
- ♦ stationmaster

Bahnhofswirtschaft, f
- → Bahnhofsgaststätte

Bahnhotel, n
- ♦ rail hotel

Bahnlinie, f
- ♦ rail line

Bahnmuseum, n
- ♦ rail museum

Bahnnetz, n
- ♦ rail network

Bahnpauschale, f
- ♦ rail package

Bahnpauschalreise, f
- Eisenbahnpauschalreise, f
- ♦ rail package tour
- ♦ rail-inclusive tour
- ♦ RIT
- ♦ package tour by rail
- ♦ inclusive tour by rail

Bahnpauschalsegment, n
- ♦ rail package segment

Bahnpauschalurlaub, m
- Bahnpauschalferien, pl
- ♦ rail-inclusive vacation AE
- ♦ rail-inclusive holiday BE

Bahnreise, f
- ♦ rail tour
- ♦ rail journey
- ♦ rail trip

Bahnreise dauert drei Stunden
- ♦ rail tour takes three hours
- ♦ rail journey takes three hours
- ♦ rail trip takes three hours
- ♦ rail tour lasts three hours
- ♦ rail journey lasts three hours

Bahnreisen, n
- Bahnreiseverkehr, m
- ♦ rail travel

Bahnreisender m
- ♦ rail traveler AE
- ♦ rail traveller BE

Bahnreiseveranstalter, m
- ♦ rail tour operator

Bahnrestaurant, n
- ♦ rail restaurant

Bahnstation, f
- ♦ rail station
- ♦ railroad station AE
- ♦ railway station BE

Bahnsteig, m
- ♦ platform
- ♦ station platform
- ♦ track AE

Bahnsteigkarte, f
- ♦ platform ticket

Bahnsteigpersonal, n
- ♦ platform staff

Bahnstrecke, f
- Bahnroute, f
- ♦ rail route

Bahnstreik, m
- ♦ rail strike

Bahntourismus, m
- ♦ rail tourism

Bahntourist, m
- ♦ rail tourist

Bahntransport, m
- Bahnbeförderung, f
- ♦ rail transportation AE
- ♦ rail transport BE

Bahntunnel, m
- ♦ rail tunnel

Bahnübergang, m
- ♦ grade crossing AE
- ♦ level crossing BE

Bahnumsatz, m
- ♦ rail sales pl
- ♦ rail turnover

Bahnurlaub, m
- Bahnferien, pl
- ♦ rail vacation AE
- ♦ rail holiday BE

Bahnurlaub machen
- ♦ take a rail vacation AE
- ♦ take a rail holiday BE

Bahnverbindung, f
(Zug)
- ♦ rail connection
- ♦ rail link

Bahnverbindung nach X, f
- ♦ rail link to X
- ♦ rail connection to X

Bahnverkehr, m
- ♦ rail traffic

Bahnzentrum, n
- ♦ rail center AE
- ♦ rail centre BE

Bahrain
- Bahrain
- ♦ Bahrain
- ♦ Bahrein

Bahrainer, m
- Bahreiner, m
- ♦ Bahraini
- ♦ Bahreini

Bahrainerin, f
Bahreinerin, f
♦ Bahraini girl
♦ Bahraini woman
♦ Bahreini
♦ Bahreini girl
♦ Bahreini woman
bahrainisch, adj
bahreinisch, adj
♦ Bahraini, adj
♦ Bahreini, adj
♦ Bahrain, adj
♦ Bahrain, adj
Bakkarat, n
♦ baccarat
Bakkarat spielen
♦ play baccarat
Bakschisch, n
♦ baksheesh
♦ bakshish
Bakschisch geben (jm)
♦ baksheesh (s.o.)
♦ bakshish (s.o.)
♦ give (s.o.) a baksheesh
♦ give (s.o.) a bakshish
Baldachinbett, n
Himmelbett n
♦ canopy bed
♦ four-poster bed
♦ testerbed *obsol*
Baldachin eines Betts, m
♦ canopy of a bed
baldmöglichst, adv
→ so bald wie möglich
Balearen, die, pl
(Inselgruppe)
♦ Balearic Islands, the *pl*
♦ Balearics, the *pl*
Bali
♦ Bali
Balinese, m
♦ Balinese
balinesisch, adj
♦ Balinese, adj
Balk., m
Balkon, m
♦ balc.
♦ balcony
Balkan, m
Balkangebirge, n
♦ Balkans, the *pl*
♦ Balkan Mountains *pl*
Balkanland, n
♦ Balkan country
Balkendecke, f
♦ beamed ceiling
♦ timbered ceiling
Balkon, m (Gebäudeteil)
Balk., m
♦ balcony
♦ balc.
Balkon, m (Theater)
erster Rang, m
♦ first balcony *AE*
♦ balcony *AE*
♦ dress circle *BE*
Balkonappartement, n
♦ balcony apartment
Balkon geht auf die Straße
♦ balcony looks onto the street

Balkon hat Blick über den See
♦ balcony overlooks the lake
Balkon liegt nach Norden
♦ balcony faces north
Balkon liegt nach Osten
♦ balcony faces east
Balkon liegt nach Süden
♦ balcony faces south
Balkon liegt nach Westen
♦ balcony faces west
Balkon liegt zur Landseite
♦ balcony faces inland
♦ balcony overlooking s.th.
Balkon mit Meeresblick, m
Balkon mit Meerblick, m
♦ seaview balcony *AE*
♦ sea-view balcony *BE*
♦ balcony with seaview *AE*
♦ balcony with sea view *BE*
Balkon mit seitlichem Meeresblick, m
♦ balcony with side sea-view
Balkon mit Sitzmöbel, m
♦ balcony with seating equipment
Balkonschlafzimmer, n
♦ balcony bedroom
Balkonstuhl, m
♦ balcony chair
Balkontisch, m
♦ balcony table
Balkontür, f
♦ balcony door
Balkonwohnung, f
♦ balcony flat *BE*
♦ balcony apartment *AE*
Balkonzimmer, n
Zimmer mit (einem) Balkon, n
♦ room with (a) balcony
♦ balcony room
Balkonzimmerzuschlag m
♦ supplement for a room with balcony
Balkon zur Landseite, m
♦ landfront balcony *AE*
♦ land-front balcony *BE*
♦ balcony facing inland
Balkon zur Meerseite, m
→ Balkon zur Seeseite
Balkon zur Ozeanseite, m
♦ oceanfront balcony *AE*
♦ ocean-front balcony *BE*
♦ balcony facing the ocean
Balkon zur Seeseite, m (Binnensee)
♦ lakefront balcony *AE*
♦ lake-front balcony *BE*
♦ balcony facing the lake
Balkon zur Seeseite, m (Meer)
Balkon zur Meerseite, m
♦ seafront balcony *AE*
♦ sea-front balcony *BE*
♦ balcony facing the sea
Ball, m (Spielball)
♦ ball
Ball, m (Veranstaltung)
♦ ball
Ballabend, m
♦ evening of the ball
Ballaststoff, m
(in Speisen)
♦ fibre
ballaststoffreiche Kost, f
Schlackenkost, f

♦ high-fiber diet *AE*
♦ high-fibre diet *BE*
Ball ausrichten (als Gastgeber)
♦ host a ball
Ball besuchen
auf einen Ball gehen
♦ go to a ball
Ballbesucher, m
♦ person visiting a ball
♦ person invited to a ball
Ballerina, f
Ballettänzerin, f
♦ ballerina
Ball eröffnen
♦ open a ball
Ballett, n
♦ ballet
Ballettabend, m
♦ ballet evening
Ballettänzer, m
♦ ballet dancer
Ballettänzerin, f
→ Ballerina
Ballettaufführung, f
Ballettdarbietung f
♦ ballet performance
Ballettmatinee, f
♦ ballet matinee *AE*
♦ ballet matinée *BE*
Ballgast, m
♦ guest at a ball
Ball geben
♦ give a ball
Ballkarte, f
♦ dance card
Ballkleid, n
♦ ball dress
Ballkönigin, f
♦ queen of the ball
♦ belle of the ball
Ball-Lokal, n
→ Tanzsaal, Ballsaal
Ballmädchen, n
(Tennis)
♦ ball girl
Ballmann, m (Kricket)
Werfer, m
♦ bowler
Ballnacht, f
♦ night of the ball
Ballon, m
Luftballon, m
♦ balloon
Ballon fahren
mit dem Ballon fahren
♦ ride a balloon
♦ balloon
Ballonfahren, n
Ballonsport, m
♦ ballooning
Ballonfahrer, m
♦ balloonist
Ballonfahrt, f
♦ balloon trip
♦ balloon ride
Ballonflug, m
♦ balloon flight
Ballonführer, m
♦ balloon pilot
Ballonkorb, m
♦ balloon basket

Ballonrennen

Ballonrennen, n
♦ balloon race
Ballon starten
♦ launch a balloon
Ballsaal m
♦ ballroom
Ballsaalraum, m
Ballsaalfläche, f
♦ ballroom space
Ballsaison f
♦ ball season
Ballsouper, n
♦ supper ball
Ballspiel, n
♦ ball game
Ballspiele machen
♦ play ball games
Ball spielen
♦ play ball
Ballspielen verboten
♦ No ball games
Ballungsgebiet, n
♦ conurbation
Ball veranstalten
♦ organise a ball
♦ organize a ball
Ballveranstaltung, f
→ Ball
Balneologe, m
♦ balneologist
Balneologie, f
Bäderwesen, n
♦ balneology
balneologisch, adj
♦ balneological, adj
balneologische Behandlung, f
Bäderkur, f
♦ balneological treatment
balneologischer Tourismus, m
Bädertourismus, m
♦ baneological tourism
balneologischer Tourist, m
Bädertourist, m
♦ balneological tourist
balneotherapeutische Einrichtung, f
♦ balneo-therapeutical facility
Balneotherapie, f
Heilbehandlung durch Bäder f
♦ balneotherapy
Bal paré, m *FR. m*
festlicher Ball, m
Prunkball, m
Festball, m
♦ bal paré *FR*
♦ festive ball
Balte, m
♦ Balt
Baltikum, n
♦ Baltic, the
Baltin, f
♦ Baltic woman
♦ Baltic girl
♦ Balt
baltisch, adj
♦ Baltic, adj
Baltischen Staaten, die, m pl
♦ Baltic states, the *pl*
Balustrade, f
♦ balustrade
Bambusfloß, n
♦ bamboo raft

Bambushütte, f
♦ bamboo hut
Bambusvorhang, m
♦ bamboo curtain
Banane, f
♦ banana
Bananenbier, n
♦ banana beer
Bananeneiskrem, f
Bananeneis, n
♦ banana ice cream *AE*
♦ banana ice-cream *BE*
Bananenhain, m
♦ banana grove
Bananenkuchen, m
♦ banana cake
Bananenlikör, m
♦ banana liqueur
Bananenmilchmixgetränk, n
♦ banana milk shake
Bananenrepublik, f
♦ banana republic
Bananenschale, f
♦ banana skin
Bananenscheibe, f
♦ banana slice
♦ slice of banana
Bananensorbet, n
♦ banana sorbet
Bananensoufflé, n
Bananenauflauf, m
♦ banana soufflé *BE*
♦ banana souffle *AE*
Bananenwein, m
♦ banana wine
Band, f (Musikkapelle)
→ Kapelle
Band engagieren
Kapelle engagieren
♦ engage a band
♦ hire a band
Bandleiter, m
Bandleader, m
♦ band leader
Bandscheibenmatratze, f
♦ orthopaedic mattress
Band spielt
♦ band plays
♦ band is playing
Bandwurm, m
♦ tapeworm
Bangladesch
♦ Bangladesh
Bangladescher, m
♦ Bangladeshi
Bangladescherin, f
♦ Bangladeshi girl
♦ Bangladeshi woman
♦ Bangladeshi
bangladeschisch, adj
♦ Bangladeshi, adj
Bank, f (Geschäft)
♦ bank
Bankett, n
Festessen, n
Festmahl, n
Gastmahl, n *obs*
♦ banquet
Bankettabteilung f
♦ banquet department
♦ banqueting department *BE*

Bankett abwickeln
♦ handle a banquet
Bankettanforderung, f
♦ banquet requirement
♦ banqueting requirement *BE*
Bankettarrangement, n
Bankettvereinbarung f
♦ banquet arrangement
♦ banqueting arrangement *BE*
♦ arrangement of a banquet
♦ arranging a banquet
Bankett arrangieren
♦ arrange a banquet
Bankettaufbau, m
♦ banquet set-up
♦ setting up a banquet
Bankett aufbauen
♦ set up a banquet
Bankettaufwand, m
♦ banquet expense *AE*
♦ banquet expenditure
♦ banqueting expenditure *BE*
Bankettaufwendungen, f pl
♦ banquet expenses *pl*
♦ banqueting expenses *BE pl*
Bankettauslastung, f
Bankettbelegung, f
♦ banquet occupancy
♦ banqueting occupancy *BE*
Bankettauslastungsrate f
Bankettauslastungsquote f
♦ banquet occupancy rate
♦ banqueting occupancy rate *BE*
Bankettbar, f
♦ banquet bar
♦ banqueting bar *BE*
Bankettbereich, m (abstrakt)
Bankettsektor, m
♦ banquet sector
♦ banqueting sector *BE*
Bankettbereich, m (Abteilung)
→ Bankettabteilung
Bankettbereich, m (konkret)
♦ banquet area
♦ banqueting area *BE*
Bankettbericht, m
♦ banquet report
♦ banqueting report *BE*
Bankett bestellen
Bankett buchen
Festessen bestellen
♦ book a banquet
Bankettbestellung, f
Bankettbuchung f
♦ banquet booking
♦ booking (of) a banquet
Bankettbestuhlung f
♦ banquet-style seating
♦ banquet seating
Bankettbetreuung, f
→ Bankettservice
Bankettbetrieb, m
♦ banquet establishment
♦ banquet operation
Bankettbrigade, f
♦ banquet brigade
♦ banqueting brigade *BE*
Bankettbuch, n
♦ banquet function book
Bankettbuchung, f
Bankettbestellung, f

♦ booking (of) a banquet
♦ banquet booking
Bankettbüro n
♦ banquet office
♦ banqueting office BE
Bankettchef, m
♦ banquet chef
Bankett dauert zwei Tage (lang)
♦ banquet lasts (for) two days
Bankettteilnehmer, m
Teilnehmer an einem Bankett, m
♦ banqueter
Banketteinnahmen, f pl
♦ banquet revenues pl
♦ banquet receipts pl
♦ income from a banquet
♦ takings from a banquet pl
Banketteinrichtung f
♦ banquet facility
♦ banqueting facility BE
Banketterlös, m
♦ banquet revenue
♦ banqueting revenue BE
Bankettertrag, m (GuV)
(Gewinn- und Verlustrechnung)
♦ banquet income
♦ banqueting income BE
Bankettessen n
♦ banquet meal
Bankett findet statt
♦ banquet takes place
Bankettfläche, f
♦ banqueting area
♦ banquet area
Bankettform, f
(Bestuhlung)
♦ banquet style
Bankettfoyer, n
♦ banquet foyer
♦ banqueting foyer BE
Bankettgast m
♦ banquet guest
Bankett geben
Festessen geben
Essen geben
♦ give a banquet
Bankettgeschäft n
♦ banquet business
♦ banqueting business BE
bankettieren
schmausen
sich gütlich tun
♦ banquet
♦ feast
♦ dine
Bankettinformation, f
♦ banquet information
♦ banqueting information
Bankettisch, m
♦ banquet table
♦ banqueting table BE
Bankettjournal, n
♦ banquet diary
♦ banqueting diary BE
Bankettkapazität, f
♦ banquet capacity
♦ banqueting capacity BE
Bankettkellner, m
♦ banquet waiter
Bankettkellnerin, f
♦ banquet waitress

Bankettkoch, m
♦ banquet cook
Bankettkoordination, f
♦ banquet coordination
Bankettkoordinator, m
♦ banquet coordinator
Bankettküche f (Raum)
♦ banquet kitchen
Bankettküchenchef, m
♦ banquet kitchen chef
Bankettleiter, m
Bankettmanager m
♦ banquet manager
Bankettleitung, f
♦ banquet management
♦ managing a banquet
Bankettmarkt m
♦ banquet market
♦ banqueting market BE
Bankettmenü, n
Festmenü, n
♦ banquet menu
Bankettoberkellner, m
♦ banquet headwaiter
♦ banquet captain AE
Bankettordner, m
Bankettordnungskraft, f
♦ banquet steward
Bankettorganisation, f
♦ banquet organisation
♦ banquet organization
bankettorientiertes Hotel n
♦ banquet-oriented hotel AE
♦ banquet-orientated hotel BE
Bankettpersonal, n
♦ banquet staff
♦ banquet personnel
♦ banqueting staff BE
♦ banqueting personnel BE
Bankettportier, m
♦ banquet porter
♦ banqueting porter BE
Bankettprospekt, m
♦ banquet prospectus
♦ banqueting prospectus BE
Bankettraum, m (Saal)
Festraum, m
Festsaal, m
♦ banquet room
♦ banqueting room BE
Bankettraum, m (Volumen, Fläche)
Bankettfläche, f
♦ banquet space
♦ banqueting space BE
Bankettträumlichkeiten, f pl
♦ banquet facilities pl
♦ banqueting facilities BE pl
Bankettrechnung, f
♦ banquet bill
♦ banquet check AE
♦ banqueting bill BE
Bankettsaal, m
Bankettshalle, f
♦ banquet hall
♦ banqueting hall BE
Bankettservice m
Bankettdienst m
♦ banquet service
♦ banqueting service BE
Bankettspeisekarte, f
Tafelkarte, f

♦ banquet menu
♦ banqueting menu BE
Bankett sponsern
Festessen sponsern
♦ sponsor a banquet
Bankettsuite, f
Festsuite, f
♦ banquet suite
♦ banqueting suite BE
Bankettumsatz, m
♦ banquet sales pl
♦ banqueting sales BE pl
♦ banquet turnover
♦ banqueting turnover BE
Bankett veranstalten (für jn)
♦ organise a banquet (for s.o.)
♦ organize a banquet (for s.o.)
♦ give a banquet (for s.o.)
Bankettveranstalter, m
Bankettorganisator, m
♦ banquet organiser
♦ banquet organizer
Bankettveranstaltung f
♦ banquet function
♦ banquet
Bankett verkaufen
Festessen verkaufen
♦ sell a banquet
Bankettvertrag, m
♦ banquet contract
♦ banqueting contract BE
Bankett vorbereiten
Festessen vorbereiten
♦ prepare a banquet
Bankettzimmer n
→ Bankettraum
Bankett zu Ehren von jm, n
Bankett zu js Ehren, n
Festessen zu Ehren von jm, n
♦ banquet in honor of s.o. AE
♦ banquet in honour of s.o. BE
♦ banquet in s.o.'s honor AE
♦ banquet in s.o.'s honour BE
Bankettzwecke, m pl
♦ banqueting purposes pl
Bankfeiertag, m
offizieller Feiertag, m
♦ bank holiday BE
Bankfeiertagsverkehr, m
♦ bank holiday traffic BE
Bankfeiertagwochenende, n
♦ bank holiday weekend BE
Bank f (Möbelstück)
♦ bench
Bankgebühr, f
Bankgebühren, f pl
Bankspesen, pl
♦ bank charge
♦ bank charges pl
Bankkonto, n
♦ bank account
Bankleitzahl, f
♦ bank code number
Banknote f
♦ bank bill AE
♦ bill AE abbr
♦ bank note BE
♦ note BE abbr
bankrott, adj
♦ bankrupt, adj

bankrottes Hotel, n
 ♦ bankrupt hotel
Bankrott machen
 ♦ go bankrupt
bankrott sein
 ♦ be bankrupt
Bankschalter, m
 ♦ bank counter
Bankwechselkurs, m
 ♦ bank exchange rate
bar, adj
 ♦ cash, adj
bar, adv
 ♦ in cash, adv
Bar, an der man soviel essen kann, wie man will
 Soviel-man-essen-kann-Bar, f
 ♦ all-you-can-eat bar
Bar, f (generell)
 ♦ bar
 taproom AE
Bar, f (Nachtbar)
 → Nachtbar
Barabteilung, f
 ♦ bars department
Baracke, f
 ♦ barrack
Barackenwohnung, f
 ♦ barrack apartment AE
 ♦ barrack flat BE
Bar am Meer, f
 ♦ bar by the sea
Bar am Wasser, f
 ♦ waterfront bar
Bar an der Ecke, f
 ♦ bar on the corner
 ♦ corner bar
Baranteil, m
 (z.B. an Einnahmen, Kosten)
 ♦ bar proportion
 ♦ bars proportion
Baranzahlung f
 ♦ cash deposit
Bararbeit, f
 ♦ barman's work
Bar aufbauen
 ♦ set up a bar
bar auf den Tisch zahlen
 ♦ pay money down
 ♦ plank down AE sl
Barausstattung, f
 Barausrüstung f
 ♦ bar equipment
Barbadier, m
 ♦ Barbadian
Barbadierin, f
 ♦ Barbadian girl
 ♦ Barbadian woman
 ♦ Barbadian
barbadisch, adj
 ♦ Barbadian, adj
Barbados
 ♦ Barbados
Barbar, m
 ♦ barbarian
Bar beaufsichtigen
 Aufsicht haben über eine Bar
 sich kümmern um eine Bar
 ♦ tend a bar
Barbecue-Abend, m
 → Grillabend

Barbecue machen
 → grillen
Barbereich, m (Raum)
 ♦ bar area
Barbesitzer, m (generell)
 ♦ bar owner
 ♦ owner of a bar
Barbesitzer, m (Nachtbar)
 ♦ nightclub owner AE
 ♦ owner of a nightclub AE
 ♦ night-club owner BE
 ♦ owner of a night-club BE
Barbestand, m (in der Bar)
 Barvorrat m
 ♦ bar stock
Bar besuchen
 ♦ visit a bar
Barbesucher, m (in der Bar)
 ♦ bar visitor
 ♦ visitor to a bar
Barbetrieb, m (Betriebsführung)
 ♦ bar operation
 ♦ operating a bar
Bar bewirtschaften
 ♦ operate a bar
bar bezahlen
 → bar zahlen
Barbüfett, n
 ♦ bar buffet
Barbummel, m
 → Kneipenbummel
Bar-Cafeteria, f
 ♦ bar-cafeteria
Barchef, m
 Chef de bar, m FR
 ♦ bar chef
 ♦ chef de bar FR
Barcommis, m
 Commis de bar, m FR
 Bargehilfe, m
 ♦ bar commis
 ♦ commis de bar FR
Bardame f
 ♦ barmaid
Bardame in der Public Bar, f
 ♦ public barmaid
Bardamen gesucht
 ♦ Barmaids wanted
Bar des Jahres, f
 ♦ Bar of the Year
Bardolino, m ITAL
 Bardolinowein, m
 ♦ Bardolino ITAL
 ♦ Bardolino wine
Bareigentümer, m
 ♦ bar proprietor
 ♦ proprietor of a bar
Bareinnahmen, f pl (in der Bar)
 ♦ bar takings pl
 ♦ bar receipts pl
 ♦ bar income
 ♦ bar revenues pl
Bärenhunger haben
 ♦ have a wolf in one's stomach
 ♦ I could eat a horse
Barerlös, m (in der Bar)
 ♦ bar revenue
Barertrag, m (in der Bar)
 (Gewinn- und Verlustrechnung)
 ♦ bar income

Baressen, n (in der Bar)
 ♦ bar meal
Barfläche f
 ♦ bar area
 ♦ area of a bar
Bar führen
 ♦ keep a bar
Barführung, f
 ♦ barkeeping
 ♦ keeping a bar
Bar für Hausgäste, f
 ♦ bar for residents
 ♦ residents' bar
 ♦ residential bar
barfuß, adj
 ♦ barefoot, adj
 ♦ barefooted, adj
barfuß gehen
 ♦ walk barefoot
Bargast, m (in der Bar)
 ♦ bar patron
 ♦ bar customer
 ♦ bar visitor
Bargeld, n
 ♦ cash
Bargeldautomat, m
 ♦ cash machine
Bargeldkasse, f (Portokasse)
 → Portokasse
Bargeldreserven, f pl
 ♦ cash reserves pl
Bargeld wechseln
 ♦ change cash
Bargericht, n
 ♦ bar dish
Bargeschäft, n (in der Bar)
 ♦ bar business
Bargetränk, n
 ♦ bar drink
 ♦ bar beverage
Bargewinn, m (in Bar)
 ♦ bar profit
Barhocker m
 (Stuhl)
 ♦ bar stool
Barimbiß, m
 ♦ bar snack
Bar im Clubstil f
 ♦ club-style bar
Bar im Westernstil, f
 ♦ western bar
Bar ist ein beliebter Treffpunkt für einen Aperitif
 ♦ bar is a popular meeting place for an aperitif
Barjargon, m
 ♦ bar jargon
Barkarte, f (Speisekarte)
 Barspeisekarte, f
 ♦ bar menu
Barkasse, f
 ♦ launch
 ♦ motor launch
Barkassierer m (in der Bar)
 Barkassier, m ÖST/SCHW
 ♦ bar cashier
Barkaution, f
 ♦ cash security deposit
Barkeeper, m
 ♦ barkeeper

Barkeeperassistent, m
　Barassistent, m
　♦ assistant barkeeper
Barkeeper mußte die Polizei anfordern
　Barkeeper mußte die Polizei rufen
　♦ barkeeper had to call the police
Barkellner, m
　♦ bar waiter
Barkellnerin, f
　♦ bar waitress
　♦ barmaid
Barkontrolle, f (in der Bar)
　♦ bar control
Barkonzession, f
　♦ bar licence
　♦ bar license
Barkosten, pl (in der Bar)
　♦ bar costs pl
　♦ bar cost
Barkunde, m (in der Bar)
　♦ bar customer
　♦ bar patron
Barlehrling, m
　♦ apprentice barman
Bar leiten
　♦ manage a bar
　♦ run a bar
Barleiter, m (einer Bar)
　Barmanager, m
　♦ bar manager
　♦ manager of a bar
Barleiter, m (mehrerer Bars)
　♦ bars manager
Barleitung, f
　Barmanagement n
　♦ bar management
　♦ bars management
　♦ managing a bar
　♦ managing bars
Barleute pl
　→ Barpersonal
Barlöffel, m
　♦ bar spoon
Barlöhne, m pl (in der Bar)
　♦ bar wages pl
Barlounge, f
　♦ bar lounge
Barmädchen, n
　♦ bargirl
Barman, m
　Barmann m
　♦ barman
　♦ bartender AE
　♦ barkeep AE coll
Barmanager, m
　Barleiter, m
　♦ manager of a bar
　♦ bar manager
Barman in der Public Bar, m
　♦ public barman
Barman/Kellner, m
　♦ barman/waiter
　♦ barman-cum-waiter
Barmann, m
　→ Barman
Barmantätigkeit, f
　♦ bartending
Barmeister, m
　Chef de bar, m FR
　♦ bar manager
　♦ chef de bar FR

Barmesser, n
　♦ bar knife
Bar mit 50 Plätzen, f
　♦ bar with 50 seats
　♦ 50-seater bar
Bar mit Bedienung, f
　♦ service bar
Bar mit Kellnerbedienung, f
　♦ bar with waiter service
Bar mit Kellnerinnenbedienung, f
　♦ bar with waitress service
Bar mit Live-Musik, f
　♦ bar with live music
Bar mit Schankerlaubnis, f
　(für alkoholische Getränke)
　♦ licensed bar
　♦ licenced bar
Barmittagessen, n
　♦ bar lunch
　♦ bar luncheon
Bar mit unverwechselbarem Charakter, f
　♦ character bar
Barmixer m
　♦ bar mixer
Barockabtei, f
　♦ baroque abbey
Barockarchitektur, f
　♦ baroque architecture
Barockfassade, f
　barocke Fassade, f
　♦ baroque façade
　♦ baroque facade AE
Barockfest, n
　♦ baroque festival
Barockgarten, m
　♦ baroque garden
Barockgebäude, n
　Barockbau, m
　♦ baroque building
Barockhaus, n
　barockes Haus, n
　♦ baroque house
　♦ house in the baroque style
Barockkathedrale, f
　Barockdom, m
　♦ baroque cathedral
Barockkirche, f
　♦ baroque church
Barockkunst, f
　♦ baroque art
Barockmöbel, n pl
　♦ baroque furniture sg
Barockmusik, f
　♦ baroque music
Barockpalast, m
　♦ baroque palace
Barockrathaus, n (Großstadt)
　barockes Rathaus, n (Großstadt)
　♦ baroque city hall
Barockrathaus, n (kleine Stadt)
　barockes Rathaus, n (kleine Stadt)
　♦ baroque town hall
Barockschloß, n
　♦ baroque castle
　♦ baroque palace
　♦ baroque château
Barockstadt, f (Großstadt)
　♦ baroque city
Barockstadt, f (kleine Stadt)
　♦ baroque town

Barockstraße, f
　(Ferienstraße)
　♦ Baroque Route, the
Barockstukkatur, f
　♦ baroque stucco work
　♦ baroque plaster work
Barockturm, m
　♦ baroque tower
Bar ohne Bedienung, f
　♦ cash bar
　♦ no-host bar AE
Barolo, m ITAL
　(Wein)
　♦ Barolo ITAL
Bar pachten (von jm)
　♦ lease a bar (from s.o.)
Barpersonal, n
　♦ bar staff
　♦ bar personnel
Barpianist, m
　♦ bar pianist
Barpreis, m (Auszeichnung)
　♦ cash prize
Barpreis, m (Barzahlung)
　→ Barzahlungspreis
Barpreis m (in der Bar)
　♦ bar price
Barräumlichkeiten, f pl
　♦ bar facilities pl
Barrechnung f (in der Bar)
　♦ bar check AE
　♦ bar bill BE
Barren, m
　(Sportgerät)
　♦ parallel bars pl
Bar-Restaurant n
　Barrestaurant n
　♦ bar-restaurant
Barrückerstattung, f (in bar)
　♦ cash refund
Barrückerstattung erhalten
　♦ receive a cash refund
Barrückerstattung leisten
　Barerstattung leisten
　♦ give a cash refund
Barscheck, m
　(Gegensatz zu Verrechnungsscheck)
　♦ cashable check AE
　♦ uncrossed check AE
　♦ open cheque BE
　♦ uncrossed cheque BE
　♦ cashable cheque BE
Barschrank, m
　(im Gästezimmer)
　♦ drinks cabinet BE
Barschrank mit Kühlanlage, m
　(im Gästezimmer)
　♦ refrigerated drinks cabinet BE
Barservice, m
　♦ bar service
Bars für jeden Geschmack, f pl
　♦ bars to suit every taste pl
Barsieb, n
　♦ bar strainer
　♦ strainer
Barsteward, m
　♦ bar steward
　♦ bars steward
Barteam, n
　Barmannschaft, f
　♦ bar team

Barterrasse

Barterrasse, f
 ♦ bar terrace
 ♦ bar patio
Bartisch, m
 ♦ bar table
Bartochter f SCHW
 → Bardame
Bartresen, m
 Bartheke f
 ♦ bar counter
Bartyp, m
 Barart, f
 ♦ bar type
 ♦ type of bar
Bar um die Ecke, f
 ♦ bar round the corner
Barumsatz, m (in der Bar)
 ♦ bar sales pl
 ♦ bar turnover
Barumsatz, m (Kassa)
 ♦ cash sales pl
 ♦ cash turnover
Barveranda, f
 ♦ bar veranda
 ♦ bar verandah
Bar verpachten (an jn)
 ♦ lease a bar (to s.o.)
Barvorrat, m (in der Bar)
 → Barbestand
Barwagen, m
 ♦ bar cart AE
 ♦ bar trolley BE
Barwert, m (bar)
 ♦ cash value
bar zahlen
 bar bezahlen
 ♦ pay cash
 ♦ pay in cash
bar zahlen etw
 ♦ pay cash for s.th.
bar zahlen im voraus
 ♦ pay cash in advance
Barzahlung f
 ♦ cash payment
Barzahlungsgast m
 ♦ cash guest
Barzahlungskunde, m
 ♦ cash customer
 ♦ cash client
Barzahlungspreis, m
 Barpreis, m
 ♦ cash price
 ♦ cash rate
Barzahlungsrabatt, m
 → Skonto
Barzange, f
 ♦ bar tongs pl
Basar m
 ♦ bazar
 ♦ bazaar
Basar veranstalten
 ♦ organise a basar
 ♦ organise a bazaar
Baseball, m
 ♦ baseball
Baseballfan, m
 ♦ baseball fan
Baseballplatz, m
 ♦ baseball grounds
 ♦ baseball field

 ♦ ballpark AE
 ♦ baseball pitch
Baseballspiel, n
 ♦ baseball game
 ♦ baseball match
Baseball spielen
 ♦ play baseball
Baseballspieler, m
 ♦ baseball player
Baseballstadion, n
 ♦ baseball stadium
Basic price, m
 → Grundpreis, Grundtarif
Basilika, f
 ♦ basilica
Basilikum, n
 Basilienkraut, n
 Basilie, f
 ♦ basil
Basisfahrzeug, n
 ♦ base vehicle
Basishotel, n
 ♦ base hotel
Basislager, n
 ♦ base camp
Basisprovision, f
 → Grundprovision
Basisquartier, n
 ♦ base quarters pl
 ♦ base camp
Basissaison, f
 ♦ basic season
Baske, m
 ♦ Basque
Baskenland, n
 ♦ Basque Country, the
Basketball, m
 ♦ basketball
Basketballplatz, m
 ♦ basketball court
Basketball spielen
 ♦ play basketball
Basketballspieler, m
 Basketballspielerin f
 ♦ basketball player
Baskin, f
 ♦ Basque girl
 ♦ Basque woman
 ♦ Basque
baskisch, adj
 ♦ Basque, adj
Bastardsoße, f
 ♦ bastard sauce
Bauarbeit, f
 ♦ construction work
Bauarbeiten, f pl
 ♦ building work sg
Bauchladen, m
 ♦ vendor's tray
Bauch pflegen
 → prassen
Bauchtanz, m
 ♦ belly dance
Bauchtanzen, n
 ♦ belly dancing
Bauchtänzerin, f
 ♦ belly dancer
Bauch vollschlagen sich
 ♦ stodge one's stomach sl
Bauchweh haben fam
 ♦ have a tummy-ache fam

Baude, f dial
 Berghütte, f
 Sennhütte, f
 ♦ bothy
 ♦ bothie
 ♦ mountain bothy
Bau der Eisenbahnlinie, m
 ♦ construction of the railroad line AE
 ♦ construction of the railway line BE
Bau eines Hotel, m
 ♦ construction of a hotel
Bau eines neuen Hotels, m
 ♦ construction of a new hotel
 ♦ building (of) a new hotel
bauen etw nach den Plänen von jm
 ♦ build s.th. to the plans of s.o.
Bäuerinart, adv gastr
 bäuerliche Art, adv gastr
 ♦ farmer's style, adv gastr
Bauernbett, n
 ♦ farmer's bed AE
 ♦ peasant's bed BE
Bauernbüfett, n
 ♦ country buffet
 ♦ farmhouse-style buffet
Bauerndorf, n
 ♦ farming village
Bauernessen, n
 ♦ country meal
Bauernfrühstück, n
 ♦ farmer's breakfast
 ♦ farmhouse breakfast
 ♦ peasant-style breakfast
 ♦ country breakfast
Bauernfrühstücksbüfett, n
 ♦ farmhouse-style buffet breakfast
 ♦ farmhouse-style breakfast buffet AE
Bauernhaus, n
 ♦ farmhouse
Bauernhof, m
 ♦ farmstead
 ♦ farm
 ♦ farmhouse
Bauernhofbereich, m (abstrakt)
 Bauernhofsektor, m
 ♦ farmhouse sector
Bauernhofbereich, m (konkret)
 ♦ farmhouse area
Bauernhofmuseum, n
 Bauernmuseum, n
 ♦ farm museum
 ♦ farming museum
Bauernhofpark, m
 ♦ farm park
Bauernhofpension, f
 ♦ farm guesthouse AE
 ♦ farm guest-house BE
Bauernhoftourismus, m
 ♦ farm tourism
Bauernhoftourist, m
 ♦ farm tourist
Bauernhofunterkunft, f
 Bauernhausunterkunft, f
 Unterkunft in einem Bauernhof, f
 Unterbringung in einem Bauernhaus, f
 ♦ farmhouse lodging AE
 ♦ farmhouse accommodation
Bauernhofurlaub, m
 Urlaub auf dem Bauernhof, m
 ♦ farm holiday BE
 ♦ farmhouse holiday BE

- farm vacation *AE*
- farmhouse vacation *AE*

Bauernhofurlaubsführer, m
- farm holiday guide *BE*
- farm vacation guide *AE*

Bauernimbiß, m
Bauernvesper, f
- ploughman's lunch *BE*

Bauernküche, f (Speisen)
Bauernhofküche, f
- farm cooking

Bauernmöbel, n pl
- rustic furniture *sg*
- farmhouse furniture *sg*
- country furniture *sg*

Bauernstube, f
- farmhouse room

Bauerntisch, m
- farmhouse table

Bauernvesper, f
→ Bauernimbiß

baufällig, adj
- dilapidated, adj
- ramshackle, adj
- out of repair, adj

baufälliges Haus, n
- dilapidated house
- ramshackle house

baufälliges Hotel, n
- dilapidated hotel
- ramshackle hotel

baufällig werden
- fall into disrepair

Baufirma, f
- construction company

Baugenehmigung, f
- planning permission *BE*

Bauherr, m
- builder-owner
- property developer
- developer

Baukastensystem, n
- modular system

Baukosten, pl
- building costs *pl*
- building cost
- construction costs *pl*
- construction cost
- hard costs *pl*

Bauland zu verkaufen
- land for sale

Baulärm, m
- building noise

baulicher Zustand, m
- state of repair

bauliche Verbesserung, f
- structural improvement

Baumgrenze, f
- treeline *AE*
- tree-line *BE*
- timberline *AE*
- timber-line *BE*

Baumhaus, n
- tree house *AE*
- tree-house *BE*

baumlos, adj
- treeless, adj

baumlose Insel, f
- treeless island

Baumwolle, f
- cotton

Baumwoll-Laken, n
- cotton sheet

Baumwollstadt, f (Großstadt)
- cotton city

Baumwollstadt, f (kleine Stadt)
- cotton town

Bau neuer Hotels, m
- building of new hotels
- construction of new hotels

Bau neuer Zimmer, m
- building of new rooms
- construction of new rooms

Baupacht, f
(mit Nutzung von 99 Jahren und mehr)
- building lease

Bauplatz, m
Baustelle, f
- building site
- construction site
- building plot
- plot

Bauplatzlärm, m
- building site noise

Bauprogramm, n
- building program *AE*
- building programme *BE*
- construction program *AE*
- construction programme *BE*

Bauprojekt, n
- building project

baureif, adj
- ripe for development, adj
- ready for building, adj
- developed, adj

baureifer Bauplatz, m
- developed site
- site ready for building

baureifes Land, n
- developed land

Bausachverständiger, m
(berechnet Volumen, Baumaterial)
- quantity surveyor *BE*

Bausaison, f
Bauzeit, f
- building season

Baustelle, f
- construction site
- building site
- site

Baustopp, m
- building freeze

Bauträger, m
- property developer
- developer
- developing company

Bauträgergesellschaft, f
- property development company
- development company

Bauunternehmer, m
- building contractor
- property developer
- developer

Bauverbot, n
- building ban
- ban on building

Bauvertrag, m
- construction contract

Bauvorschriften, f pl
- building regulations *pl*

Bauwerk, n
- edifice

bayerische Küche, f (Speisen)
- Bavarian cuisine
- Bavarian cooking

Bayerischen Alpen, die, pl
- Bavarian Alps, the *pl*

Bayerischer Abend, m
- Bavarian Evening
- Bavarian Night

Bayerisches Allgäu, n
(Region)
- Bavarian Allgäu
- Bavarian Algäu

bayerische Spezialität, f
- Bavarian specialty *AE*
- Bavarian speciality *BE*

Bayerische Wald, der, m
- Bavarian Forest, the

Bayern
(Land)
- Bavaria

beabsichtigte Abreise, f
- intended departure

beabsichtigter Aufenthalt, m
- intended stay

beabsichtigte Reise, f
- intended journey
- intended tour
- intended trip

Beachball, m
- beach ball *AE*
- beach-ball *BE*

Beachball spielen
- play beach ball

Beachbar, f
→ Strandbar

beachten etw
- note s.th.

beanspruchen etw
- claim s.th.

Beanspruchung, f (Forderung)
- claiming s.th.
- claim

Beanspruchung, f (Kapazität)
- utilising s.th.
- utilizing s.th.
- utilisation
- utilization

Beanspruchung von Kapazität, f
Nutzung von Kapazität, f
Kapazitätsnutzung, f
- utilisation of capacity
- utilization of capacity

beanstanden etw
reklamieren etw
beschweren sich über etw
- complain about s.th.
- make a complaint about s.th.

Beanstandung, f
Reklamation, f
Beschwerde, f
- objection
- complaint

beantragen etw
- apply for s.th.

beantworten etw
antworten auf etw
- answer s.th.
- reply to s.th.

Beantwortung, f
Antwort f

Beantwortung einer Anfrage 74

♦ answer
♦ reply
Beantwortung einer Anfrage, f
  ♦ reply to an inquiry
  ♦ reply to an enquiry
  ♦ answering an inquiry
  ♦ answering an enquiry
Bearbeitungsentgelt, n
  Bearbeitungsgebühr, f
  ♦ processing fee
  ♦ processing charge
  ♦ handling fee
  ♦ handling charge
Bearbeitungsgebühr, f
  ♦ handling charge
  ♦ handling fee
  ♦ processing charge
  ♦ processing fee
Bearbeitungszeit f
  (z.B. Buchung)
  ♦ handling time
  ♦ processing time
Bearbeitung von etw, f
  ♦ dealing with s.th.
  ♦ handling s.th.
  ♦ processing s.th.
Bearnerart, adv *gastr*
  nach Bearnerart, adv *gastr*
  ♦ bearnese style, adv *gastr*
beaufsichtigen etw
  Aufsicht haben über etw
  ♦ supervise s.th.
  ♦ be in charge of s.th.
beaufsichtigen jn
  → Aufsicht haben über jn
Beaujolais, m *FR*
  ♦ Beaujolais *FR*
Beaujolaisdorf, n
  ♦ Beaujolais village
Beaujolais-Gegend, f
  ♦ Beaujolais country
Beaujolais Nouveau, m *FR*
  ♦ Beaujolais Nouveau *FR*
Beauty Farm, f
  → Schönheitsfarm
bebaubar, adj
  ♦ developable, adj
bebilderter Führer, m
  Bildführer, m
  ♦ illustrated guide
  ♦ pictorial guide
Béchamelsoße, f
  ♦ béchamel sauce
  ♦ bechamel sauce *AE*
Becher, m (mit Henkel)
  Henkelbecher, m
  hohe Tasse, f
  ♦ mug
Becher leeren bis zur Neige
  Becher leeren bis zum Boden
  ♦ drain a cup to the dregs
bechern *coll*
  schnell etw trinken
  ♦ knock back a few bottles *inform*
Becherpastete, f
  → Füllpastete
Bed&Breakfast, n
  Übernachtung mit Frühstück, f
  Zimmer mit Frühstück, n
  ♦ bed&breakfast

♦ b&b
♦ B&B
Bed-and-Breakfast-Führer, m
  ♦ bed-and-breakfast guide
Bed&Breakfast-Pension, f
  ♦ bed-and-breakfast place
  ♦ bed-and-breakfast hotel
  ♦ b&b place
  ♦ b&b hotel
Bed-and-Breakfast-Unternehmen, n
  ♦ bed-and-breakfast enterprise
Bed-and-Breakfast-Unternehmung, f
  ♦ bed-and-breakfast venture
Bed-and-Breakfast-Verzeichnis, n
  ♦ bed-and-breakfast directory
  ♦ B&B directory
bedanken sich für eine Einladung
  ♦ express one's thanks for an invitation
Bedarf an etw, m
  ♦ need for s.th.
Bedarfshaltestelle, f
  ♦ request stop
bedauern etw
  ♦ regret s.th.
bedienen jn
  ♦ serve s.o.
  ♦ wait on s.o.
  ♦ attend to s.o.
bedienen lassen sich wie ein Pascha
  wie ein Pascha sich bedienen lassen
  ♦ let oneself be waited on hand and foot
bedienen sich selbst
  ♦ serve oneself
  ♦ help oneself
Bedienen Sie sich, bitte!
  Nehmen Sie sich, bitte!
  ♦ Help yourself, please
Bedienerin, f
  → Kellnerin
Bediensetenunterkunft, f
  ♦ servants' accommodation
bedient werden als erster
  ♦ be served first
bedient werden als letzter
  ♦ be served last
Bedienung, f (Person)
  → Kellner, Kellnerin
Bedienung, f (Service)
  ♦ service
Bedienung der Gäste, f
  ♦ serving guests
  ♦ guest service
Bedienung durch Kellner, f
  → Kellnerbedienung
Bedienung durch Kellnerinnen, f
  → Kellnerinnenbedienung
Bedienung inbegriffen
  einschließlich Bedienung
  mit Bedienung
  ♦ service included
Bedienung nicht inbegriffen
  ♦ Service not included
Bedienungsabgabe, f
  → Bedienungsgeld
Bedienungsanleitung, f
  (für Geräte)
  ♦ operating instruction
Bedienungsgeld, n
  Bedienungszuschlag m
  Bedienung f
  ♦ service charge

Bedienungsgeldanteil, m
  ♦ share of the service charge
Bedienungsgeld erheben
  Bedienungsgeld fordern
  ♦ levy a service charge
Bedienungsgeld inbegriffen
  → Einschließlich Bedienungsgeld
Bedienungsgeld nicht inbegriffen
  Bedienungsgeld nicht einbegriffen
  Ohne Bedienungsgeld
  Preis ohne Bedienungsgeld
  ♦ Service charge not included
Bedienungsgeld wird verlangt
  ♦ service charge is levied
  ♦ service charge is required
Bedienungsgeldzuschlag, m
  → Bedienungsgeld
Bedienungskapazität, f
  Servicekapazität, f
  ♦ capacity of service
  ♦ service capacity
Bedienungskraft, f
  → Kellner, Kellnerin
Bedienungsperson, f
  → Bedienungskraft
bedienungspersonal, n
  ♦ waiting personnel
  ♦ waiting staff
  ♦ service personnel
  ♦ service staff
Bedienungspersonal bereitstellen
  Bedienungspersonal zur Verfügung stellen
  ♦ provide service staff
  ♦ provide service personnel
Bedienungszuschlag, m
  Bedienungsgeld, m
  ♦ extra charge for service
  ♦ extra fee for service
  ♦ service charge
Bedienung und Taxen inbegriffen
  ♦ Service and taxes included
Bedienung à la carte, f
  → Service à la carte
bedrängen jn
  bestürmen jn
  hartnäckig fordern von jm
  ♦ importune s.o.
bedrohtes Tier, n
  ♦ endangered animal
Beduine, m
  ♦ Bedouin
  ♦ Beduin
  ♦ Bedoui
Beduinenzelt, n
  ♦ Bedouin tent
  ♦ Beduin tent
  ♦ Bedoui tent
Bedürfnis, n
  Wunsch, m
  Verlangen, n
  ♦ desire
Bedürfnis des Gasts, n
  ♦ requirement of a guest
  ♦ guest's requirement
Bedürfnisse eines Gastes erfüllen
  ♦ meet the requirements of a guest
beehren jn mit einem Besuch
  ♦ honor s.o. with a visit *AE*
  ♦ honour s.o. with a visit *BE*
beehren sich, jn einzuladen
  Ehre haben, jn einzuladen

Ehre geben sich, jn einzuladen
- ♦ have the honor of inviting s.o. *AE*
- ♦ have the honor to invite s.o. *AE*
- ♦ have the honour of inviting s.o. *BE*
- ♦ have the honour to invite s.o. *BE*

Beeil' Dich!
Beeilt Euch!
- ♦ Hurry up!

beeilen sich
- ♦ hurry up
- ♦ hurry

beeilen sich mit etw
- ♦ hurry up with s.th.

Beeilung, bitte!
- ♦ Get a move on!
- ♦ Get a move on, will you!

beengte Unterkunft, f
- ♦ cramped accommodation

beengt fühlen sich
- ♦ feel cramped

Beere, f
- ♦ berry

Beerensaft, m
- ♦ berry juice

Beet, n
Blumenbeet, n
- ♦ bed
- ♦ bed of flowers

befestigt, adj
gestärkt, adj
- ♦ fortified, adj

befestigte Kirche, f
- ♦ fortified church

befestigte Stadt, f (Großstadt)
- ♦ fortified city

befestigte Stadt, f (kleine Stadt)
- ♦ fortified town

Beförderer, m
- ♦ carrier

befördern etw
- ♦ carry s.th.
- ♦ transport s.th.
- ♦ convey s.th.

befördern jn
- ♦ carry s.o.
- ♦ transport s.o.
- ♦ convey s.o.

befördern jn an die frische Luft
hinauswerfen jn
hinausschmeißen jn *vulg*
- ♦ fling s.o. out
- ♦ chuck s.o. out *coll*

beförderte Fracht, f
- ♦ freight carried
- ♦ carried freight
- ♦ cargo carried
- ♦ carried cargo

beförderter Passagier, m
- ♦ passenger carried
- ♦ carried passenger

Beförderung, f
- ♦ transport *BE*
- ♦ transportation *AE*
- ♦ carriage
- ♦ conveyance

Beförderung, f (Sachgüter)
- ♦ carriage
- ♦ transport
- ♦ transportation
- ♦ conveyance
- ♦ haulage

Beförderung des Autos, f
- ♦ conveyance of the car

Beförderung in der Luft, f
Luftbeförderung, f
- ♦ transportation by air *AE*
- ♦ transport by air *BE*
- ♦ air transportation *AE*
- ♦ air transport *BE*
- ♦ air carriage

Beförderungsanbieter, m
- ♦ transport provider *BE*
- ♦ provider of transport *BE*
- ♦ transportation supplier *AE*
- ♦ supplier of transportation *AE*

Beförderungsart, f
Transportart, f
- ♦ transport mode *BE*
- ♦ mode of transport *BE*
- ♦ transportation mode *AE*
- ♦ mode of transportation *AE*

Beförderungsbedingungen, f pl
- ♦ conditions of carriage *pl*

Beförderungsbereich, m
Beförderungssektor, m
- ♦ transport sector *BE*
- ♦ transportation sector *AE*

Beförderungsmittel, n
Transportmittel, n
Verkehrsmittel, n
- ♦ means of transport *BE sg*
- ♦ means of transportation *AE sg*

Beförderungstarif, m
- ♦ transport tariff *BE*

Beförderungsunternehmen, n
- ♦ carrier

Beförderungsvertrag, m
- ♦ contract of carriage

Beförderungsvorkehrungen, f pl
Transportvorkehrungen, f pl
- ♦ transport arrangements *BE pl*
- ♦ transportation arrangements *AE pl*

Beförderung von A nach B und zurück, f
Transport von A nach B und zurück, m
- ♦ transport from A to B and return

Beförderung zu und von einem Hotel, f
- ♦ transport to and from a hotel *BE*
- ♦ transportation to and from a hotel *AE*

befrackt, adj
im Frack, adv
- ♦ tailcoated, adj
- ♦ in tails, adv
- ♦ wearing tails, adj
- ♦ tuxedoed, adj *AE*

befrackter Kellner, m
- ♦ tailcoated waiter
- ♦ tuxedoed waiter *AE*

befrackter Oberkellner, m
- ♦ tailcoated headwaiter
- ♦ tuxedoed headwaiter *AE*

Befragter, m
Interviter, m
- ♦ interviewee

befreit sein von der Fremdensteuer
- ♦ be exempted from the visitors' tax

befreit sein von einer Gebühr
- ♦ be exempted from a charge
- ♦ be exempted from a fee

befriedigender Service, m
→ zufriedenstellender Service

Begasung, f
- ♦ fumigation

begeben sich auf eine lange Reise
lange Reise unternehmen
- ♦ embark on a long journey

Begegnung, f
- ♦ encounter

Begegnung mit etw, f
- ♦ encounter with s.th.

Begegnungsstätte, f
- ♦ social center *AE*
- ♦ social centre *BE*
- ♦ meeting place

begehbarer Schrank, m
- ♦ walk-in closet

begehen etw feierlich
→ feiern etw

begehen etw mit einem Fest
- ♦ mark s.th. with a party

begeisterte Begrüßung, f
- ♦ enthusiastic welcome

begeistert empfangen werden
- ♦ be received with enthusiasm

begeisterter Empfang, m
- ♦ enthusiastic reception

begeisterter Reisender, m
Reisebegeisterter, m
- ♦ keen traveller
- ♦ keen traveler *AE*

begeisterter Schwimmer, m
- ♦ keen swimmer

begeistertes Publikum, n
- ♦ enthusiastic audience

Begießen, n (Braten)
- ♦ basting

begießen etw (Braten)
- ♦ baste s.th.

begießen etw (feiern)
- ♦ celebrate s.th. (with a drink)

begießen etw mit etw *gastr*
- ♦ baste s.th. with s.th. *gastr*

begießen etw mit Wein (Braten)
- ♦ baste s.th. with wine

begießen etw mit Wein (feiern)
- ♦ celebrate s.th. with wine

Beginn, m
- ♦ beginning
- ♦ start
- ♦ commencement *form*

Beginn der Fahrt, m
- ♦ beginning of the trip

Beginn der Reise, m
Reisebeginn, m
Reiseantritt, m
- ♦ start of the tour
- ♦ start of the journey
- ♦ start of the trip
- ♦ beginning of the tour
- ♦ commencement of the journey *form*

Beginn der Saison vorverlegen
Saisonbeginn vorverlegen
- ♦ bring forward the beginning of the season
- ♦ advance the beginning of the season

beginnend mit 1 und endend mit 2
- ♦ beginning with 1 and ending with 2

beginnend mit etw
- ♦ starting with s.th.
- ♦ beginning with s.th.
- ♦ commencing with s.th.

beginnen etw
- ♦ start s.th.
- ♦ begin s.th.
- ♦ commence s.th. *form*

Begleitboot

Begleitboot, n
- escort boat

Begleitbrief, m
Begleitschreiben, n
- accompanying letter

Begleitbus, m
Geleitbus, m
- escort bus
- escort coach *BE*

begleitende Ehefrau, f
- accompanying wife

begleitende Person, f
→ Begleitperson

begleitender Ehegatte, m
- accompanying spouse

begleitender Ehemann, m
- accompanying husband

begleitetes Kind, n
mitreisendes Kind, n
- accompanying child

begleiten jn
- accompany s.o.
- escort s.o.

begleiten jn auf dem Besuch von X
- accompany s.o. on the visit to X

begleiten jn auf dem Klavier
- accompany s.o. at the piano
- accompany s.o. on the piano

begleiten jn auf der Reise nach X
- accompany s.o. on his/her journey to X

begleiten jn auf einer Expedition
- accompany s.o. on an expedition

begleiten jn nach X
- accompany s.o. to X

begleiten jn zum Bahnhof
- accompany s.o. to the station
- see s.o. (off) to the station

begleiten jn zum Flughafen
- accompany s.o. to the airport
- see s.o. (off) to the airport

begleiten jn zur Polizeiwache
- accompany s.o. to the police station

Begleiter, m (bei Musik)
- accompanist

Begleiter, m (Eskorte)
- escort

Begleiter, m (generell)
Begleitperson, f
- companion
- accompanying person
- company

Begleitergebühr, f
- charge for accompanying person

Begleiterin, f
- woman companion
- woman escort

Begleitervermittlung, f
Begleiteragentur, f
- escort agency

begleitet, adj
geleitet, adj
- escorted, adj
- accompanied, adj

begleitete Bahnreise, f
- escorted rail tour

begleitete Busreise, f
- escorted bus tour
- escorted coach tour *BE*

begleiteter Ausflug nach X, m
- escorted excursion to X
- escorted trip to X

begleitete Reise, f
Reise mit Begleitung f
- escorted tour
- escorted trip

begleiteter Spaziergang, m
- escorted walk
- escorted stroll

begleitet von jm
- accompanied by s.o.

begleitet werden von der Ehefrau
- be accompanied by one's wife

begleitet werden von jm
- be accompanied by s.o.

Begleitfahrzeug, n
- escort vehicle

Begleitflugzeug, n
- escort plane

Begleitpapiere, n pl
- accompanying documents *pl*

Begleitperson, f (bei Jugendlichen)
→ Chaperon

Begleitperson, f (generell)
begleitende Person, f
Begleitung, f
- accompanying person
- escort

Begleitperson, f (Konferenz)
Begleitung, f
- accompanying delegate

Begleitpersonengebühr, f
- fee for accompanying person
- charge for accompanying person

Begleitpersonenprogramm, n
- accompanying persons' program *AE*
- accompanying persons' programme *BE*

Begleitprogramm, n
- accompanying program *AE*
- accompanying programme *BE*

Begleitschiff, n
→ Geleitschiff

Begleitservice, m
Begleitdienst, m
Begleitungsdienst, m *ÖST*
Begleitungsservice, m *ÖST*
- escort service

Begleitservice bieten
Begleitdienst anbieten
- offer escort service

Begleitung, f (Person)
→ Begleitperson

Begleitung, f (Service)
→ Begleitservice

Begleitungsdienst, m
→ Begleitungsservice

Begleitwagen, m
- escort car

Begleitwagen, m
Begleitauto, n
Geleitwagen, m
Geleitauto, n
- escorting car
- escort car

begraben liegen
- lie buried

Begräbnis, n
- funeral

Begräbnisfeier, f
Trauerfeier, f
- funeral celebration

begrenzt, adj
beschränkt, adj
- limited, adj

begrenzte Aufenthaltsdauer, f
- limited length of stay

begrenzte Menüwahl, f
- limited menu choice

begrenzte Parkmöglichkeiten, f pl
- limited parking

begrenzter Service, m
eingeschränkter Service, m
beschränkter Service, m
- restricted service
- limited service

begrenzte Saison, f
- limited season

begrenzte Stellplatzzahl, f
(Camping)
- limited number of pitches

begrenztes Urlaubsbudget, n
beschränktes Urlaubsbudget, n
- limited vacation budget *AE*
- limited holiday budget *BE*

begrüßen als Gäste
- welcome as guests

begrüßen jn
willkommen heißen jn
- welcome s.o.

begrüßen jn an Bord
- welcome s.o. on board

begrüßen jn mit Handschlag
Hand geben jm
- shake hands with s.o.

Begrüßer, m
Person, die willkommen heißt, f
- welcomer

Begrüßung, f
Willkommensgruß, m *form*
Willkommen, n *form*
- welcome

Begrüßungsansprache, f
Begrüßung, f
- welcome address
- welcoming address *BE*
- address of welcome

Begrüßungsaperitif m
- welcome aperitif
- welcoming aperitif *BE*

Begrüßungschampagner, m
Begrüßungssekt, m
- welcome champagne
- welcoming champagne *BE*

Begrüßungscocktail, m
Empfangscocktail, m
- welcome cocktail
- welcoming cocktail *BE*

Begrüßungscocktailempfang, m
- welcome cocktail reception

Begrüßungscocktailparty, f
- welcome cocktail party
- welcoming cocktail party *BE*

Begrüßungsdrink, m
→ Begrüßungsgetränk

Begrüßungsempfang m
(z.B. bei Konferenz)
- welcome reception
- welcoming reception *BE*

Begrüßungsessen, n (Dinner)
- welcome dinner
- welcoming dinner *BE*

Begrüßungsessen, n (generell)
  ◆ welcome meal
  ◆ welcoming meal *BE*
Begrüßungsessen, n (Lunch)
  ◆ welcome lunch
  ◆ welcome luncheon
  ◆ welcoming lunch *BE*
  ◆ welcoming luncheon *BE*
Begrüßungsfeier, f
  ◆ welcome party
  ◆ welcoming party *BE*
Begrüßungsgeschenk, n
  Begrüßungspräsent, n
  ◆ welcome gift
  ◆ welcoming gift
  ◆ welcome present
  ◆ welcoming present
Begrüßungsgetränk, n
  Begrüßungsschluck, m *form*
  ◆ welcome drink
  ◆ welcoming drink *BE*
Begrüßungsmahlzeit, f
  Begrüßungsmahl, n
  ◆ welcoming meal
  ◆ welcome meal
Begrüßungspaket, n
  ◆ welcome pack
Begrüßungsrede, f
  ◆ welcome speech
  ◆ welcoming speech *BE*
  ◆ speech of welcome
Begrüßungsschluck, m *form*
  Begrüßungsgetränk, n
  ◆ welcoming drink *BE*
  ◆ welcome drink
Begrüßungssherry, m
  ◆ welcome sherry
  ◆ welcoming sherry
Begrüßungstablett, n
  ◆ welcome tray
  ◆ hospitality tray
Begrüßungstafel, f (Information)
  ◆ welcome plaque
  ◆ welcoming plaque
Begrüßungstee, m
  ◆ welcome tea
  ◆ welcoming tea
Begrüßungstrunk, m
  → Begrüßungsgetränk
Begrüßungswort n
  Begrüßungsworte n pl
  ◆ word of welcome
  ◆ words of welcome *pl*
Begrüßung und Einführung, f
  (Programm)
  ◆ welcome and introduction
Begrüßung zuteil werden lassen
  ◆ extend a welcome to s.o.
behaglich, adj
  ◆ **snug, adj**
  ◆ cosy, adj
  ◆ cozy, adj *AE*
  ◆ comfortable, adj
behagliche Atmosphäre, f
  gemütliche Atmosphäre, f
  ◆ **comfortable atmosphere**
  ◆ cosy atmosphere
  ◆ cozy atmosphere *AE*
behaglicher Aufenthalt, m
  sorgenfreier Aufenthalt, m
  ◆ **comfortable stay**

behagliches Zimmer, n
  → komfortables Zimmer
Behaglichkeit, f
  ◆ **comfortableness**
  ◆ cosiness
  ◆ coziness *AE*
  ◆ snugness
Behalten Sie den Rest!
  (Wechselgeld)
  Der Rest ist für Sie!
  ◆ **Keep the change!**
behandeln etw
  (Krankheit)
  ◆ **treat s.th.**
behandeln jn als Gast
  ◆ **treat s.o. as a guest**
behandeln jn als Gast und nicht als Kunden
  ◆ treat s.o. as a guest and not as a customer
behandeln jn mit Samthandschuhen *coll*
  ◆ **handle s.o. with kid gloves** *coll*
behandeln jn wie den letzten Dreck
  ◆ **treat s.o. like dirt**
behandeln jn wie Vieh
  ◆ treat s.o. like cattle
behandelt werden als Bürger zweiter Klasse
  ◆ be treated as second-class citizen
behandelt werden als Gast
  ◆ be treated as a guest
behandelt werden wie ein Paria
  ◆ be treated as a pariah
Behandlung, f
  ◆ treatment
Behandlung auswählen
  ◆ select a treatment
Behandlung bestimmter Gebrechen, f
  ◆ treatment of certain ailments
Behandlung dauert 30 Minuten
  ◆ treatment takes 30 minutes
Behandlung durchführen
  ◆ carry out a treatment
Behandlung kostet DM 123
  ◆ treatment costs DM 123
Behandlungsangebot, n (Palette)
  ◆ range of treatments
Behandlungsart, f
  ◆ type of treatment
Behandlungsauswahl, f
  ◆ choice of treatments
Behandlungsberatung, f
  ◆ treatment consultation
Behandlungsbereich, m
  ◆ treatment area
Behandlungseinrichtung, f
  ◆ treatment facility
Behandlungsklinik, f
  ◆ treatment clinic
Behandlungskosten, pl
  ◆ treatment costs *pl*
  ◆ costs of treatment *pl*
  ◆ cost of treatment
Behandlungsmethode, f
  Behandlungsart, f
  ◆ **treatment method**
  ◆ method of treatment
Behandlungspauschale, f
  ◆ treatment package
  ◆ treatments package
Behandlungsplan, m
  ◆ treatment plan
Behandlungsprogramm, n
  Kurprogramm, n

  ◆ program of treatments *AE*
  ◆ programme of treatments *BE*
Behandlungsraum, m
  Behandlungszimmer, n
  ◆ **treatment room**
Behandlungsreihe, f
  ◆ **series of treatments**
Behandlungstag, m
  ◆ day of treatment
Behandlungszahl, f
  Zahl der Behandlungen, f
  ◆ **number of treatments**
Behandlungszeit, f
  ◆ treatment time
Behandlungszeitplan, m
  ◆ timetable of treatments
Behandlungszeitraum, m
  ◆ treatment period
Behandlungszentrum, n
  ◆ treatment center *AE*
  ◆ treatment centre *BE*
Behandlung verabreichen
  Behandlung geben
  ◆ give a treatment
Behandlung verordnen *med*
  ◆ **prescribe a treatment** *med*
Behang, m
  Wandbehang, m
  ◆ **hanging**
Behausung, f
  Wohnung f
  ◆ **dwelling**
  ◆ home
beheizen etw
  → heizen etw
beheizte Garage, f
  → geheizte Garage
beheiztes Bad, n
  geheiztes Becken, n
  ◆ **heated pool**
  ◆ heated swimming pool *AE*
  ◆ heated swimming-pool *BE*
beheiztes Freibad, n
  beheiztes Freischwimmbad, n
  ◆ **heated outdoor swimming pool** *AE*
  ◆ heated outdoor swimming-pool *BE*
  ◆ heated outdoor pool
beheiztes Freischwimmbad, n
  → beheiztes Freibad
beheiztes Hallenbad, n
  beheiztes Hallenschwimmbad, n
  ◆ **heated indoor swimming pool** *AE*
  ◆ heated indoor swimming-pool *BE*
  ◆ heated indoor pool
beheiztes Hallenschwimmbad, n
  → beheiztes Hallenbad
beheizte Terrasse, f
  ◆ **heated terrace**
  ◆ heated patio
Behelfsbett, n
  → behelfsmäßiges Bett
Behelfslandeplatz, m
  (für Flugzeuge)
  ◆ **air strip** *AE*
behelfsmäßig eingerichtetes Zimmer, n
  ◆ room furnished temporarily
behelfsmäßiges Bett, n
  Behelfsbett, n
  ◆ **makeshift bed**
  ◆ shakedown

behelfsmäßiges Nachtlager

behelfsmäßiges Nachtlager, n
  Strohlager, n
  behelfsmäßiges Bett, n
  Notlager, n
  ◆ **shakedown**
behelfsmäßige Unterkunft, f
  → Behelfsunterkunft
behelfsmäßig unterbringen jn
  ◆ **provide s.o. with temporary accommodation**
behelfsmäßig untergebracht sein
  ◆ **live in temporary accommodation**
Behelfsobdach, n
  behelfsmäßiges Obdach, n
  Behelfsunterkunft, f
  ◆ **makeshift shelter**
Behelfstisch, m
  ◆ **makeshift table**
Behelfsunterkunft, f
  behelfsmäßige Unterkunft, f
  ◆ **makeshift accommodation**
  ◆ **temporary accommodation**
belligen jn
  verärgern jn
  ◆ **annoy s.o.**
beherbergen etw (z.B. Konferenz)
  ◆ **harbor s.th.** *AE*
  ◆ **harbour s.th.** *BE*
beherbergen etw (z.B. Museum)
  ◆ **house s.th.**
beherbergen jn
  unterbringen jn
  aufnehmen jn
  ◆ **accommodate s.o.**
  ◆ lodge s.o.
  ◆ put s.o. up *BE coll*
  ◆ fix s.o. (up) *AE coll*
Beherbergen n
  → Beherbergung
Beherbergung, f
  Unterbringung, f
  Logement, n
  ◆ **lodging** *AE*
  ◆ accommodation
  ◆ putting s.o. up
Beherbergungsabteilung, f
  (Gegensatz zu Gastronomieabteilung)
  Logisabteilung, f
  ◆ **rooms department**
  ◆ accommodation department
  ◆ rooms division
Beherbergungsabteilungsausgaben, f pl
  ◆ **rooms division expenses** *pl*
  ◆ rooms department expenses *pl*
Beherbergungsabteilungsertrag, m
  ◆ **rooms division income**
  ◆ rooms department income
Beherbergungsabteilungsgewinn, m
  ◆ **rooms division profit**
  ◆ rooms department profit
Beherbergungsabteilungskosten, pl
  ◆ **rooms division costs** *pl*
  ◆ rooms department costs *pl*
Beherbergungsanbieter, m
  Unterkunftsanbieter, m
  ◆ **provider of lodgings** *AE*
  ◆ provider of accommodation
  ◆ provider of accommodations *AE*
  ◆ accommodation provider
  ◆ acommodation supplier

Beherbergungsangebot, n (Gegensatz zu Nachfrage)
  Logisangebot, n
  Unterkunftsangebot, n
  ◆ **supply of lodging** *AE*
  ◆ supply of lodgings *AE*
  ◆ supply of accommodation
  ◆ supply of accommodations *AE*
  ◆ accommodation supply
Beherbergungsangebot, n (Offerte)
  Logisangebot, n
  Unterkunftsangebot, n
  ◆ **accommodation offered**
  ◆ offering accommodation
  ◆ offer of accommodation
Beherbergungsangebot, n (Palette)
  Logisangebot, n
  Unterkunftsangebot, n
  ◆ **range of lodgings** *AE*
  ◆ range of accommodation
  ◆ range of accommodations *AE*
  ◆ variety of lodging(s) *AE*
Beherbergungsanteil, m
  Zimmeranteil, m
  ◆ **rooms proportion**
Beherbergungsart, f
  Unterkunftsart, f
  Unterbringungsart, f
  ◆ **type of lodging** *AE*
  ◆ kind of lodging *AE*
  ◆ type of accommodation
  ◆ accommodation type
Beherbergungsaufwand, m
  ◆ **rooms expense** *AE*
  ◆ rooms expenditure
Beherbergungsbeispiel, n
  Unterkunftsbeispiel, n
  ◆ **lodging example** *AE*
  ◆ accommodation example
Beherbergungsbereich, m (generell)
  Beherbergungssektor, m
  Unterkunftsbereich, m
  Unterkunftssektor, m
  ◆ **lodging field** *AE*
  ◆ lodging sector *AE*
  ◆ accommodation field
  ◆ accommodation sector
Beherbergungsbereich, m (im Hotel)
  (Gegensatz zu Gastronomiebereich)
  Logisbereich, m
  ◆ **rooms division**
  ◆ rooms department
  ◆ accommodation department
Beherbergungsbetrieb, m
  Unterkunftsbetrieb, m
  ◆ **lodging establishment** *AE*
  ◆ lodging operation *AE*
  ◆ accommodation establishment
  ◆ accommodation operation
  ◆ establishment of the hotel trade
Beherbergungsdienstleistung, f
  Beherbergungsleistung, f
  Beherbergungsservice, m
  Unterkunftsdienstleistung,.f
  Unterkunftsleistung, f
  ◆ **lodging service** *AE*
  ◆ accommodation service
Beherbergungseinheit, f
  (Statistik)
  Unterkunftseinheit, f

  ◆ **lodging unit** *AE*
  ◆ accommodation unit
Beherbergungseinrichtung, f
  Unterkunftseinrichtung, f
  Beherbergungsstätte, f
  ◆ **lodging facility** *AE*
  ◆ accommodation facility
Beherbergungseinrichtung nutzen
  Beherbergungsmöglichkeit nutzen
  ◆ **use an accommodation facilty**
  ◆ use a lodging facility *AE*
Beherbergungsengpaß, m
  Unterkunftsengpaß, m
  ◆ **lodging bottleneck** *AE*
  ◆ accommodation bottleneck
Beherbergungsengpässe vermeiden
  ◆ **avoid accommodation bottlenecks**
Beherbergungserlös, m
  Unterkunftserlös, m
  Logementerlös, m
  ◆ **accommodation revenue**
  ◆ room sales revenue
  ◆ revenue from room sales
  ◆ proceeds from accommodation *pl*
Beherbergungsertrag, m
  (Gewinn- und Verlustrechnung)
  Ertrag aus Beherbergung, m
  ◆ **rooms income**
  ◆ income from rooms
Beherbergungsfunktion, f
  Unterkunftsfunktion, f
  ◆ **lodging function** *AE*
  ◆ accommodation function
Beherbergungsgeschäft, n
  Unterkunftsgeschäft, n
  ◆ **lodging business** *AE*
  ◆ accommodation business
Beherbergungsgewerbe, n
  Übernachtungsgewerbe, n
  ◆ **lodging trade** *AE*
  ◆ accommodation trade
Beherbergungsgewinn, m
  Beherbergungsprofit m
  ◆ **rooms profit**
  ◆ room profit
Beherbergungsindustrie, f
  Beherbergungsbranche, f
  Beherbergungswesen, n
  ◆ **lodging industry** *AE*
  ◆ accommodation industry
  ◆ accommodations industry *AE*
Beherbergungsinstitution, f
  ◆ **lodging institution** *AE*
Beherbergungskapazität, f
  Unterkunftskapazität, f
  ◆ **lodging capacity** *AE*
  ◆ accommodation capacity
  ◆ capacity of accommodation
Beherbergungskategorie, f
  Unterkunftskategorie, f
  ◆ **lodging category** *AE*
  ◆ accommodation category
Beherbergungskosten, pl
  Unterkunftskosten, pl
  Logementkosten, pl
  Logiskosten, pl
  ◆ **lodging costs** *AE pl*
  ◆ lodging cost *AE*
  ◆ accommodation costs *pl*
  ◆ accommodation cost

Beherbergungsleistung, f
→ Beherbergungsdienstleistung
Beherbergungsmöglichkeit, f
♦ **accommodation possibility**
♦ possibility of accommodation
♦ possibility of accommodating s.o.
Beherbergungsnachfrage, f
Unterkunftsnachfrage, f
♦ **lodging demand** *AE*
♦ accommodation demand
♦ demand for lodging *AE*
♦ demand for accommodation
Beherbergungsnachfrage schaffen
Unterkunftsnachfrage schaffen
♦ **create loging demand** *AE*
♦ create demand for lodging *AE*
♦ create accommodation demand
♦ create demand for accommodation
Beherbergungsnachweis, m
→ Zimmernachweis
Beherbergungsorganisation, f
Unterkunftsorganisation, f
♦ **lodging organisation** *AE*
♦ lodging organization *AE*
♦ accommodation organisation
Beherbergungsproblem, n
Unterkunftsproblem, n
♦ **lodging problem** *AE*
♦ accommodation problem
Beherbergungsprodukt, n
Unterkunftsprodukt, n
♦ **lodging product** *AE*
♦ accommodation product
Beherbergungsrechnung, f
Unterkunftsrechnung, f
♦ **bill for accommodation**
♦ accommodation bill
Beherbergungssektor, m
Unterkunftssektor, m
♦ **lodging sector** *AE*
♦ accommodation sector
Beherbergungsservice, m
→ Beherbergungsdienstleistung
Beherbergungsstatistik f
♦ **accommodation statistics** *pl*
♦ rooms statistics *pl*
Beherbergungsstätte, f
→ Beherbergungseinrichtung
Beherbergungsumsatz, m
Unterkunftsumsatz, m
♦ **accommodation sales** *pl*
♦ room sales *pl*
♦ accommodation turnover
Beherbergungsunternehmen, n
♦ **accommodation enterprise**
Beherbergungsunternehmer, m
♦ **accommodation operator**
Beherbergungsunternehmung, f
♦ **accommodation venture**
Beherbergungsunternehmung betreiben
♦ **operate an accommodation venture**
Beherbergungsvertrag, m
(Teil des Gastaufnahmevertrags)
♦ **contract of accommodation**
♦ accommodation contract
Beherbergungsvertrag abschließen
♦ **sign an accommodation contract**
♦ conclude an accommodation contract
Beherbergungswesen, n
→ Beherbergungsindustrie

behilflich sein jm bei den Reisevorkehrungen
behilflich sein jm bei den Reisevorbereitungen
♦ **assist s.o. with the travel arrangements**
♦ assist s.o. with his/her tour arrangements
behilflich sein jm bei der Unterkunftssuche
♦ **assist s.o. in finding accommodation**
behilflich sein jm bei der Zimmervermittlung
♦ **help s.o. arrange accommodation**
behindert, adj
♦ **disabled, adj**
♦ handicapped, adj
Behinderte, m/f pl
♦ **disabled people** *pl*
♦ disabled persons *pl*
♦ handicapped people *pl*
♦ handicapped persons *pl*
Behinderten, m pl
♦ **disabled, the** *pl*
Behindertenausweis, m
♦ **disabled pass**
Behindertendusche, f
♦ **disabled shower**
♦ shower suitable for disabled persons
♦ shower suitable for a handicapped person
Behinderteneinrichtung, f
♦ **facility for the disabled**
Behinderteneinrichtungen, f pl
♦ **facilities for handicapped persons** *pl*
♦ facilities for disabled persons *pl*
♦ facilities for the handicapped *pl*
♦ facilities for the disabled *pl*
Behindertenfahrt, f
♦ **disabled trip**
♦ trip for disabled people
behindertenfreundlich, adj
behindertengerecht, adj
♦ **suitable for handicapped persons, adj**
♦ suitable for disabled persons, adj
behindertengerecht, adj
♦ **geared to handicapped persons, adj**
♦ geared to disabled persons, adj
Behindertenheim, n
♦ **home for the disabled**
Behindertenhotel, n
♦ **hotel suitable for a disabled person**
♦ hotel suitable for disabled persons
♦ hotel suitable for a handicapped person
♦ hotel suitable for handicapped persons
Behindertenreise, f
♦ **disabled tour**
♦ tour for disabled people
Behindertentoilette, f
♦ **disabled toilet**
♦ toilet suitable for disabled persons
♦ toilet suitable for a handicapped person
Behindertenumkleideraum, m
♦ **disabled changing room**
♦ changing room suitable for disabled persons
♦ changing room suitable for handicapped persons
Behindertenunterkunft, f
♦ **disabled accommodation**
♦ accommodation suitable for a disabled person
Behindertenurlaub, m
♦ **vacation suitable for a disabled person** *AE*
♦ vacation suitable for a handicapped person *AE*
♦ holiday suitable for a disabled person *BE*
♦ holiday suitable for a handicapped person *BE*
♦ disabled holiday *BE*
Behindertenzimmer, n
♦ **disabled room**

♦ room suitable for disabled persons
♦ room suitable for a handicapped person
Behinderter, m (körperlich)
♦ **disabled person**
♦ physically handicapped person
Behinderter, m (körperlich und/oder geistig)
♦ **handicapped person**
behinderter Besucher, m (körperlich)
♦ **disabled visitor**
behinderter Besucher, m (körperlich oder geistig)
♦ **handicapped visitor**
behinderter Fahrgast, m
♦ **disabled passenger**
♦ handicapped passenger
behinderter Reisender, m
♦ **disabled traveller**
♦ disabled traveler *AE*
♦ handicapped traveller
♦ handicapped traveler *AE*
Behinderung, f
(einer Person)
♦ **disability**
Behörde, f
Behörden, f pl
♦ **authority**
♦ authorities *pl*
behördlich eingestuftes Hotel, n
behördlich bewertetes Hotel n
♦ **officially graded hotel**
behördlich genehmigter Campingplatz, m
♦ **officially approved campsite**
♦ officially approved campground *AE*
♦ officially approved camping site *BE*
♦ officially approved camping ground *BE*
behördlich genehmigtes Hotel, n
♦ **officially approved hotel**
bei 90%iger Belegung
bei 90%iger Auslastung
♦ **at 90% occupancy**
bei Ankunft
→ bei der Ankunft
bei besonderen Anlässen
♦ **on special occasions**
bei dem Frühstück sein
♦ **be at breakfast**
bei der Abreise
♦ **on departure**
♦ upon departure
bei der Ankunft
bei Ankunft
♦ **on arrival**
♦ upon arrival
bei der Ankunft am Flughafen
♦ **on arrival at the airport**
♦ upon arrival at the airport
bei der Ankunft im Hotel
♦ **on arrival at the hotel**
♦ upon arrival at the hotel
bei der Anmietung
♦ **at the time of hiring** *AE*
♦ at the time of rental *AE*
bei der Ausreise
♦ **on leaving the country**
♦ on departure
bei der Buchung
♦ **on booking**
♦ at the time of booking
bei der Einreise
♦ **on entering (a country)**
♦ when entering
♦ on arrival

bei der Ein- und Ausreise

bei der Ein- und Ausreise
 ◆ on entry and departure
 ◆ upon entry and departure
bei der Hinreise
 auf der Hinreise
 ◆ on the outward journey
bei der Rückreise
 auf der Rückreise
 ◆ on the return journey
Bei diesem Hotel ist an nichts gespart worden
 ◆ Nothing has been spared at this hotel
bei einem Glas Wein
 ◆ over a glass of wine
bei einem Glas Wein sitzen
 beim Wein sitzen
 ◆ sit over a glass of wine
bei einem Treffen sein
 ◆ be at a meeting
bei einer Konferenz
 auf einer Konferenz
 ◆ at a conference
bei einer Konferenz sein
 auf einer Konferenz sein
 ◆ be at a conference
bei einer Party
 auf einer Party
 ◆ at a party
bei einer Sitzung
 auf einer Sitzung
 in einer Sitzung
 ◆ at a meeting
bei einer Teilnahme von 95 Personen
 ◆ with an attendance of 95 persons
Beifahrertür, f (Auto)
 ◆ passenger door
bei feierlichen Anlässen
 ◆ on ceremonial occasions
bei festlichen Anlässen
 ◆ on festive occasions
Beigericht, n
 → Zwischengang
Beignet, m FR
 Krapfen, m
 ◆ fritter
 ◆ beignet FR
bei günstiger Witterung
 → bei gutem Wetter
bei gutem Wetter
 bei günstigem Wetter
 bei günstiger Witterung
 ◆ weather permitting
bei guten Bedingungen
 ◆ circumstances permitting
bei guter Gesundheit
 ◆ in good health
bei guter Gesundheit sein
 ◆ be in good health
bei höherer Gewalt
 ◆ in the case of acts of God
bei klarem Wetter
 ◆ in clear weather
Beikoch, m
 Aide-cuisinier, m/f FR
 ◆ assistant cook
 ◆ aide-cuisinier FR
Beikost, f
 ◆ supplementary food
Beilage, f (Gemüse)
 ◆ vegetables pl
Beilage, f (Speise)
 ◆ vegetables and trimmings pl

 ◆ side-dish BE
 ◆ side dish AE
 ◆ trimmings pl
 ◆ entremets FR
Beilage, f (Zeitung)
 → Zeitungsbeilage
Beilageschale, f
 (Geschirr)
 ◆ pickle dish
bei Laune halten jn
 ◆ keep s.o. happy
beim Abendessen sein (Dinner)
 ◆ be at dinner
beim Abendessen sein (Supper)
 ◆ be at supper
beim Auszug (aus der Unterkunft)
 ◆ on moving out
 ◆ on leaving
beim Auszug aus der Wohnung
 ◆ on moving out of the apartment AE
 ◆ on moving out of the flat BE
beim Bier sitzen
 bei einem Glas Bier sitzen
 ◆ sit over a glass of beer
bei meinem ersten Besuch
 ◆ on my first visit
bei meinem letzten Besuch in X
 ◆ on my last visit to X
bei meiner Abreise (von X)
 ◆ on my departure (from X)
 ◆ upon my departure (from X)
bei meiner Ankunft (in X)
 ◆ on my arrival (in X)
 ◆ upon my arrival (in X)
 ◆ on my arrival (at X)
 ◆ upon my arrival (at X)
bei meiner Rückkehr (von X)
 bei meiner Rückkehr (aus X)
 ◆ on my return (from X)
 ◆ upon my return (from X)
beim ersten Besuch
 bei dem ersten Besuch
 ◆ on the first visit
beim Essen sein
 ◆ be having one's lunch
 ◆ be having one's dinner
beim Frühstück
 ◆ at breakfast
beim letzten Besuch
 bei dem letzten Besuch
 ◆ on the last visit
beim Mittagessen sein
 ◆ be at lunch
bei Nacht
 ◆ by night
 ◆ at night
Beinbehandlung, f
 ◆ leg treatment
Beine ausstrecken
 ◆ stretch one's legs
Beine unter einen fremden Tisch stecken
 nassauern bei jm
 schnorren bei jm
 ◆ sponge upon other people
Beinfreiheit, f
 ◆ legroom
Beinfreiheit bieten
 mehr Beinfreiheit bieten
 ◆ provide legroom
 ◆ provide more legroom

bei Nichtinanspruchnahme
 ◆ if not used
 ◆ if not claimed
bei Nichtinanspruchnahme eines Zimmers
 ◆ if a room is not used
 ◆ if a room is not claimed
Beinmassage, f
 ◆ leg massage
Beinpackung, f med
 ◆ leg wrap med
Beinpflege, f
 ◆ leg care
Beiprogramm, n
 (parallel zur Veranstaltung)
 ergänzendes Programm, n
 Ergänzungsprogramm, n
 ◆ complementary program AE
 ◆ complementary programme BE
 ◆ supporting program AE
 ◆ supporting programme BE
Beirat, m
 ◆ advisory board
bei Saisonbeginn
 am Saisonbeginn
 zum Saisonbeginn
 ◆ at the start of the season
 ◆ at the beginning of the season
 ◆ at the commencement of the season form
Beisammensein, n
 Zusammensein, n
 zwanglose Zusammenkunft, f
 ◆ get-together
beisammensitzen in fröhlicher Runde
 zusammensitzen in fröhlicher Runde
 ◆ sit together in a merry circle
bei schlechtem Wetter
 ◆ in bad weather
Beisel, n ÖST/BAY
 → Kneipe
beißen
 ◆ bite
Beistellbett, n
 Zustellbett, n
 Schiebebett, n
 ◆ rollaway bed AE
 ◆ rollaway AE coll
 ◆ roll-away bed BE
 ◆ roll-away BE coll
Beistelltisch, m (generell)
 Nebentisch, m
 ◆ side table
Beistelltisch, m (Service)
 → Servicetisch
bei Stoßbetrieb
 ◆ at peak times
 ◆ at the peak times of business
bei Tagesanbruch
 ◆ at daybreak
beitragen zu dem Vergnügen
 beitragen zum Vergnügen
 ◆ add to the pleasure
 ◆ contribute to the pleasure
beitragen zu der Atmosphäre
 ◆ add to the atmosphere
beitragen zum Komfort
 ◆ add to the comfort
 ◆ contribute to the comfort
bei unfreundlichem Wetter
 ◆ in inclement weather
bei Vorlage, adv
 gegen Vorlage, adv

- ◆ on presentation, adv
- ◆ upon presentation, adv

beiwohnen etw (als Zeuge)
- ◆ witness s.th.

Beiz, f
→ Kneipe

bekannt, adj
- ◆ known, adj
- ◆ well-known, adj
- ◆ renowned, adj
- ◆ noted, adj

bekanntes Hotel n
- ◆ well-known hotel

bekanntestes Hotel, n
am meisten bekanntes Hotel, n
- ◆ best-known hotel
- ◆ most well-known hotel

bekannt für sein ausgezeichnetes Essen
- ◆ noted for its excellent food

Bekanntheitsgrad, m
Beliebtheitsgrad, m
- ◆ degree of popularity
- ◆ degree of familiarity

bekannt in der ganzen Welt
in der ganzen Welt bekannt
- ◆ well-known throughout the world
- ◆ well-known all over the world

Bekanntmachung, f
- ◆ announcement

Bekanntschaft, f
- ◆ acquaintance

Bekanntschaft für eine Nacht, f
Sexpartner für eine Nacht, m
- ◆ one-night stand coll

Bekanntschaft machen von jm
kennenlernen jn
- ◆ make the acquaintance of s.o.
- ◆ make s.o's acquaintance

Bekanntschaft wieder auffrischen
- ◆ renew an acquaintance

bekannt sein für etw
- ◆ be known for s.th.
- ◆ be well-known for s.th.
- ◆ be renowned for s.th.
- ◆ be noted for s.th.

bekannt sein für sein ausgezeichnetes Essen
- ◆ be noted for its excellent food

bekannt sein für seine Atmosphäre
- ◆ be known for its atmosphere

bekannt sein für seine Gastlichkeit
bekannt sein für seine Gastfreundschaft
- ◆ be known for one's hospitality

bekannt sein für seine gute Küche
- ◆ be renowned for its good cuisine
- ◆ be renowned for its good cooking
- ◆ be known for its good cuisine
- ◆ be known for its good cooking

bekannt werden für etw
- ◆ become known for s.th.

beklagen sich über das Haar in der Suppe
- ◆ complain about the hair in the soup

beklagen sich über den schlechten Service
- ◆ complain of the poor service
- ◆ complain about the poor service

beklagen sich über etw
- ◆ complain of s.th.
- ◆ complain about s.th.

bekömmlich, adj
gesund, adj
- ◆ wholesome, adj

bekömmliche Kost, f
gesunde Kost, f
- ◆ wholesome fare
- ◆ wholesome food
- ◆ wholesome diet

bekömmliche Mahlzeit, f
gesunde Mahlzeit, f
- ◆ wholesome meal

bekömmliche Nahrung, f
gesunde Nahrung, f
bekömmliches Essen, n
gesundes Essen, n
- ◆ wholesome food

Bekömmlichkeit, f
- ◆ wholesomeness

beköstigen jn
→ verpflegen jn

beköstigen und beherbergen jn
- ◆ provide board and lodging to s.o.

Beköstigung, f
→ Verpflegung

belästigen jn
- ◆ inconvenience s.o.
- ◆ disturb s.o.

Beleg, m (Buchhaltung)
Belegschein m
- ◆ voucher

belegbar, adj
- ◆ available for occupancy, adj

Belege abheften
- ◆ file vouchers

Belege überprüfen
- ◆ audit vouchers

Beleg für die Portokasse, m
- ◆ petty-cash voucher

Belegquote, f
→ Auslastungsquote

Belegrate, f
→ Auslastungsquote

Belegschaft, f
Personal, n
- ◆ work force
- ◆ personnel
- ◆ staff
- ◆ employees
- ◆ workers

Belegt
(Hinweisschild)
- ◆ No vacancy
- ◆ Full up

belegt, adj (Sitz, Raum etc)
besetzt, adj
- ◆ taken, adj
- ◆ occupied, adj

belegt, adj (Unterkunft, Sitz etc)
besetzt, adj
- ◆ occupied, adj
- ◆ booked, adj
- ◆ taken, adj

belegter Stellplatz, m (Camping)
- ◆ occupied pitch

belegtes Bett, n
(Statistik)
- ◆ occupied bed
- ◆ bed occupied

belegtes Brot, n
- ◆ open sandwich

belegtes Zimmer, n
(Statistik)
- ◆ occupied room
- ◆ room occupied

belegt sein 100%ig
100%ig ausgelastet sein
- ◆ be 100% occupied

belegt sein mit jm
- ◆ be occupied by s.o.
- ◆ be booked by s.o.

belegt sein zu 30 %
ausgelastet sein zu 30 %
- ◆ have a 30 % occupancy
- ◆ have an occupancy of 30 %
- ◆ be 30 % occupied

Belegung, f
Auslastung, f
- ◆ occupancy

Belegung beläuft sich auf 60 %
Auslastung beläuft sich auf 60 %
- ◆ occupancy amounts to 60 %

Belegung berechnen
Auslastung berechnen
- ◆ calculate occupancy

Belegung beschränken auf 80 Gäste
Auslastung beschränken auf 80 Gäste
- ◆ limit occupancy to 80 guests

Belegung beträgt 70 %
Auslastung beträgt 70 %
- ◆ occupancy is 70 %

Belegung bleibt unter 70 %
Auslastung bleibt unter 70 %
- ◆ occupancy remains under 70 %

Belegung erhöhen
Auslastung erhöhen
- ◆ raise occupancy

Belegung erreichen von 90 %
90%ige Belegung erreichen
Auslastung erreichen von 90 %
90%ige Auslastung erreichen
- ◆ achieve 90 % occupancy

Belegung erreicht eine Höhe von 55 %
Auslastung erreicht eine Höhe von 55 %
- ◆ occupancy reaches a level of 55 %

Belegung erreicht im Durchschnitt 40 %
Auslastung erreicht im Durchschnitt 40 %
- ◆ occupancy averages 40 %

Belegung erzielen von 80 %
Auslastung erzielen von 80 %
- ◆ experience 80 % occupancy

Belegung fällt auf 40 %
Auslastung fällt auf 40 %
- ◆ occupancy decreases to 40 %
- ◆ occupancy drops to 40 %
- ◆ occupancy falls to 40 %

Belegung fällt um 4 %
Auslastung fällt um 4 %
- ◆ occupancy decreases by 4 %
- ◆ occupancy drops by 4 %
- ◆ occupancy falls by 4 %

Belegung fällt unter 40 %
Auslastung fällt unter 40 %
- ◆ occupancy falls below 40 %
- ◆ occupancy drops below 40 %

Belegung fiel von 60 % auf 55 %
Auslastung fiel von 60 % auf 55 %
- ◆ occupancy dropped from 60 % to 55 %
- ◆ occupancy decreased from 60 % to 55%
- ◆ occupancy fell from 60 % to 55 %

Belegung haben
Auslastung haben
- ◆ have an occupancy
- ◆ enjoy an occupancy

Belegung halten

Belegung halten
Auslastung halten
♦ **maintain occupancy**
Belegung im Herbst, f
Auslastung im Herbst, f
♦ **occupancy in fall** AE
♦ occupancy in autumn BE
Belegung im Januar, f
Auslastung im Januar, f
Januarbelegung, f
Januarauslastung, f
♦ **occupancy in January**
♦ January occupancy
Belegung in der Wochenmitte, f
Auslastung in der Wochenmitte, f
♦ **midweek occupancy**
Belegung ist gleichmäßig
Auslastung ist gleichmäßig
♦ **occupancy is even**
Belegung ist rückläufig
Auslastung ist rückläufig
♦ **occupancy is decreasing**
Belegung ist steigend
Auslastung ist steigend
♦ **occupancy is increasing**
Belegung ist überdurchschnittlich
Auslastung ist überdurchschnittlich
♦ **occupancy is above average**
♦ occupancy is higher than average
Belegung ist ungleichmäßig
Auslastung ist ungleichmäßig
♦ **occupancy is uneven**
Belegung ist unterdurchschnittlich
Auslastung ist unterdurchschnittlich
♦ **occupancy is below average**
♦ occupancy is lower than average
Belegung ist zufriedenstellend
Auslastung ist zufriedenstellend
Belegung ist befriedigend
Auslastung ist befriedigend
♦ **occupancy is satisfactory**
Belegung läßt (viel) zu wünschen übrig
Auslastung läßt (viel) zu wünschen übrig
♦ **occupancy leaves much to be desired**
♦ occupancy leaves a lot to be desired
Belegung liegt bei 50 %
Auslastung liegt bei 50 %
♦ **occupancy is approximately 50 %**
♦ occupancy is about 50 %
Belegung melden von 80 %
Auslastung melden von 80 %
♦ **report 80 % occupancy**
Belegung nähert sich 70 %
Auslastung nähert sich 70 %
♦ **occupancy approaches 70 %**
Belegung optimieren
Auslastung optimieren
♦ **maximise occupancy**
♦ maximize occupancy
Belegung prognostizieren
Belegung vorhersagen
Auslastung prognostizieren
Auslastung vorhersagen
♦ **forecast occupancy**
Belegung pro Jahr, f
Auslastung pro Jahr, f
♦ **occupancy per year**
Belegung pro Monat, f
Auslastung pro Monat, f
♦ **occupancy per month**

Belegung pro Tag, f
Auslastung pro Tag, f
♦ **occupancy per day**
Belegung pro Woche, f
Auslastung pro Woche, f
♦ **occupancy per week**
Belegungsabfall, m
Belegungsrückgang, m
Auslastungsabfall, m
Auslastungsrückgang, m
♦ **fall in occupancy**
♦ drop in occupancy
♦ decrease in occupancy
belegungsabhängig, adj
auslastungsabhängig, adj
♦ **occupancy-sensitive, adj**
belegungsabhängige Kosten, pl
auslastungsabhängige Kosten, pl
♦ **occupancy-sensitive costs** pl
♦ occupancy-sensitive cost
belegungsabhängige variable Aufwendungen, f pl
auslastungsabhängige variable Aufwendungen, f pl
♦ **occupancy-sensitive variable expenses** pl
Belegungsänderung, f
Auslastungsänderung, f
♦ **occupancy change**
♦ change in occupancy
Belegungsberechnung, f
Auslastungsberechnung, f
♦ **calculation of occupancy**
♦ calculating occupancy
Belegung schätzen
Auslastung schätzen
♦ **estimate occupancy**
Belegungsdaten, pl
Auslastungsdaten, pl
♦ **occupancy data**
Belegungseinbruch, m
Auslastungseinbruch, m
♦ **slump in occupancy**
Belegungsergebnis, n
Auslastungsergebnis, n
♦ **occupancy result**
♦ occupancy achieved
Belegungsflaute, f
Auslastungsflaute, f
schwache Belegungszeit, f
schwache Auslastungszeit, f
♦ **slack period of occupancy**
Belegungsfrequenz, f
→ Belegungsquote
Belegungsgewinnschwelle, f
Auslastungsgewinnschwelle, f
♦ **occupancy breakeven point**
Belegungsgewinnschwelle, f
Auslastungsgewinnschwelle, f
♦ **break-even occupancy**
Belegungsgrad von 80 % erzielen
Auslastungsgrad von 80 % erzielen
♦ **achieve an 80 % occupancy**
Belegung sichern
Auslastung sichern
♦ **secure occupancy**
Belegung sinkt
Belegung geht zurück
Belegung fällt
Belegung nimmt ab
♦ **occupancy drops**
♦ occupancy decreases
♦ occupancy falls
♦ occupancy diminishes

Belegungskontrolle, f
Auslastungskontrolle, f
♦ **occupancy control**
♦ control of occupancy
Belegungskrise, f
Auslastungskrise, f
♦ **occupancy crisis**
Belegungskrise stoppen
Auslastungskrise stoppen
♦ **halt the occupancy crisis**
Belegungskurve, f
Auslastungskurve, f
♦ **occupancy graph**
Belegungsliste, f
Belegungsverzeichnis, n
Logiergästeverzeichnis, n
♦ **occupancy list**
♦ sleepers' list
Belegungslücke, f
Auslastungslücke, f
♦ **occupancy gap**
♦ gap in occupancy
Belegungsmuster, m
Belegungsschema, n
Auslastungsmuster, n
Auslastungsschema, n
♦ **occupancy pattern**
♦ pattern of occupancy
Belegungsniveau halten
Auslastungsniveau halten
Belegungsstand halten
Auslastungsstand halten
♦ **maintain the occupancy level**
♦ maintain the level of occupancy
Belegungsniveau übersteigt 90 %
Belegungsstand übersteigt 90 %
Auslastungsstand übersteigt 90 %
Auslastungsniveau übersteigt 90 %
♦ **occupancy level exceeds 90 %**
Belegungsplan, m
Auslastungsplan, m
♦ **occupancy plan**
Belegungsproblem, n
Auslastungsproblem, n
♦ **occupancy problem**
Belegungsproblem haben
Auslastungsproblem haben
♦ **have an occupancy problem**
Belegungsprognose, f
Auslastungsprognose, f
Belegungsvorhersage, f
Auslastungsvorhersage, f
♦ **forecast of occupancy**
♦ occupancy forecast
♦ forecasting occupancy
Belegungsprozent, n
→ Belegungsprozentsatz, prozentuale Belegung
Belegungsprozentsatz, m
Auslastungsprozentsatz, m
prozentuale Belegung, f
prozentuale Auslastung, f
Frequenzprozentsatz, m
♦ **percentage (of) occupancy**
Belegungsquote, f
Belegungsrate, f
Auslastungsquote, f
Auslastungsrate, f
Belegungsfrequenz, f
♦ **occupancy rate**
♦ rate of occupancy

Belegungsquote anheben
Belegungsrate anheben
Auslastungsquote anheben
Auslastungsrate anheben
♦ raise the occupancy rate
Belegungsquoten aufschlüsseln
Belegungsraten aufschlüsseln
Auslastungsquoten aufschlüsseln
Auslastungsraten aufschlüsseln
♦ give a breakdown of (the) occupancy rates
Belegungsrate steigern auf 80 %
Belegungsquote steigern auf 80 %
Auslastungsrate steigern auf 80 %
Auslastungsquote steigern auf 80 %
♦ increase the occupancy rate to 80 %
Belegungsrate verbessern
Belegungsquote verbessern
Auslastungsrate verbessern
Auslastungsquote verbessern
♦ improve the occupancy rate
Belegungsrisiko, n
Auslastungsrisiko, n
♦ occupancy risk
Belegungsrisiko tragen
Auslastungsrisiko tragen
♦ bear the occupancy risk
Belegungsrückgang, m
Auslastungsrückgang, m
♦ drop in occupancy
♦ decrease in occupancy
♦ fall in occupancy
Belegungsschätzung, f
Auslastungsschätzung, f
♦ estimate of occupancy
♦ estimating occupancy
Belegungsschema, n
Belegungsmuster, n
Auslastungsschema, n
Auslastungsmuster, n
♦ pattern of occupancy
♦ occupancy pattern
Belegungsschwankung, f
Auslastungsschwankung, f
♦ fluctuation in occupancy
♦ variation in occupancy
Belegungssituation, f
→ Auslastungssituation
Belegungsstand, m
Belegungsniveau, n
Auslastungsstand, m
Auslastungsniveau, n
♦ occupancy level
♦ level of occupancy
♦ occupancy state
Belegungsstatistik, f
Auslastungsstatistik, f
♦ occupancy statistics pl
Belegungsstatitik erstellen
Auslastungsstatistik erstellen
♦ compile occupancy statistics
Belegungsstatus, m
Belegungsstand, m
Auslastungsstatus, m
Auslastungsstand, m
♦ occupancy state
Belegungssteigerung, f
Auslastungssteigerung, f
♦ increase in occupancy
♦ rise in occupancy

Belegungssteigerung um 5 % von 60 auf 65 %
Auslastungssteigerung um 5 % von 60 auf 65 %
♦ increase in occupancy by 5 % from 60 to 65 %
Belegungssteigerung von 10 %, f
Auslastungssteigerung von 10 %, f
♦ increase in occupancy by 10 %
♦ 10 % increase in occupancy
Belegungssteuer, f
Belegungsabgabe f
♦ occupancy tax AE
Belegungsstopp, m
♦ occupancy freeze
♦ freeze on bookings
Belegungsstopp anordnen
Buchungsstopp anordnen
♦ impose a freeze on bookings
Belegungstabelle, f
Auslastungstabelle, f
♦ occupancy table
Belegung steigt
Belegung nimmt zu
Belegung erhöht sich
Auslastung steigt
Auslastung nimmt zu
♦ occupancy increases
♦ occupancy grows
♦ occupancy rises
Belegungstrend, m
Auslastungstrend, m
♦ occupancy trend
Belegungsüberblick, m
Belegungsübersicht, f
Auslastungsüberblick, m
Auslastungsübersicht, f
♦ occupancy survey
Belegungsunterlagen, f pl
Auslastungsunterlagen, f pl
♦ occupancy records pl
♦ booking records pl
Belegungsverhältnis, n
Auslastungsverhältnis, n
♦ occupancy ratio
♦ ratio of occupancy
Belegungsverringerung, f
Belegungssenkung, f
Auslastungsverringerung, f
Auslastungssenkung, f
♦ reduction of occupancy
Belegungsverzeichnis erstellen
♦ compile an occupancy list
Belegungsvorhersage, f
Belegungsprognose, f
Auslastungsvorhersage, f
Auslastungsprognose, f
♦ occupancy forecast
♦ forecast of occupancy
Belegungszahl, f
Auslastungszahl, f
♦ occupancy figure
Belegungszeit, f
Belegzeit, f
Auslastungszeit, f
♦ occupancy time
♦ occupancy period
♦ period of occupancy
Belegungszeitpunkt, m (Check-in)
Bezugszeitpunkt, m
♦ check-in time
♦ time of checking in

Belegungszeitraum, m
Auslastungszeitraum, m
♦ occupancy period
♦ period of occupancy
Belegungsziel, n
Auslastungsziel, n
♦ targeted occupancy
Belegungszusammensetzung, f
Auslastungszusammensetzung, f
♦ occupancy mix
Belegungszustand, m
Auslastungszustand, m
♦ occupancy status
Belegung übersteigt 50 %
Auslastung übersteigt 50 %
♦ occupancy exceeds 50 %
Belegung übersteigt eine bestimmte Zahl
Auslastung übersteigt eine bestimmte Zahl
♦ occupancy exceeds a certain figure
Belegung verbessern
Auslastung verbessern
♦ improve occupancy
♦ increase occupancy
Belegung von 30 % durch Stammgäste erzielen
Auslastung von 30 % durch Stammgäste erzielen
♦ derive 30 % occupancy from regular guests
Belegung von 70 % haben
Auslastung von 70 % haben
♦ have 70 % occupancy
Belegung von 80 % überschreiten
Auslastung von 80 % übersteigen
♦ exceed 80 % occupancy
♦ surpass 80 % occupancy
Belegung von 90 % verzeichnen
Auslastung von 90 % verzeichnen
♦ record 90 % occupancy
♦ record occupancy of 90 %
Belegwesen, n (Buchhaltung)
♦ voucher system
Beletage, f
bel étage m FR
♦ bel étage FR
♦ second floor AE
♦ second story AE
♦ first floor BE
♦ first storey BE
beleuchten etw
illuminieren etw
♦ light s.th.
♦ illuminate s.th.
beleuchten mit Flutlicht
♦ floodlight
Beleuchter, m
♦ lighting technician
beleuchtet, adj (Flutlicht)
♦ floodlit, adj
♦ floodlighted, adj
beleuchtet, adj (illuminiert)
illuminiert, adj
♦ illuminated, adj
beleuchteter Tennisplatz, m
→ Flutlichttennisplatz
beleuchtetes Schloß, n
illuminiertes Schloß, n
♦ illuminated castle
♦ illuminated palace
beleuchtet sein am Abend
♦ be illuminated in the evening
♦ be floodlit in the evening
♦ be floodlighted in the evening

Beleuchtung

84

Beleuchtung, f (Ausleuchtung)
- lighting

Beleuchtung, f (generell)
- lighting

Beleuchtung, f (Illumination)
→ Illumination

Beleuchtungsanlage, f
- lighting system

Beleuchtungsdauer, f
- duration of lighting

Beleuchtungskosten, pl
- lighting costs *pl*
- cost of lighting

Beleuchtungsvorrichtung, f
Beleuchtungsausrüstung, f
- lighting rig

Belgien
- Belgium

Belgier, m
- Belgian

Belgierin, f
- Belgian girl
- Belgian woman
- Belgian

belgisch, adj
- Belgian, adj

belgische Riviera, f
- Belgian Riviera, the

beliebt, adj
- popular, adj
- well-liked, adj
- favorite, adj *AE*
- favourite, adj *BE*

beliebt bei jm
- popular with s.o.

beliebter Abstecher, m
- popular detour
- popular side trip

beliebter Ausflugsort, m
beliebtes Ausflugsziel, n
- popular place for excursions

beliebter Treffpunkt, m
- popular venue
- popular meeting place

beliebter Treffpunkt sein für jn
- be a popular venue for s.o.

beliebter Zeitvertreib, m
Lieblingszeitvertreib, m
- favorite pastime *AE*
- favourite pastime *BE*

beliebtes Gericht, n
- popular dish

beliebtes Getränk, n
- popular drink
- popular beverage

beliebtes Reiseziel, n
- popular destination

beliebtes Touristenzentrum, n
- popular tourist center *AE*
- popular tourist centre *BE*

beliebtes Urlaubsziel, n
- popular vacation destination *AE*
- popular holiday destination *BE*

Beliebtheit, f
- popularity

beliebt sein
großen Zuspruch haben
- be popular

beliebt werden bei jm
Anklang finden bei jm
- become popular with s.o.

beliefern jn mit etw
zukommen lassen jm etw
- supply s.o. with s.th.

Belize
- Belize

Belizer, m
- Belizean

Belizerin, f
- Belizean girl
- Belizean woman
- Belizean

belizisch, adj
- Belizean, adj

belüften etw
- ventilate s.th.
- air s.th.

belüftet, adj
- ventilated, adj

Belüftung, f
- ventilation

Belüftungsanlage, f
- ventilation system

Belugakaviar, m
Beluga, m
- Beluga caviar
- Beluga caviare

Belustigung, f
Lustbarkeit, f
- merrymaking *AE*
- marry-making *BE*

bemalte Fassade, f
- painted front
- painted facade

bemängeln etw
kritisieren etw
- critisize s.th.
- criticise s.th.
- find fault with s.th.

bemannte Jacht, f
- crewed yacht

bemannt oder unbemannt, adj (Schiff)
- crewed or bareboat, adj

bemerkenswertes Hotel, n
- remarkable hotel

benachbart, adj
- neighboring, adj *AE*
- neighbouring, adj *BE*
- adjoining, adj
- adjacent, adj
- next, adj

benachrichtigen jn von etw
- inform s.o. of s.th.
- notify s.o. of s.th.
- advise s.o. of s.th.

Benachrichtigung, f
Mitteilung, f
Avisierung, f
- notification
- advice

Benachrichtigungsdienst, m
Mitteilungsdienst, m
- message service

Benachrichtigungsformular, n
→ Mitteilungsformular

Benachrichtigung von etw, f
Mitteilung über etw, f
- notification of s.th.

benannt sein nach etw
- be named after s.th.

Benediktiner, m (Kräuterlikör)
- Benedictine

Benediktiner, m (Person)
- Benedictine

Benediktinerabtei, f
- Benedictine abbey

Benediktinerart, adv *gastr*
nach Benediktinerart, adv *gastr*
- Benedictine style, adv *gastr*

Benediktinerkapelle, f
- Benedictine chapel

Benediktinerkloster, n (Frauen)
- Benedictine convent
- Bendedictine nunnery

Benediktinerkloster, n (Männer)
- Benedictine monastery

Benediktinermönch, m
- Benedictine monk

Benediktinernonne, f
- Benedictine nun

Benediktinerpriorei, f
- Benedictine priory

Benefizbankett, n
- benefit banquet

Benefizkonzert, n
- benefit concert

Benefizveranstaltung, f
(z.B. im Theater)
Benefizvorstellung f
- benefit performance
- benefit night
- ticket night
- benefit

beneidenswerte Lage, f
- enviable situation
- enviable position
- enviable location
- enviable setting

Benelux-Land, n
- Benelux country

bengalisch, adj
- Bengali, adj

bengalische Küche, f
- Bengali cooking
- Bengali cuisine

Benin
- Benin

Beniner, m
- Beninese

Beninerin, f
- Beninese girl
- Beninese woman
- Beninese

beninisch, adj
- Beninese, adj

benötigen etw
verlangen etw
fordern etw
- require s.th.
- need s.th.

benötigen etw im Urlaub
- require s.th. on a vacation *AE*
- require s.th. on a holiday *BE*

benötigt, adj
- required, adj

benötigte Leistung, f
benötigte Dienstleistung, f
benötigter Service, m
- required service
- service required

benötigte Parkmöglichkeit, f
- type of parking required

benötigtes Zimmer n
♦ required room
benötigte Unterkunft, f
♦ required accommodation
♦ accommodation required
♦ needed accommodation
♦ accommodation needed
benutzen etw
nutzen etw
♦ use s.th.
♦ make use of s.th.
benutzen etw ganzheitlich
ganzheitlich beutzen etw
♦ use s.th. holistically
benutzen etw sparsam
♦ use s.th. sparingly
Benutzer, m
Anwender, m
♦ user
♦ person using s.th.
benutzerfreundlich, adj
♦ user-friendly, adj
Benutzerfreundlichkeit, f
♦ user-friendliness
Benutzergebühr, f
♦ user fee
♦ user charge
Benutzergebühr zahlen
♦ pay a user fee
♦ pay a user charge
benutztes Glas, n
♦ used glass
benutzte Wäsche f
gebrauchte Wäsche f
♦ used linen
Benutzung, f
Nutzung, f
Anwendung, f
Gebrauch, m
♦ use
♦ utilization
♦ utilisation
Benutzung der Clubeinrichtungen, f
♦ use of the club facilities
♦ using the club facilities
Benutzung der Freizeitanlagen, f
♦ use of the leisure facilities
Benutzung der Sporteinrichtungen, f
♦ use of the sports facilities
♦ using the sports facilities
Benutzung des Privatwagens, f
♦ use of the private car
Benutzung des Tennisplatzes, f
→ Tennisplatzbenutzung
Benutzung eines Campingplatzes, f
♦ use of a campsite
♦ use of a campground AE
♦ use of a camping site BE
♦ use of a camping ground BE
♦ using a campsite
Benutzung ist unentgeltlich
♦ use of this service is free of charge
♦ use is free of charge
Benutzungsbeschränkung, f
♦ restriction in the use of s.th.
Benutzungsentgelt, n
→ Benutzungsgebühr
Benutzungsgebühr, f
♦ charge for the use of s.th.
♦ fee for the use of s.th.

♦ charge for using s.th.
♦ fee for using s.th.
Benutzungsgebühr verlangen
♦ levy a charge for the use of s.th.
♦ require a charge for the use of s.th.
Benutzungszuschlag, m
♦ supplement for the use of s.th.
Benutzungszuschlag für etw, m
♦ supplement for the use of s.th.
Benutzung von etw, f
Nutzung von etw, f
Anwendung von etw, f
Gebrauch von etw, m
♦ use of s.th.
♦ using s.th.
Benzin, n
♦ gasoline AE
♦ gas AE
♦ petrol BE
Benzincoupon, m
♦ gasoline coupon AE
♦ gas coupon AE
♦ petrol coupon BE
Benzingeld, n
♦ gasoline money AE
♦ gas money AE
♦ petrol money BE
Benzingutschein, m
♦ gasoline voucher AE
♦ gas voucher AE
♦ petrol voucher BE
Benzingutschein ausgeben
♦ issue a gasoline voucher AE
♦ issue a petrol voucher BE
Benzingutschein beantragen
♦ apply for a gasoline voucher AE
♦ apply for a petrol voucher BE
Benzinmotor, m
♦ petrol engine AE
♦ gasoline engine AE
Benzinpreis, m
♦ gasoline price AE
♦ gas price AE
♦ petrol price BE
Benzinverbrauch, m
♦ gasoline consumption AE
♦ gas consumption AE
♦ petrol consumption BE
bequem, adj
leicht, adj
gemütlich, adj
komfortabel, adj
♦ easy, adj
♦ comfortable, adj
♦ cosy, adj
♦ cozy, adj AE
bequem, adv
♦ in comfort, adv
♦ easily, adv
♦ comfortably, adv
bequem erreichbar, adj
♦ easily accessible, adj
♦ easy to reach, adj
♦ convenient, adj
bequemer Sitz, m
bequemer Sitzplatz, m
bequemer Platz, m
♦ comfortable seat
bequemes Bett, n
komfortables Bett, n
♦ comfortable bed

bequeme Wohnung, f
♦ comfortable apartment AE
♦ comfortable flat BE
♦ cosy apartment AE
♦ cozy apartment AE
♦ cosy flat BE
bequem gelegen, adj
♦ handy, adj
♦ convenient, adj
♦ conveniently situated, adj
Bequemlichkeit, f
♦ convenience
♦ ease
♦ comfort
bequem machen es sich
es sich bequem machen
♦ make oneself comfortable
♦ make oneself at home
bequem reisen
♦ travel in comfort
berappen etw
→ bezahlen etw
beraten jn bei der Auswahl der Speisen/Getränke
♦ advise s.o. on the choice of food and drink
♦ advise s.o. on the selection of food and drink
♦ advise s.o. about the choice of food and drink
♦ advise s.o. about the selection of food and drink
beraten jn bei der Weinauswahl
♦ advise s.o. on the choice of wines
♦ advise s.o. about the choice of wines
♦ advise s.o. on the selection of wines
♦ advise s.o. about the selection of wines
beraten jn bei etw
♦ advise s.o. on s.th.
♦ advise s.o. about s.th.
Berater engagieren
♦ hire a consultant
♦ engage a consultant
Beratungsbüro, n
♦ advice bureau
Beratungsdienst, m
♦ advisory service
♦ consultative service
♦ consultancy service
♦ consulting service
Beratungsfirma, f
Consultingfirma, f
♦ consulting company
♦ consulting firm
♦ consultancy firm
♦ consultancy
Beratungshonorar, n
(eines Arztes etc.)
Beratungshonorar, f
♦ consultation fee
Beratungskosten, pl
(für Steuerberater, Rechtsanwalt etc.)
♦ professional fees pl
Beratungssitzung, f
♦ counselling session
berauschend, adj
♦ intoxicating, adj
berauschendes Getränk, n
♦ intoxicating drink
♦ intoxicating beverage
♦ intoxicant
Berber, m
♦ Berber
♦ Kabyle
Berberin, f
♦ Berber girl

Berchtesgadener Alpen

- Berber woman
- Berber
- Kabyle girl
- Kabyle (woman)

Berchtesgadener Alpen, pl
- **Berchtesgaden Alps, the** pl

berechnen etw (fordern)
- **charge s.th.**

berechnen etw gesondert
- **charge s.th. extra**

berechnen etw jm
- **charge s.o. for s.th.**
- charge s.o. with s.th.
- charge s.th. to s.o.

berechnen etw (kalkulieren)
→ kalkulieren etw

berechnet nach Verzehr
nach Verzehr berechnet
- **charged as taken**

Berechnung, f (Kalkulation)
Kalkulation, f
- **calculation**

berechtigen jn zu etw
Recht geben jm zu etw
- **qualify s.o. for s.th.**

berechtigt sein zu etw
Anspruch haben auf etw
- **be eligible for s.th.**

berechtigt sein zur Stornierung
berechtigt sein zum Rücktritt
berechtigt sein zur Annullierung
- **be entitled to cancel s.th.**

berechtigt zu einer Ermäßigung
- **eligible for a reduction**

berechtigt zu etw, adj
- **eligible for s.th., adj**

Bereichsaufwendungen, f pl
- **departmental expenses** pl

Bereichsbericht, m
- **departmental report**

Bereichsergebnis, n
- **departmental result**

Bereichsertrag, m
- **departmental income**

Bereichsgewinn, m
- **departmental profit**

Bereichskosten, pl
- **departmental costs** pl
- departmental cost

Bereichsleiter, m
→ Abteilungsleiter

Bereichsumsatz, m
- **departmental sales** pl
- departmental turnover

Bereichsverlust, m
- **departmental loss**

bereisen etw
reisen durch etw
- **tour s.th.**

bereist, adj
gereist, adj
- **travelled, adj**
- traveled, adj AE

bereiste Welt, f
- **travelled world**
- traveled world AE

bereithalten etw
- **hold s.th. ready**
- keep s.th. at hand
- reserve s.th.

Bereithaltezeit,
(Zeit, bis zu der Zimmer bereitgehalten wird)
Annahmezeit, f
- **holding time**

Bereithaltung, f (Reservierung)
→ Reservierung

Bereithaltung eines Zimmers, f
Reservierung eines Zimmers, f
- **reservation of a room**
- holding a room

Bereithaltung von etw, f
Reservierung von etw, f
- **reservation of s.th.**

bereitmachen sich für die Abreise
- **get ready for (the) departure**

Bereitschaftsdienst, m
- **standby duty** AE
- stand-by duty BE

Bereitschaftskosten pl
→ Fixkosten

bereit sein zur Abreise
fertig sein für die Abreise
abreisebereit sein
- **be ready for departure**
- be ready to depart
- be ready to leave

bereitstellen etw
zur Verfügung stellen etw
bieten etw
- **provide s.th.**

Bereitstellung, f
- **provision**
- supply

Bereitstellung eines Zimmers, f
- **provision of a room**
- providing a room

Bereitstellungspflicht, f (Zimmer)
- **obligation to provide a room**

Bereitstellung von Essen, Trinken und Unterkunft, f
- **provision of food, drink and accommodation**
- provision of food, drink and lodging AE
- providing food, drink and accommodation
- providing food, drink and lodging AE

Bereitstellung von Getränken, f
- **provision of drinks**
- provision of beverages

Bereitstellung von Speisen, f
- **provision of meals**
- provision of food
- providing meals
- providing food

Bereitstellung von Speisen und Getränken, f
- **provision of food and drink**
- providing food and drink

Bereitstellung von Unterkunft, f
→ Unterkunftsbereitstellung

Bereitstellung von Verpflegung, f
- **provision of food**
- providing catering

bergab, adv
- **downhill, adv**

Berg Athos, m
- **Mount Athos**

bergauf, adv
- **uphill, adv**

Bergbach, m
- **mountain stream**

Bergbahn f (Eisenbahn)
- **mountain railroad** AE
- mountain railway BE

Bergbahnstation f (Eisenbahn)
- **mountain railroad station** AE
- mountain railway station BE

Bergbau, m
- **mining**

Bergbauernhof, m
- **mountain farm**

Bergbaumuseum, n
Bergwerksmuseum, n
- **mining museum**

Bergbaustadt, f
Bergwerksstadt, f
Grubenstadt, f
- **mining town**

Berg besteigen
auf einen Berg steigen
- **climb a mountain**

Berg bezwingen
- **conquer a mountain**

Bergblick, m
- **mountain view**
- view of the mountains

Bergblickzuschlag m
- **mountain-view supplement**

Bergcafé, n
- **mountain cafe** AE
- mountain café BE

Bergcampingplatz, m
Gebirgscampingplatz, m
- **mountain campsite**
- mountain campground AE
- mountain camping site BE
- mountain camping ground BE
- mountain site

Bergchalet, n
Gebirgschalet n
- **mountain chalet**

Bergdorf n
- **mountain village**

Berge eignen sich zum Wandern
Berge bieten sich zum Wandern an
- **mountains lend themselves to walking**

Berg erklimmen
Berg erklettern
- **scale a mountain**

Berge vor der Haustür haben
- **have the mountains on one's doorstep**

Bergferien, pl
Bergurlaub, m
Gebirgsferien, pl
Gebirgsurlaub, m
- **mountain holiday** BE
- mountain vacation AE
- holiday in the mountains BE
- vacation in the mountains AE

Bergferienort, m
Bergurlaubsort, m
Bergort, m
- **mountain resort**

Bergfried, m hist
- **keep** hist

Bergführer, m
(Person)
- **mountain guide**
- mountain leader

Berggasthaus, n
Berggaststätte, f
- **mountain bar** AE
- mountain pub BE

Berggasthof m
Gebirgsgasthof m

- ♦ mountain inn
- ♦ mountain lodge

Berggebiet, n (groß)
- ♦ mountain region

Berggebiet, n (klein)
- ♦ mountain area

Berggipfel, m
- Bergspitze, f
- ♦ mountain peak
- ♦ mountain summit
- ♦ mountain top

Berghang, m
- ♦ mountain slope

Berghaus, n
- *(Cottage)*
- kleines Berghaus, m
- kleines Gebirgshaus, n
- ♦ mountain cottage

Berghospiz n
- Gebirgshospiz n
- ♦ mountain hospice

Berghotel, n
- Gebirgshotel, n
- ♦ mountain hotel

Berghütte, f
- ♦ mountain cabin
- mountain hut
- mountain bothy
- ♦ mountain lodge *AE*
- ♦ mountain shelter

Bergische Land, das, n
- ♦ Bergisch Land, the

Bergkamm, m
- ♦ mountain crest
- ♦ crest

Bergkletterer, m
- Bergsteiger, m
- ♦ mountain climber

Bergland, n
- Berggebiet, n
- ♦ mountain country

Berglandschaft, f
- Gebirgslandschaft, f
- ♦ mountain scenery
- mountain countryside
- mountain landscape
- mountainscape

Berglehrer, m
- ♦ mountaineering instructor

Berglehrerschein, m
- Berglehrerzertifikat, n
- ♦ mountaineering instructor's certificate

Berglodge, f
- Gebirgslodge, f
- Berghütte, f
- Gebirgshütte, f
- Berggasthof, f
- ♦ mountain lodge

Bergluft, f
- ♦ mountain air

Bergluft genießen
- ♦ enjoy the mountain air

Bergmarathon, m
- ♦ mountain marathon

Bergpark, m
- ♦ hill park

Bergpaß, m
- Gebirgspaß, m
- ♦ mountain pass
- ♦ pass

Bergpension, f
- ♦ mountain guesthouse *AE*
- ♦ mountain guest-house *BE*
- ♦ private hotel in the mountains

Bergpfad, m
- Bergweg, m
- ♦ mountain path

Bergplatz, m
- *(z.B. Campingplatz)*
- ♦ mountain site

Bergroute, f
- Bergstrecke, f
- ♦ mountain route

Bergrücken, m
- ♦ mountain ridge

Bergschlucht, f
- enges Tal, n
- ♦ glen

Bergschuhe, m pl
- ♦ mountain boots *pl*
- ♦ mountaineering boots *pl*

Bergschule, f
- ♦ mountain school

Bergschutzhütte, f
- Berghütte, f
- ♦ mountain shelter
- ♦ mountain refuge

Bergsee, m
- Gebirgssee m
- ♦ mountain lake

Bergski, m
- ♦ upper ski

Bergspitze, f
- Berggipfel, m
- ♦ mountain top
- ♦ mountain summit
- ♦ mountain peak

Bergsport, m
- → Bergsteigen

Bergstadt, f (Großstadt)
- Gebirgsstadt, f
- ♦ mountain city

Bergstadt, f (kleine Stadt)
- Gebirgsstadt, f
- ♦ mountain town

Bergstation f
- *(Lift)*
- ♦ top station

Bergsteigen, n
- Bergsport, m
- ♦ mountain climbing
- ♦ mountaineering
- ♦ alpinism

Bergsteiger, m
- ♦ mountain climber
- ♦ climber
- ♦ mountaineer
- ♦ alpinist

Bergsteigerexpedition, f
- ♦ mountaineering expedition

Bergsteigerlehrgang, m
- Bergsteigerkurs, m
- ♦ mountaineering course

Bergsteigermuseum, n
- ♦ mountaineering museum

Bergsteigerschule, f
- ♦ mountaineering school

Bergsteigerverein, m
- ♦ mountaineering club

Bergsteigerzelt, n
- ♦ mountaineer's tent

Bergstraße, f
- Gebirgsstraße f
- ♦ mountain road

Bergstraße, f (Eigenname)
- ♦ Mountain Road, the

Bergstube, f
- *(Lokal)*
- Gebirgsstube, f
- ♦ mountain tavern

Bergtal, n
- Gebirgstal, n
- ♦ mountain valley

Bergtour, f
- ♦ mountain tour

Bergtourismuszentrum, n
- Gebirgstourismuszentrum, n
- ♦ mountain tourism center *AE*
- ♦ mountain tourism centre *BE*

Bergtourismus, m
- Gebirgstourismus, m
- ♦ mountain tourism

Bergtourist, m
- Gebirgstourist, m
- ♦ mountain tourist

Berg überqueren
- ♦ cross a mountain

Berg- und Skiführer, m
- ♦ mountain and ski guide

Berg- und Talbahn, f
- *(Jahrmarkt)*
- Achterbahn, f
- ♦ switchback *BE*
- ♦ roller coaster

Berg- und Talbahnfahrt, f
- Achterbahnfahrt, f
- ♦ switchback ride *BE*
- ♦ roller-coaster ride

Bergurlaub, m
- Bergferien, pl
- Gebirgsurlaub, m
- Gebirgsferien, pl
- ♦ mountain vacation *AE*
- ♦ vacation in the mountains *AE*
- ♦ mountain holiday *BE*
- ♦ holiday in the mountains *BE*

Bergurlaubsort, m
- → Bergferienort

Bergurlaubsregion, f
- Gebirgsurlaubsregion, f
- ♦ mountain vacation region *AE*
- ♦ mountain holiday region *BE*

Bergverkehr, m (Fluß)
- ♦ upstream traffic
- ♦ upstream navigation

Bergwacht, f (Dienst)
- ♦ mountain rescue service

Bergwacht, f (Personen)
- ♦ mountain rescue team

Bergwachtposten, m
- ♦ mountain rescue post

Bergwald, m
- ♦ hill forest

Bergwanderer, m
- ♦ mountain hiker
- ♦ mountain walker

Bergwanderfan, m
- ♦ mountain hiking fan
- ♦ mountain walking fan

Bergwanderfreund, m
- ♦ mountain hiking enthusiast
- ♦ mountain walking enthusiast

Bergwandern

Bergwandern, n
♦ mountain hiking
♦ mountain walking
hiking in the mountains
walking in the mountains
Bergwanderung, f
♦ mountain hike
♦ mountain walk
♦ mountain hiking
♦ mountain walking
Bergwanderweg, m
♦ mountain trail
Bergweg, m
♦ mountain track
Bergwerksdorf, n
Bergbaudorf, n
Grubendorf, n
♦ mining village
Berichtsjahr, n
♦ year under review
Berichtsmonat m
♦ month under review
Berichtswoche f
♦ week under review
Berichtszeitraum, m
♦ period under review
♦ review period
Berieselungsapparat, m
♦ sprinkler
Beringstraße, f
♦ Bering Straits, the *pl*
♦ Bering Strait, the *sg*
Berlinerart, adv *gastr*
nach Berlinerart, adv *gastr*
♦ Berlin style, adv *gastr*
Berliner Mauer, f
♦ Berlin Wall, the
Berliner Messegelände, n
♦ Berlin fairground
Bermuda
♦ Bermuda
Bermuda-Dreieck, n
♦ Bermuda Triangle, the
Bermudainseln, f pl
♦ Bermuda Islands, the *pl*
Bermuda Plan, m
(Zimmer mit Frühstück)
BP
♦ Bermuda Plan
♦ BP
Bermudashorts, pl
♦ bermuda shorts *pl*
Bermuder, m
♦ Bermudian
♦ Bermudan
Bermuderin, f
♦ Bermudian girl
♦ Bermudian woman
♦ Bermudian
♦ Bermudan girl
♦ Bermudan woman
bermudisch, adj
♦ Bermudian, adj
♦ Bermudan, adj
Berner Alpen, die, pl
♦ Bernese Alps, the *pl*
Berner Oberland n
(Region)
♦ Bernese Oberland
Berninapaß, m
♦ Bernina Pass, the

Bernstein, m
♦ amber
Bernsteinmuseum, n
♦ amber museum
berufen werden zum Hoteldirektor
ernannt werden zum Hoteldirektor
♦ be appointed hotel manager
berufliche Haftpflichtversicherung, f
♦ professional liability insurance
Berufsausbildung, f
♦ vocational training
♦ professional training
Berufserfahrung, f
♦ work experience
♦ working experience
♦ professional experience
Berufsgeheimnis, n
♦ trade secret
Berufsgruppe, f
♦ professional group
Berufskleidung, f
♦ work clothes *pl*
♦ working clothes *pl*
Berufskoch, m
Profikoch, m *coll*
♦ professional cook
berufsmäßiger Glücksspieler, m
♦ professional gambler
berufsmäßiger Reisender, m
professioneller Reisender, m
Profireisender, m *coll*
♦ professional traveller
♦ professional traveler *AE*
Berufsmusiker, m
♦ professional musician
Berufsverband, m
♦ professional association
berühmt, adj
♦ famous, adj
berühmter Besucher, m
♦ famous visitor
♦ distinguished visitor
berühmter Name, m
♦ famous name
berühmtes Hotel, n
♦ famous hotel
Berühmtheit, f (Person)
→ Prominenter
berühmt sein für etw
♦ be famous for s.th.
berühmt sein für seine Atmosphäre
♦ be renowned for its atmosphere
Besatzung, f
Mannschaft, f
♦ crew
Besatzungsmitglied, n
♦ crew member
♦ member of the crew
besaufen sich *vulg*
♦ get tight *coll*
♦ get drunk
Besäufnis, f
Saufgelage, n
♦ booze *coll*
♦ booze-up *BE coll*
♦ drinking bout *BE coll*
♦ drinking binge *BE coll*
beschädigtes Gepäck, n
♦ damaged baggage *AE*
♦ damaged luggage *BE*

beschäftigen jn (Personal)
♦ employ s.o.
beschäftigt sein im Hotel- und Gastgewerbe
♦ be employed in the hotel and foodservice industry *AE*
♦ be employed in the hotel and catering industry *BE*
beschäftigt sein mit den Abreisevorbereitungen
♦ be engaged in the preparations for departure
Beschäftigung im Freien, f
♦ outdoor pursuit
Beschäftigungserlaubnis, f
→ Arbeitsgenehmigung
bescheiden ausgestattet, adj
♦ modestly equipped, adj
bescheiden ausgestattetes Zimmer, n
♦ modestly equipped room
bescheidene Gebühr, f
♦ modest charge
♦ modest fee
bescheidene Größe, f
♦ modest size
bescheidenen Komfort bieten
♦ provide moderate comfort
bescheidene Rechnung, f
♦ modest bill
♦ modest check *AE*
bescheidener Imbiß, m
♦ modest snack
♦ humble snack
bescheidener Komfort, m
♦ moderate comfort
bescheidener Urlaub, m
bescheidene Ferien, pl
♦ modest vacation *AE*
♦ modest holiday *BE*
bescheidenes Hotel, n
♦ modest hotel
bescheidenes Mahl, n
bescheidenes Essen, n
bescheidene Mahlzeit, f
♦ modest meal
♦ humble meal
bescheiden möbliert, adj
bescheiden eingerichtet, adj
♦ modestly furnished, adj
♦ modestly appointed, adj
bescheiden möbliertes Zimmer n
♦ modestly furnished room
bescheißen jn *coll*
neppen jn
♦ gyp s.o. *AE coll*
♦ clip s.o.
beschleunigen etw
♦ expedite s.th. *form*
Beschließer, m (Concierge)
→ Concierge
Beschließerin, f (Hotel)
→ Hausdame
Beschneiungsausrüstung, f
Beschneiungsgerät, n
♦ snow-making equipment
beschränkter Service, m
begrenzter Service, m
eingeschränkter Service, m
♦ limited service
♦ restricted service
beschränkte Speisekarte, f
begrenzte Speisekarte f
♦ limited menu

Beschränkung der Aufenthaltsdauer, f
Begrenzung der Aufenthaltsdauer, f
♦ restriction in the length of stay
♦ restriction of the length of stay
♦ restricting the length of stay
beschreiben etw genau
♦ describe s.th. accurately
Beschreibung der Wanderroute, f
Beschreibung der Wanderstrecke, f
Wanderroutenbeschreibung, f
Wanderstreckenbeschreibung, f
♦ description of the hiking route
♦ description of the walking route
♦ hiking route description
♦ walking route description
Beschreibung eines Hotels, f
Hotelbeschreibung, f
♦ description of a hotel
♦ hotel description
Beschreibung verifizieren
♦ verify a description
Beschwerde, f (Krankheit)
♦ ailment
Beschwerde, f (Reklamation)
→ Reklamation
Beschwerde bearbeiten
Reklamation bearbeiten
♦ deal with a complaint
♦ handle a complaint
Beschwerdebrief, m
♦ letter complaining about s.th.
♦ letter of complaint
Beschwerdebrief schreiben
♦ write a letter of complaint
♦ write a letter complaining about s.th.
Beschwerdebuch n
♦ complaints book
Beschwerdeformular, n
♦ complaints form
Beschwerdeführer, m
♦ complainant
Beschwerde gütlich beilegen
Reklamation gütlich beilegen
♦ settle a complaint amicably
Beschwerde nachgehen
Beschwerde untersuchen
♦ investigate a complaint
Beschwerdenbearbeitung f
♦ dealing with a complaint
♦ handling a complaint
Beschwerdeursache, f
→ Ursache einer Beschwerde
beschweren sich bei jm über etw
♦ complain to s.o. about s.th.
beschweren sich über das Essen
♦ complain about the food
beschweren sich über den schlechten Service
schlechten Service reklamieren
♦ complain about the poor service
beschwipst, adj
♦ tipsy, adj
♦ tiddly, adj *coll*
♦ squiffy, adj *sl*
♦ slightly sozzled, adj
Beschwipstheit, f
♦ tipsiness
beschwipst sein
Schwips haben
♦ be tipsy
Beseitigung, f
Entfernung, f

Entzug, m
♦ removal
Besen, m
♦ broom
Besenbrigade, f *humor*
Putzkolonne, f
Besengarde, f *humor*
♦ bucket brigade
Besenschrank, m
♦ broom closet
♦ broom cupboard
♦ broom cabinet
besetzen etw
(Haus, Anwesen)
♦ squat s.th.
besetzt, adj (Personal)
♦ staffed, adj
besetzt, adj (Sitz)
→ belegt
besetzter Tisch m
belegter Tisch m
♦ occupied table
Besetzung, f (Auslastung)
→ Auslastung
Besetzung, f (Theater)
♦ cast
besichtigen
♦ sightsee
♦ see the sights
besichtigen etw auf einer Reise
♦ visit s.th. on a tour
besichtigen etw (in Augenschein nehmen)
etw in Augenschein nehmen
♦ view s.th.
besichtigen etw (inspizieren)
→ inspizieren
besichtigen etw (Sehenswürdigkeit)
♦ see s.th.
♦ see the sights
♦ visit s.th.
Besichtiger, m
♦ sightseer
Besichtigung, f (Besuch)
→ Besuch
Besichtigung der Einrichtung, f
(z.B. vor einem Kongreß)
Ortsbesichtigung, f
♦ facility visit
Besichtigung der Sehenswürdigkeiten, f
♦ sightseeing
♦ seeing the sights
Besichtigungen machen
♦ go sightseeing
Besichtigungsattraktion, f
♦ sightseeing attraction
Besichtigungsausflug, m
♦ sightseeing excursion
Besichtigungsbootsfahrt, f
♦ sightseeing boat trip
Besichtigungsbus, m
♦ sightseeing bus
♦ sightseeing coach *BE*
Besichtigungsdienst, m
♦ sightseeing service
Besichtigungsfahrt, f
♦ sightseeing trip
♦ sightseeing trip
♦ sightseeing tour
Besichtigungsfahrt auf die Beine stellen *fam*
Besichtigungsfahrt organisieren
♦ lay on a sightseeing tour

Besichtigungsfahrt in die nähere Umgebung, f
♦ tour of the surrounding area
Besichtigungsfahrt machen
♦ go on a sightseeing tour
Besichtigungskreuzfahrt, f
♦ sightseeing cruise
Besichtigungsort, m
♦ sightseeing place
♦ sightseeing spot
Besichtigungsplattform, f
♦ viewing platform
Besichtigungsprogramm n
♦ sightseeing program *AE*
♦ sightseeing programme *BE*
Besichtigungsreise, f
Besichtigungstour, f
♦ sightseeing tour
Besichtigungsroute, f
Besichtigungsstrecke, f
♦ sightseeing route
Besichtigungssaison, f
Besichtigungszeit, f
♦ sightseeing season
Besichtigungstermin, m
(für Wohnung etc)
♦ appointment to view s.th.
Besichtigungstour, f
→ Besichtigungsreise
Besichtigungstourismus, m
♦ sightseeing tourism
Besichtigungstourist, m
♦ sightseeing tourist
♦ sightseer
Besichtigungsurlaub, m
Besichtigungsferien, pl
♦ sightseeing vacation *AE*
♦ sightseeing holiday *BE*
Besichtigungsurlauber, m
♦ sightseeing vacationer *AE*
♦ sightseeing holidaymaker *BE*
Besichtigungswanderweg, m
Besichtigungsweg, m
♦ sightseeing trail
Besichtigungszeit, f
♦ sightseeing time
Besiedelung des Gebiets, f
♦ occupancy of the area
♦ occupation of the area
Besitz, m
♦ ownership
besitzen etw
♦ own s.th.
♦ possess s.th.
♦ have s.th.
Besitzer, m
♦ owner
♦ proprietor
Besitzer einer Gaststätte, m
Gaststättenbesitzer, m
♦ owner of a public house *BE*
♦ owner of a pub *BE coll*
♦ owner of a bar *AE*
♦ public (house) owner *BE*
♦ bar owner *AE*
Besitzer eines Cafés, m
♦ owner of a café
♦ owner of a cafe *AE*
Besitzer eines Campingplatzes, m
♦ owner of a campsite
♦ owner of a campground *AE*

Besitzer eines Hotels

- ◆ owner of a camping site *BE*
- ◆ owner of a camping ground *BE*

Besitzer eines Hotels, m
Hotelbesitzer, m
Inhaber eines Hotels, m
Hotelinhaber, m
- ◆ owner of a hotel
- ◆ hotel owner

Besitzer eines Motels, m
- ◆ owner of a motel

Besitzer eines Restaurants, m
Restaurantbesitzer, m
- ◆ owner of a restaurant
- ◆ restaurant owner

Besitz ergreifen von einem Zimmer
Zimmer in Besitz nehmen
- ◆ take possession of a room

Besitzerin eines Hotels, f
→ Hotelbesitzerin

Besitzerin eines Motels, f
- ◆ proprietress of a motel

Besitzerin eines Restaurants, f
- ◆ proprietress of a restaurant

Besitzer-Koch, m
- ◆ owner-chef

Besitzer wechseln
- ◆ change owners
- ◆ change hands

Besitzrecht, n
- ◆ ownership right

besoffen, adj *coll*
betrunken, adj
- ◆ sloshed, adj *BE sl*
- ◆ tight, adj *coll*
- ◆ canned, adj *sl*
- ◆ drunk, adj
- ◆ stewed, adj *sl*

besoffen machen jn *coll*
betrunken machen jn
- ◆ get s.o. drunk
- ◆ make s.o. drunk

besoffen sein
- ◆ be boozed (up) *coll*
- ◆ be sloshed *BE sl*
- ◆ be stewed *sl*
- ◆ be plastered *pl*

besondere Annehmlichkeiten, f pl
spezielle Annehmlichkeiten, f pl
- ◆ special amenities *pl*

besondere Atmosphäre, f
spezielle Atmosphäre f
- ◆ special atmosphere

besondere Aussicht, f
- ◆ special view

besonderen Service anbieten
- ◆ offer special service

besonderen Service bieten
- ◆ provide special service

besonderer Anlaß, m
- ◆ special occasion

besonderer Gast, m
- ◆ special guest

besonderes Ereignis, n
Sonderveranstaltung, f
- ◆ special event

besonderes Essen, n
besondere Mahlzeit, f
Sonderessen, n
Spezialessen, n
- ◆ special meal

besondere Vorliebe haben für etw
- ◆ have a special liking for s.th.
- ◆ have a preference for s.th.

Besondere Wünsche können nicht berücksichtigt werden
- ◆ Individual wishes cannot be considered

besonders großes Bett n
- ◆ extra large bed

besonders langes Bett, n
überlanges Bett, n
Bett mit Überlänge, n
- ◆ long boy *AE*
- ◆ long-boy bed *AE*
- ◆ extra long bed

besonders ruhige Lage, f
- ◆ very quiet location
- ◆ very quiet position
- ◆ very quiet situation

besonders ruhiges Zimmer, n
- ◆ very quiet room

besorgt sein um das Wohl eines Gasts
- ◆ take an interest in the welfare of a guest

besprechen etw bei einem Getränk
- ◆ discuss s.th. over a drink

besprechen etw bei einer Flasche Wein
- ◆ discuss s.th. over a bottle of wine

Besprechung, f
- ◆ meeting
- ◆ conference

Besprechung abhalten
- ◆ hold a meeting

Besprechungen führen mit jm
- ◆ hold talks with s.o.

Besprechung findet statt
- ◆ meeting is (being) held

Besprechungssitzung, f
Besprechung, f
- ◆ syndicate session

Besprechungszimmer, n
Besprechungsraum m
- ◆ huddle room *AE sl*
- ◆ syndicate room

bessere Ernährung, f
- ◆ better nutrition

besseren Service benötigen
bessere Leistung verlangen
- ◆ require better service

besseres Hotel, n
gehobenes Hotel, n
- ◆ superior hotel

bessere Tage gesehen haben
- ◆ have seen better days

besser schlafen
- ◆ sleep better

Bestand, m (Vorräte)
- ◆ supply
- ◆ stores *pl*

Bestand, m (Waren)
- ◆ stock
- ◆ stock in hand
- ◆ inventory

Bestand an Hotels, m
Hotelbestand m
- ◆ stock of hotels
- ◆ hotel stock

Bestand an Hotelunterkünften, m
- ◆ stock of hotel accommodations *AE*
- ◆ stock of hotel accommodation *BE*

Bestandsaufnahme, f
- ◆ stocktaking

- ◆ taking an inventory
- ◆ inventory (taking)

Bestandsaufnahme machen
Inventur machen
- ◆ take an inventory *AE*
- ◆ take stock
- ◆ make an inventory

Bestandskontrolle, f (Inventar)
- ◆ inventory control
- ◆ inventory check

Bestandskontrolle, f (Waren)
- ◆ stock control
- ◆ stocktaking

Bestandsposten, m
→ Inventarposten

Bestandsveränderung, f
Inventarveränderung, f
- ◆ change in inventory
- ◆ change in stock

Bestandteil, m (generell)
- ◆ component
- ◆ part
- ◆ constituent part

Bestandteil, m (Merkmal)
→ Merkmal

Bestandteil des Reiseverlaufs, m
Teil des Reiseverlaufs, m
- ◆ part of the itinerary

Bestandteil des Reiseverlaufs sein
Teil des Reiseverlaufs sein
- ◆ be part of the itinerary

bestätigen etw
zusagen etw
- ◆ confirm s.th.

bestätigen etw mündlich
- ◆ confirm s.th. orally
- ◆ confirm s.th. verbally

bestätigen etw unverzüglich
zusagen etw unverzüglich
- ◆ confirm s.th. without delay

bestätigen jm etw
zusagen jm etw
- ◆ confirm s.th. to s.o.

bestätigt, adj
zugesagt, adj
- ◆ confirmed, adj

bestätigte Anmeldung, f
- ◆ confirmed registration

bestätigte Buchung, f
- ◆ confirmed booking

bestätigte Reservierung, f
- ◆ confirmed reservation

bestätigter Preis, m
- ◆ confirmed price
- ◆ confirmed rate

bestätigter Sitzplatz, m
bestätigter Platz, m
bestätigter Sitz, m
- ◆ confirmed seat

bestätigte Stornierung, f
bestätigter Rücktritt, m
bestätigte Absage, f
bestätigte Annullierung, f
- ◆ confirmed cancellation
- ◆ confirmed cancelation *AE*

bestätigtes Zimmer, n
zugesagtes Zimmer n
- ◆ confirmed room

bestätigte Unterkunft, f
zugesagte Unterkunft, f
zugesagte Unterbringung, f

90

♦ confirmed accommodation
♦ confirmed lodging *AE*
Bestätigung, f
Zusage, f
♦ confirmation
Bestätigung ausstellen
♦ issue a confirmation
Bestätigungsformular, n
♦ confirmation form
Bestätigungsnummer, f
♦ confirmation reference number
♦ confirmation number
Bestätigungsschreiben n
♦ letter of confirmation
♦ confirmation letter
♦ letter confirming s.th.
Bestätigungszeitpunkt, m
♦ time of confirmation
Bestätigung verlangen
Bestätigung benötigen
♦ require a confirmation
Bestätigung vornehmen
Zusage machen
bestätigen etw
zusagen etw
♦ make a confirmation
♦ confirm s.th.
Bestätigung wünschen
♦ request a confirmation
Beste, was Küche und Keller bieten, das
♦ best from kitchen and cellar
Beste an Luxus, Komfort und Service bieten, das
♦ offer the ultimate in luxury, comfort and service
Beste an Luxus bieten, das
♦ offer the ultimate in luxury
beste Aussicht, f
bester Ausblick, m
♦ best view
beste Aussicht haben auf etw
♦ have the best view of s.th.
Besteck, n (einzeln)
♦ knife, fork and spoon
♦ set of knife, fork and spoon
Besteck, n (Sammelbegriff)
Eßbesteck, n
♦ cutlery
♦ flatware *AE*
Besteckersatz, m
Ersetzung von Besteck, f
♦ replacement of cutlery
Besteckschrank, m
♦ cutlery cupboard
Besteck spülen
♦ wash up the cutlery
Besteckstück, n
♦ piece of cutlery
Besteck und Geschirr werden gestellt
♦ cutlery and crockery are provided
♦ cutlery and crockery will be provided
beste Empfehlung für ein Restaurant, f
♦ best recommendation for a restaurant
bestehen auf einem Zimmer
♦ insist on a room
bestehen auf einer Anzahlung
♦ insist on a deposit
bestehen auf etw
♦ insist on s.th.
bestehendes Hotel, n
♦ existing hotel

bestehendes Zimmer, n
♦ existing room
bestehende Unterkunft, f
♦ existing accommodation
bestehende Zimmerpreisstrukur, f
♦ existing room rate structure
Besteigung, f
♦ ascent
Besteigung des Matterhorn, f
♦ ascent of the Matterhorn
beste internationale Küche, f
♦ international cuisine of the highest standard
beste internationale Küche anbieten
♦ offer international cuisine of the highest
♦ standard
beste Lage, f
♦ prime location
♦ prime situation
bestellbar, adj
→ buchbar
Bestellblock m
(z.B. im Restaurant)
♦ order pad
Bestelldienst, m
→ Buchungsdienst
bestellen etw
♦ order s.th.
bestellen etw bei dem Kellner
etw bei dem Kellner bestellen
♦ order s.th. from the waiter
♦ place an order with the waiter
bestellen etw telefonisch
telefonisch bestellen etw
♦ order s.th. by telephone
♦ order s.th. by phone
bestellen etw zu essen
etw zu essen bestellen
♦ order s.th. to eat
bestellen etw zum Mittagessen
♦ order s.th. for lunch
bestellen etw zu trinken
etw zu trinken bestellen
♦ order s.th. to drink
bestellen nach der Karte
nach der Karte bestellen
à la carte bestellen
♦ order from the menu
♦ order a la carte *AE*
♦ order à la carte *BE*
Bestellkarte, f
(z.B. für Speisen)
♦ order card
Bestellschein, m (Buchung)
→ Buchungsformular
Bestellschein, m (generell)
♦ docket
bestellter Tisch, m
♦ booked table
♦ reserved table *AE*
bestelltes Zimmer, n
gebuchtes Zimmer, n
♦ room booked
♦ booked room
bestelltes Zimmer stornieren
♦ cancel a booked room
Bestellung, f
♦ order
Bestellung ablehnen
Bestellung zurückweisen
♦ reject an order

Bestellung annehmen
♦ accept an order
Bestellung aufgeben bei dem Kellner
♦ place an order with the waiter
Bestellung aufgeben bei jm
♦ place an order with s.o.
Bestellung aufgeben (für etw)
♦ place an order (for s.th.)
Bestellung aufnehmen für etw
(z.B. im Restaurant)
Bestellung annehmen für etw
♦ take an order for s.th.
Bestellungen aufnehmen
(z.B. im Restaurant)
Bestellungen entgegennehmen
♦ take orders
Bestellungen entgegennehmen
→ Bestellungen aufnehmen
Bestellung entgegennehmen
Bestellung aufnehmen
♦ take an order
Bestellungen werden gerne entgegengenommen
♦ Orders welcome
Bestellung erhalten
(Restaurant)
♦ receive an order
Bestellung machen
♦ give an order
Bestellung notieren
(z.B. im Restaurant)
♦ record an order
Bestellungsänderung, f
→ Buchungsänderung
Bestellungsannahme, f
→ Buchungsannahme
Bestellungsaufnahme f
(z.B. im Restaurant)
♦ taking (of) an order
♦ taking (of) orders
Bestellung verweigern
♦ refuse an order
Bestellung von etw, f
♦ order for s.th.
Bestellung von Wein, f
♦ order for wine
bestens, adv
in idealer Weise, adv
♦ ideally, adv
♦ to the highest standard, adv
bestens geeignet für etw
♦ ideally suited for s.th.
♦ ideal for s.th.
bestens geeignet sein für die Bedürfnisse von jm
♦ be ideally suited to the needs of s.o.
bestens geeignet sein für etw
♦ be ideally suited for s.th.
bestens möbliert, adj
♦ furnished to the highest standard, adj
bester Ort, um sich zu betrinken, m
♦ best place to get drunk
bestes Essen, n
♦ best food
bestes Hotel am Ort, n
♦ best hotel in town
bestes Hotel am Platz, n
♦ best hotel in the place
bestes Hotel in England, n
♦ best hotel in England
bestes Hotel in Paris, n
♦ best hotel in Paris

bestes Preis-/Leistungsverhältnis

bestes Preis-/Leistungsverhältnis, n
♦ best value for money
bestes Restaurant in der Region, n
♦ best restaurant in the region
bestes Zimmer, n
♦ best room
Beste vom Besten, das, n
♦ pick of the bunch, the *inform*
beste Wohnlage, f
♦ prime residential situation
♦ first-class residential situation
♦ first-rate residential situation *coll*
bestgelegen, adj
♦ best-situated, adj
♦ best-located, adj
♦ best-sited, adj
♦ best-positioned, adj
bestgelegenes Hotel, n
♦ best-situated hotel
♦ best-located hotel
♦ best-sited hotel
♦ best-positioned hotel
bestimmte Atmosphäre geben etw
♦ give s.th. a certain atmosphere
bestimmte Atmosphäre verleihen etw
♦ lend s.th. a certain atmosphere
bestimmte Lage einnehmen
♦ occupy a certain position
♦ occupy a certain situation
♦ occupy a certain location
bestimmten Gästekreis anziehen
♦ attract a certain clientele
♦ attract a certain type of clientele
bestimmten Gasttyp ansprechen
(Produktpolitik)
♦ appeal to a certain type of customer
bestimmter Termin, m
bestimmtes Datum, n
♦ specific date
bestimmtes Zimmer wünschen
♦ request a certain room
bestimmt nach X, adv
unterwegs nach X, adv
auf dem Weg nach X, adv
auf dem Flug nach X, adv
♦ bound for X, adv
Bestimmung, f *jur*
Vorschrift, m
♦ provision *jur*
Bestimmungen entsprechen
♦ conform with the regulations
Bestimmungsbahnhof, m
Zielbahnhof, m
♦ station of destination
♦ destination station
Bestimmungsland, n
♦ country of destination
Bestimmungsort, m
Zielort, m
Ziel, n
♦ place of destination
♦ destination
Bestimmungsort erreichen
Zielort erreichen
am Zielort ankommen
♦ reach one's destination
♦ arrive at one's destination
bestmöglichen Service bieten
♦ provide the best possible service
bestmöglicher Service, m
♦ best possible service

bestreuen etw mit etw
♦ sprinkle s.th. with s.th.
bestreuen etw mit Salz
♦ sprinkle s.th. with salt
bestuhlen etw
♦ equip s.th. with seats
Bestuhlung, f
♦ seating
♦ seating arrangement
Bestuhlungsart, f
♦ seating arrangement
Bestuhlungsform, f
♦ seating style
Bestuhlungsplan, m
Sitzplan, m
♦ seating plan
♦ plan of the seating arrangement
Bestuhlungsplan erstellen
♦ make a seating plan
Besuch, m
♦ visit
Besuch abkürzen
♦ cut short a visit
♦ curtail a visit
Besuch absagen
♦ cancel a visit
Besuch abstatten etw
♦ pay a visit to s.th.
♦ make a call at s.th.
♦ pay a call to s.th.
Besuch abstatten (jm)
♦ pay a visit (to s.o.)
♦ make a visit (to s.o.)
♦ pay a call (to s.o.)
Besuch am Rhein, m
♦ visit to the Rhine
Besuch arrangieren (bei etw)
Besuch arrangieren (von etw)
♦ arrange a visit (to s.th.)
Besuch beenden in X mit etw
♦ end a visit to X with s.th.
♦ end one's visit to X with s.th.
Besuch beginnen in X
♦ begin one's visit in X
♦ begin one's visit at X
Besuch bei Bekannten und Verwandten, m
Verwandtschafts- und Freundesbesuch, m
♦ visit to friends and relatives
♦ visiting friends and relatives
♦ VFR
Besuch bei etw, m
Besuch von etw m
♦ visit to s.th.
Besuch bei jm, m
♦ visit to s.o.
Besuch einer Ausstellung, m
Ausstellungsbesuch, m
♦ visit to an exhibition
visit to an exhibit *AE*
♦ exhibition visit
Besuch eines Museums, m
Museumsbesuch, m
♦ visit to a museum
♦ museum visit
Besuch einstellen
Besuche einstellen
♦ stop one's visit
♦ discontinue one's visit
♦ stop one's visits
♦ discontinue one's visits

Besuch empfangen
♦ receive a visit
♦ receive a visitor
♦ receive visitors
Besuche nach 22 Uhr sind untersagt
♦ There are no visitors allowed after 10 p.m.
♦ There are no visitors allowed after 22 hours
Besuch endet am 22. September
♦ visit ends on 22nd September
Besuch endet mit etw
♦ visit ends with s.th.
besuchen etw (ansehen)
♦ visit s.th.
♦ go to s.th.
♦ do s.th. *coll*
♦ call at s.th.
♦ call to see s.th.
besuchen etw auf Einladung von jm
♦ visit s.th. at the invitation of s.o.
besuchen etw kostenlos
♦ visit s.th. free of charge
besuchen etw mit dem Auto
♦ visit s.th. by car
besuchen etw persönlich
♦ visit s.th. in person
besuchen etw regelmäßig (Lokal)
häufig besuchen etw
♦ patronise s.th.
♦ patronize s.th.
♦ frequent s.th.
besuchen etw zum erstenmal
♦ visit s.th. for the first time
besuchen jn
♦ visit s.o.
♦ call on s.o.
besuchen jn gelegentlich
♦ visit s.o. occasionally
Besuchen Sie mich einmal!
♦ Come and see me some time!
Besuchen Sie uns auf Stand 123
(Messe)
♦ Visit us at stand 123
Besuchen Sie X zum ersten Mal?
♦ Is this your first visit to X ?
besuchenswert, adj
♦ worth visiting, adj
♦ worth a visit, adj
♦ well worth visiting, adj
♦ well worth a visit, adj
besuchenswert sein (wegen etw)
Besuch wert sein (wegen etw)
♦ be worth visiting (for s.th.)
♦ be worth a visit (for s.th.)
♦ be well worth visiting (for s.th.)
♦ be well worth a visit (for s.th.)
Besucher, der viel Geld ausgibt, m
♦ high-spending visitor
Besucher, m
Besucherin, f
♦ visitor
♦ guest
Besucher abfertigen
♦ handle visitors
Besucheranalyse, f
♦ visitor analysis
Besucherandrang, m
Besucheransturm m
♦ inrush of visitors
♦ influx of visitors
Besucheranforderung, f
♦ visitor requirement

Besucherankunft, f
(Statistik)
♦ visitor arrival
Besucherankunftszahl, f
♦ visitor arrivals figure
Besucher anlocken
Besucher herbeilocken
♦ lure visitors
Besucheranmeldung, f
♦ registration of a visitor
♦ registration of visitors
♦ registrating a visitor
♦ registrating visitors
Besucheranstieg, m
Besucherzunahme, f
♦ rise in the number of visitors
♦ increase in visitors
Besucheransturm, m
Besucherandrang, m
♦ throng of visitors
♦ large number of visitors
♦ influx of visitors
♦ crowd of visitors
♦ inrush of visitors
Besucheransturm erwarten
♦ expect a large number of visitors
Besucher anziehen
♦ attract visitors
♦ draw visitors
Besucherattraktion, f
♦ visitor attraction
Besucheraufkommen, n
Besuchervolumen, n
♦ volume of visitors
♦ visitor volume
Besucher aufnehmen
→ Besucher empfangen
Besucher aus dem In- und Ausland, m pl
♦ visitors from home and abroad pl
Besucherausgaben, f pl
Ausgaben durch Besucher, f pl
♦ visitor expenses pl
♦ visitor expenditures pl
♦ visitor spending
♦ visitors' spending
Besucherausgabenhöhe, f
♦ level of visitor expenses
♦ level of visitor expenditures
♦ level of visitor spending
Besucherausgaben maximieren
♦ maximise visitor spending
♦ maximize visitor spending
Besucher aus nah und fern, m pl
Besucher von nah und fern, m pl
♦ visitors from far and near pl
Besucher aus nah und fern anziehen
♦ attract visitors from far and wide
♦ draw visitors from far and wide
Besucher außerhalb der Saison, m
♦ out-of-season visitor
Besucher aus Übersee, m
Überseebesucher, m
♦ visitor from overseas
♦ overseas visitor
Besucher aus X stellen das Gros der Gäste
Besucher aus X stellen des Hauptkontingent
♦ visitors from X form the bulk of the clientele
Besucherbedürfnis, n
♦ visitor need
Besucher beeindrucken
♦ impress the visitor

Besucher benötigt ein Visum
♦ visitor requires a visa
Besucherbergwerk, n
♦ visitor mine
♦ visitors' mine
Besucherbett, n
♦ visitor bed
Besucherboom, m
♦ visitor boom
♦ boom of visitors
Besucher bringen
♦ bring visitors
Besucherbuch, n
→ Gästebuch
Besucherbüro, n
♦ visitor bureau
♦ visitors bureau
Besucherdaten, pl
♦ visitor data
♦ visitors' data
♦ visitor details pl
Besucherdelegation, f
♦ visiting delegation
Besucherdienst, m
Besucherservice, m
Besucherbetreuung, f
♦ visitor service
Besucherdruck, m
♦ visitor pressure
Besuchereingang, m
♦ visitor entrance
Besuchereinnahme, f
Besuchereinnahmen, f pl
♦ visitor revenue
♦ visitor revenues pl
Besuchereinrichtung, f
♦ visitor facility
Besucherempfang, m
♦ visitor reception
♦ receiving a visitor
♦ receiving visitors
Besucher empfangen
♦ receive a visitor
♦ receive visitors
Besuchererlebnis, n
♦ visitor experience
♦ visitors' experience
Besucher erwarten (Besuch)
→ Besuch erwarten
Besucher erwarten (Zahl)
123 Besucher erwarten
♦ expect visitors
♦ be expecting visitors
♦ expect 123 visitors
♦ be expecting 123 visitors
Besucherfamilie, f
Gastfamilie, f
♦ visiting family
Besucherflut, f
Besucherschwemme, f
♦ flood of visitors
♦ floodtide of visitors
Besucherfrequenz, f
♦ visitor number
♦ number of visitors
Besucher führen
♦ conduct visitors
Besucher führen durch ein Museum
♦ conduct (the) visitors round a museum
Besucherführer, m
♦ visitors guide

♦ visitor guide
♦ visitor's guide
Besucherführer von X, m
♦ visitors guide to X
Besuchergalerie, f
♦ visitors' gallery
Besuchergeschäft, n
♦ visitor business
Besuchergruppe, f
Besuchsgruppe, f
♦ group of visitors
♦ visitor group
♦ visiting group
Besucher haben
12345 Besucher haben jedes Jahr
♦ have visitors
♦ have 12345 visitors each year
Besuch erhalten von jm
♦ receive a visit from s.o.
♦ be visited by s.o.
Besucherinformation, f
♦ visitor information
Besucherinformationszentrum, n
♦ visitor information center AE
♦ visitors' information center AE
♦ visitor information centre BE
♦ visitors' information centre BE
Besucherkarte f
♦ visitor's card
Besucherkategorie, f
♦ visitor category
♦ category of visitor
Besucher kommen aus aller Welt
♦ visitors come from all over the world
Besucherkontingent, n
♦ visitor quota
Besucherkontingent erhöhen
♦ increase the visitor quota
Besucherliste, f
♦ visitors' list
♦ list of visitors
♦ visitor list
Besucher machen 10 % der Nachfrage aus
♦ visitors account for 10 % of demand
Besuchermagnet, m
♦ magnet for visitors
♦ magnet to visitors
♦ tourist attraction
♦ visitor attraction
Besuchermarkt, m
♦ visitor market
Besucher melden
123 Besucher melden
♦ report visitors
♦ report 123 visitors
Besucher mit hohem Einkommen, m
Besucher mit einem hohen Einkommen, m
♦ high-income visitor
Besuchermix, m
♦ visitor mix
Besucherparkplatz, m
Gästeparkplatz m
♦ visitors' parking lot AE
♦ visitors' car park BE
Besucherpotential, n
♦ visitor potential
Besucherprofil, n
♦ visitor profile
Besucherregistrierung, f
→ Besucheranmeldung

93 **Besucherregistrierung**

Besucherrekord

Besucherrekord, m (Teilnahme)
→ Rekordbesuch
Besucherrekord, m (Zahl)
♦ record number of visitors
Besucherrekord erwarten
♦ expect a record number of visitors
♦ anticipate a record number of visitors
Besucherrekord verzeichnen
♦ report an attendance record
Besucherrückgang, m (Teilnahme)
♦ decline in attendance
♦ decrease in attendance
♦ fall in attendance
♦ drop in attendance
Besucherrückgang, m (Zahl)
♦ decline in the number of visitors
♦ decrease in the number of visitors
♦ fall in the number of visitors
♦ drop in the number of visitors
Besuchersegment, n
♦ visitor segment
Besucherstatistik, f
♦ visitor statistics pl
Besuchersteuer, f
♦ visitor tax
Besucherstrecke, f
Besucherroute, f
♦ visitor route
Besucherstrom, m
♦ flow of visitors
♦ stream of visitors
♦ visitor flow
Besucherterrasse, f
♦ visitor terrace
♦ visitors' terrace
Besuchertisch, m
♦ visitors' table
♦ visitor's table
Besuchertrakt, m
♦ visitor wing
♦ visitors' wing
Besucherübernachtung, f
(Statistik)
♦ visitor night
Besucher überwachen
♦ monitor visitors
Besucherumfrage, f
♦ visitor survey
♦ survey of visitors
Besucher und Einheimische, m pl
♦ visitors and residents pl
Besucherunterkunft, f
Besucherunterbringung, f
♦ visitor accommodation
Besucherunterstützung, f
♦ visitor assistance
Besucherverkehr, m
♦ visitor traffic
♦ traffic of visitors
Besucher verteilen
♦ disperse visitors
Besuchervisum, n
Besuchsvisum n
♦ visitor visa
♦ visa to visit (a country)
♦ visitor's visa
Besucher von allen Gegenden des Globus, m pl
♦ visitors from around the globe pl
Besuch erwarten
Besucher erwarten

♦ expect a visitor
♦ expect visitors
Besucher werden erwartet
1234 Besucher werden erwartet
♦ visitors are expected
♦ 1234 visitors are expected
Besucher willkommen heißen
Besucher begrüßen
♦ welcome a visitor
♦ welcome visitors
Besucherzahl, f (generell)
Zahl der Besucher, f
♦ number of visitors
♦ visitor number
Besucherzahl, f (Teilnehmer)
Teilnehmerzahl, f
♦ attendance
Besucherzahlanstieg, m
♦ increase in the number of visitors
Besucherzahlen, f pl (generell)
♦ visitor figures pl
♦ visitor numbers pl
Besucherzahlen, f pl (Teilnehmer)
♦ attendances pl
Besucherzahlen fallen (um 100 von 800 auf 700)
♦ attendances fall (by 100 from 800 to 700)
♦ visitor numbers fall (by 100 from 800 to 700)
Besucherzahlen gehen zurück (um 10 von 100 auf 90)
♦ attendances drop (by 10 from 100 to 90)
Besucherzahlen haben um 500 abgenommen (Teilnehmer)
♦ attendances (have) decreased by 500
Besucherzahlen machten insgesamt 50.000 aus (Teilnehmerzahlen)
♦ attendances totaled 50,000 AE
♦ attendances totalled 50,000 BE
Besucherzahlen nehmen ab (um 100 von 1000 auf 900)
♦ attendances decrease (by 100 from 1000 to 900)
Besucherzahlen sind ständig gestiegen
♦ visitor numbers have been rising steadily
Besucherzahlen sind um 200 gefallen
♦ attendances have fallen by 200
♦ attendances fell by 200
Besucherzahlen sind um 300 zurückgegangen
♦ attendances (have) dropped by 300
Besucherzahlen veröffentlichen
♦ publish visitor figures
Besucherzahl erhöhen
Besucherzahlen erhöhen
♦ increase the number of visitors
♦ increase visitor figures
Besucherzahl fällt
♦ number of visitors is decreasing
Besucherzahl halten
♦ maintain the number of visitors
Besucherzahl hochtreiben
♦ boost the number of visitors
Besucherzahl ist zurückgegangen um 12 %
♦ number of visitors has declined by 12 %
Besucherzahl steigern um 10 %
♦ increase the number of visitors by 10 %
Besucherzahl übertrifft alle Rekorde
♦ number of visitors exceeds all records
Besucherzentrum, n
♦ visitor center AE
♦ visitors center AE
♦ visitor centre BE
♦ visitors centre BE

Besucherziel, n
♦ visitor destination
Besucherzimmer, n (in Gefängnis)
♦ visitors' room
Besucherzimmer, n (in Heim)
♦ reception room
Besucherzimmer, n (in Privathaus)
♦ drawing room
Besucherzufriedenheit, f
♦ visitor satisfaction
Besucherzunahme, f
Besucheranstieg, m
♦ increase in visitors
Besucherzustrom, m
Besucherandrang, m
♦ influx of visitors
Besuch genießen
♦ enjoy one's visit
♦ enjoy a visit
Besuch gern entgegensehen von jm
js Besuch gern entgegensehen
♦ look forward to s.o.'s visit
Besuch haben
♦ have a visitor
♦ have visitors
Besuch haben von jm
→ besucht werden von jm
Besuch im Freibad, m
Freibadbesuch, m
♦ visit to the outdoor pool
Besuch in einem Club, m
Besuch in einem Verein, m
Clubbesuch, m
Vereinsbesuch, m
♦ visit to a club
♦ club visit
Besuch in einem Hotel, m
♦ visit to a hotel
♦ visiting a hotel
Besuch in einem Restaurant, m
♦ visit to a restaurant
♦ visiting a restaurant
Besuch in X lohnenswert machen
♦ make a visit to X worthwhile
Besuch in X verbinden mit etw
♦ combine a visit to X with s.th.
Besuch ist fakultativ
♦ visit is optional
Besuch ist nicht komplett ohne ...
♦ visit is not complete without ...
Besuch ist obligatorisch
Besuch ist Pflicht
♦ visit is obligatory
Besuch kurzfristig absagen
♦ cancel a visit at short notice
♦ call off a visit at short notice
Besuch lohnenswert machen
♦ make a visit worthwhile
Besuch machen bei etw
♦ make a visit to s.th.
Besuch machen bei jm
(kurz)
♦ make a call on s.o.
♦ call at s.o.'s house
Besuch machen in einem Hotel
(kurz)
♦ make a call at a hotel
Besuch machen in England
♦ make a visit to England
Besuch machen in X
♦ make a visit to X

Besuch mit Führung, m
 ♦ conducted visit
Besuch mit Unterkunft, m
 Besuch mit Unterbringung, m
 ♦ residential visit
Besuch möglich machen
 ♦ make a visit possible
Besuch planen
 ♦ plan a visit
Besuchsdauer, f
 ♦ duration of a visit
Besuchsgrund, m
 Grund, um etw zu besuchen, m
 Grund, um jn zu besuchen, m
 ♦ reason for visiting s.th.
 ♦ reason for visiting s.o.
Besuchsland, n (bereist besucht)
 → besuchtes Land
Besuchsland, n (zukünftig)
 ♦ country to visit
Besuchsplanung, f
 Besuchsgestaltung, f
 ♦ planning (of) a visit
 ♦ planning (of) visits
Besuchsprogramm, n
 ♦ program of visits AE
 ♦ programme of visits BE
Besuchsprogramm bei etw, n
 Besuchsprogramm von etw, n
 ♦ program of visits to s.th. AE
 ♦ programme of visits to s.th. BE
Besuchsreihe, f
 ♦ series of visits
Besuchszahl, f
 → Zahl der Besuche
Besuchszeit, f
 (z.B. in Krankenhaus)
 ♦ visiting hours pl
Besuchszweck, m
 ♦ purpose of visit
 ♦ purpose of one's visit
besucht, adj (generell)
 ♦ visited, adj
besucht, adj (Lokal)
 ♦ patronised, adj
 ♦ patronized, adj
 ♦ frequented, adj
besucht, adj (Veranstaltung)
 ♦ attended, adj
Besucht endet (mit etw)
 ♦ visit ends (with s.th.)
besuchtes Land, n
 Besuchsland, n
 ♦ country visited
besucht werden von jm (Lokal)
 ♦ be patronised by s.o.
 ♦ be patronized by s.o.
 ♦ be frequented by s.o.
besucht werden von jm (privat)
 Besuch haben von jm
 ♦ have a visit from s.o.
besucht werden von jm (Veranstaltung)
 ♦ be attended by s.o.
Besuch verbinden mit etw
 ♦ combine a visit with s.th.
Besuch verderben
 ♦ spoil s.o.'s visit
 ♦ spoil one's visit
Besuch verlängern
 ♦ extend a visit

 ♦ extend one's visit
 ♦ prolong a visit
Besuch verlängern um eine Woche
 ♦ extend a visit by one week
 ♦ extend one's visit by one week
 ♦ prolong a visit by one week
 ♦ prolong one's visit by one week
Besuch verlängern um einige Tage
 ♦ extend a visit by a few days
 ♦ extend one's visit by a few days
 ♦ prolong a visit by a few days
 ♦ prolong one's visit by a few days
Besuch versäumen von etw
 ♦ miss a visit to s.th.
Besuch verschieben
 ♦ postpone a visit
 ♦ put off a visit
Besuch verschieben auf unbestimmte Zeit
 ♦ postpone a visit indefinitely
Besuch verschieben bis auf weiteres
 ♦ postpone a visit until further notice
Besuch von etw, m
 ♦ visit to s.th.
Besuch von jm, m
 ♦ visit by s.o.
 ♦ visit from s.o.
Besuch von X gehört unbedingt dazu
 ♦ visit to X is a must
Besuch vorverlegen
 ♦ advance a visit
 ♦ advance one's visit
Besuch wert sein
 besuchenswert sein
 ♦ be worth a visit
 ♦ be worth the visit
 ♦ be well worth a visit
 ♦ be well worth visiting
Besuch wiederholen
 wiederkommen
 ♦ repeat a visit
 ♦ call again
 ♦ come again
betagter Gast, m
 älterer Gast, m
 ♦ elderly guest
Betätigung im Freien, f
 Veranstaltung im Freien, f
 ♦ outdoor activity
beteiligt sein an einem Programm
 ♦ be involved in a program AE
 ♦ be involved in a programme BE
Beteiligung (an etw), f ökon
 ♦ interest (in s.th.) ökon
 ♦ stake (in s.th.) ökon
Betischung, f
 ♦ equipping s.th. with tables
Betischungsplan, m
 → Tischplan
Betonbettenburg, f derog
 ♦ concrete skyscraper hotel BE
Betonburg, n
 → Betonbettenburg
Betongebäude, n
 Betonbau, m
 ♦ concrete building
Betonstellplatz, m
 (Camping)
 ♦ concrete pitch
Betonstrand, m
 ♦ concrete beach

Betonstraße, f
 ♦ concrete road
 ♦ concrete street
Betontennisplatz, m
 ♦ concrete tennis court
Betonung liegt auf dem gesunden Essen
 ♦ emphasis is on healthy eating
Betonung liegt auf der Gastlichkeit
 ♦ emphasis is on hospitality
Betrag, m
 ♦ amount
Betrag in Rechnung stellen jm
 ♦ charge an amount to s.o.
Betrag in Zahlen, m
 ♦ amount in figures
Betrag pro Gedeck, m
 Rechnungsbetrag pro Gedeck, m
 ♦ amount per cover
Betrag zahlen
 ♦ pay an amount
 ♦ pay a sum
betreffend, adj
 entsprechend, adj
 passend, adj
 angemessen, adj
 ♦ appropriate, adj
betreiben etw (Firma)
 ♦ operate s.th.
 ♦ run s.th.
Betreiber einer Appartementanlage, m
 ♦ operator of an apartment complex
Betreiber einer Sehenswürdigkeit, m
 ♦ operator of an attraction
 ♦ attraction operator
Betreiber eines Campingplatzes, m
 ♦ operator of a campsite
 ♦ operator of a campground AE
 ♦ operator of a camping site BE
 ♦ operator of a camping ground BE
Betreiberfirma, f
 ♦ operating firm
 ♦ operating company
Betreiber m
 ♦ operator
betreuen jn
 ♦ look after s.o.
 ♦ take care of s.o.
 ♦ attend to s.o.
 ♦ cater for s.o.
Betreuer, m
 ♦ person looking after s.o.
 ♦ person looking after s.th.
 ♦ person in charge
Betreuung, f
 ♦ care
 ♦ attention
 ♦ looking after s.o.
 ♦ taking care of s.o.
 ♦ assistance
Betreuung bei dem Einchecken, f
 Hilfe bei der Anmeldung, f
 ♦ assistance with check-in
Betreuung von jm, f
 ♦ service provided to s.o.
 ♦ services provided to s.o.
Betrieb, m
 ♦ establishment
 ♦ operation
Betrieb aufnehmen
 Dienst aufnehmen
 ♦ start a service

Betrieb besitzen

Betrieb besitzen
♦ own an establishment
Betrieb betreiben
   Betrieb unterhalten
   Betrieb bewirtschaften
♦ operate an establishment
Betrieb bleibt geöffnet
♦ establishment remains open
Betrieb bleibt geschlossen
♦ establishment remains closed
Betrieb führen
♦ run an establishment
Betrieb ist aufgenommen worden
♦ services are operating
Betrieb leiten
♦ manage an establishment
betriebliche Aufwendungen, f pl
   Betriebsaufwand, m
♦ operating expenses *pl*
betrieblicher Lehrgang, m
   innerbetrieblicher Kurs, m
♦ in-service course
betriebliche Schulung, f
(innerhalb der Arbeitszeit/des Betriebs)
♦ in-service training
♦ in-plant training
Betrieb mit neun oder mehr Betten, m
♦ establishment with nine or more beds
♦ operation with nine or more beds
Betrieb mit Schankerlaubnis, m
(für alkoholische Getränke)
♦ licensed establishment
♦ licenced establishment
♦ licensed premises *pl*
♦ licenced premises *pl*
Betrieb ohne Schankerlaubnis, m
(für alkoholische Getränke)
♦ unlicensed establishment
♦ unlicenced establishment
♦ unlicensed premises *pl*
♦ unlicenced premises *pl*
Betriebsabrechnungsbogen, m
   BAB m
♦ departmental cost distribution summary
Betriebsabteilung, f (Firma)
♦ department of a firm
♦ operated department
Betriebsabteilung, f (generell)
♦ operational department
betriebsame Atmosphäre, f
   geschäftige Atmosphäre f
♦ businesslike atmosphere
♦ business atmosphere
Betriebsanleitung, f
   Betriebsanweisung f
♦ operation manual
Betriebsaufwand, m
   betrieblicher Aufwand, m
♦ operating expense *AE*
♦ operating expenditure
Betriebsausflug, m
♦ office outing
♦ business outing
♦ company outing
Betriebsbesichtigung, f (Fabrik)
   Rundgang durch die Fabrik, m
♦ tour of the factory
♦ tour of the plant
Betriebsbewilligung, f
→ Betriebserlaubnis

Betriebscatering, n
   Belieferung von Betriebskantinen, f
♦ industrial catering *AE*
♦ industrial contract foodservice *AE*
♦ industrial contract catering *BE*
Betrieb schließen
♦ close an establishment
Betriebseinnahme, f
   Betriebseinnahmen, f pl
♦ operating income
Betriebserfahrung, f
♦ operating experience
Betriebsergebnis, n (generell)
♦ operating result
Betriebsergebnis I, n
(Betriebsumsatz minus betriebsbedingte Kosten)
   Bruttobetriebsergebnis, n
   Bruttobetriebsgewinn, n
♦ gross operating profit *AE*
♦ GOP
♦ hotel operating profit
♦ gross profit
Betriebsergebnis II, n
(Betriebsergebnis I minus anlagebedingte Kosten)
   Nettobetriebsergebnis n
   Nettobetriebsgewinn m
♦ net operating profit
♦ NOP
♦ net profit
Betriebsergebnisrechnung, f
♦ operating statement
Betriebsergebnis vor Abschreibung, n
♦ profit before depreciation
Betriebsergebnis vor Zinsen, n
♦ profit before interest
Betriebsergebnis vor Zinsen und Abschreibung, n
♦ profit before interest and depreciation
Betriebserlaubnis, f
   Betriebsbewilligung, f
♦ business permit
Betriebserlös, m
♦ operating revenue
Betriebsferien
(Hinweisschild)
♦ Closed for vacation *AE*
♦ Closed for holidays *BE*
Betriebsferien, pl
♦ staff vacation *AE*
♦ staff holiday *BE*
Betriebsfest, n (des Personals)
♦ staff party
♦ office party
Betriebsfest, n (Fabrik)
(jährlich)
♦ annual works holiday *BE*
Betriebsführungsvereinbarung, f
♦ operating agreement
♦ management agreement
♦ operating arrangement
Betriebsgastronomie, f
→ Betriebsverpflegung
Betriebsgesellschaft, f
♦ operating company
♦ management company
Betriebsgewinn, m
♦ operating profit
Betriebsinhaber, m
♦ owner of an establishment

Betriebsjahr n
♦ operating year
♦ year of operation
Betriebskantine, f
♦ office canteen
♦ works canteen
♦ industrial staff canteen
Betriebskantinenverpflegung, f
   Betriebskantinenwesen, n
   Betriebsverpflegung, f
   betriebliche Verpflegung, f
♦ industrial catering *BE*
♦ industrial foodservice *AE*
Betriebskapital, n
   investiertes Kapital n
♦ capital employed
♦ operating capital
Betriebskonzession, f
   Betriebserlaubnis, f
♦ operation licence
♦ operation license
Betriebskosten, pl
♦ operating costs *pl*
♦ operating cost
♦ costs of operation *pl*
♦ cost of operation
Betriebskosten decken
♦ cover (the) operating costs
Betriebskosten pro Zimmer, pl
♦ operating costs per room *pl*
♦ operating cost per room
Betriebsmittel, n
♦ operating equipment
Betriebsmonat m
♦ operating month
♦ month of operation
Betriebspersonal, n
♦ operating staff
♦ operating personnel
Betriebspolitik, f
♦ operating policy
Betriebsrestaurant, n
♦ ticket restaurant
♦ staff restaurant
Betriebsrestaurantleiter, m
♦ staff restaurant manager
♦ ticket restaurant manager
Betriebssaison f
♦ operating season
Betriebsstatistik, f
♦ operating statistics *pl*
Betriebsstunde f
♦ operating hour
♦ hour of operation
Betriebstag m
♦ operating day
♦ day of operation
Betriebstyp, m
♦ establishment type
♦ type of establishment
♦ type of operation
Betriebsvergleich, m
♦ intercompany comparison
Betriebsverlust, m
♦ operating loss
Betriebsvermögen, n
♦ operating assets *pl*
Betriebsverpflegung, f
   betriebliche Verpflegung, f
   Betriebsgastronomie, f

♦ industrial foodservice *AE*
♦ industrial catering *BE*
Betriebsvoranschlag, m
Budget der betrieblichen Aufwendungen und Erträge, n
♦ **operating budget**
Betriebswirt, m
♦ **business administrator**
Betriebswoche f
♦ **operating week**
♦ week of operation
Betriebszeit, f
♦ **operating time**
♦ operating period
Betriebszeitraum, m
Betriebszeit, f
♦ **operating period**
♦ operation period
♦ period of operation
Betrieb wieder aufnehmen
♦ **resume operation**
betrinken sich
♦ **get drunk**
betrinken wollen sich
sich betrinken wollen
♦ **want to get drunk**
betrügen jn
♦ **defraud s.o.**
Betrüger, m
♦ **swindler**
♦ cheat
♦ trickster
Betrugswirt, m *derog*
→ Betriebswirt
Betrugswirtschaft, f *derog*
→ Betriebswirtschaft
betrunken, adj
♦ **drunk, adj**
♦ intoxicated, adj
Betrunkener, m
♦ **drunken person**
♦ drunk
betrunkener Fahrer, m
♦ **drunken driver**
betrunkener Mann, m
♦ **drunken man**
betrunken machen jn
♦ **make s.o. drunk**
♦ get s.o. drunk
betrunken sein
Rausch haben
♦ **be drunk**
Bett, n
♦ **bed**
Bettablett, n
Bett-Tablett, n
♦ **bed tray**
Bett abziehen
♦ **strip a bed**
Bettart f
♦ **bed type**
♦ type of bed
Bett aufdecken
♦ **turn down the bed**
Bett aufstellen
♦ **set up a bed**
Bett bereitstellen
Bett zur Verfügung stellen
♦ **provide a bed**
♦ supply a bed

Bett bereitstellen für jn
♦ **provide s.o. with a bed**
♦ supply a bed to s.o.
Bett beziehen
Bett frisch beziehen
♦ **change a bed**
♦ put clean sheets on a bed
Bettbezüge, m pl
♦ **bedclothes** *pl*
Bett bieten für die Nacht
Bett bereitstellen für die Nacht
♦ **provide a bed for the night**
♦ supply a bed for the night
Bett bleibt frei
♦ **bed remains vacant**
Bett bleibt leer
♦ **bed remains empty**
Bettchen n
♦ **bedlet**
♦ small bed
♦ cot *BE*
Bettcouch, f
♦ **couch bed**
♦ sofa-bed
♦ bed-settee *BE*
♦ studio couch
♦ put-you-up *BE*
Bettenabbau, m
Bettenreduzierung f
♦ **reduction of the number of beds**
♦ reducing the number of beds
Bettenanbieter, m
♦ **supplier of beds**
Bettenangebot, n (Gegensatz zu Nachfrage)
♦ **bed supply**
♦ supply of beds
Bettenangebot, n (Palette)
♦ **range of beds**
Bettenanordnung f
♦ **bed arrangement**
♦ arrangement of (the) beds
Bettenart f
→ s. Bettart
Bettenauslastung, f
Bettenbelegung f
♦ **bed occupancy**
♦ sleeper occupancy
♦ guest occupancy
Bettenauslastung in Prozent pro Jahr, f
♦ **percentage bed occupancy per year**
Bettenauslastungsquote, f
Bettenbelegungsquote f
♦ **bed occupancy rate**
→ Bettenauslastungsquote
Bettenauslastungsrückgang, m
Rückgang der Bettenauslastung, m
♦ **drop in bed occupancy**
♦ fall in bed occupancy
♦ decrease in bed occupancy
Bettenauslastungszahl, f
Bettenbelegungszahl, f
♦ **bed occupancy figure**
Bettenauslastungszuwachs m
Bettenauslastungsanstieg m
♦ **increase in bed occupancy**
Bettenbelegung, f
→ Bettenauslastung
Bettenbelegungskurve, f
♦ **bed occupancy graph**

Bettenbelegungsliste, f
Bettenbelegungsverzeichnis, n
♦ **bed occupancy list**
♦ sleepers' list
Bettenbelegungsliste erstellen
♦ **compile a bed occupany list**
♦ compile a sleepers' list
Bettenbesetzung, f *SCHW*
→ Bettenauslastung
Bettenbestand, m
→ Bettenzahl
Betten bieten
123 Betten bieten
♦ **provide beds**
♦ provide 123 beds
Bettenboom, m
♦ **bed boom**
Bettenbörse, f
→ Zimmernachweis
Bettenbuchung, f
♦ **bed booking**
♦ booking (of) a bed
Bettenburg, f *derog*
♦ **skyscraper hotel**
Bettenfrequenz, f
→ Bettenbelegung
Bettengeschoß, n
→ Schlafraumetage
Bettenhaus, n
→ Schlafhaus
Betten in Reserve halten
♦ **hold beds in reserve**
betten jn weich
♦ **make s.o. a soft bed**
Bettenkapazität, f
♦ **bed capacity**
Bettenkapazität erhöhen
♦ **increase the bed capacity**
Bettenkapazitätserweiterung, f
♦ **bed capacity expansion**
Bettenkapazität verringern
♦ **reduce the bed capacity**
Bettenknappheit, f
♦ **bed shortage**
♦ shortage of beds
Bettenknappheit verursachen
♦ **cause a shortage of beds**
Bettenkontingent, n
♦ **bed quota**
♦ quota of beds
♦ allocation of beds
♦ number of beds available to s.o.
♦ bed space allocated to s.o.
Bettenkontingent buchen
Bettenkontingent bestellen
♦ **book a quota of beds**
♦ book an allocation of beds
♦ book an allotment of beds
Bettenkontingent kaufen
♦ **buy a quota of beds**
♦ buy an allocation of beds
♦ buy an allotment of beds
Bettenkontingent reduzieren
♦ **reduce the bed quota**
Bettenkontingent reservieren
♦ **reserve a quota of beds**
♦ reserve an allocation of beds
♦ reserve an allotment of beds
Bettenkontrolle, f
(Kontrolle der anwesenden Schläfer)
♦ **bed check**

Betten machen

Betten machen
- make the beds

Bettenmachen, n
- bed making

Bettenmangel, m (Knappheit)
→ Bettenknappheit

Bettenmangel, m (völliges Fehlen)
- lack of beds

Bettennot, f
→ Bettenmangel, Bettenknappheit

Bettenreservierung, f
- bed reservation
- reservation of a bed
- reservation of beds
- reserving a bed
- reserving beds

Betten richten für die Gäste
- get the beds ready for the guests
- make the beds ready for the guests

Betten sind knapp
- beds are in short supply
- beds are scarce

Betten sind Mangelware
- there is a shortage of beds

Bettensteuer, f
Bettenabgabe, f
- bed tax

Bettentrakt, m
→ Schlafraumtrakt

Bettenüberangebot, n
- surplus of beds
- oversupply of beds

Bettenüberhang, m
überschüssige Betten, n pl
überzählige Betten, n pl
- surplus beds pl
- oversupply of beds
- surplus of beds

Betten verfügbar haben
- have beds available

Bettenverkauf, m
- sale of a bed
- sale of beds
- selling a bed
- selling beds

Bettenvermittlung, f
- bed-booking service

Bettenzahl, f
- number of beds

Bettenzahlanstieg, m
Bettenzahlzuwachs, m
- increase in the number of beds

Bettenzahl erhöhen
- increase the number of beds

Betten zurückhalten
Betten nicht anbieten
Betten in Reserve halten
- hedge beds BE
- hold beds in reserve

Bettenzuwachs, m
Bettenanstieg, m
- increase in beds

Bettfeder, f
(Matratze)
- bedspring

Bett finden
- find a bed

Bettflasche, f
Wärmflasche f
- hot-water bottle

Bett frisch beziehen
Bett beziehen
- put clean sheets on a bed
- change a bed

Bett füllen
Betten füllen
- fill a bed
- fill (the) beds

Bett für die Nacht (her)richten
- make up a bed for the night

Bettgenosse m
Schlafkamerad m
- bedfellow

Bettgestell, n
- bedstead

Bettgetränk, n
Schlafgetränk, n
- bedtime drink

Bettgröße f
- bedsize
- size of a bed

Bett hat Übergröße
- bed is extra-long

Betthimmel, m
- canopy
- testers obsol

Betthupfer, m
Betthupferl, n
- bedtime candy AE
- bedtime sweets BE pl

Betthüpferl, n
Betthupfer, m
- chocolate on one's pillow
- bedtime treat

Bett hüten
- keep one's bed

Bett in Anspruch nehmen
Bett beanspruchen
- claim a bed
- occupy a bed

Bett ist 1,5 m breit und 2 m lang
- bed is 1.5m wide and 2m long

Bett ist belegt
- bed is occupied

Bett ist breit
- bed is wide

Bett ist frei
- bed is vacant

Bett ist komfortabel
Bett ist bequem
- bed is comfortable

Bett ist leer
- bed is empty

Bett ist monumental
- bed is monumental

Bett ist nicht gemacht worden
- bed has not been made

Bett ist schmal
- bed is narrow

Bettkamerad, m
- bedmate

Bettkante, f
Bettrand, m
- edge of the bed

Bettkasten, m
- bedding box
- bedding drawer
- ottoman

Bettkissen, n
→ Kopfkissen

Bett klappt in die Wand zurück
- bed folds away into the wall

Bettkopfende, n
Kopfende des Bettes, n
- bedhead

bettlägerig, adj
- bedridden, adj

Bettlaken, n
Bettuch n
- bed sheet
- sheet

Bettlaken glattziehen
- tug a sheet smooth AE
- draw a sheet smooth

Bettlaken wechseln
- change the sheets

Bett läßt sich zurückklappen
Bett klappt zurück
- bed folds away

Bettleiter, f
(z.B. für Etagenbett)
- bed steps pl

Bettlektüre, f
- bedtime reading
- bedside reading
- bedside book

Bettleuchte, f
- bedside light

Bettliege, f
- lounger bed AE
- divan bed
- convertible divan

bettlos, adj
- bedless, adj
- without a bed

Bett lüften
- air a bed

Bett machen
- make the bed
- make a bed

Bett mieten
- rent a bed AE
- hire a bed BE

Bett mißt 2 m mal 1,5 m
- bed measures 2m by 1.5m

Bett mit Federmatratze, n
- feather bed

Bett mit Überlänge n
- extra long bed

Bettnacht, f
(Statistik)
- bed-night

Bettnachtangebot, n
- bed-night supply

Bettnachtkapazität, f
- bed-night capacity

Bettnachtnachfrage, f
- bed-night demand

Bettnachtstatistik, f
- bed-night statistics pl
- statistics of bed-nights pl

Bettnachtzahl, f
- bed-night figure

Bett nässen
ins Bett nässen
- wet the bed
- wet one's bed

Bettnässen, n
- bed-wetting

Bettnässer, m
♦ bed wetter *AE*
♦ bed-wetter *BE*
Bett naßmachen
→ Bett nässen
Bettpfanne, f
(zum Bettwärmen, mit Stiel)
♦ warming pan *AE*
♦ warming-pan *BE*
♦ bed warmer *AE*
Bettpfosten m
♦ bed post
Bettplatz, m
(Statistik)
♦ bedspace
Bettplatzauslastung, f
Bettplatzauslastung, f
♦ bedspace occupancy
Bettplatzkapazität, f
♦ bedspace capacity
Bett quietscht
♦ bed squeaks
Bettrahmen, m
♦ bed frame
Bettrost, m
Matratzenrost, m
♦ mattress frame *BE*
♦ mattressboard *AE*
Bettruhe, f
(bei Krankheiten)
♦ bed rest
Bettruhe verordnen jm
♦ order s.o. to stay in bed
Bettseite, f
Seite des Bettes, f
♦ bedside
Bettsofa, n
Sofabett, n
♦ sofa-bed
♦ duplex bed *AE*
♦ put-you-up *BE*
♦ put-u-up *BE coll*
♦ settee-bed *BE*
Bett steht zur Verfügung
♦ bed is available
Bett suchen
♦ look for a bed
Bett teilen mit jm
♦ share a bed with s.o.
Bett überziehen
♦ change bed linen
♦ change linen
♦ change sheets
Bettuch n
→ Bettlaken
Bettuch straffen
♦ tighten a sheet
♦ pull a sheet tight
Bett und Bettzeug, n
♦ bed and bedding
Bett unter Vertrag nehmen
Betten unter Vertrag nehmen
♦ contract a bed
♦ contract beds
Bett verkaufen
Betten verkaufen
♦ sell a bed
♦ sell beds
Bett verlängern
(wegen Übergröße)

♦ extend a bed
♦ lenghten a bed
Bettverlängerung, f
♦ extension of a bed
♦ extending a bed
♦ lengthening a bed
Bett vermieten
♦ rent (out) a bed
♦ let a bed *BE*
♦ hire out a bed *BE*
Bettvorleger, m
Bettvorlage, f
♦ bedside rug
Bettwäsche, f
♦ bed linen
Bettwäsche kann gegen Aufpreis ausgeliehen werden
♦ Bed linen can be rented at an extra charge *AE*
♦ Bed linen can be hired at an extra charge *BE*
Bettwäsche kann gegen Gebühr gemietet werden
Bettwäsche kann gegen Gebühr geliehen werden
♦ Bed linen can be rented at a charge *AE*
♦ Bed linen can be hired at a charge *BE*
Bettwäsche mieten
♦ rent bed linen *AE*
♦ hire bed linen *BE*
Bettwäsche mitbringen
→ eigene Bettwäsche mitbringen
Bettwäsche steht zur Verfügung
♦ bed linen is available
Bettwäsche stellen
♦ provide bed linen
Bettwäsche und Handtücher werden kostenlos zur
Verfügung gestellt
♦ Bed linen and towels are provided free of charge
Bettwäsche vermieten
→ Bettwäsche verleihen
Bettwäsche vermieten
Bettwäsche verleihen
♦ rent (out) bed linen
♦ hire out bed linen *BE*
Bettwäschevermietung, f
♦ renting (of) bed linen *AE*
♦ hiring out (of) bed linen *BE*
Bettwäschewechsel, m
Wechsel der Bettwäsche, m
♦ change of bed linen
Bettwäsche wechseln
♦ change the bed linen
Bettwäsche wird gestellt
♦ Bed linen will be provided
♦ Be linen is provided
Bettwäsche wird nicht gestellt
♦ Bed linen will not be provided
♦ Bed linen is not provided
Bettwäsche wird während der Aufenthaltsdauer
kostenlos gestellt
♦ Bed linen is provided free of charge during the
duration of stay
Bettzeug, n
♦ bedding
Bettzeug wird gestellt
♦ bedding is supplied
♦ bedding is provided
Bettzeug wird gestellt, jedoch keine Bettwäsche
♦ bedding is provided, but no linen
♦ beeding is supplied, but no linen

Bett zur Verfügung stellen
Bett stellen
♦ supply a bed
♦ provide a bed
Bett zuteilen jm
Bett zuweisen jm
Bett vergeben an jn
♦ allocate a bed to s.o.
betuppen jn *sl*
betrügen jn
übers Ohr hauen jn
♦ cheat s.o.
♦ take advantage of s.o.
beurlauben jn (Beamter)
in Urlaub schicken jn
beurlauben jn
♦ furlough s.o.
Beurlaubung, f (Arbeitnehmer)
♦ leave of absence
Beurlaubung verweigern jm (Arbeitnehmer)
♦ refuse s.o. leave of absence
Beurteilungsformular, n
(wird von Gast ausgefüllt)
♦ complaints/satisfaction form
Bevollmächtigter, m *jur*
♦ agent *jur*
bevorstehende Konferenz, f
♦ forthcoming conference
bevorstehendes Ereignis, n
bevorstehende Veranstaltung, f
♦ forthcoming event
Bevorzugen Sie eine bestimmte Aussicht?
♦ Do you prefer any particular view?
bevorzugte Lage, f
privilegierte Lage, f
Vorzugslage, f
♦ privileged position
♦ privileged location
♦ preferred location
♦ favored position *AE*
♦ favoured position *BE*
bevorzugte Lage genießen
♦ enjoy a privileged position
♦ enjoy a privileged location
♦ enjoy a privileged situation
bevorzugte Route, f
bevorzugte Strecke, f
♦ preferred route
bevorzugter Zielort, m
bevorzugtes Ziel, n
♦ preferred destination
bevorzugte Wohnlage, f
♦ favored residential location *AE*
♦ favoured residential location *BE*
♦ privileged residential location
bewachter Campingplatz, m
♦ guarded campsite
♦ guarded campground *AE*
♦ guarded camping site *BE*
♦ guarded camping ground *BE*
bewachter Parkplatz, m (für mehrere Autos)
♦ supervised parking lot *AE*
♦ supervised car park *BE*
bewachter Platz, m
(Camping)
♦ guarded site
Bewachungsdienst, m
→ Wachdienst
bewährtes Gericht, n
♦ standing dish

bewaldet, adj
 ♦ wooded, adj
bewegen sich mehr
 mehr Bewegung haben
 ♦ take mor exercise
beweglicher Festtag, m
 bewegliches Fest, n
 ♦ movable feast
bewegliche und unbewegliche Einrichtungsgegenstände, m pl
 ♦ fixtures and fittings pl
Bewegung, f (Sport)
 Übung, f
 Turnübung, f
 ♦ exercise
Bewegung im Freien, f
 ♦ outdoor exercise
Bewegungsbad, n
 ♦ movement bath
Bewegungsbecken, n
 Gymnastikbecken, n
 ♦ exercise pool
Bewegungsbecken mit Gegenstromanlage, n
 ♦ exercise pool with jet-stream system
 ♦ jet-stream exercise pool
Bewegungsmangel, m
 Mangel an Bewegung, m
 ♦ lack of exercise
Bewegungsprogramm, n
 ♦ exercise program AE
 ♦ exercise programme BE
Bewegungstherapie, f
 ♦ exercise therapy
 ♦ motion therapy
 ♦ therapeutic exercises pl
bewerben sich um etw
 ♦ apply for s.th.
Bewerber, m
 Antragsteller, m
 ♦ applicant
Bewerbung, f
 ♦ application
Bewerbungsschreiben, n
 ♦ letter of application
 ♦ application letter
bewerten etw (nach Noten)
 → einstufen etw
bewerten etw (Qualität, Wert)
 ♦ rate s.th.
Bewertung, f
 (z.B. eines Hotels)
 ♦ rating
Bewertungsformular, n
 ♦ rating form
Bewertungsformular ausfüllen
 ♦ complete a rating form
Bewertungssystem, n
 ♦ rating system
bewirten bis zu 123 Personen
 ♦ cater for up to 123 persons
bewirten jn (bes. in Privathaus)
 (mit Speisen und Getränken)
 gastlich aufnehmen jn
 ♦ entertain s.o.
bewirten jn fürstlich
 ♦ treat s.o. like a lord
 ♦ entertain s.o. lavishly
bewirten jn fürstlich
 ♦ entertain s.o. lavishly
 ♦ treat s.o. like a lord

bewirten jn (generell)
 verköstigen jn
 verpflegen jn
 ♦ cater for s.o.
 ♦ entertain s.o.
 ♦ treat s.o.
 ♦ regale s.o. lit
bewirten jn königlich
 ♦ entertain s.o. regally
bewirten jn mit etw (kostenlos)
 einladen jn zu etw
 ♦ treat s.o. to s.th.
bewirten jn mit Speisen and Getränken (kostenlos)
 ♦ treat s.o. to food and drink
bewirten jn mit Wein (kostenlos)
 einladen jn zum Wein
 ♦ treat s.o. to wine
 ♦ wine (and dine) s.o.
bewirtet werden
 ♦ be entertained
 ♦ be catered for
bewirtschaften etw
 ♦ operate s.th.
 ♦ run s.th.
bewirtschaftet, adj (Betrieb)
 ♦ operated, adj
 ♦ open, adj
bewirtschafteter Bauernhof, m
 (in Betrieb)
 ♦ working farm
bewirtschaftet sein (Betrieb)
 bewirtschaftet werden
 ♦ be operated
 ♦ be open
Bewirtschaftung, f
 Betrieb, m
 ♦ operation
Bewirtung, f (bes. in Privathaus)
 gastliche Aufnahme, f
 Gastlichkeit, f
 ♦ entertainment
Bewirtung, f (Lokal)
 ♦ food and service
Bewirtungsbereich, m
 (z.B. bei einer Konferenz)
 ♦ hospitality area
Bewirtungsbetrieb, m
 ♦ foodservice establishment AE
 ♦ catering establishment BE
 ♦ establishment in the catering trade BE
Bewirtungskosten, pl
 Kosten für Geschäftsbewirtung, pl
 ♦ entertainment expenses pl
 ♦ entertaining expenses pl
 ♦ cost of business entertainment
Bewirtungsstand, m
 → Verpflegungsstand
Bewirtungstablett, n
 Begrüßungstablett, n
 ♦ hospitality tray
Bewirtungsveranstaltung, f
 Veranstaltung mit Bewirtung, f
 ♦ hospitality function
 ♦ hospitality event
 ♦ function with catering BE
 ♦ function with foodservice AE
 ♦ event with catering BE
Bewirtungsvertrag, m
 (Teil eines Gastaufnahmevertrags)

 ♦ foodservice contract AE
 ♦ catering contract BE
Bewirtung von Gästen, f
 ♦ entertainment of guests
 ♦ entertaining guests
 ♦ catering for guests
Bewirtung von Geschäftskunden, f
 ♦ entertaining customers
 ♦ business entertainment
bewohnbar, adj
 (Unterkunft)
 ♦ habitable, adj
bewohnbare Fläche, f
 Wohnraum, m
 Wohnfläche, f
 ♦ habitable space
 ♦ habitable area
bewohnbares Zimmer, n
 ♦ habitable room
Bewohnbarkeit, f
 ♦ habitability
bewohnbar sein
 ♦ be habitable
bewohnen etw (Land)
 ♦ inhabit s.th.
bewohnen etw (langfristig)
 ♦ live in s.th.
 ♦ reside in s.th.
bewohnen etw (Unterkunft)
 ♦ occupy s.th.
bewohnen etw (vorübergehend)
 wohnen in etw
 logieren in etw
 ♦ stay in s.th.
Bewohner, m (Land, Stadt)
 ♦ inhabitant
 ♦ resident
Bewohner, m (Mieter)
 → Mieter
Bewohner, m (Unterkunft, generell)
 ♦ occupant
 ♦ occupier
 ♦ inhabitant
 ♦ resident
 ♦ dweller
Bewohner, m (Untermieter)
 → Untermieter
Bewohner der Insel Man, m
 ♦ Manxman
Bewohner einer Mietwohnung, m
 ♦ apartment dweller AE
 ♦ flat dweller BE
bewohnt, adj
 belegt, adj
 ♦ inhabited, adj
 ♦ occupied, adj
 ♦ lived-in, adj
bewohnte Insel, f
 ♦ inhabited island
bewohntes Gebäude, n
 ♦ occupied building
bewohntes Haus, n
 ♦ occupied house
 ♦ inhabited house
bewohntes Zimmer, n
 ♦ room occupied
 ♦ occupied room
bezahlen für einen Fahrgast
 ♦ pay for a fare
 ♦ pay for a passenger

bezahlter Flug, m
   Flug gegen Entgelt, m
   ♦ revenue flight
bezahlter Heimaturlaub, m (Arbeitnehmer)
   ♦ paid home leave
bezahlter Passagierkilometer, m
   bezahlter Fluggastkilometer, m
   ♦ revenue passenger-kilometer AE
   ♦ revenue passenger-kilometre BE
bezahlter Tonnenkilometer, m
   ♦ revenue ton-kilometer AE
   ♦ revenue ton-kilometre BE
bezahlter Urlaub, m
   (für Arbeitnehmer)
   ♦ paid vacation AE
   ♦ paid holiday BE
   ♦ holidays with pay BE pl
   ♦ paid leave
bezahlte Überstunden, f pl
   ♦ paid overtime
bezaubernde Atmosphäre, f
   ♦ charming atmosphere
bezaubernder Ort, m
   ♦ charming place
bezaubernde Umgebung, f
   ♦ charming surroundings pl
bezaubernd möbliert, adj
   ♦ charmingly furnished, adj
bezaubernd möbliertes Zimmer, n
   ♦ charmingly furnished room
beziehbar, adj (Unterkunft)
   ♦ ready to move in(to), adj
   ♦ available, adj
beziehen etw (Unterkunft)
   einziehen in etw
   ♦ move in(to) s.th.
   ♦ occupy s.th.
   ♦ claim s.th.
Bezug, m (Ankunft)
   → Ankunft, Anmeldung
Bezug, m (Einzug)
   ♦ moving in(to)
   ♦ occupation
Bezug, m (Kissen etc.)
   ♦ cover
Bezug eines Zimmers, m
   ♦ moving into a room
   ♦ occupation of a room
bezugsbereit, adj
   → beziehbar
bezugsfähig adj
   → bezugsfertig
Bezugsfertig
   (Hinweis auf Zimmerstatus)
   ♦ Ready to rent AE
   ♦ Ready to let BE
bezugsfertig, adj
   bezugsfähig, adj
   ♦ ready for occupancy, adj
   ♦ ready for occupation, adj
   ♦ ready to move in(to), adj
   ♦ ready to occupy, adj
Bezugszeit, f
   Bezugszeitraum, m
   Belegungszeit, f
   Auslastungszeit, f
   ♦ period of occupancy
   ♦ occupancy period
   ♦ time during which a room is occupied
Bezugszeitpunkt, m (Check-in)
   (Gegensatz zu Räumungszeitpunkt)

   ♦ check-in time
   ♦ time at which a room is occupied
Bezwinger des Matterhorn, m
   ♦ conqueror of the Matterhorn
BGW, m
   → Bungalow
Bhf.
   Bahnhof m
   ♦ stn.
   ♦ station
Bhutan
   ♦ Bhutan
Bhutaner, m
   ♦ Bhutani
   ♦ Bhutanese
Bhutanerin, f
   ♦ Bhutani girl
   ♦ Bhutani woman
   ♦ Bhutani
   ♦ Bhutanese girl
   ♦ Bhutanese woman
bhutanisch, adj
   ♦ Bhutani, adj
   ♦ Bhutanese, adj
   ♦ Bhutan, adj
Bibliothek, f
   Bücherei, f
   ♦ library
Bibliothekbar, f
   ♦ library bar
Bidet, n
   ♦ bidet
Bieler See, m
   Bielersee, m
   ♦ Lake of Biel, the
   ♦ Lake Biel
bien cuit, adj FR
   durchgebraten, adj
   ♦ bien cuit, adj FR
   ♦ well done, adj
Bier, n
   ♦ beer
Bierabend m
   ♦ beer evening
Bierangebot, n (Gegensatz zu Nachfrage)
   ♦ beer supply
Bierangebot, n (Palette)
   ♦ range of beers
   ♦ range of beer
   ♦ choice of beer(s)
Bier aus dem Keller holen
   ♦ fetch beer (up) from the cellar
Bierausschank, m (Lokal)
   → Bierlokal
Bierausschank, m (Raum)
   → Schankraum
Bierausschank, m (Verkauf)
   ♦ sale of beer
   ♦ beer sale
Bierauswahl, f
   Auswahl an Bier, f
   ♦ selection of beer
   ♦ selection of beers
   ♦ beer selection
   ♦ choice of beer(s)
   ♦ beer choice
Bierbar, f
   ♦ beer bar
Bierbauch, m
   ♦ beer belly

Bier besteuern
   ♦ tax beer
Bierbrauer, m
   → Brauer
Bierbrauerei, f
   → Brauerei
Bierbuch, n
   (Buch über Biere)
   ♦ beer book
Bierchen, n coll
   ♦ jar BE coll
Bierdeckel, m
   Bierfilz m
   ♦ beer mat
   ♦ coaster AE
Bierdeckel sammeln
   ♦ collect beer mats
   ♦ collect coasters AE
Bierdeckelsammlung, f
   ♦ collection of beer mats
   ♦ collection of coasters AE
Bierdose, f
   ♦ beer can
Bieretikett, n
   ♦ beer label
Bierfaß, n (groß)
   ♦ beer barrel
Bierfaß, n (klein)
   ♦ beer keg
Bierfest, n
   ♦ beer festival
Bierfilz, m
   → Bierdeckel
Bierflasche, f
   ♦ beer bottle
Bierfrau, f hist
   ♦ ale-wife hist
Bierfreak, m
   ♦ beer freak
Bierfreund, m
   → Bierliebhaber
Bierführer, m
   (Buch)
   ♦ beer guide
Biergarten, m
   ♦ beer garden
Biergartenterrasse, f
   ♦ beer garden terrace
Biergeld, n
   ♦ beer money
Biergeruch, m
   ♦ smell of beer
Bierglas n
   ♦ beer glass
Bierhahn, m
   ♦ beer tap
Bierhalle, f
   Biersaal, m
   ♦ beer hall
Bierhaus, n
   Speisehaus, n
   ♦ porterhouse AE
Bierhefe, f
   ♦ beer yeast
Bierhersteller, m
   ♦ beer producer
Bierherstellung, f
   ♦ beer production
Bier ist gut gegen den Durst
   ♦ beer is good for (the) thirst

Bierkarte

Bierkarte, f
♦ beer list
Bierkasten, m
♦ beer crate
♦ beer case
Bierkeller, m
♦ beer cellar
Bierkneipe, f
Bierpinte, f
♦ beer dive *inform*
♦ beer bar *AE*
♦ beer pub *BE*
♦ dive *inform*
♦ tavern
Bierkosten, pl
♦ beer costs *pl*
♦ beer cost
Bierkrug, m (mit Deckel)
♦ beer tankard
Bierkrug, m (offen)
Bierseidel, m
♦ beer mug
Bierkutscher, m
♦ brewer's drayman
♦ drayman
Bierliebhaber, m
Bierfreund, m
♦ beer lover
Bierlieferant, m
♦ beer supplier
Bier liefern an jn
♦ supply beer to s.o.
Bierlokal, n
♦ beer parlor *AE*
♦ beer bar *AE*
♦ tavern *AE*
♦ public house *BE*
♦ pub *BE coll*
Bier macht einen müde
♦ beer makes one sleepy
Biermarkt, m
♦ beer market
Biermuseum, n
♦ beer museum
Biernarr, m
Bierfan, m
♦ beer buff
Bierpalast, m
♦ beer palace
Bierpinte, f
→ Bierkneipe
Bierpreis, m
♦ beer price
Bierpreis erhöhen
♦ increase the beer price
Bierpreiserhöhung, f
♦ beer price increase
♦ increase in the beer price
Bierpreisliste, f
♦ beer price list
Bierprobe, f
♦ beer tasting
Bier probieren
♦ sample beer
Bier probieren
♦ taste the beer
♦ taste beers
Bierpumpe, f
♦ beer pump
Bierreise machen
Kneipenbummel machen

Zechtour machen
♦ barhop *AE*
♦ be on a spree
♦ go on a pub crawl *BE*
Bierreklame, f
♦ beer advertisement
Bierrestaurant, n
Brasserie f
♦ restaurant serving beer
♦ brasserie *FR*
Bier saufen
♦ guzzle beer
♦ swill beer
Bierschaum, m
♦ beer froth
Bierschenke, f
♦ beerhouse *BE*
Bierseidel, m
→ Bierkrug
bierselig, adj
♦ happy from beer, adj
♦ merry from beer, adj
♦ merry with beer, adj
Bierservice n
♦ beer service
Biersorte, f
♦ type of beer
♦ beer type
Bier spendieren jm
Bier zahlen jm
♦ stand s.o. a beer
Bierstand, m
♦ beer stand
♦ beer stall
Biersteuer, f
♦ beer tax
Bierstube, f (generell)
→ Bierbar, Biergaststätte
Bierstube, f (im Hotel)
Bierbar, f
♦ beverage room *CAN*
Bier trinken
♦ drink beer
♦ have a beer
Biertrinken, n
♦ beer drinking
Biertrinker, m
♦ beer drinker
Biertulpe, f
Bierkelch, m
♦ beer goblet
♦ schooner
♦ tall beer glass
Bierumsatz, m
♦ beer sales *pl*
Bierverbrauch, m
Bierkonsum, m
Bierverzehr, m
♦ beer consumption
♦ consumption of beer
Bierverlag, m
♦ beer depot
♦ beer store
Bierverleger, m
♦ retailer of beer
♦ beer retailer
Bierverzehr m
→ Bierverbrauch
Bier vom Faß, n
Faßbier, n
offenes Bier, n

♦ beer from the wood
♦ beer drawn from the wood
♦ beer from the barrel
♦ draft beer *AE*
♦ draught beer *BE*
Bierwagen, m
Brauereiwagen, m
♦ beer waggon
♦ brewer's dray
Bierwärmer, m
♦ beer warmer
Bierwoche, f
♦ beer week
Bier zapfen
♦ tap beer
♦ draw beer
Bier zapfen aus dem Faß
♦ tap beer from the barrel
♦ draw beer from the barrel
Bierzelt, n
♦ beer tent
bieten für jeden etw
♦ offer s.th. for everyone
bieten für jeden Geschmack etw
♦ cater for every taste
♦ cater for every palate
Big Band, f
♦ big band
Big-Band-Unterhaltung, f
♦ big band entertainment
Bikini, m
♦ bikini
Bikinioberteil, m
♦ bikini top
Bilanz, f
♦ balance sheet
Bilanzbuchhalter, m
♦ accountant
Bild abrunden
♦ round off the picture
Bilderausstellung, f
♦ exhibition of pictures
Bilderbuch, n
♦ illustrated book
♦ picture-book
Bilderbuchbayer, m
♦ picture-book Bavarian
Bilderbuchdorf, n
♦ picture-book village
Bilderbuchpanorama, n
♦ picture-book panorama
Bilderbuchparadies, n
♦ picture-book paradise
Bilderbuchschloß, n
♦ picture-book castle
Bilderbuchstadt, f
♦ picture-book town
Bilderbuchurlaub, m
Bilderbuchferien, pl
♦ picture-book vacation *AE*
♦ picture-book holiday *BE*
Bildergalerie, f
♦ picture gallery
Bildersammlung, f
♦ collection of pictures
Bildführer, m
bebilderter Führer, m
♦ pictorial guide
♦ illustrated guide
Bildkarte, f
♦ pictorial map

Bildkatalog, m
  ♦ illustrated catalogue
  ♦ illustrated catalog *AE*
Bildkonferenz, f
  → Bildschirmkonferenz
Bildplatte, f
  ♦ videodisc
Bildprospekt, m
  bebilderter Prospekt, m
  ♦ illustrated brochure
Bildschirmkonferenz, f
  → Videokonferenz
Bildschirmkonferenzeinrichtung, f
  ♦ video-conference facility
Bildschirmtelefon, n
  (Telefon mit Bild)
  ♦ video telephone
  ♦ video phone
Bildschirmtext, m
  BTX m
  ♦ viewdata
  ♦ Prestel *BE*
Bildschirmtextbuchung f
  BTX-Buchung f
  ♦ viewdata booking *BE*
  ♦ Prestel booking *BE*
Bildschirmtextbuchungsservice m
  BTX-Buchungsservice m
  ♦ viewdata booking service
  ♦ Prestel booking service *BE*
Bild schmückt die Wand
  ♦ picture decorates the wall
Bildstock, m
  ♦ wayside shrine
Bildungsabend, m
  ♦ educational evening
  ♦ evening class
Bildungsaufenthalt m
  ♦ educational stay
  ♦ educational visit
Bildungsbesuch, m
  ♦ educational visit
Bildungsbesucher, m
  ♦ educational visitor
Bildungsfahrt, f
  ♦ educational trip
Bildungskurs, m
  Bildungslehrgang, m
  ♦ educational course
Bildungsprogramm, n
  ♦ educational program *AE*
  ♦ educational programme *BE*
Bildungsreise, f
  ♦ educational tour
  ♦ Grand Tour *BE hist*
Bildungsreisen, n
  Bildungsreiseverkehr, m
  ♦ educational travel
Bildungsreisender m
  ♦ person on an educational tour
  ♦ person taking part in an educational tour
Bildungsseminar, n
  ♦ educational seminar
Bildungstagung, f
  Bildungskonferenz, f
  ♦ educational conference
Bildungstourismus m
  ♦ educational tourism
Bildungstourist, m
  ♦ educational tourist

Bildungsurlaub, m (Arbeitnehmer)
  ♦ educational leave
  ♦ study leave
Bildungsurlaub, m (Ferien)
  ♦ educational vacation *AE*
  ♦ educational holiday *BE*
Bildungsurlauber, m
  Bildungsurlauberin f
  ♦ educational vacationer *AE*
  ♦ educational holidaymaker *BE*
Bildvortrag, m
  Bildervortrag, m
  Vortrag mit Bildern, m
  ♦ illustrated lecture
Bildwand, f
  → Leinwand
Bild ziert die Wand
  ♦ picture adorns the wall
Billard, n
  ♦ billiards *pl = sg*
Billardcafé, n
  ♦ billiard café *BE*
  ♦ billard cafe *AE*
Billardclub, m
  Billardverein m
  ♦ billiard club
Billardkonzession, f
  ♦ billiards license
  ♦ billiards licence
Billardkugel, f
  ♦ billiard ball
Billardqueue, m
  ♦ billiard cue
Billardraum, m
  → Billardzimmer
Billardsaal, m
  Billardhalle, f
  ♦ billiard hall
Billardsalon, m
  ♦ billiard saloon
Billardspiel, n
  ♦ game of billiards
Billard spielen
  ♦ play billiards
  ♦ have a game of billiards
Billardspieler, m
  ♦ billiard player
Billardtisch, m (generell)
  ♦ billiard table
Billardtisch, m (Poolbillard)
  → Poolbillardtisch
Billardzimmer, n
  Billardraum, m
  Billardstube, f
  ♦ billiard room
  ♦ billiard parlor *AE*
  ♦ poolroom *AE*
  ♦ billiard saloon *BE*
Billett, n
  → Karte
billig, adj
  ♦ cheap, adj
  ♦ low-cost, adj
  ♦ budget, adj
Billiganbieter, m
  ♦ cut-price supplier
billige Fahrt, f
  ♦ cheap trip
  ♦ cheap ride
billige Miete, f
  ♦ cheap rent

billiger Fahrpreis, m
  ♦ cheap fare
billiger Fusel, m
  ♦ cheap rotgut *AE sl*
  ♦ cheap rot-gut *BE sl*
billiger Mittagstisch, m
  ♦ sloppy Joe *sl*
billiger Sitzplatz, m
  billiger Platz, m
  ♦ cheap seat
billiger Wein m
  ♦ cheap wine
  ♦ plonk *BE coll*
billiges Gesöff, n *derog*
  ♦ cheap booze *derog*
  ♦ cheap rotgut *AE derog*
billiges Logierhaus, n
  ♦ cheap lodging house
  ♦ doss-house *BE*
  ♦ cheap rooming house *AE*
billiges Restaurant, n
  Billigrestaurant, n
  ♦ cheap restaurant
  ♦ beanery *AE sl*
  ♦ hash house *AE sl*
billig essen
  ♦ eat cheaply
billiges Speisehaus n
  ♦ hash house *AE sl*
billiges Werbemätzchen, n
  ♦ cheap publicity gimmick
billiges Zimmer, n
  Billigzimmer n
  ♦ cheap room
  ♦ budget room
  ♦ economy room
billige Unterkunft, f
  billige Unterbringung, f
  ♦ cheap accommodation
  ♦ cheap lodging *AE*
billige Wochenendpreise anbieten
  ♦ offer cheap weekend rates
  ♦ offer cheap weekend prices
Billigflug, m
  ♦ cheap flight
  ♦ economy flight
  ♦ budget flight
Billighotel, n
  ♦ low-budget hotel
  ♦ budget hotel
  ♦ economy hotel
  ♦ cheap hotel
Billigladen, m
  ♦ cut-price store *AE*
billig leben
  ♦ live cheaply
Billigmenü, n
  ♦ low-budget menu
  ♦ budget menu
  ♦ economy menu
  ♦ cheap menu
billig möbliert, adj
  ♦ cheaply furnished, adj
billig möbliertes Zimmer n
  ♦ cheaply furnished room
Billigmotel, n
  ♦ low-budget motel
  ♦ budget motel
  ♦ economy motel
  ♦ cheap motel

Billigreise

Billigreise, f
  billige Reise, f
  ♦ cheap tour
billig reisen
  ♦ travel cheaply
Billigreisender, m
  ♦ low-budget traveller
  ♦ low-budget traveler *AE*
Billigrestaurant, n
  billiges Restaurant n
  ♦ low-budget restaurant
  ♦ budget restaurant
  ♦ economy restaurant
  ♦ cheap restaurant
  ♦ chophouse *neg*
Billigsegment, n
  Economy-Segment, n
  ♦ economy segment
Billigtarif, m
  Spartarif, m
  ♦ economy rates *pl*
  ♦ economy rate
  ♦ economy terms *pl*
  ♦ economy tariff
Billigtourismus, m
  ♦ cheap tourism
  ♦ economy tourism
Billigunterkunft, f
  ♦ low-budget accommodation
  ♦ budget lodging *AE*
  ♦ economy accommodation
  ♦ economy lodging *AE*
  ♦ cheap accommodation
Billigurlaub, m
  billiger Urlaub, m
  Billigferien, pl
  billige Ferien, pl
  ♦ cheap vacation *AE*
  ♦ cheap holiday *BE*
Billigzimmer, n
  billiges Zimmer n
  ♦ low-budget room
  ♦ budget room
  ♦ economy room
  ♦ cheap room
Billion, f
  ♦ trillion
binden etw *gastr*
  ♦ bind s.th. *gastr*
Binger Loch, n
  ♦ Bingen Hole, the
Bingo, n
  ♦ bingo
Bingoabend, m
  ♦ bingo evening
  ♦ bingo night
Bingoraum, m
  Bingozimmer, n
  ♦ bingo room
Bingorunde, f
  ♦ bingo session
Bingosaal, m
  Bingohalle, f
  ♦ bingo hall
Bingospiel, n
  ♦ game of bingo
  ♦ bingo game
Bingo spielen
  ♦ play bingo
Binnengrenze, f
  Innengrenze, f
  ♦ internal frontier
  ♦ internal border
Binnenmarketing, n
  → Innenmarketing
Binnenreiseverkehr, m
  inländischer Reiseverkehr, m
  ♦ internal travel
Binnensee, m
  ♦ inland lake
Binnentourismus, m
  Inlandstourismus, m
  Fremdenverkehr, m
  ♦ internal tourism
  ♦ domestic tourism
Bioarchitektur, f
  ♦ bio-architecture
Biokost, f
  ♦ organic fare
  ♦ organic diet
Bioladen, m
  ♦ whole food shop *BE*
Biolebensmittel, n pl
  ♦ organic food *sg*
Bioporridge, m/n
  ♦ organic porridge *BE*
Biosauna, f
  ♦ bio sauna
Biosphäre, f
  ♦ biosphere
Biowein, m
  → organisch-biologischer Wein
Birma
  Burma
  ♦ Burma
Birmane, m
  ♦ Burmese
Birmanin, f
  ♦ Burmese girl
  ♦ Burmese woman
  ♦ Burmese
birmanisch, adj
  ♦ Burmese, adj
  ♦ Burman, adj
Birne, f (Frucht)
  ♦ pear
Birne, f (Lampe)
  ♦ bulb
Birneneis, n
  ♦ pear ice cream *AE*
  ♦ pear ice-cream *BE*
Birnengeschmack, m
  ♦ pear flavor *AE*
  ♦ pear flavour *BE*
Birnenkompott, n
  ♦ pear compôte
  ♦ pear compote *AE*
  ♦ stewed pears *pl*
Birnenkruste, f
  ♦ pear crust
Birnenlikör, m
  ♦ pear liqueur
Birnenmilchmixgetränk, n
  ♦ pear milk shake
Birnenmost, m
  vergorener Birnensaft, m
  ♦ perry
  ♦ fermented pear juice
Birnenparfait, n
  ♦ pear parfait
Birnensaft, m
  ♦ pear juice
Birnensorbet, n
  ♦ pear sorbet
Birnensoufflé, n
  Birnenauflauf, m
  ♦ pear souffle *AE*
  ♦ pear soufflé *BE*
Birnenwein, m
  ♦ pear wine
bis auf den letzten Tropfen
  ♦ to the last drop
bis auf weiteres
  ♦ until further notice
bis auf Widerruf (einer Erlaubnis)
  ♦ until revoked
  ♦ unless revoked
bis auf Widerruf (generell)
  ♦ until cancelled
  ♦ until canceled *AE*
bis auf Widerruf (Stornierung)
  ♦ unless cancelled
  ♦ unless canceled *AE*
  ♦ until cancelled
  ♦ until canceled *AE*
Bischofspalast, m
  ♦ bishop's palace
bis einschließlich
  ♦ until ... inclusive
  ♦ through *AE*
  ♦ up to and including
bis einschließlich 31. Januar
  ♦ until 31 January inclusive
  ♦ through 31 January *AE*
  ♦ up to and including 31 January
bis einschließlich Freitag
  ♦ until Friday inclusive
  ♦ through Friday *AE*
  ♦ up to and including Friday
bisheriger Preis, m
  früherer Preis, m
  ♦ previous price
  ♦ previous rate
bis in die entferntesten Ecken der Welt
  ♦ to the furthest corners of the globe
bis in die frühen Morgenstunden
  ♦ until the early hours
  ♦ until the small hours
bis in die Puppen
  → bis in die frühen Morgenstunden
bis in die späte Nacht
  bis spät in die Nacht
  bis spät in der Nacht
  ♦ until late at night
bis ins kleinste Detail
  bis in die kleinste Einzelheit
  ♦ down to the minutest detail
Biskuitrolle, f
  ♦ jam roll
bißchen Appetit haben
  ♦ feel a bit peckish
bißchen betrunken werden
  ♦ get a bit tight *inform*
Bissen, m
  ♦ bite
bis spätestens Mittwoch
  ♦ by Wednesday at the latest
bis spät in die Nacht, adv
  ♦ far into the night, adv
  ♦ until late at night, adv
Bistro, n
  ♦ bistro

Bistroabendessen, n
 ♦ bistro dinner
Bistroatmosphäre, f
 ♦ bistro atmosphere
Bistrobesitzer, m
 ♦ bistro owner
 ♦ owner of a bistro
Bistro-Café, n
 ♦ bistro/café BE
 ♦ bistro/cafe AE
 ♦ bistro cum café BE
 ♦ bistro cum cafe AE
Bistroessen, n
 ♦ bistro food
Bistromittagessen, n
 ♦ bistro luncehon
Bistro-Restaurant, n
 ♦ bistro/restaurant
 ♦ bistro cum restaurant
Bistrospeisekarte, f
 Bistrokarte, f
 ♦ bistro menu
Bistrotisch, m
 ♦ bistro table
Bis wann müssen wir das Zimmer freimachen?
 Bis wieviel Uhr müssen wir das Zimmer räumen?
 ♦ By what time must we vacate the room?
bis zum Saisonende
 ♦ until the end of the season
Bitte bedienen Sie sich!
 Bitte greifen Sie zu!
 ♦ Please help yourself!
 ♦ Please help yourselves!
Bitte begleichen Sie Ihre Rechnung vor dem
 Auszug aus dem Hotel
 ♦ Please settle your bill before leaving the hotel
Bitte behalten Sie das immer bei sich
 (z.B. Schlüssel)
 ♦ Please carry it at all times
Bitte bezahlen Sie später
 ♦ Please pay later
Bitte entschuldigen Sie!
 ♦ Excuse me, please
Bitte fordern Sie Prospekt an! (schriftlich)
 ♦ Please write for brochure!
Bitte fordern Sie Prospekt an! (telefonisch)
 ♦ Please phone for brochure!
Bitte fordern Sie unseren Hausprospekt an
 (schriftlich, bei Hotel)
 ♦ Please write for our hotel brochure
Bitte fordern Sie unseren Hausprospekt an
 (telefonisch, bei Hotel)
 ♦ Please phone for our hotel brochure
Bitte füllen Sie Ihre Gläser
 ♦ Please fill your glasses
 ♦ Please charge your glasses coll
Bitte geben Sie Ihren Schlüssel bei der Rezeption
 ab
 ♦ Please leave your key with reception
Bitte geben Sie Ihre voraussichtliche
 Ankunftszeit
 auf dem Buchungsformular an
 ♦ Please indicate your estimated time of arrival
 on
 ♦ the booking form
Bitte greifen Sie zu!
 Bitte bedienen Sie sich!
 ♦ Please help yourselves!
 ♦ Please help yourself!

Bitte in Blockschrift schreiben
 ♦ Please write in capital letters
Bitte kümmern Sie sich selbst um die Unterkunft
 ♦ Please make your own arrangements for
 accommo-
 ♦ dation
Bitte nicht berühren
 ♦ Please do not touch
Bitte nicht rauchen
 ♦ No smoking, please
Bitte nicht stören
 (Hinweisschild)
 ♦ Please do not disturb
bitten jn, leise zu sein
 ♦ ask s.o. to be quiet
bitten um Asyl
 nachsuchen um Asyl
 ♦ ask for asylum
bitten um Beurlaubung
 ♦ ask for leave of absence
bitten um eine Audienz bei jm
 um eine Audienz bei jm nachsuchen
 ♦ request an audience with s.o.
bitten um einen Service
 Service verlangen
 Leistung verlangen
 ♦ ask for a service
bitten um ein spezielles Arrangement
 Spezialarrangement verlangen
 ♦ ask for a special arrangement
bitten um ein Trinkgeld
 ♦ solicit a gratuity
 ♦ solicit a tip
bitten um etw
 ♦ ask for s.th.
 ♦ request s.th.
bitten um politisches Asyl
 ♦ ask for political asylum
bitter, adj
 ♦ bitter, adj
bitteren Geschmack haben
 ♦ have a bitter taste
bitter enttäuscht, adj
 ♦ bitterly disappointed, adj
bitter enttäuscht sein
 ♦ be bitterly disappointed
bitter schmecken
 ♦ taste bitter
Bitte schenken Sie mir das Glas voll
 ♦ Please fill me this glass
 ♦ Please fill this glass for me
Bitte setzen Sie es auf meine Rechnung
 ♦ Please charge it to my account
Bitte tun Sie mir einen Gefallen und schließen
 Sie die Tür
 ♦ Please oblige me by closing the door
Bitte Tür schließen
 ♦ Please close the door
Bitte wecken Sie mich um acht Uhr
 ♦ Please wake me at eight o'clock
 ♦ Please call me at eight o'clock
Bitte wecken Sie mich um sieben Uhr morgen
 früh
 ♦ Please wake me at seven o'clock tomorrow
 morning
 ♦ Please call me at seven o'clock tomorrow
 morning
Bitte zahlen Sie an der Kasse
 ♦ Please pay at the cash desk
Bitzler, m
 → neuer Wein

Biwak, n
 ♦ bivouac
Biwak errichten
 ♦ establish a bivouac
Biwakfeuer, n
 ♦ bivouac fire
biwakieren
 ♦ bivouac
 ♦ siwash AE
biwakieren bei einem See
 ♦ bivouac by a lake
Biwakplatz, m
 ♦ bivouac site
Blackjack, m/n
 ♦ blackjack
Blackjack spielen
 ♦ play blackjack
Blackjacktisch, m
 ♦ blackjack table
blanchieren (etw)
 ♦ blanch (s.th.)
blanchiert, adj
 ♦ blanched, adj
Blanc-manger, m FR
 Mandelpudding, m
 ♦ blanc-manger, m FR
Blankoformular, n
 ♦ blank form
Blase, f (Harn)
 ♦ bladder
Blase, f (Haut)
 ♦ blister
blasiert, adj
 ♦ blasé, adj FR
Blaskapelle, f
 ♦ brass band
Blaskapellenkonzert, n
 ♦ brass band concert
Blattgemüse, n
 grünes Gemüse, n
 ♦ green vegetables pl
Blattsalat, m
 ♦ leaf salad
blau, adj (betrunken) coll
 betrunken, adj
 besoffen, adj
 voll, adj sl
 ♦ boozed, adj coll
 ♦ tight, adj inform
 ♦ sloshed, adj sl
Blaue Abfahrt, f
 (Ski)
 Blaue Piste, f
 ♦ blue run
Blaue Donau, die, f
 ♦ Blue Danube, the
blaue Flagge, f
 Blaue Flagge, f (Umweltgüte)
 ♦ blue flag
 ♦ Blue Flag, the
Blaue Grotte, f
 (Capri)
 ♦ Blue Grotto, the
blauer Montag, m
 ♦ St Monday BE
Blauer Portugieser, m
 (Wein)
 ♦ Blue Portugieser
Blaufelche, f
 Felche, f

Blei

- surface whitefish
- whitefish

Blei, n
- lead

Bleibe, f (Gasttyp) *sl*
→ Verlängerer

Bleibe, f (Unterkunft) *coll*
Unterkunft, f
- place to stay
- lodging
- pad *sl*

Bleibe, f (Zimmertyp)
→ Bleibezimmer

Bleibe finden
- find a place (where) to stay

bleiben bis zum Mittag
- stay until noon
- stay till noon *coll*

bleiben bis zum Wochenende
- stay until the weekend
- stay till the weekend *coll*

bleiben ein oder zwei Tage
- stay a day or two

Bleiben Sie zuhause oder fahren Sie weg?
- Are you staying at home or are you going away?
- Will you be staying at home or will you be going away?

bleiben so lange wie man will
- stay as long as one likes

bleiben über die ursprünglich angegebene Abreisezeit
- stay beyond the originally stated departure time

bleiben über Nacht
übernachten
- stay (for) the night
- stay overnight

bleiben über Weihnachten
- stay over Christmas

bleiben zum Abendessen (Dinner)
- stay for dinner
- stay to dinner
- stop for dinner *inform*

bleiben zum Abendessen (Supper)
- stay for supper
- stay to supper
- stop for supper *inform*

bleiben zum Mittagessen
- stay for lunch
- stay to lunch
- stop for lunch *inform*

Bleibergwerk, n
- lead mine

Bleibe suchen *coll*
- look for a place to stay *coll*

Bleibezimmer, n
(Gegenteil: Abreisezimmer)
Bleibe, f *sl*
- room of a staying guest

Bleikristall, n
- lead crystal

bleu, adj *FR*
(Fleisch)
fast roh, adj
- bleu, adj *FR*
- very underdone, adj
- very red, adj

Blick auf das Gebirge, m
Bergblick m

- view of the mountains
- mountain view

Blick auf das Schloß, m
Schloßblick m
Blick auf die Burg, m
- view of the castle
- castle view

Blick auf das Schwimmbad, m
Schwimmbadblick m
- view of the swimming pool
- view of the pool
- swimming pool view

Blick auf das Tal, m
Talblick m
- view of the valley
- valley view

Blick auf das Wasser, m
- view of the water
- water view

Blick auf den Fluß, m
Flußblick m
- view of the river
- river view

Blick auf den Garten, m
- view of the garden
- garden view

Blick auf den Hafen, m
Hafenblick m
- view of the harbor *AE*
- view of the harbour *BE*
- harbor view *AE*
- harbour view *BE*

Blick auf den Jachthafen, m
- view of the marina
- marina view

Blick auf den Ozean, m
Meeresblick m
- view of the ocean
- ocean view

Blick auf den Park, m
Parkblick m
- view of the park
- park view

Blick auf den See, m
Seeblick m
- view of the lake
- lake view

Blick auf die Alpen, m
- view of the Alps

Blick auf die Bucht, f
- view of the bay
- view of the cove
- bay view

Blick auf die Burg, m
→ Blick auf das Schloß

Blick auf die ganze Stadt, m (Großstadt)
Ausblick auf die ganze Stadt, m
Aussicht auf die ganze Stadt, f
- view of the whole city
- overlooking the whole city

Blick auf die ganze Stadt, m (kleine Stadt)
Ausblick auf die ganze Stadt, m
Aussicht auf die ganze Stadt, f
- view of the whole town
- overlooking the whole town

Blick auf die Lagune, f
Lagunenblick m
- view of the lagoon
- lagoon view

Blick auf die Landschaft ringsumher, m
- view of the surrounding countryside

Blick auf die See, m
Seeblick, m
Meeresblick, m
- view of the sea
- sea view

Blick auf die Stadt, f (Großstadt)
- view of the city
- overlooking the city

Blick auf die Stadt, m (kleine Stadt)
- view of the town
- overlooking the town

Blick auf etw, m
Ausblick auf etw
Aussicht auf etw
- view of s.th.

Blick aus dem Zimmer, m
- view from the room

Blick aus dem Zimmer ist großartig
- view from the room is superb

Blick bieten auf etw
Ausblick bieten auf etw
Aussicht bieten auf etw
- offer a view of s.th.
- provide a view of s.th.

Blick bieten über etw
Blick gewähren über etw
- afford a view over s.th.

Blick entlang von etw, m
- view along s.th.

Blick genießen (von etw)
Ausblick genießen (von etw)
Aussicht genießen (von etw)
- enjoy a view (from s.th.)
- enjoy the view (from s.th.)

Blick gewähren auf etw
Blick bieten auf etw
- afford a view of s.th.

Blick haben auf etw
Aussicht haben auf etw
Ausblick haben auf etw
- have a view of s.th.

Blick haben über etw
Blick haben auf etw
- overlook s.th.
- have a view over s.th.

Blick haben über etw von etw
- have a view over s.th. from s.th.

Blick hinüber auf das Meer, m
Ausblick hinüber auf das Meer, m
- view towards the sea
- view to the sea

Blick hinüber auf etw, m
Ausblick hinüber auf etw, m
Aussicht hinüber auf etw, f
Blicke hinüber auf etw, m pl
- view towards s.th.
- view to s.th.
- views to s.th. *pl*

Blick in das Land, m
Blick ins Land, m
Blick auf das Land, m
- view of the country
- country view

Blick ins Land, m
→ Blick in das Land

Blick über den See, m
- view over the lake

Blick über die Bucht, m
- bay view
- view of the bay

Blick über etw hinweg, m (gerade)
　Ausblick über etw, m
　Aussicht über etw, f
　♦ view over s.th.
Blick über etw hinweg, m (quer)
　Ausblick über etw
　Aussicht über etw
　♦ view across s.th.
Blick versperren
　Ausblick versperren
　Aussicht versperren
　♦ obstruct one's view
　♦ obstruct s.o.'s view
Blick vom Gipfel, m
　Gipfelblick, m
　♦ view from the summit
　♦ view from the peak
　♦ view from the top
Blick vom Schloß, m
　Blick von dem Schloß, m
　♦ view from the castle
Blick von etw, m
　♦ view from s.th.
Blick zur Landseite, m
　(Gegensatz zur Meerseite)
　Landblick m
　♦ view of the land
　♦ land view
Blindenheim, n
　♦ home for the blind
　♦ asylum for the blind
Blindenhund, m
　♦ guide dog
　♦ Seeing Eye dog *AE*
blinder Passagier, m
　♦ stowaway
Blindprobe, f
　(z.B. Wein)
　♦ blind tasting
Blindprobe geben jm
　(z.B. Wein)
　♦ give s.o. a blind tasting
Blitzbesuch, m
　♦ lightning visit
Blitzreise, f
　♦ lightning tour
Blitzreise durch das Land, f
　♦ lightning tour of the country
blitzsauber, adj
　♦ spotlessly clean, adj
　♦ immaculately clean, adj
blitzsaubere Sanitäreinrichtungen, f pl
　♦ spotlessly clean sanitary facilities *pl*
Blockade, f
　♦ blockade
Blockade beenden
　♦ end a blockade
Blockanmeldung, f
　→ Blockbuchung
Blockbestellung, f
　→ Blockbuchung
Blockbuchstabe, m
　Blockschrift, f
　♦ capital letter
Blockbuchung, f
　Blockbestellung, f
　♦ block booking
Blockhaus, n
　♦ log house
　♦ log cabin
　♦ log hut

Blockhütte, f
　Blockhaus, n
　♦ log cabin
　♦ log hut
Blockhüttenzimmer, n
　Blockhauszimmer, n
　♦ log cabin room
　♦ log hut room
Blockstand, m
　♦ block stand
Bluesschuppen, m
　♦ juke joint *AE sl*
blühend, adj
　in (der) Blüte, adv
　♦ in bloom, adv
blühende Heide, f
　♦ heather in bloom
Blühendes Britannien
　(Slogan)
　♦ Britain in Bloom
Blühendes London
　(Slogan)
　♦ London in Bloom
Blume, f (Bier)
　♦ head
　♦ froth
Blume, f (Pflanze)
　Blüte, f
　♦ flower
Blumenabteilung, f
　♦ flower department
Blumenarrangement, n
　Blumengesteck n
　♦ flower arrangement
　♦ floral arrangement
　♦ arrangement of flowers
Blumenarrangeur, m
　♦ flower arranger
Blumenausstattung, f
　Blumenschmuck, m
　♦ floral display
Blumenbalkon, m
　♦ flower balcony
　♦ balcony with flowers
Blumenbeet, n
　♦ flower bed *AE*
　♦ flower-bed *BE*
Blumenbinder, m
　→ Florist
Blumendorf, n
　♦ flower village
Blumenfest, n
　Blütenfest, n
　♦ flower festival
Blumengarten, m
　♦ flower garden
　♦ floral garden
Blumengeschäft, n
　Blumenladen m
　♦ flower shop
　♦ florist's shop
　♦ florist's
blumengeschmückt, adj
　♦ decorated with flowers, adj
blumengeschmückter Balkon, m
　♦ flowered balcony
blumengeschmückte Terrasse, f
　♦ flowered terrace
Blumenhändler, m
　→ Florist

Blumeninsel, f
　♦ island of flowers
Blumenkasten, m
　♦ flower box
Blumenkiosk, m
　♦ flower kiosk
Blumenkohl, m
　Karfiol, m *ÖST*
　♦ cauliflower
Blumenkohlsalat, m
　♦ cauliflower salad
Blumenkohlsoufflé, n
　Blumenkohlauflauf, m
　♦ cauliflower soufflé *BE*
　♦ cauliflower souffle *AE*
Blumenkohlsuppe, f
　♦ cauliflower soup
Blumenkorb, m
　♦ flower basket
　♦ floral basket
Blumenkübel, m
　♦ flower tub
Blumenmarkt, m
　♦ flower market
Blumenmotiv, n
　♦ flower motif
Blumenraum, m
　(zur Aufbewahrung von Blumen)
　♦ flower room
Blumenschau, f
　♦ flower show
Blumenschmuck, m
　Blumendekoration, f
　♦ floral decoration
　♦ floral decor *AE*
　♦ floral décor *BE*
Blumenstadt, f
　♦ floral town
Blumenstand, m
　♦ flower stand *AE*
　♦ flower stall *BE*
Blumenstrauß, m
　Strauß Blumen, m
　♦ bunch of flowers
Blumenterrasse f
　♦ flower terrace
Blumentopf, m
　♦ flowerpot
Blumenuhr, f
　♦ floral clock
Blumenvase, f
　♦ flower vase
blumiger Wein, m
　♦ flowery wine
blumiges Bukett, n
　(Wein)
　blumiges Bouquet, n
　♦ flowery bouquet
Blutdruck, m
　♦ blood pressure
Blutdruckprüfung, f
　♦ blood pressure test
Blütenfest, n
　♦ blossom festival
Blütenmeer, n
　Meer von Blüten, n
　♦ sea of blossoms
blutig gebraten, adj *gastr*
　(Fleisch)
　blutend, adj *gastr*

Blutprobe

- underdone, adj *gastr*
- rare, adj *gastr*

Blutprobe, f
- blood test

BMX-Rad, n
- BMX bike

Bob, m
Bobschlitten, m
- bobsleigh
- bobsled
- bob

Bobabfahrt, f (Strecke)
Bobabfahrtstrecke, f
Bobbahn, f
- bob run
- bobsleigh run
- bobsled run

Bobbahn, f
Bobabfahrtsstrecke, f
Bobabfahrt, f
- bobsleigh run
- bobsled run
- bob run

Bobfahren, n
Bobsport, m
- bobsleighing

Bobfahrer, m
- bobber

Bobfahrt, f
- bobsleigh ride
- bobsled ride
- bob ride

Bobmannschaft, f
- bobsleigh team
- bobsled team
- bob team

Bobrennen, n
- bobsleigh race
- bobsled race
- bob race

Boccia, n/f
- boccie
- bocci
- bocce
- boccia

Bocciabahn, f
Bocciaplatz, m
- boccie court
- boccia court

Bocciaspiel, n
- game of boccie
- boccie

Boccia spielen
- play boccie
- play boccia

Bockbier, n
- bock beer
- bock

Bocksbeutel, m
- Bocksbeutel bottle
- Bocksbeutel flagon

Bodega, f *SPAN*
Weinkeller, m
Weinschenke, f
- bodega *SPAN*
- wine cellar
- wine tavern

Boden, m
- floor

Bodenanschluß, m
Bodensteckdose, f

- floor outlet
- floor socket

Boden aufwischen
- wipe the floor

Boden auslegen mit einem Teppich
Boden belegen mit einem Teppich
- lay the floor with a carpet

Bodenbeförderung, f
Bodentransport, m
Landtransport, m
- surface transportation *AE*
- surface transport *BE*

Bodenbelag, m
→ Fußbodenbelag

Bodenbelastung, f
Bodenbelastbarkeit, f
- floor load
- floor loading

Bodendiele, f
Bodenbrett, n
- floorboard *AE*
- floor-board *BE*

Bodendienst, m
- ground service

Bodendienstpersonal, n
- ground service personnel

Boden fegen
- sweep the floor

Bodenfläche, f
- floor area
- floor space

Bodenfliese, f
- floor tile

Bodenheizung, f
→ Fußbodenheizung

Bodenhöhe, f
- floor level

Boden ist beheizt
- floor is heated

Boden ist mit Teppich ausgelegt
- floor is carpeted

Bodenmaterial, n
- floor material

Bodenmikrofon, n
- floor microphone

Boden naß aufwischen
- mop up a floor

Bodenpersonal, n
(einer Fluggesellschaft)
- ground personnel
- ground staff
- ground crew

Boden reinigen
- clean a floor

Bodenreinigung, f
- floor cleaning
- cleaning (of) a floor

Bodenreinigungsmaschine, f
- floor-cleaning machine

Bodensatz, m
(in Gefäß)
- dregs *pl*
- dreg

Boden schrubben
Boden scheuern
- scrub the floor

Bodensee, m
- Lake Constance
- Lake of Constance, the

Bodenseegebiet, n
- Lake Constance area

Bodenseemuseum, n
- Lake Constance museum

Bodenseeregion, f
- Lake Constance region

Bodenseeufer, n
- shores of Lake Constance *pl*

Bodenseewein, m
- Lake Constance wine

Bodenstation, f
(Skilift)
- bottom station
- valley station

Boden staubsaugen
- vacuum-clean a floor
- vacuum a floor
- hoover a floor *BE*

Bodensteckdose, f
Bodenanschluß, m
- floor socket
- floor outlet

Bodenstecker, m
- floor plug

Bodenstewardeß, f
- ground stewardess

Bodenteppich, m
- floor carpet

Bodyboard, n
kleines Surfbrett, n
- body board

Bogenfenster, n
- arched window

Bogenschießen, n
Bogenschießsport, m
- archery

Bogenschießplatz, m
- archery court

Bogenschießwettbewerb, m
- archery competition

Bogenschießwettkampf, m
- archery contest

Bogenschütze, m
- archer

Boheme, f
- bohemian society

Bohemeferienort, m
- bohemian resort

Bohemetreffpunkt, m
- bohemian haunt

Bohemien, m
- bohemian

Böhme, m
- Bohemian

Böhmen
(Land)
- Bohemia

Böhmin, f
- Bohemian woman
- Bohemian girl
- Bohemian

böhmisch, adj
- Bohemian, adj

böhmische Art, adv *gastr*
nach böhmischer Art, adv *gastr*
- Bohemian style, adv *gastr*

Bohne, f
- bean

Bohneneintopf, m
- bean stew

Bohnenkaffee, m
- real coffee

Bohnenkraut, n
♦ savory
Bohnenpüree, n
♦ bean purée BE
♦ bean puree AE
Bohnenpüreesuppe, f
♦ bean purée soup BE
♦ bean puree soup AE
Bohnensalat, m
♦ bean salad
Bohnensuppe, f
♦ bean soup
Boistellesoße, f
♦ Boistelle sauce
Bolivien
♦ Bolivia
Bolivier, m
Bolivianer, m
♦ Bolivian
Bolivierin, f
Bolivianerin, f
♦ Bolivian girl
♦ Bolivian woman
♦ Bolivian
bolivisch, adj
♦ Bolivian, adj
Bologneserart, adv gastr
nach Bologneserart, adv gastr
♦ Bolognese style, adv gastr
Bolzplatz, m
→ Fußballplatz
Bombengeschäft, n
♦ roaring business
♦ roaring trade
Bombengeschäft machen
♦ do a roaring trade
Bon, m
♦ voucher
♦ check
Bona-Fide-Gast, m
♦ bona fide guest BE
Bona-Fide-Hausgast m
→ Bona-Fide-Reisender
♦ bona fide resident BE
Bona-Fide-Reisender, m
(in Großbritannien)
(Hat sonntags nach einer Reise von drei Meilen Anspruch auf Bewirtung in einem Gasthaus)
♦ bona fide traveller BE
Bona-Fide-Tourist, m
♦ bona fide tourist BE
Bonart, f
(z.B. im Restaurant)
♦ type of voucher
♦ voucher type
Bonbon, n
♦ candy AE
♦ sweet BE
Bonbonladen, m
Bonbongeschäft n
♦ candy store AE
♦ sweetshop BE
Bonbuch, n
♦ book of vouchers
♦ voucher book
Bondurchschrift, f
Bondurchschlag, m
♦ duplicate check
♦ duplicate voucher
Bonität, f
→ Zahlungsfähigkeit

Bonkontrolle, f
♦ voucher control
Bonsaimuseum, n
♦ bonsai museum
Bonus, m
♦ bonus
Bonusprogramm, n
♦ bonus program AE
♦ bonus programme BE
Bonvivant, m FR
Lebemann, n
♦ bon vivant FR
♦ viveur FR
Boom, m
♦ boom
boomendes Urlaubsjahr, n
boomendes Ferienjahr, n
♦ booming vacation year AE
♦ booming holiday year BE
Boom erleben
♦ experience a boom
Boomjahr, n
♦ boom year
Boomsaison f
♦ boom season
Boot, n
Schiff, n
♦ boat
Boot besteigen
Schiff besteigen
an Bord eines Boots gehen
an Bord eines Schiffs gehen
♦ board a boat
Bootcamper, m
♦ boat camper
Boot chartern
♦ charter a boat
Bootel, n
→ Schiffshotel
Boot erreichen nach X
Schiff erreichen nach X
♦ catch the boat to X
Boot fahren
♦ go boating
Bootfahren, n
Bootssport, m
♦ boating
Boot kentern
♦ boat capsized
Boot mieten
♦ rent a boat AE
♦ hire a boat BE
Bootsanhänger, m
Boottrailer m
♦ boat trailer
Bootsanlegeplatz, m
Bootsanlegesteg m
♦ boat moorage
♦ boat moorings pl
Bootsausflug, m
Schiffsausflug, m
♦ boat excursion
♦ boat trip
Bootsausstellung, f
♦ boat show
Bootsbegeisterter, m
♦ boating enthusiast
Bootsbesitzer, m
♦ boat owner
Bootscamping, n
♦ boat camping

Bootscharter, m
♦ boat charter
Bootsdeck, n
♦ boat deck
Boot segeln
♦ sail a boat
Bootseigentümer, m
♦ boat proprietor
Bootseinrichtung, f
♦ boating facility
Bootsfahrkarte, f
Bootsfahrschein, m
Bootskarte, f
Schiffsfahrkarte, f
Schiffskarte, f
♦ boat ticket
Bootsfahrt, f
♦ boat ride
♦ trip by boat
♦ boat trip
Bootsfahrt bei Mondschein, f
♦ moonlight boat trip
Bootsfahrt machen
♦ go on a boat trip
♦ go on a boat ride
♦ go boating
Bootsfahrt um die Insel, f
♦ boat trip (a)round the island
♦ boat ride (a)round the island
Bootsfahrt unternehmen
Bootsfahrt machen
♦ take a boat trip
♦ take a boat ride
Bootsfahrt veranstalten
♦ organise a boat trip
Bootsferien, pl
Bootsurlaub, m
♦ boat holiday BE
♦ boating holiday BE
♦ boat vacation AE
Bootshafen, m
♦ boat harbor AE
♦ boat harbour BE
♦ marina
Bootshaus, n
♦ boathouse
Bootsladung (von Touristen), f
♦ boatload (of tourists)
Bootsliegeplatz, m
Anlegeplatz, m
♦ mooring place
Bootslip, m
♦ boat launching facility
Bootsmole, f
Schiffsmole, f
♦ boat jetty
Bootsmuseum, n
Schiffsmuseum, n
♦ boat museum
Bootsreisender, m
Schiffsreisender, m
♦ boat traveller
♦ boat traveler AE
Bootsrennen, n
♦ boat race
Bootssee, m
Rudersee, m
♦ boat lake
♦ boating lake BE
Bootsspaß, m
♦ boating fun

Bootssteg

Bootssteg, m
→ Landungssteg
Bootstour, f
♦ boat tour
Bootstrekking, n
♦ boat trekking
Bootsurlaub, m
Bootsferien, pl
♦ boat vacation AE
♦ boat holiday BE
♦ boating holiday BE
Bootsverkehr, m
Schiffsverkehr, m
♦ boat traffic
Bootsverleih
(Hinweisschild)
♦ Boats for rent AE
♦ Boats for hire BE
Bootsverleih, m
Bootsvermietung, f
♦ boat hire BE
♦ boat rental AE
♦ renting boats AE
♦ hiring out boats BE
Bootsvermietung, f
Bootsverleih, m
♦ boat rental AE
♦ boat hire BE
♦ renting boats AE
♦ hiring out boats BE
Bootswerft, f
Werft, f
♦ boatyard
Bootszentrum, n
Bootssportzentrum, n
♦ boating center AE
♦ boating centre BE
Boottrailer, m
→ Bootsanhänger
Boot verleihen
Boot vermieten
♦ hire out a boat BE
♦ rent (out) a boat
Boot vermieten an jn
♦ rent (out) a boat to s.o.
♦ hire (out) a boat to s.o. BE
Boot zu vermieten
(Hinweisschild)
♦ Boat for rent AE
♦ Boat for hire BE
Bordausgaben, f pl (Schiff)
♦ on-board expenses pl
♦ on-board expenditure sg
Bordausrüstung, f (Schiff)
♦ on-board equipment
Bordbibliothek, f (Schiff)
Bordbücherei, f
♦ ship's library
Borddurchsage, f (Flugzeug)
♦ in-flight announcement
Bordeauxglas, n
♦ claret glass
Bordeauxwein, m
♦ Bordeaux wine
♦ Bordeaux
♦ claret
Bordeinnahme, f (Schiff)
♦ on-board revenue
Bordeinrichtung, f (Schiff)
♦ on-board facility
♦ facility on board (ship)

Bordeleserart, adv gastr
nach Bordeleserart, adv gastr
♦ Bordelese style, adv gastr
Bordell, n
öffentliches Haus, n
Puff, m inform
♦ brothel
Bordellviertel, n
Rotlichtviertel, n
♦ red-light district
Bordfilm, m (Flugzeug)
♦ in-flight film
Bordgepäck, n
Kabinengepäck, n
♦ cabin baggage AE
♦ cabin luggage BE
Bordgeschäft, n (Schiff)
Bordladen, m
♦ ship's store AE
♦ ship's shop BE
♦ store on board AE
♦ shop on board BE
Bordkarte, f
(Flugzeug)
♦ boarding pass
♦ boarding card
Bordkino, n (Flugzeug)
♦ in-flight movie AE
♦ in-flight cinema BE
Bordkino, n (Schiff)
♦ movies on board AE
♦ cinema on board BE
♦ on-board cinema BE
Bordküche, f (Flugzeugverpflegung)
♦ in-flight kitchen
♦ in-flight cuisine
Bordküche, f (in Verkehrsmitteln)
♦ galley
Bordleben, n
→ Leben an Bord
Bordmagazin, n (Flugzeug)
♦ in-flight magazine
Bordmahlzeit, f (Flugzeug)
Bordessen, n
♦ in-flight meal
Bordmechaniker, m (Flugzeug)
Bordwart, m
Bordingenieur, m
Flugingenieur, m
♦ flight engineer
Bordorchester, n (Schiff)
♦ ship's orchestra
Bordpersonal, n (Schiff)
♦ on-board staff
♦ on-board personnel
Bordrestaurant, n (Schiff)
♦ on-board restaurant
♦ restaurant on board
Bordseminar, n (Schiff)
♦ on-board seminar
Bordservice, m (Flugzeug)
Service während des Fluges, m
♦ in-flight service
Bordservice, m (Schiff)
♦ on-board service
Bordstein, m
Randstein, m
Straßenkante, f
♦ curb AE
♦ curbstone AE

♦ kerb BE
♦ kerbstone BE
Bordsteward, m (Flugzeug)
♦ cabin attendant
Bordumsatz, m (Schiff)
Umsatz an Bord, m
♦ on-board sales pl
♦ sales on board pl
Bordunterhaltung, f (Flugzeug)
♦ in-flight entertainment
Bordunterhaltung, f (Schiff)
♦ entertainment on board
♦ on-board entertainment
Bordunterkunft, f (Schiff)
♦ on-board accommodation
Bordveranstaltung, f (Schiff)
♦ event on board
♦ function on board
Bordverpflegung, f (Flugzeug)
♦ in-flight catering
♦ flight catering
♦ in-flight food
Bordverpflegung, f (Schiff)
♦ catering on board
Bordvortrag, m (Schiff)
♦ on-board lecture
Bordwährung, f (Schiff)
♦ ship's currency
♦ on-board currency
♦ currency on board
Borretsch, m
♦ borage
Borschtsch, m
♦ bortch
♦ beetroot soup
Bosnien
♦ Bosnia
Bosnier, m
Bosniak, m
♦ Bosnian
Bosnierin, f
Bosniakin, f
♦ Bosnian girl
♦ Bosnian woman
♦ Bosnian
bosnisch, adj
♦ Bosnian, adj
botanische Reise, f
♦ botanical tour
♦ botanical journey
♦ botanical trip
Botanischer Garten, m
♦ botanical garden
♦ botanical gardens pl
♦ botanic garden
♦ botanic gardens pl
botanische Wanderreise, f
♦ botanical walking tour
♦ botanic hiking tour
Bote, m
♦ messenger
Botendienst, m
Botenservice m
♦ messenger service
Botengang für einen Gast erledigen
♦ run an errand for a guest
Botrytis, f
Edelfäule, f
♦ botrytis
♦ noble rot

Botschaft, f (eines Landes)
 ♦ embassy
Botschaft, f (Mitteilung)
 → Mitteilung
Botschafter, m
 ♦ ambassador
Botsuana
 Botswana
 ♦ Botswana
Botsuaner, m
 ♦ Botswanan
Botsuanerin, f
 ♦ Botswanan girl
 ♦ Botswanan woman
 ♦ Botswanan
botsuanisch, adj
 ♦ Botswanan, adj
 ♦ Botswana, adj
Boudoir, n
 ♦ boudoir
Bouillabaise, f *FR*
 ♦ bouillabaise *FR*
Boule, n/f *FR*
 ♦ boule *FR*
 ♦ boules *pl*
Boulekugel, f
 ♦ boule ball
Bouleplatz, m
 ♦ boule court
 ♦ boules court
 ♦ boule pitch
 ♦ boules pitch
Bouleset, n
 Boulespiel, n
 ♦ boule set
 ♦ boules set
Boulespiel, n
 ♦ game of boule
 ♦ game of boules
 ♦ boule game
 ♦ boules game
Boule spielen
 ♦ play boule
 ♦ play boules
Bouleturnier, n
 ♦ boule tournament
 ♦ boules tournament
Boulevard, m
 ♦ boulevard
Boulevardcafé, n
 ♦ boulevard café *BE*
 ♦ boulevard cafe *AE*
Bouquet, n
 → Bukett
Bouquet garni, n *FR m*
 ♦ bouquet garni *FR*
Bourbon, m
 ♦ bourbon
Bourbon Whiskey, m
 ♦ bourbon whiskey
Boutique f
 ♦ boutique
Bowle, f (Getränk)
 ♦ cold punch
 ♦ punch
 ♦ cup
 ♦ bowl
Bowle, f (Schüssel)
 Bowlenschüssel, f
 Bowleschüssel, f
 ♦ punch-bowl

Bowle ansetzen
 ♦ make the punch
bowlen
 Bowling spielen
 Bowls spielen
 kegeln
 ♦ bowl
 ♦ play (at) bowls
Bowling, n (generell)
 ♦ bowling
Bowling, n (mit zehn Kegeln)
 ♦ ten-pin bowling
Bowling, n (Rasen)
 → Bowls, Rasenkegeln
Bowlinganlage, f
 Bowlingkomplex, m
 Kegelanlage, f
 Kegelkomplex, m
 ♦ bowling complex
Bowlingbahn, f
 ♦ bowling alley
 ♦ tenpin bowling alley
Bowls, n
 Bowlsspiel, n
 Rasenkegeln, n
 ♦ bowls *pl=sg*
Bowlsplatz, m
 Rasenplatz, m
 ♦ bowling green
Bowls spielen
 ♦ play bowls
Box für ein Fahrzeug, f
 ♦ box for car *AE*
 ♦ lock-up garage *BE*
Boxkampf, m
 ♦ boxing match
Boy, m
 Türboy, m
 ♦ bellhop *AE sl*
 ♦ page
 ♦ bellboy *AE*
Boykott, m
 ♦ boycott
boykottieren etw
 ♦ boycott s.th.
BP, m
 (Zimmer mit Frühstück)
 Bermuda Plan, m
 ♦ BP
 ♦ Bermuda Plan
BR
 British Rail
 ♦ BR
 ♦ British Rail
braisiert, adj *gastr*
 ♦ braised, adj *gastr*
Branchendurchnitt, m
 ♦ industry average
Branchenführer, m
 ♦ industry leader
Branchenrabatt, m
 ♦ trade discount
Brandanschlag, m
 ♦ arson attack
Brandenburg
 (Land)
 ♦ Brandenburg
brandenburgisch, adj
 ♦ Brandenburg, adj
Brandmeldeanlage, f
 Feuermeldeanlage, f

 ♦ fire detection system
 ♦ fire alarm system
Brandschutz, m
 Feuerschutz, m
 ♦ fire protection
Brandschutzbestimmungen, f pl
 ♦ fire regulations *pl*
Brandschutztür, f
 ♦ fire door
Brandstifter, m
 ♦ arsonist
 ♦ fire-raiser *BE*
Brandstiftung, f
 ♦ arson
 ♦ fire-raising *BE*
Brandverhütung, f
 Feuerverhütung, n
 ♦ precautions against fire *pl*
 ♦ fire prevention
Brandverhütungsmaßnahme, f
 Brandschutzmaßnahme, f
 ♦ fire prevention measure
Brandversicherung, f
 Feuerversicherung f
 ♦ fire insurance
Branntwein, m
 → Weinbrand
Branntweinausschank, m (Verkauf)
 Spirituosenverkauf, m
 ♦ liquor sale
 ♦ sale of liquor
Branntweinbrenner, m
 ♦ brandy distiller
Branntweinbrennerei, f
 ♦ brandy distillery
Branntweinkirsche, f
 ♦ brandy cherry
Branntweinsteuer, f
 Steuer auf alkoholische Getränke, f
 ♦ liquor tax
 ♦ tax on liquor
 ♦ liquor excise *AE*
Brasilianer, m
 ♦ Brazilian
Brasilianerin, f
 ♦ Brazilian girl
 ♦ Brazilian woman
 ♦ Brazilian
brasilianisch, adj
 ♦ Brazilian, adj
brasilianische Art, adv *gastr*
 nach brasilianischer Art, adv *gastr*
 ♦ Brazilian style, adv *gastr*
Brasilien
 ♦ Brazil
Brasse, f
 Brachse, f
 Brachsen, m
 Blei, m
 ♦ bream
Brasserie, f *FR*
 ♦ brasserie *FR*
brasserieartige Gaststätte, f
 Gaststätte im Brasseriestil, f
 ♦ brasserie-style bar *AE*
 ♦ brasserie-style pub *BE*
Bratapfel, m
 ♦ roasted apple
 ♦ roast apple

Braten

Braten, m
  gebratenes Fleisch, n
  ♦ roast meat
braten etw am Spieß
  ♦ roast s.th. on the spit
braten etw (im Ofen)
  ♦ roast s.th.
braten etw (in der Pfanne)
  ♦ fry s.th.
Bratenfett, n
  ♦ dripping
Bratengabel, f
  ♦ joint fork
Bratenkoch, m
  Rôtisseur, m *FR*
  Rotisseur, m
  ♦ roast cook
  ♦ rôtisseur *FR*
braten lassen sich in der Sonne
  sich in der Sonne braten lassen
  ♦ roast (oneself) in the sun
Bratenmesser, n
  ♦ joint knife
Bratensoße, f
  Fleischsaft, m
  ♦ gravy
Bratenstück, n (roh) *gastr*
  Stück zum Braten, n *gastr*
  ♦ joint *gastr*
Bräter, m
  ♦ roasting pan
  ♦ roasting tin *BE*
Bratfisch, m
  gebratener Fisch, m
  ♦ fried fish
Brathähnchen, n (im Backofen gebraten)
  gebratenes Hähnchen, n
  ♦ roast chicken
Brathähnchen, n (in der Bratpfane gebraten)
  gebratenes Hähnchen, n
  ♦ fried chicken
Brathähnchenbude, f
  Brathähnchenstand, m
  ♦ fried-chicken stand
  ♦ fried-chicken stall *BE*
Bratkartoffeln, f pl
  ♦ fried potatoes *pl*
  ♦ roast potatoes *pl*
Bratküche, f
  → Garküche
Bratpfanne, f
  ♦ frying pan *AE*
  ♦ frying-pan *BE*
  ♦ skillet *AE*
Bratspieß, m
  Drehgrill, m
  ♦ spit
Bratwurst, f
  ♦ fried sausage
  ♦ grilled sausage
Bratwürstchen, n
  Würstchen, n
  ♦ banger *BE inform*
Bratwürstchen mit Kartoffelbrei, n pl
  ♦ bangers and mash *BE inform pl*
brauchen etw
  benötigen etw
  ♦ need s.th.
  ♦ require s.th.
Brauchtum, n
  ♦ local culture

  ♦ tradition
  ♦ folklore
Brauchtumsabend, m
  Heimatabend, m
  ♦ evening of traditional music and dance
  ♦ evening of local culture
Brauer, m
  Bierbrauer, m
  ♦ brewer
Brauerei, f
  Bierbrauerei, f
  ♦ brewery
brauereiabhängige Verkaufsstelle, f
  Vertragsverkaufsstelle, f
  ♦ tied outlet
brauereibetriebenes Restaurant, n
  ♦ brewery-operated restaurant
brauerei-eigene Gaststätte, f
  ♦ brewery-owned bar *AE*
  ♦ brewery-owned public house *BE*
  ♦ brewery-owned pub *BE*
Brauereigaststätte, f
  brauereigebundene Gaststätte, f
  ♦ tied house
Brauereigaststätte, f
  (braut und verkauft eigenes Bier)
  ♦ brewpub *AE*
Brauereigaul, m
  ♦ dray horse *AE*
  ♦ dray-horse *BE*
Brauereigeschäft, n
  Brauereibranche, f
  Braubranche, f
  ♦ brewery business
Brauereigesellschaft, f
  Brauereiunternehmen n
  ♦ brewery company
Brauereiindustrie, f
  Brauereibranche, f
  ♦ brewery industry
  ♦ brewing industry
Brauereimuseum, n
  (in Brauerei)
  ♦ brewery museum
Brauereipferd, n
  Brauereigaul, m *coll*
  ♦ brewer's dray horse *AE*
  ♦ brewer's dray-horse *BE*
  ♦ dray horse *AE*
  ♦ dray-horse *BE*
brauereiunabhängige Gaststätte, f
  ♦ free house
Brauereiwagen, m
  ♦ brewer's dray
Braugeschäft, n
  ♦ brewing business
Braugesellschaft, f
  Braufirma, f
  ♦ brewing company
Braugewerbe, f
  ♦ brewing trade
Brauhaus, n
  ♦ brewhouse
Brauhefe, f
  ♦ brewer's yeast
Brauindustrie, f
  Braubranche, f
  ♦ brewing industry
Braumarkt, m
  ♦ brewing market

bräunen etw *gastr*
  ♦ brown s.th. *gastr*
braungebrannt, adj
  ♦ bronzed, adj
  ♦ tanned, adj
Bräunungsbehandlung, f
  ♦ tanning treatment
Bräunungsliege, f
  → Sonnenbank
Bräunungsmassage, f
  ♦ tanning massage
Bräunungsraum, m
  Bräunungszimmer, n
  ♦ suntanning room *AE*
  ♦ sun-tanning room *BE*
Bräunungsstudio, n
  ♦ solarium
braun werden
  ♦ get a tan
Brause f
  → Dusche
Brauselimonde, f
  ♦ sherbet
Brausepulver, n
  ♦ sherbet powder
  ♦ lemonade powder
Braut, f
  ♦ bride
Bräutigam, m
  ♦ bridegroom
Brautpaar, n
  ♦ bride and groom
Braut und Bräutigam zutrinken
  ♦ toast the bride and the groom
Brauverfahren, n
  ♦ brewing method
Break-even-Analyse, f
  Gewinnschwellenanalyse, f
  ♦ break-even analysis
Break-even-Auslastungsgrad, m
  ♦ break-even occupancy level
  ♦ break-even level of occupancy
Break-even-Punkt, m
  → Gewinnschwelle
Break-even-Umsatz, m
  → Gewinnschwellenumsatz
brechend voll, adj (Raum)
  ♦ jammed, adj
  ♦ packed, adj
  ♦ jam-packed, adj *coll*
  ♦ crowded to capacity, adj
brechend voll sein
  ♦ be jammed
  ♦ be packed
  ♦ be crowded to capacity
Brechreiz, m
  Ekel, m
  ♦ nausea
Bregenzer Festspiele, n pl
  ♦ Bregenz Festival, the
breit, adj (Maßangabe)
  ♦ wide, adj
Breite, f (Maßangabe)
  ♦ width
  ♦ breadth
breiter Korridor, m
  breiter Flur, m
  ♦ wide corridor
breiter Sandstrand m
  ♦ wide sandy beach

breiter Strand, m
♦ wide beach
breites Bett, n
♦ wide bed
Breitwand, f
Breitleinwand f
♦ wide screen
brennender Durst, m
♦ burning thirst
brennendes Hotel, n
♦ burning hotel
Brennerei, f
Schnapsbrennerei, f
♦ distillery
♦ still
Brennerpaß m
(Eigenname)
♦ Brenner Pass
Brennesselsuppe, f
♦ nettle soup
Brennholz, n
Feuerholz, n
♦ firewood
Brennmaterialkosten, pl
→ Brennstoffkosten
Brennpunkt, m
♦ focus
♦ focal point
Brennpunkt des kulturellen Lebens, m
♦ focus of cultural life
♦ focal point of cultural life
Brennstoff, m
Brennmaterial, n
Heizmaterial, n
♦ fuel
Brennstoffkosten, pl
Brennmaterialkosten, pl
♦ fuel costs pl
♦ fuel cost
Brennstoff- und Energiekosten, pl
♦ fuel and energy costs pl
♦ fuel and energy cost
Brennstoffverbrauch, m
♦ consumption of fuel
♦ fuel consumption
brenzlige Ecke, f
(Gebiet)
ungemütliche Ecke, f
♦ warm corner
Bretagne, f
♦ Britanny
Bretone, m
♦ Breton
Bretonin, f
♦ Breton girl
♦ Breton woman
♦ Breton
bretonisch, adj
♦ Breton, adj
bretonische Art, adv gastr
nach bretonischer Art, adv gastr
♦ Breton style, adv gastr
Bretterweg, m
Gehsteig aus Brettern, m
♦ boardwalk
Brettlfan, m coll
Skifan, m
♦ ski buff coll
Brettspiel, n
♦ board game

Brezel, f
Salzbrezel, f
♦ pretzel
♦ salt pretzel
Bridge, n
♦ bridge
Bridgebegeisterter, m
♦ bridge enthusiast
Bridgeclub, m
♦ bridge club
Bridgekarte f
♦ bridge card
Bridgemeisterschaft, f
♦ bridge championship
Bridgenachmittag m
♦ bridge afternoon
♦ afternoon devoted to playing bridge
Bridgepartie, f
♦ bridge party
♦ game of bridge
♦ bridge game
Bridgepartie machen
♦ hold a bridge party
Bridgepartner m
♦ bridge partner
Bridgerunde f
♦ rubber of bridge
Bridgesalon, m
♦ bridge lounge
♦ bridge room
Bridgespiel, n
♦ game of bridge
♦ bridge game
Bridge spielen
Partie Bridge spielen
♦ play bridge
♦ play a game of bridge
Bridgespieler m
♦ bridge player
Bridgetisch, m
♦ bridge table
Bridgeturnier, n
♦ bridge tournament
Bridgeveranstaltung, f
♦ bridge event
Bridgewettbewerb m
♦ bridge competition
Bridgezimmer n
Bridgeraum m
♦ bridge room
Brief, m
♦ letter
Briefablage, f
Brieffach n
♦ letter rack
Briefbeschwerer, m
♦ paper weight
Brieffächer, n pl
(in der Rezeption)
Postablagefächer, n pl
♦ mail rack
Briefkasten, m
Postkasten, m
♦ letter-box BE
♦ mailbox AE
brieflich, adv
♦ by letter, adv
brieflich bestätigen etw
brieflich zusagen etw
♦ confirm s.th. by letter

briefliche Anfrage, f
♦ letter of inquiry
♦ letter of enquiry
♦ letter inquiring about s.th.
♦ letter enquiring about s.th.
briefliche Buchung, f
♦ letter booking
♦ booking by letter
briefliche Reservierung, f
♦ letter reservation
♦ reservation by letter
brieflich reservieren etw
♦ reserve s.th. by letter
♦ make a reservation by letter
brieflich stornieren
♦ cancel s.th. by letter
♦ make a cancellation by letter
♦ make a cancelation by letter AE
Briefmarke, f
♦ postage stamp
♦ stamp
Briefmarkenausstellung, f
♦ stamp exhibition
♦ stamp exhibit AE
Briefmarkensammler, m
♦ stamp collector
Briefmarkensammlung, f
♦ stamp collection
Briefrack, n
→ Briefablage
Brieftasche, f
♦ billfold AE
♦ wallet BE
Briekäse, m
Brie, m
♦ Brie cheese
♦ Brie
Brienzer See, m
♦ Lake of Brienz, the
Bries, n
♦ sweetbread
Brigade f
♦ brigade
Brigadesystem, n
♦ brigade system
bringen etw durch den Zoll
♦ bring s.th. through customs
bringen jn an den Konferenztisch
♦ bring s.o. to the conference table
bringen jn über die Grenze
über die Grenze jn bringen
♦ take s.o. across the border
Bringen Sie mir bitte die Rechnung!
♦ Bring me my bill, please
♦ Bring me my check, please AE
Bringen Sie uns fürs erste eine Flasche Wein
♦ Bring us a bottle of wine to begin with
Brioche, f FR
♦ brioche FR
Britannien
♦ Britain
Brite, m
♦ British man
♦ Briton
♦ Britisher humor
Britin, f
♦ British girl
♦ British woman
♦ Briton
britisch, adj
♦ British, adj

Britische Eisenbahn

Britische Eisenbahn, f
　British Rail
　♦ British Rail
　♦ BR
britische Kost, f
　♦ British fare
Britischen Inseln, die, f pl
　♦ British Isles, the pl
Britischen Jungferninseln, die, pl
　♦ British Virgin Islands, the pl
britischen Markt bedienen
　♦ serve the British market
Britischer Jugendherbergsverband, m
　♦ British Youth Hostels Association
Brokkoli, m
　♦ broccoli
Brokkolisuppe, f
　♦ broccoli soup
Brombeere, f
　♦ blackberry
Brombeereiskrem, f
　Brombeereis, n
　♦ blackberry ice cream AE
　♦ blackberry ice-cream BE
　♦ blackberry ice
Brombeergelee, n
　♦ blackberry jelly
　♦ bramble jelly
Brombeerkonfitüre, f
　♦ blackberry jam
Brombeermilchmixgetränk, n
　♦ blackberry milk shake
Brombeersirup, m
　♦ blackberry syrup
Brombeersorbet, n
　♦ blackberry sorbet
Brombeerwein, m
　♦ blackberry wine
Bronze, f
　♦ bronze
Bronzemedaille, f
　♦ bronze medal
Bronzeplakette, f
　♦ bronze plaque
Bronzestatue, f
　♦ bronze statue
Bronzezeit, f
　♦ Bronze Age, the
Bronzezeitsiedlung, f
　♦ Bronze Age settlement
Broschüre, f
　→ Prospekt
Broschüre anfordern
　→ Prospekt anfordern
Brot, n
　♦ bread
Brot backen
　♦ bake bread
Brot brechen mit jm
　♦ break bread with s.o.
Brotbrett, n
　(zum Schneiden von Brot)
　♦ breadboard
Brötchen, n
　Semmel, f
　Weck, m
　♦ roll
Brote machen coll
　belegte Brote machen
　♦ make sandwiches

Brotkasten, m
　♦ bread box AE
　♦ bread-bin BE
Brot kaufen
　♦ buy some bread
　♦ buy a loaf of bread
Brotkonsum, m
　Brotverbrauch, m
　♦ bread consumption
　♦ consumption of bread
Brotkorb, m
　♦ bread basket
Brotkrume, f
　♦ bread crumb AE
　♦ breadcrumb BE
brotlos, adj
　♦ breadless, adj
brotlos, adv
　ohne Brot, adv
　♦ without bread, adv
　♦ out of bread, adv
Brotmesser, n
　♦ bread knife
Brotofen, m
　♦ bread oven
Brotpudding, m
　♦ bread pudding
Brotröster, m
　♦ bread toaster
Brotscheibe, f
　♦ bread slice
　♦ slice of bread
Brotschneidemaschine, f
　♦ bread cutter
Brotsoße, f
　♦ bread sauce
Brotsuppe, f
　♦ bread soup
Brotteig, m
　♦ bread dough
Brotteller, m
　♦ bread plate
Brot toasten
　Brot rösten
　♦ toast bread
Brot verdienen
　sein Brot verdienen
　♦ earn one's bread
Brot vom Mund absparen
　♦ stint oneself of food
Brotwürfel, m
　♦ bread cube
Brotzeit, f (nachmittags)
　→ Nachmittagsimbiß
Brotzeit, f (vormittags)
　Vormittagsimbiß, m
　Vormittagsvesper, f
　♦ midmorning snack AE
　♦ mid-morning snack
　♦ elevenses BE coll
Brotzeit machen (nachmittags)
　vespern
　♦ have one's afternoon snack
Brotzeit machen (vormittags)
　vespern
　♦ have one's mid-morning snack
　♦ have one's elevenses BE
Bruch, m (Geschirr)
　♦ breakage

Bruchbude, f
　(unsolide gebautes Haus)
　♦ jerry-built house
Bruch von Porzellan und Glas, m
　♦ breakage of porcelain and glass
　♦ breakage of china and glass
Brücke, f (Bauwerk, Schiffsteil)
　♦ bridge
Brücke, f (Vorleger)
　→ Vorleger
Brückendeck, n
　♦ bridge deck
Brückentor, n
　♦ bridge gate
Brückenzoll, m
　♦ bridge toll
Brunch, m
　(Breakfast und Lunch)
　Frümi, n
　♦ brunch
Brunchbüfett, n
　♦ buffet brunch
　♦ brunch buffet AE
Brunei
　♦ Brunei
Bruneier, m
　♦ Bruneian
Bruneierin, f
　♦ Bruneian girl
　♦ Bruneian woman
　♦ Bruneian
bruneisch, adj
　♦ Bruneian, adj
　♦ Brunei, adj
Brunnen, m
　♦ fountain
　♦ well
　♦ spring
Brunnen aus rotem Sandstein, m
　♦ fountain of red sandstone
Brunnenbecken, n
　♦ fountain pool
Brunnenfest, n
　♦ fountain festival
Brunnenhalle, f
　(in Kurort)
　♦ wellroom
Brunnenhof, m
　♦ fountain court
Brunnenhofsuite, f
　♦ fountain court suite
Brunnenhofzimmer, n
　♦ fountain court room
Brunnenkresse, f
　♦ watercress
Brunnenkressesalat, m
　♦ watercress salad
Brunnenrestaurant, n
　♦ fountain restaurant
Brüsselerart, adv gastr
　nach Brüsselerart, adv gastr
　♦ Brussels style, adv gastr
Bruttoausstellungsfläche, f
　♦ overall exhibition area
　♦ overall exhibition space
Bruttobereichsergebnis, n
　♦ gross departmental result
Bruttobetrag, m
　♦ gross amount
Bruttobetriebsergebnis, n
　Bruttobetriebsgewinn, m

114

Betriebsergebnis l, n
♦ **GOP**
♦ **gross operating profit**
Bruttobetriebsertrag, m
(GuV)
♦ **gross operating income**
Bruttoeinkommen, n
♦ **gross income**
Bruttoeinnahmen, f pl
♦ **gross revenues** pl
♦ gross revenue
♦ gross income
♦ gross takings pl
♦ gross receipts pl
Bruttoerlös, m (aus Veräußerung)
♦ **gross proceeds** pl
Bruttoerlös, m (generell)
♦ **gross revenue**
Bruttoertrag, m
Rohertrag, m
♦ **gross yield**
♦ gross earning
Bruttofläche, f
♦ **gross area**
♦ gross space
Bruttogewicht, n
♦ **gross weight**
Bruttogewinn, m
Rohgewinn m
♦ **gross profit**
Bruttogewinn pro Gedeck, m
Rohgewinn pro Gedeck m
♦ **gross profit per cover**
Bruttogewinn pro Zimmer, m
♦ **gross profit per room**
Bruttohallenfläche, f
Bruttosaalfläche, f
♦ **gross hall area**
♦ gross hall space
♦ gross area of (the) hall
Bruttomiete, f
♦ **gross rental**
Bruttomieteinnahmen, f pl
♦ **gross rental income** AE
♦ gross rent income
Bruttomietkosten, pl (Mobilien)
♦ **overall rental costs** AE pl
♦ overall rental cost AE
♦ overall hire costs BE pl
♦ overall hire cost BE
Bruttopreis, m
♦ **gross price**
♦ gross rate
Bruttoprovision, f
♦ **gross commission**
Bruttoquadratmeter, m
♦ **gross square meter** AE
♦ gross square metre BE
Bruttoreiseintensität, f
♦ **gross travel intensity**
Bruttospeisenerlös, m
♦ **gross proceeds from food sales** pl
♦ gross proceeds from catering pl
Bruttoumsatz, m
♦ **gross sales** pl
♦ gross turnover
Bruttoverbrauch, m
♦ **gross consumption**
Bruttoverkaufspreis, m
♦ **gross selling price**
♦ gross selling rate

Bruttozimmererlös, m
Bruttobeherbergungserlös, m
♦ **gross room revenue**
♦ gross rooms revenue
Bruttozimmerumsatz, m
♦ **gross room sales** pl
♦ gross rooms sales pl
♦ gross room turnover
♦ gross rooms turnover
Brutzeit, f
♦ **breeding season**
brutzeln
zischen
♦ **sizzle**
BTX, m
Bildschirmtext, m
♦ **Prestel** BE
♦ viewdata
BTX-Buchung, f
♦ **Prestel booking** BE
♦ viewdata booking
BTX-Buchungsservice m
BTX-Buchungsdienst m
♦ **viewdata booking service**
♦ Prestel booking service BE
buchbar, adj
bestellbar, adj
♦ **bookable, adj**
buchbarer Stellplatz, m
(Camping)
♦ **bookable pitch**
buchbar sein
♦ **be bookable**
Buchclub, m
♦ **book club**
Buche, f
♦ **beech**
buchen
♦ **make a booking**
♦ book s.th.
♦ make a reservation AE
Buchenallee, f
♦ **beech avenue**
Buchenbaum, m
Buche, f
♦ **beech tree**
buchen bei jm
♦ **book with s.o.**
buchen bis New York
(Fahrkarte)
♦ **book to New York**
buchen bis spätestens 10. Mai
♦ **book by 10 May at the latest**
buchen bis X
(bis zu einem Ort)
buchen bis nach X
♦ **book to X**
buchen bis zu (einem bestimmten Termin)
♦ **book by (a certain date)**
Buchender, m
Bucher, m
Besteller, m
Anmelder, m
♦ **person booking s.th.**
♦ person making a booking
♦ person booking in
♦ booker
buchen etw
♦ **book s.th.**
buchen etw an Ort und Stelle
♦ **book s.th. on the spot**

buchen etw bei jm
♦ **book s.th. with s.o.**
buchen etw bis (spätestens) 3. Mai
(Buchungszeitpunkt)
♦ **book s.th. by 3 May (at the latest)**
buchen etw bis zu 14 Tagen im voraus
♦ **book s.th. up to 14 days in advance**
buchen etw brieflich
♦ **book s.th. by letter**
buchen etw direkt
♦ **book s.th. directly**
♦ book s.th. direct
buchen etw durch jn
buchen etw über jn
♦ **book s.th. through s.o.**
buchen etw frühzeitig
♦ **book s.th. early**
♦ book s.th. well in advance
buchen etw für einen bestimmten Zeitraum
♦ **book s.th. for a certain period of time**
buchen etw für jn
jm etw buchen
♦ **book s.th. for s.o.**
♦ book s.o. s.th.
buchen etw für zwei Wochen
♦ **book s.th. for two weeks**
buchen etw im voraus
vorbuchen etw
vorbestellen etw
♦ **book s.th. in advance**
♦ book s.th. ahead
♦ prebook s.th.
buchen etw in Eile
buchen etw übereilt
♦ **book s.th. in a hurry**
buchen etw in gutem Glauben
♦ **book s.th. in good faith**
buchen etw pauschal
buchen etw zum Pauschalpreis
♦ **book s.th. on inclusive terms**
buchen etw persönlich
♦ **book s.th. in person**
buchen etw per Telegramm
♦ **book s.th. by telegram**
buchen etw per Telex
♦ **book s.th. by telex**
buchen etw privat
♦ **book s.th. privately**
buchen etw provisorisch
♦ **book s.th. provisionally**
buchen etw rechtzeitig
♦ **book s.th. in good time**
buchen etw schriftlich
♦ **book s.th. in writing**
buchen etw separat
♦ **book s.th. separately**
buchen etw telefonisch
♦ **book s.th. by telephone**
♦ book s.th. by phone
♦ make a telephone booking
buchen etw verbindlich
♦ **book s.th. definitely**
buchen (etw) zwei Wochen im voraus
♦ **book (s.th.) two weeks in advance**
buchen im Namen von jm
buchen im Auftrag von jm
♦ **book on behalf of s.o.**
♦ book on s.o.'s behalf
buchen im voraus
♦ **book in advance**

buchen in letzter Minute

- ♦ book ahead
- ♦ prebook s.th.

buchen in letzter Minute
- ♦ make a last-minute booking

buchen jm etw
  buchen etw für jn
- ♦ book s.o. s.th.
- ♦ book s.th. for s.o.

Buchenmöbel, n pl
- ♦ beech furniture *sg*

buchen nach München
  (Fahrkarte)
- ♦ book for Munich

buchen nach X
  (nach einem Ort)
- ♦ book for X

buchen sehr frühzeitig
- ♦ book well in advance

Buchen Sie jetzt!
- ♦ Book now!

Buchen Sie rechtzeitig!
- ♦ Make your reservations well in advance!

Buchenstuhl, m
- ♦ beech chair

Buchentisch, m
- ♦ beech table

Buchenwald, m
- ♦ beech forest
- ♦ beech wood

buchen zu den Preisen von 1999
- ♦ book at the prices of 1999
- ♦ book at the rates of 1999

Bucher, m
  Buchender, m
  Anmelder, m
  Besteller, m
- ♦ booker
- ♦ person booking s.th.
- ♦ person making a booking
- ♦ person booking in

Bücherschrank, m
- ♦ bookcase

Bücherstand, m
  Bücherverkaufsstand, m
- ♦ bookstand
- ♦ bookstall *BE*

Buchhalter, m
- ♦ bookkeeper
- ♦ accountant

Buchhaltung, f (Aktivität)
- ♦ accounting
- ♦ bookkeeping

Buchhaltung, f (Raum)
- ♦ accounts office

Buchhaltungsabteilung, f
- ♦ accounts department
- ♦ accounting department
- ♦ bookkeeping department

Buchhaltungsautomat, m
- → Buchungsautomat

Buchhaltungsleiter, m
- ♦ accounts manager

Buchhaltungsmitarbeiter, m
  Buchhalter, m
- ♦ accounts clerk

Buchhaltungspersonal n
- ♦ accounts staff
- ♦ accounts personnel

Buchhändler m
- ♦ bookseller

Buchhandlung, f
  Buchladen, m
  Buchgeschäft, n
- ♦ bookstore *AE*
- ♦ bookshop *BE*

Buchladen, m
  Buchhandlung, f
- ♦ bookshop *BE*
- ♦ bookstore *AE*

Buchmacher, m
- ♦ bookmaker
- ♦ bookie *coll*

buchmäßiges Inventar, n
- ♦ book inventory

Buchmesse, f
- ♦ bookfair *AE*
- ♦ book fair *BE*

Buch mitnehmen in den Urlaub
  Buch mitnehmen in die Ferien
- ♦ take a book on vacation *AE*
- ♦ take a book on holiday *BE*

Büchsenbier, n
  Dosenbier, n
- ♦ tinned beer *BE*
- ♦ canned beer *AE*

Büchsenfleisch, n
  Dosenfleisch, n
- ♦ canned meat *AE*
- ♦ tinned meat *BE*

Büchsenöffner, m
  Dosenöffner, m
- ♦ tin-opener *BE*
- ♦ can opener *AE*

Bucht, f (groß)
- ♦ bay

Bucht, f (klein)
  kleine Bucht, f
- ♦ cove

Buchung, f (Bestellung)
  Bestellung, f
  Anmeldung, f
- ♦ booking
- ♦ reservation *AE*

Buchung, f (in Buchhaltung)
- ♦ entry

Buchung ablehnen
  Buchung abweisen
- ♦ decline a booking
- ♦ refuse a booking
- ♦ turn down a booking

Buchung abrufen
  (aus Computer)
- ♦ call a booking
- ♦ retrieve a booking

Buchung abrufen über den Computer
  Buchung abrufen auf dem Computer
- ♦ retrieve a booking on the computer
- ♦ call up a booking on the computer

Buchung abwickeln
  Buchung bearbeiten
- ♦ handle a booking
- ♦ process a booking

Buchung als storniert ansehen
- ♦ regard the booking as (having been) cancelled
- ♦ regard the booking as (having been) canceled *AE*

Buchung als storniert behandeln
  Buchung als annulliert betrachten
- ♦ treat a booking as canceled *AE*
- ♦ treat a booking as cancelled *BE*

Buchung ändern (geringfügig)
- ♦ alter a booking
- ♦ modify a booking

Buchung ändern (umfassend)
- ♦ change a booking

Buchung annehmen
  Buchung akzeptieren
- ♦ accept a booking

Buchung annullieren
- → Buchung stornieren

Buchung auf den Namen Peter Smith
- ♦ booking in the name of Peter Smith

Buchung aufgeben
- → Buchung vornehmen

Buchung aufheben
  Buchung freigeben
- ♦ release a booking

Buchung aufrechterhalten für zwei Tage
  Buchung zwei Tage aufrechterhalten
- ♦ hold a booking for two days

Buchung bearbeiten
- ♦ deal with a booking
- ♦ process a booking

Buchung bei einem Hotel vornehmen
- ♦ place a booking with a hotel

Buchung bestätigen
- ♦ confirm a booking

Buchung bestätigen jm
  Anmeldung bestätigen jm
- ♦ confirm a booking to s.o.

Buchung einer Dienstleistung, f
  Buchung eines Service f
- ♦ booking (of) a service

Buchung einer Garage, f
  Garagenbuchung, f
- ♦ booking (of) a garage

Buchung einer Reise, f
  Reisebuchung, f
- ♦ booking (of) a tour
- ♦ booking (of) a trip
- ♦ booking (of) a journey
- ♦ tour booking
- ♦ travel booking

Buchung einhalten
  Buch anerkennen
- ♦ honor a booking *AE*
- ♦ honour a booking *BE*

Buchungen erzeugen
- ♦ generate bookings

Buchungen gehen zurück
- ♦ bookings fall

Buchungen hochtreiben
- ♦ boost (the) bookings
- ♦ beef up (the) bookings *coll*

Buchungen liegen 10 % niedriger als letztes Jahr
- ♦ bookings are 10 % down on last year

Buchungen schließen am 30. Juni
- ♦ bookings close by 30 June

Buchungen sind enttäuschend
- ♦ bookings are disappointing

Buchungen stiegen um das Fünffache an
- ♦ bookings grew five-fold

Buchung entgegennehmen
- ♦ take a booking

Buchung entgegensehen
- ♦ look forward to receiving a booking

Buchungen verwalten
- ♦ manage the bookings

Buchung erhalten (von jm)
- ♦ receive a booking (from s.o.)

Buchung fest vereinbaren
♦ make a booking firm
♦ make a booking definite
Buchung frühzeitig erhalten
♦ receive a booking in good time
Buchung für ein Land, f
♦ booking for a country
Buchung für etw, f
♦ booking for s.th.
Buchung gegenbestätigen
♦ reconfirm a booking
Buchung geht am 7. März ein
♦ booking is received on 7 March
♦ booking comes in on 7 March
Buchung geht ein
♦ booking is received
♦ booking comes in
Buchung hinausschieben
♦ postpone a booking
♦ delay a booking
♦ put off a booking
Buchung im Auftrag von jm, f
Buchung in js Auftrag f
♦ booking on s.o.'s behalf
Buchung im Namen von jm, f
Buchung in js Namen, f
Buchung auf js Namen, f
♦ booking in s.o.'s name
Buchung in der Wochenmitte, f
Buchung unter der Woche, f
♦ midweek booking
Buchung in letzter Minute, f
Buchung in letzter Sekunde f
♦ last-minute booking
Buchung in letzter Sekunde, f
→ Buchung in letzter Minute
Buchung innerhalb von 10 Sekunden
♦ booking within 10 seconds
Buchung ist fest
♦ booking is firm
Buchung ist gesichert
♦ booking is secured
Buchung ist gültig
♦ booking is valid
Buchung ist notwendig bei diesem Restaurant
Reservierung ist notwendig bei diesem Restaurant
♦ booking is essential for this restaurant
♦ reservation is essential for this restaurant
Buchung ist provisorisch
♦ booking is provisional
Buchung ist unverbindlich
Buchung ist nicht verbindlich
♦ booking is not binding
Buchung ist verbindlich
♦ booking is binding
♦ booking is definite
Buchung ist verbindlich für eine Person
♦ booking is binding upon a person
Buchung ist vorläufig
♦ booking is tentative
♦ booking is provisional
Buchung kontrollieren
♦ control a booking
Buchung kostenlos vornehmen
♦ make a booking free of charge
Buchung machen über Bildschirmtext
♦ make a booking through viewdata
♦ make a booking through Prestel BE
Buchung modifizieren
Buchung leicht ändern
♦ modify a booking

Buchung muß 24 Stunden vorher gemacht werden
♦ booking must be made 24 hours in advance
Buchung muß bis zum 8. November gemacht werden
♦ booking must be made by 8 November
Buchung nicht einhalten
♦ dishonor a booking AE
♦ dishonour a booking BE
Buchung persönlich vornehmen
persönlich buchen
♦ make a booking in person
Buchung rechtzeitig erhalten
♦ receive a booking in due time
Buchung rückgängig machen
→ Buchung stornieren
Buchungsablehnung, f
♦ refusal of a booking
♦ refusing a booking
Buchungsabteilung f
♦ booking department
Buchungsabwicklung, f
Buchungsbearbeitung, f
♦ processing a booking
♦ handling a booking
♦ dealing with a booking
Buchungsagent, m
♦ booking agent
Buchungsagentur, f
Vermittlungsagentur, f
Buchungsvermittlung, f
♦ booking agency
Buchungsanalyse, f
♦ bookings analysis
♦ analysis of the bookings
Buchungsänderung, f (geringfügig)
♦ booking alteration
♦ alteration of a booking
♦ modification of a booking
Buchungsänderung, f (umfassend)
♦ change of booking
Buchungsanfrage, f
♦ booking inquiry
♦ booking enquiry
Buchungsanfrage beantworten
♦ answer a booking inquiry
♦ answer a booking enquiry
Buchungsanfragecoupon, m
♦ booking inquiry coupon
♦ booking enquiry coupon
Buchungsanfrage erhalten
♦ receive a booking inquiry
♦ receive a booking enquiry
Buchungsangaben, f pl
→ Buchungsdetails
Buchungsangebot, n
♦ booking offer
♦ offer of a booking
♦ offering a booking
Buchungsangebot erhalten von jm
♦ receive the offer of a booking from s.o.
Buchungsannahme, f
♦ acceptance of a booking
♦ accepting a booking
Buchungsanreiz, m
♦ booking incentive
Buchungsanstieg, m
♦ rise in bookings
♦ bookings rise
Buchungsansturm, m
♦ rush for bookings

Buchungsantrag m
♦ booking application
♦ application for booking
Buchungsanzahlung f
♦ booking deposit
Buchungsanzahlung ist nicht rückerstattbar und verfällt bei Stornierung
♦ booking deposit is non-refundable and is forfeited BE
♦ on cancellation
♦ booking deposit is nonrefundable and is forfeited
♦ on cancelation AE
Buchungsanzahlung leisten
♦ make a booking deposit AE
♦ pay a booking deposit BE
Buchungsanzahlung schicken jm
♦ send a booking deposit to s.o.
Buchungsanzahlung verlangen
Buchungsanzahlung fordern
♦ require a booking deposit
Buchungsanzahlung wünschen
♦ request a booking deposit
Buchungsarbeit, f
♦ booking work
♦ work in a booking office
♦ work entailed in making a booking
Buchungsart f
♦ booking type
♦ type of booking
Buchungsaufkommen, n
Buchungsvolumen n
♦ booking volume
♦ volume of bookings
Buchungsaufschwung, m
♦ upswing in bookings
Buchungsauftakt, m
♦ start to bookings
Buchungsaufwendungen, f pl
♦ booking expenses pl
Buchungsautomat, m
(Buchhaltung)
♦ automatic booking machine
♦ automatic accounting machine
Buchungsbearbeiter, m
Buchungssachbearbeiter, m
♦ booking clerk
♦ bookings clerk
Buchungsbearbeitung, f
Buchungsabwicklung, f
♦ dealing with a booking
♦ handling a booking
♦ processing a booking
Buchungsbedingungen, f pl
♦ booking conditions pl
♦ conditions of booking pl
Buchungsbedingungen sind verbindlich
♦ booking conditions are binding
Buchungsbestätigung, f
♦ booking confirmation
♦ confirmation of a booking
♦ confirming a booking
Buchungsbestätigung ausstellen
♦ issue a booking confirmation
♦ issue a confirmation of the booking
Buchungsbestätigung erhalten
♦ receive a booking confirmation
Buchungsbestätigung senden
Buchungsbestätigung schicken jm
♦ send a booking confirmation
♦ send s.o. confirmation of the booking

Buchungsboom

Buchungsboom, m
- booking boom

Buchungsbüro, n
- booking office
- bookings office

Buchungsbüro betreiben
- operate a booking office
- operate a bookings office

Buchungsbüro unterhalten
- run a booking office
- run a bookings office

Buchung schriftlich bestätigen
- confirm a booking in writing

Buchungscode, m
- → Buchungsschlüssel

Buchungsdaten, f pl
- booking details pl
- details of a booking pl

Buchungsdatum, n
Buchungstermin, m
- date of booking
- booking date

Buchungsdauer f
(Länge des gebuchten Aufenthalts)
- length of booking

Buchungsdetails, n pl
Buchungsangaben, f pl
- details of a booking pl
- booking details pl

Buchungsdienst, m
Buchungsservice, m
Vermittlungsdienst, m
Bestelldienst, m
- booking service
- reservation service AE

Buchungseingang, m (Erhalt)
- receipt of a booking
- receiving a booking

Buchungseingang, m (Zahl)
- inflow of bookings
- booking inflow
- bookings inflow

Buchungseingang ist gut
- inflow of bookings is good

Buchungseingang ist zufriedenstellend
- inflow of bookings is satisfactory

Buchungseinrichtung, f
Buchungsmöglichkeit, f
- booking facility

Buchungseinzelheiten, f pl
- booking particulars pl
- particulars of a booking pl

Buchungsentgegennahme f
- taking (of) a booking

Buchungsfluß, m
- flow of bookings
- stream of bookings

Buchungsflut, f
Buchungsschwemme, f
- flood of bookings

Buchungsformular, n
Anmeldeformular, n
- booking form

Buchungsformular ausfüllen
- fill out a booking form AE
- fill in a booking form BE
- complete a booking form

Buchungsformular erhalten
- receive a booking form

Buchungsformular zurücksenden an jn
- return a booking form to s.o.

Buchungsgarantie, f
- booking guarantee

Buchungsgebühr, f
- booking charge
- booking fee

Buchungsgebühr berechnen
Buchungsgebühr erheben
- charge a booking fee

Buchungsgebühr zahlen
- pay a booking fee

Buchungsgewohnheit, f
- booking habit

Buchungsinformation f
- booking information

Buchungsjahr n
- year of booking

Buchungsjournal, n
- booking diary
- bookings diary
- booking journal
- bookings journal

Buchungskarte, f
- booking card

Buchungsklasse, f
- booking class

Buchungsknappheit, f
- shortage of bookings

Buchungskraft, f
- → Buchungsbearbeiter

Buchungslage, f
Buchungssituation, f
Buchungsstand, m
- booking situation

Buchungslage ist ausgezeichnet
- booking situation is excellent

Buchungslage ist schlecht
- booking situation is poor

Buchungsleitung, f (Telefon)
- booking line

Buchungsliste, f
- booking list
- list of bookings

Buchungslücke, f
- booking gap

Buchungslücke füllen
- fill a booking gap

Buchungsmangel, m (Knappheit)
- → Buchungsknappheit

Buchungsmangel, m (völliges Fehlen)
- lack of bookings

Buchungsmaschine f
(Buchhaltung)
- billing machine

Buchungsmethode, f
Buchungsweise, f
- method of booking
- booking method

Buchungsmöglichkeit f
- booking possibility
- possibility of booking s.th.
- booking facility

Buchungsmonat m
- month of booking

Buchungsmonopol, n
- booking monopoly

Buchungsnetz n
- booking network

Buchungsniveau, n
Buchungshöhe, f
Buchungsstand, m
- booking level

- level of bookings
- level of booking

Buchungsnummer, f
- booking reference number
- reference number

Buchungsnummer angeben
- quote the booking reference number

Buchung sofort bestätigen
- confirm a booking instantly
- confirm a booking immediately

Buchungsperiode, f
- → Buchungszeitraum

Buchungspersonal, n
- booking staff
- booking personnel

Buchungsphase, f
Bestellphase f
- booking phase

Buchungsplus, n
- → Buchungszuwachs

Buchungsposten, m
- booking entry

Buchungspraxis, f
- booking practice

Buchungsproblem, n
- booking problem

Buchungsproblem haben
- have a booking problem

Buchungsproblem lösen
- solve a booking problem

Buchungsproblem taucht auf
- booking problem occurs

Buchungsprospekt, m
Buchungsbroschüre, f
- booking brochure

Buchungsprovision, f
- booking commission

Buchungsresonanz, f
- booking response

Buchungsrückgang, m
- decrease in bookings
- decline in bookings
- fall in bookings
- drop in bookings
- downturn in bookings

Buchungsrückgang erwarten
- expect a decrease in bookings
- expect a decline in bookings
- expect a fall in bookings
- expect a drop in bookings

Buchungssaison, f
Buchungszeit f
- booking season

Buchungsschlüssel, m
Buchungscode m
- booking code

Buchungsschreiben, n
Buchungsbrief m
- booking letter
- letter booking s.th.

Buchungsservice, m
- → Buchungsdienst

Buchungssituation, f
- → Buchungslage

Buchungsstand, m
- booking situation
- booking level
- level of bookings

Buchungsstand ist hoch
- level of bookings is high

Buchungsstand ist niedrig
♦ level of bookings is low
Buchungsstand ist zufriedenstellend
♦ booking situation is satisfactory
Buchungsstatistik, f
♦ booking statistics *pl*
Buchungsstatus, m
♦ booking status
Buchungssteigerung, f
Buchungszuwachs, m
♦ increase in bookings
Buchungssteigerungen melden
♦ report increases in bookings
Buchungsstelle, f
♦ booking point
Buchungsstopp, m
Belegungsstopp, m
♦ booking freeze
♦ freeze on bookings
Buchungsstornierung, f
Buchungsrücktritt, m
Buchungsannullierung, f
♦ cancellation of a booking
♦ cancelation of a booking *AE*
Buchungssystem n
♦ booking system
♦ bookings system
Buchungstafel, f
Buchungsschaubild, n
Buchungsdiagramm, n
♦ booking chart
Buchungstag, m
♦ day of booking
Buchungstermin, m
Buchungsdatum, n
♦ booking date
♦ date of booking
Buchungsterminal, n
♦ booking terminal
Buchung stornieren
Buchung rückgängig machen
Buchung annullieren
von einer Buchung zurücktreten
♦ cancel a booking
Buchungstrend, m
♦ booking trend
Buchungsüberhang, m
unerledigter Buchungsbestand, m
♦ backlog of bookings
Buchungsunterlagen, f pl
Buchungsaufzeichnungen, f pl
♦ booking documents *pl*
♦ booking records *pl*
Buchungsvereinbarung, f
♦ booking agreement
Buchungsvereinbarung einhalten
Buchungsvereinbarung anerkennen
♦ honor a booking agreement *AE*
♦ honour a booking agreement *BE*
Buchungsverfahren, n
Buchungsvorgang, m
Buchungsprozedur, f
♦ booking procedure
Buchungsverhalten, n
♦ booking pattern
Buchungsvertrag m
♦ booking contract
Buchungsverweigerung, f
♦ rejection of a booking
♦ rejecting a booking

Buchungsvolumen, n
Buchungsaufkommen, n
♦ volume of bookings
♦ booking volume
Buchungsvorrang, m
Buchungsvortritt, m
Buchungspriorität, f
♦ booking priority
Buchungsvorrang erhalten
♦ get booking priority
Buchungswachstum, n
♦ growth in bookings
Buchungsweg, m
♦ booking channel
Buchungsweise, f
Buchungsmethode f
♦ booking method
♦ method of booking
Buchungswelle, f
♦ wave of bookings
Buchungswettbewerb, m
♦ booking competition
Buchungswoche f
♦ week of booking
Buchungswunsch, m
♦ booking request
♦ request for booking
♦ booking requirement
Buchungswunsch erfüllen
♦ meet a booking request
♦ meet a booking requirement
Buchungszahl, f
Buchungsanzahl, f
♦ number of bookings
Buchungszahl bleibt gleich
♦ number of bookings remains constant
Buchungszahlen, f pl
♦ bokking figures *pl*
Buchungszahl geht zurück
Buchungszahl fällt
♦ number of bookings is decreasing
Buchungszahl stagniert
♦ number of bookings stagnates
Buchungszahl steigt
♦ number of bookings is increasing
Buchungszeichen, n
♦ booking reference
Buchungszeit, f
→ Buchungszeitpunkt, Buchungszeitraum
Buchungszeitpunkt, m
Buchungszeit f
♦ time of booking
Buchungszeitraum, m
Buchungsperiode, f
Buchungszeit, f
♦ booking period
Buchungszentrale, f
♦ central booking office
♦ central bookings office
Buchungszentrale unterhalten
♦ operate a central booking office
♦ operate a central bookings office
Buchungszustand, m
→ Buchungsstand
Buchungszuwachs, m
♦ increase in the number of bookings
♦ increase in bookings
Buchungszweck, m
♦ booking purpose

Buchung tätigen
♦ effect a booking
♦ make a booking
Buchung telefonisch bestätigen
♦ confirm a booking by telephone
Buchung überprüfen
Buchung prüfen
♦ check a booking
Buchung übertragen auf jn
♦ transfer a booking to s.o.
Buchung umfaßt das Zimmer und eine Mahlzeit
♦ booking covers the room and one meal
Buchung unmittelbar bei einem Hotel vornehmen
♦ make a booking directly with a hotel
Buchung unterzeichnen
Buchung unterschreiben
♦ sign a booking
Buchung unverzüglich bestätigen
♦ confirm a booking without delay
Buchung verbindlich vereinbaren
Buchung fest vereinbaren
♦ make a booking definite
Buchung vermitteln
Buchung arrangieren
♦ arrange a booking
Buchung verweigern
Buchung ablehnen
♦ refuse a booking
Buchung von etw, f
Bestellung von etw f
♦ booking (of) s.th.
Buchung vornehmen
♦ make a booking
♦ make a reservation *AE*
Buchung wird automatisch storniert
♦ booking will be cancelled automatically
♦ booking will be canceled automatically *AE*
Buchung wird automatisch storniert, falls die Anzahlung nicht innerhalb von 7 Tagen bei uns eingeht
♦ Booking will automatically be cancelled if we do not receive the deposit within 7 days
♦ Booking will automatically be canceled if we do not receive the deposit within 7 days *AE*
Buchung wünschen für den 20. Mai
♦ request a booking for 20 May
Buchung zurückweisen
♦ reject a booking
Buchweizen, m
♦ buckwheat
Buchweizenkloß, m
♦ buckwheat dumpling
Buchwert, m
♦ book value
♦ written-down value
Buckingham-Palast, m
♦ Buckingham Palace
Bude, f (bes. für Studenten) *coll*
♦ digs *BE pl*
Bude, f (Haus) *derog*
Bretterbude, f
♦ shack *AE*
♦ ramshackle house
♦ hovel
♦ hole
♦ shanty
Bude, f (Verkaufsstand)
Verkaufsstand, m
♦ booth
♦ stand

Bude

- ♦ stall
- ♦ kiosk

Bude, f (Wohnung)
- ♦ hangout *AE sl*
- ♦ hang-out *BE sl*

Bude, f (Zimmer)
→ Zimmer

Bude aufgeben (bes. Studenten)
- ♦ give up digs *BE*

Bude aufstellen
Bude aufschlagen
- ♦ set up a booth

Bude bewohnen (bes. Studenten)
- ♦ live in digs *BE*

Bude nehmen (bes. Studenten)
- ♦ take digs *BE*

Budget, n
Etat, m
- ♦ budget

Budget erstellen
- ♦ prepare a budget

Budget-Tarif, m
Billigtarif, m
Spartarif, m
- ♦ budget tariff
- ♦ economy tariff

Budike, f
→ Kneipe

Büfett, n (für Speisen)
- ♦ buffet
- ♦ snack counter
- ♦ counter

Büfett, n (Speisen)
- ♦ buffet

Büfett, n (Theke)
- ♦ buffet
- ♦ counter

Büfett am zweiten Weihnachtstag, n (26. Dezember)
- ♦ Boxing Day buffet

Büfettangestellter, m
- ♦ buffet employee

büfettartig, adj
im Büfettstil
- ♦ buffet-style, adj

büfettartiges Essen, n
- ♦ buffet-style meal

Büfettaufbau, m
- ♦ setting up a buffet

Büfett aufbauen
- ♦ set up a buffet

Büfettaushilfe, f
- ♦ casual barmaid
- ♦ casual barman

Büfettbar, f
- ♦ buffet bar

Büfett beim Schwimmbad, n
Büfett am Schwimmbecken, n
- ♦ buffet by the swimming pool *AE*
- ♦ buffet by the swimming-pool *BE*

Büfettbereich, m
- ♦ buffet area

Büfettbetrieb, m
- ♦ buffet operation
- ♦ buffet establishment

Büfettdame, f (in Bar)
- ♦ barmaid

Büfettempfang, m
- ♦ buffet reception

Büfettessen, n
Büfettmahlzeit f
- ♦ buffet meal

Büfettessen auf der Terrasse, n
- ♦ terrace buffet meal

Büfettessen im Freien, n
- ♦ outdoor buffet meal

Büfettfläche, f
- ♦ buffet space
- ♦ buffet area

Büfettfräulein, n (an Theke)
- ♦ counter girl
- ♦ girl at the (buffet) counter

Büfettfräulein, n (in Bar)
Büfettmädchen n
- ♦ barmaid

Büfettfrühstück, n
Frühstücksbüfett, n
- ♦ breakfast buffet

Büfettgericht, n
- ♦ buffet dish

Büfetthilfe, f
→ Büfettaushilfe

Büfettier, m (in Bar)
Buffetier, m
- ♦ counterman
- ♦ bartender
- ♦ barman

Büfettimbiß, m
- ♦ buffet snack

Büfett im Freien, n
- ♦ open-air buffet

Büfettisch, m
- ♦ buffet table

Büfettkellner, m
- ♦ bartender
- ♦ barman

Büfettleiter, m
- ♦ buffet manager

Büfettleitung, f
- ♦ buffet management

Büfettmädchen, n
→ Büfettdame

Büfettmanagement, n
Büfettleitung, f
- ♦ buffet management

Büfettmenü, n
- ♦ buffet menu

Büfettochter, f SCHW
→ Büfettfräulein, Fille de buffet

Büfettpersonal, n
- ♦ buffet staff
- ♦ buffet personnel

Büfettpräsentation, f
- ♦ buffet presentation
- ♦ presentation of a buffet

Büfettrestaurant, n
- ♦ buffet
- ♦ snack bar

Büfettservice, m
Büfettdienst m
- ♦ buffet service

Büfettwagen, m (Eisenbahn)
Speisewagen m
- ♦ buffet car

Büfettwagen, m (Restaurant)
- ♦ buffet cart *AE*
- ♦ buffet trolley *BE*

Buffet, n
→ Büfett

Buffetier, m
→ Büfettier, m

Buffetküche f SCHW
→ Büfettküche

Buffet roulant, n *FR*
fahrbares Büfett, n
- ♦ buffet roulant *FR*
- ♦ mobile buffet

Bug, m
- ♦ bow

Bugbett, n (Wohnwagen)
- ♦ front bed
- ♦ front bunk

Bugdoppelbett, n (Wohnwagen)
- ♦ front double bed
- ♦ front double bunk

Bügel, m (Kleiderbügel)
- ♦ hanger

Bügelbrett, n
- ♦ ironing board

Bügeldienst m
Bügelservice m
- ♦ pressing service
- ♦ ironing service

Bügelei, f
Plätterei f
- ♦ ironing

Bügeleisen n
- ♦ iron

Bügelgelegenheit, f
Bügeleinrichtung, f
Bügelmöglichkeit, f
- ♦ ironing facility

bügeln (etw)
plätten (etw)
- ♦ iron (s.th.)
- ♦ press (s.th.)

Bügelraum, m
Bügelzimmer, n
- ♦ ironing room

Bügelservice, m
Bügeldienst, m
- ♦ ironing service
- ♦ pressing service

Bügeltisch m
- ♦ ironing table

Bügelzimmer, n
→ Bügelraum

Bügler, m
Plätter, m
Büglerin, f
Plätterin, f
- ♦ ironer

Bugsitzgruppe, f (Wohnwagen)
- ♦ front dinette

Bugsitzplatz, m (Schiff)
Bugsitz, m
- ♦ bow seat

Bugtisch, m (Wohnwagen)
- ♦ front table

Bühne, f
- ♦ stage

Bühnenausstattung, f
- ♦ stage set
- ♦ set

Bühnenbeleuchtung, f
 ♦ stage lighting
Bühnendebut, n
 ♦ stage debut
Bühnendekoration, f
 ♦ stage decoration
Bühnenerweiterung, f
 ♦ stage extension
Bühnenfläche, f
 ♦ stage area
Bühnenhelfer, m
 ♦ stagehand *AE*
 ♦ stage-hand *BE*
Bühnenleiter, m
 ♦ stage manager *AE*
 ♦ stage-manager *BE*
Bühnenmikrofon, n
 ♦ stage microphone
Bühnenmikrofonanschluß, m
 ♦ stage microphone point
Bühnensaal, m
 (Saal mit Bühne)
 ♦ room with a stage
Bühnenzugang, m
 ♦ stage access
Bukett, n
 Bouquet, n
 Blume, f (Wein)
 ♦ bouquet
bukettreich, adj
 ♦ rich in bouquet, adj
bukettreich sein
 ♦ have a full bouquet
Bulgare, m
 ♦ Bulgarian
Bulgarien
 ♦ Bulgaria
Bulgarin, f
 ♦ Bulgarian woman
 ♦ Bulgarian girl
 ♦ Bulgarian
bulgarisch, adj
 ♦ Bulgarian, adj
Bulimie, f *med*
 Eß-Brechsucht, f *med*
 ♦ bulimia *med*
 ♦ boulimia *med*
Bullauge, n
 (Schiff)
 ♦ porthole
Bulle, m (Polizist) *sl*
 ♦ cop *sl*
Bummel, m
 ♦ stroll
 ♦ walk
Bummel machen
 ♦ go for a stroll
 ♦ take a stroll
 ♦ have a stroll
Bummel machen durch die Altstadt
 ♦ take a stroll through the Old Town
 ♦ go for a stroll through the Old Town
Bummel machen durch eine Stadt
 ♦ take a stroll through a town
 ♦ take a stroll around a town
Bummel machen in dem Park
 ♦ go for a stroll in the park
 ♦ take a stroll in the park
 ♦ have a stroll in the park
 ♦ stroll in the park

Bummel machen zu etw
 Bummel machen nach etw
 ♦ take a stroll to s.th.
bummeln durch die Altstadt
 ♦ stroll through the Old Town
bummeln durch die Straßen
 ♦ stroll through the streets
 ♦ stroll through the roads
Bummelstreik, m
 ♦ go-slow *BE*
Bummelzug, m
 ♦ way train *AE*
 ♦ slow train
 ♦ accommodation train *AE dial*
Bummler, m
 ♦ stroller *BE*
Bumslokal, n (Gaststätte)
 Spelunke, f
 ♦ gin mill *AE*
 ♦ joint *AE sl*
 ♦ low dive *sl*
 ♦ dive *sl*
B&B, n
 Bed and Breakfast, n
 ♦ b&b
 ♦ bed and breakfast
 ♦ b and b
 ♦ B and B
B&B-Agentur, f
 ♦ b&b agency
B&B-Angebot, n
 ♦ b&b offer
B&B-Betrieb, m
 Bed-and-Breakfast-Betrieb, m
 ♦ b&b establishment
 ♦ b&b operation
 ♦ bed-and-breakfast establishment
 ♦ bed-and-breakfast operation
B&B buchen
 ♦ book b&b
B&B-Einnahme, f pl
 ♦ b&b revenue
 ♦ b&b income
B&B-Ertrag, m
 (Gewinn- und Verlustrechnung)
 ♦ b&b income
B&B-Führer, m
 ♦ b&b guide
B&B-Haus, n
 ♦ b&b house
 ♦ bed-and-breakfast house
B&B-Kurzurlaub, m
 ♦ b&b break
B&B-Netz, n
 ♦ b&b network
B&B-Quartier, n
 ♦ b&b quarters *pl*
Bund Brunnenkresse, m
 ♦ bunch of watercress
B&B-Schild, n
 ♦ b&b sign
 ♦ bed-and-breakfast sign
B&B-Tarif, m
 ♦ b&b tariff
 ♦ b&b terms *pl*
 ♦ b&b rates *pl*
 ♦ b&b rate
B&B-Umsatz, m
 ♦ b&b sales *pl*
 ♦ b&b turnover

B&B-Unterkunft, f
 ♦ b&b accommodation
 ♦ bed-and-breakfast accommodation
B&B-Vereinbarung, f
 ♦ b&b arrangement
 ♦ bed-and-breakfast arrangement
B&B-Wohnung, f
 ♦ b&b apartment *AE*
 ♦ b&b flat *BE*
Bundesrepublik Deutschland f
 ♦ Federal Republic of Germany
Bundesverkehrsministerium, n
 ♦ Federal Ministry of Transport
Bund Petersilie, m
 ♦ bunch of parsley
Bungalow, m
 BGW, m
 ♦ bungalow
Bungalowanlage, f
 Bungalowkomplex m
 ♦ bungalow complex
Bungalowappartement, n
 ♦ bungalow apartment
Bungalowdorf, n
 ♦ bungalow village
Bungalowferienanlage, f
 Bungalowferienkomplex, m
 ♦ bungalow vacation complex *AE*
 ♦ bungalow holiday complex *BE*
Bungalowferiendorf, n
 Bungalowurlaubsdorf, n
 ♦ bungalow vacation village *AE*
 ♦ bungalow holiday village *BE*
Bungalowferienort, m
 Bungalowurlaubsort, m
 ♦ bungalow vacation resort *AE*
 ♦ bungalow holiday resort *BE*
Bungalowhotel n
 ♦ bungalow hotel
Bungalow mit zwei Schlafzimmern, m
 ♦ two-bedroom bungalow
 ♦ bungalow with two bedrooms
Bungalowort, m
 ♦ bungalow resort
Bungalowpark, m
 ♦ bungalow park
Bungalowstil, m
 ♦ bungalow style
Bungalowsuite f
 ♦ bungalow suite
Bungalowwohnung, f
 ♦ bungalow flat *BE*
 ♦ bungalow apartment *AE*
Bungalowzimmer n
 ♦ bungalow room
Bunter Abend, m
 bunter Unterhaltungsabend m
 ♦ varied evening entertainment
 ♦ variety show *AE*
 ♦ variety evening
Bunter Festabend, m
 ♦ gala variety evening
buntes Programm, n
 ♦ variety program *AE*
 ♦ varied program *AE*
 ♦ varied programme *BE*
 ♦ colorful program *AE*
 ♦ colourful programme *BE*
Burg, f
 → Schloß

Burgblick

Burgblick, m
- → Schloßblick

bürgen für etw
- → verbürgen sich für etw

Burgenland
- ♦ Burgenland

Burgenstraße, f
- *(Ferienstraße)*
- ♦ Castle Road, the
- ♦ Castle Route, the

Bürgerempfang, m
- ♦ civic reception

Bürgerfest, n
- ♦ civic festival
- ♦ townsmen's festival

bürgerliche Art, adv *gastr*
- nach bürgerlicher Art, adv *gastr*
- ♦ bourgeois style, adv *gastr*

bürgerliche Gaststätte, f
- ♦ traditional pub BE *coll*
- ♦ restaurant offering traditional fare
- ♦ middle-class restaurant

bürgerliche Kost, f
- herkömmliche Kost, f
- ♦ traditional food
- ♦ plain food

bürgerliche Küche, f
- ♦ plain cooking
- ♦ home cooking
- ♦ traditional cooking

bürgerliche Küche bieten
- ♦ offer plain food
- ♦ offer traditional food

Bürgermeister, m
- ♦ mayor

Bürgermeisterin, f
- ♦ lady mayoress

Bürgersteig, m
- Gehsteig, m
- ♦ sidewalk AE
- ♦ pavement BE

Burgfest, n
- → Schloßfest

Burgfrauenart, adv *gastr*
- nach Burgfrauenart, adv *gastr*
- ♦ chatelaine style, adv *gastr*

Burggasthof, m
- Schloßgasthof, m
- ♦ castle inn

Burghotel, n
- → Schloßhotel

Burgruine, f
- Schloßruine, f
- ♦ ruined castle
- ♦ castle ruins *pl*

Burgschenke, f
- Schloßschenke, f
- ♦ castle bar AE
- ♦ castle tavern
- ♦ castle pub BE

Burgund
- ♦ Burgundy

Burgunder, m (Wein)
- ♦ Burgundy wine
- ♦ Burgundy

Burgunderart, adv *gastr*
- nach Burgunderart, adv *gastr*
- ♦ burgundy style, adv *gastr*

Burgunderglas, n
- ♦ Burgundy glass
- ♦ Burgundy balloon

Burgunderrebe, f
- ♦ Burgundy vine

Burgundersoße, f
- ♦ Burgundy sauce

Burgundertraube, f
- ♦ Burgundy grape

burgundisch, adj
- ♦ Burgundian, adj

Burgverlies, n
- Verlies, n
- ♦ dungeon

Burkina Faso
- ♦ Burkina Faso

Burkiner, m
- ♦ Burkinese

Burkinerin, f
- ♦ Burkinese girl
- ♦ Burkinese woman
- ♦ Burkinese

burkinisch, adj
- ♦ Burkinese, adj

Büro, n
- ♦ office

Bürofest, n
- Betriebsfest, n
- ♦ office party

Bürofläche, f
- Büroraum, m
- ♦ office space

Büro für Kultur und Erholung, n
- ♦ office of culture and recreation

Büro für Tourismus, n
- ♦ office for tourism

Bürogehilfe, m
- Bürogehilfin f
- ♦ office clerk
- ♦ clerk

Bürohaus, n
- ♦ office block

Büro ist 24 Stunden lang besetzt
- ♦ office is staffed 24 hours

Büroklammer, f
- ♦ paper clip AE
- ♦ paper-clip BE

Bürokosten, pl
- ♦ office costs *pl*
- ♦ office cost

Büromaterial, n
- Bürobedarf, m
- ♦ office supplies *pl*
- ♦ stationery

Büropersonal, n
- ♦ office staff
- ♦ office personnel

Büroraum vermieten
- ♦ rent (out) an office
- ♦ let an office BE

Bürotag, m
- ♦ office day

Büro unterhalten
- ♦ operate an office
- ♦ run an office

Bürovermietung, f
- ♦ office renting AE
- ♦ renting (of) an office AE
- ♦ renting (of) offices AE
- ♦ office letting BE
- ♦ letting (of) an office BE

Burundi
- ♦ Burundi

Burundier, m
- Burunder, m
- ♦ Burundian

Burundierin, f
- Burunderin, f
- ♦ Burundian girl
- ♦ Burundian woman
- ♦ Burundian

burundisch, adj
- ♦ Burundian, adj
- ♦ Burundi, adj

Bürzel, m *gastr*
- *(Schwanzende von Geflügel)*
- ♦ pope's nose AE *gastr*
- ♦ parson's nose BE *gastr*

Bus, m (örtlich)
- ♦ bus
- ♦ charabanc *obsol*

Bus, m (Überland)
- ♦ coach BE
- ♦ motorcoach BE
- ♦ bus AE

Busanbindung (an etw), f
- ♦ bus access (to s.th.)
- ♦ coach access (to s.th.) BE

Busankunfts- und -abfahrtszeiten, f pl
- ♦ bus arrival and departure times *pl*
- ♦ coach arrival and departure times BE *pl*

Busanreise
- → Kapitelüberschrift
- ♦ How to Get to X by Bus
- ♦ How to Get to X by Coach BE
- ♦ Getting There by Bus
- ♦ Getting There by Coach BE

Busanreise, f
- Bushinreise, f
- ♦ outward journey by bus
- ♦ outward journey by coach BE

Busausflug, m
- ♦ bus excursion
- ♦ bus trip
- ♦ coach excursion BE
- ♦ coach trip BE
- ♦ bus outing

Busbahnhof, m
- ♦ bus station
- ♦ coach station BE

Busbeförderung, f
- Bustransport, m
- ♦ bus transport
- ♦ bus transportation AE
- ♦ coach transport BE

Busbesitzer, m
- ♦ bus owner
- ♦ coach owner BE

Bus besteigen
- einsteigen in einen Bus
- ♦ board a bus
- ♦ board a coach BE

Busbesuch, m
- ♦ visit by bus
- ♦ visit by coach BE

Busbetrieb, m
- ♦ bus operation
- ♦ bus operating
- ♦ coach operation BE
- ♦ coach operating BE

Busbranche, f
- Busgewerbe, n
- ♦ bus trade
- ♦ coach trade BE

♦ bus industry
♦ coach industry BE
♦ bus business
Bus bringt uns nach Rom
♦ **bus takes us to Rome**
♦ coach takes us to Rome BE
Buscharterdienst, m
Buschartservice, m
♦ **bus charter service**
♦ coach charter service BE
Bus chartern
♦ **charter a bus**
♦ charter a coach BE
Buschkneipe, f
(z.B. in Australien)
♦ **bush pub** BE
Busdepot, n
♦ **bus depot**
Busdienst, m
Busservice, m
Busverbindung, f
Busverkehr, m
♦ **bus service**
♦ coach service BE
Busdienst betreiben
♦ **operate a bus service**
♦ operate a coach service BE
Busdienst unterhalten
Busdienst betreiben
♦ **run a bus service**
♦ operate a bus service
♦ run a coach service BE
♦ operate a coach service BE
Busendhaltestelle, f
Busendstation, f
♦ **bus terminus**
♦ coach terminus BE
Bus erreichen
Bus nehmen
♦ **catch a bus**
♦ catch a coach BE
busfahrende Nation, f
♦ **bus-taking nation**
Bus fahren (Fahrer)
♦ **drive a bus**
♦ drive a coach BE
Bus fahren (Fahrgast)
→ fahren mit dem Bus
Busfahrer m
♦ **bus driver**
♦ coach driver BE
Busfahrgast, m
♦ **bus passenger**
♦ coach passenger BE
Busfahrplan, m
♦ **bus timetable**
Busfahrpreis, m
♦ **bus fare**
♦ coach fare BE
Busfahrschein, m
Busfahrkarte, f
♦ **bus ticket**
Busfahrschein lösen
Busfahrschein kaufen
Busfahrkarte kaufen
♦ **buy a bus ticket**
Busfahrt, f (kurz)
♦ **bus ride**
♦ coach ride BE
Busfahrt, f (Reise)
Busreise, f

♦ **bus journey**
♦ bus trip
♦ bus tour
♦ coach tour BE
♦ coach trip BE
Bus fährt alle fünf Minuten
♦ **bus goes every five minutes**
♦ bus runs every five minutes
Busfenster, n
♦ **bus window**
♦ coach window BE
Busfernreiseverkehr, m
Busfernreisen, n
♦ **long-distance bus travel**
♦ long-distance coach travel BE
Busfirma, f
Busgesellschaft, f
Busunternehmen, n
♦ **bus company** BE
♦ bus corporation AE
♦ coach company BE
♦ coaching company BE
Busflotte, f
Busfuhrpark, m
♦ **fleet of buses**
♦ fleet of busses AE
♦ fleet of coaches BE
♦ bus fleet
♦ coach fleet BE
Busfuhrpark, m
→ Busflotte
Busgeschäft, n
Busbranche, f
♦ **bus business**
♦ coach business BE
Busgesellschaft, f
Busfirma, f
♦ **coach company** BE
♦ bus company BE
♦ bus corporation AE
Busgruppe, f
→ Busreisegesellschaft
Busgruppe, f
Buskonzern, m
♦ **bus group**
♦ coach group BE
Busgruppenservice m
(Busgruppen werden versorgst)
♦ **bus tour service** AE
♦ coach party service BE
Bus hält direkt vor dem Hotel
♦ **bus stops in front of the hotel**
♦ bus stops just outside the hotel
Bushaltestelle, f
♦ **bus stop**
♦ coach stop BE
Bushaltestellenschild, n
♦ **bus stop sign**
♦ coach stop sign BE
Bus hält vor dem Hotel
♦ **bus stops outside the hotel**
Busindustrie, f
♦ **bus industry**
♦ coach industry BE
Business Class, f
♦ **business class**
Business-Class-Fahrpreis, m
♦ **business-class fare**
Business Class fliegen
in der Business Class fliegen
♦ **fly business class**

Business-Class-Flug, m
♦ **business-class flight**
Business-Class-Passagier, m
Business-Class-Fahrgast, m
♦ **business-class passenger**
Bus ist halb leer
♦ **bus is half empty**
♦ coach is half empty BE
Busladung, f
♦ **busload** AE
♦ bus-load BE
♦ coach-load BE
Busladung von Touristen, f
♦ **busload of tourists** AE
♦ bus-load of tourists BE
♦ coach-load of tourists BE
Buslinie, f
♦ **bus line**
♦ coach line BE
Busliniendienst, m
→ Linienbusdienst
Busmiete, f
♦ **bus hire** BE
♦ bus rental AE
♦ coach hire BE
Bus mieten
♦ **rent a bus** AE
♦ hire a bus BE
♦ hire a coach BE
Busmieter, m
♦ **bus renter** AE
♦ bus hirer BE
♦ coach hirer BE
Busminute, f
♦ **one minute by bus**
Busminute entfernt sein von X
♦ **be one minute by bus distant from X**
Bus mit Vierradantrieb, m
♦ **four-wheel-drive bus**
♦ four-wheel-drive coach BE
Busmuseum, n
♦ **bus museum**
♦ coach museum BE
Bus mußte umkehren
♦ **bus had to turn round**
♦ coach had to turn round BE
Bus nehmen
♦ **take a bus**
♦ catch the bus
Bus nehmen (in die Stadt)
♦ **take a bus (into town)**
♦ take a coach (into town) BE
Bus nehmen nach X
♦ **take a bus to X**
♦ take a coach to X BE
Bus nehmen nach X hinein
♦ **take a bus into X**
♦ take a coach into X BE
Busnummer, f
♦ **bus number**
♦ coach number BE
Buspark, m
♦ **bus fleet**
♦ coach fleet BE
♦ fleet of buses
♦ fleet of busses AE
♦ fleet of coaches BE
Busparkgebühr, f
♦ **bus parking charge**
♦ bus parking fee

Busparkplatz

- coach parking charge *BE*
- coach parking fee *BE*

Busparkplatz, m (1 Bus)
- **bus parking space**
- bus parking lot *AE*
- coach parking space *BE*

Busparkplatz, m (mehrere Busse)
- **bus parking lot** *AE*
- bus park *BE*
- coach park *BE*

Buspauschalreise, f
- **bus package tour**
- coach package tour *BE*
- bus-inclusive tour
- coach-inclusive tour *BE*

Buspendeldienst, m
Buspendelverkehr, m
Pendelbusdienst, m
- **bus shuttle service**
- coach shuttle service *BE*

Bus pendelt von A nach B
- **bus shuttles from A to B**
- bus runs between A and B
- coach shuttles from A to B *BE*
- coach runs between A and B *BE*

Bus pendelt zwischen A und B
- **bus shuttles between A and B**
- coach shuttles between A and B *BE*

Busreise, f
- **bus tour**
- bus journey
- bus trip
- coach tour *BE*
- coach journey *BE*

Busreisegeschäft, n
- **bus tour business**
- coach tour business *BE*

Busreisegesellschaft, f
Busreisegruppe, f
- **bus party** *AE*
- coach tour *BE*
- bus tour *AE*
- coach party *BE*

Busreisegesellschaften angenehm
- **Bus tours accepted** *AE*
- Coach parties accepted *BE*

Busreisegesellschaften willkommen
- **Bus parties welcome** *AE*
- Bus tours welcome *AE*
- Coach parties welcome *BE*

Busreisegruppe, f
Busreisegesellschaft, f
- **bus tour** *AE*
- coach tour *BE*
- coach touring party *BE*
- bus party *AE*
- coach party *BE*

Busreisegruppengast, m
Busreisegast m
- **bus tour guest** *AE*
- coach party guest *BE*

Busreisegruppen willkommen
- **Bus tours welcome** *AE*
- Coach parties welcome *BE*

Busreise machen
- **do a bus tour**
- do a coach tour *BE*
- go on a bus tour
- go on a coach tour *BE*

Busreisen, n
Busreiseverkehr, m

- **bus travel**
- coach travel *BE*
- traveling by bus *AE*
- travelling by bus (coach) *BE*
- traveling on a bus *AE*

Busreisender, m
- **bus traveler** *AE*
- bus traveller *BE*
- coach traveller *BE*

Busreiseprogramm, n
- **bus tour program** *AE*
- bus tour programme *BE*
- coach tour programm *BE*

Busreisespezialist, m
- **bus travel specialist**
- coach travel specialist *BE*

Busreise unternehmen nach X
- **take a bus tour to X**
- take a coach tour to X *BE*

Busreiseurlaub, m
Busreiseferien, pl
- **bus tour vacation** *AE*
- coach tour holiday *BE*

Busreise veranstalten
- **operate a bus tour**
- operate a coach tour *BE*

Busreiseveranstalter, m
- **bus tour operator** *AE*
- coach tour operator *BE*

Busreise zusammenstellen
- **put together a bus tour**
- put together a coach tour *BE*

Busroute, f
Busstrecke, f
- **coach route** *BE*
- bus route

Busrückfahrt, f
Rückfahrt mit dem Bus, f
- **return bus trip**
- return coach trip *BE*
- return trip by bus
- return trip by coach *BE*

Busrückreise, f
- **return bus journey**
- return bus tour
- return bus trip
- return coach journey *BE*
- return coach tour *BE*

Busschaffner, m
- **bus conductor**

Busschaffnerin, f
- **bus conductress**

Bussektor, m
- **bus sector**
- coach sector *BE*

Busservice, m
Busdienst, m
- **coach service** *BE*
- bus service

Busse willkommen
- **Buses welcome** *AE*
- Busses welcome *AE*
- Coaches welcome *BE*

Busstrecke, f
Busroute f
- **bus route**
- coach route *BE*

Büste, f
Brustbild, n
- **bust**

Büstenbehandlung, f
- **bust treatment**

Busterminal n
Busendstation f
- **bus terminal**
- coach terminal *BE*

Bustourismus, m
- **bus tourism** *AE*
- coach tourism *BE*

Bustourist m
- **bus tourist** *AE*
- coach tourist *AE*

Bustransfer, m
- **bus transfer**
- coach transfer *BE*
- transfer by bus
- transfer by coach *BE*

Bus umbauen in etw
Bus umrüsten zu etw
- **convert a bus (in)to s.th.**
- convert a coach (in)to s.th. *BE*

Busunglück, n
- **bus crash**
- coach crash *BE*
- bus accident
- coach accident *BE*

Busunternehmen, n
Busfirma, f
- **bus corporation** *AE*
- bus company *BE*
- coach company *BE*
- coaching company *BE*

Busunternehmer, m
- **bus operator**
- coach operator *BE*

Busunterstand, m
- **bus shelter**

Busurlaub m
- **bus vacation** *AE*
- coach holiday *BE*
- coaching holiday *BE*

Busurlaub machen
- **take a bus vacation** *AE*
- take a coach holiday *BE*
- take a coaching holiday *BE*

Busurlaubsveranstalter, m
- **bus vacation operator** *AE*
- coach holiday operator *BE*

Busveranstalter, m
- **bus operator**
- coach operator *BE*

Busverbindung, f
- **bus connection**
- bus connexion *BE*
- coach connection *BE*
- bus link
- bus service

Busverkehr, m (Service)
→ Busservice

Busverkehr, m (Verkehr)
- **bus traffic**
- coach traffic *BE*

Bus verkehrt zwischen A und B
- **bus runs between A and B**
- coach runs between A and B *BE*

Bus vermieten
- **rent (out) a bus**
- hire out a bus *BE*
- hire out a coach *BE*

Busvermietung, f
Busverleih, m

- ◆ bus rental *AE*
- ◆ bus hire *BE*
- ◆ coach hire *BE*

Bus verpassen
   Bus versäumen
- ◆ miss the bus
- ◆ miss the coach *BE*

Bus war verspätet,und ich verpaßte meinen Anschluß
- ◆ bus was late and I missed my connection

Butangas, n
- ◆ butane gas

Butike, f
  → Kneipe

Butler, m
- ◆ butler

Butlerdienst, m
   Butlerservice, m
- ◆ butler service

Büttenrede, f
- ◆ carnival speech

Büttenredner, m
- ◆ carnival orator

Butter, f
- ◆ butter

Butterbohnen, f pl
- ◆ beans with butter *pl*
- ◆ French beans with butter *pl*

Butterbrot, n
- ◆ bread and butter
- ◆ sandwich
- ◆ slice of bread and butter

Buttercreme, f
- ◆ butter cream

Buttercremetorte, f
- ◆ buttercream cake

Butterdose, f
   Butterschale, f
- ◆ butter dish

Butter erhitzen
- ◆ heat the butter

Butterfahrt, f (Schiff)
- ◆ duty-free cruise

Butterfaß, n
- ◆ butter churn *BE*

Buttergebäck, n
- ◆ rich cookies *AE pl*
- ◆ rich biscuits *BE pl*

Butterkartoffeln, f pl
- ◆ potatoes with butter *pl*
- ◆ buttered potatoes *pl*

Butterkeks, m
- ◆ rich tea biscuit

Butter Maître d'hôtel, f
   Maître-Butter, f
- ◆ butter maître d'hôtel

Buttermesser, n
- ◆ butter knife

Buttermilch, f
- ◆ buttermilk

Butterplatte, f
  → Buttterschale

Butterreis, m
- ◆ rice with butter

Butterschmalz, n
- ◆ clarified buttter

Buttersoße, f
- ◆ butter sauce

Butterstülpe, f
   Butterdose, f

- ◆ covered butter dish
- ◆ butter dish

Butterteig, m
- ◆ butter paste

Buttery Bar, f
- ◆ buttery bar

Buttery Restaurant, n
- ◆ buttery restaurant

Butter zergehen lassen
- ◆ melt the butter

Byronkartoffeln, f pl
- ◆ Byron potatoes *pl*

Byronsoße, f
- ◆ Byron sauce

C

Cabana, f
 Badehütte, f
 ◆ cabana *AE*
 ◆ bathing hut
Cabernet, m *FR*
 ◆ **Cabernet** *FR*
Cabernet Sauvignon, m *FR*
 ◆ **Cabernet Sauvignon** *FR*
Cabriolet, n
 ◆ cabriolet
Caddie, m
 Golfjunge, m
 Golfträger, m
 ◆ caddie
 ◆ caddy
Café, n
 ◆ café
 ◆ cafe *AE*
 ◆ coffee shop *AE*
 ◆ coffee bar *AE*
Café-Bar, f
 ◆ café-bar
 ◆ cafe-bar *AE*
Cafébereich, m
 ◆ café area
 ◆ cafe area *AE*
Cafébesitzer, m
 Besitzer eines Cafés, m
 ◆ café owner
 ◆ cafe owner *AE*
 ◆ owner of a café
 ◆ owner of a cafe *AE*
Cafe-Bistro, n
 ◆ café-bistro
 ◆ cafe-bistro *AE*
Café des artistes, n *FR m*
 Künstlercafé, n
 ◆ **café des artistes** *FR*
 ◆ artists' cafe *AE*
 ◆ artists' café *BE*
Caféeigentümer, m
 Eigentümer eines Cafés, m
 ◆ café proprietor
 ◆ cafe proprietor *AE*
 ◆ proprietor of a café
 ◆ proprietor of a cafe *AE*
Café führen
 ◆ run a cafe *AE*
 ◆ run a café *BE*
Cafégarten, m
 ◆ café garden
 ◆ cafe garden *AE*
Cafégast, m
 ◆ café guest
 ◆ cafe guest *AE*
Café häufig besuchen
 Café frequentieren

 ◆ frequent a café *BE*
 ◆ frequent a cafe *AE*
Café im Freien, n
 Freiluftcafé, n
 ◆ **outdoor café**
 ◆ open-air café
 ◆ outdoor cafe *AE*
 ◆ open-air cafe *AE*
Cafékunde, m
 ◆ **café customer**
 ◆ cafe customer *AE*
Café-Restaurant, n
 Caférestaurant, n
 ◆ **café-restaurant**
 ◆ cafe-restaurant *AE*
 ◆ café cum restaurant
 ◆ cafe cum restaurant *AE*
Cafeteria, f
 ◆ **cafeteria**
Cafeteriadienst, m
 → Cafeteriaservice
Cafeteriaservice, m
 Cafeteriadienst, m
 Cafeteriabedienung, f
 ◆ **cafeteria service**
Caféterrasse, f
 ◆ **café terrace**
 ◆ cafe terrace *AE*
Cafetier, m *ÖST*
 Inhaber eines Kaffeehauses, m
 ◆ **proprietor of a coffeehouse**
Cafetiere, f *ÖST*
 Inhaberin eines Kaffeehauses, f
 ◆ **proprietress of a coffeehouse**
Cafétisch, m
 ◆ **café table**
 ◆ cafe table *AE*
Caissier, m *FR*
 Kassierer, m
 Kassier, m *ÖST/SCHW*
 ◆ **caissier** *FR*
 ◆ cashier
Calaiserart, adv *gastr*
 nach Calaiserart, adv *gastr*
 ◆ **Calais style, adv** *gastr*
Callboy, m
 ◆ **call boy**
Callgirl, n
 ◆ **call girl**
Calvados, m
 ◆ **Calvados**
Calvadossoße, f
 ◆ **calvados sauce**
Calypsoband,
 Calypsokapelle, f
 ◆ **calypso band**
Calypsomusik, f
 ◆ **calypso music**

Camargue, die, f *FR*
 (Region)
 ◆ **Camargue, the** *FR*
Camembert, m
 ◆ **camembert**
 ◆ camembert cheese
Campari, m
 ◆ **Campari**
campen
 zelten
 ◆ **camp**
campen am Ufer (Fluß)
 ◆ **camp on the bank**
campen am Ufer (Meer, Binnensee)
 ◆ **camp on the shore**
campen auf dem Strand
 ◆ **camp on the beach**
campen auf einem Campingplatz
 ◆ **camp at a campsite**
 ◆ camp at a campground *AE*
 ◆ camp at a camping site *BE*
 ◆ camp at a camping ground *BE*
campen auf Privatgelände
 campen auf Privatland
 zelten auf Privatgelände
 zelten auf Privatland
 ◆ **camp on private land**
campen gehen
 → zelten gehen
campen ohne Genehmigung
 zelten ohne Erlaubnis
 ◆ **camp without permission**
Camper, m
 ◆ **camper**
Camper mit Fahrzeug, m
 ◆ **vehicle camper**
Camperparadies, n
 Campingparadies, n
 ◆ **camper's paradise**
Camper willkommen
 (Hinweisschild)
 ◆ **Campers welcome**
campieren
 → campen
Camping, n
 Zelten, n
 ◆ **camping**
Campingarrangement, n
 Campingvereinbarung, f
 ◆ **camping arrangement**
Campingartikel, m
 ◆ **camping article**
 ◆ camping item
Campingaufenthalt, m
 Zeltaufenthalt, m
 ◆ **camping stay**

Campingausrüstung

Campingausrüstung, f
♦ camping equipment
♦ camping gear
Campingausstattung, f (Kleider)
♦ camping outfit
Campingausstellung, f
♦ camping exhibition
♦ camping exhibit *AE*
♦ camping show
Campingauto, n
♦ camping car
Campingbedarf, m
♦ camping supplies *pl*
Campingbegeisterter, m
♦ camping enthusiast
Campingbereich, m (abstrakt)
Campingsektor, m
♦ camping sector
Campingbereich, m (konkret)
♦ camping area
Campingbett, n
Campingliege, f
♦ camping bed
♦ campbed
Campingbus, m
♦ campervan
♦ camper
Campingbusverleih, m
Campingbusvermietung, f
♦ campervan hire *BE*
♦ camper hire *BE*
♦ campervan rental *AE*
Campingcaravan, m
Campingwohnwagen, m
♦ camping caravan *BE*
♦ camping trailer *AE*
Camping-Carnet, n
♦ camping carnet
Campingclub, m
♦ camping club
Campingclub beitreten
♦ join a camping club
Campingclubmitglied, n
♦ camping club member
♦ member of a camping club
Campingdorf, n
♦ camping village
Campingeinrichtung, f
♦ camping facility
Campingerfahrung, f
♦ camping experience
Campingerfahrung haben
♦ have camping experience
Campingexpedition, f
→ Zeltexpedition
Campingexperte, m
♦ camping expert
Campingfahrt, f
Zeltfahrt, f
♦ camping trip
Campingfahrt machen
♦ go on a camping trip
Campingfahrzeug, n
♦ camping vehicle
♦ recreational vehicle *AE*
♦ RV *AE*
Campingfan, m
♦ camping fan
Campingferien, pl
Campingurlaub, m

♦ camping holiday *BE*
♦ camping vacation *AE*
Campingferiengast, m
Campingurlauber, m
♦ camping holidaymaker *BE*
♦ camping vacationer *AE*
Campingfläche, f
♦ camping area
Campingfreuden, f pl
♦ joys of camping *pl*
Campingführer, m
(Information)
♦ camping guide
Campinggebiet, n (groß)
♦ camping region
Campinggebiet, n (klein)
♦ camping area
Campinggebühr, f
♦ camping fee
♦ camping charge
Campinggegenstand, m
Campingartikel, m
♦ camping item
Campinggelegenheit, f
♦ possibility of camping
Campinggenehmigung, f
Erlaubnis zu zelten, f
♦ permission to camp
Campinggewerbe, n
♦ camping trade
Campinggruppe, f
(Touristen)
Campinggesellschaft f
♦ camping party
♦ camping group
Campinggutschein, m
♦ camping voucher
Campingherd, m
♦ camping stove *AE*
♦ camping cooker *BE*
Campingillustrierte, f
Campingmagazin, n
♦ camping magazine
Campingindustrie, f
♦ camping industry
Campinginformation, f
♦ camping information
Camping ist erlaubt
Zelten ist erlaubt
♦ camping is allowed
Camping ist gestattet
Zelten ist erlaubt
♦ camping is permitted
Camping ist nicht erlaubt
Zelten ist nicht erlaubt
♦ camping is not allowed
Camping ist nicht gestattet
Zelten ist nicht erlaubt
♦ camping is not permitted
Camping ist untersagt
Zelten ist untersagt
♦ camping is prohibited
Camping ist verboten
Zelten ist verboten
♦ camping is forbidden
Campingkocher, m
♦ camping cooker
Campingkurs, m
Campinglehrgang, m
♦ camping course

Campingkurs besuchen
♦ attend a camping course
Campingkurzurlaub, m
♦ camping break
Campinglager, n
→ Zeltlager
Campingleben, n
♦ camping life
Campingliege, f
Campingbett, n
♦ campbed
♦ camping bed
Campingmarkt, m
♦ camping market
Campingmesse, f
♦ camping fair
♦ camping trade fair
Campingneuling, m
♦ camping novice
♦ first-time camper
Campingorganisation, f
♦ camping organisation
♦ camping organization
Campingparadies, n
♦ camping paradise
Campingpark, m
♦ camping park
Campingparzelle, f
♦ camping pitch
♦ camping lot
Campingpaß, m
→ Campingcarnet
Campingpauschale, f
♦ camping package
Campingpauschalurlaub, m
♦ camping package vacation *AE*
♦ inclusive camping vacation *AE*
♦ camping package holiday *BE*
♦ inclusive camping holiday *BE*
Campingplatz, m (für Wohnwagen)
→ Wohnwagenplatz
Campingplatz, m (generell)
♦ campsite
♦ campground *AE*
♦ camping site *BE*
♦ camping ground *BE*
Campingplatzadresse, f
Campingplatzanschrift, f
♦ campsite address
♦ campground address *AE*
♦ camping site address *BE*
♦ camping ground address *BE*
Campingplatzanlage, f
Campingplatzkomplex, m
♦ campsite complex
♦ campground complex *AE*
♦ camping site complex *BE*
♦ camping ground complex *BE*
Campingplatzanmeldung, f
♦ campsite registration
♦ campground registration *AE*
♦ camping site registration *BE*
♦ camping ground registration *BE*
Campingplatzart, f
Campingplatztyp, m
♦ campsite type
♦ type of campsite
♦ type of campground *AE*
♦ type of camping site *BE*
♦ type of camping ground *BE*

128

Campingplatzliste

Campingplatz benutzen
- **use a campsite**
- use a campground *AE*
- use a camping site *BE*
- use a camping ground *BE*

Campingplatzbenutzer, m
- **campsite user**
- user of a campsite
- campground user *AE*
- user of a campground
- camping site user *BE*

Campingplatzbericht, m
- **campsite report**
- campground report *AE*
- camping site report *BE*
- camping ground report *BE*

Campingplatzbeschreibung, f
- **campsite description**
- campground description *AE*
- camping site description *BE*
- camping ground description *BE*
- description of the campsite

Campingplatz besichtigen
- → Campingplatz inspizieren

Campingplatzbesitzer, m
- **campsite owner**
- campground owner *AE*
- camping site owner *BE*
- camping ground owner *BE*

Campingplatzbesuch, m
- **campsite visit**
- visit to a campsite
- camping ground visit *BE*
- campground visit *AE*
- visit to a campground

Campingplatzbesucher, m
- **campsite visitor**
- campground visitor *AE*
- camping site visitor *BE*
- camping ground visitor *BE*
- visitor to a campsite

Campingplatz betreiben
- Campingplatz bewirtschaften
- **operate a campsite**
- operate a campground *AE*
- operate a camping site *BE*
- operate a camping ground *BE*

Campingplatzbetreiber, m
- **campsite operator**
- campground operator *AE*
- camping site operator *BE*
- camping ground operator *BE*

Campingplatzbetreuer, m
- Campingplatzgästebetreuer, m
- **campsite courier** *BE*

Campingplatzbüro, n
- **campsite office**
- campground office *AE*
- camping site office *BE*
- camping ground office *BE*
- site office

Campingplatzeigentümer, m
- **campsite proprietor**
- campground proprietor *AE*
- camping site proprietor *BE*
- camping ground proprietor *BE*

Campingplatzeingang, m
- **campsite entrance**
- campground entrance *AE*
- camping site entrance *BE*
- camping ground entrance *BE*

Campingplatz einstufen
- **grade a campsite**
- grade a campground *AE*
- grade a camping site *BE*
- grade a camping ground *BE*
- grade a site

Campingplatzferien, pl
- Campingplatzurlaub, m
- **campsite holiday** *BE*
- camping site holiday *BE*
- camping ground holiday *BE*
- campsite vacation *AE*
- campground vacation *AE*

Campingplatzführer, m
(Information)
- **campsite guide**
- campsites guide
- campground(s) guide *AE*
- camping site(s) guide *BE*
- camping ground(s) guide *BE*

Campingplatzgast, m
- **campsite guest**
- campground guest *AE*
- camping site guest *BE*
- camping ground guest *BE*

Campingplatzgebühr, f
- **campsite fee**
- campsite charge
- campground fee *AE*
- campground charge *AE*
- camping site fee *BE*

Campingplatzgeschäft, n
- **campsite store** *AE*
- campsite shop *BE*
- campground store *AE*
- camping site shop *BE*
- camping ground shop *BE*

Campingplatzgutschein, m
- **campsite voucher**
- campground voucher *AE*
- camping site voucher *BE*
- camping ground voucher *BE*

Campingplatzhalter, m
- **campsite warden**
- campground warden *AE*
- camping site warden *BE*
- camping ground warden *BE*

Campingplatzinspizient, m
- Campingplatzinspekteur, m
- **campsite inspector**
- campground inspector *AE*
- camping site inspector *BE*
- camping ground inspector *BE*
- site inspector

Campingplatz inspizieren
- Campingplatz besichtigen
- **inspect a campsite**
- inspect a campground *AE*
- inspect a camping site *BE*
- inspect a camping ground *BE*

Campingplatz ist belegt
- Campingplatz ist voll
- **campsite is full (up)**
- campground is full (up) *AE*
- camping site is full (up) *BE*
- camping ground is full (up) *BE*

Campingplatz ist bewirtschaftet von 1. März bis 31. Oktober
Campingplatz ist geöffnet vom 1. März bis 31. Oktober
- **campsite is open from 1 March to 31 October**
- campground is open from 1 March to 31 October *AE*
- camping site is open from 1 March to 31 October *BE*
- camping ground is open from 1 March to 31 October

Campingplatzkapazität, f
- **campsite capacity**
- campground capacity *AE*
- camping site capacity *BE*
- camping ground capacity *BE*

Campingplatzkarte, f (Landkarte)
- **campsite(s) map**
- campground(s) map *AE*
- camping site(s) map *BE*
- camping ground(s) map *BE*

Campingplatzkategorie, f
- **campsite category**
- campground category *AE*
- camping site category *BE*
- camping ground category *BE*

Campingplatzkette, f
- **campsite chain**
- campground chain *AE*
- camping site chain *BE*
- camping ground chain *BE*

Campingplatzkiosk, m
- **campsite kiosk**
- campground kiosk *AE*
- camping site kiosk *BE*
- camping ground kiosk *BE*

Campingplatz klassifizieren
- **classify a campsite**
- classify a campground *AE*
- classify a camping site *BE*
- classify a camping ground *BE*

Campingplatzklassifizierung, f
- **classification of a campsite**
- classification of a campground *AE*
- classification of a camping site *BE*
- classification of a camping ground *BE*

Campingplatzkonzession, f
- **campsite license**
- campground license *AE*
- camping site license *BE*
- camping ground license *BE*

Campingplatzlage, f
- Campingplatzstandort, m
- **campsite location**
- location of the campsite
- camping site location *BE*
- location of the camping site *BE*
- campsite situation

Campingplatzleiter, m
- **campsite manager**
- campground manager *AE*
- camping site manager *BE*
- camping ground manager *BE*
- site manager

Campingplatzleitung, f
- **campsite management**
- campground management *AE*
- camping site management *BE*
- camping ground management *BE*
- managing a campsite

Campingplatzliste, f
- **campsite(s) list**
- campground(s) list *AE*
- camping site(s) list *BE*
- camping ground(s) list *BE*

Campingplatzmiete

Campingplatzmiete, f
- **campsite rent**
- campground rent *AE*
- camping site rent *BE*
- camping ground rent *BE*

Campingplatzmietgebühr, f
- **campsite rental fee** *AE*
- campsite rental charge *AE*
- campsite hire charge *BE*
- camping site hire charge *BE*
- camping ground hire charge *BE*

Campingplatznachbar, m
- **campsite neighbor** *AE*
- campsite neighbour *BE*
- campground neighbor *AE*
- camping site neighbour *BE*
- camping ground neighbour *BE*

Campingplatzname, m
- **campsite name**
- campground name *AE*
- camping site name *BE*
- camping ground name *BE*
- name of the campsite

Campingplatznetz, n
- **campsite network**
- campground network *AE*
- camping site network *BE*
- camping ground network *BE*

Campingplatzpächter, m
- **campsite leaseholder**
- campground leaseholder *AE*
- camping site tenant *BE*
- camping ground tenant *BE*

Campingplatzpersonal, n
- **campsite staff**
- campsite personnel
- campground staff *AE*
- campground personnel *AE*
- camping site staff *BE*

Campingplatzprospekt, m
  Campingplatzbroschüre, f
- **campsite brochure**
- campground brochure *AE*
- camping site brochure *BE*
- camping ground brochure *BE*

Campingplatzrezeption, f
  Campingplatzempfang, m
- **campsite reception**
- campground reception *AE*
- camping site reception *BE*
- camping ground reception *BE*

Campingplatzservice, m
  Campingplatzdienst, m
  Campingplatzdienstleistung, f
- **campsite service**
- campground service *AE*
- camping site service *BE*
- camping ground service *BE*
- site service

Campingplatztester, m
  → Campingplatzinspizient

Campingplatztoilette, f
- **campsite toilet**
- campground toilet *AE*
- camping site toilet *BE*
- camping ground toilet *BE*

Campingplatzunterkunft, f
  Campingplatzunterbringung, f
- **campsite accommodation**
- campground accommodation *AE*

- camping site accommodation *BE*
- camping ground accommodation *BE*

Campingplatzurlaub, m
  Campingplatzferien, pl
- **campsite vacation** *AE*
- campsite holiday *BE*
- campground vacation *AE*
- camping site holiday *BE*
- camping ground holiday *BE*

Campingplatzurlaub machen
- **take a campsite vacation** *AE*
- take a campground vacation *AE*
- take a campsite holiday *BE*
- take a camping ground holiday *BE*
- take a camping site holiday *BE*

Campingplatz verpachten (an jn)
- **lease a campsite (to s.o.)**
- lease a campground (to s.o.) *AE*
- lease a camping site (to s.o.) *BE*
- lease a camping ground (to s.o.) *BE*
- lease a site (to s.o.)

Campingplatzverwaltung, f
- **campsite administration**
- campground administration *AE*
- camping site administration *BE*
- camping ground administration *BE*
- administering a campsite *AE*

Campingplatzverzeichnis, n
- **campsite directory**
- campground directory *AE*
- camping site directory *BE*
- camping ground directory *BE*

Campingplatzwart, m
- **campsite steward**
- campground steward *AE*
- camping site steward *BE*
- camping ground steward *BE*

Campingprospekt, m
- **camping brochure**

Campingreise, f
  Campingtour, f
- **camping tour**
- camping trip
- camping journey

Campingreise machen
- **go on a camping tour**
- go on a camping trip

Campingreiseveranstalter, m
- **camping tour operator**

Campingsafari, f
  → Zeltsafari

Campingschau, f
  Campingausstellung, f
- **camping show**

Campingsektor, m
  → Campingbereich

Campingspezialist, m
- **camping specialist**

Campingstellplatz, m
- **camping pitch**

Campingtechnik, f
- **camping technique**

Campingtourismus, m
  Zelttourismus, m
- **camping tourism**
- touring and camping

Campingtourist, m
  Zelttourist, m
- **camping tourist**
- camper

Campingübernachtung, f (generell)
- **overnight stay at a campsite**
- staying overnight at a campsite
- overnight stay at a campground *AE*
- staying overnight at a campground *AE*
- overnight stay at a camping site *BE*

Campingübernachtung, f (Statistik)
- **camping night**

Camping- und Caravanclub, m
- **camping and caravanning club** *BE*

Camping- und Caravanplatz, m
  Camping- und Wohnwagenplatz, m
- **camping and trailer site** *AE*
- camping and caravan site *BE*

Campingunterkunft, f
- **camping accommodation**

Campingunternehmen, n
- **camping enterprise**

Campingurlaub, m
  Campingferien, pl
- **camping vacation** *AE*
- camping holiday *BE*

Campingurlauber, m
  Campingferiengast, m
- **camping vacationer** *AE*
- camping holidaymaker *BE*

Campingurlaub für Selbstfahrer, m
  Campingferien für Selbstfahrer, pl
- **self-drive camping vacation** *AE*
- self-drive camping holiday *BE*
- self-driving camping holiday *BE*

Campingurlaub machen
- **go on a camping vacation** *AE*
- go on a camping holiday *BE*
- take a camping vacation *AE*
- take a camping holiday *BE*
- go camping

Campingveranstalter, m
  (Reiseveranstalter)
- **camping operator**

Campingverband, m
- **camping association**

Campingversicherung, f
- **camping insurance**

Campingvertrag, m
- **camping contract**

Campingwochenende, n
- **camping weekend**

Campingwohnwagen, m
  Campingcaravan, m
- **camping trailer** *AE*
- camping caravan *BE*

Campingzentrum, n
- **camping center** *AE*
- camping centre *BE*

Campingzubehör, n
- **camping accessories** *pl*
- camping equipment
- camping gear

Campus, m
  Hochschulgelände, n
- **campus**

Campustourismus, m
- **campus tourism**

Campustourist, m
- **campus tourist**

Campusunterkunft, f
  Campusunterbringung, f
- **campus accommodation**

Campusurlaub, m
  Urlaub auf dem Campus m

- ◆ campus vacation *AE*
- ◆ campus holiday *BE*

Campusurlauber, m
Campusurlauberin f
- ◆ campus vacationer *AE*
- ◆ campus holidaymaker *BE*

Canale Grande, m *ITAL*
(Venedig)
- ◆ Grand Canal, the
- ◆ Canale Grande, the *ITAL*

Canapé, n
→ Kanapee

Cancellation, f
→ Stornierung

canceln etw
→ stornieren etw

Candle-Light-Dinner, n
→ Abendessen bei Kerzenlicht

Canneloni, pl *ITAL gastr*
- ◆ canneloni, pl *ITAL gastr*

Caravan, m
Wohnwagen, m
- ◆ caravan *BE*
- ◆ trailer *AE*

Caravanabholstelle, f
Wohnwagenabholstelle, f
- ◆ caravan pick-up point *BE*
- ◆ trailer pick-up point *AE*

Caravanarrangement, n
Caravanvereinbarung, f
Wohnwagenarrangement, n
Wohnwagenvereinbarung, f
- ◆ caravanning arrangement *BE*
- ◆ trailer arrangement *AE*

Caravanausrüstung, f
Caravanausstattung, f
Wohnwagenausrüstung, f
Wohnwagenausstattung, f
- ◆ caravan equipment *BE*
- ◆ trailer equipment *AE*

Caravanbenutzer, m
Wohnwagenbenutzer, m
- ◆ caravan user *BE*
- ◆ person using a caravan *BE*
- ◆ trailer user *AE*
- ◆ person using a trailer *AE*

Caravanbereich, m (konkret)
Wohnwagenbereich, m
- ◆ caravan area *BE*
- ◆ trailer area *AE*

Caravanbereich, m (Sektor)
→ Caravansektor

Caravanbesitzer, m
Wohnwagenbesitzer, m
- ◆ caravan owner *BE*
- ◆ owner of a caravan *BE*
- ◆ trailer owner *AE*
- ◆ owner of a trailer *AE*

Caravan bietet drei Personen Schlafmöglichkeiten
Wohnwagen bietet drei Personen Schlafmöglichkeiten
- ◆ caravan sleeps three persons *BE*
- ◆ trailer sleeps three persons *AE*

Caravancamper, m
Wohnwagencamper, m
- ◆ caravan camper *BE*
- ◆ trailer camper *AE*

Caravanclub, m
Wohnwagenclub, m
- ◆ caravan club *BE*
- ◆ trailer club *AE*

Caravaneigentümer, m
Wohnwageneigentümer, m
- ◆ caravan proprietor *BE*
- ◆ trailer proprietor *AE*

Caravaneinheit, f
(Statistik)
Wohnwageneinheit, f
- ◆ caravan unit *BE*
- ◆ trailer unit *AE*

Caravaner, m
Caravanfahrer, m
Caravanbenutzer,
Wohnwagenfahrer, m
Wohnwagenbenutzer, m
- ◆ caravanner *BE*
- ◆ trailerite *AE*
- ◆ trailerist *AE*

Caravanfahrer, m
→ Wohnwagenfahrer

Caravanfahrpreis, m
Fahrpreis für einen Caravan, m
Wohnwagenfahrpreis, m
Fahrpreis für einen Wohnwagen, m
- ◆ caravan fare *BE*
- ◆ trailer fare *AE*

Caravangröße, f
Wohnwagengröße, f
- ◆ caravan size *BE*
- ◆ size of a caravan *BE*
- ◆ trailer size *AE*
- ◆ size of a trailer *AE*

Caravanindustrie, f
Wohnwagenindustrie, f
- ◆ caravan industry *BE*
- ◆ caravanning industry *BE*
- ◆ trailer industry *AE*

Caravaning, n
- ◆ caravanning *BE*

Caravan ist untervermietet
Wohnwagen ist untervermietet
- ◆ caravan is sublet *BE*
- ◆ trailer is sublet *AE*
- ◆ trailer is underlet *AE*
- ◆ trailer is subleased *AE*
- ◆ caravan is subleased *BE*

Caravan kann bis zu sieben Personen aufnehmen
Wohnwagen kann bis zu sieben Personen aufnehmen
- ◆ caravan can accommodate up to seven persons *BE*
- ◆ trailer can accommodate up to seven persons *AE*

Caravankurzurlaub, m
Wohnwagenkurzurlaub, m
- ◆ caravan break *BE*
- ◆ caravanning break *BE*
- ◆ trailer break *AE*

Caravanmarke, f
Wohnwagenmarke, f
- ◆ caravan make *BE*
- ◆ trailer make *AE*

Caravanmiete, f
Wohnwagenmiete, f
- ◆ caravan hire *BE*
- ◆ trailer rental *AE*

Caravan mieten
Wohnwagen mieten
- ◆ hire a caravan *BE*
- ◆ rent a trailer *AE*

Caravanmietgebühr, f
Wohnwagenmietgebühr, f
- ◆ caravan hire charge *BE*
- ◆ trailer rental charge *AE*

Caravanmodell, n
Wohnwagenmodell, n
- ◆ caravan model *BE*
- ◆ trailer model *AE*

Caravanpark, m
Wohnwagenpark, m
- ◆ caravan park *BE*
- ◆ trailer park *AE*

Caravanparkleiter, m
Wohnwagenparkleiter, m
- ◆ caravan park manager *BE*
- ◆ trailer park manager *AE*

Caravanpauschale, f
Wohnwagenpauschale, f
- ◆ caravan package *BE*
- ◆ trailer package *AE*

Caravanplatz, m
Wohnwagenplatz, m
- ◆ caravan site *BE*
- ◆ trailer site *AE*

Caravanplatzbetreiber, m
Wohnwagenplatzbetreiber, m
- ◆ caravan site operator *BE*
- ◆ caravanning site operator *BE*
- ◆ trailer site operator *AE*
- ◆ trailer camp operator *AE*

Caravanplatzklassifizierung, f
Wohnwagenplatzklassifizierung, f
- ◆ caravan site classification *BE*
- ◆ trailer site classification *AE*

Caravanplatzverzeichnis, n
Wohnwagenplatzverzeichnis, n
- ◆ caravan site directory *BE*
- ◆ trailer site directory *AE*

Caravan pro Nacht, m
Wohnwagen pro Nacht, m
- ◆ caravan per night *BE*
- ◆ trailer per night *AE*

Caravanreise, f
- ◆ caravanning tour *BE*
- ◆ trailer tour *BE*

Caravanrückgabestelle, f
Wohnwagenrückgabestelle, f
- ◆ caravan drop-off point *BE*
- ◆ trailer drop-off point *AE*

Caravanschau, f
Wohnwagenschau, f
- ◆ caravan show *BE*
- ◆ trailer show *AE*

Caravansektor, m
Caravanbereich, m
Wohnwagensektor, m
Wohnwagenbereich, m
- ◆ caravan sector *BE*
- ◆ caravanning sector *BE*
- ◆ trailer sector *AE*

Caravanstellplatz, m
(für einen Caravan)
Wohnwagenstellplatz, m
- ◆ caravan pitch *BE*
- ◆ trailer pitch *AE*

Caravantyp, m
Wohnwagentyp, m
- ◆ caravan type *BE*
- ◆ type of caravan *BE*
- ◆ trailer type *AE*
- ◆ type of trailer *AE*

Caravan- und Campingclub

Caravan- und Campingclub, m
- caravan and camping club *BE*

Caravanunterkunft, f
Caravanunterbringung, f
Wohnwagenunterkunft, f
Wohnwagenunterbringung, f
- **caravan accommodation** *BE*
- trailer accommodation *AE*
- trailer lodging *AE*

Caravanunternehmen, n
Wohnwagenunternehmen, n
- **caravan enterprise** *BE*
- caravanning enterprise *BE*
- trailer enterprise *AE*

Caravan untervermieten
Wohnwagen untervermieten
- **sublet a caravan** *BE*
- sublease a caravan *BE*
- underlet a trailer *AE*
- sublet a trailer *AE*
- sublease a trailer *AE*

Caravanuntervermietung, f
Wohnwagenuntervermietung, f
- **caravan subletting** *BE*
- subletting (of) a caravan *BE*
- trailer sublease *AE*
- subletting (of) a trailer *AE*

Caravanurlaub, m
Caravanferien, pl
Wohnwagenurlaub, m
Wohnwagenferien, pl
- **caravan holiday** *BE*
- caravanning holiday *BE*
- trailer vacation *AE*

Caravanurlauber, m
Wohnwagenurlauber, m
- **caravan holidaymaker** *BE*
- trailer vacationer *AE*

Caravan vermieten
Wohnwagen vermieten
- **hire out a caravan** *BE*
- let a caravan *BE*
- rent a trailer *AE*

Caravanvermietung, f
Wohnwagenvermietung, f
- **caravan hire** *BE*
- hiring out a caravan *BE*
- letting a caravan *BE*
- trailer rental *AE*
- renting a trailer *AE*

Caravanvorzelt, n
Wohnwagenvorzelt, n
- **caravan awning** *BE*
- trailer awning *AE*

Caravanzentrum, n
Wohnwagenzentrum, n
- **caravan centre** *BE*
- trailer center *AE*

Caravan zu vermieten (Schild)
Wohnwagen zu vermieten
- **Caravan for hire (sign)** *BE*
- Caravan to let *BE*
- Trailer for rent *AE*

Carnet, n
- carnet

Carnet de passage, n *FR m*
(für Land- und Wasserfahrzeuge)
Zollpassierschein m
Triptik n
Triptyk n
- **carnet de passage** *FR*

- customs pass
- triptyque
- tryptique
- tryptyque

Carport m
(für Auto)
- **car port**

Carrier, m
→ Verkehrsträger

Carte du jour, f *FR*
Tageskarte, f
- **carte du jour** *FR*
- (special) menu of the day
- daily menu
- daily bill of fare
- today's menu

Casino, n
→ Spielkasino

Casserolier, m *FR*
- **casserolier** *FR*

Cassette, f
→ Kassette

Caterer, m
Lieferant von Speisen und Getränken, m
- **caterer**

Catering, n
- **catering** *AE*
- contract foodservice *AE*
- outside catering *BE*
- contract catering *BE*
- off-premises catering *BE*

Cateringabteilung, f
- **catering department** *AE*
- contract foodservice department *AE*
- outside catering department *BE*
- contract catering department *BE*

Cateringaufwand, m
Cateringaufwendung, f
- **catering expense** *AE*
- catering expenditure *AE*
- contract foodservice expenditure *AE*
- contract catering expenditure *BE*
- outside catering expenditure *BE*

Cateringbereich, m (abstrakt)
- **catering field** *AE*
- contract foodservice field *AE*
- outside catering field *BE*
- contract catering field *BE*
- contract catering sector *BE*

Cateringbereich, m (einer Firma)
- **catering division** *AE*
- contract foodservice division *AE*
- outside catering division *BE*
- contract catering division *BE*

Cateringbereich, m (konkret)
- **catering area** *AE*
- contract foodservice area *AE*
- contract catering area *BE*

Cateringbetrieb, m
- **catering establishment** *AE*
- catering operation *AE*
- contract foodservice operation *AE*
- contract catering operation *BE*
- outside catering operation *BE*

Cateringerlös, m
- **catering revenue** *AE*
- contract foodservice revenue *AE*
- contract catering revenue *BE*
- outside catering revenue *BE*

Catering für Fluggesellschaften, n
- **airline catering** *AE*
- airline contract catering *BE*

Cateringgeschäft, n
- **catering business** *AE*
- contract foodservice business *AE*
- contract catering business *BE*
- outside catering business *BE*

Cateringgesellschaft, f
Cateringfirma, f
- **catering company** *AE*
- catering firm *AE*
- contract foodservice company *AE*
- contract catering company *BE*
- contrcat catering firm *BE*

Cateringgewerbe, n
Cateringbranche, f
- **catering trade** *AE*
- contract catering trade *BE*

Cateringkontrolle, f
- **catering control** *AE*
- contract catering control *BE*

Cateringkonzept, n
- **catering concept** *AE*
- contract catering concept *BE*

Cateringkosten, pl
- **catering costs** *AE pl*
- catering cost *AE*
- contract catering costs *BE pl*
- contract catering cost *BE*

Cateringleiter, m
Cateringmanager, m
- **catering manager** *AE*
- contract foodservice manager *BE*
- contract catering manager *BE*

Cateringmarkt, m
- **catering market** *AE*
- contract foodservice market *AE*
- contract catering market *BE*

Cateringorganisation, f
- **catering organisation** *AE*
- contract foodservice organisation *AE*
- contract catering organisation *BE*

Cateringpersonal, n
- **catering staff** *AE*
- catering personnel *AE*
- contract catering staff *BE*
- contract catering personnel *BE*
- contract foodservice staff *AE*

Cateringprodukt, n
- **catering product** *AE*
- contract foodservice product *AE*
- contract catering product *BE*
- outside catering product *BE*

Cateringservice, m
- **catering service** *AE*
- contract food service *AE*
- contract catering service *BE*
- outside catering service *BE*

Cateringstandard, m
- **catering standard** *AE*
- contract foodservice standard *AE*
- contract catering standard *BE*
- outside catering standard *BE*

Cateringumsatz, m
- **catering sales** *AE pl*
- catering turnover *AE*
- contract catering sales *BE pl*
- contract catering turnover *BE*
- outside catering sales *BE pl*

Cateringunternehmer, m
♦ catering contractor *AE*
♦ contract foodservice operator *AE*
♦ contract catering contractor *BE*
♦ contract catering operator *BE*
Cateringvolumen, n
Cateringumfang, m
♦ catering volume *AE*
♦ contract foodservice volume *AE*
♦ contract catering volume *BE*
Cayennepfeffer, m
♦ cayenne pepper
♦ cayenne
♦ red pepper
CD, f
CD-Platte, f
Compact Disc, f
♦ CD
♦ compact disc
CD-Spieler, m
♦ CD player
♦ compact disc player
CD-Video, n
♦ CD video
Celsius
(Temperaturangabe)
♦ centigrade
♦ Celsius
C-förmig, adj
♦ C-shaped, adj
Chacun à son goût *FR*
Jedem nach seinem Geschmack
♦ Chacun à son goût *FR*
Chaiselongue, f/n *FR*
♦ chaise longue *FR*
♦ divan
♦ couch
Chalet, n
♦ chalet
Chaletanlage, f
Chaletkomplex m
♦ chalet complex
chaletartig, adj
im Chaletstil
♦ chalet-style, adj
Chalethotel, n
♦ chalet hotel
Chalet im Privatbesitz, n
♦ privately owned chalet
♦ chalet in private ownership
Chaletpark, m
♦ chalet park
Chaletplatz, m
♦ chalet site
Chaletsuite, f
♦ chalet suite
Chaletunterkunft, f
Chaletunterbringung, f
♦ chalet accommodation
♦ chalet lodging *AE*
Chaleturlaub, m
♦ chalet vacation *AE*
♦ chalet holiday *BE*
Chaletzimmer, n
♦ chalet room
Chalet zu vermieten
(Hinweisschild)
♦ Chalet for rent *AE*
♦ Chalet to let *BE*
chambré, adj *Fr*
→ chambriert

Chambre séparée, n *FR*
♦ chambre séparée *FR*
chambrieren
(Rotwein auf Zimmertemperatur bringen)
♦ room a wine
♦ bring to room temperature
♦ see that the wine is chambré
♦ see that the wine is roomed
chambriert, adj
(Rotwein)
chambré, adj *FR*
♦ chambré, adj *FR*
♦ roomed, adj
Champagne, f
(Region)
♦ Champagne
Champagner, m
♦ champagne
♦ bubbly *BE coll*
♦ fizz *BE coll*
Champagneraperitif, m
♦ pre-dinner champagne
Champagnerflasche, f
→ Sektflasche
Champagnerfrühstück, n
→ Sektfrühstück
Champagner nach dem Essen, m
♦ after-dinner champagne
Champagnerpicknick, n
Sektpicknick, n
♦ champagne picnic
♦ champagne picknick *AE*
Champagnerprobe, f
→ Sektprobe
Champagnersorbet, n
Sektsorbet, n
♦ champagne sorbet
Champagnersoße, f
♦ champagne sauce
Champagner trinken
♦ drink champagne
♦ have a glass of champagne
Champagnerzimmer, n
♦ Champagne Room, the
Champignon, m
♦ champignon
Champignonaufstrich, m
♦ champignon spread
Champignoncremesuppe, f
♦ champignon cream soup
Champignon-Kräutersoße, f
♦ sauce with champignons and herbs
Champignonomelett, n
Champignonomelette, f *SCHW/ÖST*
♦ champignon omelet
♦ champignon omelette
Champignonpastete, f
♦ champignon pie
♦ champignon pâté
Champignonpüree, n
♦ champignon purée
♦ champignon puree *AE*
Champignonsalat, m
♦ champignon salad
Champignonschiffchen, n
♦ champignon barquette
Champignonsoße, f
♦ champignon sauce
Champignontoast, m
♦ champignon toast

Champignontörtchen, n
♦ champignon tartlet
Changement n
→ Zimmerwechsel
Chaperon, m
Begleitperson (bei Jugendlichen), m
Anstandsdame, f
♦ chaperon
♦ chaperone
Charaban, m
Kremser, m
♦ char à bancs *FR*
♦ wagonette
♦ waggonette *BE*
Chardonnay, m *FR*
♦ Chardonnay, the *FR*
Charter, m
♦ charter
Charterbasis, f
♦ charter basis
Charterbestimmungen, f pl
Chartervorschriften, f pl
♦ charter regulations *pl*
Charterboot, n
Charterschiff, n
♦ charter boat
Charterbus, m
♦ charter bus
♦ charter coach *BE*
Charterdienst, f
Charterservice m
♦ charter service
Charterer, m
♦ charterer
Charterfahrt, f
♦ charter trip
Charterfirma, f
♦ charter firm
Charterflug, m
Charterflugreise f
♦ charter flight
Charterfluggesellschaft, f
♦ charter airline
♦ charter line
Charterflugpassagier, m
♦ charter flight passenger
Charterflugpreis, m
♦ charter air fare
♦ charter fare
Charterflugschein, m
♦ charter flight ticket
Charterflugverkehr, m
♦ charter flight traffic
♦ charter air traffic
Charterflugzeug, n
♦ charter plane
♦ chartered plane
♦ charter aircraft
♦ chartered aircraft
Chartergeschäft, n
♦ charter business
Chartergesellschaft, f
Charterfirma, f
♦ charter company
Chartergruppe, f
(Gasttyp)
♦ charter group
Charterhausboot, n
♦ charter houseboat
Charterjacht, f
Charteryacht, f

Charterkette 134

- ♦ charter yacht
- ♦ chartered yacht

Charterkette, f
- ♦ charter chain

Charterkosten, pl
- ♦ charter costs *pl*
- ♦ charter cost

Charterkreuzfahrtschiff, n
- ♦ charter cruise ship
- ♦ chartered cruise ship

Charterluftverkehr, m
- ♦ charter air travel

Chartermaschine, f
Charterflugzeug, n
- ♦ charter aircraft
- ♦ chartered aircraft

chartern etw (von jm)
- ♦ charter s.th. (from s.o.)

Charterpauschalreise, f
CIT, f
- ♦ charter-inclusive tour
- ♦ CIT
- ♦ charter package tour

Charterplatz, m
Chartersitzplatz, m
- ♦ charter seat

Charterpreis m
- ♦ charter rate
- ♦ charter price

Charterreise, f
- ♦ charter tour
- ♦ charter trip

Charterreise veranstalten
- ♦ operate a charter tour
- ♦ operate a charter trip

Charterreiseveranstalter, m
- ♦ charter tour operator

Charterreiseveranstaltung, f
- ♦ charter tour operation
- ♦ charter tour operating

Charterroute, f
Charterstrecke, f
- ♦ charter route

Charterschiff, n
- ♦ charter ship
- ♦ chartered ship
- ♦ charter boat
- ♦ chartered boat

Charterservice, m
→ Charterdienst

Chartersteuer, f
- ♦ charter tax

Chartertochtergesellschaft, f
Chartertochter, f
- ♦ charter subsidiary

Chartertourismus, m
- ♦ charter tourism

Chartertourist, m
- ♦ charter tourist

Charterveranstalter, m
- ♦ charter operator

Chartervereinbarung, f
- ♦ charter agreement

Charterverkehr, m
- ♦ charter traffic

Chartervertrag, m
- ♦ charter contract

Chartervertrag machen
- ♦ make a charter contract

Chartervertrag unterzeichnen
Chartervertrag unterschreiben
- ♦ sign a charter contract

Charterzeitraum, m
Charterperiode, f
- ♦ charter period

Charterzug, m
- ♦ charter train
- ♦ chartered train

Chasseur, m *FR*
Hotelbote, m
- ♦ chasseur *FR*
- ♦ messenger boy

Chasseur de restaurant, m *FR*
Restaurantpage, m
- ♦ chasseur de restaurant *FR*
- ♦ pageboy
- ♦ page

Chasseur d'hôtel, m *FR*
Chasseur, m
Hotelbote, m
- ♦ chasseur d'hôtel *FR*
- ♦ chasseur

Château, n *FR*
- ♦ château *FR*

Châteauservice, m *FR*
(Essen wird dargereicht, Gast nimmt selbst)
- ♦ château service *FR*

Chauffeur, m
- ♦ chauffeur

Chauffeurdienst, m
Chauffeurservice m
- ♦ chauffeur service

Chauffeur engagieren
Chauffeur einstellen
- ♦ hire a chauffeur
- ♦ engage a chauffeur

Chauffeur stellen
- ♦ provide a chauffeur

Chauffeurwohnung, f
- ♦ chauffeur's apartment *AE*
- ♦ chauffeur's flat *BE*

chauffieren (jn)
fahren (jn)
- ♦ chauffeur (s.o.)
- ♦ drive (s.o.)

Check-in, m
→ Anmeldung

Checkliste, f
→ Prüfliste

Check-out, m
→ Abmeldung

Cheddarkäse, m
Cheddar, m
- ♦ Cheddar cheese
- ♦ Cheddar

Chef, m (Küche)
→ Chef de cuisine

Chefbarman, m
Chefbarmann, m
- ♦ chief barman

Chef communar, m *FR*
Leiter der Personalküche, m
- ♦ chef communar *FR*
- ♦ staff chef
- ♦ personnel chef

Chefconcierge, m/f
- ♦ chief concierge *AE*
- ♦ head concierge

Chef de bar, m *FR*
Barmeister, m
Barchef, m
- ♦ chef de bar *FR*
- ♦ bar manager

Chef de brigade, m *FR*
Stationsoberkellner, m
- ♦ chef de brigade *FR*
- ♦ captain *AE*
- ♦ station headwaiter

Chef de cuisine, m *FR*
Küchenchef, m
Chefkoch, m *ÖST*
- ♦ chef de cuisine *FR*
- ♦ chef
- ♦ head cook
- ♦ chief cook *AE*

Chef de partie, m *FR*
Partiechef, m
- ♦ chef de partie *FR*
- ♦ section head

Chef de partie garde-manger, m *FR*
- ♦ chef de partie garde-manger *FR*

Chef de partie tournant, m *FR*
(Küche)
- ♦ chef de partie tournant *FR*

Chef de rang, m *FR*
Stationskellner, m
Revierkellner, m
Rayonkellner, m
- ♦ chef de rang *FR*
- ♦ station waiter
- ♦ section waiter

Chef de rang d'étage, m *FR*
Etagenstationskellner, m
Etagenrevierkellner, m
- ♦ chef de rang d'étage *FR*
- ♦ floor section waiter
- ♦ floor station waiter *AE*

Chef de réception, m *FR*
Empfangschef, m
- ♦ chef de réception *FR*
- ♦ chief receptionist *AE*
- ♦ head receptionist *BE*

Chef de restaurant, m *FR*
Restaurantchef, m
Restaurantdirektor, m
- ♦ chef de restaurant *FR*
- ♦ restaurant manager

Chef der Rezeption m
→ Chef de réception

Chef de service, m FR
Serviceleiter, m
- ♦ chef de service *FR*
- ♦ service manager

Chef des Protokolls, m
(bei offiziellen Empfängen)
- ♦ chief of protocol
- ♦ master of ceremonies
- ♦ emcee *coll*
- ♦ MC

Chef d'étage, m *FR*
Etagenoberkellner, m
- ♦ chef d'étage *FR*
- ♦ head floor waiter
- ♦ floor headwaiter

Chef de vin, m *FR*
Weinkellner, m
Sommelier, m *FR*
- ♦ chef de vin *FR*
- ♦ wine waiter
- ♦ wine steward *AE*

- wine butler
- sommelier *FR*

Chefdirigent, m
- chief director *AE*
- chief conductor *BE*

Chef du Froid m *FR*
→ Chef garde-manger

Chef entremetier, m *FR*
- chef entremetier *FR*

Chefetage, f (Hotel)
(mit Büroeinrichtungen)
Executive Floor, m
Executive-Etage, f
- executive floor

Chef garde-manger, m *FR*
Leiter der Kalten Küche, m
Chef Gardemanger, m *FR*
- chef garde-manger *FR*
- larder chef

Chef grilleur, m *FR*
Grillpartiechef, m
- chef grilleur *FR*
- grill chef

Chef hors d'oeuvrier, m *FR*
Vorspeisenkoch, m
- chef hors d'oeuvrier *FR*

Chefkellner, m
- chief waiter *AE*
- headwaiter *BE*

Chefkoch, m *ÖST*
Küchenchef, m
Chef de cuisine, m *FR*
- chief cook *AE*
- head cook *BE*
- head chef
- chef de cuisine *FR*
- chef

Chef kocht selbst
Der Chef kocht selbst
- owner does the cooking
- The owner does the cooking

Cheforganisator, m
- chief organiser
- chief organizer

Chef pâtissier, m *FR*
- chef pâtissier *FR*
- pastry chef

Chef poissonnier, m *FR*
- chef poissonnier *FR*
- fish chef

Chefportier, m
- bell captain *AE*
- head porter *BE*

Chef potager, m *FR*
Partiechef Suppen, m
Suppenpartiechef, m
- chef potager *FR*
- soup chef

Chef rôtisseur, m *FR*
Bratenpartiechef, m
- chef rôtisseur *FR*
- roast chef

Chef saucier, m *FR*
Partiechef Soßen, m
Soßenpartiechef, m
- chef saucier *FR*
- sauce chef

Chefsteward, m (Flugzeug)
→ Purser

Chefsteward, m (generell)
Obersteward, m

- chief steward
- head steward

Chefstewardeß, f (Schiff und Flugzeug)
Oberstewardeß, f
- chief stewardess

Chef tournant, m *FR*
- chef tournant *FR*

Cheftrainer, m
- head coach
- chief coach

Chef vom Dienst, m
- duty manager

Chemikaltoilette, f
→ chemische Toilette

Chemikaltoilette leeren
- empty a chemical toilet

chemische Reinigung f
- dry cleaning

chemischer Reinigungsdienst m
chemische Reinigung f
- dry-cleaning service

chemische Toilette, f
Chemikaltoilette, f
Trockenklosett, n
- chemical toilet

chemisch reinigen etw
- dry-clean s.th.

Chesterkäse, m
- Cheshire cheese

Chianti, m *ITAL*
Chiantiwein, m *ITAL*
- Chianti *ITAL*
- Chianti wine *ITAL*

Chianti Classico, m *ITAL*
- Chianti Classico *ITAL*

Chicagoer Luftfahrtabkommen, n
- Chicago Aviation Agreement

Chicorée, m/f
- chicory
- chiccory *AE*
- chickory *AE*

Chicoréesalat, m
- chicory salad
- chiccory salad *AE*
- chickory salad *AE*

Chiemgauer Alpen, die, pl
- Chiemgau Alps, the *pl*

Chiemsee m
- Lake Chiem

Chile
- Chile

Chilene, m
- Chilean

Chilenin, f
- Chilean girl
- Chilean woman
- Chilean

chilenisch, adj
- Chilean, adj

Chili, m *SPAN*
roter Cayennpfeffer, m
- chilli *SPAN*

Chili con carne, m *SPAN*
- chilli con carne *SPAN*

Chilipulver, n
- chilli powder

Chilisoße, f
- chilli sauce

China
- China

Chinakohl, m
- Chinese cabbage

Chinaprospekt, m
- China brochure

Chinareise, f (generell)
- China tour

Chinareise, f (in China)
Chinarundreise, f
- tour of China
- tour through China
- Chinese tour

Chinareise, f (nach China)
Reise nach China, f
- tour to China
- journey to China
- trip to China

Chinareisen, n
Chinareiseverkehr, m
- travel to China

China-Restaurant, n
chinesisches Restaurant, m
Chinese, der *coll*
- Chinese restaurant

Chinatourismus, m
- Chinese tourism
- tourism to China

Chinese, m
- Chinese

Chinesenviertel, n
- Chinese quarter

Chinesin, f
- Chinese girl
- Chinese woman
- Chinese

chinesisch, adj
- Chinese, adj

chinesische Küche, f
- Chinese cooking
- Chinese cuisine

Chinesische Mauer, f
- Great Wall, the
- Great Wall of China, the

chinesisches Essen, n (generell)
- Chinese food

chinesisches Essen, n (Mahlzeit)
- Chinese meal

chinesisch essen
- have a Chinese meal

Chip, m
(Spielkasino)
Spielmarke, f
- chip

Chippendale-Möbel, n pl
- Chippendale furniture *sg*

Chips, pl
Kartoffelchips, pl
- chips *AE pl*
- potato chips *AE pl*
- crisps *BE pl*

Chipspäckchen, n
- chips packet *AE*
- crisp packet *BE*

Chlor, n
- chlorine

chloren (etw)
chlorieren (etw)
- chlorinate (s.th.)

chlorfrei, adj
- chlorine-free, adj

chlorfreies Schwimmbad, n
- chlorine-free swimming pool *AE*
- chlorine-free swimming-pool *BE*

Cholera, f
- cholera

Choleraimpfung, f
- cholera vaccination

Cholesterinprüfung, f
Cholesterintest, m
- cholesterol test

Chomage, m
(Arbeitslosigkeit, Erwerbslosigkeit)
→ Betriebsunterbrechung

Chor, m
(Sänger und Gebäudeteil)
- choir

Chorempore, f
Chorgalerie, f
- choir loft

Choreographie, f
- choreography

Chorfest, n
- choir festival

Chorgitter, n
- choir screen

Chor leiten
Chor dirigieren
- conduct a choir

Chormusik, f
- choral music

Chorstuhl, m
Chorherrenstuhl, m
Chorgestühl, n
- choir stall
- choir stalls *pl*

Chowder, n *gastr*
- chowder *gastr*

Chowdersuppe, f
- chowder soup

Christkindlmarkt, m *dial*
Weihnachtsmarkt, m
- Christmas market
- Xmas market
- Christmas fair
- Xmas fair

christliches Hospiz, n
- Christian hospice

Christophorus
Hl. Christophorus
- St. Christopher *AE*
- St Christopher *BE*

chronische Arthritis, f
- chronic arthritis

chronische Bronchitis, f
- chronic bronchitis

chronische Krankheit, f
- chronic disease
- chronic illness

chronischer Zimmermangel, m (Knappheit)
- chronic shortage of rooms

chronischer Zimmermangel, m (völliges Fehlen)
- chronic lack of rooms

Chutney, n
- chutney

Cicerone, m
(Buch oder Person)
Fremdenführer m
Reiseführer m
- cicerone *humor*

Cider, m
- cider
- cyder

Cideressig, m
- cider vinegar
- cyder vinegar

Ciderflasche, f
- cider bottle

Ciderherstellung, f
- cider making

Cidermuseum, n
- cider museum

Ciderpunsch, m
- cider punch

Cidersoße, f
- cider sauce
- cyder sauce

Cineast, m
- movie buff *AE*

CIP, m
(Gasttyp, erhält Vorzugsbehandlung)
- CIP
- Commercially Important Person

Cipollata, f *ITAL*
(Zwiebelgericht)
- cipollata *ITAL*

Cipollatawürstchen, n *ITAL*
- cipollata sausage *ITAL*

circa, adv
ca., adv
- about, adv
- approximately, adv
- circa, adv
- ca, adv
- c, adv

circa 600 v. Chr.
- circa 600 BC

CIT, f
(Pauschalreise mit Charterflugzeug)
Charter Inclusive Tour, f
Charterpauschalreise, f
- CIT
- charter-inclusive tour

Civet, n *FR*
- civet *FR*

Clef d'Or, f *FR*
(internationale Vereinigung der Portiers)
- Clef d'Or *FR*

Cloche, f *FR*
Glocke f
- cover

Clou des Abends, m
Höhepunkt des Abends m
- highlight of the evening

Club, m
Klub, m
Verein, m
- club

Clubabend, m
Vereinsabend, m
- club evening
- club night

Clubanlage, f
Clubkomplex, m
Vereinsanlage, f
Vereinskomplex, m
- club complex

clubartiges Hotel, n
- clublike hotel

Clubatmosphäre, f
Vereinsatmosphäre, f
- club atmosphere

Clubausflug, m
Vereinsausflug, m
- club outing
- club excursion

Clubausweis, m
Vereinsausweis, m
- club membership card
- membership card

Clubbar, f (generell)
- club bar

Clubbar, f (in der Lounge)
Salonbar f
Loungebar f
- lounge bar

Clubbeitrag, m
Vereinsbeitrag, m
Mitgliedsbeitrag, m
- membership dues *pl*
- dues *pl*

Club beitreten
Verein beitreten
Mitglied werden in einem Club
Mitglied werden in einem Verein
- join a club

Clubbesitzer, m
- club owner
- owner of a club

Clubbesuch, m
Vereinsbesuch, m
- club visit
- visit to a club

Clubbesucher, m
Vereinsbesucher, m
- club visitor
- visitor to a club

Clubbetrieb, m
Vereinsbetrieb m
- club establishment
- club operation

Clubbuchung, f
Vereinsbuchung f
- club booking

Clubcafé, n
Vereinscafé, n
- club cafe *AE*
- club café *BE*

Clubcampingplatz, m
Vereinscampingplatz, m
- club campsite
- club campground *AE*
- club camping site *BE*
- club camping ground *BE*
- club site

Club der Einsamen Herzen, m
- Lonely Hearts Club

Club der Köche, m
- club of chefs
- club of cooks

Clubdorf n
- club village

Clubeinrichtung, f
Vereinseinrichtung, f
- club facility

Club eintragen lassen
(ins Vereinsregister)
Verein eintragen lassen
- incorporate a club *AE*
- register a club *BE*

Club eröffnen
  Verein eröffnen
  ♦ open a club
Clubetage, f
  (im Hotel)
  ♦ club floor
Clubfahrt, f
  Vereinsfahrt, f
  ♦ club trip
Clubfarben, f pl
  Vereinsfarben, f pl
  ♦ club colors AE pl
  ♦ club colours BE pl
Clubfeier, f
  Vereinsfeier, f
  Clubfest, n
  Vereinsfest, n
  ♦ club party
Clubferien, pl
  Cluburlaub, m
  ♦ club holidays BE pl
  ♦ club vacation AE
Clubferiengast, m
  Cluburlauber, m
  ♦ club holidaymaker BE
  ♦ club vacationer AE
Clubferienort, m
  Cluburlaubsort, m
  Clubferiendorf, n
  ♦ club resort
Clubferienveranstalter, m
  Cluburlaubsveranstalter, m
  ♦ club holiday operator BE
  ♦ club vacation operator AE
Clubfest, n
  Vereinsfest, n
  Clubfeier, f
  Vereinsfeier, f
  ♦ club celebration
Clubfête, f
  Clubfete, f
  ♦ club fête
  ♦ club fete AE
Club führen
  ♦ run a club
Clubgast, m
  Vereinsgast, m
  ♦ club guest
  ♦ club visitor
Clubgaststätte, f
  Vereinsgaststätte, f
  ♦ club pub BE coll
  ♦ club bar AE
Club hat 123 Mitglieder
  Verein hat 123 Mitglieder
  ♦ club has 123 members
Clubhaus, n (Sport)
  ♦ pavilion
Clubhaus, n (Verein)
  Vereinshaus, n
  Vereinsheim, n
  ♦ clubhouse
Clubhosteß, f
  Vereinshosteß, f
  ♦ club hostess
Clubhotel, n
  Vereinshotel, n
  ♦ club hotel
Clubkarte, f
  Vereinskarte, f
  ♦ club card

Clubkassierer, m
  Vereinskassierer, m
  ♦ club treasurer
Clubklasse, f
  Club Class, f
  ♦ club class
Clubkreuzfahrt, f
  ♦ club cruise
Clubleben, n
  Vereinsleben, n
  ♦ club life
Club leiten
  ♦ manage a club
  ♦ run a club
Clubleiter, m
  Vereinsgeschäftsführer, m
  ♦ club manager
Clubleitung, f (Aktivität)
  Vereinsgeschäftsleitung, f
  ♦ club management
  ♦ managing a club
Clubleitung, f (Person)
  → Clubleiter
Clublokal, n
  Vereinslokal, n
  ♦ club premises pl
Clubmitglied, n
  Vereinsmitglied, n
  ♦ club member
  ♦ member of a club
Clubmitgliedschaft, f
  Vereinsmitgliedschaft, f
  ♦ club membership
Club mit Schankkonzession, m
  (für alkoholische Getränke)
  Verein mit Schankkonzession, m
  ♦ licensed club
  ♦ licenced club
Clubpaß, m
  ♦ club pass
Clubplatz, m
  (z.B. Camping)
  Vereinsplatz, m
  ♦ club site
Clubprogramm, n
  Vereinsprogramm, n
  ♦ club program AE
  ♦ club programme BE
Clubrabatt Verhandlungssache
  Vereinsrabatt VHS
  ♦ club discount by negotiation
Clubraum, m
  Clubzimmer, n
  Vereinsraum, m
  Vereinszimmer, n
  ♦ clubroom
Clubreise, f
  Vereinsreise, f
  ♦ club tour
  ♦ club trip
  ♦ club journey
Clubreiseveranstalter, m
  Vereinsreiseveranstalter, m
  ♦ club tour operator
Clubsandwich, n
  (drei Brotscheiben und zwei Scheiben Belag)
  ♦ club sandwich
Club schließen
  ♦ close a club
  ♦ close down a club

Clubsessel, m
  ♦ club chair
  ♦ easy chair
  ♦ lounge chair
  ♦ big armchair
Clubsitzung, f
  Vereinssitzung, f
  ♦ club session
Clubtag, m
  ♦ club day
Clubtreffen, n
  Clubversammlung, f
  Vereinstreffen, n
  Vereinsversammlung, f
  ♦ club meeting
Clubunterhaltung, f
  Vereinsunterhaltung f
  Clubamüsement n
  ♦ club entertainment
Cluburlaub, m
  Clubferien, pl
  ♦ club vacation AE
  ♦ club holiday BE
Cluburlauber, m
  Clubferiengast, m
  ♦ club vacationer AE
  ♦ club holidaymaker BE
Cluburlaubsanbieter, m
  Clubferienanbieter, m
  ♦ club vacation supplier AE
  ♦ club holiday supplier BE
  ♦ supplier of club vacation AE
  ♦ supplier of club holidays BE
Cluburlaubsveranstalter, m
  Clubferienveranstalter, m
  ♦ club vacation operator AE
  ♦ club holiday operator BE
Clubveranstaltung, f
  Vereinsveranstaltung, f
  ♦ club function
  ♦ club event
Clubvorsitzender, m
  Vereinsvorsitzender, m
  ♦ club chairman
Clubwagen, m
  (Zug)
  ♦ club car
Clubwesen, n
  Vereinswesen, n
  ♦ clubs pl
  ♦ societies pl
  ♦ associations pl
Clubwettbewerb, m
  Vereinswettbewerb, m
  ♦ club competition
Clubwirt, m
  Vereinswirt, m
  ♦ club barman
Clubwoche, f
  ♦ club week
Clubwochenende, n
  ♦ club weekend
Clubzimmer, n (in Club)
  → Clubraum
Clubzimmer, n (Lounge)
  → Lounge
Coca-Cola regist
  ♦ Coke-Cola regist
  ♦ Coke regist

Coca-Cola-Dose

Coca-Cola-Dose, f
 ♦ Coca-Cola can *AE*
 ♦ Coca-Cola tin *BE*
Cockpit, n
 Kanzel, f
 ♦ cockpit
Cockpitpersonal, n
 ♦ cockpit personnel
 ♦ cockpit staff
Cocktail, m
 ♦ cocktail
Cocktailbar f
 ♦ cocktail bar
Cocktailbarfrau, f
 ♦ cocktail barmaid
Cocktailbar für Hausgäste, f
 ♦ residents' cocktail bar
 ♦ cocktail bar for residents
Cocktailbarman, m
 ♦ cocktail barman
Cocktailempfang, m
 ♦ cocktail reception
Cocktailempfang geben
 ♦ give a cocktail reception
Cocktailglas, n
 ♦ cocktail glass
Cocktailkarte, f
 (Getränkekarte)
 ♦ cocktail menu
Cocktailkeks, m
 ♦ cocktail biscuit
Cocktailkellner, m
 Getränkekellner, m
 ♦ cocktail waiter
Cocktailkirsche, f
 ♦ cocktail cherry
Cocktailkleid, n
 ♦ cocktail dress
Cocktaillounge, f
 Cocktailsalon, m
 ♦ cocktail lounge
Cocktail mixen
 ♦ mix a cocktail
Cocktail nach dem Essen, m
 ♦ after-dinner cocktail
Cocktailparty, f
 ♦ cocktail party
Cocktailparty ausrichten
 ♦ host a cocktail party
Cocktailrezept, n
 ♦ cocktail recipe
Cocktailschrank, m
 ♦ cocktail cabinet
Cocktailserviette, f
 ♦ cocktail napkin
Cocktailshaker, m
 ♦ cocktail shaker
Cocktailspieß, m
 Cocktailspießchen, n
 ♦ cocktail stick
Cocktailstunde, f
 ♦ cocktail hour
Cocktailterrasse f
 ♦ cocktail terrace
Cocktailveranstaltung, f
 ♦ cocktail function
Cocktailwettbewerb, m
 ♦ cocktail competition
Cocktailwürstchen, n
 ♦ cocktail sausage

Cocktailzeit, f
 ♦ cocktail time
Cocktailzwiebel, f
 ♦ cocktail onion
Code, m
 Kennung, f
 ♦ code
Code benutzen
 ♦ use a code
Codenummer, f
 ♦ code number
Codenummer benutzen
 ♦ use a code number
Coffeeshop, m
 ♦ coffee shop
Coffeeshopkellner, m
 ♦ coffee-shop waiter
Coffeeshopkellnerin, f
 ♦ coffee-shop waitress
Coffeeshopumsatz, m
 ♦ coffee-shop sales *pl*
 ♦ coffee-shop turnover
Cognac, m *FR m regist*
 ♦ cognac *FR m regist*
Cognacflasche, f
 ♦ cognac bottle
Cognacglas, n
 ♦ cognac glass
Cognackonsum, m
 Cognacverbrauch, m
 ♦ cognac consumption
Cognacliebhaber, m
 Cognacfreund, m
 ♦ cognac lover
Cognacparfait, n
 ♦ cognac parfait
Cognacschwenker, m
 ♦ cognac balloon
 ♦ cognac snifter
Cognacsoße, f
 ♦ cognac sauce
Coiffeur, m *FR*
 Friseur, m
 ♦ coiffeur *FR*
 ♦ hairdresser
 ♦ hair stylist
Cointreau, m *FR regist*
 ♦ Cointreau *FR regist*
Cola, f
 ♦ Coke
Colaautomat, m
 ♦ cola machine
Coladose, f
 ♦ Coke can *AE*
 ♦ Coke tin *BE*
Colaflasche, f
 ♦ Coke bottle
College, n
 ♦ college
Collegekantine, f
 ♦ college canteen
 ♦ buttery *BE*
Collegeunterkunft, f
 Collegeunterbringung, f
 ♦ college accommodation
Collegeverpflegung, f
 ♦ college foodservice *AE*
 ♦ college catering *BE*
Collegezimmer, n
 ♦ college room

Combo, f
 ♦ combo
Comer See, m
 ♦ Lake Como
Commis, m *FR*
 (Gehilfe in Küche oder Restaurant)
 Gehilfe, m
 ♦ commis *FR*
 ♦ assistant
Commis de bar, m *FR*
 Barcommis, m
 ♦ commis de bar *FR*
 ♦ bar commis
 ♦ assistant bar waiter
Commis débarasseur, m *FR*
 Abräumcommis, m
 ♦ commis débarasseur *FR*
 ♦ assistant clearing waiter
 ♦ busboy *AE*
Commis de cuisine, m *FR*
 Küchencommis, m
 Küchengehilfe, m
 ♦ commis de cuisine *FR*
 ♦ kitchen commis
Commis de partie, m *FR*
 Gehilfe des Stationskochs, m
 Gehilfe des Chef de partie, m
 ♦ commis de partie *FR*
Commis de rang, m *FR*
 (untergeordnet dem Chef de rang)
 Kellnergehilfe, m
 Serviergehilfe, m
 ♦ commis de rang *FR*
 ♦ assistant station waiter
 ♦ commis station waiter
 ♦ commis waiter
Commis de restaurant, m *FR*
 Restaurantcommis, m
 Restaurantgehilfe, m
 ♦ commis de restaurant *FR*
 ♦ restaurant commis
 ♦ assistant restaurant waiter
Commis de suite, m *FR*
 ♦ commis de suite *FR*
Commis d'étage, m *FR*
 Etagencommis, m
 ♦ commis d'étage *FR*
 ♦ commis floor waiter
 ♦ assistant floor waiter
Commis de vin, m *FR*
 Weincommis, m
 ♦ commis de vin *FR*
 ♦ assistant wine waiter
 ♦ commis wine waiter
Commis de wagon, m *FR*
 Wagencommis, m
 ♦ commis de wagon *FR*
 ♦ assistant cart waiter *AE*
 ♦ assistant trolley waiter *BE*
Commis entremetier, m *FR*
 Zwischenspeisencommis, m
 ♦ commis entremetier *FR*
Commis garde-manger, m *FR*
 Kaltkochcommis, m
 ♦ commis garde-manger *FR*
 ♦ assistant larder cook
Commis pâtissier, m *FR*
 Konditorcommis, m
 ♦ commis pâtissier *FR*
 ♦ pastry commis

- ♦ assistant pastrycook *AE*
- ♦ assistant pastry-cook *BE*

Commis restaurateur au grill m *FR*
- ♦ commis restaurateur au grill *FR*

Commis rôtisseur, m *FR*
Bratencommis, m
Gehilfe des Bratenkochs, m
- ♦ **commis rôtisseur** *FR*
- ♦ commis roast cook
- ♦ assistant roast cook

Commis saucier, m *FR*
Soßencommis, m
Soßenhilfskoch, m
- ♦ **commis saucier** *FR*
- ♦ assistant sauce cook

Commission, f
→ Provision

Commissionaire, m *FR*
→ Kommissionär

Commis tournant, m *FR*
- ♦ **commis tournant** *FR*

Compact Disc, f
CD, f
CD-Platte, f
- ♦ **compact disc**
- ♦ **CD**

Company Rate, f
→ Firmenpreis

Computer, m
- ♦ **computer**

Computeranlage, f
Computersystem, n
- ♦ **computer system**

Computeranmeldung, f (generell)
Computerregistrierung, f
- ♦ **computer registration**

Computeranmeldung, f (Hotel)
- ♦ **computer check-in**

Computer benutzen
- ♦ **use a computer**

Computerbuchung, f
- ♦ **computer booking**
- ♦ booking by computer

Computerbuchungssystem, n
CBS, n
- ♦ **computer booking system**
- ♦ **CBS**

Computerfahrkarte, f
Computerfahrschein, m
- ♦ **computer ticket**

Computerfahrkartenausstellung, f
Computerfahrscheinausstellung, f
- ♦ **computer ticketing**

computergesteuert, adj
- ♦ **computer-controlled, adj**

computergestütztes Reservierungssystem, n
- ♦ **computer-assisted reservation system**
- ♦ computer-assisted reservations system

Computer installieren
- ♦ **install a computer**
- ♦ instal a computer *AE*

Computerkenntnisse, f pl
- ♦ **computer skills** *pl*

Computerkurs, m
Computerlehrgang, m
- ♦ **computer course**

Computerrechnung, f
- ♦ **computer bill**
- ♦ computer check *AE*
- ♦ computer invoice

Computerregistrierungsanlage, f
Computeranmeldungsanlage, f
- ♦ **computer registration system**

Computerreservierung, f
- ♦ **computer reservation**
- ♦ reservation by computer

Computerreservierungssystem, n
CRS n
- ♦ **computer reservation system**
- ♦ **CRS**

Computerspiel, n
- ♦ **computer game**

Computersystem, n
→ Computeranlage

Computerzentrum, n
- ♦ **computer center** *AE*
- ♦ computer centre *BE*

Computerzimmersuchdienst, m
- ♦ **computer room-finding service**

Concierge, m/f
- ♦ **concierge**

Concierge de nuit, m/f *FR*
Nachtconcierge m/f
- ♦ **concierge de nuit** *FR*
- ♦ night concierge

Conciergedienst, m
Conciergeservice, m
- ♦ **concierge service**

Conciergeloge, f
- ♦ **concierge's lodge**

Conciergepersonal, n
- ♦ **concierge staff**
- ♦ concierge personnel

Conciergeschalter, m
- ♦ **concierge desk**

Conciergeservice, m
→ Conciergedienst

Concorde, f
(Flugzeug)
- ♦ **Concorde, the**

Condominium, n
→ Eigentumswohnung

Conducteur, m *SCHW*
→ Conducteur d'hôtel

Conducteur d'hôtel, m *FR*
Hausdiener, m
- ♦ **conducteur d'hôtel** *FR*
- ♦ hotel porter
- ♦ house porter

Conférence machen bei einem Konzert
durch ein Konzert führen
Ansagen machen bei einem Konzert
- ♦ **compère a concert** *BE*
- ♦ compere a concert *AE*

Conférence machen (bei etw)
Conférence haben (bei etw)
durch ein Programm führen (bei etw)
conferieren (etw) *ÖST*
Ansage machen (bei etw)
- ♦ **compère (s.th.)** *BE*
- ♦ compere (s.th.) *AE*

Conférencier, m *FR*
Ansager, m
- ♦ **conférencier** *AE*
- ♦ compère *BE*
- ♦ master of ceremonies
- ♦ emcee *AE sl*
- ♦ M.C.

Confiserie, f
→ Konditorei

Consolidator, m
- ♦ **consolidator**

Consommé, f *FR*
klare Kraftbrühe, f
- ♦ **consommé** *BE*
- ♦ consomme *AE*

Consultant, m
Berater m
- ♦ **consultant**

Consultingfirma, f
Beratungsfirma f
- ♦ **consulting firm**
- ♦ consulting company

Consultingunternehmen, n
Beratungsunternehmen, n
- ♦ **consulting enterprise**

Containerschiff, n
- ♦ **container ship**
- ♦ container vessel

Continental Breakfast, n
→ kontinentales Frühstück

Continental Plan, m
CP, m
Übernachtung mit Frühstück, f
- ♦ **Continental Plan**
- ♦ **CP**

Controller, m
- ♦ **controller**
- ♦ comptroller

Controlling, n
- ♦ **controlling**

Cordon bleu, n *FR m*
- ♦ **cordon bleu** *FR*

Corporate Design, n
Unternehmenserscheinungsbild, n
- ♦ **corporate design**

Corporate Identity, f
CI, f
Unternehmensidentität, f
- ♦ **corporate identity**
- ♦ **CI**

Corporate Image, n
Unternehmensimage, n
- ♦ **corporate image**

Corporate Rate, f
→ Firmenpreis

Costa Brava, f
- ♦ **Costa Brava, the**

Côte d'Azur, f
- ♦ **Côte d'Azur, the**

Côtes du Rhône, m *FR*
- ♦ **Côtes du Rhône** *FR*

Cotswolds, pl
- ♦ **Cotswolds, the** *pl*

Cottage, f
Kate, f
Landhäuschen, n
kleines Haus, n
- ♦ **cottage**

Cottage am Meer, f
- ♦ **seaside cottage**

Cottage am See, f
- ♦ **lakeside cottage**

Cottage am Wasser, f
- ♦ **waterfront cottage**

Cottage am Wasser, f
- ♦ **waterside cottage**

Cottageanlage, f
Cottagekomplex, m
- ♦ **cottage complex**

Cottage aus roh behauenem Holz

Cottage aus roh behauenem Holz, f
♦ timber cottage
Cottagebewohner, m
♦ cottage resident
Cottage für zwei Familien, f
Zweifamiliencottage, f
♦ duplex cottage AE
♦ two-family cottage
♦ cottage for two families
Cottagehotel, n
♦ cottage hotel
Cottage ist reetgedeckt
♦ cottage is thatched
Cottage mieten
♦ rent a cottage
Cottagerestaurant, n
♦ cottage restaurant
Cottagestil, m
♦ cottage style
Cottagesuite, f
Suite in einer Cottage, f
♦ cottage suite
Cottageurlaub, m
♦ cottage vacation AE
♦ cottage holiday BE
Cottage vermieten
♦ rent (out) a cottage
♦ let (out) a cottage BE
Cottage zu vermieten
(Hinweisschild)
♦ Cottage for rent AE
♦ Cottage to let BE
Couch, f
♦ couch
♦ davenport AE
Couchbett, n
Bettcouch, f
♦ day bed
♦ couch bed
Couchette, f
→ Liegebett
Couch in ein Bett verwandeln
→ Couch umwandeln in ein Bett
Couch läßt sich in ein Bett verwandeln
♦ couch converts into a bed
Couchtisch, m
♦ coffee table
Couch umwandeln in ein Bett
Couch in ein Bett verwandeln
♦ convert a couch into a bed
Counter, m
→ Schalter, Theke, Tresen
Counter auflösen
Counter schließen
♦ close down a counter
Counterdienst, m
→ Schalterdienst, Thekendienst
Counterpersonal, n
→ Schalterpersonal, Tresenpersonal
Country Club, m
(für Stadtbewohner)
Sport- und Gesellschaftsclub, m
♦ country club
Country-Musik, f
♦ country music
Coupe, f
Eisbecher, m
♦ coupe
Coupé, n (Abteil)
→ Abteil

Coupé, n (Auto)
♦ coupe AE
♦ coupé BE
Coupon, m
♦ coupon
Coupon ausfüllen
♦ complete a coupon
♦ fill out a coupon AE
♦ fill in a coupon BE
Couponbuch, n
♦ book of coupons
Coupon einsenden an jn
♦ mail a coupon to s.o. AE
♦ post a coupon to s.o. BE
Coupon vorlegen
Coupon vorzeigen
♦ present a coupon
Couponwert, m
♦ coupon value
Coupon zurücksenden an jn
Coupon einsenden an jn
♦ return a coupon to s.o.
♦ send a coupon back to s.o.
Coupon zusenden jm mit der Post
♦ post a coupon to s.o. BE
♦ mail a coupon to s.o. AE
Couvert, n (Briefumschlag)
♦ envelope
Couvert, n FR (Gedeck)
Gedeck, n
Kuvert, n
♦ couvert FR
♦ cover
♦ place
Couvertanzahl, f
Couvertzahl f
Kuvertzahl f
Gedeckzahl f
♦ number of places laid
♦ number of covers
Couverts pro Jahr, n pl
→ Gedecke pro Jahr
Couverts pro Monat, n pl
→ Gedecke pro Monat
Couverts pro Tag, n pl
→ Gedecke pro Tag
Couverts pro Woche, n pl
→ Gedecke pro Woche
Cowboy, m
♦ cowboy
♦ puncher AE coll
Cowboyhut, m
♦ cowboy hat
CP, m
Continental Plan, m
Übernachtung mit Frühstück, f
♦ CP
♦ Continental Plan
♦ bed and breakfast
Cremeschnitte, f
♦ cream slice
Cremetorte, f
→ Sahnetorte
Crêpe, f FR
♦ crepe AE
♦ crêpe BE
Crêpe machen
♦ make a crepe AE
♦ make a crêpe BE

Crêpe Suzette, f gastr
♦ crepe suzette AE gastr
♦ crêpe suzette BE gastr
Crew, f
→ Besatzung, Mannschaft
Crewhotel, n
(für Flugzeugbesatzungen)
♦ crew hotel
Croissant, n FR m gastr
Hörnchen, n gastr
♦ croissant FR m gastr
Croupier, m
♦ croupier
Crouton, m FR m gastr
♦ crouton FR m gastr
CRS, n
Computerreservierungssystem n
♦ CRS
♦ computer reservation system
♦ computer reservations system
Cuisine, f FR (Speisen)
Küche f
♦ cuisine FR
♦ cooking
Cuisine du marché, f FR
♦ cuisine du marché, f FR
Cuisinier, m FR
Koch, m
♦ cuisinier FR
♦ cook
Cumberlandsoße, f
♦ Cumberland sauce
Curling, n
♦ curling
Curlinghalle f
♦ indoor curling rink
Curlingplatz, m
Curlingbahn, f
♦ curling arena
Curlingspiel, n
♦ game of curling
Curling spielen
♦ play curling
Curry, m/n
♦ curry
Currybutter, f
♦ curry butter
Curryhaus, n
Curryrestaurant, n
♦ curry house
Currypulver, n
♦ curry powder
Curryreis, m
♦ curry rice
Currysoße, f
♦ curry sauce
Currytruthahn, m
Currypute, f
♦ curried turkey
Currywurst, f
♦ curried sausage
CVJF, m
Christlicher Verein Junger Frauen, m
♦ YWCA
♦ Young Women's Christian Association
CVJF-Heim, n
Heim des Vereins Christlicher Junger Frauen, n
♦ YWCA hostel
♦ Young Women's Christian Association hostel
CVJM, m
Christlicher Verein Junger Männer, m

Christlicher Verein Junger Menschen, m
- ♦ **YMCA**
- ♦ Young Men's Christian Association

CVJM-Heim, n
Heim des Vereins Christlicher Junger Männer, n
Heim des Vereins Christlicher Junger Menschen, n
- ♦ **YMCA hostel**
- ♦ Young Men's Christian Association hostel

CVJM-Urlaub, m
- ♦ **YMCA vacation** *AE*
- ♦ YMCA holiday *BE*

D

Dach, n
- ♦ roof

Dachappartement, n
- → Mansardenappartement

Dachbad, n
- ♦ rooftop pool *AE*
- ♦ roof-top pool *BE*

Dachbar, f
- ♦ rooftop bar *AE*
- ♦ roof-top bar *BE*

Dachbett, n
- (Reisemobil)
- ♦ roof bed
- ♦ roof bunk

Dachcafé, n
- ♦ rooftop café *AE*
- ♦ roof-top café *BE*

Dach der Welt, n
- (Tibet)
- ♦ roof of the world, the

Dachdrehrestaurant, n
- ♦ revolving rooftop restaurant *AE*
- ♦ revolving roof-top restaurant *BE*

Dachfenster, n
- ♦ skylight
- ♦ roof window

Dachflugplatz, m
- ♦ roof aerodrome

Dachfreibad, n
- ♦ rooftop outdoor swimming pool *AE*
- ♦ roof-top outdoor swimming-pool *BE*

Dachgarage, f
- ♦ rooftop garage *AE*
- ♦ roof-top garage *BE*
- ♦ roof garage

Dachgarten, m
- ♦ roof garden
- ♦ rooftop garden *AE*
- ♦ roof-top garden *BE*

Dachgartenbar f
- ♦ roof-garden bar

Dachgartencafé, n
- ♦ roof-garden cafe *AE*
- ♦ roof-garden café *BE*

Dachgartenrestaurant, n
- ♦ roof-garden restaurant

Dachgartensuite, f
- ♦ roof-garden suite

Dachgartenterrasse f
- ♦ roof-garden terrace

Dachgeschoß, n
- DG, n
- ♦ top story *AE*
- ♦ top storey *BE*
- ♦ top floor
- ♦ attic story (storey)
- ♦ attic

Dachgeschoßfreiluftrestaurant, n
- Freiluftrestaurant im obersten Stockwerk, n
- ♦ top-floor open-air restaurant

Dachgeschoßgrill, m
- Grill im obersten Stockwerk, m
- ♦ top-floor grill

Dachgeschoßrestaurant, n
- Restaurant im obersten Stockwerk, n
- ♦ top-floor restaurant

Dachgeschoßschwimmbad, n
- Schwimmbad im obersten Stockwerk, n
- ♦ top-floor swimming pool *AE*
- ♦ top-floor swimming-pool *BE*
- ♦ top-floor pool

Dachgeschoßspeisesaal, m
- Speisesaal im obersten Stockwerk, m
- ♦ top-floor dining room

Dachgeschoßsuite, f
- (in Flachdachhaus)
- Suite im obersten Stockwerk, f
- ♦ top-floor suite

Dachgeschoßwohnung, f
- Mansardenwohnung, f
- DG-Wohnung, f
- Dachwohnung, f
- ♦ dormer flat *BE euph*
- ♦ dormer apartment *AE euph*
- ♦ attic apartment *AE*
- ♦ attic flat *BE*

Dachgeschoßzimmer, n
- (in Flachdachhaus)
- Zimmer im obersten Stockwerk, n
- ♦ top-floor room

Dachhallenbad, n
- ♦ rooftop indoor pool *AE*
- ♦ roof-top indoor pool *BE*

Dachhallenschwimmbad, n
- ♦ rooftop indoor swimming pool *AE*
- ♦ roof-top indoor swimming-pool *BE*

Dachhängebett, n
- (Wohnwagen)
- ♦ roof hammock

Dachhubschrauberlandeplatz, m
- Dachlandeplatz für Hubschrauber, m
- ♦ rooftop heliport *AE*
- ♦ roof-top heliport *BE*

Dachkammer, f
- Mansarde f
- ♦ garret
- ♦ attic

Dachlounge, f
- ♦ rooftop lounge *AE*
- ♦ roof-top lounge *BE*

Dachmeerwasserschwimmbad, n
- ♦ rooftop seawater swimming pool *AE*
- ♦ roof-top sea-water swimming-pool *BE*

Dachparkplatz, m (für 1 Auto)
- ♦ rooftop parking place *AE*

Dachparkplatz, m (für mehrere Autos)
- ♦ rooftop parking lot *AE*
- ♦ roof-top car park *BE*

Dachparkraum, m
- Dachparkfläche, f
- ♦ rooftop parking area *AE*
- ♦ rooftop parking space *AE*
- ♦ roof-top parking area *BE*
- ♦ roof-top parking space *BE*

Dachpianobar, f
- ♦ rooftop piano bar *AE*
- ♦ roof-top piano bar *BE*

Dachpool, m
- → Dachbad

Dachputtinggrün, n
- ♦ rooftop putting green *AE*
- ♦ roof-top putting green *BE*

Dachrestaurant, n
- ♦ rooftop restaurant *AE*
- ♦ roof-top restaurant *BE*

Dachschwimmbad, n
- Dachschwimmbecken, n
- ♦ rooftop swimming pool *AE*
- ♦ roof-top swimming-pool *BE*

Dachschwimmbecken, n
- → Dachschwimmbad

Dachsolarium, n
- ♦ rooftop solarium *AE*
- ♦ roof-top solarium *BE*

Dachspeisesaal, m
- ♦ rooftop dining room *AE*
- ♦ roof-top dining room *BE*

Dachstudio, n
- ♦ rooftop studio *AE*
- ♦ roof-top studio *BE*

Dachstudiowohnung, f
- ♦ rooftop studio apartment *AE*
- ♦ roof-top studio flat *BE*

Dachterrasse, f
- ♦ rooftop terrace *AE*
- ♦ roof-top terrace *BE*
- ♦ roof terrace
- ♦ roof patio

Dachterrassenappartement, n
- → Penthouseappartement

Dachterrassengarten, m
- ♦ roof terrace garden

Dachterrassenrestaurant, n
- → Penthouserestaurant

Dachterrassensuite f
- → Penthousesuite

Dachterrassenwohnung, f
- → Penthousewohnung

Dachterrassenzimmer

Dachterrassenzimmer, n
→ Penthousezimmer
Dachterrasse zum Sonnenbaden, f
♦ **rooftop sunbathing terrace** AE
♦ **roof-top sunbathing terrace** BE
♦ **sun deck** AE
♦ **sun-deck** BE
Dach über dem Kopf, n
♦ **roof over one's head**
Dach über dem Kopf haben
♦ **have a roof over one's head**
Dachwohnung, f
→ Mansardenwohnung
Dachzimmer, n
→ Mansardenzimmer
daheim bleiben
zuhause bleiben
♦ **stay at home**
Daheim ist es am schönsten
Daheim ist daheim
♦ **There is no place like home**
dahinschreiten
♦ **stride along**
Daiquiri, m
♦ **daiquiri**
Da ist die Tür!
♦ **You know the way out!**
Dalmatien
♦ **Dalmatia**
dalmatinisch, adj
♦ **Dalmatian, adj**
dalmatinische Küste, f
Küste von Dalmatien, f
♦ **Dalmatian coast**
Damasttischdecke, f
Damastdecke f
♦ **damask tablecloth**
Damebrett, n
(für das Damespiel)
♦ **checkerboard** AE
♦ **draught-board** BE
Dame de buffet, f FR
Buffetdame, f SCHW
♦ **dame de buffet** FR
Dame des Hauses, f
Hausherrin, f
♦ **lady of the house**
♦ **hostess**
Damen
(Hinweisschild vor Toiletten)
♦ **Ladies** pl = sg
Damenabend, m
♦ **ladies' evening**
♦ ladies' night
♦ **hen night** BE
Damenbesuch, m (Aktivität)
♦ **visit from a lady**
♦ **visit from a woman**
Damenbesuch, m (Person)
♦ **lady visitor**
♦ lady visitors pl
♦ **woman visitor**
♦ woman visitors pl
Damenbinde, f
Monatsbinde, f
Binde, f
♦ **sanitary napkin** AE
♦ **sanitary towel** BE
♦ **sanitary pad** BE
Damendusche, f
♦ **ladies' shower**

Damenduschraum, m
♦ **ladies' shower room**
Damenfriseur, m
(Person)
Damencoiffeur m
♦ **ladies' hairdresser**
Damengesellschaft, f (Party)
Damenparty, f
♦ **party for ladies**
♦ **hen-party** fam
Damenkaffeekränzchen, n
Kaffeekränzchen, n
Kaffeeklatsch, m
♦ **ladies' coffee party**
♦ ladies' coffee circle
♦ coffee party
♦ coffee klatsch AE fam
Damenklo, n coll
♦ **ladies' loo** BE coll
Damenmarathonlauf, m
Damenmarathon, m
♦ **women's marathon**
Damenparty, f
Party nur für Frauen, f
Damenfeier, f
♦ **hen-party** fam
Damenprogramm, n
♦ **ladies' program** AE
♦ **ladies' programme** BE
♦ **spouse program** AE
Damensalon m
Damenfriseursalon m
♦ **ladies' hairdressing salon**
♦ ladies' hairdresser's
♦ hair stylist's
♦ **ladies' salon**
Damensattel, m
♦ **side saddle**
♦ woman's saddle
Damensauna, f
♦ **ladies' sauna**
Damenschneiderin, f
♦ **ladies' tailor**
♦ **ladies' dressmaker**
Damenteil, m
(bei Sauna etc)
Damenabteil m
♦ **ladies' section**
Damentoilette, f
Damen-WC, n
♦ **ladies' toilet**
♦ **ladies' rest room** AE euph
♦ **ladies' room**
♦ **ladies' lavatory** euph
♦ **ladies' cloakroom** BE euph
Damenverein, m
Damenclub, m
♦ **ladies' club**
Damenwahl, f (beim Tanz)
♦ **ladies' choice**
♦ **ladies' turn**
Damen-WC, n
→ Damentoilette
Damenzimmer, n (vormittags)
(am Vormittag benutzt)
♦ **morning room**
Damespiel, n
(Brettspiel)
♦ **checkers** AE
♦ **game of checkers** AE

♦ **draughts** BE
♦ **game of draughts** BE
Dame spielen (Brettspiel)
♦ **play checkers** AE
♦ **have a game of checkers** AE
♦ **play draughts** BE
♦ **have a game of draughts** BE
Dämmerschoppen, m
♦ **sundowner**
Dammweg, m
Damm, m
♦ **causeway**
Dampfbad, n (Aktivität)
♦ **steam bath**
♦ vapor bath AE
♦ vapour bath BE
♦ **Turkish bath**
♦ Russian bath
Dampfbad, n (Raum)
♦ **hot room**
Dampfbad nehmen
♦ **take a steam bath**
♦ **have a steam bath**
Dampfbehandlung, f
♦ **steam treatment**
Dampfboot, n
♦ **steamboat**
Dampfbügeleisen n
♦ **steam iron**
Dampfeisenbahn, f
♦ **steam railroad** AE
♦ **steam railway** BE
dampfend heiß, adj
→ kochendheiß
Dampfer, m
Dampfschiff n
♦ **steamer**
♦ steamship
♦ **steamboat**
Dampferanlegestelle, f
♦ **steamer landing-place**
Dampferfahrt, f
♦ **steamer trip**
♦ **steamer tour**
Dampferkabine, f
♦ **steamship cabin**
Dampferreise, f
♦ **steamer journey**
♦ steamer tour
♦ steamer trip
Dampfkabine, f med
♦ **steam cubicle** med
Dampflokomotive, f
Dampflok, f coll
♦ **steam engine**
♦ **steam locomotive**
♦ **steam loco** coll
Dampfraum, m
♦ **steam room**
Dampfschiff, n
Dampfer, m
♦ **steamship**
♦ steamboat
♦ steamer
Dampfwagen, m hist
♦ **steam carriage** hist
Dampfwanne, f
♦ **steam tub**
Dampfzeitalter, n
♦ **age of steam**

Dampfzug, m
  ♦ steam train
Dampfzugbegeisterter, m
  ♦ steam train enthusiast
Dampfzugfahrt, f
  ♦ steam train ride
  ♦ steam train trip
Däne, m
  ♦ Dane
daneben liegendes Hotel, n
  → Nachbarhotel
Dänemark
  ♦ Denmark
Dänin, f
  ♦ Danish girl
  ♦ Danish woman
  ♦ Dane
dänisch, adj
  ♦ Danish, adj
dänische Art, adv gastr
  nach dänischer Art, adv gastr
  ♦ Danish style, adv gastr
dänisches Gebäck, n
  ♦ Danish pastries pl
Dankadresse, f
  ♦ message of thanks
Dankadresse verlesen
  ♦ read the message of thanks
dankbar, adj
  ♦ grateful, adj
dankbarer Gast, m
  ♦ grateful guest
dankbar sein jm für etw
  ♦ be grateful to s.o. for s.th.
Dankbrief, m
  ♦ letter of thanks
  ♦ letter thanking for s.th.
  ♦ thank-you letter coll
Danke, gern
  (Annahme einer Einladung etc)
  ♦ Thank you, with pleasure
Dankend erhalten
  (Quittung)
  ♦ Received with thanks
danken jm für die freundliche Betreuung
  ♦ thank s.o. for his/her kind attention
danken jm für eine Prospektanfrage
  ♦ thank s.o. for a brochure request
  ♦ thank s.o. for a letter requesting a brochure
danken jm für seine Gastfreundschaft
  ♦ thank s.o. for his/her hospitality
Dankesbrief für empfangene Gastfreundschaft, m
  (meist an private Gastgeber)
  ♦ bread-and-butter letter coll
Dankeschön, n
  ♦ thank-you
Danke sehr!
  ♦ Thank you very much!
Danktelegramm, f
  ♦ thank-you telegram
Danziger Bucht, f
  ♦ Bay of Danzig, the
Darauf trinke ich!
  ♦ I'll drink to that!
Darauf trinken wir einen!
  Laßt uns darauf trinken!
  ♦ Let's drink to that!
Darbietung, f
  Aufführung, f
  Vorstellung, f
  ♦ performance
  ♦ show
  ♦ entertainment
Darf es noch etwas sein?
  (Frage z.B. in Restaurant)
  ♦ Is there anything else, Sir?
  ♦ Is there anything else, Madam?
Darf ich bitten?
  (bei Tanz)
  ♦ May I have the pleasure?
  ♦ May I have the pleasure of the next dance?
Darf ich eintreten?
  ♦ May I come in?
Darf ich Ihnen Gesellschaft leisten?
  ♦ May I join you?
Darf ich Ihnen noch etwas Fisch anbieten?
  ♦ May I help you to some more fish?
Darf ich Ihnen nochmals eingießen?
  ♦ May I pour you another glass?
  ♦ May I pour you another cup?
Darf ich Ihre Bestellung aufnehmen?
  (Restaurant)
  ♦ May I have your order, Sir?
  ♦ May I have your order, Madam?
Darf ich jetzt bitte kassieren?
  ♦ Would you mind paying now, please?
Darf ich mich für einen Augenblick entschuldigen?
  ♦ May I excuse myself for a minute?
Darf ich um den nächsten Tanz bitten?
  ♦ May I have the next dance?
darstellen etw
  zeigen etw
  ♦ depict s.th.
  ♦ show s.th.
Darsteller, m
  ♦ performer
Dartmoor, n
  ♦ Dartmoor
Dartmoor Nationalpark, m
  ♦ Dartmoor National Park, the
Darts, pl
  ♦ darts pl
Dartsbrett, n
  ♦ dartboard
Dartsraum, m
  Dartszimmer, n
  ♦ darts room
Dartsspiel, n
  ♦ game of darts
  ♦ darts pl
Darts spielen
  ♦ play darts
Das geht auf mich! (Rechnung)
  ♦ That's on me!
Das geht auf mich! (Runde)
  ♦ This is my treat!
Das gleiche nochmal, bitte!
  ♦ The same again, please!
Das habe ich nicht bestellt
  ♦ This isn't what I ordered
Das ist das gleiche Zimmer, das wir letztes Jahr hatten
  ♦ This is the same room we stayed in last year
  ♦ This is the identical room we stayed in last year
Das ist ein Grund zum Feiern!
  ♦ That's a reason to celebrate!
Das ist ein Hochgenuß!
  ♦ This is a (real) treat!
Das ist mir egal
  ♦ I don't care
Das kümmert mich nicht im geringsten
  Das ist mir egal coll
  ♦ I couldn't care less
Das muß gefeiert werden!
  ♦ This calls for a celebration!
  ♦ That calls for a celebration!
Das schmeckt!
  ♦ That's delicious!
Das schmeckt nach mehr
  ♦ It tastes so good as to make one want more (of it)
Das schmeckt nach nichts
  ♦ It has no taste whatever
  ♦ It tastes like nothing
Das tut mir leid
  ♦ I'm sorry to hear this
Daten, pl
  ♦ data
Datenbank, f
  ♦ database
  ♦ databank
Datenmonitor, m
  ♦ data monitor
Datenprojektion, f
  ♦ data projection
Datensammlung, f
  ♦ compilation of data
Datenschutz, m
  ♦ data protection
Datenschutzgesetz, n
  ♦ data protection law
Datensichtgerät, n
  ♦ visual display unit
  ♦ VDU
Daten speichern
  ♦ store data
Datentechnik, f
  ♦ data systems technology
  ♦ data technology
Datenterminal n
  ♦ data terminal
Datenträger, m
  ♦ data medium
  ♦ data carrier
Datenübertragung, f
  ♦ data transfer
Datenverarbeitung, f
  ♦ data processing
Datscha, f
  Datsche f
  ♦ datcha
  ♦ dacha
Dattel, f
  ♦ date
Dattelbrot, n
  ♦ date bread
Dattel entsteinen
  ♦ stone a date
Dattelkuchen, m
  ♦ date cake
Dattelpalme, f
  ♦ date palm
Datum, n
  ♦ date
Dau, f
  (Schiffstyp)
  Dhau, f
  ♦ dhow
Dauer, f
  ♦ duration

Dauerauftrag

Dauerauftrag, m
 ♦ standing order
Dauerauslastung, f
 ♦ permanent load factor
Dauerausstellung, f
 ♦ permanent exhibition
 ♦ permanent exhibit *AE*
Dauerbelegung, f
 Dauerauslastung, f
 ♦ permanent occupancy
Dauerbesucher m
 ständiger Besucher m
 ♦ permanent visitor
 ♦ permanent guest
Dauerbetrieb, m
 ♦ continuous operation
 ♦ continuous service
 ♦ operating all the year round
 ♦ operating throughout the year
Dauercamper, m
 ♦ permanent camper
Dauercamping, n
 ♦ permanent camping
Dauercampingplatz, m
 ♦ static campsite
 ♦ static campground *AE*
 ♦ static camping site *BE*
 ♦ static camping ground *BE*
 ♦ permanent camping site *BE*
Dauer der Konferenz, f
 ♦ duration of the conference
Dauer des Urlaubsaufenthalts, f
 → Urlaubsverweildauer
Dauerermäßigung f
 ♦ permanent reduction
Dauergast, m
 ständiger Gast, m
 ♦ permanent guest
 ♦ permanent resident
 ♦ permanent fixture *coll*
Dauerhausgast, m
 Dauerresident, m
 ♦ permanent resident
Dauerkarte, f
 ♦ commutation ticket *AE*
 ♦ season ticket
 ♦ ticket giving continuous entrance
Dauerkunde, m
 → Stammkunde
Dauerlager, n
 ♦ permanent camp
Dauerlauf, m
 → Jogging
Dauermieter, m
 ♦ permanent tenant
dauern
 ♦ last
 ♦ go on
 ♦ take
dauernd unterwegs sein
 ♦ be constantly on the move
dauernd wohnen in einem Hotel
 ständig wohnen in einem Hotel
 ♦ live permanently in a hotel
Dauerparker, m
 ♦ long-term parker
Dauerplatz, m
 (z.B. Camping)
 ♦ static site
 ♦ permanent site

Dauerresident, m
 → Dauerhausgast
Dauersammlung, f
 ♦ permanent collection
Dauerstellplatz, m
 (Camping)
 ♦ permanent pitch
 ♦ static pitch
Dauerteilnehmer, m (aktiv)
 ♦ permanent participant
Dauerteilnehmer, m (passiv)
 ♦ permanent attendant
Dauerunterkunft, f
 Dauerunterbringung, f
 ♦ permanent accommodation
Dauervisum, n
 ♦ permanent visa
Dauerwohnrecht, n
 ♦ permanent residential rights *pl*
Dauerwohnsitz, m
 ♦ permanent domicile
 ♦ permanent residence
Dauerwohnsitz haben
 ♦ have a permanent residence
Dauerwohnung, f
 dauernd vermietete Wohnung, f
 ♦ apartment rented on a permanent basis *AE*
 ♦ flat let on a permanent basis *BE*
Dauerwurst, f
 ♦ hard sausage
Daune, f
 Daunen, f pl
 ♦ downy feather
 ♦ down *sg*
Daunendecke, f
 ♦ eiderdown
 ♦ down comforter
Daunenkissen, n
 ♦ down pillow
Daunensteppdecke, f
 ♦ eiderdown quilt
 ♦ eiderdown
 ♦ down quilt
Dauphinéart, adv *gastr*
 nach Dauphinéart, adv *gastr*
 ♦ dauphine style, adv *AE gastr*
 ♦ dauphiné style, adv *BE gastr*
davonmachen sich
 ♦ make off
 ♦ make away
davonmachen sich mit etw
 ♦ make off with s.th.
 ♦ make away with s.th.
DB-Lizenz, f
 Deutsche-Bahn-Lizenz, f
 ♦ DB licence
 ♦ DB license
 ♦ German Rail licence
 ♦ German Rail license
 ♦ GR licence
Deadline, f
 → Frist, Stichtag
Débarrasseur, m FR
 (im Restaurant)
 Abräumer, m
 ♦ débarrasseur *FR*
 ♦ clearing waiter
 ♦ busboy *AE*
 ♦ clearer
Debatte, f
 ♦ debate

Debatte abhalten
 ♦ hold a debate
debitieren
 ♦ debit
Debut, n
 ♦ debut *AE*
 ♦ début *BE*
Debütantinnenball, m
 ♦ debutante ball
Debut auf der internationalen Bühne, n
 ♦ debut on the international stage
 ♦ début on the international stage *BE*
Debut geben (mit etw)
 sein Debut geben (mit etw)
 ♦ make one's debut (with s.th.) *AE*
 ♦ make one's début (with s.th.) *BE*
Deck, n
 ♦ deck
Deckadresse, f
 ♦ cover address
 ♦ accommodation address
Deckbüfett, n
 ♦ deck buffet
Deckchen, n
 Zierdeckchen, n
 ♦ doily
Decke, f (Zimmerdecke)
 ♦ ceiling
Decke, f (zum Zudecken)
 ♦ blanket
Decke ist hoch
 ♦ ceiling is high
Decke ist niedrig
 ♦ ceiling is low
Deckel, m
 ♦ lid
 ♦ cover
 ♦ top
Deckenbeleuchtung, f
 ♦ ceiling lighting
Deckenbrause, f
 (in Dusche)
 ♦ ceiling shower
Deckenfresko, n
 Deckenfreske, f
 ♦ ceiling fresco
decken für zwei Personen
 Tisch decken für zwei Personen
 ♦ set the table for two persons
 ♦ lay the table for two persons
 ♦ lay covers for two persons
Deckengemälde, n
 ♦ ceiling painting
 ♦ painted ceiling
Deckenhöhe, f
 ♦ ceiling height
Deckeninstallation, f
 ♦ ceiling installation
Deckenlampe, f
 ♦ ceiling lamp
Deckentäfelung, f
 Deckenpaneel, n
 ♦ ceiling panelling
 ♦ ceiling paneling *AE*
decken (Tisch)
 Tisch decken
 Tisch eindecken
 ♦ lay the cloth
 ♦ lay the table
 ♦ set the table

Decken und Kissen werden gestellt
- ♦ Blankets and pillows are provided
- ♦ Blankets and pillows will be provided

Deckenventilator, m
- ♦ ceiling fan
- ♦ ceiling ventilator

Deckkabine, f
- Touristenkabine, f
- ♦ deck cabin

Deckmöbel, n pl
- ♦ deck furniture sg

Deckname, m
- angenommener Name, m
- ♦ alias
- ♦ assumed name

Deckpassagier, m
- ♦ deck passenger

Deckplan, m
- (Schiff)
- ♦ deck plan

Deckserviette, f
- Serviette, f
- ♦ serviette
- ♦ napkin

Deckspiel, n
- ♦ deck game
- ♦ game on deck

Deckspiele machen
- ♦ play deck games

Decksport, m
- ♦ deck sports
- ♦ deck sport

Decksteward, m
- ♦ deck steward

Deckungsbeitrag, m
- ♦ contribution
- ♦ variable gross margin
- ♦ profit contribution
- ♦ marginal income
- ♦ contribution margin

Deckungsbeitrag pro Essen, m
- ♦ contribution per meal

Deckungsbeitrag pro Gast, m
- ♦ contribution per guest

Deckungsbeitrag pro Gast pro Tag m
- ♦ contribution per guest per day

Deckungsbeitrag pro Zimmer, m
- ♦ contribution per room

Deckungsbeitragsrechnung, f
- ♦ break-even analysis
- ♦ contribution margin accounting

Defekt
- (Hinweisschild)
- → Außer Betrieb

defekt, adj
- ♦ out of order, adj
- ♦ damaged, adj
- ♦ faulty, adj

defekt sein
- nicht gehen coll
- ♦ be out of order

Defizit, n
- ♦ deficit

Defizit haben
- ♦ have a deficit

deftig, adj gastr
- ♦ solid, adj gastr
- ♦ hefty, adj coll

deftige Kost, f
- ♦ solid fare
- ♦ solid diet

deftige Küche, f
- ♦ solid cooking
- ♦ solid cuisine
- ♦ hearty cuisine
- ♦ hearty cooking

deftiges Essen, n
- ♦ solid meal
- ♦ hefty meal coll

Degenerationskrankheit, f
- ♦ degenerative disease

Degustationsmenü, n
- ♦ food-tasting menu

DEHOGA, m
- → Deutscher Hotel- und Gaststättenverband

Déjeuner, n FR
- Mittagessen n
- ♦ déjeuner FR
- ♦ luncheon
- ♦ lunch

Déjeuner dînatoire, n FR m
- Déjeuner dîner, n FR m
- Paradefrühstück, n
- ♦ déjeuner dînatoire FR

Déjeuner dîner, n FR m
- Déjeuner dînatoire, n FR m
- Paradefrühstück, n
- ♦ déjeuner dîner FR

Déjeuner à la fourchette, n FR
- Gabelfrühstück, n
- ♦ déjeuner à la fourchette FR

Dekanter, m
- Dekantierkaraffe f
- Dekantiergefäß n
- ♦ decanter

dekantieren
- ♦ decant

Dekantierkaraffe, f
- → Dekanter

Dekor, m/n
- ♦ decor AE
- ♦ décor BE

Dekorateur, m
- ♦ decorator

Dekoration, f
- ♦ decoration

Dekorationsfenster, n
- Schaufenster n
- ♦ display window

dekoratives Zimmer, n
- ♦ decorative room

Dekor entwerfen
- Dekor gestalten
- ♦ design the decor AE
- ♦ design the décor BE

Dekorgestaltung, f
- ♦ décor scheme
- ♦ decor scheme AE

dekoriert, adj
- geschmückt, adj
- ♦ decorated, adj

Delegation, f
- ♦ delegation

Delegation leiten
- Delegation anführen
- ♦ lead a delegation

Delegationsleiter, m
- Leiter einer Delegation, m
- ♦ head of a delegation
- ♦ leader of a delegation
- ♦ delegation head
- ♦ delegation leader

Delegationsmitglied, n
- Delegationsteilnehmer m
- ♦ member of a delegation

Delegation unter der Leitung von Herrn X, f
- ♦ delegation led by Mr X

delegieren jn zu einer Konferenz
- → entsenden jn zu einer Konferenz

Delegiertenkonferenz, f
- ♦ delegate conference

Delegierter, f
- Konferenzteilnehmer m
- Tagungsteilnehmer m
- Kongreßteilnehmer m
- ♦ delegate

delikat, adj (Speisen)
- schmackhaft, adj
- lecker, adj
- ♦ delicate, adj
- ♦ savory, adj AE
- ♦ savoury, adj BE
- ♦ exquisite, adj
- ♦ delicious, adj

delikates Essen, n
- leckeres Essen, n
- schmackhaftes Essen, n
- ♦ delicate food

Delikatesse, f
- Leckerbissen, m
- ♦ delicacy
- ♦ dainty

Delikatessen, f pl
- ♦ delicatessen pl

Delikatesse sein
- ♦ be a delicacy

Delikateßgeschäft, n
- Delikatessengeschäft, n
- Delikatessenhandlung, f
- Feinkosthandlung, f
- Feinkostgeschäft, n
- ♦ delicatessen shop BE
- ♦ delicatessen store AE
- ♦ delicatessen
- ♦ deli coll

Delkredereprovision, f
- ♦ del-credere commission
- ♦ guaranteed commission

delogieren jn ÖST
- ausquartieren jn
- ♦ dislodge s.o.
- ♦ drive s.o. out
- ♦ turn s.o. out
- ♦ evict s.o.

Delphinarium, n
- ♦ dolphinarium

Delphinschau, f
- Delphinvorführung f
- ♦ dolphin show

Delta, n
- ♦ delta

Deluxe-Kategorie, f
- Luxuskategorie, f
- ♦ deluxe category AE
- ♦ luxury category

De-Luxe-Zimmer, n
- → Luxuszimmer

Demi-chef, m FR
- ♦ demi-chef FR

Demi-chef de cuisine, m FR
- ♦ demi-chef de cuisine FR

Demi-chef de partie, m FR
- ♦ demi-chef de partie FR

Demi-chef de rang

Demi-chef de rang, m FR
  Demichef, m
  ♦ demi-chef de rang FR
  ♦ demi-chef FR
  ♦ junior station waiter
Demi-chef entremetier, m FR
  ♦ demi-chef entremetier FR
Demi-chef pâtissier, m FR
  ♦ demi-chef pâtissier FR
Demi-chef saucier, m FR
  ♦ demi-chef saucier FR
Demijohn, m
  Korbflasche f
  ♦ demijohn
  ♦ carboy AE
demnächst stattfindend, adj
  kommend, adj
  bevorstehend, adj
  ♦ forthcoming, adj
Demonstration, f
  Vorführung, f
  ♦ demonstration
Denkmal, n
  ♦ monument
Denkmal besuchen
  ♦ visit a monument
Denkmäler aus verschiedenen Bauepochen, n pl
  ♦ monuments from various architectural periods pl
Denkmal erinnert an jn
  ♦ monument commemorates s.o.
denkmalgeschütztes Gebäude, n
  denkmalgeschützter historischer Bau, m
  ♦ listed building
  ♦ listed historic building
denkmalgeschütztes Haus, n
  ♦ listed house
denkmalgeschütztes Hotel, n
  ♦ listed hotel
denkmalgeschützt sein
  → unter Denkmalschutz stehen
Denkmalschutz, m
  ♦ protection of historic buildings and monuments
  ♦ listing of a building
Denkmalschützer, m
  ♦ preservationist
denkwürdig, adj
  ♦ memorable, adj
denkwürdige Veranstaltung, f
  ♦ memorable event
  ♦ memorable function
Dependance, f
  Nebengebäude, n
  Anbau, m
  ♦ annex AE
  ♦ annexe BE
Dependanceunterkunft, f
  Dependanceunterbringung, f
  ♦ annex accommodation AE
  ♦ annexe accommodation BE
Dependancezimmer n
  Zimmer in der Dependance n
  ♦ annex room AE
  ♦ annexe room BE
deponieren etw in einem Safe
  ♦ deposit s.th. in a safe
Deposit, n
  → Anzahlung
Depotbuch, n
  ♦ safe deposit book

Depotquittung, f
  (bei Deponierung von Wertsachen)
  ♦ safe deposit receipt
Depotquittung ausstellen
  ♦ make out a safe deposit receipt
Depotquittung erhalten
  ♦ receive a safe deposit receipt
Depotquittung verlieren
  ♦ lose the safe deposit receipt
Depotquittung vorzeigen
  ♦ present the safe deposit receipt
  ♦ produce the safe deposit receipt
Depotschein, m
  (bei Deponierung von Wertsachen)
  ♦ safe deposit slip
Derbysuppe, f
  ♦ Derby soup
derzeitiger Aufenthaltsort, m
  zeitweiliger Aufenthaltsort, m
  ♦ whereabouts pl and sg
derzeitiger Aufenthaltsort ist unbekannt
  ♦ his/her whereabouts is unknown
  ♦ his/her whereabouts are unknown
derzeitiger Wohnsitz, m
  ♦ present address
derzeit vorhandene Kapazität, d
  → vorhandene Kapazität
Des einen Brot ist des anderen Tod
  ♦ One man's meat is another man's poison
Design, n
  Gestaltung, f
  ♦ design
Designerbett, n
  ♦ designer bed
Designerbier, n
  ♦ designer beer
Designerboutique, f
  ♦ designer boutique
Designermöbel, n pl
  ♦ designer furniture sg
Designernachtlokal, n
  ♦ designer nightspot
Designerteppich, m
  ♦ designer carpet
Desinfektion, f (durch Dämpfe)
  → Begasung
Desinfektion, f (generell)
  Desinfizierung, f
  ♦ disinfection
Desinfektionsapparat, m
  ♦ disinfector
Desinfektionsgerät, n
  ♦ disinfection appliance
Desinfektionsmittel, n (durch Dämpfe)
  ♦ fumigant
Desinfektionsmittel, n (generell)
  ♦ disinfectant
Desinfektor, m (Person)
  ♦ disinfector
desinfizieren etw (durch Dämpfe)
  begasen etw
  ausräuchern etw
  ♦ fumigate s.th.
desinfizieren etw (generell)
  ♦ disinfect s.th.
Dessert, n
  Nachtisch, m
  Nachspeise, f
  ♦ dessert
  ♦ sweet dish BE

  ♦ sweet BE
  ♦ afters BE coll sg
Dessertapfel, m
  ♦ dessert apple
Dessertbar, f
  ♦ dessert bar
Dessertbesteck, n (ein Satz)
  ♦ dessertspoon and fork AE
  ♦ dessert-spoon and fork BE
Dessertbesteck, n (generell)
  ♦ dessert set
  ♦ dessert cutlery
Dessertbirne, f
  ♦ dessert pear
Dessertbüfett, n
  Nachspeisenbüfett, n
  Nachtischbüfett, n
  ♦ buffet dessert
  ♦ dessert buffet
Dessertgabel, f
  ♦ dessert fork
Dessertgang, m
  ♦ dessert course
  ♦ sweet course BE
Dessertglas, n
  ♦ dessert glass
Dessertkarte f
  (Speisekarte)
  ♦ dessert menu
Dessertlikör, m
  ♦ dessert liqueur
Dessertlöffel, m
  ♦ dessertspoon AE
  ♦ dessert-spoon BE
Dessertmesser n
  ♦ dessert knife
Dessertteller m
  ♦ dessert plate
Dessertumsatz, m
  ♦ dessert sales pl
  ♦ dessert turnover
Dessertwagen, m
  (im Restaurant)
  ♦ dessert cart AE
  ♦ dessert wagon AE
  ♦ dessert trolley BE
  ♦ sweet trolley BE
Dessertwahl, f
  ♦ choice of dessert
  ♦ selection of dessert
Dessertwein, m
  Süßwein, m
  ♦ dessert wine
Destination, f
  Zielort, m
  Ziel, n
  ♦ destination
Destination buchen
  Zielort buchen
  Ziel buchen
  ♦ book a destination
detaillierte Streckenbeschreibung, f
  detaillierte Routenbeschreibung, f
  ♦ detailed route description
Detektiv, m
  ♦ detective
  ♦ dick coll
Detektivdienst, m
  Detektivservice, m
  ♦ detective service

Devisenbeschränkungen aufheben

deutliche Spuren hinterlassen auf etw
 ♦ leave distinctive marks on s.th.
deutsch, adj
 ♦ German, adj
Deutsche, f
 ♦ German girl
 ♦ German woman
 ♦ German
Deutsche Alpen, pl
 ♦ German Alps, the pl
Deutsche Alpenstraße, f
 ♦ German Alpine Road, the
 ♦ German Alpine Route, the
deutsche Art, adv gastr
 nach deutscher Art, adv gastr
 ♦ German style, adv gastr
Deutsche Bahn AG, f
 Deutsche Bahn, f
 ♦ German Rail plc
 ♦ German Rail PLC
 ♦ German Rail
Deutsche Barkeeper Union, f
 DBU, f
 ♦ German Barkeepers Union
Deutsche Bucht, f
 ♦ German Bay, the
 ♦ Heligoland Bight
Deutsche Bundesbahn, f
 DB, f
 ♦ German Federal Railroad AE
 ♦ German Federal Railways BE pl
 ♦ German Rail
Deutsche Bundesbank, f
 ♦ German Federal Bank, the
Deutsche Ferienstraße, f
 ♦ German Vacation Road, the AE
 ♦ German Vacation Route, the AE
 ♦ German Holiday Road, the BE
 ♦ German Holiday Route, the BE
deutsche Gastlichkeit, f
 deutsche Gastfreundschaft f
 ♦ German hospitality
deutsche Kost, f
 ♦ German fare
deutsche Küche, f (Speisen)
 ♦ German cooking
 ♦ German cuisine
Deutsche Landwirtschafts-Gesellschaft, f
 DLG, f
 ♦ German Agricultural Association
 ♦ GAA, the
Deutsche Märchenstraße, f
 (Ferienstraße)
 ♦ German Fairy-Tale Road, the
Deutscher, m
 ♦ German
Deutscher Camping Club, m
 DCC, m
 ♦ German Camping Club
deutsche Reiseleitung, f
 ♦ German tour guide
 ♦ German tour manager
Deutscher Fremdenverkehrsverband, m
 DFV, m
 ♦ German National Tourist Association, the
 ♦ German National Tourism Association, the
Deutscher Hotel- und Gaststättenverband, m
 DEHOGA, m
 ♦ German Hotel and Catering Association, the
 ♦ German Hotels and Restaurants Association, the

deutscher Wein, m
 ♦ German wine
deutsches Bier, n
 ♦ German beer
deutsches Essen, n
 ♦ German food
deutsches Gericht, n
 ♦ German dish
deutsches Menü, n
 ♦ German menu
Deutsches Museum, n
 ♦ German Museum, the
deutsche Speisekarte, f
 ♦ German menu
deutsches Recht, n
 ♦ German law
Deutsches Weinsiegel, n
 ♦ German wine seal
Deutsches Weintor, n
 (an der Deutschen Weinstraße)
 ♦ German Wine Gate, the
deutsche und französische Küche, f (Speisen)
 ♦ German and French kitchens pl
Deutsche Weinakademie, f
 ♦ German Wine Academy, the
Deutsche Weinstraße, f
 ♦ German Wine Road, the
 ♦ German Wine Route, the
Deutsche Zentrale für Tourismus, f
 DZT, f
 ♦ German National Tourist Board, the
 ♦ GNTB, the
Deutschland
 ♦ Germany
Deutschlandbesuch, m
 ♦ visit to Germany
Deutschlandbesucher, m
 Deutschlandbesucherin, f
 ♦ visitor to Germany
Deutschlandbesuch in Hamburg beginnen
 ♦ begin one's visit to Germany in Hamburg
Deutschlandbuchung, f
 ♦ booking for Germany
Deutschlandprogramm, n
 ♦ German program AE
 ♦ German programme BE
Deutschlandprospekt, m
 ♦ Germany brochure
Deutschlandreise, f (generell)
 ♦ German tour
 ♦ German trip
 ♦ German journey
Deutschlandreise, f (in Deutschland)
 Deutschlandrundreise, f
 ♦ tour of Germany
 ♦ tour through Germany
 ♦ German tour
Deutschlandreise, f (nach Deutschland)
 ♦ journey to Germany
 ♦ tour to Germany
 ♦ trip to Germany
Deutschlandreise machen (generell)
 ♦ make a German tour
 ♦ make a German trip
 ♦ make a German journey
Deutschlandreise verkaufen
 ♦ sell a German tour
Deutschlandtourist, m
 ♦ tourist to Germany
Deutschlandtournee, f
 ♦ German tour

Deutschlandurlaub, m
 ♦ German vacation AE
 ♦ German holiday BE
Deutschlandurlaub machen
 Urlaub in Deutschland machen
 ♦ take a vacation in Germany AE
 ♦ take a holiday in Germany BE
Deutschlandurlaub verkaufen
 ♦ sell a German vacation AE
 ♦ sell a German holiday BE
Deutschland von seiner besten Seite
 ♦ Germany at its best
Deutschordensritter, m pl hist
 Deutschherren, m pl hist
 ♦ Teutonic Knights, the, pl hist
 ♦ Knights of the Teutonic Order pl
Deutschritterorden, m hist
 Deutscher Ritterorden, m hist
 Deutscher Orden, m hist
 ♦ Teutonic Order, the hist
deutschsprachig, adj (Person)
 deutschsprechend, adj
 ♦ German-speaking, adj
deutschsprachig, adj (Sache)
 ♦ German-language, adj
deutschsprachige Reiseleitung, f
 deutschsprechende Reiseleitung, f
 ♦ German-speaking tour guide
deutschsprachiger Film, m
 ♦ German-language film
deutschsprachiger Führer, m (Information)
 ♦ German-language guide
deutschsprachiger Führer, m (Person)
 deutschsprechender Führer, m
 ♦ German-speaking guide
deutschsprachiger Prospekt, m
 ♦ German-language brochure
deutschsprachiges Land, n
 ♦ German-speaking country
deutschsprechend, adj
 → deutschsprachig
Devisen, pl
 ♦ foreign exchange
 ♦ foreign currency
Devisenabgänge, m pl
 ♦ foreign exchange outflow
Devisen ausführen
 ♦ take out foreign currency
 ♦ take out foreign currencies
 ♦ export foreign currency
 ♦ export foreign currencies
Devisen ausführen aus einem Land
 ♦ take foreign currency out of a country
 ♦ take foreign currencies out of a country
 ♦ export foreign currency from a country
 ♦ export foreign currencies from a country
Devisen ausführen bis zum Wert von DM 123
 ♦ take out foreign currency to the value of DM 123
 ♦ take out foreign currencies to the value of DM 123
 ♦ export foreign currency to the value of DM 123
 ♦ export foreign currencies to the value of DM 123
Devisenausgaben, f pl
 Devisenaufwand, m
 ♦ foreign exchange expenditure
 ♦ foreign exchange outflow
Devisenbeschränkungen, f pl
 ♦ foreign exchange restrictions pl
Devisenbeschränkungen aufheben
 ♦ lift foreign currency restrictions

Devisenbestimmungen

Devisenbestimmungen, f pl
- ♦ foreign currency regulations pl
- ♦ currency regulations pl

Devisenbewirtschaftung, f
- Devisenkontrolle, f
- ♦ foreign exchange control
- ♦ currency control

Devisenbilanz, f
- ♦ balance of foreign exchange payments

devisenbringend, adj
- ♦ exchange-earning, adj

Devisenbringer, m
- ♦ foreign exchange earner
- ♦ foreign currency earner

Devisen einführen
- ♦ take in foreign currency
- ♦ take in foreign currencies
- ♦ import foreign currency
- ♦ import foreign currencies

Devisen einführen in ein Land
- ♦ take foreign currency into a country
- ♦ take foreign currencies into a country
- ♦ import foreign currency into a country
- ♦ import foreign currencies into a country

Deviseneinnahmen, f pl
- ♦ foreign currency earnings pl
- ♦ foreign exchange earnings pl
- ♦ foreign currency receipts pl
- ♦ foreign exchange receipts pl
- ♦ foreign currency takings pl

Devisenerlös, m
- ♦ foreign exchange proceeds pl

Devisenertrag, m
- ♦ foreign exchange earnings pl

Devisenformular, n
- ♦ currency form

Devisengebühr, f
- ♦ exchange fee

Devisengewinn, m
- ♦ foreign exchange profit
- ♦ foreign currency profit

Devisenkontingent, n
- ♦ foreign exchange quota

Devisenkontrolle, f
- Devisenbewirtschaftung, f
- ♦ currency control
- ♦ foreign-exchange control

Devisenmarkt, m
- ♦ foreign exchange market

Devisentransfer, m
- ♦ transfer of foreign currency

Devisen verdienen
- ♦ earn foreign currency

Devisenverlust, m
- ♦ foreign exchange loss
- ♦ exchange loss
- ♦ foreign currency loss
- ♦ currency loss

Devisenvorschriften, f pl
- Devisenbestimmungen, f pl
- ♦ foreign exchange regulations pl
- ♦ foreign currency regulations pl

Devisenzwangsumtausch, m
- ♦ obligatory exchange of foreign currency

Dezember, m
- ♦ December

Dezemberauslastung, f
- Auslastung im Dezember, f
- ♦ December load factor
- ♦ load factor in December

Dezemberbelegung, f
- Dezemberauslastung, f
- ♦ December occupancy
- ♦ occupancy in December

Dezemberfeier, f
- ♦ December celebration

Dezembertagung, f
- Dezembertreffen, n
- ♦ December meeting

Dezemberurlaub, m
- ♦ December vacation AE
- ♦ December holiday BE

Dezemberwoche, f
- ♦ December week

dezente Beleuchtung, f
- gedämpfte Beleuchtung, f
- ♦ soft lighting

dezent möbliert, adj
- ♦ discreetly furnished, adj

dezent möbliertes Zimmer, n
- ♦ discreetly furnished room

DG, n
- → Dachgeschoß

DH, n
- → Doppelhaus

Dia, n
- Diapositiv, n
- Lichtbild, n
- ♦ slide
- ♦ transparency

Dia-Abend, m
- ♦ slide show in the evening

Diabetes, m
- ♦ diabetes

Diabetesdiät f
- ♦ diabetic diet

Diabetiker, m
- Zuckerkranker, m coll
- ♦ diabetic

Diabetikeressen, n
- Diabetikermahlzeit, f
- ♦ diabetic meal

Diabetikerwein, m
- ♦ diabetic wine

Diagnosesitzung, f med
- ♦ diagnostic session med

Dia herstellen
- ♦ produce a slide

Diaherstellung, f
- ♦ slide production

Diamagazin, n
- ♦ slide tray

Diamagazin laden
- ♦ load a slide tray

diamantene Hochzeit, f
- ♦ diamond wedding

diamantenes Hochzeitsjubiläum, n
- ♦ diamond wedding anniversary

Dianasoße, f
- ♦ Diana sauce

Dianasuppe, f
- ♦ Diana soup

Diapositiv, n
- → Dia

Diapräsentation, f
- ♦ slide presentation

Diaprogramm, n
- ♦ slide program AE
- ♦ slide programme BE

Diaprojektion f
- ♦ slide projection

Diaprojektor, m
- ♦ slide projector

Diaprojektor kann gegen eine geringe Gebühr zur Verfügung gestellt werden
- ♦ slide projector can be provided at a nominal fee

Diarahmen, m
- Diarähmchen, n
- ♦ slide frame

Diarrhö, f
- → Durchfall

Diaschau, f
- → Diavorführung

Diät, f
- Schonkost, f
- Diätspeise, f
- ♦ diet

Diätabteilung, f
- ♦ dietary department

Diätanforderung, f
- ♦ dietary requirement

Diätart, f
- ♦ type of diet

Diätbedürfnis, n
- ♦ dietary need

Diätbedürfnisse erfüllen
- ♦ cater for dietary needs

Diätbehandlung, f
- ♦ diet treatment

Diätberatung, f
- ♦ dietary counselling
- ♦ dietary advice

diätbewußt, adj
- ♦ diet-conscious, adj

Diätbuch, n
- ♦ diet book

Diätcola, f
- ♦ diet cola

Diäteinrichtung, f
- ♦ dietary facility

Diäteinschränkung, f
- Essenseinschränkung, f
- ♦ dietary restriction

Diätempfehlung, f
- ♦ dietary recommendation

Diätessen, n (Mahlzeit)
- → Diätmahlzeit

Diätessen, n (Speisen)
- ♦ dietary food

Diätetik, f
- Diätlehre, f
- Diätkunde, f
- Ernährungslehre, f
- ♦ dietetics pl = sg

Diätetiker, m
- Diätetikerin f
- Diätspezialist m
- ♦ dietitian
- ♦ dietician

Diätfachmann, m
- Diätexperte, m
- ♦ dietetic professional
- ♦ diet expert

Diätgast, m
- → Gast, der Diät hält

Diätgetränk, n
- ♦ dietetic drink
- ♦ dietetic beverage

Diät halten
- Diät einhalten

- ♦ keep to a diet
- ♦ diet

Diätkoch, m
Diätköchin f
- ♦ diet cook

Diätkost, f
- ♦ dietary cuisine
- dietary cooking
- dietary food
- ♦ diet

Diätkost auf Wunsch
- ♦ Special diets on request

Diätküche, f (Raum)
- ♦ diet kitchen

Diätküche, f (Speisen)
- ♦ dietary cooking
- dietary cuisine
- dietary food

Diätküche auf Anfrage
- ♦ Dietary food on request

Diätkur, f
- ♦ diet cure
- ♦ diet treatment

diät leben
Diät mächen
- ♦ be on a diet
- ♦ take a diet
- ♦ diet

Diät machen
- ♦ go on a diet

Diätmahlzeit, f
Diätessen, n
- ♦ diet meal

Diätnahrung, f
Diätlebensmittel, n pl
- ♦ diet food

Diätplan, m
- ♦ diet plan

Diätproblem, n
- ♦ dietary problem

Diätprodukt, n
- ♦ diet product

Diätprogramm, n
- ♦ program of diet AE
- ♦ programme of diets BE

Diätprogramm verordnen
- ♦ prescribe a program of diet AE
- ♦ prescribe a programme of diet BE

Diätratschlag, m
Diätrat, m
- ♦ dietary advice

Diätrestaurant, n
- ♦ dietary restaurant

Diätrichtlinien, f pl
- ♦ dietary guidelines pl

Diätspeise, f
→ Diät

Diätspezialist, m
→ Diätetiker

Diättherapie, f
- ♦ dietary therapy

Diätverpflegung, f
- ♦ catering for special dietary needs

Diätvorschrift, f
(medizinisch)
- ♦ dietary

Diätvorschriften, f pl
(rituelle und religiöse)
- ♦ dietary laws pl

Diätwahl, f
- ♦ diet choice
- choice of diet

Diätwechsel, m
- ♦ diet change
- change of diet

Diätwunsch, m
- ♦ dietary request
- dietary need

Diätziel, n
- ♦ dietary goal

Diavorführung, f
→ Lichtbilderschau, f

Diavortrag m
- ♦ slide lecture
- ♦ slide show with lecture

Dia zeigen
Dias zeigen
Dias vorführen
- ♦ show a slide
- ♦ show slides

dichtbewaldet, adj
- ♦ densely wooded, adj
- densely forested, adj
- ♦ thickly wooded, adj

dichtbewaldeter Hügel, m
- ♦ thickly-wooded hill
- densely wooded hill

dichtbewaldetes Gebiet, n
- ♦ densely wooded area
- densely forested area

Dieb, m
Langfinger, m fam
- ♦ thief

Diebeshöhle, f
- ♦ den of thieves

Diebstahl, m
- ♦ theft
- ♦ larceny jur

Diebstahlversicherung, f
- ♦ theft insurance

Diebstahlversicherung abschließen
- ♦ take out a theft insurance (policy)

Diele, f (Fußboden)
→ Fußbodendiele

Diele, f (Vorraum)
(meist in Privathäusern)
- ♦ hallway AE
- ♦ vestibule
- ♦ entrance hall

Dielengarderobe, f
(mit Spiegel etc.)
- ♦ hallstand AE

Dielenschlafzimmer, n
Schlafzimmer mit Zugang von der Diele, n
- ♦ hall room AE
- ♦ hall bedroom AE

dienen
- ♦ serve

dienen als etw
- ♦ serve as s.th.
- ♦ be used as s.th.

dienen als Führer
- ♦ serve as a guide

dienen als Kommunikationszentrum
- ♦ serve as a communication center AE
- ♦ serve as a communication centre BE

dienen als vorübergehendes Zuhause
- ♦ serve as a temporary home

Diener, m
Dienstbote, m
Bediensteter, m
- ♦ servant

Diener in Livree, m
- ♦ servant in livery

Dienst, m (Arbeit)
- ♦ duty

Dienst, m (Service)
→ Service

Dienstag, m
- ♦ Tuesday

Dienstag nachts, adv
- ♦ on Tuesday night, adv
- ♦ on Tuesday nights, adv

dienstags, adv
- ♦ on Tuesdays, adv
- ♦ on Tuesday, adv

Dienstags Ruhetag
(Schild)
Dienstag Ruhetag
- ♦ Closed on Tuesdays
- ♦ Closed on Tuesday

Dienstags Tanz
(Hinweisschild)
- ♦ Dancing on Tuesday
- ♦ Dancing on Tuesdays

Dienst am Gast, m
- ♦ service to the guest

Dienst am Kunden, m
- ♦ service to the customer

Dienst aufnehmen
Service aufnehmen
Verkehr aufnehmen
- ♦ launch a service

dienstbarer Geist, m humor
- ♦ ministering angel humor

Dienst beenden
(Personal)
- ♦ go off duty

Dienst betreiben
Service betreiben
- ♦ operate a service

Dienstboteneingang, m
- ♦ service entrance

Dienstbotentreppe, f
Hintertreppe, f
- ♦ backstairs pl
- ♦ back staircase

Dienstbotenzimmer, n
Kurierzimmer n
- ♦ servant's room

Dienst erweisen
- ♦ render a service
- ♦ provide a service

Dienst erweisen jm
- ♦ do s.o. a service
- ♦ render s.o. a service
- ♦ render a service to s.o.

dienstfrei, adj
- ♦ off duty, adv

dienstfrei haben
frei haben
- ♦ be off duty
- ♦ be off
- ♦ be free

diensthabender Nachtmanager, m
- ♦ night manager on duty

diensthabender Oberkellner, m
- ♦ headwaiter on duty

Dienst im Empfang haben
- ♦ be on duty in reception

Dienst leisten jm

Dienst leisten jm
   Dienst erweisen jm
   ♦ render s.o. a service
   ♦ render a service to s.o.
   ♦ do s.o. a service
Dienstleistung, f
   ♦ service
Dienstleistung ausführen
   Leistung ausführen
   Service ausführen
   ♦ perform a service
Dienstleistung buchen
   → Service buchen
Dienstleistungen anbieten
   ♦ offer services
Dienstleistungen ausweiten
   ♦ extend the services
   ♦ extend services
Dienstleistung erbringen
   Service erbringen
   Serviceleistung erbringen
   ♦ provide a service
   ♦ render a service
   ♦ produce a service
Dienstleistung erstellen
   Leistung erstellen
   ♦ produce a service
Dienstleistung erwerben
   ♦ purchase a service
Dienstleistung kaufen
   → Leistung kaufen
Dienstleistung produzieren
   → Dienstleistung erstellen
Dienstleistungsabkommen, n
   → Dienstleistungsvereinbarung
Dienstleistungsanbieter, m
   → Leistungsanbieter
Dienstleistungsangebot, n (Bereitstellung)
   ♦ provision of services
Dienstleistungsangebot, n (Palette)
   ♦ range of services (offered)
Dienstleistungsbereich, m
   ♦ services field
   ♦ service sector
Dienstleistungsberuf, m
   ♦ service job
Dienstleistungsberufe, m pl
   ♦ service occupations *pl*
Dienstleistungsbetrieb, m
   ♦ service operation
   ♦ service establishment
Dienstleistungsbilanz, f
   ♦ balance of services
   ♦ invisible balance
Dienstleistungsbranche, f
   → Dienstleistungsindustrie
Dienstleistungsentzug, m
   ♦ service withdrawal
   ♦ withdrawal of a service
Dienstleistungserbringer, m
   Leistungserbringer, m
   Leistungsträger, m
   ♦ provider of a service
   ♦ provider of services
   ♦ service provider
Dienstleistungserbringung, f
   ♦ providing a service
   ♦ rendering a service
Dienstleistungsfirma, f
   ♦ service firm
   ♦ service company

Dienstleistungsfunktion, f
   ♦ service function
Dienstleistungsgeschäft, n
   ♦ service business
Dienstleistungsgesellschaft, f (Firma)
   ♦ service company
Dienstleistungsgesellschaft, f (Nation)
   ♦ service society
Dienstleistungsgewerbe, n
   ♦ service trade
Dienstleistungsindustrie, f
   ♦ service industry
   ♦ service industries *pl*
Dienstleistungskäufer, m
   ♦ service buyer
   ♦ buyer of a service
Dienstleistungskonzept, n
   Servicekonzept, n
   ♦ service concept
Dienstleistungskosten, pl
   ♦ service costs *pl*
   ♦ service cost
Dienstleistungsmanagement, n
   ♦ service management
Dienstleistungsmarketing, n
   ♦ service marketing
   ♦ marketing a service
   ♦ marketing services
dienstleistungsorientiert, adj
   ♦ service-oriented, adj *AE*
   ♦ service-orientated, adj *BE*
Dienstleistungspaket, n
   Leistungspaket, n
   Servicepaket, n
   ♦ service package
Dienstleistungspalette, f
   → Leistungspalette
Dienstleistungspflicht, f
   ♦ obligation to render a service
   ♦ obligation to render services
Dienstleistungsprodukt, n
   ♦ service product
Dienstleistungsproduktion, f
   Dienstleistungserstellung, f
   ♦ service production
Dienstleistungsproduktivität, f
   ♦ service productivity
Dienstleistungsproduzent, m
   Dienstleistungsersteller, m
   ♦ service producer
   ♦ producer of a service
   ♦ producer of services
Dienstleistungssektor, m
   ♦ services sector
   ♦ service sector
dienstleistungsspezifisch, adj
   ♦ service-specific, adj
Dienstleistungsstörung, f
   → Leistungsstörung
Dienstleistungsumfang, m
   → Serviceumfang
Dienstleistungsunternehmen, n
   ♦ service enterprise
Dienstleistungsvereinbarung, f
   → Leistungsvereinbarung
Dienstleistungsverkäufer, m
   ♦ service seller
   ♦ seller of a service
Dienstleistungsverkehr, m
   ♦ invisible trade

Dienstleistungsvertrag, m
   ♦ service contract
Dienstleistung verkaufen
   → Service verkaufen
Dienstleistung vermarkten
   Leistung vermarkten
   Service vermarkten
   ♦ market a service
dienstlich reisen
   dienstlich verreisen
   ♦ travel in an official capacity
   ♦ travel on business
dienstlich verreisen
   → dienstlich reisen
Dienstmädchen, n
   (in Privathaushalt)
   ♦ maidservant
   ♦ maid
Dienstmädchen ist ein Juwel
   ♦ maid is a jewel
   ♦ maid is a treasure
Dienstmann, m *ÖST*
   ♦ street porter
   ♦ commissionaire
Dienstplan, m
   ♦ work timetable
   ♦ staffing plan
Dienstplan erstellen
   ♦ draw up a staffing plan
Dienstreise, f
   ♦ official tour
   ♦ official journey
   ♦ official trip
   ♦ business trip
   ♦ business journey
Dienstreisen, n
   Dienstreiseverkehr, m
   ♦ official travel
   ♦ business travel
Dienstreisender, m
   Geschäftsreisender, m
   ♦ person travelling on business
   ♦ business traveller *BE*
   ♦ business traveler *AE*
   ♦ person traveling on business *AE*
Dienststunden, f pl
   ♦ office hours *pl*
diensttuend, adj
   diensthabend, adj
   ♦ on duty, adv
diensttuender Arzt, m
   ♦ doctor on duty
diensttuender Manager, m
   ♦ manager on duty
Dienstvertrag, m
   ♦ contract of service
   ♦ service contract
   ♦ contract of employment
Dienstvorschriften, f pl
   ♦ service regulations *pl*
Dienstwohnung, f (Haus)
   ♦ official residence
Dienstwohnung, f (Wohnung)
   ♦ official apartment *AE*
   ♦ official flat *BE*
Diepperart, adv *gastr*
   nach Diepperart, adv *gastr*
   ♦ Dieppe style, adv *gastr*
Diesellokomotive, f
   ♦ diesel locomotive
   ♦ diesel engine

Dieselmotor, m
♦ diesel engine
♦ diesel motor
Dieselzug, m
♦ diesel train
diesjährig, adj
♦ this year's, adj
Dietrich, m
(Schlüssel)
♦ skeleton key
Digestif, m FR
♦ digestif FR
Diktaphon, n
→ Diktiergerät
Diktiergerät, n
♦ dictating machine
♦ dictaphone
Dill, m
♦ dill
Dillbutter, f
♦ dill butter
Dillessig, m
♦ dill vinegar
Dillkartoffeln, f pl
♦ dill potatoes pl
Dillsoße, f
♦ dill sauce
Dillzweigchen, n
Dillzweig, m
♦ dill sprig
Dimmer, m
→ Helligkeitsregler
Diner, n
♦ formal dinner
♦ dinner party
♦ dinner
Diner bei Kerzenlicht, n
→ Abendessen bei Kerzenlicht
Diner de gala, n FR m
Galadiner, n
♦ dîner de gala FR
♦ gala dinner
Diner geben
♦ give a dinner party
♦ give a dinner
Diner geben für jn
Essen geben für jn
♦ give a dinner for s.o.
Diner geben zu Ehren von jm
Essen geben zu js Ehren
♦ give a dinner in honor of s.o. AE
♦ give a dinner in honour of s.o. BE
♦ give a dinner in s.o.'s honor AE
♦ give a dinner in s.o.'s honour BE
Diner Maison, n FR
(Essen)
♦ dîner maison FR
Diner veranstalten zu Ehren von jm
♦ hold a dinner in honor of s.o. AE
♦ hold a dinner in honour of s.o. BE
♦ hold a dinner in s.o.'s honor AE
♦ hold a dinner in s.o.'s honour BE
Dinette, f
→ Sitzgruppe
Dingi, n
Beiboot, n
Schlauchboot, n
♦ dinghy
Dinieren, n form
Speisen, n
♦ dining

dinieren mit jm
→ speisen mit jm
Dinnerbüfett, n
→ Abendbüfett
Dinnerjacket, n
♦ dinner jacket
♦ DJ
Dinosaurier, m
♦ dinosaur
Dinosaurierausstellung, f
♦ dinosaur exhibition
♦ exhibition of dinosaurs
Dinosauriererlebnispark, m
♦ dinosaur theme park
Dinosauriermuseum, n
♦ dinosaur museum
Dinosaurierpark, m
♦ dinosaur park
Diözesanmuseum, n
♦ diocesan museum
Diözese, f
♦ diocese
Diplomatenart, adv gastr
nach Diplomatenart, adv gastr
♦ diplomat style, adv gastr
Diplomatenempfang, m
diplomatischer Empfang, m
♦ diplomatic reception
Diplomatenvisum, n
♦ diplomatic visa
diplomatische Beziehungen, f pl
♦ diplomatic relations pl
diplomatische Beziehungen abbrechen
♦ break off diplomatic relations
Directeur de cuisine, m FR
Küchendirektor, m
Küchenleiter, m
♦ directeur de cuisine FR
♦ kitchen director
♦ kitchen manager
Directeur de restaurant, m FR
Restaurantdirektor m
♦ directeur de restaurant FR
♦ restaurant director
♦ restaurant manager
Direct Mailing, n
♦ direct mailing
direkt am Bahnhof
♦ directly beside the station
♦ immediately at the station
direkt am Meer
♦ directly at the seaside
direkt am See
♦ directly at the lake
♦ directly on the lake AE
direkt am Strand
♦ directly on the beach
direkt am Waldrand gelegen
♦ situated directly at the edge of the forest
♦ situated directly on the edge of the forest AE
♦ situated directly at the edge of the wood
♦ situated directly on the edge of the wood AE
direkt an der See
direkt am Meer
♦ directly at the sea
Direktaussteller, m
♦ direct exhibitor
Direktbelegung, f
→ Direktbuchung
Direktbestellung, f
→ Direktbuchung

Direktbucher, m
direkter Bucher m
♦ direct booker
Direktbuchung, f
direkte Buchung f
♦ direct booking
Direktbuchungspreis, m
♦ direct booking price
♦ direct booking rate
Direktbuchungssystem, n
♦ direct booking system
direkte Aufwendungen, f pl
♦ direct expenses pl
♦ direct costs pl
direkte Bahnverbindung, f
♦ direct rail link
♦ direct rail connection
direkte Buchung, f
→ Direktbuchung
direkte Kosten, pl
Direktkosten pl
♦ direct costs pl
♦ direct cost
direkten Kontakt haben mit einem Gast
♦ have direct contact with a guest
direkten Zugang haben zu etw
♦ have direct access to s.th.
direkter Zugang (zu etw), m
♦ direct access (to s.th.)
direkter Zugang zum Garten, m
♦ direct access to the garden
direkter Zugang zum Meer, m
direkter Zugang zur See, m
♦ direct access to the sea
direkter Zugang zum See, m
♦ direct access to the lake
direkter Zugang zum Strand, m
♦ direct access to the beach
direkte Verbindung zwischen A und B, f
♦ direct link between A and B
♦ direct connection between A and B
direkte Wareneinsatzkosten, pl
♦ direct cost of sales
direkte Zimmerkosten, pl
♦ direct room costs pl
♦ direct room cost
Direktfähre, f
♦ direct ferry
Direktflug, m
♦ direct flight
♦ through flight
Direktflug nach X, m
♦ direct flight to X
direkt gegenüber von etw
♦ directly opposite s.th.
direkt im Stadtzentrum
♦ directly downtown AE
direkt in der Innenstadt (Großstadt)
♦ directly in the city center AE
♦ directly in the city centre BE
direkt in der Innenstadt (kleine Stadt)
♦ directly in the town center AE
♦ directly in the town centre BE
Direktion, f
♦ directors pl
♦ board of directors
Direktionsassistent, m
♦ assistant director
♦ assistant manager
♦ assistant to the director
♦ assistant to the manager

Direktionsgehälter

Direktionsgehälter, n pl
→ Direktorengehälter
Direktionssekretärin, f
♦ director's secretary
♦ executive secretary
Direktionswohnung, f
(Wohnung für Hoteldirektor)
♦ manager's apartment *AE*
♦ manager's flat *BE*
Direktkontakt, m
direkter Kontakt, m
♦ direct contact
direkt Kontakt aufnehmen mit jm
♦ contact s.o. direct
Direktkontakt herstellen mit jm
direkten Kontakt herstellen mit jm
♦ establish direct contact with s.o.
Direktkosten, pl
→ direkte Kosten
direkt neben etw
unmittelbar neben etw
♦ directly beside s.th.
Direktor, m
♦ director
♦ manager
Direktor der Personal- und Ausbildungsabteilung, m
♦ personnel and training director
Direktorenbezüge, m pl
♦ director's emoluments *pl*
♦ directors' emoluments *pl*
Direktorengehalt, n
Direktorenhonorar, n
♦ director's salary
♦ manager's salary
♦ director's fees *pl*
Direktorengehälter, n pl
Direktorenhonorare, n
♦ directors' fees *pl*
♦ directors' emoluments *pl*
Direktorenkasino, n
(in Fabriken etc.)
♦ executive dining room
Direktreservierung, f
direkte Reservierung, f
♦ direct reservation
Direktrice, f
♦ directress
♦ directrice
Direkttelefon, n
→ Direktwahltelefon
Direktverbindung, f
direkte Verbindung, f
♦ direct connection
♦ through connection
♦ direct link
Direktvermietung, f
♦ direct rental *AE*
♦ direct letting *BE*
Direktvertrieb, m
♦ direct selling
♦ direct distribution
Direktwahltelefon, n
Direkttelefon, n
Durchwahltelefon, n
♦ direct-dial telephone
♦ d.d. telephone
♦ subscriber's trunk dialling telephone *BE*
♦ s.t.d. telephone *BE*
♦ direct-dial(ling) phone

Direktwerbung, f
♦ direct advertising
Dirigent, m
♦ director *AE*
♦ conductor *BE*
Dirigentenkurs, m
Dirigentenlehrgang, m
♦ conductors' course *BE*
dirigieren (etw)
♦ conduct (s.th.) *BE*
Dirndlrock, m
♦ dirndl skirt
Dirne, f
→ Prostituierte
Disco, f
→ Diskothek
Diskette, f
♦ diskette
Diskjockey, m
DJ, m
♦ disc jockey
♦ pancake turner *sl*
♦ DJ
Disko, f
Diskothek f
♦ disco
♦ discotheque
Diskoabend m
♦ disco evening
♦ evening in the discotheque
Diskobar f
♦ disco bar
Diskoclub, m
♦ disco club
Disko ist jede Nacht geöffnet
♦ disco is open nightly
♦ disco is open every night
Diskomusik, f
♦ disco music
Diskont, m
♦ discount
diskontieren
♦ discount
Diskotanzen, n
♦ disco dancing
Diskothek, f
Disko f
♦ discotheque
♦ disco
Diskothekenbesitzer, m
♦ owner of a discotheque
Diskothekenbesuch, m
♦ visit to a discotheque
♦ visit to a disco
Diskothekenbesucher m
Diskobesucher m
♦ discotheque visitor
♦ visitor to a discotheque
♦ disco visitor *coll*
Diskothekenbetreiber, m
Diskobetreiber, m
♦ discotheque operator
♦ disco operator
Diskowagen, m (Zug)
♦ disco car *AE*
♦ disco carriage *BE*
Diskozug, m
♦ disco train
diskret, adj
taktvoll, adj

♦ discreet, adj
♦ tactful, adj
diskrete Erkundigung, f
diskrete Anfrage, f
♦ discreet inquiry
♦ discreet enquiry
diskreter Kellner, m
♦ discreet waiter
diskreter Service, m
♦ discreet service
diskretes Hotel, n
♦ discreet hotel
Diskretion, f
♦ discretion
diskret sein
♦ be discreet
Diskussion, f
♦ discussion
Diskussion abbrechen
♦ break off the discussion
Diskussion leiten (Ton angeben)
Diskussion anführen
♦ lead a discussion
Diskussion leiten (Vorsitz haben)
♦ chair a discussion
Diskussionsabend, m
♦ evening of discussion
Diskussionsanlage, f
(Konferenz)
♦ discussion system
Diskussionsbeitrag, m
♦ contribution to the discussion
Diskussionsforum, n
♦ discussion forum
Diskussionsleiter, m (generell)
♦ discussion leader
Diskussionsleiter, m (Podiumsdiskussion)
♦ panel chairman
♦ chairman of the panel
Diskussionsredner, m
♦ speaker (in a discussion)
Diskussionsrunde, f (Serie)
♦ round of discussions
Diskussionsrunde, f (Teilnehmer)
♦ discussion group
Diskussionsteilnehmer, m
(auf Podium)
♦ member of the panel
♦ panelist *AE*
♦ panellist *BE*
♦ guest
Diskussionsthema, n
♦ subject for discussion
Diskussionsveranstaltung, f
→ Forum
Diskussion veranstalten
♦ organise a discussion
♦ organize a discussion
Disneyland, n
♦ Disneyland
Dispenser, m
♦ dispenser
Display, n
→ Zurschaustellung
distinguiert, adj
vornehm, adj
♦ distinguished, adj
Dithmarschen
(Region)
♦ Ditmarsh

divers, adj (Speisen)
- assorted, adj
- choice of

diverse Ausgaben, f pl
sonstige Ausgaben, f pl
- sundry expenses pl
- sundries pl

Diwan, m
- divan
- davenport AE

DJ, m
Diskjockey, m
- DJ
- disk jockey

DJH-Ausweis, m
Deutscher Jugendherbergs-Ausweis m
- DJH membership card
- German Youth Hostel membership card

DM 123 für das Essen pro Woche zahlen
- pay DM 123 for the meals per week
- pay DM 123 for the meals a week

Do.
Doppel
- dbl.
- double

Dogcart, m
einspänniger zweirädriger hoher Pferdewagen, m
- dogcart

Dokument, n
- document

Dokumentarfilm, m
- documentary film

Dolcefarniente, n ITAL
süßes Nichtstun, n
- dolce far niente ITAL

Dolcetto, m ITAL
(Wein)
- Dolcetto ITAL

Dolce vita, n ITAL
- dolce vita ITAL

Dollar, m
- dollar
- buck AE coll

Dollars umtauschen in Mark
Dollars umwechseln in Mark
- change dollars into marks

Dolmetschanlage, f
- interpretation facilities pl

dolmetschen
- interpret

dolmetschen aus dem Englischen ins Deutsche
- interpret from English into German

Dolmetscher, m
- interpreter

Dolmetscherausstattung, f
Dolmetscherausrüstung, f
Dolmetschertechnik, f
- interpretation equipment

Dolmetscherdienst, m
Dolmetscherservice m
- interpreter service

Dolmetscherin, f
- woman interpreter
- interpretress

Dolmetscherkabine f
- interpreter's booth

Dolmetscherschule, f
- interpreters' school

Dolmetschservice, m
→ Dolmetscherdienst

Dolomiten, die, pl
- Dolomites, the pl

Dom, m
- cathedral

Domäne, f
- domain

domartig, adj
kathedralenartig, adj
- cathedral-like, adj

Domblick, m
- view of the cathedral
- cathedral view

Domführer, m
- cathedral guide

Domführung, f
Führung durch den Dom, f
Führung durch die Kathedrale, f
- tour of the cathedral

Dominikanerkirche, f
- Dominican church

Dominikanerkloster, n (Frauen)
- Dominican convent

Dominikanerkloster, n (Männer)
- Dominican monastery

Dominikanische Republik, f
- Dominican Republic, the

Domizil, n lit/humor
Wohnsitz, m
- abode
- domicil AE
- domicile

Domizil aufschlagen in X humor
sich niederlassen in X
- settle in X
- settle at X

domizilieren
→ logieren, wohnen

Domplatz, m
- cathedral square

Domstadt, f (Großstadt)
- cathedral city

Domstadt, f (kleine Stadt)
- cathedral town

Donau, f
- Danube River, the
- River Danube, the
- Danube, the

Donaudelta, n
- Danube delta

Donaukreuzfahrt, f
- Danube cruise
- cruise on the Danube

Donauquelle, f
- source of the Danube

Donautal n
- Danube valley

donnernder Applaus, m
rasender Applaus, m
- thunderous applause

Donnerstag, m
- Thursday

Donnerstag nachts, adv
- on Thursday night, adv
- on Thursday nights, adv

donnerstags, adv
- on Thursdays, adv
- on Thursday, adv

Donnerstags Ruhetag
(Schild)
Donnerstag Ruhetag
- Closed on Thursdays
- Closed on Thursday

Donnerstags Tanz
(Hinweisschild)
- Dancing on Thursday
- Dancing on Thursdays

Doppel, n
→ Doppelzimmer

Doppelausziehcouch f
→ ausziehbare Doppelcouch

Doppelausziehliege f
→ ausziehbare Doppelliege

Doppelbecken, f
Doppelwaschbecken n
- double basin

Doppelbelegung, f (Belegung mit 2 Personen)
Belegung mit zwei Personen, f
Zweierbelegung, f
- double occupancy

Doppelbelegung, f (Buchungsfehler)
→ Doppelbuchung

Doppelbelegungszuschlag, m
(für Belegung eines Zimmers mit zwei Personen)
Doppelbenutzungszuschlag m
- double-occupancy supplement

Doppelbenutzungszuschlag, m
→ Doppelbelegungszuschlag

Doppelbett, n
- double bed
- double

Doppelbettcouch, f
- double couch bed
- double bed-settee BE
- double put-you-up BE
- double put-u-up BE
- studio couch

doppelbettig, adj
- double-bedded, adj

doppelbettig belegbar, adj
- available for double-bed occupancy, adj
- available for double occupancy, adj

Doppelbettkabine, f (Bett)
- double-bed cabin

Doppelbettkabine, f (Koje)
- double-berth cabin

Doppelbettliege, f
- double divan-bed
- double divan

Doppelbettsofa, n
- double sofa-bed
- duplex bed AE

Doppelbettzimmer, n
- double-bed room
- double-bedded room
- double

Doppelbettzimmerbelegung f
- double room occupancy
- double occupancy

Doppelbogen, m
- double arch

Doppelbuchung, f
- double booking

Doppelbuchung klären
- resolve a double booking

Doppelbungalow m
- semi-detached bungalow

Doppelcarport, m
- double car port

Doppelcouch, f
- double settee BE

Doppeldeckbus

Doppeldeckbus, m
♦ double-decker bus
♦ double-decker coach BE
♦ double-deck bus
♦ double-deck coach BE
♦ double-decked bus
Doppelfeier, f
♦ double celebration
Doppelfenster, n
♦ double window
♦ double-glazed window
doppelflammig, adj
♦ double-burner, adj
doppelflammiger Gasherd, m
♦ double-burner gas stove
Doppelgarage, f (generell)
♦ double garage
♦ dbl. gge.
Doppelgarage, f (hintereinander)
♦ tandem garage
Doppelhaus, n
DH, n
♦ semi-detached house
Doppelinnenkabine, f
♦ double inside cabin
Doppeljubiläum, n
♦ double jubilee
Doppeljubiläum feiern
♦ celebrate a double jubilee
Doppelkabine, f
(in Verkehrsmittel)
♦ double cabin
Doppelkoje, f
Doppelbett, n
♦ double berth
Doppelliege f
♦ double divan
Doppelloipe, f
♦ double-track cross-country trail
♦ double-track cross-country ski trail
Doppelluftmatratze, f
♦ double air mattress
♦ double air bed BE
Doppelportion, f
→ doppelte Portion
Doppelprogramm, n
♦ two-feature program AE
♦ two-feature programme BE
Doppelprojektion, f
♦ double projection
Doppelreise, f
zweimalige Reise, f
♦ double journey
♦ double tour
♦ double trip
Doppelrundloipe, f
♦ double cross-country circuit
♦ double cross-country ski trail
Doppelsaison, f
(Winter- und Sommersaison)
♦ double season
Doppelsaison haben
♦ have a double season
Doppelscheiben, f pl
♦ double-glazed window
Doppelschlafcouch, f
♦ double sleeping couch
Doppelschlafzimmer, n
♦ double bedroom
♦ dbl bdrm

Doppelschrankbett, n
♦ double fold-up bed
Doppelsessellift m
(Ski)
♦ double chair lift
doppelsitzig, adj
♦ double-seated, adj
Doppelsitzplatz, m
Doppelsitz, m
Doppelplatz, m
♦ double seat
Doppelstadt, f
♦ double town
Doppelstockbett, n
→ doppelstöckiges Etagenbett
doppelstöckig, adj attr (Gebäude)
♦ double-story, adj attr AE
♦ double-storey, adj attr BE
♦ double-floor, adj attr
doppelstöckig, adj (Bett)
♦ double-tier, adj
♦ double-tiered, adj
doppelstöckig, adj prd (Gebäude)
♦ double-storied, adj prd AE
♦ double-storeyed, adj prd BE
doppelstöckiges Bett, n
→ doppelstöckiges Etagenbett
doppelstöckiges Etagenbett, n
Doppelstockbett, n
doppelstöckiges Bett, n
♦ double-tier bunk bed
♦ double-tiered bunk bed
doppelstöckiges Hotel, n
zweistöckiges Hotel, n
zweigeschossiges Hotel, n
♦ two-floor hotel
♦ two-story hotel AE
♦ two-storey hotel BE
doppelstöckig sein (Gebäude)
♦ be double-storied AE
♦ be double-storeyed BE
Doppelstudio, n
♦ double studio
doppelt, adj
♦ double, adj
Doppeltarif, m
♦ maximum and minimum tariff
doppelt buchen (etw)
zweimal buchen (etw)
zweimal bestellen (etw)
zweimal vergeben (etw)
♦ double book (s.th.)
doppelte Portion, f
Doppelportion, f
♦ double portion
doppelter Meeresblick, m
(auf einer Halbinsel)
♦ double seaview AE
♦ double sea view BE
doppelter Whisky, m
♦ double whisky
doppeltkohlensaures Natrium, n
Natriumbikarbonat, n
Natron, n coll
♦ bicarbonate of soda
♦ baking soda
♦ cooking soda
Doppeltür, f
♦ double door
Doppelturm, m
♦ double tower

doppelt verglast, adj
♦ double glazed, adj
Doppelveranstaltung, f
Veranstaltung mit zwei Teilen, f
♦ double bill
Doppelverglasung, f
Isolierverglasung, f
♦ double glazing
Doppelvermietung, f
♦ simultaneous renting AE
♦ simultaneous letting BE
Doppelwaschbecken, n
Doppelwaschtisch m
♦ double wash-basin
♦ twin wash-basin
Doppelzelt, n
♦ double tent
Doppelzimmer, n
♦ double room
♦ double
Doppelzimmer als Einzelzimmer vermieten
♦ rent (out) a double room as single room
♦ let a double room as single room BE
Doppelzimmer behalten
♦ keep a double room
Doppelzimmerbelegung, f
Doppelzimmerauslastung f
♦ double-room occupancy
Doppelzimmer benötigen
♦ require a double room
Doppelzimmer buchen
♦ book a double room
Doppelzimmerbuchung, f
♦ double-room booking
♦ booking (of) a double room
Doppelzimmerchalet, n
♦ double-room chalet
doppelzimmerig, adj
♦ double-roomed, adj
doppelzimmeriges Chalet, n
♦ double-roomed chalet
Doppelzimmer in Anspruch nehmen
Doppelzimmer beanspruchen
♦ claim a double room
Doppelzimmer mieten
♦ rent a double room
♦ hire a double room BE
Doppelzimmer mit Frühstück, n
♦ double room and breakfast
Doppelzimmer mit zwei Doppelbetten, n
♦ twin double room
♦ twin double-bedded room
♦ twin double
♦ double-double
Doppelzimmernachfrage, f
Nachfrage nach Doppelzimmern, f
♦ demand for double rooms
♦ demand for doubles
Doppelzimmer nehmen
♦ take a double room
Doppelzimmerpreis, m
♦ double-room rate
♦ double-room price
Doppelzimmer reservieren
♦ reserve a double room
Doppelzimmer umwandeln in ein Einzelzimmer
♦ convert a double room into a single room
♦ convert a double into a single
Doppelzimmerunterkunft, f
Doppelzimmerunterbringung, f
♦ double-room accommodation

Doppelzimmer untervermieten an jn
- sublease a double room to s.o.
- sublet a double room to s.o.
- underlet a double room to s.o.

Doppelzimmer vermieten
- rent (out) a double room
- let a double room *BE*

Doppelzimmer wünschen
- request a double room
- request a double

Doppelzimmerzuschlag m
- double-room supplement

Doppelzimmer zuweisen jm
Doppelzimmer zuteilen jm
Doppelzimmer vergeben an jn
- allocate a double room to s.o.
- assign a double room to s.o. *AE*

Dordogne, f
(Region)
- Dordogne, the

Dorf an der Donau, n
- village on the Danube

Dorfanfang m
- beginning of a village

Dorfanger, m
- village green

Dorfanlage, f
Dorfkomplex m
- village complex

Dorfatmosphäre, f
- village atmosphere

Dorfbäckerei, f
- village bakery

Dorfbewohner, m
- villager

Dorfende, n
- end of a village

Dorffest n
- village festival
- village fete

Dorffete, f
- village fete
- village fête *Be*

Dorfgasthaus, n
Dorfwirtschaft f
Dorfschenke f
Dorfgaststätte, f
- village bar *AE*
- village pub *BE*

Dorfgasthof, m
- village inn

Dorfgaststätte, f
→ Dorfgasthaus

Dorfhaus, n
- village house

Dorfhotel n
- village hotel

Dorfidylle, f
- village idyll

Dorfkirche, f
- village church

Dorfkneipe, f
→ Dorfgasthaus

Dorfkrug, m
→ Dorfgasthaus

Dorfladen, m
- village store *AE*
- village shop *BE*

Dorflage, f
- village location

Dorfleben, n
- village life

Dorfmitte, f
Ortsmitte, f
Ortszentrum, n
- center of the village *AE*
- centre of the village *BE*
- village center *AE*
- village centre *BE*

Dorfmuseum, n
- village museum

Dorfpension, f
- village guesthouse *AE*
- village guest-house *BE*
- village boardinghouse *AE*
- village boarding-house *BE*

Dorfplatz, m
- village square

Dorfrand, m
Rand des Dorfes m
- edge of a village
- outskirts of a village *pl*

Dorfrestaurant n
- village restaurant

Dorfsaal, m
Dorfhalle, f
- village hall

Dorfschenke, f
→ Dorfgasthaus

Dorfschule, f
- village school

Dorfstraße, f (generell)
- village road

Dorfstraße, f (mit Geschäften)
- village street

Dorfurlaub, m
- village vacation *AE*
- village holiday *BE*

Dorfwirtschaft, f
Dorfgaststätte f
Dorfgasthaus n
- village bar *AE*
- village pub *BE*

Dorfwirtshaus, n
→ Dorfgasthaus

dorische Säule, f
- Doric column

Dornfelder, m
(Wein)
- Dornfelder

Dornfelderrebe, f
- Dornfelder vine

Dornfeldertraube, f
- Dornfelder grape

Dornfelderwein, m
- Dornfelder wine

Dornhai, m
Katzenhai, m
- dogfish

Dörrpflaume, f
Backpflaume, f
- prune

Dorsch, m
Kabeljau, m
- codfish *AE*
- cod

Dose, f
Konservendose, f
- can *AE*
- tin *BE*

dösen
- snooze

Dosenbier, n
Büchsenbier n
- canned beer *AE*
- tinned beer *BE*

Dosenfleisch, n
Büchsenfleisch, n
- tinned meat *BE*
- canned meat *AE*

Dosengemüse, n
- canned vegetable *AE*
- tinned vegetable *BE*

Dosenöffner, m
Büchsenöffner m
- can opener *AE*
- tin-opener *BE*

Dosenpfirsiche, m pl
- canned peaches *AE pl*
- tinned peaches *BE pl*

Dosensirup, m
- tin syrup *BE*
- can syrup *AE*

Douche, f *SCHW*
→ Dusche

Downgrade, m
Tieferstufung f
- downgrade
- downgrading

Downgrading, n
→ Tieferstufung

Drachenboot, n
- dragon boat

Drachenbootrennen, n
- dragon boat race
- dragon boat racing

Drachenfliegen, n
- hang-gliding

Drachenflieger, m
- hang-glider

Drachenfliegerkurs, m
Drachenfliegerlehrgang, m
- hang-gliding course
- course in hang-gliding

Drachme, f
- drachma

Drahtesel, m *humor*
Fahrrad, n
- iron steed *humor*
- steed *humor*
- iron horse *BE humor*
- bicycle

Drahtkleiderbügel, m
- wire hanger

drahtlose Infrarotübertragung, f
- wireless infrared transmission *AE*
- wireless infra-red transmission *BE*

drahtlose Mikrofonanlage, f
- radio microphone system
- wireless microphone system

drahtlose Simultandolmetscheranlage, f
- radio simultaneous interpretation system
- wireless simultaneous interpretation system

drahtlose Simultanübersetzungsanlage, f
- radio simultaneous translation system
- wireless simultaneous translation system

Drahtmatratze, f
- wire mattress

Drahtseilbahn, f
Standseilbahn, f
Kabinenbahn, f

dramatischer Buchungsrückgang

- ♦ cable railroad *AE*
- ♦ cable railway *BE*
- ♦ funicular railroad *AE*
- ♦ funicular railway *BE*
- ♦ funicular

dramatischer Buchungsrückgang, m
- ♦ dramatic decrease in bookings
- ♦ dramatic decline in bookings
- ♦ dramatic fall in bookings

drastische Preissenkung, f
- ♦ drastic price cut

draufmachen einen
  Sauftour machen
- ♦ go on a jag

draußen essen
- ♦ eat outside

draußen schlafen
  im Freien schlafen
- ♦ sleep rough
- ♦ sleep outdoors

Dreck, m
- ♦ filth

dreckig, adj
  verdreckt, adj
  sehr schmutzig, adj
- ♦ filthy, adj

dreckige Sanitäreinrichtungen, f pl
  verschmutzte Sanitäreinrichtungen, f pl
- ♦ filthy sanitary facilities *pl*

dreckiges Zimmer, n
  verdrecktes Zimmer n
- ♦ filthy room

Drehbrücke, f
- ♦ swing bridge

Drehbühne, f
- ♦ revolving stage

Drehfenster, n
- ♦ swivel window
- ♦ pivoted window

Drehgrill, m
- → Bratspieß

Drehkreisel, m
  (Spielzeug)
- ♦ top

Drehkreuz, n
  (am Eingang)
  Drehgitter, n
- ♦ turnstile

Drehrestaurant n
  sich drehendes Restaurant n
- ♦ revolving restaurant
- ♦ rotating restaurant

Drehscheibe, f *figur*
  Drehkreuz, n
- ♦ hub

Drehstuhl, m
- ♦ swivel chair
- ♦ revolving chair

Drehtür, f
- ♦ revolving door

dreibeiniger Tisch, m
  dreifüßiger Tisch, m
- ♦ three-legged table

Dreibettappartement, n
- ♦ three-bed apartment

Dreibettbelegung, f
- → dreibettige Belegung

Dreibettcaravan, m (Bett)
  Dreibettwohnwagen, m
- ♦ three-bed caravan *BE*

- ♦ three-bed van *BE coll*
- ♦ three-bed trailer *AE*

Dreibettcaravan, m (Koje)
  Dreibettwohnwagen, m
- ♦ three-berth caravan *BE*
- ♦ three-berth van *BE coll*
- ♦ three-berth trailer *AE*

Dreibetthaus, n
- ♦ three bedroomed house
- ♦ house with three bedrooms

dreibettig, adj
- ♦ three-bedded, adj
- ♦ triple-bedded, adj

dreibettig belegbar, adj
- ♦ available for triple occupancy, adj

dreibettige Belegung, f
  Dreierbelegung, f
  Belegung mit drei Personen, f
- ♦ triple occupancy

dreibettiges Zimmer, n
- ♦ three-bedded room
- ♦ triple-bedded room

Dreibettkabine, f (Bett)
- ♦ three-bed cabin

Dreibettkabine, f (Koje)
- ♦ three-berth cabin

Dreibettschlafzimmer, n
- ♦ triple bedroom

Dreibettvilla, f
- ♦ three-bed villa

Dreibettwohnung, f
- ♦ three-bed flat *BE*
- ♦ three-bed apartment *AE*

Dreibettwohnwagen, m
  Dreibettcaravan, m
- ♦ three-berth trailer *AE*
- ♦ three-berth caravan *BE*
- ♦ three-berth van *BE coll*

Dreibettzimmer, n
- ♦ three-bed room
- ♦ three-bedded room
- ♦ triple-bedded room
- ♦ triple room
- ♦ triple

Dreibettzimmerbelegung, f
- ♦ triple-room occupancy

Dreibettzimmerpreis, m
- ♦ triple-room rate
- ♦ triple-room price

Dreibettzimmerunterkunft, f
  Dreibettzimmerunterbringung, f
- ♦ triple-room accommodation

Dreidecker, m
- ♦ triplane

dreieckiger Tisch, m
- ♦ triangular table

Dreierappartement, n
- → Dreibettappartement

Dreierbelegung, f
- → dreibettige Belegung

Dreierbett, n
- ♦ triple bed

Dreiertisch, m
  Dreipersonentisch, m
- ♦ table for three persons
- ♦ table for three
- ♦ table to seat three persons

Dreierzimmer, n
  Dreibettzimmer n
- ♦ triple room
- ♦ triple

- ♦ three-bed room
- ♦ three-bedded room

dreifach, adj
- ♦ triple, adj
- ♦ treble, adj

dreifache Portion, f
- ♦ treble portion

dreifacher Whisky, m
- ♦ triple whisky

dreifach verglast adj
- ♦ triple glazed, adj

dreifach verglastes Fenster n
- ♦ triple glazed window

dreiflammig, adj
  (Gasherd)
- ♦ three-burner, adj

dreiflammige Kochplatte, f
- ♦ three-burner hob

dreiflammiger Gaskocher, m
  dreiflammiger Gasherd, m
- ♦ three-burner gas cooker

dreiflammiger Herd, m
- ♦ three-burner stove

Dreigangfahrrad, n
- ♦ three-speed bicycle

dreigängig, adj (Essen)
- ♦ three-course, adj
- ♦ consisting of three courses

dreigängige Mahlzeit, f
  dreigängiges Essen, n
- ♦ three-course meal

dreigängiges Abendessen, n (Supper)
- ♦ three-course supper

dreigängiges Abendessen n (Dinner)
- ♦ three-course dinner

dreigängiges Essen, n
- → dreigängige Mahlzeit

dreigängiges Menü, n
- ♦ three-course menu

dreigängiges Mittagessen, n
- ♦ three-course luncheon
- ♦ three-course lunch

Dreigangmenü, n
- → dreigängiges Menü

Drei-Gang-Menü, n
- → dreigängiges Menü

Dreigangrad, n
  Rad mit drei Gängen, n
- ♦ three-gear bike

Drei-Gipfel-Wanderung, f
- ♦ three-peaks walk
- ♦ three-peaks hike

Dreihundertjahrfeier, f
- ♦ tercentenary celebration

Dreihundertjahrjubiläum, n
  dreihundertster Jahrstag, m
- ♦ tercentenary
- ♦ tercentennial

dreijährig, adj
- ♦ three-year, adj
- ♦ three years', adj
- ♦ of three years' duration
- ♦ lasting three years

dreijähriger Aufenthalt, m
- ♦ three-year stay
- ♦ three years' stay
- ♦ stay of three years

Dreiklassensitzplatzsystem, n
  Dreiklassensitzsystem, n
- ♦ three-class seating system

158

Dreikönigsfest, n
♦ Epiphany
Dreikönigstag, m
♦ Twelfth Night
♦ Epiphany
dreiköpfige Familie, f
♦ family of three
Dreikornbrot, n
♦ three-cereal bread
Dreiländerreise, f
♦ three-country tour
♦ tour of three countries
♦ tour through three countries
Dreiliterflasche, f
♦ three-liter bottle *AE*
♦ three-litre bottle *BE*
drei Mahlzeiten am Tag, f pl
♦ three meals a day *pl*
dreimalige Reise, f
♦ triple journey
♦ triple tour
♦ triple trip
dreimal täglich, adv
♦ three times daily, adv
♦ three times a day, adv
♦ three times per day, adv
Dreimannorchester, n
♦ three-man orchestra
Dreimannzelt, n
♦ three-man tent
Dreimaster, m
♦ three-master
Dreiminutenei n
♦ three-minute egg
♦ soft-boiled egg
dreimonatig, adj
♦ three-month, adj
♦ lasting three months
♦ of three months' duration
♦ three months', adj
dreimonatiger Aufenthalt, m
♦ three-month stay
♦ three months' stay
♦ stay of three months
dreimonatige Reise, f
♦ three-month journey
♦ three-month trip
♦ three-month tour
dreimotorig, adj
♦ three-engine(d), adj
dreimotoriges Flugzeug, n
♦ three-engine(d) plane
♦ three-engine(d) aeroplane *BE*
♦ three-engine(d) airplane *AE*
Dreipersonenbett, n
♦ three-person bed
Dreipersonenzelt, n
♦ three-person tent
Dreirad, n
♦ tricycle
♦ trike *coll*
Dreiradfahrer, m
♦ tricycle rider
Dreiraumwohnung, f
→ Dreizimmerwohnung
Dreisatztisch, m
Satz Tische, m
♦ nest of tables
dreischiffige Kirche, f
♦ three-nave church
♦ three-naved church

Dreisitzer, m
♦ three-seater
dreisitzig, adj
♦ three-seater, adj
dreisitziges Sofa, n
♦ three-seater sofa
dreisprachig, adj
♦ trilingual, adj
Dreisprung, m
♦ hop, step and jump
dreispurig, adj
♦ three-lane, adj
dreispurige Straße, f
♦ three-lane road
♦ three-lane street
dreißigstes Stockwerk, n
dreißigste Etage, f
dreißigstes Geschoß, n
♦ thirty-first floor *AE*
♦ thirty-first story *AE*
♦ thirtieth floor *BE*
♦ thirtieth storey *BE*
Drei-Sterne-Anlage, f
Drei-Sterne-Komplex m
♦ three-star complex
Drei-Sterne-Anwesen, n
Drei-Sterne-Objekt, n
♦ three-star property
Drei-Sterne-Appartement, n
♦ three-star apartment
Drei-Sterne-Appartementanlage, f
Drei-Sterne-Appartementkomplex, m
♦ three-star apartment complex
Drei-Sterne-Attraktion, f
♦ three-star attraction
Drei-Sterne-Aufenthalt, m
♦ three-star stay
Drei-Sterne-Bereich, m
Drei-Sterne-Sektor, m
♦ three-star sector
Drei-Sterne-Betrieb, m
♦ three-star establishment
♦ three-star operation
Drei-Sterne-Bewertung, f
♦ three-star rating
Drei-Sterne-Campingplatz, m
♦ three-star campsite
♦ three-star campground *AE*
♦ three-star camping site *BE*
♦ three-star camping ground *BE*
♦ three-star site
Drei-Sterne-Caravanplatz, m
♦ three-star caravan site *BE*
♦ three-star trailer site *AE*
Drei-Sterne-Club, m
♦ three-star club
Drei-Sterne-Einrichtung, f
♦ three-star facility
Drei-Sterne-Einstufung, f
♦ three-star grading
Drei-Sterne-Ferienwohnung, f
Drei-Sterne-Fewo f
♦ three-star vacation apartment *AE*
♦ three-star holiday flat *BE*
Drei-Sterne-Haus, n
→ Drei-Sterne-Hotel
Drei-Sterne-Hotel, n
♦ three-star hotel
Drei-Sterne-Hotelanlage, f
Drei-Sterne-Hotelkomplex m
♦ three-star hotel complex

Drei-Sterne-Hotelservice, m
♦ three-star hotel service
Dreisternekategorie, f
→ Drei-Sterne-Kategorie
Drei-Sterne-Kategorie f
♦ three-star category
Drei-Sterne-Koch, m
♦ three-star cook
Drei-Sterne-Komfort, m
♦ three-star comfort
♦ three-star amenities *pl*
Drei-Sterne-Kreuzfahrtschiff, n
♦ three-star cruise ship
♦ three-star cruise liner
Drei-Sterne-Küchenchef, m
♦ three-star chef
Drei-Sterne-Lokal, n (generell)
♦ three-star place
♦ three-star spot
Drei-Sterne-Lokal, n (Restaurant)
→ Drei-Sterne-Restaurant
Drei-Sterne-Luxus, m
♦ three-star luxury
Drei-Sterne-Luxushaus, n
→ Drei-Sterne-Luxushotel
Drei-Sterne-Luxushotel, n
♦ three-star deluxe hotel *AE*
♦ three-star luxury hotel
Drei-Sterne-Niveau, n
♦ three-star level
Drei-Sterne-Platz, m (Camping)
♦ three-star site
Drei-Sterne-Platz, m (Tennis)
♦ three-star court
Drei-Sterne-Preis, m
♦ three-star price
♦ three-star rate
Drei-Sterne-Qualität, f
♦ three-star quality
Drei-Sterne-Residenz, f
♦ three-star residence
Drei-Sterne-Restaurant n
♦ three-star restaurant
Drei-Sterne-Segment, n
♦ three-star segment
Drei-Sterne-Sektor, m
→ Drei-Sterne-Bereich
Drei-Sterne-Service, m
♦ three-star service
Drei-Sterne-Stadthotel, n (Großstadt)
♦ three-star city hotel
Drei-Sterne-Stadthotel, n (kleine Stadt)
♦ three-star town hotel
Drei-Sterne-Standard m
♦ three-star standard
Drei-Sterne-System, n
♦ three-star system
Drei-Sterne-Tagungsort, m
Drei-Sterne-Austragungsort, m
♦ three-star venue
Drei-Sterne-Unterbringung, f
→ Drei-Sterne-Unterkunft
Drei-Sterne-Unterkunft, f
Drei-Sterne-Unterbringung, f
♦ three-star accommodation
♦ three-star lodging *AE*
Drei-Sterne-Wohnwagenplatz, m
♦ three-star trailer site *AE*
♦ three-star caravan site *BE*
Drei-Sterne-Zimmer, n
♦ three-star room

dreistöckig

dreistöckig, adj attr (Gebäude)
- three-story, adj attr
- three-storey, adj attr *BE*
- three-floor, adj attr

dreistöckig, adj (Bett, Kuchen)
- three-tier, adj
- three-tiered, adj

dreistöckig, adj prd (Gebäude)
- three-storied, adj prd *AE*
- three-storeyed, adj prd *BE*

dreistöckiges Bett, n
- three-tier bed
- three-tiered bed

dreistöckiges Etagenbett n
- three-tier bunk bed
- three-tiered bunk bed

dreistöckiges Hotel, n
- three-story hotel *AE*
- three-storey hotel *BE*
- three-floor hotel

dreistündig, adj
- three-hour, adj
- lasting three hours
- of three hours' duration
- three hours', adj

dreistündiger Marsch, m
- three hours' march

dreistündiges Programm, n
- three-hour program *AE*
- three-hour programme *BE*

dreistündige Verspätung, f
- three-hour delay

Dreitagearrangement, n
- three-day arrangement

Dreitageaufenthalt, m
dreitägiger Aufenthalt, m
- three-day stay
- three days' stay
- stay of three days

Dreitagepaß, m
- three-day pass

Dreitagepauschale, f
- three-day package

Dreitagepauschalpreis, m
- three-day inclusive price
- three-day inclusive rate
- three-day package price
- three-day package rate

Dreitagepreis, m
- three-day rate
- three-day price
- rate for three days
- price for three days

Dreitageprogramm, n
dreitägiges Programm n
- three-day program *AE*
- three-day programme *BE*
- three days' program *AE*
- three days' programme *BE*
- program of three days *AE*

Dreitagerechnung, f
- three-day bill
- three-day check *AE*

Dreitagerennen, n
- three-day race

Dreitageskipaß, m
- three-day ski pass

dreitägig, adj
- three-day, adj
- three days', adj

- of three days' duration
- lasting three days

dreitägige Reise, f
- three-day journey
- three-day tour
- three-day trip
- three days' journey

dreitägiger Hotelaufenthalt, m
- three-day hotel stay
- three-day stay at a hotel
- three-day stay in a hotel

dreitägiger Urlaub, m
- three-day vacation *AE*
- three-day holiday *BE*

dreitägige Veranstaltung, f
- three-day event
- event lasting three days
- three-day function
- function lasting three days

dreitüriges Auto, n
- three-door car

Dreiviertelliterflasche Wein, f
- quart bottle of wine

Dreiwochenpauschale, f
- three-week package

Dreiwochenpauschalpreis, m
- three-week inclusive price
- three-week inclusive rate
- three-week package price
- three-week package rate

Dreiwochenpreis, m
- three-week price
- three-week rate
- rate for three weeks
- price for three weeks

dreiwöchig, adj
- three-week, adj
- three weeks', adj
- of three weeks' duration
- lasting three weeks

dreiwöchiger Aufenthalt, m
- three-week stay
- three weeks' stay
- stay of three weeks

dreiwöchige Reise, f
- three-week tour
- three-week journey
- three-week trip

dreiwöchige Tournee, f
- three-week tour

dreizehntes Stockwerk, n
dreizehnte Etage, f
dreizehntes Geschoß, n
- fourteenth floor *AE*
- fourteenth story *AE*
- thirteenth floor *BE*
- thirteenth storey *BE*

Dreizimmerappartement n
- three-room apartment

Dreizimmerferienwohnung, f
- three-room vacation apartment *AE*
- three-room holiday flat *BE*

dreizimmerig, adj
- three-roomed, adj

dreizimmeriges Appartement, n
- three-roomed apartment
- three-room apartment

dreizimmerige Suite, f
- three-roomed suite

dreizimmerige Wohnung, f
- three-roomed flat *BE*
- three-roomed apartment *AE*

Dreizimmersuite, f
- three-room suite

Dreizimmerwohnung, f
Dreiraumwohnung, f *dial*
- three-room flat *BE*
- three-room apartment *AE*

Dressing, n *gastr*
Salatsoße, n *gastr*
- dressing *gastr*

dringend, adj
- urgent, adj

dringend benötigen etw
- require s.th. urgently

dringende Einladung, f
- pressing invitation

Dringlichkeitsliste f
- priority list

Dringlichkeitssitzung, f
Notsitzung, f
- emergency meeting

Drink, m
→ Getränk

Drink genießen
Getränk genießen
- enjoy a drink
- enjoy a beverage

Drink genießen auf der Terrasse
- enjoy a drink on the terrace
- enjoy a drink on the patio

Drink mixen
→ Getränk mixen

Drink mixen jm
- fix s.o. a drink

Drink nehmen
trinken etw
- have a drink
- take a drink

Drink servieren
Drink reichen
Getränk servieren
Getränk reichen
- serve a drink

dritte Etage, f
→ drittes Stockwerk

dritte Klasse, f
- third class

Dritte-Klasse-Rückfahrkarte, f
- third-class return ticket

dritter Gang, m (Menü)
- third course

dritter Gang, m (Motor)
- third gear

dritter Klasse reisen
dritter Klasse fahren
- travel third class

Dritter Oberkellner, m
- third headwaiter

dritter Rang, m (Theater)
- gallery

drittes Bett wird, wie gewünscht, zur Verfügung gestellt
- third bed will be provided as requested

drittes Stockwerk, n
dritte Etage, f
drittes Obergeschoß, n
- fourth floor *AE*
- fourth story *AE*

◆ third floor BE
◆ third storey BE
drittes Vierteljahr, n
 ◆ **third quarter**
dritte Welt, f
 ◆ **third world**
Dritte-Welt-Tourismus, m
 Tourismus in die dritte Welt, m
 ◆ **third world tourism**
Dritte-Welt-Tourist, m
 ◆ **third world tourist**
Dritte-Welt-Ziel, n
 ◆ **third world destination**
Dritthaus, n
 drittes Haus, n
 ◆ **third home**
 ◆ **third house**
drittklassig, adj
 ◆ **third-class, adj**
 ◆ **third-rate, adj** coll
drittklassiges Hotel, n
 ◆ **third-class hotel**
 ◆ **third-rate hotel** coll
drittklassiges Zimmer, n
 ◆ **third-class room**
 ◆ **third-rate room** coll
Drittreise, f
 dritte Reise, f
 ◆ **third trip**
 ◆ **third journey**
 ◆ **third tour**
Dritturlaub, m
 dritter Urlaub, m
 ◆ **third vacation** AE
 ◆ **third holiday** BE
Drive-in-Einrichtung, f
 ◆ **drive-in facility**
Driving Range, f
 (Golf)
 ◆ **driving range**
Drogenverkäufer, m
 ◆ **drug dealer**
 ◆ **drug pusher**
Drogerie, f
 ◆ **drugstore** AE
 ◆ **chemist's shop** BE
 ◆ **chemist's** BE
Droschke, f
 Pferdedroschke, f hist
 ◆ **hackney coach** hist
 ◆ **hackney carriage** hist
 ◆ **hackney cab** hist
 ◆ **cab**
Droschkenmuseum, n
 ◆ **hackney carriage museum**
 ◆ **hackney cab museum**
Druckbuchstaben, m pl
 Druckschrift, f
 ◆ **block letters** pl
drückende Atmosphäre, f
 ◆ **stifling atmosphere**
drucken etw
 ◆ **print s.th.**
Drucker, m
 (Person oder Gerät)
 ◆ **printer**
Druckerei, f
 ◆ **printing office**
 ◆ **print shop**
Druckfahne, f
 ◆ **proof**

Druckkosten, pl
 ◆ **printing costs** pl
 ◆ **printing cost**
 ◆ **cost of printing**
 ◆ **printing expenses** pl
Drucksache, f
 ◆ **printed matter**
 ◆ **second class matter** AE
 ◆ **second class** AE
Druckschrift, f
 → Druckbuchstaben
Druckstück, n
 ◆ **piece of print**
Druck- und Büromaterial, n
 ◆ **printing and stationery**
Dschungelfieber, n
 ◆ **jungle fever**
Dschungeltour, f
 Dschungelreise, f
 ◆ **jungle tour**
Dschunke, f
 ◆ **junk**
Dubai
 ◆ **Dubai**
 ◆ **Dibai**
Dubonnet, m FR
 ◆ **Dubonnet** FR
Dudelsack, m
 ◆ **bagpipes** pl
Dudelsackmuseum, n
 ◆ **bagpipe museum**
Dudelsackpfeifer, m
 → Dudelsackspieler
Dudelsacksammlung, f
 ◆ **bagpipe collection**
Dudelsackspieler, m
 Dudelsackpfeifer, m
 ◆ **bagpiper**
 ◆ **piper**
Duft, m
 Wohlgeruch, m
 ◆ **fragrance**
duftend, adj
 ◆ **fragrant, adj**
Duftkissen, n
 ◆ **sachet**
Dumpingpreis, m
 ◆ **dumping price**
 ◆ **dumping rate**
 ◆ **cut price**
Düne, f
 ◆ **dune**
Dünenbuggy, m
 (Auto)
 ◆ **dune buggy**
Dünenbuggyfahrt, f
 ◆ **dune-buggy trip**
 ◆ **dune-buggy ride**
 ◆ **dune-buggy tour**
Dünenstrand, m
 ◆ **beach with dunes**
dunkler Anzug, m
 ◆ **dark suit**
dunkler Sirup, m
 Rübensirup, m
 Melasse, f
 ◆ **treacle**
dunkles Bier, n
 ◆ **dark beer**
 ◆ **porter**

 ◆ **brown ale** BE
 ◆ **mild** BE
dunkles Brot, n
 Schwarzbrot, n
 ◆ **dark bread**
dünnbesiedelt, adj
 ◆ **sparsely populated, adj**
dünnbesiedeltes Gebiet, n
 ◆ **sparsely populated area**
Dünnbier, n
 → Lagerbier
dünner Kaffee, m
 ◆ **thin coffee**
dünner Tee, m
 ◆ **weak tea**
dünn geschnitten, adj
 dünn in Scheiben geschnitten, adj
 ◆ **thinly sliced, adj**
Dünnpfiff, m sl
 flotter Otto, m sl
 Durchmarsch, m fam
 Diarrhö, f
 ◆ **trots, the** BE pl sl
 ◆ **runs, the** BE pl sl
Dünnpfiff bekommen
 Durchfall bekommen
 ◆ **get the trots**
 ◆ **get the runs**
Dünnschiß, m vulg
 Diarrhö, f
 ◆ **shits, the, pl** vulg
dünsten (etw)
 ◆ **steam (s.th.)**
Duplex-Wohnung, f
 → Maisonettewohnung
Durchblick, m
 Vista f
 ◆ **vista**
Durchblick haben auf etw
 ◆ **have a vista of s.th.**
durchbuchen
 ◆ **book through**
durch die Paßkontrolle gehen
 ◆ **pass through passport control**
durchfahren die ganze Nacht
 die ganze Nacht durchfahren
 ◆ **travel all night**
Durchfall, m
 Diarrhö, f
 Diarrhöe, f
 ◆ **diarrhoea**
 ◆ **diarrhea**
Durchfall haben
 ◆ **have diarrhoea**
 ◆ **have diarrhea**
durchfeiern bis zum Morgen
 ◆ **make a night of it**
 ◆ **feast away the night**
durchfeiern die ganze Nacht
 durchzechen die ganze Nacht
 bis zum Morgen durchfeiern
 bis zum Morgen durchzechen
 ◆ **feast away the night**
 ◆ **make a night of it** coll
durchfliegen (generell)
 ◆ **fly through**
durchfliegen (nonstop)
 → nonstop fliegen
durchfressen sich bei jm vulg
 einnisten sich bei jm

durchführbar

nassauern bei jm
- ♦ sponge on s.o.

durchführbar, adj
machbar, adj
- ♦ feasible, adj

Durchführbarkeitsstudie, f
- ♦ feasibility study

Durchführbarkeitsstudie in Auftrag geben
- ♦ commission a feasibility study

Durchführbarkeitsstudie machen
- ♦ undertake a feasibility study
- ♦ carry out a feasibility study

durchführen etw
- ♦ run s.th.
- ♦ operate s.th.
- ♦ organise s.th.

Durchführung, f
Umsetzung, f
Ausführung, f
- ♦ implementation

Durchführung einer Veranstaltung, f
- ♦ running (of) an event
- ♦ organisation of an event

Durchgangsbahnhof, m
- ♦ through station

Durchgangscampingplatz, m
Durchgangsplatz, m
- ♦ transit campsite
- ♦ transit campground AE
- ♦ transit camping site BE
- ♦ transit camping ground BE
- ♦ transit site

Durchgangscaravan, m
Durchgangswohnwagen, m
Caravan auf der Durchreise, m
Wohnwagen auf der Durchreise, m
- ♦ transit caravan BE
- ♦ transit trailer AE

Durchgangsgast, m
Durchreisender, m
- ♦ transient AE
- ♦ transient guest AE

Durchgangshotel, n
→ Transithotel

Durchgangskunde, m
Passant m
- ♦ transient customer
- ♦ transient guest
- ♦ customer passing through

Durchgangslager, n
Transitlager, n
- ♦ transit camp

Durchgangsland, n
Transitland n
- ♦ transit country

Durchgangsplatz, m
(Camping)
- ♦ transit site

Durchgangsstraße, f
- ♦ thoroughfare
- ♦ through road BE

Durchgangstür, f
→ Verbindungstür

Durchgangsverkehr, m
- ♦ through traffic

Durchgangsvisum, n
→ Transitvisum

Durchgangswohnwagen, m
Durchgangscaravan, m
Wohnwagen auf der Durchreise, m
Caravan auf der Durchreise, m

- ♦ transit trailer AE
- ♦ transit caravan BE

durchgebraten, adj
bien cuit, adj FR
- ♦ well done, adj
- ♦ done, adj
- ♦ bien cuit, adj FR

durchgehender Zug, m
D-Zug m
- ♦ through train
- ♦ direct train

durchgehend geöffnet, adj
- ♦ permanently open, adj
- ♦ open 24 hours, adj
- ♦ open all day, adj

durchgekocht, adj
- ♦ cooked through, adj

durchgelegen, adj (Matratze, Bett)
- ♦ worn, adj

durchgelegene Matratze f
- ♦ worn mattress

durchgelegenes Bett n
- ♦ worn bed

durchhängendes Bett, n
- ♦ sagging bed

Durchlauferhitzer, m
Warmwasserbereiter, m
Heißwasserbereiter, m
- ♦ geyser BE
- ♦ water heater

durchlüften ein Zimmer
Durchzug machen in einem Zimmer
- ♦ ventilate a room
- ♦ air a room thoroughly

durchlüften etw
- ♦ air s.th. thoroughly
- ♦ ventilate s.th.

durchqueren etw (von A nach B)
- ♦ traverse s.th. (from A to B)

Durchreiche f
- ♦ service hatch
- ♦ hatch

durchreisen
auf der Durchreise sein
- ♦ travel through
- ♦ pass through

Durchreisender, m (Gasttyp)
Durchreisende, f
- ♦ transient guest AE
- ♦ transient AE
- ♦ chance guest
- ♦ temporary guest

Durchreisender, m (generell)
- ♦ passing traveller
- ♦ passing traveler AE

Durchreisender, m (Transitreisender)
Transitreisender, m
- ♦ passenger in transit

durchreisender Autofahrer m
- ♦ motorist passing through
- ♦ motorist en route

durchreisender Besucher, m
vorbeireisender Besucher, m
- ♦ passing visitor

durchreisender Tourist, m
vorbeireisender Tourist, m
- ♦ passing tourist
- ♦ transient tourist

durchreisen durch eine Stadt
durch eine Stadt fahren
- ♦ pass through a town

Durchreisetourist, m
durchreisender Tourist, m
- ♦ transient tourist

Durchreisevisum, n
→ Transitvisum

Durchsage, f
Ansage, f
- ♦ announcement

Durchsage machen
Ansage machen
- ♦ make an announcement

Durchsage machen über die Lautsprecheranlage
Durchsage machen über den Lautsprecher
- ♦ make an announcement on the intercom
- ♦ make an announcement over the intercom

durchschlafen
- ♦ sleep through
- ♦ sleep without waking

durchschlafen bei etw
(z.B. Lärm)
- ♦ sleep through s.th.

Durchschlag, m gastr
→ Siebschüssel

Durchschnitt, m
- ♦ average

durchschnittlich, adj
- ♦ average, adj

durchschnittlich 10 Minuten Verspätung haben
- ♦ be delayed by an average of 10 minutes

durchschnittliche Aufenthaltsdauer, f
durchschnittliche Verweildauer, f
- ♦ average length of stay

durchschnittliche Aufenthaltsdauer fiel von 2 auf 1 Tag
- ♦ average length of stay dropped from 2 to 1 day

durchschnittliche Aufenthaltsdauer ging von 5 auf 3 Tage zurück
- ♦ average length of stay declined from 5 to 3 days

durchschnittliche Aufenthaltsdauer nahm von 6 auf 5 Tage ab
- ♦ average length of stay decreased from 6 to 5 days

durchschnittliche Aufenthaltsdauer stieg von 8 auf 10 Tage
- ♦ average length of stay increased from 8 to 10 days

durchschnittliche Auslandsankünfte, f pl
(aus dem Ausland)
- ♦ average foreign arrivals pl
- ♦ average overseas arrivals BE pl

durchschnittliche Auslastung, f
Durchschnittsauslastung, f
- ♦ average load factor

durchschnittliche Belegungsrate haben von 60%
durchschnittliche Auslastungsrate haben von 60%
- ♦ average a 60% occupancy rate

durchschnittliche Bettenauslastung, f
durchschnittliche Bettenbelegung, f
- ♦ average bed occupancy

durchschnittliche Bettenauslastungsquote, f
durchschnittliche Bettenauslastungsrate, f
- ♦ average bed occupancy rate

durchschnittliche Bettenbelegung, f
→ durchschnittliche Bettenauslastung

durchschnittliche Bettenzahl f
- ♦ average number of beds

durchschnittliche Einnahmen, f pl
- ♦ **average takings** *pl*
- ♦ average receipts *pl*

durchschnittliche Einnahme pro Hotelzimmer, f
- ♦ **average income per hotel room**
- ♦ average revenue per hotel room

durchschnittliche Fixkosten, pl
- ♦ **average fixed cost**
- ♦ average fixed costs *pl*

durchschnittliche Gebühr, f
- ♦ **average charge**
- ♦ average fee

durchschnittliche Gesamtauslastung, f
- ♦ **average total load factor**

durchschnittliche Gesamtbelegung, f
  durchschnittliche Gesamtauslastung, f
- ♦ **average total occupancy**

durchschnittliche Gesamtkundenzahl, f
- ♦ **average client total**
- ♦ average customer total

durchschnittliche Hotelauslastung, f
  durchschnittliche Hotelbelegung, f
- ♦ **average hotel occupancy**

durchschnittliche Jahresauslastung, f
  durchschnittliche jährliche Auslastung, f
- ♦ **average annual load factor**

durchschnittliche Jahresbelegung, f
  durchschnittliche jährliche Auslastung, f
  durchschnittliche Jahresauslastung, f
  durchschnittliche jährliche Belegung, f
- ♦ **average annual occupancy**

durchschnittliche Jahresfrequenz, f
  → durchschnittliche Jahresauslastung

durchschnittliche jährliche Wochenendauslastung, f
- ♦ **average annual weekend load factor**

durchschnittliche jährliche Wochenendbelegung, f
  durchschnittliche jährliche Wochenendauslastung, f
- ♦ **average annual weekend occupancy**

durchschnittliche jährliche Zimmerauslastung, f
  durchschnittliche jährliche Zimmerbelegung, f
- ♦ **average annual room occupancy**

durchschnittliche Kosten pro Übernachtung, pl
- ♦ **average costs per night** *pl*
- ♦ average cost per night

durchschnittliche monatliche Auslastung, f
  durchschnittliche Monatsauslastung, f
- ♦ **average monthly load factor**

durchschnittliche monatliche Nachfrage, f
- ♦ **average monthly demand**

durchschnittliche monatliche Verweildauer, f
- ♦ **average monthly length of stay**

durchschnittliche Monatsauslastung, f
- ♦ **average monthly load factor**
- ♦ average load factor per month

durchschnittliche Monatsbelegung, f
  durchschnittliche monatliche Auslastung, f
  durchschnittliche Monatsauslastung, f
  durchschnittliche monatliche Belegung, f
- ♦ **average monthly occupancy**
- ♦ average occupancy per month

durchschnittlichen Komfort anbieten
- ♦ **offer average comfort**

durchschnittliche Qualität, f
  Durchschnittsqualität, f
- ♦ **average quality**

durchschnittlicher Anteil, m
  Durchschnittsanteil, m
- ♦ **average proportion**

durchschnittlicher Beherbergungserlös, m
- ♦ **average room revenue**
- ♦ average rooms revenue

durchschnittlicher Beherbergungsertrag, m
- ♦ **average room income**
- ♦ average rooms income
- ♦ average room revenue
- ♦ average rooms revenue

durchschnittlicher Buchungseingang, m
- ♦ **average receipt of bookings**

durchschnittliche Reise, f
  Durchschnittsreise, f
- ♦ **average tour**
- ♦ average trip
- ♦ average journey

durchschnittliche Reisegeschwindigkeit, f (Flug)
- ♦ **average cruising speed**
- ♦ average cruise speed

durchschnittlicher Gewinn pro Essen, m
- ♦ **average profit per meal**

durchschnittlicher Komfort, m
- ♦ **average comfort**

durchschnittlicher Lagerbestand, m
  Lagerdurchschnittsbestand, m
- ♦ **average stock**

durchschnittlicher Mittagessenbetrag, m
- ♦ **average lunch check** *AE*

durchschnittlicher Rechnungsbetrag, m
  (Restaurant)
- ♦ **average check** *AE*

durchschnittlicher Rechnungsbetrag, m
  (Restaurantumsatz durch Zahl der
  Gästerechnungen)
- ♦ **check average**

durchschnittlicher Rechnungsbetrag für Getränke, m
  (vgl. Check Average)
- ♦ **beverage check average** *AE*

durchschnittlicher Rechnungsbetrag für Speisen, m
  (vgl. Check Average)
- ♦ **food check average** *AE*

durchschnittlicher Rechnungsgesamtbetrag, m
  (Restaurant)
- ♦ **total check average** *AE*

durchschnittlicher Reisepreis, m
  Durchschnittsreisepreis, m
- ♦ **average tour price**

durchschnittlicher Restaurantrechnungsbetrag, m
- ♦ **average restaurant check** *AE*

durchschnittlicher Speisenbetrag, m
- ♦ **average food check** *AE*

durchschnittlicher Speisenerlös, m
- ♦ **average food revenue**
- ♦ average food sales *pl*
- ♦ average food proceeds *pl*

durchschnittlicher Speisenerlös pro Gast, m
- ♦ **average food revenue per guest**
- ♦ average food sales per guest *pl*
- ♦ average food proceeds per guest *pl*

durchschnittlicher Speisenumsatz, m
- ♦ **average food sales** *pl*

durchschnittlicher Tagespreis, m
  Tagesdurchschnittspreis, m
- ♦ **average daily rate**
- ♦ average daily price

durchschnittlicher Umsatz pro Verkaufsstelle, m
- ♦ **average turnover per sales outlet**

durchschnittlicher Urlaubsaufwand pro Person, m
  durchschnittlicher Ferienaufwand pro Person, m
- ♦ **average vacation expenditure per person** *AE*
- ♦ average holiday expenditure per person *BE*

durchschnittlicher Verkaufspreis, m
- ♦ **average selling price**
- ♦ average selling rate

durchschnittlich erzielter Zimmerpreis, m
- ♦ **average room rate achieved**
- ♦ average room rate
- ♦ average rate per room

durchschnittlicher Zimmerpreis, m
  Durchschnittszimmerpreis, m
- ♦ **average room rate**

durchschnittliches Appartement n
  Durchschnittsappartement n
- ♦ **average apartment**

durchschnittliches Hotel, n
  Durchschnittshotel, n
- ♦ **average hotel**

durchschnittliche Sitzauslastung, f
- ♦ **average seat load factor**

durchschnittliches Zimmer n
  Durchschnittszimmer n
- ♦ **average room**

durchschnittliche Tagesausgabe, f
  Durchschnittsausgabe pro Tag, m
- ♦ **average daily expenditure**
- ♦ average expenditure per day

durchschnittliche Tagesauslastung, f
- ♦ **average daily load factor**

durchschnittliche Tagesbelegung, f
  durchschnittliche tägliche Auslastung, f
  durchschnittliche Tagesauslastung, f
  durchschnittliche tägliche Belegung, f
- ♦ **average daily occupancy**

durchschnittliche tägliche Auslastung, f
  → durchschnittliche Tagesauslastung

durchschnittliche tägliche Zimmerauslastung, f
  durchschnittliche tägliche Zimmerbelegung, f
- ♦ **average daily room occupancy**

durchschnittliche Verweildauer, f
  → durchschnittliche Aufenthaltsdauer

durchschnittliche Verweildauer der Besucher, f
- ♦ **average length of stay of visitors**

durchschnittliche Warenkosten, pl
- ♦ **average cost of sale**

durchschnittliche Warenkosten pro Essen, pl
- ♦ **average cost of sale per meal**

durchschnittliche Wochenauslastung, f
  → durchschnittliche Wochenauslastung

durchschnittliche Wochenbelegung, f
  durchschnittliche wöchentliche Auslastung, f
  durchschnittliche Wochenauslastung, f
  durchschnittliche wöchentliche Belegung, f
- ♦ **average weekly occupancy**

durchschnittliche Wochenendbelegung, f
  durchschnittliche Wochenendauslastung, f
- ♦ **average weekend occupancy**

durchschnittliche wöchentliche Auslastung, f
  → durchschnittliche Wochenauslastung

durchschnittliche wöchentliche Verweildauer, f
- ♦ **average weekly length of stay**

durchschnittliche Wohnung, f
  Durchschnittswohnung, f
- ♦ **average flat** *BE*
- ♦ average apartment *AE*

durchschnittliche Zimmerauslastung, f
  durchschnittliche Zimmerbelegung, f
- ♦ **average room occupancy**

durchschnittliche Zimmerauslastungsrate

durchschnittliche Zimmerauslastungsrate, f
 ♦ average room occupancy rate
durchschnittliche Zimmerbelegung, f
 → durchschnittliche Zimmerauslastung
durchschnittliche Zimmerkosten, pl
 ♦ average room costs *pl*
 ♦ average room cost
durchschnittliche Zimmerzahl pro Hotel, f
 ♦ average number of rooms per hotel
Durchschnittsalter, n
 ♦ average age
Durchschnittsappartement n
 → durchschnittliches Appartement
Durchschnittsausgabe, f
 durchschnittliche Ausgabe, f
 ♦ average expenditure
 ♦ average spending
 ♦ average spend
Durchschnittsausgabe für Getränke, f
 ♦ average spending on drink
 ♦ average spend on drink
Durchschnittsausgabe für Speisen, f
 ♦ average spending on food
 ♦ average spend on food
Durchschnittsausgabe pro Besuch, f
 durchschnittliche Ausgabe pro Besuch, f
 ♦ average expenditure per visit
Durchschnittsausgabe pro Besucher, f
 durchschnittliche Ausgabe pro Besucher, f
 ♦ average expenditure per visitor
Durchschnittsausgabe pro Gast, f
 durchschnittliche Ausgabe pro Gast, f
 ♦ average expenditure per guest
 ♦ average guest expenditure
 ♦ average spending per guest
 ♦ average spend per guest
Durchschnittsausgabe pro Gedeck, f
 ♦ average spending per cover
 ♦ average spend per cover
Durchschnittsausgabe pro Kunde, f
 durchschnittliche Ausgabe pro Kunde, f
 ♦ average expenditure per customer
 ♦ average spending per customer
 ♦ average spend per customer
Durchschnittsausgabe pro Person, f
 ♦ average spending per person
Durchschnittsausgabe pro Tag, f
 durchschnittliche Ausgabe pro Tag, f
 ♦ average expenditure per day
 ♦ average daily expenditure
Durchschnittsausgabe pro Tag und Person, f
 durchschnittliche Ausgabe pro Tag und Person, f
 ♦ average expenditure per day per person
Durchschnittsauslastung, f
 → durchschnittliche Auslastung
Durchschnittsauslastung betrug 50 Gäste pro Woche
 ♦ average occupancy was 20 guests per week
Durchschnittsbeherbergungserlös, m
 → durchschnittlicher Beherbergungserlös
Durchschnittsbelegung, f
 durchschnittliche Auslastung, f
 Durchschnittsauslastung, f
 durchschnittliche Belegung, f
 ♦ average occupancy
Durchschnittsbelegung von 60%, f
 durchschnittliche Auslastung von 60%, f
 Durchschnittsauslastung von 60%, f
 durchschnittliche Belegung von 60%, f
 ♦ average occupancy of 60%

Durchschnittsbesucher, m
 durchschnittlicher Besucher, m
 ♦ average visitor
Durchschnittseinkommen, n
 durchschnittlichen Einkommen, n
 ♦ average income
Durchschnittseinnahmen, f pl
 durchschnittlichen Einnahmen f pl
 ♦ average receipts *pl*
 ♦ average takings *pl*
 ♦ average income
 ♦ average revenue
Durchschnittserlös, m
 durchschnittlicher Erlös, m
 ♦ average proceeds *pl*
 ♦ average revenue
Durchschnittserlös pro Gedeck, m
 durchschnittlicher Erlös pro Gedeck m
 ♦ average receipt per food cover
 ♦ average check per cover *AE*
Durchschnittsertrag, m
 durchschnittlicher Ertrag, m
 ♦ average earning
 ♦ average earnings *pl*
 ♦ average income
Durchschnittsgast m
 ♦ average guest
 ♦ average visitor
Durchschnittsgeschwindigkeit, f
 ♦ average speed
Durchschnittsgewinn, m
 durchschnittlicher Gewinn, m
 ♦ average profit
Durchschnittsgröße f
 (von Zimmer etc.)
 ♦ average size
Durchschnittshotel, n
 → durchschnittliches Hotel
Durchschnittskosten, pl
 durchschnittliche Kosten, pl
 ♦ average costs *pl*
 ♦ average cost
Durchschnittskosten pro Einheit, pl
 durchschnittliche Kosten pro Einheit, pl
 Durchschnittskosten pro Stück, pl
 durchschnittliche Kosten pro Stück, pl
 ♦ average unit costs *pl*
 ♦ average unit cost
Durchschnittsmiete, f
 durchschnittliche Miete f
 ♦ average rent
Durchschnittsmonat, m
 durchschnittlicher Monat, m
 ♦ average month
Durchschnittspreis, m
 ♦ average price
 ♦ average rate
 ♦ average charge
Durchschnittspreis pro belegtes Zimmer, m
 ♦ average rate per occupied room
 ♦ average price per occupied room
Durchschnittspreis pro Gast, m
 ♦ average rate per guest
 ♦ average price per guest
Durchschnittspreis pro Mahlzeit, m
 durchschnittlicher Preis pro Mahlzeit, m
 ♦ average price per meal
 ♦ average price of a meal
Durchschnittspreis pro Zimmer, m
 ♦ average rate per room
 ♦ average price per room

Durchschnittsrate, f
 → Durchschnittspreis
Durchschnittsrendite, f
 ♦ average return
 ♦ average yield
Durchschnittssaison f
 durchschnittliche Saison f
 ♦ average season
Durchschnittstag, m
 durchschnittlicher Tag, m
 ♦ average day
Durchschnittstemperatur, f
 durchschnittliche Temperatur f
 ♦ average temperature
Durchschnittstourist, m
 durchschnittlicher Tourist, m
 ♦ average tourist
Durchschnittsumsatz, m
 durchschnittlicher Umsatz, m
 ♦ average sales *pl*
 ♦ average turnover
Durchschnittsumsatz pro Gast, m
 durchschnittlicher Umsatz pro Gast m
 ♦ average sales per guest *pl*
 ♦ average turnover per guest
Durchschnittsumsatz pro Jahr, m
 durchschnittlicher Umsatz pro Jahr m
 ♦ average sales per year *pl*
 ♦ average turnover per year
Durchschnittsumsatz pro Monat, m
 durchschnittlicher Umsatz pro Monat m
 ♦ average sales per month *pl*
 ♦ average turnover per month
Durchschnittsumsatz pro Tag, m
 durchschnittlicher Umsatz pro Tag m
 ♦ average sales per day *pl*
 ♦ average turnover per day
Durchschnittsumsatz pro Woche, m
 durchschnittlicher Umsatz pro Woche m
 ♦ average sales per week *pl*
 ♦ average turnover per week
Durchschnittsurlauber m
 ♦ average vacationer *AE*
 ♦ average holidaymaker *BE*
Durchschnittswoche, f
 durchschnittliche Woche, f
 ♦ average week
Durchschnittswohnung f
 → durchschnittliche Wohnung f
Durchschnittszahl, f
 ♦ average number
Durchschnittszimmer n
 → durchschnittliches Zimmer
Durchschnittszimmerpreis, m
 → durchschnittlicher Zimmerpreis
durchsuchen jn
 ♦ search s.o.
durchwachsener Speck, m
 ♦ streaky bacon
durchwachsenes Fleisch, n
 ♦ marbled meat
Durchwahltelefon, n
 → Direktwahltelefon
Durchwahlzimmertelefon, n
 Direktwahlzimmertelefon, n
 ♦ direct-dial room telephone
 ♦ direct-dialling room telephone
 ♦ direct-dial room phone
dürftige Mahlzeit, f
 kärgliche Mahlzeit, f

♦ scanty meal
♦ scrap meal
dürftiger Vorrat an etw, m
♦ scanty supply of s.th.
dürftiges Essen, n
dürftige Mahlzeit, f
♦ scrap meal
♦ scanty meal
dürftiges Frühstück, n
kärgliches Frühstück, n
♦ scanty breakfast
dürftig möbliert, adj
schlecht möbliert, adj
♦ poorly furnished, adj
dürftig möbliertes Zimmer n
♦ poorly furnished room
Dürkheimer Faß, n
♦ Dürkheim barrel
Durschnittsreisender, m
durschschnittlicher Reisender, m
♦ average traveller
♦ average traveler AE
Durst, m
♦ thirst
Durst bekommen
♦ get thirsty
♦ become thirsty
Durst haben
durstig sein
♦ be thirsty
Durst haben auf ein Glas Bier
♦ be thirsty for a glass of beer
♦ fancy a glass of beer
durstig, adj
♦ thirsty, adj
durstiger und hungriger Reisender, m
♦ thirsty and hungry traveler AE
♦ thirsty and hungry traveller BE
durstig sein
→ Durst haben
durstig und hungrig, adj
♦ thirsty and hungry, adj
durstig weggehen
♦ go thirsty
♦ leave thirsty
Durst löschen
Durst stillen
♦ quench one's thirst
♦ quench the thirst
♦ slake one's thirst
♦ slake the thirst
durstlöschend, adj
durststillend, adj
♦ thirst-quenching, adj
durstlöschendes Getränk, n
durststillendes Getränk, n
♦ thirst-quenching drink
♦ thirst-quenching beverage
Durstlöscher, m
durstlöschendes Getränk n
♦ thirst-quencher fam
Durst machen
♦ make one thirsty
durstmachender Marsch, m
♦ thirst-making march
durststillend, adj
→ durstlöschend
Durst stillen (mit etw)
Durst löschen (mit etw)
♦ slake one's thirst (with s.th.)
♦ quench one's thirst (with s.th.)

Duschanlage, f
Duschbäder n pl
♦ shower facilities pl
♦ shower baths pl
Duscharmaturen, f pl
♦ shower fittings pl
Duschbad n
→ Dusche
Duschbecken, n
♦ shower base AE
♦ shower basin BE
Duschbenutzung, f
♦ use of the shower
♦ using the shower
Duschbereich, m
♦ shower area
Duschblock, m
(z.B. auf Campingplatz)
♦ shower block
Dusche, f
(Ort und Aktivität)
Douche, f SCHW
♦ shower
♦ shower bath
Dusche benutzen
♦ use a shower
Dusche einbauen
Dusche installieren
♦ install a shower
♦ instal a shower AE
Dusche funktioniert nicht
♦ shower does not work
Duscheinheit f
♦ shower unit
Duscheinrichtung, f
→ Duschgelegenheit
Dusche ist kaputt coll
♦ shower is broken
Dusche ist verstopft
♦ shower is blocked
Dusche mit Kaltwasser, f
♦ shower with cold water
Dusche mit Warmwasser, f
♦ shower with hot water
Dusche nehmen
♦ take a shower
duschen (sich)
♦ have a shower
♦ take a shower
♦ shower
Dusche teilen mit jm
Dusche gemeinsam benutzen mit jm
Dusche mitbenutzen
♦ share a shower with s.o.
Dusche wird von vier Personen benutzt
♦ shower is shared by four persons
Duschgarnitur, f
(Brause, Duschstange etc.)
♦ shower attachment
Duschgebühr, f
♦ shower fee
♦ shower charge
Duschgel, n
♦ shower gel
Duschgelegenheit, f
Duschmöglichkeit, f
Duschvorrichtung, f
Duscheinrichtung, f
♦ shower facility
Duschhaube, f
♦ shower cap

Duschkabine, f (generell)
♦ shower cubicle
Duschkabine, f (Wohnwagen)
→ Duschzelle
Duschlotion, f
♦ shower lotion
Duschraum m
♦ shower room
Duschtür f
♦ shower door
Duschvorhang m
♦ shower curtain
Duschvorrichtung, f
→ Duschgelegenheit
Duschwanne, f
♦ shower tray
Duschzelle, f
(Wohnwagen)
♦ shower compartment
duselig, adj
♦ slaphappy, adj
Duseligkeit, f
♦ slaphappiness
Düsenantrieb, m
Düsenmotor, m
♦ jet engine
Düsenbelüftung, f
(Bus)
♦ jet air ventilation
Düsenflugzeug, n
♦ jet aircraft
♦ jet plane
♦ jet airplane AE
♦ jet aeroplane BE
Düsenlinienflugzeug, n
Düsenjet, m
♦ jet airliner
♦ jetliner
Düsentragflächenboot, n
Düsentragflügelboot, n
♦ jetfoil
düstere Atmosphäre, f
♦ sinister atmosphere
Duty-Free-Geschäft n
Duty-Free-Laden m
♦ duty-free store AE
♦ duty-free shop BE
Dutzend, n
♦ dozen
Duvet, n
→ Federbett
DZ, n
Doppelzimmer, n
♦ d/r
♦ double room
♦ dbl. rm.
DZ-Preis, m
→ Doppelzimmerpreis
DZT, f
Deutsche Zentrale für Tourismus, f
♦ GNTB, the
♦ German National Tourist Board, the
D-Zug, m
durchgehender Zug, m
♦ direct train
♦ through train
D-Zugverbindung, f
♦ direct train connection
♦ direct train link

eben, adj
  ♦ level, adj
ebenerdige Suite, f
  → Erdgeschoßsuite
ebenerdig gelegen, adj
  ♦ situated on the first floor, adj AE
  ♦ situated on the ground floor, adj BE
ebenerdig liegen
  ♦ be located on the first floor AE
  ♦ be situated on the first floor AE
  ♦ be situated on the ground floor BE
  ♦ be located on the ground floor BE
ebener Spazierweg, m
  ebener Wanderweg, m
  ♦ level walk
ebener Stellplatz, m
  (Camping)
  ♦ level pitch
Ebertdenkmal, n
  ♦ Ebert monument
EBK, f
  Einbauküche, f
  ♦ ftd. k.
  ♦ f.k.
  ♦ fitted kitchen
echt chinesische Küche, f
  ♦ authentic Chinese cooking
  ♦ authentic Chinese cuisine
  ♦ genuine Chinese cooking
  ♦ genuine Chinese cuisine
echte Gastfreundschaft, f
  echte Gastlichkeit f
  ♦ true hospitality
echt französische Küche anbieten
  ♦ offer authentic French cuisine
echt französische Küche bieten
  ♦ provide authentic French cuisine
Eckbadewanne, f
  ♦ corner bathtub
  ♦ corner tub
Eckbank, f
  ♦ corner bench
  ♦ nook bench
Eckcafé, n
  Café an der Ecke, n
  ♦ corner cafe AE
  ♦ corner café BE
Eckfenster, n
  ♦ corner window
Eckhaus, n
  ♦ corner house
  ♦ house at a corner
  ♦ house on a corner
Eckhotel, n
  Hotel an der Ecke, n
  ♦ corner hotel

eckiger Tisch, m
  (nicht rund)
  ♦ square table
Eckkamin, m
  ♦ corner fireplace
Eckkneipe, f coll
  Kneipe an der Ecke, f coll
  ♦ bar at the corner AE
  ♦ bar on the corner AE
  ♦ pub at the corner BE coll
Ecklage, f
  ♦ corner location
  ♦ corner position
Eckplatz, m
  (Sitzplatz)
  ♦ corner seat
Eckpreis, m
  → Grundpreis
Eckschrank, m (bes. für Geschirr)
  ♦ corner cupboard
Eckschrank, m (bes. für Kleider)
  ♦ corner wardrobe
Ecksofa, n
  ♦ corner sofa
  ♦ corner couch
  ♦ corner settee
Eckstand, m
  ♦ corner stand
  ♦ corner stall BE
Eckstellplatz, m
  (Camping)
  ♦ corner pitch
Ecktisch, m
  ♦ corner table
Ecktürmchen, n
  ♦ corner turret
Eckzimmer, n
  ♦ corner room
Economat, m SCHW
  → Magazin
Economatgouvernante, f SCHW
  → Magazinverwalterin
Economatverwaltung, f SCHW
  → Magazinverwaltung
Econome, m FR
  Magazinverwalter, m
  Lagerverwalter, m
  ♦ économe FR
  ♦ storekeeper
  ♦ store clerk BE
Economy Class, f
  Economy-Klasse, f
  ♦ economy class
Economy-Class-Buchung, f
  ♦ economy-class booking
Economy-Class-Fahrpreis, m
  ♦ economy-class fare

Economy Class fliegen
  in der Economy Class fliegen
  ♦ fly economy class
Economy-Class-Flug, m
  ♦ economy-class flight
Economy-Class-Passagier, m
  Economy-Class-Fahrgast, m
  ♦ economy-class passenger
Economy-Class-Reservierung, f
  ♦ economy-class reservation
Economyklasse, f
  → Economy Class
Economy-Klasse, f
  → Economy Class
Ecu, m
  European currency unit, f
  ♦ ECU
  ♦ ecu
  ♦ European currency unit
Ecuador
  Ekuador
  ♦ Ecuador
Ecuadorianer, m
  Ekuadorianer, m
  ♦ Ecuadorian
  ♦ Ecuadorean
Ecuadorianerin, f
  Ekuadorianerin, f
  ♦ Ecuadorian girl
  ♦ Ecuadorian woman
  ♦ Ecuadorean
  ♦ Ecuadorean girl
  ♦ Ecuadorean woman
ecuadorianisch, adj
  ekuadorianisch, adj
  ♦ Ecuadorian, adj
  ♦ Ecuadorean, adj
Edamer, m
  ♦ Edam cheese
Edelfäule, f
  Botrytis, f
  ♦ noble rot
  ♦ botrytis
Edelnutte, f fam
  ♦ high-class tart fam
Edelpilzkäse, m
  ♦ blue-veined cheese
Edelstein, m
  ♦ precious stone
Edelsteinausstellung, f
  ♦ exhibition of precious stones
  ♦ exhibit of precious stones AE
edelsüßer Paprika, m
  ♦ sweet paprika
Edeltanne, f
  ♦ silver fir
Edelweiß, n
  ♦ edelweiss

edler Tropfen, m (generell)
 ♦ noble drink
edler Tropfen, m (Wein)
 ♦ noble wine
EDV, f
 elektronische Datenverarbeitung f
 ♦ EDP
 ♦ electronic data processing
EDV-Ausstattung, f
 elektronische Datenverarbeitungsausstattung, f
 ♦ EDP equipment
 ♦ electronic data processing equipment
EDV-Buchungssystem, n
 → Computerbuchungssystem
EDV-Reservierungssystem, n
 → Computerreservierungssystem
EDV-Service, m
 ♦ EDP service
EDV-System, n
 elektronisches Datenverarbeitungssystem, n
 ♦ EDP system
 ♦ electronic data processing system
Effektivbestand, m
 Ist-Bestand, m
 ♦ actual inventory
 ♦ actual stock
effektive Auslastungsquote, f
 effektive Auslastungsrate, f
 tatsächliche Auslastungsquote, f
 tatsächliche Auslastungsrate, f
 ♦ effective occupancy rate
effizienter Service, m
 → leistungsstarker Service
effizientes Personal, n
 ♦ efficient staff
 ♦ efficient personnel
EFH, n
 → Einfamilienhaus
EG, f
 Europäische Gemeinschaft, f
 ♦ EC, the
 ♦ European Community, the
EG, n
 → Erdgeschoß
EG-Bewohner, m
 ♦ EC resident
EG-Land, n
 ♦ EC country
EG-Pauschalreiserichtlinie, f
 ♦ EC package travel directive
 ♦ EC package tour directive
EG-Richtlinie für Pauschalreisen, f
 EG-Richtlinie für Pauschalurlaubsreisen, f
 ♦ EC directive on package tours
 ♦ EC directive on package travel
 ♦ EC directive on package holiday travel BE
EG-Staatsangehöriger, m
 ♦ EC national
Ehefrau, f
 ♦ wife
Ehegatte, m
 ♦ spouse
Ehegattenermäßigung, f
 ♦ spouse reduction
Ehegattenfahrpreis, m
 ♦ spouse fare
Ehegattentarif, m
 ♦ spouse tariff
 ♦ spouse rates pl
 ♦ spouse rate

Ehegattenzuschlag, m
 ♦ spouse supplement
E-Heizung, f
 → Elektroheizung
ehemaliges Hotel, n
 ♦ onetime hotel
 ♦ former hotel
Ehemann, m
 ♦ husband
Ehepaar n
 ♦ married couple
Ehepartner, m
 Ehepartnerin, f
 ♦ marriage partner
 ♦ spouse jur/humor
Ehre haben
 beehren sich (etw zu tun)
 ♦ have the honor AE
 ♦ have the honour (of doing s.th.) BE
Ehrenabend, m
 ♦ evening party in s.o.'s honor AE
 ♦ evening party in s.o.'s honour BE
Ehrengarde, f
 ♦ guard of honor AE
 ♦ guard of honour BE
Ehrengast, m
 ♦ guest of honor AE
 ♦ guest of honour BE
Ehrengast sein bei einem Empfang
 ♦ be guest of honor at a reception AE
 ♦ be guest of honour at a reception BE
Ehrenhof, m
 ♦ court of honor AE
 ♦ court of honour BE
ehren jn
 beehren jn
 ♦ honor s.o. AE
 ♦ honour s.o. BE
Ehrenkarte, f
 → Freikarte, Gratiskarte
Ehrenmitglied, n
 ♦ honorary member
Ehrenplatz, m
 ♦ seat of honor AE
 ♦ seat of honour BE
 ♦ place of honor AE
 ♦ place of honour BE
Ehrenplatz einnehmen
 ♦ occupy the seat of honor AE
 ♦ occupy the seat of honour BE
Ehrenplatz erhalten
 ♦ be given the seat of honor AE
 ♦ be given the seat of honour BE
 ♦ be seated at the place of honor AE
 ♦ be seated at the place of honour BE
Ehrenplatz rechts von jm, m
 ♦ seat of honor to the right of s.o. AE
 ♦ seat of honour to the right of s.o. BE
Ehrenpreis, m (Auszeichnung)
 ♦ prize of honor AE
 ♦ prize of honour BE
 ♦ prize
Ehrenpreis, m (Trostpreis)
 → Trostpreis
Ehrenpreis vergeben (Auszeichnung)
 ♦ award a prize of honor AE
 ♦ award a prize of honour BE
Ehrentisch m
 ♦ honorary table
ehrfurchtgebietend, adj
 ♦ awe-inspiring, adj

ehrfurchtgebietender Berg, m
 ♦ awe-inspiring mountain
Eichamt, n
 (staatlich)
 ♦ Bureau of Standards AE
 ♦ Office of Weights and Measures BE
 ♦ gauging office
Eiche, f
 ♦ oak
Eichenbalken, m
 ♦ oak beam
Eichenbank, f
 ♦ oak bench
Eichenbaum, m
 Eichbaum, m
 Eiche, f
 ♦ oak tree
Eichenboden, m
 ♦ oak floor
Eichendach, n
 ♦ oak roof
eichen etw
 (Meßgeräte)
 ♦ calibrate s.th.
 ♦ gauge s.th.
 ♦ gage s.th.
Eichenfaß, n
 ♦ oak barrel
eichengetäfelt, adj
 ♦ oak-panelled, adj
 ♦ oak-paneled, adj AE
eichengetäfeltes Zimmer, n
 ♦ oak-panelled room
 ♦ oak-paneled room AE
eichengetäfelte Wand, f
 ♦ oak-panelled wall
 ♦ oak-paneled wall AE
Eichenholz, n
 ♦ oakwood
Eichenküche, f
 ♦ oak kitchen
Eichenmöbel, n pl
 ♦ oak furniture sg
Eichenstuhl, m
 ♦ oak chair
Eichentäfelung, f
 ♦ oak paneling AE
 ♦ oak panelling BE
Eichentisch, m
 ♦ oak table
Eichentür, f
 ♦ oak door
Eichenwald, m
 ♦ oak forest
 ♦ oakwood
Eichmarke, f
 (z.B. auf Bierglas)
 Eichstrich m
 ♦ calibration mark
 ♦ calibrating mark
Eichmaß, n
 ♦ calibrating measure
 ♦ gauge
Eichung, f
 ♦ calibration
 ♦ calibrating
Eidophorübertragung f
 (Konferenz)
 ♦ eidophor transmission
Eidophorwand, f
 ♦ eidophor wall

Eidotter, m
  Dotter, m
  ♦ egg yolk
  ♦ yolk
Eierauflauf, m
  → Eiersoufflé
Eierbecher, m
  ♦ eggcup AE
  ♦ egg-cup BE
Eierbuttersoße, f
  ♦ egg and butter sauce
Eierflip, m
  ♦ egg flip
Eierfrucht, f
  Aubergine, f
  ♦ egg-plant
  ♦ aubergine
Eiergericht, n
  Eierspeise f
  ♦ egg dish
Eiergrog, m
  ♦ egg toddy
Eierkotelett, n
  ♦ egg cutlet
Eierkrokette, f
  ♦ egg croquette
Eierkuchen, m
  → Omelett
Eierlaufen, n
  ♦ egg-and-spoon race
Eierlöffel, m
  ♦ egg spoon AE
  ♦ egg-spoon BE
Eiernudel, f
  ♦ egg noodle
Eierpastetchen, n
  ♦ egg patty
Eiersalat, m
  ♦ egg salad
Eiersoße, f
  ♦ egg sauce
Eiersoufflé, n
  Eierauflauf, m
  ♦ egg soufflé
  ♦ egg souffle AE
Eieruhr, f
  ♦ egg timer AE
  ♦ egg-timer BE
Eiervorspeise, f
  ♦ egg entrée
  ♦ egg entree AE
Eierwärmer, m
  ♦ egg cosy AE
  ♦ egg cozy AE
  ♦ egg-cosy BE
Eifel, f
  (Region)
  ♦ Eifel, the
Eifelsee, m
  ♦ Eifel lake
Eiffelturm, m
  ♦ Eiffel Tower, the
Eigelb, n
  Eidotter, m
  Dotter, m
  ♦ yolk
  ♦ egg yolk
Eigelb schlagen
  ♦ beat the yolk
eigenbewirtschaftet, adj
  ♦ owner-managed, adj

eigenbewirtschaftetes Hotel, n
  (vom Eigentümer geführt)
  ♦ owner-managed hotel
eigene Badebucht f
  ♦ private bathing cove
  ♦ private cove
eigene Bettwäsche, f
  ♦ one's own bed linen
eigene Bettwäsche mitbringen
  ♦ bring one's own bed linen
eigene Decken mitbringen
  ♦ bring one's own blankets
eigene Führung, f
  ♦ self-guided tour
eigene Führung machen
  ♦ go on a self-guided tour
eigene Garage, f
  ♦ one's own garage
  ♦ private garage
  ♦ garage of one's own
eigene Küche, f
  ♦ own kitchen
eigene Laken mitbringen
  eigene Bettlaken mitbringen
  ♦ bring one's own sheets
eigenen Restaurantbetrieb führen
  ♦ run one's own restaurant operation
eigenen Schlafsack mitbringen
  ♦ bring one's own sleeping bag
eigenen Wein mitbringen
  ♦ bring one's own wine
eigener Badestrand, m
  → Privatbadestrand
eigener Basketballplatz, m
  ♦ private basketball court
  ♦ basketball court on the premises
eigener Eingang, m
  Privateingang m
  ♦ private entrance
eigener Garten m
  ♦ one's own garden
  ♦ garden of one's own
  ♦ private garden
eigener Safe, m
  eigener Tresor, m
  ♦ safe of one's own
  ♦ private safe
eigener Tresor, m
  → eigener Safe
eigenes Badezimmer, n
  → Privatbadezimmer
eigenes Bettzeug mitbringen
  ♦ bring one's own bedding
eigenes Essen und Trinken stellen
  ♦ provide one's own food and drink
eigenes Gepäck mitbringen
  ♦ bring one's own baggage AE
  ♦ bring one's own luggage BE
eigenes Geschäft haben
  ♦ have a business of one's own
eigenes Haus, n
  ♦ house of one's own
  ♦ one's own house
eigenes Haus haben
  ♦ have a house of one's own
  ♦ have one's own house
eigenes Heim, n
  ♦ home of one's own
  ♦ one's own home
eigenes Heim haben
  eigenes Haus haben

  ♦ have a home of one's own
  ♦ have one's own home
eigene Sportausrüstung mitbringen
  ♦ bring one's own sports equipment
eigenes Restaurant, n
  ♦ one's own restaurant
eigenes Restaurant aufmachen
  ♦ set up one's own restaurant
eigenes Restaurant führen
  ♦ run one's own restaurant
  ♦ manage one's own restaurant
eigenes Schwimmbad, n
  ♦ own swimming pool AE
  ♦ own swimming-pool BE
  ♦ swimming pool of one's own AE
  ♦ private swimming pool AE
  ♦ private swimming-pool BE
eigenes Unterhaltungsprogramm haben
  ♦ have one's own entertainment program AE
  ♦ have one's own entertainment programme BE
eigenes Urteil bilden
  ♦ form one's own judgement
  ♦ form one's own judgment
eigenes Zimmer, n
  Zimmer für sich, n
  ♦ room of one's own
  ♦ one's own room
  ♦ room to oneself
eigenes Zimmer haben
  ♦ have a room of one's own
  ♦ have one's own room
  ♦ have a room to oneself
eigene Wohnung, f
  ♦ one's own apartment AE
  ♦ apartment of one's own AE
  ♦ one's own flat BE
  ♦ flat of one's own BE
eigengenutzt, adj
  (Unterkunft)
  ♦ owner-occupied, adj
eigengenutztes Appartement n
  ♦ owner-occupied apartment
eigengenutztes Haus, n
  Eigenheim n
  ♦ owner-occupied house
eigengenutzte Wohnung, f
  ♦ owner-occupied flat BE
  ♦ owner-occupied apartment AE
Eigenheim, n
  ♦ one's own home
  ♦ one's own house
Eigenheimbesitzer, m
  ♦ owner of a house
Eigenheiminteressent, m
  Eigenheiminteressentin f
  ♦ home seeker
Eigenhotel, n
  ♦ one's own hotel
  ♦ hotel of one's own
  ♦ privately owned hotel
Eigennutzer, m
  (einer Unterkunft)
  ♦ owner-occupier
Eigennutzung, f
  ♦ owner-occupancy
  ♦ own occupation
eigen sein, was das Essen angeht
  ♦ be particular about one's food
Eigentümer, m
  ♦ proprietor

Eigentümer-Betreiber

Eigentümer-Betreiber, m
- owner/operator

Eigentümer-Betreiberlohn, m
- owner/operator salary

Eigentümer der Hotelanlage, m
- proprietor of the hotel complex
- owner of the hotel complex

Eigentümer eines Hotels, m
→ Hoteleigentümer

Eigentümerfamilie, f
- owning family

Eigentümer-Geschäftsführer, m
- owner/manager

Eigentümergesellschaft, f
Eigentümerfirma, f
Besitzergesellschaft, f
Besitzerfirma, f
- owning corporation AE
- owning company BE

Eigentümerin, f
- proprietress

Eigentümersuite, f
- owner's suite

Eigentum kaufen (an Wohnung etc.)
- buy the freehold

eigentümlicher Geschmack m
- strange taste
- odd taste

Eigentumsanlage, f
→ Wohneigentumsanlage

Eigentumsbetrieb, m (Gegensatz zu Kettenbetrieb)
- independent establishment
- independent operation

Eigentumsbetrieb, m (Gegensatz zu Pachtbetrieb)
Eigentümerbetrieb m
- freehold establishment
- freehold operation

Eigentumshaus, n
- freehold house
- one's own house

Eigentumshotel n
(Gegensatz zu Pachthotel)
Eigentümerhotel n
- freehold hotel

Eigentumslokal, n
- freehold premises pl

Eigentumsrecht an Grundbesitz, n
- freehold

Eigentumsurlaubsanlage, f
Eigentumsurlaubskomplex, m
- freehold vacation complex AE
- freehold holiday complex BE

Eigentumsvilla, f
- freehold villa

Eigentumswohnsitz, m
- condominium residence AE

Eigentumswohnung, f (Condominium)
(gehört Privatperson)
- condominium apartment AE
- condominium
- condo AE coll
- condominium residence AE

Eigentumswohnung, f (generell)
ETW, f
- freehold apartment AE
- freehold flat BE

Eigentumswohnung, f (genossenschaftlich)
(gehört Genossenschaft mit Anteilen der Eigentümer)

- cooperative home AE
- co-op AE coll

Eigenverbrauch, m
- one's own consumption

eignen sich zu etw
(Dinge)
anbieten sich zu etw
- lend itself to s.th.

eignen sich zum Wandern
(z.B. Gebirge)
anbieten sich zum Wandern
- lend itself to walking

Eignung, f
- suitability

Eignungsprüfung, f
- qualifying examination

Eignungstest, m
- qualifying test
- qualification test

Ei hart kochen
- hard-cook an egg AE
- hard-boil an egg BE

Ei kochen
- boil an egg

eilen
hasten
- hurry

eiliger Reisender, m
- hurried traveller BE
- hurried traveler AE

eiliges Mittagessen, n
- on-the-run lunch
- hurried lunch

eilig haben
es eilig haben
- be in a hurry

einachsiger Caravan, m
einachsiger Wohnwagen, m
- single-axle caravan BE
- single-axle trailer AE

Einbahnstraße, f
- one-way street
- one-way road

Einbahnverkehr, m
- one-way traffic

einbauen lassen etw
installieren lassen etw
- have s.th. installed

Einbaugarage, f
→ eingebaute Garage

Einbaukleiderschrank, m
- fitted closet AE
- fitted wardrobe BE
- built-in wardrobe BE

Einbaukosten, pl
Installationskosten, pl
- installation costs pl
- installation cost
- installation charges pl

Einbauküche, f
EBK, f
- fitted kitchen
- ftd. k.
- f.k.

Einbaukühlschrank, m
eingebauter Kühlschrank, m
- built-in refrigerator
- built-in fridge

Einbauleinwand, f
- built-in screen

Einbaum, m
- dugout AE
- dug-out BE

Einbaumöbel, n pl
eingebaute Möbel, n pl
- built-in furniture sg
- fitted furniture sg

Einbauschrank, m (bes. für Geschirr)
- built-in cupboard
- fitted cupboard

Einbauschrank, m (bes. für Kleider)
- built-in wardrobe
- fitted wardrobe

Einbauwand, f
(Möbel)
- wall-to-wall cupboard
- wall unit

einberufen etw (amtlich)
- convoke s.th.

einberufen etw (generell)
- convene s.th.

Einberufer, m
- convenor
- convener

Einberufer der Konferenz, m
- convenor of the conference
- convener of the conference

Einbettappartement, n
- one-bed apartment

Einbettcaravan, m
Einbettwohnwagen, m
- one-berth caravan BE
- one-berth van BE coll
- one-berth trailer AE

einbettig, adj
- one-bedded, adj
- one-bed, adj
- with one bed
- single-bed, adj

einbettig belegbar, adj
- available for single-bed occupancy, adj
- available for single occupancy, adj

einbettige Belegung, f
- single-bed occupancy
- single occupancy

einbettiges Zimmer, n
- one-bedded room
- one-bed room

Einbettwohnung, f
Wohnung mit einem Bett, f
- one-bed flat BE
- one-bed apartment AE

Einbettwohnwagen, m
Einbettcaravan, m
- one-berth trailer AE
- one-berth caravan BE
- one-berth van BE coll

Einbettzelt, n
- one-berth tent

Einbettzimmer, n
→ Einzelzimmer, Einzelschlafzimmer

einbrechen in eine Wohnung
- burglarize an apartment AE
- break into an apartment AE
- burgle a flat BE
- break into a flat BE

einbrechen in ein Geschäft
- burglarize a store AE
- break into a store AE
- burgle a shop BE
- break into a shop BE

einbrechen in ein Haus
- ♦ burglarize a house AE
- ♦ burgle a house BE
- ♦ break into a house

einbrechen in ein Zimmer
- ♦ burglarize a room AE
- ♦ burgle a room BE
- ♦ break into a room

einbrechen in etw
- ♦ burglarize s.th. AE
- ♦ burgle s.th. BE
- ♦ break into s.th.

Einbrecher, m
- ♦ burglar

Einbrecherbande, f
- ♦ gang of burglars

Einbruch, m (in Gebäude)
- ♦ break-in
- ♦ burglary

Einbruch, m (starker Rückgang)
- ♦ slump

Einbruch bei den Gästezahlen, m
- ♦ slump in the number of guests
- ♦ reduction in the number of guests

Einbruch bei den Übernachtungszahlen, m
- ♦ slump in the number of nights spent
- ♦ reduction in the number of nights spent

Einbruchdiebstahl, m
- ♦ burglary

einbruchsicher, adj
- ♦ burglarproof, adj AE
- ♦ burglar-proof, adj BE

einbruchsicherer Tresor, m
- ♦ burglarproof safe AE
- ♦ burglar-proof safe BE

Einbruchversicherung, f
- ♦ burglary insurance

Einbruchversicherung abschließen
- ♦ take out a burglary insurance (policy)

Einbruchwarnanlage, f
Alarmanlage, f
- ♦ burglar alarm system AE
- ♦ burglar alarm AE
- ♦ burglar-alarm system BE
- ♦ burglar-alarm BE

einbuchen bei jm
sich anmelden bei jm
- ♦ book in with s.o.

einbuchen (jn)
- ♦ book in (s.o.)

einbuchen jn
anmelden jn
unterbringen jn
- ♦ book s.o. in

einbuchen jn in etw
anmelden jn bei etw
unterbringen jn in etw
- ♦ book s.o. into s.th.

einbürgern jn
- ♦ naturalize s.o.
- ♦ naturalise s.o.

Einbürgerung, f
- ♦ naturalization

Einbürgerungsnachweis, m
- ♦ naturalization certificate

Einchecken, n
→ Anmeldung

einchecken (jn)
- ♦ check in (s.o.)

Eindruck, m
- ♦ impression

Eindruck behalten
- ♦ retain an impression

Eindruck der Unterkunft, m
- ♦ impression of the accommodation

ein Einzel- und zwei Doppelzimmer reservieren
- ♦ reserve one single and two double rooms

einen heben coll
einen trinken coll
- ♦ have a wet coll
- ♦ wet one's whistle coll
- ♦ liquor up sl

einen im Tee haben coll
- ♦ have had one over the eight coll
- ♦ be in one's cups coll

einen in der Krone haben
zuviel getrunken haben
- ♦ have a jag on

einen Tag länger bleiben
einen weiteren Tag bleiben
- ♦ stay on a day
- ♦ stay one more day

einen trinken gehen coll
- ♦ go for a pint coll
- ♦ go for a drink

einen über den Durst trinken coll
ein Glas über den Durst trinken coll
- ♦ have one drink too many coll
- ♦ have a drop too much coll
- ♦ have one too many coll

Einerappartement, n
→ Einbettappartement

Einerzimmer, n
→ Einzelzimmer

eines der ersten Hotels
eines der ersten Häuser
- ♦ one of the best hotels
- ♦ one of the foremost hotels

eine warme Mahlzeit pro Tag, f
- ♦ one hot meal per day

einfache Fahrkarte, f
- ♦ one-way ticket AE
- ♦ single ticket BE

einfache Fahrkarte nach Madrid, f
- ♦ one-way ticket to Madrid AE
- ♦ single ticket to Madrid BE

einfache Fahrt, f
(Gegensatz zu Rückfahrt)
- ♦ single journey BE
- ♦ one-way journey AE
- ♦ one-way trip AE

einfache Kost, f
- ♦ plain food
- ♦ plain fare
- ♦ simple diet
- ♦ coarse fare

einfache Kreuzfahrt, f
(nur Hinfahrt)
- ♦ one-way cruise

einfache Küche, f (Speisen)
- ♦ simple cuisine
- ♦ simple cooking
- ♦ basic cooking
- ♦ basic cuisine

einfache Mahlzeit, f
einfaches Essen, n
- ♦ simple meal
- ♦ bread and cheese

einfacher Fahrpreis, m
- ♦ single fare BE
- ♦ one-way fare AE

einfacher Flug, m
Hinflug, m
- ♦ one-way flight

einfacher Platz, m
(Camping)
- ♦ simple site

einfacher Stand, m (Messe)
- ♦ basic stand

einfache Sanitäreinrichtungen, f pl
- ♦ basic sanitary facilities pl

einfaches Appartement, n
- ♦ simple apartment

einfaches Essen, n
- ♦ simple food

einfaches Frühstück n
- ♦ plain breakfast
- ♦ simple breakfast
- ♦ continental breakfast

einfaches Gericht, n
- ♦ simple dish

einfaches Hotel n
- ♦ simple hotel

einfaches Leben führen
- ♦ live a simple life

einfaches Leben genießen
- ♦ enjoy the simple life

einfaches Lokal, n
- ♦ simple place

einfaches Mahl, n
einfaches Essen, n
- ♦ bread and cheese
- ♦ simple meal

einfaches Mittagessen, n
- ♦ simple lunch

einfaches Mobiliar, n
einfache Möbel, n pl
- ♦ simple furniture sg
- ♦ plain furniture sg

einfaches Rezept, n
- ♦ simple recipe

einfaches Sandwich, n
- ♦ plain sandwich

einfaches Zimmer, n
- ♦ basic room
- ♦ plain room
- ♦ simple room

einfache Unterkunft, f
- ♦ simple accommodation
- ♦ basic accommodation

einfache Unterkunft anbieten
- ♦ offer simple accommodation
- ♦ offer basic accommodation

einfach möbliert, adj
- ♦ simply furnished, adj

einfach möbliertes Zimmer n
- ♦ simply furnished room

einfach oder üppig speisen
- ♦ dine simply or sumptuously

Einfachreise, f
Hinreise, f
- ♦ one-way trip

einfach speisen
- ♦ dine simply

einfach verglast, adj
- ♦ single glazed, adj

einfallslose Kost, f
einfallsloses Essen, n
- ♦ unimaginative diet
- ♦ unimaginative food
- ♦ unimaginative menu
- ♦ unimaginative meals pl

einfallslose Speisekarte, f
  phantasielose Speisekarte, f
  ♦ **unimaginative menu**
einfallsreiche Küche, f
  (Speisen)
  phantasievolle Küche f
  ♦ **imaginative cooking**
  ♦ imaginative cuisine
Einfamilienhaus, n
  EFH, n
  ♦ **one-family house**
  ♦ single-family house
  ♦ self-contained house
Einfamilienheim, n
  ♦ **single-family home**
einfinden sich
  kommen
  ♦ **turn up** coll
  ♦ come
  ♦ appear coll
einfinden sich an einem Platz
  sich an einem Ort einfinden
  zu einem Ort kommen
  ♦ **come to a place**
  ♦ appear at a place
  ♦ turn up at a place coll
einfinden sich bei jm
  zu jm kommen
  ♦ **come to s.o.**
einfinden sich zu einer Party (für kurze Zeit)
  sich kurz bei einer Party sehen lassen
  ♦ **put in an appearance at a party**
einfinden sich zu etw (für kurze Zeit)
  (z.B. bei einer Veranstaltung)
  sich kurz sehen lassen
  ♦ **put in an appearance at s.th.**
einfinden sich zu etw (generell)
  ♦ **arrive at s.th.**
  ♦ turn up at s.th. coll
einflammig, adj
  (Gasherd, Gaskocher)
  ♦ **one-burner, adj**
  ♦ single-burner, adj
einflammiger Herd, m
  ♦ **one-burner stove**
  ♦ single-burner stove
einfliegen jn
  ♦ **fly s.o. in**
Einfluß des Tourismus auf die Umwelt, m
  Auswirkung des Tourismus auf die Umwelt, f
  ♦ **impact of tourism on the environment**
einfrieren etw
  tiefgefrieren etw
  tiefkühlen etw
  ♦ **freeze s.th.**
  ♦ deep-freeze s.th.
einfügen sich in die Umgebung
  sich in die Umgebung einpassen
  ♦ **blend with the surroundings**
  ♦ blend into the surrounding landscape
  ♦ blend into the environment
einführen etw
  ♦ **bring s.th. in**
  ♦ take s.th. in
einführen etw in ein Land
  ♦ **bring s.th. into a country**
einführen etw zollfrei
  ♦ **bring s.th. in duty free**
  ♦ take s.th. in duty free
Einführung in etw, f
  ♦ **introduction to s.th.**

Einführungsangebot, n
  ♦ **introductory offer**
Einführungsfahrpreis, m
  ♦ **introductory fare**
Einführungsgespräch, m
  Einführungsvortrag, m
  ♦ **introductory talk**
Einführungskurs, m
  Einführungslehrgang, m
  ♦ **introductory course**
Einführungspauschale, f
  ♦ **introductory package**
Einführungspreis, m
  ♦ **introductory price**
  ♦ introductory rate
Einführungsrabatt, m
  ♦ **introductory discount**
Einfuhr von Devisen, f
  Deviseneinfuhr, f
  ♦ **import of foreign currency**
  ♦ import of foreign currencies
Eingang, m (Gebäude)
  ♦ **entrance**
  ♦ entry
  ♦ way in
Eingang, m (Zahlung, Dokument)
  Empfang, m
  ♦ **receipt**
eingängig, adj (Essen)
  ♦ **one-course, adj**
  ♦ consisting of one course, adj
Eingangsbereich, m
  ♦ **entrance area**
Eingangsdatum, n
  → Eingangstermin
Eingangsfassade, f
  ♦ **entrance façade**
  ♦ entrance facade AE
Eingangsflur, m
  Eingangskorridor, m
  ♦ **entrance corridor**
Eingangsfoyer n
  ♦ **entrance foyer**
Eingangshalle, f
  ♦ **entrance hall**
  ♦ hallway AE
  ♦ entrance lobby
Eingangsrede, f
  → Eröffnungsrede
Eingangssalon, m
  ♦ **entrance lounge**
Eingangstag, m
  (einer Buchung etc)
  ♦ **day of receipt**
Eingangstermin, m
  Eingangsdatum n
  ♦ **date of receipt**
Eingangstor, n
  ♦ **entrance gate**
  ♦ entry gate
Eingangstür, f
  ♦ **entrance door**
Eingang zu etw, m
  ♦ **entrance to s.th.**
eingebaute Garage, f
  Einbaugarage, f
  ♦ **built-in garage**
Eingeborener, m
  ♦ **native**
eingegangene Bestätigung, f
  ♦ **confirmation received**

eingegangene Buchung, f
  ♦ **booking received**
eingegangene Reservierung, f
  ♦ **reservation received**
eingegangene Stornierung, f
  eingegangene Absage, f
  ♦ **cancellation received**
  ♦ cancelation received AE
eingehen auf js Wünsche
  sich nach js Wünschen richten
  js Wünschen entgegenkommen
  ♦ **comply with s.o.'s requests**
  ♦ comply with s.o.'s wishes
eingehend, adj (Post)
  ♦ **incoming, adj**
eingehende Buchung, f
  ♦ **incoming booking**
eingehende Reservierung, f
  ♦ **incoming reservation**
eingehende Stornierung, f
  eingehende Absage, m
  eingehende Annullierung, f
  eingehende Rücktrittserklärung, f
  ♦ **incoming cancellation**
  ♦ incoming cancelation AE
eingeladen, adj
  geladen, adj
  ♦ **invited, adj**
eingeladener Referent, m
  (z.B. bei Konferenz)
  ♦ **invited speaker**
eingeladen sein bei Hof
  ♦ **be invited at court**
eingeladen sein zu etw
  ♦ **be invited to s.th.**
eingeladen werden
  ♦ **be invited**
eingemacht, adj gastr
  ♦ **preserved, adj** gastr
Eingemachtes, n
  ♦ **preserves** pl
eingerichtet, adj
  → möbliert
eingeschlossen sein in einem brennenden Hotel
  ♦ **be trapped in a burning hotel**
eingeschlossen sein vom Schnee
  eingeschneit sein
  ♦ **be snowbound** AE
  ♦ be snow-bound BE
eingeschlossen vom Schnee, adj
  ♦ **snowbound, adj** AE
  ♦ snow-bound, adj BE
eingeschneites Haus, n
  ♦ **snowbound house** AE
  ♦ snow-bound house BE
eingeschneit sein
  ♦ **be snowed in**
  ♦ be snowed up
  ♦ be snowbound AE
  ♦ be snow-bound BE
eingeschossig, adj
  → einstöckig
eingeschränkt, adj
  begrenzt, adj
  beschränkt, adj
  ♦ **restricted, adj**
eingeschränkter Campingplatzservice, m
  eingeschränkter Campingplatzdienst, m
  ♦ **restricted campsite service**
  ♦ restricted campground service AE

- ♦ restricted camping site service *BE*
- ♦ restricted camping ground service *BE*

eingeschränkter Service m
- ♦ restricted service

eingestellt auf jn
- ♦ adapted to s.o.
- ♦ adjusted to s.o.
- ♦ geared to s.o.
- ♦ oriented to s.o. *AE*
- ♦ orientated to s.o. *BE*

eingestellt auf Kinder
- ♦ adapted to children

eingestellt auf touristische Bedürfnisse
- ♦ be geared to tourist needs

eingestellt sein auf die Bedürfnisse von jm
- ♦ be adapted to the needs of s.o.
- ♦ be geared to the requirements of s.o.

eingestellt sein auf etw
  vorbereitet sein auf etw
  rechnen mit etw
- ♦ be prepared for s.th.
- ♦ be geared to s.th.

eingestellt sein auf jn
- ♦ be adapted to s.o.
- ♦ be adjusted to s.o.
- ♦ be geared to s.o.
- ♦ be oriented to s.o. *AE*
- ♦ be orientated to s.o. *BE*

eingestürztes Hotel, n
- ♦ collapsed hotel

eingetragener Verein, m
- ♦ registered club

eingezäunter Spielplatz, m
- ♦ fenced playground

eingießen etw
  → einschenken etw

Einhaltung der Essenszeiten f
- ♦ observation of the mealtimes *AE*
- ♦ observation of the meal times *BE*
- ♦ keeping (to) the mealtimes *AE*
- ♦ keeping (to) the meal times *BE*

einheimische Bevölkerung, f
- ♦ resident population
- ♦ local populace *AE*

einheimische Gerichte probieren
- ♦ sample the local dishes

einheimische Klientel, f
  einheimische Gästeschar f
  Gästeschar am Ort f
- ♦ local clientele

einheimische Küche, f (Speisen)
- ♦ local cooking
- ♦ local cuisine
- ♦ local fare

einheimische Küche anbieten
- ♦ offer local cuisine
- ♦ offer local cooking
- ♦ offer local fare

Einheimischer, m
  Einheimische, f
- ♦ local resident
- ♦ resident
- ♦ native
- ♦ local *coll*

einheimischer Gast, m
- ♦ local guest

einheimisches Essen, n
- ♦ local food

einheimisches Gericht, n
- ♦ local dish

einheimisches Getränk, n
- ♦ local drink

einheimische Spezialität, f
  heimische Spezialität, f
- ♦ local specialty *AE*
- ♦ local speciality *BE*

Einheit, f (Statistik)
- ♦ unit

einheitlich, adj
  gleich, adj
  gleichbleibend, adj
- ♦ uniform, adj

einheitlicher Preis, m
- ♦ uniform rate
- ♦ uniform price

einheitlicher Trend, m
- ♦ uniform trend

Einheit mit einem Schlafzimmer, f
- ♦ one-bedroom unit

Einheit mit Service, f
  (Statistik)
- ♦ serviced unit

Einheit mit zwei Schlafzimmern, f
- ♦ two-bedroom unit

Einheit ohne Service, f
  (Statistik)
  Einheit ohne Bedienung, f
- ♦ nonserviced unit *AE*
- ♦ non-serviced unit *BE*

Einheitscharter, f
- ♦ uniform charter

Einheitscouvert, n
  → Einheitsgedeck

Einheitsfrühstück, n
  → Standardfrühstück

Einheitsgedeck, n
  Einheitskuvert, n
  Einheitscouvert, n
- ♦ standard cover

Einheitsgericht, n
  → Standardgericht

Einheitsgröße, f
  einheitliche Größe, f
  Standardgröße, f
- ♦ standard size

Einheitsklassekabine, f
- ♦ single-class cabin

Einheitsklassepassagier, m
- ♦ single-class passenger

Einheitskuvert, n
  → Einheitsgedeck

Einheitsmenü, n
  → Standardmenü

Einheitspreis, m (einheitlich)
  Einheitsrate, f
- ♦ uniform price
- ♦ uniform rate

Einheitspreis, m (pauschal)
  Pauschalpreis, m
- ♦ flat rate

Einheitstarif, m
- ♦ uniform tariff

einholen etw
  gleichziehen mit etw
- ♦ catch up with s.th.

einige Bier trinken
- ♦ drink a couple of beers

einige Tage Ruhe sich gönnen
- ♦ allow oneself a few days' rest
- ♦ give oneself a few days' rest

einkaufen
- ♦ shop
- ♦ do some shopping

einkaufen am Sonntag
- ♦ shop on Sundays

einkaufen gehen
- ♦ go shopping

einkaufen sich in ein Hotel
- ♦ buy into a hotel

Einkäufer, m
- ♦ shopper

Einkaufsabteilung f
- ♦ purchasing department

Einkaufsauftrag, m
- ♦ purchase order

Einkaufsausflug, m
- ♦ shopping excursion
- ♦ shopping trip

Einkaufsbereich, m
  Einkaufsgelände, n
- ♦ shopping area

Einkaufsbummel, m
- ♦ shopping stroll

Einkaufsbummel machen (generell)
  einkaufen gehen
- ♦ do some shopping
- ♦ have a look around the stores *AE*
- ♦ have a look around the shops *BE*

Einkaufsbummel machen (groß)
  Einkaufsorgie veranstalten
- ♦ go on a shopping spree

Einkaufsbüro, n
- ♦ purchasing office
- ♦ buying office

Einkaufscenter, n
  Einkaufszentrum, n
- ♦ plaza *AE*

Einkaufseinrichtung, f
- ♦ shopping facility

Einkaufsermäßigung, f
- ♦ shopping reduction

Einkaufsexpedition, f *humor*
  Einkaufsbummel, m
- ♦ shopping expedition *humor*

Einkaufsfahrt, f
- ♦ shopping trip

Einkaufsfahrt machen
- ♦ go on a shopping trip

Einkaufsfahrt mit Begleitung, f
- ♦ escorted shopping trip

Einkaufsgenossenschaft, f
- ♦ cooperative buying association

Einkaufsgutschein, m
- ♦ shopping voucher

Einkaufshinweis, m
- ♦ shopping hint

Einkaufsinformation, f
- ♦ shopping information

Einkaufskomplex m
  Einkaufsanlage f
  Einkaufsbereich m
- ♦ shopping complex

Einkaufsleiter, m
  Leiter der Einkaufsabteilung m
- ♦ chief buyer
- ♦ purchasing manager

Einkaufsliste, f
- ♦ shopping list

Einkaufsmöglichkeit, f (Aktivität)
- ♦ possibility of doing some shopping

Einkaufsmöglichkeit

Einkaufsmöglichkeit, f (Einrichtung)
→ Einkaufseinrichtung
Einkaufsorgie, f
  großer Einkaufsbummel m
  ◆ shopping spree
Einkaufsparadies, n
  ◆ shopper's paradise
  ◆ shopping paradise
Einkaufspassage, f
  Einkaufsarkade f
  ◆ shopping arcade
  ◆ shopping mall BE
Einkaufspersonal, n
  ◆ purchasing staff
  ◆ buying staff
Einkaufspreis, m
  ◆ cost price
  ◆ purchase price
  ◆ buying price
Einkaufsreise, f
  ◆ shopping tour
Einkaufsstadt, f (Großstadt)
  ◆ shopping city
Einkaufsstadt, f (kleine Stadt)
  ◆ shopping town
Einkaufsstraße, f
  Geschäftsstraße, f
  ◆ shopping street
Einkaufstasche, f
  ◆ shopping bag
Einkaufstourismus, m
  ◆ shopping tourism
Einkaufstourist, m
  ◆ shopping tourist
Einkaufstrip, m
  → Einkaufsfahrt
Einkaufsurlaub, m
  ◆ shopping-spree vacation AE
  ◆ shopping-spree holiday BE
Einkaufsviertel, n
  ◆ shopping district
  ◆ shopping quarter BE
  ◆ shopping precinct BE
Einkaufswochenende, n
  ◆ shopping weekend
Einkaufszeit, f (der Kunden)
  ◆ shopping time
  ◆ time for shopping
Einkaufszeit, f (Öffnungszeit)
  Öffnungszeit der Geschäfte, f
  ◆ shopping hours pl
Einkaufszentrum, n
  Einkaufscenter n
  ◆ shopping center AE
  ◆ shopping centre BE
  ◆ plaza AE
Einkaufszone, f
  ◆ shopping precinct BE
  ◆ shopping area BE
Einkehr, f
  ◆ stop
einkehren, um etw zu essen und zu trinken
  ◆ stop for a drink and a snack
einkehren in einem Hotel
  ◆ stop at a hotel
einkehren in einer Wirtschaft
  einkehren in einer Gaststätte
  ◆ stop at a bar AE
  ◆ stop at a pub BE

einkehren in etw
  einkehren bei etw
  ◆ stop at s.th.
einkehren zum Abendessen (Dinner)
  anhalten zum Abendessen
  ◆ stop for dinner
einkehren zum Abendessen (Supper)
  anhalten zum Abendessen
  ◆ stop for supper
einkehren zum Essen
  anhalten zum Essen
  ◆ stop for a meal
einkehren zum Mittagessen
  anhalten zum Mittagessen
  ◆ stop for lunch
Einkehr halten
  Einkehr machen
  anhalten
  ◆ stop
  ◆ make a stop
Einkehr in einem Hotel, f
  Hoteleinkehr, f
  ◆ stop at a hotel
  ◆ hotel stop
Einkehr in einem Hotel zum Essen, f
  ◆ stop at a hotel for a meal
Einkehr in einem Motel, f
  Moteleinkehr, f
  ◆ stop at a motel
  ◆ motel stop
Einkehr in einer Gaststätte, f
  Einkehr in einer Bar, f
  ◆ stop at a pub BE
  ◆ stop at a bar AE
Einkehr machen bei etw.
  ◆ make a stop at s.th.
einkellern etw
  einlagern etw
  ◆ cellar s.th.
Einkommen, n
  ◆ income
Einkommensteuer, f
  Einkommenssteuer, f
  ◆ income tax
Einkünfte, f pl
  Erlöse, m pl
  ◆ revenues pl
  ◆ receipts pl
  ◆ takings pl
  ◆ income
  ◆ earnings pl
einladend, adj
  ◆ inviting, adj
  ◆ welcoming, adj
einladend aussehen
  ◆ look inviting
einladende Atmosphäre, f
  ◆ inviting atmosphere
  ◆ friendly atmosphere
  ◆ welcoming atmosphere
einladende Lounge, f
  einladender Salon, m
  ◆ inviting lounge
  ◆ welcoming lounge
einladender Ort, m
  einladender Platz, m
  ◆ inviting place
  ◆ welcoming place
einladendes Essen, n
  ◆ inviting meal

einladendes Hotel, n
  ◆ inviting hotel
  ◆ welcoming hotel
einladendes Land, n
  ◆ inviting country
einladendes Restaurant, n
  ◆ inviting restaurant
  ◆ welcoming restaurant
einladende Umgebung, f
  ◆ welcoming environment
einladend sein
  ◆ be welcoming
  ◆ be inviting
einladen jn, zum Mittagessen zu bleiben
  ◆ ask s.o. to stay for lunch
einladen jn in sein Haus
  einladen jn nach Hause
  ◆ invite s.o. to one's home
  ◆ invite s.o. to one's house
einladen jn mitzukommen
  ◆ invite s.o. along
  ◆ invite s.o. to come along
einladen jn nach Hause
  einladen jn zu sich nach Hause
  ◆ invite s.o. home
  ◆ invite s.o. to one's house
einladen jn nach Hause zu etw
  ◆ invite s.o. over to s.th.
  ◆ invite s.o. round to s.th.
einladen jn nach oben (zu kommen)
  ◆ invite s.o. up
einladen jn offiziell
  ◆ invite s.o. officially
einladen jn wegzufahren
  ◆ invite s.o. away
einladen jn wieder mit nach Hause zu kommen
  (z.B. nach Besuch einer Veranstaltung)
  ◆ invite s.o. back
einladen jn zu einem Begrüßungsgetränk
  einladen jn zu einem Willkommenstrunk form
  ◆ invite s.o. to a welcome drink
einladen jn zu einem Empfang
  ◆ invite s.o. to a reception
einladen jn zu einem Essen
  ◆ invite s.o. for a meal
einladen jn zu einem Gegenbesuch nach X
  ◆ invite s.o. to a return visit to X
einladen jn zu einem Getränk
  ◆ invite s.o. to a drink
  ◆ invite s.o. for a drink
einladen jn zu einem Glas Wein
  (in Weinstube o.ä.)
  ◆ treat s.o. to a glass of wine
einladen jn zu einem Kongreß
  ◆ invite s.o. to a convention
  ◆ invite s.o. to a congress
  ◆ ask s.o. to a convention
  ◆ ask s.o. to a congress
einladen jn zu einer Konferenz
  einladen jn zu einer Tagung
  ◆ invite s.o. to a conference
  ◆ ask s.o. to a conference
einladen jn zu einer Party
  ◆ invite s.o. to a party
  ◆ invite s.o. to come to a party
einladen jn zu einer Probefahrt
  (Auto)
  ◆ invite s.o. to test-drive a car
einladen jn zu einer Tasse Tee
  (ins Café o.ä.)
  ◆ treat s.o. to a cup of tea

einladen jn zu etw
♦ invite s.o. to s.th.
♦ invite s.o. for s.th.
♦ invite s.o. to do s.th.
einladen jn zum Abendessen (Dinner)
♦ invite s.o. to dinner
♦ invite s.o. for dinner
♦ invite s.o. to have dinner
♦ treat s.o. to dinner
einladen jn zum Abendessen im XYZ Hotel
♦ invite s.o. to dinner at the XYZ hotel
einladen jn zum Abendessen (Supper)
♦ invite s.o. to supper
♦ invite s.o. for supper
♦ invite s.o. to have supper
einladen jn zum Ball
♦ invite s.o. to a ball
einladen jn zum Essen
→ einladen jn zum Abendessen etc
einladen jn zum Essen und Trinken
bewirten jn mit Essen und Trinken
♦ wine and dine s.o.
einladen jn zum Frühstück
♦ invite s.o. to breakfast
♦ ask s.o. for breakfast
einladen jn zum Kaffee
(zu sich nach Hause)
♦ invite s.o. over for coffee
♦ ask s.o. in for coffee
einladen jn zum Mitmachen
♦ ask s.o. to join in
einladen jn zum Mittagessen
♦ invite s.o. to lunch
♦ invite s.o. for lunch
♦ invite s.o. to have lunch
einladen jn zum Tee
♦ invite s.o. to tea
♦ ask s.o. to tea
einladen jn zwei Wochen im voraus
♦ invite s.o. two weeks in advance
einladen sich selbst (zu etw)
sich selbst einladen (zu etw)
♦ invite oneself (to s.th.)
einladen zur Erkundung
♦ invite exploration
Einladung, f
♦ invitation
♦ invite BE inform
Einladung ablehnen (zu etw)
♦ decline an invitation (to s.th.)
Einladung annehmen
Einladung Folge leisten
Einladung folgen
zusagen
♦ accept an invitation
♦ accept the invitation
Einladung aussprechen etw zu tun
♦ extend an invitation to do s.th.
Einladung bekommen
♦ get an invitation
♦ get an invite BE inform
Einladungen ausgeben
Einladungen verteilen
♦ issue invitations
Einladungen verschicken
Einladungen versenden
♦ send out invitations
Einladung erhalten für etw
Einladung erhalten zu etw
♦ receive an invitation to s.th.

Einladung erhalten von jm
♦ receive an invitation from s.o.
Einladung Folge leisten
→ Einladung annehmen
Einladung folgen
→ Einladung annehmen
Einladung gilt als Eintrittskarte
♦ Please use this card as admission ticket
Einladung nicht annehmen
♦ not accept an invitation
Einladungsbrief, m
Einladungsschreiben, n
♦ letter inviting s.o.
♦ letter of invitation
Einladung senden an jn
Einladung verschicken an jn
♦ send an invitation to s.o.
Einladung sich entgehen lassen
♦ pass up an invitation inform
Einladungskarte, f
♦ invitation card
♦ card inviting s.o.
Einladungsliste, f
♦ invitation list
♦ list of invitees
Einladungsschreiben n
Einladungsbrief m
♦ letter of invitation
♦ letter inviting s.o.
Einladung trifft ein
Einladung kommt an
♦ invitation arrives
Einladung wiederholen (an jn)
♦ renew an invitation (to s.o.)
Einladung zu einem Konzert, f
Konzerteinladung, f
♦ invitation to a concert
Einladung zu einer Hochzeit, f
→ Hochzeitseinladung
Einladung zu einer Party, f
Partyeinladung, f
Festeinladung, f
♦ invitation to a party
Einladung zu etw, f
♦ invitation to s.th.
♦ invitation to do s.th.
Einladung zum Abendessen, f (Dinner)
Abendesseneinladung, f
♦ invitation to dinner
Einladung zum Abendessen, f (Supper)
♦ invitation to supper
Einladung zum Frühstück, f
♦ invitation to breakfast
Einladung zum Mittagessen, f
♦ invitation to lunch
♦ invitation to luncheon
Einladung zum Tanz, f
Einladung zur Tanzveranstaltung, f
♦ invitation to the dance
Einladung zum Tee, f
♦ invitation to tea
Einladung zurückziehen
→ ausladen jn
Einlaß, m
♦ admittance
♦ admission
Einlaß ab 18 Uhr
(Hinweis bei Veranstaltung)
♦ Doors open at 6 p.m.
Einlaßkarte, f
→ Eintrittskarte

Einlaß nur nach Einladung
♦ Admission is by invitation only
♦ Admission by invitation only
Einlaß zu etw, m
♦ admittance to s.th.
♦ admission to s.th.
einleben sich in einem Hotel
♦ settle down in a hotel
einlegen etw (in Essig)
♦ pickle s.th.
Einliegerwohnung, f
(für ältere Verwandte)
ELW, f
♦ granny flat BE inform
♦ granny annexe BE inform
Einliterflasche, f
♦ one-liter bottle AE
♦ one-litre bottle BE
einlogieren jn in einem Hotel
♦ lodge s.o. in a hotel
♦ lodge s.o. at a hotel
♦ put s.o. up at a hotel
♦ put s.o. up in a hotel
einlogieren sich bei jm
♦ take rooms with s.o.
♦ take a room with s.o.
♦ take lodgings with s.o.
♦ establish oneself in s.o.'s house
einlogieren sich in einem Hotel
♦ take a room at a hotel
♦ take a room in a hotel
♦ take rooms at a hotel
♦ take rooms in a hotel
♦ put up in a hotel
einlösbar, adj
(Gutschein)
♦ redeemable, adj
einlösbar sein
(Gutschein)
♦ be redeemable
Einmachzucker, m
♦ preserving sugar
einmal anders
(Werbeslogan)
♦ with a difference
einmalige Hotelübernachtung, f
Hotelübernachtung, f
♦ one-night hotel stay
einmaliges Erlebnis, n
einzigartiges Erlebnis, n
♦ unique experience
einmaliges Gastspiel, n
einmalige Vorstellung, f
♦ one-night stand
♦ one-night show
einmalige Übernachtung, f
Übernachtung, f
♦ one-night stay
einmalige Vorstellung, f
(z.B. in Theater)
einmaliges Gastspiel, n
♦ one-night show
♦ one-night stand
einmalige Zahlung, f
♦ nonrecurrent payment AE
♦ non-recurrent payment BE
einmal pro Woche
♦ once a week
Einmal pro Woche gibt es eine Filmvorführung
♦ Once a week there is a film show

Einmannkapelle

Einmannkapelle, f *humor*
- one-man band *humor*

Ein-Mann-Zelt, n
- one-man tent

Einmietbetrug, m (Hotel)
→ Hotelbetrug

Einmietbetrüger, m (Hotel)
Hotelbetrüger, m
Hoteleinmietbetrüger, m
- hotel defrauder
- hotel swindler

Einmietbetrügerei, f
→ Einmietbetrug

einmieten sich bei jm (Privathaus)
- take lodgings with s.o.
- lodge with s.o. *AE*
- room with s.o. *AE*

einmieten sich für die Nacht (Hotel)
- book in for the night

einmieten sich (Hotel)
Zimmer nehmen
sich in das Fremdenbuch eintragen
- book in

Einnahme, f (bes. Firma)
Einnahmen, f pl
- takings *pl*
- receipts *pl*

Einnahme, f (bes. Person)
Einnahmen, f pl
- income
- earnings *pl*

Einnahme, f (bes. Staat)
Einnahmen, f pl
- revenue
- revenues *pl*

Einnahme aus der Vermietung von Flächen, f
- income from (the) rental of space *AE*
- income from letting space *BE*

Einnahme aus etw, f
Erlös aus etw, m
- revenue from s.th.
- income from s.th.

Einnahme aus Vermietung, f
Erlös aus Vermietung, m
- revenue from renting *AE*
- revenue from rental(s) *AE*
- income from renting *AE*
- income from rental(s) *AE*
- income from letting *BE*

Einnahmen aus dem Geschäftstourismus, f pl
- receipts from business tourism *pl*
- business tourism receipts *pl*

Einnahmen aus dem Tourismus, f pl
Einnahmen aus dem Fremdenverkehr, f pl
- income from tourism
- revenues from tourism *pl*

**Einnahmen aus der Verpachtung von Geschäftsräumen
und von Ausstellungsvitrinen, f pl**
- income from leasing stores and showcases *AE*
- income from leasing shops and showcases *BE*
- revenue from leasing stores and showcases *AE*
- revenue from leasing shops and showcases *BE*

Einnahmen aus Vermietung, f pl
- income from renting *AE*
- income from rental(s) *AE*
- income from letting *BE*

Einnahmen belaufen sich auf DM 123
- takings amount to DM 123
- revenue amounts to DM 123

Einnahmen in harter Währung, f pl
- hard-currency revenues *pl*

Einnahmen maximieren
- maximise revenue
- maximize revenue

Einnahmen pro Tag, f pl
- takings per day *pl*
- receipts per day *pl*
- revenue per day
- income per day

Einnahmen sind hoch
- takings are high
- receipts are high

Einnahmen sind niedrig
- takings are low
- receipts are low

Einnahmequelle, f
- source of income
- source of revenue

Einnahmeverlust, m
- loss in income
- loss in revenue

einnehmen etw (Fläche, Raum)
- occupy s.th.

einnehmen etw (Geld)
- take s.th. in
- receive s.th.
- cash s.th.

einnehmen etw (Mahlzeit)
- take s.th.
- have s.th.

einnehmen seinen Platz
seinen Platz einnehmen
- take one's seat

einnisten sich *humor*
niederlassen sich
einleben sich
- install oneself
- instal oneself *AE*
- settle down
- park oneself *coll*

einnisten sich bei jm
- park oneself on s.o. *coll*
- live off s.o.
- sponge on s.o.

ein paar Tage bleiben
- stay a few days
- stay a couple of days

einpacken etw in etw
- pack s.th. in s.th.

einpacken (Gepäck)
- pack
- pack up

einpassieren (Hotel)
sich anmelden
sich in das Meldebuch eintragen
- check in

einpennen *coll*
- drop off *coll*

Einpersonenpreis, m
- one-person rate
- one-person price
- single-person rate
- single-person price

einpferchen jn in ein Zimmer
- crowd people into a room

einpökeln (etw)
- corn (s.th.)
- pickle (s.th.)

einquartieren jn bei einem Freund (Besuch)
- get lodgings for s.o. with a friend
- put s.o. up with a friend *coll*

einquartieren jn bei jm (Besuch)
- put s.o. up with s.o.
- get lodgings for s.o. with s.o.

einquartieren jn bei jm (Militär)
- quarter s.o. on s.o.

einquartieren jn bei sich (Besuch)
- put s.o. up (at one's place) *coll*
- put s.o. up

einquartieren jn in einem Hotel
unterbringen jn in einem Hotel
- put s.o. up at a hotel
- book s.o. into a hotel

einquartieren jn (Militär)
- billet s.o.
- quarter s.o.

einquartieren sich bei jm
- take up lodgings with s.o.
- take up quarters with s.o.
- lodge with s.o.
- put oneself up with s.o. *coll*

einquartiert, adj (Militär)
- quartered, adj

Einquartierter, m (Militär)
- billetee

einquartiert sein bei jm (Militär)
- be quartered (up)on s.o.
- be quartered with s.o.
- be billeted (up)on s.o.
- be billeted with s.o.

einquartiert sein in einem Haus
- be quartered in a house

einquartiert sein (Militär)
- be quartered
- be billeted

Einquartierung, f (Militär)
- billeting
- quartering

Einquartierungsschein, m (Militär)
- billeting order
- billet

Einrad, n
- unicycle

Einradfahren, n
Einradsport, m
- unicycling

Einradfahrer, m
- unicyclist

Einraumwohnung, f
→ Einzimmerwohnung

Einreise, f
(in ein Land)
- entry

Einreisebedingungen, f pl
- conditions of entry *pl*

Einreisebeschränkung, f
- entry restriction
- restricted entry

Einreisebestimmungen, f pl
- entry regulations *pl*
- entry requirements *pl*

Einreisedatum, n
- entry date
- date of entry

Einreiseerlaubnis, f
Einreisegenehmigung, f
- entry permit
- entry permission
- permission to enter

Einreiseerlaubnis verweigern jm
 ♦ refuse s.o. permission to enter (a country)
Einreiseflughafen, m
 ♦ airport of entry
Einreiseformalität, f
 ♦ entry formality
Einreisegebühr, f
 ♦ entry fee
Einreisegenehmigung, f
 Einreiseerlaubnis, f
 ♦ permission to enter
 ♦ entry permission
 ♦ entry permit
Einreisegesetz, n
 ♦ entry law
Einreisegesetze mildern
 ♦ relax entry laws
Einreisehafen, m
 ♦ port of entry
 ♦ entry port
Einreise in ein Land, f
 ♦ entry into a country
Einreise nach Deutschland, f
 ♦ entry into Germany
einreisen auf dem Landweg
 ♦ enter by land
einreisen aus X
 ♦ enter from X
einreisen in ein Land (aus X)
 ♦ enter a country (from X)
einreisen in ein Land illegal
 ♦ enter a country illegally
einreisen nach England
 ♦ enter England
Einreiseort, m
 Einreisepunkt, m
 ♦ entry point
 ♦ point of entry
Einreiseort in ein Land, m
 Einreisepunkt in ein Land, m
 ♦ entry point into a country
Einreisepapier, n
 Einreisedokument, n
 ♦ entry document
Einreiseposten, m
 Grenzposten, m
 ♦ entry post
Einreiseproblem, n
 ♦ entry problem
Einreiseschwierigkeit, f
 ♦ entry difficulty
Einreisesichtvermerk, m
 → Einreisevisum
Einreisestatistik, f
 ♦ entry statistics pl
Einreisestelle, f
 (in ein Land)
 Einreisepunkt, m
 Einreiseort, m
 ♦ point of entry
Einreisetaxe, f
 Einreiseabgabe, f
 ♦ entry tax
Einreiseverbot haben
 ♦ have been refused entry (to the country)
 ♦ not be allowed to enter (the country)
Einreise verweigern jm
 ♦ refuse s.o. entry (into a country)
Einreisevisum n
 Einreisesichtvermerk m jur
 ♦ entry visa

Einreisezeit, f
 Einreisezeitpunkt, m
 ♦ time of entry
einrichten etw (Ausstattung)
 ausstatten etw
 ♦ equip s.th.
 ♦ fit out s.th.
 ♦ fit up s.th.
einrichten etw (Unterkunft)
 ♦ furnish s.th.
einrichten sich häuslich
 es sich bequem machen
 ♦ make oneself at home
einrichten sich (in neuer Umgebung)
 ♦ get settled
 ♦ establish oneself
Einrichtung, f (Fazilität)
 Fazilität, f
 ♦ facility
Einrichtung, f (Mobiliar)
 ♦ furnishings pl
Einrichtungen für die Erholung, f pl
 Einrichtungen zur Erholung, f pl
 ♦ facilities for recreation pl
Einrichtung höherstufen
 Einrichtung verbessern
 ♦ upgrade a facility
Einrichtung mit dem neuesten Stand der Technik, f
 ♦ state-of-the-art facility
Einrichtungsbesitzer, m
 Besitzer der Einrichtung, m
 ♦ facility owner
Einrichtungsgegenstand, m
 ♦ item of furniture
 ♦ piece of furniture
Einrichtungskosten, pl
 Möblierungskosten, pl
 ♦ furnishing costs pl
 ♦ furnishing cost
Einrichtung tieferstufen
 Einrichtung niedriger einstufen
 ♦ downgrade a facility
Einrichtung und Mobiliar
 Einrichtung (f) und Mobiliar (n)
 ♦ furnishings and furniture pl
Einrichtung vermieten an jn
 ♦ hire out a facility to s.o. BE
 ♦ rent a facility to s.o. AE
Einrichtung verpachten (an jn)
 ♦ lease a facility (to s.o.)
Einrichtung zum Selbstkochen, f
 ♦ self-cooking facility
einrühren etw
 ♦ stir in s.th.
Einsaisonbetrieb, m
 ♦ one-season establishment
 ♦ one-season operation
Einsaisonferienort, m
 Einsaisonurlaubsort, m
 ♦ one-season resort
Einsaisonhotel n
 ♦ one-season hotel
einsame Lage, f
 ♦ lonely location
 ♦ lonely setting
einsame Mahlzeit, f
 ♦ solitary meal
einsamer Bauernhof, m
 ♦ isolated farm

einsamer Ort, m
 ♦ secluded place
 ♦ lonely place
einsamer Reisender, m
 ♦ lonely traveller
 ♦ lonely traveler AE
einsames Bauernhaus, n
 ♦ isolated farmhouse
Einsamkeit, f
 ♦ solitude
Einsamkeit suchen
 ♦ seek solitude
Einsamkeit und Ruhe suchen
 ♦ seek seclusion and peace
Einsamkeit vorziehen
 ♦ prefer solitude
einsammeln jn coll
 (z.B. Touristen)
 auflesen jn coll
 ♦ gather (people) together
einschenken etw
 eingießen etw
 ♦ pour s.th.
 ♦ pour out s.th.
einschenken jm
 ♦ pour s.o. a glass
 ♦ pour s.o. a cup
 ♦ fill s.o.'s glass
 ♦ fill s.o.'s cup
einschenken jm noch einmal
 nochmals einschenken jm
 ♦ pour s.o. another glass
 ♦ pour s.o. another cup
 ♦ refill s.o.'s glass
 ♦ refill s.o.'s cup
Einschienenbahn, f
 ♦ monorail
einschiffen sich auf der Fähre
 ♦ embark on the ferry
einschiffige Kirche, f
 ♦ one-nave church
 ♦ one-naved church
Einschiffung, f
 ♦ embarkation
Einschiffung beginnt um 15 Uhr
 ♦ embarkation commences at 3 p.m.
Einschiffungsgebühr, f
 ♦ embarkation charge
 ♦ embarkation fee
Einschiffungshafen, m
 ♦ embarkation port
 ♦ port of embarkation
Einschiffungskarte, f
 ♦ embarkation card
Einschiffungsstelle, f
 Einschiffungspunkt, m
 ♦ embarkation point
 ♦ point of embarkation
einschlafen
 in Schlaf sinken
 ♦ fall asleep
 ♦ go off inform
einschläfriges Bett n
 → Einzelbett
einschließen jn in einem Zimmer
 ♦ shut s.o. up in a room
 ♦ lock s.o. up in a room
einschließen sich in einem Zimmer
 ♦ lock oneself up in a room
einschließlich Bedienung
 → Bedienung inbegriffen

Einschließlich Bedienungsgeld

Einschließlich Bedienungsgeld
Bedienungsgeld inbegriffen
♦ **Service charge included**
einschließlich Freitag
inklusive Freitag
♦ **including Friday**
♦ **up to and including Friday**
♦ **through Friday** AE
einschließlich Mehrwertsteuer
einschließlich Mwst.
♦ **including value added tax**
♦ **including VAT**
♦ **inclusive of value added tax**
♦ **inclusive of VAT**
einschließlich Mehrwertsteuer und Bedienung
einschließlich Mwst. und Bedienung
♦ **including value added tax and service**
♦ **including VAT and service**
♦ **inclusive of value added tax and service**
♦ **inclusive of VAT and service**
einschließlich Mwst. und Bedienung
♦ **including VAT and service**
♦ **inclusive of VAT and service**
einschränken etw
begrenzen etw
beschränken etw
♦ **restrict s.th.**
Einschränkung, f
Beschränkung, f
Begrenzung, f
♦ **restriction**
einschreiben sich (anmelden)
→ anmelden sich
einschreiben sich auf einer Liste
♦ **enroll on a list** AE
♦ **enrol on a list** BE
einschreiben sich für einen Kurs
anmelden sich zu einem Kurs
♦ **enroll for a course** AE
♦ **enrol for a course** BE
♦ **register for a course**
einschreiben sich für etw
(z.B. Kurs)
anmelden sich zu etw
♦ **enroll for s.th.**
♦ **enrol for s.th.**
♦ **register for s.th.**
einschreiben sich in etw
♦ **enroll in s.th.** AE
♦ **enrol in s.th.** BE
Einschreibgebühr, f
→ Anmeldungsgebühr
Einschreibung, f
→ Anmeldung
Einschreibung der Gäste, f
♦ **registration of guests**
♦ **registering guests**
Einsiedelei, f
♦ **hermitage**
Einsiedler, m
♦ **hermit**
♦ **recluse**
Einsiedlerzelle, f
Einsiedelei, f
♦ **hermit's cell**
Einsparung, f
♦ **saving**
Einsparung von 40%, f
♦ **saving of 40%**
♦ **40% saving**

Einsparung von Geld, f
♦ **saving of money**
Einsparung von Raum, f
♦ **saving of space**
einspringen für jn
♦ **substitute for s.o.**
♦ **take s.o.'s place**
♦ **step in for s.o.**
einspurig, adj
♦ **one-lane, adj**
♦ **single-track, adj**
einspurige Straße, f
♦ **one-lane road**
eins sein mit der Natur
♦ **be at one with nature**
Einstandspreis der Waren, m
♦ **cost of goods purchased**
einsteigen (Flugzeug)
♦ **emplane**
♦ **embark**
einsteigen in ein Auto
♦ **get in a car**
einsteigen in einen Bus
♦ **get on a bus**
♦ **get onto a bus**
♦ **get on a coach** BE
♦ **get onto a coach** BE
einsteigen in einen Fahrstuhl
einsteigen in einen Aufzug
einsteigen in einen Lift
♦ **get into an elevator** AE
♦ **get into a lift** BE
einsteigen in einen Zug
♦ **get on a train**
einsteigen in ein Flugzeug
♦ **get on a plane**
♦ **board a plane**
einsteigen in etw (Verkehrsmittel)
♦ **get in s.th.**
♦ **get into s.th.**
♦ **get on s.th.**
♦ **board s.th.**
einstellen sich auf den individuellen Geschmack
♦ **adapt (oneself) to individual tastes**
einstellen sich auf etw
♦ **adapt (oneself) to s.th.**
Einstellraum, m
Lagerraum m
♦ **storage room**
Einstellraum für Skis, m
Skiraum, m
♦ **ski storage room**
♦ **ski room**
Einstellung zum Tourismus, f
Einstellung zum Fremdenverkehr, f
♦ **attitude to tourism**
Ein-Stern-Anlage, f
Ein-Stern-Komplex, m
Anlage mit einem Stern, f
Komplex mit einem Stern, m
♦ **one-star complex**
Ein-Stern-Anwesen, n
Ein-Stern-Objekt, n
Anwesen mit einem Stern, n
Objekt mit einem Stern, n
♦ **one-star property**
Ein-Stern-Appartement, n
Appartement mit einem Stern, n
♦ **one-star apartment**
Ein-Stern-Appartementanlage, f
Ein-Stern-Appartementkomplex, m

178

Appartementanlage mit einem Stern, f
Appartementkomplex mit einem Stern, m
♦ **one-star apartment complex**
Ein-Stern-Attraktion, f
Attraktion mit einem Stern, f
♦ **one-star attraction**
Ein-Stern-Bereich, m
Ein-Stern-Sektor, m
♦ **one-star sector**
Ein-Stern-Betrieb, m
Betrieb mit einem Stern, m
♦ **one-star establishment**
♦ **one-star operation**
Ein-Stern-Bewertung, f
♦ **one-star rating**
Ein-Stern-Campingplatz, m
Campingplatz mit einem Stern, m
♦ **one-star campsite**
♦ **one-star campground** AE
♦ **one-star camping site** BE
♦ **one-star camping ground** BE
♦ **one-star site**
Ein-Stern-Caravanplatz, m
Ein-Stern-Wohnwagenplatz, m
Caravanplatz mit einem Stern, m
Wohnwagenplatz mit einem Stern, m
♦ **one-star caravan site** BE
♦ **one-star trailer site** AE
Ein-Stern-Club, m
Club mit einem Stern, m
♦ **one-star club**
Ein-Stern-Einrichtung, f
♦ **one-star facility**
Ein-Stern-Einstufung, f
♦ **one-star grading**
Ein-Stern-Ferienwohnung, f
Ein-Stern-Fewo, f coll
Ferienwohnung mit einem Stern, f
Fewo mit einem Stern, f coll
♦ **one-star vacation apartment** AE
♦ **one-star holiday flat** BE
Ein-Stern-Haus, n
→ Ein-Stern-Hotel
Einsternhotel, n
→ Ein-Stern-Hotel
Ein-Stern-Hotel, n
Hotel mit einem Stern, n
♦ **one-star hotel**
Ein-Stern-Hotelanlage, f
Ein-Stern-Hotelkomplex, m
Hotelanlage mit einem Stern, f
Hotelkomplex mit einem Stern, m
♦ **one-star hotel complex**
Ein-Stern-Hotelservice, m
♦ **one-star hotel service**
Ein-Stern-Kategorie f
♦ **one-star category**
Ein-Stern-Koch, m
♦ **one-star cook**
Ein-Stern-Komfort, m
♦ **one-star comfort**
♦ **one-star amenities** pl
Ein-Stern-Komplex, m
→ Ein-Stern-Anlage
Ein-Stern-Kreuzfahrtschiff, n
Kreuzfahrtschiff mit einem Stern, n
♦ **one-star cruise ship**
♦ **one-star cruise liner**
Ein-Stern-Küchenchef, m
♦ **one-star chef**

Eintritt ist frei

Ein-Stern-Luxus, m
♦ one-star luxury
Ein-Stern-Niveau, n
♦ one-star level
Ein-Stern-Platz, m (Camping)
Platz mit einem Stern, m
♦ one-star site
Ein-Stern-Platz, m (Tennis)
Platz mit einem Stern, m
♦ one-star court
Ein-Stern-Preis, m
♦ one-star price
♦ one-star rate
Ein-Stern-Qualität, f
♦ one-star quality
Ein-Stern-Residenz, f
Residenz mit einem Stern, f
♦ one-star residence
Ein-Stern-Restaurant, n
Restaurant mit einem Stern, n
♦ one-star restaurant
Ein-Stern-Segment, n
♦ one-star segment
Ein-Stern-Sektor, m
→ Ein-Stern-Bereich
Ein-Stern-Service, m
♦ one-star service
Ein-Stern-Service anbieten
♦ offer one-star service
Ein-Stern-Stadthotel, n (Großstadt)
Stadthotel mit einem Stern, n
♦ one-star city hotel
Ein-Stern-Stadthotel, n (kleine Stadt)
Stadthotel mit einem Stern, n
♦ one-star town hotel
Ein-Stern-Standard m
♦ one-star standard
Ein-Stern-System, n
♦ one-star system
Ein-Stern-Tagungsort, m
Ein-Stern-Austragungsort, m
♦ one-star venue
Ein-Stern-Unterkunft, f
Unterkunft mit einem Stern, f
♦ one-star accommodation
♦ one-star lodging AE
Ein-Stern-Wohnwagenplatz, m
Ein-Stern-Caravanplatz, m
Wohnwagenplatz mit einem Stern, m
Caravanplatz mit einem Stern, m
♦ one-star trailer site AE
♦ one-star caravan site BE
Ein-Stern-Zimmer, n
Zimmer mit einem Stern, n
♦ one-star room
einstöckig, adj attr (Gebäude)
eingeschossig, adj, attr
♦ one-story, adj attr AE
♦ one-storey, adr attr BE
♦ one-floor, adj attr
♦ single-storey, adj attr BE
einstöckig, adj (Bett, Kuchen)
♦ one-tier, adj
♦ one-tiered, adj
einstöckig, adj prd (Gebäude)
♦ one-storied, adj prd AE
♦ one-storeyed, adj prd BE
einstöckiges Haus, n
♦ one-story house AE
♦ one-storey house BE
♦ one-floor house

einstöckig sein (Gebäude)
♦ be one-storied AE
♦ be one-storeyed BE
einstufen etw (nach Qualität, Leistung)
♦ grade s.th.
Einstufung, f (nach Qualität, Leistung)
♦ grading
Einstufung geben (nach Qualität, Leistung)
♦ award a grading
Einstufungssystem, n (nach Qualität, Leistung)
♦ grading system
Einstufungssystem nach Sternen, n
♦ star grading system
einstündig, adj
♦ one-hour, adj
♦ one hour's, adj
♦ of one hour's duration
♦ lasting one hour
einstündiger Marsch, m
♦ one hour's march
einstündiges Programm, n
♦ one-hour program AE
♦ one-hour programme BE
einstündige Verspätung, f
♦ one-hour delay
Eintagesaufenthalt, m
eintägiger Aufenthalt, m
Tagesaufenthalt, m
Aufenthalt von einem Tag, m
♦ stay of one day
♦ one-day stay
Eintageshotelaufenthalt, m
→ eintägiger Hotelaufenthalt
Eintagespreis, m
♦ one-day price
♦ one-day rate
Eintagesreise, f
→ Tagesreise
eintägig, adj
♦ one-day, adj
♦ one day's, adj
♦ lasting one day
♦ of one day's duration
eintägiger Aufenthalt, m
Eintagesaufenthalt m
Tagesaufenthalt m
♦ one-day stay
eintägiger Hotelaufenthalt, m
Eintageshotelaufenthalt m
Tageshotelaufenthalt m
♦ one-day hotel stay
♦ one-day stay at a hotel
♦ one-day stay in a hotel
eintägiger Urlaub, m
Tagesurlaub, m
♦ one-day vacation AE
♦ one-day holiday BE
eintägige Veranstaltung, f
♦ one-day event
♦ one-day function
einteilen etw
klassifizieren etw
♦ classify s.th.
einteilen jn zu einem bestimmten Service
♦ detail s.o. for a particular service
einteilen jn zu etw
♦ detail s.o. for s.th.
eintöniges Essen, n
eintönige Nahrung, f
♦ monotonous food
♦ monotonous meal

Eintopf, m
Eintopfgericht, n
Eintopfessen, n
Schmorgericht, n
♦ stew
♦ hot pot AE
♦ hotpot BE
Eintrag, m (in Buch etc)
♦ entry
eintragen einen Namen in ein Formular
♦ enter a name in a form
eintragen etw (in Buch etc)
♦ enter s.th.
eintragen etw in das Buchungsformular
♦ enter s.th. on the booking form
eintragen jn in eine Liste
♦ enter s.o. in a list
♦ put s.o. on a list
eintragen sich in das Gästebuch
eintragen sich ins Gästebuch
♦ sign the visitors' book
♦ sign the guest book
eintragen sich ins Fremdenbuch (im Hotel)
♦ sign the hotel register
Eintreffen, n (Ankunft)
→ Ankunft
Eintreffen, n (Check-in)
→ Ankunft, Anmeldung
eintreffen im Hotel
♦ check-in at the hotel
♦ arrive at the hotel
eintreffen (Personen)
ankommen
♦ show up coll
♦ arrive
♦ come in
♦ check in
♦ get in
Eintreffenszeit, f
Zeitpunkt des Eintreffens, m
Zeitpunkt des Einpassierens, m
Belegungszeitpunkt, m
♦ check-in time
eintreffen zu einem offiziellen Besuch
♦ arrive for an official visit
eintreffen zu einem privaten Besuch
♦ arrive for a private visit
eintreffen zur verabredeten Zeit
→ ankommen zur verabredeten Zeit
eintreten (Ereignis)
♦ occur
Eintritt, m (Gebühr)
→ Eintrittsgebühr
Eintritt, m (generell)
Einlaß, m
♦ admission
♦ entrance
♦ entry
Eintritt DM 12
♦ Admission DM 12
Eintritt frei
(Hinweisschild)
Eintritt gratis
♦ Admission free
♦ Entrance free
Eintritt für etw, m
♦ entrance fee to s.th.
♦ admission fee to s.th.
Eintritt ist frei
Der Eintritt ist frei

Eintritt kostet DM 12 für Erwachsene

- ♦ Admission is free
- ♦ Entrance is free

Eintritt kostet DM 12 für Erwachsene
- ♦ Admission is DM 12 for adults

Eintritt kostet DM 12 für Kinder
- ♦ Admission is DM 12 for children

Eintrittschip, m
(Art Münze)
- ♦ entrance token
- ♦ entry token

Eintrittseinnahmen, f pl
- ♦ admission revenues pl
- ♦ entrance revenues pl
- ♦ admission income

Eintrittserlös, m
- ♦ admission revenue
- ♦ admission income

Eintrittsgebühr, f
Eintrittsgeld n
- ♦ entrance fee
- ♦ admission fee
- ♦ entrance
- ♦ admission (charge)
- ♦ entry fee

Eintrittsgebühr für etw, f
- ♦ admission fee to s.th.
- ♦ entrance fee to s.th.

Eintrittsgebühr halten
Eintrittsgebühr beibehalten
- ♦ retain the admission fee
- ♦ retain the admission charge

Eintrittsgebühr verlangen
→ Eintritt verlangen

Eintrittsgebühr zahlen
- ♦ pay an entrance fee
- ♦ pay admission

Eintrittsgeld, n
→ Eintrittsgebühr

Eintrittsgeld zahlen
Eintrittsgebühr zahlen
- ♦ pay the entrance fee
- ♦ pay the admission fee

Eintrittsgutschein, m
- ♦ admission charge voucher

Eintrittskarte, f
- ♦ admission ticket
- ♦ entrance ticket
- ♦ ticket of admission
- ♦ ticket

Eintrittskarte kaufen
- ♦ buy an admission ticket
- ♦ buy an entrance ticket
- ♦ buy a ticket

Eintrittspreis, m
- ♦ admission price
- ♦ price of admission
- ♦ admission
- ♦ admission fee
- ♦ entrance fee

Eintrittspreis senken
- ♦ cut the admission price

Eintritt verlangen
Eintrittsgebühr verlangen
- ♦ charge admission
- ♦ charge an entrance fee

Eintritt zahlen
DM 10 Eintritt zahlen
- ♦ pay admission
- ♦ pay DM 10 admission

Eintritt zu etw, m
Eintritt für etw m

- ♦ admission to s.th.
- ♦ entrance to s.th.

eintrudeln coll
(Personen)
- ♦ take one's time arriving

Ein- und Ausführung von Devisen, f
- ♦ import and export of foreign currency
- ♦ import and export of foreign currencies

Ein- und Ausreise, f
- ♦ entry and departure

einverstanden sein mit den Buchungsbedingungen
- ♦ accept the booking conditions

Einwanderer, m
- ♦ immigrant

einwandern (aus einem Land)
- ♦ immigrate (from a country)

Einwanderung, f
- ♦ immigration

Einwanderungsabfertigung, f
- ♦ immigration clearance

Einwanderungsbestimmungen, f pl
- ♦ immigration regulations pl

Einwanderungsvisum, n
- ♦ immigrant visa

Einweckglas, n
- ♦ fruit jar

Einwegbecher, m
- ♦ disposable cup

Einwegbenutzung, f
(z.B. von Servietten)
- ♦ single service

Einwegbesteck, n
- ♦ disposable cutlery

Einwegflasche, f
- ♦ nondeposit bottle AE
- ♦ no-return bottle AE
- ♦ non-returnable bottle BE

Einweggeschirr, n
- ♦ disposable tableware

Einweghandtuch, n
- ♦ disposable towel

Einwegserviette, f
- ♦ disposable napkin

Einwegteller, m
- ♦ disposable plate

Einwegtischwäsche, f
- ♦ disposable table linen

Einwegvermietung, f (Fahrzeug)
(wird nicht an den Abholpunkt zurückgebracht)
- ♦ one-way rental
- ♦ one-way hire BE

Einwegwäsche, f
- ♦ disposable linen

einweihen etw
feierlich eröffnen etw
- ♦ inaugurate s.th.

einweihen etw offiziell
- ♦ inaugurate s.th. officially

Einweihung, f
feierliche Eröffnung, f
- ♦ inauguration

Einwochenpreis, m
Wochenpreis, m
- ♦ one-week rate
- ♦ one-week price
- ♦ weekly rate
- ♦ weekly price

einwöchig, adj
- ♦ one-week, adj
- ♦ lasting one week

- ♦ of one week's duration
- ♦ one week's, adj

einwöchiger Aufenthalt, m
Wochenaufenthalt, m
- ♦ one-week stay
- ♦ one week's stay
- ♦ stay of one week

einwöchige Reise, f
- ♦ one-week journey
- ♦ one-week tour
- ♦ one-week trip

einwöchige Tournee, f
Wochentournee, f
- ♦ one-week tour

Einzahlung machen (Bank)
- ♦ make a deposit BE

Einzelappartement, n
→ Einzimmerappartement

Einzelausflug, m
- ♦ individual excursion

Einzelauslandsreise, f
(individueller Reiseverlauf; Vorauszahlung)
FIT, f
- ♦ independent foreign tour
- ♦ FIT

Einzelauslandsreiseveranstalter, m
FIT-Veranstalter, m
- ♦ foreign independent tour operator
- ♦ FIT operator

Einzelaussteller, m
- ♦ individual exhibitor
- ♦ individual exhibitor AE
- ♦ individual exhibiting company
- ♦ individual exhibiting firm

Einzelausstellung, f (generell)
- ♦ individual exhibition
- ♦ individual exhibit AE

Einzelausstellung, f (z.B. Werke eines Künstlers)
- ♦ solo exhibition
- ♦ solo exhibit AE

Einzelbad, n
→ Privatbad

Einzelbadzuschlag, m
→ Privatbadzuschlag

Einzelbalkon, m
- ♦ individual balcony
- ♦ separate balcony

Einzelbecken, n
(Waschbecken)
- ♦ single basin

Einzelbehandlung, f
→ individuelle Behandlung

Einzelbelegung, f
Belegung mit einer Person, f
Einzelbenutzung, f
- ♦ single occupancy

Einzelbelegungspreis, m
Preis bei Einzelbelegung, f
Preis bei einbettiger Belegung, m
- ♦ single-occupancy rate
- ♦ single-occupancy price

Einzelbenutzung eines Zimmers, f
→ Alleinbenutzung eines Zimmers

Einzelbesitzer, m
einzelner Besitzer, m
- ♦ individual owner

Einzelbesucher, m
- ♦ individual visitor

Einzelbetreuung, f
individuelle Betreuung, f

180

◆ **individual care**
◆ individual attention
Einzelbetrieb, m
◆ **single establishment**
◆ individual establishment
◆ independent establishment
Einzelbett, n
einschläfriges Bett, n
◆ **single bed**
◆ single
Einzelbettcouch f
◆ **single couch bed**
Einzelbettkabine, f
→ Einzelkabine
Einzelbettzimmer, n
→ Einzelzimmer
Einzelbuchung f
◆ **individual booking**
◆ single booking
Einzelbungalow, m
freistehender Bungalow, m
einzelner Bungalow, m
◆ **detached bungalow**
◆ single bungalow
◆ freestanding bungalow
◆ individual bungalow
Einzelcouch, f
◆ **single couch**
Einzelfahrt, f
◆ **individual trip**
Einzelfirma, f
Einzelunternehmen n
◆ **one-man business**
Einzelgarage, f (allein im Freien stehend)
freistehende Garage, f
◆ **freestanding garage**
Einzelgarage f (für 1 Pkw)
◆ **single garage**
◆ lock-up garage BE
Einzelgast, m
einzelner Gast, m
◆ **single guest**
◆ individual guest
Einzelgericht n
einzelnes Gericht n
◆ **individual dish**
◆ single dish
Einzelgeschäft, n
(mit Einzelkunden)
◆ **individual business**
Einzelhandelsgeschäft, n
Einzelhandelsladen, m
◆ **retail store** AE
◆ retail shop BE
Einzelhandelsreisebüro, n
◆ **retail travel agency**
Einzelhaus, n
einzelnes Haus, n
◆ **single house**
◆ detached house
◆ freestanding house
Einzelheit, f
◆ **detail**
◆ particular
Einzelheiten auf Anfrage
◆ **Details on application**
Einzelheiten werden noch bekanntgegeben
◆ **Details to be announced**
Einzelheiten zusenden auf Anfrage
◆ **send details on request**

Einzelhotel, n
(kein Kettenhotel)
selbständiges Hotel, n
eigenständiges Hotel, n
◆ **independent hotel**
◆ individual hotel
◆ individually run hotel
Einzelhotelier n
einzelner Hotelier m
unabhängiger Hotelier m
◆ **individual hotelier**
◆ independent hotelier
◆ individual hotelier
◆ independent hotelkeeper
Einzeljacuzzi, m
◆ **individual jacuzzi**
Einzelkabine, f
◆ **single cabin**
Einzelkabinenzuschlag, m
◆ **single-cabin supplement**
Einzelkoje, f
Einzelbett, n
◆ **single berth**
Einzelkosten, pl
◆ **itemized costs** pl
◆ itemised costs pl
Einzelkunde m
einzelner Kunde m
◆ **individual customer**
◆ individual client
◆ single customer
Einzellage, f (Weinberg)
◆ **individual vineyard**
Einzelleistung, f
einzelne Leistung f
◆ **individual service**
Einzelliege f
◆ **single divan**
einzelnes Appartement, n
◆ **individual apartment**
einzelnes Bett, n
→ Einzelbett
einzelnes Gericht, n
Einzelgericht, n
◆ **single dish**
◆ individual dish
einzelne Sitzung, f
◆ **individual session**
◆ single session
einzeln reisend, adj
◆ **traveling single, adj** AE
◆ travelling single, adj BE
◆ touring on one's own, adj
einzeln verreisen
(nicht in einer Gruppe)
einzeln reisen
◆ **travel independently**
Einzelpackung, f
Einzelportion, f
◆ **individual pack**
Einzelpassagier, m
einzelner Passagier, m
◆ **individual passenger**
Einzelpauschale, f
◆ **individual package**
Einzelperson, f
◆ **individual person**
◆ single person
Einzelplatz, m (Sitzplatz)
einzelner Platz, m
Einzelsitzplatz, m

Einzelsitz, m
◆ **single seat**
◆ individual seat
Einzelplatzverkauf, m
◆ **seat-only sale**
Einzelportion, f
einzelne Portion, f
◆ **individual portion**
◆ single portion
◆ serving
Einzelpreis, m (für Einzelstück)
◆ **price of each item**
◆ price per unit
Einzelpreis, m (Gegensatz zu Gruppenpreis)
Individualpreis, m
◆ **individual rate**
◆ individual price
◆ single rate
◆ single price
Einzelquartier, n (Militär)
(Gegensatz zu Familienquartier)
◆ **single quarters** pl
Einzelreise, f
◆ **independent tour**
◆ individual tour
Einzelreisender, m
◆ **single traveler** AE
◆ single traveller BE
◆ individual traveler AE
◆ individual traveller BE
Einzelreservierung f
◆ **individual reservation**
Einzelrestaurant, n
◆ **individual restaurant**
◆ single restaurant
Einzelschlafzimmer, n
Einzelschlafraum, m
◆ **single bedroom**
Einzelsessellift m
(Ski)
◆ **single chair lift**
Einzelsitzplatz, m
Einzelsitz, m
Einzelplatz, m
◆ **individual seat**
◆ single seat
Einzelsitzung, f
Einzeltermin, m
einzelne Behandlungssitzung, f
◆ **single session**
◆ individual session
Einzelstand, m
◆ **individual stand**
Einzelstellplatz, m
(Camping)
◆ **individual pitch**
Einzelterrasse, f
◆ **separate terrace**
◆ single terrace
◆ private terrace
◆ individual terrace
Einzeltherapie, f
individuelle Therapie, f
◆ **individual therapy**
Einzeltisch, m (für eine Person)
◆ **table for one person**
◆ table for one
Einzeltisch, m (separater Tisch)
◆ **separate table**
◆ individual table

Einzeltischzeit

Einzeltischzeit, f
  einzelne Tischzeit, f
  einzige Tischzeit, f
  ♦ **single sitting, f**
Einzeltransfer, m
  (eine Person)
  ♦ **individual transfer**
  ♦ single transfer
Einzelübernachtungspreis, m
  ♦ **single night price**
  ♦ single night rate
Einzelübernachtungstarif, m
  ♦ **single night tariff**
  ♦ single night rates *pl*
  ♦ single night rate
  ♦ single night terms *pl*
Einzelunterbringung, f
  → Einzelunterkunft
Einzelunterhalter, m
  → Alleinunterhalter
Einzelunterkunft, f
  Einzelunterbringung, f
  ♦ **single accommodation**
  ♦ individual accommodation
Einzelunterkunft steht zur Verfügung
  ♦ **single accommodation is available**
Einzelunternehmen, n
  → Einzelfirma
Einzelunternehmer, m
  ♦ **sole trader**
  ♦ sole proprietor *AE*
Einzelunterricht, m (generell)
  ♦ **individual instruction**
  ♦ individual course
  ♦ individual tuition
  ♦ one-to-one-teaching
  ♦ one-to-one tuition
Einzelunterricht, m (Sport)
  Einzeltraining, n
  ♦ **individual coaching**
Einzelveranstalter, m
  unabhängiger Reiseveranstalter, m
  ♦ **independent operator**
Einzelveranstaltung, f (einmalig)
  (es gibt keine zweite davon)
  einmalige Veranstaltung f
  ♦ **one-off function**
Einzelveranstaltung, f (einzelne)
  ♦ **single function**
Einzelverpackung, f
  ♦ **individual packaging**
Einzelversicherung, f
  ♦ **individual insurance**
Einzelvilla, f
  freistehende Villa, f
  einzelne Villa, f
  ♦ **detached villa**
  ♦ single villa
  ♦ freestanding villa
  ♦ individual villa
Einzelvisum, n
  ♦ **individual visa**
  ♦ single visa
Einzelvoucher, m
  Einzelgutschein m
  ♦ **single voucher**
Einzelzimmer, n
  EZ, n
  ♦ **single room**
  ♦ single

♦ SR
♦ sr
Einzelzimmerappartement, n
  → Einzimmerappartement
Einzelzimmeraufschlag, m
  → Einzelzimmerzuschlag
Einzelzimmerauslastung f
  Einzelzimmerbelegung f
  ♦ **single-room occupancy**
Einzelzimmerbelegung, f
  → Einzelzimmerauslastung
Einzelzimmer benötigen
  ♦ **require a single room**
  ♦ require a single
Einzelzimmerbestellung, f
  → Einzelzimmerbuchung
Einzelzimmer brauchen
  ♦ **need a single room**
  ♦ need a single
Einzelzimmer buchen
  Einzelzimmer bestellen
  ♦ **book a single room**
  ♦ book a single
Einzelzimmerbuchung, f
  Einzelzimmerbestellung, f
  ♦ **single-room booking**
  ♦ booking (of) a single room
Einzelzimmer mieten
  ♦ **rent a single room**
  ♦ rent a single
Einzelzimmer mit Frühstück, n
  ♦ **single room and breakfast**
Einzelzimmernachfrage, f
  Nachfrage nach Einzelzimmern, f
  ♦ **demand for single rooms**
  ♦ demand for singles
Einzelzimmer nehmen
  ♦ **take a single room**
  ♦ take a single
Einzelzimmerpreis m
  ♦ **single-room rate**
  ♦ single-room price
Einzelzimmer sind knapp
  ♦ **single rooms are scarce**
Einzelzimmerunterkunft, f
  Einzelzimmerunterbringung, f
  ♦ **single-room accommodation**
Einzelzimmer vermieten
  ♦ **rent (out) a single room**
  ♦ rent (out) a single
  ♦ let a single room *BE*
  ♦ let a single *BE*
Einzelzimmer wünschen
  ♦ **request a single room**
  ♦ request a single
Einzelzimmerzuschlag m
  ♦ **single-room supplement**
Einzelzuschlag, m
  ♦ **single supplement**
einziehen bei jm
  ♦ **move into s.o.'s house**
  ♦ take lodgings with s.o.
einziehen (in Unterkunft)
  ♦ **move in**
einzigartige Atmosphäre, f
  ♦ **unique atmosphere**
einzigartige Ausstellung, f
  ♦ **unique exhibition**
einzigartige Gastlichkeit, f
  einzigartige Gastfreundschaft, f
  ♦ **unique hospitality**

einzigartige Lage, f
  ♦ **unique position**
  ♦ unique situation
  ♦ unique location
einzigartige Lage genießen
  ♦ **enjoy a unique position**
  ♦ enjoy a unique situation
  ♦ enjoy a unique location
einziges bewohnbares Zimmer, n
  ♦ **only habitable room**
Einzimmerappartement n
  ♦ **one-room apartment**
Einzimmerchalet, n
  ♦ **one-room chalet**
  ♦ single-room chalet
Einzimmerferienwohnung, f
  ♦ **one-room vacation apartment** *AE*
  ♦ one-room holiday flat *BE*
einzimmerig, adj
  ♦ **one-roomed, adj**
einzimmeriges Appartement, n
  Einzimmerappartement, n
  ♦ **one-roomed apartment**
Einzimmersuite, f
  ♦ **one-room suite**
  ♦ one-roomed suite
Einzimmerwohnung, f
  ♦ **one-room flat** *BE*
  ♦ one-room apartment *AE*
Einzug, m (in Unterkunft)
  ♦ **moving (in s.th.)**
  ♦ occupation (of s.th.)
Einzug feiern
  (in neue Wohnung, neues Haus)
  ♦ **give a housewarming party**
  ♦ have a housewarming party
  ♦ hold a housewarming party
  ♦ throw a housewarming party *coll*
Einzugsfest, n
  (nach dem Einzug in neue Wohnung)
  Einzugsfeier, f
  Wohnungseinweihung, f
  Hauseinweihung, f
  ♦ **housewarming party** *AE*
  ♦ housewarming *AE*
  ♦ house-warming party *BE*
  ♦ house-warming *BE*
Einzugsfest feiern
  Wohnungseinweihung feiern
  Hauseinweihung feiern
  ♦ **have a housewarming party** *AE*
  ♦ have a house-warming party *BE*
Einzugsgebiet, n
  ♦ **catchment area**
Einzugstag, m (in Unterkunft)
  ♦ **day of moving in**
  ♦ moving-in day
Ei pochieren
  ♦ **poach an egg**
Eipulver n
  ♦ **egg powder**
  ♦ dried egg
Eis, n (generell)
  ♦ **ice**
Eis, n (Speiseeis)
  → Eiskrem
Eis am Stiel, n
  ♦ **ice lolly**
  ♦ lollipop *BE*
Eisbahn, f
  Eislaufbahn, f

- ♦ ice rink *AE*
- ♦ ice-rink *BE*

Eisbaiser, n *FR m*
- ♦ ice meringue

Eisbar, f
→ Eisdiele

Eisbecher, m
Eis mit Früchten, n
- ♦ sundae
- ♦ coupe
- ♦ ice-cream cup

Eisbehälter, m
- ♦ ice container

Eisbombe, f
Bombe glacée, f *FR*
- ♦ ice-bomb
- ♦ bombe glacée *FR*

Eis brechen
das Eis brechen
- ♦ break the ice

Eisbrecher, m
- ♦ icebreaker *AE*
- ♦ ice-breaker *BE*

Eisbüfett, n (Theke)
Eistheke, f
- ♦ ice-cream counter

Eiscafé, n
→ Eisdiele

Eiscafé-Pizzeria
- ♦ ice-cream parlor cum pizzeria *AE*
- ♦ ice-cream parlour cum pizzeria *BE*

Ei schälen
- ♦ shell an egg

Ei schlagen
- ♦ beat an egg

Eischnee, m
- ♦ whipped egg white

Eisdiele, f
Eiscafé, n
- ♦ ice-cream parlor *AE*
- ♦ ice-cream parlour *BE*

Eisenbahn, f
- ♦ railroad *AE*
- ♦ railway *BE*
- ♦ rly. *BE*

Eisenbahnabteil, n
- ♦ railroad compartment *AE*
- ♦ railway compartment *BE*

Eisenbahnausflug, m
- ♦ railroad excursion *AE*
- ♦ railroad trip *AE*
- ♦ railway excursion *BE*
- ♦ railway trip *BE*

Eisenbahnausstellung, f
- ♦ railroad exhibition *AE*
- ♦ railroad exhibit *AE*
- ♦ railway exhibition *BE*

Eisenbahnbegeisterter, m
Eisenbahnfan, m
- ♦ railroad enthusiast *AE*
- ♦ railway enthusiast *BE*
- ♦ rail enthusiast

Eisenbahnbrücke, f
- ♦ railroad bridge *AE*
- ♦ railway bridge *BE*

Eisenbahnendstation, f
Eisenbahnendhaltestelle, f
- ♦ railroad terminus *AE*
- ♦ railway terminus *BE*
- ♦ terminus of the railroad *AE*
- ♦ terminus of the railway *BE*

Eisenbahner, m
- ♦ railroadman *AE*
- ♦ railroader *AE*
- ♦ railwayman *BE*

Eisenbahnfähre, f
- ♦ railroad ferry *AE*
- ♦ railway ferry *BE*

Eisenbahn fahren
- ♦ ride the railroad *AE*
- ♦ ride the railway *BE*

Eisenbahnfahrkarte, f
Eisenbahnfahrschein, m
- ♦ railroad ticket *AE*
- ♦ railway ticket *BE*

Eisenbahnfahrpreis, m
- ♦ railroad fare *AE*
- ♦ railway fare *BE*

Eisenbahnfahrt, f
- ♦ railroad trip *AE*
- ♦ railroad ride *AE*
- ♦ railway trip *BE*
- ♦ railway ride *BE*

Eisenbahnfreak, m
- ♦ railroad freak *AE*
- ♦ railway freak *BE*

Eisenbahnführer, m
(Information)
- ♦ railroad guide *AE*
- ♦ railway guide *BE*

Eisenbahngesellschaft, f
- ♦ railroad company *AE*
- ♦ railway company *BE*

Eisenbahngleis, n
- ♦ railroad track *AE*
- ♦ railway track *BE*

Eisenbahnhotel n
- ♦ railroad hotel *AE*
- ♦ railway hotel *BE*
- ♦ rail hotel

Eisenbahnlinie, f
- ♦ railroad line *AE*
- ♦ railway line *BE*

Eisenbahnlokomotive, f
- ♦ railroad engine *AE*
- ♦ railroad locomotive *AE*
- ♦ railway engine *BE*
- ♦ railway locomotive *BE*

Eisenbahnmanagement, n
- ♦ railroad management *AE*
- ♦ railway management *BE*

Eisenbahnmuseum, n
- ♦ railroad museum *AE*
- ♦ railway museum *BE*

Eisenbahn nehmen (nach X)
- ♦ take the railroad (to X) *AE*
- ♦ take the railway (to X) *BE*

Eisenbahnpauschalreise, f
Bahnpauschalreise, f
- ♦ rail-inclusive tour
- ♦ RIT
- ♦ rail package tour
- ♦ package tour by rail
- ♦ inclusive tour by rail

Eisenbahnreise, f
- ♦ railroad journey *AE*
- ♦ railroad trip *AE*
- ♦ railroad tour *AE*
- ♦ railway journey *BE*
- ♦ railway trip *BE*

Eisenbahnreisen, n
Eisenbahnreiseverkehr, m

- ♦ railroad travel *AE*
- ♦ railway travel *BE*

Eisenbahnreisender, m
- ♦ railroad traveler *AE*
- ♦ railway traveller *BE*

Eisenbahnrestaurant, n
- ♦ railroad restaurant *AE*
- ♦ railway restaurant *BE*

Eisenbahnstadt, f
- ♦ railroad town *AE*
- ♦ railway town *BE*

Eisenbahnstation, f
- ♦ railroad station *AE*
- ♦ railway station *BE*
- ♦ rail station

Eisenbahnstrecke, f
- ♦ railroad route *AE*
- ♦ railway route *BE*

Eisenbahnstreik, m
- ♦ railroad strike *AE*
- ♦ railway strike *BE*

Eisenbahntourismus, m
- ♦ railroad tourism *AE*
- ♦ railway tourism *BE*

Eisenbahntourist, m
- ♦ railroad tourist *AE*
- ♦ railway tourist *BE*

Eisenbahntransport, m
Eisenbahnbeförderung, f
- ♦ railroad transportation *AE*
- ♦ railway transport *BE*

Eisenbahntunnel, m
- ♦ railroad tunnel *AE*
- ♦ railway tunnel *BE*

Eisenbahnüberführung, f
Eisenbahnviadukt, m
- ♦ railroad viaduct *AE*
- ♦ railway viaduct *BE*

Eisenbahnverkehr, m
- ♦ railroad traffic *AE*
- ♦ railway traffic *BE*

Eisenbahnwagen, m (Personen)
- ♦ railroad car *AE*
- ♦ railway carriage *BE*
- ♦ railway coach *BE*

Eisenbahnzeitalter, n
- ♦ railroad age *AE*
- ♦ railway age *BE*

Eisenbahnzentrum, n
- ♦ railroad center *BE*
- ♦ railway centre *BE*

Eisenbahnzug, m
- ♦ railroad train *AE*
- ♦ railway train *BE*

Eisenbett, n
- ♦ iron bed

Eisenzeit, f
- ♦ Iron Age, the

Eisenzeitsiedlung, f
- ♦ Iron Age settlement

eiserne Ration, f
Notration, f
- ♦ iron rations *pl*
- ♦ emergency rations *pl*

Eis essen
(Eiskrem)
- ♦ eat an ice cream *AE*
- ♦ eat an ice-cream *BE*
- ♦ eat an ice *BE*

eisfrei, adj
- ♦ icefree, adj

eisgekühlt

♦ free from ice, adj
♦ clear of ice, adj
eisgekühlt, adj
♦ iced, adj
♦ ice-cooled, adj
♦ ice-cold, adj
eisgekühlt servieren etw
→ gekühlt servieren etw
Eisgeschäft, n
♦ ice-cream business
Eisgeschmack, m
♦ ice-cream flavor *AE*
♦ ice-cream flavour *BE*
Eishockey, n
♦ ice hockey
Eishockey spielen
♦ play ice hockey
Eishockeyspieler, m
♦ ice-hockey player
eisige Begrüßung, f
♦ chilly welcome
eisiger Empfang, m
♦ chilly reception
Eisjacht, f
Eissegelschlitten, m
♦ iceboat *AE*
♦ ice-boat *BE*
♦ ice yacht
Eiskaffee, m
♦ iced coffee
♦ ice coffee
eiskalt, adj
♦ ice-cold, adj
eiskaltes Bier, n
♦ ice-cold beer
eiskaltes Getränk, n
♦ ice-cold drink
♦ ice-cold beverage
eiskalt servieren etw
♦ serve s.th. ice-cold
Eiskarte, f
(Speisekarte)
♦ ice-cream menu
Eiskeller, m
♦ ice cellar
Eiskletterer, m
♦ ice climber
Eisklettern, n
♦ ice climbing
Eiskrem, f
Eiscreme, f
Eis, n
♦ ice cream *AE*
♦ ice-cream *BE*
♦ ice
Eiskremmaschine, f
Eismaschine f
♦ ice-cream freezer
♦ ice-cream machine
Eiskremspezialität, f
→ Eisspezialität
Eiskremverkäufer, m
Eisverkäufer, m
Eismann, m
♦ ice-cream vendor
♦ ice-cream seller
♦ iceman *AE*
Eiskübel, m
Eiskühler, m
♦ ice pail
♦ ice bucket

Eiskunstläufer, m
♦ figure skater
Eisladen, m
Eisgeschäft, n
♦ ice-cream shop *BE*
♦ ice-cream store *AE*
Eislaufbahn, f
→ Eislaufplatz
eislaufen
Schlittschuh laufen
Schlittschuh fahren
♦ skate
♦ ice-skate
Eislaufen, n
Eislaufsport, m
Schlittschuhlaufen, n
Schlittschuhfahren, m
Schlittschuhsport, m
♦ skating
♦ ice-skating
Eisläufer, m
Schlittschuhläufer, m
Schlittschuhfahrer, m
♦ skater
♦ ice skater *AE*
♦ ice-skater *BE*
Eislaufhalle, f
Halleneisbahn, f
♦ indoor ice rink *AE*
♦ indoor ice-rink *BE*
Eislaufkurs, m
Eislauflehrgang, m
Schlittschuhkurs, m
Schlittschuhlehrgang, m
♦ ice-skating course
Eislaufplatz, m
Eislaufbahn, f
Schlittschuhbahn, f
Schlittschuhplatz, m
♦ skating rink
♦ ice-skating rink
♦ ice rink *AE*
♦ ice-rink *BE*
Eisloch, n
♦ ice hole
Eislöffel, m
♦ ice spoon
Eismann, m
Eisverkäufer m
♦ iceman
Eismaschine, f
(für Herstellung von Eis)
♦ ice machine
Eis mit Früchten, n
→ Eisbecher
Eisrevue, f
♦ ice show *AE*
♦ ice-show *BE*
♦ ice revue
Eisschale, f
♦ ice-cream dish
Eisschießen, n
→ Eisstockschießen
Eisschnellauf, m
♦ speed skating
Eissegeln, n (mit Segelschlitten)
♦ ice-boating
♦ iceboat sailing *AE*
♦ ice-boat sailing *BE*
♦ ice yachting
♦ ice-sailing

Eissegeln, n (ohne Schlitten)
♦ skate sailing
Eissegelschlitten, m
→ Eisjacht
Eis spendieren jm
♦ treat s.o. to an ice
♦ treat s.o. to an ice-cream *BE*
Eisspezialität, f
Eiskremspezialität, f
♦ ice-cream specialty *AE*
♦ ice-cream speciality *BE*
Eissport, m
♦ ice sports
♦ ice sport
Eissportzentrum, n
♦ ice-sport center *AE*
♦ ice-sports center *AE*
♦ ice-sport centre *BE*
♦ ice-sports centre *BE*
Eisstadion n
♦ ice stadium
Eisstand, m
Eiskiosk, m
♦ ice-cream kiosk
Eisstockbahn n
(ähnlich wie Curling)
♦ eisstock rink
♦ curling rink
Eisstockschießen, n
(ähnlich wie Curling)
Eisschießen, n
♦ eisstock game
♦ curling
Eistanz, m
♦ ice dance
♦ ice dancing
Eistänzer, m
♦ ice dancer
Eistee, m
♦ iced tea
♦ ice tea
Eistorte, f
♦ ice-cream gateau
Eistüte, f
♦ ice-cream cone
Eisverkäufer, m
Eismann, m
♦ ice-cream seller
♦ ice-cream vendor
♦ iceman
Eiswaffel, f
♦ ice-cream wafer
Eiswasser, n
(stark gekühltes Wasser)
♦ ice water *AE*
♦ ice-water *BE*
Eiswein, m
(Trauben werden nach Frost geerntet)
♦ ice wine
Eiswürfel, m
♦ ice cube *AE*
♦ ice-cube *BE*
Eiswürfeleimer, m
♦ ice bucket
Eiswürfelmaschine, f
♦ ice-cube machine
Eiswürfelschale, f
(im Kühlschrank)
♦ ice-cube tray
Eiswürfelzange, f
♦ ice-cube tongs *pl*

184

Eiszange, f
♦ ice tongs *pl*
Eiszeit, f
♦ ice age, the
Eiszeitsiedlung, f
♦ ice age settlement
Ei weich kochen
♦ soft-cook an egg *AE*
♦ soft-boil an egg *BE*
Eiweiß, n (Ei)
♦ egg white
♦ white of (an) egg
♦ white
Eiweiß, n (Protein)
→ Protein
eiweißarm, adj
♦ low-protein, adj
♦ low in protein
eiweißarme Kost, f
♦ low-protein diet
eiweißreich, adj
♦ rich in protein, adj
♦ high-protein, adj
eiweißreiche Kost, f
♦ high-protein diet
ekelerregend, adj
ekelhaft, adj
♦ disgusting, adj
♦ nauseating, adj
♦ repulsive, adj
EKG, n
Elektrokardiogramm, n
♦ ECG
♦ electrocardiogram
Ekuador
→ Ecuador
elastische Nachfrage, f
♦ elastic demand
Elbe, f
♦ Elbe River
♦ River Elbe
♦ Elbe
Elbling, m
(Wein)
♦ Elbling
Elblingrebe, f
♦ Elbling vine
Elblingtraube, f
♦ Elbling grape
Elblingwein, m
♦ Elbling wine
Eldorado, n
♦ eldorado
♦ happy hunting ground *figur*
Eldorado für Taschendiebe, n
♦ happy hunting ground for pickpockets
Elefantenritt, m
♦ elephant ride
Elefantensafari, f
♦ elephant safari
elegant, adj
♦ elegant, adj
♦ fashionable, adj
♦ smart, adj
♦ posh, adj *coll*
♦ stylish, adj
elegant eingerichtetes Zimmer n
♦ elegantly appointed room
eleganter Wein, m
♦ elegant wine

elegantes Dekor, n
♦ stylish decor *AE*
♦ stylish décor *BE*
elegantes Haus, n
(privat)
♦ elegant house
♦ posh house *coll*
elegantes Hotel, n
♦ elegant hotel
♦ posh hotel *coll*
elegantes Leben, n
kultivierter Luxus, m
♦ gracious living
elegantes Viertel, n
(einer Stadt)
♦ fashionable area
♦ posh area *coll*
elegantes Zimmer, n
♦ elegant room
elegante Umgebung, f
♦ elegant surroundings *pl*
elegante Welt, f
♦ fashionable world
elegant gekleidet sein
♦ be elegantly dressed
elegant möbliert, adj
♦ elegantly furnished, adj
elegant möbliertes Zimmer n
♦ elegantly furnished room
Elektriker, m
♦ electrician
elektrische Heizung, f
→ Elektroheizung
elektrischer Grill, m
♦ electric grill
elektrischer Heizofen, m
elektrisches Heizgerät, n
Elektroheizofen, n
Elektroheizgerät, n
♦ electric heater
♦ electric fire *BE*
elektrischer Hosenbügler m
(Gerät)
♦ electric trouser press *BE*
elektrischer Mixer, m
elektrische Rührmaschine, f
♦ electric mixer
elektrischer Rasierapparat, m
Elektrorasierer, m
♦ electric razor
♦ electric shaver
elektrischer Strom, m
♦ electric current
elektrischer Ventilator, m
Elektroventilator, m
♦ electric fan
elektrisches Bügeleisen n
♦ electric iron
elektrisches Heizgerät, n
→ elektrischer Heizofen
elektrisches Kaminfeuer, n
♦ electric log fire
elektrisches Licht, n
♦ electric light
Elektroanschluß, m
(Camping)
Stromanschluß, m
♦ electric hook-up
♦ mains electricity
Elektroauto, n
♦ electric car

Elektrobus, m
♦ electric bus
Elektroeisenbahn, f
♦ electric railroad *AE*
♦ electric railway *BE*
Elektrofahrzeug, n
♦ electric vehicle
Elektrogerät, n
♦ electrical appliance
Elektroheizofen, m
→ elektrischer Heizofen
Elektroheizung, f
elektrische Heizung, f
E-Heizung, f
♦ electric heating
Elektroherd, m
elektrischer Herd, m
♦ electric range
♦ electric cooker
Elektrokardiogramm, n
EKG, n
♦ electrocardiogram
♦ ECG
Elektrokocher, m
♦ electric cooker
Elektrolokomotive, f
elektrische Lokomotive, f
♦ electric engine
♦ electric locomotive
Elektrolyse, f *med*
♦ electrolysis *med*
Elektrolysebehandlung, f
♦ electrolysis treatment
Elektromixer, m
♦ electric blender
elektronisch, adj
♦ electronic, adj
elektronische Abstimmung, f
(bei Konferenzen etc.)
♦ electronic vote counting
elektronische Abstimmungsanlage, f
(bei Konferenzen etc.)
elektronische Abstimmanlage, f
♦ electronic voting system
♦ electronic vote counting system
elektronische Buchung, f
♦ electronic booking
elektronische Datenverarbeitung, f
EDV, f
♦ electronic data processing
♦ EDP
elektronische Registrierkasse, f
♦ electronic cash register
elektronische Reservierung, f
♦ electronic reservation
elektronischer Schlüssel, m
♦ electronic key
elektronisches Buchungssystem, n
♦ electronic booking system
elektronische Schlüsselanlage, f
♦ electronic key system
elektronisches Informationssystem, n
♦ electronic information system
elektronisches Schloß, n
♦ electronic lock
elektronisches Spiel, n
♦ electronic game
elektronisches Zimmerreservierungssystem, n
♦ electronic room reservation system

elektronische Zimmerreservierung, f
- electronic room reservation
- electronic rooms reservation

elektronische Zimmerstatusanlage, f
- electronic room status system

elektronische Zimmerstatustafel, f
- electronic room status board

Elektroofen, m
(Heizung)
elektrischer Ofen, m
- electric stove

Elektrorasierer, m
elektrischer Rasierapparat, m
- electric shaver
- electric razor

elektrotherapeutische Behandlung, f
- electrotherapeutic treatment

Elektrotherapie, f
- electrotherapy

Elektrozug, m
- electric train

elende Bude, f (Haus) *coll*
- old shack *AE coll*
- old ramshackle house

Elendsviertel, n
- slum quarter
- slum area
- slums *pl*

Elfenbein, n
- ivory

Elfenbeinküste, f
- Ivory Coast, the

Elfenbeinmuseum, n
- ivory museum

elfte Etage, f
→ elftes Stockwerk

elftes Geschoß, n
→ elftes Stockwerk

elftes Stockwerk, n
elfte Etage, f
elftes Geschoß, n
- twelfth floor *AE*
- twelfth story *AE*
- eleventh floor *BE*
- eleventh storey *BE*

elfwöchig, adj
- eleven-week, adj
- lasting eleven weeks
- of eleven weeks' duration

elisabethanische Zeit, f
- Elizabethan times *pl*

elitäres Reiseziel, n
- elitist travel destination
- elitist destination

Elitehotel n
- elite hotel

Elsaß, n
(Region)
- Alsace

Elsässer, m
- Alsatian

Elsässerart, adv *gastr*
nach Elsässer Art, adv *gastr*
- Alsatian style, adv *gastr*

Elsässerin, f
- Alsatian woman
- Alsatian girl
- Alsatian

Elsässer Wein, m
elsässischer Wein, m
- Alsace wine

- Alsatian wine
- wine from Alsace

elsässisch, adj
- Alsatian, adj

elsässischer Wein, m
Elsässer Wein, m
- Alsatian wine
- Alsace wine

Elsaß-Lothringen
(Region)
- Alsace-Lorraine

Eltern, pl
- parents *pl*

Elternabend m
- parents' evening

Elternappartement n
- parents' apartment

Elternschlafzimmer n
Elternzimmer n
- parents' bedroom

Elternzimmer, n
- parents' room

Elternzimmer mitbenutzen
(Kinder)
Elternzimmer teilen
- share the parents' bedroom

ELW, f
→ Einliegerwohnung

Empfang, m (Begrüßung)
→ Begrüßung

Empfang, m (Büro)
→ Empfangsbüro

Empfang, m (Eingang)
→ Eingang

Empfang, m (Rezeption)
- reception
- front desk *AE*

Empfang abhalten (für jn)
Empfang halten (für jn)
- hold a reception (for s.o.)

Empfang ausrichten (als Gastgeber)
Gastgeber sein bei einem Empfang
- host a reception

Empfang bei dem Bürgermeister, m
- reception with the mayor

Empfang bereiten jm
- give s.o. a welcome
- give s.o. a reception

Empfang bestätigen (von etw)
- acknowledge receipt (of s.th.)

Empfang durch den Bürgermeister, m
- reception by the mayor

Empfang durch den Oberbürgermeister, m
- reception by the Lord Mayor *BE*

Empfang eines Briefes bestätigen
- acknowledge receipt of a letter

empfangen jn
aufnehmen jn
- receive s.o.

empfangen jn feierlich
- receive s.o. with ceremony

empfangen jn kühl
kühlen Empfang jm bereiten
- give s.o. a cool reception

empfangen jn mit offenen Armen
- receive s.o. with open arms

empfangen werden
- be received

empfangen werden mit allen Ehren
- enjoy full red-carpet treatment

Empfänger, m (generell)
- recipient
- receiver

Empfänger, m (Post)
Adressat, m
- addressee

Empfängerland, n
→ Aufnahmeland

Empfang findet statt
- reception takes place

Empfang geben (für jn)
- give a reception (for s.o.)

Empfang geben zu Ehren von jm
Empfang geben zu js Ehren
- give a reception in honor of s.o. *AE*
- give a reception in honour of s.o. *BE*

Empfang mit Getränken und Imbiß, m
- reception with drinks and snacks

Empfang mit offenen Armen, m
herzlicher Empfang m
- open-armed reception
- being received with open arms
- receiving s.o. with open arms

Empfang planen (für jn)
- plan a reception (for s.o.)

Empfangsabteilung, f
- front-office department
- reception department

Empfangsangestellter, m
Empfangsangestellte f
- reception employee
- front-desk clerk *AE*
- room clerk *AE*
- reception clerk
- front-desk employee *AE*

Empfangsarbeit, f
Rezeptionsarbeit, f
- front-office work
- reception work

Empfangsassistent m
Empfangsassistentin f
- assistant receptionist

Empfangsbereich, m
- front-desk area *AE*
- front-office area *AE*
- reception area

empfangsbereit, adj
- ready for check-in, adj

empfangsbereit sein
- be open to receive guests
- be ready for check-in

Empfangsbestätigung, f
- acknowledgment of receipt
- acknowledgement of receipt
- receipt

Empfangsbrett, n
Rezeptionsbrett, n
- reception board

Empfangsbuchhalter, m
- front-office accountant
- front-office bookkeeper

Empfangsbuchhaltung, f
- front-office accounting

Empfangsbüro, n
Frontbüro, n
- reception office
- front office

Empfangschef, m (Hotel)
Chef de réception, m *FR*
- chief receptionist *AE*
- head receptionist *BE*

- reception manager
- chef de réception *FR*
- rooms division manager *AE*

Empfangschef, m (Restaurant)
(empfängt und plaziert Gäste)
Maître d'hôtel de réception, m *FR*
- reception headwaiter
- maître d'hôtel de réception *FR*

Empfang schloß den Tag ab
- reception concluded the day

Empfangscocktail, m
Begrüßungscocktail, m
- welcoming cocktail
- welcome cocktail

Empfangscomputer, m
- front-desk computer *AE*
- reception computer

Empfangsdame, f (Hotel)
- female receptionist
- receptionist
- female front-desk clerk *AE*
- front-desk clerk *AE*

Empfangsdame, f (Restaurant)
- greeter *AE*
- hostess *AE*

Empfangsdienst, m
Empfangsservice, m
- front-office service
- reception service
- front-desk service *AE*

Empfangsdirektor, m
Leiter der Empfangsdirektion, m
- reception manager
- front-office manager
- front-desk manager *AE*
- rooms director *AE*

Empfangseinrichtungen f pl
- reception facilities pl

Empfangsfoyer, n
- reception foyer

Empfangsgebäude, n
Rezeptionsgebäude, n
- reception building

Empfangsgehilfe, m
Aide de réception, m/f *FR*
Empfangspraktikant, m
Empfangscommis, m
Réceptionscommis, m *SCHW*
- trainee receptionist
- junior receptionist
- aide de réception *FR*
- commis de réception *FR*

Empfangshalle, f
- reception lobby *AE*
- reception hall
- front lobby *AE*

Empfangsherr, m
- receptionist
- front-desk clerk *AE*
- reception clerk

Empfangsjournal n
- reception diary
- reception journal

Empfangskasse, f
- front-office cash register
- front-office cash till

Empfangskassierer, m
Empfangskassenführer, m
Empfangskassier, m *ÖST/SCHW*
- front-office cashier

Empfangskellner, m
(im Restaurant)
- reception waiter

Empfangskomitee n
- reception committee

Empfangskraft, f
- reception clerk
- reception employee

Empfangsleiter, m
- front-desk manager *AE*
- front-office manager
- reception manager

Empfangsleitung, f
Empfangsdirektion, f
- front-office management *AE*
- reception management
- front-desk management *AE*

Empfangsleute, pl
Empfang, m
- front-office people *pl*
- front-desk people *pl*

Empfangsloge, f
→ Portiersloge

Empfangspavillon m
- reception pavilion

Empfangsperson, f
→ Empfangsangestellter

Empfangspersonal, n
- reception staff
- reception personnel
- front-desk staff *AE*
- front-desk personnel *AE*
- front-office staff

Empfangsportier, m
- front hall porter

Empfangsraum, m
Empfangszimmer, n
Empfangssalon, m
- reception room

Empfangssaal, m
Empfangshalle, f
- reception hall

Empfangssalon, m
→ Empfangsraum

Empfangsschalter, m
Rezeptionsschalter, m
- reception desk
- front desk *AE*
- reception counter

Empfangsschalterpersonal, n
Empfangspersonal, n
- front-desk staff *AE*
- front-desk personnel *AE*

Empfangsschichtleiter m
- reception shift leader

Empfangssekretär, m
Anfangsrezeptionist, m
- junior receptionist

Empfangsservice, m
Empfangsdienst m
- reception service
- front-office service

Empfangstresen, n
- reception counter
- reception desk

Empfangsverwaltung, f
→ Empfang

Empfangsvolontär, m
- unpaid front-desk trainee *AE*
- unpaid reception trainee

Empfangszelt, n
- reception tent

Empfangszimmer, n
→ Empfangsraum, Empfangssalon

Empfang und Auskunft
- reception and information office

Empfang von Waren quittieren
Empfang von Waren bestätigen
- acknowledge receipt of goods

Empfang zu Ehren von jm, m
- reception in s.o.'s honor *AE*
- reception in s.o.'s honour *AE*

empfehlen als Tagungsort
- recommend as a venue
- recommend as the venue for s.th.

empfehlen etw jm wärmstens
- recommend s.th. to s.o. warmly

empfehlen etw zu etw
(z.B. Speisen)
- recommend s.th. with s.th.

empfehlen jm etw
- recommend s.th. to s.o.

empfehlen sich auf französisch
→ Abschied nehmen auf französisch

empfehlenswert, adj
- recommendable, adj
- recommended, adj

empfehlenswerter Platz, m
(Camping)
- recommendable site

empfehlenswertes Hotel, n
- recommendable hotel
- commendable hotel
- recommended hotel

empfehlenswertes Restaurant, n
- recommendable restaurant
- recommended restaurant
- commendable restaurant

Empfehlenswert (Plakette)
Empfohlen (Plakette)
- Commended

Empfehlung, f
- recommendation

Empfehlungsschreiben, n
Empfehlungsbrief m
- letter of recommendation
- letter recommending s.o.

empfindlicher Magen, m
- sensitive stomach

empfindsame Reise, f
- sentimental journey

empfohlen, adj
- recommended, adj

Empfohlene Häuser
(Hinweisschild)
- Commended Houses

empfohlener Anfangstermin, m
- recommended starting date

Empfohlener Betrieb (Plakette)
- Commended Establishment

empfohlene Route, f
- recommended route

empfohlener Platz, m
(Camping)
- recommended site

empfohlener Preis, m
Richtpreis, m
- recommended price
- recommended rate

empfohlenes Hotel, n
- recommended hotel

Empfohlenes Hotel (Plakette)

Empfohlenes Hotel (Plakette)
 ♦ Commended Hotel
empfohlenes Restaurant, n
 ♦ recommended restaurant
Empfohlenes Restaurant (Plakette)
 ♦ Commended Restaurant
Empore, f (generell)
 ♦ gallery
Empore, f (Kirche)
 ♦ loft
Emsland, n
 ♦ Emsland, the
E-Musik, f
 ernste Musik, f
 ♦ serious music
Endbestand m
 (Lager)
 Schlußbestand m
 ♦ closing stock
Ende der Durchsage!
 ♦ End of the message
Ende der Fahrt, n
 Fahrtende, n
 ♦ end of the trip
 ♦ end of the ride
Ende der Reise, n
 Reiseende, n
 Endstation, f
 ♦ journey's end
Ende des Besuchs, n
 ♦ end of the visit
 ♦ end of one's visit
Ende nähern sich
 dem Ende sich nähern
 zu Ende gehen
 ♦ draw to a close
 ♦ come to an end
enden (generell)
 ♦ end
enden (Vertrag)
 auslaufen
 ♦ expire
 ♦ end
Endgebühr f
 ♦ final charge
 ♦ final fee
endgültige Buchung, f
 endgültige Bestellung, f
 ♦ final booking
 ♦ definitive booking
endgültige Reservierung, f
 ♦ final reservation
 ♦ definitive reservation
endgültige Zusage, f
 endgültige Bestätigung, f
 ♦ final confirmation
 ♦ definitive confirmation
Endhafen, m
 ♦ ultimate port
Endhaltestelle, f
 → Endstation
Endiviensalat, m
 ♦ endive salad
Endloshandtuch, n
 Rollhandtuch, n
 ♦ jack-towel
 ♦ roller-towel
Endpreis, m
 (endgültiger Preis)
 ♦ final price
 ♦ final rate

Endpreis wird nach der Zahl der tatsächlichen
 Gäste berechnet
 ♦ final price will be calculated on the actual
 number of guests
Endrechnung, f (Faktur)
 Abschlußrechnung, f
 Schlußrechnung, f
 ♦ final invoice
Endrechnung, f (generell)
 Schlußrechnung, f
 ♦ final bill
 ♦ final check AE
Endreinigung, f
 ♦ cleaning on departure
 ♦ end-of-let cleaning BE
 ♦ end-of-contract cleaning
Endreinigung durchführen
 ♦ do the cleaning on departure
 ♦ do the end-of-let cleaning BE
Endreinigung selbst durchführen
 ♦ do the cleaning on departure oneself
 ♦ do the end-of-let cleaning oneself BE
Endreinigungsgebühr, f
 ♦ charge for cleaning on departure
 ♦ fee for cleaning on departure
 ♦ end-of-contract cleaning charge
 ♦ end-of-let cleaning charge BE
Endspiel, n
 ♦ final game
 ♦ final match
Endstation, f
 Endhaltestelle, f
 ♦ terminus
Endstation der Eisenbahn, f
 Endhaltestelle der Eisenbahn, f
 Eisenbahnendstation, f
 Eisenbahnendhaltestelle, f
 ♦ terminus of the railroad AE
 ♦ terminus of the railway BE
 ♦ railroad terminus AE
 ♦ railway terminus BE
Endverbraucher, m
 ♦ end consumer
Endzahlung, f
 → Abschlußzahlung
Endzielort, m
 Endziel, n
 ♦ final destination
Energieaufwendungen, f pl
 ♦ energy expenses pl
Energiekosten, pl
 ♦ energy costs pl
 ♦ energy cost
Energieverbrauch, m
 ♦ energy consumption
 ♦ consumption of energy
Engadin, n
 (Region)
 ♦ Engadine, the
engagieren jn
 ♦ hire s.o.
 ♦ engage s.o.
enge kleine Wohnung, f
 ♦ poky little apartment AE
 ♦ poky little flat BE
enges kleines Zimmer, n
 ♦ poky little room
enge Straße, f
 ♦ narrow street
 ♦ narrow road

enges Zimmer, n
 ♦ poky room
 ♦ cramped room
eng gedrängt, adj
 eng, adj
 beengt, adj
 ♦ cramped, adj
 ♦ crowded, adj
England
 ♦ England
England besuchen
 ♦ visit England
Engländer, m
 ♦ Englishman
Engländerin, f
 ♦ Englishwoman
 ♦ English girl
Englandprospekt, m
 ♦ England brochure
Englandurlaub, m
 ♦ English holiday BE
 ♦ English vacation AE
englisch, adj
 ♦ English, adj
englische Art, adv gastr
 ♦ English style gastr
englische Küche, f
 ♦ English cuisine
 ♦ English cooking
englischem Recht unterliegen
 (Vertrag)
 ♦ be governed by English law
englischer Garten, m
 ♦ English garden
englischer Service, m
 Service à l'anglaise m FR
 ♦ English service
 ♦ service à l'anglaise FR
 ♦ silver service
englisches Essen, n
 ♦ English food
englisches Frühstück n
 ♦ English breakfast
englisches Gericht, n
 ♦ English dish
englisches Menü, n
 ♦ English menu
englische Speisekarte, f
 ♦ English menu
englisches Recht, n
 ♦ English law
englischsprachig, adj (Person)
 ♦ English-speaking, adj
englischsprachig, adj (Sache)
 ♦ English-language, adj
 ♦ in English
englischsprachiger Fremdenführer, m
 (Person)
 ♦ English-speaking tour guide
englischsprachiger Prospekt, m
 ♦ English-language brochure
 ♦ brochure in English
englischsprachiges Land, n
 ♦ English-speaking country
Engpaß m
 ♦ bottleneck
Engpaß vermeiden
 ♦ avoid a bottleneck
en gros einkaufen
 ♦ buy in bulk

eng werden
(Unterkunft)
♦ get cramped
♦ get crowded
enormer Appetit, m
Riesenappetit, m
Riesenhunger, m
♦ enormous appetite
enormes Frühstück, n
♦ enormous breakfast
en pension, FR
♦ en pension FR
en place, FR
(Gast wünscht andere, gleich teuere Leistung)
♦ en place FR
♦ instead of
En-place-Bon, m FR
♦ en place voucher
♦ en place check
♦ en place chit
en route, adv FR
unterwegs, adv
♦ en route, adv
♦ on the way, adv
Ensemble, n
♦ ensemble
♦ company
♦ cast
en suite, adv FR
hintereinander, adv
miteinander verbunden, adv
mit dem Schlafzimmer verbunden, adv
innenliegend, adv
♦ en suite, adv FR
♦ in series, adv
♦ in a set, adv
entdecken etw mit dem Rad coll
mit dem Rad entdecken etw
mit dem Fahrrad entdecken etw
♦ discover s.th. by bike coll
♦ discover s.th. by bicycle
entdecken etw zufällig
zufällig entdecken etw
durch Zufall entdecken etw
♦ discover s.th. by accident
entdecken etw zu Fuß
zu Fuß entdecken etw
♦ discover s.th. on foot
Entdeckung einer Heilquelle, f
♦ discovery of a medicinal spring
Entdeckung einer Quelle, f
♦ discocery of a spring
♦ discovery of a well
Entdeckungskreuzfahrt, f
♦ discovery cruise
Entdeckungsreise, f (Land)
♦ journey of discovery
Entdeckungsreise, f (Meer)
♦ voyage of discovery
Entdeckungsurlaub, m
♦ discovery vacation AE
♦ discovery holiday BE
Ente, f
♦ duck
Entenbraten, m
♦ roast duck
Entenfüllpastete, f
♦ duckling timbale
Entengericht, n
♦ duck dish

Ententeich, m
♦ duck pond
Entertainer, m
♦ entertainer
Entertainerin, f
♦ female entertainer
entfernen etw
♦ remove s.th.
entfernteste Ecken der Welt, f pl
♦ furthest corners of the globe pl
entfernt sein nur einen Katzensprung
♦ be only a stone's throw away
entfernt sein nur ein paar Gehminuten
♦ be only a few minutes' walk away
entfernt sein nur ein paar Schritte
♦ be just a short walk away
entfernt sein (von etw)
♦ be distant (from s.th.)
♦ be away
Entfernung f
♦ distance
Entfernung vom Flughafen, f
♦ distance from the airport
Entfernung vom Strand, f
♦ distance from the beach
Entfernung von etw, f
♦ distance from s.th.
Entfernung von Zubehör, f
(aus einer Unterkunft)
♦ removal of fixtures
Entfernung zu dem nächsten Dorf beträgt 5 km
♦ distance to the nearest village is 5 km
♦ distance to the next village is 5 km
Entfernung zu den Geschäften, f
♦ distance to the stores AE
♦ distance to the shops BE
Entfernung zu etw, f
♦ distance to s.th.
Entfernung zum Strand, f
♦ distance to the beach
entgangener Gewinn, m
♦ lost profit
entgegengesetzte Richtung, f
♦ opposite direction
entgegenkommender Verkehr, m
♦ oncoming traffic
entgegensehen etw (mit Erwartung)
♦ await s.th.
♦ expect s.th.
entgegensehen etw (mit Freude)
gern etw entgegensehen
♦ look forward to s.th.
entgehen lassen sich etw
♦ miss s.th.
Entgelt, n
Vergütung, f
Gegenleistung, f
Gegenwert, m
♦ consideration
entgiften (den Körper)
♦ detoxify (the body)
Entgiftung, f
Entschlackung, f
♦ detoxification
entgleisen
♦ derail
Entgleisung, f
♦ derailment
entgräten etw
Gräten entfernen von etw

♦ bone s.th.
♦ fillet s.th.
entgrätet, adj
♦ boned, adj
♦ filleted, adj
entgräteter Lachs, m
♦ boned salmon
Enthaarungsbehandlung, f
♦ depilatory treatment
enthalten sein im Grundpreis
♦ be included in the basic price
♦ be included in the basic rate
enthäuten etw gastr
abhäuten etw gastr
♦ skin s.th. gastr
enthäutet, adj gastr
abgehäutet, adj gastr
♦ skinned, adj gastr
entkernen etw gastr
Kern entfernen aus etw gastr
♦ core s.th. gastr
entkoffeiniert, adj
♦ decaffeinated, adj
entkoffeinierter Kaffee, m
♦ decaffeinated coffee
entkorken etw
♦ uncork s.th.
entkorkte Flasche, f
♦ uncorked bottle
Entladeeinrichtung, f
♦ unloading facility
entlang reisen an etw
♦ travel along s.th.
entlassen jn aus der Quarantäne
♦ discharge s.o. from quarantine
♦ release s.o. from quarantine
entlassen jn fristlos
(Arbeitnehmer)
♦ dismiss s.o. without notice
entlassen jn (generell)
(Personal)
♦ dismiss s.o.
♦ make s.o. redundant
entlassen jn (vorübergehend)
(Personal)
♦ lay off s.o.
entlegener Ort, m
abgelegener Ort, m
♦ out-of-the-way place
♦ remote place
entlegener Weiler, m
abgelegener Weiler, m
♦ remote hamlet
entleihen etw für eine Ausstellung
♦ loan s.th. to an exhibition
Entlüftung, f
♦ ventilation
Entlüftungsanlage, f
♦ ventilation system
Entree, n
Zwischengericht, n
♦ entree AE
♦ entrée BE
Entremetier, m FR
Zwischenspeisenkoch, m
♦ entremetier FR
Entremets, n FR m
(frz: Süßspeise nach dem Käse und vor dem Obst)
(süßes) Zwischengericht, n
♦ entremets FR m

Entremetsbesteck

Entremetsbesteck, n
- entremets cutlery

Entresol, n
→ Zwischengeschoß

entrichten etw
→ zahlen etw

Entsafter, m
- juice extractor

entschädigen jn für etw
- compensate s.o. for s.th.

entschädigt werden für etw
- be recompensed for s.th.

Entschädigung, f
Schadensersatz, m
Schadenersatz, m
- damages pl
- compensation

entscheiden sich für das Frühstück
Frühstück wählen
- opt for breakfast

entscheiden sich für ein Land
- opt for a country

Entschlackung, f (Darm)
- purging
- purge

Entschlackung, f (generell)
- purification

Entschlackung des Körpers, f
- detoxification of the body

Entschlackungsdiät, f
- detoxification diet

entschuldigen etw
- excuse s.th.

entschuldigen sich bei dem Gastgeber
(nicht kommen können)
- excuse oneself to the host

entschuldigen sich für etw
- apologize for s.th.
- apologise for s.th.

Entschuldigen Sie!
- Excuse me!
- I beg your pardon!
- Pardon!
- Sorry!

Entschuldigen Sie die Verspätung!
- Sorry, I'm late.
- I apologize for being late. form

Entschuldigung!
Pardon!
- Sorry!
- Excuse me!

Entschuldigung, Sie haben Ihr Bier nicht bezahlt
- Excuse me, you haven't paid for your beer

Entschuldigungsschreiben, n
Entschuldigungsbrief m
- letter of apology

entschuppen etw gastr
abschuppen etw gastr
Schuppen entfernen von etw gastr
- scale s.th. gastr

entsenden jn zu einem Kongreß
(als Delegierter)
- delegate s.o. to a convention
- delegate s.o. to a congress

entsenden jn zu einer Konferenz
delegieren jn zu einer Konferenz
- delegate s.o. to a conference

Entsenderland, n
→ Ausgangsland, Aufkommensland

entspannen
entspannen sich

- relax
- unwind coll

entspannendes Ambiente, n
- relaxing ambience
- relaxing ambiance

entspannendes Getränk, n
- relaxing drink

entspannen sich am Schwimmbecken
- relax by the pool

entspannen sich bei einem Glas Wein
- relax over a glass of wine

entspannen (sich) im Hotelschwimmbad
- relax in the hotel's swimming pool

entspannt, adj
ausgeruht, adj
- relaxed, adj
- at ease, adj
- rested, adj

entspannt ankommen
- arrive relaxed

entspannte Atmosphäre, f
gelöste Atmosphäre, f
ungezwungene Atmosphäre, f
- relaxed atmosphere

entspanntes Abendessen, n
zwangloses Abendessen, n
- relaxed dinner

Entspannung, f
- relaxation
- rest

Entspannung finden
- find relaxation

Entspannungsbecken, n
- relaxation pool

Entspannungsbereich, m
- relaxation area

Entspannungskur, f
Entspannungsbehandlung, f
- relaxing treatment
- relaxation cure

Entspannungskurs, m
- relaxation class

Entspannungsmassage, f
- relaxing massage

Entspannungsprogramm, n
- relaxation program AE
- relaxation programme BE

Entspannungsraum, m
- relaxing room

Entspannungsseminar, n
- relaxation seminar

Entspannungssitzung, f
Entsspannungsstunde, f
- relaxation session

Entspannungstherapie, f
- relaxation therapy

Entspannungsübung, f
- relaxation exercise

Entspannung suchen
- seek relaxation

Entspannungsunterricht, m
- relaxation tuition

Entspannungsurlaub, m
- relaxing vacation AE
- relaxing holiday BE

Entspannungszeit, f
- relaxing time

Entspannungszentrum, n
- relaxation center AE
- relaxation centre BE

entsprechend, adj
- corresponding, adj

entsprechend den Bestimmungen, adv
- according to the regulations, adv
- in accordance with the regulations, adv

entsprechende Anzahlung, f
angemessene Anzahlung, f
angemessene Kaution, f
- appropriate deposit

entsprechender Vorjahresmonat m
- corresponding month of the previous year

entsprechender Vorjahreszeitraum, m
- corresponding period in the previous year
- corresponding period the year before
- corresponding period in ...

entsprechende Vorbereitungen treffen
notwendige Vorkehrungen treffen
- make the necessary arrangements

entsprechende Vorjahressaison, f
- corresponding season in the previous year
- corresponding season the year before
- corresponding season in ....

entsteinen etw gastr
Kerne entfernen gastr
- stone s.th. gastr

entsteint, adj gastr
- stoned, adj gastr

entsteinte Kirschen, f pl
- stoned cherries pl

enttäuschen jn
- disappoint s.o.

enttäuschter Gast, m
→ unzufriedener Gast

entwenden etw
stehlen etw
klauen etw coll
- pilfer s.th.

entwickeln etw
- develop s.th.

Entwicklung der Hotelauslastung, f
- development of hotel occupancy
- development of the hotel's occupancy

Entwicklung des Fremdenverkehrs, f
Aufbau des Fremdenverkehrs, m
Tourismusaufbau, m
- development of tourism

Entwicklungsland, n
- developing country

Entwicklungsstadium des Tourismus, n
- development stage of tourism

Entwöhnungskur, f
- withdrawal treatment

Entwurf, m
- draft

entzückende Lage, f
- delightful situation
- delightful position
- delightful location
- delightful setting

entzückend gelegen, adj
- delightfully situated, adj
- delightfully positioned, adj
- delightfully located, adj

entzückend gelegenes Hotel, n
- delightfully situated hotel
- delightfully positioned hotel
- delightfully located hotel

EP, m
European Plan, m
nur Übernachtung
Unterkunft ohne Verpflegung

♦ EP
♦ European Plan
Epidiaskop n
 ♦ epidiascope
Epikur
 ♦ Epicurus
Epikureer, m *philos*
 ♦ epicurean *philos*
 ♦ epicure
epikureisch, adj
 ♦ epicurean, adj
Erbbauzins, m
 (für Pachtgrundstück)
 Erbpachtzins, m
 ♦ ground rent *AE*
 ♦ ground-rent *BE*
Erbpacht, f
 ♦ hereditary leasehold
 ♦ hereditary tenancy
 ♦ 99-year leasehold
 ♦ 99-year lease
Erbpächter, m
 ♦ hereditary long-leaseholder
erbrechen
 ♦ vomit
 ♦ throw up
Erbse, f
 ♦ pea
Erbsensuppe, f
 ♦ pea soup
Erdbeerbowle, f
 ♦ strawberry cup
 ♦ strawberry bowl
Erdbeere, f
 ♦ strawberry
Erdbeereis, n
 ♦ strawberry ice cream *AE*
 ♦ strawberry ice-cream *BE*
Erdbeeren pflücken
 ♦ pick strawberries
Erdbeerfest, n
 ♦ strawberry festival
Erdbeergelee, n
 ♦ strawberry jelly
Erdbeergeschmack, m
 ♦ strawberry flavor *AE*
 ♦ strawberry flavour *BE*
Erdbeerkaltschale, f
 ♦ cold strawberry soup
Erdbeerkompott, n
 ♦ strawberry compôte *BE*
 ♦ strawberry compote *AE*
 ♦ stewed strawberries *pl*
Erdbeerkonfitüre, f
 ♦ strawberry jam
Erdbeerkuchen, m
 ♦ strawberry cake
Erdbeermilchmixgetränk, n
 ♦ strawberry milk shake
Erdbeermousse, f
 ♦ strawberry mousse
Erdbeerparfait, n
 ♦ strawberry parfait
Erdbeerpudding, m
 ♦ strawberry pudding
Erdbeersirup, m
 ♦ strawberry syrup
Erdbeersorbet, f
 ♦ strawberry sorbet
Erdbeersoße, f
 ♦ strawberry sauce

Erdbeertörtchen, n
 ♦ strawberry tartlet
Erdbeertorte, f (flach)
 ♦ strawberry tart
Erdbeertorte, f (Sahne)
 ♦ strawberry gâteau *BE*
 ♦ strawberry gateau *AE*
Erdbeerwein, m
 ♦ strawberry wine
Erdgeschoß, n
 Parterregeschoß, n
 Parterre, n
 EG, n
 ♦ first floor *AE*
 ♦ ground floor *BE*
 ♦ street floor *AE*
 ♦ English basement *AE*
 ♦ ground storey *BE*
Erdgeschoßappartement, n
 Parterreappartement, n
 ♦ first-floor apartment *AE*
 ♦ ground-floor apartment *BE*
Erdgeschoßbadezimmer, n
 Parterrebadezimmer, n
 ♦ ground-floor bathroom *BE*
 ♦ first-floor bathroom *AE*
Erdgeschoß bewohnen
 ♦ occupy the first floor *AE*
 ♦ occupy the ground floor *BE*
Erdgeschoßcafé, n
 Parterrecafé, n
 ♦ first-floor cafe *AE*
 ♦ ground-floor café *BE*
Erdgeschoß eines Gebäudes, n
 ♦ first floor of a building *AE*
 ♦ ground floor of a building *BE*
Erdgeschoßfenster, n
 Parterrefenster, n
 ♦ first-floor window *AE*
 ♦ ground-floor window *BE*
Erdgeschoßhöhe, f
 Erdgeschoßniveau, n
 ♦ first-floor level *AE*
 ♦ ground-floor level *BE*
Erdgeschoßrestaurant, n
 Parterrerestaurant, n
 ♦ first-floor restaurant *AE*
 ♦ ground-floor restaurant *BE*
Erdgeschoßschlafzimmer, n
 Parterreschlafzimmer, n
 ♦ first-floor bedroom *AE*
 ♦ ground-floor bedroom *BE*
Erdgeschoßsuite, f
 Parterresuite f
 ♦ first-floor suite *AE*
 ♦ ground-floor suite *BE*
Erdgeschoßterrasse, f
 ♦ first-floor terrace *AE*
 ♦ ground-floor terrace *BE*
Erdgeschoßveranstaltungsraum, m
 ♦ first-floor function room *AE*
 ♦ ground-floor function room *BE*
Erdgeschoßwand, f
 Parterrewand, f
 Erdgeschoßmauer, f
 Parterremauer, f
 ♦ first-floor wall *AE*
 ♦ ground-floor wall *BE*
Erdgeschoßwohnung, f
 Parterrewohnung, f

 ♦ ground-floor flat *BE*
 ♦ first-floor apartment *AE*
Erdgeschoßzimmer, n
 Parterrezimmer n
 ♦ first-floor room *AE*
 ♦ ground-floor room *BE*
Erdnuß, f
 ♦ peanut
Erdnußbutter, f
 ♦ peanut butter
Erdwall, m
 ♦ earth wall
ereignisreich, adj
 ♦ eventful, adj
erfahren, adj
 ♦ experienced, adj
 ♦ seasoned, adj
erfahrene Führungsmannschaft, f
 ♦ experienced management team
erfahrene Hotelfachleute, pl
 ♦ experienced hotelmen *pl*
erfahrene Leitung, f
 ♦ experienced management
erfahrener Camper, m
 ♦ experienced camper
erfahrener Gast, m
 ♦ seasoned guest
erfahrener Hotelier, m
 ♦ experienced hotelier
 ♦ experienced hotelkeeper
erfahrener Kellner, m
 ♦ experienced waiter
erfahrener Küchenchef, m
 ♦ experienced chef
erfahrener Reisender m
 ♦ seasoned traveler *AE*
 ♦ seasoned traveller *BE*
 ♦ experienced traveler *AE*
 ♦ experienced traveller *BE*
erfahrener Skiläufer, m
 ♦ experienced skier
 ♦ experienced skiier *AE*
Erfahrungen sammeln in einem Hotel
 ♦ gain experience at a hotel
 ♦ gain experience in a hotel
 ♦ gather experience at a hotel
 ♦ gather experience in a hotel
Erfahrung im Gastgewerbe, f
 ♦ experience in the hospitality industry
 ♦ hospitality experience
Erfahrung im Gastgewerbe haben
 ♦ have experience in the hospitality industry
 ♦ have hospitality experience
Erfahrung im Gaststättengewerbe, f
 ♦ experience in the foodservice industry *AE*
 ♦ experience in the catering industry *BE*
Erfahrung im Gaststättengewerbe haben
 ♦ have experience in the foodservice industry *AE*
 ♦ have experience in the catering industry *BE*
Erfahrung im Hotelgewerbe, f
 ♦ experience in the hotel industry
 ♦ experience in the hotel trade
Erfahrung im Hotelgewerbe haben
 ♦ have experience in the hotel trade
 ♦ have experience in the hotel industry
erfolglos, adj
 ♦ unsuccessful, adj
erfolglose Ausstellung, f
 ♦ unsuccessful exhibition

erfolgreiche Ausstellung, f
- successful exhibition
- successful exhibit *AE*

erfolgreiche Konferenz, f
- successful conference

erfolgreicher Kongreß, m
- successful convention
- successful congress

erfolgreiche Saison, f
- successful season

erfolgreiche Tagung, f
- successful meeting

Erfolgsgastronom, m
erfolgreicher Gastronom, m
- successful restaurateur
- successful restauranteur *AE*

Erfolgsquote, f
Erfolgsrate, f
- success rate

Erfolgsrezept, n
Rezept für den Erfolg, n
- recipe of success

erfrischend, adj
- refreshing, adj

erfrischender Schlaf, m
- refreshing sleep

erfrischendes Bad, n
- refreshing bath

erfrischendes Getränk, n
→ Erfrischungsgetränk

erfrischend sein
- be refreshing

erfrischen sich
- refresh oneself

erfrischen sich mit einem Bad
- refresh oneself with a bath

erfrischen sich mit einer Tasse Tee
- refresh oneself with a cup of tea

erfrischt fühlen sich
- feel refreshed

erfrischt und ausgeruht, adj
- refreshed and rested, adj

Erfrischung, f (generell)
- refreshment

Erfrischung, f (kleine Speise oder Getränk)
- refreshment

Erfrischung anbieten
- offer a refreshment

Erfrischung bieten jm
- provide refreshment to s.o.

Erfrischungen reichen
Erfrischungen servieren
- serve refreshments

Erfrischungen werden gereicht
- refreshments are served

Erfrischungsbar, f
- refreshment bar

Erfrischungsbereich, m
- refreshment area

Erfrischungsdienst, m
Erfrischungsservice, m
- refreshment service

Erfrischungsgetränk, n
erfrischendes Getränk, n
- refreshing drink
- refreshing beverage
- refreshment
- soft drink

Erfrischungsgetränkemarkt, m
- refreshment market

Erfrischungsgetränk servieren
- serve a refreshment

Erfrischungshalle, f
(Kiosk etc.)
- soda fountain *AE*

Erfrischungspause, f
(bei Veranstaltungen)
- refreshment break

Erfrischungspavillon, m
- refreshment pavilion

Erfrischungsrast, f
- refreshment stop

Erfrischungsrast machen
- make a refreshment stop

Erfrischungsraum, m
(z.B. in Bahnhof, Theater mit Verkauf)
Büfett, n
Buffet n
- refreshment room
- buffet

Erfrischungsraum (Hinweisschild)
- Refreshments

Erfrischungsservice, m
→ Erfrischungsdienst

Erfrischungsstand, m
Erfrischungsbude, f
- refreshment stand *AE*
- refreshment stall *BE*

Erfrischungstablett, n
- refreshments tray

Erfrischung suchen
- seek refreshment

Erfrischung zu sich nehmen
- have a refreshment
- take a refreshment

Erfüllung eines Traums, f
- fulfillment of a dream *AE*
- fulfilment of a dream *BE*

Erfüllungsgehilfe, m *jur*
- agent *jur*

Erfüllungsort, m *jur*
- place of performance *jur*
- place of fulfillment *AE jur*
- place of fulfilment *BE jur*

Ergänzungsprogramm, n
→ Beiprogramm

ergaunern sich etw bei jm
- cheat s.o. out of s.th.
- swindle s.th. out of s.o.
- chisel s.o. out of s.th. *coll*
- chisel s.th. out of s.o. *coll*
- swindle s.o. (out) of s.th.

Erhalt der Schlüssel, m
- receipt of the keys

erhalten etw in gutem Zustand
pflegen etw
- maintain s.th. in good condition
- keep s.th. in good repair
- maintain s.th.

erhältlich auf Anfrage, adj
- available on request, adj

Erhaltung der Umwelt, f
Umwelterhaltung, f
- conservation of the environment
- preservation of the environment

erhebliche Ermäßigung, f
- substantial reduction

erhebliche Preismäßigung, f
- substantial price reduction

erhebliche Preismäßigung erhalten
- obtain a substantial price reduction

erhitzen etw (auf 190° C)
- heat s.th. (to 190° C)

erhoffter Besucher, m
- prospected visitor

erhöht gelegener Stellplatz, m
(Camping)
erhöhter Stellplatz, m
- elevated pitch

erholen sich (genesen)
genesen
- recover
- recuperate
- convalesce
- get well

erholen sich im Urlaub
- have a restful and relaxing vacation *AE*
- have a restful and relaxing holiday *BE*

erholen sich von dem Streß
- recover from stress

erholen sich von einer Krankheit
von einer Krankheit genesen
- recover from an illness

erholsam, adj
- restful, adj
- relaxing, adj

erholsame Atmosphäre, f
- restful atmosphere

erholsamer Aufenthalt, m
- restful stay
- relaxing stay

erholsame Reise haben
- have a relaxing journey

erholsamer Urlaub, m
- restful vacation *AE*
- restful holiday *BE*

erholsames Wochenende, n
- restful weekend

erholt, adj
ausgeruht, adj
- rested, adj
- well-rested, adj
- relaxed, adj

Erholung, f (Entspannung)
→ Entspannung

Erholung, f (Ferien, Urlaub)
- recreation
- vacation *AE*
- holiday *BE*

Erholung, f (nach Krankheit)
- recovery
- recuperation
- convalescence

Erholung anbieten
- offer recreation

Erholung finden
- find recreation

Erholungsaktivität, f
- recreational activity
- recreation activity

Erholungsanlage, f
Erholungskomplex m
- recreation complex
- recreational complex

Erholungsattraktion, f
- recreational attraction
- recreation attraction

Erholungsaufenthalt, m
erholsamer Aufenthalt, m
- relaxing stay
- holiday stay *BE*
- vacation stay *AE*

Erholungsbecken, n
 ◆ recreational pool
erholungsbedürftig, adj
 erholungsreif, adj
 urlaubsbedürftig, adj
 ◆ in need of (a) holiday BE
 ◆ in need of (a) vacation AE
 ◆ in need of (a) rest
Erholungsbedürftiger, m
 Urlaubsbedürftiger, m
 ◆ person in need of rest
 ◆ person in need of vacation AE
 ◆ person in need of holiday BE
Erholungsbeschäftigung, f
 ◆ recreational pursuit
 ◆ recreational activity
Erholungsbesuch, m
 ◆ recreational visit
Erholungsbesucher, m
 ◆ recreational visitor
Erholungscamping, n
 ◆ recreational camping
Erholungsdorf, n
 ◆ resort village
 ◆ holiday village BE
 ◆ vacation village AE
 ◆ resort
Erholungseinrichtung, f
 ◆ recreation facility
 ◆ recreational facility
Erholungsfahrt, f
 ◆ recreational trip
Erholungsfläche, f
 ◆ recreational area
 ◆ recreation area
 ◆ recreational space
Erholungsführer, m
 ◆ recreation guide
Erholungsfunktion, f
 ◆ recreational function
Erholungsgast, m
 ◆ recreationist AE
Erholungsgebiet, n
 ◆ recreation area
 ◆ recreational area
Erholungsheim, n (für Rekonvaleszenten)
 → Genesungsheim
Erholungsheim, n (generell)
 ◆ recreation home
 ◆ rest house AE
 ◆ rest home BE
Erholungshotel, n
 → Ferienhotel, Urlaubshotel
Erholungskiläufer, m
 Erholungsskifahrer, m
 ◆ recreational skier
Erholungskur, f
 → Liegekur, Ruhekur
Erholungslandschaft, f
 (Gebiet)
 ◆ recreational area
Erholungsmanagement, n
 ◆ recreation management
Erholungsmöglichkeit, f
 Erholungsgelegenheit, f
 ◆ recreation opportunity
 ◆ recreational opportunity
 ◆ recreation facility
 ◆ recreational facility
Erholungsnachfrage, f
 ◆ recreational demand

Erholungsort, m
 Fremdenort, m
 Ferienort, m
 Urlaubsort, m
 ◆ resort
 ◆ vacation resort AE
 ◆ holiday resort BE
Erholungsparadies, n
 ◆ recreational paradise
Erholungspark, m
 ◆ recreation park
Erholungsplatz, m
 (Camping)
 ◆ recreational site
Erholungsprogramm n
 ◆ recreational program AE
 ◆ recreational programme BE
Erholungsprospekt, m
 → Freizeitprospekt
Erholungsraum, m (Gebiet)
 Erholungsgebiet, n
 Erholungsfläche, f
 ◆ recreational space
 ◆ recreational area
 ◆ recreation area
Erholungsraum, m (Zimmer)
 ◆ recovery room
erholungsreif, adj
 → erholungsbedürftig
Erholungsreise, f
 ◆ recreational tour
 ◆ recreational journey
 ◆ recreational trip
Erholungsreisen, n
 Erholungsreiseverkehr, m
 ◆ recreational travel
 ◆ recreation travel
Erholungssaison, f
 ◆ recreational season
 ◆ vacation season AE
 ◆ holiday season BE
erholungssuchend, adj
 ◆ seeking relaxation, adj
 ◆ seeking rest and relaxation, adj
Erholungssuchender, m
 ◆ person seeking recreation
 ◆ person seeking relaxation
Erholungstag, m
 → Ferientag, Ruhetag
Erholungstourismus, m
 ◆ recreational tourism
Erholungstourist, m
 ◆ recreational tourist
Erholung suchen
 ◆ seek recreation
Erholungs- und Freizeitabteilung, f
 ◆ recreation and leisure department
Erholungsunterkunft, f
 ◆ recreational accommodation
 ◆ recreational lodging AE
Erholungsunternehmen, n
 ◆ recreation enterprise
Erholungsurlaub, m (generell)
 erholsamer Urlaub, m
 ◆ recreative vacation AE
 ◆ recreative holiday BE
Erholungsurlaub, m (Krankenurlaub)
 (für Arbeitnehmer)
 Genesungsurlaub, m
 ◆ sick leave AE

 ◆ sick-leave BE
 ◆ convalescent leave
Erholungsurlaub, m (Rekonvaleszenz)
 Genesungsurlaub, m
 ◆ convalescent vacation AE
 ◆ convalescent holiday BE
Erholungsurlauber, m
 ◆ recreational vacationer AE
 ◆ recreational holidaymaker BE
Erholungswert, m
 → Freizeitwert
Erholungszeit, f
 ◆ recreation time
 ◆ recreational time
 ◆ recreational period
Erholungszeitraum, m
 ◆ recreational period
 ◆ recreation period
Erholungszentrum, n
 Freizeitzentrum, n
 ◆ recreation center AE
 ◆ recreational center AE
 ◆ recreation centre BE
 ◆ recreational centre BE
 ◆ relaxation centre BE
Erholungszone, f
 Erholungsbereich, m
 ◆ recreational zone
 ◆ recreation zone
Erholungszweck, m
 ◆ recreational purpose
 ◆ recreation purposes
Eriesee, m
 ◆ Lake Erie
Erinnerungen an eine Reise, f pl
 ◆ memories of a journey pl
 ◆ memories of a trip pl
 ◆ memories of a tour pl
Erinnerungsfoto, n
 ◆ souvenir photo
Erinnerungssouvenir, n
 ◆ commemorative souvenir
 ◆ souvenir
Erinnerungstafel, f
 Gedenktafel, f
 ◆ memorial plaque
 ◆ commemorative plaque
Eritrea
 ◆ Eritrea
Eritreer, m
 ◆ Eritrean
eritreisch, adj
 ◆ Eritrean, adj
erkenntlich zeigen sich
 ◆ show one's appreciation
Erker, m
 ◆ bay
 ◆ bay window
Erkerfenster, n (generell)
 ◆ bay window
Erkerfenster, n (im Dachgeschoß)
 ◆ oriel window
 ◆ oriel
Erkerzimmer, n (generell)
 Zimmer mit einem Erkerfenster, n
 ◆ room with a bay window
 ◆ bay-windowed room
Erkerzimmer, n (im Dachgeschoß)
 Zimmer mit einem Erkerfenster, n
 ◆ room with an oriel

erkranken
krank werden
♦ fall ill
♦ fall sick *AE*
♦ be taken ill
♦ become ill
erkunden etw
♦ explore s.th.
erkunden etw mit dem Auto
erkunden etw mit dem Wagen
♦ explore s.th. by car
erkunden etw zu Fuß
♦ explore s.th. on foot
erkundenswert, adj
♦ worth exploring, adj
erkundenswert sein
♦ be worth exploring
erkundigen sich am Informationsschalter
erkundigen sich bei der Information
♦ inquire at the information desk
♦ enquire at the information desk
erkundigen sich nach dem Preis
nach dem Preis fragen
♦ inquire about the rate
♦ enquire about the rate
♦ inquire about the price
♦ inquire about the price
erkundigen sich nach der Zimmerverfügbarkeit
♦ inquire about room availability
♦ enquire about room availability
erkundigen sich nach einem Zimmer
nach einem Zimmer fragen
♦ inquire about a room
♦ enquire about a room
♦ ask about a room
erkundigen sich nach einer Unterkunft
♦ inquire about accommodation
♦ enquire about accommodation
erkundigen sich nach etw
erkundigen sich über etw
♦ inquire about s.th.
♦ enquire about s.th.
erkundigen sich nach Unterkunftsmöglichkeiten
♦ inquire about accommodation possibilities
♦ enquire about accommodation possibilities
Erkundungsausflug, m
♦ exploration trip
♦ trip of exploration
erlassen etw
verzichten auf etw
♦ waive s.th.
Erlebnisabend, m
♦ theme evening
♦ theme night
Erlebnisbad, n
Erlebnisbecken, n
♦ theme pool
Erlebnisbad, n (Anlage)
♦ hydro spa
Erlebnis des Lebens, n
♦ experience of a lifetime
♦ experience of one's lifetime
Erlebniseinkaufszone, f
♦ theme shopping area
♦ theme shopping precinct
Erlebnisfreizeitpark, m
♦ theme leisure park
Erlebnisgarten, m
♦ theme garden
Erlebnisgastronomie, f
♦ atmosphere dining *AE*

♦ specialty dining *AE*
♦ theme catering *BE*
Erlebnisgebiet, n
Erlebnisbereich, m
♦ theme area
Erlebnishallenbad, n
♦ theme indoor swimming pool *AE*
♦ theme indoor swimming-pool *BE*
Erlebnishotel, n
♦ theme hotel
♦ themed hotel
Erlebnisküche, f (Speisen)
♦ theme cooking
♦ theme cuisine
Erlebnisnacht, f
Erlebnisabend, m
♦ theme night
Erlebnispark, m
♦ theme park
Erlebnisparkbetreiber, m
♦ theme park operator
Erlebnisparty, f
Erlebnisfest, n
♦ theme party
Erlebnisprogramm, n
♦ theme program *AE*
♦ theme programme *BE*
erlebnisreicher Abend, m
♦ exciting evening
Erlebnisreise, f
♦ theme tour
Erlebnisrestaurant, n
♦ theme restaurant
♦ themed restaurant
Erlebnissaal, m
Erlebnishalle, f
♦ theme hall
Erlebnisschau, f
Erlebnisshow, f
♦ theme show
Erlebnis sein
♦ be an experience
Erlebnistourismus, m
♦ theme tourism
Erlebnistourist, m
♦ theme tourist
Erlebnisurlaub, m
♦ theme vacation *AE*
♦ theme holiday *BE*
Erlebnisurlauber, m
♦ theme vacationer *AE*
♦ theme holidaymaker *BE*
Erlebnisveranstaltung, f
♦ theme event
♦ theme function
♦ theme activity
Erlebnisweg, m
Erlebnispfad, m
♦ theme trail
Erlebniswoche, f
♦ theme week
erleichtern etw
leichter machen etw
fördern etw
♦ facilitate s.th.
♦ make s.th. easier
erleichtern jn um etw
→ leichter machen jn um etw
erlesen, adj
♦ choice, adj
♦ exquisite, adj

erlesene Gerichte, n pl
♦ choice dishes *pl*
erlesene Speise, f
♦ exquisite food
erlesene Speisen, f pl
♦ choice food
♦ exquisite food
erlesene Tafelfreuden, f pl
♦ exquisite cuisine
♦ exquisite cooking
erlesene Tafelfreuden bieten
♦ offer exquisite cuisine
♦ offer exquisite cooking
erlesene Tafelfreuden genießen
♦ enjoy the exquisite cuisine
♦ enjoy the exquisite cooking
erlesen möbliert, adj
exquisit möbliert, adj
♦ exquisitely furnished, adj
erlesen möbliertes Zimmer, n
exquisit möbliertes Zimmer, n
♦ exquisitely furnished room
Erlös, m (aus Verkauf)
♦ proceeds *pl*
Erlös, m (Kostenrechnung)
♦ revenue
Erlös, m (Reingewinn)
→ Reingewinn
erloschener Vulkan, m
♦ extinct volcano
Erlös des Konzerts, m
Konzerterlös, m
♦ proceeds of the concert *pl*
Erlöse aus etw, m pl (Verkauf)
♦ proceeds from s.th. *pl*
Erlös einer Tombola, m
Tombolaerlös, m
♦ proceeds of a raffle *pl*
Erlös eines Fests, m
Festerlös, m
♦ proceeds of a festival *pl*
Erlöse pro Zimmer, m pl
♦ revenues per rooms *pl*
Erlöskategorie, f
Erlösklasse, f
♦ revenue category
Erlösklasse, f
→ Erlöskategorie
Erlöskonto, n
♦ revenue account
Erlös pro belegtes Zimmer, m
♦ revenue per occupied room
Erlös pro Bettnacht, m
♦ revenue per bed-night
Erlös pro Gästenacht, m
Erlös pro Logiernacht, m
♦ revenue per guest-night
♦ revenue per sleeper-night
Erlös pro Gast pro Tag m
♦ revenue per guest per day
Erlös pro Logiernacht, m
→ Erlös pro Gästenacht
Erlös pro Übernachtung, m
(Beherbergungsumsatz geteilt durch Zahl der Übernachtungen)
♦ revenue per night
♦ revenue per guest per night
Erlös pro Zimmer, m
♦ revenue per room
Erlös pro Zimmernacht, m
♦ revenue per room-night

Erlösquelle, f
  ♦ source of revenue
Erlös steigern
  ♦ increase revenue
Erlösüberschuß, m
  ♦ revenue surplus
ermäßigen etw
  herabsetzen etw
  verringern etw
  senken etw
  reduzieren etw
  ♦ reduce s.th.
  ♦ lower s.th.
  ♦ cut s.th.
ermäßigt, adj
  ♦ reduced, adj
  ♦ discounted, adj
ermäßigte Früh- und Spätsaisonpreise, m pl
  ♦ reduced early and late season prices *pl*
  ♦ reduced early and late season rates *pl*
ermäßigte Karte, f
  ermäßigte Fahrkarte, f
  ♦ discounted ticket
ermäßigte Leistung, f
  (zu einem reduzierten Preis)
  ermäßigter Service m
  ♦ service at a reduced price
ermäßigte Miete, f
  ♦ reduced rent
ermäßigte Preise für Gruppen, m pl
  ♦ reduced prices for groups *pl*
  ♦ reduced prices for parties *pl*
  ♦ reduced rates for groups *pl*
  ♦ reduced rates for parties *pl*
ermäßigte Preise für Kinder, m pl
  ♦ reduced prices for children *pl*
  ♦ reduced rates for children *pl*
ermäßigte Preise für Pensionäre, m pl
  ermäßigte Preise für Pensionisten, m pl ÖST
  ermäßigte Preise für Rentner, m pl
  ♦ reduced prices for old-age pensioners *pl*
  ♦ reduced rates for old-age pensioners *pl*
  ♦ reduced prices for OAPs *pl*
  ♦ reduced rates for OAPs *pl*
ermäßigte Preise für Rentner, m pl
  → ermäßigte Preise für Pensionäre
ermäßigte Preise für Senioren, m pl
  ♦ reduced prices for senior citizens *pl*
  ♦ reduced rates for senior citizens *pl*
ermäßigter Fahrpreis, m
  ♦ reduced fare
ermäßigter Preis, m
  ♦ reduced price
  ♦ reduced rate
ermäßigter Tarif, m
  ♦ reduced tariff
  ♦ reduced rates *pl*
  ♦ reduced rate
  ♦ reduced terms *pl*
ermäßigter Übernachtungspreis, m
  ♦ reduced price per night
  ♦ reduced rate per night
  ♦ reduced charge per night
  ♦ reduced overnight rate
  ♦ reduced overnight charge
ermäßigter Zimmerpreis, m
  ♦ reduced room rate
  ♦ reduced room price
  ♦ reduced room charge
Ermäßigung, f
  ♦ reduction

  ♦ allowance
  ♦ rebate
Ermäßigung anbieten
  ♦ offer a reduction
Ermäßigung auf den Zimmerpreis, f
  ♦ reduction on the room rate
  ♦ reduction on the room price
Ermäßigung außerhalb der Spitzenzeit, f
  ♦ off-peak reduction
Ermäßigung beanspruchen
  → Ermäßigung verlangen
Ermäßigung beantragen
  ♦ apply for a reduction
Ermäßigung erhalten
  Ermäßigung bekommen
  ♦ get a reduction
  ♦ be given a reduction
  ♦ obtain a reduction
Ermäßigung erhalten auf etw
  ♦ obtain a reduction on s.th.
Ermäßigung für Behinderte, f
  ♦ reduction for disabled persons
  ♦ reduction for handicapped persons
Ermäßigung für etw, f
  ♦ reduction for s.th.
Ermäßigung für Hausgäste, f
  (im Hotel)
  ♦ reduction for residents
Ermäßigung für Hotelgäste, f
  ♦ reduction for hotel guests
Ermäßigung für jn, f
  ♦ reduction for s.o.
Ermäßigung für Kinder, f
  ♦ reduction for children
Ermäßigung für Senioren, f
  ♦ reduction for senior citizens
Ermäßigung geben auf etw
  ♦ give a reduction on s.th.
  ♦ make an allowance on s.th.
Ermäßigung geben für etw
  ♦ give a reduction for s.th.
  ♦ make an allowance for s.th.
Ermäßigung gewähren auf etw
  ♦ grant a reduction on s.th.
Ermäßigung gilt für etw
  ♦ reduction applies for s.th.
Ermäßigung gilt für jn
  ♦ reduction applies for s.o.
Ermäßigung ist erhältlich
  ♦ reduction is obtainable
Ermäßigungsantrag, m
  Antrag auf Ermäßigung, m
  ♦ application for a reduction
Ermäßigungsart, f
  ♦ type of reduction
  ♦ reduction type
Ermäßigungsberechtigter, m
  Ermäßigungsberechtigte, f
  ♦ person eligible for a reduction
Ermäßigungskategorie, f
  Ermäßigungsklasse, f
  ♦ reduction category
Ermäßigungskategorie angeben
  ♦ state the reduction category
Ermäßigungsklasse, f
  → Ermäßigungskategorie
Ermäßigungspreis, m
  → ermäßigter Preis
Ermäßigung verlangen
  Ermäßigung beanspruchen
  ♦ claim a reduction

Ermäßigung von 10 % anbieten auf etw
  ♦ offer a 10 % reduction on s.th.
  ♦ offer a reduction of 10 % on s.th.
Ermäßigung von 10% geben auf alle Zimmer
  ♦ give a reduction of 10% on all rooms
  ♦ give a 10% reduction on all rooms
Ermäßigung von DM 12 auf den Prospektpreis, f
  ♦ reduction of DM 12 off the brochure price
Ermessen, n
  ♦ discretion
  ♦ judgement
  ♦ judgment
Ermessen überlassen von jm
  js Ermessen überlassen
  ♦ leave s.th. to s.o.'s discretion
ermüdend, adj
  ♦ tiring, adj
ermüdende Reise, f
  ♦ tiring journey
  ♦ tiring tour
  ♦ tiring trip
ernähren jn
  nähren jn
  ♦ nourish s.o.
  ♦ feed s.o.
ernähren sich von etw
  (Essen)
  ♦ live on s.th.
Ernährer, m
  (einer Familie)
  Geldverdiener, m
  ♦ breadwinner
Ernährung, f (Nahrung)
  ♦ nutrition
  ♦ food
  ♦ diet
  ♦ nourishment
Ernährungsanleitung, f
  ♦ nutritional guidance
Ernährungsbedürfnisse, n pl
  ♦ nutritional needs *pl*
Ernährungsberater, m
  ♦ nutritional adviser
Ernährungsberatung, f
  ♦ nutritional advice
  ♦ nutritional counselling
  ♦ advice on nutrition
Ernährungsberatung geben
  ♦ give nutritional advice
ernährungsbewußt, adj
  ♦ nutrition-conscious, adj
ernährungsbewußter Gast, m
  ♦ nutrition-conscious guest
Ernährungsfachmann, m
  Ernährungsexperte, m
  ♦ nutritional expert
  ♦ nutrition expert
  ♦ nutritionist
Ernährungsforschung, f
  ♦ food research
Ernährungsgewohnheit, f
  → Eßgewohnheit
Ernährungsgüter, n pl
  ♦ foodstuffs *pl*
Ernährungslehre, f
  → Diätetik
Ernährungsprogramm, n
  ♦ nutritional program *AE*
  ♦ nutritional programme *BE*
Ernährungstherapie, f
  ♦ nutritional therapy

Ernährungswissenschaft

Ernährungswissenschaft, f
  ♦ nutritional science
  ♦ dietetics *pl as sg*
Ernährungswissenschaftler, m
  ♦ nutritionist
ernennen jn zum Vorsitzenden
  ♦ appoint s.o. chairman
Ernennung zum Geschäftsführer, f
  ♦ appointment as manager
erneuern etw
  verlängern etw
  ♦ renew s.th.
Erneuerung, f
  Verlängerung, f
  Wiederaufnahme, f
  ♦ renewal
erneut einberufen etw
  wieder einberufen etw
  ♦ reconvene s.th.
erneut tagen (in ungefähr sechs Monaten)
  wieder tagen (in ungefähr sechs Monaten)
  erneut zusammenkommen (in ungefähr sechs Monaten)
  wieder zusammenkommen (in ungefähr sechs Monaten)
  ♦ reconvene (in approximately six months)
erneut vermieten etw
  (z.B. Zimmer)
  neu vermieten etw
  wieder vermieten etw
  ♦ rerent s.th. *AE*
  ♦ relet s.th. *BE*
Erntedankfest, n
  (In USA: 4. Donnerstag im November;
  in Kanada: 2. Montag im Oktober)
  ♦ Thanksgiving Day
  ♦ Thanksgiving
  ♦ harvest festival
  ♦ harvest home *BE*
  ♦ thanksgiving festival
Erntedanktag, m
  ♦ turkey day *AE coll*
Erntefest, n
  ♦ harvest festival
eröffnen etw (einweihen)
  → einweihen etw
eröffnen etw (generell)
  → öffnen
Eröffnung, f (Einweihung)
  → Einweihung
Eröffnung, f (generell)
  Neueröffnung, f
  ♦ opening
Eröffnung eines Hotels, f (feierlich)
  feierliche Eröffnung eines Hotels, f
  ♦ inauguration of a hotel
Eröffnung eines Kongresses, f
  Kongreßeröffnung, f
  ♦ opening of a convention
  ♦ opening of a congress
Eröffnung findet statt
  ♦ opening takes place
Eröffnung ist ins Auge gefaßt für (Datum)
  ♦ opening is targeted for (date)
Eröffnungsabend, m
  ♦ opening evening
Eröffnungsansprache, f
  Eröffnungsrede f
  ♦ opening address
  ♦ opening speech

  ♦ inaugural address
  ♦ inaugural speech
Eröffnungsball, m
  (einer Saison)
  ♦ opening ball (of the season)
Eröffnungsbestand m
  → Anfangsbestand
Eröffnungsbüfett, n
  ♦ opening buffet
  ♦ inaugural buffet
Eröffnungsempfang, m
  ♦ opening reception
Eröffnungsfahrt, f
  ♦ opening trip
Eröffnungsfeier, f
  Einweihungsfeier, f
  ♦ inaugural ceremony
  ♦ opening ceremony
Eröffnungsfeierlichkeiten, f pl
  ♦ opening ceremonies *pl*
  ♦ inaugural ceremonies *pl*
Eröffnungsfest, n
  Eröffnungsgala, f
  ♦ opening gala
Eröffnungsfrühstück, n
  ♦ opening breakfast
Eröffnungsgaladiner, n
  Eröffnungsfestessen, n
  ♦ opening gala dinner
Eröffnungskonzert, n
  ♦ opening concert
Eröffnungsmusik, f
  ♦ opening music
Eröffnungspreis, m
  ♦ inaugural price
  ♦ inaugural rate
Eröffnungsprogramm, n
  ♦ opening program *AE*
  ♦ opening programme *BE*
Eröffnungsrede, f
  Eröffnungsansprache f
  ♦ inaugural address
  ♦ inaugural speech
  ♦ opening address
  ♦ opening speech
Eröffnungssitzung, f
  ♦ opening session
  ♦ initial meeting
Eröffnungsspiel, n
  ♦ opening game
  ♦ opening match
Eröffnungstag, m
  ♦ opening day
Eröffnungstermin, m
  ♦ opening date
  → date of opening
Eröffnungsumzug, m
  ♦ opening procession
  ♦ opening parade
Eröffnungsveranstaltung f
  ♦ opening ceremony
Eröffnungswanderung, f
  ♦ inaugural walk
Eröffnungswoche, f
  ♦ opening week
Eröffnungszeremonie f
  ♦ opening ceremony
Eröffnung verschieben
  ♦ postpone the opening
Eröffnung vornehmen von etw
  ♦ perform the opening of s.th.

Eroscenter, n
  ♦ Eros center *AE*
  ♦ Eros centre *BE*
erprobtes Franchisepaket, n
  ♦ tested franchise package
erreichbar, adj (Distanz)
  ♦ accessible, adj
  ♦ reachable, adj
  ♦ within reach
Erreichbarkeit, f
  Zugänglichkeit, f
  ♦ accessibility
erreichbar mit dem Auto
  ♦ accessible by car
erreichbar mit dem Bus
  ♦ accessible by bus
  ♦ accessible by coach *BE*
erreichbar mit dem Taxi
  ♦ accessible by taxi
  ♦ accessible by cab
erreichbar mit der U-Bahn
  ♦ accessible by subway *AE*
  ♦ accessible by underground *BE*
erreichbar sein
  ♦ be accessible
  ♦ be reachable
  ♦ be within reach
erreichen etw mit dem Zug
  ♦ reach s.th. by train
erreichen etw zu Fuß
  ♦ reach s.th. on foot
errichten etw
  ♦ erect s.th.
errichten etw zur Erinnerung an jn
  ♦ erect s.th. to the memory of s.o.
Ersatz, m (Alternative)
  ♦ alternative
  ♦ ersatz
Ersatz, m (kurzfristig)
  ♦ substitute
Ersatz, m (langfristig)
  ♦ replacement
Ersatzadresse, f
  ♦ alternate address *AE*
  ♦ alternative address *BE*
Ersatz anbieten jm
  ♦ offer a substitute to s.o.
Ersatzangebot, n
  Alternativangebot, n
  anderweitiges Angebot, n
  Ausweichangebot, n
  ♦ alternate offer *AE*
  ♦ alternative offer *BE*
Ersatzanspruch, m *jur*
  → Schadensersatzanspruch
Ersatzappartement, n
  anderweitiges Appartement, n
  ♦ alternate apartment *AE*
  ♦ alternative apartment *BE*
Ersatzarrangement n
  Ersatzvereinbarung f
  ♦ alternate arrangement *AE*
  ♦ alternative arrangement *BE*
  ♦ substitute arrangement
Ersatzbeförderung, f
  Ersatztransport, m
  ♦ alternate transportation *AE*
  ♦ alternative transport *BE*
Ersatzbeförderung bieten
  Ersatztransport bieten

♦ provide alternate transportation *AE*
♦ provide alternative transport *BE*
Ersatzbesucher, m
♦ **alternate visitor** *AE*
♦ alternative visitor *BE*
Ersatzbett, n
Ausweichbett, n
anderweitiges Bett, n
♦ **alternate bed** *AE*
♦ alternative bed *BE*
♦ spare bed
Ersatzbus, m
♦ **replacement bus**
♦ replacement coach *BE*
Ersatzdatum, n
Ersatztermin, m
♦ **alternative date** *BE*
♦ alternate date *AE*
Ersatzdatum angeben
Ersatztermin angeben
♦ **give an alternative date** *BE*
♦ give an alternate date *AE*
Ersatzdienst, m
Ersatzdienstleistung, f
Ersatzleistung, f
Ersatzservice, m
anderweitiger Dienst, m
♦ **alternative service** *BE*
♦ alternate service *AE*
Ersatz finden
Ersatzperson finden
♦ **find a replacement**
Ersatzflug, m
♦ **alternate flight** *AE*
♦ alternative flight *BE*
Ersatzhotel, n
Ausweichhotel, n
anderweitiges Hotel, n
♦ **alternate hotel** *AE*
♦ alternative hotel *BE*
♦ substitute hotel
Ersatzhotel angeben
♦ **give an alternate hotel** *AE*
♦ give an alternative hotel *BE*
Ersatzhotel finden
♦ **find an alternate hotel** *AE*
♦ find an alternative hotel *BE*
Ersatzhotelunterkunft, f
Ersatzhotelunterbringung, f
anderweitige Hotelunterkunft, f
anderweitige Hotelunterbringung, f
♦ **alternate hotel accommodation** *AE*
♦ alternative hotel accommodation *BE*
Ersatzkarte, f (generell)
Ersatzfahrkarte, f
♦ **replacement ticket**
Ersatzkarte, f (Kreditkarte)
♦ **replacement card**
Ersatzkreditkarte, f
♦ **replacement credit card**
Ersatz leisten
→ Schadensersatz leisten
Ersatzleistung, f
→ Ersatzdienst
Ersatzmahlzeit f
♦ **alternate meal** *AE*
♦ alternative meal *BE*
Ersatzmodell, n
♦ **alternate model** *AE*
♦ alternative model *BE*

Ersatzort, m
Ersatzzielort, m
Ersatzziel, n
anderweitiges Ziel, n
♦ **alternative destination** *BE*
♦ alternate destination *AE*
Ersatzparkplatz, m (für 1 Auto)
♦ **alternate parking space** *AE*
♦ alternate parking place *AE*
♦ alternative parking space *BE*
♦ alternative parking place *BE*
Ersatzparkplatz, m (für mehrere Autos)
Ausweichparkplatz, m
♦ **alternate parking lot** *AE*
♦ alternative car park *BE*
Ersatzpauschalreise, f
♦ **substitute package tour**
Ersatzpauschalreise von vergleichbarer Qualität, f
♦ **substitute package tour of comparable quality**
Ersatzperson, f
Ersatzübernehmer, m
♦ **substitute person**
♦ person replacing s.o.
♦ replacement
♦ substitute
♦ alternate *AE*
Ersatzperson finden
♦ **find a replacement**
Ersatzperson suchen
♦ **look for a replacement**
Ersatzprogramm, n
anderweitiges Programm, n
Alternativprogramm, n
♦ **alternate program** *AE*
♦ alternative programme *BE*
♦ substitute program *AE*
♦ substitute programme *BE*
Ersatzprogramm anbieten
♦ **offer an alternate program** *AE*
♦ offer a substitute program *AE*
♦ offer an alternative programme *BE*
♦ offer a substitute programme *BE*
Ersatzrad, n
♦ **spare wheel**
Ersatzreifen, m
♦ **spare tire** *AE*
♦ spare tyre *BE*
Ersatzreise, f
♦ **alternate tour** *AE*
♦ alternative tour *BE*
♦ substitute tour
Ersatzroute, f
Ersatzstrecke, f
♦ **alternate route** *AE*
♦ alternative route *BE*
Ersatzservice, m
Ersatzdienst, m
Ersatzdienstleistung, f
Ersatzleistung, f
anderweitiger Service, m
♦ **alternate service** *AE*
♦ alternative service *BE*
Ersatzsitzplatz, m
Ersatzplatz, m
♦ **alternate seat** *AE*
♦ alternative seat *BE*
Ersatztermin, m
Ersatzdatum, n
Ausweichtermin, m

♦ **alternate date** *AE*
♦ alternative date *BE*
Ersatztermin angeben
Ersatzdatum angeben
♦ **give an alternate date** *AE*
♦ give an alternative date *BE*
Ersatztermin benennen
Ersatztermin angeben
♦ **indicate an alternate date** *AE*
♦ indicate an alternative date *BE*
Ersatzunterkunft, f
Ausweichunterkunft, f
anderweitige Unterkunft, f
anderweitige Unterbringung, f
♦ **alternate accommodation** *AE*
♦ alternative accommodation *BE*
Ersatzurlaub, m
Ersatzferien, pl
anderweitiger Urlaub, m
anderweitige Ferien, pl
♦ **alternate vacation** *AE*
♦ alternative holiday *BE*
♦ replacement vacation *AE*
♦ replacement holiday *BE*
Ersatz von etw
(z.B. Wäsche)
Ersetzung von etw
♦ **replacement of s.th.**
Ersatz von Porzellan, m
Ersetzung von Porzellan, f
♦ **replacement of porcelain**
Ersatzwagen, m
(z.B. nach einem Unfall)
Ersatzauto, n
♦ **replacement car**
Ersatzwagen erhalten
♦ **obtain a replacement car**
Ersatzwagenmiete, f
♦ **replacement car rental** *AE*
♦ replacement car hire *BE*
Ersatzwohnung, f
anderweitige Wohnung, f
♦ **alternative flat** *BE*
♦ alternate apartment *AE*
Ersatzziel, n
Ersatzzielort, m
anderweitiges Ziel, n
♦ **alternate destination** *AE*
♦ alternative destination *BE*
Ersatzzimmer, n
Ersatzraum, m
anderweitiges Zimmer, n
anderweitiger Raum, m
♦ **alternate room** *AE*
♦ alternative room *BE*
♦ substitute room
Ersatzzimmer angeben
♦ **give an alternate room** *AE*
♦ give an alternative room *BE*
Ersatzzimmer benennen
Ersatzzimmer angeben
♦ **indicate an alternate room** *AE*
♦ indicate an alternative room *BE*
Ersatzzimmer finden
♦ **find an alternate room** *AE*
♦ find an alternative room *BE*
erscheinen auf der Speisekarte
♦ **appear on the menu**
erscheinen auf der Speisekarte als ABC
♦ **appear on the menu as ABC**

erschießen sich in einem Hotelzimmer
- shoot oneself in a hotel room

erschließen etw (Baugelände)
- develop s.th.

erschließen etw für Besucher
- open s.th. up for visitors

erschließen etw (generell)
- open s.th. up

Erschließung, f (Baugelände, Wirtschaft)
- development

Erschließungskosten, pl (bei Bauprojekt)
- development costs *pl*
- development cost

erschlossen, adj
entwickelt, adj
- developed, adj

erschlossenes Skigebiet, n (groß)
- developed ski region
- developed skiing region

erschlossenes Skigebiet, n (klein)
- developed ski area
- developed skiing area

erschöpft, adj
- exhausted, adj

erschöpfter Reisender, m
- exhausted traveler *AE*
- exhausted traveller *BE*

erschöpft sein
- be exhausted

Erschöpfung, f
- exhaustion

erschwinglich, adj
- affordable, adj

erschwinglicher Preis, m
ziviler Preis, m
- reasonable price
- reasonable rate

erschwingliches Zimmer, n
- affordable room

erschwingliche Unterkunft, f
- affordable accommodation

ersehnte Ruhepause, f
ersehnte Ruhe f
- longed-for rest

ersetzen etw
- replace s.th.
- substitute s.th.
- supersede s.th.

erstattbar, adj
erstattungsfähig, adj
rückgabefähig, adj
- returnable, adj
- refundable, adj

erstatten etw
→ zurückerstatten etw

Erstattung, f
→ Rückerstattung

Erstattung des Rücktritts, f
→ Stornierungsrückzahlung

Erstattung des vollen Preises zusprechen jm (Gericht)
- award s.o. reimbursement of the full price

erstattungsfähig, adj
→ erstattbar

Erstattungsformular, n
- refund form

Erstaufenthalt, m
erstmaliger Aufenthalt, m
erster Aufenthalt, m
- first-time stay

erstbestes Hotel, n
- first hotel one comes to
- first hotel one comes across

Erstbesuch, m
erstmaliger Besuch, m
erster Besuch, m
- first-time visit
- first visit

Erstbesucher, m
erstmaliger Besucher, m
- first-time visitor
- first-time guest
- first-timer *coll*

Erstbuchung, f
erste Buchung, f
erstmalige Buchung, f
- first booking
- initial booking

Erstcamper, m
erstmaliger Camper, m
- first-time camper

Erste Bardame, f SCHW
- first barmaid
- head barmaid
- chief barmaid

erste Begegnung mit etw, f
- first encounter with s.th.

Erste Etagengouvernante, f
Erste Etagenhausdame, f
- executive floor housekeeper *AE*
- head floor housekeeper *BE*

erste Etappe der Reise, f
- first leg of the journey
- first leg of the tour
- first leg of the trip

Erste Hausdame, f
Leiterin der Hausdamenabteilung, f
Generalgouvernante, f SCHW
- executive housekeeper *AE*
- head housekeeper *BE*

Erste Hilfe f
- first aid

Erste Hilfe leisten jm
- render first aid to s.o.
- render s.o. first aid

erste Hoteladresse, f
→ Erstes Haus am Ort

erste Hypothek, f
- first mortgage

erste Klasse, f
- first class

Erste-Klasse-Abteil, n (Zug)
Erster-Klasse-Abteil, n
Abteil in der ersten Klasse, n
Erstklaßabteil, n SCHW
- first-class compartment

Erste-Klasse-Fahrpreis, m
Erster-Klasse-Fahrpreis, m
Fahrpreis in der ersten Klasse, m
- first-class fare

Erste-Klasse-Flug, m
Erster-Klasse-Flug, m
Flug in der ersten Klasse, m
- first-class flight

Erste-Klasse-Kabine, f
Erster-Klasse-Kabine, f
Kabine erster Klasse, f
Kabine in der ersten Klasse, f
Erstklaßkabine, f SCHW
- first-class cabin

Erste-Klasse-Rückfahrkarte, f
Erster-Klasse-Rückfahrkarte, f
Rückfahrkarte für die erste Klasse, f
Rückfahrkarte in der ersten Klasse, f
Rückfahrkarte erster Klasse, f
- first-class return ticket *BE*
- first-class round-trip ticket *AE*

Erste-Klasse-Rückflug, m
Erster-Klasse-Rückflug, m
Rückflug in der ersten Klasse, m
- first-class return flight

Erste-Klasse-Sitzplatz, m
Erste-Klasse-Sitz, m
Erste-Klasse-Platz, m
Erster-Klasse-Platz, m
- first-class seat

Erste-Klasse-Tarif, m
Erster-Klasse-Tarif, m
Tarif für die erste Klasse, m
- first-class tariff
- first-class rates *pl*
- first-class rate
- first-class terms *pl*

Erste Lingeriegouvernante, f SCHW
Erste Wäschebeschließerin, f
- head linen keeper
- executive linen keeper *AE*

ersten Gang bilden (Menü)
- form the first course

erste Qualität, f
- choice quality

Erster Barman, m
Erster Barmann m
- head barman

erster Besuch in Amerika, m
- first visit to America

Erster Commis, m
Premier Commis, m *FR m*
- first commis
- senior commis
- premier commis *FR m*

Erster Concierge, m
Erste Concierge, f
- head concierge
- chief concierge

Erster Empfangssekretär, m
Erste Empfangssekretärin, f
- chief reception clerk

Erste Rezeptionssekretärin, f
→ Erste Empfangssekretärin

erster Gang, m (Menü)
- first course

erster Gang, m (Motor)
- first gear
- bottom gear

erster Gang beim Abendessen, m (Dinner)
- first course at dinner

erster Gang beim Abendessen, m (Supper)
- first course at supper

erster Gang beim Mittagessen, m
- first course at lunch

Erster Hallenportier, m
Erster Saalportier, m
- head hall porter

Erster Hausdiener, m
- head valet

erster Klasse fliegen
- fly first class

erster Klasse logieren
  erster Klasse wohnen
  ♦ **stay first class**
erster Klasse reisen
  erster Klasse fahren
  ♦ **travel first class**
erster Koch, m
  ♦ **head cook**
  ♦ first cook
erster Konferenztag, m
  ♦ **first day of a conference**
Erster Mai, m
  Maifeiertag, m
  ♦ **May Day**
Erster Maître d'hôtel, m
  → Premier maître d'hôtel
Erster Nachtportier, m
  ♦ **head night porter**
Erster Oberkellner, m
  Premier maître d'hôtel, m *FR*
  ♦ **first headwaiter**
  ♦ premier maître d'hôtel *FR*
Ersteröffnung, f
  erste Eröffnung, f
  ♦ **first opening**
Erster Portier, m
  ♦ **head porter**
erster Preis, m (Auszeichnung)
  ♦ **first prize**
erster Programmpunkt m
  ♦ **first item on the program** *AE*
  ♦ first item on the programme *BE*
erster Rang, m (Theater)
  Balkon, m
  ♦ **dress circle** *BE*
  ♦ first balcony *AE*
  ♦ balcony *AE*
Erster Saalportier, m
  → Erster Hallenportier
Erster Souschef, m
  Premier sous-chef, m *FR*
  ♦ **premier sous-chef** *FR*
  ♦ head sous-chef
erster Teil der Reise, m
  ♦ **first part of the journey**
  ♦ first part of the trip
  ♦ first part of the tour
Erster Weinkellner, m
  ♦ **head wine waiter**
  ♦ head wine steward *AE*
Erster Weinsteward, m
  ♦ **head wine steward**
  ♦ chief wine steward
Erste Saaltochter, f *SCHW*
  ♦ **senior waitress**
erstes Frühstück, n
  → Morgenfrühstück
Erstes Haus, n (Hotel)
  ♦ **premier hotel** *FR*
  ♦ best hotel
  ♦ leading hotel
  ♦ foremost hotel
Erstes Haus am Ort, n
  Erstes Haus am Platz, n
  ♦ **leading hotel in X**
  ♦ best hotel in X
  ♦ premier hotel of X *FR*
  ♦ foremost hotel in X
  ♦ finest hotel in town
Erstes Haus am Platz, n
  → Erstes Haus am Ort

erstes Haus am Platz sein
  ♦ **be the foremost hotel in a place**
  ♦ be the premier hotel of X
erstes Hotel, n
  → Erstes Haus
erste Sitzung f
  (im Speisesaal)
  ♦ **first sitting**
erstes Stockwerk, n
  erste Etage, f
  erstes Obergeschoß, n
  ♦ **second floor** *AE*
  ♦ second story *AE*
  ♦ first floor *BE*
  ♦ first storey *BE*
erstes Vierteljahr, n
  erstes Quartal, n
  ♦ **first quarter**
erste Übernachtung vorauszahlen
  ♦ **prepay the first night**
erste Wahl, f
  ♦ **first choice**
erste Wegetappe, f
  ♦ **first leg of the trail**
Erstflug, m
  erster Flug, m
  ♦ **first flight**
Erstgast, m
  erstmaliger Gast, m
  ♦ **first-time guest**
  ♦ first-timer *inform*
Ersthaus, n
  (Gegensatz zu Zweithaus)
  erstes Haus, n
  ♦ **first home**
Erstkäufer, m
  ♦ **first-time buyer**
Erstklaßappartement, n *SCHW*
  → erstklassiges Appartement
Erstklaßhotel, n *SCHW*
  → erstklassiges Hotel
erstklassig, adj
  ♦ **first-class, adj**
  ♦ first-rate, adj *coll*
erstklassige Einrichtung, f
  ♦ **first-class facility**
  ♦ first-rate facility *coll*
erstklassige Küche, f
  ♦ **cordon bleu cookery** *humor*
  ♦ cordon bleu cooking *humor*
  ♦ first-class cooking
  ♦ first-class cuisine
erstklassige Küche, f (Raum)
  ♦ **first-class kitchen**
  ♦ first-rate kitchen *coll*
erstklassige Küche, f (Speisen)
  ♦ **first-class cuisine**
  ♦ first-rate cuisine *coll*
  ♦ first-class cooking
  ♦ first-rate cooking *coll*
  ♦ cordon bleu cuisine *humor*
erstklassigen Service anbieten
  ♦ **offer first-class service**
  ♦ offer first-rate service *coll*
erstklassigen Service bieten
  ♦ **provide first-class service**
  ♦ provide first-rate service
erstklassigen Service garantieren
  erstklassigen Service gewährleisten
  ♦ **guarantee first-class service**
  ♦ guarantee first-rate service

erstklassiger Gästekreis, m
  erstklassiger Gästestamm, m
  ♦ **first-class clientele**
  ♦ first-rate clientele *coll*
erstklassiger Koch, m
  ♦ **cordon bleu cook** *humor*
  ♦ cordon bleu *humor*
  ♦ first-class cook
erstklassiger Küchenchef, m
  ♦ **cordon bleu chef** *humor*
  ♦ first-class chef
erstklassiger Service, m
  Erstklaßservice, m *SCHW*
  erstklassiger Dienst, m
  Erstklaßdienst, m *SCHW*
  ♦ **first-class service**
  ♦ first-rate service *coll*
  ♦ top-notch service *BE coll*
erstklassiges Abendessen, n (Dinner)
  ♦ **first-class dinner**
erstklassiges Abendessen, n (Supper)
  ♦ **first-class supper**
erstklassige Sanitäreinrichtungen, f pl
  ♦ **first-class sanitary facilities** *pl*
erstklassiges Appartement, n
  Erstklaßappartement, n *SCHW*
  ♦ **first-class apartment**
erstklassiges Essen, n (Kost)
  ♦ **first-class food**
  ♦ cordon bleu food *humor*
erstklassiges Essen, n (Mahlzeit)
  erstklassige Mahlzeit, f
  erstklassiges Mahl, n
  ♦ **first-class meal**
  ♦ cordon bleu meal *humor*
erstklassiges Frühstück, n
  ♦ **first-class breakfast**
erstklassiges Gericht, n
  ♦ **cordon bleu dish** *humor*
  ♦ first-class dish
erstklassiges Hotel, n
  (gewöhnlich mit zwei Sternen)
  Hotel erster Klasse, n
  Erstklaßhotel, n *SCHW*
  First-class-Hotel, n
  ♦ **first-class hotel**
  ♦ first-rate hotel *coll*
erstklassiges Mittagessen, n
  ♦ **first-class luncheon**
  ♦ first-class lunch
erstklassiges Restaurant, n
  Erstklaßrestaurant, n *SCHW*
  Restaurant erster Klasse, n
  ♦ **first-class restaurant**
erstklassige Suite, f
  ♦ **first-class suite**
erstklassiges Zimmer, n
  Erstklaßzimmer, n *SCHW*
  ♦ **first-class room**
  ♦ first-rate room *coll*
erstklassige Unterkunft, f
  erstklassige Unterbringung, f
  Erstklaßunterkunft, f *SCHW*
  ♦ **first-class accommodation**
  ♦ first-class lodging *AE*
erstklassige Unterkunft bieten
  erstklassige Unterbringung bieten
  ♦ **provide first-class accommodation**
erstklassige Verpflegung, f
  ♦ **first-class foodservice** *AE*

Erstklaßrestaurant

- ♦ first-class catering BE
- ♦ first-class food

Erstklaßrestaurant, n SCHW
→ erstklassiges Restaurant

Erstklaßwagen, m
→ Wagen erster Klasse

Erstklaßzimmer n
→ erstklassiges Zimmer

Erstkunde, m
erstmaliger Kunde, m
- ♦ first-time customer
- ♦ first-time client

erstmalig, adj
- ♦ first-time, adj

Erstpassagier, m
erstmaliger Passagier, m
- ♦ fist-time passenger

erstrangig, adj
erstklassig, adj
- ♦ first-rate, adj coll
- ♦ first-class, adj

erstrecken sich von A nach B
- ♦ extend from A to B
- ♦ stretch from A to B
- ♦ run from A to B

Erstreisen, n
erstmaliges Reisen, n
erstes Reisen, n
Erstreiseverkehr, m
- ♦ first-time travel

Erstreisender, m
- ♦ first-time traveler AE
- ♦ first-time traveller BE

Ertrag, m
- ♦ earning

Ertrag, m (aus einem Geschäft)
Rendite, f
- ♦ return
- ♦ returns pl

Ertrag, m (Erlös)
→ Erlös

Ertrag, m (Gewinn)
→ Gewinn

Ertrag, m (Gewinne)
- ♦ gains pl
- ♦ gainings pl

Ertrag, m (Gewinn- und Verlustrechnung)
- ♦ income

Ertrag, m (Produktionsergebnis)
- ♦ yield
- ♦ output

Ertrag aus Beherbergung, m
→ Beherbergungsertrag

Ertrag aus Verpflegung, m
→ Verpflegungsertrag

Erträge ansteigen lassen
- ♦ boost earnings

Erträge aus Beherbergung, m pl
→ Beherbergungsertrag

Erträge aus Dienstleistungen, m pl
- ♦ service earnings pl
- ♦ earnings on services pl

Erträge aus Verpflegung, m pl
→ Verpflegungsertrag

Erträge nach Steuern, m pl
- ♦ after-tax earnings pl
- ♦ after-tax profits pl

Erträgnisse, n pl
- ♦ earnings pl

Ertrag pro belegtes Zimmer, m
- ♦ income per occupied room

Ertragseite, f (GuV)
(Gewinn- und Verlustrechnung)
- ♦ income side

Ertragskraft, f
Ertragsfähigkeit f
- ♦ earning power
- ♦ earnings power
- ♦ earning capacity
- ♦ earnings capacity

Ertragskurve, f
- ♦ earnings curve

Ertragsleistung, f
Ertragskraft f
- ♦ earnings performance

Ertragsmiete, f
reine Miete f
- ♦ break-even rent

Ertragsposten, m
(Gewinn- und Verlustrechnung)
Ertragsposition f
- ♦ income item

Ertragsverbesserung, f
- ♦ improvement in earnings
- ♦ earnings improvement

Ertrag und Aufwand, m (GuV)
(Gewinn- und Verlustrechnung)
- ♦ income and expenditure

Ertrag vor Steuern, m (Gewinn- u. Verlustrechnung)
- ♦ income before tax

Erwachsenenbad, n
Erwachsenenbecken, n
- ♦ adults' pool

Erwachsenenbecken, n
→ Erwachsenenbad

Erwachsenenbett n
- ♦ adult's bed
- ♦ adults' bed

Erwachseneneintritt, m
Erwachseneneintrittspreis, m
- ♦ adult admission

Erwachsenenessen, n
- ♦ adult meal

Erwachsenenfahrpreis, m
- ♦ adult fare

Erwachsenengruppe, f
- ♦ adult group
- ♦ group of adults

Erwachsenenkarte, f
Erwachsenenfahrkarte, f
- ♦ adult ticket

Erwachsenenkurs, m
Erwachsenenlehrgang, m
- ♦ adult course

Erwachsenenliftpaß, m
- ♦ adults' lift pass

Erwachsenenpreis, m
- ♦ adult price
- ♦ adult rate
- ♦ adults' rate
- ♦ adults' price
- ♦ rate for adults

Erwachsenenprogramm, n
- ♦ adult program AE
- ♦ adult programme BE

Erwachsenenrad, n coll
- ♦ adult bike coll

Erwachsenenschwimmbad, n
Erwachsenenschwimmbecken, n
- ♦ adults' swimming pool AE
- ♦ adults' swimming-pool BE

Erwachsenenschwimmbecken, n
→ Erwachsenenschwimmbad

Erwachsenentoilette f
- ♦ adults' toilet

Erwachsenenunterkunft f
- ♦ adult accommodation
- ♦ accommodation for adults

Erwachsenenzimmer n
- ♦ adults' room

Erwachsener, m
- ♦ adult
- ♦ grown-up person
- ♦ grown-up

erwähnenswert, adj
- ♦ worth mentioning, adj

erwähnenswert sein
- ♦ be worth mentioning

erwähnt werden zum erstenmal offiziell
- ♦ be first mentioned in official documents
- ♦ be mentioned in official documents for the first time

Erwähnung verdienen
- ♦ deserve mention

erwarten etw für sein Geld
- ♦ expect s.th. for one's money

erwarten etw von seinem Urlaub
- ♦ expect s.th. from one's vacation AE
- ♦ expect s.th. from one's holiday BE

erwarten jn (generell)
- ♦ expect s.o.

erwarten jn (warten auf jn)
- ♦ await s.o.
- ♦ wait for s.o.

erwarten jn zum Abendessen
- ♦ expect s.o. for dinner

erwartete Auslastung, f
- ♦ expected load factor

erwartete Belegung, f
erwartete Auslastung, f
- ♦ expected occupancy

erwarteter Besucher, m
- ♦ expected visitor

erwarteter Gast m
- ♦ expected guest

erwarteter Umsatz, m
- ♦ projected sales pl
- ♦ projected turnover

Erwartung, f
- ♦ expectation

Erwartungen entsprechen von jm
js Erwartungen erfüllen
- ♦ come up to s.o.'s expectations

Erwartungen erfüllen von jm
js Erwartungen erfüllen
- ♦ fulfill s.o.'s expectations AE
- ♦ fulfil s.o.'s expectations BE

Erwartungen nicht entsprechen von jm
- ♦ not come up to s.o.'s expectations

Erwartungen sind hoch
- ♦ expectations are high

Erwartungen sind niedrig
- ♦ expectations are low

Erwartungen standhalten von jm
- ♦ match s.o.'s expectations

Erwartungen übertreffen
alle unsere Erwartungen übertreffen
- ♦ surpass one's expectations
- ♦ surpass all our expectations

erweisen sich als Besuchermagnet
- ♦ prove a magnet to visitors

erweitern etw (Gebäude)
vergrößern etw
♦ enlarge s.th.
♦ extend s.th.
erweitern etw (Geschäft)
♦ expand s.th.
♦ enlarge s.th.
♦ extend s.th.
erweitertes Frühstück, n
♦ supplemented breakfast
erweitertes Frühstück n
♦ brunch
Erweiterung, f
♦ extension
♦ expansion
Erweiterung der Konferenzräumlichkeiten, f
♦ extension of the conference facilities
♦ expansion of the conference facilities
Erweiterungsbau, m
→ Anbau
Erweiterungsbau erstellen zu etw
♦ build an extension to s.th.
Erweiterungsbau mit 12 Schlafzimmern, m
♦ extension with 12 bedrooms
♦ 12-bedroom extension
Erweiterungsplan, m
♦ extension plan
♦ expansion plan
Erweiterungsprogramm, n
♦ extension program *AE*
♦ extension programme *BE*
♦ expansion program *AE*
♦ expansion programme *BE*
Erweiterungstrakt, m
♦ wing extension
Erwerb eines Hotels, m
Kauf eines Hotels m
♦ acquisition of a hotel
Erzbergwerk, n
♦ ore mine
Erzgebirge n
(Region)
♦ Erzgebirge
♦ Erz Mountains *pl*
♦ Ore Mountains *pl*
Erzherzogsart, adv *gastr*
nach Erzherzogsart, adv *gastr*
♦ grand duke's style, adv *gastr*
Erziehungsurlaub, m (Mutter)
→ Mutterschaftsurlaub
Erziehungsurlaub, m (Vater)
♦ paternity leave
erzielbarer Zimmerpreis, m
♦ achievable room rate
♦ achievable room price
erzwungene Abreise, f
erzwungene Abfahrt, f
♦ forced departure
es allen recht machen wollen
♦ try to please everybody
Eselkarren, m
♦ donkey cart
Eselreiten, n
♦ donkey riding
♦ riding a donkey
Eselritt, m
♦ donkey ride
Es empfiehlt sich, den Zug zu nehmen
♦ It is recommended to go by train
♦ It is advisable to go by train

Es gibt ein eigenes Schwimmbecken für Kinder
♦ There is a separate swimming pool for children
Es gibt für jeden etwas
♦ There's something for everyone
Es gibt heute Fisch zum Abendessen (Dinner)
♦ There's fish for dinner today
Es gibt keinen Zimmerservice
♦ There is no room service
Es gibt keine Überfüllung
♦ There is no overcrowding
Es herrscht eine angenehme Atmosphäre
♦ There is a pleasant atmosphere
Es ist hier langweilig
♦ It's boring here
Es ist immer Ferienzeit
♦ It is always vacation time *AE*
♦ It is always holiday time *BE*
Es ist kein Tisch frei
♦ There is no table free
Es ist serviert! (Dinner)
♦ Dinner is served!
Es ist serviert! (Lunch)
♦ Lunch is served!
Es ist serviert! (Supper)
♦ Supper is served!
Eskapismus, m
♦ escapism
eskapistisch, adj
♦ escapist, adj
Eskimo, m
♦ Eskimo
Eskorte, f
♦ escort
Es lebe der Präsident!
♦ Long live the president!
Es macht Appetit
♦ It gives you an appetite
Espe, f
Zitterpappel, f
♦ aspen
Espenbaum, m
Espe, f
Zitterpappel, f
♦ aspen tree
Esplanade, f
(offener Platz)
♦ esplanade
Espresso, m *ITAL*
♦ espresso *ITAL*
Espresso, n *ÖST*
→ Espressobar
Espressobar f
♦ espresso bar
♦ coffee bar
Espressocafé, n
♦ espresso cafe *AE*
♦ espresso café *BE*
Espressokaffee, m
♦ espresso coffee
Espressolokal, n
♦ espresso place
Espressomaschine, f
♦ espresso machine
♦ espresso
Espressostube, f
→ Espressobar
Espressotasse, f
♦ espresso cup
Eßapfel, m
♦ eating apple

eßbar, adj
♦ eatable, adj
♦ edible, adj
eßbarer Pilz, m
(d.h. nicht giftig)
♦ edible mushroom
Eßbarkeit, f
♦ edibility
Eßbereich, m
♦ eating area
♦ dining area
Eßbesteck, n
(Löffel, Gabel, Messer)
Besteck, n
♦ cutlery set
♦ set of knife, fork and spoon
♦ table cutlery
♦ flatware *AE*
Eß-Brechsucht, f
→ Bulimie
Es schmeckt mir gut
♦ I like it
♦ It tastes good to me
Es schmeckt mir nicht
♦ I don't like it
♦ It doesn't taste good to me
Eßclub, m
→ Speiseclub
Eßecke, f
Eßnische f
♦ dining recess
♦ dining alcove
♦ eating nook *BE*
♦ dinette *AE*
essen
♦ eat
♦ have a meal
Essen, n (Aktivität)
♦ eating
Essen, n (Nahrung)
♦ food
♦ fare
♦ victuals *pl*
♦ meal
essen, trinken und fröhlich sein
♦ eat, drink and be merry
Essen abschließen mit etw
Mahl abrunden mit etw
♦ complete a meal with s.th.
♦ top a meal with s.th.
Essen abschließen mit Kaffee
Mahlzeit abschließen mit Kaffee
♦ top a meal with coffee
Essen allein ist die Fahrt wert
♦ food alone is worth the trip
Essenanteil, m
(z.B. an Einnahmen, Kosten)
♦ meals proportion
Essen arrangieren
♦ arrange a meal
essen auf dem Zimmer
→ auf dem Zimmer essen
Essen auftragen
♦ dish up a meal
♦ serve a meal
Essen ausgeben
Essen austeilen
♦ issue a meal
♦ issue meals

Essen außer Haus

Essen außer Haus, n
- eating out
- dining out

Essen auswählen
(Mahlzeit)
- select a meal

Essen beginnen mit etw
- start one's meal with s.th.
- begin one's meal with s.th.
- commence one's meal with s.th. *form*

Essen bekommt mir nicht
- food does not agree with me

Essen besteht aus sechs Gängen
Mahlzeit besteht aus sechs Gängen
- meal consists of six courses

Essen bestellen
Mahlzeit bestellen
- order a meal

Essenbestellung, f
- food order
- ordering food

Essenbestellung aufgeben
- place a food order

Essen bezahlen
(Mahlzeit)
- pay for a meal

Essenbon, m (Gutschein)
Essencoupon, m
Essenkarte, f
- meal coupon *AE*
- meal ticket *AE*
- meal voucher
- lunch(eon) voucher *BE*
- LV *BE*

Esseneinnahmen, f pl
- meals takings *pl*

Essen ekelt mich
- dish makes me (feel) sick
- dish nauseates me

Essen erfreut das Auge
- food delights the eye
- food pleases the eye

Essen erhalten (Speisen)
- obtain food

essen etw mit Appetit
genießen etw mit Appetit
- eat s.th. with relish

essen etw mit einem Bissen
- eat s.th. in one bite

essen etw mit Ekel
- eat s.th. with distaste

essen etw zum Abendessen (Dinner)
- have s.th. for dinner
- eat s.th. for dinner

essen etw zum Abendessen (Supper)
- have s.th. for supper
- eat s.th. for supper

essen etw zum Frühstück
- have s.th. for (one's) breakfast
- eat s.th. for breakfast
- breakfast on s.th.

essen für drei *coll*
- eat enough for three

Essen für drei Personen, n
Essen für drei, n
Mahlzeit für drei (Personen), f
- meal for three persons
- meal for three

essen für zwei *coll*
- eat enough for two

Essen geben für jn
Festessen geben für jn
Bankett geben für jn
- give a banquet for s.o.

Essen geben zu Ehren von jm
Festessen geben zu Ehren von jm
Bankett geben zu Ehren von jm
- give a banquet in honor of s.o. *AE*
- give a banquet in honour of s.o. *BE*

essen gehen
(in einem Lokal essen)
- eat out

Essen genießen
Mahlzeit genießen
- enjoy a meal
- enjoy one's meal

Essengeruch, m
Essensgeruch, m
- smell of food
- smell of cooking

Essengong, m
- dinner gong

Essengutschein, m
Verzehrgutschein, m
Essenbon, m
Essenkarte, f
Essenmarke, f
- LV *BE*
- luncheon voucher *BE*
- lunch voucher *BE*
- meal voucher
- meal ticket *AE*

Essen hat keinen Geschmack
- food has no taste
- food is tasteless

Essen hinunterschlingen
- wolf down one's food *inform*
- bolt one's food

essen im Bett
- eat in (one's) bed

essen im Freien
- eat alfresco
- eat outside

Essen im Freien, n (Aktivität)
- eating alfresco
- dining alfresco

Essen im Freien, n (Mahlzeit)
- open-air meal
- meal in the open air

essen im Garten
- eat in the garden

Essen improvisieren
- improvise a meal

Essen im Sitzen, n
- sit-down meal

Essen im Stehen, n
→ Stehessen

Essen in der Tüte, n
Futtersack, m
- nosebag

essen in einem Restaurant
- eat in a restaurant

Essen ist abwechslungsreich
- food is varied

Essen ist akzeptabel
- food is acceptable

Essen ist appetitlich
Essen ist appetitanregend
- food is appetising
- food is appetizing

Essen ist ausgezeichnet
- food is excellent

Essen ist bekömmlich
Essen ist gesund
- food is wholesome

Essen ist bereit (Dinner)
Essen wartet (Dinner)
- dinner is waiting

Essen ist bereit (Mittagessen)
Essen wartet (Mittagessen)
- lunch is waiting

Essen ist bereit (Supper)
Essen wartet (Supper)
- supper is waiting

Essen ist berühmt
- food is celebrated

Essen ist besser geworden
- food has improved

Essen ist delikat
- food is delicate

Essen ist einfach
- food is plain
- food is simple

Essen ist eintönig
- food is dull
- food is monotonous

Essen ist erstklassig
Verpflegung ist erstklassig
- food is first-class
- food is first-rate *coll*

Essen ist fantasievoll
- food is imaginative

Essen ist fertig
Das Essen ist fertig!
- meal is ready
- The meal is ready!
- Grub's up! *inform*

Essen ist fertig (Dinner)
→ Abendessen ist fertig

Essen ist fertig (Lunch)
→ Mittagessen ist fertig

Essen ist fertig (Supper)
→ Abendessen ist fertig

Essen ist frisch
- food is fresh

Essen ist fürchterlich
- food is dreadful

Essen ist genießbar
- food is palatable

Essen ist geschmackvoll
- food is tasty

Essen ist gesund
- food is healthy

Essen ist grauenhaft
- food is awful

Essen ist großartig
- food is great

Essen ist gut
- food is good
- food is fine

Essen ist gut und reichlich
- food is good and plentiful

Essen ist herrlich
- food is superb

Essen ist hervorragend
- food is outstanding

Essen ist international
- food is international

Essen ist köstlich
- food is delicious

Essen und Trinken

Essen ist mir zuwider
♦ I loathe the food
Essen ist mittelmäßig
Essen ist nicht besonders gut
♦ food is indifferent
Essen ist nicht klassifizierbar
Speisen sind sehr durchschnittlich
♦ food is nondescript
Essen ist passabel
das Essen geht *coll*
♦ food is adequate
♦ food is fair
Essen ist preiswert
♦ food is inexpensive
Essen ist reichlich
♦ food is plentiful
Essen ist schlecht
Verpflegung ist schlecht
♦ food is of poor quality
♦ food is poor
♦ food is bad
Essen ist schrecklich
♦ food is horrible
Essen ist sehr gut
♦ food is very good
Essen ist sehr reichlich
♦ food is generous
Essen ist sein Geld wert
♦ food is good value
Essen ist traditionell
♦ food is traditional
Essen ist überdurchschnittlich
Verpflegung ist überdurchschnittlich
♦ food is above average
Essen ist ungenießbar
♦ food is unpalatable
Essen ist unvergleichlich
♦ food is matchless
Essen ist verdorben
Speise ist verdorben
♦ food has gone bad
♦ food has gone off
Essen ist vergleichsweise einfach
♦ food is relatively plain
♦ food is relatively simple
Essen ist von hoher Qualität
♦ food is of high standard
Essen kalt werden lassen
♦ let the food get cold
Essenkarte, f
Essenbon, m
Essenmarke, f
Essengutschein, m
Verzehrgutschein, m
♦ meal ticket *AE*
♦ meal voucher
♦ luncheon voucher *BE*
♦ lunch voucher *BE*
♦ LV *BE*
Essen kaufen
♦ buy a meal
Essen kochen
♦ cook a meal
Essen kochen auf dem Holzkohlengrill
♦ cook food on the charcoal grill
Essenkorb, m
♦ food basket
Essenkosten, pl
♦ cost of meals

Essen liefern
Mahlzeit liefern
♦ supply a meal
Essenmarke, f
→ Essenkarte
Essen mit Abendgarderobe, n
Diner, n
♦ formal dinner party
♦ formal dinner
essen mit Eßstäbchen
♦ eat with chopsticks
essen mit jm
mitessen mit jm
♦ eat with s.o.
♦ have a meal with s.o.
Essen mit mehreren Gängen, n
Mahlzeit mit mehreren Gängen, f
♦ meal of several courses
♦ multi-course meal
essen mit Messer und Gabel
♦ eat with knife and fork
Essen mit Tischbedienung, n
♦ table-service meal
♦ silver-service meal *BE*
essen nach der Karte
→ essen à la carte
Essen nach der Karte, n
♦ à-la-carte meal
♦ eating à la carte
♦ dining à la carte
Essenpause, f
(Pause zum Essen)
♦ meal break
Essenpreis, m
Essenspreis, m
♦ meal price
♦ price for a meal
♦ meal charge
Essenpreis ändern (geringfügig)
♦ alter the price of a meal
♦ alter the menu charges
Essenpreis ändern (umfassend)
♦ change the price of a meal
Essenpreisänderung, f (geringfügig)
♦ alteration of the food price
Essenpreisänderung, f (umfassend)
♦ change in the food price
Essenpreiserhöhung, f
♦ meal price increase
♦ meal price rise
♦ increase in meal prices
♦ rise in meal prices
Essen probieren
Essen ausprobieren
♦ try the food
Essenproduktion, f
♦ meal production
Essenrechnung, f
♦ meal bill
Essen richten
→ Essen zubereiten
Essensausgabe, f (Aktivität)
Essenausgabe f
♦ meal issue
♦ issuing a meal
♦ issuing meals
Essensausgabe, f (Stelle)
Essenausgabe f
♦ food station *AE*
♦ place where food is issued

Essen schmeckt vorzüglich
♦ meal is excellent
♦ meal tastes excellent
Essen selbst kochen
♦ cook one's meals
♦ cook one's own meals
Essenservice, m
Essensdienst, m
♦ food service
Essen servieren
Mahlzeit servieren
♦ serve a meal
Essensfest, n
♦ food festival
Essensgast, m
Speisegast m
Tischgast m
Essengast m
♦ diner
Essen Sie gern Schokolade?
♦ Do you like chocolate?
Essensmenge, f
Menge des Essens, f
♦ quantity of food
Essen spendieren jm
♦ treat s.o. to a meal
Essenstand, m
Verpflegungsstand, m
♦ food stand
♦ food stall *BE*
Essensveranstaltung, f
Veranstaltung mit Essen, f
♦ meal event
♦ meal function
Essenszeit, f (abends)
→ Abendessenzeit
Essenszeit, f (generell)
♦ mealtime
♦ meal hours *pl*
Essenszeit, f (mittags)
→ Mittagessenszeit
♦ lunchtime
Essenszeiten einhalten
♦ observe the mealtimes
Essenszeiten sind flexibel
♦ mealtimes are flexible
Essenszeit von 13 bis 14 Uhr
(Hinweis)
♦ Meals served from 1 p.m to 2 p.m.
Essenszuschlag, m
Verpflegungszuschlag, m
♦ meal supplement
♦ catering supplement
♦ board supplement
Essenszuschuß, m (generell)
♦ meal allowance
Essenszuschuß, m (Mittagessen)
→ Mittagessenszuschuß
Essen umfaßt fünf Gänge
Mahlzeit umfaßt fünf Gänge
♦ meal comprises five courses
Essen und Schutz bieten jm
Essen und Unterkunft geben jm
♦ provide s.o. with food and shelter
essen und trinken
♦ eat and drink
♦ wine and dine
Essen und Trinken, n (Aktivität)
♦ eating and drinking
♦ wining and dining

Essen und Trinken

Essen und Trinken, n (Verpflegung)
- food and drink
- food and beverage

Essen und Trinken bestellen
- order food and drink

Essen und Trinken bieten
für das leibliche Wohl sorgen
- provide food and drink

Essen und Trinken einnehmen
- take food and drink

Essen und Trinken erhalten von jm
- receive food and drink from s.o.

Essen und Trinken hält Leib und Seele zusammen
- Eating and drinking keeps body and soul together

Essen und Trinken ist ausgezeichnet
- food and drink are excellent

Essen und Trinken organisieren *fam*
- lay on food and drink *fam*

Essen und Trinken vorsetzen jm
- set food and drink before s.o.

Essen unterwegs, n
- meal en route
- meal on the way
- en route meal

Essen verkaufen
Mahlzeit verkaufen
- sell a meal

Essen verzehren
Mahlzeit verzehren
- consume a meal

Essen vom Einfachen bis zum Ausgefallenen, n
einfache bis ausgefallene Speisen, f pl
- food from simple to fancy

Essen vorbestellen
Mahlzeit vorbestellen
- preorder a meal *AE*
- order a meal in advance

Essenwahl, f
Essenauswahl, f
- food choice
- choice of food

Essen warm halten
- keep food warm

essen wie ein Scheunendrescher
fressen wie ein Scheunendrescher *vulg*
- eat like a horse

essen wie ein Spatz *coll*
- eat like a bird *coll*

Essen wird liebevoll serviert
- food is lovingly served

Essen wird von der Küche ausgegeben
- meal is issued from the kitchen

Essen zaubern
- conjure up a meal

Essenzeitraum, m
- meal period

Essen zubereiten
Essen richten
Mahlzeit zubereiten
- prepare a meal

Essen zu DM 123 pro Person, n
- meal at DM 123 a plate *AE*
- meal at DM 123 per person

Essen zum festen Preis, n
Festpreisessen, n
- meal at (a) fixed price
- fixed-price meal

Essen zum halben Preis, n
- half-price meal
- meal at half (the) price

Essen zum Mitnehmen, n
(Verkauf über die Straße)
- take-away meal
- take-away
- take-out *AE*

Essen zum vollen Preis, n
Mahlzeit zum vollen Preis, f
- full-price meal
- meal at full price

Essen zusprechen
- do justice to the food

essen à la carte
essen nach der Karte
- eat à la carte
- eat a la carte *AE*

Essen à la carte, n
- à-la-carte meal

Esser, m
Esserin f
- eater

Esserei, f neg
- eating

Eßerlebnis, n
- eating experience

Eßführer, m
(Information)
- eating guide
- food guide

Eßgeschirr, n
Tafelgeschirr, n
Speiseservice, n
- dinner service
- dinner set

Eßgewohnheit, f
- eating habit

es sich schmecken lassen
- enjoy one's meal

Essig, m
- vinegar

Essigfläschchen, n
→ Ölfläschchen

Essigflasche, f
- vinegar bottle

Essiggurke, f
- gherkin

Essig- und Ölständer, m
Menage, f
Gewürzständer, m
- cruet stand
- cruet
- caster *AE*
- castor *AE*

Eßlöffel, m
Tafellöffel, m
- tablespoon
- large spoon

Eßlöffelvoll, m
- tablespoonful
- tbsp.

Eßlokal, n
- eating establishment
- eating place
- eating spot *BE coll*
- eatery *AE*
- restaurant

Eßlokalvorschlag, m
(Vorschlag, wo man essen gehen soll)
- dining suggestion

Eßlust, f
→ Appetit

Eßnische, f
- dining alcove
- eating nook

Eßplatz, m
Eßlokal, n
- eating place
- eating spot *BE coll*

Eßritual, n
- eating ritual

Eßstäbchen, n pl
- chopsticks *pl*

Eßstörung, f
- eating disorder

Eßsüchtiger, m
Schlemmer, m
- foodie *coll*
- foody *coll*

Es steht nicht auf der Speisekarte, aber ich kann es empfehlen
- It's not on the menu, but I can recommend it

Eßteller, m
Speiseteller, m
- dinner plate

Eßtisch, m
Eßzimmertisch, m
- dining table *AE*
- dining-table *BE*
- dinner table

Eßutensilien, n pl
- eating utensils *pl*

Eßverhalten, n
- eating pattern

Eß-Wohnzimmer, n
- dining-sitting room
- dining-living room

Eßzeiten, f pl
- eating hours *pl*

Eßzimmer, n (in Wohnung)
- dining room
- dining-room *BE*

Eßzimmerstuhl, m
Eßstuhl, m
- dining chair *AE*
- dining-chair *BE*

Estland
- Estonia

Estländer, m
Este m
- Estonian

Estländerin, f
Estin, f
- Estonian girl
- Estonian woman
- Estonian

estländisch, adj
estnisch, adj
- Estonian, adj

Estragon, m
- tarragon

Estragonbutter, f
- tarragon butter

Estragonessig, m
- tarragon vinegar

Estragonsoße, f
- tarragon sauce

Es tut mir schrecklich leid. Wir haben keinen Fisch mehr
- I'm terribly sorry. We've run out of fish

Es war mir ein Vergnügen
♦ It was a pleasure
Es werden mehrere Sprachen gesprochen
Man spricht mehrere Sprachen
♦ Several languages are spoken
Es will mir heute nicht so recht schmecken
♦ I don't feel like eating today
Es zieht
(Luftzug)
♦ There is a draft *AE*
♦ There is a draught *BE*
Et., f
Etage, f
♦ flr.
♦ fl.
♦ floor
etablieren sich in einem Zimmer
♦ settle down in a room
Etablissement, n
(Bordell)
♦ cheap establishment
♦ joint *AE coll*
♦ establishment
Etablissement besuchen
♦ visit a cheap establishment
♦ visit a joint *AE coll*
♦ visit an establishment
Etage, f (Hotelbereich)
♦ floor
Etage, f (Personal)
→ Etagenpersonal
Etage, f (Stockwerk)
Et., f
Stockwerk, n
Geschoß, n
♦ floor
♦ story *AE*
♦ storey *BE*
♦ flr.
♦ fl.
Etage für Geschäftsreisende, f
♦ floor for business people
Etagenanzeiger m
(Lift)
♦ floor indicator
Etagenarbeit, f
♦ work on the first (second etc.) floor
♦ floor work
Etagenbad, n
Stockwerksbad, n
♦ bathroom on floor
Etagenbeschließerin, f
→ Etagenhausdame
Etagenbett, n
Stockbett, n
Kojenbett, n
Kajütenbett, n
♦ bunk bed
Etagenbettunterkunft, f
♦ bunk-bed accommodation
♦ bunk-bedded accommodation
Etagenbogen, m
(für Etagenservice)
♦ floor summary sheet
Etagenbon, m
Etagenbeleg, m
♦ floor check
Etagenbuch, n
♦ floor summary book
Etagenbüro, n
→ Etageoffice

Etagenchef, m
Chef d'étage, m *FR*
Etagenoberkellner, m
♦ floor headwaiter
♦ head floor waiter
♦ chef d'étage *FR*
Etagencommis, m
Commis d'étage, m *FR*
♦ commis floor waiter
♦ assistant floor waiter
♦ commis d'étage *FR*
Etagendame, f
→ Etagenhausdame
Etagendiener, m
Etagenhausdiener, m
♦ floor valet
♦ floor servant
♦ floor houseman
Etagendienst, m (Personal)
♦ floor duty
Etagendienst, m (Service)
→ Etagenservice
Etagendusche, f
♦ shower on floor
♦ shower on the floor
Etagenflur, m
Etagenkorridor m
♦ floor corridor
Etagenfrühstück, n
♦ floor breakfast
Etagengeneralgouvernante, f *SCHW*
Erste Etagenhausdame, f
♦ head floor housekeeper *BE*
♦ executive floor housekeeper *AE*
Etagengouvernante, f *SCHW*
→ Etagenhausdame
Etagenhausdame, f
Etagenbeschließerin, f
Etagengouvernante, f *SCHW*
♦ floor housekeeper
Etagenhausdiener, m
Etagendiener, m
♦ floor houseman
♦ floor valet
♦ floor servant
Etagenheizung, f
ETH, f
♦ single-story heating system *AE*
♦ single-storey heating *AE*
♦ single-storey heating system *BE*
♦ single-storey heating *BE*
Etagenhotel, n
♦ single-story hotel *AE*
♦ single-storey hotel *BE*
Etagenkellner, m
♦ floor waiter
Etagenkellnerin, f
♦ floor waitress
Etagennebenkosten, pl
♦ additional floor expenses *pl*
Etagenoberkellner, m
♦ head floor waiter
♦ floor headwaiter
Etagenoffice, f
Etagenbüro, n
♦ floor office
Etagenpantry, f
♦ floor pantry
Etagenpersonal, n
Etage, f

♦ floor personnel
♦ floor staff
Etagenportier, m
Portier d'étage, m *FR*
♦ floor porter
♦ portier d'étage *FR*
Etagenservice, m
Etagendienst m
♦ floor service
Etagenservicegebühr, f
♦ floor service charge
♦ floor service fee
Etagenservicekarte, f
♦ floor service card
Etagenservicekellner, m
♦ floor service waiter
Etagenservicekellnerin, f
♦ floor service waitress
Etagenserviceleiter, m
Etagenservicedirektor m
♦ floor superintendent
Etagenserviceleute, pl
Etagenservice, m
♦ floor service people *pl*
Etagenstationskellner, m
Etagenrevierkellner, m
Chef de rang d'étage, m *FR*
♦ floor station waiter *AE*
♦ floor section waiter *BE*
♦ chef de rang d'étage *FR*
Etagentoilette, f
♦ toilet on floor
♦ lavatory on floor *AE*
Etagenwohnung, f
♦ apartment (comprising a whole floor) *AE*
♦ flat (comprising a whole floor) *BE*
Etagenwohnung mit Bedienung, f
→ Wohnung mit Bedienung
Etappe, f (generell)
♦ stage
Etappe, f (Reise, Sport)
♦ leg
Etappe der Reise, f
♦ leg of the journey
♦ leg of the tour
♦ leg of the trip
ETH, f
(Etagenheizung)
ethnischer Tourismus, m
♦ ethnic tourism
ethnographische Sammlung, f
♦ ethnographic collection
Etikett, n
♦ label
Etikettiervorschrift, f
♦ labelling regulation
♦ labeling regulation *AE*
Etiquette, f
♦ etiquette
Etrusker, m
♦ Etruscan
etruskisch, adj
♦ Etruscan, adj
ETW, f (Eigentumswohnung)
→ Eigentumswohnung
ETW, f (Etagenwohnung)
Etagenwohnung, f
♦ flt. *BE*
♦ apt. *AE*
♦ apartment *AE*
♦ flat *BE*

etwas Besonderes anzubieten haben
  ◆ have something special to offer
etwas betrunken sein
  ◆ be a little drunk
etwas Eßbares, n
  → etwas zu essen
Etwas ist besser als nichts
  ◆ Half a loaf is better than none
  ◆ Half a loaf is better than no loaf
etwas renovierungsbedürftig, adj
  ◆ in need of some refurbishment
etwas zu essen
  etwas Eßbares, n
  ◆ something to eat
EU, f
  Europäische Union, f
  ◆ EU, the
  ◆ European Union, the
Europa
  ◆ Europe
Europa bereisen
  durch Europa reisen
  ◆ tour Europe
Europabrücke, f
  (Straßburg)
  ◆ European Bridge, the
Europa durchstreifen
  durch Europa ziehen
  ◆ roam Europe
Europäer, m
  ◆ European
Europäerin, f
  ◆ European
Europa in 24 Stunden machen coll
  Europa in 24 Stunden bereisen
  ◆ do Europe in 24 hours coll
europäisch, adj
  ◆ European, adj
Europäische Gemeinschaft, f
  EG, f
  ◆ European Community, the
  ◆ EC, the
europäisches Essen, n
  ◆ European food
europäisches Festland, n
  ◆ European mainland
  ◆ European continent
Europäisches Jahr des Tourismus, n
  ◆ European Year of Tourism
Europäisches Tourismusjahr, n
  ◆ European Tourism Year
Europareise, f (in Europa)
  Europarundreise, f
  ◆ tour of Europe
  ◆ European tour
Europareise machen
  ◆ make a tour through Europe
  ◆ make a trip through Europe
  ◆ make a journey through Europe
  ◆ do Europe coll
Europatournee, f
  ◆ European tour
Europatournee unternehmen (Künstler)
  Europareise machen (Tourist)
  ◆ undertake a European tour
Europaurlaub, m
  ◆ European vacation AE
  ◆ European holiday BE
europaweit, adj
  ◆ Europe-wide, adj

European Plan, m
  (Übernachtung ohne Frühstück)
  EP, m
  ◆ European Plan
  ◆ EP
Euro-Reisescheck, m
  ◆ Euro Traveller Cheque BE
Euroscheck, m
  ◆ Eurocheque
Euroscheckkarte, f
  ◆ Eurocheque card
Eurotunnel, m
  ◆ Eurotunnel, the
evakuieren jn
  ◆ evacuate s.o.
Evakuierter, m
  Evakuierte f
  ◆ evacuee
Evakuierung, f
  ◆ evacuation
Everglades, pl
  ◆ Everglades, the pl
Everglades Nationalpark, m
  ◆ Everglades National Park, the
Ewige Stadt, die, f
  (Rom)
  ◆ Eternal City, the
Ex!
  (Trinkspruch)
  ◆ Bottoms up!
  ◆ Down the hatch! inform
Excursion-Preis, m
  ◆ excursion fare
Excursion-Tarif, m
  ◆ excursion tariff
Executive Floor, m
  → Manageretage
Executivesuite, f
  → Managersuite
Exekutivausschuß, m
  ◆ executive committee
ex in einem Schluck
  runter in einem Schluck
  ◆ down the hatch in one gulp
exklusiv, adj
  ◆ exclusive, adj
  ◆ select, adj
Exklusivangebot, n
  exklusives Angebot, n
  ◆ exclusive offer
exklusiv etw
  ◆ exclusive of s.th.
exklusive Gesellschaft, f
  ◆ select party
exklusive Getränke
  ◆ exclusive of drinks
  ◆ exclusive of beverages
  ◆ not including drinks
  ◆ not including beverages
exklusive Möblierung, f
  ◆ exclusive furnishing
  ◆ exlusive furnishings pl
exklusiver Club, m
  exklusiver Klub m
  ◆ exclusive club
exklusiver Gästekreis, m
  ◆ exclusive clientele
exklusiver Gesellschaftskreis, m
  ◆ exclusive social circle
exklusiver Komfort, m
  ◆ exclusive comfort

exklusiver Kreis, m
  ◆ exclusive circle
exklusiver Nachtclub, m
  ◆ supper club AE
exklusives Ambiente, n
  ◆ exclusive ambience
  ◆ exclusive ambiance
exklusives Hotel, n
  ◆ exclusive hotel
exklusives Luxushotel, n
  ◆ exclusive deluxe hotel AE
  ◆ exclusive luxury hotel BE
exklusives Menü, n
  ◆ exclusive menu
exklusives Restaurant, n
  ◆ exclusive restaurant
exklusive Umgebung, f
  ◆ exclusive surroundings pl
Exklusivität, f
  ◆ exclusiveness
  ◆ exclusivity
Exklusivort, m
  exklusiver Ferienort, m
  ◆ exclusive resort
Exkursion, f
  ◆ excursion
Exkursion machen
  ◆ make an excursion
  ◆ go on an excursion
Exkursionsleiter, m
  ◆ excursion leader
Exkursionsteilnehmer, m
  ◆ person taking part in an excursion
  ◆ person going on an excursion
Exmoor, n
  ◆ Exmoor
Exmoor Nationalpark, m
  ◆ Exmoor National Park, the
Exmoorurlaub, m
  ◆ Exmoor holiday BE
  ◆ Exmoor vacation AE
exotisch, adj
  ◆ exotic, adj
exotische Kost, f
  ◆ exotic fare
  ◆ exotic food
exotischer Urlaub, m
  ◆ exotic vacation AE
  ◆ exotic holiday BE
exotisches Gericht, n
  ◆ exotic dish
exotisches Land, n
  ◆ exotic country
exotisches Menü, n
  ◆ exotic menu
exotische Speisekarte, f
  ◆ exotic menu
exotische Umgebung, f
  ◆ exotic surroundings pl
Expansionsplan, m
  ◆ plan for expansion
  ◆ plans for expansion pl
  ◆ expansion plan
Expedient, m (in Reisebüro)
  ◆ counter clerk
Expedient, m (in Transportunternehmen)
  ◆ forwarding clerk
  ◆ shipping clerk AE
expedieren etw
  ◆ expedite s.th.

Expedition, f
  Expeditionsreise, f
  ♦ expedition
Expedition leiten
  Expedition nach X leiten
  Expedition nach X anführen
  ♦ **lead an expedition**
  ♦ lead an expedition to X
Expedition machen
  ♦ **make an expedition**
Expedition nach X, f
  ♦ **expedition to X**
Expeditionsfirma, f
  Expeditionsgesellschaft, f
  ♦ **expedition firm**
  ♦ expedition company
Expeditionskreuzfahrt, f
  ♦ **expedition cruise**
Expeditionskreuzfahrtschiff, n
  ♦ **expedition cruise ship**
Expeditionsleiter, m
  Leiter der Expedition, m
  ♦ **expedition leader**
  ♦ leader of the expedition
Expeditionsmitglied, n
  ♦ **expedition member**
  ♦ member of the expedition
Expeditionsreise, f
  → Expedition
Expeditionsreisender, m
  ♦ **expedition traveller**
  ♦ expedition traveler AE
Expeditionsschiff, n
  ♦ **expedition ship**
  ♦ expedition vessel
Expedition unternehmen
  ♦ **undertake an expedition**
Expedition zum Nordpol, f
  Nordpolexpedition, f
  ♦ **expedition to the North Pole**
Expo, f
  Ausstellung, f
  ♦ **expo**
  ♦ exposition
Exponat, n
  Ausstellungsstück, n
  ♦ **exhibited item**
  ♦ exhibited article
  ♦ exhibit
Exponat ist ausgestellt
  ♦ **exhibit is on show**
  ♦ exhibit is displayed
Export, m
  Ausfuhr, f
  ♦ **export**
Exportmesse, f
  ♦ **export trade fair**
  ♦ export fair
Exportzoll, m
  Ausfuhrzoll, m
  ♦ **export duty**
Expreßaufzug, m
  Expreßlift, m
  Schnellaufzug, m
  Schnell-Lift, m
  ♦ **high-speed lift** BE
  ♦ high-speed elevator AE
Expreß-Checkin, m
  ♦ **express check-in**
Expreß-Checkin-Schalter, m
  ♦ **express-checkin desk**

Expreß-Checkout, m
  ♦ **express check-out**
Express-Checkout-Schalter, m
  ♦ **express-checkout desk**
Expreßdienst, m
  Expreßservice, m
  Schnelldienst, m
  Schnellservice, m
  ♦ **express service**
  ♦ quick service
Expreßlift, m
  → Expreßaufzug
Expreßservice, m
  → Expreßdienst
Expreßwäsche, f
  ♦ **express laundry**
exquisit, adj
  ♦ **exquisite, adj**
exquisiter Service, m
  auserlesener Service m
  ♦ **exquisite service**
exquisites Zimmer, n
  erlesenes Zimmer, n
  ♦ **exquisite room**
exquisit zubereitet, adj
  ♦ **exquisitely prepared, adj**
exquisit zubereitetes Essen, n
  ♦ **exquisitely prepared food**
externer Gast, m
  Nichthausgast, m
  ♦ **nonresident** AE
  ♦ nonresident guest AE
  ♦ non-resident guest BE
  ♦ non-resident BE
externe Schulung, f
  ♦ **external training**
  ♦ external training course
externes Telefon, n
  ♦ **external telephone**
Extra, n
  ♦ **extra**
Extraausgaben, f pl
  zusätzliche Ausgaben, f pl
  Nebenkosten, pl
  NK, pl
  ♦ **extra expenses** pl
  ♦ extras pl
  ♦ extra costs pl
extra berechnet werden
  gesondert berechnet werden
  ♦ **be charged for separately**
Extraessen, n
  (Bankett)
  ♦ **extra meal**
  ♦ special meal
Extrafahrpreis, m
  ♦ **extra fare**
Extragedeck, n
  zusätzliches Gedeck, n
  ♦ **extra cover**
Extrakellner, m
  Aushilfskellner, m
  Hilfskellner, m
  ♦ **extra waiter**
  ♦ relief waiter
  ♦ temporary waiter
Extrakomfort, m
  Sonderkomfort, m
  ♦ **extra comfort**
extralanges Bett, n
  → überlanges Bett

Extraleistung, f
  Extraservice, m
  Extradienstleistung, f
  ♦ **extra service**
  ♦ additional service
Extraprovision, f
  ♦ **extra commission**
  ♦ overriding commission
  ♦ override AE
Extraservice, m
  → Extraleistung
Extras inbegriffen
  → Nebenkosten inbegriffen
Extras nicht inbegriffen
  ♦ **extras not included**
Extratisch, m
  zusätzlicher Tisch m
  ♦ **extra table**
  ♦ additional table
Extratour, f
  ♦ **extra tour**
Extratrinkgeld n
  ♦ **extra tip**
extravagant, adj
  ♦ **extravagant, adj**
extravagante Party, f
  ♦ **extravagant party**
Extraveranstaltung, f
  ♦ **extra function**
ex trinken
  → austrinken
exzellente Küche, f (Speisen)
  ♦ **excellent cuisine**
  ♦ excellent cooking
EZ, n
  Einzelzimmer, n
  ♦ **SR**
  ♦ sr
  ♦ single room
  ♦ single
  ♦ sgl. rm.
EZ-Preis, m
  → Einzelzimmerpreis

fabelhaft, adj
  ◆ **fabulous**, adj
fabelhafter Blick, m
  fabelhafte Aussicht, f
  fabelhafter Ausblick, m
  ◆ **fabulous view**
fabelhaftes Essen, n
  (Mahlzeit)
  ◆ **fabulous meal**
fabelhaftes Haus, n
  ◆ **fabulous house**
  ◆ fabulous home
fabelhaft möbliert, adj
  fabelhaft eingerichtet, adj
  ◆ **fabulously furnished**, adj
fabelhaft möbliertes Zimmer, n
  ◆ **fabulously furnished room**
Fabrik besichtigen
  ◆ **visit the factory**
  ◆ visit the works BE
  ◆ visit the plant
Fabrikbesuch, m
  ◆ **factory visit**
  ◆ visit to a factory
Fabrikkantine, f
  Werkskantine, f
  ◆ **factory canteen**
  ◆ works canteen
Fachabend, m
  ◆ **trade evening**
Facharbeiter, m
  Fachkraft, f
  ◆ **skilled worker**
  ◆ trained worker
Fachaussteller, m
  ◆ **trade exhibitor**
Fachausstellung, f
  Gewerbeausstellung, f
  ◆ **trade exhibition**
  ◆ trade show
  ◆ trade exhibit AE
  ◆ specialised exhibition
  ◆ specialised exhibit AE
Fachausstellungsteilnehmer, m
  Fachschauteilnehmer, m
  ◆ **trade show delegate**
Fachberatung, f
  → fachmännische Beratung
Fachbesucher, m
  ◆ **trade visitor**
Fachbesucheranteil, m
  ◆ **proportion of trade visitors**
Fachbesucherprogramm, n
  ◆ **trade visitor program** AE
  ◆ trade visitor programme BE
  ◆ program for (the) trade visitors AE
  ◆ programme for (the) trade visitors BE

Fachbesuchertag, m
  ◆ **trade visitor day**
  ◆ trade visitors' day
Facheinkäufer, m
  (z.B auf einer Messe)
  Fachkäufer, m
  ◆ **trade buyer**
Fachempfang, m
  Fachbesucherempfang, m
  ◆ **trade reception**
Fächer, m
  ◆ **fan**
fächerförmig, adj
  ◆ **fan-shaped**, adj
Fächermuseum, n
  ◆ **fan museum**
Fächerpalme, f
  ◆ **fan palm**
Fächersammlung, f
  ◆ **collection of fans**
  ◆ fan collection
Fachexkursion, f
  ◆ **specialised excursion**
Fachgeschäft, n
  Fachladen, m
  ◆ **specialist store** AE
  ◆ specialist shop BE
Fachhandbuch, n
  ◆ **trade manual**
Fachhändlerausstellung, f
  ◆ **dealer show** AE
Fachhändlertreffen, n
  ◆ **dealer meeting** AE
Fachhochschule, f
  FH, f
  ◆ **polytechnic**
Fachjargon, m
  ◆ **trade jargon**
Fachkenntnisse, f pl
  ◆ **expert knowledge** sg
Fachkonferenz, f
  Fachtagung, f
  ◆ **trade conference**
Fachkongreß, m
  ◆ **trade convention**
  ◆ trade congress
  ◆ professional convention
Fachkraft, f
  Facharbeitter, m
  ◆ **trained worker**
  ◆ skilled worker
Fachkräfte, f pl
  Fachpersonal, n
  fachkundiges Personal, n
  ◆ **qualified staff**
  ◆ qualified personnel
  ◆ skilled workers pl

  ◆ trained workers pl
  ◆ skilled labo(u)r
Fachkräftemangel, m (Knappheit)
  ◆ **shortage of skilled workers**
  ◆ shortage of trained workers
  ◆ shortage of skilled staff
  ◆ shortage of trained staff
Fachkräftemangel, m (völliges Fehlen)
  ◆ **lack of skilled workers**
  ◆ lack of trained workers
  ◆ lack of skilled staff
  ◆ lack of trained staff
fachkundiger Führer, m
  ◆ **expert guide**
Fachkurs, m
  Fachlehrgang m
  ◆ **technical course**
fachliche Qualifikation, f
  ◆ **professional qualification**
Fachmagazin, n
  ◆ **trade magazine**
Fachmann, m
  Experte, m
  ◆ **expert**
  ◆ specialist
fachmännisch, adj
  fachkundig, adj
  ◆ **expert**, adj
fachmännische Beratung, f
  ◆ **expert advice**
fachmännischen Service bieten
  ◆ **provide expert service**
fachmännischer Service m
  ◆ **expert service**
fachmännisch möbliert, adj
  professionell möbliert, adj
  ◆ **professionally furnished**, adj
fachmännisch möbliertes Hotelzimmer, n
  ◆ **professionally furnished hotel room**
Fachmesse, f
  ◆ **trade fair**
Fachmesse abhalten
  ◆ **hold a trade fair**
Fachmesse für etw, f
  ◆ **trade fair for s.th.**
Fachmesse organisieren
  Fachmesse veranstalten
  ◆ **organise a trade fair**
  ◆ organize a trade fair
Fachmesse veranstalten
  Fachmesse inszenieren
  Fachmesse ausrichten
  ◆ **stage a trade fair**
  ◆ stage a fair
Fachpersonal, n
  ausgebildetes Personal, n
  ◆ **trained staff**
  ◆ trained personnel

Fachpresse

Fachpresse, f
♦ trade press
Fachpublikum, n
♦ trade, the
♦ trade audience
Fachschau, f
Gewerbeschau, f
♦ trade show
Fachseminar, n
♦ trade seminar
♦ technical seminar
Fachsitzung, f
♦ trade session
Fachstand m
(Ausstellung)
♦ trade stand
Fachtag, m
(Messe)
♦ trade day
Fachtagung, f (für eine Branche)
♦ trade meeting
♦ trade conference
Fachtagung, f (generell)
Fachkonferenz, f
♦ technical conference
♦ professional meeting
Fachteilnehmer, pl
♦ trade attendee
Fachveranstaltung f
♦ trade event
Fachverband m
♦ trade association
Fachverbandsabonnement, n
♦ trade association subscription
Fachwerkarchitektur, f
♦ half-timbered architecture
Fachwerkfassade, f
♦ half-timbered façade
♦ half-timbered facade *AE*
Fachwerkgebäude, n
Fachwerkbau, m
♦ half-timbered building
Fachwerkgeschoß, n
Fachwerkstockwerk, n
Fachwerketage, f
♦ half-timbered floor
♦ half-timbered story *AE*
♦ half-timbered storey *BE*
Fachwerkhaus, n
♦ half-timbered house
Fachwerkmauer, f
Fachwerkwand, f
♦ half-timbered wall
Fachwissen, n
♦ expertise
♦ expert knowledge *sg*
Facility, f
→ Fazilität
Fackellicht, n
♦ torchlight
Fackelzug, m
♦ torchlight procession
Fackelzug veranstalten
♦ organise a torchlight procession
♦ organize a torchlight procession
♦ hold a torchlight procession
fad, adj
schal, adj
geschmacklos, adj
♦ insipid, adj
♦ flat, adj

♦ tasteless, adj
♦ stale, adj
♦ flavorless, adj *AE*
fader Geschmack, m
♦ insipid taste
♦ stale taste
♦ flat taste
fades Essen, n
♦ insipid food
Fadheit, f
♦ insipidity
♦ insipidness
♦ flavorlessness *AE*
♦ flavourlessness *BE*
♦ tastelessness
Fado, m *PORT*
(Tanzlied)
♦ fado *PORT*
Fadoschau, f *PORT*
♦ fado show *PORT*
Fagott, n
♦ bassoon
Fagottist, m
♦ bassoonist
Fahne, f
♦ flag
♦ banner
Fahne haben *coll*
(Alkohol getrunken haben)
Schnapsfahne haben
♦ smell of drink
♦ reek of alcohol
♦ reek of drink
Fahnenstange, f
Fahnenmast, m
♦ flagpole
Fahrausweis, m
→ Fahrkarte
fahrbar, adj
mobil, adj
♦ mobile, adj
♦ movable, adj
♦ moveable, adj
♦ traveling, adj *AE*
♦ travelling, adj *BE*
fahrbarer Serviertisch, m
♦ dinner wagon
♦ dinner waggon
♦ dinner table
fahrbarer Wohnwagen, m
fahrbarer Caravan, m
♦ mobile trailer *AE*
♦ mobile caravan *BE*
fahrbares Büfett, n
Buffet roulant, n *FR*
♦ mobile buffet
♦ buffet roulant *FR*
fahrbares Ferienhaus, n
♦ mobile summer house *AE*
♦ mobile holiday home *BE*
fahrbares Heim, n
→ Mobilheim, Heim auf Rädern
fahrbare Toilette, f
→ Toilettenwagen
Fährbetrieb, f
♦ ferry operation
Fährdienst, m
Fährservice, m
Fährverkehr, m
♦ ferry service

Fähre, f
♦ ferry
Fähre buchen
♦ book a ferry
Fähre erreichen
♦ catch the ferry
♦ catch a ferry
fahren auf das Land
auf das Land hinausfahren
♦ go into the country
♦ go out into the country
fahren auf der linken Straßenseite
♦ drive on the left-hand side of the road
fahren auf einem Schiff
♦ sail on a ship
♦ sail on a boat
Fahrender, m (Umherziehender)
Umherziehender, m
Zigeuner, m
♦ traveler *AE*
♦ traveller *BE*
fahrender Ritter, m *hist*
♦ knight errant *hist*
fahrender Scholar, m *hist*
♦ wandering scholar *hist*
fahrendes Volk, n
♦ vagrants *pl*
fahren durch etw
♦ pass through s.th.
♦ travel through s.th.
♦ go through s.th.
fahren durch X (Auto)
♦ drive through X
Fähre nehmen
♦ take the ferry
fahren (Fahrzeug)
♦ go
♦ run
♦ travel
fahren in die falsche Richtung (Auto)
fahren in der falschen Richtung
♦ drive in the wrong direction
fahren in einem Auto
fahren mit einem Auto
♦ ride in a car
fahren in einem Bus
fahren mit einem Bus
♦ ride in a bus
fahren in einem Kanu
♦ go in a canoe
fahren in einem Zug
fahren mit einem Zug
♦ ride on a train
♦ ride a train
fahren jn zum Hotel (Auto)
♦ drive s.o. to the hotel
fahren mit dem Bus
Bus fahren
♦ go by bus
♦ go by coach *BE*
fahren mit dem Fahrstuhl
fahren mit dem Aufzug
fahren mit dem Lift
♦ go by elevator *AE*
♦ go by lift *BE*
fahren mit den öffentlichen Verkehrsmitteln
mit den öffentlichen Verkehrsmitteln reisen
♦ travel by public transport *BE*
♦ travel on public transport *BE*

fahren mit der Rikscha
- ride in a ricksha *AE*
- ride in a rickshaw *BE*

fahren mit der Seilbahn
- ride the cable car *AE*
- ride the cable-car *BE*

fahren mit der U-Bahn
 mit der U-Bahn fahren
- travel by underground
- go by underground
- travel by tube *BE*
- go by tube *BE*

fahren mit halsbrecherischer Geschwindigkeit
- travel at breakneck speed

fahren nach C über B (Auto)
- drive to C via B

fahren nach C über B (generell)
- go to C via B

fahren (Person)
- go
- travel
- ride
- drive

fahren quer durch das Land (Auto)
- drive across the country

fahren um die Welt
 um die Welt fahren
- go around the world
- go round the world
- travel around the world
- travel round the world

Fahrer, m (Auto)
 Kraftfahrer, m
- driver

Fahrer, m (Rad)
- rider
- biker

Fahrerhaus, n
- cab
 driver's cab

Fahrerhausbett, n
 (im Wohnmobil)
- cab bed

Fahrerhaushängebett, n
 (Reisemobil)
- cab hammock

Fahrerin, f (Auto)
- woman driver

Fahrer in einer Motorradeskorte, m
- motorcycle outrider *AE*
- motor-cycle outrider *BE*

fahrerlos, adj
- driverless, adj

Fahrerplatz, m (Auto)
 Fahrersitz, m
- driving seat
 driver's seat

Fahrersitz, m (Auto)
 Fahrerplatz, m
- driver's seat
 driving seat

Fahrer stellen
- provide a driver

Fahrertrinkgeld, n (Auto)
- driver's tip
 driver's gratuity

Fahrertür, f
- driver's door

Fähre setzt jn über
- ferry takes s.o. across

Fähre über den Rhein, f
 Rheinfähre, f
- ferry across the Rhine

Fähre verkehrt von A nach B
- ferry crosses from A to B

Fährfahrplan, m
- ferry timetable
- ferry schedule *AE*

Fährfahrpreis, m
 Fährpreis, m
- ferry fare

Fährfahrschein, m
 Fährfahrkarte, f
 Fährkarte, f
- ferry ticket

Fährfahrt, f
- ferry trip
- ferry ride

Fährführer, m
 (Information)
- ferry guide

Fahrgast, m
- fare
- passenger

Fahrgast befördern
 Passagier befördern
- carry a passenger
- convey a passenger
- transport a passenger

Fahrgastbeschwerde, f
 Passagierbeschwerde, f
- passenger complaint

Fahrgäste mit Behinderungen, m pl
- passengers with disabilities *pl*

Fahrgeld, n
 Fahrpreis, m
- carfare *AE*
- fare

Fahrgemeinschaft, f
- car pool
 car sharing
- ride sharing *AE*

Fährgeschäft, n
- ferry business

Fährgesellschaft, f
- ferry company

Fährhafen, m
- ferry port

Fahrkarte, f
 Fahrschein, m
 Flugkarte, f
 Flugschein, m
- ticket

Fahrkarte abholen
 Karte abholen
- pick up a ticket
 collect a ticket

Fahrkarte ausstellen
 Karte ausstellen
- issue a ticket
 make out a ticket

Fahrkarte bestellen
→ Karte bestellen

Fahrkarte erster Klasse, f
 Erste-Klasse-Fahrkarte, f
 Erster-Klasse-Fahrkarte, f
- first-class ticket

Fahrkarte erwerben
 Karte erwerben
- purchase a ticket

Fahrkarte ist übertragbar
→ Karte ist übertragbar

Fahrkarte kaufen
 Fahrkarte lösen
 Fahrschein kaufen
 Karte kaufen
- buy a ticket

Fahrkarte knipsen
- clip a ticket

Fahrkarte lochen
 Karte lochen
- punch a ticket

Fahrkarte nachlösen
- buy a ticket en route
- buy a ticket on the train (bus etc)
- buy a ticket on arrival

Fahrkarte nach X, f
- ticket for X

Fahrkartenausgabe, f
 Kartenausgabe, f
 Fahrscheinausgabe, f
- ticket issue
 issue of tickets
 issue of a ticket
 issuing a ticket
 issuing tickets

Fahrkartenaussteller, m
→ Schalterbeamter

Fahrkartenausstellung, f
 Fahrscheinausstellung, f
 Flugscheinausstellung, f
- ticketing
- ticketing procedure

Fahrkartenautomat, m
 Kartenautomat, m
- ticket machine
- automatic ticket machine

Fahrkartenkontrolle, f
- ticket inspection

Fahrkartenkontrolleur, m
- ticket collector
 ticket inspector

Fahrkartennummer, f
 Kartennummer, f
- ticket number

Fahrkartenschalter, m
 Kartenschalter, m
- ticket counter
 ticket office

Fahrkartentyp, m
 Fahrkartenart, f
 Kartentyp, m
 Fahrkartenart, m
- ticket type
 type of ticket

Fahrkartenüberprüfung, f
 Fahrscheinüberprüfung, f
- ticket examination

Fahrkarte überprüfen
 Fahrschein überprüfen
- examine a ticket

Fahrkarte verlieren
- lose a ticket

Fahrkarte von A nach B, f
- ticket from A to B

Fahrkarte zum halben Preis, m
- half-fare ticket

Fahrkarte zweiter Klasse, f
 Zweite-Klasse-Fahrkarte, f
- second class ticket

Fahrlehrer

Fahrlehrer, m
- ♦ driving instructor

Fährmarkt, m
- ♦ ferry market

Fährpassagier, m
- Fährfahrgast, m
- ♦ ferry passenger

Fahrplan, m
- ♦ timetable
- ♦ schedule AE

Fahrplan, m (Zug)
- Zugfahrplan, m
- ♦ train timetable BE
- ♦ train schedule AE

Fahrplanänderung, f
- ♦ schedule change AE
- ♦ timetable change BE

Fahrplanauskunft, f
- ♦ timetable information BE

fahrplanmäßig, adj
- planmäßig, adj
- ♦ scheduled, adj

fahrplanmäßig, adv
- planmäßig, adv
- ♦ on schedule, adv

fahrplanmäßig abfahren um 11 Uhr
- ♦ be scheduled to leave at 11 o'clock

fahrplanmäßig ankommen um 22 Uhr
- ♦ be due at 10 p.m.
- ♦ be scheduled to arrive at 10 p.m.

fahrplanmäßig eintreffen
- fahrplanmäßig ankommen
- ♦ arrive on schedule

fahrplanmäßiges Schiff, n
- ♦ scheduled ship

Fahrplan studieren
- Flugplan studieren
- ♦ study the timetable
- ♦ study the schedule AE

Fahrpreis, m
- ♦ fare

Fährpreis, m
- ♦ ferry price
- ♦ ferry fare

Fahrpreis ausarbeiten
- ♦ work out the fare

Fahrpreis berechnen
- Fahrpreis ausrechnen
- ♦ calculate the fare

Fahrpreisberechnung, f
- ♦ fare calculation

Fahrpreisbestimmungen, f pl
- Fahrpreisvorschriften, f pl
- ♦ fare regulations pl

Fahrpreiserhöhung, f
- ♦ fare increase
- ♦ fare rise

Fahrpreis ermäßigen
- Fahrpreis senken
- ♦ reduce the fare

Fahrpreisermäßigung, f
- ♦ fare reduction

Fahrpreise senken
- ♦ cut fares
- ♦ reduce the fares

Fahrpreis für unbegrenztes Reisen, m
- ♦ go-as-you-please fare
- ♦ unlimited mileage fare
- ♦ unlimited milage fare AE

Fahrpreis geht hoch
- ♦ fare goes up

Fahrpreis genehmigen
- ♦ approve the fare
- ♦ approve a fare

Fahrpreis in der Wochenmitte, m
- ♦ midweek fare

Fahrpreis ist gültig vom 1. März bis 30. Juli
- ♦ fare is valid from 1 March until 30 July

Fahrpreis ist verloren
- ♦ fare is forfeit
- ♦ fare is forfeited

Fahrpreiskategorie, f
- ♦ fare category

Fahrpreisniveau, n
- Fahrpreishöhe, f
- ♦ fare level

Fahrpreisrevolution, f
- ♦ fare revolution
- ♦ fares revolution

Fahrpreisstruktur, f
- Fahrpreisgefüge, n
- ♦ fare structure

Fahrpreistabelle, f
- ♦ fares table

Fahrpreisvereinbarung, f
- ♦ fare agreement

Fahrpreisvereinbarung aushandeln
- ♦ negotiate a fare agreement

Fahrpreis veröffentlichen
- ♦ publish the fare
- ♦ publish a fare

Fahrpreis zahlen
- ♦ pay the fare

Fahrpreiszone, f
- ♦ fare stage

Fahrrad, n
- Rad, n coll
- ♦ bicycle
- ♦ bike coll
- ♦ cycle
- ♦ push-bike BE coll
- ♦ wheel AE coll

Fahrradausflug, m
- Radausflug, m
- ♦ bicycle excursion
- ♦ cycling excursion

Fahrrad ausleihen an jn
- (gewöhnlich ohne Entgelt)
- Fahrrad leihen jm
- ♦ lend a bicycle to s.o.
- ♦ lend s.o. a bicycle
- ♦ lend a bike to s.o. coll
- ♦ lend s.o. a bike coll

Fahrrad benutzen
- Rad benutzen coll
- ♦ use a bicycle
- ♦ use a bike coll

Fahrradcamper, m
- ♦ bicycle camper
- ♦ cycle camper

Fahrradcamping, n
- ♦ bicycle camping
- ♦ cycle camping

Fahrräder gratis
- (Hinweisschild)
- ♦ Bicycles free of charge

Fahrräder können geliehen werden
- (gegen Gebühr)
- Fahrräder können gemietet werden
- ♦ Bicycles can be rented AE
- ♦ Bicycles can be hired BE

Fahrrad fahren
- ♦ ride a bicycle
- ♦ ride a cycle
- ♦ cycle
- ♦ bicycle

Fahrradfahren, n
- Fahrradsport, m
- ♦ riding a bicycle
- ♦ bicycle riding
- ♦ bicycling
- ♦ cycling

Fahrradfahrer, m
- ♦ bicycle rider
- ♦ bicyclist
- ♦ biker coll

Fahrradfahrt, f
- Radfahrt, f
- ♦ bicycle ride
- ♦ bicycle trip

Fahrradferien, pl
- Radferien, pl
- Fahrradurlaub, m
- Radurlaub, m
- ♦ cycling holidays BE pl
- ♦ cycling holiday BE
- ♦ cycling vacation AE

Fahrrad kostenlos zur Verfügung stellen
- ♦ provide a bicycle free of charge

Fahrrad leihen von jm (uentgeltich)
- Fahrrad borgen
- Rad leihen
- Rad borgen
- ♦ borrow a bicycle from s.o.
- ♦ borrow a bike from s.o. coll

Fahrrad mieten
- ♦ rent a bicycle AE
- ♦ rent a bike AE coll
- ♦ hire a bicycle BE
- ♦ hire a bike BE coll

Fahrradmuseum, n
- ♦ cycle museum

Fahrradreifen, m
- ♦ bicycle tire AE
- ♦ bicycle tyre BE

Fahrradrennen, n
- Radrennen, n
- ♦ bicycle race
- ♦ cycle race
- ♦ bike race coll

Fahrradrikscha, f
- ♦ pedicab
- ♦ bicycle-drawn pedicab
- ♦ bicycle rickshaw

Fahrradschuppen, m
- ♦ bicycle shed

Fahrradständer, m
- ♦ bicycle stand

Fahrrad stellen
- Rad stellen coll
- ♦ provide a bicycle
- ♦ provide a bike coll

Fahrradtour, f
- Radtour, f
- Fahrradreise, f
- Radreise, f
- ♦ bicycle tour
- ♦ cycling tour
- ♦ cycle tour

Fahrradtourist, m
- ♦ touring cyclist

- ♦ tourist travelling by bicycle
- ♦ tourist traveling by bicycle AE

Fahrradtour machen
Radtour machen
- ♦ go on a cycling tour

Fahrradtransfer, m
Radtransfer, m
- ♦ bicycle transfer
- ♦ cycle transfer
- ♦ bike transfer coll

Fahrradurlaub, m
Radurlaub, m
Fahrradferien, pl
Radferien, pl
- ♦ cycling vacation AE
- ♦ cycling holidays BE pl
- ♦ cycling holiday BE

Fahrradverein, m
Fahrradclub, m
- ♦ bicycle club
- ♦ bicycling club

Fahrradverleih, m
Fahrradvermietung, f
Radverleih, m
Radvermietung, f
- ♦ bicycle rental AE
- ♦ bike rental AE coll
- ♦ bicycle hire BE
- ♦ bike hire BE coll
- ♦ cycle hire BE

Fahrrad vermieten
Fahrrad verleihen
Rad vermieten
Rad verleihen
- ♦ rent (out) a bicycle
- ♦ hire out a bicycle BE
- ♦ rent (out) a bike coll
- ♦ hire out a bike BE coll

Fahrradvermietung, f
Fahrradverleih, m
- ♦ cycle rental AE
- ♦ cycle hire BE

Fahrradwandern, n
Radwandern, n
- ♦ cycle touring

Fahrradwanderung, f
Radwanderung, f
- ♦ cycle tour
- ♦ cycle touring

Fahrradweg, m
Radweg, m
Radfahrweg, m
- ♦ cycle track
- ♦ cycle path
- ♦ cycling path
- ♦ bicycle path
- ♦ cycleway

Fährreservierung, f
- ♦ ferry reservation

Fahrrinne, f
- ♦ shipping lane

Fahrschein, m
→ Fahrkarte

Fahrscheinausgabe, f
→ Fahrkartenausgabe

Fährschiff, n
Fährboot, n
- ♦ ferry boat

Fährschiffbuchung, f
- ♦ ferry boat booking
- ♦ booking a ferry boat

Fährschiffpassagier, m
- ♦ ferry boat passenger

Fährschiffreservierung, f
- ♦ ferry boat reservation

Fahrschulkurs, m
Fahrschullehrgang, m
- ♦ driving course

Fahrschulkurs machen
- ♦ take a driving course

Fahrstuhl, m
- ♦ elevator AE
- ♦ lift BE

Fahrstuhlanlage f
- ♦ elevator system AE
- ♦ lift system BE

Fahrstuhlart, f
- ♦ lift type BE
- ♦ elevator type AE

Fahrstuhl bedienen
Aufzug bedienen
Lift bedienen
- ♦ operate an elevator AE
- ♦ operate a lift BE

Fahrstuhl benutzen
Aufzug benutzen
Lift benutzen
- ♦ use the elevator AE
- ♦ use the lift BE

Fahrstuhlbenutzer m
- ♦ person using an elevator AE
- ♦ person using a lift BE

Fahrstuhlbenutzung, f
Aufzugbenutzung, f
Liftbenutzung, f
- ♦ using an elevator AE
- ♦ use of the elevator AE
- ♦ using a lift BE
- ♦ use of the lift BE

Fahrstuhl bleibt stecken
Aufzug bleibt stecken
Lift bleibt stecken
- ♦ elevator is stuck AE
- ♦ lift is stuck BE

Fahrstuhl einbauen
Aufzug einbauen
- ♦ instal an elevator AE
- ♦ install a lift BE

Fahrstuhlführer m
- ♦ elevator attendant AE
- ♦ lift attendant BE

Fahrstuhlgebühr f
- ♦ elevator fee AE
- ♦ elevator charge AE
- ♦ lift fee BE
- ♦ lift charge BE

Fahrstuhl geht zu allen Stockwerken
Aufzug geht zu allen Stockwerken
Lift geht zu allen Stockwerken
- ♦ elevator serves all floors AE
- ♦ lift serves all floors BE

Fahrstuhlhalle, f
- ♦ elevator lobby AE
- ♦ lift lobby BE

Fahrstuhl hält auf einem Stockwerk
Aufzug hält auf einem Stockwerk
Lift hält auf einem Stockwerk
- ♦ elevator stops at a floor AE
- ♦ lift stops at a floor BE

Fahrstuhl ist ausgefallen
- ♦ elevator isn't working AE
- ♦ lift isn't working BE

Fahrstuhl ist außer Betrieb
Aufzug ist außer Betrieb
Lift ist außer Betrieb
- ♦ elevator is out of order AE
- ♦ lift is out of order BE

Fahrstuhl ist kaputt
Aufzug ist kaputt
Lift ist kaputt
- ♦ elevator has broken down AE
- ♦ lift has broken down BE

Fahrstuhljunge m
- ♦ elevator boy AE
- ♦ lift boy BE

Fahrstuhl nehmen
Aufzug nehmen
Lift nehmen
- ♦ take the elevator AE
- ♦ take the lift BE

Fahrstuhlpersonal n
Aufzugspersonal n
Liftpersonal n
- ♦ elevator personnel AE
- ♦ elevator staff AE
- ♦ lift personnel BE
- ♦ lift staff BE

Fahrstuhlschacht, m
- ♦ lift shaft BE
- ♦ elevator shaft AE

Fahrstuhlservice, m
Liftservice m
Aufzugsservice m
- ♦ elevator service AE
- ♦ lift service BE

Fahrstuhlservice haben
Liftservice haben
- ♦ have elevator service AE
- ♦ have lift service BE

Fahrstuhltyp m
- ♦ elevator type AE
- ♦ type of elevator AE
- ♦ lift type BE
- ♦ type of lift BE

Fahrstuhl zu allen Etagen
Aufzug zu allen Etagen
Lift zu allen Etagen
- ♦ elevator to all floors AE
- ♦ lift to all floors BE

Fahrstuhl zum Strand
Aufzug zum Strand
Lift zum Strand
- ♦ elevator to the beach AE
- ♦ lift to the beach BE

Fahrstunde f (Entfernung)
- ♦ hour's drive

Fahrstunde f (Schule)
- ♦ driving lesson

Fahrt, f
- ♦ trip
- ♦ ride

Fahrt absagen
Fahrt stornieren
- ♦ cancel a trip

Fahrt abschreiben
- ♦ write off a trip
- ♦ write off the trip

Fahrt allein machen
- ♦ make the trip alone

Fahrt anbieten nach X
- ♦ offer a trip to X

Fahrt an die See, f
Fahrt ans Meer, f

Fahrt ans Meer

Fahrt ans Meer
- trip to the sea
- journey to the sea
- tour to the sea
- trip to the seaside

Fahrt ans Meer, f
→ Fahrt an die See

Fahrt arrangieren
- arrange a trip
- arrange a ride

Fahrt auf dem Fluß, f
- trip on the river

Fahrt auf die Beine stellen *fam*
Fahrt organisieren
- lay on a trip *fam*

Fahrt auf einem Motorrad, f
- ride on a motorcycle *AE*
- ride on a motor-cycle *BE*
- ride on a motorbike *coll*

Fahrt aufs Land, f
- trip into the countryside
- tour into the countryside

Fahrt beenden
- end a trip
- end a ride
- finish a trip
- finish a ride

Fahrt beginnt in X
- trip starts at X
- trip starts in X
- trip begins at X
- trip begins in X

Fahrt beschreiben
- describe a trip

Fahrt bezahlen
- pay for a trip
- pay for a ride

Fahrt buchen
- book a trip

Fahrtdauer, f
- duration of a trip

Fahrt durch die literarische Landschaft, f
- trip through the literary landscape

Fahrt durchführen (Veranstalter)
- run a trip

Fahrtende, n
Ende der Fahrt, n
- end of the ride
- end of the trip

Fahrt endet abrupt
- trip ends abruptly

Fahrt entwerfen
Fahrt gestalten
- design a trip

Fahrt erledigen in 20 Minuten
Fahrt schaffen in 20 Minuten
- do the trip in 20 minutes

Fährterminal, n
Fährabfertigungsgebäude, n
- ferry terminal

Fahrt fällt aus
Fahrt fällt ins Wasser *coll*
- trip falls through

Fahrt fortsetzen nach X mit dem Bus
- continue the trip to X by bus
- continue the trip to X by coach *BE*

Fahrt genießen
- enjoy a trip

Fahrt im voraus buchen
- book a trip in advance

Fahrt in die Berge, f
Reise ins Gebirge, f
- trip to the mountains
- journey to the mountains
- tour to the mountains

Fahrt in die Stadt, f (Großstadt)
- trip into (the) city
- ride into (the) city

Fahrt in die Stadt, f (kleine Stadt)
- trip into (the) town
- ride into (the) town

Fahrt ins Ausland, f
→ Auslandsfahrt

Fahrt ins Blaue, f
- mystery tour

Fahrt ins Paradies, f
- trip to paradise

Fahrt ist gefährlich
- trip is dangerous

Fahrt ist die Mühe wert
- trip is worth the effort

Fahrt ist kurz
- trip is short
- trip is brief

Fahrt kaufen
- buy a trip

Fahrtkosten, pl
Fahrkosten, pl
- travel costs *pl*
- travel cost
- traveling costs *AE pl*
- travelling costs *BE pl*

Fahrtlänge, f
- length of a trip

Fahrt leisten sich
Fahrt sich leisten können
- afford a trip

Fahrt machen
- make a trip
- go for a ride
- take a ride

Fahrt machen mit der Eisenbahn
- take a ride on the railroad *AE*
- take a ride on the railway *BE*

Fahrt mit der Bergbahn, f
- trip on the mountain railroad *AE*
- trip on the mountain railway *BE*

Fahrt nach X, f
- trip to X

Fahrt organisieren
Fahrt veranstalten
- organise a trip
- organize a trip

Fahrt planen
- plan a trip

Fahrtplanung, f
Planung einer Fahrt, f
- trip planning
- planning (of) a trip

Fahrt schließt mit etw ab
- trip concludes with s.th.

Fahrt stornieren
→ Fahrt absagen

Fahrtteilnehmer, m
Reiseteilnehmer, m
- participant in a tour
- person taking part in a tour
- person participating in a tour

Fahrttermin, m
- date of the trip

Fahrt um den Hafen, f
- trip round the harbor *AE*
- trip round the harbour *BE*

Fahrt um die Welt, f
- trip round the world

Fahrt um die Welt machen
- take a trip round the world

Fahrt unterbrechen
- break a trip
- break a journey

Fahrtunterbrechung, f
→ Reiseunterbrechung

Fahrt unternehmen
- take a trip
- take a ride
- undertake a trip

Fahrt unternehmen nach X
- take a trip to X
- take a tour to X
- take a journey to X

Fahrt unternehmen von X
- take a trip from X
- take a tour from X
- take a journey from X

Fahrtvergnügen, n
- trip enjoyment
- enjoyment of the trip

Fahrt verkaufen jm
- sell a trip to s.o.
- sell s.o. a trip

Fahrt verlängern
- extend a trip
- prolong a trip

Fahrt vorbereiten
- prepare a trip

Fahrt vorschlagen
- suggest a trip

Fahrt wert sein
- be (well) worth the trip
- be (well) worth a trip

Fahrtziel, n
- destination of a trip
- destination of the trip
- destination

Fahrtzone, f
Reisezone, f
- travel zone

Fahrt zum Fischen, f
Ausflug zum Fischen, m
Angelausflug, m
Angelpartie, f
- fishing trip

Fahrt zunichtemachen
- ruin a trip

Fahrt zur Arbeitsstelle, f
Fahrt zum Arbeitsplatz f
- journey to work

Fahrt zusammenstellen
- fix up a trip *AE coll*

Fahrtzweck, m
Zweck der Fahrt, m
- purpose of the trip

Fahrt zwischen A und B, f
- trip between A and B
- ride between A and B

Fährüberfahrt, f
- ferry crossing

Fährunternehmen, n
- ferry enterprise

Fährunternehmer, m
- ferry operator

Fährverbindung, f
- ferry link
- ferry connection

Fährverbindung nach X, f
  ♦ ferry link with X
  ♦ ferry connection with X
Fahrverbot, n
  ♦ ban on driving
Fahrverbot erhalten
  ♦ be banned from driving
Fahrwerk, n (Flugzeug)
  ♦ landing gear
Fahrzeit, f (Auto)
  ♦ driving time
Fahrzeit, f (generell)
  Wegezeit, f
  ♦ travelling time BE
  ♦ travel time
Fahrzeit, f (Reisezeit)
  ♦ journey time
Fahrzeug, n
  ♦ vehicle
Fahrzeugaufzug, m
  ♦ vehicle elevator AE
  ♦ vehicle lift BE
Fahrzeugausgaben, f pl
  ♦ vehicle expenses pl
Fahrzeug befördern
  Fahrzeug transportieren
  ♦ carry a vehicle
  ♦ transport a vehicle
Fahrzeug benutzen
  ♦ use a vehicle
Fahrzeugdeck, n
  ♦ vehicle deck
Fahrzeugeskorte, f
  Wageneskorte, f (z.B. durch Polizisten)
  ♦ motorcade
Fahrzeugfähre, f
  ♦ vehicle ferry
Fahrzeugkosten, pl
  ♦ vehicle costs pl
  ♦ vehicle cost
Fahrzeugmiete, f
  ♦ vehicle rent AE
  ♦ vehicle rental
  ♦ vehicle hire BE
Fahrzeug mit Kraftstoffeinspritzung, n
  ♦ vehicle with fuel injection
Fahrzeug mit Vierradantrieb, n
  ♦ four-wheel-drive vehicle
Fahrzeugpark, m
  Fahrzeugflotte f
  ♦ vehicle fleet
  ♦ fleet of vehicles
  ♦ automobile park AE
Fahrzeugrallye, f
  ♦ vehicle rally
Fahrzeugrückholung, f
  (ins Heimatland)
  ♦ vehicle repatriation
Fahrzeugzahl, f
  Zahl der Fahrzeuge, f
  ♦ number of vehicles
Fahrzeugzufahrt, f
  ♦ vehicle access
Fakir, m
  ♦ fakir
Fakirvorstellung, f
  ♦ fakir show
Faktotum, n humor
  ♦ factotum
  ♦ handyman
  ♦ handywoman

Faktur, f
  Warenrechnung, f
  ♦ invoice
fakturieren etw
  ♦ invoice s.th.
  ♦ bill s.th.
  ♦ charge s.th.
Fakturierung, f
  ♦ invoicing
Fakturist, m
  ♦ invoice clerk
fakultativ, adj
  nicht obligatorisch, adj
  ♦ optional, adj
fakultative Behandlung, f
  ♦ optional treatment
fakultative Besichtigung, f
  ♦ optional sightseeing
fakultative Besichtigungsfahrt, f
  ♦ optional sightseeing tour
fakultative Fahrt, f
  ♦ optional trip
fakultativer Ausflug, m
  Fakultativausflug m
  ♦ optional excursion
  ♦ optional trip
fakultativer Besuch, m
  ♦ optional visit
fakultativer Landausflug, m
  (Kreuzfahrt)
  ♦ optional shore excursion
fakultatives Abendessen, n (Dinner)
  ♦ optional dinner
fakultatives Abendessen, n (Supper)
  ♦ optional supper
fakultatives Essen, n
  ♦ optional meal
fakultatives Frühstück, n
  ♦ optional breakfast
fakultatives Mittagessen, n
  ♦ optional lunch
  ♦ optional luncheon
fakultative Stadtrundfahrt, f (Bus)
  ♦ optional city sightseeing tour
  ♦ optional sightseeing tour of the city
  ♦ optional city tour
fakultative Teilnahme, f (aktiv)
  ♦ optional participation
fakultative Teilnahme, f (passiv)
  ♦ optional attendance
fakultative Tour, f
  ♦ optional tour
fakultative Zusatzleistung, f
  ♦ optional extra service
  ♦ optional extra
Falkenjagd, f
  ♦ falconry
Falle, f figur
  (Bett, Schlafplatz)
  Klappe, f figur
  ♦ sack AE sl
  ♦ kip BE sl
  ♦ doss
fällig, adj (Zahlung)
  sofort zahlbar, adj
  ♦ due, adj
  ♦ payable, adj
fällige Miete, f
  geschuldete Miete, f
  ♦ rent due

Fälligkeitsdatum, n
  (Schulden)
  ♦ maturity date
fällig sein
  sofort zahlbar sein
  ♦ be due
fällig werden
  ♦ become due
  ♦ become payable
  ♦ fall due
Fallreep, n
  (Schiff)
  ♦ accommodation ladder
Fallschirm, m
  ♦ parachute
  ♦ chute sl
Fallschirmgleiten, n
  Gleitschirmfliegen, n
  ♦ parachute gliding
  ♦ paragliding
Fallschirmsegeln, n
  ♦ parachute sailing
  ♦ parasailing
Fallschirmspringen, n
  ♦ parachute jumping
  ♦ parachuting
Fallschirmspringer, m
  ♦ parachutist
  ♦ parachuter
Fallschirmsprung, m
  ♦ parachute jump
falls gewünscht
  ♦ if requested
falls verlangt
  ♦ if desired
Falltür, f
  ♦ trapdoor
  ♦ trap
falsch, adj
  ♦ wrong, adj
  ♦ false, adj
falsche Adresse, f
  ♦ wrong address
falsche Angabe, f
  ♦ false statement
falsche Angabe machen
  ♦ make a false statement
falsche Auskunft geben jm
  ♦ give s.o. (the) wrong information
  ♦ misinform s.o.
falsche Ernährung, f
  Fehlernährung f
  ♦ false nutrition
falsche Informationen geben jm
  falsche Auskünfte geben jm
  ♦ give s.o. false information
falschen Namen angeben
  ♦ give a false name
falsche Richtung, f
  ♦ wrong direction
falscher Luxus, m
  ♦ false luxury
falscher Name, m
  ♦ false name
falsche Route nehmen
  falschen Weg nehmen
  ♦ take the wrong route
falsches Reisepapier, n
  falsches Reisedokument, n
  ♦ false travel document

falsch informieren jn (über etw)

falsch informieren jn (über etw)
- misinform s.o. (about s.th.)

faltbar, adj
klappbar, adj
- folding, adj
- foldable, adj
- collapsible, adj

Faltbett, n (generell)
Klappbett, n
- folding bed
- foldaway bed

Faltbett, n (Rollbett)
→ Rollbett

Faltblatt, n
Blatt, n
Informationsblatt, n
- leaflet

Faltboot, n
- folding boat
- folding canoe
- collapsible boat

Faltcaravan, m
Faltwohnwagen, m
- folding caravan BE
- folding trailer AE

Faltgarage, f
- collapsible garage

Faltliege, f
- folding divan

Faltprospekt, m
Mappe, f
- folder
- kit AE

Faltstuhl, m (generell)
Klappstuhl, m
- collapsible chair
- folding chair

Faltstuhl, m (ohne Lehnen/Rückenteil)
Klappstuhl, m
- folding stool
- campstool AE
- camp-stool BE

Falttreppe, f
- foldaway stairs pl
- trap stairs pl

Falttür, f
- folding door
- accordion door

Faltwand, f
spanische Wand, f
- folding partition

Faltwohnwagen, m
Faltcaravan, m
- folding trailer AE
- folding caravan BE
- folder BE coll

familiäre Atmosphäre, f
- family atmosphere

familiär geführtes Hotel, n
von einer Familie geführtes Hotel, n
- family-run hotel

Familie besteht aus vier Personen
- family consists of four persons

Familie mit zwei Kindern, f
- family of two children

Familienaktivität, f
- family activity

Familienaktivurlaub, m
- family activity vacation AE
- family activity holiday BE

Familienanschluß haben
(als Gast)
- be treated as one of the family

Familienappartement n
- family apartment

Familienaufenthalt, m
- family stay

Familienausflug, m
- family outing
- family excursion

Familienbad, n (Aktivität, Männer und Frauen)
- mixed bathing

Familienbad, n (Schwimmbad)
- swimming pool for mixed bathing AE
- swimming-pool for mixed bathing BE

Familienbad, n (Strand)
- bathing beach for mixed bathing

Familienbadezimmer, n
Familienbad n
- family bathroom
- family bath

Familienbahncard, f
- family railcard
- family card

Familienbecken, n
- family pool

Familienbenutzung, f
Familiennutzung, f
- family use

Familienbesitz, m
- family ownership

Familienbetrieb, m (Betriebsart)
- family operation
- family establishment

Familienbetrieb, m (Hotel für Familien)
Familienhotel, n
- hotel suitable for families
- hotel for families
- family hotel

Familienbetrieb m (von Familie geleitet)
- family-run establishment
- family-run operation
- family business

Familienbuchung, f
- family booking

Familiencamper, m
- family camper

Familiencamping, n
- family camping

Familiencampingpark, m
- family camping park

Familiencampingplatz, m
- family campsite
- family campground AE
- family camping site BE
- family camping ground BE
- family site

Familienclub, m
- family club

Familieneinheit, f (Statistik)
(Unterkunft)
- family unit

Familieneinrichtung, f
- family facility

Familienerholung, f (Urlaub)
→ Familienurlaub

Familienermäßigung, f
Ermäßigung für Familien, f
- family reduction
- reduction for families

Familienessen, n (generell)
- family food

Familienessen, n (Mahlzeit)
Familienmahlzeit, f
- family meal

Familienfahrt, f
- family trip
- family ride

Familienfeier, f
- family party
- family celebration

Familienferien, pl
Familienurlaub, m
Ferien mit der Familie, pl
Urlaub mit der Familie, m
- family holiday BE
- family holidays BE pl
- family vacation AE

Familienferienhaus, n
Familienurlaubshaus, n
- family holiday home BE
- family vacation home AE

Familienferienhotel, n
Familienurlaubshotel, n
- family holiday hotel BE
- family vacation hotel AE

Familienferienort, m
Familienurlaubsort, m
Familienort, m
- family holiday resort BE
- family vacation resort AE
- family resort

Familienferienwohnung, f
- family vacation apartment AE
- family holiday flat BE

Familienfest, n (Feier)
- family celebration

Familienfest, n (Festival)
Fest für Familien, n
Festspiele für Familien, n pl
- family festival

Familienfest, n (Party)
Familienparty, f
- family party

Familienfestlichkeit, f
Familienfeier, f
- family festivity
- family celebration

Familienfete, f
- family fete AE
- family fête BE

Familienfreizeit, f
- family leisure

Familienfreizeiteinrichtung, f
- family leisure facility

Familienfreizeitpaß, m
- family leisure pass

familienfreundlich, adj
- family-friendly, adj
- family-oriented, adj AE
- family-orientated, adj BE

familienfreundliches Hotel, n
- family-oriented hotel AE
- family-orientated hotel BE
- hotel welcoming families
- family-friendly hotel

Familienfrühstück, n
- family breakfast

Familiengästezimmer, n
- family guest room AE
- family guest-room BE

familiengeführtes Haus, n (Hotel)
→ familiengeführtes Hotel
familiengerecht, adj
♦ suitable for families, adj
Familiengeschäft, n
Familienbetrieb m
♦ family business
Familiengröße, f
♦ size of the family
Familiengruppe, f
♦ family group
♦ family party
Familienhaus, n
FH, n
♦ family house
♦ family home
Familienhauszelt, n
♦ family ridge tent
Familienhotel, n (für Familiengäste)
♦ family hotel
Familienhotel, n (von einer Familie geführt)
familiär geführtes Hotel, n
♦ family-operated hotel
♦ family-run hotel
Familienkarte, f
Familienfahrkarte, f
♦ family ticket
Familienkreuzfahrt, f
♦ family cruise
Familienkurs, m
Familienlehrgang, m
♦ family course
Familienkurzurlaub, m
♦ family break
Familienlokal, n
♦ family place
♦ family spot
♦ family restaurant
Familienmitglied n
♦ family member
♦ member of the family
Familienmittagessen, n
♦ family lunch
♦ family luncheon
Familienmuseum, n
♦ family museum
Familiennachmittag, m
♦ afternoon for families
Familienname, m
♦ family name
Familienoberhaupt, n
♦ head of family
Familienort, m
♦ family resort
Familienpauschale, f
♦ family package
Familienpauschalpreis, m
♦ family package price
♦ family package rate
Familienpauschalurlaub, m
Familienpauschalferien, pl
♦ family package vacation AE
♦ family package holiday BE
Familienpension, f (für Familien)
♦ family guesthouse AE
♦ family guest-house BE
♦ family boardinghouse AE
♦ family boarding-house BE
♦ family pension AE
Familienpension, f (von Familie geführt)
♦ family-run guesthouse AE

♦ family-run guest-house BE
♦ family-run boardinghouse AE
♦ family-run boarding-house BE
Familienpicknick, n
♦ family picnic
Familienplatz, m
(Camping)
♦ family site
Familienpreis, m
♦ family price
♦ family rate
Familienquartier, n (Militär)
(Gegensatz zu Einzelquartier)
♦ married quarters pl
Familienrabatt m
♦ family discount
Familienrate, f
→ Familienpreis
Familienreise, f
♦ family journey
♦ family trip
♦ family tour
Familienreservierung, f
♦ family reservation
Familienrestaurant n
♦ family restaurant
Familienrezept, n
(für Speisen)
♦ family recipe
Familiensauna, f
→ Gemeinschaftssauna
Familienschlafzimmer, n
Familienschlafraum, m
♦ family bedroom
Familienseebad, n
Familienseebadeort m
♦ family seaside resort
Familienservice, m
Familienbedienung, f
Familienbetreuung, f
Familiendienst, m
♦ family service
Familiensitz, m
♦ family seat
Familiensitzung, f
Familienstunde, f
♦ family session
Familienspaß, m
♦ family fun
Familienspaßpark, m
♦ family funpark
Familienspieltisch, m
♦ family games table
Familienstand, m
(ledig, verheiratet etc.)
♦ marital status
Familiensuite, f
♦ family suite
Familientag, m
♦ family day
Familientarif, m
♦ family tariff
♦ family rates pl
♦ family rate
♦ family terms pl
Familientourismus, m
♦ family tourism
Familientourist, m
♦ family tourist
Familientradition, f
♦ family tradition

Familientreffen n
♦ family reunion
♦ reunion
Familienumzug, m
♦ family move
Familienunterbringung, f
(in einer Familie)
♦ family accommodation
Familienunterbringung mit Vollpension, f
♦ family accommodation with full board
♦ family accommodation with full pension AE
Familienunterhaltung, f
Unterhaltung für Familien, f
♦ family entertainment
Familienunterhaltungsgeschäft, n
♦ family entertainment business
Familienunterkunft, f
Familienunterbringung, f
♦ family lodging AE
♦ family accommodation
Familienurlaub, m
Familienferien, pl
Urlaub mit der Familie, m
Ferien mit der Familie, pl
♦ family vacation AE
♦ family holiday BE
♦ family holidays BE pl
Familienurlaub auf dem Bauernhof, m
Familienferien auf dem Bauernhof, pl
♦ family farmhouse vacation AE
♦ family farm vacation AE
♦ family farmhouse holiday BE
♦ family farm holiday BE
Familienurlauber, m
Familienferiengast, m
♦ family vacationer AE
♦ family holidaymaker BE
Familienurlaub mit Selbstverpflegung, m
Familienurlaub mit Selbstversorgung, m
Familienferien mit Selbstverpflegung, pl
Familienferien mit Selbstversorgung, pl
♦ self-catering family vacation AE
♦ self-catering family holiday BE
Familienurlaubshaus, n
Familienferienhaus, n
♦ family vacation home AE
♦ family vacation house AE
♦ family holiday home BE
♦ family holiday house BE
Familienurlaubshotel, n
Familienferienhotel, n
♦ family vacation hotel AE
♦ family holiday hotel BE
Familienurlaubsmarkt, m
Familienferienmarkt, m
♦ family vacation market AE
♦ family holiday market BE
Familienurlaubsort, m
Familienferienort, m
Familienort, m
♦ family vacation resort AE
♦ family holiday resort BE
♦ family resort
Familienveranstaltung, f
♦ family function
Familien verpflegen
Familien bewirten
♦ cater for families
Familienversicherung, f
♦ family insurance

Familienvilla

Familienvilla, f
 ◆ **family villa**
Familienvollpension, f
 Familienvollverpflegung, f
 ◆ **family full board**
 ◆ family full pension *AE*
Familienvorführung, f
 Familiendarbietung f
 Vorstellung für Familien, f
 ◆ **family show**
Familienwagen, m
 Familienauto, n
 Familien-Pkw, m
 ◆ **family car**
Familien willkommen
 Familien sind willkommen
 ◆ **Families welcome**
 ◆ Families are welcome
Familienwintersporturlaub, m
 Familienwintersportferien, pl
 ◆ **family wintersport vacation** *AE*
 ◆ family wintersports vacation *AE*
 ◆ family wintersport holiday *BE*
 ◆ family wintersports holiday *BE*
Familienwohnsitz, m
 Familienresidenz, f
 ◆ **family residence**
Familienwohnung, f
 ◆ **family flat** *AE*
 ◆ family apartment *AE*
Familienzentrum, n
 ◆ **family center** *AE*
 ◆ family centre *BE*
Familienzimmer n
 ◆ **family room**
Familienzusammenkunft, f
 → Familientreffen
Familienzuschlag, m
 Zuschlag für Familien m
 ◆ **family supplement**
 ◆ supplement for families
Family Plan, m
 (Kinder kostenfrei im Elternzimmer)
 FP, m
 ◆ **Family Plan**
 ◆ FP
Fan, m
 ◆ **fan**
 ◆ fanatic
 ◆ buff
Fanclub, m
 ◆ **fan club**
 ◆ enthusiasts' club
Fango, m
 Moor, n
 ◆ **fango**
 ◆ mud
Fangobad, n (Aktivität)
 ◆ **fango bath**
 ◆ mud bath *AE*
 ◆ mud-bath *BE*
Fangobehandlung, f
 ◆ **fango treatment**
Fangokur, f
 ◆ **fango cure**
 ◆ fango treatment
Fangopackung, f
 Moorpackung, f
 ◆ **fango pack**
 ◆ mudpack *AE*
 ◆ mud pack *BE*

Fangotherapie, f
 ◆ **fango therapy**
FAP, m
 (Zimmer mit allen Mahlzeiten)
 Full American Plan, m
 ◆ **FAP**
 ◆ Full American Plan
Farbanstrich, m
 ◆ **coat of paint**
Farbband, m (Buch)
 ◆ **color book** *AE*
 ◆ colour book *BE*
Farbbild, n
 ◆ **color picture** *AE*
 ◆ colour picture *BE*
Farbbroschüre, f
 → Farbprospekt
Farbdia, n
 ◆ **color slide** *AE*
 ◆ colour slide *BE*
Farbe in den Alltag bringen
 ◆ **bring a little color into everyday life** *AE*
 ◆ bring a little colour into everyday life *BE*
farbenprächtig möbliert, adj
 auffallend möbliert, adj
 ◆ **flamboyantly furnished, adj**
farbenprächtig möbliertes Zimmer, n
 auffallend möbliertes Zimmer, n
 ◆ **flamboyantly furnished room**
Färberbrunnen, m
 ◆ **dyers' fountain**
Farbfaltblatt, n
 Farbblatt, n
 ◆ **color leaflet** *AE*
 ◆ colour leaflet *BE*
Farbfernsehen n
 ◆ **color TV** *AE*
 ◆ colour TV *BE*
 ◆ colour television *BE*
Farbfernseher m
 ◆ **color TV set** *AE*
 ◆ color television set *AE*
 ◆ colour TV set *BE*
 ◆ colour television set *BE*
Farbfernsehraum, m
 ◆ **color TV room** *AE*
 ◆ color television room *AE*
 ◆ colour TV room *BE*
 ◆ colour television room *BE*
Farbfernsehsalon, m
 ◆ **color TV lounge** *AE*
 ◆ color television lounge *AE*
 ◆ colour TV lounge *BE*
 ◆ colour television lounge *BE*
Farbfilm, m
 ◆ **color film** *AE*
 ◆ colour film *BE*
Farbfolie, f
 ◆ **color transparency** *AE*
 ◆ colour transparency *BE*
Farbfoto, n
 Farbfotografie, f
 ◆ **color photograph** *AE*
 ◆ color photo *AE*
 ◆ colour photograph *BE*
 ◆ colour photo *BE*
Farbführer, m
 ◆ **color guide** *AE*
 ◆ colour guide *BE*

Farbgefühl, n
 Farbempfinden, n
 ◆ **color sense** *AE*
 ◆ colour sense *BE*
Farbgestaltung, f
 → Farbzusammenstellung
Farbkatalog, m
 ◆ **color catalogue** *AE*
 ◆ color catalog *AE*
 ◆ colour catalogue *BE*
Farbkopierer, m
 Farbkopiergerät, n
 ◆ **color copier** *AE*
 ◆ colour copier *BE*
Farblandkarte, f
 Farbkarte, f
 ◆ **color map** *AE*
 ◆ colour map *BE*
Farbmonitor, m
 ◆ **color monitor** *AE*
 ◆ colour monitor *BE*
Farbnegativ, n
 Farbbildnegativ, n
 ◆ **color negative** *AE*
 ◆ colour negative *BE*
Farbprospekt, m
 Farbbroschüre, f
 ◆ **color brochure** *AE*
 ◆ colour brochure *BE*
Farbstift, m (Bleistift)
 ◆ **colored pencil** *AE*
 ◆ coloured pencil *BE*
 ◆ crayon
Farbstift, m (Filzstift)
 ◆ **colored pen** *AE*
 ◆ coloured pen *BE*
Farbtherapie, f
 ◆ **color therapy** *AE*
 ◆ colour therapy
Farb-TV, n
 → Farbfernsehen
Farbzusammenstellung, f
 Farbgestaltung, f
 ◆ **color scheme** *AE*
 ◆ colour scheme *BE*
Farm, f
 Bauernhof, m
 Bauernhaus, n
 ◆ **farm**
Farmcampingplatz, m
 Bauernhofcampingplatz, m
 ◆ **farm campsite**
 ◆ farm campground *AE*
 ◆ farm camping site *BE*
 ◆ farm camping ground *BE*
Farmferien, pl
 → Ferien auf dem Bauernhof
Farmhotel, n
 Bauernhofhotel, n
 ◆ **farm hotel**
Farmplatz, m
 (Camping)
 Bauernhofplatz, m
 ◆ **farm site**
Farmurlaub, m
 → Urlaub auf dem Bauernhof
Fasan, m
 ◆ **pheasant**
Fasanenbraten, m
 ◆ **roast pheasant**

218

Fasanenbrust, f
   Fasanenbrüstchen, n
   ♦ pheasant breast
Fasanenfleisch, n
   ♦ pheasant meat
Fasanenpastete, f
   ♦ pheasant pâté
   ♦ pheasant pie
Fasanenragout, n/m
   ♦ pheasant stew
Fasanensalmi, n
   ♦ pheasant salmi
Fasching, m
   → Karneval
Faschingsball, m
   → Karnevalsball
Faschingsdienstag, m
   Fastnachtsdienstag m
   ♦ Shrove Tuesday
   ♦ mardi gras *AE*
   ♦ Pancake Tuesday
   ♦ Pancake Day
Faschingssaison, f
   → Karnevalsaison
Faschingssonntag, m
   Fastnachtssonntag, m
   Karnevalssonntag, m
   ♦ Shrove Sunday
Faschingstreiben, n
   → Karnevalstreiben
Faschingsumzug, m
   → Karnevalsumzug
Faschingszug, m
   → Karnevalszug
Fasnet, f *dial*
   → Karneval
Faß, n
   (aus Holz)
   ♦ barrel
   ♦ cask
Faß, n (Butter, Milch)
   ♦ churn *BE*
Fassade, f
   ♦ façade
   ♦ facade *AE*
   ♦ front
   ♦ frontage
Faß anstechen
   Faß anzapfen
   ♦ broach a barrel
   ♦ tap a barrel
   ♦ tap a cask
Faßaufzug, m
   ♦ barrel hoist
Faß Bier, n
   ♦ barrel of beer
Faßbier, n
   ♦ draft beer *AE*
   ♦ draft *AE*
   ♦ draught beer *BE*
   ♦ draught *BE*
   ♦ beer (drawn) from the wood
Fäßchen, n
   kleines Faß n
   ♦ keg
Faßcider, m
   ♦ draft cider *AE*
   ♦ draught cider *BE*
   ♦ draught cyder *BE*

fassen (aufnehmen)
   aufnehmen können
   ♦ hold
fassen bis zu 500 Personen
   bis zu 500 Personen Sitzplätze bieten
   ♦ hold up to 500 persons
   ♦ seat up to 500 persons
fassen (Saal)
   Platz bieten
   Sitzplatz bieten
   ♦ seat (s.o.)
   ♦ accommodate (s.o.)
fässerweise, adv
   faßweise, adv
   ♦ by the barrel, adv
   ♦ by the cask, adv
Faßgärung, f
   ♦ barrel fermentation
Faßinhalt, m
   Faßvolumen, n
   ♦ contents of a barrel *pl*
   ♦ volume of a barrel
Faß leer laufen lassen
   ♦ run a barrel dry
Fassung, f
   (einer Lampe etc.)
   ♦ socket
Fassungsvermögen, n
   → Kapazität
Faßwein, m
   ♦ draft wine *AE*
   ♦ draught wine *BE*
   ♦ wine from the cask
   ♦ wine (drawn) from the wood
Faß Wein, n
   ♦ barrel of wine
Faß Whisky, n
   ♦ cask of whisky
Fastage, f
   → Leergut
fasten
   ♦ fast
Fasten, n
   ♦ fasting
fasten bei Wasser und Brot
   ♦ fast on bread and water
Fastengericht, n
   (in Fastenzeit)
   ♦ Lenten dish
   ♦ meatless dish
Fastenkost, f
   (in Fastenzeit)
   ♦ Lenten diet
   ♦ Lenten fare
Fastenkur, f
   ♦ fasting cure
   ♦ fasting
   ♦ hunger cure
   ♦ therapeutic fasting
   ♦ starvation cure
Fastenmahlzeit, f
   ♦ Lenten meal
   ♦ meatless meal
Fastenzeit, f (generell)
   ♦ period of fasting
   ♦ fast
Fastenzeit, f (religiös)
   ♦ Lenten season
   ♦ season of Lent
Fast Food, n
   ♦ fast food

Fast-Food-Betrieb m
   ♦ fast-food establishment
   ♦ fast-food operation
Fast-Food-Einheit, f
   (Statistik)
   ♦ fast-food unit
Fast-Food-Firma, f
   ♦ fast-food corporation *AE*
   ♦ fast-food company
   ♦ fast-food firm
Fast-Food-Gaststätte, f
   ♦ fast-food bar *AE*
Fast-Food-Geschäft, n
   ♦ fast-food business
Fast-Food-Industrie f
   ♦ fast-food industry
Fast-Food-Kette, f
   ♦ fast-food chain
Fast-Food-Kneipe, f
   ♦ fast-food joint
Fast-Food-Kunde, m
   ♦ fast-food customer
Fast-Food-Lokal, n
   ♦ fast-food place
   ♦ fast-food spot
Fast-Food-Messe, f
   ♦ fast-food fair
Fast-Food-Restaurant, n
   ♦ fast-food diner *AE*
   ♦ fast-food restaurant
Fast-Food-Service, m
   ♦ fast-food service
Fast-Food-Umsatz, m
   ♦ fast-food sales *pl*
   ♦ fast-food turnover
Fastnacht, f
   → Fasching
Fastnachtsumzug, m
   → Karnevalsumzug
Fasttag, m
   ♦ fasting day
faul am Strand liegen
   faulenzen am Strand
   ♦ laze on the beach
faulenzen
   nichts tun
   ♦ laze
   ♦ do nothing
   ♦ be lazy
Faulenzer, m
   ♦ lazybones *pl = sg*
Faulenzerleben, n
   ♦ life of Riley
   ♦ idle life
   ♦ lazy life
   ♦ life of idleness
Faulenzerleben führen
   ♦ live the life of Riley
faules Ei, n
   ♦ rotten egg
faules Leben führen
   ♦ eat the bread of idleness
faul in der Sonne liegen
   ♦ laze in the sun
Fauna, f
   ♦ fauna
Faustkeil, m *hist*
   ♦ celt *hist*
Fauxpas, m *FR*
   ♦ fauxpas *FR*
   ♦ indiscretion

Fax

Fax, n
  Telefax n
  ♦ fax
  ♦ telefax
Faxanschluß, m
  ♦ fax connection
faxen etw an jn
  ♦ telefax s.th. to s.o.
  ♦ fax s.th. to s.o.
Faxgerät, n
  ♦ fax machine
Faxmitteilung, f
  Faxnachricht, f
  ♦ fax message
Faxmöglichkeit, f
  Faxeinrichtung, f
  ♦ fax facility
Faxnummer, f
  ♦ fax number
Faxservice, m
  Telefaxservice, m
  ♦ fax service
  ♦ telefax service
Fazilität, f
  → Einrichtung
Februar, m
  ♦ February
Februarauslastung, f
  Auslastung im Februar, f
  ♦ February load factor
  ♦ load factor in February
Februarbelegung, f
  Februarauslastung, f
  ♦ February occupancy
  ♦ occupancy in February
Februarfeier, f
  ♦ February celebration
Februartagung, f
  Februartreffen, n
  ♦ February meeting
Februarurlaub, m
  ♦ February vacation *AE*
  ♦ February holiday *BE*
Februarwoche, f
  ♦ February week
Fechtclub, m
  Fechtverein, m
  ♦ fencing club
fechten
  (Sport)
  ♦ fence
Fechten, n
  Fechtsport, m
  ♦ fencing
Fechter, m
  ♦ fencer
Fechtmeisterschaft, f
  ♦ fencing championship
Fechtschule, f
  ♦ school of fencing
Fechtturnier, n
  ♦ fencing tournament
Fechtwettbewerb, m
  ♦ fencing competition
Federball, m
  ♦ shuttle
  ♦ shuttlecock
Federballplatz, m
  ♦ shuttlecock pitch
Federbett, n
  Duvet, n *SCHW*

  ♦ duvet
  ♦ eiderdown
Federdecke, f
  ♦ featherquilt
  ♦ eiderdown
Federkernmatratze, f
  ♦ innerspring mattress *AE*
  ♦ interior spring mattress *BE*
  ♦ interior-sprung mattress *BE*
Federmatratze, f (Federfüllung)
  Matratze mit Federfüllung, f
  Matratze, die mit Federn gefüllt ist, f
  ♦ feather bed
Federmatratze, f (gefedert)
  ♦ spring mattress
Federweißer, m
  ♦ fermenting new wine
  ♦ Federweisser
  ♦ new wine
Fehlbestand, m
  (in Warenlager)
  ♦ shortfall *AE*
  ♦ shortage
  ♦ deficiency
Fehlbetrag, m
  ♦ deficient amount
Fehlbuchung, f
  fehlerhafte Buchung, f
  ♦ incorrect booking
  ♦ wrong booking
fehlender Geschmack, m
  Mangel an Geschmack, m
  ♦ lack of taste
fehlendes Gepäck, n
  ♦ missing baggage *AE*
  ♦ missing luggage *BE*
fehlende Wäsche f
  ♦ missing linen
fehlerfreier Service, m
  fehlerloser Service, m
  ♦ faultless service
fehlerloser Service, m
  → fehlerfreier Service
Fehlernährung, f
  falsche Ernährung, f
  ♦ wrong nutrition
Feier, f (Fest)
  Fest, n
  ♦ celebration
Feier, f (Festakt)
  → Zeremonie
Feier absagen
  ♦ cancel a celebration
Feier begehen
  ♦ hold a celebration
Feier bezahlen
  ♦ pay for a celebration
Feier eines Jubiläums, f
  ♦ celebration of an anniversary
  ♦ anniversary celebration
Feier klingt harmonisch aus
  Fest klingt harmonisch aus
  ♦ celebration is coming to a(n) harmonious end
Feier koordinieren
  Fest koordinieren
  ♦ coordinate a celebration
feierlich, adj
  festlich, adj
  ♦ solemn, adj
  ♦ ceremonial, adj

feierlich, adv
  ♦ ceremonially, adv
  ♦ formally, adv
  ♦ with ceremony, adv
  ♦ with great ceremony, adv
feierlicher Anlaß, m
  ♦ ceremonial occasion
  ♦ formal occasion
feierlicher Empfang, m
  ♦ ceremonial reception
  ♦ formal reception
feierlich eröffnen etw
  ♦ open s.th. with ceremony
  ♦ inaugurate s.th.
  ♦ open s.th. ceremonially
feierlicher Umzug, m
  ♦ ceremonial parade
feierliches Kleid, n
  ♦ ceremonial dress
Feierlichkeit, f (Ernst)
  ♦ solemnity
Feierlichkeit, f (Pomp)
  → Pomp
Feierlichkeit, f (Zeremonie)
  → Zeremonie
feiern
  ♦ fete *AE*
  ♦ fête *BE*
  ♦ celebrate
  ♦ party
Feiern, n
  ♦ celebrating
Feiern, n (mit viel Essen und Trinken)
  ♦ feasting
feiern bis in die Puppen
  bis in die frühen Morgenstunden feiern
  ♦ celebrate into the small hours
feiernd, adj
  ♦ celebrating, adj
Feiernder, m
  ♦ celebrator
  ♦ person taking part in a celebration
  ♦ person taking part in a festivity
feiern etw
  ♦ celebrate s.th.
  ♦ fete s.th.
  ♦ fête s.th.
feiern etw festlich
  etw festlich begehen
  ♦ celebrate s.th. festively
  ♦ celebrate s.th.
feiern etw jährlich (am 25. November)
  ♦ celebrate s.th. annually (on 25 November)
feiern etw mit einem Festessen
  feiern etw mit einem Bankett
  ♦ celebrate s.th. with a banquet
feiern etw mit einer Ausstellung
  ♦ celebrate s.th. with an exhibition
  ♦ celebrate s.th. with an exhibit *AE*
feiern etw mit einer Party
  ♦ celebrate s.th. with a party
feiern etw mit jm
  ♦ celebrate s.th. with s.o.
feiern etw still
  ♦ celebrate s.th. quietly
feiern (etw) stilvoll
  ♦ celebrate (s.th.) in style
feiern etw stilvoll
  ♦ celebrate s.th. in style
feiern jn
  ♦ celebrate s.o.

feiernswert, adj
♦ worth celebrating, adj
feiernswert sein
Feier wert sein
♦ be worth celebrating
feiern zusammen
zusammen feiern
♦ celebrate together
Feier planen
♦ plan a celebration
♦ plan a ceremony
Feier planen für das Wochenende
♦ plan a celebration for the weekend
♦ plan a party for the weekend
♦ plan a festival for the weekend
♦ plan a ceremony for the weekend
Feierplatz, m
Festplatz, m
♦ ceremonial site
Feierschicht, f
(keine Arbeitsschicht)
♦ idle shift
Feier stören
♦ disturb a celebration
Feierstunde, f
→ Zeremonie
Feiertag, m (Festtag)
♦ day of celebration
Feiertag, m (kein Werktag)
♦ holiday
Feiertag, m (religiös)
♦ holy day
♦ high day
♦ feast day
feiertags, adv
♦ on holidays, adv
Feiertagsarbeit, f
♦ Sunday and holiday work
Feiertagsgeld, n
(Arbeitnehmer)
♦ holiday pay
Feier veranstalten
Feier organisieren
♦ organise a celebration
♦ organize a celebration
Feier zu etw, f
Feier, mit der etw begangen wird, f
♦ celebration to mark s.th.
Feier zum hundertjährigen Jubiläum von etw, f
♦ celebration to mark the centenary of s.th.
Feier zur Erinnerung an etw, f
Feier zu etw, f
♦ celebration commemorating s.th.
♦ celebration to commemorate s.th.
Feige, f
♦ fig
Feigenbaum, m
♦ fig tree
feilschen mit jm um etw
feilschen mit jm wegen etw
♦ haggle with s.o. about s.th.
♦ haggle with s.o. over s.th.
feilschen um die Übernachtungspreise
♦ haggle about overnight rates
feine Küche, f
Haute Cuisine, f FR
♦ fine cuisine
♦ haute cuisine FR
feinen Gaumen haben
♦ have a fine palate

feinen Geschmackssinn haben
♦ have a fine sense of taste
feiner Pinkel, m
♦ dude AE sl
♦ toff dandy BE sl
feines Aroma, n
♦ delicate flavor AE
♦ delicate flavour BE
feines Essen, n
♦ fine food
Feingebäck, n
♦ pastry
feingehackt, adj
fein gehackt, adj
♦ finely chopped, adj
feingehackte Petersilie, f
♦ finely chopped parsley
feingerieben, adj
fein gerieben, adj
♦ finely grated, adj
feingeschnitten, adj
fein geschnitten, adj
fein in Scheiben geschnitten, adj
♦ finely sliced, adj
Feinkies, m
♦ fine shingle
Feinkiesstrand, m
♦ fine-shingle beach
♦ beach of fine shingle
Feinkost, f
♦ delicatessen pl
Feinkostgeschäft, n
Feinkosthandlung, f
Delikateßgeschäft, n
Delikatessengeschäft, n
Delikatessenhandlung, f
♦ delicatessen store AE
♦ delicatessen shop BE
♦ delicatessen
♦ deli coll
Feinkristallzucker, m
Kastorzucker, m
♦ castor sugar
♦ caster sugar
feinmachen sich
(gut anziehen)
♦ get dressed up
♦ dress up
feinsandige Bucht, f (groß)
♦ fine sandy bay
feinsandige Bucht, f (klein)
♦ fine sandy cove
feinsandiger Strand, m
♦ fine sand beach AE
♦ fine sand beach BE
fein schmecken
gut schmecken
♦ taste fine
♦ taste good
Feinschmecker, m
♦ gourmet
♦ gastronome
Feinschmeckerabendessen, n (Dinner)
Gourmetabendessen, n
♦ gourmet dinner
Feinschmeckerarrangement, n
Gourmetarrangement, n
♦ gourmet arrangement
Feinschmeckerart, adv gastr
nach Feinschmeckerart, adv gastr
♦ gourmet style, adv gastr

Feinschmeckerbankett, n
Feinschmeckerfestessen, n
Feinschmeckerfestmahl, n
♦ gourmet banquet
Feinschmeckerbistro, n
Gourmetbistro, n
♦ gourmet bistro
Feinschmeckerboutique, f
Gourmetboutique, f
♦ gourmet boutique
Feinschmeckerbuch, n
Gourmetbuch, n
♦ gourmet book
Feinschmeckerbüfett, n
Gourmetbüfett, n
♦ gourmet buffet
Feinschmeckeressen, n (generell)
Gourmetessen, n
♦ gourmet food
Feinschmeckeressen, n (Mahlzeit)
Feinschmeckermahl, n
Gourmetessen, n
Gourmetmahl, n
♦ gourmet meal
Feinschmeckerfest, n
Gourmetfest, n
♦ gourmet festival
Feinschmeckerfrühstück n
→ Gourmetfrühstück
Feinschmeckerführer, m
(Information)
Gourmetführer, m
♦ gourmet guide
Feinschmeckergaumen, m
Gourmetgaumen, m
Feinschmeckergeschmack, m
Gourmetgeschmack, m
♦ gourmet's palate
Feinschmeckergericht, n
Gourmetgericht, n
♦ gourmet dish
Feinschmeckergeschäft, n
Feinschmeckerladen, m
♦ gourmet store AE
♦ gourmet shop BE
Feinschmeckerköstlichkeiten, f pl
♦ gourmet delicacies pl
Feinschmeckerkreis m
♦ gastronomic circle
Feinschmeckerküche, f (Speisen)
Gourmetküche, f
♦ gourmet cooking
♦ gourmet cuisine
♦ gourmet gastronomy
Feinschmeckerkurzurlaub, m
Gourmetkurzurlaub, m
♦ gourmet break
Feinschmeckerlokal, n
Gourmetlokal, n
♦ gourmet place
♦ gourmet restaurant
Feinschmeckermahlzeit, f
→ Feinschmeckeressen
Feinschmeckermarkt, m
Gourmetmarkt, m
♦ gourmet market
Feinschmeckermenü, n
Gourmetmenü, n
♦ gourmet menu
Feinschmeckermittagessen, n
Gourmetmittagessen, n

Feinschmeckerparadies

- ◆ gourmet lunch
- ◆ gourmet luncheon

Feinschmeckerparadies, n
Gourmetparadies n
- ◆ gourmet's paradise

Feinschmeckerpicknick, n
Gourmetpicknick, n
- ◆ gourmet picnic

Feinschmeckerrestaurant, n
Gourmetrestaurant, n
- ◆ gourmet restaurant

Feinschmeckerrezept, n
Gourmetrezept n
- ◆ gourmet recipe

Feinschmeckerservice, m
Gourmetservice, m
- ◆ gourmet service

Feinschmeckertreff, m
Feinschmeckertreffpunkt, m
Gourmettreff, m
Gourmettreffpunkt, m
- ◆ gourmet haunt

Feinste vom Feinen, das, n
- ◆ very best, the
- ◆ the best that money can buy

Feldbett, n
- ◆ campcot AE
- ◆ cot AE
- ◆ camp-bed BE
- ◆ charpoy BE IND

Feldküche, f mil
- ◆ rolling kitchen mil

Fell über die Ohren ziehen jm
neppen jn
- ◆ fleece s.o.

Fels, m
- ◆ rock

Felsenbucht f (groß)
Felsbucht f
- ◆ rocky bay

Felsenbucht f (klein)
Felsbucht f
- ◆ rocky cove

Felsendom, m
(Jerusalem)
- ◆ Dome of the Rock, the

Felsgruppe, f
- ◆ group of rocks

felsig, adj
- ◆ rocky, adj

felsige Bucht, f
→ Felsenbucht

felsiger Strand, m
- ◆ rocky beach
- ◆ beach with rocks

felsiges Badeufer, n
(am Meer)
- ◆ rocky bathing shore

felsiges Moorland, n
- ◆ fell

Felsküste, f
- ◆ rocky coast

Felsmalerei, f
- ◆ rock painting

Felsmauer, f
- ◆ rock wall

Felsstrand, m
felsiger Strand, m
- ◆ beach with rocks
- ◆ rocky beach

Felsufer, n (Meer, Binnensee)
felsiges Ufer, n
- ◆ rocky shore

Felswand, f
- ◆ rock wall

Felsweg, m
- ◆ rock path

Fenchel, m
- ◆ fennel

Fenchelsalat, m
- ◆ fennel salad

Fenchelsoße, f
- ◆ fennel sauce

Fenchelsuppe, f
- ◆ fennel soup

Fenn, n
Marschland, n
Sumpfland, n
Flachmoor, n
Niedermoor, n
- ◆ fen

Fenster, n
- ◆ window

Fensterblick, m
- ◆ window view

fensterlos, adj
- ◆ windowless, adj

fensterlos, adv
- ◆ without a window, adv

fensterloses Zimmer, n
fensterloser Raum, m
- ◆ windowless room

Fenstermarkise, f
- ◆ window awning

Fenster mit buntem Glas, n
Buntglasfenster, n
- ◆ stained-glass window

Fenster mit Mittelpfosten, n
- ◆ mullioned window

Fenster muß offenbleiben
- ◆ window must stay open
- ◆ window has to stay open

Fensterplatz, m
- ◆ window seat
- ◆ seat by the window
- ◆ seat at the window

Fenster putzen
- ◆ clean a window
- ◆ wash a window AE

Fensterputzer m
- ◆ window cleaner
- ◆ window washer AE

Fensterrahmen, m
- ◆ window frame

Fenster schließt nicht richtig
- ◆ window won't close properly

Fenster steht offen
- ◆ window is open
- ◆ window stands open

Fenstertisch, m
- ◆ window table
- ◆ table at the window
- ◆ table by the window

Fenstertür, f
Verandatür, f
- ◆ French door AE
- ◆ French window BE
- ◆ floor-to-ceiling window

Ferien, pl (generell)
Urlaub, m
- ◆ holidays BE pl

- ◆ holiday BE
- ◆ vacation AE

Ferien, pl (Gericht, Hochschule, Parlament)
- ◆ vacation
- ◆ recess

Ferien, pl (Hochschule, Institution)
- ◆ recess

Ferienadresse, f
Urlaubsadresse, f
Ferienanschrift, f
Urlaubsanschrift, f
- ◆ holiday address BE
- ◆ vacation address AE

Ferienagentur, f
Urlaubsagentur, f
Ferienvermittlung, f
Urlaubsvermittlung, f
- ◆ holiday agency BE
- ◆ vacation agency AE

ferienähnlich, adj
urlaubsähnlich, adj
- ◆ holiday-like, adj BE
- ◆ vacation-like, adj AE

ferienähnliche Atmosphäre, f
urlaubsähnliche Atmosphäre, f
- ◆ holiday-like atmosphere BE
- ◆ vacation-like atmosphere AE

Ferienangebot, n (Palette)
Urlaubsangebot, n
- ◆ range of holidays BE
- ◆ range of vacations AE

Ferienanlage, f
Ferienkomplex, m
Urlaubsanlage, f
Urlaubskomplex, m
- ◆ holiday complex BE
- ◆ vacation complex AE
- ◆ resort AE
- ◆ resort complex

Ferienanlage mit Eigentumswohnungen, f
Ferienkomplex mit Eigentumswohnungen, m
- ◆ condominium resort AE

Ferienanlagenleiter, m
Leiter einer Ferienanlage, m
- ◆ resort manager

Ferienannehmlichkeit, f
Urlaubsannehmlichkeit, f
- ◆ holiday amenity BE
- ◆ vacation amenity AE

Ferienannonce, f
Ferienreklame, f
Urlaubsannonce, f
Urlaubsreklame, f
- ◆ holiday advertisement BE
- ◆ vacation advertisement AE

Ferienappartement, n
Urlaubsappartement, n
- ◆ holiday apartment BE
- ◆ vacation apartment AE

Ferienarrangement, n
Urlaubsarrangement, n
- ◆ holiday arrangement BE
- ◆ vacation arrangement AE

Ferienart, f
Urlaubsart, f
- ◆ holiday type BE
- ◆ type of holiday BE
- ◆ vacation type AE
- ◆ type of vacation AE

Ferienatmosphäre, f
Urlaubsatmosphäre, f

Ferienstimmung, f
Urlaubsstimmung, f
♦ holiday atmosphere BE
♦ vacation atmosphere AE
Ferien auf dem Bauernhof, pl
Urlaub auf dem Bauernhof, m
Urlaub am Bauernhof, m ÖST
Bauernhofurlaub, m
♦ farmhouse holiday BE
♦ farmhouse vacation AE
♦ farmhouse holidays BE pl
♦ farm holidays BE pl
♦ farm vacation AE
Ferien auf dem Wasser, pl
Urlaub auf dem Wasser, m
♦ holidays afloat BE pl
♦ water-borne holiday BE
♦ vacation afloat AE
♦ water-borne vacation AE
Ferienaufenthalt, m
Urlaubsaufenthalt, m
♦ holiday stay BE
♦ vacation stay AE
Ferienaufenthalt organisieren
Urlaubsaufenthalt organisieren
♦ organise a holiday stay BE
♦ organize a holiday stay BE
♦ organise a vacation stay AE
♦ organize a vacation stay AE
Ferien aufteilen
Urlaub aufteilen
♦ split holidays BE
♦ split vacations AE
Ferienausflug, m
Urlaubsausflug, m
♦ holiday excursion BE
♦ holiday outing BE
♦ vacation excursion AE
♦ vacation outing AE
Ferienausgaben, f pl
Urlaubsausgaben, f pl
♦ holiday spending BE
♦ holiday expenses BE pl
♦ vacation spending AE
♦ vacation expenses AE pl
Ferienbeschäftigung, f
Ferienaktivität, f
Urlaubsbeschäftigung, f
Urlaubsaktivität, f
♦ holiday activity BE
♦ vacation activity AE
Ferienbesucher, m
Urlaubsbesucher, m
♦ holiday visitor BE
♦ vacation visitor AE
Ferienbetreuungsdienst, m
(z.B. für Behinderte)
Urlaubsbetreuungsdienst, m
♦ holiday care service AE
♦ vacation care service BE
Ferienbuchung, f
Urlaubsbuchung, f
♦ holiday booking BE
♦ booking (of) a holiday BE
♦ vacation booking AE
♦ booking (of) a vacation AE
♦ vacation reservation AE
Ferienbudget, n
Urlaubsbudget, n
Ferienkasse, f
Urlaubskasse, f

♦ holiday budget BE
♦ vacation budget AE
Ferienbungalow, m
Urlaubsbungalow, m
♦ holiday bungalow BE
♦ vacation bungalow AE
Feriencamp, n
→ Ferienlager
Feriencamper, m
Urlaubscamper, m
♦ holiday camper BE
♦ vacation camper AE
Feriencamping, n
Urlaubscamping, n
♦ holiday camping BE
♦ vacation camping AE
Feriencampingplatz, m
Urlaubscampingplatz, m
♦ holiday campsite BE
♦ holiday camping site BE
♦ holiday camping ground BE
♦ vacation campsite AE
♦ vacation campground AE
Feriencaravan, m
Ferienwohnwagen, m
Urlaubscaravan, m
Urlaubswohnwagen, m
♦ holiday caravan BE
♦ vacation trailer AE
Ferienchalet, n
Urlaubschalet, n
♦ holiday chalet BE
♦ vacation chalet AE
Ferienclub, m
Urlaubsclub, m
♦ holiday club BE
♦ vacation club AE
Ferienclubbetreiber, m
Urlaubsclubbetreiber, m
♦ holiday club operator BE
♦ vacation club operator AE
Ferienclubdorf, n
Urlaubsclubdorf, n
♦ holiday club resort BE
♦ vacation club resort AE
Ferienclubgast, m
Urlaubsclubgast, m
♦ holiday club guest BE
♦ vacation club guest AE
Ferienclubmitglied, n
Urlaubsclubmitglied, n
♦ holiday club member BE
♦ vacation club member AE
Ferienclubmitgliedschaft, f
Urlaubsclubmitgliedschaft, f
♦ holiday club membership BE
♦ vacation club membership AE
Feriendia, n
Urlaubsdia, n
♦ holiday slide BE
♦ vacation slide AE
Feriendienst, m
Ferienservice, m
Urlaubsdienst, m
Urlaubsservice, m
Urlaubsdienstleistung, f
♦ holiday service BE
♦ vacation service AE
Feriendomizil, n
Urlaubsdomizil, n
♦ holiday domicile BE

♦ holiday residence BE
♦ vacation domicile AE
♦ vacation residence AE
Feriendorf, n
Urlaubsdorf, n
♦ holiday village BE
♦ resort village AE
♦ vacation village AE
♦ resort AE
Feriendorfanlage, f
Urlaubsdorfanlage, f
♦ holiday village complex BE
♦ vacation village complex AE
♦ resort complex
Feriendorf betreiben
Urlaubsdorf bestreiben
♦ operate a holiday village BE
♦ operate a resort village AE
♦ operate a resort AE
♦ operate a vacation village AE
♦ run a holiday village BE
Feriendorfbetreiber, m
Urlaubsdorfbetreiber, m
♦ holiday village operator BE
♦ resort village operator AE
♦ resort operator AE
♦ vacation village operator AE
Ferieneigentumswohnung, f
Urlaubseigentumswohnung, f
♦ freehold holiday flat BE
♦ freehold vacation apartment AE
Ferieneinrichtung, f
Urlaubseinrichtung, f
♦ holiday facility BE
♦ vacation facility AE
Ferienende, n
Urlaubsende, n
♦ end of the holiday BE
♦ end of one's holiday BE
♦ end of the vacation AE
♦ end of one's vacation AE
♦ end of a holiday
Ferienerfahrung, f
Urlaubserfahrung, f
♦ holiday experience BE
♦ vacation experience AE
Ferienerfahrung haben
Ferienerfahrung besitzen
Urlaubserfahrung haben
Urlaubserfahrung besitzen
♦ have holiday experience BE
♦ have vacation experience AE
Ferienerholungsort, m
→ Ferienort
Ferienerlebnis, n
Urlaubserlebnis, n
♦ holiday experience BE
♦ vacation experience AE
Ferienerwartung, f
Urlaubserwartung, f
♦ holiday expectation BE
♦ vacation expectation AE
Ferienessen, n
Urlaubsessen, n
♦ holiday meal BE
♦ vacation meal AE
Ferienfahrzeug, n
Urlaubsfahrzeug, n
♦ holiday vehicle BE
♦ vacation vehicle AE

Ferienfamilie

Ferienfamilie, f
Urlaubsfamilie, f
Urlauberfamilie, f
- **family on holiday** *BE*
- **family on vacation** *AE*

Ferienfieber, n
Urlaubsfieber, n
Reisefieber, n
- **holiday fever** *BE*
- **vacation fever** *AE*
- **travel nerves** *pl*

Ferienflug, m
Urlaubsflug, m
- **holiday flight** *BE*
- **vacation flight** *AE*

Ferienführer, m
(Information)
Urlaubsführer, m
- **vacation guide** *AE*
- **holiday guide** *BE*

Ferien für alle Preislagen, pl
Urlaube in allen Preislagen, m pl
- **holidays to suit every budget** *BE pl*
- **holidays to suit all pockets** *BE pl*
- **vacations to suit every budget** *AE pl*
- **vacations to suit all pockets** *AE pl*

Feriengast, f
Urlaubsgast, m
Urlauber, m
- **holiday guest** *BE*
- **vacation guest** *AE*
- **holidaymaker** *BE*
- **vacationer** *AE*

Feriengebiet, n
→ Ferienregion

Ferien gehen zu schnell vorbei
Urlaub geht zu schnell vorbei
- **holidays go too fast** *BE*
- **vacation goes too fast** *AE*

Feriengelegenheit, f
Urlaubsgelegenheit, f
- **holiday opportunity** *BE*
- **vacation opportunity** *AE*

Ferien genießen
Urlaub genießen
- **enjoy a holiday** *BE*
- **enjoy one's holiday** *BE*
- **enjoy a vacation** *AE*
- **enjoy one's vacation** *AE*

Feriengepäck, n
Urlaubsgepäck, n
- **holiday luggage** *BE*
- **vacation baggage** *AE*

Feriengeschäft, n
Urlaubsgeschäft, n
- **holiday business** *BE*
- **vacation business** *AE*

Feriengestaltung, f
Urlaubsgestaltung, f
- **organisation of a holiday** *BE*
- organisation of a holiday *BE*
- organisation of a vacation *AE*
- organization of a vacation *AE*
- use of one's holiday *BE*

Feriengesundheitsprüfliste, f
Urlaubsgesundheitsprüfliste, f
- **holiday healthcare checklist** *BE*
- vacation healthcare checklist *AE*

Feriengruppe, f
Urlaubergruppe, f

- **group of holidaymakers** *BE*
- group of vacationers *AE*

Ferien haben
Urlaub haben
- **have a holiday** *BE*
- have holidays *BE*
- have a vacation *AE*

Ferienhaus, n (Cottage)
Urlaubshaus, n
- **holiday cottage** *BE*
- vacation cottage *AE*
- cottage *AE*

Ferienhaus, n (generell)
Urlaubshaus, n
- **holiday home** *BE*
- vacation home *AE*

Ferienhaus, n (im Sommer)
→ Sommerhaus

Ferienhausanbieter, m
Urlaubshausanbieter, m
- **holiday home supplier** *BE*
- supplier of holiday homes *BE*
- vacation home supplier *AE*
- supplier of vacation homes *AE*

Ferienhausanlage, f
Ferienhauskomplex, m
Urlaubshausanlage, f
Urlaubshauskomplex, m
- **holiday home complex** *BE*
- vacation home complex *AE*
- summer house complex *AE*

Ferienhaus bauen
Urlaubshaus bauen
- **build a holiday home** *BE*
- build a vacation home *AE*

Ferienhausbesitz, m
Urlaubshausbesitz, m
- **holiday home ownership** *BE*
- vacation home ownership *AE*

Ferienhausbesitzer, m
Urlaubshausbesitzer, m
- **holiday home owner** *BE*
- owner of a holiday home *BE*
- vacation home owner *AE*
- owner of a vacation home *AE*

Ferienhaus buchen
Urlaubshaus buchen
- **book a holiday home** *BE*
- reserve a vacation home *AE*

Ferienhaus für Selbstversorger, n
Selbstverpflegungsferienhaus, n
- **self-catering holiday home** *BE*
- self-catering vacation home *AE*

Ferienhausgebiet, n
Urlaubshausgebiet, n
- **holiday home area** *BE*
- vacation home area *AE*
- summer house area *AE*

Ferienhauskatalog, m
Urlaubshauskatalog, m
- **holiday home catalogue** *BE*
- vacation home catalogue *AE*
- vacation home catalog *AE*

Ferienhausmarkt, m
Urlaubshausmarkt, m
- **holiday-home market** *BE*
- vacation-home market *AE*

Ferienhaus mieten
Urlaubshaus mieten
- **hire a holiday home** *BE*

- rent a holiday home *BE*
- rent a vacation home *AE*

Ferienhausprospekt, m
Urlaubshausprospekt, m
- **holiday home brochure** *BE*
- vacation home brochure *AE*

Ferienhaus reservieren
Urlaubshaus reservieren
- **reserve a holiday home** *BE*
- reserve a vacation home *AE*

Ferienhaustausch, m
Urlaubshaustausch, m
- **holiday home exchange** *BE*
- vacation home exchange *AE*

Ferienhaus vermieten
Urlaubshaus vermieten
- **let a holiday home** *BE*
- hire out a holiday home *BE*
- rent (out) a vacation home *AE*

Ferienhausvermietung, f
Urlaubshausvermietung, f
- **letting a holiday home** *BE*
- vacation home rental *AE*
- renting a vacation home *AE*

Ferienhausvermittler, m
Urlaubshausvermittler, m
- **holiday home agent** *BE*
- vacation home agent *AE*

Ferienhausvermittlung, f (Agentur)
Urlaubshausvermittlung, f
- **holiday home agency** *BE*
- vacation home agency *AE*

Ferienhausvermittlung, f (Tätigkeit)
Urlaubshausvermittlung, f
- **holiday home booking service** *BE*
- vacation home reservation service *AE*

Ferienheim, n
→ Ferienhaus

Ferienhochburg, f *humor*
Urlaubshochburg, f *humor*
- **popular holiday resort** *BE*
- popular vacation resort *AE*
- popular resort

Ferienhotel, n
Urlaubshotel, n
- **holiday hotel** *BE*
- vacation hotel *AE*

Ferienhotellerie, f
Urlaubshotellerie, f
- **holiday hotel industry** *BE*
- holiday hotel business *BE*
- vacation hotel industry *AE*
- vacation hotel business *AE*

Ferienhütte, f (Cottage)
- **vacation cottage** *AE*
- holiday cottage *BE*

Ferienhütte, f (Lodge)
Ferienlodge, f
Urlaubshütte, f
Urlaubslodge, f
- **holiday lodge** *BE*
- vacation lodge *AE*

Ferienidee, f
Urlaubsidee, f
- **holiday idea** *BE*
- vacation idea *AE*
- idea about/for/of a holiday *BE*
- idea about/for/of a vacation *BE*

Ferienimmobilie, f
Urlaubsimmobilie, f

◆ holiday property *BE*
◆ vacation property *AE*
Ferien in der Karibik, pl
Karibikferien, pl
Urlaub in der Karibik, m
Karibikurlaub, m
◆ **holiday in the Caribbean** *BE*
◆ vacation in the Caribbean *AE*
Ferien in der Sonne, pl
Urlaub in der Sonne, m
◆ **holiday in the sun** *BE*
◆ vacation in the sun *AE*
Ferien in freier Natur, pl
Urlaub in freier Natur, m
Ferien im Freien, pl
Urlaub im Freien, m
◆ **outdoor holiday** *BE*
◆ outdoor vacation *AE*
Ferieninsel, f
Urlaubsinsel, f
◆ **holiday island** *BE*
◆ vacation island *AE*
Ferienjet, m
Urlaubsjet, m
◆ **holiday jet** *BE*
◆ vacation jet *AE*
Ferienjob, m
Ferienarbeit, f
Urlaubsjob, m
Urlaubsarbeit, f
◆ **holiday job** *BE*
◆ vacation job *AE*
Ferienkarte, f (Fahrkarte, Eintritt)
Ferienfahrkarte, f
Urlaubskarte, f
Urlaubsfahrkarte, f
◆ **holiday ticket** *BE*
◆ vacation ticket *AE*
Ferienkarte, f (Postkarte)
→ Ferienpostkarte
Ferienkatalog, m
Urlaubskatalog, m
◆ **holiday catalogue** *BE*
◆ vacation catalogue *AE*
◆ vacation catalog *AE*
Ferienkatzenjammer, m
Feriendepression, f
Urlaubskatzenjammer, m
Urlaubsdepression, f
◆ **holiday blues** *BE*
◆ vacation blues *AE pl*
Ferienkind, n
Urlaubskind, n
◆ **child on holiday** *BE*
◆ child on vacation *AE*
Ferienkolonie, f
Ferienlager, n
Urlaubslager, n
Sommerlager, n
◆ **summer camp** *AE*
◆ vacation camp *AE*
◆ holiday camp *BE*
Ferienkreuzfahrt, f
Urlaubskreuzfahrt, f
◆ **holiday cruise** *BE*
◆ vacation cruise *AE*
Ferienkunde, m
Urlaubskunde, m
◆ **holiday customer** *BE*
◆ vacation customer *AE*
◆ vacation client *AE*

Ferienkurs, m
Urlaubskurs, m
Sommerkurs, m
Ferienlehrgang, m
Urlaubslehrgang, m
◆ **holiday course** *BE*
◆ vacation course *AE*
◆ summer course
Ferienkurs besuchen
Urlaubskurs besuchen
◆ **attend a holiday course** *BE*
◆ attend a vacation course *AE*
◆ attend a summer course
Ferienlager, n
Freizeitlager, n
Urlaubslager, n
◆ **holiday camp** *BE*
◆ summer camp *AE*
◆ vacation camp *AE*
Ferienlager betreiben
Urlaubslager betreiben
◆ **operate a holiday camp** *BE*
◆ operate a vacation camp *AE*
◆ operate a summer camp
Ferienlagerbetreiber, m
Urlaubslagerbetreiber, m
◆ **holiday camp operator** *BE*
◆ summer camp operator *AE*
◆ vacation camp operator *AE*
Ferienlagerleiter, m
Urlaubslagerleiter, m
◆ **holiday camp manager** *BE*
◆ summer camp director *AE*
◆ vacation camp director *AE*
Ferienlager organisieren
Ferienlager veranstalten
Urlaubslager organisieren
Urlaubslager veranstalten
◆ **organise a holiday camp** *BE*
◆ organise a summer camp *AE*
◆ organise a vacation camp *AE*
Ferienland, n
Urlaubsland, n
◆ **holiday country** *BE*
◆ vacation country *AE*
Ferienleben, n
Urlaubsleben, n
◆ **holiday life** *BE*
◆ vacation life *AE*
Ferien machen
Urlaub machen
◆ **take a holiday** *BE*
◆ holiday *BE*
◆ go vacationing *AE*
◆ be vacationing *AE*
◆ take a vacation *AE*
Ferienmarkt, m
Urlaubsmarkt, m
◆ **holiday market** *BE*
◆ vacation market *AE*
Ferienmarktanteil, m
Urlaubsmarktanteil, m
◆ **holiday market share** *BE*
◆ vacation market share *AE*
Ferienmiete, f
Urlaubsmiete, f
◆ **holiday rent** *BE*
◆ vacation rent *AE*
Ferien mit dem Auto, pl
Urlaub mit dem Auto, m
Autoferien, pl

Autourlaub, m
◆ **holiday by car** *BE*
◆ vacation by car *AE*
Ferien mit der Familie, pl
→ Familienferien
Ferienmonat, m
Urlaubsmonat, m
◆ **holiday month** *BE*
◆ vacation month *AE*
Ferienmotel, n
Urlaubsmotel, n
◆ **holiday motel** *BE*
◆ vacation motel *AE*
Feriennachfrage, f
Urlaubsnachfrage, f
◆ **holiday demand** *BE*
◆ demand for holidays *BE*
◆ vacation demand *AE*
◆ demand for vacations *AE*
Feriennachrichten, f pl
Urlaubsnachrichten, f pl
◆ **holiday news** *BE pl = sg*
◆ vacation news *AE pl = sg*
Ferienort, m (generell)
Urlaubsort, m
◆ **holiday resort** *BE*
◆ vacation resort *AE*
◆ resort
Ferienort, m (wo man gerade Ferien macht)
Urlaubsort, m
◆ **holiday place** *BE*
◆ vacation spot *AE*
◆ vacation place *BE*
◆ holiday spot *BE*
Ferienortabgabe, f
Urlaubsortabgabe, f
◆ **resort tax**
◆ resort levy
◆ local tax
◆ local levy
Ferienortanalyse, f
Urlaubsortanalyse, f
◆ **resort analysis**
◆ analysis of a resort
Ferienortanlage, f
Ferienortkomplex, m
Ferienanlage, f
Urlaubsortanlage, f
Urlaubsanlage, f
◆ **resort complex**
ferienortartiges Hotel, n
urlaubsortartiges Hotel, n
◆ **resort-type hotel**
Ferienortatmosphäre, f
Urlaubsortatmosphäre, f
◆ **holiday resort atmosphere** *BE*
◆ vacation resort atmosphere *AE*
◆ resort atmosphere
Ferienortaufenthalt, m
Urlaubsortaufenthalt, m
◆ **resort stay**
◆ stay at a resort
◆ stay in a resort
Ferienortbericht, m
Urlaubsortbericht, m
◆ **resort report**
Ferienortbeschreibung, f
Urlaubsortbeschreibung, f
◆ **description of a resort**
◆ resort description
◆ describing a resort

Ferienorthotel

Ferienorthotel, n
  Urlaubsorthotel, n
  ♦ resort hotel
Ferienortinformation, f
  Urlaubsortinformation, f
  Ortsinformation, f
  ♦ resort information
  ♦ information about a resort
  ♦ information on a resort
Ferienortlandhaus, n
  Landhaus in einem Ferienort, n
  Urlaubsortlandhaus, n
  Landhaus in einem Urlaubsort, n
  ♦ resort cottage
Ferienort mit Campingeinrichtungen, m
  Urlaubsort mit Campingeinrichtungen, m
  ♦ resort with camping facilities
Ferienort planen
  Urlaubsort planen
  ♦ plan a resort
Ferienortplanung, f
  Urlaubsortplanung, f
  ♦ resort planning
  ♦ planning a resort
Ferienortreferent, m
  Urlaubsortreferent, m
  ♦ resort officer
Ferienortwerbung, f
  Urlaubsortwerbung, f
  ♦ resort promotion
  ♦ promotion of a resort
Ferienortzentrum, n
  Urlaubsortzentrum, n
  ♦ resort center AE
  ♦ resort centre BE
Ferienpaket, n
  (Information)
  Urlaubspaket, n
  ♦ holiday pack BE
  ♦ vacation pack AE
Ferienparadies, n
  Urlaubsparadies, n
  ♦ holiday paradise BE
  ♦ vacation paradise AE
Ferienpark, m
  Urlaubspark, m
  ♦ holiday park BE
  ♦ vacation park AE
Ferienpension, f
  Urlaubspension, f
  ♦ holiday guest-house BE
  ♦ vacation guesthouse AE
  ♦ private vacation hotel AE
  ♦ private holiday hotel BE
Ferien planen
  Urlaub planen
  ♦ plan a holiday BE
  ♦ plan a vacation AE
Ferienplatz, m (Camping)
  Urlaubsplatz, m
  ♦ holiday site BE
  ♦ vacation site AE
Ferienplatz, m (Ort)
  Ferienort, m
  Urlaubsplatz, m
  Urlaubsort, m
  ♦ holiday spot BE
  ♦ holiday place BE
  ♦ vacation spot AE
  ♦ vacation place AE

Ferienpostkarte, f
  Ferienkarte, f
  Urlaubspostkarte, f
  Urlaubskarte, f
  ♦ holiday postcard BE
  ♦ vacation postcard AE
  ♦ card from s.o. on holiday BE
  ♦ card from s.o. on vacation AE
Ferienpreis, m (Auszeichnung)
  Urlaubspreis, m
  ♦ holiday prize BE
  ♦ vacation prize AE
Ferienpreis, m (Kosten)
  Urlaubspreis, m
  ♦ holiday price BE
  ♦ holiday rate BE
  ♦ vacation price AE
  ♦ vacation rate AE
  ♦ price of a holiday BE
Ferienpriorität, f
  Urlaubspriorität, f
  ♦ holiday priority BE
  ♦ vacation priority AE
Ferienprogramm, n
  Urlaubsprogramm, n
  ♦ holiday programme BE
  ♦ vacation program AE
Ferienprospekt, m
  Urlaubsprospekt, m
  ♦ holiday brochure BE
  ♦ vacation brochure AE
Ferienquartier, n
  Ferienunterkunft, f
  Urlaubsquartier, n
  ♦ holiday quarters BE pl
  ♦ vacation quarters AE pl
Ferienrabatt, m
  Urlaubsrabatt, m
  ♦ holiday discount BE
  ♦ vacation discount AE
Ferienregion, f (groß)
  Urlaubsregion, f
  Feriengebiet, n
  Urlaubsgebiet, n
  ♦ holiday region BE
  ♦ vacation region AE
Ferienregion, f (klein)
  Urlaubsregion, f
  Feriengebiet, n
  Urlaubsgebiet, n
  ♦ holiday area BE
  ♦ vacation area AE
Ferienreise, f
  Urlaubsreise, f
  ♦ holiday trip BE
  ♦ vacation trip AE
  ♦ holiday tour BE
  ♦ vacation tour AE
Ferienreisemarkt, m
  Urlaubsreisemarkt, m
  ♦ holiday travel market BE
  ♦ vacation travel market AE
Ferienreisemesse, f
  Urlaubsreisemesse, f
  ♦ holiday travel fair BE
  ♦ vacation travel fair AE
Ferienreisen, n
  Ferienreiseverkehr, m
  Urlaubsreisen, n
  Urlaubsreiseverkehr, m

  ♦ holiday travel BE
  ♦ vacation travel AE
Ferienreisender, m
  Urlaubsreisender, m
  ♦ holiday traveller BE
  ♦ vacation traveler AE
Ferienreise stornieren
  Ferienreise streichen
  Ferienreise absagen
  Urlaubsreise stornieren
  Urlaubsreise absagen
  ♦ cancel a holiday trip BE
  ♦ cancel a holiday tour BE
  ♦ cancel a vacation trip AE
  ♦ cancel a vacation tour AE
Ferienreiseverkehrsmittel, n
  Urlaubsreiseverkehrsmittel, n
  ♦ means of holiday transport BE
  ♦ means of vacation transportation AE
Ferienresidenz, f
  Urlaubsresidenz, f
  ♦ holiday residence BE
  ♦ vacation residence AE
Ferienrest, m
  Urlaubsrest, m
  Rest der Ferien, m
  Rest des Urlaubs, m
  ♦ rest of the holiday BE
  ♦ remainder of one's holiday BE
  ♦ rest of the vacation AE
  ♦ remainder of one's vacation AE
Ferienritual, n
  Urlaubsritual, n
  ♦ holiday ritual BE
  ♦ vacation ritual AE
Ferienromanze, f
  Urlaubsromanze, f
  ♦ holiday romance BE
  ♦ vacation romance AE
Ferienroutine, f
  Urlaubsroutine, f
  ♦ holiday routine BE
  ♦ vacation routine AE
Feriensaison, f
  Urlaubssaison, f
  ♦ holiday season BE
  ♦ vacation season AE
Ferienschlafraum, m
  Urlaubsschlafraum, m
  ♦ holiday bedroom BE
  ♦ vacation bedroom AE
Feriensegment, n
  Urlaubssegment, n
  ♦ holiday segment BE
  ♦ vacation segment AE
Ferienservice, m
  → Feriendienst
Feriensex, m
  Urlaubssex, m
  ♦ holiday sex BE
  ♦ vacation sex AE
Ferien sind voll abgesichert
  (bei Insolvenz des Reiseveranstalters)
  Urlaub ist voll abgesichert
  ♦ holiday is fully bonded BE
Feriensommer, m
  Urlaubssommer, m
  ♦ holiday summer BE
  ♦ vacation summer AE

Ferienwohnungskatalog

Ferienstadt, f (Großstadt)
Urlaubsstadt, f
♦ resort city
Ferienstadt, f (kleine Stadt)
Urlaubsstadt, f
♦ resort town
Ferienstimmung, f (Atmosphäre)
→ Ferienatmosphäre
Ferienstimmung, f (einer Person)
Urlaubsstimmung, f
♦ holiday mood BE
♦ vacation mood AE
Ferien stornieren
Urlaub stornieren
Ferien absagen
Urlaub absagen
♦ cancel a holiday BE
♦ cancel a vacation AE
Ferienstraße, f
Urlaubsstraße, f
♦ holiday road BE
♦ holiday route BE
♦ vacation road AE
♦ vacation route AE
Ferienstudie, f
Urlaubsstudie, f
♦ holiday study BE
♦ vacation study AE
Ferientag, m
Urlaubstag, m
♦ day of one's holiday BE
♦ holiday BE
♦ day of one's vacation AE
♦ vacation day AE
Ferientarif, m
Urlaubstarif, m
♦ holiday tariff BE
♦ holiday rates BE pl
♦ holiday rate BE
♦ holiday terms BE pl
♦ vacation tariff AE
Ferientermin, m
Feriendatum, n
Urlaubstermin, m
Urlaubsdatum, n
♦ holiday date BE
♦ date of holiday BE
♦ vacation date AE
♦ date of vacation AE
Ferientourismus, m
Urlaubstourismus, m
♦ holiday tourism BE
♦ vacation tourism AE
Ferientourist, m
Urlaubstourist, m
♦ holiday tourist BE
♦ vacation tourist AE
Ferientrip, m
→ Ferienreise
Ferienübernachtung, f (generell)
Urlaubsübernachtung, f
♦ holiday night BE
♦ vacation night AE
Ferienübernachtung, f (Statistik)
Urlaubsübernachtung, f
♦ holiday night spent BE
♦ vacation night spent AE
Ferienumgebung, f
Urlaubsumgebung, f
♦ holiday environment BE
♦ holiday setting BE

♦ vacation environment AE
♦ vacation setting AE
Ferien unterbrechen
Urlaub unterbrechen
♦ interrupt one's holiday BE
♦ break one's holiday BE
♦ interrupt one's vacation AE
♦ break one's vacation AE
Ferienunterhaltung, f
Urlaubsunterhaltung, f
♦ holiday entertainment BE
♦ vacation entertainment AE
Ferienunterkunft, f
Urlaubsunterkunft, f
♦ holiday accommodation BE
♦ vacation accommodation AE
♦ vacation lodging AE
Ferienunterkunft für Selbstversorger, f
Ferienunterkunft für Selbstverpfleger, f
Urlaubsunterkunft für Selbstversorger, f
Urlaubsunterkunft für Selbstverpfleger, f
♦ self-catering holiday accommodation BE
♦ self-catering vacation accommodation AE
Ferienurlauber, m
Urlauber, m
Feriengast, m
♦ holidaymaker BE
♦ vacationer AE
Ferienverbrechen, n
Urlaubsverbrechen, n
♦ holiday crime BE
♦ vacation crime AE
Ferien verbringen in X
Urlaub verbringen in X
♦ spend one's holiday in X BE
♦ spend one's holiday at X BE
♦ spend one's vacation in X AE
♦ spend one's vacation at X AE
♦ spend a holiday in/at X BE
Ferienvergnügen, n
Urlaubsvergnügen, n
♦ holiday pleasure BE
♦ vacation pleasure AE
♦ holiday enjoyment BE
♦ vacation enjoyment AE
Ferienverkehr, m
Urlaubsverkehr, m
♦ holiday traffic BE
♦ vacation traffic AE
Ferien verleben
Ferien verbringen
Urlaub verleben
Urlaub verbringen
♦ spend a holiday BE
♦ have a holiday BE
♦ spend a vacation AE
♦ have a vacation AE
Ferienvermittlung, f (Agentur)
→ Ferienagentur
Ferienvilla, f
Urlaubsvilla, f
♦ holiday villa BE
♦ vacation villa AE
Ferienvorschlag, m
Urlaubsvorschlag, m
♦ holiday suggestion BE
♦ vacation suggestion AE
Ferienvorschlag machen
Urlaubsvorschlag machen
♦ make a holiday suggestion BE
♦ make a vacation suggestion AE

Ferienwagen, m
Ferienauto, n
Ferien-Pkw, m
Urlaubswagen, m
Urlaubsauto, n
♦ holiday car BE
♦ vacation car AE
Ferienwetter, n
Urlaubswetter, n
♦ holiday weather BE
♦ vacation weather AE
Ferienwinter, m
Urlaubswinter, m
♦ holiday winter BE
♦ vacation winter AE
Ferienwoche, f
Urlaubswoche, f
♦ holiday week BE
♦ vacation week AE
Ferienwochenende, n
Urlaubswochenende, n
♦ holiday weekend BE
♦ vacation weekend AE
Ferienwohnanlage, f
Urlaubswohnanlage, f
♦ holiday housing estate BE
♦ vacation resort AE
♦ vacation condominium AE
Ferienwohnung, f
Fewo, f
Urlaubswohnung, f
♦ holiday flat BE
♦ vacation apartment AE
Ferienwohnung mit allem Komfort, f
Fewo mit allem Komfort, f
Urlaubswohnung mit allem Komfort, f
♦ holiday flat with all modern conveniences BE
♦ holiday apartment with all modern conveniences AE
Ferienwohnung mit Selbstversorgung, f
Fewo mit Selbstversorgung, f
Urlaubswohnung mit Selbstversorgung, f
♦ self-catering holiday flat BE
♦ self-catering vacation apartment AE
Ferienwohnungsanbieter, m
Fewo-Anbieter, m
Urlaubswohnungsanbieter, m
♦ holiday flat supplier BE
♦ supplier of holiday flats BE
♦ vacation apartment supplier AE
♦ supplier of vacation apartments AE
Ferienwohnungsanlage, f
Ferienwohnungskomplex, m
Urlaubswohnungsanlage, f
Urlaubswohnungskomplex, m
♦ holiday flat complex BE
♦ vacation apartment complex AE
Ferienwohnungsbereich, m (konkret)
Ferienwohnungsgebiet, n
Urlaubswohnungsbereich, m
Urlaubswohnungsgebiet, n
♦ holiday flat area BE
♦ vacation apartment area AE
Ferienwohnungsbereich, m (Sektor)
→ Ferienwohnungssektor
Ferienwohnungsgeschäft, n
Urlaubswohnungsgeschäft, n
♦ holiday flat business BE
♦ vacation apartment business AE
Ferienwohnungskatalog, m
Fewo-Katalog, m

Ferienwohnungsprospekt

Urlaubswohnungskatalog, m
- holiday flat catalogue BE
- vacation apartment catalogue AE
- vacation apartment catalog AE

Ferienwohnungsprospekt, m
Fewo-Prospekt, m
Urlaubswohnungsprospekt, m
- holiday flat brochure BE
- vacation apartment brochure AE

Ferienwohnungssektor, m
Ferienwohnungsbereich, m
Urlaubswohnungssektor, m
Urlaubswohnungsbereich, m
- holiday flat sector BE
- vacation apartment sector AE

Ferienwohnwagenpark, m
Feriencaravanpark, m
Urlaubswohnwagenpark, m
Urlaubscaravanpark, m
- holiday caravan park BE
- vacation trailer park AE

Ferienzeit, f
Urlaubszeit, f
- holiday time Be
- holiday period BE
- holiday season BE
- vacation time AE
- vacation period AE

Ferienzeitraum, m
Ferienzeit, f
Urlaubszeitraum, m
Urlaubszeit, f
- holiday period BE
- vacation period AE

Ferienzentrum, n
Urlaubszentrum, n
- holiday centre BE
- vacation center AE

Ferienzentrum betreiben
Urlaubszentrum betreiben
- operate a holiday centre BE
- operate a vacation center AE

Ferienzentrumbetreiber, m
Urlaubszentrumbetreiber, m
- holiday centre operator BE
- vacation center operator AE

Fernbedienung, f
(für technische Geräte)
- remote control

Fernbus m
- long-distance bus AE
- long-distance coach BE

Ferner Osten, m
Fernost
- Far East, the

Fernfahrer, m
(Lkw-Fahrer)
- long-distance truck driver AE
- long-distance trucker AE
- long-haul truck driver AE
- (long-haul) trucker AE
- long-distance lorry driver BE

Fernfahrercafé, n
Fernfahrerimbißstube, f
- truck stop cafe AE
- truckers' cafe AE
- lorry drivers' café BE
- transport café BE

Fernfahrergaststätte, f
- truck stop restaurant AE
- lorry drivers' restaurant BE

- lorry drivers' café BE
- truckers' restaurant AE

Fernfahrt, f
- long-haul trip
- long-distance trip

Fernflug, m
Langstreckenflug, m
- long-haul flight
- long-distance flight

Ferngespräch, n
- long-distance call AE
- trunk call BE

Fernmarkt, m
- long-haul market

Fernost
→ Ferner Osten

fernöstliche Spezialität, f
- Far East speciality
- Far East specialty AE

Fernosturlaub, m
- Far East vacation AE
- Far East holiday BE

Fernostziel, n
- Far East destination

Fernpauschalreise, f
- long-distance package tour
- long-haul package tour

Fernreise, f
- long-distance tour
- long-haul tour
- long-distance journey
- long-haul journey

Fernreisebus m
- long-distance tour bus AE
- long-distance touring coach BE

Fernreisen, n
Fernreiseverkehr, m
- long-distance travel
- long-haul travel

Fernreisender, m
- long-distance traveller
- long-distance traveler AE

Fernreisespezialist, m
- long-distance travel specialist
- long-haul travel specialist

Fernreiseurlaub, m
- long-distance vacation AE
- long-haul vacation AE
- long-distance holiday BE
- long-haul holiday BE

Fernreiseveranstalter, m
- long-distance tour operator
- long-haul tour operator

Fernreiseverkehr, m
- long-haul travel
- long-distance travel

Fernreiseziel, n
Ferndestination, f
- long-distance travel destination
- long-distance destination
- long-haul destination

Fernschreibdienst, m
→ Telexdienst

Fernschreiber, m
- teletypewriter
- teleprinter
- telex

Fernschreibraum, m
→ Telexraum

Fernschreibzimmer n
→ s. Fernschreibraum

fernschriftlich stornieren etw
- cancel s.th. by telex
- make a cancellation by telex
- make a cancelation by telex AE

Fernsehanschluß, m
(Antennensteckdose)
TV-Anschluß, m
- TV connection
- TV socket BE
- television connection
- television socket BE

Fernsehantenne, f
- television antenna AE
- TV antenna AE
- television aerial BE
- TV aerial BE

Fernsehapparat, m
→ Fernsehempfänger

Fernsehbenutzung, f
- use of TV

Fernsehbenutzungsgebühr f
- charge for the use of TV
- fee for the use of TV

Fernsehbereich, m
- television area
- TV area

Fernsehclubzimmer, n
→ Fernsehsalon

Fernsehecke, f
- TV corner
- television corner

Fernsehempfänger, m
Fernsehgerät, n
Fernsehapparat, m
- television set
- TV set

fernsehen
- watch TV
- watch television

Fernsehen, n
- television
- TV
- telly coll

Fernseher, m
- TV set
- television set
- TV

Fernseher hat den Geist aufgegeben
- television has packed up
- TV has packed up

Fernseher in allen Zimmern
- All rooms with TV
- All rooms with television

Fernseher ist kaputt coll
- TV is broken
- television is broken

Fernseh-Film-Raum, m
- TV/movie room AE
- television/movie room AE
- TV/cinema room BE
- television/cinema room BE

Fernsehgebühr, f
- television fee
- TV fee

Fernsehgerät mieten
Fernseher mieten
- rent a television set
- rent a TV
- hire a television set BE
- hire a TV BE

Fernsehgerät vermieten
Fernseher vermieten
♦ **rent (out) a television set**
♦ **rent (out) a TV**
♦ **hire out a television set** *BE*
♦ **hire out a TV** *BE*
Fernsehgroßprojektion, f
♦ **large screen TV projection**
Fernsehkamera, f
♦ **television camera**
♦ **TV camera**
Fernsehkoch, m
♦ **TV cook**
Fernsehmietgebühr, f
♦ **television rental charge** *AE*
♦ **TV rental charge** *AE*
♦ **television hire charge** *BE*
♦ **TV hire charge** *BE*
Fernsehmoderator, m
♦ **presenter** *BE*
Fernsehmöglichkeit, f
♦ **possibility of watching TV**
♦ possibility of watching television
Fernsehmonitor, m
♦ **TV monitor**
Fernsehprogramm, n
♦ **TV program** *AE*
♦ television program *AE*
♦ **TV programme** *BE*
♦ television programme *BE*
Fernsehprogramm ansehen
♦ **watch a TV program** *AE*
♦ watch a television program *AE*
♦ **watch a TV programme** *BE*
♦ watch a television programme *BE*
Fernsehrechte, n pl
♦ **television rights** *pl*
♦ **TV rights** *pl*
Fernsehrechte verkaufen
♦ **sell television rights**
♦ sell TV rights
Fernsehreklame, f
→ Fernwehwerbung
Fernsehsalon, m
♦ **TV lounge**
♦ television lounge
Fernsehsalon für Hausgäste, m
♦ **residents' TV lounge**
♦ residents' television lounge
♦ TV lounge for residents
Fernsehturm, m
♦ **television tower**
♦ **TV tower**
Fernsehturmrestaurant, n
♦ **TV-tower restaurant**
♦ television-tower restaurant
Fernsehübertragungsanlage, f
hausinterne Fernsehübertragung, f
♦ **closed-circuit television**
♦ closed-circuit TV
Fernseh-Video-Raum, m
♦ **TV/video room**
♦ television/video room
Fernsehwerbung, f
Fernsehreklame, f
♦ **television advertising**
♦ TV advertising
Fernsehzimmer für Hausgäste, n
♦ **residents' TV room**
♦ residents' television room
♦ TV room for residents

Fernsprechamt, n (Postamt)
Fernsprechvermittlung, f
♦ **telephone exchange**
♦ **exchange**
Fernsprechanschluß, m
→ Telefonanschluß
Fernsprechraum, m
→ Telefonraum
Fernsprechvermittlung, f (eines Unternehmens)
Fernsprechzentrale, f
♦ **telephone switchboard**
♦ **switchboard**
Fernsprechvermittlungsdienst, m (Hotel)
Fernsprechvermittlung f
Telefonvermittlung f
♦ **switchboard service**
Fernsprechzelle, f
♦ **telephone box**
♦ telephone booth *BE*
♦ telephone call box *BE*
Fernsprechzentrale, f (Postamt)
→ Fernsprechvermittlung
Fernstraße, f
♦ **trunk road**
Fernstrecke, f
Fernroute, f
♦ **long-distance route**
♦ long-haul route
♦ trunk route *BE*
Fernstreckenkarte, f
♦ **long-haul ticket**
Ferntourismus, m
♦ **long-haul tourism**
Ferntourist, m
♦ **long-haul tourist**
Fernurlaub, m
♦ **long-haul vacation** *AE*
♦ long-haul holiday *BE*
Fernurlaubsreisen, n
Fernurlaubsreiseverkehr, m
♦ **long-haul vacation traffic** *AE*
♦ long-haul holiday traffic *BE*
Fernurlaubsspezialist, m
♦ **long-haul vacation specialist** *AE*
♦ long-haul holiday specialist *BE*
Fernveranstalter, m
(Reiseveranstalter)
♦ **long-haul operator**
♦ long-distance operator
Fernwanderer, m
→ Langstreckenwanderer
Fernwanderung, f
♦ **long-distance walk**
♦ long-distance hike
Fernwanderweg, m
♦ **long-distance walkers' route**
♦ long-distance footpath
♦ long-distance trail
♦ long-distance hiking route
Fernweg, m
♦ **long-distance path**
♦ long-distance trail
♦ long-distance footpath
Fernziel, n
Ferndestination, f
♦ **long-distance destination**
♦ long-haul destination
Fernzug, m
♦ **long-distance train**
♦ long-haul train

fertig aufgeschlagenes Zelt, n
♦ **ready-erected tent**
Fertigbauweise, f
♦ **prefabricated construction**
Fertiggericht, n
fertiges Gericht, n
♦ **ready-cooked dish**
♦ ready-to-serve dish
♦ ready dish
♦ ready-to-serve meal
♦ instant meal
Fertighaus, n
♦ **prefabricated house**
♦ prefab *coll*
Fertigmenü n
♦ **ready-to-serve menu**
♦ ready menu
♦ instant menu
Fertignahrung, f
♦ **convenience food**
♦ convenience foods *pl*
Fertignahrungsindustrie, f
♦ **convenience food industry**
Fertigprodukt, n (Speise)
♦ **convenience product**
Fertigstand m
(Ausstellung)
♦ **prefabricated stand**
fertigstellen etw termingerecht
♦ **complete s.th. on schedule**
fertigwerden mit dem Jetlag
♦ **cope with jetlag**
fertigwerden mit einer Reisegruppenankunft
♦ **cope with a tour arrival**
Fesselballon, m
♦ **captive balloon**
Fest, n (Feier)
→ Feier
Fest, n (Feiertag)
→ Feiertag
Fest, n (kirchlich)
Festtag, m
kirchlicher Feiertag, m
♦ **feast**
Fest, n (Party)
→ Party
Festabend, m (festlich)
festlicher Abend m
♦ **festive evening**
♦ festive night
Festabend, m (Party)
→ Partyabend
Fest abhalten (Festival)
Festival abhalten
Festspiele abhalten
♦ **hold a festival**
Fest abhalten (Party)
Party abhalten
♦ **hold a party**
Fest absagen (Festival)
Festival absagen
♦ **cancel a festival**
Festakt, m
festliche Zeremonie, f
♦ **solemn ceremony**
♦ ceremonial act
♦ ceremony
Festakt ausrichten (als Gastgeber)
Gastgeber sein bei einer Feierlichkeit
Feierstunde ausrichten
♦ **host a ceremony**

festangestellt

festangestellt, adj
  fest angestellt, adj
  ♦ permanently employed, adj
festangestelltes Personal, n
  ♦ permanently employed staff
  ♦ permanently employed personnel
Festanlaß, m
  festlicher Anlaß, m
  ♦ gala occasion
  ♦ festive occasion
Festansprache, f
  Festrede f
  ♦ ceremonial address
  ♦ ceremonial speech
Festansprache halten
  → Ansprache halten
Fest arrangieren (Feier)
  Feier arrangieren
  ♦ arrange a celebration
Fest auf die Beine stellen *fam*
  Fest organisieren
  Party auf die Beine stellen *fam*
  ♦ lay on a party *fam*
Festaufführung, f (im Theater etc.)
  → Galaaufführung
Fest aufpeppen, sl
  Fest aufmöbeln, coll
  Fest lebhafter machen
  ♦ jazz up a party *sl*
Festauftakt, m
  → Festbeginn
Festausklang, m
  → Festende
Festausschuß, m
  Festkomitee, n
  Festspielausschuß, m
  Festspielkomitee, n
  ♦ festival committee
Festausstellung, f
  ♦ festival exhibition
  ♦ festival exhibit *AE*
Festbankett, n
  ♦ gala banquet
Festbankett zum Gedenken an etw, n
  Festbankett zu etw
  ♦ gala banquet to commemorate s.th.
  ♦ gala banquet commemorating s.th.
Fest begehen
  feiern
  ♦ celebrate
Festbeleuchtung, f
  festliche Beleuchtung, f
  ♦ gala illumination
  ♦ festive illumination
Festbesuch, m (Festival)
  ♦ festival visit
  ♦ visit to a festival
Festbesucher, m (Festival)
  Festivalbesucher, m
  Festspielbesucher, m
  ♦ festival visitor
  ♦ visitor to a festival
  ♦ festivalgoer *AE*
  ♦ festival-goer *BE*
Festbesucher, m (Party)
  → Partybesucher
Festbuchung, f
  → feste Buchung
Festdekoration, f
  → Festschmuck

feste Anmeldung, f
  ♦ firm registration
  ♦ definite registration
feste Buchung f
  Festbuchung f
  ♦ firm booking
  ♦ definite booking
feste Gebühr f
  Festgebühr f
  ♦ fixed charge
  ♦ fixed fee
festeingebaut, adj
  eingebaut, adj
  ♦ built-in, adj
  ♦ fixed, adj
fest eingebautes Mobiliar, n
  fest eingebaute Möbel, n pl
  ♦ fixed furniture *sg*
  ♦ fitted furniture *sg*
Festeinladung, f
  Einladung zu einem Fest, f
  ♦ invitation to a festival
feste Kundschaft, f
  ♦ permanent customers *pl*
  ♦ regulars customers *pl*
Festempfang, m
  festlicher Empfang, m
  ♦ festive reception
  ♦ gala reception
feste Nahrung, f
  ♦ solid food
festen Bestandteil der Veranstaltung bilden
  ♦ form an integral part of the event
  ♦ form an integral part of the function
Festende, n
  ♦ end of a festival
  ♦ end of a fête (fete)
  ♦ end of a celebration
  ♦ end of a party
fester Bestandteil der Veranstaltung, m
  ♦ integral part of the event
  ♦ integral part of the function
feste Reservierung, f
  ♦ firm reservation
  ♦ definite reservation
Festerlös, m
  → Erlös eines Fests
feste Route, f
  feste Strecke, f
  ♦ set route
fester Preis, m
  Festpreis, m
  ♦ set price
  ♦ fixed price
  ♦ fixed rate
  ♦ firm price
fester Reisetermin, m
  festes Reisedatum, n
  ♦ fixed travel date
fester Trend, m
  ♦ firm trend
fester Wohnsitz, m *jur*
  ♦ permanent residence
  ♦ fixed abode *jur*
  ♦ fixed address
festes Inventar, n
  fest installierte Gegenstände, m pl
  eingebaute Anlagen, f pl
  festes Zubehör, n
  feste Einbauten, m pl
  ♦ fixtures *pl*

festes Menü, n
  ♦ set menu
festes Partymenü, n
  ♦ set party menu
festes Personal, n
  Stammpersonal, n
  ♦ permanent staff
  ♦ permanent personnel
festes Programm, n
  ♦ set program *AE*
  ♦ set programme *BE*
festes Schuhwerk, n
  feste Schuhe, m pl
  ♦ sturdy shoes *pl*
Festessen, n (Bankett)
  → Bankett
Festessen, n (Galadiner)
  → Galadiner
Festessen, n (generell)
  ♦ celebration dinner
Festessen, n (Schmaus)
  → Schmaus
Festessen geben für jn
  → Bankett geben für jn
feste Stiefel, m pl
  kräftige Stiefel, m pl
  ♦ sturdy boots *pl*
feste Unterkunft haben
  (Gegensatz zu Zelt etc)
  ♦ sleep under a roof
feste Wand, f
  steife Wand, f
  ♦ rigid wall
Fest findet statt (Festival)
  → Festival findet statt
Festgast, m (Party)
  ♦ guest at a party
  ♦ partygoer *AE*
  ♦ party-goer *BE*
Festgebühr, f
  feste Gebühr, f
  ♦ fixed fee
  ♦ fixed charge
Festgelage, n
  → Festessen
Festgelände, n
  Festspielgelände, n
  Festivalgelände, n
  ♦ festival ground
  ♦ festival grounds *AE pl = sg*
Festgericht, n
  festliches Gericht, n
  ♦ festive dish
Festgesang, n
  ♦ festive singing
  ♦ festive song
festgesetzt, adj
  vereinbart, adj
  ♦ stipulated, adj
festgesetzte Anmeldungszeit, f
  ♦ stipulated registration period
festgesetzter Aufenthaltsbeginn, m
  ♦ date fixed for (the) start of (the) stay
Fest gestalten (Festival)
  Fest arrangieren
  Festspiele gestalten
  Fest gestalten
  ♦ arrange a festival
Festgrüße, m pl
  (Aufschrift auf Karten)

Grüße zum Fest, m pl
 ♦ season's greetings
Festhalle, f (generell)
Festsaal, m
 ♦ auditorium AE
 ♦ hall
Festhalle, f (hist. für Bankette)
Bankhalle, f
 ♦ banqueting hall
Fest hat eine besondere Note
 ♦ celebration has a special flavor AE
 ♦ celebration has a special flavour BE
Festhaus, n
 ♦ banquet house
 ♦ banqueting house BE
fest installierter Caravan, m
 → stationärer Caravan
Festival, n
Festspiele, n pl
Festwoche, f
Festspielwoche, f
 ♦ festival
Festival besuchen
 ♦ visit a festival
Festival bringt 123 Besucher
Festspiele bringen 123 Besucher
Fest bringt 123 Besucher
 ♦ festival brings 123 visitors
Festival eröffnen
Festspiele eröffnen
 ♦ open a festival
Festival findet statt (im September)
Festspiele finden statt (im September)
Fest findet statt (im September)
 ♦ festival takes place (in September)
Festival findet statt vom 20. bis 27. Juni
Festspiele finden vom 20. bis 27. Juni statt
Fest findet vom 20. bis 27. Juni statt
 ♦ festival takes place from 20 to 27 June
Festival geht vom 1. bis 10. Mai
 ♦ festival runs from 1 to 10 May
Festival inszenieren
Festspiele inszenieren
Fest inszenieren
Festival ausrichten
 ♦ stage a festival
Festival organisieren
 → Festival veranstalten
Festival planen
Fest planen
Festspiele planen
 ♦ plan a festival
Festivalreise, f
 → Festspielreise
Festival veranstalten
Festival organisieren
Festspiele veranstalten
Festspiele organisieren
 ♦ organise a festival
 ♦ organize a festival
Festivität, f *humor*
 → Festlichkeit
Festkalender, m
Festspielkalender, m
 ♦ festival calendar
Fest klang aus mit etw
Fest endete mit etw
Festspiele klangen aus mit etw
Festspiele endeten mit etw
 ♦ festival ended with s.th.
 ♦ festival ended in s.th.

Festkleid, n
 ♦ festive dress
 ♦ gala dress
Fest klingt aus
 ♦ festival is coming to an end
 ♦ festivity is coming to an end
 ♦ fête (fete) is coming to an end
 ♦ celebration is coming to an end
 ♦ party is coming to an end
Fest klingt harmonisch aus
 ♦ festival is coming to a(n) harmonious end
 ♦ festivity is coming to a(n) harmonious end
 ♦ fête (fete) is coming to a(n) harmonious end
 ♦ celebration is coming to a(n) harmonious end
 ♦ party is coming to a(n) harmonious end
Festkomitee, n
Festausschuß, m
Fetenkomitee, n
Fetenausschuß, m
 ♦ fete committee AE
 ♦ fête committee BE
Festkonzert, n (Festspiel)
 ♦ festival concert
 ♦ gala concert
 ♦ festive concert
Festkonzession, f (Festival)
Festspielkonzession, f
Festivalkonzession, f
 ♦ festival license
 ♦ festival licence
Festkoordination, f
 (bei Festival)
 ♦ festival management
Festkoordinator, m
Festspielkoordinator, m
 ♦ festival co-ordinator
 ♦ coordinator of a festival
Fest koordinieren
Festspiele koordinieren
 ♦ coordinate a festival
Festland, n
 (Gegensatz zu Insel)
 ♦ mainland
Festlandsfrühstück, n
 → kontinentales Frühstück
Festlandsküste, f
 ♦ mainland coast
Festlandurlaub, m
 (Gegensatz zu Inselurlaub)
 ♦ mainland vacation AE
 ♦ mainland holiday BE
festlich, adj (generell)
 ♦ festive, adj
 ♦ festival, adj
festlich bewirten jn mit etw
 ♦ feast s.o. with s.th.
 ♦ regale s.o. with s.th.
festlich bewirtet werden
 ♦ be lavishly entertained
 ♦ be feasted
festliche Beleuchtung, f
Festbeleuchtung f
 ♦ festive illumination
 ♦ gala illumination
festliche Dekoration, f
 → Festdekoration
festliche Mahlzeit, f
 → festliches Essen
festlicher Abend, m
 → Festabend

festlicher Anlaß, m
Festanlaß, m
 ♦ festive occasion
 ♦ gala occasion
festlicher Auftakt, m
festlicher Beginn, m
 ♦ festive start
 ♦ festive beginning
festlicher Rahmen, m
Festrahmen, m
 ♦ festive setting
festlicher Tag, m
Festtag, m
 ♦ festive day
 ♦ festival day
 ♦ feast day
festliches Abendessen, n (Dinner)
festliches Diner, n
Festabendessen, n
Festdiner, n
 ♦ festive dinner
festliches Abendessen, n (Supper)
Festabendessen, n
 ♦ festive supper
festliches Bankett, n
Festbankett, n
 ♦ festive banquet
festliches Essen, n
Festessen, n
festliche Mahlzeit, f
festliches Mahl, n
 ♦ festive meal
festliches Konzert, n
 ♦ festive concert
 ♦ gala concert
festliches Mittagessen, n
Festmittagessen, n
 ♦ festive luncheon
 ♦ festive lunch
festliche Veranstaltung, f
Festveranstaltung, f
 ♦ festive function
 ♦ festive event
 ♦ gala function
 ♦ gala event
 ♦ festivity
festlich gedeckter Tisch, m
Festtisch, m
 ♦ festive board
 ♦ festive table
festlich gedeckte Tafel, f
Festtafel f
 ♦ festive table
festlich gekleidet sein
 ♦ be festively dressed
 ♦ be in festive dress
 ♦ be in gala dress
festlich geschmückt, adj
festlich, adj
 ♦ festively decorated, adj
 ♦ festive, adj
festlich geschmückter Raum, m
festlich geschmücktes Zimmer, n
Festraum, m
Festzimmer, n
 ♦ festive room
 ♦ room which is festively decorated
festlich geschmückter Saal, m
festlich geschmückte Halle, f
 ♦ festive hall
 ♦ festive room

festlich geschmückt sein

- hall which is festively decorated
- room which is festively decorated

festlich geschmückt sein
- be festively decorated

Festlichkeit, f
Festivität, f *humor*
- festivity
- junket *humor*

Festlichkeit abhalten
Festlichkeit veranstalten
- hold a festivity

Festlichkeit anläßlich von etw, f
- festivity on the occasion of s.th.

Festlichkeit arrangieren
- arrange a festivity

Festlichkeit ausrichten (als Gastgeber)
Fest ausrichten
- host a festivity

Festlichkeit begehen
Fest feiern
- celebrate a festivity

Festlichkeiten jeder Art, f pl
- festivities of all kinds *pl*

Festlichkeit klang aus mit etw
- festivity ended with s.th.

Festlichkeit klingt harmonisch aus
- festivity comes to a(n) harmonious end

Festlichkeit stören
- disturb a festivity

Festlichkeit veranstalten
Festlichkeit organisieren
Fest veranstalten
Fest organisieren
- organise a festivity
- organize a festivity

Festlied, n
- festive song

Festmahl, n (Bankett)
→ Bankett

Festmahlzeit, f
→ Festessen

Festmeile, f
- festival mile

Festmenge, f
Festmasse, f
Festspielmasse, f
- festival crowd

Festmenü, n (Bankett)
→ Bankettmenü

Festmenü, n (generell)
festliches Menü, n
- festive menu

Festnacht, f (Festival)
Festspielnacht, f
Festivalnacht, f
- festival night

Festnacht, f (festlich)
festliche Nacht f
- festive night

Festnacht, f (Party)
→ Partynacht

Festordner, m
- steward (of the festival)

Festorganisation, f (Festival)
- festival organisation
- festival organization
- organisation of a festival
- organization of a festival
- organising a festival

Festorganisator, m (Festival)
- organiser of a festival
- organizer of a festival

Festorganisator, m (Party)
Veranstalter einer Party, m
Partyveranstalter, m
Festveranstalter, m
- organiser of a party
- organizer of a party

Fest organisieren (Feier)
→ Feier organisieren

Fest organisieren (Festival)
→ Fest veranstalten

Fest organisieren (Festlichkeit)
→ Festlichkeit organisieren

Fest organisieren (Fête)
→ Fête organiseren

Fest planen (Party)
Party planen
- plan a party

Festplaner, m
Partyplaner, m
- party planner

Festplanung, f (Party)
Partyplanung, f
- party planning
- planning (of) a party

Festplatz, m (generell)
- festival site
- festival ground
- festival grounds

Festplatz, m (Marktplatz)
- festival square

Festpreis, m
fester Preis, m
- fixed price
- fixed rate
- firm price
- firm rate
- set price

Festpreisessen, n
Essen zum festen Preis, n
- fixed-price meal
- set-price meal

Festpreisgarantie, f
- fixed-price guarantee
- fixed-rate guarantee

Festpreisgarantie geben
- give a fixed-price guarantee
- give a fixed-rate guarantee

Festpreismahlzeit, f
→ Festpreisessen

Festpreismenü, n
Festpreismahlzeit f
Festpreisessen n
Menü zum festen Preis n
- fixed-price menu

Festpreismenü anbieten
Menü zum festen Preis anbieten
- offer a fixed-price menu

Festpreismenü bestellen
- order a fixed-price menu

Festpreismittagessen, n
Mittagessen zum festen Preis, n
- fixed-price lunch
- fixed-price luncheon
- set price lunch(eon)
- prix-fixe lunch *FR*
- prix-fixe luncheon *FR*

Festpreis pro Essen, m
- fixed price per meal

Festpreistarif, m
- fixed-price tariff
- fixed rates *pl*
- fixed rate

Festpreisvertrag, m
- fixed-price contract

Festprogramm, n (Festival)
- festival program *AE*
- festival programme *BE*

Festprogramm, n (generell)
(z.B. an Weihnachten)
festliches Programm, n
- festive program *AE*
- festive programme *BE*

Festprogramm, n (Veranstaltungen)
Veranstaltungsprogramm, n
- events' program *AE*
- events' programme *BE*
- program of events *AE*
- programme of events *BE*

Festrahmen, m
→ festlicher Rahmen

Festraum, m
Bankettraum, m
- banqueting room
- banquet room

Festrede, f
- ceremonial speech
- ceremonial address
- speech of the day
- speech

Festredner, m
- official speaker
- speaker
- speaker on this occasion

fest reservieren etw
feste Reservierung vornehmen
- make a firm reservation

Festreservierung, f
(Kunde zahlt voll, selbst wenn Leistung nicht in Anspruch genommen wird)
feste Reservierung f
- guaranteed payment reservation
- definite reservation

Festsaal, m (Bankett)
→ Bankettsaal

Festsaal, m (generell)
Festhalle, f
- festival hall

Festsaal, m (im Hotel)
→ Bankettraum

Festsaal, m (in Heim, Schule)
Aula f
- assembly hall
- auditorium *AE*

Festsaalmikrofonanschluß, m
- auditorium microphone point

Festsaison, f
→ Festzeit, Festspielsaison

Festschmaus, m
Schmaus, m
Hochgenuß, m
- treat

Festschmuck, m
Festdekoration, f
festlicher Schmuck, m
festliche Dekoration, f
- festive decoration
- festive decorations *pl*

festsitzen in einem Verkehrsstau
 ♦ be stuck in a traffic jam
 ♦ be stuck in a traffic congestion
festsitzen (Person)
 ♦ be stuck
 ♦ be stranded
Festspiel, n (Aufführung)
 Festspielaufführung, f
 ♦ festival performance
Festspiel, n (Festival)
 → Festival
Festspielbesucher, m
 Festivalbesucher, m
 Festbesucher, m
 ♦ festivalgoer AE
 ♦ festival-goer BE
 ♦ festival visitor
 ♦ visitor to a festival
Festspielbulletin, n
 Festbulletin, n
 ♦ festival bulletin
Festspieldauer, f
 Festdauer, f
 Festivaldauer, f
 ♦ festival duration
 ♦ duration of the festival
Festspieldirektor, m
 ♦ festival director
Festspiele ausrichten (als Gastgeber)
 Fest ausrichten
 Festival ausrichten
 ♦ host a festival
Festspiele feierlich eröffnen
 Festival feierlich eröffnen
 ♦ inaugurate the festival
Festspiele gründen
 Fest gründen
 ♦ found a festival
Festspielerlebnis, n
 Festerlebnis, n
 Festivalerlebnis, n
 ♦ festival experience
Festspielfahrt, f
 ♦ festival trip
 ♦ trip to a festival
Festspielführer, m
 (Information)
 Festführer, m
 Festivalführer, m
 ♦ festival guide
Festspielgast, m
 Festgast, m
 Festivalgast, m
 ♦ festival guest
Festspielhaus, n (Oper)
 ♦ festival opera house
Festspielhaus, n (Theater)
 Festspieltheater n
 ♦ festival theater AE
 ♦ festival theatre BE
Festspielkarte, f
 Festivalkarte, f
 Festkarte, f
 ♦ festival ticket
Festspielkatalog, m
 Festkatalog, m
 Festivalkatalog, m
 ♦ festival catalogue
 ♦ festival catalog AE
Festspielkurzurlaub, m
 ♦ festival break

Festspielkurzurlaub machen
 ♦ take a festival break
Festspiellogo, n
 ♦ festival logo
Festspielort, m
 ♦ festival venue
Festspielpauschale, f
 ♦ festival package
Festspielplakat, n
 ♦ festival poster
Festspielplaner, m
 ♦ festival planner
Festspielreise, f
 Festivalreise, f
 Festivaltour, f
 ♦ festival tour
 ♦ tour to a festival
Festspielsaison, f
 Festspielzeit, f
 Festsaison, f
 Festzeit, f
 ♦ festival season
Festspielservice, m
 Festspieldienst, m
 Festivalservice, m
 Festivaldienst, m
 ♦ festival service
Festspielstadt, f (Großstadt)
 ♦ festival city
Festspielstadt, f (kleine Stadt)
 ♦ festival town
Festspieltag, m
 Festtag, m
 Festivaltag, m
 ♦ festival day
Festspieltagebuch, n
 ♦ festival diary
Festspieltheater, n
 → Festspielhaus
Festspieltitel, m
 Festtitel, m
 Festivaltitel, m
 ♦ festival title
Festspielzeit, f
 Festzeit, f
 Festspielzeitraum, m
 Festzeitraum, m
 ♦ festival time
 ♦ festival period
Festspielzeitraum, m
 Festspielzeit, f
 ♦ festival period
feststellen etw
 ermitteln etw
 ♦ ascertain s.th.
Feststimmung, f (Atmosphäre)
 festliche Atmosphäre, f
 Festatmosphäre, f
 ♦ festive atmosphere
Feststimmung, f (Person)
 Festfreude f
 ♦ festive mood
Festsuite, f
 Bankettsuite, f
 ♦ banqueting suite
 ♦ banquet suite
Festtafel, f
 ♦ festive dinner table
Festtag, m (Feiertag)
 → Feiertag

Festtag, m (generell)
 ♦ feast day
 ♦ festive day
 ♦ holiday
 ♦ high day
 ♦ gala day
Festtag, m (im Kalender)
 ♦ red-letter day
festtäglich, adj
 → festlich
festtags, adv
 ♦ on a festival day, adv
 ♦ on festival days, adv
 ♦ on a legal holiday, adv AE
 ♦ on legal holidays, adv AE
 ♦ on a public holiday, adv BE
Festtagsmenü, n
 ♦ holiday menu
Festtagsstimmung, f
 → Feststimmung
Festtagszuschlag m
 ♦ public-holiday supplement
Festtarif, m (Feier)
 ♦ celebration tariff
 ♦ celebration rates pl
 ♦ celebration rate
 ♦ celebration terms pl
Festtarif, m (fester Tarif)
 fester Tarif, m
 ♦ fixed tariff
 ♦ fixed rates pl
 ♦ fixed rate
Festteilnehmer, m (Feier)
 ♦ participant in a celebration
Festteilnehmer, m (Festival)
 Festspielteilnehmer, m
 ♦ participant in a festival
Festteilnehmer, m (Festlichkeit)
 ♦ participant in a festivity
Festteilnehmer, m (Fete)
 ♦ participant in a fete AE
 ♦ participant in a fête BE
Festteilnehmer, m (Party)
 ♦ participant in a party
Festtisch, m
 → festlich gedeckter Tisch, m
Festtracht, f
 ♦ festive costume
 ♦ festive dress
Festtrubel, m
 ♦ festive turmoil
Festumzug, m
 → Festzug
Festung, f
 ♦ fortress
Festungsruine, f
 ♦ ruined fortress
Festungswall, m
 Wall, m
 ♦ rampart
Festung und Schloß
 ♦ fortress and castle
Festunterhaltung, f
 festliche Unterhaltung f
 ♦ festive entertainment
Festveranstalter, m (Festival)
 → Festorganisator
Festveranstalter, m (Party)
 ♦ party organiser
 ♦ party organizer

Festveranstaltung

- organiser of a party
- organizer of a party

Festveranstaltung, f (Aktivität)
- **organisation of a festival**
- organisation of a party
- **organising a festival**
- organising a party

Festveranstaltung, f (Fest)
festliche Veranstaltung f
- **festive event**
- festive function
- gala event
- gala function
- festivity

Festversammlung, f
- **festive gathering**

Fest vorbereiten (Feier)
- **prepare a celebration**

Fest vorbereiten (Festival)
Festival vorbereiten
Festspiele vorbereiten
- **prepare a festival**

Fest vorbereiten (Festlichkeit)
- **prepare a festivity**

Fest vorbereiten (Fete)
Fete vorbereiten
- **prepare a fete** AE
- prepare a fête BE

Fest vorbereiten (Party)
Party vorbereiten
- **prepare a party**

Festvorbereitung, f (Feier)
- **preparation of a celebration**

Festvorbereitung, f (Feierlichkeit)
- **preparation of a festivity**

Festvorbereitung, f (Festival)
- **preparation of a festival**

Festvorbereitung, f (Fete)
- **preparation of a fete** AE
- preparation of a fête BE

Festvorbereitung, f (Party)
- **preparation of a party**

Festvorstellung, f
→ Festaufführung

Festwagen, m
Umzugsfestwagen, m
- **float**
- decorated carriage
- decorated cart

Festwoche, f (Festival)
Festspielwoche, f
- **festival week**

Festwoche, f (Festival)
→ Festival

Festwoche, f (generell)
- **gala week**

Festzeit, f (Festspiel)
→ Festspielzeit

Festzeit, f (generell)
festliche Zeit, f
Festsaison, f
- **festive season**

Festzelt, n (generell)
großes Zelt, n
- **marquee**

Festzelt, n (Jahrmarkt)
→ Jahrmarktzelt

Festzelt errichten
- **erect a marquee**

Festzeltfläche, f
- **marquee space**
- marquee area

Festzeltverleih, m
Zeltverleih, m
- **marquee rental** AE
- marquee hire BE

Festzeltverpflegung, f
- **marquee catering**
- marquee foodservice AE

Festzug, m (generell)
festlicher Umzug, m
festlicher Zug, m
- **festive procession**
- festive parade
- procession
- parade

Festzug, m (mit historischen Kostümen)
- **pageant**

Fest zur Erinnerung an etw, n
Fest zu etw, n
- **celebration to commemorate s.th.**
- celebration commemorating s.th.

fest zusagen jm etw
jm etw gewährleisten
- **guarantee s.o. s.th.**

Fete, f
- **fete** AE
- fête BE

Fete abhalten
Fete veranstalten
- **hold a fete** AE
- hold a fête BE

Fete absagen
- **cancel a fete**
- cancel a fête BE

Fete eröffnen
- **open a fete** AE
- open a fête BE

Fete klang aus mit etw
Fete endete mit etw
- **fete ended with s.th.** AE
- fête ended with s.th. BE

Fete klingt harmonisch aus
- **fete is coming to a(n) harmonious end** AE
- fête is coming to a(n) harmonious end BE

Fete koordinieren
- **coordinate a fete** AE
- coordinate a fête BE

Fetenkeller, m
→ Partykeller

Fete veranstalten
Fete organisieren
- **organise a fete** AE
- organise a fête BE
- organize a fete AE
- organize a fête BE

fettarm, adj
- **low-fat, adj**
- low in fat, adj

fettarme Kost, f
- **low-fat diet**
- diet containing little fat

fettarmes Gericht, n
- **low-fat dish**

fettarmes Menü, n
- **low-fat menu**

fette Kost, f
fette Speisen f pl
- **fat food**

- fatty food
- greasy food

fettes Fleisch, n
- **fat meat**

fettfrei, adj
- **fat-free, adj**

fettfreie Diät, f
→ fettfreie Kost

fettfreie Kost, f
fettfreie Diät, f
- **fat-free diet**

Fettgehalt, m
- **fat content**

fettiges Essen, n
- **greasy food**

feuchtes Zimmer, n
naßkaltes Zimmer, n
- **damp room**

feuchtfröhlich, adj coll
- **merry, adj**
- jolly, adj
- convivial, adj

feuchtfröhliche Feier, f
(bes. für die Belegschaft)
feuchtfröhliches Fest, n
- **beanfeast** BE inform
- beano BE inform

feuchtfröhlicher Abend, m
Sauferei, f
- **bender** AE sl
- spree
- binge coll
- dinking bout BE coll

feuchtkaltes Zimmer, n
naßkaltes Zimmer, n
- **dank room**

feudal bewirtet werden coll
- **be entertained sumptuously**

feudales Essen, n coll
- **sumptuous meal**

feudale Unterkunft, f coll
prachtvolle Unterkunft, f
- **sumptuous accommodation**

feudale Wohnung, f coll
prachtvolle Wohnung, f
- **sumptuous apartment** AE
- sumptuous flat BE
- swanky apartment AE coll
- swanky flat BE coll

feudal leben coll
→ in Luxus leben

Feueralarm, m
- **fire alarm** AE
- fire-alarm BE

Feueralarm geben
- **raise the fire alarm** AE
- raise the fire-alarm BE
- sound the fire alarm AE
- sound the fire-alarm BE

Feuer bemerken
- **notice the fire**

feuerbeständig, adj
feuerfest, adj
- **fire-resistant, adj**
- fireproof, adj AE
- fire-proof, adj BE
- flame-resistant, adj

Feuerbohne, f
grüne Bohne, f
- **French bean**

feuerfest, adj *gastr*
♦ **ovenproof, adj** *gastr*
♦ flameproof, adj *gastr*
feuerfeste Kasserolle, f
♦ **flameproof casserole**
feuerfeste Schüssel, f
♦ **ovenproof dish**
feuerfestes Geschirr, n
♦ **ovenware**
Feuerfresser, m
Feuerschlucker, m
♦ **fire-eater**
Feuerglocke, f
♦ **fire bell**
feuerhemmend, adj
♦ **fire-retardant, adj**
♦ flame-retardant, adj
Feuer legen in etw
Brand legen in etw
in Brand setzen etw
♦ **set fire to s.th.**
Feuerleiter, f
→ Feuertreppe
Feuerlöschanlage, f
Sprinkleranlage, f
automatische Feuerlöschanlage, f
♦ **sprinkler system**
Feuerlöscher, m
Löschgerät, n
♦ **fire extinguisher**
♦ extinguisher
Feuermeldeanlage, f
Brandmeldeanlage, f
♦ **fire alarm system**
♦ fire detection system
Feuermelder, m
Brandmelder, m
♦ **fire alarm** *AE*
♦ fire-alarm *BE*
Feuermeldestelle, f
♦ **fire alarm point**
feuerpolizeiliches Zeugnis, n
♦ **fire certificate**
feuerpolizeiliches Zeugnis erhalten
♦ **receive a fire certificate**
Feuerschutz, m
→ Brandschutz
Feuerstätte, f
♦ **fireplace**
Feuertreppe, f
Feuerleiter, f
♦ **fire escape** *AE*
♦ fire-escape *BE*
Feuerverhütung, f
→ Brandverhütung
Feuerversicherung, f
→ Brandversicherung
Feuervorhang, m
(Theater)
♦ **fire curtain**
Feuerwasser, n *humor*
starkes alkoholisches Getränk, n
♦ **firewater** *AE*
♦ fire-water *BE*
Feuerwehr, f
♦ **fire department** *AE*
♦ fire brigade *BE*
♦ fire service *BE*
Feuerwehrmann, m
♦ **fireman**

Feuerwerk, n
♦ **fireworks** *pl*
♦ display of fireworks
♦ fireworks display
Feuerwerk veranstalten
♦ **put on a fireworks display**
Feuerzeug, n
♦ **lighter**
♦ cigarette lighter
Fewo, f *sl*
→ Ferienwohnung
FF, n
Farbfernsehen, n
♦ **CTV**
♦ color television *AE*
♦ colour television *BE*
FH, f
→ Fachhochschule
FH, n
→ Familienhaus
Fichtelgebirge, n
(Region)
♦ **Fichtelgebirge, the**
♦ Fichtel Gebirge, the
Fichtenwald, m
♦ **spruce forest**
fidel, adj *coll*
♦ **jolly, adj**
♦ jovial, adj
♦ cheerful, adj
♦ merry, adj
fidele Korona, f *coll*
♦ **merry crew**
fideler Zecher, m
♦ **jolly piddler**
Fidschiinseln, die, f *pl*
♦ **Fiji Islands, the** *pl*
Fieber, n
♦ **fever**
Figurproblem, n
♦ **figure problem**
Filet, n
♦ **fillet**
♦ filet
filetieren etw
♦ **fillet s.th.**
♦ filet s.th. *AE*
filetiert, adj
♦ **filleted, adj**
♦ fileted, adj *AE*
Filetsteak, n
♦ **fillet steak**
♦ filet steak *AE*
Filetstück, n
♦ **piece of sirloin**
Filia hospitalis, f *LAT*
(Studentenjargon)
Tochter der Vermieterin, f
♦ **filia hospitalis** *LAT*
Filiale, f
Geschäftsstelle, f
♦ **outlet**
♦ branch
Filialgeschäft, n
Filialladen, m
♦ **branch store** *AE*
♦ branch shop *BE*
Filialleiter, m
→ Geschäftsstellenleiter
Filialnetz, n
♦ **branch network**

Filipino, m
→ Philippiner
Fille de buffet, f *FR*
Büfettochter f *SCHW*
Büfettfräulein n
♦ **fille de buffet** *FR*
♦ counter girl
♦ barmaid
Film, m
♦ **film**
♦ movie *AE*
Filmabend, m
♦ **film show in the evening**
♦ film evening
Filmbar f
♦ **movie bar** *AE*
♦ video bar *BE*
Filmbesucher, m
♦ **film-goer** *BE*
Filmfan, m
♦ **film fan**
♦ movie fan *AE*
Filmfestival, n
Filmfestspiele, n pl
♦ **film festival**
Filmführer, m
(Information)
♦ **film guide**
Filmkassette, f
♦ **film cartridge**
♦ film magazine
Filmkonzession, f
♦ **movie license** *AE*
♦ movie licence *AE*
♦ cinematograph licence *BE*
Film läuft in einem Kino
♦ **film is playing in a cinema** *BE*
♦ film is showing in a cinema *BE*
Filmleihgebühr, f
♦ **film rental**
Filmleinwand, f
♦ **silver screen**
♦ motion-picture screen
♦ movie screen *AE*
Filmmuseum, n
♦ **movie museum** *AE*
♦ film museum *BE*
Filmpremiere, f
♦ **film première** *BE*
Filmprojektor, m
♦ **film projector**
♦ cineprojector
♦ movie projector *AE*
♦ motion-picture projector *AE*
♦ cinematograph *BE*
Filmraum, m
Kinoraum, m
♦ **movie room** *AE*
♦ cinema room *BE*
Filmregisseur, m
♦ **film director**
Film sehen
♦ **see a film**
Filmstar, m
♦ **film star**
♦ movie star *AE*
Filmstarhotel, n
♦ **movie star hotel** *AE*
♦ film star hotel

Filmsternchen

Filmsternchen, n
- movie starlet *AE*
- film starlet

Filmstudio, n
- film studio

Filmtag, m
- film day

Filmtheater, n
Kino, n
Lichtspieltheater, n
- movie theater *AE*
- motion-picture theater *AE*
- cinema *BE*
- film theatre *BE*
- movies *AE pl coll*

Filmunterhaltung, f
- film entertainment

Film vorführen
Film zeigen
- show a film

Filmvorführer, m
- movie projectionist *AE*
- projectionist

Filmvorführkonzession, f
Filmkonzession, f
- cinematograph license *BE*
- cinematograph licence *BE*
- cinema license *BE*
- cinema licence *BE*
- movie license *AE*

Filmvorführraum, m
- film projection room
- movie projection room *AE*

Filmvorführung, f (Projektion)
Filmprojektion, f
- film projection
- projecting a film
- movie projection *AE*
- projecting a movie *AE*

Filmvorführung, f (Veranstaltung)
- film show
- film performance

Filmwoche, f
- film week
- movie week *AE*

Film zeigen
→ Film vorführen

Filterkaffee, m
- percolated coffee
- filtered coffee
- filter coffee
- drip coffee *AE*

Filzlaus, f
- crab louse

Filzschreiber m
→ s. Filzstift

Filzstift, m
- felt-tip pen
- felt-tipped pen

Finale, n
- finale

Finanzbericht, m
- financial report

finanzieren etw
- finance s.th.

Finanzierungsaufwand, m
- financial expense

finden etw
- find s.th.

Finder, m
- finder

Finderlohn, m
- finder's reward

Finder wird um Rückgabe des Schlüssels gebeten
- Will finder please return the key

Finne, m
- Finn
- Finlander

Finnin, f
- Finnish girl
- Finnish woman
- Finn

finnisch, adj
- Finnish, adj

finnische Sauna, f
- Finnish sauna

Finnland
- Finland

Firlefanz, m *coll*
Schnickschnack, m *coll*
- frills *pl*

Firma, f
- firm
- company
- concern

Firmenausflug, m
- corporate outing *AE*
- company outing *BE*

Firmenausstellungsstand, m
- corporate exhibition stand *AE*
- company exhibition stand *BE*

Firmenbesucher, m
- corporate visitor *AE*
- company visitor *BE*

Firmenbewirtung, f
- corporate hospitality *AE*
- corporate entertaining *AE*

Firmenbuchung, f
Geschäftsbuchung, f
- company booking *BE*
- corporate booking *AE*

Firmenemblem, n
Logo, n
- logo

Firmenempfang, m
- corporate reception *AE*
- company reception *BE*

Firmenempfang abhalten
- hold a corporate reception *AE*
- hold a company reception *BE*

Firmenessen, n
- company dinner *BE*
- corporate dinner *AE*

Firmengarantie, f
- corporate guarantee *AE*
- company guarantee *BE*

Firmengast, m
- corporate guest *AE*
- company guest *BE*
- company's guest *BE*

Firmenjahrestag, m
Firmenjubiläum, n
- company anniversary

Firmenkantine, f
- company canteen
- company's canteen

Firmenkonferenz, f
- corporate conference *AE*
- company conference *BE*

Firmenkultur, f
- corporate culture

Firmenkunde, m
- corporate customer *AE*
- corporate client *AE*

Firmenlogo, n
- company logo

Firmenmarkt, m
- corporate market *AE*
- company market

Firmenmittagessen, n
- corporate lunch *AE*
- corporate luncheon *AE*
- company lunch *BE*
- company luncheon *BE*

Firmenname, m
- company name

Firmenpräsentation, f
- company presentation
- corporate presentation *AE*

Firmenpreis, m
Firmenrate, f
- corporate rate *AE*
- corporate price *AE*
- company rate *BE*
- company price *BE*

Firmenpreis zahlen
- pay the corporate rate *AE*
- pay the corporate price *AE*
- pay the company rate *BE*
- pay the company price *BE*

Firmenrabatt, m
- corporate discount *AE*
- company discount *BE*
- company reduction *BE*

Firmenrate, f
Firmenpreis, m
- company price *BE*
- company rate *BE*
- corporate rate *AE*
- coporate price *AE*

Firmenreisen, n
Firmenreiseverkehr, m
- corporate travel *AE*
- company travel *BE*

Firmenreisestelle, f
- corporate travel agency *AE*
- company travel agency *BE*

Firmenreisestellenexpedient, m
- corporate travel agent *AE*
- company travel agent *BE*

Firmenreisestellenleiter, m
- corporate travel executive *AE*
- manager of a company travel agency *BE*

Firmenreiseverkehr, m
Firmenreisen, n
- company travel *BE*
- corporate travel *AE*

Firmenseminar, n
- in-house seminar

Firmenservice, m
- corporate service *AE*
- company service *BE*

Firmenstand, m
- company stand
- corporate stand

Firmentagung, f
- corporate meeting *AE*
- company meeting *BE*

Firmentagungsgeschäft, n
- corporate meetings business *Ae*
- company meetings business

Firmentreffen, n
♦ company gathering
♦ corporate gathering AE
Firmenveranstaltung, f
♦ corporate event AE
♦ corporate function AE
♦ company event
♦ company function
Firmenverpflegung, f
♦ corporate foodservice AE
♦ company catering BE
Firmenverzeichnis, n
♦ list of firms
♦ list of companies
Firmenwagen, m
Firmenauto, n
♦ company car
Firmenwohnung, f
♦ corporate apartment AE
♦ company flat BE
♦ company dwelling
Firmenzentrale, f
♦ corporate headquarters AE pl + sg
♦ company headquarters BE pl + sg
Firn, m
Firnschnee, m
♦ old snow
♦ hard snow
Firnschnee, m
Firn, m
♦ hard snow
♦ old snow
Fisch, m
♦ fish
Fischaspik, m/n
♦ fish jelly
Fischbestand, m
♦ fish stock
Fischbesteck, n (ein Satz)
♦ fish knife and fork
Fischbesteck, n (generell)
♦ fish cutlery
Fischbräterei, f
(Laden)
♦ fried-fish shop
♦ fish-and-chip shop BE
Fischbrühe, f
♦ fish broth
Fischcanapé, n
♦ fish canapé
♦ fish canape AE
Fischcocktail, m
♦ fish cocktail
Fische füttern
(seekrank sein)
♦ feed the fishes
fischen
angeln
♦ fish
♦ angle
fischen gehen
♦ go fishing
fischen nach etw
♦ fish for s.th.
Fischen verboten
(Hinweis)
♦ No fishing
♦ Fishing prohibited
Fischer, m
♦ fisherman

Fischerboot, n
♦ fishing boat
Fischerdorf, n
♦ fishing village
Fischereibegeisterter, m
begeisterter Fischer, m
♦ fishing enthusiast
Fischereihafen, m
♦ fishing port
♦ fishing harbor AE
♦ fishing harbour BE
Fischereischein, m
♦ fishing license
♦ fishing licence
Fischerfest, n
♦ fishermen's festival
Fischerhaus, n
♦ fisherman's house
Fischerhäuschen, n
Fischerkate, f
♦ fisherman's cottage
Fischerhütte, f
♦ fisherman's hut
♦ fishing lodge
Fischerkneipe, f coll
Fischergaststätte, f
♦ fishermen's pub BE
♦ fishermen's bar AE
Fischerlaubnis, f
Angelerlaubnis, f
Erlaubnis zu fischen, f
♦ permit to fish
Fischernetz, n
Fischnetz, n
♦ fishing net
♦ fish-net
Fischerort, m
♦ fishing resort
Fischerparadies, n
♦ fisherman's paradise
Fischerpatent, n
Angelerlaubnis, f
♦ fishing permit
Fischerstadt, f
♦ fishing town
Fischerurlaub, m
Angelurlaub, m
Angelferien, pl
♦ fishing vacation AE
♦ fishing holiday BE
Fisch essen
♦ eat fish
Fischesser, m
♦ fish eater
Fischfanggelegenheit, f
Angelgelegenheit, f
♦ opportunity for fishing
Fischfest, n
♦ fish festival
Fischfilet, n
♦ fish fillet
♦ fish filet AE
Fischfond, m gastr
♦ fish stock gastr
Fischfondue, n
♦ fish fondue
♦ fish fondu AE
Fischfüllung, f
Fischfarce, f
♦ fish stuffing

Fischgabel f
♦ fish fork
Fischgang, m
(Mahlzeit)
♦ fish course
Fischgericht n
♦ fish dish
Fischgeruch, m
♦ fishy smell
♦ smell of fish
Fischgeschäft, n
Fischladen, m
♦ fish shop
Fischgeschmack, m
♦ fishy taste
Fischgräte, f
♦ fishbone
Fischhändler, m
♦ fish dealer AE
♦ fishmonger BE
Fischkarte, f
→ Fischspeisekarte
Fischklößchen, n
♦ fish dumpling
Fischkoch, m
Poissonnier, m FR
♦ fish cook
♦ poissonnier FR
Fischkrokette, f
♦ fish croquette
Fischküche, f (Raum)
♦ fish kitchen
Fischküche, f (Speisen)
Fischspeisen f pl
♦ fish food
Fischleiter, f
Fischtreppe, f
♦ fish ladder
♦ fish lift
Fischmarinade, f
Fischsud, m
♦ fish marinade
Fischmarkt, m
♦ fish market
Fischmayonnaise, f
♦ fish mayonnaise
Fischmenü, n
♦ fish menu
♦ set fish meal
Fischmesser, n
♦ fish knife
♦ fish-knife BE
Fischpastete, f
♦ fish pie
♦ fish pâté
Fischplatte, f (Gang)
♦ plate of fish
Fischportion, f
♦ fish portion
Fischragout, n/m
♦ fish stew
Fischrestaurant, n
Fischlokal, n
♦ fish restaurant
♦ seafood restaurant
Fischrezept, n
Fischrezeptur, f
♦ fish recipe
Fischrisotto, m/n
♦ fish risotto

Fischsalat

Fischsalat, m
♦ fish salad
Fischscheibe, f
♦ fish slice
♦ slice of fish
Fischsoße, f
♦ fish sauce
Fischsoufflé, n
Fischauflauf, m
♦ fish soufflé BE
♦ fish souffle AE
Fischspeisekarte, f
Fischkarte, f
♦ fish menu
Fischspezialität, f
♦ fish specialty AE
♦ fish speciality BE
Fischspezialitätenrestaurant, n
♦ restaurant serving fish specialties AE
♦ restaurant offering fish specialities BE
Fischstäbchen, n
♦ fish stick AE
♦ fish finger BE
Fischsud, m
→ Fischmarinade
Fischsuppe, f
♦ fish soup
Fischteich, m
♦ fishpond AE
♦ fish-pond BE
♦ fishing pond
Fischteller, m
♦ fish plate
Fischterrine, f
♦ fish terrine
Fischvergiftung, f
♦ fish poisoning
Fischzucht, f (Aktivität)
♦ fish-farming
Fischzucht, f (Ort)
♦ fish-farm
Fish-and-Chip-Laden, m
Fish-and-Chip-Geschäft, n
♦ fish and chip shop BE
♦ chip shop BE coll
♦ chippy BE coll
Fish-and-Chips, pl
♦ fish and chips pl
Fish-and-Chips essen aus einer Zeitung
♦ eat fish and chips out of a newspaper
FIT, f
Flugpauschalreise, f
♦ FIT
♦ flight-inclusive tour
FIT, f
(individueller Reiseverlauf; Vorauszahlung)
Einzelauslandsreise, f
♦ FIT
♦ foreign independent tour
fit bleiben
in Form bleiben
♦ keep fit
♦ stay fit
♦ stay in shape
FIT-Gutschein, m
Flugpauschalreisegutschein, m
♦ FIT voucher
♦ flight-inclusive tour voucher
Fitneß, f
♦ fitness

Fitneßannehmlichkeit, f
Trimmannehmlichkeit, f
♦ fitness amenity
♦ keep-fit amenity
Fitneßarrangement, n
Trimm-dich-Arrangement, n
Trimmarrangement, n
♦ fitness arrangement
♦ keep-fit arrangement
Fitneßbegeisterter, m
Trimmbegeisterter, m
♦ fitness enthusiast
♦ keep-fit enthusiast
Fitneßbehandlung, f
Trimmbehandlung, f
♦ fitness treatment
♦ keep-fit treatment
Fitneßbereich, m
Trimm-dich-Bereich, m
Trimmbereich, m
♦ fitness area
♦ keep-fit area
Fitneßbeurteilung, f
♦ fitness assessment
Fitneßbewertung, f
♦ fitness evaluation
Fitneßcenter, n
Fitneßzentrum, n
Trimm-dich-Zentrum, n
Trimmzentrum, n
♦ fitness center AE
♦ fitness centre BE
♦ keep-fit center AE
♦ keep-fit centre BE
Fitneßclub, m
Trimm-dich-Club, m
Trimmclub, m
♦ fitness club
♦ keep-fit club
Fitneßclubleiter, m
Trimmclubleiter, m
♦ fitness club manager
♦ keep-fit club manager
Fitneßeinrichtung, f
Timm-dich-Einrichtung, f
Trimmeinrichtung, f
♦ fitness facility
♦ keep-fit facility
Fitneßgymnastik, f
♦ fitness exercises pl
Fitneßkurs, m
Trimmkurs, m
♦ fitness class
♦ keep-fit class
Fitneßparcours, m
Trimmbahn, f
Trimmparcours, m
♦ fitness track
♦ keep-fit track
♦ fitness trail
♦ keep-fit trail
Fitneßpauschale, f
Trimm-dich-Pauschale, f
Trimmpauschale, f
♦ fitness package
♦ keep-fit package
Fitneßprogramm, n
Trimmprogramm, n
Trimm-dich-Programm, n
♦ fitness program AE
♦ fitness programme BE

♦ keep-fit program AE
♦ keep-fit programme BE
Fitneßraum, m
Trimmraum, m
Trimm-dich-Raum, m
♦ fitness room
♦ keep-fit room
Fitneßsitzung, f
Fitneßstunde, f
Trimm-dich-Stunde, f
Trimmstunde, f
♦ fitness session
♦ keep-fit session
Fitneßstation, f
Trimm-dich-Station, f
Trimmstation, f
♦ fitness station
♦ keep-fit station
Fitneßstudio, n
Trimm-dich-Studio, n
Trimmstudio, n
♦ fitness studio
♦ keep-fit studio
Fitneßsuite, f
mehrere Fitneßräume, m pl
mehrere Trimm-dich-Räume, m pl
mehrere Trimmräume, m pl
♦ fitness suite
♦ keep-fit suite
Fitneßtag, m
Trimmtag, m
Trimm-dich-Tag, m
♦ fitness day
♦ keep-fit day
Fitneßtrainer, m
Trimmtrainer, m
♦ fitness trainer
♦ keep-fit trainer
Fitneßtraining, n
Trimmtraining, n
♦ fitness training
♦ keep-fit training
Fitneßübung, f
Trimmübung, f
Trimm-dich-Übung, f
♦ fitness exercise
♦ keep-fit exercise
Fitneßunterricht, m
Trimmunterricht, m
Trimm-dich-Unterricht, m
♦ fitness lessons pl
♦ keep-fit lessons pl
Fitneßurlaub, m
Trimmurlaub, m
Trimm-dich-Urlaub, m
Fitneßferien, pl
Trimmferien, pl
♦ fitness vacation AE
♦ fitness holiday BE
♦ keep-fit vacation AE
♦ keep-fit holiday BE
Fitneßwoche, f
Trimm-dich-Woche, f
Trimmwoche, f
♦ fitness week
♦ keep-fit week
Fitneßzone, f
Trimm-dich-Zone, f
Trimmzone, f
♦ fitness zone
♦ keep-fit zone

FIT-Veranstalter, m
Einzelauslandsreiseveranstalter, m
- ♦ **FIT operator**
- ♦ foreign independent tour operator

fixe Aufwendungen, f pl
- ♦ **fixed expenses** *pl*

fixe Betriebskosten, pl
- ♦ **fixed operating cost**
- ♦ fixed operating costs *pl*
- ♦ fixed costs of operating *pl*
- ♦ fixed costs of operation *pl*
- ♦ fixed cost of operation

fixe Buchung, f
→ feste Buchung

fixe Kosten, pl
→ Fixkosten

fixer Erlös, m
- ♦ **fixed revenue**

Fixkosten, pl
fixe Kosten, pl
- ♦ **fixed costs** *pl*
- ♦ fixed cost

Fixkostenanteil, m
- ♦ **proportion of fixed costs**

Fixkosten pro Zimmer, pl
- ♦ **fixed costs per room** *pl*
- ♦ fixed cost per room

Fjord, m
- ♦ **fiord**
- ♦ fjord

Fjordhotel, n
- ♦ **fiord hotel**
- ♦ fjord hotel

FKK, f
Freikörperkultur, f
- ♦ **nudism**
- ♦ naturism

FKK-Anhänger, m
- ♦ **naturist**
- ♦ nudist

FKK-Campingplatz, m
- ♦ **naturist campsite**
- ♦ naturist campground *AE*
- ♦ naturist camping site *BE*
- ♦ naturist camping ground *BE*
- ♦ naturist site

FKK-Club, m
- ♦ **naturist club**
- ♦ nudist club

FKK-Ferien, pl
FKK-Urlaub, m
- ♦ **nudist holiday** *BE*
- ♦ naturist holiday *BE*
- ♦ nudist vacation *AE*
- ♦ naturist vacation *AE*

FKK-Gast, m
- ♦ **naturist guest**
- ♦ nudist guest

FKK-Gelände, n
- ♦ **naturist area**
- ♦ nudist area

FKK-Hotel, n
Freikörperkulturhotel, n
- ♦ **naturist hotel**
- ♦ nudist hotel

FKK-Kolonie, f
- ♦ **nudist colony**
- ♦ naturist colony

FKK-Lager, n
FKK-Gelände, n

- ♦ **nudist camp**
- ♦ naturist camp

FKK-Platz, m
(Camping)
- ♦ **naturist site**
- ♦ nudist site

FKK praktizieren
- ♦ **practice naturism**
- ♦ practice nudism

FKK-Strand, m
- ♦ **nudist beach**
- ♦ nude-bathing beach
- ♦ naturist beach

FKK-Terrasse, f
- ♦ **naturist terrace**
- ♦ nudist terrace
- ♦ nudists' terrace
- ♦ naturist's terrace

FKK-Urlaub, m
- ♦ **naturist vacation** *AE*
- ♦ nudist vacation *AE*
- ♦ naturist holiday *BE*
- ♦ nudist holiday *BE*

Flachbau, m
- ♦ **flat building**
- ♦ low building

Flachbauhotel, n
- ♦ **low-rise hotel**

Flachdach, n
- ♦ **flat roof**

Flachdachgebäude, n
- ♦ **flat-roofed building**

Fläche, f
- ♦ **area**

Fläche bedecken von 123 Quadratmeilen
- ♦ **cover an area of 123 square miles**

Fläche belegen
- ♦ **occupy space**

Fläche beträgt 123 Quadratmeter
→ Fläche ist 123 Quadratmeter

Fläche buchen
(Ausstellung)
- ♦ **book space**

Fläche des Raumes, f
- ♦ **area of the room**
- ♦ floor area of the room

Fläche in qm, f
- ♦ **area in sq.m.**

Fläche in Quadratmetern, f
- ♦ **area in square meters** *AE*
- ♦ area in square metres *BE*

Fläche ist 123 Quadratmeter
Fläche ist 123 qm
Fläche beträgt 123 Quadratmeter
Fläche beträgt 123 qm
- ♦ **area is 123 square meters** *AE*
- ♦ area is 123 square metres *BE*
- ♦ area is 123 sq.m.

Fläche mit flachem Boden, f
Bereich mit flachem Boden, m
- ♦ **flat-floor area**

Flächenzuteilung, f
(Ausstellung)
Flächenvergabe, f
- ♦ **allocation of space**
- ♦ assignment of space *AE*
- ♦ space allocation
- ♦ space assignment *AE*

flache Platte, f
(Geschirr)
- ♦ **flat platter**

Fläche pro Stand, f
- ♦ **area per stand**
- ♦ area per stall *BE*

flacher Boden, m
- ♦ **flat floor**

flacher Kuchen, m
- ♦ **flat cake**

flacher Stellplatz, m
(Camping)
- ♦ **flat pitch**

flacher Strand, m
- ♦ **flat beach**

flacher Teller, m
- ♦ **flat plate**
- ♦ dinner plate

flaches Becken, n
- ♦ **shallow pool**

flache Schüssel, f
- ♦ **shallow bowl**
- ♦ shallow dish

flaches Ende, n
(im Schwimmbecken)
- ♦ **shallow end**

flaches Geschirr, n
- ♦ **flatware** *BE*

flaches Land, n
- ♦ **flat country**
- ♦ flat land

Fläche von 25 Quadratmetern haben
Fläche von 25 qm haben
- ♦ **have an area of 25 square meters** *AE*
- ♦ have an area of 25 square metres *BE*
- ♦ have an area of 25 sq.m.

Fläche zuteilen jm
(Ausstellung)
Fläche vergeben an jn
- ♦ **allocate space to s.o.**
- ♦ assign space to s.o. *AE*

Flachland, n
Tiefland, n
- ♦ **lowland**

flachlegen sich
- ♦ **lie down for a bit**

Flachmann, m
(Flasche)
- ♦ **hip flask**

Flachsitzanordnung, f
- ♦ **flat-floor seating**

Flachsitzplatz, m
Sitzplatz auf flachem Boden, m
- ♦ **flat-floor seat**

Flambiergericht, n
- ♦ **flambé dish**

flambiert, adj
- ♦ **flambé, adj**
- ♦ flambée, adj
- ♦ flambéed, adj *AE*
- ♦ flamed, adj

flambiertes Fleisch, n
- ♦ **flamed meat**
- ♦ meat flambé

flambiertes Steak, n
- ♦ **steak flambé**
- ♦ flamed steak

Flambierwagen, m
- ♦ **flambé cart** *AE*
- ♦ flambé trolley *BE*

Flame, m
- ♦ **Fleming**

Flamenco, m
- ♦ **flamenco**

Flamenco tanzen
 ♦ dance the flamenco
Flamencotänzer, m
 ♦ flamenco dancer
Flamencovorführung, f
 Flamencodarbietung, f
 ♦ flamenco show
Flämin, f
 ♦ Flemish girl
 ♦ Flemish woman
 ♦ Fleming
Flamingo, m
 ♦ flamingo
Flamingopark, m
 ♦ flamingo park
 ♦ flamingo gardens pl
flämisch, adj
 ♦ Flemish, adj
flämische Art, adv gastr
 nach flämischer Art, adv gastr
 ♦ flemish style, adv gastr
Flandern
 (Region)
 ♦ Flanders
flankieren etw
 ♦ flank s.th.
Flasche, f
 ♦ bottle
Flasche Bier, f
 ♦ bottle of beer
Flasche Champagner, f
 Flasche Sekt, f
 ♦ bottle of champagne
Flasche Champagner sich gönnen
 ♦ treat oneself to a bottle of champagne
Flasche entkorken
 ♦ uncork a bottle
Flasche Essig, f
 ♦ bottle of vinegar
Flasche ist halb leer
 ♦ bottle is half empty
Flasche ist halb voll
 ♦ bottle is half full
Flasche ist leer
 ♦ bottle is empty
Flasche ist voll
 ♦ bottle is full
Flaschenbier n
 ♦ bottled beer
Flaschenbürste, f
 ♦ bottle brush
Flaschenetikett, n
 ♦ bottle label
Flaschengärung, f
 ♦ bottle fermentation
 ♦ fermentation in the bottle
Flaschengröße, f
 ♦ bottle size
 ♦ size of a bottle
Flaschenhals, m
 ♦ neck of the bottle
Flaschenmilch, f
 ♦ bottled milk
Flaschenöffner m
 ♦ bottle opener
Flaschenpfand, n
 ♦ bottle deposit
 ♦ deposit on the bottle
 ♦ deposit on a bottle
 ♦ deposit

Flaschenpreis, m
 Preis pro Flasche, m
 ♦ bottle price
 ♦ price per bottle
Flaschenständer, m
 Flaschengestell, n
 ♦ bottle rack
 ♦ bottle stand
Flaschenverschluß, m
 ♦ bottle top
Flaschenwärmer, m
 ♦ bottle warmer
Flaschenwein m
 ♦ bottled wine
 ♦ bottle wine
flaschenweise, adv
 ♦ by the bottle, adv
Flasche öffnen
 ♦ open a bottle
Flasche Sekt, f
 → Flasche Champagner
Flasche teilen mit jm
 (Verbrauch und Kosten teilen)
 ♦ split a bottle with s.o.
Flasche Wein, f
 ♦ bottle of wine
Flasche Wein bestellen
 ♦ order a bottle of wine
Flasche Wein sich gönnen
 Flasche Wein sich leisten
 ♦ treat oneself to a bottle of wine
Flasche Wein trinken
 ♦ have a bottle of wine
 ♦ drink a bottle of wine
Flasche Whisky, f
 ♦ bottle of whisky
 ♦ bottle of Scotch
 ♦ bottle of whiskey
flaue Nachfrage, f
 ♦ slack demand
flaue Zeit, f
 verkehrsschwache Zeit, f
 Flaute, f
 ♦ dull period
 ♦ slack period
flaue Zeit haben
 ♦ have a slack period
Flaute, f ökon
 ♦ slack period
 ♦ lull
 ♦ trough
Flautenmonat, m
 ♦ slack month
 ♦ poor month
Flautenzeit, f
 ♦ trough period
Fleck entfernen
 ♦ remove a stain
fleckige Wäsche f
 ♦ stained linen
Fleisch, Fisch und Geflügel
 (auf Speisekarte)
 ♦ Meat, fish and poultry
Fleisch, n
 ♦ meat
Fleischaspik, m
 Fleischsülze, f
 ♦ meat jelly
Fleischbesteck, n (ein Satz)
 ♦ meat knife and fork

Fleischbesteck, n (generell)
 ♦ meat cutlery
Fleischbon, m
 (bei Lagerung von Fleisch)
 ♦ meat ticket
Fleischeintopf, m
 ♦ meat stew
Fleisch essen
 ♦ eat meat
Fleischesser, m
 ♦ meat eater
Fleischextrakt, m/n
 ♦ meat extract
Fleischfondue, n
 ♦ meat fondue
 ♦ meat fondu AE
fleischfrei, adj
 fleischlos, adj
 ♦ meatfree, adj
 ♦ meatless, adj
Fleischfrühstück, n
 Frühstück mit Fleisch, n
 ♦ meat breakfast
Fleischgabel, f
 ♦ meat fork
Fleischgang, m
 (Mahlzeit)
 ♦ meat course
Fleischgericht, n
 Fleischspeise, f
 ♦ meat dish
Fleischgerichte
 (auf der Speisekarte)
 ♦ Meat dishes
Fleischhauptgericht, n
 (bei Speisefolge)
 Grande pièce f FR
 Grosse pièce f FR
 ♦ main meat course
 ♦ grande pièce FR
 ♦ grosse pièce FR
Fleisch ist schlecht geworden
 ♦ meat is off
 ♦ meat has gone off
Fleisch ist zäh wie Leder
 ♦ meat is tough as leather
Fleischkloß, m
 ♦ meat dumpling
Fleischkosten, pl
 ♦ meat costs pl
 ♦ meat cost
fleischlos, adj
 fleischfrei, adj
 ♦ meatless, adj
 ♦ meatfree, adj
fleischlose Kost f
 ♦ meatless diet
fleischloser Tag, m
 ♦ meatless day
 ♦ day on which no meat is eaten
fleischloses Gericht, n
 Gericht ohne Fleisch, n
 ♦ meatless dish
 ♦ dish without meat
fleischlose Vorspeise f
 ♦ meatless hors d'oeuvre
fleischlos leben
 sich fleischlos ernähren
 ♦ eat no meat
 ♦ live without meat

Fleischmahlzeit f
 ♦ meal with meat
Fleischmarkt, m
 ♦ meat market
Fleischmesser, n
 ♦ meat knife
Fleisch mit Beilage, n
 ♦ meat with vegetables
Fleischpastete, f
 ♦ meat pie
 ♦ meat pâté
Fleischplatte, f
 ♦ meat platter
Fleischsalat, m
 ♦ meat salad
Fleischspieß, m
 Fleischspießchen, n
 Spieß, m
 Spießchen, n
 ♦ meat skewer
 ♦ skewer
Fleischteller, m
 ♦ meat plate
Fleischverbrauch, m
 Fleischkonsum, m
 ♦ meat consumption
 ♦ consumption of meat
Fleischvergiftung, f
 ♦ meat poisoning
 ♦ ptomaine poisoning
 ♦ botulism *scient*
Fleischwaren, f pl
 ♦ meat products *pl*
 ♦ meat goods *pl*
 ♦ meats *pl*
Fleischwolf, m
 ♦ mincer
 ♦ meat grinder
Flensburger Förde, f
 ♦ Flensburg Förde, the
Flexenpaß, m
 (Eigenname)
 ♦ Flexen Pass, the
flexibel, adj
 ♦ flexible, adj
Flexibilität, f
 ♦ flexibility
flexible Essenszeiten, f pl
 ♦ flexible mealtimes *pl*
flexibler Urlaub, m
 flexible Ferien, pl
 ♦ flexible vacation *AE*
 ♦ flexible holiday *BE*
flexible Speisekarte, f
 ♦ flexible menu
flexible Tischanordnung, f
 ♦ flexible table system
flexible Tischanordnung benutzen
 ♦ use a flexible table system
Flickendecke, f
 ♦ patchwork quilt
Fliegender, m
 → Chef tournant, Tournant
Fliegender Teppich m
 ♦ magic carpet
fliegendes Personal, n
 Flugpersonal, n
 ♦ flying staff
 ♦ flying personnel
 ♦ flight personnel
 ♦ flight crew

fliegen direkt nach X
 ♦ fly direct to X
Fliegenfischen, n
 ♦ fly fishing
fliegen mit British Airways
 British Airways fliegen
 ♦ fly with British Airways
 ♦ fly British Airways
fliegen (mit dem Flugzeug)
 ♦ fly
 ♦ go by air
 ♦ travel by air
 ♦ go by plane
 ♦ travel by plane
fliegen mit Reisegeschwindigkeit
 fahren mit Reisegeschwindigkeit
 ♦ cruise
fliegen nach X
 ♦ fly to X
fliegen ohne Begleitung
 ♦ fly unaccompanied
fliegen von A nach C über B
 ♦ fly from a to C via B
fliegen zwischen A und B
 ♦ fly between A and B
Flieger, m (Flugzeug)
 Flugzeug, n
 ♦ plane
 ♦ airplane *AE*
 ♦ aeroplane *BE*
 ♦ aircraft *sg*
Flieger, m (generell)
 ♦ flier
 ♦ flyer
Flieger, m (Militär)
 ♦ airman
Flieg-und-Spar-Tarif, m
 PEX-Tarif, m
 Holiday-Tarif, m
 ♦ purchase excursion tariff
 ♦ PEX tariff
Fliesenboden, m
 → gefliester Boden
Fliesenleger, m
 ♦ tile setter
Fliesenmuseum, n
 Kachelmuseum, n
 ♦ tile museum
fließendes warmes und kaltes Wasser, n
 fließendes Warm- und Kaltwasser n
 ♦ hot and cold running water
fließendes Wasser, n
 Fließwasser, n ÖST
 ♦ running water
fließend Französisch sprechen
 ♦ speak French fluently
 ♦ speak fluent French
Fließheck, n
 ♦ hatchback
Fließwasser, n ÖST
 → fließendes Wasser
flinker Service, m
 ♦ swift service
Flip, m
 ♦ flip
Flipchart, f
 ♦ flipchart
Flipper, m
 → Flippertisch
flippern
 ♦ play pinball

Flippertisch, m
 Flipperautomat, m
 Flipper, m
 ♦ pinball machine
Flitterwochen, f pl
 ♦ honeymoon
Flitterwochenangebot, n
 Flitterwochenofferte, f
 ♦ honeymoon offer
Flitterwochenhotel n
 ♦ honeymoon hotel
Flitterwochenpauschale, f
 ♦ honeymoon package
Flitterwochenpauschaltourist, m
 ♦ honeymoon package tourist
Flitterwochenservice, m
 Flitterwochendienst, m
 ♦ honeymoon service
Flitterwochen verbringen in X
 ♦ spend one's honeymoon in X
 ♦ spend one's honeymoon at X
 ♦ honeymoon in X
 ♦ honeymoon at X
Flitterwöchner, m
 Hochzeitsreisender, m
 ♦ honeymooner
Floh, m
 ♦ flea
Flohbiß, m
 ♦ flea bite
Flohkiste, f neg (Bett)
 (auch Schlafsack)
 ♦ fleabag *AE sl*
 ♦ doss *BE sl*
Flohkiste, f neg (Pension etc)
 (schlechte Unterkunft)
 ♦ fleabag *AE sl*
Flohmarkt m
 ♦ flea market
Flohzirkus, m
 ♦ flea circus
Flora, f
 ♦ flora
Flora und Fauna, f pl
 ♦ flora and fauna
Florentinerart, adv *gastr*
 nach Florentinerart, adv *gastr*
 ♦ Florentine style, adv *gastr*
Floridareisender, m
 ♦ Florida traveller
 ♦ Florida traveler *AE*
Florida-Salat, m
 ♦ Florida salad
Floridastand, m
 (Messe)
 ♦ Florida stand
Florist, m
 Floristin, f
 Blumenhändler, m
 Blumenhändlerin, f
 Blumenbinderin, f
 ♦ florist
Floß, n
 Raft, n
 ♦ raft
Floßbrücke, f
 ♦ float bridge
Floß fahren
 Floß fahren gehen
 ♦ go rafting

Floßfahren

Floßfahren, n
♦ rafting
Floßfahrt, f
♦ raft trip
♦ rafting trip
Floßreise, f
♦ raft journey
♦ raft tour
Floßreise machen
♦ make a raft journey
♦ go on a raft journey
♦ make a raft tour
Flöte, f
♦ flute
Flötenunterricht, m
♦ flute tuition
flotten Otto haben *sl*
Durchfall haben
♦ have the runs *sl*
flotter Otto, m *sl*
Diarrhö, f
Durchfall, m
Dünnpfiff, m *sl*
Durchmarsch, m *fam*
♦ runs, the *pl sl*
♦ trots, the *pl sl*
fluchtartig verlassen etw
♦ leave s.th. in a hurry
flüchtige Bekanntschaft, f
♦ casual acquaintance
flüchtigen Besuch machen bei jm
♦ pay s.o. a fleeting visit
flüchtiger Besuch, m
♦ fleeting visit
Flüchtling, m (auf der Flucht)
♦ fugitive
Flüchtling, m (nach der Flucht)
Geflüchteter, m
♦ refugee
Flüchtlingslager, n
♦ refugee camp
Fluchttür, f
♦ emergency door
Fluchtweg, m
♦ escape route
Flug, m
♦ flight
Flug abbrechen
♦ abort a flight
Flug absagen
Flug stornieren
Flug streichen
♦ cancel a flight
Fluganfrage, f
♦ flight inquiry
♦ flight enquiry
Flugangebot, n (Gegensatz zu Nachfrage)
♦ flights available *pl*
Flugangst, f
Angst vor dem Fliegen, f
♦ fear of flying
♦ plane phobia
♦ pterophobia *scient*
Flugangst haben
→ Angst haben vor dem Fliegen
Flugarrangement, n
♦ flight arrangement
Flugbedingungen, f pl
♦ flight conditions *pl*
Flugbegleiter, m
♦ flight attendant

Flugbereich, m
Flugsektor, m
♦ flight sector
Flug bestätigen
♦ confirm a flight
Flugbestätigung, f
♦ flight confirmation
♦ confirmation of a flight
Flug bezahlen
♦ pay for a flight
Flugblatt, n
Reklamezettel, m
♦ flier
♦ flyer
Flugboot, n
♦ flying boat
Flug buchen
♦ book a flight
Flugbuchung, f
♦ flight booking
♦ booking a flight
Flugcateringpersonal, n
♦ commissary personnel
♦ commissary staff
Flugcateringstelle, f
♦ commissary
Flugcharter, m
♦ air charter
Flugchartergesellschaft, f
♦ air charter comopany
Flugchartermarkt, m
♦ air charter market
Flugcoupon, m
♦ flight coupon
Flug dauert 30 Minuten
♦ flight lasts 30 minutes
♦ flight takes 30 minutes
Flugdokument, n
♦ flight document
Flugdurchsage, f
♦ flight announcement
Flügel, m (Gebäudeteil)
Trakt m
♦ wing
Flügel, m (Musikinstrument)
♦ grand piano
Flug erreichen
Flugzeug erreichen
Flugzeug nehmen
♦ catch a flight
♦ catch the flight
Flugfähigkeit, f
♦ fitness to fly
Flug fortsetzen (nach X)
weiterfliegen (nach X)
♦ continue one's flight (to X)
♦ fly on (to X)
Flugfrequenz, f
♦ flight frequency
Flugführer, m
(Information)
♦ flight guide
Fluggast, m
Flugpassagier, m
Luftpassagier, m
♦ aircraft passenger
♦ air passenger
Fluggastauslastung, f
♦ passenger load factor
Fluggastbodendienst, m
♦ ground passenger service

Fluggastversicherung, f
♦ air passenger insurance
Fluggepäck, n
♦ airplane baggage *AE*
♦ aeroplane luggage *BE*
Fluggesellschaft, f
Fluglinie, f
Luftfahrtgesellschaft, f
Luftverkehrsunternehmen, n
♦ airline
♦ airline company *BE*
Fluggesellschaftspersonal, n
♦ airline staff
♦ airline personnel
Flughafen, m
♦ airport
Flughafenabholdienst, m
Flughafenabholungsdienst, m
♦ airport pick-up service
♦ airport collection service
♦ airport limousine service
Flughafenabholgebühr, f
♦ airport pick-up fee
♦ airport pick-up charge
Flughafenabholung, f
(mit Pkw)
♦ collection from the airport
♦ airport collection
♦ airport limousine service
♦ airport pick-up
Flughafenabholung mit Pkw, f
Pkw-Flughafenabholdienst m
♦ airport limousine service
Flughafenabholungsdienst, m
(mit Pkw)
Flughafenabholdienst, m
♦ airport collection service
♦ airport pick-up service
♦ airport limousine service
Flughafenabholung veranlassen
♦ arrange for airport pick-up
Flughafen anfliegen
♦ serve an airport
Flughafenaufpreis, m
♦ airport surcharge
Flughafenbahnhof, m
♦ airport station
Flughafenbehörde, f
Flughafenbehörden, f pl
♦ airport authority
♦ airport authorities *pl*
Flughafen benutzen
♦ use an airport
Flughafenbereich, m
♦ airport area
Flughafenbus, m
Zubringerbus, m
♦ airport bus
♦ airport coach *BE*
♦ transfer bus
♦ transfer coach *BE*
Flughafencode, m
♦ airport code
Flughafendirektor, m
♦ airport director
♦ airport manager
Flughafenendhaltestelle, f
Flughafenendstation, f
♦ airport terminus

242

Flughafengebühr, f
♦ airport tax
♦ airport fee
Flughafengeschäft, n
♦ airport store AE
♦ airport shop BE
Flughafenhotel n
♦ airport hotel
Flughafeninformation, f
♦ airport information
Flughafen ist geschloßen
♦ airport is closed
Flughafen ist nur fünf Meilen entfernt
♦ airport is only five miles away
Flughafenkapazität, f
♦ airport capacity
Flughafenlärm, m
♦ airport noise
Flughafenmotel, n
♦ airport motel
Flughafennähe, f
Nähe zum Flughafen, f
♦ proximity to the airport
♦ closeness of the airport
Flughafennähe ist von Vorteil
♦ proximity to the airport is an advantage
Flughafenparken, n
Parken am Flughafen, n
♦ airport parking
Flughafenparkplatz, m
♦ airport parking lot AE
♦ airport car park BE
Flughafenpersonal, n
♦ airport staff
♦ airport personnel
Flughafenplanung, f
♦ airport planning
♦ planning of an airport
Flughafenrestaurant n
♦ airport restaurant
Flughafen schließen
♦ close an airport
Flughafenservice m
(Beförderung zum und vom Flughafen)
♦ airport service
Flughafensicherheitsgebühr, f
♦ airport security charge
♦ airport security fee
Flughafensprecher, m
♦ airport spokesman
Flughafentaxe, f
→ Flughafengebühr
Flughafenterminal, m/n
♦ airport terminal
Flughafentransfer, m
♦ airport transfer
♦ transfer to/from the airport
Flug hat Verspätung
Flugzeug hat Verspätung
♦ flight is delayed
♦ flight is late
Fluginformation, f
♦ flight information
Flug ist ausgebucht
♦ flight is fully booked
Flug ist ausverkauft
♦ flight is sold out
Flugkapazität, f
♦ flight capacity
Flugkarte, f
Flugticket, n

Flugschein, m
♦ flight ticket
Flugkatastrophe, f
♦ air disaster
♦ plane disaster
Flugkunde, m
♦ airline customer
Fluglehrer, m
♦ flight instructor
♦ flying instructor BE
Fluglotse, m
♦ air-traffic controller
Fluglotsenstreik, m
♦ strike of the air-traffic controllers
Flugmannschaft, f
♦ flight crew
Flugmarkt, m
♦ airline market
Flugmaschine, f *hist*
♦ flying machine *hist*
Flug mit Abendessen, m
♦ dinner flight
Flug mit Lufthansa, m
♦ flight with Lufthansa
Flug mit Wildbeobachtung, m
♦ game-viewing flight
Flug nach Norden, m
♦ northbound flight
Flug nach Osten, m
♦ eastbound flight
Flug nach Süden, m
♦ southbound flight
Flug nach Westen, m
♦ westbound flight
Flug nach X, m
♦ flight to X
♦ flight for X
Flug nehmen (von A nach B)
Flugzeug nehmen (von A nach B)
♦ take a flight (from A to B)
Flugnummer, f
♦ flight number
Flugpauschale, f
♦ flight package
♦ air package
Flugpauschalpreis, m
♦ inclusive air fare
♦ inclusive fare
Flugpauschalreise, f
FIT, f
♦ flight-inclusive tour
♦ FIT
♦ air-inclusive tour
Flugpauschalurlaub, m
Flugpauschalferien, pl
♦ package vacation by air AE
♦ package holiday by air BE
Flugpersonal, n
♦ flight personnel
♦ flight crew
♦ flying staff
♦ flying personnel
♦ air staff
Flugplan, m
♦ flight schedule AE
♦ air (service) schedule AE
♦ (flying) schedule AE
♦ air(line) timetable BE
♦ timetable BE
Flug planen
♦ plan a flight

Flugplanung, f
♦ flight planning
Flugplatz, m
♦ airfield
♦ airdrome AE
Flugplatzfest, n
♦ airfield festival
♦ aerdrome festival AE
Flugpreis, m
♦ air fare
♦ airline fare
♦ fare
♦ flight price
Flugrabatt, m
♦ flight discount
Flugreise, f
♦ air tour
♦ air journey
♦ air trip
Flugreiseführer, m
♦ air travel guide
Flugreisegeschäft, n
♦ air travel business
Flugreisemarkt, m
♦ air travel market
Flugreisen, n
Flugreiseverkehr, m
♦ air travel
Flugreisender, m
♦ air traveller
♦ air traveler AE
♦ traveller by air
♦ traveler by air AE
Flugreisespezialist, m
♦ air travel specialist
Flugreiseveranstalter, m
Luftreiseveranstalter, m
♦ air tour operator
Flugreiseveranstalterlizenz, f
♦ air travel organiser's license BE
♦ ATOL BE
Flugreiseverkehr, m
Luftreiseverkehr, m
♦ air passenger traffic
Flug reservieren
♦ reserve a flight
Flugreservierung, f
♦ flight reservation
♦ reserving a flight
Flugroute, f
Flugstrecke, f
♦ air route
Flugsafari, f
♦ air safari
Flugsaison, f
♦ flying season
Flugschau, f
Luftschau, f
♦ air circus
♦ air show
Flugschein, m
♦ air ticket
♦ airline ticket
♦ plane ticket
Flugschein kaufen
♦ buy an air ticket
Flugscheinnummer, f
♦ air ticket number
♦ ticket number
Flugscheinschalter, m
(Verkaufsstelle)

Flugscheinumsatz 244

Flugschalter m
♦ **airline ticket desk**
♦ airline ticket office
♦ airline travel desk
♦ airline desk *abbr*
Flugscheinumsatz, m
♦ **airline ticket sales** *pl*
♦ airline ticket turnover
Flugscheinverkauf, m
♦ **airline ticket sale**
♦ air ticket sale
♦ selling an airline ticket
♦ selling air tickets
Flug-Schiffsreise, f
kombinierte Flug-Schiffsreise, f
♦ **air-steamer voyage**
Flugschneise, f
♦ **flight lane**
♦ flight corridor
Flugschule, f
♦ **flying school**
Flugsicherheit, f
♦ **air safety**
Flugsicherung, f
♦ **air-traffic control**
Flugspezialist, m
♦ **flight specialist**
Flugstatistik, f
♦ **flight statistics** *pl*
Flugsteig, m
♦ **gate**
Flugsteignummer, f
♦ **gate number**
Flugstornierung, f
Flugannullierung, f
♦ **flight cancellation**
♦ flight cancelation *AE*
♦ cancellation of a flight
♦ cancelation of a flight *AE*
Flugstrecke, f
Flugroute, f
♦ **flight route**
Flugstreckennetz, n
Flugnetz, n
♦ **network of air routes**
Flugstunde, f (Entfernung)
♦ **one-hour flight**
♦ one hour's flight
Flugstunde, f (Unterricht)
♦ **flying lesson**
Flugstunde, f (Zeit)
♦ **flying hour**
Flugtarif, m
♦ **air fares** *pl*
Flugtaxi, n
→ Lufttaxi
Flugticket, n
→ Flugkarte
Flugtourismus, m
Flugtouristik, f
♦ **air tourism**
Flugtourist, m
♦ **air tourist**
Flug überbuchen
♦ **overbook a flight**
Flug umleiten zu einem anderen Flughafen
♦ **divert a flight to another airport**
Flugunfall, m
♦ **air crash**
Flugunglück, n
♦ **aviation accident**

Flugunterbrechung, f
♦ **stopover**
Flugunterbrechungsgebühr, f
♦ **stopover fee**
Flugunterbrechungspunkt, m
Stopoverpunkt, m
♦ **stopover point**
Flugurlaub, m
Urlaub mit dem Flugzeug, m
Flugferien, pl
Ferien mit dem Flugzeug, pl
♦ **air vacation** *AE*
♦ vacation by air *AE*
♦ holiday by air *BE*
♦ air holiday *BE*
Flugurlaubsspezialist, m
♦ **air vacation specialist** *AE*
♦ air holiday specialist *BE*
Flugveranstalter, m
♦ **air operator**
Flugverbindung, f
♦ **flight connection**
♦ air link
♦ air connection
Flugverbot, n
♦ **flight ban**
♦ ban on flights
♦ ban on flying
Flugverkehr, m
→ Luftverkehr
Flugverpflegung, f
♦ **in-flight foodservice** *AE*
♦ in-flight catering *BE*
♦ flight catering
Flug versäumen
Flug verpassen
♦ **miss the flight**
♦ miss a flight
Flugversicherung, f
♦ **flight insurance**
Flugverspätung, f
♦ **flight delay**
Flug von A nach B, m
♦ **flight from A to B**
Flug von B (zurück nach A), m
♦ **flight from B (back to A)**
Flugzeit, f
♦ **flight time**
♦ flying time
Flugzeug, n
♦ **airplane** *AE*
♦ aeroplane *BE*
♦ plane
♦ aircraft *sg*
♦ craft
Flugzeugabsturz, m
♦ **air crash**
♦ plane crash
Flugzeugankunft, f
Flugankunft, f
♦ **flight arrival**
Flugzeug auf dem Weg nach Spanien, n
Flugzeug auf dem Flug nach Spanien, n
♦ **plane bound for Spain**
♦ plane for Spain
Flugzeug benutzen
♦ **use an airplane** *AE*
♦ use an aeroplane *BE*
♦ use a plane
Flugzeugbesatzung, f
♦ **air crew**

♦ aircraft crew
♦ crew
Flugzeug buchen
♦ **book a plane**
Flugzeugbuchung, f
♦ **plane booking**
♦ booking a plane
Flugzeug chartern
♦ **charter a plane**
♦ charter an airplane *AE*
♦ charter an aeroplane *AE*
♦ charter an aircraft
Flugzeug entführen
♦ **hijack a plane**
Flugzeugentführer, m
♦ **hijacker**
Flugzeugentführung, f
♦ **hijacking**
♦ airplane hijacking *AE*
Flugzeug erreichen
Flugzeug nehmen
♦ **catch a plane**
♦ catch an airplane *AE*
♦ catch an aeroplane *BE*
Flugzeugessen, n
Flugzeugmahlzeit, f
♦ **aircraft meal**
Flugzeug fliegen (als Pilot)
♦ **fly an aeroplane** *BE*
♦ pilot an aeroplane *BE*
♦ fly an airplane *AE*
♦ fly a plane
♦ fly an aircraft
Flugzeugführer, m
Pilot, m
♦ **aircraft pilot**
Flugzeughangar, m
♦ **aircraft hangar**
Flugzeug hat Verspätung
Flug hat Verspätung
♦ **flight is late**
♦ flight is delayed
Flugzeughersteller, m
♦ **aircraft manufacturer**
Flugzeugindustrie, f
♦ **aircraft industry**
Flugzeug ist startbereit
♦ **airplane is ready to take off** *AE*
♦ aeroplane is ready to take off *BE*
♦ plane is ready to take off
Flugzeug ist überbucht
♦ **plane is overbooked**
Flugzeugkabine, f
♦ **aircraft cabin**
Flugzeugkatastrophe, f
Flugkatastrophe, f
♦ **plane disaster**
♦ air disaster
Flugzeug landet
♦ **plane lands**
♦ plane is landing
Flugzeug mieten
♦ **rent a plane** *AE*
♦ hire a plane *BE*
♦ rent an aircraft *AE*
♦ hire an aircraft *BE*
Flugzeugmotor, m
♦ **aircraft engine**
♦ airplane engine *AE*
♦ aeroplane engine *BE*

Flugzeugmuseum, n
Luftfahrtmuseum, n
♦ aircraft museum
♦ air museum
Flugzeug nach New York, n
♦ plane to New York
Flugzeug nehmen (nach X)
♦ take a plane (for X)
♦ take the plane (for X)
Flugzeugpark, m
♦ aircraft fleet
Flugzeugpassagier, m
♦ aircraft passenger
♦ air passenger
Flugzeugpersonal, n
♦ aircraft staff
♦ aircraft personnel
Flugzeugpilot, m
♦ airplane pilot AE
♦ aeroplane pilot BE
Flugzeugplatz, m (Sitzplatz)
Flugzeugsitzplatz, m
Flugzeugsitz, m
♦ plane seat
♦ air seat
♦ aircraft seat
Flugzeugplatz buchen (Sitzplatz)
♦ book a plane seat
♦ book an air seat
♦ book an aircraft seat
Flugzeugreise, f
♦ plane trip
Flugzeugreisender, m
♦ plane traveller
♦ plane traveler AE
Flugzeugreservierung, f
♦ plane reservation
Flugzeugträger, m
♦ aircraft carrier
Flugzeugtyp, m
♦ aircraft type
♦ type of aircraft
Flugzeug überbuchen
♦ overbook a plane
♦ overbook an airplane AE
♦ overbook an aeroplane BE
♦ overbook an aircraft
Flugzeug versäumen
Flugzeug verpassen
♦ miss the plane
Flugzeugwartung, f
♦ aircraft maintenance
Flugzeugwechsel, m
♦ change of plane
Flug zum halben Preis, m
♦ half-price flight
Flugzuschlag m
♦ flight supplement
Fluktuation, f
→ Schwankung, Personalfluktuation
Flunder, f
Plattfisch, m
♦ flounder
Flur, m (Kurridor)
→ Flur
Flur, m (Vestibül)
→ Vestibül
Flurbeleuchtung, f
Korridorbeleuchtung, f
♦ corridor lighting

Flurgarderobe, f
♦ hall tree AE
♦ hallstand
Flurwand, f
Korridorwand, f
♦ corridor wall
Fluß, m
♦ river
flußabwärts, adv
♦ downriver, adv
♦ downstream, adv
♦ down the river, adv
♦ down the stream, adv
flußabwärts fahren nach X
♦ go downriver to X
flußabwärts segeln
flußabwärts fahren
♦ sail downriver
♦ sail downstream
flußabwärts von etw
♦ downstream from s.th.
♦ downriver from s.th.
Flußappartement, n
♦ riverside apartment
Flußappartement, n (direkt am Fluß)
Appartement am Fluß, n
♦ riverfront apartment
flußaufwärts, adv
stromaufwärts, adv
♦ upriver, adv
♦ upstream, adv
♦ up the river, adv
♦ up the stream, adv
flußaufwärts fahren nach X
♦ go upriver to X
flußaufwärts segeln
flußaufwärts fahren
♦ sail upriver
♦ sail upstream
flußaufwärts von etw
♦ upstream from s.th.
♦ upriver from s.th.
Flußbalkon, m
♦ riverside balcony
Fluß befahren
♦ ply a river
Flußblick, m
Blick auf den Fluß m
♦ river view
♦ view of the river
Flußblickrestaurant, n
♦ river-view restaurant
Flußblickzimmer, n
♦ river-view room
♦ room with river view
Flußcampingplatz, m
♦ riverside campsite
♦ riverside campground AE
♦ riverside camping site BE
♦ riverside camping ground BE
♦ riverside site
Flußcaravanpark, m
Flußwohnwagenpark, m
♦ riverside caravan park BE
♦ riverside trailer park AE
Flußcaravanplatz, m
Flußwohnwagenplatz, m
♦ riverside caravan site BE
♦ riverside trailer site AE
Flüßchen, n
kleiner Fluß, m

♦ rivulet
♦ creek AE
Flußdampfer, m
♦ river steamer
Flußdorf, n
♦ riverside village
Flußexpedition, f
♦ river expedition
Flußfähre, f
♦ river ferry
Flußfahrt, f
♦ river trip
Flußfahrzeug, n
♦ river craft
♦ river vessel
Flußferienort, m
♦ riverside resort
Flußgaststätte, f
♦ riverside bar AE
♦ riverside pub BE
Flußhafen, m
♦ river port
Fluß hinuntersegeln
Fluß hinunterfahren
♦ sail down a river
Flußhotel n (direkt am Fluß)
Hotel am Fluß, n
♦ riverfront hotel
Flußhotel n (zur Flußseite gelegen)
♦ riverside hotel
flüssig, adj
♦ liquid, adj
flüssige Nahrung, f
♦ liquid food
Flüssigseife, f
♦ liquid soap
Flußinsel, f
♦ river island
Flußkrebs, m
Edelkrebs, m
♦ crayfish
♦ crawfish
Flußkreuzer, m
♦ river cruiser
Flußkreuzfahrt f
♦ river cruise
Flußkreuzfahrtschiff, n
♦ river cruise boat
Flußlandschaft, f
♦ river scenery
♦ river landscape
♦ riverscape
Flußlauf, m
Lauf des Flusses, m
♦ river course
♦ course of the river
Flußlauf folgen
♦ follow the course of the river
♦ follow the river course
Fluß macht eine Kurve
♦ river makes a bend
Flußmündung, f (generell)
Mündung eines Flusses, f
♦ mouth of a river
Flußmündung, f (mit Gezeiten)
♦ estuary
Flußpark, m
♦ riverside park
Flußplatz, m
(z.B. Camping)
♦ riverside site

Flußreise   246

Flußreise, f
 ♦ river tour
 ♦ river journey
 ♦ river trip
Flußreiseveranstalter, m
 ♦ river tour operator
Flußrestaurant n (direkt am Fluß)
 Restaurant am Fluß, n
 ♦ riverfront restaurant
Flußrestaurant n (zur Flußseite gelegen)
 ♦ riverside restaurant
Flußschiff, n
 Flußboot, n
 ♦ riverboat
 ♦ river vessel
Flußspaziergang, m
 Spaziergang entlang des Flusses, m
 ♦ walk along the riverside
 ♦ riverside walk
Flußspazierweg, m
 Spazierweg entlang des Flusses, m
 ♦ riverside walk
 ♦ walk along the riverside
Flußstadt, f
 ♦ riverside town
Flußtal, n
 ♦ river valley
Flußtaverne, f
 Taverne am Fluß, f
 Weinstube am Fluß, f
 ♦ riverside tavern
Flußterrasse, f
 ♦ riverside terrace
 ♦ river terrace
Fluß überqueren
 ♦ cross a river
Flußufer, n
 ♦ riverbank
 ♦ bank of a river
 ♦ riverside
Flußurlaub, m
 Flußferien, pl
 ♦ river vacation *AE*
 ♦ river holiday *BE*
Flußveranda, f
 ♦ riverside veranda
 ♦ riverside verandah
Flußverkehr, m
 ♦ river traffic
Flußwiese, f
 ♦ riverside meadow
Flußwohnung, f (direkt am Fluß)
 Wohnung am Fluß, f
 ♦ riverfront flat *BE*
 ♦ riverfront apartment *AE*
Flußwohnwagenpark, m
 Flußcaravanpark, m
 ♦ riverside trailer park *AE*
 ♦ riverside caravan park *BE*
Flußwohnwagenplatz, m
 Flußcaravanplatz, m
 ♦ riverside trailer site *AE*
 ♦ riverside caravan site *BE*
Fluthafen, m
 ♦ tidal harbor *AE*
 ♦ tidal harbour *BE*
Flutlicht, n
 ♦ floodlight
Flutlichtanlage, f
 ♦ floodlights *pl*
 ♦ floodlighting

Flutlichtbeleuchtung, f
 ♦ floodlighting
Flutlichthang, m
 ♦ floodlit slope
Flutlichtpiste f
 (Ski)
 ♦ floodlit piste
 ♦ floodlit run
Flutlichttennisplatz, m
 Tennisplatz mit Flutlicht, m
 beleuchteter Tennisplatz, m
 ♦ floodlit tennis court
Fly-Cruise-Arrangement, n
 Kreuzfahrtarrangement mit Flug, n
 ♦ fly-cruise arrangement
Fly-Cruise-Pauschalreise, f
 Kreuzfahrtpauschalreise mit Flug, f
 ♦ fly-cruise package tour
 ♦ fly-cruise package
Fly-Cruise-Programm, n
 Kreuzfahrtprogramm mit Flug, n
 ♦ fly-cruise program *AE*
 ♦ fly-cruise programme *BE*
Fly-Cruise-Urlaub, m
 Kreuzfahrturlaub mit Flug, m
 Kreuzfahrtferien mit Flug, pl
 ♦ fly-cruise vacation *AE*
 ♦ fly-cruise holiday *BE*
Fly-Drive-Pauschale, f
 Pauschale für Urlaub mit Flug und Landfahrzeug, f
 ♦ fly-drive package
Fly-Drive-Urlaub, m
 Urlaub mit Flug und Landfahrzeug, m
 Ferien mit Flug und Landfahrzeug, pl
 ♦ fly-drive vacation *AE*
 ♦ fly-drive holiday *BE*
Folder, m
 → Faltprospekt, Mappe
Folgebuchung f
 folgende Buchung, f
 Nachbuchung, f
 ♦ subsequent booking
Folie, f (Projektor, beschriftet)
 Lichtbild, n
 ♦ transparency
Folie, f (Projektor, leer)
 ♦ acetate *BE*
Folie, f (Verpackung)
 ♦ foil
 ♦ plastic wrap *AE*
 ♦ cling film *BE*
Folklore, f
 ♦ folklore
Folkloreabend, m
 ♦ folklore evening
 ♦ evening of local culture
 ♦ evening of traditional music and dance
Folkloredarbietung, f
 Folkloreaufführung f
 ♦ folklore performance
Folklorefest, n
 Folklorefestival, n
 ♦ folklore festival
 ♦ folkloric festival *AE*
Folkloregruppe, f
 ♦ folklore group
Folkloreprogramm, n
 ♦ folklore program *AE*
 ♦ folklore programme *BE*
Folkloreschau, f
 ♦ folklore show

Folkloreveranstaltung, f
 ♦ folklore event
Folklorevorführung, f
 Folkloredarbietung f
 ♦ folklore show
folkloristisch, adj
 ♦ folkloric, adj
folkloristischer Abend, m
 ♦ folkloric evening
folkloristische Vorstellung, f
 folkloristische Aufführung, f
 ♦ folkloric performance
Folterkammer, f
 ♦ torture chamber
Fön, m
 (zum Trocknen der Haare)
 ♦ hair-drier
 ♦ hair-dryer
Fond, m *gastr*
 ♦ stock *gastr*
Fondue, n
 ♦ fondue
 ♦ fondu *AE*
Fondueabend, m
 ♦ fondue evening
 ♦ fondu evening *AE*
Fondueparty, f
 ♦ fondue party
 ♦ fondu party *AE*
Fonduetopf, m
 ♦ fondue pot
 ♦ fondu pot *AE*
Fontäne, f
 → Springbrunnen
Food and Beverage
 F&B
 Verpflegung, f
 Gastronomie, f
 Speisen und Getränke, pl
 ♦ food and beverage
 ♦ f&b
Food and Beverage Manager, m
 → Wirtschaftsdirektor
Football, m
 (amerikanisch)
 ♦ football *AE*
Force majeure, f FR
 höhere Gewalt f
 ♦ force majeure *FR*
 ♦ act of God
fordern etw
 ♦ demand s.th.
 ♦ require s.th.
Fordern Sie (einen) kostenlosen Prospekt an
 (telefonisch)
 ♦ Ring for (a) free brochure
 ♦ Call for (a) free brochure
 ♦ Phone for (a) free brochure
Fordern Sie Infopaket an (schriftlich)
 ♦ Write for info pack
Fordern Sie Infopaket an (telefonisch)
 ♦ Call for info pack
 ♦ Phone for info pack
Fordern Sie unseren Prospekt an! (schriftlich)
 ♦ Write for our brochure
Fordern Sie unseren Prospekt an! (telefonisch)
 ♦ Ring for our brochure
 ♦ Call for our brochure
 ♦ Telephone for our brochure
 ♦ Phone for our brochure

Forelle, f
 ◆ trout
Forelle nach Müllerinart, f
 Forelle Müllerinart, f
 ◆ trout a la meuniere *AE*
 ◆ trout (à la) meunière *BE*
Forellenbach, m
 ◆ trout stream
 ◆ trout creek *AE*
Forellenbecken, n
 ◆ trout pool
forellenbesetzter Teich, m
 mit Forellen besetzter Teich, m
 ◆ trout-stocked lake
Forellenfang, m
 Forellenfangen, n
 ◆ trout fishing
Forellen fangen
 Forellen fischen
 ◆ go trout fishing
Forellenfilet, n
 ◆ trout fillet
 ◆ trout filet
Forellenfluß, m
 ◆ trout river
Forellengericht, n
 ◆ trout dish
Forellenpastete, f
 ◆ trout pie
 ◆ trout pâté
Forellensee, m
 ◆ trout lake
Forellenteich, m
 ◆ trout pond
Forellenzucht, f
 ◆ trout farm
Forint, m
 Ft
 ◆ Forint
 ◆ Ft
Form, f (für Speisen)
 ◆ mould
formal
 (Kleiderangabe bei Einladungen)
 ◆ formal
 ◆ black tie
Formalität, f
 ◆ formality
Form des Reisens, f
 → Reiseform
Form des Übernachtens, f
 ◆ form of overnighting
formell, adj
 ◆ formal, adj
formelle Begrüßung, f
 ◆ formal welcome
formelle Einladung, f
 ◆ formal invitation
formellen Besuch abstatten jm
 ◆ pay a formal visit to s.o.
formeller Besuch, m
 ◆ formal visit
 ◆ formal call
formeller Empfang, m
 feierlicher Empfang m
 ◆ formal reception
formeller Vertrag, m
 ◆ formal contract
Formular, n
 Formblatt n
 ◆ form

 ◆ printed form
 ◆ blank *AE*
Formular ausfüllen
 ◆ fill out a form *AE*
 ◆ fill in a form *BE*
 ◆ complete a form
 ◆ fill out a blank *AE*
 ◆ complete a blank *AE*
Formular erstellen
 ◆ draw up a form
 ◆ draw up a blank *AE*
Formular zurücksenden
 ◆ return a form
Forstamt, n
 ◆ forestry office
Försterinart, adv *gastr*
 nach Försterinart, adv *gastr*
 ◆ forester's style, adv *gastr*
Forsthaus, n
 ◆ forester's house
 ◆ forester's lodge
 ◆ ranger's house *AE*
 ◆ ranger's lodge *AE*
Fortbildung, f
 ◆ continuing education
Fortbildungskurs, n
 Fortbildungslehrgang, m
 ◆ further training course
Fortbildungsprogramm, n
 ◆ continuing education program *AE*
 ◆ continuing education programme *BE*
fortbleiben
 wegbleiben
 ausbleiben
 ◆ stay away
 ◆ fail to come
Fortgeschrittenenkurs, m
 Fortgeschrittenenlehrgang, m
 ◆ advanced course
 ◆ course for the advanced
 ◆ course for advanced students
 ◆ advanced class
Fortgeschrittenenniveau, n
 ◆ advanced level
Fortgeschrittenenprogramm, n
 ◆ advanced program *AE*
 ◆ advanced programme *BE*
Fortgeschrittenenseminar n
 ◆ advanced seminar
 ◆ seminar for advanced students
Fortgeschrittener, m (Student)
 ◆ advanced student
 ◆ advanced
fortgeschrittener Skiläufer m
 ◆ advanced skier
 ◆ advanced skiier *AE*
fortreisen
 → verreisen
Forum, n (für Diskussion)
 ◆ platform
Forum, n (generell)
 ◆ forum
Forum, n (Podiumsdiskussion)
 → Podiumsdiskussion
Forum bieten für etw
 ◆ provide a forum for s.th.
Fossil, n
 ◆ fossil
Fossilienbörse, f
 ◆ fossil exchange

Fossiliensammlung, f
 ◆ fossil collection
 ◆ collection of fossils
Foto, n
 Fotografie, f
 ◆ photo
 ◆ photograph
Fotoausstellung, f
 ◆ photo exhibition
 ◆ photo exhibit *AE*
 ◆ photographic exhibition
 ◆ photographic exhibit *AE*
 ◆ exhibition of photographs
Fotobibliothek, f
 ◆ photographic library
Fotodienst, m
 ◆ photographic service
Fotofestival, n
 ◆ photography festival
Fotoflugsafari, f
 ◆ air photo safari
fotogen, adj
 ◆ photogenic, adj
fotogenes Dorf, n
 ◆ photogenic village
fotogene Stadt, f
 ◆ photogenic town
Fotogeschäft, n
 Fotoladen, m
 ◆ photographer's shop
 ◆ photographer's
Fotograf, m
 ◆ photographer
fotografieren etw
 ◆ take a photograph of s.th.
 ◆ take a photo of s.th.
 ◆ take a picture of s.th.
Fotographiewettbewerb, m
 ◆ photography competition
Fotokopie, f
 Kopie, f
 ◆ photocopy
 ◆ copy
 ◆ photostat
Fotokopie machen
 Kopie machen
 ◆ make a photocopy
 ◆ make a copy
Fotokopierdienst, m
 ◆ photocopying service
Fotokopiereinrichtung, f
 ◆ photocopying facility
fotokopieren etw
 kopieren etw
 ◆ photocopy s.th.
 ◆ copy s.th.
Fotokopierer, m
 ◆ photocopier
Fotokopiergerät, n
 ◆ photocopying machine
Foto machen
 ◆ take a picture
 ◆ take a photo(graph)
Fotoparadies, n
 ◆ photographer's paradise
Fotosafari, f
 ◆ photo safari
 ◆ photographic safari
 ◆ camera safari
Fotospaziergang, m
 ◆ photo walk

Fotostand

Fotostand, m
- ◆ photo stall *BE*

Fotostudio, n
- ◆ photographer's studio
- ◆ photographic studio
- ◆ photography studio

Fotowerkstatt, f
- ◆ photography workshop

Fotowettbewerb, m
- ◆ photo competition
- ◆ photographic competition
- ◆ photo contest
- ◆ photographic contest

Foyer, n
- ◆ foyer
- ◆ lobby *AE*
- ◆ entrance hall
- ◆ lounge

Foyerausstellung, f
- ◆ foyer exhibition
- ◆ foyer exhibit *AE*

Foyerbar, f
- ◆ foyer bar

Foyerbereich, m
Foyerfläche, f
- ◆ foyer area
- ◆ foyer space

Foyerfläche, f
- → Foyerbereich

Foyerkaffeebar, f
- ◆ foyer coffee bar

Foyerraum, m (Volumen, Fläche)
- ◆ foyer space
- ◆ foyer area

Foyer reinigen
- ◆ clean the foyer
- ◆ clean the lobby *AE*
- ◆ clean the entrance hall

Foyerveranstaltung, f
- ◆ foyer event

FP, m
(Kinder kostenfrei im Elternzimmer)
Family Plan, m
- ◆ FP
- ◆ Family Plan

Fracht, f
- ◆ cargo
- ◆ freight

Frachtabfertigung, f
- ◆ cargo handling
- ◆ freight handling

Fracht befördern
- ◆ carry cargo
- ◆ carry freight

Frachtbestimmungen, f pl
Frachtvorschriften, f pl
- ◆ freight regulations *pl*
- ◆ cargo regulations *pl*

Frachtbrief, m
Frachtschein, m
Begleitschein, m
- ◆ waybill *AE*
- ◆ freight bill *AE*
- ◆ consignment note

Frachtcontainer, m
- ◆ cargo container
- ◆ freight container

Frachtdienst, m
- ◆ freight service
- ◆ cargo service

Frachter, m
Frachtschiff, n
- ◆ freighter
- ◆ cargo ship

Frachterfahrt, f
Frachterreise, f
- ◆ freighter trip

Frachterreisen, n
Frachterreiseverkehr, m
- ◆ freighter travel

Frachterreisender, m
- ◆ freighter traveller
- ◆ freighter traveler *AE*

Frachtflug, m
- ◆ cargo flight
- ◆ freight flight

Frachtflugzeug, n
Transportflugzeug, n
- ◆ cargo aircraft
- ◆ cargo plane
- ◆ freight plane
- ◆ airfreighter

Frachtraum, m
Frachtfläche, f
- ◆ cargo space

Frachtschein, m
Frachtbrief, m
Begleitbrief, m
- ◆ freight bill *AE*
- ◆ waybill *AE*
- ◆ consignment note

Frachtschiff, n
Frachter, m
- ◆ cargo ship
- ◆ cargo boat
- ◆ freight ship
- ◆ cargo vessel
- ◆ freighter

Frachttarif, m
- ◆ cargo tariff
- ◆ freight tariff

Fracht transportieren
Fracht befördern
- ◆ transport freight
- ◆ transport cargo

Frachtverkehr, m
Güterverkehr, m
- ◆ freigt traffic
- ◆ goods traffic

Frack
(auf Einladungen)
- ◆ Tails
- ◆ White tie

Frack, m
- ◆ tails *pl*
- ◆ tailcoat

Frackhemd, n
- ◆ dress shirt

Frack tragen
- ◆ wear tails

Frack und Dekorationen
(auf Einladungen)
- ◆ Tails and decorations

Frackzwang
(auf Einladungen)
- ◆ Evening dress

Frackzwang herrschen
- ◆ tails are compulsory

Frage, f
- ◆ question

Fragebogen, m
- ◆ questionnaire
- ◆ questionaire *AE*
- ◆ questionary *AE*

Fragebogen ausfüllen
- ◆ complete a questionnaire
- ◆ fill out a questionnaire *AE*
- ◆ fill out a questionaire *AE*
- ◆ fill out a questionary *AE*
- ◆ fill in a questionnaire *BE*

Fragebogen verteilen
- ◆ distribute a questionnaire
- ◆ distribute a questionaire *AE*
- ◆ distribute a questionary *AE*

Fragebogen zurücksenden
- ◆ return a questionnaire
- ◆ return a questionaire *AE*
- ◆ return a questionary *AE*

fragen, ob sie ein Zimmer frei haben
- ◆ ask if they have a room free

fragen nach dem Weg
nach dem Weg fragen
- ◆ ask the way
- ◆ ask one's way

fragen nach einem Zimmer
nach einem Zimmer fragen
nach einem Zimmer sich erkundigen
- ◆ ask about a room
- ◆ enquire about a room
- ◆ inquire about a room

Frage zu einer Rechnung haben
Rückfrage zu einer Rechnung haben
- ◆ have a query about a bill
- ◆ have a query about a check *AE*

Franchise, n
Franchising, n
Franchise, f (Versicherung)
- ◆ franchise
- ◆ franchising

Franchiseabkommen, n
- → Franchisevereinbarung

Franchiseabteilung, f *(eines Unternehmens)*
- ◆ franchise division

Franchiseabteilung, f *(generell)*
- ◆ franchise department

Franchiseaktivität, f
- ◆ franchise activity

Franchisearrangement, n
Franchisevereinbarung, f
- ◆ franchise arrangement

Franchiseausstellung, f
- ◆ franchise show

Franchiseberater, m
- ◆ franchise consultant

Franchisebetreiber, m
Franchiseunternehmer, m
- ◆ franchise operator

Franchisebetrieb, m
- ◆ franchise establishment
- ◆ franchise operation
- ◆ franchise

Franchisebüro, n
- ◆ franchise office

Franchiseeinheit, f
(Statistik)
- ◆ franchise unit

Franchiseeinnahme, f
- ◆ franchise revenue
- ◆ franchise income

Franchiseertrag, m (Guv)
  (Gewinn- und Verlustrechnung)
  ◆ franchise income
Franchisefirma, f
  Firma mit einer Franchisevereinbarung, f
  ◆ franchised firm
  ◆ franchised company
Franchisegeber, m
  ◆ franchiser
  ◆ franchisor
  ◆ franchise-giver
Franchisegebiet, n (abstrakt)
  Franchisesektor, m
  ◆ franchise sector
  ◆ franchise field
Franchisegebiet, n (konkret)
  ◆ franchise area
Franchisegebühr f
  ◆ franchise fee
  ◆ franchise charge
Franchisegeschäft n
  ◆ franchise business
Franchisegesellschaft, f
  ◆ franchise corporation *AE*
  ◆ franchise company *BE*
Franchisegruppe f
  ◆ franchise group
Franchisehaus, n
  ◆ franchise house
Franchisehotel, n
  Hotel mit einer Franchisevereinbarung, n
  ◆ franchise hotel
  ◆ franchised hotel
Franchisehotelkette, f
  ◆ franchise hotel chain
Franchiseimmobilie, f
  ◆ franchise property
  ◆ franchised property
Franchiseinhaber, m
  ◆ franchise owner
  ◆ owner of a franchise
Franchise kaufen
  ◆ buy a franchise
Franchisekette f
  ◆ franchise chain
Franchisekonzept, n
  ◆ franchise concept
Franchisekonzern, m
  ◆ franchise group
Franchisemanagement, n
  ◆ franchise management
Franchisemarketing, n
  ◆ franchise marketing
Franchisemotel, n
  Motel mit einer Franchisevereinbarung, n
  ◆ franchise motel
  ◆ franchised motel
Franchise nehmen
  ◆ take up a franchise
Franchisenehmer, m
  Franchiseträger, m
  ◆ franchisee
Franchisenetz, n
  ◆ franchise network
Franchiseorganisation, f
  ◆ franchise organisation
Franchisepaket, n
  ◆ franchise package
Franchisepartner, m
  ◆ franchise partner

Franchisepraxis, f
  ◆ franchise practice
Franchiseprogramm, n
  ◆ franchise program *AE*
  ◆ franchise programme *BE*
Franchiserestaurant, n
  Restaurant mit einer Franchisevereinbarung, n
  ◆ franchise restaurant
  ◆ franchised restaurant
Franchisesektor, m
  → Franchisegebiet
Franchisesystem n
  ◆ franchise system
Franchiseträger, m
  → Franchisenehmer
Franchisetrend, m
  ◆ franchise trend
Franchisetrend folgen
  ◆ follow the franchise trend
Franchiseumsatz, m
  ◆ franchise sales *pl*
  ◆ franchise turnover
Franchiseverband, m
  Franchiseassoziation f
  ◆ franchise association
Franchisevereinbarung f
  Franchiseabkommen f
  ◆ franchise agreement
Franchise vergeben an jn
  ◆ grant a franchise to s.o.
Franchise verkaufen
  ◆ sell a franchise
Franchiseverkaufsstelle, f
  ◆ franchise outlet
Franchise verlieren
  ◆ lose one's franchise
  ◆ lose a franchise
Franchisevertrag m
  ◆ franchise contract
  ◆ franchise agreement
Franchisevertrag verlängern
  ◆ renew a franchise contract
Franchisewerbung, f
  ◆ franchise advertising
Franchising n
  ◆ franchising
Franke, m (generell)
  ◆ Franconian
Franke, m (historisch)
  ◆ Frank
Franken
  (Land)
  ◆ Franconia
Frankenwald m
  (Region)
  ◆ Franconian Forest, the
Frankenwein, n
  fränkischer Wein, m
  ◆ Franconian wine
Frankfurter Messe, f
  ◆ Frankfurt Fair, the
Frankfurter Würstchen, n
  Frankfurter Wurst, f
  Frankfurter, f
  Knackwurst, f
  ◆ frankfurter sausage
  ◆ frankfurter
  ◆ frank *AE inform*
frankierter adressierter Briefumschlag, m
  → Freiumschlag

frankierter Briefumschlag, m
  frankierter Umschlag, m
  ◆ stamped envelope
frankierter Umschlag, m
  → frankierter Briefumschlag
frankierter und adressierter Umschlag, m
  → Freiumschlag
Fränkin, f (generell)
  ◆ Franconian girl
  ◆ Franconian woman
  ◆ Franconian
  ◆ girl from Franconia
  ◆ woman from Franconia
Fränkin, f (historisch)
  ◆ Frankish girl
  ◆ Frankish woman
  ◆ Frank
fränkisch, adj (generell)
  ◆ Franconian, adj
fränkisch, adj (historisch)
  ◆ Frankish, adj
Fränkische Alb, f
  (Region)
  Fränkischer Jura, m
  ◆ Franconian Jura, the
Fränkischer Jura, m
  → Fränkische Alb
Fränkische Schweiz f
  (Region)
  ◆ Franconian Switzerland
fränkische Zeit, f *hist*
  ◆ Frankish times, pl *hist*
Frankreich
  ◆ France
Frankreichprospekt, m
  ◆ France brochure
Frankreichurlaub, m
  ◆ French vacation *AE*
  ◆ French holiday *BE*
Franziskanerkirche, f
  ◆ Franciscan church
Franziskanerkloster, n (Frauen)
  Franziskanerinnenkloster, n
  ◆ Franciscan convent
Franziskanerkloster, n (Männer)
  ◆ Franciscan monastery
  ◆ Franciscan friary
Franziskanermuseum, n
  ◆ Franciscan Museum
Franzose, m
  ◆ Frenchman
Französin, f
  ◆ Frenchwoman
französisch, adj
  ◆ French, adj
französisch-deutsche Grenze, f
  ◆ Franco-German border
  ◆ Franco-German frontier
französische Art, adv *gastr*
  nach französischer Art, adv *gastr*
  ◆ French style, adv *gastr*
französische Küche f
  ◆ French cuisine
  ◆ French cooking
Französischen Alpen, die, pl
  ◆ French Alps, the *pl*
französischer Abschied m
  Abschied auf französisch m
  ◆ French leave
Französische Riviera, f
  ◆ French Riviera, the

französischer Service

französischer Service, m
　Service à la française m FR
　♦ French service
　♦ service à la française FR
französischer Wein, m
　♦ French wine
französisches Bett n
　Grand lit n
　♦ French double bed FR
　♦ grand lit FR
französisches Château, n
　♦ French château
französisches Gericht, n
　♦ French dish
französische Toilette, f
　sitzlose Toilette, f
　Stehtoilette, f
　♦ French-style toilet
　♦ seatless toilet
　♦ squatter BE coll
Französische Woche, f
　♦ French Week
französisch kochen
　französische Gerichte kochen
　♦ cook French dishes
　♦ prepare French cuisine
Frascati, m ITAL
　♦ Frascati ITAL
Fraß, m coll
　♦ chow AE sl
　♦ grub sl
　♦ muck vulg
　♦ swill fam
　♦ poison coll
Frau
　(Anrede)
　♦ Mrs. AE
　♦ Mrs BE
Frau, f
　♦ woman
Frauenhotel, n
　♦ ladies' hotel
　♦ women's hotel
Frauenkirche, f
　♦ Church of Our Lady
　♦ Our Lady's Church
Frauenklinik, f
　♦ gynaecological clinic
　♦ gynecological clinic
Frauenkongreß, m
　♦ women's congress
Frauenleiden, n
　♦ gynaecological disorder
　♦ gynecological disorder
Fräulein!
　(Anrede an Kellnerin)
　♦ Waitress!
Fräulein, n
　junge Frau, f
　♦ young lady
Fräulein Stadtfeld
　♦ Miss Stadtfeld
　♦ Ms. Stadtfeld AE
　♦ Ms Stadtfeld BE
Frau Peters
　♦ Mrs. Peters AE
　♦ Mrs Peters BE
Free-flow-Theke, f
　♦ free-flow counter

Freeholder, m hist
　(in England früher lehensfreier Grundeigentümer)
　♦ freeholder hist
Frei
　(Hinweisschild an Toilette, Taxi)
　♦ Vacant
frei, adj (Straße)
　♦ clear, adj
frei, adj (Unterkunft)
　→ leerstehend
Freibad, n
　♦ outdoor swimming pool AE
　♦ outdoor swimming-pool BE
　♦ outdoor pool
　♦ open-air swimming pool AE
　♦ open-air swimming-pool BE
Freibadanlage, f
　♦ outdoor swimming pool complex AE
　♦ outdoor swimming-pool complex BE
　♦ outdoor pool complex
Freibadbecken, n
　Schwimmbecken im Freien, n
　♦ outdoor bathing pool
　♦ outdoor swimming pool AE
　♦ outdoor swimming-pool BE
Freibadbenutzung, f
　♦ use of the outdoor swimming pool AE
　♦ use of the outdoor swimming-pool BE
　♦ use of the outdoor pool
　♦ using the outdoor swimming pool AE
　♦ using the outdoor swimming-pool BE
Freibadbesuch, m
　♦ visit to the outdoor swimming pool AE
　♦ visit to the outdoor swimming-pool BE
　♦ visit to the outdoor pool
Freibar, f
　(Veranstalter zahlt gesamte Rechnung)
　♦ free bar
　♦ open bar
Freibett, n
　kostenloses Bett, n
　♦ free bed
　♦ bed free of charge
Freibier, n
　kostenloses Bier, n
　♦ free beer
freie Ausreise, f
　(aus einem Land)
　♦ free exit
freie Betten füllen
　♦ fill vacant beds
freie Einreise, f
　(in ein Land)
　♦ free entry
freie Hotelwahl, f
　♦ choice of hotel
freie Kapazität haben
　♦ have spare capacity
freie Marktwirtschaft, f
　♦ free-enterprise economy
freie Menüwahl, f
　♦ free choice of menu
freien Eintritt haben
　♦ have free admission
　♦ have free entrance
　♦ be admitted gratis
freien Tag haben
　Tag frei haben
　♦ have a day off
freien Tag nehmen (sich)
　(Personal)

Tag frei nehmen (sich)
　♦ take a day off
freien Zugang haben zu etw
　♦ have free access to s.th.
freie Plätze haben
　♦ have vacancies
freier Blick auf etw, m
　♦ uninterrupted view of s.th.
　♦ unrestricted view of s.th.
freie Reichsstadt, f hist
　♦ free imperial city hist
freier Eintritt zu etw, m
　freier Eintritt in etw, m
　♦ free admission to s.th.
　♦ free entrance to s.th.
freier Grundeigentümer, m
　Eigentümer, m
　Grund- und Hauseigentümer, m
　♦ freeholder
freier Platz in letzter Sekunde, m
　Last-Minute-Platz, m
　♦ last-minute vacancy
freier Sitzplatz, m
　♦ vacant seat
freier Stellplatz, m
　(Camping)
　♦ vacant pitch
　♦ empty pitch
freier Stuhl, m
　♦ vacant chair
freier Tag, m (Arbeitnehmer)
　♦ day off
freier Tag, m (Tourist)
　→ programmfreier Tag
freier Tisch, m
　♦ free table
　♦ vacant table
　♦ unoccupied table
freier Zugang zur Sauna, m
　♦ free access to the sauna
freier Zutritt zu etw., m
　♦ free access to s.th.
freies Appartement, n
　♦ vacant apartment
　♦ vacancy
freies Bett, n
　♦ vacant bed
　♦ empty bed
freies Geleit, n jur
　♦ safe conduct jur
freies Geleit geben jm jur
　♦ give s.o. safe conduct jur
freie Sicht, f
　freier Blick, m
　freier Ausblick, m
　♦ unobstructed view
　♦ uninterrupted view
freies Quartier, n
　kostenloses Quartier, n
　♦ quarters free of charge pl
　♦ free quarters pl
freies Quartier haben
　kostenloses Quartier haben
　umsonst wohnen
　♦ have free quarters
freie Station, f
　♦ free room and board with all bills paid AE
　♦ free board and lodging, everything found BE
　♦ free board and lodging, all found BE
freies Taxi, n
　leeres Taxi, n

250

- empty taxi
- vacant taxi
- empty cab

freies Zimmer, n
vakantes Zimmer, n
- **vacancy**
- vacant room

Freie Verpflegungswahl möglich
- **Choice of board available**

freie Wahl haben
- **be free to choose**
- have the liberty to choose

freie Wohnung, f
- **vacant flat** BE
- vacant apartment AE
- vacancy

freie Zeit, f
- **free time**
- spare time
- leisure time
- time off

freie Zimmer haben
- **have vacancies**

Freifahrschein, m
→ Freikarte

Freifahrt, f
kostenlose Fahrt, f
- **free ride**
- free trip

Freiflug, m
→ kostenloser Flug

Freiflugschein, m
→ kostenloser Flugschein

Freigabe unverkaufter Zimmer, f
Rückgabe unverkaufter Zimmer, f
- **release of unsold rooms**

Freigast, m
nichtzahlender Gast, m
umsonst wohnender Gast, m
- **deadhead** coll
- nonpaying guest AE
- non-paying guest BE

freigeben etw
aufheben etw
zurückgeben etw
- **release s.th.**

freigeben etw aus dem Kontingent
zurückgeben etw aus dem Kontingent
- **release s.th. from the allocation**
- release s.th. from the allotment

freigebig, adj
freigiebig, adj
- **generous, adj**
- openhanded, adj AE
- open-handed, adj BE
- lavish, adj

Freigehege, n
(für Tiere)
- **outdoor enclosure**
- outdoor inclosure
- open-air enclosure
- open-air inclosure

Freigelände, n
- **open-air grounds** pl

Freigepäck, n
Freigepäckgrenze, f
- **baggage allowance** AE
- allowed baggage AE
- luggage allowance BE
- allowed luggage BE
- free baggage allowance AE

Freigepäckgrenze, f
Freigepäck, n
- **luggage allowance** BE
- baggage allowance AE

frei haben
nicht arbeiten
- **be free**
- be off (duty)

Freihafen, m
- **free port**

Frei-/Hallenbad, n
(Kombination)
- **outdoor-indoor swimming pool** AE
- outdoor-indoor swimming-pool BE
- outdoor-indoor pool

Freiheitsstatue, f
- **Statue of Liberty, the**

Freihof, m
nicht überdachter Innenhof, m
Freisitz, m
- **open-air patio**

Freikarte, f
kostenlose Karte, f
Ehrenkarte, f
- **free ticket**
- complimentary ticket

Freikörperkultur, f
→ FKK

Freilichtbühne, f
- **open-air stage**

Freilichtbühnenvorstellung, f
- **open-air theater performance** AE
- open-air theatre performance BE

Freilichtkino, n
- **open-air cinema** Be
- open-air movie AE

Freilichtmuseum n
- **open-air museum**

Freilichttheater, n
Freilichtbühne, f
- **open-air theater** AE
- open-air theatre BE

Freiluftbar f
- **open-air bar**

Freiluftbecken, n
Freibecken, n
Freibad, n
- **open-air pool**
- outdoor pool

Freiluftcafé, n
Café im Freien, n
- **open-air cafe**
- open-air café BE
- outdoor cafe
- outdoor café BE

Freiluftdisko, f
Freiluftdiskothek, f
- **open-air disco**
- open-air discotheque

Freiluftdiskothek, f
Freiluftdisko, f
- **open-air discotheque**
- open-air disco

Freilufteisbahn, f
- **open-air ice-skating rink**
- open-air skating rink

Freiluftfestival n
→ Open-air-Festival

Freiluftgrill, m
- **open-air grill**
- open-air barbecue

Freiluftimbißstand, m
- **open-air snack bar**

Freiluftnachtbar, f
- **open-air nightclub** AE
- open-air night-club BE

Freiluftrestaurant n
Restaurant im Freien n
Gartenrestaurant n
- **open-air restaurant**

Freiluftsaison, f
- **outdoor season**

Freiluftspeisesaal, m
→ Speisesaal im Freien

Freiluft-Spezialitätenrestaurant, n
- **open-air specialty restaurant** AE
- open-air speciality restaurant BE

Freiluftthermalbecken, n
- **open-air thermal pool**

Freiluftveranstaltung, f
- **open-air event**
- open-air function

frei machen etw (Unterkunft)
→ räumen etw

Freimaurerkongreß, m
- **masonic convention**
- masonic congress

Freiplatz, m (Sitzplatz)
kostenloser Platz, m
kostenloser Sitzplatz, m
- **free seat**

Freiplatz, m (Unterkunft)
(in Heim etc)
kostenloser Platz, m
Freistelle, f
- **free quarters** pl

frei reisen in Europa
ungehindert reisen in Europa
- **travel freely in Europe**

Freischach, n
Freilandschach, n
Gartenschach, n
- **open-air chess**
- outdoor chess

freisetzen jn euph
entlassen jn
- **make s.o. redundant**
- dismiss s.o.
- lay s.o. off

Freisitz, m (Sitzplatz)
→ Freiplatz

Freisitz, m (Terrasse)
→ Freiterrasse

Freisolebad n
→ s. Solefreibad n

frei sprechen
ohne Manuskript sprechen
- **speak extempore**

freistehend, adj (einzeln stehend)
- **freestanding, adj**

freistehend, adj (leerstehend)
→ leerstehend

freistehende Garage f
Einzelgarage f
- **detached garage**

freistehende Möbel, n pl
(Gegensatz zu Einbaumöbel)
- **freestanding furniture** sg

freistehendes Chalet, n
- **detached chalet**

freistehendes Haus

freistehendes Haus, n
- freestanding house
- fully detached house

freistehen (leerstehen)
(Unterkunft)
  leerstehen
- be vacant
- be unoccupied
- be empty

Freistelle, f
→ Freiplatz

Freitag, m
- Friday

Freitagabend, m
- Friday evening
- Friday night

freitagabends, adv
- on Friday evenings, adv
- friday evenings, adv
- on Friday evening, adv
- Friday evening, adv

Freitag morgens
- on Friday morning
- Friday morning

Freitag nachts
- on Friday night
- on Friday nights

freitags, adv
- on Fridays, adv
- on Friday, adv
- every Friday, adv
- each Friday, adv
- Fridays, adv *AE*

freitags Fisch essen
- eat fish on Fridays

Freitags Ruhetag
(Schild)
  Freitag Ruhetag
- Closed on Fridays
- Closed on Friday

Freitags Tanz
(Hinweisschild)
- Dancing on Friday
- Dancing on Fridays

Freiterrasse, f
  Freisitz, m
  offene Terrasse, f
- open-air terrace
- open-air patio

Freithermalschwimmbad n
→ s. Thermalfreibad n

Freitisch, m
  kostenlose Verpflegung, f
- free board
- free meals *pl*

Freiumschlag, m
  Rückumschlag, m
- stamped addressed envelope
- SAE

Freiumschlag beifügen
(frankiert und adressiert)
- enclose a stamped addressed envelope
- enclose an SAE

frei verfügbares Einkommen, n
  verfügbares Einkommen, n
- disposable income
- discretionary income *AE*

frei verfügbare Zeit, f
- leisure time

frei werden
  leer werden

  vakant werden
- become vacant
- become empty

Freizeit, f (generell)
- leisure
- leisure time
- free time
- spare time

Freizeit, f (religiös)
  Ferien, pl
- retreat

Freizeitabteilung, f (Behörde)
- recreation department

Freizeitabteilung, f (eines Unternehmens)
- leisure division

Freizeitaktivität, f
  Freizeitveranstaltung, f
- leisure activity

Freizeitangebot, n (Einrichtungen)
  Freizeiteinrichtungen, f pl
- leisure amenities *pl*
- leisure facilities *pl*

Freizeitangebot, n (Palette)
- range of leisure facilities

Freizeitangler, m
- leisure angler

Freizeitanlage, f
  Freizeitkomplex m
- leisure complex

Freizeitannehmlichkeit, f
- leisure amenity

Freizeitansatz, m
- leisure approach

Freizeitanteil, m
- amount of leisure time

Freizeitartikel, m
- leisure item

Freizeitattraktion, f
- leisure attraction

Freizeitaufenthalt, m
- leisure stay

Freizeitausgaben, f pl
- leisure spending
- leisure expenses *pl*

Freizeitausrüstung, f
  Freizeitausstattung, f
- leisure equipment

Freizeitausschuß, m
- leisure committee

Freizeitausstellung, f
- leisure exhibition
- leisure show
- leisure exhibit *AE*

Freizeitbad, n
  Freizeitschwimmbad, n
- leisure swimming pool *AE*
- leisure swimming-pool *BE*
- leisure pool

Freizeitbecken n
- leisure pool

Freizeitbedürfnis, n
- leisure need

Freizeitbenutzer, m
  Freizeitnutzer, m
- leisure user

Freizeitberater, m
- leisure consultant

Freizeitberatung, f
- leisure counseling *AE*
- leisure counselling *BE*

Freizeitberatungsfirma, f
- leisure consultancy

Freizeitberatungsfirma gründen
- form a leisure consultancy

Freizeitbereich, m (abstrakt)
  Freizeitsektor, m
- leisure field
- leisure sector

Freizeitbereich, m (Gelände)
- leisure area

Freizeitbeschäftigung, f
- leisure pursuit
- leisure-time pursuit
- leisure(-time) activity
- leisure(-time) occupation

Freizeitbeschäftigung im Freien, f
- outdoor leisure pursuit

Freizeitbeschäftigung nachgehen
- follow leisure pursuits

Freizeitbesuch, m
- leisure visit

Freizeitbesucher, m
- leisure visitor

freizeitbezogen, adj
- leisure-related, adj

freizeitbezogene Infrastruktur, f
- leisure-related infrastructure

Freizeitclub, m
- leisure club

Freizeitdienstleistung, f
→ Freizeitservice

Freizeitdistrikt, m
  Freizeitviertel, n
- leisure district

Freizeitdorf, n
- leisure village

Freizeiteinrichtung, f
- leisure facility

Freizeiteinrichtungen verbessern
- improve the leisure facilities

Freizeiterlebnis, n
  Freizeiterfahrung, f
- leisure experience

Freizeitfahrzeug, n
(z.B. Reisemobil)
- recreational vehicle *AE*
- RV *AE*
- leisure vehicle

Freizeitfirma, f
- leisure company
- leisure firm

Freizeitforschung f
- leisure research

Freizeitführer, m
(Information)
- leisure guide

Freizeitgast, m
- leisure guest

Freizeitgebiet, n (abstrakt)
→ Freizeitsektor

Freizeitgebiet, n (konkret)
  Freizeitgelände, n
- leisure area

Freizeitgelegenheit, f
  Freizeitmöglichkeit, f
- leisure opportunity

Freizeitgeschäft, n
  Freizeitbranche, f
- leisure business

Freizeitgesellschaft, f (Firma)
→ Freizeitfirma

Freizeitgesellschaft, f (Nation)
- leisure society
- leisure-oriented society *AE*
- leisure-orientated society *BE*

Freizeitgestaltung, f
- use of one's leisure time
- use of one's leisure

Freizeitgewerbe, n
Freizeitbranche, f
- leisure trade

Freizeitgewohnheit, f
- leisure habit

Freizeithaus, n
→ Urlaubshaus

Freizeitheim, n
→ Urlaubsheim

Freizeithof, m
Freizeitbauernhof, m
- leisure farm

Freizeithotel n
- leisure hotel

Freizeitindustrie, f
Freizeitbranche, f
- leisure industry

Freizeitkarte, f (Landkarte)
- leisure map

Freizeitkatalog, m
- leisure catalogue
- leisure catalog *AE*

Freizeitkleidung, f
- leisurewear
- casual wear

Freizeitkomplex, m
→ Freizeitanlage

Freizeitkonzept, n
- leisure concept

Freizeitkonzern, m
- leisure group

Freizeitkurzurlaub, m
- leisure break

Freizeitlager, n
→ Ferienlager

Freizeitlebensstil, m
- leisure lifestyle

Freizeitleistung, f
→ Freizeitdienstleistung

Freizeitliege, f
(Möbelstück)
- leisure lounger

Freizeitmaler, m
- leisure painter

Freizeitmanagement, n
- leisure management

Freizeitmanager, m
- leisure manager

Freizeitmarketing, n
- leisure marketing

Freizeitmarkt m
- leisure market

Freizeitmesse, f
- leisure fair

Freizeitnutzung, f
- leisure use
- use of one's leisure (time)

Freizeitorganisation, f
- leisure organisation
- leisure organization

freizeitorientiert, adj
- leisure-oriented, adj *AE*
- leisure-orientated, adj *BE*

Freizeitort, m
- leisure resort

Freizeitparadies, n
- leisure paradise

Freizeitpark, m
- leisure park

Freizeitplaner, m
- leisure planner

Freizeitplanung, f
- leisure planning

Freizeitplatz, m
Freizeitort, m
- leisure venue

Freizeitpolitik, f
- leisure policy

Freizeitpotential, n
- leisure potential

Freizeitprodukt, n
- leisure product

Freizeitprogramm, n
- leisure program *AE*
- leisure programme *BE*

Freizeitprojekt, n
- leisure project

Freizeitprospekt, m
Erholungsprospekt, m
- recreation brochure

Freizeitraum, m
→ Aufenthaltsraum

Freizeitreferent, m
(in Gemeinde)
- leisure officer

Freizeitreiseindustrie, f
Freizeitreisegewerbe, n
- leisure travel industry

Freizeitreisen, n
Freizeitreiseverkehr, m
- leisure travel
- leisure traveling *AE*
- leisure travelling *BE*

Freizeitreisender, m
- leisure traveller
- leisure traveler *AE*

freizeitrelevant, adj
- leisure-relevant, adj

Freizeitschwimmbad, n
→ Freizeitbad

Freizeitsee, m (Binnensee)
- leisure lake

Freizeitsegment, n
- leisure segment

Freizeitsegmentierung, f
- leisure segmentation

Freizeitsektor, m
Freizeitbereich, m
- leisure sector

Freizeitservice, m
Freizeitdienst, m
Freizeitdienstleistung, f
Freizeitleistung, f
- leisure service

Freizeitspezialist, m
- leisure specialist

Freizeitstadt, f (Großstadt)
- leisure city

Freizeitstadt, f (kleine Stadt)
- leisure town

Freizeitstätte, f
→ Freizeiteinrichtung

Freizeitstudien, f pl
- leisure studies *pl*

Freizeittag, m
- leisure day

Freizeittip, m
- leisure tip

Freizeittourismus, m
- leisure tourism

Freizeittourist, m
- leisure tourist

Freizeitumwelt, f
- leisure environment

Freizeit und Vergnügen
Freizeit (f) und Vergnügen (n)
- leisure and pleasure

Freizeitunterkunft, f
- leisure accommodation

Freizeitunternehmen, n
- leisure enterprise

Freizeituntersuchung, f
(zur Freizeit)
Freizeitstudie f
- leisure study

Freizeitverhalten, n
- leisure pattern
- leisure routine

Freizeitverkaufsstelle, f
- leisure outlet

Freizeitverkehr, m
- leisure traffic

Freizeitwert, m
Erholungswert, m
- recreational value

Freizeitwochenende, n
- leisure weekend

Freizeitzentrum, n
- leisure center *AE*
- leisure centre *BE*

Freizeitzentrumleiter, m
- leisure center manager *AE*
- leisure centre manager *BE*

Freizeitzielort, m
Freizeitziel, n
Freizeitdestination, f
- leisure destination

Freizeitzweck, m
- leisure purpose

Freizimmer, n
Gratiszimmer, n
kostenloses Zimmer, n
- courtesy room *AE*
- room free of charge
- free room
- complimentary room

Fremdagentur, f
Fremdvermittlung, f
- outside agency

Fremdberater, m
außerbetrieblicher Berater, m
- outside consultant

Fremdberatungsdienst, m
außerbetrieblicher Beratungsdienst, m
- outside consultancy service

Fremdcaterer, m
Drittcaterer, m
Fremdverpflegungslieferant, m
- outside catering contractor
- outside caterer

fremde Leistung, f
→ Fremdleistung

Fremdenabgabe, f
→ Fremdensteuer

Fremdenankünfte

Fremdenankünfte, f pl
(Statistik)
Touristenankünfte, f pl
♦ tourist arrivals *pl*

Fremdenaufenthalt, m
Touristenaufenthalt, m
♦ tourist stay

Fremdenbett, n (allgemein)
♦ bed available to tourists
♦ hotel bed
♦ bed
♦ bed for a paying guest

Fremdenbett, n (für Touristen)
♦ tourist bed
♦ bed available to a tourist

Fremdenbett, n (in Hotel)
→ Hotelbett

Fremdenbuch, n (Gästebuch)
→ Gästebuch

Fremdenbuch, n (Hotel)
Fremdenregister, n
Fremdenverzeichnis, n
♦ hotel register
♦ guest book

Fremdenbuch führen (generell)
♦ keep a visitors' book

Fremdenbuch führen (Hotel)
♦ keep a hotel register

Fremdenessen, n
→ Touristenessen

fremdenfeindlich, adj
xenophob, adj
♦ hostile to strangers, adj
♦ hostile to foreigners, adj
♦ xenophobic, adj

Fremdenführer, m (Buch)
♦ guidebook
♦ guide
♦ cicerone *humor*

Fremdenführer, m (Person)
♦ tourist guide
♦ guide
♦ cicerone *humor*

Fremdenführerdienst, m
Fremdenführerservice m
Fremdenführer m
♦ guide service
♦ guide available

Fremdenführer engagieren
Fremdenführer anheuern *coll*
♦ engage a tourist guide
♦ hire a tourist guide *BE*

Fremdenführergebühr, f
♦ tourist guide fee
♦ guide fee

Fremdenführerlohn, m
♦ tourist guide charge
♦ tourist guide fee
♦ guide charge
♦ guide fee
♦ charge for the guide

Fremdenführerservice, m
→ Fremdenführerdienst

Fremdenführer vor Ort, m
Reiseleiter vor Ort, m
Standortsreiseleiter, m
♦ local tourist guide
♦ local guide

Fremdenführerzuschlag m
♦ guide supplement

Fremdenführung, f
→ Führung

Fremdenhaß, m
♦ hatred of strangers
♦ hatred of foreigners
♦ xenophobia

Fremdenheim, n
(ohne Restaurant und ohne Passanten)
Pension, f
♦ tourist home *AE*
♦ bed-and-board house *AE*
♦ rooming house *AE*
♦ boardinghouse *AE*
♦ tourist hostel

Fremdenindustrie, f
→ Fremdenverkehrsindustrie

Fremdenliste, f
Ankunftsliste f
♦ list of arrivals
♦ arrivals list

Fremdenmenü, n
→ Touristenmenü

Fremdenpension, f
♦ guesthouse *AE*
♦ guest-house *BE*

Fremdenpolizei, f (für Touristen)
♦ tourist police

Fremdenregister, n (Hotel)
→ Fremdenbuch

Fremdenschein, m (Hotel)
Meldeschein, m
♦ registration form

Fremdensteuer, f
Fremdenabgabe, f
♦ visitors' tax
♦ tourist tax
♦ non-resident tax *BE*

Fremdenübernachtung, f (Statistik)
Fremdenbettnacht, f
Touristenübernachtung, f
♦ tourist bed-night

Fremdenunterkunft, f
Touristenunterkunft, f
♦ accommodation for tourists
♦ tourist accommodation

Fremdenunterkunft mit Service, f
♦ serviced tourist accommodation

Fremdenunterkunft ohne Service, f
Fremdenunterkunft ohne Bedienung, f
♦ nonserviced tourist accommodation *AE*
♦ non-serviced tourist accommodation *BE*

Fremdenunterkunftsbereich, m
Touristenunterkunftssektor, m
♦ tourist accommodation sector

Fremdenverkehr, m (Inlandstourismus)
→ Inlandstourismus

Fremdenverkehr, m (Reiseverkehr)
→ Reiseverkehr

Fremdenverkehr, m (Tourismus)
→ Tourismus

Fremdenverkehr fördern (Reiseverkehr)
Reiseverkehr fördern
♦ promote tourist traffic

Fremdenverkehr fördern (Tourismus)
Tourismus fördern
♦ further tourism
♦ promote tourism

Fremdenverkehr gleichmäßiger verteilen
Tourismus gleichmäßiger verteilen
♦ spread tourism more evenly

Fremdenverkehr innerhalb Europas, m (Reiseverkehr)
→ Reiseverkehr innerhalb Europas

Fremdenverkehr innerhalb Europas, m (Tourismus)
Tourismus innerhalb Europas, m
♦ tourism within Europe

Fremdenverkehrsabgabe, f
Fremdenabgabe, f
Fremdensteuer, f
♦ non-residents tax *BE*
♦ tourist tax
♦ visitors' tax

Fremdenverkehrsabteilung, f (eines Unternehmens)
touristische Abteilung, f
Tourismusabteilung, f
♦ tourist division
♦ tourism division

Fremdenverkehrsamt, n
Verkehrsamt, n
FVA, f
♦ tourist office

Fremdenverkehrsamtsdame, f
Dame vom Fremdenverkehrsamt, f
♦ tourist office lady
♦ lady at the tourist office

Fremdenverkehrsamtsmitarbeiter, m
♦ tourist official
♦ tourism official

Fremdenverkehrsanbieter, m
Tourismusanbieter, m
touristischer Anbieter, m
♦ tourist supplier
♦ tourism supplier

Fremdenverkehrsangebot, n (Gegensatz zu Nachfrage)
touristisches Angebot, n
Tourismusangebot, n
♦ tourist supply
♦ tourism supply

Fremdenverkehrsangelegenheit, f
Tourismusangelegenheit, f
♦ tourist matter
♦ tourism matter
♦ matter of tourism

Fremdenverkehrsattraktion, f
→ Touristenattraktion

Fremdenverkehrsaufkommen, n
Fremdenverkehrsvolumen, n
♦ tourist volume
♦ tourism volume
♦ volume of tourism

Fremdenverkehrsaufwand, m
touristischer Aufwand, m
Tourismusaufwand, m
♦ tourist expenditure
♦ tourist expense *AE*

Fremdenverkehrsausgaben, f pl
(durch Touristen)
♦ tourist expenses *pl*
♦ tourist expenditures *pl*
♦ tourism spend

Fremdenverkehrsausschuß, m
Tourismusausschuß, m
♦ tourist committee
♦ tourism committee
♦ committee for tourism

Fremdenverkehrsausschuß gründen
Tourismusausschuß gründen
♦ set up a tourist committee

- ♦ set up a tourism committee
- ♦ set up a committee for tourism

Fremdenverkehrsbasis, f
Fremdenverkehrsgrundlage, f
touristische Basis, f
Tourismusgrundlage, f
- ♦ **tourist base**
- ♦ basis of tourism

Fremdenverkehrsbehörde, f
Tourismusbehörde, f
- ♦ **tourist authority**
- ♦ tourism authority

Fremdenverkehrsbereich, m (Sektor)
Fremdenverkehrssektor, m
Tourismusbereich, m
Tourismussektor, m
- ♦ **tourist field**
- ♦ tourism field
- ♦ tourist sector
- ♦ tourism sector

Fremdenverkehrsbetrieb, m
touristischer Betrieb, m
Tourismusbetrieb, m
- ♦ **tourist establishment**
- ♦ tourism establishment
- ♦ tourist operation
- ♦ tourism operation

Fremdenverkehrsbilanz, f
Tourismusbilanz, f
- ♦ **tourist balance**
- ♦ tourism balance

Fremdenverkehrsboom, m
Tourismusboom, m
- ♦ **tourist boom**
- ♦ tourism boom

Fremdenverkehrsbüro, n
Fremdenverkehrsstelle, f
- ♦ **tourist bureau** AE
- ♦ tourist information office
- ♦ tourist agency
- ♦ tourist office

Fremdenverkehrsbürokratie, f
Tourismusbürokratie, f
- ♦ **tourist bureaucracy**
- ♦ tourism bureaucracy

Fremdenverkehrsdaten, pl
- ♦ **tourism data**

Fremdenverkehrsdienstleistung, f
Fremdenverkehrsleistung, f
Fremdenverkehrsservice, m
touristische Dienstleistung, f
Tourismusleistung, f
- ♦ **tourist service**
- ♦ tourism service

Fremdenverkehrsdirektor, m
- ♦ **director of the tourist office**
- ♦ head of the tourist office

Fremdenverkehrsdorf, n
Touristendorf, n
- ♦ **tourist village**
- ♦ tourism village

Fremdenverkehrseinnahme, f
Tourismuseinnahme, f
- ♦ **tourist revenue**
- ♦ tourism revenue
- ♦ tourist receipt
- ♦ tourist income
- ♦ revenue from tourism

Fremdenverkehrseinnahmen, f pl
Einnahmen aus dem Fremdenverkehr, f pl
- ♦ **tourist receipts** pl

- ♦ receipts from tourism pl
- ♦ earnings from tourism pl
- ♦ revenues from tourism pl
- ♦ tourist income

Fremdenverkehrseinrichtung, f
Tourismuseinrichtung, f
touristische Einrichtung, f
- ♦ **tourist facility**
- ♦ tourism facility

Fremdenverkehrsentwicklung, f (generell)
Ausbau des Fremdenverkehrs, m
Tourismusentwicklung, f
Ausbau des Tourismus, m
- ♦ **tourism development**
- ♦ development of tourism

Fremdenverkehrsentwicklung, f (historisch)
Tourismusentwicklung, f
- ♦ **evolution of tourism**

Fremdenverkehrsentwicklungsprojekt, n
Tourismusentwicklungsprojekt, n
- ♦ **tourism development project**

Fremdenverkehrsentwicklungsstrategie, f
Tourismusentwicklungsstrategie, f
- ♦ **tourism development strategy**

Fremdenverkehrsexperte, m
Tourismusexperte, m
- ♦ **tourist expert**
- ♦ tourism expert
- ♦ expert in tourism
- ♦ expert from the tourism industry

Fremdenverkehrsfachmann, m
- ♦ **specialist in tourism**

Fremdenverkehrsfirma, f
- ♦ **tourism company**
- ♦ tourism firm

Fremdenverkehrsförderung, f
Tourismusförderung, f
- ♦ **tourist promotion**
- ♦ tourism promotion
- ♦ promotion of tourism
- ♦ promotion of the tourism industry
- ♦ promotion of the tourism trade

Fremdenverkehrsförderungsbüro, n
Tourismusförderungsbüro, n
- ♦ **tourist promotion office**
- ♦ tourism promotion office

Fremdenverkehrsförderungsfonds, m
- ♦ **tourism promotion fund**

Fremdenverkehrsforschung, f
Tourismusforschung, f
- ♦ **tourist research**
- ♦ tourism research
- ♦ research in the field of tourism

Fremdenverkehrsforschungsprogramm, n
- ♦ **tourism research program** AE
- ♦ tourism research programme BE

Fremdenverkehrsgebiet, n (groß)
Fremdenverkehrsregion, f
Tourismusgebiet, n
Tourismusregion, f
- ♦ **tourist region**
- ♦ tourism region

Fremdenverkehrsgebiet, n (klein)
Tourismusgebiet, n
- ♦ **tourist area**
- ♦ tourism area

Fremdenverkehrsgemeinde, f
- ♦ **tourist community**
- ♦ tourist resort

Fremdenverkehrsgeschäft, n
Tourismusgeschäft, n

Fremdenverkehrsbranche, f
Tourismusbranche, f
- ♦ **tourist business**
- ♦ tourism business

Fremdenverkehrsgesellschaft, f
(zur Förderung des Tourismus)
- ♦ **tourist society**
- ♦ tourism society

Fremdenverkehrsgesetzgebung, f
Tourismusgesetzgebung, f
- ♦ **tourist legislation**
- ♦ tourism legislation
- ♦ legislation regarding tourism

Fremdenverkehrsgewerbe, n
Tourismusgewerbe, n
Fremdenverkehrsbranche, f
Tourismusbranche, f
- ♦ **tourist trade**
- ♦ tourism trade

Fremdenverkehrsgremium, n
Tourismusgremium, n
- ♦ **tourist body**
- ♦ tourism body

Fremdenverkehrsindustrie, f
Fremdenindustrie, f
Tourismusindustrie, f
Fremdenverkehrsbranche, f
Tourismusbranche, f
- ♦ **tourist industry**
- ♦ tourism industry
- ♦ hotel and tourism industry

Fremdenverkehrsinfrastruktur aufbauen
Tourismusinfrastruktur aufbauen
- ♦ **develop a tourist infrastructure**
- ♦ develop a tourism infrastructure

Fremdenverkehrsinstitution, f
Tourismusinstitution, f
- ♦ **tourist institution**
- ♦ tourism institution

Fremdenverkehrsinvestition, f
Tourismusinvestition, f
- ♦ **tourism investment**
- ♦ investment in tourism

Fremdenverkehrsjahr, n
touristisches Jahr, n
Tourismusjahr, n
- ♦ **tourist year**
- ♦ tourism year

Fremdenverkehrskapazität, f
Tourismuskapazität, f
- ♦ **tourist capacity**
- ♦ tourism capacity

Fremdenverkehrskonferenz, f
Tourismuskonferenz, f
- ♦ **conference on tourism**
- ♦ tourism conference

Fremdenverkehrskonzentration, f
Tourismuskonzentration, f
- ♦ **concentration of tourism**

Fremdenverkehrskooperation, f
- ♦ **tourism cooperation**
- ♦ cooperation in tourism

Fremdenverkehrsleute, pl
Tourismusleute, pl
- ♦ **tourist people** pl
- ♦ tourism people pl

Fremdenverkehrslobby, f
Tourismuslobby, f
- ♦ **tourist lobby**
- ♦ tourism lobby

Fremdenverkehrsmanager

Fremdenverkehrsmanager, m
  Tourismusmanager, m
  ♦ tourist manager
  ♦ tourism manager
  ♦ tourist executive
  ♦ tourism executive
Fremdenverkehrsmarkt, m
  → touristischer Markt
Fremdenverkehrsmetropole, f
  → Fremdenverkehrszentrum
Fremdenverkehrsminister, m
  → Tourismusminister
Fremdenverkehrsministerium, n
  → Tourismusministerium
Fremdenverkehrsnachfrage, f
  touristische Nachfrage, f
  Tourismusnachfrage, f
  ♦ tourist demand
  ♦ tourism demand
  ♦ demand for tourism
Fremdenverkehrsnation, f
  Fremdenverkehrsvolk, n
  ♦ tourist nation
Fremdenverkehrsort, m
  ♦ tourist resort
  ♦ tourism resort
Fremdenverkehrsortentwicklung, f
  ♦ development of a tourist resort
  ♦ resort development
Fremdenverkehrsortmarketing, n
  → Zielortmarketing
Fremdenverkehrsplakat, n
  Tourismusplakat, n
  ♦ tourist poster
  ♦ tourism poster
Fremdenverkehrsplanung, f
  Tourismusplanung, f
  ♦ tourist planning
  ♦ tourism planning
  ♦ planning (of) tourism
Fremdenverkehrsplatz, m
  Fremdenverkehrsort, m
  Touristenplatz, m
  Touristenort, m
  ♦ tourist site
Fremdenverkehrspluspunkt, m
  Fremdenverkehrsstärke, f
  ♦ tourist asset
  ♦ tourism asset
Fremdenverkehrspolitik, f
  Tourismuspolitik, f
  ♦ tourist policy
  ♦ tourism policy
Fremdenverkehrspotential, n
  Tourismuspotential, n
  ♦ tourist potential
  ♦ tourism potential
Fremdenverkehrspreis, m (Auszeichnung)
  Tourismuspreis, m
  ♦ tourism prize
  ♦ tourism award
Fremdenverkehrspreis gewinnen
  Tourismuspreis gewinnen
  ♦ win a tourism award
  ♦ win a tourism prize
Fremdenverkehrsprodukt, n
  touristisches Produkt, n
  Tourismusprodukt, n
  ♦ tourist product
  ♦ tourism product

Fremdenverkehrsprogramm, n
  touristisches Programm, n
  Tourismusprogramm, n
  ♦ tourist program *AE*
  ♦ tourist programme *BE*
  ♦ tourism program *AE*
  ♦ tourism programme *BE*
Fremdenverkehrsprojekt, n
  Fremdenverkehrsvorhaben, n
  Tourismusprojekt, n
  Tourismusvorhaben, n
  ♦ tourist project
  ♦ tourism project
Fremdenverkehrsrat, m (Gremium)
  Tourismusrat, m
  ♦ tourist council
  ♦ tourism council
Fremdenverkehrsreferent, m
  (z.B. in einer Gemeinde)
  Tourismusreferent, m
  ♦ tourist officer
  ♦ tourism officer
  ♦ tourist official
  ♦ tourism official
Fremdenverkehrsrezession, f
  Tourismusrezession, f
  ♦ tourism recession
Fremdenverkehrssaison, f
  Touristensaison, f
  Tourismussaison, f
  ♦ tourist season
Fremdenverkehrssaison verlängern
  Tourismussaison verlängern
  ♦ extend the tourist season
  ♦ lengthen the tourist season
Fremdenverkehrssektor, m
  Fremdenverkehrsbereich, m
  Tourismussektor, m
  Tourismusbereich, m
  ♦ tourist sector
  ♦ tourism sector
Fremdenverkehrsseminar, n
  Tourismusseminar, n
  ♦ seminar on tourism
  ♦ tourism seminar
Fremdenverkehrsseminar abhalten
  ♦ hold a tourism seminar
  ♦ hold a seminar on tourism
Fremdenverkehrsstadt, f (Großstadt)
  → Touristenstadt
Fremdenverkehrsstatistik, f
  Tourismusstatistik, f
  ♦ tourist statistics *pl*
  ♦ tourism statistics *pl*
Fremdenverkehrsstatistik erstellen
  Tourismusstatistik erstellen
  ♦ compile tourist statistics
  ♦ compile tourism statistics
Fremdenverkehrsstelle, f
  ♦ tourist information office
  ♦ tourist bureau *AE*
  ♦ tourist office
Fremdenverkehrsstrategie, f
  touristische Strategie, f
  Tourismusstrategie, f
  ♦ tourist strategy
  ♦ tourism strategy
Fremdenverkehrsstreitfrage, f
  strittiges Tourismusproblem, n
  ♦ tourist issue
  ♦ tourism issue

Fremdenverkehr staffeln
  Tourismus staffeln
  ♦ stagger tourism
Fremdenverkehr stimulieren
  → Tourismus anregen
Fremdenverkehrstrend, m
  Tourismustrend, m
  ♦ tourist trend
  ♦ tourism trend
  ♦ trend in tourism
Fremdenverkehrsumfrage, f
  Tourismusumfrage, f
  Fremdenverkehrsüberblick, m
  Tourismusüberblick, m
  ♦ tourist survey
  ♦ tourism survey
Fremdenverkehrsunternehmen, n
  Tourismusunternehmen, n
  ♦ tourist enterprise
  ♦ tourism enterprise
Fremdenverkehrsunternehmer, m
  Tourismusunternehmer, m
  ♦ tourist operator
  ♦ tourism operator
  ♦ tourism entrepreneur
Fremdenverkehrsverband, m
  Tourismusverband, m
  ♦ tourist board
  ♦ tourism board
Fremdenverkehrsverbandsvorsitzender, m
  ♦ tourist board chairman
  ♦ chairman of the tourist board
Fremdenverkehrsverein, m
  Verkehrsverein, m
  ♦ tourist association
  ♦ tourism association
Fremdenverkehrsverwaltung, f
  Tourismusverwaltung, f
  ♦ tourism administration
Fremdenverkehrsvolumen, n
  Tourismusvolumen, n
  ♦ tourism volume
  ♦ volume of tourism
Fremdenverkehrswachstum, n
  Tourismuswachstum, n
  ♦ tourist growth
  ♦ tourism growth
  ♦ increase in tourism
  ♦ growth of tourism
Fremdenverkehrswerbung, f
  Tourismuswerbung, f
  ♦ tourist advertising
  ♦ tourism advertising
Fremdenverkehrswesen, n
  → Tourismus
Fremdenverkehrswirtschaft, f
  Tourismuswirtschaft, f
  ♦ tourist economy
  ♦ tourism economy
  ♦ economics of tourism
Fremdenverkehrszeitschrift, f
  Tourismuszeitschrift, f
  ♦ tourist journal
  ♦ tourism journal
  ♦ journal of tourism
Fremdenverkehrszentrum, n
  Fremdenverkehrsmetropole, f
  Tourismuszentrum, n
  ♦ tourist centre *BE*
  ♦ tourist center *AE*

- tourism center *AE*
- tourism centre *BE*

Fremdenverkehr zeitlich und räumlich entzerren
- stagger tourist traffic in time and space

Fremdenverzeichnis, n
→ Fremdenbuch

Fremdenwohnung, f
Touristenwohnung, f
- tourist flat *BE*
- tourist apartment *AE*

Fremdenzimmer, n (gewerblich)
- room available to tourists
- room to let *BE*

Fremdenzimmer, n (in Privathaus)
→ Gästezimmer

Fremdenzimmer (ein Zimmer)
(Hinweisschild)
- Room to rent *AE*
- Room to let *BE*

Fremdenzimmer (mehrere Zimmer)
(Hinweisschild)
- Rooms to rent *AE pl*
- Rooms to let *BE pl*

Fremder, m (Besucher)
→ Besucher

Fremder, m (Tourist)
→ Tourist

Fremder, m (Unbekannter)
- stranger

fremdes Land, n
Ausland, n
- foreign land
- foreign country

Fremdfirma, f
- outside company
- contract company

Fremdhersteller, m
- outside producer

Fremdkosten, pl
→ Fremdleistungskosten

Fremdleistung, f
- outside service
- contract service
- service provided by others
- service rendered by others

Fremdleistung vergeben (an jn)
- contract out a service (to s.o.)

Fremdpersonal, n
- outside personnel
- outside labor *AE*
- outside labour *BE*

Fremdpersonalkosten, pl
- outside personnel costs *pl*
- outside personnel cost

Fremdreinigung, f
(durch Dritte)
- contract cleaning
- cleaning by a third party

Fremdreinigungsaufwendungen, f pl
- contract-cleaning expenses *pl*

Fremdreinigungsfirma, f
- contract-cleaning company

Fremdreinigung vergeben
- contract out cleaning

Fremdreservierung, f (Flug)
Reservierung bei einer anderen Fluggesellschaft, f
- offline reservation

Fremdsprachinstitut, n
- foreign language institute
- institute of foreign languages

Fremdsprachenkenntnisse, f pl
- knowledge of foreign languages *sg*
- foreign language skills *pl*

Fremdsprachenkenntnisse verbessern
- improve one's (foreign) language skills

Fremdsprache sprechen
- speak a foreign language

Fremdunternehmen, n
- outside concern

Fremdveranstaltung, f
- outside event
- outside function

fremdvergeben etw an jn
- contract s.th. out to s.o.

Fremdverpflegung, f
(durch Personen außerhalb der eigenen Firma etc)
Fremdcatering n
Fremdversorgung f
- outside catering

Fremdvertriebsstelle, f
- outside distribution office
- outside distribution point

Fremdwährung, f
- foreign currency

Fremdwäscherei, f
- outside laundry

frequentieren etw
(Lokal)
- frequent s.th.
- patronise s.th.
- patronize s.th.

Frequentierung, f
→ Auslastung, Belegung

Frequenz, f *SCHW*
→ Belegung, Auslastung

frequenzabhängig, adj *SCHW*
→ belegungsabhängig

freskengeschmückte Decke, f
- frescoed ceiling

freskengeschmückte Wand, f
- frescoed wall

Fresko, n
Freske, f
- fresco

Fressalien, f pl *humor*
- eats *pl coll*
- eatables *pl*
- provisions *pl*
- victuals *pl*

Fressen und Saufen, n vulg
- eating and drinking

fressen wie ein Scheunendrescher *vulg*
→ essen wie ein Scheunendrescher

Fresser, m
→ Vielfraß

Fresserei, f (Völlerei) *vulg*
Völlerei, f
Gefräßigkeit, f
- gormandizing
- gormandizing *BE*
- guzzling
- gluttony

Fresserei, f vulg (Aktivität)
- tuck-in *coll*
- greedy eating

Freßgelage, n
Saufgelage, n
- binge

Freßgier, f vulg
→ Bulimie

Freßkorb, m *coll*
→ Proviantkorb

Freßorgie, f *derog*
großes Essen, n
Veranstaltung mit einem großen Essen, f
- blowout *AE sl*
- blow-out *BE sl*

Freßpaket, n *coll*
- food parcel

Freuden des Lebens genießen
- savor the joys of life *AE*
- savour the joys of life *BE*
- enjoy the pleasures of life

Freudenfest, n
- joyful celebration
- celebration

Freudenfest, n (Jubiläum)
→ Jubiläum

Freudenhaus, n
Bordell n
- house of ill fame
- brothel

freudiger Anlaß, m
- joyful occasion

freuen sich auf einen Besuch
sich auf einen Besuch freuen
- look forward to a visit

freuen sich auf js Gesellschaft
- look forward to the pleasure of s.o.'s company

Freunde einladen zum Abendessen (Dinner)
- invite friends to dinner

Freunde einladen zum Abendessen (Supper)
- invite friends to supper

Freunde einladen zum Mittagessen
- invite friends to lunch

Freundesgruppe, f
- group of friends

Freunde treffen
- meet one's friends

freundlich, adj
- friendly, adj
- kind, adj
- pleasant, adj

freundlich aufgenommen werden
- find a ready welcome

freundlich begrüßen jn
- give s.o. a friendly welcome
- give s.o. a warm welcome

freundlich begrüßt werden
- receive a warm welcome

freundliche Atmosphäre, f
- friendly atmosphere

freundliche Atmosphäre durchdringt das Hotel
- friendly atmosphere pervades the hotel

freundliche Atmosphäre schaffen
- create a friendly atmosphere

freundliche Begrüßung, f
- friendly welcome
- warm welcome

freundliche Begrüßung versprechen
- promise a warm welcome

freundliche Leitung, f
- friendly management

freundlich empfangen jn
- give s.o. a friendly reception
- give s.o. a warm reception

freundlichen Empfang erhalten
- receive a friendly welcome

freundlichen Empfang erleben
- experience a friendly reception

freundlichen Service sicherstellen für alle Gäste
♦ ensure a friendly service to all guests
freundlicher, aber unaufdringlicher Service, m
♦ friendly but unobtrusive service
freundlicher Empfang, m
freundliche Aufnahme, f
♦ friendly reception
♦ kind reception
freundlicher Service m
♦ friendly service
freundliches Hotel, n
♦ friendly hotel
freundliches Lächeln, n
♦ friendly smile
freundliches Zimmer, n
♦ cheerful room
♦ bright room
Freundlichkeit, f
♦ friendliness
Freundlichkeit des Personals f
♦ friendliness of (the) staff
♦ friendliness of (the) personnel
freundlich machen etw
(z.B. Zimmer)
freundliche Atmosphäre geben etw
♦ brighten up s.th.
freundlich sein zu jedem
♦ be friendly to everyone
freundlich zulächeln jm
♦ give s.o. a friendly smile
Freundschaftsbesuch, m
(Politiker etc)
♦ goodwill visit
Freundschaftsspiel, n
♦ friendly match
♦ friendly game
Friedenskonferenz, f
♦ peace conference
Friedenskongreß, m
♦ peace congress
Frieden und Heiterkeit finden
♦ find peace and serenity
Frieden und Stille
Frieden (m) und Stille (f)
♦ peace and quiet
♦ peace and tranquillity BE
♦ peace and tranquility AE
Frieden und Stille finden
♦ find peace and quiet
Frieden und Stille suchen
♦ seek peace and quiet
♦ look for peace and tranquility BE
♦ look for peace and tranquility AE
friedlichen Urlaub suchen
friedliche Ferien suchen
♦ seek a peaceful vacation AE
♦ seek a peaceful holiday BE
friedlicher Abend, m
♦ peaceful evening
friedliches Wochenende, n
♦ peaceful weekend
friedlich schlafen
♦ sleep peacefully
frieren (Person)
♦ be cold
♦ feel cold
♦ be freezing
frieren wie ein Schneider coll
♦ be cold as a brass monkey coll

Friese, m
♦ Frisian
♦ Friesian
Friesin, f
♦ Frisian girl
♦ Frisian woman
♦ Friesian
♦ Friesian girl
♦ Friesian woman
friesisch, adj
♦ Frisian, adj
♦ Friesian, adj
friesische Küste, f
♦ Frisian coast
♦ Friesian coast
Friesischen Inseln, die, f pl
♦ Frisian Islands, the pl
Friesland
♦ Frisia
♦ Friesland
Frigidaire, m ÖST
→ Kühlschrank
Frigobar, f
→ Kühlbar
Frikassee, n
♦ fricassee
frikassieren (etw)
♦ fricassee (s.th.)
frisch aus dem Ofen
♦ fresh from the oven
frisch aus der Küche
♦ fresh from the kitchen
♦ freshly made
frisch belegtes Sandwich, n/m
♦ freshly made sandwich
frisch bezogenes Bett, n
♦ bed with clean sheets
frische Blumen, f pl
♦ fresh flowers pl
frische grüne Kräuter, n pl
♦ fresh green herbs pl
frische Lebensmittel, n pl
♦ fresh food
frischer Fisch, m
♦ fresh fish
frischer Orangensaft, m
♦ fresh orange juice
frischer Salat, m
♦ fresh salad
frisches Ei, n
♦ fresh egg
frisches Essen, n
♦ fresh food
frisches Obst, n
Frischobst, n
♦ fresh fruit
frische Wäsche, f
saubere Wäsche, f
♦ clean linen
frische Wäsche aufziehen
♦ put on fresh linen
♦ put on fresh sheets
frische Zutat, f
♦ fresh ingredient
frisch fühlen sich
♦ feel fresh
frisch gebacken, adj
♦ freshly baked, adj
♦ newly baked, adj
frisch gebackenes Brot, n
♦ fresh-baked bread

♦ freshly baked bread
♦ newly baked bread
frisch gefangener Fisch, m
♦ freshly caught fish
frisch gehackte Petersilie, f
♦ freshly chopped parsley
frisch gekocht, adj (generell)
♦ freshly cooked, adj
frisch gekocht, adj (in Wasser)
♦ freshly boiled, adj
frisch gekochte Nudeln, f pl
♦ freshly boiled noodles pl
frisch gekochtes Essen, n
♦ freshly cooked meal
♦ freshly cooked food
frisch gekochtes Gericht, n
♦ freshly cooked dish
frisch gelegtes Ei, n
♦ newlaid egg
frisch gemahlen, adj
♦ freshly ground, adj
♦ fresh-ground, adj AE
frisch gemahlener Kaffee, m
♦ freshly ground coffee
♦ fresh-ground coffee AE
frisch gemahlener Pfeffer, m
♦ freshly ground pepper
frisch gepflücktes Obst, n
♦ freshly picked fruit
frisch gepresst, adj
♦ freshly pressed, adj
frisch gepresster Orangensaft, m
♦ freshly pressed orange juice
Frisch gestrichen!
(Hinweisschild)
♦ Fresh paint! AE
♦ Wet paint! BE
Frischgewicht, n
(von Waren)
♦ fresh weight
♦ green weight
frisch halten etw
♦ keep s.th. fresh
Frischkost, f
♦ fresh fruit and vegetables pl
Frischmilch, f
frische Milch, f
♦ fresh milk
Frischvermählte, pl
♦ newly married couple
Frischwaren, f pl
♦ fresh produce
♦ perishables pl
frisch zubereitet, adj
♦ freshly prepared, adj
frisch zubereitetes Essen, n
♦ freshly prepared meal
frisch zubereitetes Gericht, n
♦ freshly prepared dish
Friseur, m (für Damen)
♦ hairdresser
Friseur, m (für Herren)
Herrenfriseur, m
♦ barber
♦ gentlemen's hairdresser BE
♦ gents' hairdresser BE
♦ men's hairdresser BE
♦ hairdresser BE
Friseurgeschäft, n
→ Friseursalon

Friseur im Haus
(im Hotel)
♦ hairdresser at the hotel
♦ hairdresser in the hotel
Friseursalon, m (für Damen)
♦ hairdresser's shop
Friseursalon, m (für Damen und Herren)
♦ hairdresser's salon
♦ hairdressing salon
♦ hairdressing saloon *AE*
Friseursalon, m (für Herren)
Herrenfriseursalon, m
♦ hairdresser's shop *BE*
♦ barber's shop *BE*
♦ barbershop *AE*
♦ barber's
Frisierkommode, f
→ Frisiertisch
Frisiertisch, m
Frisierkommode, f
♦ dressing table *AE*
♦ dressing-table *BE*
♦ dresser *coll*
♦ vanity table *AE*
♦ vanity *AE*
Frist, f (Aufschub)
Aufschub, m
Verlängerung, f
♦ prolongation
♦ extension
♦ time allowed
Frist, f (Zeitpunkt)
♦ deadline
♦ time limit *AE*
♦ time-limit *BE*
Frist, f (Zeitraum)
→ Zeitraum
Fristablauf, m
♦ expiry
♦ end of a period of time
Frist einhalten
Termin einhalten
♦ meet a deadline
fristgemäß, adv
fristgerecht, adv
♦ within the period prescribed, adv
♦ in time, adv
♦ punctually, adv
fristgerechte Ankunft, f
→ termingerechte Ankunft
Frist gewähren jm von zehn Tagen
♦ grant s.o. an extension of ten days
♦ give s.o. ten days
fristlos, adv
♦ without notice, adv
♦ without giving notice, adv
fristlose Entlassung, f
(von Personal)
♦ immediate dismissal
fristlose Kündigung, f (Personal)
♦ dismissal without notice
♦ summary dismissal
fristlos kündigen jm
fristlos entlassen jn
♦ dismiss s.o. without notice
Frist setzen (für etw)
♦ set a deadline (for s.th.)
♦ fix a deadline (for s.th.)
♦ set a time limit (for s.th.) *AE*
♦ set a time-limit (for s.th.) *BE*
♦ fix a time limit (for s.th.) *AE*

Frist verlängern vom 1. Mai bis zum 1. Juni
Frist verlängern vom 1. Mai zum 1. Juni
♦ extend the deadline from 1 May to 1 June
Frist versäumen
♦ miss a deadline
Friteuse, f
♦ deep fryer *AE*
♦ deep fat fryer *BE*
♦ deep frying pan
fritieren etw
in schwimmendem Fett braten etw
♦ deep-fry s.th.
fritiert, adj
♦ deep-fried, adj
fritierte Speise, f
♦ deep-fried food
Fritten, pl
Pommes frites, pl
Pommes, pl *coll*
♦ fries *AE pl*
♦ French fries *AE pl*
♦ chips *BE pl*
Frl. Peters
Fräulein Peters
Frau Peters
♦ Ms. Peters *AE*
♦ Ms Peters *BE*
Frohe Feiertage!
♦ Have a pleasant holiday!
♦ Have a nice holiday!
Frohe Ostern!
♦ Happy Easter!
Frohe Pfingsten!
♦ Happy Whitsun!
Frohe Weihnacht!
Frohe Weihnachten!
♦ Merry Christmas!
♦ Happy Christmas!
fröhliche Atmosphäre, f
♦ bright atmosphere
fröhliche Runde, f
♦ circle of merry friends
♦ merry company
fröhliche Stimmung, f
♦ happy mood
Fronleichnam, m
♦ Corpus Christi
Frontbüro, n
→ Front-Office
Front-Office, n
Frontbüro, n
Empfangsbüro, n
♦ front office
♦ reception office
Front-Office-Angestellter, m
Front-Office-Angestellte f
♦ front-office employee
Front-Office-Betrieb, m
♦ front-office operation
Front-Office-Manager, m
♦ front-office manager
Front-Office-Personal, n
Empfangspersonal, n
Gastkontaktpersonal, n
♦ front-office staff
♦ front-office personnel
♦ reception staff
♦ reception personnel
Front-Office-Sekretärin f
♦ front-office secretary

Front-Office-System, n
♦ front-office system
Front-of-the-House, f
(Gegensatz zu Back-of-the-House)
Gästekontaktbereich m
♦ front of the house
Front-of-the-House-Personal, n
Personal im Gästekontaktbereich n
♦ front-of-the-house staff
♦ front-of-the-house personnel
Frontportier, m
→ Türsteher
Frontprojektion f
(bei Dias etc.)
♦ front projection
Frontprojektionsleinwand, f
Leinwand für Frontprojektion, f
♦ front projection screen
Froschschenkel, m pl *gastr*
♦ frog legs, pl *gastr*
frostige Begrüßung, f
♦ frosty welcome
frostiger Empfang m
♦ frosty reception
Frottee, n/m
♦ terrycloth
♦ terry
Frotteebademantel, m
♦ terrycloth bathrobe
♦ terry bathrobe
Frotteebettuch, n
Frotteebettlaken, n
♦ terrycloth sheet
♦ terry sheet
Frotteehandtuch, n
♦ terrycloth towel
♦ terry towel
Fruchtcocktail, m
♦ fruit cocktail
Früchte, f pl
♦ fruits, pl
Früchteauflauf, m
Fruchtauflauf, m
Obstauflauf, m
♦ fruit soufflé
Früchtebecher, m
Fruchtbecher, m
♦ fruit cup
Früchte der Saison, f pl
♦ fruits in season *pl*
Früchtegelee, n
Fruchtgelee, n
♦ fruit jelly
Fruchteis, n
Früchteis, n
♦ fruit ice cream *AE*
♦ fruit ice-cream *BE*
Früchtekaltschale, f
kalte Fruchtsuppe, f
Fruchtkaltschale, f
♦ cold fruit soup
Früchtekonfitüre, f
Fruchtkonfitüre, f
♦ fruit jam
Früchtekorb, m
Obstkorb, m
♦ fruit basket
Fruchtfüllpastete, f
♦ fruit timbale

Fruchtgehalt

Fruchtgehalt, m
 (von Getränken)
 ♦ fruit content
Fruchtgetränk, n
 ♦ fruit drink
fruchtiger Wein, m
 ♦ fruity wine
Fruchtlikör, m
 → Obstlikör
Fruchtsaft, m
 ♦ fruit juice
 ♦ squash BE
Fruchtsaftgetränk, n
 ♦ fruit juice drink
 ♦ fruit juice beverage
Fruchtsafthersteller, m
 ♦ fruit juice manufacturer
Fruchtsaftumsatz, m
 ♦ fruit juice sales pl
Fruchtsaftverbrauch, m
 Fruchtsaftkonsum, m
 ♦ fruit juice consumption
 ♦ consumption of fruit juice
Fruchtsorbet, n
 ♦ fruit sorbet
Fruchtsoße, f
 ♦ fruit sauce
frugal, adj
 karg, adj
 kärglich, adj
 ♦ frugal, adj
frugales Mahl, n
 → karge Mahlzeit
Frühanmeldung, f
 → frühe Anmeldung
früh aufstehen
 ♦ rise early
 ♦ get up early
früh aufstehen und früh zu Bett gehen
 ♦ keep early hours
Frühaufsteher m
 ♦ early riser
 ♦ early bird coll
früh buchen
 → frühzeitig buchen
Frühbucher m
 ♦ early booker
Frühbuchung, f
 frühzeitige Buchung, f
 ♦ early booking
Frühbuchungsangebot, n
 Frühbuchungsofferte, f
 ♦ early-booking offer
Frühbuchungsermäßigung f
 ♦ early-booking reduction
 ♦ reduction for booking early
Frühbuchungsgeschäft, n
 ♦ early-booking business
Frühbuchungsrabatt, m
 Frühbucherrabatt, m
 ♦ early-booking discount
Frühburgunder, m
 ♦ Frühburgunder
frühe Anmeldung, f
 → frühzeitige Anmeldung
frühe Morgenstunden, f pl
 ♦ early hours pl
 ♦ small hours pl
 ♦ wee hours pl
früher abreisen als erwartet
 früher abfahren als erwartet

 ♦ depart earlier than expected
 ♦ leave earlier than expected
früher ankommen als erwartet
 ♦ arrive earlier than expected
früher Checkout, m
 ♦ early checkout
früheren Ankunftstermin wählen
 früheres Ankunftsdatum wählen
 ♦ choose an earlier arrival date
frühere Reise, f
 vorherige Reise, f
 ♦ previous journey
 ♦ previous tour
 ♦ previous trip
früher zurückkommen als erwartet
 ♦ return earlier than expected
frühes Abendessen, n (Dinner)
 ♦ early dinner
frühes Abendessen, n (Supper)
 ♦ early supper
frühes Frühstück, n
 → vorzeitiges Frühstück
frühes Kinderabendessen n (Dinner)
 frühzeitiges Kinderabendessen n
 ♦ early children's dinner
 ♦ early dinner for children
frühes Mittagessen, n
 ♦ early lunch
 ♦ early luncheon
früh essen
 frühzeitig essen
 ♦ eat early
frühestens, adv
 ♦ at the earliest, adv
frühestmöglich, adv
 ♦ at your earliest convenience
 ♦ as soon as possible
Frühflug, m
 Flug am frühen Morgen, m
 Morgenflug, m
 ♦ early-morning flight
Frühgeschichte, f
 ♦ early history
Frühgotik, f (Stil)
 ♦ early Gothic style
 ♦ early Gothic
Frühgotik, f (Zeit)
 ♦ early Gothic period
frühgotisch, adj
 ♦ early Gothic, adj
frühgotische Kirche, f
 ♦ early Gothic church
Frühgymnastik, f
 Morgengymnastik, f
 Morgensport, m
 Frühsport, m
 ♦ early-morning gymnastics pl
 ♦ early-morning exercises pl
Frühherbst, m
 ♦ early fall AE
 ♦ early autumn BE
früh in der Saison
 frühzeitig in der Saison
 ♦ early in the season
Frühjahr, n
 Frühling, m
 ♦ spring
Frühjahrsabend, m
 ♦ spring evening

Frühjahrsangebot, n
 Frühjahrsofferte, f
 ♦ spring offer
Frühjahrsarrangement, n
 ♦ spring arrangement
Frühjahrsaufenthalt, m
 ♦ spring stay
Frühjahrsauslastung, f
 ♦ spring load factor
Frühjahrsausstellung, f
 ♦ spring exhibition
 ♦ spring exhibit AE
 ♦ spring show
Frühjahrsball, m
 ♦ spring ball
Frühjahrsbelegung, f
 Frühjahrsauslastung, f
 ♦ spring occupancy
 ♦ occupancy in spring
Frühjahrsbesuch, m
 ♦ spring visit
Frühjahrsbesucher m
 ♦ spring visitor
 ♦ spring guest
Frühjahrsbuchung, f
 ♦ spring booking
 ♦ spring reservation AE
Frühjahrscamper, m
 ♦ spring camper
Frühjahrscamping, n
 ♦ spring camping
Frühjahrscampingplatz, m
 ♦ spring campsite
 ♦ spring campground AE
 ♦ spring camping site BE
 ♦ spring camping ground BE
 ♦ spring site
Frühjahrsfahrplan, m
 Frühjahrsflugplan, m
 ♦ spring schedule AE
 ♦ spring timetable
Frühjahrsfahrt, f
 ♦ spring trip
Frühjahrsferien, pl
 Frühjahrsurlaub, m
 ♦ spring holidays BE pl
 ♦ spring holiday BE
 ♦ spring vacation
Frühjahrsfestlichkeit, f
 Frühjahrsfest, n
 ♦ spring festivity
Frühjahrsgast, m
 ♦ spring guest
 ♦ spring visitor
Frühjahrsgeschäft, n
 ♦ spring business
Frühjahrskatalog, m
 ♦ spring catalogue
 ♦ spring catalog AE
Frühjahrskonferenz, f
 ♦ spring conference
Frühjahrskonzert, n (Veranstaltung)
 ♦ spring concert
Frühjahrskreuzfahrt, f
 ♦ spring cruise
Frühjahrskur, f
 ♦ spring treatment
 ♦ spring cure
Frühjahrskurzurlaub, m
 ♦ spring break

Frühstück

Frühjahrsmarkt, m
 ♦ spring market
Frühjahrsmesse, f
 ♦ spring fair
 ♦ spring trade fair
Frühjahrsmonat, m
 ♦ spring month
Frühjahrsparadies, n
 Frühlingsparadies, n
 ♦ spring paradise
Frühjahrsparty, f
 Frühjahrsfest, n
 ♦ spring party
Frühjahrspause, f
 ♦ spring break
Frühjahrspreis, m
 ♦ spring price
 ♦ spring rate
Frühjahrspreisliste, f
 ♦ spring tariff
Frühjahrsprogramm n
 ♦ spring program AE
 ♦ spring programme BE
Frühjahrsprospekt m
 ♦ spring brochure
Frühjahrsputz, m
 ♦ spring-cleaning AE
 ♦ spring-clean BE
Frühjahrsputz machen in einem Haus
 ♦ spring-clean a house
Frühjahrsputz machen in einem Zimmer
 ♦ spring-clean a room
Frühjahrsputz machen in etw
 ♦ spring-clean s.th.
 ♦ give s.th. a spring-cleaning AE
 ♦ give s.th. a spring-clean BE
Frühjahrsrabatt, m
 ♦ spring discount
Frühjahrsreise, f
 ♦ spring journey
 ♦ spring tour
 ♦ spring trip
Frühjahrsreisen, n
 Frühjahrsverkehr, m
 ♦ spring travel
Frühjahrsreisender, m
 ♦ spring traveler AE
 ♦ spring traveller BE
Frühjahrsreservierung f
 ♦ spring reservation
Frühjahrssaison, f
 ♦ spring season
Frühjahrssaisonauslastung, f
 ♦ spring-season load factor
Frühjahrssaisonbuchung, f
 ♦ spring-season booking
Frühjahrssaisonermäßigung f
 ♦ spring-season reduction
Frühjahrssaisoneröffnung, f
 ♦ spring-season opening
 ♦ opening of the spring season
Frühjahrssaisonpreis, m
 ♦ spring-season price
 ♦ spring-season rate
Frühjahrssaisonreservierung, f
 ♦ spring-season reservation
Frühjahrssaisonwoche, f
 ♦ spring-season week
 ♦ week in the spring season
Frühjahrssaisonzuschlag m
 ♦ spring-season supplement

Frühjahrsschau, f
 Frühjahrsausstellung, f
 ♦ spring show
Frühjahrsseminar, n
 ♦ spring seminar
Frühjahrssitzung, f
 ♦ spring meeting
Frühjahrsskilauf, m
 Frühjahrsskilaufen, n
 Frühjahrsskifahren, n
 ♦ spring skiing
Frühjahrssonderangebot, n
 ♦ special spring offer
Frühjahrsstellplatz, m
 (Camping)
 ♦ spring pitch
Frühjahrssymposion, n
 ♦ spring symposium
Frühjahrstag, m
 ♦ spring day
Frühjahrstagung, f
 Frühjahrstreffen, n
 ♦ spring meeting
Frühjahrstourismus, m
 Frühjahrsfremdenverkehr, m
 ♦ spring tourism
Frühjahrstourist, m
 ♦ spring tourist
Frühjahrstournee, f
 ♦ spring tour
Frühjahrsurlaub, m
 Frühjahrsferien, pl
 ♦ spring vacation AE
 ♦ spring holiday BE
Frühjahrsurlauber, m
 Frühjahrsferiengast, m
 ♦ spring vacationer AE
 ♦ spring holidaymaker BE
Frühjahrsurlaubsprogramm, n
 Frühjahrsferienprogramm, n
 ♦ spring vacation program AE
 ♦ spring holiday programme BE
Frühjahrsurlaubssaison, f
 Frühjahrsferiensaison, f
 ♦ spring vacation season AE
 ♦ spring holiday season BE
Frühjahrsveranstaltung, f
 ♦ spring event
 ♦ spring function
Frühjahrswandern, n
 ♦ spring walking
 ♦ spring hiking
Frühjahrswanderung, f
 ♦ spring walk
 ♦ spring hike
Frühjahrswoche, f
 ♦ spring week
Frühjahrswochenende, n
 ♦ spring weekend
Frühjahrszeit, f
 ♦ spring period
Frühjahrsziel, n
 ♦ spring destination
Frühjahrszuschlag m
 ♦ spring supplement
Frühkonzert, m
 Morgenkonzert, n
 ♦ early-morning concert
Frühlingsart, adv gastr
 nach Frühlingsart, adv gastr
 ♦ spring style, adv gastr

Frühlingsblume, f
 ♦ spring flower
Frühlingsfest, n (Festival)
 ♦ spring festival
Frühlingsfest, n (Party)
 → Frühjahrsparty
Frühlingssoße, f
 ♦ spring sauce
Frühlingszwiebel, f
 ♦ spring onion
 ♦ scallion AE
frühmorgens aufbrechen
 ♦ start (off) early in the morning
Frühnebel, m
 Morgennebel, m
 ♦ early-morning mist
Frühreservierung, f
 → frühzeitige Reservierung
Frühsaison, f
 ♦ early season
Frühsaisonbesucher m
 ♦ early-season visitor
 ♦ early-season guest
Frühsaisonbuchung f
 ♦ early-season booking
Frühsaisonermäßigung f
 ♦ early-season reduction
Frühsaisongast m
 ♦ early-season guest
Frühsaisonmonat, m
 ♦ early-season month
 ♦ month in the early season
Frühsaisonpreis m
 ♦ early-season rate
 ♦ early-season price
Frühsaisonrabatt m
 ♦ early-season discount
Frühsaisonreservierung, f
 ♦ early-season reservation
Frühsaisontag, m
 ♦ early-season day
 ♦ day in the early season
Frühsaisonwoche, f
 ♦ early-season week
 ♦ week in the early season
Frühschicht, f
 ♦ early shift
 ♦ morning shift
Frühschicht haben
 Frühschicht arbeiten
 ♦ work an early shift
Frühschoppen, m coll
 ♦ early-morning drink
 ♦ morning drink
 ♦ morning pint
 ♦ breakfast party
Frühsommer, m
 ♦ early summer
Frühsport, m
 Morgensport, m
 Frühgymnastik, f
 Morgengymnastik, f
 ♦ early-morning exercises pl
 ♦ early-morning exercises pl
Frühsport machen
 ♦ do early morning exercises
Frühstück, n (generell)
 ♦ breakfast
Frühstück, n (Veranstaltung)
 Frühstücksempfang, m
 ♦ breakfast party

Frühstück anbieten

- breakfast
- midmorning reception *AE*
- mid-morning reception *BE*

Frühstück anbieten
- offer breakfast

Frühstück auf Bestellung, n
- cooked-to-order breakfast

Frühstück auf das Zimmer eines Gastes bringen
- bring breakfast to a guest's room

Frühstück auf das Zimmer servieren
- serve breakfast in the room

Frühstück auf dem Zimmer, n
- breakfast in one's room

Frühstück auf dem Zimmer einnehmen
- take one's breakfast in one's room

Frühstück auslassen
Frühstück nicht einnehmen
- skip breakfast
- not take breakfast

Frühstück bekommen
- get breakfast

Frühstück bestellen
- order (a) breakfast

Frühstück bestellen für 8 Uhr
- order breakfast for 8 o'clock

Frühstück einnehmen
- take (one's) breakfast
- have (one's) breakfast
- eat (one's) breakfast

frühstücken
Frühstück einnehmen
- have breakfast
- breakfast
- have (one's) breakfast
- take (one's) breakfast
- eat (one's) breakfast

frühstücken auf dem Zimmer
- have breakfast in one's room

frühstücken auf dem Zimmer
Frühstück auf dem Zimmer einnehmen
auf dem Zimmer frühstücken
- have (one's) breakfast in one's room
- breakfast in one's room

frühstücken auf seinem Balkon
- have breakfast on one's balcony

frühstücken im Bett
im Bett frühstücken
- have (one's) breakfast in (one's) bed
- breakfast in bed

frühstücken mit jm
- have breakfast with s.o.
- breakfast with s.o.

frühstücken um 8 Uhr
- have breakfast at 8 o'clock

Frühstück für eine Person, n
- breakfast for one person

Frühstück geben
Frühstücksempfang geben
- give a breakfast
- give a midmorning reception
- give a breakfast party

Frühstück gemeinsam einnehmen
zusammen frühstücken
- take breakfast together
- have breakfast together

Frühstück gibt es von 7 bis 10 Uhr
- breakfast is from 7 to 10 o'clock

Frühstück im Bett, n
- breakfast in bed

Frühstück im Hotel, n
- breakfast at the hotel
- breakfast in the hotel

Frühstück im Zimmer, n
Frühstück auf dem Zimmer n
- breakfast in the room

Frühstück ist angesetzt für 8 Uhr
- breakfast is scheduled for 8 o'clock

Frühstück ist im Preis eingeschlossen
Frühstück ist im Preis inbegriffen
Preis enthält Frühstück
- breakfast is included in the price
- breakfast is included in the rate
- price includes breakfast
- rate includes breakfast

Frühstück ist im Preis inbegriffen
→ Frühstück ist im Preis eingeschlossen

Frühstück kommt mit einer frischen Rose
- breakfast arrives with a fresh rose
- breakfast comes with a fresh rose

Frühstück kostenlos abgeben
- give away a breakfast

Frühstück machen
- make breakfast

Frühstück nicht einnehmen
- not take breakfast
- not have breakfast

Frühstück richten
- fix breakfast *AE*
- prepare breakfast *BE*

Frühstücksart f
- breakfast type
- type of breakfast

Frühstücksartikel, m
- breakfast item

Frühstücksautomat, m
(in Hotelzimmer)
- breakfast machine

Frühstücksbalkon m
- breakfast balcony

Frühstücksbar f
- breakfast bar

Frühstücksbarraumteiler, m
- breakfast bar divider

Frühstücksbedienungspersonal n
- breakfast waiting staff
- breakfast waiting personnel

Frühstücksbereich, m (abstrakt)
Frühstückssektor, m
- breakfast sector

Frühstücksbereich, m (konkret)
- breakfast area

Frühstücksbesprechung, f
Besprechung beim Frühstück, f
Frühstückstreffen, n
- breakfast meeting

Frühstücksbestellschein, m
Frühstücksbestellzettel m
- breakfast order form

Frühstücksbestellung, f
- breakfast order
- ordering (of) breakfast
- order for breakfast

Frühstücksbrett, n
- bread-cheese board

Frühstücksbrötchen n
- breakfast roll

Frühstücksbüfett, n
- buffet breakfast
- breakfast buffet *AE*

Frühstücksbüfett ausrichten
(z.B. bei einem Kongreß)
Gastgeber sein bei einem Frühstücksbüfett
- host a buffet breakfast
- host a breakfast buffet *AE*

Frühstücksbüfettservice m
Frühstücksbüfettdienst m
- buffet-breakfast service

Frühstücksclub, m
- breakfast club

Frühstückscouvert, n
→ Frühstücksgedeck

Frühstücksecke f
Frühstücksnische f
- breakfast nook

Frühstückseinladung, f
- breakfast invitation
- invitation to breakfast

Frühstückseinnahmen, f pl
- breakfast revenues *pl*
- breakfast revenue
- breakfast income
- breakfast takings *pl*

Frühstück selbst machen
- make one's own breakfast
- cook one's own breakfast

Frühstück selbst zubereiten
- prepare one's own breakfast

Frühstücksempfang, m
- midmorning reception *AE*
- mid-morning reception *BE*

Frühstücksempfang findet um 10 Uhr statt
- midmorning reception will be held at 10 o'clock *AE*
- mid-morning reception will be held at 10 o'clock *BE*

Frühstücksempfang geben
Frühstück geben
- give a midmorning reception *AE*
- give a mid-morning reception *BE*
- give a breakfast

Frühstücksertrag, m (Guv)
(Gewinn- und Verlustrechung)
- breakfast income

Frühstück servieren
- serve breakfast

Frühstück servieren jm
- serve breakfast to s.o.
- serve s.o. breakfast

Frühstücksessen, n
- breakfast meal

Frühstücksfernsehen, n
- breakfast television
- breakfast TV

Frühstücksfleisch, n
(Konserve)
- luncheon meat

Frühstücksflocken, f pl
(Getreide)
- breakfast cereal

Frühstücksgabel, f
- breakfast fork

Frühstücksgast, m
Frühstückskunde, m
- breakfast customer
- breakfaster

Frühstücksgedeck n
Frühstückscouvert n
Frühstückskuvert n
- breakfast cover

Frühstücksgericht, n
♦ breakfast dish
Frühstücksgeschirr, n
Frühstücksservice, n
♦ breakfast dishes pl
♦ breakfast service
♦ breakfast set
Frühstücksgutschein, m
♦ breakfast voucher
Frühstückshaus, n
(Betriebstyp)
♦ bed-and-breakfast house
♦ B&B house
♦ b&b house
Frühstückshotel, n
Hotel garni, n FR
Garnihotel, n
♦ bed-and-breakfast hotel
♦ b&b hotel
♦ hotel garni FR
♦ hotel offering breakfast only
Frühstück sich auf dem Zimmer servieren lassen
♦ have breakfast served in one's room
Frühstücksidee, f
♦ breakfast idea
Frühstückskarte, f
(Speisekarte)
♦ breakfast menu
Frühstückskellnerin, f
♦ breakfast waitress
Frühstückskellner m
♦ breakfast waiter
Frühstückskoch, m
♦ breakfast cook
Frühstückskost, f (aus Getreide)
♦ breakfast cereals pl
♦ cereals pl
Frühstückskosten, pl
♦ breakfast costs pl
♦ breakfast cost
Frühstücksküche, f (Raum)
♦ breakfast kitchen
Frühstückskuvert, n
→ Frühstücksgedeck
Frühstücksleistung, f
→ Frühstücksservice
Frühstückslöffel, m
♦ breakfast spoon
Frühstücksloggia f
♦ breakfast loggia
Frühstückslokal, n
♦ breakfast place
♦ breakfast spot
frühstückslos, adj
♦ breakfastless, adj
♦ breakfastless
Frühstückslounge, f
♦ breakfast lounge
Frühstücksmarkt, m
♦ breakfast market
Frühstücksmenü, n
♦ breakfast menu
Frühstücks-Mise-en-place, f
♦ breakfast mise en place
Frühstücksnachrichten, f pl
(TV, Radio)
♦ breakfast news sg
Frühstücksoberkellner m
♦ breakfast head waiter
Frühstücksomelett, n
Frühstücksomelette, f SCHW/ÖST

♦ breakfast omelette
♦ breakfast omelet
Frühstücksoption, f
Frühstücksmöglichkeit f
♦ breakfast option
Frühstückspause f
♦ breakfast break
Frühstückspension, f
♦ residential hotel (offering breakfast)
♦ bed-and-breakfast pension BE/FR
♦ bed-and-breakfast place BE
Frühstückspensionbetreiber, m
♦ bed-and-breakfast operator
♦ b&b operator
♦ B&B operator
Frühstückspersonal n
♦ breakfast personnel
♦ breakfast staff
Frühstückspreis, m
♦ breakfast price
♦ breakfast charge
♦ breakfast rate
♦ price of breakfast
Frühstücksraum, m
Frühstückszimmer, n
♦ breakfast room
♦ bfst room
Frühstücksraumbedienung, f
→ Frühstücksraumservice
Frühstücksraumservice, m
Frühstücksraumbedienung, f
♦ breakfast-room service
Frühstückssaal m
♦ breakfast room
♦ large breakfast room
Frühstückssalon, m
♦ breakfast salon AE
♦ breakfast lounge
Frühstückssandwich, n
♦ breakfast sandwich
Frühstücksseminar n
♦ breakfast seminar
Frühstücksservice, m
Frühstücksdienst, m
Frühstücksbewirtung, f
Frühstücksleistung, f
♦ breakfast service
Frühstücksservice, n
Frühstücksgeschirr, n
♦ breakfast set
♦ breakfast service
Frühstücksspeise, f
→ Frühstückskost
Frühstücksspezialität, f
♦ breakfast specialty AE
♦ breakfast speciality BE
Frühstücksstandard, m
♦ breakfast standard
Frühstücksstube, f
→ Frühstücksraum
Frühstückstablett n
♦ breakfast tray
Frühstückstasse, f
obere Frühstückstasse, f
♦ breakfast cup
Frühstücksteller, m
♦ breakfast plate
Frühstücksterrasse f
♦ breakfast terrace

Frühstückstisch, m
♦ breakfast table
♦ table laid for breakfast
Frühstückstisch decken
♦ lay the table for breakfast
Frühstückstischeindeckung, f
♦ breakfast table setting
Frühstückstischzeit, f
♦ breakfast sitting
Frühstückstreff, m
Frühstückstreffpunkt, m
♦ breakfast haunt
Frühstückstreffen, n
→ Frühstücksbesprechung
Frühstücksumsatz, m
♦ breakfast sales pl
♦ breakfast turnover
Frühstücksumsatz erhöhen
♦ increase breakfast sales
♦ increase breakfast turnover
Frühstücksuntertasse, f
untere Frühstückstasse, f
♦ breakfast saucer
Frühstücksveranda, f
♦ breakfast veranda
♦ breakfast verandah
Frühstückszeit, f (Zeitpunkt)
♦ breakfast time
Frühstückszeit, f (Zeitraum)
♦ breakfast period
Frühstückszimmer, n
→ Frühstücksraum
Frühstückszimmerservice, m (auf dem Zimmer)
→ Zimmerfrühstück
Frühstückszimmerservice, m (im Frühstücksraum)
→ Frühstücksraumservice
Frühstückszubereitung, f
♦ preparation of breakfast
♦ breakfast preparation
♦ preparing breakfast
Frühstückszusammenstellung, f
♦ breakfast composition
♦ composition of a breakfast
Frühstückszuschlag m
(Preis)
♦ breakfast supplement
♦ supplement for breakfast
Frühstück und Abendessen, n
♦ breakfast and evening meal
Frühstück war verspätet
♦ breakfast was tardy
Frühstück wird auf dem Zimmer serviert
♦ breakfast is served in the room
Frühstück wird auf einem Tablett im Zimmer serviert
♦ breakfast is served on a tray in the room
Frühstück wird gemeinsam eingenommen
♦ breakfast will be taken together
♦ breakfast is taken together
Frühstück wird im Bett serviert
♦ breakfast is served in bed
Frühstück wird im Frühstücksraum serviert
♦ breakfast is served in the breakfast room
Frühstück wird von 7 bis 9 Uhr serviert
♦ breakfast is served from 7 to 9 o'clock
Frühstück zubereiten
♦ prepare breakfast
Frühstück zu zweit, n
♦ breakfast à deux

frühzeitig ankommen
  ♦ arrive in good time
frühzeitig buchen
  früh buchen
  ♦ book early
  ♦ book well in advance
  ♦ make a reservation well in advance AE
frühzeitige Abbestellung, f
  → frühzeitige Stornierung
frühzeitige Absage, f
  → frühzeitige Stornierung
frühzeitige Ankunft, f
  ♦ early arrival
frühzeitige Anmeldung, f
  frühe Anmeldung, f
  Frühanmeldung, f
  ♦ early registration
frühzeitige Anmeldung wird empfohlen
  ♦ early registration is recommended
frühzeitige Besichtigung sehr empfohlen
  ♦ early viewing strongly recommended
  ♦ early inspection highly recommended
frühzeitige Buchung, f
  → Frühbuchung
frühzeitige Reservierung, f
  frühe Reservierung, f
  Frühreservierung, f
  ♦ early reservation
Frühzeitige Reservierung ratsam
  ♦ Early reservation advisable
frühzeitige Stornierung, f
  frühzeitige Abbestellung, f
  frühzeitige Absage, f
  frühzeitiger Rücktritt, m
  ♦ early cancellation
  ♦ early cancelation AE
frühzeitig in der Saison
  → früh in der Saison
frühzeitig stornieren
  frühzeitig absagen
  frühzeitig zurücktreten
  ♦ cancel early
frühzeitig vor Saisonbeginn
  ♦ well in advance of the start of the season
  ♦ well in advance of the season
früh zu Bett gehen
  früh ins Bett gehen
  ♦ go to bed early
Frühzug, m
  ♦ early train
  ♦ early-morning train
  ♦ morning train
Frümi, n
  (Frühstück/Mittagessen)
  → Brunch
Fühlen Sie sich wie zu Hause!
  ♦ Make yourself at home!
führender Reiseveranstalter, m
  ♦ leading tour operator
führendes Hotel, n
  ♦ leading hotel
führendes Hotel in X sein
  ♦ be the leading hotel in X
führen durch ein Programm
  → Conférence machen
führen etw als Museum
  betreiben etw als Museum
  ♦ run s.th. as a museum
führen jn
  ♦ conduct s.o.
  ♦ guide s.o.

führen jn durch das Museum
  ♦ conduct s.o. round the museum
  ♦ guide s.o. through the museum
führen jn durch die Zimmer
  führen jn durch die Räume
  ♦ guide s.o. through the rooms
  ♦ conduct s.o. through the rooms
führen zu einer Auslastungsrate von 60 %
  ♦ result in a load factor of 60 %
führen zu einer Belegungsrate von 60 %
  führen zu einer Auslastungsrate von 60 %
  ♦ result in an occupancy rate of 60 %
führen zu Überkapazität
  zu Überkapazität führen
  ♦ lead to overcapacity
  ♦ result in overcapacity
Führer, m (Anführer)
  (z.B. bei Wanderungen)
  ♦ leader
Führer, m (Buch)
  ♦ guide
  ♦ guidebook
Führer, m (Person)
  ♦ guide
Führer beschreibt eine große Zahl von Hotels
  ♦ guide describes a large number of hotels
Führer bestellen
  (Person)
  ♦ book a guide
Führer engagieren
  (Person)
  ♦ engage a guide
  ♦ hire a guide BE
Führer enthält 1234 Hotels
  ♦ guide lists 1234 hotels
Führer für etw
  ♦ guide to s.th.
Führergebühr, f
  ♦ guide fee
Führer herausgeben
  ♦ issue a guide
Führer nehmen
  ♦ take a guide
Führerschein, m
  ♦ driver's license AE
  ♦ driving licence BE
Führer und Fahrer, m
  ♦ driver guide
Führer vermitteln
  (Person)
  Führer besorgen
  ♦ arrange a guide
Führer veröffentlichen
  ♦ publish a guide
Führer zusammenstellen
  ♦ compile a guide
Fuhrlohn, m
  Rollgeld, n
  ♦ cartage
Fuhrmann, m hist
  ♦ wagoner
  ♦ waggoner BE
Fuhrpark, m
  ♦ fleet of vehicles
Führung, f (Besuch)
  ♦ guided visit
Führung, f (Touristen)
  ♦ guided tour
  ♦ conducted tour
  ♦ tour

Führung durch die Innenstadt, f (Großstadt)
  ♦ guided tour of the city center AE
  ♦ guided tour of the city centre BE
Führung durch die Innenstadt, f (kleine Stadt)
  ♦ guided tour of the town center AE
  ♦ guided tour of the tour centre BE
Führung durch etw, f
  ♦ guided tour of s.th.
  ♦ guided tour through s.th.
  ♦ conducted tour of s.th.
  ♦ conducted tour through s.th.
  ♦ tour of s.th.
Führung durch etw, f (Besuch)
  ♦ guided visit to s.th.
Führungen anbieten
  ♦ offer guided tours
Führungen arrangieren für Besucher
  ♦ arrange guided tours for visitors
Führungen werden durchgeführt von 9 bis 10 Uhr
  ♦ guided tours are given from 9 to 10 a.m.
Führung erhalten durch den Dom
  ♦ be given a conducted tour of the cathedral
  ♦ be given a guided tour of the cathedral
Führung hinter den Kulissen, f
  ♦ behind-the-scenes tour
Führung machen durch das historische Viertel
  (Tourist)
  ♦ take a guided tour of the historic quarter
Führung machen durch die Altstadt (Tourist)
  ♦ take a guided tour of the Old Town
Führung machen durch X (Führer)
  Führung leiten durch X
  ♦ conduct a tour of X
Führung machen (Führer)
  Führung leiten
  ♦ conduct a tour
  ♦ give a tour
Führung machen für jn durch X
  ♦ lead s.o. on a tour of X
Führung machen für jn persönlich
  persönlich führen jn
  ♦ give s.o. a personal tour
Führung machen (generell)
  ♦ do a tour
Führung machen mit jm durch etw
  ♦ take s.o. on a tour of s.th.
Führung machen (Tourist)
  ♦ take a guided tour
  ♦ go on a guided tour
Führungskräfte, f pl
  ♦ managerial staff
  ♦ managerial personnel
Führungsmannschaft, f
  Führungsteam n
  ♦ management team
Führungspersonal, n
  ♦ management personnel
  ♦ management staff
  ♦ management
Führungsseminar, n
  ♦ management seminar
Führungsteam, n
  → Führungsmannschaft
Führung unter Tage, f
  (im Bergwerk)
  Unter-Tage-Führung, f
  ♦ guided underground tour
  ♦ guided tour underground
Führung zu Fuß, f
  → geführter Spaziergang

Fuhrwerk, n
  Gespann, n
  ◆ rig *AE coll*
Full American Plan, m
  (Zimmer mit allen Mahlzeiten)
  FAP, m
  ◆ Full American Plan
  ◆ FAP
füllen etw (gastronomisch)
  ◆ stuff s.th.
füllen etw (generell)
  ◆ fill s.th.
Fülle von Ausstellungsgegenständen, f
  ◆ array of exhibits
Füllpastete, f
  Becherpastete, f
  Timbale, f
  ◆ timbale
Füllung, f *gastr*
  Füllsel, n *gastr*
  Farce, f *gastr*
  ◆ stuffing *gastr*
Füllung machen *gastr*
  ◆ make the filling *gastr*
Fundabteilung, f
  → Fundbüro
F&B-Anforderung, f
  ◆ f&b requirement
F&B-Assistent,m
  Food-and-Beverage-Assistent, m
  ◆ f&b assistant
  ◆ food and beverage assistant
F&B-Bereich, m (abstrakt)
  F&B-Sektor, m
  ◆ f&b sector
F&B-Lehrgang, m
  F&B-Kurs, m
  ◆ f&b course
F&B-Leiter, m
  → F&B-Manager
  F&B-Leiterin f
F&B-Manager, m
  → Wirtschaftsdirektor
F&B-Sekretärin, f
  Food-and-Beverage-Sekretärin, f
  ◆ f&b secretary
  ◆ food and beverage secretary
Fundbuch, n
  → Fundsachenbuch
Fundbüro, n
  ◆ lost and found office *AE*
  ◆ lost-property office *BE*
Fundsache, f
  ◆ lost property
  ◆ object found
  ◆ piece of lost property
Fundsachenbuch, n
  ◆ lost-property book
Fundsachenbuch führen
  ◆ keep a lost-property book
Fünfbettappartement, n
  ◆ five-bed apartment
  ◆ five-bedded apartment
Fünfbettcaravan, m
  Fünfbettwohnwagen, m
  ◆ five-berth caravan *BE*
  ◆ five-berth van *BE coll*
  ◆ five-berth trailer *AE*
fünfbettig, adj
  ◆ five-bedded, adj

fünfbettiges Zimmer, n
  ◆ five-bedded room
Fünfbettvilla, f
  ◆ five-bed villa
Fünfbettwohnung, f
  ◆ five-bed flat *BE*
  ◆ five-bed apartment *AE*
Fünfbettwohnwagen, m
  Fünfbettcaravan, m
  ◆ five-berth trailer *AE*
  ◆ five-berth caravan *BE*
  ◆ five-berth van *BE coll*
Fünfbettzimmer, n
  ◆ five-bed room
  ◆ five-bedded room
  ◆ quintuple room
  ◆ quintuple
Fünfertisch, m
  Fünfpersonentisch, m
  ◆ table for five persons
  ◆ table for five
  ◆ table to seat five persons
Fünferzimmer, n
  Fünfbettzimmer, n
  ◆ quintuple room
  ◆ quintuple
  ◆ five-bed room
  ◆ five-bedded room
Fünfgangfahrrad, n
  ◆ five-speed bicycle
fünfgängig, adj (Essen)
  ◆ five-course, adj
  ◆ consisting of five courses
fünfgängiges Abendessen, n (Supper)
  ◆ five-course supper
fünfgängiges Abendessen n (Dinner)
  ◆ five-course dinner
fünfgängiges Menü, n
  Fünfgangmenü, n
  ◆ five-course menu
fünfgängiges Mittagessen, n
  ◆ five-course luncheon
  ◆ five-course lunch
fünfgängiges Schlemmermenü, n
  ◆ five-course gourmet menu
Fünf-Gang-Menü, n
  → fünfgängiges Menü
Fünfgangrad, n
  Rad mit fünf Gängen, n
  ◆ five-gear bike
Fünfhundertjahrfeier, f
  ◆ quincentenary celebration
Fünfhundertjahrjubiläum, n
  ◆ quincentenary
  ◆ quingentenary
fünfköpfige Familie, f
  ◆ family of five
Fünfkornbrot, n
  ◆ five-cereal bread
Fünfliterflasche, f
  ◆ five-liter bottle *AE*
  ◆ five-litre bottle *BE*
Fünf-Mann-Zelt, n
  ◆ five-man tent
Fünfpersonenzelt, n
  ◆ five-person tent
Fünfraumwohnung, f
  → Fünfzimmerwohnung
Fünf-Sterne-Anlage, f
  Fünf-Sterne-Komplex m
  ◆ five-star complex

Fünf-Sterne-Anwesen, n
  Fünf-Sterne-Objekt, n
  ◆ five-star property
Fünf-Sterne-Appartement, n
  ◆ five-star apartment
Fünf-Sterne-Appartementanlage, f
  Fünf-Sterne-Appartementkomplex, m
  ◆ five-star apartment complex
Fünf-Sterne-Attraktion, f
  ◆ five-star attraction
Fünf-Sterne-Aufenthalt, m
  ◆ five-star stay
Fünf-Sterne-Bereich, m
  Fünf-Sterne-Sektor, m
  ◆ five-star sector
Fünf-Sterne-Betrieb, m
  ◆ five-star establishment
  ◆ five-star operation
Fünf-Sterne-Bewertung, f
  ◆ five-star rating
Fünf-Sterne-Campingplatz, m
  ◆ five-star campsite
  ◆ five-star campground *AE*
  ◆ five-star camping site *BE*
  ◆ five-star camping ground *BE*
Fünf-Sterne-Caravanplatz, m
  Fünf-Sterne-Wohnwagenplatz, m
  ◆ five-star caravan site *BE*
  ◆ five-star trailer site *AE*
Fünf-Sterne-Club, m
  ◆ five-star club
Fünf-Sterne-Einrichtung, f
  ◆ five-star facility
Fünf-Sterne-Einstufung, f
  ◆ five-star grading
Fünf-Sterne-Ferienwohnung, f
  Fünf-Sterne-Fewo f
  ◆ five-star vacation apartment *AE*
  ◆ five-star holiday flat *BE*
Fünf-Sterne-Grandhotel, n
  ◆ five-star grand hotel
Fünf-Sterne-Haus, n (Hotel)
  → Fünf-Sterne-Hotel
Fünf-Sterne-Hotel, n
  ◆ five-star hotel
Fünf-Sterne-Hotelanlage, f
  Fünf-Sterne-Hotelkomplex m
  ◆ five-star hotel complex
Fünf-Sterne-Hotelservice, m
  ◆ five-star hotel service
Fünf-Sterne-Kategorie f
  ◆ five-star category
Fünf-Sterne-Koch, m
  ◆ five-star cook
Fünf-Sterne-Komfort, m
  ◆ five-star comfort
  ◆ five-star amenities *pl*
Fünf-Sterne-Komplex, m
  → Fünf-Sterne-Anlage
Fünf-Sterne-Kreuzfahrtschiff, n
  ◆ five-star cruise ship
  ◆ five-star cruise liner
Fünf-Sterne-Küchenchef, m
  ◆ five-star chef
Fünf-Sterne-Luxus, m
  ◆ five-star luxury
Fünf-Sterne-Luxushaus, n (Hotel)
  → Fünf-Sterne-Luxushotel
Fünf-Sterne-Luxushotel, n
  ◆ five-star deluxe hotel *AE*
  ◆ five-star luxury hotel *BE*

Fünf-Sterne-Niveau

Fünf-Sterne-Niveau, n
- ◆ five-star level

Fünf-Sterne-Platz, m (Camping)
- ◆ five-star site

Fünf-Sterne-Preis, m
- ◆ five-star price
- ◆ five-star rate

Fünf-Sterne-Qualität, f
- ◆ five-star quality

Fünf-Sterne-Residenz, f
- ◆ five-star residence

Fünf-Sterne-Restaurant n
- ◆ five-star restaurant

Fünf-Sterne-Segment, n
- ◆ five-star segment

Fünf-Sterne-Sektor, m
- → Fünf-Sterne-Bereich

Fünf-Sterne-Service, m
- ◆ five-star service

Fünf-Sterne-Stadthotel, n (Großstadt)
- ◆ five-star city hotel

Fünf-Sterne-Stadthotel, n (kleine Stadt)
- ◆ five-star town hotel

Fünf-Sterne-Standard m
- ◆ five-star standard

Fünf-Sterne-System, n
- ◆ five-star system

Fünf-Sterne-Tagungsort, m
  Fünf-Sterne-Austragungsort, m
- ◆ five-star venue

Fünf-Sterne-Unterkunft, f
  Fünf-Sterne-Unterbringung, f
- ◆ five-star accommodation
- ◆ five-star lodging *AE*

Fünf-Sterne-Wohnwagenplatz, m
  Fünf-Sterne-Caravanplatz, m
- ◆ five-star trailer site *AE*
- ◆ five-star caravan site *BE*

Fünf-Sterne-Zimmer, n
- ◆ five-star room

fünfstöckig, adj attr (Gebäude)
  fünfgeschoßig, adj attr
- ◆ five-floor, adj attr
- ◆ five-story, adj attr *AE*
- ◆ five-storey, adj attr *BE*

fünfstöckig, adj (Bett, Kuchen)
- ◆ five-tier, adj
- ◆ five-tiered, adj

fünfstöckig, adj prd (Gebäude)
- ◆ five-storied, adj prd *AE*
- ◆ five-storeyed, adj prd *BE*

fünfstöckiges Bett, n
- ◆ five-tier bed
- ◆ five-tiered bed

fünfstöckiges Gebäude, n
- ◆ five-floor building
- ◆ five-story-building *AE*
- ◆ five-storey building *BE*

fünfstöckig sein (Gebäude)
- ◆ be five-storied *AE*
- ◆ be five-storeyed *BE*

fünfstündig, adj
- ◆ five-hour, adj
- ◆ lasting five hours
- ◆ of five hours' duration
- ◆ five hours', adj

fünfstündiger Marsch, m
- ◆ five hours' march

fünfstündiges Programm, n
  Fünfstundenprogramm, n

- ◆ five-hour program *AE*
- ◆ five-hour programme *BE*

fünfstündige Verspätung, f
- ◆ five-hour delay

Fünftagearrangement, n
- ◆ five-day arrangement
- ◆ five days' arrangement

Fünftageaufenthalt, m
  fünftägiger Aufenthalt, m
- ◆ five-day stay
- ◆ five days' stay
- ◆ stay of five days

Fünftagepaß, m
- ◆ five-day pass

Fünftagepauschale, f
- ◆ five-day package

Fünftagepauschalpreis, m
- ◆ five-day inclusive price
- ◆ five-day inclusive rate
- ◆ five-day package price
- ◆ five-day package rate

Fünftagepreis, m
- ◆ five-day rate
- ◆ five-day price
- ◆ rate for five days
- ◆ price for five days

Fünftageprogramm, n
  fünftägiges Programm n
- ◆ five-day program *AE*
- ◆ five-day programme *BE*
- ◆ five days' program *AE*
- ◆ five days' programme *BE*
- ◆ program of five days *AE*

Fünftagereise, f
  fünftägige Reise, f
- ◆ five-day tour
- ◆ five-day trip
- ◆ five-day journey

Fünf-Tage-Skipaß, m
- ◆ five-day ski pass

fünftägig, adj
- ◆ five-day, adj
- ◆ five days', adj
- ◆ lasting five days
- ◆ of five days' duration

fünftägiger Aufenthalt, m
- → Fünftageaufenthalt

fünftägiger Urlaub, m
  Fünftageurlaub, m
  fünftägige Ferien, pl
- ◆ five-day vacation *AE*
- ◆ five-day holiday *BE*

fünftägige Veranstaltung, f
  Fünftageveranstaltung, f
- ◆ five-day event
- ◆ five-day function

fünfte Etage, f
- → fünftes Stockwerk

fünfter Gang, m (Menü)
- ◆ fifth course

fünfter Gang, m (Motor)
- ◆ fifth gear

fünftes Stockwerk, n
  fünfte Etage, f
  fünftes Obergeschoß, n
- ◆ sixth floor *AE*
- ◆ sixth story *AE*
- ◆ fifth floor *BE*
- ◆ fifth storey *BE*

Fünfuhrtanztee, m
- ◆ tea-dance

Fünfuhrtee m
- ◆ five-o'clock tea

fünfwöchig, adj
- ◆ five-week, adj
- ◆ of five weeks
- ◆ lasting five weeks
- ◆ five weeks', adj

fünfwöchige Reise, f
- ◆ five-week journey
- ◆ five-week tour
- ◆ five-week trip

fünfwöchige Tournee, f
- ◆ five-week tour

fünfzehntes Stockwerk, n
  fünfzehnte Etage, f
  fünfzehntes Geschoß, n
- ◆ sixteenth floor *AE*
- ◆ sixteenth story *AE*
- ◆ fifteenth floor *BE*
- ◆ fifteenth storey *BE*

fünfzigste Etage, f
- → fünfzigstes Stockwerk

fünfzigstes Stockwerk, n
  fünfzigste Etage, f
  fünfzigstes Geschoß, n
- ◆ fifty-first floor *AE*
- ◆ fifty-first story *AE*
- ◆ fiftieth floor *BE*
- ◆ fiftieth storey *BE*

Fünfzimmerappartement, n
- ◆ five-room apartment

Fünfzimmerferienwohnung, f
  Fünfzimmerurlaubswohnung, f
- ◆ five-room vacation apartment *AE*
- ◆ five-room holiday flat *BE*

fünfzimmerig, adj
- ◆ five-roomed, adj

fünfzimmeriges Appartment, n
- ◆ five-roomed apartment

fünfzimmerige Wohnung, f
- ◆ five-roomed flat *BE*
- ◆ five-roomed apartment *AE*

Fünfzimmerwohnung, f
- ◆ five-room flat *BE*
- ◆ five-room apartment *AE*

fungieren als Führer
  als Führer dienen
- ◆ act as a guide

funken um Hilfe
- ◆ radio for help

Funkmikrofon, n
- ◆ radio microphone

Funktaxi, n
- ◆ radio taxi

Funktelefon, n
- ◆ radio telephone
- ◆ portable telephone

Funktion, f
- ◆ function

funktionierender Lift, m
- ◆ working elevator *AE*
- ◆ working lift *BE*

Funktionsraum, m
- → Veranstaltungsraum

für Bankettzwecke
- ◆ for banqueting purposes

für besondere Anlässe
- ◆ for special occasions

für Buchungszwecke
- ◆ for booking purposes

für den genannten Termin
♦ for the date mentioned
für den halben Preis
♦ for half the price
♦ for half the rate
für den Rest des Urlaubs
für den Rest der Ferien
♦ for the rest of the vacation AE
♦ for the rest of the holiday BE
für denselben Zeitraum
♦ for the same period (of time)
Für den Verkehr gesperrt
♦ Closed to All Traffic
für die Dauer des Aufenthalts
♦ for the duration of the stay
für die Dauer des Urlaubs
♦ for the duration of the vacation AE
♦ for the duration of the holiday BE
für die genannte Zeit
für die angegebene Zeit
♦ for the period mentioned
für die Nacht
♦ for the night
für die Nacht vom 21. auf 22. August
♦ for the night of 21 August
für die Woche vom 7. bis 14. April
♦ for the week of 7 to 14 April
♦ for the week beginning on 7 and ending on 14 April
für drei Nächte ab 5. August
♦ for three nights beginning on 5 August
♦ for three nights from 5 August
für eine bescheidene Gebühr
gegen eine bescheidene Gebühr
♦ for a modest fee
Für einen Besichtigungstermin rufen Sie 123 an
♦ For an appointment to view, please call 123
Für ein unverbindliches Preisangebot wenden Sie
sich bitte an Herrn X
♦ For a quotation without obligation please contact
♦ Mr X
für Erholungszwecke
♦ for recreation purposes
für Ferienzwecke
für Urlaubszwecke
♦ for holiday purposes BE
♦ for vacation purposes AE
für Freizeitzwecke
♦ for leisure purposes
für Ihren Komfort
♦ for your comfort
für jede Jahreszeit
♦ for all seasons
für jeden Anlaß
♦ for any occasion
für jeden etwas
♦ something for everyone
für jeden etwas bieten
♦ offer something for everyone
für jeden Geschmack
♦ for every taste
♦ to suit every taste
♦ to suit every palate
♦ for all tastes
♦ to suit all tastes
für jeden Geschmack etw bieten
♦ cater for all tastes
♦ cater for every taste

für jeden Geschmack und Geldbeutel
♦ for every palate and purse
♦ to suit every palate and purse
♦ to suit every palate and purse
♦ for all tastes and pockets
♦ for all tastes and budgets
für jeden Geschmack und jedes Alter
♦ for every taste and age
für jeden Geschmack wird etw geboten
♦ every palate is catered for
♦ all tastes are catered for
Für nähere Einzelheiten wenden Sie sich
bitte an Herrn X
♦ For further particulars please apply to Mr X
Für nicht eingenommene Mahlzeiten gibt es keine
Erstattung
♦ There is no refund for meals not taken
Fürsorgeheim, n
Fürsorgeanstalt, f
♦ welfare home
fürsorgend, adj
fürsorglich, adj
♦ caring, adj
fürsorgendes Personal, n
fürsorgliches Personal, n
♦ caring staff
♦ caring personnel
Fürstbischof, m
♦ prince-bishop
Fürstentum Liechtenstein, n
♦ Principality of Liechtenstein, the
Fürstentum Monaco, n
♦ Principality of Monaco, the
fürstlich eingerichtet, adj
♦ splendidly furnished, adj
fürstlich eingerichtetes Zimmer, n
♦ splendidly furnished room
fürstlicher Empfang, m
königlicher Empfang m
♦ royal reception figur/lit
♦ royal welcome figur/lit
♦ princely welcome figur
fürstliches Mahl, n
♦ meal fit for a king
fürstlich leben
♦ live in grand style
♦ live like a king
fürstlich übernachten
♦ spend the night in luxury
Furt, f
♦ ford
für Trinkzwecke
♦ for drinking purposes
für unseren Komfort
♦ for our comfort
für vier Nächte
♦ for four nights
Für weitere Auskünfte wenden Sie sich an Frl. Y
♦ For further details contact Miss Y
Für weitere Auskünfte wenden Sie sich bitte an Frl. X
♦ For further information please contact Miss X
Für weitere Einzelheiten wenden Sie sich an XYZ
♦ For further information contact XYZ
♦ For further information write to XYZ
Für weitere Informationen wenden Sie sich bitte
direkt an das Hotel oder an die Reservierungszentrale

♦ For further information please contact the hotel
♦ direct or the central reservation office
Für wie viele Personen ist diese Buchung?
♦ How many persons does this reservation cover? AE
♦ How many persons does this booking cover? BE
für Wohnzwecke
♦ for residential purposes
für zwei Wochen ab 10 März
♦ for two weeks beginning on 10 March
♦ for two weeks from 10 March
Fusel, m
(billiger Schnaps)
♦ rotgut AE sl
♦ rot-gut BE sl
♦ hooch AE
♦ bad liquor AE
Fuselwein, m
billiger Wein, m
♦ plonk BE coll
♦ cheap wine
Fußbad, n
♦ footbath AE
♦ foot-bath BE
Fußball, m (amerikanisch)
→ Football
Fußball, m (europäisch)
♦ soccer AE
♦ football BE
Fußballfan, m
♦ soccer fan AE
♦ football fan BE
Fußballfeld, n
♦ football pitch BE
Fußballmannschaft, f
♦ soccer team AE
♦ football team BE
Fußballmeisterschaft, f
♦ soccer championship AE
♦ football championship BE
Fußballplatz, m
♦ soccer field AE
♦ soccer ground AE
♦ football field BE
♦ football ground BE
Fußballreise, f
♦ soccer tour AE
♦ football tour BE
Fußballrowdy, m
♦ football hooligan BE
Fußballsaison, f
♦ soccer season AE
♦ football season BE
Fußballschuh, m
♦ soccer shoe AE
♦ football shoe BE
Fußballspiel, n
♦ soccer match AE
♦ football match BE
♦ football game BE
Fußball spielen
♦ play soccer AE
♦ play football BE
Fußballspieler, m
♦ soccer player AE
♦ football player BE
Fußballstadion, n
♦ soccer stadium AE
♦ football stadium BE

Fußballtrainer

Fußballtrainer, m
- soccer coach *AE*
- football coach *BE*

Fußballtraining, f
- soccer coaching *AE*
- football coaching *BE*

Fußballturnier, n
- soccer tournament *AE*
- football tournament *BE*

Fußballverein, m
Fußballclub, m
- soccer club *AE*
- football club *BE*

Fußballweltmeister, m
- world soccer champion *AE*
- world football champion *BE*

Fußballweltmeisterschaft, f
- world soccer championship *AE*
- world football championship *BE*
- World Cup

Fußbecken, n
(Waschbecken)
- foot basin

Fußbehandlung, f
- foot treatment

Fußbodenbelag, m
Bodenbelag, m
- floor covering
- flooring

Fußbodenfläche, f
Bodenfläche, f
- floorage
- floor space

Fußbodenheizung, f
Bodenheizung, f
- underfloor heating

Fußgänger, m
- pedestrian
- walker

Fußgängerbrücke, f
Fußbrücke, f
- footbridge *AE*
- foot-bridge *BE*

Fußgängereinkaufszone, f
- pedestrian shopping area
- pedestrian shopping zone
- pedestrian shopping precinct *BE*

Fußgängerstraße, f
- pedestrian road
- pedestrian street

Fußgängertunnel, m
- pedestrian tunnel
- underpass *AE*
- pedestrian subway *BE*
- subway *BE*

Fußgängerzone, f
- pedestrian area
- pedestrian zone
- pedestrian precinct *BE*

Fußleiste, f
- baseboard *AE*
- skirting-board *BE*

Fußmarsch, m
- march
- walk

Fußmassage, f
- foot massage

Fußmatte, f
- doormat

Fußpflege, f
→ Pediküre

Fußpflegerin, f
→ Pediküre

Fußreisender, m
→ Fußwanderer

Fußsafari, f
→ Wandersafari

Fußschemel, m
Fußbank, f
- footstool

Fußstütze, f
- footrest

Fußwanderer, m
Fußreisender, m
- wayfarer

Fußwandern, n
Fußreisen, n
- wayfaring *form*

fußwandernd, adj
fußreisend, adj
- wayfaring, adj *form*

Fußwanderung, f
→ Wanderung

Fustage, f
→ Leergut

Futonbett, n
- futon bed

Futter, n (Essen) *coll*
- grub *inform*
- chow *AE sl*
- food
- eats *coll*

Futter, n (Tier)
- fodder

futtern *inform*
tüchtig essen
tüchtig zugreifen *fam*
spachteln *fam*
- tuck in *inform*
- dig in *inform*

futtern etw *inform*
(essen)
verdrücken etw *inform*
wegputzen etw *inform*
- put s.th. away *inform*

füttern jn (z.B. Kinder, Kranke)
- feed s.o.

Futtersack, m
(z.B. für ein Pferd)
- feedbag *AE*
- nosebag

FV, m
→ Fremdenverkehr

FVA, n
→ Fremdenverkehrsamt

FVV, m
Fremdenverkehrsverband, m
- RTB
- regional tourist board

G

Gabel, f
 ◆ fork
Gabelbüfett, n
 ◆ fork buffet
Gabelfrühstück, n
 Déjeuner à la fourchette, n *FR m*
 Zweites Frühstück, n
 ◆ fork lunch
 ◆ déjeuner à la fourchette *FR m*
 ◆ brunch
 ◆ elevenses *BE pl*
 ◆ meat breakfast
Gabelfrühstück einnehmen
 ◆ have a fork lunch
 ◆ take a fork lunch
Gabelreise, f
 ◆ open jaw tour
Gabun
 ◆ Gabon
Gabuner, m
 ◆ Gabonese
Gabunerin, f
 ◆ Gabonese girl
 ◆ Gabonese woman
 ◆ Gabonese
gabunisch, adj
 ◆ Gabonese, adj
Gag, m
 ◆ gag
Gage, f (einmalige)
 ◆ fee
 ◆ honorarium
Gage, f (generell)
 ◆ salary
gähnend leer, adj
 ◆ completely empty, adj
Gala, f *SPAN*
 Fest, n
 ◆ gala *SPAN*
Galaabend, m
 Festabend, m
 ◆ gala evening
 ◆ gala night
Galaabendessen, n
 → Galadiner
Galaabschiedsfeier, f
 Festabschiedsfeier, f
 festliche Abschiedsfeier, f
 ◆ gala farewell party
Galaaufführung, f
 (Theater)
 Galavorstellung, f
 Festaufführung, f
 Festvorstellung, f
 ◆ gala performance
Galaball, m
 Festball, m
 ◆ gala ball

Galabüfett, n
 Festbüfett, n
 ◆ gala buffet
Galadiner, n
 Galaessen, n
 Galaabendessen, n
 Festessen, n
 ◆ gala dinner
Galadiner bei Kerzenlicht, n
 Galadiner bei Kerzenschein, n
 Festessen bei Kerzenlicht, n
 Festessen bei Kerzenschein, n
 ◆ candle-light gala dinner
Galadinerkapazität, f
 Festessenkapazität, f
 ◆ gala-dinner capacity
Galaempfang, m
 Festempfang, m
 ◆ gala reception
Galaeröffnung, f
 festliche Eröffnung, f
 Festeröffnung, f
 ◆ gala opening
Galaessen, n (Diner)
 → Galadiner
Galaessen, n (Lunch)
 festliches Mittagessen, n
 Festmittagessen, n
 ◆ gala luncheon
 ◆ gala lunch
Galafest, n
 ◆ gala festivity
Galafestabend, m
 ◆ gala party night
Galafeuerwerk, n
 festliches Feuerwerk, n
 Festfeuerwerk, n
 ◆ gala fireworks *pl*
 ◆ gala fireworks display
Galakonzert, n
 Festkonzert n
 ◆ gala concert
Galanacht, f
 Festnacht, f
 ◆ gala night
Galapagosinseln, f pl
 ◆ Galapagos Islands, the *pl*
Galatanzdiner, n
 festliches Tanzdiner, n
 ◆ gala dinner dance
Galaveranstaltung, f
 festliche Veranstaltung, f
 Festveranstaltung, f
 ◆ gala function
 ◆ gala event
 ◆ gala
Galaveranstaltung organisieren
 festliche Veranstaltung organisieren

Festveranstaltung organisieren
 ◆ organise a gala function
 ◆ organise a gala event
 ◆ organise a gala
Galavorstellung, f
 → Galaveranstaltung
Galerie, f
 ◆ gallery
Galeriebar, f
 ◆ gallery bar
Galeriebesuch, m
 (Kunstgalerie)
 ◆ visit to a gallery
 ◆ gallery visit
Galerie besuchen
 ◆ visit a gallery
Galerieführung, f
 ◆ guided tour of the gallery
 ◆ guided gallery tour
Galicien
 (Region in Spanien)
 ◆ Galicia
Galizien
 (Region in Mitteleuropa)
 ◆ Galicia
Gallenbeschwerden, f pl
 ◆ bilious complaints *pl*
Gallenbeschwerden behandeln
 ◆ treat bilious complaints
Gallenleiden, n
 ◆ bilious complaint
Gambia
 ◆ Gambia, the
Gambier, m
 ◆ Gambian
Gambierin, f
 ◆ Gambian girl
 ◆ Gambian woman
 ◆ Gambian
gambisch, adj
 ◆ Gambian, adj
Gambrinus
 (angeblicher Erfinder des Biers)
 ◆ Gambrinus
Gang, m (Essen)
 Menügang, m
 ◆ course
Gang, m (Korridor)
 → Korridor
Gang, m (Motor)
 ◆ gear
Gang auslassen
 (bei Mahlzeit)
 Gang überspringen
 ◆ skip a course
Gang beenden
 ◆ finish the course

Gang bilden

Gang bilden
(Menü)
♦ form a course
Ganges, m
♦ Ganges River, the
♦ River Ganges, the
♦ Ganges, the
Gangfolge, f
(bei Mahlzeit)
Speisefolge f
♦ sequence of courses
♦ order of courses
gängiger Marktpreis, m
♦ going market price
Gangkabine, f
♦ court cabin
Gangway, f
(Schiff oder Flugzeug)
Laufgang, m
Landungsbrücke, f
♦ gangway
Gang wechseln (Motor)
schalten *coll*
♦ change gears
♦ swift gears *AE*
Gänsebraten, m
♦ roast goose
Gänsebrust, f
♦ goose breast
Gänsewein, m *humor*
Wasser, n
♦ Adam's ale *humor*
♦ Adam's wine *humor*
♦ water
ganze Fahrt, f
♦ whole trip
♦ whole journey
ganze Fahrt nochmals machen
ganze Fahrt noch einmal machen
♦ do the whole trip again
ganze Familie, f
♦ whole family, the
ganze Nacht geöffnet
♦ open all night
ganze Nacht hindurch
♦ all night long
ganzen Monat bleiben
♦ stay for a whole month
♦ stay the whole month
ganzen Tag im Bett liegen
♦ lie in bed all day
ganzen Tag im Gasthaus sitzen
ganzen Tag in der Bar sitzen
♦ sit around in the bar all day *AE*
♦ sit around in the pub all day *BE*
ganzen Tag unterwegs sein
♦ be out and about all day
ganze Portion, f
→ volle Portion
ganze Welt bereisen
♦ travel the whole world
ganz früh abreisen
sehr früh abfahren
♦ leave very early
ganz geschafft sein *coll*
ganz kaputt sein *coll*
♦ be badly cut
ganzheitlich, adj
holistisch, adj
♦ holistic, adj

ganzheitliche Behandlung, f
♦ holistic treatment
ganzheitlicher Urlaub, m
ganzheitliche Ferien, pl
♦ holistic vacation *AE*
♦ holistic holiday *BE*
ganzheitliche Therapie, f *med*
Ganzheitstherapie, f *med*
♦ holistic therapy *med*
ganz in der Nähe ist XYZ
♦ nearby is XYZ
Ganzjahresanlage, f
Ganzjahreskomplex, m
♦ year-round complex
♦ all-year-round complex
Ganzjahresauslastung, f
Ganzjahresbelegung, f
ganzjährige Auslastung, f
ganzjährige Belegung, f
♦ year-round occupancy
♦ annual occupancy
Ganzjahresbetrieb, m
ganzjähriger Betrieb, m
♦ year-round operation
♦ year-round service
Ganzjahrescampingplatz, m
♦ year-round campsite
♦ year-round campground *AE*
♦ year-round camping site *BE*
♦ year-round camping ground *BE*
♦ year-round site
Ganzjahresdestination, f
Ganzjahresziel, n
Ganzjahreszielort, m
♦ year-round destination
♦ whole-year destination
Ganzjahresdienst m
ganzjähriger Dienst m
Ganzjahresservice m
ganzjähriger Service m
ganzjähriger Betrieb m
♦ year-round service
Ganzjahresferienort, m
Ganzjahresurlaubsort m
♦ year-round vacation resort *AE*
♦ year-round holiday resort *BE*
♦ year-round resort
Ganzjahreshotel, n
♦ year-round hotel
♦ hotel open all year round
♦ hotel open throughout the year
Ganzjahreskreuzfahrt, f
Jahreskreuzfahrt, f
♦ year-round cruise
Ganzjahreskurort, m
Jahreskurort, m
♦ year-round spa
♦ year-round health resort
Ganzjahresplatz, m
(Camping)
♦ year-round site
♦ site open all year round
♦ site open throughout the year
♦ site open all over the year
Ganzjahrespreis, m
das ganze Jahr gültiger Preis, m
♦ year-round price
♦ year-round rate
Ganzjahresziel, n
→ Ganzjahresdestination

ganzjährig, adv
♦ all over the year, adv
♦ throughout the year, adv
♦ all year round, adv
♦ during the whole year, adv
♦ all year, adv
ganzjährig bewirtschaftet sein
ganzjährig geöffnet haben
♦ be operated throughout the year
♦ be open throughout the year
ganzjährige Belegung, f
→ Ganzjahresauslastung
ganzjähriger Betrieb, m
→ Ganzjahresbetrieb
ganzjähriger Dienst, m
ganzjähriger Service, m
♦ service throughout the year
♦ year-round service
ganzjähriger Service, m
→ ganzjähriger Dienst
ganzjähriger Tourismus, m
♦ year-round tourism
Ganzjährig geöffnet
(Hinweisschild)
♦ Open all year round
♦ Open throughout the year
♦ Open all over the year
♦ Open all year
ganzjährig geöffnet bleiben
♦ remain open throughout the year
♦ remain open all over the year
♦ remain open all year round
ganz oben wohnen
♦ live on the top floor
ganztägig, adj
♦ full-day, adj
♦ whole-day, adj
♦ one-day, adj
♦ all-day, adj
ganztägige Busreise, f
Ganztagsbusreise, f
♦ full-day bus tour *AE*
♦ whole-day bus tour *AE*
♦ one-day bus tour *AE*
♦ all-day bus tour *AE*
♦ full-day coach tour *BE*
ganztägige Stadtbesichtigung f
♦ one-day city sightseeing tour
♦ one-day city tour
Ganztägig geöffnet
(Hinweisschild)
♦ Open all day
ganztägig geöffnet, adj
♦ open all day, adj
Ganztägig geschlossen
(Hinweisschild)
♦ Closed all day
Ganztagsaufsicht, f
ganztägige Aufsicht, f
♦ full-day supervision
Ganztagsausflug, m
ganztägiger Ausflug, m
♦ full-day excursion
♦ whole-day excursion
♦ one-day excursion
♦ all-day excursion
♦ full-day trip
Ganztagsbesichtigung, f
♦ full-day sightseeing
♦ whole-day sightseeing
♦ one-day sightseeing

Ganztagsbesichtigungsfahrt, f
♦ full-day sightseeing trip
♦ whole-day sightseeing trip
♦ one-day sightseeing trip
Ganztagsbesuch, m
ganztägiger Besuch, m
♦ full-day visit
♦ whole-day visit
♦ one-day visit
Ganztagsfahrt, f
ganztägige Fahrt, f
♦ full-day trip
♦ whole-day tour
♦ one-day tour
♦ all-day tour
♦ full-day tour
Ganztagskreuzfahrt, f
♦ full-day cruise
♦ whole-day cruise
♦ one-day cruise
Ganztagsprogramm, n
ganztägiges Programm, n
♦ full-day program *AE*
♦ whole-day program *AE*
♦ full-day programme *BE*
♦ whole-day programme *BE*
Ganztagsseminar, n
ganztägiges Seminar, n
♦ full-day seminar
♦ whole-day seminar
♦ one-day seminar
Ganztagssitzung, f
ganztägige Sitzung, f
♦ full-day session
♦ whole-day session
♦ one-day session
♦ all-day session
Ganztagstour, f
ganztägige Tour, f
♦ full-day tour
♦ whole-day tour
♦ one-day tour
♦ full day's touring
Ganztagsveranstaltung, f
ganztägige Veranstaltung, f
♦ full-day function
♦ whole-day function
♦ one-day function
♦ full-day event
♦ whole-day event
Ganztagswanderung, f
♦ full-day walk
♦ full-day hike
♦ full day's ramble
Garage, f
♦ garage
Garage benutzen
♦ use a garage
Garage bereithalten
→ Garage reservieren
Garage bereitstellen
Garage zur Verfügung stellen
♦ provide a garage
Garage betreiben
♦ operate a garage
Garage buchen
Garage bestellen
♦ book a garage
Garage gratis
♦ garage free of charge
♦ free garage

Garage ist die ganze Nacht geöffnet
♦ garage is open all night
Garage leiten
♦ manage a garage
Garage mieten
♦ rent a garage
♦ hire a garage *BE*
Garagenabstellung, f
♦ garage parking
Garagenanlage, f
Garagenblock m
♦ block of garages
♦ garage block
Garagenarbeiter, m
♦ garageman
Garagenarrangement, n
♦ garage arrangement
Garagenbenutzer, m
♦ user of a garage
♦ person using a garage
Garagenbenutzung, f
Benutzung einer Garage f
♦ use of a garage
♦ using a garage
Garagenbereich, m
♦ garage area
Garagenbetreiber, m
♦ garage operator
Garagenbetrieb, m
♦ operation of a garage
Garagenblock, m
Garagenanlage f
♦ garage block
Garagenbuchung, f
♦ garage booking
♦ booking of a garage
Garageneinstellung, f
(für Auto)
Garagenabstellung f
Garagenunterbringung f
♦ garage accommodation
Garagenfläche, f
♦ garage area
Garagengebühr, f
Garagenpreis m
♦ garage charge
♦ garage fee
Garagenkosten, pl
♦ garage costs *pl*
♦ garage cost
Garagenleitung, f
♦ management of a garage
Garagenmiete, f
♦ garage rent
Garagenpersonal, n
♦ garage staff
♦ garage personnel
Garagenplatz, m (für 1 Auto)
♦ garage space
♦ garaging space *BE*
Garagenplatz bestellen (für 1 Auto)
Garagenplatz buchen
♦ book garage space (for one car)
♦ book garaging space (for one car) *BE*
Garagenraum, m
Garagenfläche, f
♦ garaging space
♦ garage space
Garagenreservierung, f
♦ garage reservation

♦ reservation of a garage
♦ reserving a garage
Garagenschlüssel, m
Schlüssel zur Garage m
♦ garage key
♦ key to the garage
Garagenstellplatz, m (für 1 Auto)
→ Garagenplatz
Garagenstellplätze für 80 Wagen, m pl
♦ garage facilities for 80 cars *pl*
♦ garaging facilities for 80 cars *BE pl*
Garagentür, f
♦ garage door
Garagenunterstellmöglichkeit kann arrangiert werden
♦ Garaging cars can be arranged
Garagenwart, m
Garagenaufseher m
Garagenwärter m
♦ garage attendant
♦ garage warden *BE*
Garage reservieren
Garagge bereithalten
♦ reserve a garage
Garage vermieten
♦ rent (out) a garage
♦ let a garage *BE*
Garage zur Verfügung stellen
→ Garage bereitstellen
Garantie, f
♦ guarantee
Garantiebelegung, f
♦ guaranteed occupancy
Garantiebuchung f
♦ guaranteed booking
Garantiefonds, m
(Schutz bei Firmenzusammenbruch)
♦ bonding scheme *BE*
Garantiegutschein, m
Gutschein mit Garantie, m
garantierter Gutschein, m
♦ guaranteed voucher
Garantiehotel n
♦ guaranteed hotel
Garantiepreis m
♦ guaranteed rate
♦ guaranteed price
Garantieprovision, f
♦ guaranteed commission
garantieren etw
gewährleisten etw
fest zusagen etw
♦ guarantee s.th.
garantierter Gutschein, m
→ Garantiegutschein
garantierter Sitzplatz, m
garantierter Platz, m
♦ guaranteed seat
garantierte Zimmerreservierung, f
♦ guaranteed room reservation
Garçon, m *FR*
Kellner, m
Gehilfe, m
Geselle, m
♦ garçon *FR*
♦ waiter
Garçon de salle, m *FR*
Hallenkellner, m
Saalkellner, m
♦ garçon de salle *FR*

Garçon d'hôtel

♦ lounge waiter
♦ hall waiter
Garçon d'hôtel, m *FR*
Hotelkellner, m
♦ garçon d'hôtel *FR*
♦ hotel waiter
Gardasee, m
♦ Lake Garda
Gardemanger, m (Koch)
Kalter Koch, m
Garde-manger, m *FR*
Kaltkoch, m
♦ garde-manger *FR*
♦ larder cook
Gardemanger, m (Küche)
(frz: Fliegenschrank für Speisen)
Kalte Küche f
Garde-manger, m *FR*
♦ garde-manger *FR*
♦ cold kitchen
♦ larder
Garderobe, f (Kleiderständer)
→ Kleiderständer
Garderobe, f (Kleidung)
♦ wardrobe
♦ clothes
Garderobe, f (Raum in Hotel, Restaurant etc.)
♦ checkroom *AE*
♦ cloakroom
Garderobe, f (Raum in Theater)
♦ dressing room *AE*
♦ dressing-room *BE*
♦ tiring room
Garderobe abgeben
♦ check one's things
♦ deposit one's things
Garderobendienst, m
Garderobenservice m
♦ checkroom service *AE*
♦ cloakroom service
Garderobenfrau, f
Garderobendame, f
Garderobiere, f *FR*
♦ cloakroom attendant
♦ cloakroom girl
♦ cloakroom woman
♦ checkroom attendant *AE*
♦ checkroom girl *AE*
Garderobengebühr, f
♦ checkroom charge *AE*
♦ checkroom fee *AE*
♦ cloakroom charge
♦ cloakroom fee
Garderobenmarke, f
(Quittung für abgegebene Kleider)
Garderobenschein m
Garderobenzettel m
♦ cloakroom check *AE*
♦ check *AE*
♦ cloakroom ticket
♦ checkroom ticket *AE*
Garderobenpauschale f
♦ group cloakroom charge *BE*
♦ group charge for (the) use of (the) cloakroom *BE*
Garderobenraum, m
→ Garderobe
Garderobenschein, m
→ Garderobenmarke
Garderobenzettel, m
→ Garderobenmarke

Garderobier, m
Garderobiere f
♦ checkroom attendant *AE*
♦ cloakroom attendant
Gardinen und Behänge, pl
♦ curtains and draperies *pl*
gären
♦ ferment
garen etw
garen lassen etw
♦ cook s.th. slowly
Gargantua
♦ Gargantua
gargantuanischer Appetit, m
Riesenappetit, m
♦ gargantuan appetite
gargantuanisches Essen, n
Riesenessen, n
♦ gargantuan meal
Garkoch m
Rotisseur m
♦ rotisseur m
Garküche, f
♦ cookshop
♦ cheap eating house
Garnele, f
(gewöhnlich größer als eine Krevette)
Steingarnele, f
Krevette, f
♦ prawn
♦ shrimp
Garnelensoße, f
Krevettensoße, f
♦ prawn sauce
♦ shrimp sauce
Garnibetrieb, m
♦ bed-and-breakfast establishment
♦ bed-and-breakfast operation
♦ b&b establishment
♦ b&b operation
Garni-Buchung, f
♦ bed-and-breakfast booking
garnieren etw mit etw
(Speisen)
♦ garnish s.th. with s.th.
Garnierlös, m
♦ bed-and-breakfast revenue
♦ b&b revenue
♦ B&B revenue
garniert mit etw
♦ garnished with s.th.
Garniertrag, m (Guv)
(Gewinn- und Verlustrechnung)
♦ bed-and-breakfast income
♦ b&b income
♦ B&B income
Garnierung, f *gastr*
Verzierung, f
Zutaten, f pl
♦ garnishing *gastr*
♦ trimmings *pl*
Garnihotel, n
→ Hotel garni
Garnivereinbarung, f
Garni-Arrangement, n
♦ bed-and-breakfast arrangement
♦ b&b arrangement
♦ B&B arrangement
Gartenabteilung, f
♦ grounds department

Gartenanlage f
♦ garden
♦ gardens *pl*
Garten anlegen
♦ lay out a garden
Gartenarchitekt, m
♦ landscape gardener
Gartenausstellung, f
Gartenschau, f
♦ horticultural exhibition
♦ horticultural show
♦ garden show
Gartenbank, f
♦ garden bench
Gartenbar f
♦ garden bar
Gartenbau, m
♦ horticulture
Gartenbauausstellung, f
♦ horticultural show
♦ horticultural exhibition
Gartenbedienung, f
Gartenbewirtung f
♦ garden service
Gartenbegeisterter, m
♦ garden enthusiast
Gartenbereich, m
♦ garden area
Gartenbesuch, m
♦ garden visit
♦ visit to a garden
Gartenblick, m
Blick auf den Garten m
♦ garden view
♦ view of the garden
Gartenbohne, f
♦ haricot bean
♦ haricot
♦ string bean
Gartenbohnensalat, m
♦ haricot bean salad
Gartenbüfett, n
♦ garden buffet
Gartenbungalow, m
♦ garden bungalow
Gartencafé, n
♦ garden café
♦ garden cafe *AE*
♦ open-air café
♦ open-air cafe *AE*
♦ outdoor café
Gartencoffeeshop, m
♦ garden coffee shop
Gartenfassade, f
♦ garden façade
♦ garden facade *AE*
Gartenferienort, m
Gartenurlaubsort, m
Gartenort, m
♦ garden resort
Gartenfest, n (Festival)
♦ garden festival
Gartenfest, n (Party)
→ Gartenparty
Gartenfete, f
Gartenfête f
♦ garden fete
♦ garden fête
Gartenfläche, f
♦ garden space
♦ garden area

Gartenflügel, m
→ Gartentrakt
Gartenfreund, m
→ Gartenliebhaber
Gartengemüse, n
♦ garden vegetable
Gartengeschoß, n
(euphemistisch für Souterrain)
♦ garden floor
Gartengeschoßappartement, n
♦ garden-floor apartment
Gartengeschoßsuite, f
♦ garden-floor suite
♦ garden-level suite
Gartengeschoßwohnung, f
♦ garden-floor flat BE
♦ garden-floor apartment AE
Gartengeschoßzimmer, n
♦ garden-floor room
Gartengrillfest, n
♦ garden barbecue
♦ barbecue
Gartenhaus, n
(ähnlich wie Laube)
♦ garden house AE
Gartenhof, m
♦ garden court
Gartenhofrestaurant, n
♦ garden court restaurant
Gartenhotel n
♦ garden hotel
Garten ist gepflegt
♦ garden is well kept
♦ garden is well tended
♦ garden is well maintained
Garten ist schön angelegt
♦ garden is beautifully laid out
Gartenkresse, f
♦ garden cress
Gartenliebhaber, m
Gartenfreund, m
♦ garden lover
Gartenliege, f
Liege, f
♦ sunlounger
♦ sunbed
Gartenlokal, n
→ Biergarten, Heurigenlokal
Gartenlokal, n (Café)
→ Gartencafé
Gartenlokal, n (Restaurant)
→ Gartenrestaurant
Gartenmaisonette, f
Maisonette mit Gartenbenutzung, f
♦ garden duplex AE
♦ garden maisonette BE
Gartenmöbel, n pl
♦ garden furniture sg
Gartenparty, f
Gartenfest, n
Gartengesellschaft, f obs
♦ garden party
Gartenpatio, m
♦ garden patio
Gartenpavillon, m
♦ garden pavilion
Gartenrestaurant n
♦ garden restaurant
♦ open-air restaurant
Gartensalon, m
♦ garden lounge

Gartenschach, n
Freischach, n
Freilandschach, n
♦ outdoor chess
♦ open-air chess
Gartenschau, f
♦ garden show
♦ horticultural show
♦ garden festival
Gartenschirm, m
♦ garden umbrella
Gartenschlauch, m
♦ garden hose
Gartenschwimmbad, n
Gartenschwimmbecken, n
♦ garden swimming pool AE
♦ garden swimming-pool BE
♦ garden pool
Gartenschwimmbecken, n
→ Gartenschwimmbad
Gartenspielplatz, m
♦ garden playground
Gartenstadt, f (Großstadt)
♦ garden city
Gartenstadt, f (kleine Stadt)
♦ garden town
Gartenstuhl, m
♦ garden chair
Gartensuite, f
Suite mit Gartenbenutzung, f
♦ garden suite
Gartenteich, m
♦ garden pond
Gartenterrasse f
♦ garden terrace
Gartentor, n
♦ garden gate
Gartentrakt, m
Gartenflügel m
♦ garden wing
Gartenveranstaltung, f
♦ garden event
♦ garden function
Gartenvorstadt, f
♦ garden suburb
Gartenwirtschaft, f
→ Gartenlokal
Gartenwohnung, f
Wohnung mit Gartenbenutzung, f
♦ garden apartment AE
♦ garden flat BE
Gartenzelt, n
(zum Feiern)
♦ garden marquee
Gartenzelt mieten
♦ rent a garden marquee AE
♦ hire a garden marquee BE
Gartenzelt vermieten
♦ rent (out) a garden marquee
♦ hire out a garden marquee BE
Garten zum Entspannen, m
♦ garden for relaxing
Garten zur Gästebenutzung, m
♦ garden for guests' use
Gärtner, m
♦ gardener
♦ ground keeper
Gärtner/Chauffeur, m
♦ gardener-chauffeur
Gärtnerinart, adv gastr
nach Gärtnerinart, adv gastr

♦ gardener's style, adv gastr
♦ à la jardinière, adv gastr
Gärung, f
♦ fermentation
Gärungsprozeß, m
♦ fermentation process
Gas abstellen
♦ cut off gas
Gas aus der Leitung, n
→ Leitungsgas
Gasboiler, m
♦ gas heater
Gasfeuerzeug, n
♦ gas lighter
Gasflasche, f
(Camping, Ballonfahrt)
♦ gas cylinder
♦ gas bottle
Gasheizung, f
GH, f
♦ gas heating
♦ GH
Gasherd, m
♦ gas range AE
♦ gas cooker
♦ gas stove
♦ gas oven
Gaskocher, m
Gasherd, m
♦ gas cooker
Gaskosten, pl
♦ gas costs pl
♦ gas cost
Gasofen, m
Gasheizofen, m
♦ gas stove
Gasrechnung, f
♦ gas bill
Gast, der Diät hält, m
Diätgast, m
♦ dieting guest
Gast, der keine Diät hält, m
Nicht-Diätgast, m
♦ nondieting guest AE
♦ non-dieting guest BE
Gast, der vorausbezahlt hat, m
P.I.A.-Gast, m
♦ P.I.A. guest
♦ guest who has paid in advance
Gast, m (Besucher)
♦ visitor
♦ caller
Gast, m (generell)
♦ guest
Gast, m (Kunde)
→ Kunde
Gast, m (Mieter)
→ Mieter
Gast, m (Tourist)
→ Tourist
Gast abfertigen
Gast bedienen
sich kümmern um einen Gast
♦ attend to a guest
♦ serve a guest
Gast abschrecken
♦ frighten a guest away
Gast abweisen
Gast wegschicken
♦ turn away a guest
♦ send away a guest

Gast als VIP behandeln

Gast als VIP behandeln
- give a guest VIP treatment

Gastanalyse, f
→ Gästeanalyse

Gastanspruch, m
Gästeanspruch m
Gastbedürfnis n
Gästebedürfnis n
- guest requirement
- guest's requirement
- guests' requirement

Gastanspruch zufriedenstellen
Gastanspruch erfüllen
- meet a guest requirement
- meet a guest's requirement

Gastarbeiter, m
Gastarbeiterin f
- immigrant worker
- guest worker

Gastarif, m
- gas tariff
- gas rates *pl*
- gas rate

Gast auf das Zimmer begleiten
- accompany a guest to his/her room

Gastaufenthalt, m
→ Gästeaufenthalt

Gast auffordern, das Hotel zu verlassen
- ask a guest to leave the hotel

Gastaufführung, f
- guest performance

Gastaufführung geben
→ Gastspiel geben

Gastaufführung mit internationalen Künstlern, f
- guest performance by international artists

Gastaufnahme, f
- receiving (of) a guest
- receiving (of) guests
- reception

Gastaufnahmevertrag, m
(umfaßt Beherbergung und Bewirtung)
- guest reception contract
- reception contract

Gastaufnahmevertrag abschließen
- conclude a guest reception contract

Gastaufnahmevertrag unterzeichnen
Gastaufnahmevertrag unterschreiben
- sign a guest reception contract

Gast aufnehmen
→ Gast empfangen

Gastauftritt geben
- make a guest performance

Gast auschecken
- check-out a guest

Gast aus dem Ausland, m
ausländischer Gast, m
- guest from abroad
- foreign guest

Gast außerhalb der Spitzenzeit, m
- off-peak guest

Gast aussperren aus seinem Zimmer
- lock a guest out of his/her room

Gast aus Übersee, m
Überseegast, m
- guest from overseas
- overseas guest

Gast bedienen
- serve a guest
- attend to a guest
- wait on a guest

Gast begrüßen mit einem Glas Wodka
- greet a guest with a glass of vodka

Gast beleidigen
Gast beschimpfen
- insult a guest

Gastbetrieb, m
→ Gastgewerbetrieb

Gastbett n
→ Gästebett

Gastbevölkerung, f
gastgebende Bevölkerung, f
- host population

Gast bewirten
- cater for a guest
- entertain a guest

Gast der Regierung, m
Regierungsgast m
- guest of the government

Gast des Hauses, m
Hausgast, m
- house guest
- guest of the management

Gast des Hauses sein
- be a guest of the house
- be a guest of the management

Gast die Zimmernummer sagen
- tell a guest his (her) room number

Gastdirigent, m
- guest director *AE*
- guest conductor *BE*
- visiting director *AE*
- visiting conductor *BE*

Gastdozent, m
- guest lecturer

Gästeabend, m (in Club etc.)
(Gäste können eingeladen werden)
- guest night *AE*
- guest-night *BE*

Gäste abfragen
(im Restaurant)
- inquire about a guest's wishes
- enquire about a guest's wishes
- inquire about guests' wishes
- enquire about guests' wishes

Gästeabrechnung, f
Gastabrechnung f
- guest billing
- guest's billing
- guests' billing

Gästeanalyse, f
Gastanalyse, f
- guest analysis

Gästeandrang, m
- inrush of guests
- influx of guests

Gästeanfrage, f
Gastanfrage, f
- guest's inquiry
- guest's enquiry
- guests' inquiry
- guests' enquiry

Gästeanfragen bearbeiten
- deal with guests' inquiries
- deal with guests' enquiries
- handle guests' inquiries
- handle guests' enquiries

Gästeankunft, f
- guest arrival
- arrival of a guest
- arrival of guests

- guest's arrival
- guests' arrival

Gästeankunft bearbeiten
- process a guest arrival
- deal with a guest arrival

Gäste anlocken
Gäste herbeilocken
- lure guests
- attract guests

Gäste ansagen
(bei einem Fest)
- announce the guests

Gästeanstieg, m
Gästezahlanstieg m
- increase in guests
- increasing number of guests

Gästeansturm, m
Gästeandrang, m
- throng of guests

Gäste anziehen
Gäste gewinnen
- attract guests

Gästeart, f
Gasttyp, m
- type of guest
- guest type

Gästeartikel, m pl
- guest supplies *pl*

Gästeaufenthalt, m
- stay of a guest
- stay of guests

Gästeaufenthaltsraum, m (Hotel)
Gästesalon, m
- lounge for residents
- residents' lounge

Gästeaufkommen, n
- guest turnover

Gäste aufnehmen
- take in guests

Gästeaufzug, m
→ Gästefahrstuhl

Gäste aus aller Welt, m pl
- guests from all over the world *pl*

Gästeausgaben, f pl
Ausgaben durch Gäste, f pl
- guest expenses *pl*
- guest expenditures *pl*
- guest spending
- guests' spending

Gästeauslastung f
Gästebelegung f
- guest occupancy

Gästebad, n
- guest bath
- guest's bath

Gästebadezimmer, n
Gästebad, n
- guest bathroom
- guest's bathroom
- guest bath
- guest's bath

Gästebar, f
→ Hausgästebar

Gästebedürfnis, n
- guest need
- guest's need
- guest requirement
- guest's requirement

Gästebeförderung, f
- guest transportation *AE*
- guest's transportation *AE*

- ♦ guest transport *BE*
- ♦ guest's transport *BE*

Gäste begrüßen
- Gäste willkommen heißen
- ♦ welcome guests
- ♦ welcome the guests

Gäste begrüßen mit einem Glas Gratiswein
- ♦ welcome guests with a complimentary glass of wine
- ♦ welcome guests with a free glass of wine

Gästebegrüßung, f
- Begrüßung der Gäste, f
- ♦ welcoming (of) a guest
- ♦ welcoming (of the) guests

Gästebeherbergung, f
- ♦ accommodation of guests
- ♦ accommodating guests

Gästebenutzung, f
- ♦ guests' use
- ♦ guest use
- ♦ guest's use

Gästebeschwerde f
- ♦ guest complaint
- ♦ guest's complaint

Gästebetreuer, m
- ♦ guest host
- ♦ courier

Gästebetreuung, f
- ♦ hosting a guest
- ♦ looking after a guest
- ♦ taking care of a guest

Gästebetreuungsprogramm, n
- ♦ guest entertainment program *AE*
- ♦ guest entertainment programme *BE*

Gästebetrieb, m
- → Gastbetrieb

Gästebett, n (allgemein)
- Gastbett, n
- ♦ guest bed

Gästebett, n (bestimmter Gast)
- Gastbett, n
- ♦ guest's bed

Gäste bewirten
- ♦ cater for guests
- ♦ cater to guests

Gästebewirtung, f
- ♦ guest entertainment
- ♦ entertaining guests
- ♦ catering for guests

Gästebeziehung, f
- Gästeverhältnis, n
- Beziehung zu den Gästen, f
- ♦ guest relations *pl*

Gästebibliothek, f
- ♦ guest library

Gäste bleiben aus
- Gäste bleiben weg
- ♦ guests stay away

Gästebriefpapier, n
- ♦ guest stationery

Gästebuch, n (generell)
- Besucherbuch, n
- Goldenes Buch, n
- ♦ visitors' book

Gästebuch, n (Hotel)
- → Fremdenbuch

Gästebuch führen (Hotel)
- → Fremdenbuch führen

Gästebuchführung, f
- ♦ guest bookkeeping

Gästebuchhaltung, f
- ♦ guest accounting

Gästebungalow, m
- ♦ guest bungalow
- ♦ guest's bungalow
- ♦ guests' bungalow

Gästecottage, f
- ♦ guest cottage

Gästedatei, f
- Gästekartei, f
- ♦ guest index

Gästedatei auf den neuesten Stand bringen
- ♦ update the guest index

Gästeeinrichtung, f
- ♦ guest facility

Gästeempfang, m
- ♦ reception of guests
- ♦ reception of a guest
- ♦ guest reception
- ♦ guest's reception
- ♦ guests' reception

Gäste empfangen
- ♦ receive guests

Gäste erwarten
- ♦ expect guests
- ♦ be expecting guests

Gästeerwartung, f
- ♦ guest expectation
- ♦ guests' expectations
- ♦ guest's expectation

Gästeerwartung erfüllen
- ♦ satisfy guests' expectations
- ♦ satisfy a guest's expectations

Gäste evakuieren
- ♦ evacuate (the) guests

Gästefahrrad, n
- ♦ guest bicycle
- ♦ guest's bicycle

Gästefahrstuhl m
- ♦ guest elevator *AE*
- ♦ guest lift *BE*

Gästefarm, f
- ♦ guest farm

Gästeflügel, m
- Gästetrakt, m
- ♦ guest-room wing
- ♦ guest wing

Gästefragebogen, m
- ♦ guest questionnaire
- ♦ guest questionaire *AE*
- ♦ guest questionary *AE*

Gästefrequenz, f
- → Gästeauslastung

Gästefrühstück, n
- ♦ guest's breakfast

Gäste fühlen sich in der ungezwungenen Atmosphäre
- unseres Hauses wohl
- ♦ guests feel at home in the casual atmosphere of our hotel

Gästeführer, m
- → Führer

Gästegarderobe, f (Raum)
- ♦ guest checkroom *AE*
- ♦ guest cloakroom *BE*

Gästegarten, m
- Gastgarten, m
- ♦ guest's garden
- ♦ guests' garden

Gästegeneration, f
- ♦ generation of guests

Gästegepäck, n
- ♦ guest baggage *AE*
- ♦ guest's baggage *AE*
- ♦ guests' baggage *AE*
- ♦ guest's luggage *BE*
- ♦ guests' luggage *BE*

Gästegepäck freigeben
- *(nach Rechnungszahlung)*
- ♦ release a guest's baggage *AE*
- ♦ release a guest's luggage *BE*

Gästegeschmack, m
- Gastgeschmack, m
- ♦ guest's taste
- ♦ guests' taste

Gäste gewinnen
- → Gäste anziehen

Gästegruppe, f
- ♦ guest group
- ♦ group of guests
- ♦ group of visitors
- ♦ group

Gäste haben
- ♦ have guests

Gäste haben zum Tee (privat)
- Gast haben zum Tee
- ♦ have company for tea

Gäste halten
- Gäste behalten
- ♦ keep guests

Gästehandtuch, n
- ♦ guest towel
- ♦ guest's towel

Gästehaus, n (von Regierung, Institution)
- ♦ guesthouse *AE*
- ♦ guest-house *BE*

Gästeheim, n
- ♦ guests' hostel
- ♦ guest hostel

Gäste herbeilocken
- → Gäste anlocken

Gast einbuchen
- Gast anmelden
- ♦ book in a guest

Gast einchecken
- Gast in das Hotel aufnehmen
- ♦ check in a guest

Gast eines Hotels, m
- ♦ guest of a hotel

Gästeinformation, f
- ♦ guest information
- ♦ information of guests
- ♦ informing guests

Gästeinformationsdienst m
- Gästeinformationsservice m
- Gästeinformation f
- ♦ guest information service

Gästeinformationskarte, f
- ♦ guest information card

Gästeinformationsprogramm, n
- ♦ guest information program *AE*
- ♦ guest information programme *BE*

Gast einquartieren in einem Hotel
- ♦ book a guest into a hotel
- ♦ put a guest up at a hotel
- ♦ put a guest up in a hotel

Gast eintragen in das Meldebuch
- Gast einschreiben
- Gast registrieren
- ♦ register a guest

Gästejournal, n
- *(enthält alle Gästerechnungen)*

Gästejournal führen

Hoteljournal n
♦ visitor's tabular ledger
♦ tab
Gästejournal führen
♦ keep a visitors' tabular ledger
Gästejournal täglich saldieren
♦ balance the visitors' tabular ledger daily
Gästekapazität, f
♦ guest capacity
Gästekarte, f (generell)
Gastkarte, f
♦ guest card
Gästekarte, f (Kartei)
(mit Eigenheiten der Gäste)
Gästekarteikarte, f
♦ guest index card
Gästekartei, f
♦ card index of guests
♦ guest index
Gästekarteikarte anlegen
♦ open a guest index card
Gästekarteikarte f
→ Gästekarte
Gästekategorie f
♦ guest category
Gästeklientel, f
→ Kundenstamm
Gästekomfort, m
♦ guest comfort
♦ guest's comfort
♦ guests' comfort
Gästekommentarkarte f
(enthält Eigenheiten der Gäste)
Gästekarte f
♦ guest record card
Gäste kommen von fern und nah
♦ guests come from far and near
Gästekommission, f
♦ errand for a guest
Gästekommission erledigen
(durch Pagen)
♦ run errands for a guest
Gästekontakt, m
Gastkontakt m
♦ guest contact
♦ contact with guests
♦ contact with visitors
Gästekontaktpersonal, n
♦ guest-contact staff
♦ guest-contact personnel
Gästekonto, n
♦ guest account
♦ guest's account
Gästekonto anlegen
→ Gästekonto eröffnen
Gästekonto eröffnen
Gästekonto anlegen
♦ open a guest account
♦ open a guest's account
Gästekontokarte, f
♦ guest account card
Gästekonto schließen
♦ close a guest's account
♦ close a guest account
Gästekorrespondenz, f
♦ guest correspondence
♦ guest's correspondence
♦ guests' correspondence
Gästekorrespondenz erledigen
♦ deal with guest correspondence
♦ deal with guests' correspondence
♦ deal with a guest's correspondence
Gästekreis, m
→ Kundenstamm
Gästekreis besteht aus Touristen
♦ clientele is composed of tourists
Gästekreis eines Kurorts, m
Publikum eines Kurorts, n
♦ clientele of a spa
Gästekreis eines Restaurants, m
Publikum eines Restaurants, n
♦ clientele of a restaurant
Gästeküche, f (Raum)
♦ guest's kitchen
♦ guests' kitchen
Gästelift, m
♦ guest elevator AE
♦ guest lift BE
♦ visitors' elevator AE
♦ visitors' lift BE
Gästeliste f
Gästeverzeichnis n
♦ guest list
♦ list of (the) guests
Gästeliste zusammenstellen
♦ compile a guest list
Gästelob, n
♦ guest's praise
♦ guests' praise
♦ approval of (the) visitors
Gästelogiernacht, f
→ Gästenacht
Gasteltern, pl
(in Familie)
♦ host parents pl
Gästemehrheit, f
♦ majority of guests
Gästemeldekarte, f
♦ guest registration card
Gästemix, m
♦ guest mix
Gast empfangen
♦ receive a guest
Gästen absagen
seinen Gästen absagen
♦ put off one's guests
Gästenachfrage, f
♦ guest demand
Gästenachlaß, m
Nachlaß an einen Gast, m
♦ allowance (made) to a guest
Gästenacht, f (Statistik)
Gastnacht, f
Logiernacht, f ÖST/SCHW
Gästelogiernacht, f ÖST/SCHW
Logisnacht, f ÖST/SCHW
♦ guest-night
♦ sleeper-night
Gästename m
♦ guest's name
♦ name of a guest
Gästen persönlichen Service bieten
♦ provide personal service for one's guests
Gast enttäuschen
♦ disappoint a guest
Gästen wird jeder Komfort und Service geboten
♦ guests receive every comfort and service
Gästen zur Verfügung stehen
♦ be available to guests
♦ be available for guests AE
♦ be at the guests' disposal

Gästeordnung, f
(Hausordnung)
♦ guest regulations pl
Gästeparkplatz
(Hinweisschild)
♦ Parking for guests
Gästepaß, m
♦ guest pass
Gästepauschale, f
♦ guest package
Gästepavillon, m
♦ guest pavilion
♦ guests' pavilion
Gästepost, f
♦ guest mail
♦ guests' mail
♦ guest's mail
Gästepost ausgeben
♦ issue the guests' mail
Gästepost sortieren
♦ sort the guests' mail
Gästepotential, n
potentielle Gäste, m pl
♦ guest potential
♦ potential guests pl
Gästeprogramm n
♦ guests' program AE
♦ guest program AE
♦ guests' programme BE
♦ guest programme BE
Gästepublikum, n
→ Gästekreis
Gästeranch, f
♦ guest ranch
♦ dude ranch AE humor
Gästerechnung, f
♦ guest's bill
♦ guests' bill
♦ guest bill
♦ guest check AE
♦ guest account
Gästerechnung erstellen
♦ make out a guest's bill
♦ issue a guest's bill
Gästeregistrierung, f
♦ guest registration
♦ registration of guests
♦ registering guests
Gästerückgang, m
Gästezahlrückgang m
♦ decrease in the number of guests
♦ drop in the number of guests
♦ fall in the number of guests
♦ decline in the number of guests
Gast erwarten
♦ expect a guest
♦ be expecting a guest
Gästeschaft f
→ Gästekreis
Gästeschar, f
→ Kundenstamm
Gästeschicht, f
♦ class of guests
♦ class of guest
Gästeschwimmbad, n
♦ swimming pool for guests AE
♦ swimming pool for guests' use AE
♦ swimming-pool for guests BE
♦ swimming-pool for guests' use BE
Gästeseife, f
♦ guest soap

Gästeservice, m
  Gastservice m
  ♦ guest service
Gästeserviceangebot, n (Palette)
  ♦ range of guest services
  ♦ range of guest services offered
Gästeserviceangebot erweitern
  Gästeserviceangebot vergrößern
  Gästeserviceangebot ausweiten
  ♦ broaden the range of guest services
  ♦ enlarge the range of guest services
  ♦ extend the range of guest services
  ♦ expand the range of guest services
Gästeserviette, f
  ♦ guest napkin
  ♦ guest's napkin
Gästesicherheit, f
  ♦ guest safety
Gäste sind handverlesen
  Gäste sind sorgfältig ausgesucht
  ♦ guests are hand-picked
Gäste sind in Feststimmung
  Gäste sind festlich gestimmt
  ♦ guests are in a festive mood
Gästespeisesaal m
  ♦ guests' dining room
Gästestamm, m
  → Kundenstamm
Gästestammdatei, f
  Gästehauptkartei, f
  ♦ guest master file
Gästestatistik, f
  ♦ guest statistics pl
  ♦ statistics of guests pl
  ♦ statistics of visitors pl
Gästestrom, m
  ♦ flow of guests
  ♦ stream of guests
  ♦ guest flow
Gästestruktur, f
  ♦ guest structure
Gästestrukturanalyse f
  ♦ guest structure analysis
  ♦ analysis of the guest structure
Gästestruktur untersuchen
  Gästestruktur analysieren
  ♦ analyse the guest structure
  ♦ analyze the guest structure AE
Gästesuite, f
  Gastsuite, f
  ♦ guest suite
  ♦ guest's suite
  ♦ guests' suite
Gästesuite mit eigenem Eingang, f
  → abgeschlossene Gästesuite
Gästetisch, m
  Gasttisch, m
  ♦ guest table
  ♦ guest's table
  ♦ guests' table
  ♦ visitor's table
  ♦ visitors' table
Gästetoilette, f
  ♦ guest cloakroom BE euph
  ♦ guest toilet
Gästetrakt, m
  → Gästeflügel
Gäste treffen ein
  ♦ guests are arriving
  ♦ guests come in AE

Gästetreue, f
  Gästeloyalität f
  ♦ guest loyalty
Gästeturnier, n
  Gästewettkampf m
  ♦ guest tournament
  ♦ guests' tournament
Gästeturnier veranstalten
  ♦ hold a guest tournament
  ♦ organise a guest tournament
Gästetyp m
  → Gästeart
Gästeübernachtung, f (generell)
  ♦ overnight accommodation of a guest
  ♦ overnight accommodation for a guest
  ♦ overnight accommodation of guests
  ♦ overnight accommodation for guests
Gästeübernachtung, f (Statistik)
  ♦ guest night
Gästeübernachtungen melden
  ♦ report the number of guest nights
Gästeübernachtung vermitteln
  ♦ arrange overnight accommodation for a guest
  ♦ arrange overnight accommodation for guests
Gäste überwachen
  ♦ monitor guests
Gästeunterhaltung f
  ♦ guest entertainment
Gästeunterhaltungsabteilung, f
  ♦ guest entertainment department
Gästeunterhaltungsaufwendungen, f pl
  ♦ guest entertainment expenses pl
Gästeunterhaltungskosten, pl
  ♦ guest entertainment costs pl
  ♦ guest entertainment cost
Gästeunterkunft, f
  ♦ guest's accommodation
  ♦ guests' accommodation
  ♦ guest accommodation
Gästeverhalten, n
  ♦ guest behavior AE
  ♦ guest behaviour BE
  ♦ guest's behavio(u)r
  ♦ guests' behavio(u)r
Gästevermittlung, f
  Gästevermittlungsstelle, f
  ♦ guest agency
Gästeverpflegung, f (Aktivität)
  ♦ catering to guests
  ♦ catering to a guest
  ♦ feeding guests
  ♦ feeding a guest
Gästeverpflegung, f (Nahrungsmittel)
  ♦ guest provisions pl
  ♦ guest's provisions pl
  ♦ guests' provisions pl
Gästeverzeichnis, n
  ♦ guest register
Gästevolumen, n
  ♦ volume of guests
Gästevorliebe, f
  ♦ guest preference
Gästewäsche, f
  ♦ guest laundry
  ♦ guest's laundry
  ♦ guests' laundry
  ♦ visitors' laundry
Gästewäscherei, f
  Wäscherei für Gäste f
  ♦ guest laundry
  ♦ visitors' laundry

Gästewaschsalon m
  (Selbstbedienung)
  ♦ guest laundromat AE
  ♦ guest launderette BE
Gäste-WC, n
  ♦ guest WC
  ♦ guest's WC
  ♦ guests' WC
Gästewerbung, f
  ♦ attracting guests
Gäste werden am Bahnhof abgeholt
  ♦ guests will be met at the station
Gäste werden auf Wunsch abgeholt
  ♦ guests will be met on request
Gäste werden gebeten, ihr Zimmer bis 11 Uhr zu räumen
  ♦ guests are requested to vacate their rooms by
  ♦ 11 a.m.
Gäste werden höflichst gebeten
  ♦ guests are kindly requested
Gäste werden kostenlos vom Bahnhof abgeholt
  ♦ guests are collected from the station free of
  ♦ charge
Gästewohnung, f
  Gastwohnung, f
  ♦ guest's apartment AE
  ♦ guests' apartment AE
  ♦ guest's flat BE
  ♦ guests' flat BE
Gästewunsch, m
  ♦ guest request
  ♦ guest's request
  ♦ guests' request
  ♦ request by a guest
Gästezahl, f
  Gästeanzahl f
  ♦ number of guests
Gästezahlanstieg, m
  → Gästezuwachs
Gästezahlen hochtreiben
  ♦ boost the guest numbers
Gästezahl geht zurück
  Gästezahl sinkt
  Gästezahl nimmt ab
  ♦ number of guests is decreasing
  ♦ number of guests is falling
  ♦ number of guests is dropping
Gästezahl halten
  ♦ maintain the number of guests
  ♦ maintain the number of visitors
Gästezahlrückgang, m
  Gästerückgang, m
  ♦ fall in the number of guests
  ♦ drop in the number of guests
  ♦ decrease in the number of guests
  ♦ decline in the number of guests
Gästezahl steigern
  Gästezahl erhöhen
  ♦ increase the number of guests
Gästezahl steigt (an)
  ♦ number of guests is increasing
  ♦ number of guests is rising
Gästezahl verringern
  Gästezahl herabsetzen
  ♦ reduce the number of guests
  ♦ reduce the number of visitors
Gästezielgruppe, f
  ♦ target guest group
  ♦ target clientele

Gästezielgruppe ansprechen

Gästezielgruppe ansprechen
♦ appeal to the targeted guest group
Gästezimmer, n (in Privatwohnung)
♦ spare room
♦ spare bedroom
♦ guest room *AE*
♦ guest-room *BE*
Gästezimmer, n (kommerziell oder nichtkommerziell)
♦ guest room *AE*
♦ guest-room *BE*
♦ guestchamber *AE*
Gästezimmer betreten
♦ enter a guest's room
♦ enter the room of a guest
Gästezimmernachweis, m
Gästezimmervermittlung, f
Zimmernachweis, m
Zimmervermittlung, f
Unterkunftsnachweis, m
♦ tourist accommodations office *AE*
♦ accommodations office *AE*
♦ accommodation agency
♦ accommodation bureau
♦ room agency
Gästezimmernutzung, f
♦ use of a guest room *AE*
♦ use of a guest-room *BE*
♦ guest-room use
♦ using a guest room *AE*
♦ using guest-rooms *BE*
Gästezimmertresor, m
Gästezimmersafe m
♦ guest-room safe
Gästezimmerumsatz, m
♦ guest-room sales *pl*
♦ guest-room turnover
Gästezimmervermietung, f
♦ guest-room rental *AE*
♦ renting (out) a guest room *AE*
♦ letting a guest-room *BE*
♦ letting guest-rooms *BE*
Gästezimmerverzeichnis, n
♦ list of guest rooms *AE*
♦ list of guest-rooms *BE*
Gästezufriedenheit, f
Gastzufriedenheit, f
♦ guest satisfaction
♦ guests' satisfaction
♦ guest's satisfaction
Gästezufriedenheit steigern
♦ increase guest satisfaction
♦ increase guests' satisfaction
Gästezufriedenheit verbessern
♦ improve guest satisfaction
Gästezuwachs, m
Gästezahlanstieg, m
♦ increase in the number of guests
♦ rise in the number of guests
Gästezuwachs verzeichnen
♦ record an increase in the number of guests
♦ record a rise in the number of guests
Gastfamilie, f
Gastgeberfamilie, f
gastgebende Familie, f
♦ host family
Gast festlich bewirten
♦ feast a guest
Gastfirma, f
gastgebende Firma, f

Gastgeberfirma, f
♦ host firm
Gastforschung, f
♦ guest research
gastfrei, adj
→ gastfreundlich
gastfrei sein
gastfreundlich sein
♦ keep an open house
♦ be hospitable
gastfreundlich, adj
gastfrei, adj
♦ hospitable, adj
gastfreundliche Atmosphäre, f
gastliche Atmosphäre f
♦ hospitable atmosphere
♦ friendly atmosphere
gastfreundliche Leute, pl
♦ hospitable people *pl*
gastfreundlicher Service, m
♦ hospitable service
gastfreundliches Hotel, n
gastliches Hotel, n
♦ hospitable hotel
♦ friendly hotel
gastfreundliches Volk, n
♦ hospitable people *sg*
gastfreundliches Zimmer, n
♦ hospitable room
Gastfreundlichkeit f
→ Gastfreundschaft
gastfreundlich sein zu jm
♦ be hospitable to s.o.
♦ be hospitable towards s.o.
Gastfreundschaft, f
Gastlichkeit, f
♦ hospitality
Gastfreundschaft ablehnen
Gastfreundschaft ausschlagen
♦ refuse hospitality
Gastfreundschaft ausnutzen von jm
js Gastfreundschaft übermäßig beanspruchen
js Gastlichkeit übermäßig in Anspruch nehmen
♦ impose on s.o.'s hospitality
♦ be imposing on s.o.'s hospitality
Gastfreundschaft erfahren
Gastfreundschaft erleben
♦ experience hospitality
Gastfreundschaft erwidern von jm
js Gastfreundschaft erwidern
js großzügige Gastfreundschaft erwidern
♦ reciprocate s.o.'s hospitality
♦ reciprocate s.o.'s generous hospitality
Gastfreundschaft genießen von jm
♦ enjoy s.o.'s hospitality
♦ enjoy the hospitality of s.o.
Gastfreundschaft gewähren
♦ extend hospitality
Gastfreundschaft kennenlernen
Gastfreundschaft erfahren
Gastfreundschaft ausprobieren
♦ sample hospitality
Gastfreundschaft mißbrauchen von jm
js Gastfreundschaft mißbrauchen
♦ abuse s.o.'s hospitality
Gastfreundschaft verletzen
♦ insult the hospitality
gastgebend, adj
♦ host, adj
♦ acting as host, adj

gastgebende Familie, f
→ Gastfamilie
gastgebende Gemeinde, f
Gastgemeinde, f
♦ host community
gastgebender Verein, m
Gastverein, m
♦ host club
gastgebendes Hotel, n
→ Gasthotel
gastgebende Stadt, f (Großstadt)
Gastgeberstadt, f
Gaststadt, f
♦ host city
gastgebende Stadt, f (kleine Stadt)
Gastgeberstadt, f
Gaststadt, f
♦ host town
Gastgeber, m
Ausrichter, m
♦ host
Gastgeberfamilie, f
→ Gastfamilie
Gastgeberin, f
♦ hostess
Gastgeber sein
♦ be host
Gastgeber sein bei einem Diner
♦ be host at a dinner
Gastgeber sein bei einem Empfang
♦ be host at a reception
♦ host a reception
Gastgeber sein bei einer Party
Gastgeber sein bei einem Fest
♦ host a party
♦ be host at a party
Gastgeber sein bei einer Pressekonferenz
Pressekonferenz ausrichten
♦ host a press conference
Gastgeber sein bei einer Schau
Schau ausrichten
♦ host a show
Gastgeber sein für jn
♦ be host to s.o.
♦ host s.o.
Gastgeber spielen (bei etw)
♦ play host (at s.th.)
Gastgeber spielen für einen Besucher
♦ play host to a visitor
Gastgeber spielen für jn
♦ play host to s.o.
Gastgeberstadt, f
→ gastgebende Stadt
Gastgebersuite, f
Hospitality Suite f
♦ hospitality suite
Gastgeberverzeichnis, n
Unterkunftsverzeichnis, n
Unterkunftsliste, f
♦ list of accommodation
♦ list of accommodations *AE*
♦ accommodation list
Gast Gefallen erweisen
Gast gefällig sein
entgegenkommend sein bei einem Gast
♦ oblige a guest
Gastgemeinde, f
→ gastgebende Gemeinde
Gast gern entgegensehen
♦ look forward to welcoming a guest

278

Gastgeschäft, n
 Geschäft mit dem Gast, n
 ♦ hospitality business
Gastgewerbe, n
 ♦ hospitality industry
Gastgewerbeabteilung, f (eines Unternehmens)
 ♦ hospitality division
Gastgewerbeausbilder, m (akademisch)
 Gastgewerbedozent, m
 ♦ hospitality educator
Gastgewerbeausbildung, f (akademisch)
 ♦ hospitality education
Gastgewerbeausbildung, f (nicht akademisch)
 ♦ hospitality training
Gastgewerbebereich, m
 Gatsgewerbesektor, m
 ♦ hospitality field
 ♦ hospitality sector
Gastgewerbebetrieb, m
 ♦ hospitality establishment
 ♦ hospitality operation
Gastgewerbeerfahrung, f
 ♦ hospitality experience
Gastgewerbefirma, f
 ♦ hospitality firm
 ♦ hospitality corporation AE
 ♦ hospitality company
 ♦ hospitality concern
Gastgewerbeforum, n
 ♦ hospitality forum
Gastgewerbefranchise, n
 ♦ hospitality franchise
Gastgewerbefranchisesystem, n
 ♦ hospitality franchise system
Gastgewerbegeschäft, n
 Gastgeschäft, n
 ♦ hotel and restaurant business
 ♦ hospitality business
Gastgewerbeinfrastruktur, f
 ♦ hospitality infrastructure
Gastgewerbeinstitut, n
 ♦ hospitality institute
Gastgewerbekenntnisse, f pl
 gastgewerbliche Fachkenntnisse, f pl
 ♦ hospitality skills pl
Gastgewerbekonzern, m
 ♦ hospitality group
Gastgewerbekurs, m
 Gastgewerbelehrgang, m
 ♦ hospitality course
Gastgewerbemanagement, n
 ♦ hospitality management
Gastgewerbemanager, m
 Manager im Gastgewerbe m
 ♦ hospitality manager
Gastgewerbemarketing, n
 ♦ hospitality marketing
Gastgewerbemarkt, m
 ♦ hospitality market
Gastgewerbeorganisation, f
 ♦ hospitality organisation
 ♦ hospitality organization
Gastgewerbeort, m
 ♦ hospitality venue
Gastgewerbepraktiker, m
 ♦ hospitality practitioner
Gastgewerbeprodukt, n
 gastgewerbliches Produkt n
 ♦ hospitality product
Gastgewerbeprofi, m
 ♦ hospitality professional

Gastgewerbeschule, f
 Gastronomieschule, f
 ♦ school of hospitality
 ♦ hospitality school
Gastgewerbesektor, m
 ♦ hospitality sector
 ♦ hospitality field
Gastgewerbeservice, m
 gastgewerblicher Service, m
 gastgewerbliche Dienstleistung, f
 gastgewerbliche Leistung, f
 Gastronomieleistung, f
 ♦ hospitality service
Gastgewerbestudiengang, m
 Gastgewerbeprogramm, n
 ♦ hospitality program AE
 ♦ hospitality programme BE
Gastgewerbe- und Tourismusausbildung, f (akadem.)
 ♦ hospitality and tourism education
Gastgewerbe- und Tourismusausbildung, f (unakadem.)
 ♦ hospitality and tourism training
Gastgewerbeunternehmen, n
 ♦ hospitality enterprise
Gastgewerbeveranstaltung, f
 Veranstaltung mit Bewirtung, f
 ♦ hospitality event
 ♦ hospitality function
Gastgewerbezentrum, n
 ♦ hospitality center AE
 ♦ hospitality centre BE
gastgewerbliche Dienstleistung, f
 → Gastgewerbeservice
gastgewerblicher Arbeitnehmer, m
 Arbeitnehmer im Gastgewerbe m
 ♦ employee in the hospitality industry
 ♦ employee in the hotel and catering trade BE
gastgewerblicher Betrieb, m
 Gastgewerbebetrieb, m
 ♦ hospitality operation
 ♦ hospitality establishment
gastgewerbliche Schule, f
 ♦ catering school
Gast gratis aufnehmen
 Gast gratis unterbringen
 ♦ accommodate a guest free of charge
Gast hat zuviel gezahlt
 ♦ guest has overpaid
Gast hat zuwenig gezahlt
 ♦ guest has underpaid
Gasthaus, das auf halbem Weg liegt, n
 ♦ halfway house AE
 ♦ half-way house BE
Gasthaus, n
 → Gaststätte
Gasthaus am Ort, n
 Ortsgasthaus, n
 ♦ local public house BE
 ♦ local pub BE coll
 ♦ local bar AE
 ♦ local coll
Gasthaus benutzen
 Gaststätte benutzen
 ♦ use a bar AE
 ♦ use a public house BE
 ♦ use a pub BE coll
Gasthaus-Pension, f
 ♦ bar/guesthouse AE
 ♦ bar cum guesthouse AE
 ♦ pub cum guest-house BE

Gasthausspiel, m
 Wirtshausspiel, m
 ♦ bar game AE
 ♦ pub game BE
Gast herzlich willkommen heißen
 ♦ extend a warm welcome to a guest
 ♦ give a warm welcome to a guest
Gast hinhalten
 ♦ keep a guest hanging
Gasthof, m
 ♦ inn
Gasthof am Meer, m
 ♦ inn by the sea
 ♦ seaside inn
Gasthof am Weg, m
 ♦ wayside inn
Gasthofangestellter, m
 Gasthofangestellte f
 ♦ inn employee
Gasthofbesitzer, m
 Gastwirt, m
 ♦ innkeeper
 ♦ owner of an inn
Gasthof erreichen
 ♦ reach an inn
Gasthofgast, m
 ♦ inn guest
Gasthof hält bis 23 Uhr offen
 ♦ inn is open until 11 p.m.
Gasthofschild, n
 ♦ inn sign
Gasthof sieht sehr einladend aus
 ♦ inn looks very inviting
Gasthofzimmer, n
 ♦ inn room
Gasthof zum Roten Ochsen, m
 Gasthaus zum Roten Ochsen, n
 ♦ Red Ox Inn, the
 ♦ Red Ox, the
Gasthof zur Sonne, m
 ♦ Sun Inn, the
Gasthörer, m
 (an Hochschule)
 ♦ auditor
Gasthotel, n
 gastgebendes Hotel, n
 ♦ host hotel
Gast ignorieren
 Gast übersehen
 keine Notiz von einem Gast nehmen
 ♦ ignore a guest
 ♦ overlook a guest
 ♦ take no notice of a guest
Gast individuelle Betreuung geben
 Gast individuell betreuen
 ♦ provide individual attention to a guest
Gast in einem Hotel willkommen heißen
 ♦ welcome a guest to a hotel
Gast in einem Zimmer unterbringen
 ♦ room a guest
Gast irrtümlich in Rechnung stellen etw
 ♦ charge a guest wrongly for s.th.
Gast ist betrunken
 ♦ guest is drunk
Gastkarte, f
 → Gästekarte
Gastkoch, m
 ♦ guest cook
Gast kommt an
 ♦ guest is arriving

Gastkontakt

- guest shows up *sl*
- guest is checking in

Gastkontakt, m
Gästekontakt, m
- contact with guests
- guest contact
- contact with visitors

Gastkontaktbereich, m
Empfangsbereich, m
- front-office area
- reception area

Gastkontaktpersonal n
- front-office personnel
- front-office staff

Gastkonzert, n
- guest concert

Gast kränken
- offend a guest

Gastküchenchef, m
- guest chef

Gastland, n
gastgebendes Land, n
Gastgeberland, n
- host country

gastliche Atmosphäre, f
heitere Atmosphäre f
- convivial atmosphere

gastliches Haus, n
→ gastfreundliches Hotel

gastliches Hotel, n
- convivial hotel

gastliche Umgebung, f
heitere Umgebung f
- convivial surroundings *pl*

gastliche Veranstaltung, f
gesellige Veranstaltung, f
- convivial event
- convivial function

Gastlichkeit, f
→ Gastfreundschaft

Gastlichkeit anbieten
Gastfreundschaft anbieten
- offer hospitality

Gastlichkeit ist Trumpf
Gastlichkeit kommt zuerst
- hospitality is foremost

Gastlichkeit kennt keine Grenzen
Gastfreundschaft kennt keine Grenzen
- hospitality knows no limits

Gastlichkeit von ihrer besten Seite, f
- hospitality at its best
- hospitality at its finest

gastlich sein
gastfreundlich sein
- be hospitable

Gast links liegenlassen
- slight a guest
- cold-shoulder a guest

Gastlokal, n
→ Gaststätte

gastlos, adj
- guestless, adj

Gastmahl, n
→ Bankett

Gast meldet sich an
Gast trägt sich in das Meldebuch ein
- guest registers

Gast mitbringen in einen Club
- bring a guest into a club

Gast mit Halbpension, m
- guest on half-board terms

- guest on half board
- guest on demi-pension terms
- guest on demi-pension

Gast mit seinem Namen begrüßen
- greet a guest by his/her name

Gast mit Teilpension, m
- guest on part-board terms
- guest on part board
- guest on partial board

Gast mit Vollpension, m
- guest on full-board terms
- guest on full board
- guest on full-pension terms
- guest on full pension

Gastnation, f
gastgebende Nation, f
Gastgebernation, f
- host nation

Gast nehmen
Gast aufnehmen
- take a guest

Gastorchester, n
- visiting orchestra

Gastorganisation, f
gastgebende Organisation, f
Gastgeberorganisation, f
- host organisation

Gast persönlich begrüßen
- give a guest a personal welcome

Gast plazieren
→ Platz zuweisen einem Gast

Gastprofessor, m
- visiting professor
- guest professor

Gastrechnung, f
- guest bill
- guest's bill
- guest check *AE*
- guest's check *AE*

Gastrechnung vorbereiten
- prepare a guest's account
- prepare a guest's bill
- prepare a guest's check *AE*

Gastrecht, n
- right of hospitality
- right to hospitality
- hospitality

Gastrecht genießen
Gastfreundschaft genießen
- enjoy the hospitality of s.o.
- enjoy s.o.'s hospitality

Gastrecht gewähren jm
- grant s.o. hospitality

Gastredner, m
(bei einer Veranstaltung)
- guest speaker
- visiting speaker

Gastreferent, m
Gastredner, m
- visiting speaker
- guest speaker

Gast reist ab
- guest is departing
- guest is leaving

Gastritis, f
Magenentzündung, f
- gastritis

Gastronom, m (Feinschmecker)
Feinschmecker, m
- gastronome
- gastronomist

Gastronom, m (generell)
- restaurant owner
- innkeeper
- hotelier
- hotelkeeper
- publican *BE*

Gastronomie
(Überschrift in Führern)
- Where to eat

Gastronomie, f (generell)
- foodservice *AE*
- catering

Gastronomie, f (Hotel)
→ Food-and-Beverage

Gastronomie, f (Kochkunst)
höhere Kochkunst, f
Küche, f
- gastronomy

Gastronomieabteilung, f
(eines Unternehmens)
- foodservice division *AE*
- catering division

Gastronomieangebot, n (Gegensatz zu Nachfrage)
gastronomisches Angebot n
- foodservice supply *AE*
- catering supply *BE*

Gastronomieangebot, n (Offerte)
gastronomisches Angebot n
- foodservice offer *AE*
- catering offer *BE*

Gastronomieangebot, n (Palette)
gastronomisches Angebot n
- foodservice range *AE*
- catering range *BE*

Gastronomieangestellter, m
- foodservice employee *AE*
- catering employee *BE*

Gastronomieausbildung, f (akademisch)
- foodservice education *AE*
- catering education *BE*

Gastronomieausbildung, f (nicht akademisch)
- foodservice training *AE*
- catering training *BE*

Gastronomieausstellung, f
- foodservice show *AE*
- catering show *BE*

Gastronomieberater, m
Gastronomieconsultant, m
- foodservice consultant *AE*
- catering consultant *BE*

Gastronomiebereich, m (Hotel, abstrakt)
Verpflegungsbereich, m
Wirtschaftsbereich, m
- food and beverage field
- f&b field
- food and beverage sector
- f&b sector

Gastronomiebereich, m (Hotel, konkret)
Verpflegungsbereich, m
Wirtschaftsbereich, m
- food and beverage area
- f&b area

Gastronomiebereich, m (Wirtschaftszweig)
- foodservice sector *AE*
- catering sector *BE*

Gastronomiebetrieb, m
gastronomischer Betrieb m
Restaurationsbetrieb, m *ÖST/SCHW*
- foodservice establishment *AE*
- foodservice operation *AE*

- ♦ catering establishment BE
- ♦ catering operation BE

Gastronomieconsultant, m
→ Gastronomieberater

Gastronomiedozent, m
Gastgewerbedozent, m
- ♦ **lecturer in catering**

Gastronomieeinnahmen, f pl (Hotel)
Verpflegungseinnahmen, f pl
Einnahmen aus Verpflegung, f pl
- ♦ **food and beverage takings** pl
- ♦ food and beverage receipts pl
- ♦ food and beverage income
- ♦ f&b takings pl
- ♦ f&b receipts pl

Gastronomieeinrichtung, f (Hotel)
gastronomische Einrichtung, f
Verpflegungseinrichtung, f
- ♦ **food and beverage facility**
- ♦ f&b facility

Gastronomiefiliale, f
- ♦ **foodservice outlet** AE
- ♦ catering outlet BE

Gastronomiefirma, f
- ♦ **foodservice firm** AE
- ♦ catering firm BE
- ♦ foodservice company AE
- ♦ catering company BE

Gastronomieführer, m
(Buch)
Restaurantführer, m
- ♦ **food guide**
- ♦ restaurant guide
- ♦ guide to the restaurants

Gastronomiegeschäft, n
Restaurationsgeschäft, n ÖST/SCHW
- ♦ **foodservice business** AE
- ♦ catering business BE
- ♦ restaurant business

Gastronomiegewerbe, n
- ♦ **foodservice trade** AE
- ♦ catering trade BE

Gastronomiegewinn, m (Hotel)
Verpflegungsgewinn, m
Gewinn aus Verpflegungsleistungen, m
- ♦ **food and beverage profit**
- ♦ f&b profit

Gastronomieimmobilie, f
gastgewerbliche Immobilie, f
- ♦ **foodservice property** AE
- ♦ catering property BE

Gastronomieindustrie, f
Gastronomiebranche, f
- ♦ **foodservice industry** AE
- ♦ catering industry BE

Gastronomiekarriere, f
Karriere in der Gastronomie, f
- ♦ **foodservice career** AE
- ♦ catering career BE

Gastronomiekette, f
- ♦ **foodservice chain** AE
- ♦ catering chain AE

Gastronomiekonzept, n
- ♦ **foodservice concept** AE
- ♦ catering concept BE

Gastronomiekosten, pl (Hotel)
Verpflegungskosten, pl
Lebensmittel- und Getränkekosten, pl
Speisen- und Getränkekosten, pl
- ♦ **food and beverage cost**
- ♦ food and beverage costs pl

- ♦ f&b cost
- ♦ f&b costs pl

Gastronomiekritiker, m
- ♦ **food critic**

Gastronomieleistung, f (Hotel)
Gastronomiedienstleistung, f
gastronomische (Dienst-)Leistung, f
Gastronomieservice, m
Verpflegungsleistung, f
- ♦ **food and beverage service**
- ♦ f&b service

Gastronomieleiter, m
Gastronomiemanager, m
Restaurationsleiter, m ÖST/SCHW
- ♦ **foodservice manager** AE
- ♦ catering manager BE

Gastronomieleitung, f
Gastronomiemanagement, n
- ♦ **foodservice management** AE
- ♦ catering management BE

Gastronomiemanagement, n
Gastronomieleitung, f
- ♦ **catering management** BE
- ♦ foodservice management AE

Gastronomiemanager, m
Gastronomieleiter, m
- ♦ **catering manager** BE
- ♦ foodservice manager AE

Gastronomiemarkt, m
gastronomischer Markt m
- ♦ **foodservice market** AE
- ♦ catering market BE

Gastronomienachfrage, f
gastronomische Nachfrage f
- ♦ **foodservice demand** AE
- ♦ catering demand BE

Gastronomiepersonal, n (Hotel)
gastronomisches Personal, n
Verpflegungspersonal, n
Wirtschaftspersonal, n
- ♦ **food and beverage staff**
- ♦ food and beverage personnel
- ♦ f&b staff
- ♦ f&b personnel

Gastronomiepolitik, f
- ♦ **foodservice policy** AE
- ♦ catering policy BE

Gastronomieschriftsteller, m
Gastronomieautor, m
- ♦ **food writer**

Gastronomiesektor, m (generell)
- ♦ **foodservice sector** AE
- ♦ catering sector BE
- ♦ restaurant sector

Gastronomiesektor, m (Hotel)
Gastronomiebereich, m
gastronomischer Bereich, m
Verpflegungssektor, m
Verpflegungsbereich, m
- ♦ **food and beverage sector**
- ♦ f&b sector

Gastronomieservice, m
Restaurationsservice, m ÖST/SCHW
- ♦ **foodservice** AE
- ♦ catering service BE

Gastronomiesituation, f
gastronomische Situation f
- ♦ **foodservice situation** AE
- ♦ catering situation BE

Gastronomieszene, f
→ Restaurantszene

Gastronomietempel, m humor
- ♦ **temple of gastronomy** humor
- ♦ gastronomic shrine humor

Gastronomieumsatz, m (generell)
gastronomischer Umsatz, m
Verpflegungsumsatz, m
- ♦ **foodservice sales** AE pl
- ♦ catering sales BE pl

Gastronomieumsatz, m (Hotel)
gastronomischer Umsatz, m
Verpflegungsumsatz, m
- ♦ **food and beverage turnover**
- ♦ food and beverage sales pl
- ♦ f&b turnover
- ♦ f&b sales pl

Gastronomieunternehmer, m
- ♦ **foodservice operator** AE
- ♦ catering operator BE

gastronomisch, adj (feinschmeckerisch)
feinschmeckerisch, adj
- ♦ **gastronomic, adj**
- ♦ gastronomical, adj

gastronomische Erfahrung, f
Gastronomieerfahrung, f
Feinschmeckererfahrung, f
Feinschmeckererlebnis, n
- ♦ **gastronomic experience**

gastronomische Gründe, m pl
Feinschmeckergründe, m pl
- ♦ **gastronomic reasons** pl

gastronomische Hauptstadt, f
Feinschmeckerhauptstadt, f
- ♦ **gastronomic capital**

gastronomische Orgie, f
Feinschmeckerorgie, f
- ♦ **gastronomic orgy**

gastronomischer Betrieb, m
→ Gastronomiebetrieb

gastronomische Region, f
Feinschmeckerregion, f
- ♦ **gastronomic region**

gastronomischer Standard, m
Gastronomiestandard, m
Feinschmeckerstandard, m
Küchenstandard, m
- ♦ **gastronomic standard**

gastronomisches Abenteuer, n
Feinschmeckerabenteuer, n
- ♦ **gastronomic adventure**

Gastronomisches Angebot
(Überschrift in Prospekten)
- ♦ **Restaurants**

gastronomisches Angebot, n
→ Gastronomieangebot

gastronomisches Festmahl, n
gastronomischer Festschmaus, m
Feinschmeckerfestmahl, n
Feinschmeckerfestschmaus, m
- ♦ **gastronomic feast**

gastronomisches Personal, n
Gastronomiepersonal, n
gastgewerbliches Personal, n
Gastgewerbepersonal, n
- ♦ **foodservice staff** AE
- ♦ foodservice personnel AE
- ♦ catering staff BE
- ♦ catering personnel BE

gastronomisches Wochenende, n
Feinschmeckerwochenende, n
- ♦ **gastronomic weekend**

gastronomische Tradition

gastronomische Tradition, f
  gastronomische Überlieferung, f
  Feinschmeckertradition, f
  Küchentradition, f
  ♦ **gastronomic tradition**
gastronomische Veranstaltung, f
  (Feinschmecker)
  Feinschmeckerveranstaltung, f
  ♦ **gastronomic event**
  ♦ **gastronomic function**
gastronomische Veranstaltung, f (generell)
  Gastronomieveranstaltung, f
  Veranstaltung mit Verpflegung, f
  Veranstaltung mit Essen, f
  ♦ **foodservice function** *AE*
  ♦ **foodservice event** *AE*
  ♦ **catering function** *BE*
  ♦ **catering event** *BE*
Gastschule, f
  gastgebende Schule, f
  ♦ **host school**
Gastsegment, n
  ♦ **guest segment**
  ♦ **visitor segment**
Gast sein bei jm
  js Gast sein
  ♦ **be s.o.'s guest**
Gast sein Zimmer zuweisen
  Gast sein Zimmer anweisen
  ♦ **assign a guest to his/her room**
Gastservice, m
  → Gästeservice
Gastspiel, n (Sport)
  ♦ **away game**
Gastspiel, n (Stippvisite)
  → Stippvisite
Gastspiel, n (Theater)
  ♦ **guest performance**
Gastspiel absolvieren
  Gastspiel geben
  Gastaufführung geben
  ♦ **give a guest performance**
Gastspielreise, f
  → Tournee
Gastspieltruppe, f
  (Theater)
  ♦ **touring company**
Gaststadt, f
  → gastgebende Stadt
Gaststar, m
  Stargast, m
  ♦ **star guest**
Gaststätte, f
  Gastwirtschaft, f
  Wirtschaft, f
  ♦ **public house** *BE*
  ♦ **pub** *BE*
  ♦ **bar** *AE*
  ♦ **saloon** *AE*
  ♦ **restaurant**
Gaststätte besuchen
  Wirtschaft besuchen
  ♦ **visit a pub** *BE*
  ♦ **visit a bar** *AE*
Gaststätte betreiben
  ♦ **keep a public house** *BE*
  ♦ **keep a pub** *BE coll*
  ♦ **keep a bar** *AE*
  ♦ **keep a saloon** *AE coll*

Gaststätte des Jahres, f
  ♦ **Pub of the Year** *BE*
  ♦ **Bar of the Year** *AE*
Gaststätte führen
  Gaststätte leiten
  ♦ **run a public house** *BE*
  ♦ **run a pub** *BE coll*
  ♦ **run a bar** *AE*
Gaststätte ist verpachtet
  ♦ **bar is leased** *AE*
  ♦ **public house is tenanted** *BE*
  ♦ **pub is tenanted** *BE coll*
Gaststätte mit Charakter, f
  ♦ **bar of character** *AE*
  ♦ **pub of character** *BE*
Gaststätte mit einer Bar, f
  ♦ **one-bar saloon** *AE*
  ♦ **one-bar pub** *BE*
Gaststätte mit zwei Bars, f
  ♦ **two-bar saloon** *AE*
  ♦ **two-bar pub** *BE*
Gaststättenbesucher, m
  Wirtshausbesucher, m
  Gasthausbesucher, m
  ♦ **pub visitor** *BE*
  ♦ **bar visitor** *AE*
  ♦ **pub-goer** *BE*
Gaststättenbetreiber, m
  ♦ **public house operator** *BE*
  ♦ **pub operator** *BE*
Gaststättenbetrieb, m
  ♦ **foodservice establishment** *AE*
  ♦ **foodservice operation** *AE*
  ♦ **catering establishment** *BE*
  ♦ **catering operation** *BE*
Gaststättenessen, n (generell)
  ♦ **pub food** *BE*
  ♦ **bar food** *AE*
  ♦ **pub grub** *BE inform*
Gaststättenessen, n (Mahlzeit)
  Gaststättenmahlzeit, f
  ♦ **pub meal** *BE*
  ♦ **bar meal** *AE*
Gaststättenführer, m
  ♦ **pub guide** *BE*
Gaststättengehilfin, f *form*
  → Kellnerin
Gaststättengewerbe, n
  ♦ **catering trade**
Gaststättenkette, f
  ♦ **pub chain** *BE*
  ♦ **chain of pubs** *BE*
  ♦ **bar chain** *AE*
  ♦ **chain of bars** *AE*
Gaststättenkonzession, f
  ♦ **public house licence** *BE*
  ♦ **public house license** *BE*
  ♦ **bar license** *AE*
  ♦ **bar licence** *AE*
Gaststättennebenzimmer, n
  ♦ **function room in a bar** *AE*
  ♦ **function room in a pub** *BE*
  ♦ **bar's side room** *AE*
  ♦ **pub's side room** *BE*
Gaststättenparkplatz, m
  ♦ **bar parking lot** *AE*
  ♦ **pub car park** *BE*
Gaststättenrecht, n
  ♦ **restaurant law**

Gaststättenrestaurant, n
  ♦ **pub restaurant** *BE*
  ♦ **bar restaurant** *AE*
Gaststättentisch, m
  Gasthaustisch, m
  Wirtshaustisch, m
  ♦ **pub table** *BE coll*
  ♦ **bar table** *AE*
Gaststättentrakt, m
  → Restauranttrakt
Gaststättenunterhaltung, f
  ♦ **bar entertainment** *AE*
  ♦ **pub entertainment** *BE*
Gaststättenverband, m
  ♦ **catering association**
  ♦ **restaurant association**
Gaststätte schließt um 23 Uhr
  ♦ **bar closes at 11 p.m.** *AE*
  ♦ **restaurant closes at 11 p.m.**
  ♦ **saloon closes at 11 p.m.** *AE*
  ♦ **public house closes at 11 p.m.** *BE*
  ♦ **pub closes at 11 p.m.** *BE*
Gaststatus, m
  (politisch)
  ♦ **guest status**
Gaststatus erhalten
  (politisch)
  ♦ **receive guest status**
Gaststatus gewähren jm
  (politisch)
  ♦ **grant s.o. guest status**
Gast stören
  ♦ **disturb a guest**
Gasttelefonnummer, f
  ♦ **guest's telephone number**
Gasttisch, m
  → Gästetisch
Gasttyp m
  ♦ **guest type**
  ♦ **type of guest**
Gast- und Fremdenverkehrsgewerbe, n
  ♦ **hospitality and tourism industry**
Gast- und Reisegewerbe, n
  ♦ **hospitality and travel trade**
Gast- und Reiseindustrie, f
  ♦ **hospitality and travel industry**
Gast- und Reiseorganisation, f
  ♦ **hospitality and travel organisation**
Gast unterbringen
  Gast aufnehmen
  ♦ **accommodate a guest**
  ♦ **put up a guest** *BE coll*
Gast unterhalten
  ♦ **entertain a guest**
Gasturbine, f
  ♦ **gas turbine**
Gasturbinenmotor, m
  ♦ **gas-turbine engine**
Gastveranstaltung, f
  ♦ **guest event**
  ♦ **guest function**
Gast verköstigen
  Gast bewirten
  ♦ **feed a guest**
  ♦ **cater for a guest**
Gast verlegen
  (in anderes Zimmer)
  Gast umlegen *sl*
  Gast umquartieren
  ♦ **move a guest**
  ♦ **transfer a guest**

Gast verlegen in anderes Zimmer
- transfer a guest to another room
- move a guest to another room

Gast verlegen in ein anderes Hotel
- transfer a guest to another hotel
- switch a guest to another hotel *coll*

Gast vom Hotel zum Bahnhof befördern
- transport a guest from the hotel to the station
- carry a guest from the hotel to the station

Gast von einem Zimmer in ein anderes verlegen
Gast umquartieren in ein anderes Zimmer
- move a guest from one room to another
- transfer a guest from one room to another

Gastvorlesung, f
- guest lecture

Gastvorrechte, n pl
- guest privileges *pl*

Gastvorrechte genießen
- enjoy guest privileges

Gastvorstellung, f
Gastauftritt, m
- guest appearance
- guest performance

Gast wecken
- wake a guest
- call a guest

Gast willkommen heißen
Gast begrüßen
- welcome a guest

Gastwirt, m
→ Wirt
- public house keeper *BE*
- pub keeper *BE*
- innkeeper
- landlord

Gastwirtin, f
Wirtin, f
- female innkeeper
- female publican *BE*
- female saloonkeeper *AE*
- lady innkeeper
- landlady

Gastwirtschaft, f
→ Gaststätte

Gastwirtshaftung, f
- innkeeper's liability
- liability of an innkeeper

Gastwirtspfandrecht, n
Pfandrecht des Gastwirts, n
- innkeeper's lien

Gastwohnung, f
Gästewohnung, f
- guest's flat *BE*
- guest's apartment *AE*
- guests' flat *BE*
- guests' apartment *AE*

Gastwunsch, m
- guest's request

Gast zufriedenstellen
- satisfy a guest
- please a guest

Gast zur Räumung seines Zimmers zwingen *jur*
Gast hinaussetzen
- evict a guest from his (her) room *jur*

Gast zur Räumung zwingen *jur*
Gast hinaussetzen
- evict a guest *jur*

Gast zurückweisen
Gast abweisen
- reject a guest
- turn away a guest

Gast zu seinem Tisch führen
- show a guest to his/her table
- conduct a guest to his/her table

Gast zu seinem Zimmer bringen
- show a guest to his/her room

Gast zu seinem Zimmer führen
- take a guest to his (her) room

Gast zu seinem Zimmer geleiten
- escort a guest to his (her) room

Gas und Strom sind in der Miete enthalten
- gas and electricity are included in the rent

Gasverbrauch, m
- gas consumption
- consumption of gas

Gas verbrauchen
- consume gas

Gasversorgung, f
- gas supply

Gaszähler, m
Gasuhr, f
- gas meter

Gaszähler ablesen
Gasuhr ablesen
- read the gas meter

Gaszentralheizung, f
GZH, f
- gas central heating
- GCH

Gaudi, f *coll*
Spaß m
Vergnügen n
- fun
- good time

Gaudi haben *fam*
→ Mordsspaß haben

Gaumen, m
- palate

Gaumen beleidigen
- offend s.o.'s palate

Gaumenfreuden, f pl
- gastronomic delights *pl*
- culinary delights *pl*

Gaumen kitzeln
- tickle s.o.'s palate
- tickle one's palate

Gaumen verwöhnen
- pamper s.o.'s palate
- pamper one's palate

Gazastreifen, m
- Gaza Strip, the

Gebäude, n
- building

Gebäudeabschreibung, f
- building depreciation
- depreciation of a building

Gebäudebewertung, f
- assessment of a building
- building survey *BE*

Gebäudebewohner, m
- building resident

Gebäudeertragswert, m
- annual value of a building

Gebäude erwerben
- acquire a building

Gebäudegutachten, n
(über den Zustand des Gebäudes)
- surveyor's report

Gebäudeheizung, f
Heizung eines Gebäudes, f
- heating of a building
- heating a building

Gebäude in gutem Zustand erhalten
Gebäude instandhalten
Gebäude unterhalten
- keep a building in good repair

Gebäudeinstandhaltung, f
- building maintenance
- property maintenance
- maintenance of a building

Gebäudeinstandhaltungskosten, pl
Gebäudeunterhaltungskosten, pl
- costs of building maintenance *pl*
- cost of building maintenance

Gebäude kaufen
- buy a building

Gebäudekosten, pl
- buildings costs *pl*
- building cost

Gebäude mit Eigentumswohnungen, n
- condominium building *AE*

Gebäude modernisieren
- modernise a building
- modernize a building
- update a building

Gebäude nach Abschreibung, n
(Bilanz)
- building less depreciation

Gebäudenutzfläche, f
- useful area of a building

Gebäude renovieren
- renovate a bulding
- refurbish a building

Gebäudereparaturen, f pl
- building repairs *pl*
- repairs of structure *pl*

Gebäuderohbau, m
- building shell

Gebäudesanierung, f
Restaurierung eines Gebäudes, f
- restoration of a building

Gebäude stammen hauptsächlich aus dem 13. Jahrhundert
- buildings date mainly from the 13th century

Gebäude stammt aus dem 18. Jahrhundert
- building dates from the 18th century

Gebäude stammt aus dem letzten Jahrhundert
- building dates back to the last century

Gebäudeunterhaltung, f
→ Gebäudeinstandhaltung

Gebäude unterteilen
- subdivide a building

Gebäude unterteilen in Büros
- subdivide a building into offices

Gebäude versichern gegen etw
- insure a building against s.th.

Gebäudeversicherung f
- building insurance
- insurance of a building

Gebäude von historischem Interesse, n
- building of historical interest

Gebäude wird nachts angestrahlt
- building is floodlit at night

Gebäude zu einem Hotel umbauen
Gebäude in ein Hotel umwandeln
- convert a building into a hotel

Geben Sie mir bitte nochmal das gleiche!
(Bestellung)
- Give me the same again, please!

Gebiet, n (klein)
- area

Gebiet

Gebiet, n (Region)
→ Region
Gebiet ausweisen
♦ designate an area
Gebiet bereisen
♦ tour the area
♦ tour the region
Gebiet bietet ausgezeichnete Skibedingungen auf leichten bis mittelschweren Abfahrten
♦ area offers excellent skiing on easy to medium-grade runs
Gebiet erkunden
♦ explore the area
♦ explore the region
Gebiet erschließen für den Tourismus
♦ open up a region for tourism
♦ open up an area for tourism
Gebiet ist unberührt
♦ area is unspoiled
♦ area is unspoilt BE
Gebiet meiden
♦ avoid an area
Gebietsbeschreibung, f
♦ description of an area
description of a region
describing an area
describing a region
Gebietscharakter, m
♦ character of the area
♦ character of the region
Gebietsdirektor, m
♦ area director
Gebietsfranchise, n
♦ area franchise
Gebietsfranchisenehmer, m
♦ area franchisee
Gebietsfremder, m
♦ stranger to the area
Gebietsführer, m
Regionalführer, m
♦ area guide
♦ guide to the area
♦ regional guide
Gebietsimage, n
♦ area image
♦ image of an area
Gebietsleiter, m
♦ area manager
Gebietsreiseleiter, m
♦ local area guide
Gebietswanderführer, f
♦ area walking guide
Gebietswanderkarte, f (Landkarte)
♦ walking map of the area
♦ hiking map of the area
Gebietswerbung, f
♦ advertising for a region
♦ publicity for a region
♦ advertising campaign for a region
♦ publicity campaign for a region
Gebinde, n
♦ consignment
♦ package
gebirgig, adj
♦ mountainous, adj
gebirgige Landschaft, f
♦ mountainous countryside
Gebirgsblick, m
→ Bergblick
Gebirgsferienort, m
Gebirgsurlaubsort, m

Bergferienort, m
Bergurlaubsort, m
♦ mountain holiday resort BE
♦ mountain vacation resort AE
♦ mountain resort
gebirgsgasthof, m
→ Berggasthof
Gebirgsheilbad, n
Gebirgskurort, m
♦ mountain health resort
♦ mountain spa
Gebirgshotel, n
→ Berghotel
Gebirgskette, f
♦ mountain chain
♦ chain of mountains
Gebirgsklima, n
♦ mountain climate
Gebirgskurort, m
Gebirgsheilbad, n
♦ mountain spa
♦ mountain health resort
Gebirgslandschaft, f
Berglandschaft, f
♦ mountain countryside
♦ mountain scenery
♦ mountain landscape
♦ mountainscape
Gebirgsspaß, m
→ Bergpaß, m
Gebirgsrefugium, n
Bergrefugium, n
♦ mountain retreat
Gebirgsregion, f
gebirgige Region, f
♦ mountainous region
Gebirgsurlaubsort, m
Gebirgsferienort, m
Bergurlaubsort, m
Bergferienort, m
♦ mountain vacation resort AE
♦ mountain holiday resort BE
♦ mountain resort
geborene, adj
geborene Peters
♦ nee, adj AE
♦ née , adj BE
♦ nee Peters AE
♦ née Peters BE
geborener Wanderer, m
♦ born walker
♦ born hiker
♦ born rambler
gebraten, adj
♦ roasted, adj
♦ roast, adj
gebratene Ente, f
♦ roasted duck
gebratenes Hähnchen, n
→ Brathähnchen
gebratene Tauben, f pl
Tauben gebraten
♦ roast pigeons pl
Gebräu, n
♦ brew, the
Gebrauch, m
→ Benutzung
gebrauchen etw
Gebrauch von etw machen
♦ make use of s.th.
♦ use s.th.

Gebrauch machen von einem Service
♦ avail oneself of a service
Gebrauch machen von etw
♦ avail oneself of s.th.
♦ use s.th.
♦ make use of s.th.
Gebrauchsfahrzeug, n
♦ utility craft
gebraucht, adj
benutzt, adj
genutzt, adj
♦ used, adj
Gebrauchtcaravan, m
Gebrauchtwohnwagen, m
♦ used caravan BE
♦ used trailer AE
Gebrauchtfahrzeug, n
♦ used vehicle
Gebrauchtwagen, m
♦ used car
Gebrauchtwohnwagen, m
Gebrauchtcaravan, m
♦ used trailer AE
♦ used caravan BE
Gebrauch von den Hoteleinrichtungen machen
♦ make use of the hotel facilities
♦ make use of the hotel's facilities
gebräunt, adj
(Person)
♦ tanned, adj
gebräunt zurückkommen
♦ come back with a tan
gebucht adj
angemeldet, adj
bestellt, adj
♦ booked, adj
gebuchte Destination, f
gebuchter Zielort, m
gebuchtes Ziel, n
♦ booked destination
♦ destination booked
gebuchte Hotelkategorie, f
♦ booked hotel category
♦ hotel category booked
gebuchte Kategorie, f
♦ booked category
♦ category booked
gebuchte Klasse, f
♦ booked class
♦ class booked
gebuchte Nacht, f
gebuchte Übernachtung, f
♦ night booked
♦ booked night
gebuchte Person, f
♦ booked person
♦ person booked
gebuchter Monat m
♦ booked month
♦ month booked
gebuchter Stellplatz, m
(Camping)
♦ booked pitch
♦ pitch booked
gebuchter Tag m
♦ booked day
♦ day booked
gebuchter Zeitraum, m
♦ booked period
♦ period booked

gebuchtes Zimmer, n
  bestelltes Zimmer, n
  ♦ booked room
  ♦ room booked
gebuchte Übernachtung, f
  gebuchte Nacht, f
  ♦ booked night
  ♦ night booked
gebuchte Unterkunft, f
  ♦ booked accommodation
  ♦ booked lodging AE
  ♦ accommodation booked
  ♦ lodging booked AE
gebuchte Unterkunft zurückgeben an das Hotel
  ♦ release booked accommodation back to the hotel
gebuchte Woche, f
  ♦ booked week
  ♦ week booked
gebucht nach Rom, adj
  ♦ booked to Rome, adj
gebucht sein auf etw
  gebucht sein bei etw
  angemeldet sein für etw
  ♦ be booked on s.th.
gebucht sein auf Linienmaschinen
  ♦ be booked on scheduled services
Gebühr, f
  ♦ charge
  ♦ fee
Gebühr ausrechnen
  Gebühr berechnen
  ♦ calculate a charge
  ♦ calculate a fee
Gebühr bei vorzeitiger Abreise, f
  ♦ curtailment charge
  ♦ curtailment fee
Gebühr einziehen
  ♦ collect a charge
  ♦ collect a fee
Gebühren, f pl
  Beiträge, m pl
  ♦ dues pl
Gebühren auf Anfrage
  ♦ Fees on application
  ♦ Charges on application
Gebührenberechnung f
  ♦ calculation of a charge
  ♦ calculation of charges
  ♦ calculation of a fee
  ♦ calculation of fees
Gebührenblatt, n
  Gebührenverzeichnis, n
  ♦ fee sheet
Gebühreneinheit, f
  Gebühr pro Einheit, f
  ♦ unit charge
  ♦ unit fee
  ♦ charge per unit
  ♦ fee per unit
Gebühreneinzug m
  ♦ collection of a charge
  ♦ collection of a fee
  ♦ collecting (of) charges
  ♦ collecting (of) fees
Gebührenerhöhung f
  ♦ increase in fees
  ♦ fee increase
  ♦ increase in charges

gebührenfrei, adj (generell)
  ♦ free of charge, adj
  ♦ free, adj
gebührenfrei, adj (Telefon)
  ♦ toll-free, adj
gebührenfrei anrufen
  ♦ call toll-free
gebührenfreie Buchung, f
  (ohne Telefongebühren)
  ♦ toll-free booking
gebührenfreie Nummer, f
  (Telefon)
  ♦ toll-free number
gebührenfreier Anruf, m
  ♦ toll-free call
gebührenfreie Reservierung, f
  (ohne Telefongebühren)
  ♦ toll-free reservation
gebührenfreier Parkplatz, m (für 1 Auto)
  kostenloser Parkplatz, m
  ♦ free parking space
  ♦ free parking place
  ♦ free parking lot AE
gebührenfreier Parkplatz, m (für mehrere Autos)
  kostenloser Parkplatz, m
  ♦ free parking lot AE
  ♦ free car park BE
gebührenfreier Reservierungsdienst, m
  (ohne Telefongebühren)
  gebührenfreier Reservierungsservice, m
  ♦ toll-free reservation service
  ♦ toll-free reservations service
gebührenfreier Telefonanruf, m
  ♦ toll-free telephone call
gebührenfreies Parken, n
  kostenloses Parken, n
  ♦ free parking
  ♦ complimentary parking
  ♦ parking free of charge
  ♦ courtesy parking AE
gebührenfreies Reservierungssystem, n
  (ohne Telefongebühren)
  ♦ toll-free reservation system
  ♦ toll-free reservations system
gebührenfreie Telefonnummer, f
  ♦ toll-free telephone number
  ♦ toll-free phone number
Gebührenliste, f
  ♦ fee list
  ♦ fee sheet
Gebühren niedrig halten
  ♦ keep charges down
  ♦ keep fees down
Gebührenpauschale, f
  ♦ fee package
gebührenpflichtig, adj
  ♦ liable to a charge, adj
  ♦ liable to charges, adj
  ♦ liable to a fee, adj
  ♦ liable to fees, adj
  ♦ subject to a charge, adj
gebührenpflichtige Garage, f
  ♦ pay garage AE
  ♦ paying garage BE
gebührenpflichtiger Parkplatz, m (für 1 Auto)
  ♦ pay parking space
  ♦ pay parking place
  ♦ pay parking lot AE
  ♦ paying parking space BE
  ♦ paying parking place BE

gebührenpflichtiger Parkplatz, m (mehrere Autos)
  ♦ pay parking lot AE
  ♦ paying car park BE
gebührenpflichtige Straße, f
  Mautstraße, f
  ♦ turnpike road AE
  ♦ toll road BE
gebührenpflichtige Veranstaltung f
  ♦ ticketed function
gebührenpflichtige Verwarnung, f
  (für Kfz)
  ♦ ticket
Gebührenrückerstattung, f
  ♦ refund of a fee
  ♦ refund of a charge
  ♦ refunding a fee
  ♦ refunding a charge
Gebührensenkung, f
  ♦ decrease in charges
  ♦ decrease in fees
Gebührentabelle, f
  ♦ table of charges
  ♦ table of fees
Gebührentarif m
  ♦ tariff of charges
  ♦ tariff of fees
Gebühr entrichten
  → Gebühr zahlen
gebührenzahlend, adj
  ♦ fee-paying, adj
Gebühr erheben
  Gebühr verlangen
  ♦ charge a fee
  ♦ levy a charge
  ♦ levy a fee
  ♦ make a charge
Gebühr erlassen
  ♦ waive a fee
  ♦ waive a charge
  ♦ remit a fee
  ♦ remit a charge
Gebühr ermäßigen
  ♦ reduce a fee
  ♦ reduce a charge
  ♦ abate a charge
  ♦ abate a fee
Gebühr erstatten
  → Gebühr zurückerstatten
Gebühr festsetzen
  Gebühr festlegen
  ♦ fix a charge
  ♦ fix a fee
Gebühr in Rechnung stellen
  ♦ make a charge
  ♦ levy a charge
  ♦ charge a fee
Gebühr ist rückerstattbar
  ♦ charge is returnable
  ♦ fee is returnable
Gebühr pro Einheit, f
  ♦ charge per unit
  ♦ fee per unit
  ♦ unit charge
  ♦ unit fee
Gebühr pro Jahr, f
  Jahresgebühr, f
  ♦ charge per year
  ♦ fee per year
Gebühr pro Monat, f
  Monatsgebühr, f

- ◆ charge per month
- ◆ fee per month

Gebühr pro Person, f
- Personengebühr, f
- ◆ charge per person
- ◆ fee per person

Gebühr pro Tag, f
- Tagesgebühr, f
- ◆ charge per day
- ◆ fee per day

Gebühr wird erhoben für etw
- ◆ fee is charged for s.th.
- ◆ charge is made for s.th.

Gebühr zahlen
- Gebühr entrichten
- ◆ pay a fee
- ◆ pay a charge

Gebühr zahlen für etw
- ◆ pay a charge for s.th.
- ◆ pay a fee for s.th.

Gebühr zurückbehalten
- Gebühr einbehalten
- ◆ withhold a fee
- ◆ withhold a charge

Gebühr zurückerstatten
- Gebühr erstatten
- ◆ refund a charge
- ◆ refund a fee

gebundener Preis m
- ◆ controled price AE
- ◆ controled rate AE
- ◆ controlled rate BE
- ◆ controlled price BE

gebürtiger Kölner, m
- ◆ native of Cologne

Geburtsdatum, n
- ◆ birth date
- ◆ date of birth

Geburtsfest mit Geschenken, n
- ◆ baby shower AE

Geburtshaus, n
- ◆ birthplace
- ◆ house where s.o. was born

Geburtsjahr, n
- ◆ year of birth
- ◆ birth year coll

Geburtsland, n (amtlich)
- Heimatland, n
- ◆ country of birth

Geburtsland, n (generell)
- ◆ native country
- ◆ native land

Geburtsname, m
- Mädchenname, m
- ◆ birth name
- ◆ maiden name

Geburtsort, m (amtlich)
- ◆ place of birth

Geburtsort, m (generell)
- ◆ birthplace

Geburtsstadt, f (Großstadt)
- ◆ native city

Geburtsstadt, f (kleine Stadt)
- ◆ native town

Geburtstag, m (amtlich)
- Tag der Geburt, m
- ◆ date of birth

Geburtstag, m (generell)
- ◆ birthplace

Geburtstagsessen, n (Dinner)
- Geburtstagsessen, n
- ◆ birthday dinner

Geburtstagsessen, n (generell)
- Geburtstagsessen, n
- ◆ birthday meal

Geburtstagsessen, n (Lunch)
- Geburtstagsessen, n
- ◆ birthday luncheon
- ◆ birthday lunch

Geburtstagsessen, n (Supper)
- Geburtstagsessen, n
- ◆ birthday supper

Geburtstag feiern
- ◆ celebrate one's birthday
- ◆ celebrate s.o.'s birthday

Geburtstagsfeier, f
- ◆ birthday celebration
- ◆ birthday party

Geburtstagsfestschmaus, m
- Geburtstagsschmaus, m
- ◆ birthday treat

Geburtstagsgeschenk, n
- ◆ birthday present

Geburtstagskarte, f
- ◆ birthday card

Geburtstagskind, n
- ◆ birthday boy
- ◆ birthday girl

Geburtstagskuchen, m
- ◆ birthday cake

Geburtstagsliste, f
- ◆ birthday list

Geburtstagsparty, f
- Geburtstagsfeier, f
- ◆ birthday party

Geburtstagsständchen, n
- ◆ birthday serenade

Geburtstagstorte, f
- ◆ birthday gateau AE
- ◆ birthday gâteau BE

Geburtsurkunde, f
- ◆ birth certificate

gechartert, adj
- ◆ chartered, adj

Gedächtnisfest, n
- Gedächntisfestspiele, n pl
- ◆ memorial festival

Gedächtniskirche, f
- ◆ memorial church

Gedächtniszimmer, n
- Gedächtnisraum, m
- ◆ memorial room

gedämpfte Beleuchtung, f
- → dezente Beleuchtung

Gedeck, n (Kuvert)
- Kuvert, n
- Couvert, n FR
- ◆ cover
- ◆ couvert FR
- ◆ place setting AE
- ◆ place-setting BE
- ◆ place (at a table)

Gedeck, n (Menü)
- Menü, n
- ◆ set meal
- ◆ menu

Gedeck auflegen
- ◆ lay a place

Gedeckendpreis, m
- ◆ final cover charge

Gedecke pro Jahr, n pl
- Couverts pro Jahr, n pl
- Kuverts pro Jahr, n pl
- ◆ covers per year pl

Gedecke pro Monat, n pl
- Couverts pro Monat, n pl
- Kuverts pro Monat, n pl
- ◆ covers per month pl

Gedecke pro Tag, n pl
- Couverts pro Tag, n pl
- Kuverts pro Tag, n pl
- ◆ covers per day pl

Gedecke pro Woche, n pl
- Couverts pro Woche, n pl
- Kuverts pro Woche, n pl
- ◆ covers per week pl

Gedeck für eine Person, n
- (mit Bedienung)
- ◆ plate AE
- ◆ cover

Gedeckgebühr f
- Kuvertgebühr f
- ◆ cover charge

Gedeckpreis, m
- → Preis pro Gedeck

Gedeckzahl, f
- Kuvertzahl, f
- Couvertzahl, f
- ◆ number of covers
- ◆ number of places laid

Gedeckzwang, m
- → Verzehrzwang

Gedenkfeier, f
- ◆ commemoration ceremony
- ◆ commemoration
- ◆ celebration commemorating s.th.
- ◆ celebration to commemorate s.th.
- ◆ shindig AE inform

Gedenkstätte, f
- Gedenkplatz, m
- ◆ memorial site
- ◆ memorial

Gedenkstatue, f
- ◆ commemorative statue

Gedenktafel, f
- Erinnerungstafel, f
- ◆ commemorative plaque
- ◆ memorial plaque

Gedenktafel an ein Haus anbringen
- Erinnerungstafel an ein Haus anbringen
- ◆ mark a house with a commemorative plaque

Gedenkveranstaltung, f
- Gedächtnisveranstaltung, f
- ◆ memorial event

gediegene Atmosphäre, f
- häusliche Atmosphäre
- ◆ homely atmosphere

Gedränge, n
- Menschenmenge, f
- ◆ throng

gedruckte Preisliste, f
- ◆ printed tariff

gedruckte Speisekarte f
- ◆ printed menu

gedünstet, adj
- ◆ steamed, adj

gedünsteter Fisch, m
- ◆ steamed fish

geeignete anderweitige Unterkunft, f
- ◆ suitable alternate accommodation AE
- ◆ suitable alternative accommodation BE

geeignete Ersatzvorkehrungen treffen
- make suitable alternate arrangements *AE*
- make suitable alternative arrangements *BE*

geeigneten Ersatz bieten jm
- offer a suitable alternative to s.o.

geeigneten Ort suchen für eine Konferenz
passenden Ort suchen für eine Tagung
- look for a suitable venue for a conference

geeignete Räumlichkeiten, f pl
- suitable facilities *pl*

geeignete Räumlichkeiten suchen
- look for suitable facilities
- seek suitable facilities

geeigneter Veranstaltungsort, m
geeigneter Austragungsort, m
- suitable venue

geeignetes Zimmer, n
- suitable room

geeignetes Zimmer finden
- find a suitable room

geeignetes Zimmer suchen
- look for a suitable room
- seek a suitable room

geeignet sein für etw
- be suitable for s.th.
- qualify for s.th.

gefährliche Reise, f
- dangerous journey
- dangerous trip
- dangerous tour

gefallen dem anspruchsvollsten Gaumen
- please the most discriminate palate

Gefallen erweisen einem Freund
Freund gefällig sein
- oblige a friend

gefallen jm
- like s.th.
- enjoy s.th.

Gefälligkeitsadresse, f
→ Hilfsadresse

gefällig sein jm
Gefallen erweisen jm
entgegenkommend sein bei jm
- oblige s.o.

Gefällt es Ihnen?
- Do you like it?
- Are you enjoying it?

Gefällt es Ihnen hier?
- Do you like it here?

Gefängnis, n
- prison
- jail
- gaol *BE*

Gefängnismuseum, n
- prison museum

Gefängniszelle, f
- prison cell

gefederter Fußboden, m
gefederter Boden, m
- sprung floor

gefeiert, adj
- celebrated, adj

gefeiert werden
- be celebrated
- be fêted *BE*
- be feted *AE*

gefliest, adj
gekachelt, adj
- tiled, adj

gefliese Küche, f
- tiled kitchen

gefliester Boden, m
Fliesenboden, m
- tiled floor

gefliestes Badezimmer, n
gefliestes Bad, n
- tiled bathroom
- tiled bath

Geflügel, n
- poultry
- chicken

Geflügelbraten, m
- roast poultry

Geflügelcocktail, m
- poultry cocktail

Geflügelfarce, f
- poultry stuffing

Geflügelgericht, n
- poultry dish

Geflügelhaschee, n
- minced chicken

Geflügelmarkt, m
- poultry market

Geflügelsalpikon, m
- poultry salpicon

Geflügelsoße, f
- poultry sauce

Geflügelspezialität, f
- poultry specialty *AE*
- poultry speciality *BE*

Gefolge, n
(z.B. beim Besuch eines Staatsmanns)
- entourage

gefragt sein
- be in demand

gefräßig, adj
unersättlich, adj
- gluttonous, adj

Gefräßigkeit, f
Unersättlichkeit, f
Völlerei, f
- gluttony

Gefrierfach, n
- freezer compartment
- freezer
- freezing compartment

Gefrierfleisch, n
- frozen meat

Gefrierraum, m
- refrigerating room
- refrigeration room
- freezing room
- freezer
- chillroom

Gefriertruhe, f
→ Tiefkühltruhe

gefroren, adj
- frozen, adj

Gefühl der guten Lebensart vermitteln
- convey a sense of gracious living

Gefühl geben jm, daß er/sie willkommen ist
- make s.o. feel welcome

Gefühl geben jm, daß er/sie zu Hause ist
- make s.o. feel at home

geführte Bergwanderung, f
- guided mountain walk
- guided mountain hike

geführte Besichtigung, f
- guided sightseeing tour
- guided sightseeing

geführte Gruppe, f
- guided group
- guided party

geführte Radtour, f
→ geführte Radwanderung

geführte Radwanderung, f
geführte Radtour, f
- guided bicycle tour
- guided cycle tour
- guided cycling tour

geführter Ausflug, m
Ausflug mit Führung, m
- guided excursion

geführter Fahrradausflug, m
geführter Radausflug, m
- guided bicycle excursion
- guided cycling excursion

geführter Radausflug, m
geführter Fahrradausflug, m
- guided cycling excursion
- guided bicycle excursion

geführter Ritt, m
- conducted ride
- guided ride

geführter Rundgang, m
Rundgang mit Führung, m
- conducted tour
- guided tour

geführter Rundgang durch den Dom, m
Rundgang mit Führung durch die Kathedrale, m
- conducted tour of the cathedral

geführter Rundgang durch etw, m
- conducted tour of s.th.
- conducted tour through s.th.

geführter Spaziergang, m
Führung zu Fuß, f
- guided walk
- conducted walk
- guided walking tour

geführter Stadtrundgang, m
geführter Rundgang durch die Stadt, m
Rundgang durch die Stadt mit Führung, m
- guided walk around the town
- guided walk around the city
- guided walking tour of the town
- guided walking tour of the city

geführter Untertagerundgang durch das Bergwerk, m
- guided underground tour of the mine

geführte Safari, f
- guided safari

geführte Skitour, f
→ geführte Skiwanderung

geführte Skiwanderung, f
geführte Skitour, f
- guided ski tour

geführte Stadtrundfahrt, f
- guided city sightseeing tour
- guided city tour

geführte Wanderung, f
Wanderführung, f
- guided hike
- guided walk(ing tour)
- guided ramble
- guided hiking tour
- conducted walk

gefüllt, adj *gastr*
ausgestopft, adj
gestopft, adj *gastr*
- stuffed, adj *gastr*

gefüllte Eier

gefüllte Eier, n pl
 ♦ **stuffed eggs** *pl*
gefüllte Olive, f
 ♦ **stuffed olive**
gefüllte Paprika, f
 ♦ **stuffed pepper**
gefülltes Weinblatt, n
 ♦ **stuffed vine leaf**
gefüllte Tomate, f
 ♦ **stuffed tomato**
 ♦ **filled tomato**
Gegenanspruch, m *jur*
 ♦ **counterclaim** *jur*
gegen Aufpreis
 ♦ **at a supplementary charge**
 ♦ at an extra charge
 ♦ at extra cost
gegen Aufpreis erhältlich sein
 ♦ **be available at extra cost**
gegen Berechnung
 → gegen Gebühr
gegenbestätigen etw
 rückbestätigen etw
 ♦ **reconfirm s.th.**
Gegenbestätigung, f
 Rückbestätigung, f
 ♦ **reconfirmation**
Gegenbesuch, m
 ♦ **return visit**
Gegenbesuch abstatten jm
 Gegenbesuch machen (bei) jm
 ♦ **pay a return visit to s.o.**
 ♦ return s.o.'s visit
Gegenbesucher, m
 ♦ **return visitor**
Gegenbesuch machen (in X)
 ♦ **make a return visit (to X)**
 ♦ pay a return visit (to X)
Gegenbuchung, f (Buchhaltung)
 ♦ **contra entry** *AE*
 ♦ cross entry
gegen eine geringe Gebühr
 gegen eine geringfügige Gebühr
 ♦ **at a nominal charge**
 ♦ at a nominal fee
 ♦ for a small fee
gegen einen Aufpreis von $ 123
 ♦ **for an extra charge of $ 123**
 ♦ at an extra charge of $ 123
gegen einen Baum fahren (Auto)
 ♦ **drive into a tree**
gegen einen geringen Preis
 gegen einen geringfügigen Preis
 ♦ **at a nominal price**
gegen einen Zuschlag
 ♦ **for a supplement**
gegen einen Zuschlag von $ 123
 ♦ **at a supplementary charge of $ 123**
gegen eine Pauschale von DM 123
 ♦ **at an inclusive price of DM 123**
 ♦ at an inclusive rate of DM 123
gegen eine zusätzliche Gebühr
 ♦ **for an additional charge**
gegen Entgelt
 gegen Zahlung
 ♦ **against payment**
gegen Gebühr
 gegen eine Gebühr
 gegen Berechnung
 ♦ **at a charge**

Gegenleistung, f (generell)
 ♦ **return service**
 ♦ service in return
 ♦ quid pro quo
Gegenleistung, f (Preis/Leistung)
 ♦ **value for money**
gegen Mehrkosten
 → gegen Gebühr
gegen Provision
 ♦ **on commission**
gegen Quittung
 ♦ **against receipt**
 ♦ on receipt
gegenseitiger Besuch, m
 ♦ **reciprocal visit**
gegenseitiges Verständnis, n
 ♦ **mutual understanding**
Gegensprechanlage, f
 Wechselsprechanlage, f
 ♦ **intercom**
 ♦ intercom system
Gegenstromanlage, f
 (im Schwimmbad)
 ♦ **jet-stream system**
 ♦ jet stream
 ♦ counter current jet
Gegenstromschwimmanlage, f
 → Gegenstromanlage
gegenüberliegendes Zimmer n
 ♦ **opposite room**
gegen Vorkasse
 ♦ **on advance payment**
 ♦ against advance payment
 ♦ against prepayment
gegen Vorlage, adv
 bei Vorlage, adv
 ♦ **upon presentation, adv**
 ♦ on presentation, adv
gegenwärtiger Besitzer, m
 ♦ **current owner**
 ♦ present owner
gegenwärtige Saison, f
 → laufende Saison
Gegenwert, m
 ♦ **equivalent**
gegen Zahlung der Gebühren
 nach Zahlung der Gebühren
 ♦ **on payment of the fees**
 ♦ on payment of the charges
gegenzeichnen etw
 ♦ **countersign s.th.**
gegen Zuschlag
 ♦ **at a supplement**
gegoren, adj
 vergoren, adj
 ♦ **fermented, adj**
gegrillt, adj
 ♦ **grilled, adj**
 ♦ barbecued, adj
 ♦ broiled, adj *AE*
gegrilltes Steak, n
 ♦ **broiled steak** *AE*
 ♦ grilled steak *BE*
gehackt, adj *gastr*
 ♦ **chopped, adj** *gastr*
gehackte Kräuter, n pl
 ♦ **chopped herbs** *pl*
gehackte Petersilie, f
 ♦ **chopped parsley**
gehackte Zwiebel, f
 ♦ **chopped onion**

Gehalt, m (Inhalt)
 Inhalt, m
 ♦ **content**
Gehalt, n (Entlohnung)
 Gehälter, n pl
 ♦ **salary**
 ♦ salaries *pl*
Gehalt zahlen
 ♦ **pay a salary**
Geheimbesprechung, f
 geheime Besprechung, f
 ♦ **huddle** *coll*
Geheimbesuch, m
 geheimer Besuch, m
 ♦ **secret visit**
Geheimrezept n
 ♦ **secret recipe**
Geheimtip, m
 (Ratschlag)
 ♦ **personal tip**
 ♦ private tip
Geheimtreffen, n
 geheimes Treffen, n
 ♦ **secret meeting**
geheizt, adj
 beheizt, adj
 ♦ **heated, adj**
geheizte Garage, f
 beheizte Garage, f
 heizbare Garage, f
 ♦ **heated garage**
geheiztes Schwimmbad, n
 beheiztes Schwimmbad, n
 ♦ **heated swimming pool** *AE*
 ♦ heated swimming-pool *BE*
 ♦ heated pool
geheiztes Zimmer, n
 beheiztes Zimmer, n
 ♦ **heated room**
gehen auf eine Konferenz
 ♦ **go on a conference**
gehen auf einen Kongreß
 ♦ **go on a convention**
 ♦ go on a congress
gehen lassen sich
 ♦ **let one's hair down** *coll*
gehen mit der Zeit
 mit der Zeit gehen
 ♦ **march with the times**
 ♦ move with the times
Gehen Sie bitte zur Rezeption
 ♦ **Please go to reception**
gehfähig, adj
 ♦ **ambulant, adj**
gehfähiger Patient, m
 ♦ **ambulant patient**
Gehilfe, m
 (in Küche und Restaurant)
 Commis, m *FR*
 ♦ **assistant**
 ♦ commis *FR*
Gehminute, f
 ♦ **one-minute walk**
 ♦ minute's walk
Gehsteig, m
 Bürgersteig, m
 ♦ **pavement** *BE*
 ♦ sidewalk *AE*
Gehstunde, f
 ♦ **hour's walk**
 ♦ one hour's walk

Gehweg, m
　Weg, m
　Pfad, m
　♦ footpath
Geisha, f
　♦ geisha
Geisterdorf, n
　♦ ghost village
Geisterstadt, f
　♦ ghost town
Geisterzimmer, n
　♦ ghost room
geistig behindert, adj
　♦ mentally handicapped, adj
geistige Getränke, n pl
　→ Spirituosen
geistige Nahrung, f
　♦ spiritual nourishment
geistige Reise, f
　♦ spiritual journey
gekocht, adj (generell)
　♦ cooked, adj
gekocht, adj (in Wasser)
　gesotten, adj
　♦ boiled, adj
gekochte Lebensmittel, n pl (generell)
　♦ cooked food
gekochte Lebensmittel, n pl (in Wasser)
　♦ boiled food
gekochter Reis, m
　♦ boiled rice
gekochter Schinken, m
　Kochschinken, m
　♦ cooked ham AE
　♦ boiled ham BE
gekochtes Ei, n
　♦ cooked egg AE
　♦ boiled egg BE
gekochtes Ei zum Frühstück essen
　♦ have a cooked egg for breakfast AE
　♦ have a boiled egg for breakfast BE
gekochtes Essen, n
　(Mahlzeit)
　♦ cooked meal
gekochtes Frühstück n
　♦ cooked breakfast
gekochtes Gericht, n
　♦ cooked dish
gekochtes Wasser, n
　abgekochtes Wasser, n
　♦ boiled water
gekocht vor Ihren Augen
　zubereitet vor Ihren Augen
　♦ cooked before your eyes
gekröntes Haupt, n
　♦ crowned head
gekühlt, adj
　tiefgekühlt, adj
　♦ chilled, adj
gekühlter Weißwein m
　♦ chilled white wine
gekühltes Getränk, n
　kühles Getränk, n
　♦ chilled drink
　♦ chilled beverage
gekühlt servieren etw
　♦ serve s.th. chilled
geladener Gast, m
　♦ invited guest
Geländefahrzeug, n
　geländegängiges Fahrzeug, n

　♦ off-road vehicle
　♦ cross-country vehicle
　♦ all-terrain vehicle
　♦ ATV
geländegängiges Fahrzeug, n
　Geländefahrzeug, n
　♦ all-terrain vehicle
　♦ ATV
geländegängiges Motorrad, n
　♦ trailbike
Geländekur, f
　→ Terrainkur
Geländeschach, n
　→ Freischach
Gelatine, f
　♦ gelatine
　♦ gelatin AE
Gelbe Meer, das, n
　♦ Yellow Sea, the
Gelbfieber, n
　♦ yellow fever
Gelbfieberimpfung, f
　♦ yellow fever vaccination
Gelbwurz, f
　♦ turmeric
Gelbwurzpulver, m
　♦ turmeric powder
Geld, n
　♦ money
Geldangabe, f
　(z.B. bei der Einreise in ein Land)
　♦ money declaration
Geld ausführen aus einem Land
　♦ take money out of a country
　♦ export money from a country
Geld ausgeben für etw
　♦ spend money for s.th. AE
　♦ spend money on s.th. BE
Geld einführen in ein Land
　♦ take money into a country
　♦ import money into a country
Geld für den eigenen Bedarf, n
　♦ money for one's own use
Geld investieren in ein Hotel
　♦ invest money in a hotel
Geld investieren in Renovierungen
　♦ invest money in renovations
Geldschrank m
　→ Safe, Tresor
Geldstrafe für falsches Parken, f
　♦ parking fine
Geld verlieren beim Spielen
　Geld verlieren beim Glücksspiel
　♦ lose money gambling
Geld verspielen
　♦ gamble away one's money
Geld waschen
　♦ launder money
Geldwechsel, m
　Geldumtausch, m
　♦ money exchange
　♦ changing money
　♦ money changing
Geldwechselautomat, m
　Geldwechsler m
　♦ change-giving machine
　♦ coin changer AE
Geldwechselmöglichkeit, f
　♦ money changing facility
　♦ facility for changing money

　♦ bureau de change facility
　♦ currency exchange facility
Geld wechseln
　♦ change money
Geldwechselstube, f
　Wechselstube, f
　Wechselbüro, n
　♦ exchange office
　♦ money changing facility
　♦ exchange bureau
　♦ bureau de change
Geldwechsler, m
　(Person oder Gerät)
　♦ money changer AE
　♦ money-changer BE
Geld zurückerstatten an jn
　♦ refund money to s.o.
Geld-zurück-Garantie, f
　♦ money-back guarantee
Geldzuwendung f
　Trinkgeld n
　♦ gratuity
Gelee, n
　♦ jelly
Gelegenheit, f
　♦ opportunity
Gelegenheit bieten für etw
　♦ provide the opportunity for s.th.
Gelegenheit für etw, f
　♦ opportunity for s.th.
Gelegenheit geben jm, etw zu tun
　♦ give s.o. the opportunity of doing s.th.
Gelegenheit haben zu einer Führung durch etw
　♦ have the opportunity of a guided tour of s.th.
　♦ have the opportunity of a guided visit to s.th.
Gelegenheit haben zu etw
　Gelegenheit haben für etw
　♦ have the opportunity of doing s.th.
Gelegenheitsarbeiter, m
　♦ casual worker
Gelegenheitsbekanntschaft, f
　Flittchen, n
　♦ pick-up
Gelegenheitsbeschäftigung, f
　gelegentliche Beschäftigung, f
　♦ casual employment
Gelegenheitsbesucher, m
　→ gelegentlicher Besucher
Gelegenheitscamper, m
　♦ occasional camper
Gelegenheitsgast, m
　→ gelegentlicher Gast
Gelegenheitsgeschäft, n
　Passantengeschäft n
　♦ casual trade
Gelegenheitskunde, m
　gelegentlicher Kunde m
　♦ casual customer
　♦ casual client
Gelegenheitsreiseveranstalter, m
　♦ occasional tour operator
　♦ ad hoc tour operator
Gelegenheitswerbung, f
　♦ opportunity advertising
Gelegenheit wahrnehmen zum Besuch von etw
　♦ take the opportunity of visiting s.th.
Gelegenheit zu einem Bummel (durch die Altstadt)
　♦ opportunity for a stroll (through the Old Town)
　♦ opportunity for a stroll (round the Old Town)

Gelegenheit zum Besuch von etw

- opportunity for a walk (through the Old Town)
- opportunity for a walk (round the Old Town)

Gelegenheit zum Besuch von etw, f
- opportunity to visit s.th.

Gelegenheit zum Parken, f
- opportunity to park (a car)

Gelegenheit zum Reisen, f
Reisegelegenheit, f
- chance to travel

gelegen sein
liegen
- be situated
- be located
- be positioned
- be sited
- be placed

gelegen sein in Bahnhofsnähe
in Bahnhofsnähe liegen
- be situated close to the station
- be conveniently situated for the station

gelegentlicher Besucher, m
- casual visitor
- occasional visitor

gelegentlicher Dienst, m
gelegentlicher Service, m
Gelegenheitsdienst, m
- occasional service

gelegentlicher Gast, m
Gelegenheitsgast, m
- casual guest
- occasional guest

gelegentlicher Kunde, m
Gelegenheitskunde, m
- casual client
- casual customer

gelegentlicher Unterkunftsanbieter, m
- occasional accommodation provider
- occasional accommodation supplier

gelegentlich umrühren etw
- stir s.th. occasionally

geleisteter Dienst, m
erbrachte Leistung, d
- service rendered
- service provided

Geleitfahrzeug, n
- escorting vehicle

Geleitschiff, n
Begleitschiff, n
- escort vessel

gelernter Koch, m
- trained cook

geliehenes Fahrrad, n (gegen Entgelt)
→ gemietetes Fahrrad

geliehenes Fahrrad, n (unentgeltlich)
geliehenes Rad, n
- borrowed bicycle
- borrowed bike

gelockerte Atmosphäre, f
→ lockere Atmosphäre

geltend, adj
- applicable, adj
- valid, adj

geltender Tarif, m
- applicable rate

gelungener Beginn, m
gelungener Auftakt, m
gelungener Start, m
erfolgreicher Beginn, m
- successful beginning
- successful start

gelungener Urlaub, m
gelungene Ferien, pl
- successful vacation AE
- successful holiday BE

gelungenes Fest, n
- successful festival
- successful fete (fête)
- successful celebration
- successful party
- successful festivity

GEMA, f
Gesellschaft für musikalische Aufführungs- und mechanische Vervielfältigungsrechte, f
- PRS BE
- Performing Right Society BE

Gemach, n obs
- chamber obs

gemahlener Zimt, m
- ground cinnamon

Gemälde, n
- painting

Gemäldeausstellung, f
- exhibition of paintings
- exhibit of paintings AE
- display of paintings

Gemäldegalerie, f
- painting gallery
- picture gallery

Gemäldesammlung, f
- collection of paintings
- paintings collection

Gemäldeschau, f
- display of paintings

Gemälde von Rubens, n
- painting by Rubens

gemalzt, adj
- malted, adj

gemäßigtes Klima, n
- temperate climate

Gemeinde, f
- community
- town
- village

Gemeindeabgaben, f pl
Kommunalabgaben, f pl
Gemeindesteuern, f pl
Kommunalsteuern, f pl
- municipal taxes AE pl

Gemeindebehörde, f
Körperschaft des öffentlichen Rechts, f
- municipal corporation

Gemeindefest, n
- community festival

Gemeindefestlichkeit, f
Gemeindefeier, f
- village festivity
- village fete
- village fête BE
- village festival

Gemeindegasthaus, n
- community bar AE
- community pub BE

Gemeindesteuer, f
Gemeindeabgabe, f
städtische Abgabe, f
- community tax
- municipal tax

Gemeindezentrum, n
- community center AE
- community centre BE

Gemeinkosten, pl
- overhead costs pl
- overhead cost
- overheads pl
- overhead expenses pl

gemeinnützige Fahrt, f
- nonprofit trip AE
- non-profit trip BE

gemeinnütziger Verein, m
- service club

gemeinsam benutztes Haus, n
Gemeinschaftshaus, n
- shared house

gemeinsame Dusche, f
Gemeinschaftsdusche, f
- shared shower
- communal shower

gemeinsame Kaffeetafel, f
- table d'hôte coffee
- coffee taken together

gemeinsame Konferenz, f
- joint conference

gemeinsame Küche, f
Gemeinschaftsküche, f
- shared kitchen
- communal kitchen

gemeinsame Mahlzeit, f
Gemeinschaftsessen, n
- meal taken together
- table d'hôte meal
- communal meal

gemeinsame Mittagstafel, f
→ gemeinsamer Mittagstisch

gemeinsame Option, f
gemeinsam ausgeübte Option, f
- joint option

gemeinsame Pressekonferenz, f
- joint press conference

gemeinsamer Balkon, m
- shared balcony

gemeinsamer Besitz, m
- joint ownership

gemeinsamer Garten, m
Gemeinschaftsgarten, n
- shared garden
- communal garden

gemeinsamer Mittagstisch, m
Table d'hôte, f FR
gemeinsame Mittagstafel, f
- table d'hôte lunch
- table d'hôte luncheon
- lunch taken together

gemeinsames Abendessen, n (Dinner)
- dinner taken together
- table d'hôte dinner

gemeinsames Abendessen, n (Supper)
- supper taken together
- table d'hôte supper

gemeinsames Badezimmer, n
gemeinsames Bad, n
- shared bathroom
- shared bath

gemeinsame Schirmherrschaft, f
- joint auspices pl
- joint patronage

gemeinsames Essen, bei dem jeder für sich zahlt, n
- Dutch treat

gemeinsames Frühstück, n
- table d'hôte breakfast
- breakfast taken together

gemeinsame Sitzung, f
♦ joint meeting
gemeinsames Marketing, n
♦ joint marketing
gemeinsames Mittagessen, n
♦ lunch taken together
♦ table d'hôte luncheon
♦ table d'hôte lunch
gemeinsames Reservierungssystem, n
♦ joint reservation system
gemeinsames Zimmer, n
Zimmer, das mit jm geteilt wird, n
♦ shared room
gemeinsame Tagung, f
♦ joint meeting
gemeinsame Unterkunft, f
Gemeinschaftsunterkunft, f
♦ shared lodging AE
♦ shared accommodation
gemeinschaftliche Tafel, f
→ gemeinsamer Mittagstisch
Gemeinschaftsannonce, f
Gemeinschaftsinserat, n
gemeinsame Annonce, f
♦ joint advertisement
Gemeinschaftsarrangement, n
♦ joint arrangement
Gemeinschaftsbad, n
gemeinsames Bad, m
♦ communal bath
♦ shared bath
Gemeinschaftsbadezimmer, n
gemeinsames Badezimmer, n
♦ communal bathroom
♦ shared bathroom
♦ shared bath
Gemeinschaftsbadezimmerbenutzung f
♦ use of the communal bathroom
♦ using the communal bathroom
Gemeinschaftsbecken, n
♦ shared pool
♦ communal pool
Gemeinschaftsbecken, n
Gemeinschaftsbad, n
gemeinsames Becken, n
gemeinsames Bad, n
♦ communal pool
♦ shared pool
Gemeinschaftsbereich, m
Gemeinschaftsfläche, f
♦ communal area
Gemeinschaftsbuchung, f (generell)
gemeinsame Buchung, f
♦ joint booking
Gemeinschaftsbuchung, f (Gruppe)
♦ party booking
Gemeinschaftsdusche, f
gemeinsame Dusche f
♦ communal shower
♦ shared shower
Gemeinschaftsduschraum, m
gemeinsamer Duschraum, m
♦ communal shower room
♦ shared shower room
Gemeinschaftseinrichtung, f
gemeinsame Einrichtung, f
♦ communal facility
♦ shared facility
Gemeinschaftsessen, n
Table d'hôte, f FR
gemeinsame Mahlzeit, f

♦ communal meal
♦ table d'hôte FR
♦ group meal
Gemeinschaftsfaltblatt, n
Gemeinschaftsblatt, n
♦ joint leaflet
Gemeinschaftsgarten, m
gemeinsamer Garten, m
♦ communal garden
♦ shared garden
Gemeinschaftsgeist, m
♦ communal spirit
Gemeinschaftskampagne, f
♦ joint campaign
Gemeinschaftskatalog, m
♦ joint catalogue
♦ joint catalog AE
Gemeinschaftsküche, f
gemeinsame Küche, f
♦ communal kitchen
♦ shared kitchen
Gemeinschaftslounge, f
Gemeinschaftsaufenthaltsraum m
Gemeinschaftsraum m
♦ communal lounge
Gemeinschafts-PR, f
♦ joint PR
♦ joint public relations pl
Gemeinschaftsprojekt, n
♦ joint project
Gemeinschaftsprospekt, m
♦ joint brochure
Gemeinschaftsraum, m (in Heim etc)
Gemeinschaftszimmer, n
♦ communal room
Gemeinschaftsraum, m (in Hotel)
→ Aufenthaltsraum
Gemeinschaftsräumlichkeiten, f pl
Gemeinschaftseinrichtungen, f pl
♦ communal facilities pl
Gemeinschaftssalon, m
gemeinsamer Salon, m
♦ communal parlor AE
♦ communal parlour BE
♦ communal lounge
♦ shared parlor AE
♦ shared parlour BE
Gemeinschaftssauna, f (für mehrere)
gemeinsame Sauna, f
♦ communal sauna
♦ shared sauna
Gemeinschaftssauna, f (Männer und Frauen)
♦ mixed sauna
Gemeinschaftsschau, f
♦ joint show
♦ show jointly organised by ...
Gemeinschaftsschlafquartier, n
♦ communal sleeping quarters pl
Gemeinschaftsschlafraum, m
Gemeinschaftsschlafzimmer, n
♦ communal bedroom
Gemeinschaftsschwimmbad, n
Gemeinschaftsschwimmbecken, n
♦ communal swimming pool AE
♦ communal swimming-pool BE
♦ communal pool
Gemeinschaftsschwimmbecken, n
→ Gemeinschaftsschwimmbad
Gemeinschaftssitzplätze, m pl
♦ communal seating

Gemeinschaftsspeisesaal m
gemeinschaftlicher Speisesaal m
♦ communal dining room
Gemeinschaftsstand, m
♦ joint stand
Gemeinschaftstaxi, n
♦ communal taxi
Gemeinschaftstaxifahrt, f
♦ communal taxi ride
Gemeinschaftstisch, m (Möbelstück)
♦ communal table
Gemeinschaftstoilette, f
gemeinsame Toilette, f
♦ shared toilet
Gemeinschaftsunterbringung, f
Gemeinschaftsunterkunft, f
♦ shared accommodation
♦ shared lodging AE
Gemeinschaftsunterkunft, f
Gemeinschaftsunterbringung, f
♦ communal lodging AE
♦ shared accommodation
♦ shared lodging AE
♦ communal accommodation
Gemeinschaftsunternehmen, n
Joint Venture n
♦ joint venture
Gemeinschaftsveranstaltung, f
♦ joint event
♦ joint function
Gemeinschaftsverpflegung, f (Aktivität)
♦ communal feeding
Gemeinschaftsverpflegung, f (Kantine)
♦ canteen meals pl
♦ canteen food
Gemeinschaftsverpflegung, f (Nahrung)
♦ communal provisions pl
Gemeinschaftswerbung, f
♦ joint advertising
♦ cooperative advertising
Gemeinschaftswohnung, f
gemeinsame Wohnung, f
♦ shared apartment AE
♦ shared flat BE
Gemeinschaftszimmer, n
♦ communal room
Gemeinschaft Unabhängiger Staaten, f
GUS, f
♦ Commonwealth of Independent States
♦ CIS
gemeldeter Bettplatz, m
(Statistik)
registrierter Bettplatz, m
♦ registered bedspace
gemietet, adj (Immobilie)
♦ rented, adj
♦ leased, adj
gemietet, adj (Mobilie)
♦ hired, adj BE
♦ rented, adj AE
gemieteter Bungalow, m
♦ rented bungalow
gemieteter Bus, m
Mietbus, m
♦ hired bus BE
♦ hired coach BE
♦ rented bus AE
gemieteter Saal, m
♦ rented hall AE
♦ hired hall BE

gemietetes Appartement, n
  Mietappartement, n
  ♦ rented apartment
gemietetes Auto, n
  Mietauto, n
  Leihauto, n
  geliehenes Auto, n
  ♦ rented car *AE*
  ♦ hired car *BE*
gemietetes Boot, n
  Mietboot, n
  ♦ hired boat *BE*
  ♦ rented boat *AE*
gemietetes Chalet, n
  Mietchalet, n
  ♦ hired chalet *BE*
  ♦ rented chalet
gemietetes Fahrrad, n
  Leihrad, n
  Mietrad, n
  ♦ hired bicycle *BE*
  ♦ hired bike *BE coll*
  ♦ rented bicycle *AE*
  ♦ rented bike *AE coll*
gemietetes Haus, n
  Mietshaus, n
  ♦ rented home
  ♦ rented house
gemietetes Hotel, n
  ♦ rented hotel
gemietetes Hotelzimmer, n
  ♦ rented hotel room
  ♦ hired hotel room *BE*
gemietetes Motorboot, n
  ♦ rented motorboat *AE*
  ♦ hired motor boat *BE*
gemietetes Zimmer, n
  Mietzimmer, n
  Mietraum, m
  gemieteter Raum, m
  ♦ rented room
  ♦ hired room *BE*
gemietete Unterkunft, f
  Mietunterkunft f
  ♦ rented accommodation
gemietete Villa, f
  ♦ rented villa
gemietete Wohnung, f
  Mietwohnung, f
  ♦ rented flat *BE*
  ♦ flat *BE*
  ♦ rented apartment *AE*
  ♦ lodging
  ♦ lodgement
gemischter Salat, m
  ♦ mixed salad
gemischtes Programm, n
  ♦ mixed program *AE*
  ♦ mixed programme *BE*
Gemischtwarenladen, m
  ♦ general store *AE*
Gemüse, n sg
  ♦ vegetable
  ♦ vegetables *pl*
  ♦ veg *coll*
Gemüsebeilage, f
  ♦ vegetable side dish *AE*
  ♦ vegetable side-dish *BE*
Gemüsebrühe, f
  ♦ vegetable broth

Gemüsebüfett, n
  ♦ vegetable buffet
Gemüsebutter, f
  ♦ vegetable butter
Gemüsecanapé, n
  ♦ vegetable canapé
  ♦ vegetable canape *AE*
Gemüsecremesuppe, f
  ♦ vegetable cream soup
Gemüse der Saison, n
  ♦ seasonal vegetable
  ♦ seasonal vegetables *pl*
Gemüseeintopf, m
  ♦ vegetable stew
  ♦ boiled dinner *AE*
Gemüsefarce, f
  Gemüsefüllung, f
  ♦ vegetable farce
  ♦ vegetable filling
Gemüsefond, m
  ♦ vegetable fond
Gemüsefüllung, f
  Gemüsefarce, f
  ♦ vegetable filling
  ♦ vegetable farce
Gemüsegang, m
  ♦ vegetable course
Gemüsegarten, m
  ♦ vegetable garden
Gemüsegericht, n
  ♦ vegetable dish
Gemüsehändler, m
  ♦ vegetable dealer *AE*
  ♦ greengrocer *BE*
Gemüsekeller, m
  ♦ vegetable cellar
Gemüsekoch, m
  ♦ vegetable cook
Gemüsekonserve, f
  ♦ tinned vegetable *BE*
  ♦ canned vegetable *AE*
Gemüsekost, f
  ♦ vegetable diet
Gemüsemarinade, f
  Gemüsesud, m
  ♦ vegetable marinade
Gemüsemarkt, m
  ♦ vegetable market
Gemüsepartiechef, m
  Partiechef Gemüse, m
  ♦ vegetable chef
Gemüsepastetchen, n
  ♦ vegetable patty
Gemüsepastete, f
  ♦ vegetable pie
Gemüseplatte, f
  ♦ vegetable platter
Gemüsepüree, n
  ♦ vegetable purée
  ♦ vegetable puree *AE*
Gemüsepüreesuppe, f
  ♦ vegetable-purée soup
  ♦ vegetable-puree soup *AE*
Gemüse putzen
  ♦ clean vegetable
Gemüseputzer, m
  ♦ vegetable cleaner
Gemüsesaft, m
  ♦ vegetable juice
Gemüsesalat, m
  ♦ vegetable salad

Gemüseschüssel, f
  ♦ vegetable bowl
  ♦ vegetable dish
Gemüsesoufflé, n
  Gemüseauflauf, m
  ♦ vegetable soufflé
Gemüsesud, m
  → Gemüsemarinade
Gemüsesuppe, f
  ♦ vegetable soup
Gemüseterrine, f
  ♦ vegetable terrine
Gemüsetoast, m
  ♦ vegetable toast
Gemüsetörtchen, n
  ♦ vegetable tartlet
Gemüsevorspeise, f
  ♦ vegetable hors d'hoeuvre
Gemüsewürstchen, n
  → Chipolata
gemütlich, adj
  behaglich, adj
  ♦ cosy, adj
  ♦ cozy, adj *AE*
  ♦ comfortable, adj
gemütliche Atmosphäre, f
  behagliche Atmosphäre, f
  ♦ cosy atmosphere
  ♦ cozy atmosphere *AE*
  ♦ comfortable atmosphere
gemütliche Atmosphäre bieten
  behagliche Atmosphäre bieten
  ♦ offer a cosy atmosphere
  ♦ offer a comfortable atmosphere
  ♦ provide a cosy atmosphere
  ♦ provide a comfortable atmosphere
gemütliche Dorfkneipe, f
  ♦ cosy village bar *AE*
  ♦ cozy village bar *AE*
  ♦ cosy village pub *BE*
gemütliche Ecke, f
  ♦ cosy corner
  ♦ cozy corner *AE*
gemütliche Fahrt, f (Auto)
  ♦ leisurely drive
gemütliche Fahrt, f (generell)
  ♦ leisurely trip
  ♦ leisurely ride
gemütlich eingerichtet, adj
  ♦ cosily furnished, adj
  ♦ cozily furnished, adj *AE*
  ♦ comfortably furnished, adj
gemütlich eingerichtetes Zimmer, n
  ♦ cosily furnished room
  ♦ cozily furnished room
  ♦ comfortably furnished room
gemütliche Nacht verbringen
  ♦ spend a comfortable night
  ♦ pass a comfortable night *AE*
gemütlicher Abend, m
  ♦ leisurely evening
gemütlicher Aufenthaltsraum, m
  (in Hotel)
  ♦ comfortable lounge
gemütlicher Bummel, m
  ♦ leisurely stroll
gemütlicher Spaziergang, m
  ♦ leisurely walk
gemütlicher Urlaub, m
  ♦ leisurely vacation *AE*
  ♦ leisurely holiday *BE*

gemütliches Beisammensein, n
  gemütliches Zusammensein, n
  ♦ cosy get-together
  ♦ cozy get-together AE
gemütliches Essen, n
  gemütliche Mahlzeit, f
  ♦ leisurely meal
gemütliches Frühstück, n
  ♦ leisurely breakfast
gemütliches Haus, n
  (privat)
  ♦ cosy house
  ♦ cozy house AE
  ♦ comfortable house
gemütliches Hotel, n
  ♦ cosy hotel
  ♦ cozy hotel AE
  ♦ comfortable hotel
gemütliches Restaurant, n
  ♦ cosy restaurant
  ♦ cozy restaurant AE
  ♦ comfortable restaurant
gemütlich essen etw
  ♦ eat s.th. in a cosy atmosphere
  ♦ eat s.th. in a comfortable atmosphere
  ♦ eat s.th. in a cozy atmosphere AE
gemütliches Zimmer, n
  ♦ cosy room
  ♦ cozy room AE
  ♦ comfortable room
gemütliches Zusammensein, n
  → gemütliches Beisammensein
gemütliche Umgebung, f
  ♦ comfortable surroundings pl
Gemütlichkeit, f
  ♦ cosiness
  ♦ coziness AE
  ♦ cosy atmosphere
  ♦ cozy atmosphere AE
  ♦ comfortableness
genannte Leistung, f
  ♦ service mentioned
  ♦ stated service
genannter Termin, m
  genanntes Datum, n
  ♦ date mentioned
genaue Beschreibung, f
  ♦ accurate description
  ♦ detailed description
genaue Information, f
  genaue Auskunft, f
  ♦ accurate information
genaue Route, f
  genaue Strecke, f
  ♦ exact route
genauer Preis, m
  ♦ exact price
  ♦ exact rate
genau fahrplanmäßig eintreffen
  genau fahrplanmäßig ankommen
  ♦ arrive right on schedule
genau nach Westen, adv
  ♦ due west, adv
genau nach Westen segeln
  ♦ sail due west
genehmigte Fremdenunterkunft, f
  ♦ approved tourist accommodation
genehmigte Piste, f (Ski)
  ♦ approved ski run
genehmigtes Hotel, n
  ♦ approved hotel

Genehmigung, f
  Erlaubnis, f
  ♦ permission
  ♦ permit
Genehmigung erhalten
  Erlaubnis erhalten
  ♦ obtain a permit
Genehmigung verlängern
  Erlaubnis verlängern
  ♦ renew a permit
geneigter Boden, m
  Boden mit Neigung, f
  ♦ raked floor
geneppt werden
  ♦ be ripped off BE coll
  ♦ be fleeced
  ♦ be rooked
Generalagent, m
  ♦ general agent
Generalagentur, f
  ♦ general agency
Generaldirektor, m
  ♦ director general AE
  ♦ direcor-general BE
  ♦ general manager
  ♦ GM
Generalgouvernante, f SCHW
  Erste Hausdame, f
  ♦ head housekeeper BE
  ♦ executive housekeeper AE
Generalkonsul, m
  ♦ consul general
Generalkonsulat, n
  ♦ consulate general
General Manager, m
  → Generaldirektor
Generalprobe, f
  (Theater)
  ♦ dress rehearsal
Generalquartiermeister, m (Militär)
  ♦ quartermaster general
  ♦ Quartermaster General
Generalreinigung, f
  ♦ general cleaning
Generalschlüssel, m
  ♦ grand master key
  ♦ grand master
Generalsekretär, m
  ♦ secretary general
Generalüberholung, f
  ♦ major overhaul
Generalversammlung, f (Aktionäre)
  Aktionärsversammlung, f
  ♦ shareholders' meeting BE
  ♦ stockholders' meeting AE
Generalversammlung, f (generell)
  Hauptversammlung, f
  ♦ general meeting
Generalversammlung, f (Politik)
  ♦ general assembly
Generationen von Reisenden, f pl
  ♦ generations of travellers pl
  ♦ generations of travelers AE pl
Genesungsheim, n
  Erholungsheim, n (für Rekonvaleszenten)
  ♦ convalescent home
Genesungsurlaub, m
  Erholungsurlaub m
  Krankenurlaub m
  ♦ convalescent leave

♦ sick leave
♦ sick-leave BE
Genever, m
  ♦ geneva
Genf
  ♦ Geneva
Genfer See, m
  ♦ Lake Geneva
  ♦ Lake of Geneva, the
  ♦ Lake Leman
genießbar, adj
  schmackhaft, adj
  wohlschmeckend, adj
  ♦ toothsome, adj fam
  ♦ palatable, adj
  ♦ tasty, adj
Genießbarkeit, f
  Eßbarkeit, f
  ♦ palatability
genießen etw
  (Geschmack, Geruch)
  ♦ savour s.th.
  ♦ savor s.th. AE
genießen etw in Ruhe
  genießen etw mit Ruhe
  ♦ enjoy s.th. with peace of mind
genießen etw in vollen Zügen
  ♦ enjoy s.th. to the full
genießen etw mit Appetit
  → essen etw mit Appetit
Genießer, m
  ♦ savourer
  ♦ savorer AE
  ♦ epicure
Genossenschaft, f
  ♦ cooperative association AE
  ♦ cooperative
genossenschaftlicher Wohnungsbau, m
  ♦ cooperative housing
Genossenschaftsweingut, n
  ♦ cooperative winery
genügend Hotelzimmer bereitstellen
  genügend Hotelzimmer zur Verfügung stellen
  ♦ provide sufficient hotel rooms
Genußmensch, m
  ♦ man of pleasure
  ♦ epicure
Genußsucht, f
  Epikureimus, m philos
  ♦ epicureism philos
Genuß- und Nahrungsmittelmesse, f
  ♦ food and drink fair
geöffnet, adj
  ♦ open, adj
geöffnete Flasche, f
  ♦ opened bottle
geöffnet für Besucher
  ♦ open to visitors
geöffnet haben
  ♦ be open
geöffnet haben am Montag
  ♦ be open on Monday
geöffnet haben bis Mitternacht
  (Geschäft)
  ♦ be open until midnight
geöffnet nur während der örtlichen Ausschankzeit
  ♦ open only during local licensing hours
  ♦ open only during local licencing hours
geöffnet sein für Besucher
  ♦ be open to visitors

Geöffnet vom 1. April bis 31. Oktober

Geöffnet vom 1. April bis 31. Oktober
- Open from 1 April until 31 October

Geöffnet von Mai bis einschließlich September
- Open from May through September *AE*
- Open from May until September inclusive *BE*

Geograph, m
- geographer

Geographie, f
- geography

geographisch, adj
- geographic, adj
- geographical, adj

geographische Lage, f
- geographic(al) location
- geographic(al) situation
- geographic(al) position

geographischer Mittelpunkt (von England), m
- geographic center (of England) *AE*
- geographical centre (of England) *BE*

geographische Verteilung, f
(z.B. des Tourismus)
- geographic spread
- geographical spread

geologischer Lehrpfad, m
- geological trail

geologisches Museum, n
- geological museum

Georgien
- Georgia

Georgier, m
- Georgian

Georgierin, f
- Georgian girl
- Georgian woman
- Georgian

georgisch, adj
- Georgian, adj

gepachtet, adj
- leased, adj
- rented, adj

gepachteter Grundbesitz, m
gepachtete Immobilie f
Pachtimmobilie f
- leasehold property

gepachteter Raum, m (Volumen)
- leased space

gepachtetes Hotel, n
- leased hotel
- leasehold hotel

gepachtetes Land, n
- leased land

gepachtetes Restaurant, n
- leased restaurant
- leasehold restaurant

Gepäck, n
Reisegepäck, n
- baggage *AE*
- luggage *BE*

Gepäckabfertiger, m
- baggage handler *AE*
- luggage handler *BE*

Gepäckabfertigung, f
- baggage handling *AE*
- luggage handling *BE*

Gepäckabfertigungsgebühr f
- baggage-handling charge *AE*
- baggage-handling fee *AE*
- luggage-handling charge *BE*
- luggage-handling fee *BE*

Gepäckabfertigungsservice m
Gepäckabfertigung f

Gepäckdienst m
- baggage-handling service *AE*
- luggage-handling service *BE*

Gepäckabholdienst m
Gepäckabholung f
Gepäckabholservice m
- baggage pick-up service *AE*
- luggage pick-up service *BE*

Gepäck abholen
- collect one's baggage *AE*
- collect one's luggage *BE*
- pick up (one's) baggage *AE*
- pick up (one's) luggage *BE*

Gepäck abholen von der Gepäckaufbewahrung
- claim one's baggage from the baggage room *AE*
- claim one's luggage from the left-luggage office *BE*

Gepäckabholung, f
- baggage collection *AE*
- luggage collection *BE*

Gepäckablage, f
Kofferablage, f
- baggage rack *AE*
- baggage stand *AE*
- luggage rack *BE*
- luggage stand *BE*

Gepäckabteil, n
- baggage compartment *AE*
- luggage compartment *BE*

Gepäckanhänger, m (Fahrzeug)
- baggage trailer *AE*
- luggage trailer *BE*

Gepäckanhänger, m (Karte)
- baggage tag *AE*
- luggage tag *BE*

Gepäck annehmen (zur Beförderung)
- check baggage *AE*

Gepäckaufbewahrung, f (in Bahnhof etc.)
- baggage room *AE*
- checkroom *AE*
- left-luggage office *BE*

Gepäckaufbewahrungsdienst m
Gepäckaufbewahrungsservice m
Gepäckaufbewahrung f
- baggage storage service *AE*
- luggage storage service *BE*

Gepäckaufgabe, f
- baggage check-in *AE*
- baggage check *AE*
- luggage registration *BE*

Gepäckaufgabestelle, f
- baggage check-in facility *AE*

Gepäck aufgeben
- check one's baggage (in the baggage room) *AE*
- leave one's luggage at the (left-)luggage office *BE*

Gepäckaufkleber, m
Gepäckzettel, m
- luggage label *BE*
- baggage label *AE*

Gepäck ausfindig machen
- locate the baggage *AE*
- locate the luggage *BE*

Gepäckausgabe, f
- baggage claim *AE*
- luggage claim *BE*

Gepäckausgabebereich, m
- baggage claim area *AE*
- luggage claim area *BE*

Gepäck ausladen (aus etw)
- unload baggage (from s.th.) *AE*
- unload luggage (from s.th.) *BE*

Gepäck ausliefern
Gepäck abliefern
- deliver (s.o.'s) baggage *AE*
- deliver (s.o.'s) luggage *BE*

Gepäck befördern (schnell)
- expedite baggage *AE*
- expedite luggage *AE*

Gepäckberg, m
- mountain of baggage *AE*
- mountain of luggage *BE*

Gepäckbesorgung, f
→ Gepäckabfertigung

Gepäckbestimmungen, f pl
Gepäckvorschriften, f pl
- baggage regulations *AE pl*
- luggage regulations *BE pl*

Gepäckbuch, n
- baggage book *AE*
- luggage book *BE*

Gepäckbuch führen
- keep a baggage book *AE*
- keep a luggage book *BE*

Gepäckdienst m
Gepäckservice m
- baggage service *AE*
- luggage service *BE*

Gepäckdurchsuchung, f
- baggage search *AE*
- luggage search *BE*

Gepäck erleichtern
- lighten one's baggage *AE*
- lighten one's luggage *BE*

Gepäckermittlung, f
- lost and found baggage *AE*
- lost and found luggage *BE*

Gepäckförderband, n
- baggage conveyor belt *AE*
- luggage conveyor belt *BE*

Gepäckgewicht, n
- baggage weight *AE*
- luggage weight *BE*

Gepäckhaftung, f
Gepäckhaftpflicht, f
- baggage liability *AE*
- luggage liability *BE*

Gepäck im Auge behalten
- keep an eye on the baggage *AE*
- keep an eye on the luggage *BE*

Gepäckinspektion, f
- baggage inspection *AE*
- luggage inspection *BE*

Gepäckkapazität, f
- baggage capacity *AE*
- luggage capacity *BE*

Gepäckkarren, m
Gepäckwagen, m
Kofferkuli, m
Kofferwagen, m
- luggage trolley *BE*
- baggage cart *AE*

Gepäckkarte, f
Gepäckschein, m
- baggage ticket *AE*
- luggage ticket *BE*

Gepäck kommt an
- baggage arrives *AE*
- luggage arrives *BE*

Gepäckkontrolle, f
- luggage check *BE*
- baggage check *AE*

Gepäcklogbuch, n
→ Gepäckbuch

Gepäckmann, m
Gepäckangestellte, m
- baggage clerk *AE*
- luggage clerk *BE*

Gepäck mit einem Gepäckanhänger versehen
Gepäck auszeichnen
- label one's baggage *AE*
- label one's luggage *BE*

Gepäckpaß, m
(erhältlich nach Rechnungsbegleichung)
- baggage pass *AE*
- luggage pass *BE*

Gepäckpaß ausgeben
- issue a baggage pass *AE*
- issue a luggage pass *BE*

Gepäckpaß ausstellen
- make out a baggage pass *AE*
- make out a luggage pass *BE*
- issue a baggage pass *AE*
- issue a luggage pass *BE*

Gepäckraum, m (generell)
- checkroom *AE*
- baggage room *AE*
- luggage room *BE*

Gepäckraum, m (Stauraum)
- baggage space *AE*
- luggage space *BE*

Gepäckschalter, m
- baggage counter *AE*
- baggage desk *AE*
- luggage counter
- left-luggage counter *BE*

Gepäckschein, m
→ Gepäckkarte

Gepäckschließfach, n
Gepäckfach, n
- baggage locker *AE*
- luggage locker *BE*
- left-luggage locker *BE*

Gepäckschließfachgebühr, f
Gepäckfachgebühr f
- baggage locker fee *AE*
- baggage locker charge *AE*
- luggage locker fee *BE*
- luggage locker charge *BE*

Gepäckschutz, m
(Versicherung)
- baggage cover *AE*
- luggage cover *BE*

Gepäckservice, m
→ Gepäckdienst

Gepäckständer, m (im Zimmer)
→ Kofferbock

Gepäckstück, n
- piece of baggage *AE*
- item of baggage *AE*
- piece of luggage *BE*
- item of luggage *BE*

Gepäckstück aufgeben
- check (in) a piece of baggage *AE*
- check (in) a piece of luggage *BE*

Gepäckstücke sind erlaubt
drei Gepäckstücke sind erlaubt
- pieces of baggage are allowed *AE*
- pieces of luggage are allowed *BE*
- three pieces of baggage are allowed *AE*
- three pieces of luggage are allowed *BE*

Gepäck tragen
- carry baggage *AE*
- carry luggage *BE*

Gepäckträger, m (Bahnhof, Flughafen)
- porter
- redcap *AE*
- skycap *BE*

Gepäckträger, m (Person)
- baggage porter *AE*
- luggage porter *BE*

Gepäckträger, m (Vorrichtung)
(z.B. auf Autodach)
- luggage rack *BE*
- baggage rack *AE*

Gepäckträgerdienst, m
- porterage service

Gepäckträgergebühr, f
→ Gepäckträgerlohn

Gepäckträgerlohn, m
Gepäckträgergebühr, f
- porterage

Gepäckträger rufen
- call the baggage porter *AE*
- call the luggage porter *BE*

Gepäcktransfer, m
- baggage transfer *AE*
- luggage transfer *BE*

Gepäcktransport, m
- porterage *AE*

Gepäckverlust, m
- loss of (one's) baggage *AE*
- loss of (one's) luggage *BE*

Gepäck versichern
- insure (one's) baggage *AE*
- insure (one's) luggage *BE*

Gepäckversicherung, f
Reisegepäckversicherung, f
- baggage insurance *AE*
- luggage insurance *BE*

Gepäckversicherung abschließen
- take out a luggage insurance *BE*
- take out a baggage insurance *AE*

Gepäck voraussenden
Gepäck vorausschicken
- send one's baggage in advance *AE*
- send one's luggage in advance *BE*
- send one's baggage ahead *AE*
- send one's luggage ahead *BE*

Gepäckwagen, m
→ Gepäckkarren

Gepäck wird in das Hotel befördert
- luggage is transported to the hotel *BE*
- baggage is transported to the hotel *AE*

Gepäck wird von Ort zu Ort befördert
- baggage is transferred from place to place *AE*
- baggage is transported from place to place *AE*
- luggage is transferred from place to place *BE*
- luggage is transported from place to place *BE*
- luggage is conveyed from place to place *BE*

Gepäckzettel, m
Gepäckaufkleber, m
- baggage label *AE*
- luggage label *BE*

Gepäck zurückbehalten
- keep back baggage *AE*
- keep back luggage *BE*

Gepäckzustellung, f
- delivery of baggage *AE*
- delivery of luggage *BE*

gepanscht, adj
- adulterated, adj

gepanschter Flaschenwein, m
- adulterated bottled wine

gepanschter Wein, m
- adulterated wine

geparkt, adj
parkend, adj
- parked, adj

gepfefferter Preis, m
gesalzener Preis, m
- steep price
- steep rate

gepflasterter Hof, m
- paved courtyard
- cobbled courtyard

gepflegt, adj (generell)
gut instandgehalten, adj
- well-kept, adj
- well-maintained, adj
- well-looked-after, adj
- well-groomed, adj

gepflegt, adj (kultiviert)
kultiviert, adj
- refined, adj
- cultivated, adj

gepflegt ankommen
- arrive in style

gepflegt ausgehen
- eat out in style
- dine out in style

gepflegte Abfahrt f
(Ski)
- well-maintained run

gepflegte Anlage, f
- well-tended grounds *pl*

gepflegte Atmosphäre, f
kultivierte Atmosphäre, f
- refined atmosphere
- cultivated atmosphere

gepflegte Gastlichkeit bieten
- provide refined hospitality

gepflegte Piste, f
- well-groomed piste

gepflegter Boden, m
- well-kept floor

gepflegter Garten, m
- well-kept garden
- well-tended garden
- well-maintained garden

gepflegter Platz, m
(Camping)
- well-kept site
- well-maintained site

gepflegter Pub, m
- well-looked-after pub
- well-maintained pub

gepflegter Rasen, m
- well-kept lawn

gepflegter Service, m
kultivierter Service, m
- sophisticated service

gepflegtes Essen, n
- eating in style
- dining in style

gepflegtes Haus, n
- well-kept house
- well-looked-after house
- well-maintained house

gepflegtes Hotel, n
- well-kept hotel

♦ well-maintained hotel
♦ well-looked-after hotel
gepflegte Skipiste, f
♦ well-groomed ski run
gepflegt essen
♦ eat in style
gepflegtes Zimmer, n
♦ well-maintained room
♦ well-kept room
gepflegte Weine, m pl
♦ select wines *pl*
gepflegt reisen
♦ travel in style
gepflegt speisen
♦ dine in style
gepflegt tun etw
♦ do s.th. in style
geplant, adj
♦ planned, adj
geplanten Besuch absagen
♦ cancel a planned visit
geplanter Besuch, m
♦ planned visit
geplantes Hotelzimmer, n
♦ planned hotel room
geplantes Programm, n
♦ planned program *AE*
♦ planned programme *BE*
geplante Veranstaltung, f
♦ planned event
♦ planned function
geplatzter Reifen, m
♦ burst tire *AE*
♦ burst tyre *BE*
gepökelt, adj
♦ pickled, adj
♦ salted , adj
♦ cured, adj
gepökeltes Rindfleisch, n
♦ pickled beef
geprellt, adj
♦ swindled, adj
♦ defrauded, adj
geprellter Gast, m
♦ swindled guest
♦ swindled visitor
gerade noch rechtzeitig ankommen für etw
♦ arrive just in time for s.th.
gerade zur rechten Zeit
just zur rechten zeit
♦ just at the right time
♦ just in time
Gerance, f SCHW
→ Geschäftsführung
Gerant, m SCHW
→ Geschäftsführer
Gerantenpaar, n
→ Geschäftsführerehepaar
Gerantin, f SCHW
→ Geschäftsführerin
Gerätemiete, f
♦ equipment rental *AE*
♦ equipment hire *BE*
Geräteverleih, m
Ausrüstungsverleih, m
♦ equipment hire *BE*
♦ equipment rental *AE*
geräuchert, adj
♦ smoked, adj
geräucherter Kabeljau, m
♦ smoked cod

geräucherter Lachs, m
Räucherlachs, m
♦ smoked salmon
geräucherter Schellfisch, m
♦ finnan
♦ smoked haddock
geräucherter Schinken, m
Räucherschinken, m
♦ smoked ham
geräucherter Schinken, m
schwach geräucherter Schinken, m
♦ gammon
geräumig, adj
weiträumig, adj
♦ spacious, adj
♦ roomy, adj
geräumiger Stellplatz, m
(Camping)
♦ spacious pitch
♦ roomy pitch
geräumiges Appartement, n
♦ spacious apartment
geräumiges Haus, n
♦ spacious house
geräumiges Zimmer, n
♦ spacious room
geräumige Unterkunft, f
♦ spacious accommodation
geräumige Wohnung, f
♦ spacious flat *BE*
♦ spacious apartment *AE*
Geräumigkeit, f
♦ roominess
♦ spaciousness
geräumt, adj (Unterkunft)
frei gemacht, adj
♦ vacated, adj
geräumt, adj (Weg)
♦ cleared, adj
geräumter und markierter Weg, m
♦ cleared and marked path
geräumter Wanderweg, m
♦ cleared walking path
♦ cleared walking trail
♦ cleared hiking trail
geräumter Weg, m
♦ cleared path
geräumtes Zimmer, n
frei gemachtes Zimmer n
♦ vacated room
Gerber, m
♦ tanner
Gerberbrunnen, m
♦ tanners' fountain
Gerberviertel, n
♦ tanners' quarter
♦ tanners' district
Gericht, n (Gang)
→ Gang
Gericht, n (Speise)
♦ dish
Gericht auf Bestellung, n
♦ dish prepared to order
Gericht aufmöbeln
(durch Zusätze)
♦ doctor a dish
Gericht auftragen
Gericht servieren
Gericht vorsetzen
♦ serve a dish

Gericht aus Italien, n
♦ dish from Italy
Gericht auswählen
Gericht wählen
♦ choose a dish
♦ select a dish
Gericht des Tages, n
Tagesgericht, n
Plat du jour, f *FR m*
♦ special dish of the day
♦ dish of the day
♦ plat du jour *FR m*
♦ today's special
Gerichte aus aller Welt, n pl
♦ dishes from all over the world *pl*
Gericht empfehlen
♦ recommend a dish
Gericht enthält viele Kalorien
♦ dish is high in calories
Gericht essen
♦ eat a dish
♦ have a dish
Gerichtfolge, f
♦ order of (the) dishes
Gericht macht schnell satt
♦ dish is very filling
Gericht probieren
Gericht versuchen
♦ sample a dish
♦ try a dish
Gericht reicht für sechs Personen
♦ dish serves six persons
♦ dish serves six
Gericht sieht appetitlich aus
♦ dish looks delicious
Gerichtskosten, pl *jur*
♦ court fees *pl jur*
Gerichtssaal, m
♦ court room
Gericht verkaufen
♦ sell a dish
Gericht vorbestellen
♦ preorder a dish *AE*
♦ order a dish in advance
Gericht zubereiten
♦ prepare a dish
gerieben, adj *gastr*
♦ grated, adj *gastr*
geriebene Muskatnuß, f
♦ grated nutmeg
geriebener Käse, m
♦ grated cheese
geriebene Zitronenschale, f
♦ grated lemon rind
geringe Auslastung, f (Transport)
♦ low load factor
geringe Auslastung haben
geringe Auslastung erzielen
schwache Auslastung haben
schwache Auslastung erzielen
♦ have a low load factor
geringe Gebühr f
♦ nominal charge
♦ nominal fee
geringer Preis, m
geringfügiger Preis, m
♦ nominal price
♦ nominal rate
geringfügige Änderung, f
kleine Änderung, f
♦ minor alteration

geringfügige Unbequemlichkeiten, f pl
- ♦ little discomforts pl

Gern!
- ♦ My pleasure!
- ♦ With pleasure!
- ♦ Of course!

gern, adv
- gerne, adv
- ♦ gladly, adv
- ♦ with pleasure, adv
- ♦ willingly, adj

gern einen trinken
- gerne einen heben coll
- ♦ like a drop
- ♦ be fond of a drop

gerngesehener Gast, m
- → willkommener Gast

gern gut essen und trinken
- ♦ have a liking for good food and drink

gern hart liegen
- gerne hart liegen
- ♦ like a hard bed

gern picheln coll
- gern trinken
- ♦ be fond of the bottle

gern reisen
- ♦ love travelling
- ♦ love traveling AE

gern süß essen
- Zuckermäulchen sein fam
- ♦ have a sweet tooth

Gerste, f
- ♦ barley

Gerstenbrot, n
- ♦ barley bread

Gerstencremesuppe, f
- ♦ barley cream soup

Gerstenmalz, n
- ♦ barley malt

Gerstenmehl, n
- ♦ barley flower

Gerstenpolenta, f
- ♦ barley polenta

Gerstensaft, m humor
- ♦ juice of the barley humor

Gerstensuppe, f
- ♦ barley soup

geruhsam, adj
- gemächlich, adj
- gemütlich, adj
- ♦ leisurely, adj

geruhsame Atmosphäre, f
- ♦ leisurely atmosphere

gerupft, adj
- ♦ plucked, adj

gerupfte Gans, f
- ♦ plucked goose

gesalzen, adj
- ♦ salted, adj

gesalzene Rechnung, f coll
- ♦ hefty bill coll

Gesamtangebot, n
- ♦ total supply

Gesamtankünfte, f pl
- ♦ total arrivals pl

Gesamtaufenthalt, m
- ♦ total stay

Gesamtaufwand, m
- gesamter Aufwand, m
- ♦ total expenditure

Gesamtausgaben, f pl
- ♦ total expenses pl
- ♦ total spending

Gesamtauslastung, f (Beförderung)
- ♦ overall load factor

Gesamtauslastung, f (Unterkunft)
- gesamte Auslastung f
- Gesamtbelegung f
- gesamte Belegung f
- ♦ overall occupancy
- ♦ total occupancy

Gesamtauslastungsniveau n
- Gesamtbelegungsniveau n
- ♦ overall occupancy level
- ♦ overall level of occupancy

Gesamtauslastungsrate f
- Gesamtauslastungsquote f
- Gesamtbelegungsrate f
- Gesamtbelegungsquote f
- ♦ overall occupancy rate
- ♦ overall rate of occupancy
- ♦ total occupancy rate
- ♦ rate of total occupancy

Gesamtauslastungszahl, f
- Gesamtbelegungszahl, f
- ♦ total occupancy figure
- ♦ overall occupancy figure

Gesamtausstellungsfläche, f
- ♦ total exhibition area
- ♦ overall exhibition area

Gesamtbeherbergungserlös, m
- ♦ total rooms revenue

Gesamtbeherbergungsertrag, m
- ♦ total rooms income

Gesamtbelegung, f
- → Gesamtauslastung

Gesamtbelegung von durchschnittlich 80% erzielen
- Gesamtauslastung von durchschnittlich 80% erzielen
- ♦ achieve an average total occupancy of 80%

Gesamtbereichsrechnung, f
- ♦ statement of income AE

Gesamtbesucher, m pl
- gesamte Besucher, m pl
- ♦ total visitors pl
- ♦ total number of visitors

Gesamtbesucherzahl, f
- ♦ visitor total
- ♦ total number of visitors

Gesamtbettenkapazität, f
- gesamte Bettenkapazität, f
- ♦ total bed capacity

Gesamtbettenzahl, f
- ♦ total number of beds

Gesamtbettenzahl erhöhen
- ♦ increase the total number of beds

Gesamtbewertung, f
- ♦ overall rating

Gesamtbodenfläche, f
- Gesamtfläche, f
- ♦ total floor area

Gesamtbuchungszahl, f
- ♦ booking total
- ♦ total number of bookings

Gesamtdauer der Konferenz, f
- gesamte Dauer der Konferenz f
- ♦ entire length of the conference

Gesamtdimensionen eines Zimmers, f pl
- Gesamtmaße eines Zimmers, n pl
- ♦ overall measurements of a room pl

gesamte Auslastung, f
- → Gesamtauslastung

gesamte Fahrt, f
- ♦ entire trip

gesamte Gebühr, f
- Gesamtgebühr, f
- ♦ overall charge
- ♦ overall fee
- ♦ total charge
- ♦ total fee

Gesamteinnahme, f
- ♦ total income
- ♦ total revenue

Gesamteinnahmen, f pl
- gesamte Einnahmen, f pl
- ♦ total takings pl
- ♦ total revenues pl
- ♦ total receipts pl
- ♦ total income

Gesamteinrichtung, f
- ♦ overall furnishings pl

gesamte Instandhaltungsausgaben, f pl
- ♦ total maintenance expenses pl

gesamte Jahresnachfrage nach Unterkünften, f
- gesamte Unterkunftsjahresnachfrage, f
- ♦ total annual demand for accommodations AE
- ♦ total annual demand for accommodation BE

gesamte Mahlzeit, f
- ♦ entire meal
- ♦ total meal

Gesamtentfernung, f
- ♦ total distance

gesamter Aufenthalt, m
- ♦ entire stay
- ♦ whole stay

gesamte Reise, f
- ♦ entire journey
- ♦ entire trip
- ♦ entire tour

Gesamterlebnis, n
- ♦ total experience

Gesamterlebnis suchen
- ♦ seek a total experience

Gesamterlös, m
- ♦ total proceeds pl
- ♦ total revenue

Gesamterlös der Küche, m
- ♦ total kitchen revenue

Gesamterlös pro Gast, m
- ♦ total revenue per guest

Gesamterlös pro Tag pro Gast m
- ♦ total revenue per day per guest

Gesamterscheinung, f
- ♦ overall appearance

gesamter Speisen- und Getränkeerlös, m
- ♦ total food and beverage revenue

gesamter Speisen- und Getränkeertrag, m
- ♦ total food and beverage income

Gesamtertrag, m (Gewinn- und Verlustrechnung)
- ♦ total income

gesamtes Anlagevermögen, n
- ♦ total fixed assets pl

gesamtes Umlaufvermögen, n
- ♦ total current assets pl

gesamte Übernachtungskapazität f
- ♦ total bedroom capacity

gesamteuropäisch, adj
- ♦ pan-European, adj

gesamte Veranstaltung, f
- ♦ entire event
- ♦ entire function

Gesamtfahrgastzahl

Gesamtfahrgastzahl, f
  Gesamtpassagierzahl, f
  ♦ passenger total
  ♦ total number of passengers
Gesamtfahrt, f
  ♦ overall trip
Gesamtfahrzeit, f
  Gesamtreisezeit, f
  ♦ total journey time
  ♦ overall journey time
Gesamtferienpreis, m
  Gesamturlaubspreis, m
  ♦ overall holiday price *BE*
  ♦ overall vacation price *AE*
Gesamtfläche, f
  gesamte Fläche, f
  ♦ total area
Gesamtfläche beträgt 123 Quadratfuß
  ♦ total area is 123 square feet
Gesamtfläche von 123 Quadratmetern, f
  ♦ total area of 123 square meters *AE*
  ♦ total area of 123 square metres *BE*
  ♦ total area of 123 sq.m.
Gesamtgästezahl, f (generell)
  Gesamtzahl der Gäste, f
  ♦ guest count
  ♦ total number of guests
Gesamtgästezahl, f (Hotel)
  Gesamtzahl der Hotelgäste, f
  ♦ hotel count
  ♦ house count
  ♦ total number of guests
Gesamtgästezahl, f (Restaurant)
  Gesamtzahl der Gäste, f
  ♦ total covers *pl*
  ♦ total number of guests
Gesamtgästezahl, f (Unterkunft)
  Gesamtzahl der Gäste, f
  ♦ house count
  ♦ total number of guests
Gesamtgebühr, f
  gesamte Gebühr, f
  ♦ total charge
  ♦ total fee
  ♦ overall charge
  ♦ overall fee
Gesamtgedeckgebühr, f
  ♦ overall cover charge
Gesamtgedeckzahl, f
  Gesamtzahl der Gedecke, f
  ♦ cover count
  ♦ total number of covers
Gesamtgepäck, n
  gesamtes Gepäck, n
  ♦ total baggage *AE*
  ♦ total luggage *BE*
Gesamtgetränkeumsatz, m
  ♦ total beverage sales *pl*
  ♦ total beverage turnover
Gesamtgewicht, n
  ♦ total weight
Gesamtgewinn, m
  ♦ total profit
Gesamthallenfläche, f
  Gesamtsaalfläche, f
  ♦ total hall area
  ♦ overall hall area
Gesamtkapazität, f
  ♦ total capacity
Gesamtkonzept, n
  ♦ overall concept

Gesamtkosten, pl
  ♦ total cost
  ♦ total costs *pl*
  ♦ overall cost
  ♦ overall costs *pl*
Gesamtkosten pro Bettnacht, pl
  Gesamtkosten pro Logiernacht pl
  ♦ total cost per bed-night
Gesamtkosten pro Tag, pl
  ♦ total cost per day
  ♦ overall costs per day *pl*
Gesamtkosten pro Zimmer, pl
  ♦ total cost per room
Gesamtkundenzahl, f
  Gesamtzahl der Kunden, f
  ♦ customer count
  ♦ client count
  ♦ total number of clients
  ♦ total numer of customers
  ♦ client total
Gesamtkundenzahl halten
  ♦ maintain client total
Gesamtlandfläche, f
  gesamte Landfläche, f
  ♦ total land area
Gesamtlänge, f
  ♦ overall length
Gesamtleistung, f (Person, Gerät)
  ♦ overall performance
Gesamtleistung, f (Produktion)
  ♦ total output
Gesamtleistung, f (Service)
  ♦ total service
Gesamtmarktnachfrage, f
  ♦ total market demand
  ♦ overall market demand
Gesamtmiete, f
  ♦ total rent
Gesamtnachfrage, f
  gesamte Nachfrage, f
  ♦ total demand
Gesamtpassagierverkehr, m
  ♦ overall passenger traffic
  ♦ total passenger traffic
Gesamtpassagierzahl, f
  ♦ total number of passengers
  ♦ passenger total
Gesamtpersonalbestand, m
  ♦ total number of staff
  ♦ total number of personnel
  ♦ total number of employees
Gesamtpersonalzahl, f
  ♦ staff total
  ♦ total number of staff
Gesamtpersonenverkehr, m
  ♦ total passenger traffic
Gesamtplan, m
  ♦ master plan
Gesamtplan des Gebäudes, m
  ♦ master plan of the building
Gesamtplanung, f
  ♦ overall planning
Gesamtpreis, m
  gesamter Preis m
  ♦ total price
  ♦ total rate
Gesamtprogramm, n
  ♦ complete program *AE*
  ♦ complete programme *BE*
Gesamtprospekt, m
  ♦ complete brochure

Gesamtrechnung, f
  ♦ total bill
  ♦ total check *AE*
Gesamtreise, f
  ♦ total journey
  ♦ total tour
  ♦ total trip
Gesamtreisepreis, m
  ♦ total tour price
Gesamtreiseprogramm, n
  ♦ overall tour program *AE*
  ♦ overall tour programme *BE*
Gesamtreiseverkehr, m
  Gesamtreisen, n
  ♦ total travel
Gesamtreisezeit, f
  ♦ total traveling time *AE*
  ♦ total travelling time *BE*
  ♦ total travel time
  ♦ total journey time
  ♦ overall journey time
Gesamtsitzplatzkapazität f
  gesamte Sitzplatzkapazität f
  ♦ total seating capacity
Gesamtspeisenkosten, pl
  ♦ total food costs *pl*
  ♦ total food cost
Gesamtspeisenumsatz, m
  gesamter Speisenumsatz, m
  ♦ total food sales *pl*
  ♦ total food turnover
Gesamttarif, m
  ♦ overall tariff
Gesamtteilnahmezahl, f
  Gesamtteilnehmerzahl, f
  ♦ total attendance
Gesamtteilnehmerzahl, f (aktive Teilnehmer)
  ♦ total number of participants
  ♦ total number of persons participating in s.th.
  ♦ total number of persons taking part in s.th.
Gesamtteilnehmerzahl, f (passive Teilnehmer)
  ♦ total number of attendants
  ♦ total number of persons attending s.th.
Gesamtthema, f
  ♦ overall theme
Gesamttrend, m
  ♦ overall trend
Gesamtübernachtungen, f pl
  (Statistik)
  ♦ total nights spent *pl*
Gesamtübernachtungszahl f
  (Statistik)
  ♦ total number of nights spent
Gesamtumsatz, m
  ♦ total sales *pl*
  ♦ total turnover
  ♦ overall sales *pl*
  ♦ overall turnover
Gesamtumsatz steigern
  Gesamtumsatz erhöhen
  ♦ increase total sales
  ♦ increase total turnover
  ♦ increase overall sales
  ♦ increase overall turnover
Gesamturlaubspreis, m
  ♦ overall vacation price *AE*
  ♦ overall holiday price *BE*
Gesamtverbrauch, m
  Gesamtkonsum, m
  ♦ total consumption

Gesamtvergatterung, f
 ♦ final briefing
Gesamtverkehr, m
 ♦ total traffic
Gesamtverlust, m
 ♦ total loss
Gesamtverpflegungserlös, m
 gesamter Verpflegungserlös, m
 ♦ total food and beverage revenue
Gesamtvolumen, n
 Gesamtaufkommen, n
 ♦ total volume
Gesamtwarenaufwand, m
 ♦ total cost of sales
Gesamtwert, m
 ♦ total value
Gesamtwert der Vorräte, m
 ♦ total value of stock
Gesamtwohnfläche, f
 ♦ total living space
 ♦ overall living space
Gesamtzahl der Aussteller, f
 ♦ total number of exhibitors
 ♦ exhibitor total
Gesamtzahl der Bettnächte, f
 Gesamtzahl der Logiernächte, f
 ♦ total number of bed-nights
Gesamtzahl der Essen, f
 ♦ total number of meals
Gesamtzahl der Gäste, f
 Gesamtgästezahl, f
 ♦ total number of guests
 ♦ guest count
Gesamtzahl der Kunden, f
 Gesamtkundenzahl, f
 ♦ total number of customers
 ♦ total number of clients
 ♦ customer count
 ♦ client count
Gesamtzahl der Logiernächte, f
 → Gesamtzahl der Bettnächte
Gesamtzahl der Stellplätze, f
 (Camping)
 ♦ total number of pitches
Gesamtzahl der Zimmer, f
 Gesamtzimmerzahl, f
 ♦ total number of rooms
 ♦ room count
Gesamtzahl der Zimmernächte f
 ♦ total number of room-nights
Gesamtzimmerangebot, n
 ♦ total rooms available pl
 ♦ total available rooms pl
Gesamtzimmerkapazität f
 gesamte Zimmerkapazität f
 ♦ total room capacity
Gesamtzimmerumsatz, m
 gesamter Zimmerumsatz, m
 ♦ total room sales pl
 ♦ total rooms sales pl
Gesamtzimmerzahl, f
 Gesamtzahl der Zimmer, f
 ♦ room count
 ♦ total number of rooms
Gesamtzuwachs, m
 ♦ overall increase
Gesangskonzert, n
 ♦ singing concert
gesattelt, adj
 ♦ saddled, adj

gesatteltes Pferd, n
 ♦ saddled horse
geschabt, adj gastr
 ♦ scraped, adj gastr
geschabte Karotte, f
 ♦ scraped carrot
Geschäft außerhalb der Saison, n
 ♦ out-of-season business
Geschäft geht gut
 ♦ business is good
geschäftiges Hotel, n
 lebhaftes Hotel, n
 ♦ busy hotel
Geschäft ist flau
 ♦ business is slack
Geschäft ist ruhig
 ♦ business is quiet
geschäftliche Besprechung, f
 → Geschäftsbesprechung
Geschäftliches mit Vergnügen verbinden
 Angenehmes mit dem Nützlichen verbinden
 ♦ combine business and pleasure
geschäftliche Verabredung, f
 ♦ business appointment
geschäftlich oder zum Vergnügen nach X fahren
 ♦ go to X on business or for pleasure
geschäftlich reisen
 geschäftlich verreisen
 geschäftlich unterwegs sein
 ♦ travel on business
 ♦ travel in an official capacity
geschäftlich Reisender m
 (Gegensatz zu Urlaubsreisender)
 dienstlich Reisender m
 ♦ commercial traveler AE
 ♦ commercial traveller BE
geschäftlich unterwegs sein
 ♦ be on business
 ♦ travel on business
geschäftlich zusammenarbeiten mit jm
 Geschäfte machen mit jm
 ♦ do business with s.o.
Geschäft mit dem Gast, n
 → Gastgeschäft
Geschäftsadresse, f
 ♦ business address
Geschäftsaufenthalt, m
 geschäftlicher Aufenthalt
 ♦ business stay
Geschäftsauslastung, f
 ♦ business occupancy
Geschäftsbedingungen, f pl
 ♦ terms of trade pl
 ♦ terms of business pl
 ♦ trade conditions pl
 ♦ business conditions pl
 ♦ trading conditions pl
Geschäftsbesprechung, f
 geschäftliche Besprechung, f
 ♦ business discussion
 ♦ business meeting
Geschäftsbesuch, m
 geschäftlicher Besuch, m
 ♦ business visit
Geschäftsbesucher, m
 geschäftlicher Besucher, m
 ♦ business visitor
Geschäftsbetrieb, m
 ♦ business establishment
 ♦ business operation

Geschäftsbewirtung, f
 geschäftliche Bewirtung, f
 ♦ business entertaining
 ♦ business entertainment
Geschäftsbuchung, f
 Firmenbuchung, f
 ♦ corporate booking AE
 ♦ company booking BE
Geschäftsdiner, n
 → Geschäftsessen
Geschäftsdüsenflugzeug, n
 Geschäftsjet, m
 ♦ business jet
Geschäftsessen, n (abends)
 Geschäftsdiner, n form
 ♦ business dinner
Geschäftsessen, n (mittags)
 ♦ business luncheon
 ♦ business lunch
Geschäftsflug, m
 ♦ business flight
Geschäftsfrau f
 ♦ businesswoman
 ♦ female executive
geschäftsführender Direktor, m
 ♦ managing director
 ♦ MD
Geschäftsführung, f
 Geschäftsleitung f
 ♦ management
Geschäftsführungshonorar, n
 ♦ management fee
Geschäftsführungsvereinbarung, f
 ♦ management agreement
Geschäftsführungsvertrag, m
 Betriebsführungsvertrag, m
 Managementvertrag, m
 ♦ management contract
Geschäftsgast, m
 Firmengast m
 ♦ business guest
 ♦ business visitor
Geschäftsgäste bewirten
 ♦ entertain business guests
 ♦ entertain business visitors
Geschäftsjahr, n
 ♦ business year
Geschäftsjubiläum n
 ♦ business anniversary
Geschäftsklientel f
 (Geschäftsleute)
 ♦ business clientele
Geschäftskonferenz, f
 ♦ business conference
Geschäftskunde m
 ♦ business client
Geschäftsleitung, f (Aktivität)
 → Geschäftsführung
Geschäftsleitung, f (Personal)
 ♦ management staff
 ♦ management personnel
 ♦ management
Geschäftsleute, pl
 ♦ business people pl
Geschäftslokal, n
 Ladenlokal, n
 ♦ shop premises pl
 ♦ business premises pl
Geschäftsmieter, m
 ♦ business tenant

Geschäftspartner

Geschäftspartner, m
- business partner

Geschäftspolitik, f
- business policy

Geschäftsräume, m pl
  Geschäftslokal, n
- business premises *pl*
- shop premises *pl*

Geschäftsreise, f
- business trip
- business tour

Geschäftsreisebereich, m
  Geschäftsreisesektor, m
- business trip sector
- business travel sector
- business tour sector

Geschäftsreisebüro, n
  Reisebüro, das auf Geschäftsreisen spezialisiert ist, n
- business travel agency
- business travel agent

Geschäftsreiseflugverkehr, m
- business air travel

Geschäftsreisemarkt, m
- business trip market
- business tour market
- business travel market

Geschäftsreisemittler, m
- business travel agent

Geschäftsreisen, n
  Geschäftsreiseverkehr, m
- business travel

Geschäftsreisende, f
  Dienstreisende, f
- woman business traveller
- woman business traveler *AE*
- travelling business woman
- traveling business woman *AE*

Geschäftsreisendenhotel, n
  Geschäftshotel, n
- business hotel

Geschäftsreisender, m
  Dienstreisender, m
- business traveler *AE*
- business traveller *BE*
- business visitor
- traveling businessman *AE*
- travelling businessman *BE*

Geschäftsreiseorganisation, f
- business travel organisation
- business travel organization

Geschäftsreisesektor, m
  Geschäftsreisebereich, m
- business travel sector
- business tour sector
- business trip sector

Geschäftsreisestellenleiter, m
- business travel manager

Geschäftssaison, f
- business season

Geschäftsseminar, n
- business seminar

Geschäftsservice m
- business service

Geschäftssitzung, f
  geschäftliche Sitzung, f
- business session

Geschäftsstelle, f
  Filiale, f
- branch office

Geschäftsstellenleiter, m
  Filialleiter, m
- branch manager

Geschäftsstraße, f
→ Einkaufsstraße

Geschäftsstrategie, f
- business strategy

Geschäftsstunden, f pl
  Bürozeit, f
- office hours *pl*

Geschäftstag, m
- business day
- trading day

Geschäft stagniert
- business is stagnant

Geschäftstagung, f
  geschäftliche Tagung, f
  Geschäftstreffen, n
- business meeting

Geschäftstourismus, m
- business tourism

Geschäftstourismuseinnahmen, f pl
- business tourism receipts *pl*

Geschäftstourist, m
- business tourist

Geschäftsübernachtung, f
  (Statistik)
- business bed-night

Geschäftsumfang, m
→ Geschäftsvolumen

Geschäftsumfeld, n
- business environment

Geschäftsunternehmen, n
- business enterprise

Geschäftsveranstaltung, f
- business function
- business event

Geschäftsverkehr, m
- business traffic

Geschäftsviertel, n
- business quarter
- business district

Geschäftsvisum, n
- business visa

Geschäftsvolumen n
  Geschäftsumfang m
- business volume
- volume of business

Geschäftszeit, f
  Geschäftsstunden, f pl
- business hours *pl*
- hours of business *pl*
- office hours *pl*

Geschäftszentrum, n (Einkauf)
→ Einkaufszentrum

Geschäftszentrum, n (generell)
- business center *AE*
- business centre *BE*

Geschäftszielort, m
  Geschäftsziel, n
- business destination

Geschäftszusammenkunft, f
  geschäftliche Zusammenkunft, f
- business gathering

geschält, adj (Ei)
- shelled, adj

geschält, adj (generell)
- peeled, adj

geschälte Mandel, f
- blanched almond

geschältes Ei, n
- shelled egg

geschältes Obst, n
- peeled fruit

geschälte Zwiebel, f
- peeled onion

geschätzte Auslastungsquote f
  geschätzte Belegungsquote f
- estimated occupancy rate

geschätzte Besucherzahl, f
- estimated number of visitors
- estimated visitor number(s)

geschätzte Jahreseinnahmen, f pl
- estimated annual receipts *pl*
- estimated annual revenue
- estimated annual income
- estimated annual takings *pl*

geschätzte Nutzungsdauer des Hotelgebäudes, f
- estimated useful life of the hotel building

geschätzter Beherbergungserlös, m
- estimated accommodation revenue

Geschenk, n
  Präsent, n
- gift
- present

Geschenkboutique, f
- gift boutique
- gift shop

Geschenkeausstellung, f
- collection of presents
- presents collection

Geschenke austauschen
- exchange gifts
- exchange presents

Geschenkgutschein, m
- gift voucher

Geschenkidee, f
- gift idea

Geschenkkorb, m
  Präsentkorb, m
- gift basket

Geschenkladen, m
- gift shop

Geschichtsfan, m
  Geschichtsnarr, m
- history buff

Geschicklichkeitsspiel, n
- game of skill

Geschirr, n (irdenes)
- crockery

Geschirr, n (Küchengeschirr)
- kitchen utensils *pl*
- kitchen things *pl*
- pots and pans *pl*

Geschirr, n (Porzellan)
→ Porzellan

Geschirr, n (Steingut)
→ Steingut

Geschirr abräumen
  Geschirr abdecken
  Geschirr abtragen
- clear away the dishes
- clear the table
- remove the dishes
- carry away the dishes

Geschirraum, m
  Glasraum, m
- pantry

Geschirrersatz, m (irdenes)
  Ersetzung von Geschirr, f
- replacement of crockery

Geschirrschrank, m
♦ dresser
Geschirrspülautomat, m
♦ automatic dishwasher
♦ dishwasher
Geschirrspüle, f (Becken)
Geschirrspülbecken, n
♦ dishwashing sink
Geschirrspüle, f (Raum)
→ Geschirrspülraum
Geschirr spülen
Geschirr abwaschen
♦ do the dishes AE
♦ wash the dishes AE
♦ do the washing-up BE
♦ wash up BE
Geschirrspülmaschine, f
→ Spülmaschine
Geschirrspülraum, m
♦ dishwashing room
♦ washing-up room BE
Geschirrstück, n (Irdenes)
♦ piece of crockery
Geschirrstück, n (Porzellan)
♦ piece of china
Geschirrtuch, n
♦ tea towel AE
♦ dish towel AE
♦ tea-towel BE
♦ tea-cloth BE
♦ dishcloth
Geschirrwäscher, m
Geschirrspüler, m
♦ washer-up BE coll
♦ dishwasher
geschlagenes Ei, n
♦ beaten egg
Geschlecht, n
Sex, m
♦ sex
geschlossen, adj
♦ closed, adj
geschlossen ankommen
♦ arrive in a body
Geschlossen an öffentlichen Feiertagen
(Hinweisschild)
♦ Closed on public holidays
geschlossen bleiben
♦ stay closed
♦ remain closed
geschlossene Gesellschaft f
♦ private party
geschlossener Ball, m
privater Ball, m
Privatball, m
♦ private ball
geschlossener Service, m
→ Bankettservice
geschlossene Speisefolge, f
→ Menü
geschlossene Veranstaltung, f
private Veranstaltung, f
Privatveranstaltung, f
♦ private function
♦ private event
♦ private party
geschlossene Versammlung, f
♦ indoor meeting
geschlossene Vorstellung, f (Theater)
♦ private performance
♦ performance for season-ticket holders

geschlossen für die Öffentlichkeit
♦ closed to the public
geschlossen sein bis auf weiteres
♦ be closed until further notice
geschlossen sein für die Öffentlichkeit
♦ be closed to the public
geschlossen sein wegen Renovierung
wegen Renovierung geschlossen haben
♦ be closed for refurbishment
♦ be closed for renovation
Geschlossen über Weihnachten
(Hinweisschild)
Über Weihnachten geschlossen
♦ Closed over Christmas
Geschlossen wegen Betriebsferien
(Hinweisschild)
♦ Closed for staff vacation AE
♦ Closed for staff holidays BE
Geschmack, m (Aroma)
♦ flavor AE
♦ flavour BE
♦ taste
♦ savor AE
♦ savour BE
Geschmack, m (eines Essens)
♦ taste
Geschmack, m (generell)
Geschmacksrichtung, f
♦ taste
Geschmäcker sind verschieden
♦ tastes differ
Geschmack genießen von etw
♦ savor the taste of s.th. AE
♦ savour the taste of s.th. BE
Geschmack haben
♦ have taste
geschmacklos, adj (ohne Aroma)
♦ flavorless, adj AE
♦ flavourless, adj BE
♦ savorless, adj AE
♦ savourless, adj BE
geschmacklos, adj (Speise, Getränk)
♦ tasteless, adj
♦ insipid, adj
♦ flat, adj
Geschmacksempfindung, f
♦ taste sensation
Geschmacksknospe, f
♦ taste bud AE
♦ taste-bud BE
Geschmacksknospen kitzeln
♦ titillate one's taste buds AE
♦ titillate one's taste-buds BE
Geschmacksrichtung, f
→ Geschmack
Geschmackssache, f
♦ matter of taste
Geschmackssinn, m
♦ sense of taste
♦ taste
Geschmackssinn verlieren
Geschmack verlieren
♦ lose one's palate
Geschmacksverstärker, m
♦ flavor enhancer AE
♦ flavour enhancer BE
Geschmack treffen von jm
js Geschmack treffen
♦ meet s.o.'s taste

Geschmack verlieren an etw
♦ lose one's taste for s.th.
♦ lose one's palate for s.th.
geschmackvoll, adj
♦ tasteful, adj
geschmackvolle Dekoration, f
♦ tasteful decoration
geschmackvolles Ambiente, n
♦ tasteful ambiance
♦ tasteful ambience
geschmackvolles Zimmer, n
♦ tasteful room
geschmackvoll mit Blumen dekoriert
♦ tastefully decorated with flowers
geschmackvoll möbliert, adj
♦ tastefully furnished, adj
♦ furnished in good taste, adj
geschmackvoll möbliertes Zimmer n
♦ tastefully furnished room
geschmackvoll modernisiert, adj
♦ tastefully modernised
♦ tastefully modernized
geschmackvoll modernisiert, adj
♦ tastefully modernised, adj
♦ tastefully modernized, adj
geschmackvoll modernisiertes Zimmer, n
♦ tastefully modernised room
♦ tastefully modernized room
geschmackvoll renoviert, adj
♦ tastefully refurbished, adj
♦ tastefully renovated, adj
geschmackvoll restauriert, adj
♦ tastefully restored, adj
geschmackvoll tapeziert, adj
geschmackvoll gestrichen, adj
♦ tastefully decorated, adj
geschmort, adj
♦ stewed, adj
♦ braised, adj
geschmuggelte Spirituosen, f pl
illegal verkaufte Spirituosen, f pl
♦ bootlegged liquor
geschnitzt, adj
♦ carved, adj
geschnitzte Decke, f
♦ carved ceiling
geschnitzte Figur, f
♦ carved figure
geschnitzter Altar, m
♦ carved altar
Geschoß, n
→ Stockwerk
geschossig, adj
→ stöckig
geschuldete Miete, f
→ fällige Miete
geschulter Gaumen, m
♦ trained palate
geschultes Personal, n
ausgebildetes Personal, n
Fachpersonal, n
♦ trained personnel
♦ trained staff
geschützt, adj
♦ sheltered, adj
geschützte Lage, f
♦ sheltered location
♦ sheltered position
♦ sheltered situation
♦ sheltered setting

geschützter Ort

geschützter Ort, m
 ◆ sheltered place
geschützter Stellplatz, m
 (Camping)
 ◆ sheltered pitch
geschützte Terrasse f
 ◆ sheltered terrace
geschützt sein gegen etw
 abgesichert sein gegen etw
 ◆ be guaranteed against s.th.
Geschwindigkeitsbegrenzung, f
 Tempolimit, n
 ◆ speed limit
gesegneten Appetit haben
 ◆ have a good appetite
 ◆ have a hearty appetite
 ◆ eat well
Geselle, m
 Handwerksgeselle, m
 ◆ journeyman
Gesellenherberge, f
 Herberge f
 Gasthaus n
 ◆ house of call
gesellig, adj
 ◆ sociable, adj
gesellige Atmosphäre, f
 ◆ sociable atmosphere
geselligen Abend abhalten
 ◆ hold a social evening
geselliger Abend, m
 ◆ social evening
geselliger Urlaub, m
 gesellige Ferien, pl
 ◆ sociable vacation AE
 ◆ sociable holiday BE
geselliges Zusammensein, n
 geselliges Beisammensein, n
 ◆ social get-together
gesellig sein
 ◆ be sociable
Gesellschaft, f (Gäste)
 ◆ company
Gesellschaft, f (Staat)
 ◆ society
Gesellschaften bis zu 90 Personen bewirten
 ◆ cater for parties of up to 90 persons
Gesellschaft genießen von jm
 ◆ enjoy the company of s.o.
Gesellschaft haben
 Besuch haben
 ◆ have company
Gesellschaft leisten jm beim Frühstück
 frühstücken mit jm
 ◆ join s.o. for breakfast
Gesellschaft leisten jm beim Kaffee
 Kaffee trinken mit jm
 ◆ join s.o. for coffee
 ◆ take coffee with s.o.
Gesellschaft leisten jm beim Mittagessen
 zu Mittag essen mit jm
 ◆ join s.o. for lunch
 ◆ join s.o. for luncheon
gesellschaftlicher Anlaß, m
 ◆ social occasion
gesellschaftliches Ereignis, n
 Gesellschaftsereignis, n
 ◆ society event
gesellschaftliches Zentrum, n
 ◆ social center AE
 ◆ social centre BE

gesellschaftliche Veranstaltung, f
 Gesellschaftsveranstaltung, f
 ◆ social function
 ◆ social event
gesellschaftliche Veranstaltungen, f pl
 gesellschaftliche Aktivitäten, f pl
 ◆ social activities pl
Gesellschaftsabend, m
 Abendfest, n
 ◆ evening
 ◆ evening party
 ◆ soirée
 ◆ soiree AE
Gesellschaftsausflug, m
 (ins Grüne)
 Gruppenausflug m
 ◆ party outing
 ◆ social outing
Gesellschaftskalender, m
 gesellschaftlicher Kalender, m
 ◆ social calendar
Gesellschaftskleid, n
 ◆ evening dress
Gesellschaftsleben, n
 gesellschaftliches Leben, n
 ◆ social life
Gesellschaftsprogramm, n
 → Rahmenprogramm
Gesellschaftsraum, m
 Gesellschaftszimmer n
 ◆ lounge
 ◆ public room
Gesellschaftsreise, f
 organisierte Reise, f
 ◆ organised tour
 ◆ organized tour
Gesellschaftsreisen, n
 Gesellschaftsreiseverkehr, m
 organisiertes Reisen, n
 organisierter Reiseverkehr, m
 ◆ organised travel
 ◆ organized travel
Gesellschaftsspiel, n
 ◆ parlor game AE
 ◆ parlour game BE
Gesellschaftsveranstaltung, f
 gesellschaftliche Veranstaltung, f
 ◆ social event
 ◆ social function
gesetzliche Haftpflicht, f
 gesetzliche Haftung, f
 ◆ legal liability
gesetzliche Miete, f
 ◆ legal rent
gesetzlicher Feiertag, m
 ◆ statutory holiday BE
 ◆ legal holiday
 ◆ public holiday BE
 ◆ official holiday
gesetzlicher Urlaub, m
 ◆ legal vacation AE
 ◆ legal holiday BE
gesetzliches Zahlungsmittel, n
 ◆ legal tender
 ◆ lawful money
Gesichtsbehandlung, f med
 ◆ facial treatment med
Gesichtshandtuch n
 ◆ face towel
Gesichtsmaske, f
 ◆ facial masque

302

Gesichtsmassage, f
 ◆ facial massage
Gesindel ins Haus bringen
 ◆ bring riff-raff into one's house
Gesöff, n derog
 ◆ poison derog
 ◆ swill derog
 ◆ dishwater AE derog
 ◆ dish-water BE derog
 ◆ rotgut AE derog
gesondert aufgeführt, adj
 ◆ specially indicated, adj
gesondert berechnen jm
 ◆ charge s.o. extra
gesondert servieren etw
 ◆ serve s.th. separately
 ◆ serve s.th. extra
gesondert zahlen für etw
 etw extra bezahlen
 ◆ pay for s.th. separately
 ◆ pay for s.th. extra
 ◆ pay extra for s.th.
gesotten, adj
 → gekocht
Gespann, n
 Pkw mit Wohnwagen, m
 ◆ outfit
gespannte Atmosphäre, f
 angespannte Atmosphäre f
 ◆ strained atmosphere
gesperrt (für etw), adj
 gesperrt (für jn), adj
 ◆ closed (to sth.), adj
 ◆ closed (to s.o.), adj
gespickt, adj
 ◆ larded, adj
gesponsert, adj
 ◆ sponsored, adj
gesponserte Essensveranstaltung, f
 ◆ sponsored meal event
 ◆ sponsored meal function
gesponserte Reise, f
 ◆ sponsored journey
 ◆ sponsored tour
 ◆ sponsored trip
gesponserte Tournee, f
 ◆ sponsored tour
gesponserte Wanderung, f
 ◆ sponsored walk
 ◆ sponsored hike
Gespräche ausrichten (als Gastgeber)
 Gastgeber sein bei Gesprächen
 ◆ host talks
Gesprächsrunde, f
 ◆ discussion meeting
Gespür für Gastlichkeit, n
 Gefühl für Gastlichkeit, n
 ◆ sense of hospitality
gespurte Langlaufloipe, f
 gespurte Loipe, f
 ◆ prepared cross-country ski trail
 ◆ prepared cross-country trail
gespurte Loipe, f
 ◆ prepared ski track
 ◆ prepared ski trail
gestaffelte Ferien, pl
 gestaffelter Urlaub, m
 Staffelferien, pl
 Staffelurlaub, m
 ◆ staggered vacation AE
 ◆ staggered holidays BE pl

gestaffelter Preis, m
  Staffelpreis, m
  ♦ staggered price
  ♦ staggered rate
Gestalter, m
  Designer, m
  ♦ designer
Gestaltung der Speisekarte, f
  → Speisekartengestaltung
Gestaltungsmuseum, n
  ♦ design museum
gestärkt mit etw
  (z.B. Speisen, Getränke)
  ♦ fortified with s.th.
gestärkt sein von etw
  (durch Speisen oder Getränke)
  ♦ be fortified by s.th.
gestärkt von etw
  (durch Speisen oder Getränke)
  ♦ fortified by s.th.
Geste der Anerkennung, f
  ♦ gesture of appreciation
Gestehungskosten, pl
  Wareneinsatz plus produktive Löhne, m
  ♦ prime cost
gestern, adv
  ♦ yesterday, adv
gestern abend, adv
  ♦ yesterday evening, adv
gestern morgen, adv
  gestern früh, adv
  ♦ yesterday morning, adv
gestern nachmittag, adv
  ♦ yesterday afternoon, adv
gestiegene Energiekosten, pl
  ♦ increased energy costs pl
  ♦ increased energy cost
gestillter Durst, m
  ♦ quenched thirst
gestoßen, adj gastr
  ♦ crushed, adj gastr
gestoßenes Eis, n
  ♦ crushed ice
gestreift, adj
  ♦ striped, adj
gestreifter Teppich, m
  ♦ striped carpet
gestreifte Tapete, f
  ♦ striped wallpaper
  ♦ striped paper
gestrichen, adj
  tapeziert, adj
  ♦ decorated, adj
gesuchte Lage f
  ♦ sought-after location
gesuchte Wohnlage f
  ♦ sought-after residential location
gesülzt, adj
  gesulzt, adj
  ♦ jellied, adj
gesülzt, adv
  gesülzt, adv
  ♦ in jelly, adv
Gesundbrunnen, m
  → Jungbrunnen
gesunde Entspannung, f
  ♦ healthy relaxation
gesunde Ernährung, f
  ♦ sound nutrition
gesunde Kost, f
  bekömmliche Kost, f

  ♦ wholesome diet
  ♦ wholesome fare
  ♦ healthy fare
gesunde Landkost, f
  ♦ sound country fare
  ♦ sound country diet
gesunde Luft, f
  ♦ healthy air
gesunde Nahrung, f
  ♦ healthy fare
  ♦ wholesome diet
  ♦ healthy food
  ♦ wholesome food
gesunden Appetit haben
  ♦ have a healthy appetite
gesunder Appetit, m
  ♦ healthy appetite
gesündere Kost, f
  ♦ healthier fare
gesunder Imbiß, m
  ♦ healthy snack
gesunder Ort, m
  heilsamer Ort, m
  ♦ salubrious place
gesundes Essen, n (Aktivität)
  ♦ healthy eating
gesundes Essen, n (Kost)
  ♦ healthy food
gesundes Gericht, n
  ♦ healthy dish
gesundes Klima, n
  ♦ healthy climate
gesundes Mahl, n
  gesunde Mahlzeit f
  ♦ healthy meal
  ♦ sound meal
gesunde Sonnenbräune, f
  ♦ healthy suntan AE
  ♦ healthy sun-tan BE
gesunde Umwelt, f
  ♦ healthy environment
Gesundheit, f
  ♦ health
Gesundheitsabteilung, f
  ♦ health department
Gesundheitsanlage, f
  Gesundheitskomplex, m
  ♦ health complex
Gesundheitsannehmlichkeit, f
  ♦ health amenity
Gesundheitsapostel, m humor
  ♦ health freak
  ♦ keep-fit freak
  ♦ health faddist
Gesundheitsbar, f
  ♦ health bar
Gesundheitsbehörde, f
  ♦ health authorities pl
Gesundheitsberater, m
  ♦ health consultant
Gesundheitsberatung, f
  ♦ health consultation
Gesundheitsberatung geben
  ♦ give health advice
Gesundheitsbestimmungen, f pl
  Gesundheitsvorschriften, f pl
  ♦ public health regulations pl
  ♦ health regulations pl
Gesundheitsbetrieb, m
  ♦ health establishment

gesundheitsbewußt, adj
  ♦ health-conscious, adj
gesundheitsbewußter Gast, m
  ♦ health-conscious guest
Gesundheitsbewußtsein, n
  ♦ health consciousness
  ♦ health awareness
Gesundheitsclub, m
  ♦ health club
Gesundheitsclub auf dem neuesten Stand der Technik
  ♦ state-of-the-art health club
Gesundheitsclubdorf, n
  ♦ health club village
Gesundheitsclubleiter, m
  ♦ health club manager
Gesundheitseinrichtung, f
  ♦ health facility
Gesundheitsfanatiker, m
  ♦ health fanatic
  ♦ health freak
  ♦ health maniac
Gesundheitsfarm, f
  Health Farm, f
  ♦ health farm
Gesundheitsfarmtag, m
  ♦ health farm day
Gesundheitsfarmwoche, f
  ♦ health farm week
Gesundheitsferien, pl
  Gesundheitsurlaub, m
  ♦ health holiday BE
  ♦ health vacation AE
Gesundheitsferiengast, m
  Gesundheitsurlauber, m
  ♦ health holidaymaker BE
  ♦ health vacationer AE
Gesundheitsformalitäten, f pl
  ♦ health formalities pl
Gesundheitsfürsorge, f
  Gesundheitswesen, n
  ♦ health care
Gesundheitsgefahr, f
  ♦ health danger
Gesundheitsgründe, m pl
  ♦ health reasons pl
Gesundheitshotel n
  ♦ health hotel
Gesundheitsklinik, f
  ♦ health clinic
Gesundheitskontrolle, f
  ♦ health control
Gesundheitskost, f
  ♦ health diet
Gesundheitskur, f
  Gesundheitsbehandlung, f
  Kur, f
  ♦ health treatment
Gesundheitskurzurlaub, m
  ♦ health break
gesundheitsorientiert, adj
  ♦ health-oriented, adj AE
  ♦ health-orientated, adj BE
gesundheitsorientierter Urlaub, m
  gesundheitsorientierte Ferien, pl
  ♦ health-oriented vacation AE
  ♦ health-orientated holiday BE
Gesundheitspauschale, f
  ♦ health package
Gesundheitsproblem, n
  ♦ health problem

Gesundheitsprodukt

Gesundheitsprodukt, n
  ♦ health product
Gesundheitsprogramm, n
  ♦ health program *AE*
  ♦ health programme *BE*
Gesundheitsraum, m
  ♦ health room
Gesundheitsrisiko, n
  ♦ health hazard
  ♦ health risk
Gesundheitsstudio, n
  ♦ health studio
Gesundheitssuppe, f
  ♦ health soup
Gesundheitstag, m
  ♦ health day
Gesundheitstourismus, m
  ♦ health tourism
Gesundheitstourist, m
  ♦ health tourist
Gesundheits- und Fitneßeinrichtung, f
  ♦ health and fitness facility
Gesundheits- und Freizeitzentrum, n
  ♦ health and leisure center *AE*
  ♦ health and leisure centre *BE*
Gesundheitsurlaub, m
  Gesundheitsferien, pl
  ♦ health vacation *AE*
  ♦ health holiday *BE*
Gesundheitsurlauber, m
  Gesundheitsferiengast, m
  ♦ health vacationer *AE*
  ♦ health holidaymaker *BE*
Gesundheitsverbesserung, f
  Gesundheitssteigerung, f
  ♦ health improvement
Gesundheitsvorkehrungen, f pl
  ♦ health precautions *pl*
Gesundheitsvorschrift, f
  ♦ health requirement
Gesundheitswiederherstellung, f
  Wiederherstellung der Gesundheit, f
  ♦ health restoration
  ♦ restoration of one's health
  ♦ restoration of s.o.'s health
Gesundheitswoche, f
  ♦ health week
Gesundheitswochenendkurzurlaub, m
  ♦ health weekend break
Gesundheitszentrum n
  Gesundheitscenter n
  ♦ health center *AE*
  ♦ health centre *BE*
Gesundheitszeugnis, n
  ♦ health certificate
Gesundheit wiederherstellen
  ♦ restore one's health
  ♦ restore s.o.'s health
gesund schlafen
  ♦ sleep soundly
gesund und munter, adj
  ♦ safe and sound, adj
  ♦ hale and hearty, adj
gesund und munter zurückkommen
  gesund und munter zurückkehren
  ♦ return safe and sound
getäfelt, adj
  holzgetäfelt, adj
  ♦ panelled, adj
  ♦ paneled, adj *AE*

getäfelte Bar, f
  ♦ panelled bar
  ♦ paneled bar *AE*
getäfelte Decke, f
  ♦ panelled ceiling
  ♦ paneled ceiling *AE*
getäfeltes Zimmer, n
  ♦ panelled room
  ♦ paneled room *AE*
getäfelte Wand, f
  ♦ panelled wall
  ♦ paneled wall *AE*
geteert, adj
  ♦ tarred, adj
getippte Speisekarte f
  ♦ typed menu
getoastet, adj
  geröstet, adj
  ♦ toasted, adj *BE*
  ♦ grilled, adj *AE*
Getränk, n (außer Wasser)
  ♦ beverage *form or humor*
Getränk, n (generell)
  ♦ drink
Getränk anbieten jm
  etwas zu trinken anbieten jm
  ♦ offer s.o. a drink
  ♦ offer a drink to s.o.
Getränk auf das Zimmer bringen
  ♦ bring a drink to the room
Getränk aufdrängen jm
  ♦ press a drink on s.o.
Getränk auf Kosten des Hauses, n
  ♦ drink on the house
Getränk auf Kosten des Hauses spendieren jm
  ♦ give s.o. a drink on the house
Getränk aufmöbeln
  (z.T. durch Drogen)
  ♦ doctor a drink
  ♦ doctor a beverage
Getränk aufzwingen jm
  (alkoholisch)
  ♦ ply s.o. with a drink
Getränk bekommen
  ♦ get a drink
Getränk bestellen
  ♦ order a drink
  ♦ order a beverage
  ♦ order a refreshment
Getränk bezahlen
  Getränk zahlen
  ♦ pay for a beverage
  ♦ pay for a drink
Getränkeabteilung, f
  ♦ beverage department
  ♦ drinks department
Getränkeangabe, f
  ♦ beverage specification
Getränkeangebot, n (Gegensatz zu Nachfrage)
  ♦ beverage supply
  ♦ supply of beverages
  ♦ drinks supply
  ♦ supply of drinks
Getränkeangebot, n (Palette)
  ♦ range of drinks (offered)
  ♦ range of beverages (offered)
Getränkeart, f
  ♦ beverage type
  ♦ type of beverage
  ♦ drinks type
  ♦ type of drinks

Getränkeart, f
  ♦ type of drink
  ♦ type of beverage
  ♦ drink type
  ♦ beverage type
Getränkeartikel, m
  ♦ beverage item
  ♦ drink(s) item
Getränkeaufwendungen, f pl
  ♦ beverage expenses *pl*
  ♦ drinks expenses *pl*
Getränkeausgabe, f (Aktivität)
  ♦ dispensing drinks
  ♦ dispensing beverages
Getränkeausgabe, f (Aufwand)
  ♦ expenditure on beverages
  ♦ expenditure on drinks
  ♦ beverages expenditure
  ♦ expenses for beverages *AE*
Getränkeausgabe, f (Raum)
  (den Gästen nicht zugänglich)
  ♦ dispense bar
Getränkeausschank, m (Kiosk)
  ♦ refreshment kiosk
Getränkeausschank, m (Tresen)
  Getränketresen, m
  Getränketheke, f
  ♦ beverage counter
  ♦ drinks counter
  ♦ bar
Getränkeausschank, m (Verkauf)
  → Verkauf von Getränken
Getränkeauswahl, f
  Auswahl an Getränken, f
  ♦ choice of drinks
  ♦ choice of beverages
  ♦ selection of drinks
  ♦ selection of beverages
Getränkeautomat, m
  Ausschankautomat, m
  ♦ automatic drinks dispenser
  ♦ drink(s) dispenser
  ♦ drink vending machine
  ♦ drink(s) machine
  ♦ beverage dispenser
Getränkeautomat, m (in Gastzimmer)
  ♦ bell captain
Getränkebar, f
  Trinkbar f
  ♦ drinks' bar
  ♦ drinking bar
  ♦ wet bar
Getränkebereich, m (abstrakt)
  Getränkesektor m
  ♦ beverage sector
  ♦ drinks sector
Getränkebereich, m (konkret)
  ♦ beverage area
  ♦ drinks area
Getränkebestellung, f
  ♦ drink order
  ♦ drinks order
  ♦ ordering a drink
  ♦ ordering drinks
Getränkebestellung aufgeben
  ♦ place a drinks order
Getränkebetrieb, m
  ♦ beverage establishment
  ♦ beverage operation
  ♦ drinks establishment
  ♦ drinks operation

Getränkebudget, n
  Getränkeetat, m
  ◆ beverage budget
  ◆ drinks budget
Getränkebüfett, n
  ◆ drinks buffet
Getränkedose, f
  ◆ drink can
Getränkeeinkauf, m
  ◆ beverage purchase
  ◆ purchase of beverages
  ◆ purchasing beverages
  ◆ drinks purchase
  ◆ purchase of drinks
Getränkeeinrichtung, f
  ◆ beverage facility
Getränkeeinzelhandel, m
  ◆ beverage retailing company
Getränkeerlös, m
  ◆ beverage revenue
  ◆ beverages revenue
  ◆ drinks revenue
Getränkeetikett, n
  ◆ beverage label
  ◆ drink label
Getränkefirma, f
  ◆ beverage company
  ◆ beverage firm
  ◆ drinks company
Getränke fließen in Strömen
  ◆ drinks flow freely
  ◆ beverages flow freely
Getränkefolge, f
  ◆ sequence of beverages
  ◆ sequence of drinks
Getränkeführer, m
  ◆ drinks guide
Getränke gehen auf das Haus
  ◆ drinks are on the house
Getränke gehen auf mich
  ◆ drinks are on me
Getränkegeld, n
  Geld für (die) Getränke, n
  Trinkgeld, n
  ◆ drinks money
  ◆ drink money
Getränkegeschäft, n
  ◆ beverage business
  ◆ drinks business
Getränkegroßhändler, m
  ◆ drinks wholesaler
  ◆ beverages wholesaler
Getränkegutschein, m
  Getränkebon, m
  ◆ beverage voucher
  ◆ drink voucher
  ◆ drinks voucher
Getränkehersteller, m
  ◆ beverage manufacturer
  ◆ drinks manufacturer
Getränkeherstellung, f
  ◆ beverage manufacturing
  ◆ beverage production
  ◆ drinks manufacturing
  ◆ drinks production
Getränkeindustrie, f
  Getränkebranche, f
  ◆ drinks industry
  ◆ beverage industry
Getränkekalkulation, f
  ◆ calculation of beverages

  ◆ calculation of drinks
  ◆ calculating beverages
  ◆ calculating drinks
Getränkekarte, f
  ◆ beverage list
  ◆ list of beverages
  ◆ drinks list
  ◆ list of drinks
Getränkekategorie, f
  ◆ beverage category
  ◆ drinks category
Getränkekauf, m
  → Getränkeeinkauf
Getränkekeller, m
  → Weinkeller
Getränkekellner m
  ◆ wine waiter
  ◆ cocktail waiter
Getränkekonsum, m
  ◆ consumption of drinks
  ◆ consumption of beverages
Getränkekontrollbuch, n
  ◆ beverage control book
  ◆ drinks control book
Getränkekontrolle, f
  ◆ beverage control
Getränkekonzern, m
  ◆ drinks group
  ◆ beverage group
Getränkekonzession, f
  ◆ beverage license
  ◆ beverage licence
  ◆ drinks license
  ◆ drinks licence
Getränkekosten, pl
  ◆ beverage costs *pl*
  ◆ beverage cost
  ◆ drinks costs *pl*
  ◆ drinks cost
  ◆ cost of beverages
Getränkeladen, m
  Getränkegeschäft, n
  ◆ beverage store *AE*
  ◆ drinks shop *BE*
Getränkelager, n
  ◆ drinks store
  ◆ beverage store
Getränkelagerraum, m
  ◆ drinks storage room
  ◆ beverage storage room
Getränkelieferant, m
  ◆ drinks supplier
Getränkeliste f
  → Getränkekarte
Getränkelöffel, m
  ◆ beverage spoon
Getränkemanagement, n
  Getränkewirtschaft, f
  Getränkeverwaltung, f
  ◆ beverage management
  ◆ drinks management
Getränkemanager, m
  ◆ beverage manager
  ◆ drinks manager
Getränkemarketing, n
  ◆ beverage marketing
  ◆ drinks marketing
Getränkemarkt, m
  ◆ drinks market
  ◆ beverage market

Getränkemixer, m
  ◆ beverage mixer
Getränke nicht inbegriffen
  ◆ Drinks not included
  ◆ Not including drinks
  ◆ Drinks extra
getränkeorientiert, adj
  ◆ beverage-oriented, adj *AE*
  ◆ drinks-oriented, adj *AE*
  ◆ beverage-orientated, adj *BE*
  ◆ drinks-orientated, adj *BE*
getränkeorientiertes Hotel n
  ◆ drink-oriented hotel *AE*
  ◆ drink-orientated hotel *BE*
Getränkepreis, m
  ◆ beverage price
  ◆ price of a beverage
  ◆ drink price
  ◆ price of a drink
Getränkeproduktion, f
  Getränkeherstellung, f
  ◆ beverage production
  ◆ drinks production
  ◆ producing of beverages
  ◆ producing drinks
Getränkeproduzent, m
  Getränkehersteller, m
  ◆ beverage producer
  ◆ drinks producer
Getränkequalität, f
  ◆ beverage quality
  ◆ drinks quality
Getränkequalitätsstandard, m
  ◆ beverage quality standard
  ◆ drinks quality standard
Getränkeraum, m
  ◆ beverage room
  ◆ drinks room
Getränkerechnung, f
  ◆ beverage check *AE*
  ◆ beverage bill
  ◆ drink(s) check *AE*
  ◆ drink(s) bill
Getränkerezeptur, f
  Getränkerezept, n
  ◆ drink recipe
  ◆ beverage recipe
Getränkerohertrag, m
  ◆ gross beverage(s) income
  ◆ gross drinks income
  ◆ gross beverage(s) revenue
  ◆ gross drinks revenue
Getränkeschieberei, f
  illegaler Getränkehandel, m
  ◆ drinks racket
Getränkeschrank, m
  ◆ drinks cabinet
  ◆ drinks cupboard
  ◆ bell captain *BE*
Getränkeservice, m
  Getränkedienst m
  ◆ beverage service
  ◆ drinks service
  ◆ drink service
Getränkeservicepersonal, n
  ◆ beverage service staff
  ◆ beverage service personnel
  ◆ drinks service staff
  ◆ drinks service personnel
Getränke sind gratis
  ◆ Drinks are complimentary

Getränkesorte

Getränkesorte, f
- sort of drink
- sort of beverage

Getränkespender, m
(Gerät)
- drinks dispenser
- drink dispenser

Getränkestand, m
- beverage stand
- beverage stall
- drinks stand
- drinks stall

Getränkesteuer f
- beverage tax

getränkesteuerfrei, adj
- exempt from beverage tax, adj

Getränkesteuer inbegriffen
- beverage tax included
- including beverage tax

getränkesteuerpflichtig, adj
- subject to beverage tax, adj

getränkesteuerpflichtige Erlöse, m pl
- revenue subject to beverage tax

getränkesteuerpflichtiges Getränk, n
- drink subject to beverage tax
- drink carrying beverage tax

Getränketablett, n
- beverage tray

Getränketerrasse, f
- drinks terrace
- drinks patio

Getränketrend, m
- beverage trend
- drinks trend

Getränkeumsatz, m
- beverage sales pl
- drinks sales pl
- drink sales pl
- beverage turnover
- drinks turnover

Getränkeumsatz pro Gedeck, m
Getränkeumsatz je Gedeck, m
- beverage sales per cover pl
- drink sales per cover pl
- beverage turnover per cover
- drinks turnover per cover

Getränkeverbrauch, m
Getränkekonsum, m
Getränkeverzehr, m
- beverage consumption
- consumption of beverages
- drink consumption
- consumption of drinks

Getränkeverkauf, m
Verkauf von Getränken, m
Ausschank, m
- sale of drinks
- sale of beverages
- selling beverages
- selling drinks

Getränkeverwaltung, f
Getränkemanagement, n
- drinks management
- beverage management

Getränkeverzehr m
→ Getränkeverbrauch

Getränkevorrat, m
- beverage stock
- stock of beverages
- drinks stock
- stock of drinks

Getränkevorschlag, m
- beverage suggestion
- drink suggestion

Getränkewagen, m
(z.B. im Restaurant)
- drinks' cart AE
- drinks' trolley BE

Getränke werden extra berechnet
- drinks are charged for separately
- beverages are charged for separately

Getränkezelt, n
- beverage tent
- drinks tent

Getränkezusammensetzung, f ökon
Getränkemix, m
- beverage mix

Getränkezwang, m
- obligation to order drinks
- obligation to order beverages

Getränk genießen
Drink genießen
- enjoy a beverage
- enjoy a drink

Getränk hinunterstürzen
- down a drink

Getränk inbegriffen
- drink included
- beverage included
- b.i.

Getränk kaufen
- buy a drink
- buy a beverage

Getränk konsumieren
- consume a drink
- consume a beverage

Getränk mixen
Getränk mischen
- mix a drink

Getränk nach dem Essen, n
Digestif m
- after-dinner drink
- digestif FR

Getränk ohne Zutaten, n
Getränk pur, n
unverdünntes Getränk, n
- straight drink

Getränk probieren
Getränk versuchen
- try a drink
- try a beverage

Getränk selbst bezahlen
- pay for one's drink

Getränk servieren
Getränk verabreichen
- serve a beverage
- serve a drink
- serve a refreshment

Getränk spendieren jm
- buy s.o. a drink

Getränk trinken
- drink a beverage
- have a drink

Getränk verabreichen
→ Getränk servieren

Getränk verkaufen
- sell a drink
- sell a beverage

Getränk vor dem Essen, n (abends)
Aperitif, m
- pre-dinner drink
- before-dinner drink
- aperitif

Getränk vor dem Essen, n (mittags)
Aperitif, m
- pre-luncheon drink
- pre-lunch drink
- before-lunch drink
- aperitif

Getränk vorschlagen
- suggest a drink
- suggest a beverage

Getränk wird Sie erfrischen
- drink will refresh you

Getränk zahlen
Getränk bezahlen
- pay for a drink
- pay for a beverage

Getränk zubereiten
- prepare a drink
- prepare a beverage

Getränk zum Essen, n
Getränk beim Essen, n
- with-dinner drink

Getreidekost, f
(bes. zum Frühstück)
- cereals pl

getrennt, adj
separat, adj
- divided, adj
- separate, adj

getrennt abreisen
- leave separately

getrennt ankommen
- arrive separately

getrennte Kasse, f
(bei gemeinsamem Essen etc)
- separate account
- Dutch treat

getrennte Kasse machen
(bei Essen, Einladung etc.)
Kosten teilen
- go Dutch coll

getrennten Urlaub machen
- take separate vacations AE
- take separate holidays BE

getrenntes Bett, n
→ separates Bett

getrenntes Schlafzimmer, n
separates Schlafzimmer, n
separater Schlafraum, m
- separate bedroom

getrennte Toilette, f
separate Toilette f
- separate toilet

getrennte Zimmer buchen
getrennte Zimmer bestellen
- book separate rooms

getrennte Zimmer haben
- have separate rooms

getrennt schlafen
- sleep apart

getrocknet, adj
- dried, adj

getrocknete Kräuter, n pl
- dried herbs pl

getrockneter Salbei, m
- dried sage

getrockneter Thymian, m
- dried thyme

getrüffelt, adj
- truffled, adj

Getto, n
Ghetto, n
♦ ghetto
geübter Skiläufer, m
♦ proficient skier
geviertelt, adj gastr
♦ quartered, adj gastr
Gewächshaus, n
♦ greenhouse
♦ conservatory BE
gewählte Hotelkategorie, f
♦ selected hotel category
♦ chosen hotel category
gewaltsame Auflösung eines Treffens, f
Sprengung einer Versammlung, f
♦ breakup of a meeting
geweckt werden
♦ be waked
♦ have a call
Gewehr, n
♦ shotgun
Gewerbeausstellung, f
→ Fachausstellung
Gewerbebetrieb, m
gewerblicher Betrieb, m
♦ commercial operation
♦ commercial establishment
Gewerberaum, m
→ gewerblicher Raum
Gewerbeschau, f
→ Fachschau
Gewerbesteuer, f
♦ trade tax
gewerblich, adj
gewerbsmäßig, adj
kommerziell, adj
♦ commercial, adj
gewerbliche Beherbergung, f
gewerbliche Unterkunft, f
♦ commercial lodging AE
♦ commercial accommodation
gewerbliche Gastronomie, f
♦ commercial catering BE
♦ commercial foodservice AE
gewerbliche Immobilie, f
Gewerbeimmobilie, f
♦ commercial property
gewerblicher Anbieter, m
♦ commercial supplier
♦ commercial provider
gewerblicher Beherbergungssektor, m
gewerblicher Beherbergungsbereich, m
♦ commercial lodging sector AE
♦ commercial accommodation sector
gewerblicher Betreiber, m
gewerblicher Veranstalter, m
♦ commercial operator
gewerblicher Campingplatz, m
gewerbsmäßig betriebener Campingplatz m
♦ commercial campsite
♦ commercial campground AE
♦ commercial camping site BE
♦ commercial camping ground BE
gewerblicher Gast, m
♦ commercial guest
gewerblicher Gastronomiebetrieb, m
♦ commercial foodservice establishment AE
♦ commercial foodservice operation BE
gewerblicher Mieter, m
♦ commercial tenant

gewerblicher Platz, m
(Camping)
♦ commercial site
gewerblicher Preis, m
♦ commercial price
♦ commercial rate
gewerblicher Raum, m
Gewerberaum, m
♦ commercial room
gewerblicher Unterkunftsanbieter, m
gewerblicher Beherbergungsanbieter, m
♦ commercial accommodation supplier
gewerblicher Unterkunftsbereich, m
gewerblicher Beherbergungsbereich, m
♦ commercial accommodation sector
♦ commercial lodging sector AE
gewerbliches Anwesen, n
♦ commercial premises pl
gewerbliches Bett, n
♦ commercial bed
gewerbliches Dienstleistungsunternehmen, n
♦ commercial service enterprise
gewerbliches Fremdenverkehrsunternehmen, n
gewerbliches Tourismusunternehmen, n
♦ commercial tourism enterprise
♦ commercial tourist enterprise
gewerbliches Hotel, n
gewerbsmäßig betriebenes Hotel n
♦ commercial hotel
gewerbliches Restaurant, n
gewerbsmäßig betriebenes Restaurant n
♦ commercial restaurant
gewerbliche Unterkunft, f
gewerbliche Beherbergung, f
♦ commercial accommodation
♦ commercial lodging AE
gewerbsmäßiger Caterer m
♦ institutional caterer
♦ industrial caterer
Gewerkschaft, f
♦ labor union AE
♦ trade union BE
Gewerkschaftsheim, n
♦ trade union hostel
Gewerkschaftshotel, n
♦ trade union hotel
Gewerkschaftskongreß, m
♦ Trades Union Congress BE
♦ TUC BE
Gewichtheben, n
♦ weight lifting
Gewichtheber, m
♦ weight lifter
Gewichtsobergrenze, f
Gewichtsgrenze, f
♦ weight limit
Gewichtsreduzierung, f
♦ weight reduction
Gewichtstraining, n
♦ weight training
Gewinn, m
Profit m
♦ profit
Gewinn abwerfen
Profit abwerfen
♦ yield a profit
Gewinnaufschlag, m
Aufschlag, m
♦ markup
gewinnbringend, adj
♦ profit-earning, adj

♦ revenue-earning, adj
♦ moneymaking, adj
gewinnen an Beliebtheit
gewinnen an Popularität
♦ win in popularity
gewinnen etw bei einer Verlosung
♦ win s.th. in a draw
gewinnen etw in einer Tombola
♦ win s.th. in a raffle
Gewinner eines Wettbewerbs, m
♦ winner of a competition
Gewinn machen
Profit machen
♦ make a profit
Gewinn nach Steuern, m
Gewinn nach Steuer, m
♦ profit after taxes
♦ after-tax profit
♦ profit after tax
Gewinnpotential, n
Profitpotential, n
♦ profit potential
Gewinn pro Gast, m
♦ profit per guest
Gewinn pro Übernachtung, m
♦ profit per night
Gewinn pro Zimmer, m
♦ profit per room
Gewinnschwelle, f
Rentabilitätsschwelle, f
Rentabilitätsgrenze, f
♦ break-even point
Gewinnschwelle berechnen
♦ calculate the break-even point
Gewinnschwelle erreichen
Rentabilitätsschwelle erreichen
Rentabilitätsgrenze erreichen
♦ reach the break-even point
Gewinnschwellenanalyse, f
♦ break-even analysis
Gewinnschwellendiagramm, n
♦ break-even chart
Gewinnschwellenpreis, m
♦ break-even price
♦ break-even rate
Gewinnschwellenumsatz, m
♦ break-even sales pl
♦ break-even turnover
Gewinnspanne, f
♦ profit margin
♦ margin
Gewinnsträhne, f
(Spielkasino)
♦ winning streak
Gewinn- und Verlustrechnung, f
GuV, f
♦ statement of income and expenses AE
♦ profit and loss statement AE
♦ profit and loss account BE
gewohnheitsmäßiger Reisender, m
♦ habitual traveller
♦ habitual traveler AE
gewohnheitsmäßiger Spieler, m
♦ habitual gambler
gewohnheitsmäßiger Trinker, m
Gewohnheitstrinker, m
♦ habitual drinker
♦ habitual drunkard
gewöhnliche Kost, f
♦ ordinary fare
♦ ordinary food

gewöhnlicher Service

gewöhnlicher Service, m
  (negativ)
  ♦ ordinary service
gewohnte Kost, f
  ♦ one's accustomed diet
gewohntes Appartement, n
  ♦ usual apartment
gewohnte Suite, f
  ♦ usual suite
gewohntes Zimmer, n
  ♦ usual room
gewohnte Umgebung, f
  ♦ one's accustomed environment
Gewölbe, n
  ♦ vault
Gewölbedecke, f
  ♦ vaulted ceiling
Gewölbekeller, m
  ♦ vaulted cellar
Gewölbesaal, m
  ♦ vaulted hall
Gewölbespeisesaal, m
  ♦ vaulted dining room
Gewölbezimmer, n
  ♦ vaulted room
gewünscht, adj
  ♦ requested, adj
gewünschte Aufenthaltsdauer, f
  ♦ requested length of stay
gewünschte Aufenthaltsdauer angeben
  gewünschte Aufenthaltsdauer nennen
  ♦ state the requested length of stay
  ♦ indicate the requested length of stay
gewünschten Garagenplatz reservieren
  ♦ reserve the requested garage space
  ♦ reserve the requested garaging space
gewünschten Parkplatz reservieren (für 1 Auto)
  ♦ reserve the requested parking place
  ♦ reserve the requested parking space
  ♦ reserve the requested parking lot *AE*
gewünschte Parkmöglichkeit, f
  ♦ type of parking requested
gewünschter Sitzplatz, m
  gewünschter Platz, m
  gewünschter Sitz, m
  ♦ requested seat
gewünschter Termin, m
  gewünschtes Datum, n
  ♦ desired date
gewünschtes Appartement, n
  ♦ requested apartment
gewünschtes Hotel, n
  Hotel der Wahl, n
  ♦ hotel of one's choice
gewünschte Suite, f
  ♦ requested suite
gewünschtes Zimmer, n
  ♦ requested room
gewünschte Unterkunft, f
  ♦ requested accommodation
gewünschte Zimmerart, f
  gewünschter Zimmertyp m
  ♦ requested room type
gewünschte Zimmerart angeben
  ♦ state the requested room type
gewünschte Zimmerart mitteilen
  gewünschte Zimmerart angeben
  ♦ indicate the requested room type
  ♦ state the requested room type
gewünschte Zimmerzahl, f
  ♦ requested number of rooms

gewürfelt, adj *gastr*
  in Würfel geschnitten, adj *gastr*
  ♦ diced, adj *gastr*
  ♦ cubed, adj *gastr*
gewürfelte Gurke, f
  in Würfel geschnittene Gurke, f
  ♦ diced cucumber
Gewürz, n (generell)
  ♦ spice
Gewürz, n (würzende Zutat)
  ♦ seasoning
  ♦ condiment
Gewürzinseln, die, f pl
  ♦ Spice Islands, the, pl
Gewürzregal, n
  ♦ spice rack
Gewürzset, n
  ♦ spice set
gewürzt, adj
  ♦ spiced, adj
  ♦ seasoned, adj
Gewürztopf, m
  ♦ spice jar
Gewürztraminer, m
  (Wein)
  ♦ Gewuerztraminer
Geysir, m
  ♦ geyser
gezeigte Preise sind nur Richtpreise
  ♦ prices shown are for guidance only
  ♦ rates shown are for guidance only
gezeigt werden
  ausgestellt sein
  ♦ be on show
  ♦ be on display
  ♦ be on view
Gezeiten, f pl
  ♦ tides pl
Gezeitendammweg, m
  ♦ tidal causeway
gezogener Wohnwagen, m
  gezogener Caravan, m
  ♦ towed trailer *AE*
  ♦ towed caravan *BE*
gezuckert, adj
  ♦ sugared, adj
Gge., f
  Garage, f
  ♦ gge
  ♦ garage
GH, f
  Gasheizung, f
  ♦ GH
  ♦ gas heating
Ghana
  ♦ Ghana
Ghanaer, m
  ♦ Ghanaian
Ghanaerin, f
  ♦ Ghanaian girl
  ♦ Ghanaian woman
  ♦ Ghanaian
ghanaisch, adj
  ♦ Ghanaian, adj
Gibraltar
  ♦ Gibraltar
Gibt es eine Ermäßigung für Kinder?
  ♦ Is there a reduction for children?
Gibt es hier in der Nähe einen Parkplatz?
  ♦ Is there a parking lot near here? *AE*
  ♦ Is there a car park near here? *BE*

Gibt es hier in der Nähe eine Reparaturwerkstatt?
  (für Autos)
  ♦ Is there a garage near here?
Giebel, m
  ♦ gable
Giebeldach, n
  ♦ gable roof
  ♦ gabled roof
Giebelfenster, n
  ♦ gable window
  ♦ gabled window
Giebelhaus, n
  ♦ gable house
  ♦ gabled house
Giebelseite, f
  ♦ gable end
Gießer, m
  Sahnekännchen, n
  ♦ creamer *AE*
  ♦ cream jug
Gießkanne, f
  (für Garten)
  ♦ sprinkling can
gigantisches Zimmer, n
  ♦ gigantic room
Gin, m
  ♦ gin
Ginflasche, f
  ♦ gin bottle
Ginger Ale, n
  ♦ ginger ale
Ginschenke, f
  ♦ gin-shop
Gipfel, m
  ♦ summit
  ♦ peak
  ♦ top
Gipfelblick, m
  Blick vom Gipfel, m
  ♦ summit view
  ♦ view from the summit
Gipfelclub, m
  ♦ summit club
Gipfel erreichen
  ♦ reach the summit
Gipfelfrühstück, n (Berg)
  ♦ breakfast on the summit
Gipfelfrühstück, n (Politik)
  ♦ summit breakfast
Gipfelgespräch, n
  (Politiker)
  ♦ summit talk
Gipfelkonferenz, f
  (Politiker)
  ♦ summit conference
Gipfelkreuz, n
  (Berg)
  ♦ cross at the summit
  ♦ cross at the top
Gipfelpunkt, m
  Scheitelpunkt, m
  Gipfel, m
  Spitze, m
  ♦ apex
Gipfeltreffen, n
  (Politiker)
  ♦ summit meeting
Gipfeltreffen ausrichten (als Gastgeber)
  ♦ host a summit meeting
  ♦ host a summit

308

Gipfelweg, m
   Weg zum Gipfel, m
   ♦ path to the summit
   ♦ trail to the summit
GIT, f
   Gruppenpauschalreise, f
   ♦ GIT
   ♦ group inclusive tour
Gitarre, f
   ♦ guitar
Gitarrenkonzert, n (Musikstück)
   ♦ guitar concerto
Gitarrenkonzert, n (Veranstaltung)
   ♦ guitar concert
Gitarrenspieler, m
   ♦ guitarist
   ♦ guitar player
Gitarre spielen
   ♦ play the guitar
Gîte, m *FR*
   Unterkunft, f
   Quartier, n
   ♦ gîte *FR*
Glanznummer, f
   ♦ party number
Glarner Alpen, pl
   ♦ Glarus Alps, the *pl*
Glas, n (generell)
   ♦ glass
Glas, n (mit Verschluß)
   ♦ jar
Glas an die Lippen setzen
   ♦ set the glass on one's lips
Glasatrium, n
   ♦ glass atrium
Glas auffüllen
   ♦ top up a glass
   ♦ refill a glass
Glas austrinken in einem Zug
   ♦ empty one's glass in one go
Glasbecher, m
   ♦ glass tumbler
Glas Bier, n
   ♦ glass of beer
Glas Bier einschenken jm
   ♦ pour s.o. a glass of beer
   ♦ pour s.o. a beer
Glasbläser, m
   ♦ glass-blower
Glasbläserei, f
   ♦ glass-blowing
Glasbläserindustrie, f
   ♦ glass-blowing industry
Glasbodenboot, n
   ♦ glass-bottom boat
Glasbruch, m
   ♦ glass breakage
Gläschen Gin, n
   ♦ shot of gin
Gläschen Schnaps, n
   ♦ tot
Gläschen Whisky und Soda, n
   ♦ peg
Gläschen zur Stärkung, n
   (Alkohol)
   ♦ pick-me-up
Glasdach, n
   ♦ glass roof
Glasdachlobby, f
   glasüberdachte Halle, f
   ♦ glass-roofed lobby

Gläser anstoßen
   ♦ chink glasses
Glas erheben
   ♦ raise one's glass
   ♦ raise a glass
Gläserkühler, m
   ♦ glass cooler
Gläser polieren
   ♦ polish (the) glasses
Gläserspüler m
   ♦ glass-rinser
Glasflasche, f
   ♦ glass bottle
Glas füllen
   ♦ fill a glass
   ♦ charge a glass *coll*
Glas füllen bis an den Rand
   Glas füllen bis oben
   ♦ fill a glass to the brim
   ♦ fill a glass brimfull *AE*
   ♦ fill a glass brimful *BE*
Glas füllen bis oben
   → Glas füllen bis an den Rand
Glasgebäude, n
   Glasbau, m
   ♦ glass building
Glasgefäß, n
   ♦ glass vessel
Glasgeschirr, n
   Glaswaren, f pl
   ♦ glass dishes *pl*
   ♦ glasses *pl*
   ♦ glassware
Glas Gratiswein, n
   kostenloses Glas Wein, n
   ♦ complimentary glass of wine
   ♦ free glass of wine
Glas hat einen Sprung
   ♦ glass is cracked
Glashütte, f
   ♦ glassworks *pl=sg*
   ♦ glass factory
glasieren etw *gastr*
   mit Glasur überziehen etw *gastr*
   ♦ glaze s.th. *gastr*
Glas immer wieder füllen
   ♦ charge a glass again and again
   ♦ fill a glass again and again
   ♦ keep refilling the glass
   ♦ keep topping up s.o.'s glass
Glas ist halb leer
   ♦ glass is half empty
Glas ist halb voll
   ♦ glass is half full
Glas ist leer
   ♦ glass is empty
Glas ist voll
   ♦ glass is full
Glaskasten, m
   ♦ glass case
glasklares Wasser, n
   → kristallklares Wasser
Glaskrug, m
   ♦ glass jug
Glaskuppel, f
   ♦ glass dome
Glas leeren auf einen Zug
   ♦ empty a glass at a gulp
   ♦ empty a glass at a draught *BE*
   ♦ empty a glass at a draft *AE*

Glas leeren bis auf den Grund
   ♦ empty one's glass completely
   ♦ drain one's glass
Glas leeren mit einem Schluck
   Glas leeren in einem Schluck
   ♦ empty a glass at one draft *AE*
   ♦ empty a glass at one draught *BE*
   ♦ empty a glass at a gulp
Glasmalerei, f
   buntes Fensterglas, n
   ♦ stained glass
Glasmuseum, n
   ♦ glass museum
Glasschrank, m
   ♦ glass cabinet
Glasschüssel, f
   ♦ glass bowl
   ♦ glass dish
Glas Sekt, n
   ♦ glass of champagne
Glas Sekt bestellen
   Glas Champagner bestellen
   ♦ order a glass of champagne
Glastablett, n
   ♦ glass tray
Glastheke, f
   ♦ glass counter
Glastisch, m
   ♦ glass table
Glastür, f
   ♦ glass door
Glasturm, m
   ♦ glass tower
glasüberdachtes Atrium, n
   Glasdachatrium, n
   ♦ glass-roofed atrium
Glas über den Durst trinken *coll*
   einen über den Durst trinken
   ♦ have one too many *coll*
   ♦ have one drop too much *coll*
   ♦ have one drink too many *coll*
Glasvase, f
   ♦ glass vase
Glasveranda, f
   verglaste Veranda f
   ♦ glass veranda
   ♦ glass verandah
   ♦ glassed-in veranda
   ♦ glassed-in verandah
   ♦ sun parlor *AE*
Glasvoll, n
   ♦ glassfull
Glaswand, f
   ♦ glass wall
Glaswaren, f pl
   Glasgeschirr n
   ♦ glassware
Glas Wasser n
   ♦ glass of water
Glas Wein, n
   ♦ glass of wine
Glas Wein jm kredenzen
   ♦ present s.o. with a glass of wine
Glas Wein trinken
   ♦ drink a glass of wine
   ♦ have a glass of wine
glasweise, adv
   ♦ by the glass, adv
Glaswintergarten, m
   ♦ glass conservatory

Glattrochen

Glattrochen, m
  Rochen, m
  ♦ skate
gleichbleibende Nachfrage, f
  ♦ static demand
gleiche Qualität, f
  ♦ same quality
  ♦ equivalent quality
gleiches Zimmer, n
  ♦ same room
  ♦ identical room
gleichgroß, adj
  ♦ even-sized, adj
gleichgroße Portionen, f pl
  ♦ even-sized portions pl
gleichgültiger Service, m
  oberflächlicher Service, m
  ♦ casual service
gleichmäßige Auslastung, f
  ♦ even occupancy
gleichmäßige Verteilung der Besucher, f
  ♦ even spread of visitors
gleich möbliert, adj
  → identisch möbliert
Gleich und gleich gesellt sich gern
  ♦ Birds of a feather flock together
gleich weit entfernt, adj
  ♦ equidistant, adj
gleich weit entfernt sein von A und B
  ♦ be equidistant from A and B
gleichwertig, adj
  ♦ equivalent, adj
  ♦ of the same standard
  ♦ of similar standard
gleichwertige Qualität, f
  gleiche Qualität, f
  ♦ equivalent quality
gleichwertiges Hotel, n
  ♦ hotel of similar category
  ♦ alternate hotel of similar category AE
  ♦ alternative hotel of similar category BE
  ♦ hotel of similar standard and price
  ♦ hotel of similar standard
gleichwertiges Hotel finden
  ♦ find an alternate hotel of similar category AE
  ♦ find an alternative hotel of similar category BE
gleichwertiges Zimmer n
  ♦ room of similar standard
gleichzeitig buchen und zahlen
  ♦ book and pay at the same time
gleitende Arbeitszeit, f
  ♦ flexitime
Gleitschirm, m
  ♦ paraglider
Gleitschirmfliegen, n
  Gleitschirmsport, m
  ♦ paragliding
  ♦ parascending
Gleitschirmflieger, m
  ♦ paraglider
Gletscher, m
  ♦ glacier
Gletscherblick, m
  ♦ glacier view
  ♦ view of the glacier
Gletscherdorf, n
  ♦ glacier village
  ♦ village near a glacier
Gletschersee, m
  ♦ glacial lake

Gletscherskigebiet, n
  ♦ glacier ski area
  ♦ glacier skiing area
Gletscherskilauf, m
  Gletscherskilaufen, n
  Gletscherskifahren, n
  ♦ glacier skiing
Gletschertal, n
  ♦ glacial valley
Gletscher überqueren
  ♦ cross a glacier
Globalpreis m
  ♦ total inclusive rate
  ♦ total inclusive price
Globetrotter, m
  → Weltenbummler
Globus, m
  ♦ globe
Glocke, f
  ♦ bell
glockenförmiges Zelt, n
  ♦ bell tent
Glockenspiel, n
  ♦ carillon
  ♦ glockenspiel
Glockenspiel mit 123 Glocken, n
  ♦ carillon of 123 bells
  ♦ glockenspiel of 123 bells
Glockenturm, m
  ♦ belfry
  ♦ bell tower
Glockentürmchen, n
  ♦ bell turret
Glück bringen
  ♦ bring good luck
glücklichen Urlaub jm wünschen
  ♦ wish s.o. a happy vacation AE
  ♦ wish s.o. a happy holiday BE
Glückliche Reise!
  Gute Fahrt!
  ♦ Have a good journey!
  ♦ Have a nice trip!
  ♦ Bon voyage! FR
glücklicher Gewinner, m
  ♦ lucky winner
glücklicher Kunde, m
  ♦ happy customer
  ♦ happy client
glückliches Ereignis, n
  (z.B. Hochzeitsfest)
  ♦ happy event
Glück probieren (bei etw)
  sein Glück probieren (bei etw)
  ♦ try one's luck (at s.th.)
Glücksspiel, n
  ♦ game of chance
  ♦ gambling game
Glücksspielautomat, m
  ♦ one-armed bandit coll
  ♦ one-arm bandit coll
  ♦ automatic gambling machine
  ♦ fruit machine BE
  ♦ slot machine AE
Glücksspielautomat betreiben
  ♦ operate a one-arm bandit coll
  ♦ operate a one-armed bandit coll
  ♦ operate an automatic gambling machine
Glücksspieleinnahme, f
  ♦ gambling revenue
  ♦ gaming revenue

Glücksspiele spielen
  ♦ play games of chance
Glücksspielgeschäft, n
  ♦ gambling business
  ♦ gaming business
Glücksspielkonzession, f
  ♦ gambling license
  ♦ gambling licence
  ♦ gaming license
  ♦ gaming licence
Glücksspielparadies, n
  ♦ gambler's paradise
  ♦ gambling paradise
Glückwunschkarte, f
  ♦ congratulatory card
Glückwunschkarte, f
  ♦ greetings card
Glückwunschschreiben, n
  ♦ letter of congratulation
Glückwunschtelegramm, n
  ♦ congratulatory telegram
Glückwunschtelegramm, n
  ♦ greetings telegram
Glühbirne, f
  ♦ light bulb
  ♦ electric bulb
  ♦ bulb
Glühwein, m
  ♦ mulled wine
  ♦ gluhwein AE
Glühweinparty, f
  ♦ mulled-wine party
  ♦ gluhwein party AE
Glühweinstand, m
  ♦ mulled-wine stand
  ♦ mulled-wine stall BE
  ♦ stand serving mulled wine
  ♦ stall serving mulled wine BE
  ♦ gluhwein stand AE
glutenfreie Diät, f
  ♦ gluten-free diet
Glyndebourner Festspiele, n pl
  ♦ Glyndebourne Festival, the
GM, m
  General Manager, m
  ♦ GM
  ♦ general manager
GmbH, f
  Gesellschaft mit beschränkter Haftung f
  ♦ Ltd.
  ♦ Limited liability company
gnädige Frau
  (Anrede)
  ♦ madam
  ♦ ma'am coll
gnädiges Fräulein
  (Anrede)
  ♦ madam
  ♦ ma'am coll
Gobelin, m
  ♦ Gobelin
Gobelinwandteppich, m
  Gobelinteppich, m
  ♦ Gobelin tapestry
Go-go-Girl, n
  ♦ go-go girl
Go-go-Tänzerin, f
  ♦ go-go dancer
Go-Kart, m
  ♦ go-cart AE
  ♦ go-kart BE

310

Go-Kart-Bahn, f
  ♦ go-cart track AE
  ♦ go-kart track
Go-Kart-Fahren, n
  ♦ go-carting AE
  ♦ carting AE
  ♦ go-karting BE
  ♦ karting BE
Go-Kart-Rennen, n
  ♦ go-cart race AE
  ♦ go-kart race BE
Go-Kart-Sport, m
  ♦ go-cart racing AE
  ♦ go-kart racing BE
goldbraun, adj
  ♦ golden brown, adj
goldene Hochzeit, f
  ♦ golden wedding
goldener Sandstrand, m
  ♦ golden sandy beach
Goldenes Buch, n
  (bei Empfang von besonderen Gästen)
  → Gästebuch
goldenes Hochzeitsjubiläum, n
  ♦ golden wedding anniversary
Goldfischteich, m
  ♦ goldfish pond
Goldküste, f
  ♦ Gold Coast, the
Goldmedaille, f
  ♦ gold medal
Goldstadt, f (Großstadt)
  ♦ gold city
Goldstadt, f (kleine Stadt)
  ♦ gold town
Goldstrand, m
  goldener Strand, m
  ♦ golden beach
Golf, m (Meer)
  ♦ gulf
Golf, n (Sport)
  ♦ golf
Golfanlage, f
  Golfkomplex, m
  ♦ golf complex
Golfarrangement, n
  ♦ golf arrangement
  ♦ golfing arrangement
Golfaufenthalt, m
  ♦ golf stay
  ♦ golfing stay
Golfausrüstung, f
  ♦ golf equipment
  ♦ golfing equipment
Golfausstellung, f
  ♦ golf show
Golfball, m
  ♦ golf ball
Golfbegeisterter, m
  ♦ golf enthusiast
  ♦ golfing enthusiast
Golfclub, m
  Golfverein m
  ♦ golf club
Golfclub beitreten
  Mitglied werden in einem Golfclub
  ♦ join a golf club
Golfeinrichtung, f
  ♦ golf facility
Golfer, m
  Golfspieler, m

  ♦ golfer
  ♦ golf player
Golffachgeschäft, n
  ♦ golf pro shop
  ♦ pro shop
Golfferien, pl
  Golfurlaub, m
  ♦ golf holiday BE
  ♦ golfing holiday BE
  ♦ golf vacation AE
Golfferienort, m
  Golfurlaubsort, m
  ♦ golfing resort
  ♦ golf resort
Golffirma, f
  ♦ golf company
Golffreund, m
  Golfliebhaber, m
  ♦ golf lover
Golfhotel, n
  ♦ golf hotel
  ♦ golfing hotel
Golfincentivereise, f
  ♦ golf incentive tour
Golfkurs, m
  Golflehrgang, m
  ♦ golf course
  ♦ golfing course
Golfkurzurlaub, m
  ♦ golf break
  ♦ golfing break
Golfküste, f
  ♦ Gulf coast, the
Golflehrer, m
  ♦ golf instructor
Golfmeister, m
  ♦ golf champion
Golfmeisterschaft, f
  ♦ golf championship
Golfmöglichkeiten, f pl
  Golfeinrichtungen, pl
  ♦ golf facilities pl
  ♦ golfing facilities pl
Golfmütze, f
  Golfkappe, f
  ♦ golfing cap
  ♦ golfer's cap
Golfoase, f
  ♦ golf oasis
  ♦ golfing oasis
Golfort, m
  ♦ golf resort
  ♦ golfing resort
Golfparadies, n
  ♦ golfer's paradise
Golfpauschale, f
  ♦ golf package
  ♦ golfing package
Golfplatz, m
  ♦ golf course
  ♦ golf-course BE
  ♦ golf links AE pl
  ♦ golf-links BE pl
Golfplatzbenutzung, f
  ♦ use of the golf course
  ♦ using the golf course
Golfplatzbenutzungszuschlag, m
  → Golfplatzzuschlag
Golfplatz betreiben
  ♦ operate a golf course

Golfplatzbetrieb, m
  ♦ operation of a golf course
  ♦ golf course operation
Golfplatzgebühr f
  ♦ golf-course fee
  ♦ fee for the use of the golf course
  ♦ charge for the use of the golf course
Golfplatzhotel, n
  ♦ golf course hotel
Golfplatz ist gut angelegt
  ♦ golf course is well laid out
Golfplatz mit 18 Löchern, m
  ♦ golf course with 18 holes
  ♦ golf-links with 18 holes pl
  ♦ links with 18 holes pl
Golfplatzzuschlag m
  ♦ supplement for the use of the golf course
Golfpreis, m (Auszeichnung)
  Golfauszeichnung, f
  ♦ golf prize
Golfpreis, m (Kosten)
  ♦ golf price
Golfprofi, m
  ♦ golf professional
  ♦ golf pro
Golfreise, f
  ♦ golf tour
  ♦ golfing tour
Golfresort, m
  → Golfort
Golfsack, m
  Golftasche, f
  ♦ golf bag
Golfschläger, m
  ♦ golf-club
Golfschläger mieten
  ♦ rent a golf-club AE
  ♦ hire a golf-club BE
Golfschläger vermieten
  ♦ rent (out) a golf-club
  ♦ hire out a golf-club BE
Golfschuh, m
  ♦ golf shoe
Golfschule, f
  ♦ golfing school
Golfspiel, n
  ♦ game of golf
  ♦ golf
  ♦ match of golf
Golf spielen
  ♦ play golf
  ♦ golf
Golfspielen, n
  Golfsport, m
  Golfen, n
  ♦ golfing
Golfspieler, m
  Golfer, m
  ♦ golf player
  ♦ golfer
Golfstar, m
  ♦ golf star
Golfstrom, m
  ♦ Gulf Stream, the
Golfstunde, f
  ♦ golf lesson
Golftag, m
  ♦ golf day
  ♦ golfing day
Golftasche, f
  → Golfsack

Golftrainer

Golftrainer, m
- ♦ golf coach

Golfturnier, n
- ♦ golf tournament

Golfübungsbereich, m
- ♦ golf practice area

Golfübungsloch, n
- ♦ golf practice hole

Golf und Tennis in der Nähe
- ♦ golf and tennis nearby

Golfunterricht, m
- ♦ golf tuition
- golf lessons *pl*
- golfing lessons *pl*

Golfurlaub, m
- ♦ golf vacation *AE*
- golfing vacation *AE*
- ♦ golf holiday *BE*
- golfing holiday *BE*

Golfverband, m
- ♦ golf association

Golf von Biskaya, m
- Biskaya, f
- ♦ Bay of Biscay, the

Golf von Mexiko, m
- ♦ Gulf of Mexico, the

Golf von Triest, m
- ♦ Gulf of Trieste, the

Golfwagen, m (Auto)
- Golfauto, n
- ♦ golf car

Golfwagen, m (Karren)
- ♦ golf cart *AE*
- ♦ golf trolley *BE*

Golfwettbewerb, m
- Golfwettkampf, m
- ♦ golf competition
- golfing competition
- ♦ golf contest

Golfwoche, f
- ♦ golf week
- golfing week

Golfwochenende, n
- ♦ golf weekend
- golfing weekend

Golfzentrum, n
- ♦ golf center *AE*
- ♦ golf centre *BE*
- golfing centre *BE*

Golfzuschlag m
- ♦ golf supplement

Gondel, f
- ♦ gondola

Gondelbahn f
- *(im Gebirge)*
- ♦ gondola lift

Gondelfahrt, f
- ♦ gondola ride
- ride in a gondola

Gondoliere, m *ITAL*
- Gondelführer, m
- ♦ gondolier *ITAL*

Gong m
- ♦ gong

gönnen sich ein gutes Hotel
- sich ein gutes Hotel gönnen
- ♦ treat oneself to a good hotel

gönnen sich etw (Schönes leisten)
- leisten sich etw
- ♦ treat oneself for s.th. *AE*
- ♦ treat oneself to s.th. *BE*

gönnen sich etw (zugestehen)
- sich etw genehmigen
- ♦ allow oneself s.th.
- ♦ permit oneself s.th.

Gönnen Sie sich das Beste!
- ♦ Treat yourself to the best

gönnen Sie sich etw
- ♦ treat yourself for s.th. *AE*
- ♦ treat yourself to s.th. *BE*

Gönnen Sie sich und Ihrer Familie ein gutes Hotel
- ♦ Treat yourself and your family to a good hotel

Gorgonzola, m *ITAL*
- Gorgonzolakäse, m *ITAL*
- ♦ Gorgonzola *ITAL*
- ♦ Gorgonzola cheese *ITAL*

Go-show, m
- Passagier ohne Reservierung, m
- ♦ go-show

Gote, m
- ♦ Goth

Gotik, f (Epoche)
- ♦ Gothic period

Gotik, f (Stil)
- ♦ Gothic style
- ♦ Gothic

gotisch, adj
- ♦ Gothic, adj

gotische Architektur, f
- ♦ Gothic architecture

gotische Kathedrale, f
- gotischer Dom, m
- ♦ Gothic cathedral

gotische Kirche, f
- ♦ Gothic church

gotischer Chor, m
- ♦ Gothic choir

gotischer Kreuzgang, m
- ♦ Gothic closters *pl*

gotisches Fresko, n
- ♦ Gothic fresco

Gott des Weins, m
- Weingott, m
- ♦ god of wine
- ♦ wine god

Gottesdienst m
- ♦ church service
- ♦ divine service

Gotthardtunnel, m
- ♦ Gotthard Tunnel, the
- ♦ St Gotthard Tunnel, the *BE*
- ♦ St. Gotthard Tunnel, the *AE*

Goudakäse, m
- Gouda, m
- ♦ Gouda cheese
- ♦ Gouda

Gourmand, m
- Vielesser, m
- Schlemmer, m
- ♦ gourmand
- ♦ gourmandizer
- ♦ gormandizer *BE*
- ♦ glutton

Gourmet, m
- → Feinschmecker

Gourmetdiner, n
- ♦ gourmet dinner

Gourmetkoch, m
- ♦ gourmet cook

Gourmet-Kritiker, m
- ♦ gourmet-critic

Gourmetküche, f (Speisen)
- Feinschmeckerküche, f
- ♦ gourmet cuisine
- ♦ gourmet cooking
- ♦ gourmet gastronomy

Gourmetküchenchef, m
- ♦ gourmet chef

Gourmetrestaurant n
- → Feinschmeckerrestaurant

Gourmettempel, m
- → Schlemmertempel

Gouvernante, f (Erzieherin) *obs*
- ♦ governess *obs*

Gouvernante, f (Hausdame) *SCHW*
- → Hausdame

gr.
- groß, adj
- ♦ lge.
- ♦ large, adj

Grabräuber, m
- ♦ grave robber

Gracht, f
- ♦ canal

Grachtenmuseum, n
- ♦ canal museum

Graf, m
- ♦ count

Gräfinart, adv *gastr*
- nach Gräfinart, adv *gastr*
- ♦ countess style, adv *gastr*

Grafschaft, f
- ♦ county

Grafschaftsmuseum, n
- ♦ county museum

Gramm, m
- ♦ gram
- ♦ gramme *BE*

Granatapfel, m
- ♦ pomegranate
- ♦ pomegranate apple

Granatapfelbaum, m
- ♦ pomegranate tree
- ♦ pomegranate

Granatapfelsaft, m
- ♦ pomegranate juice

Granatapfelsirup, m
- Grenadine, f *FR*
- ♦ grenadine *FR*

Grand Canyon, m
- ♦ Grand Canyon, the

Grande pièce, f FR
- *(bei Speisefolge)*
- Fleischhauptgericht, n
- Grosse pièce, f *FR*
- ♦ grande pièce *FR*
- ♦ main meat course
- ♦ grosse pièce *FR*

Grand Gala-Dîner, n *FR*
- ♦ grand gala dîner *FR*

Grandhotel, n
- ♦ grand hotel

Grand Hotel, n (Eigenname)
- ♦ Grand Hotel, the

Grandhotelier, m
- ♦ owner of a grand hotel
- ♦ proprietor of a grand hotel

Grandhotelkomfort, m
- ♦ grand-hotel comfort
- ♦ grand-hotel amenities *pl*

Grand lit, n *FR*
- *(Doppelbett oder übergroßes Einzelbett)*

Gratisessen

französisches Bett, n
♦ **grand lit** FR
♦ French double bed
Grandsuite, f
♦ **grand suite**
Grand Tour, f hist
große Bildungsreise, f hist
♦ **grand tour, the** hist
Grapefruit, f
Pampelmuse, f
♦ **grapefruit**
Grapefruitcocktail, m
Pampelmusencocktail, m
♦ **grapefruit cocktail**
Grapefruitcoupe, f
Grapefruiteisbecher, m
Pampelmusencoupe, f
Pampelmuseneisbecher, m
♦ **grapefruit coupe**
Grapefruiteiskrem, f
Grapefruiteis, n
Pampelmuseneiskrem, f
Pampelmuseneis, n
♦ **grapefruit ice cream** AE
♦ grapefruit ice-cream BE
♦ grapefruit ice
Grapefruitglas, n
Pampelmusenglas, n
♦ **grapefruit glass**
Grapefruitsaft, m
Pampelmusensaft, m
♦ **grapefruit juice**
Grapefruitschale, f
Pampelmusenschale, f
♦ **grapefruit rind**
♦ grapefruit peel
Grapefruitschnitz, m
Pampelmusenschnitz, m
♦ **grapefruit wedge**
Grapefruitsirup, m
Pampelmusensirup, m
♦ **grapefruit syrup**
Grapefruitsorbet, n
Pampelmusensorbet, n
♦ **grapefruit sorbet**
Graphik, f
graphische Darstellung, f
♦ **graph**
♦ diagram
Graphiksammlung, f
♦ **collection of graphic art**
Grappa, f ITAL
♦ **Grappa** ITAL
Grascampingplatz, m
♦ **grass campsite**
♦ grass campground AE
♦ grass camping site BE
♦ grass camping ground BE
♦ grassy campsite
Grasdach, n
♦ **turf roof**
Grasflugplatz, m
♦ **grass airfield**
Grashang, m
♦ **grass slope**
Grasplatz, m (Camping)
♦ **grass site**
♦ grassy site
Grasplatz, m (Tennis)
♦ **grass court**

Grasschlittenfahren, n
♦ **grass tobogganing**
Grasskilaufen, n
Grasskilauf, m
Grasskifahren, n
♦ **grass skiing**
Grasskiläufer, m
Grasskifahrer, m
♦ **grass skier**
Grasstellplatz, m
(Camping)
♦ **grass pitch**
♦ grassy pitch
Grastennisplatz, m
♦ **grass tennis court**
Gratifikation, f
Sondervergütung, f
♦ **bonus**
Gratin, n
gratinierte Speise, f
überbackenes Gericht, n
♦ **gratin**
gratiniert, adj
überbacken, adj
überkrustet, adj
♦ **gratinated, adj**
gratis, adv
zum Nulltarif, adv
kostenlos, adv
♦ **gratis, adv**
♦ on a gratis basis, adv
♦ free (of charge), adv
Gratisabendessen, n (Dinner)
kostenloses Abendessen, n
♦ **complimentary dinner**
♦ free dinner
♦ courtesy dinner AE
Gratisabendessen, n (Supper)
kostenloses Abendessen, n
♦ **complimentary supper**
♦ free supper
♦ courtesy supper AE
gratis abgeben etw an jn
♦ **furnish s.th. gratis to s.o.**
Gratisangebot, n
Angebot ohne Kosten, n
♦ **free offer**
♦ gratuitous offer
Gratisartikel, m
kostenloser Artikel, m
♦ **complimentary item**
♦ free item
Gratisaufenthalt, m
kostenloser Aufenthalt, m
♦ **complimentary stay**
♦ free stay
Gratisauto, n
kostenloses Auto, n
Gratis-Pkw, m
Gratiswagen, m
♦ **complimentary car**
♦ courtesy car AE
♦ free car
Gratisauto stellen
kostenloses Auto stellen
kostenlos ein Auto stellen
♦ **furnish a complimentary car**
♦ furnish a courtesy car AE
♦ provide a free car
♦ provide a complimentary car

Gratisbar, f
Freibar, f
♦ **complimentary bar**
♦ free bar
Gratisbeförderung, f
Gratistransfer, m
kostenlose Beförderung, f
kostenloser Transfer, m
♦ **free transfer**
♦ complimentary transfer
♦ courtesy transfer AE
♦ free transfer service
♦ complimentary transfer service
Gratisbenutzung, f
kostenlose Benutzung, f
unentgeltliche Benutzung, f
♦ **complimentary use (of s.th.)**
♦ courtesy use (of s.th.) AE
♦ free use (of s.th.)
Gratisberatung, f
Gratiskonsultation, f
kostenlose Beratung, f
♦ **complimentary consultation**
♦ free consultation
Gratisbier, n
Freibier, n
kostenloses Bier, n
♦ **complimentary beer**
♦ free beer
Gratisbonbons, n pl
kostenlose Bonbons, n pl
♦ **complimentary candies** AE pl
♦ complimentary sweets BE pl
♦ free candies AE pl
♦ free sweets BE pl
Gratisbus, m
kostenloser Bus, m
♦ **complimentary bus**
♦ complimentary coach BE
♦ courtesy bus AE
♦ free bus
♦ free coach BE
Gratisbusdienst, m
kostenloser Busdienst, m
♦ **complimentary bus service**
♦ complimentary coach service BE
♦ courtesy bus service AE
Gratiscocktail, m
kostenloser Cocktail, m
♦ **complimentary cocktail**
♦ free cocktail
Gratisdienst, m
Gratisservice, m
kostenloser Service, m
kostenloser Dienst, m
♦ **courtesy service** AE
♦ free service
♦ service (provided) free of charge
♦ complimentary service
gratis erhalten etw
kostenlos erhalten etw
♦ **get s.th. gratis**
♦ get s.th. free (of charge)
♦ receive s.th. free (of charge)
Gratisessen, n (Mahlzeit)
kostenloses Essen, n
♦ **complimentary meal**
♦ free meal
Gratisessen, n (Mittagessen)
Gratismittagessen, n
kostenloses Mittagessen, n

Gratisfahrzeug

- ♦ complimentary lunch
- ♦ complimentary luncheon
- ♦ free lunch
- ♦ free luncheon

Gratisfahrzeug, n
- kostenloses Fahrzeug, n
- unentgeltliches Fahrzeug, n
- ♦ complimentary vehicle
- ♦ courtesy vehicle AE
- ♦ free vehicle

Gratisflasche, f
- kostenlose Flasche, f
- ♦ complimentary bottle
- ♦ free bottle

Gratisfrüchte, f pl
- Gratisobst, n
- kostenlose Früchte, f pl
- kostenloses Obst, n
- ♦ complimentary fruit
- ♦ free fruit

Gratisfrühstück, n
- kostenloses Frühstück n
- ♦ complimentary breakfast
- ♦ free breakfast

Gratisgetränk, n
- kostenloses Getränk, n
- ♦ complimentary drink
- ♦ free drink
- ♦ free beverage
- ♦ complimentary beverage

Gratiskaffee, m
- kostenloser Kaffee, m
- ♦ complimentary coffee
- ♦ free coffee
- ♦ courtesy coffee AE

Gratiskarte, f
- Freikarte, f
- Ehrenkarte, f
- ♦ complimentary ticket
- ♦ free ticket

Gratiskatalog, m
- kostenloser Katalog, m
- ♦ complimentary catalogue
- ♦ free catalogue
- ♦ complimentary catalog AE
- ♦ free catalog AE

Gratisleistung, f
- Gratisservice, m
- kostenlose Leistung, f
- kostenloser Service, m
- ♦ complimentary service
- ♦ service free of charge
- ♦ free service
- ♦ courtesy service AE
- ♦ comp service AE sl

Gratisleistungen, f pl
- Gratisdienstleistungen, f pl
- Gratisdienste, m pl
- ♦ comps AE pl sl
- ♦ complimentary services pl

Gratislikör, m
- kostenloser Likör, m
- ♦ complimentary liqueur
- ♦ free liqueur

gratis logieren
- kostenlos wohnen
- ♦ stay free

Gratismitgliedschaft, f
- kostenlose Mitgliedschaft, f
- ♦ complimentary membership
- ♦ free membership

Gratisparken, n
- kostenloses Parken, n
- ♦ complimentary parking
- ♦ free parking
- ♦ courtesy parking AE

Gratisparkplatz, m
- gebührenfreier Parkplatz, m
- ♦ free car park BE
- ♦ free parking lot AE

Gratis-Pkw-Dienst, m
- kostenloser Pkw-Dienst, m
- ♦ complimentary car service
- ♦ courtesy car service AE
- ♦ free car service

Gratisprospekt, m
- kostenloser Prospekt, m
- ♦ complimentary brochure
- ♦ brochure free of charge
- ♦ free brochure

Gratissauna, f
- → kostenlose Saunabenutzung

Gratisservice, m
- → Gratisdienst

Gratissherry, m
- kostenloser Sherry, m
- ♦ complimentary sherry
- ♦ free sherry

Gratisskibus, m
- kostenloser Skibus, m
- ♦ complimentary ski bus
- ♦ free ski bus
- ♦ courtesy ski bus AE

Gratisspeisen, f pl
- Gratisessen, n
- kostenlose Speisen, f pl
- kostenloses Essen, n
- ♦ complimentary food
- ♦ free food

Gratistee, m
- kostenloser Tee, m
- ♦ complimentary tea
- ♦ free tea
- ♦ courtesy tea AE

Gratistelefonanruf, m
- kostenloser Telefonanruf, m
- ♦ complimentary telephone call
- ♦ free telephone call

Gratistransport, m
- Gratisbeförderung, f
- kostenloser Transport, m
- kostenlose Beförderung, f
- ♦ complimentary transportation AE
- ♦ complimentary transport BE

Gratisübernachtung, f
- kostenlose Übernachtung, f
- ♦ complimentary overnight stay
- ♦ complimentary night
- ♦ complimentary overnight stay
- ♦ free night
- ♦ free bed

Gratisunterbringung, f
- kostenlose Unterbringung f
- ♦ free accommodation
- ♦ free lodging AE

Gratisunterhaltung, f
- kostenlose Unterhaltung, f
- ♦ complimentary entertainment
- ♦ free entertainment

Gratisunterkunft, f
- kostenlose Unterkunft, f
- kostenlose Unterbringung, f

- ♦ complimentary accommodation
- ♦ free lodging AE
- ♦ free accommodation

Gratisurlaub, m
- Gratisferien, pl
- kostenloser Urlaub, m
- kostenlose Ferien, pl
- ♦ complimentary vacation AE
- ♦ complimentary holiday BE
- ♦ free vacation AE
- ♦ free holiday BE

Gratiswagen holt die Gäste am Bahnhof ab
- Wagen holt die Gäste gratis am Bahnhof ab
- ♦ courtesy car meets the guests at the station AE

Gratiswein, m
- kostenloser Wein, m
- ♦ complimentary wine
- ♦ free wine
- ♦ wine free of charge

gratis wohnen
- → kostenlos logieren

Gratiszeitung, f
- kostenlose Zeitung, f
- ♦ complimentary newspaper
- ♦ free newspaper
- ♦ free paper

Gratiszimmer, n
- Freizimmer, n
- kostenloses Zimmer, n
- ♦ complimentary room
- ♦ room free of charge
- ♦ free room
- ♦ courtesy room AE

Graubünden
- Bünden SCHW
- ♦ Grisons, the pl

Graubündner Alpen, die, pl
- Bündner Alpen, die, pl SCHW
- ♦ Grisons Alps, the, pl

Grauburgunder, m
- ♦ Grey Burgundy
- ♦ Gray Burgundy

grauenhaftes Essen, n
- schreckliches Essen, n
- ♦ awful food

grauer Markt, m
- Graumarkt, m
- ♦ gray market
- ♦ grey market

Graumarktfahrkarte, f
- Graumarktflugschein, m
- Graumarktkarte, f
- ♦ bucket-shop ticket BE

Graumarktpreis, m
- ♦ bucket-shop price BE
- ♦ price under the counter

Grauzone, f
- ♦ grey area
- ♦ gray area AE

gravierender Mangel, m jur
- ♦ serious shortcoming jur

graziös möbliert, adj
- anmutig möbliert, adj
- ♦ gracefully furnished, adj

Grd., n
- → Grundstück

Greenfee, f
- → Grüngebühr

Greifen Sie tüchtig zu! (Speisen)
- ♦ Cut and come again!

Grenadine, f FR
→ Granatapfelsirup
Grenzabfertigung, f
→ Zollabfertigung
Grenzbahnhof, m
 ♦ border station
 ♦ frontier station
Grenzbetriebskosten, pl
 ♦ marginal costs of operation pl
Grenzdorf, n
 ♦ border village
 ♦ frontier village
Grenze, f (Staatsgrenze)
 ♦ border
 ♦ frontier
Grenze ist geschlossen
 ♦ border is closed
 ♦ frontier is closed
Grenze ist offen
 ♦ border is open
 ♦ frontier is open
grenzenlose Gastfreundschaft, f
 grenzenlose Gastlichkeit, f
 ♦ unbounded hospitality
grenzenlose Gastfreundschaft anbieten
 grenzenlose Gastlichkeit anbieten
 ♦ offer unbounded hospitality
Grenze öffnen
 ♦ open the border
 ♦ open the frontier
Grenze passieren
 ♦ pass over a frontier
 ♦ pass over a border
Grenzerlös, m
 ♦ marginal revenue
Grenzertrag, m
 ♦ marginal income
Grenze schließen
 Grenzen schließen
 ♦ close the border
 ♦ close the borders
Grenze überschreiten (bei X nach Jordanien)
 Grenze überqueren (bei X nach Jordanien)
 ♦ cross the border (at X into Jordan)
 ♦ cross the frontier (in X into Jordan)
Grenze von England, f
 ♦ border of England
Grenze zu Belgien, f
 ♦ border with Belgium
 ♦ frontier with Belgium
Grenzformalitäten, f pl
 ♦ border formalities pl
 ♦ frontier formalities pl
Grenzformalitäten vereinfachen
 ♦ simplify border formalities
 ♦ simplify frontier formalities
Grenzgänger, m (Arbeit)
 ♦ cross-border commuter
Grenzgänger, m (illegal)
 illegaler Grenzgänger, m
 ♦ illegal border crosser
Grenzgebiet, n
 ♦ border area
 ♦ frontier area
Grenzgebirge, n
 ♦ frontier mountains pl
Grenzhafen, m
 ♦ frontier port
Grenzkontrolle, f
 ♦ border control

 ♦ border check
 ♦ frontier control
Grenzkontrollen abbauen
 ♦ dismantle border controls
 ♦ dismantle frontier controls
Grenzkosten, pl
 ♦ marginal costs pl
 marginal cost
Grenzkostenrechnung, f
 ♦ marginal costing
Grenzland, n
 Grenzgebiet, n
 ♦ border country
Grenzöffnung, f
 Öffnung der Grenze, f
 ♦ opening of the frontier
 ♦ opening of the border
Grenzposten, m
 ♦ border post
 ♦ frontier post
Grenzregion, f
 ♦ border region
Grenzstadt, f (Großstadt)
 ♦ border city
 ♦ frontier city
Grenzstadt, f (kleine Stadt)
 ♦ border town
 ♦ frontier town
Grenzstraße, f
 ♦ border road
 ♦ frontier road
Grenzübergang, m
 (Ort und Aktivität)
 ♦ border crossing
 ♦ frontier crossing
Grenzübergang schließen
 ♦ close a border crossing
Grenzübergangsschließung, f
 ♦ closure of a border crossing
Grenzübergangsstelle, f
 ♦ border crossing point
 ♦ frontier crossing point
 ♦ checkpoint AE
 ♦ check-point BE
grenzüberschreitender Luftverkehr, m
 ♦ border-crossing air traffic
 ♦ frontier-crossing air traffic
 ♦ international air traffic
grenzüberschreitender Tourismus, m
 ♦ border-crossing tourism
 ♦ frontier-crossing tourism
 ♦ international tourism
grenzüberschreitender Verkehr, m
 ♦ frontier-crossing traffic
 ♦ border-crossing traffic
 ♦ international traffic
Grenzübertritt, m
 → Grenzübergang
Grieben, f pl
 ♦ greaves pl
 ♦ crackling sg
Griebenschmalz, n
 ♦ dripping with greaves
 ♦ dripping with crackling
Grieche, m (Person)
 ♦ Greek
Grieche, m (Restaurant) coll
 griechisches Restaurant, n
 ♦ Greek restaurant
Griechenland
 ♦ Greece

Griechenlandspezialist, m
 ♦ specialist in Greece
 ♦ firm specialising in Greece
 ♦ tour operator specializing in Greece
Griechenlandurlaub, m
 ♦ Greek vacation AE
 ♦ Greek holiday BE
Griechin, f
 ♦ Greek girl
 ♦ Greek woman
 ♦ Greek
griechisch, adj
 ♦ Greek, adj
griechische Art, adv gastr
 nach griechischer Art, adv gastr
 ♦ Greek style, adv gastr
griechische Drachme, f
 ♦ Greek drachma
griechische Insel, f
 ♦ Greek island
griechische Küche, f (Speisen)
 ♦ Greek cooking
 ♦ Greek cuisine
griechischer Wein, m
 ♦ Greek wine
griesgrämiges Personal, n
 ♦ sullen staff
 ♦ sullen personnel
Grießkloß, m
 Grießklößchen, n
 ♦ semolina dumpling
Grieß, m
 Grießbrei, m
 ♦ semolina
Grießpudding, m
 ♦ semolina pudding
Grießsoufflé, n
 Grießauflauf, m
 ♦ semolina soufflé
Grießstrudel, m
 ♦ semolina strudel
Grießsuppe, f
 ♦ semolina soup
Grill, m (Bratrost)
 ♦ grill
Grill, m (Bratrost mit Spieß)
 ♦ barbecue
 ♦ bbq
Grillabend, m
 ♦ barbecue evening
 ♦ grill evening
 ♦ evening barbecue
Grillade, f FR
 Gegrilltes, n
 gegrilltes Fleisch, n
 ♦ grillade FR
Grillardin, m FR
 Grillkoch, m
 Grilleur, m FR
 ♦ grillardin FR
 ♦ grill cook
 ♦ roast cook
 ♦ grilleur FR
Grillbar, f
 ♦ grill-bar
grillen
 ♦ have a barbecue
grillen etw (am Spieß)
 (oft ganzes Tier)
 ♦ barbecue s.th.

grillen etw (auf dem Bratrost)
    auf dem Grill braten etw
    grillieren etw
    ♦ **grill s.th.**
grillen etw auf Holzkohle
    ♦ **charbroil s.th.**
grillen lassen sich
    in der Sonne sich bräunen
    ♦ **grill oneself**
grillen lassen sich in der Sonne
    sich in der Sonne grillen lassen
    ♦ **grill (oneself) in the sun**
Grillessen, n
    ♦ **barbecued meal**
Grillfest, n
    Grillparty, f
    ♦ **barbecue party**
    ♦ **barbecue**
    ♦ **bbq party**
    ♦ **bbq**
    ♦ **grill party**
Grillfete, f
    → Grillfest
Grillfleisch, n (gegrillt)
    gegrilltes Fleisch, n
    ♦ **grilled meat**
    ♦ **barbecued meat**
Grillfleisch, n (zum Grillen)
    ♦ **meat for grilling**
Grillgarten, m
    ♦ **grill garden**
    ♦ **barbecue garden**
Grillgelände, n
    Grillbereich, m
    ♦ **barbecue area**
Grillgericht, n
    gegrilltes Gericht, n
    ♦ **grilled dish**
Grillgestell, n
    ♦ **grill rack**
Grillholzkohle, f
    ♦ **barbecue charcoal**
Grillhütte, f
    ♦ **barbecue hut**
Grillkoch, m
    Grilleur, m *FR*
    ♦ **grill cook**
    ♦ grilleur *FR*
    ♦ **roast cook**
Grillmenü, n
    ♦ **barbecue menu**
Grillmittagessen, n
    ♦ **barbecue lunch**
    ♦ **barbecue luncheon**
Grillmöglichkeit, f
    Grilleinrichtung f
    ♦ **grill facility**
    ♦ **barbecue facility**
Grillofen, m
    ♦ **barbecue oven**
Grillparty, f
    Grillfest, n
    ♦ **grill party**
    ♦ **barbecue party**
    ♦ **barbecue**
    ♦ **bbq**
Grillpfanne, f
    ♦ **grill pan**
Grillpicknick, n
    ♦ **barbecue picnic**
    ♦ barbecue picknick *AE*

♦ **bbq picnic**
♦ **grill picnic**
Grillplatz, m
    ♦ **barbecue pit**
    ♦ **barbecue site**
    ♦ **grill pit**
    ♦ **barbecue spot**
    ♦ **barbecue**
Grillplatz im Freien, m
    ♦ **open-air barbecue pit**
Grillrestaurant, n
    Grillroom, m
    ♦ **grill restaurant**
    ♦ grill-room *BE*
    ♦ grillroom *AE*
Grillroom, m
    Grillrestaurant, n
    Grill, m *coll*
    ♦ **grillroom** *AE*
    ♦ grill-room *BE*
    ♦ grill *coll*
    ♦ griller *coll*
Grillsoße, f
    ♦ **barbecue sauce**
Grillspeisen, f pl
    ♦ **barbecued food**
    ♦ grilled food
Grillspezialität, f
    ♦ **barbecue specialty** *AE*
    ♦ **barbecued specialty** *AE*
    ♦ **barbecue speciality** *BE*
    ♦ **barbecued speciality** *BE*
    ♦ grilled specialty *AE*
Grillsteak, n
    gegrilltes Steak, n
    ♦ **grilled steak**
    ♦ **barbecued steak**
Grillstein, m
    ♦ **hot stone**
Grillstelle, f
    ♦ **grill pit**
    ♦ **barbecue pit**
Grilltunke, f
    ♦ **barbecue dip**
Grillvorrichtung, f
    ♦ **griller**
    ♦ **grill**
    ♦ **barbecue**
Grillwein, m
    ♦ **barbecue wine**
Grillwurst, f
    gegrillte Wurst, f
    ♦ **grilled sausage**
grobe Fahrlässigkeit, f *jur*
    ♦ **wanton negligence** *jur*
grobe Kost, f
    einfache Kost, f
    ♦ **rough food**
    ♦ coarse fare
grober Sand, m
    ♦ **coarse sand**
grobgehackt, adj *gastr*
    grob gehackt, adj *gastr*
    ♦ **roughly chopped, adj** *gastr*
    ♦ coarsely chopped, adj *gastr*
Grobsandstrand, m
    ♦ **coarse-sand beach**
grob werden
    sehr unfreundlich werden
    massiv werden
    ♦ **cut rough**

Grog, m
    ♦ **grog**
    ♦ **toddy**
Grogglas, n
    ♦ **grog glass**
Grogparty, f
    ♦ **grog** *BE*
Grönland
    ♦ **Greenland**
Grönländer, m
    Grönländerin, f
    ♦ **Greenlander**
grönländisch, adj
    ♦ **Greenland, adj**
    ♦ **Greenlandic, adj**
Gros der Besucher, n
    Masse der Besucher, f
    Mehrheit der Besucher, f
    ♦ **bulk of the visitors**
Gros der Gäste, n
    Mehrzahl der Gäste f
    Hauptkontingent der Gäste, n
    ♦ **bulk of the clientele**
    ♦ **bulk of (the) guests**
    ♦ **majority of (the) guests**
Großabnehmer, m
    ♦ **bulk buyer**
    ♦ **bulk purchaser**
Großabnehmertarif, m
    ♦ **bulk-buyer tariff**
großartig, adj
    ♦ **grand, adj**
    ♦ **great, adj**
großartigen Komfort erwarten
    ♦ **expect great comfort**
großartiger Komfort, m
    ♦ **great comfort**
großartiger Urlaub, m
    großartige Ferien, pl
    ♦ **grand vacation** *AE*
    ♦ **grand holiday** *BE*
großartiges Hotel, n
    ♦ **great hotel**
    ♦ magnificent hotel
großartig möbliert, adj
    ♦ **magnificently furnished, adj**
großartig möbliertes Zimmer, n
    ♦ **magnificently furnished room**
Großausstellung, f
    große Ausstellung, f
    ♦ **big exibition**
    ♦ **large exhibition**
    ♦ **big exhibit** *AE*
    ♦ **large exhibit** *BE*
Großbetrieb, m
    ♦ **large establishment**
    ♦ large operation
Großbildfernsehvorführung, f
    ♦ **giant-screen TV show**
Großbildprojektion, f
    ♦ **large screen projection**
Großbildprojektor m
    ♦ **large screen projector**
Großbildschirm, m
    ♦ **large screen**
Großbildvideo, n
    ♦ **large screen video**
Großbrauerei, f
    ♦ **large brewery**
    ♦ **big brewery**

Großbritannien
♦ Great Britain
Großdiskothek, f
Großdisko, f
♦ large discotheque
♦ large disco
Größe, f
♦ size
große Auswahl, f
♦ wide choice
♦ wide range
♦ great variety
große Auswahl an Bieren, f
♦ wide choice of beers
♦ wide selection of beers
große Auswahl an Essen, f
♦ wide choice of meals
große Auswahl an etw, f
♦ great variety of s.th.
♦ wide selection of s.th.
♦ wide range of s.th.
große Auswahl an Menüs, f
♦ wide choice of menus
♦ wide selection of menus
große Auswahl an Restaurants, f
♦ wide selection of restaurants
♦ wide choice of restaurants
große Auswahl an Speisen, f
große Auswahl an Gerichten, f
♦ wide choice of dishes
♦ wide range of dishes
♦ big choice of dishes
große Auswahl an Unterkünften, f
♦ wide choice of accommodations *AE*
♦ wide choice of accommodation *BE*
♦ great variety of accommodations *AE*
♦ great variety of accommodation *BE*
♦ wide range of accommodations *AE*
große Auswahl an Unterkunftsmöglichkeiten anbieten
♦ offer a wide range of accommodation possibilities
♦ offer a wide choice of accommodation possibilities
große Auswahl an Weinen, f
♦ wide choice of wines
♦ wide selection of wines
große Auswahl an Wohnungen, f
♦ wide selection of apartments *AE*
♦ wide choice of apartments *AE*
♦ wide selection of flats *BE*
♦ wide choice of flats *BE*
große Auswahl an Zimmern erwartet unsere Gäste
♦ wide selection of rooms awaits our guests
♦ wide choice of rooms awaits our guests
große Besuchergruppen anziehen
♦ attract large contingents
Größe der Gruppe, f
Gruppengröße, f
♦ size of the group
♦ size of the party
Größe des Zimmers, f
Zimmergröße, f
♦ size of the room
große Ferien, pl (Gericht, Hochschule)
(im Sommer)
♦ long vacation
große Ferien, pl (Schule)
♦ long school vacation *AE*
♦ long school holiday *BE*

große Garage, f
Großgarage, f
♦ large garage
♦ big garage
große Gastlichkeit, f
große Gastfreundschaft, f
♦ warm hospitality
große Kanne, f
♦ large pot
große Kanne Kaffee, f
♦ large pot of coffee
große Kanne Tee, f
♦ large pot of tea
Große Karte, f
→ A-la-carte-Speisekarte
große Konferenz, f
♦ large conference
♦ big conference
große Küche, f (generell)
Großküche, f
♦ large kitchen
♦ big kitchen
Große Küche, f (Hauptküche)
♦ main kitchen
große landschaftliche Vielfalt, f
♦ great diversity of landscape
große Menschenmengen anlocken
♦ attract large crowds
große Menüwahl anbieten
große Auswahl an Menüs anbieten
♦ offer a wide choice of menu
große Nachfrage, f
♦ great demand
♦ heavy demand
großen Anklang finden
♦ be much in demand
♦ be very popular
großen Appetit haben
♦ have a large appetite
♦ have hollow legs *humor*
großen Bahnhof haben
♦ receive the red-carpet treatment
großen Bahnhof veranstalten für jn
♦ give s.o. the red-carpet treatment
großen Hunger haben
kräftigen Hunger haben
♦ be very hungry
Größenkategorie f
♦ size category
großen Schluck nehmen
♦ take a big swig
großen Spaß haben
♦ have great fun
großen Wert legen auf etw
♦ lay great emphasis on s.th.
großen Zuspruch haben von jm
großen Zuspruch haben durch jn
beliebt sein bei jm
♦ be popular with s.o.
großen Zuspruchs sich erfreuen
♦ be well-frequented
♦ receive a warm response
große Pause, f (Schule)
♦ long break
große Pause, f (Theater)
♦ long interval
großer Appetit, m
♦ large appetite
großer Balkon, m
♦ large balcony

Großer Ballsaal, m (Eigenname)
♦ Grand Ballroom, the
großer Ballsaal, m (generell)
♦ large ballroom
großer Beliebtheit sich erfreuen
♦ enjoy great popularity
♦ be very popular
großer Campingbus, m
♦ camper
großer Durst, m
♦ big thirst
größere Bequemlichkeit, f
♦ higher standard of comfort
Großereignis, n
Großveranstaltung, f
große Veranstaltung, f
♦ big event
♦ large event
♦ big function
♦ large function
große Reise, f
♦ long journey
große Reisegruppe, f
♦ large tour group
größere Veranstaltung, f
♦ major event
♦ major function
großer Festsaal, m
♦ large banquet hall
♦ large banqueting hall *BE*
großer Kongreß, m
♦ large convention
♦ large congress
♦ big convention
♦ big congress
großer Löffel, m
♦ large spoon
großer Nachfrage erfreuen sich
regen Zuspruch finden
großen Zuspruch finden
♦ be in great demand
großer Name, m
♦ big name
großer Park, m
♦ large park
♦ large gardens *pl*
Großer Saal, m
(Eigenname)
♦ Grand Hall, the
♦ Great Hall, the
großer Saal, m (generell)
♦ large hall
♦ big hall
♦ great hall
Großer Saal bietet 800 Personen Platz
Der Große Saal bietet 800 Personen Platz
♦ Great Hall has seating for 800 persons
♦ The Great Hall has seating for 800 persons
großer Schluck, m
♦ big swig
großer Stand, m
(Messe)
♦ large stand
großer Stellplatz, m
(Camping)
♦ large pitch
großer Tisch, m
♦ large table
großes Abendessen, n (Dinner)
♦ big dinner

großes Abendessen, n (Supper)
  ◆ big supper
großes Angebot an Bieren, n
  ◆ wide range of beers
großes Bankett, n
  ◆ great banquet
Großes Barriere-Riff, n
  ◆ Great Barrier Reef, the
großes Besäufnis, n
  Zecherei, f
  ◆ carousal
  ◆ spree
großes Bett, n
  ◆ large bed
  ◆ big bed
großes Dankeschön, n
  ◆ big thank you
großes Essen, n
  große Mahlzeit, f
  ◆ big meal
  ◆ tuck-in BE inform
großes Finale, n
  ◆ grand finale
großes Freizeitangebot, n
  (Einrichtungen)
  ◆ wide range of leisure facilities
großes Freizeitangebot haben
  ◆ offer a lot of leisure amenities
großes Frühstück, n
  ◆ large breakfast
  ◆ big breakfast
großes Haus, n
  ◆ big house
großes Herrenhaus, n
  Landsitz m
  ◆ stately home
großes Hotelangebot n
  ◆ wide range of hotels
  ◆ array of hotels
großes Mahl essen
  ◆ eat a large meal
großes Mittagessen, n
  ◆ large luncheon
  ◆ large lunch
  ◆ big luncheon
  ◆ big lunch
Große Speisekarte, f
  → A-la-carte-Speisekarte
großes Personal erfordern
  ◆ demand a large staff
großes Trinkgeld, n
  ◆ big tip
  ◆ large tip
großes Trinkgeld geben (jm)
  ◆ tip (s.o.) heavily
großes Urlaubsangebot bieten
  großes Ferienangebot bieten
  ◆ provide a wide variety of vacations AE
  ◆ provide a wide variety of holidays BE
großes Zelt, n
  ◆ large tent
  ◆ big tent
große Tagung, f
  ◆ large meeting
große Veranstaltung, f
  ◆ large event
  ◆ big event
  ◆ large function
  ◆ big function
große Zahl von Besuchern, f
  ◆ large number of visitors

große Zeche machen
  ◆ run up a big bill
groß feiern coll
  ◆ have a do coll
Großflugzeug, n
  ◆ large aircraft
  ◆ large airplane AE
  ◆ large aeroplane BE
  ◆ large plane
Großgaststätte, f
  ◆ large bar AE
  ◆ large public house BE
  ◆ large pub BE coll
Großgedrucktes, n
  (in Verträgen)
  ◆ bold print
  ◆ big print
Großgedrucktes lesen
  (in Verträgen)
  ◆ read the bold print
Großhalle, f
  ◆ big hall
  ◆ large hall
Großhändler, m
  Grossist, m
  ◆ wholesaler
Großherzog, m
  ◆ Grand Duke
Großherzogin, f
  ◆ Grand Duchess
großherzoglich, adj
  ◆ grand ducal, adj
großherzoglicher Palast, m
  ◆ grand ducal palace
großherzogliches Schloß, m
  ◆ grand ducal castle
  ◆ grand ducal palace
Großherzogtum, n
  ◆ Grand Duchy
Großherzogtum Luxemburg, n
  ◆ Grand Duchy of Luxemburg
  ◆ Grand Duchy of Luxembourg
Großhotel n
  großes Hotel
  ◆ big hotel
  ◆ large hotel
Grossist, m
  → Großhändler, m
Großkongreß, m
  großer Kongreß, m
  ◆ big convention
  ◆ big congress
Großküche, f (Betrieb)
  ◆ canteen
Großküche, f (Raum)
  große Küche, f
  ◆ big kitchen
  ◆ large kitchen
Großkunde, m
  ◆ big customer
Großkundennachlaß, m
  → Großkundenrabatt
Großkundenrabatt, m
  → Mengenrabatt
Großkundgebung, f
  Massenkundgebung, f
  ◆ mass rally
Großlage, f
  (Weinberg)
  ◆ collective site

Großmesse, f
  große Messe, f
  ◆ big fair
Großparkhaus, n
  ◆ big parking garage AE
  ◆ big multi-story parking garage AE
  ◆ big multi-storey car park BE
Großparkplatz, m
  großer Parkplatz, m
  ◆ large parking lot AE
  ◆ large car park BE
Großputz, m
  ◆ large-scale house cleaning
  ◆ thorough cleaning
Großraumdüsenflugzeug, n
  Großraumjet, m
  ◆ wide-bodied jet
Großraumflugzeug, n
  ◆ wide-bodied aircraft
Großraumgaststätte, f
  ◆ open-plan bar AE
  ◆ open-plan pub BE
Großraumlimousine, f
  ◆ minivan
Großrazzia, f
  ◆ large-scale raid
  ◆ large-scale swoop coll
Großreiseveranstalter, m
  (mit Großhandelscharakter)
  Großveranstalter m
  ◆ wholesale tour operator
großspurig, adj
  arrogant, adj
  angeberisch, adj
  ◆ overbearing, adj
  ◆ arrogant, adj
  ◆ pretentious, adj
Großstadt, f
  ◆ city
  ◆ big city
  ◆ large city
Großstadthotel, n
  ◆ city hotel
Großstadthotelier, m
  ◆ city hotelier
Großstadtlage f
  (Standort)
  ◆ city location
Großstadtleben, n
  ◆ city life
Großveranstaltung, f
  große Veranstaltung, f
  ◆ big function
  ◆ large function
  ◆ big event
  ◆ large event
  ◆ mass rally polit
Großwild, n
  ◆ big game
Großwildjagd, f
  ◆ big-game hunting
  ◆ big-game shooting
Großwildjäger, m
  ◆ big-game hunter
Großwildsafari, f
  ◆ big-game safari
großzügig angelegt, adj
  ◆ generously laid-out, adj
großzügig angelegter Platz, m
  (Camping)
  ◆ generously laid-out site

großzügige Ermäßigung, f
♦ generous reduction
großzügige Gastfreundschaft, f
  großzügige Gastlichkeit, f
♦ generous hospitality
großzügige Kinderermäßigung, f
♦ generous child reduction
  generous children's reduction
  generous reduction for children
großzügige Parkmöglichkeiten, f pl
  großzügige Parkflächen f pl
  großzügiger Parkraum m
♦ plenty of parking space
großzügige Parkmöglichkeiten haben
♦ have plenty of car parking space
großzügige Portion, f (1 Person)
♦ generous serving
großzügige Portion, f (ausgeteilt)
♦ generous helping
großzügige Portion, f (generell)
♦ generous portion
großzügige Provision, f
♦ generous commission
großzügiges Büfett, n
♦ generous buffet
großzügiges Trinkgeld, n
♦ generous tip
großzügige Urlaubsbedingungen, f pl
  (Arbeitnehmer)
♦ generous leave conditions pl
großzügig proportioniertes Zimmer, n
  großzügig bemessenes Zimmer, n
♦ amply proportioned room
großzügig Trinkgeld geben
♦ tip generously
Grotte, f
♦ grotto
Groupie, n
  (meist weibl. Anhänger eines Popstars)
♦ groupie
Grst., n
→ Grundstück
Grün, n
  (auf Golfplatz)
♦ green
Grünanlagen, f pl
♦ green spaces pl
Grundabgabe, f
→ Grundpacht
Grundanforderung, f
♦ basic requirement
Grundanforderungen genügen
♦ meet the basic requirements
Grundaufenthalt, m
♦ basic stay
Grundausbildung, f
♦ basic training
Grundausstattung, f
♦ basic equipment
Grundbesteck, n
♦ basic cutlery
Grundbuch, n
♦ real-estate register AE
♦ land register BE
Grundeinrichtung, f
♦ basic facility
Grundfahrpreis, m
♦ basic fare
grundfläche, f
♦ floor space
♦ surface area

Grundgebühr f
♦ basic charge
♦ basic fee
Grundinformation, f
♦ basic information
Grundkosten, pl
♦ basic cost
♦ basic costs pl
Grundkosten der Reise betragen $ 123
♦ basic cost of the tour is $ 123
Grundkurs, m
  Grundlehrgang, m
♦ basic course
♦ foundation course
Grundlagenkurs, m
  Grundlagenlehrgang m
♦ foundation course
Grundlagenseminar, n
♦ foundation seminar
♦ foundation course
Grundlebensmittel, n pl
♦ basic foodstuffs pl
Grundleihgebühr, f
  Grundmietgebühr, f
♦ basic hire charge BE
♦ basic hire fee BE
♦ basic rental charge AE
♦ basic rental fee AE
gründliche Reinigung, f
♦ thorough cleaning
gründlich gereinigt, adj
♦ thoroughly cleaned, adj
gründlich reinigen etw
♦ clean s.th. thoroughly
Grundlohn, m
♦ basic wage
♦ basic wages pl
Grundmietgebühr, f
  Grundleihgebühr, f
♦ basic rental charge AE
♦ basic rental fee AE
♦ basic hire charge BE
♦ basic hire fee BE
Grundnahrungsmittel, n
♦ basic food
Gründonnerstag, m
  (Donnerstag vor Ostern)
♦ Maundy Thursday
♦ Holy Thursday
Grundpreis, m
♦ basic price
♦ basic rate
♦ base price
♦ base rate
Grundpreis pro Monat, m
  Monatsgrundpreis m
♦ basic price per month
♦ basic rate per month
Grundpreis pro Person, m
♦ basic rate per person
♦ basic price per person
Grundpreis pro Tag, m
  Tagesgrundpreis m
♦ basic price per day
♦ basic rate per day
Grundpreis pro Woche, m
  Wochengrundpreis, m
♦ basic price per week
♦ basic rate per week
Grundpreis pro Zimmer, m
  Zimmergrundpreis, m

♦ basic price per room
♦ basic rate per room
♦ basic room price
♦ basic room rate
Grundprogramm, n
♦ basic program AE
♦ basic programme BE
Grundprovision, f
  Basisprovision, f
♦ basic commission
Grundreinigung, f
♦ basic cleaning
Grundrezeptur, f
  Grundrezept, n
♦ basic recipe
Grundriß, m
  (eines Gebäudes)
♦ ground plan AE
♦ ground-plan BE
♦ plan
♦ layout
Grundsoße, f
♦ basic sauce
Grundstein, m
♦ foundation stone
Grundstein legen
♦ lay the foundation stone
Grundstück, n
  Grd., n
  Grst., n
♦ plot of land
♦ piece of land
Grundstücke und Gebäude, n pl
♦ land and buildings pl
Grundstückserschließer, m
  Bauunternehmer, m
♦ developer
Grundstückskosten, pl
♦ land costs pl
♦ land cost
Grundstückspreis, m
♦ land price
Grundstücksübertragungsurkunde, f
♦ warranty deed AE
Grundtarif, m
♦ basic tariff
♦ basic rates pl
♦ basic rate
Grund- und Hauseigentum, n
  Eigentum an Grund und Gebäuden, n
♦ freehold property
Gründung, f
♦ foundation
Gründungsfeier, f
  Einweihungsfeier, f
♦ inaugural celebrations pl
♦ inaugural ceremony
Gründungsfest, n
  Gründungsfeier f
♦ foundation ceremony
Gründungssitzung f
  (von Vereinen etc.)
♦ inaugural meeting
Grundverpflegungsausrüstung, f
  Grundverpflegungsausstattung, f
♦ basic catering equipment
Grundzins, m
  Grundpacht, f
  Grundabgabe, f
  Erbpachtzins, m

Grund zum Feiern

Reallast, f
- ground rent

Grund zum Feiern, m
- reason to celebrate

Grund zur Unzufriedenheit, m
Grund der Unzufriedenheit m
- cause for dissatisfaction
- cause of dissatisfaction

Grund zur Unzufriedenheit beseitigen
- remedy the cause of dissatisfaction

Grund zur Unzufriedenheit haben
- have a cause for dissatisfaction

grüne Abfahrt, f (Ski)
- green run

grüne Bohne, f
- green bean
- French bean

grüne Erbsen, f pl
- green peas pl

Grüne Insel, die, f
(Irland)
- Emerald Isle, the

grüne Kräuter, n pl
- green herbs pl

grüne Lunge, f
- green lung

grüne Olive, f
- green olive

grüner Bohnensalat, m
- green bean salad

grüner Pfeffer, m
- green pepper

grüner Salat, m
- green salad
- lettuce

grüner Tee, m
- green tea

grüner Tourismus, m
sanfter Tourismus, m
Ökotourismus, m
ökologischer Tourismus, m
- green tourism
- soft tourism
- ecotourism
- ecological tourism
- sustainable tourism

grünes Gemüse, n
→ Blattgemüse

grüne Trauben, f pl
- green grapes pl

grüne Weihnacht, f
(ohne Schnee)
- green Christmas
- green Xmas

Grünfläche, f
- green
- park

Grüngebühr, f
(Golfplatz)
Greenfee, f
- green fee

Grüngürtel, m
- greenbelt AE
- green belt BE

Grüppchen, n
kleine Gruppe, f
- small group
- small party

Gruppe, f
- group
- party

Gruppe bilden
- make up a party

Gruppe leiten
Gruppe führen
Gruppe anführen
- lead a group
- lead a party

Gruppe mit Spezialinteresse, f
→ Special-Interest-Gruppe

Gruppenabend, m
- group get-together
- group meeting

Gruppenabend, m (von Jugendlichen)
- youth evening

Gruppenabendessen, n (Dinner)
- group dinner

Gruppenabendessen, n (Supper)
- group supper

Gruppenabfertigung, f
- group handling
- handling a group

Gruppenankunft, f
Reisegruppenankunft, f
- tour arrival
- arrival of a tour

Gruppenanmeldung, f
- group registration

Gruppenarbeit, f
- group work

Gruppenarbeitsraum, m
- room suitable for work in groups

Gruppenarbeitssitzung, f
- group work session

Gruppenarbeitstreffen, n
- group work meeting

Gruppenarbeit zu etw, f
- group work on s.th.

Gruppenarrangement, n
- group arrangement

Gruppen aufnehmen
- welcome groups
- cater for groups

Gruppenausflug, m
- group excursion
- party outing

Gruppenausstellung, f
- group exhibition
- group exhibit AE

Gruppenbelegung, f
- group occupancy
- occupancy by a group
- group booking

Gruppenbesichtigung, f
→ Gruppenbesuch

Gruppenbesuch, m
Gruppenbesichtigung, f
- group visit

Gruppenbesucher, m
- group visitor

Gruppenbuchung, f (generell)
- group booking

Gruppenbuchung f (private Gruppe)
- party booking

Gruppenbuchung machen
- make a group booking

Gruppencampingreise, f
- group camping tour

Gruppenempfang, m
- group reception

Gruppenermäßigung, f
Gruppennachlaß m
- group reduction

Gruppenessen n
- group meal

Gruppenfahrkarte, f
Gruppenkarte, f
Gruppenfahrschein, m
- group ticket

Gruppenfahrt, f
- party trip

Gruppenflug, m
- group flight

Gruppenfoto, n
- group photo
- photo of the group

Gruppenfrühstück, n
- group breakfast

Gruppenführer, m
- group leader

Gruppengeschäft, n
(mit Gruppen)
- group business
- party business

Gruppengröße, f
- group size
- number in party
- size of the party

Gruppengröße angeben
(bei Buchung)
- give the number in party

Gruppengröße mitteilen
(bei Buchung)
- indicate the number in party

Gruppenkarte, f
- party ticket

Gruppenleiter, m
(oft nicht professionell organisierte Gruppe)
- party leader

Gruppenliste
→ s. Reisegruppenliste

Gruppenmenü n
(Menü für eine Gruppe)
- group menu

Gruppenmitglied, n
- group member

Gruppenmittagessen, n
- group lunch
- group luncheon

Gruppen nur nach Vereinbarung
- parties only by arrangement

Gruppen nur nach vorheriger Vereinbarung
- parties only by prior arrangement

Gruppenpauschale, f
- group package

Gruppenpauschalreise, f
GIT f
- group inclusive tour
- GIT

Gruppenpreis, m
- group price
- group rate
- party price
- party rate

Gruppenpreisliste, f
- group tariff

Gruppenprogramm, n
- group's program AE
- group's programme BE

Gruppenrabatt, m
- ◆ group discount
- ◆ discount for a group

Gruppenrate, f
- → Gruppenpreis

Gruppenraum, m
- ◆ room assigned for the use of a group
- ◆ room assigned for the use of a party

Gruppenreise, f
- ◆ group tour
- ◆ party tour

Gruppenreise für Alleinstehende, f
- ◆ group tour for singles

Gruppenreisen, n
Gruppenreiseverkehr, m
- ◆ group travel
- ◆ party travel

Gruppenreisender, m
- ◆ group traveller
- ◆ group traveler AE
- ◆ group tourist

Gruppenreisenorganisator, m
- ◆ group travel organiser

Gruppenreiseprogramm, n
- ◆ group travel program AE
- ◆ group travel programme BE

Gruppenreisespezialist, m
Spezialist für Gruppenreisen, m
- ◆ group travel specialist
- ◆ party travel specialist

Gruppenreiseveranstalter m
- ◆ group tour operator

Gruppenreservierung f
- ◆ group reservation

Gruppensitzung, f
- ◆ group meeting

Gruppenspiel, n
- ◆ group game

Gruppenstand, m
(bei Ausstellung etc)
- ◆ group stand

Gruppenstellplatz, m
(Camping)
- ◆ group pitch

Gruppenstornierung, f
Gruppenrücktritt, m
- ◆ group cancellation
- ◆ group cancelation AE

Gruppentarif, m
- ◆ group tariff
- ◆ tariff for groups
- ◆ party tariff
- ◆ tariff for parties

Gruppentaxi, n
Sammeltaxi, n
- ◆ collective taxi

Gruppenteilnahme, f (aktiv)
- ◆ group participation
- ◆ participation of a group

Gruppenteilnahme, f (passiv)
- ◆ group attendance
- ◆ attendance of a group

Gruppentourist m
- ◆ group tourist

Gruppentransfer m
(Personengruppe)
- ◆ group transfer

Gruppenunterbringung, f
- → Gruppenunterkunft

Gruppenunterkunft, f
Gruppenunterbringung, f
- ◆ group accommodation

Gruppenunterricht, m
- ◆ group instruction
- ◆ group lessons pl

Gruppenveranstalter, m
- ◆ group operator

Gruppenveranstaltung, f
- ◆ group function
- ◆ group event
- ◆ group activity

Gruppenvereinbarung f
Gruppenarrangement n
- ◆ group arrangement

Gruppenverkehr, m
- ◆ group traffic

Gruppenverpflegung, f
- ◆ group catering

Gruppenversicherung, f
- ◆ group insurance

Gruppenvisum, n
- ◆ party travel visa

Gruppen von jeder Größe, f pl
- ◆ groups of all sizes pl
- ◆ parties of all sizes pl

Gruppenwanderung, f
- ◆ group walk
- ◆ group hike
- ◆ group ramble

Gruppenwerbung, f
- ◆ group advertisement

Gruppen willkommen
(Hinweisschild)
- ◆ Parties welcome

Gruppenzimmer n
(für Besprechungen etc)
Gruppenraum m
- ◆ group room

Gruppe von Touristen, f
Touristengruppe, f
- ◆ group of tourists
- ◆ party of tourists
- ◆ tourist group
- ◆ tourist party

Grußadresse, f
- → Grußbotschaft

Grußbekanntschaft, f
- ◆ nodding acquaintance

Grußbotschaft, f
Grußadresse, f
- ◆ message of greeting

grüßen jn (generell)
jm guten Tag sagen
- ◆ greet s.o.
- ◆ say hello to s.o. coll

grüßen jn (Grüße bestellen lassen)
Grüße bestellen lassen an jn
- ◆ give my regards to s.o.
- ◆ give our regards to s.o.
- ◆ give s.o.'s regards to s.o.

grüßen jn mit dem Namen
- ◆ greet s.o. by name

Grußwort, n
- ◆ word of welcome
- ◆ words of welcome pl
- ◆ word of greeting
- ◆ greeting
- ◆ opening words pl

Grußwort sagen
- ◆ deliver a message of greeting

Gruyèrekäse, m
Gruyere, m
Greyerzer Käse, m
Greyerzer, m
- ◆ Gruyere cheese AE
- ◆ Gruyère cheese BE
- ◆ Gruyere AE
- ◆ Gruyère BE

Guatemala
- ◆ Guatemala

Guatemalteke, m
- ◆ Guatemalan
- ◆ Guatemaltekan

Guatemaltekin, f
- ◆ Guatemalan girl
- ◆ Guatemalan woman
- ◆ Guatemalan
- ◆ Guatemaltekan girl
- ◆ Guatemaltekan woman

guatemaltekisch, adj
- ◆ Guatemalan, adj

Guckloch, n
(in der Tür)
- ◆ peephole AE
- ◆ peep-hole BE
- ◆ spyhole

Guéridon, m FR
(im Restaurant)
kleiner Serviertisch m
Beistelltisch m
- ◆ guéridon FR
- ◆ side table

Guéridonkellner, m
- ◆ guéridon waiter

Guéridonservice, m
(in Restaurant)
- ◆ guéridon service
- ◆ cart service AE
- ◆ trolley service BE
- ◆ wagon service
- ◆ side-table service

Guernsey
- ◆ Guernsey

Guinea
- ◆ Guinea

Guineer, m
- ◆ Guinean

Guineerin, f
- ◆ Guinean girl
- ◆ Guinean woman
- ◆ Guinean

guineisch, adj
- ◆ Guinean, adj

Gulasch, m/n
- ◆ goulash

Gulaschkanone, f coll
Feldküche, f
- ◆ field kitchen

Gulaschsuppe, f
- ◆ goulash soup

gültig, adj
- ◆ valid, adj
- ◆ in force, adj
- ◆ good, adj

gültig ab 7. März
- ◆ valid from 7 March

gültig bleiben (für ein Jahr)
- ◆ remain valid (for one year)

gültige Bescheinigung, f
- ◆ valid certificate

gültige internationale Impfbescheinigung

gültige internationale Impfbescheinigung, f
- ♦ valid international certificate of vaccination
- ♦ valid international vaccination certificate
- ♦ valid international certificate of inoculation
- ♦ valid international inoculation certificate

gültige Karte, f
- ♦ valid ticket

gültiger Reisepaß, m
- ♦ valid passport

gültiger Tarif, m
- ♦ tariff in force
- ♦ applicable tariff
- ♦ valid tariff
- ♦ valid rate(s)
- ♦ applicable rate(s)

gültige Stornierung, f
- ♦ valid cancellation
- ♦ valid cancelation AE

gültiges Visum, n
- ♦ valid visa

gültiges Visum benötigen
- ♦ require a valid visa

gültiges Visum haben
- ♦ have a valid visa

Gültigkeit, f
- ♦ validity

Gültigkeit der Reisepapiere, f
- ♦ validity of (the) travel documents

Gültigkeitsdauer, f
- ♦ period of validity
- ♦ validity period
- ♦ validity

Gültigkeitstag, m
- ♦ day of validity

gültig sein
- ♦ be valid
- ♦ be in force
- ♦ apply

gültig werden
- ♦ become valid

Gummiboot, n
  Schlauchboot, n
- ♦ rubber boat
- ♦ rubber dinghy

Gummiseilspringen, n
  (z.B. von Brücken)
  Bungeespringen, n
- ♦ bungee jumping
- ♦ bungee diving

Gummiseilspringer, m
  Bungeespringer, m
- ♦ bungee jumper

Gummizelle, f
- ♦ padded cell

günstig, adj
- ♦ favorable, adj AE
- ♦ favourable, adj BE

günstigen Preis aushandeln
- ♦ negotiate a favorable price AE
- ♦ negotiate a favorable rate AE
- ♦ negotiate a favourable price BE
- ♦ negotiate a favourable rate BE

günstige Preise bieten
→ konkurrenzfähige Preise anbieten

günstiger Preis, m
- ♦ favorable rate AE
- ♦ favorable price AE
- ♦ favourable rate BE
- ♦ favourable price BE

günstiger Wechselkurs, m
- ♦ favorable exchange rate AE
- ♦ favourable exchange rate BE

günstiges Angebot, n
- ♦ favorable offer AE
- ♦ favourable offer BE

günstiges Klima, n
- ♦ favorable climate AE
- ♦ favourable climate BE

günstig gelegen, adj
  vorteilhaft gelegen, adj
- ♦ conveniently situated, adj
- ♦ conveniently located, adj
- ♦ handy, adj
- ♦ advantageously situated, adj
- ♦ advantageously located, adj

günstig gelegen in Flughafennähe
- ♦ convenient for the airport
- ♦ close to the airport

günstig gelegen sein für etw
  günstig liegen für etw
  verkehrsgünstig liegen für etw
- ♦ be conveniently situated for s.th.
- ♦ be conveniently located for s.th.
- ♦ be in a convenient position for s.th.

Gurgel spülen (sich) humor
→ Kehle anfeuchten

Gurke, f (Essiggurke)
→ Essiggurke

Gurke, f (Salatgurke)
  Salatgurke, f
  Schlangengurke, f
- ♦ cucumber

Gurkenbowle, f
- ♦ cucumber cup
- ♦ cucumber bowl

Gurkenhälfte, f
- ♦ cucumber half

Gurkenhobel, m
- ♦ cucumber slicer

Gurkensaft, m
- ♦ cucumber juice

Gurkensalat, m
- ♦ cucumber salad

Gurkensandwich, n/m
- ♦ cucumber sandwich

Gurkenschale, f
- ♦ cucumber peel

Gurkenscheibe, f
- ♦ cucumber slice
- ♦ slice of cucumber

Gurkensoße, f
- ♦ cucumber sauce

Gurkensuppe, f
- ♦ cucumber soup

Gurke schälen
- ♦ peel a cucumber

Gurt, m
- ♦ strap

Gürteltasche, f
- ♦ belt pouch

GUS, f
  Gemeinschaft Unabhängiger Staaten, f
- ♦ CIS
- ♦ Commonwealth of Independent States

gußeisernes Bett, n
- ♦ cast-iron bed

Gut, n
→ Gutshof

gutachtliche Schätzung, f
  fachmännische Schätzung f

gutachterliche Schätzung, f
- ♦ expert appraisal

gutangelegt, adj
- ♦ well-laid out, adj

gutangelegter Garten, m
  hübsch angelegter Garten m
- ♦ well-laid out garden

gut ankommen
- ♦ arrive safely

gut aufgehoben sein coll
→ gut betreut werden

gutausgelastetes Hotel, n
- ♦ highly utilised hotel

gut ausgeruht ankommen
- ♦ arrive well rested

gutausgeschildert, adj
- ♦ well-signposted, adj

gutausgeschildertes Besucherzentrum, n
- ♦ well-signposted visitor center AE
- ♦ well-signposted visitor centre BE

gutausgestattet, adj
- ♦ well-equipped, adj
- ♦ well-appointed, adj

gutausgestatteter Platz, m
  (Camping)
- ♦ well-equipped site

gutausgestattetes Zimmer, n
- ♦ well-equipped room
- ♦ well-appointed room

gut behandeln jn
- ♦ treat s.o. well

gutbelegt, adj
  gutausgelastet, adj
- ♦ well-occupied, adj
- ♦ well-booked, adj

gutbemessen, adj
- ♦ good-sized, adj

gutbemessener Balkon, m
- ♦ good-sized balcony

gutbemessenes Zimmer, n
- ♦ good-sized room

gutbesetzt, adj (Haus, Lokal)
- ♦ well-filled, adj

gutbesetztes Café, n
- ♦ well-filled cafe AE
- ♦ well-filled café BE

gutbestückt, adj
  wohlassortiert, adj
- ♦ well-stocked, adj

gutbestücktes Lager, n
  wohlassortiertes Lager, n
- ♦ well-assorted stock

gutbesucht, adj (Lokal)
- ♦ well-patronised, adj
- ♦ well-frequented, adj

gutbesucht, adj (Veranstaltung)
- ♦ well-attended, adj

gutbesuchte Ausstellung, f
- ♦ well-attended exhibition
- ♦ well-attended exhibit AE

gutbesuchte Bar f
- ♦ well-patronised bar

gutbesuchter Ball, m
- ♦ well-attended ball

gutbesuchtes Hotel, n
- ♦ well-patronised hotel
- ♦ well-frequented hotel

gutbesuchte Vorstellung, f
- ♦ well-attended performance

gutbesucht sein (Lokal)
  ♦ be well patronised
  ♦ be well frequented
gutbesucht sein von jm (Veranstaltung)
  ♦ be well attended by s.o.
gut betreut werden
  gut aufgehoben sein *coll*
  ♦ be well looked after
  ♦ be well cared for
gut bewirtet werden
  gut verpflegt werden
  ♦ be well catered for
gut bezahlt sein
  gut bezahlt werden
  ♦ be well paid
gutbürgerlich, adj
  bürgerlich, adj
  ♦ middle-class, adj
  ♦ plain, adj
  ♦ home, adj
  ♦ one-star, adj
gutbürgerliche Küche, f (Speisen)
  ♦ home cooking
  ♦ plain cooking
  ♦ traditional cooking
gutbürgerliches Hotel, n
  → Hotel der Mittelklasse
gutbürgerliches Restaurant, n
  gutbürgerliches Lokal, n
  ♦ middle-class restaurant
gutbürgerlich essen
  ♦ eat plain food
gutbürgerlich kochen
  ♦ cook traditional dishes
gutdimensioniert, adj
  ♦ well-dimensioned, adj
gutdimensioniertes Zimmer n
  ♦ well-dimensioned room
gut durchgebraten, adj
  durchgebraten, adj
  bien cuit, adj *FR*
  ♦ well-done, adj
  ♦ bien cuit, adj *FR*
gute alte Zeit, f
  ♦ good old days, the *pl*
gute Auslastung, f
  ♦ good load factor
gute Auswahl von etw bieten
  ♦ offer a good choice of s.th.
  ♦ provide a good choice of s.th.
gute Belegung, f
  gute Auslastung, f
  ♦ good occupancy
gute Belegung erreichen im ganzen Jahr
  gute Auslastung erreichen während des ganzen Jahrs
  ♦ achieve good occupancy all year round
  ♦ achieve good occupancy throughout the year
gute englische Kost f
  ♦ honest English fare
Gute Fahrt!
  ♦ Have a good trip!
gute Gastgeber sein
  ♦ be good hosts
gute Gebirgsluft genießen
  gute Bergluft genießen
  ♦ enjoy the good mountain air
gute Gesellschaft, f
  ♦ good company
guteingeführt, adj
  alteingeführt, adj

  ♦ well-established, adj
  ♦ old-established, adj
guteingeführtes Hotel n
  ♦ well-established hotel
guteingerichtet, adj
  (Unterkunft)
  gutausgestattet, adj
  ♦ well-appointed, adj
  ♦ well-furnished, adj
guteingerichtetes Appartement, n
  ♦ well-appointed apartment
  ♦ well-furnished apartment
guteingerichtetes Haus, n
  ♦ well-appointed house
  ♦ well-furnished house
guteingerichtetes Hotel, n
  ♦ well-appointed hotel
  ♦ well-furnished hotel
guteingerichtetes Zimmer, n
  ♦ well-appointed room
  ♦ well-furnished room
guteingerichtete Villa, f
  ♦ well-appointed villa
Güteklasse, f
  ♦ quality category
  ♦ grade
gute körperliche Verfassung, f
  ♦ good physical fitness
gute Kost, f
  ♦ good fare
gute Küche, f
  (Speisen)
  ♦ good cooking
  ♦ good cuisine
  ♦ good food
gute Lage, f
  ♦ good location
  ♦ good situation
  ♦ good position
gute Laune haben
  bei guter Laune sein
  ♦ be in a good mood
  ♦ be in good spirits
gute Lebensart, f
  Kunst des guten Lebens, f
  ♦ good living
  ♦ art of good living
gute Manieren, f pl
  gute Umgangsformen, f pl
  ♦ good manners *pl*
gute Manieren haben
  gute Umgangsformen haben
  ♦ have good manners
gut empfangen werden
  (Gäste)
  gut aufgenommen werden
  ♦ be well received
Guten Abend!
  ♦ Good evening!
Gute Nacht!
  ♦ Good night!
gute Nacht, f
  ♦ good night
gute Nacht haben
  ♦ have a good night
Gute Nacht sagen
  ♦ say Good Night
Guten Appetit!
  ♦ Bon appétit! *FR*
guten Auslastungsgrad garantieren
  ♦ guarantee a good occupancy rate

Gutenbergbibel, f
  ♦ Gutenberg bible
guten Empfang bekommen
  ♦ get a good reception
guten Magen haben
  ♦ have a good stomach
Guten Morgen!
  ♦ Good morning!
Guten Morgen. Ihr Weckruf
  ♦ Good morning, Sir. This is your wake-up call
  ♦ Good morning, Madam. This is your wake-up call
guten Preis erzielen
  ♦ obtain a good price
  ♦ get a good price
guten Ruf genießen
  ♦ enjoy a good reputation
  ♦ have a good reputation
guten Ruf haben
  ♦ have a good reputation
guten Schlaf haben
  gut schlafen
  ♦ have a good sleep
guten Schluck nehmen
  ♦ take a good swig *coll*
  ♦ take a good drink
guten Service anbieten
  ♦ offer good service
guten Service bekommen
  ♦ get good service
guten Service bieten
  ♦ provide good service
guten Service erfahren
  guten Service erleben
  ♦ experience good service
guten Service geben jm
  ♦ give s.o. good service
Guten Tag! (morgens, abends)
  → Guten Morgen, Guten Abend
Guten Tag! (nachmittags)
  ♦ Good afternoon!
guten Wein schätzen
  guten Wein zu schätzen wissen
  ♦ appreciate (a) good wine
Güter, n pl
  ♦ goods *pl*
guter Appetit, m
  ♦ good appetite
Gute Reise!
  Glückliche Reise!
  ♦ Have a pleasant journey!
  ♦ Have a good journey!
  ♦ Have a nice trip!
  ♦ Bon voyage!
gute Reise wünschen jm
  ♦ wish s.o. a good journey
  ♦ wish s.o. bon voyage
guter Gasthof, m
  ♦ good inn
guter Geschmack, m
  ♦ good taste
guterhalten, adj
  ♦ well-maintained, adj
  ♦ well-kept, adj
  ♦ well-preserved, adj
  ♦ in good condition, adv
  ♦ in good repair, adv
guterhaltener Tempel, m
  ♦ well-preserved temple
guterhaltener Turm, m
  ♦ well-preserved tower

guterhaltenes Gebäude, n
- building in good condition
- building in good repair
- well-preserved building

guterhaltenes Haus, n
- well-preserved house

guterhaltenes Hotel, n
- hotel in good condition
- hotel in good repair
- well-kept hotel
- well-maintained hotel
- well-preserved hotel

guter Magen, m
- good stomach

guter Ort für einen Urlaub, m
- good place for a vacation *AE*
- good place for a holiday *BE*

guter Ruf (für etw), m
- good reputation (for s.th.)
- high reputation (for s.th.)

guter Schläfer, m
- good sleeper

guter Service, m
- good service

guter Strand, m
- good beach

Güterverkehr, m
- goods traffic
- freight traffic

Güterwagen, m (Zug)
- freight car *AE*
- goods wagon *BE*
- goods waggon *BE*

guter Wein, m
  edler Wein, m
  nobler Wein, m *form*
- fine wine

Güterzug, m
- freight train *AE*
- waggon train *AE*
- goods train *BE*

gute Saison, f
- good season

gute Saison haben
- have a good season

gute Schneebedingungen bieten
- offer good snow conditions

gutes Essen, n
- good food

gutes Essen mögen
- like good food

gutes Frühstück, n
- good breakfast

gutes Frühstück machen
- make a good breakfast

gutes Haus führen
- keep a good house

gutes Hotel, n
- good hotel

gutes Mittelklassehotel, n
  gutes Mittelklaßhotel, n *SCHW*
  gutbürgerliches Hotel, n
- good middle-class hotel

gutes Preis-/Leistungsverhältnis, n
- good value for money

gutes Preis-/Leistungsverhältnis anbieten
- offer good value for money

gutes Preis-/Leistungsverhältnis bieten
- give good value for money
- provide good value for money

gutes Preis-/Leistungsverhältnis erhalten
  Gegenleistung erhalten
- get value for money

gutes Restaurant, n
- good restaurant

gut essen
  (gutes Essen bekommen)
- eat well

gute Stelle zum Campen, f
  guter Platz zum Campen, m
- good place for camping
- good spot for camping

gute Stimmung, f
- happy atmosphere

gute Stube, f (in Privathaus)
- bets room
- front room
- parlor *AE*
- parlour *BE*

gutes Weinjahr, n
- good year for wine

gutes Zimmer, n
- good room

gutes Zimmer bekommen
- get a good room

gute Unterkunft, f
  gute Unterbringung, f
- good accommodation

gute Weinkarte, f
- good wine list

Gütezeichen, n
- quality label

gutgebräunt, adj (Person)
- well-tanned, adj

gutgebräunt, adj (Speise)
- well-browned, adj

gutgefedert, adj
- well-sprung, adj

gutgefedertes Bett, n
- well-sprung bed

gutgeführt, adj
  (Betrieb)
- well-managed, adj
- well-run, adj

gutgeführter Betrieb, m
- well-run establishment
- well-run operation

gutgeführter Platz, m
  (Camping)
- well-run site
- well-managed site

gutgeführtes Hotel n
- well-managed hotel
- well-run hotel
- hotel under good management

gutgehend, adj
  prosperierend, adj
  florierend, adj
- flourishing, adj
- thriving, adj
- prosperous, adj

gutgehendes Hotel, n
- flourishing hotel
- thriving hotel

gutgekochtes Gericht, n
- well-cooked dish

gutgekühlt, adj
- well-chilled, adj

gutgelaunt, adj
- good-humored, adj *AE*
- good-humoured, adj *BE*
- in a good mood
- in good spirits

gutgelegen, adj
- well-located, adj
- well-situated, adj
- well-positioned, adj
- well-placed, adj
- well-sited, adj

gutgelegenes Hotel n
- well-located hotel

gutgelegene Wohnung, f
- well-situated apartment *AE*
- well-situated flat *BE*

gutgelegen sein
  gut liegen
- be well situated
- be well located
- be well sited
- be well positioned

gutgenährt, adj
- well-fed, adj
- well-nourished, adj

gutgeplant, adj
- well-planned, adj

gutgeplantes Zimmer, n
- well-planned room

gut geschriebener Führer, m
- well-written guide

gutgewählt, adj
- well-chosen, adj
- well-selected, adj

gutgewählte Möbel, n pl
- well-chosen furniture *sg*

gutgewürzt, adj
- well-seasoned, adj

gut kochen
- be a good cook
- cook well

gut leben
  (bes. Ernährung)
- live well

gütliche Beilegung einer Beschwerde vereinbaren
- agree an amicable settlement to a complaint

gütlicher Vergleich, m *jur*
- amicable agreement *jur*
- amicable settlement *jur*

gut liegen für etw
  gut gelegen sein für etw
- be well situated for s.th.
- be well positioned for s.th.
- be well placed for s.th.
- be well sited for s.th.

gutmarkiert, adj
- well-marked, adj

gutmarkierte Piste, f
  (Ski)
- well-marked piste
- well-marked run

gutmarkierter Weg, m
- well-marked footpath
- well-marked path

gutmarkiert sein
- be well marked

gutmöbliert, adj
- well-furnished, adj

gutmöbliertes Zimmer n
  gut eingerichtetes Zimmer n
- well-furnished room

gutorganisiert, adj
♦ well-organised, adj
♦ well-organized, adj
gutorganisierter Urlaub, m
♦ well-organised vacation AE
♦ well-organized vacation AE
♦ well-organised holiday BE
♦ well-organized holiday BE
gutpräparierte Loipe f
(Ski)
♦ well-prepared trail
♦ well-prepared track
gut proportioniert, adj
♦ well-proportioned, adj
gut proportioniertes Zimmer, n
♦ well-proportioned room
gut riechen
♦ smell good
Gutsappartement, n
Gutshausappartement, n
♦ manor-house apartment
Gutschein, m
♦ voucher
Gutschein ablehnen
Gutschein zurückweisen
♦ refuse a voucher
Gutschein anerkennen
Gutschein akzeptieren
Gutschein in Zahlung nehmen
♦ honour a voucher AE
♦ honour a voucher BE
Gutschein annehmen
Gutschein akzeptieren
♦ accept a voucher
Gutscheinart, f
Gutscheintyp m
♦ voucher type
♦ type of voucher
Gutscheinausgabe, f
♦ issue of a voucher
♦ issuing a voucher
Gutschein ausgeben
♦ issue a voucher
Gutschein ausgeben für etw
♦ spend a voucher on s.th.
♦ spend a voucher for s.th. AE
Gutschein ausstellen
♦ make out a voucher
♦ issue a voucher
Gutschein bekommen für etw
♦ get a voucher for s.th.
Gutschein benutzen (für etw)
♦ use a voucher (for s.th.)
Gutschein bestellen
Gutschein buchen
♦ book a voucher
Gutscheinbetrag, m
♦ voucher amount
♦ amount of a voucher
Gutscheinbetrag von einer Gästerechnung abziehen
Gutscheindurchschrift, f
→ Gutscheinduplikat
Gutscheindurchschrift, f
Gutscheinduplikat, n
♦ duplicate voucher
Gutschein einlösen (gegen Bargeld)
♦ cash a voucher
Gutschein einlösen (gegen Service oder Ware)
♦ trade in a voucher

Gutschein einlösen (generell)
Gutschein eintauschen
♦ exchange a voucher
Gutschein einlösen in einem Restaurant
♦ exchange a voucher at a restaurant
Gutschein einsammeln
Gutschein an sich nehmen
♦ collect a voucher
Gutschein erhalten
Gutschein erhalten für etw
♦ receive a voucher
♦ receive a voucher entitling to s.th.
Gutschein für Abendessen, m (Supper)
→ Abendessengutschein
Gutschein für ein kostenloses Getränk, m
♦ voucher for a free drink
♦ voucher for a free beverage
Gutschein für ermäßigten Eintritt, m
♦ reduced admission charge voucher
Gutschein für Frühstück, m
→ Frühstücksgutschein
Gutschein für Mittagessen, m
♦ luncheon voucher
♦ lunch voucher
Gutscheinheft, n
♦ voucher book
♦ book of vouchers
Gutschein ist einlösbar in einem Hotel
♦ voucher is redeemable at a hotel
Gutschein ist gültig für etw
♦ voucher is valid for s.th.
Gutschein ist ungültig
♦ voucher is void
Gutschein kaufen (von jm)
♦ buy a voucher (from s.o.)
Gutscheinkunde, m
♦ voucher customer
♦ voucher client
Gutscheinnummer, f
♦ voucher number
Gutscheinpreis m
♦ voucher rate
♦ voucher price
Gutscheinprogramm, n
♦ voucher scheme
Gutscheinseriennummer, f
♦ voucher serial number
Gutschein stiften
♦ donate a voucher
Gutscheinsystem, n (generell)
♦ voucher system
Gutschein über DM 123, m
Gutschein für DM 123 m
♦ voucher for DM 123
Gutschein verkaufen (an jn)
♦ sell a voucher (to s.o.)
Gutschein verrechnen mit der Endrechnung
♦ check a voucher against the final bill
Gutschein vorlegen
Gutschein vorweisen
♦ present a voucher
Gutscheinwert, m
♦ voucher value
♦ value of a voucher
Gutschein zurückweisen
Gutschein ablehnen
♦ reject a voucher
gut schlafen
♦ sleep well
gut schlafen die ganze Nacht
♦ sleep well all night

gut schmecken
fein schmecken
♦ taste good
♦ taste fine
gutschmeckend, adj
→ wohlschmeckend
gutschreiben etw jm
♦ credit s.th. to s.o.
♦ credit s.o. with s.th.
Gutschrift, f (generell)
♦ credit
Gutschrift, f (in Gutscheinform)
♦ credit voucher
Gutschriftanzeige, f
♦ credit note
Gutshaus, n
Herrenhaus n
♦ manor house AE
♦ manor-house BE
♦ manor
Gutshof, m
Gut, n
Landgut, n
Weingut, n
♦ estate
gutsortiert, adj
♦ well-stocked, adj
♦ well-assorted, adj
gutsortierte Bar f
♦ well-stocked bar
gutsortierten Weinkeller haben
♦ have a well-stocked wine cellar
♦ keep a well-stocked wine cellar
gutsortierter Weinkeller m
♦ well-stocked wine cellar
gutsortiertes Geschäft, n
gutsortierter Laden m
♦ well-stocked store AE
♦ well-stocked shop BE
Gutswohnung, f
Gutshauswohnung, f
♦ manor-house flat BE
♦ manor-house apartment AE
gut temperiert, adj
richtig temperiert, adj
♦ at the right temperature
gut untergebracht, adj
♦ well-lodged, adj
♦ well-accommodated, adj
♦ well-put up, adj AE coll
♦ well-fixed (up), adj AE sl
gut untergebracht sein
♦ be well lodged AE
♦ be well accommodated
♦ be well put up BE coll
♦ be well fixed (up) AE
♦ have good accommodation
gut vermieten lassen sich
♦ rent well AE
♦ let well BE
gutversorgt, adj
♦ well-cared for, adj
gut versorgt werden
gut betreut werden
♦ be well cared for
gut würzen etw
♦ season s.th. well
Guyana
♦ Guiana
Guyaner, m
♦ Guyanese

Guyanerin, f
♦ **Guyanese girl**
♦ Guyanese woman
♦ Guyanese
guyanisch, adj
♦ **Guyanese, adj**
Gymkhana, n
Geschicklichkeitswettbewerb, m
♦ **gymkhana**
Gymnastik, f
Kunstturnen, n
♦ **gymnastics** *pl = sg*
Gymnastikbereich, m
♦ **exercise area**
Gymnastikeinrichtung, f
Bewegungseinrichtung, f
♦ **exercise facility**
Gymnastikgerät, n
♦ **exercise machine**
Gymnastikhalle, f
Gymnastiksaal, m
Turnhalle, f
Turnsaal, m
♦ **gymnasium**
♦ gym
Gymnastikkonditionstraining, n
♦ **gym workout**
Gymnastikkurs, m
♦ **exercise class**
Gymnastik machen
♦ **do one's exercises**
Gymnastikprogramm, n
Bewegungsprogramm, n
♦ **exercise program** *AE*
♦ exercise programme *BE*
Gymnastikrad, m
Heimtrainer, m
♦ **exercise bike**
Gymnastikraum, m
Trimmraum, m
Trainingsraum, m
♦ **exercise room**
Gymnastikräume, m pl
♦ **exercise suite**
Gymnastiksaal, m
♦ **large exercise room**
Gymnastikstudio, n
♦ **exercise studio**
Gymnastikstunde, f
♦ **exercise session**
GZH, f
Gaszentralheizung, f
♦ **GCH**
♦ gas central heating

Haarbehandlung, f
 ♦ hair treatment
Haar in der Suppe, n
 (konkret)
 ♦ hair in the soup
Haar in der Suppe finden
 nörgeln
 ♦ find s.th. to criticise
 ♦ find s.th. to moan about *coll*
Haarpflege, f
 ♦ hair care
Haarpflegebehandlung, f
 ♦ hair care treatment
Haarstudio, n
 ♦ hair studio
Haben Sie das Formular ausgefüllt?
 ♦ Have you completed the form?
 ♦ Have you filled in the form? *BE*
 ♦ Have you filled out the form? *AE*
Haben Sie ein Einzelzimmer frei?
 ♦ Do you have a single room free?
Haben Sie ein Einzelzimmer mit Bad?
 ♦ Have you a single room with bath?
Haben Sie einen Tisch für drei Personen?
 ♦ Have you a table for three persons?
 ♦ Have you a table for three?
Haben Sie einen Tisch reserviert?
 ♦ Have you reserved a table?
Haben Sie ein Zimmer frei?
 Haben Sie ein Zimmer?
 ♦ Have you a room vacant?
Haben Sie ein Zimmer (für mich)?
 ♦ Do you have a room (for me)?
Haben Sie etwas dagegen, wenn ich mich
 hier hinsetze?
 ♦ Do you mind if I sit here?
Haben Sie gebucht?
 ♦ Have you booked?
Haben Sie geläutet?
 ♦ Did you ring the bell?
Haben Sie gewählt?
 (im Restaurant)
 ♦ Have you decided?
Haben Sie heute nacht ein Zimmer frei?
 ♦ Have you got a room free for tonight?
 ♦ Have you a room free for tonight?
Haben Sie Ihren Schlüssel abgegeben?
 ♦ Did you give back your key?
Haben Sie nichts vergessen?
 ♦ Have you not left anything?
Haben Sie noch eine Box frei?
 (Garage)
 ♦ Have you got a box free?
Haben Sie noch eine Garage frei?
 ♦ Have you got a garage free?
Haben Sie noch einen Wunsch?
 ♦ Is there anything else I can do for you?

Haben Sie noch eine Unterkunft frei?
 ♦ Do you have any accommodation available?
Haben Sie noch Zimmer frei?
 ♦ Do you have any rooms free?
Haben Sie reserviert?
 ♦ Have you made a reservation?
Haben Sie richtig geschlafen?
 ♦ Did you sleep all right?
Haben Sie schon bestellt?
 (z.B. im Restaurant)
 ♦ Have you ordered yet?
Haben Sie schon eine Unterkunft?
 ♦ Are you fixed up with accommodation? *coll*
Haben Sie schon ein Quartier?
 ♦ Have you got somewhere to stay?
Haben Sie schon gegessen?
 ♦ Have you eaten (yet)?
 ♦ Have you already eaten?
Haben Sie schon gewählt?
 (z.B. im Restaurant)
 ♦ Have you decided yet?
Habitué, m *FR*
 ständiger Besucher, m
 ständiger Gast, m
 Stammgast, m
 ♦ habitué *FR*
 ♦ regular guest
 ♦ regular customer
Habituée, f *FR*
 ständige Besucherin f
 ständiger Gast m
 ♦ habituée *FR*
 ♦ regular guest
 ♦ regular customer
Habitué eines Cafés, m *FR*
 Stammgast eines Cafés, m
 ♦ habitué of a café *FR*
Haché, n
 → Haschee
Hackblock, m
 ♦ chopping block
Hackbraten, m
 ♦ meat loaf
Hackbrett, n *gastr*
 Küchenbrett, n *gastr*
 ♦ chopping board *gastr*
hacken (etw)
 ♦ chop (s.th.)
Hadrianswall, m
 ♦ Hadrian's Wall, the
Hadsch, f
 Pilgerfahrt nach Mekka, f
 ♦ hadj
Hafen, m
 ♦ port
 ♦ harbor *AE*
 ♦ harbour *BE*

Hafen anlaufen
 ♦ call at a port
 ♦ make a call at a port
Hafenbesuch, m
 ♦ port visit
 ♦ port call
Hafen besuchen
 ♦ visit a port
Hafenblick, m
 Blick auf den Hafen m
 ♦ harbor view *AE*
 ♦ harbour view *BE*
 ♦ view of the harbor *AE*
 ♦ view of the harbour *BE*
Hafendamm, m
 Mole, f
 ♦ jetty
Hafeneinrichtung, f
 ♦ port facility
Hafenfahrt, f
 ♦ dock trip
 ♦ trip around the docks
Hafenfahrt, f
 Hafenrundfahrtt, f
 ♦ harbor tour *AE*
 ♦ harbour tour *BE*
 ♦ tour of the harbor *AE*
 ♦ tour of the harbour *BE*
Hafenfest, n
 ♦ harbor festival *AE*
 ♦ harbour festival *BE*
Hafenfete, f
 Hafenfest, n
 ♦ harbor fete *AE*
 ♦ harbour fête *BE*
 ♦ harbor gala *AE*
 ♦ harbour gala *BE*
Hafengebühr, f
 ♦ port charge
 ♦ port fee
Hafenhotel n
 ♦ harbor hotel *AE*
 ♦ harbour hotel *BE*
 ♦ port hotel
Hafenkonzert, n
 ♦ harbor concert *AE*
 ♦ harbour concert *BE*
Hafenmeister, m
 ♦ harbor master *AE*
 ♦ harbour-master *BE*
Hafenpolizei, f
 ♦ harbor police *AE*
 ♦ harbour police *BE*
Hafenrundfahrt, f
 ♦ trip around the docks
 ♦ tour of the port
 ♦ tour of the harbor *AE*

Hafenseite 328

- ♦ tour of the harbour *BE*
- ♦ harbor tour *AE*

Hafenseite, f
- ♦ harbor side *AE*
- ♦ harbour side *BE*

Hafenstadt, f (Großstadt)
- ♦ port city
- ♦ harbor city *AE*
- ♦ harbour city *BE*

Hafenstadt, f (kleine Stadt)
- ♦ port town
- ♦ harbor town *AE*
- ♦ harbour town *BE*

Hafensteuer, f
Hafentaxe f
- ♦ port tax
- ♦ harbor tax *AE*
- ♦ harbour tax *BE*

Hafenviertel, n
- ♦ harbor quarter *AE*
- ♦ harbour quarter *BE*
- ♦ harbor district *AE*
- ♦ harbour district *BE*

Hafenvortrag, m
Vortrag über den Hafen, m
- ♦ port lecture
- ♦ lecture on the port

Hafenwohnung, f
- ♦ harborside apartment *AE*
- ♦ harbourside flat *BE*

Haferbrei, m
Porridge, m/n
- ♦ cooked oatmeal *AE*
- ♦ oatmeal *AE*
- ♦ porridge *BE*

Haferbrot, n
- ♦ oatmeal bread

Haferflocken, f pl
- ♦ porridge oats *BE pl*
- ♦ oatmeal *AE sg*

Hafergrütze, f
- ♦ groats *pl*

Haferkeks, m
- ♦ oat biscuit

Haferkleie, f
- ♦ oat bran

Hafermehl, n
- ♦ oatmeal

Haferschleim, m
Haferschleimsuppe, f
- ♦ gruel

Haferschrot, m/n
Hafergrütze, f
- ♦ grits *pl*

haftbar, adj *jur*
haftbar für etw, adj
- ♦ liable, adj *jur*
- ♦ responsible, adj
- ♦ liable for s.th., adj *jur*
- ♦ responsible for s.th., adj

haftbar sein für etw
haftpflichtig sein für etw
- ♦ be liable for s.th.

haften für die Garderobe
- ♦ be responsible for articles of clothing

haften für Mängel
- ♦ be liable for defects

Haftpflicht, f
- ♦ liability
- ♦ third party liability

haftpflichtig für etw
- ♦ liable for s.th.

Haftpflichtversicherung, f
(des Geschädigten gegenüber Dritten)
- ♦ third party insurance
- ♦ liability insurance

Haftpflichtversicherung abschließen
- ♦ take out a third party insurance

Haftung, f
- ♦ liability

Haftungsausschluß, m
(bei einer Haftpflichtversicherung)
- ♦ collision damage waiver

Hafturlaub, m
- ♦ prisoner's leave

Hagebutte, f
- ♦ rose hip

Hagebuttenkaltschale, f
- ♦ cold rose-hip soup

Hagebuttensoße, f
- ♦ rose hip sauce

Hagebuttentee, m
- ♦ rose hip tea

Hahn, m (Technik)
Zapfhahn, m
- ♦ tap *BE*
- ♦ faucet *AE*

Hahn, m (Tier)
- ♦ rooster
- ♦ cock

Hahn abdrehen
Wasserhahn zudrehen
- ♦ turn off a faucet *AE*
- ♦ turn off a tap *BE*

Hahn aufdrehen
Wasserhahn aufdrehen
- ♦ turn on a faucet *AE*
- ♦ turn on a tap *BE*

Hähnchen, n *gastr*
Brathähnchen, n
- ♦ broiler
- ♦ chicken
- ♦ fryer *AE*

Hähnchenrestaurant, n
- ♦ chicken restaurant

Hahnenkampf, m
- ♦ cockfight

Hahnenkampfplatz, m
- ♦ cockpit

Haifischbecken, n
- ♦ shark tank

haifischfrei, adj
- ♦ shark-free, adj
- ♦ free from shark, adj

haifischfreier Strand, m
- ♦ shark-free beach

Hain, m
- ♦ grove

Haiti
- ♦ Haiti

Haitianer, m
Haitier, m
- ♦ Haitian

Haitianerin, f
Haitierin, f
- ♦ Haitian girl
- ♦ Haitian woman
- ♦ Haitian

haitianisch, adj
haitisch, adj
- ♦ Haitian, adj

Halbe Bier, f
- ♦ pint of beer

Halbedelstein, m
- ♦ semi-precious stone

halbe Flasche, f
- ♦ half a bottle
- ♦ half bottle

halben Fahrpreis zahlen
- ♦ pay half fare

halben Preis zahlen
- ♦ pay half price
- ♦ pay half rate

halbe Portion, f
- ♦ half a portion

halber Fahrpreis, m
- ♦ half fare

halber Liter, m
- ♦ half a liter *AE*
- ♦ half a litre *BE*
- ♦ pint *coll*

halber Preis, m
- ♦ half price
- ♦ half rate

halber Preis für Kinder, m
- ♦ half price for children
- ♦ half rate for children

halber Tarif m
- ♦ half rate
- ♦ half price

halbes Dutzend, n
- ♦ half a dozen

halbes Hähnchen, n
- ♦ half a chicken

halbfertiges Hotel, n
- ♦ half-completed hotel

Halbfinale, n
- ♦ semifinal *AE*
- ♦ semi-final *BE*

Halbfinale gewinnen
- ♦ win the semifinal *AE*
- ♦ win the semi-final *BE*

halbgekocht, adj
- ♦ half-cooked, adj

Halbgeschoß, n
Zwischengeschoß, n
- ♦ entresol
- ♦ mezzanine floor

halbieren etw
in zwei Hälften schneiden etw
- ♦ cut s.th. in half
- ♦ cut s.th. into halves

halbiert, adj
- ♦ halved, adj

halbierter Apfel, m
- ♦ halved apple

Halbinsel, f
- ♦ peninsula

Halbinsel Yucatan, f
→ Yucatan-Halbinsel

halbjährige Kündigung, f
- ♦ six months' notice
- ♦ giving six months' notice

halbjährlich, adj
- ♦ half-yearly, adj
- ♦ semi-annual, adj

halbleer, adj
halb leer, adj
- ♦ half-empty, adj

halbleere Bar, f
- ♦ half-empty bar

halbleere Flasche, f
 ♦ half-empty bottle
halbleeres Hotel, n
 ♦ half-empty hotel
halb leer sein
 ♦ be half empty
Halbliterflasche, f
 ♦ half-liter bottle AE
 ♦ half-litre bottle BE
halbmonatlich, adj/adv
 ♦ half-monthly, adj/adv
 ♦ fortnightly, adj/adv BE
Halbpension, f
 ♦ half board
 ♦ demipension AE
 ♦ demi-pension FR
 ♦ half pension AE
 ♦ Modified American Plan (MAP)
Halbpension anbieten
 ♦ offer half board
 ♦ offer demipension AE
 ♦ offer half pension AE
Halbpension bieten
 ♦ provide half board
 ♦ provide demipension AE
 ♦ provide half pension AE
Halbpension buchen
 ♦ book half board
 ♦ book demipension AE
 ♦ book half pension AE
Halbpensionbuchung, f
 ♦ half-board booking
 ♦ demipension booking AE
 ♦ half-pension reservation AE
Halbpensioneinnahmen, f pl
 Halbpensionseinnahmen, f pl
 ♦ half-board revenue
 ♦ half-board income
 ♦ demipension revenue AE
 ♦ demipension income AE
Halbpensiongast, m
 Halbpensionsgast, m
 Gast mit Halbpension, m
 ♦ half-board guest
 ♦ half-board client
 ♦ demipension guest AE
 ♦ demipension client AE
 ♦ guest on half board
Halbpension haben
 ♦ stay on half board
 ♦ be on half board
 ♦ stay on demipension AE
 ♦ be on demipension AE
 ♦ stay on half pension AE
Halbpensionhotelunterkunft, f
 ♦ half-board hotel accommodation
 ♦ demipension hotel accommodation AE
 ♦ half-pension hotel accommodation AE
Halbpension mit Frühstücksbüfett, f
 Halbpension inklusive Frühstücksbüfett, f
 ♦ half board including buffet breakfast
 ♦ demipension including buffet breakfast AE
 ♦ half pension including buffet breakfast AE
Halbpension nehmen
 ♦ take half board
 ♦ take half pension AE
 ♦ take demipension AE
Halbpensionpauschale, f
 ♦ half-board package
 ♦ demipension package AE
 ♦ half-pension package AE

Halbpensionpreis, m
 HP-Preis, m
 ♦ half-board rate
 ♦ half-board price
 ♦ demipension rate AE
 ♦ demipension price BE
 ♦ half-pension price AE
Halbpensionsangebot, n
 ♦ half-board offer
 ♦ demipension offer AE
 ♦ half-pension offer AE
Halbpensionsarrangement, n
 Halbpensionsvereinbarung, f
 ♦ half-board arrangement
 ♦ demipension arrangement AE
 ♦ MAP arrangement
 ♦ half-pension arrangement AE
Halbpensionsgutschein, m
 ♦ half-board voucher
 ♦ demipension voucher AE
 ♦ MAP voucher
 ♦ half-pension voucher AE
Halbpensionstarif, m
 ♦ half-board tariff
 ♦ demipension tariff AE
 ♦ half-board rates pl
 ♦ MAP tariff
 ♦ half-board terms pl
Halbpensionsunterkunft, f
 Halbpensionsunterbringung, f
 ♦ half-board accommodation
 ♦ demipension accommodation AE
 ♦ half-pension accommodation AE
Halbpensionsvereinbarung, f
 Halbpensionsarrangement, n
 ♦ demipension arrangement AE
 ♦ half-board arrangement
 ♦ half-pension arrangement AE
 ♦ MAP arrangement
Halbpensiontagespreis, m
 Tagespreis für Halbpension, m
 ♦ daily half-board rate
 ♦ daily half-board price
 ♦ daily demipension rate AE
 ♦ daily demipension price AE
 ♦ daily half-pension rate AE
Halbpension umfaßt Zimmer, Frühstück und Abendessen
 ♦ half board includes room, breakfast and dinner
 ♦ demipension includes room, breakfast and dinner AE
 ♦ half pension includes room, breakfast and dinner AE
Halbpensionumsatz, m
 ♦ half-board sales pl
 ♦ demipension sales AE pl
 ♦ half-pension sales AE pl
Halbpensionurlaub, m
 Halbpensionferien, pl
 ♦ demipension vacation AE
 ♦ half-pension vacation AE
 ♦ half-board holiday BE
Halbpensionwochenpreis, m
 Wochenpreis für Halbpension, m
 ♦ weekly half-board rate
 ♦ weekly half-board price
 ♦ weekly demipension rate AE
 ♦ weekly demipension price AE
 ♦ weekly half-pension price AE

Halbpensionzuschlag, m
 ♦ half-board supplement
 ♦ demipension supplement AE
 ♦ supplement for half board
 ♦ supplement for demipension AE
 ♦ half-pension supplement AE
halbstündig, adj
 ♦ half-hour, adj
halbstündige Fahrt, f (Auto)
 ♦ half-hour drive
 ♦ half-hour ride
 ♦ half hour's drive
 ♦ half hour's ride
halbstündige Fahrt, f (generell)
 ♦ half-hour trip
 ♦ half-hour ride
halbstündlich, adv
 ♦ half-hourly, adv
 ♦ every half hour, adv
 ♦ every 30 minutes, adj
halbtägig, adj
 ♦ half-day, adj
 ♦ half a day's, adj
 ♦ lasting half a day
 ♦ of half day's duration
halbtägige Busreise, f
 ♦ half-day bus tour
 ♦ half-day bus trip
 ♦ half-day coach tour BE
 ♦ half-day coach trip BE
halbtägige Stadtbesichtigung f
 ♦ half-day city sightseeing tour
 ♦ half-day city tour
halbtägige Veranstaltung, f
 ♦ half-day function
 ♦ half-day event
halbtags arbeiten
 ♦ work part-time
Halbtagsausflug, m
 ♦ half-day outing
 ♦ half-day excursion
 ♦ half-day trip
Halbtagsbesichtigung, f
 ♦ half-day sightseeing
Halbtagsbesichtigungsfahrt, f
 ♦ half-day sightseeing trip
 ♦ half-day sightseeing tour
Halbtagsbesuch, m
 ♦ half-day visit
 ♦ half day's visit
Halbtagsbesuch bei etw, m
 Halbtagsbesuch in etw, m
 ♦ half-day visit to s.th.
Halbtagsexkursion, f
 Halbtagsausflug, m
 ♦ half-day excursion
Halbtagsfahrt, f
 ♦ half-day trip
 ♦ half-day ride
Halbtagsprogramm, n
 ♦ half-day program AE
 ♦ half-day programme BE
Halbtagsreise, f
 ♦ half-day journey
 ♦ half-day tour
 ♦ half-day trip
Halbtagssitzung, f
 ♦ half-day session
Halbtagswanderung, f
 ♦ half-day walk

halbtrocken

- half-day hike
- half day's ramble

halbtrocken, adj *gastr*
(Wein, Sekt)
- medium dry, adj *gastr*
- demi-sec, adj *FR gastr*

halbverfallenes Dorf, m
- half-ruined village

halbvoll, adj
halb voll, adj
- half-full, adj

halbvolle Flasche, f
- half-full bottle

halb voll sein
- be half full

Halbwelt, f
- demimonde *AE*
- demi-monde *BE*

Hälfte, f
- half

Halle, f
- hall
- large room

Halle anmieten
Halle mieten
Saal mieten
- hire a hall *BE*
- rent a hall

Halle besichtigen
Saal besichtigen
- view a hall

Hallenbad, n
Schwimmhalle, f
- indoor swimming pool *AE*
- indoor swimming-pool *BE*
- indoor pool
- swimming-bath *BE*

Hallenbadanlage, f
Hallenbadkomplex, m
- indoor swimming-pool complex
- indoor pool complex

Hallenbadbenutzung, f
- use of the indoor swimming pool *AE*
- use of the indoor swimming-pool *BE*
- using the indoor swimming pool *AE*
- using the indoor swimming-pool *BE*

Hallenbadbesuch, m
- visit to the indoor swimming pool *AE*
- visit to the indoor swimming-pool *BE*
- visit to the indoor pool

Hallenbadgebühr, f
Hallenbadbenutzungsgebühr, f
- charge for the use of the indoor swimming pool *AE*
- fee for the use of the indoor swimming pool *AE*
- charge for the use of the indoor swimming-pool *BE*
- fee for the use of the indoor swimming-pool *BE*
- charge for using the indoor swimming pool *AE*

Hallenbad mit Gegenstromanlage, n
- indoor swimming pool with jet stream *AE*
- indoor-swimming pool with jet stream *BE*
- indoor pool with jet stream

Hallenbar, f
Lobbybar, f
- lobby bar

Hallenbecken, n
Innenbecken, n
- indoor pool

Hallenbesitzer, m
Saalbesitzer, m
- hall owner

Hallenbestuhlung, f
Saalbestuhlung, f
- hall seating

Hallenbühne, f
Saalbühne, f
- hall stage

Hallenchef, m
- lobby manager

Hallencommis, m
- commis hall waiter
- commis lobby waiter *AE*
- assistant hall waiter
- assistant lobby waiter *AE*

Halleneingang, m (im Hotel)
- lobby entrance *AE*
- hall entrance

Halleneinrichtung, f (Fazilität)
- hall facility
- lobby facility *AE*

Halleneinrichtung, f (Mobiliar)
- hall furniture *sg*
- lobby furniture *AE sg*
- hall furnishings *pl*
- lobby furnishings *AE pl*

Halleneisbahn, f
→ Eislaufhalle

Hallenfläche, f
Saalfläche, f
- hall area

Hallenfußball, m
- five-a-side football *BE*
- indoor football *BE*
- indoor soccer *AE*

Hallengolf, m/n
- indoor golf

Hallenimbißstand, m
Hallenimbiß, m
Saalimbißstand, m
Saalimbiß, m
- hall snackbar

Hallenkapazität, f
Saalkapazität, f
- hall capacity
- capacity of a hall

Hallenkegelbahn, f
- indoor bowling alley

Hallenkellner, m
- hall waiter
- lounge waiter
- lobby waiter *AE*

Hallenkellnerin, f
- hall waitress
- lounge waitress
- lobby waitress *AE*

Hallenkorridor, m
Saalkorridor, m
- hall corridor

Hallenkosten, pl
→ Saalkosten

Hallenmarkt, m
- indoor market

Hallenmeister, m
(bei Kongreß)
- hall manager

Hallenmeisterschaft, f
- indoor championship

Hallenmiete, f
Saalmiete, f

- hall hire *BE*
- hall rental *AE*
- hall rent

Hallenmieter, m
Saalmieter, m
- hall hirer *BE*
- hall renter *AE*

Hallenpersonal, n
(Portiers etc)
- lobby staff *BE*
- lobby personnel *AE*
- hall staff *BE*
- hall personnel *BE*

Hallenplan, m
Saalplan, m
- plan of the hall
- hall plan

Hallenplatz, m (Tennis)
- indoor court

Hallenportier, m
- hall porter

Hallen-Putting-Grün, n
Putting-Grün im Innern, n
- indoor putting green

Hallenrestaurant, n (Hotellobby)
- lobby restaurant *AE*

Hallenrestaurant, n (Messe)
- in-hall restaurant

Hallensalon, m
Hallenlounge, f
Lobbylounge, f
- lobby lounge

Hallenschwimmbad, n
→ Hallenbad

Hallenservice, m
- hall service
- lobby service *AE*

Hallensolebad, n
→ s. Solehallenbad n

Hallensport, m
- indoor sports
- indoor sport

hallensportveranstaltung, f
- indoor sports event
- indoor sport event

Hallensportzentrum, n
- indoor sports center *AE*
- indoor sports centre *BE*

Hallentennis, n
- indoor tennis

Hallentennisplatz, m
→ Tennishalle

Hallentennisplatzbenutzung, f
- use of the indoor tennis court
- using the indoor tennis court

Hallentennisturnier, n
- indoor tennis tournament

Hallentenniszentrum, n
- indoor tennis center *AE*
- indoor tennis centre *BE*

Hallentournant, m
- relief hall porter

Hallenveranstaltung, f
Innenveranstaltung, f
- indoor event
- indoor function

Hallenvermieter, m
Saalvermieter, m
- hall lessor *jur*
- hall renter *AE*

- ◆ person renting a hall *AE*
- ◆ person letting a hall *BE*

Hallenwellenbad n
Wellenhallenbad n
- ◆ indoor swimming pool with artificial waves
- ◆ indoor pool with artificial waves

Hallstätter See, m
- ◆ Lake of Hallstatt, the

Halogenbeleuchtung, f
- ◆ halogen lighting

Hals über Kopf, adv
- ◆ pell-mell, adv

haltbar gemachte Lebensmittel, n pl
- ◆ processed food

haltbar machen etw *gastr*
einsalzen etw *gastr*
pökeln etw *gastr*
räuchern etw *gastr*
- ◆ cure s.th. *gastr*

Haltebucht, f (an Landstraße)
- ◆ rest area *AE*
- ◆ lay-by *BE*

halten etw auf Zimmertemperatur
auf Zimmertemperatur halten etw
- ◆ keep s.th. at room temperature

halten etw in bewohnbarem Zustand
in bewohnbarem Zustand halten etw
- ◆ keep s.th. in habitable repair

Halten verboten
(Hinweisschild)
- ◆ No Stopping

Halteplatz, m
(z.B. an der Straße)
- ◆ stopping place

Haltepunkt, m
Haltestelle, f
- ◆ stop
- ◆ stopping place
- ◆ stopping-off point

Haltepunkt für die Dampferfahrten, m
- ◆ stopping-off point for the steamer tours

Halteverbot, n
- ◆ prohibition of stopping
- ◆ ban on stopping
- ◆ stopping ban

Halteverbotsschild, n
(für Autos)
- ◆ no-stopping sign
- ◆ 'no stopping' sign

haltmachen auf einem Campingplatz
bleiben auf einem Campingplatz
- ◆ stop at a campsite
- ◆ stop at a campground *AE*
- ◆ stop at a camping site *BE*
- ◆ stop at a camping ground *BE*

haltmachen bei etw
- ◆ pause at s.th.
- ◆ make a stop at s.th.
- ◆ stop at s.th.

haltmachen in X
- ◆ stop in X
- ◆ stop at X
- ◆ make a stop in X
- ◆ make a stop at X

Halt machen in X für zwei Stunden
- ◆ make a stop in X for two hours
- ◆ make a stop at X for two hours

Halt unterwegs, m
Stopp unterwegs, m
Rast unterwegs, f
- ◆ stop en route
- ◆ en route stop

Halt zum Essen, m
- ◆ mealstop

Hamburger, m (Speise)
- ◆ hamburger

Hamburger bestellen
- ◆ order a hamburger

Hamburgerkette, f
- ◆ hamburger chain

Hamburgerstand, m
- ◆ hamburger stand
- ◆ burger stand

Hamburgerstube, f
- ◆ hamburger restaurant

Hammelbraten, m
- ◆ roast mutton

Hammelbrust, f
- ◆ mutton breast

Hammelcurry, m/n
- ◆ mutton curry

Hammelfilet, n
- ◆ mutton fillet
- ◆ mutton filet

Hammelfleisch, n
- ◆ mutton

Hammelgulasch, m/n
- ◆ mutton goulash

Hammelkeule, f
- ◆ mutton leg

Hammelkotelett, n
- ◆ mutton cutlet

Hammellende, f
- ◆ tenderloin of mutton

Hammelniere, f
- ◆ mutton kidney

Hammelpastete, f
- ◆ mutton pie
- ◆ mutton pâté

Hammelragout, n/m
- ◆ mutton stew

Hammelschnitzel, n
- ◆ mutton escalope

Hammelschulter, f
- ◆ mutton shoulder

Hammelspießchen, n
- ◆ mutton skewer

Hammelsuppe, f
- ◆ mutton soup

Hammelzunge, f
- ◆ mutton tongue

Hammer, m (für den Vorsitzenden)
Hämmerchen, n
- ◆ gavel

Handball, m
- ◆ handball

Handballer, m
- ◆ handballer

Handballmannschaft, f
- ◆ handball team

Handballplatz, m
- ◆ handball court

Handball spielen
- ◆ play handball

Handbecken, n
(Waschbecken)
- ◆ hand basin

Handbuch, n (generell)
- ◆ handbook

Handbuch, n (Leitfaden)
- ◆ manual

Handbuch des Reisens, n
- ◆ handbook of travel

Hände abtrocknen sich
- ◆ dry one's hands

Handel, m
Gewerbe, n
- ◆ trade

Handelsdelegation, f
- ◆ trade delegation

Handelshafen, m
- ◆ commercial port
- ◆ trading port

Handelsmesse, f
- ◆ trade fair

Handelsreisender m
Handlungsreisender m
Vertreter m
- ◆ traveling salesman *AE*
- ◆ travelling salesman *BE*

Handelsschiff, n
- ◆ merchant ship
- ◆ trading ship
- ◆ trading vessel

Handelsstraße, f
- ◆ trade route

Handelsvertreter, m *jur*
- ◆ commercial agent *jur*

Handelsvertreterstatus, m *jur*
- ◆ commercial agent status *jur*

Hände sich waschen
sich die Hände waschen
- ◆ wash one's hands

handgeblasen, adj
- ◆ hand-blown, adj

handgeblasenes Glas, n
- ◆ hand-blown glass

Handgepäck, n (Flug)
- ◆ carry-on baggage *AE*
- ◆ carry-on luggage *BE*

Handgepäck, n (generell)
- ◆ hand-baggage *AE*
- ◆ hand-luggage *BE*

handgeschnitzt, adj
- ◆ hand-carved, adj

handgeschnitzter Altar, m
- ◆ hand-carved altar

handgeschriebene Speisekarte f
- ◆ handwritten menu

handgezapft, adj
- ◆ hand-pulled, adj

handgezapftes Ale, n
- ◆ hand-pulled ale

Handkamera, f
- ◆ hand-held camera

Handkarren, m
Handkarre, f
- ◆ handcart

Handkoffer, m
- ◆ small suitcase

Handling Agent, m
(für Personen und Güter)
- ◆ handling agent

Handling Agentur, f
(für Personen und Güter)
- ◆ handling agency

Handlungsreisender m
→ Handelsreisender

Handmassage, f (der Hand)
Massage der Hand, f
- ◆ hand massage

Handmassage 332

Handmassage, f (mit der Hand)
 ♦ manual massage
Handmikrofon, n
 ♦ hand-held microphone
Handschuhfach, n
 ♦ glove compartment
Handtuch, n
 ♦ towel
Handtücher werden täglich gewechselt
 ♦ towels are changed daily
Handtuch für die Hände, n
 ♦ hand towel
Handtuchhaken, m
 ♦ towel hook
 ♦ hook for a towel
Handtuch leihen
 Handtuch mieten
 ♦ rent a towel AE
 ♦ hire a towel BE
Handtuchspender, m
 ♦ towel dispenser
 ♦ paper towel dispenser
Handtuchstange, f
 ♦ towel rail
Handtuch stellen
 Handtuch bereitstellen
 ♦ provide a towel
Handtuchwärmer, m
 ♦ towel warmer
Handtuchwechsel, m
 Wechsel der Handtücher, m
 ♦ change of towels
Handtuch wechseln
 Handtücher wechseln
 ♦ change towels
 ♦ change the towels
Handwaschbecken, n
 ♦ wash-hand-basin BE
 ♦ hand-wash-basin BE
 ♦ hand basin
Handwäsche, f
 ♦ hand wash
 ♦ hand washing
Handzettel, m
 (für Werbung oder Information)
 Flugblatt, n
 ♦ handbill
Hang, m
 (Berghang)
 ♦ slope
Hängebett, n
 (Wohnwagen)
 ♦ hammock bunk
Hängekorb, m
 (z.B. für Blumen)
 ♦ hanging basket
Hängelampe, f
 ♦ hanging lamp
Hängematte f
 ♦ hammock
Hängenden Gärten, die, m pl
 ♦ Hanging Gardens, the pl
Hängestuhl, m
 ♦ hanging chair
Hanglage f
 ♦ hillside position
 ♦ hillside location
 ♦ hillside situation
Hanse, f
 ♦ Hanseatic League, the
 ♦ Hansa, the

Hansestadt, f
 (Eigenname)
 ♦ Hansa Town
 ♦ Hanseatic town
 ♦ Hansa City
 ♦ Hanseatic city
Hansestadt Rostock, f
 ♦ Hanseatic city of Rostock
Hansom, m
 (zweirädrige Kutsche)
 ♦ hansom cab
Happening, n
 ♦ happening
Happy Hour f
 (ermäßigte Getränkepreise)
 ♦ Happy Hour
Hardtwald, m
 ♦ Hardt Forest, the
Harlekinsart, adv gastr
 nach Harlekinsart, adv gastr
 ♦ harlequin's style, adv gastr
harmonische Atmosphäre, f
 ♦ harmonious atmosphere
harmonischer Wein, m
 ♦ well-balanced wine
hartes Bett, n
 ♦ hard bed
hartgekocht, adj
 ♦ hard-cooked, adj AE
 ♦ hard-boiled, adj BE
hartgekochtes Ei, n
 ♦ hard-cooked egg AE
 ♦ hard-boiled egg BE
Hartplatz, m
 (Tennis)
 ♦ hard court
Harttennisplatz, m
 ♦ hard tennis court
 ♦ hard-top tennis court
 ♦ hard-surface tennis court
Harz, m
 (Region)
 ♦ Harz Mountains, the pl
 ♦ Harz, the
Harzreise, f
 (Heinrich Heine)
 ♦ Journey through the Harz Mountains
Haschee, n
 Haché, n
 ♦ hash
 ♦ minced meat
Haschisch, n/m
 ♦ hashish
 ♦ hasheesh
 ♦ haschisch
Hase, m
 ♦ hare
Haselnuß, f
 ♦ hazelnut
Haselnußbutter, f
 ♦ hazelnut butter
Hasenbraten, m
 ♦ roast hare
Hasenfilet, n
 ♦ fillet of hare
 ♦ filet of hare
Hasenfleisch, n
 ♦ hare meat
Hasenkeule, f
 ♦ leg of hare

Hasenkotelett, n
 ♦ hare cutlet
Hasenpastete, f
 ♦ hare pie
 ♦ hare pâté
Hasenpfeffer, m
 ♦ jugged hare
Hasenragout, n/m
 ♦ hare stew
Hasenrücken, m
 ♦ saddle of hare
Hasensoufflé, n
 Hasenauflauf, n
 ♦ hare soufflé
 ♦ hare souffle AE
Hasensuppe, f
 ♦ hare soup
hastig, adj
 ♦ hasty, adj
hastig abreisen
 ♦ leave in a hurry
 ♦ depart in a hurry
hastig absagen etw
 hastig stornieren etw
 ♦ cancel s.th. hastily
hastige Abreise, f
 eilige Abreise f
 ♦ hasty departure
hastiger Abschied, m
 eiliger Abschied m
 ♦ hasty farewell
hastiges Frühstück, n
 ♦ hurry-up breakfast AE
hastig essen
 ♦ eat hastily
 ♦ eat in a hurry
hastig improvisiert, adj
 ♦ hastily improvised, adj
hastig improvisiertes Essen, n
 ♦ hastily improvised meal
Hat es Ihnen geschmeckt?
 ♦ Did you enjoy your meal?
 ♦ Did you like your meal?
Hat Ihnen das Abendessen geschmeckt? (Dinner)
 ♦ Did you enjoy dinner?
Hat Ihnen das Abendessen geschmeckt? (Supper)
 ♦ Did you enjoy supper?
Hat Ihnen das Frühstück geschmeckt?
 ♦ Did you enjoy your breakfast?
Hat jemand abgesagt?
 ♦ Have you got a cancellation?
 ♦ Have you got a cancelation? AE
Hatten Sie eine angenehme Reise?
 ♦ Did you have a pleasant journey?
Hatten Sie eine gute Fahrt?
 ♦ Did you have a pleasant trip?
Hatten Sie eine gute Reise?
 ♦ Did you have a good journey?
Hatten Sie einen angenehmen Flug?
 ♦ Did you have a pleasant flight?
Hätten Sie morgens gern eine Zeitung?
 ♦ Would you like a morning paper?
hauchdünn, adj
 ♦ wafer-thin, adj
hauchdünnes Sandwich, n
 ♦ wafer-thin sandwich
Hauch von Luxus, m
 ♦ touch of luxury
häufig befahrene Strecke, f
 häufig genommene Route, f

- frequently travelled route
- frequently traveled route *AE*

häufig besuchen etw (Lokal)
→ besuchen etw regelmäßig

häufiger Benutzer, m
- frequent user

häufiger Besucher, m
- frequent visitor

häufiger Gast m
- frequent guest

häufiger Geschäftskunde, m
- frequent business customer
- frequent business client

häufiger Kunde, m
- frequent customer
- frequent client

häufig variierte Speisekarte, f
- frequently varied menu

Hauptabfahrtsort, m
Hauptabfahrtsstelle, f
- main departure point

Hauptaltar, m
- main altar

Hauptanziehungspunkt, m
Hauptattraktion f
- main attraction

Hauptapsis, f
- main apsis

Hauptaufenthaltsraum, m
→ Hauptgastraum

Hauptbahnhof, m
- main station

Hauptbar f
- main bar

Hauptbecken n
(Schwimmbad)
- main pool

Hauptbesuchergruppe, f
- main visitor group

Hauptbesuchszeit, f
- main visitor season

Hauptbesuchszweck, m
- main purpose of (the) visit

Hauptbühne, f
- main stage

Hauptcampingplatz, m
- main campsite
- main campground *AE*
- main camping site *BE*
- main camping ground *BE*
- main site

Hauptdeck, n
- main deck

Hauptdorf, n
- main village

Haupteingang, m
- main entrance
- grand entrance

Haupteingangsfoyer, n
- main entrance foyer

Haupteingangshalle, f
- main entrance hall

Haupteisenbahnstrecke, f
- main railroad line *AE*
- main railway line *BE*

Hauptessen, n
→ Hauptmahlzeit

Hauptetage, f
Hauptgeschoß, n
- main floor

Hauptfassade, f
- main façade
- main facade *AE*
- main front
- main frontage

Hauptferien, pl
Haupturlaub, m
- main holiday *BE*
- main holidays *BE* pl
- main vacation *AE*

Hauptferienland, n
Haupturlaubsland, n
- main holiday country *BE*
- main vacation country *AE*

Hauptferienmarkt, m
Haupturlaubsmarkt, m
- main holiday market *BE*
- main vacation market *AE*

Hauptferienort, m
Haupturlaubsort, m
Hauptort, m
- main resort

Hauptferienreise, f
Haupturlaubsreise, f
- main holiday trip *BE*
- principal holiday trip *BE*
- main vacation trip *AE*
- principal vacation trip *AE*

Hauptferienreiseziel, n
Hauptferienziel, n
Haupturlaubsreiseziel, n
Haupturlaubsziel, n
- main holiday destination *BE*
- main vacaction destination *AE*

Hauptferiensaison, f
Haupturlaubssaison, f
- main holiday season *BE*
- main vacation season *AE*

Hauptferienwoche, f
Haupturlaubswoche, f
- main holiday week *BE*
- main vacation week *AE*

Hauptferienzeit, f
Haupturlaubszeit, f
- main holiday period *BE*
- main holiday season *BE*
- main vacation period *AE*
- main vacation season *AE*

Hauptfestsaal, m
- main auditorium

Hauptfleischgang m
- main meat course

Hauptfoyer n
- main foyer

Hauptfremdenverkehrsgebiet, n (groß)
Haupttouristengebiet, n
- main tourist region
- main tourism region

Hauptfremdenverkehrsgebiet, n (klein)
Haupttouristengebiet, n
- main tourist area
- main tourism area

Hauptfremdenverkehrsort, m
- main tourist resort

Hauptgang, m
(Essen)
Hauptspeise, f
- main course

Hauptganggericht, n
- main-course dish

Hauptgang kommt
- main course arrives

Hauptgast, m
- chief guest
- principal guest

Hauptgastraum, m
Hauptaufenthaltsraum, m
- main public room
- main lounge

Hauptgebäude, n
- main building

Hauptgebiet, n (groß)
- main region

Hauptgebiet, n (klein)
- main area

Hauptgepäckträger, m
Erster Gepäckträger m
- chief baggage porter *AE*
- head luggage porter *BE*

Hauptgericht, n
- main dish
- entree *AE*

Hauptgetränk, n
(in einem Land)
- staple beverage

Hauptgetränkekeller, m
- main cellar

Hauptgruppe, f (Gäste)
- main group
- main party

Hauptgutschein, m
(berechtigt zum Empfang der Einzelvoucher)
Generalgutschein, m
Mastervoucher, m
- master voucher

Haupthafen, m
- main port
- main harbor *AE*
- main harbour *BE*

Haupthalle, f (Lobby)
→ Hauptlobby

Haupthaus, n
- main house

Haupthotel, n
- main hotel

Haupthotelgebäude, n
- main hotel building

Haupthotelrestaurant, n
- main hotel restaurant

Hauptinsel, f
- main island
- principal island

Hauptkartei, f
→ Stammdatei

Hauptkatalog, m
- main catalogue
- main catalog *AE*

Hauptkirche, f
- main church

Hauptkonferenzraum, m
- main conference room

Hauptkonferenzsaal, m
- main conference auditorium
- main conference room

Hauptkonferenzsaal faßt bis zu 300 Personen
- main conference room seats up to 300 persons

Hauptkontingent, n (Gäste)
- main party

Hauptkontingent der Gäste, n
Gros der Gäste, n

Hauptkontingent der Gäste stellen

- main party of guests
- main party of visitors
- bulk of (the) guests
- bulk of the clientele

Hauptkontingent der Gäste stellen
- form the main party of guests
- form the main party of visitors

Hauptkunde, m
- main customer

Hauptleistung, f
Hauptdienstleistung, f
Hauptservice, m
- principal service
- main service

Hauptlift, m (Haus)
Hauptfahrstuhl, m
Hauptaufzug, m
- main elevator AE
- main lift BE

Hauptlift, m (Ski)
- main lift

Hauptlobby, f
- main lobby

Hauptmahlzeit, f
Hauptessen, n
Hauptmahl, m
- main meal

Hauptmarkt, m
- main market

Hauptmast, m
- mainmast

Hauptmenü, n
- main menu

Hauptmieter, m
- main tenant

Hauptmietvertrag, m (Immobilien)
- master lease

Hauptmietvertrag haben
- hold the master lease
- have the master lease

Hauptmietvertrag unterzeichnen (Immobilien)
- sign a master lease

Hauptnachfrage, f
- main demand
- principal demand

Hauptnahrung, f
- staple diet
- staple food

Hauptpavillon, m
- main pavilion

Hauptplatz, m (Camping)
- main site

Hauptplatz, m (generell)
- main square

Hauptprogramm, n
- main program AE
- main programme BE

Hauptprospekt, m
- main brochure

Hauptpublikum, n
Hauptzuhörerschaft, f
Hauptzuhörer, m pl
- main audience

Hauptquerhaus, n
Hauptquerschiff, n
Haupttransept, m/n
- main transept

Hauptraum, m
→ Hauptzimmer

Hauptredner, m
- main speaker

Hauptreisegrund, m
- principal reason for travel
- principal reason for traveling AE
- principal reason for travelling BE
- primary reason for travel
- primary reason for traveling AE

Hauptreisemarkt, m
- main travel market

Hauptreisemotiv, n
- principal travel motivation
- principal motivation for traveling AE
- principal motivation for travelling BE
- principal motivation for travel

Hauptreisesaison, f
Hauptreisezeit, f
- main travel season
- main travel period

Hauptreisezeit, f
- main travel period
- main travel season

Hauptreiseziel, n
- main travel destination
- main destination
- principal travel destination
- principal destination

Hauptrestaurant, n
- main restaurant
- principal restaurant

Hauptrezeption f
(Gebäudeteil)
- main reception

Hauptrolle, f
- leading role
- principal role

Hauptroute, f
Hauptstrecke, f
- principal route
- main route

Hauptsaal, m
Haupthalle, f
- main hall

Hauptsaison, f
- main season

Hauptsaisoncamper, m
- main season camper

Hauptsaisoncamping, n
- main season camping

Hauptsaisonkontingent, n
- main season allocation
- main season allotment

Hauptsaisonmonat, m
- main season month
- month in the main season

Hauptsaisonreise, f
- main season tour
- main season journey
- main season trip

Hauptsaisonreiseverkehr, m
Hauptsaisonreisen, n
- main season travel

Hauptsaisontag, m
- main season day
- day in the main season

Hauptsaisonunterkunft, f
- main season accommodation

Hauptsaisonwoche, f
- main season week
- week in the main season

Hauptsalon, m
Hauptaufenthaltsraum, m

Hauptgastraum, m
- main lounge

Hauptschlafzimmer, n (für Hausherrn)
- master bedroom

Hauptschlafzimmer, n (generell)
- main bedroom
- principal bedroom

Hauptschlüssel, m
- passkey
- master key
- master
- passe-partout FR

Hauptsegel, n
- mainsail

Hauptsehenswürdigkeit, f
- main sight
- main attraction

Hauptsehenswürdigkeiten besichtigen
- see the main attractions
- see the main sights

Hauptservice, m
Hauptleistung, f
Hauptdienstleistung, f
- main service
- principal service

Hauptsommerurlaub, m
Hauptsommerferien, pl
- main summer vacation AE
- main summer holiday BE

Hauptspeise, f
→ Hauptgang

Hauptspeisesaal m
- main dining room

Hauptstadt, f
- capital city
- capital

Hauptstrand, m
- main beach

Hauptstraße, f
- main road
- main street

Hauptstrecke, f
Hauptroute, f
- main route
- principal route

Hauptterrasse, f
- main terrace

Haupttisch, m
- main table

Haupttischzeit f
- main sitting

Haupttor, n
- main gate

Haupttouristengebiet, n
→ Hauptfremdenverkehrsgebiet

Haupttouristenstrecke, f
Haupttouristenroute, f
- main tourist route

Haupttreppenhaus, n
- main staircase
- grand staircase

Haupttribüne, f
- grandstand

Haupttribünenplatz, m
Haupttribünensitzplatz, m
Haupttribünensitz, m
- grandstand seat
- seat in the grandstand

Hauptunterkunft, f
- main accommodation

334

Haupturlaub, m
  Hauptferien, pl
  ♦ **principal vacation** AE
  ♦ **main vacation** AE
  ♦ **principal holiday** BE
  ♦ **main holiday** BE
Haupturlaubsdestination, f
  → Haupturlaubsreiseziel
Haupturlaubsland, n
  Hauptferienland, n
  ♦ **main vacation country** AE
  ♦ **main holiday country** BE
Haupturlaubsmarkt, m
  Hauptferienmarkt, m
  ♦ **main vacation market** AE
  ♦ **main holiday market** BE
Haupturlaubsreise, f
  Hauptferienreise, f
  ♦ **main vacation trip** AE
  ♦ **principal vacation trip** AE
  ♦ **main holiday trip** BE
  ♦ **principal holiday trip** BE
Haupturlaubsreiseziel, n
  Haupturlaubsziel, n
  Hauptferienreiseziel, n
  Hauptferienziel, n
  ♦ **main vacation destination** AE
  ♦ **main holiday destination** BE
Haupturlaubssaison, f
  Hauptferiensaison, f
  ♦ **main vacation season** AE
  ♦ **main holiday season** BE
Haupturlaubswoche, f
  Hauptferienwoche, f
  ♦ **main vacation week** AE
  ♦ **main holiday week** BE
Haupturlaubszeit, f
  Hauptferienzeit, f
  ♦ **main vacation period** AE
  ♦ **main vacation season** AE
  ♦ **main holiday period** BE
  ♦ **main holiday season** BE
Hauptveranstaltung, f
  ♦ **main event**
  ♦ **main function**
Hauptveranstaltungsort, m
  ♦ **principal venue**
Hauptveranstaltungsraum, m
  ♦ **main function room**
Hauptvermieter, m jur
  ♦ **master lessor** jur
Hauptwäschekammer, f
  ♦ **main linen room**
Hauptwohnsitz, m
  Hauptwohnort, m
  ♦ **principal residence**
Hauptzelt, n
  ♦ **main tent**
Hauptzielort, m
  Hauptziel, n
  ♦ **main destination**
  ♦ **principal destination**
  ♦ **chief destination**
Hauptzimmer, n
  Hauptraum, m
  ♦ **main room**
Haus, das früher eine Stallung war, n
  ♦ **mews house**
Haus, n
  ♦ **house**
  ♦ **home**

Haus abreißen
  ♦ **knock down a house**
  ♦ **pull down a house**
  ♦ **dismantle a house**
Haus am Meer, n
  Haus an der See, n
  ♦ **house at the seaside**
  ♦ **house by the seaside**
Haus am Wasser, n
  ♦ **waterside house**
Hausangestellter, m
  → Hotelangestellter
Hausarbeit, f
  häusliche Arbeit, f
  ♦ **housework**
  ♦ **household chores** pl
  ♦ **domestic chores** pl
Hausarbeit erledigen
  Hausarbeit verrichten
  ♦ **do the housework**
  ♦ **do the household chores**
  ♦ **do the domestic chores**
Hausarbeitsraum, m
  Wirtschaftsraum, m
  ♦ **utility room**
Hausarrest, m
  ♦ **house arrest**
Hausarzt, m (generell)
  ♦ **house doctor**
Hausarzt, m (wohnt im selben Haus)
  ♦ **resident practioner**
Haus auf dem Land, n
  Landhaus, n
  ♦ **house in the country**
  ♦ **country house**
  ♦ **rural home**
  ♦ **rural retreat**
Haus auf Rädern, n
  ♦ **house on wheels**
Haus aus dem fünfzehnten Jahrhundert, n
  ♦ **fifteenth-century house**
Hausball, m
  Privatball, m
  ♦ **dinner and dance**
  ♦ **private ball**
Hausband, f
  Hauskapelle f
  ♦ **resident band**
Hausbank, f
  (Geldgeschäfte)
  ♦ **house bank**
Hausbar, f (im Hotel)
  Hausgästebar, f
  ♦ **residential bar**
  ♦ **bar for residents**
  ♦ **residents' bar**
Hausbar, f (im Privathaus)
  ♦ **liquor cabinet**
Hausbau, m
  ♦ **housebuilding**
Hausbauer, m
  Hauserbauer, m
  ♦ **housebuilder**
Hausbeschreibung, f (Hotel)
  → Hotelbeschreibung
Haus besetzen
  ♦ **squat**
Hausbesetzer, m
  ♦ **squatter**
Hausbesetzung, f
  ♦ **squatting**

Haus besichtigen
  ♦ **view a house**
Hausbesitzer, m
  ♦ **house owner**
  ♦ **landlord**
  ♦ **homeowner**
  ♦ **property owner**
Hausbesitzerverband, m
  ♦ **property owners' association**
Hausbesuch, m
  (z.B. durch einen Arzt)
  ♦ **home visit**
Haus besuchen
  ♦ **visit a house**
Hausbesucher, m
  (z.B. Arzt)
  ♦ **home visitor**
Haus bewohnen
  ♦ **occupy a house**
  ♦ **live in a house**
Hausbier, n
  ♦ **house beer**
Hausboot, n
  ♦ **houseboat**
Hausbootbesitzer, m
  ♦ **houseboat owner**
  ♦ **owner of a houseboat**
Hausbootfahren, n
  ♦ **houseboating**
Hausbootsteuer, f
  ♦ **houseboat tax**
Hausbooturlaub, m
  Hausbootferien, pl
  ♦ **houseboat holiday** BE
  ♦ **houseboating holiday** BE
  ♦ **houseboat vacation** AE
Hausboy, m
  ♦ **houseboy**
Hausbursche, m SCHW
  → Hoteldiener
Häuschen, n
  kleines Haus, n
  ♦ **maisonette**
  ♦ **maisonnette**
  ♦ **small house**
Hausdame, f
  (im Hotel)
  Gouvernante, f SCHW
  Beschließerin, f obs
  ♦ **housekeeper**
Hausdamenabteilung, f (Hotel)
  ♦ **housekeeping department**
Hausdamenarbeit f
  ♦ **housekeeping**
Hausdamenassistentin, f
  Assistentin der Hausdame, f
  Hilfsgouvernante, f SCHW
  ♦ **assistant housekeeper**
  ♦ **assistant to the housekeeper**
Hausdamenbereich m
  ♦ **housekeeping area**
Hausdamenbericht m
  ♦ **housekeeper's report**
  ♦ **housekeeping report**
Hausdamenbüro, n
  ♦ **housekeeper's office**
Hausdamenpersonal, n
  ♦ **housekeeping personnel**
  ♦ **housekeeping staff**

Hausdamentafel

Hausdamentafel, f
  Hausdamenbrett n
  ♦ housekeeper's board
Haus der A-Kategorie, n (Hotel)
  Hotel (in) der A-Kategorie, n
  ♦ hotel of the A-category
  ♦ hotel in the A-category
Haus der Kunst, n
  ♦ House of Art, the
Haus der Luxusklasse, n (Hotel)
  → Hotel der Luxusklasse
Haus der Spitzenklasse, n (Hotel)
  → Hotel der Spitzenklasse
Haus des Deutschen Weins, n
  ♦ House of the German Wine, the
Hausdetektiv, m
  ♦ house detective
Hausdiätetiker, m
  ♦ resident dietitian
  ♦ resident dietician
Hausdiener, m (Hotel)
  Hoteldiener, m
  ♦ houseman AE
  ♦ valet
Hausdiener, m (Privathaus)
  ♦ domestic servant
Hausdienst, m
  ♦ cleaning and maintenance
Haus durchsuchen
  ♦ search the house
hauseigen, adj (generell)
  ♦ in-house, adj
hauseigen, adj (Hotel)
  → hoteleigen
hauseigene Freizeiteinrichtung, f
  ♦ in-house leisure facility
Hauseigentümer, m
  ♦ home proprietor
Hauseinweihung, f
  → Einzugsfest
hausen wie die Vandalen
  ♦ wreak havoc
Häusermakler, m
  ♦ house agent BE
Hausfest, n
  Hausparty f
  ♦ house party
Hausfilm, m
  ♦ in-house film
  ♦ in-house movie AE
Hausfrauenart, adv gastr
  nach Hausfrauenart, adv gastr
  ♦ bonne femme, adv gastr
Hausfriedensbruch m jur
  ♦ disturbance of domestic peace and security jur
Hausführer, m
  (Person oder Information)
  ♦ house guide
  ♦ in-house guide
Haus füllen mit Kunstgegenständen und Antiquitäten
  ♦ fill a house with art and antiques
Haus für gehobene Ansprüche, n
  (Privathaus)
  ♦ executive-level house
  ♦ executive house
Haus für zwei Familien, n
  Zweifamilienhaus, n
  ♦ duplex house AE

  ♦ two-family house
  ♦ house for two families
Hausgast, m (generell)
  → Gast des Hauses
Hausgast, m (Hotel)
  im Hotel wohnender Gast m
  ♦ resident guest
  ♦ (hotel) resident
  ♦ in-house guest AE
  ♦ boarder
  ♦ house guest
Hausgästebar, f
  Hausbar, f
  ♦ residents' bar
  ♦ bar for residents
  ♦ residential bar
Hausgäste können die Sauna gratis benutzen
  ♦ Resident guests have free use of the sauna
Hausgästesalon, m
  ♦ residents' lounge
  ♦ lounge for residents
Hausgeist, m
  Hausspuk, m
  ♦ resident ghost
hausgemacht, adj
  zuhause gemacht, adj
  selbst gemacht, adj
  selbstgebacken, adj
  ♦ homemade, adj AE
  ♦ home-made, adj BE
hausgemachtes Gericht, n
  ♦ homemade dish AE
  ♦ home-made dish BE
hausgemachte Spezialität, f
  ♦ homemade specialty AE
  ♦ home-made speciality BE
Hausgenosse, m
  → Mitbewohner
Hausgespräch, n
  (Telefon)
  ♦ house call
Haus haben in X
  ♦ have a house at X
  ♦ have a house in X
Haushalt führen
  ♦ keep house
Haushaltsausstellung, f
  ♦ exhibition of household appliances
Haushaltsbesteck, n
  Eßbesteck, n
  Besteck, n
  ♦ flatware AE
Haushaltsgegenstand, m
  ♦ household utensil
Haushaltsgeld, n
  Wirtschaftsgeld, n
  ♦ housekeeping money
Haushaltshilfe, f
  ♦ household help
  ♦ domestic help
Haushaltshilfe gesucht
  (Hinweisschild)
  ♦ Household help wanted
Haushaltspflichten, f pl
  (in Privathaus)
  Hausarbeiten, f pl
  ♦ household chores pl
Haus hat allen modernen Komfort
  ♦ house has all (the) modern conveniences
Haus hat vier Schlafzimmer
  ♦ house has four bedrooms

Haus hüten
  nicht ausgehen
  ♦ keep the house
Haushüten, n
  ♦ homesitting
  ♦ house sitting
Haushüter, m
  ♦ homesitter
  ♦ house sitter
  ♦ sitter
Hausierer, m
  ♦ peddlar
Haus im Stil der Zeit, n
  ♦ period house
Haus in bewohnbarem Zustand halten
  ♦ keep a house in habitable repair
Hausinhaber, m (Bewohner)
  Hausbewohner m
  ♦ occupant of a house
  ♦ occupier of a house
Hausinneres, n
  Innere eines Hauses, das
  ♦ interior of a house
hausinterne Fernsehübertragung, f
  Fernsehübertragungsanlage, f
  ♦ closed-circuit TV
  ♦ closed-circuit television
hausinterne Fernsehübertragungsanlage f
  ♦ closed-circuit TV system
  ♦ closed-circuit television system
Haus ist eigengenutzt
  ♦ house is owner-occupied
Haus ist leer
  ♦ house is empty
Haus ist nicht länger bewohnbar
  ♦ house is no longer habitable
Haus ist schön gelegen
  ♦ house is beautifully situated
  ♦ house is beautifully located
Haus ist voll belegt
  Haus ist voll besetzt
  ♦ house is fully booked
  ♦ house is full (up)
Haus kann besichtigt werden
  Haus kann besucht werden
  ♦ house can be visited
Hauskapelle, f (Musik)
  → Hausband
Hauskino, n
  ♦ in-house cinema BE
  ♦ in-house movie AE
Hauskonferenz, f
  (wohnen und tagen im selben Hotel)
  ♦ in-house conference AE
  ♦ residential conference BE
Hauskongreß, m
  (wohnen und tagen im selben Hotel)
  ♦ in-house convention AE
  ♦ in-house congress AE
  ♦ residential convention BE
  ♦ residential congress BE
Hauskosmetikerin, f
  ♦ resident beautician
Haus läßt sich gut vermieten
  Haus vermietet sich gut
  ♦ house rents well AE
  ♦ house lets well BE
häusliche Bequemlichkeit, f
  ♦ home comforts pl
häuslich einrichten sich in einem Hotel
  es sich in einem Hotel bequem machen

◆ make oneself at home in a hotel
◆ settle down in a hotel
häuslicher Komfort, m
  Wohnkomfort, m
  ◆ domestic comfort
häuslich niederlassen sich in einer Wohnung
  ◆ instal oneself in an apartment *AE*
  ◆ install oneself in a flat *BE*
häuslich niederlassen sich in etw
  (Zimmer, Wohnung)
  ◆ settle down in s.th.
  ◆ instal oneself in s.th. *AE*
  ◆ install oneself in s.th. *BE*
  ◆ ensconce oneself in s.th.
Hausmädchen, n
  (für grobe Arbeiten)
  ◆ housemaid
  ◆ maid
  ◆ domestic help *BE*
Hausmädchenservice, m
  Hausmädchendienst, m
  ◆ housemaid service
Hausmagazin, n
  Hauszeitschrift, f
  ◆ in-house magazine
Hausmann, m
  ◆ house husband
Hausmannsgericht, n
  ◆ plain dish
  ◆ ordinary dish
Hausmannskost, f
  ◆ plain fare
  ◆ ordinary fare
  ◆ good plain cooking
  ◆ plain cooking
Hausmannsküche, f (Speisen)
  → gutbürgerliche Küche
Hausmeister, m
  ◆ janitor *AE*
  ◆ caretaker *BE*
Hausmeisterbetreuung, f
  Hausmeisterservice, m
  Hausmeisterdienst, m
  ◆ janitor service *AE*
  ◆ caretaker service *BE*
Hausmeisterdienst, m
  Hausmeisterservice, m
  ◆ caretaker service *BE*
  ◆ janitor service *AE*
Hausmeisterin, f
  ◆ janitress *AE*
  ◆ female caretaker *BE*
Haus mieten
  ◆ rent a house
  ◆ hire a house *BE*
Haus mietfrei bewohnen
  ◆ live in a house rent-free
Haus mit allem Komfort, n
  ◆ house with all modern conveniences
  ◆ house with all mod cons
Haus mit Charakter, n
  ◆ house with character
Haus mit einem Schlafzimmer, n
  ◆ one-bedroom house
  ◆ house with one bedroom
Haus mit fünf Schlafzimmern, n
  ◆ five-bedroom house
  ◆ house with five bedrooms
Haus mit sieben Schlafzimmern, n
  ◆ seven-bedroom house
  ◆ house with seven bedrooms

Haus mit unverwechselbarem Charakter, n
  ◆ character house
Haus mit vier Schlafzimmern, n
  ◆ house with four bedrooms
  ◆ four-bedroom house
Haus mit zwei Schlafzimmern, n
  ◆ two-bedroom house
  ◆ house with two bedrooms
Haus möblieren
  ◆ furnish a house
Hausmusik, f
  ◆ house music
Haus nehmen
  ◆ take a house
Hausnummer, f
  ◆ house number
Haus ohne fließendes Wasser, n
  Haus ohne Fließwasser, n *ÖST*
  ◆ house without running water
Hausorchester, n
  ◆ resident orchestra
Hausordnung, f
  ◆ house rules *pl*
  ◆ house regulations *pl*
Haus pachten (von jm)
  ◆ lease a house (from s.o.)
Hausparty, f
  → Hausfest
Hauspersonal, n
  (in Hotel)
  ◆ house staff
  ◆ house personnel
  ◆ internal staff
Hauspianist, m
  im Haus wohnender Pianist, m
  ◆ resident pianist
Hausportier, m
  ◆ house porter
Hauspreis, m
  ◆ house price
Hausprogramm, n
  ◆ in-house program *AE*
  ◆ in-house programme *BE*
Hausprospekt, m (von Hotel)
  → Hotelprospekt
Hausprospekt anfordern (mündlich)
  Hotelprospekt anfordern
  ◆ ask for a hotel brochure
Hausprospekt anfordern (schriftlich)
  Hotelprospekt anfordern
  ◆ write for a hotel brochure
Hausprospekt anfordern (telefonisch)
  Hotelprospekt anfordern
  ◆ phone for a hotel brochure
Haus putzen
  ◆ clean the house
  ◆ clean the place up *coll*
Hausradio, f
  → Musikanlage
Hausrat, m
  ◆ household equipment
  ◆ household effects *pl*
  ◆ household goods *pl*
  ◆ contents of a house *pl*
Hausrat inventarisieren
  ◆ inventory the contents of a house
Hausratversicherung, f
  ◆ insurance of household equipment
  ◆ house contents insurance

Haus räumen
  Haus frei machen
  ◆ vacate a house
Hausrechnung, f
  ◆ house bill
Hausreinigung, f
  Großputz, m
  ◆ house cleaning
Haus schätzen
  (durch Gutachter)
  ◆ appraise a house
Haus schätzen lassen
  (durch Gutachter)
  ◆ have a house appraised
Hausschlüssel, m
  ◆ house key
Hausseminar, n
  (Gäste wohnen und tagen im selben Haus)
  ◆ in-house seminar *AE*
  ◆ residential seminar *BE*
Hausspezialität, f
  (Essen)
  ◆ house specialty *AE*
  ◆ house speciality *BE*
  ◆ specialty of the house *AE*
  ◆ speciality of the house *BE*
  ◆ spécialité de la maison *FR*
Hausspiel, n
  (nicht im Freien)
  Spiel im Haus, n
  ◆ indoor game
Haussprechanlage, f
  Wechselsprechanlage, f
  ◆ intercom system
  ◆ intercom
Hausstauballergie, f
  ◆ dust mite allergy
Haus steht leer
  ◆ house stands empty
Haussteuer, f
  Gebäudesteuer f
  ◆ house tax
Haus suchen
  ◆ look for a house
Haustagung, f
  (Gäste wohnen und tagen im selben Hotel)
  ◆ in-house meeting *AE*
  ◆ residential meeting *BE*
Haustausch, m
  ◆ house swapping
  ◆ home swopping
  ◆ home exchange
  ◆ house exchange
Haustauschclub, m
  ◆ home exchange club
Haus tauschen
  Häuser tauschen
  Haus tauschen mit jm
  ◆ swap homes
  ◆ swop homes
  ◆ exchange homes
  ◆ swap one's home with s.o.
  ◆ exchange one's home with s.o.
Haustauschvermittlung, f
  Hausvermittlung, f
  ◆ house exchange service
  ◆ home exchange service
Haustechniker, m
  (in Hotel)
  ◆ resident technician
  ◆ technician

Haus teilen mit jm

Haus teilen mit jm
  Haus mitbenutzen mit jm
  ♦ share a house with s.o.
Haustelefon, n (Fernsprechanlage)
  ♦ house telephone
  ♦ housephone
  ♦ internal telephone
Haustelefon, n (Sprechanlage)
  → Haussprechanlage
Haustherapeut, m
  ♦ resident therapist
Haustier, n
  ♦ pet
Haustiere angenehm
  (Hinweisschild)
  ♦ Pets accepted
Haustierecke, f
  (z.B. im Park)
  ♦ pets corner
Haustiere erlaubt
  ♦ Pets allowed
Haustiere nicht erlaubt
  (Hinweisschild)
  ♦ No pets admitted
Haustiere nur nach Absprache
  ♦ Pets by arrangement only
Haustiere sind willkommen
  ♦ Pets are welcome
Haustiere verboten
  (Hinweisschild)
  ♦ No pets
Haustiere willkommen
  (Hinweisschild)
  ♦ Pets welcome
Haustierhaltung, f
  ♦ keeping of pets
Haustradition, f
  Hausbrauch, m
  ♦ house custom
Haustürschlüssel, m
  ♦ front-door key
  ♦ key to the front door
Haustyp, m
  Hausart, f
  ♦ house type
  ♦ type of house
Haus überfallen
  ♦ raid a house
  ♦ raid a home
Haus umbauen zu einem Hotel
  ♦ convert a house into a hotel
Hausunterbringung, f
  Unterbringung im Haus, f
  ♦ residential accommodation
Hausunterhaltung, f (Amüsement)
  Unterhaltung im Haus f
  ♦ in-house entertainment
Hausvater, m
  (z.B. in Jugendheimen)
  ♦ house warden
  ♦ warden
  ♦ housefather AE
Hausverbot, n (Hotel)
  ♦ order to stay away from a hotel
Hausverbot erteilen jm (Hotel)
  ♦ order s.o. to stay away from a hotel
Haus vermieten
  ♦ rent (out) a house
  ♦ let (out) a house BE

Hausvermietung, f
  Immobilienvermietung, f
  ♦ property letting BE
Hausvermittlung, f
  Wohnungsvermittlung, f
  ♦ house agency
Haus verpachten (an jn)
  ♦ lease a house (to s.o.)
Hausverpflegung, f
  ♦ in-house catering
Haus verwalten
  ♦ manage a house
Hausverwalter, m
  ♦ property manager
Hausverwaltung, f
  Immobilienverwaltung f
  ♦ property management
Hausverwaltungsbüro, n
  ♦ property management office
Hausverwaltungsdienst, m
  Hausverwaltungsservice, m
  ♦ property management service
  ♦ management service
Hausvideo, n
  ♦ in-house video
Haus voller Gäste haben
  ♦ have a houseful of guests
Hausvoll Gäste, n
  ♦ houseful of guests
Hauswäsche, f
  (Gegensatz zu Gästewäsche)
  ♦ house laundry
  ♦ in-house laundry
Hauswäscherei f
  Eigenwäscherei f
  Wäscherei im Haus f
  ♦ in-house laundry
Hauswein m
  ♦ house wine
Haus wiederaufbauen
  ♦ reconstruct a house
  ♦ rebuild a house
Haus wird leer
  Haus wird frei
  ♦ house falls vacant
Hauswirt, m
  (Privathaus)
  ♦ landlord
Hauswirtin f
  (Privathaus)
  ♦ landlady
Hauswirtschaft, f
  Hauswirtschaftslehre, f
  Hauswirtschaftskunde, f
  ♦ domestic economy
  ♦ home economics pl
  ♦ domestic science
Hauswirtschaftsabteilung, f (Haus)
  ♦ housekeeping department
Hauswirtschaftslehre, f
  Hauswirtschaft, f
  ♦ home economics pl=sg
  ♦ domestic economy
  ♦ domestic science
Hauswirtschaftslehrer, m
  Hauswirtschaftslehrerin, f
  ♦ home economist
Hauswohnwagen, m
  (sehr groß)
  ♦ house trailer AE

Hauszeitschrift, f (Firma)
  Firmenzeitschrift, f
  ♦ company magazine
Hauszelt, n
  ♦ ridge tent
Haus zur Miete haben
  ♦ tenant a house
  ♦ be tenant of a house
Haus zu vermieten
  (Hinweisschild)
  ♦ House for rent AE
  ♦ House to let BE
Haus zu Wohnungen umbauen
  Haus zu Einzelwohnungen umbauen
  ♦ convert a house into apartments AE
  ♦ turn a house into apartments AE
  ♦ convert a house into flats BE
  ♦ turn a house into flats BE
Hautart, f
  Hauttyp, m
  ♦ skin type
Hautbeschwerden, f pl
  ♦ skin disorders pl
Hautbeschwerden behandeln
  ♦ treat skin disorders
Haute cuisine, f FR
  feine Küche, f
  ♦ haute cuisine FR
  ♦ fine cuisine
  ♦ high gastronomy
Haute-cuisine-Betrieb, m
  ♦ haute-cuisine establishment
  ♦ haute-cuisine operation
Haute-cuisine-Restaurant, n
  ♦ haute-cuisine restaurant
Hautgout, m FR
  ♦ haut goût FR
  ♦ high flavor AE
  ♦ high flavour BE
Hautkrankheit, f
  ♦ skin disease
Hautpflege, f
  ♦ skin care
Hautpflegebehandlung, f
  ♦ skin care treatment
Hautpflegeprogramm, n
  ♦ skin care program AE
  ♦ skin care programme BE
Hautproblem, n
  ♦ skin problem
Hautreinigung, f med
  ♦ skin purification med
Hawaii
  ♦ Hawaii
Hawaiianer, m
  ♦ Hawaiian
Hawaiianerin, f
  ♦ Hawaiian girl
  ♦ Hawaiian woman
  ♦ Hawaiian
Hawaii-Inseln, die, f pl
  ♦ Hawaiian Islands, the pl
hawaiisch, adj
  hawaiianisch, a dj
  ♦ Hawaiian, adj
Haxe, f
  ♦ knuckle
Hazienda, f SPAN
  (Landgut in Süd- oder Mittelamerika)
  ♦ hacienda SPAN

Haziendastil, m
 ♦ hacienda style
Health Farm, f
 → Gesundheitsfarm
Hebriden, die, pl
 ♦ Hebrides, the pl
Hebrideninsel, f
 ♦ Hebridean island
Heckbett, n
 (in Wohnwagen)
 ♦ rear bed
 ♦ rear bunk
Heckfenster, n
 ♦ rear window
Hecksitzbank, f
 (Wohnwagen)
 ♦ rear bench seat
Hecksitzgruppe, f
 (Wohnwagen)
 ♦ rear dinette
Hecktisch, m
 (Wohnwagen)
 ♦ rear table
Hefe, f
 ♦ yeast
Hefepfannkuchen, m
 ♦ yeast pancake
Heide, f
 ♦ heath
Heidedorf n
 ♦ heath village
Heidegolfplatz, m
 ♦ heathland golf course
Heidekraut, n
 ♦ heather
Heideland, n
 Heide f
 ♦ heathland
 ♦ heath
Heidelbeere, f
 Blaubeere, f
 ♦ bilberry
 ♦ blueberry
Heidelbeerkompott, n
 ♦ blueberry compote AE
 ♦ blueberry compôte BE
Heidelbeerkuchen, m
 ♦ blueberry cake
Heidelbeermilchmixgetränk, n
 ♦ blueberry milk shake
Heidelbeermuffin, n
 ♦ blueberry muffin
Heidelbeersorbet, n
 ♦ blueberry sorbet
Heidelberger Schloß, n
 ♦ Heidelberg Castle
Heidemoor, n
 ♦ heather moor
 moorland
Heidemoorland, n
 ♦ heather moorland
 ♦ moorland
Heidenlärm machen
 ♦ raise hell
Heidschnucke, f
 Heideschaf, n
 ♦ heath sheep
 ♦ moorland sheep
heikel im Essen
 ♦ pernicky about one's food

Heilanzeige, f
 → Indikation
Heilbad, n (Aktivität)
 ♦ curative bath
Heilbad, n (Ort)
 ♦ health resort
Heilbadbesucher m
 ♦ health-resort visitor
 ♦ visitor to a health resort
Heilbadsektor, m
 ♦ health resort sector
Heilbadtradition haben
 ♦ have a tradition as a health resort
Heilbehandlung, f
 ♦ curative treatment
Heilbrunnen, m
 ♦ healing well
 ♦ medicinal spring
Heilbutt, m
 ♦ halibut
Heildiät, f
 Heilnahrung f
 ♦ therapeutic diet
Heileigenschaft, f
 ♦ curative property
Heilerde, f
 ♦ healing earth
Heilerfolg, m
 erfolgreiche Behandlung, f
 ♦ successful treatment
 ♦ successful cure
 ♦ success
Heilfasten, n
 ♦ therapeutic fasting
Heilgymnastik, f
 ♦ remedial exercises pl
 ♦ remedial gymnastics pl
 ♦ therapeutic exercise
Heilgymnastikkurs, f
 ♦ remedial exercise class
Heiligabend, m
 (24. Dezember)
 Heiliger Abend, m
 Weihnachtsabend, m
 ♦ Christmas Eve
 ♦ Xmas Eve
Heiligabendessen, n (Dinner)
 ♦ Christmas Eve dinner
Heiligabendessen, n (generell)
 ♦ Christmas Eve meal
Heiligabendessen, n (mittags)
 ♦ Christmas Eve lunch
 ♦ Christmas Eve luncheon
Heiligabendessen, n (Supper)
 ♦ Christmas Eve supper
heilige Quelle, f
 ♦ holy well
Heiliger Abend, m
 → Heiligabend
Heilige Römische Reich, das
 ♦ Holy Roman Empire, the
heiliger Ort, m
 ♦ sacred site
Heilige Stadt, f
 ♦ Holy City, the
Heilklima, n
 ♦ salubrious climate
 ♦ healthy climate
heilklimatischer Kurort, m
 Klimakurort, m

 ♦ climatic health resort
 ♦ climatic resort
Heilkraft, f
 ♦ curative power
 ♦ healing power
 ♦ healing force
Heilkraft des Schlafes, f
 ♦ curative power of sleep
 ♦ healing power of sleep
Heilkraft des Wassers, f
 ♦ curative power of water
 ♦ healing power of water
Heilkraut, n
 ♦ medicinal herb
Heilkräuterfachmann, m
 ♦ medical herbalist
Heilkur, f
 Kur, f
 ♦ health cure
 ♦ cure
Heilkurwasser, n
 Heilwasser, n
 ♦ therapeutic spa water
Heilmassage, f
 ♦ therapeutic massage
 ♦ remedial massage
Heilmittel, n
 ♦ remedy
 ♦ cure
 ♦ treatment
 ♦ medicine
Heilort, m
 → Heilbad
Heilpflanze, f
 ♦ medicinal plant
 ♦ medicinal herb
Heilpraktiker, m
 Naturheilkundiger, m
 ♦ naturopath
Heilquelle, f
 ♦ medicinal spring
 ♦ healing well
 ♦ therapeutic spring
Heilschlaf, m
 ♦ healing sleep
 ♦ hypnotherapy
Heilstätte, f
 → Sanatorium
Heil- und Kurort m
 ♦ health resort and spa town
Heilung, f
 ♦ cure
Heilungsprozeß, m
 ♦ healing process
Heilwasser, n
 heilendes Wasser, n
 ♦ healing water
 ♦ healing waters pl
 ♦ medicinal water
 ♦ spa water
 ♦ curative water
Heilwirkung, f
 ♦ therapeutic effect
Heilzwecke, m pl
 ♦ therapeutic purposes pl
Heim, n (Institution)
 ♦ home
 ♦ hostel
 ♦ dormitory AE

Heim

Heim, n (Privathaus)
- home
- house

Heimatabend, m
- Brauchtumsabend, m
- Folkloreabend, m
- evening of local culture

Heimatadresse, f
- Heimatanschrift, f
- home address

Heimatadresse angeben
- give one's home address
- state one's home address

Heimatdorf, n
- home village

Heimatflughafen, m
- home airport

Heimatgeschichte, f
- Ortsgeschichte, f
- local history

Heimatgeschichtemuseum, n
- heimatgeschichtliches Museum, n
- local history museum

Heimathafen, m
- home port
- port of registry
- registered port

Heimatkundemuseum, n
- Museum für Ortsgeschichte, n
- museum of local history
- local history museum

Heimatland, n
- homeland
- home country

Heimatlosigkeit, f
- homelessness

Heimatmuseum, n
- local heritage museum
- local history museum
- local museum

Heimatprogramm, n
- program of local culture *AE*
- programme of local culture *BE*

Heimatstadt, f (Großstadt)
- home city

Heimatstadt, f (kleine Stadt)
- hometown *AE*
- home town *BE*

Heimaturlaub, m (Arbeitnehmer)
- home leave

Heimaturlaub, m (Ferien)
- Heimatferien, pl
- home vacation *AE*
- vacation at home *AE*
- home holiday *BE*
- holiday at home *BE*

Heimaturlaub antreten (Beamter)
- auf Urlaub nach Hause fahren
- go home on furlough

Heimaturlaub bekommen (Arbeitnehmer)
- Heimaturlaub erhalten
- get home leave
- get leave to go home

Heim auf Rädern, n
- (z.B. Caravan)
- home on wheels

Heimfahrt, f
- journey home
- return journey

heimfliegen
- nach Hause fliegen
- fly home

heimfliegen nach X
- fly home to X

Heimflug, m
- homeward flight
- flight home

heimische Küche, f
- → einheimische Küche

heimischer Markt, m
- Inlandsmarkt, m
- home market
- domestic market

heimischer Urlaubsmarkt, m
- → Inlandsurlaubsmarkt

Heimkehr, f
- homecoming

Heim leiten
- Heim führen
- manage a home
- run a home
- manage a hostel
- run a hostel

heimliche Hauptstadt, f
- secret capital

heimlicher Trinker, m
- secret drinker

heimlich trinken
- drink stealthily
- have a drink on the quiet

heimlich verschwinden
- (weggehen)
- do a bunk *coll*

Heimreise, f (generell)
- Rückreise, f
- homeward journey
- journey home
- home journey
- journey back home

Heimreise, f (Seereise)
- homeward voyage
- voyage home
- home voyage

Heimreisen, n
- Heimreiseverkehr, m
- homeward travel

Heimreisestrecke, f
- Rückreiseroute, f
- homeward route

Heimreisetermin, m
- Heimreisedatum n
- homeward travel date
- date of the homeward journey

Heimspiel, n
- home match
- home game

Heimtrainer, m
- (Gerät)
- home exerciser
- exercise bike *coll*
- exerciser

heimwärts, adv
- homewards, adv
- homeward, adv

Heimweh, n
- homesickness

Heimweh haben
- be homesick

heiß, adj
- warm, adj
- hot, adj

heiße Milch, f
- hot milk

heiße Quelle, f
- (Heilbad)
- hot spring

heißer Draht, m
- hot line

heißer Draht für Karten, m
- ticket hotline

heißer Draht für Prospekte, m
- brochure hotline

heißer Tip, m
- hot tip

heißes Gericht, n
- → warmes Gericht

heißes Getränk, n
- Heißgetränk, n
- warmes Getränk, n
- Warmgetränk, n
- hot drink
- hot beverage

heißes Land, n
- hot country

heißes Würstchen, n
- (Frankfurter Würstchen mit Brötchen)
- warmes Würstchen, n
- hot dog *coll*
- frankfurter
- frank *inform*

Heißgetränk, n
- → heißes Getränk

Heißgetränkeverkaufsautomat, m
- Heißgetränkeautomat, m
- hot drink vending nachine
- hot drink machine

Heißluft, f
- Warmluft, f
- hot air

Heißluftbad, n
- hot-air bath

Heißluftballon, m
- hot-air balloon

Heißluftballonabenteuer, n
- hot-air balloon adventure

Heißluftballonfahren, n
- Heißluftballonsport, m
- hot-air ballooning

Heißluftballonfahrt, f
- hot-air balloon ride
- hot-air balloon trip

Heißluftbehandlung, f
- Warmluftbehandlung, f
- hot-air treatment

heiß servieren etw
- serve s.th. hot

heiß serviert, adj
- served hot, adj

Heißwasser, n
- heißes Wasser, n
- hot water

Heißwasserbereiter, m
- → Warmwasserbereiter

Heißwassersprudelbad, n
- Heißwassersprudelbecken, n
- hot whirlpool

Heißwassersprudelbecken, n
- → Heißwassersprudelbad

heizbar, adj
  beheizbar, adj
  ♦ heatable, adj
heizbares Zimmer, n
  Zimmer mit Heizung, n
  ♦ room with heating
Heizdecke, f
  (im Bett)
  ♦ electric blanket
Heizelement, n
  ♦ heating element
Heizenergie, f
  ♦ heating energy
heizen etw
  beheizen etw
  ♦ heat s.th.
heizen mit Kohle
  mit festem Brennstoff heizen
  ♦ have solid fuel heating
heizen mit Öl
  mit Öl heizen
  ♦ have oil-fired heating
Heizgerät, n
  → Heizofen
Heizkeller, m
  ♦ boiler room
Heizkissen, n
  ♦ electric pad
Heizkörper m
  ♦ radiator
Heizkosten, pl
  Heizungskosten, pl
  ♦ heating costs pl
  ♦ heating cost
Heizkostenzuschlag, m
  Heizungszuschlag, m
  ♦ heating supplement
Heizlüfter, m
  ♦ fan heater
Heizmaterial, n
  → Brennstoff
Heizofen, m
  Heizgerät, n
  ♦ heater
  ♦ stove
Heizperiode, f
  ♦ heating period
Heizstoff, m
  → Heizmaterial
Heizung, f
  HZ, f
  ♦ heating
Heizung abstellen
  ♦ switch off the heating
  ♦ turn off the heating
Heizung funktioniert nicht
  (dauernd)
  ♦ heating does not work
Heizung funktioniert nicht richtig
  (vorübergehend)
  ♦ heating isn't working properly
Heizung geht nachts aus
  ♦ heating goes off at night
Heizung inbegriffen
  (im Preis)
  Heizung eingeschlossen
  ♦ heating included
Heizung ist an
  ♦ heating is on
Heizung ist aus
  ♦ heating is off

Heizungsanlage, f
  Heizanlage f
  ♦ heating system
Heizungsanlage einbauen
  Heizungsanlage installieren
  ♦ install a heating system
  ♦ instal a heating system AE
Heizung scheint außer Betrieb zu sein
  ♦ heating seems to be out of order
Heizungseinbau, m
  Einbau einer Heizanlage, m
  ♦ installation of a heating system
  ♦ heating installation
Heizungsrechnung, f
  ♦ heating bill
Heizung und Beleuchtung f
  ♦ heating and lighting
  ♦ heat and light abbr
Hektik des Alltagslebens, f
  ♦ hustle and bustle of everyday life
  ♦ everyday hustle and bustle
Hektoliter, m
  ♦ hectoliter AE
  ♦ hectolitre BE
helfen jm bei der Unterbringung
  behilflich sein jm bei der Unterbringung
  ♦ help s.o. with accommodation
Helgoland
  (Insel)
  ♦ Helgoland
  ♦ Heligoland
Helgoländer Bucht f
  ♦ Helgoland Bight
  ♦ Heligoland Bight
Helikopter, m
  → Hubschrauber
Helikopterservice, m
  → Hubschrauberservice
Helikopterskilauf m
  ♦ helicopter skiing
  ♦ heli-skiing abbr
helles, freundliches Zimmer, n
  ♦ bright room
helles Bier, n
  ♦ pale beer AE
  ♦ pale ale BE
  ♦ bitter BE
  ♦ light beer AE
helles Zimmer, n
  lichtes Zimmer, n
  ♦ light room
  ♦ bright room
hellhörig, adj (Zimmer)
  ♦ poorly soundproofed, adj
  ♦ not soundproof, adj
Helligkeitsregler, m
  Dimmer, m
  ♦ dimmer
Henkel, m
  ♦ handle
Henkelkrug, m
  ♦ jug
  ♦ pitcher AE
Hepatitis, f
  Gelbsucht, f
  ♦ hepatitis
herabgesetzter Preis, m
  ♦ discounted price
  ♦ discounted rate
Herabstufung, f
  → Tieferstufung

herausfordernde Abfahrt, f
  (Ski)
  ♦ challenging run
herbeischaffen jn mit dem Bus
  ♦ bus s.o.
Herberge, f (Heim)
  ♦ hostel
Herberge, f (humor)
  ♦ hostelry AE
Herberge, f (Obdach)
  → Obdach
Herberge betreiben
  (z.B. Jugendherberge)
  ♦ operate a hostel
Herberge finden bei jm
  Quartier finden bei jm
  ♦ find lodging in s.o.'s house
  ♦ find lodging with s.o.
Herbergsatmosphäre, f
  ♦ hostel atmosphere
Herbergsbesucher, m
  ♦ hosteler AE
  ♦ hosteller BE
Herbergsleiter, m
  Heimleiter, m
  ♦ hostel manager
  ♦ manager of a hostel
Herbergsmutter, f
  ♦ hostel warden
  ♦ warden (of a hostel)
  ♦ housemother
Herbergsnetz, n
  ♦ hostel network
Herbergssuche, f
  → Unterkunftssuche
Herbergsunterkunft, f
  Herbergsunterbringung, f
  Heimunterkunft, f
  Heimunterbringung, f
  ♦ hostel accommodation
  ♦ hostel lodging AE
Herbergsvater, m (einer 'Penne')
  Inhaber einer billigen Herberge m
  ♦ warden of a dosshouse
  ♦ dossman BE sl
Herbergsvater, m (generell)
  ♦ hostel warden
  ♦ warden (of a hostel)
  ♦ housefather
herber Wein, m
  saurer Wein m
  ♦ rough wine
Herbst, m
  ♦ fall AE
  ♦ autumn BE
Herbstabend, m
  ♦ fall evening AE
  ♦ autumn evening BE
Herbstangebot, n
  Herbstofferte, f
  ♦ fall offer AE
  ♦ autumn offer BE
Herbstarrangement, n
  ♦ fall arrangement AE
  ♦ autumn arrangement BE
Herbstausflug, m
  ♦ fall excursion AE
  ♦ autumn excursion BE
Herbstauslastung, f
  ♦ fall load factor AE
  ♦ autumn load factor BE

Herbstausstellung

Herbstausstellung, f
- fall exhibition *AE*
- fall exhibit *AE*
- autumn exhibition *BE*
- fall show *AE*
- autumn show *BE*

Herbstball, m
- fall ball *AE*
- autumn ball *BE*

Herbstbelegung, f
Herbstauslastung, f
- fall occupancy *AE*
- autumn occupancy *BE*

Herbstbesuch, m
- fall visit *AE*
- autumn visit *BE*

Herbstbesucher, m
- fall visitor *AE*
- fall guest *AE*
- autumn visitor *BE*
- autumn guest *BE*

Herbstbuchung, f
- fall booking *AE*
- autumn booking *BE*
- fall reservation *AE*

Herbstcamper, m
- fall camper *AE*
- autumn camper *BE*

Herbstcamping, n
- fall camping *AE*
- autumn camping *BE*

Herbstcampingplatz, m
- fall campsite *AE*
- fall campground *AE*
- autumn campsite *BE*
- autumn camping site *BE*
- autumn camping ground *BE*

Herbstfahrplan, m
- fall schedule *AE*
- autumn timetable *BE*

Herbstfahrt, f
- fall trip *AE*
- autumn trip *BE*

Herbstferien, pl
Herbsturlaub, m
- autumn holidays *BE pl*
- autumn holiday *BE*
- fall vacation *AE*

Herbstferiengast, m
Herbsturlauber, m
- autumn holidaymaker *BE*
- fall vacationer *AE*

Herbstfestival, n
Herbstfestspiele, n pl
Herbstfest, n
- fall festival *AE*
- autumn festival *BE*

Herbstfestlichkeit, f
Herbstfest, n
- fall festivity *AE*
- autumn festivity *BE*

Herbstflug, m
- autumn flight *BE*
- fall flight *AE*

Herbstgast, m
- fall guest *AE*
- fall visitor *AE*
- autumn guest *BE*
- autumn visitor *BE*

Herbstgeschäft, n
- fall business *AE*
- autumn business *BE*

Herbstkatalog, m
- fall catalogue *AE*
- fall catalog *AE*
- autumn catalogue *BE*

Herbstkonferenz, f
- fall conference *AE*
- autumn conference *BE*

Herbstkongreß, m
- fall convention *AE*
- fall congress *AE*
- autumn convention *BE*
- autumn congress *BE*

Herbstkonzert, n (Veranstaltung)
- fall concert *AE*
- autumn concert *BE*

Herbstkreuzfahrt, f
- fall cruise *AE*
- autumn cruise *BE*

Herbstkur, f
Herbstbehandlung, f
- fall treatment *AE*
- fall cure *AE*
- autumn treatment *BE*
- autumn cure *BE*

Herbstkurzurlaub, m
- fall break *AE*
- autumn break *BE*

Herbstmarkt, m
- fall market *AE*
- autumn market *BE*

Herbstmesse, f
- fall fair *AE*
- fall trade fair *AE*
- autumn fair *BE*
- autumn trade fair *BE*

Herbstmonat, m
- fall month *AE*
- autumn month *BE*

Herbstparadies, n
- fall paradise *AE*
- autumn paradise *BE*

Herbstparty, f
- fall party *AE*
- autumn party *BE*

Herbstpauschale, f
- fall package *AE*
- autumn package *BE*

Herbstpauschalpreis, m
Herbstpauschale, f
- inclusive fall price *AE*
- inclusive fall rate *AE*
- inclusive autumn price *BE*
- inclusive autumn rate *BE*

Herbstpause, f
- fall break *AE*
- autumn break *BE*

Herbstpreis, m
- fall rate *AE*
- fall price *AE*
- autumn rate *BE*
- autumn price *BE*

Herbstpreisliste, f
Herbsttarif, m
- fall tariff *AE*
- autumn tariff *BE*

Herbstprogramm n
- fall program *AE*
- autumn programme *BE*

Herbstprospekt, m
- fall brochure *AE*
- autumn brochure *BE*

Herbstrabatt, m
- fall discount *AE*
- autumn discount *BE*

Herbstreise, f
- fall journey *AE*
- fall tour *AE*
- autumn journey *BE*
- autumn tour *BE*
- fall trip *AE*

Herbstreisen, n
Herbstreiseverkehr, m
- fall travel *AE*
- autumn travel *BE*

Herbstreisender, m
- fall traveler *AE*
- autumn traveller *BE*

Herbstreiseverkehr, m
Herbstreisen, n
- autumn travel *BE*
- fall travel *AE*

Herbstreservierung, f
- fall reservation *AE*
- autumn reservation *BE*

Herbstsaison, f
- fall season *AE*
- autumn season *BE*

Herbstsaisonauslastung, f
- fall-season load factor *AE*
- autumn-season load factor *BE*

Herbstsaisonbelegung, f
Herbstsaisonauslastung, f
- fall-season occupancy *AE*
- autumn-season occupancy *BE*

Herbstsaisonbuchung, f
- fall-season booking *AE*
- fall-season reservation *AE*
- autumn-season booking *BE*

Herbstsaisonermäßigung f
- fall-season reduction *AE*
- autumn-season reduction *BE*

Herbstsaisoneröffnung, f
- fall-season opening *AE*
- opening of the fall season *AE*
- autumn-season opening *BE*
- opening of the autumn season *BE*

Herbstsaisonmonat, m
- fall-season month *AE*
- month in the fall season *AE*
- autumn-season month *BE*
- month in the autumn season *BE*

Herbstsaisonpreis, m
- fall-season rate *AE*
- fall-season price *AE*
- autumn-season rate *BE*
- autumn-season price *BE*

Herbstsaisonreservierung, f
- fall-season reservation *AE*
- autumn-season reservation *BE*

Herbstsaisonwoche, f
- fall-season week *AE*
- week in the fall season *AE*
- autumn-season week *BE*
- week in the autumn season *BE*

Herbstsaisonzeit, f
- fall-season period *AE*
- autumn-season period *BE*

Herbstsaisonzuschlag, m
- fall-season supplement *AE*
- autumn-season supplement *BE*

Herbstschau, f
Herbstausstellung, f
- fall show *AE*
- autumn show *BE*

Herbstseminar, n
- fall seminar *AE*
- autumn seminar *BE*

Herbstsitzung, f
- fall meeting *AE*
- autumn meeting *BE*

Herbstsonderangebot, n
- special fall offer *AE*
- special autumn offer *BE*

Herbstsymposium, n
- fall symposium *AE*
- autumn symposium *BE*

Herbsttag, m
- fall day *AE*
- autumn day *BE*

Herbsttagung, f
Herbsttreffen, n
- autumn meeting *BE*
- fall meeting *AE*

Herbsttourismus, m
Herbstfremdenverkehr, m
- fall tourism *AE*
- autumn tourism *BE*

Herbsttourist, m
- fall tourist *AE*
- autumn tourist *BE*

Herbsttournee, f
- autumn tour *BE*
- fall tour *AE*

Herbsturlaub, m
Herbstferien, pl
- fall vacation *AE*
- autumn holidays *BE pl*
- autumn holiday *BE*

Herbsturlauber, m
Herbstferiengast, m
- fall vacationer *AE*
- autumn holidaymaker *BE*

Herbsturlaubsprogramm, n
- fall vacation program *AE*
- autumn holiday programme *BE*

Herbsturlaubssaison, f
- fall vacation season *AE*
- autumn holiday season *BE*

Herbstveranstaltung, f
- fall event *AE*
- fall function *AE*
- autumn event *BE*
- autumn function *BE*

Herbstwandern, n
- fall walking *AE*
- fall hiking *AE*
- autumn walking *BE*
- autumn hiking *BE*

Herbstwanderung, f
- fall walk *AE*
- fall hike *AE*
- autumn walk *BE*
- autumn hike *BE*

Herbstwoche, f
- fall week *AE*
- autumn week *BE*

Herbstwochenende, n
- fall weekend *AE*
- autumn weekend *BE*

Herbstzeit, f
- fall period *AE*
- autumn period *BE*

Herbstziel, n
Herbstzielort m
- fall destination *AE*
- autumn destination *BE*

Herd, m
- stove *AE*
- range
- cooker *BE*

Herdmädchen, n
- cook's help
- cook's assistant

hereinbitten jn
(in die Unterkunft)
- invite s.o. in

hereinbitten jn zu einem Aperitif
- ask s.o. in for an aperitif

hergestellt mit Qualitätszutaten
- made with quality ingredients

Hering, m (Fisch)
- herring

Hering, m (Zelt)
- peg

Heringsbutter, f
- herring butter

Heringssalat, m
- herring salad

herkömmliche Kost, f
→ traditionelle Kost

herkömmliche Route, f
herkömmliche Strecke, f
- traditional route

herkömmliches Hotel, n
→ konventionelles Hotel

herkömmliche Speisekarte, f
→ traditionelle Speisekarte

Herkunftsgebiet, n
- area of origin
- country of origin

Herkunftsland, n
Ursprungsland n
- country of origin
- origin country *AE*

Herkunftsmarkt, m
→ Aufkommensmarkt

Herr
(Anrede)
- Mr. *AE*
- Mr *BE*

Herren
(Hinweisschild an Toiletten)
- Gentlemen
- Gents *pl = sg*

Herrenabend, m
Männerabend, m
- stag night *BE*
- gentlemen's evening party

Herrenbereich, m
(z.B. bei Sauna)
- gentlemen's sector

Herrenbesuch, m (Aktivität)
- visit from a gentleman
- visit from a man

Herrenbesuch, m (Person)
- gentleman visitor
- gentleman visitors *pl*
- man visitor
- man visitors *pl*

Herrenduschraum, m
- gentlemen's shower room
- gents' shower room

Herrenfahrrad, n
- men's bicycle

Herrenfriseur, m (Person)
- gentlemen's hairdresser *BE*
- gents' hairdresser *BE*
- men's hairdresser *BE*
- barber

Herrenfriseur m (Laden)
→ Herrenfriseursalon

Herrenfriseursalon, m
Herrensalon m
- barbershop *AE*
- barber's shop *BE*
- barber's

Herrenhaus, n
Herrensitz, m
- mansion house *BE*

herrenlos, adj
- ownerless, adj

herrenloser Hund, m
- ownerless dog

herrenloses Auto, n
- ownerless car

Herrenmarathonlauf, m
Herrenmarathon, m
- men's marathon

Herrenparty, f
Männerparty, f
Polterabend, m
- stag-party *BE*

Herrensalon m
→ Herrenfriseur

Herrensauna, f
- gentlemen's sauna

Herrensitz, m
Herrenhaus n
- manor

Herrentoilette, f (Raum)
Herren-WC, n
- gentlemen's toilet
- gents' toilet
- men's room *AE*

Herrentoilette, f (Schild)
→ Herren

Herren-WC, n
→ Herrentoilette

herrichten etw
(tapezieren etc.)
- fix s.th. up

Herr im Haus sein
- rule the roost

Herr in seinem eigenen Haus sein
- be master in one's own house

Herr in seinem Haus, m
- master in one's own house

herrlichen Blick bieten auf etw
- command a wonderful view of s.th.

herrlichen Blick haben auf etw
- have a wonderful view of s.th.

herrlicher Blick, m
herrlicher Ausblick, m
herrliche Aussicht, f
- splendid view
- wonderful view

herrliches Essen, n
- superb food

herrliches Haus, n
- superb house
- superb home

herrlich möbliert, adj
- superbly furnished, adj

herrlich möbliertes Zimmer, n
- superbly furnished room

herrlich möblierte Wohnung, f
- superbly furnished apartment AE
- superbly furnished flat BE

Herr Ober!
Ober!
- Waiter!

Herr Ober, bitte die Karte
- Waiter, the menu, please

Herr Ober, könnte ich bitte die Karte haben?
- Waiter, could I have the menu, please?

Herr Peters
- Mr. Peters AE
- Mr Peters BE

Herr und Frau Peters
- Mr. and Mrs. Peters AE
- Mr and Mrs Peters BE

Herr X, bitte melden. Herr X, bitte melden
(Ausruf)
- Paging Mr X. Paging Mr X AE
- Paging Mr. X. Paging Mr. X BE

Herr X wird sich der Angelegenheit annehmen
- Mr X will sort the matter out AE
- Mr X. will sort the matter out BE

Herr X wird sich sofort darum kümmern
- Mr X will attend to this immediately AE
- Mr X. will attend to this immediately BE

herumchauffiert werden
- be chauffeured around

herumfahren
- cruise

herumfahrendes Taxi, n (auf Fahrgastsuche)
- cruising taxi

herumkommen
- get around

herumstochern in seinem Essen
- nibble at one's food

heruntergekommenes Hotel, n
- down-at-heel hotel
- run-down hotel

heruntergewirtschaftetes Hotel, n
- run-down hotel

hervorragende Qualität, f
- outstanding quality

hervorragender Service, m
herausragender Service, m
- outstanding service
- excellent service

hervorragende Servicequalität anbieten
- offer outstanding quality of service

Herzbeschwerden, f pl
- heart complaints pl

Herzgefäßbeschwerden, f pl
- cardiovascular disorders pl

herzhaft, adj (Speisen)
- hearty, adj

herzhafte Kost, f
- hearty fare

herzhafte Küche, f
- hearty cuisine
- hearty cooking

herzhafter Wein, m
- hearty wine

herzhaftes Essen n
- hearty meal

herzhaftes Frühstück n
- hearty breakfast

herzhaftes Gericht, n
- hearty dish

herzhaftes Mittagessen, n
- hearty lunch
- hearty luncheon

Herzkrankheit, f
- heart disease

herzliche Atmosphäre, f
- cordial atmosphere

herzliche Begrüßung, f
herzliche Begrüßung in X, f
- warm welcome
- hearty welcome
- warm welcome at X
- hearty welcome at X

herzliche Begrüßung erwartet Sie
- hearty welcome awaits you

herzliche Gastlichkeit, f
herzliche Gastfreundschaft, f
- cordial hospitality

herzlich eingeladen, adj
- cordially invited, adj

herzlich eingeladen sein
- be cordially invited

herzlich empfangen werden
- be given a cordial reception
- be given a warm welcome

herzlichen Empfang jm bereiten
- give s.o. a cordial reception

Herzlichen Glückwunsch!
- Congratulations!

herzlicher Empfang, m (Aufnahme)
- cordial reception
- warm reception

herzlicher Empfang, m (Willkommen)
- hearty welcome
- warm welcome

herzliches Willkommen, n
herzliche Begrüßung, f
- cordial welcome

Herzlichkeit, f
- cordiality

Herzlich willkommen!
- Welcome!

herzlich willkommen, adj
- cordially welcome, adj

herzlich willkommen heißen
- bid s.o. a cordial welcome

herzlich willkommen heißen jn
- extend a warm welcome to s.o.
- welcome s.o. cordially

Herzoginart, adv gastr
nach Herzoginart, adv gastr
- duchess style, adv gastr

Herzogsart, adv gastr
nach Herzogsart, adv gastr
- duke's style, adv gastr

Herzogspalast, m
herzoglicher Palast, m
- ducal palace

Herzog von Schwaben, m
- Duke of Swabia, the

Herzog von Württemberg, m
- Duke of Wuerttemberg, the

Herz verlieren an etw
- lose one's heart to s.th.

Hesse, m
- Hessian

Hessen
(Land)
- Hesse

Hessin, f
- Hessian girl
- Hessian woman
- Hessian

hessisch, adj
- Hessian, adj

Hetze entkommen
der Hektik entkommen
- escape the hustle and bustle
- escape the hassle BE

Heurigenlokal, n ÖST
Gartenlokal mit Weinausschank, n
- wine garden

Heuschnupfen, m
- hay fever

Heute Betriebsruhe
→ Heute Geschlossen

Heute Geschlossen
(Schild)
Heute Betriebsruhe
- Closed Today

Heute hat mir das Essen geschmeckt
Heute hat es mir geschmeckt
- I enjoyed the meal today

Heute hier, morgen dort
- Here today, gone tomorrow

Hexenmuseum, n
- witchcraft museum

H-förmiges Hotel, n
- H-shaped hotel

Hier entlang, bitte
- This way, please

Hier ist Ihr Schlüssel
- Here's your key

Hier ist Ihr Schlüssel. Zimmer 123
- Here's your key. Room 123

Hier läßt es sich aushalten
- This is a place to live

Hier lebt es sich gut
- It's a good life here

Hier sind Ihre Schlüssel
- Here are your keys
- Here's your keys inform

Hier sind Sie gut aufgehoben
Hier werden Sie gut bewirtet
- They do you very well here
- They treat you (very) well here

Hifi-Anlage, f
- hifi system

Highball, m
- highball

Highballglas, n
- highball glass

Highlife, n sl
tolle Party, f
- high jinks pl sl

high sein
(durch Drogenkonsum)
- be high

High Society, f
- high society

High Tea, m
(bes. in Nordengland und Schottland)
frühes Abendessen mit Tee n
- high tea

Hilfe, f (Person)
- helper AE
- help

Hilfsabteilung, f
♦ support department
Hilfsadresse, f
(z.B. bei Wechselgeschäft)
Deckadresse, f
Gefälligkeitsdresse, f
♦ accommodation address
♦ address in case of need
hilfsbereit, adj
♦ helpful, adj
hilfsbereites Personal, n
♦ helpful staff
♦ helpful personnel
Hilfsbereitschaft des Personals, f
♦ helpfulness of (the) staff
Hilfsbett, n
→ behelfsmäßiges Bett
Hilfsbuchhalter, m
♦ assistant accountant
♦ assistant bookkeeper
Hilfsdienst, m
Hilfsleistung, f
♦ support service
♦ ancillary service
Hilfsfahrzeug, n
Begleitfahrzeug, n
♦ back-up vehicle
Hilfsfonds, m
♦ back-up fund
Hilfsgouvernante, f SCHW
→ Hausdamenassistentin
Hilfskellner, m
Aushilfskellner, m
Servicehilfe, f
♦ relief waiter
♦ extra waiter
Hilfskellnerin, f
Aushilfskellnerin f
♦ relief waitress
♦ extra waitress
Hilfskoch, m
Aushilfskoch, m
Kochtournant, m
Tournant, m FR
Fliegender, m sl
♦ relief cook
♦ tournant FR
Hilfskraft, f
♦ help
♦ helper
♦ assistant
♦ auxiliary worker
♦ casual worker
Hilfsleistung, f
Nebenleistung f
♦ ancillary service
♦ auxiliary service
Hilfsmittel n
♦ aid
Hilfspersonal n (für Hilfstätigkeiten)
♦ ancillary personnel
♦ ancillary staff
Hilfspersonal n (Gelegenheitskräfte)
Aushilfspersonal n
♦ casual personnel
♦ casual staff
Hilfsschwimmeister, m
♦ assistant swimming pool attendant
♦ assistant pool attendant
Hilfs- und Betriebsstoffe, m pl
♦ operating supplies pl

Hilfswäscheraum, m
♦ auxiliary linen room
Hilfszimmermädchen n
♦ extra chambermaid
♦ relief chambermaid
Himalaja, m
♦ Himalayas, the pl
Himalaja besteigen
♦ climb the Himalayas
Himalajagebirge, n
♦ Himalayan Mountains, the pl
Himbeerbowle, f
♦ raspberry cup
♦ raspberry bowl
Himbeercreme, f
♦ raspberry cream
Himbeere, f
♦ raspberry
Himbeereiskrem, f
Himbeereis, n
♦ raspberry ice cream AE
♦ raspberry ice-cream BE
♦ raspberry ice
Himbeeressig, m
♦ raspberry vinegar
Himbeergeist, m
♦ raspberry brandy
Himbeergelee, n
♦ raspberry jelly
Himbeergeschmack, m
♦ raspberry flavor AE
♦ raspberry flavour BE
Himbeerkaltschale, f
♦ cold raspberry soup
Himbeerkompott, n
♦ raspberry compote
♦ stewed raspberries pl
Himbeerkonfitüre, f
♦ raspberry jam
Himbeerkuchen, m
♦ raspberry cake
Himbeermilchmixgetränk, n
♦ raspberry milk shake
Himbeerparfait, n
♦ raspberry parfait
Himbeerpudding, m
♦ raspberry pudding
Himbeerpüree, n
Himbeermus, n
♦ raspberry purée
♦ raspberry puree AE
Himbeersaft, m
♦ raspberry juice
Himbeersirup, m
♦ raspberry syrup
Himbeersorbet, n
♦ raspberry sorbet
Himbeersoße, f
♦ raspberry sauce
Himbeersoufflé, n
Himbeerauflauf, m
♦ raspberry soufflé BE
♦ raspberry souffle AE
Himbeertorte, f (flach)
♦ raspberry tart
Himbeertorte, f (Sahne)
♦ raspberry gâteau BE
♦ raspberry gateau AE
Himmelbett, n
(mit hohen Eckpfosten)

♦ four-poster bed
♦ four-poster abbr
Himmelbettzimmer, n
♦ four-poster room
hinabblicken auf etw
♦ look down to s.th.
hinauffahren mit dem Fahrstuhl
hinauffahren mit dem Lift
hinauffahren mit dem Aufzug
♦ go up by elevator AE
♦ go up by lift BE
hinaufführen jn
(in höhere Etage)
♦ show s.o. up
♦ show s.o. upstairs
hinausführen jn
♦ show s.o. out
♦ conduct s.o. out
hinauskomplimentieren jn
♦ usher s.o. out
hinaussetzen jn (Räumung)
zur Räumung zwingen jn
♦ evict s.o.
hinauswerfen jn
♦ throw s.o. out
♦ chuck s.o. out coll
hinauswerfen jn auf die Straße
♦ throw s.o. into the street
♦ chuck s.o. into the street sl
hinauswerfen jn aus dem Hotel
♦ throw s.o. out of the hotel
♦ chuck s.o. out of the hotel sl
hinauswerfen jn aus der Gaststätte
♦ throw s.o. out of the bar AE
♦ throw s.o. out of the pub BE
♦ chuck s.o. out of the bar AE sl
♦ chuck s.o. out of the pub BE sl
hinauswerfen jn aus etw
♦ throw s.o. out of s.th.
♦ chuck s.o. out of s.th. sl
Hindenburgdamm, m
♦ Hindenburg Causeway, the
Hindernislauf, m
♦ steeplechase
Hindu-Essen, n
Hindu-Mahlzeit, f
♦ Hindu meal
Hindukusch, m
♦ Hindu Kush, the
hineinplatzen in eine Party
♦ crash a party
hinfahren
→ hinreisen
Hinfahrt, f
→ Hinreise
Hinflug, m
♦ outward flight
hinhalten jn
♦ keep s.o. hanging
hinlegen sich
♦ lie down
Hinreise, f (generell)
Hinfahrt, f
♦ outward journey
♦ outbound journey
Hinreise, f (Meer)
♦ outward voyage
♦ voyage out
Hinreise mit dem Flugzeug machen
♦ make the outward journey by plane

hinreisen
    hinfahren
    ♦ travel out
Hinreisen, n
    Hinreiseverkehr, m
    ♦ outward travel
Hinreiseroute, f
    Hinreisestrecke, f
    ♦ outward route
hinter den Kulissen
    ♦ behind the scenes
Hintereingang, m
    ♦ back entrance
Hintereingang benutzen
    ♦ use the back entrance
    ♦ use the back door
hinteres Parkett, n (Theater)
    ♦ rear orchestra AE
    ♦ orchestra circle
    ♦ circle
    ♦ back stalls BE pl
    ♦ rear stalls BE pl
Hintergrundmusik f
    ♦ background music
Hinterhaus, n
    ♦ rear building
    ♦ back building
    ♦ house at the back
    ♦ building at the back
Hinterhauswohnung, f
    ♦ apartment in the building at the back AE
    ♦ flat in the building at the back BE
Hinterhof, m
    ♦ backyard
Hinterhofzimmer, n
    ♦ backyard room
Hinterland, n
    ♦ hinterland
Hinterland erkunden
    ♦ explore the hinterland
hinterlegen etw (bei jm)
    ♦ deposit s.th. (with s.o.)
Hinterlegung einer Kaution, f
    ♦ payment of a deposit as a security
Hinterpommern
    (Region)
    Ostpommern
    ♦ Eastern Pomerania
Hinterrad, n
    ♦ rear wheel
    ♦ back wheel
Hinterrhein, m
    ♦ Hinter Rhine, the
Hintertür, f
    ♦ back door
hinter verschlossenen Türen
    hinter geschlossenen Türen
    unter Ausschluß der Öffentlichkeit
    ♦ behind closed doors
    ♦ in camera jur
Hinterzimmer, n
    Hinterraum, m
    rückwärtiges Zimmer, n
    Zimmer nach hinten, n
    Nebenzimmer, n
    ♦ back room
    ♦ room at the back
Hin- und Rückfahrt, f
    ♦ outward and return trip
    ♦ round trip AE

Hin- und Rückflug, m
    ♦ round-trip flight AE
    ♦ round trip AE
Hin- und Rückflugpreis, m
    ♦ round-trip fare AE
Hin- und Rückkreuzfahrt, f
    Rundkreuzfahrt, f
    ♦ round-trip cruise
Hin- und Rückreise, f
    ♦ outward and return journey
    ♦ round trip AE
Hin- und Rückreiseroute, f
    ♦ outward and return route
hin und zurück
    ♦ out and back
    ♦ there and back
hin- und zurückreisen
    ♦ travel out and back
hinunterfahren mit dem Fahrstuhl
    hinunterfahren mit dem Lift
    hinunterfahren mit dem Aufzug
    ♦ go down by elevator AE
    ♦ go down by lift BE
hinunterschlingen etw (Essen)
    ♦ bolt s.th. down
    ♦ bolt s.th.
    ♦ gobble s.th.
    ♦ wolf s.th. down
    ♦ wolf s.th.
hinunterspülen etw mit einem Bier coll
    ♦ rinse s.th. down with a beer coll
hinunterspülen etw mit etw
    (Speisen/Getränke)
    ♦ wash s.th. down with s.th.
hinunterstürzen etw (Getränk)
    ♦ gulp s.th. down
Hinweise für Touristen, m pl
    ♦ hints for tourists pl
hinzumieten etw (langzeitig, Immobilien)
    ♦ rent s.th. in addition to s.th.
hinzumieten etw (Mobilien)
    ♦ hire s.th. in addition to s.th. BE
    ♦ rent s.th. in addition to s.th. AE
Hippie, m
    ♦ hippie
    ♦ hippy
Hippodrom, n/m
    Reitbahn, f
    ♦ hippodrome
Hirschragout, n/m
    ♦ deer stew
Hirse, f
    ♦ millet
Hirsebrei, m
    ♦ millet gruel
Hirsekorn, n
    ♦ millet seed
    ♦ millet
Hirsemehl, n
    ♦ millet flour
historisch, adj (alt)
    ♦ historical, adj
historisch, adj (bedeutsam)
    historischen Wert habend, adj
    mit historischem Wert
    historisch bedeutsam, adj
    ♦ historic, adj
historisch bedeutsame Architektur, f
    ♦ historic architecture
historisch bedeutsame Attraktion, f
    ♦ historic attraction

historisch bedeutsame Gaststätte, f
    ♦ historic bar AE
    ♦ historic pub BE
historisch bedeutsamer Platz, m
    historisch bedeutsamer Ort, m
    ♦ historic place
historisch bedeutsames Denkmal, n
    ♦ historic monument
historisch bedeutsames Haus, n
    ♦ historic house
historisch bedeutsame Stadt, f (Großstadt)
    ♦ historic city
historisch bedeutsame Stadt, f (kleine Stadt)
    ♦ historic town
historisch bedeutsames Treffen, n
    ♦ historic meeting
historisch bedeutsames Viertel, n
    (einer Stadt)
    ♦ historic quarter
historische Atmosphäre, f
    ♦ historical atmosphere
historische Attraktion, f
    ♦ historical attraction
historischen Ort besichtigen
    ♦ view a historic place
historischer Rahmen, m
    ♦ historical setting
historischer Umzug, m
    ♦ historical parade
historisches Denkmal, n
    ♦ historical monument
historische Sehenswürdigkeit, f
    ♦ historical sight
historische Sehenswürdigkeiten besichtigen
    ♦ see the historical sights
historisches Fest, n
    historische Festspiele, n pl
    ♦ historical festival
historisches Gebäude, n (bedeutsam)
    historisch bedeutsames Gebäude, n
    ♦ historic building
historisches Gebäude, n (generell)
    ♦ historical building
Historisches Museum n
    ♦ Historical Museum
historische Stadt, f (alt, Großstadt)
    ♦ historical city
historische Stadt, f (alt, kleine Stadt)
    ♦ historical town
historische Stätte, f
    historisch bedeutsame Stätte, f
    ♦ historic site
Hitze, f
    ♦ heat
hitzebeständig, adj
    hitzefest, adj
    ♦ heatproof, adj
    ♦ heat-resistant, adj
hitzebeständiges Glas, n
    ♦ heatproof glass
Hitzewelle, f
    ♦ heatwave
Hitzschlag, m
    ♦ heat stroke
H-Milch, f
    ♦ long-life milk
Hobby, n
    Liebhaberei, f
    ♦ hobby

Hobbyarchäologe, m
 ♦ amateur archaeologist
 ♦ amateur archeologist
Hobbyferien, pl
 Hobbyurlaub, m
 ♦ hobby holidays BE pl
 ♦ hobby holiday BE
 ♦ hobby vacation AE
Hobbygärtner, m
 ♦ amateur gardener
Hobbygeologe, m
 ♦ amateur geologist
Hobbygolfspieler, m
 Amateurgolfspieler, m
 ♦ amateur golfer
Hobbygruppe, f
 ♦ hobby group
Hobbykoch, m
 ♦ amateur cook
 ♦ amateur chef
Hobbykoch des Jahres, m
 ♦ Amateur Chef of the Year
Hobbykochwettbewerb, m
 Hobbykochwettkampf, m
 ♦ amateur chef competition
Hobbykochwettkampf, m
 ♦ amateur chef contest
Hobbykünstler, m
 ♦ amateur artist
Hobbymaler, m
 ♦ amateur painter
Hobbymesse, f
 ♦ hobby fair
Hobbynachmittag, m
 ♦ hobby afternoon
Hobbysegler, m
 ♦ amateur sailor
Hobby- und Freizeiteinrichtung, f
 ♦ hobby and leisure facility
Hobbyurlaub, m
 Hobbyferien, pl
 ♦ hobby vacation AE
 ♦ hobby holiday(s) BE (pl)
Hobel, m gastr
 ♦ slicer gastr
Hochalpen, pl
 ♦ High Alps, the pl
Hochaltar, m
 ♦ high altar
Hochbetrieb, m
 Stoßzeit, f
 ♦ peak hours pl
 ♦ peak season
 ♦ rush hour
Hochbetrieb herrschen
 ♦ business is booming
 ♦ be really busy
Hochbetriebstag, m
 → Spitzentag
Hochburg des Tourismus, f
 ♦ stronghold of tourism
 ♦ tourist center AE
 ♦ tourist centre BE
Hochgebirge, n
 Hochgebirgsregion, f
 ♦ high mountain area
 ♦ high mountain region
Hochgebirgskurort, m
 ♦ high-altitude mountain spa
Hochgebirgsregion, f
 Hochgebirge, n

 ♦ high mountain region
 ♦ high mountain area
Hochgebirgstreck, m
 ♦ high mountain trek
Hochgebirgstrekking, n
 ♦ high mountain trekking
Hochgebirgstrekkingtour, f
 ♦ high mountain trekking tour
 ♦ high mountain trek
Hochgenuß, m
 ♦ great delight
 ♦ real delight
 ♦ treat coll
Hochgenuß sein
 ♦ be a treat
Hochgeschwindigkeitsbahndienst, m
 Hochgeschwindigkeitsbahnverkehr, m
 ♦ high-speed rail service
Hochgeschwindigkeitsbahnnetz, n
 ♦ high-speed rail network
Hochgeschwindigkeitslinie, f
 ♦ high-speed line
Hochgeschwindigkeitszug, m
 ♦ high-speed train
Hochgeschwindigkeitszugdienst, m
 Hochgeschwindigkeitszugverkehr, m
 ♦ high-speed train service
Hochglanzbroschüre, f
 ♦ glossy brochure
Hochglanzfaltblatt, n
 Hochglanzblatt, n
 ♦ glossy leaflet
Hochhaus, n
 ♦ high-rise building
Hochhausblock, m
 Hochhaus, n
 ♦ high-rise block
Hochhaushotel, n
 ♦ high-rise hotel
Hochhauswohnung, f
 ♦ high-rise apartment AE
 ♦ high-rise flat BE
hoch im Preis stehen
 ♦ command a high price
 ♦ command a high rate
hochkarätige Delegation, f
 hochrangige Delegation, f
 ♦ high-ranking delegation
 ♦ VIP delegation
hochkarätige Konferenz, f
 ♦ high-level conference
hochklappbarer Sitz, m
 aufklappbarer Sitz, m
 Klappsitz, m
 ♦ tip-up seat
hochklassig, adj
 ♦ high-class, adj
hochklassiger Betrieb, m
 ♦ high-class establishment
 ♦ high-class operation
hochklassiges Hotel, n
 ♦ high-class hotel
hochklassiges Restaurant, n
 ♦ high-class restaurant
Hochlandstraße, f
 ♦ upland road
hochlandweg, m
 ♦ upland trail
Hochmoor, n
 ♦ sphagnum bog

Hochmoorland, n
 ♦ bog land
hoch oben wohnen
 hoch wohnen
 ♦ live high up
Hochparterre, n
 ♦ raised ground floor
Hochplateau, n
 ♦ high plateau
hochprozentig, adj
 (Getränk)
 ♦ high-proof, adj
hochprozentige alkoholische Getränke, n pl
 ♦ high-proof spirits pl
hochprozentiges Getränk, n
 ♦ high-proof drink
 ♦ high-proof beverage
Hochrad, n
 (alter Fahrradtyp)
 ♦ penny farthing
 ♦ penny farthing bicycle
Hochsaison, f
 ♦ high season
Hochsaisonaufschlag, m
 → Hochsaisonzuschlag
Hochsaisonauslastung, f
 ♦ high-season load factor
Hochsaisonbelegung, f
 Hochsaisonauslastung, f
 ♦ high-season occupancy
Hochsaisonbesucher m
 ♦ high-season visitor
Hochsaisonbuchung f
 ♦ high-season booking
Hochsaisoncamper, m
 ♦ high-season camper
Hochsaisoncamping, n
 ♦ high-season camping
Hochsaisonermäßigung f
 ♦ high-season reduction
Hochsaisonfahrpreis, m
 ♦ high-season fare
Hochsaisonferien, pl
 Hochsaisonurlaub, m
 ♦ high-season holiday BE
 ♦ high-season vacation AE
Hochsaisongast m
 ♦ high-season guest
 ♦ high-season visitor
Hochsaison haben
 ♦ have its high season
Hochsaisonmonat m
 ♦ high-season month
 ♦ month in the high season
Hochsaisonnachfrage, f
 ♦ high-season demand
 ♦ demand in the high season
Hochsaisonpreis, m
 ♦ high-season price
 ♦ high-season rate
Hochsaisonreiseverkehr, m
 Hochsaisonreisen, n
 ♦ high-season travel
Hochsaisonreservierung, f
 ♦ high-season reservation
Hochsaisonumsatz, m
 ♦ high-season sales pl
 ♦ high-season turnover
Hochsaisonunterkunft, f
 ♦ high-season accommodation

Hochsaisonurlaub

Hochsaisonurlaub, m
  Hochsaisonferien, pl
  ♦ high-season vacation *AE*
  ♦ high-season holiday *BE*
Hochsaisonwoche, f
  ♦ high-season week
  ♦ week in the high season
Hochsaisonzeit f
  ♦ high-season period
Hochsaisonzuschlag m
  ♦ high-season supplement
Hochschwarzwald, m
  ♦ Upper Black Forest
Hochseeangelausflug, m
  ♦ sea angling excursion
Hochseeangeln, n
  ♦ sea angling
Hochseeangelzentrum, n
  ♦ sea angling center *AE*
  ♦ sea angling centre *BE*
Hochseefischen, n
  Hochseefischerei, f
  ♦ deep-sea fishing
Hochseeschiff, n
  ♦ seagoing vessel
Hochsommer, m
  ♦ high summer
Hochsommerwoche, f
  ♦ high summer week
  ♦ week in (the) high summer
Hochsprung, m
  ♦ high jump
Hochstapelei, f
  ♦ confidence game
  ♦ confidence trick *BE*
  ♦ swindle
  ♦ fraud
hochstapeln
  ♦ play a confidence trick *BE*
  ♦ swindle
  ♦ deceive
Hochstapler, m
  ♦ confidence man *AE*
  ♦ confidence trickster *BE*
  ♦ con man *coll*
  ♦ impostor
  ♦ swindler
Höchstauslastung, f
  höchste Auslastung, f
  ♦ highest load factor
  ♦ maximum load factor
Höchstbelegung, f
  höchste Belegung, f
  Höchstauslastung, f
  höchste Auslastung, f
  ♦ highest occupancy
  ♦ maximum occupancy
Höchstdauer, f
  ♦ maximum duration
  ♦ maximum length
  höchste Auslastung am Mittwoch haben
  ♦ have the highest load factor on Wednesday
  höchste Belegung am Mittwoch haben
  höchste Auslastung am Mittwoch haben
  ♦ have the highest occupancy on Wednesday
  höchste Durchschnittsausgabe pro Tag, f
  (z.B. durch Tourist)
  ♦ highest average expenditure per day
  höchsten Komfort bieten
  ♦ provide maximum comfort

höchsten Komfort genießen
  ♦ enjoy the ultimate in comfort
höchsten Komfort- und Luxusstandard anbieten
  ♦ offer the highest standards of comfort and luxury
höchsten Luxus bieten
  größten Luxus bieten
  ♦ provide the ultimate in luxury
höchsten Service- und Unterkunftsstandard anbieten
  ♦ offer the highest possible standards of service
  ♦ and accommodation
höchstes Hotel, n
  ♦ tallest hotel
höchstes Personal-Gäste-Verhältnis haben
  höchstes Personal-Gast-Verhältnis haben
  ♦ have the highest staff/guest ratio
  ♦ have the highest staff-to-guest ratio
höchstes Service- und Komfortniveau bieten
  ♦ provide the highest levels of service and comfort
Höchstfahrpreis, m
  ♦ maximum fare
Höchstgebühr f
  ♦ maximum charge
  ♦ maximum fee
Höchstgeschwindigkeit, f
  ♦ maximum speed
Höchstgewicht, n
  ♦ maximum weight
Höchstmaß an modernem Komfort bieten
  ♦ offer all the best of modern comfort
höchstmöglichen Servicestandard anbieten
  ♦ offer the highest possible standard of service
Höchstpauschale, f
  ♦ maximum package
Höchstpreis, m
  Spitzenpreis, m
  ♦ maximum price
  ♦ maximum rate
  ♦ top price
  ♦ top rate
Höchstpreise zahlen
  ♦ pay top prices
  ♦ pay top rates
Höchstquote, f
  ♦ maximum quota
Hochstraße, f
  Überführung, f
  ♦ overpass *AE*
  ♦ flyover *BE*
Hochstuhl, m
  Kinderhochstuhl, m
  ♦ high chair
Hochwald, m
  ♦ timber forest
hochwertige Küche, f (Speisen)
  ♦ high-quality cuisine
  ♦ high-quality cooking
hochwertige Küche anbieten
  ♦ offer high-quality cuisine
  ♦ offer high-quality cooking
hochwertiges Produkt, n
  ♦ high-quality product
hochwertige Unterkunft, f
  ♦ high-quality accommodation
  ♦ quality accommodation
Hochwiese, f
  Hochlandwiese, f

  ♦ upland meadow
  ♦ high meadow
hochwillkommen, adj
  ♦ most welcome, adj
hochwillkommener Gast, m
  ♦ most welcome guest
hochwillkommen sein
  ♦ be most welcome
Hochzeit, f
  ♦ wedding
Hochzeit feiern
  ♦ celebrate one's wedding
  ♦ get married
Hochzeitsarrangement, n
  ♦ wedding arrangement
Hochzeitsbankett, n
  Hochzeitsmahl, n
  ♦ wedding banquet
Hochzeitseinladung, f
  Einladung zu einer Hochzeit, f
  ♦ invitation to a wedding
Hochzeitsempfang m
  ♦ wedding reception
Hochzeitsessen, n (generell)
  ♦ wedding dinner
  ♦ wedding banquet
  ♦ wedding feast
Hochzeitsessen, n (vormittags)
  ♦ wedding breakfast
Hochzeitsfeier, f (Veranstaltung)
  → Hochzeitsveranstaltung
Hochzeitsfeier, f (Zeremonie)
  ♦ wedding ceremony
  ♦ marriage ceremony
Hochzeitsfeierlichkeiten, f pl
  ♦ wedding festivities *pl*
Hochzeitsfest, n
  ♦ wedding celebration
  ♦ wedding
Hochzeitsfestschmaus, m
  Hochzeitsfestessen, n
  ♦ wedding feast
  ♦ wedding banquet
Hochzeitsgast m
  ♦ wedding guest
Hochzeitsgesellschaft f
  ♦ wedding party
Hochzeitsjubiläum, n
  Hochzeitstag, m
  ♦ wedding anniversary
Hochzeitsjubiläum feiern
  ♦ celebrate one's wedding anniversary
  ♦ celebrate a wedding anniversary
Hochzeitskuchen, m
  ♦ wedding cake
  ♦ bridecake *AE*
Hochzeitsmahlzeit, f
  ♦ wedding meal
Hochzeitspauschale, f
  ♦ wedding package
Hochzeitsreise, f
  ♦ honeymoon trip
  ♦ honeymoon
Hochzeitsreisende, pl
  Flitterwöchner, pl
  ♦ honeymooners *pl*
  ♦ honeymoon couple
Hochzeitssuite f
  Suite für Hochzeitsreisende f
  ♦ bridal suite

Hochzeitstag, m
 ♦ wedding day
Hochzeitsurlaub, m (Arbeitnehmer)
 ♦ wedding leave
Hochzeitsveranstaltung f
 ♦ wedding function
Hochzeitszimmer, n
 ♦ bridal room
Hocker m
 ♦ stool
Hockey, n
 ♦ hockey
Hockeyplatz, m
 ♦ hockey field
 ♦ hockey arena AE
Hockeyschläger, m
 ♦ hockey stick
Hockey spielen
 ♦ play hockey
Hockeyspieler, m
 ♦ hockey player
Hocktoilette, f
 Sitztoilette, f
 ♦ American-style toilet
 ♦ British-style toilet
Hof, m
 ♦ court
Hofa, n
 → Hotelfach
hoffen auf mehr Buchungen
 ♦ hope for more bookings
hofhalten
 ♦ hold court
Hofkirche, f
 ♦ court church
Hofleben, f
 ♦ life at court
höfliche Bedienung, f
 höflicher Service, m
 ♦ polite service
 ♦ courteous service
höflich empfangen werden
 ♦ be received courteously
höflicher Service, m
 höfliche Bedienung, f
 ♦ courteous service
 ♦ polite service
Höflichkeit, f
 höfliches Benehmen, n
 ♦ courtesy
 ♦ politeness
Höflichkeitsbesuch, m
 Anstandsbesuch, m
 ♦ courtesy visit
 ♦ courtesy call
Höflichkeitskampagne, f
 ♦ courtesy campaign
höflich sein zu den Gästen
 ♦ be polite to the guests
Hofraum, m
 Hof, m
 ♦ courtyard
Hofrestaurant n
 Innenhofrestaurant n
 ♦ courtyard restaurant
 ♦ patio restaurant
Hoftheater, n
 ♦ court theater AE
 ♦ court theatre BE
Hofzimmer, n
 Zimmer zum Hof, n

 ♦ courtyard room
 ♦ room facing the courtyard
Höhe, f
 ♦ altitude
 ♦ height
Hohe Atlas, der, m
 ♦ High Atlas, the
hohe Auslastung, f
 starke Auslastung, f
 ♦ high load factor
hohe Auslastung erreichen
 ♦ achieve a high load factor
hohe Auslastung erwarten
 ♦ expect a high load factor
hohe Auslastung garantieren
 ♦ guarantee a high load factor
hohe Auslastung haben
 ♦ have a high load factor
hohe Belegung, f
 starke Belegung, f
 hohe Auslastung, f
 starke Auslastung, f
 ♦ high occupancy
hohe Belegung erreichen
 hohe Auslastung erreichen
 ♦ achieve a high occupancy
hohe Belegung erwarten
 hohe Auslastung erwarten
 ♦ expect a high occupancy
 ♦ expect a high level of occupancy
hohe Belegung garantieren
 hohe Auslastung garantieren
 ♦ guarantee high occupancy
 ♦ guarantee a high level of occupancy
hohe Belegung haben
 hohe Auslastung haben
 ♦ have a high occupancy
hohe Betriebskosten, pl
 ♦ high costs of operation pl
 ♦ high costs of operating pl
hohe Decke, f
 ♦ high ceiling
hohe Erfolgsquote erreichen
 hohe Erfolgsrate erzielen
 ♦ achieve a high success rate
hohe Erwartung, f
 ♦ high expectation
hohe fixe Betriebskosten, pl
 ♦ high fixed costs of operation pl
hohe Kilometerzahl, f
 ♦ high mileage
 ♦ high milage
hohe Kochkunst, f
 → Haute Cuisine
hohe Miete, f (für Immobilien)
 ♦ high rent
hohe Miete erzielen (Immobilien)
 ♦ command a high rent
hohe Miete zahlen für etw
 ♦ pay a high rent for s.th.
hohen Alkoholgehalt haben
 ♦ have a high alcohol content
hohen Auslastungsstand erreichen
 hohes Auslastungsniveau erreichen
 ♦ reach a high load factor level
hohen Bekanntheitsgrad haben
 ♦ be widely known
hohen Belegungsstand erzielen
 hohes Belegungsniveau erreichen
 hohen Auslastungsstand erzielen
 hohes Auslastungsniveau erreichen

 ♦ achieve a high occupancy level
 ♦ achieve a high level of occupancy
hohen Erholungswert haben
 ♦ have a high recreational value
 ♦ be of high recreational value
Höhenhotel, n
 → Berghotel
Höhenklima, n
 ♦ high-altitude climate
hohen Komfort bieten
 ♦ provide a high standard of comfort
hohen Komfortgrad anbieten
 ♦ offer a high degree of comfort
Höhenkrankheit, f
 ♦ altitude sickness
hohen Küchenstandard bieten
 ♦ provide a high standard of cuisine
 ♦ provide a high standard of cooking
Höhenkurort, m
 ♦ high-altitude health resort
Höhenlage, f
 ♦ situation at high altitude
Höhenlinienkarte, f
 ♦ contour map
Höhenluft, f
 → Bergluft
Höhenort, m
 hochgelegener Ort m
 ♦ high-altitude resort
 ♦ mountain resort
Höhenpark, m
 ♦ high-altitude nature park
hohen Preis fordern für etw
 ♦ charge a high price for s.th.
Höhenrestaurant, n
 → Bergrestaurant
hohen Ruf genießen für etw
 ♦ enjoy a high reputation for s.th.
hohen Servicestandard anbieten
 ♦ offer a high service standard
 ♦ offer a high standard of service
hohen Servicestandard bieten
 ♦ provide a high service standard
 ♦ provide a high standard of service
hohen Servicestandard halten
 ♦ maintain a high service standard
 ♦ maintain a high standard of service
Höhenskiort, m
 ♦ high-altitude ski resort
Höhensonne, f
 (Lampe)
 ♦ sunlamp AE
 ♦ sun-lamp BE
hohen Standard halten
 ♦ maintain a high standard
Höhenstraße, f
 → Bergstraße
Höhen und Tiefen, f pl
 (z.B. Nachfrage)
 ♦ peaks and troughs pl
Höhepunkt, m (Programm)
 ♦ highlight
 ♦ climax
Höhepunkt bildet X
 Höhepunkt ist X
 ♦ highlight is X
Höhepunkt der Fahrt, m
 Fahrthöhepunkt, m
 ♦ highlight of the trip
Höhepunkt der Fremdenverkehrssaison, m
 ♦ height of the tourist season

Höhepunkt der Reise

Höhepunkt der Reise, m
Reisehöhepunkt, m
♦ highlight of the journey
♦ highlight of the tour
♦ highlight of the trip
Höhepunkt der Saison, m
Saisonhöhepunkt, m
♦ height of the season
Höhepunkt der Tournee, m
Tourneehöhepunkt, m
♦ highlight of the tour
Höhepunkt der Urlaubszeit, m
♦ height of the vacation season AE
♦ height of the holiday season BE
Höhepunkt des Abends, m
♦ climax of the evening
♦ highlight of the evening
Höhepunkt des Tages, m
♦ highlight of the day
Höhepunkt einer Veranstaltung, m
♦ highlight of an event
♦ highlight of a function
Höhepunkt kommt am Montag
♦ highlight will be on Monday
hoher Alkoholgehalt, m
♦ high alcohol content
höhere Auslastung erzielen
♦ experience a higher occupancy
♦ achieve a higher occupancy
höhere Besucherzahlen erwarten
♦ anticipate higher visitor figures
Höhere Gewalt, f
♦ act of God
♦ force majeure FR
höher einstufen etw
höherstufen etw
verbessern etw
♦ upgrade s.th.
höheren Komfortstandard verlangen
♦ demand a higher standard of comfort
höhere Qualität, f
♦ superior quality
höherer Freizeitanteil, m
♦ increased amount of leisure time
hoher Erlös, m
♦ high revenue
hoher Gast, m
distinguierter Gast, m
vornehmer Gast, m
♦ distinguished guest
hoher Grad an Komfort, m
hoher Grad von Komfort m
♦ high degree of comfort
♦ high level of comfort
hoher Grad von Kapazitätsnutzung m
♦ high degree of capacity utilization
♦ high degree of capacity utilisation
hoher Komfortstandard, m
♦ high standard of comfort
♦ high comfort standard
hoher Küchenstandard, m
♦ high standard of cuisine
♦ high standard of cooking
hoher Nutzungsgrad, m
♦ high level of utilisation
♦ high level of utilization
hoher Preis, m
♦ high price
♦ high rate

hoher Servicestandard, m
♦ high standard of service
♦ high service standard
höherstufen etw
→ höher einstufen etw
Höherstufung, f
(gewöhnlich ohne Preisänderung für den Kunden)
Raufstufung, f coll
♦ upgrading
♦ upgrade
Höherstufung fordern
Höherstufung verlangen
♦ require an upgrade
♦ demand an upgrade
hohes Auslastungsniveau sicherstellen
♦ ensure a high occupancy level
hohes Belegungsniveau erreichen
hohes Auslastungsniveau erreichen
♦ reach a high occupancy level
hohes Bierglas, n
Biertulpe, f
♦ tall beer glass
♦ schooner AE
hohes Buchungsniveau, n
♦ high level of bookings
hohes Buchungsniveau haben
♦ have a high level of bookings
hohes Glas, n
♦ tall glass
hohes Glas, n (für Bier)
hohes Bierglas, n
Biertulpe, f
♦ schooner AE
♦ tall beer glass
♦ beer goblet
hohes Reiseinteresse haben
♦ have a high propensity to travel
hohes Serviceniveau bieten
♦ provide a high level of service
hohes Serviceniveau erwarten
hohes Leistungsniveau erwarten
♦ expect a high service level
♦ expect a high level of service
hohes Umsatzvolumen, n
♦ high sales volume
hohes Umsatzvolumen haben
♦ have a high sales volume
hohes Weinglas, n
♦ tall wine glass
hohes Zimmer, n
Zimmer mit hoher Decke, n
♦ high-ceilinged room
hohes Zimmerumsatzvolumen haben
♦ have a high volume of room sales
Hohe Tatra, die, f
♦ High Tatra, the
hohe Teilnehmerzahl, f
♦ high attendance figure
♦ high number of participants
♦ high number of attendants
hohe variable Betriebskosten, pl
♦ high variable costs of operation pl
hohe Verkehrsdichte, f
♦ high traffic density
Höhle, f (konkret)
♦ cave
Höhle, f (Lasterhöhle)
♦ den
Höhle bewohnen
♦ inhabit a cave

Höhle des Lasters, f
Lasterhöhle f
♦ den of iniquity
♦ den of vice
Höhle erforschen
Höhle erkunden
♦ explore a cave
Höhlenbehandlung, f
♦ speleological treatment
Höhlenbewohner, m
♦ cave-dweller
♦ troglodyte scient
Höhlenforscher, m
♦ speleologist
♦ potholer
Höhlenforschung, f
Speläologie, f
♦ speleology
Höhlenrestaurant, n
♦ cave restaurant
Höhlentherapie, f
♦ speleological therapy
Holdinggesellschaft, f
♦ holding company
holen etw aus dem Backofen
aus dem Ofen holen etw
♦ remove s.th. from the oven
Holland
♦ Holland
hollandaise, adj FR
♦ hollandaise, adj FR
Holländer, m
♦ Dutchman
Holländerin, f
♦ Dutchwoman
holländisch, adj
♦ Dutch, adj
holländische Küste, f
♦ Dutch coast
holländischer Käse, m
♦ Dutch cheese
Hölle heiß machen jm
♦ make it warm for s.o.
♦ make things warm for s.o.
Höllenlärm machen
Höllenkrach machen fam
♦ make a hell of a noise
♦ make a (hell of a) racket
Hollywoodbett, n
(ohne Seitenrahmen)
♦ Hollywood bed
Holstein
(Region)
♦ Holstein
Holsteinische Schweiz f
(Region)
♦ Holstein Switzerland
Holunder, m
♦ elder
Holunderblütentee, m
♦ elderflower tea
Holzbalken, m
♦ wooden beam
♦ wood beam
Holzbalkendecke, f
♦ wood-beamed ceiling
Holzbank, f
♦ wooden bench
♦ wood bench
Holzbaracke, f
♦ wooden barack AE

- ♦ shanty
- ♦ shack
- ♦ shed

Holzbett n
- ♦ wooden bed

Holzboden, m
→ Holzfußboden

Holzbrett, n
- ♦ wooden board

Holzchalet, n
- ♦ wooden chalet

Holzdecke, f
- ♦ wooden ceiling

hölzerne Trennwand, f
- ♦ wooden partition

Holzfaß, n
- ♦ wooden barrel
- ♦ wooden cask

Holzfloß, n
- ♦ timber raft

Holzfußboden, m
Holzboden, m
- ♦ wooden floor

Holzgebäude, n
- ♦ wooden building

holzgetäfelt, adj
→ getäfelt

Holzhaus, n
- ♦ wooden house
- timber house
- ♦ frame house AE

Holzhütte, f
- ♦ wooden hut

Holzkirche, f
- ♦ wooden church

Holzkiste, f
- ♦ wooden box
- ♦ wooden crate

Holzkohle, f
- ♦ charcoal

Holzkohlenfeuer, n
- ♦ charcoal fire

Holzkohlengrill m
- ♦ charcoal grill
- ♦ charcoal barbecue

Holzkohlenofen, m
- ♦ charcoal stove

Holzlöffel, m
Kochlöffel, m
- ♦ wooden spoon

Holzofen, m
- ♦ wood stove

Holzplatte, f
(Restaurant)
- ♦ wooden platter

Holzpritsche, f
(zum Schlafen)
- ♦ plank bed
- ♦ pallet

Holzschemel, m
- ♦ wooden stool

Holzschnitzer, m
- ♦ wood-carver

Holzschnitzerei, f
Holzschnitzereien, f pl
- ♦ wood carving
- ♦ wood carvings pl

Holzschüssel, f
- ♦ wooden bowl
- ♦ wooden dish

Holzsitz, m
- ♦ wooden seat

Holzstuhl, m
- ♦ wooden chair
- ♦ wood chair

Holztäfelung, f
- ♦ wood panelling
- ♦ wood paneling AE

Holztisch, m
- ♦ wooden table
- ♦ wood table

Holztreppe, f
Holztreppenhaus, n
- ♦ wooden staircase

Holzweg, m
- ♦ logging track

Homöopath, m
- ♦ homoeopath

Homöopathie, f
- ♦ homoeopathy

homöopathisch, adj
- ♦ homoeopathic, adj

Homosexuellennachtbar, f
Homosexuellennachtclub, m
Schwulennachtbar, f
- ♦ gay nightclub AE
- ♦ gay night-club BE

Hongkong
- ♦ Hong Kong

Honig, m
- ♦ honey

Honigglas, n
- ♦ honey jar

Honorar, n
- ♦ fee

Hopfen, m
- ♦ hop

Hopfenfest, n
- ♦ hop festival

Horde von Pauschaltouristen, f
- ♦ horde of package tourists

Hornbläser, m
- ♦ hornblower

Horn von Afrika, n
- ♦ Horn of Africa, the

horrende Miete, f
- ♦ exorbitant rent

Hörsaal m
(wie in Hochschule)
- ♦ lecture room
- ♦ lecture hall rare

Hors d'oeuvre, n FR m
Vorspeise, f
- ♦ hors d'oeuvre FR m
- ♦ starter

Hors d'oeuvre chaud, n FR m
warme Vorspeise, f
- ♦ hors-d'oeuvre chaud FR
- ♦ hot hors d'oeuvre
- ♦ hot starter

Hors d'oeuvre froid, n FR m
kalte Vorspeise, f
- ♦ hors-d'oeuvre froid FR
- ♦ cold hors d'oeuvre
- ♦ cold starter

Hors-d'oeuvre-Schälchen, n
(Geschirr)
- ♦ hors-d'oeuvre dish

Hors-d'oeuvre-Service, n
- ♦ hors-d'oeuvre set

Hors-d'oeuvre-Spezialität, f
- ♦ hors-d'oeuvre specialty AE
- ♦ hors-d'oeuvre speciality BE

Hors-d'oeuvres variés, n pl FR m pl
verschiedene Vorspeisen, f pl
- ♦ hors-d'oeuvres variés FR pl
- ♦ various hors d'oeuvres pl
- ♦ various starters pl

Hors-d'oeuvre-Wagen, m
Vorspeisenwagen m
- ♦ hors d'oeuvre cart AE
- ♦ hors d'oeuvre trolley BE

Hors d'oeuvrier, m FR
→ Vorspeisenkoch

Hörweite f
- ♦ hearing distance

Hosenbügler m
(Gerät)
- ♦ trouser press

Hospitalityroom, m
→ Hospitality-Zimmer

Hospitality Suite, f
→ Gastgebersuite

Hospitality-Zimmer, n
Gastgeberzimmer, n
- ♦ hospitality room

Hospiz n
(gehört Kirche oder ähnlichem)
- ♦ hospice

Hosteß, f
- ♦ hostess

Hosteß-Service, m
Hosteß-Dienst, m
Hosteß-Betreuung, f
- ♦ hostess service

Hotelabbestellung, f
→ Hotelstornierung

Hotelabgabe, f
→ Hotelsteuer

Hotelabholdienst, m
Hotelabholung, f
- ♦ hotel pick-up service

Hotelabholung, f
→ Hotelabholdienst

Hotel abreißen
- ♦ knock down a hotel
- ♦ pull down a hotel
- ♦ dismantle a hotel

Hotelabteilung, f (eines Hotels)
- ♦ hotel department
- ♦ department of a hotel

Hotelabteilung, f (eines Unternehmens)
- ♦ hotel division

Hoteladministration, f
Hotelverwaltung, f
- ♦ hotel administration

Hoteladministrator, m
- ♦ hotel administrator

Hotelagent m
- ♦ hotel agent

Hotelaktie, f
- ♦ hotel stock AE
- ♦ hotel share BE

Hotelaktionär, m
- ♦ hotel stockholder AE
- ♦ hotel shareholder BE

Hotelaktivität, f
- ♦ hotel activity

Hotel als eigenständige Einheit führen
- ♦ run an hotel as an autonomous unit

Hotel am Meer

Hotel am Meer, n
♦ hotel at the seaside
Hotel am Ort, n
örtliches Hotel, n
Ortshotel, n
♦ local hotel
Hotel am Seeufer, n (Binnensee)
♦ hotel on the lakeshore *AE*
♦ hotel on the lake-shore *BE*
Hotel am Seeufer, n (Meer)
Hotel am Meerufer, n
Hotel am Meeresufer, n
♦ hotel on the seashore *AE*
♦ hotel on the sea-shore *BE*
Hotel am Zielort, n
♦ hotel of your destination
♦ destination hotel
Hotelanalytiker, m
♦ hotel analyst
Hotelanbau, m
Hoteldependance, f
♦ hotel addition
♦ hotel annexe *BE*
♦ hotel annex *AE*
Hotel anbieten zum Verkauf
Hotel zum Verkauf anbieten
♦ offer a hotel for sale
Hotel an einer Endstation, n
♦ terminal hotel
Hotelangebot, n (Gegensatz zu Nachfrage)
♦ hotel supply
♦ supply of hotels
Hotelangebot, n (Palette)
♦ range of hotels
♦ choice of hotels
♦ available hotels *pl*
Hotelangestellter, m
→ Hotelbeschäftigter
Hotelankunft, f
♦ hotel arrival
Hotelanlage, f
Hotelkomplex m
♦ hotel complex
Hotelanmeldeformular, n
→ Hotelmeldezettel
Hotelanmeldung, f (Buchung)
→ Hotelbuchung
Hotelanmeldung, f (Registrierung)
♦ hotel registration
Hotelanmeldung, f (Rezeption)
→ Rezeption, Empfang
Hotel anmieten
→ Hotel mieten
Hotelannex, m
→ Hotelanbau
Hotelanonymität, f
♦ hotel anonymity
Hotelanteil, m
Hotelbeteiligung, f
♦ hotel stake
♦ stake in a hotel
♦ hotel interest
Hotelanwesen, n
Hotellokal, n
Hotelareal, n
♦ hotel premises *pl*
Hotelanzahlung, f
♦ hotel deposit
Hotelanzeiger, m
Hotelverzeichnis, n
♦ hotel list

♦ list of hotels
♦ hotel directory
Hotelappartement, n
♦ hotel apartment
Hotelappartementanlage, f
Hotelappartementkomplex m
♦ hotel apartment complex
Hotelarbeit, f
♦ hotel work
Hotel arbeitet mit 30 % der Kapazität
♦ hotel runs at 30 % capacity
Hotel arbeitet mit einem Gutscheinsystem
♦ hotel operates a voucher system
Hotel arbeitet mit Verlust
♦ hotel operates at a loss
Hotel arbeitet mit voller Auslastung
♦ hotel operates at full occupancy
Hotel arbeitet saisonal
♦ hotel operates seasonally
Hotelarbeitskräfteknappheit f
♦ hotel labor shortage *AE*
♦ shortage of hotel labor *AE*
♦ hotel labour shortage *BE*
♦ shortage of hotel labour *BE*
Hotelarbeitskräftemarkt, m
♦ hotel labor market *AE*
♦ hotel labour market *BE*
Hotelarbeitsplatz, m
Hoteljob m
♦ hotel job
Hotelarchitekt, m
♦ hotel architect
Hotelarchitektur, f
♦ hotel architecture
Hotelareal, n
Hotelgelände, n
♦ hotel grounds *pl*
♦ hotel premises *pl*
Hotelarrangement, n
Hotelvereinbarung, f
♦ hotel arrangement
♦ arrangement with a hotel
Hotelart, f
Hoteltyp, m
♦ type of hotel
♦ hotel type
Hotelarzt, m
♦ hotel doctor
Hotelassoziation f
→ Hotelverband
Hotelatmosphäre, f
♦ hotel atmosphere
Hotel auf dem neuesten Stand der Technik, n
♦ state-of-the-art hotel
Hotelaufenthalt, m
Aufenthalt in einem Hotel, m
♦ hotel stay
♦ stay at a hotel
♦ stay in a hotel
♦ staying at a hotel
♦ staying in a hotel
Hotelaufenthalt mit Halbpension, m
♦ hotel stay on half board
♦ hotel stay on demipension *AE*
♦ hotel stay on half pension *AE*
Hotelaufenthalt mit Teilpension, m
♦ hotel stay on partial board
Hotelaufenthalt mit Vollpension, m
Hotelaufenthalt mit Vollverpflegung, m
♦ hotel stay on full board
♦ hotel stay on full pension *AE*

Hotelauffahrt, f
Hotelzufahrt f
♦ hotel drive
Hotel auflisten
(z.B. in einem Prospekt)
Hotel aufführen
♦ list a hotel
♦ list hotels
Hotelaufnahme f
→ Einchecken
Hotelaufnahmevertrag, m
♦ hotel reception contract
Hotel aufnehmen in einen Prospekt
♦ include a hotel in a brochure
Hotel auf Rädern, n
Rotel, n
rollendes Hotel, n
♦ hotel on wheels
Hotelaufzug, m
→ Hotelfahrstuhl, Hotellift
Hotel ausbauen
Hotel erweitern
Hotel verlängern
♦ extend a hotel
♦ expand a hotel
♦ enlarge a hotel
Hotelausbilder, m (akademisch)
♦ hotel educator
Hotelausbilder, m (nicht akademisch)
♦ hotel trainer
Hotelausbildung, f (akademisch)
♦ hotel education
Hotelausbildung, f (nicht akademisch)
♦ hotel training
Hotel aus der guten alten Zeit, n
♦ old-world hotel
♦ olde-worlde hotel *humor*
Hotelauslastung, f
Hotelbelegung, f
♦ hotel occupancy
Hotelauslastung optimieren
Hotelbelegung optimieren
♦ maximise hotel occupancy
♦ maximize the hotel's occupancy
Hotelauslastungsrückgang, m
Hotelbelegungsrückgang, m
♦ decrease in hotel occupancy
♦ decrease in the hotel's occupancy
♦ drop in (the) hotel('s) occupancy
♦ fall in (the) hotel('s) occupancy
Hotelauslastungsüberblick, m
→ Hotelauslastungsübersicht
Hotelauslastungsübersicht, f
Hotelauslastungsüberblick, m
♦ hotel occupancy survey
Hotel ausprobieren
♦ try a hotel
Hotelausstattung f
♦ hotel equipment
Hotelausstellung, f
♦ hotel show
Hotel aussuchen
♦ pick a hotel *coll*
♦ select a hotel
♦ choose a hotel
Hotel auswählen
Hotel wählen
♦ select a hotel
♦ choose a hotel
Hotelauto, n
Hotelwagen, m

Hotelbetrieb

Hotel-Pkw, m
♦ **hotel car**
♦ hotel limousine
Hotelbabysitter, m
♦ **hotel babysitter**
Hotelbad, n (Badezimmer)
♦ **hotel bath**
Hotelbad, n (Schwimmbad)
Hotelbecken, n
♦ **hotel pool**
Hotelbadewanne, f
♦ **hotel bathtub**
♦ hotel tub
Hotelbadezimmer, n
♦ **hotel bathroom**
Hotelbalkon m
♦ **hotel balcony**
Hotelballsaal, m
♦ **hotel ballroom**
Hotelbar f
♦ **hotel bar**
Hotelbau, m
♦ **hotel construction**
♦ construction of a hotel
♦ constructing a hotel
♦ building a hotel
Hotelbauboom, m
♦ **hotel building boom**
♦ boom in hotel building
♦ boom in hotel construction
Hotel bauen
♦ **build a hotel**
♦ construct a hotel
Hotelbauplan, m
♦ **hotel building plan**
Hotelbauprogramm n
♦ **hotel building program** AE
♦ hotel building programme BE
Hotelbausektor, m
Hotelbaubereich, m
♦ **hotel building sector**
Hotelbeanspruchung, f
Hotelnutzung, f
♦ **hotel utilisation**
♦ utilisation of a hotel
♦ hotel use
Hotelbecken, n
→ Hotelpool
Hotelbedarf, m
♦ **hotel supplies** pl
♦ needs of the hotel pl
Hotelbediensteter, m
→ Hotelangestellter
Hotelbedienung, f (Bedienungszuschlag)
→ Hotelbedienungszuschlag
Hotelbedienung, f (Person)
→ Hotelkellner
Hotelbedienung, f (Service)
→ Hotelservice
Hotelbedienungsgeld, n
→ Hotelbedienungszuschlag
Hotelbedienungszuschlag, m
Hotelbedienungsgeld, n
♦ **hotel service charge**
Hotel begutachten
Hotel schätzen
♦ **survey a hotel**
Hotel begutachten lassen
(z.B. vor Kauf)
♦ **have a hotel surveyed**

Hotelbelegung, f
→ Hotelauslastung
Hotelbelegungsrückgang, m
→ Hotelauslastungsrückgang
Hotel benachrichtigen von etw
♦ **notify a hotel of s.th.**
Hotel benennen (nach etw)
♦ **name a hotel (after s.th.)**
Hotel benutzen
Hotel in Anspruch nehmen
♦ **use a hotel**
Hotelbenutzer m
♦ **hotel user**
♦ person using a hotel
Hotelbenutzung, f
♦ **use of a hotel**
♦ hotel use
♦ using a hotel
Hotelberater, m
♦ **hotel consultant**
Hotelberatung, f
♦ **hotel consulting**
Hotelberatungsfirma, f
♦ **hotel consulting firm**
♦ hotel consultancy
Hotelberatungsgesellschaft, f
Hotelberatungsfirma, f
♦ **hotel consulting company**
Hotelbereich, m (Gelände)
Hotelgebiet, n
Hotelgelände, n
♦ **hotel area**
Hotelbereich, m (Sektor)
→ Hotelsektor
Hotelberuf, m
Hotelkarriere, f
♦ **career in the hotel trade**
♦ hotel career
Hotelbesatzung, f
→ Hotelpersonal
Hotelbeschäftigter, m
♦ **hotel employee**
♦ person employed in a hotel
Hotelbeschäftigung, f
♦ **hotel employment**
Hotel beschreiben
♦ **describe a hotel**
Hotelbeschreibung f
♦ **hotel description**
♦ description of a hotel
♦ describing a hotel
Hotel besichtigen
→ Hotel inspizieren
Hotelbesitz, m
♦ **hotel ownership**
Hotel besitzen
♦ **own a hotel**
Hotelbesitzer, m
Hotelinhaber, m
♦ **hotel owner**
♦ owner of a hotel
Hotelbesitzerin, f
♦ **proprietress of a hotel**
♦ hotel proprietress
Hotel besitzt drei Räume für Privatveranstaltungen
♦ **hotel has three private function rooms**
Hotel besitzt eine komfortable Tagungssuite mit sechs Zimmern
♦ **hotel has a comfortable conference suite of six rooms**

Hotel besitzt eine Tiefgarage
♦ **hotel has an underground parking lot** AE
♦ hotel has an underground car park BE
Hotel besitzt fünf Stockwerke
♦ **hotel has five floors**
♦ hotel comprises five floors
♦ hotel consists of five floors
Hotel besitzt Räume für Privatveranstaltungen
♦ **hotel has private function rooms**
Hotel besitzt Räumlichkeiten für Geschäftsbesprechungen
♦ **hotel has facilities for business meetings**
Hotelbestand, m (generell)
♦ **hotel stock**
♦ hotel inventory AE
♦ stock of hotels
Hotelbestand, m (Hotelbesitz)
♦ **hotel portfolio**
♦ portfolio of hotels
Hotelbestand erhöhen
♦ **increase the hotel stock**
Hotelbestätigung, f
→ Hotelzusage
Hotelbesteck n
♦ **hotel cutlery**
Hotelbestellung, f
→ Hotelbuchung
Hotel besuchen
Hotel Besuch abstatten
♦ **visit a hotel**
♦ call at a hotel
Hotelbesucher m
♦ **hotel visitor**
♦ person visiting a hotel
♦ hotel guest
Hotelbeteiligung, f
♦ **hotel interest**
♦ interest in a hotel
♦ hotel stake
♦ stake in a hotel
Hotelbeteiligung haben
Hotelbeteiligungen haben
♦ **have an interest in a hotel**
♦ have interests in hotels
♦ have hotel interests
Hotelbeteiligungsgesellschaft, f
♦ **hotel investment company**
Hotel betreiben
Hotel führen
Hotel bewirtschaften
♦ **operate a hotel**
♦ run a hotel
♦ manage a hotel
Hotel betreiben mit einem Geschäftsführungsvertrag
♦ **operate a hotel under a management agreement**
Hotelbetreiber, m
♦ **hotel operator**
Hotelbetreibergesellschaft, f
→ Hotelbetriebsgesellschaft
Hotel betreten
♦ **enter a hotel**
♦ walk into a hotel
Hotelbetrieb, m (Aktivität)
♦ **managing (of) a hotel**
♦ running (of) a hotel
♦ operating (of) a hotel
Hotelbetrieb, m (Unternehmen)
♦ **hotel establishment**

Hotelbetriebsführung

- hotel operation
- hotel

Hotelbetriebsführung, f
- hotel operation
- hotel management
- operating a hotel
- managing a hotel
- running a hotel

Hotelbetriebsgesellschaft, f
- hotel management company
- hotel operating company

Hotelbetriebsvereinbarung, f
- hotel operating arrangement
- arrangement to operate a hotel
- arrangement for operating a hotel

Hotelbetriebswirt, m
- graduate of a hotel college
- graduate of a hotel school
- person holding a diploma in hotel management
- person having a diploma in hotel administration

Hotelbetriebswirtschaft studieren
- take a course in hotel management
- study hotel management

Hotelbetrug, m
  Einmietbetrug, m
- hotel fraud

Hotelbetrug begehen
  Hotelbetrügerei begehen
  Zechprellerei begehen
- commit a hotel fraud

Hotel betrügen
  Hotel prellen
  Einmietbetrug begehen
- defraud a hotel

Hotelbetrüger, m
  Einmietbetrüger, m
- hotel swindler
- hotel defrauder

Hotelbett, n
  Fremdenbett, n
- hotel bed

Hotelbettenangebot n
- hotel bed supply
- supply of hotel beds

Hotelbettenboom, m
- hotel bed boom

Hotelbettenkapazität, f
- hotel bed capacity
- hotel sleeping capacity

Hotelbettenknappheit, f
- hotel bed shortage
- shortage of hotel beds

Hotelbettenmangel, m (Knappheit)
  → Hotelbettenknappheit

Hotelbettenmangel, m (völliges Fehlen)
- lack of hotel beds

Hotelbettennachfrage f
- hotel bed demand
- demand for hotel beds

Hotelbettnacht, f
  (Statistik)
- hotel bed-night

Hotel beurteilen
- judge a hotel

Hotel bewerten
- rate a hotel

Hotelbewertung, f
- hotel rating
- rating (of) a hotel

Hotel bewirtschaften
  → Hotel betreiben

Hotelbewohner m
- hotel resident
- person staying at a hotel
- hotel guest

Hotelbezirk, m
  Hotelviertel, n
- hotel district

Hotelbibliothek, f
- hotel library

Hotel bietet 123 Betten
- hotel provides 123 beds

Hotel bietet allen Komfort
- hotel offers all comforts
- hotel offers all conveniences

Hotel bietet Beherbergung für 123 Personen
  Hotel bietet Schlafmöglichkeiten für 123 Personen
- hotel sleeps 123 persons

Hotel bietet einen freien Blick auf den Strand
- hotel has unrestricted views of the beach

Hotel bietet einen idealen Rahmen für
  geschäftliche und gesellschaftliche
  Veranstaltungen
- hotel offers an ideal setting for business
  and social activities

Hotel bietet einen idealen Rahmen für etw
- hotel offers an ideal setting for s.th.

Hotel bietet eine zwanglose Atmosphäre,
  in der man entspannen kann
- hotel provides an informal atmosphere,
  in which one can relax

Hotel bietet jede Annehmlichkeit
- hotel affords every convenience
- hotel offers every convenience

Hotel bietet jede Bequemlichkeit
- hotel offers every convenience

Hotel bietet jeden Komfort
- hotel affords every comfort
- hotel offers every comfort

Hotel bietet nur Übernachtung und Frühstück
- hotel provides bed and breakfast only
- hotel caters for bed and breakfast only

Hotel bietet Übernachtungsunterkünfte
- hotel provides overnight accommodations AE
- hotel provides overnight accommodation BE

Hotelboom, m
- hotel boom

Hotelbote, m
  Chasseur, m FR
  Chasseur d'hôtel, m FR
- messenger boy
- chasseur FR
- chasseur d'hôtel FR

Hotelboutique f
- hotel boutique

Hotelbranche, f
- hotel line
- hotel industry
- hotel trade

Hotelbranche boomt
  Hotelgewerbe boomt
- hotel industry is booming
- hotel trade is booming

Hotelbrand, m
- hotel fire

Hotelbrand auslösen
- start a hotel fire

Hotelbrand forderte 123 Leben
- hotel fire claimed 123 lives

Hotelbrand löschen
- extinguish a hotel fire

Hotel buchen
  (das gesamte Hotel)
- book a hotel

Hotelbücher, n pl
  (Buchhaltung)
- hotel records pl

Hotelbücherei, f
  → Hotelbibliothek

Hotelbuchführung, f
  Hotelbuchhaltung, f
- hotel bookkeeping
- hotel accounting

Hotelbuchhalter, m
- hotel accountant
- hotel bookkeeper

Hotelbuchhaltung f
- hotel accounting
- hotel bookkeeping

Hotelbuchung, f
  Hotelbestellung, f
- hotel booking

Hotelbuchungen steigern
- increase the hotel bookings

Hotelbuchungsdienst, m
  → Hotelvermittlung

Hotelbuchungsformular n
- hotel booking form

Hotelbuchungsmaschine, f
  (Buchhaltung)
- hotel booking machine

Hotelbuchungsservice, m
  → Hotelvermittlung

Hotelbuchungsvertrag, m
- hotel booking contract

Hotelbungalow, m
- hotel bungalow

Hotelbüro, n
- hotel office

Hotelbus, m
- hotel bus

Hotelbusdienst m
  Hotelbusservice m
  Hotelbusverbindung f
  Hotelbusverkehr m
  Hotelbus m
- hotel bus service

Hotelbusservice, m
  → Hotelbusdienst

Hotelbustransfer m
- hotel bus transfer

Hotelbusverbindung, f
  → Hotelbusdienst

Hotelcafé, n
  (Café in Hotel)
- hotel café
- hotel cafe AE
- hotel coffee shop AE
- hotel coffee bar AE

Hotel-Café, n (Betriebstyp)
  (Hotel und Café)
- hotel and café
- hotel/café

Hotelcharakter, m
- character of the hotel

Hotelchen, n humor
  Kleinsthotel, n
  Minihotel, n
- minihotel
- tiny hotel

Hotelclub, m
♦ hotel club
♦ hotel's club
Hotelclubanlage, f
Hotelclubkomplex m
♦ hotel club complex
Hotelcomputeranlage, f
Hotelcomputersystem n
♦ hotel computer system
Hotelconcierge, m/f
♦ hotel concierge
Hotelconsulting, n
→ Hotelberatung
Hotelcoupon, m
♦ hotel coupon
Hoteldach, n
♦ hotel roof
Hoteldekor, m/n
♦ hotel decor AE
♦ hotel décor BE
Hoteldependance, f
♦ hotel annex AE
♦ hotel annexe BE
Hotel der A-Kategorie, n
♦ A-category hotel
Hotel der B-Kategorie, n
♦ B-category hotel
Hotel der C-Kategorie, n
♦ C-category hotel
Hotel der D-Kategorie, n
♦ D-category hotel
Hotel der E-Kategorie, n
♦ E-category hotel
Hotel der ersten Kategorie, n
→ Hotel der ersten Klasse
Hotel der ersten Klasse, n
→ erstklassiges Hotel
Hotel der ersten Wahl, n
(z.B. bei Buchung)
♦ first choice hotel
Hotel der gehobenen Kategorie, n
♦ quality hotel
Hotel der gehobenen Mittelklasse, n
gutes Mittelklassehotel, n
gutbürgerliches Hotel, n
♦ good medium-range hotel
♦ good middle-class hotel
Hotel der Komfortklasse, n
♦ comfort-class hotel
Hotel der Luxuskategorie, n
♦ deluxe-category hotel AE
♦ luxury-category hotel
Hotel der Luxusklasse, n
♦ luxury-class hotel
♦ deluxe-class hotel AE
Hotel der Mittelklasse n
gutbürgerliches Hotel, n
♦ middle-class hotel
Hotel der mittleren Kategorie, n
♦ medium-category hotel
♦ medium-range hotel
♦ mid-market hotel
Hotel der oberen Kategorie, n
Hotel der oberen Klasse, n
♦ up-market hotel
♦ superior hotel
Hotel der oberen Klasse, n
♦ upmarket hotel
♦ superior hotel
Hotel der Spitzenkategorie, n
♦ top-category hotel

Hotel der Spitzenklasse n
♦ top-class hotel
Hotel der Touristenklasse, n
Touristenklassehotel, n
♦ economy-class hotel
♦ tourist-class hotel
Hotel der unteren Kategorie, n
Touristenhotel, n
♦ economy hotel
Hotel der Vier-Sterne-Kategorie, n
♦ hotel in the four-star category
Hotel der zweiten Wahl, n
(z.B. bei Buchung)
♦ second choice hotel
Hotel des Jahres, n
(Auszeichnung)
♦ Hotel of the Year
Hoteldetektiv m
♦ hotel detective
♦ hotel dick sl
Hoteldieb, m
♦ hotel thief
Hoteldiebstahl m
♦ hotel theft
Hoteldiener, m
♦ hotel servant
♦ houseman AE
♦ valet
Hoteldienergebühr, f
→ Hoteldienerlohn
Hoteldienerlohn m
Hoteldienergebühr f
♦ hotel porterage
Hoteldienstleistung, f
→ Hotelservice
Hoteldienstleistung in Anspruch nehmen
Hotelservice in Anspruch nehmen
♦ make use of a hotel service
♦ use a hotel service
Hoteldienstleistungsangebot, n
Hotleistungsangebot, n
Hotelserviceangebot, n
♦ range of the hotel services
♦ range of hotel services
♦ hotel service range
Hoteldienstleistungsgewerbe n
♦ hotel service industry
Hoteldirectrice, f
→ Hoteldirektorin
Hotel direkt am Strand, n
♦ beachfront hotel
♦ hotel (situated) directly on the beach
Hoteldirektion, f
♦ hotel management
Hoteldirektor, m
♦ hotel director
Hoteldirektorin, f
♦ hotel manageress
♦ female hotel manager
Hotel direkt zahlen
♦ pay the hotel direct
Hoteldisko, f
♦ hotel disco
Hoteldiskothek, f
♦ hotel discotheque
Hoteldiskothek macht zuviel Lärm
♦ hotel discotheque is too loud
Hoteldorf, n
♦ hotel village
Hoteldozent, m
♦ lecturer in hotel studies

Hoteldruckerei, f
♦ hotel's print shop
Hoteldusche f
♦ hotel shower
Hoteldynastie, f
♦ hotel dynasty
hoteleigen, adj
hauseigen, adj
♦ hotel's own, adj
♦ own, adj
♦ private, adj
hoteleigene Garage, f
♦ hotel's own garage
hoteleigener Parkplatz, m (für mehrere Autos)
♦ hotel's own parking lot AE
♦ hotel's private parking lot AE
♦ hotel's own car park BE
♦ hotel's private car park BE
hoteleigener Strand, m
♦ hotel's own beach
hoteleigenes Hallenbad, n
♦ hotel's own indoor swimming pool AE
♦ hotel's own indoor swimming-pool BE
♦ hotel's own indoor pool
hoteleigene Wäscherei, f
♦ hotel's own laundry
Hoteleigentum, n
♦ hotel property
Hoteleigentümer, m
♦ hotel proprietor
♦ proprietor of a hotel
Hoteleigentümerin, f
♦ hotel proprietress
♦ proprietress of a hotel
Hotel eignet sich (sehr gut) für Tagungen
♦ hotel is (very) suitable for conferences
Hoteleingang, m
♦ hotel entrance
Hoteleingangshalle, f
♦ hotel entrance hall
Hoteleinheit f
(Statistik)
♦ hotel unit
Hoteleinkehr, f
→ Einkehr in einem Hotel
Hoteleinnahmen, f pl
♦ hotel income
♦ hotel takings pl
♦ hotel revenues pl
♦ hotel receipts pl
Hotel einrichten
→ Hotel möblieren
Hoteleinrichtung, f (Fazilität)
♦ hotel facility
Hoteleinrichtung, f (Möbel)
Hotelmöbel, n pl
Hotelmobiliar, n
♦ hotel furnishings pl
♦ hotel furniture sg
Hoteleinrichtungen benutzen
♦ use the hotel facilities
♦ use the hotel's facilities
Hotel einstufen (nach etw)
♦ grade a hotel (according to s.th.)
Hoteleinstufung f
♦ hotel grading
♦ grading (of) a hotel
Hoteleinteilung, f
Hotelklassifizierung, f
♦ hotel classification

Hoteleinteilungssystem

Hoteleinteilungssystem, n
Hotelklassifizierungssystem, n
♦ hotel classification system
Hotel einweihen
Hotel feierlich eröffnen
♦ inaugurate a hotel
Hoteleinweihung, f
feierliche Hoteleröffnung, f
♦ hotel inauguration
Hotelektriker, m
Hauselektriker, m
♦ hotel electrician
♦ our own electrician
Hotelemblem, n
♦ hotel emblem
Hotelempfang, m
Hotelrezeption, f
♦ hotel reception
Hotelempfangsabteilung f
♦ hotel reception department
Hotelempfangsabteilung leiten
♦ be in charge of the hotel reception department
Hotelempfangsabteilungsleiter m
→ Hotelempfangschef
Hotelempfangsdame, f
Hotelrezeptionistin, f
♦ female hotel receptionist
Hotelempfangsherr, m
Hotelrezeptionist, m
♦ hotel receptionist
♦ male hotel receptionist
Hotel empfehlen
Hotelempfehlung geben
♦ recommend a hotel
Hotel empfehlen jm wärmstens
♦ recommend a hotel warmly to s.o.
Hotelempfehlung, f
♦ recommendation of a hotel
♦ hotel recommendation
♦ recommending a hotel
Hotelempfehlung geben
→ Hotel empfehlen
Hotelengagement, n
Hotelbeteiligung, f
♦ hotel engagement
♦ interest in a hotel
♦ interests in hotels *pl*
Hotelengpaß, m
(Kapazität)
♦ hotel bottleneck
♦ accommodation bottleneck
Hotelengpaß vermeiden
♦ avoid a hotel bottleneck
Hotel entwerfen
Hotel gestalten
♦ design a hotel
Hotelentwicklung, f
Hotelerschließung, f
♦ hotel development
Hotelentwicklungen ermutigen
♦ encourage hotel developments
Hotelerbauer, m
Hotelbauer m
♦ hotel builder
Hotel erben von jm
♦ inherit a hotel from s.o.
Hotelerfahrung, f
♦ hotel experience
Hotelerfahrung haben
♦ have hotel experience

Hotelermäßigung f
♦ hotel reduction
Hotel eröffnen
♦ open a hotel
Hoteleröffnung, f
Eröffnung eines Hotels, f
♦ opening of a hotel
♦ opening a hotel
Hotel erreichen
♦ reach a hotel
Hotel errichten
♦ erect a hotel
Hotel erstehen
Hotel kaufen
♦ purchase a hotel
♦ buy a hotel
♦ acquire a hotel
Hotel ersteigern
♦ buy a hotel at an auction
Hotelersteller, m
Hotelbauträger, m
Hotelbauunternehmer, m
♦ hotel developer
Hotel erster Klasse, n
→ erstklassiges Hotel
Hotel erweitern
♦ expand a hotel
♦ enlarge a hotel
♦ extend a hotel
Hotel erweitern um 20 Zimmer
♦ add 20 rooms to the hotel
Hotelerweiterung, f
Hotelvergrößerung f
♦ hotel extension
♦ extension of a hotel
♦ hotel expansion
♦ expansion of a hotel
Hotelerweiterungsprogramm, n
♦ program of hotel extension *AE*
♦ program of hotel extensions *AE*
♦ programme of hotel extension *BE*
♦ programme of hotel extensions *BE*
Hotel erwerben
♦ acquire a hotel
Hotelerwerb m
♦ hotel acquisition
♦ acquisition of a hotel
♦ acquiring a hotel
Hotel erzielt 50 % seiner Auslastung durch Frauen
♦ hotel derives 50 % of its occupancy from women
Hotelessen, n (generell)
Hotelverpflegung, f
♦ hotel food
Hotelessen, n (Mahlzeit)
→ Hotelmahlzeit
Hoteleßlokal, n
Hotelspeiselokal, n
♦ hotel eating place
Hoteletage, f
Hotelstockwerk, n
Hotelgeschoß, n
♦ hotel floor
Hotel evakuieren
♦ evacuate a hotel
Hotelexperte, m
♦ hotel expert
♦ hotel professional
Hotelfach, n (Geschäft)
→ Hotelgeschäft

Hotelfach, n (Studienfach)
♦ hotel subject
Hotelfach einschlagen
♦ enter the hotel business
♦ go into the hotel business
Hotelfachkenntnisse, f pl
Hotelkenntnisse, f pl
♦ hotel expertise *sg*
♦ hotel skills *pl*
Hotelfachkenntnisse besitzen
♦ have hotel expertise
Hotelfachkraft, f
♦ trained hotel employee
♦ skilled hotel employee
Hotelfachleute, pl
♦ hotelmen *pl*
♦ professional hotel people *pl*
♦ hotel people *pl*
Hotelfachschule, f
Hotelschule, f
♦ hotel school
♦ school of hotel management
Hotelfahrstuhl, m
Hotelaufzug, m
Hotellift, m
♦ hotel elevator *AE*
♦ hotel lift *BE*
Hotelfahrzeug, n
♦ hotel vehicle
Hotelfassade, f
♦ hotel façade
♦ hotel's façade
♦ hotel facade *AE*
♦ hotel's facade *AE*
♦ hotel front
Hotelfenster, n
♦ hotel window
Hotelferien, pl
Hotelurlaub, m
♦ hotel holiday *BE*
♦ hotel vacation *AE*
Hotelferienort, m
Hotelurlaubsort, m
Hotelferienanlage, f
♦ hotel resort
Hotel fertigstellen
(Bau)
♦ complete a hotel
Hotel feuerversichern
Hotel gegen Feuer versichern
Hotel gegen Brand versichern
♦ insure a hotel against fire
Hotel finden
♦ find a hotel
Hotelfirma, f
♦ hotel firm
Hotelfirmenpreis, m
Hotelfirmenrate, f
♦ hotel company rate *BE*
♦ hotel corporate rate *AE*
Hotelfirmenrate, f
Hotelfirmenpreis, m
♦ hotel corporate rate *AE*
♦ hotel company rate *BE*
Hotelflur, m
Hotelkorridor, m
♦ hotel corridor
Hotelfoyer, n
♦ hotel foyer
Hotelfragebogen, m
♦ hotel questionnaire

- hotel questionaire *AE*
- hotel questionary *AE*

Hotelfragebogen ausfüllen
- **fill out a hotel questionnaire** *AE*
- fill out a hotel questionaire *AE*
- fill out a hotel questionary *AE*
- fill in a hotel questionnaire *BE*
- complete a hotel questionnaire

Hotelfranchise, n
- **hotel franchise**

Hotelfranchisekette, f
- **hotel franchise chain**

Hotelfranchisesystem, n
- **hotel franchise system**

Hotelfranchising, n
- **hotel franchising**

Hotelfreizeitclub, m
- **hotel leisure club**
- hotel's leisure club

Hotel frequentieren
- **frequent a hotel**
- patronise a hotel

Hotelfriseur, m (für Damen)
- **hotel hairdresser**
- hotel hair stylist

Hotelfriseur, m (für Herren)
- **hotel barber**
- hotel hairdresser *BE*

Hotelfront, f
(bei Gebäude)
Hotelfrontlänge f
- **hotel frontage**

Hotelfrühstück n
- **hotel breakfast**

Hotelfrühstücksraum, m
Hotelfrühstückssaal, m
- **hotel breakfast room**

Hotelfrühstückszimmer, n
→ Hotelfrühstücksraum

Hotel führen
Hotel leiten
- **run a hotel**
- manage a hotel
- keep a hotel

Hotel führen (für jn)
- **keep a hotel (for s.o.)**
- run a hotel (for s.o.)
- manage a hotel (for s.o.)

Hotel führen mit einer persönlichen Note
- **run a hotel on personal lines**

Hotelführer, m
(Buch)
- **hotel guide**
- guide to the hotels

Hotelführer führt 123 Hotels auf
- **hotel guide lists 123 hotels**

Hotelführer veröffentlichen
- **publish a hotel guide**

Hotelführer zu Rat ziehen
(Buch)
- **consult a hotel guide**

Hotelführung, f
- **hotelkeeping**
- managing a hotel
- running a hotel
- hotel management

Hotelführungskraft, f
- **hotel executive**
- hotel manager

Hotelführungsmannschaft, f
Hotelführungsteam n
- **hotel management team**

Hotelführungspersonal, n
- **hotel management staff**
- hotel management personnel

Hotel füllen
- **fill a hotel**

Hotel für alle Jahreszeiten, n
- **hotel for all seasons**

Hotel für anspruchsvolle Gäste, n
- **hotel for demanding guests**
- hotel for discerning guests

Hotel für Durchreisende, n
→ Passantenhotel

Hotel für gehobene Ansprüche, n
- **hotel for discerning guests**

Hotel für jedermann, n
- **hotel for everybody**

Hotelgarage, f
- **hotel garage**

Hotelgarantie, f
- **hotel guarantee**

Hotel garni, n *FR*
Garnihotel, n
Frühstückshotel, n
- **hotel garni** *FR*
- bed-and-breakfast hotel
- hotel providing bed and breakfast
- residential hotel

Hotelgarten, m
- **hotel garden**

Hotelgast, m
- **hotel guest**
- guest staying at a hotel

Hotelgast ausrufen lassen
Hotelgast suchen lassen
- **page a hotel guest**

Hotelgästeliste, f
Hotelgästeverzeichnis, n
- **hotel guest list**

Hotelgästeverzeichnis, n
→ Hotelgästeliste

Hotelgastfreundschaft, f
Hotelgastlichkeit, f
- **hotel hospitality**
- hospitality at the hotel
- hospitality of the hotel

Hotel-Gasthof, m
- **hotel/inn**
- private hotel

Hotelgastlichkeit genießen
- **enjoy the hotel's hospitality**

Hotelgastronomie, f
Hotelverpflegung, f
- **hotel foodservice** *AE*
- hotel catering *BE*

Hotelgebäude, n
Hotelbau, n
- **hotel building**

Hotelgebiet, n
Hotelsektor m
- **hotel field**
- hotel sector

Hotelgebühr f
- **hotel charge**
- hotel fee

Hotelgehälter, n pl
- **hotel salaries** *pl*

Hotel gehört zu den ersten Häusern in X
- **hotel is one of the foremost in X**

Hotel gehört zu einer Preiskategorie
- **hotel belongs to a price category**

Hotel geht in Konkurs
- **hotel is going into receivership**

Hotelgelände, n
- **hotel terrain**

Hotel genießt einen guten Ruf
- **hotel enjoys a good reputation**

Hotelgenossenschaft, f
- **hotel cooperative** *AE*
- hotel co-operative *BE*

Hotelgeschäft, n
Hotelbranche, f
Hotelwesen, n
Hotelfach, n
- **hotel business**

Hotelgeschenkgutschein, m
- **hotel gift voucher**

Hotelgeschirr, n (irdenes)
- **hotel crockery**

Hotelgeschirr, n (Porzellan)
→ Hotelporzellan

Hotelgesellschaft, f
- **hotel corporation** *AE*
- hotel company

Hotelgestaltung, f
- **hotel design**

Hotelgewerbe, n
Hotelbranche, f
Hotelwesen, n
- **hotel trade**

Hotelgewinn, m
Hotelprofit, m
- **hotel profit**
- profit made by a hotel

Hotelgolfplatz, m
- **hotel golf course**

Hotelgröße f
- **hotel size**
- size of a hotel

Hotelgrundstück, n
- **hotel site**
- hotel premises *pl*

Hotelgründung, f
- **establishment of a hotel**
- establishing a hotel

Hotelgruppe, f
- **group of hotels**
- hotel group

Hotelgutachten, f
Hotelschätzung, f
- **hotel appraisal**

Hotelgutachter, m
Hotelschätzer m
- **hotel appraiser**

Hotelgutschein, m
Hotelvoucher, m
- **hotel voucher**

Hotelgutschein an Abrechnungsstelle weitergeben
- **pass a hotel voucher to the bills office**

Hotelgutschein erhalten
- **receive a hotel voucher**

Hotelgutscheinpreis m
- **hotel voucher rate**
- hotel voucher price

Hotelgutscheinprogramm, n
- **hotel voucher scheme**

Hotelgutschein vorlegen
- **present a hotel voucher**

Hotelhalle

- produce a hotel voucher
- show a hotel voucher

Hotelhalle, f
- hotel lobby *AE*
- hotel hall

Hotelhandbuch, n
(für Betriebsführung)
- hotel manual

Hotel hat 123 Zimmer
- hotel has 123 rooms

Hotel hat Atmosphäre
- hotel has atmosphere

Hotel hat besondere Annehmlichkeiten für Kinder
- hotel has special amenities for children

Hotel hat eine eigene Garage für 50 Pkws
- hotel has its own garage for 50 cars

Hotel hat eine ideale Lage
- hotel has an ideal situation
- hotel is ideally situated

Hotel hat eine intime Atmosphäre
- hotel has an intimate atmosphere

Hotel hat einen eigenen Parkplatz
- hotel has its own parking lot *AE*
- hotel has its own car park *BE*

Hotel hat einen eigenen Strand
- hotel has its own beach

Hotel hat einen großen Gästekreis
- hotel has a large clientele

Hotel hat einen neuen Besitzer
- hotel is under new ownership

Hotel hat einen Ruf für Gastlichkeit und Service
- hotel has a reputation for hospitality and service

Hotel hat einen Ruf für seine Gastlichkeit und seinen Service
- hotel has a reputation for its hospitality and service

Hotel hat eine Zwei-Sterne-Bewertung
- hotel has a two-star rating

Hotel hat etwas Anheimelndes an sich
- hotel has a homely air about it

Hotel hat keine Atmosphäre
- hotel lacks atmosphere

Hotel hat Konferenzmöglichkeiten für bis zu 30 Teilnehmer
- hotel has conference facilities for up to 30 delegates

Hotel hat seinen viktorianischen Charakter bewahrt
- hotel has retained its Victorian character

Hotel hat uns geneppt *inform*
- hotel has rooked us *inform*
- hotel has overcharged us

Hotel hat vier Zimmer belegt
- hotel has four rooms occupied

Hotel hat wenige Zimmer
- hotel has few rooms

Hotel hat zehn Etagen
Hotel hat zehn Stockwerke
Hotel hat zehn Geschosse
- hotel has ten floors
- hotel has ten stories *AE*
- hotel has ten storeys *BE*

Hotel hat zehn Stockwerke
→ Hotel hat zehn Etagen

Hotelhöherstufung, f
Hotelverbesserung, f
Bereitstellung einer höheren Hotelleistung, f
- hotel upgrade
- hotel upgrading

Hotelhypothek f
- hotel mortgage

Hotelier, m
- hotelier
- hotelkeeper

Hotelier des Jahres, m
(Auszeichnung)
- Hotelier of the Year

Hotelier direkt zahlen
- pay the hotelier direct

Hotelierehepaar, n
- couple running the hotel

Hoteliergruppe, f
- group of hoteliers

Hotelierkollege, m
- fellow hotelier

Hoteliersfamilie, f
Hotelierfamilie, f
- family running the hotel

Hotelierspfandrecht, n
Pfandrecht des Hoteliers, n
- hotelkeeper's lien
- hotelier's lien

Hotelierverband, m
→ Hoteliervereinigung

Hotelierverein, m
→ Hotelvereinigung

Hoteliervereinigung, f
Hotelierverein, m
Hotelierverband, m
- hoteliers' association

Hotel Ihrer Wahl, n
- hotel of your choice

Hotelimage, n
- hotel image
- hotel's image

Hotel im Atriumstil, n
- atrium-style hotel

Hotel im Bau, n
→ Hotelneubau

Hotel im Bungalowstil, n
- bungalow-style hotel

Hotel im Chaletstil, n
- chalet-style hotel

Hotel im Cottagestil, n
- cottage-style hotel

Hotel im Hotel, n
- hotel within the hotel
- hotel in the hotel
- hotel within a hotel
- hotel in a hotel

Hotelimmobilie, f
Hotelanwesen, n
- hotel property

Hotel im spanischen Stil, n
- Spanish-style hotel

Hotel im Stil der Zeit, n
- period hotel

Hotel in Betrieb nehmen
→ Hotel eröffnen

Hotel in Brand stecken
Hotel in Brand setzen
- set fire to a hotel

Hotel in der mittleren Kategorie, n
- medium-range hotel
- medium-category hotel

Hotel in der mittleren Preisklasse, n
- middle-bracket hotel
- hotel in the middle price category

Hotel in der oberen Preisklasse, n
- upper-bracket hotel
- hotel in the upper price category

Hotel in der unteren Preisklasse, n
- lower-bracket hotel
- hotel in the lower price category

Hotel in eine höhere Kategorie einstufen
Hotel höher einstufen
Hotel höherstufen
Hotel verbessern
- upgrade a hotel

Hotel in Familienbesitz, n
- family-owned hotel

Hotelinfrastruktur, f
- hotel infrastructure

Hotelinhaber, m
→ Hotelbesitzer

Hotel in idyllischer Lage, n
idyllisch gelegenes Hotel, n
- idyllically located hotel
- idyllically situated hotel

Hotelinklusivarrangement, n
Hotelpauschalarrangement n
- hotel inclusive arrangement
- arrangement including hotel

Hotel inkognito besuchen
- visit a hotel incognito
- pay a hotel an incognito visit

Hotel innen und außen renovieren
- renovate a hotel inside and out
- refurbish a hotel inside and outside

Hotelinnere, n
Innere eines Hotels, das
- interior of a hotel

Hotel in Pacht haben
- have the lease of a hotel

Hotel in Privatbesitz, n
Privathotel, n
- privately owned hotel
- hotel in private ownership
- individually owned hotel
- independently owned hotel

Hotelinspizient m
- hotel inspector

Hotel inspizieren
Hotel überprüfen
- inspect a hotel

Hotelinstandhaltung, f
- hotel maintenance
- maintenance of a hotel

Hotel instandsetzen
- fix a hotel *AE*
- restore a hotel
- renovate a hotel
- refurbish a hotel
- repair a hotel

Hotel in Übersee, n
- hotel overseas
- overseas hotel

Hotel in verkehrsgünstiger Lage, n
günstig gelegenes Hotel, n
- conveniently situated hotel
- conveniently located hotel

Hotel in Verruf bringen
- bring a hotel into disrepute

Hotelinvestition f
- hotel investment
- investment in a hotel
- investing in a hotel

Hotelinvestor, m
- hotel investor
- investor in hotel(s)

Hotel in zentraler Lage, n
- centrally situated hotel
- centrally located hotel
- centrally placed hotel

Hotel ist 100%ig belegt
- hotel is 100 % occupied

Hotel ist 12 Jahre alt
- hotel is 12 years old

Hotel ist ab dem 1. Mai belegt
- hotel is booked from 1 May (onwards)

Hotel ist abgebrannt
Hotel brannte ab
- hotel burned down
- hotel burnt down

Hotel ist anders
- hotel is different

Hotel ist ausgebucht
Hotel ist vollbelegt
- hotel is fully booked
- hotel is booked to capacity
- hotel is booked up

Hotel ist bei den Gästen sehr beliebt
- hotel is very popular with (the) guests

Hotel ist bekannt
- hotel is well known

Hotel ist bekannt für seine Gastlichkeit
- hotel is renowned for its hospitality
- hotel is noted for its hospitality

Hotel ist belegt
Hotel ist voll
- hotel is full
- hotel is full up

Hotel ist besonders für Familien geeignet
- hotel is especially suited for families
- hotel is especially suitable for families

Hotel ist bestens geeignet für etw
- hotel is ideally suited for s.th.

Hotel ist bestens geeignet für kleine Tagungen
- hotel is ideally suited for small meetings
- hotel is ideally suited for small conferences

Hotel ist bis September belegt
- hotel is booked until September

Hotel ist das erste Haus in X
- hotel is the premier hotel in X
- hotel is the leading hotel in X

Hotel ist das ganze Jahr über geöffnet
- hotel is open all year round
- hotel is open throughout the year

Hotel ist der Mittelpunkt des Gemeindelebens
- hotel is the center of community life AE
- hotel is the center of local life AE
- hotel is the centre of community life BE
- hotel is the centre of local life BE

Hotel ist ein Saisonbetrieb
- hotel is seasonal
- hotel is run on a seasonal basis

Hotel ist ein Zweckbau
Hotel wurde als Hotel gebaut
- hotel is purpose built

Hotel ist ein zweites Zuhause
- hotel is a home from home
- hotel is a home away from home

Hotel ist familienfreundlich
Familien sind in dem Hotel willkommen
- hotel welcomes families
- hotel is family-friendly

Hotel ist für Behinderte geeignet
- hotel is suitable for disabled persons

Hotel ist für die Qualität seines Service bekannt
- hotel is renowned for the quality of its service

Hotel ist für Familien geeignet
- hotel is suitable for families

Hotel ist für Kinder nicht geeignet
- hotel is not suitable for children

Hotel ist für Monate im voraus gebucht
Hotel ist für Monate im voraus belegt
- hotel is booked months in advance

Hotel ist für Rollstuhlfahrer geeignet
- hotel is suitable for wheelchairs

Hotel ist für seine ausgezeichnete Küche bekannt
- hotel is noted for its excellent cuisine

Hotel ist für seine familiäre Atmosphäre bekannt
- hotel is known for its family atmosphere

Hotel ist für seinen ausgezeichneten Service bekannt
- hotel is renowned for its excellent service

Hotel ist ganzjährig geöffnet
- hotel is open throughout the year
- hotel is open all over the year
- hotel is open all (the) year round
- hotel is open all year

Hotel ist gebucht
(vollständig)
- hotel has been booked

Hotel ist gebucht von einem Reiseveranstalter
- hotel has been booked by a tour operator

Hotel ist gut eingeführt
- hotel is well established

Hotel ist halb leer
- hotel is half empty

Hotel ist heruntergekommen
- hotel is run-down

Hotel ist hervorragend geeignet für Bergsteiger und Wanderer
- hotel is admirably suited for climbers and hikers

Hotel ist im Bau
- hotel is being built
- hotel is being constructed
- hotel is under construction

Hotel ist in Bahnhofsnähe gelegen
- hotel is situated close to the station
- hotel is conveniently situated for the station

Hotel ist in Betrieb seit 1990
- hotel has been in operation since 1990

Hotel ist in britischem Besitz
- hotel is in British ownership

Hotel ist in dem Prospekt aufgeführt
- hotel is listed in the brochure

Hotel ist in Privatbesitz
- hotel is independently owned

Hotel ist kinderfreundlich
- hotel welcomes children
- hotel is child-friendly

Hotel ist komplett renoviert worden
- hotel has been completely renovated
- hotel has been completely refurbished

Hotel ist kultiviert
- hotel is refined

Hotel ist miserabel
Hotel ist mies
- hotel is wretched

Hotel ist mittelgroß
- hotel is medium-sized

Hotel ist modern eingerichtet
- hotel is appointed with all modern conveniences
- hotel is modernly appointed

Hotel ist neu
- hotel is new

Hotel ist nicht ganz voll
- hotel is not quite full

Hotel ist nicht weit entfernt vom Stadtzentrum
- hotel is not far from the city center AE
- hotel is not far from the city centre BE
- hotel is not far from the town center AE
- hotel is not far from the town centre BE

Hotel ist ruhig
- hotel is quiet

Hotel ist rustikal
- hotel is rustic

Hotel ist sauber
- hotel is clean

Hotel ist schlecht geführt
- hotel is badly managed

Hotel ist schrecklich
- hotel is terrible

Hotel ist schwer zu finden
- hotel is difficult to find

Hotel ist sechs Monate im Jahr geöffnet
- hotel is open for six months of the year
- hotel is open for six months in the year

Hotel ist sehr beliebt für Tanzdiners und Hochzeitsfeste
- hotel is very popular for dinner dances and
- wedding receptions

Hotel ist stark gebucht
Hotel ist stark belegt
- hotel is heavily booked

Hotel ist überbeansprucht
- hotel is overutilised
- hotel is overutilized
- hotel is overused

Hotel ist überbelegt
- hotel is filled beyond capacity
- hotel is overbooked
- hotel is overcrowded

Hotel ist überbucht
- hotel is overbooked

Hotel ist überfüllt
Hotel ist überbelegt
- hotel is overcrowded

Hotel ist unkonventionell
- hotel is unconventional

Hotel ist unterbeansprucht
- hotel is underutilised
- hotel is underutilized
- hotel is underused
- hotel is not used to capacity

Hotel ist unterbelegt
- hotel is underbooked
- hotel is booked below capacity
- hotel is underutilised
- hotel is underutilized
- hotel is underused

Hotel ist vergleichsweise neu
- hotel is comparatively new

Hotel ist voll
- hotel is packed *coll*
- hotel is full up *coll*
- hotel is full

Hotel ist vollbelegt
Hotel ist ausgebucht
- hotel is booked to capacity
- hotel is full

Hotel ist vollgestopft mit Gästen
- hotel is packed with guests

Hotel ist vom Strand durch eine Straße getrennt
- hotel is separated from the beach by a road

Hotel ist von der Straße zurückgesetzt

Hotel ist von der Straße zurückgesetzt
- hotel is set back from the road
- hotel is set back from the street

Hotel ist wieder in Betrieb
- hotel is running again
- hotel is operating again

Hotel ist zu 90 % gebucht
- hotel is 90 % booked

Hotel ist zugeschnitten auf die Bedürfnisse von jn
- hotel is geared to the requirements of s.o.

Hotel ist zu jeder Zeit einen Besuch wert
- hotel is worth a visit during any season

Hotel ist zu verkaufen
- hotel is for sale

Hotel ist zu wenig auf Kinder eingestellt
- hotel is too little adapted to children

Hotel ist zweistöckig
- hotel is two-storied *AE*
- hotel is two-storeyed *BE*

Hoteljargon m
- hotel jargon

Hoteljob, m
→ Hotelarbeitsplatz

Hoteljournal, n
  Recettenbuch, n
  Main-courante, f *FR*
  Gästejournal, n
- hotel diary
- visitors' tabular ledger

Hoteljournal führen
  Recettenbuch führen
- keep a hotel diary

Hoteljournalführer, m
- hotel ledger clerk

Hotelkabarett, n
- hotel cabaret

Hotel kann 123 Gäste beherbergen
- hotel accommodates 123 guests
- hotel sleeps 123 guests

Hotel kann ganzjährig benutzt werden
- hotel can be used all year round

Hotel kann leicht verfehlt werden
- hotel can easily be missed

Hotel kann maximal 123 Gäste pro Nacht beherbergen
- hotel can accommodate a maximum of 123 guests per night

Hotel kann nicht verfehlt werden
- hotel cannot be missed

Hotelkapazität, f
- hotel capacity
- capacity of a hotel

Hotelkapazität ist nicht voll ausgelastet
- hotel capacity is not used to the full
- hotel capacity is not fully utilised

Hotelkapazität steigern
- increase (the) hotel capacity

Hotelkapelle, f (Kirche)
- hotel chapel

Hotelkapelle, f (Musik)
- hotel band

Hotelkapitalist, m
  Hotellöwe m *humor*
- hotel tycoon

Hotelkarriere, f
→ Hotellaufbahn

Hotelkarte, f
- hotel map

Hotelkasino, n
  (im Hotel)
- hotel casino

Hotelkasse, f
- hotel cash
- hotel till *BE*

Hotelkassierer, m
  Hotelkassenführer, m
  Hotelkassier, m *ÖST/SCHW*
- hotel cashier

Hotelkategorie f
- hotel category

Hotelkategorisierung, f
- hotel categorisation

Hotel kaufen
- buy a hotel

Hotelkaufleute, pl
- people in the hotel trade *pl*

Hotelkaufmann, m
  (offizieller Beruf)
- man in the hotel trade

Hotelkenntnisse, f pl
  Hotelfachkenntnisse, f pl
- hotel skills *pl*

Hotelkette, f
- hotel chain
- chain of hotels

Hotelkino n
- hotel cinema
- hotel movie *AE coll*

Hotelkiosk m
- hotel kiosk

Hotelklasse, f
- hotel class

Hotel klassifizieren
- classify a hotel

Hotelklassifizierung, f
→ Hoteleinteilung

Hotelklotz, m
  Hotelkasten, m
  Hotelblock, m
- hotel block

Hotelkomfort, m
- hotel comforts *pl*
- hotel amenities *pl*

Hotelkomplex, m
→ Hotelanlage

Hotelkonferenz, f
- hotel conference

Hotelkonferenzleiter, m
  Hotelkonferenzmanager m
- hotel conference manager

Hotelkonsortium n
- hotel consortium
- consortium of hotels

Hotelkontingent, n
- hotel allocation
- hotel allotment

Hotelkontingent einhalten
  Hotelkontingent anerkennen
- honor a hotel allocation *AE*
- honour an hotel allocation *BE*

Hotelkontrolleur, m
- hotel control clerk

Hotelkonzept, n
- hotel concept

Hotelkonzern m
- hotel group

Hotelkonzession, f
- hotel license

- hotel licence
- hotel concession *AE*

Hotelkonzession verlieren
- lose a hotel license
- lose a hotel licence
- lose a hotel concession *AE*

Hotelkooperation, f
- hotel cooperation

Hotelkorrespondenz, f
- hotel correspondence
- hotel's correspondence

Hotelkorrespondenz erledigen
- deal with the hotel's correspondence
- handle the hotel's correspondence

Hotelkosmetikerin, f
- hotel beautician

Hotelkosten, pl
- hotel costs *pl*
- hotel cost
- hotel expenses *pl*

Hotelkosten senken
- reduce the hotel costs
- reduce the hotel cost

Hotelkosten zurückerstatten
- refund the hotels costs

Hotelkreise, m pl
  (Personen)
- hotel circles *pl*

Hotelküche, f (Raum)
- hotel kitchen
- hotel's kitchen

Hotelküche, f (Speisen)
- hotel cooking
- hotel cuisine

Hotelküchenpersonal, n
- hotel kitchen staff
- hotel kitchen personnel

Hotelkunde m
- hotel client
- hotel customer

Hotelkundschaft, f
- hotel customers *pl*
- customs of the hotel *pl*
- hotel clientele

Hotelkurs, m
  Hotellehrgang m
  Hotelstudiengang m
- hotel course

Hotelkurzurlaub, m
- hotel break
- short hotel break

Hotelladen, m
  (Laden in Hotel)
  Hotelladengeschäft n
  Hotelgeschäft n
- hotel store *AE*
- hotel shop *BE*

Hotellage, f
- hotel position
- hotel location
- hotel setting
- hotel situation

Hotellaufbahn, f
  Hotelkarriere f
- hotel career

Hotellaufbahn einschlagen
- embark on a hotel career

Hotel lebt von seinem Namen
- hotel lives on its name

Hotelleistung, f (Dienstleistung)
→ Hoteldienstleistung

Hotelleistung, f (Leistungskraft)
Hotelleistungskraft, f
♦ hotel performance
♦ hotel's performance
Hotelleistungsangebot, n
→ Hoteldienstleistungsangebot
Hotel leiten
Hotel führen
♦ manage a hotel
♦ run a hotel
♦ keep a hotel
Hotelleiter, m
♦ hotel manager
♦ hotelkeeper
Hotelleiterin, f
♦ female hotel manager
♦ hotel manageress
Hotelleitung, f (Management)
♦ hotel management
♦ management of a hotel
♦ managing a hotel
Hotelleitung, f (Person)
→ Hotelleiter
Hotelleitung übernehmen
→ Leitung eines Hotels übernehmen
Hotellerie, f
Hotelbranche, f
Hotelwesen, n
♦ hotel industry
♦ hotel trade
♦ hotel business
♦ hotelkeeping
Hotellerieprodukt, n
Hotelprodukt n
♦ product for the hotel trade
Hotelleriestandard, m
Standard der Hotelführung, m
♦ standard of hotelkeeping
Hotellerie (Überschrift)
→ Unterkunftshinweise
Hotel liegt 200 m über dem Meeresspiegel
♦ hotel lies 200 m above sea level
Hotel liegt abseits der Straße
♦ hotel is off the road
Hotel liegt an der Busstrecke
♦ hotel is on the bus route
Hotel liegt an der Hauptstrecke nach Y
♦ hotel is situated on the main route to Y
♦ hotel lies on the main route to Y
Hotel liegt an einer Busstrecke
♦ hotel lies on a bus route
Hotel liegt außerhalb des Stadtzentrums
♦ hotel is situated outside the city center AE
♦ hotel is situated outside the city centre BE
♦ hotel is situated outside the town center AE
♦ hotel is situated outside the town centre BE
Hotel liegt ein bißchen abseits
♦ hotel is a bit out of the way
Hotel liegt gut
♦ hotel is well situated
Hotel liegt ideal für etw
♦ hotel is ideally situated for s.th.
♦ hotel is ideally located for s.th.
♦ hotel is ideally positioned for s.th.
♦ hotel is ideally sited for s.th.
Hotel liegt in der mittleren Preisklasse
♦ hotel is in the medium price range
Hotel liegt in der Nähe des Theaters
♦ hotel is close to the theater AE
♦ hotel is close to the theatre BE

Hotel liegt in einem parkähnlichen Gelände
♦ hotel is set in landscaped grounds
Hotel liegt in einer Sackgasse
♦ hotel is situated in a cul-de-sac
Hotel liegt nach Norden
♦ hotel faces north
Hotel liegt nach Osten
♦ hotel faces east
Hotel liegt nach Süden
♦ hotel faces south
Hotel liegt nach Westen
♦ hotel faces west
Hotel liegt neben dem Zoo
♦ hotel is situated next to the zoological gardens
♦ hotel is situated next to the zoo
Hotel liegt ruhig
♦ hotel is in a quiet area
Hotel liegt zum Meer hin
♦ hotel faces the sea
Hotel liegt zwei Meilen nördlich von X
♦ hotel is situated two miles north of X
♦ hotel lies two miles north of X
Hotellift, m
Hotelfahrstuhl, m
Hotelaufzug, m
♦ hotel lift BE
♦ hotel elevator AE
Hotelliste, f
♦ list of hotels
♦ hotel list
Hotelloggia f
♦ hotel loggia
Hotellogiernacht, f
(Statistik)
Hotelgästenacht, f
♦ hotel sleeper-night
♦ hotel guest-night
Hotellogo, n
♦ hotel logo
Hotellöhne, m pl
♦ hotel wages pl
Hotellokal, n
(z.B. Nachtclub im Hotel)
♦ hotel spot coll
hotellos, adj
hotelfrei, adj
♦ hoteless, adj
♦ without hotels
♦ devoid of hotels, adj
Hotelmagazin, n
♦ hotel store
Hotelmagnat, m
♦ hotel magnate
Hotelmahlzeit, f
Hotelessen, n
Hotelmahl, n form
♦ hotel meal
Hotelmakler m
♦ hotel broker
Hotelmanagement, n
→ Hotelleitung
Hotelmanagementlehrgang, m
Hotelmanagementkurs, m
♦ hotel management course
Hotelmanagementlehrgang machen
♦ do a hotel management course
♦ take a hotel management course
Hotelmanager, m
→ Hotelleiter

Hotelmarke, f
♦ hotel brand
Hotelmarketing n
♦ hotel marketing
♦ marketing (of) a hotel
Hotelmarkt, m
♦ hotel market
Hotel meiden
♦ avoid a hotel
♦ stay away from a hotel
hotelmeldeschein, m
→ Hotelmeldezettel
Hotel meldet eine 80%ige Auslastung
Hotel meldet eine 80%ige Belegung
♦ hotel reports 80 % occupancy
Hotelmeldezettel, m
Hotelmeldeschein, m
♦ hotel registration form
Hotel mieten
Hotel anmieten
♦ rent a hotel
Hotel mit 123 Zimmern, n
♦ hotel with 123 bedrooms
♦ 123-bedroom hotel
Hotel mit allem Komfort ausstatten
♦ fit out a hotel with all comforts and conveniences
Hotelmitbewerber, m
→ Hotelkonkurrent
Hotel mit Blick auf etw, n
♦ hotel overlooking s.th.
♦ hotel offering a view of s.th.
Hotel mit Charakter, n
♦ hotel of character
Hotel mit Charakter und Charme, n
♦ hotel of character and charm
Hotel mit drei Sternen, n
→ Drei-Sterne-Hotel
Hotel mit einem Stern, n
→ Ein-Stern-Hotel
Hotel mit einer großen Tradition, n
♦ hotel with a great tradition
Hotel mit europäischem Standard, n
♦ hotel of European standard
Hotel mit fünf Sternen, n
→ Fünf-Sterne-Hotel
Hotel mit hohem Standard, n
♦ high-standard hotel
Hotel mit hoher Auslastung, n
Hotel mit hoher Belegung, n
♦ hotel with high occupancy
Hotel mit internationalem Standard, n
♦ hotel of international standard
Hotel mit Jahresbetrieb, n
♦ hotel open all the year round
♦ hotel open all year round
Hotel mit jedem Komfort, n
♦ hotel with every comfort
Hotel mit niedriger Auslastung, n
Hotel mit niedriger Belegung, n
♦ hotel with low occupancy
Hotel mit Pfiff, n
♦ hotel with a difference
Hotel mittlerer Preislage, n
♦ medium-priced hotel
Hotel mit Tradition, n
→ Traditionshotel
Hotel mit vergleichbarem Standard und Preis, n
♦ hotel of similar standard and price
Hotel mit viel Charakter, n
♦ hotel with a lot of character

Hotel mit vier Sternen

Hotel mit vier Sternen, n
  Vier-Sterne-Hotel, n
  ♦ four-star hotel
Hotel mit vollem Service, n
  ♦ hotel offering full service
  ♦ full-service hotel
Hotel mit vollem Serviceangebot, n
  ♦ hotel offering a full range of services
  ♦ hotel offering full service
  ♦ full-service hotel
Hotel mit voller Schankerlaubnis, n
  (für alkoholische Getränke)
  ♦ fully licensed hotel *BE*
  ♦ fully licenced hotel
  ♦ hotel holding a full-on license
Hotel mit zwei Sternen, n
  → Zwei-Sterne-Hotel
Hotelmöbel, n pl
  Hoteleinrichtung; f
  Hotelmobiliar, n
  ♦ hotel furniture *sg*
  ♦ hotel furnishings *pl*
Hotelmobiliar, n
  → Hotelmöbel
Hotel möblieren
  Hotel einrichten
  ♦ furnish a hotel
Hotelmöblierung, f
  → Hotelmöbel
Hotel modernisieren
  ♦ modernise a hotel
  ♦ modernize a hotel
  ♦ update a hotel
Hotelmodernisierung, f
  ♦ hotel modernisation
  ♦ modernisation of a hotel
Hotelnachfrage, f
  Nachfrage nach Hotels, f
  ♦ hotel demand
  ♦ demand for hotels
  ♦ demand for hotel rooms
Hotelnachtbar, f
  Hotelnachtclub, m
  ♦ hotel nightclub *AE*
  ♦ hotel night-club *BE*
Hotelnachweis, m
  (Service)
  ♦ hotel information service
  ♦ hotel information
Hotelname, m
  ♦ hotel name
  ♦ name of a hotel
Hotelnebenkosten, pl
  ♦ hotel extras *pl*
  ♦ hotel extra expenses *pl*
  ♦ hotel extra costs *pl*
Hotelnebenzimmer, n
  → Nebenzimmer
Hotelneubau, m (fertig)
  ♦ newly built hotel
  ♦ newly constructed hotel
Hotelneubau, m (im Bau)
  Hotel im Bau, n
  ♦ hotel under construction
  ♦ hotel which is being built
Hotel neu einstufen
  ♦ regrade a hotel
Hotel neu klassifizieren
  ♦ reclassify a hotel
Hotel niedriger Kategorie, n
  ♦ lower-class hotel

Hotel nimmt Haustiere auf
  ♦ hotel accepts pets
  ♦ hotel caters for pets
Hotel nimmt Kinder auf
  ♦ hotel accepts children
  ♦ hotel caters for children
Hotel nimmt Kinder unter 10 Jahren nicht auf
  ♦ hotel does not accept children under 10 years
Hotel offenhalten
  Hotel geöffnet halten
  ♦ keep a hotel open
Hotel öffnet am 29 Mai
  ♦ hotel opens on 29 May
  ♦ hotel will open on 29 May
Hotel öffnet seine Pforten
  ♦ hotel opens its doors
Hotel ohne Ausschank alkoholischer Getränke, n
  ♦ temperance hotel
Hotel ohne Konferenzräume, n
  Hotel ohne Tagungsräume n
  ♦ hotel without conference facilities
Hotel ohne Kongreßräumlichkeiten, n
  ♦ hotel without convention facilities
  ♦ hotel without congress facilities
Hotel ohne Schankerlaubnis, n
  (für alkoholische Getränke)
  ♦ unlicensed hotel
  ♦ unlicenced hotel
Hotelökologie, f
  ♦ hotel ecology
Hotelordnung, f
  Hausordnung, f
  ♦ hotel regulations *pl*
Hotelorganisation, f (Verband etc.)
  ♦ hotel organisation
Hotelpacht, f
  ♦ hotel lease
  ♦ hotel leasehold
Hotel pachten (von jm)
  ♦ lease a hotel (from s.o.)
Hotelpächter, m
  ♦ hotel tenant
  ♦ hotel lessee *jur*
  ♦ hotel leaseholder
Hotelpachtvertrag, m
  ♦ hotel lease contract
  ♦ hotel lease
Hotelpage m
  ♦ hotel page
Hotelpalast, m
  ♦ hotel palace
Hotelpark, m
  ♦ hotel gardens *pl*
Hotelparkplatz, m (für mehrere Autos)
  ♦ hotel parking lot *AE*
  ♦ hotel car park *BE*
Hotelpaß, m
  ♦ hotel pass
Hotelpauschalarrangement n
  ♦ hotel package arrangement
  ♦ hotel inclusive arrangement
Hotelpavillon, m
  ♦ hotel pavilion
Hotelpendelbus, m
  ♦ hotel shuttle bus
Hotelpendelbusdienst m
  Hotelpendelbusservice m
  Hotelpendelbusverbindung f
  Hotelpendelbus m
  ♦ hotel shuttle-bus service

Hotelpendelbusservice, m
  → Hotelpendelbusdienst
Hotelpendelbusverbindung, f
  ♦ hotel shuttle-bus connection
  ♦ hotel shuttle-bus service
Hotelpension, f
  → Pension
Hotelpersonal, n
  ♦ hotel personnel
  ♦ hotel staff
Hotelpersonalknappheit, f
  ♦ hotel staff shortage
Hotelpersonaltrinkgelder, n pl
  ♦ hotel staff gratuities *pl*
Hotelpianist, m
  ♦ hotel pianist
Hotelpionier m
  ♦ hotel pioneer
Hotel-Pkw, m
  Hotelwagen, m
  Hotelauto, n
Hotellimousine, f
  ♦ hotel limousine
  ♦ hotel limo *coll*
  ♦ hotel car
Hotel planen
  ♦ plan a hotel
Hotelplanung, f
  ♦ planning (of) a hotel
  ♦ hotel planning
Hotel platzt aus den Nähten
  ♦ hotel is bursting at the seams
Hotelpolitik f
  ♦ hotel policy
Hotelportier, m
  ♦ hotel porter
  ♦ hotel bellman *AE*
Hotelporzellan, n
  Hotelporzellangeschirr, n
  ♦ hotel china
Hotelpotential, n
  ♦ hotel potential
Hotelpräferenz, f
  → Hotelwunsch
Hotelpraktikant, m
  Hoteltrainee, m
  ♦ hotel trainee
Hotelpraktiker, m
  ♦ hotel practitioner
Hotelpraxis, f
  ♦ hotel practice
Hotelpreis, m (Auszeichnung)
  ♦ hotel award
Hotelpreis, m (Betrag)
  ♦ hotel rate
  ♦ hotel price
  ♦ hotel charge
Hotelpreise aushandeln
  verhandeln über die Hotelpreise
  ♦ negotiate hotel rates
  ♦ negotiate hotel prices
Hotelpreise aushängen
  ♦ display the hotel prices
  ♦ display the hotel rates
Hotelpreis fällt
  ♦ hotel rate is falling
  ♦ hotel price is falling
Hotelpreis festsetzen
  Hotelpreis festlegen
  ♦ fix a hotel price

♦ fix a hotel rate
♦ fix a hotel charge
Hotelpreisgarantie, f
♦ hotel rate guarantee
♦ hotel price guarantee
Hotelpreis gewinnen
♦ win a hotel award
Hotelpreiskategorie f
♦ hotel price category
Hotelpreisliste, f
♦ hotel tariff
Hotelpreisliste aushängen
♦ display the hotel tariff
Hotelpremiere f
→ s. Hoteleröffnung f
Hotel privatisieren
♦ privatise a hotel
♦ privatize a hotel
Hotelproblem n
♦ hotel problem
Hotelprodukt, n
♦ hotel product
♦ product for the hotel trade
Hotelprodukt auf den Markt zuschneiden
♦ gear a hotel product to the market
Hotelproduktivität, f
♦ hotel productivity
Hotelprofi, m coll
♦ hotel professional
Hotelprofit, m
→ Hotelgewinn
Hotelprogramm, n
♦ hotel program AE
♦ hotel programme BE
Hotelprojekt n
♦ hotel project
Hotelprospekt, m
Hotelbroschüre, f
Hausprospekt, m
♦ hotel brochure
Hotelprospekt herausgeben
♦ issue a hotel brochure
Hotelprovision, f
♦ hotel commission
Hotel prüfen
♦ check a hotel
♦ examine a hotel
♦ inspect a hotel
Hotelprüfliste, f
♦ hotel checklist
Hotelpublikum, n
Hotelkundschaft, f
Hotelgästekreis, m
♦ hotel clientele
Hotelratte, f sl
rat d'hôtel, m FR
Hoteldieb, m
♦ hotel rat sl
♦ hotel thief
♦ rat d'hôtel FR
Hotelraum, m
→ Hotelzimmer
Hotel räumen
(das gesamte Hotel)
Hotel frei machen
♦ vacate a hotel
Hotelrechnung, f
♦ hotel bill
♦ hotel check AE
Hotelrechnung ausstellen
♦ make out a hotel bill

Hotelrechnung begleichen
♦ settle the hotel bill
♦ settle the hotel check AE
Hotelrechnung quittieren
♦ receipt a hotel bill
Hotelrechnung verlangen
♦ ask for the hotel bill
♦ ask for the hotel check AE
Hotelrechnung vorbereiten
♦ prepare a hotel bill
Hotelrechnung zahlen
♦ pay the hotel bill
Hotelrechnung zahlen bei Vorlage
♦ pay the hotel bill on presentation
Hotelrecht, n
♦ hotel law
Hotel renovieren
♦ renovate a hotel
♦ refurbish a hotel
Hotelrentabilität, f
♦ hotel profitability
Hotelrepräsentant, m
Hotelvertreter, m
♦ hotel representative
Hotelrepräsentanz, f
Hotelvertretung, f
♦ hotel representation
Hotelreservation, f SCHW
→ Hotelreservierung
Hotel reservieren lassen
♦ make a hotel reservation
Hotelreservierung, f
Hotelreservation, f SCHW
♦ hotel reservation
♦ reservation of a hotel
♦ reserving a hotel
Hotelreservierungsdienst, m
Hotelreservierungsservice, m
♦ hotel reservation service
Hotelreservierungsformular, n
♦ hotel reservation form
Hotelreservierungsservice, m
→ Hotelreservierungsdienst
Hotelreservierungssystem, n
♦ hotel reservation system
Hotelreservierungsvertrag, m
♦ hotel reservation contract
Hotelreservierungsvertrag abschließen
♦ make a hotel reservation contract
Hotelreservierungsvertrag unterzeichnen
♦ sign a hotel reservation contract
Hotelreservierungsvorgang, m
Hotelreservierungsprozedur, f
♦ hotel reservation procedure
Hotelreservierungszentrale, f
♦ hotel reservations center AE
♦ hotel reservations centre BE
♦ central hotel reservations office
Hotelrestaurant, n (Betriebstyp)
♦ hotel and restaurant
Hotelrestaurant, n (im Hotel)
♦ hotel restaurant
♦ hotel's restaurant
Hotelrestaurantkellner, m
♦ hotel restaurant waiter
Hotelrestaurantkellnerin, f
♦ hotel restaurant waitress
Hotel-Restaurantkette, f
♦ hotel-restaurant chain
Hotelrezeption, f
→ Hotelempfang

Hotelsafe, m
→ Hoteltresor
Hotelsaison f
♦ hotel season
Hotel schätzen
(durch Gutachter)
♦ appraise a hotel
Hotel schätzen lassen
(durch Gutachter)
♦ have a hotel appraised
Hotelschiff, n
schwimmendes Hotel, n
♦ boatel humor
♦ botel BE humor
♦ floating hotel
Hotelschild, n
♦ hotel sign
Hotelschlafraumbestand, m
Hotelgästezimmerbestand, m
♦ hotel bedroom stock
Hotel schließen
♦ close a hotel
♦ close down a hotel
Hotel schließt im Oktober
♦ hotel closes down in October
Hotel schließt seine Pforten
♦ hotel closes its doors
Hotel schließt wegen Renovierung
♦ hotel closes for renovation
Hotelschließung f
♦ hotel closure
♦ closure of a hotel
♦ closing a hotel
Hotelschreibpapier, n
♦ hotel stationery
♦ hotel writing paper
♦ hotel note paper BE
Hotelschule, f
→ Hotelfachschule
Hotelschule besuchen
♦ attend a hotel school
Hotelschwimmbad, n
Hotelschwimmbecken, n
♦ hotel swimming pool AE
♦ hotel swimming-pool BE
♦ hotel pool
Hotelschwimmbecken, n
→ Hotelschwimmbad
Hotelsegment, n
♦ hotel segment
Hotelsegmentierung, f
♦ hotel segmentation
Hotelsekretär, m
♦ hotel secretary
♦ male hotel secretary
Hotelsekretärin, f
♦ hotel secretary
♦ female hotel secretary
Hotelsektor, m
Hotelbereich, m
♦ hotel sector
Hotelservice, m
Hoteldienst, m
Hoteldienstleistung, f
Hotelleistung, f
♦ hotel service
Hotelserviceangebot, n
Hotelservicepalette, f
Hotelleistungsangebot, n
♦ hotel service range
♦ range of (the) hotel services

Hotelservice in Anspruch nehmen

Hotelservice in Anspruch nehmen
   Hoteldienstleistung in Anspruch nehmen
   ♦ use a hotel service
   ♦ make use of a hotel service
Hotelservicepalette, f
   → Hotelserviceangebot
Hotelsicherheitsbeauftragter, m
   ♦ hotel security officer
Hotelsituation, f
   Hotellage f
   ♦ hotel situation
Hotelspeisesaal m
   ♦ hotel dining room
Hotelspesen, pl
   ♦ hotel expenses *pl*
Hotelspesen haben
   ♦ incur hotel expenses
Hotelsprecher, m
   (bei Pressekonferenz etc)
   ♦ hotel spokesman
Hotelsprecherin, f
   (bei Pressekonferenz etc.)
   ♦ hotel spokeswoman
Hotelstadt, f (Großstadt)
   ♦ hotel city
Hotelstadt, f (kleine Stadt)
   ♦ hotel town
Hotelstammgast m
   ♦ regular hotel guest
Hotel stammt aus dem 18. Jahrhundert
   ♦ hotel dates back to the 18th century
Hotel stammt aus dem Jahr 1944
   ♦ hotel dates from 1944
Hotelstandard m
   ♦ hotel standard
   ♦ hotel's standard
Hotelstandort m
   ♦ hotel location
   ♦ hotel's location
   ♦ location of a hotel
Hotelstatistik, f
   ♦ hotel statistics *pl*
Hotel steht auf einer Anhöhe
   ♦ hotel stands on a promontory
Hotel steht auf einer kleinen Anhöhe
   ♦ hotel stands on a slight rise
Hotel steht in bevorzugter Lage
   ♦ hotel stands in a privileged position
Hotel steht in Brand
   ♦ hotel is on fire
Hotel steht in einem parkartigen Gelände
   ♦ hotel stands in parkland
Hotel steht ungefähr in der Mitte zwischen A und B
   ♦ hotel stands about midway between A and B
Hotel steht unter englischer Leitung
   ♦ hotel is under English management
Hotel steht unter Vertrag mit jm
   ♦ hotel is under contract with s.o.
Hotel steht zum Verkauf
   ♦ hotel is up for sale
Hotelsteuer, f
   Hotelabgabe, f
   ♦ hotel tax
Hotelstornierung, f
   Hotelabbestellung, f
   Hotelabsage, f
   ♦ hotel cancellation
   ♦ hotel cancelation *AE*
   ♦ cancelling a hotel *BE*
   ♦ canceling a hotel *AE*

Hotelstrand m
   ♦ hotel beach
Hotelstrategie, f
   ♦ hotel strategy
Hotelstreik, m
   ♦ hotel strike
Hotelstreik ist im Gang
   ♦ hotel strike is on
Hotel stürzt ein
   ♦ hotel collapses
Hotel suchen
   ♦ look for a hotel
   ♦ seek a hotel
Hotelsuite f
   ♦ hotel suite
Hotelsuitenart f
   Hotelsuitentyp m
   ♦ hotel suite type
   ♦ type of hotel suite
Hotelsuitenbeschreibung f
   ♦ hotel suite description
   ♦ description of a hotel suite
Hotels und ähnliche Betriebe, pl
   ♦ hotels and similar establishments *pl*
Hotelszene f
   ♦ hotel scene
Hoteltabakwarenhändler, m
   ♦ hotel tobacconist
Hoteltag, m
   ♦ hotel day
   ♦ day at a hotel
Hoteltag beginnt um 5 Uhr morgens
   ♦ hotel day begins at 5 a.m.
Hoteltarif, m
   ♦ hotel tariff
   ♦ hotel rates *pl*
   ♦ hotel rate
   ♦ hotel terms *pl*
Hoteltaverne f
   ♦ hotel tavern
Hoteltaxi, n
   → Hotellimousine
Hoteltelefon, n
   ♦ hotel telephone
   ♦ hotel phone
Hoteltelefonist, m
   ♦ hotel telephonist
   ♦ male hotel telephonist
Hoteltelefonistin, f
   ♦ hotel telephonist
   ♦ female hotel telephonist
Hoteltelefonverzeichnis, n
   ♦ hotel telephone directory
Hoteltelefonzentrale, f
   Hotelnachrichtenzentrale f
   ♦ hotel switchboard
Hoteltelexnummer, f
   ♦ hotel telex number
   ♦ hotel's telex number
Hoteltennisplatz, m
   ♦ hotel tennis court
Hotelterrasse f
   ♦ hotel terrace
Hotel tieferstufen
   Hotel niedriger einstufen
   Hotel runterstufen *coll*
   ♦ downgrade a hotel
Hoteltieferstufung, f
   ♦ hotel downgrade
   ♦ hotel downgrading

Hoteltochterfirma f
   ♦ hotel subsidiary
Hoteltoilette f
   ♦ hotel toilet
Hoteltradition f
   ♦ hotel tradition
Hoteltrainee, m
   → Hotelpraktikant
Hoteltrakt, m
   (Gebäudeteil)
   Hotelflügel m
   ♦ hotel wing
Hoteltransfer, m
   ♦ hotel transfer
   ♦ transfer to a hotel
   ♦ transfer from a hotel
   ♦ transfer to or from a hotel
Hoteltresor, m
   Hotelsafe m
   ♦ hotel safe
Hoteltreuhandgesellschaft, f
   ♦ hotel trust company
Hoteltrinkgeld n
   ♦ hotel tip
   ♦ hotel gratuity
Hotelturm, m
   ♦ hotel tower
Hoteltürsteher, m
   ♦ hotel doorman
Hoteltyp, m
   Hotelart, f
   ♦ hotel type
   ♦ type of hotel
Hotelüberangebot, n
   ♦ surplus of hotels
   ♦ oversupply of hotels
Hotel überbewerten
   ♦ overrate a hotel
Hotel überbuchen
   ♦ overbook a hotel
Hotelüberbuchung f
   ♦ hotel overbooking
Hotelübernachtung, f (eine Nacht)
   einmalige Hotelübernachtung, f
   ♦ one-night stay at a hotel
   ♦ one-night stay in a hotel
   ♦ staying at a hotel for one night
   ♦ staying in a hotel for one night
Hotelübernachtung, f (generell)
   ♦ overnight stay at a hotel
   ♦ overnight stay in a hotel
Hotelübernachtung, f (Statistik)
   ♦ night spent at a hotel
   ♦ night spent in a hotel
   ♦ hotel night
Hotelübernachtungszahl f
   (Statistik)
   ♦ number of nights spent in a hotel
Hotelübernahme, f
   ♦ hotel takeover
   ♦ taking over a hotel
Hotel übernehmen
   ♦ take over a hotel
Hotel übernehmen von jm
   ♦ take a hotel over from s.o.
Hotel umbauen (in etw)
   ♦ turn a hotel (into s.th.)
   ♦ convert a hotel (into s.th.)
Hotel umbauen (teilweise)
   ♦ make structural alterations to a hotel

Hotel umbauen (völlig)
- ◆ **rebuild a hotel**

Hotel umbenennen
- Hotel neuen Namen geben
- ◆ **rename a hotel**

Hotelumsatz, m
- ◆ **hotel sales** *pl*
- ◆ hotel turnover

Hotelumsatz optimieren
- ◆ **maximise hotel sales**
- ◆ maximize hotel turnover

Hotel- und Campingführer, m
- (Buch)
- ◆ **hotel and camping guide**

Hotel- und Freizeitgewerbe, n
- ◆ **hotel and leisure industry**

Hotel- und Gastgewerbe, n
- ◆ **hotel and foodservice industry** *AE*
- ◆ hotel and catering industry *BE*
- ◆ hotel and catering trade *BE*

Hotel- und Gastronomieangebot, n
- ◆ **hotels and restaurants available** *pl*
- ◆ hotel and restaurants *pl*

Hotel- und Gastronomiekonzern, m
- ◆ **hotel and catering group**

Hotel- und Gastronomiemanagement studieren
- ◆ **do a course in hotel and catering management**
- ◆ take a course in hotel and catering management
- ◆ study hotel and catering management

Hotel- und Gaststättenbetrieb, m
- ◆ **hotel and foodservice establishment** *AE*
- ◆ hotel and foodservice operation *AE*
- ◆ hotel and catering establishment *BE*
- ◆ hotel and catering operation *BE*

Hotel- und Gaststättenführer, m
- ◆ **hotel and restaurant guide**

Hotel- und Gaststättengewerbe, n
- Hotel- und Gaststättenwesen, n
- ◆ **hotel and catering trade**
- ◆ hotel and catering industry
- ◆ hospitality industry

Hotel- und Gaststättenumsatz, m
- ◆ **hotel and catering sales** *pl*
- ◆ hotel and catering turnover

Hotel- und Gaststättenverband m
- ◆ **hotel and catering association**

Hotel- und Gaststättenwesen, n
- → Hotel- und Gaststättengewerbe

Hotel- und Restaurantadministration, f
- ◆ **hotel and restaurant administration**

Hotel- und Restaurantkette, f
- ◆ **hotel and restaurant chain**

Hotel- und Restaurationsbetrieb m
- ◆ **hotel and restaurant**

Hotel- und Zimmernachweis, m
- ◆ **hotel and accommodation agency**
- ◆ hotel and accommodation bureau

Hoteluniform, f
- ◆ **hotel uniform**

Hotel unterbewerten
- ◆ **underrate a hotel**
- ◆ undervalue a hotel

Hotelunterbringung, f
- Hotelunterkunft, f
- ◆ **hotel lodging** *AE*
- ◆ hotel accommodation

Hotelunterbringung mit Halbpension, f
- → Hotelunterkunft mit Halbpension

Hotelunterbringung mit Teilpension, f
- → Hotelunterkunft mit Teilpension

Hotelunterbringung mit Vollpension, f
- → Hotelunterkunft mit Vollpension

Hotel unter Choleraquarantäne, n
- ◆ **hotel in quarantine for cholera**

Hotel unterhält einen kostenlosen Busdienst
- ◆ **hotel runs a free bus service**
- ◆ hotel operates a free bus service

Hotel unterhalten (instandhalten)
- ◆ **keep a hotel in good repair**

Hotelunterhaltung, f (Amüsement)
- ◆ **hotel entertainment**

Hotelunterhaltung, f (Instandhaltung)
- → Hotelinstandhaltung

Hotelunterkunft, f
- Hotelunterbringung, f
- ◆ **hotel accommodation**
- ◆ hotel lodging *AE*

Hotelunterkunft benötigen
- ◆ **require hotel accommodation**

Hotelunterkunft buchen
- ◆ **book hotel accommodation**

Hotelunterkünfte sind knapp
- ◆ **hotel accommodations are scarce** *AE*
- ◆ hotel accommodation is scarce *BE*

Hotelunterkunft mit Halbpension, f
- Hotelunterbringung mit Halbpension, f
- ◆ **hotel accommodation with half board**
- ◆ half-board hotel accommodation
- ◆ hotel accommodation with demipension *AE*
- ◆ demipension hotel accommodation *AE*

Hotelunterkunft mit Teilpension, f
- Hotelunterbringung mit Teilpension f
- ◆ **hotel accommodation with partial board**
- ◆ partial-board hotel accommodation

Hotelunterkunft mit Vollpension, f
- Hotelunterbringung mit Vollpension, f
- ◆ **hotel accommodation with full board**
- ◆ full-board hotel accommodation
- ◆ hotel accommodation with full pension *AE*
- ◆ full-pension hotel accommodation *AE*

Hotelunterkunft reservieren
- ◆ **reserve hotel accommodation**

Hotelunterkunftskapazität, f
- ◆ **hotel accommodation capacity**

Hotelunterkunft stornieren
- Hotelunterkunft absagen
- ◆ **cancel hotel accommodation**

Hotelunternehmen, n
- ◆ **hotel enterprise**

Hotelunternehmer, m
- ◆ **hotel entrepreneur**

Hotel unter Vertrag nehmen
- ◆ **contract a hotel**

Hotel unterwegs, n
- ◆ **hotel en route**
- ◆ en-route hotel

Hotelurlaub, m
- Hotelferien, pl
- ◆ **hotel vacation** *AE*
- ◆ hotel holiday *BE*

Hotelurlaub machen
- ◆ **take a hotel vacation** *AE*
- ◆ take a hotel holiday *BE*

Hotelurlaub verbringen
- Hotelferien verbringen
- ◆ **spend a hotel vacation** *AE*
- ◆ spend a hotel holiday *BE*

Hotelvakanz, f
- ◆ **hotel vacancy**

Hotelveranda f
- ◆ **hotel veranda**
- ◆ hotel verandah

Hotelverband, m
- Hotelassoziation, f
- Hotelvereinigung, f
- ◆ **hotel association**

Hotelverbesserung, f
- Hotelverschönerung, f
- ◆ **hotel improvement**
- ◆ hotel upgrade
- ◆ hotel upgrading

Hotel verbindet den Charme der guten alten Zeit
- mit modernem Komfort
- ◆ **hotel combines old-world charm with modern**
- ◆ comforts

Hotelvereinbarung, f
- → Hotelarrangement

Hotelvereinigung, f
- → Hotelverband

Hotel vereint modernen Komfort mit einer
- historischen Atmosphäre
- ◆ **hotel combines modern comforts with an**
- ◆ historic atmosphere

Hotel verfallen lassen
- ◆ **dilapidate a hotel**

Hotelverfügbarkeit, f
- ◆ **hotel availability**
- ◆ availability of hotels

Hotel verfügt über ausgezeichnete Räumlich-
- keiten für kleine und große gesell-
- schaftliche Treffen und Zusammenkünfte
- von 20 bis 350 Personen
- ◆ **hotel has excellent facilities for handling**
- ◆ small and large social gatherings
- ◆ and meetings from 20 to 350 persons

Hotel verfügt über etw
- ◆ **hotel has s.th.**
- ◆ hotel provides s.th.

Hotel verfügt über jeden modernen Komfort
- ◆ **hotel has all modern comforts**
- ◆ hotel has every modern comfort

Hotel verfügt über jede nur denkbare Annehmlich-
- keit für Kinder
- ◆ **hotel has every conceivable amenity for children**

Hotel vergleichen mit einem anderen
- ◆ **compare a hotel with another one**

Hotel vergrößern
- ◆ **enlarge a hotel**

Hotel verkaufen
- ◆ **sell a hotel**

Hotelverkaufsdirektor, m
- ◆ **hotel sales executive**

Hotelverkaufshandbuch, n
- ◆ **hotel sales manual**

Hotelverkaufsleiter m
- ◆ **hotel sales manager**

Hotel verlassen
- ◆ **leave a hotel**
- ◆ walk out of a hotel
- ◆ check out of a hotel

Hotel verlassen ohne zu zahlen
- ◆ **leave a hotel without paying**
- ◆ depart from a hotel without paying

Hotel vermarkten
- ◆ **market a hotel**

Hotel vermieten an jn
- ◆ **rent a hotel to s.o.** *AE*
- ◆ let a hotel to s.o. *BE*

Hotelvermittlung

Hotelvermittlung, f
  Hotelvermittlungsdienst, m
  Hotelbuchungsdienst, m
  Hotelbuchungsservice, m
  ♦ hotel booking service
  ♦ hotel reservation service *AE*
  ♦ hotel accommodation service
Hotelvermittlungsdienst, m
  Hotelvermittlung, f
  Hotelbuchungsdienst, m
  Hotelreservierungsdienst, m
  ♦ hotel accommodation service
  ♦ hotel booking service
  ♦ hotel reservation service
Hotel verpachten
  ♦ lease out a hotel
  ♦ lease a hotel
Hotel verpachten an jn
  ♦ lease a hotel to s.o.
Hotel verpachten an jn zum Betrieb
  Hotel verpachten an jn zur Bewirtschaftung
  ♦ lease a hotel to s.o. for operation
Hotelverpflegung, f
  ♦ hotel catering *BE*
  ♦ hotel food
  ♦ hotel foodservice *AE*
  ♦ hotel board
Hotelversicherung, f
  ♦ hotel insurance
Hotel versteigern
  ♦ auction a hotel
  ♦ sell a hotel at auction
  ♦ sell a hotel by auction *BE*
Hotelversteigerung, f
  ♦ sale of a hotel at auction
  ♦ selling a hotel at auction
  ♦ sale of a hotel by auction *BE*
  ♦ selling a hotel by auction *BE*
Hotelvertrag, m
  ♦ hotel contract
  ♦ hotel agreement
Hotelvertrag abschließen
  Hotelvertrag machen
  ♦ make a hotel contract
Hotelvertrag aushandeln
  ♦ negotiate a hotel contract
Hotelvertrag kündigen
  Hotelvertrag aufkündigen
  zurücktreten von einem Hotelvertrag
  Hotelvertrag stornieren
  ♦ cancel a hotel contract
Hotelvertrag stornieren
  → Hotelvertrag kündigen
Hotelvertrag unterzeichnen
  ♦ sign a hotel contract
Hotelvertreter, m
  → Hotelrepräsentant
Hotelvertretung, f
  → Hotelrepräsentanz
Hotelverwaltung, f
  → Hoteladministration
Hotelverzeichnis, n
  Hotelliste, f
  Hotelanzeiger, m
  ♦ hotel directory
  ♦ hotel list
  ♦ list of hotels
Hotelvestibül, n
  ♦ hotel vestibule
Hotel vier Sterne zuerkennen
  ♦ award four stars to a hotel

Hotelviertel, n
  (in einem Ort)
  ♦ hotel area
  ♦ hotel district
Hotelviertel besuchen
  ♦ visit the hotel area
  ♦ visit the hotel district
Hotelvollpension, f
  ♦ hotel full board
  ♦ hotel full pension *AE*
Hotel von internationalem Ruf, n
  ♦ hotel of international reputation
  ♦ hotel with international reputation
  ♦ hotel of international repute
  ♦ internationally renowned hotel
Hotel von mittlerer Größe, n
  mittelgroßes Hotel, n
  ♦ hotel of medium size
  ♦ medium-size hotel
Hotel von vergleichbarer Qualität, n
  ♦ hotel of comparable quality
Hotel vorausreservieren
  Hotel im voraus reservieren
  ♦ reserve a hotel in advance
Hotelvorplatz, m
  Hotelvorhof, m
  ♦ hotel forecourt
Hotel vorschlagen
  ♦ suggest a hotel
Hotelvoucher, m
  → Hotelgutschein
Hotelvoucherpreis, m
  → Hotelgutscheinpreis
Hotelwahl, f
  Wahl des Hotels, f
  ♦ choice of the hotel
  ♦ selection of the hotel
  ♦ choosing a hotel
  ♦ selecting a hotel
Hotel wählen
  Hotel auswählen
  ♦ choose a hotel
  ♦ select a hotel
Hotel war früher ein Schloß
  ♦ hotel was formerly a castle
Hotelwäsche, f
  ♦ hotel linen
Hotelwäscherei, f
  ♦ hotel laundry
Hotelwaschsalon, m
  ♦ hotel laundromat *AE*
  ♦ hotel launderette *BE*
  ♦ hotel laundrette *BE*
Hotelwechsel, m
  (Gast zieht in anderes Hotel)
  ♦ hotel change
  ♦ change of hotel
  ♦ change of hotels
  ♦ changing hotels
Hotelwechsel bewerkstelligen
  ♦ effect a hotel change
Hotelwechsel genehmigen
  ♦ approve (of) the change of hotels
Hotel wechseln
  ♦ change hotels
Hotelwelt, f
  ♦ hotel world
  ♦ world of hotels
Hotelwerbung f
  ♦ hotel promotion
  ♦ promotion of a hotel

Hotelwesen, n
  → Hotelgewerbe, Hotelgeschäft
Hotel wiederaufbauen
  ♦ reconstruct a hotel
  ♦ rebuild a hotel
Hotel wiedereröffnen
  ♦ reopen a hotel
Hotel wird im Sommer bewirtschaftet
  ♦ hotel is operated during the summer
Hotel wird voll
  ♦ hotel becomes crowded
Hotel wird vom Besitzer geleitet
  ♦ hotel is owner-managed
Hotelwirtschaftsabteilung, f
  ♦ hotel food and beverage department
Hotelwohnung, f
  ♦ hotel flat *BE*
  ♦ hotel apartment *AE*
Hotelwörterbuch, n
  ♦ hotel dictionary
Hotelwunsch, m (allgemein)
  ♦ hotel request
  ♦ request for a hotel
Hotelwunsch, m (Präferenz)
  Vorliebe für ein bestimmtes Hotel f
  Hotelvorliebe f
  Hotelpräferenz f
  ♦ hotel preference
  ♦ preference for a hotel
Hotelwunsch angeben (Präferenz)
  (bei Auswahl von Hotel)
  ♦ indicate one's hotel preference
  ♦ state one's hotel preference
Hotelwunsch haben (Präferenz)
  eine Vorliebe haben für ein Hotel
  ♦ have a hotel preference
Hotel wurde 1990 eröffnet
  ♦ hotel was opened in 1990
Hotel wurde 1990 fertiggestellt
  ♦ hotel was completed in 1990
Hotel wurde mir empfohlen
  ♦ hotel was recommended to me
Hotel wurde total renoviert
  ♦ hotel was totally renovated
  ♦ hotel was totally refurbished
Hotelzentrale, f
  Hotelhauptverwaltung, f
  ♦ hotel headquarters *pl + sg*
Hotelzentrum, n
  ♦ hotel center *AE*
  ♦ hotel centre *BE*
Hotelzettel m
  (Gepäck)
  ♦ hotel label
Hotelzimmer, n
  Hotelraum, m
  ♦ hotel room
Hotelzimmer abbestellen
  Hotelzimmer stornieren
  Hotelzimmer absagen
  ♦ cancel a hotel room
Hotelzimmerabgabe, f
  → Hotelzimmersteuer
Hotelzimmer absagen
  → Hottelzimmer abbestellen
Hotelzimmerangebot, n
  ♦ number of hotel rooms offered
  ♦ number of hotel rooms
Hotelzimmerangebot erhöhen
  ♦ increase the number of hotel rooms

Hotelzimmerart f
 Hotelzimmertyp m
 ♦ hotel room type
 ♦ type of hotel room
Hotelzimmerauslastung f
 Hotelzimmerbelegung f
 ♦ hotel room occupancy
 ♦ occupancy of (the) hotel rooms
Hotelzimmerbeschreibung f
 ♦ hotel room description
 ♦ description of a hotel room
Hotelzimmerboom, m
 ♦ hotel room boom
Hotelzimmer buchen
 ♦ book a hotel room
Hotelzimmereinstufung, f
 ♦ hotel room grade
 ♦ hotel room grading
 ♦ grading a hotel room
 ♦ grading hotel rooms
Hotelzimmerimbiß, m
 Hotelzimmervesper, f
 ♦ hotel-room snack
Hotelzimmer ist ab 18 Uhr gebucht
 ♦ hotel room is booked from 6 p.m.
Hotelzimmer ist ab 2. Mai gebucht
 ♦ hotel room is booked from 2 May
Hotelzimmer ist belegt
 ♦ hotel room is occupied
Hotelzimmer ist besetzt
 ♦ hotel room is taken
Hotelzimmer ist beziehbar
 ♦ hotel room is available
Hotelzimmer ist frei
 ♦ hotel room is free
 ♦ hotel room is vacant
Hotelzimmer ist unbelegt
 Hotelzimmer ist nicht belegt
 ♦ hotel room is unoccupied
 ♦ hotel room is not occupied
Hotelzimmer ist vakant
 Hotelzimmer ist frei
 ♦ hotel room is vacant
Hotelzimmerlage, f
 ♦ hotel room location
 ♦ hotel room position
 ♦ location of a hotel room
 ♦ position of a hotel room
Hotelzimmer mieten
 ♦ rent a hotel room
Hotelzimmer modernisieren
 ♦ update a hotel room
Hotelzimmermodernisierung f
 ♦ hotel room modernisation
 ♦ modernisation of a hotel room
Hotelzimmernachfrage, f
 ♦ hotel room demand
 ♦ demand for hotel rooms
Hotelzimmernachfrage befriedigen
 Hotelzimmernachfrage nachkommen
 Hotelzimmernachfrage erfüllen
 ♦ meet the hotel room demand
 ♦ meet the demand for hotel rooms
Hotelzimmernachfragezuwachs, m
 Steigerung der Hotelzimmernachfrage, f
 ♦ increase in hotel room demand
 ♦ increase in demand for hotel rooms
Hotelzimmernachfragezuwachs erfüllen
 ♦ meet the increase in hotel room demand
Hotelzimmer nehmen
 ♦ take a hotel room

Hotelzimmernummer, f
 ♦ hotel room number
Hotelzimmerplan, m
 Hotelzimmerlageplan, m
 Hotelzimmerspiegel, m
 ♦ hotel floor plan
Hotelzimmerpreis m
 ♦ hotel room rate
 ♦ hotel room charge
 ♦ hotel room price
Hotelzimmer reservieren (für jn)
 ♦ reserve a hotel room (for s.o.)
Hotelzimmerreservierung, f
 ♦ hotel room reservation
 ♦ reservation of a hotel room
 ♦ reserving a hotel room
Hotelzimmer sich sichern
 ♦ secure a hotel room
Hotelzimmerspiegel, m
 → Hotelzimmerplan
Hotelzimmerstandard m
 ♦ hotel room standard
 ♦ standard of hotel rooms
Hotelzimmersteuer, f
 Hotelzimmerabgabe, f
 ♦ hotel room tax
Hotelzimmer stornieren
 → Hotelzimmer abbestellen
Hotelzimmer teilen mit jm
 ♦ share a hotel room with s.o.
 ♦ share a hotel bedroom with s.o.
Hotelzimmertyp, m
 → Hotelzimmerart
Hotelzimmerüberangebot, n
 ♦ excess of hotel rooms
Hotelzimmerzahl, f
 Zahl der Hotelzimmer, f
 ♦ number of hotel rooms
Hotelzimmer zu DM 123 bis DM 213
 ♦ hotel room at DM 123 to DM 213
Hotelzimmerzuschlag m
 ♦ hotel room supplement
Hotel zu einem 5-Sterne-Hotel aufwerten
 ♦ upgrade a hotel to a 5-star hotel
Hotelzufahrt, f
 → Hotelauffahrt
Hotel zum Verkauf anbieten
 ♦ put a hotel up for sale
Hotelzusage, f
 Hotelbestätigung, f
 ♦ hotel confirmation
Hotelzusammenarbeit, f
 Hotelkooperation, f
 ♦ cooperation between hotels
 ♦ hotel cooperation
Hotelzusammenschluß, m
 Zusammenschluß von Hotels, m
 ♦ affiliation of hotels
Hotelzuschlag m
 ♦ hotel supplement
Hotel zu verkaufen
 (Hinweisschild)
 ♦ Hotel for sale
Hotelzuweisung, f
 Hotelzuteilung, f
 ♦ hotel allocation
 ♦ allocation of a hotel
 ♦ hotel assignment *AE*
Hotel zweiter Klasse, n
 zweitklassiges Hotel, n

 ♦ second-rate hotel *coll*
 ♦ second-class hotel
Hot Tub, m
 (Wanne für mehrere Personen zum Entspannen im warmen Wasser, oft im Garten installiert)
 ♦ hot tub *AE*
HP, f
 Halbpension, f
 ♦ HB
 ♦ half board
 ♦ MAP
 ♦ Modified American Plan
 ♦ demipension *AE*
HP-Preis, m
 Halbpensionpreis, m
 ♦ HB price
 ♦ HB rate
 ♦ MAP price
 ♦ MAP rate
Hs.
 Haus, n
 ♦ hse.
 ♦ house
Hubbart Formel, f
 (für Hotelklassifizierung)
 ♦ Hubbart formula
hübsch ausgestattet, adj
 ♦ handsomely equipped, adj
hübsch ausgestattetes Zimmer, n
 ♦ handsomely equipped room
hübsch eingerichtet, adj
 hübsch möbliert, adj
 ♦ prettily furnished, adj
hübsch eingerichtetes Zimmer, n
 hübsch möbliertes Zimmer, n
 ♦ prettily furnished room
hübsche Möbel, n pl
 ♦ handsome furniture *sg*
hübsches Hotel, n
 ♦ handsome hotel
hübsches Zimmer, n
 ♦ handsome room
hübsche Umgebung, f
 ♦ lovely surroundings *pl*
hübsch möbliert, adj
 ♦ handsomely furnished, adj
hübsch möbliertes Zimmer n
 ♦ handsomely furnished room
Hubschrauber, m
 Helikopter m
 ♦ helicopter
 ♦ chopper *coll*
Hubschrauberabsturz, m
 ♦ helicopter crash
Hubschrauberdienst, m
 Hubschrauberverbindung, f
 ♦ helicopter service
Hubschrauberflug, m
 ♦ helicopter flight
Hubschrauberlandeplatz, m
 Heliport, m
 ♦ heliport
Hubschrauberlandestelle, f
 Hubschrauberlandeplatz, m
 ♦ helipad
 ♦ helicopter pad
Hubschrauberliniendienst, m
 ♦ scheduled helicopter service

Hubschraubermannschaft, f
  ♦ helicopter crew
  ♦ chopper crew *coll*
Hubschrauber mieten
  ♦ hire a helicopter *BE*
  ♦ rent a helicopter *AE*
Hubschraubermuseum, n
  ♦ helicopter museum
Hubschrauberrundflug unternehmen
  Hubschrauberrundflug machen
  ♦ take a helicopter tour
Hubschrauberservice, m
  Hubschrauberdienst, m
  ♦ chopper service *coll*
  ♦ helicopter service
Hubschraubertaxi, n
  ♦ helicopter taxi
Hubschraubertour, f
  ♦ helicopter tour
Hubschraubertransfer, m
  ♦ helicopter transfer
Hubschrauberverbindung, f
  ♦ helicopter connection
  connection by helicopter
  ♦ chopper connection *coll*
  ♦ chopper service *coll*
  ♦ helicopter service
hübsch restauriert, adj
  ♦ handsomely restored, adj
  nicely restored, adj
Hudson, m
  ♦ Hudson River, the
  ♦ River Hudson, the
  ♦ Hudson, the
Hufeisenbestuhlung f
  hufeisenförmige Bestuhlung
  ♦ horseshoe-style seating
  ♦ horseshoe seating
Hufeisenform, f
  (Bestuhlung)
  ♦ horseshoe style
hufeisenförmig, adj
  ♦ horseshoe-shaped, adj
hufeisenförmige Eßecke, f
  ♦ horseshoe-shaped dinette
  ♦ U-shaped dinette
Hügel, m
  kleiner Berg, m
  ♦ hill
hügelig, adj
  ♦ hilly, adj
hügeliger Campingplatz, m
  ♦ hilly campsite
  ♦ hilly campground *AE*
  ♦ hilly camping site *BE*
  ♦ hilly camping ground *BE*
  ♦ hilly site
hügeliger Platz, m
  (z.B. Campingplatz)
  ♦ hilly site
hügeliges Gebiet, n
  hügeliges Gelände, n
  ♦ hilly country
HUGO *sl derog*
  heute unbekannt gestorbenes Objekt, n *sl derog*
  verstorbener Tourist, m
  ♦ dead tourist
Huhn, n (generell)
  ♦ hen
Huhn, n (Speise)
  ♦ chicken

Huhn ausbeinen
  ♦ bone a chicken
Hühnchen, n
  ♦ pullet
Hühnenbratenstück, n
  Hühnerbraten, m
  ♦ chicken joint
Hühnerbrühe, f
  ♦ chicken broth
Hühnerbrust, f
  ♦ chicken breast *AE*
  ♦ chicken-breast *BE*
Hühnercremesuppe, f
  ♦ chicken cream soup
  ♦ cream of chicken soup
Hühnerfleisch, n
  ♦ chicken meat
  ♦ chicken
  ♦ chicken flesh
Hühnerflügel, m
  ♦ chicken wing
Hühnerfond, m
  ♦ chicken fond
Hühnerfrikassee, n
  ♦ chicken fricassee
Hühnergericht, n
  ♦ chicken dish
Hühnergulasch, m/n
  ♦ chicken goulash
Hühnerklein, n
  (Innereien)
  ♦ chicken giblets *pl*
Hühnerleber, f
  ♦ chicken liver
  ♦ chicken livers *pl gastr*
Hühnerpastete, f
  ♦ chicken pie
  ♦ chicken pâté
Hühnerragout, n/m
  Geflügelragout, n/m
  ♦ chicken stew
Hühnersalat, m
  ♦ chicken salad
Hühnersalpikon, m
  ♦ chicken salpicon
Hühnersuppe, f
  ♦ chicken soup
Hummer, m
  ♦ lobster
Hummeraspik, m
  ♦ lobster jelly
Hummeraufstrich, m
  ♦ lobster spread
Hummerbar, f
  ♦ lobster bar
Hummerbutter, f
  ♦ lobster butter
Hummercanapé, n
  ♦ lobster canapé *BE*
  ♦ lobster canape *AE*
Hummercocktail, m
  ♦ lobster cocktail
Hummercremesoße, f
  ♦ lobster cream sauce
Hummercremesuppe, f
  ♦ lobster cream soup
Hummergericht, n
  ♦ lobster dish
Hummer in Aspik, m
  ♦ lobster in jelly

Hummerkrokette, f
  ♦ lobster croquette
Hummermayonnaise, f
  ♦ lobster mayonnaise
Hummermedaillon, n
  ♦ lobster medallion
Hummerparfait, n
  ♦ lobster parfait
Hummerragout, n/m
  ♦ lobster stew
Hummersalat, m
  ♦ lobster salad
Hummersalpikon, m
  ♦ lobster salpicon
Hummerschiffchen, n
  ♦ lobster barquette
Hummersoße, f
  ♦ lobster sauce
Hummersoufflé, n
  Hummerauflauf, m
  ♦ lobster soufflé *BE*
  ♦ lobster souffle *AE*
Hummersuppe, f
  ♦ lobster soup
Hund, m
  ♦ dog
Hund ausführen
  ♦ walk a dog
Hundeausstellung, f
  ♦ dog show
Hundebesitzer, m
  ♦ dog owner
  ♦ owner of a dog
Hundefreund, m
  Hundeliebhaber, m
  ♦ dog lover
hundefreundlich, adj
  ♦ dogs (are) welcome
hundefreundliches Hotel n
  ♦ hotel (which) accepts dogs
Hundefutter, n
  ♦ dog food
Hundehütte, f
  ♦ doghouse *AE*
  ♦ dog kennel
Hundekarren, m
  Hundekarre, f
  ♦ dogcart
Hundeliebhaber, m
  ♦ dog-lover
Hunde nicht erwünscht
  (Hinweisschild)
  ♦ No dogs admitted
Hundepension, f
  ♦ boarding home for dogs
Hundertjahrfeier, f
  ♦ centennial celebration
  ♦ centenary celebration
Hundertjahrjubiläum, n
  ♦ centennial anniversary
  ♦ centennial
hundertprozentige Tochtergesellschaft, f
  ♦ wholly-owned subsidiary
Hundeschlitten, m
  ♦ dog sleigh
  ♦ dog sled
Hundeschlittenrennen, n
  ♦ dog sled race
Hunde sind an der Leine zu führen
  ♦ Dogs must be kept on a leash *AE*
  ♦ Dogs must be kept on a lead *BE*

Hundetoilette, f
♦ dogs' toilet
Hunde unerwünscht
♦ No dogs accepted
Hundeverbot
(Hinweisschild)
♦ No dogs allowed
Hunde willkommen
(Hinweisschild)
♦ Dogs welcome
Hundezwinger, m
♦ dog kennel
♦ kennel
Hund pro Nacht, m
♦ dog per night
Hunger, m
♦ hunger
Hunger bekommen
→ hungrig werden
Hunger haben
hungrig sein
♦ feel hungry
♦ be hungry
Hunger ist der beste Koch
♦ Hunger is the best sauce
♦ A good appetite is the best sauce
♦ A good appetite needs no sauce
Hungerkur, f
Nulldiät, f
Hungerdiät, f
♦ starvation diet
♦ hunger cure
♦ calorie-free diet
Hungerkur machen
♦ go on a starvation diet
♦ be on a starvation diet
hungern
♦ starve
♦ go hungry
Hungersnot, f
♦ famine
Hunger stillen
♦ satisfy one's hunger
♦ appease one's hunger
Hungerstreik, m
♦ hunger strike
Hungerstreik machen
in den Hungerstreik treten
♦ go on hunger strike
Hungrigen, die, pl
♦ hungry, the *pl*
hungrig sein
Hunger haben
♦ be hungry
♦ feel hungry
hungrig weggehen
♦ go hungry
♦ leave hungry
hungrig werden
Hunger bekommen
♦ get hungry
hungrig wie ein Wolf
♦ hungry as a wolf
♦ hungry as a bear
♦ hungry as a hunter
Hunsrück, m
(Region)
♦ Hunsrück, the
Hunsrückhöhen, f pl
♦ Hunsrück heights *pl*

Husarenart, adv *gastr*
nach Husarenart, adv *gast*
♦ hussar's style, adv *gastr*
♦ hussar style, adv *gastr*
Husarensoße, f
♦ hussar sauce
Hut, m
♦ hat
Hutablage f
♦ hat rack
Huthaken, m
♦ hat-peg
Hutmarke, f
(Garderobe)
♦ hat check *AE*
Hutschachtel, f
♦ hatbox
Hutständer, m
♦ hatstand *AE*
♦ hat stand *BE*
♦ hat tree *AE*
Hütte, f
♦ hut
♦ cabin
♦ bothy *SCOT*
Hütte bewirtschaften
♦ run a hut
Hütte ist von Mai bis August bewirtschaftet
♦ hut is open from May to August
Hüttenhotel, n (im Gebirge)
♦ small mountain hotel
♦ mountain lodge *AE*
Hüttenkäse, m
♦ cottage cheese
Hüttenrestaurant, n (im Gebirge)
♦ small mountain restaurant
Hüttenzelt, n
♦ umbrella tent
Huxelrebe, f
(Wein)
♦ Huxelrebe
Hydrant, m
♦ fire hydrant
♦ hydrant
♦ fire-plug *AE*
Hydraulikbett, n
(wie in Krankenhaus)
♦ hydraulic bed
Hydrotherapie, f
♦ hydrotherapy
Hydrotherapiebereich, m
♦ hydrotherapy area
Hydrotherapiezentrum, n
♦ hydrotherapy center *AE*
♦ hydrotherapy centre *BE*
Hygiene, f
♦ hygiene
Hygieneartikel, m pl
♦ toiletries *pl*
Hygienebestimmungen, f pl
♦ hygiene regulations *pl*
Hygienebeutel, m
(für Damenbinden)
♦ bag for sanitary napkins *AE*
♦ bag for sanitary towels *BE*
♦ bag for sanitary pads *BE*
Hygienegesetze einhalten
♦ comply with the hygiene laws
Hygienestandard, m
♦ hygiene standard

Hygienestandards erfüllen
♦ meet hygiene standards
Hygienestandard überwachen
♦ monitor the hygiene standard
Hygienevorschriften, f pl
♦ rules of hygiene *pl*
hygienisch, adj
♦ hygienic, adj
hygienische Verhältnisse, n pl
♦ hygienic conditions *pl*
hypermodern, adj
ultramodern, adj
♦ ultra-modern, adj
hypermoderner Saal, m
ultramoderner Saal, m
hypermoderne Halle, f
ultramoderne Halle, f
♦ ultra-modern hall
Hypnotherapie, f
♦ hynotherapy
Hypothek, f
Grundschuld f
♦ mortgage
Hypothek auf eine Wohnung, f
♦ mortgage on an apartment *AE*
♦ mortgage on a flat *BE*
Hypothek aufnehmen
♦ take out a mortgage
Hypothekengeber, m
♦ mortgage lender
Hypothekenzins, m
Hypothekenzinsen, m pl
♦ mortgage interest *sg*
HZ, f
→ Heizung

I

IATA, f
   International Air Transport Association, f
   ♦ IATA
   ♦ International Air Transport Association
IATA-Agent, m
   ♦ IATA agent
IATA-Agentur, f
   ♦ IATA agency
IATA-Bestimmungen, f pl
   IATA-Vorschriften, f pl
   ♦ IATA regulations *pl*
IATA-Fluggesellschaft, f
   ♦ IATA airline
IATA-Flugschein, m
   ♦ IATA ticket
IATA-Lizenz, f
   ♦ IATA licence
   ♦ IATA license
IATA-Lizenz haben
   ♦ hold a IATA license
   ♦ hold a IATA licence
   ♦ have a IATA license
   ♦ have a IATA licence
Iberische Halbinsel, die, f
   ♦ Iberian Peninsula, the
Ibiza
   ♦ Ibiza
ICE-Zug, m
   ♦ ICE train
Ich begrüße Sie im Namen des Direktors
   ♦ I welcome you on behalf of the director
Ich bin Ihnen sehr verbunden
   ♦ I am much obliged to you
Ich bin satt
   ♦ I have had enough
   ♦ I have had sufficient
   ♦ I am full
   ♦ I am full up *coll*
Ich brauche hier noch eine Unterschrift
   ♦ I need one more signature here
Ich bringe gleich das Wechselgeld
   ♦ I'll bring the change in a moment
Ich freue mich, Sie in unserem Hotel begrüßen zu können
   ♦ I am pleased to welcome you to our hotel
Ich freue mich auf Ihren nächsten Besuch
   ♦ I look forward to your next visit
   ♦ I'm looking forward to your next visit *inform*
Ich habe nichts dagegen, wenn Sie hier bleiben
   Es macht mir nichts aus, wenn Sie hier bleiben
   ♦ I don't care if you stay here
Ich habe noch nicht ausgeschlafen
   ♦ I haven't had enough sleep yet
Ich habe noch nicht gewählt
   (im Restaurant)
   ♦ I haven't decided yet

Ich habe reservieren lassen
   Ich habe reserviert
   ♦ I have a reservation
Ich heiße Sie alle herzlich willkommen
   ♦ I bid you all a hearty welcome
Ich hoffe, Sie hatten eine gute Reise
   ♦ I hope you had a good journey
Ich hole schnell einen Portier
   ♦ I'll just get a porter
Ich kann empfehlen ...
   ♦ I can recommend ...
Ich mache mir das Frühstück selbst
   ♦ I cook my own breakfast
Ich mache mir nichts aus Bier
   ♦ I don't care for beer
Ich möchte abreisen
   ♦ I'd like to check out
Ich möchte lieber etwas essen
   ♦ I'd rather have something to eat
Ich möchte lieber etwas trinken
   ♦ I'd rather have something to drink
Ich möchte mich anmelden
   ♦ I'd like to register
Ich möchte mich beschweren
   ♦ I have a complaint to make
Ich möchte mit Kreditkarte zahlen
   ♦ I'd like to pay by credit card
Ich möchte morgen früh geweckt werden
   ♦ I'd like an early call tomorrow morning
Ich möchte umbuchen
   ♦ I would like to make a change in reservation *AE*
Ich nehme Kaffee
   ♦ I'll have coffee
Ich schmecke nichts
   ♦ I can't taste anything
   ♦ I don't taste anything
Ich stehe Ihnen ganz zu Diensten
   Ich stehe ganz zu Ihrer Verfügung
   ♦ I am entirely at your service
Ich trinke auf Ihr Wohl!
   Ich trinke auf Ihre Gesundheit!
   ♦ I drink (to) your health!
Ich wäre Ihnen sehr dankbar, wenn ...
   ♦ I would be very grateful to you if ...
Ich wäre Ihnen sehr verbunden, wenn ...
   ♦ I would be much obliged to you if ...
Ich werde das probieren
   ♦ I'll try that
Ich werde Ihnen einen Platz reservieren
   ♦ I'll reserve a seat for you
Ich werde mich darum so bald wie möglich kümmern
   ♦ I'll attend to it as soon as possible
Ich werde mich persönlich um die Angelegenheit kümmern
   ♦ I will give the matter my personal attention

Ich werde mich selbst darum kümmern
   ♦ I'll see to that myself
Ich werde veranlassen, daß ein Wagen Sie abholt
   ♦ I will arrange for a car to meet you
Ich werde veranlassen, daß sich sofort jemand darum kümmert
   ♦ I'll have that seen to right away
Ich will abreisen. Kann ich die Rechnung haben?
   ♦ I want to check out. Can I have the bill, please?
Ich wohne in Zimmer 103
   ♦ I'm staying in room 103
Ich wünsche Ihnen eine gute Reise
   ♦ I hope you will have a pleasant journey
IC-Zug, m
   Intercity-Zug, m
   ♦ IC train
   ♦ intercity train *AE*
   ♦ inter-city train *BE*
IDD
   → internationaler Selbstwählverkehr
ideal, adj
   ♦ ideal, adj
ideale Gegend für Wanderer und Kletterer, f
   ♦ ideal country for walkers and climbers
ideale Lage, f
   Ideallage, f
   ♦ ideal location
   ♦ ideal position
   ♦ ideal setting
   ♦ ideal situation
ideale Lage für Bergwanderungen, f
   ideale Lage für Gebirgswanderungen, f
   ♦ ideal location for mountain walks
   ♦ ideal situation for mountain hikes
idealen Ausgangspunkt für Reisen darstellen
   ♦ make an ideal touring base
idealen Rahmen bieten für etw
   ♦ offer the ideal setting for s.th.
   ♦ provide the ideal setting for s.th.
   ♦ provide the ideal framework for s.th.
idealen Rahmen für etw abgeben
   idealen Rahmen für etw bieten
   ♦ provide the ideal setting for s.th.
idealen Veranstaltungsrahmen bieten
   ♦ provide an ideal setting for a function
idealer Ausgangspunkt (für etw), m
   idealer Ausgangsort (für etw), m
   ♦ ideal starting point (for s.th.)
   ♦ ideal base (for s.th.)
idealer Ausgangspunkt sein für etw
   ♦ be an ideal base for s.th.
   ♦ be an ideal starting point for s.th.
idealer Ort für etw, m
   ♦ ideal place for s.th.
   ♦ ideal site for s.th.
idealer Quartierort (für etw), m
   idealer Ausgangsort (für etw), m

idealer Rahmen (für etw)

- ♦ ideal base (for s.th.)
- ♦ ideal starting point (for s.th.)

idealer Rahmen (für etw), m
- ♦ ideal setting (for s.th.)

idealer Rahmen sein für etw
- ♦ be the ideal setting for s.th.

idealer Veranstaltungsrahmen sein
  idealer Rahmen für eine Veranstaltung sein
- ♦ be the ideal setting for a function

ideales Hotel, n
  Idealhotel, n
- ♦ ideal hotel

ideal für einen Erholungsurlaub
- ♦ ideal for a relaxing vacation AE
- ♦ ideal for a relaxing holiday BE

ideal für etw
- ♦ ideal for s.th.

ideal für Familienbetrieb
  (Geschäft)
- ♦ ideal for family operation

ideal gelegen, adj
- ♦ ideally situated, adj
- ♦ ideally located, adj
- ♦ ideally positioned, adj
- ♦ ideally placed, adj
- ♦ ideally set, adj

ideal gelegen sein für etw
  ideal liegen für etw
- ♦ be ideally situated for s.th.
- ♦ be ideally located for s.th.
- ♦ be ideally positioned for s.th.
- ♦ be ideally placed for s.th.
- ♦ be ideally set for s.th.

Ideallage, f
  → ideale Lage

ideal sein für etw
- ♦ be ideal for s.th.

Ideal von einem Hotel, n
- ♦ ideal of a hotel
- ♦ ideal hotel

ideal zum Ausspannen
- ♦ ideal for relaxing

ideal zum Wandern und Radfahren
- ♦ ideal for hiking and biking

identifizieren jn
- ♦ identify s.o.

Identifizierung, f
- ♦ identification

identisch, adj
- ♦ identical, adj

identisches Zimmer, n
  gleiches Zimmer n
- ♦ identical room

identisch mit etw
- ♦ identical with s.th.
- ♦ identical to s.th.

identisch möbliert, adj
  gleich möbliert, adj
- ♦ identically furnished, adj

identisch möbliertes Zimmer, n
  gleich möbliertes Zimmer n
- ♦ identically furnished room

Identität, f
- ♦ identity

Identität feststellen von jm
- ♦ establish the identity of s.o.

Identität preisgeben von jm
- ♦ reveal the identity of s.o.

Identitätsprüfung, f
- ♦ identity check

Identität verheimlichen
  Identität verbergen
- ♦ conceal one's identity

Idiotenhügel, m (Ski) humor
  Anfängerhügel, m
- ♦ nursery slope
- ♦ beginners' slope

IDS
  → internationaler Selbstwählverkehr

Idylle, f
- ♦ idyll
- ♦ idyl AE

idyllisch, adj
- ♦ idyllic, adj

idyllische Ferien, pl
  idyllischer Urlaub, m
- ♦ idyllic holidays BE pl
- ♦ idyllic holiday BE
- ♦ idyllic vacation AE

idyllische Lage f
- ♦ idyllic location
- ♦ idyllic position
- ♦ idyllic setting
- ♦ idyllic situation

idyllische Landschaft, f
- ♦ idyllic landscape
- ♦ idyllic scenery
- ♦ idyllic countryside

idyllischer Rahmen, m
- ♦ idyllic setting

idyllischer See, m
- ♦ idyllic lake

idyllischer Tag, m
- ♦ idyllic day

idyllischer Urlaub, m
  idyllische Ferien, pl
- ♦ idyllic vacation AE
- ♦ idyllic holiday BE
- ♦ idyllic holidays BE pl

idyllisches Dorf, n
- ♦ idyllic village

idyllische Umgebung, f
- ♦ idyllic surroundings pl

idyllisch gelegen, adj
- ♦ idyllically situated, adj
- ♦ idyllically located, adj

idyllisch gelegenes Hotel, n
  Hotel in idyllischer Lage, m
- ♦ idyllically situated hotel
- ♦ idyllically located hotel

Iglu, n
  Schneehütte, f
- ♦ igloo
- ♦ iglu AE

ignorieren etw
  übersehen etw
- ♦ ignore s.th.

ignorieren jn
  übersehen jn
- ♦ ignore s.o.

Ihnen zu Gefallen
- ♦ to oblige you

Ihr Auto versperrt den Eingang
- ♦ Your car is blocking the entrance

Ihr Geschäft ist unser Vergnügen
- ♦ Your business is our pleasure

Ihr Wunsch ist mir Befehl
- ♦ Your wish is my command

Ikone, f
- ♦ icon

illegal, adj
  ungesetzmäßig, adj
- ♦ illegal, adj
- ♦ unlawful, adj

illegale Einwanderung, f
- ♦ illegal immigration

illegaler Ausländer, m
- ♦ illegal alien

illegaler Einwanderer, m
- ♦ illegal immigrant

illegaler Spielbetrieb, m
  illegaler Glücksspielbetrieb m
- ♦ illegal gambling establishment
- ♦ illegal gambling operation

illegales Glücksspiel, n
- ♦ illegal gambling

Illumination, f
  Illuminierung, f
  Beleuchtung, f
  Anstrahlung, f
- ♦ illumination

illuminieren etw
  beleuchten etw
  anstrahlen etw
- ♦ illuminate s.th.

illuminieren etw festlich
  festlich illuminieren etw
  festlich beleuchten etw
- ♦ illuminate s.th. festively

illuster, adj
- ♦ illustrious, adj

illustre Gesellschaft, f
- ♦ illustrious company

illustre Persönlichkeit, f
- ♦ illustrious personality

illustre Weinkarte, f
- ♦ illustrious wine list

illustriert, adj
  bebildert, adj
- ♦ illustrated, adj

im Adamskostüm
- ♦ in the buff

Image, n
- ♦ image

Imageanalyse, f
- ♦ image analysis

Image behalten
- ♦ retain an image

Imagebroschüre, f
  → Imageprospekt

Image der Unterkunft, n
- ♦ image of the accommodation

Image erhalten
- ♦ maintain an image

Image erzeugen
  Image schaffen
- ♦ create an image

Image fördern
- ♦ promote an image

Imagekampagne, f
- ♦ image campaign

Imagepflege, f
- ♦ cultivation of one's image
- ♦ image polishing

Image pflegen
- ♦ cultivate an image
- ♦ cultivate one's image

Imageproblem, n
- ♦ image problem

Imageproblem haben
  Problem mit dem Image haben

♦ have an image problem
♦ have a problem with one's image
Imageprospekt, m
 Imagebroschüre f
 ♦ image brochure
Image schädigen
 ♦ damage one's image
 ♦ damage s.o.'s image
Image schaffen
 → Image erzeugen
Imageübertragung, f
 ♦ image transfer
Image verbessern
 ♦ improve one's image
 ♦ improve s.o.'s image
Imageverbesserung, f
 ♦ image improvement
 ♦ improvement of one's image
Image verstärken von etw
 ♦ enhance the image of s.th.
Image von Luxus, n
 ♦ image of luxury
Image von Luxus fördern
 ♦ promote an image of luxury
Imagewerbung, f
 ♦ image promotion
 ♦ image advertising
im Angebot
 ♦ on offer
im Angebot sein
 ♦ be on offer
im Anschluß an den Vortrag gab es ...
 ♦ subsequent to the lecture there was ...
im Anschluß an etw
 ♦ following s.th.
 ♦ subsequent to s.th.
im Anschluß daran
 ♦ following this
 ♦ subsequent to this
Im Anschluß daran findet ein Empfang im Hauptfoyer
 statt
 ♦ Following this, a reception will be given in the
 ♦ main foyer
Im Anschluß daran findet ein Empfang statt
 ♦ Following this, there will be a reception
im Ausland, adv
 ♦ abroad, adv
im Ausland Urlaub machen
 ♦ vacation abroad AE
 ♦ spend one's vacation abroad AE
 ♦ holiday abroad BE
 ♦ spend one's holiday abroad BE
im Barockstil, adv
 im barocken Stil, adv
 ♦ in baroque style, adv
 ♦ in the baroque style, adv
im Bau sein
 ♦ be under construction
im Besitz sein von etw
 ♦ be in possession of s.th.
im Bett
 ♦ in bed
im Bett bleiben
 liegenbleiben
 ♦ stay in bed
 ♦ stop in bed
im Bett frühstücken
 ♦ have breakfast in bed
 ♦ breakfast in bed

im Bett liegen
 ♦ lie in bed
im Bett liegen mit jm
 ♦ be in bed with s.o.
im Bett liegen mit Kopfschmerzen
 ♦ be in bed with a headache
Imbiß, m
 Jause, f ÖST
 Vesper, f dial
 ♦ snack
 ♦ light meal
 ♦ bite coll
Imbißbude, f
 ♦ snack booth
 ♦ hot-dog stand
 ♦ hot-dog stall
Imbißcafé in einer Parkbucht, n
 (an einer Landstraße)
 ♦ lay-by café BE
Imbiß einnehmen
 Imbiß essen
 ♦ have a snack
 ♦ take a snack
 ♦ snack inform
Imbißkette, f
 Kette von Imbißstuben, f
 ♦ snack-bar chain
 ♦ snack chain
Imbißlokal, n
 ♦ snack place
Imbißpaket, n
 ♦ lunch packet
 ♦ packed lunch
 ♦ food pack
Imbiß reichen
 Imbiß servieren
 ♦ serve a snack
Imbißrestaurant, n
 Imbißstube, f
 ♦ snack restaurant
 ♦ snack bar AE
 ♦ snack-bar BE
Imbißservice m
 ♦ snack service
Imbißstand, m
 Fast-Food-Stand, m
 ♦ fast-food stand
 ♦ fast-food stall BE
Imbißstätte, f jur
 → Imbißstube
Imbißstube, f
 ♦ snack bar AE
 ♦ snack-bar BE
 ♦ lunchroom/luncheonette AE
 ♦ lunch counter AE
 ♦ lunch(eon) bar BE
Imbißstube mit Verkauf über die Straße, f
 ♦ take-away snack bar AE
 ♦ take-away snack-bar BE
Imbißstubeneigentümer, m
 ♦ snack-bar proprietor
Imbißstubenkonzession, f
 Imbißkonzession, f
 ♦ snack-bar concession
 ♦ snack-bar licence
 ♦ snack-bar license
Imbißtablett, n
 ♦ snack tray
Imbißtheke, f
 ♦ snack counter

Imbißwagen, m
 ♦ mobile snack bar AE
 ♦ mobile snack-bar BE
Imbiß zu sich nehmen
 Imbiß einnehmen
 ♦ take a snack
 ♦ have a snack
im Bus, adv
 in dem Bus, adv
 ♦ on the bus, adv
 ♦ on the coach, adv BE
im Dienst
 ♦ in attendance
 ♦ on duty
im dritten Vierteljahr
 ♦ in the third quarter
im Durchschnitt
 ♦ on average
im Einklang sein mit etw
 (Farben, Architektur etc)
 ♦ be in keeping with s.th.
im Einvernehmen mit jm
 ♦ in consultation with s.o.
im Elsaß
 ♦ in Alsace
im Ermessen liegen von jm
 im Ermessen stehen von jm
 ♦ lie within s.o.'s discretion
 ♦ be within s.o.'s discretion
im ersten Vierteljahr
 ♦ in the first quarter
 ♦ in the first three months
im Evaskostüm
 ♦ in the buff
im Falle des Rücktritts
 im Falle einer Stornierung
 ♦ in (the) case of (a) cancellation
 ♦ in (the) case of (a) cancelation AE
 ♦ in the event of (a) cancellation
 ♦ in the event of (a) cancelation AE
im Falle einer Panne
 ♦ in the event of a breakdown
 ♦ in the case of a breakdown
im Falle einer Stornierung
 → im Falles des Rücktritts
im falschen Zug sein
 ♦ be on the wrong train
im Flugzeug
 ♦ on the plane
im Frack, adv
 ♦ in tails, adv
 ♦ wearing tails
im Freien
 ♦ in the open air
 ♦ in the open
im Freien bleiben
 draußen bleiben
 ♦ stay outdoors
im Freien essen
 ♦ eat in the open air
 ♦ eat in the open
 ♦ eat alfresco
im Freien lagern
 im Freien campen
 ♦ camp out
im Freien schlafen
 ♦ sleep outdoors
 ♦ sleep rough
 ♦ sleep out
im Freien speisen
 ♦ dine outdoors

im Freien übernachten 374

- dine in the open air
- dine in the open
- dine alfresco

im Freien übernachten
- sleep in the open
- sleep outdoors
- sleep under the open sky

im Freien zu Mittag essen
- lunch alfresco
- lunch in the open air
- lunch in the open

im Frühjahr
- in spring
- in the spring

im Haus, adv
- indoors, adv
- in the house, adv

im Haus bleiben
drinnen bleiben
- stay indoors

im Haus schlafen
zu Hause schlafen
- sleep in

im Haus wohnende Eigentümerin, f
- resident proprietress

im Haus wohnender Besitzer, m
- resident owner

im Haus wohnender Eigentümer, m
- resident proprietor

im Haus wohnender geschäftsführender Direktor, m
- resident managing director

im Haus wohnender Geschäftsführer, m
- resident manager

im Haus wohnender Lehrgangsteilnehmer, m
- resident student

im Haus wohnender Platzwart, m (z.B. Camping)
- resident warden

im Haus wohnender Portier, m
- resident porter

im Haus wohnendes Unterhaltungsteam, n
Hausunterhaltungsteam, n
- resident entertainment team

im Herbst
- in the fall AE
- in fall AE
- in autumn BE
- in the autumn BE

im Herzen der Stadt (Großstadt)
- in the heart of the city

im Herzen der Stadt (Kleinstadt)
- in the heart of the town

im Herzen von etw
- at the heart of s.th.

im Hintergrund
- in the background

im Hotel bleiben
- stay in the hotel

im Hotelfach arbeiten
- be in the hotel business

im Hotelfach tätig sein
- be working in the hotel business

im Hotelgewerbe arbeiten
- be in the hotel trade

im Hotel wohnen, (dauernd)
- live at a hotel
- live in a hotel

im Hotel wohnen, (vorübergehend)
im Hotel logieren

- stay at a hotel
- stay in a hotel

im Hungerstreik sein
- be on (a) hunger strike

im In- und Ausland
- at home and abroad

im Kasino spielen
- gamble in the casino
- gamble at the casino

im klassischen Stil
- in classical style

im Land bleiben
- remain in the country
- stay in the country

im Landhausstil
- in country-house style

im Land umherwandern
- ramble around the country
- ramble about the country
- ramble in the country

im Laufe des Nachmittags
- during the afternoon
- in the afternoon

im Laufe des Vormittags
- during the morning
- in the morning

im Leerlauf fahren (Auto)
im Freilauf fahren (Fahrrad)
- coast

im Libanon
- in Lebanon

im Lokal
im Haus
- on the premises

im März
- in March

immaterieller Firmenwert, m ökon
- goodwill ökon

immenses Frühstück, n
- immense breakfast

Immer mit der Ruhe! coll
- Hold your horses! AE coll

immer wieder kommen
- keep coming back

immer willkommen sein
jederzeit willkommen sein
- be always welcome

im Mietzinsbereich von $ 123 - 321 pro Woche
- in the rent range of $ 123 - 321 per week

im Mittelalter, adv
- in the Middle Ages, adv
- in medieval times, adv
- in the medieval period, adv

Immobilien, f pl jur
- immovables pl jur

Immobilien, f pl ökon
- real estate AE sg
- landed property BE sg
- property BE sg

Immobilienangebot, n (Palette)
- range of properties

Immobilienberater, m
- property consultant

Immobilienberatung, f
- property consultancy

Immobilienbesitz, m
- property ownership

Immobilienbesitzer, m
Hausbesitzer, m
- property owner

Immobilienboom, m
- property boom

Immobilienbüro, n
- real-estate agency AE
- estate agency BE

Immobiliendienst, m
Immobilienservice, m
- real-estate service AE
- property service BE

Immobilienerwerb, m
Immobilienkauf, m
- porperty purchase
- purchase of a property

Immobilienexperte, m
- real-estate expert AE
- property expert BE

Immobiliengeschäft, n
- real-estate business AE
- property business BE

Immobiliengesellschaft, f
- real-estate company AE
- property company BE

Immobiliengewerbe, n
- real-estate trade AE
- property trade BE

Immobilienhändler, m
→ Immobilienmakler

Immobilienkonzern, m
- real-estate group AE
- property group BE

Immobilienmagnat, m
- real-estate magnate AE
- property magnate BE

Immobilienmakler, m
Immobilienhändler, m
- real-estate agent AE
- real-estate broker AE
- realtor AE
- estate agent BE
- house agent BE

Immobilienmarkt, m
- real-estate market AE
- property market BE

Immobilienpreis, m
- real-estate price AE
- property price BE

Immobilienspekulant, m
- property speculator

Immobilien- und Wohnungsmakler, m (bei Firmenverlegungen)
- relocating agent

Immobilienunternehmer, m
- real-estate developer AE

Immobilienversicherung, f
- insurance of real estate

Immobilienverwaltung, f
- real-estate management AE
- property management BE

Immobilienverwaltungsgesellschaft, f
- real-estate management company BE
- property management company BE

Immobilienwert, m
- property value
- value of the property

Immobilie vermieten
- let a property BE
- rent out a property AE

im Nachbarzimmer, adv
- in the adjoining room, adv
- in the next room, adv

im Namen von jm
  namens jm
  ♦ on behalf of s.o.
im Norden liegen von etw
  ♦ be situated to the north of s.th.
  ♦ lie to the north of s.th.
im Norden von etw, adv
  ♦ to the north of s.th., adv
im Notfall
  ♦ in the case of (an) emergency
im Osten liegen von etw
  ♦ be situated to the east of s.th.
  ♦ lie to the east of s.th.
im Osten von etw, adv
  ♦ to the east of s.th., adv
im Paradies leben
  ♦ live in paradise
Impfaktion, f
  ♦ vaccination program AE
  ♦ vaccination programme BE
Impfbescheinigung, f
  ♦ vaccination certificate
  ♦ certificate of vaccination
  ♦ inoculation certificate
  ♦ certificate of inoculation
Impfbestimmungen, f pl
  ♦ inoculation regulations pl
  ♦ vaccination regulations pl
Impfdienst, m
  ♦ vaccination service
impfen jn gegen etw
  ♦ inoculate s.o. against s.th.
  ♦ vaccinate s.o. against s.th.
impfen lassen sich
  ♦ have a vaccination
  ♦ get a vaccination
  ♦ be vaccinated
impfen lassen sich gegen Typhus
  ♦ have a typhoid vaccination
Impfnachweis, m
  ♦ evidence of vaccination
  ♦ evidence of inoculation
Impfnachweis verlangen
  ♦ require evidence of vaccination
  ♦ require evidence of inoculation
Impfpaß, m
  ♦ vaccination card
Impfstoff, m
  ♦ vaccine
  ♦ serum
Impfung, f
  ♦ vaccination
  ♦ inoculation
  ♦ shot sl
Impfung gegen Cholera, f
  ♦ vaccination against cholera
Impfung gegen Gelbfieber, f
  ♦ vaccination against yellow fever
Impfung gegen Pocken, f
  ♦ vaccination against smallpox
  ♦ inoculation against smallpox
Impfung gegen Tetanus, f
  ♦ vaccination against tetanus
Impfung gegen Typhus, f
  ♦ vaccination against typhoid
Impfvorschriften, f pl
  ♦ inoculation requirements pl
  ♦ vaccination requirements pl
Impfzwang, m
  ♦ compulsory vaccination

Import, m
  Einfuhr, f
  ♦ import
Importlizenz, f
  Einfuhrlizenz, f
  ♦ import license
  ♦ import licence
Importzoll, m
  Einfuhrzoll, m
  ♦ import duty
Im Preis enthalten sind ...
  ♦ The price includes ...
im Preis ist alles inbegriffen
  ♦ price includes everything
  ♦ price is inclusive of everything
im Privatquartier wohnen (dauernd)
  ♦ live in private accommodation
im Privatquartier wohnen (vorübergehend)
  im Privatquartier logieren
  ♦ stay in private accommodation
im Programm haben
  im Programm sein
  ♦ be on the program AE
  ♦ be on the programme BE
Improvisation, f (aus Gedächtnis)
  (z.B. Rede)
  ♦ extemporisation
  ♦ extemporization
  ♦ extemporising
  ♦ extemporizing
Improvisation, f (generell)
  ♦ improvisation
  ♦ improvising
improvisieren etw
  ♦ improvise s.th.
improvisieren etw aus Zeitmangel
  ♦ improvise s.th. for lack of time
improvisieren etw hastig
  hastig improvisieren etw
  ♦ improvise s.th. hastily
improvisieren etw schnell
  schnell improvisieren etw
  ♦ improvise s.th. quickly
improvisiert, adj
  ♦ improvised, adj
improvisierter Ausflug, m
  ♦ improvised excursion
  ♦ improvised trip
  ♦ improvised outing
improvisierte Rede, f
  improvisierte Ansprache f
  ♦ improvised speech
improvisiertes Bett, n
  ♦ improvised bed
improvisiertes Essen, n
  ♦ improvised meal
improvisiertes Programm, n
  ♦ improvised program AE
  ♦ improvised programme BE
im Quartier liegen bei jm (Militär)
  ♦ be billeted (up)on s.o. mil
  ♦ be quartered (up)on s.o. mil
im Quartier liegen in X (Militär)
  ♦ be quartered at X
  ♦ be quartered in X
im Rahmen der Ausstellung zeigen etw
  ♦ exhibition includes s.th.
im Rahmen eines Festes
  im Verlauf eines Festes
  ♦ in the course of a celebration

im Reisepreis enthalten
  ♦ included in the tour price
im Rokokostil
  ♦ in rococo style
  ♦ in the rococo style
im siebten Himmel sein
  ♦ be in one's seventh heaven
im Skiurlaub sein
  Skiurlaub machen
  ♦ be on a ski(ing) vacation AE
  ♦ be on a ski(ing) holiday BE
im Sommer, adv
  ♦ in summer, adv
  ♦ in the summer, adv
im Stil der Zeit
  ♦ in the style of the period
  ♦ in period style
im Streik sein
  → streiken
im Stundentakt
  ♦ at hourly intervals
im Süden liegen von etw
  ♦ be situated to the south of s.th.
  ♦ lie to the south of s.th.
im Süden von etw, adv
  ♦ to the south of s.th., adv
im Turnus
  ♦ in rotation
  ♦ in turns
  ♦ by turns
im Urlaub (beurlaubt)
  ♦ on leave
im Urlaub etw tun
  ♦ do s.th. on one's vacation AE
  ♦ do s.th. on one's holiday BE
im Urlaub (Ferien)
  ♦ on vacation AE
  ♦ on holiday BE
im Urlaub fühlen sich
  sich in (den) Ferien fühlen
  ♦ feel on vacation AE
  ♦ feel on holiday BE
im Urlaub sein (Arbeitnehmer)
  ♦ be on leave
im Urlaub sein (Ferien)
  in Ferien sein
  ♦ be on vacation AE
  ♦ be on holiday BE
im Urlaub sein für einen Monat
  in Ferien sein für einen Monat
  ♦ be on vacation for a month AE
  ♦ be on holiday for a month BE
im Verlauf der Reise
  während der Reise
  ♦ in the course of the tour
  ♦ during the tour
im Verlauf des Aufenthalts
  ♦ in the course of the stay
  ♦ during the course of the stay
im vierten Vierteljahr
  ♦ in the fourth quarter
im voraus bezahlt, adj
  im voraus gezahlt, adj
  vorbezahlt, adj
  ♦ paid in advance, adj
  ♦ prepaid, adj
im voraus buchbar, adj
  vorausbuchbar, adj
  ♦ bookable in advance, adj
  ♦ prebookable, adj

im voraus buchen   376

im voraus buchen
  vorbestellen
  vorbuchen
  ♦ book ahead
  ♦ book in advance
  ♦ prebook s.th.
im voraus etw zuteilen jm
  im voraus etw zuweisen jm
  im voraus etw verteilen an jn
  ♦ pre-allocate s.th. to s.o.
  ♦ earmark s.th. for s.o.
im voraus stornieren etw
  vorher absagen etw
  vorher zurücktreten von etw
  ♦ precancel s.th.
  ♦ cancel s.th. in advance
im voraus zubereiten etw
  im voraus richten etw
  ♦ pre-prepare s.th.
im Vordergrund, adv
  ♦ in the foreground, adv
Im Wein ist Wahrheit
  ♦ In wine is truth
im Wert von DM 123
  ♦ to the value of DM 123
im Westen liegen von etw
  ♦ be situated to the west of s.th.
  ♦ lie to the west of s.th.
im Westen von etw, adv
  ♦ to the west of s.th., adv
im Winter
  ♦ in winter
  ♦ in the winter
im zeitgenössischen Stil möbliert, adj
  ♦ contemporarily furnished, adj
im Zelt schlafen
  ♦ sleep in a tent
  ♦ sleep under canvas
im Zimmer
  auf dem Zimmer
  ♦ in the room
im Zimmer nebenan
  ♦ in the next room
im Zug
  ♦ on the train
im zweiten Vierteljahr
  ♦ in the second quarter
In achtzig Tagen um die Welt
  (Roman von Jules Verne)
  ♦ Around the World in Eighty Days
inakzeptabel, adj
  ♦ unacceptable, adj
inakzeptabel sein
  ♦ be unacceptable
in allen Altersgruppen
  ♦ in all age groups
in allen Preislagen
  ♦ in every price range
in aller Frühe
  ♦ very early in the morning
in alphabetischer Reihenfolge
  ♦ in alphabetical order
in angenehmer Umgebung
  ♦ in pleasant surroundings
in angenehmer Wohnlage
  ♦ in a pleasant residential location
in anmutiger Umgebung
  ♦ in gracious surroundings
in Anspruch genommene Leistung, f
  ♦ service used
  utilised service

Inanspruchnahme, f
  ♦ utilisation
  utilization
  ♦ use
  utilising s.th.
  using s.th.
Inanspruchnahme der vertraglichen Leistungen, f
  ♦ use of the services stated in the contract
  utilisation of the services stated in the contract
  utilization of the services stated in the contract
Inanspruchnahme einer Leistung, f
  Leistungsinanspruchnahme, f
  ♦ utilisation of a service
  utilization of a service
  use of a service
Inanspruchnahme einer Unterkunft, f
  ♦ utilisation of accommodation
  utilization of accommodation
  use of accommodation
Inanspruchnahme eines Zimmers, f
  ♦ utilisation of a room
  utilization of a room
  utilising a room
  use of a room
  using a room
Inanspruchnahme von etw, f
  Nutzung von etw, f
  ♦ utilisation of s.th.
  utilization of s.th.
  utilising s.th.
  using s.th.
  use of s.th.
Inanspruchnahme von Raum, f
  ♦ occupancy of space
in Arenaform
  (Bestuhlung)
  ♦ in arena style
in Bahnhofsnähe
  ♦ close to the station
  ♦ near the station
in Bankettform
  (Bestuhlung)
  ♦ in banquet style
in Begleitung von Freunden
  in Gesellschaft von Freunden
  ♦ in the company of friends
inbegriffen im Preis
  im Preis enthalten
  ♦ included in the price
in Betrieb befindliches Hotel, n
  ♦ operating hotel
in Betrieb bleiben
  ♦ remain in operation
in Betrieb haben etw
  ♦ have s.th. in operation
Inbetriebnahme, f (Eröffnung)
  ♦ opening
  beginning of work
Inbetriebnahme, f (generell)
  Inbetriebsetzung, f
  ♦ setting in operation
  setting in action
  putting in(to) operation
  beginning to run
in Betrieb sein
  ♦ be in operation
in betrunkenem Zustand
  ♦ in a state of intoxication
in bewohnbarem Zustand
  ♦ in habitable repair

in Bildern
  ♦ in pictures
in Blockschrift schreiben
  ♦ write in capital letters
in Brand stecken etw
  ♦ set s.th. on fire
in Butter coll
  in Ordnung
  ♦ in apple-pie order coll
Incentive, m
  Leistungsanreiz, m
  Anreiz, m
  Leistungsprämie, f
  ♦ incentive
Incentivebereich, m
  Incentivesektor, m
  ♦ incentive sector
Incentivebüro, n
  ♦ incentive bureau
Incentivefahrt, f
  ♦ incentive trip
Incentivegruppe, f
  ♦ incentive group
Incentivemarkt, m
  ♦ incentive market
Incentiveprofi, m
  ♦ incentive professional
  incentive specialist
Incentiveprogramm, n
  ♦ incentive program AE
  ♦ incentive programme BE
Incentivereise, f
  ♦ incentive tour
  ♦ incentive trip
Incentivereisen, n
  Incentivereiseverkehr, m
  ♦ incentive travel
Incentivereiseveranstalter, m
  ♦ incentive tour operator
Incentivespezialist, m
  ♦ incentive specialist
Incentivetour, f
  → Incentivereise
Incentivetourismus, m
  ♦ incentive tourism
Incentivetourist, m
  Teilnehmer an einer Incentivereise, m
  ♦ incentive tourist
Incentiveurlaub, m
  ♦ incentive vacation AE
  ♦ incentive holiday BE
Incentiveverkehr, m
  ♦ incentive traffic
Incentiveziel, m
  Incentivezielort, n
  ♦ incentive destination
Incoming, n
  (vom Ausland in das Inland)
  ♦ incoming
Incoming-Agent, m
  ♦ incoming agent
Incoming-Agentur, f
  ♦ incoming agency
Incoming-Aktivität, f
  ♦ incoming activity
Incoming-Büro, n
  ♦ incoming office
Incoming-Forum, n
  ♦ incoming forum
Incoming-Geschäft, n
  ♦ incoming business

Incoming-Markt, m
- ◆ incoming market

Incoming-Partner, m
- ◆ incoming partner

Incoming-Reiseveranstalter, m
- ◆ incoming tour operator

Incoming-Tochtergesellschaft, f
- ◆ incoming subsidiary

Incoming-Tourismus, m
Tourismus aus dem Ausland, m
- ◆ incoming tourism
- ◆ inbound tourism

Incoming-Tourist, m
- ◆ incoming tourist

Incoming-Veranstalter, m
- ◆ incoming operator

Incoming-Workshop, m
- ◆ incoming workshop

in das Haus wurde eingebrochen
- ◆ house was burglarized AE
- ◆ house was burgled BE

in dem Bus, adv
im Bus, adv
- ◆ on the coach, adv BE
- ◆ on the bus, adv

In dem Zimmer kann für 20 Personen gedeckt werden
- ◆ This room dines 20 persons

in den Außenbezirken (eines Ortes)
- ◆ on the outskirts

in den nächsten Tagen
- ◆ during the next few days
- ◆ in the next few days

in den Schlaf singen jn
- ◆ sing s.o. to sleep
- ◆ lull s.o. to sleep

in den Tropen
- ◆ in the tropics

Inder, m
- ◆ Indian

in der besten englischen Tradition
- ◆ in the best English tradition

in der falschen Richtung
- ◆ in the wrong direction

in der ganzen Welt
- ◆ all over the world
- ◆ throughout the world

in der Hauptrolle
- ◆ in the leading role

in der Hochsaison
- ◆ in the high season
- ◆ in high season

Inderin, f
- ◆ Indian girl
- ◆ Indian woman
- ◆ Indian

in der kommenden Saison
- ◆ in the coming season
- ◆ in the upcoming season

in der kommenden Wintersaison
- ◆ in the coming winter season

in der Mansarde wohnen (dauernd)
- ◆ live in the attic
- ◆ live in the garret

in der Mansarde wohnen (vorübergehend)
in der Mansarde logieren
- ◆ stay in the attic
- ◆ stay in the garret

in der Mittagspause
- ◆ at the luncheon interval

- ◆ at the lunch interval
- ◆ at lunchtime

in der mittleren Preisklasse
- ◆ in the medium price range
- ◆ in the medium price bracket

in der Nachbarschaft (von X)
- ◆ in the neighborhood (of X) AE
- ◆ in the neighbourhood (of X) BE

in der Nacht von Montag auf Dienstag
- ◆ during the night from Monday to Tuesday

in der Nähe
- ◆ in the vicinity
- ◆ nearby

in der Nähe sein
- ◆ be close by
- ◆ be near by

in der Nähe von etw
- ◆ close to s.th.
- ◆ in the vicinity of s.th.

in der Nebensaison
- ◆ in the off-season

in der oberen Preisklasse
- ◆ in the top price range
- ◆ in the top price bracket

in der Osterwoche
- ◆ in the Easter week

in der Planung befindliches Hotel, n
- ◆ projected hotel

in der Provence
- ◆ in Provence

in der Renaissance
- ◆ in Renaissance times

in der Saison
- ◆ in the season
- ◆ in season
- ◆ during the season

in der Saisonmitte
- ◆ in mid-season
- ◆ at mid-season

in der Sauregurkenzeit coll
in der schlechten Geschäftszeit
- ◆ in the slack season
- ◆ in the dull season
- ◆ in the dead season

in der Sonne liegen
- ◆ lie in the sun

in der Sonne sitzen
- ◆ sit in the sun

in der Spitzenzeit
- ◆ in peak time

in der Teepause
zur Teepause
- ◆ at tea-break

in der Umgebung
- ◆ in the surrounding area
- ◆ in the surroundings

in der unteren Preisklasse
- ◆ in the bottom price range
- ◆ in the bottom price bracket

in der Urlaubssaison
in der Urlaubszeit
in der Feriensaison
in der Ferienzeit
- ◆ in the vacation season AE
- ◆ in the holiday season BE

in der zweiten Reihe parken
- ◆ double-park

in der Zwischensaison
- ◆ in the shoulder season
- ◆ between the seasons
- ◆ between seasons

Indianer, m
- ◆ Red Indian
- ◆ Indian

Indianerland, n
Indianergebiet, n
- ◆ Indian country

Indianerreservat, n
- ◆ Indian reservation

Indianertanz, m
- ◆ Indian dance

Indianerzelt, n
→ Wigwam

in die Berge fahren
- ◆ go to the mountains

in die Falle gehen sl
(zu Bett gehen)
- ◆ hit the sack sl

Indien
- ◆ India

in Dienst gehen
- ◆ enter service

in Dienst sein
- ◆ be in service

in die Oper gehen
- ◆ go to the opera

in die Sauna gehen
- ◆ go to the sauna

in diesem Haus spukt es
- ◆ this house is haunted

In diesem Hotel herrscht eine freundliche Atmosphäre
- ◆ There is a friendly atmosphere at this hotel

in diesem Teil von Italien
- ◆ in this part of Italy

in diesem Zimmer spukt es
- ◆ this room is haunted

in die Wanne steigen
in die Badewanne steigen
- ◆ get into the bath

in die Wohnung wurde eingebrochen
- ◆ apartment was burglarized AE
- ◆ flat was burgled BE

Indikation, f
Heilanzeige, f
- ◆ indication

indirekte Aufwendungen, f pl
- ◆ indirect expenses pl

indirekte Beleuchtung, f
- ◆ indirect lighting

indirekte Buchung, f
- ◆ indirect booking

indirekte Kosten, pl
- ◆ indirect costs pl
- ◆ indirect cost

indirekter Bucher, m
- ◆ indirect booker

indirekte Steuern, f pl
- ◆ indirect taxes pl

indisch, adj
- ◆ Indian, adj

indische Art, adv gastr
nach indischer Art, adv gastr
- ◆ Indian style, adv gastr

Indischer Ozean, m
- ◆ Indian Ocean, the

indisches Feldbett, n
- ◆ charpoy

indisches Restaurant, n
- ◆ Indian restaurant

indiskret, adj
- ◆ indiscreet, adj

Indiskretion, f
- indiscretion
- indiscreetness

Indiskretion begehen
- commit an indiscretion

indiskret sein
- be indiscreet

Individualgast, m
  Einzelgast, m
  einzelner Gast, m
- individual guest

Individualhotel, n
- individual hotel
- independent hotel

Individualist, m
  Individualistin f
- individualist

Individualität, f
- individuality

Individualpreis, m
  → Einzelpreis

Individualreise, f
  (Gegensatz zu Pauschalreise)
- individual tour
- individual trip
- individual journey
- independent tour

Individualreisen, n
  Individualreiseverkehr, m
- individual travel

Individualreisender, m
  Individualreisende, f
- individual traveler AE
- individual traveller BE
- single traveler AE
- single traveller BE

Individualtarif, m
  (Gegensatz zu Gruppentarif)
- individual tariff
- individual rates pl
- individual rate
- individual terms pl

Individualtourismus, m
- individual tourism

Individualtourist, m
- individual tourist

individuell, adj
- individual, adj

individuelle Bedürfnisse erfüllen
- meet individual requirements

individuelle Behandlung, f
  Einzelbehandlung, f
- individual treatment

individuelle Betreuung, f
  Einzelbetreuung, f
- individual attention
- individual care

individuelle Betreuung eines Gasts, f
- individual attention to a guest

individuelle Betreuung zusichern jm
- guarantee s.o. individual attention

individueller Geschmack, m
- personal taste

individueller Gymnastikzeitplan, m
- individual exercise schedule

individueller Service m
- individual service

individuelles Bedürfnis, n
- individual requirement
- individual need

individuelle Wünsche angeben
- indicate one's individual requirements
- state one's individual requirements

individuell gestalteter Urlaub, m
  individuell geplanter Urlaub, m
- individually designed vacation AE
- individually designed holiday BE

individuell gestaltetes Programm, n
- individually designed program AE
- individually designed programme BE

individuell regulierbare Klimaanlage, f
- individually controlled air conditioning AE
- individually controlled air-conditioning BE
- individually controlled air-conditioner

Indonesien
- Indonesia

Indonesier, m
- Indonesian

Indonesierin, f
- Indonesian girl
- Indonesian woman
- Indonesian

indonesisch, adj
- Indonesian, adj

Industriearchäologie, f
- industrial archaeology
- industrial archeology

Industrieausstellung, f
- industrial exhibition
- industrial exhibit AE

Industrieerbe, n
- industrial heritage

Industrieerbepark, m
- industrial heritage park

Industrieerfahrung, f
  Industriepraxis, f
- industrial practice

Industriehafen, m
- industrial port

Industriekantine, f
  Werkskantine, f
- industrial canteen

Industrielandschaft, f
- industrial landscape

Industriemesse, f
- industrial fair
- industries fair

Industriemuseum, n
- industrial museum

Industriestadt, f (Großstadt)
- industrial city

Industriestadt, f (kleine Stadt)
- industrial town

Industrie- und Handelskammer, f
  IHK, f
- Chamber of Industry and Commerce, the
- CIC, the

ineinandergehende Hallen, f pl
- interconnecting halls pl
- connecting halls pl

ineinandergehende Zimmer, n pl
- interconnecting rooms pl
- connecting rooms pl

in eine Bar gehen
  zu einer Bar gehen
- go to a bar

in einem ansprechenden Rahmen
- in a congenial setting

in einem engen Zimmer wohnen (vorübergehend)
- stay in a cramped room

in einem entspannten Rahmen
- in a relaxed setting

in einem Gasthof logieren
  in einem Gasthof wohnen
- stay at an inn

in einem Haus wohnen (dauernd)
- live in a house

in einem Haus wohnen (vorübergehend)
- stay at a house
- stay in a house

in einem Hotel leben
  in einem Hotel permanent wohnen
  in einem Hotel dauernd wohnen
- live in a hotel

in einem Hotel logieren
  → in einem Hotel wohnen

in einem ländlichen Rahmen
  in einer ländlichen Umgebung
- in a rural setting

in einem Privathaus logieren
- stay in a private house

in einem Restaurant essen
- eat at a restaurant
- eat in a restaurant

in einem sauberen und aufgeräumten Zustand
  (Zimmer)
- in a clean and tidy condition

in einem Schluck
  in einem Zug
- in one gulp
- at a gulp
- at one draft AE
- at one draught BE

in einer Besprechung sein (mit jm)
- be in conference (with s.o.)

in einer Farbzusammenstellung gehalten sein
- be decorated in a (certain) color scheme AE
- be decorated in a (certain) colour scheme BE

in einer Höhe von 2000 Metern
- at an altitude of 2000 meters AE
- at an altitude of 2000 metres BE

in einer idyllischen Umgebung
  in einer idyllischen Lage
- in an idyllic setting

in einer Jugendherberge wohnen
  (vorübergehend)
- stay at a youth hostel
- stay in a youth hostel

in einer malerischen Umgebung
  in einem malerischen Rahmen
- in a picturesque setting
- in picturesque surroundings

in einer Pizzeria essen
- eat in a pizza parlor AE
- eat in a pizza parlour BE
- eat in a pizzeria

in einer romantischen Umgebung
- romantic surroundings
- in a romantic setting

in einer Schlange stehen
- stand in a queue

in einer schönen Landschaft
- in a beautiful scenery

in einer Tischzeit
- at one sitting

in ein Hotel bringen jn
- take s.o. to a hotel

in ein Hotel gehen
  zu einem Hotel gehen
- go to a hotel

in eleganter Umgebung
- ♦ in elegant surroundings
in Empfang nehmen jn
- treffen jn
- abholen jn
- ♦ meet s.o.
in Empfang nehmen jn am Bahnhof
- → abholen jn am Bahnhof
in England bleiben
- ♦ stay in England
in entgegengesetzter Richtung
- ♦ in the opposite direction
in Erwartung Ihrer Antwort
  (Brief)
- ♦ looking forward to your reply
- ♦ awaiting your reply
in Fahrtweite
- mit dem Auto erreichbar
- ♦ within driving distance
in Fahrtweite sein
- mit dem Auto erreichbar sein
- ♦ be within driving distance
in Farbe, adv
- ♦ in color, adv AE
- ♦ in colour, adv BE
Infektionskrankheit, f
- ♦ infectious disease
in Ferien fahren
- in die Ferien fahren
- ♦ go on holiday BE
- ♦ go on vacation AE
in Ferien sein (in X)
- in den Ferien sein (in X)
- ♦ be on holiday (in X) BE
- ♦ be on vacation (in X) AE
in Ferienstimmung
  (Person)
- in Urlaubsstimmung
- ♦ in a holiday mood BE
- ♦ in a vacation mood AE
in Feststimmung
  (Person)
- ♦ in a festive mood
in Feststimmung sein
  (Person)
- festlich gestimmt sein
- ♦ be in a festive mood
inflationsbereinigt, adj
- ♦ inflation-adjusted, adj
Inflationsrate, f
- Preissteigerungsrate, f
- Teuerungsrate, f
- ♦ inflation rate
- ♦ rate of inflation
Infodienst, m
- Infoservice, m
- ♦ info service
Infopaket, n
- Informationspaket, n
- ♦ info pack
- ♦ info kit AE
- ♦ information pack
- ♦ information kit AE
Inforeise, f (Reisebüro)
- Informationsreise, f
- ♦ fam trip
- ♦ familiarisation trip
Information, f (Auskunft)
- Auskunft, f
- i

- ♦ information sg
- ♦ i
Information, f (Schalter)
- → Informationsschalter
Informationen austauschen
- ♦ exchange information
Informationen bieten
- Informationen geben
- ♦ provide information
- ♦ give information
Informationen erhalten über etw
- Auskünfte erhalten über etw
- ♦ receive information about s.th.
- ♦ receive information on s.th.
- ♦ obtain information about s.th.
- ♦ obtain information on s.th.
Informationen geben über etw
- Informationen geben zu etw
- ♦ give information about s.th.
- ♦ give information on s.th.
Informationen in mehreren Sprachen, f pl
- ♦ information in several languages
Informationsabend, m
- ♦ evening briefing
Informationsabteilung, f
- ♦ information department
Informationsanbieter, m
- ♦ information provider
Informationsanfrage, f
- ♦ inquiry for information
- ♦ enquiry for information
Informationsanfrage richten an jn
- ♦ address an inquiry for information to s.o.
- ♦ address an enquiry for information to s.o.
Informationsangebot, n
- ♦ availability of information
Informationsangestellter, m
- Informationsangestellte, f
- ♦ inquiry clerk
- ♦ enquiry clerk
Informationsaustausch, m
- ♦ exchange of information
Informationsbesprechung, f (für Mitarbeiter)
- Informationssitzung f
- ♦ briefing meeting
- ♦ briefing conference
Informationsbesuch, m (generell)
- ♦ fact-finding visit
Informationsbesuch, m (Reisebüro)
- ♦ familiarisation visit
- ♦ fam visit coll
Informationsblatt, n
- ♦ information sheet
- ♦ information leaflet
- ♦ sheet giving information
- ♦ leaflet giving information
Informationsbrett, n
- → Informationstafel
Informationsbroschüre, f
- ♦ brochure of information
- ♦ brochure giving information on s.th.
- ♦ brochure giving information about s.th.
- ♦ informative brochure
Informationsbüro, n
- ♦ information bureau
- ♦ information office
- ♦ inquiry office
- ♦ enquiry office
Informationscoupon, m
- Informationsscheck m
- ♦ information coupon

Informationsdienst, m
- Informationsservice, m
- Information, f
- Nachweis, m
- ♦ information service
Informationseinrichtung, f
- ♦ information facility
Informationsfahrt, f
- ♦ fact-finding trip
Informationsfaltblatt, n
- Informationsblatt, n
- ♦ information leaflet
- ♦ leaflet giving information
Informationsführer, m
- ♦ information guide
Informationsgespräch, n
  (über ein Projekt)
- ♦ briefing
- ♦ giving information
Informationsgutschein m
- ♦ information voucher
Informationshandbuch, n
- Info-Handbuch n
- ♦ information manual
Informationshosteß, f
- ♦ information hostess
- ♦ hostess giving information
Informationskiosk, m
- ♦ information kiosk
Informationskraft, f
- Informationsangestellter m
- Informationsangestellte f
- ♦ information clerk
Informationsliteratur, f
- ♦ informative literature
Informationsmangel, m (Knappheit)
- ♦ shortage of information
Informationsmangel, m (völliges Fehlen)
- ♦ lack of information
Informationsmappe, f
- ♦ information folder
- ♦ information kit
- ♦ information pack
Informationsmaterial, n
- ♦ information sg
- ♦ informative literature
Informationsmaterial anfordern über etw bei jm
  (per Telefon)
- ♦ phone s.o. for information about s.th.
- ♦ phone s.o. for information on s.th.
Informationsmaterial anfordern über etw bei jm
  (schriftlich)
- ♦ write to s.o. for information about s.th.
- ♦ write to s.o. for information on s.th.
Informationsmaterial anfordern über etw (Brief)
- ♦ write for information about s.th.
- ♦ write for information on s.th.
Informationsmaterial anfordern über etw
  (Telefon)
- ♦ phone for information about s.th.
- ♦ phone for information on s.th.
Informationsmaterial verteilen
- ♦ distribute informative literature
Informationsmesse, f
- ♦ information fair
Informationspaket, n
- Infopaket, n
- ♦ information pack
- ♦ pack of information
- ♦ information kit AE

Informationspavillon

- ♦ packet of information *AE*
- ♦ info pack

Informationspavillon, m
- ♦ information pavilion

Informationsprogramm, n
- ♦ information program *AE*
- ♦ information programme *BE*

Informationsprospekt, m
- Informationsbrochüre, f
- ♦ information brochure
- ♦ informative brochure

Informationspunkt, m
- Informationsstelle, f
- ♦ information point

Informationsquelle, f
- ♦ information source
- ♦ source of information

Informationsreise, f (generell)
- ♦ fact-finding journey
- ♦ fact-finding trip
- ♦ fact-finding tour

Informationsreise, f (Reisebüro)
- ♦ familiarisation tour
- ♦ familiarization tour
- ♦ fam tour
- ♦ fam trip
- ♦ fam

Informationsrücklauf, m
- ♦ debriefing

Informationsschalter, m
- ♦ information desk
- ♦ information counter
- ♦ inquiry desk
- ♦ enquiry desk

Informationsscheck, m
- → Informationscoupon

Informationsschrift, f
- ♦ information booklet

Informationsschrift mit dem Titel X
- ♦ information booklet entitled X

Informationsstand, m
- Infostand m
- ♦ information stand
- ♦ info stand

Informationsstelle, f
- Informationsbüro, n
- ♦ information office
- ♦ information bureau
- ♦ inquiry office
- ♦ enquiry office

Informationssystem, n
- ♦ information system

Informationstafel, f
- Informationsbrett n
- ♦ information board
- ♦ bulletin board *AE*

Informationstechnologie, f
- ♦ information technology

Informationstour, f
- → Informationsreise

Informationstreffen, n
- ♦ information meeting

Informations- und Kommunikationssystem, n
- ♦ information and communications system

Informations- und Kommunikationstechnologie, f
- ♦ information and communications technology

Informations- und Reservierungssystem, n
- ♦ information and reservations system
- ♦ information and reservation system

Informations- und Vertriebssystem, n
- ♦ information and distribution system

Informationsveranstaltung, f (für Mitarbeiter)
- ♦ briefing conference
- ♦ briefing meeting

Informationszentrale, f
- Informationszentrum n
- ♦ information center *AE*
- ♦ information centre *BE*
- ♦ central office of information

Informationszentrum, n
- → Informationszentrale

Informationszentrum einrichten
- ♦ establish an information center *AE*
- ♦ establish an information centre *BE*

Information über die Reise, f
- *(Instruktion)*
- ♦ tour briefing

Information über ein Hotel, f
- Informationen über ein Hotel, f pl
- ♦ information about a hotel
- ♦ information on a hotel

Information über etw, f
- Informationen über etw, f pl
- ♦ information about s.th.
- ♦ information on s.th.

informativ, adj
- ♦ informative, adj

informativer Führer, m
- ♦ informative guide

informativer Prospekt, m
- ♦ informative brochure

informell, adj
- ♦ informal, adj

informieren jn über etw
- ♦ inform s.o. about s.th.
- ♦ inform s.o. on s.th.

informieren sich über etw
- erkundigen sich über etw
- ♦ make enquiries about s.th.
- ♦ make inquiries about s.th.
- ♦ inquire about s.th.
- ♦ enquire about s.th.

in Form sein
- ♦ be in shape

Infostand, m
- Informationsstand, m
- ♦ info stand
- ♦ information stand

in Frage kommen für eine Ermäßigung
- berechtigt sein zu einer Ermäßigung
- ermäßigungsberechtigt sein
- ♦ be eligible for a reduction

in Frage stellen etw
- ♦ query s.th.
- ♦ call s.th. in question

Infrarotbehandlung, f
- ♦ infrared treatment *AE*
- ♦ infra-red treatment *BE*

Infrarotstrahler, m
- ♦ infrared heater *AE*
- ♦ infra-red heater *BE*

Infrarottherapie, f
- ♦ infrared therapy *AE*
- ♦ infra-red therapy *BE*

Infrarotübertragung, f
- Infrarotlichtübertragung, f
- ♦ infrared transmission *AE*
- ♦ infra-red transmission *BE*

Infrarotübertragungsanlage, f
- ♦ infrared transmission system *AE*
- ♦ infra-red transmission system *BE*

Infrastruktur, f
- ♦ infrastructure

Infrastrukturprogramm, n
- ♦ infrastructure program *AE*
- ♦ infrastructure programme *BE*

Infrastrukturprojekt, n
- ♦ infrastructure project

in freundlicher Umgebung
- ♦ in friendly surroundings

in fröhlicher Runde
- ♦ in a merry circle of friends
- ♦ in merry company

in fröhlicher Runde beisammensitzen
- ♦ sit in a merry circle of friends
- ♦ sit in merry company

in ganz Europa
- ♦ in the whole of Europe
- ♦ all over Europe

in ganz Frankreich
- ♦ in the whole of France
- ♦ all over France

in Gebrauch
- ♦ in use

in Gebrauch sein
- ♦ be in use

in gelockerter Stimmung
- ♦ in a relaxed mood

in gemütlicher Umgebung
- ♦ in cosy surroundings
- ♦ in cozy surroundings *AE*

in geringer Zahl
- ♦ in small numbers

in Gesellschaft von jm
- in Begleitung von jm
- ♦ in s.o.'s company
- ♦ in company with s.o.
- ♦ in company of s.o.

in glänzender Stimmung
- in glänzender Laune
- ♦ in high spirits

in großer Zahl
- ♦ in large numbers

in günstiger Lage
- ♦ in a convenient location
- ♦ in a convenient situation
- ♦ in a convenient position

in gutem baulichen Zustand
- ♦ in good repair

in gutem Zustand
- ♦ in good condition
- ♦ in good shape
- ♦ in good repair

in guten Händen sein
- ♦ be in good hands

in guter Gesellschaft sein
- ♦ be in good company

in guter Laune
- bei guter Laune
- ♦ in a good mood

Ingwer, m
- ♦ ginger

Inhaber, m (Bewohner)
- ♦ occupant
- ♦ possessor

Inhaber, m (Eigentümer)
- → Eigentümer

Inhaber, m (eines Dokuments)
- ♦ holder

Inhaber, m (juristisch)
- ♦ tenant

Inhaber eines Gasthofs, m (Eigentümer)
- proprietor of an inn
- owner of an inn

Inhaber eines Hauses, m (Bewohner)
Hausbewohner, m
- occupier of a house
- occupant of a house

Inhaber eines Hotels, m (Eigentümer)
- proprietor of a hotel
- owner of a hotel

Inhaber eines Zimmers, m (Bewohner)
→ Zimmerinhaber

Inhaberin, f (Eigentümerin)
→ Eigentümerin

Inhaberin eines Gasthofs, f (Eigentümerin)
- proprietress of an inn

Inhaberin eines Hotels, f (Eigentümerin)
→ Hoteleigentümerin

Inhalation, f
- inhalation

Inhalationskur, f
- inhalation cure

Inhalationstherapie, f
- inhalation therapy

inhalieren etw
einatmen etw
- inhale s.th.

Inhalt einer Flasche, m
Flascheninhalt, m
- contents of a bottle pl

in Harmonie mit der Umwelt
- in harmony with the environment

in herrlicher Umgebung
- in superb surroundings
- in a superb setting

in Höhe von DM 123
- at a level of DM 123
- of DM 123

in Hörweite
- within hearing distance

in hübscher Umgebung
- in lovely surroundings

in Hufeisenform
(Bestuhlung)
- in horseshoe style
- in horseshoe shape

in Hungerstreik treten
- go on (a) hunger strike

in Hütten wohnen
(dauernd)
- live in huts

Injektion, f
- injection

in js Ermessen
- within s.o.'s discretion
- at s.o.'s discretion

Inka, m
- Inca

Inkakultur, f
- Inca civilisation
- Inca civilization

Inkareich, n
- Inca Empire, the

Inkassoaufwand, m
- collection expense

Inkassogebühr, f
- collection charge
- collection fee

in keltischer Zeit
- in Celtic times

in Kenntnis setzen jn von etw
- notify s.o. of s.th.

in Kenntnis setzen jn von seiner beabsichtigten Abreise
- inform s.o. of one's intended departure

inkl., prep
inklusive, prep
einschließlich, prep
- incl., prep
- inc., prep
- inclusive, prep
- including, prep

in Klassenzimmerform
(Bestuhlung)
in Tischform
- in classroom style
- in schoolroom style

Inklusivarrangement n
Inklusivvereinbarung f
- inclusive arrangement
- package arrangement

inklusive, prep
inkl., prep
einschließlich, prep
- incl., prep
- including, prep
- inclusive, prep
- inc., prep

inklusive aller Eintrittsgebühren
einschließlich aller Eintrittsgebühren
- including all admissions
- including all entrance fees

inklusive etw
inclusive von etw
- inclusive of s.th.
- including s.th.

inklusive Getränke
einschließlich Getränke
- including drinks
- including beverages
- inclusive of drinks
- inclusive of beverages

inklusive von etw
inklusive etw
- including s.th.
- inclusive of s.th.

Inklusivgebühr, f
Pauschalgebühr, f
- inclusive fee
- inclusive charge

Inklusivmiete, f
- inclusive rent

Inklusivpreis, m
Pauschalpreis, m
- inclusive price
- inclusive rate

Inklusivpreise, m pl
Pauschalpreise, m pl
- inclusive terms pl
- inclusive prices pl
- inclusive rates pl

Inklusivpreis pro Person, m
- inclusive price per person
- inclusive rate per person

inkognito, adv
- incognito, adv

Inkognito, n
- incognito

Inkognitobesuch, m
- incognito visit

inkognito besuchen etw
- pay an incognito visit to s.th.

inkognito in einem Hotel logieren
- stay incognito at a hotel
- stay incognito in a hotel

inkognito logieren
inkognito wohnen
- stay incognito

Inkognito preisgeben
Inkognito lüften
- reveal one's identity

inkognito reisen
- travel incognito

inkognito sein
- be incognito

inkognito übernachten
- overnight incognito AE
- spend the night incognito
- stay the night incognito

Inkognito wahren
- preserve one's incognito
- preserve one's anonymity

inkognito wohnen in einem Hotel
inkognito logieren in einem Hotel
- stay at a hotel incognito
- stay in a hotel incognito

inkommodieren jn obs
belästigen jn
- bother s.o.
- trouble s.o.
- inconvenience s.o.

inkompetent, adj
- incompetent, adj

inkompetenter Service, m
- incompetent service

inkompetentes Personal, n
- incompetent staff
- incompetent personnel

in Konferenzform
(Bestuhlung)
- in conference form

in Konkurrenz stehen mit etw
konkurrieren mit etw
- be in competition with s.th.
- compete with s.th.

inkorrekt gekleidet sein
- be incorrectly dressed
- be improperly dressed

in Kraft sein
- be in force

in Kur gehen
zur Kur gehen
- go for a cure
- go for the cure

in Kur sein
- be on a cure
- take a cure

Inland, n
(Gegensatz zu Ausland)
- home

Inländer, m
Landeskind, n
- native
- national
- resident

inländisch, adj
- domestic, adj

inländische Ferienunterkunft, f
Inlandsferienunterkunft, f
inländische Urlaubsunterkunft, f
Inlandsurlaubsunterkunft, f
- domestic holiday accommodation BE

inländischer Besucher

- ♦ domestic vacation accommodation *AE*
- ♦ domestic vacation lodging *AE*

inländischer Besucher, m
→ Inlandsbesucher

inländischer Freizeitmarkt, m
→ Inlandsfreizeitmarkt

inländischer Gast, m
→ Inlandsgast

inländischer Tourismus, m
→ Inlandstourismus

inländische Urlaubsunterkunft, f
Inlandsurlaubsunterkunft, f
inländische Ferienunterkunft, f
Inlandsferienunterkunft, f
- ♦ domestic vacation accommodation *AE*
- ♦ domestic vacation lodging *AE*
- ♦ domestic holiday accommodation *BE*

in ländlicher Abgeschiedenheit
- ♦ in rural seclusion

in ländlicher Umgebung
in ländlicher Lage
- ♦ in rural surroundings
- ♦ in a rural setting

Inlandsaufenthalt, m
- ♦ stay within one's country

Inlandsbesucher, m
inländischer Besucher, m
- ♦ domestic visitor
- ♦ internal visitor *AE*

Inlandscampingplatz, m
(Gegensatz zu Seecampingplatz)
- ♦ inland campsite
- ♦ inland campground *AE*
- ♦ inland camping site *BE*
- ♦ inland camping ground *BE*
- ♦ inland site

Inlandsdienst, m
Inlandsservice, m
- ♦ domestic service

Inlandsfahrpreis, m
- ♦ domestic fare

Inlandsfahrt, f
- ♦ domestic trip

Inlandsferien, pl
Inlandsurlaub, m
- ♦ domestic holiday *BE*
- ♦ home holiday *BE*
- ♦ domestic vacation *AE*

Inlandsferiengast, m
Inlandsurlauber, m
- ♦ domestic holidaymaker *BE*
- ♦ domestic vacationer *AE*

Inlandsferienmarkt, m
inländischer Ferienmarkt, m
Inlandsurlaubsmarkt, m
inländischer Urlaubsmarkt, m
- ♦ domestic holiday market *BE*
- ♦ domestic vacation market *AE*

Inlandsflug, m
- ♦ domestic flight
- ♦ internal flight

Inlandsfluggeschäft, n
- ♦ domestic airline business

Inlandsfluggesellschaft, f
- ♦ domestic airline

Inlandsflughafen, m
inländischer Flughafen, m
Binnenflughafen, m
- ♦ domestic airport

Inlandsflugpreis, m
- ♦ domestic air fare
- ♦ domestic fare

Inlandsfreizeitmarkt, m
inländischer Freizeitmarkt, m
- ♦ domestic leisure market

Inlandsfremdenverkehr, m
→ Inlandstourismus

Inlandsgast, m
inländischer Gast, m
- ♦ internal visitor *AE*
- ♦ home visitor
- ♦ national tourist
- ♦ domestic visitor

Inlandsgebiet, n (groß)
- ♦ inland region

Inlandsgebiet, n (klein)
- ♦ inland area

Inlandshotel, n
- ♦ hotel in one's home country
- ♦ hotel in the home country

Inlandskurort, m
inländischer Kurort, m
- ♦ inland spa

Inlandsmarkt, m
heimischer Markt, m
- ♦ domestic market
- ♦ home market

Inlandsmesse, f
- ♦ domestic fair
- ♦ domestic trade fair

Inlandsnachfrage, f
- ♦ domestic demand
- ♦ internal demand *AE*

Inlandsnachfrage machte 70 % aller Besuche aus
- ♦ domestic demand accounted for 70 % of all visits
- ♦ domestic demand made up 70 % of all visits

Inlandspassagier, m
Inlandsfluggast, m
- ♦ domestic passenger

Inlandspauschalurlaub, m
- ♦ domestic package vacation *AE*
- ♦ domestic package holiday *BE*

Inlandsplatz, m
(Camping; Gegensatz zu Seeplatz)
- ♦ inland site

Inlandsreise, f
- ♦ domestic journey
- ♦ domestic trip
- ♦ domestic tour

Inlandsreisemarkt, m
- ♦ domestic travel market

Inlandsreisen, n
Inlandsreiseverkehr, m
Binnenreiseverkehr, m
- ♦ domestic travel

Inlandsreisender, m
- ♦ domestic traveler *AE*
- ♦ domestic traveller *BE*

Inlandsreiseziel, n
Inlandsreisezielort, m
- ♦ domestic travel destination
- ♦ domestic destination

Inlandsstrecke, f
Inlandsroute, f
- ♦ domestic route

Inlandstourismus, m
Inlandsfremdenverkehr, m
Fremdenverkehr, m
- ♦ domestic tourism
- ♦ internal tourism *AE*

Inlandstourismusnachfrage, f
inländische Tourismusnachfrage, f
- ♦ domestic demand for tourism
- ♦ domestic tourism demand

Inlandstourist, m
- ♦ domestic tourist
- ♦ national tourist
- ♦ internal tourist *AE*

Inlandstouristenreise, f
- ♦ domestic tourist trip

Inlandsübernachtung, f (generell)
- ♦ overnight stay in one's home country
- ♦ overnight stay in the home country

Inlandsübernachtung, f (Statistik)
- ♦ domestic night spent

Inlandsumsatz, m
- ♦ domestic sales *pl*
- ♦ domestic turnover
- ♦ home sales *pl*

Inlandsunterkunft, f
- ♦ domestic accommodation

Inlandsurlaub, m
Inlandsferien, pl
- ♦ domestic vacation *AE*
- ♦ domestic holiday *BE*
- ♦ home holiday *BE*

Inlandsurlauber, m
- ♦ domestic vacationer *AE*
- ♦ domestic holidaymaker *BE*
- ♦ internal vacationer *AE*

Inlandsurlaub machen
- ♦ take a domestic vacation *AE*
- ♦ take a domestic holiday *BE*

Inlandsurlaubsmarkt, m
inländischer Urlaubsmarkt, m
Inlandsferienmarkt, m
inländischer Ferienmarkt, m
- ♦ domestic vacation market *AE*
- ♦ domestic holiday market *BE*

Inlandsurlaubsübernachtung, f
- ♦ domestic vacation night *AE*
- ♦ domestic holiday night *BE*

Inlandsveranstaltung, f
- ♦ domestic event
- ♦ domestic function

Inlandsverkehr, m
inländischer Verkehr, m
Binnenverkehr, m
- ♦ domestic traffic

Inlandsziel, n
Inlandszielort, m
- ♦ domestic destination

in Leihpacht überlassen etw
- ♦ lend-lease s.th.

Inlett, n
- ♦ ticking
- ♦ tick
- ♦ bed ticking

in letzter Sekunde
- ♦ at the last minute

in Livree, adv
livriert, adj
- ♦ in livery, adv

in Logis, adv
→ in Untermiete

in Logis nehmen jn
vorübergehend unterbringen jn
- ♦ lodge s.o.

in Lothringen
- in Lorraine

in luxuriöser Umgebung
- in luxurious surroundings

in Luxus leben
- live in luxury

in malerischer Umgebung
- in picturesque surroundings

In meinem Zimmer ist es nicht warm genug.
Kann die Heizung angestellt werden?
- My room isn't warm enough. Can the heating be turned on?

In meinem Zimmer wird es nicht richtig warm.
Kann die Heizung größer gestellt werden?
- My room isn't warm enough. Can the heating be turned up?

In meinem Zimmer zieht es
- There is a draft in my room AE
- There is a draught in my room BE

In meiner Suppe ist ein Haar!
- There's a hair in my soup!

in möblierten Zimmern wohnen
→ zur Untermiete wohnen

in Mode bleiben
- remain in fashion

in Morpheus' Armen
(schlafen)
- in the arms of Morpheus

in Morpheus' Armen ruhen
(schlafen)
- lie in the arms of Morpheus

Inn, m
- Inn River, the
- River Inn, the
- Inn, the

in natürlicher Umgebung
- in natural surroundings

Innenarchitekt, m
- interior designer
- interior decorator

Innenarchitektur, f
- interior design

Innenaufteilung, f
(eines Raums)
- interior layout

Innenausstattung, f (Aktivität)
- interior decorating

Innenausstattung, f (einer Unterkunft)
Inneneinrichtung f
- interior decoration

Innenausstattung, f (Technik)
- interior equipment
- interior fitting

Innenbecken, n
Hallenbecken, n
- interior pool
- indoor pool

Innenbeleuchtung, f
- interior lighting

Innencafé, n
- indoor cafe AE
- indoor café BE

Innendekor, m/n
- interior decor AE
- interior décor BE

Innendoppelzimmer, n
nach innen liegendes Doppelzimmer, n
- inside double room

Inneneinrichtung, f
(Unterkunft)
- interior furnishings pl

Inneneinzelzimmer, n
(Schiff)
- inside single room

Innengang, m
Innenkorridor m
- interior corridor

Innengarten, m
- interior garden
- inner garden

Innengrenze, f
→ Binnengrenze

Innenhafen, m
- inner harbor AE
- inner harbour BE

Innenhof, m
- inner courtyard
- interior court
- patio
- inner court

Innenhofappartement, n
Terrassenappartement, n
- patio apartment AE

Innenhofbereich, m
Terrassenbereich, m
- patio area

Innenhofgarten, m
Terrassengarten, m
- patio garden

Innenhofrestaurant, n
Hofrestaurant, n
Terrassenrestaurant, n
- patio restaurant

Innenhofterrasse f
- patio terrace

Innenhofwohnung, f
Terrassenwohnung, f
- patio flat BE
- patio apartment AE

Innenjacuzzi, m
- indoor jacuzzi

Innenkabine, f
- inside cabin

innenliegendes Badezimmer n
→ integriertes Badezimmer

innenliegendes Privatbadezimmer, n
(mit Zimmer verbunden)
integriertes Privatbadezimmer, n
innenliegendes Privatbad, n
integriertes Privatbad, n
- private bathroom en suite
- private bath en suite

innenliegende Toilette f
→ integrierte Toilette

Innenmarketing, n
Binnenmarketing, n
- internal marketing

Innenplatz, m
- seat inside
- inside seat
- seat at the inside

Innenprivatsalon, m (Schiff)
- inside state-room AE
- inside stateroom BE

Innenraum, m
innenliegendes Zimmer n
- interior room

Innenschwimmbad, n
→ Hallenschwimmbad

Innensitzplatz, m
Innenplatz, m
Platz im Innern, m
- inside seat

Innenspültoilette, f
(Wohnwagen)
- inside flush toilet

Innenstadt, f (Großstadt)
- city center AE
- city centre BE
- downtown AE

Innenstadt, f (kleinere Stadt)
- town center AE
- town centre BE
- downtown AE

Innenstadtbetrieb, m (Großstadt)
- city-center establishment AE
- city-centre establishment BE
- downtown establishment AE

Innenstadtbetrieb, m (kleine Stadt)
- downtown establishment AE
- town-center establishment AE
- town-centre establishment BE

Innenstadthotel, n (Großstadt)
- city-center hotel AE
- downtown hotel AE
- city-centre hotel BE

Innenstadthotel, n (kleine Stadt)
- town-center hotel AE
- downtown hotel AE
- town-centre hotel BE

Innenstadthotelzimmer, n (Großstadt)
- city-center hotel room AE
- downtown hotel room AE
- city-centre hotel room BE

Innenstadthotelzimmer, n (kleine Stadt)
- town-center hotel room AE
- downtown hotel room AE
- town-centre hotel room BE

Innenstadtlage, f (Großstadt)
- city-center location AE
- downtown location AE
- city-centre location BE

Innenstadtlage, f (kleine Stadt)
- town-center location AE
- town-centre location BE
- downtown location AE

Innenstadtlokal, n (Großstadt)
- downtown establishment AE
- city-center establishment AE
- city-centre establishment BE

Innenstadtlokal, n (kleine Stadt)
- town-center establishment AE
- downtown establishment AE
- town-centre establishment BE

Innenstadtmiete, f (Großstadt)
- city-center rent AE
- downtown rent AE
- city-centre rent BE

Innenstadtmiete, f (kleine Stadt)
- town-center rent AE
- downtown rent AE
- town-centre rent BE

Innenstadtparkplatz, m (mehrere Autos)
- downtown parking lot AE
- town-centre car park BE

Innenstadtrestaurant, n (Großstadt)
- city-center restaurant AE
- downtown restaurant AE
- city-centre restaurant BE

Innenstadtrestaurant

Innenstadtrestaurant, n (kleine Stadt)
- town-center restaurant *AE*
- downtown restaurant *AE*
- town-centre restaurant *BE*

Innenstadtunterkunft, f (Großstadt)
Innenstadtunterbringung, f
- city-center accommodation *AE*
- downtown accommodation *AE*
- downtown lodging *AE*
- city-centre accommodation *BE*

Innenstadtunterkunft, f (kleine Stadt)
Innenstadtunterbringung, f
- town-center accommodation *AE*
- downtown accommodation *AE*
- downtown lodging *AE*
- town-centre accommodation *BE*

Innensuite, f
(Schiff)
- inside suite

Innentemperatur, f
(in Gebäude)
- indoor temperature

Innentisch, m
Tisch im Innern, m
- indoor table

Innentür, f
- inner door

Innenwand, f
- interior wall

Innenwasserfall, m
- interior waterfall

Innenzelt, n
- inner tent

Innenzimmer, n
nach innen gelegenes Zimmer n
- inside room

innereien, f pl (Fisch)
- guts *pl*

Innereien, f pl (Geflügel)
- giblets *pl*

Innere Mongolei, die, f
- Inner Mongolia

Inneren Hebriden, die, pl
- Inner Hebrides, the *pl*

Inneres, n (Gebäud)
- inside
- interior

innereuropäisch, adj
- inter-European, adj
- intra-European, adj

innereuropäischer Reiseverkehr, m
innereuropäisches Reisen, n
- intra-European travel
- inter-European travel

innereuropäischer Tourismus, m
innereuropäischer Fremdenverkehr, m
- inter-European tourism
- intra-European tourism

innerhalb der Gültigkeitsdauer von etw
- within the validity of s.th.
- while s.th. is still valid
- before the expiry date

innerhalb der Saison
- within the season

innerhalb des Hotels
- in the hotel
- inside the hotel

innerhalb einer Frist von sieben Tagen
- within a period of seven days
- within a seven-day period

innerhalb einer Woche
- within a week

innerhalb einer Woche nach meiner Ankunft
- within a week of my arrival

innerhalb einer Woche vor meiner Ankunft
- within a week of my arrival

innerhalb eines Radius von 12 km
- within a radius of 12 km

innerhalb kurzer Zeit nach der Ankunft
- within a short time of (one's) arrival

innerhalb oder außerhalb des Lokals
- on or off the premises

innerhalb sieben Tage nach Buchungsbestätigung
- within seven days of confirmation of booking

innerhalb und außerhalb der Saison
in und außer der Saison
- in and out of season

Inntal, n
- Inn valley, the

Innung der Geschäftsreisestellen, f
- Guild of Business Travel Agents *BE*

in öffentlichen Verkehrsmitteln
- on public transport

inoffiziell, adj
- unofficial, adj
- informal, adj
- inofficial, adj *AE*

inoffizieller Besuch, m
- unofficial visit
- inofficial visit *AE*

inoffizieller Besucher, m
- unofficial visitor
- inofficial visitor *AE*

inoffizieller Empfang, m
- unofficial reception
- inofficial reception *AE*

inoffizieller Teil einer Veranstaltung, m
- unofficial part of an event
- unofficial part of a meeting
- inofficial part of an event *AE*
- inoffcial partt of a meeting *AE*

in Ordnung, adv
- in order, adv

in Ordnung halten etw
- keep s.th. in order

in Pacht haben etw
- have the lease of s.th.
- tenant s.th. *jur*
- hold s.th. under a lease
- have the leasehold of s.th. *BE*
- have the leasehold on s.th. *BE*

in Pacht nehmen etw
- take a lease of s.th.
- take out a lease on s.th.

in Pacht vergeben auf 10 Jahre
- put out to a lease of 10 years

in Panik geraten
- panic
- get into a panic

in parkartiger Umgebung
- in parkland setting

in Parlamentsform
(Bestuhlung)
- in Parliamentary style

in Partnerschaft mit jm
- in partnership with s.o.

in Pension sein bei jm
- board with s.o.

in Quarantäne gehen
- go into quarantine

in Quarantäne halten jn
- keep s.o. in quarantine
- hold s.o. in quarantine

in Quarantäne legen
- put under quarantine

in Quarantäne legen jn
- put s.o. in(to) quarantine
- place s.o. in(to) quarantine

in Quarantäne sein
- be in quarantine
- be under quarantine

in Quartier legen jn bei jm (Militär)
- billet s.o. (up)on s.o.
- billet s.o. with s.o.

in Rechnung stellen etw
- bill s.th.
- charge s.th.
- invoice s.th.

in Rechnung stellen etw jm
- charge s.th. to s.o's account
- debit s.th. to s.o.'s account
- put s.th. on s.o.'s account

in regelmäßigen Zügen
(trinken)
- in regular drafts *AE*
- in regular draughts *BE*

in Reichweite
- within reach

in Reichweite sein
- be within one's reach

in Reihenform
→ in Theaterform

in Richtung von X, adv
- in the direction of X, adv
- in the X direction, adv

in römischer Zeit
- in Roman times

in ruhiger Lage
- in a quiet location
- in peaceful surroundings
- in a peaceful position
- in a quiet position

in ruhiger Lage liegen
- be situated in a quiet location

in ruhiger Umgebung
- in peaceful surroundings
- in a peaceful setting
- in tranquil surroundings

in ruhiger und abgeschiedener Lage
- in a quiet and secluded location
- in a quiet and secluded position

in ruhiger Wohnlage
- in a quiet residential area

in Rundtischform
(Bestuhlung)
- in roundtable style

in sächsischer Zeit
- in Saxon times

Insasse, m (Fahrzeug)
- passenger

Insasse, m (Heim, Gefängnis etc.)
- inmate

Insassenhaftpflichtversicherung, f
(Auto)
- passenger liability insurance

ins Auge gefaßte Fahrt, f
vorgesehene Fahrt, f
- projected trip

ins Ausland reisen
- travel abroad
- go abroad

♦ take a trip abroad
♦ travel overseas BE
in Saus und Braus
♦ in the lap of luxury
in Saus und Braus leben
♦ live in the lap of luxury
♦ be in the lap of luxury
♦ live high
ins Bett bringen jn
ins Bett legen jn
♦ put s.o. to bed
♦ bed s.o.
ins Bett fallen
♦ collapse into bed
♦ fall into bed
ins Bett gehen
sich schlafen legen
♦ go to bed
ins Bett kuscheln sich
♦ snuggle down in bed
ins Bett steigen mit jm
♦ sleep around
in Scharen kommen
♦ come in droves
♦ flock
in Scharen logieren
in Scharen wohnen
♦ stay in droves
in Scheiben geschnitten, adj
♦ sliced, adj
in Scheiben geschnittene Zwiebel, f
♦ sliced onion
in Scheiben schneiden etw
aufschneiden etw
♦ slice s.th.
in Schlaf sinken
→ einschlafen
in schlechtem baulichen Zustand
♦ in bad repair
in schlechter Laune
bei schlechter Laune
♦ in a bad temper
in schöner Landschaft
♦ in beautiful countryside
in Schwung kommen
(Feier)
♦ warm up
in See stechen (nach X)
lossegeln (nach x)
losfahren (nach X)
♦ set sail (for X)
in sein
in Mode sein
♦ be in
in seinem Schlafquartier sein
♦ be in one's sleeping quarter
in seinen eigenen vier Wänden
♦ within one's own four walls
in seinen Mußestunden
♦ in one's idle hours
in sein Zimmer gehen
auf sein Zimmer gehen
♦ go to one's room
Insekt, n
♦ insect
Insektenbekämpfung, f
♦ insect control
Insektenbekämpfungsmittel, n
♦ insecticide
♦ insect repellent

Insel, f
♦ island
Insel Anglesey, f
♦ Isle of Anglesey, the
Inselbewohner, m
Insulaner, m
♦ islander
inselchen, n
♦ islet
♦ small island
Insel der Ruhe und des Friedens, f
♦ oasis of rest and peace
Inselferien, pl
Inselurlaub, m
♦ island holiday BE
♦ island vacation AE
Inselgruppe, f
♦ island group
♦ group of islands
Insel Harris, f
♦ Isle of Harris, the
Inselhotel n
♦ island hotel
Inselhüpfen, n
Reisen von Insel zu Insel, n
♦ island hopping
Insel im Privatbesitz, f
♦ privately owned island
Insel im Rhein, f
♦ island in the Rhine
Insel im See, f
♦ island in the lake
Insel ist bewohnt
♦ island is inhabited
Insel ist unbewohnt
♦ island is uninhabited
Insel Lewis, f
♦ Isle of Lewis, the
Insel Mainau, f
♦ Mainau Island
♦ island of Mainau
Insel Man, f
♦ Isle of Man, the
Inselparadies, n
♦ island paradise
Inselrundfahrt, f
♦ tour of an island
♦ tour of the island
♦ island tour
Insel Skye, f
♦ Isle of Skye, the
Inselstaat, m
♦ island state
Insel Sylt, f
♦ island of Sylt
Inseltourismus, m
♦ island tourism
Inseltourist, m
♦ island tourist
Inselurlaub, m
Inselferien, pl
♦ island vacation AE
♦ island holiday BE
Inselurlaubsort, m
Inselferienort, m
Inselort, m
♦ island resort
Inselvogelschutzgebiet, n
♦ island bird sanctuary

Insel vor der Küste, f
Küsteninsel, f
♦ offshore island
Insel vor der Küste von Cornwall, f
♦ island off the coast of Cornwall
Insel Wight, f
♦ Isle of Wight, the
Inselziel, n
♦ island destination
Inselzuschlag m
♦ island supplement
Inserat, n
Annonce, f
Anzeige, f
♦ ad BE coll
♦ advertisement
♦ advert BE coll
Inserent, m
♦ advertiser
ins Gebirge reisen
♦ travel to the mountains
♦ go to the mountains
insgesamt 123 Zimmer haben
♦ have a total of 123 rooms
insgesamt können 123 Personen bewirtet werden
♦ a total of 123 persons can be catered for
ins Haus lassen jn
♦ let s.o. into the house
ins Haus platzen jm
♦ burst in on s.o.
in sich geschlossene Wohnung, f
abgeschlossene Wohnung f
♦ self-contained apartment AE
♦ self-contained flat BE
in Sicht, adv
in Sichtweite, adv
♦ in sight, adv
in Sicht kommen
♦ come into view
♦ come into sight
in Sichtweite sein von etw
♦ be within sight of s.th.
♦ be in sight of s.th.
ins Kino gehen
♦ go to the movies AE
♦ go to the cinema BE
♦ go to the pictures
in Skiurlaub gehen
♦ go on a ski vacation AE
♦ go on a skiing vacation AE
♦ go on a ski holiday BE
♦ go on a skiing holiday BE
ins Konzert gehen
♦ go to a concert
ins Konzert schleppen jn
♦ drag s.o. along to a concert
ins Meer fließen
♦ flow into the sea
♦ enter the sea
insolvenzabgesicherter Pauschalurlaub, m
♦ bonded package holiday BE
insolvenzabgesichertes Reisebüro, n
♦ bonded travel agency
Inspektionsbesuch, m
♦ inspection visit
Inspektionsreise, f
Inspektionstour f
♦ tour of inspection
Inspektionsreise machen
♦ make a tour of inspection

in Spitzenstunden

in Spitzenstunden
- at peak hours

inspizieren etw
   in Augenschein nehmen etw
   überprüfen etw
- inspect s.th.

ins Quartier rücken, *mil*
- move to quarters *mil*

ins Röhrchen blasen (müssen) *coll*
   Promilletest machen (müssen)
- be breath-tested
- be breathalyzed

ins Ausland, adv
   in das Ausland, adv
- abroad, adv

Installateur, m
- plumber
- fitter

Installation, f
   Einbau, m
- installation

Installationsdienst, m
- installation service

Installationskosten, pl
   → Einbaukosten

installieren etw
   einbauen etw
- instal s.th. *AE*
- install s.th. *BE*

installieren lassen etw
   → einbauen lassen etw

instandhalten etw (Gebäude)
- maintain s.th.

instandhalten etw (generell)
- keep s.th. in good repair
- maintain s.th. in good condition

instandhalten etw (warten)
   → warten etw

Instandhaltung, f (Gebäude)
   Wartung, f (Gerät)
- maintenance

Instandhaltungsarbeit, f
- maintenance work

Instandhaltungsauftrag, m
- maintenance work order

Instandhaltungsaufwand, m
- maintenance expense *AE*
- maintenance expenditure *BE*

Instandhaltungsausgaben, f pl
- maintenance expenses *pl*

Instandhaltungskosten, pl
- maintenance costs *pl*
- maintenance cost

Instandhaltungskosten senken
- cut maintenance costs
- reduce maintenance costs

Instandhaltungspersonal, n
   Wartungspersonal, n
- maintenance staff
- maintenance personnel

Instandhaltungsprogramm, n
- maintenance program *AE*
- maintenance programme *BE*

Instandhaltungsrechnung, f
- maintenance bill

Instandhaltungsvertrag, m
   Wartungsvertrag, m
- maintenance contract

Instandhaltung und Reparaturen, pl
- maintenance and repair

instandsetzen etw
   reparieren etw
- fix s.th.
- repair s.th.

ins Theater gehen
- go to the theater *AE*
- go to the theatre *BE*

in Stimmung bringen jn
- liven s.o. up

in Stimmung kommen nach drei Gläsern
- liven up after the third glass

Institut für Freizeitmanagement, n
- institute of leisure management

Institut für Tourismus, n
   Institut für Fremdenverkehr, n
- institute of tourism

in Strandnähe
- near the beach

in Streik treten
- go on strike

instruieren jn
- instruct s.o.
- brief s.o.

Instruktion, f (für bestimmtes Projekt)
   Anweisung f
   Vergatterung f
- briefing

Instruktion, f (generell)
   Anweisung, f
- instruction

instruktiv, adj
- instructive, adj

instruktiver Führer, m
   (Buch oder Person)
- instructive guide

instruktiver Prospekt, m
- instructive brochure

in Stücke schneiden etw
- cut s.th. into pieces

Insulaner, m pl
- island people *pl*
- islanders *pl*

inszenieren etw (Theater)
- stage s.th.
- put s.th. on the stage
- mount s.th. *AE*
- produce s.th.

ins Zimmer platzen
   in das Zimmer platzen
- burst into the room

intakte mittelalterliche Stadt, f
- intact medieval town

integriert, adj
   (Bad, Dusche etc.)
   innenliegend, adj
   miteinander verbunden, adj
- en suite, adj
- e/s

integrierte Einrichtung, f
   (insbesondere Bad/WC)
- en-suite facility

integrierte Garage f
   (Garage im Haus)
- integral garage
- built-in garage

integrierter Duschraum, m
- shower room en suite
- en-suite shower room

integrierte sanitäre Einrichtungen, f pl
- en-suite facilities *pl*

integriertes Bad, n
   innenliegendes Bad, n
- en-suite bath
- bath en suite
- e/s bath

integriertes Badezimmer, n
   (mit Zimmer verbunden)
   innenliegendes Badezimmer, n
- bathroom en suite
- en-suite bathroom
- e/s bathroom

integriertes Schlafzimmer, n
- bedroom en suite
- en-suite bedroom

integriertes Wohnzimmer, n
   (mit Schlafzimmer verbunden)
- living room en suite
- sitting room en suite

integriertes Zimmer, n
- room en suite
- en suite room

integrierte Toilette f
   (mit Zimmer verbunden)
   innenliegende Toilette f
- toilet en suite
- en suite toilet

intelligent möbliert, adj
- intelligently furnished, adj

intelligent möbliertes Zimmer, n
- intelligently furnished room

Intensivkurs, m
   Intensivlehrgang, m
- intensive course
- crash course

Intensivlehrgang, m
   → Intensivkurs

Intensivprogramm, n
- intensive program *AE*
- intensive programme *BE*

Intensivseminar n
- intensive seminar

Intensivsprachkurs, m
- intensive language course

Intercity, m (Zug) *coll*
   IC, m
- intercity *AE coll*
- inter-city *BE coll*
- IC

Intercity-Bus, m
- intercity bus *AE*
- inter-city coach *BE*

Intercity-Verbindung, f
- intercity connection *AE*
- inter-city connection *BE*

Intercity-Verbindung im Stundentakt, f
- intercity connections at hourly intervals *AE pl*
- inter-city connections at hourly intervals *BE pl*

Intercity-Zug, m
   IC-Zug, m
- intercity train *AE*
- inter-city train *BE*
- IC train
- intercity *AE inform*
- inter-city *BE inform*

interessante Speisekarte, f
- interesting menu

interessante Veranstaltung, f
- interesting event
- interesting activity
- interesting function

Interesse für das Wohlbefinden seiner Gäste

zeigen
Interessengruppe, f
- ◆ pressure group
- ◆ interest group

Interferenztherapie, f
- ◆ interferential therapy

Interieur, n
- ◆ interior
- ◆ interior decoration

Interimsquartier, n
- ◆ interim quarters *pl*

Interimsunterkunft, f
- ◆ interim accommodation

Interkontinentalflug, m
- ◆ intercontinental flight

Interkontinentalreise, f
- ◆ intercontinental journey
- ◆ intercontinental trip
- ◆ intercontinental tour

Interkontinentalstrecke, f
Interkontinentalroute, f
- ◆ intercontinental route

Interline-Abkommen, n
Interline-Vereinbarung, f
- ◆ interline agreement

Interline-Arrangement, n
- ◆ interline arrangement

Interline-Gepäck, n
- ◆ interline baggage *AE*
- ◆ interline luggage *BE*

Interline-Passagier, m
Interline-Fluggast, m
- ◆ interline passenger

Interliner, m
Mitarbeiter von internationalen Fluggesellschaften, m
- ◆ interliner

Interline-Schalter, m
- ◆ interline counter

Interline-System, n
- ◆ interline system

Interline-Verbindung, f
- ◆ interline connection

Interlining, n
Zusammenarbeit von internationalen Fluggesellschaften, f
Wechsel zu einer anderen Fluggesellschaft bei einem Transfer, m
- ◆ interlining

Internat, n
Internatsschule, f
Pensionat, n
- ◆ boarding school *AE*
- ◆ boarding-school *BE*

Internat besuchen
- ◆ go to boarding school *AE*
- ◆ go to boarding-school *BE*

international, adj
- ◆ international, adj

international bekannt, adj
- ◆ internationally renowned, adj
- ◆ internationally known, adj

international bekanntes Hotel, n
- ◆ internationally renowned hotel

international berühmt, adj
- ◆ internationally famous, adj

international berühmter Star, m
- ◆ internationally famous star

internationale Atmosphäre, f
- ◆ international atmosphere

internationale Ausstellung, f
- ◆ international exhibition
- ◆ international exhibit *AE*
- ◆ international show

Internationale Filmwoche, f
- ◆ International Film Week, the

Internationale Hotelordnung f
(Hausordnung)
- ◆ International Hotel Regulations *pl*

internationale Impfbescheinigung, f
- ◆ international certificate of vaccination

Internationale Jugendherbergsföderation, f
- ◆ International Youth Hostel Federation, the

internationale Jugendmusikwoche, f
- ◆ international youth music week

internationale Konferenz, f
internationale Tagung f
- ◆ international conference

internationale Konzertreihe, f
- ◆ series of international concerts

internationale Küche, f (Speisen)
- ◆ international cuisine
- ◆ international cooking

internationale Küche servieren
internationale Speisen servieren
- ◆ serve international cuisine
- ◆ serve international food

internationale Messe, f
- ◆ international fair
- ◆ international trade fair

internationale Messestadt, f (Großstadt)
- ◆ international fair city

internationale Messestadt, f (kleine Stadt)
- ◆ international fair town

internationalen Ruhm beanspruchen
- ◆ claim international fame

internationalen Ruhm erlangen
- ◆ gain international fame

Internationalen Telegrammcode für Hotels benutzen
- ◆ use the International Hotel Telegraph Code

Internationaler Antwortschein m
- ◆ international reply coupon
- ◆ international reply voucher

internationaler Austausch, m
- ◆ international exchange

internationaler Busverkehr, m
- ◆ international bus traffic *AE*
- ◆ international coach traffic *BE*

internationaler Ferienkurs, m
- ◆ international vacation course *AE*
- ◆ international holiday course *BE*

internationaler Flughafen, m
- ◆ international airport

internationaler Fremdenverkehr, m (Reiseverkehr)
internationaler Reiseverkehr, m
- ◆ international tourist traffic

internationaler Fremdenverkehr, m (Tourismus)
→ internationaler Tourismus

internationaler Fremdenverkehrsort, m
- ◆ international tourist resort

internationaler Führerschein, m
- ◆ international driving permit

Internationaler Hotelier-Verband, m
- ◆ International Hotel Association
- ◆ IHA

internationaler Hotelkonzern, m
- ◆ international hotel group

Internationaler Hotelschlüssel m
- ◆ International Hotel Booking Code

internationaler Jetreiseverkehr, m
- ◆ international jet travel

internationaler Kongreß m
- ◆ international congress
- ◆ international convention

internationaler Kundenkreis, m
- ◆ international clientele

Internationaler Luftverkehrsverband, m
IATA, f
- ◆ International Air Transport Association
- ◆ IATA

internationaler Ruf m
- ◆ international reputation

internationaler Ruhm, m
- ◆ international fame

internationaler Selbstwählverkehr, m (Telefon)
- ◆ international susbscriber telephone *AE*
- ◆ international direct dialing telephone *AE*
- ◆ international direct dialling telephone *BE*
- ◆ IDD
- ◆ IDS

internationaler Star, m
- ◆ international star

internationaler Tarif, m
- ◆ international tariff
- ◆ international terms *pl*
- ◆ international rates *pl*
- ◆ international rate

internationaler Teilnehmer, m (Konferenz)
- ◆ international delegate

Internationaler Telegrammcode für Hotels, m
- ◆ International Hotel Telegraph Code

Internationaler Touring-Verband, m
- ◆ International Touring Association

internationaler Tourismus, m
internationaler Fremdenverkehr, m
- ◆ international tourism

Internationaler Verband der Jugendherbergen, m
- ◆ International Youth Hostel Association

internationaler Verkehr, m
- ◆ international traffic

internationales Bewertungssystem n
internationales Einstufungssystem n
- ◆ international grading system

Internationales Camping-Carnet, n
- ◆ international camping carnet

internationale Schau, f
internationale Darbietung, f
internationale Ausstellung, f
- ◆ international show

internationales Essen, n
- ◆ international food

internationales Flair, n
- ◆ international charm

internationales Flair haben
- ◆ have an international charm

internationales Gericht, n
- ◆ international dish

internationales Jugendlager, n
- ◆ international youth camp

internationales Publikum, n
internationale Zuhörerschaft, f
- ◆ international audience

internationales Reisen, n
internationaler Reiseverkehr, m
- ◆ international travel

internationales Renommee, n
- ◆ international renown
- ◆ international reputation

internationales Selbstwähltelefon, n
- ◆ international direct dialing telephone *AE*

internationales Volksfest

- ♦ international direct dialling telephone BE
- ♦ international subscriber telephone
- ♦ IDD telephone
- ♦ IDS telephone

internationales Volksfest, n
- ♦ international folk festival

internationale Tagung, f
internationales Treffen, n
- ♦ international meeting

Internationale Tourismus-Börse, f
ITB, f
- ♦ International Tourism Exchange, the
- ♦ ITB, the

internationale Tourismuseinnahmen, f pl
- ♦ international tourism receipts pl

internationale Touristenströme, m pl
- ♦ international tourist flows pl
- ♦ international tourism flows pl

internationale Veranstaltung, f
- ♦ international event
- ♦ international function

Internationale Woche, f
- ♦ International Week

Internatsuniversität, f
- ♦ residential university

interne Rechnungsprüfung, f
- ♦ internal audit

interne Schulung, f
- ♦ internal training
- ♦ internal training course

Interrailkarte, f
- ♦ inter-rail card

Intervallentimesharing, n
(mit Grundstücksübertragungsurkunde)
- ♦ interval timesharing AE

Interview, n
Befragung, f
- ♦ interview

in Theaterform
→ in Vortragsform

intim, adj
gemütlich, adj
- ♦ intimate, adj
- ♦ cosy, adj
- ♦ cozy, adj AE

intime Atmosphäre, f
- ♦ intimate atmosphere

intime Beleuchtung, f
- ♦ intimate lighting
- ♦ soft lighting

intime Ecke, f
- ♦ intimate corner

intime kleine Bar, f
- ♦ intimate little bar

intimen Rahmen bieten für etw
- ♦ provide an intimate setting for s.th.

intimer Rahmen, m
- ♦ intimate setting

intimes Ambiente, n
- ♦ intimate ambience
- ♦ intimate ambiance

intimes Hotel, n
- ♦ intimate hotel

intimes Restaurant, n
- ♦ intimate restaurant

intimes Zimmer, n
- ♦ intimate room

in Tischform
(Bestuhlung)
in Klassenzimmerform

- ♦ in schoolroom style
- ♦ in classroom style

in U-Form
(Bestuhlung)
- ♦ in U-form style

in umgekehrter Richtung
in der umgekehrten Richtung
- ♦ in reverse direction
- ♦ in the reverse direction

in und um London
- ♦ in and around London

in unmittelbarer Nachbarschaft
- ♦ in close vicinity

in unmittelbarer Nähe, adv
- ♦ close at hand, adv
- ♦ in the immediate vicinity, adv

in unmittelbarer Nähe sein
- ♦ be close at hand
- ♦ be in the immediate vicinity

in unmittelbarer Nähe von etw
- ♦ in the immediate vicinity of s.th.

in Untermiete
zur Untermiete
- ♦ in lodgings

in Untermiete wohnen
→ zur Untermiete wohnen

in unvergleichlich schöner Umgebung
- ♦ in incomparably beautiful surroundings

in Urlaub fahren (Ferien)
in Urlaub gehen
- ♦ go on vacation AE
- ♦ go on holiday BE

in Urlaub fahren nach X
- ♦ go to X for a vacation AE
- ♦ go to X for a holiday BE

in Urlaub gehen (Arbeitnehmer)
Urlaub antreten
- ♦ go on leave

in Urlaubsstimmung
(Person)
in Ferienstimmung
- ♦ in a vacation mood AE
- ♦ in a holiday mood BE

Invalide, m
- ♦ invalid

Invalidenheim, n
- ♦ home for the disabled
- ♦ asylum for invalids

Inventar, n (Bestand)
- ♦ inventory

Inventar, n (Möbel und Ausstattung)
- ♦ furniture and equipment

Inventar abschreiben
- ♦ depreciate inventory
- ♦ write down inventory

Inventarabschreibung, f
- ♦ inventory writedown
- ♦ depreciation of inventory

Inventar aufstellen
Inventar aufnehmen
- ♦ make an inventory of s.th.
- ♦ take an inventory of s.th.
- ♦ draw up an inventory of s.th.

Inventarbewertung, f
- ♦ inventory valuation
- ♦ valuation of inventory
- ♦ inventory evaluation

Inventarblatt, n
- ♦ inventory sheet

Inventarbuch, n
- ♦ inventory book

- ♦ inventory
- ♦ stock ledger

Inventarfehlbetrag, m
- ♦ inventory shortage

Inventargegenstand, m
Inventarposten m
- ♦ inventory item
- ♦ item of inventory

Inventarherabsetzung, f
- ♦ inventory reduction
- ♦ reduction of inventory

Inventarinstandhaltung, f
- ♦ inventory maintenance

inventarisieren etw
- ♦ inventory s.th.
- ♦ take an inventory
- ♦ make an inventory
- ♦ draw up an inventory
- ♦ take stock

Inventarkarte, f
Inventarkarteikarte f
- ♦ inventory card
- ♦ stock card

Inventarkonto, n
- ♦ inventory account
- ♦ furniture and fixture account

Inventarkontrolle, f
- ♦ inventory checking
- ♦ checking (of) inventory

Inventarliste, f
- ♦ inventory list
- ♦ inventory

Inventarliste führen
- ♦ keep an inventory

Inventarposten, m
Inventargegenstand, m
Bestandsposten, m
- ♦ item of inventory
- ♦ inventory item

Inventarpreis, m
- ♦ inventory price

Inventarprüfung, f (Buchhaltung)
Inventarüberprüfung f
- ♦ inventory audit
- ♦ auditing inventory

Inventarschwankung, f
- ♦ inventory fluctuation
- ♦ fluctuation in inventory

Inventarstück, n
- ♦ fixture
- ♦ inventory item

Inventar überprüfen
- ♦ check the inventory

Inventarveränderung, f
- ♦ inventory change
- ♦ change in inventory

Inventarverlust, m
- ♦ inventory loss

Inventarverzeichnis, n
- ♦ inventory register
- ♦ inventory

Inventarwert, m
Lagerwert, m
- ♦ value of inventory
- ♦ inventory value

Inventarwertberichtigung, f
- ♦ inventory valuation adjustment

Inventar zu Beginn des Geschäftsjahrs, n
- ♦ beginning inventory

Inventar zu Ende des Geschäftsjahrs, n
- ♦ closing inventory

Inventar zum Anschaffungspreis, n
♦ inventory at cost
Inventur, f
Inventuraufnahme f
♦ inventory
♦ stock-taking
Inventurberichtigung, f
Bestandsberichtigung f
♦ inventory adjustment
♦ stock adjustment
Inventurkosten, pl
♦ inventory costs *pl*
♦ inventory cost
Inventur machen
♦ make an inventory
♦ take stock
♦ take an inventory *AE*
in Verbindung mit jm
♦ in conjunction with s.o.
♦ in association with s.o.
in vermietungsfähigem Zustand
♦ in tenantable repair
in Verruf bringen etw
♦ bring s.th. into disrepute
investieren in die Tourismusindustrie
in die Fremdenverkehrsindustrie investieren
♦ invest in the tourism industry
investieren in etw
♦ invest in s.th.
Investition, f
♦ investment
Investitionskosten, pl
♦ investment costs *pl*
♦ investment cost
Investitionsprogramm, n
♦ investment program *AE*
♦ investment programme *BE*
Investitionsprogramm zur Renovierung, n
♦ investment program of refurbishment *AE*
♦ investment programme of refurbishment *BE*
Investitionsprojekt, n
♦ investment project
Investitionssteuer, f
♦ investment tax
Investmentgesellschaft, f
♦ investment company
♦ investment trust
In vino veritas *LAT*
Im Wein ist Wahrheit
♦ In vino veritas *LAT*
♦ In wine is truth
in vorgeschichtlicher Zeit
in prähistorischer Zeit
♦ in prehistoric times
in Vortragsform
(Bestuhlung)
in Theaterform
♦ in theater style *AE*
♦ in theatre style *BE*
In welchem Zimmer wohnen Sie?
♦ Which room are you staying in?
In welcher Preisklasse?
♦ In what price category?
in Winterurlaub gehen
♦ go on a winter vacation *AE*
♦ go on a winter holiday *BE*
in Wohlfahrtsunterkünften schlafen
♦ sleep in charity lodgings
in Würfel schneiden etw
würfeln etw
♦ cut s.th. into dice

in X ist viel los
♦ there's going on a lot in X
in zentraler Lage, adv
♦ centrally situated, adj
♦ situated in the center, adv *AE*
♦ situated in the centre, adv *BE*
in Zimmern wohnen
(zeitweise)
♦ stay in rooms
in Zusammenarbeit mit jm
♦ in cooperation with s.o.
ionischer Tempel, m
♦ Ionic temple
ionische Säule, f
♦ Ionic column
♦ ionic pillar
Ionisches Meer, n
♦ Ionian Sea, the
Irak, m
♦ Iraq
♦ Irak
Iraker, m
♦ Iraqi
♦ Iraki
Irakerin, f
♦ Iraqi girl
♦ Iraqi woman
♦ Iraqi
♦ Iraki girl
♦ Iraki woman
irakisch, adj
♦ Iraqi, adj
♦ Iraki, adj
Iran, m
♦ Iran
Iraner, m
♦ Iranian
Iranerin, f
♦ Iranian girl
♦ Iranian woman
♦ Iranian
iranisch, adj
♦ Iranian, adj
Ire, m
Irländer m
♦ Irishman
Irin, f
Irländerin f
♦ Irishwoman
irisch, adj
♦ Irish, adj
irische Art, adv *gastr*
nach irischer Art, adv *gastr*
♦ Irish style, adv *gastr*
irischer Pub, m
♦ Irish pub
irisch-römisches Bad, n
♦ Irish-Roman bath
♦ hot-air bath
Irland
♦ Ireland
♦ Eire
Irlandprospekt, m
♦ Ireland brochure
Irlandurlaub, m
♦ Irish vacation *AE*
♦ Irish holiday *BE*
irreführend, adj
♦ misleading, adj
irreführende Beschreibung, f
♦ misleading description

irreführende Information, f
irreführende Auskunft, f
♦ misleading information
irreführender Prospekt, m
irreführende Broschüre, f
♦ misleading brochure
irren sich in der Person
Person verwechseln
♦ mistake s.o.'s identity
Irrfahrt, f
→ Odyssee
Irrtümer vorbehalten
♦ Errors excepted
Islam, m
♦ Islam
islamisch, adj
♦ Islamic, adj
Island
♦ Iceland
Isländer, m
Isländerin, f
♦ Icelander
isländisch, adj
♦ Icelandic, adj
Isolierkanne, f
Thermoskanne, f
♦ thermos jug
isolierte Lage, f
einsame Lage, f
♦ isolated position
♦ isolated location
♦ isolated situation
Isolierverglasung, f
→ Doppelverglasung
Isolierzimmer, n *med*
(z.B. bei Seuchenkranken)
♦ isolation room *med*
Israel
♦ Israel
Israeli, m/f
♦ Israeli
israelisch, adj
♦ Israeli, adj
Iß es und beklag' Dich nicht!
♦ Eat it and like it!
Ist alles zu Ihrer Zufriedenheit?
♦ Is everything to your liking?
Ist-Auslastung f
tatsächliche Auslastung, f
♦ actual load factor
Ist-Belegung f
tatsächliche Belegung f
Ist-Auslastung f
tatsächliche Auslastung f
♦ actual occupancy
Ist-Bestand, m
Effektivbestand, m
♦ actual stock
♦ actual inventory
Ist darin das Frühstück enthalten?
Ist das mit Frühstück?
♦ Does that include breakfast?
Ist das alles, was Sie an Gepäck haben?
♦ Is that all you have in the way of baggage? *AE*
♦ Is that all you have in the way of luggage? *BE*
Ist das inklusive Frühstück?
♦ Is that with breakfast?
♦ Does that include breakfast?
Ist das mit Bedienung?
→ Ist das mit Bedienungsgeld?

Ist das mit Bedienungsgeld?

Ist das mit Bedienungsgeld?
  Ist das mit Bedienung?
  ♦ **Is that with service charge?**
  ♦ Does that include service charge?
Ist das Zimmer klimatisiert?
  ♦ **Is the room air-conditioned?**
Ist der Parkplatz bewacht?
  ♦ **Is there an attendant?**
  ♦ Is there a car park attendant? *BE*
Ist der Parkplatz die ganze Nacht geöffnet?
  ♦ **Is the parking lot open all night?** *AE*
  ♦ Is the car park open all night? *BE*
Ist die Garage die ganze Nacht geöffnet?
  ♦ **Is the garage open all night?**
Ist dieser Platz besetzt?
  (Sitzplatz)
  ♦ **Is this seat taken?**
Ist dieser Platz frei?
  (Sitzplatz)
  ♦ **Is this seat free?**
  ♦ Is this seat vacant?
Ist er auf seinem Zimmer?
  Ist er in seinem Zimmer?
  ♦ **Is he in his room?**
Ist es möglich, so spät noch etwas zu essen
  zu bekommen?
  ♦ **Is it possible to get something to eat this late?**
Ist-Gedeckzahl, f
  ♦ **actual number of covers**
Ist Ihr Zimmer in Ordnung?
  ♦ **Is your room okay?**
Ist-Kosten, pl
  tatsächliche Kosten, pl
  ♦ **actual costs** *pl*
  ♦ actual cost
Ist Post für mich da?
  ♦ **Is there any mail for me?** *AE*
  ♦ Is there any post for me? *BE*
  ♦ Are there any letters for me?
Istrien
  ♦ **Istria**
istrisch, adj
  ♦ **Istrian, adj**
Ist-Umsatz, m
  tatsächlicher Umsatz, m
  ♦ **actual sales** *pl*
  ♦ actual turnover
Ist-Verbrauch, m
  tatsächlicher Verbrauch, m
  Ist-Konsum, m
  tatsächlicher Konsum, m
  ♦ **actual consumption**
Ist-Wareneinsatz Getränke, m
  ♦ **actual beverage cost**
  ♦ actual drinks cost
Ist-Wareneinsatz Speisen, m
  ♦ **actual food cost**
Ist-Zahl, f
  ♦ **actual figure**
IT, f
  Inclusive Tour, f
  ♦ **IT**
  ♦ inclusive tour
Italien
  ♦ **Italy**
Italienbuchung, f
  ♦ **booking for Italy**
Italiener, m
  ♦ **Italian**

Italienerin, f
  ♦ **Italian girl**
  ♦ Italian woman
  ♦ Italian
italienisch, adj
  ♦ **Italian, adj**
italienische Art, adv *gastr*
  nach italienischer Art, adv *gastr*
  ♦ **italian style, adv** *gastr*
italienische Küche, f (Speisen)
  ♦ **Italian cuisine**
  ♦ Italian cooking
  ♦ Italian gastronomy
Italienischen Alpen, die, pl
  ♦ **Italian Alps, the** *pl*
Italienischen Dolomiten, die, pl
  ♦ **Italian Dolomites, the** *pl*
Italienische Riviera, f
  ♦ **Italian Riviera, the**
italienischer Wein, m
  ♦ **Italian wine**
italienisches Gericht, n
  ♦ **Italian dish**
italienische Spezialität, f
  ♦ **Italian specialty** *AE*
  ♦ Italian speciality *BE*
italienisches Restaurant, n
  ♦ **Italian restaurant**
Italienprogramm, n
  ♦ **Italian program** *AE*
  ♦ Italian programme *BE*
Italienreise, f (in Italien)
  Italienrundreise, f
  ♦ **tour of Italy**
  ♦ tour through Italy
  ♦ Italian tour
Italienreise, f (nach Italien)
  ♦ **journey to Italy**
  ♦ tour to Italy
  ♦ trip to Italy
Italientourist, m
  ♦ **tourist to Italy**
Italienurlaub, m
  ♦ **Italian vacation** *AE*
  ♦ Italian holiday *BE*
ITB, f
  Internationale Tourismus-Börse, f
  ♦ **ITB, the**
  ♦ International Tourism Exchange, the
IT-Flugschein, m
  Inclusive-Tour-Flugschein, m
  Pauschalreiseflugschein, m
  ♦ **IT air ticket**
  ♦ IT ticket
IT-Reisender, m
  Pauschalreisender, m
  ♦ **IT tourist**
  ♦ IT traveler *AE*
  ♦ IT traveller *BE*
  ♦ inclusive tour traveler *AE*
IT-Tarif, m
  Pauschalreisetarif, m
  ♦ **IT tariff**
  ♦ inclusive tour tariff
IT-Urlaub, m
  ♦ **inclusive tour vacation** *AE*
  ♦ inclusive tour holiday *BE*

J

Jacht, f
   Yacht, f
   ♦ yacht
Jachtausflug, m
   Yachtausflug, m
   ♦ yacht excursion
Jachtbegeisterter, m
   Yachtbegeisterter, m
   ♦ yachting enthusiast
Jachtbesitzer, m
   Yachtbesitzer, m
   ♦ yacht owner
Jacht chartern
   Yacht chartern
   ♦ charter a yacht
Jachtclub, m
   Jachtverein, m
   Yachtclub, m
   Yachtverein, m
   ♦ yacht club *AE*
   ♦ yacht-club *BE*
   ♦ yachting club
Jachtclubhaus, n
   Yachtclubhaus, n
   ♦ yacht clubhouse
Jachtclubhotel, n
   Yachtclubhotel, n
   ♦ yacht club hotel
Jachtfirma, f
   Yachtfirma, f
   ♦ yacht company
   ♦ yachting company
Jachtflotte, f
   Yachtflotte, f
   ♦ fleet of yachts
   ♦ yacht fleet
Jachtführer, m
   Jachtkapitän, m
   Yachtführer, m
   Yachtkapitän, m
   ♦ yacht skipper
Jachtgeschäft, n
   Yachtgeschäft, n
   ♦ yacht business
   ♦ yachting business
Jachthafen, m
   Yachthafen, m
   Segelhafen, m
   ♦ yacht harbor *AE*
   ♦ yacht(ing) harbour *BE*
   ♦ yacht port
   ♦ yacht(ing) marina
   ♦ marina
Jachtkreuzfahrt, f
   Yachtkreuzfahrt, f
   ♦ yacht cruise
Jachtlehrgang, m
   Jachtkurs, m

   Yachtlehrgang, m
   Yachtkurs, m
   ♦ yachting course
Jachtmarina, f
   Yachtmarina, f
   ♦ yacht marina
   ♦ yachting marina
Jachtort, m
   Yachtort, m
   ♦ yacht resort
   ♦ yachting resort
Jachtregatta, f
   Yachtregatta, f
   ♦ yacht regatta
   ♦ yachting regatta
Jachtreise, f
   Yachtreise, f
   ♦ yacht voyage
Jachtrennen, n
   Yachtrennen, n
   Jachtrennsport, m
   Yachtrennsport, m
   Wettsegeln, n
   ♦ yacht race
   ♦ yacht racing
Jachtschoner, m
   Yachtschoner, m
   ♦ yacht schooner
Jachtsegeln, n
   Jachtsegelsport, n
   Yachtsegeln, n
   Yachtsegelsport, m
   ♦ yacht sailing
Jachtsport, m
   Yachtsport, m
   Wettsegeln, n
   ♦ yachting
Jachttourismus, m
   Yachttourismus, m
   Segeltourismus, m
   ♦ yacht tourism
   ♦ yachting tourism
Jachttourist, m
   Yachttourist, m
   Segeltourist, m
   ♦ yacht tourist
   ♦ yachting tourist
Jachtumsatz, m
   Yachtumsatz, m
   ♦ yacht sales *pl*
Jachturlaub, m
   Yachturlaub, m
   ♦ yacht vacation *AE*
   ♦ yacht holiday *BE*
   ♦ yachting holiday *BE*
Jachtwerft, f
   Yachtwerft, f
   ♦ yacht building yard

Jachtzentrum, n
   Yachtzentrum, n
   ♦ yacht center *AE*
   ♦ yacht centre *BE*
   ♦ yachting center *AE*
   ♦ yachting centre *BE*
Jacht zu vermieten (Hinweisschild)
   Yacht zu vermieten
   ♦ **Yacht for rent (sign)** *AE*
   ♦ Yacht for hire *BE*
Jackpot, m
   ♦ jackpot
Jackpot gewinnen
   ♦ hit the jackpot
Jacuzzi, m *regist*
   ♦ jacuzzi *regist*
Jacuzzibad, n *regist*
   Jacuzzibecken, n *regist*
   ♦ jacuzzi pool *regist*
   ♦ jacuzzi *regist*
Jacuzzibecken, n
   → Jacuzzibad
Jadebusen, m
   (Region)
   ♦ Jade Bay, the
Jagdausflug, m
   ♦ hunting excursion
Jagdbild, n
   (Wandschmuck)
   ♦ hunting picture
Jagdessen, n
   ♦ hunting meal
   ♦ game meal
Jagdexpedition, f
   ♦ hunting expedition
Jagdfahrt, f
   ♦ hunting trip
Jagdgesellschaft, f
   ♦ hunting party
   ♦ shooting party
   ♦ hunt
   ♦ shoot
Jagdhaus n
   Jagdschloß n
   Jagdhütte f
   ♦ hunting lodge
   ♦ lodge
Jagdhorn, n
   ♦ hunting horn
Jagdkurzurlaub, m
   ♦ shooting break
Jagdlodge, f
   ♦ game lodge
   ♦ hunting lodge
Jagdmenü, n
   ♦ game menu
Jagdmuseum, n
   ♦ hunting museum

Jagdpächter

Jagdpächter, m
- game tenant

Jagdpartie, f
- shooting party

Jagdreise, f
- hunting tour
- hunting trip
- hunting journey

Jagdreservat, n
Wildreservat, n
- game preserve
- game reserve

Jagdrevier, n
Jagdgebiet, n
- hunting ground

Jagdsafari, f
- hunting safari

Jagdsaison, f
Jagdzeit, f
- hunting season
- shooting season
- open season

Jagdschein, m
- game license BE
- game licence BE
- shooting license
- hunting license

Jagdschloß, n
Jagdschlößchen, n
- hunting castle
- hunting seat BE
- hunting lodge
- shooting lodge
- hunting palace

Jagdtourismus, m
- hunting tourism

Jagdtourist, m
- hunting tourist

Jagdzeit, f
Jagdsaison, f
- shooting season
- hunting season

jagen
(Tiere jagen)
- hunt
- shoot

Jäger, m
- hunter
- huntsman

Jägerart, adv *gastr*
nach Jägerart, adv *gastr*
- hunter's style, adv *gastr*

Jägersoße, f
- hunter's sauce

Jahr, n
- year

Jahresanfang, m
- beginning of the year

Jahresärztekongreß, m
jährlicher Ärztekongreß, m
- annual medical convention

Jahresaufwand, m
jährlicher Aufwand, m
- annual expenditure

Jahresausflug, m
(eines Betriebs etc. ins Grüne)
alljährlicher Ausflug, m
jährlicher Ausflug m
- annual outing

Jahresauslastung, f
jährliche Auslastung, f
- annual load factor

Jahresauslastung in Prozent, f
prozentuale Jahresauslastung, f
- annual load factor percentage

Jahresauslastungsrate, f
→ Jahresauslastungsquote

Jahresausstellung, f
jährliche Ausstellung, f
- annual exhibition
- annual show
- annual exhibit AE

Jahresball, m
- annual ball

Jahresbeitrag, m
- yearly subscription
- annual subscription

Jahresbelegung, f
jährliche Auslastung, f
Jahresauslastung, f
jährliche Belegung, f
- annual occupancy

Jahresbelegung, f
→ Jahresauslastung

Jahresbelegungsquote, f
jährliche Auslastungsquote, f
Jahresauslastungsrate, f
jährliche Auslastungsrate, f
- annual occupancy rate

Jahresbesuch, m
jährlicher Besuch m
- annual visit

Jahresbetrieb, m (Betrieb)
- establishment operating all the year round
- establishment open all over the year

Jahresbetrieb, m (Service)
- service available throughout the year
- year-round service

Jahresbettenauslastung, f
jährliche Bettenauslastung, f
Jahresbettenbelegung, f
jährliche Bettenbelegung, f
- annual bed occupancy
- yearly bed occupancy

Jahresbilanz, f
- annual balance sheet

Jahresdiner, n
jährliches Diner, n
Jahresessen, n
- annual dinner

Jahresdurchschnitt, m
- annual average
- yearly average
- average of the year

Jahreseinnahme, f
jährliche Einnahme, f
- annual revenue

Jahreseinnahmen, f pl
jährliche Einnahmen f pl
- annual revenues pl
- annual income
- annual takings pl
- annual receipts pl
- yearly receipts pl

Jahresende, n
- end of the year
- year's end
- year end

Jahresertrag, m
jährlicher Ertrag, m
- annual return
- annual yield

Jahresessen, n (Dinner)
- yearly dinner
- annual dinner

Jahresessen, n (Lunch)
- annual luncheon
- annual lunch

Jahresetat, m
Jahresbudget, n
- annual budget

Jahresfahrkarte, f
Jahreskarte, f
- annual ticket

Jahresfahrt, f
jährliche Fahrt, f
- annual trip

Jahresfeier, f
jährliche Feier f
- annual celebration
- anniversary

Jahresfeier abhalten
Jahrestag feiern
- celebrate an anniversary

Jahresferien, pl
jährliche Ferien, pl
- annual holidays BE pl
- annual vacation AE

Jahresfest, n
→ jährliches Fest

Jahresgebühr, f
jährliche Gebühr, f
- annual fee
- annual charge

Jahresgehalt, n
jährliches Gehalt, n
- annual salary

Jahresgesamtdurchschnitt, m
- total annual average
- overall annual average

Jahresgesamtumsatz, m
- annual total sales pl
- annual overall turnover

Jahreshauptversammlung, f
- annual general meeting
- AGM

Jahresinventur, f
Jahresbestandsaufnahme f
- annual stocktaking
- annual inventory

Jahresinventur durchführen
- take the annual inventory

Jahresjubiläum, n
→ Jahrestag

Jahreskapazität f
- annual capacity

Jahreskonferenz, f
jährliche Konferenz, f
- annual conference

Jahreskonferenz abhalten
- hold an annual conference

Jahreskongreß, m
jährlicher Kongreß, m
- annual convention
- annual congress

Jahreskongreß abhalten
- hold an annual convention
- hold an annual congress

Jahreskurort, m
→ Ganzjahreskurort

Jahresmiete, f
  JM, f
  Miete pro Jahr, f
  ♦ **yearly rent**
  ♦ rent per year
  ♦ per annum rent
  ♦ pa rent
Jahresmietwert m
  ♦ **annual rental**
  ♦ yearly rental
Jahresmitgliedsbeitrag, m
  jährlicher Mitgliedsbeitrag, m
  ♦ **annual membership fee**
Jahresmitte, f
  ♦ **middle of the year**
  ♦ midyear
Jahresnachfrage, f
  jährlich Nachfrage, f
  ♦ **annual demand**
  ♦ yearly demand
Jahrespressekonferenz, f
  ♦ **annual press conference**
Jahresschau, f
  Jahresausstellung, f
  jährliche Schau, f
  jährliche Ausstellung, f
  ♦ **annual show**
Jahressitzung, f
  jährliche Sitzung, f
  ♦ **annual session**
Jahresstatistik f
  ♦ **annual statistics** *pl*
  ♦ statistics covering one year *pl*
Jahresstelle f
  (Arbeitszeit)
  ♦ **job held on a one-year contract**
Jahrestag, m
  Jubiläum, n
  Jubelfeier, f
  Jubelfest, n
  ♦ **anniversary**
Jahrestag der Stadtgründung, m
  ♦ **anniversary of the town's foundation**
Jahrestagung, f
  jährliche Tagung, f
  ♦ **annual meeting**
Jahrestagung abhalten
  ♦ **hold an annual meeting**
Jahrestreffen, n
  → Jahresversammlung
Jahresturnier, n
  jährliches Turnier n
  ♦ **annual tournament**
Jahresumsatz, m
  jährlicher Umsatz, m
  ♦ **annual turnover**
  ♦ yearly turnover
  ♦ annual sales *pl*
  ♦ yearly sales *pl*
Jahresumsatz haben von DM 123456
  ♦ **have an annual turnover of DM 123456**
  ♦ have a yearly turnover of DM 123456
  ♦ have annual sales of DM 123456
  ♦ have yearly sales of DM 123456
Jahresurlaub, m (Arbeitnehmer)
  ♦ **annual leave**
Jahresurlaub, m (Ferien)
  jährlicher Urlaub, m
  Jahresferien, pl
  jährliche Ferien, pl
  ♦ **annual vacation** *AE*

  ♦ yearly vacation *AE*
  ♦ annual holiday *BE*
  ♦ yearly holiday *BE*
Jahresveranstaltung, f
  jährliche Veranstaltung f
  ♦ **annual event**
Jahresversammlung, f
  jährliche Versammlung, f
  Jahrestreffen, n
  jährliches Treffen, n
  ♦ **annual meeting**
Jahresvisum, n
  ♦ **one-year visa**
Jahreszeit, f (generell)
  ♦ **time of the year**
  ♦ time of year
Jahreszeit, f (Saison)
  → Saison
jahreszeitlich, adj
  → saisonal
jahreszeitlichen Schwankungen unterliegen
  saisonalen Schwankungen unterliegen
  ♦ **be subject to seasonal fluctuations**
jahreszeitlicher Rückgang, m
  saisonale Rezession f
  ♦ **seasonal recession**
jahreszeitliche Schwankung, f
  → saisonale Schwankung
jahreszeitlich verschieden sein
  ♦ **change with the season**
  ♦ vary with the season
  ♦ depend on the season
Jahreszimmerauslastung, f
  → jährliche Zimmerauslastung
Jahreszimmerbelegung, f
  → jährliche Zimmerbelegung
Jahrgang, m (Wein)
  ♦ **wine of one year**
  ♦ vintage of one year
  ♦ vintage
Jahrgangssekt, m
  ♦ **vintage champagne**
Jahrgangswein, m
  ♦ **vintage wine**
  ♦ vintage
jahrhundertealt, adj
  ♦ **centuries-old, adj**
jahrhundertealte Geschichte, f
  ♦ **centuries-old history**
jahrhundertealtes Hotel, n
  ♦ **centuries-old hotel**
jahrhundertealte Tradition, f
  ♦ **centuries-old tradition**
jahrhundertealte Tradition aufrechterhalten
  ♦ **keep up the centuries-old tradition**
Jahrhundertfeier, f
  Hundertjahrfeier f
  ♦ **centenary**
  ♦ centennial
Jahrhundertwein, m
  ♦ **vintage of the century**
  ♦ rare vintage
jährlich, adj
  ♦ **annual, adj**
  ♦ yearly, adj
jährlich, adv
  ♦ **by the year, adv**
  ♦ on a yearly basis, adv
  ♦ yearly, adv
  ♦ every year, adv
  ♦ per annum, adv

jährliche Auslastung, f
  → Jahresauslastung
jährliche Auslastungsquote, f
  → Jahresauslastungsquote
jährliche Bettenauslastung, f
  → Jahresbettenauslastung
jährliche Nachfrage, f
  → Jahresnachfrage
jährlicher Umsatz, m
  Jahresumsatz, m
  ♦ **annual sales** *pl*
  ♦ annual turnover
  ♦ yearly sales *pl*
  ♦ yearly turnover
jährliches Besucheraufkommen, n
  jährliches Besuchervolumen, n
  ♦ **annual volume of visitors**
  ♦ annual visitor volume
jährliches Fest, n (Festival)
  Jahresfest, n
  ♦ **annual festival**
jährliches Fest, n (Party)
  Jahresfest, n
  ♦ **annual party**
jährliches Wiedersehen, n
  ♦ **annual reunion**
jährliche Vorstandssitzung, f
  (Vorstand und Aufsichtsrat)
  ♦ **annual board meeting**
jährliche Wochenendbelegung, f
  jährliche Wochenendauslastung, f
  ♦ **annual weekend occupancy**
jährliche Zimmerauslastung, f
  Jahreszimmerauslastung, f
  ♦ **annual room occupancy**
  ♦ yearly room occupancy
Jahrmarkt, m
  ♦ **fair**
  ♦ fun-fair *BE*
  ♦ amusement park *AE*
Jahrmarkt abhalten
  ♦ **hold a fair**
Jahrmarktaussteller, m
  ♦ **fairground showman**
Jahrmarktbude, f
  Rummelplatzbude, f
  ♦ **fairground booth**
  ♦ fairground stall *BE*
  ♦ fairground stand *AE*
Jahrmarkt der Eitelkeiten, m
  ♦ **vanity fair**
Jahrmarktplatz, m
  Festplatz, m
  ♦ **fairground**
Jahrmarktzelt, n
  Festzelt, n
  ♦ **fairground tent**
Jahrtausend, n
  ♦ **millenium**
Jahrtausendfeier, f
  Tausendjahrfeier f
  ♦ **millenary celebration**
  ♦ thousand-year celebration
  ♦ millenium celebration
Jalousie, f (generell)
  ♦ **venetian blind**
  ♦ Venetian blind *AE rare*
  ♦ jalousie
  ♦ (sun)-blind *BE*
  ♦ window shade *AE*

Jalousie

Jalousie, f (Rolljalousie)
 ♦ blind
Jalousietür, f
 ♦ louvre door
Jamaika
 ♦ Jamaica
Jamaikaner, m
 ♦ Jamaican
Jamaikanerin, f
 ♦ Jamaican girl
 ♦ Jamaican woman
 ♦ Jamaican
jamaikanisch, adj
 ♦ Jamaican, adj
Jamaika-Rum, m
 ♦ Jamaica rum
Jamboree, n
 Festzusammenkunft f
 Pfadfindertreffen n
 lautes Gelage n
 buntes Unterhaltungsprogramm n
 ♦ jamboree
Jamsession, f
 (Treffen mit improvisierter Jazzmusik)
 ♦ jam session
Januar, m
 ♦ January
Januarauslastung, f
 Auslastung im Januar, f
 ♦ January load factor
 ♦ load factor in January
Januarbelegung, f
 Januarauslastung, f
 ♦ January occupancy
 ♦ occupancy in January
Januarfeier, f
 ♦ January celebration
Januartagung, f
 Januartreffen, n
 ♦ January meeting
Januarurlaub, m
 ♦ January vacation AE
 ♦ January holiday BE
Januarwoche, f
 ♦ January week
Japan
 ♦ Japan
Japaner, m
 ♦ Japanese
Japanerin, f
 ♦ Japanese girl
 ♦ Japanese woman
 ♦ Japanese
japanisch, adj
 ♦ Japanese, adj
japanische Art, adv gastr
 nach japanischer Art, adv gastr
 ♦ Japanese style, adv gastr
japanische Küche, f (Speisen)
 ♦ Japanese cuisine
 ♦ Japanese cooking
Japanische Meer, das, n
 ♦ Japan Sea, the
japanischer Garten, m
 ♦ Japanese garden
Jardiniere, f
 Blumenschale, f
 Blumenständer, m
 ♦ jardiniere AE
 ♦ jardinière BE

Jasmintee, m
 ♦ jasmine tea
Jause, f ÖST
 → Imbiß
jausen ÖST
 → vespern
Jausenstation, f ÖST
 kleiner Gasthof, m
 ♦ small inn
Java
 ♦ Java
Javaner, m
 ♦ Javanese
Javanerin, f
 ♦ Javanese girl
 ♦ Javanese woman
 ♦ Javanese
javanisch, adj
 ♦ Javanese, adj
 ♦ Javan, adj
javanische Art, adv gastr
 nach javanischer Art, adv gastr
 ♦ Javanese style gastr
Jazz, m
 ♦ jazz
Jazzabend, m
 ♦ jazz evening
 ♦ jazz night
Jazzballett, n
 ♦ jazz ballet
Jazzband, f
 Jazzkapelle f
 ♦ jazz band
Jazzbrunch, m
 ♦ jazz brunch
Jazzclub, m
 Jazzklub m
 ♦ jazz club
Jazzfestival, n
 Jazzfest n
 ♦ jazz festival
Jazzkeller, m
 ♦ jazz cellar
 ♦ jazz club
Jazzkonzert, n
 ♦ jazz concert
Jazzmatinée, f
 ♦ jazz matinée
 ♦ jazz matinee AE
Jazzmusik, f
 ♦ jazz music
Jazzmusiker, m
 ♦ jazz musician
Jazzpianist, m
 ♦ jazz pianist
Jazzreise, f
 ♦ jazz tour
Jazzreise, f
 ♦ journey through jazz
Jazzsänger, m
 ♦ jazz singer
Jazzveranstaltung, f
 ♦ jazz show
Jazzwochenende, n
 ♦ jazz weekend
jede denkbare Art Bier, f
 ♦ every conceivable type of beer
jede Einrichtung für jeden Anlaß
 ♦ every facility for every occasion
jedem Geschmack gefallen
 ♦ suit every palate

jedem Geschmack kann etwas geboten werden
 ♦ every taste can be catered for
jedem möglichen Geschmack gerecht werden
 ♦ cater for all possible tastes
jeden nach seinem Geschmack
 ♦ everybody to his taste
jeden Abend außer montags
 ♦ every night except Mondays
 ♦ every evening except Mondays
jede Nacht, adv
 jeden Abend, adv
 ♦ every night, adv
 ♦ nightly, adv
jeden denkbaren Luxus und Komfort bieten
 ♦ offer every conceivable luxury and comfort
jeden Geschmack zufriedenstellen
 ♦ satisfy all tastes
 ♦ satisfy every palate
jeden Komfort und Luxus genießen
 ♦ enjoy all the comforts and luxuries
jeden modernen Komfort anbieten
 ♦ offer all modern comforts
 ♦ offer all modern conveniences
 ♦ offer all mod. cons.
jeden modernen Luxus und Komfort anbieten
 ♦ offer every modern luxury and comfort
jeden Tag
 ♦ every day
jeden Tag seiner Ferien genießen
 jeden Tag seines Urlaubs genießen
 ♦ enjoy every day of one's vacation AE
 ♦ enjoy every day of one's holiday BE
jeden vorstellbaren Luxus und Komfort bieten
 ♦ offer every imaginable luxury and comfort
jeden Wunsch jm von den Augen ablesen
 ♦ anticipate s.o.'s every wish
jeden zweiten Montag, adv
 ♦ every other Monday, adv
 ♦ on alternate Mondays, adv AE
jeden zweiten Tag, adv
 an jedem zweiten Tag, adv
 ♦ every other day, adv
jeder denkbare Komfort, m
 jeder vorstellbare Komfort m
 ♦ every conceivable comfort
 ♦ every imaginable comfort
jeder kann teilnehmen
 jeder kann mitmachen
 ♦ everyone can take part
 ♦ everybody can join in
jeder Komfort, m
 jeglicher Komfort, m
 ♦ every comfort
jeder moderne Komfort, m
 jeglicher moderne Komfort, m
 ♦ all modern comforts pl
 ♦ every modern comfort
 ♦ all modern conveniences pl
 ♦ all modern amenities pl
 ♦ all mod. cons. pl
jeder moderne Luxus und Komfort, m
 ♦ every modern luxury and comfort
jeder nur denkbare Komfort und Service, m
 ♦ every imaginable comfort and service
 ♦ every conceivable comfort and service
Jeder Tag ein Ferientag
 (Slogan)
 ♦ Every day a holiday
jeder weitere Tag
 jeder zusätzliche Tag
 ♦ each additional day

jederzeit, adv
♦ at any time, adv
♦ at all times, adv
♦ always, adv
jederzeit willkommen sein
zu jeder Zeit willkommen sein
♦ be welcome any time
♦ be welcome at all times
♦ be always welcome
jeder zweite Tag, m
♦ every other day
Jedes der 123 Zimmer ist verschieden in Form und
Stil
♦ Each of the 123 rooms is different in shape and
♦ style
Jedes Zimmer ist individuell eingerichtet und gehalten
♦ Each room is furnished and decorated in an in-
♦ dividual style
jedes zusätzliche Kind, n
jedes weitere Kind, n
♦ each additional child
Jeep, m
♦ jeep
Jeepfahrt, f
♦ jeep trip
♦ jeep ride
Jeep mieten
♦ rent a jeep AE
♦ hire a jeep BE
Jeepreise, f
♦ jeep journey
♦ jeep tour
♦ jeep trip
Jeepsafari, f
♦ jeep safari
Jeeptour, f
Jeepfahrt, f
♦ jeep tour
♦ jeep trip
Jeepverleih, m
♦ jeep rental AE
♦ jeep hire BE
je früher desto besser
♦ the earlier the better
jeglicher Komfort, m
→ jeglicher Komfort
jeglicher Komfort wird geboten
♦ every comfort is catered for
Jemen, m
♦ Yemen, the
Jemenit, m
Jemenite, m
♦ Yemenite
Jemenitin, f
♦ Yemenite girl
♦ Yemenite woman
♦ Yemenite
jemenitisch, adj
♦ Yemenite, adj
je nach Bestuhlung, adv
♦ according to the seating arrangement, adv
♦ depending on the seating arrangement, adv
je nach Geschmack
♦ according to taste
je nach Jahreszeit
♦ depending on the season
♦ according to the season

je nach Laune, adv
♦ according to one's mood, adv
♦ depending on one's mood, adv
je nach Saison, adv
entsprechend der Saison, adv
♦ according to the season, adv
♦ depending on the season, adv
je nach Tageszeit, adv
♦ according to the time of day, adv
je nach Unterkunft
♦ depending on accommodation
Jesuitenkirche, f
♦ Jesuit Church, the
Jet, m
(Flugzeug)
♦ jet
Jet-Anlage, f
→ Gegenstromanlage
Jetflugzeug, n
Düsenflugzeug, n
♦ jet plane
♦ jet airplane AE
♦ jet aeroplane BE
♦ jet aircraft
Jetlag, m
(Müdigkeit nach langer Flugreise)
♦ jet lag
Jetlag überstehen
fertigwerden mit dem Jetlag
♦ overcome jetlag
Jetset, m
(reiche Reisende, oft Schickeria)
♦ jet set
Jetsetort, m
♦ jet-set place
Jetsetter, m
(Mitglied des Jetsets)
♦ jet-setter
jetten um die Welt
um die Welt jetten
♦ jet around the world
♦ jet round the world
Jetzeitalter, n
♦ jet age
jetzige Saison, f
♦ present season
♦ current season
Jiu-Jitsu, n
♦ jujitsu
♦ jiujitsu
JM, f
→ Jahresmiete
Job, m
Arbeitsplatz m
♦ job
joggen
♦ jog
Joggen, n
→ Jogging
Jogger, m
Joggerin f
♦ jogger
Jogging, n
Joggen, n
♦ jogging
Joggingeinrichtung, f
♦ jogging facility
Joggingkarte, f (Landkarte)
♦ jogging map
Joggingkleidung, f
♦ jogging outfit

Jogginglauf, m
Lauf, m
♦ jog
Jogginglauf machen
Lauf machen
♦ go on a jog
Joggingpfad, m
♦ jogging track
♦ jogging trail
Joggingrundweg, m
♦ jogging circuit
Joghurt, m
♦ yoghurt
♦ yogurt
♦ yoghourt
Joghurtdressing, n
♦ yoghurt dressing
♦ yogurt dressing
♦ yoghourt dressing
Joghurtsoße, f
♦ yoghurt sauce
♦ yogurt sauce
♦ yoghourt sauce
Joghurtsuppe, f
♦ yoghurt soup
♦ yogurt soup
♦ yoghourt soup
Johann (Dienername)
♦ Jack (servant's name)
Johannisbeergelee, n (rot)
♦ redcurrant jelly
Johannisbeergelee, n (schwarz)
♦ blackcurrant jelly
Johannisbeerkonfitüre, f (rot)
♦ redcurrant jam
Johannisbeersaft, m (rot)
♦ redcurrant juice
Johannisbeersorbet, n
Cassissorbet, n
♦ blackcurrant sorbet
Johannisbeerwein, m (rot)
♦ redcurrant wine
Joie de vivre, f FR
Lebensfreude f
♦ joie de vivre FR
♦ enjoyment of life
Joiner, m sl
(wird von Hotelgast heimlich mitgebracht)
unangemeldeter Gast, m
♦ joiner sl
♦ unregistered guest
Joint, m
(Zigarette mit Marihuana)
♦ joint
Joint Venture, n
→ Gemeinschaftsunternehmen
Joint-Venture-Hotel, n
♦ joint venture hotel
Joint-Venture-Vereinbarung, f
♦ joint venture agreement
Joint-Venture-Vereinbarung unterzeichnen
♦ sign a joint venture agreement
Jolle, f
♦ jolly boat AE
♦ jolly-boat BE
♦ jolly
♦ wherry
♦ dinghy
Jollenführer, m
♦ wherry-man

Jollenkreuzer, m
♦ jolly cruiser
Jollensegeln, n
Jollensegelsport, m
♦ jolly sailing
Jongleur, m
♦ juggler
jonglieren (mit etw)
♦ juggle (with s.th.)
Jordan, m
♦ Jordan River, the
♦ River Jordan, the
♦ Jordan, the
Jordanien
♦ Jordan
Jordanier, m
♦ Jordanian
Jordanierin, f
♦ Jordanian girl
♦ Jordanian woman
♦ Jordanian
jordanisch, adj
♦ Jordanian, adj
Journal, n ökon
♦ diary
♦ journal
♦ daybook
♦ day-book BE
♦ tabular ledger
Journalbüro, n
♦ ledger office
Journaleintrag, m
♦ journal entry
♦ ledger entry
Journal führen
♦ keep a diary
♦ keep a journal
♦ keep a (tabular) ledger
Journalführer, m
♦ ledger clerk
Journalführung, f
♦ keeping a diary
♦ keeping a journal
♦ keeping a (tabular) ledger
Journalist, m
♦ journalist
jovial, adj
leutselig, adj
♦ jovial, adj
joviale Begrüßung, f
freundliche Begrüßung, f
♦ jovial welcome
Jovialität, f
Leutseligkeit, f
Freundlichkeit, f
♦ joviality
Jubelempfang, m
→ jubelnder Empfang
Jubelfeier, f (Jahrestag)
→ Jahrestag
jubelnd, adj
♦ jubilant, adj
jubelnden Empfang bereiten jm
♦ give s.o. a jubilant reception
jubelnder Empfang, m
Jubelempfang m humor
♦ jubilant reception
Jubel und Trubel, m
Trubel, m
Hektik, f

Rummel, m derog
♦ hustle and bustle
Jubiläum, n
♦ jubilee
♦ anniversary
Jubiläum feiern
Jubiläum begehen
♦ celebrate a jubilee
♦ celebrate an anniversary
Jubiläumsball m
♦ anniversary ball
Jubiläumsempfang, m
♦ anniversary reception
Jubiläumsessen, n (Dinner)
Gedächtnisessen, n
Jubiläumsdiner, n
♦ anniversary dinner
Jubiläumsessen, n (generell)
Gedächtnisessen, n
♦ anniversary meal
Jubiläumsessen, n (Lunch)
Gedächtnisessen, n
♦ anniversary lunch
♦ anniversary luncheon
Jubiläumsessen, n (Supper)
Gedächtnisessen n
♦ anniversary supper
Jubiläumsfahrt, f
♦ anniversary trip
Jubiläumsfeier, f
♦ anniversary celebration
♦ celebration of an anniversary
♦ celebration of a jubilee
Jubiläumsfest, n
Jubiläumsparty, f
♦ anniversary party
Jubiläumsgeschenk, n
♦ anniversary present
♦ anniversary gift
Jubiläumskonzert, n
♦ anniversary concert
Jubiläumskreuzfahrt, f
♦ anniversary cruise
Jubiläumspreis, m
♦ anniversary price
♦ anniversary rate
Jubiläumsprogramm, n
♦ anniversary program AE
♦ anniversary programme BE
Jubiläumsreise, f
♦ anniversary tour
♦ anniversary trip
♦ anniversary journey
Jubiläumssäule, f
♦ jubilee column
Jubiläumsveranstaltung, f
♦ anniversary event
♦ anniversary function
♦ anniversary
Jude, m
♦ Jew
Judenviertel, n
♦ Jewish quarter
Jüdin, f
♦ Jewish girl
♦ Jewish woman
♦ Jew
jüdisch, adj
♦ Jewish, adj

jüdische Art, adv gastr
nach jüdischer Art, adv gastr
♦ Jewish style, adv gastr
Judo, n
♦ judo
Jugendaustauschprogramm, n
♦ youth exchange program AE
♦ youth exchange programme BE
Jugendcampingplatz, m
♦ youth campsite
♦ youth campground AE
♦ youth camping site BE
♦ youth camping ground BE
♦ youth site
Jugendchor, m
♦ youth choir
Jugendclub, m
♦ youth club
Jugendfahrpreis, m
♦ youth fare
Jugendgruppe f
♦ youth group
Jugendgruppenabend, m
Gruppenabend m
♦ young people's evening
♦ youth evening
Jugendgruppenreise, f
Jugendgruppenfahrt f
♦ youth group journey
♦ youth group tour
Jugendheim, n
♦ hostel for young people
Jugendherberge f
♦ youth hostel
Jugendherberge mit 123 Betten, f
♦ youth hostel with 123 beds
Jugendherbergsbewohner, m
Jugendherbergsbesucher m
♦ youth hosteler AE
♦ youth hosteller BE
Jugendherbergsfahrt, f
♦ youth hosteling tour AE
♦ hosteling tour AE
♦ youth hostelling tour BE
♦ hostelling tour BE
Jugendherbergsleiter, m
♦ youth hostel warden
♦ warden of a youth hostel
♦ youth hosteler AE
Jugendherbergsmitglied, n
♦ youth hostel member
Jugendherbergsorganisation, f
♦ youth hostel organisation
♦ youth hostel organization
Jugendherbergsreise machen
♦ go youth hostelling
Jugendherbergsverband, m
♦ Youth Hostel Association, the
♦ Youth Hostels Association, the
♦ YHA, the
Jugendherbergsverbandsmitglied, n
♦ Youth Hostel Association member
♦ Youth Hostels Association member
♦ YHA member
Jugendhotel, n
♦ hotel for young people
♦ young people's hotel
♦ youth hotel
Jugendlager, n
♦ youth camp

Jugendlicher, m/f
Jugendliche, m/f pl
♦ young person
♦ juvenile
♦ young people *pl*
Jugendliche unter 16 Jahren, m/f pl
♦ young persons under 16 years of age *pl*
♦ young persons under 16 *pl*
Jugendmeisterschaft, f
♦ youth championship
Jugendmusikfest, n
♦ youth music festival
Jugendmusikwoche, f
♦ youth music week
Jugendorchester, n
♦ youth orchestra
Jugendpension, f
♦ youth guesthouse *AE*
♦ youth guest-house *BE*
Jugendplatz, m
(Camping)
♦ youth site
Jugendpreis, m
♦ youth price
♦ youth rate
Jugendprogramm, n
♦ youth program *AE*
♦ youth programme *BE*
Jugendreise, f
Jugendfahrt f
♦ journey of young people
♦ journey for young people
♦ youth travel *coll*
Jugendreiseleiter, m
♦ youth tour guide
♦ youth travel guide
Jugendreisen, n
Jugendreiseverkehr, m
♦ youth travel
Jugendreiseorganisation, f
♦ youth travel organisation
♦ youth travel organization
Jugendschutz, m
♦ protection of children and young people
Jugendschutzgesetz, n
♦ law for the protection of children and young people
Jugendsegment, n
(Marketing)
♦ youth segment
Jugend-Stand-by-Preis, m
♦ youth standby fare *AE*
♦ youth stand-by fare *BE*
Jugendstil, m
(Kunststil zu Beginn des 20. Jahrhunderts)
♦ Jugendstil
♦ Art Nouveau
Jugendtarif, m
♦ youth tariff
♦ youth rates *pl*
♦ youth rate
♦ youth terms *pl*
Jugendtheater, n
♦ theater for young people *AE*
♦ theatre for young people *BE*
♦ young people theater *AE*
♦ young people theatre *BE*
Jugendtourismus, m
♦ youth tourism
Jugendtourist, m
♦ youth tourist

Jugendtreffen, n
♦ youth meeting
Jugendunterkunft, f
♦ youth accommodation
Jugendvorstellung, f
♦ performance for young people
Jugendwohnheim, n
♦ hostel for apprentices and young workers
Jugendzentrum, n
Jugendhaus n
Jugendheim n
♦ youth center *AE*
♦ youth centre *BE*
Jugendzimmer, n
→ Kinderzimmer
Jugoslawe, m
♦ Jugoslav
♦ Jugoslavian
♦ Yugoslav
♦ Yugoslavian
Jugoslawien
♦ Jugoslavia
♦ Yugoslavia
Jugoslawin, f
♦ Jugoslav
♦ Jugoslavian
♦ Yugoslav
♦ Yugoslavian
jugoslawisch, adj
♦ Jugoslav, adj
♦ Jugoslavian, adj
♦ Yugoslav, adj
♦ Yugoslavian, adj
Julep, m (Eisgetränk)
alkoholisches Eisgetränk, n
♦ julep *AE*
Julep, m (medizinisch) *hist*
medizinisches Getränk, n
♦ julep *hist*
Juli, m
♦ July
Juliauslastung, f
Auslastung im Juli, f
♦ July load factor
♦ load factor in July
Julibelegung, f
Juliauslastung, f
♦ July occupancy
♦ occupancy in July
Julifeier, f
♦ July celebration
Julitagung, f
Julitreffen, n
♦ July meeting
Juliurlaub, m
♦ July vacation *AE*
♦ July holiday *BE*
Juliwoche, f
♦ July week
Jumbo, m
♦ jumbo
Jumbofähre, f
♦ jumbo ferry
Jumbojet, m
♦ jumbo jet
Jumboladung, f
♦ jumboload *AE*
♦ jumbo-load *BE*
Jungbier, n
♦ freshly brewed beer

Jungbrunnen, m *humor*
Gesundbrunnen, m
♦ fountain of youth
Junge, m
♦ boy
junge Familie, f
♦ young family
junger Besucher, m
junge Besucherin f
♦ young visitor
junger Gast, m
♦ young guest
junger Kellner, m
♦ young waiter
junger Pilz, m
kleiner Pilz, m
♦ button mushroom
junger Wein, m
Jungwein, m
♦ young wine
♦ new wine
junges verheiratetes Paar, n
♦ young married couple
Jungfernfahrt, f (generell)
♦ inaugural journey
♦ maiden journey
Jungfernfahrt, f (Meer)
♦ maiden voyage
♦ inaugural voyage
Jungfernflug, m
♦ maiden flight
♦ inaugural flight
Jungferninseln, f pl
♦ Virgin Islands, the *pl*
Jungfernwein, m
♦ virgin wine
Junggebliebener, m
Junggebliebene f
♦ young-at-heart
Junggehilfe, m (Kellner)
→ Jungkellner
Junggeselle, m
♦ bachelor
♦ single man
♦ single
♦ unmarried man
♦ bach *AE sl*
Junggesellenbude, f *coll*
♦ bachelor's den *coll*
♦ bachelor's digs *BE pl coll*
Junggesellenfest, n
Junggesellenparty, f
Junggesellenfeier, f
♦ bachelor party
Junggesellenwohnung, f
Wohnung für Alleinstehende, f
♦ bachelor apartment *AE*
♦ bachelor's apartment *AE*
♦ bachelor flat *BE*
♦ bachelor's flat *BE*
Junggesellin, f
♦ bachelor girl
♦ single woman
♦ unmarried woman
Jungkellner, m
Commis de rang m *FR*
♦ junior waiter
♦ commis de rang *FR*
♦ junior commis
Jungkoch, m
Juniorkoch, m

Anfangskoch, m
- ♦ junior cook

jung trinken etw
(z.B. jungen Wein)
- ♦ drink s.th. young

jung und alt, pl
die Jungen und die Alten, pl
- ♦ young and old pl

Jungverheiratete, m/f pl
Jungvermählte m/f pl
- ♦ newly-wed couple
- ♦ newlywed couple
- ♦ newly-weds pl
- ♦ newlyweds pl

Jungwein, m
→ junger Wein

Juni, m
- ♦ June

Juniauslastung, f
Auslastung im Juni, f
- ♦ June load factor
- ♦ load factor in June

Junibelegung, f
Juniauslastung, f
- ♦ June occupancy
- ♦ occupancy in June

Junifeier, f
- ♦ June celebration

Junior, m
- ♦ junior

Juniorappartement, n
- ♦ junior apartment

Juniorchef, m
- ♦ junior manager

Juniorenbahnkarte, f
- ♦ young persons' railcard

Juniorenkurs, m
Juniorenlehrgang, m
- ♦ junior course

Juniorenurlaub, m
- ♦ young people's vacation AE
- ♦ vacation for young people AE
- ♦ young people's holiday BE
- ♦ holiday for young people BE

Juniorenzelt, n
- ♦ junior tent

Juniorkoch, m
→ Jungkoch

Juniorskischule, f
- ♦ junior ski school

Juniorsuite, f
(im Gegensatz zur Vollsuite)
- ♦ junior suite
- ♦ jr suite

Junitagung, f
Junitreffen, n
- ♦ June meeting

Juniurlaub, m
- ♦ June vacation AE
- ♦ June holiday BE

Juniwoche, f
- ♦ June week

Junk Food, n
→ minderwertiges Essen

Junkie, m
Fixer, m
Drogenabhängiger, m
- ♦ junkie
- ♦ junky

Jupiterlampe, f
(bei Ausstellungen etc)
- ♦ sun lamp
- ♦ floodlight

Jura, m
- ♦ Jura, the

Jurte, f
(großes Rundzelt in Asien)
- ♦ yurt
- ♦ yurta

Jüte, m
- ♦ Jute
- ♦ Jutlander
- ♦ inhabitant of Jutland

Jütin, f
- ♦ Jute
- ♦ Jutlander
- ♦ inhabitant of Jutland

jütisch, adj
- ♦ Jutish, adj
- ♦ Jutlandic, adj

Jütland
- ♦ Jutland

Juwelier, m
Goldschmied m
- ♦ jeweler AE
- ♦ jeweller BE

Juwelierladen m
Juweliergeschäft n
Schmuckgeschäft n
- ♦ jewelry store AE
- ♦ jeweler's store AE
- ♦ jewellery shop BE
- ♦ jeweller's shop BE
- ♦ jeweller's BE abbr

jwd
→ tiefste Provinz

jwd wohnen coll
in der tiefsten Provinz wohnen
- ♦ live out in the sticks AE
- ♦ live at the back of beyond

K

Kabarett, n
 ♦ cabaret
Kabarettanordnung, f (Bestuhlung)
 (mehrere Einzeltische)
 ♦ cabaret arrangement
Kabarettclub, m
 Nachtclub mit Varietédarbietungen, m
 ♦ cabaret club
Kabarett-Kneipe, f
 ♦ cabaret-bar AE
 ♦ cabaret-pub BE
Kabarett machen
 ♦ do cabaret
Kabarettrevue, f
 ♦ cabaret revue
Kabarettunterhaltung f
 ♦ cabaret entertainment
Kabarettveranstaltung, f
 ♦ cabaret show
Kabarettveranstaltung präsentieren
 ♦ feature a cabaret show
Kabarettvorstellung, f
 Kabarettsatire, f
 ♦ revue
Kabelfarbfernsehen n
 ♦ cable color TV AE
 ♦ cable color television AE
 ♦ cable colour TV BE
 ♦ cable colour television BE
Kabelfarbfernseher, m
 ♦ cable color TV set AE
 ♦ cable colour TV set BE
 ♦ cable color television AE
 ♦ cable colour television BE
Kabelfernsehen, n
 ♦ cable TV
 ♦ cable television
Kabelfernseher, m
 ♦ cable TV set
 ♦ cable television set
 ♦ cable TV
 ♦ cable television
Kabeljau, m
 Dorsch, m
 ♦ cod
 ♦ codfish AE
Kabeljaufilet, n
 ♦ cod fillet
 ♦ cod filet
Kabeljausteak, n
 ♦ cod steak
Kabelkanal, m
 (z.B. in einer Ausstellungshalle)
 ♦ cable duct
Kabine, f (in Schwimmbad etc.)
 ♦ cubicle
Kabine, f (in Verkehrsmitteln)
 ♦ cabin

Kabine belegen
 Kabine bewohnen
 ♦ occupy a cabin
Kabinenbreite, f
 ♦ cabin width
 ♦ width of the cabin
Kabinenbuchung, f
 ♦ cabin booking
 ♦ booking a cabin
Kabinendecke, f
 ♦ cabin ceiling
Kabinenfahrgast, m (Schiff)
 ♦ saloon passenger
Kabinenfenster, n
 ♦ cabin window
Kabinenfernsehen, n
 ♦ cabin television
 ♦ cabin TV
Kabinengepäck, n
 Bordgepäck, n
 ♦ cabin luggage BE
 ♦ cabin baggage AE
Kabinengröße, f
 ♦ cabin size
 ♦ size of the cabin
Kabinengrundriß, m
 ♦ cabin layout
 ♦ layout of the cabin
Kabinenhöhe, f
 ♦ cabin height
 ♦ height of the cabin
Kabinenhosteß, f
 (Flugzeug)
 ♦ cabin hostess
Kabinenkategorie, f
 ♦ cabin category
Kabinenklasse, f
 ♦ cabin class
 ♦ cabin category
Kabinenkomfort, m
 ♦ cabin comfort
Kabinenkonfiguration, f
 ♦ cabin configuration
Kabinenkreuzer, m
 Kajütboot, n
 ♦ cabin cruiser
Kabinenlage, f
 ♦ cabin location
 ♦ location of the cabin
Kabinenlänge, f
 ♦ cabin length
 ♦ length of the cabin
Kabinenlift, m
 → Kabinenseilbahn
Kabinenmannschaft, f
 ♦ cabin crew
Kabinennummer, f
 ♦ cabin number

Kabinenpersonal, n
 ♦ cabin staff
 ♦ cabin personnel
Kabinenplan, m
 ♦ cabin plan
Kabinenseilbahn, f
 Kabinenlift, m
 ♦ cabin lift
Kabinenservice, m
 Kabinendienst, m
 ♦ cabin service
Kabinensitzplatz, m
 Kabinenplatz, m
 ♦ cabin seat
Kabinensteward, m
 ♦ cabin steward
Kabinenstewardeß, f
 ♦ cabin stewardess
Kabinentemperatur, f
 ♦ cabin temperature
Kabinentür, f
 ♦ cabin door
Kabinentyp, m
 Kabinenart, f
 ♦ cabin type
 ♦ type of cabin
Kabinenüberprüfung, f
 Kabinenkontrolle, f
 ♦ cabin check
Kabinenunterkunft, f
 Kabinenunterbringung, f
 ♦ cabin accommodation
Kabinenwand, f
 ♦ cabin wall
Kabinenzuweisung, f
 Kabinenzuteilung, f
 ♦ cabin allocation
 ♦ cabin assignment AE
 ♦ allocation of cabins
 ♦ assignment of cabins AE
Kabinettwein, m
 ♦ cabinet wine
 ♦ Kabinett wine
Kabotage, f
 ♦ cabotage
Kabotagestrecke, f
 Kabotageroute, f
 ♦ cabotage route
Kabuff, n derog
 winziger Raum, m
 ♦ cubby
 ♦ cubbyhole AE
 ♦ cubby-hole BE
 ♦ tiny room
Kachelofen, m
 ♦ tiled stove
Kachelofenheizung, f
 ♦ tiled-stove heating

Kaderangestellter, m
  Führungskraft, f
  ♦ employee in managerial job
Kadermitarbeiter, m
  Führungskraft, f
  ♦ employee in managerial post
Kaderpersonal n
  Führungspersonal n
  ♦ executive staff
  ♦ executive personnel
  ♦ managerial staff
  ♦ managerial personnel
Kafeneion, n GR
  ♦ kafeneion GR
Kaffee, m
  ♦ coffee
Kaffee auf Bestellung
  ♦ coffee to order
Kaffee aufgießen
  ♦ brew coffee
Kaffeeausgabestelle, f
  ♦ coffee point
Kaffee ausschenken
  ♦ pour coffee
Kaffeeautomat, m
  ♦ coffee-making machine
  ♦ coffee machine
Kaffeebar f
  ♦ coffee bar
Kaffee bestellen
  ♦ order coffee
Kaffeebestellung, f
  ♦ coffee order
  ♦ ordering coffee
Kaffeebeutel, m
  ♦ coffee bag
  ♦ coffee sachet
Kaffeebohne, f
  ♦ coffee bean
Kaffee-Ersatz, m
  ♦ coffee substitute
  ♦ ersatz coffee
Kaffeefilter, m
  ♦ coffee filter
Kaffee für vier Personen, m
  ♦ coffee for four persons
  ♦ coffee for four
Kaffeegast, m
  ♦ coffee customer
Kaffeegedeck, n
  ♦ coffee cover
  ♦ place laid for coffee
Kaffeegeschirr, n
  ♦ coffee things pl
  ♦ coffee service
Kaffeegeschmack, m
  ♦ coffee flavor AE
  ♦ coffee flavour BE
Kaffeehaus, n
  ♦ coffee house
Kaffeehausliterat, m
  ♦ coffee-house writer
Kaffeehausmusik, f
  ♦ coffee-house music
Kaffeehausphilosoph, m
  ♦ coffee-house philosopher
Kaffee heiß servieren
  ♦ serve the coffee hot
Kaffee im Bett, m
  ♦ coffee in bed

Kaffeekanne, f
  ♦ coffeepot
Kaffeekarte, f
  (Speisekarte)
  ♦ coffee menu
Kaffeeklatsch, m
  → Kaffeekränzchen
Kaffeekoch, m
  Kaffeeköchin, f
  ♦ coffee-maker
Kaffee kochen
  Kaffee machen
  ♦ make coffee
  ♦ make the coffee
  ♦ make some coffee
Kaffeekränzchen, n
  Kaffeeklatsch, m
  ♦ coffee party
  ♦ ladies' coffee party
  ♦ ladies' coffee circle
  ♦ afternoon coffee party
  ♦ coffee klatsch AE fam
Kaffeekrug, m
  Kaffeekanne, f
  ♦ coffee jug
Kaffeeküche, f
  ♦ coffee pantry
  ♦ stillroom BE
Kaffeelöffel, m
  ♦ teaspoon
Kaffee machen
  → Kaffee kochen
Kaffee mahlen
  ♦ grind coffee
Kaffeemarke, f
  (wie eine Münze)
  Kaffeechip, m
  ♦ coffee token
Kaffeemaschine, f (groß)
  ♦ coffee urn
Kaffeemaschine, f (klein)
  ♦ coffee maker
  ♦ coffee machine
Kaffee mit Milch, m
  Milchkaffee, m
  Café au lait, m FR m
  ♦ coffee with milk AE
  ♦ white coffee BE
  ♦ café au lait FR
  ♦ milky coffee
Kaffeemühle, f
  ♦ coffee-grinder
  ♦ coffee mill AE
Kaffee ohne Milch, m
  schwarzer Kaffee, m
  ♦ black coffee
Kaffeepause, f
  ♦ coffee break
Kaffeepause machen
  ♦ have a coffee break
  ♦ take a coffee break
Kaffeepausenverpflegung, f
  Kaffeepausenbewirtung, f
  ♦ coffee-break foodservice AE
  ♦ coffee-break catering BE
Kaffeepulver, n
  ♦ coffee powder
Kaffeerestaurant n
  → Café-Restaurant
Kaffee rösten
  ♦ roast coffee

Kaffeesahne, f
  Kaffeeobers, n ÖST
  ♦ coffee cream
  ♦ cream
Kaffeesalon, m
  ♦ coffee lounge
Kaffeesatz, m
  ♦ coffee grounds pl
  ♦ coffee dregs pl
Kaffee schmeckt wie Spülwasser
  ♦ coffee tastes like dishwater AE
  ♦ coffee tastes like dish-water BE
Kaffeeservice, m (Dienstleistung)
  Kaffeeverpflegung, f
  ♦ coffee service
Kaffeeservice, n (Geschirr)
  ♦ coffee set
  ♦ coffee service
Kaffeestand, m
  ♦ coffee stand
  ♦ coffee stall BE
Kaffeestube, f
  Kaffeezimmer, n
  ♦ coffee room
  ♦ coffeeshop AE
Kaffeestunde, f
  Kaffeezeit, f
  ♦ coffeetime AE
  ♦ coffee-time BE
  ♦ coffee hour
Kaffeetablett, n
  ♦ coffee tray
Kaffeetafel, f
  → Kaffeetisch
Kaffeetante, f
  starker Kaffeetrinker, m
  ♦ coffee freak
  ♦ coffee addict
Kaffeetasse, f
  ♦ coffee cup
Kaffeeterrasse, f
  ♦ coffee terrace
Kaffeetisch, m
  Kaffeetafel, f
  ♦ table laid for coffee
Kaffeetisch decken
  ♦ lay the table for coffee
Kaffee trinken
  ♦ have (a) coffee
  ♦ drink coffee
Kaffeetrinken, n
  ♦ coffee drinking
Kaffeetrinker, m
  ♦ coffee drinker
Kaffee und Kuchen, m
  ♦ coffee and cake
Kaffee und Kuchen servieren
  ♦ serve coffee and cake
Kaffee- und Teefilter, m
  Kaffee- und Teemaschine, f
  ♦ coffee and tea maker
Kaffee- und Teemaschine, f (Filter)
  → Kaffee- und Teefilter
Kaffeeverbrauch, m
  Kaffeekonsum, m
  ♦ coffee consumption
  ♦ consumption of coffee
Kaffeeverpflegung, f
  → Kaffeeservice

Kaffeewärmer, m
　Kaffeemütze, f
　♦ coffee-pot cosy
Kaffeeweißer, m
　♦ coffee whitener
　♦ coffee creamer AE
Kaffee zubereiten
　♦ prepare coffee
Kai, m
　Quai, m
　♦ quay
　♦ quayside
　♦ wharf
Kaianlage, f
　♦ wharf
　♦ wharves pl
Kaimaninseln, die, f pl
　♦ Cayman Islands, the pl
kaiserliches Hotel, n
　♦ imperial hotel
kaiserliche Suite, f
　Kaisersuite, f
　♦ imperial suite
Kaiserpalast, m
　♦ imperial palace
Kaiserresidenz, f
　kaiserliche Residenz, f
　♦ imperial residence
Kaisersaal, m
　♦ imperial hall
Kaiserschloß, n
　kaiserliches Schloß, n
　♦ imperial castle
　♦ imperial palace
Kaiserstuhl, m
　(Region)
　♦ Kaiserstuhl, the
Kajak, m
　♦ kayak
　♦ kajak AE
　♦ kyak AE
　♦ cajak AE
Kajakfahren, n
　Kajaksport, m
　♦ kayaking
　♦ kajaking AE
　♦ kyaking AE
Kajakfahrt, f
　♦ kayak trip
　♦ kajak trip AE
　♦ kyak trip AE
Kajakreise, f
　♦ kayak tour
　♦ kajak tour AE
　♦ kyak tour AE
Kajütboot, n
　→ Kabinenkreuzer
Kajüte, f
　♦ cabin
Kajütenbett n
　→ Etagenbett
Kakao, m
　♦ cocoa
Kakaobecher, m
　♦ chocolate tumbler
Kakaopulver, n
　♦ cocoa powder
Kakerlak, m
　Schabe, f
　♦ roach AE
　♦ cockroach

Kalabrien
　♦ Calabria
kalabrisch, adj
　♦ Calabrian, adj
Kalb, n
　♦ calf
Kalbfleisch, n
　♦ veal
Kalbfleischgericht, n
　♦ veal dish
Kalbsbraten, m
　♦ roast veal
Kalbsbratenstück, n (roh)
　(Stück zum Braten)
　♦ joint of veal
Kalbsbries, n
　♦ calf's sweetbread
　♦ sweetbread
Kalbsbriesfüllpastete, f
　♦ sweetbread timbale
Kalbsbrust, f
　♦ breast of veal
Kalbsfarce, f
　♦ veal stuffing
Kalbsfilet, n
　♦ veal fillet
　♦ veal filet AE
　♦ fillet of veal
　♦ filet of veal AE
Kalbsfrikassee, n
　♦ veal fricassee
Kalbsfüllpastete, f
　♦ veal timbale
Kalbshaxe, f
　♦ knuckle of veal
　♦ veal knuckle
Kalbshirn, n
　♦ calf's brain
Kalbskotelett, n
　♦ veal cutlet
Kalbsleber, f
　♦ calf's liver
Kalbsniere, f
　♦ veal kidney
Kalbsragout, n/m
　♦ veal stew
Kalbsschnitzel, n
　♦ veal escalope
Kalbsspezialität, f
　♦ veal specialty AE
　♦ veal speciality BE
Kalbssteak, n
　♦ veal steak
Kalbswurst, f
　♦ veal sausage
Kaldaunen, f pl
　→ Kutteln
Kalender, m
　♦ calendar
Kalenderjahr, n
　♦ calendar year
Kalendermonat m
　♦ calendar month
Kalendertag, m
　♦ calendar day
Kalifornien
　♦ California
Kalifornienreise, f
　♦ Californian tour

Kalifornienurlaub, m
　♦ Californian vacation AE
　♦ Californian holiday BE
Kalifornier, m
　♦ Californian
kalifornisch, adj
　♦ Californian, adj
kalifornischer Wein, m
　♦ Californian wine
Kalksteinhöhle, f
　♦ limestone cave
Kalkulation beruht auf etw
　Berechnung beruht auf etw
　♦ calculation is based on s.th.
kalkulieren etw
　ausrechnen etw
　berechnen etw
　♦ calculate s.th.
Kalorie, f
　♦ calorie
　♦ calory
kalorienarm, adj
　♦ low-calorie, adj
　♦ low in calories, adj
kalorienarme Kost f
　♦ low-calorie diet
kalorienarme Lebensmittel, n pl
　♦ low-calorie food
kalorienarmes Bier n
　♦ low-calorie beer
kalorienarmes Getränk, n
　♦ low-calorie drink
　♦ low-calorie beverage
kalorienarmes Menü, n
　♦ low-calorie menu
Kalorienbedarf m
　♦ calorie requirement
kalorienbewußt, adj
　♦ calorie-conscious, adj
kalorienbewußte Küche, f
　♦ calorie-conscious cooking
　♦ calorie-conscious cuisine
kalorienfrei, adj
　♦ calorie-free, adj
Kaloriengehalt, m
　♦ caloric content
　♦ calorific content
Kalorienmenge f
　♦ number of calories
kalorienreich, adj
　♦ high-calorie, adj
　♦ rich in calories, adj
Kalorientabelle f
　♦ table of calorific values
kalorienüberwacht, adj
　♦ calorie-controlled, adj
kalorienüberwachte Kost, f
　♦ calorie-controlled diet
kalorienüberwachtes Menü, n
　♦ calorie-controlled menu
Kalorienwert, m
　♦ calorific value
　♦ calorific power
Kalorien zählen
　♦ count the calories
Kaltdusche f
　kalte Dusche f
　♦ cold shower
kalt duschen (sich)
　♦ have a cold shower
　♦ take a cold shower

kalte Dusche, f
→ Kaltdusche
kalte Jahreszeit f
♦ cold season
Kalte Küche, f (Ort)
Garde-manger f FR
♦ cold larder
♦ garde-manger FR
♦ larder
kalte Mahlzeit, f
→ kaltes Essen
kalte Platte, f
♦ plate of cold meats BE
♦ cold cuts AE pl
kalter Braten, m
♦ cold meat
kalter Imbiß, m
♦ cold snack
Kalter Koch, m
→ Kaltkoch
kaltes Bad nehmen
kalt baden
♦ have a cold bath
kaltes Büfett, n
♦ cold buffet
kalte Schulter zeigen jm
♦ give s.o. the cold shoulder
Kälteschutzanzug, m sport
Taucheranzug, m
♦ wetsuit
kaltes Essen, n
kalte Mahlzeit, f
♦ cold meal
kaltes Gericht, n
Kaltgericht n
♦ cold dish
kaltes Getränk, n
Kaltgetränk, n
♦ cold drink
♦ cold beverage
kalte Speisen, f pl
♦ cold dishes pl
♦ cold meals pl
kalt essen
♦ have a cold meal
kaltes und warmes Büfett, n
♦ hot and cold buffet
kaltes und warmes Wasser, n
KWW
♦ cold and hot water
♦ CHW
kalte Suppe, f
Kaltschale, f
♦ cold soup
Kalte und warme Küche zu jeder Tageszeit
♦ Hot and cold meals at any time of the day
Kaltgericht, n
→ kaltes Gericht
Kaltgetränk, n
→ kaltes Getränk
Kaltgetränkeverkaufsautomat, m
Kaltgetränkeautomat, m
♦ cold drink vending machine
♦ cold drink machine
kalt halten etw
♦ keep s.th. cold
Kaltkoch, m
Kalter Koch, m
♦ larder cook
♦ garde-manger FR

Kaltlagerung, f
♦ cold storage
Kaltmiete, f
kalte Miete f
♦ rent exclusive of heating
♦ basic rent (without heating)
Kaltschale, f
süße Suppe, f
♦ sweet soup
♦ cold soup
♦ fruit soup
kalt servieren etw
♦ serve s.th. cold
kalt serviert, adj
♦ served cold, adj
Kalttauchbecken, n
♦ cold plunge pool
kalt-warmes Büfett, n
♦ cold-hot buffet
Kaltwasser, n
kaltes Wasser n
♦ cold water
Kaltwasserbehandlung, f
♦ cold-water treatment
Kaltwasserdusche f
♦ cold-water shower
Kaltwasserhahn, m
♦ cold-water faucet AE
♦ cold-water tap BE
Kaltwasserkur, f
♦ cold-water therapy
♦ cold-water cure
Kambodscha
♦ Cambodia
Kambodschaner, m
♦ Cambodian
Kambodschanerin, f
♦ Cambodian girl
♦ Cambodian woman
♦ Cambodian
kambodschanisch, adj
♦ Cambodian, adj
Kamel, n
♦ camel
Kamelkarawane, f
♦ camel caravan
Kamel reiten
♦ ride a camel
Kamelreiten, n
♦ camel riding
Kamelritt, m
♦ camel ride
Kamelroute, f
Kamelstrecke, f
♦ camel route
Kamelsafari, f
♦ camel safari
Kamerun
♦ Cameroon
♦ Cameroun
Kameruner, m
♦ Cameroonian
♦ Camerounian
Kamerunerin, f
♦ Cameroonian girl
♦ Cameroonian woman
♦ Cameroonian
♦ Camerounian girl
♦ Camerounian woman
kamerunisch, adj
♦ Cameroon, adj

♦ Cameroonian, adj
♦ Camerounian, adj
Kamillentee, m
♦ camomile tea
Kamin, m (im Zimmer)
offener Kamin, m
♦ fireplace
Kamin, m (Schornstein)
→ Schornstein
Kaminbar, f
♦ bar with open fireplace
♦ bar with a log fire
Kaminecke, f
♦ chimney nook
♦ chimney corner
Kaminessen, n
Essen am Kamin, n
Mahlzeit am Kamin, f
♦ fireside meal
Kaminfeuer, n
♦ open fire
Kaminhalle, f
♦ lobby with open fireplace
♦ lobby with open log fire
Kamin mit Sitzecke, m
Kamin mit Sitzplatz, m
Kaminecke, f
♦ inglenook fireplace AE
♦ ingle-nook fireplace BE
Kaminplatz, m
(Sitzplatz am Kamin)
Kaminecke, f
♦ inglenook AE
♦ ingle-nook BE
Kaminstube, f
→ Kaminzimmer
Kaminstuhl, m
Stuhl am Kamin, m
Stuhl am offenen Kamin, m
♦ fireside chair
Kaminzimmer, n (generell)
♦ room with log fire
♦ room with open fireplace
♦ room with open fire
Kaminzimmer, n (Salon)
♦ lounge with log fire
♦ lounge with open fire
Kammer, f (Abstellkammer)
♦ boxroom
Kammerjäger, m
♦ vermin exterminator
♦ exterminator
♦ pest controller
Kammerkonzert, n (Musikstück)
♦ chamber concerto
Kammerkonzert, n (Veranstaltung)
♦ concert of chamber music
♦ chamber music concert
Kammerkonzertabend, m
♦ chamber music evening
Kammermusik, f
♦ chamber music
Kammermusikaufführung, f
Kammermusikdarbietung, f
♦ chamber music performance
Kammerorchester, n
♦ chamber orchestra
Kammerzofe, f
♦ waiting maid
♦ waiting girl

Kammstraße, f
♦ crest road
Kammuschel, f
Jakobsmuschel, f
♦ scallop
♦ scollop
Kampagne, f
♦ campaign
Kampagne starten
♦ launch a campaign
Kampanien
♦ Campania
Kampf um Marktanteile, m
♦ fight for market shares
Kanada
♦ Canada
Kanadaurlaub, m
♦ Canadian vacation *AE*
♦ Canadian holiday *BE*
Kanadier, m
♦ Canadian
Kanadierin, f
♦ Canadian girl
♦ Canadian woman
♦ Canadian
kanadisch, adj
♦ Canadian, adj
Kanal, m (Abwasser)
♦ drain
Kanal, m (generell)
♦ canal
Kanal, m (natürlich)
♦ channel
Kanal, m (TV)
♦ channel
Kanalboot, n
♦ narrowboat
♦ canal boat
Kanalbootreise, f
♦ narrowboat tour
Kanalfahrt, f
♦ canal trip
♦ canal ride
Kanalinseln, f pl
Ärmelkanalinseln, f pl
♦ Channel Islands, the *pl*
Kanalisierung, f
♦ canalisation
♦ canalization
Kanalkreuzfahrt, f
♦ canal cruise
♦ canal cruising
Kanalküste, f
Ärmelkanalküste, f
♦ Channel coast
Kanalmuseum, n
♦ canal museum
Kanalrestaurant, n
Grachtenrestaurant, n
♦ canalside restaurant
Kanaltunnel, m
Ärmelkanaltunnel, m
♦ Channel tunnel
Kanalufer, n
♦ canal bank
Kanalurlaub, m
Kanalferien, pl
♦ canal vacation *AE*
♦ canal holiday *BE*

Kanalverbindung, f
♦ canal connection
♦ canal link
Kanal von Korinth, m
♦ Corinth Canal, the
Kanapee, n (Möbelstück)
Sofa, n
♦ davenport
♦ settee *BE*
♦ sofa
Kanapee, n (Speise)
Canapé, n *FR m*
♦ canapé *FR m*
Kanaren, die, pl
Kanarischen Inseln, die, f pl
♦ Canaries, the *pl*
♦ Canary Islands, the *pl*
Kanarischen Inseln, die, f pl
Kanaren, die, pl
♦ Canary Islands, the *pl*
♦ Canaries, the *pl*
Kandelaber, m
♦ candelabrum
♦ candelabra
kandieren (etw)
♦ candy (s.th.)
kandiert, adj
♦ candied, adj
kandierte Früchte, f pl
♦ candied fruits *pl*
Kandiszucker, m
♦ candy sugar
Kaninchen, n
♦ rabbit
Kaninchenbraten, m
Kaninchen gebraten, n
♦ roast rabbit
Kaninchenfleisch, n
♦ rabbit meat
Kaninchenfrikassee, n
♦ rabbit fricassee
Kaninchenkasserolle, f
♦ rabbit casserole
Kaninchenpastete, f
♦ rabbit pie
♦ rabbit pâté
Kaninchenpfeffer, m
♦ jugged rabbit
Kaninchenragout, n/m
♦ rabbit stew
Kaninchenterrine, f
♦ rabbit terrine
Kännchen, n
♦ small jug
♦ pot
Kännchen Kaffee, n
Kanne Kaffee, f
Portion Kaffee, f
♦ pot of coffee
Kännchen Tee, n
Kanne Tee, f
Portion Tee, f
♦ pot of tea
Kann ich bitte Ihre Bestellung aufnehmen?
♦ Can I take your order, please?
Kann ich bitte Ihren Paß sehen?
♦ Can I see your passport, please?
Kann ich bitte kassieren?
♦ Can I have your payment, please?
Kann ich etwas ausrichten?
♦ Can I take a message?

Kann ich etwas zu trinken haben?
♦ Can I have something to drink?
Kann ich hier parken?
♦ Can I park here?
Kann ich Ihnen behilflich sein?
♦ Can I be of help to you?
Kann ich Ihnen ein Mittagessen spendieren?
♦ Can I buy you a lunch?
Kann ich Ihnen helfen?
♦ Can I help you?
Kann ich mit Reiseschecks zahlen?
♦ Can I pay by traveler's checks? *AE*
♦ Can I pay with traveler's checks? *AE*
♦ Can I pay by traveller's cheques? *BE*
♦ Can I pay with traveller's cheques? *BE*
Kann ich neben Ihnen sitzen?
♦ Can I sit next to you?
Kannst Du mir ein Bier zahlen?
♦ Can you stand me a beer?
Kantine, f (generell)
♦ canteen
Kantine, f (Hochschule)
♦ buttery *BE*
Kantine führen
♦ run a canteen
Kantinenessen, n
♦ canteen food
Kantinenfraß, m *derog*
♦ canteen slop *derog*
Kantinengast, m
♦ canteen guest
Kantinenmahlzeit, f
Kantinenessen, n
♦ canteen meal
Kantinenverpflegung, f
♦ canteen catering
♦ canteen meals *pl*
Kanton, m
♦ canton
Kanu, n
♦ canoe
Kanucamper, m
♦ canoe camper
Kanucamping, n
♦ canoe camping
Kanu fahren
♦ canoe
♦ go canoeing
Kanufahren, n
Kanusport, m
♦ canoeing
Kanufahrer, m
Kanute m
♦ canoeist
Kanufahrt, f
♦ canoe trip
♦ canoeing trip
♦ trip by canoe
Kanuferien, pl
Kanuurlaub, m
♦ canoe holiday *BE*
♦ canoeing holiday *BE*
♦ canoe vacation *AE*
Kanufreizeit, f
→ Kanuurlaub
Kanulager, n
♦ canoe camp
Kanumietgebühr, f
♦ canoe rental charge *AE*
♦ canoe rental fee *AE*

♦ canoe hire charge *BE*
♦ canoe hire fee *BE*
Kanumietservice, m
Kanuvermietungsdienst, m
Kanuvermietung, f
♦ canoe rental service *AE*
♦ canoe hire service *BE*
Kanuregatta, f
♦ canoe regatta
Kanureise, f
Kanutour, f
♦ canoe tour
Kanusport, m
→ Kanufahren
Kanutour, f
♦ trip by canoe
Kanuurlaub, m
Kanuferien, pl
♦ canoe vacation *AE*
♦ canoe holiday *BE*
♦ canoeing holiday *BE*
Kanuverleih, m
♦ canoe rental *AE*
♦ canoe hire *BE*
Kanzel, f (Flugzeug)
→ Cockpit
Kanzel, f (Kirche)
♦ pulpit
Kapaun, m
♦ capon
Kapazität, f
Fassungsvermögen, n
♦ capacity
Kapazität begrenzen
♦ restrict (the) capacity
♦ limit (the) capacity
Kapazität belegen
♦ fill capacity
Kapazität bleibt ungenutzt
♦ capacity remains idle
Kapazität erhöhen
♦ increase capacity
♦ augment capacity
Kapazität füllen
Kapazität auffüllen
♦ fill to capacity
Kapazität haben von ...
über eine Kapazität verfügen von ...
♦ have a capacity of ...
Kapazität hochtreiben
Kapazität stark erhöhen
♦ boost capacity
Kapazität nutzen
♦ utilise capacity
♦ utilize capacity
Kapazität reduzieren
Kapazität mindern
Kapazität senken
♦ reduce capacity
Kapazitätsauslastung, f
→ Kapazitätsnutzung
Kapazitätsbegrenzung, f
Kapazitätsbeschränkung, f
♦ capacity restriction
♦ restriction of (the) capacity
Kapazitätsbegrenzung untersagen
♦ forbid the restriction of capacity
Kapazitätsengpaß, m
♦ capacity bottleneck
♦ capacity squeeze

Kapazitätserweiterung, f
♦ capacity expansion
♦ expansion of capacity
Kapazitätsgrenze erreichen
♦ reach the limit of one's capacity
Kapazitätsniveau, n
♦ capacity level
Kapazitätsnutzung, f
Kapazitätsausnutzung, f
Kapazitätsbeanspruchung, f
Kapazitätsauslastung, f
♦ capacity utilisation
♦ capacity utilization
♦ utilisation of capacity
♦ utilization of capacity
Kapazitätssteigerung, f
Kapazitätserweiterung, f
♦ increase in capacity
Kapazitätsüberbeanspruchung, f
Überbeanspruchung von Kapazität, f
♦ capacity overutilisation
♦ capacity overutilization
♦ overutilisation of capacity
♦ overutilization of capacity
Kapazitätsunterbeanspruchung, f
♦ underutilisation of capacity
♦ underutilization of capacity
♦ capacity underutilisation
♦ capacity underutilization
Kap der Guten Hoffnung, n
♦ Cape of Good Hope, the
Kapelle, f (Kirche)
♦ chapel
Kapelle, f (Musik)
→ Musikkapelle
Kapelle engagieren
→ Band engagieren
Kaper, f
♦ caper
Kapernsoße, f
♦ caper sauce
Kapitalertrag, m
♦ capital yield
Kapitalertragsteuer, f
♦ capital gains tax
kapitalintensiv, adj
♦ capital-intensive, adj
Kapitän, m (Schiff)
♦ captain
Kapitänscocktailparty, f
♦ captain's cocktail party
Kapitänsempfang, m
♦ captain's reception
Kapitänskajüte, f
♦ captain's cabin
Kapitell, n
♦ capital
Kapselschneider, m
(z.B. für Weinflaschen)
♦ foil cutter
Kapstadt
♦ Cape Town
Karaffe, f
♦ carafe
♦ decanter
Karaffenwein, m
♦ carafe wine
Karate, n
♦ karate
Karawane, f
♦ caravan

Karawanenherberge, f
→ Karawanserei
Karawanserei, f
Karawanenherberge f
♦ caravansary
♦ caravanserai
♦ khan
Kardinalsart, adv *gastr*
nach Kardinalsart, adv
♦ cardinal's style, adv *gastr*
Karelien
♦ Karelia
♦ Carelia
karelisch, adj
♦ Karelian, adj
♦ Carelian, adj
Karfreitag, m
♦ Good Friday
karge Mahlzeit, f
kärgliche Mahlzeit, f
frugales Mahl, n
♦ frugal meal
Karibik, f
♦ Caribbean, the
Karibikhotel, n
♦ Caribbean hotel
Karibikinsel, f
♦ Caribbean island
Karibikkreuzfahrt, f
♦ Caribbean cruise
Karibikküste, f
♦ Caribbean coast
Karibikland, n
♦ Caribbean country
Karibikreise, f (generell)
♦ tour to the Caribbean
♦ journey to the Caribbean
♦ trip to the Caribbean
Karibikreise, f (Seereise)
♦ voyage to the Carribbean
Karibiktörn, m
♦ Caribbean turn
Karibiktraum, m
♦ Caribbean dream
Karibikurlaub, m
Urlaub in der Karibik, m
Karibikferien, pl
Ferien in der Karibik, pl
♦ Caribbean vacation *AE*
♦ Caribbean holiday *BE*
Karibikwoche, f
♦ Caribbean Week
karibisch, adj
♦ Caribbean, adj
Karibisches Meer, n
Karibische See, f
♦ Caribbean Sea, the
Karneval, m
Fasching m
Fastnacht f
♦ carnival
Karnevalbegeisterter, m
♦ carnival enthusiast
Karnevalfan, m
♦ carnival fan
Karnevalfestlichkeit, f
Karnevalfestivität, f
Faschingsfestlichkeit, f
Fastnachtsfestlichkeit, f
♦ carnival festivity

Karnevalmuseum, n
  Fastnachtsmuseum, n
  Faschingsmuseum, n
Karnevalsaison, f
  ♦ carnival season
Karnevalsatmosphäre, f
  Karnevalsstimmung, f
  Faschingsatmopshäre, f
  Faschingsstimmung, f
  Fastnachtsatmosphäre, f
  ♦ carnival atmosphere
Karnevalsball, m
  Faschingsball m
  Fastnachtsball m
  ♦ carnival ball
Karnevalsdienstag, m
  Faschingsdienstag, m
  Fastnachtsdienstag, m
  ♦ Pancake Day
Karnevalsfeier, f
  ♦ carnival celebration
Karnevalsgesellschaft, f
  Faschingsgesellschaft, f
  Fastnachtsgesellschaft, f
  ♦ carnival company
Karnevalskampagne, f
  Faschingskampgane, f
  Fastnachtskampagne, f
  ♦ carnival campaign
Karnevalskapelle, f
  ♦ carnival band
Karnevalskostüm, n
  Faschingskostüm, n
  Fastnachtskostüm, n
  ♦ carnival costume
Karnevalsmaske, f
  Fastnachtsmaske, f
  Faschingsmaske, f
  ♦ carnival mask
Karnevalsprinz, m
  Faschingsprinz, m
  Fastnachtsprinz, m
  ♦ carnival prince
  ♦ carnival king *BE*
Karnevalsprinzessin, f
  Faschingsprinzessin, f
  Fastnachtsprinzessin, f
  ♦ carnival princess
  ♦ carnival queen *BE*
Karnevalsprogramm, n
  Faschingsprogramm, n
  Fastnachtsprogramm, n
  ♦ carnival program *AE*
  ♦ carnival programme *BE*
Karnevalssitzung, f
  Faschingssitzung, f
  Fastnachtssitzung, f
  ♦ carnival meeting
Karnevalstanz, m
  Faschingstanz, m
  Fastnachtstanz, m
  ♦ carnival dance
Karnevalstreiben, n
  Faschingstreiben, n
  Fastnachtstreiben, n
  ♦ carnival activities *pl*
Karnevalsumzug, m
  Faschingsumzug, m
  Fastnachtsumzug, m
  ♦ carnival parade
  ♦ carnival procession

Karnevalsveranstaltung, f
  Faschingsveranstaltung, f
  Fastnachtsveranstaltung, f
  ♦ carnival function
  ♦ carnival event
  ♦ function in the carnival
  ♦ event in the carnival
Karnevalsverein, m
  Karnevalsclub, m
  Faschingsverein, m
  Fastnachtsverein, m
  ♦ carnival club
Karnevalsvereinigung, f
  Faschingsvereinigung, f
  Fastnachtsvereinigung, f
  ♦ carnival association
Karnevalsvorstellung, f
  Fastnachtsvorstellung, f
  Faschingsvorstellung, f
  ♦ carnival performance
Karnevalszeit, f
  Karnevalzeit, f
  Fastnachtszeit, f
  Faschingszeit, f
  ♦ carnival period
  ♦ carnival season
  ♦ carnival time
  ♦ Shrovetide
  ♦ carnival
Karnevalszug, m
  Faschingszug, m
  Fastnachtszug, m
  ♦ carnival procession
  ♦ carnival parade
Karnischen Alpen, die, pl
  ♦ Carnic Alps, the *pl*
Kärnten
  ♦ Carinthia
kärntisch, adj
  kärntnerisch, adj
  ♦ Carinthian, adj
Kärntner, m
  Kärntener, m
  ♦ Carinthian
Kärntnerin, f
  Kärntenerin, f
  ♦ Carinthian girl
  ♦ Carinthian woman
  ♦ Carinthian
karolingische Zeit, f *hist*
  ♦ Carolingian times *pl*
Karosse, f
  ♦ state coach
Karosserie, f
  ♦ car body
Karotte, f
  Mohrrübe, f
  ♦ carrot
Karottenkuchen, m
  ♦ carrot cake
Karottensaft, m
  ♦ carrot juice
Karottensalat, m
  ♦ carrot salad
Karottensoufflé, n
  Karottenauflauf, m
  ♦ carrot soufflé
  ♦ carrot souffle *AE*
Karottensuppe, f
  ♦ carrot soup

Karpaten, die, pl
  ♦ Carpathians, the *pl*
Karpatengebirge, n
  ♦ Carpathian Mountains, the *pl*
Karpfen, m
  ♦ carp
Karpfenteich, m
  ♦ carp pond
Karren, m
  ♦ cart
Karrenfahrt, f
  ♦ cart ride
  ♦ cart trip
Karsamstag, m
  Ostersamstag, m
  Ostersonnabend, m
  ♦ Holy Saturday
  ♦ Easter Saturday
Kartäuser, m
  ♦ Carthusian
Kartäuserart, adv *gastr*
  nach Kartäuserart, adv *gastr*
  ♦ chartreuse style, adv *gastr*
Kartäuserkirche, f
  ♦ Carthusian church
Kartäuserkloster, n (Frauen)
  Kartause, f
  ♦ Carthusian convent
Kartäuserkloster, n (Männer)
  Kartause, f
  ♦ Carthusian monastery
Kartäusermönch, m
  ♦ Carthusian monk
Kartbahn, f
  → Go-kart-Bahn
Karte, f (Eintrittskarte)
  Eintrittskarte f
  ♦ ticket
  ♦ admission ticket
  ♦ entrance ticket
  ♦ ticket of admission
Karte, f (Fahrkarte)
  → Fahrkarte
Karte, f (Landkarte)
  → Landkarte
Karte, f (Postkarte)
  ♦ card
  ♦ postcard
  ♦ postal card *AE*
Karte, f (Rationierungskarte)
  → Rationierungskarte
Karte, f (Speisekarte)
  → Speisekarte
Karte, f (Spielkarte)
  → Spielkarte
Karte, f (Visitenkarte)
  → Visitenkarte
Karte, f (Weinkarte)
  → Weinkarte
Karte abholen
  Fahrkarte abholen
  ♦ collect a ticket
Karte ausstellen
  Fahrkarte ausstellen
  ♦ make out a ticket
  ♦ issue a ticket
Karte bekommen
  Fahrkarte bekommen
  ♦ get a ticket

Karte besorgen für jn

Karte besorgen für jn
  Fahrkarte besorgen für jn
  ♦ arrange a ticket for s.o.
Karte bestellen
  Fahrkarte bestellen
  ♦ book a ticket
Karte bezahlen
  Fahrkarte bezahlen
  ♦ pay for a ticket
Karte der Rad- und Wanderwege, f
  ♦ map of (the) biking and hiking paths
Karte erhalten
  Fahrkarte erhalten
  ♦ obtain a ticket
  ♦ get a ticket
  ♦ receive a ticket
Karte für ein Konzert, f
  ♦ ticket for a concert
Kartei, f
  ♦ card index
  ♦ index
Karteikarte, f
  ♦ index card
  ♦ file card
Karte ist herabgesetzt von DM 123 auf DM 12
  ♦ ticket is reduced from DM 123 to DM 12
Karte ist nicht übertragbar
  Fahrkarte ist nicht übertragbar
  ♦ ticket is not transferable
Karte ist übertragbar
  Fahrkarte ist übertragbar
  ♦ ticket is transferable
Karte kaufen an der Kasse
  (Theater)
  ♦ buy a ticket at the door
  ♦ purchase a ticket at the door
Karte kaufen für ein Konzert
  ♦ buy a ticket for a concert
Karte kostet DM 12
  Fahrkarte kostet DM 12
  ♦ ticket costs DM 12
Karte lesen
  Landkarte lesen
  ♦ read a map
Kartellamt, n
  ♦ Monopolies and Mergers Commission, the BE
Kartenausgabe, f
  → Fahrkartenausgabe
Karten bei Einlaß
  (z.B. Theater)
  ♦ Pay at the doors
Kartenbude, f
  Kartenverkaufsstelle, f
  ♦ ticket booth
Karten im Vorverkauf besorgen
  ♦ buy tickets in advance
  ♦ book in advance
Karteninhaber, m (Fahrkarte)
  Fahrkarteninhaber, m
  ♦ ticket holder
Karteninhaber, m (Scheckkarte etc.)
  ♦ cardholder
Kartenkontingent, n
  ♦ allotment of tickets
  ♦ allocation of tickets
Kartenkontingent haben
  ♦ have an allotment of tickets
  ♦ have an allocation of tickets
Kartenkontingent sich sichern
  ♦ secure an allotment of tickets
  ♦ secure an allocation of tickets

Kartenlesen, n
  ♦ map reading
  ♦ reading a map
Kartenpreis, m (Eintritt, Fahrkarte)
  Fahrkartenpreis, m
  Fahrscheinpreis, m
  ♦ ticket price
Kartenpreis, m (Speisekarte)
  → Speisekartenpreis
Kartenpreis hochsetzen (Eintritt etc.)
  ♦ raise the ticket price
Kartenschalter, m
  (z.B. für Theaterkarten)
  ♦ ticket desk
Kartenspiel, n
  ♦ game of cards
  ♦ card-game BE
Karten spielen
  ♦ play cards
Kartenspieler, m
  ♦ cardplayer AE
  ♦ card-player BE
Kartenspielwettbewerb, m
  ♦ card competition
Kartenspielzimmer, n
  ♦ cardroom AE
  ♦ card-room BE
Kartenumsatz, m
  Fahrkartenumsatz, m
  ♦ ticket sales pl
Kartenverkauf, m
  Fahrkartenverkauf, m
  ♦ ticket sale
  ♦ sale of tickets
Kartenverkäufer, m
  ♦ ticket sales agent
Kartenverkaufsstelle, f
  ♦ ticket bureau
  ♦ ticket office
  ♦ ticket desk
  ♦ ticket agency
  ♦ ticket booth
Kartenverkaufszeit, f
  (Theater)
  ♦ box-office hours pl
Kartenverlosung, f
  ♦ ticket raffle
Kartenvorverkauf, m
  Vorverkauf von Karten, m
  ♦ advance ticket sale
  ♦ presale of tickets
Kartenwucherer, m
  (verkauft Karten zu überhöhten Preisen)
  ♦ ticket tout
Karte reservieren (für etw)
  Karte reservieren lassen (für etw)
  ♦ reserve a ticket (for s.th.)
Karte reservieren für jn
  Fahrkarte reservieren für jn
  ♦ reserve a ticket for s.o.
Karte senden jm
  Karte senden an jn
  Karte schicken jm
  Karte schicken an jn
  ♦ send a card to s.o.
  ♦ send s.o. a card
Karte verkaufen jm
  Karte verkaufen an jn
  Fahrkarte verkaufen jm
  Fahrkarte verkaufen an jn

♦ sell a ticket to s.o.
♦ sell s.o. a ticket
Karte verlosen
  Fahrkarte verlosen
  ♦ raffle a ticket
Karte weiterverkaufen an jn
  Karte wieder verkaufen an jn
  Fahrkarte weiterverkaufen an jn
  Fahrkarte wieder verkaufen an jn
  ♦ resell a ticket
Karte zurückgeben
  Fahrkarte zurückgeben
  ♦ return a ticket
Karte zuschicken jm per Post
  Fahrkarte zusenden jm mit der Post
  ♦ post a ticket to s.o. BE
  ♦ mail a ticket to s.o. AE
Kartoffelbrei, m
  ♦ mashed potatoes pl
Kartoffelchips, pl
  ♦ potato chips AE pl
  ♦ potato crisps BE pl
Kartoffelmuseum, n
  ♦ potato museum
Kartoffeln schälen
  ♦ peel potatoes
Kartoffelpastete, f
  ♦ potato pie
Kartoffelpüree, n
  ♦ potato purée
  ♦ potato puree AE
Kartoffelsalat, m
  ♦ potato salad
Kartoffelschalen, f pl
  ♦ potato peelings pl
Kartoffelschäler, m
  Kartoffelschälmesser, n
  ♦ potato peeler
Kartoffelscheibe, f
  ♦ potato slice
  ♦ slice of potato
Kartoffelstärke, f
  ♦ potato starch
Kartoffelsuppe, f
  ♦ potato soup
Karussell, n
  ♦ merry-go-round
  ♦ carrousel AE
  ♦ carousal AE
  ♦ roundabout
Karussellmagazin, n
  ♦ carousel tray
Karussellprojektor m
  (für Dias)
  ♦ carousel projector
Karwendelgebirge, n
  ♦ Karwendel Mountains, the pl
Karwoche, f
  Passionswoche, f
  ♦ Holy Week
Kasache, m
  ♦ Kazak
  ♦ Kazakh
Kasachin, f
  ♦ Kazak girl
  ♦ Kazak woman
  ♦ Kazak
  ♦ Kazakh girl
  ♦ Kazakh woman

kasachisch, adj
 ♦ Kazak, adj
 ♦ Kazakh, adj
Kasachstan
 ♦ Kazakhstan
Kaschemme, f *derog*
 Spelunke, f *derog*
 ♦ beer joint
 ♦ dive *inform*
 ♦ pothouse
Kaschmir
 ♦ Kashmir
Käse, m
 ♦ cheese
Käseaufschnitt, m
 ♦ assorted cheese slices *pl*
 ♦ cheese platter
Käseauswahl, f
 ♦ cheese selection
Käsebrett, n
 ♦ cheese board
Käsebüfett, n
 ♦ cheese buffet
Käsecanapé, n
 ♦ cheese canapé
Käsedessert, n
 ♦ cheese dessert
Käsefondue, n
 ♦ cheese fondue
 ♦ cheese fondu *AE*
Käsegang, m
 (Speisefolge)
 ♦ cheese course
Käsegericht, n
 ♦ cheese dish
Käseglocke, f
 ♦ cheese cover
Käsehobel, m
 ♦ cheese slicer
Käsekuchen, m
 ♦ cheesecake
Käse läuft
 ♦ cheese has gone runny
Käseplatte, f
 ♦ selection of cheeses
 ♦ cheese platter
Käsereibe, f
 ♦ cheese grater
Kaserne, f
 ♦ barracks *sg + pl*
Käsesalat, m
 ♦ cheese salad
Käsesandwich, n
 Käsebrot, n
 ♦ cheese sandwich
Käsescheibe, f
 ♦ cheese slice
 ♦ slice of cheese
Käse schließt den Magen
 ♦ Cheese is the best dessert
Käsesorte, f
 ♦ type of cheese
 ♦ cheese
Käsesoße, f
 ♦ cheese sauce
Käsesoufflé, n
 Käseauflauf, m
 ♦ cheese soufflé *BE*
Käseteller, m
 ♦ cheese plate

Käse- und Weinabend, m
 ♦ cheese and wine evening
Käse- und Weinprobe, f
 ♦ cheese and wine tasting
Kasino, n (Militär)
 ♦ mess
 ♦ officers' mess
 ♦ officers' club
Kasino, n (Spielkasino)
 Spielkasino, n
 ♦ casino
Kasinoabteilung, f
 Spielkasinoabteilung, f
 ♦ casino department
Kasinoausweis, m
 Spielkasinoausweis, m
 ♦ casino card
Kasinobesuch, m
 ♦ visit to the casino
Kasino betreiben
 ♦ operate a casino
Kasinobetrieb, m
 ♦ casino operation
Kasinoeinnahmen, f pl
 Spielkasinoeinnahmen, f pl
 ♦ casino income
 ♦ casino revenue
 ♦ casino revenues *pl*
 ♦ casino receipts *pl*
Kasinogeschäft, n
 ♦ casino business
Kasinoglücksspiel, n
 ♦ casino gambling
Kasinohotel, n
 Spielkasinohotel, n
 ♦ casino hotel
Kasinokonzession, f
 Kasinolizenz, f
 Spielkasinokonzession, f
 Spielkasinolizenz, f
 ♦ casino license
 ♦ casino licence
Kasinoleitung, f
 Spielkasinoleitung, f
 ♦ casino management
Kasinolizenz, f
 → Kasinokonzession
Kasinovertrag, m
 Spielkasinovertrag, m
 ♦ casino contract
Kaspische Meer, das, n
 ♦ Caspian Sea, the
Kasse, f (Kassenschalter)
 ♦ cash desk
 ♦ cashier's desk
 ♦ cashier's counter
 ♦ cash till
Kasse, f (Raum in Geschäft)
 Kassenraum m
 ♦ cash room
 ♦ cashier's office
Kasse, f (Registrierkasse)
 → Registrierkasse
Kassenbeleg, m
 ♦ cash voucher
Kassenbericht, m (generell)
 ♦ cash report
Kassenbericht, m (Verein)
 Bericht des Kassenwarts, m
 ♦ treasurer's report

Kassenbogen, m
 ♦ cash sheet
Kassenbuch, n
 ♦ cashbook
 ♦ cash-book *BE*
 ♦ daybook
 ♦ day-book *BE*
Kassendefizit, n
 ♦ cash shortfall
Kasseneingänge, m pl
 ♦ cash receipts *pl*
 ♦ takings *pl*
Kasseneingangsbuch, n
 ♦ cash received book
Kasseneinnahmen, f pl (Theater)
 ♦ box-office takings *pl*
 ♦ box-office receipts *pl*
Kassenfehlbetrag, m
 (Gegensatz zu Kassenüberschuß)
 ♦ cash shortage
 ♦ unders *pl*
 ♦ shortage
Kassenfehlbetragsbuch, n
 Buch mit den Kassenfehlbeträgen, n
 ♦ unders book *BE*
Kassenführer, m
 → Kassierer
Kassenführung, f
 ♦ cashkeeping
Kassenmagnet, m (Theater, Kino)
 Kassenerfolg, m
 Kassenschlager, m
 ♦ box-office hit
Kassenpatient, m
 ♦ National Health Service patient *BE*
 ♦ NHS patient *BE*
Kassenpreis, m (Theater)
 ♦ box office price
 ♦ box office rate
 ♦ price at the door
Kassenschlager, m
 → Kassenmagnet
Kassensturz machen
 ♦ count one's cash
Kassenüberschuß, m
 (Gegensatz zu Kassenfehlbetrag)
 ♦ cash overage
 ♦ overs *pl*
 ♦ overage
Kassenüberschußbuch, n
 Buch mit den Kassenüberschüssen, n
 ♦ overs book *BE*
Kassenüberschüsse und -fehlbeträge, m pl
 ♦ cash overages and shortages *pl*
Kassenwart, m (Verein)
 → Kassierer
Kasserolle, f
 Schmortopf, m
 Schmorpfanne, f
 ♦ casserole
Kassette, f
 Cassette, f
 ♦ cassette
Kassettenaufnahme, f
 Casettenaufnahme f
 ♦ cassette recording
Kassettengerät, n
 → Kassettenrecorder
Kassettenrecorder, m
 Cassettenrecorder, m
 ♦ cassette recorder

Kassettenspieler

Kassettenspieler, m
♦ cassette player
Kassierer, m (generell)
Kassenführer, m
Kassier, m ÖST/SCHW
♦ cashier
♦ teller AE
Kassierer, m (Theater, Kino)
Kassier, m ÖST
♦ box-office clerk
Kassierer, m (Verein)
Kassenführer, m
Kassenwart, m
♦ treasurer
Kastanienpüree, n
♦ chestnut purée BE
♦ chestnut puree AE
Kasten, m
♦ crate
♦ box
Kastenbett, n
(mit Staukasten)
Truhenbett, n
♦ storage bed
Kasten Bier, m
♦ crate of beer
Kasten Wein, m
♦ crate of wine
Kastenweißbrot, n (Toast)
Toastbrot, n
♦ sandwich loaf
kastilische Art, adv gastr
nach kastilischer Art, adv gastr
♦ Castilian style, adv gastr
Kastorzucker, m
→ Feinkristallzucker
Katalane, m
♦ Catalan
Katalanin, f
♦ Catalan girl
♦ Catalan woman
♦ Catalan
katalanisch, adj
♦ Catalan, adj
Katalog, m
♦ catalogue
♦ catalog AE
Katalogkosten, pl
♦ catalogue costs pl
♦ catalogue cost
♦ catalog costs AE pl
♦ catalog cost AE
Katalogpreis, m
(im Katalog angegeben)
♦ catalogue price
♦ catalogue rate
♦ catalog price AE
♦ catalog rate AE
♦ brochure price
Katalog publizieren
Katalog veröffentlichen
♦ publish a catalogue
♦ publish a catalog AE
Katalog verteilen
♦ distribute a catalogue
♦ distribute a catalog AE
Katalonien
♦ Catalonia
Katamaran, m
♦ catamaran

Katar
♦ Qatar
♦ Katar
Katarer, m
♦ Qatari
♦ Katari
Katarerin, f
♦ Qatari girl
♦ Qatari woman
♦ Qatari
♦ Katari girl
♦ Katari woman
katarisch, adj
♦ Qatari, adj
♦ Katari, adj
Katastrophentourismus, m
♦ disaster tourism
Katastrophentourist, m
♦ disaster tourist
Kate, f
→ Cottage
Kategorie f
♦ category
Kategorisierung, f
(Unterscheidung: Hotel, Pension etc.)
♦ categorisation
Kater, m figur
♦ hangover
Kater auskurieren figur
Kater heilen figur
♦ cure a hangover
Kater ausschlafen
♦ sleep off one's hangover
Katerfrühstück n
♦ hangover breakfast
Kater haben figur
♦ have a hangover
♦ be hung over AE
Kathedrale, f
Dom, m
♦ cathedral
Kathedrale wurde im Jahr 1234 geweiht
♦ cathedral was consecrated in 1234
Katzenfisch, m
Wels, m
♦ catfish
♦ sheat fish
Katzenfutter, n
♦ cat food
Katzenpension, f
♦ boarding home for cats
Katzensprung, m coll
(kleine Entfernung)
♦ stone's throw coll
♦ short distance
Katzensprung entfernt sein von etw
♦ be a stone's throw away from s.th.
♦ be a short distance from s.th.
Katzentisch, m
♦ side table
kauen etw
♦ chew s.th.
kaufen etw
♦ buy s.th.
kaufen etw in letzter Sekunde
♦ buy s.th. at the last minute
kaufen etw über die Theke
♦ buy s.th. over the counter
Käufer, m
♦ buyer

Käufermarkt, m
♦ buyer's market
Käuferverhalten, n
♦ buyer behavior AE
♦ buyer behaviour BE
Kaufkraft, f
♦ purchasing power
Kaufpreis, m
♦ purchase price
Kaufverhalten, n
♦ purchasing behavior AE
♦ purchasing behaviour BE
Kaugummi, n
♦ chewing gum
Kaukasier, m
♦ Caucasian
Kaukasierin, f
♦ Caucasian girl
♦ Caucasian woman
♦ Caucasian
kaukasisch, adj
♦ Caucasian, adj
Kaukasus, m
♦ Caucasus, the
♦ Caucasus Mountains, the pl
Kaukasusland, n
♦ Caucasian country
kaum die Augen offenhalten
♦ hardly keep one's eyes open
kaum etw essen
♦ hardly eat a thing
kaum möbliert, adj
kaum eingerichtet, adj
♦ barely furnished, adj
Kaution, f (Haft)
♦ bail
Kaution, f ökon (Anzahlung)
Kt., f
♦ deposit
♦ security deposit
Kaution, f ökon (Sicherheit)
♦ security
♦ surety
♦ guarantee
Kaution fordern (Anzahlung)
♦ require a deposit
Kaution für einen Schlüssel, f
♦ deposit for a key
Kaution hinterlegen (Anzahlung)
♦ leave a deposit
Kaution leisten (Anzahlung)
Kaution zahlen
♦ make a deposit AE
♦ pay a deposit BE
Kaution stellen (Anzahlung)
♦ provide a deposit
Kaution zurückgeben
♦ return a deposit
Kavalier der alten Schule, m
♦ gentleman of the old school
Kaviar, m
♦ caviar
♦ caviare
Kaviarbutter, f
♦ caviar butter
♦ caviare butter
Kaviarcanapé, n
♦ caviar canapé
♦ caviare canapé

Kaviarsoße, f
♦ caviar sauce
♦ caviare sauce
Kebab, m
♦ kebab
Keeper, m
→ Barkeeper
Kegel, m
(einzelner Kegel)
♦ pin
♦ skittle
Kegelabend, m
Bowlingabend, m
♦ bowling evening
Kegelbahn, f
♦ skittle alley BE
♦ skittle alley BE
♦ ninepin(s) alley
♦ bowling alley
Kegelbahn im Freien, f
♦ outdoor bowling alley
Kegelbahn mit vier Bahnen, f
♦ four-lane bowling alley
♦ bowling alley with four lanes
Kegelbegeisterter, m
Bowlingbegeisterter, m
♦ bowling enthusiast
Kegelbruder, m
♦ bowling mate
Kegelcenter, n
Kegelzentrum, n
Bowlingcenter, n
Bowlingzentrum, n
♦ bowling center AE
♦ bowling centre BE
Kegelclub, m
Kegelverein, m
Bowlingclub, m
Bowlingverein, m
♦ skittle club
♦ bowling club
Kegelfan, m
Bowlingfan, m
♦ bowling fan
♦ bowling freak
Kegelfreund, m
♦ bowls lover
Kegeljunge, m
♦ pin boy
Kegelkugel, f
Bowlingkugel, f
♦ bowling ball
Kegelkurzurlaub, m
Bowlingkurzurlaub, m
♦ bowling break
kegeln
Kegel spielen
♦ play (at) skittles BE
♦ skittle BE
♦ play (at) ninepins BE
♦ bowl AE
Kegeln, n
Kegelspiel, n
Kegelsport, m
♦ skittles pl = sg
♦ bowling
kegeln gehen
♦ go bowling
Kegelpartie, f
♦ game of bowling

♦ game of skittles BE
♦ game of ninepins BE
Kegelraum, m
Bowlingraum, m
♦ bowling room
Kegelspaß, m
Bowlingspaß, m
♦ bowling fun
Kegelsport, m
→ Kegeln
Kegelwettbewerb, m
Bowlingwettbewerb, m
♦ bowling competition
Kegelwettkampf, m
Bowlingwettkampf, m
♦ bowling contest
Kegelwochenende, n
Bowlingwochenende, n
♦ bowling weekend
Kegler, m
♦ bowler
Kehle anfeuchten sich humor
einen heben coll
♦ whet one's whistle humor
Kehraus, m
♦ last dance
♦ finale figur
♦ grand finale figur
Keilkopfkissen, n
Nackenkissen, n
♦ bolster
kein Aufpreis
♦ no surcharge
Kein-Aufpreis-Garantie, f
♦ no-surcharge guarantee
kein Auge zutun
♦ not sleep a wink
♦ not get a wink
♦ not have a wink
kein Bissen zu essen
♦ not a bite to eat
kein Dach über dem Kopf haben
♦ have no roof over one's head
Kein Durchgangsverkehr
(Hinweisschild)
♦ No thoroughfare
keine Atmosphäre haben
♦ lack atmosphere
keine Ausgabe scheuen
♦ spare no expense
keine Bleibe haben coll
♦ have nowhere to stay coll
keine Eintrittsgebühr
♦ no charge for admission
keine ermäßigten Preise
♦ no reduced prices
♦ no reduced rates
Keine Haustiere
(Hinweisschild)
♦ No pets, please
♦ Pets not accepted
♦ No pets
Keine Kinder
(Angabe im Prospekt)
♦ Children not accepted
keine Mühe scheuen
♦ go out of one's way
keinen Appetit haben
♦ have no appetite
♦ be off one's food

keinen festen Wohnsitz haben
♦ have no fixed residence
keinen Grund zur Klage haben
♦ have no cause to complain
♦ have no cause for complaining
♦ have no cause for complaint
keine Notiz nehmen von einem Gast
Gast ignorieren
♦ take no notice of a guest
♦ ignore a guest
keinen Parkraum haben
♦ lack parking space
keinen Pfifferling wert
♦ not worth a pin
keinen Service erhalten
nicht bedient werden
♦ be refused service
keinen Wunsch offen lassen
♦ leave no wish unsatisfied
Keine Reservierung erforderlich
♦ No reservations required
Keine Reservierung notwendig
Reservierung nicht notwendig
♦ No reservations necessary
keine Vermittlungsgebühr
♦ no booking fee
Keine Zelte!
(Hinweis)
♦ No tents admitted
keine zwei Zimmer sind gleich
♦ no two rooms are alike
kein Firlefanz
♦ no frills
kein Obdach haben
♦ have no shelter
♦ be homeless
Kein Pfand, keine Rücknahme
(Flaschen)
♦ No deposit, no return
kein Rabatt möglich
♦ no discount possible
kein Service
♦ no service
♦ no service provided
Kein Trinkgeld, bitte!
(Verbot)
♦ No tipping!
♦ Gratuities prohibited
Kein Verzehrzwang
(Hinweis)
♦ Nondiners welcome AE
♦ Non-diners welcome BE
kein Zimmer finden
♦ fail to find a room
♦ not find a room
kein Zuckerlecken sein
♦ it's not all beer and skittles
♦ it's not a picnic
Kein Zutritt
(Hinweisschild)
♦ No admittance
Keks, m
♦ biscuit BE
♦ biscuits BE pl
♦ cookie AE
Kelch, m (generell)
Kelchglas, n
♦ goblet
♦ cup
Kelch, m (Kirche)
♦ chalice

Keller

Keller, m (generell)
♦ cellar
Keller, m (Souterrain)
→ Souterrain
Kellerassel, f
Assel, f
♦ woodlouse
Kellerbad, n
Kellerpool, m
♦ cellar pool
Kellerbar, f
♦ cellar bar
♦ dive bar *coll*
♦ basement bar
Kellerbestand, m
Kellervorrat, m
♦ cellar stock
Keller bewohnen
(dauernd)
♦ live in a basement apartment *AE*
♦ live in a basement flat *BE*
Kellerbuch, n
♦ cellar book
Kellerbursche, m *SCHW*
→ Kellergehilfe
Kellerclub, m
♦ cellar club
♦ basement club
Kellerdiskothek, f
Kellerdisko, f
♦ cellar discotheque
♦ cellar disco
Kellerei, f
Weinkellerei, f
♦ cellars *pl*
♦ wine cellars *AE pl*
♦ wine-cellars *BE pl*
Kellereiführung, f
Führung durch die Kellerei, f
♦ tour of the wine cellars
♦ tour of the cellars
Kellereitechnologie, f
♦ cellar technology
Kellerfenster, n
♦ cellar window
Kellerfläche, f
♦ cellar area
Kellerführung, f
♦ tour of the cellars
Kellergarage, f
→ Souterraingarage
Kellergaststätte, f
Kellerwirtschaft, f
♦ cellar pub *BE*
♦ cellar bar *AE*
Kellergehilfe, m
♦ cellarman's assistant
Kellergeschoß, n (Keller)
→ Keller
Kellergeschoß, n (Souterrain)
→ Souterrain
Kellergewölbe, n
♦ cellar vault
kellerkühl, adj
♦ cellar-cool, adj
Kellerlokal, n (Bar)
♦ night cellar *BE*
Kellerlokal, n (Nachtbar)
♦ cellar nightclub *AE*
♦ cellar night-club *BE*

Kellerlokal, n (Restaurant)
→ Kellerrestaurant
Kellermeister, m
♦ head cellarman
♦ cellarman
♦ cellar master
Kellerpersonal n
♦ cellar staff
♦ cellar personnel
Kellerraum, m (Raum)
♦ cellar room
Kellerraum, m (Volumen)
♦ cellar space
Kellerrestaurant, n
♦ basement restaurant
♦ cellar restaurant
♦ underground restaurant
Kellerschwimmbad, n
♦ cellar swimming pool *AE*
♦ cellar swimming-pool *BE*
♦ cellar pool
Kellerspielraum, m
(für Erwachsene)
Kellerspielzimmer, n
♦ cellar games room
Kellertank, m
♦ cellar tank
Kellertaverne, f
♦ cellar tavern
Kellertemperatur, f
♦ cellar temperature
Kellertreppe, f
♦ cellar steps *pl*
♦ cellar stairs *pl*
Kellerwirtschaft, f
♦ cellar economy
Kellerwohnung, f
→ Souterrainwohnung
Kellner, bitte zahlen!
Ober, bitte zahlen!
♦ Waiter, the bill please! *BE*
♦ Waiter, the check please! *AE*
Kellner, m
♦ waiter
Kellnerbedienung f
Kellnerservice, m
Bedienung durch Kellner, f
♦ waiter service
Kellnerbericht, m
♦ waiter's report
Kellnerbrigade, f
Kellnerriege, f
♦ brigade of waiters
♦ waiting brigade
Kellnerbuch, n
♦ waiter's book
Kellnercommis, m
→ Kellnergehilfe
Kellnergehilfe, m
Kellnercommis, m
Serviergehilfe, m
♦ assistant waiter
♦ commis waiter
Kellnergeselle, m
→ Kellnergehilfe
Kellner herbeirufen
♦ beckon (to) a waiter
♦ call a waiter
Kellnerin, f
Gaststättengehilfin, f *form*
♦ waitress

Kellner in einem Drive-in-Restaurant, m
♦ carhop *AE*
Kellnerin gesucht
(Hinweisschild)
♦ Waitress wanted
Kellner in Livree, m
→ livrierter Kellner
Kellnerinnenbedienung, f
Kellnerinnenservice, m
Bedienung durch Kellnerinnen, f
♦ waitress service
Kellnerinnenservice, m
→ Kellnerinnenbedienung
Kellnerinnenservice bieten
♦ provide waitress service
Kellnerinnen werden angelernt
♦ waitresses are trained on the job
Kellner ist diskret
♦ waiter is discreet
Kellnerlehre, f
♦ apprenticeship as a waiter
♦ training as a waiter
Kellnerlehre abschließen
♦ finish an apprenticeship as a waiter
Kellnerlehre absolvieren
♦ do an apprenticeship as a waiter
Kellnerlehrling, m
Servicelehrling, m
♦ apprentice waiter
♦ apprentice waitress
kellnern *coll*
♦ work as a waiter
♦ work as a waitress
♦ job around as a waiter
♦ job around as a waitress
♦ waitress
Kellneroffice, n
♦ waiter's pantry
Kellnerpraktikum, n
♦ practical training as a waiter
Kellnerpraktikum machen
♦ do a practical training as a waiter
Kellnerriege, f
→ Kellnerbrigade
Kellnerservice, m
→ Kellnerbedienung
Kellnertablett, n
♦ waiter's tray
♦ waiters' tray
Kelte, m
♦ Celt
Keltin, f
♦ Celtic girl
♦ Celtic woman
♦ Celt
keltisch, adj
♦ Celtic, adj
keltisches Kreuz, n
♦ Celtic cross
keltische Zeit, f
Keltenzeit, f
♦ Celtic times *pl*
Kemenate, f *hist*
♦ bower *hist*
♦ lady's room *coll*
Kenia
♦ Kenya
Kenianer, m
♦ Kenyan
Kenianerin, f
♦ Kenyan girl

410

◆ Kenyan woman
◆ Kenyan
kenianisch, adj
  ◆ Kenyan, adj
kennen jn namentlich
  ◆ know s.o. by name
kennen jn nur dem Namen nach
  ◆ know s.o. only by the name
kennen jn persönlich
  persönlich kennen jn
  ◆ know s.o. personally
Kennenlernparty, f
  Party zum Kennenlernen, f
  ◆ get-together party
Kenner, m (Experte)
  ◆ authority
  ◆ expert
Kenner, m (Liebhaber von Wein, Kunst etc)
  ◆ connoisseur
kenntnisreich, adj
  ◆ knowledgeable, adj
kenntnisreicher Führer, m
  ◆ knowledgeable guide
Kennung, f
  → Code
Kennzeichen, n
  Prägezeichen, n
  ◆ hallmark
kentern
  ◆ capsize
Keramikmuseum, n
  ◆ ceramics museum
Keramiksammlung, f
  ◆ collection of ceramics
  ◆ ceramics collection
Keramikteller, m
  ◆ ceramic plate
Keramiktischgeschirr, n
  Keramikeßgeschirr, n
  ◆ ceramic tableware
Keramikwaren, f pl
  ◆ ceramics pl
keramisch, adj
  ◆ ceramic, adj
Kerbel, m
  ◆ chervil
Kern, m (Obst)
  ◆ stone
  ◆ pit AE
Kerner, m
  (Wein)
  ◆ Kerner
Kernfach, n
  ◆ core subject
Kernstück des Programms, n
  ◆ core of the program AE
  ◆ core of the programme BE
Kernstück des Programms bilden
  ◆ form the core of the program AE
  ◆ form the core of the programme BE
Kerze, f
  ◆ candle
Kerzenleuchter, m
  Kerzenständer, m
  Kerzenhalter, m
  ◆ candlestick
Kessel, m (groß, oben offen)
  ◆ cauldron
  ◆ caldron
Kessel, m (z.B. für Tee)
  ◆ kettle

Ketchup, n/m
  ◆ ketchup
Kette, f
  ◆ chain
Kettenbetrieb, m
  ◆ chain establishment
  ◆ chain operation
Kettenbuchung, f
  ◆ chain booking
Ketteneinheit, f
  (Statistik)
  ◆ chain unit
Kettengeschäft, n
  Kettenladen, m
  ◆ multiple store AE
  ◆ multiple shop BE
Kettenhotel, n
  ◆ chain hotel
  ◆ chain-operated hotel
Kettenhotellerie, f
  ◆ chain hotel trade
  ◆ chain hotel business
Kettenmanagement, n
  Kettenleitung, f
  ◆ chain management
Kettenmitglied, n
  ◆ chain member
Kettenreisebüro, n
  ◆ chain travel agency
  ◆ multiple travel agency
Kettenrestaurant n
  ◆ chain restaurant
Kettensystem, n
  ◆ chain system
Key- und Letter-Rack n
  (Rezeption)
  Schlüssel- und Brieffach n
  ◆ key and letter rack
Key- und Mail-Rack n
  (Rezeption)
  Schlüssel- und Postfach n
  ◆ key and mail rack
Kfz-Ausstellung, f
  Autoausstellung, f
  Automobilausstellung, f
  ◆ car show
  ◆ automobile show AE
  ◆ motor show BE
kg
  Kilogramm, n
  ◆ kg
  ◆ kilogram
  ◆ kilogramme
Kichererbse, f
  ◆ chick-pea
Kiefer, f
  ◆ pine
  ◆ pine tree
Kiefernwald, m
  ◆ pinewood
  ◆ pine forest
Kieler Bucht f
  (Region)
  ◆ Kiel Bay
Kies, m
  ◆ gravel
  ◆ grit
Kieselbucht, f (groß)
  ◆ shingle bay
Kieselbucht, f (klein)
  ◆ shingle cove

Kieselbucht, f (klein, grob)
  ◆ pebble cove AE
  ◆ pebbly cove BE
Kieselstrand, m (fein)
  ◆ shingle beach AE
  ◆ shingly beach BE
Kieselstrand, m (grob)
  ◆ pebble beach AE
  ◆ pebbly beach BE
Kiesel- und Sandstrand, m (fein)
  ◆ shingle and sand beach
Kiesel- und Sandstrand, m (grob)
  ◆ pebble and sand beach
Kiesstrand, m
  → Kieselstrand
Kilimandscharo, m
  ◆ Mount Kilimanjaro
Kilo, n
  ◆ kilo
Kilogramm, n
  kg
  ◆ kilogram
  ◆ kilogramme
  ◆ kg
Kilometer, m
  km
  ◆ kilometer AE
  ◆ kilometre BE
  ◆ km
Kilometergebühr, f
  → Kilometergeld
Kilometergeld, n (Forderung)
  (in Meilen berechnet)
  Kilometergebühr, f
  ◆ mileage charge
  ◆ milage charge
Kilometergeld, n (Zuschuß)
  (wird z.B. an Arbeitnehmer gezahlt)
  ◆ mileage allowance
  ◆ milage allowance
  ◆ allowance for traveling expenses AE
  ◆ allowance for travelling expenses BE
Kilometerzahl, f
  (eines Fahrzeugs)
  ◆ mileage
  ◆ milage
Kind, n
  ◆ child
Kinderabendessen n (Dinner)
  ◆ children's dinner
  ◆ child's dinner
  ◆ dinner for children
Kinderabenteuerpark, m
  ◆ children's adventure park
Kinderappartement n
  ◆ child's apartment
  ◆ children's apartment
Kinderarzt, m
  ◆ paediatrician
  ◆ pediatrician
Kinderattraktion, f
  ◆ children's attraction
Kinderaufsicht, f
  Kinderbeaufsichtigung, f
  ◆ children's supervision
Kinderausflug, m
  ◆ children's outing
Kinderbad, n
  → Kinderschwimmbad
Kinderbadewanne, f
  ◆ children's bath

Kinderball

Kinderball, m
 (Veranstaltung)
 ♦ children's ball
Kinderbauernhof, m
 ♦ children's farm
Kinder beaufsichtigen
 ♦ look after (the) children
Kinderbeaufsichtigung f
 ♦ child minding
 ♦ child-minding service
Kinderbecken, n
 Kinderbad, n
 ♦ children's pool
 kids' pool *coll*
 kiddies' pool *coll*
Kinderbegleitdienst, m
 ♦ child escort service
Kinderbesteck, n
 ♦ child's cutlery
 children's cutlery
Kinderbetreuerin, f
 Tagesmutter, f
 Kinderbetreuer, m
 ♦ child minder
Kinderbetreuung, f
 ♦ child care
 child-minding service
 ♦ child minding
Kinderbetreuungsdienst, m
 Kinderbeaufsichtigungsdienst, m
 Kinderbetreuung, f
 Kinderbeaufsichtigung, f
 ♦ child-minding service
Kinderbetreuungspersonal, n
 ♦ child-care staff
 ♦ child-care personnel
Kinderbett n
 ♦ child's bed
 ♦ children's bed
Kinder bewirten
 Kinder aufnehmen
 ♦ cater for children
Kinderbuchung f
 ♦ child's booking
 ♦ children's booking
Kinderbüfett, n
 ♦ children's buffet
Kinderchor, m
 ♦ children's choir
Kinderclub, m
 ♦ children's club
Kinderdeck, n
 (Schiff)
 ♦ children's deck
Kinderdorf, n
 ♦ children's village
Kinderecke, f
 (im Schwimmbad etc.)
 ♦ children's corner
Kindereinrichtung, f
 ♦ children's facility
Kinder erhalten großzügige Ermäßigungen
 ♦ Children are given generous reductions
Kinder erhalten Vorzugsbehandlung
 Kinder bekommen Vorzugsbehandlung
 ♦ Children receive preferential treatment
 ♦ Children get preferential treatment
Kindererholungsheim, n
 ♦ children's recreation home
 recreation home for children

Kinderermäßigung, f
 Kindernachlaß, m
 ♦ child reduction
 ♦ children's reduction
 ♦ reduction for children
Kinderessen, n
 Kindermahlzeit, f
 Kinderteller, m
 ♦ child's meal
 ♦ children's meal
Kinderetagenbett, n
 Kinderkojenbett, n
 Kinderstockbett, n
 ♦ children's bunk bed
 ♦ child's bunk bed
Kinderfahrpreis, m
 ♦ children's fare
 ♦ child fare
Kinderfahrt, f
 ♦ children's ride
 ♦ children's trip
Kinderfeier, f
 ♦ child's party
 ♦ children's party
 ♦ kids' party *coll*
Kinderferien, pl
 Kinderurlaub, m
 ♦ children's holiday BE
 ♦ child's holiday BE
 ♦ children's vacation AE
 ♦ child's vacation AE
Kinderferienprogramm, n
 Kinderurlaubsprogramm, n
 ♦ children's holiday programme BE
 ♦ children's vacation program AE
Kinderfest, n
 Kinderfeier, f
 Kinderparty, f
 ♦ kids' party *coll*
 ♦ children's party
 ♦ child's party
Kinderfestival, n
 Kinderfest, n
 ♦ children's festival
Kinderfrau, f
 Kindermädchen, n
 ♦ nurse
 ♦ dry nurse
 ♦ nanny BE
 ♦ child-minder
Kinderfreizeit, f
 (kirchlich organisiert)
 → Kinderurlaub
kinderfreundlich, adj
 ♦ child-friendly, adj
 ♦ suitable for children, adj
 ♦ welcoming children, adj
kinderfreundliches Hotel, n
 ♦ hotel welcoming children
 ♦ hotel which is suitable for children
 ♦ child-friendly hotel
Kinderfrühstück, n
 ♦ children's breakfast
 ♦ child's breakfast
Kindergarten, m
 ♦ kindergarten
 ♦ nursery school
 ♦ nursery
Kindergeburtstag m
 ♦ child's birthday party
 ♦ children's birthday party

Kindergedeck n
 Kinderkuvert n
 Kindercouvert n
 ♦ child's cover
 ♦ children's cover
kindergerechte Verpflegung, f
 ♦ meals suitable for children *pl*
Kindergetränk, n
 ♦ children's drink
 ♦ children's beverage
Kindergruppe, f
 ♦ children's group
 ♦ group of children
Kinder haben freien Eintritt
 ♦ Children are admitted free
Kinder haben ihr eigenes Programm
 ♦ Children have their own special program AE
 ♦ Children have their own special programme BE
Kinderheilstätte, f
 Kindersanatorium n
 Kinderheim n
 ♦ children's sanatorium
 ♦ sanatorium AE
Kinderheim, n (generell)
 ♦ children's home
Kinderheim, n (Sanatorium)
 → Kinderheilstätte
Kinderhochstuhl, m
 Hochstuhl, m
 ♦ baby's high chair
 ♦ high chair
Kinderhosteß, f
 ♦ children's hostess
Kinderhotel, n
 ♦ hotel suitable for children
 ♦ hotel for children
Kinderhütedienst, m
 → Kinderbeaufsichtigung
Kinder im Elternzimmer, n pl
 ♦ children sharing (their) parents' room
Kinder im Elternzimmer kostenlos
 → Kinder im Elternzimmer wohnen kostenlos
Kinder im Elternzimmer wohnen kostenlos
 Kinder gratis im Elternzimmer
 ♦ Children sharing their parents' room stay free
Kinder im Erwachsenenzimmer wohnen kostenfrei
 Kinder gratis im Erwachsenenzimmer
 ♦ Children sharing the adults' room stay free
Kinderkarneval, m
 Kinderfasching, m
 Kinderfastnacht, f
 ♦ children's carnival
Kinderkarte, f
 ♦ child's ticket
Kinderkojenbett, n
 Kinderetagenbett, n
 ♦ child's bunk bed
 ♦ children's bunk bed
Kinderkrippe, f
 ♦ day nursery
 ♦ crèche BE
 ♦ children's crèche BE
Kinderkrippeneinrichtung, f
 ♦ crèche facility BE
Kinderladen, m
 (zum Einkaufen für Kinder)
 Kindergeschäft, n
 ♦ children's store AE
 ♦ children's shop BE

412

Kinderlager, n
♦ children's camp
♦ summer camp
Kinderlätzchen, n
Lätzchen, n
♦ child's bib
♦ bib
Kinderlift, m
♦ child's lift
♦ children's lift
Kinderliftpaß, m
♦ child's lift pass
♦ children's lift pass
kinderlos, adj
♦ childless, adj
kinderloses Paar, n
♦ childless couple
Kindermädchen, n
Kinderfrau, f
♦ nanny BE
♦ nursery maid
♦ child-minder
Kindermahlzeit, f
→ Kinderessen
Kindermalwettbewerb m
♦ children's painting competition
Kindermaskenfest, n
♦ children's fancy-dress party
Kindermenü n
♦ child's menu
♦ children's menu
Kindernachlaß, m
→ Kinderermäßigung
Kindernachmittag, m
♦ children's afternoon
kinderorientiert, adj
♦ child-oriented, adj AE
♦ child-orientated, adj BE
Kinderparadies n
♦ child's paradise
♦ children's paradise
Kinderpark, m
♦ children's park
Kinderparty, f
Kinderfeier, f
♦ children's party
♦ child's party
♦ kids' party coll
Kinderplanschbecken n
♦ children's wading pool AE
♦ children's paddling pool BE
Kinderplatz, m (am Tisch)
Kindersitzplatz m
♦ child's seat at table
Kinderplatz, m (generell)
♦ children's place
♦ child's place
Kinderpool, m
→ Kinderschwimmbecken
Kinderportion f
♦ child's portion
♦ children's portion
Kinderpreis m
♦ child's rate
♦ child's price
♦ children's rate
♦ children's price
Kinderprogramm, n
♦ children's program AE
♦ kids' program coll
♦ children's programme BE

♦ program for children AE
♦ programme for children BE
Kinderrabatt, m
♦ children's discount
♦ child's discount
Kinderrad, n coll
♦ child's bike coll
♦ children's bike coll
kinderreiche Familie, f
♦ large family
Kinderreise, f
♦ children's trip
♦ children's tour
♦ children's journey
Kinderreitschule, f
♦ children's riding school
Kinderrestaurant, n
♦ children's restaurant
Kinderroller, m
Roller, m
♦ child's scooter
Kinderschau, f
Kindervorstellung, f
♦ children's show
♦ kids' show coll
Kinderschlafzimmer n
♦ child's bedroom
♦ children's bedroom
Kinderschlitten, m
♦ children's toboggan
♦ child's toboggan
Kinderschwester, f
(z.B. im Krankenhaus)
♦ children's nurse
Kinderschwimmbad, n
Kinderschwimmbecken, n
Kinderbad, n
♦ children's swimming pool AE
♦ children's swimming-pool BE
♦ children's pool
♦ kids' pool coll
♦ kiddies' pool coll
Kinderschwimmbecken, n
→ Kinderschwimmbad
Kinderservice, m
Kinderdienst m
♦ children's service
♦ catering for children
Kinder sind willkommen
♦ Children are welcome
Kindersitzplatz, m
Kindersitz, m
Kinderplatz, m
♦ child seat
♦ child's seat
Kinderskikurs, m
Kinderskilehrgang, m
♦ children's ski course
Kinderskischule f
♦ children's ski school
Kindersonderermäßigung, f
Sonderermäßigung für Kinder, f
♦ special reduction for children
Kinderspaßbecken, n
♦ children's fun pool
Kinderspeisekarte, f
♦ children's menu
♦ kids' menu coll
Kinderspeisesaal m
♦ children's dining room

Kinderspiel, n
♦ children's game
Kinderspielbecken, n
♦ children's play pool
Kinderspielecke, f
♦ children's play-corner
♦ children's corner
♦ play-corner
Kinderspielgelände, n
♦ children's play area
Kinderspielplatz, m
♦ children's playground
♦ playground
Kinderspielplatz mit Betreuung, m
→ überwachter Kinderspielplatz
Kinderspielzimmer n
♦ children's play room
♦ children's playing room BE
Kinderstuhl, m (generell)
♦ children's chair
♦ child's chair
Kinderstuhl, m (Hochstuhl)
→ Hochstuhl
Kindertag, m
♦ children's day
Kindertagesstätte, f
Kindertagesheim, n
♦ day-care center AE
♦ day-care centre BE
♦ day nursery
♦ crèche BE
Kindertarif, m
♦ tariff for children
Kinderteil, m
(z.B. im Schwimmbad)
Kinderabschnitt, m
♦ children's section
♦ section for children
Kinderteller, m (Mahlzeit)
Kinderessen, n
♦ children's meal
♦ child's meal
Kinderteller, m (Teller)
♦ child's plate
♦ children's plate
Kinderteller erhältlich
♦ Children's meals available
Kindertheater, n
♦ children's theater AE
♦ children's theatre BE
Kindertisch, m
♦ child's table
♦ children's table
Kindertoilette, f
♦ children's toilet
♦ child's toilet
Kinderunterhalter, m
♦ children's entertainer
Kinderunterhaltung, f
♦ children's entertainment
Kinderunterkunft, f
Kinderunterbringung, f
♦ children's accommodation
♦ accommodation for children
♦ accommodating children
Kinder unter sechs Jahren werden nicht verköstigt
♦ Children under six years are not catered for
Kinder unter vier Jahren erhalten eine Ermäßigung
♦ Children under four years receive a reduction

Kinderurlaub

Kinderurlaub, m
  Kinderferien, pl
  ♦ children's vacation *AE*
  ♦ child's vacation *AE*
  ♦ children's holiday *BE*
  ♦ child's holiday *BE*
Kinderurlaubsprogramm, n
  Kinderferienprogramm, n
  ♦ children's vacation program *AE*
  ♦ child's vacation program *AE*
  ♦ children's holiday programme *BE*
  ♦ child's holiday programme *BE*
Kinderveranstaltung, f
  ♦ children's event
  ♦ children's activity
Kinderwagen, m
  ♦ baby carriage *AE*
  ♦ perambulator *BE*
  ♦ pram *BE*
Kinderwaschbecken n
  ♦ children's washbasin
Kinder werden kostenlos untergebracht
  ♦ Children stay free
Kinder werden nicht aufgenommen
  ♦ Children are not catered for
Kinderwettbewerb m
  ♦ children's competition
Kinderwettkampf m
  ♦ children's contest
Kinder willkommen
  ♦ Children welcome
Kinder zahlen (den) halben Preis
  ♦ Children are (admitted) half price
Kinder zahlen die Hälfte
  (Hinweisschild)
  ♦ Children half price
Kinderzimmer, n (für Kleinkind)
  ♦ nursery
Kinderzimmer, n (generell)
  ♦ child's room
  ♦ children's room
  ♦ kids' room *coll*
Kinderzoo, m
  ♦ children's zoo
kindgerecht, adj
  kindgerecht, adj
  ♦ geared to children, adj
  ♦ suitable for children, adj
Kind ins Bett bringen
  ♦ put a child to bed
  ♦ pack a child off to bed
Kind ins Bett jagen
  ♦ pack a child off to bed
Kind mit Begleitung, n
  ♦ accompanied child
Kind ohne Begleitung, n
  → unbegleitetes Kind
Kind pro Nacht, n
  Kind pro Übernachtung, n
  ♦ child per night
Kind über sechs Jahren, n
  ♦ child over six (years of age)
Kind unter zwölf Jahren, n
  ♦ child under twelve (years of age)
King Room, m
  (Zimmer mit King-Size-Bett)
  ♦ king room
  ♦ king
King-Size-Bett, n
  ♦ king-size bed
  ♦ king bed *sl*

King-Size-Doppelbett n
  ♦ king-size double bed
King-Size-Wohnwagen, m
  King-Size-Caravan, m
  ♦ king-size trailer *AE*
  ♦ king-size caravan *BE*
Kino, n (Gebäude)
  Filmtheater n
  ♦ cinema
  ♦ motion-picture theater *AE*
  ♦ movie theater *AE coll*
  ♦ movie *AE abbr*
  ♦ movie house *AE coll*
Kino, n (Vorstellung)
  ♦ movies *AE*
  ♦ cinema
Kinobesitzer, m
  ♦ movie owner *AE*
  ♦ cinema owner *BE*
Kinobesuch, m
  ♦ visit to the movie *AE*
  ♦ visit to the cinema *BE*
Kino besuchen
  ♦ visit a movie *AE*
  ♦ visit a cinema *BE*
Kinobesucher, m
  Kinogänger, m
  ♦ moviegoer *AE*
  ♦ cinema-goer *BE*
Kinoclub, m
  ♦ cinema club *BE*
  ♦ movie club *AE*
Kinofilm, m
  ♦ movie film *AE*
  ♦ cinema film *BE*
  ♦ motion picture *AE*
Kinoführer, m
  (Information)
  ♦ movie guide *AE*
  ♦ cinema guide *BE*
Kinogänger, m
  Kinobesucher, m
  ♦ cinema-goer *BE*
  ♦ moviegoer *AE*
Kino ist halb leer
  ♦ movie is half empty *AE*
  ♦ cinema is half empty *BE*
Kinokarte, f
  ♦ movie ticket *AE*
  ♦ cinema ticket *BE*
Kinokarte kostet DM 12
  ♦ movie ticket costs DM 12 *AE*
  ♦ cinema ticket costs DM 12 *BE*
Kinokasse, f
  ♦ cinema box office *BE*
  ♦ box office
Kinopreis, m
  ♦ movie price *AE*
  ♦ cinema price *BE*
Kinoprogramm, n
  ♦ movie program *AE*
  ♦ cinema programme *BE*
Kinoraum, m
  → Filmraum
Kiosk, m
  ♦ kiosk
Kioskbesitzer, m
  ♦ kiosk owner
Kiosk betreiben
  ♦ operate a kiosk

Kioskbetreiber, m
  ♦ kiosk operator
Kipptisch, m
  ♦ tilt-top table
  ♦ tip-top table
  ♦ tip table
Kirche, f
  ♦ church
Kirche besichtigen
  Kirche besuchen
  ♦ visit a church
Kirche ist romanisch
  ♦ church is Romanesque
Kirchenarchitektur, f
  Kirchenbaukunst, f
  ♦ church architecture
Kirchenfest, n
  ♦ church fete *AE*
  ♦ church fête *BE*
Kirchenkongreß m
  ♦ church congress
Kirchenkonzert, n
  ♦ church concert
Kirchenmusik, f
  ♦ church music
Kirchensaal, m
  ♦ church hall
Kirchenstuhl, m
  Kirchenbank, f
  ♦ pew
kirchlicher Feiertag, m
  ♦ religious holiday
  ♦ church holy day
Kirchplatz, m
  ♦ church square
Kirchturm, m (mit Spitze)
  ♦ church steeple
Kirchturm, m (ohne Spitze)
  ♦ church tower
Kirgise, m
  ♦ Kirghiz
  ♦ Kirghis
  ♦ Kirgis
Kirgisien
  ♦ Kirghizia
kirgisisch, adj
  ♦ Kirghizian, adj
Kirschblüte, f
  ♦ cherry blossom
Kirschblütenfest, n
  ♦ cherry blossom festival
Kirsche, f
  ♦ cherry
Kirscheis, n
  ♦ cherry ice cream *AE*
  ♦ cherry ice-cream *BE*
Kirschenfüllpastete, f
  ♦ cherry timbale
Kirschenkaltschale, f
  ♦ cold cherry soup
Kirschenmilchmixgetränk, n
  ♦ cherry milk shake
Kirschholztäfelung, f
  Kirschholzpaneel, n
  ♦ cherrywood panelling
  ♦ cherrywood paneling *AE*
Kirschkuchen, m
  ♦ cherry cake
Kirschkuchen, m (gedeckt)
  ♦ cherry pie

Kirschlikör, m
♦ cherry brandy
Kirschparfait, n
♦ cherry parfait
Kirschsaft, m
♦ cherry juice
Kirschsorbet, n
♦ cherry sorbet
Kirschsoße, f
♦ cherry sauce
Kirschstrudel, m
♦ cherry strudel
Kirschtomate, f
♦ cherry tomato
Kirschtorte, f
♦ cherry gateau
Kirschwasser, n
♦ kirsch
Kissen, n (generell)
♦ cushion
Kissen, n (Kopfkissen)
→ Kopfkissen
Kissenbezug, m (generell)
♦ cushion cover
Kissenbezug, m (Kopfkissen)
♦ pillowcase
♦ pillowslip
Kissenschlacht, f
♦ pillow fight
Kiste, f
♦ case
♦ crate
Kiste Bier, f
♦ case of beer
kistenweise, adv
♦ by the crate, adv
Kiste Wein, f
♦ case of wine
Kittel, m
Arbeitskittel, m
Kittelschürze, f
♦ smock
Kitzbraten, m
♦ roast kid
Kiwi, f
♦ kiwi fruit
Kiwi, m inform
Neuseeländer, m
♦ Kiwi inform
Kiwieis, n
♦ kiwi ice cream AE
♦ kiwi ice-cream BE
Kiwisalat, m
♦ kiwi salad
Kiwisorbet, n
♦ kiwi sorbet
Klagemauer, f
(in Jerusalem)
♦ Wailing Wall, the
klagen auf Räumung
Räumungsklage erheben
♦ sue for eviction
♦ sue for ejection AE
klagen über Appetitlosigkeit
♦ complain of lack of appetite
Klamauk, m
Krawall, m
♦ row
♦ shindy
Klamm, f
♦ flume

Klappbett, n
wegklappbares Bett, n
♦ foldaway bed
♦ folding bed
Klappboot, n
♦ collapsible boat
Klappcaravan, m
Klappwohnwagen, m
♦ collapsible caravan BE
♦ collapsible trailer AE
Klappcouch f
♦ folding couch
Klappfahrrad, n
♦ folding bicycle
♦ folding cycle
Klappmöbel, n pl
♦ folding furniture sg
♦ collapsible furniture sg
♦ trestle furniture sg
Klappmotorrad, n
♦ folding motorcycle AE
♦ folding motor cycle BE
Klapprad, n
♦ folding bike
Klappsessel, m
→ Klappstuhl
Klappsitz, m
♦ folding seat
♦ tip-up seat
Klappsofa, n
♦ folding sofa
Klappstuhl, m (mit Rückenlehne)
♦ folding chair
♦ camp chair
♦ camp-chair BE
♦ collapsible chair
Klappstuhl, m (ohne Rückenlehne)
♦ campstool
♦ camp-stool BE
Klapptisch, m (generell)
♦ folding table
♦ collapsible table
Klapptisch, m (mit Seitenbeinen)
♦ gateleg table
♦ gatelegged table
Klapptisch, m (mit Tischbock)
♦ trestle table
Klappwohnwagen, m
Klappcaravan, m
♦ collapsible trailer AE
♦ collapsible caravan BE
Klapsmühle, f sl
♦ nuthouse sl
♦ bin sl
Kläranlage, f
♦ sewage plant
klare Suppe, f
♦ clear soup
klarspülen etw
→ nachspülen etw
Klassenausflug, m
(Schulklasse)
♦ class excursion
♦ class outing
Klassenfahrt, f
(Schulklasse)
♦ class trip
Klassenreise, f
(Schulklasse)
♦ class tour

Klassentreffen, n
(Treffen ehemaliger Schüler)
♦ class reunion
Klassenzimmerbestuhlung, f
♦ classroom seating
♦ classroom-style seating
Klassenzimmerform, f (Bestuhlung)
Klassenzimmerstil, m
Tischform, f
♦ classroom style
♦ schoolroom style
Klassenzimmerstil, m
→ Klassenzimmerform
Klassifikation f
→ Klassifizierung
Klassifikationssystem n
→ Klassifizierungssystem
Klassifizierung f
♦ classification
Klassifizierungsschema, n
♦ classification scheme
Klassifizierungssystem, n
♦ classification system
♦ system of classification
klassisch, adj (Antike oder Klassik des 18. Jhr)
♦ classical, adj
klassisch, adj (vorbildhaft)
♦ classic, adj
klassische französische Küche, f (18. Jahrhundert)
♦ classical French cuisine
♦ classical French cooking
klassische französische Küche, f (vorbildhaft)
♦ classic French cuisine
♦ classic French cooking
klassische Küche f (Essen)
♦ classical cuisine
♦ classical cooking
klassische Musik, f
♦ classical music
klassischer französischer Wein, m
♦ classic French wine
klassische Route, f
♦ classic route
klassische Seereise, f
♦ classic voyage
klassisches Gericht, n
♦ classic dish
klassisches Rezept, n
klassische Rezeptur, f
♦ classic recipe
Klausel, f
♦ clause
♦ provision
Klausel enthalten
♦ contain a clause
♦ contain a provision
Klausurtagung, f
♦ closed conference
Klavier, n
Piano n
♦ piano
Klavierabend, m
♦ piano recital (in the evening)
♦ piano concert (in the evening)
Klavierabend veranstalten
♦ organise a piano recital (in the evening)
♦ organize a piano recital (in the evening)
♦ organise a piano concert (in the evening)
♦ organize a piano concert (in the evening)

Klavierkonzert

Klavierkonzert, n (Musikstück)
 ♦ piano concerto
Klavierkonzert, n (Veranstaltung)
 ♦ piano recital
 ♦ piano concert
Klaviermiete, f
 → Klaviermietgebühr
Klaviermietgebühr, f
 Klaviermiete, f
 ♦ piano rental AE
 ♦ piano hire BE
Klaviermusik f
 ♦ piano music
Klavier spielen
 ♦ play the piano
Klavierspieler, m
 ♦ piano player
Klavier stimmen
 ♦ tune the piano
Klavierstuhl, m
 Klavierschemel, m
 ♦ piano stool
 ♦ music stool
Klavierwettbewerb, m
 ♦ piano competition
Klavierzimmer, n
 ♦ piano room
Kleider anziehen
 ♦ put on one's clothes
Kleider ausziehen
 ♦ take off one's clothes
Kleiderbügel m
 ♦ clothes hanger
 ♦ hanger
 ♦ coat hanger
Kleider bügeln
 ♦ iron clothes
Kleiderbürste, f
 ♦ clothesbrush AE
 ♦ clothes-brush BE
Kleider bürsten
 ♦ brush one's clothes
 ♦ brush s.o.'s clothes
Kleiderhaken, m
 Mantelhaken, m
 Haken, m
 ♦ coat hook
 ♦ coat peg
 ♦ peg
Kleiderhakenbrett, n
 ♦ coatrack AE
 ♦ coat-rack BE
Kleiderkorb, m
 ♦ clothes basket AE
 ♦ clothes-basket BE
Kleider lüften
 ♦ air clothes
Kleidermotte, f
 ♦ clothes moth
Kleiderordnung, f
 Bekleidungsvorschrift, f
 ♦ dress code
Kleider packen
 ♦ pack one's clothes
Kleiderpflegedienst, m
 Kleider- und Bügeldienst, m
 Kleider- und Bügelservice, m
 Kleiderpflege, f
 Kleiderdienst, m
 ♦ valet service

Kleiderschrank, m
 ♦ closet AE
 ♦ wardrobe BE
 ♦ clothespress AE
 ♦ clothes closet AE
Kleiderschranktür, f
 ♦ closet door AE
 ♦ wardrobe door BE
Kleiderservice, m
 → Kleiderpflegedienst
Kleiderständer, m
 Garderobe, f
 ♦ clothes tree
 ♦ coat stand
 ♦ coatrack AE
 ♦ clothes rack
 ♦ coat-rack BE
Kleidertrockenmöglichkeit, f
 ♦ clothes drying facility
Kleider trocknen
 ♦ dry clothes
Kleider- und Bügeldienst m
 → Kleiderpflegedienst
Kleider verstauen in einem Schrankkoffer
 ♦ stow clothes (away) into a trunk
Kleider waschen
 ♦ wash one's clothes
Kleider waschen und bügeln
 ♦ launder clothes
Kleiderwaschgelegenheit, f
 ♦ clothes washing facility
Kleidung im Stil der Zeit, f
 ♦ period dress
Kleidungsstück, n
 ♦ piece of clothing
Kleie, f
 ♦ bran
klein, aber fein
 ♦ small is beautiful
kleinasiatisch, adj
 ♦ from Asia Minor, adv
 ♦ of Asia Minor, adv
Kleinasien
 ♦ Asia Minor
Kleinbahn, f
 → Schmalspurbahn
Kleinbauer, m
 ♦ crofter BE
Kleinbauernkate, f
 Bauernkate, f
 ♦ croft cottage
Kleinbetrieb, m
 kleiner Betrieb, m
 ♦ small establishment
 ♦ small business
 ♦ small hotel
 ♦ small restaurant
Kleinbus, m
 Minibus, m
 ♦ minibus
 ♦ minicoach BE
 ♦ passenger van AE
Kleinbusdienst, m
 Kleinbusservice, m
 Kleinbusverbindung, m
 Kleinbusverkehr, m
 ♦ minibus service
 ♦ minicoach service BE
 ♦ passenger van service AE

Kleinbus für Selbstfahrer, m
 ♦ self-drive minibus
 ♦ self-drive passenger van AE
Kleinbus mieten
 ♦ rent a minibus AE
 ♦ rent a passenger van AE
 ♦ hire a minibus BE
Kleinbus mit 12 Plätzen, m
 ♦ minibus with 12 seats
 ♦ 12-seater minibus
 ♦ passenger van with 12 seats AE
 ♦ 12-seater passenger van AE
 ♦ minicoach with 12 seats BE
kleine Ausstellung, f
 ♦ small exhibition
 ♦ small exhibit AE
kleine Couch f
 ♦ settee
kleine Dienste erbringen für die Gäste
 kleine Dienste erweisen den Gästen
 ♦ render small services to guests
kleine Etagenwohnung, f
 kleine Wohnung, f
 ♦ small apartment AE
 ♦ small flat BE
kleine Feier, f (Festival)
 kleines Fest, n
 ♦ small festival
kleine Feier, f (Party)
 ♦ small party
kleine Flasche, f
 ♦ small bottle
kleine Gebühr, f
 ♦ small fee
kleine Gebühr berechnen
 kleine Gebühr fordern
 ♦ charge a small fee
kleine Insel, f
 ♦ small island
 ♦ little island
kleine Inventarstücke, n pl
 ♦ small fixtures pl
kleine Konferenz, f
 ♦ small conference
kleine Küche, f (Raum)
 Kleinküche, f
 ♦ small kitchen
 ♦ kitchenette
kleinen Diebstahl begehen
 ♦ pilfer
kleine Pause, f (Schule)
 ♦ short break
 ♦ recess AE
kleine Pause, f (Theater)
 ♦ short interval
kleine Pfanne, f
 ♦ small pan
kleiner Bauernhof, m
 ♦ croft BE
kleiner Dieb, m (generell)
 ♦ petty thief
kleiner Dieb, m (Hotel)
 ♦ pilferer
kleiner Diebstahl, m
 Schwund, m euph
 ♦ pilfering
 ♦ pilferage
kleine Reise, f
 ♦ small tour
 ♦ small trip
 ♦ small journey

kleine Reisegruppe, f
 ♦ small tour group
kleiner Flugplatz, m
 ♦ aerodrome BE obs
 ♦ drome sl
 ♦ small airfield
kleiner Gast, m (Kind)
 → Kind
kleiner gemütlicher Raum, m
 kleines gemütliches Plätzchen, n
 kleine Kammer, f
 ♦ cubbyhole AE
 ♦ cubby-hole BE
 ♦ cubby
kleiner Happen, m
 → kleiner Imbiß
kleiner Imbiß, m
 kleiner Happen, m
 ♦ small snack
kleiner Parkplatz, m
 ♦ small parking lot AE
 ♦ small car park BE
kleiner Reiseveranstalter, m
 ♦ small tour operator
Kleiner Saal, m (Eigenname)
 ♦ Little Hall, the
kleiner Saal, m (generell)
 ♦ small auditorium
 ♦ little hall
kleiner Stellplatz, m
 (Camping)
 ♦ small pitch
kleiner Strand, m
 ♦ small beach
kleiner Umweg, m
 ♦ little detour
 ♦ slight detour
kleines Badezimmer, n
 kleines Bad, n
 ♦ small bathroom
 ♦ small bath
kleine Serviette, f
 ♦ small napkin
 ♦ small serviette
kleines Frühstück, n
 ♦ small breakfast
kleines Geschenk, n
 ♦ little present
kleines Geschenk geben jm
 ♦ give s.o. a little present
kleines Haus, n
 ♦ small house
 ♦ maisonette
kleines Hotel, n
 Kleinhotel, n
 Minihotel, n
 ♦ small hotel
 ♦ minihotel
kleines Messer, n
 ♦ small knife
kleines Orchester, n
 ♦ small orchestra
kleine Speisekarte, f
 ♦ small menu
kleines Restaurant, n
 ♦ small restaurant
kleines Trinkgeld n
 ♦ small tip
kleines Zimmer, n
 Zimmerchen, n
 ♦ small room

kleine Tagung, f
 kleines Treffen, n
 ♦ small meeting
kleine Tischdecke, f
 kleines Tischtuch, n
 ♦ tea cloth AE
 ♦ tea-cloth BE
kleine Überraschung, f
 (Geschenk)
 ♦ little something
kleine Veranstaltung, f
 ♦ small function
 ♦ small event
Kleingedrucktes, n
 (Vertrag)
 ♦ small print
 ♦ little print
Kleingedrucktes ansehen sich
 ♦ look at the small print
Kleingedrucktes lesen
 ♦ read the small print
kleinhacken (etw)
 kleinschneiden (etw)
 ♦ mince (s.th.)
Kleinhotel, n
 → kleines Hotel
Kleinigkeit, f (Imbiß)
 ♦ bite
 ♦ snack
Kleinigkeit essen
 ♦ have a bite
 ♦ have a snack
 ♦ eat a snack
Kleinkind, n (2 bis 6 Jahre)
 ♦ small child
 ♦ young child
Kleinkind, n (unter 4 Jahren)
 ♦ infant
 ♦ baby
Kleinkinderbecken n
 → s. Kleinkinderschwimmbecken
Kleinkinderbett n
 ♦ infant's bed
Kleinkinderkorb, m
 Kleinkinderbett, n
 Babybett, n
 ♦ bassinet
 ♦ bassinette
Kleinkindernahrung, f
 ♦ infants' food
Kleinkinderschwimmbecken n
 ♦ toddlers' swimming pool AE
 ♦ toddlers' swimming-pool BE
 ♦ toddlers' pool
Kleinkind unter zwei Jahren, n
 ♦ infant under the age of two years
Kleinklima, n
 → Mikroklima
Kleinkriminalität, f
 ♦ petty crime
Kleinküche, f
 → kleine Küche
Kleinod, n
 Juwel, n
 Glanzstück, n
 Prachtstück, n
 ♦ gem
Kleinreiseveranstalter, m
 (mit Einzelhandelscharakter)
 Kleinveranstalter, m
 ♦ retail tour operator

Kleinstadt, f
 ♦ small town
Kleinstadthotel, n
 ♦ small-town hotel
 ♦ town hotel
kleinstes Detail, n
 kleinste Einzelheit, f
 ♦ minutest detail
Kleinstwohnung, f
 ♦ miniflat BE
 ♦ miniapartment AE
Klein Venedig
 ♦ Little Venice
Kleinwagen, m
 ♦ minicar
 ♦ runabout BE coll
 ♦ small car
Kleinwohnung, f
 kleine Wohnung, f
 ♦ small flat BE
 ♦ small apartment AE
 ♦ flatlet BE
Klepper, m
 Schindmähre, f
 ♦ jade
Kletterei, f
 → Klettern
Kletterer, m
 ♦ climber
 ♦ rock climber
Kletterfahrt, f
 ♦ climbing trip
Klettergebiet, n
 Klettergelände, n
 ♦ climbing country
 ♦ climbing area
Klettergerüst, n
 (auf Spielplatz für Kinder)
 ♦ climbing-frame
 ♦ jungle gym AE
Klettergestell, n
 (für Kinder)
 Klettergerüst, n
 ♦ jungle gym AE
 ♦ climbing-frame BE
Kletterkurs, m
 ♦ rock climbing course
klettern
 ♦ climb
Klettern, n
 Klettersport, m
 Kletterei, f
 ♦ climbing
Kletterpartie, f
 → Klettertour
Kletterschuh, m
 ♦ climbing shoe
Kletterseil, n
 ♦ climbing rope
Klettersport, m
 → Klettern
Kletterstange, f
 ♦ climbing pole
Klettertour, f
 Kletterpartie, f
 ♦ climbing tour
Kletterzentrum, n
 ♦ climbing center AE
 ♦ climbing centre BE
Klient, m
 Kunde, m

Klientel 418

- client
- customer

Klientel, f
→ Kundenstamm

Klimaänderung, f
→ Klimawechsel

Klimaanlage, f
- air-conditioning system *AE*
- air conditioning *AE*
- air-conditioning *BE*
- air-conditioner

Klimaanlage funktioniert nicht
(dauernd)
- air conditioning does not work *AE*
- air-conditioning does not work *BE*

Klimaanlage funktioniert nicht richtig
- air conditioning is not working properly *AE*
- air-conditioning is not working properly *BE*

Klimaanlage ist abgestellt
- air conditioning is turned off *AE*
- air-conditioning is turned off *BE*
- air-condtioner is turned off

Klimaanlage scheint außer Betrieb zu sein
- air conditioning seems to be out of order *AE*
- air-conditioning seems to be out of order *BE*

Klimakammer, f
- climatic chamber

Klimakurort, m
Klimaort, m
- climatic resort

klimatisch begünstigter Ort, m
- climatically favored place *AE*
- climatically favoured place *BE*

klimatisieren etw
- air-condition s.th.

klimatisiert, adj
- air-conditioned, adj

klimatisierter Bus, m
- air-conditioned bus
- air-conditioned coach *BE*

klimatisiertes Auto, n
- air-conditioned car

klimatisiertes Zimmer, n
klimatisierter Raum, m
- air-conditioned room

klimatisiert sein
- be air-conditioned

Klimatisierungskosten, pl
- costs of air conditioning *AE pl*
- costs of air-conditioning *BE pl*

Klimatologie, f
Klimakunde, f
Klimaforschung, f
- climatology

Klimaverhältnisse, n pl
- climatic conditions *pl*

Klimawechsel, m
Klimaänderung, f
- change of climate

Klimazone, f
- climatic zone
- climate zone

Klippe, f
- cliff

Klippenwanderung, f
Wanderung entlang der Klippen, f
Wanderung auf den Klippen, f
- cliff walk
- cliff walking

Klippfisch, m
- cured cod

Klo, n *coll*
- john *AE coll*
- loo *BE coll*

Klopapier, n *coll*
- loo paper *coll*
- toilet paper

Klopfmassage, f
- percussion massage

Klosett, n
- lavatory
- toilet

Kloster, n (Frauen)
- convent
- nunnery

Kloster, n (Männer)
- monastery

Kloster Ettal, n
- Ettal Monastery

Klostergarten, m (Frauenkloster)
- convent garden

Klostergarten, m (Männerkloster)
- monastery garden

Kloster gründen (Frauenkloster)
- found a convent

Kloster gründen (Männerkloster)
- found a monastery

Klosterkirche, f (Frauenkloster)
- convent church

Klosterkirche, f (Männerkloster)
- monastery church

Klosterruine, f (Frauenkloster)
- ruins of a convent *pl*
- convent ruins *pl*

Klosterruine, f (Männerkloster)
- ruins of a monastery *pl*
- monastery ruins *pl*
- monastic ruins *pl*

Klub, m
→ Club, Verein

km
Kilometer, m
- km
- kilometer *AE*
- kilometre *BE*

Knäckebrot, n
- crispbread

Knackwürstchen, n
→ Frankfurter Würstchen

knapp bei Kasse sein
- be short of money

Knappheit an erschwinglichen Unterkünften, f
- shortage of affordable accommodations *AE*
- shortage of affordable accommodation *BE*

Knappheit an Hotelunterkünften, f
- shortage of hotel accommodations *AE*
- shortage of hotel accommodation *BE*

Knappheit an Hotelzimmern, f
- shortage of hotel rooms

knapp kalkulierter Preis, m
scharf kalkulierter Preis, m
- keenly calculated price

knapp sein
(z.B. Zimmer)
- be scarce
- be in short supply

knauserig, adj
- stingy, adj

Kneipe, f (Gaststätte)
- boozer *BE sl*
- pub *BE*
- bar *AE*

Kneipe, f (Spelunke)
Spelunke, f *derog*
Kaschemme, f *derog*
- dive *inform*
- (beer) joint *AE*
- gin mill *AE*
- saloon *AE*

Kneipe an der Ecke, f
Gaststätte an der Ecke, f
Eckkneipe, f
Eckgaststätte, f
- corner bar *AE*
- corner pub *BE*

Kneipe mit Musikautomat, f
Lokal mit Musikbox, n
Bluesschuppen, m
- juke joint *AE sl*

Kneipenbesitzer, m *neg*
- owner of a dive *neg*

Kneipenbesuch, m
- visit to a dive
- visit to a beer joint *AE*
- visit to a saloon *AE*

Kneipenbummel, m
Sauftour, f *vulg*
Zechtour, f
- barhop *AE*
- pub crawl *BE*

Kneipenbummel machen
Bierreise machen
- be on a spree
- go barhopping
- go on a pub crawl *BE*

Kneipenhocker, m
Säufer m
- barfly

Kneipenleben, n
- bar life *AE*
- pub life *BE coll*

Kneipenschlägerei, f
Kneipenkrach, m
Kneipenstreit, m
- pub rumpus *BE*

Kneipenwirt, m
Gastwirt, m
- saloonkeeper *AE*
- barkeeper *AE*
- pub-owner *BE*
- publican *BE*

Kneipier, m
→ Kneipenwirt

Kneippbad, n
(Aktivität)
- Kneipp bath
- hydropathic bath

kneippen
→ Kneippkur machen

Kneippheilbad, n
(war vorher Kneippkurort)
- health resort offering Kneipp treatment
- hydropathic spa offering Kneipp treatment

Kneippkur, f
- hydropathic Kneipp treatment
- hydropathic treatment
- Kneipp cure

Kneippkurhotel n
- hotel offering Kneipp treatment
- hotel offering hydropathic treatment

Kneippkur machen
kneippen

Kochkunst

- take a hydropathic Kneipp cure
- take a Kneipp cure

Kneippkurort, m
(kann später Kneippheilbad werden)
- spa offering Kneipp treatment
- spa offering hydropathic treatment
- Kneipp spa

Kneippmassage, f
- Kneipp massage
- hydrotherapy massage

Kneipptherapie, f
- Kneipp therapy
- Kneipp treatment
- hydropathy

kneten (etw)
- knead (s.th.)

Knicks, m
- curtsey
- curtsy

knicksen (vor jm)
- curtsey (to s.o.)
- curtsy (to s.o.)

Knicks machen (vor jm)
- make a curtsey (to s.o.)
- make a curtsy (to s.o.)
- bob a curts(e)y (to s.o.)
- drop a curts(e)y (to s.o.)

Kniebundhosen, f pl
- breeches pl

Knie verstauchen sich
- wrench one's knee

Knoblauch, m
- garlic

Knoblauchbrot, n
- garlic bread

Knoblauchbutter, f
- garlic butter

Knoblauchgeruch, m
- smell of garlic

Knoblauchpresse, f
- garlic press

Knoblauchsalz, n
- garlic salt

Knoblauchsoße, f
- garlic sauce

Knoblauchsuppe, f
- garlic soup

Knoblauchwurst, f
- garlic sausage

Knoblauchzehe, f
Zehe Knoblauch, f
- garlic clove
- clove of garlic

Knoblauchzwiebel, f
- garlic bulb

Knöchelmassage, f
- ankle massage

Knotenpunkt, m (Eisenbahn)
- junction

knusprig, adj
- crisp, adj

Koalabär, m
- koala bear

Koch, m
- cook
- male cook

Kochanleitung, f
- cooking instructions pl

Kochapfel, m
- cooking apple

Kochart, f
Kochmethode, f
- cooking method

Kochassistent, m
→ Kochgehilfe

Kochaushilfe, f
- cook's helper AE
- cooking help

Kochausrüstung, f
- cooking equipment
- cooking gear

Kochausstellung, f
- culinary exhibition AE
- cookery exhibition BE

Koch-Auszubildender, m off
(früher: Kochlehrling)
Koch-Azubi, m coll
- trainee cook
- apprentice cook

Kochberuf, m
- career of a cook
- career as a cook

Kochbuch, n
- cookbook AE
- cookery book BE

Kochbuch schreiben
- write a cookbook AE
- write a cookery book BE

Kochcommis, m
→ Kochgehilfe

Kochecke, f
(in Wohnung)
Kochnische f
- kitchenette

Köcheclub, m
Club der Köche, m
- cooks' club

Kocheleve, m
Kochlehrling, m
- student cook
- trainee cook
- apprentice cook

Kochen, n
- cooking

kochen auf Bestellung
- cook to order

Kochen besorgen
das Kochen besorgen
kochen
- do the cooking

kochend, adj
- boiling, adj

kochendes Wasser, n
- boiling water

kochendheiß, adj
kochend heiß, adj
- piping hot
- boiling hot

kochend heiß servieren etw
dampfend heiß servieren etw
- serve s.th. piping hot

kochen etw am Tisch
- cook s.th. at the table

kochen etw auf Bestellung
- cook s.th. to order

kochen etw bei mäßiger Hitze
- cook s.th. under moderate heat

kochen für die Schule
- cook for the school

kochen für jn
- cook for s.o.

kochen für sich selbst
- cook for oneself

kochen im Freien
im Freien kochen
- cook out

Kochen im Freien, n
- alfresco cooking

Kochen ist eine Kunst
- cooking is an art

kochen lernen
- learn to cook

kochen (Speise)
- be cooking

kochen (Speisen zubereiten)
- cook
- do the cooking

kochen vor Wut
- seethe with rage

kochfertig, adj
- ready-to-cook, adj

Kochfest, n
- cookery festival BE

Kochfett, n
Speisefett, n
- cooking fat
- edible fat

Kochflüssigkeit, f
- cooking fluid

Kochgehilfe, m
Kochcommis, m
Koch-Commis, m
- commis cook
- assistant cook
- commis chef

Kochgelegenheit, f
Kochmöglichkeit, f
- cooking facility

Kochgerät, n
Kochausrüstung, f
- cooking gear

Kochgeruch, m
- smell of cooking

Kochgeschirr, n
- cooking utensils pl
- kitchenware
- kitchen utensils pl
- cookware AE

Kochherd, m
- cooking stove
- cookstove AE
- cooker

Kochhilfe, f
Küchenhilfe, f
- cooking help
- cook's help
- cook's helper AE
- cookee AE

Köchin, f
Küchenfee, f humor
- woman cook
- female cook
- cooky coll
- cook

Kochkenntnisse, f pl
- knowledge of cooking
- knowledge of cookery
- cookery knowledge
- cookings skills pl

Kochkunst, f
- culinary art
- art of cooking

Kochkunstmekka

- cookery
- cooking

Kochkunstmekka, n
Mekka der Kochkunst, n
- culinary Mecca

Kochkunstschau, f
- culinary food show
- cookery show BE

Kochkunststudien, f pl
- culinary arts studies pl

Kochkurs, m
- cooking course AE
- cookery course BE
- course in cooking
- cookery class BE

Kochlehre, f
- apprenticeship as a cook
- training as a cook

Kochlehre absolvieren
- do an apprenticeship as cook
- train as a cook

Kochlehrling, m
- apprentice cook
- apprentice chef

Kochlöffel, m
- cooking spoon
- wooden spoon

Kochlöffel schwingen humor
- be busy cooking

Kochmannschaft, f
Kochteam, n
- cookery team BE

Kochmöglichkeit, f
→ Kochgelegenheit

Kochmütze, f
Toque de cuisinier, f FR
- chef's hat
- toque de cuisinier FR

Kochnische, f
→ Kochecke

Kochofen, m
- cookstove AE
- cooking stove
- cooker

Kochöl, n
→ Speiseöl

Kochpersonal, n
- cooking staff
- cooking personnel

Kochplatte, f
(auf Herd)
- hot plate AE
- hotplate BE
- ring BE
- hob

Kochrezept, n
→ Rezept

Kochsalz, n
- cooking salt

Kochschinken, m
gekochter Schinken, m
- boiled ham BE
- cooked ham AE

Kochschule, f
- cookery school BE
- cooking school AE
- school of cookery BE

Kochshelfer, m
→ Küchenhelfer

Kochsjunge, m
→ Küchenjunge

Kochstunde, f
- cookery lesson BE
- cookery session BE
- cooking lesson AE
- cooking session BE

Kochtopf, m
- cooking pot

Kochtournant, m
→ Hilfskoch

Kochunterricht, m
- cooking lessons AE pl
- cookery lessons BE pl

Kochvolontär, m
- unpaid trainee cook

Kochvorführung, f
- cookery demonstration BE

Kochwasser, n
- cooking water

Kochwein, m
- cooking wine

Kochweise, f
- way of cooking
- cuisine

Kochwettbewerb, m
Wettkochen, n
- cooking contest AE
- cooking competition AE
- cookery contest BE
- cookery competition BE

Kochwettkampf, m
Wettkochen, n
- cookery contest BE
- cooking contest AE

Kochzeit, f
- cooking time

Kochzeit berechnen
- calculate the cooking time

Kochzeit verkürzen
- reduce (the) cooking time

Koffein, n
- caffeine

Koffer, m (großer)
Überseekoffer m
Schrankkoffer m
- trunk

Koffer, m (Reisekoffer)
→ Reisekoffer

Koffer abholen aus einem Gepäckschließfach
- collect a suitcase from a baggage locker AE
- collect a suitcase from a luggage locker BE

Kofferablage, f
Kofferbank, f
- luggage rack AE
- luggage stand BE
- baggage stand AE
- baggage rack AE

Kofferbank, f
Kofferablage, f
Kofferboy, m
- luggage stand BE
- luggage rack BE
- baggage stand AE
- baggage rack AE

Kofferbock, f
- baggage stand AE
- luggage stand BE

Kofferboy, m
→ Kofferbank

Koffer deponieren in einem Gepäckschließfach
Koffer abstellen in einem Gepäckfach

- deposit a suitcase in a baggage locker AE
- deposit a suitcase in a luggage locker BE

Koffer die Treppen hochschleppen
- lug a suitcase up the stairs

Kofferkuli, m
Kofferwagen, m
Gepäckwagen, m
Gepäckkarren, m
- baggage cart AE
- luggage trolley BE

Koffer packen
Sachen packen coll
- pack a suitcase
- pack one's bags coll

Kognak, m (Cognac)
→ Cognac

Kognak, m (Weinbrand)
→ Weinbrand

Kognakglas, n
- brandy glass

Kognakschwenker, m
Kognakglas, n
- brandy balloon
- brandy swifter

Kohldampf, m sl
rasender Hunger, m
- ravenous hunger sl

Kohldampf haben sl
- be dying of hunger sl

Kohleheizung, f
- solid fuel heating

Köhlerfisch, m
Köhler, m
Seelachs, m
Gründorsch, m
- coalfish AE
- coal-fish BE
- black cod
- pollock AE

Kohlsalat, m
- cabbage salad
- coleslaw AE

Koje, f (Bett)
Wandbett, n
- bunk

Koje, f (Messe)
- booth

Kojenbett, n
→ Etagenbett

Kojennummer, f
- berth number

Kojenreinigung, f (Messe)
- cleaning of the booth

Kojenunterkunft, f
Kojenunterbringung, f
- berth accommodation

Kojenzuweisung, f
Kojenzuteilung, f
Kojenverteilung, f
- allocation of a berth
- allocation of berths
- assignment of a berth AE

Koje reinigen (Messe)
- clean a booth

Kokosbutter, f
- coconut butter

Kokospalme, f
- coconut palm

Kolbenmotor, m
- piston engine

Kollation, f obs
  Imbiß, m
  leichte Zwischenmahlzeit, f
  ♦ collation obs
  ♦ light meal
Kollektivversicherung, f
  ♦ blanket insurance
Kollektivversicherungsschutz, m
  ♦ blanket insurance cover
Kolloquium, n
  ♦ colloquium
Kolloquium abhalten
  Kolloquium veranstalten
  ♦ hold a colloquium
Köln
  ♦ Cologne
Kölner Dom, m
  ♦ Cologne Cathedral
Kolonialhaus, n
  ♦ colonial house
Kolonialhotel, n
  ♦ colonial hotel
Kolumbien
  ♦ Colombia
Kolumbier, m
  Kolumbianer, m
  ♦ Colombian
Kolumbierin, f
  Kolumbianerin, f
  ♦ Colombian girl
  ♦ Colombian woman
  ♦ Colombian
kolumbisch, adj
  kolumbianisch, adj
  ♦ Colombian, adj
Kombi, m
  Kombiwagen, m
  ♦ estate car BE
  ♦ estate BE coll
  ♦ station wagon AE
Kombinationsfahrt, f
  ♦ combination trip
Kombinationsmöbel, n pl
  ♦ unit furniture sg
Kombinationsreise, f
  ♦ combination tour
Kombinationsschloß, n
  ♦ combination lock
Kombinationstarif, m
  ♦ combination tariff
kombinierte Badewanne/Dusche, f
  ♦ tub/shower combination
Kombiwagen, m
  Kombi, m
  ♦ station wagon AE
  ♦ estate car BE
  ♦ estate BE coll
Kombüse, f
  Schiffsküche, f
  ♦ caboose
  ♦ galley
Komfort, der Sie erwartet, m
  ♦ comfort that awaits you
Komfort, m
  ♦ comfort
  ♦ comforts pl
  ♦ modern conveniences pl
  ♦ conveniences pl
  ♦ amenities pl
komfortabel, adj
  bequem, adj

  gemütlich, adj
  behaglich, adj
  ♦ comfortable, adj
  ♦ cosy, aadj
  ♦ cozy, adj AE
  ♦ snug, adj
komfortabel ausgestattet, adj
  ♦ comfortably appointed, adj
komfortabel ausgestattetes Zimmer, n
  ♦ comfortably appointed room
komfortabel leben
  ♦ live in comfort
  ♦ live in comfortable circumstances
  ♦ live at ease
komfortabel möbliert, adj
  ♦ comfortably furnished, adj
komfortabel möbliertes Zimmer n
  ♦ comfortably furnished room
komfortabel sitzen
  bequem sitzen
  ♦ sit in comfort
komfortabel wohnen
  bequem wohnen
  ♦ be comfortably housed
komfortable Eigentumswohnung, f
  ♦ comfortable condominium apartment AE
  ♦ comfortable condominium AE
  ♦ comfortable freehold apartment AE
  ♦ comfortable freehold flat BE
komfortable Ferienwohnung, f
  Komfortferienwohnung, f
  komfortable Urlaubswohnung, f
  Komforturlaubswohnung, f
  ♦ comfortable holiday flat BE
  ♦ comfortable vacation apartment AE
komfortable Möbel, n pl
  ♦ comfortable furniture sg
komfortables Ferienappartement n
  ♦ comfortable vacation apartment AE
  ♦ comfortable holiday apartment BE
komfortables Hotel n
  ♦ comfortable hotel
komfortables Leben, n
  ♦ comfortable life
komfortables Quartier, n
  ♦ comfortable quarters pl
komfortables Wohnen, n
  ♦ comfortable living
komfortables Zimmer, n
  ♦ comfortable room
komfortable Unterkunft, f
  komfortable Unterbringung, f
  Komfortunterkunft, f
  Komfortunterbringung, f
  ♦ comfortable accommodation
  ♦ comfortable lodging AE
Komfort anbieten
  ♦ offer modern conveniences
  ♦ offer comfort
Komfortanforderung, f
  ♦ level of comfort required
  ♦ standard of comfort required
Komfortanspruch, m
  gewünschter Komfort, m
  ♦ requested level of comfort
  ♦ required level of comfort
  ♦ requested standard of comfort
  ♦ required standard of comfort
  ♦ level of comfort required
Komfortanspruch genügen
  ♦ meet the required level of comfort

  ♦ meet the required standard of comfort
  ♦ meet the requested level of comfort
  ♦ meet the requested standard of comfort
Komfortappartement, n
  ♦ apartment with all modern conveniences
  ♦ apartment with all modern amenities
Komfortausstattung, f
  ♦ comfortable appointments pl
  ♦ comfortably appointed
Komfortbett n
  → komfortables Bett n
Komfort bieten
  Komfort anbieten
  ♦ offer comfort
Komfort des Zimmers, m
  ♦ comfort of the room
Komforteigentumswohnung, f
  ♦ freehold apartment with all modern conveniences AE
  ♦ freehold flat with all modern conveniences BE
Komfortferienappartement n
  → komfortables Ferienappartement
Komfortferienhaus, n
  komfortables Ferienhaus, n
  Komforturlaubshaus, n
  komfortables Urlaubshaus, n
  ♦ comfortable holiday home BE
  ♦ comfortable vacation home AE
Komfortferienwohnung f
  → komfortable Ferienwohnung
Komfortgrad, m
  ♦ degree of comfort
Komforthotel, n
  komfortables Hotel, n
  ♦ hotel offering all modern conveniences
  ♦ comfortable hotel
Komfortkategorie f
  ♦ comfort category
  ♦ category of comfort
Komfortklasse, f
  ♦ comfort class
Komfort läßt viel zu wünschen übrig
  ♦ comfort leaves much to be desired
komfortlos, adj
  ohne Komfort
  ♦ comfortless, adj
Komfortniveau, n
  ♦ level of comfort
  ♦ comfort level
Komfortpension, f
  ♦ comfortable private hotel
Komfortstandard m
  ♦ standard of comfort
Komfort und Bequemlichkeit
  Komfort (m) und Bequemlichkeit (f)
  ♦ comfort and convenience
Komfort und Bequemlichkeit verbessern
  ♦ improve comfort and convenience
Komfortunterkunft, f
  komfortable Unterkunft, f
  ♦ comfortable lodging AE
  ♦ comfortable accommodation
Komforturlaubsappartement n
  → komfortables Ferienappartement
Komforturlaubshaus, n
  komfortables Urlaubshaus, n
  Komfortferienhaus, n
  komfortables Ferienhaus, n
  ♦ comfortable vacation home AE
  ♦ comfortable holiday home BE

Komfortvilla, f
  komfortable Villa f
  ♦ comfortable villa
  ♦ villa with all modern conveniences
  ♦ villa with all modern comforts
  ♦ villa with all modern amenities
  ♦ villa with every modern comfort
Komfortwohnung, f
  komfortable Wohnung f
  ♦ flat with all modern conveniences BE
  ♦ apartment with all modern amenities AE
  ♦ apartment with all modern conveniences AE
  ♦ flat with all mod. amenities BE
  ♦ flat with all mod. cons. BE
Komfortzimmer, n
  komfortables Zimmer, n
  ♦ room with all modern conveniences
  ♦ comfortable room
Komitee, n
  → Ausschuß
kommen
  ♦ come
kommen als Besucher
  ♦ come as a visitor
kommen auf Einladung von jm
  ♦ come at the invitation of s.o.
kommende Saison f
  ♦ coming season
kommendes Jahr, n
  ♦ coming year
kommende Veranstaltung, f
  ♦ coming event
  ♦ upcoming event
  ♦ coming function
  ♦ upcoming function
kommende Wintersaison, f
  ♦ coming winter season
kommen mit dem Auto
  mit dem Auto kommen
  per Auto kommen
  ♦ come by car
kommen mit dem Dampfer
  ♦ come by steamer
kommen mit dem eigenen Auto
  ♦ come in one's own car
kommen mit dem Flugzeug
  ♦ come by air
kommen mit dem Zug
  ♦ come by train
kommen mit jm
  ♦ come with s.o.
Kommen Sie und entspannen Sie sich bei uns!
  ♦ Come and unwind with us
Kommen Sie und lassen Sie sich verwöhnen!
  ♦ Come and let us spoil you BE
Kommen Sie und sehen Sie selbst!
  ♦ Come and see for yourself!
kommen und gehen nach Belieben
  ♦ come and go at pleasure
kommen von fern und nah
  ♦ come from far and near
kommen zu einer Stippvisite
  ♦ come on a flying visit
kommen zur Kur
  zur Kur kommen
  ♦ come for a cure
kommerziell, adj
  → gewerblich
kommerzielle Konferenz, f
  ♦ commercial conference

kommerzieller Luftverkehr, m
  ♦ commercial air traffic
kommerzieller Reiseveranstalter, m
  gewerblicher Reiseveranstalter, m
  ♦ commercial tour operator
kommerzielles Catering, n
  gewerbliche Gastronomie, f
  ♦ commercial catering AE
  ♦ commercial contract catering BE
kommerzielle Unterkunft, f
  → gewerbliche Unterkunft
Kommis, m
  → Commis
Kommissionär, m
  (im Hotel und Restaurant)
  Bote, m
  Botengänger, m
  Laufbursche, m
  Commissionnaire, m FR
  ♦ commissionaire
  ♦ errand boy
  ♦ commissionnaire FR
Kommissionszahlung, f
  ♦ commission payment
Kommission zahlen
  ♦ pay a commission
Kommode, f
  ♦ chest of drawers
Kommunalabgaben, f pl
  ♦ local rates pl
  ♦ local taxes pl
Kommunikationskosten, pl
  ♦ communication costs pl
  ♦ communication cost
Kommunikationstechnik, f
  ♦ communication technique
Kommunikationszentrum, n
  ♦ communication center AE
  ♦ communication centre BE
kompakte Wohnung, f
  Kompaktwohnung, f
  ♦ compact apartment AE
  ♦ compact flat BE
Kompaktseminar, n
  ♦ compact seminar
kompetenter Service, m
  ♦ competent service
Komplettarrangement, n
  komplettes Arrangement, n
  ♦ complete arrangement
komplett ausgestattet, adj
  vollständig ausgestattet, adj
  ♦ fully equipped, adj
  ♦ completely equipped, adj
komplett ausgestattete Küche, f
  ♦ fully equipped kitchen
komplett ausgestattetes Zelt, n
  ♦ fully equipped tent
komplett eingerichtet, adj
  vollständig eingerichtet, adj
  ♦ fully appointed, adj
  ♦ fully fitted, adj
komplett eingerichtete Küche, f
  → komplett ausgestattete Küche
komplette Mahlzeit, f
  komplettes Essen, n
  vollständiges Essen, n
  ♦ complete meal
  ♦ full meal
komplette Pauschale, f
  ♦ complete package

kompletter Service, m
  → Komplettservice
komplettes Abendessen, n (Dinner)
  ♦ full-course dinner
komplettes Abendessen, n (Supper)
  ♦ full-course supper
komplettes englisches Frühstück, n
  → volles englisches Frühstück
komplettes Essen, n
  ♦ full-course meal
komplettes Frühstück n
  ♦ complete breakfast
  ♦ full breakfast
komplettes Mittagessen, n
  ♦ full-course lunch
  ♦ full-course luncheon
komplett möbliert, adj
  vollständig möbliert, adj
  ♦ completely furnished, adj
  ♦ fully furnished, adj
komplett möbliertes Appartement, n
  vollständig möbliertes Appartement, n
  ♦ completely furnished apartment
  ♦ fully furnished apartment
komplett möblierte Wohnung, f
  ♦ completely furnished flat BE
  ♦ completely furnished apartment AE
komplett modernisiert, adj
  vollständig modernisiert, adj
  ♦ completely modernised, adj
  ♦ completely modernized, adj
  ♦ fully modernised, adj
  ♦ fully modernized, adj
komplett renoviert, adj
  vollständig renoviert, adj
  ♦ completely refurbished, adj
  ♦ completely renovated, adj
komplett renoviertes Hotel, n
  vollständig renoviertes Hotel, n
  ♦ completely refurbished hotel
  ♦ completely renovated hotel
Komplettservice, m
  kompletter Service, m
  voller Service, m
  ♦ complete service
  ♦ full service
Kompliment, n
  ♦ compliment
Komplimente machen jm
  ♦ pay s.o. compliments
komplimentieren jn in das Zimmer
  ins Zimmer komplimentieren jn
  ♦ usher s.o. into a room
Komponist, m
  ♦ composer
Komponistenkurs, m
  Komponistenlehrgang, m
  ♦ composers' course
Kompott, n
  ♦ compôte BE
  ♦ compote AE
  ♦ stewed fruit
Kompottschale, f
  ♦ compôte BE
  ♦ compote AE
Kompottschüssel, f
  Kompottschale, f
  ♦ dessert bowl
Kondensmilch, f (generell)
  ♦ evaporated milk

Kondensmilch, f (gesüßt)
  ♦ condensed milk *AE*
Konditionstraining, n
  ♦ workout
Konditionstraining machen
  ♦ work out
Konditionstrainingsprogramm, n
  ♦ workout program *AE*
  ♦ workout programme *BE*
Konditor, m
  Pâtissier, m *FR*
  Patissier, m
  Zuckerbäcker, m *ÖST*
  ♦ confectioner
  ♦ pâtissier *FR*
  ♦ pastrycook *AE*
  ♦ pastry-cook *BE*
Konditorei, f (Café)
  → Café
Konditorei, f (Laden)
  Konditorladen m
  Konditorgeschäft n
  ♦ confectionery
  ♦ confectionary *AE*
  ♦ cake shop
Konditoreiabteilung, f
  → Patisserieabteilung
Konditoreiumsatz, m
  Konditoreiwarenumsatz, m
  ♦ confectionery sales *pl*
  ♦ confectionery turnover
  ♦ confectionary sales *AE pl*
  ♦ confectionary turnover *AE*
Konditoreiwaren, f pl
  ♦ cakes and pastry
  ♦ confectionary *AE*
  ♦ confectionery *BE*
Konditoreiwarenumsatz, m
  → Konditoreiumsatz
Konditorladen, m
  → Konditorei
Kondolenzbesuch, m
  ♦ visit of condolence
Kondukteur, m
  → Conducteur d'hôtel, Hausdiener
Konferenz, f
  ♦ conference
Konferenz abhalten
  ♦ hold a conference
Konferenz absagen
  ♦ cancel a conference
Konferenz abschließen
  Konferenz schließen
  ♦ close a conference
  ♦ conclude a conference
Konferenzabschluß, m
  Konferenzschluß, m
  ♦ close of a conference
  ♦ end of a conference
Konferenz abwickeln
  ♦ handle a conference
Konferenz am runden Tisch, f
  ♦ round-table conference
Konferenzanforderung, f
  ♦ conference requirement
Konferenzanfrage, f
  ♦ conference inquiry
  ♦ conference enquiry
  ♦ inquiry about the conference
  ♦ enquiry about the conference

Konferenzanfrage erhalten
  ♦ receive a conference inquiry
  ♦ receive a conference enquiry
Konferenzangebot, n (Offerte)
  ♦ conference offer
Konferenzangebot, n (Palette)
  ♦ range of conferences
Konferenzanlage, f
  Konferenzkomplex, m
  ♦ conference complex
Konferenzanmelder, m
  ♦ conference registrant
Konferenzanmeldung, f
  (Anmeldung zu einer Konferenz)
  ♦ conference registration
Konferenzanmeldungskosten, pl
  ♦ conference registration costs *pl*
  ♦ conference registration cost
Konferenzanmeldungsschalter, m
  Konferenzanmeldung, f
  ♦ conference registration desk
Konferenzarrangement, n
  Konferenzvereinbarung, f
  ♦ conference arrangement
Konferenz arrangieren (für jn)
  ♦ arrange a conference (for s.o.)
Konferenzatmosphäre, f
  ♦ conference atmosphere
Konferenzaufwand, m
  ♦ conference expenditure
Konferenzausgaben, f pl
  Konferenzspesen, pl
  ♦ conference expenses *pl*
Konferenz ausrichten (als Gastgeber)
  ♦ host a conference
Konferenzausrichter, m (Gastgeber)
  ♦ host of a conference
  ♦ conference host
Konferenzausschuß, m
  ♦ conference committee
Konferenzausschußvorsitzender, m
  Vorsitzender des Konferenzausschusses, m
  ♦ conference committee chairman
  ♦ chairman of the conference committee
Konferenzausstatter, m
  ♦ conference contractor
Konferenzausstattung, f
  (Technik)
  ♦ conference set
Konferenzausstellung, f
  ♦ conference exhibition
  ♦ conference exhibit *AE*
Konferenzausweis, m
  ♦ conference ticket
  ♦ conference card
Konferenzbankett, n
  ♦ conference banquet
Konferenzbedürfnis, n
  ♦ conference need
Konferenz befindet sich im Planungsstadium
  ♦ conference is in the planning stage
Konferenzbeginn, m
  ♦ start of a conference
  ♦ beginning of a conference
Konferenz beherbergen
  ♦ harbor a conference *AE*
  ♦ harbour a conference *BE*
Konferenzbereich, m (Abteilung)
  Konferenzabteilung, f
  ♦ conference department

Konferenzbereich, m (Sektor)
  Konferenzsektor, m
  ♦ conference sector
Konferenzbereich m (abstrakt)
  ♦ conference field
Konferenzbericht, m (Sitzungsbericht)
  ♦ conference proceedings *pl*
  ♦ proceedings of a conference *pl*
Konferenzbericht, m (über die Konferenz)
  ♦ report of a conference
  ♦ conference report
Konferenzbericht veröffentlichen
  ♦ publish the conference proceedings
Konferenzbestuhlung, f
  ♦ conference-style seating
  ♦ conference seating
Konferenzbesuch, m
  ♦ conference visit
  ♦ visit to a conference
Konferenzbesucher, m
  ♦ conference visitor
Konferenzbuchung, f
  ♦ conference booking
  ♦ booking (of) a conference
Konferenzbudget, n
  Konferenzetat, m
  ♦ conference budget
Konferenzbühne, f
  ♦ conference stage
Konferenzbühnenausstattung, f
  ♦ conference stage set
Konferenzbüro n
  ♦ conference office
Konferenzdatenbank, f
  ♦ conference database
  ♦ conference databank
Konferenzdatum, n
  Konferenztermin, m
  ♦ date of a conference
  ♦ conference date
Konferenzdauer, f
  ♦ duration of a conference
Konferenz dauert fünf Tage
  ♦ conference lasts (for) five days
Konferenzdienst, m
  Konferenzservice, m
  Konferenzdienstleistung, f
  ♦ conference service
Konferenzdiner, n
  Konferenzessen, n
  ♦ conference dinner
Konferenzdokumentation, f
  ♦ conference documentation
Konferenzdolmetschen, n
  ♦ conference interpreting
Konferenzdolmetscher, m
  ♦ conference interpreter
Konferenzdolmetscherdienst, m
  ♦ conference interpreting service
Konferenzdraht, m
  heißer Draht für Konferenzen, m
  ♦ conference hot line
Konferenz durchführen
  ♦ run a conference
Konferenz einberufen
  ♦ convene a conference
Konferenzeinrichtung, f
  Konferenzfazilität, f
  ♦ conference facility

Konferenzeinrichtungen bieten 424

Konferenzeinrichtungen bieten
  Konferenzeinrichtungen bereitstellen
  ♦ provide conference facilities
Konferenzende, n
  ♦ end of a conference
  ♦ close of a conference
Konferenzerlös, m
  ♦ conference revenue
Konferenz eröffnen
  ♦ open a conference
Konferenzeröffnung, f
  Eröffnung einer Konferenz, f
  ♦ opening of a conference
Konferenzertrag, m (GuV)
  (Gewinn- und Verlustrechnung)
  ♦ conference income
Konferenzetage, f
  ♦ conference floor
Konferenzfachmann, m
  Konferenzprofi, m *coll*
  ♦ conference professional
Konferenzfazilität, f
  → Konferenzeinrichtung
Konferenzferienort, m
  Konferenzurlaubsort m
  Konferenzort m
  ♦ conference resort
Konferenz findet statt
  ♦ conference takes place
Konferenzfirma, f
  ♦ conference firm
Konferenzfläche, f
  Konferenzbereich, m
  ♦ conference area
  ♦ conference space
Konferenzform f
  (Bestuhlung)
  ♦ conference style
Konferenzfotograf, m
  ♦ conference photographer
Konferenz für eröffnet erklären
  ♦ declare the conference open
Konferenzgast, m
  ♦ conference guest
Konferenzgastgeber, m
  Konferenzausrichter, m (Gastgeber)
  ♦ conference host
  ♦ host of a conference
Konferenzgebäude, n
  ♦ conference building
Konferenzgebühr f
  ♦ conference charge
  ♦ conference fee
Konferenz geht von Montag bis Freitag
  ♦ conference runs from Monday to Friday
Konferenzgeneralsekretär, m
  ♦ conference secretary general
Konferenzgeschäft n
  ♦ conference business
Konferenzgespräch, n (Telefon)
  Sammelgespräch, n
  ♦ conference call
Konferenzgestaltung, f
  ♦ conference design
Konferenzgewerbe, n
  ♦ conference trade
Konferenzgröße, f
  ♦ size of a conference
Konferenzgruppe, f
  ♦ conference group

Konferenzhandbuch, n
  ♦ conference handbook
Konferenzhauptstadt, f
  ♦ conference capital
Konferenzhaus, n
  ♦ conference house
Konferenzhaus, n (Hotel)
  → Konferenzhotel
Konferenzhotel n
  ♦ conference hotel
Konferenzindustrie, f
  Konferenzwesen, n
  ♦ conference industry
Konferenzinformation, f
  ♦ conference information
Konferenz inszenieren
  Konferenz ausrichten
  ♦ stage a conference
Konferenz ist festgesetzt für den 8. November
  Konferenz ist für den 8. November terminiert
  ♦ conference is scheduled for (the) 8 November
Konferenzkalender, m
  ♦ conference calendar
Konferenzkapazität, f
  ♦ conference capacity
Konferenzkapazität erhöhen
  ♦ increase the conference capacity
Konferenzkäufer, m
  ♦ conference buyer
Konferenzklientel, f
  Konferenzkundenstamm, m
  Konferenzkundenkreis, m
  ♦ conference clientele
Konferenzkomfort, m
  ♦ conference comfort
  ♦ conference amenities *pl*
Konferenzkomplex, m
  → Konferenzanlage
Konferenzkonzept, n
  Konferenzkonzeption, f
  ♦ conference concept
Konferenzkoordinator, m
  ♦ conference coordinator
Konferenz koordinieren
  ♦ coordinate a conference
Konferenzkosten, pl
  ♦ conference costs *pl*
  ♦ conference cost
Konferenzkunde, m
  ♦ conference customer
  ♦ conference client
Konferenzland, n
  ♦ conference country
Konferenz läuft perfekt
  ♦ conference runs perfectly
Konferenz läuft reibungslos
  ♦ conference runs smoothly
Konferenz leiten (generell)
  ♦ conduct a conference
  ♦ lead a conference
Konferenz leiten (Vorsitz)
  Konferenz vorsitzen
  ♦ chair a conference
Konferenzleiter, m
  ♦ conference leader
  leader of a conference
Konferenzleitung, f (Aktivität)
  ♦ leading a conference
Konferenzleitung, f (Organisatoren)
  ♦ conference organisers *pl*

Konferenzmanagement, n
  ♦ conference management
Konferenzmanager, m
  (zuständig für Konferenzabwicklung)
  ♦ conference manager
Konferenzmannschaft, f
  Konferenzteam, n
  ♦ conference team
Konferenzmappe, f
  ♦ conference folder
  ♦ conference kit *AE*
Konferenzmarketing, n
  ♦ conference marketing
Konferenzmarkt m
  ♦ conference market
Konferenz mit Teilnehmern aus X, f
  ♦ conference with delegates from X
Konferenzmöglichkeiten schaffen
  Konferenzräumlichkeiten schaffen
  ♦ establish conference facilities
Konferenznachfrage, f
  ♦ conference demand
  ♦ demand for conferences
Konferenznamensschild, n
  (am Revers)
  ♦ conference badge
Konferenzobjekt, n
  Konferenzimmobilie, f
  Konferenzanwesen, n
  ♦ conference property
Konferenzorganisator, m
  ♦ organiser of a conference
  ♦ organizer of a conference
  ♦ conference organiser
  ♦ conference organizer
Konferenz organisieren
  Konferenz veranstalten
  ♦ organise a conference
  ♦ organize a conference
konferenzorientiertes Hotel n
  ♦ conference-oriented hotel *AE*
  ♦ conference-orientated hotel *BE*
Konferenzort, m
  ♦ conference venue
  ♦ conference site
  ♦ place of a conference
Konferenzort bestimmen
  ♦ decide the conference venue
  ♦ decide the venue
Konferenzpaket, n
  (Informationen)
  ♦ conference pack
Konferenzpauschale, f
  ♦ conference package
Konferenzpauschalpreis, m
  ♦ conference package price
  ♦ conference package rate
Konferenzpause, f
  ♦ conference break
Konferenz planen
  ♦ plan a conference
Konferenzplaner, m
  (Person)
  ♦ conference planner
Konferenzplanung, f
  ♦ conference planning
  ♦ planning (of) a conference
Konferenzpotential, n
  ♦ conference potential

Konferenzpreis m
♦ conference rate
♦ conference price
Konferenzprobe, f
♦ conference rehearsal
Konferenz proben
♦ rehearse a conference
Konferenzprodukt, n
♦ conference product
Konferenzprogramm, n
♦ conference program AE
♦ conference programme BE
Konferenzprogramm ausarbeiten
♦ work out a conference program AE
♦ work out a conference programme BE
Konferenzprogrammausschuß, m
Konferenzprogrammkomitee, n
♦ conference program committee AE
♦ conference programme committee BE
Konferenzprogramm zusenden jm
♦ send s.o. the conference program AE
♦ send s.o. the conference programme BE
Konferenzprospekt, m
Konferenzbroschüre, f
♦ conference brochure
Konferenzprospekt versenden an jn
Konferenzbroschüre verschicken an jn
♦ mail a conference brochure to s.o.
Konferenzpublikum, n
♦ conference audience
Konferenzrahmen, m
Rahmen einer Konferenz, m
♦ setting of a conference
Konferenzraum, m (Volumen, Fläche)
♦ conference space
Konferenzraum, m (Zimmer)
Konferenzzimmer, n
♦ conference room
Konferenzraumeinnahme, f
♦ conference-room revenue
Konferenzraumkapazität f
Konferenzzimmerkapazität f
♦ conference room capacity
♦ capacity of a conference room
Konferenzräumlichkeiten, f pl
♦ conference facilities pl
Konferenzraum vergrößern
♦ enlarge the conference room
♦ enlarge a conference room
Konferenzraumvermietung, f
♦ conference-room rental AE
♦ conference-room hire BE
♦ renting (of) a conference room AE
♦ letting (of) a conference room BE
♦ hiring (of) a conference room BE
Konferenzredner, m
Tagungsredner, m
♦ conference speaker
Konferenzreise, f
♦ conference tour
♦ conference trip
♦ conference journey
♦ trip to a conference
♦ tour to a conference
Konferenzreisen, n
Konferenzreiseverkehr, m
♦ conference travel
Konferenzreisender, m
→ Konferenztourist
Konferenzreisespezialist, m
♦ conference travel specialist

Konferenzsaal m
♦ conference hall
♦ large conference room
Konferenz sabotieren
♦ sabotage a conference
Konferenzsaison f
♦ conference season
Konferenzsekretär, m
Konferenzsekretärin, f
♦ conference secretary
Konferenzservice, m
→ Konferenzdienst
Konferenzsitzung, f
♦ conference session
Konferenzspesen, pl
→ Konferenzausgaben
Konferenzspezialist, m
♦ conference specialist
Konferenz sponsern
♦ sponsor a conference
Konferenzsponsor m
♦ conference sponsor
Konferenzsprache, f
♦ conference language
Konferenzstadt, f (Großstadt)
Tagungsstadt f
♦ conference city
Konferenzstadt, f (kleine Stadt)
♦ conference town
Konferenzstandort, m
♦ conference location
Konferenzstätte, f
→ Konferenzort
Konferenzstuhl, m
♦ conference chair
Konferenzstuhl hat eine Schreibauflage
♦ conference chair has a writing tablet
Konferenzsuite f
♦ conference suite
Konferenzszene, f
♦ conference scene
Konferenztarif, m
♦ conference tariff
♦ conference rates pl
♦ conference rate
♦ conference terms pl
Konferenztechnik, f
♦ conference equipment
Konferenztechnik umfaßt Lautsprecheranlage
♦ conference equipment includes p.a. system
♦ conference equipment includes public address system
Konferenztechnologie, f
♦ conference technology
Konferenzteilnahmegebühr, f
♦ conference registration fee
Konferenzteilnehmer, m (aktiv)
♦ conference participant
♦ person participating in a conference
Konferenzteilnehmer, m (passiv)
♦ conference delegate
♦ person attending a conference
♦ person taking part in a conference
♦ conferee AE
Konferenzteilnehmer aus aller Welt, m pl
♦ conference delegates from all over the world
♦ conference participants from all over the world
Konferenzteilnehmerverkehr, m
♦ conference delegate traffic
Konferenztermin, m
Konferenzdatum, n

♦ conference date
♦ date of a conference
Konferenztermin festlegen
♦ fix the conference date
Konferenz terminieren für September
Konferenz festlegen auf September
♦ schedule a conference for September
Konferenztisch, m
Verhandlungstisch, m
♦ conference table
Konferenztourismus, m
♦ conference tourism
Konferenztourist m
♦ conference tourist
Konferenztrakt, m
Konferenzflügel, m
♦ conference wing
Konferenz über etw, f
Konferenz zu etw, f
♦ conference on s.th.
Konferenzumsatz, m
♦ conference sales pl
♦ conference turnover
Konferenz- und Ausstellungszentrum, n
♦ conference and exhibition center AE
♦ conference and exhibition centre BE
Konferenzunterkunft, f
♦ conference accommodation
Konferenz untersucht etw
(Thema)
♦ conference examines s.th.
Konferenz veranstalten
Konferenz organisieren
♦ put on a conference
♦ organise a conference
♦ organize a conference
Konferenzveranstalter, m
Konferenzorganisator, m
♦ conference organiser
♦ conference organizer
♦ organiser of a conference
♦ organizer of a conference
Konferenzvereinbarung, f
♦ conference agreement
Konferenzverkäufer, m
♦ conference seller
Konferenzverkaufsmannschaft, f
♦ conference sales team
Konferenzverkehr, m
♦ conference traffic
Konferenzverleihfirma, f
♦ conference rental firm AE
♦ conference hire company BE
Konferenz vermarkten
♦ market a conference
Konferenzvermarkter, m
♦ conference marketer
Konferenz vorbereiten
♦ prepare a conference
Konferenzvorbereitung, f
♦ preparation of a conference
♦ preparing a conference
Konferenzvorbesprechung, f
♦ pre-conference discussion
Konferenzvorprogramm, n
♦ pre-conference program AE
♦ pre-conference programme BE
Konferenzvorsitzende, f
♦ conference chairwoman
♦ conference chairperson

Konferenzvorsitzender, m
♦ conference chairman
♦ conference chairperson
Konferenzvortrag, m
Konferenzbeitrag, m
♦ conference paper
Konferenzvorträge veröffentlichen
♦ publish the conference papers
Konferenzwesen, n
→ Konferenzindustrie
Konferenz wird geleitet von jm
Konferenzvorsitz hat jm
♦ conference is chaired by s.o.
Konferenzzeitraum, m
♦ conference period
Konferenzzentrum, n
♦ conference center AE
♦ conference centre BE
Konferenzzentrum leiten
♦ manage a conference center AE
♦ manage a conference centre BE
♦ be the manager of a conference center AE
♦ be the manager of a conference centre BE
Konferenzzentrummanagement, n
♦ conference center management AE
♦ conference centre management BE
Konferenzzentrummanager, m
Konferenzzentrumleiter, m
♦ conference center manager AE
♦ conference centre manager BE
Konferenzziel, n
♦ conference objective
Konferenzzielort, m
Konferenzziel, n
Konferenzdestination, f
♦ conference destination
Konferenzzimmer, n
→ Konferenzraum
Konferenz zu einem bestimmten Thema, f
♦ conference on a certain subject
Konferenzzweck, m
♦ purpose of the conference
konferieren (über etw)
♦ confer (on s.th.)
♦ confer (about s.th.)
Konfetti, n
♦ confetti
Konfirmation, f relig
♦ confirmation relig
Konfirmationsfeier, f (Zeremonie) relig
♦ confirmation ceremony relig
Konfiserie, f SCHW
→ Konditorei
Konfiseur, m SCHW
→ Konditor
Konfitüre, f
♦ jam
Konfitüreglas, n
♦ jam jar
Kongo, m
♦ Congo River, the
♦ River Congo, the
♦ Congo, the
Kongreß, m (politisch und Veranstaltung)
♦ congress
Kongreß, m (Veranstaltung)
♦ convention
Kongreß abhalten
♦ hold a congress
♦ hold a convention

Kongreß absagen
♦ cancel a convention
♦ cancel a congress
Kongreßabteilung f
♦ convention department
♦ congress department
Kongreß abwickeln
♦ handle a convention
♦ handle a congress
Kongreßadministration, f
♦ convention administration
♦ congress administration
Kongreßanbieter m
♦ convention supplier
♦ congress supplier
Kongreßanforderung, f
♦ convention requirement
♦ congress requirement
Kongreßanfrage, f
♦ convention inquiry
♦ convention enquiry
♦ congress inquiry
♦ congress enquiry
♦ inquiry about the convention
Kongreßanfrage erhalten
♦ receive a convention inquiry
♦ receive a congress enquiry
Kongreßangebot, n (Offerte)
♦ convention offer
♦ congress offer
Kongreßangebot, n (Palette)
♦ range of conventions
♦ range of congresses
Kongreßanlage, f
Kongreßkomplex, m
♦ convention complex
♦ congress complex
Kongreßanmeldungskosten, pl
♦ convention registration costs pl
♦ convention registration cost
♦ congress registration costs pl
♦ congress registration cost
Kongreßanschlußprogramm n
♦ post-convention program AE
♦ post-convention programme BE
Kongreßarrangement, n
Kongreßvereinbarung, f
♦ convention arrangement
♦ congress arrangement
Kongreß arrangieren (für jn)
♦ arrange a convention (for s.o.)
♦ arrange a congress (for s.o.)
Kongreßart, f
Kongreßtyp, m
♦ type of convention
♦ convention type
♦ type of congress
♦ congress type
Kongreß aufnehmen
♦ accommodate a convention
♦ accommodate a congress
Kongreßaufwand, m
♦ convention expenditure
♦ congress expenditure
Kongreßausgaben, f pl
Kongreßspesen, f pl
♦ convention expenses pl
♦ congress expenses pl
Kongreßauslastungsrate f
Kongreßauslastungsquote f

♦ congress occupancy rate
♦ convention occupancy rate
Kongreßausrichter, m (Gastgeber)
♦ host of a convention
♦ convention host
♦ host of a congress
♦ congress host
Kongreßausschuß, m
♦ convention committee
♦ congress committee
Kongreßausschußvorsitzender, m
Vorsitzender des Kongreßausschusses, m
♦ convention committee chairman
♦ congress committee chairman
♦ chairman of the convention committee
♦ chairman of the congress committee
Kongreßausstatter, m
♦ convention contractor
♦ congress contractor
Kongreßausstattung, f
(Technik)
♦ convention set
♦ congress set
Kongreßaustragungsort, m
Kongreßort, m
♦ convention venue
♦ congress venue
Kongreßausweis, m
♦ convention ticket
♦ convention card
♦ congress ticket
♦ congress card
Kongreßbankett, n
♦ convention banquet
♦ congress banquet
Kongreßbedürfnis, n
♦ convention need
♦ congress need
Kongreßbeginn, m
♦ beginning of a convention
♦ start of a convention
♦ commencement of a convention
♦ beginning of a congress
♦ start of a congress
Kongreßbereich, m (abstrakt)
♦ convention field
♦ congress field
♦ convention sector
♦ congress sector
Kongreßbereich, m (Abteilung)
Kongreßabteilung, f
♦ congress department
♦ convention department
Kongreßbereich m (Fläche)
♦ congress area
♦ convention area
Kongreßbereich m (Sektor)
♦ congress sector
♦ convention sector
Kongreßbericht, m (Sitzungsbericht)
♦ congress proceedings pl
♦ convention proceedings pl
Kongreßbericht, m (über den Kongreß)
♦ report of the convention
♦ report of the congress
Kongreßbericht veröffentlichen
♦ publish the convention proceedings
♦ publish the congress proceedings
Kongreßbestuhlung, f
♦ convention seating
♦ convention-style seating

Kongreßkosten

Kongreßbesucher, m
- ◆ convention visitor
- ◆ congress visitor

Kongreßbranche, f
- → Kongreßindustrie, Kongreßgeschäft

Kongreßbudget, n
Kongreßetat, m
- ◆ convention budget
- ◆ congress budget

Kongreßbühne, f
- ◆ convention stage
- ◆ congress stage

Kongreßbühnenausstattung, f
- ◆ convention stage set
- ◆ congress stage set

Kongreßbüro, n (beim Kongreß)
- ◆ convention office
- ◆ congress office

Kongreßbüro, n (Vermittlungsstelle)
- ◆ convention bureau

Kongreßdatum, n
Kongreßtermin, m
- ◆ date of a convention
- ◆ date of the congress
- ◆ convention date
- ◆ congress date

Kongreßdatum festlegen
Kongreßdatum bestimmen
- ◆ determine the convention date
- ◆ determine the congress date

Kongreßdauer, f
- ◆ duration of a convention
- ◆ duration of a congress

Kongreß dauert vier Tage
- ◆ convention lasts (for) four days
- ◆ congress lasts (for) four days

Kongreßdienst, m
- → Kongreßservice

Kongreßdienstleistung, f
- → Kongreßservice

Kongreßdirektor, m
Kongreßleiter, m
- ◆ conventions director
- ◆ convention director

Kongreßdokumentation, f
- ◆ congress documentation
- ◆ convention documentation

Kongreß einberufen
- ◆ convene a congress
- ◆ convene a convention

Kongreßeinrichtung, f
Kongreßfazilität, f
- ◆ convention facility
- ◆ congress facility

Kongreßende, n
- ◆ end of a convention
- ◆ end of a congress

Kongreßerlös, m
- ◆ congress revenue
- ◆ convention revenue

Kongreß eröffnen
- ◆ open a congress
- ◆ open a convention

Kongreßeröffnung, f
Eröffnung eines Kongresses, f
- ◆ opening of a congress
- ◆ opening of a convention

Kongreßertrag, m (GuV)
(Gewinn- und Verlustrechnung)
- ◆ congress income
- ◆ income from a congress

- ◆ convention income
- ◆ income from a convention

Kongreßetage f
- ◆ convention floor
- ◆ congress floor

Kongreßfachmann, m
Kongreßprofi, m *coll*
- ◆ convention professional
- ◆ congress professional

Kongreßfazilität, f
- → Kongreßeinrichtung

Kongreß findet statt
- ◆ convention takes place
- ◆ congress takes place

Kongreßfirma, f
- ◆ convention firm
- ◆ congress firm

Kongreßfläche, f
- ◆ convention area
- ◆ congress area

Kongreßform, f
- → Kongreßart

Kongreßfotograf, m
- ◆ convention photographer
- ◆ congress photographer

Kongreßführer, m
- ◆ convention leader
- ◆ congress leader

Kongreßgast, m
- ◆ congress guest
- ◆ congress visitor
- ◆ convention guest
- ◆ convention visitor

Kongreßgastgeber, m
Kongreßausrichter, m
- ◆ convention host
- ◆ host of a convention
- ◆ congress host
- ◆ host of a congress

Kongreßgebäude, n
- ◆ convention building
- ◆ congress building

Kongreßgebühr, f
- ◆ convention charge
- ◆ convention fee
- ◆ congress charge
- ◆ congress fee

Kongreßgebühr entrichten
- ◆ pay the convention charge
- ◆ pay the convention fee
- ◆ pay the congress charge
- ◆ pay the congress fee

Kongreßgeneralsekretär, m
- ◆ convention secretary general
- ◆ congress secretary general

Kongreßgeschäft n
- ◆ convention business
- ◆ congress business

Kongreßgestaltung, f
- ◆ convention design
- ◆ congress design

Kongreßgewerbe, n
- ◆ convention trade
- ◆ conventions trade

Kongreßgröße, f
- ◆ size of a convention
- ◆ size of a congress

Kongreßgruppe, f
- ◆ convention group
- ◆ congress group

Kongreßhalle, f
Kongreßsaal, m
- ◆ convention hall
- ◆ congress hall

Kongreßhalle mieten
- ◆ rent a congress hall
- ◆ rent a convention hall
- ◆ hire a congress hall *BE*
- ◆ hire a convention hall *BE*

Kongreßhauptstadt, f
- ◆ convention capital
- ◆ congress capital

Kongreßhaus, n
- ◆ convention house
- ◆ congress house

Kongreßhaus, n (Hotel)
- → Kongreßhotel

Kongreßhotel n
- ◆ convention hotel
- ◆ congress hotel

Kongreßindustrie, f
Kongreßbranche, f
- ◆ convention industry
- ◆ congress industry

Kongreßinformationsdienst, m
- ◆ congress information service
- ◆ convention information service

Kongreß inszenieren
Kongreß ausrichten
- ◆ stage a convention
- ◆ stage a congress

Kongreß ist festgesetzt für den 22. September
Kongreß ist festgelegt für den 22. September
- ◆ convention is scheduled for (the) 22 September
- ◆ congress is scheduled for (the) 22 September

Kongressistik, f
- ◆ conventioneering

Kongreßkapazität, f
- ◆ convention capacity
- ◆ congress capacity

Kongreßklientel, f
Kongreßkundenstamm, m
Kongreßkundenkreis, m
- ◆ convention clientele
- ◆ congress clientele

Kongreßkomfort, m
- ◆ convention comfort
- ◆ congress comfort
- ◆ convention amenities *pl*
- ◆ congress amenities *pl*

Kongreßkomplex, m
Kongreßanlage, f
- ◆ congress complex
- ◆ convention complex

Kongreßkonzept, n
Kongreßkonzeption, f
- ◆ convention concept
- ◆ congress concept

Kongreßkoordinator, m
- ◆ convention coordinator
- ◆ congress coordinator

Kongreß koordinieren
- ◆ coordinate a convention
- ◆ coordinate a congress

Kongreßkosten, pl
- ◆ convention costs *pl*
- ◆ convention cost
- ◆ congress costs *pl*
- ◆ congress cost

Kongreßkunde

Kongreßkunde, m
- convention customer
- congress customer
- convention customer
- convention client

Kongreßland, n
- convention country
- congress country

Kongreß leiten
- conduct a convention
- conduct a congress
- lead a convention
- lead a congress

Kongreßleiter m
- congress leader
- convention leader

Kongreßleitung, f (Aktivität)
- leading a convention
- leading a congress

Kongreßleitung, f (Organisatoren)
- convention organisers *pl*
- congress organisers *pl*

Kongreßmanagement, n
Kongreßleitung, f
- convention management
- conventions management
- congress management

Kongreßmanager, m
Kongreßleiter, m
- convention manager
- congress manager

Kongreßmannschaft, f
Kongreßteam, n
- convention team
- congress team

Kongreßmappe, f
- convention folder
- convention kit *AE*
- congress folder
- congress kit *AE*

Kongreßmarketing, n
- convention marketing
- congress marketing

Kongreßmarkt m
- convention market
- congress market

Kongreßnachfrage, f
- convention demand
- congress demand
- demand for conventions
- demand for congresses

Kongreßobjekt, n
Kongreßimmobilie, f
Kongreßanwesen, n
- convention property
- congress property

Kongreßorganisation f
- congress organisation
- organisation of a congress
- organisation of a convention
- organising a congress
- organising a convention

Kongreßorganisator, m
- organiser of a convention
- organiser of a congress
- convention organiser
- congress organiser

Kongreß organisieren
- organise a congress
- organise a convention

kongreßorientiertes Hotel n
- convention-oriented hotel *AE*
- congress-oriented hotel *AE*
- convention-orientated hotel *BE*
- congress-orientated hotel *BE*

Kongreßort, m
Kongreßplatz, m
- convention site
- congress site
- convention venue
- congress venue

Kongreßort auswählen
Kongreßplatz auswählen
- select a convention site
- select a congress site
- select a convention venue
- select a congress venue

Kongreßpaket, n
(Informationen)
- convention pack
- congress pack

Kongreßpauschale, f
- convention package
- congress package

Kongreßpauschalpreis m
- convention package rate
- convention package price
- congress package rate
- congress package price

Kongreßpause, f
- convention break
- congress break

Kongreß planen
- plan a congress
- plan a convention

Kongreßplaner, m
- convention planner
- congress planner

Kongreßplanung, f
- convention planning
- congress planning
- planning (of) a convention
- planning (of) a congress

Kongreßpolitik f
- convention policy

Kongreßpotential, n
- convention potential
- congress potential

Kongreßpreis, m
(Preis während eines Kongresses)
- convention rate
- convention price
- congress rate
- congress price

Kongreßprodukt, n
- convention product
- congress product

Kongreßprogramm, n
- convention program *AE*
- convention programme *BE*
- congress program *AE*
- congress programme *BE*

Kongreßprogrammausschuß, m
Kongreßprogrammkomitee, n
- convention program committee *AE*
- congress program committee *AE*
- convention programme committee *BE*
- convention programme committee *BE*

Kongreßprospekt, m
- convention brochure
- congress brochure

Kongreßrahmen, m
Rahmen eines Kongresses, m
- setting of a convention
- setting of a congress

Kongreßraum, m
- convention room
- congress room

Kongreßräumlichkeiten, f pl
- convention facilities *pl*
- congress facilities *pl*

Kongreßraum mieten
- rent a convention room
- rent a congress room
- hire a convention room *BE*
- hire a congress room *BE*

Kongreßraum vermieten
- rent (out) a convention room
- rent (out) a congress room
- hire out a convention room *BE*
- hire out a congress room *BE*
- let a convention room *BE*

Kongreßraumvermietung, f
- convention-room rental *AE*
- convention-room hire *BE*
- renting (of) a convention room *AE*
- letting (of) a convention room *BE*
- hiring (of) a convention room *BE*

Kongreßredner, m
- convention speaker
- congress speaker

Kongreßreise, f
- convention tour
- convention trip
- congress tour
- congress trip

Kongreßreisen, n
Kongreßreiseverkehr, m
- congress travel
- congressional travel
- convention travel

Kongreßreisender m
- convention traveler *AE*
- congress traveler *AE*
- convention traveller *BE*
- congress traveller *BE*

Kongreßreiseverkehr, m
Kongreßreisen, n
- convention travel
- congressional travel
- congress travel

Kongreßreisezentrum, n
- convention travel center *AE*
- congress travel center *AE*
- convention travel centre *AE*
- congress travel centre *BE*

Kongreßsaal, m
- congress hall
- convention hall

Kongreßsaal bietet 1500 Personen Platz
- congress hall seats 1500 persons
- convention hall seats 1500 persons

Kongreßsaal faßt 2000 Personen
- congress hall holds 2000 persons
- convention hall holds 2000 persons

Kongreßsaal kann 1000 Personen aufnehmen
- congress hall can accommodate 1000 persons
- convention hall can accommodate 1000 persons

Kongreßsaison f
- congress season
- convention season

Kongreßsekretär, m
  Kongreßsekretärin, f
  ◆ convention secretary
  ◆ congress secretary
Kongreßsektor m
  ◆ convention sector
  ◆ congress sector
Kongreßservice, m
  Kongreßdienst, m
  Kongreßdienstleistung, f
  ◆ convention service
  ◆ congress service
Kongreßsitzung, f
  ◆ convention session
  ◆ congress session
Kongreßspesen, pl
  → Kongreßausgaben
Kongreßspezialist, m
  ◆ convention specialist
  ◆ congress specialist
Kongreß sponsern
  ◆ sponsor a convention
  ◆ sponsor a congress
Kongreßsprache, f
  ◆ convention language
  ◆ congress language
  ◆ language of the convention
  ◆ language of the congress
Kongreßstadt, f (Großstadt)
  ◆ convention city
  ◆ congress city
Kongreßstadt, f (Kleinstadt)
  ◆ convention town
  ◆ congress town
Kongreßstandort, m
  ◆ convention location
  ◆ congress location
Kongreßstätte, f
  → Kongreßort
Kongreßszene, f
  ◆ convention scene
  ◆ congress scene
Kongreßtechnik, f
  ◆ convention equipment
  ◆ congress equipment
Kongreßtechnologie, f
  ◆ convention technology
  ◆ congress technology
Kongreßteilnehmer, m
  Kongreßdelegierter, m
  ◆ convention delegate
  ◆ congress delegate
  ◆ conventioneer *AE*
  ◆ convention participant
Kongreßteilnehmer aus aller Welt, m pl
  ◆ convention delegates from all over the world
  ◆ convention participants from all over the world
Kongreßtermin, m
  Kongreßdatum, n
  ◆ convention date
  ◆ congress date
  ◆ date of the convention
  ◆ date of a congress
Kongreßtermin festlegen
  ◆ fix the convention date
  ◆ fix the congress date
Kongreßtourismus m
  ◆ convention tourism
  ◆ congress tourism
Kongreßtourist, m
  ◆ convention tourist

  ◆ convention visitor
  ◆ congress tourist
  ◆ congress visitor
Kongreßtrakt, m
  Kongreßflügel, m
  ◆ convention wing
  ◆ congress wing
Kongreßtyp, m
  → Kongreßart
Kongreß über etw, m
  Kongreß zu etw, m
  ◆ convention on s.th.
  ◆ congress on s.th.
Kongreßumsatz, m
  ◆ congress sales *pl*
  ◆ convention sales *pl*
Kongreß- und Besucherbüro, n
  Kongreß- und Gästebüro, n
  ◆ **Convention and Visitors Bureau**
  ◆ **CVP**
Kongreß- und Kulturzentrum, n
  ◆ congress and cultural center *AE*
  ◆ congress and cultural centre *BE*
Kongreß- und Tagungsmanagement, n
  ◆ conventions and meetings management
  ◆ convention and meetings management
Kongreßveranstalter m
  ◆ congress organiser
  ◆ convention organiser
Kongreßveranstaltung, f
  (Veranstaltung während eines Kongresses)
  ◆ congress event
  ◆ convention event
Kongreßveranstaltung, f (Kongreß)
  → Kongreß
Kongreßverkäufer, m
  ◆ convention salesman
  ◆ congress salesman
Kongreßverkaufsmannschaft, f
  ◆ convention sales team
  ◆ congress sales team
Kongreßverkehr, m
  ◆ convention traffic
  ◆ congress traffic
Kongreß vermarkten
  ◆ market a convention
  ◆ market a congress
Kongreßvermarkter, m
  ◆ convention marketer
  ◆ conventions marketer
  ◆ congress marketer
Kongreß vorbereiten
  ◆ prepare a convention
  ◆ prepare a congress
Kongreßvorbereitung, f
  ◆ preparation of a convention
  ◆ preparation of a congress
  ◆ preparing a convention
  ◆ preparing a congress
Kongreßvorbesprechung, f
  ◆ pre-convention discussion
  ◆ pre-congress discussion
Kongreßvorprogramm n
  ◆ pre-convention program *AE*
  ◆ pre-convention programme *BE*
Kongreßvortrag, m
  Kongreßbeitrag, m
  ◆ convention paper
  ◆ congress paper

Kongreßvorträge veröffentlichen
  ◆ publish the convention papers
  ◆ publish the congress papers
Kongreßwesen, n
  → Kongreßindustrie, Kongreßgeschäft
Kongreß wird feierlich eröffnet
  ◆ congress is opened ceremonially
  ◆ convention is opened ceremonially
Kongreßzeitraum, m
  ◆ convention period
  ◆ congress period
Kongreßzentrum, n
  ◆ convention center *AE*
  ◆ convention centre *BE*
  ◆ congress center *AE*
  ◆ congress centre *BE*
Kongreßzentrum leiten
  ◆ manage a convention center *AE*
  ◆ manage a congress center *AE*
  ◆ manage a convention centre *BE*
  ◆ manage a congress centre *BE*
  ◆ be the manager of a convention center *AE*
Kongreßzentrummanagement, n
  Kongreßzentrumleitung, f
  ◆ convention center management *AE*
  ◆ congress center management *AE*
  ◆ convention centre management *BE*
  ◆ congress center management *BE*
Kongreßzentrummanager, m
  Kongreßzentrumleiter, m
  ◆ convention center manager *AE*
  ◆ congress center manager *AE*
  ◆ convention centre manager *BE*
  ◆ congress centre manager *BE*
Kongreßziel, n
  ◆ convention objective
  ◆ congress objective
Kongreßzielort, m
  Kongreßziel, n
  ◆ convention destination
  ◆ congress destination
Kongreßzimmer n
  → s. Kongreßraum
Kongreßzweck, m
  ◆ purpose of the convention
  ◆ purpose of the congress
Königinart, adv *gastr*
  ◆ queen's style, adv *gastr*
königliche Art, adv *gastr*
  ◆ royal style, adv *gastr*
königlicher Besucher, m
  ◆ royal visitor
königlicher Empfang m
  fürstlicher Empfang m
  ◆ royal welcome
königliche Suite, f
  Königssuite, f
  ◆ royal suite
königlich speisen
  ◆ dine royally (on s.th.)
Königspalast, m
  königlicher Palast, m
  ◆ royal palace
Königsresidenz, f
  königliche Residenz, f
  ◆ royal residence
Königssaal, m
  ◆ King's Hall
Königsschloß, n
  königliches Schloß, n
  Königsburg, f

Konkurrent

königliche Burg, f
♦ royal castle
Konkurrent, m
Mitbewerber, m
♦ competitor
Konkurrenz, f
Wettbewerb, m
Konkurrenzkampf, m
♦ rivalry
♦ competition
Konkurrenzangebot, n
♦ rival offer
Konkurrenzbetrieb m
♦ competing establishment
♦ competing operation
konkurrenzfähig, adj
♦ competitive, adj
♦ able to compete, adj pred
konkurrenzfähig bleiben
♦ remain competitive
konkurrenzfähige Preise anbieten
günstige Preise anbieten
♦ offer competitive prices
♦ offer competitive rates
♦ offer competitive terms
konkurrenzfähiger Preis, m
♦ competitive price
♦ competitive rate
konkurrenzfähiger Tarif, m
♦ competitive terms pl
♦ competitive rates pl
♦ competitive terms pl
♦ competitive tariff
Konkurrenzhotel, n
♦ competing hotel
♦ rival hotel
Konkurrenzkampf entkommen
Hektik entkommen
♦ escape the rat race coll
Konkurrenzprodukt, n
Konkurrenzerzeugnis, n
♦ rival product
konkurrieren mit jm
Konkurrenz machen jm
♦ compete with s.o.
Konkurs anmelden
♦ file for bankruptcy
Konkurs machen
♦ go into receivership
Können Sie das für mich reinigen lassen?
♦ Can you have this cleaned for me?
Können Sie ihm etwas ausrichten?
Können Sie ihm etwas mitteilen?
♦ Can you give him a message?
Können Sie Ihr Gepäck identifizieren?
♦ Can you identify your baggage? AE
♦ Can you identify your luggage? BE
Können Sie mich einen Augenblick entschuldigen?
♦ Would you excuse me for a minute?
Können Sie mir diesen Anzug reinigen?
♦ Can I have this suit cleaned, please?
Können Sie mir dieses Kleid reinigen?
♦ Can I have this dress cleaned, please?
Können Sie mir meine Post an diese
Adresse nachsenden?
♦ Can you forward my mail to this address? AE
♦ Can you forward my post to this address? BE
Können Sie mir mit meinem Gepäck helfen?
♦ Can you help me with my baggage? AE
♦ Can you help me with my luggage? BE

Können Sie mir mit meinem Koffer helfen?
♦ Can you help me with my case?
Können Sie mir sagen, was das ist?
♦ Can you tell me what this is?
Können Sie umbuchen?
♦ Can you change the booking?
♦ Can you change the reservation? AE
Können Sie uns noch ein anderes Zimmer zeigen?
♦ Can you show us another room, please?
Können wir das Zimmer sehen?
♦ Can we see the room?
Können wir eine getrennte Rechnung haben?
♦ Can we have separate bills?
Können wir hier zelten?
♦ Can we camp here?
Könnte ich die Speisekarte haben?
Die Speisekarte, bitte!
♦ Could I have the menu, please?
Könnte ich geweckt werden?
♦ Could I have an early call, please?
♦ Could I have a call in the morning, please?
Könnten Sie dafür sorgen, daß mein Gepäck hinunter
gebracht wird?
♦ Could you arrange for my baggage to be brought
down? AE
♦ Could you arrange for my luggage to be brought
down? BE
Könnten Sie ein gutes Hotel in X empfehlen?
♦ Could you recommend a good hotel in X?
Könnten Sie meine Rechnung so schnell wie möglich
fertigmachen?
♦ Could you get my bill ready as soon as possible?
Könnten Sie mich bei dem Gastgeber entschuldigen?
Ich kann nicht kommen.
♦ Would you excuse me to the host? I can't come.
Könnten Sie mich bitte um sieben Uhr wecken?
♦ Could you wake me up at seven, please?
♦ Could I have a call at seven o'clock, please?
♦ Could I have a seven o'clock call, please?
Könnten Sie mir bitte Ihren Namen nennen?
♦ Could you give me your name, please?
Könnten Sie mir ein Taxi bestellen?
♦ Could you order a taxi for me?
Könnten Sie uns ein Lied singen?
Könnten Sie uns ein Lied zum besten geben?
♦ Could you oblige us with a song?
Könnten wir bitte noch etwas Brot haben?
♦ Could we have some more bread, please?
Konservendose, f
Dose, f
♦ tin BE
♦ can AE
konserviert, adj (Dose)
♦ canned, adj AE
♦ tinned, adj BE
Konsortium, n
♦ consortium
Konsortium bilden
♦ form a consortium
Konsortiumsbildung, f
♦ formation of a consortium
Konsortium von Hotels, n
♦ consortium of hotels

Konsul, m
♦ consul
konsularisch, adj
♦ consular, adj
Konsulat, n
♦ consulate
Konsulat eröffnen
♦ open a consulate
Konsulatsbeamter, m
♦ consulate official
Konsulatsbüro, n
♦ consulate office
Konsulat schließen
♦ close a consulate
Konsultation, f
Beratung, f
♦ consultation
Konsumation, f
→ Verbrauch, Verzehr
Konsumationszwang, m
→ Verzehrzwang
Konsument, m
→ Verbraucher
Konsumgeschäft, n
Konsumladen, m
♦ cooperative retail store AE
♦ cooperative store AE
♦ cooperative retail shop BE
♦ cooperative shop BE
konsumierbar, adj
verzehrbar, adj
verbrauchbar, adj
♦ consumable, adj
konsumieren etw
♦ consume s.th.
konsumieren etw beim Frühstück
verzehren etw bei dem Frühstück
♦ consume s.th. at breakfast
konsumiert, adj
verzehrt, adj
verbraucht, adj
♦ consumed, adj
konsumierte Speisen, f pl
♦ food consumed
Kontakt, m
♦ contact
Kontaktadresse, f
♦ contact address
Kontakte knüpfen
Kontakte aufbauen
♦ establish contacts
Kontakte pflegen
♦ cultivate (one's) contacts
Kontakt haben mit den Gästen
♦ have contact with the guests
Kontakt mit seinen Gästen verlieren
♦ lose touch with one's guests
Kontaktname, m
♦ contact name
Kontaktperson, f
♦ contact person
Kontaktpersonal, n
♦ contact staff
♦ contact personnel
Kontaktstelle, f
♦ contact point
Kontaktzentrum, n
♦ contact center AE
♦ contact centre BE

Kontakt zwischen (dem) Gastgeber und (den) Gästen
♦ contact between (the) host and (the) guests
Konten abstimmen
♦ balance accounts
kontinentale Art, adv *gastr*
♦ continental style, adv *gastr*
kontinentale Küche, f (Speisen)
europäische Festlandsküche, f
♦ continental cuisine
♦ continental cooking
kontinentales Frühstück, n
(wie in Mitteleuropa)
♦ continental breakfast
Kontinentaleuropa
♦ continental Europe
Kontinentalfrühstück, n
→ kontinentales Frühstück
Kontinentalklima, n
kontinentales Klima, n
♦ continental climate
Kontingent, n
♦ allotment
♦ allocation
♦ quota
♦ contingent *mil*
Kontingent haben (von etw)
♦ have an allotment (of s.th.)
♦ have an allocation (of s.th.)
Kontingent halten (von zehn Einheiten)
♦ hold an allocation (of ten units)
♦ hold an allotment (of ten units)
kontingentieren (Quote festsetzen)
Quote festsetzen
♦ establish a quota
♦ fix a quota
kontingentieren (zuteilen)
zuteilen
zuweisen
♦ allocate
♦ apportion
kontingentiert, adj
♦ subject to quota, adj
♦ subject to allocation, adj
♦ subject to restriction, adj
Kontingent reduzieren um 20%
♦ reduce an allocation by 20 %
♦ reduce an allotment by 20%
♦ reduce a quota by 20%
Kontingent steht zur Verfügung
♦ allotment is available
♦ allocation is available
♦ quota is available
Kontingent von 123 Karten, n
♦ allocation of 123 tickets
♦ quota of 123 tickets
♦ allotment of 123 tickets
Kontingent zurückgeben
♦ give back an allotment
♦ give back an allocation
Konto, n
♦ account
Konto eröffnen
♦ open an account
Kontonummer, f
♦ account number
Kontraindikation, f
Gegenindikation, f
♦ contraindication
kontraindizieren (etw)
♦ contraindicate (s.th.)

Kontrast bieten zu etw
♦ provide a contrast to s.th.
Kontrollabschnitt, m (einer Karte)
♦ stub
Kontrollbüro, n
♦ control office
Kontrollliste, f
→ Prüfliste
Kontrollpunkt, m
Kontrollstelle, f
♦ control point
♦ checkpoint
Kontrollraum, m
♦ control room
Kontrollstelle, f
Kontrollpunkt, m
♦ checkpoint
♦ control point
Kontrollturm, m
(Flughafen)
♦ control tower
Konvention, f
♦ convention
konventioneller Bus, m
♦ conventional bus
♦ conventional coach *BE*
konventionelles Hotel, n
herkömmliches Hotel, n
♦ conventional hotel
Konvoi, m
♦ convoy
Konzept, n
Konzeption, f
♦ concept
Konzern, m
♦ group
Konzernhotel, n
♦ group hotel
Konzernhotellerie, f
♦ group hotel business
♦ group hotel trade
♦ group hotels *pl*
Konzernumsatz, m
♦ group sales *pl*
♦ group turnover
Konzert, n (Musikstück)
♦ concerto
Konzert, n (Solovortrag)
♦ recital
Konzert, n (Veranstaltung)
Konzertveranstaltung, f
♦ concert
♦ recital
Konzertabend, m
♦ concert evening
♦ concert night
Konzert abhalten
♦ hold a concert
Konzert absagen
♦ cancel a concert
Konzertagent, m
♦ concert agent
Konzertagentur, f
♦ concert agency
Konzertaufführung, f
♦ concert performance
Konzert ausrichten (als Gastgeber)
♦ host a concert
Konzertbeginn, m
♦ beginning of a concert

♦ start of a concert
♦ commencement of a concert *form*
Konzertbestuhlung, f
♦ concert-style seating
♦ concert seating
Konzertbesuch, m
♦ visit to a concert
♦ concert visit
Konzert besuchen
teilnehmen an einem Konzert
♦ visit a concert
♦ attend a concert
Konzertbesucher, m
♦ concertgoer *AE*
♦ concert-goer *BE*
♦ visitor to a concert
♦ concert visitor
♦ audience
Konzert eröffnen
♦ open a concert
Konzert findet statt
♦ concert takes place
Konzertflügel, m
♦ concert grand
♦ classical grand
Konzert geben
konzertieren
♦ give a concert
♦ give concerts
Konzerthalle, f
♦ concert hall
♦ music-hall
Konzerthaus, n
♦ concert house
konzertieren
Konzert(e) geben
♦ give concerts
♦ give a concert
Konzertkarte, f
♦ concert ticket
Konzertmuschel, f
♦ band shell
Konzertort, m
♦ concert venue
Konzertpause, f
♦ concert interval
Konzert planen
♦ plan a concert
Konzert proben
♦ rehearse a concert
Konzertprogramm, n (Information)
♦ concert program *AE*
♦ concert programme *BE*
Konzertprogramm, n (Veranstaltungen)
♦ program of concerts *AE*
♦ programme of concerts *BE*
Konzertraum, m
♦ concert room
Konzertreihe, f
♦ series of concerts
♦ concert series
Konzertreise, f
♦ concert tour
♦ concert trip
♦ concert journey
♦ journey to a concert
♦ trip to a concert
Konzertsaal, m
♦ concert hall

Konzertsaal mit 2000 Plätzen 432

Konzertsaal mit 2000 Plätzen, m
- ◆ concert hall with 2000 seats
- ◆ 2000-seat concert hall

Konzertsaison, f
- ◆ concert season

Konzertsänger, m
- ◆ concert singer

Konzerttournee, f
- ◆ concert tour

Konzert veranstalten
- ◆ organise a concert
- ◆ organize a concert
- ◆ put on a concert
- ◆ promote a concert

Konzertveranstalter, m
- ◆ concert promoter

Konzertveranstaltung, f
- → Konzert

Konzert verschieben
- ◆ postpone a concert

Konzession, f
  Erlaubnis, f
  Lizenz, f
- ◆ concession
- ◆ license
- ◆ licence

Konzessionär, m
- → Konzessionsinhaber

Konzession beantragen
- ◆ apply for a concession
- ◆ apply for a licence
- ◆ apply for license

Konzession entziehen jm
  Lizenz entziehen jm
- ◆ cancel s.o.'s license
- ◆ cancel s.o.'s concession
- ◆ revoke s.o.'s license
- ◆ revoke s.o.'s concession
- ◆ withdraw s.o.'s license

Konzession erteilen an jn
  Konzession vergeben an jn
  Lizenz vergeben an jn
- ◆ grant a concession to s.o.
- ◆ grant a licence to s.o.
- ◆ grant s.o. a license

Konzession erwerben
- ◆ acquire a concession

Konzession für Alkoholausschank an Hausgäste, f
- ◆ residential licence
- ◆ residential license

konzessionieren etw
- ◆ license s.th.
- ◆ licence s.th.

konzessioniert, adj (Alkoholausschank)
  berechtigt zum Ausschank von alkoholischen Getränken, adj
- ◆ licensed, adj
- ◆ licenced, adj

konzessionierter Betrieb, m (Alkoholausschank)
  Betrieb mit Konzession für den Ausschank alkoholischer Getränke, m
- ◆ licensed operation
- ◆ licenced operation
- ◆ licensed establishment
- ◆ licenced establishment

konzessionierter Campingplatz, m
- ◆ licensed campsite
- ◆ licensed campground AE
- ◆ licenced camping site BE

- ◆ licenced camping ground BE
- ◆ licensed site

konzessionierter Führer, m
- ◆ licensed guide
- ◆ licenced guide

konzessionierter Platz, m (Camping)
- ◆ licensed site
- ◆ licenced site

konzessioniertes Hotel, n (Alkoholausschank)
  Hotel mit Konzession für den Ausschank alkoholischer Getränke, n
- ◆ licensed hotel
- ◆ licenced hotel

konzessioniertes Restaurant, n (Alkoholausschank)
- ◆ licensed restaurant
- ◆ licenced restaurant

konzessioniert sein für den Verkauf von etw
  Erlaubnis haben für den Verkauf von etw
- ◆ be licensed for the sale of s.th.
- ◆ be licenced for the sale of s.th.

Konzessionsfirma, f
  konzessionsgebende Firma, f
- ◆ licensing company
- ◆ licencing company
- ◆ licensing corporation AE
- ◆ licencing corporation AE

Konzessionsgebühr, f
- → Lizenzgebühr

Konzessionsinhaber, m
  Konzessionär, m
  Konzessionsträger, m
  Lizenzinhaber, m
- ◆ concessionaire
- ◆ concessionnaire AE
- ◆ concessionary AE
- ◆ licencee
- ◆ licensee

Konzessionsübertragung, f
  Lizenzübertragung, f
- ◆ transfer of a license
- ◆ transfer of a licence
- ◆ transfer of a concession

Konzessionsvereinbarung, f
- ◆ concession agreement

Konzession übertragen
  Lizenz übertragen
- ◆ transfer a concession
- ◆ transfer a licence
- ◆ transfer a license

Konzession verlieren
  Lizenz verlieren
- ◆ lose one's license
- ◆ lose one's licence
- ◆ lose one's concession

Konzession zum Verkauf alkoholischer Getränke, f
  (zum Konsum innerhalb des Lokals)
- ◆ on-license
- ◆ on-licence

Konzession zum Verkauf alkoholischer Getränke, f
  (zum Konsum außerhalb des Lokals)
  Schankkonzession über die Straße, f
- ◆ off-licence BE

Konzil von Konstanz, n
- ◆ Council of Constance, the

Koordinator, m
- ◆ coordinator

koordinieren etw
- ◆ coordinate s.th.

Kopfbahnhof, m
- ◆ stub station AE
- ◆ loop station

Kopf-bis-Fuß-Behandlung, f med
- ◆ top-to-toe treatment med

Kopf-bis-Fuß-Pauschale, f med
- ◆ top-to-toe package med
- ◆ head-to-toe package med

Kopf-bis-Fuß-Programm, n med
- ◆ top-to-toe program AE med
- ◆ top-to-toe programme BE med

Kopffreiheit, f
  (z.B. im Bus)
- ◆ headroom

Kopfhautbehandlung, f
- ◆ scalp treatment

Kopfhautmassage, f
- ◆ scalp massage

Kopfkissen, n
  Bettkissen, n
- ◆ pillow

Kopfkissenbezug, m
- ◆ pillowslip
- ◆ pillowcase

Kopfkissen ist (seit über einer Woche) nicht neu bezogen worden.
- ◆ pillowcase hasn't been changed (for over a week)

Kopfsalat, m
- ◆ lettuce
- ◆ head of lettuce

Kopfstand, m (Messe)
- ◆ end-of-row stand

Kopfsteinplatz, m
- ◆ cobbled square

Kopfsteinstraße, f
  Pflasterstraße, f
- ◆ cobbled street
- ◆ cobbled road

Kopfstütze, f
- ◆ headrest

Kopie machen
- ◆ make a copy

Kopierdienst, m
  Kopierservice, m
- ◆ copying service
- ◆ facsimile service

kopieren etw
  fotokopieren etw
- ◆ copy s.th.
- ◆ photocopy s.th.

Kopiergerät, n
- ◆ copying machine

Kopilot, m
- ◆ copilot AE
- ◆ co-pilot BE
- ◆ second pilot

Koralleninsel, f
- ◆ coral island

Korallenküste, f
- ◆ coral coast

Korallenriff, n
- ◆ coral reef

Korallenstrand, m
- ◆ coral beach

Korbball, m
- ◆ korfball

Korbball spielen
- ◆ play korfball

Korblift, m
(z.B. Skilift)
 ♦ basket lift
Korbmöbel, n pl
 ♦ wicker furniture *sg*
Korbsessel, m
 ♦ wicker chair
 ♦ basket chair
Korea
 ♦ Korea
Koreaner, m
 ♦ Korean
 ♦ Corean
Koreanerin, f
 ♦ Korean girl
 ♦ Korean woman
 ♦ Korean
 ♦ Corean girl
 ♦ Corean woman
koreanisch, adj
 ♦ Korean, adj
 ♦ Corean, adj
Korfu
 ♦ Corfu
Koriander, m
 ♦ coriander
Korinthe, f
 ♦ currant
korinthische Säule, f
 ♦ Corinthian column
Kork, m
 Korken m
 ♦ cork
Korkeiche, f
 ♦ cork oak
Korken entfernen
 ♦ remove a cork
Korkengeld n
 → s. Korkgeld
Korken knallen lassen
 ♦ pop a cork
Korken ziehen
 ♦ draw a cork
Korkenzieher m
 ♦ corkscrew
Korkgebühr, f
 Korkgeld, n
 ♦ corkage charge
 ♦ corkage
Korkgebühr erheben
 Korkgeld erheben
 ♦ charge corkage
Korkgeld, n
 → Korkgebühr
Körnchen Salz, n
 → Salzkorn
kornisch, adj
 ♦ Cornish, adj
kornische Küste, f
 Küste von Cornwall, f
 ♦ Cornish coast
 ♦ Cornish coastline
Kornische Riviera, f
 ♦ Cornish Riviera, the
Kornkammer, f
 Kornspeicher, m
 ♦ granary
Körper, m (generell)
 Leib, m
 ♦ body

Körper, m (Wein)
 ♦ body
Körperbehandlung, f
 ♦ body treatment
Körperbehinderter, m
 ♦ physically handicapped person
 ♦ physically disabled person
Körperflüssigkeit, f
 ♦ body fluid
körpergerechter Stuhl, m
 ♦ contour chair
 ♦ formfitting chair
Körper kräftigen
 Körper stärken
 ♦ invigorate the body
körperlich behindert, adj
 ♦ physically handicapped, adj
körperlich und geistig behindert, adj
 ♦ physically and mentally handicapped, adj
Körpermassage, f
 ♦ body massage
Körpermassagebehandlung, f
 ♦ body massage treatment
Körperpackung, f
 ♦ body pack
Körperprogramm, n
 ♦ body program *AE*
 ♦ body programme *BE*
Körperschaft, f *jur*
 ♦ corporation *jur*
Körperschaft des öffentlichen Rechts, f *jur*
 ♦ statutory corporation *jur*
 ♦ municipal corporation *jur*
Körpertherapie, f
 ♦ body therapy
Körper verjüngen
 ♦ rejuvenate the body
Körperwickel, m
 ♦ body wrap
korrekt, adj
 ♦ correct, adj
korrekte Information, f
 richtige Auskunft, f
 ♦ correct information
korrektes Verhalten, n
 ♦ correct behavior *AE*
 ♦ correct behaviour *BE*
Korrespondenz, f
 Schriftwechsel, m
 ♦ correspondence
Korrespondenz erledigen
 ♦ deal with correspondence
Korridor, m
 ♦ corridor
Korse, m
 ♦ Corsican
Korsika
 ♦ Corsica
korsisch, adj
 ♦ Corsican, adj
koscher, adj
 ♦ kosher, adj
koschere Kost, f
 ♦ kosher diet
koschere Küche, f (Speisen)
 ♦ kosher cooking
 ♦ kosher cuisine
koschere Lebensmittel, n pl
 ♦ kosher food

koscheres Essen, n
 koschere Mahlzeit, f
 ♦ kosher meal
koscheres Fest, n (Party)
 ♦ kosher party
koscheres Gericht, n
 ♦ kosher dish
koscheres Hotel, n
 ♦ kosher hotel
koscheres Restaurant, n
 ♦ kosher restaurant
koschere Veranstaltung, f
 ♦ kosher function
 ♦ kosher event
Kosmetika, pl
 Kosmetikartikel, m pl
 ♦ cosmetics *pl*
Kosmetikbeutel, m
 Schminktasche, f
 ♦ vanity bag
Kosmetikerin, f
 ♦ beautician
 ♦ cosmetician
Kosmetikfarm, f
 → Schönheitsfarm
Kosmetikgeschäft, n
 ♦ cosmetics store *AE*
 ♦ cosmetics shop *BE*
Kosmetiksalon, m
 Schönheitssalon, m
 ♦ beauty parlor *AE*
 ♦ beauty parlour *BE*
 ♦ beauty salon
 ♦ beauty shop *AE*
Kosmetikschule, f
 ♦ beauty school
kosmopolitisch, adj
 weltstädtisch, adj
 weltoffen, adj
 ♦ cosmopolitan, adj
kosmopolitische Atmosphäre, f
 weltstädtische Atmosphäre, f
 ♦ cosmopolitan atmosphere
kosmopolitisches Flair, n
 weltstädtisches Flair, n
 ♦ cosmopolitan flair
Kost, f (Speisen)
 ♦ diet
 ♦ fare
Kost, f (Verköstigung)
 → Verköstigung
Kost ändern
 ♦ change the diet
Kost bieten
 ♦ provide board
Kosten, pl
 ♦ costs *pl*
 ♦ cost
Kostenanalyse, f
 ♦ cost analysis
 ♦ analysis of costs
 ♦ analysis of expenses
 ♦ systems analysis
Kostenanstieg, m
 Kostensteigerung, f
 ♦ cost increase
 ♦ increase in costs
 ♦ rise in costs
Kostenart, f
 ♦ type of costs
 ♦ expense category *BE*

Kosten aufgliedern
- itemize costs

Kostenaufgliederung, f
- itemization of costs

Kosten aufschlüsseln
- break down costs

Kosten belaufen sich auf DM 123
- costs run to DM 123
- cost runs to DM 123

Kosten berechnen
- cost s.th.
- calculate the costs of s.th.

Kostenbeteiligung, f
Kostenbeitrag, m
- contribution towards expenses
- contribution

kostenbewußt, adj
- cost-conscious, adj

kostenbewußter Reisender, m
- cost-conscious traveler AE
- cost-conscious traveller BE

Kostenblatt, n
- cost sheet

Kosten decken
- cover costs
- cover cost

Kosten der Behandlung, pl
- cost of treatment
- costs of treatment pl

Kosten der Spirituosen, pl
- liquor costs pl
- liquor cost

Kosten des Urlaubs, pl
- cost of one's vacation AE
- costs of the vacation AE pl
- cost of one's holiday BE
- costs of the holiday BE pl

kosteneffektiv, adj
- cost effective, adj

Kosteneffektivität, f
- cost effectiveness

Kosten eines Besuchs, pl
- costs of a visit pl
- cost of a visit

Kosten eines Essens teilen
(Gast)
- split the cost of a meal
- share the cost of a meal

Kostenentwicklung, f
- cost trend

Kosten ermitteln
- ascertain the costs

kosten etw (probieren)
probieren etw
verkosten etw
- taste s.th.
- try s.th.
- sample s.th.

kostenfrei, adj
→ kostenlos

kostenfreie Stornierung, f
kostenlose Abbestellung, f
kostenfreier Rücktritt, m
- free cancellation
- free cancelation AE
- cancellation free of charge
- cancelation free of charge AE

kostenfrei logieren
kostenlos logieren
kostenfrei wohnen
kostenlos wohnen

- stay free of charge
- stay free

Kostenkontrolle, f
- cost control
- control of costs
- cost controlling

Kostenkontrolleur, m
- cost controller

kostenlos, adj
ohne Berechnung
kostenfrei, adj
- free of charge, adj
- free, adj
- complimentary, adj
- courtesy, adj AE

kostenlos bekommen etw
frei bekommen etw
- get s.th. free (of charge)
- get s.th. gratis

kostenlos bewohnt, adj
- occupied rent-free, adj

kostenlose Abholung, f
- free collection

kostenlose Beförderung, f
kostenloser Transport, m
- free transport BE
- free transportation AE
- free carriage
- complimentary tranportation AE
- free conveyance

kostenlose Benutzung aller Clubeinrichtungen, f
- free use of all club facilities
- complimentary use of all club facilities

kostenlose Benutzung des Geschirrspülers f
- free use of (the) dishwasher

kostenlose Beratung, f
- free advice

kostenlose Busverbindung nach X, f
- free bus service to X
- free bus link to X
- free coach service to X BE
- free coach link to X BE

kostenlose Duschbenutzung f
- free use of the shower

kostenlose Fahrt, f
Freifahrt, f
- free trip
- free ride

kostenlose Garagenbenutzung, f
- free use of the garage
- complimentary use of the garage
- courtesy use of the garage AE

kostenlose Hallenbadbenutzung, f
- free use of the indoor swimming pool AE
- free use of the indoor swimming-pool BE
- free use of the indoor pool

kostenlose Leistung, f
kostenlose Dienstleistung, f
kostenloser Dienst, m
kostenloser Service, m
Gratisleistung, f
- free service
- service free of charge
- complimentary service
- courtesy service AE

kostenlose Mitfahrt gewähren jm
kostenlos befördern jn
- deadhead s.o.

kostenlosen Eintritt gewähren jm
- deadhead s.o.

kostenlosen Urlaub verbringen
kostenlose Ferien verbringen
- spend a free vacation AE
- spend a free holiday BE

kostenlose Parkplatzbenutzung, f
- free use of the parking lot AE
- complimentary use of the parking lot AE
- courtesy use of the parking lot AE
- free use of the car park BE
- complimentary use of the car park BE

kostenlose Probe, f
(von Speise, Getränk)
- free tasting

kostenloser Aufenthalt, m
- free stay
- stay free of charge

kostenloser Ausflug, m
- free excursion

kostenloser Babysitterdienst, m
kostenloser Babysitterservice, m
kostenloser Babysitter, m
- free baby-sitting service

kostenloser Besuch, m
- free visit

kostenloser Besuch im Schwimmbad, m
- free visit to the swimming pool AE
- free visit to the swimming-pool BE

kostenloser Diskoeintritt, m
- free entrance to a disco
- free admission to the disco

kostenloser Eintritt, m
- free entrance
- free admission

kostenloser Flug, m
Freiflug, m
- free flight

kostenloser Flugschein, m
Freiflugschein, m
- free air ticket
- free ticket

kostenlos erhältlich auf Wunsch
- available free of charge on request
- available free on request

kostenlos erhältlich sein bei jm
(z.B. Prospekt)
- be available free from s.o.
- be available free of charge from s.o.

kostenloser Pendeldienst, m
- free shuttle service

kostenloser Platz, m
(z.B. bei einer Reise)
- free place

kostenloser Probehappen, m
(von Speisen)
- free taster

kostenloser Prospekt, m
- free brochure

kostenloser Reservierungsdienst, m
kostenloser Reservierungsservice, m
- free reservation service
- free reservations service

kostenloser Service, m
kostenloser Dienst, m
kostenlose Dienstleistung, f
kostenlose Leistung, f
Gratisservice, m
- service free of charge
- complimentary service
- courtesy service AE
- free service

kostenloser Skipaß, m
♦ free ski pass
kostenloser Unterricht, m
♦ free lessons pl
kostenloser Versicherungsschutz, m
♦ free insurance cover
kostenlose Saunabenutzung, f
Gratissauna, f
♦ free use of the sauna
kostenlose Schwimmbadbenutzung, f
♦ free use of the swimming pool AE
♦ free use of the swimming-pool BE
♦ free use of the pool
kostenloses Essen erhalten
♦ receive a free meal
kostenloses Frühstück, n
Gratisfrühstück, n
♦ free breakfast
♦ complimentary breakfast
kostenloses Frühstücksbüfett, n
♦ free buffet breakfast
♦ free breakfast buffet AE
kostenloses Geschenk, n
♦ free gift
♦ free present
kostenloses Geschenk erhalten
♦ receive a free gift
♦ receive a free present
kostenloses Getränk, n
Gratisgetränk, n
♦ free drink
♦ free beverage
♦ complimentary drink
♦ complimentary beverage
kostenloses Informationspaket, n
♦ free information pack
kostenlose Skibeförderung, f
♦ free transportation of skis AE
♦ free carriage of skis
♦ free transport of skis BE
kostenloses Parken, n
→ gebührenfreies Parken
kostenloses Preisangebot, n
♦ free quotation
kostenlos essen
♦ eat free
kostenloses Wochenende, n
♦ free weekend
kostenloses Zimmer, n
Freizimmer, n
Gratiszimmer, n
♦ free room
♦ room free of charge
♦ complimentary room
kostenlose Tennisplatzbenutzung, f
♦ free use of (the) tennis court
kostenlose Überlassung aller Lehrgangsbücher, f
♦ free loan of all course books
kostenlose Überlassung von etw, f
♦ free loan of s.th.
kostenlose Übernachtung, f
♦ free night
kostenlose Unterkunft, f
kostenlose Unterbringung, f
♦ free accommodation
♦ accommodation free of charge
♦ free lodging AE
kostenlose Verlängerungswoche, f
♦ extra week free of charge
♦ additional week free of charge

kostenlose Verpflegung, f
♦ free meals pl
♦ free board
kostenlose Verpflegung erhalten
♦ receive free board
kostenlose Woche, f
♦ free week
kostenlos fliegen
♦ fly free
kostenlos für alle
♦ free for all
kostenlos reisen
♦ travel free
♦ travel free of charge
kostenlos übernachten
♦ spend the night free of charge
♦ stay (for) the night free of charge
Kosten minimieren
♦ minimise costs
♦ minimize costs
Kosten niedrig halten
♦ keep costs down
Kosten-Nutzen-Analyse, f
♦ cost-benefit analysis
Kosten-Nutzen-Analyse durchführen
♦ carry out a cost-benefit analysis
kosten (Preis)
♦ cost
Kosten pro Beschäftigtem, pl
♦ costs per employee pl
♦ cost per employee
Kosten pro Gast pro Tag, pl
♦ costs per guest per day pl
♦ cost per guest per day
Kosten pro Logiernacht, pl
Kosten pro Logisnacht, pl
Kosten pro Person pro Übernachtung, pl
♦ cost per bed per night
♦ cost per person per night
♦ costs per person per night pl
Kosten pro Person pro Übernachtung, pl
Kosten pro Logiernacht, pl
Kosten pro Logisnacht, pl
♦ costs per person per night pl
♦ cost per person per night
Kosten pro Stellplatz, pl
(Camping)
♦ costs per pitch pl
♦ cost per pitch
Kosten pro Zimmer, pl
♦ costs per room pl
♦ cost per room
Kostenpunkt, m
♦ cost item
Kostenquelle, f
♦ source of cost
♦ source of costs
Kostenrechnung, f
♦ cost accounting
♦ costing
Kostensenkung, f
♦ cost cutting
♦ cost reduction
Kosten sind minimal
♦ costs are minimal
Kostensteigerung an den Kunden weitergeben
♦ pass on a cost increase to the customer
Kostenstelle, f
♦ cost center AE
♦ cost centre BE

Kostenstellenrechnung, f
♦ cost location accounting AE
♦ cost centre accounting BE
Kostenstruktur, f
♦ cost structure
♦ structure of costs
Kostenstruktur eines Hotels, f
♦ cost structure of a hotel
Kosten teilen
♦ share the costs
Kostenträger, m
♦ cost unit
♦ unit of cost
♦ costing unit
Kostenträgerrechnung, f
♦ cost unit accounting
Kosten umlegen auf etw
Kosten aufteilen auf etw
♦ apportion costs to s.th.
Kosten umlegen auf jn
Kosten aufteilen auf jn
♦ allocate costs to s.o.
Kostenvoranschlag, m
♦ cost estimate
♦ estimate of costs
♦ estimate
♦ quotation
Kostenvoranschlag zusenden jm
♦ send s.o. an estimate
♦ send s.o. a quotation
Kosten zahlen
♦ pay for the costs
Kosten zuordnen etw
Kosten zuweisen etw
Kosten umlegen auf etw
♦ allocate costs to s.th.
Koster, m
→ Verkoster
Kostgänger, m
→ Pensionsgast
Kost ist abwechslungsreich und reichhaltig
♦ cuisine is varied and plentiful
köstlich, adj (Speise)
♦ delicious, adj
♦ tasty, adj
♦ savory, adj AE
♦ savoury, adj BE
♦ palatable, adj
köstlich amüsieren sich
♦ enjoy oneself tremendously
♦ have a great time
♦ have great fun
♦ enjoy oneself immensely
köstlichen Geschmack haben (Aroma)
♦ have a delicious flavor AE
♦ have a delicious flavour BE
köstliches Dessert, n
♦ delicious dessert
köstliches Frühstück n
♦ delicious breakfast
Köstlichkeit, f (Delikatesse)
→ Delikatesse
Köstlichkeit, f (Qualität)
♦ deliciousness
♦ tastiness
♦ savor AE
♦ savour BE
Köstlichkeiten der französischen Küche probieren
♦ sample the delights of French food

Köstlichkeiten der internationalen Küche 436

♦ sample the delights of French cooking
♦ sample the delights of French cuisine
Köstlichkeiten der internationalen Küche, f pl
  ♦ international specialties *AE pl*
  ♦ international specialities *BE pl*
köstlich schmecken
  köstlichen Geschmack haben
  ♦ taste delicious
kostspielig, adj
  ♦ costly, adj
Kostümabend, m
  ♦ fancy-dress evening
Kostümball, m
  ♦ fancy-dress ball
Kostümfest, n
  ♦ fancy-dress party
  ♦ fancy-dress gala
  ♦ fancy-dress ball
  ♦ fancy ball
kostümiert, adv
  ♦ in costume, adv
Kostümverleih, m
  ♦ fancy-dress rental *AE*
  ♦ fancy-dress hire *BE*
Kostümwettbewerb, m
  ♦ fancy-dress competition
Kost und Logis
  Kost (f) und Logis (n)
  ♦ board and lodging
Kost und Logis bieten
  Unterkunft und Verpflegung bieten
  ♦ provide board and lodging
Kost und Logis frei haben
  ♦ have free board and lodging
Kost und Logis geben jm
  ♦ provide s.o. with board and lodging
Kost und Quartier
  → Kost und Logis
Kost und Unterkunft
  → Kost und Logis
Kotelett, n (entbeint)
  Chop, m
  ♦ chop
Kotelett, n (generell)
  ♦ cutlet
krabbeln
  klettern
  ♦ scramble
Krach, m
  Krawall, m
  Krakeel, m *coll*
  ♦ shindy *inform*
  ♦ racket
  ♦ noise
  ♦ rumpus
Krach anfangen
  Krawall anfangen
  anfangen zu krakeelen
  ♦ create a shindy *inform*
  ♦ make a racket
Kraftbrühe, f
  Beeftea, m
  ♦ beef tea
Kraft durch Freude
  ♦ strength through joy
Kraftfahrer, m
  → Fahrer, Autofahrer
Kraftfahrzeug, n
  Kfz, n
  ♦ motorcar *AE*
  ♦ motor car *BE*

Kraftfahrzeugversicherung, f
  Kfz-Versicherung, f
  Autoversicherung, f
  ♦ automobile insurance *AE*
  ♦ motorcar insurance *AE*
  ♦ motor car insurance *BE*
  ♦ car insurance
kräftiger Wein, m
  ♦ vigorous wine
  ♦ powerful wine
kräftiges Schuhwerk, n
  festes Schuhwerk, n
  ♦ sturdy footwear
Kraftstoffeinspritzung, f
  ♦ fuel injection
krakeelen
  ♦ brawl
Krakeeler, m
  Ruhestörer, m
  ♦ brawler
Krankenbett, n
  ♦ sickbed
Krankengeld, n
  ♦ sickness benefit
Krankengymnast, m
  Physiotherapeut, m
  ♦ physiotherapist
Krankengymnastik, f
  → Physiotherapie
Krankenhaus, n
  ♦ hospital
Krankenhausbett, n
  ♦ hospital bed
Krankenhausessen, n
  ♦ hospital meal
Krankenhausverpflegung, f
  Krankenhauscatering, n
  ♦ hospital foodservice *AE*
  ♦ hospital catering *BE*
Krankenkost, f
  ♦ convalescent diet
  ♦ light foods *pl*
Krankenschwester, f
  ♦ sick nurse
  ♦ nurse
Krankenversicherung, f
  ♦ health insurance
  ♦ medical insurance
Krankenversicherung abschließen
  ♦ take out a medical insurance policy
  ♦ take out a medical insurance
Krankenversicherungspolice, f
  ♦ medical insurance policy
  ♦ health insurance policy
Krankenversicherungsschutz, m
  ♦ medical insurance cover
  ♦ health cover
Krankenwagen, m
  Sanitätswagen, m
  ♦ ambulance
Krankenzimmer, n (generell)
  ♦ sickroom
Krankenzimmer, n (Heim, Schule etc.)
  ♦ infirmary
krank essen sich
  krank fressen sich *vulg*
  ♦ eat oneself sick
Krankheit, f
  ♦ illness
  ♦ disease
  ♦ medical conditions *pl euph*

Krankheiten heilen
  ♦ cure illnesses
krank im Bett liegen
  ♦ be lying ill in bed
  ♦ be laid up
krank machen jn
  ♦ make s.o. sick
krank sein
  ♦ be ill
krank werden
  erkranken
  ♦ become ill
  ♦ fall ill
  ♦ fall sick *AE*
krank werden an etw
  an etw erkranken
  ♦ fall sick with s.th.
krank werden an Malaria
  an Malaria erkranken
  ♦ fall sick with malaria
Kränzchen, n
  Damenkränzchen, n
  Kaffeekränzchen, n
  ♦ bee *AE*
  ♦ ladies' circle
  ♦ ladies' coffee circle
Krapfen, m
  ♦ doughnut
Kräuter, n pl
  ♦ herbs *pl*
Kräuterbad, n
  (Aktivität)
  ♦ herbal bath
Kräuterbutter, f
  ♦ herb butter
Kräuterdressing, f
  ♦ herb dressing
Kräutergarten, m
  ♦ herb garden
Kräuterlikör, m
  ♦ herb-flavored liqueur *AE*
  ♦ herb-flavoured liqueur *BE*
Kräutersoße, f
  ♦ herb sauce
Kräutertee, m
  ♦ herb tea
  ♦ herbal tea
Krautsuppe, f
  ♦ cabbage soup
Krawall, m
  Krach, m
  Streit, m
  ♦ rumpus
Krawallokal, n
  gefährlicher Ort, m
  ♦ hot spot *sl*
  ♦ rough joint *AE sl*
Krawatte, f
  ♦ tie
Krawattenzwang
  ♦ collar and tie compulsory
Krawatte tragen
  ♦ wear a tie
kraxeln
  → klettern
Kraxier, m
  → Kletterer, Bergsteiger
kreative Küche, f (Speisen)
  ♦ creative cooking
  ♦ creative cuisine

Kreativkurs, m
 ♦ creative course
Kreativurlaub, m
 Kreativferien, pl
 ♦ creative vacation *AE*
 ♦ creative holiday *BE*
kredenzen etw jm
 ♦ present s.o. with s.th.
 ♦ offer s.th. to s.o.
Kredit, m
 Darlehen, n
 ♦ credit
 ♦ loan
Krediterweiterung, f
 ♦ extension of credit
Kredit gewähren
 ♦ grant credit
Kreditkarte, f
 ♦ credit card
Kreditkarte ablehnen
 Kreditkarte zurückweisen
 ♦ reject a credit card
Kreditkarte anerkennen
 ♦ honor a credit card *AE*
 ♦ honour a credit card *BE*
Kreditkarten annehmen
 Kreditkarten akzeptieren
 ♦ accept credit cards
Kreditkartenbetrüger, m
 ♦ credit card swindler
Kreditkartengebühr, f
 ♦ credit card charge
 ♦ credit card fee
Kreditkartengesellschaft, f
 ♦ credit card company
Kreditkarteninhaber, m
 ♦ holder of a credit card
Kreditkartennummer, f
 ♦ credit card number
Kreditkartenorganisation, f
 ♦ credit card organisation
 ♦ credit card organization
Kreditkartensystem n
 ♦ credit card system
Kreditkarten werden angenommen
 ♦ credit cards are accepted
Kreditkarten werden nicht angenommen
 ♦ credit cards are not accepted
Kreditkartenzahlung, f
 Zahlung mit Kreditkarte, f
 ♦ credit card payment
Kreditkontrolle, f
 ♦ credit control
Kreditobergrenze, f
 Kreditlimit, n
 ♦ credit line
 ♦ credit limit
Kreditpolitik, f
 ♦ credit policy
Kreditprüfung, f
 ♦ credit investigation
Kreditumsatz, m
 (Gegensatz zu Barumsatz)
 ♦ credit sales *pl*
 ♦ credit turnover
Kreditwürdigkeit, f
 ♦ creditworthiness
Kreditwürdigkeit prüfen
 ♦ investigate creditworthiness
Kreide, f
 ♦ chalk

Kreideklippe, f
 Kreidefels, m
 ♦ chalk cliff
Kreisel, m (Straße)
 Piccadillykreisel, m
 ♦ circus
 ♦ Piccadilly Circus
Kreisel, m (Verkehr)
 Verkehrskreisel, m
 ♦ roundabout *BE*
 ♦ rotary *AE*
kreisförmiger Tisch, m
 ♦ circular table
Kreislauf anregen *med*
 ♦ stimulate (the) circulation *med*
Kreislaufproblem, n
 ♦ circulatory problem
Kreislauf verbessern *med*
 ♦ improve (the) circulation *med*
Kreisstadt, f
 ♦ district town
 ♦ county town *BE*
Kremser, m (Kutsche)
 ♦ wagonette
 ♦ wagonette *BE*
 ♦ charabanc *BE*
 ♦ char à bancs *FR*
Kren, m *ÖST*
 → Meerrettich
Kreppapier, n
 ♦ crepe paper
Kreta
 ♦ Crete
Kreter, m
 ♦ Cretan
Kreterin, f
 ♦ Cretan girl
 ♦ Cretan woman
 ♦ Cretan
kretisch, adj
 ♦ Cretan, adj
kreuzen
 segeln
 ♦ cruise
kreuzen durch die Karibik
 ♦ cruise the Caribbean
Kreuzfahrer, m (Passagier)
 Kreuzfahrtteilnehmer, m
 ♦ cruise passenger
 ♦ cruising passenger
Kreuzfahrer, m (Religionskrieg) *hist*
 ♦ crusader *hist*
Kreuzfahrerschloß, n *hist*
 ♦ crusader castle *hist*
 ♦ crusader's castle *hist*
Kreuzfahrt, f
 ♦ cruise
Kreuzfahrtanbieter, m
 ♦ cruise supplier
 ♦ cruise provider
Kreuzfahrtangebot, n
 Kreuzfahrtofferte, f
 ♦ cruise offer
Kreuzfahrtarrangement, n
 ♦ cruise arrangement
Kreuzfahrt auf dem Rhein, f
 ♦ cruise on the Rhine
Kreuzfahrtbeginn, m
 ♦ start of the cruise
 ♦ beginning of the cruise
 ♦ commencement of the cruise *form*

Kreuzfahrtbestandteil, m
 Kreuzfahrtkomponente, f
 ♦ cruise component
Kreuzfahrtbesucher, m
 Kreuzfahrtgast, m
 ♦ cruise visitor
Kreuzfahrtboot, n
 Kreuzfahrtschiff, n
 ♦ cruise boat
Kreuzfahrt buchen
 ♦ book a cruise
Kreuzfahrtbuchung, f
 ♦ cruise booking
 ♦ booking a cruise
Kreuzfahrtdatum, n
 Kreuzfahrttermin, m
 ♦ cruise date
 ♦ date of the cruise
Kreuzfahrtdirektor, m
 ♦ cruise director
Kreuzfahrt durchführen
 ♦ run a cruise
Kreuzfahrtende, n
 ♦ end of the cruise
Kreuzfahrterfahrung, f
 ♦ cruise experience
 ♦ cruising experience
Kreuzfahrterlebnis, n
 ♦ cruise experience
 ♦ cruising experience
Kreuzfahrtexperte, m
 ♦ cruise expert
Kreuzfahrtflotte, f
 ♦ cruise fleet
Kreuzfahrt/Flug-Pauschale, f
 ♦ fly/cruise package
Kreuzfahrt/Flug-Pauschalreise, f
 ♦ fly/cruise package tour
Kreuzfahrtführer, m
 ♦ cruise guide
Kreuzfahrtgebiet, n (groß)
 ♦ cruise region
 ♦ cruising region
Kreuzfahrtgebiet, n (klein)
 ♦ cruise area
 ♦ cruising area
Kreuzfahrt geht ab X
 ♦ cruise departs from X
Kreuzfahrt genießen
 ♦ enjoy a cruise
Kreuzfahrtgeschäft n
 ♦ cruise business
Kreuzfahrtgesellschaft, f
 Kreuzfahrtlinie, f
 ♦ cruise line
Kreuzfahrthafen, m
 ♦ cruise port
Kreuzfahrt in die Antarktis, f
 ♦ cruise to Antarctica
Kreuzfahrtindustrie, f
 ♦ cruise industry
Kreuzfahrtkapazität, f
 ♦ cruise capacity
 ♦ cruising capacity
Kreuzfahrtkunde, m
 ♦ cruise customer
 ♦ cruise client
Kreuzfahrtleitung, f
 ♦ cruise management
Kreuzfahrtliebhaber, m
 ♦ cruise lover

Kreuzfahrt machen

Kreuzfahrt machen
- ♦ go on a cruise
- ♦ take a cruise
- ♦ cruise

Kreuzfahrtmarkt, m
- ♦ cruise market
- ♦ cruising market

Kreuzfahrt mit Flug, f
- ♦ fly-cruise

Kreuzfahrt nach Norden, f
- ♦ northbound cruise

Kreuzfahrt nach Osten, f
- ♦ eastbound cruise

Kreuzfahrt nach Süden, f
- ♦ southbound cruise

Kreuzfahrt nach Westen, f
- ♦ westbound cruise

Kreuzfahrtpassagier, m
- → Kreuzfahrer

Kreuzfahrtpauschale, f
- ♦ cruise package

Kreuzfahrtpauschalreise, f
- ♦ cruise package tour

Kreuzfahrtpersonal, n
- ♦ cruise personnel
- ♦ cruise staff

Kreuzfahrt/Pkw-Arrangement, n
- ♦ cruise/drive arrangement

Kreuzfahrtplan, m
- ♦ cruise plan

Kreuzfahrtpreis, m
- ♦ cruise price
- ♦ cruise fare
- ♦ cruise rate

Kreuzfahrtprodukt, n
- ♦ cruise product

Kreuzfahrtprogramm, n
- ♦ cruise program *AE*
- ♦ cruise programme *BE*
- ♦ cruising programme *BE*

Kreuzfahrtprospekt, m
- ♦ cruise brochure

Kreuzfahrtreservierung, f
- ♦ cruise reservation

Kreuzfahrtroute, f
- Keruzfahrtstrecke, f
- ♦ cruise route

Kreuzfahrtrundstrecke, f
- ♦ cruise circuit

Kreuzfahrtsaison, f
- ♦ cruise season
- ♦ cruising season

Kreuzfahrtschiff, n
- ♦ cruise ship
- ♦ cruise liner
- ♦ cruise vessel

Kreuzfahrttag, m
- ♦ cruise day

Kreuzfahrtteilnehmer, m
- ♦ cruise taker
- ♦ cruiser *sl*
- ♦ cruisegoer *AE*
- ♦ cruise-goer *BE*

Kreuzfahrttermin, m
- Kreuzfahrtdatum, n
- ♦ date of the cruise
- ♦ cruise date

Kreuzfahrt um die Welt, f
- Weltkreuzfahrt, f
- ♦ round-the-world cruise

- ♦ cruise (a)round the world
- ♦ world cruise

Kreuzfahrt um die Welt machen
- ♦ go on a world cruise

Kreuzfahrtumsatz, m
- ♦ cruise sales *pl*
- ♦ cruise turnover

Kreuzfahrt unternehmen
- ♦ take a cruise
- ♦ undertake a cruise

Kreuzfahrturlaub, m
- ♦ cruise vacation *AE*
- ♦ cruise holiday *BE*
- ♦ cruising holiday *BE*

Kreuzfahrturlauber, m
- ♦ cruise vacationer *AE*
- ♦ cruise holidaymaker *BE*

Kreuzfahrturlaub machen
- ♦ go on a cruise vacation *AE*
- ♦ take a cruise vacation *AE*
- ♦ go on a cruise holiday *BE*
- ♦ take a cruise holiday *BE*
- ♦ take a cruising holiday *BE*

Kreuzfahrt veranstalten
- ♦ operate a cruise

Kreuzfahrtveranstalter, m
- ♦ cruise operator

Kreuzfahrtveranstaltung, f
- Veranstaltung einer Kreuzfahrt, f
- ♦ cruise operation
- ♦ cruise operating

Kreuzfahrtverkehr, m
- ♦ cruise traffic

Kreuzfahrt von A nach B, f
- ♦ cruise from A to B
- ♦ cruise out of A to B

Kreuzfahrtziel, n
- ♦ cruise destination

Kreuzfahrt zwischen A und B, f
- ♦ cruise between A and B

Kreuzgang, m
- ♦ cloisters *pl*

Kreuzkümmel, m
- Kümmel, m
- ♦ cumin

Kreuzkümmelkorn, n
- Kümmelkorn, n
- ♦ cumin seed

kreuz und quer durch die Stadt
- in der ganzen Stadt
- ♦ all over town

Kreuzung, f (Straße)
- ♦ crossroads *pl=sg*
- ♦ intersection
- ♦ junction

Kreuzung, f (Straße oder Eisenbahn)
- ♦ junction

Kreuzzug, m
- Kreuzfahrt, f
- ♦ crusade

Krevette, f
- *(gewöhnlich kleiner als eine Garnele)*
- Garnele, f
- ♦ shrimp
- ♦ prawn

Krevettenbutter, f
- Garnelenbutter, f
- ♦ shrimp butter

Krevettencocktail, m
- Garnelencocktail, m
- ♦ shrimp cocktail

Krevettensalpikon, m
- Garnelensalpikon, m
- ♦ shrimp salpicon

Krevettensoße, f
- Garnelensoße, f
- ♦ shrimp sauce

Kricket, n
- *(Sportart)*
- ♦ cricket

Kricketball, m
- ♦ cricket ball

Kricketclub, m
- Kricketverein, m
- ♦ cricket club

Kricketclubhaus, n
- Kricketvereinshaus, n
- ♦ cricket pavilion

Kricketfan, m
- ♦ cricket fan
- ♦ cricket buff

Kricketfeld, n
- Kricketplatz, m
- ♦ cricket pitch
- ♦ cricket field

Kricketfest, n
- ♦ cricket festival

Kricketmannschaft, f
- ♦ cricket team

Kricketplatz, m
- Kricketspielfeld, n
- ♦ cricket ground

Kricketsaison, f
- ♦ cricket season

Kricketschläger, m
- ♦ cricket bat

Kricketspiel, n
- ♦ game of cricket
- ♦ cricket match

Kricket spielen
- ♦ play cricket

Kricketspieler, m
- ♦ cricket player
- ♦ cricketer

Kriegerdenkmal, n
- ♦ war memorial

Kriegsmuseum, n
- ♦ war museum
- ♦ wartime museum

Kriegsschaden, m
- ♦ war damage

Kriegstanz, m
- ♦ war dance

Kriegstanz aufführen
- ♦ perform a war dance

Krim, f
- ♦ Crimea, the

Krimhauptstadt, f
- ♦ Crimean capital

Krimsekt, m
- ♦ Crimean champagne
- ♦ champagne from the Crimea

Krisenmanagement, n
- ♦ crisis management

Kristall, n
- ♦ crystal

Kristalleuchter, m
- ♦ crystal chandelier

Kristallglas, n
- ♦ crystal glass

Kristallglaswaren, f pl
- ♦ crystal glassware

kristallklares Wasser, n
  glasklares Wasser, n
  ♦ crystal-clear water
Kristallvase, f
  ♦ crystal vase
Kriterium erfüllen
  ♦ meet a criterion
Kroate, m
  ♦ Croat
  ♦ Croatian
Kroatien
  ♦ Croatia
Kroatin, f
  ♦ Croat girl
  ♦ Croatian girl
  ♦ Croat woman
  ♦ Croatian woman
  ♦ Croat
kroatisch, adj
  ♦ Croat , adj
  ♦ Croatian, adj
Krocket, n
  ♦ croquet
Krocketfeld, n
  ♦ croquet green
Krockethammer m
  Krocketschläger m
  ♦ croquet mallet
  ♦ mallet
Krocketrasen, m
  ♦ croquet lawn
Krocketspiel, n (Aktivität)
  ♦ game of croquet
  ♦ croquet
Krocketspiel, n (Ausrüstung)
  ♦ croquet set
Krocket spielen
  ♦ play croquet
Krocketspieler, m
  ♦ croquet player
Krocketverband, m
  ♦ croquet association
Krokette, f *gastr*
  ♦ croquette *gastr*
Krönungsfeier, f
  (eines Königs/einer Königin)
  Krönungsfeierlichkeit, f
  ♦ coronation ceremony
Krug, m (Bierkrug)
  Bierkrug, m
  Humpen, m
  ♦ tankard
  ♦ stein *AE*
Krug, m (ohne oder mit Henkel)
  (oft aus Glas)
  ♦ jar
Krug Bier, m
  ♦ mug of beer
Krug Wasser, m
  ♦ jug of water
Kruste, f
  Rinde, f
  ♦ crust
Krypta, f
  ♦ crypt
Kt., f
  → Kaution
Kü., f
  Küche, f
  ♦ kit.
  ♦ kitchen

Kuba
  ♦ Cuba
Kubaner, m
  ♦ Cuban
Kubanerin, f
  ♦ Cuban girl
  ♦ Cuban woman
  ♦ Cuban
kubanisch, adj
  ♦ Cuban, adj
Kubikmeter, m
  ♦ cubic meter *AE*
  ♦ cubic metre *BE*
Küche, f (Militär, Lager)
  ♦ cookhouse
Küche, f (Raum)
  Kü.
  ♦ kitchen
  ♦ kit.
Küche, f (Raum in Verkehrsmitteln)
  → Bordküche
Küche, f (Speisen)
  ♦ cooking
  ♦ cuisine *FR*
  ♦ kitchens *pl*
  ♦ gastronomy
Küche ausprobieren (Speisen)
  Speisen probieren
  ♦ try the cuisine
  ♦ try the cooking
Küche-Eßzimmer, n
  (z.B. in Ferienhaus)
  ♦ kitchen/dining room
  ♦ kitchen/diner
Küche-Frühstückszimmer
  ♦ kitchen/breakfast room
Küche hat geschlossen
  ♦ kitchen has closed
Küche ist ausgezeichnet (Speisen)
  ♦ cooking is excellent
  ♦ cuisine is excellent
Küche ist die beste in Irland
  ♦ cuisine is the best in Ireland
  ♦ cooking is the best in Ireland
Küche ist gefliest
  ♦ kitchen is tiled
Küche ist geschlossen
  Küche ist zu *coll*
  ♦ kitchen is shut
Küche ist gut (Speisen)
  ♦ cooking is good
  ♦ cuisine is good
Küche ist (jetzt) geschlossen
  ♦ kitchen is closed (now)
Küche ist nicht geheizt
  ♦ there is no heating in the kitchen
Küche ist überdurchschnittlich (Speisen)
  ♦ cooking is above average
  ♦ cuisine is above average
Küche ist vegetarisch
  ♦ cuisine is vegetarian
  ♦ cooking is vegetarian
Küche mit Eßbar, f
  Küche mit Frühstücksbar, f
  ♦ kitchen with breakfast bar
Kuchen, m
  ♦ cake
Küchenabfall, m
  Küchenabfälle, m pl
  ♦ kitchen waste
  ♦ kitchen refuse

  ♦ kitchen scrap
  ♦ kitchen stuff
Küchenabteilung f
  ♦ kitchen department
Küchenangebot, n
  → Speisenangebot
Küchenangestellter, m
  Küchenmitarbeiter, m
  ♦ kitchen employee
Küchenanrichte, f
  ♦ kitchen dresser
  ♦ kitchen cabinet
Küchenansager, m
  → Aboyeur
Küchenarbeit, f
  ♦ kitchen work
  ♦ work in the kitchen
Küchenarbeiter, m
  ♦ kitchen worker
Küchenaufwand, m
  ♦ kitchen expenditure
Küchenaufzug, m
  → Speisenaufzug
Küchenausstattung, f
  Küchenausrüstung, f
  ♦ kitchen equipment
Kuchen backen
  ♦ bake a cake
Küchenbäcker, m
  → Konditor
Küchenbank f
  ♦ kitchen bench
Küchenbar, f
  ♦ kitchen bar
Küchenbedarf, m (Lebensmittel)
  ♦ kitchen requisition
Küchenbenutzung, f
  ♦ use of the kitchen
  ♦ using the kitchen
  ♦ use of kitchen
Küchenbereich, m (konkret)
  ♦ kitchen area
Küchenbetrieb, m
  ♦ kitchen operation
Küchenblock, m
  ♦ kitchen block
Küchenbon, m
  Küchenbeleg, m
  ♦ kitchen voucher
Küchenbrennstoff, m
  ♦ kitchen fuel
Küchenbrett, n
  → Hackbrett
Küchenbrigade f
  ♦ kitchen brigade
Kuchenbrötchen, n (mit Rosinen)
  Rosinenbrötchen, n
  ♦ bun
Kuchenbüfett, n
  ♦ cake buffet
Küchenbüfett, n
  Küchenanrichte, f
  ♦ kitchen cabinet
  ♦ kitchen dresser
Küchenbulle, m *mil derog*
  ♦ kitchen wallah *inform*
Küchenbursche, m *SCHW*
  → Küchenjunge
Küchenchef, m
  Chef de cuisine, m *FR*
  ♦ chef

Küchenchef des Jahres

♦ chef de cuisine *FR*
♦ chief cook *AE*
♦ head cook *BE*
♦ executive chef *AE*
Küchenchef des Jahres, m
♦ Chef of the Year
Küchenchef-Eigentümer, m
♦ chef-proprietor
Küchenchef empfiehlt
der Küchenchef empfiehlt
♦ chef recommends
♦ the chef recommends
Küchenchefin, f
♦ lady chef
♦ woman chef
Küchencommis, m
Küchengehilfe, m
Commis de cuisine, m *FR*
♦ kitchen commis
♦ commis de cuisine *FR*
Küchendienst, m (generell)
♦ kitchen duties *pl*
Küchendienst, m (Militär)
♦ kitchen police *AE*
♦ K.P. *AE*
♦ jankers *BE*
Küchendirektor, m
(Küchenchef in großen Küchen)
Directeur de cuisine, m *FR*
♦ kitchen director
♦ kitchen manager
♦ directeur de cuisine *FR*
Kücheneinheit, f
(Statistik)
♦ kitchen unit
Kücheneinnahmen, f pl
♦ kitchen receipts *pl*
♦ kitchen income
♦ kitchen revenue
♦ kitchen revenues *pl*
Küchenerlös, m
♦ kitchen revenue
Küchenertrag, m (GuV)
(Gewinn- und Verlustrechnung)
♦ kitchen income
Küchenfachmann, m
♦ expert cook
Küchenfenster, n
♦ kitchen window
Küchenfertigkeiten, f pl
Küchenkenntnisse, f pl
♦ kitchen skills *pl*
Kuchenfest, n
♦ cake festival
Kuchenform, f
♦ cake tray
♦ cake tin
Küchenfrau, f
Küchenhelferin, f
Küchenhilfe, f
♦ kitchen woman
Küchenführung, f
→ Küchenleitung
Kuchenfüllung, f
♦ cake filling
Kuchengabel, f
♦ cake fork
Küchengabel, f
♦ kitchen fork
Küchengarten, m
Gemüsegarten, m

Nutzgarten, m
♦ kitchen garden
Küchengemeinkosten, pl
♦ kitchen overhead costs *pl*
♦ kitchen overheads *pl*
Küchengerät, n (bes. Maschinen)
♦ kitchen appliance
Küchengerät, n (generell)
♦ kitchen utensil
Küchengeruch m
♦ kitchen smell
Kuchengeschäft, n
Kuchenladen, m
♦ cake store *AE*
♦ cake shop *BE*
Küchengeschirr, n (generell)
♦ kitchenware
♦ kitchen things *pl*
♦ pots and pans *pl*
Küchengeschirr, n (irdenes)
♦ kitchen crockery
Küchengewinn, m
♦ kitchen profit
Küchenhandtuch n
♦ kitchen towel
Küchenhelfer, m
Küchenhilfe, f
♦ kitchen helper *AE*
♦ kitchen hand
♦ kitchen help
Küchenherd m
♦ kitchen range
Küchenhilfspersonal n
♦ ancillary kitchen personnel
♦ ancillary kitchen staff
Küchenjargon, m
♦ kitchen jargon
Küchenjunge, m
Kochsjunge, m
Küchenbursche, m *SCHW*
♦ kitchen boy
Küchenkapazität f
♦ kitchen capacity
♦ capacity of a kitchen
Küchenkenntnisse, f pl
Kochkenntnisse, f pl
♦ cooking skills *pl*
Küchenkomplex, m
Küchenanlage, f
♦ kitchen complex
Küchenkonditor, m
Patissier, m
Pâtissier, m *FR*
Süßspeisenkoch, m
♦ pâtissier *FR*
♦ pastrycook *AE*
♦ pastry-cook *BE*
♦ confectioner
Küchenkontrolle, f
♦ kitchen control
Küchenkosten, pl
♦ kitchen costs *pl*
♦ kitchen cost
Küchenkraut, n
♦ potherb
Küchenkrepp, m
→ Küchenpapier
Küchenlatein, n
♦ dog Latin

Küchenleistung, f (Output)
♦ kitchen output
♦ kitchen's performance
Küchenleistung, f (Service)
♦ kitchen service
Küchenleiter, m
(z.B. in Firmenkantine, Heim)
♦ kitchen manager
♦ catering manager
Küchenleitung, f
Küchenführung, f
♦ kitchen management
Küchenlöffel, m
♦ kitchen spoon
Küchenlöhne, m pl
♦ kitchen wages *pl*
Kuchen machen
♦ make a cake
Küchenmädchen, n
♦ kitchen maid
♦ cook maid
Küchenmannschaft, f
♦ kitchen crew
♦ kitchen team
Küchenmaschine, f
♦ food processor
Küchenmeister, m
→ Maître de cuisine
Küchenmeister, m (Kloster)
♦ kitchener
Kuchenmesser, n
♦ cake knife
Küchenmesser, n
♦ kitchen knife
Küchenmitarbeiter, m
♦ kitchen clerk
Küchenmöbel, n pl
♦ kitchen furniture *sg*
Küchennebenkosten, pl
♦ incidental kitchen expenses *pl*
♦ incidental catering expenses *pl*
Küchenorganisation, f
♦ kitchen organisation
♦ kitchen organization
Küchenpapier, n
Küchenkrepp, m
♦ kitchen paper
Küchenpersonal n
♦ kitchen personnel
♦ kitchen staff
Küchenportier, m
♦ kitchen porter
Küchenpraktikant, m
angehender Koch, m
Kochgehilfe, m
♦ trainee cook
Küchenproduktion, f
♦ kitchen production
Küchenprofi, m *coll*
Küchenfachmann, m
♦ kitchen professional
Küchenqualität, f
→ Speisenqualität
Küchenrenovierung, f
♦ kitchen renovation
♦ kitchen refurbishment
♦ renovation of the kitchen
♦ refurbishment of the kitchen
Küchenrentabilität, f
♦ kitchen profitability

Küchenreste, m pl
  Speisereste, m pl
  ◆ kitchen leftovers pl
  ◆ leftovers pl
Kuchenschlacht, f
  ◆ cake orgy
Küchenschöpflöffel, m
  Küchenkelle, f
  ◆ kitchen ladle
Küchenschrank, m
  ◆ kitchen cupboard
  ◆ kitchen cabinet
  ◆ dresser BE
Kuchenschüssel, f
  ◆ cake dish
Küchensprache, f
  → Küchenjargon
Küchenspüle, f
  Küchenspülstein, m
  ◆ kitchen sink
Kuchenstand, m
  ◆ cake stand
  ◆ cake stall BE
Küchenstandard, m
  ◆ standard of cuisine
  ◆ standard of cooking
Küchenstuhl m
  ◆ kitchen chair
Küchenteam, n
  Küchenmannschaft, f
  ◆ kitchen team
  ◆ kitchen crew
Kuchenteller, m
  ◆ cake plate
Küchentisch m
  ◆ kitchen table
Küchentür, f
  ◆ kitchen door
Küchenuhr, f
  ◆ kitchen clock
Küchenumsatz, m
  ◆ kitchen sales pl
Küchenverbrauch, m
  Küchenkonsum, m
  ◆ kitchen consumption
Küchenwaage, f
  ◆ kitchen scales pl
  ◆ pair of kitchen scales
Küchenwagen, m
  → mobile Küche
Küchenwaren, f pl
  ◆ kitchen supplies pl
Küchenwäsche f
  ◆ kitchen linen
Küchenzeile, f
  ◆ kitchen units pl
Küchenzelt, n
  ◆ kitchen tent
  ◆ cookhouse tent
Küchenzettel m
  → Speisekarte
Küche probieren (Speisen)
  Speisen probieren
  ◆ sample the cuisine
  ◆ sample the cooking
Kuckucksuhr, f
  ◆ cuckoo clock
Küfer, m (generell)
  ◆ cooper
Küfer, m (Kellermeister)
  → Kellermeister

kugelsicher, adj
  ◆ bulletproof, adj AE
  ◆ bullet-proof, adj BE
Kühlanlage, f
  ◆ cooling system
  ◆ cold-storage plant
Kühlbar, f
  Bar mit Kühlvorrichtung, f
  Frigorbar, f
  ◆ refrigerated bar
kühl behandeln jn
  ◆ treat s.o. coolly
Kühleinrichtung, f
  ◆ refrigeration facility
kühl empfangen werden
  ◆ meet with a cool reception
kühlen etw
  abkühlen etw
  ◆ cool s.th.
  ◆ chill s.th.
kühlen etw im Kühlschrank
  ◆ chill s.th. in the refrigerator
kühler Empfang, m
  ◆ cool reception
  ◆ cold reception
kühler Keller, m
  ◆ cool cellar
kühles Bier, n
  ◆ cool beer
kühles Getränk, n
  ◆ cool drink
  ◆ cool beverage
kühl lagern etw
  ◆ keep s.th. in a cool place
Kühlmittel, n pl
  ◆ refrigeration supplies pl
Kühlraum, m
  ◆ cold room
  ◆ cold store
Kühlschrank, m
  ◆ refrigerator
  ◆ fridge coll
Kühlschrank ist kaputt coll
  ◆ fridge is broken coll
  ◆ refrigerator is broken
Kühltheke, f
  ◆ refrigerated counter
Kühltruhe, f
  ◆ chest freezer
  ◆ freezer
  ◆ deep freeze
Kühlung, f
  ◆ refrigeration
  ◆ cooling
Kuhmilch, f
  ◆ cow's milk
kulante Bedingungen, f pl
  großzügige Bedingungen, f pl
  ◆ accommodating terms pl
  ◆ generous terms pl
kulant sein
  verbindlich sein
  ◆ be obliging
kulinarisch, adj
  ◆ culinary, adj
kulinarische Ausbildung, f
  ◆ culinary training
kulinarische Ausbildung haben
  kulinarische Ausbildung besitzen
  ◆ have culinary training

kulinarische Ausstattung, f
  kulinarische Ausrüstung, f
  ◆ culinary equipment
kulinarische Fertigkeiten, f pl
  kulinarische Kenntnisse, f pl
  ◆ culinary skills pl
kulinarische Freuden genießen
  ◆ enjoy culinary pleasures
kulinarische Genüsse aufgeben
  ◆ abandon culinary delights
kulinarische Genüsse genießen
  ◆ enjoy (the) culinary pleasures
  ◆ enjoy (the) culinary delights
kulinarische Köstlichkeiten, f pl
  kulinarische Genüsse, m pl
  Gaumenfreuden, f pl
  ◆ culinary delights pl
kulinarische Mühen, f pl
  kulinarische Bemühungen, f pl
  ◆ culinary efforts pl
kulinarischen Standard anheben
  ◆ raise the culinary standard
kulinarische Reise, f
  ◆ culinary tour
  ◆ culinary journey
  ◆ culinary trip
kulinarischer Genuß, m
  ◆ culinary pleasure
  ◆ culinary delight
kulinarischer Höhepunkt m
  ◆ culinary highlight
  ◆ culinary triumph
kulinarischer Leckerbissen, m
  ◆ culinary delicacy
kulinarischer Standard, m
  ◆ culinary standard
kulinarischer Wettbewerb, m
  ◆ culinary competition
kulinarisches Angebot, n
  kulinarische Offerte, f
  ◆ culinary offer
kulinarisches Bewußtsein, n
  ◆ culinary awareness
kulinarisches Erlebnis, n
  ◆ culinary experience
kulinarische Spezialität, f
  ◆ culinary specialty AE
  ◆ culinary speciality BE
kulinarisches Programm, n
  ◆ culinary program AE
  ◆ culinary programme BE
kulinarische Szene, f
  ◆ culinary scene
kulinarische Tradition, f
  ◆ culinary tradition
kulinarische Tradition pflegen
  ◆ cultivate one's culinary tradition
kulinarische Überraschung, f
  ◆ culinary surprise
kulinarische Vielfalt, f
  kulinarische Abwechslung, f
  ◆ culinary variety
kulinarische Woche, f
  ◆ culinary week
Kulisse, f
  (Theater)
  ◆ flat
kultiviert, adj
  gepflegt, adj
  ◆ cultivated, adj
  ◆ refined, adj

kultivierte Atmosphäre

kultivierte Atmosphäre, f
   gepflegte Atmosphäre, f
   ♦ cultivated atmosphere
   ♦ refined atmosphere
kultivierte Gastlichkeit, f
   ♦ refined hospitality
kultivierter Luxus, m
   ♦ civilised luxury
   ♦ gracious living
kultivierter Service, m
   gepflegter Service, m
   ♦ refined service
kultiviertes Hotel, n
   ♦ refined hotel
   ♦ civilised hotel
Kultiviertheit, f
   ♦ refinement
   ♦ culture
Kultur, f
   ♦ culture
   ♦ civilisation
Kulturabend, m
   ♦ cultural evening
Kulturbesuch, m
   ♦ cultural visit
Kulturbesucher, m
   ♦ cultural visitor
Kulturdenkmal, n
   ♦ cultural monument
Kultureinrichtung, f
   kulturelle Einrichtung, f
   ♦ cultural facility
kulturelle Aktivität, f
   ♦ cultural activity
kulturelle Attraktion, f
   ♦ cultural attraction
kulturelle Mannigfaltigkeit, f
   ♦ cultural diversity
kultureller Austausch, m
   Kulturaustausch, m
   ♦ cultural exchange
kultureller Treffpunkt, m
   ♦ cultural meeting point
kulturelle Sehenswürdigkeit, f
   ♦ cultural sight
   ♦ cultural attraction
kulturelles Programm, n
   → Kulturprogramm
kulturelle Unversehrtheit, f
   kulturelle Integrität, f
   ♦ cultural integrity
kulturelle Veranstaltung, f
   Kulturveranstaltung, f
   ♦ cultural event
kulturelle Vielfalt, f
   ♦ cultural variety
kulturelles Zentrum, n
   → Kulturzentrum
Kulturerbe, n
   ♦ cultural heritage
   ♦ heritage
   ♦ cultural inheritance
Kulturerbe erhalten
   ♦ preserve one's cultural heritage
Kulturerbeerhaltung, f
   ♦ cultural heritage preservation
   ♦ preservation of one's cultural heritage
Kulturexpedition, f
   ♦ cultural expedition
Kulturfahrt, f
   ♦ cultural trip

Kulturfest, n
   → Kulturfestival
Kulturfestival, n
   Kulturfest, n
   Kulturfestspiele, n pl
   ♦ cultural festival
   ♦ culture festival
Kulturgeschichte, f
   ♦ cultural history
Kulturgeschichtemuseum, n
   kulturgeschichtliches Museum, n
   ♦ heritage museum
Kulturgeschichtepark, m
   ♦ heritage park
Kulturgeschichtetag, m
   ♦ heritage day
Kulturgeschichtetourismus, m
   Kulturerbetourismus, m
   ♦ heritage tourism
Kulturgeschichtetourist, m
   Kulturerbetourist, m
   ♦ heritage tourist
Kulturgeschichteweg, m
   ♦ heritage trail
Kulturgeschichtewoche, f
   ♦ heritage week
Kulturgeschichtezentrum, n
   ♦ heritage centre BE
kulturgeschichtliche Reise, f
   kulturgschichtlicher Rundgang, m
   ♦ heritage tour
Kulturinstitut, n
   ♦ cultural institute
Kulturkalender, m
   ♦ cultural calendar
Kulturlandschaft, f
   ♦ man-made landscape
   ♦ cultural landscape
Kulturleben, n
   kulturelles Leben, n
   ♦ cultural life
Kulturliebhaber, m
   ♦ culture lover
Kulturmesse, f
   ♦ cultural fair
Kulturprogramm, n (Aktivtität)
   kulturelles Programm, n
   ♦ cultural program AE
   ♦ cultural programme BE
Kulturprogramm, n (Liste)
   ♦ program of cultural events AE
   ♦ programme of cultural events BE
Kulturraum, m
   ♦ culture area
   ♦ area of culture
Kulturreise, f
   ♦ cultural tour
   ♦ cultural trip
   ♦ cultural journey
Kulturschatz, m
   ♦ cultural treasure
Kulturschau, f
   ♦ cultural show
Kulturschock, m
   ♦ culture shock
Kulturstadt, f
   ♦ culture city
Kulturstudie, f
   ♦ cultural study
Kulturszene, f
   ♦ cultural scene

Kulturtourismus, m
   kultureller Tourismus, m
   ♦ cultural tourism
Kulturtourist, m
   ♦ cultural tourist
Kulturtradition, f
   kulturelle Tradition, f
   ♦ cultural tradition
Kultur- und Fremdenverkehrsamt, n
   ♦ office of culture and tourism
Kulturlaub, m
   ♦ cultural vacation AE
   ♦ cultural holiday BE
Kultururlauber, m
   ♦ cultural vacationer AE
   ♦ cultural holidaymaker BE
Kulturwochenende, n
   ♦ cultural weekend
Kulturzentrum, n
   Zentrum der Kultur, n
   ♦ cultural center AE
   ♦ cultural centre BE
   ♦ center of culture AE
   ♦ centre of culture BE
Kümmel, m
   ♦ caraway
Kümmelbrötchen, n
   ♦ caraway roll
Kümmelkorn, n
   ♦ caraway seed
Kummer hinunterspülen
   ♦ drown one's sorrows
kümmerlichen Empfang jm bereiten
   ♦ give s.o. a poor reception
kümmerlicher Empfang m
   ♦ poor reception
kümmern sich um das Gepäck
   ♦ take care of the baggage AE
   ♦ take care of the luggage BE
kümmern sich um das Wohlergehen eines Gasts
   ♦ take care of a guest's well-being
   ♦ look after a guest's well-being
kümmern sich um die Unterkunft
   ♦ make arrangements for accommodation
kümmern sich um einen Gast
   sich um einen Gast kümmern
   ♦ look after a guest
   ♦ take care of a guest
kümmern sich um etw
   ♦ look after s.th.
   ♦ take care of s.th.
   ♦ attend to s.th.
kümmern sich um jn
   ♦ take care of s.o.
   ♦ look after s.o.
Kunde, m
   ♦ customer
   ♦ client
Kunde hat immer recht
   Der Kunde hat immer recht
   ♦ customer is always right
   ♦ The customer is always right
Kunde ist König
   Der Kunde ist König
   ♦ customer comes first
   ♦ The customer comes first
Kunden abweisen
   Kunden wegschicken
   ♦ turn away a customer
   ♦ send away a customer

Kundenanfrage, f
 ♦ client inquiry
 ♦ client enquiry
Kunden anlocken
 Kunden herbeilocken
 ♦ lure customers
 ♦ attract customers
 ♦ entice customers
Kunden anziehen
 Kunden anlocken
 ♦ attract customers
 ♦ attract clients
Kundenart f
 → Kundentyp
Kundenausgaben, f pl
 ♦ customer spending
Kundenausgabenverhalten, n
 Kundenausgabengewohnheit, f
 ♦ customer spending habit
Kundenbedürfnisse, n pl
 ♦ customer needs pl
 ♦ customer's needs pl
 ♦ customers' needs pl
Kunden beraten
 ♦ advise a customer
Kundenbestellung, f
 ♦ customer's order
 ♦ client's order
Kundenbetreuung, f
 Kundenservice, m
 ♦ customer service
Kunden bewirten
 ♦ entertain a customer
 ♦ entertain customers
Kundenbewirtung, f
 (z.B. durch Firma)
 ♦ entertainment of customers
Kundendienst, m
 ♦ after-sales service
 ♦ back-up service
 ♦ customer service
Kundendossier, n
 Kundenakte, f
 ♦ customer file
Kunden entfremden
 ♦ alienate customers
kundenfreundlich, adj
 ♦ customer-friendly, adj
Kundengepäck, n
 ♦ client's baggage AE
 ♦ clients' baggage AE
 ♦ baggage of a client AE
 ♦ client's luggage BE
 ♦ clients' luggage BE
Kundengruppe, f
 ♦ customer group
 ♦ client group
Kundenkartei, f
 ♦ customers' index
 ♦ index of customers
Kundenkomfort, m
 ♦ comfort of the customer
 ♦ comfort of the client
Kundenkreis, m
 → Kundenstamm
Kundenkreis erhalten
 Kundenkreis behalten
 ♦ retain one's clientele
Kundenliste, f
 Kundenverzeichnis, n
 ♦ customer list

♦ client list
 ♦ list of customers
 ♦ list of clients
Kundenmix, m
 ♦ customer mix
Kundennachfrage, f
 Nachfrage durch Kunden, f
 ♦ customer demand
Kundennachlaß f
 (Preisermäßigung)
 ♦ allowance (made) to a customer
kundenorientiert, adj
 ♦ customer-oriented, adj AE
 ♦ customer-orientated, adj BE
 ♦ client-oriented, adj AE
 ♦ customer-orientated, adj BE
Kundenprofil, n
 ♦ customer profile
Kundenrechnung, f
 ♦ customer's bill
 ♦ customer's check AE
 ♦ client's bill
 ♦ client's check AE
Kundenrechnung ändern (geringfügig)
 ♦ alter a customer's bill
Kundenrechnung vorbereiten
 ♦ prepare a customer's bill
Kundenreklamation, f
 ♦ customer complaint
 ♦ complaint by a customer
Kundensegment, n
 ♦ customer segment
Kundenstamm, m
 Gästestamm, m
 Gästeklientel, f
 Gästekreis, m
 Klientel, f
 ♦ clientele
Kundenstamm aufbauen
 ♦ build up a clientele
Kundenstrom, m
 ♦ customer flow
 ♦ flow of customers
Kundentreue, f
 ♦ customer loyalty
 ♦ customers' loyalty
Kundentyp m
 Kundenart f
 ♦ customer type
 ♦ type of customer
kundenunfreundlich, adj
 kundenfeindlich, adj
 ♦ customer-unfriendly, adj
Kundenunzufriedenheit f
 ♦ customer dissatisfaction
Kundenverhalten, n
 ♦ customer behavior AE
 ♦ customer behaviour BE
 ♦ customers' behavior AE
 ♦ customers' behaviour BE
Kunden verlieren
 ♦ lose a customer
 ♦ lose customers
 ♦ lose a client
 ♦ lose clients
Kunden vertreiben
 ♦ drive customers away
Kundenvorliebe, f
 Kundenpräferenz, f
 ♦ customer preference

Kundenwahl, f
 ♦ customer choice
 ♦ customer's choice
Kundenwunsch, m
 ♦ customer's request
 ♦ client's request
Kundenzahl, f
 ♦ number of customers
 ♦ number of clients
Kundenzufriedenheit f
 ♦ customer satisfaction
Kundenzufriedenheit steht an oberster Stelle
 ♦ customer satisfaction is paramount
Kundenzufriedenheit steigern
 ♦ increase customer satisfaction
Kundenzufriedenheit verbessern
 ♦ improve customer satisfaction
Kunden zufriedenstellen
 ♦ please a customer
 ♦ please a client
Kunde zweiter Klasse, m
 ♦ second-category customer
 ♦ second-category client
Kundgebung, f
 ♦ rally
kündigen
 ♦ give notice
kündigen jm (generell)
 ♦ give s.o. notice
kündigen jm mit einer Frist von zwei Wochen
 ♦ give s.o. two weeks' notice
kündigen jm (Unterkunft)
 ♦ give notice to quit
kündigen mit einer Frist von einer Woche
 ♦ give one week's notice
kündigen zum Quartalsende
 ♦ give notice for the end of the quarter
Kündigung, f (durch Vermieter)
 ♦ notice to quit
Kündigung, f (generell)
 ♦ notice (of termination)
 ♦ notice
Kündigung der Mietvereinbarung, f
 ♦ cancellation of the tenancy agreement
 ♦ cancelation of the tenancy agreement AE
 ♦ cancel(l)ation of the rent(al) agreement
 ♦ cancel(l)ation of the lease agreement
 ♦ cancellation of the letting agreement BE
Kündigungsfrist, f
 ♦ period of notice
 ♦ notice period
 ♦ term of notice
 ♦ length of notice
 ♦ notice
Kündigungsfrist beträgt 7 Tage
 ♦ notice for leaving is 7 days
Kündigungsfrist von einer Woche, f
 ♦ week's notice
 ♦ a week's notice
Kündigungsrecht, n
 ♦ right to notice
Kündigungsschreiben, n
 → schriftliche Kündigung
Kundin, f
 ♦ woman customer
 ♦ female customer
 ♦ woman client
 ♦ female client
Kundschaft verlieren
 ♦ lose custom

Kunst

Kunst, f
- ◆ art

Kunstauktion, f
- Kunstversteigerung, f
- ◆ art auction

Kunstausstellung, f
- ◆ art exhibition
- ◆ art exhibit *AE*

Kunst der Hotelführung, f
- Hotelkunst, f
- ◆ hotelmanship

Kunst des Reisens, f
- Reisekunst, f
- ◆ art of travelling
- ◆ art of traveling *AE*

Kunsteis, n
- ◆ artificial ice

Kunsteisbahn f
- ◆ artificial ice rink

Kunsteisstockbahn, f
- ◆ artificial eisstock rink

Kunstfest, n
- ◆ arts festival
- ◆ art festival

Kunstform, f
- ◆ form of art
- ◆ arts form

Kunstfreund, m
- → Kunstliebhaber

Kunstführer, m
- ◆ art guide
- ◆ arts guide

Kunstgalerie f
- ◆ art gallery

Kunstgeschäft, n
- Kunstladen, m
- ◆ art store *AE*
- ◆ art shop *BE*

Kunstgeschichte, f
- ◆ history of art
- ◆ art history

Kunstgewerbe, n
- Kunsthandwerk, n
- ◆ arts and crafts *pl*

Kunstgewerbebedorf, n
- ◆ craft village

Kunstgewerbefest, n
- ◆ crafts festival

Kunstgewerbefest, n
- Kunstgewerbefestival, n
- ◆ arts and crafts festival

Kunstgewerbegalerie, f
- ◆ craft gallery

Kunstgewerbejahrmarkt, m
- ◆ crafts fair

Kunstgewerbeladen, m
- Kunstgewerbegeschäft n
- ◆ craft shop

Kunstgewerbemesse, f
- ◆ craft fair

Kunstgewerbeschau, f
- Kunstgewerbeausstellung, f
- ◆ craft show

Kunstgewerbewerkstatt, m
- ◆ craft workshop

Kunstgewerbezentrum, n
- ◆ craft center *AE*
- ◆ craft centre *BE*

Kunsthandwerk, n
- → Kunstgewerbe

Kunsthandwerkausstellung, f
- ◆ handicraft exhibition

Kunsthandwerker, m
- ◆ artist-craftsman

Kunsthandwerkgeschäft, n
- ◆ handicraft shop

Kunsthistoriker, m
- ◆ art historian

Kunsthonig, m
- ◆ artificial honey

Kunstkenner, m
- ◆ art connoisseur
- ◆ connoisseur

Kunstlandschaft, f
- Kunstszene, f
- ◆ art landscape

Kunstleder, n
- ◆ imitation leather

Künstler, m
- ◆ artist

Künstleratelier, n
- ◆ artist's studio
- ◆ artist's atelier
- ◆ atelier

Künstlercafé, n
- ◆ artists' cafe *AE*
- ◆ artists' café *BE*

Künstlerdorf, n
- ◆ artists' village

Künstlerfest, n (Festival)
- ◆ artists' festival

Künstlerfest, n (Party)
- ◆ artists' party

Künstlergarderobe, f
- (im Theater)
- Künstlerzimmer, n
- ◆ greenroom

Künstlergilde, f
- ◆ fellowship of artists

künstlerisch, adj
- ◆ artistic, adj

künstlerischer Leiter, m
- künstlerischer Direktor, m
- ◆ artistic director
- ◆ art director

Künstlerkneipe, f
- Künstlerbar, f
- ◆ artists' pub *BE coll*
- ◆ artists' bar *AE*

Künstlerkolonie, f
- ◆ artists' colony

Künstlerlokal, n
- Künstlerkneipe, f
- ◆ artists' bar *AE*
- ◆ artists' pub *BE coll*

Künstlername, m
- ◆ stage name
- ◆ pen name

Künstlerschule, f
- Kunstschule, f
- ◆ artists' school

Künstlertreffpunkt, m
- Künstlertreff, m
- ◆ artists' haunt
- ◆ haunt of artists

Künstlerveranstaltung, f
- künstlerische Veranstaltung, f
- ◆ artistic event

Künstlerviertel, n
- ◆ artists' quarter

künstliche Blume, f
- Kunstblume, f
- ◆ artificial flower

künstliche Düne, f
- ◆ artificial dune

künstliche Insel, f
- ◆ man-made island
- ◆ artificial island

künstlicher See, m
- ◆ man-made lake
- ◆ artificial lake

künstlicher Strand m
- ◆ man-made beach

Kunstlicht, n
- ◆ artificial light

Kunstliebhaber, m
- Kunstfreund, m
- ◆ art lover

Kunstmarkt, m
- ◆ art market

Kunstmarkt abhalten
- ◆ hold an art market

Kunstmäzen, m
- ◆ patron of the arts

Kunstmesse, f
- ◆ art fair

Kunstmuseum, n
- ◆ art museum

Kunstobjekt, n
- ◆ art object

Kunstrasen, m
- künstlicher Rasen, m
- ◆ artificial turf

Kunstreise, f
- ◆ art tour
- ◆ arts tour

Kunstreiter, m
- ◆ trick rider

Kunstsammler, m
- ◆ art collector

Kunstsammlung, f
- ◆ art collection
- ◆ collection of works of art

Kunstschatz, m
- ◆ art treasure

Kunstschau, f
- Kunstausstellung, f
- ◆ art show
- ◆ art exhibition

Kunstschnee, m
- künstlicher Schnee, m
- ◆ artificial snow

Kunstskihang, m
- künstlicher Skihang, m
- ◆ artificial ski slope

Kunstsponsoring, f
- ◆ arts sponsorship

Kunstspringen, n
- ◆ springboard diving

Kunstspringer, m
- ◆ springboard diver

Kunststoffschlüssel, m
- → Plastikschlüssel

Kunst- und Kulturfest, f
- Kunst- und Kulturfestival, n
- ◆ arts and culture festival

Kunst- und Kunstgewerbemarkt, m
- ◆ arts and crafts market

Kunsturlaub, m
- Kunstferien, pl

Kurkonzert

- ♦ art vacation *AE*
- ♦ art holiday *BE*

Kunstveranstaltung, f
- ♦ art event
- ♦ arts event
- ♦ arts activity

Kunstverein, m
- ♦ arts society

Kunstwerk, n
- ♦ work of art

Kunstzentrum, n
Kunst- und Veranstaltungszentrum, n
- ♦ arts center *AE*
- ♦ arts centre *BE*

Kupee, n
→ Abteil

Kupferbergwerk, n
- ♦ copper mine

Kupferkessel, m (groß)
(oben offen)
- ♦ copper cauldron
- ♦ copper caldron

Kupferkessel, m (klein)
- ♦ copper kettle

Kupferpfanne, f
- ♦ copper pan

Kupon, m
→ Coupon

Kuppe, f
Bergkuppe, f
- ♦ hilltop

Kuppel, f
- ♦ dome

Kuppeldach, n
- ♦ domed roof

Kuppelei, f *jur*
- ♦ procuration *jur*

Kuppelzelt, n
- ♦ dome tent

Kuppler, m *jur*
- ♦ procurer *jur*

Kupplerin, f *jur*
- ♦ procuress *jur*

Kur, f
- ♦ cure
- ♦ treatment
- ♦ course of treatment
- ♦ health cure
- ♦ health treatment

Kurabgabe, f
→ Kurtaxe

kurabgabenfrei, adj
- ♦ exempt from spa tax, adj

Kuramt, n *obs*
→ Kurverwaltung

Kuramt, n *obs*
→ Kurverwaltung

Kurangebot, n (generell)
- ♦ spa treatments available *pl*
- ♦ treatments available *BE*

Kurangebot, n (Offerte)
- ♦ offer of spa treatments
- ♦ offer of treatments

Kurangebot, n (Palette)
- ♦ range of spa treatments
- ♦ range of treatments

Kuranlage, f
Kurkomplex, m
- ♦ spa complex

Kurannehmlichkeit, f
- ♦ spa amenity

Kurarzt, m
Badearzt, m
- ♦ spa doctor

Kuraufenthalt, m
- ♦ stay at a spa
- ♦ stay at a spa town

Kurbad, n (Stadt)
→ Kurstadt

Kurbehandlung, f
- ♦ spa treatment

Kurbehandlungszentrum, n
- ♦ spa treatment center *AE*
- ♦ spa treatment centre *BE*

Kurbehörde, f
- ♦ spa authorities *pl*

Kurbereich, m (abstrakt)
Kursektor, m
- ♦ spa field
- ♦ spa sector

Kurbereich, m (konkret)
Kurgebiet, n
- ♦ spa area

Kurbetrieb, m
- ♦ spa establishment
- ♦ spa operation

Kürbis, m
- ♦ pumpkin

Kürbiskern, m
- ♦ pumpkin seed

Kürbiskuchen, m
- ♦ pumpkin cake

Kürbispastete, f
- ♦ pumpkin pie

Kürbissuppe, f
- ♦ pumpkin soup

Kurde, m
- ♦ Kurd

Kurdirektor, m
- ♦ head of the spa administration
- ♦ spa director

kurdisch, adj
- ♦ Kurdish, adj

Kurdistan
- ♦ Kurdistan

Kurdorf, n
- ♦ spa village

Kur durchführen
- ♦ receive treatment
- ♦ take a cure

Kureinrichtung, f
- ♦ spa facility

kuren
→ Kur machen

Kuren, n
- ♦ taking a cure
- ♦ taking the waters

Kurender, m
- ♦ person taking a cure

Kurerfolg, m
erfolgreiche Kur, f
- ♦ successful cure
- ♦ successful treatment

Kurfachmann, m
Kurexperte, m
- ♦ spa expert

Kurferien, pl
Kururlaub, m
Kurlaub, m
- ♦ spa holidays *BE pl*
- ♦ spa holiday *BE*
- ♦ holiday-cum-cure *BE*

- ♦ spa vacation *AE*
- ♦ vacation-cum-cure *AE*

Kurform, f
- ♦ form of spa treatment
- ♦ form of treatment

Kurfürst, m
- ♦ elector
- ♦ prince elector

Kurfürstin, f
- ♦ electress

kurfürstlich, adj
- ♦ electoral, adj

Kurgarten, m
→ Kurpark

Kurgast m
- ♦ spa visitor
- ♦ visitor to a spa
- ♦ health-resort visitor
- ♦ visitor to a health resort
- ♦ person visiting a spa (a health resort)

Kurgastzahl, f
Zahl der Kurgäste, f
- ♦ number of spa visitors

Kurgebäude, n
- ♦ spa building

Kurgebiet, n
→ Kurbereich

Kurgegend, f
- ♦ spa region

Kurhaus, n
- ♦ main spa building
- ♦ kurhaus
- ♦ spa center *AE*
- ♦ spa centre *BE*

Kurheim, n
- ♦ hostel in a spa town

Kurhotel, n
Kurorthotel, n
- ♦ spa hotel

Kurhotellerie, f
- ♦ spa hotel trade
- ♦ spa hotels *pl*
- ♦ hotels in a spa *pl*
- ♦ spa hotel business

Kurier, m
- ♦ courier

Kurierdienst, m
Kurierservice m
- ♦ courier service

kurieren etw
heilen etw
- ♦ cure s.th.
- ♦ heal s.th.

Kuriergepäck, n
- ♦ courier baggage *AE*
- ♦ courier luggage *BE*

Kurierzimmer, n
- ♦ courier's room

Kuriositätengeschäft, n
- ♦ curiosity shop *BE*
- ♦ curio shop *BE inform*

Kurkapelle, f
- ♦ spa band
- ♦ spa orchestra

Kurkarte, f
Besucherkarte, f
- ♦ visitor's card

Kurklinik f
- ♦ spa clinic

Kurkonzert, n
- ♦ spa concert

Kurkrankengymnast

Kurkrankengymnast, m
  Kurphysiotherapeut, m
  ♦ spa physiotherapist
Kurland
  ♦ Kurland
  ♦ Courland
Kurlaub, m
  Kururlaub, m
  Kurferien, pl
  ♦ spa vacation *AE*
  ♦ vacation-cum-cure *AE*
  ♦ spa holiday *BE*
  ♦ holiday-cum-cure *BE*
  ♦ spa holidays *BE pl*
Kur machen (generell)
  ♦ take a cure
  ♦ be on a cure
  ♦ go for a cure
Kur machen (Trinkkur)
  → Trinkkur machen
Kurmarkt, m
  ♦ spa market
Kurmittelhaus, n
  ♦ health treatment center *AE*
  ♦ health treatment centre *BE*
Kurmusik, f
  ♦ spa music
Kurmusiker, m
  ♦ spa musician
Kurorchester, n
  ♦ spa orchestra
Kurort, m
  ♦ spa
  ♦ spa town
  ♦ spa city
  ♦ health resort
  ♦ spa resort
Kurortatmosphäre, f
  ♦ spa atmosphere
Kurortbuchung, f
  Kurbuchung, f
  ♦ spa booking
Kurortentwicklung, f
  ♦ spa development
  ♦ development of a spa
Kurorterbe, n
  Kurerbe, n
  ♦ spa heritage
Kurorthotel, n
  → Kurhotel
Kurortmarketing, n
  ♦ spa marketing
Kurortmuseum, n
  Kurmuseum, n
  ♦ spa museum
Kurortstandort, m
  Kurortlage, f
  ♦ spa location
  ♦ location of the spa
Kurorttradition, f
  Kurtradition, f
  ♦ spa tradition
  ♦ tradition as a spa
Kurorttyp, m
  ♦ spa type
  ♦ type of spa
Kurpackung, f (Haare)
  ♦ conditioner
Kurpark, m
  ♦ spa gardens *pl*

Kurpatient, m
  Kurpatientin, f
  ♦ patient taking a cure
  ♦ patient at a spa
  ♦ patient at a health resort
Kurpauschale, f
  ♦ health cure package
Kurpauschalreise, f
  ♦ health cure package tour
  ♦ health cure inclusive tour
Kurpauschalurlaub, m
  ♦ health cure package vacation *AE*
  ♦ health cure package holiday *BE*
Kurpavillon, m
  ♦ spa pavilion
Kurpension, f
  ♦ guesthouse in a spa town *AE*
  ♦ guesthouse in a spa *AE*
  ♦ guest-house in a spa town *BE*
  ♦ guest-house in a spa *BE*
Kurpfuscher, m
  (schlechter Arzt)
  ♦ quack
  ♦ quack doctor
Kurpfuscherei, f
  ♦ quackery
Kurprogramm, n
  ♦ spa program *AE*
  ♦ spa programme *BE*
  ♦ program of treatments *AE*
  ♦ programme of treatments *BE*
Kurpromenade, f
  ♦ spa promenade
Kurreiseverkehr, m
  ♦ spa travel
Kurs, m (Weg)
  ♦ course
Kursaal, m
  ♦ spa assembly hall
  ♦ spa assembly room
  ♦ assembly room
  ♦ kursaal
Kurs abhalten
  Kurs halten
  Lehrgang abhalten
  Lehrgang halten
  ♦ hold a course
Kurs abschließen
  Lehrgang abschließen
  Kurs bis zum Ende besuchen
  Lehrgang bis zum Ende besuchen
  ♦ complete a course
Kurs absolvieren
  Kurs machen
  Lehrgang absolvieren
  Lehrgang machen
  ♦ do a course
  ♦ take a course
Kursabweichung, f
  ♦ deviation from the course
Kursaison f
  ♦ spa season
  ♦ season at a spa
  ♦ season at a health resort
Kurs anbieten über etw
  ♦ offer a course on s.th.
Kurs ändern (Schiff)
  ♦ change course
Kursänderung, f
  ♦ change of course

Kurs arrangieren
  Lehrgang einrichten
  ♦ arrange a course
Kursbaustein, m
  Kursmodul, m
  Lehrgangsbaustein, m
  Lehrgangsmodul, n
  ♦ course module
Kursbeginn, m
  ♦ beginning of the course
  ♦ commencement of the course *form*
  ♦ start of the course
Kurs belegen
  ♦ take a course
Kurs besuchen
  ♦ attend a course
Kursbuch, n (Lehrgang)
  Lehrgangsbuch, n
  Kursbegleitbuch, n
  ♦ course book
Kursbuch, n (Zug)
  ♦ railroad timetable *AE*
  ♦ railway timetable *BE*
  ♦ timetable
  ♦ railway guide *BE*
Kürschner, m
  ♦ furrier
Kurschwimmbad, n
  Kurbad, n
  ♦ spa swimming pool *AE*
  ♦ spa swimming-pool *BE*
  ♦ spa pool
Kursdauer, f
  Dauer eines Kurses, f
  Lehrgangsdauer, f
  Dauer eines Lehrgangs, f
  ♦ duration of a course
Kurs durchführen (für jn)
  Lehrgang durchführen (für jn)
  ♦ run a course (for s.o.)
Kurse anbieten für jn
  ♦ offer courses for s.o.
Kursektor, m
  Kurortbereich, m
  ♦ spa sector
  ♦ health resort sector
Kurs für Anfänger, m
  Lehrgang für (die) Anfänger, m
  Anfängerkurs, m
  Anfängerlehrgang, m
  ♦ course for beginners
  ♦ course for the beginners
  ♦ beginners' course
  ♦ beginners' class
Kurs für Fortgeschrittene, m
  Lehrgang für Fortgeschrittene, m
  Fortgeschrittenenkurs, m
  Fortgeschrittenenlehrgang, m
  ♦ course for the advanced
  ♦ course for advanced students
  ♦ advanced course
Kursgebühr, f
  Lehrgangsgebühr, f
  ♦ course charge
  ♦ course fee
Kurs geht von Montag bis Freitag
  Lehrgang geht von Montag bis Freitag
  ♦ course runs from Monday to Friday
Kurs halten
  ♦ stay on course

Kursinhalt, m
  Lehrgangsinhalt, m
  ♦ content of a course
Kurs inszenieren
  Kurs ausrichten
  ♦ stage a course
Kurslänge, f
  ♦ length of the course
Kurs mit Unterkunft, m
  Lehrgang mit Unterkunft, m
  ♦ residential course
Kurs mit Unterkunft durchführen
  Lehrgang mit Unterkunft durchführen
  ♦ run a residential course
Kurs ohne Unterkunft, m
  Lehrgang ohne Unterkunft, m
  ♦ nonresidential course *AE*
  ♦ non-residential course *BE*
Kurspauschale, f
  Lehrgangspauschale, f
  ♦ course package
Kursprogramm, n
  Lehrgangsprogramm, n
  ♦ course program *AE*
  ♦ course programme *BE*
Kurstadt, f (Großstadt)
  ♦ spa city
  ♦ spa
Kurstadt, f (Kleinstadt)
  ♦ spa town
  ♦ spa
Kurstadthotel, n (Großstadt)
  ♦ spa-city hotel
Kurstadthotel, n (Kleinstadt)
  ♦ spa-town hotel
Kursteilnahme, f
  Lehrgangsteilnahme, f
  ♦ course attendance
  ♦ class attendance
Kursteilnehmer, m
  Lehrgangsteilnehmer, m
  ♦ course participant
  ♦ person taking part in a course
Kurswagen, m
  ♦ through carriage
  ♦ through coach
Kurszeit, f
  Lehrgangszeit, f
  ♦ course time
Kursziel, n
  Lehrgangsziel, n
  ♦ objective of a course
  ♦ course objective
  ♦ aim of a course
Kursziel erreichen
  Lehrgangsziel erreichen
  ♦ attain the course objective
Kurs zuschneiden auf js Bedürfnisse
  Lehrgang zuschneiden auf js Bedürfnisse
  ♦ tailor a course to s.o.'s needs
Kurtaxe, f
  ♦ spa tax
  ♦ health resort tax
Kurtheater, n
  ♦ spa theater *AE*
  ♦ spa theatre *BE*
Kurtherapie, f
  ♦ spa therapy
Kurtourismus, m
  ♦ spa tourism

Kurtourist, m
  ♦ spa tourist
  ♦ visitor to a spa
Kurtradition haben
  ♦ have a tradition as a spa town
Kur- und Erholungsort, m
  ♦ spa resort
Kur- und Ferienhotel, n
  Kur- und Urlaubshotel, n
  ♦ spa and vacation hotel *AE*
  ♦ spa and holiday hotel *BE*
Kur- und Freizeitanlage, f
  Kur- und Freizeitkomplex, m
  ♦ spa and leisure complex
Kur- und Sporthotel, n
  ♦ spa and sports hotel
Kur- und Tennishotel, n
  ♦ spa and tennis hotel
Kurve machen
  ♦ make a bend
Kurverein, m
  ♦ spa association
  ♦ spa club
Kurverein gründen
  ♦ form a spa association
Kurverwaltung, f
  Kuramt, n *obs*
  ♦ spa administration
Kurviertel, n
  ♦ spa district
  ♦ spa quarter
Kurwasser, n
  ♦ spa water
Kurwasser probieren
  ♦ sample the spa water
Kurwerbung, f
  Kurortwerbung, f
  ♦ spa advertising
Kurwesen, n
  ♦ spa industry
  ♦ spa business
Kurzaufenthalt, m
  kurzer Aufenthalt, m
  ♦ short stay
  ♦ brief stay
Kurzaufenthalt planen
  ♦ plan a short stay
  ♦ plan a brief stay
Kurzaufenthaltsarrangement n
  ♦ short-stay arrangement
Kurzaufenthaltsbuchung f
  ♦ short-stay booking
Kurzaufenthaltsgruppe, f
  ♦ short-stay group
  ♦ short-stay party
Kurzaufenthaltsreise, f
  ♦ short-stay journey
  ♦ short-stay tour
  ♦ short-stay trip
Kurzaufenthaltsunterkunft, f
  ♦ short-stay accommodation
Kurzaufenthaltsurlaub, m
  Kurzurlaub, m
  Kurzaufenthaltsferien, pl
  Kurzferien, pl
  ♦ short-stay vacation *AE*
  ♦ short-stay holiday *BE*
Kurzaufenthaltszuschlag m
  ♦ short-stay supplement
Kurzbesuch, m
  kurzer Besuch, m

  ♦ brief visit
  ♦ short visit
kurz besuchen etw
  ♦ visit s.th. briefly
kurz besuchen jn
  vorbeikommen bei jm
  vorbeigehen bei jm *coll*
  vorbeischauen bei jm
  ♦ call in on s.o.
  ♦ call in at s.o.'s house
Kurzbesucher, m
  ♦ short-stay visitor
Kurzbesuch in den USA, m
  ♦ short visit to the US
Kurzbuchung, f (für kurze Zeit)
  Buchung für eine kurze Zeit, f
  kurzzeitige Buchung, f
  ♦ short-term booking
Kurzbuchung, f (kurzfristig)
  kurzfristige Buchung, f
  ♦ booking at short notice
Kurzcamper, m
  → Kurzzeitcamper
kurze Busfahrt, f
  ♦ short bus ride
  ♦ short bus trip
kurze Etappe, f
  ♦ short lap
  ♦ short stage
  ♦ short hop
kurze Fahrt, f (Auto)
  ♦ short drive
kurze Fahrt, f (generell)
  ♦ short ride
  ♦ short trip
kurze Fahrt machen nach X
  ♦ take a short trip to X
kurze Fahrt von X, f (Auto)
  ♦ short drive from X
kurzen Besuch im Krankenhaus machen
  ♦ make a call at the hospital
  ♦ call at the hospital
kurzen Besuch im Museum machen
  ♦ make a call at the museum
  ♦ call at the museum
kurzen Spaziergang machen
  ♦ take a turn
Kurzentrum, n
  Kurhaus, n
  ♦ spa center *AE*
  ♦ spa centre *BE*
kurze Rast, f
  ♦ short rest
  ♦ brief rest
kurzer Aufenthalt, m (Verkehrsmittel)
  ♦ short halt
  ♦ short stop
kurzer Aufenthalt, m (Wohnen)
  → Kurzaufenthalt
kurzer Besuch, m
  Kurzbesuch, m
  ♦ short visit
  ♦ brief visit
kurzer Bummel, m
  ♦ short stroll
kurze Reise, f (Auto)
  → kurze Fahrt
kurze Reise, f (generell)
  Kurzreise, f
  ♦ short journey
  ♦ short trip

kurze Reise

kurze Reise, f (Seereise)
- ♦ short tour
- ♦ brief journey
- ♦ brief trip

kurze Reise, f (Seereise)
- ♦ short voyage

kurzer Erholungsurlaub, m
- ♦ short relaxing break

kurzer Rundgang, m
  kurze Rundfahrt, f
  kurzer Spaziergang, m
  kurze Spazierfahrt, f
- ♦ turn

kurzer Schlaf, m
  Schläfchen, n
- ♦ short sleep

kurzer Schlaf nach dem Mittagessen, m
  Schläfchen nach dem Mittagessen, n
- ♦ short sleep after lunch

kurzer Spaziergang, m
- ♦ short walk
- ♦ turn

kurzer Stopp, m
  kurzer Halt, m
- ♦ brief stop
- ♦ short stop

kurzer Umweg, m
- ♦ short detour

kurzer Urlaub, m
→ Kurzurlaub

kurze Saison, f
  Kurzsaison, f
- ♦ short season

kurze Saison haben
- ♦ have a short season

kurze Seereise, f
- ♦ short sea journey
- ♦ short voyage

kurze Sitzung, f
- ♦ brief meeting

kurze Sitzung abhalten
- ♦ hold a brief meeting

kurze Speisekarte f
- ♦ short menu

kurze Strecke, f
- ♦ short distance
- ♦ short route

kurze Strecke reisen
- ♦ travel a short distance

kurze Wanderung, f
- ♦ short ramble
- ♦ short hike
- ♦ short walk

kurze Weinkarte, f
- ♦ short wine list

Kurzflug, m
  kurzer Flug, m
- ♦ short flight

Kurzfreizeit, f
→ Kurzurlaub

kurzfristig, adj
- ♦ short-term, adj

kurzfristig, adv
- ♦ in the short term, adv
- ♦ at short notice, adv

kurzfristig abbestellen
→ kurzfristig stornieren

kurzfristig abreisen
- ♦ leave at short notice

kurzfristig absagen
→ kurzfristig stornieren

kurzfristig buchen
- ♦ book at short notice

kurzfristige Abbestellung, f
→ kurzfristige Stornierung

kurzfristige Absage, f
→ kurzfristige Stornierung

kurzfristige Buchung, f
- ♦ booking at short notice

kurzfristige Fremdenverkehrsnachfrage, f
  kurzfristige Tourismusnachfrage, f
- ♦ short-term tourism demand
- ♦ short-term tourist demand

kurzfristiger Mietvertrag, m
  kurzer Mietvertrag, m
- ♦ short-term lease
- ♦ short lease

kurzfristige Stornierung, f
  kurzfristige Abbestellung, f
  kurzfristige Absage, f
  kurzfristiger Rücktritt, m
- ♦ short-term cancellation
- ♦ cancellation at short notice
- ♦ short-term cancelation AE
- ♦ cancelation at short notice AE

kurzfristig stornieren
  kurzfristig abbestellen
  kurzfristig absagen
  kurzfristig zurücktreten
- ♦ cancel at short notice

kurzfristig storniertes Zimmer, n
  kurzfristig abbestelltes Zimmer, n
- ♦ room canceled at short notice AE
- ♦ room cancelled at short notice BE

kurz haltmachen in X
  Zwischenstation machen in X
- ♦ stop off in X
- ♦ stop off at X

Kurzlehrgang, m
- ♦ short course

Kurzlehrgang besuchen
- ♦ attend a short course

Kurzlehrgang machen (in etw)
- ♦ take a short course (in s.th.)
- ♦ do a short course (in s.th.)

Kurzlehrgang mit Unterkunft, m
- ♦ residential short course

kürzlicher Besuch, m
- ♦ recent visit

kürzlich renoviert, adj
  vor kurzem renoviert, adj
- ♦ recently refurbished, adj
- ♦ recently renovated, adj

Kurzmassage, f
  kurze Massage, f
- ♦ short massage

kurz- oder langzeitig vermieten etw
- ♦ rent s.th. short or long term AE
- ♦ let s.th. short or long term BE

Kurzone, f
- ♦ spa zone

Kurzparker, m
→ Kurzzeitparker

Kurzprogramm, n
  kurzes Programm, n
- ♦ short program AE
- ♦ short programme BE

Kurzreise, f
  kurze Reise, f
- ♦ short trip
- ♦ short tour

Kurzreisemarkt, m
- ♦ short-trip market
- ♦ short-tour market

Kurzreiseprogramm, n
- ♦ short-trip program AE
- ♦ short-trip programme BE

Kurzreiseveranstalter, m
- ♦ short-haul tour operator
- ♦ short-distance tour operator

kurz schlafen nach dem Mittagessen
- ♦ have a short sleep after lunch

Kurzschluß, m
- ♦ short circuit

Kurzstrecke, f
  kurze Strecke, f
- ♦ short-haul route
- ♦ short-range route
- ♦ short haul

Kurzstreckenbereich, m
- ♦ short-haul sector

Kurzstreckenchartverkehr, m
- ♦ short-haul charter traffic

Kurzstreckendienst, m
  Kurzstreckenservice, m
- ♦ short-haul service

Kurzstreckendüsenflugzeug, n
  Kurzstreckenjet, m
- ♦ short-haul jet
- ♦ short-range jet
- ♦ short-distance jet

Kurzstreckenflug, m
- ♦ short-haul flight
- ♦ short-range flight

Kurzstreckenflugzeug, n
- ♦ short-haul aircraft
- ♦ short-range aircraft

Kurzstreckenmarkt, m
- ♦ short-haul market

Kurzstreckenpauschale, f
- ♦ short-haul package

Kurzstreckenpauschalreise, f
- ♦ short-haul package tour

Kurzstreckenreise, f
  Kurzreise, f
- ♦ short-haul tour
- ♦ short-distance tour
- ♦ short-haul journey
- ♦ short-distance journey

Kurzstreckenreiseverkehr, m
  Kurzstreckenreisen, n
- ♦ short-haul travel
- ♦ short-distance travel

Kurzstreckenroute, f
  Kurzstrecke, f
  kurze Strecke, f
- ♦ short-range route
- ♦ short-haul route
- ♦ short haul

Kurzstreckensegment, n
- ♦ short-haul segment

Kurzstreckenurlaub, m
  Kurzstreckenferien, pl
- ♦ short-haul vacation AE
- ♦ short-haul holiday BE

Kurzstreckenurlauber, m
- ♦ short-haul vacationer AE
- ♦ short-haul holidaymaker BE

Kurzstreckenverkehr, m
- ♦ short-haul traffic

Kurzstreckenziel, n
- ♦ short-haul destination

Kürzung, f
  Verkürzung, f
  Abkürzung, f
  Beschränkung, f
  Herabsetzung, f
  ♦ curtailment
Kurzurlaub, m (Arbeitnehmer)
  ♦ short leave
  ♦ pass AE
Kurzurlaub, m (Ferien)
  kurzer Urlaub, m
  Kurzferien, pl
  kurze Ferien, pl
  ♦ short vacation AE
  ♦ short holiday BE
  ♦ short-break holiday BE
  ♦ short break
  ♦ break
Kurzurlaub auf dem Land, m
  ♦ short vacation in the country AE
  ♦ short holiday in the country BE
  ♦ break in the country
Kurzurlauber, m
  ♦ short-stay vacationer AE
  ♦ short-stay holidaymaker BE
Kurzurlaub in der Wochenmitte, m
  Kurzurlaub unter der Woche, m
  ♦ midweek short break
  ♦ midweek break
Kurzurlaub machen
  kurzen Urlaub machen
  ♦ take a short vacation AE
  ♦ take a short holiday BE
  ♦ take a short break
  ♦ take a break
Kurzurlaub mit drei Übernachtungen, m
  ♦ three-night break
Kurzurlaubsgeschäft, n
  ♦ short-vacation business AE
  ♦ short-holiday business BE
  ♦ short-break business
Kurzurlaubsland, n
  ♦ short vacation country AE
  ♦ short holiday country BE
Kurzurlaubsmarkt, m
  ♦ short vacation market AE
  ♦ short holiday market BE
Kurzurlaubspauschale, f
  ♦ short break package
Kurzurlaubsreise, f
  kurze Urlaubsreise, f
  ♦ short vacation trip AE
  ♦ short holiday trip BE
Kurzurlaubsreisender, m
  ♦ short break traveller
  ♦ short break traveler AE
Kurzurlaubsziel, n
  Kurzurlaubsdestination, f
  ♦ short-vacation destination AE
  ♦ short-holiday destination BE
  ♦ short break destination
Kurzurlaub verbringen
  ♦ spend a short vacation AE
  ♦ spend a short holiday BE
Kurzurlaub verlängern
  ♦ extend a short vacation AE
  ♦ extend a short holiday BE
  ♦ extend a short-break holiday BE
Kurzveranstalter, m
  (Reiseveranstalter)

  ♦ short-haul operator
  ♦ short-distance operator
Kurzvisite, f
  → kurzer Besuch
kurz vorsprechen bei jm
  kurz aufsuchen jn
  ♦ call on s.o.
Kurzzeitaufenthalt, m
  Kurzaufenthalt, m
  ♦ short-term stay
Kurzzeitbesucher, m
  Kurzbesucher, m
  ♦ short-term visitor
Kurzzeitcamper, m
  Kurzcamper, m
  ♦ short-term camper
  ♦ short-stay camper
Kurzzeitferien, pl
  Kurzferien, pl
  Kurzzeiturlaub, m
  Kurzurlaub, m
  ♦ short-stay holiday BE
  ♦ short-stay vacation AE
Kurzzeitgast, m
  ♦ short-stay guest
  ♦ short-term guest
kurzzeitige Buchung, f
  → Kurzbuchung
kurzzeitig gepachtete Immobilie, f
  ♦ short leasehold property
kurzzeitig vermietetes Zimmer, n
  ♦ room rented on a short-term basis AE
  ♦ room let on a short-term basis BE
Kurzzeitmieter, m
  ♦ short-term tenant
Kurzzeitparken, n
  Kurzparken, n
  ♦ short-time parking
Kurzzeitparker, m
  Kurzparker m
  ♦ short-term parker
Kurzzeitpreis, m
  Kurzpreis, m
  ♦ short-term price
  ♦ short-term rate
kuscheln sich in ein Bett
  ♦ snuggle up in a bed
Kuskus, m
  ♦ couscous
Küste, f
  ♦ coast
Küstencampingplatz, m
  ♦ coastal campsite
  ♦ coastal campground AE
  ♦ coastal camping site BE
  ♦ coastal camping ground BE
Küstendampfer, m
  ♦ coaster
  ♦ coasting steamer
Küstendorf, n
  ♦ coast village
  ♦ coastal village
Küstenfähre, f
  ♦ coastal ferry
Küstenferien, pl
  Küstenurlaub, m
  ♦ coast holiday BE
  ♦ coast vacation AE
Küstenferienort, m
  Küstenurlaubsort, m

  ♦ coastal resort
  ♦ coast resort
Küstengebiet, n (groß)
  ♦ coastal region
Küstengebiet, n (klein)
  ♦ coastal area
Küstengesundheitsfarm, f
  ♦ coastal health farm
Küstenhafen, m
  ♦ coastal port
Küstenhaus, n
  ♦ coastal house
Küstenhotel n
  ♦ coastal hotel
Küsteninsel, f
  ♦ coastal island
Küstenkreuzfahrt, f
  ♦ coast cruise
  ♦ coastal cruise
Küstenlage, f
  ♦ coastal location
Küstenlagune, f
  ♦ coastal lagoon
Küstenland, n
  Küstengegend, f
  ♦ coastal country
  ♦ coastal land
Küstenlandhaus, n
  kleines Küstenhaus, n
  ♦ coastal cottage
Küstenlandschaft, f
  ♦ coastal scenery
  ♦ coastal countryside
Küstenlinie, f
  ♦ coastline
Küstenort, m
  → Küstenferienort, Küstenstadt
Küstenpark, m
  ♦ coastal park
Küstenpfad, m
  Küstenweg, m
  ♦ coastal path
  ♦ coast path
Küstenplatz, m
  (Camping)
  ♦ coastal site
Küstenschiff, n
  ♦ coastal ship
  ♦ coastal boat
  ♦ coastal vessel
Küstenspazierweg, m
  Küstenwanderweg, m
  ♦ coastal walk
  ♦ walk along the coast
Küstenstaat, m
  ♦ coastal state
Küstenstadt, f (Großstadt)
  ♦ coastal city
  ♦ city on the coast
  ♦ coast city
Küstenstadt, f (Kleinstadt)
  ♦ coastal town
  ♦ town on the coast
  ♦ coast town
Küstenstrand, m
  ♦ coastal beach
Küstenstraße, f
  ♦ coast road
  ♦ coastal road
  ♦ road along the coast

Küstenstrecke

Küstenstrecke, f
  Küstenroute, f
  ♦ coastal route
Küstenstreifen, m
  ♦ coastal strip
Küstentourismus, m
  ♦ coastal tourism
Küstentourist, m
  ♦ coast tourist
Küstenurlaub, m
  Küstenferien, pl
  ♦ coastal vacation AE
  ♦ coastal holiday BE
Küstenurlaubsort, m
  → Küstenferienort
Küstenverschmutzung, f
  ♦ coastal pollution
  ♦ pollution of the coast
Küstenvilla, f
  ♦ coastal villa
Küstenwache, f
  ♦ coastguard
Küstenwanderung, f
  ♦ coastal hike
  ♦ coastal walk
  ♦ hike along the coast
  ♦ walk along the coast
Küstenweg, m
  Küstenpfad, m
  ♦ coast path
  ♦ coastal path
Kutschbock, m
  ♦ coach box
Kutsche, f
  ♦ coach
  ♦ carriage
Kutsche mieten für einen Tagesausflug
  ♦ hire a carriage for a day excursion BE
  ♦ rent a coach for a day excursion AE
Kutschenhaus, n *hist*
  ♦ coach house *hist*
  ♦ carriage house *hist*
Kutschenmuseum, n
  ♦ coach museum
  ♦ carriage museum
  ♦ museum of coaches
Kutscher, m
  ♦ coachman
Kutschfahren, n
  ♦ carriage driving
Kutschfahrt, f
  ♦ coach ride
  ♦ carriage ride
Kutschfahrt machen (gefahren werden)
  ♦ drive in a coach
  ♦ ride in a coach
Kutschfahrt machen (selbst fahren)
  ♦ drive a coach
Kutschfahrt unternehmen
  ♦ take a coach ride
  ♦ take a carriage ride
kutschieren
  → Kutschfahrt machen
kutschieren jn
  Chauffeur spielen für jn
  ♦ act as s.o.'s chauffeur
Kutteln, f pl
  Kaldaunen, f pl
  ♦ tripe *sg*
Kuttelsalat, m
  ♦ tripe salad

Kuttelsuppe, f
  ♦ tripe soup
Kutter, m
  ♦ cutter
Kuvert, n (Briefumschlag)
  → Couvert
Kuvert, n (Gedeck)
  → Gedeck
Kuvertüre, f *gastr*
  ♦ coating *gastr*
Kuwait
  ♦ Kuwait
Kuwaiter, m
  ♦ Kuwaiti
Kuwaiterin, f
  ♦ Kuwaiti girl
  ♦ Kuwaiti woman
  ♦ Kuwaiti
kuwaitisch, adj
  ♦ Kuwaiti, adj
Kwaß, m
  (Getränk)
  ♦ kvass
  ♦ kvas
  ♦ quass
  ♦ quas
kyrillisch, adj
  ♦ Cyrillic, adj

L

Laacher See m
- ♦ Lake Laach

Lab, n
- ♦ rennet

laben sich (an etw)
- sich ergötzen (an etw)
- sich gütlich tun (an etw)
- ♦ regale oneself (on s.th.)
- ♦ regale oneself (with s.th.)

Laberdan, m
- gesalzener Kabeljau, m
- ♦ salted cod

Labrador
- ♦ Labrador

Lache, f
- ♦ puddle

lächeln
- ♦ smile

Lachen ist die beste Medizin
- ♦ Laughter is the best medicine

Lachs, m
- ♦ salmon

Lachsaufstrich, m
- ♦ salmon spread

Lachsbrötchen, n
- Lachsbrot, n
- ♦ salmon sandwich

Lachsersatz, m
- Seelachs, m
- ♦ smoked salmon substitute
- ♦ mock salmon
- ♦ rock salmon

Lachsfang, m
- Lachsfischerei, f
- ♦ salmon fishing

Lachsforelle, f
- ♦ salmon trout

Lachskotelett, n
- ♦ salmon cutlet

Lachsmayonnaise, f
- ♦ salmon mayonnaise

Lachsmedaillon, n
- ♦ salmon medallion

Lachspastete, f
- ♦ salmon pie
- ♦ salmon pâté

Lachssalat, m
- ♦ salmon salad

Lachssteak, n
- Lachsmittelstück, n
- ♦ salmon steak

Ladebucht, f
- ♦ loading bay
- ♦ service bay

Ladeeinrichtung, f
- ♦ loading facility

Ladefläche, f
- ♦ load area

Laden, m
- Ladenlokal n
- Geschäftsraum m
- Geschäft n
- ♦ store *AE*
- ♦ shop *BE*

Laden, m (Spelunke) *derog*
- Schuppen, m *derog*
- Spelunke, f *derog*
- ♦ joint *derog*

Laden führen
- Geschäft führen
- ♦ run a store *AE*
- ♦ run a shop *BE*

Ladengeschäft, n
- → Laden

Ladeninhaber, m
- Ladenbesitzer, m
- ♦ storekeeper *AE*
- ♦ shopkeeper *BE*

Ladenlokal, n
- → Geschäftslokal

Ladenmiete, f
- ♦ store rental *AE*
- ♦ shop rent *BE*
- ♦ shop hire *BE*

Ladenpassage, f
- Ladenzeile, f
- Ladenstraße, f
- Einkaufspassage, f
- ♦ shopping mall *AE*
- ♦ shopping arcade

Ladentheke, f
- Ladentisch, m
- ♦ shop counter

Ladogasee, m
- ♦ Lake Ladoga

Ladysuite, f
- ♦ lady suite

Lage, f (konkret)
- ♦ situation
- ♦ location
- ♦ position
- ♦ site
- ♦ setting

Lage, f (Weinlage)
- ♦ site

Lage an der Seeseite, f (Meer)
- seeseitige Lage, f
- Lage zur Seeseite hin, f
- ♦ seafront location *AE*
- ♦ seafront position *AE*
- ♦ seafront situation *AE*
- ♦ sea-front location *BE*
- ♦ sea-front position *BE*

Lage Bier, f
- ♦ round of beer

Lage Bier ausgeben
- ♦ pay for a round of beer

Lagename, m (Wein)
- ♦ site name

Lageplan, m (generell)
- ♦ location plan

Lageplan, m (Zimmer)
- → Zimmerlageplan

Lager, n (Unterkunft)
- ♦ camp

Lager, n (Vorrat)
- → Lagervorrat

Lager abbauen (Vorräte)
- ♦ run down stock
- ♦ reduce inventory *AE*

Lager abbrechen
- Lager abschlagen
- ♦ strike camp
- ♦ break camp

Lager abschlagen
- Lager abbauen
- ♦ break up camp

Lager anlegen (Unterkunft)
- ♦ make a camp
- ♦ pitch camp

Lager anlegen (Vorräte)
- ♦ lay in stock

Lagerarbeiten, f pl
- ♦ camp chores *pl*

Lagerarbeiter, m
- ♦ storeman
- ♦ stock boy

Lagerartikel, m pl
- ♦ stock articles *pl*
- ♦ articles in stock *pl*
- ♦ articles on stocklist *pl*

Lageraufbau, m
- Bestandsaufbau, m
- ♦ store building
- ♦ stock building
- ♦ stockpiling

Lageraufbau, m (Vorräte)
- ♦ stock building
- ♦ store building
- ♦ building of stocks

Lager aufbauen (Vorräte)
- ♦ build up stock
- ♦ build up an inventory *AE*

Lager auffrischen (Vorräte)
- Lager wieder auffüllen
- ♦ renew one's stock

Lager aufschlagen
- ♦ pitch a camp
- ♦ establish one's camp
- ♦ encamp
- ♦ set up (a) camp

Lagerausstattung

Lagerausstattung, f
  Lagerausrüstung, f
  ♦ storage equipment
Lager aus Stroh, n
  → Strohlager
lagerbar, adj
  lagerfähig, adj
  ♦ storable, adj
Lagerbeamter, m (Unterkunft)
  ♦ camp official
Lagerbedarf, m
  ♦ stock requirements pl
Lagerbedingungen, f pl
  Lagerungsverhältnisse, f pl
  ♦ storage conditions pl
Lagerbehälter, m
  ♦ storage container
Lager bereiten jm
  (Bett)
  ♦ make the bed for s.o.
Lagerbestand, m
  Warenbestand, m
  ♦ stock on hand
  ♦ stock
  ♦ stock in hand
  ♦ stockpile
Lagerbestandskarte, f
  ♦ stock record card
  ♦ stock ledger card
Lagerbestandsprüfung, f
  ♦ inventory verification
Lagerbestandsveränderungen, f pl
  ♦ stock changes pl
  ♦ inventory changes AE pl
Lagerbewertung, f
  ♦ stock valuation
  ♦ inventory valuation AE
Lagerbier, n
  (leichtes, helles Bier)
  ♦ lager
  ♦ lager beer
Lagerbon, m
  Lagerbeleg, m
  ♦ stock voucher
  ♦ stores voucher
Lagerbuch, n
  ♦ stock book
  ♦ stock ledger
  ♦ store book
Lagerbuchführung, f
  ♦ stock bookkeeping
  ♦ stock accounting
Lagerbuchhalter, m
  ♦ stores ledger clerk
Lagerbüro, n
  ♦ camp office
Lagerdisponibilität, f
  ♦ stock availability
Lagerdurchschnittsbestand, m
  → durchschnittlicher Lagerbestand
Lagereinrichtung, f
  Lagermöglichkeit, f
  ♦ storage facility
Lagerfeuer, n
  ♦ camp fire
Lagerfläche, f (Unterkunft)
  ♦ camp area
  ♦ camp space
Lagerfläche, f (Vorrat)
  ♦ storage area
  ♦ storage space

Lagergebäude, n
  ♦ storage building
Lagergebühr, f
  ♦ storage charge
  ♦ storage fee
Lagergestell, n
  Lagerregal, n
  ♦ storage rack
Lagergröße, f
  ♦ stock size
  ♦ inventory size AE
Lagerhalter, m
  → Lagerist
Lagerhaltung, f
  ♦ stockkeeping
  ♦ storekeeping
  ♦ storing
Lagerhauptbuch, n
  ♦ stores ledger
  ♦ stock record
Lagerhaus, n
  ♦ warehouse
  ♦ storehouse
  ♦ store
Lagerhauswohnung, f
  (war früher Lager)
  ♦ warehouse apartment AE
  ♦ warehouse flat BE
Lagerist, m
  Lagerhalter, m
  Lagerverwalter, m
  ♦ stockman AE
  ♦ storeman
  ♦ stock clerk
  ♦ storekeeper BE
  ♦ store clerk BE
Lagerkapazität, f
  ♦ storage capacity
Lagerkarte, f
  Inventarkarte, f
  ♦ stock card
  ♦ inventory card
  ♦ bin card
Lagerkartei, f
  ♦ inventory record
Lagerkeller, m
  ♦ storage cellar
Lagerkoller, m
  ♦ camp psychosis
Lagerkontrolle, f
  ♦ stores control
  ♦ stock control
  ♦ inventory control AE
  ♦ inventory checking AE
Lagerkontrollführer, m
  ♦ stock clerk
  ♦ store clerk AE
Lagerkosten, pl
  ♦ storage costs pl
  ♦ storage cost
  ♦ costs of storing s.th. pl
  ♦ cost of storage
  ♦ storage
Lagerleben, n
  ♦ life in a camp
  ♦ camp life
Lager leeren (Unterkunft)
  (von Personen)
  ♦ empty a camp

Lagerleiter, m (Unterkunft)
  ♦ camp supervisor AE
  ♦ camp warden BE
Lagerleiter, m (Vorräte)
  ♦ stock manager
  ♦ warehouse manager
Lager machen
  ♦ make camp
Lagermädchen, n
  Lagerarbeiterin, f
  ♦ stock girl
Lagermindestbestand, m
  ♦ minimum stock
lagern etw
  einlagern etw
  ♦ store s.th.
  ♦ stock s.th.
  ♦ keep s.th. in stock
lagern etw in einem kühlen Keller
  ♦ store s.th. in a cool cellar
  ♦ keep s.th. in a cool cellar
lagern (Unterkunft)
  ♦ camp
Lagerordnung, f
  ♦ camp rules pl
Lagerplanung, f
  ♦ stock planning
Lagerplatz, m (Unterkunft)
  ♦ camp site
lagerraum, m (Ort)
  Lager, n
  ♦ stockroom
  ♦ store-room BE
  ♦ storeroom AE
Lagerraum, m (Volumen, Fläche)
  Stauraum, m
  Lagerfläche, f
  ♦ storage space
Lager räumen (Unterkunft)
  Lager frei machen
  ♦ vacate a camp
  ♦ clear a camp
Lagerräumlichkeiten, f pl
  ♦ storage facilities pl
Lagerraumpersonal, n
  ♦ storeroom staff AE
  ♦ storeroom personnel AE
  ♦ store-room staff BE
  ♦ store-room personell BE
Lagerrisiko, n
  ♦ storage risk
Lager schließen
  Lager auflösen
  ♦ close down a camp
Lagerschuppen, m
  ♦ storage shed
Lagerteilnehmer, m
  ♦ camper
Lagerüberwachung, f
  → Lagerkontrolle
Lagerumschlag, m
  ♦ stock turnover
  ♦ inventory turnover AE
Lagerumschlagsgeschwindigkeit, f
  ♦ rate of stock turnover
Lagerumschlagsverhältnis, n
  ♦ stock-sales ratio
  ♦ inventory-sales ratio
Lagerung, f
  ♦ storage
  ♦ storing s.th.

Lagerungskosten, pl
→ Lagerkosten
Lagerungsmöglichkeit, f
→ Lagereinrichtung
Lagerunterkunft, f
Lagerunterbringung, f
♦ camp accommodation
Lagerveränderung, f
Bestandsveränderung, f
♦ change in stock
♦ change in inventory
Lagerverlust, m
♦ shrinkage of stocks
Lagerverwalter, m
Lagerist, m
♦ stockkeeper
♦ storekeeper
Lagerverzeichnis, n
♦ stock register
♦ inventory register
♦ inventory
♦ stock list
Lagervorrat, m
♦ stock
♦ supply
Lagerwert, m
Inventarwert, m
♦ inventory value
♦ value of inventory
♦ stock figure
Lager wieder auffüllen (Vorräte)
♦ replenish the stock
♦ refill the stock
Lagerzeit, f
♦ storing time
♦ time of storing
Lagerzugang, m
♦ incoming stock
♦ addition to stock
Lage zur Landseite hin, f
♦ landfront location AE
♦ landfront position AE
♦ landfront situation AE
♦ land-front location BE
♦ land-front position BE
Lage zur Seeseite hin, f (Binnensee)
♦ lakefront position AE
♦ lakefront situation AE
♦ lakefront location AE
♦ lake-front position BE
♦ lake-front location BE
Lage zur Seeseite hin, f (Meer)
→ Lage an der Seeseite
Lago Maggiore m
♦ Lake Maggiore
Lagune, f
♦ lagoon
Lagunenblick, m
Blick auf die Lagune, m
♦ lagoon view
♦ view of the lagoon
Lagunenrestaurant, n
♦ lagoonside restaurant
Laib Brot, m
♦ loaf of bread
Laib Käse, m
♦ whole cheese
Laientheater, n
♦ amateur theater AE
♦ amateur theatre BE

Lakai, m
livrierter Diener, m
♦ lackey
♦ flunkey derog
♦ flunky derog
Laken, n
♦ sheet
lallen
(Betrunkener)
♦ blabber
♦ mumble
Lama, m
♦ lama
Lama, n
♦ llama
Lamakloster, n
♦ lamasery
Lambrusco, m ITAL
♦ Lambrusco ITAL
Lametta, n humor
Orden, m pl
♦ fruit salad humor
Lamm, n
♦ lamb
Lammbraten, m
♦ roast lamb
Lammbrust, f
♦ lamb breast
♦ breast of lamb
Lammeintopf, m
♦ lamb hot pot AE
♦ lamb hotpot BE
Lammfilet, n
♦ lamb fillet
♦ lamb filet AE
Lammfleisch, n
♦ lamb meat
Lammfrikassee, n
♦ lamb fricassee
Lammgericht, n
♦ lamb dish
Lammgulasch, m/n
♦ lamb goulash
Lammkasserolle, f
♦ lamb casserole
Lammkebab, m
♦ lamb kebab
Lammkeule, f
♦ lamb's leg
♦ gigot FR
Lammkotelett, n
♦ lamb cutlet
Lammlendenstück, n
Lammlende, f
♦ loin of lamb
Lammnüßchen, n
♦ medallion of lamb
Lammpastete, f
♦ lamb pie
♦ lamb pâté
Lammpilaw, m
Lammpilau, m
♦ lamb pilaff
♦ lamb pilaf
♦ lamb pilau
♦ lamb pilaw
♦ pilaf of lamb
Lammragout, n/m
♦ lamb stew
Lammschaschlik, m
♦ lamb shashlik

Lammschnitzel, n
♦ lamb escalope
Lammschulter, f
♦ lamb shoulder
Lammschulterbraten, m
Lammschulter gebraten, f
♦ roast lamb shoulder
♦ roast shoulder of lamb
Lammsteak, n
♦ lamb steak
Lammwürfel, m
♦ lamb cube
Lampe f
♦ lamp
Lampenfieber, n
♦ stage fright
Lampenschirm, m
♦ lamp shade
Lampion, m
♦ Chinese lantern
Land, n
♦ country
Land, wo Milch und Honig fließt, n
♦ land flowing with milk and honey
♦ land of milk and honey
Landarrangement, n (generell)
♦ land arrangement
Landarrangement, n (nicht Flug)
♦ ground arrangement
Landatmosphäre, f
♦ country atmosphere
Landaufenthalt, m (an Land)
♦ land stay
Landaufenthalt, m (außerhalb der Stadt)
♦ stay in the country
Landaufenthalt, m (nicht auf See)
♦ stay ashore
Landausflug, m (außerhalb der Stadt)
♦ excursion to the country
♦ outing in the country
♦ country excursion
Landausflug, m (bei Kreuzfahrt)
♦ shore excursion
♦ land excursion
Landausflug machen (bei Kreuzfahrt)
♦ take a shore excursion
♦ take a land excursion
Landausflugsabteilung, f
♦ shore excursion department
Landausflugsbüro, n
♦ shore excursion office
Landausflugsdirektor, m
♦ shore excursion director
Landausflugskarte, f
♦ shore excursion ticket
Landausflugsmanager, m
♦ shore excursion manager
Landausflugspreis, m
♦ shore excursion price
Landausflugsprogramm, n (bei Kreuzfahrt)
♦ shore excursion program AE
♦ land excursion program BE
♦ shore excursion programme BE
♦ land excursion programme BE
Landausflugsveranstalter, m
♦ shore excursion operator
Land bereisen
♦ tour a country
♦ travel through a country
♦ travel the country

Landbesitz

Landbesitz, m
 ♦ landed property
 ♦ real estate
Landbesitzer, m
 ♦ landowner
Land besuchen als Tourist
 ♦ visit a country as a tourist
Land besuchen (Dörfer)
 ♦ visit the countryside
Land besuchen (Nation)
 ♦ visit a country
Landbewohner, m
 ♦ country dweller
 ♦ rural resident
Landbezirk, m
 ländlicher Bezirk, m
 ♦ rural district
Landblick, m
 Blick auf das Land, m
 ♦ landview *AE*
 ♦ land view *BE*
 ♦ view of the land
Landbrot, n
 ♦ country bread
Landcampingplatz, m
 Campingplatz im Land, m
 ♦ country campsite
 ♦ country campground *AE*
 ♦ country camping site *BE*
 ♦ country camping ground *BE*
Landclubleiter, m
 → Country Club Manager
Landcottage, f
 → Landhaus
Land der Inkas, n
 ♦ land of the Incas
Land der Mitternachtssonne, n
 ♦ land of the midnight sun
Land der Träume, n
 Schlaf m
 Schlummer m
 ♦ land of Nod
Land des Wohnsitzes, n
 ♦ country of established residence
Land durchstreifen
 ♦ roam a country
Landeabgabe, f
 Landesteuer, f
 ♦ landing tax
Landebahn, f
 (für Flugzeuge)
 Landepiste, f
 ♦ landing runway
 ♦ runway
Landegebühr, f
 ♦ landing fee
 ♦ landing charge
Landegenehmigung, f
 ♦ clearance for landing
 ♦ landing clearance
Landegeschwindigkeit, f
 ♦ landing speed
Landegewicht, n
 ♦ landing weight
Landekarte, f
 ♦ landing map
Landekarte, f
 ♦ landing card
landen
 ♦ land
 ♦ touch down

landen auf einem Flughafen
 ♦ land at an airport
landen mit dem Fallschirm
 ♦ land by parachute
landen mit dem Hubschrauber
 ♦ land by helicopter
Landeort, m
 Landeplatz, m
 ♦ landing site
Landepiste, f
 (für Flugzeuge)
 Rollbahn, f
 Startbahn, f
 ♦ landing strip
 ♦ air strip
Landeplatz, m
 ♦ landing pad
Länderarrangement, n
 ♦ arrangements for individual countries *pl*
Ländercode, m
 Länderkennzeichen, n
 ♦ country code
Landerechte, n pl
 ♦ landing rights *pl*
Länderführer, m
 (Information)
 ♦ country guide
Landerholung, f
 Erholung auf dem Land, f
 ♦ countryside recreation
Land erkunden
 Land erforschen
 ♦ explore a country
 ♦ explore the country
Landesfest, n
 → Staatsfest, Regionalfest
Landesfremdenverkehrsverband, m
 (Gesamtstaat)
 ♦ national tourist office
 ♦ national tourist board
Landesfremdenverkehrsverband, m (Region)
 → regionaler Fremdenverkehrsverband
Landeshauptstadt, f
 ♦ state capital
Landesinnere, n
 ♦ interior of the country
 ♦ hinterland
Landeslot, m
 ♦ landing slot
Landessprache, f
 ♦ national language
Landestracht, f
 Nationaltracht, f
 Tracht, f
 ♦ national costume
Landestreifen, m
 ♦ landing strip
 ♦ air strip
landestypische Küche, f
 ♦ ethnic cuisine
 ♦ ethnic cooking
landestypisches Gericht, n
 ♦ ethnic dish
landesüblich, adj
 ♦ customary in the country, adj
 ♦ customary in a country, adj
 ♦ customary, adj
Landesverkehrsamt, n (Gesamtstaat)
 LVA, n
 ♦ national tourist board
 ♦ n.t.b.

Landesverkehrsamt, n (Region)
 → regionaler Fremdenverkehrsverband
Landeswährung, f
 ♦ national currency
 ♦ currency of the country
Landeverbot, n
 ♦ landing ban
 ♦ ban on landing
Landexpedition, f (bei Kreuzfahrt)
 ♦ shore expedition
Landezeit, f
 ♦ landing time
 ♦ time of landing
Landferienort, m
 Landurlaubsort, m
 Landort, m
 ♦ country resort
Landfläche, f
 ♦ land area
Landfrühstück, n
 Bauernfrühstück, n
 ♦ country breakfast
Landgasthaus, n
 Landgaststätte, f
 ♦ country bar *AE*
 ♦ country pub *BE*
Landgasthof, m
 ♦ country inn
Landgaststätte, f
 Landgasthaus, n
 ♦ country pub *BE*
 ♦ country bar *AE*
Landgericht, n *gastr*
 Bauerngericht, n *gastr*
 ♦ country dish *gastr*
Landgut, n
 Gut, n
 ♦ country estate
 ♦ estate
Landhaus, n (Familie)
 ♦ country home
Landhaus, n (generell)
 Haus auf dem Land, n
 ♦ country house
 ♦ house in the country
 ♦ rural retreat
 ♦ rural home
Landhaus, n (klein)
 kleines Landhaus, n
 Landcottage, f
 ♦ country cottage
 ♦ cottage
Landhausambiente, n
 ♦ country-house ambience
 ♦ country-house ambience
Landhausatmosphäre, f
 ♦ country-house atmosphere
Landhaushotel, n
 ♦ country-house hotel
Landhausküche, f (Speisen)
 ♦ country-house cooking
 ♦ country-house cuisine
Landhausrestaurant, n
 ♦ country-house restaurant
 ♦ cottage restaurant
Landhausstil, m
 ♦ country-house style
Landhausurlaub, m
 ♦ country cottage vacation *AE*
 ♦ country cottage holiday *BE*

Landherberge, f
  Landheim, n
  ♦ country hostel
Landherrenhaus, n
  Herrenhaus auf dem Land, n
  ♦ country mansion
Landhotel n
  ♦ country hotel
Landjahrmarkt, m
  ♦ country fair
Landkarte, f
  Karte, f
  ♦ map
Landkost f
  ♦ country food
  ♦ country fare
Landkreis, m
  ♦ country district
  ♦ district
Landküche, f
  Bauernküche, f
  ♦ country cooking
  ♦ country cuisine
Landlage, f
  (im Landesinnern)
  ♦ country location
  ♦ countryside location
Landleben, n
  ländliches Leben, n
  ♦ country life
  ♦ rural life
ländlich, adj
  ♦ rural, adj
ländliche Gegend, f
  ländliches Gebiet, n
  ♦ rural region
ländliche Idylle, f
  ♦ rural idyll
  ♦ rural idyl AE
ländliche Lage, f
  Landlage, f
  ♦ rural location
  ♦ rural situation
  ♦ rural position
  ♦ rural setting
ländliche Landschaft, f
  ♦ rural landscape
ländlicher Gasthof, m
  Landgasthof, m
  ♦ rural inn
ländlicher Rahmen, m
  ländliche Umgebung, f
  ♦ rural setting
ländlicher Tourismus, m
  ländlicher Fremdenverkehr, m
  Tourismus auf dem Land, m
  Fremdenverkehr auf dem Land, m
  ♦ tourism in the countryside
  ♦ rural tourism
ländlicher Urlaub, m
  → Landurlaub
ländliches Gebiet, n
  Landgebiet, n
  ♦ rural area
  ♦ country area
ländliches Leben, n
  Landleben, n
  ♦ rural life
  ♦ country life
ländliches Restaurant, n
  Landrestaurant, n

  ♦ rural restaurant
  ♦ country restaurant
ländliche Umgebung, f
  ♦ rural surroundings pl
  ♦ rural setting
Landluft, f
  ♦ country air
Landmaschinenausstellung, f
  ♦ agricultural machinery exhibition
  ♦ exhibition of agricultural machinery
Landmuseum, n
  ♦ country museum
Landpark, m
  Landerholungsgebiet, n
  ♦ country park
Landpartie, f
  Ausflug ins Freie m
  Ausflug ins Grüne m
  ♦ outing in the country
  ♦ outing
  ♦ junketing
Landpartie machen
  ♦ make an excursion to the country
  ♦ make a sally to the country humor
  ♦ go junketing
Landpension, f
  ♦ country guesthouse AE
  ♦ country guest-house BE
Landplatz, m (Camping)
  Platz im Land, m
  ♦ country site
Landratte, f humor
  ♦ landlubber
  ♦ lubber
Landrefugium, n
  Tuskulum, n
  ♦ country retreat
Landreise, f
  ♦ land journey
  ♦ land tour
  ♦ land trip
Landresidenz, f
  Landsitz, m
  ♦ country residence
  ♦ country seat
  ♦ rural seat
Landrestaurant, n
  ländliches Restaurant, n
  ♦ country restaurant
  ♦ rural restaurant
Landschaft, f
  ♦ scenery
  ♦ countryside
  ♦ landscape
Landschaft beherrschen
  ♦ dominate the countryside
Landschaft besichtigen
  ♦ view the scenery
  ♦ view the landscape
  ♦ view the countryside
Landschaft bewundern
  ♦ admire the scenery
  ♦ admire the countryside
  ♦ admire the landscape
Landschaft erhalten
  ♦ preserve the countryside
Landschaft erkunden
  ♦ explore the countryside
Landschaft genießen
  ♦ enjoy the scenery

  ♦ enjoy the countryside
  ♦ enjoy the landscape
Landschaft ist abwechslungsreich
  ♦ scenery is varied
  ♦ landscape is varied
  ♦ countryside is varied
Landschaft ist besonders schön
  ♦ scenery is particularly beautiful
  ♦ countryside is particularly beautiful
  ♦ landscape is particularly beautiful
Landschaft ist romantisch
  ♦ scenery is romantic
  ♦ countryside is romantic
  ♦ landscape is romantic
Landschaft ist wild
  ♦ scenery is wild
  ♦ countryside is wild
  ♦ landscape is wild
landschaftliche Schönheit, f
  ♦ scenic beauty
landschaftliche Schönheit genießen (von etw)
  ♦ enjoy the scenic beauty (of s.th.)
landschaftliche Vielfalt, f
  Abwechslungsreichtum der Landschaft, m
  ♦ diversity of landscape
  ♦ diversity of scenery
landschaftlich schön, adj
  ♦ scenic, adj
landschaftlich schöne Aussicht, f
  landschaftlich schöner Ausblick, m
  landschaftlich schöner Blick, m
  ♦ scenic view
landschaftlich schöne Fahrt, f (Auto)
  Fahrt durch (eine) schöne Landschaft, f
  ♦ scenic drive
landschaftlich schöne Lage, f
  landschaftlich schöner Standort, m
  ♦ scenic location
landschaftlich schöner Spazierweg, m
  Spazierweg in schöner Landschaft, m
  ♦ scenic walk
landschaftlich schöner Weg, m
  landschaftlich schöner Pfad, m
  Weg in schöner Landschaft, m
  Pfad in schöner Landschaft, m
  ♦ scenic path
  ♦ scenic trail
landschaftlich schönes Gebiet, n
  ♦ scenic area
landschaftlich schöne Straße, f
  ♦ scenic road
landschaftlich schöne Strecke, f
  landschaftlich schöne Route, f
  ♦ scenic route
landschaftlich schöne Tour, f
  Fahrt durch eine schöne Landschaft, f
  ♦ scenic tour
landschaftlich schönstes Gebiet, n
  ♦ most scenic area
Landschaft prägen
  ♦ characterize the landscape
  ♦ characterise the landscape
Landschaftsarchitekt, m
  ♦ landscape architect
Landschaftserhaltung, f
  ♦ countryside conservation
  ♦ conservation of the countryside
Landschaftsgärtner, m
  ♦ landscape gardener
Landschaftsgenuß, m
  ♦ enjoyment of (the) scenery

Landschaftsmalerei

Landschaftsmalerei, f
- ♦ landscape painting

Landschaftsschutz, m
- Schutz der Landschaft, m
- ♦ conservation of the countryside
- ♦ protection of the countryside

Landschaftsschutzgebiet, n
- ♦ conservation area

Landschloß, n
- ♦ country castle

Landseite, f
- (Gegensatz zu Meerseite)
- ♦ landfront AE
- ♦ land front BE

landseitig, adj
- ♦ landfront, adj AE
- ♦ land-front, adj BE

landseitig gelegen, adj
- ♦ land-front position

Landsitz, m
- ♦ country seat
- ♦ country residence
- ♦ rural seat

Landsmann, m
- ♦ fellow-countryman
- ♦ compatriot

Landsmännin, f
- ♦ fellow-countrywoman

Landspazierweg, m
- ♦ country walk

Landstadt, f
- ♦ country town

Landstadthotel, n
- ♦ country town hotel

Landstraße, f
- ♦ country road
- ♦ road

Landstraßencafé, n
- Café an einer Landstraße, n
- Imbißstube an einer Landstraße, f
- ♦ roadside cafe AE
- ♦ roadside café BE

Landstraßengasthof, m
- Gasthof an einer Landstraße m
- ♦ roadside inn

Landstraßengastronomie, f
- Landstraßenverpflegung, f
- ♦ roadside foodservice AE
- ♦ roadside catering BE

Landstraßenhotel, n
- Hotel an einer Landstraße, n
- ♦ roadside hotel

Landstraßenrasthaus, n
- Landstraßenwirtshaus n
- Gaststätte an einer Landstraße f
- Hotel an einer Landstraße n
- ♦ roadhouse AE
- ♦ road-house BE

Landstraßenrestaurant, n
- Restaurant an einer Landstraße n
- ♦ roadside restaurant
- ♦ roadside diner AE

Landstrecke, f
- Landroute, f
- ♦ land route

Landstreicher, m
- Tippelbruder, m
- Penner, m
- Pennbruder, m
- ♦ hobo AE sl
- ♦ bum AE sl
- ♦ tramp
- ♦ vagabond
- ♦ vagrant

Landstreicherei, f
- ♦ vagabondage
- ♦ vagrancy
- ♦ hoboism AE

Landstreicherlager, m
- ♦ hobo camp AE
- ♦ jungle AE sl

Landtourismus, m
- ländlicher Tourismus, m
- ländlicher Fremdenverkehr, m
- Tourismus auf dem Land, m
- ♦ rural tourism
- ♦ tourism in the countryside

Landtransport, m
- ♦ land transportation AE
- ♦ land transport BE

Landtransportgesellschaft, f
- ♦ land carrier

Land und Leute
- das Land und die Leute
- ♦ land and the people, the

Landung, f (Flugzeug)
- Aufsetzen, n
- ♦ touchdown

Landung, f (generell)
- (Luft- und Wasserfahrzeuge)
- ♦ landing

Landung machen
- ♦ make a landing

Landungsbrücke, f
- (für Wasserfahrzeuge)
- ♦ landing pier
- ♦ pier
- ♦ landing stage

Landungsplatz, m
- ♦ landing place

Landungssteg, m
- Bootssteg, m
- Bootsanlegeplatz, m
- ♦ landing stage
- ♦ jetty

Landunterkunft, f
- Landunterbringung, f
- ♦ land accommodation

Landurlaub, m (Ferien)
- Urlaub auf dem Land, m
- Landferien, pl
- Ferien auf dem Land, pl
- ♦ rural vacation AE
- ♦ rural holiday BE
- ♦ country vacation AE
- ♦ country holiday BE

Landurlaub, m (Seeleute)
- ♦ shore leave

Landurlaub genießen
- ♦ enjoy a country vacation AE
- ♦ enjoy a country holiday BE

Landurlaub machen
- ♦ take a country vacation AE
- ♦ take a country holiday BE

Landvilla, f
- ♦ country villa

Landwanderung, f
- ♦ country ramble
- ♦ country walk
- ♦ country hike

Landwein, m
- Wein der Gegend, m
- ♦ local wine
- ♦ country wine

Landwirtschaftsausstellung, f
- ♦ agricultural exhibition
- ♦ agricultural show

Landwirtschaftsgebiet, n
- ♦ agricultural area
- ♦ agricultural region

Landwirtschaftsmesse, f
- ♦ agricultural fair
- ♦ agricultural show

Landwirtschaftsmuseum, n
- ♦ agricultural museum

Landwirtschaftsschau f
- ♦ agricultural show

lang anhaltender Beifall, m
- ♦ prolongued applause

Langaufenthalt, m
- → langer Aufenthalt

Langaufenthaltsbesucher, m
- ♦ long-stay visitor

Langaufenthaltsgast, m
- ♦ long-stay guest

Langaufenthaltsurlaub, m
- ♦ long-stay vacation AE
- ♦ long-stay holiday BE

Langaufenthaltsurlauber, m
- ♦ long-stay vacationer AE
- ♦ long-stay holidaymaker BE

lang bleiben (an einem Ort)
- ♦ stay long (in one place)

Länge, f
- ♦ length

lange aufbleiben
- bis spät aufbleiben
- ♦ stay up late

lange ausgesprochene Einladung, f
- ♦ long-standing invitation

Länge der Weinkarte, f
- ♦ length of the wine list

Länge des Urlaubsaufenthalts, f
- ♦ length of the vacation stay AE
- ♦ length of the holiday stay BE

lange Fahrt, f (Auto)
- ♦ long drive

lange Fahrt, f (generell)
- ♦ long trip
- ♦ long journey

lange Ferien, pl
- langer Urlaub, m
- ♦ long holidays BE pl
- ♦ long holiday BE
- ♦ long vacation AE

lange geplanter Urlaub, m
- ♦ long-planned vacation AE
- ♦ long-planned holiday BE

langen Schluck nehmen
- ♦ take a long draft AE
- ♦ take a long draught BE

langen Spaziergang machen
- ♦ go for a long walk

langer Aufenthalt, m
- Langaufenthalt m
- ♦ long stay

langer Besuch, m
- ♦ long visit
- ♦ extended visit

länger bleiben
- ♦ stay longer
- ♦ stay on

länger bleiben, als man erwünscht ist
 ◆ outstay one's welcome
 ◆ overstay one's welcome
 ◆ wear out one's welcome
länger bleiben (als angegeben)
 ◆ overstay
länger bleiben als ursprünglich angenommen
 ◆ stay longer than anticipated
lange Reihe von Gästen, f
 lange Reihenfolge von Gästen, f
 ◆ long succession of guests
lange Reise, f (generell)
 ◆ long tour
 ◆ long journey
 ◆ long trip
lange Reise, f (Seereise)
 lange Seereise, f
 ◆ long voyage
lange Reise machen (generell)
 ◆ make a long tour
 ◆ make a long journey
 ◆ make a long trip
lange Reise machen (Seereise)
 ◆ make a long voyage
langer Flug, m
 ◆ long flight
langer Pachtvertrag, m
 langer Mietvertrag, m
 ◆ long lease
langer Schluck, m
 (z.B. Bier)
 ◆ long draft AE
 ◆ long draught BE
länger sitzenbleiben als die anderen Gäste
 ◆ outsit the other guests
langer Spaziergang, m
 ◆ long walk
langer Strand, m
 ◆ long beach
langer Urlaub, m
 ◆ long vacation AE
 ◆ long holiday BE
lange Saison, f
 Langsaison, f
 ◆ long season
lange Schlange, f figur
 ◆ long queue
langes Kleid, n
 ◆ long dress
lange Spaziergänge machen
 lange Wanderungen machen
 ◆ go for long walks
lange Spaziergänge unternehmen
 ◆ take long walks
lange Speisekarte f
 ◆ long menu
lange Strecke, f
 weite Strecke, f
 ◆ long route
 ◆ long distance
lange Strecken reisen
 weite Strecken reisen
 ◆ travel long distances
langes Wochenende, n
 ◆ long weekend
lange Wanderung, f
 ◆ long hike
 ◆ long walk
 ◆ long ramble

lange Warteliste, f
 ◆ long waiting list AE
 ◆ long waiting-list BE
lange Wartezeit, f
 ◆ long wait
lange Weinkarte, f
 ◆ long wine list
lange Zugreise, f
 ◆ long train journey
Langfinger, m fam
 → Dieb
langfristig, adj
 langzeitig, adj
 ◆ long-term, adj
langfristig, adv
 ◆ in the long term, adv
 ◆ in the long run, adv
langfristige Fremdenverkehrsnachfrage, f
 ◆ long-term tourism demand
 ◆ long-term tourist demand
langfristige Pacht, f
 ◆ long-term lease
langfristiger Mietvertrag m
 ◆ long-term lease
 ◆ long lease
langfristig gepachtete Immobilie, f
 ◆ long leasehold property
langfristig gepachtete Wohnung, f
 langfristig gemietete Wohnung, f
 ◆ long leasehold apartment AE
 ◆ long leasehold flat BE
langfristig vermietetes Zimmer, n
 ◆ room rented on a long-term basis AE
 ◆ room let on a long-term basis BE
lang genug bleiben
 ◆ stay long enough
Langhaus, n
 ◆ longhouse
Langkornreis, m
 ◆ long-grain rice
Langlauf, m (Dauerlauf)
 → Jogging
Langlauf, m (Ski)
 → Skilanglauf
Langlaufausrüstung, f
 ◆ cross-country equipment
Langläufer, m (Ski)
 → Skiläufer
Langlaufloipe, f
 Langlaufskiloipe, f
 ◆ cross-country trail
 cross-country track
 ◆ cross-country ski run
 cross-country circuit
Langlaufmöglichkeiten, f pl (Ski)
 ◆ cross-country facilities pl
 ◆ opportunities for cross-country skiing pl
Langlaufort, m (Ski)
 Skilanglaufort, m
 ◆ cross-country resort
 cross-country ski resort
Langlaufparadies, n (Ski)
 ◆ cross-country ski paradise
 cross-country skiing paradise
 paradise for cross-country skiing
Langlaufpauschale, f
 ◆ cross-country package
Langlaufski, m
 ◆ cross-country ski
Langlaufskiloipe, f
 Langlaufloipe, f

 ◆ cross-country ski trail
 cross-country ski track
Langlaufskistrecke, f
 Skilanglaufstrecke, f
 Langlaufstrecke, f
 ◆ cross-country ski course
 cross-country course
Langlaufskiverleih, m
 ◆ cross-country ski rental
 cross-country ski hire BE
Langlaufskizentrum, n
 ◆ cross-country ski center AE
 ◆ cross-country ski centre BE
 ◆ center of cross-country skiing AE
 ◆ centre of cross-country skiing BE
Langlaufspaß, m (Ski)
 ◆ cross-country ski fun
Langlaufstrecke, f (Ski)
 → Langlaufskistrecke
Langlauftour, f (Ski)
 ◆ cross-country ski tour
 cross-country tour
Langlaufwettbewerb, m (Ski)
 ◆ cross-country competition
 cross-country ski competition
Langlaufwettkampf, m (Ski)
 ◆ cross-country ski contest
 cross-country contest
Langlaufzentrum, n (Ski)
 ◆ cross-country center AE
 ◆ cross-country centre BE
Langlaufziel, n (Ski)
 ◆ cross-country destination
 cross-country ski destination
langlegen sich coll
 ausruhen sich
 ◆ have a little rest
Langpreis, m
 Langzeitpreis, m
 ◆ long-term price
 long-term rate
langsam, adj
 ◆ slow, adj
langsamer Service m
 ◆ slow service
langsamer Walzer, m
 ◆ slow waltz
Langsam fahren!
 ◆ Drive slowly
langsam fahren (Auto)
 ◆ drive slowly
langsam fallende Belegung, f
 langsam fallende Auslastung, f
 ◆ slowly falling occupancy
langsam reisen
 ◆ travel slowly
 go slowly
langsam steigende Belegung, f
 langsam steigende Auslastung, f
 ◆ slowly rising occupancy
lang schlafen
 ◆ sleep late
 ◆ lie in
Langschläfer, m
 ◆ lie-abed coll
 ◆ late riser
 ◆ slugabed coll
Langschläferfrühstück, n
 Frühstück für Langschläfer, n
 ◆ breakfast for late risers
 ◆ late breakfast

Langspielplatte

Langspielplatte, f
  LP, f
  ◆ long-playing record
  ◆ LP
längstens, adv
  ◆ at (the) most, adv
  ◆ at (the) longest, adv
  ◆ no more than, adv
  ◆ a maximum, adv
längstens drei Tage
  ◆ three days at the most
  ◆ three days at most
  ◆ no more than three days
  ◆ a maximum of three days
längstens drei Tage bleiben
  höchstens drei Tage bleiben
  ◆ stay three days at the most
  ◆ stay three days at most
Langstrecke, f
  ◆ long-range route
  ◆ long-haul route
  ◆ long haul
Langstreckenbereich, m
  Langstreckensektor, m
  ◆ long-haul sector
Langstreckencharter, m
  ◆ long-haul charter
  ◆ long-distance charter
Langstreckencharterverkehr, m
  ◆ long-haul charter traffic
  ◆ long-distance charter traffic
Langstreckendüsenflugzeug, n
  Langstreckenjet, m
  ◆ long-haul jet
  ◆ long-range jet
  ◆ long-distance jet
Langstreckenflug, m
  Fernflug, m
  ◆ long-distance flight
  ◆ long-haul flight
Langstreckenflugzeug, n
  ◆ long-haul aircraft
Langstreckenmarkt, m
  ◆ long-haul market
Langstreckenpauschale, f
  ◆ long-haul package
Langstreckenroute, f
  ◆ long-haul route
Langstreckensegment, n
  ◆ long-haul segment
Langstreckenspezialist, m
  ◆ long-haul specialist
Langstreckenurlaub, m
  ◆ long-haul vacation AE
  ◆ long-haul holiday BE
Langstreckenurlauber, m
  ◆ long-haul vacationer AE
  ◆ long-haul holidaymaker BE
Langstreckenwanderer, m
  ◆ long-distance walker
  ◆ long-distance hiker
Langstreckenwettrennen, n
  ◆ long-distance running race
Langstreckenziel, n
  Fernstreckenziel, n
  ◆ long-haul destination
Langurlaub, m
  → langer Urlaub
Langurlauber, m
  → Langzeiturlauber

Languste, f
  ◆ rock lobster
  ◆ spiny lobster
Langweile, f
  Langeweile, f
  ◆ boredom
Langweile haben
  → langweilen sich
langweilen jn
  ◆ bore s.o.
langweilen sich
  Langweile haben
  ◆ be bored
langweilen sich schrecklich
  ◆ be bored stiff
langweilig, adj
  ◆ boring, adj
  ◆ dull, adj
  ◆ tedious, adj
langweiliger Abend, m
  ◆ boring evening
langweilige Reise, f
  ◆ tedious journey
  ◆ tedious trip
  ◆ tedious tour
Langzeitaufenthalt, m
  ◆ long-term stay
Langzeitbesucher m
  ◆ long-term visitor
  ◆ long-term guest
Langzeitbuchung, f
  → langzeitige Buchung
Langzeitcamper, m
  ◆ long-term camper
Langzeitcamping, n
  ◆ long-term camping
Langzeitgast, m
  ◆ long-term guest
  ◆ long-stay guest
langzeitig, adj
  → langfristig
langzeitige Buchung, f
  Langzeitbuchung, f
  ◆ long-term booking
Langzeitmieter, m
  ◆ long-term tenant
Langzeitparken, n
  Langparken, n
  ◆ long-term parking
Langzeitparker, m
  → Dauerparker
Langzeitparkplatz, m
  ◆ long-term parking lot AE
  ◆ long-term car park BE
Langzeitpauschale, f
  ◆ long-term package
Langzeitpauschalpreis, m
  Langzeitpauschale, f
  ◆ long-term inclusive price
  ◆ long-term inclusive rate
  ◆ long-term package price
  ◆ long-term package rate
Langzeitpauschalpreis, m
  → Langzeitpauschale
Langzeitpreis m
  Langpreis m
  ◆ long-term rate
  ◆ long-term price
Langzeittarif, m
  ◆ long-term tariff

  ◆ long-term rates pl
  ◆ long-term rate
Langzeiturlaub, m
  ◆ long-term vacation AE
  ◆ long-term holiday BE
Langzeiturlauber, m
  Langurlauber, m
  ◆ long-term vacationer AE
  ◆ long-term holidaymaker BE
Langzeitvermietung, f (Immobilien)
  ◆ long-term rental AE
  ◆ long-term rent AE
  ◆ long-term letting BE
  ◆ long let BE coll
Langzeitvermietung, f (Mobilien)
  ◆ long-term hire BE
  ◆ long-term hiring BE
  ◆ long-term rental AE
Langzeitvermietungsbedingungen, f pl (Immobilien)
  ◆ conditions of long-term letting BE pl
  ◆ terms of long-term letting BE pl
  ◆ conditions of long-term rental AE pl
  ◆ terms of long-term rental AE pl
Langzeitvermietungsbedingungen, f pl (Mobilien)
  ◆ conditions of long-term rental AE pl
  ◆ terms of long-term rental AE pl
  ◆ conditions of long-term hire BE pl
  ◆ terms of long-term hire BE pl
Lanzarote
  ◆ Lanzarote
Laos
  ◆ Laos
Laote, m
  ◆ Laotian
Laotin, f
  ◆ Laotian girl
  ◆ Laotian woman
  ◆ Laotian
laotisch, adj
  ◆ Laotian, adj
Lappe, m
  Lappländer, m
  ◆ Lapp
Lappin, f
  ◆ Lapp girl
  ◆ Lapp woman
  ◆ Lapp
Lappland
  ◆ Lapland
Lappländer, m
  Lappe, m
  ◆ Laplander
lappländisch, adj
  ◆ Lapp, adj
Lärche, f
  ◆ larch
Lärchenwald, m
  ◆ larch forest
  ◆ larch wood
Lärm, m
  ◆ noise
Lärmbekämpfung, f
  ◆ noise control
  ◆ noise abatement
Lärmbelästigung, f
  ◆ noise pollution
lärmempfindlich, adj
  ◆ sensitive to noise, adj

lärmend, adj
  laut, adj
  ♦ **noisy, adj**
lärmende Bar, f
  laute Bar, f
  ♦ **rumbustious bar** *inform*
  ♦ **noisy bar**
lärmende Party, f
  ♦ **boisterous party**
lärmisoliert, adj
  → schalldicht
lärmisoliertes Fenster, n
  ♦ **soundproof window** *AE*
  ♦ **sound-proof window** *BE*
Lärm machen
  lärmen
  ♦ **make noise**
Lärmpegel, m
  ♦ **noise level**
Lärmschutz, m
  ♦ **noise protection**
Lärmverhinderung, f
  Lärmvermeidung, f
  ♦ **noise prevention**
Lasagne, f
  ♦ **lasagne**
  ♦ **lasagna**
Laserschau, f
  ♦ **laser show**
Lasertontaubenschießen, n
  ♦ **laser clay-pigeon shooting**
Laserzeigestock, m
  (bei Tagungen)
  Laserzeigestab, m
  ♦ **laser pointer**
Lassen Sie es sich schmecken!
  ♦ **Enjoy your meal!**
  ♦ **I hope you enjoy your meal!**
Lassen Sie Ihr Gepäck hier stehen!
  ♦ **Leave your baggage here!** *AE*
  ♦ **Leave your luggage here!** *BE*
Lassen Sie sich von uns verwöhnen!
  ♦ **Let us pamper you**
Laßt uns abhauen! *sl*
  ♦ **Let's split!** *AE sl*
  ♦ **Let's push off!** *BE sl*
Laßt uns das feiern!
  ♦ **Let's celebrate that!**
Laßt uns feiern!
  ♦ **Let's celebrate!**
Lastenaufzug, m
  Warenaufzug, m
  ♦ **goods lift** *BE*
  ♦ **freight elevator** *AE*
Lastenlift, m
  → Lastenaufzug
Lastensegler, m
  ♦ **cargo glider**
Lasterhöhle, f
  Höhle des Lasters f
  ♦ **den of vice**
  ♦ **den of iniquity**
Lasterleben, n
  ♦ **life of vice**
  ♦ **wicked life**
  ♦ **life of sin**
Lasterleben führen
  ausschweifendes Leben führen
  ♦ **lead a dissolute life**
lästiger Besucher, m
  ♦ **tiresome visitor**

lästig fallen jm
  auf die Nerven gehen jm
  ♦ **get on s.o.'s nerves**
lästig sein jm
  ♦ **be a nuisance to s.o.**
Last-Minute-Angebot, n
  → Angebot in letzter Minute
Last-Minute-Fahrt, f
  ♦ **last-minute trip**
Last-Minute-Flug, m
  Flug in letzter Minute, m
  ♦ **last-minute flight**
Last-Minute-Reise, f
  Reise in letzter Sekunde, f
  ♦ **last-minute tour**
Last-Minute-Schnäppchen, n
  Sonderangebot in letzter Minute, n
  ♦ **last-minute bargain**
Last-Minute-Ticket, n
  ♦ **last-minute ticket**
Lastschrift, f
  (Buchhaltung)
  ♦ **debit entry**
Lastwagen, m
  Lkw, m
  LKW, m
  Lastkraftwagen, m
  ♦ **truck** *AE*
  ♦ **lorry** *BE*
Lastwagenfahrer, m
  Lkw-Fahrer, m
  LKW-Fahrer, m
  ♦ **truck driver** *AE*
  ♦ **trucker** *coll*
  ♦ **lorry driver** *BE*
Lastwagenparkplatz, m
  Lkw-Parkplatz, m
  LKW-Parkplatz, m
  ♦ **truck parking lot** *AE*
  ♦ **lorry park** *BE*
Lateinamerika
  ♦ **Latin America**
Lateinamerikaner, m
  ♦ **Latin American**
Lateinamerikanerin, f
  ♦ **Latin American girl**
  ♦ **Latin American woman**
  ♦ **Latin American**
lateinamerikanisch, adj
  ♦ **Latin-American, adj**
Laterne, f
  ♦ **lantern**
Laternenfest, n
  ♦ **lantern festival**
Laternenumzug, m
  ♦ **lantern procession**
  ♦ **procession of lanterns**
Late-show, m
  zu spät ankommender Gast, m
  verspätet ankommender Gast, m
  ♦ **late-show**
Latexmatratze, f
  ♦ **latex mattress**
Latrine f
  ♦ **latrine**
Latz, m
  Eßlatz, m
  Lätzchen, n
  ♦ **bib**
Laubbaum, m
  ♦ **deciduous tree**

Laube, f
  (im Garten)
  ♦ **summerhouse** *AE*
  ♦ **summer-house** *BE*
Laubengang, m (Arkade)
  ♦ **arbored walk** *AE*
  ♦ **arboured walk** *BE*
  ♦ **covered walk**
Laubengang, m (Pergola)
  → Pergola
Laubenkolonie, f
  Schrebergärten mit Lauben, m pl
  ♦ **allotment (of) gardens with summerhouses** *AE*
  ♦ **allotment (of) gardens with summer-houses** *BE*
Laubwald, m
  ♦ **deciduous forest**
  ♦ **deciduous wood**
  ♦ **deciduous woodland**
Lauch, m
  ♦ **leek**
Lauchsoufflé, n
  Lauchauflauf, m
  ♦ **leek soufflé** *BE*
  ♦ **leek souffle** *AE*
Lauchsuppe, f
  ♦ **leek soup**
lauer Applaus, m
  ♦ **lukewarm applause**
  ♦ **tepid applause**
Laufbursche, m
  → Laufjunge
Lauf des Flusses, m
  Flußlauf, m
  ♦ **course of the river**
  ♦ **river course**
laufende Aufwendungen, f pl
  ♦ **running expenses** *pl*
laufende Ausgaben, f pl
  (gegenwärtige Ausgaben)
  ♦ **current expenses** *pl*
  ♦ **running expenses** *pl*
laufende Inventur, f
  ♦ **continuous inventory**
laufende Kosten, f
  (gegenwärtige Kosten)
  ♦ **current costs** *pl*
  ♦ **current expenses** *pl*
laufende Saison, f
  gegenwärtige Saison, f
  jetzige Saison, f
  ♦ **current season**
Läufer, m (Person)
  ♦ **runner**
Laufgang, m
  ♦ **walkway**
Laufgitter, n
  → Laufstall
Laufjunge, m
  Chasseur, m FR
  Laufbursche, m
  ♦ **errand boy**
  ♦ **messenger boy**
  ♦ **chasseur** *FR*
  ♦ **hall boy** *AE*
Laufkunde, m
  → Passant
Laufkundschaft, f
  ♦ **casual customers** *pl*
  ♦ **casual trade**

Laufkundschaft bewirten

- occasional customers *pl*
- passing trade

Laufkundschaft bewirten
- cater for the passing trade
- cater for casual customers

Laufplanke, f
- gangplank
- gangboard

Laufstall, m
(für Kleinkinder)
Laufgitter, n
- playpen
- pen

Laufsteg, m
(z.B. bei Modenschau)
- catwalk
- runway *AE*

Laufstuhl, m
(für Babys)
- baby walker

Laufzeit, f (Vertrag)
- term
- duration
- life

Laufzeit eines Mietvertrags, f
- duration of a lease
- term of a lease
- life of a lease

Laufzeit eines Pachtvertrags, f
- life of a lease

Launen haben
launig sein
- be moody
- have one's moods

Laus, f
- louse

lauschen an der Tür
- eavesdrop at the door

Lausitz, f
(Region)
- Lusatia

Lausitzer Bergland, n
- Lusatian Hills, the *pl*

laut, adj
- loud, adj
- noisy, adj
- boisterous, adj

laute Bar, f
- noisy bar

laute Begrüßung, f
stürmische Begrüßung, f
- boisterous welcome

laute Musik, f
- loud music

laute Party, f
- noisy party

lautes Zimmer n
- noisy room

Lautsprecher, m
- loudspeaker
- speaker

Lautsprecheranlage, f
- public-address system
- PA system
- Tannoy

Lautsprecherwagen, m
- sound truck *AE*

laut Vereinbarung
→ wie vereinbart

lauwarm, adj
- lukewarm, adj
- tepid, adj

lauwarmes Essen, n
- lukewarm food

lauwarmes Wasser, n
- lukewarm water
- tepid water

Lawine, f
- avalanche

Lawine auslösen
- trigger off an avalanche

Lawine bilden
- avalanche

lawinenfrei, adj
- free from avalanches, adj

Lawinengefahr, f
- danger of avalanches
- avalanche danger

lawinengefährdet, adj
- exposed to avalanches, adj

lawinengeschützt, adj
- protected from avalanches, adj
- protected against avalanches, adj

Lawinenhang, m
- avalanche slope

Lawinenkatastrophe, f
- avalanche disaster

lawinensicher, adj
- safe from avalanches, adj

Lawinenwarnung, f
- avalanche warning

Laxativ, n
Abführmittel, n
- laxative

Lay-over, m
(erzwungener Zwischenaufenthalt)
- lay-over

leasen etw
- lease s.th.

Leasing, n
- leasing

Leasinggeber, m
- leasor

Leasinggesellschaft, f
- leasing company

Leasingkosten, pl
- leasing costs *pl*
- costs of leasing *pl*

Leasingnehmer, m *jur*
- leasee *jur*

Leasingrate, f
- leasing rate

Lebedame, f
Halbweltdame, f
- demimondaine *AE*
- demi-mondaine *BE*

Lebemann, m
- man about town
- playboy

Leben an Bord, n
Bordleben, n
- life on board

leben auf anderer Leute Kosten
- live at the expense of others
- live at rack and manger *coll*
- sponge

Leben auf der Straße, n
Leben unterwegs, n
Wanderleben, n
- life on the road

leben auf großem Fuß
(auf Kosten anderer)
- live at rack and manger *coll*
- live on a large scale

leben aus dem Koffer
- live out of a suitcase

lebendes Museum, n
- living museum

Leben genießen
- enjoy life

Leben genießen in vollen Zügen
- enjoy life to the full
- enjoy one's life to the full

leben im Freien
im Freien leben
- live rough

leben in Baracken
in Baracken leben
- house in barracks

Leben in die Bude bringen *coll*
- liven the place up

leben in Harmonie mit der Umgebung
- live in harmony with the environment

leben in ländlicher Abgeschiedenheit
- live in rural seclusion

leben in Ruhe und Frieden
- live in peace and quiet

leben in Saus und Braus
aufwendiges Leben führen
- live on the fat of the land
- live in grand style
- live a riotous life

Leben ist kein Honigschlecken
Das Leben ist kein Honigschlecken
- Life is not all beer and skittles

Lebensart, f
- way of living
- manners

Lebensbereich, m
- walk of life

Lebensfreude, f
- enjoyment of life

Lebensgewohnheit, f
- living habit

Lebenshaltungskosten, pl
- cost of living
- living costs *pl*

Lebenslauf, m
- curriculum vitae
- c.v.
- resumé

Lebensmittel, n pl (generell)
- food
- foodstuffs *pl*
- victuals *pl*

Lebensmittel, n pl (Vorräte)
→ Lebensmittelvorräte

Lebensmittelallergie, f
- food allergy

Lebensmittelallergieprüfung, f *med*
- food allergy testing *med*

Lebensmittel ausgeben
- issue food

Lebensmittelausstellung, f
- food exhibition

Lebensmittelbedarf, m
Lebensmittelanforderung, f
- food requisition

Lebensmittelbestand, m
Lebensmittellager, n

- food inventory *AE*
- food stock

Lebensmitteleinkauf, m
- food purchase
- purchase of food
- purchasing food

Lebensmitteleinkäufer, m
- food purchasing agent

Lebensmitteleinzelhändler, m
- food retailer

Lebensmitteletikett, n
- food label

Lebensmittelfarbe, f
- food coloring *AE*
- food colouring *BE*

Lebensmittel für 12 Tage, n pl
- food for 12 days

Lebensmittelgeschäft, n (Handel)
- food business

Lebensmittelgeschäft, n (Laden)
Lebensmittelladen, m
- food store *AE*
- food shop *BE*
- general food store *AE*
- grocery
- grocer's shop *BE*

Lebensmittelgeschäft mit Selbstbedienung, n
- groceteria *AE*
- self-service grocery

Lebensmittelgroßhändler, m
- food wholesaler

Lebensmittel haben für 12 Tage
- have food for 12 days

Lebensmittelhändler, m
- grocer

Lebensmittelhersteller, m
- food manufacturer

Lebensmittelherstellung, f
- food manufacturing

Lebensmittelhilfe, f
- food aid

Lebensmittelhilfe schicken jm
- send food aid to s.o.

Lebensmittelhygiene, f
- food hygiene

Lebensmittelindustrie, f
Lebensmittelbranche, f
- food industry

Lebensmittelkäufer, m
- food purchaser
- food buyer

Lebensmittelknappheit, f
Lebensmittelmangel, m
- food shortage
- shortage of food

Lebensmittelkonservierung, f
- food conservation
- conserving food

Lebensmittelkonzern, m
- food group

Lebensmittelkosten, pl
- food costs *pl*
- food cost

Lebensmittelkosten in Prozent, pl
prozentuale Lebensmittelkosten, pl
- food cost percentage

Lebensmittelladen, m
Lebensmittelgeschäft, n
- grocery
- grocer's store *AE*

- grocer's shop *BE*
- grocer's

Lebensmittellager, n
Lebensmittellagerraum, m
- food store

Lebensmittel lagern
- store food

Lebensmittellagerungsvorschriften, f pl
- food storage regulations *pl*

Lebensmittellieferant, m
Lebensmittellieferer, m
- food supplier
- victualler
- victualer *AE*

Lebensmittellieferung, f
- food supply

Lebensmittelmarkt, m
- food market

Lebensmittelmesse, f
- food fair

Lebensmittel mit einem hohen Fettgehalt, n pl
- food with a high fat content

Lebensmittelpreis m
- food price

Lebensmittelproduktion, f
Lebensmittelherstellung, f
- food production

Lebensmittelproduzent, m
Lebensmittelhersteller, m
- food producer

Lebensmittelprüfer, m
- food inspector

Lebensmittelrationierung, f
- food rationing

Lebensmittelrechnung, f
- food bill

Lebensmittelstand, m
- food stall *BE*
- food stand *AE*

Lebensmittelsubvention, f
- food subsidy

Lebensmitteltechnologie, f
- food technology

Lebensmittelumsatz, m
- food turnover
- food sales *pl*

Lebensmittel- und Getränkeeinkauf, m
Einkauf von Lebensmitteln und Getränken, m
Einkauf von Speisen und Getränken, m
- food and beverage purchase
- purchase of food and beverages
- purchasing food and beverages

Lebensmittel- und Getränkekosten, pl
→ Food-and-Beverage-Kosten

Lebensmittel- und Verpflegungsindustrie, f
- food and catering industry

Lebensmittel verarbeiten
- process food

Lebensmittelverarbeitung, f
- food processing
- processing of food

Lebensmittelverarbeitungsfirma, f
- food-processing company
- food-processing firm

Lebensmittelverarbeitungsindustrie, f
- food-processing industry

Lebensmittelverbrauch, m
Lebensmittelkonsum, m
Lebensmittelverzehr, m
- food consumption
- consumption of food

Lebensmittelvergiftung, f
- food poisoning

Lebensmittelvergiftung bekommen
- get food poisoning

Lebensmittelvorrat, m
- food stock
- stock of food

Lebensmittelvorräte, m pl
- food supplies *pl*
- provisions *pl*

Lebensmittelvorräte auffüllen
- replenish food

Lebensmittelwaren, f pl
Lebensmittel, n pl
- groceries *pl*
- grocery *sg*

Lebensphilosophie, f
- philosophy of life

Lebensstandard, m
- living standard
- standard of living

Lebensstil, m
- lifestyle
- style of living

Lebensstilberater, m
- lifestyle consultant

Lebensstilberatung, f
- lifestyle counselling

Lebensstilgewohnheit, f
- lifestyle habit

Lebensstilverbesserung, f
- lifestyle improvement

Lebensversicherung, f
- life insurance
- life assurance

Lebensweise, f
- way of life
- lifestyle

leben und leben lassen
- live and let live

leben vom Fremdenverkehr
leben von Tourismus
- live on tourism
- live on holiday trade *BE*
- depend on tourism for one's livelihood

leben vom Tourismus
- depend on tourism for one's livelihood
- live on tourism
- live on holiday trade *BE*

leben von der Hand in den Mund
- live from hand to mouth

leben von etw
sich nähren von etw
- live on s.th.

leben von Luft und Liebe
- live on air
- hardly eat a thing

leben von Wasser und Brot
von Brot und Wasser leben
- live on bread and water

leben wie ein König
- live like a king

leben wie Gott in Frankreich
- be in clover
- live in the lap of luxury
- live like a king
- live the life of Riley *coll*

Leber, f
- liver

Leberkebab, m
- liver kebab

Leberpastete 462

Leberpastete, f
♦ liver pâté
♦ liver pie
Leberschaden, m
♦ liver damage
Leberwurst, f
♦ liver sausage
Lebewelt, f
♦ fast set
Lebewohl, n
♦ farewell
♦ good-bye AE
♦ good-by AE
♦ goodbye BE
Lebewohl sagen etw
♦ bid farewell to s.th.
♦ say farewell to s.th.
♦ say good-bye to s.th. AE
♦ say good-by to s.th. AE
♦ say goodbye to s.th. BE
Lebewohl sagen jm
♦ bid farewell to s.o.
♦ say farewell to s.o.
♦ say good-bye to s.o. AE
♦ say good-by to s.o. AE
♦ say goodbye to s.o. BE
Lebewohl sagen jm im Namen von jm
♦ bid s.o. farewell in the name of s.o.
♦ say good-bye to s.o. in the name of s.o. AE
♦ say good-by to s.o. in the name of s.o. AE
♦ say goodbye to s.o. in the name of s.o. BE
lebhaft, adj
♦ lively, adj
♦ buoyant, adj ökon
lebhafte Atmosphäre, f
geschäftige Atmosphäre f
♦ lively atmosphere
lebhafte Buchungen, f pl
♦ buoyant bookings pl
lebhafter Buchungsauftakt, m
♦ buoyant start to bookings
lebhaftes Hotel, n
(meist laut und überfüllt)
♦ lively hotel
♦ busy hotel
lebhaftes Interesse finden
auf lebhaftes Interesse stoßen
♦ meet with a lively interest
Lebkuchen, m
♦ gingerbread
Lechtaler Alpen, die, pl
♦ Lechtal Alps, the, pl
lecker, adj
köstlich, adj
♦ savory, adj
♦ savoury, adj
♦ delicious, adj
♦ tasty, adj
Leckerbissen, m
Leckerei, f
Delikatesse, f
♦ titbit
♦ tidbit AE
♦ dainty (morsel)
♦ delicacy
Leckerei, f
Leckerbissen, m
Delikatesse, f
♦ dainty
♦ dainty morsel
♦ delicacy

♦ titbit
♦ tidbit AE
Ledermöbel, n pl
♦ leather furniture sg
Ledersessel, m
♦ leather armchair
ledig, adj
unverheiratet, adj
alleinstehend, adj
♦ single, adj
♦ unmarried, adj
ledige Frau, f
♦ single woman
lediger Mann, m
♦ single man
ledig sein
♦ be single
leer, adj
♦ empty, adj
Leerbett, n
→ leeres Bett
Leerbettgebühr, f (Kabine)
♦ charge for (an) unoccupied berth
Leerbettgebühr, f (Zimmer)
♦ charge for (an) unoccupied bed
leer bleiben
♦ remain empty
♦ stay empty
leere Bank, f
leere Sitzbank, f
♦ empty bench
leeren etw
♦ empty s.th.
leeren etw bis zur Neige
(trinken)
leeren etw bis zum Boden
♦ drain s.th. to the dregs
leeren etw mit einem Schluck
♦ empty s.th. at one draft AE
♦ empty s.th. at one draught BE
leeren etw mit wenigen Schlucken
♦ quaff s.th. obs
leerer Bus, m
♦ empty bus
♦ empty coach BE
leerer Magen, m
nüchterner Magen, m
♦ empty stomach
leerer Sitzplatz, m
leerer Platz, m
leerer Sitz, m
Leerplatz, m
♦ empty seat
leerer Strand, m
♦ empty beach
leerer Stuhl, m
♦ empty chair
leeres Bett n
Leerbett n
♦ empty bed
♦ bed not occupied
♦ unoccupied bed
leeres Glas, n
♦ empty glass
leeres Haus, n
♦ empty house
♦ unoccupied house
♦ vacant house
leeres Hotelzimmer, n
♦ empty hotel room
♦ unoccupied hotel room

♦ hotel room not occupied
♦ vacant hotel room
leeres Zimmer, n
Leerzimmer, n
♦ empty room
♦ unoccupied room
♦ room not occupied
♦ vacant room
leere Wohnung, f
♦ empty apartment AE
♦ empty flat BE
Leergut, n
Fustage f FR
Fastage f FR
♦ empties pl
Leergut wird nicht zurückgenommen
♦ empties are not taken back
♦ bottles are not taken back
♦ bottles nonreturnable AE
♦ bottles non-returnable BE
Leergut wird zurückgenommen
♦ empties are taken back
♦ bottles returnable
Leerkapazität, f
freie Kapazität, f
♦ spare capacity
♦ unused capacity
Leerplatz, m
→ leerer Sitzplatz
Leerplatzzahl, f
Zahl der leeren Sitzplätze, f
♦ number of empty seats
leer sein
♦ be empty
Leerstand m
(Ausstellung)
leerer Stand m
♦ empty stand
leer stehen
♦ stand empty
♦ be unoccupied
♦ be vacant
leerstehend, adj
frei, adj
vakant, adj
freistehend, adj
♦ vacant, adj
♦ unoccupied, adj
♦ empty, adj
♦ free, adj
♦ available, adj
leerstehendes Appartement, n
unbelegtes Appartement, n
♦ unoccupied apartment
♦ vacant apartment
♦ empty apartment
leerstehendes Bett n
→ leeres Bett
leerstehendes Gebäude, n
♦ vacant building
♦ empty building
♦ building standing empty
leerstehendes Haus, n
♦ vacant house
♦ unoccupied house
♦ empty house
leerstehendes Zimmer, n
♦ vacant room
♦ unoccupied room
♦ empty room

leerstehende Wohnung, f
  ♦ unoccupied flat BE
  ♦ vacant flat BE
  ♦ unoccupied apartment AE
  ♦ vacant apartment AE
  ♦ empty apartment AE
leer werden
  frei werden
  ♦ become empty
  ♦ become vacant
Leerzimmer, n
  leeres Zimmer, n
  ♦ unoccupied room
  ♦ room not occupied
  ♦ empty room
  ♦ vacant room
Legende lebt weiter
  ♦ legend lives on
leger, adj
  zwanglos, adj
  gelegentlich, adj
  ♦ casual, adj
legere Atmosphäre, f
  → lockere Atmosphäre
legiert, adj gastr
  gebunden, adj gastr
  ♦ bound, adj gastr
  ♦ thickened, adj gastr
legierte Suppe, f
  ♦ bound soup
Lehmhaus, n
  ♦ clay house
Lehmhütte, f
  ♦ mud hut
Lehmofen, m
  ♦ clay oven
Lehmziegelhaus, n
  ♦ adobe house
Lehmziegelhütte, f
  ♦ adobe hut
Lehnstuhl, m
  Lehnsessel, m
  ♦ easy chair
Lehnstuhl, m (hohe runde Lehne)
  ♦ barrel chair
Lehnstuhlarchäologe, m
  ♦ armchair archaeologist
  ♦ armchair archeologist
Lehnstuhl mit verstellbarer Rückenlehne, m
  ♦ reclining chair
  ♦ recliner
Lehnstuhlreisender, m
  ♦ armchair traveller
  ♦ armchair traveler AE
Lehre, f
  Lehrzeit, f
  ♦ apprenticeship
Lehre machen
  Lehre absolvieren
  ♦ do an apprenticeship
Lehrer, m
  ♦ instructor
  ♦ teacher
Lehrerfahrung, f
  ♦ teaching experience
Lehrerin, f
  ♦ instructress
  ♦ female teacher
Lehrgang, m
  Kurs, m
  Klasse, f

  ♦ course
  ♦ class
Lehrgang in Gastronomiemanagement, m
  ♦ course in foodservice management AE
  ♦ course in catering management BE
Lehrgang machen in etw
  Lehrgang absolvieren in etw
  Kurs machen in etw
  Kurs absolvieren in etw
  ♦ do a course in s.th.
  ♦ take a course in s.th.
Lehrgang planen
  Kurs planen
  ♦ plan a course
Lehrgangsgebühr, f
  Kursgebühr, f
  ♦ course fee
  ♦ course charge
Lehrgarten, m
  ♦ teaching garden
Lehrgaststätte, f
  Ausbildungsgaststätte, f
  ♦ training bar AE
  ♦ training public house BE
  ♦ training pub BE coll
Lehrhotel, n
  Schulhotel, n SCHW
  Ausbildungshotel, n
  ♦ teaching hotel
  ♦ training hotel
Lehrküche, f
  ♦ training kitchen
Lehrling, m obs
  → Auszubildender
Lehrmädchen, n
  ♦ girl apprentice
Lehrpfad, m
  ♦ instructional path
Lehrrestaurant, n
  ♦ training restaurant
Lehrsaal, m
  → Unterrichtsraum, Vortragsraum
Lehrseminar, n
  ♦ teaching seminar
Lehrtochter, f SCHW
  (weiblicher Lehrling)
  → Lehrling
Lehrvertrag, m
  ♦ contract of apprenticeship
Lehrzeit, f
  → Lehre
Leibarzt, m
  ♦ personal physician
  ♦ private physician
Leibgericht, n
  → Lieblingsgericht
Leibkoch, m
  ♦ personal chef
leibliche Genüsse, m pl
  ♦ physical comforts pl
leibliches Wohl, n (Essen und Trinken)
  ♦ wining and dining
leibliches Wohl, n (Gesundheitszustand)
  ♦ physical well-being
leibliches Wohl, n (Redewendung)
  für das leibliche Wohl sorgen
  ♦ food and drink
  ♦ provide food and drink
leibliches Wohlergehen, n
  (Nahrung und Kleidung)

  materielle Annehmlichkeiten, f pl
  ♦ creature comforts pl
Leibspeise, f
  → Lieblingsgericht
Leibwächter, m
  ♦ bodyguard
Leichenschmaus, m
  ♦ funeral meal
leicht abfallender Stellplatz, m
  (Camping)
  ♦ gently sloping pitch
  ♦ slightly sloping pitch
Leichtathlet, m
  ♦ track-and-field athlete
  ♦ athlete BE
Leichtathletik, f
  ♦ athletics pl
Leichtathletikbahn, f
  ♦ athletics track
Leichtathletiktreffen, n
  Leichtathletikveranstaltung, f
  ♦ athletics meeting
Leichtathletikveranstaltung, f
  ♦ track-and-field event
  ♦ athletic event BE
Leichtathletikwettbewerb, m
  ♦ track-and-field competition
  ♦ atletic competition BE
Leichtathletikwettkampf, m
  ♦ track-and-field contest
  ♦ athletic contest BE
Leichtatletik, f
  ♦ track-and-field sports pl
  ♦ athletic sports BE pl=sg
  ♦ athletics BE pl=sg
Leichtbauweise, f
  ♦ lightweight construction
leichte Abfahrt, f (Ski)
  (meist blau gekennzeichnet)
  ♦ easy run
leichte Erfrischung, f
  (Getränk oder Speise)
  ♦ light refreshment
leichte Kost, f
  ♦ light diet
  ♦ light fare
leichte Mahlzeit, f
  leichtes Mahl, n
  leichtes Essen, n
  Imbiß, m
  ♦ light meal
  ♦ light repast form
leichte Musik, f
  ♦ light music
leichten Schlaf haben
  leisen Schlaf haben
  ♦ be a light sleeper
leichte Piste, f (Ski)
  ♦ easy ski run
  ♦ easy run
leichter Imbiß, m
  ♦ light snack
leichter machen jn um $ 123
  erleichtern jn um $ 123
  ♦ relieve s.o. of $ 123
leicht erreichbar, adj
  leicht zugänglich, adj
  ♦ easy to reach, adj
  ♦ easy to get to, adj
  ♦ easily accessible, adj

leicht erreichbar sein
  leicht zu erreichen sein
  ♦ be within easy reach
  ♦ can easily be reached
  ♦ be easy to reach
  ♦ be easily accessible
leicht erreichbar sein von X aus
  ♦ be easily accessible from X
leichter Schläfer, m
  ♦ light sleeper
leichter Wein, m
  ♦ light wine
leichtes Bier, n
  ♦ light beer
leichtes Büfett, n
  ♦ light buffet
leichtes Frühstück, n
  ♦ light breakfast
leichtes Handgepäck, n
  ♦ light hand baggage AE
  ♦ light hand luggage BE
leichtes Mädchen, n
  ♦ fast girl
leichtes Mittagessen, n
  ♦ light lunch
  ♦ light luncheon
leichte Unterhaltung, f
  ♦ light entertainment
leichte Zugänglichkeit, f
  ♦ easy accessibility
Leichtflugzeug, n
  Sportflugzeug, n
  ♦ light plane
  ♦ light aircraft
leichtgebaut, adj
  ♦ lightly built, adj
leicht kochen
  köcheln (lassen)
  ♦ simmer
leicht seekrank werden
  ♦ be a bad sailor
leichtverdaulich, adj
  ♦ easy to digest, adj
leicht würzen etw (mit etw)
  ♦ season s.th. lightly (with s.th.)
Leichtzelt, n
  ♦ lightweight tent
leicht zu erreichen, adj
  ♦ easy to reach, adj
leicht zu erreichen sein
  leicht erreichbar sein
  ♦ be easy to reach
  ♦ be easily accessible
leicht zugängliche Lage, f
  leicht zugänglicher Standort, m
  ♦ easily accessible location
leiden an Flugangst
  ♦ suffer from fear of flying
leiden an Heimweh
  ♦ suffer from homesickness
leiden an Schlaflosigkeit
  ♦ suffer from sleeplessness
  ♦ suffer from insomnia
leidenschaftlicher Skiläufer, m
  ♦ passionate skier
leidenschaftlich gern essen etw
  ♦ have a passion for s.th.
leiden unter einem Hotelmangel (völliges Fehlen)
  ♦ suffer from a lack of hotels
leiden unter einer Hotelknappheit
  leiden an einer Hotelknappheit

leiden unter einem Hotelmangel
leiden an einem Hotelmangel
  ♦ suffer from a shortage of hotels
Leierkasten, m
  ♦ barrel organ AE
  ♦ barrel-organ BE
Leierkastenmann, m
  Leiermann, m
  ♦ barrel-organ man
  ♦ barrel-organ grinder
Leihangelgerät, n
  Leihfischereigerät, n
  ♦ fishing tackle for hire BE
  ♦ fishing tackle for rent AE
Leihbibliothek, f
  Leihbücherei, f
  ♦ lending library BE
  ♦ rental library AE
Leihbücherei, f
  Leihbibliothek, f
  ♦ rental library AE
  ♦ lending library BE
Leihcaravan, m (gemietet)
  Leihwohnwagen, m
  Mietcaravan, m
  Mietwohnwagen, m
  ♦ hired caravan BE
  ♦ rented trailer AE
Leihcaravan, m (generell)
  Leihwohnwagen, m
  Mietcaravan, m
  Mietwohnwagen, m
  ♦ hire caravan BE
  ♦ rental trailer AE
  ♦ letting caravan BE
Leihdienst, m
  Mietdienst, m
  ♦ hire service AE
  ♦ rental service BE
leihen etw jm
  verleihen etw an jn
  ausleihen etw an jn
  ♦ loan s.th. to s.o. AE
  ♦ lend s.th. to s.o.
leihen etw jm (gegen Gebühr)
  → vermieten etw
leihen etw von jm
  ausleihen etw von jm
  ♦ borrow s.th. from s.o.
Leiher, m (Entleiher)
  ♦ borrower
Leiher, m (Verleiher)
  ♦ lender
  ♦ loaner
Leihfahrrad, n
  → Mietfahrrad
Leihfirma, f
  ♦ hire company BE
  ♦ hire firm BE
  ♦ rental company AE
  ♦ rental firm AE
Leihfrist, f
  ♦ lending period
  ♦ rental period
  ♦ hire period BE
Leihgabe, f
  (z.B. für Kunstausstellung)
  ♦ object on loan
  ♦ loan

Leihgaben, f pl
  (Kunstwerke)
  ♦ loan-collection
Leihgebühr, f (Bücher)
  ♦ lending fee
Leihgebühr, f (generell)
  Mietgebühr, f
  ♦ hire charge BE
  ♦ hire fee BE
  ♦ hiring charge BE
  ♦ rental charge AE
  ♦ rental fee AE
Leihpacht, f
  ♦ lend-lease
Leihrad, n
  → Mietfahrrad
Leihski, m (gemietet)
  Mietski, m
  ♦ hired ski BE
  ♦ rented ski AE
Leihski, m (generell)
  Mietski, m
  ♦ hire ski BE
  ♦ rental ski AE
Leihski, m (zu vermieten)
  Mietski, m
  ♦ ski for hire BE
  ♦ ski for rent AE
Leihwagen, m (gemietet)
  Leihauto, n
  Leihwagen, m
  Leihauto, n
  ♦ hired car BE
  ♦ rented car AE
Leihwagen, m (generell)
  Mietwagen, m
  Mietauto, n
  ♦ hire car BE
  ♦ rental car AE
Leihwagen, m (zu vermieten)
  ♦ car for hire BE
  ♦ car for rent AE
Leihwagenagentur, f
  Leihwagenvermittlung, f
  Mietwagenagentur, f
  Mietwagenvermittlung, f
  ♦ car hire agency BE
  ♦ rental car agency AE
Leihwagenfirma, f
  Mietwagenfirma, f
  ♦ car hire firm BE
  ♦ car rental firm AE
Leihwagengeschäft, n
  Mietwagengeschäft, n
  ♦ car hire business BE
  ♦ car rental business AE
Leihwagengesellschaft, f
  Mietwagengesellschaft, f
  ♦ car hire company BE
  ♦ car rental company AE
Leihwagenkosten, pl
  Mietwagenkosten, pl
  ♦ car hire costs BE pl
  ♦ car hire charges BE pl
  ♦ car rental costs AE pl
Leihwagenmarkt, m
  Mietwagenmarkt, m
  ♦ car hire market BE
  ♦ car rental market AE
Leihwagenorganisation, f
  Mietwagenorganisation, f

- ♦ car hire organisation BE
- ♦ car rental organisation AE

Leihwagenprospekt, m
   Mietwagenprospekt, m
- ♦ car hire brochure BE
- ♦ car rental brochure AE

Leihwagenschalter, m
   Mietwagenschalter, m
- ♦ car hire desk BE
- ♦ car rental desk AE

Leihwagenservice, m
   Leihwagenvermietung, f
   Leihwagendienst, m
   Mietwagenservice, m
   Mietwagendienst, m
- ♦ car hire service BE
- ♦ car rental service AE

Leihwagenunternehmen, n
   Leihwagenbetrieb, m
   Mietwagenunternehmen, n
   Mietwagenbetrieb, m
- ♦ car rental operation AE
- ♦ car hire operation BE

Leihwagenunternehmer, m
   Mietwagenunternehmer, m
- ♦ car hire operator BE
- ♦ car rental operator AE

Leihwäsche, f (gemietet)
   Mietwäsche, f
- ♦ hired linen BE
- ♦ rented linen AE

Leihwäsche, f (generell)
   Mietwäsche, f
- ♦ hire linen BE
- ♦ rental linen AE

leihweise, adv (gegen Geld)
- ♦ on hire, adv

leihweise, adv (generell)
- ♦ by way of loan, adv
- ♦ as a loan, adv
- ♦ on loan, adv

leihweise erbitten etw
- ♦ ask for the loan of s.th.

leihweise haben etw
- ♦ have s.th. on loan

leihweise überlassen jm etw
→ ausleihen jm etw

Leihzeit, f
   Mietzeit, f
- ♦ hire period BE
- ♦ hire time BE
- ♦ rental period AE
- ♦ period of rental AE

Leihzeit, n (gemietet)
   Mietzeit, n
- ♦ hired tent BE
- ♦ rented tent AE

Leihzeit, n (generell)
   Mietzeit, n
- ♦ hire tent BE
- ♦ rental tent AE

Leihzeit, n (zu vermieten)
   Mietzeit, n
- ♦ tent for hire BE
- ♦ tent for rent AE

Leinenwäsche, f
- ♦ linen

Leintuch, n
   Leinentuch, n
- ♦ linen sheet
- ♦ linen

Leinwand, f
   Bildwand, f
- ♦ screen

Leipziger Messe, f
- ♦ Leipzig Fair, the

leise, adj
- ♦ soft, adj
- ♦ quiet, adj

leise Musik, f
- ♦ soft music
- ♦ quiet music

leise sein
- ♦ be quiet

leise sein nach Mitternacht
- ♦ be quiet after midnight

leise sprechen
- ♦ talk quietly
- ♦ talk in a low voice

leisten können sich etw
- ♦ be able to afford s.th.
- ♦ can afford s.th.

leisten sich etw
- ♦ afford s.th.

leisten sich etw (gönnen)
→ gönnen sich etw

Leistung, f (Arbeitsleistung)
   Arbeitsleistung, f
- ♦ performance

Leistung, f (Dienstleistung)
→ Dienstleistung

Leistung anbieten jm
   Service anbieten jm
- ♦ offer a service to s.o.

Leistung benötigen
   Service benötigen
- ♦ require a service

Leistung bestellen
- ♦ order a service

Leistung bezahlen
   Dienstleistung bezahlen
- ♦ pay for a service

Leistung bieten
→ Service bieten

Leistung einkaufen
→ Leistung kaufen

Leistung einschränken
   Service einschränken
- ♦ cut a service
- ♦ reduce a service
- ♦ curtail a service

Leistungen
   (Prospektüberschrift)
- ♦ The price includes

Leistungen erbringen
- ♦ render services

Leistungen erweitern
- ♦ expand services

Leistung entfallen lassen
   Leistung streichen
   Dienst entfallen lassen
   Dienst streichen
- ♦ withdraw a service

Leistungen vergleichen
- ♦ compare services

Leistung erhalten
   Dienstleistung erhalten
- ♦ receive a service

Leistung erstellen
→ Dienstleistung erstellen

Leistung in Anspruch nehmen
- ♦ use a service

- ♦ utilise a service
- ♦ utilize a service
- ♦ make use of a service

Leistung kaufen
   Leistung einkaufen
   Dienstleistung (ein)kaufen
- ♦ buy a service

Leistung kürzen
→ Service kürzen

Leistung reduzieren
→ Service einschränken

Leistungsanbieter, m
→ Leistungsträger

Leistungsänderung, f
- ♦ change in service
- ♦ change in the service
- ♦ change in services
- ♦ change in the services

Leistungsanforderung, f
   Serviceanforderung, f
- ♦ rervice required
- ♦ service requirement

Leistungsanforderungen erfüllen
- ♦ meet the service requirements

Leistungsangebot, n (Offerte)
- ♦ service offer
- ♦ services offered

Leistungsangebot, n (Palette)
   Servicepalette f
   Serviceangebot n
   Leistungspalette f
- ♦ service range
- ♦ range of services offered
- ♦ range of services

Leistungsangebot umfaßt etw
- ♦ service comprises s.th.

leistungsberechtigt, adj
- ♦ eligible for benefit, adj

Leistungsberechtigter, m
- ♦ beneficiary

Leistungsbeschreibung, f
- ♦ service description
- ♦ description of (a) service

Leistungseinschränkung, f
   Serviceeinschränkung, f
- ♦ cut in service
- ♦ cut in services
- ♦ curtailment of service

Leistungsempfänger, m
- ♦ recipient of a service
- ♦ recipient of services

Leistungsentzug, m
- ♦ withdrawal of a service

Leistungserbringung, f
- ♦ rendering a service

Leistungsfähigkeit, f
- ♦ efficiency

Leistungsgeber, m
   Leistungsanbieter, m
   Leistungsträger, m
- ♦ supplier of a service
- ♦ service supplier

Leistungsgutschein, m
   Servicegutschein m
   Dienstleistungsgutschein m
- ♦ service voucher

Leistungsinanspruchnahme, f
- ♦ use of a service
- ♦ utilisation of a service
- ♦ utilization of a service

Leistungskatalog

Leistungskatalog, m
♦ service catalogue
♦ service catalog *AE*
♦ catalogue of services
♦ catalog of services *AE*
Leistungskosten pl
→ variable Kosten
Leistungsmangel, m
♦ shortcoming in service
Leistungsminderung, f
♦ service reduction
♦ reduction of service
Leistungsniveau, n
→ Serviceniveau
Leistungsniveau steigern
Serviceniveau verbessern
♦ improve the service level
Leistungspaket, n
♦ package of services
Leistungspalette, f
→ Leistungsangebot
Leistungsprogramm, n
Serviceprogramm n
Leistungspalette f
♦ services available *pl*
♦ service range
♦ range of services
Leistungsprogramm erweitern
♦ increase the service range
♦ increase the range of services
Leistungsschau, f
♦ competitive exhibition
♦ trade show
♦ trade exhibition
♦ show
Leistungsschwund, m
Leistungsrückgang, m
♦ decline in service
♦ decline in services
Leistungsspektrum, n
→ Leistungspalette
Leistungsstandard, m
Servicestandard, m
♦ standard of service
♦ service standard
leistungsstark, adj
♦ efficient, adj
leistungsstarker Service, m
effizienter Service, m
♦ efficient service
leistungsstarkes Hotel, n
♦ efficient hotel
Leistungssteigerung, f
Leistungsausweitung, f
♦ increase in the range of services
♦ increase in the range of services offered
Leistungsstopp m
♦ halt in services
Leistungsstornierung, f
♦ cancellation of a service
♦ cancellation of services
♦ cancelation of a service *AE*
♦ cancelation of services *AE*
Leistungsstörung, f
♦ hitch in service
♦ disruption of service
Leistungsstörung beheben
♦ eliminate a hitch in service
♦ deal with a hitch in service
Leistung stornieren
Dienstleistung stornieren

Dienst stornieren
♦ cancel a service
Leistungsträger, m
Leistungsanbieter, m
♦ service provider
♦ provider of a service
♦ corporation providing a service *AE*
♦ company providing a service *BE*
♦ service supplier
Leistungsträgervertrag, m
♦ contract for provision of services
♦ contract for the provision of the service
Leistungsumfang, m
→ Serviceumfang
Leistungsunterschied, m
♦ difference in service
Leistungsvereinbarung, f
Dienstleistungsvereinbarung, f
Servicevereinbarung, f
♦ service agreement
Leistungsvergleich, m
♦ comparison of services
♦ comparing services
Leistungsverzeichnis n
♦ service directory
♦ service list
♦ list of (the) services
♦ list of the services offered
Leistung verkaufen
→ Service verkaufen
Leistung wünschen
Service wünschen
Dienst wünschen
♦ request a service
leitende Angestellte, pl
♦ senior staff
♦ executives *pl*
leitender Angestellter, m
Führungskraft, m
♦ executive
♦ exec. *abbr*
leitender Empfangschef, m
♦ head receptionist
♦ executive receptionist *AE*
leitender Ingenieur, m
♦ chief engineer
leiten etw (Firma)
♦ manage s.th.
♦ run s.th.
Leiter der Beherbergungsabteilung, m
Empfangschef, m
♦ rooms division manager
♦ manager of the rooms division
Leiter der Einkaufsabteilung, m
♦ purchasing manager
Leiter der Finanzabteilung, m
♦ financial controller
Leiter der Gästeinformation, m
♦ guest information manager
Leiter der Informationsabteilung, m
♦ information manager
Leiter der Instandhaltungsabteilung, m
♦ maintenance manager
Leiter der Öffentlichkeitsarbeit, m
PR-Leiter, m
♦ public relations manager
♦ PR manager
Leiter der Personal- und Ausbildungsabteilung, m
♦ personnel and training manager

Leiter der Reservierungsabteilung, m
Reservierungsleiter, m
♦ reservations manager
♦ reservation manager
Leiter der Verkaufsförderung, m
♦ sales promotion manager
Leiter der Wareneinsatzkontrolle, m
→ Wirtschaftskontrolleur
Leiter der Wareneinsatzkontrolle Getränke, m
♦ beverage cost controller
Leiter der Wareneinsatzkontrolle Speisen, m
♦ food cost controller
Leiter der Werbeabteilung, m
♦ advertising manager
♦ publicity manager
Leiter des Finanzwesens, m
♦ finance manager
♦ financial director *BE*
Leiter des Kurorchesters, m
♦ conductor of the spa orchestra
Leiter einer Abteilung, m
Abteilungsleiter, m
♦ head of a department
♦ department head
♦ departmental manager
Leiter einer Delegation, m
♦ leader of a delegation
♦ head of a delegation
Leiter einer Jugendherberge, m
Jugendherbergsleiter, m
♦ warden of a youth hostel
♦ youth hostel warden
Leiter einer Reisegruppe, m
♦ leader of a tour group
♦ leader of a tour
Leiter einer Versammlung, m
(Vorsitzender)
♦ chairman of a meeting
Leiterin der Hausdamenabteilung, f
→ Erste Hausdame
Leiterin der Wäscherei, f
♦ head laundress
Leithammel, m *humor*
♦ boss of a group
♦ boss
Leitung, f (Aufsicht)
→ Aufsicht
Leitung, f (Veranstaltung)
♦ conduct
Leitung einer Hauptversammlung, f
♦ conduct of a general meeting
Leitung einer Konferenz, f
♦ conduct of a conference
Leitung einer Sitzung, f
♦ conduct of a meeting
Leitung eines Hotels, f
Hotelleitung, f
♦ management of a hotel
♦ hotel management
♦ managing a hotel
Leitung eines Hotels übernehmen
Management eines Hotels übernehmen
♦ take over the management of a hotel
Leitung eines Kongresses, f
♦ conduct of a convention
♦ conduct of a congress
Leitung haben von etw
leiten etw
Aufsicht haben über etw
♦ be in charge of s.th.

Leitung ist in europäischer Hand
♦ management is in European hands
Leitung neu verlegen
♦ relay a pipe
Leitungsgas, n
Gas aus der Leitung, n
♦ mains gas
Leitungstrinkwasserversorgung, f
♦ piped drinking water supply
Leitungswasser, n
♦ tap water AE
♦ tap-water BE
♦ piped water
Leitungswasserversorgung, f
Leitungswasseranschluß, m
♦ piped water supply
Leitweg, m
Routing, n
♦ routing
Lektüre, f
♦ reading
♦ reading matter
Lemberger, m
(Wein)
Limberger, m
♦ Lemberger
Lembergerrebe, f
♦ Lemberger vine
Lembergertraube, f
♦ Lemberger grape
Leng, m
Lengfisch, m
♦ ling
Lenkungsausschuß, m
♦ steering committee
Lernurlaub, m
Lernferien, pl
♦ learning vacation AE
♦ learning holiday BE
Lernzentrum, n
♦ learning center AE
♦ learning centre BE
Leselampe, f
♦ reading lamp
♦ reading light
lesen etw
♦ read s.th.
Lesepult, n
Vortragspult, n
Rednerpult, n
♦ lectern
Leseratte, f humor
Bücherwurm, m humor
♦ bookworm humor
Leseraum, m
Lesezimmer, n
♦ reading room
Lesesaal, m
♦ large reading room
♦ reading room
Lesesalon, m
♦ reading lounge
Lesezimmer, n
→ Leseraum
Lesotho
♦ Lesotho
Lette, m
♦ Latvian
Lettin, f
♦ Latvian girl

♦ Latvian woman
♦ Latvian
lettisch, adj
♦ Latvian, adj
Lettland
♦ Latvia
Letzte Abendmahl, das, n relig
♦ Last Supper, the relig
letzte Bestellungen werden um 21 Uhr aufgenommen
♦ last orders will be taken at 9 p.m.
letzte Etappe der Reise, f
♦ last leg of the journey
♦ last leg of the tour
♦ last leg of the trip
letzte Nacht, adv
♦ last night, adv
letzter Besuch in X, m
♦ last visit to X
♦ most recent visit to X
letzte Reise, f
♦ last journey
♦ most recent journey
♦ last trip
♦ most recent trip
♦ last tour
letzter Gültigkeitstag, m
♦ last day of validity
letzter Programmpunkt m
♦ last item on the program AE
♦ last item on the programme BE
letzte Saison, f
♦ last season
letzte Sommersaison, f
♦ last summer season
letztes Quartal, n
letztes Vierteljahr, n
♦ last quarter
letzte Wegetappe, f
letzte Etappe des Weges, f
♦ last leg of the trail
letztjährige Saison, f
♦ last year's season
leuchten jm zu seinem Zimmer
♦ light s.o. to his room
♦ light s.o. to her room
Leuchter, m (Kerzenleuchter)
→ Kerzenleuchter
Leuchter, m (Lüster)
→ Lüster
Leuchtturm, m
♦ lighthouse
Leute, pl
♦ people pl
Leute kennenlernen
♦ meet people
Leute nach X bringen
♦ bring people to X
Leute nebenan, pl
♦ people next door pl
Levante, f
♦ Levant, the
L-förmig, adj
♦ L-shaped, adj
L-förmige Eßecke, f
L-förmige Sitzgruppe, f
♦ L-shaped dinette
L-förmiger Tisch, m
♦ L-shaped table
LFV, m
→ Landesfremdenverkehrsverband

Libanese, m
♦ Lebanese
Libanesin, f
♦ Lebanese girl
♦ Lebanese woman
♦ Lebanese
libanesisch, adj
♦ Lebanese, adj
Libanon, m
♦ Lebanon, (the)
liberalisieren etw
♦ liberalise s.th.
♦ liberalize s.th.
Liberalisierung, f
♦ liberalisation
♦ liberalization
Liberalisierung der Tarife, f
♦ liberalisation of tariffs
♦ liberalization of tariffs
Liberia
♦ Liberia
Liberianer, m
♦ Liberian
Liberianerin, f
♦ Liberian girl
♦ Liberian woman
♦ Liberian
liberianisch, adj
♦ Liberian, adj
Libyen
♦ Libya
Libyer, m
♦ Libyan
Libyerin, f
♦ Libyan girl
♦ Libyan woman
♦ Libyan
libysch, adj
♦ Libyan, adj
Licht, n
♦ light
Licht an lassen
Licht brennen lassen
♦ leave the light on
Licht anmachen
♦ switch on the light
Licht ausmachen
Licht ausschalten
♦ switch out the light
♦ switch off the light
Lichtbild, n
→ Dia
Lichtbilderschau, f
Diaschau, f
Lichtbildschau, f
Lichtbildervorführung, f
♦ slide show
Lichtbildervorführung, f
→ Lichtbilderschau
Lichtbildervortrag, m
Diavortrag, m
♦ lecture with slides
♦ slide lecture
Lichtbildprojektion, f
Lichtbilderprojektion, f
Diaprojektion, f
♦ transparency projection
♦ slide projection
Lichteffekt, m
♦ lighting effect

lichte Hallenhöhe in m, f
  ♦ hall clearance in m
lichte Höhe, f
  ♦ headroom
  ♦ headway
lichtes Zimmer, n
  helles Zimmer, n
  ♦ light room
  ♦ bright room
Lichthof, m
  Innenhof, m
  ♦ patio
Lichtrufanlage, f
  ♦ luminous calling system
  ♦ light indicator
Lichtschacht, m
  ♦ light shaft
  ♦ well
Lichtschalter, m
  ♦ light switch
  ♦ switch
Lichtspielhaus, n
  Lichtspieltheater, n
  Kino, n
  ♦ motion-picture theater AE
  ♦ movie theater AE
  ♦ cinema BE
  ♦ movies AE pl coll
Licht und Ton
  Son et lumière, FR
  ♦ light and sound
  ♦ son et lumière FR
Lichtung, f
  Rodung, f
  ♦ clearing
Lido, m
  Strandbad, n
  Freibad, n
  Strandort, m
  ♦ lido
Liebe auf den ersten Blick, f
  ♦ love at first sight
Liebe geht durch den Magen, die
  ♦ The way to a man's heart is through his stomach
lieben langen Tag nichts tun
  ♦ laze away one's time
liebenswürdig, adj
  hilfsbereit, adj
  ♦ kind, adj
  ♦ friendly, adj
Liebenswürdigkeit, f
  ♦ kindness
lieber zu Hause bleiben
  ♦ prefer to stay at home
lieber zu Hause essen
  ♦ prefer to eat at home
Liebesnest, n
  ♦ love nest AE
  ♦ love-nest BE
Liebespaar, n
  ♦ pair of lovers
liebevoll erhalten, adj
  liebevoll gepflegt, adj
  ♦ lovingly preserved, adj
liebevoll gepflegt, adj
  ♦ lovingly tended, adj
  ♦ lovingly preserved, adj
liebevoll gepflegter Garten, m
  ♦ lovingly tended garden

liebevoll gepflegte Tradition, f
  ♦ lovingly preserved tradition
liebevoll möbliert, adj
  ♦ lovingly furnished, adj
liebevoll möbliertes Zimmer, n
  ♦ lovingly furnished room
liebevoll restauriert, adj
  ♦ lovingly restored, adj
liebevoll zubereitet, adj
  ♦ lovingly prepared, adj
liebevoll zubereitetes Essen, n
  ♦ lovingly prepared meal
Liebfraumilch, f
  (Wein)
  ♦ Liebfraumilch
Liebhaber, m
  ♦ lover
Liebhaber des guten Essens, m
  ♦ lover of fine food
Liebhaberei, f
  → Hobby
Liebhaber guter Weine, m
  Freund guter Weine, m
  ♦ lover of good wines
  ♦ lover of good wine
Liebhabertheater, n
  → Privattheater
Lieblingsart, adv gastr
  ♦ favorite style, adv AE gastr
  ♦ favourite style, adv BE gastr
Lieblingsbeschäftigung, f
  ♦ favorite occupation AE
  ♦ favourite occupation BE
Lieblingscafé, n
  ♦ favorite cafe AE
  ♦ favourite café BE
Lieblingsecke, f
  ♦ favorite corner AE
  ♦ favourite corner BE
Lieblingsessen, n
  Lieblingsspeise, f
  ♦ favorite food AE
  ♦ favourite food BE
Lieblingsferienort, m
  Lieblingsurlaubsort, m
  Lieblingsort, m
  ♦ favorite resort AE
  ♦ favourite resort BE
Lieblingsgaststätte, f
  Lieblingskneipe, f coll
  ♦ favorite bar AE
  ♦ favourite public house BE
  ♦ favourite pub BE coll
Lieblingsgericht, n
  Leibgericht, n
  Leibspeise, f
  ♦ favorite dish AE
  ♦ favourite dish BE
Lieblingsgetränk, n
  ♦ favorite drink AE
  ♦ favorite beverage AE
  ♦ favourite drink BE
  ♦ favourite beverage BE
Lieblingshotel n
  ♦ favorite hotel AE
  ♦ favourite hotel BE
Lieblingskneipe, f
  → Lieblingsgaststätte
Lieblingsmahl, n
  Lieblingsessen, n

♦ favorite meal AE
♦ favourite meal BE
Lieblingsort, m
  Lieblingsplatz, m
  ♦ favorite place AE
  ♦ favourite place BE
Lieblingsplatz, m
  Lieblingsort, m
  Lieblingsstätte, f
  ♦ favorite site AE
  ♦ favourite site BE
Lieblingsprogramm, n
  ♦ favorite program AE
  ♦ favourite programme BE
Lieblingsrestaurant, n
  ♦ favorite restaurant AE
  ♦ favourite restaurant BE
Lieblingsrezept, n
  ♦ favorite recipe AE
  ♦ favourite recipe BE
Lieblingssessel, m
  ♦ favorite armchair AE
  ♦ favourite armchair BE
Lieblingssitzplatz, m
  Lieblingsplatz, m
  Lieblingssitz, m
  ♦ favorite seat AE
  ♦ favourite seat BE
Lieblingsstadt, f (Großstadt)
  ♦ favorite city AE
  ♦ favourite city BE
Lieblingsstadt, f (kleine Stadt)
  ♦ favorite town AE
  ♦ favourite town BE
Lieblingsstelle, f
  Lieblingsplatz, m
  ♦ favorite spot AE
  ♦ favourite spot BE
Lieblingstreff, m
  Lieblingstreffpunkt, m
  Stammlokal, n
  ♦ favorite haunt AE
  ♦ favourite haunt BE
Lieblingstreff sein für jn
  Lieblingstreffpunkt sein für jn
  Lieblingsplatz sein für jn
  ♦ be the favorite haunt for s.o. AE
  ♦ be the favourite haunt for s.o. BE
Lieblingstropfen, m
  Lieblingsgetränk, n
  ♦ favorite tipple AE
  ♦ favourite tipple BE
Lieblingsurlaub, m
  Lieblingsferien, pl
  ♦ favorite vacation AE
  ♦ favourite holiday BE
Lieblingswein, m
  ♦ favorite wine AE
  ♦ favourite wine BE
Lieblingszimmer, n
  ♦ favorite room AE
  ♦ favourite room BE
lieblos zubereitet, adj
  ♦ prepared without proper care, adj
Liebstöckel, n/m
  ♦ lovage
Liechtenstein
  (Land)
  ♦ Liechtenstein
Liechtensteiner, m
  ♦ Liechtensteiner

Liechtensteinerin, f
♦ Liechtenstein girl
♦ Liechtenstein woman
♦ Liechtensteiner

liechtensteinisch, adj
♦ Liechtenstein, adj

Lied, n
♦ song

Liederabend, m
♦ song recital
♦ lieder recital

Liederwettbewerb, m
♦ song competition

Lied singen
♦ sing a song

Lieferant, m
Lieferer, m
♦ supplier
♦ purveyor

Lieferanteneingang, m
♦ tradesmen's entrance
♦ service entrance

lieferbar, adj
♦ available, adj

Lieferbedingungen, f pl
♦ terms of delivery pl

Lieferer, m
→ Lieferant

Lieferfrist, f
♦ period for delivery

Liefergebühr, f
♦ delivery charge

liefern etw (ausliefern)
ausliefern etw
♦ deliver s.th.

liefern etw (versorgen)
♦ supply s.th.

Lieferschein, m
♦ delivery note
♦ delivery slip

Lieferschein unterzeichnen
Lieferschein unterschreiben
♦ sign a delivery note

Liefertermin, m
♦ delivery date
♦ date of delivery

Lieferung, f (Auslieferung)
♦ delivery

Lieferung, f (Versorgung)
♦ supply

Lieferzeit, f
♦ delivery time
♦ time of delivery
♦ delivery

Liege, f
♦ lounge AE
♦ lounger BE

Liegebalkon, m (Sonnenbaden)
♦ sunbathing balcony

Liegebereich, m (Sonnenbaden)
♦ sunbathing area
♦ sunbathing space

Liegebereich grenzt an das Schwimmbad an
♦ sunbathing area borders the swimming pool

Liegedeck, n (Schiff)
♦ lounge deck
♦ sunbathing deck

Liegehalle, f med
♦ rest-cure room med

Liegekur, f
Ruhekur f

♦ rest cure AE
♦ rest-cure BE

liegen
gelegen sein
♦ lie
♦ be situated
♦ be located
♦ be placed
♦ be sited

liegenbleiben
nicht weiter kommen
festsitzen
♦ be stranded

liegenbleiben (im Bett)
→ im Bett bleiben

liegengebliebener Tourist, m
festsitzender Tourist, m
Tourist, der nicht weiterreisen kann, m
♦ stranded tourist

liegengebliebene Touristen zurückholen
(aus dem Ausland)
♦ repatriate stranded tourists

liegen im Herzen von etw
♦ lie at the heart of s.th.
♦ be located at the heart of s.th.

liegen in etw
(Grundstück)
gelegen sein in etw
♦ be set in s.th.

liegen innerhalb eines Radius von 12 km
innerhalb einer Reichweite von 12 km liegen
♦ lie within a radius of 12 km

Liegeplatz, m (Wasserfahrzeug)
♦ berth
♦ mooring
♦ slip AE

Liegeplätze für 123 Boote
♦ berths for 123 boats

Liegeplatzkapazität, f
(Hafen)
♦ berth capacity

Liegeraum, m
Ruheraum, m
♦ rest room
♦ rest-cure room med

Liegesitz, m
(in Verkehrsmittel)
Sitz mit verstellbarer Rückenlehne, m
♦ reclining seat

Liegesofa n
♦ divan

Liegestuhl, m
♦ deck chair AE
♦ deck-chair BE
♦ hammock chair BE
♦ sling chair AE

Liegestuhl abholen
♦ collect a deck chair AE
♦ collect a deck-chair BE

Liegestuhl mieten
♦ rent a deck chair AE
♦ hire a deck-chair BE

Liegestuhl vermieten
♦ rent (out) a deck chair AE
♦ hire (out) a deck-chair BE

Liegestuhl zurückbringen
Liegestuhl zurückgeben
♦ return a deck chair AE
♦ return a deck-chair BE

Liegeterrasse, f
♦ sunbathing terrace

♦ sunbathing patio
♦ rest-cure terrace

Liegewagen, m
(Zug)
♦ couchette car
♦ couchette coach BE

Liegewagenplatz, m
(Zug)
♦ couchette

Liegewagenzuschlag, m
(Zug)
♦ supplement for (a) couchette

Liegewiese, f
♦ sunbathing lawn
♦ sunbathing meadow
♦ rest-cure lawn
♦ lawn for resting
♦ lawn for sunbathing

Liegt das Zimmer zum Garten hin?
♦ Does the room look onto the garden?

Lifestyle, m
→ Lebensstil

Lift, m
♦ lift BE
♦ elevator AE

Liftanlage, f (generell)
→ Fahrstuhlanlage

Liftanlage, f (Skilift)
♦ lift system

Lift auf dem neuesten Stand der Technik, m
♦ state-of-the-art lift

Liftbenutzer m
♦ person using a lift BE
♦ person using an elevator AE

Liftbenutzung, f
Fahrstuhlbenutzung, f
♦ use of the lift BE
♦ using the lift BE
♦ use of an elevator AE
♦ using the elevator AE

Liftboy, m
Liftjunge, m
♦ lift boy BE
♦ elevator boy AE

Lift defekt
(Schild)
♦ Lift out of order

Liftführer, m
♦ lift attendant BE
♦ elevator attendant AE

Liftgebühr, f
♦ lift fee BE
♦ lift charge BE

Lift geht zu allen Stockwerken
Fahrstuhl geht zu allen Stockwerken
Aufzug geht zu allen Stockwerken
♦ elevator operates to all floors AE
♦ lift operates to all floors BE

Liftgesellschaft, f (Ski)
♦ lift company

Lift ist in Betrieb
Fahrstuhl ist in Betrieb
♦ lift is in operation BE
♦ elevator is in operation AE

Liftjunge, m
→ Liftboy

Liftkapazität, f (generell)
♦ elevator capacity AE
♦ lift capacity BE

Liftkapazität, f (Ski)
♦ lift capacity

Liftliste

Liftliste, f
→ Liftverzeichnis
Liftpaß, m
(Ski)
♦ lift pass
Liftpaß erlaubt Ihnen die unbeschränkte Benutzung
aller Lifte
♦ Lift pass gives you the unlimited use of all the
♦ lifts
Liftpaß erwerben
(Ski)
♦ purchase a lift pass
Liftpaß kaufen
(Ski)
♦ buy a lift pass
Liftservice haben
→ Fahrstuhlservice haben
Liftverzeichnis, n
(Ski)
Liftliste, f
♦ lift list
♦ list of lifts
Lift zum Strand, m
♦ elevator serving the beach AE
♦ lift serving the beach BE
Likör, m
♦ liqueur
Likörglas, n
♦ liqueur glass
Likörservice, m
♦ liqueur service
Likörwagen, m
(im Restaurant)
♦ liqueur cart AE
♦ liqueur trolley BE
Liliputaner, m
♦ midget
Limberger, m
→ Lemberger
Limes, m
♦ Limes, the
Limesmuseum, n
♦ Limes Museum, the
Limette, f
→ Limone
Limonade, f
♦ soda pop AE
♦ fizzy drink
♦ lemonade
Limonadenpulver, n
Brausepulver, n
♦ lemonade powder
Limone, f
Limette, f
♦ lime
Limonensaft, m
Limettensaft, m
♦ lime-juice
Limousine, f
♦ limousine
♦ limo
♦ sedan AE
♦ saloon car BE
Limousine mit Chauffeur, f
Limousine mit Fahrer, f
♦ chauffeur-driven limousine
Limousinenbeförderung, f
♦ limousine transportation AE
♦ limousine transport BE

Limousineservice, m
Wagendienst, m
♦ limousine service
♦ limo service coll
Limousineservice vom Flughafen, m
♦ limousine service from the airport
Limousineservice zum Flughafen, m
♦ limousine service to the airport
Limousinetransfer, m
♦ limousine transfer
♦ transfer by limousine
Linde, f
♦ lime
Lindenbaum, m
♦ lime-tree
Lindenblütentee, m
♦ lime blossom tea
Linderung bringen jm
♦ bring curative benefit to s.o.
lineare Abschreibung, f
♦ straight-line depreciation
Lingère, f FR
Wäschefrau, f
Wäschemädchen, n
♦ lingère FR
♦ linen maid
♦ linen keeper
Lingerie, f SCHW
→ Wäscheraum
Lingerieangestellte, f
→ Wäschemädchen
Lingeriemädchen, n SCHW
→ Wäschemädchen
Linienbus, m
♦ scheduled bus
♦ scheduled coach BE
Linienbusdienst, m
Linienbusverbindung f
Linienbusverkehr m
Linienbusservice m
♦ scheduled bus service
♦ scheduled coach service BE
Linienbusservice, m
→ Linienbusdienst
Linienbusverbindung, f
Linienbusdienst, m
♦ scheduled bus connection
♦ scheduled bus service
♦ scheduled coach connection BE
♦ scheduled coach service BE
Linienbusverkehr, m
♦ scheduled bus traffic
♦ scheduled coach traffic BE
♦ scheduled bus service
♦ scheduled coach service BE
Liniendienst, m
♦ scheduled service
regular service
Liniendienst betreiben
♦ operate a scheduled service
Linienfahrpreis, m
Linienflugpreis, m
Linienpreis, m
♦ scheduled fare
Linienflug, m
planmäßiger Flug, m
♦ scheduled flight
Linienflugdienst, m
♦ scheduled air service

Linienfluggesellschaft, f
Linienluftgesellschaft, f
♦ scheduled airline
Linienflugpreis, m
♦ scheduled air fare
Linienflugreiseverkehr, m
Linienflugreisen, n
♦ scheduled air travel
Linienflugschein, m
♦ scheduled air ticket
Linienflugtourismus, m
♦ scheduled airline tourism
♦ scheduled air tourism
Linienflugtourist, m
♦ scheduled airline tourist
♦ scheduled air tourist
Linienflugverkehr, m
♦ scheduled air traffic
Linienflugzeug, n
♦ airliner
Linienjet, m
Liniendüsenflugzeug, n
♦ jetliner
♦ jet airliner
Linienluftgesellschaft, f
→ Linienfluggesellschaft
Linienmaschine, f
→ Linienflugzeug
Linienpassagier, m
♦ scheduled passenger
Linienpauschalreise, f
♦ scheduled package tour
Linienschiff, n
♦ liner
Linienschiffahrtsdienst, m
♦ scheduled shipping service
Linienstrecke, f
Linienroute, f
♦ scheduled route
Linienverbindung nach X, f
♦ scheduled connection with X
♦ scheduled connection to X
Linienverkehr, m
♦ scheduled traffic
regular traffic
linkes Ufer, n (Fluß)
♦ left bank
links essen
♦ eat with one's left hand
links fahren (Auto)
♦ drive on the left
Linkshänder, m
Linkshänderin, f
♦ left-hander
♦ left-handed person
links liegenlassen jn
♦ cold-shoulder s.o.
Linse, f gastr
♦ lentil gastr
Linseneintopf, m
♦ lentil stew
Linsensuppe, f
♦ lentil soup
Lippen lecken (sich)
♦ lick one's lips
Lissabon
♦ Lisbon
Liste, f
Verzeichnis n
♦ list

Liste abrunden
- round up the list

Liste der abreisenden Gäste, f
- departure list

Liste der abreisenden Gäste erstellen
Abreiseliste erstellen
- make out a departure list
- make out a departures list

Liste der abreisenden Gäste zusammenstellen
- compile a departure list

Liste der ankommenden Gäste, f
→ Ankunftsliste

Liste der ankommenden Gäste erstellen
- make out an arrivals list
- make out an arrival list

Liste der ankommenden Gäste zusammenstellen
- compile an arrivals list
- compile an arrival list

Liste der Konferenzteilnehmer f
- list of conference delegates
- list of conference participants

Liste der Konferenzteilnehmer liegt bei der Konferenz aus
- list of conference delegates is available at the conference

Liste der Veranstaltungen abrunden
- round up the list of activities

Liste ergänzen
Verzeichnis ergänzen
- add s.th. to a list
- amend a list

Liste erstellen
Verzeichnis erstellen
- draw up a list
- compile a list
- make out a list

Liste ist endlos
- list is endless

Liste zusammenstellen
Verzeichnis zusammenstellen
Liste erstellen
- make out a list
- compile a list

Litauen
- Lithuania

Litauer, m
- Lithuanian

Litauerin, f
- Lithuanian girl
- Lithuanian woman
- Lithuanian

litauisch, adj
- Lithuanian, adj

Liter, m
- liter *AE*
- litre *BE*

literarische Führung, f
- guided literary tour
- conducted literary tour

literarische Landschaft, f
- literary landscape

literarische Reise, f
- literary tour

Literatencafé, n
- literary cafe *AE*
- literary café *BE*

Literaturfest, n
literarische Party, f
- literary party

Literaturtourismus, m
- literary tourism

Literaturtourist, m
- literary tourist

Literaturwettbewerb, m
literarischer Wettbewerb, m
- literary competition

Literflasche, f
- liter bottle *AE*
- litre bottle *BE*

literweise, adv
- by the liter, adv *AE*
- by the litre, adv *BE*

Litfaßsäule, f
→ Plakatsäule

Litschipflaume, f
Litschi, f
- litchi
- lichee
- lichi
- leechee
- lychee

live aus New York, adv
- live from New York, adv

Live-Band, f
Live-Kapelle, f
- live band

Live-Klaviermusik, f
- live piano music

Live-Musik, f
- live music

Live-Musik jeden Donnerstag abend
- Live music every Thursday night

Live-Musikunterhaltung, f
- live musical entertainment

Live-Orchester, n
- live orchestra

Live-Programm, n
- live program *AE*
- live programme *BE*

Live-Sänger, m
- live singer

Live-Tänzer, m
- live dancer

Live-Tanzmusik, f
- live music for dancing
- live dance music

Live-Theater, n
- live theater *AE*
- live-theatre *BE*

live übertragen etw im Radio
- broadcast s.th. live on radio

Live-Übertragung, f
(TV, Radio)
- live transmission

Live-Unterhaltung, f
- live entertainment

Live-Unterhaltung bieten
- provide live entertainment

Live-Unterhaltung wird dreimal die Woche geboten
Live-Unterhaltung dreimal pro Woche
- live entertainment is provided three times a week
- live entertainment three times a week

Live-Vorstellung, f
Live-Auftritt, m
- live performance

Livland
- Livonia

Livländer, m
- Livonian

Livländerin, f
- Livonian girl
- Livonian woman
- Livonian

livländisch, adj
- Livonian, adj

Livree, f
- livery

livriert, adj
- liveried, adj
- dressed in livery, adj

livrierter Kellner, m
Kellner in Livree, m
- liveried waiter

livriertes Personal, n
Personal in Livree, n
- liveried staff
- liveried personnel

lizensierter Agent, m
- licensed agent
- licenced agent

Lizenz, f
Erlaubnis, f
Konzession, f
- license
- licence

Lizenzabkommen, n
→ Lizenzvereinbarung, f

Lizenzantrag, m
- license application
- licence application
- application for a license
- application for a licence

Lizenzart, f
- license type
- licence type
- type of license
- type of licence

Lizenz ausstellen
Konzession ausstellen
- issue a license
- issue a licence

Lizenz beantragen
- apply for a license
- apply for a licence

Lizenzbedingungen, f pl
Lizenzbestimmungen, f pl
Konzessionsbedingungen, f pl
Konzessionsbestimmungen, f pl
- terms of a license *pl*
- terms of a licence *pl*

Lizenzbehörde, f
- licensing authority
- licencing authority

Lizenz benötigen
Konzession benötigen
- require a license
- require a licence

Lizenzbeschränkung, f
Lizenzauflage, f
- license restriction
- licence restriction

Lizenz besitzen
Lizenz innehaben *form*
Konzession besitzen
- hold a license
- hold a licence

Lizenzdauer, f
Lizenzzeit, f
Konzessionsdauer, f
Konzessionszeit, f

Lizenz einschränken

- period of a license
- period of a licence
- term of a license
- term of a licence

Lizenz einschränken
- Konzession einschränken
- restrict a license
- restrict a licence

Lizenz entziehen
- Konzession entziehen
- remove a license
- remove a licence

Lizenzentzug, m
- Konzessionsentzug, m
- removal of a license
- removal of a licence
- removing a license
- removing a licence

Lizenz erhalten
- Konzession erhalten
- receive a license
- receive a licence

Lizenz erneuern
- → Lizenz verlängern

Lizenzerneuerung, f
- license renewal
- licence renewal
- renewal of a license
- renewal of a licence

Lizenzerträge, m pl
- license income
- licence income
- rights earnings pl

Lizenz erwerben
- Lizenz beschaffen sich
- take out a license
- take out a licence

Lizenz geben jm für etw
- license s.o. for s.th.
- licence s.o. for s.th.

Lizenzgeber, m
- Konzessionsgeber, m
- Konzessionserteiler, m
- licensor
- licencor
- licencer
- licenser

Lizenzgebühr, f
- license fee
- licence fee
- royalty

Lizenzgebühr zahlen
- Konzessionsgebühr zahlen
- pay a license fee
- pay a licence fee

Lizenz gewähren (für etw)
- Lizenz erteilen (für etw)
- Konzession vergeben (für etw)
- grant a license (for s.th.)
- grant a licence (for s.th.)

Lizenzgewährung, f
- grant of a license
- grant of a licence
- granting a license
- granting a licence

Lizenz haben (für etw)
- Konzession haben (für etw)
- have a license (for s.th.)
- have a licence (for s.th.)

lizenziert, adj
- → konzessioniert

Lizenzierung, f
- licensing
- licencing

Lizenzinhaber, m
- license holder
- licence holder
- licensee jur
- licencee jur

Lizenz ist erloschen
- license is expired
- licence is expired
- licence has expired
- license has expired

Lizenz ist gültig
- license is valid
- licence is valid

Lizenz ist in Kraft
- license is in force
- licence is in force

Lizenz ist ungültig
- license is void
- licence is void

Lizenz ist wirksam
- license is effective
- licence is effective

Lizenz läuft aus
- license expires
- licence expires

Lizenznehmer, m
- Konzessionsnehmer, m
- Lizenzträger, m
- licensee
- licencee

Lizenz suspendieren
- Lizenz vorübergehend entziehen
- suspend a license
- suspend a licence

Lizenzträger, m
- → Lizenznehmer

Lizenz übertragen
- Konzession übertragen
- transfer a license
- transfer a licence

Lizenzübertragung, f
- license transfer
- licence transfer
- transfer of a license
- transfer of a licence

Lizenzvereinbarung, f
- Lizenzabkommen, n
- licensing agreement
- licencing agreement

Lizenz vergeben
- grant a license
- grant a licence

Lizenz verlängern
- Lizenz erneuern
- renew a license
- renew a licence

Lizenz verlieren
- lose a license
- lose a licence
- forfeit a license
- forfeit a licence

Lizenz verlustig gehen
- Lizenz verlieren
- Konzession verlieren
- Konzession einbüßen
- forfeit a license
- forfeit a licence

Lizenz versagen
- Lizenz verweigern
- Konzession versagen
- Konzession verweigern
- refuse a license
- refuse a licence

Lizenz verweigern
- → Lizenz versagen

Lizenzwiderruf, m
- license revocation
- licence revocation
- revocation of a license
- revocation of a licence
- cancellation of a licence

Lizenz widerrufen
- Konzession widerrufen
- revoke a license
- revoke a licence

Lkw, m
- LKW, m
- Lastkraftwagen, m
- Lastwagen, m
- lorry BE
- truck AE

Lkw-Parkplatz, m
- LKW-Parkplatz, m
- Lastwagenparkplatz, m
- lorry park BE
- truck parking lot AE

Lobby, f
- Wandelhalle, f
- Halle, f
- lobby

Lobbybar, f
- → Hallenbar

Lobbybereich, m
- lobby area

Loch, n
- hole

Loch, n (flaue Zeit)
- Flaute, f
- trough
- slack period

Loch, n (schlechte Unterkunft)
- dump
- hole

Loch im Magen füllen
- fill a hole in the stomach

Lochtoilette, f
- pit toilet

locken jn nach X
- lure s.o. to X

lockere Atmosphäre, f
- zwanglose Atmosphäre f
- ungezwungene Atmosphäre f
- legere Atmosphäre f
- casual atmosphere

lockerer Vogel, m humor
- loose liver humor

Lockvogelangebot, n
- loss leader

Lodge, f
- lodge

Lodgeaufenthalt, m
- lodge stay
- stay at a lodge

Lodgesafari, f
- lodge safari

Lodgeunterkunft, f
- Lodgeunterbringung, f
- lodge accommodation

Lodgeurlaub, m
◆ lodge vacation *AE*
◆ lodge holiday *BE*
Löffel, m
◆ spoon
Löffelbiskuit, m/n
◆ sponge finger
Löffelchen, n
◆ small spoon
löffeln etw
auslöffeln etw
◆ spoon s.th.
◆ spoon s.th. up
Löffelvoll, m
◆ spoonful
löffelweise, adv
◆ by the spoonful, adv
◆ in spoonfuls, adv
Löffel Zucker, m
◆ spoonful of sugar
Loft, m
(Einzimmeratelierwohnung)
◆ loft *AE*
Loge, f (Portier)
Portierloge, f
◆ lodge
◆ porter's lodge
Loge, f (Theater)
◆ box
Logement, n
→ Beherbergung
Logenkarte, f
(Theater)
◆ box ticket
Logenplatz, m (Theater)
Logensitzplatz, m
Logensitz, m
◆ box seat
Loggia f
◆ loggia
Logierbesuch, m (Aktivität)
Übernachtungsbesuch, m
◆ overnight visit
Logierbesuch, m (Person)
Übernachtungsgast, m
◆ overnight visitor
◆ overnight guest
◆ visitor staying overnight
◆ guest staying overnight
◆ staying guest
Logierbesuch haben
(privat)
◆ have friends to stay
Logieren, n
◆ lodging
logieren bei jm (Untermieter)
◆ lodge at s.o.'s (place)
◆ lodge with s.o.
◆ room with s.o. *AE*
logieren bei jm (wohnen)
→ wohnen bei jm
logieren (bes. privat)
◆ lodge
logieren (generell)
◆ stay
◆ lodge
logieren in einem Hotel
wohnen in einem Hotel
◆ lodge in a hotel
◆ lodge at a hotel

◆ stay in a hotel
◆ stay at a hotel
logieren jn
→ beherbergen jn
logieren unter einem anderen Namen
wohnen unter einem anderen Namen
◆ stay under another name
Logiergast, m
Übernachtungsgast, m
Logisgast, m
Schlafgast, m
◆ overnighter *sl*
◆ overnight visitor
◆ overnight guest
◆ sleeper
◆ house guest
Logiergästeliste, f
Belegungsliste, f
Belegungsverzeichnis, n
◆ sleepers' list
◆ occupancy list
Logierhaus, n
(Mietshaus mit möblierten Zimmern)
◆ rooming house *AE*
◆ lodging house
Logiernacht, f (allgemein) *ÖST/SCHW*
→ Übernachtung
Logiernacht, f (Statistik) *ÖST/SCHW*
Logisnacht, f
Gästenacht, f
◆ sleeper-night
◆ guest-night
Logiernächtekategorie, f
Logisnachtkategorie, f
◆ bed-night category
◆ sleeper-night category
Logiernachtzahl, f
Logisnachtzahl, f
Zahl der Logiernächte, f
Zahl der Logisnächte, f
◆ number of sleeper-nights
◆ number of bed-nights
Logierplatz, m
Logisplatz, m
◆ sleeper space
Logierzimmer, n
→ Gästezimmer
Logierzimmer, n (in Privathaus)
Gästezimmer, n
◆ spare bedroom
◆ spare room
◆ guest room *AE*
◆ guest-room *BE*
Logis, Frühstück und Abendessen, n
◆ lodging, breakfast and dinner
Logis, n (generell)
Unterkunft f
◆ lodging
◆ lodgings *pl*
◆ accommodation
◆ room
◆ rooms *pl*
Logis, n (Schiff)
Back, f
◆ fo'c's'le *BE*
◆ forecastle
Logisabteilung, f
→ Beherbergungsabteilung
Logisangebot, n
→ Beherbergungsangebot

logisbezogen, adj
unterkunftsbezogen, adj
◆ accommodation-related, adj
logisbezogenes Veranstaltungsgeschäft, n
◆ accommodation-related function business
Logisbuch n
◆ arrivals and departures book
Logis finden für die Nacht
→ Quartier finden für die Nacht
Logisgast, m
Logiergast, m
Übernachtungsgast, m
Schlafgast, m
◆ lodging guest *AE*
◆ overnight guest
◆ overnight visitor
◆ overnighter
◆ sleeper
Logisgebühr, f
→ Unterkunftsgebühr
Logisgeld, n
◆ lodging money
Logisherr, m *obs*
Untermieter, m
möblierter Herr, m *obs*
◆ roomer *AE*
◆ lodger
Logiskapazität, f
Logierkapazität, f
◆ sleeper capacity
Logisleiter, m
→ Leiter der Beherbergungsabteilung
Logisnacht, f
→ Logiernacht
Logisnachtkategorie, f
→ Logiernächtekategorie
Logispreis, m
Unterkunftspreis, m
Unterbringungspreis, m
◆ lodging price *AE*
◆ lodging rate *AE*
◆ accommodation price
◆ accommodation rate
Logistikproblem, n
logistisches Problem, n
◆ logistical problem
Logo, n
→ Firmenemblem
Lohnanstieg, m
◆ wages increase
◆ increase in wages
Lohnbuchhalter, m
◆ wages clerk
Lohnbüro, n
◆ wages office
Löhne, m pl
◆ wages *pl*
Löhne für Aushilfen, m pl
◆ extra wages *pl*
lohnend, adj
◆ rewarding, adj
◆ worthwhile, adj
lohnenden Abstecher machen nach X (Umweg)
◆ make a rewarding detour to X
lohnender Abstecher, m (Ausflug)
lohnender Ausflug, m
◆ rewarding side trip *AE*
◆ worthwhile side trip *AE*
◆ rewarding trip
◆ worthwhile trip
◆ rewarding excursion

lohnender Abstecher

lohnender Abstecher, m (Umweg)
- rewarding detour
- worthwhile detour

lohnender Ausflug, m
- rewarding excursion
- rewarding trip
- rewarding outing
- worthwhile excursion
- worthwhile trip

lohnendes Ausflugsziel, n
- rewarding place to visit

Löhne und Gehälter
Löhne (m, pl) und Gehälter (n, pl)
- wages and salaries pl

Lohnkosten, pl
- payroll costs pl
- labor cost AE
- labor costs AE
- labour cost BE
- labour costs BE pl

Lohnkostenkontrolle, f
- payroll control

Lohnkürzung, f
- wage reduction

Lohnsteuer, f
- withholding (wage) tax AE
- payroll tax AE
- PAYE tax BE
- pay-as-you-earn (income) tax BE
- income tax

Lohnsteuerkarte, f
- tax card

Lohnstopp, m
- wage freeze

Lohnsummensteuer, f
- payroll tax

Lohntarif, m
- wage rate
- wage scale

Lohn- und Gehaltsbuchhalter, m
- payroll clerk

Lohn- und Gehaltsliste f
- payroll

Lohn- und Gehaltsstruktur, f
- wage and salary structure

Lohnvorauszahlung, f
- advance wage payment

Lohnvorschuß, m
- wage advance

Loipe, f
(Ski)
- cross-country course
- cross-country (ski) track
- cross-country (ski) trail
- track
- trail

Loire-Schlösser, n pl
- Châteaux of the Loire, the pl

Loiretal, n
- Loire Valley, the

Lok, f coll
Lokomotive, f
- loco coll
- locomotive
- engine

lokal, adj
→ örtlich

Lokal, n (Anwesen)
→ Anwesen

Lokal, n (Gaststätte)
→ Gaststätte

Lokal, n (generell)
- place
- spot coll

Lokal, n (Restaurant)
→ Restaurant

Lokal, n (Versammlungsraum)
→ Versammlungsraum

Lokalbeschreibung, f
- description of the premises

lokale Schau, f
Lokalschau, f
- local show

Lokal führen
- run a place
- run the place

Lokalgröße, f
Größe eines Lokals, f
- size of the premises

Lokal hat keine Schankerlaubnis
(für alkoholische Getränke)
- place is unlicensed
- place is unlicenced

Lokalität, f
Örtlichkeit, f
- locality
- rooms pl
- premises pl

Lokalkolorit, n
- local color AE
- local colour BE

Lokal pachten
- lease the premises

Lokal räumen
- vacate the premises

Lokal verpachten
- lease the premises

Lokführer, m
Lokomotivführer, m
- engine-driver BE
- engineer

Lokomotive, f
Lok, f coll
- engine
- locomotive
- loco coll

Lokomotivführer, m
Lokführer, m
- engineer AE
- engine-driver BE

Lokus, m fam
→ Klo, Toilette

Lombardei, f
- Lombardy

Londoner Hotel, n
- London hotel

Longdrink, m
(über 5 cl)
- long drink

Longdrinkbar, f
- long-drink bar
- long-drinks bar

Longdrinkglas, n
- long-drink glass

Longdrinkrezept, n
- long-drink recipe

Lorbeerbaum, m
- bay tree
- laurel tree

Lorbeerblatt, n
Lorbeer, m
- bay leaf

Loreley, f
(Felsen am Rhein)
Lorelei, f
- Lorelei, the
- Lorelei Rock, the

Los, n (Tombola)
→ Tombolalos

Löscheimer, m
- fire bucket

löschen (Schiff)
entladen
- unship

Löschgerät, n
→ Feuerlöscher

Löschung, f (Schiff)
Löschen, n
- unshipment
- unshipping

losfahren nach Hause
- head for home

losfahren nach Norden
- head north

losfahren nach Osten
- head east

losfahren nach Süden
- head south

losfahren nach Westen
- head west

losfahren nach X
Kurs nehmen auf X
- head for X

losfahren (Person)
aufbrechen
starten
- start

losfahren zu einem Campingurlaub
- go off to a camping vacation AE
- go off to a camping holiday BE

losgehen
(zu Fuß)
- set off
- set off on foot

Los kaufen
→ Tombolalos kaufen

losradeln nach X
losfahren nach X
- cycle off to X

lostippeln (nach X)
- tramp off (to X)

lostrudeln
loszuckeln inform
- trundle off

Lösung eines Umweltproblems, f
- solution to an environmental problem

Los verkaufen
Tombolalos verkaufen
- sell a raffle ticket

loswerden etw
- get rid of s.th.

loswerden jn
- get rid of s.o.

Los ziehen
- draw a ticket

losziehen (aufbrechen)
aufbrechen
- set out

Lothringen
(Region)
- Lorraine

Lothringer, m
- Lorrainer

Lothringerart, adv *gastr*
  nach Lothringerart, adv *gastr*
  ♦ **Lorraine style, adv** *gastr*
Lothringerin, f
  ♦ **Lorrainese girl**
  ♦ **Lorrainese woman**
lothringisch, adj
  ♦ **Lorrainese, adj**
Lötschenpaß, m
  ♦ **Lötschen Pass, the**
Lotse, m
  ♦ **pilot**
Lotsengebühr, f
  ♦ **pilotage**
lotsen (jn)
  ♦ **pilot (s.o.)**
Lotterieannahmestelle, f
  ♦ **lottery office**
Lounge, f
  ♦ **lounge**
Loungebar, f (in der Lounge)
  Salonbar, f
  Clubbar, f
  ♦ **lounge bar**
Loungebar, f (in Pub)
  (Gegensatz zur Public Bar)
  ♦ **lounge bar** BE
Loungebedienung, f
  → Loungeservice
Loungebedienungspersonal, n
  ♦ **lounge waiting staff**
  ♦ **lounge waiting personnel**
Loungebereich, m
  ♦ **lounge area**
Loungefläche, f
  ♦ **lounge space**
  ♦ **lounge area**
Loungekellner, m
  ♦ **lounge waiter**
Loungekellnerin, f
  ♦ **lounge waitress**
Loungepianist, m
  Salonpianist, m
  ♦ **lounge pianist**
Loungeservice, m
  Loungebedienung, f
  Loungedienst, m
  ♦ **lounge service**
LP, f
  Langspielplatte, f
  ♦ **LP**
  ♦ **long-playing record**
Lübecker Bucht, f
  ♦ **Lübeck Bay, the**
  Bay of Lübeck, the
Luft, f
  ♦ **air**
Luftaufnahme, f
  ♦ **aerial photograph**
  ♦ **aerial photo**
Luftbad, n
  ♦ **air bath**
Luftballon, m
  → Ballon
Luftbeförderung, f
  ♦ **air carriage**
  ♦ **air transport(ation)**
  ♦ **air conveyance**
  ♦ **transportation by air** AE
  ♦ **transport by air** BE

Luftbild, n
  ♦ **aerial view**
  ♦ **aerial photograph**
Luftbrücke, f
  ♦ **airlift**
lüften etw
  ♦ **air s.th.**
  ♦ **ventilate s.th.**
Luftfahrt, f
  ♦ **aviation**
Luftfahrtausstellung, f
  ♦ **aviation exposition**
  ♦ **aviation expo**
Luftfahrtgeschichte, f
  ♦ **aviation history**
Luftfahrtgesellschft, f
  → Fluggesellschaft
Luftfahrtindustrie, f
  ♦ **aviation industry**
Luftfahrtmuseum, n
  ♦ **aviation museum**
Luftfahrtschule, f
  ♦ **aviation school**
Luftfahrtvereinbarung, f
  ♦ **aviation agreement**
Luftfahrzeug, n
  ♦ **aircraft**
  ♦ craft
Luftfederung, f
  ♦ **air suspension**
Luftfracht, f
  ♦ **air cargo**
  ♦ air freight
Luftfrachtdienst, m
  ♦ **air cargo service**
Luftfrachter, m
  ♦ **airfreighter**
Luftfrachtgeschäft, n
  ♦ **air cargo business**
  ♦ air freight business
luftgetrocknet, adj
  ♦ **air-dried, adj**
luftgetrockneter Schinken, m
  ♦ **air-dried ham**
Luftgewehr, n
  ♦ **air rifle**
luftig, adj
  ♦ **airy, adj**
luftiges Zimmer, n
  ♦ **airy room**
Luftkissen, n
  ♦ **air cushion**
Luftkissenboot, n
  ♦ **hovercraft**
Luftkissenboot befördert Passagiere und Autos
  ♦ **hovercraft carries passengers and cars**
  ♦ hovercraft transports passengers and cars
Luftkissenbootfahrt, f
  ♦ **hovercraft flight**
Luftkissenboothafen, m
  Hafen für Luftkissenboote, m
  ♦ **hoverport**
Luftkissenbootterminal, m/n
  ♦ **hovercraft terminal**
Luftkissenbootüberfahrt, f
  ♦ **hovercraft crossing**
Luftkissenfahrzeug, n
  ♦ **air-cushion vehicle**
  ♦ ACV
luftkrank, adj
  ♦ **airsick, adj**

Luftkrankheit, f
  ♦ **airsickness**
Luftkur, f
  ♦ **climate cure**
  ♦ climatic cure
Luftkurort, m
  ♦ **climatic resort**
  ♦ climatic health resort
Luftmatratze, f
  ♦ **airmattress** AE
  ♦ **air mattress** BE
  ♦ inflatable mattress
  ♦ lilo BE
  ♦ air-bed BE
Luftpassagier, m
  Flugpassagier, m
  Fluggast, m
  ♦ **air passenger**
  ♦ aircraft passenger
Luftpauschalreise, f
  ♦ **air-inclusive tour**
Luftpauschalreisemarkt, m
  ♦ **air-inclusive tour market**
Luftpauschalreiseveranstalter, m
  ♦ **air-inclusive tour operator**
Luftpost, f
  ♦ **airmail**
Luftpostbrief, m
  ♦ **air letter**
Luftqualität, f
  ♦ **air quality**
Lufttransportgesellschaft, f
  ♦ **air carrier**
Luftraum, m
  ♦ **airspace**
Luftreise, f
  ♦ **air journey**
  ♦ journey by air
Luftreisedienst, m
  Flugreisedienst, m
  ♦ **air passenger service**
Luftreiseveranstalter, m
  → Flugreiseveranstalter
Luftschau, f
  Flugschau, f
  ♦ **air show**
Luftschiff, n
  ♦ **airship**
Luftschlange, f
  ♦ **streamer**
Luft-See-Arrangement, n
  ♦ **air-sea arrangement**
Luft-Seereise, f
  ♦ **air-sea voyage**
Luftseilbahn, f
  Seilschwebebahn, f
  ♦ **aerial cableway**
Luftsprudelbad, n
  → Whirlpool
Lufttaxi, n
  Flugtaxi, n
  ♦ **air taxi**
Lufttaxidienst, m
  Lufttaxiservice, m
  Flugtaxidienst, m
  Flugtaxiservice, m
  ♦ **air-taxi service**
Lufttemperatur, f
  ♦ **air temperature**
Lufttemperatur regeln
  ♦ **control the air temperature**

Lüftung

Lüftung, f
 ♦ ventilation
Lüftungsanlage, f
 ♦ ventilation system
Luftverbesserer, m
 ♦ air-freshener
 ♦ air-purifier
Luftverbindung, f
 ♦ air link
 ♦ air connection
Luftverkehr, m
 ♦ air traffic
Luftverkehrsabkommen, n
 ♦ air service agreement
 ♦ ASA
Luftverkehrsaufkommen, n
 ♦ air traffic volume
 volume of air traffic
Luftverkehrsbestimmungen, f pl
 ♦ air-traffic regulations pl
 ♦ air-traffic rules pl
Luft verschmutzen
 Luft verpesten
 ♦ pollute the air
Luftverschmutzung, f
 Luftverunreinigung, f
 ♦ air pollution
Luganer See m
 ♦ Lake Lugano
Lügenmärchen, n
 Lügengeschichte, f (bes. von Reisenden)
 ♦ traveler's tale AE
 ♦ traveller's tale BE
lukrative Strecke, f
 lukrative Route, f
 ♦ lucrative route
lukullisch, adj
 ♦ mouth-watering, adj
 ♦ Lucullan, adj
 ♦ Lucullean, adj
 ♦ Lucullian, adj
lukullische Genüsse, m pl
 ♦ mouth-watering delicacies pl
 ♦ Lucullan delicacies pl
lukullisches Gericht, n
 ♦ mouth-watering dish
lukullisches Mahl, n
 lukullisches Essen, n
 ♦ mouth-watering meal
 ♦ gourmet meal
 ♦ Lucullan meal
lukullisches Menü, n
 ♦ mouth-watering menu
lumpiges Trinkgeld, n
 ♦ measly tip
Lunch, m AE
 (leichter Imbiß zu jeder Tageszeit)
 ♦ lunch AE
Lunch, m (Mittagessen)
 → Mittagessen
Lunchbox, f
 (tragbare Box)
 ♦ lunch box
Lunchbüfett, n
 → Mittagsbüfett
Lunchmenü, n
 → Mittagsmenü
Lunchpaket, n
 ♦ box lunch AE
 ♦ boxed lunch AE
 ♦ packed lunch BE

 ♦ lunch packet
 ♦ food pack
Lunchpaketdienst, m
 → Lunchpaketservice
Lunchpaketservice, m
 Lunchpaketdienst, m
 ♦ packed-lunch service BE
 ♦ box-lunch service BE
Lunchservice, m
 → Mittagsservice
Lunchtheke, f
 ♦ lunch counter
Lunchzeit, f
 → Mittagessenzeit
Lüneburger Heide, f
 (Region)
 ♦ Lüneburg Heath
Lustbarkeit, f
 ♦ cakes and ale
Lüster, m
 Leuchter, m
 ♦ chandelier
Lustgarten, m
 ♦ pleasure garden
Lust haben
 ♦ care to do
Lust haben auf etw (Essen)
 ♦ fancy s.th.
 ♦ have a taste for s.th.
lustige Gesellschaft, f
 ♦ merry party
lustigen Abend haben
 sich einen lustigen Abend machen
 ♦ have a spree coll
lustigen Abend sich machen
 (mit großen Geldausgaben)
 vergnügten Abend sich machen
 ausgehen
 ♦ go on a spree coll
 ♦ go out on a spree coll
lustiger Abend, m
 (mit großen Geldausgaben)
 vergnügter Abend m
 Zechgelage n
 ♦ spree coll
lustige Witwe, f
 ♦ merry widow
lustlos essen
 ♦ not enjoy one's meal
Lustpark, m
 Vergnügungspark, m
 ♦ pleasure park
Lustprinzip, n
 ♦ pleasure principle
Lustreise, f
 → Vergnügungsreise
Lustschloß, n
 ♦ pleasure palace
Lutherkirche, f
 ♦ Luther Church, the
Lutscher, m
 ♦ lollipop
 ♦ lolly coll
Luxemburg
 ♦ Luxemburg
 ♦ Luxembourg
Luxemburger, m
 Luxemburgerin, f
 ♦ Luxemburger
 ♦ Luxembourger

luxemburgisch, adj
 ♦ Luxemburg, adj
 ♦ Luxembourg, adj
 ♦ Luxemburgian, adj
 ♦ Luxembourgian, adj
 ♦ from Luxemb(o)urg
luxemburgisches Dorf, n
 ♦ Luxemburg village
 ♦ Luxembourg village
luxuriös, adj
 ♦ luxurious, adj
 ♦ deluxe, adj AE
 ♦ ritzy, adj coll
luxuriös ausgestattet, adj
 (Unterkunft)
 ♦ luxuriously appointed, adj
luxuriös ausgestattetes Zimmer n
 ♦ luxuriously appointed room
luxuriöse Atmosphäre, f
 ♦ luxurious atmosphere
luxuriöse Ausstattung, f
 ♦ luxurious equipment
luxuriös eingerichtet, adj
 ♦ furnished in deluxe style, adj AE
 ♦ luxuriously furnished, adj
 ♦ luxuriously appointed, adj
luxuriöses Ambiente, n
 ♦ luxurious ambience
 ♦ luxurious ambiance
luxuriöses Appartement n
 ♦ luxurious apartment
luxuriöses Hotel, n
 ♦ luxurious hotel
luxuriöses Leben, n
 ♦ luxurious life
 ♦ life in luxury
luxuriöses Restaurant, n
 ♦ luxurious restaurant
luxuriöses Zimmer n
 ♦ luxurious room
luxuriöse Umgebung, f
 ♦ luxurious surroundings pl
luxuriöse Unterkunft, f
 ♦ luxurious accommodation
 ♦ luxurious lodging AE
luxuriöse Villa, f
 ♦ luxurious villa
luxuriöse Wohnung, f
 ♦ luxurious apartment AE
 ♦ luxurious flat BE
luxuriös gedeckter Tisch, m
 ♦ luxuriously laid table
 ♦ table spread with luxury
luxuriös möbliert, adj
 ♦ luxuriously furnished, adj
 ♦ furnished in deluxe style, adj AE
luxuriös möbliertes Zimmer n
 ♦ luxuriously furnished room
Luxus, m
 ♦ luxury
Luxus an Bord, m
 ♦ luxury on board
Luxusanlage, f
 Luxuskomplex, m
 ♦ deluxe complex AE
 ♦ luxury complex
Luxusappartement, n
 ♦ deluxe apartment AE
 ♦ luxury apartment

Luxusappartementsuite, f
- deluxe apartment suite *AE*
- luxury apartment suite

Luxusappartementzimmer, n
- deluxe apartment room *AE*
- luxury apartment room

Luxusartikel, m
- deluxe article *AE*
- luxury article
- deluxe item *AE*
- luxury item

Luxusausrüstung, f
Luxusausstattung, f
- deluxe equipment *AE*
- luxury equipment

Luxusauto, n
- deluxe car *AE*
- luxury car

Luxusautomobil, n
- deluxe automobile *AE*
- luxury automobile

Luxusbad, n (Bad)
- deluxe bath *AE*
- luxury bath

Luxusbad, n (Schwimmbad)
Luxusbecken, n
- deluxe pool *AE*
- luxury pool

Luxusbadezimmer, n
- deluxe bathroom *AE*
- luxury bathroom

Luxusbar, f
- deluxe bar *AE*
- luxury bar

Luxusbauernhaus, n
- deluxe farmhouse *AE*
- luxury farmhouse

Luxusbecken, n
Luxusbad, n
- luxury pool
- deluxe pool *AE*

Luxusbetrieb, m
- deluxe establishment *AE*
- luxury establishment

Luxusbett n
- deluxe bed *AE*
- luxury bed

Luxusbleibe, f *humor*
→ Luxusunterkunft, Luxushotel

Luxusbungalow, m
- deluxe bungalow *AE*
- luxury bungalow

Luxusbus, m
- deluxe bus *AE*
- luxury bus
- luxury coach *BE*

Luxusbusreise, f
- deluxe bus tour *AE*
- luxury bus tour
- luxury coach tour *BE*

Luxuscamping, n
- deluxe camping *AE*
- luxury camping

Luxuscampingplatz, m
- deluxe campsite *AE*
- deluxe campground *AE*
- luxury campsite
- luxury camping ground *BE*
- luxury camping site *BE*

Luxuscampingurlaub, m
- deluxe camping vacation *AE*
- luxury camping holiday *BE*

Luxuscaravan, m
Luxuswohnwagen, m
- luxury caravan *BE*
- deluxe trailer *AE*
- luxury trailer *AE*

Luxuschalet, n
- deluxe chalet *AE*
- luxury chalet

Luxuscottage, f
- deluxe cottage *AE*
- luxury cottage

Luxusdampfer, m
- luxury liner

Luxusdoppelbett, n
- deluxe double bed *AE*
- luxury double bed

Luxusdoppelzimmer, n
- deluxe double room *AE*
- luxury double room

Luxuseigentumsvilla, f
- freehold deluxe villa *AE*
- freehold luxury villa

Luxus eines Urlaubs sich leisten
Luxus eines Urlaubs sich leisten können
- afford the luxury of a vacation *AE*
- afford the luxury of a holiday *BE*

Luxuseinrichtung, f (Fazilität)
- deluxe facility *AE*
- luxury facility

Luxuseinrichtung, f (Mobiliar)
- deluxe furniture *AE sg*
- deluxe furnishings *AE pl*
- luxury furniture *sg*
- luxury furnishings *pl*

Luxuseinzelbett n
- deluxe single bed *AE*
- luxury single bed

Luxuseinzelzimmer, n
- deluxe single room *AE*
- luxury single room

Luxusfahrt, f
- deluxe trip *AE*
- luxury trip

Luxusfamilienhaus, n
- deluxe family home *AE*
- deluxe family house *AE*
- luxury family home
- luxury family house

Luxusferienanlage, f
Luxusferienkomplex, m
- deluxe vacation complex *AE*
- luxury holiday complex *BE*

Luxusferienappartement, n
Luxusurlaubsappartement n
- deluxe vacation apartment *AE*
- luxury holiday apartment *BE*

Luxusferiencaravan, m
Luxusferienwohnwagen, m
Luxusurlaubscaravan, m
Luxusurlaubswohnwagen, m
- luxury holiday caravan *BE*
- luxury vacation trailer *AE*
- deluxe vacation trailer *AE*

Luxusferienhaus, n
- deluxe vacation home *AE*
- deluxe vacation house *AE*
- luxury holiday home *BE*
- luxury holiday house *BE*

Luxusferienort, m
Luxusurlaubsort, m
- luxury holiday resort *BE*
- deluxe vacation resort *AE*
- deluxe resort *AE*
- luxury resort

Luxusferienwohnung, f
Luxusurlaubswohnung, f
- luxury holiday flat *BE*
- deluxe vacation apartment *AE*

Luxusfernreisebus, m
- deluxe long-distance tour bus *AE*
- deluxe long-distance touring bus *AE*
- luxury long-distance touring coach *BE*

Luxusflußschiff, n
- deluxe riverboat *AE*
- luxury riverboat

Luxusfrühstück, n
- deluxe breakfast *AE*
- luxury breakfast

Luxusgästezimmer, n
Luxusgastzimmer, n
- deluxe guest room *AE*
- luxury guest room

Luxusgegenstand, m
- luxury

Luxus genießen
- enjoy luxuries

Luxusgeschäft, n
- deluxe store *AE*
- luxury shop *BE*

Luxusgüter, n pl
- luxury goods *pl*
- luxuries *pl*

Luxushauptschlafzimmer, n
- deluxe master bedroom *AE*
- luxury master bedroom *BE*

Luxushaus, n
- deluxe house *AE*
- deluxe home *AE*
- luxury house
- luxury home

Luxusherberge, f *humor*
- deluxe hostelry *AE*
- luxury hostelry

Luxushotel, n
(gewöhnlich drei Sterne)
- deluxe hotel *AE*
- luxury hotel

Luxushotelferienort, m
Luxushotelurlaubsort, m
Luxushotelferienanlage, f
- deluxe hotel resort *AE*
- luxury hotel resort

Luxushotellerie, f
- deluxe hotel trade *AE*
- deluxe hotel industry *AE*
- deluxe hotel business *AE*
- luxury hotel trade
- luxury hotel industry

Luxushotel mit drei Sternen, n
Drei-Sterne-Luxushotel, n
- three-star luxury hotel
- three-star deluxe hotel *AE*

Luxushotel mit fünf Sternen, n
Fünf-Sterne-Luxushotel, n
- five-star luxury hotel
- five-star deluxe hotel *AE*

Luxushotel mit vier Sternen, n
Vier-Sterne-Luxushotel, n

Luxushotel mit zwei Sternen

- four-star luxury hotel
- four-star deluxe hotel AE

Luxushotel mit zwei Sternen, n
- two-star luxury hotel
- two-star deluxe hotel

Luxushotelzimmer, n
- deluxe hotel room AE
- luxury hotel room

Luxusimmobilie, f
Luxusanwesen, n
- luxury property
- deluxe property AE

Luxusjacht, f
- deluxe yacht AE
- luxury yacht

Luxuskabine, f
- deluxe cabin AE
- luxury cabin
- state cabin
- stateroom

Luxuskategorie, f
- luxury category
- deluxe category AE

Luxusklasse, f
- deluxe class AE
- luxury class

Luxusklassehotel, n
Hotel der Luxusklasse, n
- deluxe-class hotel AE
- luxury-class hotel

Luxuskleinwohnung, f
kleine Luxuswohnung, f
- small deluxe apartment AE
- small luxury flat BE
- luxury flatlet BE

Luxuskomplex, m
→ Luxusanlage

Luxuskost, f
- luxury fare

Luxuskreuzfahrt, f
- deluxe cruise AE
- luxury cruise

Luxuskreuzfahrtschiff, n
- deluxe cruise ship AE
- deluxe cruise liner AE
- luxury cruise ship
- luxury cruise liner

Luxusküche, f (Raum)
- deluxe kitchen AE
- luxury kitchen

Luxuskurzurlaub, m
- deluxe short vacation AE
- luxury short break holiday BE
- luxury short break

Luxusleben, n
- life of luxury
- luxury life
- high life

Luxusleben führen
- live a life of luxury
- lead a life of luxury
- live high

Luxus leisten können sich
- be able to afford luxury
- can afford luxury

Luxus leisten sich
- afford luxury

Luxusliner, m
- deluxe liner AE
- luxury liner

Luxuslodge, f
- deluxe lodge AE
- luxury lodge

Luxusmodell, n
- deluxe model AE
- luxury model

Luxusnest, n sl
(Haus)
- luxury pad BE sl

Luxusort, m
Luxusferienort, m
Luxusurlaubsort, m
- deluxe resort AE
- luxury resort

Luxuspenthouse, n
- deluxe penthouse AE
- luxury penthouse

Luxuspenthousesuite, f
- deluxe penthouse suite AE
- luxury penthouse suite

Luxuspenthousewohnung, f
- deluxe penthouse apartment AE
- luxury penthouse flat BE

Luxusplatz, m (Camping)
- deluxe site AE
- luxury site

Luxusreise, f
- deluxe journey AE
- deluxe trip AE
- deluxe tour AE
- luxury journey
- luxury trip

Luxusreisecaravan, m
Luxusreisewohnwagen, m
- luxury touring caravan BE
- luxury tourer BE coll
- deluxe travel trailer AE

Luxusreisen, n
Luxusreiseverkehr, m
- deluxe travel AE
- luxury travel

Luxusreisender, m
- deluxe traveler AE
- luxury traveler AE
- luxury traveller BE

Luxusreisewohnwagen, m
Luxusreisecaravan, m
- deluxe travel trailer AE
- luxury touring caravan BE
- luxury tourer BE coll

Luxusrestaurant, n
- deluxe restaurant AE
- luxury restaurant

Luxusschiff, n
- deluxe ship AE
- luxury ship

Luxusschlafzimmer, n
- deluxe bedroom AE
- luxury bedroom

Luxusschwimmbad, n
- deluxe swimming pool AE
- deluxe pool AE
- luxury swimming pool
- luxury swimming-pool BE
- luxury pool

Luxussegment, n
- luxury segment
- deluxe segment AE

Luxusselbstverpflegungshaus, n
Luxusselbstversorgungshaus, n
- deluxe self-catering house AE
- luxury self-catering house

Luxusstandard, m
- deluxe standard AE
- luxury standard

Luxussteuer, f
- luxury tax

Luxusstudio, n
- deluxe studio AE
- luxury studio

Luxusstudiozimmer, n
- deluxe studio room AE
- luxury studio room

Luxus suchen
- look for luxury

Luxussuite, f
- deluxe suite AE
- luxury suite

Luxusterrasse, f
- deluxe terrace AE
- deluxe patio AE
- luxury terrace
- luxury patio

Luxustoilette, f
- deluxe toilet AE
- luxury toilet

Luxus und Komfort, m
- luxury and comfort

Luxus und Komfort anbieten
- offer luxury and comfort

Luxus und Komfort bieten
- provide luxury and comfort

Luxusunterkunft, f
- deluxe accommodation AE
- luxury accommodation

Luxusurlaub, m
- deluxe vacation AE
- luxury vacation AE
- luxury holiday BE

Luxusurlaubsappartement n
→ Luxusferienappartement

Luxusurlaubshaus, n
Luxusferienhaus, n
- luxury holiday home BE
- luxury holiday house BE
- deluxe vacation home AE
- deluxe vacation house AE

Luxusurlaubsort, m
Luxusferienort m
- deluxe vacation resort AE
- luxury holiday resort BE
- deluxe resort AE
- luxury resort

Luxusurlaubswohnung f
→ Luxusferienappartement

Luxusurlaubswohnwagen, m
Luxusurlaubscaravan, m
Luxusferienwohnwagen, m
Luxusferiencaravan, m
- deluxe vacation trailer AE
- luxury vacation trailer AE
- luxury holiday caravan BE

Luxusvilla, f
- deluxe villa AE
- luxury villa

Luxuswagen, m
Luxusauto, n
- luxury car
- deluxe car AE

478

Luxus-WC, n
- ◆ deluxe WC *AE*
- ◆ luxury WC

Luxuswochenende, n
- ◆ deluxe weekend *AE*
- ◆ luxury weekend

Luxuswohnung, f
- ◆ **luxury flat** *BE*
- ◆ deluxe apartment *AE*

Luxuswohnung mit Bedienung, f
- ◆ deluxe service apartment *AE*
- ◆ luxury service flat *BE*

Luxuswohnwagen, m
  Luxuscaravan, m
- ◆ deluxe trailer *AE*
- ◆ luxury trailer *AE*
- ◆ luxury caravan *BE*

Luxuszelt, n
- ◆ deluxe tent *AE*
- ◆ luxury tent

Luxuszimmer, n
- ◆ deluxe room *AE*
- ◆ luxury room

Luxuszug, m
- ◆ deluxe train *AE*
- ◆ luxury train

Luxuszweibettzimmer, n (generell)
- ◆ deluxe two-bedded room *AE*
- ◆ luxury two-bedded room

Luxuszweibettzimmer, n (zwei Einzelbetten)
- ◆ deluxe twin-bedded room *AE*
- ◆ deluxe twin room *AE*
- ◆ luxury twin-bedded room
- ◆ luxury twin room

LVA, n
  Landesverkehrsamt, n
- ◆ **NTB**
- ◆ national tourist board

Lymphdrainage, f
- ◆ **lymph drainage**

Lyonerart, adv *gastr*
  nach Lyonerart, adv *gastr*
- ◆ **Lyon style, adv** *gastr*

M

machbar, adj
→ durchführbar
Machen Sie uns das Vergnügen und seien Sie unser
Gast beim Abendessen
♦ Oblige us with your company at dinner
Mach-mit-Urlaub, m
♦ join-in vacation *AE*
♦ join-in holiday *BE*
Madagaskar
♦ Madagascar
Madagasse, m
♦ Madagascan
Madagassin, f
♦ Madagascan girl
♦ Madagascan woman
♦ Madagascan
madagassisch, adj
♦ Madagascan, adj
Mädchen, n (generell)
♦ girl
Mädchen, n (Zimmermädchen)
♦ maid
Mädchen für alles, n
♦ general servant
♦ Girl Friday *humor*
♦ cook-general *BE*
♦ maid of all service *iron*
♦ factotum *coll*
Mädchenname, m
(Geburtsname)
♦ maiden name
Mädchenzimmer, n (Dienstmädchen)
♦ maid's room
♦ servant's room
Mädchenzimmer, n (generell)
♦ girl's room
♦ girls' room
Mädchenzimmer, n pl (Dienstmädchen)
♦ servants' quarters *pl*
Madeira
♦ Madeira
Madeirawein, m
Madeira, m
♦ Madeira wine
♦ Madeira
Madera
→ Madeira
Magazin, n
→ Lager
Magazinpersonal, n
→ Lagerpersonal
Magazinverwalter, m
→ Lagerist, Lagerverwalter
Magen, m
♦ stomach
♦ breadbasket *AE sl*

Magenbeschwerden, f pl
♦ stomach trouble
♦ gastric trouble
♦ gastric disorder
Magenbitter, m
(Getränk)
♦ bitters *pl*
♦ bitter cordial
Magenentzündung, f
→ Gastritis
Magenfahrplan, m
♦ cuisine timetable
Magen knurrt (vor Hunger)
♦ stomach is rumbling (with hunger)
Magenkrampf, m
♦ stomach cramp
Magenschmerzen, m pl
Magenweh, n
♦ stomach pains *pl*
♦ stomach ache *AE*
♦ stomach-ache *BE*
Magen tut mir weh
♦ stomach aches
♦ my stomach aches
Magen überladen
♦ overload one's stomach
♦ overeat
Magen verdorben haben (sich)
♦ have an upset stomach
Magenverstimmung, f
♦ indigestion
♦ stomach upset
Magenverstimmung bekommen
♦ get a stomach upset
Magenweh, n
Magenschmerzen, m pl
♦ stomach ache *AE*
♦ stomach-ache *BE*
♦ stomach pains *pl*
magere Kost, f (fettarm)
fettarme Kost, f
♦ low-fat fare
magere Kost, f (nicht reichlich)
♦ meagre diet
mageres Fleisch, n
♦ lean meat
Magermilch, f
entrahmte Milch, f
♦ skimmed milk
♦ skim milk *AE*
Mahagonimöbel, n pl
♦ mahogany furniture *pl*
Mahagonitisch, m
♦ mahogany table
mähen
♦ mow

Mahl, n *form*
Mahlzeit, f
♦ repast *form*
Mahl abrunden (mit etw)
Mahlzeit abrunden (mit etw)
Essen abrunden (mit etw)
♦ round off a meal (with s.th.)
mahlen etw
♦ grind s.th.
Mahlzeit!
♦ Afternoon!
Mahlzeit, f
Essen, n
Mahl, n *form*
♦ meal
Mahlzeit an Bord, f
Essen an Bord, n
♦ meal on board
Mahlzeit auslassen
Essen auslassen
♦ skip a meal
♦ not take a meal
Mahlzeit beenden
Mahl beenden
Essen beenden
♦ finish one's meal
♦ finish a meal
Mahlzeit besteht aus etw
Essen besteht aus etw
♦ meal is composed of s.th.
Mahlzeit bestellen
→ Essen bestellen
Mahlzeit einnehmen
♦ take a meal
♦ have a meal
♦ take a repast *form*
Mahlzeit einnehmen auf dem Zimmer
auf dem Zimmer essen
auf dem Zimmer speisen
♦ take a meal in one's room
Mahlzeit einnehmen in einem Hotel
♦ have a meal at a hotel
♦ have a meal in a hotel
Mahlzeitenart f
♦ meal type
♦ type of meal
Mahlzeiten erfolgen mit Selbstbedienung
♦ meals are self-service style
Mahlzeitengutschein, m
→ Essengutschein
Mahlzeitenschnellservice, m
♦ quick meal service
Mahlzeiten von mittags bis Mitternacht, f pl
♦ meals from noon to midnight *pl*
Mahlzeiten werden auf dem Teller serviert
♦ meals are served plated
Mahlzeiten werden berechnet wie eingenommen
→ Mahlzeiten werden nach Verzehr berechnet

Mahlzeiten werden nach Verzehr berechnet
  ♦ meals are charged as taken
Mahlzeit essen
  ♦ eat a meal
Mahlzeit genießen
  → Essen genießen
Mahlzeit herstellen
  Essen herstellen
  ♦ produce a meal
Mahlzeit im Freien, f
  Essen im Freien, n
  ♦ alfresco meal
Mahlzeit improvisieren
  Essen improvisieren
  ♦ knock up a meal
  ♦ improvise a meal
Mahlzeit ist frisch gekocht
  ♦ meal is freshly cooked
Mahlzeit ist reichlich
  Essen ist reichlich
  ♦ meal is copious
Mahlzeit komponieren
  ♦ compose a meal
Mahlzeit mit mehreren Gängen, f
  → Essen mit mehreren Gängen
Mahlzeit nach der Karte, f
  → A-la-carte-Mahlzeit
Mahlzeit servieren im Freien
  Essen im Freien servieren
  ♦ serve a meal alfresco
Mahlzeit verzehren
  → Essen verzehren
Mahl zubereiten
  → Essen zubereiten
Mahl zum festen Preis, n
  Essen zum festen Preis, n
  ♦ meal at (a) fixed price
  ♦ fixed-price meal
Mahnmal, n
  Gedenkstätte, f
  ♦ memorial
Mahnschreiben, n
  (dringendes)
  ♦ dunning letter
  ♦ reminder
Mahnung, f
  Zahlungserinnerung, f
  ♦ reminder
Mähre, m
  ♦ Moravian
Mähren
  (Region)
  ♦ Moravia
mährisch, adj
  ♦ Moravian, adj
Mahut, m
  Elefantenführer, m
  ♦ mahout
Mai, m
  ♦ May
Maiauslastung, f
  Auslastung im Mai, f
  ♦ May load factor
  ♦ load factor in May
Maibaum, m
  ♦ maypole
Maibelegung, f
  Maiauslastung, f
  ♦ May occupancy
  ♦ occupancy in May

Maibowle, f
  ♦ May wine
Maifeier, f
  (am 1. Mai)
  ♦ May Day celebration
  ♦ May Day celebrations pl
Maifeiertag, m
  (am 1. Mai)
  ♦ May Bank Holiday BE
  ♦ May Day
Maiferien, pl
  Maiurlaub, m
  ♦ May holiday BE
  ♦ May vacation AE
Maifest, n
  (am 1. Mai)
  ♦ May Day festival
Maikundgebung, f
  (am 1. Mai)
  ♦ May Day rally
Mailänderart, adv gastr
  nach Mailänderart, adv gastr
  ♦ Milanese style, adv gastr
Mailing, n
  ♦ mailing
Maimarkt, m
  ♦ May market
Main-courante, f FR
  → Hoteljournal
Main-Donau-Kanal, m
  ♦ Main-Danube Canal, the
Mainquelle, f
  ♦ source of the Main
Mais, m
  ♦ maize
  ♦ corn AE
Maisbrot, n
  ♦ corn bread AE
Maische, f
  ♦ mash
  ♦ pulp
maischen (etw)
  ♦ mash (s.th.)
Maisflocken, f pl
  ♦ cornflakes pl
Maiskränzchen, n
  (Zusammenkunft zum Maisschälen)
  ♦ husking bee AE
Maiskuchen, m
  Maispfannkuchen, m
  ♦ corn cake AE
Maismehl, n
  ♦ cornmeal AE
  ♦ Indian meal BE
Maisonette, f
  Maisonettewohnung, f
  ♦ maisonette BE
  ♦ maisonette flat BE
  ♦ duplex AE
  ♦ duplex apartment AE
  ♦ maisonnette
Maisonetteappartement, n
  ♦ duplex apartment AE
  ♦ duplex AE
  ♦ maisonette apartment BE
  ♦ maisonette BE
Maisonettepenthouse, n
  ♦ duplex penthouse AE
  ♦ maisonette penthouse BE

Maisonettesuite, f
  ♦ duplex suite AE
  ♦ maisonette suite BE
Maisonettewohnung, f
  ♦ maisonette flat BE
  ♦ maisonette BE
  ♦ duplex apartment AE
  ♦ duplex AE
  ♦ split-level flat BE
Maisonettezimmer, n
  ♦ duplex room AE
  ♦ maisonette room BE
Maitagung, f
  Maitreffen, n
  ♦ May meeting
Maître chef, m FR
  ♦ maître chef FR
Maître d', m FR
  Oberkellner, m
  Ober, m coll
  ♦ maître d' FR
  ♦ headwaiter
  ♦ captain AE
Maître de cuisine, m FR
  Küchenmeister, m
  ♦ maître de cuisine FR
Maître de plaisir, m FR
  ♦ maître de plaisir FR
Maître d'hôtel, m FR
  Oberkellner, m
  Ober, m coll
  ♦ maître d'hôtel FR
  ♦ headwaiter
  ♦ captain AE
Maître d'hôtel de carré, m FR
  Stationsoberkellner, m
  Revieroberkellner, m
  ♦ maître d'hôtel de carré FR
  ♦ captain AE
  ♦ station headwaiter
  ♦ section headwaiter
Maître d'hôtel de reception, m FR
  (im Restaurant)
  Empfangschef, m
  ♦ maître d'hôtel de réception FR
  ♦ reception headwaiter
Maiurlaub, m
  ♦ May vacation AE
  ♦ May holiday BE
Maiwoche, f
  ♦ May week
majestätischer Berg, m
  ♦ majestic mountain
majestätisches Bett, n
  ♦ majestic bed
Majonäse, f
  → Mayonnaise
Majoran, m
  ♦ marjoram
Makedonien
  → Mazedonien
makellos sauber, adj
  ♦ meticulously clean, adj
  ♦ spotlessly clean, adj
Makkaroni, pl
  ♦ macaroni sg
Makkaronisalat, m
  ♦ macaroni salad
Makler, m (Börse)
  Börsenmakler, m

◆ broker
◆ stockbroker
Makler, m (Immobilien)
Immobilienmakler, m
◆ realtor *AE*
◆ real-estate agent *AE*
◆ estate agent *BE*
Maklergebühr, f (generell)
◆ broker's fee
◆ broker's charge
◆ brokerage
Maklergebühr, f (Vermietung)
◆ letting fee *BE*
◆ letting charge *BE*
Maklerprovision, f
◆ broker's commission
◆ commission
◆ brokerage
Makrele, f
◆ mackerel
makrobiotisch, adj
◆ macrobiotic, adj
makrobiotische Mahlzeit, f
makrobiotisches Mahl, n
makrobiotisches Essen, n
◆ macrobiotic meal
makrobiotisches Essen, n
◆ macrobiotic food
Makrone, f
◆ macroon
Malagawein, m
Malaga, m
◆ Malaga wine
◆ Malaga
Malaie, m
◆ Malay
◆ Malayan
Malaiin, f
◆ Malay(an) girl
◆ Malay(an) woman
◆ Malay(an)
malaiisch, adj
◆ Malay, adj
◆ Malayan, adj
Malaiische Halbinsel, f
◆ Malay Peninsula, the
◆ Malaya
Malaria, f
◆ malaria
malariafrei, adj
◆ free from malaria, adj
Malariagebiet, n
◆ malarial area
◆ malarial region
◆ malarial country
Malariapille, f
◆ malaria pill
◆ anti-malaria pill
Malariaprophylaxe, f
◆ malaria prophylaxis
Malariarisiko, n
◆ malaria risk
Malariatablette, f
◆ malaria tablet
◆ anti-malaria tablet
Malawi
◆ Malawi
Malawier, m
◆ Malawian
Malawierin, f
◆ Malawian girl

◆ Malawian woman
◆ Malawian
malawisch, adj
◆ Malawian, adj
Malaysien
◆ Malaysia
Malaysier, m
◆ Malaysian
Malaysierin, f
◆ Malaysian girl
◆ Malaysian woman
◆ Malaysian
malaysisch, adj
◆ Malaysian, adj
Malediven, pl
◆ Maldives, the *pl*
◆ Maldive Islands, the *pl*
Maler, m
◆ painter
Malerarbeiten, f pl
◆ painting and decoration
◆ painting
Maleratelier, n
◆ painter's studio
malerisch, adj
pittoresk, adj
◆ picturesque, adj
◆ scenic, adj
◆ quaint, adj
malerische Ecke, f
◆ picturesque corner
malerische Lage, f
◆ picturesque location
◆ picturesque situation
◆ picturesque position
◆ picturesque setting
malerische Landschaft, f
◆ picturesque scenery
◆ picturesque landscape
◆ picturesque countryside
malerischer Rahmen, m
malerische Umgebung, f
◆ picturesque setting
malerischer Winkel, m
◆ picturesque nook
malerisches Dorf, n
◆ picturesque village
◆ quaint village
malerische Stadt, f
◆ picturesque town
◆ quaint town
malerische Umgebung, f
◆ picturesque surroundings *pl*
◆ picturesque setting
Malferien, pl
◆ painting holidays *BE pl*
◆ painting vacation *AE*
Mali
◆ Mali
Malier, m
◆ Malian
Malierin, f
◆ Malian girl
◆ Malian woman
◆ Malian
malisch, adj
◆ Malian, adj
Malkurs, m
◆ painting course

Mallorca
◆ Majorca
◆ Mallorca
Mallorquiner, m
◆ Marjorcan
mallorquinisch, adj
◆ Majorcan, adj
Malreise, f
◆ painting tour
Malschule, f
◆ painting school
Malta
◆ Malta
Malteser, m
◆ Maltese
Malteserin, f
◆ Maltese girl
◆ Maltese woman
◆ Maltese
maltesisch, adj
◆ Maltese, adj
Malurlaub, m
Malferien, pl
◆ painting vacation *AE*
◆ painting holiday *BE*
Malve, f
◆ mallow
Malvenblütentee, m
◆ mallow leaf tea
malvenfarbig, adj
◆ mauve, adj
Malventee, m
◆ mallow tea
Malvernwasser, n
◆ Malvern water
mal verschwinden *coll*
auf die Toilette gehen
◆ pay a visit *coll*
◆ spend a penny *coll*
◆ leave the room *euph*
Malwettbewerb, m
◆ painting competition
Malwochenende, n
◆ painting weekend
Malz, n
◆ malt
Malzbier, n
◆ malt beer
Malzessig, m
◆ malt vinegar
Malzkaffee, m
◆ malt coffee
◆ coffee substitute
◆ ersatz coffee
Malzwhisky, m
◆ malt whisky
Mammuthotel n
◆ giant hotel
Mammutkonferenz, f
◆ giant conference
◆ jumbo conference *humor*
◆ mammoth conference *humor*
Mammutkongreß, m
◆ giant convention
◆ giant congress
◆ jumbo convention *humor*
◆ jumbo congress *humor*
◆ mammoth convention *humor*
Mammutmesse, f
◆ giant fair
◆ giant trade fair

Mammutprogramm

- jumbo fair *humor*
- jumbo trade fair *humor*

Mammutprogramm, n
- marathon program *AE*
- marathon programme *BE*

Mammuttagung, f
- giant meeting
- jumbo meeting *humor*

Mammutveranstaltung, f
- giant event
- jumbo event *humor*

mampfen (etw)
- munch (s.th.)
- chomp (s.th.) *fam*

Management, n
- management

Managementberater, m
- management consultant

Managementbetrieb, m
- management operation
- management establishment

Management-Buy-Out, m
(Geschäftsführung kauft Unternehmen)
Managementübernahme, f
- management buy-out

Managementclub, m
- management club

Management eines Hotels übernehmen
→ Leitung eines Hotels übernehmen

Management Fee, f
→ Managementhonorar

Managementhotel, n
- management hotel

Managementlehrgang, m
Managementkurs, m
- management course

Managementleistung, f
Managementservice, m
- management service

Managementtechnik, f
- management technique

Managementtraining, n
- management training

Managementübernahme, f
→ Management-Buy-Out

Managementvertrag unterzeichnen
- sign a management contract

Manager, m
- manager

Manager ernennen
- appoint a manager
- Geschäftsführer ernennen

Managerin, f
Leiterin, f
- lady manager
- manageress

Managerkrankheit, f
→ Streßkrankheit

Managerstudio, n
- executive studio

Managersuite, f
- executive suite

Managerzimmer, n
- executive room

Mandarine, f
- mandarin
- mandarin orange
- tangerine

Mandarineneis, n
- mandarin ice cream *AE*
- mandarin ice-cream *BE*

Mandarinenlikör, m
- mandarin liqueur

Mandarinensaft, m
- mandarin juice

Mandarinenscheibe, f
- tangerine slice
- slice of tangerine
- mandarin slice
- slice of mandarin

Mandarinenschnitz, m
- tangerine wedge
- mandarin wedge

Mandarinensorbet, m
- mandarin sorbet

Mandel, f (Frucht)
- almond

Mandelbaum, m
- almond tree

Mandelblüte, f
- almond blossom

Mandelblütenfest, n
- almond blossom festival

Mandelbutter, f
- almond butter

Mandeleiskrem, f
Mandeleis, n
- almond ice cream *AE*
- almond ice-cream *BE*
- almond ice

Mandschurei, f
- Manchuria

mandschurisch, adj
- Manchurian, adj

Manege, f
- ring
- circus ring

Mangel, f
Wäschemangel, f
- mangle

Mangel, m (Abwesenheit, Fehler)
Mangelhaftigkeit, f
- deficiency

Mangel, m (Defekt)
- defect
- shortcoming

Mangel, m (Knappheit)
Knappheit, f
- shortage
- scarcity

Mangel, m (völliges Fehlen)
- lack

Mangel an Atmosphäre, m
- lack of atmosphere

Mangel an Besuchern, m (Knappheit)
- shortage of visitors

Mangel an Besuchern, m (völliges Fehlen)
- lack of visitors

Mangel an erschwinglichen Unterkünften, m
(völliges Fehlen)
- lack of affordable accommodations *AE*
- lack of affordable accommodation *BE*

Mangel an erschwinglichen Unterkünften, m
(Knappheit)
→ Knappheit an erschwinglichen Unterkünften

Mangel an Festen und Feiern, m (Knappheit)
- shortage of festivals and celebrations

Mangel an Gästen, m (Knappheit)
- shortage of guests

Mangel an Gästen, m (völliges Fehlen)
- lack of guests

Mangel an Hotelkapazität, m (Knappheit)
- shortage of hotel capacity

Mangel an Hotelkapazität, m (völliges Fehlen)
- lack of hotel capacity

Mangel an Hotelunterkünften, m (Knappheit)
→ Knappheit an Hotelunterkünften

Mangel an Hotelunterkünften, m (völliges Fehlen)
- lack of hotel accommodations *AE*
- lack of hotel accommodation *BE*

Mangel an Hotelzimmern, m (völliges Fehlen)
- lack of hotel rooms

Mangel an Kunden, m (völliges Fehlen)
- lack of customers

Mangel an Produktionskapazität, m (Knappheit)
- shortage of production capacity

Mangel an Schlaf, m
- lack of sleep

Mangel an Unterhaltung, m (Knappheit)
- shortage of entertainment

Mängelanzeige, f
Mängelrüge, f
- notification of deficiencies
- notice of defect(s)

Mangel beanstanden
Mangel reklamieren
- complain about a defect

Mangel beseitigen
- eliminate a deficiency
- eliminate a defect

Mängelbeseitigung, f
Fehlerbeseitigung, f
- correction of faults

Mangel feststellen
- find a defect

mangelfrei, adj
- free of faults, adj
- faultless, adj
- free of defects, adj

Mängel haben
- have shortcomings
- have deficiencies
- have defects

mangelhaft, adj (fehlerhaft)
fehlerhaft, adj
- faulty, adj
- defective, adj

mangelhaft, adj (unzureichend)
- insufficient, adj
- unsatisfactory, adj

mangelhafte Information, f
mangelhafte Auskunft, f
unzureichende Information, f
- insufficient information

mangelhafte Leistung, f (Arbeitsleitung)
- poor performance

mangelhafte Leistung, f (Service)
- deficient service
- unsatisfactory service

mangelhafte Service, m
- unsatisfactory service
- deficient service

mangelhafte Sanitäreinrichtungen, f pl
unzureichende Sanitäreinrichtungen, f pl
- unsatisfactory sanitary facilities *pl*

mangelhafte Unterkunft, f
unbefriedigende Unterkunft, f
- unsatisfactory accommodation

Mangelhaftung, f
Mängelhaftung, f
- liability for defects
- warranty for defects

mangelnde Hygiene, f
 ◆ lack of hygiene
mangeln etw
 ◆ mangle s.th.
Mängelrüge, f
 → Mängelanzeige
mangels, prp
 ◆ in default of, prep
 ◆ for lack of, prep
 ◆ for want of, prep
 ◆ in the absence of, prep
Mangel taucht auf
 ◆ shortcoming occurs
Mangel verschweigen
 ◆ conceal a defect
Mangobaum, m
 ◆ mango tree
Mangochutney, n
 ◆ mango chutney
Mangold, m
 Mangoldgemüse, n
 ◆ chard
Mangosaft, m
 ◆ mango juice
Mangosorbet, n
 ◆ mango sorbet
Mangosoße, f
 ◆ mango sauce
Manieren, f pl
 Umgangsformen, f pl
 ◆ manners pl
manierlich essen
 ◆ eat nicely
Maniküre, f
 (Tätigkeit und Person)
 ◆ manicure
Maniküre machen lassen sich
 ◆ have a manicure
Man kann nicht auf zwei Hochzeiten tanzen
 ◆ You can't have your cake and eat it
Man muß die Suppe auslöffeln, die man sich eingebrockt hat
 ◆ You must drink as you have brewed
Mann, m
 ◆ man
Manna, n
 ◆ manna
Mannequin, n
 ◆ mannequin
 ◆ model
Männerabteil, n
 (z.B. in Sauna)
 Männerteil, m
 ◆ men's section
Männerchor, m
 ◆ male-voice choir
 ◆ male choir
 ◆ all-male choir
Männerverein, m
 Männerclub, m
 ◆ men's club
Mann für alles, m
 ◆ odd-job man
 ◆ Man Friday
 ◆ utility man AE
männlich, adj
 ◆ male, adj
männlicher Gast, m
 ◆ male guest
Mannschaftsspiel, n
 ◆ team game

Mansarde, f
 ◆ attic
Mansardenappartement, n
 Dachappartement n
 ◆ attic apartment
Mansardenschlafzimmer, n
 ◆ attic bedroom
 ◆ dormer bedroom euph
Mansardenstudio, n
 ◆ attic studio
 ◆ dormer studio euph
Mansardenwohnung, f
 Dachwohnung, f
 ◆ attic flat BE
 ◆ attic apartment AE
 ◆ dormer apartment AE euph
 ◆ dormer flat BE euph
Mansardenzimmer, n
 Dachzimmer n
 ◆ attic room
 ◆ room in the attic
 ◆ garret room
 ◆ dormer room euph
Mantel, m
 ◆ coat
Mantel abgeben
 (zur Aufbewahrung an Garderobe)
 ◆ check a coat AE
 ◆ leave a coat BE
Mantelhaken, m
 Kleiderhaken, m
 Haken, m
 ◆ coat peg
 ◆ coat hook
 ◆ peg
manuell, adj
 ◆ manual, adj
manuell hergestellt, adj
 manuell erstellt, adj
 ◆ made by hand, adj
MAP, m
 Modified American Plan, m
 Halbpension, f
 ◆ MAP
 ◆ Modified American Plan
 ◆ half board
 ◆ demipension AE
 ◆ half pension AE
Mappe, f
 ◆ kit AE
 ◆ folder
Maracujasaft, m
 (Saft der Passionsfrucht)
 ◆ granadilla juice
 ◆ grenadilla juice
Maraschino, m
 (Likör aus Maraskakirschen)
 ◆ maraschino
Maraskakirsche, f
 (schwarze dalmatinische Kirsche)
 ◆ marasca cherry
 ◆ maraschino cherry
Marathonlauf, m
 (42,2 km)
 Marathon, m
 ◆ marathon
 ◆ Marathon
Marathonläufer, m
 ◆ marathon runner

Marathonlauf machen
 Marathon laufen
 ◆ run a marathon
Marathonsitzung, f
 Mammutsitzung, f
 ◆ marathon session
Märchendorf, n
 ◆ fairy-tale village
Märchenfestspiele, n pl
 ◆ fairy-tale festival
Märchenland, n
 ◆ fairyland
Märchenlandschaft, f
 ◆ fairyland scenery
Märchenpalast, m
 ◆ fairy-tale palace
Märchenpark m
 ◆ fairyland park
Märchenschloß, n
 Märchenburg, f
 ◆ fairy-tale castle
Märchenwald, m
 ◆ fairy-tale wood
Margarine, f
 ◆ margarine
Marihuana, n
 ◆ marijuana
 ◆ grass coll
 ◆ tea sl
Marina, f
 ◆ marina
Marina bietet 123 Liegeplätze
 ◆ marina provides 123 berths
Marinaclub, m
 ◆ marina club
Marinade, f
 ◆ marinade
Marinadorf, n
 ◆ marina village
Marinaeinrichtung, f
 ◆ marina facility
Marinahotel, n
 ◆ marina hotel
Marina mit 123 Liegeplätzen, f
 ◆ marina with 123 berths
 ◆ 123-berth marina
Marineflugzeug, n mil
 ◆ navy plane mil
Marinemuseum, n mil
 ◆ naval museum mil
marinieren (etw)
 ◆ marinate (s.th.)
 ◆ pickle (s.th.)
 ◆ marinade (s.th.)
mariniert, adj
 ◆ marinated, adj
 ◆ pickled, adj
Marionette, f
 ◆ marionette
 ◆ puppet
Marionettentheater, n
 Puppentheater, n
 ◆ puppet theater AE
 ◆ puppet theatre BE
Mark, f (Geld)
 ◆ mark
Mark, n (Fruchtmark)
 ◆ pulp
Mark Brandenburg, f
 ◆ Brandenburg Marches, the, pl

Marke

Marke, f (Produkt)
- brand

Marke, f (statt Geld)
- token

Markenname, m
- brand name

Marketender, m *hist*
Marketenderin, f
- sutler *hist*

Marketing, n
- marketing

Marketingabteilung, f
- marketing department

Marketingagentur, f
- marketing agency

Marketingaktivität, f
- marketing activity

Marketinganstrengung, f
- marketing effort

Marketingarbeit, f
- marketing work

Marketingassistent, m
- marketing assistant
- assistant to the marketing manager

Marketingaufwand, m
- marketing expense *AE*
- marketing expenditure *BE*

Marketingaufwendungen, f pl
Marketingausgaben, f pl
- marketing expenses *pl*

Marketingausschuß, m
- marketing committee

Marketingberater, m
- marketing consultant

Marketingberatungsfirma, f
Marketingberatung, f
- marketing consultancy

Marketingbudget, n
Marketingetat, m
- marketing budget

Marketingdaten, pl
- marketing data

Marketingdirektor, m
- marketing director
- director of marketing

Marketingentscheidung, f
- marketing decision

Marketingerfolg, m
- marketing success

Marketingfirma, f
- marketing firm

Marketinggesellschaft, f
- marketing corporation *AE*
- marketing company

Marketingidee, f
- marketing idea

Marketinginitiative, f
- marketing initiative

Marketinginstrument, n
- marketing tool

Marketingkampagne, f
- marketing campaign

Marketingkampagne starten
- launch a marketing campaign

Marketingkenntnisse, f pl
- marketing skills *pl*

Marketingkonsortium, n
- marketing consortium

Marketingkonzept, n
- marketing concept

Marketingkooperation, f
- marketing cooperation

Marketingkoordinator, m
- marketing coordinator

Marketingkosten, pl
- marketing costs *pl*
- marketing cost

Marketingleiter, m
Leiter der Marketingabteilung, m
Marketingmanager, m
- marketing manager

Marketingmedium, n
- marketing medium

Marketingmißerfolg, m
- marketing failure

Marketingnachteil, m
- marketing disadvantage

Marketingnutzen, m
Marketingvorteil, m
- marketing benefit

Marketingorganisation, f
- marketing organisation
- marketing organization

Marketingpersonal, n
- marketing staff
- marketing personnel

Marketingplan, m
- marketing plan

Marketingplanung, f
- marketing planning

Marketingpraxis, f
- marketing practice

Marketingprinzip, n
- marketing principle

Marketingproblem, n
- marketing problem

Marketingprogramm, n
- marketing program *AE*
- marketing programme *BE*

Marketingreise, f
- marketing tour

Marketingseminar, n
- marketing seminar

Marketingseminar besuchen
- attend a marketing seminar

Marketingsitzung, f
- marketing session

Marketingspezialist, m
- marketing specialist

Marketingstrategie, f
- marketing strategy

Marketingtechnik, f
- marketing technique

Marketingtrend, m
- marketing trend

Marketingunternehmen, n
- marketing enterprise

Marketingvereinbarung, f
- marketing agreement

Marketingvereinigung, f
- marketing association

Marketingvorteil, m
- marketing advantage

Marketingziel, n
- marketing goal

markieren etw
- mark s.th.

markiert, adj
(Weg)
- marked, adj
- waymarked, adj

markierte Loipe f
(Ski)
- marked trail
- marked track

markierter Spazierweg, m
markierter Weg, m
- waymarked walk

markierter Stellplatz, m
parzellierter Stellplatz, m
- marked pitch

markierter Weg, m
- marked path
- waymarked path

markiert mit einem Sternchen
(z.B. in Prospekt)
- marked with an asterisk

Markierung, f
(Weg)
- marking
- signposting

Markierungssystem, n
(für Wege)
- marking system

Markise, f
- awning

Markt, m
- market

Markt abhalten
- hold a market

Marktanalyse, f
- market analysis

Marktanteil, m
- market share

Marktanteile gewinnen
- gain market shares

Marktanteil halten
- maintain one's market share

Markt bedienen
- serve a market

Markt beherrschen
- rule the market

Marktbeherrschung, f
- market monopoly

Marktbrunnen, m
- market fountain

Marktcafé, n
- market café

Marktforscher, m
- market researcher

Marktforschung, f
- market research

Marktforschungsdaten, pl
- market research data

Marktforschungsinstitut, n
- market research institute

Marktforschungsleiter, m
- market research manager

Marktführer, m
- market leader

Marktführung, f
- market leadership

Markt für etw, m
- market for s.th.

Markt für Pauschalurlaube, m
- market for package vacations *AE*
- market for inclusive vacations *AE*
- market for package holidays *BE*
- market for inclusive holidays *BE*

Marktgasthof, m
- market inn

Markthalle, f
♦ market hall
Markthaus, n
♦ market house
Markt im Freien, m
Markt unter freiem Himmel, m
♦ open-air market
Marktkirche, f
♦ market church
Marktkreuz, n
♦ market cross
Marktlücke, f
♦ market gap
Marktlücke füllen
♦ fill a market gap
Marktnachfrage, f
Marktbedarf, m
♦ market demand
Marktnische, f
♦ market niche
marktorientiert, adj
♦ market-oriented, adj AE
♦ market-orientated, adj BE
Marktplatz, m
♦ market place
♦ market square
Marktplatzbrunnen, m
♦ market square fountain
Marktplatzfest, n
♦ market square festival
♦ market place festival
Marktposition, f
♦ market position
Marktpotential, n
♦ market potential
Marktpreis, m
♦ market price
♦ market rate
Marktsättigung, f
♦ market saturation
Marktsegment, n
♦ market segment
Marktsegment auswählen
♦ select a market segment
♦ choose a market segment
Marktsegment bedienen
♦ serve a market segment
Marktsegment bilden
♦ form a market segment
Markt segmentieren
♦ segment a market
Marktsegmentierung, f
♦ market segmentation
Marktstadt, f
♦ market town
Markt stagniert
♦ market is stagnant
Marktstand, m
Stand auf dem Markt, m
♦ market stand
♦ market stall
♦ stand on the market
♦ stall on the market
Marktstudie, f
♦ market study
Markttag, m
♦ market day
Markttrend, m
♦ market trend

marktübliche Miete, f
übliche Miete, f
♦ going rent
marktüblicher Preis, m
üblicher Preis, m
♦ going price
♦ going rate
marktüblicher Provisionssatz, m
üblicher Provisionssatz, m
♦ going rate of commission
Markt versorgen
♦ cater to a market
Marktvolumen, n
♦ market volume
Marmelade, f
♦ marmalade
Marmeladesoße, f
Marmeladensoße, f
♦ marmalade sauce
Marmor, m
♦ marble
Marmorbad, n
♦ marble bath
Marmorbadezimmer, n
♦ marble bathroom
Marmorbecken, n
Marmorbad, n
♦ marble pool
Marmorboden, m
Marmorfußboden, m
♦ marble floor
Marmorkamin, m
♦ marble fireplace
Marmorlobby, f
♦ marble lobby
Marmorsaal, m
Marmorhalle, f
♦ marble hall
Marmorsäule, f
♦ marble column
Marmortisch, m
♦ marble table
Marmortreppe, f
♦ marble stairs pl
Marmortreppenhaus, n
♦ marble staircase
Marmor-WC, n
♦ marble WC
Marokkaner, m
♦ Moroccan
Marokkanerin, f
♦ Moroccan girl
♦ Moroccan woman
♦ Moroccan
marokkanisch, adj
♦ Moroccan, adj
Marokko
♦ Morocco
Marone, f
Eßkastanie, f
♦ sweet chestnut
♦ edible chestnut
Maroniverkäufer, m
♦ chestnut vendor
Marsala, m ITAL
(sizilianischer Dessertwein)
Marsalawein, m
♦ Marsala ITAL
♦ Marsala wine
Marsch, m
♦ march

Marschkapelle, f
♦ marching band
Marschland, n
Sumpfland, n
♦ fenland
Marsch über die Alpen, m
♦ march across the Alps
Marsch von A nach B, m
♦ march from A to B
Marstallhof, m
Marstall, m
♦ mews courtyard
♦ mews pl
Martini, m
♦ Martini
Martiniglas, n
♦ Martini glass
Martinischale, f
♦ Martini bowl
März, m
♦ March
Märzauslastung, f
Auslastung im März, f
♦ March load factor
♦ load factor in March
Märzbelegung, f
Märzauslastung, f
♦ March occupancy
♦ occupancy in March
Märzfeier, f
♦ March celebration
Marzipan, n/m
♦ marzipan
Märztagung, f
Märztreffen, n
♦ March meeting
Märzurlaub, m
♦ March vacation AE
♦ March holiday BE
Märzveranstaltung, f
♦ March event
♦ March meeting
Märzwoche, f
♦ March week
Maschine, f (Flugzeug, Motorrad, Fahrrad etc.)
♦ machine
Maschine, f (generell)
♦ machine
maschinelle Kücheneinrichtung, f
♦ mechanical kitchen equipment
maschinenlesbar, adj
♦ machine readable, adj
Maschinenraum, m
(Schiff)
♦ engine room
Maskenball, m
♦ masked ball
♦ fancy-dress ball
♦ fancy ball
maskieren sich
sich verkleiden
♦ mask oneself
♦ disguise oneself
Maß, n (Einheit)
Maßeinheit, f
♦ measure
Maß, n (Liter) dial
→ Liter
Massage, f
♦ massage

Massageabteilung 488

Massageabteilung, f
 ♦ massage department
Massageausstattung, f
 Massageeinrichtung, f
 ♦ massage equipment
Massagebad, n
 (Aktivität)
 ♦ massage bath
Massagebehandlung, f
 (Verkehrsmittel)
 ♦ massage treatment
Massagedienst, m
 Massageservice, m
 ♦ massage service
Massageeinrichtung, f
 ♦ massage facility
Massage erhalten
 Massage bekommen
 ♦ get a massage
 ♦ have a massage
 ♦ receive a massage
Massagegerät, n
 Massageapparat, m
 ♦ massage machine
Massage mit ätherischen Ölen, f
 ♦ massage with essential oils
Massagepersonal, n
 ♦ massage staff
 ♦ massage personnel
Massageraum, m
 Massagezimmer, n
 ♦ massage room
Massagesalon, m
 (oft zweideutig)
 ♦ massage parlor AE
 ♦ massage parlour BE
Massage von zwanzig Minuten, f
 zwanzigminütige Massage, f
 ♦ massage of twenty minutes
 ♦ twenty-minute massage
Maß Bier, f
 Liter Bier, m
 ♦ liter of beer AE
 ♦ litre of beer BE
Maße, n pl
 (Länge, Breite, Höhe)
 ♦ dimensions pl
 ♦ measurements pl
Masse der Kundschaft ausmachen
 ♦ form the bulk of the clientele
Maße eines Gebäudes, n pl
 Gebäudemaße, n pl
 ♦ dimensions of a building pl
Maße eines Zimmers, n pl
 Zimmermaße, n pl
 ♦ dimensions of a room pl
Massenabfütterung, f derog
 Massenspeisung, f
 ♦ feeding (of) the masses derog
 ♦ mass feeding derog
Massenabreise, f
 ♦ mass departure
Massenankunft, f
 ♦ bulk arrival
Massenbesuch, m
 ♦ mass visit
Massenbesucher, m
 ♦ mass visitor
Massenbuchung f
 ♦ bulk booking
Massenferien, pl
 Massenurlaub, m

 ♦ mass holiday BE
 ♦ mass vacation AE
massenhaft Whisky
 jede Menge Whisky
 ♦ whisky galore
Massenhotel n
 ♦ mass hotel
Massenkarambolage, f
 (Verkehrsmittel)
 ♦ mass collision
Massenkauf, m
 Mengenkauf, m
 ♦ bulk purchase
Massenkundgebung, f
 Großkundgebung, f
 ♦ mass demonstration
 ♦ mass meeting
 ♦ rally
Massenquartier, n
 → Massenunterkunft
Massenrabatt, m
 → Mengenrabatt
Massenreise, f
 ♦ mass tour
Massenreisen, n
 Massenreiseverkehr, m
 ♦ mass travel
Massenrestaurant, n
 ♦ mass restaurant
Massenspeisung, f
 ♦ mass feeding
Massentourismus m
 ♦ mass tourism
Massentourismusziel, n
 ♦ mass tourist destination
 ♦ mass tourism destination
Massentourist m
 ♦ mass tourist
Massentransport, m
 ♦ mass transportation AE
 ♦ mass transport
Massentransportmittel, n
 ♦ means of mass transportation AE
 ♦ means of mass transport BE
Massenunterbringung, f
 → Massenunterkunft
Massenunterhaltung, f
 ♦ mass entertainment
Massenunterkunft, f
 Sammelunterkunft, f
 Massenunterbringung, f
 Massenquartier, n
 ♦ collective accommodation
Massenurlaub, m
 Massenferien, pl
 ♦ mass vacation AE
 ♦ mass holiday BE
Massenveranstaltung, f
 ♦ mammoth event
 ♦ popular event
 ♦ mass rally
Massenverpflegung, f
 ♦ mass catering
Massenversammlung, f
 ♦ mass meeting
 ♦ rally
Maße und Gewichte, n pl
 ♦ weights and measures pl
Masseur, m
 ♦ masseur
 ♦ massager AE

Masseurin, f
 (offizielle Bezeichnung)
 ♦ female masseur
 ♦ female massager AE
Masseuse, f
 (Prostituierte)
 ♦ masseuse
maßgeschneidert, adj
 ♦ tailor-made, adj
 ♦ bespoke, adj
maßgeschneiderte Konferenzpauschale, f
 ♦ tailor-made conference package
maßgeschneiderte Leistung f
 maßgeschneiderter Service m
 auf den Kunden zugeschnittener Service m
 ♦ tailor-made service
maßgeschneiderte Reise, f
 ♦ bespoke tour
maßgeschneiderter Kurs, m
 maßgeschneiderter Lehrgang, m
 ♦ tailor-made course
maßgeschneiderter Reiseverlauf, m
 ♦ bespoke itinerary
 ♦ tailor-made itinerary
maßgeschneiderter Urlaub, m
 maßgeschneiderte Ferien, pl
 ♦ tailor-made vacation AE
 ♦ tailor-made holiday BE
maßgeschneidertes Programm, n
 ♦ tailor-made program AE
 ♦ tailor-made programme BE
massieren etw
 ♦ massage s.th.
massieren jn
 ♦ massage s.o.
massieren lassen sich
 ♦ have a massage
mäßig, adj
 maßvoll, adj
 moderat, adj
 bescheiden, adj
 ♦ moderate, adj
mäßiger Genuß von Alkohol, m
 ♦ moderate consumption of alcohol
mäßiger Preis, m
 → ziviler Preis
mäßige Zuwachsrate, f
 ♦ moderate growth rate
 ♦ moderate rate of growth
mäßig im Trinken
 maßvoll im Trinken
 ♦ moderate in drinking
massive Ermäßigung, f
 ♦ massive reduction
massive Möbel, n pl
 → Massivholzmöbel
Massivholz, n
 ♦ solid wood
Massivholzmöbel, n pl
 ♦ solid wood furniture sg
Maßstab 1 zu 50.000, m
 ♦ scale 1 to 50,000
maßstabgetreu, adv
 ♦ to scale, adv
 ♦ true to scale, adv
maßvoller Esser, m
 mäßiger Esser, m
 ♦ moderate eater
maßvoller Trinker, m
 mäßiger Trinker, m
 ♦ moderate drinker

mästen etw
♦ fatten s.th.
mästen jn
♦ fatten s.o.
Masthuhn, n
♦ fattened chicken
Masuren, die, pl
♦ Masuria
Masurische Seen, m pl
♦ Masurian Lakes, the pl
Material, n
♦ material
Materialkosten, pl
Sachkosten, pl
♦ material costs pl
♦ material cost
♦ cost of material
♦ material expenses pl
Materialkosten pro Gericht, pl
♦ material cost per dish
Materialverbrauch, m
♦ material consumption
♦ consumption of material
Matinee, f
(in GB/USA meist nachmittags)
♦ matinee AE
♦ matinée BE
Matineevorstellung, f
♦ matinee performance AE
♦ matinée performance BE
Matratze, f
♦ mattress
Matratze ist bequem
♦ mattress is comfortable
Matratze ist durchgelegen
♦ mattress is worn
Matratze ist unbequem
♦ mattress is uncomfortable
Matratze lüften
♦ air a mattress
Matratzenlager, n coll
(zum Schlafen)
♦ mattresses pl
Matratzenrost, m
Bettrost, m
♦ mattressboard AE
♦ mattress frame BE
Matratzenschoner, m
♦ mattress protector AE
♦ mattress cover
Matrose, m
♦ sailor
♦ seaman
Matrosenart, adv gastr
nach Matrosenart, adv gastr
♦ mariner's style, adv gastr
Matrosenkneipe, f
Seemannskneipe, f
♦ sailors' pub BE
♦ sailors' bar AE
Matte, f
♦ mat
Matterhorn, n
♦ Matterhorn, the
Matterhorn besteigen
♦ climb the Matterhorn
Mauer, f
♦ wall
Mauerreste, m pl
♦ remains of a wall pl
♦ remains of the wall pl

Mauerturm, m
♦ wall tower
Maulbeerbaum, m
♦ mulberry tree
Maultier, n
♦ mule
Maultierausflug, m
♦ mule trip
Maultier reiten
♦ ride a mule
Maultierreiten, n
♦ mule riding
♦ riding a mule
Maultierritt, m
♦ mule ride
Maultiertreiber, m
♦ muleteer
Mauretanien (historisch)
Marokkko
♦ Mauretania
Mauretanien (modern)
♦ Mauritania
Mauretanier, m (historisch)
Marokkaner, m
♦ Mauretanian
Mauretanier, m (modern)
♦ Mauritanian
mauretanisch, adj (historisch)
marokkanisch, adj
♦ Mauretanian, adj
mauretanisch, adj (modern)
♦ Mauritanian, adj
maurisch, adj
♦ Moorish, adj
Mauritius
♦ Mauritius
Maus, f
♦ mouse
Mausefalle, f
♦ mousetrap
Mäuseturm, m
(am Rhein)
♦ Mouse Tower, the
Mausoleum, n
♦ mausoleum
Maut, f
(Straßengebühr)
Mautgebühr, f
♦ toll
♦ road toll
Mautautobahn, f
♦ toll motorway BE
♦ turnpike AE
Mautbrücke, f
Zollbrücke, f
♦ toll bridge AE
♦ toll-bridge BE
Maut erheben auf etw
Gebühr erheben auf etw
♦ take a toll on s.th.
mautfrei, adj
♦ exempt from toll, adj
mautpflichtig, adj
♦ subject to toll, adj
Mautstation, f
♦ toll station
Mautstation einrichten
♦ establish a toll station
Mautstelle, f
♦ tollhouse AE
♦ toll-house BE

Mautstraße, f
♦ toll road BE
♦ turnpike road AE
♦ tollway
Mauttor, n
♦ tollgate AE
♦ toll-gate BE
Maut verlangen
♦ charge toll
Maut zahlen
♦ pay a toll
maximal, adj
♦ maximum, adj
maximal 123 Gäste
♦ a maximum of 123 guests
♦ up to 123 guests
Maximalaufenthalt, m
maximaler Aufenthalt m
längster Aufenthalt m
♦ maximum stay
Maximalauslastung, f
maximale Auslastung, f
♦ maximum load factor
Maximalbelegung, f
maximale Belegung, f
Maximalauslastung, f
maximale Auslastung, f
♦ maximum occupancy
Maximalbetrag, m
Höchstbetrag, m
♦ maximum amount
♦ highest amount
maximale Aufenthaltsdauer, f
Maximalaufenthaltsdauer f
maximale Verweildauer f
Maximalverweildauer f
längste Verweildauer f
♦ maximum length of stay
maximale Auslastung, f
→ Maximalauslastung
maximale Gästezahl, f
♦ maximum number of guests
maximale Personenzahl pro Zimmer, f
♦ maximum number of persons per room
maximaler Aufenthalt, m
→ Maximalaufenthalt
maximale Wartezeit, f
längste Wartezeit, f
♦ maximum waiting time
♦ maximum waiting period
Maximalgebühr, f
Höchstgebühr, f
♦ maximum fee
♦ maximum charge
Maximalhöhe, f
♦ maximum height
Maximalkapazität, f
♦ maximum capacity
Maximalpreis, m
→ Höchstpreis
Maximaltarif, m
Höchsttarif, m
♦ maximum tariff
♦ maximum rates pl
♦ maximum rate
Maximalzimmerpreis, m
höchster Zimmerpreis, m
♦ maximum room rate
♦ maximum room price
Maximumrate, f
→ Höchstpreis

Maya, m
♦ Maya
Mayapyramide, f
♦ Mayan pyramid
Mayaruine, f
♦ Mayan ruin
Mayaruinen, f pl
♦ Maya ruins pl
Mayastadt, f (Großstadt)
♦ Mayan city
Mayastadt, f (kleine Stadt)
♦ Mayan town
Mayazeit, f
♦ Mayan times pl
Mayonnaise, f
♦ mayonnaise
Mayonnaisemischung, f
♦ mayonnaise mixture
Mazedonien
Makedonien
♦ Macedonia
Mazedonier, m
Makedonier, m
♦ Macedonian
Mazedonierin, f
Makedonierin, f
♦ Macedonian girl
♦ Macedonian woman
♦ Macedonian
mazedonisch, adj
makedonisch, adj
♦ Macedonian, adj
Mäzen, m
Förderer, m
Gönner, m
♦ patron
MCO, f
(bei Luftbeförderung)
Miscellaneous Charges Order, f
♦ MCO
♦ miscellaneous charges order
M-Dach, n
Doppelsatteldach, n
♦ M roof
ME., f
→ Mieteinnahme
Mechaniker, m
♦ mechanic
Meckerei, f coll
♦ grumbling
Meckerer, m coll
Nörgler, m
♦ grumbler coll
♦ moaner
♦ nagger
meckern coll
♦ grumble coll
Mecklenburg
(Land)
♦ Mecklenburg
Mecklenburger Bucht f
♦ Mecklenburg Bay
♦ Bay of Mecklenburg
Mecklenburgische Seenplatte, f
♦ Mecklenburg Lakes pl
Mecklenburg-Vorpommern
♦ Mecklenburg/Western Pomerania
Medien, n pl
♦ media pl
Medientag, m
♦ media day

Meditation, f
♦ meditation
Medizinalbad, n
♦ medicinal bath
medizinische Behandlung, f
ärztliche Behandlung, f
♦ medical treatment
medizinischer Kongreß, m
→ Ärztekongreß
medizinischer Tourismus, m
♦ medical tourism
medizinischer Tourist, m
♦ medical tourist
medizinische Zwecke, m pl
♦ medicinal purposes pl
Meer, n
See, f
♦ sea
Meeraal, m
→ Seeaal
Meeralpen, pl
→ Seealpen
Meeräsche, f
♦ grey mullet
♦ green mullet
Meerblick, m
→ Meeresblick
Meerbrasse, f
♦ sea bream AE
♦ sea-bream BE
Meerenge, f
♦ strait
♦ straits pl
Meerenge von Gibraltar, f
♦ Straits of Gibraltar, the, pl
♦ Strait of Gibraltar, the, sg
Meeresalgen, f pl
♦ marine algae pl
Meeresaquarium, n
♦ marine aquarium
Meeresarm, m
♦ arm of the sea
♦ sea arm
♦ inlet
♦ estuary
Meeresblick, m
Meerblick, m
Seeblick, m
♦ seaview AE
♦ sea view BE
♦ view of the sea
Meeresblickbalkon m
♦ sea-view balcony
Meeresblickfenster, n
Meerblickfenster, n
♦ sea-view window
Meeresblickzimmer, n
Meerblickzimmer, n
♦ sea-view room
Meeresblickzuschlag, m
Meerblickzuschlag, m
♦ sea-view supplement
♦ supplement for sea view
Meeresfisch, m
Seefisch, m
♦ sea fish
Meeresfrüchte, f pl
♦ seafood sg
Meeresfrüchteabendessen, n
Meeresfrüchtediner, n
♦ seafood dinner

Meeresfrüchtebüfett, n
♦ seafood buffet
♦ seafood bar
Meeresfrüchtecocktail, m
♦ seafood cocktail
Meeresfrüchteessen, n
Meeresfrüchtemahlzeit, f
Meeresfrüchtemahl, n
♦ seafood meal
Meeresfrüchtegericht, n
♦ seafood dish
Meeresfrüchtejahrmarkt, m
Meeresfrüchtemarkt, m
♦ seafood fair
Meeresfrüchtemenü, n
♦ seafood menu
Meeresfrüchtemittagessen, n
♦ seafood lunch
♦ seafood luncheon
Meeresfrüchteplatte, f
♦ seafood platter
Meeresfrüchterestaurant, n
Fischrestaurant, n
♦ seafood restaurant
Meeresfrüchtesalat, m
♦ seafood salad
Meeresfrüchtestand, m
♦ seafood stand AE
♦ seafood stall BE
Meeresfrüchtetag, m
♦ seafood day
Meeresfrüchteterrine, f
♦ seafood terrine
Meeresfrüchtewoche, f
♦ seafood week
Meeresklima, n
Seeklima, n
♦ maritime climate
♦ sea climate
Meereskreuzfahrt, f
Seekreuzfahrt, f
♦ sea cruise
Meereskurort, m
Seekurort, m
♦ seaside spa
♦ seaside health resort
Meeresleben, n
♦ marine life
Meeresluft, f
Seeluft, f
♦ sea air
Meeresnaturlehrpfad, m
♦ seaside nature trail
Meeresspezialität, f
♦ seafood specialty AE
♦ seafood speciality BE
Meeresspiegel, m
♦ sea level AE
♦ sea-level BE
Meeresstrand, m
Seestrand, m
♦ sea beach
Meeresstraße, f (Küste)
Küstenstraße, f
♦ sea road
♦ marine drive
Meeresströmung, f
♦ sea current
Meerestemperatur, f
♦ sea temperature

Meerestourismus, m
- ♦ maritime tourism
- ♦ sea tourism

Meerestourist, m
- ♦ maritime tourist
- ♦ sea tourist

Meeresverschmutzung, f
- ♦ pollution of the sea
- ♦ marine pollution

Meereswellenbad, n
- ♦ seawater swimming pool with artificial waves AE
- ♦ seawater pool with artificial waves AE
- ♦ sea-water swimming-pool with artificial waves BE
- ♦ sea-water pool with artificial waves BE

Meerforelle, f
- ♦ sea trout
- ♦ bull trout BE

Meerinsel, f
Meeresinsel, f
- ♦ sea island

Meer ist 1 km entfernt
- ♦ sea is 1 km away
- ♦ sea is 1 km distant

Meerrettich, m
Kren, m ÖST
- ♦ horseradish AE
- ♦ horse-radish BE

Meerrettichbutter, f
Krenbutter, f ÖST
- ♦ horseradish butter

Meerrettichsoße, f
Krensoße, f ÖST
- ♦ horseradish sauce AE
- ♦ horse-radish sauce BE

Meerseite, f
→ Seeseite

Meerufer, n
→ Seeufer

Meerwasser, n
- ♦ seawater AE
- ♦ sea water BE

Meerwasserbad, n
Meerwasserbecken, n
- ♦ seawater swimming pool AE
- ♦ seawater pool AE
- ♦ sea-water swimming-pool BE
- ♦ sea-water pool BE

Meerwasserbecken, n
→ Meerwasserbad

Meerwasserbehandlung, f
- ♦ seawater treatment AE
- ♦ sea-water treatment BE

Meerwasserfreibad, n
- ♦ outdoor seawater swimming pool AE
- ♦ outdoor seawater pool AE
- ♦ outdoor sea-water swimming-pool BE
- ♦ outdoor sea-water pool BE

Meerwasserhallenbad, n
- ♦ seawater indoor swimming pool AE
- ♦ seawater indoor pool AE
- ♦ sea-water indoor swimming-pool BE
- ♦ sea-water indoor pool BE

Meerwasserhallenwellenbad, n
- ♦ seawater indoor wave pool AE
- ♦ sea-water indoor wave pool BE

Meerwasserinhalation, f
- ♦ seawater inhalation AE
- ♦ sea-water inhalation BE

Meerwasserkur, f
- ♦ seawater cure AE

- ♦ sea-water cure BE
- ♦ thalassotherapy
- ♦ thalassotherapy treatment

Meerwasserpool, m
→ Meerwasserbecken

Meerwasserschwimmhalle, f
- ♦ indoor seawater swimming pool AE
- ♦ indoor seawater pool AE
- ♦ indoor sea-water swimming-pool BE
- ♦ indoor sea-water pool BE

Meerwasserwellenhallenbad, n
- ♦ indoor seawater pool with artificial waves AE
- ♦ indoor sea-water pool with artificial waves BE

Megacarrier, m
- ♦ mega-carrier

Megahotel, n
- ♦ mega-hotel

Megahotellerie, f
- ♦ mega-hotel trade
- ♦ mega-hotel industry
- ♦ mega-hotel business

Megaphon, n
- ♦ megaphone
- ♦ meg coll

Megastar, m
- ♦ mega-star

Megaurlaubsort, m
Megaferienort, m
Megaort, m
- ♦ mega-resort

Megaveranstaltung, f
- ♦ mega-event

Mehl, n (fein)
- ♦ flour

Mehl, n (grob)
- ♦ meal

Mehlbutter, f
- ♦ beurre manié FR
- ♦ kneaded butter

Mehl einrühren
- ♦ stir in the flour

mehlige Kartoffel, f
- ♦ mealy potato

Mehl sieben
- ♦ sift the flour

Mehlspeise, f (generell)
- ♦ farinaceous dish

Mehlspeise, f ÖST
→ Dessert, Süßspeise

Mehrbettappartement, n
- ♦ multi-bed apartment
- ♦ multi-bedded apartment
- ♦ multiple-bedded apartment

mehrbettig, adj (Bett)
- ♦ multi-bedded, adj
- ♦ multiple-bedded, adj

mehrbettig, adj (Koje)
- ♦ multi-berth, adj

mehrbettiges Zimmer, n
- ♦ multi-bedded room

Mehrbettkabine, f
- ♦ multi-berth cabin

Mehrbettzimmer, n
- ♦ multi-bed room
- ♦ multi-bedded room
- ♦ multiple-bedded room

mehr bieten als Tisch und Bett
- ♦ offer more than bed and board

mehr Buchungen erwarten
- ♦ expect more bookings

mehrere Sprachen sprechen
- ♦ speak several languages

mehrere Zimmer, n pl
- ♦ several rooms pl

Mehrfachbelegung f
(Zimmer)
mehrfache Belegung f
- ♦ multiple occupancy

Mehrfachbuchung, n
mehrfache Buchung, f
- ♦ multiple booking

mehrfache Belegung, f
→ Mehrfachbelegung

Mehrfachkurzurlaub, m
mehrfacher Kurzurlaub, m
- ♦ multiple short vacation AE
- ♦ multiple short holiday BE

Mehrfachreisender, m
→ Vielreisender, Wiederholungsreisender

Mehrfachreservierung, f
mehrfache Reservierung, f
- ♦ multiple reservation
- ♦ scattershot reservation AE

Mehrfachurlaub, m
Mehrfachferien, pl
mehrmaliger Urlaub, m
mehrmalige Ferien, pl
- ♦ multiple vacation AE
- ♦ multiple holiday BE

Mehrfamilienhaus, n
- ♦ multiple family dwelling
- ♦ multiple dwelling unit jur
- ♦ multiple dwelling jur
- ♦ apartment house AE

mehrgängig, adj
(Mahlzeit)
- ♦ multi-course, adj

mehrgängige Mahlzeit, f
mehrgängiges Essen, n
- ♦ multi-course meal

mehrgängiges Abendessen, n (Dinner)
Abendessen mit mehreren Gängen, n
- ♦ multi-course dinner

mehrgängiges Abendessen, n (Supper)
Abendessen mit mehreren Gängen, n
- ♦ multi-course supper

mehrgängiges Essen, n
→ mehrgängige Mahlzeit

mehrgängiges Menü, n
Menü mit mehreren Gängen, n
- ♦ multi-course menu

mehrgängiges Mittagessen, n
Mittagessen mit mehreren Gängen, n
- ♦ multi-course luncheon
- ♦ multi-course lunch

mehr Geld haben als Geschmack
- ♦ have more money than taste

Mehrgepäck, n
Übergepäck, n
- ♦ excess luggage BE
- ♦ excess baggage AE

mehrgeschossig, adj
→ mehrstöckig

mehrgeschossiges Hotel, n
→ mehrstöckiges Hotel

Mehrheitsbeteiligung, f
- ♦ majority interest
- ♦ majority stake

Mehrkosten, pl
zusätzliche Kosten, pl
- ♦ additional expenses pl

mehrmotorig

- extra costs *pl*
- additional costs *pl*
- extra expenses *pl*

mehrmotorig, adj
- multiengined, adj
- multiengine, adj

mehrmotoriges Flugzeug, n
- multiengined plane
- multiengine plane

Mehrpreis, m
- additional price
- extra charge

mehrsaisonal adj
- multi-seasonal, adj

mehr schlecht als rechte Unterkunft, f
- rough and ready accommodation

mehrsprachig, adj
- multilingual, adj
- polyglot, adj

mehrsprachiger Empfangsherr, m
mehrsprachiger Rezeptionist, m
- multilingual receptionist

mehrsprachiger Führer, m
(Person oder Buch)
- multilingual guide

mehrsprachiger Prospekt m
- multilingual brochure

mehrsprachiges Personal, n
- multilingual staff
- multilingual personnel

mehrstöckig, adj attr
mehrgeschossig, adj attr
- multi-story, adj attr AE
- multi-storey, adj attr BE

mehrstöckig, adj prd
mehrgeschossig, adj prd
- multi-storied, adj prd AE
- multi-storeyed, adj prd BE

mehrstöckiges Hotel, n
mehrgeschossiges Hotel, n
- multi-story hotel AE
- multi-storey hotel BE

mehrstöckig sein (Gebäude)
- be multi-storied AE
- be multi-storeyed BE

mehrstündig, adj
- lasting several hours
- of several hours' duration

Mehrtageaufenthalt, m
→ mehrtägiger Aufenthalt

Mehrtagesgast, m
- guest staying several days

mehrtägig, adj
- lasting several days
- of several days' duration

mehrtägiger Aufenthalt, m
Mehrtageaufenthalt m
- stay of several days

mehr trinken als man verträgt
- drink more than is good for one

Mehrwertsteuer, f
MwSt., f
- value added tax
- VAT

Mehrwertsteuer erstatten
MwSt. erstatten
- refund value added tax
- refund VAT

Mehrwertsteuersatz, m
- VAT rate

mehrwöchig, adj
- lasting several weeks
- of several weeks' duration
- several-week

mehrwöchiger Aufenthalt, m
- stay of several weeks

Mehrzahl der Besucher, f
Mehrheit der Besucher, f
- majority of the visitors

Mehrzimmerappartement, n
Appartement mit mehreren Zimmern, n
- multi-room apartment

mehrzimmerig, adj
- multi-roomed, adj
- multi-room, adj

mehrzimmeriges Appartement, n
- multi-roomed apartment
- apartment with several rooms
- multi-room apartment

mehrzimmerige Wohnung, f
- multi-roomed flat BE
- multi-room flat BE
- multi-room apartment AE

Mehrzimmerwohnung, f
- multi-room flat BE
- multi-room apartment AE

Mehrzweckarena, f
- multipurpose arena AE
- multi-purpose arena BE

Mehrzweckbereich, m
- multipurpose area AE
- multi-purpose area BE

Mehrzweckeinrichtung, f
- multipurpose facility AE
- multi-purpose facility BE

Mehrzweckfahrzeug, n
- multipurpose vehicle AE
- multi-purpose vehicle BE
- utility vehicle

Mehrzweckgebäude, n
Mehrzweckbau, m
- multipurpose building AE
- multi-purpose building BE

Mehrzweckgymnastikhalle, f
Mehrzweckturnhalle, f
- multipurpose gymnasium AE
- multi-purpose gymnasium BE
- multigym coll

Mehrzweckhalle, f
Multihalle, f
- multipurpose hall AE
- multi-purpose hall BE

Mehrzweckhotel, n
- multipurpose hotel AE
- multi-purpose hotel BE

Mehrzweckmöbel, n pl
Mehrzweckmobiliar, n sg
- multipurpose furniture AE sg
- multi-purpose furniture BE sg

Mehrzweckraum, m
→ Mehrzweckzimmer

Mehrzweckrestaurant, n
- multipurpose restaurant AE
- multi-purpose restaurant BE

Mehrzwecksaal, m
- multipurpose hall AE
- multi-purpose hall BE

Mehrzwecksporthalle, f
- multipurpose sports hall
- multi-purpose sports hall BE
- multi-purpose sportsdome BE

Mehrzweckturnhalle, f
Mehrzweckgymnastikhalle, f
- multigym coll
- multipurpose gymnasium AE
- multi-purpose gymnasium BE

Mehrzweckveranstaltungsort, m
- multipurpose venue AE
- multi-purpose venue BE

Mehrzweckzelt, n
- multipurpose tent AE
- multi-purpose tent BE

Mehrzweckzimmer, n
Mehrzweckraum, m
- multipurpose room AE
- multi-purpose room BE

Meile, f
- mile

meilenlang, adj
- mile-long, adj

meilenlange Prachtstraße, f
- mile-long avenue

Meine Damen und Herren!
(Anrede bei Ansprache)
- Ladies and Gentlemen!

mein Frühstück, n
- my breakfast

Meißner Porzellan, n
- Meissen porcelain
- Meissen china

Meißner Porzellansammlung, f
- collection of Meissen porcelain
- collection of Meissen china

meistbesucht, adj (generell)
- most visited, adj

meistbesucht, adj (Lokal)
am meisten besucht, adj
- most frequented, adj

meistbesuchtes Hotel, n
am meisten besuchtes Hotel, n
- most frequented hotel

meistbesuchte Touristenattraktion, f
am meisten besuchte Touristenattraktion, f
- most visited tourist attraction

meisten Zimmer haben Flußblick
- most rooms have river views

meisten Zimmer haben zwei Vollbetten
- most rooms have two full-size beds

Meisterkoch, m
- master cook
- master chef

Meisterschaft, f (Kenntnisse)
- mastery

Meisterschaft, f (Wettkämpfe)
- championship

Meisterschaft abhalten
- hold a championship

Meisterschaft ausrichten (als Gastgeber)
- host a championship

Meisterschaft gewinnen
- win the championship
- win a championship

Meisterschaftsgolfplatz, m
- championship golf course

Meisterschaftsplatz, m (Golf)
- championship course

Meisterschaftsplatz, m (Tennis)
- championship court

Meisterschaftsspiel, n
- championship match
- championship game

Meisterschaftstennisplatz, m
 ♦ championship tennis court
Meisterwerk, n
 ♦ masterpiece
Meisterwerk der Baukunst, n
 ♦ masterpiece of architecture
 ♦ masterpiece of the art of building
Meisterwerk der gotischen Architektur, n
 ♦ masterpiece of Gothic architecture
meistgetrunken, adj
 am meisten getrunken, adj
 ♦ most widely drunk, adj
Mekka
 (Stadt)
 ♦ Mecca
Mekka für Touristen, n
 Touristenmekka, n
 ♦ mecca for tourists
 ♦ tourist mecca
Mekka sein für jn
 ♦ be a mecca for s.o.
Melanesien
 ♦ Melanesia
Melanesier, m
 ♦ Melanesian
Melanesierin, f
 ♦ Melanesian girl
 ♦ Melanesian woman
 ♦ Melanesian
melanesisch, adj
 ♦ Melanesian, adj
Meldebogen, m
 → Anmeldebogen
Meldebuch, n
 Fremdenbuch, n
 ♦ registration book
Meldedatum n
 → Anmeldedatum
Meldeformalitäten, f pl
 → Anmeldeformalitäten
Meldekarte, f
 (Rezeption)
 Meldezettel, m
 ♦ registration card
Meldekarte prüfen
 ♦ check a registration card
Meldeliste, f
 → Anmeldeliste
melden (jn)
 ausrufen (jn)
 ♦ page (s.o.)
Meldepflicht, f
 Meldezwang, m
 Anmeldepflicht, f
 Anmeldezwang, m
 ♦ obligatory registration
 ♦ compulsory registration
 ♦ obligation to register
meldepflichtig, adj
 anmeldepflichtig, adj
 ♦ subject to registration, adj
Meldeschein, m
 ♦ registration form
Meldeschein ausfüllen
 ♦ fill out a registration form AE
 ♦ fill in a registration form BE
 ♦ complete a registration form
Meldeschein signieren
 Meldeschein unterzeichnen
 sich in einem Hotel anmelden
 ♦ sign the registration form

Meldeschluß, m
 (z.B. bei Veranstaltungen)
 ♦ latest check-in time
 ♦ check-in deadline
Meldetermin m
 → Anmeldetermin
Meldevorgang, m
 → Anmeldevorgang
Meldezeit, f
 Meldefrist, f
 Anmeldungszeit, f
 Anmeldungsfrist, f
 ♦ registration period
Meldezettel, m
 → Anmeldeformular
Melone, f (Frucht)
 ♦ melon
Melone, f (Hut)
 ♦ bowler hat BE
 ♦ bowler
 ♦ derby AE
Melonenbowle, f
 ♦ melon cup
 ♦ melon bowl
Melonencocktail, m
 ♦ melon cocktail
Meloneneis, n
 ♦ melon ice cream AE
 ♦ melon ice-cream BE
Melonenkaltschale, f
 ♦ cold melon soup
Melonensorbet, n
 ♦ melon sorbet
Melonensuppe, f
 ♦ melon soup
Menage, f
 Essig- und Ölständer, m
 Gewürzständer, m
 ♦ caster AE
 ♦ castor AE
 ♦ cruet stand AE
 ♦ cruet
Menge, f (Menschen)
 ♦ crowd
Menge, f (Quantität)
 → Quantität
Mengenprämie, f
 ♦ quantity bonus
Mengenpreis, m
 ♦ bulk price
 ♦ bulk rate
Mengenpreisrabatt, m
 ♦ bulk-price discount
 ♦ bulk-rate discount
Mengenrabatt, m
 ♦ bulk discount
 ♦ quantity discount
 ♦ quantity rebate
 ♦ quantity bonus
Mengenstandard, m
 ♦ quantity standard
Menge zu essen
 ♦ lot to eat
 ♦ lots to eat
Meningitis, f med
 Hirnhautentzündung, f med
 ♦ meningitis med
Menorca
 ♦ Minorca
 ♦ Menorca

Mensa, f
 (Speisesaal in Schule, Hochschule)
 ♦ students' dining hall
 ♦ refectory BE
 ♦ commons pl=sg
Menu, n SCHW
 → Menü
Menü, n
 Speisenfolge, f
 Menu, n SCHW
 ♦ menu
 ♦ set meal
Menü aus dem Hut zaubern
 ♦ produce a menu at the drop of a hat
Menüauswahl, f
 → Menüwahl
Menübeginn, m
 ♦ beginning of the menu
Menübeliebtheit, f
 ♦ menu popularity
Menü beschreiben
 ♦ describe a menu
Menübeschreibung, f
 ♦ menu description
 ♦ description of a menu
 ♦ describing a menu
Menü besprechen
 ♦ discuss the menu
Menübesprechung, f
 ♦ discussion of the menu
Menü einnehmen
 ♦ take a menu
 ♦ have a menu
Menüende, n
 ♦ end of the menu
Menü entwerfen
 ♦ devise a menu
Menüfolge, f
 ♦ menu
Menü für Autofahrer, n
 ♦ menu for motorists
Menügang, m
 → Gang
Menu gastronomique, n FR m
 (Essen mit mehr als vier Gängen)
 ♦ menu gastronomique FR
Menügedeck, n
 Menükuvert, n
 Menücouvert, n
 ♦ menu cover
Menügestaltung, f
 → Menüplanung
Menükalkulation f
 ♦ menu calculation
 ♦ calculation of a menu
 ♦ calculating a menu
Menükarte, f
 (Speisekarte mit Menüs)
 Speisekarte, f
 ♦ menu card
Menükartenhalter, m
 Speisekartenhalter, m
 ♦ menu-card holder AE
Menükomponente, f
 ♦ menu item
Menükomposition, f
 Menüzusammenstellung, f
 ♦ composition of a menu
 ♦ menu composition
 ♦ composing a menu

Menü kredenzen 494

Menü kredenzen
→ Menü servieren
Menükritik, f
♦ criticism of a menu
Menü mit mehreren Gängen, n
♦ menu of several courses
♦ multi-course menu
Menüplan, m
♦ menu plan
Menüplan ausarbeiten
♦ work out a menu plan
Menüplaner, m
(Person)
♦ menu planner
Menüplanung, f
♦ planning (of) a menu
♦ menu planning
Menüplanung überwachen
♦ supervise menu planning
Menüpreis, m
♦ price of a menu
♦ menu price
Menüpreis festsetzen
Menüpreis festlegen
♦ fix the menu price
♦ price a menu
Menüpreis kalkulieren
♦ calculate the menu price
♦ calculate the price of a menu
Menüservice, n
♦ menu service
Menü servieren
♦ serve a menu
Menu touristique, n FR m
Touristenessen, n
♦ menu touristique FR
♦ tourist menu
Menü und Preis fest, adv
♦ table d'hôte, adv
Menüvariation, f
♦ menu variation
Menüvorschlag, m
♦ menu suggestion
♦ suggestion of a menu
♦ menu proposal
♦ suggestion for the menu
Menü vorschlagen
♦ suggest a menu
♦ propose a menu
Menüvorschlag unterbreiten
Menüvorschlag machen
♦ make a menu suggestion
Menüwahl, f
(Gast kann Speisen auswählen)
Speisewahl, f
♦ menu choice
♦ choice of menu
♦ menu selection
Menüwahl ist begrenzt
Menüwahl ist beschränkt
♦ menu choice is limited
Menü zaubern
Menü aus dem Hut zaubern
♦ create a menu
♦ produce a menu at the drop of a hat
Menü zum festen Preis, n
♦ menu at (a) fixed price
♦ fixed-price menu
Menü zusammenstellen
♦ compose a menu
♦ compile a menu

Menüzusammenstellung, f
Menükomposition, f
♦ menu composition
♦ composition of a menu
♦ composing a menu
♦ compilation of a menu
♦ compiling a menu
Merchandising, n
♦ merchandising
Meringe, f
♦ meringue
Merkmal, n
♦ feature
merkwürdigen Geschmack haben
seltsamen Geschmack haben
♦ have a queer taste
merkwürdiger Geschmack, m
seltsamer Geschmack, m
♦ queer taste
Merlan, m
Wittling, m
Weißling, m
♦ whiting
Merlot, m FR
♦ Merlot
Mesopotamien
♦ Mesopotamia
Meßbecher, m
♦ measuring cup
♦ measuring jug
Messe, f (Ausstellung)
Messeveranstaltung, f
♦ fair
♦ trade fair
Messe, f (Kirche)
♦ mass
Messe abhalten
♦ hold a trade fair
♦ hold a fair
Messe abschließen
♦ conclude a fair
♦ conclude a trade fair
Messeaktivität, f
♦ fair activity
♦ trade fair activity
Messeamt, n
Messebüro, n
♦ fair office
♦ trade fair office
Messeanfang, m
→ Messebeginn
Messeattraktion, f
♦ fair attraction
♦ fair's attraction
♦ trade fair attraction
Messeauftakt, m
→ Messebeginn
Messe aufziehen
→ Messe organisieren
Messe ausrichten (als Gastgeber)
♦ host a fair
♦ host a trade fair
Messeausschuß, m
Messekomitee, n
♦ fair committee
♦ trade fair committee
Messeausstatter, m
♦ fair contractor
♦ trade fair contractor
Messeausstellung, f
♦ fair exhibition

♦ trade fair exhibition
♦ fair exhibit AE
♦ trade fair exhibit AE
Messeausweis, m
♦ fair pass
♦ trade fair pass
Messebahnhof, m
♦ fair station
♦ trade fair station
Messebeginn, m
Messeanfang, m
♦ beginning of the fair
♦ start of the fair
♦ commencement of the fair form
♦ beginning of the trade fair
♦ start of the trade fair
Messeberater, m
♦ trade fair consultant
♦ fair consultant
Messe beschicken
♦ send goods to a fair
♦ send goods to a trade fair
Messebeschicker, m
Messeaussteller, m
♦ exhibitor (at a fair)
♦ exhibiter (at a fair) AE
♦ exhibitor (at a trade fair)
♦ exhibitor (at a trade fair) AE
Messebesuch, m
♦ visit to a fair
♦ visit to a trade fair
♦ fair visit
♦ trade fair visit
Messe besuchen (Ausstellung)
♦ visit a fair
♦ visit a trade fair
Messe besuchen (Kirche)
♦ attend mass
Messebesucher, m
♦ fair visitor
♦ trade fair visitor
♦ visitor to a fair
♦ fairgoer AE
♦ fair-goer BE
Messebesucherzahl, f
Zahl der Messebesucher, f
♦ number of fair visitors
♦ number of trade fair visitors
♦ number of fairgoers
Messebeteiligung, f (aktiv)
Messeteilnahme, f
♦ participation in a fair
♦ participation in a trade fair
Messe beziehen
→ Messe besuchen
Messebüro, n
Messeamt, n
♦ trade fair office
♦ fair office
Messechef, m
→ Messeleiter
Messedienst, m
→ Messeservice
Messedienstleistung, f
Messeleistung, f
Messedienst, m
Messeservice, m
♦ trade fair service
♦ fair service
Messedirektion, f
→ Messeleitung

Messedirektor, m
 ♦ fair director
 ♦ trade fair director
Messe durchführen
 ♦ implement a fair
 ♦ implement a trade fair
Messedurchführung, f
 ♦ implementation of a fair
 ♦ implementation of a trade fair
Messeeinrichtung, f
 ♦ fair facility
 ♦ trade fair facility
Messeende, n
 ♦ end of a fair
 ♦ end of the fair
 ♦ end of a trade fair
 ♦ end of the trade fair
Messeerfahrung, f
 ♦ fair experience
 ♦ trade fair experience
Messeerfolg, m
 ♦ success of a trade fair
 ♦ success of a fair
Messe eröffnen
 ♦ open a fair
 ♦ open a trade fair
Messeeröffnung, f
 Eröffnung einer Messe, f
 ♦ opening of a fair
 ♦ opening of a trade fair
Messefachhändler, m
 Messehändler, m
 ♦ fair dealer
 ♦ trade fair dealer
Messe findet gleichzeitig statt mit etw
 ♦ fair is running concurrently with s.th.
 ♦ trade fair is running concurrently with s.th.
Messe findet statt
 ♦ fair takes place
 ♦ trade fair takes place
Messefirma, f
 ♦ fair firm
 ♦ trade fair firm
Messefläche, f
 ♦ fair area
 ♦ fair space
 ♦ trade fair area
 ♦ trade fair space
Messe für etw, f
 ♦ fair for s.th.
 ♦ trade fair for s.th.
Messegast, m
 ♦ fair guest
 ♦ trade fair guest
Messegebäude, n
 ♦ fair building
 ♦ trade fair building
Messegelände, n
 ♦ fairgrounds AE pl = sg
 ♦ fair site
Messegeschäft, n
 Messewesen, n
 ♦ fair business
 ♦ trade fair business
Messegeschenk, n
 ♦ fairing
Messegesellschaft, f
 ♦ fair corporation AE
 ♦ fair company BE
 ♦ trade fair corporation AE
 ♦ trade fair company BE

Messehalle, f
 ♦ fair hall AE
 ♦ exhibition hall
Messe im Freigelände, f
 Messe im Freien, f
 ♦ outdoor fair
Messeindustrie, f
 Messewesen, n
 ♦ fair industry
 ♦ trade fair industry
Messeinformationsstelle, f
 ♦ fair information office
 ♦ fair information bureau
Messe inszenieren
 Messe ausrichten
 ♦ stage a fair
 ♦ stage a trade fair
Messejahr, n
 ♦ fair year
 ♦ trade fair year
Messekalender, m
 ♦ fair calendar
 ♦ trade fair calendar
Messekatalog, m
 ♦ fair catalogue
 ♦ fair catalog AE
 ♦ trade fair catalogue
 ♦ trade fair catalog AE
Messekoje, f
 ♦ fair booth
 ♦ trade fair booth
Messekonzept, n
 Messekonzeption, f
 ♦ fair concept
 ♦ trade fair concept
 ♦ concept of a fair
 ♦ concept of a trade fair
Messekunde, m
 ♦ fair customer
 ♦ trade fair customer
 ♦ fair client
 ♦ trade fair client
Messeland, n
 ♦ fair country
 ♦ trade fair country
Messelandschaft, f
 ♦ fair scenery
 ♦ trade fair scenery
Messeleiter, m
 ♦ fair manager
 ♦ trade fair manager
Messeleitung, f (Behörde)
 Messebehörde, f
 Messebehörden, f pl
 ♦ fair authority
 ♦ fair authorities pl
Messeleitung, f (Management)
 Messedirektion, f
 ♦ fair management
 ♦ trade fair management
 ♦ management of a fair
 ♦ management of a trade fair
 ♦ managing a fair
Messemanagement, n
 → Messeleitung
Messemanager, m
 → Messeleiter
Messemarketing, n
 ♦ fair marketing
 ♦ trade fair marketing

Messemarkt, m
 ♦ fair market
 ♦ trade fair market
Messemetropole, f
 ♦ fair metropolis
 ♦ trade fair metropolis
Messemonat, m
 ♦ fair month
 ♦ trade fair month
Messen besuchen
 ♦ visit fairs
 ♦ frequent fairs
Messeordnung, f
 ♦ fair regulations pl
 ♦ trade fair regulations pl
Messeorganisation, f
 Messeveranstaltung, f
 ♦ fair organisation
 ♦ trade fair organisation
 ♦ organisation of a fair
 ♦ organisation of a trade fair
 ♦ organising a fair
Messeorganisator, m
 Messeveranstalter, m
 ♦ fair organiser
 ♦ fair organizer
 ♦ trade fair organiser
 ♦ trade fair organizer
Messe organisieren
 Messe veranstalten
 ♦ organise a fair
 ♦ organize a fair
 ♦ organise a trade fair
 ♦ organize a trade fair
Messeort, m
 ♦ fair venue
 ♦ trade fair venue
Messepartner, m
 ♦ trade fair partner
 ♦ fair partner
Messepavillon, m
 ♦ fair pavilion
 ♦ trade fair pavilion
 ♦ pavilion at a fair
 ♦ pavilion at a trade fair
Messeplatz, m (Gelände)
 ♦ fair site
 ♦ trade fair site
Messeplatz, m (Ort)
 ♦ fair place
 ♦ trade fair place
Messeplatz, m (Stadt)
 → Messestadt
Messepolitik, f
 ♦ fair policy
 ♦ trade fair policy
Messeprodukt, n
 ♦ fair product
 ♦ trade fair product
Messeprogramm, n
 ♦ fair program AE
 ♦ trade fair program AE
 ♦ fair programme BE
 ♦ trade fair programme BE
Messer, Gabel, Scher' und Licht taugt für kleine Kinder nicht
 ♦ Children and fools may not play with edged tools
Messer, n
 ♦ knife

Messerabatt

Messerabatt, m
- fair rebate
- fair discount
- trade fair rebate
- trade fair discount

Messerbank, f
- knife rest

Messereise, f
- trade fair trip
- trade fair tour
- trade fair journey
- trip to a trade fair
- tour to a trade fair

Messerestaurant, n
- fair restaurant
- trade fair restaurant

Messer ist scharf
- knife is sharp

Messer ist stumpf
- knife is blunt

Messer schärfen
- sharpen a knife
- grind a knife

Messerschmied, m
- cutler

Messer und Gabel
Messer (n) und Gabel (f)
- knife and fork

Messerwaren, f pl
- cutlery

Messesaison, f
- fair season
- trade fair season

Messeservice, m
Messedienst, m
Messeleistung, f
Messedienstleistung, f
- fair service
- trade fair service

Messestadt, f (Großstadt)
- fair city
- trade fair city

Messestadt, f (kleine Stadt)
- fair town
- trade fair town

Messestand, m
- fair stand
- stand at a fair
- fair stall *BE*
- stall at a fair *BE*

Messestandgebühr, f
Messestandmiete, f
Standgebühr, f
Standmiete, f
- piccage
- pickage

Messestandort, m
- fair location
- trade fair location

Messestatistik, f
- trade fair statistics *pl*
- fair statistics *pl*

Messetag, m
- fair day
- trade fair day
- day of the fair
- day of the trade fair

Messeteilnahme, f (aktiv)
→ Messebeteiligung

Messeteilnahme, f (passiv)
- fair attendance

- trade fair attendance
- attendance at a fair
- attendance at a trade fair

Messeteilnehmer, m (aktiv)
- fair participant
- trade fair participant
- participant in a fair
- participant in a trade fair

Messeteilnehmer, m (passiv)
- fair attendant
- trade fair attendant
- attendant at a fair
- attendant at a trade fair

Messetermin, m
Messedatum, n
- fair date
- trade fair date
- date of the fair
- date of the trade fair

Messetest, m
- fair test
- trade fair test

Messetourismus m
- fair tourism
- trade fair tourism

Messetourist, m
- fair tourist
- trade fair tourist

Messetrubel m
- bustle of the fair

Messe veranstalten
→ Messe organisieren

Messeveranstalter, m
- fair operator
- trade fair operator
- fair organiser
- trade fair organiser

Messeveranstaltung, f (Ereignis)
(Veranstaltung während der Messe)
- fair event
- trade fair event
- fair function
- trade fair function

Messeveranstaltung, f (Messe)
→ Messe

Messeveranstaltung, f (Organisation)
→ Messeorganisation

Messeversicherung, f
- fair insurance
- trade fair insurance

Messevertrag, m
- fair contract
- trade fair contract

Messeverzeichnis, n
- fair directory
- trade fair directory

Messe vorbereiten
- prepare a fair
- prepare a trade fair

Messevorbereitung, f
- preparation of a fair
- preparation of a trade fair
- preparing a fair
- preparing a trade fair

Messewesen, n
→ Messeindustrie, Messegeschäft

Messewoche, f
- fair week
- trade fair week
- week of the fair
- week of the trade fair

Messezeit, f
- fair period
- trade fair period

Messezentrum, n
(Stadt)
- fair center *AE*
- trade fair center *AE*
- fair centre *BE*
- trade fair centre *BE*

Messezuschlag, m
- fair supplement
- trade fair supplement

Meßglas, n
- measuring glass

Messingbett, n
- brass bed
- brass bedstead

Messingfigur, f
- brass figure

Messinginschrift, f
- brass inscription

Messingkandelaber, m
- brass candelabrum
- brass candelabra

Messinglampe, f
- brass lamp

Meßtischkarte, f
(der nationalen Landvermessung)
Meßtischblatt, n
- Ordnance Survey map

Meßwein, m
- altar wine

Met, m
- mead

Metallbett n
- metal bed

Metallstuhl, m
- metal chair

Metalltisch, m
- metal table

Méthode champenoise, f *FR*
Champagnermethode, f
- méthode champenoise *FR*

Metropole, f
Weltstadt, f
- metropolis

Metzger, m
Fleischer, m
- butcher
- meatman *AE*

Metzgerei, f
Metzgerladen, m
- butcher store *AE*
- butcher's shop *BE*
- butcher's

Metzgereimuseum, n
- butchers' museum

Metzgerinart, adv *gastr*
nach Metzgerinart, adv *gastr*
- butcher's style, adv *gastr*

Metzgerladen, m
→ Metzgerei

Mexikaner, m
- Mexican

Mexikanerin, f
- Mexican girl
- Mexican woman
- Mexican

mexikanisch, adj
- Mexican, adj

mexikanische Art, adv *gastr*
  nach mexikanischer Art, adv *gastr*
  ♦ **Mexican style, adv** *gastr*
Mexiko
  ♦ **Mexico**
Mezzaningeschoß, n
  → Zwischengeschoß
Michelin-Führer, m
  ♦ **Michelin guide**
Michelin-Stern, m
  ♦ **Michelin star**
mickriges Essen, n
  (Quantität)
  nicht ausreichendes Essen, n
  mickrige Mahlzeit, f
  ♦ **skimpy meal**
mieser Gasthof, m
  ♦ **wretched inn**
mieser Ruf, m
  ♦ **odious reputation**
mieses Hotel, n
  ♦ **wretched hotel**
mieses Zimmer, n
  ♦ **wretched room**
miese Unterkunft, f
  ♦ **miserable lodging**
  ♦ **miserable dwelling**
Miesmacher, m
  Meckerer, m
  ♦ **moaner**
  ♦ **grumbler**
  ♦ **whinger** *inform*
Miesmuschel, f
  → Muschel
Mietanhebung, f
  → Mieterhöhung
Mietanzahlung, f
  Ablöse, f
  ♦ **key money** *BE*
  ♦ **forehand rent**
  ♦ **advance rental** *AE*
Mietappartement, n (gemietet)
  → gemietetes Appartement
Mietappartement, n (generell)
  ♦ **rental apartment** *AE*
Mietappartement, n (zu vermieten)
  ♦ **apartment for rent**
Mietaufwand, m
  Mietausgabe, f
  ♦ **rental expense** *AE*
Mietaufwendungen, f pl
  ♦ **rent expenses** *pl*
Mietausfall, m
  Mietverlust m
  ♦ **loss of rent**
  ♦ **rental loss** *AE*
  ♦ **rent deficiency** *AE*
Mietausrüstung, f (gemietet)
  ♦ **rented equipment** *AE*
  ♦ **hired equipment** *BE*
Mietausrüstung, f (generell)
  Leihausrüstung, f
  ♦ **rental equipment** *AE*
  ♦ **hire equipment** *BE*
Mietausrüstung, f (zu vermieten)
  ♦ **equipment for rent** *AE*
  ♦ **equipment for hire** *BE*
Mietauto, n
  → Mietwagen
mietbar, adj (kurzzeitig)
  ♦ **hirable, adj** *BE*
  ♦ **for rent** *AE*
  ♦ **rentable, adj** *AE*
  ♦ **for hire** *BE*
mietbar, adj (langzeitig)
  ♦ **tenantable, adj**
  ♦ **rentable, adj**
Mietbedingungen, f pl (kurz, meist Mobilien)
  ♦ **rental terms** *AE pl*
  ♦ **rental conditions** *AE pl*
  ♦ **terms of rent** *AE pl*
  ♦ **hiring conditions** *BE pl*
  ♦ **terms of hire** *BE pl*
Mietbedingungen, f pl (lang, meist Immobilien)
  ♦ **terms of tenancy** *pl*
  ♦ **terms of letting** *BE pl*
  ♦ **letting conditions** *BE pl*
  ♦ **tenancy conditions** *pl*
Mietbeginn, m (kurz, meist Mobilien)
  ♦ **beginning of (the) rental** *AE*
  ♦ **beginning of (the) rent** *AE*
  ♦ **commencement of (the) rental** *AE*
  ♦ **beginning of (the) hire** *BE*
  ♦ **commencement of (the) hire** *BE*
Mietbeginn, m (lang, meist Immobilien)
  ♦ **beginning of rent**
Mietbeihilfe, f
  Mietzuschuß, m
  ♦ **housing benefit** *BE*
  ♦ **rent allowance**
  ♦ **rent subsidy**
Mietbetrag, m
  ♦ **amount of rent**
  ♦ **rental rate**
  ♦ **rental**
  ♦ **rent**
Mietbindung, f
  ♦ **rent control**
Mietblock, m
  → Mietskaserne
Mietboot, n (gemietet)
  ♦ **rented boat** *AE*
  ♦ **hired boat** *BE*
Mietboot, n (generell)
  Leihboot, n
  ♦ **rental boat** *AE*
  ♦ **hire boat** *BE*
Mietboot, n (zu vermieten)
  ♦ **boat for hire** *BE*
  ♦ **boat for rent** *AE*
Mietboykott, m
  ♦ **rent boycott**
Mietbuch, m
  ♦ **rent book**
Mietbüro, n
  ♦ **renting office**
Mietbus, m (gemietet)
  ♦ **rented bus** *AE*
  ♦ **hired bus** *BE*
  ♦ **hired coach** *BE*
Mietbus, m (generell)
  Leihbus, m
  ♦ **rental bus** *AE*
  ♦ **hire bus** *BE*
  ♦ **hire coach** *BE*
Mietbus, m (zu vermieten)
  Leihbus, m
  ♦ **bus for rent** *AE*
  ♦ **bus for hire** *BE*
  ♦ **coach for hire** *BE*
Mietcaravan, m (gemietet)
  → gemieteter Caravan
Mietcaravan, m (generell)
  Mietwohnwagen, m
  Leihcaravan, m
  Leihwohnwagen, m
  ♦ **letting caravan** *BE*
  ♦ **rental trailer** *AE*
  ♦ **hire caravan** *BE*
Mietcaravan, m (zu vermieten)
  Mietwohnwagen, m
  ♦ **caravan for hire** *BE*
  ♦ **trailer for rent** *AE*
Mietchalet, n (gemietet)
  gemietetes Chalet, n
  ♦ **rented chalet**
  ♦ **hired chalet** *BE*
Mietchalet, n (generell)
  ♦ **rental chalet** *AE*
  ♦ **hire chalet** *BE*
Mietchalet, n (zu vermieten)
  ♦ **chalet for hire** *BE*
  ♦ **chalet for rent** *AE*
Mietdauer, f (kurz, meist Mobilien)
  ♦ **rent period** *AE*
  ♦ **rental period** *BE*
  ♦ **hire period** *BE*
  ♦ **hiring period** *BE*
Mietdauer, f (lang, meist Immobilien)
  ♦ **duration of lease**
  ♦ **term of lease**
  ♦ **period of tenancy**
  ♦ **length of let** *BE*
Miete, f (Aktivität)
  → Anmietung, f
Miete, f (kurz, meist Mobilien)
  ♦ **rent** *AE*
  ♦ **hire** *BE*
Miete, f (lang, meist Immobilien)
  ♦ **rent**
Miete abwerfen
  ♦ **yield a rent**
Miete anheben
  ♦ **raise the rent**
Miete eines Saals, f (Aktivität)
  → Anmietung eines Saals
Miete eintreiben
  ♦ **recover the rent**
Miete einziehen
  ♦ **collect the rent**
Miete erhalten
  ♦ **receive the rent**
Miete erhöhen
  ♦ **increase the rent**
Miete ermäßigen
  Miete senken
  ♦ **reduce the rent**
Miete für eine Garage, f
  ♦ **rent for a garage**
Miete für einen Parkplatz, f (1 Auto)
  ♦ **rent for a parking place**
  ♦ **rent for a parking space**
Miete für etw, f
  ♦ **rent for s.th.**
Miete herabsetzen
  ♦ **lower the rent**
Miete hochschrauben
  ♦ **rack the rent**
Miete hochsetzen
  ♦ **put up the rent**
Miete hochsetzen um $ 123
  ♦ **put the rent up by $ 123**

Mieteinnahmen

Mieteinnahmen, f pl
- ◆ rent(al) receipts *pl*
- ◆ rent(al) income
- ◆ rent(al) earnings *pl*
- ◆ rent(al) revenues *pl*
- ◆ rent(al) takings *pl*

Miete ist fällig
   Miete ist am Samstag fällig
- ◆ rent is due
- ◆ rent is due on Saturday

Miete ist fällig an jedem Quartalsende
- ◆ rent is due at the end of each quarter

Miete ist gestiegen
- ◆ rent has gone up

Miete ist hoch
- ◆ rent is high

Miete ist niedrig
- ◆ rent is low

Miete ist sprunghaft gestiegen
- ◆ rent has leapt up

Miete monatlich bezahlen
- ◆ pay the rent monthly
- ◆ pay one's rent monthly

Mieten, n
→ Anmietung

Mietende, n
- ◆ end of rent
- ◆ end of let *BE*

mieten etw für die Dauer des Aufenthalts
- ◆ rent s.th. for the length of one's stay
- ◆ hire s.th. for the length of one's stay *BE*

mieten etw für die Dauer des Urlaubs
- ◆ rent s.th. for the duration of the vacation *AE*
- ◆ rent s.th. for the duration of the holiday *BE*
- ◆ hire s.th. for the duration of the holiday *BE*

mieten etw gegen eine Gebühr
- ◆ rent s.th. for a fee
- ◆ hire s.th. for a fee *BE*

mieten etw in einem Geschäft
- ◆ rent s.th. from a store *AE*
- ◆ hire s.th. from a shop *BE*

mieten etw (kurz, meist Mobilien)
- ◆ rent s.th. *AE*
- ◆ hire s.th. *BE*

mieten etw (lang, meist Immobilien)
- ◆ rent s.th.

mieten etw (Verkehrsmittel)
→ chartern

mieten etw von jm (langzeitig, Immobilien)
- ◆ rent s.th. from s.o.

mieten etw von jm (Mobilien)
- ◆ hire s.th. from s.o. *BE*
- ◆ rent s.th. from s.o.

Mieten gehen hoch
- ◆ rents are going up

Mieten sind sprunghaft gestiegen
- ◆ rents have leapt up

Miete ohne etw, f
- ◆ rent exclusive of s.th.

Miete pro Einheit, f
- ◆ rent per unit

Miete pro Jahr, f
   Jahresmiete, f
   JM, f
- ◆ rent per year
- ◆ rent per annum
- ◆ pa rent
- ◆ yearly rent

Miete pro Monat, f
- ◆ rent per month

Miete pro Person, f
- ◆ rent per person

Miete pro Person pro Monat, f
   Monatsmiete pro Person, f
- ◆ rent per person per month

Miete pro Person pro Tag, f
   Tagesmiete pro Person, f
- ◆ rent per person per day

Miete pro Person pro Woche, f
   Wochenmiete pro Person, f
- ◆ rent per person per week

Miete pro Tag, f
   Tagesmiete, f
- ◆ rent per day

Miete pro Woche, f
- ◆ rent per week

Mieter, der bald auszieht, m
   bald ausziehender Mieter m
   ausziehender Mieter, m
- ◆ outgoing tenant

Mieter, der Kündigungsschutz genießt, m
- ◆ statutory tenant

Mieter, der Wuchermiete zahlt, m
- ◆ rack-renter *AE*

Mieter, m (kurz, meist Mobilien)
- ◆ renter *AE*
- ◆ hirer *BE*

Mieter, m (lang, meist Immobilien)
- ◆ tenant
- ◆ lessee *jur*
- ◆ renter
- ◆ leaseholder

Mieter, m (Zimmer)
→ Untermieter

Mieter einer möblierten Wohnung, m
- ◆ tenant of a furnished apartment *AE*
- ◆ renter of a furnished apartment *AE*
- ◆ tenant of a furnished flat *BE*

Mieter einer Wohnung, m
- ◆ tenant of a flat *BE*
- ◆ renter of an apartment *AE*
- ◆ tenant of an apartment *AE*

Mieter eines Appartements, m
- ◆ tenant of an apartment

Mieter eines Safe, m
   Mieter eines Schließfachs m
- ◆ renter of a safe *AE*
- ◆ hirer of a safe *BE*

Mieter finden für ein Haus
   Mieter bekommen für ein Haus
- ◆ get a renter for a house *AE*
- ◆ get a tenant for a house

Mieterhaftung, f *jur*
- ◆ tenant's liability *jur*

Mieterhöhung, f
   Mietanhebung, f
- ◆ rent increase
- ◆ increase in rent
- ◆ rise in rent

Mieter im zweiten Geschoß, m
   Mieter im zweiten Stockwerk, m
- ◆ third-floor tenant *AE*
- ◆ second-floor tenant *BE*

Mieter kündigen
- ◆ give a tenant notice to quit
- ◆ give a tenant warning

Mieter muß nur Wäsche mitbringen
   (z.B. Wohnwagenmieter)
- ◆ renter needs only bring linen *AE*
- ◆ hirer needs only bring linen *BE*

Mieterschutz, m
- ◆ protection of tenants' rights

Mieterschutzbund, m
- ◆ tenants' rights association

Mietertrag, m
   Mieteinnahme, f
- ◆ rental income
- ◆ rental return
- ◆ rental
- ◆ revenue from rentals

Mieterverband, m
- ◆ tenants' association

Miete schulden
   Miete schuldig bleiben
- ◆ owe the rent

Miete steigt
- ◆ rent is rising

Miete stunden jm
- ◆ grant s.o. a respite from payment of rent
- ◆ give s.o. time to pay the rent

Miete subventionieren
   Mieten subventionieren
- ◆ subsidise rent
- ◆ subsidize rents

Miete von $ 123 pro Quadratfuß
   Miete von $ 123 je Quadratfuß
- ◆ rent of $ 123 per square foot
- ◆ rent of $ 123 a square foot

Miete vorauszahlen
   Miete im voraus zahlen
- ◆ prepay the rent
- ◆ pay the rent in advance

Miete wird monatlich bezahlt
- ◆ rent is paid monthly

Miete zahlen
- ◆ pay rent
- ◆ pay one's rent
- ◆ pay the rent

Miete zahlen für etw
- ◆ pay rent for s.th.

Miete zahlen im voraus
   Miete im voraus zahlen
- ◆ pay the rent in advance
- ◆ prepay the rent

Miete zurückbehalten
   Miete behalten
- ◆ withhold rent

Miete zurückerstatten
- ◆ refund the rent

Miete zurückerstatten teilweise
- ◆ refund part of the rent

Mietfahrrad, n (gemietet)
   Leihfahrrad, n
   Mietrad, n
   Leihrad, n
- ◆ rented bicycle *AE*
- ◆ rented bike *AE coll*
- ◆ hired bicycle *BE*
- ◆ hired bike *BE coll*

Mietfahrrad, n (generell)
   Leihfahrrad, n
   Mietrad, n
   Leihrad, n
- ◆ rental bicycle *AE*
- ◆ rental bike *AE coll*
- ◆ hire bicycle *BE*
- ◆ hire bike *BE coll*

Mietfahrrad, n (zu vermieten)
   Leihfahrrad, n
   Mietrad, n
   Leihrad, n

- bicycle for rent AE
- bike for rent AE coll
- bicycle for hire BE
- bike for hire BE coll

Mietfahrradfirma, f
Leihfahrradfirma, f
- cycle rental firm AE
- cycle hire company BE
- cycle hire firm BE

Mietfahrradservice, m
Mietfahrraddienst, m
Leihfahrradservice, m
Leihfahrraddienst, m
- rental bicycle service AE
- bicycle hire service BE
- cycle hire service BE

Mietfirma, f
Leihfirma, f
- rental firm AE
- rental company AE
- hire firm BE
- hire company BE

Mietfläche, f (gemietet)
- rented area
- hired area BE

Mietfläche, f (generell)
- rental area AE
- hire area BE

Mietfläche, f (zu vermieten)
- area for rent
- area for hire BE

Mietflotte, f
- rental fleet AE
- hire fleet BE

mietfrei, adj
- rent-free, adj
- free of rent, adj

mietfreies Appartement, n
- rent-free apartment

mietfreie Wohnung, f
- rent-free flat BE
- rent-free apartment AE

mietfreie Zeit, f
- rent-free period

Mietfreiheit, f
- rent exemption

mietfrei in einem Haus wohnen
- live in a house free of rent
- live in a house rent-free

Mietgarantie, f
- rental guarantee

Mietgebühr, f
Leihgebühr, f
- rental charge AE
- rental fee AE
- rental AE
- hire charge BE
- hire fee BE

Mietgebühr ausrechnen
Mietgebühr berechnen
Mietgebühr kalkulieren
- calculate the rental charge AE
- calculate the rental fee AE
- calculate the rental AE
- calculate the hire charge BE
- calculate the hiring charge BE

Mietgegenstand, m jur
- leased property jur

Mietgeld, n
Miete, f

- rent money
- rent

Mietgrundlage, f
- rental basis

Miethalle, f
→ Mietsaal

Mietherabsetzung, f
→ Mietsenkung

Miethöhe, f
- level of rent
- amount of rent

Mietimmobilie, f
Mietanwesen, n
Mietobjekt, n
- rental property

Mietjacht, f (gemietet)
Mietjacht, f
- rented yacht AE
- hired yacht BE

Mietjacht, f (generell)
Mietyacht, f
Leihjacht, f
Leihyacht, f
- rental yacht AE
- hire yacht BE

Mietjacht, f (zu vermieten)
Mietyacht, f
- yacht for rent AE
- yacht for hire BE

Mietkauf, f
- lease with an option to purchase
- rent with an option to purchase

Mietkauf, m (Timesharing)
→ Timesharing

Mietkaution, f
- lease security deposit
- security deposit
- deposit
- key money BE

Mietkontrakt, m
→ Mietvertrag

Mietkosten, pl
- rental costs AE pl
- rental cost AE

Mietkutsche, f
- hired carriage
- hackney coach
- hackney carriage

Mietmarkt, m (Immobilien)
- rent market

Mietmarkt, m (Mobilien)
Leihmarkt, m
- rental market AE
- hire market BE

Mietmöbel, n pl
→ Mietmobiliar

Mietmobiliar, n (gemietet)
Mietmöbel, n pl
- rented furniture AE sg
- hired furniture BE sg

Mietmobiliar, n (generell)
Mietmöbel, n pl
Leihmöbel, n pl
- rental furniture AE sg
- hire furniture BE sg

Mietmobiliar, n (zu vermieten)
Mietmöbel, n pl
- furniture for rent AE sg
- furniture for hire BE sg

Mietmotorboot, n (gemietet)
- rented motorboat AE
- hired motor boat BE

Mietmotorboot, n (generell)
- rental motorboat AE
- hire motor boat BE

Mietmotorboot, n (zu vermieten)
- motorboat for rent AE
- motor boat for hire BE

Mietniveau, n
Mietebene f
- rent level

Mietobjekt, n (gemietet)
Mietsache, f
- leased property
- rented property

Mietobjekt, n (generell)
→ Mietimmobilie

Mietpartei, f
→ Mieter

Mietpauschale, f
pauschale Miete, f
Pauschalmiete, f
- flat rent

Mietpferd, n
- livery horse
- hired horse BE

Mietpreis, m (Immobilien)
- rent price
- rent
- amount of rent
- rental price
- letting price BE

Mietpreis, m (Mobilien)
- rental price AE
- hire price BE

Mietpreis festsetzen (Immobilie)
Miete festlegen
- fix the rent
- fix a rent

Mietpreis festsetzen (Mobilie)
Mietpreis festlegen
- fix the rental price AE
- fix the hire price BE

Mietpreisforderung, f
- asking rent

Mietpreisforderung von $ 12 pro Quadratfuß, f
- asking rent of $ 12 a square foot
- asking rent of $ 12 a sq. ft.

mietpreisgebunden, adj
dem Mieterschutz unterliegend, adj
- rent-controlled, adj

mietpreisgebundene Unterkunft, f
- rent-controlled accommodation

Mietrad, n
→ Mietfahrrad

Mietraum, m
→ gemietetes Zimmer

Mietrechnung, f
- rent bill

Mietrecht, n
- law governing tenancy
- laws governing tenancy pl

Mietrichtsatz, m
- reference rent

Mietrückstand, m
Mietrückstände, m pl
- rent arrears pl
- rent in arrears
- arrears of rent pl

Mietsaal

Mietsaal, m (gemietet)
 Miethalle, f
 gemieteter Saal, m
 gemietete Halle, f
 ♦ hired hall *BE*
 ♦ rented hall *AE*
Mietsaal, m (generell)
 Miethalle, f
 ♦ rental hall *AE*
 ♦ hire hall *BE*
Mietsaal, m (zu vermieten)
 Miethalle, f
 ♦ hall for rent *AE*
 ♦ hall for hire *BE*
Mietsatz, m
 ♦ rental rate
 ♦ rental
Mietschalter, m
 (z.B. für Mietwagen)
 ♦ rental counter *AE*
 ♦ hire counter *BE*
Mietschalter in allen größeren Flughäfen haben
 ♦ have rental counters at all major airports *AE*
 ♦ have hire counters at all major airports *BE*
Mietschein m
 → Mietvertrag
Mietschuldner, m
 ♦ defaulting tenant
Mietsenkung, f
 Mietherabsetzung, f
 ♦ reduction of rent
Mietservice, m
 Mietdienst, m
 Vermietung, f
 ♦ rental service *AE*
 ♦ hire service *BE*
Mietsgebäude, n
 ♦ multiple dwelling *jur*
Mietshaus, n (gemietet)
 gemietetes Haus, n
 ♦ rented house
 ♦ rented home
Mietshaus, n (generell)
 ♦ apartment house *AE*
 ♦ apartment building *AE*
 ♦ block of flats *BE*
 ♦ apartment block
Mietshaus, n (groß)
 ♦ mansion *BE*
 ♦ mansions *BE pl*
Mietshaus ohne Fahrstuhl, n
 Haus ohne Fahrstuhl n
 ♦ walk-up *AE coll*
Mietsitz, m
 Mietstuhl, m
 ♦ rental seat *AE*
 ♦ hire seat *BE*
Mietskaserne, f *derog*
 ♦ tenement house *AE*
 ♦ tenement block *BE*
 ♦ tenement
 ♦ barracks *pl inform*
Mietski, m (gemietet)
 Leihski, m
 ♦ rented ski *AE*
 ♦ hired ski *BE*
Mietski, m (generell)
 Leihski, m
 ♦ rental ski *AE*
 ♦ hire ski *BE*

Mietski, m (zu vermieten)
 Leihski, m
 ♦ ski for rent *AE*
 ♦ ski for hire *BE*
Mietspiegel, m
 ♦ rental table
Mietstall, m
 Mietstallung, f
 ♦ livery stable
 ♦ livery *AE*
Mietstand, m (gemietet)
 ♦ rented stand *AE*
 ♦ hired stall *BE*
Mietstand, m (generell)
 Leihstand, m
 ♦ rental stand *AE*
 ♦ hire stand *BE*
 ♦ hire stall *BE*
 ♦ rental booth *AE*
Mietstand, m (zu vermieten)
 ♦ stand for rent *AE*
 ♦ stall for hire *BE*
 ♦ booth for rent *AE*
Mietstation, f
 (z.B. für Mietautos)
 Leihstation, f
 ♦ rental station
 ♦ hire station *BE*
Mietstopp, m
 Mietzinsstopp, m
 ♦ rent freeze
Mietstopp aufheben
 Mietzinsstopp aufheben
 ♦ lift a rent freeze
Mietstreitigkeit, f
 ♦ tenancy dispute
Mietsubvention, f
 ♦ rent subsidy
Mietsumme, f
 ♦ rental
Miettennisplatz, m (gemietet)
 ♦ rented tennis court *AE*
 ♦ hired tennis court *BE*
Miettennisplatz, m (generell)
 ♦ rental tennis court *AE*
 ♦ hire tennis court *BE*
Miettennisplatz, m (zu vermieten)
 ♦ tennis court for rent *AE*
 ♦ tennis court for hire *BE*
Miettretboot, n (gemietet)
 ♦ rented pedalo *AE*
 ♦ rented pedal boat *AE*
 ♦ hired pedalo *BE*
 ♦ hired pedal boat *BE*
Miettretboot, n (generell)
 Leihtretboot, n
 Mietwasservelo, n *SCHW*
 Leihwasservelo, n *SCHW*
 ♦ rental pedalo *AE*
 ♦ rental pedal boat *AE*
 ♦ hire pedalo *BE*
 ♦ hire pedal boat *BE*
Miettretboot, n (zu vermieten)
 Mietwasservelo, n *SCHW*
 ♦ pedalo for rent *AE*
 ♦ pedal boat for rent *AE*
 ♦ pedalo for hire *BE*
 ♦ pedal boat for hire *BE*
Mietunterkunft, f (gemietet)
 → gemietete Unterkunft

Mietunterkunft, f (generell)
 ♦ rental accommodation *AE*
 ♦ letting accommodation *BE*
Mietunterkunft, f (zu vermieten)
 ♦ accommodation for rent *AE*
 ♦ accommodation to let *BE*
Mietvereinbarung, f
 ♦ tenancy agreement
 ♦ rental agreement
 ♦ rent agreement
 ♦ lease agreement
 ♦ letting agreement *BE*
Mietvereinbarung eingehen
 ♦ enter a tenancy agreement
 ♦ enter a rental agreement
 ♦ enter a rent agreement
 ♦ enter a letting agreement *BE*
Mietvereinbarung unterzeichnen
 ♦ sign a tenancy agreement
Mietverhältnis, n
 ♦ tenancy
 ♦ lease (for rent)
Mietverhältnis kündigen
 ♦ give notice of tenancy
Mietverhältnis verlängern
 ♦ extend a tenancy
Mietverlängerung, f (kurz, meist Mobilien)
 ♦ extension of rental *AE*
 ♦ extension of hire *BE*
 ♦ hire extension *BE*
Mietverlängerung, f (lang, meist Immobilien)
 ♦ lease renewal
 ♦ renewal of a lease
 ♦ extension of the lease
Mietverlust m
 → Mietausfall m
Mietverlustversicherung, f
 (für Vermieter)
 ♦ rent insurance
Mietvertrag, m (Immobilien)
 ♦ lease contract
 ♦ lease
 ♦ letting contract *BE*
Mietvertrag, m (Mobilien)
 ♦ rental contract *AE*
 ♦ hire contract *BE*
Mietvertrag abschließen
 → Mietvertrag eingehen
Mietvertrag beenden
 ♦ terminate a lease
Mietvertrag eingehen
 Mietvertrag abschließen
 ♦ enter into a lease
Mietvertrag kündigen
 ♦ cancel a lease
 ♦ give notice
Mietvertrag läuft ab
 ♦ lease expires
Mietvertragsbedingungen, f pl
 Mietbedingungen, f pl
 ♦ conditions of a lease *pl*
 ♦ terms of a lease *pl*
Mietvertragsbestimmungen, f pl
 ♦ terms of a lease *pl*
Mietvertragsdauer, f
 Laufzeit eines Mietvertrags, f
 ♦ life of a lease
Mietvertragszeit, f
 ♦ rental contract period *AE*
Mietvertrag über gewerbliche Räume, m
 ♦ commercial lease

Mietvertrag unterzeichnen
  Mietvertrag abschließen
  ♦ sign a lease
Mietvertrag verlängern
  ♦ extend a lease
  ♦ renew a lease
Mietvilla, f (gemietet)
  → gemietete Villa
Mietvilla, f (generell)
  ♦ rental villa *AE*
  ♦ hire villa *BE*
Mietvilla, f (zu vermieten)
  ♦ villa for rent *AE*
  ♦ villa to let *BE*
Mietvorauszahlung, f
  ♦ prepayment of rent
  ♦ rent (paid) in advance
  ♦ advance rent
  ♦ key money *BE*
Mietvorvertrag, m
  ♦ contract for a lease
  ♦ agreement for a lease
Mietwagen, m (gemietet)
  → gemietetes Auto
Mietwagen, m (generell)
  Leihwagen, m
  Mietauto, n
  ♦ rental car *AE*
  ♦ hire car *BE*
Mietwagen, m (zu vermieten)
  ♦ car for rent *AE*
  ♦ car for hire *BE*
Mietwagen buchen
  Mietwagen bestellen
  Leihwagen buchen
  Leihwagen bestellen
  ♦ book a rental car *AE*
  ♦ book a hire car *BE*
Mietwagenbuchung, f
  Leihwagenbuchung, f
  ♦ booking (of) a rental car *AE*
  ♦ booking (of) a hire car *BE*
Mietwagenfirma, f
  Leihwagenfirma, f
  ♦ car rental firm *AE*
  ♦ car hire firm *BE*
Mietwagen für Selbstfahrer, m
  ♦ self-drive car
  ♦ self-drive
  ♦ U-drive *AE*
Mietwagengeschäft, n
  Leihwagengeschäft, n
  ♦ car rental business *AE*
  ♦ hire car business *BE*
Mietwagengesellschaft, f
  Leihwagengesellschaft, f
  ♦ car rental company *AE*
  ♦ car hire company *BE*
Mietwagenkosten, pl
  Leihwagenkosten, pl
  ♦ car rental costs *AE pl*
  ♦ car hire costs *BE pl*
  ♦ car hire charges *BE pl*
Mietwagenmarkt, m
  Leihwagenmarkt, m
  ♦ car rental market *AE*
  ♦ car hire market *BE*
Mietwagenorganisation, f
  Leihwagenorganisation, f
  ♦ car rental organisation *AE*
  ♦ car hire organisation *BE*

Mietwagenpreis, m
  Leihwagenpreis, m
  ♦ car rental price *AE*
  ♦ car hire price *BE*
Mietwagenprospekt, m
  Leihwagenprospekt, m
  ♦ car rental brochure *AE*
  ♦ car hire brochure *BE*
Mietwagenschalter, m
  Leihwagenschalter, m
  ♦ car rental desk *AE*
  ♦ car hire desk *BE*
Mietwagenservice, m
  Mietwagendienst, m
  Leihwagenservice, m
  Leihwagendienst, m
  ♦ car rental service *AE*
  ♦ car hire service *BE*
Mietwagenunternehmen, n
  Mietwagenbetrieb, m
  Leihwagenunternehmen, n
  Leihwagenbetrieb, m
  ♦ car rental operation *AE*
  ♦ car hire operation *BE*
Mietwagenunternehmer, m
  Leihwagenunternehmer, m
  ♦ car rental operator *AE*
  ♦ car hire operator *BE*
Mietwagenvermittlung, f
  Mietwagenagentur, f
  Leihwagenvermittlung, f
  Leihwagenagentur, f
  ♦ car rental agency *AE*
  ♦ hire car agency *BE*
Mietwäsche, f (gemietet)
  Leihwäsche, f
  ♦ rented linen *AE*
  ♦ hired linen *BE*
Mietwäsche, f (generell)
  Leihwäsche, f
  ♦ rental linen *AE*
  ♦ hire linen *BE*
Mietwäsche, f (zu vermieten)
  Leihwäsche, f
  ♦ linen for rent *AE*
  ♦ linen for hire *BE*
Mietwäschedienst, m
  ♦ linen rental service *AE*
  ♦ linen hire service *BE*
mietweise, adv
  pachtweise, adv
  ♦ on lease, adv
  ♦ by way of lease, adv
  ♦ on hire, adv
  ♦ by way of hire, adv
  ♦ on a rental basis, adv
mietweise überlassen etw jm
  ♦ let s.th. out on lease to s.o. *BE*
  ♦ let s.th. to s.o. *BE*
  ♦ rent (out) s.th. out on lease to s.o.
  ♦ hire (out) s.th. to s.o. *BE*
Mietwert, m
  ♦ rental value *AE*
  ♦ renting value
  ♦ letting value *BE*
Mietwert feststellen
  ♦ ascertain the rental value *AE*
  ♦ ascertain the rent value
  ♦ ascertain the letting value *BE*

Mietwertversicherung, f
  (für Mieter)
  ♦ rental value insurance
Mietwohngrundstück, n
  vermietete Immobilie, f
  ♦ rented property
Mietwohnung, f (gemietet)
  → gemietete Wohnung
Mietwohnung, f (generell)
  MTW, f
  ♦ rental apartment *AE*
  ♦ lodging
  ♦ tenement
Mietwohnwagen, m (gemietet)
  Mietcaravan, m
  ♦ rented trailer *AE*
  ♦ hired caravan *BE*
Mietwohnwagen, m (generell)
  Mietcaravan, m
  Leihwohnwagen, m
  Leihcaravan, m
  ♦ rental trailer *AE*
  ♦ hire caravan *BE*
  ♦ letting caravan *BE*
Mietwohnwagen, m (zu vermieten)
  Mietcaravan, m
  ♦ trailer for rent *AE*
  ♦ caravan for hire *BE*
Mietwohnwagenbuchung, f
  Mietcaravanbuchung, f
  ♦ booking (of) a rental trailer *AE*
  ♦ reservation of a rental trailer *AE*
  ♦ booking (of) a hire caravan *BE*
Mietwohnwagenreservierung, f
  Mietcaravanreservierung, f
  Bereithaltung eines Mietwohnwagens, f
  ♦ reservation of a rental trailer *AE*
  ♦ reservation of a hire caravan *BE*
Mietwucher, m
  ♦ rack renting
  ♦ rack rent
Mietwucherer, m
  ♦ rent racketeer
Mietyacht, f
  → Mietjacht
Mietzahler, m
  ♦ rent payer
Mietzahlung, f
  ♦ payment of rent
  ♦ rental payment *AE*
Mietzeit, f (kurz, meist Mobilien)
  Leihzeit, f
  ♦ rental period *AE*
  ♦ period of rental *AE*
  ♦ period of rent *AE*
  ♦ hire period *BE*
  ♦ hire time *BE*
Mietzeit, f (lang, meist Immobilien)
  ♦ term of a lease
  ♦ duration of a lease
  ♦ length of a lease
  ♦ lease period
  ♦ term of tenancy
Mietzeiten kennen (kurz, meist Mobilien)
  ♦ know the rental periods *AE*
  ♦ know the rental times *AE*
  ♦ know the hire periods *BE*
  ♦ know the hire times *BE*
Mietzeit geht gewöhnlich von Samstag bis Freitag
  (z.B. bei Wohnwagen)

Mietzeit ist abgelaufen

Mietzeit ist abgelaufen
- ♦ rental period is usually from Saturday to Friday *AE*
- ♦ hire period is usually from Saturday to Friday *BE*

Mietzeit ist abgelaufen (kurz, meist Mobilien)
Leihzeit ist abgelaufen
- ♦ rental period has expired *AE*
- ♦ hire period has expired *BE*

Mietzeit ist abgelaufen (lang, meist Immobilien)
- ♦ lease period has expired
- ♦ term of lease has expired

Mietzeitpunkt, m (kurz, meist Mobilien)
- ♦ time of rental *AE*
- ♦ time of hiring *BE*

Mietzelt, n (gemietet)
- ♦ rented tent *AE*
- ♦ hired tent *BE*

Mietzelt, n (generell)
Leihzelt, n
- ♦ rental tent *AE*
- ♦ hire tent *BE*

Mietzelt, n (zu vermieten)
- ♦ tent for rent *AE*
- ♦ tent for hire *BE*

Mietzimmer n
→ gemietetes Zimmer

Mietzins, m
- ♦ rental fee
- ♦ rental
- ♦ rent

Mietzins anstelle von Dienstleistungen, m
Pachtzins anstelle von Dienstleistungen, m
- ♦ quitrent

Mietzinsbereich, m
Mietbereich, m
- ♦ rent range

Mietzinsbereich von $ 123 - 321 pro Woche, m
- ♦ rent range of $ 123 - 321 per week

Mietzins festsetzen von DM 123
- ♦ fix a rent of DM 123

Mietzinsforderung, f *jur*
Mietforderung, f
- ♦ claim for rent *jur*

mietzinspflichtig, adj
mietpflichtig, adj
- ♦ subject to rent, adj

Mietzinsstopp, m
→ Mietstopp

Mietzuschuß, m
Mietbeihilfe f
- ♦ rent allowance
- ♦ rent subsidy
- ♦ housing benefit *BE*

Migräne, f
- ♦ migraine

Mikadospiel, n
Mikado, n
- ♦ jackstraws *pl=sg*

Mikadostäbchen, n
- ♦ jackstraw

Mikrofon, n
- ♦ microphone
- ♦ mike *coll*

Mikrofonanlage f
- ♦ microphone system

Mikrofonanschluß, m
- ♦ microphone point

Mikrofondiskussionsanlage, f
- ♦ microphone discussion system

Mikrofonkabel, n
- ♦ microphone cable

Mikrofonstativ, n
Mikrofonständer, m
- ♦ microphone stand

Mikrofonverbindung, f
- ♦ microphone connection

Mikroklima, n
Kleinklima, n
- ♦ microclimate

Mikronesien
- ♦ Micronesia

Mikronesier, m
- ♦ Micronesian

Mikronesierin, f
- ♦ Micronesian girl
- ♦ Micronesian woman
- ♦ Micronesian

mikronesisch, adj
- ♦ Micronesian, adj

Mikrowelle, f
- ♦ microwave

Mikrowellenherd, m
- ♦ microwave oven
- ♦ microwave cooker

Mikrowellenküche, f
Mikrowellenkochen, n
- ♦ microwave cooking *AE*
- ♦ microwave cookery *BE*

Milbe, f
- ♦ mite

Milch, f
- ♦ milk

Milchbar f
- ♦ milk bar
- ♦ dairy bar *AE*
- ♦ dairy lunch *AE*

Milchbecher mit Ei, m
- ♦ eggnog

Milchbrot, n
- ♦ milk bread

Milchbrötchen, n
- ♦ milk roll

Milchflasche, f
- ♦ milk bottle

Milch frisch von der Kuh, f
kuhfrische Milch, f
- ♦ milk fresh from the cow

Milchgeschäft, n
Milchladen, m
- ♦ creamery
- ♦ dairy

Milchgetränk, n
- ♦ milk drink
- ♦ milk beverage
- ♦ milky drink
- ♦ milky beverage

Milchglas, n
lichtdurchlässiges Glas, n
- ♦ translucent glass

Milchkaffee, m
Kaffee mit Milch, m
- ♦ milky coffee
- ♦ white coffee *BE*
- ♦ café au lait *FR*
- ♦ coffee with milk *AE*

Milchkännchen, n
Milchgießer, m
- ♦ milk pot
- ♦ milk jug

Milchkanne, f (Bauernstall)
- ♦ milk churn *BE*

Milchkanne, f (Tisch)
Milchkännchen, n
- ♦ milk jug

Milchkur, f
- ♦ milk diet

Milchmixgetränk, n
Milchshake, m
- ♦ milk shake

Milchportion, f
- ♦ milk portion

Milchprodukt, n
Milcherzeugnis, n
- ♦ milk product

Milchschokolade, f
- ♦ milk chocolate

Milchstube, f
→ Milchbar

Milchtee, m
- ♦ milky tea
- ♦ tea with milk *AE*

Milch trinken
- ♦ drink milk

Milchtrinker, m
- ♦ milk drinker

Milchverbrauch, m
Milchkonsum, m
- ♦ milk consumption
- ♦ consumption of milk

Militärfahrpreis, m
- ♦ military fare

Militärgebiet, n
- ♦ military area

Militärkapelle, f
- ♦ military band

Militärmuseum, n
- ♦ military museum

Militärübungsgebiet, n
- ♦ military training area

Milliardär, m
- ♦ billionaire

Milliardärin, f
- ♦ billionairess

Milliarde, f
Mrd., f
- ♦ billion
- ♦ bn

Million, f
Mio., f
- ♦ million
- ♦ m

Millionär, m
- ♦ millionaire

Millionärin, f
- ♦ millionairess

Millionärsferienort, m
Millionärsurlaubsort, m
- ♦ millionaires' resort

Millstätter See m
- ♦ Lake Millstatt

Minderheitsanteil, m
Minderheitsbeteiligung, f
- ♦ minority stake
- ♦ minority interest

Minderheitsanteil halten
Minderheitsbeteiligung haben
- ♦ hold a minority stake
- ♦ have a minority stake

Minderheitsbeteiligung, f
- ♦ minority interest
- ♦ minority stake

minderjährig, adj
♦ under age, adj
♦ minor, adj
Minderjähriger, m
(Person unter 18 Jahren)
Minderjährige, f
♦ minor
♦ infant BE jur
minderjähriger Gast, m
♦ guest who is a minor
♦ minor guest
Minderjähriger ohne Begleitung, m
alleinreisender Minderjähriger, m
♦ unaccompanied minor
♦ UM
minderwertig, adj
♦ inferior, adj
♦ of inferior value
minderwertiges Essen n
Nahrung mit niedrigem Nährwert, f
♦ junk food
minderwertiges Nahrungsmittel, n
♦ inferior food
♦ inferior foodstuff
♦ junk food
minderwertige Unterkunft, f
unter der Norm liegende Unterkunft, f
♦ substandard accommodation
Mindestalkoholgehalt, m
♦ minimum alcoholic content
♦ minimum alcohol content AE
Mindestalkoholgehalt haben von 10 %
♦ have a minimum alcoholic content of 10 %
♦ have a minimum alcohol content of 10 % AE
Mindestalter, n
♦ minimum age
Mindestanforderung, f
♦ minimum requirement
Mindestanmeldezeit, f
Mindesteincheckzeit, f
♦ minimum check-in time
Mindestarbeitszeit, f
♦ minimum working hours pl
Mindestarrangement n
Mindestvereinbarung f
♦ minimum arrangement
Mindestaufenthalt, m
♦ minimum stay
Mindestaufenthaltsdauer, f
Mindestverweildauer f
♦ minimum duration of stay
♦ minimum length of stay
Mindestauslastung, f
♦ minimum load factor
Mindestausstattung f
♦ minimum equipment
♦ minimum facilities pl
Mindestbeherbergungskapazität, f
♦ minimum accommodation capacity
Mindestbelegung, f
Mindestauslastung, f
♦ minimum occupancy
Mindestbesetzung, f
(Personal)
♦ minimum manning
Mindestbestand, m
♦ minimum inventory AE
♦ minimum stock
Mindestbetrag, m
♦ minimum amount

Mindestbettenzahl f
♦ minimum number of beds
Mindestbettgröße f
♦ minimum bed size
♦ minimum size of a bed
Mindestbodenfläche, f
♦ minimum floor area
Mindestbreite, f
♦ minimum width
Mindestdauer, f
♦ minimum duration
Mindestdeckenhöhe, f
♦ minimum ceiling height
mindestens, adv
♦ at least, adv
♦ no less than, adv
♦ not under, adv
mindestens zwei Nächte bleiben
♦ stay a minimum of two nights
Mindestfahrpreis, m
♦ minimum fare
Mindestfläche, f
♦ minimum area
♦ minimum space
Mindestgebühr f
♦ minimum charge
♦ minimum fee
Mindestgehalt, n
♦ minimum salary
Mindestgeschwindigkeit, f
♦ minimum speed
Mindestgruppengröße f
♦ minimum group size
Mindesthöhe, f
♦ minimum height
Mindestkapazität f
♦ minimum capacity
Mindestkomfort, m
♦ minimum comfort
Mindestlänge, f
♦ minimum length
Mindestlohn, m
♦ minimum wage
Mindestlohnsatz, m
♦ minimum wage rate
Mindestmietdauer, f
→ Mindestmietzeit
Mindestmiete, f (kurz, meist Mobilien)
♦ minimum hire BE
♦ minimum rent AE
Mindestmiete, f (lang, meist Immobilien)
♦ minimum rent
Mindestmietzeit, f (kurz, meist Mobilien)
♦ minimum rental period AE
♦ minimum rent period AE
♦ minimum hiring period BE
♦ minimum hire period BE
Mindestmietzeit, f (lang, meist Immobilien)
♦ minimum rent period AE
♦ minimum rental period AE
♦ minimum letting period BE
♦ minimum let BE
Mindestpauschale, f
♦ minimum package
Mindestpauschalpreis, m
♦ minimum package price
♦ minimum package rate
Mindestpersonal, n
Rumpfpersonal, n
♦ skeleton staff

Mindestpreis, m
♦ minimum price
♦ minimum rate
Mindestquote, f
♦ minimum quota
Mindestreisepreis, m
♦ minimum tour price
Mindestschrankpreis, m
♦ minimum rack rate
Mindeststandard, m
♦ minimum standard
Mindeststandard erfüllen
♦ meet the minimum standard
Mindeststellfläche, f
(Camping)
Mindeststellplatz, m
♦ minimum pitch
Mindestteilnahme, f
♦ minimum attendance
Mindestteilnehmerzahl f
♦ minimum number of participants
Mindestübergangszeit, f
(Umsteigen)
♦ minimum connecting time
♦ MCT
Mindestübernachtungspreis m
Minimumrate f
♦ minimum rate
Mindestumtausch, m
♦ minimum currency exchange
Mindestverweildauer, f
Mindestaufenthaltsdauer f
♦ minimum length of stay
♦ minimum duration of stay
Mindestzahl, f
♦ minimum number
Mindestzimmerkapazität f
♦ minimum room capacity
Mindestzimmerpreis, m
♦ minimum room rate
♦ minimum room price
Mindestzimmerzahl f
♦ minimum number of rooms
Mindestzuhörerschaft, f
♦ minimum audience
Mindestzuhörerschaft garantieren jm
♦ guarantee s.o. a minimum audience
mineralarm, adj
♦ low-mineral, adj
mineralarmes Wasser, n
♦ low-mineral water
Mineralbad, n (Aktivität)
♦ mineral bath
Mineralbad, n (Ort)
→ Mineralheilbad
Mineralheilbad, n (Ort)
Mineralbad n
♦ mineral spa
Mineralienbörse, f
♦ mineral exchange
Mineraliensammlung, f
♦ collection of minerals
Mineralquelle, f
Mineralbrunnen, m
♦ mineral spring
Mineralquellwasser, n
♦ mineral spring water
mineralreich, adj
♦ rich in minerals, adj
♦ mineral rich, adj

mineralreiches Wasser, n
  ♦ mineral rich water
  ♦ water rich in minerals
Mineralwasser, n
  ♦ mineral water
Mineralwasserbehälter, m
  ♦ soda fountain
Mineralwasserindustrie, f
  ♦ mineral water industry
Minestrone, f *ITAL*
  ♦ minestrone *ITAL*
Ming-Grabmal, n
  Ming-Grab, n
  ♦ Ming tomb
Miniappartement, n
  ♦ miniapartment
Miniaturdampfeisenbahn, f
  ♦ miniature steam railroad *AE*
  ♦ miniature steam railway *BE*
Miniatureisenbahn, f
  ♦ miniature railroad *AE*
  ♦ miniature railway *BE*
Miniaturfernsehen, n
  ♦ miniature television
  ♦ miniature TV
Miniaturgolf, m/n
  Minigolf, m/n
  ♦ miniature golf
  ♦ minigolf
  ♦ crazy golf
Miniaturrasen, m
  ♦ miniature lawn
Minibadewanne, f
  Minibad, n
  ♦ minibath
Minibar, f
  ♦ minibar
Minibarfüllung, f
  Minibarbestand, m
  ♦ minibar stock
Minibarservice m
  ♦ minibar service
Minibus, m
  Kleinbus, m
  ♦ passenger van *AE*
  ♦ minibus
  ♦ minicoach *BE*
Minicar, m
  Minitaxi, n
  ♦ minicab
Minicarfahrer, m
  Minitaxifahrer, m
  ♦ minicab driver
Minicarfirma, f
  Minitaxifirma, f
  ♦ minicab firm
Miniferien, pl
  Miniurlaub, m
  ♦ miniholidays *BE pl*
  ♦ miniholiday *BE*
  ♦ minivacation *AE*
Minigolf, m/n
  Miniaturgolf, m/n
  ♦ minigolf
  ♦ miniature golf
  ♦ crazy golf
Minigolfanlage, f
  → Minigolfplatz
Minigolfplatz, m
  Minigolfanlage, f
  Miniaturgolfplatz, m

♦ minigolf course
♦ miniature golf course
♦ crazy golf course
Minigolfspiel, n
  ♦ game of minigolf
  ♦ minigolf
  ♦ game of crazy golf
Minigolf spielen
  ♦ play minigolf
  ♦ play crazy golf
Minigolfturnier, n
  ♦ minigolf tournament
  ♦ crazy golf tournament
Minikonferenz, f
  ♦ miniconference
Minikongreß, m
  ♦ miniconvention
  ♦ minicongress
Minikreuzfahrt, f
  ♦ minicruise
Minikühlschrank, m
  ♦ minirefrigerator
  ♦ minifridge *coll*
minimale Gebühr, f
  sehr kleine Gebühr, f
  ♦ minimal charge
  ♦ minimal fee
Minimumrate, f
  → Mindestübernachtungspreis
Minireise, f
  Minitour, f
  ♦ minitour
Minirestaurant, n
  ♦ minirestaurant
Minisafe, m
  Minitresor, m
  ♦ minisafe
Minishow, f
  ♦ minishow
Minister für Sport und Erholung, m
  ♦ minister for sport and recreation
Ministerium für Tourismus, n
  ♦ Ministry of Tourism
Ministerkonferenz, f
  ♦ ministerial conference
Ministudio, n
  ♦ ministudio
Minisuite, f
  ♦ minisuite
Minitaxi, n
  ♦ minitaxi
  ♦ minicab
Miniurlaub, m
  Miniferien, pl
  ♦ minivacation *AE*
  ♦ miniholiday *BE*
  ♦ miniholidays *BE pl*
Minizoo, m
  Kleinzoo, m
  ♦ minizoo
Minnesänger, m
  ♦ minnesinger
Minute, f
  ♦ minute
Minzeblatt, n
  Pfefferminzblatt, n
  ♦ mint leaf
Minzezweig, m
  Minzezweigchen, n
  ♦ mint sprig

Mio., f
  Million, f
  ♦ m
  ♦ million
Mirabelle, f
  ♦ yellow plum
Mirabellenkonfitüre, f
  ♦ yellow plum jam
Mir gefällt es hier
  ♦ I like it here
Mir hat es hier gefallen
  ♦ I have enjoyed being here
Mir ist bekannt, daß
  ♦ I understand that
Mir schmeckt das Essen (Dinner)
  ♦ I enjoy my dinner
Miscellaneous Charges Order, f
  (bei Luftbeförderung)
  MCO, f
  ♦ miscellaneous charges order
  ♦ MCO
Mischbecher, m
  → Schüttelbecher
Mischgetränk, n
  Mixgetränk, n
  ♦ mixed beverage
  ♦ mixed drink
  ♦ shake
Mischglas, n
  (Bar)
  Mixglas, n
  ♦ mixing glass
Mischkosten, pl
  → sprungfixe Kosten
Mischlöffel, m
  ♦ mixing spoon
Mischpult, n
  (Konferenztechnik)
  ♦ mixing console
  ♦ mixing desk
  ♦ mixer
Mischung von Arbeit und Vergnügen, f
  ♦ mix of work and pleasure
Mischung von Ost und West, f
  ♦ blend of East and West
Mischwald, m
  ♦ mixed forest
Mise en place, f *FR*
  ♦ mise en place *FR*
  ♦ arrangement of materials
Mise-en-place-Kosten, pl
  ♦ mise-en-place costs *pl*
  ♦ mise-en-place cost
Mise en place machen
  ♦ do the mise en place
Mise en place organisieren
  ♦ organise the mise en place
Mise-en-place-Tisch, m
  ♦ mise-en-place table
Mise en place überprüfen
  ♦ check the mise en place
Mise en place veranlassen
  ♦ induce the mise en place
Mise en place vorbereiten
  ♦ prepare the mise en place
miserablen Urlaub haben
  beschissenen Urlaub haben *vulg*
  ♦ have a lousy vacation *AE*
  ♦ have a lousy holiday *BE*
miserabler Urlaub, m
  beschissener Urlaub, m *vulg*

- ♦ **lousy vacation** *AE*
- ♦ **lousy holiday** *BE*

Mißbrauch, m
- ♦ **abuse**
- ♦ **misuse**

Mißbrauch der Gastfreundschaft, m
- ♦ **abuse of hospitality**

mißbrauchen etw
- ♦ **abuse s.th.**
- ♦ **misuse s.th.**

Mississippi, m
- ♦ **Mississippi River, the**
- ♦ River Mississippi, the
- ♦ Mississippi, the

Mißmanagement, n
Mißwirtschaft, f
- ♦ **mismanagement**
- ♦ **bad management**

Missouri, m
- ♦ **Missouri River, the**
- ♦ River Missouri, the
- ♦ Missouri, the

Mißtrauen, n
Argwohn, m
- ♦ **distrust**

Mißtrauen gegen Fremde, n
- ♦ **distrust of strangers**

mißtrauen jm
- ♦ **distrust s.o.**

Mißverhalten, n
- ♦ **misconduct**

Mißverständnis, n
- ♦ **misunderstanding**

Mißverständnis ausräumen
Mißverständnis beseitigen
- ♦ **clear up a misunderstanding**

Mißwahl, f
Schönheitswettbewerb, m
- ♦ **beauty contest**
- ♦ **beauty competition**

Mistral, m
- ♦ **mistral, the**

mit allem modernen Komfort
- → mit jedem modernen Komfort

mit allen Schikanen
(Ausstattung)
- ♦ **with all the trimmings**

Mitarbeit, f
- → Zusammenarbeit

Mitarbeitermotivation, f
- ♦ **employee motivation**

Mitarbeiterschulung, f
Mitarbeiterausbildung, f
- ♦ **employee training**

Mitarbeiterseminar n
- ♦ **staff seminar**

Mitarbeiterstab, m
Personal, n
- ♦ **personnel**
- ♦ **staff**

mit Bedienung
- → Bedienung inbegriffen

mitbenutzen etw
- ♦ **share s.th.**

Mitbenutzer, m
- ♦ **co-user**

Mitbenutzung, f
- ♦ **shared use**
- ♦ **joint use**

Mitbesitz, m
- ♦ **co-ownership**
- ♦ **joint ownership**
- ♦ **part ownership** *AE*
- ♦ **part-ownership** *BE*

Mitbesitzer, m
Mitbesitzerin, f
Miteigentümer, m
Miteigentümerin, f
- ♦ **co-owner**
- ♦ **part owner** *AE*
- ♦ **part-owner** *BE*
- ♦ **joint owner**

Mitbesitzer einer Wohnung, m
Miteigentümer einer Wohnung, m
- ♦ **part owner of an apartment** *AE*
- ♦ **part-owner of a flat** *BE*

Mitbesucher, m
- ♦ **fellow visitor**

Mitbetreiber, m
- ♦ **fellow operator**

Mitbewerber, m
- → Konkurrent

Mitbewohner, m (Haus)
Hausgenosse, m
- ♦ **fellow lodger**
- ♦ **fellow occupant**

Mitbewohner, m (Hotel)
- ♦ **fellow resident**

Mitbewohner, m (Zimmer)
- ♦ **fellow occupant**
- ♦ **roommate** *AE*
- ♦ **room-mate** *BE*

mit Blick auf etw
- ♦ **with a view of s.th.**
- ♦ with a view of s.th.

Mitbringsel, n
- ♦ **little present**
- ♦ **souvenir**

Mitcamper, m
- ♦ **fellow camper**

mit dem Auto, adv
mit dem eigenen Auto, adv
- ♦ **by car, adv**
- ♦ in one's own car, adv

mit dem Auto fahren
- ♦ **go by car**

mit dem Autozug fahren
- ♦ **go Motorail** *BE*

mit dem Boot
mit dem Schiff
- ♦ **by boat**

mit dem Boot fahren
- ♦ **go by boat**

mit dem Bus
- ♦ **by bus**
- ♦ by coach *BE*

mit dem Bus ankommen
- ♦ **arrive by coach** *BE*
- ♦ arrive by bus

mit dem Bus reisen
- ♦ **travel by coach** *BE*
- ♦ travel by bus

mit dem Dampfer
- ♦ **by steamer**

mit dem Fahrrad
mit dem Rad *coll*
- ♦ **by bicycle**
- ♦ by bike *coll*

mit dem Fahrrad fahren
mit dem Rad fahren
- ♦ **go by bicycle**
- ♦ ride a bicycle
- ♦ cycle
- ♦ bike *coll*

mit dem Fahrrad kommen
- ♦ **come by bicycle**

mit dem Fallschirm springen
- ♦ **parachute**

mit dem Flugzeug
- ♦ **by airplane** *AE*
- ♦ **by aeroplane** *BE*
- ♦ **by plane**

mit dem Flugzeug fliegen
- ♦ **go by airplane** *AE*
- ♦ **go by aeroplane** *BE*
- ♦ **go by plane**

mit dem linken Fuß zuerst aufstehen
- ♦ **get out of bed on the wrong side**
- ♦ have got out of bed on the wrong side
- ♦ have got out of the wrong side of the bed

mit dem Rad *coll*
mit dem Fahrrad
- ♦ **by bike** *coll*
- ♦ by bicycle

mit dem Rad kommen *coll*
- ♦ **come by bike** *coll*

mit dem Schiff
- ♦ **by ship**
- ♦ **by boat**

mit dem Zug
- ♦ **by train**

mit dem Zug fahren
- ♦ **go by train**

mit der Bahn
- ♦ **by rail**

mit der Bahn reisen
- → mit der Eisenbahn reisen

mit der Fähre
- ♦ **by ferry**

mit der Miete im Rückstand sein
- ♦ **be behind with the rent**
- ♦ be in arrears with the rent

mit der richtigen Temperatur
(servieren)
- ♦ **at the correct temperature**

mit der U-Bahn
- ♦ **by subway** *AE*
- ♦ **by underground** *BE*
- ♦ **by tube** *BE*
- ♦ **by metro**

mit der Zeit gehen
- ♦ **move with the times**
- ♦ march with the times

mit direktem Zugang zu etw
- ♦ **with direct access to s.th.**

Miteigentum, n
- ♦ **coproprietorship** *AE*
- ♦ **co-proprietorship** *BE*
- ♦ **joint ownership**

Miteigentümer, m (generell)
- ♦ **coproprietor** *AE*
- ♦ **co-proprietor** *BE*
- ♦ **joint proprietor**
- ♦ **joint owner**
- ♦ **tenant in common**

Miteigentümer, m (Timesharing)
Zeitmiteigentümer, m
Timesharer, m
- ♦ **time sharer**

Miteigentumsanteil, m
- ♦ **share in the property**

miteinander verbundene Doppelzimmer, n pl
- ♦ interconnected double rooms pl
- ♦ interconnecting double rooms pl

miteinander verbundene Zimner, n pl
zusammenhängende Zimmer, n pl
- ♦ rooms en suite pl
- ♦ connecting rooms pl

mit Eiswürfeln (Getränk)
- ♦ on the rocks

mitessen mit jm
→ essen mit jm

mit etw in der Hauptrolle (Programm)
- ♦ featuring s.th.

mitfahren auf dem Sozius
(Motorrad)
- ♦ ride pillion

mitfahren lassen jn (Auto)
(privat, unentgeltlich)
mitnehmen jn
- ♦ give s.o. a ride AE
- ♦ give s.o. a lift BE

mitfahren mit jm (Auto)
- ♦ drive with s.o.

mitfahren mit jm (generell)
- ♦ go with s.o.
- ♦ ride with s.o.

Mitfahrer, m (Autolenker)
- ♦ fellow driver

Mitfahrer, m (generell)
→ Mitreisender

Mitfahrgelegenheit anbieten jm
(im Auto)
- ♦ offer s.o. a ride AE
- ♦ offer s.o. a lift BE

Mitfahrzentrale, f
- ♦ car pool service

mitfeiern
mitmachen bei einer Feier
- ♦ join in a celebration

Mitflieger, m
Mitfliegender, m
- ♦ fellow flyer
- ♦ fellow flier

mit französischer Küche
- ♦ with French cuisine
- ♦ with French cooking

mit freundlicher Genehmigung von jm
durch jn
mittels jn
als Geschenk von jm
- ♦ by courtesy of s.o.
- ♦ courtesy of s.o.

Mitgast, m
- ♦ fellow guest

Mitgast behelligen
Mitgast verärgern
- ♦ annoy a fellow guest

Mitgast belästigen
- ♦ inconvenience a fellow guest

Mitgastgeber, m
- ♦ co-host

mitgehen lassen etw coll
klauen etw
stehlen etw
- ♦ pinch s.th. coll
- ♦ pilfer s.th. coll
- ♦ steal s.th.

Mitglied, n
- ♦ member

Mitglied auf Lebenszeit, n
- ♦ life member

Mitglied des Jetset, n
- ♦ member of the jet set

Mitgliederversammlung, f
- ♦ members' meeting
- ♦ meeting of the members
- ♦ assembly of the members

Mitgliederverzeichnis, n
- ♦ membership directory

Mitgliederzahl, f
- ♦ membership

Mitgliedsausweis, m
Mitgliedskarte, f
- ♦ membership card

Mitgliedsbeitrag, m
Mitgliederbeitrag, m
Vereinsbeitrag, m
- ♦ membership fee
- ♦ membership dues pl
- ♦ dues pl

Mitgliedschaft, f
- ♦ membership

Mitgliedschaft erwerben
Mitglied werden
- ♦ become a member

Mitgliedschaft in einem Club, f
- ♦ membership of a club

Mitgliedschaft in etw, f
- ♦ membership of s.th.

Mitgliedsfluggesellschaft, f
- ♦ member airline

Mitgliedsherberge, f
Mitgliedsheim, n
- ♦ member hostel

Mitgliedshotel n
- ♦ member hotel

Mitgliedskarte, f
→ Mitgliedsausweis

Mitgliedsland, n
- ♦ member country

Mitgliedsnummer, f
- ♦ membership number

Mitgliedsrestaurant, n
- ♦ member restaurant

Mitgliedsstaat, m
- ♦ member state

Mitgliedsverband, m
- ♦ member association

Mitglied werden in einem Campingclub
- ♦ become a member of a camping club

mit größtem Vergnügen
- ♦ with the greatest pleasure

mit jedem modernen Komfort
mit jeglichem modernen Komfort
mit allem modernen Komfort
- ♦ with all modern comforts
- ♦ with every modern comfort
- ♦ with all modern conveniences
- ♦ with all modern amenities
- ♦ with all mod. cons.

mit leerem Magen
- ♦ with an empty stomach
- ♦ on an empty stomach

mit leerem Magen zu Bett gehen
- ♦ go to bed with an empty stomach
- ♦ go to bed on an empty stomach

mit liebevoller Sorgfalt für jedes Detail
- ♦ with loving attention to every detail

mitmachen bei einem Angelausflug
- ♦ join a fishing trip

mitmachen bei einem fakultativen Ausflug
teilnehmen an einem fakultativen Ausflug
- ♦ join an optional excursion
- ♦ join an optional trip

mitmachen bei einer Expedition
teilnehmen an einer Expedition
- ♦ join an expedition

mitmachen bei einer Feier
→ mitfeiern

mitmachen bei einer Reise
- ♦ join a tour

mitmachen bei etw
- ♦ join s.th.
- ♦ join in s.th.

Mitmieter, m
- ♦ cotenant AE
- ♦ co-tenant BE
- ♦ joint tenant

Mitmieter, m (Immobilien)
- ♦ fellow tenant

Mitmieter, m (Mobilien)
- ♦ fellow hirer BE
- ♦ fellow renter AE

mit monatlicher Kündigung
- ♦ subject to one month's notice

mitnehmen jn (im Auto)
(privat, unentgeltlich)
mitfahren lassen jn
- ♦ give s.o. a lift BE
- ♦ give s.o. a ride AE

mitnehmen lassen sich nach X
(kostenlos als Anhalter)
- ♦ hitch a ride to X AE
- ♦ hitch a lift to X BE

mit Orchesterkonzerten
(Programm)
- ♦ featuring orchestral concerts

Mitorganisator, f
- ♦ co-organiser
- ♦ co-organizer

Mitpacht, f
- ♦ joint tenancy
- ♦ cotenancy AE
- ♦ co-tenancy BE

Mitpächter, m
- ♦ joint tenant
- ♦ cotenant AE
- ♦ co-tenant BE

mit Pack und Sack
- ♦ bag and baggage

Mitpassagier, m
Mitreisender, m
Mitfahrer, m
Mitfahrgast, m
- ♦ fellow passenger

mit Proviant versehen, adj
mit Proviant
- ♦ provisioned, adj

Mitreisegepäck, n
- ♦ accompanied baggage AE
- ♦ accompanied luggage BE

mitreisend, adj
begleitend, adj
- ♦ accompanying, adj

Mitreisender, m
Mitfahrer, m
- ♦ fellow traveler AE
- ♦ fellow traveller BE
- ♦ fellow passenger

mitreisender Partner, m
begleitender Partner, m
- ♦ accompanying partner

mit Sack und Pack
♦ with bag and baggage
mit seinem Rad fahren
♦ go on one's bike
mit Service
♦ with service
mit Sorgfalt zubereitetes Essen, n
♦ carefully prepared meal
Mitspeisegast, m
♦ fellow diner
Mitsponsor, m
♦ cosponsor AE
♦ co-sponsor BE
Mittag, m
♦ noon
♦ midday
Mittagessen, n (generell)
Mittagsmahlzeit, f
♦ midday meal
Mittagessen, n (Lunch)
Mittagsmahlzeit, f
♦ luncheon
♦ lunch
Mittagessen an Bord, n
♦ lunch on board
Mittagessen an Bord servieren
♦ serve lunch on board
Mittagessen an der Gästetafel, n
→ gemeinsamer Mittagstisch
Mittagessen ankündigen
♦ announce lunch
♦ announce luncheon
Mittagessen arrangieren
♦ arrange (a) lunch
Mittagessen ausgeben
♦ issue (a) lunch
Mittagessen auslassen
♦ skip lunch
Mittagessen ausrichten (als Gastgeber)
♦ host a lunch
♦ host a luncheon
Mittagessen außer Haus essen
♦ lunch out
Mittagessen beenden
♦ finish one's lunch
♦ finish one's luncheon
Mittagessenbuchung, f
Mittagessenbestellung, f
♦ lunch booking
♦ luncheon booking
Mittagesseneinladung, f
♦ lunch invitation
♦ invitation to lunch
Mittagessen einnehmen
♦ take lunch
♦ have lunch
Mittagessen essen
♦ eat one's lunch
Mittagessengeschäft, n
Mittagsgeschäft, n
♦ lunch business
♦ luncheon business
Mittagessen im Freien, n
♦ alfresco lunch
Mittagessen im Garten servieren
♦ serve lunch in the garden
♦ serve luncheon in the garden
Mittagessen im Hotel, n
♦ lunch at the hotel
♦ lunch in the hotel

Mittagessen im Sitzen, n
♦ sit-down lunch
♦ sit-down luncheon
Mittagessen ist fertig
♦ lunch is ready
Mittagessen kochen
♦ cook lunch
Mittagessen mit dem Bürgermeister
♦ luncheon with the mayor
♦ lunch with the mayor
Mittagessen mit vier Gängen, n
→ viergängiges Mittagessen
Mittagessenrechnung, f
♦ lunch bill
♦ luncheon bill
♦ lunch check AE
♦ luncheon check AE
Mittagessen richten
♦ fix lunch AE
♦ prepare lunch BE
♦ get lunch BE
Mittagessen servieren
♦ serve lunch
Mittagessen servieren jm
♦ serve lunch to s.o.
♦ serve s.o. lunch
Mittagessen spendieren jm
♦ buy s.o. lunch
Mittagessentour, f
Tour mit Mittagessen, f
Rundgang mit Mittagessen, m
♦ luncheon tour
♦ lunch tour
Mittagessen umfaßt vier Gänge
♦ lunch comprises four courses
Mittagessenumsatz, m
Mittagsumsatz, m
♦ luncheon sales pl
♦ lunch sales pl
Mittagessen unterwegs
♦ lunch en route
♦ lunch on the way
Mittagessen von 12 bis 13 Uhr
♦ lunch from 12 to 13
♦ luncheon from 12 o'clock to 1 p.m.
Mittagessen wird zwischen 12 und 14 Uhr serviert
♦ lunch is served between 12 o'clock and 2 p.m.
Mittagessenzeit, f (Zeitpunkt)
Mittagszeit, f
♦ lunchtime AE
♦ lunch-time BE
Mittagessenzeit, f (Zeitraum)
Mittagszeit, f
♦ lunch period
Mittagessen zubereiten
♦ prepare lunch
♦ get lunch
Mittagessen zusammen einnehmen
zusammen zu Mittag essen
♦ lunch together
♦ have lunch together
Mittagessenzuschlag, m
(Preis)
♦ luncheon supplement
♦ lunch supplement
♦ supplement for luncheon
♦ supplement for lunch
Mittagessenzuschuß, m
(von Arbeitgeber an Arbeitnehmer)

Essenzuschuß, m
♦ luncheon allowance
♦ lunch allowance
Mittagkuvert n
→ Mittagsgedeck
mittags, adv
→ am Mittag
Mittagsarrangement, n
♦ lunch arrangement
Mittagsaufführung, f
(Theater)
Mittagsvorstellung, f
♦ lunchtime performance
Mittagsbar, f
♦ lunch bar
Mittagsbesuch, m
♦ lunchtime visit
Mittagsbrot, n
belegtes Brot am Mittag, n
♦ lunchtime sandwich
Mittagsbüfett, n
♦ lunch buffet AE
♦ luncheon buffet AE
♦ buffet lunch(eon) BE
♦ lunchtime buffet AE
♦ lunch-time buffet BE
Mittagsbüfett anbieten
♦ offer a lunch buffet AE
♦ offer a buffet luncheon
♦ offer a buffet lunch
Mittagscouvert n
→ Mittagsgedeck
Mittagseinkehr, f
Halt zum Mittagessen, m
♦ lunch stop
Mittagsgast m
(im Restaurant)
♦ lunch customer
♦ luncher
Mittagsgedeck, n
Mittagkuvert, n
Mittagscouvert, n
♦ lunch cover
♦ luncheon cover
Mittagsgeschäft, n
→ Mittagessengeschäft
Mittagsgesellschaft, f (mit Essen)
Tischgesellschaft beim Mittagessen, f
Tischgesellschaft, f
♦ luncheon party
♦ lunch party
Mittagsgetränk, n
♦ lunchtime drink
♦ lunchtime tipple coll
Mittagsimbiß, m
♦ snack lunch
♦ lunch snack
♦ midday snack
Mittagskaffee, m
♦ after-lunch coffee
Mittagskarte, f
Mittagsspeisekarte, f
♦ lunchtime menu
♦ luncheon menu
♦ lunch menu
Mittagskonzert, n (generell)
♦ lunchtime concert
Mittagskonzert, n (Solomusik)
♦ lunchtime recital
Mittagskuvert, n
→ Mittagsgedeck

Mittagslektüre

Mittagslektüre, f
- ♦ lunchtime reading

Mittagsmahl, n
→ Mittagessen

Mittagsmenü, n
- ♦ lunch menu
- ♦ luncheon menu
- ♦ set lunch *BE*

Mittagspause, f
- ♦ lunchbreak *AE*
- ♦ luncheon break
- ♦ lunch-break *BE*
- ♦ lunch interval
- ♦ luncheon interval

Mittagspause machen
Mittagspause haben
- ♦ have a lunchbreak *AE*
- ♦ have a lunch-break *BE*
- ♦ take a lunchbreak *AE*
- ♦ take a lunch-break *BE*

Mittagspause von 12 bis 13 Uhr
- ♦ lunchbreak from 12 to 13 *AE*
- ♦ lunch-break from 12 to 13 *BE*
- ♦ luncheon break from 12 until 13

Mittagspicknick, n
- ♦ lunch picnic *AE*
- ♦ picnic lunch
- ♦ picnic luncheon
- ♦ basket lunch *AE*

Mittagspicknick essen
- ♦ eat one's picnic lunch

Mittagsrestaurant, n
- ♦ lunch room
- ♦ lunch bar

Mittagsruhe, f
- ♦ noon rest
- ♦ siesta

Mittagsruhe von 13 bis 14 Uhr
(Hinweisschild)
- ♦ Closed for lunch 1 - 2 p.m.

Mittagsschlaf, m
Mittagsschläfchen, n *coll*
- ♦ after-dinner nap
- ♦ siesta

Mittagsschlaf halten
- ♦ have an after-dinner nap
- ♦ have a siesta

Mittagsservice, m
- ♦ lunch service
- ♦ luncheon service

Mittagsspaziergang, m
- ♦ midday walk
- ♦ noon walk

Mittagsspeisekarte, f
Mittagskarte, f
- ♦ luncheon menu
- ♦ lunch menu
- ♦ lunchtime menu

Mittagsstunde, f
- ♦ lunch hour

Mittagstafel, f
→ gemeinsamer Mittagstisch

Mittagstisch m
→ Mittagessen n

Mittagstreffpunkt, m
- ♦ lunch venue
- ♦ luncheon venue

Mittagsverabredung, f
(von z.B. Geschäftsleuten)
Verabredung zum Mittagessen, f
- ♦ luncheon engagement

- ♦ luncheon commitment
- ♦ luncheon meeting

Mittagsvesper, f
Mittagsimbiß, m
- ♦ lunch snack
- ♦ midday snack

Mittagsvortrag, m
- ♦ lunchtime lecture

Mittagszeit, f
→ Mittagessenzeit

Mitte, f
- ♦ middle
- ♦ center *AE*
- ♦ centre *BE*

Mitte des Zimmers, f
- ♦ middle of the room

mitteilen jm etw
- ♦ tell s.o. s.th.
- ♦ inform s.o. about s.th.
- ♦ inform s.o. of s.th.

Mitteilung, f
Nachricht, f
- ♦ message
- ♦ notification

Mitteilung entgegennehmen (für jn)
Mitteilung annehmen (für jn)
- ♦ take a message (for s.o.)

Mitteilungsfach, n
- ♦ message box

Mitteilungsformular n
Benachrichtigungsformular n
- ♦ notification form

Mitteilungsschalter, m
- ♦ message desk

Mitteilungszettel, m
Benachrichtigungszettel, m
- ♦ notification slip

Mitteilung weitergeben an jn
- ♦ pass on a message to s.o.

Mitteilung zukommen lassen jm
jm etw ausrichten
- ♦ give a message to s.o.

Mittelalter, n
- ♦ Middle Ages, the *pl*

mittelalterlich, adj
- ♦ medieval, adj
- ♦ mediaeval, adj

mittelalterlichen Charakter bewahren
mittelalterlichen Charakter bewahrt haben
- ♦ retain its medieval character
- ♦ retain its mediaeval character
- ♦ have retained its medieval character
- ♦ have retained ist mediaeval character

mittelalterlicher Jahrmarkt, m
mittelalterlicher Markt, m
- ♦ medieval fair
- ♦ mediaeval fair

mittelalterlicher Markt, m
- ♦ medieval market
- ♦ mediaeval market

mittelalterlicher Marktplatz, m
- ♦ medieval market square
- ♦ mediaeval market square
- ♦ medieval market place
- ♦ mediaeval market place

mittelalterliches Bankett, n
mittelalterliches Festessen, n
- ♦ medieval banquet
- ♦ mediaeval banquet

mittelalterliches Schloß, n
mittelalterliche Burg, f

- ♦ medieval castle
- ♦ mediaeval castle

mittelalterliche Stadt, f (Großstadt)
- ♦ medieval city
- ♦ mediaeval city

mittelalterliche Stadt, f (kleine Stadt)
- ♦ medieval town
- ♦ mediaeval town

mittelalterliche Stadtmauer, f
- ♦ medieval town wall
- ♦ mediaeval town wall
- ♦ medieval city wall
- ♦ mediaeval city wall

Mittelamerika
- ♦ Central America

Mittelamerikaner, m
- ♦ Central American

mittelamerikanisch, adj
- ♦ Central American, adj

Mittelasiate, m
- ♦ Central Asian

mittelasiatisch, adj
- ♦ Central Asian, adj

Mittelasien
- ♦ Central Asia

mittelbare Arbeitskosten, pl
- ♦ indirect labor costs *AE pl*
- ♦ indirect labour costs *BE pl*

Mittelbetrieb, m
mittelgroßer Betrieb, m
- ♦ medium-sized establishment
- ♦ medium-sized operation

Mitteldeutschland
- ♦ Central Germany

Mittelengland
- ♦ Middle England
- ♦ Central England

Mitteleuropa
- ♦ Central Europe

Mitteleuropäer, m
- ♦ Central European

mitteleuropäisch, adj
- ♦ Central European, adj

Mittelfranken
(Region)
- ♦ Central Franconia

mittelfristig, adj
- ♦ medium-term, adj

mittelfristige Fremdenverkehrsnachfrage, f
mittelfristige Tourismusnachfrage, f
- ♦ medium-term tourist demand
- ♦ medium-term tourism demand

Mittelgang, m
Gang, m
- ♦ central aisle
- ♦ aisle

Mittelgangplatz, m
Mittelgangsitzplatz, m
Gangplatz, m
Gangsitz, m
- ♦ aisle seat

Mittelgangstand, m
Gangstand, m
- ♦ aisle stand

Mittelgebäude, n
Zentralgebäude, n
- ♦ central building

Mittelgebirge, n
- ♦ medium-altitude mountains *pl*

mittelgroß, adj
von mittlerer Größe

508

- **medium-sized**, adj
- of medium size

mittelgroße Halle, f
- mittelgroßer Saal, m
- **medium-sized hall**

mittelgroße Konferenz, f
- mittlere Konferenz, f
- **medium-sized conference**

mittelgroßer Stellplatz, m
- (Camping)
- mittlerer Stellplatz, m
- **medium-sized pitch**

mittelgroßer Teller, m
- **medium-sized plate**

mittelgroßes Hotel, n
- mittleres Hotel, n
- Hotel von mittlerer Größe, n
- **medium-sized hotel**
- hotel of medium size

mittelgroßes Zimmer n
- mittleres Zimmer n
- **medium-sized room**

mittelgroße Veranstaltung, f
- mittlere Veranstaltung, f
- **medium-sized event**
- medium-sized function

Mittelhaardt, f
- (Region)
- **Middle Haardt, the**

Mittelitalien
- **Central Italy**

Mittelklassehaus, n
- → Mittelklassehotel

Mittelklassehotel, n
- Mittelklaßhotel, n
- Mittelklassehaus, n
- **mid-price hotel**
- middle-class hotel

Mittelklassewagen, m
- **middle-of-the-market car**

Mittelkorridor, m
- Mittelgang, m
- **central corridor**

Mittellandkanal, m
- (Wasserstraße)
- **Mittelland Canal, the**

mittelmäßig, adj
- **mediocre,** adj
- **indifferent,** adj

mittelmäßiger Koch, m
- **indifferent cook**

mittelmäßiger Wein, m
- **mediocre wine**

mittelmäßiges Essen, n
- **mediocre food**
- **indifferent** food

mittelmäßiges Restaurant n
- **mediocre restaurant**

Mittelmeer, n
- **Mediterranean Sea, the**
- **Mediterranean, the**
- **Med, the** coll

Mittelmeerbuchung, f
- **booking for the Mediterranean**

Mittelmeerferienland, n
- Mittelmeerurlaubsland, n
- **Mediterranean holiday country**
- Mediterranean vacation country

Mittelmeerferienort, m
- Mittelmeerurlaubsort, m
- **Mediterranean resort**

Mittelmeergebiet, n (groß)
- **Mediterranean region**

Mittelmeergebiet, n (klein)
- **Mediterranean area**

Mittelmeerinsel, f
- **Mediterranean island**

Mittelmeerklima, n
- **Mediterranean climate**

Mittelmeerkreuzfahrt, f
- **Mediterranean cruise**

Mittelmeerküste, f
- **Mediterranean coast**
- Mediterranean coastline

Mittelmeerland, n
- **Mediterranean country**

Mittelmeerpauschale, f
- **Mediterranean package**

Mittelmeerplatz, m
- (Camping)
- **Mediterranean site**

Mittelmeerreise, f
- **Mediterranean tour**

Mittelmeersaison, f
- **Mediterranean season**

Mittelmeersonne, f
- **Mediterranean sun**

Mittelmeerstadt, f (Großstadt)
- **Mediterranean city**

Mittelmeerstadt, f (kleine Stadt)
- **Mediterranean town**

Mittelmeerstil, m
- **Mediterranean style**

Mittelmeerstrand, m
- **Mediterranean beach**

Mittelmeerurlaub, m
- **Mediterranean vacation** AE
- **Mediterranean holiday** BE

Mittelmeerurlauber, m
- **vacationer to the Mediterranean** AE
- holidaymaker to the Mediterranean BE
- Mediterranean vacationer AE
- Mediterranean holidaymaker BE

Mittelmeerurlaubsland, n
- Mittelmeerferienland, n
- **Mediterranean vacation country** AE
- Mediterranean holiday country BE

Mittelmeervilla, f
- **Mediterranean villa**

Mittelmeerziel, n
- Mittelmeerzielort, m
- **Mediterranean destination**

Mittelmosel, f
- **Middle Mosel, the**
- Middle Moselle, the

Mittelplatz, m
- Mittelsitzplatz, m
- Mittelsitz, m
- **middle seat**

Mittelpreis, m
- mittlerer Preis, m
- **middle price**
- middle rate

Mittelrhein, m
- (Region)
- **Middle Rhine, the**

Mittelrheingebiet n
- **Middle Rhine region**

Mittelrheinwein, m
- **Middle Rhine wine**

Mittelsaison, f
- mittlere Saison, f
- **middle season**

Mittelschiff, n (Kirche)
- Hauptschiff, n
- Längsschiff, n
- Längshaus, n
- **central nave**
- nave

mittelschwere Abfahrt, f
- → mittlere Abfahrt

Mittelsegment, n
- mittleres Segment, n
- **middle segment**

Mittelsitz, m
- Mittelsitzplatz, m
- Mittelplatz, m
- **central seat**

Mittelsitzgruppe, f
- (Wohnwagen)
- **center dinette** AE
- centre dinette BE

Mittelsitzplatz, m
- Mittelsitz, m
- Mittelplatz, m
- **center seat** AE
- centre seat Be

Mittelslowakei, f
- **Central Slovakia**

mittelständischer Hotelbetrieb, m
- → mittelständisches Hotel

mittelständischer Hotelier, m
- Privathotelier, m
- **independent hotelkeeper**
- independent hotelier

mittelständischer Reiseveranstalter, m
- **independent tour operator**

mittelständischer Unternehmer, m
- **independent operator**

mittelständisches Hotel, n
- **medium-sized independent hotel**
- independent hotel

mittelständisches Reisebüro, n
- **medium-sized independent travel agency**

Mittelstation, f (Skilift)
- **middle lift station**
- middle station

Mittelstrecke, f
- Mittelstreckenroute, f
- **medium-haul route**
- medium-range route
- medium haul

Mittelstreckenbereich, m
- Mittelstreckensektor, m
- **medium-haul sector**

Mittelstreckencharterverkehr, m
- **medium-haul charter traffic**

Mittelstreckendüsenflugzeug, n
- Mittelstreckenjet, m
- **medium-haul jet**
- medium-range jet
- medium-distance jet

Mittelstreckenferien, pl
- Mittelstreckenurlaub, m
- **medium-haul holiday** BE
- **medium-haul vacation** AE

Mittelstreckenferiengast, m
- Mittelstreckenurlauber, m
- **medium-haul holidaymaker** BE
- medium-haul vacationer AE

Mittelstreckenflug

Mittelstreckenflug, m
♦ medium-range flight
♦ medium-haul flight
Mittelstreckenflugzeug, n
♦ medium-haul aircraft
Mittelstreckenmarkt, m
♦ medium-haul market
Mittelstreckenpauschale, f
♦ medium-haul package
Mittelstreckenpauschalreise, f
♦ medium-haul package tour
Mittelstreckenreise, f
♦ medium-haul tour
Mittelstreckenreiseveranstalter, m
♦ medium-haul tour operator
Mittelstreckenroute, f
Mittelstrecke, f
♦ medium-range route
♦ medium-haul route
Mittelstreckensegment, n
♦ medium-haul segment
Mittelstreckenurlaub, m
Mittelstreckenferien, pl
♦ medium-haul vacation *AE*
♦ medium-haul holiday *BE*
Mittelstreckenurlauber, m
Mittelstreckenferiengast, m
♦ medium-haul vacationer *AE*
♦ medium-haul holidaymaker *BE*
Mittelstreckenveranstalter, m
(Reiseveranstalter)
♦ medium-haul operator
Mittelstreckenziel, n
♦ medium-haul destination
Mittelstreifen, m
(Autobahn)
♦ central reservation
Mittelstufenfranzösischkurs, m
Mittelstufenfranzösischlehrgang, m
♦ intermediate French course
Mittelstufenkurs, m
Mittelstufenlehrgang, m
♦ intermediate course
Mitteltisch, m
mittlerer Tisch, m
♦ middle table
♦ center table *AE*
♦ centre table *BE*
♦ central table
Mittelturm, m
♦ central tower
mittel- und langfristig, adj
♦ medium- and long-term, adj
Mittelvogesen, die, pl
♦ Central Vosges, the *pl*
Mittelzimmer, n
♦ central room
mitten im Nichts
mitten in der Pampa *coll*
♦ in the middle of nowhere
mit Teppich ausgelegt sein
(Raum)
♦ be carpeted
Mitternacht, f
♦ midnight
Mitternachtsbüfett, n
♦ midnight buffet
Mitternachtsimbiß, m
♦ midnight snack
Mitternachtsonne, f
♦ midnight sun

Mitternachtsserenade, f
♦ midnight serenade
Mitternachtsshow, f
♦ midnight show
Mitternachtssonne, f
♦ midnight sun
Mitternachtswanderung, f
♦ midnight ramble
Mittler, m
→ Vermittler
mittlere Abfahrt, f (Ski)
(meist rot gekennzeichnet)
mittelschwere Abfahrt, f
♦ medium-grade run
mittlere Aufenthaltsdauer, f
→ durchschnittliche Aufenthaltsdauer
mittlere Belegung, f
→ durchschnittliche Belegung
mittlere Kategorie, f
♦ medium category
♦ middle category
mittlere Logementeinnahme, f *SCHW*
→ durchschnittliche Zimmereinnahme
mittlere Ortszeit, f
MOZ
♦ local mean time
♦ LMT
mittlere Preiskategorie, f
mittlere Preislage, f
♦ medium price category
♦ medium price range
mittlere Preisklasse, f
mittlere Preiskategorie, f
♦ medium price range
♦ medium price bracket
♦ medium price category
mittlere Preislage, f
♦ medium price bracket
♦ medium price range
♦ middle price range
mittlere Qualität, f
♦ medium quality
mittlerer Preis, m
Mittelpreis, m
♦ middle rate
♦ middle price
mittlerer Reiseveranstalter, m
mittelgroßer Reiseveranstalter, m
♦ medium-sized tour operator
Mittlerer Schwarzwald, m
♦ Central Black Forest, the
mittlerer Skiläufer m
♦ intermediate skier
♦ intermediate skiier *AE*
mittleres Hotel, n
→ mittelgroßes Hotel
mittleres Management, n
♦ middle management
mittleres Preissegment, n
♦ middle price segment
♦ middle rate segment
mittleres Zimmer, n
→ mittelgroßes Zimmer
mittlere Tageseinnahme f
→ durchschnittliche Tageseinnahme
mittlere Veranstaltung, f
→ mittelgroße Veranstaltung
mittrinken
♦ join for a drink
♦ join in

mittrinken mit jm
♦ have a drink with s.o.
♦ take a drink with s.o.
♦ join s.o. for a drink
Mittschiffskabine, f
♦ midship cabin
Mittsommerfest, n
♦ midsummer festival
Mittwoch, m
♦ Wednesday
Mittwoch nachts
♦ on Wednesday night
♦ on Wednesday nights
mittwochs, adv
♦ on Wednesdays, adv
♦ on Wednesday, adv
Mittwochs Ruhetag
(Schild)
Mittwoch Ruhetag
♦ Closed on Wednesdays
♦ Closed on Wednesday
Mittwochs Tanz
(Hinweisschild)
♦ Dancing on Wednesday
♦ Dancing on Wednesdays
Mituntermieter, m
♦ fellow roomer *AE*
♦ fellow lodger
Miturlauber, m
Mitferiengast, m
♦ fellow vacationer *AE*
♦ fellow holidaymaker *BE*
Mitveranstalter, m
♦ coorganiser
♦ coorganizer
♦ joint organiser
♦ joint organizer
mit Vergnügen
♦ with pleasure
mit Verspätung, adv
♦ late, adv
mit Verspätung von einer Stunde (Flug)
mit einer Stunde Verspätung
♦ one hour behind schedule
mit Verspätung von einer Stunde (generell)
mit einer Stunde Verspätung
♦ one hour late
mit vierteljährlicher Kündigung
♦ subject to three months notice
mit vollem Magen
auf vollen Magen
♦ on a full stomach
mit von der Partie sein bei etw
→ teilnehmen an etw
Mit welcher Gruppe sind Sie gekommen?
♦ Which tour are you with, Sir?
♦ Which tour are you with, Madam?
Mitwirkender, m (generell)
♦ contributor
♦ assistant
♦ cooperator
Mitwirkender, m (Theater)
Schauspieler, m
Darsteller, m
♦ player
♦ actor
♦ performer
♦ cast
mitwirken in einer Revue
mitwirken bei einer Revue
♦ participate in a revue

mitwirken in etw
   mitwirken bei etw
   ♦ participate in s.th.
   ♦ contribute to s.th.
   ♦ assist in s.th.
Mitzecher, m
   Mittrinker, m
   Zechbruder, m
   Zechkumpan, m
   ♦ fellow drinker
   ♦ drinking companion
Mixbecher, m
   → Schüttelbecher
Mixed Grill, m
   Gemischtes vom Grill, n
   ♦ mixed grill
mixen etw
   (Getränk)
   ♦ mix s.th.
Mixer, m
   Rührmaschine, f
   Rührwerk, n
   ♦ mixer
Mixgetränk, n
   Mischgetränk, n
   ♦ mixed drink
   ♦ mixed beverage
   ♦ shake
MM, f
   → Monatsmiete
Möbel, n pl
   Mobiliar, n
   ♦ furniture sg
   ♦ furnishings pl
Möbel abstauben
   ♦ dust the furniture
Möbel ausräumen aus einem Zimmer
   Möbel entfernen aus einem Zimmer
   ♦ remove the furniture from a room
   ♦ clear the furniture out of a room
Möbelausstellung, f
   ♦ furniture exhibition
Möbel austauschen
   Mobiliar wechseln
   ♦ change the furniture
Möbel einräumen in ein Zimmer
   ♦ put the furniture in(to) a room
Möbel ersetzen
   → Mobiliar ersetzen
Möbel im Bauernstil, n pl
   ♦ country-style furniture sg
Möbel lagern
   ♦ store furniture
   ♦ put furniture into storage
Möbelmesse, f
   ♦ furniture fair
Möbel pflegen
   ♦ service (the) furniture
Möbelpolierer, m
   ♦ furniture polisher
Möbelpolitur, f
   ♦ furniture polish
Möbel polstern
   ♦ upholster furniture
Möbel reinigen
   ♦ clean (the) furniture
Möbelreparatur, f
   ♦ furniture repair
   ♦ repair of furniture
Möbel reparieren
   ♦ repair furniture

Möbelsammlung, f
   ♦ collection of furniture
Möbel sind altmodisch
   ♦ furniture is old-fashioned
Möbel sind gut gewählt
   ♦ furniture is well chosen
Möbel sind neuwertig
   ♦ furniture is as good as new
   ♦ furniture is as new
Möbel sind von hoher Qualität
   ♦ furniture is of high standard
Möbelspediteur, m
   Spediteur, m
   ♦ removal contractor BE
   ♦ remover BE
   ♦ firm of removers BE
Möbel stellen
   (im Zimmer)
   ♦ arrange the furniture
Möbelstil, m
   ♦ style of (the) furniture
Möbelstoffe, m pl
   ♦ soft furnishings pl
Möbelstück, n
   ♦ piece of furniture
Möbelstück ersetzen durch ein anderes
   ♦ change a piece of furniture for another one
   ♦ replace a piece of furniture by another one
Möbel umstellen
   Mobiliar umstellen
   ♦ rearrange the furniture
Möbel umziehen
   ♦ remove furniture
Möbelumzug, m
   Umziehen von Möbel, n
   ♦ removing furniture
Möbelverleih, m
   ♦ furniture rental AE
   ♦ furniture hire BE
Möbelverleihdienst, m
   ♦ furniture rental service AE
   ♦ furniture hire service BE
Möbelversicherung, f
   ♦ insurance of (the) furniture
mobil, adj
   → fahrbar
mobile Bühne, f
   ♦ mobile stage
mobile Küche, f
   Küchenwagen, m
   ♦ mobile kitchen
mobiles Ferienhaus, n
   mobiles Urlaubshaus, n
   ♦ mobile vacation home AE
   ♦ mobile holiday home BE
mobiles Restaurant, n
   (z.B. am Strand)
   Restaurantwagen, m
   ♦ mobile restaurant
mobile Tanzfläche, f
   ♦ mobile dance floor
mobile Trennwand, f
   ♦ movable partition
   ♦ mobile partition
Mobilheim, n
   großes Wohnmobil, n
   ♦ mobile home
Mobilheimanlage, f
   Mobilheimkomplex, m
   Wohnmobilanlage, f

   Wohnmobilkomplex, m
   ♦ mobile-home complex
Mobilheimausstattung, f
   Wohnmobilausrüstung, f
   ♦ mobile-home equipment
Mobilheimindustrie, f
   Wohnmobilindustrie, f
   ♦ mobile-home industry
Mobilheimpark, m
   Wohnmobilpark, m
   ♦ mobile-home park
Mobilheimplatz, m
   Wohnmobilplatz, m
   ♦ mobile-home site
Mobilheimstellplatz, m
   Wohnmobilstellplatz, m
   ♦ mobile-home pitch
   ♦ mobile-home site AE
Mobilheimunterkunft, f
   Mobilheimunterbringung, f
   Wohnmobilunterkunft, f
   Wohnmobilunterbringung, f
   ♦ mobile-home accommodation
   ♦ mobile-home lodging AE
Mobilheimurlaub, m
   Mobilheimferien, pl
   Wohnmobilurlaub, m
   Wohnmobilferien, pl
   ♦ mobile-home vacation AE
   ♦ mobile-home holiday BE
Mobilheimvermietung, f
   Wohnmobilvermietung, f
   ♦ mobile-home rental AE
   ♦ renting a mobile home AE
   ♦ mobile-home letting BE
   ♦ letting a mobile home BE
   ♦ hiring out a mobile home BE
Mobiliar, n
   → Möbel
Mobiliar ersetzen
   Möbel ersetzen
   Mobiliar erneuern
   Möbel erneuern
   ♦ replace the furniture
   ♦ replace furniture
Mobiliar und Zubehör, n
   Mobiliar (n) und feste Einbauten (pl)
   Mobiliar und festes Zubehör, n
   ♦ furniture and fixtures pl
   ♦ furniture and fittings pl
Mobiliarversicherung, f
   ♦ insurance of personal property
Mobilien, pl ökon/jur
   bewegliche Güter, n pl
   bewegliche Habe, f
   ♦ movable goods pl
Mobilität, f
   ♦ mobility
möbliert, adj
   eingerichtet, adj
   ♦ furnished, adj
möblierte Ferienunterkunft, f
   → möblierte Urlaubsunterkunft
möblierter Herr, m
   → Untermieter
möbliertes Appartement, n
   ♦ furnished apartment
möbliertes Haus, n
   ♦ furnished house
möblierte Suite, f
   ♦ furnished suite

möbliertes Zimmer

möbliertes Zimmer, n
- furnished room

möblierte Unterkunft, f
- furnished accommodation

möblierte Unterkunftseinheit, f
(Statistik)
- furnished accommodation unit

möblierte Urlaubsunterkunft, f
möblierte Ferienunterkunft, f
- furnished vacation accommodation *AE*
- furnished holiday accommodation *BE*

möblierte Wohnung, f
- furnished flat *BE*
- furnished apartment *AE*

möblierte Wohnung mieten
- rent a furnished apartment *AE*
- rent a furnished flat *BE*

möblierte Wohnung vermieten
- rent (out) a furnished flat *BE*
- let a furnished flat *BE*
- rent (out) a furnished apartment *AE*

möbliert im Stil der Zeit, adj
- furnished in period style, adj

möbliert mit Antiquitäten, adj
- furnished with antiques, adj
- furnished with antiquities, adj

möbliert oder unmöbliert, adj
- furnished or unfurnished, adj

möbliert sein in einem bestimmten Stil
- be furnished in a certain style

möbliert wohnen
- live in furnished rooms
- live in furnished apartments *AE*
- live in lodgings

Möblierung eines Zimmers, f
Zimmermöblierung, f
- furnishing of a room
- furnishing a room

Möblierungskosten, pl
→ Einrichtungskosten

Mocca, m *ÖST*
→ Mokka

Möchtegernbesucher, m
- would-be visitor

Möchtegerngast, m
- would-be guest

Möchtegernkellner, m
- would-be waiter

Möchtegernreisender, m
- would-be traveller
- would-be traveler *AE*

Möchten Sie das Zimmer wechseln?
- Would you like to change your room?

Möchten Sie ein anderes Zimmer?
- Would you like to have another room?

Möchten Sie eine Flasche mit mir teilen?
- Would you like to share a bottle with me?
- Would you like to go halves on a bottle with me? *coll*

Möchten Sie ein Zimmer mit Bergblick?
- Would you like a room with mountain view?

Möchten Sie etwas essen?
Möchten Sie etwas zu essen?
- Would you like something to eat?

Möchten Sie etwas Wein?
- Would you like some wine?

Möchten Sie geweckt werden?
- Do you want an early call?

Möchten Sie jetzt bestellen?
- Would you like to order now?
- Are you ready to order now?

Möchten Sie mir bitte folgen?
- Would you like to follow me, Sir?
- Would you like to follow me, Madam?

Möchten Sie mitkommen?
- Would you like to come along?

Möchten Sie morgen früh geweckt werden?
- Do you want to be called in the morning?

Möchten Sie sich bitte anmelden?
- Would you like to register, please?

Möchten Sie speisen?
Belieben Sie zu speisen? *form*
- Do you wish to dine?

Mocktail, m
(alkoholfreies Getränk)
- mocktail

Mode, f
- fashion

Modebad, n
→ Modebadeort

Modebadeort, m
Modebad, n
- fashionable health resort

Modeboutique, f
- fashion boutique

Modedesigner, m
- fashion designer

Modegalerie, f
- fashion gallery

Modegeschäft, n
- fashion store *AE*
- fashion shop *BE*

Modegetränk, n
- fashion drink

Modekurort, m
- fashionable spa
- fashionable spa town
- fashionable watering place *hist*

Modellboot, n
- model boat

Modellbootsee, m
- model boat lake
- model boating lake

Modelldorf, n
- model village

Modelleisenbahn, f
- model railroad *AE*
- model railway *BE*

Modelleisenbahnanlage, f
- model railroad layout *AE*
- model railway layout *BE*

Modelleisenbahnausstellung, f
- model railroad exhibition *AE*
- model railroad exhibit *AE*
- model railway exhibition *BE*

Modelleisenbahnmuseum, n
- model railroad museum *AE*
- model railway museum *BE*

Modellhotel, n
Musterhotel, n
- model hotel

Modelljahr, n
(z.B. bei Autos)
- model year

Modellschiff, n
- model ship

Modellsegelflugzeug, n
- model glider

Modellstadt, f
- model town

Modellzimmer, n
- model room

Modellzug, m
- model train

Modenschau, f
Modeschau, f
- fashion show
- fashion parade

Modeort, m
- fashionable resort

Moder, m
- mold *AE*
- mould *BE*

moderater Preis, m
→ mäßiger Preis

Moderator, m (Fernsehen)
→ Fernsehmoderator

Moderator, m (generell)
- moderator

Modergeruch, m
- moldy smell *AE*
- mouldy smell *BE*

moderieren (bei etw)
Moderation haben (bei etw)
- moderate (in s.th.)
- act as moderator (in s.th.)

moderieren etw
- moderate s.th.
- present s.th.

modern ausgestattet, adj
- modernly equipped, adj
- with modern furnishings
- with modern fittings

modern ausgestattetes Zimmer, n
- modernly equipped room
- room with modern furnishings
- room with modern fittings

moderne Einrichtung, f
moderne Möbel, n pl
modernes Mobiliar, n
- modern furnishings *pl*
- modern furniture *sg*

modern eingerichtet, adj
(Zimmer)
- modernly appointed, adj
- appointed in a modern style, adj

modern eingerichtetes Zimmer, n
- modernly appointed room
- room with modern furnishings
- room with modern fittings

moderne Managementtechniken, f pl
- modern management techniques *pl*

moderne Möbel, n pl
modernes Mobiliar, n
moderne Einrichtung, f
- modern furniture *sg*
- modern furnishings *pl*

modernen Komfort anbieten
- offer modern comforts

modernen Komfort genießen
- enjoy modern comfort

moderner Betrieb, m
- modern establishment
- modern operation
- up-to-date establishment
- up-to-date operation

moderner Komfort, m
- modern comforts *pl*
- modern conveniences *pl*
- mod. cons. *pl*

moderner Service, m
- modern service

moderne Sanitäreinrichtungen, f pl
♦ modern sanitary facilities pl
modernes Dekor, n
♦ modern décor
♦ modern decor AE
modernes Haus, n
♦ modern house
♦ modern home
modernes Interieur, n
♦ modern interior
modernes Mobiliar, n
→ moderne Möbel
modernes Zimmer, n
♦ modern room
modernisieren etw
♦ modernise s.th.
♦ modernize s.th.
♦ update s.th.
♦ bring s.th. up to date
modernisiert, adj
♦ modernised, adj
♦ modernized, adj
♦ updated, adj
modernisiertes Hotel, n
♦ modernised hotel
♦ modernized hotel
modernisiertes Zimmer, n
♦ modernised room
♦ modernized room
Modernisierung, f
♦ modernisation
♦ modernization
Modernisierung der bestehenden Unterkünfte, f
♦ modernisation of existing accommodations AE
♦ modernization of existing accommodations AE
♦ modernisation of existing accommodation BE
♦ modernization of existing accommodation BE
Modernisierung eines Hauses, f
♦ modernisation of a house
♦ modernization of a house
Modernisierung eines Hotels, f
♦ modernisation of a hotel
♦ modernization of a hotel
Modernisierungskredit, m
♦ modernisation credit
♦ modernization credit
Modernisierungsprogramm, n
♦ modernisation program AE
♦ modernization program AE
♦ modernisation programme BE
♦ modernization programme BE
Modernisierungsprogramm abschließen
♦ complete a modernisation program AE
♦ complete a modernization program AE
♦ complete a modernisation programme BE
♦ complete a modernization programme BE
Modernisierungszuschuß, m
(durch Behörde)
♦ modernisation grant
♦ modernization grant
modern möbliert, adj
♦ modernly furnished, adj
♦ furnished in (a) modern style, adj
modern möbliertes Zimmer, n
♦ modernly furnished room
♦ room furnished in (a) modern style
modernster Komfort, m
♦ up-to-date amenities pl
Modesaison, f
♦ fashion season

Modeveranstaltung, f
♦ fashion event
Modevorführung, f
♦ fashion display
♦ fashion parade
Modewettbewerb, m
♦ fashion contest
Modezeitschrift, f
♦ fashion magazine
Modified American Plan, m
(Zimmer mit Frühstück und weiterer Mahlzeit)
MAP
Halbpension, f
♦ Modified American Plan
♦ MAP
♦ demipension AE
♦ half board
modifizieren etw
leicht ändern etw
♦ modify s.th.
Modifizierung, f
♦ modification
modisch, adj
schick, adj
elegant, adj
♦ fashionable, adj
modrig, adj
♦ moldy, adj
♦ mouldy, adj BE
möglicher Kunde, m
zukünftiger Kunde, m
voraussichtlicher Kunde, m
♦ prospective client
♦ prospective customer
möglicher Tagungsort m
♦ possible venue (for a conference)
Möglichkeiten anbieten für etw
♦ offer opportunities for doing s.th.
♦ offer opportunities for s.th.
Möglichkeiten für etw, f pl
Einrichtungen für etw, f pl
♦ facilities for s.th. pl
♦ facilities for doing s.th. pl
Möglichkeiten zum Bootfahren bieten
♦ provide boating facilities
Möhrensuppe, f
→ Karottensuppe
Mohrrübe, f
→ Karotte
Mokka, m
♦ mocha
Mokkaeiskrem, f
♦ mocha ice cream AE
♦ mocha ice-cream BE
Mokkagetränk, n
♦ mocha drink
Mokkakaffee, m
Mokka, m
♦ mocha coffee
♦ mocha
Mokkalöffel, m
♦ demitasse spoon AE
♦ coffee spoon BE
Mokkamaschine, f
♦ mocha machine
Mokkaparfait, n
Kaffeeparfait, n
♦ coffee parfait
Mokkatasse, f
♦ demitasse AE
♦ demi-tasse BE

Moldawien
♦ Moldavia
♦ Moldova
Moldawier, m
♦ Moldovan
moldawisch, adj
♦ Moldovan, adj
Mole, f
♦ mole
♦ jetty
Molke, f
♦ whey
Molkerei, f
♦ dairy
♦ creamery
Molkereiprodukt, n
♦ dairy product
♦ dairy produce
Molton m
(Textil für Tisch)
♦ molleton
♦ swanskin
Molukken, die, pl
♦ Moluccas, the pl
Monaco
Monako
♦ Monaco
Monat, m
♦ month
monatlich, adj
♦ monthly, adj
monatlich, adv
monatsweise, adv
♦ by the month, adv
♦ on a monthly basis, adv
monatlich buchen etw
monatsweise buchen etw
♦ book s.th. on a monthly basis
monatliche Gebühr, f
→ Monatsgebühr
monatliche Inventur, f
♦ monthly inventory
♦ monthly stock-taking
monatliche Kündigung, f
♦ month's notice
♦ one month's notice
♦ monthly notice
♦ a month's warning
monatliche Miete, f
→ Monatsmiete
monatliche Rechnungsstellung f
♦ monthly billing
monatliche Rechnungstellung wünschen
♦ request (a) monthly billing
monatliche Verweildauer, f
♦ monthly length of stay
monatliche Zahlung, f
♦ monthly payment
monatlich kündbares Mietverhältnis, n
♦ monthly tenancy
monatlich mieten etw (meist Immobilien)
monatsweise mieten etw
♦ rent s.th. by the month
♦ rent s.th. on a monthly basis
monatlich mieten etw (Mobilien)
monatsweise mieten etw
♦ hire s.th. by the month BE
♦ hire s.th. on a monthly basis BE
♦ rent s.th. by the month
♦ rent s.th. on a monthly basis

monatlich vermieten etw (Immobilie)
  monatsweise vermieten etw
  ♦ **rent (out) s.th. by the month**
  ♦ rent s.th. on a monthly basis *AE*
  ♦ let s.th. by the month *BE*
  ♦ let s.th. on a monthly basis *BE*
monatlich vermieten etw (Mobilien)
  ♦ **hire (out) s.th. by the month** *BE*
  ♦ hire (out) s.th. on a monthly basis *BE*
  ♦ rent (out) s.th. by the month *AE*
  ♦ rent (out) s.th. on a monthly basis *AE*
monatlich vermietetes Zimmer, n
  ♦ **room rented on monthly basis** *AE*
  ♦ room let on a monthly basis *BE*
Monatsanfang, m
  ♦ **beginning of the month**
Monatsauslastung, f
  monatliche Auslastung, f
  ♦ **monthly load factor**
  ♦ load factor per month
Monatsbelegung, f
  monatliche Belegung, f
  Monatsauslastung, f
  monatliche Auslastung, f
  ♦ **monthly occupancy**
  ♦ occupancy per month
  ♦ occupancy in a particular month
Monatsbericht, m
  ♦ **monthly report**
  ♦ monthly statement
Monatsbinde, f
  → Damenbinde
Monatsdurchschnitt, m
  ♦ **monthly average**
Monatsende, m
  ♦ **end of the month**
Monatsfahrkarte, f
  → Monatskarte
Monatsgebühr, f
  monatliche Gebühr f
  Gebühr pro Monat f
  ♦ **monthly charge**
  ♦ monthly fee
  ♦ charge per month
  ♦ fee per month
Monatsgehalt, n
  monatliches Gehalt, n
  ♦ **monthly salary**
Monatsgrundpreis, m
  Grundpreis pro Monat, m
  ♦ **basic rate per month**
  ♦ basic price per month
Monatskapazität f
  ♦ **monthly capacity**
Monatskarte, f
  Monatsfahrkarte, f
  ♦ **monthly ticket**
Monatsmiete, f
  MM, f
  ♦ **month's rent**
  ♦ monthly rent
  ♦ rent per month
  ♦ monthly rental
  ♦ one month's rent
Monatsmiete pro Person, f
  → Miete pro Person pro Monat
Monatsmitte, f
  ♦ **middle of the month**
Monatsnachfrage, f
  monatliche Nachfrage, f
  ♦ **monthly demand**

Monatspauschale, f
  Monatspauschalpreis, m
  ♦ **package price per month**
  ♦ package rate per month
  ♦ inclusive price per month
  ♦ inclusive rate per month
Monatspauschalpreis, m
  → Monatspauschale
Monatspreis, m
  monatlicher Preis, m
  Preis pro Monat, m
  ♦ **monthly rate**
  ♦ monthly price
  ♦ rate per month
  ♦ price per month
Monatsprogramm n
  ♦ **monthly program** *AE*
  ♦ monthly programme *BE*
Monatsrechnung, f
  ♦ **monthly bill**
  ♦ monthly check *AE*
  ♦ monthly account
Monatsrückfahrkarte, f
  ♦ **monthly return ticket**
Monatssitzung f
  ♦ **monthly meeting**
Monatsspezialität, f
  → Spezialität des Monats
Monatsstatistik, f
  ♦ **monthly statistics** *pl*
Monatstarif, m
  ♦ **monthly terms** *pl*
  ♦ monthly rates *pl*
  ♦ monthly rate
Monatstreffen, n
  monatliches Treffen, n
  ♦ **monthly meeting**
Monatsumsatz, m
  monatlicher Umsatz, m
  ♦ **monthly sales** *pl*
  ♦ monthly turnover
Monatsveranstaltungen, f pl
  monatliche Veranstaltungen, f pl
  ♦ **monthly events** *pl*
Monatsverbrauch, m
  monatlicher Verbrauch, m
  ♦ **monthly consumption**
Monatsversammlung f
  ♦ **monthly meeting**
monatsweise, adv
  → monatlich, adv
monatsweise mieten etw
  → monatlich mieten etw
monatsweise vermieten etw
  → monatlich vermieten etw
Mönchssiedlung, f
  ♦ **monastic settlement**
Mondscheinspaziergang, m
  Spaziergang bei Mondschein, m
  ♦ **moonlight walk**
  ♦ walk by moonlight
Monegasse, m
  ♦ **Monacan**
  ♦ Monegasque
Monegassin, f
  ♦ **Monacan girl**
  ♦ Monacan woman
  ♦ Monegasque girl
  ♦ Monegasque woman

monegassisch, adj
  ♦ **Monacan, adj**
  ♦ Monegasque, adj
Mongole, m
  ♦ **Mongol**
  ♦ Mongolian
Mongolei, f
  ♦ **Mongolia**
Mongolin, f
  ♦ **Mongol girl**
  ♦ Mongol woman
  ♦ Mongolian girl
  ♦ Mongolian woman
mongolisch, adj
  ♦ **Mongol, adj**
  ♦ Mongolian, adj
Monitor, m
  ♦ **monitor**
Monopol, n
  ♦ **monopoly**
Monopol auf etw, n
  ♦ **monopoly of s.th.**
monopolisieren etw
  etw mit Beschlag belegen
  ♦ **monopolise s.th.**
  ♦ monopolize s.th.
monopolistische Hotelgesellschaft, f
  (z.B. Hotelgesellschaft bei Industriekonzern)
  ♦ **captive hotel company**
monopolistischer Markt, m
  ♦ **captive market**
Monoski, m
  ♦ **monoski**
Monsun, m
  ♦ **monsoon**
Montag, m
  ♦ **Monday**
Montag bis Samstag inklusive
  ♦ **Monday to Saturday inclusive**
  ♦ Monday through Saturday *AE*
Montag nachts
  ♦ **on Monday night**
  ♦ on Monday nights
montags, adv
  ♦ **on Mondays, adv**
  ♦ on Monday, adv
Montags ganztägig geschlossen
  (Hinweisschild)
  ♦ **Closed all day on Monday**
  ♦ Closed all day on Mondays
Montags haben wir nicht geöffnet
  ♦ **We are not open on Mondays**
Montags Ruhetag
  (Schild)
  Montag Ruhetag
  ♦ **Closed on Mondays**
  ♦ Closed on Monday
Montags Tanz
  (Hinweisschild)
  ♦ **Dancing on Monday**
  ♦ Dancing on Mondays
Mont Blanc, m
  ♦ **Mont Blanc**
Mont Blanc besteigen
  ♦ **climb Mont Blanc**
Montenegriner, m
  ♦ **Montenegrin**
  ♦ Montenegrine
Montenegrinerin, f
  ♦ **Montenegrin girl**
  ♦ Montenegrin woman

- Montenegrin
- Montenegrine girl
- Montenegrine woman

montenegrinisch, adj
- Montenegrin, adj

Montenegro
- Montenegro

Montezumas Rache, f *humor*
Diarrhö, f
Diarrhöe, f
- Montezuma's revenge

monumentales Bett, n
- monumental bed

Moorbad, n (Ort)
→ Moorheilbad

Moorbad, n (Vorgang)
- mud bath *AE*
- mud-bath *BE*
- moor bath

Moorbehandlung, f
- mud treatment

Moorheilbad, n (Ort)
(offizielle Bezeichnung)
- moorland spa
- spa offering fango treatment

Moorland, n
- moorland

Moorlandschaft, f
- moorland scenery

Moorlandwanderung, f
Wanderung durch felsiges Moorland, f
- fell walking

Moorpackung, f
Fangopackung, f
- mudpack *AE*
- mud pack *BE*
- fango pack

Moorspazierweg, m
Moorweg, m
- moorland walk

Moorwanderung, f
- moorland hike
- moorland walk

Moorwickel, m
Moorpackung, f
- mud wrap

Moosbeere, f
- fenberry

Moped, n
- moped *BE*

Mordsdurst, m *coll*
- almighty thirst *coll*

Mordsdurst haben *coll*
- be dying of thirst

Mordsgaudi haben *coll*
Mordsspaß haben
- have a ripping time

Mordsspaß, m *coll*
- jam *BE sl*

Mordsspaß haben
Riesenspaß haben
Gaudi haben *fam*
- have a whale of a time *obs*
- have a smashing time *coll*

morgen, adv
- tomorrow, adv

Morgen, m
Vormittag, m
- morning

Morgen beginnen mit etw
- start the morning with s.th.

- start the morning by doing s.th.
- begin the morning with s.th.

Morgenbericht m
- morning report

Morgen der Abreise, m
- morning of (the) departure

Morgen der Ankunft, m
- morning of (the) arrival

Morgenempfang, m
Vormittagsempfang, m
- morning reception

Morgenessen, n
Vormittagsessen, n
- morning meal
- breakfast

Morgenfähre, f
- early-morning ferry
- morning ferry

Morgenfrühstück, n
erstes Frühstück, n
- early-morning breakfast

Morgengetränk, n
- early-morning beverage
- early-morning drink
- morning beverage
- morning drink

Morgengymnastik, f
- morning exercises *pl*

Morgenjogging, n
- morning jogging

Morgenkaffee, m
- morning coffee
- early-morning coffee

Morgenkaffee zu sich nehmen
- take morning coffee

Morgenmahlzeit, f
Vormittagsmahlzeit, f
- midmorning meal *AE*
- mid-morning meal *BE*

Morgenmantel, m
(Herren)
- dressing gown
- wrapper

Morgenritt, m
Vormittagsritt, m
- morning ride

Morgenrock, m
(Damen)
- morning gown
- dressing gown

morgens, adv
vormittags, adv
- in the mornings, adv
- in the morning, adv
- a.m., adv

Morgenschicht f
- morning shift

Morgenservice, m
Morgendienst, m
- early-morning service

Morgensitzung, f
→ Vormittagssitzung

Morgenspaziergang, m
- morning walk
- early-morning walk
- walk in the morning

Morgenständchen, n
Morgenmusik, f
- morning music

Morgenstund hat Gold im Mund
- Early to bed and early to rise

- makes a man healthy, wealthy and wise.
- The early bird catches the worm

Morgentee, m
- morning tea
- early morning tea
- EMT

Morgenwanderung, f
- morning hike
- hike in the morning

Morgenzeitung, f
- morning paper

Morgenzimmermädchen, n
- morning chambermaid
- morning maid

Morgenzug, m
Frühzug, m
- early-morning train
- morning train
- early train

Morgen zur freien Verfügung
→ Vormittag zur freien Verfügung

Morgen zur freien Verfügung haben
→ Vormittag zur freien Verfügung haben

Morio-Muskat, m
Morio-Muskat-Wein, m
- Morio-Muscat
- Morio-Muscat wine

Morpheus, m
(Gott der Träume)
- Morpheus

morsches Gebäude, n
baufälliges Gebäude, n
- ramshackle building

Mosaik, n
- mosaic

Mosaikboden, m
- mosaic floor

Mosaikwand, f
- mosaic wall

Mosambik
- Mozambique

Moschee, f
- mosque

Mosel, f
- Mosel River, the
- Moselle River, the
- River Mosel, the
- River Moselle, the
- Mosel, the

Moseldorf, n
- Mosel village
- Moselle village
- village on the Mosel
- village on the Moselle

Moselgebiet, n (groß)
- Mosel region
- Moselle region

Moselgebiet, n (klein)
- Mosel area
- Moselle area

Moselkreuzfahrt, f
- Mosel cruise
- Moselle cruise
- cruise on the Mosel
- cruise on the Moselle

Moselschleife, f
- Mosel loop
- Moselle loop

Moselstadt, f
- Mosel town
- Moselle town

Moseltal

- ◆ town on the Mosel
- ◆ town on the Moselle

Moseltal, n
- ◆ Mosel valley
- ◆ Moselle valley

Moselwein, m
- Mosel, m
- ◆ Mosel wine
- ◆ Moselle wine
- ◆ Moselle

Moskito, m
- ◆ mosquito

Moskitonetz, n
- ◆ mosquito net

moskitosicher, adj
- ◆ mosquito-secure, adj

Moskitostich, m
- ◆ mosquito bite

Moslem, m
- ◆ Muslim

moslemisch, adj
- ◆ Muslim, adj
- ◆ Moslem, adj

moslemisches Land, n
- ◆ Muslim country
- ◆ Moslem country

Most, m (für Wein)
- ◆ must

Mostgewicht, n
- (Wein)
- ◆ grape must density
- ◆ must density

Mostrich, m
- → Senf

Motel, n
- ◆ motel

Motelanlage, f
- Motelkomplex, m
- ◆ motel complex

Motelappartement n
- Motelwohnung f
- ◆ motel apartment

Motelbau, m (Aktivität)
- ◆ motel construction
- ◆ construction of a motel
- ◆ constructing a motel
- ◆ building a motel

Motelbau, m (Gebäude)
- → Motelgebäude

Motelbenutzer m
- ◆ motel user

Motelbeschreibung f
- ◆ motel description
- ◆ description of a motel

Motelbesitzer, m
- Motelinhaber, m
- ◆ motel owner

Motel betreiben
- ◆ operate a motel

Motelbetreiber m
- ◆ motel operator

Motelbetrieb, m
- ◆ motel establishment
- ◆ motel operation

Motelbett n
- ◆ motel bed

Moteleinheit, f
- (Statistik)
- ◆ motel unit

Moteleinkehr, f
- → Einkehr in einem Motel

Motelfranchisesystem, n
- ◆ motel franchise system

Motelgast m
- ◆ motel guest

Motelgebäude, n
- Motelbau, m
- ◆ motel building

Motelgutschein, m
- ◆ motel voucher

Motelindustrie, f
- ◆ motel industry

Motelkette, f
- ◆ motel chain

Motelmahlzeit f
- ◆ motel meal

Motelrestaurant n (Betriebsart)
- ◆ motel and restaurant

Motelrestaurant n (im Motel)
- ◆ motel restaurant
- ◆ motel's restaurant

Motelunterkunft, f
- Motelunterbringung, f
- ◆ motel accommodation

Motelzimmer, n
- ◆ motel room

Motelzimmer kostet $ 123 pro Nacht
- ◆ motel room costs $ 123 per night
- ◆ motel room costs $ 123 a night

Motivforschung, f
- ◆ motivation research

Motodrom, n
- ◆ motordrome

Motorbarkasse, f
- ◆ motor launch

Motorboot, n
- ◆ motorboat AE
- ◆ motor boat BE

Motorbootausflug, m
- ◆ motorboat excursion AE
- ◆ motorboat trip AE
- ◆ powerboat excursion AE
- ◆ motor-boat excursion BE
- ◆ motor-boat trip BE

Motorboot fahren
- ◆ ride a motorboat AE
- ◆ ride a motor boat BE

Motorbootfahren, n
- Motorbootsport, m
- ◆ motorboating AE
- ◆ motor boating BE

Motorbootfahrt, f
- ◆ motorboat trip AE
- ◆ motorboat ride AE
- ◆ motor-boat trip BE
- ◆ motor-boat ride BE

Motorbootrennen, n
- ◆ motorboat race AE
- ◆ motor-boat race BE

Motorbootrennsport, m
- ◆ motorboat racing AE
- ◆ motor-boat racing BE
- ◆ powerboat racing AE
- ◆ power-boat racing BE

Motorbootverleih, m
- ◆ motorboat rental AE
- ◆ motor-boat hire BE

Motorcaravan, m
- → Reisemobil

Motorcaravaner, m
- → Wohnwagenfahrer

Motor Court, m
- Motel, n
- ◆ motor court
- ◆ auto court AE
- ◆ motel

Motordroschke, f
- → Autodroschke

Motorfahrzeug, n
- ◆ motor vehicle

Motorhome, n
- → Reisemobil

Motor Inn, m
- (Motel mit vollem Essenservice)
- ◆ motor inn

motorisieren etw
- ◆ motorise s.th.
- ◆ motorize s.th.

motorisierter Wohnwagen, m
- ◆ motorised caravan BE
- ◆ motorised trailer AE

Motorisierung, f
- ◆ motorisation
- ◆ motorization

Motorjacht, f
- Motoryacht, f
- ◆ motor yacht

Motorrad, n
- ◆ motorcycle AE
- ◆ motor bicycle AE
- ◆ motorbike AE coll
- ◆ motor cycle BE
- ◆ motor bike BE coll

Motorradbegeisterter, m
- ◆ motorcycle enthusiast AE
- ◆ motorbike enthusiast AE coll
- ◆ motor-cycle enthusiast BE
- ◆ motor-bike enthusiast BE coll

Motorradcamper, m
- ◆ motorcycle camper AE
- ◆ motorbike camper AE coll
- ◆ motor-cycle camper BE
- ◆ motor-bike camper BE coll

Motorradcamping, n
- ◆ motorcycle camping AE
- ◆ motorbike camping AE coll
- ◆ motor-cycle camping BE
- ◆ motor-bike camping BE coll

Motorradeskorte, f
- Motorradbegleitung, f
- ◆ motorcyclist escort AE
- ◆ motor-cyclist escort BE

Motorrad fahren
- ◆ ride a motorcycle AE
- ◆ ride a motorbike AE coll
- ◆ motorcycle BE
- ◆ ride a motor cycle BE

Motorradfahrer, m
- ◆ motorcyclist AE
- ◆ motorcycle rider AE
- ◆ motor-cyclist BE
- ◆ motor-cycle rider BE
- ◆ biker coll

Motorradfahrt, f
- ◆ motorcycle ride AE
- ◆ motorbike ride AE coll
- ◆ motor-cycle ride BE
- ◆ motor-bike ride BE coll

Motorradfan, m
- ◆ motorcycle fan AE
- ◆ motorbike fan AE coll

- motor-cycle fan *BE*
- motor-bike fan *BE coll*

Motorradmeisterschaft, f
- motorcycle championship *AE*
- motor-cycle championship *BE*

Motorrad mieten
- rent a motorcycle *AE*
- rent a motorbike *AE coll*
- hire a motor cycle *BE*
- hire a motorbike *BE coll*

Motorrad mit Seitenwagen, n
Motorrad mit Beiwagen, n
- motorcycle combination *AE*
- motor-cycle combination *BE*

Motorradmuseum, n
- motorcycle museum *AE*
- motorbike museum *AE coll*
- motor-cycle museum *BE*
- motor-bike museum *BE coll*

Motorradnarr, m
- motorcycle freak *AE*
- motorbike freak *AE coll*
- motor-cycle freak *BE*
- motor-bike freak *BE coll*

Motorradreise, f
- motorcycle journey *AE*
- motor-cycle journey *BE*
- motorbike journey *AE coll*
- motor-bike journey *BE coll*

Motorradrikscha, f
- motor-drawn pedicab
- pedicab

Motorradtour, f
Motorradreise, f
- motorcycle tour *AE*
- motorbike tour *AE coll*
- motor-cycle tour *BE*
- motor-bike tour *BE coll*

Motorradurlaub, m
Motorradferien, pl
- motorcycle vacation *AE*
- motorbike vacation *AE coll*
- motor-cycle holiday *BE*
- motor-bike holiday *BE coll*

Motorradurlauber, m
- motorcycle vacationer *AE*
- motorbike vacationer *AE coll*
- motor-cycle holidaymaker *BE*
- motor-bike holidaymaker *BE coll*

Motorrennsport, m
- motor racing

Motorroller, m
- motor scooter *AE*
- motor-scooter *BE*
- scooter

Motorschiff, n
- motorship
- motor vessel

Motorschlitten, m
- snowmobile
- skidoo *FR CAN*

Motorschlitten fahren
- ride a snowmobile
- snowmobile

Motorschlittenfahren, n
Motorschlittensport, m
- snowmobiling

Motorschlittenfahrt, f
- snowmobile ride
- snowmobile trip

Motorschlittenfahrt machen
- take a snowmobile ride

Motorschlittenloipe, f
Motorschlittenweg, m
- snowmobile trail
- snowmobile track

Motorschlittenrennen, n
- snowmobile race

Motorsegler, m
Motorsegelflugzeug, n
- power glider

Motorsport, m
- motor sport

Motorsportreise, f
- motor-sport tour
- motor-sport journey
- motor-sport trip

Motortourist, m
→ Autotourist

Motte, f
- moth

Mottenbekämpfung, f
- moth control

Mottenkugel, f
- mothball
- camphor ball

Mottenpulver, n
- moth powder

Mottenschutzmittel, n
- moth repellent

mottensicher, adj
- mothproof, adj

Mountainbike, n
- mountain bike

Mountainbikefahren, n
Mountainbikesport, m
- mountain-biking

Mountainbikefahrer, m
- mountain-biker

Mountainbikefahrt, f
- mountain-bike trip
- mountain-bike ride

Mountainbikeprogramm, n
- mountain-bike program *AE*
- mountain-bike programme *BE*

Mountainbikestrecke, f
- mountain-bike route

Mountainbiketour, f
- mountain-bike tour

Mount Everest, m
- Mount Everest

Mount Everest-Expedition, f
- Mount Everest expedition

Mousse, f
Schaumspeise, f
- mousse

moussierend, adj (Limonade etc.)
- fizzy, adj

moussierend, adj (Wein)
- sparkling, adj

moussieren (generell)
- fizz
- be fizzy

moussieren (Wein)
- sparkle

Mouvementliste, f
Ankunfts- und Abreiseliste f
- arrival and departure list
- A & D list

MOZ
mittlere Ortszeit, f

- LMT
- local mean time

Mozartfestspiele, n pl
- Mozart Festival, the

Mozzarella, m
Mozzarellakäse, m
- Mozzarella
- Mozzarella cheese

Mozzarellasalat, m
- Mozzarella salad

MTW, f
→ Mietwohnung

müde, adj
- tired, adj
- sleepy, adj
- weary, adj

müde Füße ausruhen
- ease one's weary feet

müde werden
- get tired

müde wie ein Hund, adj
- dog-tired, adj

Muesli, n *SCHW*
→ Müsli

muffiges Zimmer, n
stickiges Zimmer n
- musty room
- stuffy room

Muffin, n *gastr*
- muffin *gastr*

Mühe wert sein
Anstrengung wert sein
- be worth the effort

Mühlbach, m
- mill stream

Mühle, f
- mill

Müll, m
(Hausmüll)
- garbage *AE*
- dust *BE*
- rubbish
- refuse

Müllabfuhr, f
- garbage collection *AE*
- garbage disposal *AE*
- dust collection *BE*
- dust disposal *BE*

Müllabfuhrwagen, m
- garbage truck *AE*
- dustcart *BE*

Müllbeseitigung, f
- garbage removal *AE*
- removal of garbage *AE*
- waste disposal *BE*
- removal of dust *BE*
- removal of refuse

Mülleimer, m
Mülltonne, f
- garbage can *AE*
- ash can *AE*
- dustbin *BE*
- trash can *AE*

Müllerinart, adv *gastr*
nach Müllerinart, adv *gastr*
- meunière, adv *BE gastr*
- meuniere, adv *gastr*
- à la meunière *FR gastr*

Müller-Thurgau, m
Müller-Thurgau-Wein, m

Müllsack

- ♦ Mueller-Thurgau
- ♦ Mueller-Thurgau wine

Müllsack, m (leer)
- ♦ garbage bag *AE*
- ♦ dustbin liner *BE*

Müllsack, m (voll)
- ♦ sack of garbage *AE*
- ♦ sack of rubbish *BE*

Müllschlucker, m
- ♦ garbage chute *AE*
- ♦ garbage disposer *AE*
- ♦ dust shoot *BE*

Mülltonne, f
Mülleimer, m
- ♦ dust bin *BE*
- ♦ garbage can *AE*

multifunktionaler Konferenzraum, m
- ♦ multifunctional conference room
- ♦ multi-purpose conference room

multifunktionaler Saal, m
multifunktionale Halle, f
- ♦ multifunctional hall

multifunktionaler Urlaub, m
multifunktionale Ferien, pl
- ♦ multifunctional vacation *AE*
- ♦ multifunctional holiday *BE*

Multihalle, f
→ Mehrzweckhalle

multikulturell, adj
- ♦ multicultural, adj

Multimediapräsentation, f
- ♦ multi-media presentation

Multimediaprogramm, n
- ♦ multi-media program *AE*
- ♦ multi-media programme *BE*

Multimediaprojektion, f
- ♦ multi-media projection

Multimediashow, f
- ♦ multi-media show

Multimillionär, m
- ♦ multimillionaire

multinational, adj
- ♦ multinational, adj

multinationales Hotel, n
- ♦ multinational hotel

Multisporthalle, f
- ♦ multi-sports hall

Multivisionspräsentation, f
- ♦ multi-vision presentation

Multivisionsschau, f
- ♦ multi-vision show

Multivitamingetränk, n
- ♦ multivitamin drink

München
- ♦ Munich

Münchner Bier, n
- ♦ Munich beer
- ♦ beer from Munich

Münchner Oktoberfest, n
- ♦ Munich Oktoberfest, the
- ♦ Munich October festival, the

Mund, m
- ♦ mouth

munden
- ♦ be delicious
- ♦ taste good
- ♦ be to s.o.'s taste
- ♦ tickle the palate
- ♦ be palatable

mündlich abgeschlossener Mietvertrag, m
- ♦ verbal lease agreement
- ♦ parol lease

mündliche Bestätigung, f
mündliche Zusage, f
- ♦ oral confirmation

mündliche Buchung, f
- ♦ verbal booking
- ♦ oral booking
- ♦ booking by word of mouth

mündliche Einladung, f
- ♦ oral invitation
- ♦ invitation by word of mouth

mündliche Empfehlung, f
- ♦ word-of-mouth recommendation

mündliche Reservierung, f
- ♦ verbal reservation
- ♦ oral reservation
- ♦ reservation by word of mouth

mündlicher Vertrag, m
- ♦ verbal contract
- ♦ oral contract

mündliche Stornierung, f
mündliche Abbestellung, f
- ♦ verbal cancellation
- ♦ verbal cancelation *AE*
- ♦ cancellation by word of mouth
- ♦ cancelation by word of mouth *AE*
- ♦ oral cancel(l)ation

mündliche Vereinbarung, f
mündliche Zusage, f
- ♦ verbal agreement
- ♦ agreement by word of mouth
- ♦ oral agreement

Mundpropaganda, f
(Werbung)
- ♦ word-of-mouth advertising

Mundraub, m
kleiner Diebstahl, m
Schwund, m *euph*
- ♦ pilferage
- ♦ pilfering
- ♦ petty theft

Mundserviette, f
→ Serviette

Mündung, f (Fluß)
Flußmündung, f
- ♦ mouth
- ♦ mouth of a river

Mundvoll, m
Bissen, m
Brocken, m
- ♦ mouthful

Mundwasser, n
- ♦ mouthwash

Mund wässerig machen
→ Wasser im Mund zusammenlaufen lassen

Mund-zu-Mund-Propaganda, f
→ Mundpropaganda

Münster, n
- ♦ minster

Münsterland n
(Region)
- ♦ Münsterland

munter und gesund, adj
gesund und munter, adj
- ♦ hale and hearty, adj
- ♦ safe and sound, adj

Münzduschanlage, f
- ♦ coin shower facilities *AE pl*
- ♦ coin-operated shower facilities *BE pl*

Münzdusche, f
- ♦ coin shower *AE*
- ♦ coin-operated shower *BE*

Münze, f
- ♦ coin

Münzfarbfernsehen, n
- ♦ coin-operated color television *AE*
- ♦ coin-operated color TV *AE*
- ♦ coin-operated colour television *BE*
- ♦ coin-operated colour TV *BE*

Münzfernrohr, n
- ♦ coin telescope *AE*
- ♦ coin-operated telescope *BE*

Münzfernsehen, n
- ♦ coin-operated television
- ♦ coin-operated TV

Münzgeschirrspülautomat m
- ♦ coin-operated dishwasher

Münzradio, n
- ♦ coin-operated radio

Münztelefon, n
- ♦ pay telephone
- ♦ pay phone
- ♦ coinbox telephone *BE*

Münzwäscherei f
- ♦ coin laundry *AE*
- ♦ coin-operated laundry *BE*

Münzwäscheschleuder f
- ♦ coin-operated spin drier
- ♦ coin-operated spin dryer

Münzwaschgelegenheit, f (für Kleider)
Münzwaschmöglichkeit, f
Münzwaschanlage, f
- ♦ coin laundry facility *AE*
- ♦ coin-operated laundry facility *BE*

Münzwaschgelegenheit, f (für Personen)
- ♦ coin-operated washing facility

Münzwaschmaschine, f
Münzwaschautomat, m
- ♦ coin-operated washer *AE*
- ♦ coin washer *AE*
- ♦ coin-operated washing machine *BE*

Münzwechsler, m
Wechselautomat, m
- ♦ change machine
- ♦ change dispenser

Münzwhirlpool, m
- ♦ coin-operated whirlpool

Münzzähler, m
(z.B. bei Elektroheizung)
- ♦ slot meter

Mürbegebäck, n
- ♦ shortcake

mürrischer Service, m
- ♦ surly service

mürrisches Personal, n
- ♦ surly staff
- ♦ surly personnel

Muschel, f (Schale)
→ Schale

Muschel, f (Tier)
Miesmuschel, f
- ♦ mussel
- ♦ muscle *AE*

Muschelmuseum, n
- ♦ shell museum

Muschelplatte, f (generell)
- ♦ plate of mussels

Muschelplatte, f (Kammuscheln, Jakobsmuscheln)
- ♦ scallop platter
- ♦ scollop platter

Muschelsalat, m
- ♦ mussel salad

Muschelschale, f
- ♦ scallop-shell
- ♦ scollop-shell

Muschelsoße, f
- ♦ mussel sauce

Muschelsuppe, f
- ♦ mussel soup

Muschelsuppe nach amerikanischer Art, f
Muschelsuppe amerikanische Art, f
- ♦ clam chowder *AE*
- ♦ mussel soup American style

Muscheltiere, n pl
Schalenweichtiere, n pl
- ♦ shellfish

Muschelvergiftung, f
- ♦ mussel poisoning

Museum, n
- ♦ museum

Museum beherbergen
- ♦ house a museum

Museum besuchen
- ♦ visit a museum

Museum der schönen Künste, n
- ♦ museum of fine arts

Museum des Landlebens, n
- ♦ museum of rural life
- ♦ country life museum

Museum erzählt die Geschichte der Stadt
- ♦ museum tells the history of the town
- ♦ museum tells the history of the city

Museum für Arbeitsgeschichte, n
- ♦ museum of labor history *AE*
- ♦ museum of labour history *BE*

Museum für etw, n
- ♦ museum for s.th.

Museum für Frühgeschichte, n
- ♦ museum of early history

Museum für moderne Kunst, n
- ♦ museum of modern art

Museum für Naturgeschichte, n
- ♦ museum of natural history

Museum für Sozialgeschichte, n
Sozialgeschichtliches Museum, n
- ♦ museum of social history

Museum für Technologie, n
Technologiemuseum, n
- ♦ museum of technology
- ♦ technology museum

Museum für Verkehr, n
Verkehrsmuseum, n
- ♦ museum of transport *BE*
- ♦ museum of transportation *AE*
- ♦ transportation museum *AE*
- ♦ transport museum *BE*

Museum für Völkerkunde, n
- ♦ museum of ethnology

Museum für zeitgenössische Kunst, n
- ♦ museum of contemporary art

Museum präsentiert Wechselausstellungen
- ♦ museum features changing exhibitions

Museumsanlage, f
Museumskomplex, m
- ♦ museum complex

Museumsausstellung, f
- ♦ museum exhibition
- ♦ museum exhibit *AE*

Museumsbesuch, m
- ♦ museum visit
- ♦ visit to a museum

Museumsdorf, n
- ♦ museum village

Museumseingang, m
- ♦ museum entrance

Museumseintritt, m
- ♦ museum admission
- ♦ museum entrance

Museumsführer, m
- ♦ museum guide
- ♦ museums guide

Museumsreise, f
- ♦ museum tour
- ♦ museums tour

Museumsrestaurant, n
- ♦ museum restaurant

Museumsschiff, n
- ♦ museum ship

Museumsstück, n
- ♦ museum piece

Musical, n
- ♦ musical

Music Hall, f
- ♦ mucic hall

Musikabend, m
- ♦ musical evening
- ♦ musical soiree *AE*
- ♦ evening of music
- ♦ soirée musicale *FR*
- ♦ musicale

musikalisch, adj
- ♦ musical, adj

musikalische Begleitung, f
- ♦ musical accompaniment

musikalische Matinée, f
- ♦ musical matinée *BE*
- ♦ musical matinee *AE*

musikalische Reise, f
Musikreise, f
- ♦ musical journey

musikalischer Höhepunkt, m
- ♦ musical highlight

musikalischer Rahmen, m
→ musikalische Umrahmung

musikalische Soiree, f
- ♦ musical soiree *AE*
- ♦ musical soirée *BE*
- ♦ musical evening

musikalische Umrahmung, f
musikalischer Rahmen, m
- ♦ musical setting

musikalische Umrahmung besorgen
für den musikalischen Rahmen sorgen
- ♦ provide a musical setting

musikalische Umrahmung geben etw
musikalischen Rahmen etw geben
- ♦ give s.th. a musical setting

musikalische Unterhaltung, f
Musikunterhaltung, f
- ♦ musical entertainment

musikalisch umrahmen etw
- ♦ provide the music for s.th.

Musikanlage, f
Hausradio, n
- ♦ piped music

Musik aufführen von Beethoven
- ♦ perform music by Beethoven

Musikaufführung, f
- ♦ music performance

Musikautomat, m
→ Musikbox

Musikbox, f
Musikautomat, m
- ♦ jukebox *AE*
- ♦ juke-box *BE*
- ♦ juke *coll*

Musikdarbietung, f
musikalische Darbietung, f
- ♦ musical performance

Musikdirektor, m
- ♦ music director

Musiker, m
- ♦ musician

Musiker engagieren
- ♦ engage a musician
- ♦ hire a musician *BE*

Musikfan, m
- ♦ music fan

Musikfest, n
Musikfestspiele, n pl
Musikfestival, n
- ♦ music festival

Musikfestspiel, n
→ Musikfest

Musikfreund m
→ Musikliebhaber

Musikgruppe, f
- ♦ musical group

Musikhauptstadt der Welt, f
- ♦ musical capital of the world

Musikinstrument, n
- ♦ musical instrument

Musikinstrumentensammlung, f
- ♦ collection of musical instruments

Musikkapelle, f
Kapelle, f
Band, f
- ♦ band

Musikkassette, f
- ♦ music cassette

Musikkneipe, f
(z.B. in Irland)
- ♦ musical pub *BE*

Musikkonserve, f
- ♦ recorded music
- ♦ canned music *coll*

Musikkonzession, f
- ♦ music license
- ♦ music licence

Musikkurs, m
Musiklehrgang, m
- ♦ music course

Musikleben, n
- ♦ musical life

Musikliebhaber, m
Musikfreund, m
- ♦ music lover

Musik machen
- ♦ play music

Musiknacht, f
- ♦ music night

Musik nach Vereinbarung
- ♦ music by arrangement

Musikpavillon, m
- ♦ music pavilion
- ♦ bandstand

Musikprogramm

Musikprogramm, n
- ♦ music program *AE*
- ♦ music programme *BE*

Musiksaal, m
- ♦ large music room
- ♦ music room

Musiksaal, m (Konzertsaal)
→ Konzertsaal

Musiksalon, m
- ♦ music lounge

Musikschule, f
- ♦ school of music

Musikstück, n
- ♦ piece of music

Musiktag, m
- ♦ music day

Musikübertragungsanlage, f
- ♦ music transmission system

Musikübertragungseinrichtung, f
- ♦ music transmission equipment

Musik und Unterhaltung, f
- ♦ music and entertainment

Musikveranstaltung, f
- ♦ musical event
- ♦ music event

Musikwettbewerb, m
musikalischer Wettbewerb, m
- ♦ musical competition

Musikwoche, f
- ♦ music week

Musikworkshop, m
Musikwerkstatt, f
- ♦ music workshop

Musikzentrum, n
- ♦ musical center *AE*
- ♦ music center *AE*
- ♦ musical centre *BE*
- ♦ music centre *BE*

Musikzimmer, n
- ♦ music room

Musik zum Tanzen, f
- ♦ music for dancing

Muskatblüte, f *gastr*
- ♦ mace *gastr*

Muskateller, m
- ♦ muscatel

Muskatellertraube, f
- ♦ muscat grape
- ♦ muskat grape

Muskatellerwein, m
- ♦ muscatel wine

Muskatnuß, f
- ♦ nutmeg

Muskelstimulation, f *med*
- ♦ muscle stimulation *med*

Müsli, n
Muesli, n *SCHW*
- ♦ muesli

Müslifan, m
Mueslifan, m *SCHW*
- ♦ muesli fan
- ♦ muesli freak

Müslifrühstück, n
Mueslifrühstück, n *SCHW*
- ♦ muesli breakfast
- ♦ cereals *pl*

Müsliriegel, m
Muesliriegel, m *SCHW*
- ♦ muesli bar

Müslischale, f
Mueslischale, f *SCHW*

- ♦ muesli bowl
- ♦ muesli dish

Muße, f
- ♦ leisure time
- ♦ leisure

Mußestunden, f pl
- ♦ idle hours *pl*

Mußezeit, f
- ♦ idle time
- ♦ idle hours *pl*

Muß ich bar zahlen?
- ♦ Do I have to pay in cash?

Müßiggänger, m
- ♦ loafer

Musterausstellung, f
- ♦ sample exhibition
- ♦ samples exhibition

Musterausstellungsgrundriß, m
- ♦ sample exhibition layout
- ♦ sample exhibit layout *AE*

Mustergutschein, m
- ♦ sample voucher

Musterhaus, n
- ♦ model house
- ♦ showhouse
- ♦ showhome

Musterküche, f
- ♦ show kitchen

Mustermenü, n
- ♦ sample menu

Mustermesse, f
- ♦ sample fair
- ♦ samples fair
- ♦ sample trade fair

Musterpreis, m
(Preisbeispiel)
- ♦ sample price
- ♦ sample rate

Musterprogramm, n
- ♦ sample program *AE*
- ♦ sample programme *BE*

Musterschau, f
- ♦ sample show
- ♦ samples show
- ♦ sample(s) exhibition

Musterschlafzimmer, n
- ♦ show bedroom

Musterspeisekarte, f
- ♦ specimen menu
- ♦ sample menu

Musterwohnung, f
- ♦ show flat *BE*
- ♦ show apartment *AE*

Musterzimmer, n
- ♦ sample room

Mut antrinken sich
- ♦ give oneself some Dutch courage

Muttergesellschaft, f
- ♦ parent corporation *AE*
- ♦ parent company *BE*

Mutterhotel, n
(Gegensatz zu Tochterhotel)
- ♦ parent hotel

Mutterland, n
- ♦ mother country

Mutter Natur, f
- ♦ Mother Nature

Mutterschaftsurlaub, m
Erziehungsurlaub, m
- ♦ maternity leave

Mutterschaftsurlaub nehmen
- ♦ take maternity leave

Muttersprache, f
- ♦ mother tongue
- ♦ native language

Muttertag, m
- ♦ Mother's Day *AE*
- ♦ Mothering Sunday *BE*

mutwillige Sachbeschädigung, f *jur*
- ♦ wanton and wilful damage *jur*
- ♦ wilful trespass *jur*
- ♦ wilful damage *jur*

mutwillige Zerstörung, f
Vandalismus, m
- ♦ deliberate destruction
- ♦ deliberate damage
- ♦ vandalism

MwSt., f
Mehrwertsteuer, f
- ♦ VAT
- ♦ value added tax

N

nach Absprache
  nach Vereinbarung
  ♦ by appointment
  ♦ by arrangement
nach außen gelegenes Zimmer, n
  Außenzimmer n
  zur Außenseite gelegenes Zimmer n
  ♦ outward-facing room
  ♦ outward room
  ♦ outside room
Nachbar, m
  ♦ neighbor AE
  ♦ neighbour BE
Nachbardorf, n
  ♦ neighboring village AE
  ♦ neighbouring village BE
  ♦ next village
Nachbargarten, m
  ♦ neighboring garden AE
  ♦ neighbouring garden BR
  ♦ next-door garden
  ♦ adjoining garden
  ♦ adjacent garden
Nachbargebäude, n
  ♦ neighboring building AE
  ♦ neighbouring building BE
  ♦ adjoining building
  ♦ adjacent building
Nachbargemeinde, f
  ♦ neighboring community AE
  ♦ neighbouring community BE
Nachbarhaus, n (direkt nebenan)
  ♦ neighboring house AE
  ♦ neighbouring house BE
  ♦ adjoining house
  ♦ house next door
Nachbarhaus, n (in der Nähe)
  ♦ nearby house
  ♦ house nearby
Nachbarhotel, n (direkt nebenan)
  ♦ neighboring hotel AE
  ♦ neighbouring hotel BE
  ♦ adjoining hotel
  ♦ adjacent hotel
Nachbarhotel, n (in der Nähe)
  ♦ nearby hotel
  ♦ hotel nearby
Nachbarinsel, f
  ♦ neighboring island AE
  ♦ neighbouring island BE
Nachbarland, n
  ♦ neighboring country AE
  ♦ neighbouring country BE
Nachbar nebenan, m
  ♦ next-door neighbor AE
  ♦ next-door neighbour BE

Nachbarschaft, f
  ♦ neighborhood AE
  ♦ neighbourhood BE
nachbarschaftlich, adj
  ♦ neighborly, adj AE
  ♦ neighbourly, adj BE
nachbarschaftliche Hilfe, f
  ♦ neighborly help AE
  ♦ neighbourly help BE
Nachbarsitz, m
  Nachbarsitzplatz, m
  Nachbarplatz, m
  ♦ neighboring seat AE
  ♦ neighbouring seat BE
Nachbarstadt, f (Großstadt)
  ♦ neighboring city AE
  ♦ neighbouring city BE
  ♦ adjoining city
  ♦ next city
Nachbarstadt, f (kleine Stadt)
  ♦ neighboring town AE
  ♦ neighbouring town BE
  ♦ adjoining town
  ♦ next town
Nachbarstand, m
  ♦ neighboring stand AE
  ♦ neighbouring stand BE
  ♦ adjoining stand
  ♦ neighbouring stall BE
  ♦ adjoining stall
Nachbartisch, m
  ♦ neighboring table AE
  ♦ neighbouring table BE
  ♦ next table
Nachbarvolk, n
  ♦ neighboring nation AE
  ♦ neighbouring nation BE
Nachbarwohnung, f
  ♦ neighboring apartment AE
  ♦ next apartment AE
  ♦ neighbouring flat BE
  ♦ next flat BE
Nachbarzimmer, n
  ♦ adjacent room
  ♦ adjoining room
  ♦ next room
Nachbehandlung, f med
  Nachsorge, f med
  Nachkur, f med
  ♦ aftercare treatment AE med
  ♦ aftercare AE med
  ♦ after-care treatment BE med
  ♦ after-care BE med
nachbelasten
  nachberechnen
  ♦ make a subsequent addition to the bill
nach Belieben
  ♦ at pleasure

nachbestellen etw
  ♦ reorder s.th.
  ♦ order some more
Nachbestellung, f (generell)
  ♦ reorder
Nachbestellung, f (nachträglich)
  nachträgliche Bestellung, f
  ♦ subsequent order
  ♦ second order
  ♦ repeat order
Nachbestellung vornehmen
  ♦ place a repeat order
nach Bier riechen
  ♦ smell of beer
nachbuchen etw (später)
  ♦ book s.th. subsequently
nachbuchen etw (zusätzlich)
  ♦ book s.th. additionally
Nachbuchung, f (folgend)
  → Folgebuchung
Nachbuchung, f (zusätzlich)
  → Zusatzbuchung
nach dem Abendessen (Dinner)
  ♦ after dinner
nach dem Abendessen (Supper)
  ♦ after supper
nach dem Bezugstermin
  → nach der Ankunft
nach dem Eintreffen
  ♦ after check-in
  ♦ after checking in
nach dem Essen
  nach der Mahlzeit
  nach Tisch
  ♦ after the meal
Nach dem Essen sollst Du ruh'n
  oder tausend Schritte tun
  ♦ After dinner sit awhile,
  ♦ after supper walk a mile
nach dem Frühstück
  ♦ after breakfast
Nach dem Frühstück geht unsere Reise weiter
  nach X
  (Reiseverlauf)
  ♦ After breakfast our journey continues to X
nach dem Mittagessen
  ♦ after lunch
  ♦ after luncheon
nach der Ankunft
  ♦ after arriving
  ♦ after having arrived
  ♦ upon arrival form
  ♦ on arrival
nach der Ankunft im Hotel
  ♦ after arriving at the hotel
  ♦ (up)on arrival at the hotel
nach der Karte
  → à la carte

nach der Karte

nach der Kur
 ♦ after the treatment
nach der Mahlzeit
 → nach dem Essen
nach der Pause
 ♦ after the break
 ♦ after the interval
nach eigenem Belieben
 ♦ at one's own convenience
nacheilen jm
 ♦ hurry after s.o.
nach Eingang Ihrer Anzahlung
 ♦ on receipt of your deposit
nach englischem Recht
 ♦ under English law
nach Erhalt der Schlüssel
 ♦ on receipt of the keys
 ♦ upon receipt of the keys
nach Erhalt des Anmeldeformulars (Buchung)
 ♦ on receipt of the booking form
nach Erhalt des Anmeldeformulars (Kurs)
 ♦ on receipt of the enrolment form AE
 ♦ on receipt of the enrolment form BE
nach Erhalt von etw
 ♦ on receipt of s.th.
 ♦ upon receipt of s.th.
Nachfaßbesuch, m
 ♦ follow-up visit
Nachfeier, f (generell)
 ♦ subsequent celebration
Nachfeier, f (Theater)
 ♦ after-show party
Nachfolgekonferenz, f
 nachfolgende Konferenz, f
 ♦ subsequent conference
 ♦ follow-up conference
Nachfolgeleistung, f
 Nachfolgedienstleistung, f
 Nachfaßleistung, f
 ♦ follow-up service
nachfolgend, adj
 folgend, adj
 ♦ subsequent, adj
nachfolgender Monat, m
 Nachmonat, m
 ♦ subsequent month
Nachfolger, m (generell)
 ♦ successor
Nachfolger, m (Miete, Pacht)
 ♦ incomer
Nachfolgereise, f
 nachfolgende Reise, f
 ♦ follow-up tour
Nachfolgeschau, f
 nachfolgende Schau, f
 ♦ subsequent show
 ♦ following show
Nachfrage, f
 ♦ demand
Nachfrageanalyse, f
 ♦ analysis of demand
Nachfrageänderung, f
 Änderung der Nachfrage, f
 ♦ change in demand
Nachfrage ankurbeln
 ♦ boost demand
Nachfrageanstieg, m
 ♦ increase in demand
 ♦ rise in demand
 ♦ upturn in demand

Nachfrage befriedigen
 ♦ satisfy the demand
 ♦ meet the demand
 ♦ supply the demand
Nachfrage beleben
 Nachfrage anregen
 ♦ stimulate demand
Nachfrage bleibt gleich
 ♦ demand remains static
Nachfrage decken
 ♦ meet demand
Nachfrage durch jn, f
 ♦ demand from s.o.
Nachfrage durch Kunden, f
 ♦ demand from customers
Nachfrageeinbruch m
 ♦ slump in demand
Nachfrageelastizität, f
 ♦ elasticity of demand
 ♦ demand elasticity
Nachfrage erfüllen
 Nachfrage befriedigen
 ♦ meet the demand
 ♦ satisfy the demand
Nachfrage erreicht einen Höhepunkt im August
 ♦ demand reaches a peak in August
Nachfrage erzeugen für etw
 ♦ generate demand for s.th.
Nachfrage fällt
 ♦ demand falls
Nachfrage feststellen
 Nachfrage beurteilen
 ♦ assess the demand
 ♦ assess demand
Nachfrage geht zurück
 ♦ demand drops
Nachfrage gleichmäßig über die Saison verteilen
 ♦ spread demand evenly throughout the season
Nachfrage ist elastisch
 ♦ demand is elastic
Nachfrage ist flau
 ♦ demand is slack
Nachfrage ist gering
 ♦ demand is small
Nachfrage ist gleich
 ♦ demand is constant
Nachfrage ist groß
 ♦ demand is high
 ♦ demand is great
Nachfrage ist niedrig
 ♦ demand is low
Nachfrage ist saisonal
 ♦ demand is seasonal
Nachfrage ist träge
 ♦ demand is sluggish
Nachfrage ist unelastisch
 ♦ demand is inelastic
Nachfrage ist ungleichmäßig
 ♦ demand is uneven
Nachfrage ist verteilt über das ganze Jahr
 ♦ demand is spread throughout the year
Nachfrage kanalisieren
 ♦ channel demand
Nachfrage kommt (hauptsächlich) von jm
 ♦ demand comes (mainly) from s.o.
 ♦ demand is (mainly) from s.o.
Nachfrageloch, n
 Nachfrageflaute, f
 ♦ trough in demand
Nachfrage messen
 ♦ measure demand

Nachfragemuster, n
 Nachfrageverhalten, n
 ♦ demand pattern
 ♦ pattern of demand
Nachfrage nach Auslandsurlauben, f
 Nachfrage nach Urlauben im Ausland, f
 ♦ demand for vacations abroad AE
 ♦ demand for foreign vacations AE
 ♦ demand for holidays abroad BE
 ♦ demand for overseas holidays BE
 ♦ demand for foreign holidays BE
Nachfrage nach Banketten, f
 ♦ demand for banquets
Nachfrage nach Beherbergungsleistungen, f
 ♦ demand for accommodation services
 ♦ demand for lodging services AE
Nachfrage nach Doppelzimmern, f
 → Doppelzimmernachfrage
Nachfrage nach Einzelzimmern, f
 → Einzelzimmernachfrage
Nachfrage nach etw, f
 ♦ demand for s.th.
Nachfrage nach Hotelleistungen, f
 ♦ demand for hotel services
Nachfrage nach Hotels bleibt hoch
 Hotelnachfrage bleibt hoch
 ♦ demand for hotels remains high
Nachfrage nach Hotelunterkunft, f
 ♦ demand for hotel accommodation
Nachfrage nach Hotelunterkünften, f
 ♦ demand for hotel accommodations AE
 ♦ demand for hotel accommodation BE
Nachfrage nach Hotelunterkünften schätzen
 ♦ estimate the demand for hotel accommodations AE
 ♦ estimate the demand for hotel accommodation BE
Nachfrage nach Hotelzimmern, f
 ♦ demand for hotel rooms
Nachfrage nach Kurzurlauben, f
 ♦ demand for short breaks
Nachfrage nach Restaurantleistungen, f
 ♦ demand for restaurant services
Nachfrage nach Speisen und Getränken, f
 Nachfrage nach Essen und Trinken, f
 Nachfrage nach Verpflegungsleistungen, f
 ♦ demand for food and beverages
 ♦ demand for food and drink
Nachfrage nach Unterkünften, f
 ♦ demand for accommodations AE
 ♦ demand for accommodation BE
Nachfrage nach Veranstaltungen, f
 Veranstaltungsnachfrage, f
 ♦ demand for functions
 ♦ demand for events
Nachfrage nach Zimmernächten, f
 ♦ demand for room-nights
Nachfrage nimmt ab
 ♦ demand decreases
Nachfrage nimmt zu
 ♦ demand increases
 ♦ demand is increasing
Nachfrageniveau, n
 ♦ demand level
 ♦ level of demand
Nachfragepotential, n
 ♦ demand potential
Nachfragepreis, m
 ♦ bid price
Nachfrageprognose, f
 ♦ demand forecast

Nachfrage reduzieren
   Nachfrage verringern
   Nachfrage senken
   ♦ reduce demand
Nachfragerückgang, m
   ♦ decrease in demand
   ♦ decline in demand
   ♦ fall in demand
   ♦ downturn in demand
Nachfragerückgang erleben
   ♦ experience a decrease in demand
   ♦ experience a decline in demand
   ♦ experience a fall in demand
   ♦ experience a down-turn in demand
Nachfragerückgang erleiden
   ♦ suffer a decrease in demand
   ♦ suffer a decline in demand
   ♦ suffer a fall in demand
Nachfrage schaffen
   Nachfrage erzeugen
   ♦ create demand
Nachfrage schätzen
   ♦ estimate the demand
   ♦ estimate demand
Nachfrageschätzung, f
   ♦ estimation of demand
Nachfrage schwankt
   ♦ demand fluctuates
Nachfrageschwankung, f
   ♦ fluctuation in demand
Nachfrageschwankungen erfahren
   Nachfrageschwankungen erleben
   ♦ experience fluctuations in demand
Nachfrageseite, f
   ♦ demand side
Nachfragesituation, f
   ♦ demand situation
Nachfragespitze und -tiefe, f
   ♦ peak and trough in demand
Nachfrage steigt an
   ♦ demand rises
   ♦ demand increases
Nachfragestruktur, f
   ♦ demand structure
   ♦ structure of demand
Nachfragetrend, m
   Nachfragetendenz, f
   ♦ demand trend
Nachfrage übersteigen
   ♦ outstrip demand
   ♦ outpace demand
Nachfrage umleiten nach X
   ♦ divert demand to X
Nachfrage umleiten zu etw
   ♦ divert demand to s.th.
Nachfrage verdoppelt sich
   ♦ demand doubles
Nachfrage verdreifacht sich
   ♦ demand trebles
Nachfrageverhalten, n
   ♦ pattern of demand
   ♦ demand pattern
Nachfrage verlagern in die Nebensaison
   Nachfrage verschieben in die Nebensaison
   ♦ shift demand to the off season
   ♦ shift demand to the low season
Nachfrageverlagerung, f
   Nachfrageverschiebung, f
   ♦ shift in demand

Nachfrage verteilen
   ♦ spread the demand
   ♦ spread demand
Nachfragevolumen, n
   ♦ volume of demand
   ♦ demand volume
Nachfragevolumen des Auslandstourismus, n
   ♦ volume of demand for foreign tourism
   ♦ volume of demand for overseas tourism
Nachfragevolumen des Inlandstourismus, n
   ♦ volume of demand for domestic tourism
Nachfragezuwachs für Unterkünfte, m
   ♦ increasing demand for accommodations AE
   ♦ increasing demand for accommodation BE
nachfüllen etw
   (z.B. Glas)
   ♦ refill s.th.
nach Gärtnerinart, adv gastr
   ♦ à la jardinière, adv FR gastr
   ♦ gardener's style, adv gastr
nach Gebrauch
   ♦ after use
Nachgeschmack, m
   ♦ aftertaste
Nachgeschmack hinterlassen
   ♦ leave an aftertaste
nachhaltig, adj
   über lange Zeit erhaltbar, adj
   ♦ sustainable, adj
nachhaltige Entwicklung, f
   ♦ sustainable development
nachhaltiger Tourismus, m
   → umweltverträglicher Tourismus
nach Hause begleiten jn
   jn nach Hause bringen
   ♦ see s.o. home
nach Hause fahren
   ♦ go home
nach Hause fahren müssen
   ♦ have to go home
nach Hause fliegen
   → heimfliegen
nach Hause gehen
   ♦ go home
nach Hause kommen
   heimkommen
   ♦ come home
nach Hause senden jn
   nach Hause schicken jn
   ♦ send s.o. home
nach Hause telefonieren
   ♦ telephone home
   ♦ phone home
Nachhauseweg, m
   ♦ way home
nach Hause zurückgehen
   nach Hause zurückfahren
   ♦ go back home
Nach Ihnen!
   ♦ After you!
nach innen gelegenes Zimmer, n
   (Innenzimmer)
nach js Geschmack sein
   jm gefallen
   ♦ be to s.o.'s taste
Nachkonferenzreise, f
   ♦ post-conference tour
   ♦ post-conference journey
Nachkongreßreise, f
   ♦ post-convention tour
   ♦ post-convention journey

   ♦ post-congress tour
   ♦ post-congress journey
Nachkur, f
   ♦ follow-up cure
Nachkur, f
   Nachbehandlung, f
   ♦ aftertreatment AE
   ♦ after-treatment BE
   ♦ follow-up treatment
Nachlaß, m
   (Preis)
   ♦ allowance
   ♦ reduction
Nachlaß auf den Pensionspreis, m
   ♦ allowance on the cost of board
   ♦ reduction of the charge for board
Nachlaß fordern
   Nachlaß verlangen
   ♦ demand a reduction
Nachlaß gewähren
   ♦ allow a reduction
Nachlaß gewähren für nicht eingenommene Mahlzeiten
   ♦ make an allowance for meals not taken
nachlässig, adj
   ♦ negligent, adj
nachlässiger Service, m
   ♦ negligent service
Nachlaß von 10% geben auf den Zimmerpreis
   ♦ make an allowance of 10% on the room rate
nachlegen jm
   weitere Portion jm geben
   ♦ give s.o. another helping
nachlösen
   → Fahrkarte nachlösen
nach meinem letzten Besuch
   ♦ after my last visit
Nachmeldung, f
   nachträgliche Anmeldung, f
   ♦ subsequent registration
Nachmieter, m
   neuer Mieter, m
   ♦ new tenant
   ♦ subsequent tenant
   ♦ subsequent lessee iur
Nachmittag, m
   ♦ afternoon
Nachmittag frei
   (Programmhinweis)
   ♦ afternoon free
   ♦ afternoon at leisure
Nachmittag ist frei für Besichtigungen
   ♦ afternoon is free for sightseeing
Nachmittag ist frei zum Einkaufen
   ♦ afternoon is free for shopping
nachmittags, adv
   ♦ in the afternoons, adv
   ♦ in the afternoon, adv
   ♦ p.m., adv
Nachmittagsaufführung, f
   → Nachmittagsvorstellung
Nachmittagsbesuch, m
   ♦ afternoon visit
Nachmittagsfähre, f
   ♦ afternoon ferry
Nachmittagsimbiß, m
   Brotzeit, f dial
   Vesper, f dial
   ♦ afternoon snack
   ♦ snack in the afternoon

Nachmittagsjause

Nachmittagsjause, f ÖST
  → Nachmittagsimbiß
Nachmittagskaffee, m
  ♦ afternoon coffee
Nachmittagskarte, f (Speisekarte)
  Teekarte, f
  Vesperkarte, f
  ♦ tea menu
Nachmittagskonzert, n
  ♦ afternoon concert
Nachmittagsprogramm, n
  ♦ afternoon program AE
  ♦ afternoon programme BE
Nachmittagsritt, m
  ♦ afternoon ride
Nachmittagsschicht, f
  ♦ afternoon shift
Nachmittagsschlaf, m
  ♦ afternoon sleep
  ♦ siesta
Nachmittagsschläfchen, n coll
  ♦ afternoon nap coll
  ♦ siesta
Nachmittagsschläfchen machen
  Nachmittagsschläfchen halten
  ♦ have an afternoon nap
  ♦ take an afternoon nap
Nachmittagssitzung, f
  ♦ afternoon session
  ♦ afternoon meeting
Nachmittagsspaziergang, m
  ♦ afternoon walk
Nachmittagstee, m
  ♦ afternoon tea
  ♦ five o'clock tea
Nachmittagstour, f
  ♦ afternoon tour
Nachmittagsunterhaltung f
  ♦ afternoon entertainment
Nachmittagsvorstellung, f
  Nachmittagsaufführung, f
  ♦ afternoon performance
  ♦ matinee AE
  ♦ matinée BE
Nachmittag zur freien Verfügung
  ♦ afternoon at leisure
  ♦ free afternoon
  ♦ afternoon at one's disposal
Nachmittag zur freien Verfügung haben
  ♦ have the afternoon at leisure
Nachnahme, f
  ♦ collection on delivery AE
  ♦ cash on delivery BE
  ♦ c.o.d.
Nachname, m
  Zuname, m
  ♦ surname
  ♦ last name
  ♦ second name
nach Norden, adv
  ♦ to the north, adv
  ♦ north, adv
nach Norden fahren (Auto)
  ♦ drive north
nach Norden fahren (generell)
  nach Norden reisen
  ♦ travel north
  ♦ go north
nach Norden fliegen
  ♦ fly north

nach Norden gehen
  nach Norden fahren
  ♦ go north
nach Norden liegen
  ♦ face north
nach Norden liegend, adj
  nach Norden gelegen, adj
  ♦ north-facing, adj
  ♦ facing north, adj
nach Norden segeln
  ♦ sail north
nach Norden wandern
  ♦ walk north
nach Norden ziehen
  ♦ move north
nach oben gehen (Stockwerk)
  ♦ go upstairs
nach Osten, adv
  ♦ to the east, adv
  ♦ east, adv
nach Osten fahren
  nach Osten reisen
  ♦ travel east
nach Osten fahren (Auto)
  ♦ drive east
nach Osten fliegen
  ♦ fly east
nach Osten gehen
  nach Osten fahren
  ♦ go east
nach Osten liegen
  ♦ face east
nach Osten liegend, adj
  nach Osten gelegen, adj
  ♦ east-facing, adj
  ♦ facing east, adj
nach Osten wandern
  ♦ walk east
nach Osten ziehen
  ♦ move east
Nachpächter m
  ♦ subsequent tenant
  ♦ new tenant
nachprüfen etw
  überprüfen etw
  ♦ review s.th.
nachreisen jm
  ♦ follow s.o.
  ♦ go after s.o.
  ♦ follow on (later)
Nachrichtenredaktion, f
  (bei Kongreß)
  → Nachrichtenzentrale
Nachrichtenzentrale, f
  Nachrichtenraum, m
  Nachrichtenredaktion, f
  ♦ newsroom AE
  ♦ news-room BE
Nachricht hinterlassen für jn
  ♦ leave a message for s.o.
Nachsaison, f
  ♦ after-season
Nachsaisonauslastung, f
  ♦ after-season load factor
Nachsaisonbelegung, f
  Nachsaisonauslastung, f
  ♦ after-season occupancy
Nachsaisonbesuch, m
  ♦ after-season visit
Nachsaisonbesucher, m
  ♦ after-season visitor

Nachsaisonbuchung, f
  ♦ after-season booking
Nachsaisoncamper, m
  ♦ after-season camper
Nachsaisoncamping, f
  ♦ after-season camping
Nachsaisonermäßigung f
  ♦ after-season reduction
Nachsaisonfahrt, f
  ♦ after-season trip
Nachsaisongast m
  ♦ after-season guest
  ♦ after-season visitor
Nachsaisongeschäft, n
  ♦ after-season business
Nachsaisonmonat, m
  ♦ after-season month
  ♦ month in the after-season
Nachsaisonnachfrage, f
  ♦ after-season demand
Nachsaisonpreis m
  ♦ after-season rate
  ♦ after-season price
Nachsaisonrabatt, m
  ♦ after-season discount
Nachsaisonreise, f
  ♦ after-season tour
  ♦ after-season trip
  ♦ after-season journey
Nachsaisonreisen, n
  Nachsaisonreiseverkehr, m
  ♦ after-season travel
Nachsaisonreservierung, f
  ♦ after-season reservation
Nachsaisontag, m
  ♦ after-season day
  ♦ day in the after-season
Nachsaisontarif, m
  ♦ after-season tariff
  ♦ after-season rates pl
  ♦ after-season rate
  ♦ after-season terms pl
Nachsaisonumsatz, m
  ♦ after-season sales pl
  ♦ after-season turnover
Nachsaisonunterkunft, f
  ♦ after-season accommodation
Nachsaisonurlaub, m
  Nachsaisonferien, pl
  ♦ after-season vacation AE
  ♦ after-season holiday BE
Nachsaisonwoche, f
  ♦ after-season week
  ♦ week in the after-season
Nachsaisonzeit, f
  Nachsaisonzeitraum, m
  ♦ after-season period
Nachsaisonzuschlag, m
  ♦ after-season supplement
nachsalzen etw
  ♦ add more salt to s.th.
  ♦ salt s.th. afterwards
Nachschlüssel, m
  ♦ duplicate key
  ♦ skeleton key
  ♦ passkey
Nachsehen haben
  ♦ come off badly
Nachsendeadresse, f
  Nachsendeanschrift, f
  ♦ forwarding address

nachsenden etw
(Post)
♦ forward s.th.
Nachsommer, m
♦ Indian summer
Nachsorge, f med
♦ aftercare AE med
♦ after-care BE med
Nachspeise, f
→ Dessert
Nachspeisenbüfett, n
→ Dessertbüfett
Nachspeisewagen, m
Dessertwagen, m
♦ sweet trolley BE
♦ dessert trolley BE
♦ dessert cart AE
nachspülen etw
→ spülen etw
nächstbestes Hotel, n
♦ next hotel we come to
nächste Bushaltestelle ist nur 100 m entfernt
♦ nearest bus stop is only 100 m distant
nächste Eisenbahnstation, f
♦ nearest railroad station AE
♦ nearest railway station BE
nächsten Gang servieren
♦ serve the next course
nächsten Zug nehmen
♦ take the next train
nächster Gang, m
♦ next course
nächster Ort, m
♦ next town
♦ nearest town
♦ next village
♦ nearest village
nächste Runde geht auf meine Rechnung
♦ next round is on me
nächste Saison, f
♦ next season
nächstes Haus, n
nächstgelegenes Haus, n
♦ next house
♦ nearest house
nächstes Wochenende zu Hause verbringen
♦ spend next weekend at home
♦ spend the next weekend at home
nächstes Zimmer, n
Nebenzimmer, n
♦ next room
nachsuchen um Asyl
→ um Asyl bitten
nachsuchen um eine Audienz
um eine Audienz bitten
♦ request an audience
nachsuchen um eine Ermäßigung
bitten um eine Ermäßigung
♦ ask for a reduction
nach Süden, adv
♦ to the south, adv
♦ south, adv
nach Süden fahren
nach Süden reisen
♦ travel south
nach Süden fahren (Auto)
♦ drive south
nach Süden fliegen
♦ fly south

nach Süden gehen
nach Süden fahren
♦ go south
nach Süden liegen
♦ face south
nach Süden liegend, adj
nach Süden gelegen, adj
♦ south-facing, adj
♦ facing south, adj
♦ s/f
nach Süden wandern
♦ walk south
nach Süden ziehen
♦ move south
Nacht, f
♦ night
Nachtaffe, m sl
(Hotelangestellter, der Nachtdienst hat)
♦ night clerk
Nachtarbeit, f
♦ nightwork
Nachtasyl, n
♦ night refuge
♦ shelter for the night
♦ night shelter
Nacht außerhalb des Hauses, f
Übernachtung außer Haus, f
♦ night away from home
♦ night away from the house
♦ night out
Nacht außer Haus, f
♦ night out
Nachtbankett, n
♦ late-night banquet
Nachtbar, f
Nachtclub, m
♦ nightclub AE
♦ night-club BE
♦ nighterie sl
♦ nite club AE
Nachtbarangestellter, m
Nachtbarangestellte, f
♦ nightclub employee AE
♦ night-club employee BE
Nachtbarbesuch, m
♦ visit to a nightclub AE
♦ visit to a night-club BE
♦ nightclubbing AE
Nachtbarbesucher, m
♦ nightclub visitor AE
♦ visitor to a nightclub AE
♦ night-club visitor BE
♦ visitor to a night-club BE
♦ nightclubber AE
Nachtbar betreiben
♦ operate a nightclub AE
♦ operate a night-club BE
Nachtbarbummel, m
Nachtclubbummel, m
Runde durch die Nachtbars, f
Runde durch die Nachtclubs, f
♦ nightclub tour AE
♦ night-club tour BE
Nachtbargast, m
♦ nightclub guest AE
♦ night-club guest BE
♦ night-clubber BE inform
Nachtbarmieze, f sl
Nachtclubmieze, f sl
Animiermädchen, n

♦ B-girl AE sl
♦ sitter sl
Nachtbarrausschmeißer, m
Nachtclubrausschmeißer, m
♦ nightclub bouncer AE
♦ night-club bouncer BE
Nachtbarsängerin, f
Nachtbarsänger, m
♦ nightclub singer AE
♦ night-club singer BE
Nachtbarunterhaltung, f
♦ nightclub entertainment AE
♦ night-club entertainment BE
Nachtbarvorstellung, f
Nachtclubvorstellung, f
♦ floor show
Nacht bleiben
eine Nacht bleiben
einmal übernachten
♦ stay one night
Nachtbrigade, f
♦ night brigade
Nachtbumslokal, n sl
Nachtbums, m sl
♦ night trap sl
Nachtclub, m
→ Nachtbar
Nachtclubunterhaltung, f
→ Nachtbarunterhaltung
Nachtconcierge, m/f
Concierge de nuit, m/f FR
♦ night concierge
♦ concierge de nuit FR
Nachtdienst, m (Personal)
♦ night duty
Nachtdienst, m (Service)
Nachtservice, m
♦ night service
Nachtdienst haben (Personal)
♦ be on night duty
Nacht durchfeiern
durchfeiern
Nacht durchmachen
♦ celebrate all night
♦ make a night of it coll
♦ party went on all night
Nacht durchschlafen
♦ sleep through the night
Nacht durchtanzen
♦ dance the night away
♦ dance through the night
Nacht durchtrinken
♦ drink the night away
Nacht durchzechen und -trinken
Nacht durchfeiern
♦ feast the night away
nächtelang, adv
♦ for nights on end, adv
Nachtempfangsdame, f
Nachtrezeptionistin, f
♦ female night receptionist
Nachtempfangsherr m
Nachtrezeptionist m
♦ night receptionist
Nachtessen, n SCHW
♦ late-night supper
Nachtexpedition, f
♦ night expedition
Nachtfähre, f
♦ night ferry

Nachtfahrpreis

Nachtfahrpreis, m
♦ night fare
Nachtfahrt, f
♦ night trip
Nachtfahrverbot, n
♦ ban on nighttime driving
♦ all motor vehicles prohibited at night
Nachtflug, m
♦ night flight
Nachtflugpreis, m
♦ night flight fare
Nachtflugverbot, n
♦ ban on nighttime flying
♦ ban on night flights
Nachtgebühr, f
Gebühr pro Nacht, f
Übernachtungsgebühr, f
♦ charge per night
Nachtglocke, f
♦ night bell
Nachthemd, n (Damen)
♦ nightdress AE
♦ night-dress BE
♦ nightie inform
♦ nighty inform
♦ nightgown AE
Nachthemd, n (Männer)
♦ nightshirt AE
♦ night-shirt BE
Nachthemdenball, m
(Karneval)
♦ pyjama ball
Nachtigall, f
♦ nightingale
nächtigen ÖST
→ übernachten
Nächtigung, f ÖST
→ Übernachtung
Nachtimbiß, m
♦ late-night snack
nach Tisch
→ nach dem Essen
Nachtisch, m
→ Dessert
Nachtkabarett, n
♦ late-night cabaret
Nachtkellner, m
♦ night waiter
Nachtkellnerin, f
♦ night waitress
Nachtklub, m
→ Nachtbar
Nachtkoch, m
♦ night cook
♦ night chef
Nachtkonzession, f
(z.B. für Bar)
♦ late-hour license
♦ late-hour licence
Nachtlager, n (generell)
♦ place (in which) to stay the night
♦ shakedown (for the night)
♦ place where to stay the night
♦ place for the night
Nachtlager, n (Lager)
Übernachtungslager, n
♦ overnight camp
Nachtlager finden coll
♦ find a place (in which) to stay the night
Nachtlager suchen coll
♦ look for a place (in which) stay the night

Nachtlampe, f
♦ night lamp
Nachtleben, n
♦ night life AE
♦ night-life BE
Nachtleben ist gleich null
♦ nightlife is almost nonexistent AE
♦ there is hardly any night-life BE
nächtlich, adj
♦ nocturnal, adj
♦ nightly, adj
nächtlicher Auszug, m
(heimlich aus Unterkunft)
♦ moonlight flit BE inform
♦ moonlight flitting BE inform
nächtlicher Besuch, m
♦ nocturnal visit
nächtlicher Besucher, m
♦ nocturnal visitor
nächtliche Ruhestörung, f
♦ nighttime disturbance
♦ nocturnal disturbance
♦ disorderly behaviour at night BE
nächtliche Unterhaltung, f
abendliche Unterhaltung, f
♦ nightly entertainment
Nachtlicht, n
♦ night-light
Nachtlokal, n
♦ night spot AE
♦ night trap sl
Nachtmahl, n ÖST
→ Abendessen
Nachtmanager, m
(Direktionsvertreter während der Nacht)
♦ night manager
Nachtparkverbot, n
♦ night parking ban
♦ ban on night parking
Nachtpersonal, n
♦ night staff
♦ night personnel
Nachtportier, m
Portier de nuit, m FR
♦ night porter
♦ portier de nuit FR
♦ night room clerk AE
Nachtportierdienst, m
Nachtportierservice, m
♦ night-porter service
♦ night porterage
Nachtportier hat Dienst von 23 bis 8 Uhr
♦ night porter is on duty from 23.00 to 8.00
Nachtportierservice, m
→ Nachtportierdienst
Nachtprogramm, n
♦ late-night program AE
♦ late-night programme BE
♦ nighttime program AE
♦ night-time programme BE
Nachtquartier, n
♦ night's lodging
♦ place for the night
♦ accommodation for the night
Nachtquartier geben einem Reisenden
Obdach geben einem Reisenden für die Nacht
♦ take a traveler in for the night AE
♦ take a traveller in for the night BE
Nachtquartier geben jm
unterbringen jn für eine Nacht
♦ put s.o. up for a night

♦ take s.o. in for the night
♦ accommodate s.o. for a night
nachträgliche Gebühr, f
Nachgebühr, f
♦ subsequent charge
♦ subsequent fee
Nachtreinigung, f
♦ night cleaning
♦ night cleanup AE
Nachtreinigungskraft, f
Nachtputzkraft, f
♦ night cleaner
Nachtreinigungspersonal, n
♦ night cleaning staff
♦ night cleaning personnel
Nachtreise, f
♦ overnight journey
Nachtreisender, m
♦ night traveler AE
♦ night traveller BE
♦ person traveling at night AE
♦ person travelling at night BE
Nachtreiseverkehr, m
Nachtreisen, n
♦ night travel
Nachtrezeptionist, m
→ Nachtempfangsherr
Nachtruhe, f
♦ night rest
♦ night's rest
♦ night's sleep
Nachtruhe genießen
♦ enjoy one's night rest
♦ enjoy one's night's sleep
Nachtruhe halten
♦ keep silence during the night
Nachtruhe von 22 Uhr an
Nachtruhe von 22 Uhr
♦ night rest from 10 p.m.
nachts, adv
♦ at night, adv
♦ in the night, adv
♦ during the night, adv
♦ nights, adv AE
Nachtsafe, m
→ Nachttresor
nachts arbeiten
♦ work at night
nachts beleuchtet
♦ floodlit at night
Nachtschalter, m
♦ night counter
♦ night desk
Nachtschicht, f
♦ night shift
♦ graveyard shift AE hum
♦ lobster shift hum
Nachtschicht haben
Nachtschicht arbeiten
♦ be on night shift
♦ work (on) the night shift
♦ do the night shift
Nachtschiff, n
♦ night boat
♦ night ship
Nachtschlaf, m
♦ night's sleep
Nacht schlafen bei jm
♦ sleep the night with s.o.
Nachtschuhputzdienst, m
Nachtschuhputzservice, m

- night shoe cleaning service
- overnight shoeshine service AE

Nachtschwärmer, m humor
- night owl BE humor
- night moth BE
- night-bird BE

Nachtschwester, f
- night nurse

Nachtsekretär m
  Nachtsekretärin f
- night secretary

Nachtservice, m
  → Nachtdienst

nachts fahren
- go by night

Nachtsitzung, f
- night session
- all-night session

Nachtspeicherofen, m
  (für Zimmerheizung)
- night storage heater

nachts reisen
- travel by night

Nachtstunde, f
- night hour

Nachttarif, m
- night tariff
- nightly tariff

Nachttelefonist, m
  Nachttelefonistin, f
- night telephonist

Nachttemperatur, f
- night temperature

Nachttisch, m
- night table AE
- nightstand AE
- bedside table BE

Nachttischlampe, f
  Nachttischleuchte, f
- bedside lamp

Nachttischlampe funktioniert nicht
- bedside lamp is not working

Nachttischlampe ist kaputt
- bedside lamp is broken

Nachttopf, m
  Topf, m fam
- chamber pot AE
- chamber-pot BE
- jerry BE fam

Nachttresor, m
  Nachtsafe, m
- night safe
- night depository AE

Nachtüberfahrt, f
- night crossing

Nacht um die Ohren schlagen sich coll
  Nacht durchmachen
- make a night of it coll

Nacht und Tag
  Nacht (f) und Tag (m)
- night and day

Nachtunterhaltung, f
- night entertainment
- nighttime entertainment

Nachtveranstaltung, f
- night event
- night function

Nacht verbringen
- spend a night
- pass a night AE

Nacht verbringen im Freien
  Nacht im Freien verbringen
  im Freien übernachten
- spend the night in the open air
- spend the night in the open

Nacht verbringen in einem Hotel
  übernachten in einem Hotel
- spend a night in a hotel
- spend a night at a hotel

Nacht verbringen in einem Notquartier
  übernachten in einem Notquartier
- spend the night in temporary accommodation

Nacht verbringen mit jm
  (Sex)
- spend a night with s.o.
- spend the night with s.o.

Nachtverkehr, m
- night traffic

Nacht vom 10. auf 11. April, f
  Nacht vom 10. auf den 11. April, f
- night from April 10 to 11
- night of 10 April

Nacht vom 21. auf 22. August, f
  Nacht vom 21. auf den 22. August, f
- night of 21 August

Nacht von Montag auf Dienstag, f
- night from Monday to Tuesday

Nachtwache, f
- night watch AE
- night-watch BE

Nachtwächter, m
- night watchman AE
- night-watchman BE

Nachtwanderung, f
- night walk
- nighttime walk
- night hike
- nighttime hike
- nighttime ramble

Nachtwandler, m
  → Schlafwandler

Nachtzeit, f
- nighttime AE
- night-time BE

Nachtzug, m
- night train

Nacht zum Sonntagmorgen, f
  → Samtagnacht

Nacht zum Tag machen
- turn night into day

Nacht zur freien Verfügung
- night at leisure
- free night
- night at one's disposal

Nacht zur freien Verfügung haben
- have the night at leisure

Nachurlaub, m (Arbeitnehmer)
  Zusatzurlaub, m
- additional leave

Nachurlaubsunruhe, f
  Nachurlaubsdysphorie, f
- post-vacation dysphoria AE
- vacation lag AE
- post-holiday dysphoria BE
- holiday lag BE

nach Vereinbarung
  nach Absprache
- by arrangement
- by appointment

nach vorheriger Absprache
  → nach vorheriger Vereinbarung

nach vorheriger Vereinbarung
  nach vorheriger Absprache
- by prior arrangement

Nachweis, m
- evidence

Nachweis erbringen, daß …
- provide evidence that …
- produce evidence that …

Nachweis praktischer Erfahrung, m
- evidence of practical experience

nach Westen, adv
- to the west, adv
- west, adv

nach Westen fahren
  nach Westen reisen
- travel west

nach Westen fahren (Auto)
- drive west

nach Westen fliegen
- fly west

nach Westen gehen
  nach Westen fahren
- go west

nach Westen liegen
- face west

nach Westen liegend, adj
  nach Westen gelegen, adj
- west-facing, adj
- facing west, adj

nach Westen reisen mit dem Bus
- travel west by bus
- travel west by coach BE

nach Westen wandern
- walk west

nach Westen ziehen
- move west

nachwiegen etw
- reweigh s.th.

Nachwuchskraft, f
- trainee

nachzahlen etw (später)
- pay s.th. later

nachzahlen etw (zusätzlich)
- pay s.th. in addition
- pay s.th. extra
- make an additional payment

Nachzahlung, f (später)
- subsequent payment

Nachzahlung, f (zusätzlich)
- additional payment
- extra payment

Nachzahlung leisten (später)
- make a subsequent payment

Nachzahlung leisten (zusätzlich)
- make an additional payment
- make an extra payment

Nachzügler, m
  Zuspätkommender, m
- latecomer

Nackenbehandlung, f med
- neck treatment med

Nackenkissen, n
- neck cushion
- bolster

Nackenmassage, f
- neck massage

nackt baden
- bathe in the nude
- bathe nude
- swim in the nude
- bathe naked

Nacktbaden

Nacktbaden, n
- ◆ nude bathing

Nacktbadestrand, m
- Nacktstrand, m
- ◆ nude-bathing beach
- ◆ nudist beach
- ◆ naturist beach
- ◆ nude beach

nacktes Zimmer, n
- ◆ bare room

Nacktkultur, f
- → FKK

nackt schwimmen
- ◆ swim in the nude

Nacktschwimmen, n
- ◆ nude swimming

Nacktstrand, m
- (Gegensatz zu Textilstrand)
- Nacktbadestrand, m
- ◆ nude beach
- ◆ beach for nudists

Nadelwald, m
- ◆ coniferous forest
- ◆ coniferous wood
- ◆ coniferous woodland

Nagelbehandlung, f
- ◆ nail treatment

nagelneues Hotel, n
- ◆ brand-new hotel

nagen (an etw)
- knabbern (an etw)
- ◆ nibble (at s.th.)

Nahe, f
- ◆ Nahe River, the
- ◆ River Nahe, the
- ◆ Nahe, the

Nähe, f
- ◆ proximity

nahe am Meer
- ◆ near the sea

nahe am Strand, adv
- nahe bei dem Strand, adv
- strandnah, adv
- ◆ close to the beach, adv
- ◆ near the beach, adv

nahe bei allen Einrichtungen
- ◆ close to all amenities

nahe bei etw
- in der Nähe von etw
- ◆ near s.th.
- ◆ close to s.th.

nahe bevorstehende Abreise, f
- ◆ imminent departure

nahe bevorstehende Ankunft, f
- ◆ imminent arrival

nahegelegen, adj
- ◆ nearby, adj

nahegelegene Attraktion, f
- Attraktion in der Nähe, f
- ◆ nearby attraction

nahegelegene Großstadt, f
- ◆ nearby city

nahegelegene Stadt, f
- ◆ nearby town

nahende Abreise, f
- ◆ impending departure

nahende Ankunft, f
- ◆ impending arrival

nähere Angaben, f pl
- genaue Angaben, f pl
- ◆ particulars pl

- ◆ detailed information sg
- ◆ details pl

nähere Umgebung, f
- unmittelbare Umgebung, f
- ◆ immediate vicinity
- ◆ immediate surroundings, the pl

Naherholer m
- ◆ person seeking recreation in the vicinity

Naherholung, f
- ◆ recreation in the vicinity
- ◆ recreation in the immediate vicinity
- ◆ local recreation

Naherholungsangebot, n
- ◆ recreation offered in the vicinity
- ◆ recreation offered in the immediate vicinity

Naherholungseinrichtungen, f pl
- ◆ recreational facilities in the vicinity pl
- ◆ recreational facilities in the immediate vicinity pl

Naherholungsgebiet, n
- ◆ recreation area in the vicinity
- ◆ recreation area in the immediate vicinity
- ◆ recreation area for weekend trips
- ◆ greenbelt recreation area

Naherholungsurlauber, m
- ◆ vacationer seeking recreation in the vicinity AE
- ◆ recreational vacationer AE
- ◆ holidaymaker seeking recreation in the vicinity BE
- ◆ recreational holidaymaker BE

Näherin f
- ◆ seamstress
- ◆ sempstress

nähern sich etw
- ◆ approach s.th.

Naher Osten, m
- ◆ Middle East, the
- ◆ Near East, the

naher Verwandter, m
- ◆ near relative

Nahetal, n
- ◆ Nahe valley, the

Nähe von etw, f
- ◆ proximity of s.th.

Nahewein, m
- ◆ Nahe wine

Nähe zu etw, f
- ◆ proximity to s.th.

Nähe zum Flughafen, f
- Nähe zu dem Flughafen, f
- Flughafennähe, f
- ◆ closeness to the airport
- ◆ proximity to the airport

Nähe zur Großstadt, f
- Nähe zu der Großstadt, f
- Großstadtnähe, f
- ◆ proximity to the city

Nähkränzchen, n
- (Zusammenkunft)
- ◆ sewing bee AE
- ◆ sewing circle

Nährbier, n
- (nichtalkoholisch)
- Malzbier, n
- ◆ near beer

nähren jn
- speisen jn
- ◆ feed s.o.
- ◆ nourish s.o.

Nährgehalt, m
- ◆ nutritional content

nahrhaft, adj
- ◆ nourishing, adj
- ◆ nutritious, adj

nahrhafte Mahlzeit, f
- nahrhaftes Mahl, n
- nahrhaftes Essen, n
- ◆ nourishing meal

nahrhafte Mahlzeit, f
- nahrhaftes Mahl, n
- nahrhaftes Essen, n
- ◆ nutritious meal

nahrhaftes Getränk, n
- ◆ nourishing drink
- ◆ nourishing beverage

nahrhaftes Mittagessen, n
- ◆ nutritious lunch
- ◆ nutritious luncheon

nahrhafte Suppe, f
- ◆ nutritious soup
- ◆ nourishing soup

Nährstoff, m
- ◆ nutrient

Nahrungsaufnahme, f
- ◆ food intake

Nahrungsmangel, m (Knappheit)
- Nahrungsknappheit, f
- ◆ shortage of food
- ◆ scarcity of food

Nahrungsmangel, m (völliges Fehlen)
- ◆ lack of food

Nahrungsmittel, n
- Nahrungsmittel, n pl
- ◆ foodstuff
- ◆ food item
- ◆ foodstuffs pl

Nahrungsmittelchemie, f
- Lebensmittelchemie, f
- ◆ food chemistry

Nahrungsmittelchemiker, m
- Lebensmittelchemiker, m
- ◆ food chemist

Nahrungsmittelvergiftung, f
- → Lebensmittelvergiftung

Nahrungsquelle, f
- ◆ food source

Nährwert, m
- ◆ nutritional value
- ◆ food value

Nahstreckenziel, n
- → Kurzstreckenziel

Nahurlaub, m
- → Naherholung

Nahverkehr, m
- ◆ short-distance traffic
- ◆ local traffic
- ◆ short-haul traffic

Nahverkehrsbus, m
- ◆ local bus

Nahverkehrszug, m
- ◆ local train
- ◆ commuter train

Nähzeug, n
- ◆ sewing kit

Nahziel, n
- ◆ immediate objective

Name, m
- ◆ name

Name des Hotels, m
- ◆ name of the hotel

Namen angeben
  seinen Namen angeben
  ♦ give one's name
Namen der nächsten Verwandten, m pl
  ♦ names of the nearest relatives pl
Namen eines Hotels ändern
  ♦ change the name of a hotel
Namen machen sich als
  ♦ win a name as
namens
  → im Namen von jm
Namensänderung, f
  ♦ change of name
Namenskarte f
  ♦ name card
Namensliste, f
  Namensverzeichnis, n
  ♦ name list
  ♦ list of names
Namensschild, n (am Revers)
  ♦ name badge
  ♦ badge
  ♦ name tag AE
Namensschild, n (Aufkleber)
  ♦ name label
Namensschild, n (Tür, Tisch)
  ♦ nameplate
Namensverwechslung, f
  ♦ confusion of names
Namensverzeichnis, n
  ♦ register of names
Namensvetter, m
  ♦ namesake
Namen und Adresse auf das Formular schreiben
  ♦ write one's name and address on the form
Namen verwechseln
  ♦ confuse names
Name und Adresse angeben
  ♦ give one's name and address
Name und Adresse eines Gastes
  Name (m) und Adresse (f) eines Gastes
  ♦ name and address of a guest
Namibia
  ♦ Namibia
Namibier, m
  ♦ Namibian
Namibierin, f
  ♦ Namibian girl
  ♦ Namibian woman
  ♦ Namibian
namibisch, adj
  ♦ Namibian, adj
Napfpastete, f
  ♦ deep-dish pie
Napperon, m FR
  Deckserviette, f
  ♦ napperon FR
naschen an etw
  ♦ nibble at s.th.
Näscherei, f
  Süßigkeit, f
  ♦ goodies pl inform
  ♦ goody inform
  ♦ sweet BE
  ♦ candy AE
Nassauer, m
  Schnorrer, m
  ♦ sponger inform
  ♦ freeloader AE inform
  ♦ scrounger inform

  ♦ cadger inform
  ♦ dead beat AE sl
nassauern
  schnorren
  ♦ sponge inform
  ♦ freeload inform
  ♦ cadge
  ♦ scrounge inform
Nassauern, n
  Schnorren, n
  ♦ sponging
  ♦ freeloading AE inform
  ♦ free-loading BE inform
  ♦ cadging
nassauernd, adj
  schnorrend, adj
  ♦ sponging, adj
  ♦ freeloading, adj AE inform
  ♦ free-loading, adj BE inform
  ♦ cadging, adj
  ♦ scrounging, adj inform
nassauernder Besucher, m
  schnorrender Besucher, m
  ♦ freeloading visitor AE inform
  ♦ free-loading visitor BE inform
  ♦ sponging visitor
  ♦ cadging visitor
  ♦ scrounging visitor
nasses Wetter, n
  ♦ wet weather
naßkalt, adj
  ♦ damp and cold, adj
  ♦ chilly and damp, adj
naßkaltes Zimmer, n
  → feuchtes Zimmer
Naßzelle, f
  → Sanitäreinheit
national, adj
  staatlich, adj
  ♦ national, adj
Nationalbibliothek, f
  ♦ national library
Nationaldenkmal, n
  ♦ national monument
Nationalerbe, n
  nationales Erbe, n
  ♦ national heritage
nationaler Kongreß, m
  ♦ national convention
  ♦ national congress
Nationalfahne, f
  Nationalflagge, f
  Staatsflagge, f
  ♦ national flag
Nationalfeier, f
  nationale Feier, f
  ♦ national celebration
Nationalfeiertag, m
  Staatsfeiertag, m
  ♦ national holiday
Nationalfest, n
  nationales Fest, n
  ♦ national festival
Nationalgericht, n
  Nationalspeise, f ÖST
  ♦ national dish
Nationalgetränk, n
  ♦ national drink
  ♦ national beverage
Nationalhymne, f
  ♦ national anthem

Nationalhymne spielen
  ♦ play the national anthem
Nationalität, f
  ♦ nationality
Nationalitätenkennzeichen, n
  (am Auto)
  ♦ national identity plate
Nationalitätenrestaurant, n
  ♦ nationality restaurant
  ♦ ethnic restaurant
Nationalkonferenz, f
  nationale Konferenz, f
  ♦ national conference
Nationalküche, f
  (Speisen)
  ♦ national cuisine
  ♦ national cooking
  ♦ ethnic cuisine
  ♦ ethnic cooking
Nationalmuseum, n
  ♦ national museum
Nationalpark, m
  ♦ national park
Nationalparkaufseher, m
  ♦ national park warden
Nationalparkbehörde, f
  ♦ national park authority
Nationalparkbesucher, m
  ♦ national park visitor
  ♦ visitor to the national park
Nationalparkführer, m
  ♦ national park guide
Nationalparkurlaub, m
  ♦ national park vacation AE
  ♦ national park holiday BE
Nationalparkverwaltung, f
  ♦ national park administration
  ♦ national park authorities pl
Nationalspeise, f ÖST
  → Nationalgericht
Nationalsport, m
  ♦ national sport
Nationaltheater, n
  ♦ national theater AE
  ♦ national theatre BE
Nationaltracht, f
  → Landestracht
National Trust, m
  ♦ National Trust, m
Nationalwald, m
  ♦ national forest
Nationalwaldcampingplatz, m
  ♦ national forest campground AE
  ♦ national forest campsite
Nation von Feinschmeckern, f
  ♦ nation of gourmets
Natron, n coll
  doppeltkohlensaures Natrium, n
  Natriumbikarbonat, n
  ♦ baking soda
  ♦ cooking soda
  ♦ bicarbonate of soda
Naturbad, n
  Naturbecken, n
  ♦ natural pool
Naturbadesee, m
  ♦ natural bathing lake
Naturbegeisterter, m
  Naturfan, m
  ♦ nature enthusiast
  ♦ outdoor enthusiast

Naturbehandlung

Naturbehandlung, f
  natürliche Behandlung, f
  ♦ **natural treatment**
naturbewußt, adj
  ♦ **nature-conscious, adj**
Naturdenkmal, n
  ♦ **natural monument**
Natur der Behandlung, f
  Art der Behandlung, f
  ♦ **nature of (the) treatment**
Naturdüne, f
  ♦ **natural dune**
Natureisbahn, f
  Natureislaufbahn, f
  ♦ **natural ice rink**
Natureisstockbahn f
  ♦ **natural eisstock rink**
  ♦ **natural curling rink**
Naturerlebnis, n
  ♦ **outdoor experience**
Naturfango, m
  ♦ **therapeuthic mud**
Naturferien, pl
  Natururlaub, m
  ♦ **nature holiday** BE
  ♦ **nature vacation** AE
Naturforscher, m
  ♦ **naturalist**
Naturforscherparadies, n
  ♦ **naturalist's paradise**
Naturfotografie, f
  ♦ **nature photography**
Naturfreund, m
  → Naturliebhaber
Naturfreundehaus, n
  ♦ **nature lovers' refuge**
Natur genießen
  ♦ **enjoy nature**
Naturgeschichte, f
  ♦ **natural history**
Naturgeschichteliebhaber, m
  ♦ **natural history lover**
Naturgeschichtemuseum, n
  → Naturhistorisches Museum
Naturgeschichtesammlung, f
  naturgeschichtliche Sammlung, f
  ♦ **natural history collection**
Naturgeschichteweg, m
  naturgeschichtlicher Weg, m
  ♦ **natural history trail**
Naturgesundheitspflege, f
  natürliche Gesundheitspflege, f
  ♦ **natural health care**
Naturhafen, m
  ♦ **natural harbor** AE
  ♦ **natural harbour** BE
Naturheilkunde, f
  ♦ **naturopathy** AE
  ♦ **natureopathy** AE
  ♦ **nature therapy**
Naturheilkundebehandlung, f
  ♦ **naturopathic treatment**
Naturheilkundeklinik, f
  ♦ **naturopath clinic**
Naturheilkundetherapie, f
  ♦ **naturopathic therapy**
Naturheilmittel, n
  ♦ **natural remedy**
Naturheilzentrum, n
  ♦ **natural healing center** AE
  ♦ **natural healing centre** BE

Naturhistorisches Museum, n
  Naturgeschichtemuseum, n
  Museum für Naturgeschichte, n
  ♦ **Natural History Museum**
  ♦ **Museum of Natural History**
Naturhöhle, f
  ♦ **natural cave**
Naturholz, n
  ♦ **natural wood**
Naturholzmöbel, n pl
  ♦ **natural wood furniture** sg
Naturjoghurt, m
  ♦ **natural yoghurt**
  ♦ **natural yogurt**
  ♦ **natural yoghourt**
Naturkatastrophe, f
  ♦ **natural disaster**
Naturkost, f
  Naturküche, f
  ♦ **natural diet**
  ♦ **health food**
Naturküche, f
  → Naturkost
Naturkundeweg, m
  naturkundlicher Weg, m
  ♦ **nature study trail**
naturkundliche Reise, f
  ♦ **nature study tour**
Naturkurbehandlung, f
  ♦ **nature cure treatment**
Naturkurzentrum, n
  ♦ **nature cure center** AE
  ♦ **nature cure centre** BE
Naturlandschaft, f
  ♦ **natural landscape**
Naturlehrpfad, m
  ♦ **nature trail**
natürlich, adj
  ♦ **natural, adj**
natürlichen Rahmen bieten für etw
  ♦ **provide the natural setting for s.th.**
natürlicher Rahmen, m
  ♦ **natural setting**
natürlicher Strand, m
  → Naturstrand
natürliche Schönheit, f
  Naturschönheit, f
  ♦ **natural beauty**
natürliche Schönheit der Landschaft bewahren
  ♦ **conserve the natural beauty of the countryside**
natürliches Licht, n
  Tageslicht, n
  ♦ **natural light**
natürliche Umgebung, f
  ♦ **natural surroundings** pl
  ♦ **natural environment**
natürliche Umwelt, f (generell)
  ♦ **natural environment**
natürliche Umwelt, f (Tiere)
  natürlicher Lebensraum, m
  ♦ **natural habitat**
natürliche Zutat, f
  ♦ **natural ingredient**
Naturliebhaber, m
  Naturfreund, m
  ♦ **nature lover**
Naturparadies, n
  ♦ **nature paradise**
  ♦ **natural paradise**

530

Naturpark, m
  ♦ **nature park**
  ♦ **nature reserve**
naturrein, adj
  ♦ **naturally pure, adj**
  ♦ **pure, adj**
  ♦ **unadulterated, adj**
naturreiner Wein, m
  ♦ **pure wine**
  ♦ **unadulterated wine**
Naturreservat, n
  ♦ **nature reserve**
Naturschatz, m
  ♦ **natural treasure**
Naturschlittschuhbahn f
  ♦ **natural ice skating rink**
Naturschönheit, f
  → natürliche Schönheit
Naturschutz, m
  ♦ **nature conservation**
  ♦ **conservation**
  ♦ **protection of nature**
Naturschutzbehörde, f
  ♦ **Nature Conservancy** BE
Naturschützer, m
  ♦ **conservationist**
Naturschutzgebiet, n
  (steht über Landschaftsschutzgebiet)
  ♦ **nature conservation area**
  ♦ **conservation area**
  ♦ **nature reserve** BE
Naturschutzparadies, n
  ♦ **conservationist's paradise**
Naturschutzpark, m
  ♦ **conservation park**
Naturschutz und Erholung in Einklang bringen
  ♦ **reconcile conservation and recreation**
Naturschwimmbad, n
  Naturschwimmbecken, n
  ♦ **natural swimming pool** AE
  ♦ **natural swimming-pool** BE
  ♦ **natural pool**
Naturschwimmbecken, n
  → Naturschwimmbad
Natursee, m
  natürlicher See, m
  ♦ **natural lake**
Natursehenswürdigkeit, f
  ♦ **natural sight**
  ♦ **natural monument**
Naturspaziergang, m
  Spaziergang in der Natur, m
  ♦ **nature walk**
Naturstrand, m
  ♦ **natural beach**
Naturtherapie, f
  natürliche Therapie, f
  ♦ **natural therapy**
Natururlaub, m
  ♦ **nature vacation** AE
  ♦ **nature holiday** BE
Naturwein, m
  ♦ **natural wine**
Naturwunder, n
  ♦ **natural wonder**
Natur zerstören
  ♦ **destroy nature**
  ♦ **ruin nature**
Nautikunterricht, m
  ♦ **lessons in navigation** pl

Navigator, m
♦ navigator
Neapel
♦ Naples
neapolitanische Art, adv gastr
♦ Neapolitan style, adv gastr
Nebel, m
♦ fog
nebelfrei, adj
♦ free of fog, adj
nebenan, adv
♦ next door, adv
nebenan wohnen
♦ live next door
Nebenapparat, m (Telefon)
♦ extension
Nebenattraktion, f
Nebenveranstaltung, f
♦ side attraction
♦ side show
Nebenausgaben, f pl
♦ incidental expenses pl
♦ extra expenses pl
♦ incidentals pl
♦ extras pl
Nebenausgang, m
Seitenausgang, m
♦ side exit
♦ side door
Nebenbahn, f
(Eisenbahn)
♦ branch railroad AE
♦ branch railway BE
nebenbei arbeiten als Kellnerin
♦ work as a waitress in one's spare time
Nebendarsteller, m
♦ supporting actor
neben dem Hotel ist ein Restaurant
♦ next to the hotel is a restaurant
nebeneinander, adv
♦ side by side, adv
nebeneinander liegend, adj
→ angrenzend
nebeneinander liegende Einzelzimmer, n pl
♦ adjoining single rooms pl
nebeneinander liegende Zimmer, n pl
♦ adjoining rooms pl
♦ adjacent rooms pl
nebeneinander wohnen
→ Tür an Tür wohnen
neben einem Restaurant wohnen
(dauernd)
♦ live next to a restaurant
♦ live beside a restaurant
Nebeneingang, m
Seiteneingang, m
♦ side entrance
Nebeneinnahmen, f pl
♦ extra income
neben etw
♦ beside s.th.
♦ next to s.th.
Nebenfluß, m
Seitenfluß, m
♦ tributary
Nebenfluß der Themse, m
♦ tributary of the Thames
Nebengebäude, n (Dependance)
→ Dependance
Nebengebäude, n (generell)
Hintergebäude, n

♦ outhouse BE
♦ outbuilding
Nebengebühr, f
♦ incidental charge
♦ additional charge
♦ additional fee
Nebengericht, n
Zwischengericht, n
♦ side order
♦ side dish AE
♦ side-dish BE
neben jm
(Unterkunft)
♦ next door to s.o.
Nebenkasse, f (Portokasse)
→ Portokasse
Nebenkosten, pl
NK, pl
♦ extras pl
♦ extra costs pl
♦ extra expenses pl
♦ incidentals pl
Nebenkostenabrechnung f
♦ settlement of incidentals
Nebenkostenberechnung, f
♦ calculation of incidentals
Nebenkosten inbegriffen
Extras inbegriffen
♦ extras included
Nebenkostenpauschale f
♦ flat rate for additional expenses
Nebenkosten und Endreinigung inklusive
♦ including incidentals and final cleaning
Nebenleistung, f
♦ auxiliary service
♦ additional service
Nebenplatz, m
(Camping)
♦ annex site AE
♦ annexe site BE
Nebenprogramm, n
Rahmenprogramm, n
♦ fringe program AE
♦ fringe programme BE
Nebenrolle, f
♦ supporting role
♦ supporting rôle
Nebensaison, f
♦ off season
♦ low season
♦ value season advert
Nebensaisonauslastung f
Nebensaisonbelegung f
♦ off-season occupancy
♦ low-season occupancy
Nebensaisonbelegung, f
→ Nebensaisonauslastung
Nebensaisonbesuch, m
♦ off-season visit
♦ low-season visit
Nebensaisonbesucher, m
♦ off-season visitor
♦ low-season visitor
♦ off-season guest
♦ low-season guest
Nebensaisonbuchung, f
♦ off-season booking
♦ low-season booking
Nebensaisoncamper, m
♦ off-season camper
♦ low-season camper

Nebensaisoncamping, n
♦ off-season camping
♦ low-season camping
Nebensaisonermäßigung f
♦ off-season reduction
♦ low-season reduction
Nebensaisonferien, pl
Nebensaisonurlaub, m
♦ off-season holiday BE
♦ low-season holiday BE
♦ off-season vacation AE
♦ low-season vacation AE
Nebensaisonferiengast, m
Nebensaisonurlauber, m
♦ off-season holidaymaker BE
♦ low-season holidaymaker BE
♦ off-season vacationer AE
♦ low-season vacationer AE
Nebensaisongast m
♦ off-season guest
♦ low-season guest
Nebensaisongeschäft, n
♦ off-season business
♦ low-season business
Nebensaisonkurzurlaub, m
♦ off-season break
♦ low-season break
Nebensaisonmonat, m
♦ off-season month
♦ low-season month
♦ month in the off season
♦ month in the low season
Nebensaisonnachfrage, f
♦ off-season demand
♦ low-season demand
Nebensaisonpreis, m
♦ off-season price
♦ off-season rate
♦ low-season price
♦ low-season rate
Nebensaisonreise, f
♦ off-season tour
♦ low-season tour
Nebensaisonreiseverkehr, m
Nebensaisonreisen, n
♦ off-season travel
Nebensaisontag, m
♦ off-season day
♦ low-season day
♦ day in the off season
♦ day in the low season
Nebensaisontarif, m
♦ off-season tariff
♦ low-season tariff
♦ off-season rates pl
♦ low-season rates pl
♦ off-season terms pl
Nebensaisonumsatz, m
♦ off-season sales pl
♦ low-season sales pl
♦ off-season turnover
♦ low-season turnover
Nebensaisonunterkunft, f
♦ off-season accommodation
♦ low-season accommodation
Nebensaisonurlaub, m
Nebensaisonferien, pl
♦ off-season vacation AE
♦ low-season vacation AE
♦ off-season holiday BE
♦ low-season holiday BE

Nebensaisonurlauber, m
- off-season vacationer *AE*
- low-season vacationer *AE*
- off-season holidaymaker *BE*
- low-season holidaymaker *BE*

Nebensaisonwoche, f
- off-season week
- low-season week
- week in the off season
- week in the low season

Nebensaisonzeit, f
- off-season period
- low-season period

Nebensaisonzeit, f
- off-season time

Nebensaisonzuschlag m
- off-season supplement
- low-season supplement

Nebenservice, m
→ Nebenleistung

Nebenstraße, f (in Ort)
- side street *AE*
- side-street *BE*
- off-street
- street off ...

Nebenstraße, f (Land)
- branch road *AE*
- side road *BE*
- side-road *BE*
- minor road
- secondary road

Nebenstrecke, f
(Eisenbahn)
- branch line

Nebentisch, m
- adjoining table *AE*
- neighboring table *AE*
- neighbouring table *BE*
- next table
- side table

Nebentrakt, m
Seitenflügel, m
Seitentrakt, m
- side wing

Nebentür, f (an der Seite)
→ Seitentür

Nebentür, f (nächste)
- next door

Nebenveranstaltung, f
Nebenvorstellung, f
Randveranstaltung, f
- sideshow
- fringe event

Nebenvertrag, m
→ Untervertrag

Nebenwohnung, f
→ Nachbarwohnung

Nebenzeit, f
- off-peak period

Nebenzimmer, n (angrenzend)
→ angrenzendes Zimmer

Nebenzimmer, n (Hinterzimmer)
→ Hinterzimmer

Nebenzimmer, n (nächstes Zimmer)
→ nächstes Zimmer

Nebenzimmer, n (privat)
- by-room *AE*

Nebenzimmer, n (Seitenzimmer)
- side room

Nebenzimmer, n (Veranstaltungsraum)
→ Veranstaltungsraum

Necessaire, n
Kulturbeutel, m
- toilet bag
- wash bag

Neckar, m
- Neckar River, the
- River Neckar, the
- Neckar, the

Neckartal, n
- Neckar valley, the

Negativ, n
(Film)
- negative

negative Tourismuseinflüsse, m pl
- negative tourism impacts *pl*

Negativimage, n
- negative image

Negligé, n
Négligé, n *SCHW*
- negligee *AE*
- negligée *BE*
- negligé
- négligé *FR*
- neglige *AE*

nehmen etw (Speisen)
- have s.th.

Nehmen Sie bitte Platz
- Please sit down
- Please be seated

Nehmen Sie Kreditkarten an?
- Do you accept credit cards?

Nehmen Sie noch etwas Fleisch!
- Have some more meat!

Nehmen Sie Reiseschecks an?
- Do you accept travelers' checks? *AE*
- Do you accept travellers' cheques? *BE*

Nehmen Sie sich bitte!
- Help yourself!
- Help yourselves!

Nehmen Sie Zucker?
- Do you take sugar, Sir?
- Do you take sugar, Madam?
- Do you take sugar?

Nehmen Sie Zucker zum Tee?
- Do you take sugar in your tea, Sir?
- Do you take sugar with your tea, Sir?
- Do you take sugar in your tea, Madam?
- Do you take sugar with your tea, Madam?
- Do you take sugar in (with) your tea?

Neigung, f
Neigungswinkel, m
- rake

Neigung haben
(Bühne, Boden)
geneigt sein
- rake

Nektar, m
- nectar

Nelke, f (Blume)
- carnation

Nelke, f (Gewürz)
- clove

nennen jn namentlich
- mention s.o. by name

neoklassische Villa, f
- neo-classical villa

Neonlicht, n
- neon light

Neonröhre, f
- neon tube

Neonschild, n
- neon sign

Nepal
- Nepal

Nepalese, m
Nepaler, m
- Nepalese
- Nepali

Nepalesin, f
Nepalin, f
- Nepalese girl
- Nepalese woman
- Nepali
- Nepali girl
- Nepali woman

nepalesisch, adj
nepalisch, adj
- Nepalese, adj
- Nepali, adj

Nepp, m
Nepperei, f
- rip-off *BE sl*
- gyp *AE coll*
- clip
- gyp *AE coll*
- daylight robbery

Nepp, m
Nepperei, f
- rip-off *BE coll*
- clip *coll*
- gyp *AE coll*

neppen jn
ausnehmen jn *coll*
rupfen jn *coll*
- rook s.o.
- fleece s.o.
- gyp s.o. *AE*
- clip s.o.
- overcharge s.o.

neppen lassen sich
bluten *sl*
- pay through the nose

Nepperei, f
Nepp, m
- gyp *AE coll*
- clip *coll*
- rip-off *BE coll*

Neppkneipe, f
Nepplokal, m
- clip-joint *sl*
- gyp joint *AE sl*

Nepplokal, n
- rip-off place *BE sl*
- tourist trap
- clip-joint *sl*
- gyp joint *AE sl*
- skin joint *AE sl*

Nepp-Preis, m
- rip-off price *BE sl*
- rip-off *BE sl*

Nervenheilanstalt, f
- mental home
- mental hospital
- mental asylum

Nervenkitzel, m
- thrills *pl*

Nervensystem, n
- nervous system

Nest, n (Haus)
Bude, f *coll*
- pad *BE sl*

Nest, n (Ort) neg
 ♦ hole neg
nett eingerichtet, adj
 ♦ nicely appointed, adj
nett eingerichtetes Zimmer, n
 ♦ nicely appointed room
netten Abend machen sich
 ♦ have a nice evening
 ♦ have a pleasant evening
nett möbliert, adj
 ♦ nicely furnished, adj
nett möbliertes Zimmer, n
 ♦ nicely furnished room
Nettoaufwand, m
 ♦ net expenditure
Nettoausstellungsfläche, f
 ♦ net exhibition area
 ♦ net exhibition space
 ♦ net exhibit area AE
 ♦ net exhibit space AE
Nettoausstellungsraum, m
 Nettoausstellungsfläche, f
 ♦ net exhibition space
 ♦ net exhibit space AE
Nettobeherbergungsertrag, m
 ♦ net rooms income pl
 ♦ net room income
 ♦ net rooms revenue
 ♦ net room revenue
Nettobereichsergebnis, n
 ♦ net departmental result
Nettobetrag, m
 ♦ net amount
Nettobetriebsgewinn, m
 ♦ net profit from operations
 ♦ net profit on operations
Nettobetriebsverlust, m
 ♦ net operating loss
 ♦ net operating deficit
Nettoeinkommen, n
 ♦ net income
Nettoeinnahmen, f pl
 ♦ net takings pl
 ♦ net receipts pl
 ♦ net revenues pl
 ♦ net income
Nettoergebnis, n
 ♦ net result
Nettoerlös, m
 Reinerlös, m
 ♦ net revenue
 ♦ net proceeds pl
Nettoerlös Küche, m
 → Nettoküchenerlös
Nettoerlös pro Übernachtung, m
 ♦ net revenue per night
 ♦ net profit per night
Nettoertrag, m
 Reinertrag, m
 ♦ net earning
 ♦ net income
 ♦ net yield
Nettoertrag pro Übernachtung, m
 ♦ net income per night
Nettofläche, f
 ♦ net area
 ♦ net space
Nettogewicht, n
 Reingewicht, n
 ♦ net weight

Nettogewinn, m
 Reingewinn, m
 ♦ net profit
Nettogewinnspanne, f
 ♦ net margin
Nettogruppenpreis, m
 ♦ net group price
 ♦ net group rate
Nettohallenfläche, f
 Nettosaalfläche, f
 ♦ net hall area
 ♦ net hall space
 ♦ net area of (the) hall
Nettoinvestition, f
 ♦ net investment
netto Kasse, adv
 ♦ net cash, adv
Nettokasse im voraus
 ♦ net cash in advance
Nettokosten, pl
 ♦ net costs pl
 ♦ net cost
Nettoküchenerlös, m
 Nettoerlös Küche, m
 ♦ net kitchen revenue
Nettoküchenumsatz, m
 Nettoumsatz der Küche, m
 Nettoumsatz Küche, m
 ♦ net kitchen sales pl
 ♦ net kitchen turnover
Nettomiete, f (kurz, meist Mobilien)
 ♦ net rental AE
 ♦ net rent AE
 ♦ net hire BE
Nettomiete, f (lang, meist Immobilien)
 ♦ net rent
Nettomieteinnahme, f
 ♦ net rent(al) income
 ♦ net rent(al) revenue
Nettopreis, m
 ♦ net price
 ♦ net rate
Nettoprovision, f
 ♦ net commission
Nettoquadratmeter, m
 ♦ net square meter AE
 ♦ net square metre BE
Nettorate, f
 Nettopreis, m
 ♦ net rate
Nettoreiseintensität, f
 ♦ net travel intensity
Nettospeiseerlös, m
 ♦ net food revenue
Nettospeiseumsatz, m
 Nettoumsatz Speisen, m
 ♦ net food sales pl
 ♦ net food turnover
Nettoumsatz, m
 ♦ net sales pl
 ♦ net turnover
Nettoumsatz der Küche, m
 → Nettoküchenumsatz
Nettoumsatz Küche, m
 → Nettoküchenumsatz
Nettoverbindlichkeiten, f pl
 ♦ net debts pl
Nettoverbrauch, m
 ♦ net consumption

Nettoverkaufspreis, m
 ♦ net selling price
 ♦ net selling rate
Nettoverlust, m
 Reinverlust, m
 ♦ net loss
Nettovermögen, n
 ♦ net worth AE
Nettowarenaufwand, m
 ♦ net cost of sales
Nettowert, m
 ♦ net value
Nettozimmereinnahmen, f pl
 ♦ net room(s) takings pl
 ♦ net room(s) revenues pl
 ♦ net room(s) receipts pl
Nettozimmerumsatz, m
 ♦ net room sales pl
 ♦ net rooms sales pl
 ♦ net room turnover
 ♦ net rooms turnover
Nettozinsen, m pl
 ♦ net interest
Netzball, m (Tennis)
 ♦ netball
Netzballspiel, n
 ♦ netball match
Netzball spielen
 ♦ play netball
Netzgebiet, n
 Netz, n
 ♦ network area
Netzkarte, f
 (für Verkehrsmittel)
 ♦ runaround ticket
 ♦ runabout ticket BE
Netzstrom, m
 Leitungsstrom, m
 ♦ mains current
 ♦ mains electricity
neuangekommenen Gast begrüßen
 ♦ welcome a newly arrived guest
neuangekommener Gast m
 ♦ newly arrived guest
Neuankunft, f (Person)
 Neuankömmling, m
 Ankömmling, m
 ♦ new arrival
Neuanmeldung, f
 ♦ new registration
Neuanschaffung, f
 ♦ new acquisition
Neubau, m (fertig)
 ♦ new building
 ♦ new construction
 ♦ newly built house
 ♦ newly built construction
 ♦ newly constructed building
Neubau, m (im Bau)
 ♦ building under construction
Neubauhotel, n
 → Hotelneubau
Neubauwohnung, f (fertig)
 ♦ newly built apartment AE
 ♦ newly built flat BE
Neubauwohnung, f (im Bau)
 ♦ apartment under construction AE
 ♦ flat under construction BE
Neubuchung, f
 neue Buchung, f
 Neubestellung, f

neue Ankunft

neue Bestellung, f
- ◆ new booking

neue Ankunft, f
- → Neuankunft

neue Besucher gewinnen
- ◆ attract new visitors

neue Gäste gewinnen
- ◆ attract new guests

neue Gäste suchen
- ◆ look for new guests

neue Hotelzimmer finanzieren
- ◆ finance new hotel rooms

neu einstufen etw
- ◆ regrade s.th.

Neueinstufung, f
- ◆ regrading

neu einziehender Mieter, m
- ◆ incoming tenant

neu einziehender Pächter, m
- ◆ incoming tenant

neue Kontakte knüpfen
- ◆ make new contacts

neue Kontakte pflegen
- ◆ cultivate new contacts

neue Kunden gewinnen
- neuen Gästekreis erschließen
- ◆ attract new clients
- ◆ attract new customers

neue Leute kennenlernen
- ◆ meet new people

neue Märkte erschließen
- ◆ move into new markets

Neuenburger See, m
- ◆ Lake Neuchâtel
- ◆ Lake of Neuchâtel, the

neuen Gästekreis erschließen
- ◆ attract new customers
- ◆ attract new clientele

neuen Geschäftsführer ernennen
- ◆ appoint a new manager

Neuengland
- ◆ New England

neuen Ort erkunden
- ◆ explore a new place

neuen Rekord aufstellen
- ◆ set up a new record

neuen Standard setzen für die Hotelgastronomie
- ◆ set a new standard for hotel foodservice AE
- ◆ set a new standard for hotel catering BE

neuen Wein in alte Schläuche füllen
- ◆ put new wine in old bottles

neuen Wein probieren
- ◆ taste the new wine

neuen Wein verkosten
- neuen Wein probieren
- ◆ sample the new wine
- ◆ taste the new wine

neue Orte besichtigen
- neue Orte sehen
- ◆ see new places

neuerbautes Hotel, n
- → Hotelneubau

Neue Residenz, f (Eigenname)
- ◆ New Residence, the

neuer Gast, m
- ◆ new guest

neuer Kunde, m
- neue Kundin, f
- ◆ new customer
- ◆ new client

neuernannter Manager, m
- ◆ newly appointed manager

neueröffnet, adj
- neu eröffnet, adj
- ◆ newly opened, adj

neueröffneter Club, m
- ◆ newly opened club

neueröffnetes Hotel n
- ◆ newly opened hotel

Neueröffnung, f (Eröffnung)
- → Eröffnung

Neueröffnung, f (Wiedereröffnung)
- → Wiedereröffnung

neuer Pächter, m
- ◆ new tenant
- ◆ new leaseholder

neuer Trakt, m
- neuer Flügel, m
- ◆ new wing

neuer Wein, m
- ◆ new wine
- ◆ green wine

neuerworben, adj
- neu erworben, adj
- ◆ newly acquired, adj

neuerworbenes Hotel, n
- ◆ newly acquired hotel

neue Saison, f
- ◆ new season

neues Gericht, n
- ◆ new dish

neues Gericht erfinden
- ◆ invent a new dish

neues Hotel, n
- ◆ new hotel

neues Hotel bauen
- ◆ build a new hotel

neues Hotel eröffnen
- ◆ open a new hotel

neuester Stand der Technik, m
- ◆ state of the art

neues Zimmer, n
- ◆ new room

Neue Welt, die, f
- (Amerika)
- ◆ New World, the

neue Wohnung, f
- ◆ new apartment AE
- ◆ new flat BE

neue Wohnung suchen
- ◆ look for a new apartment AE
- ◆ seek a new apartment AE
- ◆ look for a new flat BE
- ◆ seek a new flat BE

neue Zielgruppen gewinnen
- ◆ attract new target groups

neue Zimmer bauen
- ◆ build new rooms
- ◆ construct new rooms

Neufundland
- ◆ Newfoundland

Neugotik, f (Epoche)
- ◆ neo-Gothic period

Neugotik, f (Stil)
- ◆ neo-Gothic style

neugotisch, adj
- ◆ neo-Gothic, adj

neugotische Architektur, f
- ◆ neo-Gothic architecture

neugotisches Schloß, n
- ◆ neo-Gothic castle
- ◆ neo-Gothic palace

neu hergerichtetes Zimmer, n
- neu tapeziertes Zimmer, n
- neu gestrichenes Zimmer, n
- renoviertes Zimmer, n
- ◆ redecorated room

Neujahr, n
- ◆ New Year

Neujahrsbuchung, f
- ◆ New Year booking

Neujahrsempfang m
- ◆ New Year reception

Neujahrsfeier, f
- ◆ New Year's celebration

Neujahrskreuzfahrt, f
- ◆ New Year cruise

Neujahrsparty, f
- ◆ New Year's party

Neujahrsprogramm, n
- ◆ New Year's program AE
- ◆ New Year's programme BE

Neujahrsreservierung, f
- ◆ New Year reservation

Neujahrstag, m
- ◆ New Year's Day

Neujahrsurlaub, m
- ◆ New Year vacation AE
- ◆ New Year holiday BE

Neujahrswoche, f
- ◆ New Year week

Neujahrswochenende, n
- ◆ New Year's weekend

Neujahrszuschlag m
- ◆ New Year's supplement

Neujahr verbringen in X
- ◆ spend New Year in X
- ◆ spend New Year at X

neu klassifizieren etw
- ◆ reclassify s.th.

Neuklassifizierung, f
- ◆ reclassification

Neuling in der Hotelszene, m
- ◆ newcomer on the hotel scene

neu möblieren etw
- wieder möblieren etw
- ◆ refurnish s.th.

neumöbliert, adj
- neu möbliert, adj
- ◆ newly furnished, adj

neumöbliertes Zimmer n
- ◆ newly furnished room

neunbettig, adj
- ◆ nine-bedded, adj

neunbettiges Zimmer, n
- ◆ nine-bedded room

Neunbettzimmer, n
- ◆ nine-bed room
- ◆ nine-bedded room

neungängig, adj (Essen)
- ◆ nine-course, adj
- ◆ consisting of nine courses

neungängiges Essen, n
- ◆ nine-course meal

neungängiges Menü, n
- ◆ nine-course menu

Neun-Loch-Golfplatz m
- 9-Loch-Golfplatz m
- ◆ nine-hole golf course
- ◆ 9-hole golf course

Neun-Loch-Pitch-und-Putt-Platz, m
  9-Loch-Pitch-und-Putt-Platz, m
  ♦ **nine-hole pitch-and-putt course**
  ♦ **9-hole pitch-and-putt course**
Neun-Loch-Puttinggrün, n
  9-Loch-Puttinggrün, n
  ♦ **nine-hole putting green** AE
  ♦ **9-hole putting green** AE
  ♦ **nine-hole putting-green** BE
  ♦ **9-hole putting-green** BE
Neun-Loch-Puttingplatz, m
  9-Loch-Puttingplatz, m
  ♦ **nine-hole putting course**
neunstündiger Marsch, m
  ♦ **nine hours' march**
neunstündige Verspätung, f
  ♦ **nine-hour delay**
Neuntagepaß, m
  ♦ **nine-day pass**
neuntägig, adj
  ♦ **nine-day, adj**
  ♦ nine days', adj
  ♦ of nine days' duration
  ♦ lasting nine days
neuntägige Wanderung, f
  Neuntagewanderung, f
  ♦ **nine-day ramble**
  ♦ nine days' walk
neunter Gang, m (Menü)
  ♦ **ninth course**
neunwöchig, adj
  ♦ **nine-week, adj**
  ♦ nine weeks', adj
  ♦ of nine weeks' duration
  ♦ lasting nine weeks
neunwöchige Reise, f
  ♦ **nine-week journey**
  ♦ nine-week tour
  ♦ nine-week trip
neunwöchige Tournee, f
  ♦ **nine-week tour**
Neunzimmerhaus, n
  ♦ **nine-room house**
  ♦ nine-room home
  ♦ nine-roomed house
  ♦ nine-roomed home
neunzimmerig, adj
  ♦ **nine-roomed, adj**
neunzimmeriges Haus, n
  ♦ **nine-roomed house**
Neun-Zimmer-Villa, f
  ♦ **nine-room villa**
neu polstern etw
  ♦ **re-upholster s.th.**
Neureichen, die, pl
  ♦ **nouveaux riches, the** FR pl
  ♦ new-rich, the AE pl
  ♦ new rich, the BE pl
Neureicher, m
  Neureiche, f
  ♦ **new-rich** AE
  ♦ new rich BE
  ♦ nouveau riche FR
  ♦ newly rich
neurenoviert, adj
  neu renoviert, adj
  ♦ **newly refurbished, adj**
  ♦ newly renovated, adj
neurenoviertes Zimmer, n (tapeziert, gestrichen)
  → neutapeziertes Zimmer

neurenoviertes Zimmer, n (umfassend)
  ♦ **newly refurbished room**
  ♦ newly renovated room
neurenovierte Wohnung, f
  ♦ **newly refurbished apartment** AE
  ♦ newly renovated apartment AE
  ♦ newly refurbished flat BE
  ♦ newly renovated flat BE
Neuschnee, m
  ♦ **new snow**
  ♦ new-fallen snow
  ♦ fresh snow
Neuschottland
  ♦ **Nova Scotia**
Neuseeland
  ♦ **New Zealand**
Neuseeländer, m
  Neuseeländerin, f
  ♦ **New Zealander**
  ♦ Kiwi inform
neuseeländisch, adj
  ♦ **New Zealand, adj**
Neusiedler See, m
  ♦ **Lake Neusiedl**
neu streichen etw
  wieder streichen etw
  ♦ **repaint s.th.**
neu tapezieren etw
  ♦ **repaper s.th.**
  ♦ redecorate s.th.
neutapeziertes Zimmer, n
  neugestrichenes Zimmer, n
  ♦ **newly decorated room**
Neuvergabe, f
  → Neuverteilung
neuvermählt, adj
  jungvermählt, adj
  neu vermählt, adj
  ♦ **newlywed, adj** AE
  ♦ newly-wed, adj BE
  ♦ newly married, adj
neuvermähltes Paar, n
  jungvermähltes Paar, n
  ♦ **newlywed couple** AE
  ♦ newly-wed couple BE
  ♦ newly married couple
neu verteilen etw
  neu zuteilen etw
  neu vergeben etw
  neu zuweisen etw
  ♦ **reallocate s.th.** AE
  ♦ re-allocate s.th. BE
Neuverteilung, f
  Neuvergabe f
  Neuzuweisung f
  Neuzuteilung f
  ♦ **reallocation** AE
  ♦ re-allocation BE
Neuwagen, m
  neues Auto, n
  ♦ **new car**
Neuwert, m
  ♦ **value as new**
neuwertig, adj
  ♦ **as good as new, adj**
  ♦ as new, adj
Neuzugänge, m pl
  neue Anmeldungen, f pl
  ♦ **new registrations** pl
Neuzuteilung, f
  → Neuverteilung

New Forest, m
  ♦ **New Forest, the**
Nfl.
  → Nutzfläche
Niagarafälle, m pl
  ♦ **Niagara Falls, the** pl
Nibelungenstraße, f
  (Ferienstraße)
  ♦ **Nibelungs' Road, the**
  ♦ Nibelungs' Route, the
Nicaragua
  ♦ **Nicaragua**
Nicaraguaner, m
  ♦ **Nicaraguan**
Nicaraguanerin, f
  ♦ **Nicaraguan girl**
  ♦ Nicaraguan woman
  ♦ Nicaraguan
nicaraguanisch, adj
  ♦ **Nicaraguan, adj**
nicht abreißender Besucherstrom, m
  unaufhörlicher Besucherstrom m
  ♦ **incessant stream of visitors**
  ♦ unceasing stream of visitors
nichtalkoholisch, adj
  ♦ **nonalcoholic, adj** BE
  ♦ non-alcoholic, adj BE
nichtalkoholische Getränke, n pl jur
  ♦ **nonalcoholic liquor** AE jur
  ♦ non-alcoholic liquor BE jur
nichtalkoholisches Getränk, n
  ♦ **nonalcoholic drink** AE
  ♦ nonalcoholic beverage AE
  ♦ non-alcoholic drink BE
  ♦ non-alcoholic beverage BE
nicht an der Arbeitsstelle schlafen
  Schlafquartier nicht an der Arbeitsstelle haben
  ♦ **sleep out**
nicht angemeldeter Gast, m
  (nicht ins Meldebuch eingetragen)
  unangemeldeter Gast, m
  ♦ **unregistered guest**
Nichtankunft, f
  ♦ **nonarrival** AE
  ♦ non-arrival BE
Nichtannahme, f
  ♦ **nonacceptance** AE
  ♦ non-acceptance BE
Nichtantritt einer Reise, m
  ♦ **failure to take a journey**
nicht anwesend sein (generell)
  ♦ **not be present**
nicht anwesend sein (Unterkunft)
  nicht dort zur Zeit wohnen
  ♦ **not be in residence**
Nichtaufführung, f
  ♦ **nonperformance** AE
  ♦ non-performance BE
nicht ausgeübte Option, f
  ♦ **unexercised option**
Nichtbehinderter, m
  ♦ **nondisabled person** AE
  ♦ nonhandicapped person AE
  ♦ non-disabled person BE
  ♦ non-handicapped person BE
nicht belegt, adj
  ♦ **not occupied, adj**
  ♦ vacant, adj
  ♦ free, adj
nicht benutzte Fahrkarte, f
  ♦ **unused ticket**

Nichtbenutzung

Nichtbenutzung, f
  Nichtinanspruchnahme, f
  ♦ **nonuse** *AE*
  ♦ non-use *BE*
Nichtbereithaltung eines Zimmers, f
  Nichtbereitstellung eines Zimmers, f
  ♦ **failure to provide a room**
  ♦ failure to have a room ready
Nichtbereitstellung einer Leistung f
  ♦ **failure to provide a service**
Nichtbereitstellung eines Zimmers, f
  Nichtbereithaltung eines Zimmers, f
  ♦ **failure to make a room available**
  ♦ failure to provide a room
Nicht berühren!
  ♦ **Do not touch**
nicht bezugsfertig, adj
  nicht bezugsfähig, adj
  ♦ **not ready for occupation, adj**
  ♦ not ready to move in(to), adj
nichtbrennbar, adj
  nicht brennbar, adj
  ♦ **nonflammable, adj** *AE*
  ♦ non-flammable, adj *BE*
  ♦ noninflammable, adj *AE*
  ♦ non-inflammable, adj *BE*
Nichtcamper, m
  Nichtzelter, m
  ♦ **noncamper** *AE*
  ♦ non-camper *BE*
Nicht-Diätgast, m
  → Gast, der nicht Diät hält
nicht durchgebraten, adj
  (Fleisch)
  englisch gebraten, adj
  englisch, adj
  ♦ **rare, adj**
  ♦ underdone, adj
Nicht-EG-Land, n
  ♦ **non-EC country**
nicht eingenommene Mahlzeit, f
  nicht eingenommenes Essen, n
  ♦ **meal not taken**
nicht eingestuftes Hotel, n
  ♦ **ungraded hotel**
nicht einschlafen können
  ♦ **not get to sleep**
nichteintreffender Gast, m
  ♦ **nonarrival** *AE*
  ♦ non-arrival *BE*
  ♦ no-show
nicht elastische Nachfrage, f
  ♦ **nonelastic demand** *AE*
  ♦ non-elastic demand *BE*
nicht erbrachte Dienstleistung, f
  nicht erbrachte Leistung f
  ♦ **service not rendered**
  ♦ service not provided
Nichterbringung, f
  Nichtleistung, f
  Nichterfüllung, f
  ♦ **nonperformance** *AE*
  ♦ non-performance *BE*
Nichterbringung einer Leistung, f
  ♦ **nonperformance of a service** *AE*
  ♦ non-performance of a service *BE*
Nichterfüllung, f
  ♦ **nonfulfillment** *AE*
  ♦ non-fulfilment *BE*
  ♦ nonperformance, *AE*
  ♦ non-performance *BE*

Nichterfüllung eines Vertrages, f
  ♦ **nonperformance of a contract** *AE*
  ♦ non-performance of a contract *BE*
  ♦ nonfulfilment of a contract *AE*
  ♦ non-fulfilment of a contract *BE*
nicht erstattbar, adj
  nicht rückerstattbar, adj
  ♦ **nonrefundable, adj** *AE*
  ♦ non-refundable, adj *BE*
  ♦ **nonreturnable, adj** *AE*
  ♦ non-returnable, adj *BE*
nicht erstattbare Anzahlung, f
  nicht erstattbare Kaution, f
  ♦ **nonrefundable deposit** *AE*
  ♦ non-refundable deposit *BE*
  ♦ nonreturnable deposit *AE*
  ♦ non-returnable deposit *BE*
nicht eßbar, adj
  ♦ **inedible, adj**
  ♦ uneatable, adj
nichteuropäisch, adj
  ♦ **non-European, adj**
nichteuropäisches Land, n
  ♦ **non-European country**
nicht fertiggestelltes Hotel, n
  ♦ **unfinished hotel**
Nichtfleischgericht, n
  fleischloses Gericht, n
  ♦ **nonmeat dish** *AE*
  ♦ non-meat dish *BE*
nicht ganz durchgebraten, adj
  → englisch gebraten
Nichtgast, m
  ♦ **nonguest** *AE*
  ♦ non-guest *BE*
nicht geeignet für Kinder
  ♦ **not suitable for children**
nichtgeladener Gast, m
  → uneingeladener Gast
nicht gemeldet, adj
  nicht angemeldet, adj
  ungemeldet, adj
  unangemeldet, adj
  ♦ **not registered, adj**
  ♦ unregistered, adj
nicht genügend Schlaf haben
  ♦ **not have enough sleep**
nicht genug reisen
  ♦ **not travel enough**
nicht genug zu essen haben
  ♦ **not to have enough to eat**
nicht geöffnet für die Öffentlichkeit
  ♦ **not open to the public**
Nichtgewünschtes streichen
  ♦ **Delete as required**
  ♦ Delete where inapplicable
nicht haltbar gemacht, adj *gastr*
  ungesalzen, adj *gastr*
  ungepökelt, adj *gastr*
  ungeräuchert, adj *gastr*
  ♦ **uncured, adj** *gastr*
Nichthausgast, m
  ♦ **nonresident guest** *AE*
  ♦ non-resident guest *BE*
  ♦ nonresident *AE*
  ♦ non-resident *BE*
Nicht hinauslehnen!
  ♦ **Do not lean out**
Nichthotel, n
  ♦ **nonhotel** *AE*
  ♦ non-hotel *BE*

Nichthotelgast, m
  ♦ **nonhotel guest** *AE*
  ♦ non-hotel guest *BE*
Nichthotelunterbringung, f
  → Nichthotelunterkunft
Nichthotelunterkunft, f
  Nichthotelunterbringung, f
  ♦ **nonhotel accommodation** *AE*
  ♦ non-hotel accommodation *BE*
nicht im Haus wohnend, adj
  extern, adj
  auswärtig, adj
  ♦ **nonresident, adj** *AE*
  ♦ non-resident, adj *BE*
nicht im Haus wohnender Gast, m
  → Nichthausgast
nicht im Preis inbegriffen
  nicht im Preis eingeschlossen
  ♦ **not included in the price**
  ♦ not included in the rate
nicht im voraus buchbar
  ♦ **not bookable in advance**
nicht im voraus reservierbar
  ♦ **not reservable in advance**
nicht in Anspruch genommene Leistung, f
  nicht in Anspruch genommener Service, m
  ♦ **service not used**
  ♦ unclaimed service
  ♦ service not claimed
nicht in Anspruch genommener Gutschein, m
  ♦ **unused voucher**
nicht in Anspruch genommenes Zimmer, n
  ♦ **unclaimed room**
  ♦ room not taken
Nichtinanspruchnahme, f
  Nichtbenutzung, f
  ♦ **nonutilisation** *AE*
  ♦ nonuse *AE*
  ♦ non-utilisation *BE*
  ♦ non-use *BE*
Nichtinanspruchnahme einer Leistung, f
  → Nichtinanspruchnahme eines Service
Nichtinanspruchnahme eines Service, f
  Nichtinanspruchnahme einer Leistung, f
  ♦ **nonutilisation of a service** *AE*
  ♦ non-utilisation of a service *BE*
Nichtinanspruchnahme eines Zimmers, f
  Nichtbenutzung eines Zimmers, f
  ♦ **nonutilisation of a room** *AE*
  ♦ non-utilisation of a room *BE*
Nichtjahrgangssekt, m
  ♦ **nonvintage champagne** *AE*
  ♦ non-vintage champagne *BE*
nicht jedermanns Geschmack sein
  ♦ **not be everyone's taste**
nicht klassifiziertes Hotel, n
  ♦ **unclassified hotel**
nichtklimatisiert, adj
  nicht klimatisiert, adj
  ♦ **nonairconditioned, adj** *AE*
  ♦ non-airconditioned, adj *BE*
nichtklimatisiertes Zimmer, n
  ♦ **nonairconditioned room** *AE*
  ♦ non-airconditioned room *BE*
nichtkommerziell, adj
  nicht kommerziell, adj
  nichtgewerblich, adj
  nicht gewerblich, adj
  ♦ **noncommercial, adj** *AE*
  ♦ non-commercial, adj *BE*

nichtkommerzieller Reiseveranstalter, m
  nichtgewerblicher Reiseveranstalter, m
  ♦ **noncommercial tour operator** *AE*
  ♦ non-commercial tour operator *BE*
nichtkommerzielle Unterkunft, f
  nichtgewerbliche Unterkunft, f
  ♦ **noncommercial accommodation** *AE*
  ♦ noncommercial lodging *AE*
  ♦ non-commercial accommodation *BE*
nicht kontingentiert, adj
  ♦ **nonquota, adj** *AE*
  ♦ non-quota, adj *BE*
nichtkonzessioniert, adj
  → nichtlizenziert
nicht länger bleiben als absolut notwendig
  ♦ **stay no longer than is absolutely necessary**
Nichtliniendienst, m
  ♦ **nonscheduled service** *AE*
  ♦ non-scheduled service *BE*
Nichtlinienflug, m
  ♦ **nonscheduled flight** *AE*
  ♦ non-scheduled flight *BE*
nichtlizenziert, adj
  nichtkonzessioniert, adj
  ♦ **nonlicensed, adj** *AE*
  ♦ nonlicenced, adj *AE*
  ♦ non-licensed, adj *BE*
  ♦ non-licenced, adj *BE*
nicht lumpen lassen sich
  großzügig sein
  ♦ **be generous**
  ♦ be open-handed
nicht markierter Stellplatz, m (Camping)
  → unparzellierter Stellplatz
nicht mehr auf der Speisekarte stehen
  ♦ **be off the menu**
nicht mehr geben
  (im Restaurant)
  ♦ **be off**
nicht mehr vorrätig
  vergriffen
  ♦ **out of stock**
nicht mehr vorrätig haben etw
  etw nicht mehr haben *coll*
  ♦ **have run out of s.th.**
  ♦ be run out of s.th.
nicht mit dem Essen warten auf jn
  ♦ **start eating without s.o.**
Nichtmitglied, n
  ♦ **nonmember** *AE*
  ♦ non-member *BE*
Nichtmitgliedschaft, f
  ♦ **nonmembership** *AE*
  ♦ non-membership *BE*
nichtöffentlich, adj
  nicht öffentlich, adj
  ♦ **nonpublic, adj** *AE*
  ♦ non-public, adj *BE*
  ♦ private, adj
  ♦ closed, adj
nichtöffentliche Konferenz, f
  ♦ **nonpublic conference** *AE*
  ♦ non-public conference *BE*
  ♦ private conference
Nicht öffnen!
  ♦ **Do not open**
nicht provisionsfähig, adj
  nicht provisionsträchtig, adj
  ♦ **noncommissionable, adj** *AE*
  ♦ non-commissionable, adj *BE*

Nichtradfahrer, m
  ♦ **nonbiker** *AE coll*
  ♦ non-biker *BE coll*
Nichtrauchen, n
  ♦ **nonsmoking** *AE*
  ♦ non-smoking *BE*
Nichtraucher, m
  Nichtraucherin f
  ♦ **nonsmoker** *AE*
  ♦ non-smoker *BE*
Nichtraucherabteil, n
  (Zug)
  ♦ **nonsmoking compartment** *AE*
  ♦ nonsmoker *AE*
  ♦ non-smoking compartment *BE*
  ♦ non-smoker *BE*
  ♦ no-smoking compartment
Nichtraucherappartement, n
  ♦ **nonsmoking apartment** *AE*
  ♦ non-smoking apartment *BE*
  ♦ no-smoking apartment
Nichtraucherbereich, m
  ♦ **nonsmoking area** *AE*
  ♦ non-smoking area *BE*
  ♦ no-smoking area
Nichtraucherbetrieb, m
  ♦ **nonsmoking establishment** *AE*
  ♦ non-smoking establishment *BE*
  ♦ no-smoking establishment
Nichtraucherflug, m
  ♦ **nonsmoking flight** *AE*
  ♦ non-smoking flight *BE*
  ♦ no-smoking flight
Nichtrauchergaststätte, f
  ♦ **nonsmoking bar** *AE*
  ♦ non-smoking pub *BE coll*
  ♦ no-smoking pub *BE coll*
Nichtraucherhotel, n
  ♦ **nonsmoking hotel** *AE*
  ♦ non-smoking hotel *BE*
  ♦ no-smoking hotel
Nichtraucherplatz, m
  ♦ **nonsmoking seat** *AE*
  ♦ non-smoking seat *BE*
  ♦ no-smoking seat
  ♦ seat for a nonsmoker *AE*
  ♦ seat for a non-smoker *BE*
Nichtraucherraum, m
  → Nichtraucherzimmer
Nichtraucherreise, f
  ♦ **nonsmoking tour** *AE*
  ♦ non-smoking tour *BE*
  ♦ no-smoking tour
Nichtraucherrestaurant, n
  ♦ **nonsmoking restaurant** *AE*
  ♦ non-smoking restaurant *BE*
  ♦ no-smoking restaurant
Nichtraucherschlafzimmer, n
  ♦ **nonsmoking bedroom** *AE*
  ♦ non-smoking bedroom *BE*
  ♦ no-smoking bedroom
Nichtraucherteil, m
  ♦ **nonsmoking section** *AE*
  ♦ non-smoking section *BE*
  ♦ no-smoking section
Nichtraucherwagen, m (Zug)
  ♦ **nonsmoking car (train)** *AE*
  ♦ non-smoking carriage *BE*
  ♦ no-smoking carriage *BE*
Nichtraucherwohnung, f
  ♦ **non-smoking flat** *BE*

  ♦ nonsmoking apartment *AE*
  ♦ no-smoking flat *BE*
Nichtraucherzimmer, n
  Nichtraucherraum, m
  ♦ **nonsmoking room** *AE*
  ♦ non-smoking room *BE*
  ♦ no-smoking room
Nichtraucherzone, f
  ♦ **nonsmoking zone** *AE*
  ♦ non-smoking zone *BE*
  ♦ no-smoking zone
Nichträumung eines Zimmers, f
  (durch Gast)
  ♦ **failure to vacate a room**
nicht reisefähig sein
  ♦ **be in no condition to travel**
Nichtreiter, m
  Nichtreiterin, f
  ♦ **nonrider** *AE*
  ♦ non-rider *BE*
nicht reserviert, adj
  ♦ **unreserved, adj**
  ♦ not reserved, adj
  ♦ nonreserved, adj *AE*
  ♦ non-reserved, adj
nicht reserviertes Zimmer, n
  ♦ **unreserved room**
Nichtreservierung, f
  ♦ **nonreservation** *AE*
  ♦ non-reservation *BE*
  ♦ failure to reserve s.th.
Nichtreservierung eines Zimmers, f
  ♦ **nonreservation of a room** *AE*
  ♦ non-reservation of a room *BE*
nicht rückerstattbar, adj
  nicht erstattbar, adj
  ♦ **nonreturnable, adj** *AE*
  ♦ non-returnable, adj *BE*
  ♦ nonrefundable, adj *AE*
  ♦ non-refundable, adj *BE*
nicht rückerstattbare Anzahlung, f
  nicht rückerstattbare Kaution, f
  ♦ **nonreturnable deposit** *AE*
  ♦ non-returnable deposit *BE*
  ♦ nonrefundable deposit *AE*
  ♦ non-refundable deposit *BE*
nicht rückerstattbarer Gutschein, m
  nicht erstattbarer Gutschein, m
  ♦ **nonrefundable voucher** *AE*
  ♦ non-refundable voucher *BE*
nichtsaisonal, adj
  nicht von der Saison abhängig, adj
  ♦ **nonseasonal, adj** *AE*
  ♦ non-seasonal, adj *BE*
nichtsaisonales Geschäft, n
  ♦ **nonseasonal business** *AE*
  ♦ non-seasonal business *BE*
nichtsaisonales Hotel, n
  ♦ **nonseasonal hotel** *AE*
  ♦ non-seasonal hotel *BE*
Nichtsaisonhotel, n
  → nichtsaisonales Hotel
nichts als Natur
  ♦ **nothing but nature**
nichts als Show
  ♦ **nothing but show**
nichts an Bequemlichkeit vermissen lassen
  ♦ **leave nothing to be desired in the way of comfort**
  ♦ offer all modern comforts

Nichtschwimmer

Nichtschwimmer, m
- nonswimmer AE
- non-swimmer BE

Nichtschwimmerbecken, n
- nonswimmers' pool AE
- non-swimmers' pool BE

nichts dem Zufall überlassen
- leave nothing to chance

nicht sehr gut schlafen
- not sleep very well

Nichtskifahrer, m
Nichtskiläufer m
- nonskier AE
- nonskiier AE
- non-skier BE

Nichtspeisegast, m
- nondiner AE
- non-diner BE

Nichtstaatsbürger, m jur
Ausländer, m
- alien jur

Nicht stören
(Hinweisschild)
- Do not disturb

nichts tun
- do nothing

Nichtstun, n
- doing nothing
- idleness
- leisure
- dolce far niente ITAL
- loafing

Nichtsuitenhotel, n
- nonsuite hotel AE
- non-suite hotel BE

nichts wird dem Zufall überlassen
nichts bleibt dem Zufall überlassen
- nothing is left to chance

nichts zu essen
nichts Eßbares, n
- nothing to eat

nichts zu wünschen übriglassen
- leave nothing to be desired

Nichttänzer, m
Nichttänzerin, f
- nondancer AE
- non-dancer BE

Nichtteilnahme, f (aktiv)
- nonparticipation AE
- non-participation BE

Nichtteilnahme, f (passiv)
Nichterscheinen, n
- nonattendance AE
- non-attendance BE

Nichtteilnehmer, m
- nonparticipant AE
- non-participant BE

nichttouristisch, adj
- nontourist, adj AE
- non-tourist, adj BE

nichttouristisches Gebiet, n (groß)
- nontourist region AE
- non-tourist region BE

nichttouristisches Gebiet, n (klein)
- nontourist area AE
- non-tourist area BE

Nichttrinker, m (Abstinenzler)
Abstinenzler, m
Alkoholgegner, m
- TT
- teetotaler AE

- teetotaller BE
- abstainer
- total abstainer

Nichttrinker, m (generell)
- nondrinker AE
- non-drinker BE

nicht übertragbar, adj
- nontransferable, adj AE
- non-transferable, adj BE
- not transferable, adj

nicht übertragbarer Gutschein, m
- nontransferable voucher AE
- non-transferable voucher BE

nichtvegetarisch, adj
- nonvegetarian, adj AE
- non-vegetarian, adj BE

nichtvegetarische Mahlzeit, f
nichtvegetarisches Mahl, n
nichtvegetarisches Essen, n
- nonvegetarian meal AE
- non-vegetarian meal BE

Nichtverfügbarkeit, f
- nonavailability AE
- non-availability BE

nicht vermietbares Zimmer, n
(z.B. wegen Reparatur)
- out-of-order room
- OOO room

nicht vermietbar sein
- not be rentable

nicht verzehrte Speisen, f pl
- food not consumed

nicht voll genutzt sein
unterbeansprucht sein
- be underutilised
- be underused
- not be used to the full
- not be used to capacity

nicht weit entfernt sein von etw
- be not far from s.th.

nicht weit gereist, adj
- untravelled, adj
- untraveled, adj AE

Nichtwohngebäude, n
- building not used for habitation

nichtzahlend, adj
- nonpaying, adj
- non-paying, adj

nichtzahlender Gast, m (Freigast)
Freigast, m
- nonpaying guest AE
- non-paying guest BE
- deadhead coll

nichtzahlender Gast, m (Zahlungsunfähiger)
- defaulting guest

Nichtzahlung, f
- nonpayment AE
- non-payment BE
- failure to pay
- default

Nichtzahlung der Miete, f
- nonpayment of rent AE
- non-payment of rent BE

Nichtzelter, m
→ Nichtcamper

nicht zum Verzehr geeignet
- not fit to eat
- inedible

Nichtzutreffendes streichen
(z.B. auf Formular)
- Delete as appropriate

- Delete as applicable
- Delete where inapplicable

Nickerchen, n coll
Schläfchen, n coll
- nap coll
- snooze coll

Nickerchen machen coll
- have a nap coll
- take a nap coll
- have a snooze coll
- take a snooze coll
- have forty winks coll

Nickerchen machen nach dem Mittagessen coll
- take a nap after lunch coll
- have a nap after lunch coll
- take a snooze after lunch coll
- have a snooze after lunch coll

Nickerchen machen nachmittags
- take a nap in the afternoon
- have a nap in the afternoon

Niederbayern
(Region)
- Lower Bavaria

Niederfranken
→ Unterfranken

Niederlande, die pl
- Netherlands, the sg

Niederländer, m
- Netherlander
- Dutchman

niederländisch, adj
- Netherlands, adj
- Dutch, adj
- Netherlandish, adj

niederlassen sich auf dem Land
- make one's home in the country

niederlassen sich in einem Land
- settle in a country

niederlassen sich in einem Ort
- settle in a place
- settle down in a place

niederlassen sich in einem Sessel
- instal oneself in an armchair AE
- install oneself in an armchair BE

niederlassen sich in X
Domizil aufschlagen in X humor
- settle at X
- settle in X

Niederlausitz f
(Region)
- Lower Lusatia

Niederösterreich
(Land)
- Lower Austria

niederreißen etw
- pull s.th. down

Niederrhein, m
- Lower Rhine, the

Niederrheingebiet, n
(Region)
- Lower-Rhine region

Niedersachse, m
- man from Lower Saxony

Niedersachsen
(Land)
- Lower Saxony

Niedersächsin, f
- girl from Lower Saxony
- woman from Lower Saxony

niedersächsisch, adj
- from Lower Saxony, adv
- of Lower Saxony, adv

Niederschlag, m
(Regen)
- precipitation
- rainfall

Niederschlesien
(Region)
- Lower Silesia

niederschreiben etw
aufschreiben etw
- write s.th. down

niedersetzen sich
setzen sich
- sit down
- take a seat

niedrige Auslastung, f
niedrige Belegung, f
geringe Auslastung, f
geringe Belegung, f
- low occupancy

niedrige Auslastung haben
→ niedrige Auslastung erreichen

niedrige Auslastungsrate f
niedrige Auslastungsquote f
niedrige Belegungsrate f
niederige Belegungsquote f
- low occupancy rate

niedrige Belegung erreichen
niedrige Belegung haben
niedrige Auslastung erzielen
niedrige Auslastung haben
- have a low occupancy

niedrige Betriebskosten, pl
- low costs of operation *pl*
- low cost of operation

niedrige Decke, f
- low ceiling

niedrige Erwartung, f
- low expectation

niedrige Kilometerzahl, f
- low mileage
- low milage

niedrige Miete, f
- low rent

niedrige Miete zahlen für etw
- pay a low rent for s.th.

niedrigen Alkoholgehalt haben
- have a low alcohol content

niedrigen Erholungswert haben
- have a low recreational value
- be of low recreational value

niedrigen Komfortstandard akzeptieren
- accept a low standard of comfort

niedriger Alkoholgehalt, m
- low alcohol content

niedriger Bekanntheitsgrad, m
- low degree of popularity

niedriger einstufen etw
→ tieferstufen etw

niedriger Erlös, m
- low revenue

niedriger Ertrag, m
- low income
- low profit
- low earning

niedriger Gewinn, m
- low profit

niedriger Komfortstandard, m
- low standard of comfort

niedriger Lohn, m
- low wage

niedriger Preis, m
- low price
- low rate
- keen price *BE inform*

niedriger Zimmerpreis, m
- low room rate
- low room price

niedriges Bett, n
- low bed

niedriges Buchungsniveau, n
- low level of bookings

niedriges Haus, n
- low-built house

niedriges Restaurantumsatzvolumen haben
- have a low volume of restaurant sales

niedriges Rollbett, n
(tagsüber unter höherem Bett)
Schiebebett, n
- truckle-bed *BE*
- trundle-bed *AE*

niedriges Umsatzvolumen, n
- low sales volume

niedriges Umsatzvolumen haben
- have a low sales volume

niedriges Zimmer, n
Zimmer mit niedriger Decke, n
- low-ceilinged room

Niedrigfahrpreis, m
Sparfahrpreis, m
- budget fare

Niedrigpreis, m
Sparpreis, m
- budget price
- budget rate

Niedrigpreisangebot, n
- budget offer

Niedrigpreisherberge, f
- budget hostel

Niedrigpreishotel n
- budget hotel

Niedrigpreismotel, n
- budget motel

Niedrigpreisrestaurant, n
- budget restaurant

Niedrigpreissektor, m
- budget sector

Niedrigpreisurlaubsziel, n
- low-price vacation destination *AE*
- low-price holiday destination *BE*

niedrigster Preis, m
Tiefstpreis, m
- lowest price
- lowest rate
- rock-bottom price *inform*
- rock-bottom rate *inform*

Niedrigtarif, m
- low rates *pl*
- low rate
- low prices *pl*
- low tariff

Nierenfett, n
- suet

nierenförmig, adj
- kidney-shaped, adj

nierenförmiger Tisch, m
- kidney-shaped table

nierenförmiges Becken, n
- kidney-shaped pool

Niete, f
(bei Verlosung)
- blank

Niger
- Niger

Nigeria
- Nigeria

Nigerianer, m
- Nigerian

Nigerianerin, f
- Nigerian girl
- Nigerian woman
- Nigerian

nigerianisch, adj
- Nigerian, adj

Night Auditor, m
- night auditor

Night Manager, m
→ Nachtmanager

Nigrer, m
(Einwohner von Niger)
- Nigerois

nigrisch, adj
- Niger, adj

Nikaragua
→ Nicaragua

Nil, m
- Nile River, the
- River Nile, the
- Nile, the

Nilkreuzfahrt, f
- Nile cruise
- cruise on the Nile

Niltal, n
- Nile valley, the

nippen an einem Glas
- sip from a glass
- take a sip from a glass

nippen an etw
- sip at s.th.
- sip from s.th.

Nische, f (Alkoven)
→ Alkoven

Nische, f (in der Wand)
Wandnische, f
- niche

Nischenbett, n
- recess bed
- wall bed *AE*

Nischenmarkt, m
- niche market

Nischentisch, m
- alcove table

nisten
- nest

Nistplatz, m
- nesting site

Niveau, n
- level

niveauvoll, adj
- of a high standard

NK
→ Nebenkosten

nobel, adj
- posh, adj
- grand, adj
- high-class, adj

Nobelhaus, n *humor*
→ Nobelhotel

Nobelherberge, f *humor*
→ Nobelhotel

Nobelhotel

Nobelhotel, n *humor*
  Nobelhaus, n *humor*
  Nobelherberge, f *humor*
  ♦ **posh hotel** *humor*
  ♦ grand hostelry *humor*
  ♦ high-class hotel
Nobelkarosse, f *humor*
  ♦ **posh car** *humor*
Nobelrestaurant, n *humor*
  ♦ **posh restaurant** *humor*
  ♦ classy restaurant *humor*
Nobelskiort, m *humor*
  ♦ **posh ski resort** *humor*
noch eine weitere Nacht bleiben
  Nacht länger bleiben
  ♦ **stay one more night**
  ♦ stay another night
noch größeres Programm anbieten
  ♦ **offer an even bigger program** *AE*
  ♦ offer an even bigger programme *BE*
noch zustehender Urlaub, m (Arbeitnehmer)
  ♦ **terminal leave**
No-go, m (Person)
  (Person, die nicht verreist)
  ♦ **no-go**
  ♦ stay-at-home
No-go, n (Verkehrsmittel)
  Verkehrsmittel, das nicht fährt oder fliegt
  ♦ **no-go**
Nomade, m
  ♦ **nomad**
  ♦ nomade *AE*
nomadenhaft, adj
  → nomadisch
Nomadenleben, n
  ♦ **nomadic life**
  ♦ unsettled life
Nomadenleben führen
  ♦ **live a nomadic life**
  ♦ lead a nomadic life
Nomadenstamm, m
  ♦ **nomadic tribe**
Nomadentum, n
  ♦ **nomadism**
Nomadenvolk, n
  ♦ **nomadic people**
Nomadenzelt, n
  ♦ **nomad tent**
  ♦ nomad's tent
nomadisch, adj
  nomadenhaft, adj
  ♦ **nomadic, adj**
  ♦ nomad, adj
nomadisieren
  ♦ **nomadise**
  ♦ nomadize
nominelle Miete, f
  symbolische Miete, f
  ♦ **peppercorn rent**
Nonchalance, f
  ♦ **nonchalance**
Non-Food-Bereich, m (abstrakt)
  ♦ **nonfood sector** *AE*
  ♦ non-food sector *BE*
Non-Food-Bereich, m (konkret)
  ♦ **nonfood area** *AE*
  ♦ non-food area *BE*
Nonnenkirche, f
  ♦ **nuns' church**

Nonnenkloster, n
  ♦ **nunnery**
  ♦ convent
nonstop, adv
  ♦ **nonstop, adv** *AE*
  ♦ non-stop, adv *BE*
Nonstopbetrieb, m
  ♦ **nonstop operation** *AE*
  ♦ non-stop operation *BE*
Nonstopdienst, m
  Nonstopservice, m
  ♦ **nonstop service** *AE*
  ♦ non-stop service *BE*
Nonstopfahrt, f
  ♦ **nonstop trip** *AE*
  ♦ non-stop trip *BE*
nonstop fliegen (nach X)
  durchfliegen (nach X)
  ohne Zwischenlandung fliegen (nach X)
  ♦ **fly nonstop (to X)** *AE*
  ♦ fly non-stop (to X) *BE*
Nonstopflug, m
  ♦ **nonstop flight** *AE*
  ♦ non-stop flight *BE*
Nonstopprogramm, n
  ♦ **nonstop program** *AE*
  ♦ non-stop programme *BE*
Nonstopreise, f
  ♦ **nonstop journey** *AE*
  ♦ nonstop tour *AE*
  ♦ nonstop trip *AE*
  ♦ non-stop journey *BE*
  ♦ non-stop tour *BE*
Nonstoptanzmusik, f
  ♦ **nonstop dance music** *AE*
  ♦ non-stop dance music
  ♦ nonstop music for dancing *AE*
  ♦ non-stop music for dancing *BE*
Nonstopüberfahrt, f
  ♦ **nonstop crossing** *AE*
  ♦ non-stop crossing *BE*
Nonstopunterhaltung, f
  ♦ **nonstop entertainment** *AE*
  ♦ non-stop entertainment *BE*
Nonstopverkehr, m
  ♦ **nonstop traffic** *AE*
  ♦ non-stop traffic *BE*
Nordafrika
  ♦ **North Africa**
  ♦ Northern Africa
Nordafrikaner, m
  ♦ **North African**
nordafrikanisch, adj
  ♦ **North African, adj**
Nordalpen, pl
  ♦ **Northern Alps, the** *pl*
Nordamerika
  ♦ **North America**
Nordamerikaner, m
  Nordamerikanerin, f
  ♦ **North American**
nordamerikanisch, adj
  ♦ **North American, adj**
Nordappartement, n
  ♦ **north-facing apartment**
  ♦ apartment facing north
Nordatlantik, m
  ♦ **North Atlantic, the**
Nordatlantikflugreise, f
  ♦ **North Atlantic air travel**

Nordatlantikflugverkehr, m
  ♦ **North Atlantic air traffic**
Nordatlantikroute, f
  Nordatlantikstrecke, f
  ♦ **North Atlantic route**
Nordatlantik überqueren
  ♦ **cross the North Atlantic**
Nordbaden
  (Region)
  ♦ **North Baden**
Nordbalkon m
  ♦ **north-facing balcony**
  ♦ balcony facing north
norddeutsch, adj
  ♦ **North German, adj**
Norddeutscher, m
  Norddeutsche, f
  ♦ **North German**
Norddeutsche Tiefebene, f
  ♦ **North German Plain, the**
Norddeutschland
  ♦ **North Germany**
  ♦ Northern Germany
Nordeingang, m
  ♦ **north entrance**
Nordengland
  ♦ **North England**
  ♦ Northern England
  ♦ North Country, the
nordenglisch, adj
  ♦ **Northern English, adj**
  ♦ northern English, adj
Nordeuropa
  ♦ **North Europe**
  ♦ Northern Europe
Nordeuropäer, m
  ♦ **North European**
  ♦ Northern European
nordeuropäisch, adj
  ♦ **North European, adj**
  ♦ Northern European, adj
Nordfassade, f
  ♦ **north façade**
  ♦ north facade *AE*
  ♦ north front
Nordfenster, n
  ♦ **north-facing window**
  ♦ window facing north
  ♦ window to the north
Nordflügel, m
  Nordtrakt, m
  ♦ **north wing**
Nordfriesische Inseln, f pl
  ♦ **North Frisians** *pl*
  ♦ North Friesian islands *pl*
Nordfriesland
  (Region)
  ♦ **North Friesland**
Nordgebäude, n
  ♦ **north building**
Nordgrenze, f
  ♦ **north border**
  ♦ northern border
Nordhang, m
  (Ski)
  ♦ **north-facing slope**
  ♦ slope facing north
Nordire, m
  ♦ **man from Northern Ireland**

Nordirin, f
- girl from Northern Ireland
- woman from Northern Ireland

Nordirland
- Northern Ireland

Nordkap, n
- north cape

Nordküste, f
- north coast
- northern coast

Nordlage, f
- north-facing position

Nordländer, m
- Northerner

Nördlichen Kalkalpen, die, pl
- Northern Limestone Alps, the, pl

nördliche Route, f
nördliche Strecke, f
- northerly route

nördliches Mittelmeer, n
- northern Mediterranean, the

nördliches Querschiff, n (Kirche)
nördliches Querhaus, n
Nordtransept, m/n
- north transept
- northern transept

nördlich liegen von etw
- lie north of s.th.
- be situated to the north of s.th.

nördlichst, adj
- northernmost, adj
- most northerly, adj

nördlichster Punkt, m
- most northerly point

nördlichste Spitze, f
- northernmost tip

nördlich von etw
- north of s.th.

Nordloggia, f
- north-facing loggia
- loggia facing north

Nordostecke, f
- northeast corner AE
- north-east corner BE

Nordosten, m
- northeast AE
- north-east BE
- North-East BE

Nordostküste, f
- northeast coast AE
- north-east coast BE

nordöstlich, adj
- northeasterly, adj AE
- north-easterly, adj BE

nordöstliche Richtung, f
- northeasterly direction AE
- north-easterly direction BE

Nord-Ostsee-Kanal, m
- Kiel Canal, the

Nordpol, m
- North Pole, the

Nordpolarkreis, m
- Arctic Circle, the

Nordpolexpedition, f
→ Expedition zum Nordpol

Nordportal, n (Kirche)
- north porch

Nordrhein-Westfalen
(Land)
- North-Rhine/Westphalia

Nordroute, f
Nordstrecke, f
nördliche Route, f
nördliche Strecke, f
- northern route

Nordschleswig
- Northern Schleswig
- North Schleswig

Nordschwarzwald, m
- Northern Black Forest, the

Nordschweiz, f
- Northern Switzerland
- North Switzerland

Nordsee, f
- North Sea, the

Nordseebad, n (Aktivität)
Bad in der Nordsee, n
- bath in the North Sea
- bathing in the North Sea

Nordseebad, n (Ort)
- North Sea resort

Nordseeferienort, m
Nordseeurlaubsort, m
- North Sea vacation resort AE
- North Sea holiday resort BE
- North Sea resort

Nordseegebiet, n
- North Sea region

Nordseehafen, m
- North Sea port

Nordseeheilbad, n
- North Sea health resort
- North Sea spa

Nordseeinsel, f
- North Sea island

Nordseekurort, m
- North Sea spa

Nordseeküste, f
- North Sea coast

Nordseite, f
- north side
- northern side

Nordstrand, m
- north beach

Nord-Süd-Richtung, f
- north to south direction
- north-south direction

Nord-Süd-Straße, f
- north-south road

Nord-Süd-Verbindung, f
- north-south link
- north-south connection

Nordtiroler Kalkalpen, die, pl
- North Tyrolean Limestone Alps, the, pl

Nordtor, n
- north gate
- northern gate

Nordtribüne, f
- north stand
- north stands pl

Nordturm, m
- north tower
- northern tower

Nordufer, n (Fluß)
- north bank

Nordufer, n (Meer, Binnensee)
- north shore
- northern shore

Nordverkehr, m
Verkehr nach Norden, m
- northbound traffic

Nordvogesen, pl
- Northern Vosges, the pl

Nordwales
- North Wales
- Northern Wales

Nordwand, f (Berg)
- north face

Nordwand, f (Mauer)
Nordmauer, f
- north wall

nordwärts, adv
nach Norden, adv
- northwards, adv
- northward, adv
- to the north, adv
- north, adv

nordwärts reisen
- travel northwards
- travel northward

nordwärts wandern
- walk northwards

nordwärts ziehen
nordwärts wandern
- migrate northwards

Nordwesten, m
- northwest AE
- north-west BE
- North-West BE

Nordwestküste, f
- northwest coast AE
- north-west coast BE

nordwestliche Richtung, f
- northwesterly direction AE
- north-westerly direction BE

Nordzimmer n
Zimmer nach Norden n
nach Norden gelegenes Zimmer n
- north-facing room
- room facing north

Nörgler, m
Meckerer, m
- faultfinder
- nagger
- moaner coll
- grumbler

Norische Alpen, pl
- Noric Alps, the pl

Normalausstattung, f
Standardausstattung, f
- standard equipment
- standard facilities pl

Normalbenzin, n
- regular gasoline AE
- regular gas AE
- regular petrol BE
- two-star petrol BE

Normalbett n
→ normalgroßes Bett

normale Abnutzung, f
- fair wear and tear

normale Buchung, f
- normal booking

normale Essenszeiten, f pl
- normal mealtimes pl

normale Reservierung, f
- normal reservation

normaler Kartenpreis, m
- normal ticket price

normaler Preis, m
Normalpreis, m
Normalrate, f

normaler Tourist 542

- normal price
- normal rate

normaler Tourist, m
gewöhnlicher Tourist, m
- ordinary tourist

normales Zimmer, n
Normalzimmer, n
- normal room

Normalfahrpreis, m
normaler Fahrpreis, m
- normal fare

normalgroß, adj
- normal-sized, adj
- of normal size

normalgroßes Bett, n
Normalbett, n
- normal-sized bed

Normalkost, f
- normal diet

Normalküche, f (Speisen)
(Gegensatz zu Diätküche)
- normal cooking

Normalpreis, m
→ normaler Preis

Normalroute, f
- normal route

Normalschwimmbecken, n
normalgroßes Schwimmbecken, n
- normal-sized swimming pool AE
- normal-sized swimming-pool BE
- normal-sized pool

Normalspureisenbahn, f
- standard gage railroad AE
- standard gauge railway BE

Normalsterblicher, m
gewöhnlicher Sterblicher, m
- ordinary mortal

Normaltarif, m
- normal tariff pl
- standard prices pl
- standard rates pl
- normal prices pl
- standard tariff

Normaltarif berechnen
Standardpreise berechnen
- charge standard rates
- charge standard prices

Normaltourist m
- standard tourist

Normalverbraucher, m
- average consumer

Normalzimmer, n
→ normales Zimmer

Normandie, f
- Normandy

Normandieart, adv gastr
nach Normandieart, adv gastr
- Normandy style, adv gastr

Normanne, m
- Norman

Normannenzeit, f
normannische Zeit, f
- Norman times pl
- Norman period

normannisch, adj (Normandie)
- Normandy, adj

normannisch, adj (Normanne) hist
- Norman, adj hist

normannische Art, adv (historisch) gastr hist
nach normannischer Art, adv gastr hist
- Norman style, adv gastr hist

normannische Küche, f
- Normandy cuisine
- Normandy cooking

normannischer Bergfried, m hist
- Norman keep hist

normannisches Schloß, n hist
Normannenschloß, n hist
- Norman castle hist

normannische Zeit, f
→ Normannenzeit

Northumbria
(Region)
- Northumbria

Norwegen
- Norway

Norweger, m
- Norwegian

Norwegerin, f
- Norwegian girl
- Norwegian woman
- Norwegian

norwegisch, adj
- Norwegian, adj

norwegische Art, adv gastr
nach norwegischer Art, adv gastr
- Norwegian style, adv gastr

No-show
nicht eintreffender Gast, m
ausbleibender Gast, m
- no-show
- non-arrival

No-show-Gebühr, f
- no-show charge
- no-show fee

No-show-Gebühr berechnen
- charge a no-show fee

No-show-Quote, f
No-show-Rate, f
- no-show rate

Nostalgie, f
- nostalgia

Nostalgiefahrt, f
- nostalgia trip
- nostalgic trip

Nostalgiefahrt machen
- make a nostalgia trip
- make a nostalgic trip

nostalgische Fahrt, f
- nostalgic trip

Notarzt, m
- emergency doctor
- doctor on call

Notarztdienst, m
Notarztservice, m
- emergency medical service

Notarztwagen, m
- emergency ambulance

Notausgang, m
- emergency exit
- emergency door
- fire exit

Notausgangstür, f
- emergency exit door

Notausstieg, m
(Flugzeug)
- escape hatch

Notbehelf, m
- makeshift measure
- temporary measure

Notbeleuchtung, f
- emergency lights pl
- emergency lighting

Notbett, n (Behelf)
- behelfsmäßiges Bett

Notbett, n (bei Katastrophen)
- emergency bed

Notdienst m
- emergency service

notdürftig, adj
behelfsmäßig, adj
- makeshift, adj

notdürftige Behausung, f
- makeshift dwelling

notdürftiges Lager, n
notdürftiges Feldlager, n mil
- makeshift encampment

notdürftige Unterkunft, f
behelfsmäßige Unterkunft, f
- makeshift lodging AE
- makeshift accommodation

Notdurft verrichten
sich erleichtern
- relieve oneself

Notenständer, m
- music stand AE
- music-stand BE

Notfalldienst, m
→ Notdienst

nötige Bettschwere haben
- be ready for bed

Notizblock, m
- memo pad
- notepad

Notlager, n (für die Nacht)
→ behelfsmäßiges Nachtlager

Notlandung, f
- emergency landing

Notlandung machen
- make an emergency landing

Notmahlzeit, f
notdürftige Mahlzeit, f
- makeshift meal

Notprogramm, n
- emergency program AE
- emergency programme BE

Notquartier, n
→ Notunterkunft

Notration, f
eiserne Ration, f
- emergency rations pl
- iron rations pl

Notruf, m
(Telefon)
- emergency call

Notrufnummer, f
(Telefon)
- emergency number

Notruftelefon, n
- emergency telephone

Notrutsche, f
(Flugzeug)
- escape chute

Notschlafsaal, m
behelfsmäßiger Schlafsaal, m
- makeshift dormitory

Notsitz, m (Fahrzeug)
Klappsitz, m
- jump seat

Notsitzung, f
→ Dringlichkeitssitzung

Nottreppe, f
♦ emergency stairs pl
♦ emergency staircase
Notunterkunft, f (Katastrophen)
Notquartier, n
♦ emergency accommodation
Notunterkunft, f (provisorisch)
provisorische Unterkunft, f
Notquartier, n
♦ temporary accommodation
♦ provisional accommodation
Notunterkünfte bereitstellen für die Obdachlosen
(z.B. nach einer Katastrophe)
♦ provide emergency accommodations for the homeless AE
♦ provide emergency accommodation for the homeless BE
notwendig sein
♦ be necessary
Notwohnung, f (Behelf)
♦ makeshift home
♦ temporary home
Notzimmer, n
♦ emergency room
Nouveau riche, m FR
→ Neureicher
Nouvelle Cuisine, f FR
♦ nouvelle cuisine FR
November, m
♦ November
Novemberauslastung, f
Auslastung im November, f
♦ November load factor
♦ load factor in November
Novemberbelegung, f
Novemberauslastung, f
♦ November occupancy
♦ occupancy in November
Novemberfeier, f
♦ November celebration
Novembertagung, f
Novembertreffen, n
♦ November meeting
Novemberurlaub, m
♦ November vacation AE
♦ November holiday BE
Novemberwoche, f
♦ November week
Nubien
♦ Nubia
Nubier, m
♦ Nubian
nubisch, adj
♦ Nubian, adj
nüchtern, adj (ohne Alkohol)
♦ sober, adj
nüchtern, adj (ohne Essen)
→ auf einen leeren Magen
nüchtern bleiben
♦ stay sober
nüchterner Magen, m
→ leerer Magen
nüchtern zu Bett gehen
♦ go to bed sober
♦ go to bed soberly
Nudel, f
♦ noodle
Nudelgericht, n
♦ noodle dish
Nudelholz, n
♦ rolling pin

Nudellokal, n
♦ noodle bar
Nudelsalat, m
♦ noodle salad
Nudelsuppe, f
♦ noodle soup
Nudismus, m
→ FKK, Freikörperkultur
Nudist, m
→ FKK-Anhänger
Nulldiät, f
♦ calorie-free diet
♦ starvation diet
Null-Null, n
→ Toilette
Nulltarif, m
♦ free fares pl
♦ free admission
null und nichtig
♦ null and void
Nullwachstum, n
♦ zero growth
numerieren etw
♦ number s.th.
numeriert, adj
♦ numbered, adj
numerierter Sitzplatz,
numerierter Sitz, m
numerierter Platz, m
♦ numbered seat
numerierter Stellplatz, m
(Camping)
♦ numbered pitch
Numerierung, f
♦ numbering
Nummer, f (generell)
♦ number
Nummer, f (Varieté, Theater)
Programmnummer, f
kurzer Auftritt, m
♦ turn
Nummernschild, n
(Auto)
♦ license plate AE
♦ licence plate AE
♦ numberplate BE
♦ registration plate BE
Nur abends geöffnet
(Hinweisschild)
♦ Open evenings only
♦ Open in the evenings only
Nur an Werktagen geöffnet
(Hinweisschild)
♦ Open on weekdays only
♦ Open weekdays only
nur das Beste servieren
nur das Beste vorlegen
♦ serve only the best
nur eine kurze Fahrtstrecke entfernt sein on etw
♦ be only a short drive away from s.th.
nur eine Nacht bleiben
nur einmal übernachten
♦ stay one night only
♦ stay overnight only
nur Frühstück
außer dem Frühstück keine Speisen
♦ breakfast only
Nur für Erwachsene
(Hinweisschild)
♦ Adults only

Nur für Gäste
(Hinweisschild)
♦ For patrons only
♦ Patrons only
nur für geladene Gäste
♦ by invitation only
Nur-Hotel, n
♦ purpose-built hotel
nur Hotels und Gaststätten beliefern
♦ supply hotels and restaurants only
♦ cater for hotels and restaurants only
♦ purvey for hotels and restaurants only
Nur im Sommer geöffnet
♦ Open in summer only
♦ Open in the summer only
Nur im Winter geöffnet
♦ Open in winter only
♦ Open in the winter only
nur mit Reservierung
nur nach Reservierung
♦ by reservation only
Nürnberg
♦ Nuremberg
Nur-Skiort, m
♦ purpose-built ski resort
Nur Stehplätze
(Hinweisschild, z.B. im Theater)
♦ Standing room only
Nur-Suiten-Einheit, f
(Statistik)
♦ all-suite unit
Nur-Suiten-Hotel n
♦ all-suite hotel
Nur-Suiten-Immobilie, f
Nur-Suiten-Anwesen, n
♦ all-suite property
Nur-Suiten-Preis, m
♦ all-suite price
♦ all-suite rate
nur über Nacht bleiben
♦ stay overnight only
nur Übernachtung
nur Unterkunft
nur Zimmer
Unterkunft ohne Verpflegung
♦ AO
♦ accommodation only
♦ room only
♦ European plan
♦ EP
nur Unterkunft
→ nur Übernachtung
Nur vormittags geöffnet
(Hinweisschild)
♦ Open mornings only
nur wenige Besucher fanden sich ein
♦ only few visitors came
nur Zimmer
nur Unterkunft
nur Übernachtung
Unterkunft ohne Verpflegung
♦ room only
♦ accommodation only
♦ AO
♦ European Plan
♦ EP
Nur-Zimmer-Tarif, m
♦ room only tariff
♦ room only rates pl
♦ room only rate
♦ room only terms pl

nur zum Vergnügen
    ♦ just for fun
Nuß, f
    ♦ nut
Nußbrot, n
    ♦ nut bread
Nußbutter, f
    ♦ nut butter
Nüsse knacken
    ♦ crack nuts
Nußgeschmack, m
    ♦ nutty flavor *AE*
    ♦ nutty flavour *BE*
Nußknacker, m
    ♦ nutcracker *AE*
    ♦ nutcrackers *BE pl*
Nußstrudel, m
    ♦ nut strudel
Nutte, f *sl*
    Prostituierte, f
    ♦ tart *sl*
    ♦ hooker *AE sl*
    ♦ whore
    ♦ pro *BE sl*
    ♦ floozie *AE sl*
nutzen etw
    benutzen etw
    ♦ utilise s.th.
    ♦ utilize s.th.
    ♦ use s.th.
nutzen etw für Heilzwecke
    ♦ use s.th. for therapeutic purposes
Nutzfahrzeug, n
    ♦ utility vehicle
    ♦ commercial vehicle
Nutzfläche, f
    ♦ useful area
    ♦ usable floor space
Nutzladefähigkeit, f
    ♦ useful load
Nutzladefaktor, m
    ♦ payload factor
Nutzlast, f
    ♦ payload
Nutzlast von 123 Passagieren und 12 Pkws, f
    ♦ payload of 123 passengers and 12 cars
nützlich, adj
    nutzbringend, adj
    ♦ useful, adj
nützliche Adresse, f
    ♦ useful address
nützliche Information, f
    nützliche Informationen, f pl
    ♦ useful information *sg*
nützlicher Führer, m
    ♦ useful guide
Nutzungsdauer, f
    ♦ useful life
Nutzungsdauer des Gebäudes, f
    ♦ useful life of the building
Nutzungsentgelt, n
    ♦ compensation for use
    ♦ hire
Nutzungsgrad, m
    ♦ utilisation level
    ♦ utilization level
    ♦ level of utilisation
    ♦ utilisation degree
    ♦ degree of utilisation
Nutzungsgrad festlegen
    ♦ determine the degree of utilisation

Nylonbettlaken, n
    Nylonlaken, n
    ♦ nylon sheet
Nylonzelt, n
    ♦ nylon tent
Nymphäum, n
    ♦ nymphaeum
    ♦ nympheum

Oase, f
- oasis
- haven *figur*

Oase der Ruhe, f
- haven of tranquillity
- haven of tranquility *AE*
- oasis of tranquillity
- oasis of tranquility *AE*

Oase der Stille, f
- oasis of tranquillity
- oasis of tranquility *AE*

Oase des Friedens, f
- oasis of peace
- haven of peace

Oase des Friedens und der Ruhe, f
- oasis of peace and tranquillity
- oasis of peace and tranquility *AE*

Oase des Komforts, f
- haven of comfort

Oasenbewohner, m
Oasenbewohnerin, f
- inhabitant of an oasis
- oasis-dweller

Oasenstadt, f
- oasis town

Obdach, n (Unterkunft)
- shelter
- lodging
- harborage *AE*
- harbourage *BE*

Obdach, n (Wohnstätte)
- housing
- dwelling
- lodging
- house

Obdach bieten jm
Obdach gewähren jm
- provide shelter for s.o.

Obdach für die Nacht, n
- shelter for the night

Obdach gewähren jm
- shelter s.o.
- give shelter to s.o.

obdachlos, adj
- homeless, adj
- without shelter
- unsheltered, adj
- roofless, adj
- unhoused, adj

Obdachlose, m/f pl
- homeless people *pl*

obdachlose Familie, f
- homeless family

Obdachlosenasyl, n
- night shelter
- shelter for the homeless
- shelter
- house of refuge

Obdachlosenfürsorge f
- relief for the homeless

Obdachlosenheim, n
- shelter for the homeless
- doss-house *BE sl*
- homeless shelter *AE*
- common lodging house
- hostel for the homeless

Obdachloser, m
Obdachlose, f
Wohnsitzloser, m
Wohnsitzlose, f
- homeless person
- homeless

Obdachlosigkeit, f
- homelessness
- houselessness

obdachlos machen jn
- make s.o. homeless

obdachlos sein
- be homeless

obdachlos werden
- be made homeless
- be left homeless

Obelisk, m
- obelisk

oben, adv (generell)
am oberen Ende, adv
- at the top, adv
- on the top, adv

oben, adv (Stockwerk)
- upstairs, adv
- abovestairs, adv *AE*

oben am Tisch sitzen
oben sitzen
- sit at the top of the table
- sit at the head of the table

oben auf der Liste
- at the top of the list

oben bleiben (Stockwerk)
- stay upstairs
- remain upstairs

obenerwähnt, adj
oben erwähnt, adj
obengenannt, adj
oben genannt, adj
- above-mentioned, adj
- above, adj
- mentioned above, adj

oben gelegenes Zimmer, n
→ Zimmer im oberen Stock

oben ohne
(Kleidung)
- topless

Oben-ohne-Badeanzug, m
einteiliger Bikini, m
- topless bathing suit
- topless bathing dress *BE*

- topless swim suit
- topless swimming suit

Oben-ohne-Baden, n
- topless bathing

Oben-ohne-Bar f
- topless bar

Oben-ohne-Bedienung, f
→ Oben-ohne-Kellnerin

Oben-ohne-Kellnerin, f
Oben-ohne-Bedienung, f
- topless waitress

Oben-ohne-Kleid, n
- topless dress

Oben-ohne-Lokal, n
- place with topless waitresses
- topless bar

Oben-ohne-Sonnenbaden, n
- topless sunbathing

Oben-ohne-Strand, m
- topless beach

Oben-ohne-Tänzerin, f
- topless dancer

oben stehen auf einer Liste
- be at the top of a list

Ober!
→ Herr Ober!

Ober, bitte zahlen!
Kellner, bitte zahlen!
- Waiter, the check please! *AE*
- Waiter, the bill please! *BE*

Ober, m *coll*
Oberkellner, m
Maître d', m *FR*
- captain *AE*
- headwaiter
- maître d' *FR*

Oberägypten
- Upper Egypt

Oberallgäu, n
- Upper Allgäu, the
- Upper Algäu, the

Oberammergauer Passionsspiel, n
- Oberammergau Passion Play, the

oberbayerisch, adj
oberbayrisch, adj
- Upper Bavarian, adj

Oberbayern
(Region)
- Upper Bavaria

Oberbett, n (bei Etagenbett)
→ oberes Bett

Oberbett, n (Federdecke)
→ Federdecke, Steppdecke

Oberbett, n (Koje)
→ obere Koje

Oberdeck, n
oberes Deck, n
- upper deck

Oberdeckkabine

Oberdeckkabine, f
♦ upper-deck cabin
obere Etage, f
→ Obergeschoß
obere Kategorie, f
♦ upper category
obere Koje, f
oberes Bett, n
Oberbett, n
♦ upper berth
Oberelsaß n
(Region)
♦ Upper Alsace
Oberengadin, n
(Region)
♦ Upper Engadine, the
oberen Zehntausend, die, pl
♦ upper ten (thousand), the pl
♦ four hundred, the AE pl
obere Preiskategorie, f
obere Preisklasse, f
♦ upper price category
♦ top price range
obere Preisklasse, f
obere Preiskategorie, f
♦ top price range
♦ top price bracket
♦ upper price category
oberer Flur, m
oberer Korridor, m
♦ upper corridor
oberes Bett, n (bei Etagenbett)
Oberbett, n
♦ upper bed
♦ upper bunk
♦ top bed
♦ top bunk
oberes Bett, n (Koje)
→ obere Koje
obere Schlafkoje, f
→ obere Koje
obere Schublade, f
♦ upper drawer
oberes Preissegment, n
♦ upper price segment
♦ upper rate segment
oberes Stockwerk, n
→ Obergeschoß
oberes Tischende n
♦ top of the table
♦ head of the table
oberes Zimmer, n
→ oben gelegenes Zimmer
Oberfläche, f (generell)
♦ surface
Oberfläche, f (wissenschaftlich)
♦ surface area
oberflächlich, adj
♦ superficial, adj
♦ slapdash, adj
oberflächlicher Service, m
♦ superficial service
Oberfranken
(Region)
♦ Upper Franconia
oberfränkisch, adj
♦ Upper Franconian, adj
obergärig, adj
♦ top-fermented, adj
obergäriges Bier, n
♦ top-fermented beer

Obergeschoß, n
oberes Stockwerk, n
obere Etage, f
oberes Geschoß, n
OG, n
♦ upper floor
♦ upper story AE
♦ upper storey BE
♦ UF
Obergeschoßappartement, n
Appartement im oberen Geschoß, n
♦ upstairs apartment
Obergeschoßwohnung, f
Wohnung im oberen Geschoß, f
♦ upstairs flat BE
♦ upstairs apartment AE
Obergewicht, n
♦ top weight
Obergrenze, f
♦ upper limit
Oberhaardt, f
(Region)
♦ Upper Haardt, the
oberhalb 1500 Meter
oberhalb 1500 m
♦ above 1500 meters AE
♦ above 1500 metres BE
♦ above 1500 m
Oberhessen
(Region)
♦ Upper Hesse
oberhessisch, adj
♦ Upper Hessian, adj
Oberin, f
→ Oberkellnerin, Kellnerin
Oberitalien
♦ Upper Italy
Oberkärnten
(Region)
♦ Upper Carinthia
Oberkellner, m
Saalchef, m SCHW
Ober, m coll
♦ headwaiter
Oberkellnerin, f
Saalchefin, f SCHW
♦ headwaitress
Oberkellnerservice, m
Oberservice, m coll
♦ headwaiter service
Oberland, n
♦ Uplands, the pl
Oberlausitz f
(Region)
♦ Upper Lusatia
Oberlicht, n (an der Tür)
♦ fanlight
Oberlicht, n (Fenster)
♦ high window
Obermietverhältnis, n
♦ concurred lease
Oberösterreich
(Region)
♦ Upper Austria
oberösterreichisch, adj
♦ Upper Austrian, adj
Oberpfalz, f
(Region)
♦ Upper Palatinate, the

Oberpfälzer Jura, m
(Region)
♦ Upper Palatinate Jura, the
Oberpfälzer Wald, m
♦ Upper Palatinate Forest
oberpfälzisch, adj
♦ Upper Palatinate, adj
Oberrhein, m
♦ Upper Rhine, the
Oberrheingebiet, n
♦ Upper Rhine region
♦ Upper Rhine area
Oberrheinische Tiefebene, f
♦ Upper Rhine Plain, the
Obers, n ÖST
→ Sahne
Obersaaltochter, f SCHW
→ Oberkellnerin
Oberschicht, f
♦ upper class
Oberschlesien
(Region)
♦ Upper Silesia
oberschlesisch, adj
♦ Upper Silesian, adj
Oberschwaben
(Region)
♦ Upper Swabia
oberschwäbisch, adj
♦ Upper Swabian, adj
Oberschwäbische Barockstraße, f
(Ferienstraße)
♦ Upper Swabian Baroque Road, the
♦ Upper Swabian Baroque Route, the
Oberseite, f
obere Seite, f
♦ topside
♦ top
♦ upper side
♦ upside
Oberstadt, f
♦ upper town
♦ High Town, the
oberste Etage, f
oberstes Stockwerk n
oberstes Geschoß n
♦ top floor
♦ topmost floor
Obersteiermark f
(Region)
♦ Upper Styria
oberste Koje, f
♦ top berth
oberstes Bett, n (bei Etagenbett)
♦ top bunk
♦ top bed
oberste Schublade, f
♦ top drawer
oberstes Stockwerk, n
→ oberste Etage
Obersteward, m
Chefsteward, m
♦ head steward
♦ chief steward
Oberstock, m
→ Obergeschoß
Obertasse, f
→ Tasse
Obertor, n
♦ upper gate

Obervolta
 ♦ Upper Volta
obige Anschrifft, f
 obige Adresse, f
 ♦ address mentioned above
Objekt, n (Vermögensobjekt)
 Immobilie, f
 ♦ property
Objet d'art, n FR m
 Kunstgegenstand, m
 ♦ objet d'art FR
Oblate, f gastr
 ♦ wafer
obligat, adj
 unverzichtbar, adj
 unerläßlich, adj
 ♦ indispensible, adj
obligates Gläschen Sekt, n
 ♦ indispensible glass of champagne
obligatorisch, adj
 ♦ obligatory, adj
 ♦ compulsory, adj
Obst, n
 ♦ fruit
Obstbaum, m
 ♦ fruit tree
Obstbesteck, n
 ♦ fruit knife and fork
Obstbrand, m
 Obstbranntwein, m
 ♦ fruit liquor
 ♦ spirits (distilled from fruit)
 ♦ fruit schnapps
Obstbranntwein, m
 Obstbrand, m
 ♦ spirits (distilled from fruit) pl
 ♦ fruit liquor
 ♦ fruit schnapps
Obstbüfett, n
 ♦ fruit buffet
Obst der Saison, n
 ♦ seasonal fruit
Obstessig, m
 ♦ fruit vinegar
Obstfleisch, n
 Fruchtfleisch, n
 ♦ fruit pulp
Obstfüllung, f
 ♦ fruit stuffing
Obstgabel, f
 ♦ fruit fork
Obstgarten, m
 ♦ orchard
 ♦ fruit garden
Obstipation, f
 Stuhlverstopfung, f
 ♦ constipation
 ♦ obstipation
obstipiert, adj
 ♦ constipated, adj
obstipiert sein
 ♦ be constipated
Obstkompott, n
 ♦ fruit compôte BE
 ♦ fruit compote AE
 ♦ stewed fruit
Obstkorb, m
 Früchtekorb, m
 ♦ basket of fruit
 ♦ fruit basket

Obstkuchen, gedeckt, m
 Obsttorte, f
 ♦ fruit pie
Obstkuchen, m
 ♦ fruit cake
Obstkuchenplatte auf Fuß, f
 ♦ footed fruitcake platter
Obstkur, f
 Obstdiät, f
 ♦ fruit diet
Obstkur machen
 ♦ be on a fruit diet
Obstler, m
 → Obstschnaps
Obstlikör, m
 Fruchtlikör, m
 ♦ fruit liqueur
Obstmesser, n
 ♦ fruit knife
Obstpudding, m
 ♦ fruit pudding
Obstsaft, m
 → Fruchtsaft
Obstsalat, m
 ♦ fruit salad
Obstschale, f
 (Gericht)
 ♦ fruit dish
Obstschnaps, m
 Obstler, m
 ♦ fruit schnapps
Obstschüssel, f
 Obstschale, f
 ♦ fruit bowl
 ♦ fruit dish
Obstsekt, m (aus Äpfeln)
 ♦ champagne cider
Obstsekt, m (aus Birnen)
 ♦ champagne perry
Obststand, m
 ♦ fruit stand AE
 ♦ fruit stall BE
Obsttag, m
 ♦ fruit diet day
Obstteller, m
 ♦ fruit plate
Obsttorte, f
 ♦ fruit tart
 ♦ fruit flan
 ♦ fruit pie
Obst- und Gemüsehändler, m
 ♦ greengrocer
Obst- und Gemüsehandlung, f
 Obst- und Gemüsegeschäft, n
 ♦ greengrocery
Obstvorspeise, f
 Früchtevorspeise, f
 Fruchtvorspeise, f
 ♦ fruit hors d'oeuvre
Obstwein, m
 ♦ fruit wine
Obstzeit, f
 ♦ fruit season
Obulus, m
 ♦ contribution
 ♦ widow's mite
Obulus beisteuern
 Obulus entrichten
 ♦ pay one's corner
O-Bus, m
 → Obus

Obus, m
 Oberleitungsomnibus, m
 Trolleybus, m
 ♦ trolleybus AE
 ♦ trolley-bus BE
Obushaltestelle, f
 ♦ trolleybus stop AE
 ♦ trolley-bus stop BE
Obuslinie, f
 ♦ trolley line
Obusstation, f
 ♦ trolleybus station AE
 ♦ trolley-bus station BE
Occupancy List, f
 → Belegungsliste
Ochsenfleisch, n
 → Rindfleisch
Ochsenkarren, m
 ♦ oxcart
Ochsentour, f
 ♦ hard graft
Öchsle, n
 (Maßeinheit für Mostgewicht)
 Öchslegrad, m
 ♦ Oechsle degree
Öchslegrad, m
 Öchsle, n
 ♦ degrees Oechsle pl
 ♦ Oechsle degree
Odenwald, m
 (Region)
 ♦ Odenwald, the
Odeon, n
 Odeum, n
 ♦ odeum
 ♦ odeon
Oder, f
 ♦ Oder River, the
 ♦ River Oder, the
 ♦ Oder, the
Odyssee, f
 Irrfahrt, f
 ♦ odyssey
Odyssee machen durch etw
 ♦ make an odyssey through s.th.
Ofen, m
 → Backofen, Heizofen, Kochofen
Ofen anheizen
 ♦ light a stove
Ofenbank, f
 ♦ bench by the stove
Ofenbürste, f
 ♦ oven brush
ofenfertig, adj
 backfertig, adj
 ♦ oven-ready, adj
ofenfrisch, adj
 ♦ oven-fresh, adj
 ♦ fresh from the oven, adj
ofenfrisches Gericht, n
 ♦ oven-fresh dish
Ofenfüllung, f
 ♦ oven charge
ofengebacken, adj
 ♦ oven-baked, adj
Ofen heizen
 ♦ heat the stove
Ofen heizt gut
 ♦ stove heats well
Ofenheizung, f
 OH, f

Ofenhocker

♦ stove heating
♦ heating by stove
♦ fuel heating
Ofenhocker, m
Stubenhocker, m
♦ stay-at-home
♦ homebody
Ofenhocker sein
♦ be a stay-at-home
♦ be a homebody
Ofen läßt sich gut heizen
♦ stove is easily heated
Ofenschirm, m
♦ fire screen
Ofentemperatur, f
Backofentemperatur, f
♦ oven temperature
Ofen vorheizen
Backofen vorheizen
♦ preheat the oven
offenbleiben
♦ stay open
♦ remain open
offenbleiben während der Nacht
♦ stay open during the night
offene Flasche, f
♦ open bottle
Offene Handelsgesellschaft, f
♦ general partnership
♦ ordinary partnership
offene Küche, f
(ohne Trennwände)
♦ open-plan kitchen
offene Lounge, f
(ohne Trennwände)
♦ open-plan lounge
offenen Wein servieren
offenen Wein ausschenken
♦ serve wine by the carafe
♦ serve wine by the glass
offener Aufenthaltsraum, m
(ohne Trennwände)
♦ open-plan public room
offene Rechnung, f
unbeglichene Rechnung, f
♦ unsettled bill
♦ unsettled account
♦ unsettled check AE
♦ open check AE
offener Flugschein, m
♦ open air-ticket
offener Gutschein, m
♦ open voucher
offener Gutschein, m (Datum)
(mit offenem Datum)
♦ open-dated voucher
offener Kamin, m
♦ open fireplace
♦ fireplace
offener Rotwein, m
♦ red wine by the carafe
♦ red wine by the glass
offener Service, m
→ Service à la carte
offener Wagen, m (Zug)
♦ open car (train) AE
♦ open carriage
♦ open coach BE
offener Wein, m
Schoppenwein, m
♦ wine by the carafe

♦ wine by the glass
♦ wine from the cask
♦ wine from the wood
♦ open wine
offener Weißwein, m
♦ white wine by the carafe
♦ white wine by the glass
offene Savanne, f
♦ open savannah
♦ open savanna
offenes Bier, n
→ Bier vom Faß
offene See, f
offenes Meer, n
♦ open sea
offenes Fahrzeug, n
Fahrzeug mit offenem Verdeck, n
♦ open-top vehicle
offenes Feuer, n
♦ open fire
offenes Geheimnis, n
♦ open secret
offenes Haus, n
gastfreies Haus, n
♦ open house
offenes Haus haben
gastfreies Haus haben
♦ keep open house
♦ have open house
offenes Land, n
♦ open countryside
offenes Licht, n
♦ naked light
offenes Meer, n
♦ high seas pl
offenes Quadrat, n
(Bestuhlung)
♦ open square
offene Veranda f
♦ open-air veranda
♦ open-air verandah
offenhalten (Lokal)
→ geöffnet sein
offenstehende Rechnung, f
♦ outstanding bill
♦ outstanding check AE
offenstehen (Rechnung)
♦ be outstanding
offenstehen (Tür etc.)
♦ stand open
♦ be open
öffentliche Anlagen, f pl
öffentlicher Park, m
♦ public gardens pl
öffentliche Annehmlichkeiten, f pl
♦ public amenities pl
öffentliche Ausgaben, f pl
♦ rates and taxes pl
öffentliche Badeanstalt, f
♦ public baths pl
öffentliche Bedürfnisanstalt, f
♦ public comfort station AE
♦ public convenience BE
öffentliche Bibliothek, f
öffentliche Bücherei, f
♦ public library
öffentliche Debatte, f
♦ public debate
öffentliche Dusche, f
♦ public shower

öffentliche Einrichtungen, f pl
♦ public facilities pl
öffentliche Halle, f
♦ public hall
öffentliche Mittel, n pl
♦ public funds pl
öffentliche Nutzung, f
♦ public use
öffentlicher Badestrand, m
♦ public bathing beach
♦ lido BE
öffentlicher Bus, m
♦ public bus
♦ public coach BE
öffentlicher Busdienst, m
öffentlicher Busverkehr, m
♦ public bus service
♦ public coach service BE
öffentlicher Campingplatz, m
♦ public campsite
♦ public campground AE
♦ public camping site BE
♦ public camping ground BE
♦ public site
öffentlicher Feiertag, m
♦ public holiday
♦ legal holiday
♦ bank holiday BE
öffentlicher Garten, m
♦ public garden
öffentlicher Golfplatz, m
♦ public golf course
♦ public golf links AE pl
♦ public golf-links BE pl
öffentlicher Grillplatz, m
♦ public barbecue pit
♦ public barbecue
öffentlicher Park, m
♦ public park
♦ public gardens pl
öffentlicher Parkplatz, m (für 1 Auto)
♦ public parking place
♦ public parking space
öffentlicher Parkplatz, m (für mehrere Autos)
♦ public parking lot AE
♦ public car park BE
öffentlicher Platz, m
♦ public place
♦ public square
öffentlicher Raum, m
→ Publikumsraum
öffentlicher Reiseverkehr, m
öffentliches Reisen, n
♦ public travel
öffentlicher Reitweg, m
♦ public bridleway
öffentlicher Saal, m
♦ public hall
öffentlicher See, m
♦ public lake
öffentlicher Sektor, m
♦ public sector
öffentlicher Strand, m
♦ public beach
♦ lido BE
öffentlicher Tanz, m
öffentliche Tanzveranstaltung, f
♦ public dance
öffentlicher Versorgungsbetrieb, m
(z.B. Wasserwerk)

- ♦ public utility
- ♦ utility
- öffentliches Ärgernis, n
  - ♦ public nuisance
- öffentliches Ärgernis erregen
  - ♦ offend public decency
- öffentliche Sauna, f
  - ♦ public sauna
- öffentliche Saunakabine, f
  - ♦ public sauna cubicle
- öffentliches Bad, n
  - ♦ public pool
- öffentliches Diner, n
  - Festessen, n
  - ♦ public dinner
- öffentliches Gebäude, n
  - ♦ public building
- öffentliches Haus, n
  - → Bordell
- öffentliche Sitzung, f
  - ♦ open session
- öffentliches Münztelefon, n
  - ♦ public pay phone
  - ♦ public coinbox telephone BE
- öffentliches Restaurant, n
  - ♦ public restaurant
- öffentliches Schwimmbad, n
  - öffentliches Schwimmbecken, n
  - öffentliches Bad, n
  - ♦ public swimming pool AE
  - ♦ public swimming-pool BE
  - ♦ public pool
- öffentliches Telefon, n
  - ♦ public telephone
  - ♦ public phone
- öffentliches Verkehrsmittel, n
  - ♦ public transport
  - ♦ public transportation AE
- öffentliches Verkehrsmittel benutzen
  - öffentliche Verkehrsmittel benutzen
  - ♦ use public transport
  - ♦ use public transportation AE
- öffentliche Telefonzelle, f
  - ♦ public call box
  - ♦ public telephone booth
- öffentliche Terrasse, f
  - ♦ public terrace
- öffentliche Toilette, f
  - ♦ public toilet
  - ♦ public rest room euph
  - ♦ public lavatory euph
  - ♦ public convenience BE euph
  - ♦ comfort station AE
- öffentliche Unterhaltung, f
  - ♦ public entertainment
- öffentliche Veranstaltung, f
  - ♦ public event
  - ♦ public function
- öffentliche Verkehrsmittel nehmen
  - ♦ take public transport
- öffentliche Versammlung, f
  - ♦ public meeting
  - ♦ open meeting
- Öffentlichkeit, f
  - ♦ public, the
- Öffentlichkeit ausschließen
  - ♦ exclude the public
- Öffentlichkeitsarbeit, f
  - PR, f
  - ♦ public relations pl

- ♦ public relations work
- ♦ PR
- öffentlich-rechtlicher Fremdenverkehr, m
  - öffentlich-rechtlicher Tourismus, m
  - ♦ public sector tourism
- öffentlich zugänglicher Bereich, m
  - ♦ public area
  - ♦ area open to the public
- öffentlich zugänglicher Raum, m
  - öffentlicher Raum, m
  - Allgemeinraum, m
  - ♦ room open to the public
  - ♦ public room
- öffentlich zugängliches Badezimmer, n
  - öffentliches Bad, n
  - ♦ public bathroom
  - ♦ public bath
- offerieren etw
  - → anbieten etw
- Offerte, f
  - → Angebot
- Office, n
  - ♦ stillroom
  - ♦ pantry
- Officeangestellter, m
  - ♦ stillroom employee
- Officeassistent, m
  - ♦ stillroom assistant
- Officebursche, m SCHW
  - ♦ stillroom boy
- Officehilfe, f
  - ♦ stillroom hand
- Officemädchen, n
  - ♦ stillroom maid
- Officepersonal, n
  - ♦ stillroom staff
  - ♦ stillroom personnel
- Officier, m FR gast
  - ♦ officier FR gast
  - ♦ clearer
  - ♦ busboy AE gast
- offiziell, adj
  - ♦ official, adj
- offiziell ankündigen etw
  - ♦ announce s.th. officially
- offizielle Begrüßung, f
  - ♦ official welcome
- offizielle Begrüßung findet statt in etw
  - ♦ official welcome takes place in s.th.
- offizielle Bewertung, f
  - ♦ official rating
- offizielle Einstufung, f
  - ♦ official grading
- offizielle Erlaubnis, f
  - behördliche Genehmigung, f
  - ♦ official permission
- offizielle Eröffnung (von etw), f
  - ♦ official opening (of s.th.)
- offiziellen Besuch abstatten bei jm
  - ♦ pay an official visit to s.o.
- offiziellen Empfang geben für jn
  - ♦ give an official reception for s.o.
- offizieller Anlaß, m
  - ♦ official occasion
- offizieller Beginn, m
  - ♦ official beginning
  - ♦ official start
  - ♦ official commencement form
- offizieller Besuch, m
  - ♦ official visit

- offizieller Besucher, m
  - ♦ official visitor
- offizieller Empfang, m
  - ♦ official reception
- offizieller Feiertag, m
  - ♦ official holiday
  - ♦ public holiday
- offizieller Führer, m
  - (Person)
  - ♦ official guide
- offizieller Gast, m
  - Staatsgast, m
  - ♦ official guest
- offiziell eröffnen etw
  - ♦ open s.th. officially
- offizieller Programmpunkt, m
  - ♦ official item on the program AE
  - ♦ official item on the programme BE
- offizieller Sponsor, m
  - ♦ official sponsor
- offizieller Stadtführer, m (Großstadt)
  - ♦ official city guide
- offizieller Stadtführer, m (kleine Stadt)
  - ♦ official town guide
- offizieller Tarif, m
  - ♦ official tariff
  - ♦ official rates pl
  - ♦ official rate
  - ♦ official terms pl
- offizieller Wechselkurs, m
  - ♦ official exchange rate
  - ♦ official rate
- offizieller Wohnsitz, m
  - ♦ official residence
- offizielles Essen, n (Diner)
  - ♦ official dinner
- offizielle Sternebewertung, f
  - offizielle Bewertung mit Sternen, f
  - ♦ official star rating
- offiziell genehmigt, adj
  - offiziell anerkannt, adj
  - behördlich genehmigt, adj
  - ♦ officially approved, adj
  - ♦ approved, adj
- offiziell sein
  - ♦ be official
- Offiziersmesse, f
  - ♦ officers' messroom
- Offiziersunterkünfte, f pl
  - ♦ officers' quarters pl
- Off-line-Betrieb, m
  - ♦ off-line operation
- Off-line-Büro, n
  - (Flugverkehr: Büro abseits der Flugstrecke)
  - ♦ off-line office
- off line (EDV)
  - (ohne Anschluß an Zentralrechner)
  - ♦ off line
- off line (Flugverkehr)
  - (abseits der festen Route)
  - ♦ off line
- Off-Line-Region, f (Flugverkehr)
  - ♦ off-line region
- öffnen etw
  - eröffnen etw
  - ♦ open s.th.
- öffnen etw für die Öffentlichkeit
  - öffnen etw für die Allgemeinheit
  - ♦ open s.th. to the public
- Öffnung, f
  - ♦ opening

Öffnung der Grenze

Öffnung der Grenze, f
  Grenzöffnung, f
  ♦ opening of the border
  ♦ opening of the frontier
Öffnungsmonat, m
  ♦ open month
  ♦ month in which s.th. is open
Öffnungstag, m
  ♦ open day
  ♦ day on which s.th. is open
Öffnungszeit, f
  (Zeit, während der etw geöffnet ist)
  ♦ opening hours pl
  ♦ hours of opening pl form
  ♦ business hours pl
Öffnungszeitpunkt, m
  (Zeitpunkt, an dem etw geöffnet wird)
  Öffnungszeit, f
  ♦ opening time
Öffnungszeit verlängern
  ♦ extend the opening hours
OG, n
  Obergeschoß, n
  ♦ UF
  ♦ upper floor
OH, f
  Ofenheizung, f
  ♦ FH
  ♦ fuel heating
  ♦ stove heating
ÖH, f
  Ölheizung, f
  ♦ OH
  ♦ oil heating
Ohio
  ♦ Ohio
Ohio, m
  ♦ Ohio River, the
  ♦ River Ohio, the
  ♦ Ohio, the
ohne Aufenthaltsgenehmigung
  ohne Aufenthaltserlaubnis
  ♦ without residence permit
ohne Aufpreis
  ♦ at no additional charge
  ♦ at no extra cost
Ohne Bedienungsgeld
  → Bedienungsgeld nicht inbegriffen
ohne Berechnung
  → kostenlos
ohne Einhaltung einer Frist, adv
  fristlos, adv
  ♦ without notice, adv
ohne Entschuldigung abwesend sein
  ohne Entschuldigung fehlen
  ohne Entschuldigung weg bleiben coll
  ♦ be absent without excuse
ohne Erfahrung
  (Reisender)
  unerfahren, adj
  ♦ unseasoned, adj
ohne Erlaubnis abwesend sein
  ♦ be absent without permission
  ♦ be absent without leave
ohne etw
  ♦ without s.th.
  ♦ excluding s.th.
  ♦ exclusive of s.th.
ohne Fahrstuhl, adv
  (Gebäude)
  ♦ walk-up, adv AE coll

ohne festen Wohnsitz jur
  ♦ of no fixed abode jur
ohne Firlefanz, adv
  ohne Brimborium, adv
  ♦ without frills, adj
ohne Gebühr
  ♦ at no charge
ohne Geschmack
  ♦ without taste
  ♦ tasteless
ohne großen häuslichen Komfort
  ♦ without great domestic comfort
ohne Kosten, adv
  ♦ without costs, adv
  ♦ free of charge, adv
  ♦ without expense, adv
ohne Luxus oder Komfort
  ♦ without luxury or comforts
ohne Meerblick
  ohne Meeresblick
  ♦ without seaview AE
  ♦ without sea view BE
ohne Mehrkosten
  ♦ at no extra cost
  ♦ at no additional charge
ohne Mehrwertsteuer
  ohne Mwst.
  ♦ without value added tax
  ♦ without VAT
  ♦ exclusive of valued added tax
  ♦ exclusive of VAT
ohne Provision, adv
  ♦ without commission, adv
ohne Service, adv
  ♦ without service, adv
  ♦ nonserviced, adj AE
  ♦ non-serviced, adj BE
ohne Sitzplatz
  ohne Sitz
  ohne Platz
  ♦ unseated, adj
ohne Trennwände
  ♦ open-plan
ohne unsere ausdrückliche Zustimmung
  ♦ without our express consent
ohne Vergleich, adv
  ♦ without comparison, adv
ohne Vergleich sein
  ♦ be without comparison
ohne Verpflichtung
  ♦ without obligation
ohne Vorankündigung
  ♦ without previous notice
ohne Vorbehalt
  ♦ without reservation
ohne vorherige Ankündigung
  ♦ without prior notice
ohne zusätzliche Kosten
  ohne Zusatzkosten
  ♦ at no additional charge
ohne Zuschlag
  ♦ without supplement
  ♦ at no extra charge
ohne Zustimmung von jm
  ohne js Zustimmung
  ♦ without the approval of s.o.
  ♦ without s.o.'s approval
ohne Zwischenlandung
  → nonstop
ohnmächtig werden
  ♦ faint

OH-Projektor, m
  Tageslichtprojektor, m
  ♦ OH projector
  ♦ overhead projector
Ohrensessel, m
  ♦ wing chair AE
  ♦ wing-chair BE
  ♦ winged chair
Ohrring, m
  ♦ earring
Ökobilanz, f
  ♦ ecological balance sheet
Ökobus, m
  ♦ eco-bus
  ♦ eco-coach BE
ökofreundlich, adj
  ♦ eco-friendly, adj
Ökohotel, n
  ♦ eco hotel
Ökologe, m
  ♦ ecologist
Ökologie, f
  ♦ ecology
Ökologiebewegung, f
  ökologische Bewegung, f
  ♦ ecological movement
ökologieorientiert, adj
  ♦ ecology-oriented, adj AE
  ♦ ecology-orientated, adj BE
ökologisch, adj
  ♦ ecological, adj
ökologische Aufnahmekapazität, f
  ♦ ecological carrying capacity
ökologische Kapazität, f
  ♦ ecological capacity
ökologische Krise, f
  ♦ ecological crisis
ökologischer Einfluß, m
  ♦ ecological impact
ökologischer Tourismus, m
  Öko-Tourismus, m
  sanfter Tourismus, m
  sanftes Reisen, n
  ♦ ecological tourism
  ♦ ecotourism
  ♦ soft tourism
  ♦ green tourism
  ♦ sustainable tourism
ökologisches Hotel, n
  ♦ ecological hotel
Ökomarketing, n
  ♦ eco marketing
Ökonom, m
  ♦ economist
Ökonomat, m SCHW
  → Lager, Magazin
Ökonomie, f (Wirtschaft)
  Wirtschaft, f
  Wirtschaftlichkeit, f
  ♦ economy
Ökonomie, f (Wissenschaft)
  ♦ economics sg
ökonomisch, adj (sparsam)
  → sparsam
ökonomisch, adj (wirtschaftlich)
  wirtschaftlich, adj
  ♦ economic, adj
Ökopark, m
  ♦ ecological park

Ökoprogramm, n
- ecological program *AE*
- ecological programme *BE*

Ökoprojekt, n
- ecological project

Ökoreise, f
sanfte Reise, f
- ecotour

Ökosystem, n
- ecosystem

Ökotourismus, m
ökologischer Tourismus, m
sanfter Tourismus, m
sanftes Reisen, n
- ecotourism
- ecological tourism
- green tourism
- soft tourism
- sustainable tourism

Ökotourismusfirma, f
- ecotourism firm
- ecotourism company

Ökotourist, m
sanfter Tourist, m
- ecotourist

ökotouristisch, adj
- ecotourist, adj

Ökourlaub, m
- ecovacation *AE*
- ecoholiday *BE*

Ökoweg, m
Ökopfad, m
- ecology trail

Oktober, m
- October

Oktoberauslastung, f
Auslastung im Oktober, f
- October load factor
- load factor in October

Oktoberbelegung, f
Oktoberauslastung, f
- October occupancy
- occupancy in October

Oktoberfeier, f
- October celebration

Oktoberferien, pl
Oktoberurlaub, m
- October holiday *BE*
- October vacation *BE*

Oktoberfest n
(München)
- Oktoberfest, the
- October festival, the

Oktobertagung, f
Oktobertreffen, n
- October meeting

Oktoberurlaub, m
- October vacation *AE*
- October holiday *BE*

Oktoberwoche, f
- October week

Öl, n
- oil

Ölbad, n *med*
- oil bath *med*

Oldenburgische Schweiz f
(Region)
- Oldenburg Switzerland

Oldtimerauto, n
Oldtimer, m

- vintage car
- veteran car

Oldtimerdampfeisenbahn, f
- vintage steam railroad *AE*
- vintage steam railway *BE*

Oldtimerfahrt, f
- veteran car run
- vintage car run

Oldtimermuseum, n
- vintage car museum
- veteran car museum

Oldtimerrallye, f
- vintage car rally
- veteran car rally

Oldtimersammlung, f
- collection of vintage cars
- collection of old cars

Oldtimerzug, m
- vintage train

Ölfläschchen oder Essigfläschchen, n
- cruet

Ölflasche, f
- oil bottle

Ölgemälde, n
Ölbild, n
- oil painting

Ölheizung, f
ÖH, f
- oil heating
- oil-fired heating
- OH

ölig, adj
- oily, adj

öliges Essen, n
- oily food

Olive, f
- olive

Olivenfüllung, f
- olive stuffing

Olivenhain, m
- olive grove

Olivenöl, n
- olive oil

Ölkrise, f
- oil crisis

Öllampe, f
Petroleumlampe, f
- oil lamp

Ölofen, m
- oil heater
- oil stove

Ölsardine, f *figur*
→ Sardine

Ölsardinen, f pl
- canned sardines *AE pl*
- tinned sardines *BE pl*

Ölstand, m
(Auto)
- oil level

Ölstand prüfen
(Auto)
- check the oil level

Öltank, m
- oil tank

Öl- und Essigdressing, n
- oil and vinegar dressing

Ölverbrauch, m
- oil consumption

Ölwechsel machen
(Auto)
- do an oil change

Ölwechsel machen lassen
- have the oil changed

Olympiade, f
(Zeitraum von vier Jahren)
- Olympiad

Olympiadorf, n
- Olympic village

Olympiamannschaft, f
- Olympic team

Olympiaort, m
- site of the Olympic Games
- site of the Olympics

Olympiastadion, n
- Olympic stadium

Olympiastadt, f (Großstadt)
- Olympic city

Olympiastadt, f (kleine Stadt)
- Olympic town

olympisch, adj
- Olympic, adj

olympische Skiabfahrt, f
- Olympic ski run

Olympische Sommerspiele, n pl
- Olympic Summer Games *pl*

Olympische Spiele, n pl
- Olympic Games *pl*
- Olympics *pl*

Olympische Spiele ausrichten (als Gastgeber)
- host the Olympic games

Olympische Winterspiele, n pl
- Olympic Winter Games *pl*

Ölzentralheizung, f
ÖZH, f
- oil central heating
- OCH

Öl-ZH
Ölzentralheizung, f
- oil CH
- oil central heating

Ölzuschlag m
- oil supplement

Oma, f
Großmutter, f
- grandma
- granny

Oman
- Oman

Omelett, n
Omelette, f *SCHW/ÖST*
- omelette
- omelet

Omen, n
- omen

Omnibus, m
- omnibus

Omnibusbahnhof, m
- omnibus station

Omnibusfahrer, m
- omnibus driver

Omnibusfahrt, f
- omnibus trip
- omnibus ride

Omnibusgruppe, f
Omnibusreisegesellschaft, f
- omnibus party
- omnibus tour

Omnibushaltestelle, f
- omnibus stop

Omnibuslinie, f
- omnibus line

Omnibusliniendienst

Omnibusliniendienst, m
- ◆ scheduled omnibus service

Omnibusreise, f
- ◆ omnibus journey
- ◆ omnibus trip
- ◆ omnibus tour

Omnibusschaffner, m
- ◆ omnibus conductor

Omnibusschaffnerin, f
- ◆ omnibus conductress

Omnibusunternehmen, n
- ◆ omnibus company
- ◆ omnibus corporation *AE*

Omnibusunternehmer, m
- ◆ omnibus operator

On-line-Bestätigung, f
(z.B. einer Reservierung)
- ◆ on-line confirmation

On-line-Betrieb, m
- ◆ on-line operation

On-line-Büro, n
(Flugverkehr: Büro an Flugstrecke)
- ◆ on-line office

On-line-Computer, m
- ◆ on-line computer

on line (EDV)
(mit Anschluß an Zentralrechner)
- ◆ on line

on line (Flugverkehr)
(auf der festen Route)
- ◆ on line

Önologe, m
- ◆ oenologist
- ◆ enologist

Önologie, f
Weinbaukunde, f
Weinkunde, f
- ◆ oenology
- ◆ enology

Ontariosee, m
- ◆ Lake Ontario

on the rocks
→ mit Eis

ooo
Außer Betrieb
Defekt
Nicht belegbar (Zimmer)
- ◆ ooo
- ◆ out of order

Opa, m
Großvater, m
- ◆ grandpa
- ◆ grandad

Open-air-Festival n
- ◆ open-air festival

Open-air-Konzert, n
Platzkonzert, n
- ◆ open-air concert

Open Bar, f
Freibar, f
- ◆ open bar
- ◆ free bar

open-end, adj
ohne vorher festgesetztes Ende
- ◆ open-ended, adj
- ◆ open-end, adj *AE*

Open-end-Diskussion, f
Diskussion ohne vorher festgesetztes Ende, f
- ◆ open-ended discussion
- ◆ open-end discussion *AE*

Open-end-Interview, n
Interview ohne vorher festgesetztes Ende, n
- ◆ open-ended interview
- ◆ open-end interview *AE*

Oper, f (Gebäude)
→ Opernhaus

Oper, f (Musik)
- ◆ opera

Operations Research
- ◆ operations research
- ◆ operational research

Oper besuchen
- ◆ visit the opera house
- ◆ go to the opera
- ◆ attend an opera

Operette, f
- ◆ operetta

Operettenabend, m
- ◆ operetta evening

Operettenwoche, f
- ◆ operetta week

Opernabend, m
- ◆ opera evening

Opernaufführung, f
- ◆ opera performance

Opernball m
- ◆ opera ball

Opernbesuch, m
- ◆ opera visit
- ◆ visit to the opera house

Opernbesucher, m
- ◆ opera visitor
- ◆ operagoer *AE*
- ◆ opera-goer *BE*

Operndiva, f
- ◆ opera diva

Opernfestabend, m
- ◆ opera gala night

Opernfestspiele, n pl
- ◆ opera festival *sg*

Opernfreund, m
Opernliebhaber, m
- ◆ opera lover

Opernglas, n
- ◆ opera glasses *pl*

Opernhaus n
Oper f
- ◆ opera house

Opernkarte, f
- ◆ opera ticket

Opernkonzert, n
- ◆ operatic concert

Opernnarr, m
- ◆ opera buff

Opernorchester, n
- ◆ opera orchestra

Opernsaison f
- ◆ opera season

Opernsänger, m
- ◆ opera singer

Opernstar, m
- ◆ opera star

Opiumhöhle, f
- ◆ opium den

opportun, adj
- ◆ opportune, adj

Opportunitätskosten, pl
→ Alternativkosten

optieren für etw
- ◆ opt for s.th.

optimal, adj
- ◆ optimum, adj
- ◆ optimal, adj

optimale Auslastung, f
optimale Belegung, f
- ◆ optimum occupancy

optimale Bedingungen, f pl
- ◆ optimum conditions *pl*

optimale Lage, f
- ◆ optimal location
- ◆ optimal position

optimalen Service bieten
- ◆ provide optimum service

optimale Raumnutzung, f
optimale Raumausnutzung, f
- ◆ optimum utilisation of space
- ◆ optimum utilization of space
- ◆ optimum use of space

optimal gelegen, adj
- ◆ optimally situated, adj
- ◆ optimally positioned, adj
- ◆ optimally located, adj
- ◆ optimally sited, adj

Optimalkost, f
- ◆ optimal diet

optimieren etw
- ◆ optimise s.th.
- ◆ optimize s.th.
- ◆ optimalise s.th.
- ◆ optimalize s.th.

optimiertes Programm, n
- ◆ optimised program *AE*
- ◆ optimized program *AE*
- ◆ optimalised programme *BE*
- ◆ optimalized programme *BE*

optimistisch, adj
- ◆ optimistic, adj

Option, f
Vormerkung, f
- ◆ option

optional, adj
freiwillig, adj
- ◆ optional, adj

Option anbieten
Option bieten
- ◆ offer an option

Option annehmen
- ◆ take up an option

Option aufgeben
- ◆ abandon an option
- ◆ renounce an option

Option aufrechthalten
→ Option halten

Option ausüben
- ◆ exercise an option
- ◆ take up an option

Option bestätigen
- ◆ confirm an option

Option einräumen
→ Option gewähren

Option gewähren
Option einräumen
- ◆ grant an option

Option haben auf etw
- ◆ have an option on s.th.

Option halten (sieben Tage)
Option aufrechthalten (für sieben Tage)
- ◆ hold an option (for seven days)

Option in eine feste Buchung umwandeln
Vormerkung in eine feste Buchung umwandeln
- ◆ convert an option into a definite booking

Option läuft aus
   Option erlischt
   ♦ option expires
Option nicht ausüben
   ♦ not exercise an option
Option offenhalten bis ...
   ♦ keep one's option open until ...
Option offenlassen
   ♦ leave one's option open
Optionsausübung, f
   ♦ exercise of an option
   ♦ option exercise
Optionsberechtigter, m
   ♦ holder of an option
   ♦ optionee
   ♦ owner of an option
Optionsbestätigung, f
   ♦ confirmation of an option
   ♦ confirming an option
Optionsbuchung, f
   ♦ optional booking
Optionsdauer, f
   → Optionsfrist
Optionsfrist, f (Dauer)
   Optionsdauer, f
   Optionszeit, f
   ♦ option period
Optionsfrist, f (Zeitpunkt)
   ♦ option date
Optionsgeber, m
   Optionsgewährer, m
   ♦ giver of an option
   ♦ optioner
Optionsgebühr, f
   ♦ option fee
Optionsgeld, n
   → Optionsgebühr
Optionsgeschäft, n
   ♦ option business
Optionsgewährer, m
   ♦ optioner
   ♦ giver of an option
Optionsgewährung, f
   ♦ granting (of) an option
Optionsklausel, f
   ♦ option clause
   ♦ optional clause
Optionsnehmer, m
   ♦ taker of an option
Optionsprovision, f
   ♦ commission on an option
   ♦ commission on options
Optionsrecht, n
   ♦ right to opt
   ♦ option
   ♦ optional right
Optionsrecht nicht in Anspruch nehmen
   verzichten auf ein Optionsrecht
   ♦ opt out
Optionsrecht vereinbaren
   ♦ stipulate an option right
Optionsvereinbarung, f
   ♦ option agreement
Optionsvertrag, m
   ♦ option contract
Optionszahlung, f
   ♦ option payment
Optionszeit, f
   → Optionsfrist
Option verfallen lassen
   ♦ let one's option slide

opulent, adj
   üppig, adj
   ♦ sumptuous, adj
   ♦ opulent, adj
opulente Mahlzeit, f
   opulentes Mahl, n
   ♦ rich meal
   ♦ sumptuous meal
   ♦ luxurious meal
opulentes Essen, n
   opulentes Mahl, n
   ♦ opulent meal
   ♦ luxurious meal
opulentes Mahl, n
   → opulentes Essen
Opulenz, f
   Üppigkeit, f
   ♦ sumptuousness
   ♦ opulence
   ♦ wealth
Orange, f
   Apfelsine, f
   ♦ orange
Orangenbaum, m
   ♦ orange tree
Orangenblüte, f
   ♦ orange blossom
Orangenchutney, n
   ♦ orange chutney
Orangeneis, n
   ♦ orange ice cream AE
   ♦ orange ice-cream BE
Orangenfüllung, f
   ♦ orange stuffing
Orangengelee, n
   ♦ orange jelly
Orangengetränk, n
   ♦ orange drink
Orangenhain, m
   ♦ orange grove
Orangenkaltschale, f
   ♦ cold orange soup
Orangenlikör, m
   ♦ orange liqueur
   ♦ orange brandy
Orangenlimonade, f
   Orangeade, f
   ♦ orangeade
Orangenmarmelade, f
   ♦ orange marmalade
   ♦ marmalade BE
Orangenmilchmixgetränk, n
   ♦ orange milk shake
Orangenparfait, n
   ♦ orange parfait
Orangenpresse, f
   ♦ orange squeezer
Orangensaft, m
   ♦ orange juice
Orangensalat, m
   ♦ orange salad
Orangenschale, f
   ♦ orange peel
   ♦ orange rind
Orangenscheibe, f
   ♦ orange slice
   ♦ slice of orange
Orangenschnitz, m
   ♦ orange wedge
Orangensorbet, n
   ♦ orange sorbet

Orangensoße, f
   ♦ orange sauce
Orangensoufflé, f
   ♦ orange soufflé BE
   ♦ orange souffle AE
Orangentee, m
   ♦ orange tea
Orangerie, f
   ♦ orangery
Orange schälen
   ♦ peel an orange
Orchester, n
   ♦ orchestra
Orchester dirigieren
   ♦ conduct an orchestra
Orchestergraben, m
   ♦ orchestra pit
   ♦ orchestra
Orchesterkonzert, n
   ♦ orchestral concert
Orchestermusik, f
   ♦ orchestral music
Orchesterplatz, m
   Orchesterpavillon, m
   ♦ bandstand
Orchidee, f
   ♦ orchid
Orchideenvase, f
   ♦ orchid vase
ordentlich, adj
   ♦ orderly, adj
ordentlicher Platz, m
   (Camping)
   ♦ orderly site
ordentlicher Schluck aus der Flasche, m
   ♦ good pull at the bottle
ordentliches Frühstück, n
   → richtiges Frühstück
ordentliches Mitglied, n
   ♦ regular member
   ♦ ordinary member
ordentliches Trinkgeld n
   ♦ good tip
   ♦ decent tip
ordentliches Zimmer, n
   → aufgeräumtes Zimmer
Ordentliches zu essen bekommen
   etw Ordentliches zu essen bekommen
   ♦ get s.th. decent to eat
   ♦ get a proper meal
Ordner, m (Aktenordner)
   Aktenordner, m
   ♦ file
Ordner, m (Person)
   (bei Veranstaltung, Fest etc)
   ♦ steward
   ♦ usher
   ♦ supervisor
Ordnungsdienst, m
   (bei Veranstaltung, Fest etc)
   ♦ stewarding service
Ordnungsdienst machen
   ♦ act as stewards
ordnungsgemäß, adv
   ♦ duly, adv
   ♦ in due order, adv
ordnungsgemäße Kündigung, f
   ♦ due and proper notice
   ♦ due and lawful notice

Ordnungsnummer 554

Ordnungsnummer, f
  Referenznummer, f
  ♦ reference number
Oregano, m
  ♦ oregano
Organigramm, n
  ♦ organisation chart
  ♦ organization chart
Organisation des Tourismus, f
  Organisation des Fremdenverkehrs, f
  ♦ organisation of tourism
  ♦ organization of tourism
Organisation einer Konferenz, f
  → Konferenzorganisation
Organisationsausschuß, m
  → Organisationskomitee
Organisationsfehler, m
  ♦ faulty organisation
  ♦ faulty organization
Organisationskomitee, n
  Organisationsausschuß, m
  ♦ organising committee
  ♦ organizing committee
Organisationskomitee einer Konferenz, n
  Organisationsausschuß einer Konferenz, m
  ♦ organising committee of a conference
  ♦ organizing committee of a conference
  ♦ steering committee of a conference
Organisationssekretariat, n
  ♦ organising secretariat
  ♦ organizing secretariat
Organisator, m
  Veranstalter, m
  ♦ organiser
  ♦ organizer
Organisator, m (Dieb) *sl*
  Dieb, m
  Klauer, m
  ♦ scrounger *inform*
Organisator einer Veranstaltung, m
  Veranstaltungsorganisator, m
  ♦ event organiser
  ♦ function organiser
  ♦ organiser of an event
  ♦ organiser of a function
organisatorisch, adj
  ♦ organisational, adj
  ♦ organizational, adj
organisch angebaute Lebensmittel, n pl
  ♦ organically grown food
organisch angebautes Gemüse, n
  ♦ organically grown vegetables *pl*
organisch-biologischer Lieferant, m
  Biolieferant, m
  ♦ organic supplier
organisch-biologischer Wein, m
  Biowein, m
  ♦ organic wine
organisch-biologisches Gemüse, n
  Biogemüse, n
  ♦ organic vegetables *pl*
organisch-biologisches Obst, n
  Bioobst, n
  ♦ organic fruit
organisch-biologisches Produkt, n
  (Landwirtschaft)
  Bioprodukt, n
  ♦ organic produce
organische Krankheit, f
  ♦ organic disease

organisierbar, adj
  ♦ organisable, adj
  ♦ organizable, adj
organisieren etw (auf die Beine stellen)
  → auf die Beine stellen etw
organisieren etw (stehlen) *sl*
  klauen etw
  stehlen etw
  ♦ scrounge s.th. *inform*
organisiert, adj
  veranstaltet, adj
  ♦ organised, adj
  ♦ organized, adj
organisierte Busreise, f
  ♦ organised bus tour
  ♦ organized bus tour
  ♦ organised coach tour *BE*
  ♦ organized coach tour *BE*
organisierte Fahrradtour, f
  organisierte Radtour, f
  ♦ organised cycling tour
  ♦ organized cycling tour
organisierte Fahrt, f
  ♦ organised trip
  ♦ organized trip
organisierter Ausflug, m
  ♦ organised excursion
  ♦ organized excursion
  ♦ organised trip
  ♦ organized trip
  ♦ organised outing
organisierter Tourismus, m
  ♦ organised tourism
  ♦ organized tourism
organisierter Urlaub, m
  organisierte Ferien, pl
  ♦ organised vacation *AE*
  ♦ organized vacation *AE*
  ♦ organised holiday *BE*
  ♦ organized holiday *BE*
organisierte Wandertour, f
  organisierte Wanderreise, f
  ♦ organised walking tour
  ♦ organized walking tour
  ♦ organised hiking tour
  ♦ organized hiking tour
organisierte Wanderung, f
  ♦ organised walk
  ♦ organized walk
  ♦ organised hike
  ♦ organized hike
Organist, m
  Organistin, f
  Orgelspieler, m
  Orgelspielerin, f
  ♦ organist
  ♦ organ player
Orgel, f
  ♦ organ
Orgelempore, f
  ♦ organ loft
Orgelkonzert, n (Musikstück)
  ♦ organ concerto
Orgelkonzert, n (Veranstaltung)
  ♦ organ recital
Orgelkonzert geben
  ♦ give an organ recital
Orgelmusik, f
  ♦ organ music
Orgel spielen
  ♦ play the organ

Orgelspieler, m
  ♦ organ player
Orgie, f
  ♦ orgy
Orgien feiern
  ♦ have orgies
Orient, m
  ♦ Orient, the
Orientale, m
  ♦ Oriental
orientalisch, adj
  ♦ oriental, adj
  ♦ Oriental, adj
orientalische Art, adv *gastr*
  nach orientalischer Art, adv *gastr*
  ♦ oriental style, adv *gastr*
orientalisches Essen, n
  ♦ oriental food
Orientexpreß, m
  ♦ Orient Express, the
orientieren etw nach etw
  ♦ orient s.th. according to s.th. *AE*
  ♦ orientate s.th. according to s.th. *BE*
orientieren sich
  ♦ orient oneself *AE*
  ♦ orientate oneself *BE*
orientiert sein an etw
  ♦ be oriented towards s.th. *AE*
  ♦ be orientated towards s.th. *BE*
Orientierung, f (abstrakt)
  ♦ guidance
  ♦ information
Orientierung, f (konkret)
  ♦ orientation
Orientierungsblatt, n
  ♦ orientation leaflet
Orientierungshilfe, f
  ♦ guideline assistance
Orientierungslauf, m
  ♦ orienteering
  ♦ orienteering race
Orientierungsmarsch, m
  ♦ orienteering march
  ♦ orienteering
Orientierungspfeil, m
  Richtungspfeil, m
  ♦ directional arrow
  ♦ direction arrow
Orientierungsplan, m
  ♦ orientation plan
Orientierungspunkt, m
  ♦ landmark
Orientierungsrennen, n
  ♦ orienteering race
Orientierungsritt, m
  ♦ orienteering trip on horseback
Orientierungsschild, n
  ♦ direction sign
Orientierungstafel, f (generell)
  Orientierungskarte, f
  ♦ orientation chart
  ♦ orientation map
  ♦ reference table
Orientierungstafel, m (Verkehr)
  → Verkehrsschild
Orientierung verlieren
  ♦ lose one's bearings
Orientläufer, m
  Orientbrücke, f
  ♦ oriental rug

Orientteppich, m
♦ oriental carpet
♦ Turkish carpet BE
original, adj
ursprünglich, adj
echt, adj
♦ original, adj
Originalexponat, n
♦ original exhibit
♦ authentic exhibit
Originalgutschein, m
♦ original voucher
original italienische Küche, f
♦ original Italian cuisine
♦ original Italian cooking
Originalkarte, f
Originalfahrkarte, f
♦ original ticket
Originalkunstwerk, n
♦ original work of art
Originalmöbel, n pl
♦ original furniture sg
Originalpreis, m
♦ original price
♦ original rate
Originalprogramm, n
♦ original program AE
♦ original programme BE
Originalquittung, f
♦ original receipt
Originalrechnung, f
♦ original bill
♦ original check AE
♦ original invoice
Originalrezept, n
Originalrezeptur, f
♦ original recipe
originelle Bar, f
♦ original bar
Orkneyinseln, f pl
♦ Orkney Islands, the pl
♦ Orkneys, the pl
Ornament, n
♦ ornament
Ornithologe, m
Vogelkundler, m
♦ ornithologist
ornithologische Wanderung, f
♦ bird-watching walk
Ort, m
Stelle, f
Platz, m
♦ place
♦ spot
♦ locality
♦ location
Ort, wo man dem Alltag entkommt, m
♦ get-away
Ort am Ende der Welt, m
Nest am Ende der Welt, n
Ende der Welt, n
♦ jumping-off place AE
Ort an der Strecke, m
♦ place on the route
Ort aufnehmen in den Reiseverlauf
♦ include a place in the itinerary
Ort benutzen als Ausgangspunkt für Reisen zu etw
♦ use a place as a touring place for s.th.

Ort besuchen
♦ visit a site
♦ visit a place
Örtchen, n coll
Klo, n
Toilette, f
♦ loo BE coll
♦ john AE coll
♦ toilet
Ort des Zwischenstopps, m
♦ place of the intermediate stop
Ort einer römischen Siedlung, m
♦ site of a Roman settlement
Ort erkunden
♦ explore a place
Orthopäde, m
♦ orthopaedist
♦ orthopedist
orthopädisch, adj
♦ orthopaedic, adj
♦ orthopedic, adj
orthopädische Behandlung, f
♦ orthopaedic treatment
♦ orthopedic treatment
Ort ist überlaufen mit Touristen
♦ place is overrun with tourists
Ortlergruppe, f
♦ Ortler Mountains, the, pl
örtlich, adj
lokal, adj
♦ local, adj
örtliche Reiseleitung, f
Ortsrepräsentanz, f
Reiseleitung vor Ort, f
♦ local rep coll
♦ local representative
örtlicher Gratisdienst, m
(z.B. Botengang)
♦ local favor AE
♦ local favour BE
♦ free service locally
örtliche Spezialität, f
Spezialität des Ortes, f
♦ local speciality BE
♦ local specialty AE
örtliches Reservierungsbüro, n
♦ local reservations office
♦ local reservation office
örtliche Veranstaltung, f
Ortsveranstaltung, f
♦ local event
♦ local function
Örtlichkeit, f
→ Lokalität
Ort meiden
Platz meiden
♦ avoid a place
♦ shun a place
Ort mit schöner Landschaft, m
landschaftlich schöner Ort, m
♦ place of scenic interest
Ortsagentur, f
Agentur am Ort, f
örtliche Agentur, f
♦ local agency
ortsansässig, adj
♦ local, adj
♦ resident, adj
Ortsansässiger, m
♦ local inhabitant

♦ local resident
♦ local coll
Ortsansässigkeit, f
♦ residence
Ortsausgang, m
♦ exit of a town
♦ exit of a village
Ortsbehörde, f
♦ local authority
♦ local authorities pl
♦ local bodies pl
Ortsbeschreibung, f
Ferienortbeschreibung, f
♦ resort description
♦ description of a resort
Ortsbesichtigung, f
Ortsbegehung, f
♦ inspection of a locality
♦ local inspection jur
Ortschaft, f
♦ place
♦ town
♦ village
Ortsdurchfahrt, f
♦ passage through a town
♦ passage through a village
Ortseingang, m
♦ entrance of a town
♦ entrance of a village
Ortsfest, n
örtliches Fest, n
♦ local festival
ortsfremd, adj
♦ nonlocal, adj AE
♦ non-local, adj BE
♦ nonresident, adj AE
♦ non-resident, adj BE
Ortsfremder, m
→ Fremder
Ortsführer m
(Buch)
♦ resort guide
Ortsgasthaus, n
örtliches Gasthaus, n
Gasthaus am Ort, n
♦ local bar AE
♦ local public house BE
♦ local pub BE coll
ortsgebunden, adj
♦ tied to a place, adj
♦ attached to a place, adj
Ortsgeschichte, f
→ Heimatgeschichte
Ortsgespräch, n
(Telefon)
♦ local call
Ortshotel, n
→ Hotel am Ort
Ortsinformation, f
→ Ferienortinformation
Ortskenntnis, f
♦ knowledge of a place
♦ familiarity with a place
♦ local knowledge
Ortskenntnisse haben
♦ know the place
♦ have knowledge of the locality
Ortskennzahl, f
(Telefon)
♦ trunk-dialling code
♦ trunk code

Ortskennzahl

Ortskennzahl, f
  (Post)
  ◆ postal area
Ortskern, m
  → Ortsmitte
ortskundig, adj
  ◆ familiar with a place, adj
  ◆ familiar with a locality, adj
Ortsmeister, m
  ◆ local champion
Ortsmeisterschaft, f
  ◆ local championship
Ortsmitte, f (Dorf)
  Ortszentrum, n
  ◆ village center *AE*
  ◆ village centre *BE*
Ortsmitte, f (Stadt)
  Ortszentrum, n
  ◆ downtown *AE*
  ◆ town centre *BE*
  ◆ town center *AE*
Ortsmuseum, n
  örtliches Museum, n
  ◆ local museum
Ortsname, m
  ◆ place-name
  ◆ name of a place
Ortspolizeibehörde, f
  örtliche Polizei, f
  Ortspolizei, f
  ◆ local police
Ortspreis, m
  Preis am Ort, m
  ◆ local price
  ◆ local rate
Ortsprospekt, m
  ◆ resort brochure
  ◆ brochure of a resort
  ◆ brochure describing a resort
Ortsrand, m
  → Dorfrand, Stadtrand
Ortsrandlage, f
  ◆ place on the outskirts
Ortsregister, n
  → Ortsverzeichnis
Ortsrepräsentanz, f
  (von Reiseveranstalter)
  örtliche Reiseleitung, f
  Reiseleiter vor Ort, m
  ◆ local representative
  ◆ local rep *coll*
  ◆ resort representative
Ortsschild, n
  ◆ place-name sign
Ortstaxe, f
  ◆ local tax
  ◆ resort tax
ortsüblich, adj
  ◆ customary in a place, adj
  ◆ local, adj
ortsüblicher Lohn, m
  ◆ local wage
ortsübliche Sätze, m pl
  ◆ local rates *pl*
Ort suchen für die nächste Konferenz
  ◆ look for a venue for the next conference
Ortsveränderung, f
  Ortswechsel, m
  ◆ change of scene
Ortsveranstaltung, f
  → örtliche Veranstaltung

Ortsverkehr, m
  örtlicher Verkehr, m
  ◆ local traffic
Ortsverzeichnis, n
  Ortsregister, n
  ◆ gazeteer
Ortswechsel, m
  ◆ change of place
Ortszeit, f
  ◆ local time
  ◆ LT
Ortszentrum, n
  → Ortsmitte
Ortszuschlag, m
  (Zuschuß)
  ◆ local bonus
  ◆ residential allowance
Ort von historischem Interesse, m
  ◆ site of historical interest
Ort wimmelt von Touristen
  ◆ place is lousy with tourists
Ossiacher See m
  ◆ Lake Ossiach
Ostafrika
  ◆ East Africa
  ◆ Eastern Africa
Ostafrikaner, m
  ◆ East African
Ostafrikanerin, f
  ◆ East African girl
  ◆ East African woman
  ◆ East African
ostafrikanisch, adj
  ◆ East African, adj
ostafrikanische Küste, f
  ◆ East African coast
Ostalpen, f pl
  (Region)
  ◆ Eastern Alps *pl*
Ostanglien
  ◆ East Anglia
Ostappartement, n
  ◆ east-facing apartment
  ◆ apartment facing east
Ostapsis, f
  ◆ east apsis
Ostasiate, m
  ◆ East Asian
Ostasiatin, f
  ◆ East Asian girl
  ◆ East Asian woman
  ◆ East Asian
ostasiatisch, adj
  ◆ East Asian, adj
Ostasien
  ◆ East Asia
  ◆ Eastern Asia
Ostbalkon m
  ◆ east-facing balcony
  ◆ balcony facing east
ostdeutsch, adj
  ◆ East German, adj
Ostdeutsche, f
  ◆ East German girl
  ◆ East German woman
  ◆ East German
Ostdeutscher, m
  ◆ East German
Ostdeutschland
  ◆ East Germany
  ◆ Eastern Germany

Osteingang, m
  ◆ east entrance
Osten, m
  ◆ east
Ostengland
  ◆ Eastern England
  ◆ East England
Osteopath, m
  ◆ osteopath
Osteopathie, f
  ◆ osteopathy
Osterangebot, n
  ◆ Easter offer
Osterarrangement n
  Ostervereinbarung f
  ◆ Easter arrangement
Osterausflug, m
  ◆ Easter excursion
Osterausflügler, m
  ◆ Easter excursionist
Osterbesucher, m
  Osterbesucherin, f
  ◆ Easter visitor
Osterbrauch, m
  ◆ Easter custom
Osterbuchung, f
  ◆ Easter booking
Osterdienstag, m
  ◆ Easter Tuesday
Osterei, n
  ◆ Easter egg
Ostereier suchen
  ◆ search for Easter eggs
Osterfahrt, f
  ◆ Easter trip
Osterfeiertag, m
  ◆ Easter holiday
Osterferien, pl (generell)
  ◆ Easter holidays *BE pl*
  ◆ Easter vacation *AE*
Osterferien, pl (Hochschule, Institutionen)
  ◆ Easter recess
Osterfest, n
  ◆ Easter festival
Ostergeschenk, n
  ◆ Easter present
Osterhase, m
  ◆ Easter rabbit
  ◆ Easter bunny
Osterkreuzfahrt, f
  ◆ Easter cruise
Ostermenü n
  ◆ Easter menu
Ostermonat, m
  ◆ Easter month
Ostermontag, m
  ◆ Easter Monday
Ostern, n
  ◆ Easter
Osternacht, f
  ◆ Easter Eve
Osternest, n
  ◆ nest for Easter eggs
Osterpause, f
  Osterkurzurlaub, m
  ◆ Easter break
Osterprogramm, n
  ◆ Easter program *AE*
  ◆ Easter programme *BE*

Österreich
(Land)
♦ Austria
Österreichbesucher, m
♦ visitor to Austria
Österreicher, m
♦ Austrian
Österreicherin, f
♦ Austrian girl
Austrian woman
♦ Austrian
österreichisch, adj
♦ Austrian, adj
Österreichische Alpen, pl
♦ Austrian Alps, the pl
österreichische Grenze, f
♦ Austrian frontier
Austrian border
österreichische Küche, f
♦ Austrian cuisine
♦ Austrian cooking
Österreichischer Alpenverein, m
♦ Austrian Alpine Club
österreichischer Schilling, m
♦ Austrian schilling
österreichischer Wein, m
♦ Austrian wine
Österreichurlaub, m
♦ Austrian vacation AE
♦ Austrian holiday BE
♦ vacation in Austria AE
♦ holiday in Austria BE
Österreichurlaub machen
Urlaub in Österreich machen
♦ take a vacation in Austria AE
♦ take a holiday in Austria BE
Osterreise, f
♦ Easter tour
♦ Easter journey
Osterreservierung, f
♦ Easter reservation
Ostersaison f
♦ Easter season
Ostersamstag, m
Ostersonnabend, m
Karsamstag, m
♦ Easter Saturday
♦ Holy Saturday
Ostersonntag, m
♦ Easter Sunday
Ostertag, m
♦ Easter day
Osterurlaub, m
♦ Easter vacation AE
♦ Easter holiday BE
Osterurlauber, m
Osterurlauberin, f
♦ Easter vacationer AE
♦ Easter holidaymaker BE
Osterverkehr, m
♦ Easter traffic
Osterwoche, f
♦ Easter week
♦ Holy Week, the BE
Osterwochenende, n
♦ Easter weekend
Osterzeit, f
österliche Zeit, f
♦ Easter time
♦ Easter season

Osterzuschlag m
♦ Easter supplement
Osteuropa
♦ East Europe
♦ Eastern Europe
Osteuropäer, m
♦ East European
Osteuropäerin, f
♦ East European girl
♦ East European woman
♦ East European
osteuropäisch, adj
♦ East European, adj
♦ Eastern European, adj
Ostfassade, f
♦ east façade
♦ east facade AE
♦ east front
Ostfenster, n
♦ east-facing window
♦ window facing east
♦ window to the east
Ostflandern
♦ East Flanders
Ostflügel, m
Ostrakt, m
♦ east wing
Ostfranke, m hist
♦ East Frank hist
Ostfriese, m
♦ East Frisian
Ostfriesische Inseln, f pl
♦ East Frisians pl
♦ East Friesian islands pl
Ostfriesland
(Region)
♦ East Friesland
Ostgebäude, n
♦ east building
Ostgrenze, f
♦ east border
♦ eastern border
Ostküste, f
♦ east coast
♦ eastern coast
Ostlage, f
♦ east-facing position
östliche Route, f
→ Ostroute
östliches Mittelmeer, n
♦ eastern Mediterranean, the
östlich liegen von etw
♦ lie east of s.th.
♦ be situated to the east of s.th.
östlichst, adj
♦ easternmost, adj
♦ most easterly, adj
östlichster Punkt, m
♦ most easterly point
östlichste Spitze, f
♦ easternmost tip
östlich von etw
♦ east of s.th.
♦ to the east of s.th.
östlich von Suez
♦ east of Suez
Ostloggia, f
♦ east-facing loggia
♦ loggia facing east
Ostpommern
→ Hinterpommern

Ostpreußen
(Region)
♦ East Prussia
ostpreußisch, adj
♦ East Prussian, adj
Ostroute, f
Oststrecke, f
östliche Route, f
östliche Strecke, f
♦ eastern route
Ostschweiz, f
♦ Eastern Switzerland
♦ East Switzerland
Ostsee, f
♦ Baltic Sea, the
♦ Baltic, the
Ostseebad, n
Seebad an der Ostsee, n
♦ Baltic resort
♦ resort on the Baltic
Ostseebad Dierhagen, n
♦ Baltic resort of Dierhagen
Ostseeheilbad, n
♦ Baltic health resort
Ostseeinsel, f
♦ Baltic island
Ostseekurort, m
♦ Baltic spa
Ostseeküste, f
♦ Baltic coast
Ostseestrand, m
♦ Baltic beach
♦ Baltic Sea beach
♦ beach of the Baltic Sea
Ostseeufer, n
Ufer der Ostsee, n
♦ shore of the Baltic (Sea)
♦ Baltic Sea shore
♦ Baltic shore
Ostseite, f
♦ east side
♦ eastern side
Oststrand, m
♦ east beach
Osttirol
(Region)
♦ East Tirol
♦ East Tyrol
Osttor, n
♦ east gate
♦ eastern gate
Osttribüne, f
♦ east stand
♦ east stands pl
Ostturm, m
♦ east tower
♦ eastern tower
Ostufer, n (Fluß)
♦ east bank
Ostufer, n (Meer, Binnensee)
♦ east shore
♦ eastern shore
Ostverkehr, m
Verkehr nach Osten, m
♦ eastbound traffic
Ostwales
♦ East Wales
ostwärts, adv
♦ eastwards, adv
♦ eastward, adv

ostwärts reisen

♦ to the east, adv
♦ east, adv
ostwärts reisen
♦ travel eastwards
♦ travel eastward
ostwärts wandern
♦ walk eastwards
ostwärts ziehen
ostwärts wandern
♦ migrate eastwards
Ost-West-Flug, m
♦ east-west flight
Ost-West-Richtung, f
♦ east to west direction
♦ east-west direction
Ost-West-Straße, f
♦ east-west road
Ost-West-Verbindung, f
♦ east-west link
♦ east-west connection
Ostzimmer n
Zimmer nach Osten n
nach Osten gelegenes Zimmer n
♦ east-facing room
♦ room facing east
Ötztaler Alpen, die, pl
♦ Oetztal Alps, the, pl
Outback, m
(in Australien)
♦ outback
Outbacksafari, f
♦ outback safari
Outfit, n (Kleidung)
(Kleidung für Tennis, Golf etc.)
♦ outfit
Outgoing, n
(vom Inland in das Ausland)
♦ outgoing
Outgoing-Agent, m
♦ outgoing agent
Outgoing-Agentur, f
♦ outgoing agency
Outgoing-Aktivität, f
♦ outgoing activity
Outgoing-Büro, n
♦ outgoing office
Outgoing-Forum, n
♦ outgoing forum
Outgoing-Geschäft, n
♦ outgoing business
Outgoing-Markt, m
♦ outgoing market
Outgoing-Partner, m
♦ outgoing partner
Outgoing-Reiseveranstalter, m
♦ outgoing tour operator
Outgoing-Tochtergesellschaft, f
♦ outgoing subsidiary
Outgoing-Tourismus, m
Tourismus in das Ausland, m
♦ outgoing tourism
♦ outbound tourism
Outgoing-Veranstalter, m
♦ outgoing operator
Outsider, m
→ Außenseiter
Ouzo, m GR
♦ ouzo GR
oval, adj
♦ oval, adj

ovale Platte, f
(Geschirr)
♦ oval platter
ovaler Tisch, m
♦ oval table
ovales Zimmer, n
ovaler Raum, m
♦ oval room
Ovation, f
♦ ovation
Ovation bereiten jm
♦ give s.o. an ovation
Ovation im Stehen, f
im Stehen gegebene Ovation, f
Beifall im Stehen, m
♦ standing ovation
Overheadfolie, f
→ Tageslichtfolie
Overheadprojektion, f
→ Tageslichtprojektion
Overheadprojektor, m
→ Tageslichtprojektor
Overheadwagen, m
Wagen für den Tageslichtprojektor, m
♦ overhead cart AE
♦ overhead trolley BE
Overriding commission, f
→ Superprovision
Overstay, m
→ Verlängerer
Ozean, m
♦ ocean
Ozeanarium, n
♦ oceanarium
Ozeanblick, m
♦ ocean view
♦ view of the ocean
Ozeandampfer, m
♦ ocean steamer
♦ ocean liner
♦ ocean-going steamer
♦ ocean-going liner
Ozeanreise, f
♦ transoceanic voyage
♦ ocean voyage
Ozeanriese, f
♦ large ocean liner
Ozeanseite, f
♦ oceanfront AE
♦ ocean front BE
Ozean überqueren
♦ cross the ocean
♦ traverse the ocean
Ozeanüberquerung, f
♦ ocean crossing
ÖZH, f
Ölzentralheizung, f
♦ OCH
♦ oil central heating
Ozon, n/m
♦ ozone
Ozonbad, n
(Vorgang)
♦ ozone bath
♦ ozonic bath
Ozonbehandlung, f med
♦ ozone treatment med
Ozonhallenbad, n
♦ ozone indoor swimming pool AE
♦ ozone indoor swimming-pool BE
♦ ozone indoor pool

Ozonkonzentration, f
Ozongehalt, m
♦ ozone concentration
Ozonloch, n
♦ hole in the ozone layer
♦ ozone hole
Ozonproblem, n
♦ ozone problem
ozonreich, adj
♦ rich in ozone, adj
♦ high in ozone, adj
Ozonschicht, f
♦ ozone layer
Ozonschwimmbad, n
♦ ozone swimming pool AE
♦ ozone swimming-pool BE
Ozontherapie, f
♦ ozone therapy

P

p.a.
  per annum
  pro Jahr
  ♦ p.a.
  ♦ per annum
  ♦ per year
  ♦ annually
paar, *pron*
  ♦ several, *pron*
  ♦ some, *pron*
  ♦ a few, *pron*
Paar, n (Mann und Frau)
  ♦ couple
Paar, n (zwei)
  ♦ pair
Paar auf der Hochzeitsreise, n
  Hochzeitsreisende, pl
  Flitterwöchner, pl
  ♦ honeymoon couple
Paar Hosen, n
  ♦ pair of trousers
Paar Schuhe, n
  ♦ pair of shoes
paar Tage Entspannung, m pl
  ♦ a few days' relaxation
paar Tage Entspannung suchen
  ♦ seek a few days' relaxation
paar Tage Ruhe, m pl
  ♦ a few days' rest
paarweise, adv
  ♦ in pairs, adv
  ♦ two by two, adv
Pacht, f
  ♦ leasehold
  ♦ lease
Pachtangebot, n
  ♦ supply of leasehold
  ♦ leasehold availability
Pacht auf Lebenszeit, f
  ♦ lease for life
Pacht auf Zeit, f
  ♦ lease for a term of year
pachtbar, adj
  ♦ leasable, adj
  ♦ tenantable, adj
Pachtbedingungen, f pl
  ♦ conditions of leasehold *pl*
  ♦ leasehold conditions *pl*
  ♦ terms of lease *pl*
Pachtbesitz, m (Bilanz)
  ♦ leasehold land and buildings *pl*
Pachtbesitz, m (generell)
  ♦ leasehold
  ♦ leasehold tenure
Pachtbetrag, m
  ♦ amount of lease

Pachtbetrieb m
  ♦ leasehold establishment
  ♦ leasehold operation
Pachtdauer, f
  ♦ length of (a) lease
  ♦ duration of (a) lease
  ♦ term of (a) lease
Pacht eines Hauses haben
  ♦ hold the tenancy of a house
  ♦ tenant a house
Pachteinnahmen, f pl
  ♦ lease income
  ♦ lease revenue
  ♦ lease receipts *pl*
  ♦ lease takings *pl*
pachten auf 99 Jahre
  ♦ take a 99 year lease
pachten etw
  ♦ take s.th. on lease
  ♦ lease s.th.
  ♦ take a lease of s.th.
  ♦ rent s.th.
pachten etw von jm
  ♦ lease s.th. from s.o.
Pächter, der bald auszieht, m
  bald ausziehender Pächter, m
  ♦ outgoing tenant
Pächter, m
  ♦ leaseholder
  ♦ tenant
  ♦ lessee *jur*
  ♦ renter
  ♦ occupier *BE*
Pächterehepaar, n
  Pächterpaar, n
  ♦ tenant couple
Pächterinart, adv *gastr*
  ♦ tenant's style, adv *gastr*
Pachtertrag, m
  ♦ rental (received)
  ♦ rent-roll
Pächter wechseln
  ♦ change leaseholders
  ♦ change tenants
Pachtgasthof, m
  gepachteter Gasthof, m
  ♦ leasehold inn
  ♦ leased inn
Pachtgebühr, f
  ♦ lease charge
Pachtgebühr erheben
  ♦ levy a lease charge
Pachtgegenstand, m
  ♦ object of lease
Pachtgeschäft, n
  ♦ leasehold business
Pachtgesuch, n
  (Gegensatz von Pachtangebot)

  ♦ demand for leasehold
  ♦ leasehold demand
Pachtgrundstück, n
  ♦ leasehold property
  ♦ leasehold
Pachthotel, n
  gepachtetes Hotel, n
  ♦ leasehold hotel
  ♦ leased hotel
Pachtimmobilie, f
  ♦ leasehold property
Pachtjahr, n
  ♦ leasehold year
  ♦ year of lease
  ♦ tenancy year
Pachtkosten, pl
  ♦ leasehold costs *pl*
  ♦ leasehold cost
  ♦ cost of leasehold
Pachtland, n
  ♦ leasehold land
  ♦ leasehold
Pacht läuft ab
  ♦ lease is running out
  ♦ lease expires
Pacht läuft noch über fünf weitere Jahre
  ♦ lease has five years left to run
Pachtlokal, n
  gepachtetes Lokal, n
  ♦ leasehold premises *pl*
  ♦ leased premises *pl*
Pachtrestaurant, n
  gepachtetes Restaurant, n
  ♦ leasehold restaurant
  ♦ leased restaurant
Pachtsystem, n
  Pachtwesen, n
  ♦ leasehold system
Pacht- und Leihgesetz, n
  ♦ Lend-Lease Act *AE*
Pacht- und Leihvertrag, m
  ♦ lend-lease contract
  ♦ lend-lease
Pachtung, f
  ♦ leasing
Pachtvereinbarung, f
  ♦ lease agreement
  ♦ leasing agreement
  ♦ tenancy agreement
Pachtvereinbarung beginnt am 1. Mai
  ♦ lease agreement begins on 1 May
  ♦ lease agreement commences on 1 May *form*
  ♦ lease agreement starts on 1 May
Pachtverhältnis, n
  ♦ lease
  ♦ tenancy

Pacht verlängern um 20 Jahre

Pacht verlängern um 20 Jahre
   Pachtvertrag verlängern um 20 Jahre
   ◆ extend a lease by 20 years
Pachtverlängerung, f
   Mietverlängerung, f
   ◆ renewal of (the) lease
Pachtversicherung, f
   ◆ leasehold insurance
Pachtvertrag, m
   Mietvertrag, m
   ◆ lease contract
   ◆ contract of lease
   ◆ lease
Pachtvertrag aufsetzen
   ◆ draw up a lease
Pachtvertrag eingehen
   Pachtvertrag abschließen
   ◆ enter into a lease
Pachtvertrag erfüllen
   ◆ fulfill the terms of the lease *AE*
   ◆ fulfil the lease *AE*
   ◆ fulfil the terms of the lease *BE*
   ◆ fulfil the lease *BE*
Pachtvertrag erneuern
   → Pachtvertrag verlängern
Pachtvertrag ist verlängerbar (um weitere 5 Jahre)
   ◆ lease is renewable (for a further 5 years)
Pachtvertrag kündigen
   Pachtvertrag beenden
   ◆ terminate a lease
   ◆ cancel a lease
Pachtvertrag läuft aus
   Pachtvertrag läuft ab
   ◆ lease expires
Pachtvertrag läuft über 10 Jahre
   ◆ lease runs over 10 years
Pachtvertragsbestimmungen, f pl
   ◆ terms of a lease *pl*
Pachtvertrag unterzeichnen
   Pachtvertrag abschließen
   ◆ sign a lease
Pachtvertrag verlängern
   ◆ renew the lease
Pacht von 99 Jahren, f
   ◆ lease of 99 years
   ◆ 99-year lease
Pacht von Jahr zu Jahr, f
   ◆ lease from year to year
Pachtvorvertrag, m
   Mietvorvertrag, m
   ◆ agreement for a lease
pachtweise, adv
   mietweise, adv
   ◆ by way of lease, adv
   ◆ on lease, adv
   ◆ on a lease basis, adv
   ◆ by lease, adv
Pachtwert, m
   ◆ lease value
   ◆ rental value
Pachtwohnung, f
   ◆ leasehold apartment *AE*
   ◆ leasehold flat *BE*
Pachtzahlung, f
   ◆ leasehold payment
Pachtzeit, f
   ◆ term of a lease
   ◆ lease term

Pachtzeitraum m
   ◆ period of a lease
   ◆ lease period
Pachtzins, m
   ◆ rent
Pachtzinsforderung, f
   ◆ claim for lease
Package, f
   ◆ package
Packagetour, f
   → Pauschalreise
Päckchen, n
   (Post)
   ◆ parcel *BE*
   ◆ package *AE*
Packen erledigen
   ◆ do one's packing
packen (etw)
   ◆ pack (s.th.)
Packesel, m
   ◆ pack mule *AE*
   ◆ pack-mule *BE*
   ◆ sumpter mule *AE*
   ◆ sumpter-mule *BE*
Packpferd, n
   ◆ packhorse *AE*
   ◆ pack-horse *BE*
Packtasche, f
   (auf Fahrrad etc)
   ◆ pannier bag
Packtier, n
   ◆ pack animal *AE*
   ◆ pack-animal *BE*
Packtier mieten
   ◆ rent a pack animal *AE*
   ◆ hire a pack-animal *BE*
Packung, f (Kosmetik)
   ◆ pack
Packung, f (Moor etc.) *med*
   ◆ wrap *med*
Packung Zigaretten, f
   → Schachtel Zigaretten
Paddel, n
   ◆ paddle
Paddelboot, n
   ◆ paddle-boat
   ◆ canoe
Paddelbootfahrt, f
   ◆ paddle-boat ride
   ◆ paddle-boat trip
paddeln
   ◆ paddle
   ◆ canoe
Paddeln, n
   Paddelsport, m
   ◆ paddling
Paddeltour f
   (mit Paddelboot)
   ◆ canoe tour
Paddler, m
   ◆ paddler
Paella, f *SPAN*
   ◆ paella *SPAN*
Page, m
   ◆ page
   ◆ page boy *AE*
   ◆ page-boy *BE*
   ◆ bellboy *AE*
   ◆ bellhop *AE sl*
Page wird Sie hinaufführen
   ◆ page will show you up

Page wird Sie zu Ihrem Zimmer bringen
   ◆ page will take you to your room
Pagode, f
   ◆ pagoda
Paketboot, n
   Postboot, n
   ◆ packet boat *AE*
   ◆ packet ship *AE*
   ◆ packet-boat *BE*
   ◆ packet
Paketreise, f
   ◆ bus-inclusive tour
Paketreiseveranstalter, m
   (verkauft Arrangements an Busreisefirmen)
   ◆ bus tour wholesaler
Pakistan
   ◆ Pakistan
Pakistaner, m
   ◆ Pakistani
Pakistanerin, f
   ◆ Pakistani girl
   ◆ Pakistani woman
   ◆ Pakistani
pakistanisch, adj
   ◆ Pakistani, adj
   ◆ Pakistan, adj
Palais, n
   Stadtpalais, n
   ◆ town mansion
palastartiges Hotel, n
   Palasthotel, n
   ◆ palatial hotel
palastartige Suite, f
   Palastsuite, f
   ◆ palatial suite
palastartiges Zimmer, n
   Palastzimmer, n
   ◆ palatial room
Palast auf Rädern, m
   ◆ palace on wheels
Palastfest, n
   Palastfestspiele, n pl
   ◆ palace festival
Palasthotel, n (Eigenname)
   ◆ Palace Hotel, the
Palasthotel, n (generell)
   ◆ palace hotel
Palästina
   ◆ Palestine
Palästinenser, m
   ◆ Palestinian
Palästinenserin, f
   ◆ Palestinian girl
   ◆ Palestinian woman
   ◆ Palestinian
palästinensisch, adj
   palästinisch, adj
   ◆ Palestinian, adj
Palastkapelle, f
   ◆ palace chapel
Palastkirche, f
   ◆ palace church
Palastpark, m
   ◆ palace gardens *pl*
Palastruine, f
   ◆ ruined palace
   ◆ palace ruins *pl*
Palasttheater, n
   Schloßtheater, n
   ◆ palace theater *AE*
   ◆ palace theatre *BE*

Paplergeld

Palasttor, n
♦ palace gate
Palaver, n
♦ palaver
Palazzo, m ITAL
♦ palazzo ITAL
Palette, f (Auswahl)
♦ range
Palette, f (Transport)
♦ pallet
Palme, f
Palmenbaum, m
♦ palm
♦ palm tree AE
♦ palm-tree BE
Palmenallee, f
♦ palm-fringed boulevard
Palmengarten, m
♦ palm garden
palmengedeckte Hütte, f
♦ palm-thatched hut
Palmenhain, m
Palmenwäldchen, n
♦ palm grove
♦ grove of palms
♦ grove of palm trees AE
♦ grove of palm-trees BE
♦ coconut grove
Palmenhaus, n
(Gewächshaus)
♦ palm house
♦ palmery
Palmenhof, m
♦ palm court
Palmenhofcafé, n
♦ palm court café BE
♦ palm court cafe AE
Palmenhofhotel, n
♦ palm court hotel
Palmenstrand, m
♦ palm-fringed beach
♦ palm beach AE
palmenumsäumt, adj
palmengesäumt, adj
♦ palm-fringed, adj
Palmsonntag, m
♦ Palm Sunday
Palmwein, m
♦ palm wine
♦ toddy
Pampelmuse, f
→ Grapefruit
Panama
♦ Panama
Panamaer, m
♦ Panamanian
♦ Panaman
Panamaerin, f
♦ Panamanian girl
♦ Panamanian woman
♦ Panaman girl
♦ Panaman woman
panamaisch, adj
♦ Panamanian, adj
♦ Panaman, adj
Panamakanal, m
♦ Panama Canal, the
Pandschab, m
♦ Punjab, the
Paneel, n
→ Täfelung

panieren etw
♦ coat s.th. with breadcrumbs
♦ bread s.th.
Paniermehl, n
♦ bread crumbs AE pl
♦ breadcrumbs BE pl
paniert, adj
♦ in bread crumbs, adv AE
♦ in breadcrumbs, adv BE
♦ breaded, adj
♦ covered with bread crumbs, adv AE
♦ covered with breadcrumbs, adv BE
Panik, f
♦ panic
Panik bricht aus
♦ panic breaks out
Panikmaßnahmen, f pl
Maßnahmen bei einer Panik, f pl
♦ panic measures pl
Panne, f (Auto)
♦ breakdown
Panne, f (Reifenpanne)
→ Reifenpanne
Panne haben (Auto)
♦ have a breakdown
Panne haben (Reifenpanne)
→ Reifenpanne haben
Pannendienst, m
Abschleppdienst, m
Pannenhilfe, f
♦ breakdown service
Pannenhelfer, m
♦ patrolman BE
Pannenhilfe, f
Abschlepphilfe, f
♦ breakdown assistance
Pannenschutz, m
Autopannenschutz, m
♦ breakdown cover
Pannenversicherung, f
Autopannenversicherung, f
♦ breakdown insurance
Panorama, n
♦ panorama
Panoramabad, n
♦ panoramic pool
Panoramablick, m
→ Rundblick
Panoramacafé, n
♦ panoramic cafe AE
♦ panoramic café BE
Panoramafahrt, f
♦ panoramic trip
Panoramafenster, n
Aussichtsfenster, n
♦ panoramic window
♦ picture window
Panoramahallenbad, n
Panoramaschwimmhalle, f
♦ panoramic indoor swimming pool AE
♦ panoramic indoor swimming-pool BE
♦ panoramic indoor pool
Panoramakarte, f
♦ panoramic map
Panoramalage, f
♦ panoramic situation
♦ panoramic position
Panoramasauna, f
♦ panoramic sauna
Panoramaschwimmbad, n
Panoramabad, n

♦ panoramic swimming pool AE
♦ panoramic swimming-pool BE
♦ panoramic pool
Panoramaspaziergang unternehmen
Panoramawanderung unternehmen
♦ take a panoramic walk
Panoramastraße, f
♦ panoramic road
Panoramaterrasse, f
Aussichtsterrasse, f
♦ panoramic patio
♦ panoramic terrace
Panoramawanderweg, m
Panoramaspazierweg, m
♦ panoramic walking trail
♦ panoramic hiking trail
♦ panoramic hiking path
♦ panoramic footpath
♦ panoramic walk
panschen etw
(Getränk)
pantschen etw
♦ adulterate s.th.
♦ doctor s.th.
♦ water s.th. down
Panscher, m
♦ adulterator
Panscherei, f
♦ adulteration
Pantoffel, m
♦ bedroom slipper
♦ slipper
Pantomime, f
♦ pantomime
Pantry, f
→ Geschirraum, Anrichteraum
Panzerauto, n
♦ armored car AE
♦ armoured car BE
Panzerglas, n
♦ bulletproof glass AE
♦ bullet-proof glass BE
Panzermuseum, n
♦ tank museum
Panzerschrank, m
→ Safe
Pap, m sl
(Luftverkehr)
zahlender Passagier, m
♦ pap sl
♦ paying passenger
Papagallo, m
♦ beach romeo
Papagei, m
♦ parrot
Papaya, f
♦ papaw
♦ pawpaw
♦ papaya
Papayasaft, m
♦ papaya juice
♦ papaw juice
♦ pawpaw juice
Papier, n
♦ paper
Papierblume, f
♦ paperflower AE
♦ paper-flower BE
Papiergeld, n
♦ paper money

Papiergeschäft

Papiergeschäft, n
  → Schreibwarengeschäft
Papierhandtuch, n
  ◆ paper towel
Papierhandtuchspender, m
  ◆ paper towel dispenser
Papierkorb, m
  ◆ wastebasket *AE*
  ◆ waste-paper basket *BE*
  ◆ waste-bin *AE*
Papierkorb leeren
  ◆ empty a wastebasket *AE*
  ◆ empty a waste-paper basket *BE*
Papierkrieg, m
  Schreibarbeit, f
  ◆ paperwork
Papierserviette f
  ◆ paper napkin
  ◆ paper serviette *BE*
Papiertischset, n
  Platzdeckchen aus Papier, n
  Papierset, n
  ◆ paper place mat *AE*
  ◆ paper place-mat *BE*
Papiertischtuch, n
  ◆ paper tablecloth
Papiertrinkhalm, m
  ◆ paper straw
Papiertüte, f
  ◆ paper bag
Papierwaren, f pl
  ◆ paper supplies *pl*
Pappmöbel, n pl
  ◆ cardboard furniture *sg*
Pappschnee, m
  ◆ sticky snow
Papptasse, f
  Papiertasse, f *neg*
  ◆ paper cup
Pappteller, m
  Papierteller, m *neg*
  ◆ paper plate
Paprika, f (Frucht)
  ◆ sweet pepper
  ◆ pepper
Paprika, m (Gewürz)
  ◆ paprika
  ◆ paprica
Paprikabutter, f
  ◆ paprika butter
Papstbesuch, m
  päpstlicher Besuch, m
  ◆ pope's visit
  ◆ papal visit
Papua-Neuguinea
  ◆ Papua New Guinea
Par, n
  (Golf)
  ◆ par
Parade, f
  Umzug, m
  ◆ parade
Paradebett, n
  Prunkbett, n
  ◆ bed of state
Paradefrühstück, n
  → Dejeuner dînatoire
Paradeplatz, m
  ◆ parade ground
paradieren
  ◆ parade

Paradies, n
  ◆ paradise
Paradies für Angler, n
  ◆ paradise for anglers
Paradies für etw, n
  ◆ paradise for s.th.
Paradies für jn, n
  ◆ paradise for s.o.
Paradies für Naturliebhaber, n
  ◆ paradise for nature lovers
  ◆ nature lover's paradise
Paradies für Skilanglauf, n
  ◆ paradise for cross-country skiing
Paradies für Urlauber, n
  ◆ paradise for vacationers *AE*
  ◆ paradise for holidaymakers *BE*
Paradies für Weinliebhaber, n
  ◆ paradise for wine lovers
  ◆ wine lover's paradise
paradiesisch, adj
  ◆ heavenly, adj
  ◆ delightful, adj
  ◆ paradisal, adj
  ◆ paradisiac, adj
paradiesische Insel, f
  ◆ paradisical island
paradiesische Umgebung, f
  ◆ heavenly surroundings *pl*
paradiesisch gelegen, adj
  ◆ magnificently situated, adj
  ◆ magnificently located, adj
Parador, m *SPAN*
  (spanisches Hotel)
  ◆ parador *SPAN*
Paraffin, n
  ◆ paraffin
  ◆ paraffine *AE*
  ◆ paraffin wax
Paraffinbad, n
  ◆ paraffin wax bath
Paraffinbehandlung, f
  ◆ paraffin wax treatment
Paraffingesichtsbehandlung, f
  ◆ paraffin wax facial treatment
Paraffinöl, n
  ◆ paraffin oil
Paraguay
  ◆ Paraguay
Paraguayer, m
  ◆ Paraguayan
Paraguayerin, f
  ◆ Paraguayan girl
  ◆ Paraguayan woman
  ◆ Paraguayan
paraguayisch, adj
  ◆ Paraguayan, adj
Parahotellerie, f
  ◆ other accommodation
  ◆ non-hotel accommodation *BE*
  ◆ other accommodations *AE pl*
  ◆ nonhotel accommodation *AE*
  ◆ other accommodation facilities *pl*
Parallelkurs, m
  gleichzeitiger Kurs, m
  ◆ simultaneous course
Parallelsitzung, f
  ◆ parallel session
Parallelveranstaltung, f
  (bei Konferenz)
  ◆ concurrent session
  ◆ concurrent sessions *pl*

Parallelvortrag, m
  ◆ concurrent lecture
Paranuß, f
  ◆ Brazil nut
Paratourismus, m
  (Leistungen für ortsansässige Nichttouristen)
  abgeleiteter Tourismus, m
  ◆ paratourism
Paratyphus, m
  ◆ paratyphoid fever
  ◆ paratyphoid
Paravent, m
  ◆ folding screen
Pärchen, n
  → Paar
Parcours, m
  (Reiten)
  ◆ course
Pardon!
  → Entschuldigung!
Parfait, n
  ◆ parfait
Parfüm, n
  ◆ perfume
Parfümerie, f
  ◆ perfume store *AE*
  ◆ scent store *AE*
  ◆ perfume shop *BE*
parfümieren etw
  ◆ perfume s.th.
parfümieren sich
  ◆ perfume oneself
Parfümzerstäuber, m
  ◆ perfume spray
Paria, n
  ◆ pariah
  ◆ outcast
Paris des Nordens, n
  ◆ Paris of the North, the
Pariserart, adv *gastr*
  ◆ Parisian style, adv *gastr*
Park, m
  Parkanlage, f
  ◆ park
  ◆ gardens *pl*
Park, m (Fuhrpark)
  → Fuhrpark
parkähnlicher Platz, m
  (z.B. Camping)
  ◆ landscaped site
Park and Ride, n
  ◆ park and ride
Park-and-ride-System, n
  ◆ park-and-ride system
Parkanlage, f
  → Park
Park anlegen
  ◆ create a park
parkartiges Gelände, n
  Parkgelände, n
  ◆ parkland
parkartige Umgebung, f
  ◆ parklike setting
Parkausweis, m
  Parkerlaubnis, f
  ◆ parking permit
Parkausweis ausstellen
  ◆ issue a parking permit
Parkbank, f
  ◆ park bench

Parkbereich, m
Parkzone f
♦ parking area
Parkblick, m
Blick auf den Park m
♦ park view
♦ view of the park
♦ view of the gardens
Parkbon, m
→ Parkgutschein
Parkbucht, f (an Landstraße)
♦ lay-by BE
♦ rest area AE
Parkbucht, f (generell)
♦ parking bay
Parkdauer bis zehn Minuten
♦ waiting limited to ten minutes
Parkdienst, m
Parkservice, m
♦ parking service
Parkeingang, m
♦ park entrance
parken
(Fahrzeug)
parkieren SCHW
abstellen
♦ park
Parken, n
♦ parking
Parken an Ort und Stelle, n
♦ on-site parking
Parken auf der Straße, n
♦ on-street parking
parken auf eigene Gefahr
♦ park at the owner's risk
♦ park at owner's risk
Parken auf eigene Gefahr, n
♦ parking at owner's risk
parkendes Auto, n
parkender Wagen m
♦ parked car
Parken für Freizeitfahrzeuge, n
Parken für Campingfahrzeuge, n
♦ RV parking AE
♦ parking for recreational vehicles AE
♦ parking for leisure vehicles
Parken gebührenfrei
♦ Free parking
Parken gestattet (für Mitarbeiter)
(Hinweisschild)
♦ Authorised parking
♦ Authorized parking
Parken gestattet (generell)
(Hinweisschild)
♦ Parking allowed
parken im Freien
♦ park in the open air
♦ park in the open
Parken im Freien, n
♦ outdoor parking
parken im Halteverbot
♦ park in a no-stopping zone
Parken im Innern, n
(im Haus)
♦ indoor parking
parken im Parkverbot
♦ park in a no-parking zone
Parken in der Tiefgarage, n
♦ underground parking
Parken in einer Nebenstraße, n
♦ off-street parking

Parken ist hier verboten
♦ parking is prohibited here
Parken ist kostenlos
♦ parking is free
Parken ist verboten
♦ parking is prohibited
Parken mit Gutschein, n
♦ voucher parking
Parken mit Parkscheibe, n
♦ disc parking AE
♦ disk parking BE
Parken verboten
(Hinweisschild)
♦ No Parking
Parkerlaubnis, f
→ Parkausweis
Parkett, n (Boden)
♦ parquet
Parkett, n (Tanzfläche)
→ Tanzfläche
Parkett, n (Theater)
Sperrsitz, m
♦ stalls BE pl
♦ orchestra AE
Parkettboden, m
♦ parquet floor
Parkettplatz, m (Theater)
Sperrsitzplatz, m
Sperrsitz, m
♦ seat in the stalls BE
♦ seat in the orchestra AE
♦ orchestra seat AE
Parkfest, n
♦ park festival
Parkfläche, f (für Autos)
Parkraum m
♦ parking area
♦ parking space
Parkgarage, f
→ Parkhaus
Parkgebühr, f
♦ parking fee
♦ parking charge
Parkgebühr erheben
Parkgebühr verlangen
♦ levy a parking charge
♦ charge a parking fee
Parkgebühr zahlen
♦ pay a parking charge
♦ pay a parking fee
Parkgelegenheit, f
Parkmöglichkeit, f
♦ parking facility
♦ opportunity to park
Parkgolfplatz, m
Golfplatz im Parkgelände, m
♦ parkland golf course AE
♦ parkland golf-course BE
Parkgutschein, m
Parkbon, m
♦ parking voucher
Parkhaus, n
Parkhochhaus n
♦ parking garage AE
♦ multi-story parking garage AE
♦ multi-storey car park BE
Parkhausbetreiber, m
♦ parking garage operator AE
♦ operator of a multi-storey car park BE
Parkhotel, n (Eigenname)
♦ Park Hotel, the

Parkhotel, n (generell)
♦ park hotel
parkieren, SCHW
→ parken
Park ist für die Öffentlichkeit geöffnet
Park ist für die Öffentlichkeit zugänglich
♦ park is open to the public
Park ist geöffnet von 8 bis 18 Uhr
♦ park is open from 8 a.m. until 6 p.m.
♦ gardens are open from 8 a.m. until 6 p.m.
Parklücke, f
♦ parking space
Parkmöglichkeiten, f pl
Parkgelegenheiten f pl
Abstellmöglichkeiten f pl
Stellmöglichkeiten f pl
♦ parking facilities pl
Parkmöglichkeiten für über 100 Autos, f pl
♦ parking facilities for over 100 cars pl
♦ parking for over 100 cars
Parkmöglichkeiten im Freien, f pl
Abstellmöglichkeiten im Freien, f pl
♦ open-air parking facilities pl
♦ open-air parking
♦ outside parking facilities pl
♦ outside parking
Parkmöglichkeiten im Freien für 100 Autos, f pl
Abstellmöglichkeiten im Freien für 100 Autos, f pl
♦ open-air parking facilities for 100 cars
♦ open-air parking for 100 cars
♦ outside parking facilities for 100 cars
♦ outside parking for 100 cars
Parkmöglichkeit in Tiefgeschoß, f
Parken im Tiefgeschoß n
♦ parking in (the) basement
parknah, adv
in Parknähe, adv
♦ close to (the) park, adv
♦ near (the) park, adv
Parkometer, m
→ Parkuhr
Parkordnung, f
(Gartenpark)
♦ park regulations pl
Parkplatz, m (für 1 Auto)
♦ parking place
♦ parking space
♦ parking lot AE
Parkplatz, m (für mehrere Autos)
♦ parking lot AE
♦ car park BE
Parkplatz anbieten (für 1 Auto)
Stellplatz anbieten
♦ offer a parking place
♦ offer a parking space
Parkplatzangebot, n (Gegensatz zu Nachfrage)
♦ supply of parking spaces
♦ supply of parking places
♦ supply of parking facilities
Parkplatzangebot, n (Palette)
♦ range of parking spaces
♦ range of parking spaces
♦ range of parking facilities
Parkplatz auf dem Grundstück, m
eigener Parkplatz m
♦ parking lot on the premises AE
♦ car park on the premises BE
Parkplatzaufseher, m
→ Parkplatzwächter

Parkplatzausfahrt

Parkplatzausfahrt, f
♦ parking lot exit AE
♦ car park exit BE
Parkplatz benutzen
♦ use a parking lot AE
♦ use a car park BE
Parkplatzbenutzer, m
Parkplatzbenutzerin f
♦ person using a parking lot AE
♦ person who uses a parking lot BE
♦ person using a car park BE
♦ person who uses a car park BE
Parkplatzbenutzung, f (für mehrere Autos)
Benutzung eines Parkplatzes f
♦ use of a parking lot AE
♦ using a parking lot AE
♦ use of a car park BE
♦ using a car park BE
Parkplatz betreiben
♦ operate a parking lot AE
♦ operate a car park BE
Parkplatzbetreiber, m
♦ parking lot operator AE
♦ car park operator BE
Parkplatzbetrieb, m
♦ operation of a parking lot AE
♦ operation of a car park BE
Parkplätze für 10 Autos haben
zehn Parkplätze frei haben
♦ have parking space available for 10 cars
Parkplatzeinfahrt, f
♦ parking lot entrance AE
♦ car park entrance BE
Parkplätze schaffen
♦ create parking places
♦ create parking space
♦ create parking lots AE
Parkplatz finden (für 1 Auto)
♦ find a parking place
♦ find a parking space
♦ find a parking lot AE
Parkplatz finden (für mehrere Autos)
♦ find a parking lot AE
♦ find a car park BE
Parkplatz für Besucher (Hinweisschild)
Besucherparkplatz (Hinweisschild)
♦ Parking for visitors (sign)
Parkplatz für Wohnwagen, m
Wohnwagenparkplatz, m
Caravanparkplatz, m
♦ trailer parking lot AE
♦ caravan park BE
Parkplatz gleich nebenan, m
♦ adjoining parking lot AE
♦ adjoining car park BE
Parkplatz ist bewacht
Parkplatz ist überwacht
♦ parking lot is supervised AE
♦ car park is guarded BE
Parkplatz ist die ganze Nacht geöffnet
♦ parking lot is open all night AE
♦ car park is open all night BE
Parkplatz ist geschlossen
♦ parking lot is closed AE
♦ car park is closed BE
Parkplatz ist offen
Parkplatz ist geöffnet
♦ parking lot is open AE
♦ car park is open BE
Parkplatz ist voll
♦ parking lot is full AE

♦ parking lot is full up AE coll
♦ car park is full BE
♦ car park is full up BE coll
Parkplatz ist von 6.00 bis 21.00 Uhr geöffnet
♦ parking lot is open from 6 a.m. to 9 p.m. AE
♦ car park is open from 6 a.m. to 9 p.m. BE
Parkplatzkapazität, f
♦ parking lot capacity AE
♦ car park capacity BE
Parkplatzknappheit, f
♦ shortage of parking space
Parkplatzmangel, m (Knappheit)
→ Parkplatzknappheit
Parkplatzmangel, m (völliges Fehlen)
♦ lack of parking space
Parkplatz mieten (für 1 Auto)
Stellplatz mieten
♦ rent a parking place
♦ rent a parking space
♦ hire a parking place BE
♦ hire a parking space BE
Parkplatz nur für Gäste (Hinweisschild)
♦ Parking for patrons only (sign)
Parkplatzpersonal, n
♦ parking lot staff AE
♦ parking lot personnel AE
♦ car park staff BE
♦ car park personnel BE
Parkplatz reservieren (für 1 Auto)
Stellplatz reservieren
♦ reserve a parking place
♦ reserve a parking space
♦ reserve a parking lot AE
Parkplatzreservierung, f (für 1 Auto)
♦ parking space reservation
♦ reservation of a parking space
♦ parking place reservation
♦ reservation of a parking place
♦ reservation of a parking lot AE
Parkplatzsicherheit, f
♦ parking lot security AE
♦ car park security BE
Parkplatzsuche, f
♦ looking for a parking place
♦ looking for a parking space
♦ looking for a parking lot AE
♦ looking for a car park BE
Parkplatz suchen (für 1 Auto)
♦ look for a parking place
♦ look for a parking space
♦ look for a parking lot AE
Parkplatz suchen (für mehrere Autos)
♦ look for a car park BE
♦ look for a parking lot AE
Parkplatz vermieten (für 1 Auto)
Stellplatz vermieten
♦ rent (out) a parking place
♦ rent (out) a parking space
♦ rent a parking lot AE
♦ let a parking place (space) BE
♦ hire out a parking place (space) BE
Parkplatzwächter, m
Parkplatzaufseher, m
Parkwächter, m
♦ parking lot attendant AE
♦ car park attendant BE
♦ car park warden BE
♦ parking attendant
Parkproblem, n
♦ parking problem

Parkraum zur Verfügung stellen
Parkmöglichkeiten zur Verfügung stellen
♦ provide parking space
Parkscheibe, f
(für Autos)
♦ parking disc AE
♦ parking disk BE
♦ parking dial
Parkschein, m
(z.B. für Garage)
♦ parking ticket
Parksituation, f
♦ parking situation
Parksünde, f
→ Parkvergehen
Parksünder, m
♦ parking offender
Parktor, n
♦ park gate
Parkuhr, f
(für Autos)
♦ parking meter
♦ parkometer BE
Parkverbot, n
♦ prohibition of parking
♦ ban on parking
♦ parking ban
Parkverbotsbereich, m
Parkverbotszone, f
♦ no-parking zone
Parkverbotsschild, n
♦ no-parking sign
♦ 'no parking' sign
Parkvergehen, n
♦ parking offence
Parkvorschriften, f pl
♦ parking regulations pl
Parkvorschriften beachten
♦ obey the parking regulations
Parkwächter, m (Park)
♦ park warden
Parkwächter, m (Parkplatz)
→ Parkplatzwächter
Parkzeit, f
♦ parking time
Parkzeitüberschreitung, f
♦ overtime parking
♦ parking over the time limit
Parkzimmer, n
→ Zimmer zum Park
Parkzone, f
Parkbereich m
♦ parking zone
parlamentarische Bestuhlung, f
→ Parlamentsbestuhlung
parlamentarische Sitzordnung, f
→ Parlamentsbestuhlung
Parlamentsbestuhlung f
parlamentarische Bestuhlung, f
parlamentarische Sitzordnung, f
♦ Parliamentary-style seating
♦ Parliamentary seating
Parlamentsferien, pl
♦ Parliamentary recess
Parlamentsform, f
(Bestuhlung)
♦ Parliamentary style
Parmaschinken, m
♦ Parma ham
Parmesankäse, m
Parmesan, m

♦ Parmesan cheese
♦ Parmesan
Parteiabend, m
♦ party evening
♦ political party evening
Parteikonferenz, f
♦ party conference
Parteikongreß, m
Parteitag, m
♦ party congress
♦ party convention
Parteitag, m
♦ party convention *AE*
♦ convention *AE*
♦ party conference *BE*
♦ party congress
Parteitag abhalten
♦ hold a convention *AE*
Parteiveranstaltung, f
♦ party function
♦ party event
Parteiversammlung, f
♦ party meeting
♦ party rally
Parterre, n (Erdgeschoß)
Erdgeschoß, n
Parterregeschoß, n
♦ ground floor *BE*
♦ first floor *AE*
Parterre, n (Theater)
♦ rear stalls *BE pl*
♦ rear orchestra *AE*
Parterreappartement, n
Erdgeschoßappartement, n
♦ ground-floor apartment *BE*
♦ first-floor apartment *AE*
Parterregeschoß, n
→ Erdgeschoß
Parterrerestaurant, n
Erdgeschoßrestaurant, n
♦ ground-floor restaurant *BE*
♦ first-floor restaurant *AE*
Parterresuite, f
Erdgeschoßsuite, f
♦ ground-floor suite *BE*
♦ first-floor suite *AE*
Parterrewohnung, f
→ Erdgeschoßwohnung
Parterrezimmer, n
Erdgeschoßzimmer, n
♦ ground-floor room *BE*
♦ first-floor room *AE*
Partiechef, m
→ Abteilungskoch, Chef de partie
Partie Schach spielen
♦ play a game of chess
Partner, m
♦ partner
Partnerhotel, n
♦ partner hotel
Partnerschaft, f
♦ partnership
Partnerstadt, f (Großstadt)
(Städtepartnerschaft)
♦ twin city
Partnerstadt, f (kleine Stadt)
(Städtepartnerschaft)
♦ twin town
Party, f
♦ party

Party absagen
♦ cancel a party
Party arrangieren
♦ arrange a party
Partybesucher, m
♦ partygoer *AE*
♦ party-goer *BE*
♦ guest at a party
Partybungalow, m
♦ party bungalow
Party dauerte die ganze Nacht
Party ging die ganze Nacht
♦ party lasted the whole night
Partyessen, n
♦ party meal
Party findet statt
♦ party takes place
Partygag, m
♦ party gag
Partygänger, m
→ Festbesucher
Partygast, m
♦ party guest
Party geben zu Ehren von jm
Party geben zu js Ehren
♦ give a party in s.o.'s honor *AE*
♦ give a party in s.o.'s honour *BE*
Party geht die ganze Nacht durch
♦ party goes on all night
Partygeschäft n
♦ party business
Partygetränk, n
♦ party drink
Party Ihrer Träume, f
♦ party of your dreams
Partykeller, m
Fetenkeller, m
♦ basement party room
♦ party room in the basement
Party klang aus mit etw
Party endete mit etw
♦ party ended with s.th.
Party klingt harmonisch aus
♦ party is coming to a(n) harmonious end
Party koordinieren
♦ coordinate a party
Party machen
Fest machen
♦ have a party
Partymädchen, n
(Prostituierte)
Partygirl, n
♦ party girl
Partynacht, f
Festnacht, f
♦ party night
Party ohne Alkohol, f
♦ dry party
Partyplaner, m
→ Festplaner
Partyraum, m
Hobbyraum, m
♦ rumpus room *AE*
Partyräumlichkeiten, f pl
♦ party facilities *pl*
Partysalat, m
♦ party salad
Party schmeißen *coll*
♦ throw a party *coll*

Partyservice, m
♦ party service
♦ party catering service
Party stören
♦ disturb a party
Party veranstalten
Fest veranstalten
♦ organise a party
♦ organize a party
Partyverleih, m
♦ party rental *AE*
♦ party hire *BE*
Party war ein Besäufnis
♦ party was a booze-up *BE inform*
Partywein, m
♦ party wine
Party zu Ehren von jm, f
♦ party in honor of s.o. *AE*
♦ party in honour of s.o. *BE*
Party zum Kennenlernen, f
→ Kennenlernparty
Parvenu, m *FR*
♦ parvenu *FR*
Parzelle, f (Camping)
→ Stellplatz
Parzelle, f (generell)
♦ lot *AE*
♦ plot (of land) *BE*
♦ allotment
parzellieren
♦ divide into lots
parzellierter Stellplatz, m
→ markierter Stellplatz
Pascha, m
♦ pasha
Paß, m (Bergpaß)
♦ pass
Paß, m (Erlaubnisschein)
♦ pass
Paß, m (Reisepaß)
→ Reisepaß
Paßabfertigung, f
♦ passport procedure
Passage, f (Durchgang)
Durchgang, m
♦ passage
♦ passageway
Passage, f (Einkaufen)
→ Einkaufspassage
Passage, f (generell)
♦ passage
Passage, f (Überfahrt)
→ Überfahrt
Passagedienst, m (Fluggesellschaft)
♦ passenger service
Passagepreis, m
♦ passage fare
Passageverkehr, m
Fluggastverkehr, m
♦ passenger traffic
Passagevertrag, m
♦ contract of passage
Passagier, m
Fahrgast, m
Fluggast, m
♦ passenger
Passagierabfertigung, f (Behörde)
♦ passenger clearance
Passagierabfertigung, f (nicht Behörde)
♦ passenger handling
♦ passenger processing

Passagierabfertigungsdienst

Passagierabfertigungsdienst, m
♦ passenger-handling service
Passagierabfertigungshalle, f
(Flughafen)
♦ passenger terminal
Passagierabteil, n
Fahrgastabteil, n
♦ passenger compartment
Passagieraufkommen, n
♦ passenger volume
Passagier befördern
♦ convey a passenger
♦ carry a passenger
♦ transport a passenger
Passagierbereich, m
Fahrgastbereich, m
♦ passenger area
passagierbezogen, adj
♦ passenger-related, adj
passagierbezogene Kosten, pl
♦ passenger-related costs pl
♦ passenger-related cost
Passagiercoupon, m
Fluggastcoupon, m
♦ passenger coupon
Passagierdampfer, m
♦ passenger steamer
♦ passenger liner
Passagierdeck, n
♦ passenger deck
Passagierdienst, m
Passagierservice, m
♦ passenger service
Passagier dritter Klasse, m
Passagier in der dritten Klasse, m
♦ third-class passenger
Passagierdüsenflugzeug, m
Passagierjet, m
♦ passenger jet
Passagiere befördern über den Atlantik
♦ carry passengers across the Atlantic
♦ transport passengers across the Atlantic
Passagier erster Klasse, m
Passagier in der ersten Klasse, m
Erste-Klasse-Passagier, m
Erster-Klasse-Passagier, m
♦ first-class passenger
Passagierflug, m
♦ passenger flight
Passagierflugzeug, n
♦ passenger plane
♦ passenger aircraft
Passagiergepäck, n
♦ passenger('s) baggage AE
♦ passengers' baggage AE
♦ passenger('s) luggage BE
♦ passengers' luggage BE
Passagierhafen, m
♦ passenger port
♦ passenger harbor AE
♦ passenger harbour BE
Passagierkabine, f
♦ passenger cabin
Passagierkapazität, f
♦ passenger capacity
Passagierkilometer, m
Fluggastkilometer, m
♦ passenger-kilometer AE
♦ passenger-kilometre BE
Passagierkomfort, m
♦ passenger comfort

Passagierliste, f
♦ list of passengers
♦ passenger list
♦ waybill obs
Passagiermarkt, m
♦ passenger market
Passagier-Meile, f
♦ passenger-mile
Passagierraum, m
Passagierfläche, f
♦ passenger space
Passagierreise, f
♦ passenger journey
♦ passenger trip
♦ passenger tour
Passagierrückgang, m
♦ decline in passengers
♦ passenger decline
Passagierschiff, n
♦ passenger ship
♦ passenger vessel
♦ passenger liner
Passagierseehafen, m
♦ sea passenger port
♦ sea passenger harbor AE
♦ sea passenger harbour BE
Passagiersitz, m
Fahrgastsitz, m
Fluggastsitz, m
♦ passenger seat
Passagier-Tonnenkilometer, m
Fluggast-Tonnenkilometer, m
♦ passenger ton-kilometre BE
Passagierunterhaltung, f
♦ passenger entertainment
Passagierunterkunft, f
♦ passenger accommodation
Passagierverkehr, m
Fluggastverkehr, m
♦ passenger traffic
Passagierverpflegung, f
♦ passenger catering
Passagierversicherung, f
(Flugverkehr)
♦ personal insurance
Passagierzahl, f
Fahrgastzahl, f
Fluggastzahl, f
Zahl der Passagiere, f
Zahl der Fahrgäste, f
♦ number of passengers
♦ passenger number
Passagierzufriedenheit, f
Fahrgastzufriedenheit, f
Fluggastzufriedenheit, f
♦ passenger satisfaction
Passagier zweiter Klasse, m
Passagier in der zweiten Klasse, m
♦ second-class passenger
Paßamt, n
♦ passport office
Passant, m (Besucher)
zufälliger Besucher, m
♦ chance visitor
Passant, m (Kunde)
unangemeldeter Gast, m
Laufkunde, m
Zufallsgast, m
♦ chance guest
♦ walk-in (guest)
♦ chance customer

♦ transient (guest)
♦ chance
Passant, m (Vorbeigehender)
♦ passerby AE
♦ passer-by BE
Passantenabendessen, n (Dinner)
♦ chance dinner
Passantenabendessen, n (Supper)
♦ chance supper
Passantenankunft f
♦ chance arrival
♦ arrival of a chance guest
Passantenbetrieb m
♦ transient establishment
♦ transient hotel
♦ transient restaurant
Passantenessen, n
♦ chance meal
Passantenfrühstück, n
♦ chance breakfast
Passantengeschäft, n
♦ walk-in business
♦ chance business
Passantenhotel, n
Durchgangshotel, n
Hotel für Durchreisende, n
♦ transient hotel
Passantenkaffee, m
♦ chance coffee
Passantenmittagessen, n
♦ chance luncheon
♦ chance lunch
Passantenrestaurant n
♦ transient restaurant
Passantentee, m
♦ chance tea
Passantenumsatz, m
♦ chance sales pl
♦ chance turnover
Passantenunterkunft, f
♦ transient accommodation
♦ transient lodging AE
Passantenverkauf, m
Verkauf an einen Passanten, m
♦ chance sale
Passantenzimmer, n
♦ transient room
Paß ausstellen
Reisepaß ausstellen
♦ issue a passport
♦ make out a passport
Paß beantragen
→ Reisepaß beantragen
Paßbild, n
♦ passport photograph
Paßbüro, n
→ Paßamt
passend, adj
→ geeignet
passenden Austragungsort finden für etw
passenden Tagungsort finden für etw
passenden Ort finden für etw
♦ find a suitable venue for s.th.
passenden Platz finden für etw
♦ find a suitable site for s.th.
passender Rahmen, m
entsprechender Rahmen, m
angemessener Rahmen, m
♦ appropriate setting

passender Rahmen sein für etw
entsprechender Rahmen sein für etw
* be the appropriate setting for s.th.

passende Unterkunft finden
* find suitable accommodation

passen in das Programm
* fit into the program *AE*
* fit into the programme *BE*

Passepartout, m
Dietrich, m
* passepartout
* skeleton key

Paßhöhe, f
* altitude of a pass

passieren etw
→ vorbeifahren

Passiermaschine, f
* food mill

Passierschein, m
* permit
* pass

Passiersieb, n
* strainer
* sieve

Paßinhaber, m (Reisepaß)
* passport holder
* holder of a passport

Passionsfrucht, f
Maracuja, f
* passion fruit *AE*
* passion-fruit *BE*
* granadilla

Passionsfruchteis, n
* passion-fruit ice cream *AE*
* passion-fruit ice-cream *BE*

Passionsfruchtsorbet, n
* passion-fruit sorbet

Passionsspiel, n
(z.B. in Oberammergau)
Passionsspiele, n pl
* Passion Play

Paß ist abgelaufen
* passport has expired

Paß ist gesperrt
Bergpaß ist für Reisende gesperrt
* pass is closed
* pass is closed to travellers *BE*
* pass is closed to travelers *AE*

Paß ist gültig
* passport is valid

Paß ist offen
Bergpaß ist geöffnet
* pass is open

Passiva, n pl
(Bilanz)
* liabilities pl

passive Dienstleistungen, f pl
unsichtbare Exporte m pl
unsichtbare Ausfuhren f pl
* invisible exports pl

Passivseite, f
(Bilanz)
* liabilities side
* debit side

Paßkontrolle, f
* passport control
* passport check
* passport inspection

Paß kontrollieren
Paß überprüfen
* inspect a passport

Paßnummer f
* passport number
* number of a passport

Paßpflicht, f
Paßzwang, m
* obligation to obtain a passport
* obligatory passport

Paß prüfen
* check the passport
* examine a passport

Paßschalter, m
* passport counter

Paß schützen (Bergpaß)
Bergpaß schützen
* protect a pass

Paßstelle, f
* passport agency

Paß stempeln
Paß abstempeln
* stamp a passport

Paßstraße, f
* pass road
* road leading over a pass
* road leading across a pass

Paß überqueren
* cross a pass

Paß ungültig erklären
Paß für ungültig erklären
* invalidate a passport

Paß verlängern
* renew a passport

Paß verlängern lassen
* have one's passport renewed

Paßvorschriften, f pl
* passport regulations pl

Paß vorzeigen
* show one's passport

Paßwort, n
(EDV)
* password

Paßzwang, m
→ Paßpflicht

Pastagericht, n
→ Nudelgericht

Paste, f
* paste

Pastetchen, n
* patty

Pastete, f (generell)
* pie

Pastete, f (Leber)
Leberpastete, f
* pâté

Pastetenkoch, m
Konditor, m
* pastrycook *AE*
* pastryman *AE*
* pastry-cook *BE*

Pastetenschüssel, f
* pie dish

pasteurisieren etw
(Milch)
* pasteurise s.th.
* pasteurize s.th.

pasteurisiert, adj
* pasteurised, adj
* pasteurized, adj

pasteurisierte Milch, f
* pasteurised milk
* pasteurized milk

Pasteurisierung, f
* pasteurisation
* pasteurization

Pasteurisierungsapparat, m
* pasteuriser
* pasteurizer

Pastinake, f
Pastinak, m
* parsnip

Pastinakensalat, m
* parsnip salad

Pastis, m *FR*
* Pastis *FR*

Patagonien
* Patagonia

patagonisch, adj
* Patagonian, adj

Paternoster, m
(Fahrstuhl)
* paternoster

Paternosteraufzug, m
Paternosterfahrstuhl, m
Paternosterlift, m
* paternoster elevator *AE*
* paternoster lift *BE*

Paternosterfahrstuhl, m
→ Paternosteraufzug

Paternosterlift, m
→ Paternosteraufzug

Patience, f
(Spiel)
* patience *BE*
* solitaire *AE*

Patience legen
* play patience *BE*
* play solitaire *AE*

Patient, m
* patient

Patio, m *SPAN*
(Innenhof eines spanischen Hauses)
* patio *SPAN*

Patisserie, f (Feingebäck)
* patisserie
* fine confectionary *AE*
* fine confectionery

Patisserie, f (Konditorei)
→ Konditorei

Patisserieabteilung, f
Konditoreiabteilung, f
* pastry department

Patisseriewagen, m
(im Restaurant)
* pastry cart *AE*
* pastry trolley *BE*

Pâtissier, m *FR*
* pâtissier *FR*

Patrizierhaus, n
* patrician house

patrouillieren
* patrol
* go on patrol

pauschal, adv
(Preis)
* inclusive, adv
* all-inclusive, adv

Pauschalangebot, n
* inclusive offer
* package offer

Pauschalarrangement, n
Pauschalvereinbarung, f
* package arrangement

Pauschalaufenthalt

- ◆ inclusive arrangement
- ◆ package deal
- ◆ inclusive terms *pl*
- ◆ package terms *pl*

Pauschalaufenthalt, m
- ◆ stay on inclusive terms
- ◆ stay on package terms

Pauschalausflug, m
- ◆ package excursion

Pauschalbasis, f
- ◆ flat-rate basis
- ◆ lump-sum basis

Pauschalbehandlung, f
- ◆ inclusive treatment

Pauschalbeitrag m
- ◆ flat-rate contribution

pauschal berechnet, adj (einheitlich)
- ◆ charged at a flat rate, adj

Pauschalbetrag, m
- ◆ flat-rate price

Pauschalcampingurlaub, m
 Campingpauschalurlaub, m
- ◆ inclusive camping holiday *BE*
- ◆ inclusive camping vacation *AE*

Pauschale, f
 Pauschalpreis, m
- ◆ inclusive rate
- ◆ inclusive price
- ◆ package rate
- ◆ package price
- ◆ inclusive terms *pl*

Pauschale beinhaltet vier Behandlungen
- ◆ package includes four treatments

Pauschale für Übernachtung mit Frühstück, f
- ◆ bed and breakfast package

pauschale Preiserhöhung f
- ◆ overall increase in prices

Pauschale pro Person und Woche, f
- ◆ inclusive rate per person per week
- ◆ inclusive price per person per week

Pauschalfahrpreis, m (einheitlich)
- ◆ flat fare

Pauschalfahrpreis, m (inklusiv)
- ◆ inclusive fare
- ◆ all-inclusive fare

Pauschalfahrt, f
- ◆ inclusive trip
- ◆ inclusive journey
- ◆ all-expense trip *AE*
- ◆ all-in trip *BE*

Pauschalferien, pl
 Pauschalurlaub, m
- ◆ package holiday *BE*
- ◆ package vacation *AE*
- ◆ inclusive holiday *BE*
- ◆ inclusive vacation *AE*

Pauschalferiengast, m
 Pauschalurlauber, m
- ◆ package holidaymaker *BE*
- ◆ package vacationer *AE*

Pauschalferienmarke, f
 Pauschalurlaubsmarke, f
- ◆ package holiday brand *BE*
- ◆ package vacation brand *AE*

Pauschalferienmarkt, m
 Pauschalurlaubsmarkt, m
- ◆ package holiday market *BE*
- ◆ inclusive holiday market *BE*
- ◆ package vacation market *AE*
- ◆ inclusive vacation market *AE*

Pauschalferienpreis, m
 Pauschalurlaubspreis, m
- ◆ package holiday price *BE*
- ◆ inclusive holiday price *BE*
- ◆ package vacation price *AE*
- ◆ inclusive vacation price *AE*

Pauschalfluggeschäft, n
- ◆ air package business

Pauschalflugmarkt, m
- ◆ air package market

Pauschalflugreise, f
- ◆ air-inclusive tour
- ◆ flight-inclusive tour

Pauschalgast, m
- ◆ package guest
- ◆ guest on inclusive terms

Pauschalgebühr, f (einheitlich)
- ◆ flat-rate fee
- ◆ flat-rate charge

Pauschalgebühr, f (inklusiv)
- ◆ inclusive charge
- ◆ inclusive fee
- ◆ comprehensive charge

Pauschalgruppe, f
 → Pauschalreisegruppe

Pauschalhochzeitsurlaub, m
- ◆ wedding package vacation *AE*
- ◆ wedding package holiday *BE*

Pauschalhotel, n
- ◆ package hotel
- ◆ all-inclusive hotel

Pauschalkonzept, n
- ◆ package scheme

Pauschalkosten, pl
- ◆ inclusive costs *pl*
- ◆ inclusive cost

Pauschalkunde, m
- ◆ package customer
- ◆ package client

Pauschalkur, f
- ◆ course of treatment on inclusive terms

Pauschalkurs, m
 Pauschallehrgang, m
- ◆ package course

Pauschalkurzurlaub, m
- ◆ inclusive break
- ◆ package break

Pauschalleistung, f
- ◆ inclusive service
- ◆ package service

Pauschalmahlzeit, f
 (zum Pauschalpreis)
 Pauschalessen, n
- ◆ inclusive-price meal
- ◆ inclusive meal

Pauschalmarkt, m
- ◆ package market

Pauschalmenü, n
 (zum Pauschalpreis)
- ◆ inclusive-price menu
- ◆ inclusive menu

Pauschalofferte, f
 → Pauschalangebot

Pauschalpreis, m (Fahrpreis)
 → Pauschalfahrpreis

Pauschalpreis, m (generell)
 Pauschale, f
- ◆ package price
- ◆ package rate
- ◆ inclusive price
- ◆ inclusive rate

Pauschalpreis pro Monat, m
- ◆ inclusive rate per month
- ◆ inclusive price per month
- ◆ package rate per month
- ◆ package price per month

Pauschalpreis pro Person, m
- ◆ inclusive rate per person
- ◆ inclusive price per person
- ◆ package rate per person
- ◆ package price per person

Pauschalpreis pro Person pro Tag, m
- ◆ inclusive rate per person per day
- ◆ inclusive price per person per day
- ◆ package rate per person per day
- ◆ package price per person per day

Pauschalpreis pro Tag, m
- ◆ inclusive rate per day
- ◆ inclusive price per day
- ◆ package rate per day
- ◆ package price per day

Pauschalpreis pro Woche, m
 Wochenpauschalpreis, m
 Wochenpauschale, f
- ◆ inclusive rate per week
- ◆ inclusive price per week
- ◆ package rate per week
- ◆ package price per week

Pauschalpreis umfaßt etw
- ◆ inclusive price covers s.th.
- ◆ inclusive rate covers s.th.

Pauschalprogramm, n
- ◆ package program *AE*
- ◆ package programme *BE*

Pauschalreise, f
- ◆ package tour
- ◆ inclusive tour
- ◆ packaged tour
- ◆ package

Pauschalreiseanbieter, m
- ◆ package-tour supplier
- ◆ package-tour provider

Pauschalreiseangebot, n
- ◆ package tours on offer *pl*
- ◆ package tours available *pl*
- ◆ range of inclusive tours (on offer)
- ◆ range of package tours (on offer)

Pauschalreisebeschreibung, f
- ◆ description of a package tour
- ◆ package tour description

Pauschalreisebestandteil, m
- ◆ package-tour component
- ◆ inclusive-tour component

Pauschalreisebestimmungen, f pl
- ◆ package travel regulations *pl*

Pauschalreise buchen
- ◆ book a package tour

Pauschalreiseeinnahmen, f pl
- ◆ package-tour receipts *pl*
- ◆ package-tour income
- ◆ package-tour takings
- ◆ inclusive-tour receipts *pl*

Pauschalreise findet statt
- ◆ package tour takes place
- ◆ inclusive tour takes place

Pauschalreisegast m
- ◆ inclusive-tour guest
- ◆ IT guest
- ◆ package-tour guest
- ◆ package guest

Pauschalreisegesetzgebung, f
- ◆ package-tour legislation

Pause für den Tee

Pauschalreisegewerbe, n
♦ package-tour trade
Pauschalreisegruppe f
♦ package group
♦ package tour
Pauschalreiseindustrie, f
♦ package tour industry
♦ package travel industry
Pauschalreise kaufen
♦ buy a package tour
♦ buy an inclusive tour
Pauschalreisekonzept, n
♦ package-tour scheme
Pauschalreisemarkt m
♦ package-tour market
♦ inclusive-tour market
♦ IT market
Pauschalreisen, n
♦ package-tour travel
♦ inclusive-tour travel
Pauschalreisender, m
♦ inclusive-tour traveler AE
♦ inclusive-tour traveller BE
♦ IT travel(l)er
♦ package tourist
♦ inclusive travel(l)er
Pauschalreisepreis, m
♦ package-tour price
♦ inclusive-tour price
♦ price of a package tour
♦ price of an inclusive tour
Pauschalreiseprodukt, n
♦ package-tour product
♦ inclusive-tour product
Pauschalreiseprogramm, n
♦ package-tour program AE
♦ package-tour programme BE
♦ inclusive-tour program AE
♦ inclusive-tour programme BE
Pauschalreiseprospekt, m
♦ package-tour brochure
♦ inclusive-tour brochure
Pauschalreisesektor, m
♦ package-tour sector
♦ inclusive-tour sector
♦ IT sector
Pauschalreiseumsatz, m
♦ package-tour turnover
♦ package-tour sales pl
♦ inclusive-tour turnover
♦ inclusive-tour sales pl
Pauschalreiseurlauber, m
♦ inclusive-tour vacationer AE
♦ IT vacationer AE
♦ package-tour vacationer AE
♦ inclusive-tour holidaymaker BE
♦ IT holidaymaker BE
Pauschalreiseveranstalter, m
♦ package-tour operator
♦ inclusive-tour operator
♦ package-tour organiser
♦ travel house AE
Pauschalreiseveranstaltung, f
♦ package-tour operation
♦ package-tour operating
Pauschalreise verkaufen
♦ sell a package tour
♦ sell an inclusive tour
Pauschalreiseverkehr, m
♦ package-tour traffic
♦ inclusive-tour traffic

Pauschalreisevertrag, m
♦ package-tour contract
♦ package travel contract
♦ inclusive-tour contract
♦ IT contract
Pauschalreise zusammenstellen
♦ put together a package tour
♦ put together an inclusive tour
♦ assemble a package tour
♦ assemble an inclusive tour
Pauschaltarif, m
♦ inclusive tariff
♦ flat-rate tariff
♦ inclusive terms pl
♦ package terms pl
Pauschaltourismus, m
♦ package tourism
♦ inclusive tourism
Pauschaltourist, m
Pauschaltouristin, f
♦ package tourist
♦ inclusive tourist
Pauschalurlaub, m
Pauschalferien, pl
♦ package vacation AE
♦ inclusive vacation AE
♦ package holiday BE
♦ inclusive holiday BE
Pauschalurlauber, m
Pauschalferiengast, m
♦ package vacationer AE
♦ package holidaymaker BE
Pauschalurlaub kaufen
Pauschalferien kaufen
♦ buy a package vacation AE
♦ buy a package holiday BE
Pauschalurlaub machen
♦ take a package vacation AE
♦ take a package holiday BE
Pauschalurlaubsanbieter, m
Pauschalferienanbieter, m
♦ supplier of package vacations AE
♦ supplier of package holidays BE
Pauschalurlaubsangebot, n (Palette)
♦ range of package vacations AE
♦ range of package holidays BE
Pauschalurlaubsbuchung, f
♦ package vacation reservation AE
♦ package holiday booking BE
Pauschalurlaubsgeschäft, n
♦ package vacation business AE
♦ package holiday business BE
Pauschalurlaubsindustrie, f
♦ package vacation industry AE
♦ package holiday industry BE
Pauschalurlaubsmarke, f
Pauschalferienmarke, f
♦ package vacation brand AE
♦ package holiday brand BE
Pauschalurlaubsmarke einführen
♦ launch a package holiday brand BE
♦ launch a package vacation brand Ae
Pauschalurlaubsmarkt, m
Pauschalferienmarkt, m
♦ package vacation market AE
♦ inclusive vacation market AE
♦ package holiday market BE
♦ inclusive holiday market BE
Pauschalurlaubspreis, m
Pauschalferienpreis, m
♦ package vacation price AE

♦ inclusive vacation price AE
♦ package holiday price BE
♦ inclusive holiday price BE
Pauschalurlaubsumsatz, m
Pauschalferienumsatz, m
♦ package vacation sales AE pl
♦ package vacation turnover AE
♦ package holiday sales BE pl
♦ package holiday turnover BE
Pauschalurlaubsveranstaltung, f
♦ package vacation operation AE
♦ package vacation operating AE
♦ package holiday operation BE
♦ package holiday operating BE
Pauschalurlaub verkaufen (an jn)
♦ sell a package vacation (to s.o.) AE
♦ sell an inclusive vacation (to s.o.) AE
♦ sell a package holiday (to s.o.) BE
♦ sell an inclusive holiday (to s.o.) BE
Pauschalveranstalter, m
♦ package operator
♦ inclusive-tour operator
Pauschalvereinbarung, f
Pauschalarrangement, n
♦ package deal
♦ package arrangement
Pauschalverpflegungsleistung, f
♦ inclusive catering service
♦ inclusive meal arrangement
Pauschalvertrag, m
♦ package contract
Pauschalweltreise, f
♦ world package tour
♦ round-the-world package tour
Pauschalwoche, f
♦ package week
♦ inclusive week
Pauschalwochenende, n
♦ package weekend
♦ inclusive weekend
Pauschalwochenendkurzurlaub, m
♦ inclusive weekend break
♦ package weekend break
Pauschalzahlung, f
(für mehrere kleine Summen)
♦ lump-sum payment
♦ lump sum
Pause, f (Frühstück etc.)
♦ break
Pause, f (Halt)
♦ stop
Pause, f (Kino)
♦ intermission AE
Pause, f (Rede, Gespräch)
♦ pause
Pause, f (Ruhepause)
♦ rest
Pause, f (Theater, Veranstaltung)
♦ interval
Pause brauchen
♦ need a break
Pause für das Abendessen, f (Dinner)
♦ break for dinner
Pause für das Abendessen, n (Supper)
♦ break for supper
Pause für das Frühstück, f
♦ break for breakfast
Pause für das Mittagessen, f
♦ break for lunch
Pause für den Tee, f
♦ break for tea

Pause machen (Frühstück etc.)

Pause machen (Frühstück etc.)
♦ take a break
Pause machen für eine Tasse Kaffee
♦ pause for a cup of coffee
Pause machen für eine Tasse Tee
♦ pause for a cup of tea
Pause machen (für etw)
♦ pause (for s.th.)
Pause machen für Kaffee und Kuchen
♦ pause for coffee and cake
Pause machen (Halt)
♦ make a stop
♦ stop
Pause machen (Ruhepause)
♦ have a rest
♦ take a rest
♦ rest
Pausenbewirtung, f
♦ refreshments during the break pl
♦ catering in the interval
♦ foodservice in the interval AE
♦ interval catering
♦ interval foodservice AE
Pausenbrot, n
♦ sandwich eaten in the break
♦ breaktime snack
Pausenbüfett, n
♦ buffet in the interval
♦ buffet in the break
Pausenfüller, m
♦ filler
Pausenraum, m
(z.B. bei Konferenz)
→ Aufenthaltsraumm
Pause von 15 Minuten, f
♦ break of 15 minutes
♦ interval of 15 minutes
♦ stop of 15 minutes
♦ intermission of 15 minutes
Pavillon, m
♦ pavilion
Pavillonrestaurant, n
♦ pavilion restaurant
Pax, m/f
♦ pax sg + pl
Pay-TV, n
♦ pay TV
♦ pay television
Pazifik, m
Pazifischer Ozean, m
♦ Pacific, the
♦ Pacific Ocean, the
Pazifikinsel, f
♦ Pacific island
Pazifikkreuzfahrt, f
♦ Pacific cruise
Pazifikküste, f
♦ Pacific coast
Pazifikstrand, m
♦ Pacific beach
Pazifikufer, n
♦ Pacific shore
♦ shore of the Pacific
Pazifischer Ozean, m
Pazifik, m
♦ Pacific Ocean, the
♦ Pacific, the
PC, m
Personalcomputer, m
♦ PC
♦ personal computer

PCO, m
Professional Conference Organiser, m
♦ PCO
♦ professional conference organiser
Peak District, m
♦ Peak District, the
Peak Nationalpark, m
♦ Peak National Park, the
Peak Season, f
→ Spitzensaison, Hauptsaison
Pech haben
♦ be unlucky
♦ be out of luck
Pedalo, n
→ Tretboot
Pedant, m
♦ pedant
Pedanterie, f
♦ pedantry
pedantisch, adj
♦ pedantic, adj
Pediküre, f (Aktivität)
Fußpflege, f
♦ pedicure
♦ chiropody
♦ podiatry AE
Pediküre, f (Person)
Fußpflegerin, f
♦ chiropodist
♦ podiatrist AE
Pediküre machen lassen sich
♦ have a pedicure
pellen (etw)
→ schälen
Pellkartoffeln, f pl
♦ jacket potatoes pl
♦ potatoes boiled in their skin pl
♦ potatoes boiled in their jackets pl
Peloponnes, m/f
♦ Peloponnesus, the
♦ Peloponesos, the
♦ Peloponnese, the
Pelota, f
(baskisches Ballspiel)
♦ pelota
Pelota spielen
♦ play pelota
Pelzgeschäft, n
♦ fur store AE
♦ fur shop BE
Pelzjäger, m
♦ fur trapper
Pelzmantel, m
♦ fur coat
Pelzmütze, f
♦ fur cap
Pelzstiefel, m
♦ fur boot
Pemmikan, m
♦ pemmican
♦ pemican
Penaten, pl
(altrömische Hausgötter)
♦ Penates pl
♦ penates pl
Pendelbus, m
♦ shuttle bus
Pendelbusdienst, m
Pendelbusverbindung, f
Pendelbusverkehr, m

Pendelbusservice, m
♦ shuttle-bus service
Pendelbusservice, m
→ Pendelbusdienst
Pendelbusverbindung, f
♦ shuttle-bus connection
♦ shuttle-bus service
Pendelbusverkehr, m
♦ shuttle-bus traffic
♦ shuttle-bus service
Pendeldienst, m
(bei Transportmitteln)
Pendelverbindung f
Pendelverkehr m
♦ shuttle service
Pendeldienst betreiben zwischen A und B
♦ operate a shuttle service between A and B
Pendeldienst zwischen A und B, m
♦ shuttle service between A and B
Pendelflug, m
♦ shuttle flight
pendeln (Fahrzeug)
♦ shuttle
pendeln (Person)
♦ commute
pendeln zwischen A und B (Fahrzeug)
♦ shuttle between A and B
Pendeltür, f
♦ swing door
Pendelverbindung, f
♦ shuttle connection
♦ shuttle service
Pendelverkehr, m
♦ shuttle traffic
♦ shuttle service
Pendelverkehr anbieten
♦ offer a shuttle service
Pendelzug, m
♦ shuttle train
Pendler, m
♦ commuter
Pendlerbus, m
♦ commuter bus
Pendlerdienst, m
Pendlerverkehr, m
♦ commuter service
Pendlerflug, m
♦ commuter flight
Pendlerreisen, n
Pendlerreiseverkehr, m
Pendlerverkehr, m
♦ commuter travel
Pendlerstrecke, f
Pendlerroute, f
♦ commuter route
Pendlerzug, m
♦ commuter train
Pennbruder, m sl
Penner, m sl
♦ vagrant
♦ vag AE sl
♦ bum AE sl
♦ dosser BE sl
Penne, f sl
(billige Herberge)
♦ flophouse AE
♦ doss-house BE
♦ kip BE sl
pennen sl
♦ kip (down) sl

♦ doss (down) BE
♦ snooze coll
pennen auf dem Boden
   niederlegen sich auf den Boden
   ♦ **doss down on the floor** BE
pennen auf dem Strand
   ♦ **kip on the beach**
Penner, m
   Pennbruder, m
   Tippelbruder, m
   Landstreicher, m
   Herumtreiber, m
   ♦ **bum** AE sl
   ♦ **dosser** BE sl
   ♦ **hobo** AE sl
   ♦ **tramp**
   ♦ **vagabond**
Penninisches Gebirge, n
   ♦ **Pennines, the** pl
Pennsylvanien
   ♦ **Pennsylvania**
pennsylvanisch, adj
   ♦ **Pennsylvanian, adj**
Penny, m
   ♦ **penny**
Pension, f (Betriebstyp)
   (bes. für Urlaubs- und Feriengäste)
   ♦ **private hotel**
   ♦ **guesthouse** AE
   ♦ **guest-house** BE
   ♦ **boardinghouse** AE
   ♦ **boarding-house** BE
Pension, f (Rente)
   ♦ **pension**
Pension, f (Unterkunft und Verpflegung)
   → Unterkunft und Verpflegung
Pensionär, m
   Pensionist, m ÖST/SCHW
   Rentner, m
   ♦ **O.A.P.**
   ♦ **old-age pensioner**
   ♦ **pensioner**
Pensionat, n
   → Internat
Pension führen
   Pension leiten
   ♦ **run a private hotel**
   ♦ **run a guesthouse** AE
   ♦ **run a guest-house** BE
   ♦ **run a boardinghouse** AE
   ♦ **run a boarding-house** BE
Pensionierungsfest, n
   (bei Erreichen des Rentenalters)
   ♦ **retirement party**
Pensionist m ÖST
   → Pensionär
Pensionsarrangement, n
   → Pensionsvereinbarung
Pensionsbereich, m
   Pensionssektor, m
   ♦ **private-hotel sector**
   ♦ **guesthouse sector** AE
   ♦ **guest-house sector** BE
   ♦ **boardinghouse sector** AE
   ♦ **boarding-house sector** BE
Pensionsbesitzer, m
   ♦ **owner of a private hotel**
   ♦ **owner of a guesthouse** AE
   ♦ **owner of a guest-house** BE
   ♦ **owner of a boardinghouse** AE
   ♦ **owner of a boarding-house** BE

Pensionsbetrieb, m
   ♦ **boarding establishment**
Pensionsführer, m
   ♦ **guesthouse guide** AE
   ♦ **guest-house guide** BE
Pensionsgast, m (in Fremdenpension)
   ♦ **guest staying at a private hotel**
   ♦ **guest staying at a guesthouse** AE
   ♦ **guest staying at a guest-house** BE
   ♦ **guest staying at a boardinghouse** AE
   ♦ **guest staying at a boarding-house** BE
Pensionsgast, m (Verpflegung)
   Verpflegungsgast, m
   ♦ **boarder**
   ♦ **food and beverage guest**
   ♦ **f&b guest**
Pensionsgäste aufnehmen
   ♦ **take in boarders**
Pensionsgeschäft, n
   ♦ **private hotel business**
   ♦ **boardinghouse business** AE
   ♦ **boarding-house business** BE
   ♦ **guesthouse business** AE
   ♦ **guest-house business** BE
Pensionskasse, f (Rentner)
   ♦ **pension fund**
Pensionskosten, pl
   ♦ **boarding costs** pl
   ♦ **cost of board**
Pensionsleistung, f (in einer Pension)
   ♦ **private-hotel service**
Pensionsliste, f
   (Rezeption)
   ♦ **list of residents**
   ♦ **list of boarders**
Pensionsmenü, n
   Hausgästemenü, n
   Stammessen, n
   ♦ **residents' menu**
Pensionspreis, m
   ♦ **price for board and lodging**
   ♦ **charge for board and lodging**
   ♦ **en pension terms** pl
   ♦ **board**
Pensionspreis, m (in Pension)
   ♦ **guesthouse price** AE
   ♦ **guesthouse rate** AE
   ♦ **guest-house price** BE
   ♦ **guest-house rate** BE
Pensionsunterkunft, f (in Pension)
   ♦ **guesthouse accommodation** AE
   ♦ **guest-house accommodation** BE
   ♦ **boardinghouse accommodation** AE
   ♦ **boarding-house accommodation** BE
Pensionsurlaub, m
   ♦ **guesthouse vacation** AE
   ♦ **guest-house holiday** BE
   ♦ **boardinghouse vacation** AE
   ♦ **boarding-house holiday** BE
Pensionsvereinbarung, f
   Pensionsarrangement, n
   Vollpensionsvereinbarung, f
   Vollpensionsarrangement, n
   ♦ **en-pension arrangement**
   ♦ **full-board terms** pl
Pensionswirtin, f
   Wirtin einer Pension, f
   ♦ **landlady of a boardinghouse** AE
   ♦ **landlady of a boarding-house** BE
   ♦ **landlady of a guesthouse** AE
   ♦ **landlady of a guest-house** BE

Penthouse, n
   ♦ **penthouse**
Penthouseappartement, n
   Dachterrassenappartement, n
   ♦ **penthouse apartment**
Penthousegrillrestaurant, n
   ♦ **penthouse grillroom** AE
   ♦ **penthouse grill-room** BE
Penthouse mit drei Schlafzimmern, n
   ♦ **three-bedroom penthouse**
Penthouse mit einem Schlafzimmer, n
   ♦ **one-bedroom penthouse**
Penthouse mit fünf Schlafzimmern, n
   ♦ **five-bedroom penthouse**
Penthouse mit vier Schlafzimmern, n
   ♦ **four-bedroom penthouse**
Penthouse mit zwei Schlafzimmern, n
   ♦ **two-bedroom penthouse**
Penthouserestaurant n
   Dachterrassenrestaurant n
   ♦ **penthouse restaurant**
Penthousesuite f
   Dachterrassensuite f
   ♦ **penthouse suite**
Penthousewohnung, f
   Dachterrassenwohnung, f
   ♦ **penthouse flat** BE
   ♦ **penthouse apartment** AE
Penthousezimmer n
   Dachterrassenzimmer n
   ♦ **penthouse room**
per Adresse
   c/o
   ♦ **care of**
   ♦ **c/o**
per Anhalter reisen
   → trampen
per diem
   → pro Tag
per Einschreiben
   ♦ **by registered mail** AE
   ♦ **by registered post** BE
perfekt, adj
   ♦ **perfect, adj**
perfekt ablaufen
   ♦ **run perfectly**
perfekte Akustik, f
   ♦ **perfect acoustics** pl
perfekte Akustik haben
   ♦ **have perfect acoustics**
perfekte Atmosphäre, f
   ♦ **perfect atmosphere**
perfekte Atmosphäre bieten
   ♦ **provide the perfect atmosphere**
perfekten Rahmen bieten für etw
   ♦ **provide the perfect setting for s.th.**
perfekten Service bieten
   ♦ **provide perfect service**
perfekten Service erwarten
   ♦ **expect perfect service**
perfekten Urlaub bereiten jm
   perfekte Ferien jm bereiten
   ♦ **provide a perfect vacation for s.o.** AE
   ♦ **provide a perfect holiday for s.o.** BE
perfekter Rahmen, m
   ♦ **perfect setting**
perfekter Service, m
   ♦ **perfect service**
perfekter Urlaub, m
   perfekte Ferien, pl

perfekte Urlaubsumgebung

- ◆ perfect vacation *AE*
- ◆ perfect holiday *BE*

perfekte Urlaubsumgebung, f
perfekte Ferienumgebung, f
- ◆ perfect vacation setting *AE*
- ◆ perfect holiday setting *BE*

perfekt möbliert, adj
- ◆ perfectly furnished, adj

perfekt möbliertes Zimmer, n
- ◆ perfectly furnished room

perfekt servieren etw
- ◆ serve s.th. perfectly
- ◆ serve s.th. in a perfect way

Pergola, f
Laubengang, m
- ◆ pergola

Periode, f
Zeitraum, m
- ◆ period

Perkolator, m
- ◆ percolator

Perle, f (Haushaltshilfe)
- ◆ treasure

Perlenkette, f
- ◆ pearl necklace

Perlhuhn, n
- ◆ guinea fowl

Perlhuhnbraten, m
- ◆ roast guinea fowl

Perlwein, m
→ Schaumwein

Perlzwiebel, f
- ◆ pearl onion

permanente Inventur, f
- ◆ perpetual inventory

per Nachnahme schicken
- ◆ send COD

Pernod, m *FR*
- ◆ Pernod *FR*

per pedes, adv *humor*
per pedes apostolorum, adv *humor*
- ◆ by shanks' pony, adv *AE humor*
- ◆ by shanks' mare, adv *AE humor*
- ◆ on Shanks's pony, adv *BE humor*
- ◆ on Shanks's mare, adv *BE humor*
- ◆ on foot, adv

per pedes reisen *humor*
- ◆ go by shanks' pony *AE humor*
- ◆ go by shanks' mare *AE humor*
- ◆ take shanks' pony *AE humor*
- ◆ take Shanks's pony *BE humor*
- ◆ foot it *coll*

Perron, m
→ Bahnsteig

per Scheck
- ◆ by check *AE*
- ◆ by cheque *BE*

Perser, m
- ◆ Persian

Perserbrücke, f
- ◆ Persian rug

Perserin, f
- ◆ Persian girl
- ◆ Persian woman
- ◆ Persian

Perserteppich, m
- ◆ Persian carpet

Persien
- ◆ Persia

Persienreise, f (generell)
- ◆ Persian journey
- ◆ Persian tour
- ◆ Persian trip

Persienreise, f (in Persien)
Persienrundreise, f
- ◆ tour of Persia
- ◆ tour through Persia
- ◆ Persian tour

Persienreise, f (nach Persien)
- ◆ journey to Persia
- ◆ tour to Persia
- ◆ trip to Persia

persisch, adj
- ◆ Persian, adj

Persischer Golf, m
- ◆ Persian Gulf, the

Person, die abnimmt, f
- ◆ slimmer

Person, die Diät hält, f
- ◆ dieter

Person, die nicht Diät hält, f
- ◆ nondieter *AE*
- ◆ non-dieter *BE*

Person, die viel Geld ausgibt, f
- ◆ big spender
- ◆ high spender

Person, die wenig Geld ausgibt, f
- ◆ low spender

Person, die willkommen heißt, f
→ Begrüßer

Person, f
- ◆ person

Persona grata, f
- ◆ persona grata

Persona ingrata, f
→ Persona non grata

Personal, n
- ◆ staff
- ◆ personnel
- ◆ labor force *AE*
- ◆ labour force *BE*

Personalabbau, m
- ◆ reduction of staff
- ◆ reduction of personnel
- ◆ personnel reduction
- ◆ staff reduction

Personal abbauen
- ◆ reduce the personnel
- ◆ reduce the number of employees

Personalabteilung, f
- ◆ staff department
- ◆ personnel department

Personalakte, f
- ◆ personal file

Personalanforderung, f
- ◆ staff requirement
- ◆ personnel requirement
- ◆ staffing requirement *BE*

Personalaufenthaltsraum, m
Personalraum, m
- ◆ personnel room
- ◆ staff room

Personalaufwand, m
- ◆ expenditure on personnel
- ◆ expenditure on staff
- ◆ personnel expenditure
- ◆ labor costs *AE pl*
- ◆ labour costs *BE pl*

Personalaufwendungen, f pl (Bilanz)
- ◆ wages and salaries *pl*

Personalaufwendungen, f pl (generell)
- ◆ personnel expenses *pl*
- ◆ staff expenses *pl*

Personalaufzug, m
- ◆ staff elevator *AE*
- ◆ personnel elevator *AE*
- ◆ personnel lift *BE*
- ◆ staff lift *BE*

Personalausbildung, f
Personalschulung, f
- ◆ personnel training
- ◆ staff training

Personalauswahl, f
- ◆ selection of staff
- ◆ selection of personnel

Personalausweis, m
Ausweis, m
- ◆ identification card *AE*
- ◆ identity card *BE*
- ◆ ID card

Personalausweisnummer, f
- ◆ identification card number *AE*
- ◆ identity card number *AE*
- ◆ ID card number

Personalausweis prüfen
- ◆ check an identification card *AE*
- ◆ check an identity card *BE*
- ◆ check an ID card

Personalbeherbergung, f
Personalunterbringung, f
- ◆ personnel accommodation
- ◆ staff accommodation

Personalbeherbergungskosten, pl
- ◆ costs of staff accommodation *pl*
- ◆ cost of staff accommodation

Personalbereich, m (Hotel)
Nicht-Gastkontaktbereich, m
- ◆ back of the house

Personalbestand, m
Personalstand, m
Personalstärke, f
- ◆ number of staff
- ◆ number of personnel

personalbezogene Kosten, pl
- ◆ staff-related costs *pl*
- ◆ personnel-related costs *pl*

Personalbildungsprogramm, n
- ◆ staff training program *AE*
- ◆ personnel training program *AE*
- ◆ employee training program *AE*
- ◆ staff training programme *BE*
- ◆ personnel training programme *BE*

Personalbrigade, f
- ◆ staff brigade

Personalbüro, n
- ◆ personnel office

Personalchef, m
Personalleiter, m
- ◆ personnel manager

Personalcomputer, m
PC, m
- ◆ personal computer
- ◆ PC

Personal der Kalten Küche, n
- ◆ cold larder staff
- ◆ cold larder personnel

Personaldiebstahl, m
Diebstahl durch das Personal, m
- ◆ pilfering by (the) employees
- ◆ pilfering by the staff

Personaldirektor, m
♦ **personnel director**
♦ staff director
Personal einsparen
♦ **cut staff**
♦ cut personnel
Personaleinsparung, f
♦ **cutting staff**
♦ cutting personnel
Personal einstellen
♦ **employ staff**
♦ employ personnel
Personal einteilen für etw
♦ **assign employees to s.th.**
Personalengpaß, m
→ Personalmangel
Personalessen, n
♦ **staff meal**
♦ employee's meal
Personaleßraum, m
Personalspeisesaal, m
♦ **personnel dining room**
♦ staff dining room
Personalfahrstuhl m
♦ **personnel elevator** AE
♦ staff elevator AE
♦ personnel lift BE
♦ staff lift BE
Personalfluktuation, f
Personalwechsel, m
♦ **staff turnover**
♦ turnover of staff
Personalführung, f
♦ **personnel management**
Personal-Gast-Verhältnis, n (zahlenmäßig)
Personal-Gäste-Verhältnis, n
♦ **staff/guest ratio**
♦ staff-to-guest ratio
♦ staff/guests ratio
♦ staff-to-guests ratio
♦ ratio of staff to guests
Personalgetränke, n pl
♦ **employees' beverages** pl
♦ employees' drinks pl
Personalhaus, n
→ Personalquartier
Personalien, f pl
persönliche Daten, pl
♦ **personal data**
Personalien angeben
♦ **give one's personal data**
Personalien aufnehmen
♦ **write down s.o.'s personal data**
♦ note s.o.'s personal data
Personal ist erfahren
♦ **staff are experienced**
♦ personnel are experienced
Personal ist freundlich
♦ **staff are friendly**
♦ personnel are friendly
Personal ist hilfsbereit
♦ **staff are helpful**
♦ personnel are helpful
Personal ist höflich
♦ **staff are polite**
♦ personnel are polite
Personal ist mehrsprachig
♦ **staff are multilingual**
♦ personnel are multilingual
Personal ist rücksichtsvoll
♦ **staff is considerate**

♦ staff are considerate
♦ personnel is considerate
♦ personnel are considerate
Personal ist sympathisch
♦ **staff is congenial**
♦ staff are congenial
♦ personnel is congenial
♦ personnel are congenial
Personal ist über jeden Tadel erhaben
♦ **staff are beyond reproach**
Personal ist unfreundlich
♦ **staff are unfriendly**
♦ staff is unfriendly
Personal ist zuvorkommend
♦ **staff are obliging**
♦ personnel are obliging
Personalkantine f
♦ **staff canteen**
Personalknappheit f
♦ **staff shortage**
♦ personnel shortage
♦ shortage of staff
♦ shortage of personnel
Personalkoch, m
♦ **staff cook**
♦ personnel cook
Personalkost, f
→ Personalverpflegung
Personalkosten, pl
♦ **staff costs** pl
♦ staff cost
♦ personnel costs pl
♦ personnel cost
♦ payroll costs pl
Personalküche, f
♦ **staff kitchen**
♦ personnel kitchen
Personallebensmittel, n pl
Personalessen, n
♦ **staff food**
♦ personnel food
Personalleiter, m
→ Personalchef
Personallift, m
Personalfahrstuhl, m
♦ **staff lift** BE
♦ personnel lift BE
♦ personnel elevator AE
♦ staff elevator AE
Personallogis n
→ Personalunterkunft
Personallöhne, m pl
♦ **staff wages** pl
♦ personnel wages pl
Personalmangel, m (Knappheit)
→ Personalknappheit
Personalmangel, m (völliges Fehlen)
♦ **lack of staff**
♦ lack of personnel
Personalnebenkosten, pl
♦ **incidental wage costs** pl
Personalproblem, n
♦ **staff problem**
♦ personnel problem
Personalprovision, f
♦ **staff commission**
♦ personnel commission
Personalquartier, n
♦ **staff quarters** pl
♦ personnel quarters pl

Personalraum, m
♦ **staff room**
Personalrestaurant n
♦ **staff restaurant**
Personalschlafraum, m
♦ **staff bedroom**
♦ personnel bedroom
Personalsituation, f
♦ **staffing situation**
Personalspeisesaal, m
♦ **staff dining room**
♦ personnel dining room
Personalstand, m
Personalbestand, m
♦ **number of employees**
♦ number of persons employed
Personalstärke, f
Personalzahl, f
Personalbestand, m
♦ **number of personnel**
♦ number of staff
Personalsteuer, f
♦ **personal tax**
Personaltoilette, f
♦ **staff toilet**
♦ personnel toilet
♦ employee rest room AE euph
Personaltrinkgeld n
♦ **staff tip**
♦ staff gratuity
Personalunterkunft, f
♦ **staff accommodation**
♦ personnel accommodation
♦ employees' lodging AE
Personalunterkunftsausgaben, f pl
Personalunterbringungsausgaben, f pl
♦ **staff accommodation expenses** pl
Personalverfügbarkeit, f
♦ **staff availability**
♦ personnel availability
Personalverpflegung, f
♦ **staff meals** pl
♦ employees' meals pl
Personalverpflegungskosten, pl
♦ **cost of staff meals**
Personalwäsche, f (generell)
♦ **staff linen**
Personalwäsche, f (zum Waschen)
♦ **staff laundry**
Personalwechsel, m
→ Personalfluktuation
Personalwohnraum, m
→ Personalunterkunft
Personalwohnung, f
♦ **staff apartment** AE
♦ staff flat BE
Personalzimmer, n
Personalschlafraum, m
♦ **personnel bedroom**
♦ staff bedroom
Personalzimmermädchen, n
♦ **staff chambermaid**
♦ personnel chambermaid
♦ staff maid
♦ personnel maid
Persona non grata, f
unerwünschte Person, f
Persona ingrata, f
♦ **persona non grata**
♦ unwanted person

Personenaufzug 574

- undesirable person
- undesirable

Personenaufzug, m
→ Personenfahrstuhl

Personenbeförderung, f
- passenger transportation AE
- transport(ation) of passengers
- passenger transport BE
- conveyance of passengers
- passenger service

Personeneisenbahn, f
- passenger railroad AE
- passenger railway BE

Personenfähre, f
Passagierfähre, f
- passenger ferry

Personenfahrstuhl, m
Personenlift, m
Personenaufzug; m
- passenger elevator AE
- passenger lift BE

Personenfahrzeug, n
- passenger vehicle

Personengebühr, f
→ Gebühr pro Person

Personenkraftfahrzeug, n
- passenger motor vehicle

Personenkraftwagen, m
→ Personenwagen

Personenlift, m
→ Personenfahrstuhl

Personennacht, f (Statistik)
(1 zahlender Gast bleibt 1 Nacht)
- person-night

Personenpauschale, f
Pauschalpreis pro Person, m
Personenpauschalpreis, m
- package price per person
- package rate per person
- inclusive price per person
- inclusive rate per person

Personenpauschalpreis, m
→ Personenpauschale

Personenreise, f (Statistik)
(eine Person macht eine Reise)
- person trip AE

Personenrufanlage, f
→ Rufanlage

Personenschiff, n
- passenger boat
- passenger ship

Personenstand, m
(z.B. verheiratet)
- civil status
- marital status
- status

Personentarif, m (Transport)
- passenger tariff
- passengers fares pl

Personentransfer, m
- passenger transfer

Personentransport, m
Personenbeförderung, f
- passenger conveyance
- conveyance of passengers
- passenger transportation AE
- passenger transport BE
- transport(ation) of passengers

Personenverkehr, m
- passenger traffic
- passenger service

Personenverkehrsstatistik, f
- passenger traffic statistics pl

Personenverwechslung, f
- mistaken identity

Personenwagen, m (Auto)
Personenkraftwagen, m
Pkw, m
PKW, m
- passenger car
- motorcar AE
- motor car BE
- auto(mobile) AE
- car

Personenwagen, m (Zug)
- passenger car AE
- passenger carriage BE
- passenger coach BE

Personenzahl, f
Anzahl der Personen, f
Zahl der Personen, f
- number of persons

Personenzug, m (nicht Güterzug)
- passenger train

Personenzug, m (nicht Schnellzug)
- slow train
- local train

persönlich, adj
- personal, adj
- person-to-person, adj

persönlich, adv
- in person, adv
- personally, adv

persönlich Anteil nehmen an etw
- take a personal interest in s.th.

persönlich ausgewählte Hotels, n pl
- personally selected hotels pl

persönlich begrüßen jn
- give s.o. a personal welcome

persönliche Ausgaben, f pl
- personal expenses pl

persönliche Begrüßung, f
- personal welcome

persönliche Begrüßung anbieten
- offer a personal welcome

persönliche Betreuung, f
- personal attention
- personal service
- personal service
- individual attention

persönliche Buchung f
- personal booking

persönliche Daten, pl
→ Personalien

persönliche Gegenstände, m pl
persönliche Habe, f
- personal belongings pl

persönliche Grüße, m pl
- personal greetings pl

persönliche Grüße richten an jn
- extend personal greetings to s.o.

persönliche Konsultation, f
persönliche Beratung, f
- personal consultation

persönliche Kreditkarte, f
- personal credit card

persönliche Mitteilung weiterleiten an jn
- pass a personal message to s.o.

persönliche Nachricht, f
persönliche Mitteilung, f
- personal message

persönliche Nachricht überbringen
persönliche Mitteilung überbringen
- deliver a personal message

persönliche Note, f
- personal touch

persönliche Note geben etw
- give s.th. a personal touch
- give a personal touch to s.th.

persönlichen Service bieten
- provide personal service

persönlichen Service garantieren
- guarantee personal service

persönlicher Besuch, m
- personal visit

persönliche Reservierung, f
- personal reservation

persönlicher Führer, m
- personal guide

persönlicher Gast, m
- personal guest

persönlich erscheinen
- appear in person
- make a personal appearance

persönlicher Service, m
persönliche Betreuung, f
- personal service
- personalised service

persönliche Sachen, f pl
- personal items pl

persönliche Sachen zurücklassen
persönliche Sachen liegenlassen
persönliche Sachen vergessen
- leave personal items behind

persönliches Gepäck, n
- personal baggage AE
- personal luggage BE

persönliche Sicherheit, f
- personal safety

persönlich geführtes Hotel, n
- personally run hotel
- personally operated hotel

Persönlichkeit, f
- personality

Persönlichkeitsschulung, f
Persönlichkeitstraining, n
- personality training

persönlich kommen
- come in person

persönlich stornieren etw
- cancel s.th. in person
- make a cancellation in person
- make a cancelation in person AE

persönlich teilnehmen an etw (aktiv)
- participate in s.th. in person
- take part in s.th. in person

persönlich teilnehmen an etw (passiv)
- attend s.th. in person

persönlich überprüft, adj
persönlich inspiziert, adj
- personally inspected, adj

persönlich überprüfte Unterkunft, f
persönlich inspizierte Unterkunft, f
- personally inspected accommodation

Person mit unbekanntem Aufenthaltsort, f
- person whose whereabouts are unknown

Person ohne Begleitung, f
→ unbegleitete Person

Person pro Nacht, f
Person pro Übernachtung, f
- person per night

Peru
- ♦ Peru

Peruaner, m
- ♦ Peruvian

Peruanerin, f
- ♦ Peruvian girl
- ♦ Peruvian woman
- ♦ Peruvian

peruanisch, adj
- ♦ Peruvian, adj

Peseta, f
Pesete, f
- ♦ peseta

Peso, m
- ♦ peso

Petersilie, f
- ♦ parsley

Petersiliensoße, f
- ♦ parsley sauce

Petersilienzweigchen, n
Petersilienzweig, m
- ♦ parsley sprig

Petit déjeuner, n FR m
Frühstück, n
- ♦ petit déjeuner FR m
- ♦ breakfast
- ♦ Continental breakfast

Petits fours, pl FR m
(Dessertgebäck zum Kaffee)
- ♦ petits fours, pl FR m

PEX-Tarif, m
Flieg-und-Spar-Tarif, m
Holiday-Tarif, m
- ♦ PEX tariff
- ♦ purchase excursion tariff

Pfad, m
Weg, m
- ♦ path
- ♦ trail

Pfadfinder, m
- ♦ boy scout
- ♦ scout

Pfadfindertreffen, n
(regional)
- ♦ camporee AE

Pfalz, f
(Region)
- ♦ Palatinate, the

Pfalz bei Kaub, f
(am Rhein)
- ♦ Pfalz of Kaub, the

Pfälzer, m
- ♦ inhabitant of the Palatinate

Pfälzer Abend, m
- ♦ Palatinate Evening
- ♦ Palatinate Night

Pfälzer Küche, f
pfälzische Küche, f
- ♦ Palatinate cuisine
- ♦ Palatinate cooking

Pfälzer Wald m
(Region)
- ♦ Palatinate Forest

Pfälzer Wein, m
- ♦ Palatinate wine
- ♦ wine of the Palatinate

Pfalzgraf, m
- ♦ Count Palatine, the

pfälzisch, adj
- ♦ Palatinate, adj

Pfand, n (Flaschen)
Pfandgeld, n
- ♦ deposit

Pfand, n (Spiel)
- ♦ forfeit

pfänden etw
- ♦ seize s.th. as security

pfänden wegen rückständiger Miete
- ♦ distrain for rent

Pfänderspiel, n
- ♦ game of forfeits
- ♦ forfeits

Pfänderspiel machen
- ♦ play forfeits

Pfandgeld, n
→ Pfand

Pfandrecht, n
Zurückbehaltungsrecht, n
- ♦ lien

Pfandrecht des Gastwirts, n
→ Gastwirtspfandrecht

Pfandrecht des Hoteliers, n
→ Hotelierspfandrecht

Pfandrecht des Vermieters, n
→ Vermieterpfandrecht

Pfandrecht geltend machen auf etw
Zurückbehaltungsrecht geltend machen bei etw
- ♦ lay a lien on s.th.

Pfand rückerstatten
- ♦ refund a deposit

Pfandrückerstattung, f (Flasche)
- ♦ deposit refund (bottle)

Pfändung, f
- ♦ seizure

Pfand zahlen
(für Flasche)
- ♦ pay a deposit

Pfanne, f
- ♦ pan

Pfannkuchen, m
- ♦ pancake

Pfannkuchenrennen, n
- ♦ pancake race

Pfarrhaus, n
- ♦ vicarage

Pfarrkirche, f
- ♦ parish church

Pfauenthron, m
- ♦ peacock throne

Pfeffer, m
- ♦ pepper

Pfefferkorn, n
- ♦ peppercorn

Pfefferminzchutney, n
- ♦ mint chutney

Pfefferminze, f
- ♦ peppermint

Pfefferminztee, m
- ♦ mint tea

Pfeffermühle, f
- ♦ pepper mill AE
- ♦ peppermill BE

pfeffern (etw)
- ♦ pepper (s.th.)

Pfeffersoße, f
- ♦ pepper sauce

Pfeffersteak, n
- ♦ pepper steak
- ♦ peppered steak

Pfefferstreuer, m
- ♦ pepperbox AE
- ♦ pepper caster
- ♦ pepper-pot BE
- ♦ peppershaker AE

Pfeife, f (Tabak)
- ♦ pipe

Pfeife, f (Trillerpfeife)
- ♦ whistle

Pfeifenraucher, m
- ♦ pipe smoker

Pfeiler, m
- ♦ pillar

Pfeilwurzpulver, n
- ♦ arrowroot powder

Pfennig, m
- ♦ pfennig

Pfennig dreimal umdrehen
- ♦ be as mean as they come

pferchen jn in etw
- ♦ cram s.o. into s.th.
- ♦ stuff s.o. into s.th.

Pferd, n
- ♦ horse

Pferdeanhänger, m
- ♦ horse trailer

Pferdebahn, f
- ♦ horse-drawn tram
- ♦ horse tram

Pferdebahnwagen, m
- ♦ horse-drawn tramcar

Pferdebox, f
- ♦ horse box

Pferdebus, m hist
- ♦ horse-drawn bus hist

Pferdedroschke, f hist
Droschke, f hist
- ♦ hackney carriage hist
- ♦ horse cab hist
- ♦ hackney cab hist
- ♦ horse-drawn cab hist

Pferdefleisch, n
- ♦ horsemeat
- ♦ horseflesh

Pferdefreund, m
Pferdeliebhaber, m
- ♦ horse lover

Pferdefuhrwerk, n
- ♦ horse-drawn vehicle

Pferdehaar, n
- ♦ horsehair

Pferdekarren, m
- ♦ horse-drawn cart

Pferdekenner, m
- ♦ horseman

Pferdekoppel, f
- ♦ paddock
- ♦ corral AE

Pferdekutsche, f
- ♦ horse-drawn carriage
- ♦ horse-drawn coach

Pferdekutschenfahrt, f
- ♦ horse-drawn coach ride
- ♦ horse-drawn carriage ride
- ♦ ride in a horse-drawn coach
- ♦ ride in a horse-drawn carriage

Pferdeliebhaber, m
→ Pferdefreund

Pferdemarkt, m
- ♦ horse market
- ♦ horse fair

Pferdenarr, m
- ♦ horsy person

Pferdeomnibus

Pferdeomnibus, m *hist*
 ♦ horse-drawn omnibus *hist*
Pferderanch, f
 ♦ horse ranch
Pferdereitbahn, f
 ♦ horseback riding arena
 ♦ riding arena
Pferderennbahn, f
 Rennbahn, f
 ♦ horse racecourse
 ♦ horse racetrack *AE*
 ♦ racecourse
 ♦ racetrack
Pferderennen, n
 ♦ horse race *AE*
 ♦ horse-race *BE*
 ♦ horse racing
 ♦ races *pl*
Pferderennsport, m
 Pferderennen, n
 ♦ horse racing *AE*
 ♦ horse-racing *BE*
Pferderitt, m
 ♦ horse ride
 ♦ ride
Pferdeschlitten, m
 ♦ horse sleigh
 ♦ horse-drawn sleigh
 ♦ horse(-drawn) sledge
 ♦ cutter *AE*
Pferdeschlittenfahren, n
 ♦ horse-sleigh riding
 ♦ sleigh riding
Pferdeschlittenfahrt, f
 ♦ horse-sleigh ride
 ♦ horse-drawn sleigh ride
 ♦ sleigh ride
 ♦ ride in a horse-drawn sleigh
Pferdeschwemme, f
 ♦ horsepond
Pferdesport, m
 Reitsport, m
 ♦ equestrian sport(s)
 ♦ riding
Pferdestall, m
 ♦ horse stable
 ♦ stable
Pferdestärke, f
 PS
 ♦ horsepower
 ♦ hp
Pferdetaxi, n *humor*
 (von Pferd gezogene Kutsche)
 ♦ horse-drawn taxi *humor*
Pferdeverleih, m
 ♦ hacking
Pferdewagen, m (Kutsche)
 → Pferdekutsche
Pferdewagen, m (Wohnwagen)
 ♦ horse-drawn caravan
Pferd mieten
 ♦ rent a horse *AE*
 ♦ hire a horse *BE*
Pferd reiten
 ♦ ride a horse
Pferd satteln
 ♦ saddle (up) a horse
Pfingstausflug, m
 ♦ Whitsun excursion
Pfingstausflügler, m
 ♦ Whitsun excursionist

Pfingstdienstag, m
 ♦ Whit-Tuesday *AE*
 ♦ Whitsun Tuesday *AE*
 ♦ Whit Tuesday *BE*
Pfingsten, n
 ♦ Whitsun
 ♦ Whitsuntide
 ♦ Whit
 ♦ Pentecost *AE*
Pfingsten in Spanien verbringen
 ♦ spend Whit(sun) in Spain
Pfingstfahrt, f
 ♦ Whitsun trip
Pfingstfeiertag, m
 ♦ Whitsun holiday
 ♦ Pentecostal holiday
Pfingstferien, pl
 ♦ Whitsun holidays *BE pl*
 ♦ Whitsun vacation *AE*
Pfingstferien, pl (Hochschule, Institution)
 ♦ Whitsun recess
Pfingstmontag, m
 ♦ Whitmonday *AE*
 ♦ Whit Monday *BE*
Pfingstreise, f
 ♦ Whitsun tour
 ♦ Whitsun journey
 ♦ Whitsun trip
Pfingstsaison, f
 ♦ Whitsun season
 ♦ Whit season
 ♦ season of Pentecost *AE*
Pfingstsonntag, m
 ♦ Whitsunday *AE*
 ♦ Whit Sunday *BE*
 ♦ Pentecost
Pfingsturlaub, m
 ♦ Whitsun vacation *AE*
 ♦ Whitsun holiday *BE*
Pfingstwoche, f
 ♦ Whit Week *AE*
 ♦ Whit week
 ♦ Whit-week
 ♦ Whitsun week
Pfingstwochenende, n
 ♦ Whit weekend
Pfingstzeit, f
 ♦ Whitsuntide
 ♦ Whitsun
 ♦ Whit
 ♦ Pentecost *AE*
 ♦ season of Pentecost *AE*
Pfirsich, m
 ♦ peach
Pfirsichbaum, m
 ♦ peach tree
Pfirsichbowle, f
 ♦ peach cup
 ♦ peach bowl
Pfirsicheis, n
 ♦ peach ice cream *AE*
 ♦ peach ice-cream *BE*
Pfirsichkern, m
 ♦ peach stone
Pfirsichkonfitüre, f
 ♦ peach jam
Pfirsichkonserve, f
 ♦ tinned peaches *BE pl*
 ♦ canned peaches *AE pl*
Pfirsichlikör, m
 ♦ peach brandy

Pfirsich Melba
 ♦ peach Melba
Pfirsichmilchmixgetränk, n
 ♦ peach milk shake
Pfirsichmousse, f
 ♦ peach mousse
Pfirsichsaft, m
 ♦ peach juice
Pfirsichsorbet, n
 ♦ peach sorbet
Pflanze, f
 ♦ plant
Pflanzenarrangement, n
 ♦ plant arrangement
Pflanzenextrakt, m
 ♦ plant extract
Pflanzengel, n
 ♦ plant gel
Pflanzenkunde, f
 ♦ phytology
Pflanzenkur, f
 ♦ phytotherapy
Pflanzenschutz, m
 ♦ plant conservation
Pflastermaler, m
 ♦ sidewalk artist *AE*
 ♦ pavement artist *BE*
Pflasterstraße, f
 → Kopfsteinstraße
Pflaume, f (generell)
 ♦ plum
Pflaume, f (getrocknet)
 → Dörrpflaume
Pflaumenbaum, m
 Zwetschgenbaum, m
 ♦ plum tree
Pflaumenfest, n
 Zwetschgenfest, n
 ♦ plum festival
Pflaumengelee, n
 ♦ plum jelly
Pflaumenkern, m
 ♦ plum stone
Pflaumenkonfitüre, f
 Zwetschgenkonfitüre, f
 ♦ plum jam
Pflaumenkuchen, m
 Zwetschgenkuchen, m
 ♦ plum pie *AE*
 ♦ plum flan
Pflaumensaft, m
 Zwetschgensaft, m
 ♦ plum juice
Pflaumenschnaps, m
 Zwetschgenschnaps, m
 Zwetschgenwasser, n
 ♦ plum brandy
Pflaumensorbet, n
 Zwetschgensorbet, n
 ♦ plum sorbet
Pflaumenstrudel, m
 Zwetschgenstrudel, m
 ♦ plum strudel
Pflege, f (Arzt)
 ♦ care
Pflege, f (Instandhaltung)
 → Instandhaltung
Pflegeanstalt, f
 Pflegeheim n
 Privatpflegeheim n
 Privatklinik f

576

Privatsanatorium n
- ♦ nursing-home *BE*

Pflegeheim, n
(für Alte und Rekonvaleszenten)
- ♦ rest home *AE*
- ♦ rest-home *BE*
- ♦ nursing-home *BE*
- ♦ care home

Pflichtfrühstück, n
- ♦ obligatory breakfast

Pflichtversicherung, f
- ♦ compulsory insurance

pflücken etw
- ♦ pick s.th.

Pforten schließen
- ♦ close down
- ♦ close

Pförtner, m (Heim, Firma)
Portier, m
- ♦ porter
- ♦ doorman *AE*
- ♦ doorkeeper

Pförtner, m (Schloß, Park)
- ♦ gatekeeper

Pförtnerhaus, n (Schloß, Park)
- ♦ gatehouse

Pförtnerin, f
- ♦ porteress
- ♦ portress

Pförtnerloge, f (Firma)
- ♦ reception (company)

Pförtnerloge, f (Haus)
- ♦ porter's lodge

Pfund, n (Gewicht)
Pfd.
- ♦ pound
- ♦ lb

Pfund, n (Währung)
- ♦ pound sterling
- ♦ pund
- ♦ quid *BE sl*

Pfund Zucker, n
- ♦ pound of sugar

P.G.
→ zahlender Gast

Phantasiegetränk, n
Fantasiegetränk, n
- ♦ fancy drink

Phantasiekostüm, n
Fantasiekostüm, n
- ♦ fancy dress

Phantasieland, n
Fantasieland, n
- ♦ fantasy land

phantasieloses Essen, n (Speisen)
einfallsloses Essen n
- ♦ unimaginative food

phantasieloses Gericht, n
einfallsloses Gericht n
- ♦ unimaginative dish

Phantasiespeisenbüfett, n
Fantasiespeisenbüfett, n
- ♦ food fantasy buffet

phantasievolles Gericht, n
einfallsreiches Gericht, n
- ♦ imaginative dish

phantastischer Urlaub, m
- ♦ fantastic vacation *AE*
- ♦ fantastic holiday *BE*

Philatelist, m
- ♦ philatelist

Philippinen, die, pl
- ♦ Philippines, the *pl*

Philippiner, m
Filipino, m
- ♦ Philippine
- ♦ Filipino

Philippinerin, f
Filipina, f
- ♦ Philippine girl
- ♦ Philippine woman
- ♦ Filipino girl
- ♦ Filipino woman
- ♦ Filipina

philippinisch, adj
- ♦ Philippine, adj
- ♦ Filipino, adj

Phönizier, m
- ♦ Phoenician

phönizisch, adj
- ♦ Phoenician, adj

Photo, n
→ Foto

Phylloxera, f
Reblaus, f
- ♦ phylloxera
- ♦ vine louse

Physiotherapeutin, f
→ Krankengymnastin

Physiotherapie, f
Krankengymnastik, f
- ♦ physiotherapy

Physiotherapieabteilung, f
Krankengymnastikabteilung, f
- ♦ physiotherapy department

P.I.A.
→ paid in advance

P.I.A.- Gast, m
→ paid in advance guest

Pianino, n
- ♦ small piano

Pianist, m
Pianistin, f
- ♦ pianist

Piano, n
→ Klavier

Pianobar f
- ♦ piano bar

Pianosalon, m
Pianolounge, f
- ♦ piano lounge

picheln *coll*
trinken
- ♦ tipple *coll*
- ♦ booze *coll*

Pichler, m *coll*
- ♦ tippler *coll*
- ♦ boozer *coll*

Picknick, n
- ♦ picnic
- ♦ picknick *AE*
- ♦ basket lunch *AE*
- ♦ basket dinner *AE*

Picknickausflug, m
- ♦ picnic excursion
- ♦ picnic outing
- ♦ picnic

Picknickausflug machen
- ♦ go for a picnic
- ♦ go on a picnic excursion
- ♦ make a picnic excursion

Picknickbank, f
- ♦ picnic bench

Picknickbeutel, m
Picknicktüte, f
- ♦ picnic bag

picknicken
Picknick machen
- ♦ picnic
- ♦ have a picnic

picknicken im Wald
im Wald ein Picknick machen
- ♦ picnic in the wood
- ♦ picnic in the forest

Picknicker, m
Picknickteilnehmer, m
- ♦ picnicker

Picknickessen, n (abends)
- ♦ basket dinner *AE*
- ♦ picnic dinner

Picknickessen, n (Dinner)
- ♦ picnic dinner
- ♦ basket dinner *AE*

Picknickessen, n (Lunch)
- ♦ picnic lunch
- ♦ basket lunch *AE*
- ♦ lunch picnic *AE*

Picknickessen, n (mittags)
- ♦ basket lunch *AE*
- ♦ picnic lunch

Picknickfahrt, f
- ♦ picnic trip

Picknickfeuer, n
- ♦ picnic fire

Picknickgebiet, n
Picknickgelände, n
Picknickbereich, m
- ♦ picnic area

Picknickhütte, f
- ♦ picnic hut

Picknickimbiß, m
- ♦ basket snack *AE*

Picknickkoffer, m
- ♦ picnic case

Picknickkorb, m
- ♦ picnic basket
- ♦ picnic hamper
- ♦ tea-basket *BE*

Picknick machen
- ♦ have a picnic
- ♦ picnic
- ♦ take a picnic
- ♦ go on a picnic
- ♦ hold a picnic *AE*

Picknickmenü, n
- ♦ picnic menu

Picknick mitnehmen
- ♦ take a picnic (with me)

Picknickmöbel, n pl
- ♦ picnic furniture *sg*

Picknickpark, m
- ♦ picnic park

Picknickpastete, f
- ♦ picnic pie

Picknickplatz, m
Picknickort, m
Picknickstelle, f
- ♦ picnic spot
- ♦ spot for a picnic
- ♦ picnic site
- ♦ picnic place

Picknickstelle

Picknickstelle, f
  Picknickplatz, m
  Picknickort, m
  ♦ picnic place
  ♦ picnic spot
  ♦ picnic site
Picknickteilnehmer, m
  → Picknicker
Picknicktisch, m
  ♦ picnic table
Picknicktüte, f
  → Picknickbeutel
Picknickveranstaltung, f
  ♦ basket meeting AE
Picknickvorräte, m pl
  ♦ picnic supplies pl
Pièce de résistance, f FR
  ♦ pièce de résistance FR
piekfein, adj
  ♦ slap-up, adj BE inform
piekfeines Abendessen, n (Dinner)
  ♦ slap-up dinner BE inform
piekfeines Abendessen, n (Supper)
  ♦ slap-up supper BE inform
piekfeines Gartenfest, n
  ♦ slap-up garden party BE inform
piekfeines Hotel, n
  ♦ slap-up hotel BE inform
piekfeines Mittagessen, n
  ♦ slap-up luncheon BE inform
  ♦ slap-up lunch BE inform
piekfeines Restaurant, n
  ♦ slap-up restaurant BE inform
Piemont
  (Region)
  ♦ Piedmont
Piemontese, m
  ♦ Piedmontese
Piemonteserart, adv gastr
  ♦ Piemontese style, adv gastr
piemontesisch, adj
  piemontisch, adj
  ♦ Piedmontese, adj
Piepser, m coll
  (elektron. Gerät für Benachrichtigung)
  ♦ beeper
  ♦ pager
Pier, m/f
  ♦ pier
pikant, adj
  (Speisen)
  ♦ piquant, adj
  ♦ spicy, adj
  ♦ highly seasoned, adj
pikante Nachspeise, f
  ♦ savory AE
  ♦ savoury BE
pikante Soße, f
  ♦ piquant sauce
pikante Speise, f
  ♦ savoury
  ♦ savory AE
pikant gewürzt, adj
  stark gewürzt, adj
  ♦ spicily flavored, adj AE
  ♦ spicily flavoured, adj BE
  ♦ highly seasoned, adj
pikant gewürzter Reis, m
  ♦ savory rice AE
  ♦ savoury rice BE

pikant schmecken
  ♦ taste spicy
Pikkolo, m (Flasche)
  → Pikkoloflasche
Pikkolo, m (Person)
  ♦ piccolo
  ♦ pageboy
  ♦ apprentice waiter
  ♦ trainee waiter
  ♦ busboy AE
Pikkoloflasche, f (Sekt)
  ♦ small bottle (of champagne)
Piktogramm, n
  ♦ pictogram AE
  ♦ pictogramme BE
Pilaw, m
  Pilau, m
  ♦ pilaff
  ♦ pilaf
  ♦ pilau
  ♦ pilaw
Pilger, m
  Wallfahrer, m
  ♦ pilgrim
Pilger aufnehmen
  ♦ take in pilgrims
Pilgerfahrt, f (generell)
  Pilgerreise, f
  Pilgerschaft, f
  ♦ pilgrimage
Pilgerfahrt machen nach Mekka
  ♦ make the hadj to Mecca
Pilgerfahrt machen nach X
  Wallfahrt machen nach X
  ♦ make a pilgrimage to X
  ♦ go on a pilgrimage to X
Pilgerfahrt machen (nach X)
  pilgern (nach X)
  ♦ go on a pilgrimage (to X)
  ♦ make a pilgrimage (to X)
Pilgerheim, n
  Pilgerherberge, f
  ♦ pilgrims' hostel
pilgern zu einem Ort
  pilgern nach einem Ort
  wallfahren zu einem Ort
  ♦ make a pilgrimage to a place
  ♦ go on a pilgrimage to a place
Pilgerort, m
  → Wallfahrtsort
Pilgerschaft, f
  → Pilgerfahrt
Pilgerstab, m
  ♦ pilgrim's staff
Pilgerstraße, f
  ♦ pilgrims' road
  ♦ pilgrim route
Pilgerstrecke, f
  Pilgerroute, f
  ♦ pilgrimage route
Pilgerweg, m
  ♦ pilgrimage road
  ♦ pilgrims' way
  ♦ pilgrim's way
Pilgerzug, m (Eisenbahn)
  ♦ pilgrim train
Pilgerzug, m (Gruppe)
  ♦ procession of pilgrims
Pilot, m
  ♦ pilot
  ♦ peelo sl

Pilothotel, n
  (bei Experiment)
  ♦ pilot hotel
Pilotprogramm, n
  ♦ pilot program AE
  ♦ pilot programme BE
Pilotprojekt, n
  ♦ pilot project
Pils, n
  Pilsbier, n
  ♦ pilsner (beer)
  ♦ pilsener (beer)
Pilsbar, f
  ♦ bar serving pilsner
  ♦ bar serving pilsener
Pilsener Bier, n
  (aus Pilsen)
  ♦ Pilsen beer
Pilsglas, n
  ♦ pilsner
Pilsstand, m
  ♦ stand serving pilsner
  ♦ stand serving pilsener
  ♦ stall serving pilsner
  ♦ stall serving pilsener
Pilsstube, f
  ♦ pub serving pilsner BE
  ♦ pub serving pilsener BE
  ♦ bar serving pilsner AE
  ♦ bar serving pilsener AE
Pilstulpe, f
  ♦ pilsner tulip
  ♦ pilsener tulip
Pilz, m (eßbar)
  ♦ mushroom
Pilz, m (giftig)
  ♦ toadstool
Pilzcocktail, m
  ♦ mushroom cocktail
Pilzcremesuppe, f
  ♦ mushroom cream soup
  ♦ cream of mushroom soup
Pilze sammeln
  ♦ collect mushrooms
Pilzfüllung, f
  ♦ mushroom stuffing
Pilzgericht, n
  ♦ mushroom dish
Pilzsalat, m
  ♦ mushroom salad
Pilzseminar, n
  Seminar über Pilze, n
  ♦ seminar on mushrooms
Pilzsoße, f
  ♦ mushroom sauce
Pilzsuppe, f
  ♦ mushroom soup
Pilzvergiftung, f
  ♦ mushroom poisoning
Piment, m/n
  ♦ pimento
  ♦ pimiento
Pinakothek, f
  ♦ pinacotheca
  ♦ picture gallery
pingeliger Gast, m
  ♦ fussy guest
Pingpong, n
  → Tischtennis
Pinie, f
  ♦ stone pine

Plakatsäule

- nut pine
- parasol pine
- pine

Pinienhain, m
Pinienwäldchen, n
- stone-pine grove
- pine grove

Pinienwald, m
- stone-pine forest
- stone-pine wood
- pinewood(s)

Pinienwäldchen, n
→ Pinienhain, m

pinkeln *coll*
- pee *coll*
- have a pee *coll*
- have a piddle *coll*
- piddle *coll*

pinkeln gehen *coll*
pieseln gehen *coll*
- fo for a pee *coll*

Pinkelpause, f
(unterwegs)
- stop for a pee
- loo stop *BE*
- pisscall *AE vulg*
- pit stop *AE sl*

Pinnwand, f
→ Anschlagtafel

Pinot blanc, m *FR*
- Pinot blanc *FR*

Pinot gris, m *FR*
- Pinot gris *FR*

Pinot noir, m *FR*
- Pinot noir *FR*

Pinottraube, f
- Pinot grape

Pinte, f (Kneipe)
→ Kneipe

Pinte, f (Maß)
(AE: 0,47 Liter; BE: 0,57 Liter))
Halbe (Bier), f
- pint

Pionier, m
- pioneer

Pionierfest, n
- pioneer festival

Pipipause, f *sl*
(z.B. bei Busreise)
- pit stop *AE sl*
- loo stop *BE*

Pirat, m
- pirate

Piratenflagge, f
Totenkopfflagge, f
- Jolly Roger, the

Piratenschlupfwinkel, m
- pirate haunt

Pirschgang, m
(Jagd)
Pirsch, f
- deer stalking
- stalking

pissen
- piss

Pissoir, n
- pissoir *AE*
- public urinal

Pistazie, f
- pistachio

Pistazienbutter, f
- pistachio butter

Pistazieneis, n
- pistachio ice cream *AE*
- pistachio ice-cream *BE*

Pistazienparfait, n
- pistachio parfait

Piste, f (Flugplatz)
→ Rollbahn

Piste, f (Rennbahn)
Rennbahn, f
Bahn, f
Weg, m
- track

Piste, f (Ski)
- piste
- ski run
- run

Piste für Anfänger, f (Ski)
- ski run for beginners
- run for beginners

Piste für Kinder, f (Ski)
- ski run for children
- run for children

Piste ist gut präpariert (Ski)
- piste is well prepared

Pistenbereich, m
- piste area
- ski run area

Pistendienst, m (Ski)
- ski run maintenance service

Pistenlänge, f (Ski)
- length of the run
- length of the piste

Pistenpflege, f (Ski)
- ski run maintenance

Pistenplan, m (Ski)
- piste plan

Pitch-und-Putt, n
- pitch-and-putt

Pitch-und-Putt-Platz, m
- pitch-and-putt course

pittoresk, adj
→ malerisch

Pizza, f
- pizza

Pizzaabend m
- pizza evening

Pizza backen
- make a pizza

Pizza essen
- eat a pizza

Pizzagastronom, m
- pizza restaurateur
- pizza restauranteur *AE*

Pizzageschäft, n
Pizzaladen, m
- pizza store *AE*
- pizza shop *BE*

Pizzakette, f
(Kette von Pizzerias)
- pizza chain

Pizzalokal, n
Pizzeria, f
- pizza parlor *AE*
- pizza parlour *BE*

Pizzaofen, m
- pizza oven

Pizzarestaurant, n
- pizza restaurant
- pizza parlor *AE*

- pizza parlour *BE*
- restaurant serving pizzas

Pizzeria, f
- pizzeria
- pizza parlor *AE*
- pizza parlour *BE*

Pkw, m
→ Personenwagen

Pkw-Abstellgebühr, f
→ Pkw-Parkgebühr

Pkw-Anhänger-Gespann, n
- car-trailer outfit

Pkw-Anhänger-Kombination, f
- car-trailer combination

Pkw-Aufzug, m
→ Autoaufzug

Pkw-Einstellplatz, m
→ Pkw-Stellplatz

Pkw in der Garage abstellen
Auto in der Garage abstellen
Wagen in die Garage fahren
- garage a car

Pkw-Parkgebühr, f
Pkw-Abstellgebühr, f
Autoparkgebühr, f
- car parking fee
- car parking charge

Pkw-Reise, f
Autoreise, f
Autotour, f
- car tour
- car journey
- car trip
- motor tour

Pkw-Stellplatz, m (für 1 Auto)
Autostellplatz m
Pkw-Parkplatz m (für 1 Auto)
Pkw-Abstellplatz m (für 1 Auto)
- parking space for one car

Pkw-Transfer, m
→ Autotransfer

Pkw- und Busparkplatz, m (für mehrere Autos)
- car and bus parking lot *AE*
- car and coach park *BE*
- car and bus park *BE*

Pkw-Wohnwagengespann, n
Pkw-Caravangespann, n
- car-trailer outfit

Plakat, n (auf Pappe)
- placard

Plakat, n (generell)
Poster, m /n
- poster
- bill

Plakatausstellung, f
- exhibition of posters
- exhibit of posters *AE*
- poster exhibition
- poster exhibit *AE*

Plakate ankleben verboten!
- Post no bills!

Plakatfläche, f
- poster space

Plakatkunst, f
- poster art

Plakatsammlung, f
- poster collection
- collection of posters

Plakatsäule, f
Litfaßsäule, f
- advertising pillar

Plakatwerbung

Plakatwerbung, f
- poster publicity
- poster advertising

Plakette, f
Tafel, f
- plaque

Plakette erhalten
- be awarded a plaque

Plakette vergeben an jn
Plakette zuerkennen jm
- award a plaque to s.o.

Pläne ändern
- change one's plans

planen etw
- plan s.th.

Planetarium n
- planetarium

planmäßig, adj (Verkehrsmittel)
→ fahrplanmäßig

planmäßige Abfahrt, f (Verkehrsmittel)
- scheduled departure

planmäßige Abfahrtszeit, f
planmäßige Abreisezeit, f
- scheduled departure time
- scheduled time of departure
- STD

planmäßige Abflugzeit, f
planmäßige Abfahrtszeit, f
- scheduled time of departure
- STD
- scheduled take-off time

planmäßige Ankunft, f (Verkehrsmittel)
- scheduled arrival

planmäßige Ankunftszeit, f
- scheduled time of arrival
- scheduled arrival time
- STA

planmäßiger Abreisetermin, m
(Person)
planmäßiger Abfahrtstermin, m
- scheduled date of departure
- scheduled departure date

planmäßiger Flug, m
→ Linienflug

planmäßiger Zielort, m
- scheduled destination

Planschbecken, n
(Schwimmbad)
- wading pool AE
- paddling pool BE
- paddler BE coll
- splash pool BE

planschen
- splash around

Plantage, f
- plantation

Planung der Speisekarte, f
→ Speisekartenplanung

Planung einer Fahrt, f
Fahrtplanung, f
- planning (of) a trip
- trip planning

Planungsphase, f
- planning phase

Planungsstadium, n
- planning stage

Plan verschieben
- postpone a plan

Planwagen, m
- covered wagon

Planwagenfahrt, f
- covered wagon trip

Planwagentour, f
- covered wagon tour

Planwagentreck, m
- covered wagon trek

Planzahl, f
- planning figure

Planziel, n
- planned target

Plastikbecher, m
- plastic mug
- plastic beaker

Plastikbehälter, m
- plastic container

Plastikbesteck, n
- plastic cutlery

Plastikflasche, f
- plastic bottle

Plastikgabel, f
- plastic fork

Plastikgeld, n
(Kreditkarten)
- plastic money

Plastikherberge, f derog
- plastic hostelry derog

Plastikkork, m
- plastic cork
- plastic stopper

Plastiklöffel, m
- plastic spoon

Plastikmesser, n
- plastic knife

Plastikschlüssel m
Kunststoffschlüssel m
- plastic key

Plastikschüssel, f
- plastic bowl
- plastic basin

Plastikstuhl, m
- plastic chair

Plastiktasche, f
- plastic bag

Plastiktasse, f
- plastic cup

Plastikteller, m
- plastic plate

Plastiktrinkhalm, m
- plastic straw

Plat du jour, f FR m
Tagesgericht, n
- plat du jour FR m
- special dish of the day
- dish of the day
- specialty of the day AE
- speciality of the day BE

Plateau, n
- plateau

Platte, f (Gang)
- plate

Platte, f (großer Teller)
- plate
- dish

Platte, f (Kochplatte)
→ Kochplatte

Platte, f (Servierplatte)
Servierplatte, f
- platter
- serving dish
- serving plate

plätten
→ bügeln

Plattensee m
- Lake Balaton

Plattenservice, m
Plattenbedienung, f
- platter service

Plattenspieler, m
→ Schallplattenspieler

Plätter, m
→ Bügler

Plätterei, f
→ Bügelei

Plätterin, f
→ Büglerin

platter Reifen, m
- flat tire AE
- flat tyre BE
- punctured tire AE
- punctured tyre BE

Platz, m (Sitzplatz)
→ Sitzplatz

Platz, m (Stelle)
- place
- spot

Platz, m (Tennis)
Tennisplatz, m
- court
- tennis court

Platz an der Sonne, m
- place in the sun

Platz anweisen jm (Sitzplatz)
- seat s.o.

Platzanweiser, m
- usher

Platzanweiserin, f
- usherette

Platzanweisung, f (Sitzplatz)
- seating s.o.
- showing s.o. to his/her seat

Platzanzahl, f
→ Sitzzahl

Platzart, f
(z.B. Camping)
Platztyp, m
- site type
- type of site

Platzaufteilung, f
(Camping)
Platzanlage, f
- site layout
- layout of a site

Platzauslastung, f (Camping)
Platzbelegung, f
- site occupancy
- occupancy of a site

Platzauslastung, f (Sitzplatz)
→ Sitzauslastung

Platz auswählen
(z.B. Campingplatz)
- select a site

Platz bekommen für das Mittagessen
- get a place for lunch

Platz belegen (Sitzplatz)
→ Sitzplatz belegen

Platz belegt
(Hinweisschild; z.B. bei Campingplatz)
- Site full

Platzbelegung, f
→ Platzauslastung

Platzbericht, m (Camping)
♦ site report
Platzbesitzer, m
(z.B. von Campingplatz)
♦ site owner
Platz bestellen (Sitzplatz)
→ Sitzplatz buchen
Platzbestellung, f (Sitzplatz)
♦ booking (of) a seat
♦ seat reservation AE
Platzbetreiber, m
(z.B. Campingplatz)
♦ site operator
Platz bieten für 123 Besucher
♦ accommodate 123 visitors
♦ hold 123 visitors
Platz bieten für 123 Personen
♦ accommodate 123 persons
♦ hold 123 persons
Platz bietet vollen Service
(z.B. Camping)
♦ site provides full service
Platz bleibt leer (Camping)
♦ site remains empty
Platz bleibt leer (Sitzplatz)
♦ seat remains empty
Platz bleibt unbesetzt (Sitzplatz)
♦ seat remains unfilled
Platzbüro, n
(Camping)
♦ site office
Plätzchen, n
(Speise)
♦ cookie AE
♦ biscuit BE
Platzdeckchen, n
(auf Tisch)
→ Tischset
Platzeigentümer, m
(z.B. von Campingplatz)
♦ site proprietor
Platz einnehmen (Gebäude)
♦ occupy a site
Platz einnehmen in einem Programm
♦ have a place in a program AE
♦ have a place in a programme BE
♦ fill a slot in a program AE
♦ fill a slot in the programme BE
Platz einnehmen (Sitzplatz)
→ Sitzplatz belegen
Platzeinrichtung, f (Camping)
♦ site facility
Platzeinrichtung, f (Golf)
♦ course facility
Platz einstufen
(Campingplatz)
♦ grade a site
platzen aus allen Nähten
♦ be bursting at the seams
platzen sich fam
sich platzen
Platz nehmen
♦ take a pew fam
♦ take a seat
platzen vor Lachen
♦ split one's sides with laughter
platzen vor Wut
♦ be seething with rage
♦ be hitting the roof
Platz finden (Camping)
♦ find a site

Platz für 123 Camper, m
♦ site for 123 campers
Platz für 123 Fahrzeuge
♦ space for 123 vehicles
Platz für ein Picknick, m
♦ spot for a picnic
Platz für Spätankünfte, m
(Camping)
♦ late arrivals enclosure
Platzgebühr, f (Camping)
♦ site fee
♦ site charge
Platzgebühr, f (Tennis)
♦ court fee
Platzgebührenermäßigung, f (Camping)
♦ site fee discount
♦ site charge discount
Platzgedeck, n
Gedeck, n
Kuvert, n
♦ place setting AE
♦ place-setting BE
♦ cover
Platzgeschäft, n
(z.B. auf Campingplatz)
Platzladen, m
♦ site store AE
♦ site shop BE
Platzgutschein, m
(Camping)
♦ site voucher
Platz haben für 20 Autos
♦ have room for 20 cars
Platzhalter, m
→ Platzwart
Platz hat 123 Einheiten
(z.B. Camping)
♦ site has 123 units
Platz hat 123 Einzelstellplätze
(Camping)
♦ site has 123 individual pitches
Platz hat 123 Stellplätze
(z.B. Camping)
♦ site has 123 pitches
Platz hat eine Konzession für 123 Zelte
(Camping)
♦ site is licensed for 123 tents
♦ site is licenced for 123 tents
Platz hat getrennte Felder
(Camping)
♦ site has separate enclosures
Platzhotel, n (Camping)
Hotel auf dem Platz, n
♦ on-site hotel
Platz Ihrer Wahl, m (Camping)
♦ site of your choice
Platz im voraus reservieren (Sitzplatz)
♦ reserve a seat in advance
Platz inspizieren
(Campingplatz)
Platz überprüfen
♦ inspect a site
Platz instandhalten (Camping)
♦ maintain a site
Platz instandhalten (Golf)
♦ maintain a course
Platz instandhalten (Tennis)
♦ maintain a court
Platzinstandhaltung, f (Camping)
♦ site maintenance

Platzinstandhaltung, f (Tennis)
♦ court maintenance
Platz ist ausgebucht
(Camping)
♦ site is fully booked
Platz ist ausgeschildert
(z.B. Campingplatz)
♦ site is signposted
Platz ist belegt
(Camping)
→ Platz ist voll
Platz ist eben
(Camping)
♦ site is level
Platz ist flach
(Camping)
♦ site is flat
Platz ist gepflegt
(z.B. Camping)
♦ site is well-maintained
♦ site is well-kept
Platz ist großzügig angelegt
(Camping)
♦ site is generously laid out
Platz ist günstig gelegen
(Camping)
♦ site is conveniently situated
Platz ist leicht abfallend
(Camping)
♦ site is gently sloping
Platz ist überfüllt
(Camping)
♦ site is overcrowded
Platz ist umzäunt
(z.B. Camping)
♦ site is fenced
Platz ist voll
(Camping)
Platz ist belegt
♦ site is full up coll
♦ site is full
Platz ist von Ostern bis Oktober in Betrieb
(Camping)
♦ site operates from Easter to October
Platz ist zwei Meilen vom Meer entfernt
(Camping)
♦ site is two miles from the sea
Platz kann 123 Zelte aufnehmen
(Camping)
Platz kann 123 Zelte fassen
♦ site accommodates 123 tents
♦ site takes 123 tents
Platzkapazität, f
(z.B. Camping)
♦ site capacity
Platzkarte, f (Camping, Landkarte)
♦ sites map
Platzkarte, f (Sitzplatz)
♦ seat ticket
Platzkarte, f (Tischplatz)
♦ place card
Platz klassifizieren
(z.B. Camping)
♦ classify a site
Platzkonzert, n
→ Open-air-Konzert
Platzleiter, m
(z.B. von Campingplatz)
♦ site manager

Platzleitung

Platzleitung, f
(Camping)
♦ site management
Platz liegt auf einer ebenen Wiese
(Camping)
♦ site lies on a level meadow
Platz machen für etw
♦ make room for s.th.
Platz machen für jn
♦ make way for s.o.
♦ make room for s.o.
Platzmangel, m (Knappheit)
♦ shortage of space
Platzmangel, m (völliges Fehlen)
♦ lack of space
Platzmeister, m (Golfplatz)
Platzwart, m
♦ greenman
Platzmiete, f (Camping)
♦ site rent
♦ site hire *BE*
Platzmiete, f (Veranstaltung)
♦ venue rent
♦ venue hire *BE*
Platz mit direktem Zugang zum Strand, m
(Camping)
♦ site with direct access to the beach
Platz modernisieren
(z.B. Camping)
♦ modernise a site
♦ modernize a site
Platzname, m (Camping)
♦ site name
♦ name of the site
Platz nehmen
sich setzen
♦ take a seat
♦ sit down
Platznummer, f
Sitzplatznummer, f
Sitznummer, f
♦ seat number
Platzordnung, f
(Camping)
♦ site rules *pl*
♦ site regulations *pl*
Platzplan, m
(z.B. von Campingplatz)
♦ site plan
Platzprospekt, m (Camping)
Platzbroschüre, f
♦ site brochure
Platz reservieren (generell)
♦ reserve a place
Platz reservieren lassen (Sitzplatz)
♦ make a seat reservation
Platz reservieren (Sitzplatz)
→ Sitzplatz reservieren
Platzreservierung, f (Sitzplatz)
Sitzplatzreservierung, f
♦ reservation of a seat
♦ seat reservation
♦ reserving a seat
Platzreservierung ist erforderlich (Sitzplatz)
♦ seat reservation is required
Platzreservierung vornehmen (Sitzplatz)
♦ make a reservation for a seat
♦ make a seat reservation
Platzrestaurant, n (Camping)
Restaurant auf dem Platz, n
♦ on-site restaurant

Platzrezeption, f
(Camping)
Platzempfang, m
♦ site reception
Platzservice, m
(Camping)
Platzdienst, m
♦ site service
Platz sichern sich
♦ secure a place
Platz suchen (Camping)
♦ look for a site
♦ seek a site
Platz suchen für die Nacht (Camping)
Platz suchen zum Übernachten
♦ look for a place for the night
♦ seek a place for the night
Platz tauschen mit jm (generell)
♦ change places with s.o.
♦ swap places with s.o.
♦ swop places with s.o.
Platz tauschen mit jm (Sitzplatz)
♦ change seats with s.o.
♦ swap seats with s.o.
♦ swop seats with s.o.
Platzteller, m
♦ service plate
Platztoilette f
(z.B. Campingplatz)
♦ site toilet
Platz umfaßt 123 Stellplätze
(z.B. Camping)
♦ site comprises 123 pitches
Platzverfügbarkeit, f (Sitzplatz)
→ Sitzplatzverfügbarkeit
Platzverzeichnis, n (Camping)
♦ sites directory
Platz vorbestellen (Sitzplatz)
Sitzplatz im voraus buchen
Sitz vorbuchen
Sitz vorbestellen
♦ prebook a seat
♦ book a seat in advance
Platzwart, m (Camping)
Platzhalter, m
♦ site warden
Platzwart, m (Sport)
♦ groundman
♦ groundsman
♦ groundkeeper
Platzwartbüro, n
(z.B. Camping)
♦ warden's office
Platzwechsel, m
→ Sitzplatzwechsel
Platzzahl, f (Sitzplatz)
→ Sitzplatzzahl
Platz zuweisen einem Gast (Restaurant)
Platz anweisen einem Gast
Gast plazieren
♦ seat a guest
Platzzuweisung, f (Sitzplatz)
Platzzuteilung, f
Platzanweisung, f
♦ seat allocation
♦ seat assignment *AE*
♦ allocation of a seat
♦ assignment of a seat *AE*
Platzzuweisungssystem, n (Sitzplatz)
♦ seat allocation system
♦ seat assignment system *AE*

Playboy, m
♦ playboy
Playgirl, n
♦ playgirl
Plaza, f *SPAN*
(in spanischen Städten)
Marktplatz, m
freier Platz, m
♦ plaza *SPAN*
plazieren jn
♦ place s.o.
plazieren sich
♦ place oneself
plaziert, adj
♦ placed, adj
♦ sited, adj
Plazierung der Gäste f
♦ seating of (the) guests
pleite, adj (Firma)
♦ bust, adj
pleite, adj (Person)
vollkommen pleite, adj
♦ broke, adj *inform*
♦ skint, adj *BE sl*
♦ stony broke, adj *inform*
♦ flat broke, adj *inform*
pleite gehen
(Firma)
♦ go bust
pleite sein (Firma)
♦ have gone bust
pleite sein (Person)
♦ be broke *inform*
♦ be skint *BE sl*
Plenarsaal, m
Plenarhalle, f
♦ plenary hall
Plenarsitzung f
♦ plenary session
Plenarvortrag, m
♦ plenary lecture
Plenumskapazität, f
♦ plenary capacity
Plenumssaal m
→ s. Plenarsaal
Plenumsversammlung, f
♦ plenary assembly
Plenumsvortrag, m
♦ lecture to conference in full session
♦ address to conference in full session
Plöner See m
♦ Lake Plön
Plonge, f *FR*
Topfspüle, f
Topfspülraum, m
♦ plonge *FR*
♦ scullery
Plongeur, m *FR*
Topfspüler, m
♦ plongeur *FR*
♦ potwasher
♦ dishwasher
Plötze, f
→ Rotauge
plötzlich abreisen
♦ leave suddenly
♦ depart suddenly
plötzliche Abreise, f
♦ sudden departure
plötzliche Stornierung, f
plötzliche Abbestellung, f

plötzlicher Rücktritt, m
plötzliche Absage, f
♦ **sudden cancellation**
♦ sudden cancelation *AE*
Plumpsklo, n *coll*
→ Latrine, Trockentoilette
Plumpudding, m
Rosinenauflauf, m
♦ **plum pudding**
Plus, n
→ Zuwachs, Anstieg
Plüsch, m
♦ **plush**
Plüschbar, f
♦ **plush bar**
Plüschdekor, n/m
♦ **plush decor** *AE*
♦ plush décor *BE*
Plüschhotel, n
Luxushotel, n
♦ **plush hotel**
PLZ, f
→ Postleitzahl
pochieren etw
(Ei)
♦ **poach s.th.**
pochiertes Ei, n
verlorenes Ei, n
♦ **poached egg**
Pockenimpfung, f
Pockenschutzimpfung, f
♦ **smallpox vaccination**
♦ vaccination against smallpox
♦ variolisation *scient*
♦ variolization *scient*
Podest, n
→ Treppenhausabsatz
Podium, n (für Redner)
♦ **rostrum**
Podium, n (generell)
♦ **dais**
♦ podium
♦ platform
Podiumkamera, f
♦ **rostrum camera**
Podiumsdiskussion, f
Podiumsgespräch, n
♦ **panel discussion**
♦ platform discussion *BE*
Podiumsdiskussion leiten
♦ **chair the panel**
Podiumsteilnehmer, m
♦ **panelist** *AE*
♦ panellist *BE*
♦ member of a panel
Podiumsteilnehmer, m pl
♦ **discussion panel**
Poissonnier, m FR
Fischkoch, m
♦ **poissonnier** *FR*
♦ fish cook
Pokal, m (Trinkgefäß) *hist*
♦ **goblet** *hist*
Pokerspiel, n
♦ **game of poker**
Polarexpedition, f
♦ **polar expedition**
Polargebiet, n
♦ **polar region**
♦ polar regions *pl*

Polarkreis, m
→ Nordpolarkreis, Südpolarkreis
Polarreise, f
♦ **polar journey**
Polarroute, f
♦ **polar route**
Pole, m
♦ **Pole**
Polen
♦ **Poland**
Polenta, f
♦ **polenta**
Polentafüllpastete, f
♦ **polenta timbale**
polieren etw
♦ **polish s.th.**
Poliermittel, n
Politur, f
♦ **polish**
polierter Tisch, m
♦ **polished table**
Poliertuch, n
♦ **polishing cloth**
Polin, f
♦ **Polish girl**
♦ Polish woman
Polio, f
Poliomyelitis, f
spinale Kinderlähmung, f
♦ **polio**
♦ poliomyelitis
Polioimpfung, f
♦ **polio vaccination**
Politesse, f
♦ **meter maid** *AE*
♦ traffic warden *BE*
Politikkonferenz, f
politische Konferenz, f
♦ **political conference**
politisches Asyl, n
♦ **political asylum**
politisches Asyl suchen
♦ **seek political asylum**
politisches Asyl wünschen
um politisches Asyl nachsuchen
♦ **request political asylum**
politisches Treffen, n
politische Tagung, f
♦ **political meeting**
politische Unruhen, f pl
♦ **political disturbances** *pl*
politische Versammlung, f
♦ **political assembly**
Politur, f
→ Poliermittel
Polizei, f
♦ **police**
Polizei anfordern
Polizei rufen
♦ **call the police**
Polizeibeamter, m
♦ **police officer**
Polizeieskorte, f
♦ **police motorcade**
Polizeikontrolle, f
♦ **police check**
polizeilich anmelden sich
→ anmelden sich bei der Polizei
polizeilicher Meldeschein, m
♦ **form for police records**

Polizeimuseum, n
♦ **police museum**
Polizeipräsidium, n
♦ **police headquarters** *pl + sg*
Polizeirazzia, f
♦ **police raid**
Polizeirazzia in einem Hotel, f
♦ **police raid on a hotel**
Polizeirevier, n
♦ **police district**
♦ police precinct *AE*
Polizeischutz, m
♦ **police protection**
Polizeistunde, f
Sperrstunde, f
♦ **closing time**
Polizeistunde beginnt um 23 Uhr
♦ **closing time begins at 11 p.m.**
Polizeistunde endet um 7 Uhr
♦ **closing time ends at 7 a.m.**
Polizeiwache, f
Polizeidienststelle, f
Polizeirevier, n
♦ **police station**
Polizist, m
Bulle, m *derog*
♦ **policeman**
♦ cop *AE coll*
Polizistin, f
♦ **policewoman**
♦ woman cop *AE coll*
♦ female cop *AE coll*
Polka, f
♦ **polka**
Pollack, m
(Fisch)
Steinköhler, m
♦ **green pollack**
♦ green pollock
polnisch, adj
♦ **Polish, adj**
polnische Art, adv *gastr*
♦ **Polish style, adv** *gastr*
Polo, n
♦ **polo**
Polofeld, n
♦ **polo field**
Polonaise, f
Polonäse, f
♦ **polonaise**
Polonaise tanzen
♦ **dance a polonaise**
♦ polonaise
Polo spielen
♦ **play polo**
Polospieler, m
♦ **polo player**
Polowochenende, n
♦ **polo weekend**
Polsterer, m
♦ **upholsterer**
Polstergarnitur, f
♦ **upholstered three-piece suite**
♦ living-room suite
Polstermöbel, n pl
♦ **upholstered furniture** *sg*
polstern etw
(Möbel)
♦ **upholster s.th.**
Polsterreinigung, f
♦ **upholstery cleaning**

Polstersitz

Polstersitz, m
♦ upholstered seat
Polsterstuhl, m
♦ upholstered chair
Polsterung, f
(Möbel)
♦ padding
Polterabend, m (Männer)
→ Herrenabend
polyglott, adj
vielsprachig, adj
♦ polyglot, adj
Polynesien
♦ Polynesia
Polynesier, m
♦ Polynesian
Polynesierin, f
♦ Polynesian girl
♦ Polynesian woman
♦ Polynesian
polynesisch, adj
♦ Polynesian, adj
Pomeranze, f
♦ bitter orange
Pommer, m
♦ Pomeranian
Pommerin, f
♦ Pomeranian girl
♦ Pomeranian woman
♦ Pomeranian
pommerisch, adj
pommersch, adj
♦ Pomeranian, adj
Pommern
(Region)
♦ Pomerania
Pommersche Bucht, die, f
♦ Bay of Pomerania, the
Pommes, pl *coll*
Pommes frites, pl
Fritten, pl
♦ chips *BE pl*
♦ French fries *AE pl*
♦ fries *AE pl*
Pommes frites, pl
Pommes, pl *coll*
Fritten, f pl
♦ French fries *AE pl*
♦ fries *AE pl*
♦ chips *BE pl*
Pomp, m
Feierlichkeit, f
♦ pomp
Pompeji
Pompei
♦ Pompeii
pompös, adj
♦ pompous, adj
Pony, n
♦ pony
Pony reiten
♦ ride a pony
Ponyreiten, n
Ponyreitsport, m
♦ pony riding
Ponyritt, m
♦ pony ride
Ponytrekker, m
Wanderreiter, m
♦ pony-trekker

Ponytrekking, n
Wanderreiten, n
♦ pony-trekking
Ponytrekkingurlaub, m
Ponytrekkingferien, pl
♦ pony-trekking vacation *AE*
♦ pony-trekking holiday *BE*
Ponytrekkingzentrum, n
♦ pony-trekking center *AE*
♦ pony-trekking centre *BE*
Pool, m
Schwimmbad, n
Schwimmbecken, n
♦ pool
Poolabkommen, n
♦ pool agreement
Poolbar, f
♦ pool bar
Poolbedienung f
Poolservice m
♦ pool service
Poolbereich, m
♦ pool area
Poolbillard, n
♦ pool
Poolbillardtisch, m
♦ pool table
Poolcafé, n
♦ pool-cum-cafe *AE*
♦ pool-cum-café *BE*
♦ poolside cafe *AE*
♦ poolside café *BE*
Poolclub, m
♦ pool club
Poolgrill, m
♦ poolside grill
♦ poolside barbecue
Poolgrillfest, n
♦ poolside barbecue
Poolluftverkehr, m
♦ pooled air traffic
Pool mit Bar, m
♦ pool with bar
Poolparty, f
♦ pool party
Poolrestaurant, n
Schwimmbadrestaurant, n
♦ pool restaurant
♦ poolside restaurant
Poolservice, m
Pooldienst, m
Poolbedienung, f
♦ poolside service
♦ swimming-pool service
♦ pool service
Poolspiel, n
♦ pool game
Poolterrasse, f
♦ pool terrace
♦ poolside terrace
Poolterrassenrestaurant, n
♦ pool terrace restaurant
Poolvereinbarung, f
♦ pool arrangement
Poolverkehr, m
♦ pooled traffic
Popcorn, n
Puffmais, m
♦ popcorn
Popfan, m
♦ pop fan

Popfestival, n
♦ pop festival
Popgruppe, f
♦ pop group
Popkonzert, n
♦ pop concert
Popmusik, f
♦ pop music
Popsänger, m
♦ pop singer
Popstar, m
♦ pop star
Popveranstaltung, f
♦ pop event
Porridge, m/n
Haferbrei, m
♦ porridge *BE*
♦ oatmeal *AE*
♦ cooked oatmeal *AE*
Porridge zum Frühstück essen
♦ have porridge for breakfast *BE*
♦ have (cooked) oatmeal for breakfast *AE*
Portal, n
(Kirchenbau)
überdachte Vorhalle, f
Vorbau, m
♦ porch
Porta Westfalica, die, f
Westfälische Pforte, die, f
♦ **Porta Westfalica**
♦ Westphalian Gate, the
♦ Westphalian Gap, the
Porter, m
→ Gepäckträger
Portier, m
Türsteher, m
♦ porter
♦ bellman *AE*
♦ doorman *AE*
♦ doorkeeper
Portierassistent, m
♦ assistant porter
Portier de nuit, m *FR m*
Nachtportier, m
♦ portier de nuit *FR m*
♦ night porter
Portier d'étage, m *FR*
Etagenportier, m
♦ portier d'étage *FR*
♦ floor porter
Portierdienst, m
Portierservice m
♦ porter service
♦ bell service *AE*
♦ porterage service *BE*
♦ portering service *BE*
♦ porterage
Portiere, f
Türvorhang, m
♦ portiere *AE*
♦ portière *BE*
♦ door curtain *AE*
♦ door-curtain *BE*
Portierloge, f
Pförtnerloge, f
♦ porter's lodge
Portierpersonal, n
♦ bell staff *AE*
♦ bell personnel *AE*
♦ porterage staff *BE*

- ♦ porterage personnel *BE*
- ♦ bellpersons *AE pl*

Portierschalter, m
- ♦ porter's desk

Portierservice, m
- → Portierdienst

Portiertournant, m
- Aushilfsportier, m
- ♦ relief porter
- ♦ relief bellman *AE*

Portier wird das Gepäck auf das Zimmer bringen
- ♦ porter will bring the baggage to the room *AE*
- ♦ porter will bring the luggage to the room *BE*

Portier wird Ihnen zeigen, wo das Zimmer ist
- ♦ porter will show you where the room is

Portier wird Ihr Gepäck hochbringen
- ♦ porter will take your baggage up(stairs) *AE*
- ♦ porter will take your luggage up(stairs) *BE*

Portikus, m
- Säulengang, m
- ♦ portico

Portion, f (ausgeteilt)
- ♦ helping

Portion, f (eine Person)
- ♦ serving

Portion, f (generell)
- ♦ portion

Portion, f (Kaffee, Tee)
- ♦ pot

Portion Eiskrem, f
- Portion Eis, f
- ♦ portion of ice cream *AE*
- ♦ portion of ice-cream *BE*

Portionen sind großzügig
- ♦ portions are lavish

portionieren etw
- ♦ portion s.th.

Portionierer, m
- (z.B. für Eiskrem)
- ♦ scoop

Portion Kaffee, f
- → Kännchen Kaffee

Portion servieren
- ♦ serve a portion

Portionsgröße f
- ♦ portion size
- ♦ size of a portion

Portionskontrolle, f
- ♦ portion control

Portionskosten, pl
- ♦ portion costs *pl*
- ♦ portion cost

Portionspackung, f
- ♦ portion packaging

portionsweise, adv
- in Portionen, adv
- ♦ in portions, adv

Portionszahl f
- ♦ number of portions

Portion Tee, f
- → Kännchen Tee

Porto, n
- ♦ postage

Portobuch, n
- ♦ petty-cash book

portofrei, adj
- ♦ post paid, adj *AE*
- ♦ postage paid, adj
- ♦ post-free, adj *BE*

Portokasse, f
- Auslagenkasse, f
- Bargeldkasse, f
- Nebenkasse, f
- ♦ petty cash

Portokassenbeleg, m
- ♦ petty cash voucher

Portraitgalerie, f
- ♦ portrait gallery

Portugal
- ♦ Portugal

Portugiese, m
- ♦ Portuguese

Portugieser, m
- (Wein)
- ♦ Portugieser

Portugieserrebe, f
- ♦ Portugieser vine

Portugiesertraube, f
- ♦ Portugieser grape

Portugieserwein, m
- ♦ Portugieser wine

Portugiesin, f
- ♦ Portuguese girl
- Portuguese woman
- ♦ Portuguese

portugiesisch, adj
- ♦ Portuguese, adj

portugiesische Art, adv *gastr*
- ♦ Portuguese style, adv *gastr*

portugiesische Küche, f (Speisen)
- ♦ Portuguese cooking
- ♦ Portuguese cuisine

portugiesischer Wein, m
- ♦ Portuguese wine

Portwein, m
- ♦ port wine
- ♦ port

Portweinglas, n
- ♦ port glass

Porzellan, n (Geschirr)
- ♦ china

Porzellan, n (Werkstoff)
- ♦ porcelain

Porzellanbecher, m
- hohe Porzellantasse, f
- ♦ china mug
- ♦ porcelain mug

Porzellanersatz, m
- Ersetzung von Porzellan f
- ♦ replacement of china
- replacement of porcelain

Porzellangeschirr, n
- ♦ china dishes *pl*
- ♦ porcelain dishes *pl*
- ♦ chinaware

Porzellansammlung, f
- ♦ collection of porcelain
- ♦ porcelain collection
- ♦ collection of china
- ♦ china collection

Porzellanschüssel, f
- ♦ china bowl
- ♦ china dish
- ♦ porcelain bowl
- ♦ porcelain dish

Porzellantablett, n
- ♦ china tray
- ♦ porcelain tray

Porzellantasse, f
- ♦ china cup
- ♦ porcelain cup

Porzellanteller, m
- ♦ china plate
- ♦ porcelain plate

Porzellan- und Glaswaren, f pl
- ♦ china and glassware

Porzellanuntertasse, f
- ♦ china saucer
- ♦ porcelain saucer

Posada, f *SPAN*
- Gasthof, m
- ♦ posada *SPAN*
- ♦ inn

Position behalten
- ♦ maintain one's position

positives Image, n
- günstiges Image, n
- ♦ favorable image *AE*
- ♦ favourable image *BE*

Post abholen
- ♦ collect one's mail *AE*
- ♦ collect one's post *BE*

postalische Buchung, f
- Buchung über die Post, f
- ♦ postal booking

Postamt, n
- Post, f
- Postschalter, m
- Poststelle, f
- ♦ post office

Postanschrift, f
- Postadresse, f
- ♦ mailing address *AE*
- ♦ postal address *BE*

Postanweisung, f
- ♦ postal order
- money order

Postbarscheck, m
- ♦ postal cheque *BE*
- ♦ postal check *AE*

Postboot, n
- Postschiff, n
- Paketboot, n
- Paketschiff, n
- ♦ mail-boat
- ♦ packet boat *AE*
- ♦ packet-boat *BE*

Postbus, m
- Postautobus, m
- Postomnibus, m
- ♦ post bus
- ♦ postal bus *BE*

Postdienst, m
- ♦ postal service

Poster, m/n
- → Plakat

Postfach, n (in Postamt)
- ♦ post-office box
- ♦ P.O. box

Postfach, n (in Rezeption)
- → Ablagefach

Posthotel n
- ♦ post hotel

Postillion, m
- ♦ postilion

Postkarte, f
- ♦ postcard

Postkarte oder Anruf genügt
- ♦ postcard or telephone call will suffice

Postkasten, m
- Briefkasten, m
- ♦ mailbox *AE*

Postkutsche

- post-box *BE*
- pillar-box *BE*

Postkutsche, f
- **stagecoach** *AE*
- **stage-coach** *BE*

Postkutschenfahrt, f
- **stagecoach ride** *AE*
- stagecoach trip *AE*
- stage-coach ride *BE*
- stage-coach trip *BE*

Postkutschengasthof, m
→ Postkutschenstation

Postkutschenreise, f
- **stagecoach journey** *AE*
- stage-coach journey *BE*

Postkutschenreisen, n
Postkutschenreiseverkehr, m
- **stagecoach travel** *AE*
- stagecoach traveling *AE*
- stage-coach travel *BE*
- stage-coach travelling *BE*

Postkutschenstation, f
- **coaching inn**
- posting inn

Postkutschenzeit, f
- **stagecoach era** *AE*
- stage-coach era *BE*

postlagernd, adv
- **poste restante, adv**
- general delivery, adv *AE*

Postleitzahl, f
PLZ, f
- **Zip code** *AE*
- postcode *BE*
- postal code *BE*

Postleitzahl angeben
- **indicate the Zip code** *AE*
- indicate the postcode *BE*
- indicate the postal code *BE*

Postmuseum, n
- **postal museum**

Postomnibus, m
→ Postbus

Post sortieren
- **sort (the) mail**

Poststation, f
- **post house**

Poststraße, f *hist*
- **post road** *hist*

Post verteilen
- **distribute (the) mail**
- hand out (the) mail

Potagier, m *FR*
Suppenkoch, m
- **potagier** *FR*
- soup cook

Potential, n
- **potential**

potentiell, adj
- **potential, adj**

potentieller Besucher, m
- **potential visitor**
- prospective visitor

potentieller Gast, m
- **potential guest**
- prospective guest

potentieller Kunde, m
- **potential customer**
- prospective customer

Pourboire, m *FR*
Trinkgeld, n

- **pourboire** *FR*
- tip

Pousada, f *PORT*
(Hotel in Portugal)
- **pousada** *PORT*

Pow-wow, n
(indianisch: Pallaver)
Touristikmesse, f
- **pow wow**

PR, f
Öffentlichkeitsarbeit, f
- **PR**
- public relations *pl*

PR-Abteilung, f
- **PR department**
- public relations department

Pracht des Orients, f
- **splendors of the Orient** *AE pl*
- splendours of the Orient *BE pl*

prächtige Suite, f
- **sumptuous suite**

Prachtstraße, f
Allee, f
Avenue, f
- **avenue**

Prachtstück der Sammlung, n
Glanzstück der Sammlung, n
- **gem of the collection**

Prachtsuite, f
Prunksuite, f
- **state suite**

prachtvolles Hotel, n
- **sumptuous hotel**

Pragerart, adv *gastr*
- **Prague style, adv** *gastr*

prähistorisch, adj
- **prehistoric, adj**

prähistorische Zeit, f
→ vorgeschichtliche Zeit

Praktikant, m
- **trainee**

Praktikantin, f
- **female trainee**

Praktikum, n
- **practical training**
- practical work

Praktikum absolvieren
Praktikum machen
- **do a practical training**
- do a practical

praktische Information, f
- **practical information** *sg*

praktische Informationen bieten über etw
praktische Informationen bieten zu etw
- **provide practical information about s.th.**
- provide practical information on s.th.

praktischer Arzt, m
- **general practitioner**
- medical practitioner

praktische Tätigkeit, f
Praxis, f
- **practical work**
- practice

Praline, f
- **chocolate**

Pralinenschachtel, f
- **chocolate box**
- box of chocolates

Prallsack, m
Luftsack, m

Airbag, m
- **airbag**

Prämie, f
- **premium**

prämieren etw
prämiieren etw
- **award a prize to s.th.**
- award s.th. a prize

prämieren jn
prämiieren jn
- **give s.o. a prize**
- give s.o. an award

prämierter Wein, m
preisgekrönter Wein, m
- **award-winning wine**
- prize-winning wine

prämiertes Restaurant, n
preisgekröntes Restaurant, n
- **award-winning restaurant**
- prize-winning restaurant

Prämie zahlen
- **pay a premium**

Prämonstratenser, m
- **Premonstratensian**

Prämonstratenserkloster, n (Frauen)
- **Premonstratensian convent**

Prämonstratenserkloster, n (Männer)
- **Premonstratensian monastery**

präpariert, adj
vorbereitet, adj
zubereitet, adj
- **prepared, adj**

präparierte Piste, f (Ski)
- **prepared piste**
- prepared ski run
- prepared run

PR-Arbeit, f
Öffentlichkeitsarbeit, f
- **PR work**
- public relations work

Präsent, n
Geschenk, n
- **present**
- gift

Präsentation, f
Vorführung, f
- **presentation**

Präsentation durchführen
- **run a presentation**

Präsentation machen
- **give a presentation**

Präsentation planen
- **plan a presentation**

Präsentation proben
- **rehearse a presentation**

Präsentationsraum, m
- **presentation room**

Präsentationssaal, m
Präsentationshalle, f
- **presentation hall**

präsentieren etw (auflisten)
- **feature s.th.**

präsentieren etw unter dem Motto XYZ
- **present s.th. under the motto XYZ**

präsentieren etw (vorstellen)
vorstellen etw
- **present s.th.**

Präsentierteller, m
- **presentation plate**

Präsentkorb, m
→ Geschenkkorb

präsent sein
  → anwesend sein
Präsenzliste, f
  ♦ list of persons present
Präsidentenbude, f *humor*
  ♦ presidential digs *sl pl*
Präsidentensuite f
  ♦ presidential suite
präsidieren bei einer Konferenz
  ♦ preside over a conference
  ♦ preside at a conference
präsidieren bei einer Tagung
  ♦ preside over a meeting
  ♦ preside at a meeting
präsidieren bei etw
  ♦ preside over s.th.
  ♦ preside at s.th.
prassen
  schlemmen
  seinen Bauch pflegen
  ♦ gormandize
  ♦ gormandise
Prasser, m
  Schlemmer, m
  ♦ gormandizer
  ♦ gormandiser
  ♦ gourmand
Prasserei, f
  ♦ high life
  ♦ gormandizing
  ♦ gormandising
  ♦ lavish lifestyle
PR-Ausgaben, f pl
  ♦ PR expenses *pl*
  ♦ public relations expenses *pl*
Praxis, f
  praktische Tätigkeit, f
  ♦ practice
Praxiserfahrung, f
  praktische Erfahrung, f
  ♦ practical experience
Praxiserfahrung sammeln
  ♦ gain practical experience
Praxisraum, m
  (eines Arztes)
  → Arztpraxis
PR-Berater, m
  ♦ PR adviser
  ♦ public relations adviser
PR-Budget, n
  PR-Etat, m
  ♦ PR budget
  ♦ public relations budget
PR-Büro, n
  ♦ PR office
  ♦ public relations office
PR-Direktor, m
  ♦ PR director
  ♦ public relations director
Preis, m (Auszeichnung)
  ♦ prize
  ♦ award
Preis, m (Rechnung)
  ♦ price
  ♦ rate
  ♦ charge
preisabhängig, adj
  ♦ price-sensitive, adj
  ♦ rate-sensitive, adj

preisabhängiger Markt, m
  ♦ price-sensitive market
  ♦ rate-sensitive market
preisabhängige variable Aufwendungen, f pl
  ♦ rate-sensitive variable expenses *pl*
  ♦ price-sensitive variable expenses *pl*
Preisabschlag, m
  → Preisermäßigung
Preis an der Kasse, m (Theater)
  Kassenpreis, m
  ♦ price at the door
  ♦ box office price
  ♦ box office rate
Preis ändern (beträchtlich)
  ♦ change a price
  ♦ change a rate
Preis ändern (geringfügig)
  ♦ alter a price
  ♦ alter a rate
Preisänderung, f (geringfügig)
  ♦ alteration of price
  ♦ alteration of rate
Preisänderung, f (umfassend)
  ♦ price change
  ♦ change in price
  ♦ rate change
  ♦ change in rate
Preisänderungen vorbehalten
  Preisänderungen möglich
  ♦ Prices (are) subject to alteration
  ♦ Rates (are) subject to alteration
  ♦ Tariff (is) subject to alteration
Preisangabe, f
  ♦ price quotation
  ♦ rate quotation
  ♦ quotation of a price
  ♦ quotation of a rate
  ♦ quotation
Preisangabe benötigen
  ♦ require a quotation
Preisangaben sind als annähernd und
unverbindlich
  zu verstehen
  ♦ Quoted prices should be treated as general
  ♦ indications
  ♦ Quoted rates should be treated as general
  ♦ indications
Preis angeben
  Preis nennen
  ♦ quote a price
  ♦ quote a rate
Preisangebot, n
  ♦ quotation
  ♦ price estimate
Preisangebot für etw, n
  ♦ quotation for s.th.
  ♦ price estimate for s.th.
Preisangebot senden jm
  ♦ send a price estimate to s.o.
  ♦ send s.o. a price estimate
Preis angleichen an etw
  ♦ adjust a price to s.th.
  ♦ adjust a rate to s.th.
Preis angleichen geringfügig
  ♦ adjust a price slightly
  ♦ adjust a rate slightly
Preis anheben
  ♦ raise a price
  ♦ raise a rate
Preis anheben um 10 %
  Preise anheben um 10 %

  ♦ raise a price by 10 %
  ♦ raise a rate by 10 %
  ♦ raise prices by 10 %
  ♦ raise rates by 10 %
Preis anheben um DM 30
  ♦ raise a price by DM 30
  ♦ raise a rate by DM 30
Preis anheben von DM 10 auf DM 20
  ♦ raise a price from DM 10 to DM 20
  ♦ raise a rate from DM 10 to DM 20
Preisanhebung, f
  ♦ price hike
  ♦ price rise
  ♦ rate rise
  ♦ rate hike
Preisanpassung, f
  ♦ price adjustment
  ♦ rate adjustment
  ♦ adjustment of rates
  ♦ adjustment of prices
Preisanstieg, m
  Preiserhöhung, f
  ♦ increase in price
  ♦ price increase
  ♦ rate increase
  ♦ increase in rate
Preis auf Anfrage
  Preis auf Verlangen
  ♦ price on application
  ♦ price on demand
Preisaufschlag, m
  → Preiszuschlag
Preis auf Wunsch
  ♦ price on request
Preis aushandeln (im voraus)
  Preis (vorher) aushandeln
  ♦ negotiate the price (in advance)
Preis aushandeln (mit jm)
  ♦ negotiate a price (with s.o.)
  ♦ negotiate a rate (with s.o.)
Preis ausrechnen
  → Preis kalkulieren
Preisausschreiben, n
  ♦ prize competition
  ♦ competition with prizes
  ♦ competition
Preis bei dreibettiger Belegung, m
  ♦ triple-occupancy rate
  ♦ triple-occupancy price
Preis bei einbettiger Belegung, m
  → Preis bei Einzelbelegung
Preis bei Einzelbelegung, m
  → Einzelbelegungspreis
Preis bei zweibettiger Belegung, m
  ♦ double-occupancy rate
  ♦ double-occupancy price
Preisberechnung f
  Preiskalkulation, f
  ♦ calculation of a price
  ♦ calculation of prices
  ♦ price calculation
  ♦ calculation of a rate
  ♦ calculation of rates
Preis bestätigen
  ♦ confirm a price
  ♦ confirm a rate
Preisbestätigung, f
  ♦ price confirmation
  ♦ confirmation of a price
  ♦ rate confirmation
  ♦ confirmation of a rate

preisbewußt

preisbewußt, adj
♦ price-conscious, adj
♦ rate-conscious, adj
♦ budget-conscious, adj
♦ budget-minded, adj
preisbewußter Gast m
♦ budget-conscious guest
Preisbewußtsein, n
♦ price-consciousness
Preisbildung, f
Preisgebung, f
Preisstellung, f
Preisgestaltung, f
♦ pricing
Preisbindung f
♦ price maintenance
♦ resale price fixing
♦ resale price maintenance BE
♦ fair trade AE
Preis bleibt stabil
♦ price remains stable
♦ rate remains stable
Preis der Reise, m
Reisepreis, m
♦ price of the tour
♦ price of the journey
♦ price of the trip
Preisdisziplin, f
♦ price restraint
♦ rate restraint
Preis drücken
♦ bring down a price
♦ bring down a rate
♦ force down a price
♦ force down a rate
Preise auf dem Tiefststand halten
♦ keep prices at rock-bottom level
♦ keep rates at rock-bottom level
Preise auf Verlangen
Preise auf Anfrage
♦ Prices on demand
♦ Rates on demand
Preise beginnen bei DM 123
♦ prices start at DM 123
♦ rates start at DM 123
Preise beginnen bei DM 123 pro Nacht
Preise beginnen bei DM 123 pro Übernachtung
♦ prices start at DM 123 per night
♦ rates start at DM 123 per night
♦ prices begin at DM 123 per night
♦ rates begin at DM 123 per night
Preise beginnen bei DM 123 pro Person und Tag
♦ prices start at DM 123 per person per day
♦ rates start at DM 123 per person per day
Preise beinhalten alle Mahlzeiten vom Abendessen
am ersten Tag bis zum Frühstück am letzten Tag
♦ prices include all meals from dinner on the first
♦ day to breakfast on the last day
Preise beinhalten Personaltrinkgelder
♦ prices include staff gratuities
♦ rates include staff gratuities
Preise beinhalten Unterkunft und Verpflegung
♦ prices cover accommodation and food
♦ rates cover accommodation and food
Preisebene, f
Preisniveau, n
♦ rate level
♦ price level

Preise einfrieren
Preisstopp durchführen
♦ freeze (the) prices
♦ freeze (the) rates
Preise einschließlich Bedienungsgeld und Mwst.
Preise einschließlich Bedienungsgeld und Mehrwertsteuer
♦ prices include service charge and VAT
♦ prices include service charge and value added tax
♦ rates include service charge and VAT
♦ rates include service charge and value added tax
Preise festsetzen
♦ fix prices
♦ fix rates
Preise für jeden Geldbeutel, m pl
♦ prices to suit every pocket pl
♦ rates to suit every pocket pl
Preise garantiert
♦ prices guaranteed
♦ rates guaranteed
Preise gehen runter coll
♦ prices come down
♦ rates come down
Preise hoch halten
♦ keep prices up
♦ keep rates up
Preis einer Portion berechnen
♦ calculate the price of one portion
Preis eines Urlaubs, m
♦ price of a vacation AE
♦ price of a holiday BE
Preis eines Zimmers erhöhen um 10 %
♦ increase the price of a room by 10 %
♦ increase the rate of a room by 10 %
Preise je nach Zimmer und Saison, m pl
♦ prices according to room and season pl
♦ rates according to room and season pl
♦ terms according to room and season pl
Preise kontrollieren
♦ control prices
♦ control rates
Preiselastizität, f
♦ price elasticity
♦ elasticity of price
Preiselbeere, f
♦ cranberry
Preiselbeerkonfitüre, f
♦ cranberry jam
Preiselbeerlikör, m
♦ cranberry liqueur
Preiselbeersoße, f
♦ cranberry sauce
Preis empfangen
Preis erhalten
♦ receive a prize
♦ receive an award
Preisempfänger, m
♦ prize recipient
♦ recipient of the prize
Preis empfehlen
♦ recommend a price
♦ recommend a rate
Preisempfehlung, f
♦ price recommendation
Preisentwicklung, f
♦ price trend
♦ rate trend
Preise ohne Gewähr
♦ prices without guarantee
♦ rates without guarantee

Preise reichen bis DM 1234 pro Nacht
♦ prices range to DM 1234 per night
♦ rates range to DM 1234 per night
Preis erhalten
Preis empfangen
♦ receive an award
♦ receive a prize
Preis erhöhen in der Hochsaison
♦ raise the price in (the) high season
♦ raise the rate in (the) high season
Preis erhöhen kräftig
Preis saftig erhöhen coll
♦ bump up a price
♦ bump up a rate
♦ make a whacking increase in/to the price
Preiserhöhung, f
♦ price rise
♦ price increase
Preiserhöhung findet statt
Preissteigerung findet statt
♦ price increase takes place
♦ rate increase takes place
Preis ermäßigen um 15 %
♦ reduce a price by 15 %
♦ reduce a rate by 15 %
Preis ermäßigen von DM 500 auf DM 300
♦ reduce a price from DM 500 to DM 300
♦ reduce a rate from DM 500 to DM 300
Preisermäßigung, f
Preisnachlaß, m
Preisabschlag, m
♦ price reduction
♦ rate reduction
♦ reduced prices pl
♦ reduced rates pl
Preisermäßigung für Rentner, f
♦ price reduction for old-age pensioners
♦ rate reduction for old-age pensioners
♦ price reduction for O.A.P.s
♦ rate reduction for O.A.P.s
Preisermäßigung in letzter Sekunde, f
♦ last-minute price reduction
♦ last-minute rate reduction
♦ last-minute reduction
Preisermäßigung weitergeben an jn
♦ pass on a price reduction to s.o.
♦ pass on a rate reduction to s.o.
Preise sind inklusive Frühstück
♦ terms are inclusive of breakfast
♦ terms include breakfast
Preise sind niedriger als in der letzten Saison
♦ prices are lower than last season
♦ rates are lower than last season
Preise vergleichen
♦ compare (the) prices
♦ compare (the) rates
Preisfahrt, f (Belohnung)
♦ award trip
Preisfehler, m
falscher Preis, m
♦ wrong price
♦ mistake in the price
Preis festlegen
♦ fix a price
♦ fix a rate
Preis festsetzen
♦ establish a price
♦ establish a rate
Preisfestsetzung, f
♦ price determination
♦ determination of price

588

Preis fordern für etw
  ♦ charge a price for s.th.
Preisforderung, f
  ♦ asking price
Preis für (das) Essen und Trinken, m
  ♦ price for food and drink
Preis für ein Einzelzimmer beträgt DM 123
  ♦ price for a single room is DM 123
  ♦ rate for a single room is DM 123
Preis für ein Einzelzimmer ist $ 123
  ♦ rate for a single room is $ 123
  ♦ price for a single room is $ 123
Preis für eine Übernachtung, m
  ♦ price for an overnight stay
  ♦ rate for an overnight stay
Preis für Übernachtungsunterkunft, m
  ♦ price for overnight accommodation
  ♦ rate for overnight accommodation
Preis für Übernachtung und Frühstück, m
  ♦ price for bed and breakfast
  ♦ European Plan price
  ♦ European Plan rate
  ♦ EP rate
Preis für weitere Übernachtung, m
  Preis für Verlängerungsübernachtung, m
  Preis für zusätzliche Übernachtung, m
  ♦ extra-night price
  ♦ extra-night rate
Preis für Zimmer mit Frühstück, m
  Garnipreis, m
  ♦ bed-and-breakfast price
  ♦ bed-and-breakfast rate
  ♦ b&b price
  ♦ b&b rate
Preis für zwei Tage, m
  Zweitagespreis, m
  ♦ price for two days
  ♦ rate for two days
  ♦ two-day price
  ♦ two-day rate
Preisgarantie, f
  ♦ price guarantee
  ♦ rate guarantee
Preisgarantie aufheben
  ♦ withdraw a price guarantee
  ♦ withdraw a rate guarantee
Preisgarantie geben
  ♦ give a price guarantee
  ♦ give a rate guarantee
Preisgarantie gilt nicht während großer Veranstaltungen
  ♦ price guarantee does not apply during major events
  ♦ rate guarantee does not apply during major events
Preisgarantie gilt nur für Familien
  ♦ price guarantee applies only for families
  ♦ rate guarantee applies only for families
Preis garantieren
  ♦ guarantee a price
  ♦ guarantee a rate
Preisgebungspolitik f
  ♦ pricing policy
  ♦ price policy
Preisgefüge, n
  → Preisstruktur
preisgekrönt, adj
  prämiert, adj
  ausgezeichnet, adj
  ♦ award-winning, adj
  ♦ prize-winning, adj

preisgekrönte Küche, f (Speisen)
  ausgezeichnete Küche, f
  ♦ award-winning cuisine
  ♦ prize-winning cuisine
  ♦ award-winning cooking
  ♦ prize-winning cooking
preisgekröntes Hotel, n
  ♦ award-winning hotel
  ♦ prize-winning hotel
preisgekröntes Menü, n
  ♦ award-winning menu
  ♦ prize-winning menu
preisgekröntes Restaurant, n
  prämiertes Restaurant, n
  ♦ prize-winning restaurant
  ♦ award-winning restaurant
Preisgeld, n
  ♦ award money
Preis genehmigen
  ♦ approve (of) a price
  ♦ approve (of) a rate
Preis gewinnen
  Auszeichnung gewinnen
  prämiiert werden
  prämiert werden
  ♦ win a prize
  ♦ win an award
Preis gewinnen in einem Preisausschreiben
  ♦ win a prize in a competition
Preis gilt für März und April
  ♦ price applies to March and April
  ♦ rate applies to March and April
Preis gilt im Juni
  ♦ price applies to June
  ♦ rate applies to June
Preis gilt während der ganzen Saison
  ♦ price applies throughout the season
  ♦ rate applies throughout the season
Preisgründe, m pl
  ♦ price reasons pl
Preisgruppe, f
  ♦ price group
  ♦ rate group
preisgünstig, adj
  ♦ attractively priced, adj
  ♦ low-cost, adj
preisgünstige Pauschale, f
  ♦ low-cost package
preisgünstige Reise, f
  ♦ low-cost tour
  ♦ low-cost journey
  ♦ low-cost trip
preisgünstiger Urlaub, m
  preisgünstige Ferien, pl
  ♦ low-cost vacation AE
  ♦ low-cost holiday BE
preisgünstiges Arrangement, n
  ♦ attractively priced arrangement
preisgünstiges Hotel, n
  ♦ low-cost hotel
preisgünstiges Reisen, n
  ♦ low-cost travel
preisgünstiges Restaurant, n
  ♦ low-cost restaurant
preisgünstiges Wochenende, n
  ♦ low-cost weekend
preisgünstige Unterkunft, f
  preisgünstige Unterbringung, f
  ♦ low-cost accommodation
  ♦ low-cost lodging AE

preisgünstigstes Hotel, n
  ♦ best-value hotel
Preis halbieren
  ♦ halve a price
  ♦ halve a rate
Preis halten
  ♦ keep a price
  ♦ keep a rate
Preis herabsetzen
  Preis ermäßigen
  Preis reduzieren
  ♦ reduce a price
  ♦ reduce a rate
Preis herabsetzen von DM 123 auf DM 121
  ♦ reduce a price from DM 123 to DM 121
  ♦ reduce a rate from DM 123 to DM 121
Preis herunterhandeln
  Preis herunterfeilschen
  ♦ haggle down a price
Preis heruntersetzen
  ♦ peg a price
  ♦ peg a rate
Preis hochsetzen
  Preise hochsetzen
  ♦ put a price up
  ♦ put a rate up
  ♦ put prices up
  ♦ put rates up
Preis hochtreiben
  ♦ boost a price
  ♦ boost a rate
  ♦ puff up a price
  ♦ puff up a rate
Preis in der Saisonmitte, m
  ♦ mid-season price
  ♦ mid-season rate
Preis in der Wochenmitte, m
  Preis unter der Woche, m
  ♦ midweek price
  ♦ midweek rate
Preisindex, m
  ♦ price index
Preis in die Höhe treiben
  ♦ drive up a price
  ♦ drive up a rate
Preis ist endgültig
  Preis ist Endpreis
  ♦ price is final
  ♦ rate is final
Preis ist fest
  ♦ price is firm
  ♦ rate is firm
Preis ist günstig
  ♦ price is favorable AE
  ♦ rate is favorable AE
  ♦ price is favourable BE
  ♦ rate is favourable BE
Preis ist hoch
  ♦ price is high
  ♦ rate is high
Preis ist niedrig
  ♦ price is low
  ♦ rate is low
Preis ist ohne Unterkunft
  ♦ price excludes accommodation
  ♦ rate excludes accommodation
Preis ist unschlagbar
  ♦ price is unbeatable
  ♦ rate is unbeatable
Preis ist Verhandlungssache
  Preis VHS

Preis je Person

- ♦ price is a matter for negotiation
- ♦ price is negotiable
- ♦ rate is negotiable

Preis je Person, m
→ Preis pro Person

Preiskalkulation, f
Preisberechnung, f
- ♦ price calculation
- ♦ rate calculation
- ♦ calculation of a price
- ♦ calculation of a rate
- ♦ calculating a price

Preis kalkulieren
Preis ausrechnen
Preis berechnen
- ♦ calculate a price
- ♦ calculate a rate

Preiskampf, m (mit Auszeichnung)
- ♦ prize-fight

Preiskampf, m (über die Preise)
- ♦ price battle

Preiskarte, f
- ♦ price card
- ♦ rate card

Preiskartell, n
- ♦ price cartel

Preiskategorie, f
Preisklasse, f
- ♦ price category
- ♦ rate category

Preisknüller, m
- ♦ super bargain price
- ♦ special bargain

Preisknüllerurlaub, m
sehr günstiger Urlaub, m
sehr günstige Ferien, pl
- ♦ bargain vacation *AE*
- ♦ bargain holiday *BE*

Preiskontrolle, f
- ♦ price control

Preiskontrollen aufheben
- ♦ lift price controls

preiskontrolliert, adj
preisüberwacht, adj
- ♦ price-controlled, adj
- ♦ rate-controlled, adj

Preiskonzession, f
Preiszugeständnis, n
- ♦ price concession
- ♦ rate concession

Preiskonzessionen machen
- ♦ make price concessions
- ♦ make rate concessions

Preiskorrektur, f
- ♦ adjustment of prices
- ♦ adjustment of rates

Preiskrieg, m
- ♦ price war

Preiskrieg anzetteln
Preiskrieg beginnen
- ♦ start a price war

Preiskrieg bricht aus
- ♦ price war breaks out

Preislage, f
Preisklasse, f
- ♦ price range
- ♦ range of prices

Preis-/Leistungsimage, n
- ♦ value-for-money image

Preis-/Leistungsverhältnis, n
- ♦ value for money

Preisliste, f
- ♦ price list
- ♦ tariff

Preisliste auf Anfrage
- ♦ Tariff on application

Preisliste aushängen in dem Zimmer
- ♦ display the tariff in the room
- ♦ put up a price list in the room

Preislücke, f
- ♦ price gap

Preisnachlaß, m
Rabatt, m
- ♦ rebate

Preis nennen
- ♦ quote the price
- ♦ quote the rate

Preis niedrig halten
- ♦ keep a price down
- ♦ hold a price down

Preisniveau, n
Preisebene, f
- ♦ price level
- ♦ rate level

Preisobergrenze, f
- ♦ price ceiling

Preis ohne Bedienungsgeld
→ Bedienungsgeld nicht inbegriffen

Preispolitik, f
- ♦ price policy

Preis pro Gedeck, m
Gedeckpreis, m
- ♦ price per cover
- ♦ charge per cover

Preis pro Mahlzeit, m
Preis pro Essen, m
- ♦ price per meal
- ♦ price charged per meal

Preis pro Person, m
- ♦ price per person
- ♦ rate per person

Preisrabatt, m
- ♦ price discount
- ♦ rebate on the price
- ♦ rebate on the rate

Preisrückgang, m
- ♦ decline in price(s)
- ♦ fall in price(s)
- ♦ drop in price(s)
- ♦ recession in price(s)

Preisschild, n
(an Ware)
- ♦ price tag

Preisschild prüfen
- ♦ check a price tag

Preis schließt etw ein
- ♦ price includes s.th.
- ♦ rate includes s.th.

Preisschwankung, f
- ♦ price fluctuation
- ♦ rate fluctuation
- ♦ price variation
- ♦ rate variation

Preissegment, n
- ♦ price segment
- ♦ rate segment

Preissegmentierung, f
- ♦ price segmentation
- ♦ rate segmentation

Preissektor, m
Preisbereich, m

- ♦ price sector
- ♦ rate sector

Preis senken
- ♦ cut a price
- ♦ cut a rate

Preissenkung, f
- ♦ price cut
- ♦ rate cut

Preisskala, f
- ♦ price scale

Preisspanne, f
- ♦ range of prices
- ♦ price range
- ♦ price bracket

Preisspanne von DM 123 bis DM 1234, f
- ♦ price range from DM 123 to DM 1234
- ♦ rates from DM 123 to DM 1234 *pl*

Preisstabilität f
- ♦ price stability

Preissteigerung, f
Preiserhöhung, f
- ♦ price increase
- ♦ rate increase
- ♦ increase in price
- ♦ increase in rate

Preissteigerung auffangen
- ♦ absorb a price increase
- ♦ absorb a rate increase

Preissteigerungsrate, f
→ Inflationsrate

Preisstopp, m
- ♦ price freeze
- ♦ rate freeze

Preisstopp durchführen
→ Preise einfrieren

Preisstruktur, f
- ♦ price structure
- ♦ rate structure
- ♦ pricing structure *BE*

Preisstufe, f
- ♦ price bracket
- ♦ price level

Preistabelle, f
- ♦ price table
- ♦ rate table
- ♦ price panel
- ♦ price list
- ♦ tariff

Preisträger, m
- ♦ prizewinner *AE*
- ♦ prize winner *BE*

Preisüberwachung, f
→ Preiskontrolle

Preis- und Komfortklasse, f
- ♦ price and comfort class

Preis unten halten
- ♦ hold a price down
- ♦ hold a rate down
- ♦ keep a price down
- ♦ keep a rate down

Preis unterbieten
- ♦ undercut a price
- ♦ undercut a rate

Preisuntergrenze, f
- ♦ price floor
- ♦ lower price limit

Preisunterschied, m
- ♦ price difference
- ♦ price variation
- ♦ difference in price(s)
- ♦ difference of price(s)

Preisveränderung, f
- change in price(s)
- change of price(s)
- change in rate(s)
- change of rate(s)

Preis verdoppeln
- double a price
- double a rate

Preis vereinbaren
- agree (up)on a price
- agree (up)on a rate

Preisvereinbarung, f
Preisarrangement, n
- price arrangement

Preisverfall, m
Preisverschlechterung, f
- price erosion
- price deterioration
- deterioration in price(s)

Preis vergeben an jn
Preis zuerkennen jm
- award a prize to s.o.

Preisvergleich, m
- price comparison
- rate comparison
- comparison of prices
- comparison of rates

Preisvergleich anstellen
Preisvergleich machen
- compare prices
- compare rates

Preisvergünstigung, f
→ Preisermäßigung

Preisverleihung, f (Feier)
- prize ceremony
- prize-giving ceremony
- awards ceremony

Preisverleihungsbankett, n
- awards banquet

Preisverleihungsessen, n (abends)
- awards dinner

Preisverleihungsessen, n (mittags)
- awards luncheon
- awards lunch

Preisverlosung, f
- prize draw

Preisverlosung durchführen
- run a prize draw

Preisverschlechterung, f
Preisverfall, m
- price deterioration
- deterioration in price(s)
- price erosion

Preisversprechen, n
- price promise

Preisverstoß, m
- offence against price regulations

Preis verteilen
Preis vergeben
- hand out a prize

Preisvorteil, m
- price advantage
- advantage in price

Preiswanderung, f
- challenge walk

preiswert, adj
- inexpensive, adj
- low-priced, adj
- low-cost, adj
- good value (for money), adj

preiswerte Ferienwohnung, f
- inexpensive vacation apartment AE
- low-priced vacation apartment AE
- inexpensive holiday flat BE
- low-priced holiday flat BE

preiswerter Aufenthalt, m
- low-priced stay
- inexpensive stay
- budget stay

preiswertes Essen, n
- inexpensive food

preiswertes Essen anbieten
- offer inexpensive food

preiswertes Familienessen, n
- low-priced family meal
- inexpensive family meal
- low-cost family meal

preiswertes Frühstück, n
- inexpensive breakfast
- low-cost breakfast
- low-priced breakfast

preiswertes Quartier, n
- inexpensive quarters pl
- low-cost quarters pl
- low-priced quarters pl

preiswerte Unterkunft, f
- inexpensive accommodation
- low-cost accommodation
- low-priced accommodation

Preiswettbewerb, m
- price competition

Preiswucher, m
- charging exorbitant prices
- charging exorbitant rates

Preis zahlen
- pay a price
- pay a rate

Preiszugeständnis, n
Preiskonzession, f
- rate concession
- price concession

Preiszugeständnis machen
- allow a price concession
- allow a rate concession

Preiszusammenbruch, m
- price collapse
- rate collapse
- collapse of prices
- collapse of rates

Preiszuschlag, m
- addition to the price
- additional charge
- extra charge
- supplementary charge

prellen jn um etw
- swindle s.o. out of s.th.
- bilk s.o. out of s.th.
- defraud s.o. of s.th.
- trick s.o. out of s.th.

Premiere, f (Film)
- first run

Premiere, f (generell)
- premiere
- première BE
- first performance

Premiere, f (Theater)
- first night

Premiereabend, m
- opening night AE
- first night

Premierefeier, f
- opening-night party
- first-night party

Premierefest, n
- opening-night gala
- first-night gala

Premieregast, m
- guest at the opening night
- guest at the first night

Premiere haben (Film)
- be the first run

Premiere haben (generell)
- have its premiere AE
- have its première BE

Premiere haben (Theater)
- be the opening night AE
- be the first night

Premierepublikum, n
- opening-night audience
- audience on the opening night
- first-night audience
- audience on the first night

Premiereveranstaltung, f
- opening-night performance
- first-night performance

Premierevorabend, m
- eve of the premiere AE
- eve of the première BE

Premier maître d'hôtel, m FR
Erster Maître d'hôtel, m
- premier maître d'hôtel FR

Pre-Opening, n
→ Voreröffnung

Presse, f
- press

Presseausweis, m
- press card
- press pass

Pressebericht, m
- press report

Pressebüro, n
- press office

Presseempfang m
- press reception

Presseinformation, f (Aktivität)
- press briefing

Presseinformation, f (Inhalt)
- press information

Presseinformation abhalten
- hold a press briefing

Pressekonferenz, f
- press conference
- news conference AE

Pressekonferenz abhalten
- hold a press conference
- hold a news conference AE

Pressekonferenz geben
- give a press conference
- give a news conference AE

Pressemappe, f
(Informationen für die Presse)
- press kit AE
- press pack BE

Pressemitteilung, f
Presseerklärung, f
- press release

Presseraum, m
(z.B. bei Kongressen)
Pressezimmer n
- press room
- briefing room

Presseräume

Presseräume, m pl
♦ press suite
Pressestelle, f
♦ news office
♦ press office
Presse- und Informationsamt, n
Presse- und Informationsbüro, n
♦ press and information office
Presseveranstaltung, f
♦ press event
Prestige, n
♦ Prestige
Prestigeaustragungsort, m
Prestigeort, m
♦ prestige venue
Prestigehotel n
♦ prestige hotel
Prestigekette, f
(von Betrieben)
♦ prestige chain
Prestigelage, f
♦ prestige location
Prestigereisender, m
♦ prestige traveler AE
♦ prestige traveller BE
prestigeträchtiges Hotel, n
→ renommiertes Hotel
Preuße, m
♦ Prussian
Preußen
♦ Prussia
preußisch, adj
♦ Prussian, adj
PR-Firma, f
♦ PR firm
♦ public relations firm
PR-Firma engagieren
♦ hire a PR firm
♦ engage a PR firm
♦ hire a public relations firm
♦ engage a public relations firm
Priel, m
♦ tidal inlet
prima vista ITAL
(ohne Proben etw spielen)
vom Blatt
♦ prima vista ITAL
♦ sight reading
primitive Sanitäreinrichtungen, f pl
♦ primitive sanitary facilities pl
primitive Unterkunft, f
♦ rough accommodation
Prinzessinart, adv gastr
♦ princess style, adv gastr
Prior, m
♦ prior
Priorei, f
♦ priory
Prioreikirche, f
♦ priory church
Priorität, f
Vorrang, m
Dringlichkeit, f
♦ priority
Prise, f gastr
♦ pinch gastr
Prise Salz, f
♦ pinch of salt
Prise Zucker, f
♦ pinch of sugar

Pritsche, f
(zum Schlafen)
♦ pallet
♦ plank bed
Pritschenwagen, m
♦ pickup truck AE
♦ pick-up truck BE
♦ pickup AE coll
♦ pick-up BE coll
Pritschenwohnwagen, m
Pritschencaravan, m
♦ pickup trailer AE
♦ pickup camper AE
♦ pick-up caravan AE
♦ topper AE coll
♦ pickup AE coll
priv.
privat, adj
♦ pvte.
♦ private, adj
Privatadresse, f
Privatanschrift, f
♦ private address
Privatangelegenheit, f
♦ personal matter
Privatanschrift, f
→ Privatadresse
Privatappartement, n
privates Appartement, n
♦ private apartment
Privataudienz, f
♦ private audience
Privatausflug, m
privater Ausflug, m
♦ private excursion
♦ private outing
Privatauto, n
privates Auto, n
Privatwagen, m
privater Wagen, m
♦ private car
♦ private motorcar AE
♦ private motor car BE
Privatbad, n (Bad)
Einzelbad, n
♦ private bath
Privatbad, n (Schwimmbad)
Privatbecken, n
♦ private pool
Privatbadeinsel, f
(Ponton)
♦ private pontoon (on the lake)
Privatbadestrand, m
privater Badestrand, m
eigener Badestrand, m
♦ private bathing beach
♦ private beach
Privatbadezimmer n
eigenes Badezimmer, n
♦ private bathroom
♦ private bath
Privatbadzuschlag, m
Einzelbadzuschlag, m
♦ private bath supplement
♦ supplement for a private bathroom
Privatbalkon m
♦ private balcony
Privatbar f
♦ private bar
Privatbesitz, m
privater Besitz, m

Privatland, n
♦ private property
Privatbesuch, m
privater Besuch m
♦ private visit
Privatbesucher m
privater Besucher m
♦ private visitor
♦ private guest
Privatbett n
♦ private bed
Privatboot, n
privates Boot, n
♦ private boat
Privatbrennerei, f
♦ private distillery
♦ private still
Privatbuchung f
(durch Privatperson)
♦ private booking
Privatbus, m
privater Bus, m
♦ private bus
♦ private coach BE
Privatcampingplatz, m
privater Campingplatz, m
♦ private campsite
♦ private campground AE
♦ private camping site BE
♦ private camping ground BE
Privatcaravanpark, m
privater Caravanpark, m
Privatwohnwagenpark, m
privater Wohnwagenpark, m
♦ private caravan park BE
♦ private trailer park AE
Privatcaravanplatz, m
privater Caravanplatz, m
Privatwohnwagenplatz, m
privater Wohnwagenplatz, m
♦ private caravan site BE
♦ private trailer site AE
Privatcharter, f
♦ private charter
Privatclub, m
privater Club, m
♦ private club
Privatcottage, f
♦ private cottage
Privatdusche, f
eigene Dusche f
private Dusche, f
♦ private shower
private Abendgesellschaft, f (mit Essen)
private Tischgesellschaft beim Abendessen, f
private Tischgesellschaft, f
♦ private dinner party
private Atmosphäre, f
♦ private atmosphere
private Essensveranstaltung, f
(mittags)
♦ private luncheon
♦ private lunch
private Mittagsgesellschaft, f (mit Essen)
private Tischgesellschaft beim Mittagessen, f
private Tischgesellschaft, f
♦ private luncheon party
♦ private lunch party
Privatempfang m
(Veranstaltung)
♦ private reception

592

privater Anlegeplatz, m
  (für Wasserfahrzeuge)
  private Anlegestelle, f
  ♦ **private moorings** *pl*
privater Badestrand, m
  → Privatbadestrand
privater Golfplatz, m
  ♦ **private golf course**
Privaterholungsheim, n (für Rekonvaleszenten)
  ♦ **private convalescent home**
Privaterholungsheim, n (generell)
  Privatpflegeheim, n
  ♦ **private recreation home**
  ♦ private rest house *AE*
  ♦ private rest home *BE*
privater Mietmarkt, m (Mobilien)
  ♦ **private rental market** *AE*
  ♦ private hire market *BE*
privater Sandstrand, m
  ♦ **private sand beach** *AE*
  ♦ private sandy beach *BE*
privater Speiseclub, m
  ♦ **private dining club**
privater Speisesaal, m
  → Privatspeisesaal
privater Sportclub, m
  ♦ **private sports club**
privates Appartement, n
  → Privatappartement
private Saunakabine, f
  ♦ **private sauna cubicle**
privates Essen, n
  → Privatessen
privates Ferienhaus, n
  privates Urlaubshaus, n
  ♦ **private vacation home** *AE*
  ♦ private holiday home *BE*
privates Flugzeug, n
  Privatflugzeug, n
  ♦ **private plane**
  ♦ private aircraft
  ♦ private airplane *AE*
  ♦ private aeroplane *BE*
private Sicherheitsfirma, f
  ♦ **private security firm**
privates Schwimmbad, n
  → Privatschwimmbad
Privatessen, n
  privates Essen, n
  Privatgastmahl, n
  ♦ **private meal**
privates Speisezimmer, n
  → Privatspeisezimmer
privates Urlaubshaus, n
  privates Ferienhaus, n
  ♦ **private holiday home** *BE*
  ♦ private vacation home *AE*
privates Verkehrsmittel, n
  ♦ **private means of transportation** *AE*
  ♦ private means of transport *BE*
privates Wohnhaus, n
  ♦ **private dwelling house**
privates Wohnheim, n
  (z.B. für Pensionäre)
  ♦ **private residential home**
private Terrasse, f
  → Privatterrasse
private Wohnanlage, f
  ♦ **private residential complex**
Privatfahrer, m (Auto)
  ♦ **private driver**

Privatfahrer, m (Reisender)
  → Privatreisender
Privatfahrt, f
  private Fahrt, f
  ♦ **private trip**
  ♦ private ride
Privatfahrzeug, n
  privates Fahrzeug, n
  ♦ **private vehicle**
Privatfeier, f
  Privatfest, n
  ♦ **private party**
  ♦ private function
Privatferien, pl
  Privaturlaub, m
  ♦ **private holiday** *BE*
  ♦ private holidays *BE pl*
  ♦ private vacation *AE*
Privatferienort, m
  privater Ferienort, m
  ♦ **private resort**
Privatfeuerwerk, n
  ♦ **private fireworks display**
Privatflugplatz, m
  privater Flugplatz, m
  ♦ **private airfield**
Privatflugzeug, n
  privates Flugzeug, n
  ♦ **private airplane** *AE*
  ♦ private aeroplane *BE*
  ♦ private plane
  ♦ private aircraft
Privatführung, f
  ♦ **private guided tour**
  ♦ private tour
Privatführung durch die Räume, f
  ♦ **private guided tour of the rooms**
  ♦ private tour of the rooms
Privatgarage, f
  private Garage f
  eigene Garage f
  ♦ **private garage**
Privatgarten m
  eigener Garten, m
  ♦ **private garden**
  ♦ garden of one's own
Privatgast m
  privater Gast m
  ♦ **private guest**
Privatgastmahl, n
  → Privatessen
Privatgelände, n
  privates Gelände, n
  ♦ **private grounds** *pl*
Privatgespräch, n
  (Telefon: Gegensatz zu Dienstgespräch)
  ♦ **private call**
  ♦ personal call
Privatgruppe, f
  ♦ **private group**
  ♦ private party
Privathaus, n
  privates Haus, n
  ♦ **private house**
  ♦ private home
Privatheim, n
  privates Heim, n
  Privathaus, n
  ♦ **private home**

Privathof, m
  privater Hof, m
  ♦ **private courtyard**
Privathotel, n
  → Hotel in Privatbesitz
Privathotelier, m
  ♦ **independent hotelier**
Privatinsel, f
  private Insel, f
  ♦ **private island**
Privatjacht, f
  Privatyacht, f
  private Jacht, f
  private Yacht, f
  ♦ **private yacht**
Privatjacuzzi, m
  privater Jacuzzi, m
  ♦ **private jacuzzi**
Privatjet, m
  privates Düsenflugzeug, n
  ♦ **private jet**
Privatkellerei, f
  ♦ **private cellars** *pl*
Privatklinik, f
  private Klinik, f
  ♦ **private nursing-home** *BE*
  ♦ nursing-home *BE*
  ♦ private clinic
Privatkonferenz, f
  private Konferenz, f
  ♦ **private conference**
Privatkrankenhaus, n
  privates Krankenhaus, n
  ♦ **private hospital**
Privatkreuzfahrt, f
  private Kreuzfahrt, f
  ♦ **private cruise**
Privatkunde, m
  ♦ **private customer**
  ♦ private client
Privatkur, f
  ♦ **private cure**
  ♦ private treatment
Privatkurgast, m
  ♦ **private visitor to a spa**
Privatland, n
  privates Land, n
  ♦ **private land**
Privatlehrer, m
  ♦ **private instructor**
  ♦ private teacher
  ♦ private tutor
Privatlehrerin, f
  ♦ **private instructress**
  ♦ private teacher
Privatliegeplatz, m (für Wasserfahrzeug)
  ♦ **private berth**
  ♦ private mooring
Privatlift, m
  privater Lift, m
  Privatfahrstuhl, m
  privater Fahrstuhl, m
  ♦ **private elevator** *AE*
  ♦ private lift *BE*
Privatmarina, f
  private Marina, f
  ♦ **private marina**
Privatmaschine, f
  → Privatflugzeug
Privatmäzen, m
  ♦ **private patron**

Privatmuseum

Privatmuseum, n
  privates Museum, n
  ♦ **private museum**
Privatpark, m
  ♦ **private park**
  ♦ private gardens *pl*
Privatparkplatz, m (für 1 Auto)
  privater Parkplatz, m
  eigener Parkplatz, m
  ♦ **private parking place**
  ♦ private parking space
  ♦ private parking lot *AE*
Privatparkplatz, m (für mehrere Autos)
  privater Parkplatz, m
  eigener Parkplatz, m
  ♦ **private parking lot** *AE*
  ♦ private car park *BE*
  ♦ private parking
Privatpatio, m
  privater Innenhof, m
  Privatterrasse, f
  ♦ **private patio**
Privatpension, f
  ♦ **private guesthouse** *AE*
  ♦ private guest-house *BE*
  ♦ private boardinghouse *AE*
  ♦ private boarding-house *BE*
  ♦ bed-and-breakfast place
Privatperson, f
  ♦ **private person**
Privatpflegeheim, n
  ♦ **private rest house** *AE*
  ♦ private rest home *BE*
  ♦ private nursing home *BE*
Privatpilot, m
  ♦ **private pilot**
Privatplatz, m
  (Camping)
  privater Platz, m
  ♦ **private site**
Privatquartier, n
  ♦ **room in a private house**
  ♦ private quarters *pl*
  ♦ private house offering bed and breakfast
  ♦ private house
Privatquartier beziehen
  einziehen in ein Privatquartier
  ♦ **move into private quarters**
Privatquartier finden
  ♦ **find a room in a private house**
Privatraum, m
  → Privatzimmer
Privatreise, f
  private Reise, f
  ♦ **private journey**
  ♦ private tour
  ♦ private trip
Privatreisen, n
  Privatreiseverkehr, m
  ♦ **private travel**
  ♦ independent travel
Privatreisender, m
  ♦ **independent traveler** *AE*
  ♦ independent traveller *BE*
Privatreiseverkehr, m
  Privatreisen, n
  ♦ **independent travel**
  ♦ private travel
Privatresidenz, f
  Privatsitz, m
  ♦ **private residence**

Privatsafe, m
  → Privattresor
Privatsalon, m (generell)
  ♦ **private parlor** *AE*
  ♦ private parlour *BE*
  ♦ private salon
Privatsalon, m (Lounge)
  ♦ **private lounge**
Privatsalon, m (Schiff)
  ♦ **stateroom** *BE*
  ♦ state-room *AE*
Privatsalon, m (Wohnzimmer)
  ♦ **private sitting room**
  ♦ private salon
Privatsammlung, f
  private Sammlung, f
  ♦ **private collection**
Privatsanatorium, n
  ♦ **private sanatorium**
  ♦ private sanatarium *AE*
  ♦ private sanitarium *AE*
  ♦ private sanitorium *AE*
Privatsauna, f
  private Sauna, f
  ♦ **private sauna**
Privatschwimmbad, n
  privates Schwimmbad, n
  Privatschwimmbecken, n
  privates Schwimmbecken, n
  ♦ **private swimming pool** *AE*
  ♦ private swimming-pool *BE*
  ♦ private pool
Privatschwimmbecken, n
  → Privatschwimmbad
Privatsee, m
  privater See, m
  ♦ **private lake**
Privatseereise, f
  private Seereise, f
  ♦ **private voyage**
Privatsektor, m
  privater Sektor, m
  ♦ **private sector**
Privatsitzung, f
  Privattreffen, n
  Privatstunde, f
  ♦ **private session**
Privatspeiseräume, m pl
  ♦ **private dining suite**
Privatspeisesaal, m
  privater Speisesaal, m
  ♦ **private dining hall**
  ♦ private dining room
Privatspeisezimmer, n
  Privatspeiseraum m
  ♦ **private dining room**
Privatstrand, m
  privater Strand, m
  ♦ **private beach**
Privatstrandbereich, m
  privater Strandbereich, m
  ♦ **private beach area**
Privatstraße, f
  private Straße, f
  ♦ **private road**
Privatsuite, f
  private Suite, f
  ♦ **private suite**
Privattennisplatz, m
  privater Tennisplatz, m
  ♦ **private tennis court**

594

Privatterrasse, f
  private Terrasse, f
  ♦ **private terrace**
  ♦ private patio
Privattheater, n
  Liebhabertheater, n
  ♦ **private theater** *AE*
  ♦ private theatre *BE*
Privattoilette, f
  private Toilette, f
  eigene Toilette, f
  ♦ **private toilet**
Privattour, f
  privater Rundgang, m
  ♦ **private tour**
Privattransport, m
  Privatbeförderung, f
  ♦ **private transportation** *AE*
  ♦ private transport *BE*
Privattreffen, n
  privates Treffen, n
  ♦ **private meeting**
Privattresor, m
  privater Tresor, m
  Privatsafe, m
  privater Safe, m
  ♦ **private safe**
privat unterbringen jn
  → unterbringen jn privat
Privatunterkunft, f
  ♦ **private accommodation**
  ♦ accommodation in a private house
  ♦ accommodation in private houses
  ♦ privately owned accommodation
Privatunternehmer, m
  privater Unternehmer, m
  ♦ **private entrepreneur**
Privatunterricht, m
  privater Unterricht, m
  ♦ **private tuition**
  ♦ private lessons *pl*
Privatunterricht haben in Russisch
  ♦ **have private tuition in Russian**
Privaturlaub, m
  privater Urlaub, m
  Privatferien, pl
  ♦ **private vacation** *AE*
  ♦ private holiday *BE*
Privatveranda, f
  private Veranda, f
  ♦ **private veranda**
  ♦ private verandah
Privatveranstalter, m
  (Reiseveranstalter)
  ♦ **private operator**
Privatveranstaltung, f
  private Veranstaltung, f
  geschlossene Veranstaltung, f
  ♦ **private event**
  ♦ private function
  ♦ private party
Privatveranstaltungsbuchung, f
  Buchung einer privaten Veranstaltung, f
  Buchung einer geschlossenen Veranstaltung, f
  ♦ **private function booking**
  ♦ booking (of) a private function
Privatverbrauch, m
  privater Verbrauch, m
  Privatverzehr, m
  privater Verzehr, m
  ♦ **private consumption**

Privatvermieter, m
 ♦ private landlord
 ♦ landlord
Privatvermieterin, f
 ♦ private landlady
 ♦ landlady
Privatvilla, f
 private Villa, f
 ♦ private villa
Privatwagen, m
 Privatauto, n
 privater Wagen, m
 privates Auto, n
 ♦ private motorcar AE
 ♦ private motor car BE
 ♦ private car
Privatwagen benutzen
 ♦ use a private car
Privat-WC, n
 Privattoilette, f
 ♦ private WC
 ♦ private toilet
Privatweg, m
 privater Weg, m
 ♦ private path
Privatwohnwagenpark, m
 privater Wohnwagenpark, m
 Privatcaravanpark, m
 privater Caravanpark, m
 ♦ private trailer park AE
 ♦ private caravan park BE
Privatwohnwagenplatz, m
 privater Wohnwagenplatz, m
 Privatcaravanplatz, m
 privater Caravanplatz, m
 ♦ private trailer site AE
 ♦ private caravan site BE
Privatyacht, f
 → Privatjacht
Privatzimmer, n
 privates Zimmer, n
 Privatraum, m
 privater Raum, m
 ♦ private room
Privatzimmervermieter, m
 → Privatvermieter
Privatzimmervermietung, f
 ♦ renting (out) a private room
 ♦ rental of private rooms AE
 ♦ letting (of) private rooms BE
Privatzimmerverzeichnis, n
 ♦ list of private rooms
 ♦ register of private rooms
Privatzoo, m
 privater Zoo, m
 ♦ private zoo
privilegiert, adj
 ♦ privileged, adj
Prix fixe, m FR
 Festpreis, m
 fester Preis, m
 ♦ prix fixe FR
 ♦ fixed price
 ♦ fixed rate
 ♦ set price
 ♦ set rate
PR-Manager, m
 Leiter für Öffentlichkeitsarbeit, m
 PR-Leiter, m
 ♦ PR manager
 ♦ public relations manager

pro Aufenthaltstag
 ♦ per day of stay
Probe, f (generell)
 → Test
Probe, f (Theater)
 ♦ rehearsal
Probe, f (Wein)
 → Weinprobe
Probebestellung, f
 ♦ trial order
Probebuchung, f
 → Testbuchung
probefahren (etw)
 ♦ test-drive (s.th.)
Probefahrt, f (Auto)
 ♦ test drive
 ♦ test run
 ♦ trial run
Probefahrt machen (Auto)
 (Auto)
 ♦ have a test drive
 ♦ take a test drive
 ♦ have a trial run
Probeflug, m
 ♦ test flight
proben etw (Theater)
 ♦ rehearse s.th.
Probereise, f
 Testreise, f
 ♦ trial tour
Probetag, m
 ♦ rehearsal day
Probezeit, f
 ♦ probationary period
 ♦ probation period
 ♦ trial period
probieren etw
 (Speisen)
 ♦ sample s.th.
 ♦ taste s.th.
Probieren geht über Studieren
 ♦ The proof of the pudding is in the eating
Probierglas, n
 ♦ tasting glass
Probiermenü, n
 ♦ tasting menu
 ♦ trial menu
Probierraum, m
 → Probierstube
Probierstube, f
 (z.B. für Wein)
 ♦ tasting room
 ♦ wine-tasting room
Probiertag, m
 ♦ tasting day
Probiertheke, f
 Probiertresen, m
 ♦ tasting counter
Probierwoche, f
 ♦ tasting week
Problem, n
 ♦ problem
Problem darstellen
 ♦ present a problem
Problem haben wegen der Unterkunft
 ♦ have a problem about accommodation
problemlos, adj
 ♦ problem-free, adj
Problem lösen
 ♦ solve a problem

problemloser Urlaub, m
 problemlose Ferien, pl
 ♦ problem-free vacation AE
 ♦ problem-free holiday BE
Problem schaffen
 ♦ create a problem
Problem sein
 ♦ be a problem
Problemstrecke, f
 ♦ problem route
Problem wegen der Unterkunft, n
 ♦ problem about accommodation
Produkt, n (generell)
 ♦ product
Produkt, n (landwirtschaftlich)
 ♦ produce
Produktangebot, n (Palette)
 ♦ product range
 ♦ range of products
Produkt ausstellen
 ♦ exhibit a product
Produktion, f
 ♦ production
Produktion kontrollieren
 ♦ control production
Produktionskapazität, f
 ♦ production capacity
Produktionskontrolle, f
 ♦ production control
Produktionsprognose, f
 ♦ production forecast
Produktivität, f
 ♦ productivity
Produktivität steigern
 ♦ increase productivity
Produktlinie, f
 ♦ product line
Produktmanagement, n
 ♦ product management
Produktmanager, m
 ♦ product manager
Produktpolitik, f
 ♦ product policy
Produktpräsentation, f
 ♦ product presentation
Produkt präsentieren
 ♦ present a product
Produktqualität, f
 ♦ product quality
Produktveranstaltung, f
 ♦ product function
Produkt vorführen
 ♦ demonstrate a product
Produktvorführung, f
 ♦ product demonstration
Produkt vorstellen
 ♦ launch a product
Produktvorstellung, f
 ♦ product launch
 ♦ launch
Produktvorstellungssitzung, f
 ♦ product launch session
Produkt zur Schau stellen
 Produkt ausstellen
 ♦ display a product
produzieren etw
 ♦ produce s.th.
Profanarchitektur, f
 ♦ secular architecture

Profanbauwerk

Profanbauwerk, n
Profangebäude, n
♦ secular building
Professional Conference Organiser, m
PCO, m
♦ professional conference organiser
♦ PCO
Professionalität, f
♦ professionalism
professionell betriebenes Hotel, n
♦ professionally operated hotel
professionelle Bedienung, f (Person)
fachmännische Bedienung, f
♦ professional waiter
♦ professional waitress
professionelle Bedienung, f (Service)
→ professioneller Service
professionelle Behandlung, f
fachmännische Behandlung, f
♦ professional treatment
professioneller Dienst, m
→ professioneller Service
professioneller Führer, m
(Person)
gewerbsmäßiger Führer m
♦ professional guide
professioneller Kongreßorganisator, m
♦ professional congress organiser
♦ PCO
professioneller Service, m
professioneller Dienst, m
professionelle Bedienung, f
Profiservice, m
♦ professional service
professioneller Service bei allen Vermietungsangelegenheiten, m
♦ professional service in all aspects of renting AE
♦ professional service in all aspects of letting BE
professioneller Tagungsplaner, m
♦ professional meeting planner
professioneller Trainer, m
Profitrainer, m
♦ professional coach
professioneller Unterhalter, m
Berufsunterhalter, m
♦ professional entertainer
professioneller Unterricht, m
♦ professional tuition
professioneller Veranstalter, m
♦ professional organiser
♦ professional organizer
professionelle Veranstaltung, f
♦ professional event
♦ professional function
professionell geführt, adj
professionell geleitet, adj
♦ professionally run, adj
♦ professionally managed, adj
professionell geführtes Hotel, n
professionell geleitetes Hotel, n
♦ professionally run hotel
♦ professionally managed hotel
professionell organisiert, adj
♦ professionally organised, adj
♦ professionally organized, adj
professionell organisierte Veranstaltung, f
♦ professionally organised event
♦ professionally organized event
♦ professionally organised function
♦ professionally organized function

professionell serviert, adj
fachmännisch serviert, adj
♦ professionally served, adj
♦ served professionally, adj
Profi, m coll
Fachmann, m
♦ professional
♦ pro coll
Profikoch, m
→ Berufskoch
Profil, n
♦ profile
Profiservice, m
→ professioneller Service
Profit, m
→ Gewinn
profitgierig, adj
♦ profit-seeking, adj
Profit maximieren
Gewinn optimieren
♦ maximise profit
♦ maximize profit
profitorientiert, adj
gewinnorientiert, adj
♦ profit-oriented, adj AE
♦ profit-orientated, adj BE
♦ profit-minded, adj
Profitrainer im Haus, m
professioneller Trainer im Haus, m
♦ resident professional coach
Proformarechnung, f
Vorfaktur, f
♦ pro forma invoice
Prognose, f
Vorhersage, f
♦ forecast
Prognose des wöchentlichen Speisenumsatzes, f
♦ forecast of weekly food sales
prognostizieren etw
vorhersagen etw
♦ forecast s.th.
Programm, n (generell)
♦ program AE
♦ programme BE
Programm, n (Theater)
→ Repertoire
Programmabfolge, f
Programmverlauf, m
♦ course of the program AE
♦ course of the programme BE
Programmablaufplan, m
♦ program flow AE
♦ programme flow AE
Programm abrunden
♦ round off a program AE
♦ round off a programme BE
Programm absagen
Programm streichen
♦ cancel a program AE
♦ cancel a programme BE
Programm abschließen
Programm zum Abschluß bringen
♦ close a program AE
♦ close a programme BE
♦ wind up a program AE
♦ wind up a programme BE
Programm abwickeln
♦ handle a program AE
♦ handle a programme BE

Programm anbieten
♦ offer a program AE
♦ offer a programme BE
Programm ändern (geringfügig)
♦ alter a program AE
♦ alter a programme BE
Programm ändern (umfassend)
♦ change a program AE
♦ change a programme BE
Programmänderung, f (geringfügig)
♦ alteration of the program AE
♦ alteration of the programme BE
Programmänderung, f (umfassend)
♦ change in the program AE
♦ change in the programme BE
♦ change of program AE
♦ change of programme BE
Programmänderung vorbehalten
(Hinweis)
Programmänderung möglich
♦ Program subject to alteration AE
♦ Programme subject to alteration BE
Programmänderung vornehmen
→ Programm ändern
Programmansage, f
♦ program announcement AE
♦ programme announcement BE
Programm ansagen
♦ announce a program AE
♦ announce a programme BE
Programm arrangieren
♦ arrange a program AE
♦ arrange a programme BE
programmatische Veranstaltung, f
Hauptveranstaltung, f
♦ keynote event
Programm aufrufen (Computer)
Programm abrufen
♦ call up a program AE
♦ call up a programme BE
Programm aufstellen
♦ set up a program AE
♦ set up a programme BE
Programm aufzeichnen
(z.B. mit Videokamera)
Programm aufnehmen
♦ record a program AE
♦ record a programme BE
Programm ausarbeiten
♦ work out a program AE
♦ work out a programme BE
Programm ausführen
Programm umsetzen
Programm durchführen
♦ implement a program AE
♦ implement a programme BE
Programmausschuß, m
Programmkomitee, n
♦ program committee AE
♦ programme committee BE
Programm austeilen
♦ hand out a program AE
♦ hand out a programme BE
Programm ausweiten
♦ extend a program AE
♦ extend a programme BE
Programm beenden
Programm abschließen
♦ end a program AE
♦ end a programme BE

Programm beginnen
- begin a program *AE*
- start a program *AE*
- commence a program *AE form*
- begin a programme *BE*
- start a programme *BE*

Programm beginnt mit etw
- program starts with s.th. *AE*
- program begins with s.th. *AE*
- program commences with s.th. *AE form*
- programme starts with s.th. *BE*
- programme begins with s.th. *BE*

Programm beginnt um 15 Uhr
- program starts at 3 p.m. *AE*
- program begins at 3 p.m. *AE*
- program commences at 3 p.m. *AE form*
- programme starts at 3 p.m. *BE*
- programme begins at 3 p.m. *BE*

Programm beinhaltet etw
- program includes s.th. *AE*
- programme includes s.th. *BE*

Programmberater, m
- program consultant *AE*
- programme consultant *BE*

Programmbeschreibung, f
- program description *AE*
- programme description *BE*
- description of the program *AE*
- description of the programme *BE*

Programm bewältigen
- do a program *AE*
- do a programme *BE*

Programm buchen
- book a program *AE*
- book a programme *BE*

Programm deckt etw ab
- program covers s.th. *AE*
- programme covers s.th. *BE*

Programm der Spitzenklasse, n
- top-class program *AE*
- top-class programme *BE*

Programm der Veranstaltungen, n
→ Veranstaltungsprogramm

Programmdirektor, m
- program director *AE*
- programme director *BE*

Programm durchführen
- run a program *AE*
- run a programme *BE*

Programm einhalten
- adhere to a program *AE*
- adhere to a programme *BE*
- stick to a program *AE*
- stick to a programme *BE*

Programmeinzelheit, f
- program detail *AE*
- programme detail *BE*

Programm endet um 22 Uhr
- program ends at 10 p.m. *AE*
- programme ends at 10 p.m. *BE*

Programm entwickeln
- develop a program *AE*
- develop a programme *BE*

Programmentwurf, m
- draft program *AE*
- draft programme *BE*

Programm ergänzen
- complement a program *AE*
- complement a programme *BE*

Programm eröffnen
Programm beginnen

- start a program *AE*
- start a programme *BE*

Programm erstellen (für jn)
- draw up a program (for s.o.) *AE*
- draw up a programme (for s.o.) *BE*

Programm erwartet die Besucher
- program awaits the visitors *AE*
- programme awaits the visitors *BE*

Programm erweitern
Programm ausweiten
- expand a program *AE*
- expand a programme *BE*
- widen a program *AE*
- widen a programme *BE*

Programm formulieren
- formulate a program *AE*
- formulate a programme *BE*

Programm fortsetzen
- continue a program *AE*
- continue a programme *BE*

programmfrei, adv
ohne Programm, adv
frei, adv
- free, adv
- at leisure, adv

programmfreier Tag, m
Tag ohne Programm, m
freier Tag, m
- free day
- day at leisure
- day at one's disposal

Programm füllen
- fill a program *AE*
- fill a programme *BE*

Programm für diesen Sommer, n
- program for this summer *AE*
- programme for this summer *BE*

Programm für Kinder, n
- program for children *AE*
- programme for children *BE*

Programm für Singles, n
- program for singles *AE*
- programme for singles *BE*
- singles' program *AE*
- singles' programme *BE*

Programm geht reibungslos über die Bühne
- program is going like clockwork *AE*
- programme is going like clockwork *BE*

programmgemäß, adv
plangemäß, adv
- according to schedule, adv
- according to plan, adv

Programm gestalten
- design a program *AE*
- design a programme *BE*

Programmgestaltung, f
- programming
- programming *AE*
- program planning *AE*
- programme planning *BE*

Programmhinweis, m
→ Programmansage

Programm in Kürze, n
Programmüberblick, m
- program at a glance *AE*
- programme at a glance *BE*

Programm ist gut
- program is good *AE*
- programme is good *BE*

Programm ist schlecht
- program is poor *AE*
- programme is poor *BE*

Programmkosten, pl
- program costs *AE pl*
- program cost *AE*
- programme costs *BE pl*
- programme cost *BE*

Programm kürzen
- make a cut in a program *AE*
- make a cut in a programme *BE*
- cut a program *AE*
- cut a programme *BE*

Programm maßgeschneidert machen für jn
maßgeschneidertes Programm machen für jn
- tailor a program for s.o. *AE*
- tailor a programme for s.o. *BE*

Programm mit 15 Nummern, n
- program featuring 15 items *AE*
- programme featuring 15 items *BE*

Programm modifizieren
Programm leicht ändern
- modify a program *AE*
- modify a programme *BE*

Programmnummer, f
Programmpunkt, m
- program item *AE*
- programme item *BE*
- item (on the program) *AE*
- item (on the programme) *BE*

Programm organisieren
- organise a program *AE*
- organize a program *AE*
- organise a programme *BE*
- organize a programme *BE*

Programm planen
- plan a program *AE*
- plan a programme *BE*

Programmplanung, f
Programmgestaltung, f
- program planning *AE*
- programme planning *BE*
- programming *BE*
- programing *AE*

Programm präsentiert etw
- program features s.th. *AE*
- programme features s.th. *BE*

Programmpunkt, m
Programmnummer, f
- item (on the program) *AE*
- item (on the programme) *BE*
- program item *AE*
- programme item *BE*

Programm reibungslos über die Bühne bringen
- make a program go like clockwork *AE*
- make a programme go like clockwork *BE*
- make a program go like a bomb *AE*
- make a programme go like a bomb *BE*

Programm revidieren
Programm überarbeiten
- revise a program *AE*
- revise a programme *BE*

Programm schaffen
- create a program *AE*
- create a programme *BE*

Programm schließt mit etw ab
- program concludes with s.th. *AE*
- programme concludes with s.th. *BE*

Programm sieht etw vor
- program provides for s.th. *AE*
- programme provides for s.th. *BE*

Programmskizze

Programmskizze, f
- outline of a program *AE*
- outline of a programme *BE*

Programm steht fest
- program has been finalised *AE*
- programme has been finalised *BE*

Programm steht jetzt fest
- program is (now) fixed *AE*
- programme is (now) fixed *BE*

Programm steht noch nicht fest
- program has not yet been finalised *AE*
- programme has not yet been finalised *BE*

Programm steht schon fest
- program is already settled *AE*
- programme is already settled *BE*

Programm straffen
- tighten a program *AE*
- tighten a programme *BE*

Programm streng einhalten
- adhere strictly to a program *AE*
- adhere strictly to a programme *BE*

Programm studieren
- study a program *AE*
- study a programme *BE*

Programm stutzen
  Programm kürzen
- cut a program *AE*
- cut a programme *BE*

Programm überarbeiten
- touch up a program *AE*
- touch up a programme *BE*
- revise a program *AE*
- revise a programme *BE*

Programmübersicht, f
- survey of the program *AE*
- survey of the programme *BE*
- program at a glance *AE*
- programme at a glance *BE*

Programm übertragen in ein Land
  (TV, Radio)
- transmit a program to a country *AE*
- transmit a programme to a country *BE*

Programm umfaßt etw
- program comprises s.th. *AE*
- programme comprises s.th. *BE*

Programmveranstaltung, f
  (Gegensatz zu fakultativer Veranstaltung)
- scheduled event
- scheduled function

Programm verbreitern
- widen a program *AE*
- widen a programme *BE*

Programm vergrößern
- enlarge a program *AE*
- enlarge a programme *BE*
- increase a program *AE*
- increase a programme *BE*

Programm versenden an jn
  Programm verschicken an jn
- mail a program to s.o. *AE*
- send a program to s.o. *AE*
- post a programme to s.o. *BE*
- send a programme to s.o. *BE*

Programm vervollständigen
  Programm komplettieren
  Programm abschließen
- complete a program *AE*
- complete a programme *BE*

Programm verwässern
- water down a program *AE*
- water down a programme *BE*

Programm (von jm) anfordern (schriftlich)
- write (to s.o.) for a program *AE*
- write (to s.o.) for a programme *BE*

Programm (von jm) anfordern (telefonisch)
- call (s.o.) for a program *AE*
- call (s.o.) for a programme *BE*
- ring (s.o.) for a programme *BE*
- telephone (s.o.) for a program *AE*
- phone (s.o.) for a program *AE*

Programmvorschau, f (Fernsehen)
- program parade *AE*
- programme parade *BE*

Programmvorschau, f (generell)
- program preview *AE*
- programme preview *BE*
- preview of forthcoming programs *AE*
- preview of forthcoming programmes *BE*

Programm vorstellen
- present a program *AE*
- present a programme *BE*

Programmwahl, f
- choice of programs *AE*
- choice of programmes *BE*
- choosing a program *AE*
- choosing a programme *BE*

Programm wählen
  Programm auswählen
- choose a program *AE*
- choose a programme *BE*
- select a program *AE*
- select a programme *BE*

Programmwechsel, m
- change of program *AE*
- change of programme *BE*
- program change *AE*
- programme change *BE*

Programm wird zur Zeit erweitert
- program is currently being expanded *AE*
- programme is currently being expanded *BE*

Programm zusammenstellen
- put together a program *AE*
- put together a programme *BE*

pro Jahr
- per year
- per annum
- p.a.

Projekt, n
- project

Projekt aufgeben
- abandon a project

Projekt durchführen
- run a project

Projektion, f
  Vorführung, f
- projection

Projektionsausrüstung, f
  Projektionstechnik, f
- projection equipment

Projektionseinrichtung, f
- projection facility

Projektionsfläche, f
- projection area

Projektionshilfsmittel, n
- projection aid

Projektionskabine, f
  → Vorführkabine

Projektionsleinwand, f
  Projektionswand, f
- projection screen

Projektionsraum, m
  (für Filme etc.)
  → Vorführraum

Projektionsschirm, m
  → Projektionsleinwand

Projektionstisch, m
- table for projector

Projektleiter, m
- project manager
- projects manager
- project leader

Projektleitung, f
- project management

Projektor, m
- projector

Projektorbirne, f
- projector bulb

Projektor mit Fernbedienung, m
- projector with remote control

projizieren etw
  vorführen etw
- project s.th.

pro Kopf
- per head
- per capita
- per person

Pro-Kopf-Einkommen aus dem Tourismus, n
  Pro-Kopf-Einnahmen aus dem Fremdenverkehr, f pl
- per capita income from tourism

Pro-Kopf-Verbrauch, m
- per capita consumption

Pro-Kopf-Verbrauch von Wein, m
- per capita consumption of wine

Prokrustesbett, n
  (griech. Mythologie)
- Procrustean bed
- Procrustes bed

Prokura, f
- power of attorney

Promenade, f (generell)
- promenade
- prom *BE inform*

Promenade, f (Meer)
  → Seepromenade

Promenadencafé, n
- promenade cafe *AE*
- promenade café *BE*

Promenadendeck, n
  (auf Schiff)
- promenade deck

Promenadenhotel, n
- promenade hotel

Promenadenkonzert, n
- promenade concert
- prom *BE inform*

Promenadenrestaurant, n
- promenade restaurant

Promenadenweg, m
- promenade walk

Promenade trennt das Hotel vom Strand
- promenade separates the hotel from the beach

Promillegrenze, f
- maximum permissible blood alcohol level
- maximum permissible level of alcohol
- permissible level of alcohol

Promilletest, m
- breathalyser test

Prominentenherberge, f *humor*
  → Prominentenhotel

Prominentenhotel, n
♦ VIP hotel
♦ hotel for VIPs
Prominentenkoch, m
♦ celebrity cook
♦ VIP cook
prominenten Platz auf dem Programm einnehmen
♦ feature on the program *AE*
♦ feature on the programme *BE*
prominenten Redner engagieren
♦ hire a celebrity speaker *BE*
Prominententribüne, f
♦ VIP stands *pl*
♦ VIP stand
Prominenter, m
Berühmtheit, f
Promi, m *sl*
♦ celebrity
♦ VIP
prominenter Gast, m
Promi, m *sl*
♦ prominent guest
♦ VIP
pro Monat
♦ per month
Promoter, m
→ Veranstalter
prompt, adj
♦ prompt, adj
♦ immediate, adj
prompter Service, m
♦ prompt service
pro Nacht
pro Übernachtung
♦ per night
propanbeheizt, adj
propangeheizt, adj
♦ propane-heated, adj
Propangas, n
♦ propane gas
Propeller, m
♦ propeller
Propellerantrieb, m
♦ propeller engine
Propellerflugzeug, n
♦ propeller plane
♦ propeller aircraft
♦ prop
pro Person
je Person
♦ per person
pro Person pro Woche
p.P.p.W.
♦ per person per week
♦ p.p.p.w.
Proportionen eines Gebäudes, f pl
♦ proportions of a building *pl*
Proportionen eines Zimmers, f pl
♦ proportions of a room *pl*
Prosit!
Prost!
♦ Your health!
♦ Cheers!
♦ Cheerio! *BE coll*
♦ Prost! *AE*
♦ Prost! *AE*
Prosit, n
→ Trinkspruch
Prosit dem Gastgeber!
♦ Here's to our host!

Prosit dem Gastgeber!
Ein Prosit dem Gastgeber!
♦ Here's a health to the host!
Prosit Neujahr!
♦ Happy New Year!
♦ Here's to the New Year!
Prospekt, m (Börse, Schule)
♦ prospectus
Prospekt, m (generell)
Broschüre, f
♦ brochure
Prospekt anfordern
♦ request a brochure
Prospekt anfordern bei jm (schriftlich)
♦ write to s.o. for a brochure
Prospekt anfordern bei jm (telefonisch)
♦ call s.o. for a brochure
♦ telephone s.o. for a brochure
♦ phone s.o. for a brochure
Prospekt anfordern (schriftlich)
♦ write for a brochure
Prospekt anfordern (telefonisch)
♦ telephone for a brochure
♦ phone for a brochure
♦ call for a brochure
Prospektanfrage, f
Prospektanforderung, f
Prospektwunsch, m
♦ brochure request
♦ letter requesting a brochure
♦ request for a brochure
♦ request for brochures
Prospektangebot, n
♦ brochure offer
Prospekt auslegen
♦ display a brochure
Prospektauswahl, f
♦ selection of brochures
Prospektbeschreibung, f
Beschreibung im Prospekt, f
♦ brochure description
Prospektdienst, m
Prospektservice, m
♦ brochure service
Prospekt drucken
♦ print a brochure
Prospekt durchsehen
Prospekt durchlesen
♦ look through a brochure
Prospekt erneut herausgeben
Prospekt wieder herausgeben
♦ reissue a brochure
Prospekt ersetzen durch einen anderen
♦ substitute a brochure by another one
♦ replace a brochure by another one
Prospekt erstellen
♦ draw up a brochure
Prospekte vergleichen
♦ compare brochures
Prospektformat, n
♦ brochure format
Prospektfoto n
♦ brochure photograph
♦ brochure photo
Prospekt freigeben
♦ release a brochure
Prospekt führt 123 Hotels auf
♦ brochure lists 123 hotels
Prospekt für 1999, m
(für das Jahr 1999)
♦ brochure for 1999

Prospektgröße, f
♦ brochure size
♦ size of a brochure
Prospekt herausbringen
♦ launch a brochure
Prospekt herstellen
♦ produce a brochure
Prospektherstellung, f
♦ brochure production
♦ production of a brochure
Prospekt holen in einem Fremdenverkehrsamt
♦ collect a brochure from a tourist office
Prospektinhalt, m
♦ brochure content
♦ content of the brochure
Prospekt in mehreren Sprachen, m
♦ brochure in several languages
Prospekt ist erhältlich durch jn
Prospekt ist erhältlich bei jm
♦ brochure can be obtained through s.o.
♦ brochure can be obtained from s.o.
Prospekt ist kostenlos erhältlich von jm
♦ brochure is available free (of charge) from s.o.
Prospekt ist (vorübergehend) vergriffen
♦ brochure is (temporarily) out of stock
Prospekt kann gegen Einsendung von DM 12 bezogen
werden
♦ brochure can be obtained by sending DM 12
Prospektkosten, pl
♦ brochures costs *pl*
♦ brochure costs *pl*
♦ brochure cost
Prospektmaterial, n
♦ brochures *pl*
♦ advertising literature
♦ literature
Prospekt postwendend
♦ brochure by return mail
Prospekt präsentiert 123 Hotels
♦ brochure features 123 hotels
Prospektpreis, m
(im Prospekt angegeben)
♦ brochure rate
♦ brochure price
♦ price quoted in the brochure
♦ rate quoted in the brochure
Prospekt richtet sich an jn
♦ brochure is aimed at s.o.
Prospekt schriftlich oder telefonisch anfordern
♦ write or call for a brochure
♦ write or phone for a brochure
Prospektständer, m
Prospektregal, n
♦ brochure rack
Prospekttelefonleitung, f
Telefonleitung für Prospekte, f
♦ brochureline
Prospekt über etw, m
Prospekt zu etw, m
♦ brochure about s.th.
♦ brochure on s.th.
Prospekt überreicht durch jn
♦ brochure presented by s.o.
Prospekt zurückziehen
♦ withdraw a brochure
Prospekt zusammenstellen
♦ put together a brochure
Prost!
→ Prosit!

prosten auf etw   600

prosten auf etw
→ trinken auf etw
Prostituierte, f
 Hure, f
 ♦ prostitute
 ♦ whore
 ♦ streetwalker
Prostitution, f
 ♦ prostitution
pro Stunde
 ♦ per hour
Proszenium, n
 Vorbühne, f
 ♦ proscenium
 ♦ forestage
pro Tag
 ♦ per day
pro Tag und pro Besuch
 ♦ per day and per visit
Protein, n
 Eiweiß, n
 ♦ protein
Protokoll, n (Bericht)
 ♦ minutes pl
Protokoll, n (Verhalten)
 ♦ protocol
Protokollchef, m
 ♦ head of protocol
 ♦ chief of protocol
Protokollfehler, m
 Protokollfauxpas, m
 ♦ protocol gaffe
Prototyp, m
 ♦ prototype
protziges Hotel, n
 ♦ swanky hotel inform
pro Übernachtung
 → pro Nacht
pro Übernachtung DM 123 verlangen
 ♦ charge DM 123 per night
Provence, f
 (Region)
 ♦ Provence
Provencedorf, n
 ♦ Provençal village
Provence entdecken
 ♦ discover Provence
Provenceküche, f
 provenzalische Küche, f
 ♦ Provençal cooking
 ♦ Provençal cuisine
Provencestadt, f
 ♦ Provençal town
provenzalisch, adj
 ♦ Provençal, adj
provenzalische Art, adv gastr
 nach provenzalischer Art, adv gastr
 ♦ Provence style, adv gastr
pro Verlängerungstag
 pro Zusatztag
 ♦ per extra day
 ♦ per additional day
Proviant, m (generell)
 ♦ provisions pl
 ♦ food supplies pl
 ♦ supplies pl
Proviant, m (Lunchpaket)
 → Lunchpaket
Proviantausgabe, f
 ♦ issue of provisions
 ♦ issue of food (supplies)

 ♦ issuance of provisions AE
 ♦ issuance of (food) supplies AE
 ♦ issuing provisions
Proviant ausgeben
 ♦ issue provisions
 ♦ issue food supplies
 ♦ issue supplies
Proviantkorb, m (generell)
 Freßkorb, m coll
 ♦ lunch basket
 ♦ luncheon basket
Proviantkorb, m (Picknick)
 Picknickkorb, m
 ♦ picnic hamper
 ♦ hamper
Provinz, f
 ♦ province
Provinzdorf, n
 ♦ provincial village
Provinzhauptstadt, f
 ♦ provincial capital
Provinzhotel, n
 provinzielles Hotel, n
 Hotel in der Provinz, n
 ♦ provincial hotel
provinziell, adj
 ♦ provincial, adj
provinzielles Hotel, n
 → Provinzhotel
Provinzstadt, f
 ♦ provincial town
Provision, f
 ♦ commission
Provision bekommen (für etw)
 ♦ get (a) commission (on s.th.)
Provision berechnen
 Provision ausrechnen
 ♦ calculate a commission
 ♦ compute a commission
Provision erhalten (von jm)
 ♦ receive commission (from s.o.)
Provision für etw, f
 ♦ commission on s.th.
Provision geben jm
 ♦ give s.o. a commission
 ♦ give a commission to s.o.
Provision ist hoch
 ♦ commission is high
Provision ist niedrig
 ♦ commission is small
 ♦ commission is low
Provisionsanreiz, m
 ♦ commission incentive
Provisionsbasis, f
 ♦ commission basis
Provisionsbetrag, m
 ♦ amount of commission
 ♦ commission amount
Provisionseinnahmen, f pl
 ♦ commission receipts pl
 ♦ commission revenues pl
 ♦ commission takings pl
 ♦ commission income
provisionsfähig, adj
 provisionsträchtig, adj
 ♦ commissionable, adj
provisionsfähige Buchung, f
 ♦ commissionable booking
provisionsfähige Reservierung, f
 ♦ commissionable reservation

provisionsfrei, adj
 ♦ commission-free, adj
 ♦ free of commission, adj
provisionsfrei, adv
 ♦ without commission, adv
Provisionsgebühr, f
 ♦ commission charge
Provisionshöhe, f
 Provisionsniveau, n
 ♦ level of commission
Provisionskosten, pl
 ♦ commission costs pl
 ♦ commission cost
provisionspflichtig, adj
 ♦ subject to (a) commission, adj
Provisionspreis, m
 ♦ commission price
 ♦ commission rate
Provisionsprogramm, n
 ♦ commission program AE
 ♦ commission programme BE
Provisionsrechnung, f
 ♦ statement of commission
 ♦ commission account
Provisionsregelung, f
 Provisionsvereinbarung, f
 ♦ commission agreement
Provisionsreisender, m
 (Handlungsreisender)
 ♦ commission traveler AE
 ♦ commission traveller BE
 ♦ traveler on commission AE
 ♦ traveller on commission BE
Provisionssatz, m
 ♦ commission rate
 ♦ rate of commission
Provisionssumme, f
 Provisionsbetrag, m
 ♦ commission amount
 ♦ amount of commission
provisionsträchtig, adj
 → provisionsfähig
Provisionszahlung, f
 ♦ commission payment
 ♦ payment of (a) commission
 ♦ paying a commission
Provision verlangen
 Provision berechnen
 ♦ charge (a) commission
Provision vom Umsatz, f
 ♦ commission on sales
 ♦ commission on turnover
Provision von 10 %, f
 ♦ commission of 10 %
 ♦ 10 % commission
Provision zahlen jm
 ♦ pay s.o. a commission
 ♦ pay a commission to s.o.
Provison verlangen
 Provision berechnen
 ♦ charge a commission
 ♦ levy a commission
provisorisch, adj
 vorläufig, adj
 ♦ provisional, adj
provisorische Buchung, f
 → vorläufige Buchung
provisorische Konzession, f
 vorläufige Konzession, f
 provisorische Lizenz, f
 vorläufige Lizenz, f

♦ provisional license
♦ provisional licence
provisorische Reservierung, f
→ vorläufige Reservierung
provisorische Reservierung vornehmen
→ vorläufige Reservierung vornehmen
provisorisches Lager aufschlagen
♦ set up a provisional camp
provisorisches Programm, n
vorläufiges Programm, n
♦ provisional program AE
♦ provisional programme BE
provisorische Toilette, f
♦ temporary toilet
provisorische Unterkunft, f
vorläufige Unterkunft, f
provisorisches Logis, n
♦ provisional accommodation
♦ provisional lodging AE
♦ temporary accommodation
♦ makeshift accommodation
provisorisch reservieren etw
→ vorläufig reservieren etw
Provisorium, n
♦ temporary arrangement
Provokation, f
♦ provocation
provozieren jn
♦ provoke s.o.
pro Woche
♦ per week
Prozent, n
♦ percent AE
♦ per cent BE
Prozentpunkt, m
♦ percentage point
Prozentsatz, m
♦ percentage
prozentuale Auslastung, f
→ Auslastung in Prozent
prozentuale Auslastung berechnen
♦ calculate the percentage load factor
prozentuale Belegung, f
prozentuale Auslastung, f
♦ percentage occupancy
prozentuale Belegung berechnen
prozentuale Auslastung berechnen
♦ calculate the percentage occupancy
prozentuale Bettenauslastung, f
prozentuale Bettenbelegung, f
♦ bed occupancy percentage
♦ sleeper occupancy percentage
prozentuale Bettenbelegung, f
→ prozentuale Bettenauslastung
prozentuale Bettenbesetzung, f SCHW
→ prozentuale Bettenauslastung
prozentuale Gebühr f
♦ percentage fee
♦ percentage charge
prozentuale Jahresbelegung, f
Jahresauslastung in Prozent, f
prozentuale Jahresauslastung, f
Jahresbelegung in Prozent, f
♦ annual occupancy percentage
prozentuale Lebensmittelkosten, pl
→ Lebensmittelkosten in Prozent
prozentualer Bruttogewinn, m
♦ percentage gross profit
prozentualer Rohertrag, m (generell)
♦ percentage gross earning AE
♦ percentage gross profit

prozentualer Rohertrag, m (GuV)
♦ percentage gross income
prozentuale Wareneinsatzkosten Getränke, pl
♦ percentage drink cost of sales
prozentuale Zimmerauslastung, f
prozentuale Zimmerbelegung, f
♦ room occupancy percentage
prozentuale Zimmerbesetzung, f SCHW
→ prozentuale Zimmerauslastung
Prozession, f
Umzug, m
♦ procession
Prozession anführen
Umzug anführen
Zug anführen
♦ lead a procession
PR-Personal, n
♦ public relations personnel
♦ public relations staff
♦ PR personnel
♦ PR staff
PR-Übung, f
♦ PR exercise
♦ public relations exercise
prüfen etw
→ überprüfen etw
Prüfliste, f
Kontrolliste, f
♦ checklist
Prüfung, f (amtlich)
♦ certification
Prügel beziehen
♦ get beaten up
Prügelei, f
Krakeelerei, f
♦ brawl
♦ fight
Prunkbett, n
→ Paradebett
Prunkgemach, n
(z.B. in einem Schloß)
♦ state apartment
♦ apartment of state
prunkhaft, adj
♦ ostentatious, adj
Prunkkarosse, f
♦ state carriage
prunklos, adj
schlicht, adj
dezent, adj
unauffällig, adj
♦ unostentatious, adj
Prunksaal, m
(z.B. in einem Schloß)
♦ large stateroom
Prunkschlafgemach, n
(z.B. in einem Schloß)
♦ state bedroom
Prunkspeisesaal m
♦ state dining room
Prunkstück, n
♦ showpiece
prunkvoll, adj
♦ splendid, adj
♦ sumptuous, adj
♦ magnificent, adj
♦ gorgeous, adj
prunkvollen Rahmen bieten für etw
♦ provide a magnificent setting for s.th.
prunkvoller Rahmen, m
♦ magnificent setting

Prunkzimmer, n
(z.B. in Schloß)
♦ stateroom
PR-Veranstaltung, f
♦ PR event
♦ public relations event
PS
Pferdestärke, f
♦ hp
♦ horsepower
Pseudoveranstaltung, f
(z.B. für Touristen)
♦ pseudo-event
♦ pageant
Psoriasis, f med
Schuppenflechte, f med
♦ psoriasis med
Psychotherapie, f
♦ psychotherapy
Pub, m
Gasthaus, n
Gaststätte, f
♦ pub BE
♦ public house BE
Pub im britischen Stil, m
♦ British-style pub BE
Public Bar, f
(Gegensatz zu Lounge Bar in Pub)
♦ public bar BE
Public Relations, f
→ Öffentlichkeitsarbeit
Public-Relations-Abteilung, f
PR-Abteilung, f
Abteilung für Öffentlichkeitsarbeit, f
♦ public relations department
♦ PR department
Public-Relations-Arbeit, f
PR-Arbeit, f
Öffentlichkeitsarbeit, f
♦ public relations work
♦ PR work
Public-Relations-Budget, n
PR-Budget, n
PR-Etat, m
Etat für die Öffentlichkeitsarbeit, m
♦ public relations budget
♦ PR budget
Public-Relations-Gesellschaft, f
PR-Gesellschaft, f
PR-Firma, f
♦ public relations company
♦ PR company
Publikum, n (Gäste)
→ Klientel
Publikum, n (Messe)
♦ interested public, the
Publikum, n (Zuhörer)
Zuhörer, m pl
♦ audience
Publikum, n (Zuschauer)
♦ spectators pl
Publikum amüsieren
♦ amuse the audience
Publikum eines Kurorts, n
→ Gästekreis eines Kurorts
Publikum eines Restaurants, n
→ Gästekreis eines Restaurants
Publikumserfolg, m
♦ popular success

Publikumsliebling 602

Publikumsliebling, m
- favorite with the public *AE*
- favourite with the public *BE*

Publikumsraum, m
(der Öffentlichkeit zugänglich)
- public room

Publikumssitzung, f
- public session

Publikumstag, m
(Messe)
- public day

Publikumsteilnahme, f
- public attendance

Publikum verärgern
Zuhörer verärgern
- annoy the audience

Pudding, m
- pudding
- flan *FR*

Puderzucker, m
Staubzucker, m
- confectioner's sugar *AE*
- icing sugar *BE*

Puertoricaner, m
- Puerto Rican
- Porto Rican

Puertoricanerin, f
- Puerto Rican girl
- Puerto Rican woman
- Porto Rican
- Porto Rican girl
- Porto Rican woman

puertoricanisch, adj
- Puerto Rican, adj
- Porto Rican, adj

Puerto Rico
- Puerto Rico
- Porto Rico

Puff, m *inform*
Bordell, n
- sporting house *AE*
- brothel

Puffbohne, f
Saubohne, f
- horse bean
- Windsor bean
- broad bean

Puffmais, m
→ Popcorn

Puffmutter, f
- madam
- brothel keeper

Puffreis, m
- puffed rice

Pulle, f
→ Flasche

Pullmanbett, n
(in Verkehrsmitteln)
- Pullman bed
- Pullman berth

Pullmanbus, m
- Pullman bus

Pullmansessel, m
- Pullman chair

Pullmanwagen, m
(Eisenbahn)
- Pullman car *AE*
- Pullman carriage *BE*
- Pullman coach *BE*
- Pullman

Pult, n (bei Vortrag)
→ Vortragspult

Pult, n (Schreibpult)
- desk

Pultmikrofon, n
- lectern microphone

Pulverkaffee, m
- instant coffee

Pulverschnee, m
- powder snow
- powdery snow

Pumpernickel, m
(Brot)
- pumpernickel

pünktlich, adj
- punctual, adj

pünktlich, adv
- on time, adv
- punctually, adv

pünktlich abfahren
(Verkehrsmittel)
- leave on time
- leave punctually
- depart on time
- depart punctually

pünktlich abreisen
(Personen)
- depart on time
- depart punctually
- leave on time
- leave punctually

pünktlich ankommen
(Person oder Verkehrsmittel)
pünktlich eintreffen
- arrive on time
- arrive punctually

pünktlich einchecken
pünktlich eintreffen
- check in punctually
- check in on time

pünktlich eintreffen
→ pünktlich ankommen

pünktlicher Zahler, m
- prompt payer

Pünktlichkeit, f
- punctuality

Pünktlichkeit ist die Höflichkeit der Könige
- Punctuality is the politeness of kings

pünktlich sein
(Person)
- be punctual

pünktlich um 5 Uhr
Punkt 5 Uhr
- at 5 o'clock sharp
- at 5 o'clock prompt
- on the stroke of 5
- on the dot of 5 *coll*

pünktlich verkehren
(Transportmittel)
- run on time

pünktlich zahlen
- pay punctually

Punsch, m
- punch

Punschabend, m
- punch evening

Punschglas, n
- punch glass

Punschschüssel, f
- punch bowl

Puppenhaus, n
- dollhouse *AE*
- doll's house *BE*

Puppenküche, f
- doll's kitchen

Puppenmöbel, n pl
- doll's furniture *sg*

Puppenmuseum, n
- dolls museum
- museum of dolls

Puppen tanzen lassen
alle Puppen tanzen lassen
- live it up
- have a fling

Puppentheater, n
Spielzeugtheater, n
- toy theater *AE*
- toy theatre *BE*
- puppet theater *AE*
- puppet theatre *BE*

pur, adj
(Getränk)
→ unverdünnt

Püree, n
- puree *AE*
- purée *BE*
- mash

pürieren (etw)
- purée (s.th.) *BE*
- puree (s.th.) *AE*
- mash (s.th.)

püriert, adj
- puréed, adj
- pureed, adj *AE*

pürierte Karotten, f pl
- puréed carots *BE pl*
- pureed carots *AE pl*

Purser, m (Flugzeug)
Chefsteward, m
- purser

pur trinken etw
- drink s.th. neat

Pußta, f
- puszta

Pute, f
→ Truthahn

Putenbraten, m
→ Truthahnbraten

putten
(Golf)
- putt

Putting, n
Putten, n
- putting

Puttinggrün, n
- putting green *AE*
- putting-green *BE*

Puttingplatz, m
- putting course

Puttingrasen, m
- putting lawn

Puttingspiel, n
- game of putting

Puttingspiel machen
- have a game of putting

Puttingturnier, n
- putting tournament

Putzbrigade, f
- cleaning brigade

Putzdienst, m
→ Reinigungsdienst

putzen
　Reinigung durchführen
　◆ **do the cleaning**
putzen etw
　→ reinigen etw
Putzfrau, f
　◆ **cleaning woman**
　◆ cleaning lady
　◆ cleaner
　◆ charwoman
　◆ charlady *BE*
Putzhilfe, f
　(Person)
　◆ **cleaning help**
Putzkolonne, f
　◆ **cleaning crew**
　◆ cleaning squad
Putzkraft, f
　Reinigungskraft, f
　◆ **charwoman**
　◆ charlady *BE*
　◆ char *coll*
　◆ cleaning woman
　◆ cleaner
Putzlappen, m
　◆ **cleaning rag**
　◆ cleaning cloth
　◆ floor cloth *BE*
Putzleder, n
　Wildleder, n
　◆ **chamois leather**
　◆ chamois
　◆ leather
Putzmaterial, n
　Reinigungsmaterial n
　Putzzeug n
　Putzmittel n
　◆ **cleaning material**
Putzzeug, n
　◆ **cleaning things** *pl*
p.W.
　pro Woche
　◆ **p.w.**
　◆ per week
Pyjama, m
　Schlafanzug, m
　◆ **pyjamas** *BE pl*
　◆ pajamas *AE pl*
Pyramide, f
　◆ **pyramid**
Pyrenäen, die, pl
　◆ **Pyrenees, the** *pl*

Q.b.A.
→ Qualitätswein bestimmter Anbaugebiete
qm
 Quadratmeter, m
 ♦ **sq.m.**
 ♦ square meter *AE*
 ♦ square metre *BE*
Quadrat, n (generell)
 ♦ **square**
Quadrat, n (Häuserblock)
 Häuserblock, m
 Block, m
 ♦ **block**
Quadratfuß, m
 ♦ **square foot**
 ♦ sq.ft.
quadratisch, adj
 rechtwinklig, adj
 eckig, adj
 ♦ **square, adj**
quadratischer Tisch, m
 ♦ **square table**
quadratisches Zimmer, n
 ♦ **square room**
Quadratkilometer, m
 ♦ **square kilometer** *AE*
 ♦ square kilometre *BE*
Quadratmeile, f
 ♦ **square mile**
Quadratmeter, m
 qm
 ♦ **square meter** *AE*
 ♦ square metre *BE*
 ♦ sq.m.
Quadratmeterpreis, m
 ♦ **price per square meter** *AE*
 ♦ price per square metre *BE*
 ♦ price per sq.m.
Quai, m
 → Kai
Qual der Wahl, f
 → Wer die Wahl hat, hat die Qual
quälend, adj
 ♦ **raging, adj**
 ♦ tormenting, adj
 ♦ agonising, adj
 ♦ gnawing, adj
quälende Hitze, f
 ♦ **tormenting heat**
quälender Durst, m
 rasender Durst, m
 ♦ **raging thirst**
quälender Hunger, m
 ♦ **gnawing hunger**
Quälgeist, m
 (Person)
 ♦ **nuisance**

 ♦ pest
 ♦ plague *coll*
Qualifikation, f
 ♦ **qualification**
Qualifikationswettbewerb, m
 ♦ **qualifying contest**
qualifizieren sich für das Finale
 ♦ **qualify for the final**
qualifizieren sich (für etw)
 ♦ **qualify (for s.th.)**
 ♦ be eligible (for s.th.)
 ♦ be suitable (for s.th.)
qualifiziert, adj
 ♦ **qualified, adj**
 ♦ eligible, adj
 ♦ skilled, adj
qualifizierte Arbeitskräfte, f pl
 ♦ **skilled workers** *pl*
qualifizierter Fremdenführer, m
 ♦ **qualified tourist guide**
qualifizierter Führer, m
 fachkundiger Führer, m
 kundiger Führer, m
 ♦ **qualified guide**
qualifizierter Reiseleiter, m
 qualifizierte Reiseleitung, f
 ♦ **qualified tour guide**
qualifiziertes Personal, n
 fachkundiges Personal, n
 Fachpersonal, n
 ♦ **qualified personnel**
 ♦ qualified staff
Qualifizierung, f
 ♦ **qualifying**
 ♦ qualification
 ♦ eligibility
Qualität, f (generell)
 ♦ **quality**
Qualität, f (Güteklasse)
 ♦ **grade**
 ♦ class
Qualität beurteilen
 ♦ **assess the quality**
Qualität bewerten
 ♦ **evaluate the quality**
Qualität der Lebensmittel, f
 ♦ **quality of (the) food**
Qualität der Speisen, f
 ♦ **quality of the meals**
Qualität der Unterkunft, f
 ♦ **quality of (the) accommodation**
Qualität der Verpflegung, f
 ♦ **quality of foodservice** *AE*
 ♦ quality of catering *BE*
Qualität des Essens, f
 Essensqualität, f
 ♦ **quality of (the) food**

Qualität des Fremdenverkehrsangebots verbessern
 Qualität des touristischen Angebots verbessern
 Qualität des Tourismusangebots verbessern
 ♦ **improve the quality of tourist supply**
 ♦ improve the quality of tourism supply
Qualität des Service, f
 ♦ **quality of service**
Qualität ist unschlagbar
 Qualität ist unübertroffen
 ♦ **quality cannot be beaten**
qualitativ, adj
 ♦ **qualitative, adj**
qualitative Analyse, f
 ♦ **qualitative analysis**
Qualität mindern
 ♦ **reduce the quality**
Qualität prüfen
 ♦ **check (the) quality**
Qualitätsanforderung, f
 ♦ **quality requirement**
Qualitätsanforderungen erfüllen
 ♦ **meet quality requirements**
Qualitätsappartement, n
 Qualitätswohnung, f
 ♦ **quality apartment**
Qualitätsbeurteilung, f
 ♦ **quality assessment**
Qualitätsbewertung, f
 ♦ **quality evaluation**
qualitätsbewußt, adj
 ♦ **quality-conscious, adj**
Qualitätsbier, n
 ♦ **quality beer**
 ♦ high-quality beer
Qualitätsessen, n (Mahlzeit)
 ♦ **quality meal**
 ♦ high-quality meal
Qualitätsessen, n (Speisen)
 ♦ **quality food**
 ♦ high-quality food
Qualitätsgarantie, f
 ♦ **quality guarantee**
Qualitätsgetränk, n
 ♦ **quality beverage**
 ♦ quality drink
 ♦ high-quality beverage
 ♦ high-quality drink
Qualitätskontrolle, f
 ♦ **quality control**
Qualitätskontrolleur, m
 ♦ **quality controller**
Qualitätslandhaus, n
 Qualitätslandhäuschen, n
 ♦ **quality cottage**
Qualitätsmangel, m
 ♦ **quality defect**

Qualitätsminderung

Qualitätsminderung, f
　Qualitätsverminderung, f
　♦ reduction in quality
　♦ loss of quality
Qualitätsmöbel, n pl
　♦ quality furniture sg
Qualitätsniveau, n
　→ Qualitätsstufe
Qualitätsprüfer, m
　♦ quality checker
Qualitätsprüfung, f
　♦ quality test
　♦ checking (of) quality
Qualitätssicherung, f
　♦ quality assurance
Qualitätssicherungsprogramm, n
　♦ quality assurance program AE
　♦ quality assurance programme BE
Qualitätssiegel, n
　(z.B. bei Wein)
　♦ seal of quality
Qualitätsstandard, m
　♦ quality standard
　♦ standard of quality
Qualitätssteigerung, f
　Qualitätsverbesserung, f
　♦ quality improvement
　♦ improvement in quality
Qualitätsstufe, f
　Qualitätsniveau, n
　♦ quality level
Qualitätstourismus, m
　♦ quality tourism
Qualitätsunterkunft, f
　hochwertige Unterkunft, f
　♦ quality accommodation
　♦ high-quality accommodation
Qualitätsunterschied, m
　♦ difference in quality
Qualitätsurlaub, m
　Qualitätsferien, pl
　♦ quality vacation AE
　♦ quality holiday BE
Qualitätsverbesserung, f
　Qualitätssteigerung, f
　♦ improvement in quality
　♦ quality improvement
Qualitätsverlust, m
　♦ loss of quality
Qualitätsverpflegung, f
　♦ quality foodservice AE
　♦ quality catering BE
Qualitätsverschlechterung, f
　♦ deterioration in quality
Qualitätsvilla, f
　♦ quality villa
Qualitätsware, f
　Qualitätsprodukt, n
　♦ quality product
　♦ high-quality product
Qualitätswein, m
　♦ quality wine
　♦ high-quality wine
　♦ vintage wine
Qualitätswein bestimmter Anbaugebiete, m
　Qualitätswein b.A., m
　Q.b.A., m
　♦ quality wine of a designated area
Qualitätsweingebiet, n
　♦ quality-wine region

Qualitätszeichen, n
　♦ mark of quality
Qualitätszertifikat, n
　♦ certificate of quality
Qualitätszielort, m
　Qualitätsdestination, f
　♦ quality destination
Qualitätszimmer, n
　♦ quality room
Qualitätszutat, f
　♦ quality ingredient
Qualität testen
　♦ test the quality
Qualität verbessern
　♦ improve the quality
Qualität zählt mehr als Quantität
　♦ quality matters more than quantity
Qualität zahlt sich aus
　♦ quality pays off
Qualle, f
　♦ jellyfish
qualvolle Enge, f
　enges Quartier, n
　♦ cramped quarters pl
quantifizieren (etw)
　♦ quantify (s.th.)
Quantifizierung, f
　♦ quantification
Quantität, f
　Menge, f
　♦ quantity
　♦ qty.
quantitativ, adj
　♦ quantitative, adj
quantitative Analyse, f
　♦ quantitative analysis
quantitative Verminderung, f
　♦ quantitative decrease
　♦ decrease in quantity
Quarantäne, f
　♦ quarantine
Quarantäne aufheben
　♦ lift the quarantine
　♦ remove the quarantine
　♦ take off the quarantine
Quarantänebeamter, m
　♦ quarantine official
Quarantäne durchmachen
　♦ perform one's quarantine
Quarantäneflagge, f
　♦ yellow flag
　♦ yellow jack sl
Quarantänegesetz, n
　♦ quarantine law
Quarantäne halten müssen
　Quarantäne unterworfen sein
　♦ be subject to quarantine
Quarantäneprüfung, f
　♦ quarantine inspection
Quarantänestation, f
　♦ quarantine ward
　♦ quarantine station
　♦ isolation ward
Quarantäne verhängen über jn
　in Quarantäne nehmen jn
　♦ quarantine s.o.
Quarantänevorschriften, f pl
　Quarantänebestimmungen, f pl
　♦ quarantine regulations pl
Quarantänevorschriften verletzen
　♦ break the quarantine regulations

Quarantänezeit, f
　♦ quarantine period
Quarantänezwinger, m
　(für Tiere)
　♦ quarantine kennel
Quark, m
　♦ curd
Quarkcreme, f
　♦ curd cream
Quarkdressing, n
　♦ curd dressing
Quarkkäse, m
　Weißkäse, m
　♦ curd cheese
Quarkkuchen, m
　♦ curd cake
Quart, f obs
　(Maß)
　♦ quart
Quartal, n
　Vierteljahr, n
　♦ quarter
Quartalsabrechnung, f
　♦ quarterly statement of account
　♦ quarterly statement
Quartalsanfang, m
　Quartalsbeginn, m
　♦ beginning of the quarter
　♦ start of the quarter
　♦ commencement of the quarter form
Quartalsäufer, m
　♦ bout drinker BE
　♦ habitual drunkard
　♦ incurable drunkard
Quartalsende, n
　♦ end of the quarter
Quartalskündigung, f
　vierteljährliche Kündigung, f
　♦ quarterly notice
　♦ notice by the quarter
Quartalsmiete, f
　Vierteljahresmiete, f
　♦ quarter's rent
Quartalsrechnung, f
　♦ quarterly bill
　♦ quarterly check AE
　♦ quarterly account
Quartalstag, m ökon
　♦ quarter day
Quartalsvergleich, m
　♦ comparison of quarters
quartalsweise, adv
　♦ quarterly, adv
　♦ by the quarter, adv
　♦ every three months, adv
quartalsweise zahlen
　vierteljährlich zahlen
　♦ pay by the quarter
Quartalszahlung, f
　Vierteljahreszahlung, f
　♦ quarterly payment
　♦ quarter's payment
Quartett, n
　♦ quartet
Quartier, n (Militär)
　♦ quarters pl
　♦ quarterage
　♦ quartering
　♦ billet

Quartier, n (Stadtviertel)
- quarter
- district

Quartier, n (Unterkunft)
- quarters *pl*
- lodging
- accommodation
- digs *BE pl coll*
- lodgings *pl*

Quartieramt, n (Militär)
Quartierbüro, n
- billet office *AE*
- billeting office *BE*

Quartier aufschlagen (in X)
- take up one's quarters (in/at X)

Quartier benötigen für jn
- require quarters for s.o.

Quartierbeschaffungsstelle, f
Quartierbüro, n
- lodging bureau

Quartier besorgen
Quartier beschaffen
Quartier vermitteln
- arrange for accommodation

Quartier besorgen für jn
→ Unterkunft besorgen für jn

Quartier beziehen
(Militär oder Privatperson)
- take up quarters

Quartier beziehen in einem Dorf
- take up quarters in a village

Quartier beziehen in einem Hotel
→ Quartier nehmen in einem Hotel

Quartierbüro, n
→ Quartieramt

Quartier finden bei jm
- find lodgings with s.o.

Quartier finden für die Nacht
Logis finden für die Nacht
- find a lodging for the night
- find lodgings for the night

Quartier für die Nacht, n
Unterkunft für die Nacht, f
- accommodation for the night
- night's lodging
- lodging for the night

Quartier geben jm
- put s.o. up

Quartiergeber m
→ Quartierwirt

Quartiergutschein, m
→ Unterkunftsgutschein

Quartier haben bei jm
- lodge with s.o.

Quartier machen
- prepare quarters

Quartiermacher, m (Militär)
- billet officer *AE*
- billeting officer *BE*

Quartiermeister, m (Militär)
- quartermaster
- billet master

Quartier nehmen
- take lodgings

Quartier nehmen in einem Hotel
Quartier beziehen in einem Hotel
- stop at a hotel

Quartierort, m
Standquartier, n
- base

Quartierproblem, n
→ Unterkunftsproblem

Quartierschein, m (Militär)
Quartierzettel, m
- billet paper *AE*
- billeting paper *BE*
- billeting slip *BE*

Quartiersuche, f
- looking for accommodation
- hunting for accommodation
- looking for quarters
- hunting for quarters

Quartier suchen
→ Unterkunft suchen

Quartier und Verpflegung
→ Kost und Logis

Quartierverteilung, f
Quartiervergabe, f
Quartierzuweisung, f
Quartierzuteilung, f
- allocation of quarters
- assignment of quarters *AE*
- allocating quarters
- assigning quarters *AE*

Quartier wechseln
umziehen
- change one's quarters

Quartierwirt, m
Quartiergeber, m
- host
- landlord

Quartierzettel, m (Militär)
- billet
- billeting slip *BE*

Quarzlampe, f
- quartz lamp

Quarzuhr, f
- quartz clock

Quasivertrag, m
- quasi-contract

Queen Room, m
(Zimmer mit Queen-Size-Bett)
- queen room
- queen

Queen-Size-Bett n
- queen-size bed
- queen bed

Quelle, f
- well
- spring

Quelle, f (Fluß und figurativ)
- source

Quelle, f (in der Erde)
- spring
- well

Quelle ausbeuten
- exploit a spring

Quell-Land, n
- source country

Quellmarkt, m
- source market

Quellwasser, n
- springwater *AE*
- spring water *BE*

Quellwasser abfüllen
- bottle springwater *AE*
- bottle spring water *BE*

Quellwasserbad, n (Aktivität)
- springwater bath *AE*
- spring-water bath *BE*

Quellwasserbad, n (Becken)
- springwater pool *AE*
- spring-water pool *BE*

Quentchen, n
- tiny bit
- pinch *gastr*

Quentchen Salz, n
- sprinkle of salt

quer auf dem Bett liegen
- lie across the bed

Querbett, n
(Wohnwagen)
- transverse bed
- transverse bunk

Querdoppelbett, n
(Wohnwagen)
- transverse double bed
- transverse double bunk

quer durch Bayern
- across Bavaria

quer durch etw
- across s.th.

querfeldein, adv
- across country, adv
- cross-country, adj
- off-piste, adv

Querfeldeinlauf, m
(Laufen)
Waldlauf, m
- cross-country run

Querfeldeinlaufen, n
Querfeldeinlauf, m
Waldlaufen, n
Waldlauf, m
- cross-country running

Querfeldeinradfahren, n
- cross-country cycling

Querfeldeinrennen, n (Radsport)
Querfeldeinfahren, n
- cyclo-cross race
- cyclo-cross

Querfeldeinritt, m
- cross-country ride

Querfeldeinskifahren, n
→ Variantenskifahren

Querfeldeinstrecke, f
- cross-country course

Querfeldeinwettkampf, m
- cross-country contest

Querhaus, n (Kirche)
Querschiff, n
Transept, m/n
- transept

quer sitzen
- sit sideways

Querstraße, f (Abzweigung)
- turning
- intersecting road

Querstraße, f (Seitenstraße)
Seitenstraße, f
- street off (another street)
- road off (another road)

Querulant, m
- troublemaker
- grouch *AE*

Quiche, f
- quiche

Quiche Lorraine, f
- quiche lorraine

Quid pro quo

Quid pro quo, n
   Gegenleistung, f
   ♦ quid pro quo
quietschendes Bett, n
   ♦ squeaking bed
Quintett, n
   ♦ quintet
Quirl, m
   ♦ beater
Quitte, f
   ♦ quince
Quittengelee, n
   ♦ quince jelly
Quittenkompott, n
   ♦ quince compote AE
   ♦ quince compôte BE
Quittenkonfitüre, f
   ♦ quince jam
Quittenlikör, m
   ♦ quince liqueur
quittieren etw (Eingang)
   bestätigen etw (Eingang)
   ♦ acknowledge s.th.
quittieren etw (Rechnung)
   ♦ receipt s.th.
   ♦ give a receipt for s.th.
quittiert, adj
   ♦ receipted, adj
quittierte Rechnung, f
   ♦ receipted bill
   ♦ receipted check AE
   ♦ receipted invoice
quitt sein (mit jm)
   ♦ be quits (with s.o.)
Quittung, f
   ♦ receipt
Quittung aufbewahren
   ♦ retain a receipt
Quittung aushändigen
   Quittung ausstellen
   ♦ issue a receipt
Quittung ausstellen
   ♦ make out a receipt
   ♦ give a receipt
Quittung ausstellen in doppelter Ausfertigung
   ♦ make out a receipt in duplicate
Quittung geben
   ♦ give a receipt
Quittungsaussteller, m
   ♦ receiptor
Quittungsbuch, n
   ♦ receipt book
Quittungsdurchschrift, f
   Quittungsduplikat, n
   ♦ duplicate receipt
Quittungsformular, n
   ♦ receipt form
Quittungsinhaber, m
   ♦ receipt holder
   ♦ holder of a receipt
Quittungskarte, f
   ♦ receipt card
Quittungsstempel, m
   ♦ receipt stamp
Quittung über den ganzen Betrag, f
   ♦ receipt in full
Quittung über den Restbetrag, f
   ♦ receipt for the balance
Quittung über DM 123, f
   ♦ receipt for DM 123

Quiz, n
   ♦ quiz
Quizabend, m
   ♦ quiz night
Quizmaster, m (generell)
   ♦ quizmaster AE
   ♦ quiz-master BE
   ♦ question master
Quizmaster, m (Sendung)
   ♦ quiz-show host
   ♦ game-show host
Quizprogramm, n
   Quizsendung, f (TV, Radio)
   ♦ quiz program AE
   ♦ quiz programme BE
Quizsendung, f (generell)
   Quizshow, f
   ♦ quiz show
Quizsendung, f (Spiele)
   ♦ game-show
Quizshow, f
   → Quizsendung
Quizspiel, n
   ♦ quiz game
Quizteilnehmer, m
   ♦ quiz panelist AE
   ♦ quiz panellist BE
Quodlibet, n
   Potpourri, m
   Allerlei, n
   ♦ quodlibet
Quote, f
   ♦ quota
   ♦ allotment
   ♦ allocation
Quote anheben
   ♦ raise the quota
Quote erhöhen
   ♦ increase the quota
Quote festsetzen
   Quote festlegen
   ♦ fix a quota
   ♦ establish a quota
Quotenanteil, m
   ♦ quota share
Quotenbeschränkung, f
   ♦ quota restriction
Quotenerhöhung, f
   ♦ quota increase
   ♦ increase in quotas
Quotenkürzung, f
   ♦ quota cut
   ♦ reduction of a quota
quotenmäßig, adj
   anteilsmäßig, adj
   ♦ pro rata, adj
   ♦ quotational, adj
quotenmäßige Verteilung, f
   ♦ pro-rata distribution
Quotensystem, n
   Zuteilungssystem, n
   Kontingentierungssystem, n
   ♦ quota system
Quotenzuteilung, f
   Quotenvergabe, f
   ♦ allocation of quotas
   ♦ assignment of quotas AE
Quote senken
   Quote kürzen
   ♦ reduce a quota

Quote überschreiten
   ♦ exceed the quota
Quote vereinbaren
   ♦ agree on a quota
Quote zuteilen
   ♦ apportion a quota
Quotient, m
   ♦ quotient
quotieren (etw)
   ♦ quota (s.th.)
   ♦ allot (s.th.)
   ♦ allocate (s.th.)

R

Rabatt, m
- discount
- rebate

Rabatt anbieten
- offer a discount

Rabatt anbieten auf etw
- offer a discount on s.th.

Rabattangebot, n
- discount offer

Rabatt auf etw, m
- discount on s.th.

Rabatt aushandeln
- negotiate a discount
- negotiate a rebate

Rabattcoupon m
- discount coupon

Rabatt erhalten
- receive a discount

Rabatt erhalten von 15 % auf den Schrankpreis
- receive a 15 % discount off the rack rate
- receive a discount of 15 % off the rack rate

Rabattfahrpreis, m
- discount fare

Rabattflug, m
- discount flight

Rabatt für Kinder unter zwölf Jahren
- discount for children under twelve years (of age)

Rabatt geben
- give a discount

Rabatt geben von DM 123 auf etw
- give a discount of DM 123 on s.th.

Rabatt gewähren
- allow a discount
- grant a discount

Rabatt gewähren auf etw
- grant a discount on s.th.
- allow a discount on s.th.

Rabatt gewähren jm
  Rabatt zugestehen jm
- grant s.o. a discount
- grant a discount to s.o.

Rabattgutschein, m
- discount voucher

Rabattpreis, m
- discount price
- discount rate

Rabatt von 7 % anbieten
- offer a discount of 7 %
- offer a 7 % discount

Rabattzahlung, f
- rebate payment

Rabatz, m coll
- racket coll
- row BE
- rowdydow AE coll
- row-de-dow AE coll
- hell of a racket

Rabatz machen coll
- make a hell of a racket coll

RAC-empfohlenes Hotel, n
  vom RAC empfohlenes Hotel, n
  vom Royal Automobile Club empfohlenes Hotel, n
- RAC Commended Hotel BE

Rack, n
- rack

Rackkarte, f
- rack card

Rackrate, f
  Standardzimmerpreis, m
  Tarifpreis, m
  Schrankpreis, m
- rack rate

Rackzettel, m
  (Rezeption)
- rack slip

Raclette, f/n
- raclette

Racletteabend m
- raclette evening

Racletteparty f
- raclette party

Rad, n (Fahrrad oder Motorrad) coll
  Fahrrad, n
  Motorrad, n
- bike coll

Radausflug, m
  Fahrradausflug, m
- cycling excursion
- bicycle excursion

Rad benutzen
  Fahrrad benutzen
- use a bike
- use a bicycle

Raddampfer, m
  Schaufelraddampfer, m
- paddle steamer AE
- paddle-wheeler AE
- paddle-steamer BE

radebrechen
- speak broken (English etc)

radeln
→ radfahren

radeln durch Europa
- cycle through Europe
- wheel through Europe AE

Radelpartie, f
→ Radtour

radfahren
  radeln
- cycle
- ride a (bi)cycle
- bicycle
- go by bicycle
- bike coll

Radfahren, n
- cycling
- bicycling

Radfahrer, m
  Radler, m
- cyclist
- bicycle rider
- bicyclist
- cycler AE
- bike rider

radfahrerfreundlich, adj
- cyclist-friendly, adj

Radfahrt, f
- bike ride
- cycle ride

Radfahrweg, m
→ Fahrradweg

Radferien, pl
→ Fahrradferien

Radgeschäft, n coll
- bike store AE coll
- bike shop BE coll

Radiator, m
→ Heizkörper

Radio, n
- radio
- radio set

Radioanschluß f
- radio connection

Radiogerät, n
- radio set

Radio in allen Zimmern
- radio sets in all rooms

Radio leiser stellen
- turn the radio down

Radio mit Wecker, n
→ Radiowecker

Radiowecker, m
  Radio mit Wecker, n
- radio alarm clock

Radius, m
- radius

Radkarte, f (Landkarte)
  Fahrradkarte, f
- cycling map

Radler, m (Getränk) BAY
  (Bier mit Limonade)
  Radlermaß, f BAY
  Alsterwasser, n
- shandy

Radler, m (Person)
  Radfahrer, m
- bike rider
- cyclist
- bicycle rider

Radlermaß, f
→ Radler

Radlermaß

Rad mieten
- ♦ rent a cycle *AE*
- ♦ rent a bike *AE coll*
- ♦ hire a cycle *BE*
- ♦ hire a bike *BE coll*

Radpauschalurlaub, m
Fahrradpauschalurlaub, m
- ♦ cycling package vacation *AE*
- ♦ cycling package holiday *BE*

Radrennbahn, f
- ♦ cycling track

Radrennen, n
Fahrradrennen, n
- ♦ cycle race
- ♦ bicycle race
- ♦ bike race *coll*

Radrennfahrer, m
- ♦ racing cyclist

Radsafari, f
- ♦ cycling safari

Radsport, m
- ♦ bicycling
- ♦ cycling

Radsportler, m
- ♦ bicyclist
- ♦ cyclist

Radtag, m
Fahrradtag, m
Radfahrtag, m
- ♦ cycling day

Radtour, f
Fahrradtour, f
- ♦ cycling tour
- ♦ cycle tour
- ♦ bicycle tour

Radtourismus, m
- ♦ cycle tourism
- ♦ cycle touring

Radtourist, m
- ♦ cycling tourist

Radurlaub, m
Fahrradurlaub, m
Radferien, pl
Fahrradferien, pl
- ♦ cycle vacation *AE*
- ♦ cycling vacation *AE*
- ♦ cycle holiday *BE*
- ♦ cycling holiday *BE*
- ♦ biking holiday *BE coll*

Radverleih, m
Radvermietung, f
Fahrradverleih, m
Fahrradvermietung, f
- ♦ bike rental *AE coll*
- ♦ cycle rental *AE*
- ♦ cycle hire *BE*
- ♦ bike hire *BE coll*
- ♦ bicycle rental *AE*

Rad vermieten
- ♦ rent (out) a bike *coll*
- ♦ hire out a bike *BE coll*

Radwanderer, m
→ Fahrradwanderer

Radwandern, n
→ Fahrradwandern

Radwanderung, f
→ Fahrradwanderung

Radwanderweg, m
Fahrradwanderweg, m
- ♦ bicycle trail
- ♦ bike trail *coll*

Radwanderwoche, f
- ♦ cycling week

Radweg, m
Fahrradweg, m
- ♦ cycle path
- ♦ cycling path
- ♦ cycleway
- ♦ cycle track
- ♦ bike path *coll*

Radwegenetz, n
- ♦ network of cycle paths
- ♦ cycle path network
- ♦ network of cycling paths
- ♦ network of cycling trails
- ♦ cycle network

Radwegenetz erweitern
- ♦ expand the network of cycle paths

Radwoche, f
- ♦ bike week *coll*

Raft, n
→ Floß

Rafting, n
→ Floßfahren

Ragout, n/m
- ♦ ragout
- ♦ stew

Ragoutschüssel, f
- ♦ vegetable tureen

Ragoutsoße, f
- ♦ ragout sauce

Rahm, m
- ♦ cream

Rahmdressing, n
Sahnedressing, n
- ♦ cream dressing

Rahmen, m (Bild)
- ♦ frame

Rahmen, m (Veranstaltung)
Umrahmung, f
- ♦ setting

Rahmen der Konferenz, m
- ♦ setting of the conference

Rahmen einer Veranstaltung, m
Veranstaltungsrahmen, m
- ♦ setting of an event
- ♦ setting of a function

Rahmen eines Kongresses, m
→ Kongreßrahmen

Rahmenprogramm, n
(außerhalb der Veranstaltung)
Gesellschaftsprogramm, n
- ♦ social program *AE*
- ♦ social programme *BE*
- ♦ fringe program *AE*
- ♦ fringe programme *BE*

Rahmenprogramm bieten
- ♦ provide a social program *AE*
- ♦ provide a social programme *BE*
- ♦ provide a fringe program *AE*
- ♦ provide a fringe programme *BE*

Rahmenprogrammveranstalter, m
- ♦ social program organiser *AE*
- ♦ social programme organiser *BE*

Rahmenveranstaltung, f
Nebenveranstaltung, f
- ♦ fringe event

rahmig, adj
sahnig, adj
cremig, adj
- ♦ creamy, adj

Rahmkäse, m
Sahnekäse, m
Vollfettkäse, m
- ♦ cream cheese

Rahmsoße, f
Sahnesoße, f
- ♦ cream sauce

Rallye, f
Sternfahrt, f
- ♦ rally

Rallyefahrer, m
- ♦ rally driver

Ramadan, m
- ♦ Ramadan

Rampe, f
(zum Laden)
- ♦ ramp

ramponiert, adj
abgenutzt, adj
verschlissen, adj
- ♦ battered, adj
- ♦ worn, adj
- ♦ run-down, adj

ramponierter Sessel, m
- ♦ battered armchair

Ramschladen, m
- ♦ jumble shop

Ranch, f
- ♦ ranch

Ranchbesitzer, m
- ♦ ranch owner

Ranchgast, m
- ♦ ranch guest

Ranchhaus, n
- ♦ ranch house

Ranchurlaub, m
Ranchferien, pl
- ♦ ranch vacation *AE*
- ♦ ranch holiday *BE*

Rand, m
- ♦ edge
- ♦ margin
- ♦ verge

randalieren
- ♦ kick up a racket *coll*
- ♦ kick up a shindy *coll*
- ♦ kick up a row *BE coll*
- ♦ raise the roof *coll*

Randalierer, m
Rowdy, m
- ♦ hooligan
- ♦ rowdy

Randlage, f
- ♦ marginal location
- ♦ marginal situation
- ♦ marginal position

Randmonat, m
- ♦ fringe month

Randstein, m
Bordstein, m
Randkante, f
Straßenkante, f
- ♦ kerb *BE*
- ♦ kerbstone *BE*
- ♦ curb *AE*
- ♦ curbstone *AE*

Randveranstaltung, f
→ Rahmenveranstaltung

randvolles Glas, n
- ♦ bumper

Rang, m
- rank
Rangierbahnhof, m
- shunting yard BE
- switchyard AE
Rangloge, f (Theater)
- dress circle
- first-balcony box AE
- first balcony AE
Rangplatz, m (Theater)
Platz im ersten Rang, m
- dress-circle seat
- seat in the dress circle
- first-balcony seat AE
- seat in the first balcony AE
rank und schlank, adj
- slim and trim, adj
rank und schlank bleiben
- stay slim and trim
ranzig, adj
- rancid, adj
ranziges Essen, n
- rancid food
ranzig werden
- turn rancid
Raritätenkabinett, n
- curiosity cabinet
rascher Service, m
schneller Service, m
- rapid service
Rasen, m
- lawn
rasenden Hunger haben
Mordshunger haben coll
- be ravenous
- feel ravenous
rasender Durst, m
→ quälender Durst
rasender Hunger, m
→ Kohldampf
Rasenkegeln, n
- lawn bowling
- bowls pl=sg
Rasen mähen
- mow the lawn
Rasenplatz, m (Tennis)
- lawn court
Rasensprenger, m
Sprenger, m
- sprinkler
Rasentennis, n
- lawn tennis
Rasentennisplatz, m
- lawn tennis court
Rasen zum Entspannen, m
- lawn for relaxing
Rasierapparat, m
- razor
- shaver
Rasiermesser, n
- razor blade
Rasierschaum, m
- shaving foam
Rasiersteckdose, f
- shaver point
- shaver socket
- razor socket BE
- razor point
- razor outlet AE

Rasierzeug, n
- shaving things pl
- shaving kit
rassiger Wein, m
- racy wine
Rasthaus, n (generell)
- rest house
Rasthaus, n (Landstraße)
→ Landstraßenrasthaus
Rasthof, m
→ Rasthaus
Rasthütte, f
- rest hut
Rastlager, n
- rest camp
Rast machen
- take a rest
- make a halt
- make a stop
- have a rest
Rastplatz, m (allgemein)
Platz zum Rasten m
Platz zum Ausruhen m
- resting place
- rest area
- stopping area
- picnic area
Raststätte, f (Autobahn)
Raststation, f ÖST
- motorway service area BE
- highway service area AE
- service area
Raststättenkonzession, f
Autobahnraststättenkonzession, f
- highway service center concession AE
- motorway service centre concession BE
Rat annehmen
Ratschlag annehmen
- accept advice
Ratatouille, f/n FR
- ratatouille FR
Rat d'hôtel, m FR
Hotelratte, f sl
Hoteldieb, m
- rat d'hôtel FR
- hotel thief
Ratenzahlung, f
Rate, f
- instalment
- installment AE
Ratgeber, m
Berater, m
- counsellor
- counselor AE
Rathaus, n (Dorf)
- village hall
Rathaus, n (Großstadt)
- city hall
Rathaus, n (kleine Stadt)
- town hall
Rathauscafé, n (Großstadt)
- city hall cafe AE
- city hall café
Rathauscafé, n (kleine Stadt)
- town hall café
Rathaus einer Grafschaft, n
- county hall BE
Rathausmuseum, n
- town hall museum
Rathausplatz, m (Großstadt)
- city hall square

Rathausplatz, m (kleine Stadt)
- town hall square
Rathausturm, m
- town hall tower
Ration, f
- ration
rationalisieren etw
- rationalise s.th.
- rationalize s.th.
- streamline s.th.
Rationalisierung, f
- rationalisation
- rationalization
Rationalisierungskosten, pl
- rationalisation cost
- rationalisation costs pl
- costs of rationalisation pl
Ration Bier, f
Quantum Bier, n
- ration of beer
Rationierung, f
- rationing
Rationierungskarte, f
- ration card
- coupon
Rätischen Alpen, die, pl
- Rhaetian Alps, the pl
ratsam, adj
empfehlenswert, adj
- advisable, adj
Ratschlag, m
Rat, m
- advice
- piece of advice
Ratschläge zur Ernährung geben
- give advice on nutrition
Ratsherr, m
- councillor
Ratsherrenstube, f
- councillors' tavern
Ratskeller, m
(Gaststätte im Rathaus)
- rathskeller AE
- restaurant in a town hall
- restaurant in a city hall
Ratssaal, m
Ratszimmer, n
- council chamber
Ratsschenke, f
→ Ratsstube
Ratssitzung, f
Ratsitzung, f
- council meeting
Ratsstube, f (Großstadt)
(Restaurant)
- City Hall restaurant
Ratsstube, f (kleine Stadt)
(Restaurant)
- town hall restaurant
Rattan, n
Peddigrohr, n
- rattan
Rattanmöbel, n pl
Peddigrohrmöbel, n pl
- rattan furniture sg
- cane furniture sg
rattanmöbliert, adj
- rattan-furnished, adj
- cane-furnished, adj
Ratte, f
- rat

Rattenfänger

Rattenfänger, m (figurativ)
 ♦ Pied Piper
Rattenfänger, m (konkret)
 ♦ ratcatcher
Rattenfänger von Hameln, m
 ♦ Pied Piper of Hamelin
Rattengift, n
 ♦ rat poison
Rattenloch, n
 (schlechte Unterkunft)
 ♦ rathole
Ratzeburger See m
 ♦ Lake Ratzeburg
Räuberhöhle, f
 ♦ robbers' den
 ♦ thieves' den
Raubritter, m
 ♦ robber baron
 ♦ robber knight
Raubritterburg, f
 ♦ robber baron's castle
 ♦ robber knight's castle
rauchen
 ♦ smoke
rauchen im Bett
 ♦ smoke in (one's) bed
Rauchen verbieten
 das Rauchen verbieten
 ♦ ban smoking
rauchen wie ein Schlot
 qualmen wie ein Schlot
 ♦ smoke like a chimney
Raucher, m
 ♦ smoker
Räucheraal, m
 geräucherter Aal, m
 ♦ smoked eel
Raucherabteil, n
 (Zug)
 ♦ smoking compartment
 ♦ smoker
Raucherentwöhnungsprogramm, n
 ♦ stop smoking program AE
 ♦ stop smoking programme BE
Räucherhering, m
 ♦ kipper
 ♦ smoked herring
Räucherkerze, f
 ♦ aromatic candle
Räucherlachs, m
 → geräucherter Lachs
Räucherlachsbrot, n
 ♦ smoked salmon sandwich
Räucherlachsbutter, f
 ♦ smoked salmon butter
räuchern etw
 ♦ smoke s.th.
 ♦ cure s.th.
Räucherofen, m
 ♦ curing furnace
Raucherplatz, m
 ♦ smoking seat
Rauchersalon, m
 ♦ smokers' lounge
Räucherschinken, m
 → geräucherter Schinken
Raucherzimmer, n
 ♦ smoke room
 ♦ smoking room

Rauchfleisch, n
 geräuchertes Fleisch, n
 ♦ smoked meat
rauchfrei, adj
 ♦ smoke-free, adj
rauchfreie Zone, f
 ♦ smoke-free zone
Rauchglas, n
 ♦ tinted glass
Rauchmelder, m
 ♦ smoke detector
 ♦ smoke detection device
Rauchmelder installieren auf jedem Stockwerk
 ♦ instal smoke detectors on every floor AE
 ♦ install smoke detectors on every floor BE
Rauchsalon, m
 Rauchzimmer, n
 ♦ smoking room
Rauchtabak, m
 ♦ smoking tobacco
Rauchverbot, n
 ♦ smoking ban
Rauchwarenumsatz, m
 ♦ tobacco sales pl
 ♦ tobacco turnover
Rauchzimmer, n
 → Rauchsalon
rauhe Begrüßung, f
 unfreundliche Begrüßung f
 ♦ rough welcome
rauhes Klima, n
 ♦ harsh climate
Rauhputz, m
 ♦ roughcast plastering
Raum, m (Volumen)
 ♦ space
Raum, m (Zimmer)
 Zimmer, n
 ♦ room
Raumangebot, n (Volumen)
 ♦ availability of space
 space available
 ♦ available space
Raumangebot, n (Zimmer)
 → Zimmerangebot
Raumanmietung, f
 → Anmietung eines Raumes
Raumausnutzung, f
 Raumnutzung, f
 ♦ utilisation of room space
 utilization of room space
 ♦ use of (available) space
Raumausstatter, m
 → Innendekorateur
Raumausstattung, f
 → Innenausstattung
Raumbedarf, m
 benötigter Raum, m
 benötigte Fläche, f
 ♦ required space
 ♦ space required
Raum bestellen für ein Abendessen
 Zimmer buchen für ein Diner
 ♦ book a room for dinner
Räume für gewerbliche Zwecke, m pl
 ♦ rooms for commercial purposes pl
räumen etw bis 11 Uhr (Unterkunft)
 frei machen etw bis 11 Uhr
 ♦ vacate s.th. by 11 o'clock
räumen etw (Straße)
 ♦ clear s.th.

räumen etw (Unterkunft)
 frei machen etw
 ♦ vacate s.th.
 ♦ leave s.th.
Räumen Sie bitte den Saal!
 ♦ Leave the room, please!
Raumfahrt, f
 ♦ space travel
Raum für geschlossene Veranstaltungen, m
 → Raum für private Veranstaltungen
Raum für private Veranstaltungen, m
 Privatveranstaltungsraum, m
 Raum für geschlossene Veranstaltungen, m
 ♦ private function room
 ♦ room for private functions
 ♦ private room
Raumgestaltung, f
 ♦ interior design
Raum hat eine Breite von 20 m, eine Länge von
 30 m und eine Höhe von 4 m
 ♦ room has a width of 20 m, a length of 30 m,
 and a height of 4 m
Raum hat (eine) ideale Akustik
 ♦ room provides ideal acoustics
Raum hat Platz für 123 Personen
 Raum bietet für 123 Personen Sitzplätze
 ♦ room seats 123 persons
Raum ist unterteilbar in zwei Einheiten
 ♦ room is divisible into two units
Raum kann durch Schiebewand unterteilt werden
 ♦ room can be partitioned by a sliding screen
Raum kann verdunkelt werden
 ♦ room can be blacked out
Raumkapazität, f
 Zimmerkapazität, f
 ♦ capacity of a room
 ♦ capacity of the rooms
 ♦ room capacity
Raumkosten, pl
 ♦ room costs pl
 ♦ room cost
Raum kostenlos zur Verfügung stellen
 Zimmer kostenlos bereitstellen
 ♦ provide a room free of charge
Räumlichkeit, f
 ♦ room
 ♦ facility
Räumlichkeiten für Geschäftsbesprechungen, f pl
 ♦ facilities for business meetings pl
Räumlichkeiten für Sitzungen und Konferenzen, f pl
 ♦ facilities for meetings and conferences pl
Räumlichkeiten haben für Geschäftsbesprechungen
 ♦ have facilities for business meetings
Räumlichkeiten zur Erholung und Unterhaltung, f pl
 ♦ facilities for recreation and entertainment pl
Raummaße, n pl
 Zimmermaße, n pl
 ♦ room measurements pl
 ♦ measurements of the room pl
Raum mieten (Fläche)
 Fläche mieten
 ♦ rent space
 ♦ hire space BE
Raum mieten (Zimmer)
 → Zimmer mieten
Raum mit flachem Boden, m
 ♦ flat-floored room

Raumnacht f
→ Zimmernacht
Raumnot, f (Knappheit)
→ Zimmerknappheit
Raumnot, f (völliges Fehlen)
→ Zimmermangel
Raumnutzung, f
→ Raumausnutzung
Raumordnungsplan, m
♦ development plan
Raumpflegerin, f
♦ cleaning lady
♦ charlady *BE*
Raumplan, m (Zimmer)
→ Zimmerlageplan
Raumschiff, n
♦ spaceship
♦ spacecraft
Raum sparen
♦ save space
raumsparend, adj
platzsparend, adj
♦ space-saving, adj
Raumteiler m
♦ room divider
Raumtemperatur, f
Zimmertemperatur, f
♦ ambient temperature
♦ room temperature
Räumung, f (Straße etc)
♦ clearance
Räumung, f (zwangsweise)
♦ ejection *AE*
♦ eviction
♦ ejectment *AE*
♦ dispossession
Räumungsbefehl, m *jur*
♦ dispossession warrant *jur*
♦ eviction warrant *jur*
Räumungsklage, f *jur*
♦ action for eviction *jur*
♦ dispossession proceedings *pl jur*
Räumungsklage erheben
klagen auf Räumung
♦ sue for ejection *AE*
♦ sue for eviction *AE*
Räumungsurteil, n *jur*
♦ eviction order *jur*
Räumungsverfahren durchführen gegen einen Mieter *jur*
→ Zwangsräumung durchführen gegen einen Mieter
Räumungsverfahren durchführen gegen jn
Enteignungsverfahren durchführen gegen jn
♦ dispossess s.o.
Räumungszeitpunkt, m
(eines Zimmers etc)
♦ time by which a room must be vacated
♦ time by which a room is vacated
♦ check-out time
Raum verdunkeln (teilweise)
♦ darken a room
Raum verdunkeln (völlig)
♦ black out a room
Raum vermieten (Fläche)
♦ rent (out) space
♦ hire out space *BE*
♦ let space *BE*
Raumverschwendung, f
♦ waste of space
Raumzahl, f
→ Zimmerzahl

Rausch, m
Betrunkenheit, f
♦ intoxication
♦ drunkenness
♦ inebriety
♦ inebriation
Rausch antrinken sich
♦ go and get drunk
♦ get drunk
Rausch ausschlafen
♦ sleep it off *coll*
♦ sleep off one's liquor
♦ sleep oneself sober
rauschendes Fest, n
♦ magnificent celebration
♦ magnificent party
♦ magnificent festival
♦ sumptuous feast
Rausch haben
→ betrunken sein
rausschmeißen jn
→ rauswerfen jn
Rausschmeißer, m
♦ bouncer *sl*
♦ chucker-out *BE sl*
Rausschmiß, m
♦ bum's rush *AE sl*
♦ chuck *BE sl*
rauswerfen jn
rausschmeißen jn
♦ kick s.o. out
♦ throw s.o. out
♦ chuck s.o. out
♦ give s.o. the bum's rush *AE sl*
rauswerfen jn aus dem Gasthaus *coll*
hinauswerfen jn aus dem Gasthaus
♦ chuck s.o. out of the bar *AE*
♦ chuck s.o. out of the pub *BE*
Ravioli, pl
♦ ravioli
Raviolifüllpastete, f
♦ ravioli timbale
Rayonkellner, m
→ Revierkellner
Razzia, f
♦ roundup *AE*
♦ round-up
♦ police raid
♦ raid
♦ swoop *coll*
Razzia in einem Haus, f
♦ raid on a house
Razzia machen gegen jn
Razzia veranstalten gegen jn
♦ make a raid on s.o.
Rebenreihe, f
♦ row of vines
♦ vine-row
Rebensaft, m *lit*
♦ juice of the grape *lit*
Rebenterrasse, f
♦ vine terrace
Rebhuhn, n
♦ partridge
Rebhuhnsalmi, n
♦ partridge salmi
Rebhuhnsuppe, f
♦ partridge soup
Reblaus, f
Phylloxera, f

♦ vine louse
♦ phylloxera
Rebschule, f
♦ vine nursery
Rebsorte, f
♦ vine variety
♦ variety of vine
Rebsortenverzeichnis, n
♦ variety register
Rebstock, m
Weinstock, m
Rebe, f
♦ vine
Réception, f *SCHW*
→ Rezeption, Empfang
Réceptionist, m *SCHW*
→ Rezeptionist, Empfangsherr
Recettenbuch, n
→ Hoteljournal
Rechaud, n/m
Wärmeplatte, f
♦ rechaud *AE*
♦ réchaud *BE*
♦ warming plate
rechnen mit 123 Besuchern
♦ anticipate 123 visitors
♦ expect 123 visitors
rechnen mit 123 Gästen
♦ anticipate 123 guests
♦ expect 123 guests
rechnen mit 25% mehr Kunden
♦ reckon with 25% more clients
♦ reckon with 25% more customers
rechnen mit einem kühlen Empfang
vorbereitet sein auf einen kühlen Empfang
♦ be prepared for a cool reception
rechnen mit einem Plus von 8%
erwarten ein Plus von 8%
♦ anticipate an 8% increase
rechnen mit einem Anstieg von 8%
♦ anticipate a plus of 8%
rechnen mit einem Rückgang der Ankünfte
erwarten einen Rückgang der Ankünfte
♦ anticipate a fall in arrivals
♦ anticipate a drop in arrivals
♦ anticipate a decrease in arrivals
rechnen mit einer Belegung von 70%
erwarten eine Auslastung von 70%
♦ anticipate 70% occupancy
rechnen müssen mit dem Pfennig
♦ have to watch every penny
Rechnung, bitte
Die Rechnung, bitte
♦ bill, please
♦ The bill, please
♦ The check, please *AE*
Rechnung, f (Faktur)
→ Faktur
Rechnung, f (generell)
♦ bill
Rechnung, f (im Lokal)
♦ bill
♦ check *AE*
♦ tab *AE sl*
Rechnung abrufen
(aus Computer)
♦ call the bill
♦ call the check *AE*
Rechnung abzeichnen
Rechnung signieren

Rechnung ausstellen

- ♦ sign the bill
- ♦ sign the check AE

Rechnung ausstellen
- ♦ make out a bill
- ♦ issue a bill
- ♦ make out a check AE
- ♦ issue a check AE

Rechnung bar begleichen
(Restaurant etc)
- ♦ settle a bill in cash
- ♦ settle a check in cash AE
- ♦ settle an account in cash

Rechnung begleichen
- ♦ settle an account
- ♦ balance an account

Rechnung bezahlen
Rechnung zahlen
- ♦ settle the bill
- ♦ settle a bill
- ♦ pay the bill
- ♦ pay a bill
- ♦ pay the check AE

Rechnung bezahlen per Kreditkarte
- ♦ pay the bill by credit card

Rechnung bezahlen per Postanweisung
- ♦ pay the bill by postal order

Rechnung bezahlen per Scheck
- ♦ pay the bill by check AE
- ♦ pay the bill by cheque BE

Rechnung bringen
- ♦ bring the bill
- ♦ bring the check AE

Rechnung fertig machen für jn
- ♦ get s.o.'s bill ready
- ♦ get s.o.'s check ready AE

Rechnung für das letzte Quartal, f
Rechnung für das letzte Vierteljahr, f
- ♦ bill for the last quarter
- ♦ check for the last quarter AE
- ♦ invoice for the last quarter

Rechnung für Essen und Trinken, f
- ♦ bill for meals and drinks
- ♦ check for meals and drinks AE

Rechnung für Zimmer 123, f
- ♦ bill for room 123
- ♦ check for room 123

Rechnung gegenzeichnen
- ♦ countersign a bill
- ♦ countersign a check AE

Rechnung geht auf das Haus
- ♦ bill is on the house
- ♦ check is on the house AE

Rechnung im voraus zahlen
- ♦ pay the bill in advance

Rechnung in dreifacher Ausfertigung, f (Faktur)
- ♦ invoice in triplicate

Rechnung in dreifacher Ausfertigung, f (Lokal)
- ♦ bill in triplicate
- ♦ check in triplicate AE

Rechnung in fünffacher Ausfertigung, f (Faktur)
- ♦ invoice in quintuplicate

Rechnung in fünffacher Ausfertigung, f (Lokal)
- ♦ bill in quintuplicate
- ♦ check in quintuplicate AE

Rechnung in vierfacher Ausfertigung, f (Faktur)
- ♦ invoice in quadruplicate

Rechnung in vierfacher Ausfertigung, f (Lokal)
- ♦ bill in quadruplicate
- ♦ check in quadruplicate AE

Rechnung in zweifacher Ausfertigung, f (Faktur)
- ♦ invoice in duplicate

Rechnung in zweifacher Ausfertigung, f (Lokal)
- ♦ bill in duplicate
- ♦ check in duplicate AE

Rechnung ist astronomisch (hoch)
- ♦ bill is astronomical

Rechnung ist ungewöhnlich hoch
- ♦ bill is unusually high
- ♦ check is unusually high AE
- ♦ account is unusually high

Rechnung ist vier Wochen vor Ankunftstermin fällig
- ♦ account is due for settlement four weeks before
- ♦ the arrival date

Rechnung kam auf $ 123
- ♦ bill came to $ 123
- ♦ check came to $ 123

Rechnung monatlich begleichen
- ♦ settle the bill monthly
- ♦ settle the check monthly AE

Rechnung nicht zahlen
- ♦ refuse to pay the bill
- ♦ not pay the bill
- ♦ refuse to pay the check AE
- ♦ not pay the check AE

Rechnung ohne den Wirt machen
- ♦ reckon without one's host

Rechnung präsentieren jm
- ♦ present s.o. with the bill
- ♦ present s.o. with the check AE

Rechnung quittieren
- ♦ receipt a bill
- ♦ receipt a check AE
- ♦ receipt an invoice

Rechnungsadresse f
- ♦ billing address

Rechnungsausstellung, f
→ Rechnungsstellung

Rechnungsbegleichung, f
- ♦ settlement of an account
- ♦ account settlement

Rechnungsbetrag, m (Faktur)
- ♦ invoice amount
- ♦ amount of (the) invoice

Rechnungsbetrag, m (Lokal)
- ♦ amount of the bill
- ♦ amount of the check AE

Rechnungsbüro, n
- ♦ bill office
- ♦ bills office
- ♦ accounting office

Rechnungsbüroangestellter, m
- ♦ bill office clerk
- ♦ bill office employee

Rechnungsdatum, n
- ♦ date of invoice
- ♦ billing date

Rechnungseingang, m (Faktur)
Rechnungserhalt, m
Rechnungsempfang, m
- ♦ receipt of invoice

Rechnungseingang, m (Lokal)
Rechnungserhalt, m
Rechnungsempfang, m
- ♦ receipt of bill
- ♦ receipt of check AE

Rechnung signieren
Rechnung abzeichnen
- ♦ sign a bill
- ♦ sign a check AE

Rechnungsnummer, f
- ♦ bill number
- ♦ check number AE
- ♦ number of (the) bill
- ♦ number of (the) check AE

Rechnung spezifizieren
- ♦ itemize a bill
- ♦ itemize a check AE
- ♦ itemize an account

Rechnungsstellung, f
Rechnungsausstellung, f
- ♦ billing

Rechnungsstellung wünschen
- ♦ request a billing

Rechnung stellen jm
- ♦ bill s.o.

Rechnungsvorbereitung, f
- ♦ preparation of an account
- ♦ preparation of accounts
- ♦ preparation of a bill
- ♦ preparation of bills

Rechnungszeitraum, m
→ Abrechnungszeitraum

Rechnung täglich begleichen
- ♦ settle the bill daily
- ♦ settle the check daily AE

Rechnung über DM 123, f
- ♦ bill for DM 123
- ♦ check for DM 123 AE

Rechnung übernehmen
- ♦ pick up a bill

Rechnung verlangen
- ♦ ask for the bill
- ♦ ask for the check AE

Rechnung vierteljährlich begleichen
- ♦ settle the bill quarterly
- ♦ settle the check quarterly AE

Rechnung vorbereiten
- ♦ prepare an account
- ♦ prepare a bill
- ♦ prepare a check AE

Rechnung vorlegen jm
- ♦ present a bill to s.o.
- ♦ present a check to s.o. AE

Rechnung wöchentlich begleichen
- ♦ settle the bill weekly
- ♦ settle the check weekly AE

Rechnung zahlen
Rechnung bezahlen
Rechnung begleichen
- ♦ pay the check AE
- ♦ pay the bill

rechteckig, adj
- ♦ rectangular, adj
- ♦ oblong, adj

rechteckiger Tisch, m
- ♦ rectangular table
- ♦ oblong table

rechtes Ufer, n (Fluß)
- ♦ right bank

Rechtsanwaltsgebühren, f pl
Anwaltsgebühren, f pl
- ♦ legal fees pl
- ♦ legal expenses pl

Rechtsausschuß, m
- ♦ legal committee

rechts fahren (Auto)
- ♦ drive on the right

Rechtsschutzversicherung, f
- ♦ legal aid insurance

Recht vorbehalten sich, den Tarif ohne Vorankündigung zu ändern
- ♦ reserve the right to alter the tariff without notice

Recht vorbehalten sich, etw zu tun
- ♦ reserve the right to do s.th.

rechtzeitig, adv
- ♦ in good time, adv
- ♦ in time, adv

rechtzeitig abreisen
- ♦ depart in time
- ♦ leave in time

rechtzeitig ankommen
- ♦ arrive in time

rechtzeitig buchen
- ♦ book in good time

rechtzeitige Buchung f
- rechtzeitige Anmeldung f
- ♦ booking in good time

rechtzeitig einchecken
- rechtzeitig eintreffen
- ♦ check in in time

rechtzeitig eintreffen für etw
- ♦ arrive in time for s.th.

rechtzeitige Kündigung, f
- termingerechte Kündigung, f
- fristgerechte Kündigung, f
- ♦ due notice

rechtzeitig eröffnen
- rechtzeitig öffnen
- ♦ open on time

rechtzeitig reservieren etw
- ♦ reserve s.th. in time

rechtzeitig stornieren etw
- ♦ cancel s.th. in time

rechtzeitig zum Abendessen (Dinner)
- ♦ in time for dinner

rechtzeitig zum Abendessen (Supper)
- ♦ in time for supper

rechtzeitig zum Frühstück
- ♦ in time for breakfast

rechtzeitig zum Mittagessen
- ♦ in time for lunch
- ♦ in time for luncheon

rechtzeitig zum Mittagessen in X sein
- ♦ be in X in time for lunch
- ♦ be in X in time for luncheon

rechtzeitig zurückkehren zum Mittagessen
- rechtzeitig zurückkommen zum Mittagessen
- rechtzeitig zurück sein zum Mittagessen
- ♦ return in time for lunch
- ♦ return in time for luncheon

recyceln etw
- ♦ recycle s.th.

Recycling, n
- ♦ recycling

Recyclingpapier, n
- ♦ recycled paper

Rede ablesen
- Rede vorlesen
- ♦ read a speech

Rede absagen
- ♦ cancel a speech

Rede halten
- ♦ make a speech
- ♦ deliver a speech

Redner, der eine programmatische Rede hält, m
- Hauptredner, m
- ♦ keynote speaker

Redner, m
- Referent, m
- ♦ speaker

Redner engagieren
- ♦ hire a speaker BE

Rednerliste, f
- ♦ list of speakers

Rednerpodium, n
- Rednerbühne, f
- ♦ speaker's rostrum
- ♦ rostrum
- ♦ speaker's platform

Rednerpult, n
- → Tischpult, Lesepult

Reeder, m
- ♦ shipowner

Reederei, f
- ♦ shipping company

Reetdach, n
- ♦ reed roof

Reetdachhaus, n
- ♦ reed-roofed house

Refektorium, n
- (Speisesaal eines Klosters)
- ♦ refectory

Refektoriumstisch, m
- ♦ refectory table

Referat, n
- ♦ paper
- ♦ report
- ♦ presentation

Referat halten
- Vortrag halten
- ♦ read a paper

Referat veröffentlichen in dem Konferenzbericht
- ♦ publish a paper in the conference proceedings

Referent, m (Redner)
- → Redner

Referenznummer, f
- → Ordnungsnummer

referieren über etw
- ♦ give a presentation on s.th.
- ♦ give a lecture on s.th.

Reflexzonenbehandlung, f
- ♦ reflexology treatment

Reformhaus, n
- Naturkostladen, m
- ♦ health food store AE
- ♦ health food shop BE

Reformkost f
- ♦ health food

Reformkostimbiß, m
- ♦ health food snack

Reformkostrestaurant, n
- ♦ health food restaurant

Refugium, n
- Zufluchtsort, m
- Zufluchtsstätte, f
- Zuflucht, f
- ♦ retreat

Regal, n
- ♦ shelf

Regatta, f
- ♦ regatta

Regatta abhalten
- ♦ hold a regatta

regelmäßig, adj
- ♦ regular, adj

regelmäßige Busverbindung, f
- ♦ regular bus service
- ♦ regular coach service BE

regelmäßige Gebühr, f
- ♦ regular charge
- ♦ regular fee

regelmäßiger Besuch, m
- ständiger Besuch, m
- ♦ regular visit

regelmäßiger Busdienst, m
- → regelmäßige Busverbindung

regelmäßige Reinigung (von etw), f
- ♦ regular cleaning (of s.th.)

regelmäßiger Handtuchwechsel, m
- ♦ regular change of towels

regelmäßiges Programm, n
- ♦ regular program AE
- ♦ regular programme BE

regelmäßiges Unterhaltungsprogramm, n
- ♦ regular program of entertainments AE
- ♦ regular programme of entertainments BE

regelmäßig trinken etw
- ♦ drink s.th. regularly

regelmäßig verkehrender Bus, m
- regelmäßig abfahrender Bus, m
- ♦ regularly departing bus
- ♦ regularly departing coach BE

regelmäßig wechselnde Speisekarte, f
- ♦ menu that is changed regularly
- ♦ regularly changed menu

Regeltarif, m
- ♦ general tariff

Regelung, f
- ♦ regulation

Regelung gilt vom 1. Mai bis 30. Juni
- ♦ regulation applies from 1 May until 30 June

Regelzug, m
- ♦ scheduled train

Regen, m
- ♦ rain

Regenbogenforelle, f
- ♦ rainbow trout

Regenbogenzimmer, n
- ♦ Rainbow Room, the

regendicht, adj
- ♦ rainproof, adj

regendichter Anorak, m
- ♦ rainproof anorak

Regeneration, f
- ♦ regeneration

regenerieren sich
- ♦ regenerate

Regenkleidung, f
- ♦ rainwear

Regenmantel, m
- ♦ raincoat
- ♦ macintosh BE
- ♦ mac BE coll

Regenschirm, m *verleih comple-*
- → Schirm *mentary umbrella*

Regentag, m *service*
- ♦ rainy day

Regenwasser, n
- ♦ rainwater AE
- ♦ rain-water BE

Regenwasserzisterne, f
- ♦ rainwater cistern AE
- ♦ rain-water cistern BE

Regenwettereinrichtung, f
- Schlechtwettereinrichtung, f
- ♦ wet-weather facility

Regenzeit

Regenzeit, f
♦ rainy season
regen Zuspruch finden
großen Zuspruch finden
♦ be much sought after
♦ be very popular
♦ be in great demand
♦ be greatly appreciated
♦ be well frequented
Reggaefestival, n
♦ reggae festival
Reggaemusik, f
♦ reggae music
regierungseigenes Hotel n
♦ government-owned hotel
Regierungsfest, n
♦ government party
Regierungsgast, m
Gast der Regierung, m
♦ government guest
♦ guest of the government
Regierungsgästehaus, n
♦ government guesthouse AE
♦ government-owned guesthouse AE
♦ government guest-house BE
♦ government-owned guest-house BE
Regierungshotel n
♦ government hotel
♦ government-owned hotel
Regierungstreffen, n
♦ government meeting
Regierungsviertel, n
♦ government quarter
♦ government district
Region, f
Gebiet, n
♦ region
regional, adj
♦ regional, adj
Regionalausstellung, f
regionale Ausstellung, f
Landesausstellung, f
♦ regional exhibition
♦ regional exhibit AE
♦ regional show
regionale Fremdenverkehrspolitik, f
regionale Tourismuspolitik, f
♦ regional tourism policy
regionale Gerichte ausprobieren
♦ sample regional dishes
♦ sample the regional dishes
regionale Küche, f (Speisen)
♦ regional cuisine
♦ regional cooking
regionaler Fremdenverkehr, m
regionaler Tourismus, m
♦ regional tourism
regionaler Fremdenverkehrsverband, m
Landesfremdenverkehrsverband, m
LVA, n
♦ regional tourist board
♦ r.t.b.
regionaler Urlaubsverkehr, m
regionaler Ferienverkehr, m
regionaler Reiseverkehr, m
♦ regional vacation traffic AE
♦ regional holiday traffic BE
regionale Speisekarte, f
♦ regional menu
regionale Spezialität, f
Regionalspezialität, f
♦ regional specialty AE
♦ regional speciality BE
regionales Seminar, n
Regionalseminar, n
♦ regional seminar
regionales Verkaufsbüro, n
♦ regional sales office
regionale Verbrauchermesse, f
♦ regional consumer fair
regionale Verteilung, f
(z.B. des Fremdenverkehrs)
♦ regional spread
Regionalfest, n
Regionalfestival, n
regionales Fest, n
regionales Festival, n
regionale Festspiele, n pl
♦ regional festival
Regionalflughafen, m
regionaler Flughafen, m
♦ regional airport
Regionalflugverkehr, m
♦ regional air traffic
Regionalführer, m
(Information)
Gebietsführer, m
♦ regional guide
Regionalgericht, n
regionales Gericht, n
♦ regional dish
Regionalkonferenz, f
regionale Konferenz, f
♦ regional conference
Regionalkongreß, m
regionaler Kongreß, m
♦ regional convention
♦ regional congress
Regionalmesse, f
regionale Messe, f
♦ regional fair
Regionalmuseum, n
Landesmuseum, n
♦ regional museum
Regionalreiseveranstalter, m
regionaler Reiseveranstalter, m
♦ regional tour operator
Regionalschau, f
regionale Schau, f
Landesschau, f
♦ regional show
Regionalspezialitätenrestaurant, n
♦ restaurant serving regional specialties AE
♦ restaurant serving regional specialities BE
Regionaltagung, f
regionale Tagung, f
Regionaltreffen, n
regionales Treffen, n
♦ regional meeting
Regionalveranstalter, m
(Reiseveranstalter)
♦ regional operator
Regionalwerbung, f
regionale Werbung, f
♦ regional advertising
Registraturangestellter, m
♦ file clerk
registrieren jn
→ anmelden jn
Registrierkasse, f
♦ cash register

616

registriert, adj
→ angemeldet
registrierte Touristenunterkunft, f
registriertes Touristenquartier, n
gemeldetes Fremdenquartier, n
♦ registered tourist accommodation
registrierte Unterkunft, f
gemeldete Unterkunft, f
♦ registered accommodation
Registrierung, f
→ Anmeldung
Registrierung eines Teilnehmers, f
(z.B. bei Konferenz)
♦ registration of a delegate
♦ registering a delegate
Registrierungsanlage, f
♦ registration system
Registrierungsformular, n
→ Anmeldeformular
Registrierungskosten, pl
→ Anmeldungskosten
Registrierungsschalter, m
→ Anmeldeschalter
reglementieren (etw)
♦ regiment (s.th.)
♦ regulate (s.th.)
Reglementierung, f
♦ regimentation
regnen
♦ rain
Regreß, m
→ Schadensersatzanspruch
regulärer Fahrpreis, m
♦ regular fare
regulärer Preis, m
♦ regular price
♦ regular rate
regulärer Tarif, m
♦ regular tariff
Rehabilitation, f
♦ rehabilitation
Rehabilitationsklinik, f
♦ rehabilitation clinic
Rehabilitationsprogramm, n
♦ rehabilitation program AE
♦ rehabilitation programme BE
Reibe, f gastr
♦ grater gastr
Reibekuchen, m
♦ potato pancake
reiben etw gastr
raspeln etw gastr
♦ grate s.th. gastr
reibungslos ablaufen
reibungslos laufen
♦ run smoothly
reibungslosen Service sicherstellen
♦ ensure smooth service
reibungsloser Service, m
♦ smooth service
reich bebildert, adj
♦ richly pictured, adj
reich bebilderter Prospekt, m
♦ richly pictured brochure
reichen etw
→ servieren etw
reichhaltige Auswahl, f
♦ wide selection
♦ wide choice
♦ wide range
♦ plenty of choice

reichhaltige Auswahl bieten
♦ offer a wide choice
♦ offer a wide selection
♦ offer a wide range
♦ offer plenty of choice
reichhaltiges Abendessen, n (Dinner)
♦ substantial dinner
reichhaltiges Abendessen, n (Supper)
♦ substantial supper
reichhaltiges Essen, n
♦ substantial meal
♦ rich meal
reichhaltiges Frühstück, n
♦ substantial breakfast
reichhaltiges Mittagessen, n
♦ substantial lunch
♦ substantial luncheon
reichhaltige Speisekarte, f
♦ comprehensive menu
reichhaltiges und abwechslungsreiches Programm, n
♦ rich and varied program AE
♦ rich and varied programme BE
reichhaltiges Weinsortiment, n
♦ great variety of wines
♦ large assortment of wines
♦ wide variety of wines
reich illustriert, adj
reich bebildert, adj
♦ richly illustrated, adj
reich illustrierter Prospekt, m
♦ richly illustrated brochure
reichliche Mahlzeit, f
reichliches Essen, n
♦ copious meal
♦ substantial meal
♦ square meal coll
reichliche Parkplätze, m pl
♦ ample parking
reichlicher Vorrat an etw, m
♦ ample supply of s.th.
reichliches Essen, n
reichliche Mahlzeit, f
♦ plentiful meal
reichliches Mittagessen, n
♦ ample lunch
Reichshauptstadt, f
♦ imperial capital
♦ capital of the empire
Reichsstadt, f
♦ imperial city
Reichweite, f
♦ range
♦ reach
reif, adj
♦ ripe, adj
Reifenpanne, f
♦ puncture
Reifenpanne haben
♦ have a puncture
reifer Wein, m
ausgereifter Wein, m
♦ ripe wine
♦ mature wine
reife Tomate, f
♦ ripe tomato
Reihe, f (Folge)
♦ series sg + pl
Reihe, f (Sitzreihe)
♦ row

Reihenbestuhlung, f
Vortragsbestuhlung, f
Theaterbestuhlung, f
♦ theater seating AE
♦ theatre seating BE
♦ theater-style seating AE
♦ theatre-style seating BE
Reihenbungalow, m
♦ terraced bungalow BE
♦ terrace-bungalow
Reiheneckhaus, n
Reihenendhaus, n
♦ end-of-row house AE
♦ end-of-terrace house BE
♦ end-of-terrace home BE
Reihenform, f
(Bestuhlung)
→ Theaterbestuhlung
Reihenhaus, n
RH, n
♦ row house AE
♦ terraced house BE
♦ terrace-house BE
♦ town house AE
Reihenimmobilie, f
Reihenanwesen, n
♦ row property AE
♦ terraced property BE
Reihenstand, m
♦ row stand
Reihe von Bars, f
♦ series of bars sg
rein ausfegen
♦ sweep clean
Reineclaude, f
♦ greengage
♦ gage
Reineclaudenkonfitüre, f
♦ gage plum jam
♦ greengage jam
reine Luft, f
♦ pure air
Reinerlös, m
→ Nettoerlös
Reinertrag, m
→ Nettoertrag
reines Vergnügen, n
♦ pure pleasure
reines Wasser, n
♦ pure water
Reinfall, m
(Veranstaltung)
♦ nonevent AE
♦ non-event BE
Reingewicht, n
→ Nettogewicht
Reingewinn, m
→ Nettogewinn
rein halten etw
♦ keep s.th. clean
reinhauen
→ tüchtig zulangen
reinigen etw
putzen etw
♦ clean s.th.
Reinigung, f
♦ cleaning
Reinigung eines Zimmers, f
♦ cleaning of a room
♦ cleaning a room

Reinigung in regelmäßigen Zeiträumen, f
Reinigung in regelmäßigen Abständen, f
♦ periodic cleaning
Reinigungsaufwendungen, f pl
Reinigungsausgaben, f pl
♦ cleaning expenses pl
Reinigungsdienst, m
Reinigungsservice, m
Putzdienst, m
♦ cleaning service
Reinigungsgebühr f
♦ cleaning charge
♦ cleaning fee
♦ charge for cleaning s.th.
♦ fee for cleaning s.th.
Reinigungsgeräte, n pl
♦ cleaning utensils pl
Reinigungskosten, pl
♦ cleaning costs pl
♦ cleaning cost
Reinigungskraft, f
♦ cleaner
Reinigungskräfte, f pl
→ Reinigungspersonal
Reinigungsmaterial, n
→ Putzmaterial
Reinigungspersonal, n
Reinigungskräfte, f pl
Putzpersonal, n
♦ cleaning personnel
♦ cleaning staff
♦ cleaners pl
Reinigungspersonal beaufsichtigen
♦ supervise the cleaning personnel
♦ supervise the cleaning staff
Reinigungsservice, m
→ Reinigungsdienst
Reinigungsunternehmer, m
♦ cleaning contractor
rein machen
→ reinigen
reinpferchen jn coll
hineinpferchen jn
♦ cram s.o. in
reinschauen bei jm inform
besuchen jn
♦ stop by s.o. AE inform
♦ pop in at s.o.'s place BE inform
Reinverlust, m
→ Nettoverlust
Reis, m
♦ rice
Reise, f (Fahrt)
→ Fahrt
Reise, f (Journey)
(Hin- bzw. Rückreise zu einem Ort)
♦ journey
Reise, f (lang, bes. Luft-, See- und Raumreise)
Seereise, f
lange Flugreise, f
Raumfahrt, f
♦ voyage
Reise, f (Tour)
(Reise mit Rückkehr zum Ausgangspunkt)
♦ tour
Reise abbrechen
♦ cut short a journey
♦ cut short a trip
♦ cut short a tour
Reiseabenteuer, n
♦ travel adventure AE

Reiseabfahrtsstelle 618

- traveler's adventure *AE*
- traveller's adventure *BE*
- travelling adventure *BE*
- adventure

Reiseabfahrtsstelle, f
- tour departure point

Reiseablauf, m
→ Reiseverlauf

Reiseabsage, f
→ Reisestornierung

Reise absagen
  Reise stornieren
- cancel a journey
- cancel a trip
- cancel a tour

Reise abschließen
  Tour abschließen
- wind up a tour

Reiseabsicht, f
- travel intention
- intention to travel

Reiseabteilung, f
- travel department

Reiseagentur, f
- travel agency

Reiseakademie, f
- travel academy

Reiseaktivität, f
  Reisetätigkeit, f
- travel activity

Reisealter, n
- travel age

Reisealtersgruppe, f
- travel age group

Reiseamateur, m
- amateur traveller
- amateur traveler *AE*

Reiseanalyse, f
- travel analysis

Reise anbieten
  Reise offerieren
- offer a tour

Reiseanbieter, m
- travel supplier
- travel provider

Reiseandenken, n
- travel souvenir
- traveling souvenir *AE*
- travelling souvenir *BE*
- souvenir of a trip
- souvenir

Reiseanforderung, f
  Reiseerfordernis, n
- travel requirement
- tour requirement

Reiseanfrage, f
- travel inquiry
- travel enquiry

Reiseangebot, n (Gegensatz zu Nachfrage)
- tours available *pl*
- journeys available *pl*
- trips available *pl*
- trips on offer *pl*
- tours offered *pl*

Reiseangebot, n (Palette)
- range of tours
- range of journeys
- range of trips

Reiseangelegenheit, f
- travel matter

Reiseanreiz, m
- travel incentive

Reise antreten
- start on a journey
- start off on a journey
- set out on a journey
- embark on a journey
- set off on a journey

Reiseantritt, m
- commencement of (the) journey *form*
- beginning of (the) journey
- setting out on a journey
- commencement of travel *form*

Reiseantrittsland, n
- country of (the) commencement of travel
- COC

Reiseanzahlung, f
- travel deposit

Reiseapotheke, f
- tourist's medicine case
- portable medicine case

Reisearchiv, n
- travel archives *pl*

Reisearrangement, n (generell)
- travel arrangement

Reisearrangement, n (speziell)
- tour arrangement

Reise arrangieren
  Reise vermitteln
- arrange a journey
- arrange a tour
- arrange a trip

Reise arrangieren für jn
- arrange a tour for s.o.

Reiseart, f
- type of travel
- type of journey
- type of trip
- type of tour

Reiseartikel, m
  Reisegegenstand, m
- travel item
- travel article

Reiseatlas, m
- touring atlas
- tourist atlas

Reise auf dem Kontinent, f
  (Festlandseuropa)
- continental tour

Reise auf der Suche nach etw, f
- journey in search of s.th.

Reiseaufkommen, n
→ Reisevolumen

Reise aufs Land, f
- tour into the countryside
- trip into the countryside

Reiseaufwand, m
  Reiseausgabe, f
- travel expenditure

Reiseaufwendungen, f pl
  Reisespesen, pl
- traveling expenses *AE pl*
- travelling expenses *BE pl*
- travel expenses *pl*
- travel expenditures *pl*

Reiseausgaben, f pl
  Reiseaufwendungen, f pl
- travel spending
- travel expenses *pl*
- travelers' expenditures *AE pl*
- spending on travel

Reiseausgabenbilanz, f
- travel expenditure balance

Reiseauskunft, f
→ Reiseinformation

Reiseausrüstung, f
  Reiseausstattung, f
- traveling equipment *AE*
- travelling equipment *BE*

Reiseausstellung, f
  (zum Reisen)
- travel exhibition
- travel show

Reiseauswahl, f
  Reisewahl, f
  Auswahl an Reisen, f
- selection of tours
- selecting a tour
- choice of tours
- choosing a tour
- tour choice

Reisebasar, m
- travel bazar
- travel bazaar

Reisebazillus, m coll
  Reisefieber, n
  Reiseleidenschaft, f
- travel bug *coll*

Reisebedarf, m
- traveling requisites *AE pl*
- travelling requisites *AE pl*
- traveling necessaries *AE pl obs*
- travelling necessaries *BE pl obs*
- travel necessaries *pl obs*

Reisebedingungen, f pl
- travel conditions *pl*
- tour conditions *pl*

Reisebedingungen anerkennen
- accept the travel conditions
- accept the tour conditions

Reisebedürfnis, n
- travel need

Reisebedürfnisse erfüllen von jm
- meet s.o.'s travel needs

Reise beenden
- end a journey
- end a tour
- end a trip

Reisebegeisterter, m
- travel enthusiast

Reisebegeisterung, f
- enthusiasm for travel

Reisebeginn, m
  Reiseantritt, m
- start of a journey
- start of the journey
- beginning of a/the journey
- commencement of a/the journey *form*
- departure

Reise beginnen
- begin a journey
- start a journey
- begin a tour
- begin a trip
- start a trip

Reise beginnt am Montag und endet am Donnerstag
- journey begins on Monday and ends on Thursday
- trip starts on Monday and ends on Thursday
- tour commences on Monday and ends on Thursday *form*

Reise beginnt in A
- journey begins at/in A
- trip starts at/in A
- tour commences at/in A *form*

Reise beginnt in A und endet in B
- journey begins at/in A and ends at/in B
- trip starts at/in A and ends at/in B
- tour commences at/in A and ends at/in B *form*

Reisebegleiter, m
Reisebegleitung, f
Reisegefährte, m
- travel companion
- traveling companion *AE*
- travelling companion *BE*

Reisebegleitung, f
Reisebegleiter, m
- tour escort
- travel companion

Reisebeilage, f
(einer Zeitung)
- travel supplement

Reisebekanntschaft, f
- traveling acquaintance *AE*
- travelling acquaintance *BE*

Reisebekanntschaft machen
- make a travelling acquaintance
- make a traveling acquaintance *AE*
- meet s.o. while travelling *AE*
- meet s.o. while traveling *AE*

Reiseberater, m
- travel consultant
- travel adviser
- travel counselor *AE*
- travel counsellor *BE*

Reiseberatung, f
- travel consultancy

Reiseberechtigung, f
- travel entitlement
- entitlement to travel

Reisebereich, m
- travel field

Reisebericht, m (generell)
- travel report
- report of a journey
- report on a tour
- account of a tour

Reisebericht, m (mit Lichtbildern oder Film)
Reisevortrag, m
- travelog *AE*
- travelogue *BE*

Reisebeschränkung, f
- travel restriction
- traveling restriction *AE*
- travelling restriction *BE*
- restriction on travel(ing) *AE*
- restriction on travel(ling) *BE*

Reise beschreiben
- describe a journey
- describe a trip
- describe a tour

Reisebeschreibung, f
- description of a journey
- description of a trip
- description of a tour

Reisebestandteil, m
Bestandteil der Reise, m
- part of the tour
- part of the trip
- part of the journey

Reise bestätigen
Reise zusagen

- confirm a tour
- confirm a trip
- confirm a journey

Reisebestätigung, f
- confirmation of a tour
- tour confirmation
- travel confirmation

Reisebestimmungen, f pl
Reisevorschriften, f pl
- travel regulations *pl*

Reisebetreuer, m (Busreise)
- courier

Reisebetreuung, f (Aktivität)
→ Reiseservice

Reisebetreuung, f (Person)
→ Reisebetreuer

Reisebetrieb, m
- travel operation
- travel establishment

Reisebetrieb führen
Reisebetrieb leiten
- run a travel operation
- run a travel establishment

Reisebett, n
- traveling bed *AE*
- travelling bed *BE*

Reise bezahlen (generell)
- pay for a journey
- pay for a tour
- pay for a trip

Reise bezahlen (Seereise)
- pay for a voyage

reisebezogen, adj
- travel-related, adj
- related to travel, adj

reisebezogenes Geschäft, n
- travel-related business

Reisebibliothek, f
Reisebücherei, f
- travel library

Reisebilanz, f
(Zahlungsbilanz)
- travel balance

Reisebiographie, f
- travel biography

Reiseboom, m
Reisewelle, f
- travel boom

Reisebranche, f
→ Reiseindustrie, Reisegeschäft

Reisebroschüre, f
→ Reiseprospekt

Reisebuch, n
- travel book
- touring book

Reisebuchautor, m
Autor eines Reisebuchs, m
- author of a travel book
- travel book author

Reise buchen
- book a tour
- book a trip
- book a journey

Reise buchen bei einem Reisebüro
- book a tour with a travel agent
- book a trip with a travel agent
- book a journey with a travel agent

Reise buchen in einem Reisebüro
- book a tour in a travel agency
- book a trip in a travel agency
- book a journey in a travel agency

Reise buchen nach X bei jm
- book a trip to X with s.o.
- book a tour to X with s.o.
- book a journey to X with s.o.

Reise buchen über ein Reisebüro
- book a tour through a travel agency
- book a trip through a travel agency
- book a journey through a travel agency

Reisebuchladen, m
Reisebuchgeschäft, n
- travel bookstore *AE*
- travel bookshop *BE*

Reisebüchlein, n
kleines Reisebuch, n
- travel booklet

Reisebuch schreiben
- write a travel book

Reisebuchung, f
- travel booking
- booking (of) a tour
- booking (of) a trip
- booking (of) a journey
- tour booking

Reisebudget, n
Reiseetat, m
- travel budget

Reisebudgetbeschränkung, f
Reisemittelbeschränkung, f
- travel budget restriction

Reisebudget drastisch kürzen
Reiseetat drastisch senken
- slash the travel budget

Reisebügeleisen, n
- travelling iron *BE*
- traveling iron *AE*

Reisebüro, n (generell)
- travel agency
- travel agent's shop *BE*
- travel agent's
- travel bureau *AE*

Reisebüro, n (Schalter)
- travel bureau *AE*
- travel desk

Reisebüro am Ort, n
- local travel agency

Reisebürobesitzer, m
- owner of a travel agency
- travel agent

Reisebüro betreiben
- operate a travel agency

Reisebürobetrieb, m
- travel agency operation

Reisebürobranche, f
→ Reisebürogewerbe

Reisebürobuchung, f
- travel agency booking
- travel agent's booking

Reisebürodienstleistung, f
Reisebüroleistung, f
- travel agency service
- travel agent's service

Reisebüro eröffnen
- open a travel agency

Reisebüro erwerben
- purchase a travel agency

Reisebüroexpedient, m
- travel agency clerk
- travel agent

Reisebürofachkraft, f
- trained travel agent

Reisebürofachverband

Reisebürofachverband, m
♦ travel agency trade association
Reisebürofiliale, f
Reisebürostelle, f
♦ travel agency outlet
Reisebürofranchising, n
♦ travel agency franchising
Reisebüroführungskraft, f
♦ travel agency executive
Reisebürogeschäft, n (abstrakt)
Reisemittlergeschäft, n
♦ travel agency business
Reisebürogeschäft, n (konkret)
Reisebüroladen, m
♦ travel agent's store *AE*
♦ travel agent's shop *BE*
♦ travel agent's
Reisebürogewerbe, n
Reisebürobranche, f
Reisemittlergewerbe, n
Reisemittlerbranche, f
♦ travel agency trade
Reisebürogutschein, m
♦ travel agency voucher
♦ agency voucher
♦ travel agent's voucher
Reisebüroinhaber, m
♦ travel agency owner
♦ owner of a travel agency
Reisebürokette, f
♦ travel agency chain
♦ chain of travel agencies
Reisebürokonzession, f
Reisebürolizenz, f
♦ travel agency license
♦ travel agency licence
Reisebürokooperation, f
♦ travel agency cooperation
Reisebürokratie, f
♦ travel bureaucracy
Reisebürokratie abbauen
♦ reduce travel bureaucracy
Reisebüro leiten
♦ run a travel agency
♦ manage a travel agency
Reisebüroleiter, m
♦ travel agency manager
Reisebürolizenz, f
→ Reisebürokonzession
Reisebüromarketing, n
♦ travel agency marketing
Reisebüromarkt, m
♦ travel agency market
Reisebüromitarbeiter, m
♦ travel agency employee
Reisebüronetz, n
♦ travel agency network
Reisebüroorganisation, f
♦ travel agency organisation
♦ travel agency organization
Reisebüropersonal, n
♦ travel agency staff
♦ travel agency personnel
Reisebüroprovision, f
Reisemittlerprovision, f
♦ travel agency commission
♦ travel agent's commission
Reisebüroreservierung, f
♦ travel agency reservation
♦ travel agent's reservation

Reisebürosektor, m
Reisebürobereich, m
♦ travel agency sector
Reisebürostatistik, f
♦ travel agency statistics *pl*
Reisebürostelle, f
(z.B. im Hotel)
Reisebüro, n
♦ travel desk
Reisebüroterminal, n
♦ travel agency terminal
Reisebürotheke, m
Reisebüroschalter, m
♦ travel agency counter
Reisebürotochtergesellschaft, f
♦ travel agency subsidiary
Reisebüroumsatz, m
♦ travel agency turnover
♦ travel agency sales *pl*
Reisebüroverband, m
♦ travel agents' association
Reisebüro wechseln
(anderes Reisebüro konsultieren)
♦ change one's travel agent
Reisebüro zu Rat ziehen
♦ consult a travel agent
Reisebus, m
♦ tour bus *AE*
♦ touring bus *AE*
♦ touring coach *BE*
♦ tour coach *BE*
♦ coach *BE*
Reisebusfahrer, m
Fahrer eines Reisebusses, m
♦ tour bus driver *AE*
♦ touring coach driver *BE*
♦ driver of a tour bus *AE*
♦ driver of a touring coach *BE*
Reisecamper, m
♦ touring camper
Reisecaravan, m
Reisewohnwagen, m
♦ touring caravan *BE*
♦ tourer *BE coll*
♦ travel trailer *AE*
Reisecaravanplatz, m
Reisewohnwagenplatz, m
♦ touring caravan site *BE*
♦ tourer site *BE coll*
♦ travel trailer site *AE*
Reiseclub, m
Reiseverein, m
♦ travel club
♦ travellers' club
♦ travelers' club *AE*
Reiseclubmitglied, n
♦ travel club member
♦ travellers' club member
♦ travelers' club member *AE*
Reisecoupon, m
♦ travel coupon
Reisedaten, pl
♦ travel data
Reisedatendienst, m
Reisedatenservice, m
♦ travel data service
Reisedatum, n
Reisetermin, m
♦ travel date
♦ date of a journey

♦ date of a tour
♦ date of a trip
Reisedatum wählen
Reisetermin wählen
♦ choose the travel date
Reisedauer, f (generell)
♦ duration of a journey
♦ duration of a tour
♦ duration of a trip
♦ length of a journey
♦ length of a tour
Reisedauer, f (Seereise)
♦ duration of a voyage
♦ length of a voyage
Reise dauert einen Tag
♦ journey lasts one day
♦ journey takes one day
♦ trip lasts one day
♦ trip takes one day
♦ tour lasts one day
Reise dauert länger als angenommen
♦ journey takes longer than anticipated
♦ trip takes longer than anticipated
♦ tour takes longer than anticipated
Reise dauert weniger als einen Tag
♦ journey lasts less than one day
♦ tour lasts less than one day
♦ trip lasts less than one day
♦ journey takes less than one day
♦ tour takes less than one day
Reisedecke, f
♦ traveling rug *AE*
♦ travelling rug *BE*
♦ lap robe *AE*
Reisedefizit, n
♦ travel deficit
Reise des Lebens, f
♦ journey of a lifetime
♦ journey of one's lifetime
♦ tour of a lifetime
♦ tour of one's lifetime
♦ trip of a/one's lifetime
Reisedevisenausgaben, f pl
Reiseausgaben im Ausland, f pl
♦ foreign travel expenditure
♦ travelers' expenditures abroad *AE pl*
Reisedevisenbilanz, f
♦ foreign travel expenditure balance
Reisedevisenfreibetrag, m
♦ travel allowance
Reisedevisenzuteilung, f
♦ foreign travel allowance
Reisedienst, m
Reiseservice, m
Reisebetreuung, f
♦ travel service
Reisedienstanbieter, m
♦ travel service supplier
Reisedienstleistung, f
→ Reiseleistung
Reisedienststellenleiter, m
(in einem Unternehmen)
♦ passenger traffic manager *AE*
♦ PTM *AE*
Reisedimension, f
♦ travel dimension
Reisediplomat, m
♦ shuttle diplomat
Reisediplomatie, f
♦ shuttle diplomacy

Reisedokument, n
→ Reisepapier
Reisedokument bearbeiten
♦ **handle a travel document**
♦ deal with a travel document
Reise durch 12 Großstädte, f
♦ **tour of 12 cities**
♦ tour through 12 cities
♦ 12-city tour
Reise durch die Geschichte, f
♦ **tour through history**
Reise durch drei Länder, f
Dreiländerreise, f
♦ **tour of three countries**
♦ tour through three countries
♦ three-country tour
Reise durch Frankreich, f
♦ **journey through France**
♦ tour of France
♦ tour through France
Reise durchführen (Seereise)
Reise unternehmen
♦ **go on a voyage**
Reise durchführen (Seereise, lt. Vertrag)
♦ **perform a voyage**
Reise durchführen (Tourist)
Reise unternehmen
♦ **undertake a journey**
♦ undertake a tour
♦ undertake a trip
♦ go on a journey
♦ go on a tour
Reise durchführen (Veranstalter)
Reise unternehmen
♦ **run a tour**
♦ perform a tour
♦ run a trip
♦ perform a trip
Reise durch Raum und Zeit, f
♦ **journey through space and time**
Reiseeindrücke, m pl
♦ **impressions of a journey** pl
♦ impressions of one's travels pl
Reiseeinzelhändler, m
Reisewiederverkäufer, m
♦ **travel retailer**
♦ tour retailer
Reiseempfehlung, f
♦ **travel recommendation**
♦ recommendation on travel
Reiseende, n
Ende der Reise, n
♦ **end of the journey**
♦ end of the tour
♦ end of the trip
♦ journey's end
Reise endet abrupt
♦ **journey ends abruptly**
♦ tour ends abruptly
♦ trip ends abruptly
Reise endet in X
♦ **journey ends at/in X**
♦ trip ends at/in X
♦ tour ends at/in X
Reiseentfernung, f
♦ **travel distance**
Reise entwerfen
Reise gestalten
♦ **design a journey**
♦ design a tour
♦ design a trip

Reiseereignis, n
Veranstaltung während der Reise, f
♦ **travel event**
Reiseerfahrung, f
♦ **travel experience**
Reiseerfahrung haben
Reiseerfahrung besitzen
♦ **have travel experience**
Reiseerfordernis, n
Reiseanforderung, f
♦ **tour requirement**
♦ travel requirement
Reiseerinnerungen, f pl
♦ **reminiscences of one's travels** pl
Reiseerlaubnis, f
♦ **permission to travel**
Reiseerlaubnis geben jm
♦ **give s.o. permission to travel**
Reiseerlebnis, n
♦ **travel experience**
Reise erleichtern
♦ **ease a journey**
♦ ease s.o.'s journey
Reiseermäßigung, f
(z.B. für Kinder)
♦ **travel reduction**
Reiseersatz, m
Ersatz für das Reisen, m
♦ **substitute for travel**
Reiseetappe, f
Etappe einer Reise, f
♦ **stage of a journey**
♦ stage of a tour
♦ stage of a trip
Reiseetat, m
→ Reisebudget
Reiseexperte, m
→ Reisefachmann
Reisefachmann, m
Reiseexperte, m
♦ **travel expert**
♦ travel specialist
Reisefachmesse, f
Reisemesse, f
♦ **travel trade fair**
Reisefachpresse, f
♦ **travel trade press**
Reisefachveranstaltung, f
♦ **travel trade event**
reisefähig, adj
♦ **fit to travel, adj**
Reisefähigkeit, f
♦ **fitness to travel**
♦ being fit to travel
reisefähig sein
♦ **be fit to travel**
Reisefahrkarte, f
♦ **travel ticket**
Reisefahrplan, m
♦ **travel schedule**
Reisefan, m
♦ **travel fan**
reisefertig, adj
♦ **ready to start, adj**
♦ ready to leave, adj
♦ ready to depart, adj
reisefertig machen sich
♦ **get ready to leave**
♦ prepare for a journey
Reisefieber, n
♦ **travel nerves** pl

♦ vacation fever AE
♦ holiday fever BE
♦ travel fever
♦ travel bug coll
Reisefieber haben
♦ **have travel nerves**
♦ have vacation fever AE
♦ have holiday fever BE
Reisefilm, m
♦ **travel film**
Reise finanzieren
♦ **finance a journey**
♦ finance a tour
♦ finance a trip
Reisefinanzierung, f
♦ **financing a journey**
♦ financing a tour
♦ financing a trip
Reise findet nicht statt (generell)
♦ **tour has been cancelled**
♦ tour has been cancelled AE
♦ trip has been cancelled
♦ trip has been canceled AE
♦ journey has been cancelled
Reise findet nicht statt (Seereise)
♦ **voyage has been cancelled**
♦ voyage has been canceled AE
Reisefirma, f
♦ **travel firm**
♦ travel company BE
♦ travel corporation AE
♦ tour company
♦ tour firm
Reiseflughöhe, f
♦ **cruising altitude**
Reiseform, f
Form des Reisens, f
♦ **form of travel**
♦ form of travelling
♦ form of traveling AE
Reiseformalität, f
♦ **travel formality**
Reiseform empfehlen
♦ **recommend a form of travel**
Reiseforschung, f
♦ **travel research**
Reise fortsetzen
♦ **continue a journey**
♦ continue a tour
♦ proceed on one's journey
♦ resume one's journey
♦ continue a trip
Reiseforum, n
♦ **travel forum**
Reisefreak, m
♦ **travel freak**
Reisefrequenz, f
→ Reisehäufigkeit
reisefreudig, adj
reiselustig, adj
♦ **fond of traveling, adj** AE
♦ fond of travelling, adj BE
reisefreudiges Volk, n
reisefreudige Nation, f
♦ **nation fond of travelling**
♦ nation fond of traveling AE
Reisefreudigkeit, f
Reiselust, f
♦ **fondness for traveling** AE
♦ fondness for travelling BE
♦ love of travel

Reiseführer

Reiseführer, m (Buch)
- ◆ guidebook
- ◆ guide
- ◆ travel directory *AE*
- ◆ touring guide

Reiseführer, m (Person)
Reiseleiter, m
- ◆ travel guide
- ◆ guide
- ◆ Cicerone *humor*
- ◆ tour escort
- ◆ tour leader

Reiseführer für Berlin, m
(Buch)
Reiseführer von Berlin, m
- ◆ guide to Berlin

Reiseführer vor Ort, m
Reiseleiter vor Ort, m
- ◆ local representative of a travel firm
- ◆ local representative
- ◆ local rep *coll*

Reise führt uns nach X
Reise bringt uns nach X
- ◆ trip takes us to X
- ◆ tour takes us to X
- ◆ journey takes us to X

Reise für zwei Personen, f
- ◆ tour for two persons
- ◆ journey for two persons
- ◆ trip for two persons
- ◆ tour for two (people)
- ◆ journey for two (people)

Reisegebiet, n (groß)
- ◆ touring region
- ◆ tourist region
- ◆ travel region

Reisegebiet, n (klein)
- ◆ touring area
- ◆ tourist area
- ◆ travel area

Reisegefährte, m
(Privatperson)
Reisebegleiter, m
- ◆ travelling companion *AE*
- ◆ travelling companion *BE*
- ◆ fellow traveler *AE*
- ◆ fellow traveller *BE*
- ◆ travel companion

Reisegefühl, n
- ◆ travel sensation

Reise geht weiter nach X
- ◆ journey continues to X
- ◆ tour continues to X
- ◆ trip continues to X
- ◆ journey proceeds to X
- ◆ tour proceeds to X

Reisegeld n
- ◆ money for traveling *AE*
- ◆ money for travelling *BE*

Reisegelegenheit, f
Reisemöglichkeit, f
- ◆ travel opportunity
- ◆ opportunity to travel
- ◆ chance to travel

Reisegenehmigung f
- ◆ travel permit

Reise genießen
- ◆ enjoy a tour
- ◆ enjoy a journey
- ◆ enjoy a trip

Reisegenosse, m
→ Reisebegleiter

Reisegeographie, f
- ◆ travel geography

Reisegepäck, n
Gepäck, n
- ◆ luggage *BE*
- ◆ baggage *AE*

Reisegepäckversicherung, f
Gepäckversicherung, f
- ◆ luggage insurance *BE*
- ◆ baggage insurance *AE*

Reisegepäckversicherung abschließen
- ◆ take out a baggage insurance *AE*
- ◆ take out a luggage insurance *BE*

Reisegeschäft, n
Reisebranche, f
- ◆ travel business

Reisegeschichte, f
Geschichte des Reisens, f
- ◆ travel history
- ◆ history of travel

Reisegeschwindigkeit, f (Flugzeug)
- ◆ cruising speed
- ◆ cruise speed

Reisegeschwindigkeit, f (generell)
- ◆ travel speed

Reisegesellschaft, f (Firma)
- ◆ travel corporation *AE*
- ◆ travel company *BE*
- ◆ travel firm

Reisegesellschaft, f (Privatpersonen)
- ◆ travel party
- ◆ tourist party
- ◆ party
- ◆ outfit *AE*

Reisegesetzgebung, f
- ◆ travel legislation

Reisegespann, n
(Pkw plus Wohnwagen)
Tourengespann, n
- ◆ touring outfit
- ◆ touring unit

Reisegewerbe, n
Reisebranche, f
- ◆ travel trade

Reisegewerbehandbuch, n
- ◆ travel trade manual

Reisegewerbemittler, m
Reisemittler, m
- ◆ travel trade intermediary
- ◆ travel agent

Reisegewerbepersonal, n
- ◆ travel trade personnel
- ◆ travel trade staff

Reisegewerbeprofi, m
- ◆ travel trade professional

Reisegewerberepräsentant, m
- ◆ travel trade representative

Reisegewerbeschau, f
- ◆ travel trade show

Reise gewinnen (bei einer Verlosung)
- ◆ win a trip (in a raffle)
- ◆ win a tour (in a raffle)

Reisegewohnheit, f
- ◆ travel habit
- ◆ traveling habit *AE*
- ◆ travelling habit *BE*

Reisegroßhändler, m
- ◆ tour wholesaler

Reisegrund, m
- ◆ reason for traveling *AE*
- ◆ reason for travelling *BE*
- ◆ reason for travel

Reisegruppe, f (generell)
- ◆ travel group

Reisegruppe, f (gewerblich)
- ◆ tour group
- ◆ tour

Reisegruppe, f (z.T. ungewerblich)
- ◆ tour party
- ◆ touring party
- ◆ party

Reisegruppe begleiten
- ◆ escort a tour group
- ◆ accompany a tour group

Reisegruppenankunft, f
- ◆ arrival of a tour
- ◆ tour arrival

Reisegruppenbuchung f
- ◆ tour booking

Reisegruppencharter, m
- ◆ travel group charter
- ◆ TGC

Reisegruppenführer, m (professionell)
- ◆ tour-group leader

Reisegruppengast m
- ◆ tour guest

Reisegruppengutschein, m
Reisegutschein, m
- ◆ tour voucher

Reisegruppenhotel, n
- ◆ tour-group hotel

Reisegruppenliste f
Gruppenliste f
- ◆ tour list

Reisegruppenmitglied, n
- ◆ tour member
- ◆ member of a tour
- ◆ member of a travel group

Reisegruppenpreis m
- ◆ tour rate
- ◆ tour price

Reisegruppenrechnung, f
- ◆ tour-group bill
- ◆ tour bill

Reisegruppenreservierung, f
- ◆ tour-group reservation
- ◆ tour reservation

Reisegruppenservice, m
- ◆ tour-group service
- ◆ tour service

Reisegruppenteilnehmer, m
- ◆ member of a tour group
- ◆ member of a travel group

Reisegruppen werden nicht aufgenommen
- ◆ Tour groups are not catered for

Reisegruppe umfaßt zehn Personen
(professionelle Reise)
- ◆ tour comprises ten persons

Reisegutschein, m
- ◆ travel voucher
- ◆ tour voucher

Reisegutschein ausgeben für etw
- ◆ spend a travel voucher on s.th.

Reisegutschein einlösen
- ◆ cash a travel voucher

Reisegutscheingast, m
- ◆ tour voucher guest

Reise hat ihren Zauber verloren
- ◆ journey has lost its magic

Reisehäufigkeit, f
Reisefrequenz, f
♦ travel frequency
Reisehelfer, m
♦ travel assistant
♦ travel help
♦ tour assistant
♦ tour help
Reisehöhepunkt, m
Höhepunkt der Reise, m
♦ highlight of the tour
♦ highlight of the journey
♦ highlight of the trip
Reisehotel, n
Tourenhotel, n
♦ touring hotel
♦ travellers' hotel *BE obs*
Reiseidee, f
♦ travel idea
Reise in den Fußstapfen von jm, f
♦ journey in the footsteps of s.o.
Reise in die Vergangenheit, f (generell)
♦ journey into the past
Reise in die Vergangenheit, f (persönlich)
♦ trip down memory lane
♦ journey down memory lane
Reise in die Vergangenheit machen (generell)
♦ make a journey into the past
Reise in die Vergangenheit machen (persönlich)
♦ take a trip down memory lane
♦ take a journey down memory lane
Reiseindustrie, f
Reisebranche, f
♦ travel industry
Reiseindustrieumsatz, m
Reisebranchenumsatz, m
♦ travel industry sales *pl*
Reiseindustrieveranstaltung, f
♦ travel industry event
Reiseinformation, f
Reiseauskunft, f
♦ travel information
♦ touring information
Reiseinformationsdienst m
Reiseinformationsservice m
Reiseinformation f
♦ travel information service
Reiseinformationshandbuch, n
♦ travel information manual
Reiseinformationspaket, n
♦ travel information pack
Reiseinformationsprogramm, n
♦ travel information program *AE*
♦ travel information programme *BE*
Reiseinformationsservice, m
→ Reiseinformationsdienst
Reiseinhalt, m
♦ tour content
♦ content of a tour
♦ travel content
Reise ins Ausland, f
♦ journey abroad
♦ trip abroad
Reise ins Ausland unternehmen
Auslandsreise unternehmen
♦ take a trip abroad
♦ take a journey abroad
♦ take a tour abroad
Reiseintensität, f
♦ travel intensity

Reiseintensität erreichen von 20%
♦ achieve a travel intensity of 20%
Reiseintensität fiel um 2% von 47% auf 45%
Reiseintensität ging um 2% von 47% auf 45% zurück
Reiseintensität verringerte sich um 2% auf 45%
♦ travel intensity dropped by 2% from 47% to 45%
♦ travel intensity fell by 2% from 47% to 45%
♦ travel intensity declined by 2% from 47% to 45%
Reiseintensitätsindex, m
♦ travel intensity index
Reiseintensität stieg um 5% von 45% auf 50%
Reiseintensität erhöhte sich um 5% von 45% auf 50%
♦ travel intensity increased by 5% from 45% to 50%
♦ travel intensity rose by 5% from 45% to 50%
Reiseinteresse, n
(Statistik)
Reiseneigung, f
Reisegeneigtheit, f
Reisefreudigkeit, f
♦ travel propensity
Reiseinteressent, m
♦ potential traveller
♦ potential traveler *AE*
Reise in Übersee, f
Überseereise, f
♦ overseas tour
Reise ist die Mühe wert
♦ journey is worth the effort
♦ trip is worth the effort
♦ tour is worth the effort
Reise ist ein Abenteuer
♦ journey is an adventure
♦ tour is an adventure
Reise ist eine Enttäuschung
♦ journey is a disappointment
♦ tour is a disappointment
♦ trip is a disappointment
Reise ist ein Mißerfolg
♦ tour is a failure
♦ journey is a failure
♦ trip is a failure
Reise ist gefährlich
♦ journey is dangerous
♦ trip is dangerous
♦ tour is dangerous
Reise ist unwiederholbar
♦ journey is unrepeatable
♦ trip is unrepeatable
♦ tour is unrepeatable
Reise ist vorbei
♦ journey is over
♦ trip is over
♦ tour is over
Reise ist zuende
♦ journey is finished
♦ trip is finished
♦ tour is finished
Reisejahr, n
♦ travel year
Reisejahre, n pl
♦ years of travelling *pl*
♦ years of traveling *AE pl*
Reisejournal, n
♦ travel journal
Reisejournalist, m
♦ travel journalist

Reise kann individuellen Bedürfnissen angepaßt werden
♦ tour can be adapted to suit individual requirements
Reisekasse, f (Geldmittel)
Reisemittel, n pl
♦ travel funds *pl*
♦ traveling funds *AE pl*
♦ travelling funds *BE pl*
Reisekatalog, m
♦ travel catalogue
♦ travel catalog *AE*
Reisekategorie, f
♦ travel category
Reise kaufen
♦ buy a tour
♦ buy a trip
Reisekäufer, m
♦ travel buyer
Reisekissen, n
♦ travel pillow
Reiseklasse, f
♦ class of travel
Reisekleid, n
♦ travel dress
♦ travelling dress *BE*
Reisekleidung, f
♦ travel clothes *pl*
♦ traveling clothes *AE pl*
♦ travelling clothes *BE pl*
♦ travel clothing
Reiseklinik, f
♦ travel clinic
Reisekoffer, m (groß)
♦ traveling case *AE*
♦ travelling case *BE*
♦ trunk
Reisekoffer, m (klein)
♦ suitcase
Reisekomfort, m (generell)
♦ travel comforts *pl*
Reisekomfort, m (speziell)
♦ touring comfort
Reisekonto, n
♦ travel account
Reisekonzept, n (generell)
♦ travel scheme
Reisekonzept, n (speziell)
♦ tour scheme
Reisekonzept entwickeln
♦ develop a travel scheme
♦ develop a tour scheme
Reisekonzern, m
♦ travel group
Reisekosten, pl
♦ travel cost
♦ travel costs *pl*
♦ travelling costs *pl*
♦ traveling costs *AE pl*
♦ journey costs *pl*
Reisekostenantrag, m
(durch Arbeitnehmer)
♦ travel expense request
♦ travel request
Reisekosten decken
♦ cover (the) travel costs
Reisekostenvergütung, f
Reisevergütung, f
♦ reimbursement of travel costs
♦ reimbursement of travel expenses

Reisekosten zahlen

Reisekosten zahlen
Reisekosten bezahlen
♦ **pay for the travel costs**
♦ pay for the traveling costs *AE*
♦ pay for the travelling costs *BE*
Reise kostet DM 1234
♦ **tour costs DM 1234**
♦ journey costs DM 1234
♦ trip costs DM 1234
reisekrank, adj
♦ **travel-sick, adj**
Reisekrankenversicherung, f
♦ **travel health insurance**
Reisekrankheit, f
♦ **travel-sickness**
Reisekreditbrief, m
Reiseakkreditiv, n
♦ **traveler's letter of credit** *AE*
♦ traveller's letter of credit *BE*
Reisekultur, f
♦ **travel culture**
Reisekurzinformation, f
♦ **travel brief**
Reisekurzurlaub, m
♦ **touring break**
Reisekutsche, f
♦ **traveling coach** *AE*
♦ travelling coach *BE*
♦ traveling carriage *AE*
♦ travelling carriage *BE*
♦ coach
Reiseladen m
Reisegeschäft n
♦ **travel store** *AE*
♦ travel shop *BE*
Reiseland n
♦ **tourist country**
♦ tourist destination
Reiselänge, f
♦ **length of the journey**
♦ length of the tour
♦ length of the trip
Reiseleben, n
♦ **traveling life, one's** *AE*
♦ one's travelling life *BE*
Reiselehrgang, m
Reisekurs, m
♦ **travel course**
Reiseleistung, f
Reisedienstleistung, f
♦ **travel service**
Reiseleiter, m
♦ **tour guide**
♦ tour manager
♦ travel supervisor
♦ courier *BE*
♦ tour conductor
Reiseleiter am Aufenthaltsort, m
Standortreiseleiter, m
♦ **local guide**
♦ local tour guide
Reiseleiterausbildung, f
Ausbildung von Reiseleitern, f
♦ **training of tour guides**
Reiseleiterservice, m
Reiseleiterdienst, m
♦ **tour-guide service**
♦ courier service *BE*
Reiseleitung, f (Aktivität)
♦ **tour management**

♦ management of a tour
♦ managing a tour
Reiseleitung, f (Person)
→ Reiseleiter
Reiseleitung vor Ort, f
→ örtliche Reiseleitung
Reiselexikon, n
Reiseenzyklopädie, f
♦ **travel encyclopedia**
Reiseliberalisierung, f
♦ **travel liberalisation**
♦ travel liberalization
♦ liberalisation of travel
♦ liberalization of travel
Reiseliteratur, f (generell)
♦ **travel literature**
♦ travel books *pl*
Reiseliteratur, f (spezielle Reise)
♦ **tour literature**
Reiselust, f
♦ **love of travel**
♦ fondness for travelling
♦ fondness for traveling *AE*
♦ itchy feet *pl coll*
♦ travel bug *coll*
reiselustig, adj
→ reisefreudig
Reiselustiger, m
Reisebegeisterter, m
♦ **person fond of traveling** *AE*
♦ person fond of travelling *BE*
♦ keen traveller
♦ keen traveler *AE*
reiselustig sein
♦ **be a keen traveller**
♦ be a keen traveler *AE*
Reise machen
♦ **make a journey**
♦ go on a journey
♦ take a trip
♦ make a trip
♦ make a tour
Reise machen durch Europa
♦ **make a journey through Europe**
♦ make a trip through Europe
♦ make a tour through Europe
♦ make a tour of Europe
Reise machen mit dem Zug
♦ **make a journey by train**
Reise machen mit jm nach X
auf die Reise mitnehmen jn nach X
♦ **take s.o. on a journey to X**
♦ take s.o. on a tour to X
Reise machen nach X (Seereise)
Seereise nach X machen
♦ **make a voyage to X**
Reise machen (Seereise)
→ Seereise machen
Reisemagazin, n
♦ **travel magazine**
Reisemakler, m
♦ **tour broker**
Reisemanagement, n
♦ **travel management**
Reisemanager, m
♦ **travel manager**
Reisemannschaft, f
Reiseteam, n
♦ **travel team**
♦ tour team

Reisemarketing, n
♦ **travel marketing**
Reisemarketingexperte, m
♦ **travel marketing expert**
Reisemarkt, m
♦ **travel market**
Reisemarkt ist gesättigt
♦ **travel market is saturated**
reisemäßig, adv
was das Reisen angeht
♦ **travel-wise, adv**
Reisemesse, f
♦ **travel fair**
♦ travel trade fair
Reisemitbringsel, n
♦ **travel gift**
Reise mit dem Auto, f
Reise im Auto, f
♦ **journey by car**
♦ motoring tour
Reise mit öffentlichen Verkehrsmitteln, f
♦ **journey by public transport**
Reisemittel, n pl
Reisegeld, n
Reisekasse, f
♦ **traveling funds** *AE pl*
♦ travelling funds *BE pl*
♦ travel funds *pl*
Reisemittler, m
Reisevermittler, m
Reisebüro, n
♦ **travel agent**
♦ travel agency
Reisemittlergewerbe, n
→ Reisebürogewerbe
Reisemobil, n
Wohnmobil, n
♦ **motor caravan** *BE*
♦ motor home *BE*
♦ motorhome *AE*
Reisemobilbegeisterter, m
Wohnmobilbegeisterter, m
♦ **motor-caravan enthusiast** *BE*
♦ motor-home enthusiast *BE*
♦ motorhome enthusiast *AE*
Reisemobilbesitzer, m
Wohnmobilbesitzer, m
♦ **motor-caravan owner** *BE*
♦ motor-home owner *BE*
♦ motorhome owner *AE*
Reisemobilfan, m
Wohnmobilfan, m
♦ **motor-caravan fan** *BE*
♦ motor-home fan *BE*
♦ motorhome fan *AE*
Reisemobilferien, pl
Reisemobilurlaub, m
Wohnmobilferien, pl
Wohnmobilurlaub, m
♦ **motor-caravan holidays** *BE pl*
♦ motor-home holidays *BE pl*
♦ motorhome vacation *AE*
Reisemobil mieten
Wohnmobil mieten
♦ **hire a motor caravan** *BE*
♦ hire a motor home *BE*
♦ rent a motorhome *AE*
Reisemobilpark, m
Wohnmobilpark, m
♦ **motor-caravan park** *BE*

- ♦ motor-home park *BE*
- ♦ motorhome park *AE*

Reisemobilplatz, m
Wohnmobilplatz, m
- ♦ motor-caravan site *BE*
- ♦ motor-home site *BE*
- ♦ motorhome site *AE*

Reisemobil pro Nacht, n
Wohnmobil pro Nacht, n
- ♦ motor caravan per night *BE*
- ♦ motor home per night *BE*
- ♦ motorhome per night *AE*

Reisemobilstellplatz, m
Wohnmobilstellplatz, m
- ♦ motor-caravan pitch *BE*
- ♦ motor-home pitch *BE*
- ♦ motorhome pitch *AE*
- ♦ motorhome site *AE*

Reisemobilurlaub, m
Reisemobilferien, pl
Wohnmobilurlaub, m
Wohnmobilferien, pl
- ♦ motor-caravan holidays *BE pl*
- ♦ motor-caravanning holiday *BE*
- ♦ motor-home holiday *BE*
- ♦ motorhome vacation *AE*

Reisemobil vermieten
Wohnmobil vermieten
- ♦ hire out a motor caravan *BE*
- ♦ let a motor caravan *BE*
- ♦ hire out a motor home *BE*
- ♦ let a motor home *BE*
- ♦ rent a motorhome *AE*

Reisemodus, m
Reiseart, f
- ♦ mode of travel

Reisemöglichkeit, f
- ♦ possibility of traveling *AE*
- ♦ possibility of travelling *BE*
- ♦ travel opportunity

Reisemonat, m
- ♦ travel month

Reisemonitor, m
- ♦ travel monitor

Reisemotiv, n
- ♦ travel motive
- ♦ motive for travel

Reisemotivation, f
- ♦ travel motivation
- ♦ trip motivation

reisemüde, adj
- ♦ tired of traveling, adj *AE*
- ♦ tired of traveling, adj *BE*
- ♦ weary of traveling, adj *AE*
- ♦ weary of travelling, adj *BE*
- ♦ travel-weary, adj

Reisemultiplikator, m
- ♦ travel multiplier

Reisemuster, n
- ♦ travel pattern

reisen
- ♦ travel
- ♦ go on a journey
- ♦ journey

Reisen, n
Reiseverkehr, m
- ♦ travel

reisen abseits der Touristenpfade
- ♦ travel off the beaten tourist tracks

Reisenachfrage, f
- ♦ travel demand
- ♦ demand for travel

Reisenachfrage erzeugen
Reisenachfrage schaffen
- ♦ create travel demand

Reise nach Frankreich, f
- ♦ trip to France
- ♦ journey to France
- ♦ tour to France

Reise nach Norden, f
- ♦ journey northwards

Reise nach Osten, f
- ♦ journey eastwards

Reisenachrichten, f pl
Verkehrsfunk, m
- ♦ travel news *sg*

Reise nach Süden, f
- ♦ journey southwards

Reise nach Westen, f
- ♦ journey westwards

reisen als blinder Passagier auf einem Schiff
- ♦ stow away on a ship

Reisenarr, m
- ♦ travel buff

reisen auf dem Land
- ♦ travel on land

reisen auf dem Luftweg
- ♦ go by air

reisen auf dem Meer
reisen auf See
- ♦ travel on sea

reisen auf dem Seeweg
- ♦ go by sea

reisen auf der Straße
auf der Straße reisen
- ♦ travel by road

reisen auf eigene Kosten
auf eigene Kosten reisen
- ♦ travel at one's own expense

reisen auf Kosten von jm
auf js Kosten reisen
- ♦ travel at the expense of s.o.
- ♦ travel at s.o.'s expense

reisen aus ethnischen Gründen
- ♦ travel for ethnic reasons

reisen aus geschäftlichen Gründen
aus geschäftlichen Gründen reisen
aus geschäftlichen Gründen verreisen
- ♦ travel for business reasons
- ♦ travel on business

reisen außerhalb von Europa
- ♦ travel outside Europe

reisen aus Vergnügen
aus Vergnügen reisen
- ♦ travel on pleasure *AE*
- ♦ travel for pleasure *BE*

reisen bei Nacht
→ nachts reisen

Reisen bildet
Reisen weitet den Horizont
- ♦ travel broadens the mind

reisen bis nach X
- ♦ travel as far as X

reisend, adj
- ♦ traveling, adj *AE*
- ♦ travelling, adj *BE*

Reisende, f
- ♦ woman traveller
- ♦ woman traveler *AE*

Reisenden auflauern
einen Reisenden überfallen
einen Reisenden ausrauben
- ♦ waylay a traveller
- ♦ waylay a traveler *AE*

Reisenden willkommen heißen
Reisenden begrüßen
- ♦ welcome a traveller
- ♦ welcome a traveler *AE*

Reisender, der viel Geld ausgibt, m
- ♦ high-spending traveller
- ♦ high-spending traveler *AE*

Reisender, der wenig Geld ausgibt, m
- ♦ low-spending traveller
- ♦ low-spending traveler *AE*

Reisender, m (generell)
- ♦ traveler *AE*
- ♦ traveller *BE*
- ♦ tourist
- ♦ passenger

Reisender, m (Handelsreisender)
→ Handelsreisender

Reisender, m (Seereise)
→ Seereisender

Reisender, m (Tourist)
→ Tourist

Reisender, m (Umherziehender)
Umherziehender, m
Fahrender, m
- ♦ itinerant
- ♦ traveller
- ♦ traveler *AE*

Reisender auf dem Weg zum Mittelmeer, m
- ♦ traveller bound for the Mediterranean
- ♦ traveler bound for the Mediterranean *AE*

Reisender aus dem Ausland, m
ausländischer Reisender, m
- ♦ traveller from abroad
- ♦ traveler from abroad *AE*
- ♦ foreign traveller
- ♦ foreign traveler *AE*

Reisender aus Europa, m
- ♦ traveler from Europe *AE*
- ♦ traveller from Europe *BE*

Reisender mit Spezialinteresse, m
Special-Interest-Reisender, m
- ♦ special interest traveller
- ♦ special interest traveler *AE*

Reisender mit wenig Geld, m
- ♦ budget traveller
- ♦ budget traveler *AE*

Reisender ohne Erfahrung, m
unerfahrener Reisender, m
- ♦ unseasoned traveller
- ♦ unseasoned traveler *AE*

Reisender von heute, m
- ♦ traveler of today *AE*
- ♦ traveller of today *BE*

Reisende werden gebeten, pünktlich zu sein
- ♦ passengers are asked to be punctual

reisen durch das ganze Land
durch das ganze Land reisen
das ganze Land bereisen
- ♦ travel all over the country

reisen durch das Land
im Landesinneren reisen
- ♦ travel the countryside

reisen durch die ganze Welt
durch die ganze Welt reisen
die ganze Welt bereisen
- ♦ travel all over the world

reisen durch die Welt
  Welt bereisen
  ♦ tour the world
  ♦ travel the world
reisen durch die Zeit
  reisen durch die Jahrhunderte
  ♦ travel through time
reisen durch ein Land
  Land bereisen
  ♦ travel through a country
  ♦ journey through a country
  ♦ tour a country
reisen durch etw
  ♦ travel through s.th.
  ♦ journey through s.th.
reisen durch Europa
  durch Europa reisen
  ♦ travel through Europe
  ♦ journey through Europe
reisen durch Raum und Zeit
  ♦ travel through space and time
Reisenecessaire, n
  Kulturbeutel, m *coll*
  ♦ toilet case
  ♦ dressing case
Reisen erster Klasse, n
  Reiseverkehr erster Klasse, m
  ♦ first-class travel
Reisenetz, n
  ♦ travel network
Reisen führen jn nach X
  ♦ travels take one to X
  ♦ one's travels take one to X
Reisen für Behinderte, n
  ♦ travel for disabled people
  ♦ travel for the disabled
  ♦ travel for handicapped people
  ♦ travel for the handicapped
reisen für eine Firma
  ♦ travel for a firm
  ♦ travel for a company
reisen für umsonst
  umsonst reisen
  ♦ travel for free
reisen im Konvoi
  ♦ travel in convoy
reisen in der Luft
  ♦ travel in the air
reisen in der Nacht
  in der Nacht reisen
  ♦ travel at night
reisen in der Touristenklasse
  in der Touristenklasse reisen
  ♦ travel economy class
  ♦ travel economy
reisen in die Ferien
  in die Ferien reisen
  in den Urlaub reisen
  ♦ go for one's vacation *AE*
  ♦ go for one's holiday *BE*
reisen in Dreiergruppen
  ♦ travel in groups of three
reisen in einem Flugzeug
  ♦ travel on a plane
  ♦ travel on an aircraft
reisen in einem Kanu
  ♦ travel in a canoe
reisen in Gruppen
  ♦ travel in groups
reisen in kurzen Etappen
  ♦ travel in short stages
  ♦ travel in short hops
reisen in langen Etappen
  ♦ travel in long stages
reisen innerhalb eines Landes
  ♦ travel within a country
reisen ins Ausland
  → ins Ausland reisen
Reisen ins Ausland, n
  Auslandsreisen, n
  Auslandsreiseverkehr, m
  ♦ travel abroad
reisen in seinem eigenen Land
  ♦ travel in one's own country
reisen in Vierergruppen
  ♦ travel in groups of four
reisen in Vietnam
  umherreisen in Vietnam
  ♦ travel in Vietnam
reisen kreuz und quer durch etw
  reisen in ganz X
  ♦ travel the length and breadth of s.th.
reisen mit 100 Meilen pro Stunde
  mit 100 Meilen pro Stunde reisen
  ♦ travel at 100 miles per hour
  ♦ travel at 100 mph
reisen mit dem Auto
  verreisen mit dem Auto
  anreisen mit dem Auto
  ♦ travel by car
  ♦ travel by automobile *AE*
reisen mit dem Boot
  mit dem Boot reisen
  mit dem Schiff reisen
  ♦ travel by boat
  ♦ travel by ship
  ♦ voyage
reisen mit dem Bus
  mit dem Bus reisen
  ♦ travel by bus
  ♦ travel by coach *BE*
reisen mit dem Dampfer
  mit dem Dampfer reisen
  ♦ travel by steamer
reisen mit dem eigenen Auto
  ♦ travel in one's own car
reisen mit dem Fahrrad
  mit dem Fahrrad reisen
  mit dem Rad reisen *coll*
  ♦ travel by bicycle
  ♦ travel by bike *coll*
reisen mit dem Flugzeug
  mit dem Flugzeug reisen
  anreisen mit dem Flugzeug
  ♦ travel by air
  ♦ travel by plane
  ♦ go by plane
reisen mit dem Kanu
  mit dem Kanu reisen
  ♦ travel by canoe
reisen mit dem Rad *coll*
  mit dem Fahrrad reisen
  ♦ travel by bike *coll*
  ♦ travel by bicycle
reisen mit dem Schiff
  mit dem Schiff reisen
  ♦ travel by ship
  ♦ travel by boat
  ♦ voyage
reisen mit dem Zug
  mit dem Zug reisen
  ♦ travel by train
reisen mit der Bahn
  mit der Bahn reisen
  ♦ travel by rail
reisen mit einem bestimmten Zug
  ♦ travel on a specific train
reisen mit einer Reisegesellschaft
  ♦ travel with a tourist party
reisen mit Einsicht
  ♦ travel with insight
reisen mit Flug Nr. 125
  fliegen mit Flug Nr. 125
  ♦ travel on flight no. 125
reisen mit jm
  ♦ travel with s.o.
reisen mit Kindern
  ♦ travel with children
reisen mit wenig Gepäck
  ♦ travel light
reisen nach exotischen Orten
  reisen zu exotischen Orten
  ♦ travel to exotic places
reisen nach Übersee
  nach Übersee reisen
  nach Übersee verreisen
  ♦ travel overseas
reisen nach X
  ♦ travel to X
  ♦ go to X
  ♦ make a trip to X
Reisenotiz, f
  ♦ travel note
Reisenotwendigkeit, f
  ♦ travel necessity
reisen per Schiff
  per Schiff reisen
  mit dem Schiff reisen
  ♦ voyage
  ♦ travel by ship
Reisen sagt ihr zu
  das Reisen sagt ihr zu
  ♦ traveling is congenial to her taste *AE*
  ♦ travelling is congenial to her taste *BE*
Reisen Sie allein?
  ♦ Are you travelling on your own?
  ♦ Are you traveling on your own? *AE*
Reisen Sie mit dem Zug oder dem Flugzeug?
  ♦ Are you travelling by train or by air?
  ♦ Are you traveling by train or by air? *AE*
reisen über den Atlantik
  über den Atlantik reisen
  ♦ travel across the Atlantic
reisen über Land
  über Land reisen
  ♦ travel over land
reisen über Rom
  über Rom reisen
  ♦ travel via Rome
reisen um die Welt
  um die Welt reisen
  ♦ travel around the world
  ♦ travel round the world
  ♦ make a (round-the) world trip
Reisen um die Welt, f pl
  ♦ travels (a)round the world *pl*
Reisen um die Welt, n
  Reiseverkehr um die Welt, m
  ♦ travel (a)round the world

- ♦ traveling (a)round the world *AE*
- ♦ travelling (a)round the world *BE*

reisen unter einem Decknamen
- ♦ travel under an alias

reisen unter einem falschen Namen
- ♦ travel under a false name

reisen unter einem fremden Namen
- ♦ travel under an assumed name

reisen von A nach C über B
- ♦ travel from A to C via B
- ♦ travel from A to C by way of B
- ♦ journey from A to C via B
- ♦ journey from A to C by way of B

reisen von Ort zu Ort
- ♦ travel from place to place

reisen weit und breit
- nach nah und fern reisen
- ♦ travel far and wide

reisen zu Land
- zu Land reisen
- ♦ travel by land

reisen zum halben Preis
- zum halben Preis reisen
- ♦ travel at half (the) fare

reisen zum Vergnügen
- zum Vergnügen reisen
- zum Vergnügen verreisen
- ♦ travel for pleasure
- ♦ travel on pleasure *AE*

reisen zum vollen Preis
- zum vollen Preis reisen
- ♦ travel at (the) full fare

reisen zu Wasser
- zu Wasser reisen
- ♦ travel by sea

Reisen zweiter Klasse, n
- Reiseverkehr zweiter Klasse, m
- ♦ second-class travel

reisen zwischen A und B
- ♦ travel between A and B

Reise offerieren
- → Reise anbieten

Reise ohne Begleitung, f
- → unbegleitete Reise

Reiseonkel, m *humor*
- → Weltenbummler

Reiseoption, f
- ♦ tour option
- ♦ travel option

Reiseorganisation, f (Firma)
- ♦ travel organisation
- ♦ travel organization

Reiseorganisator, m
- Reiseveranstalter, m
- ♦ tour organiser
- ♦ tour organizer
- ♦ organiser of a tour
- ♦ organizer of a tour
- ♦ travel organiser

Reise organisieren
- Reise veranstalten
- ♦ organise a tour
- ♦ organize a tour
- ♦ organise a journey
- ♦ organize a journey
- ♦ organise a trip

Reisepaket, n
- (Information)
- ♦ travel pack

Reisepapier, n
- Reisedokument, n
- Reiseunterlage, f
- ♦ travel document

Reisepapiere ausstellen
- Reisedokumente ausstellen
- ♦ issue the travel documents

Reisepapiere prüfen
- Reisepapiere kontrollieren
- ♦ check the travel documents

Reisepartner, m
- ♦ travel partner

Reisepaß, m (Fahrschein)
- ♦ travel pass

Reisepaß, m (staatliches Dokument)
- Paß, m
- ♦ passport

Reisepaß beantragen
- Paß beantragen
- ♦ apply for a passport

Reisepaß bekommen
- Paß bekommen
- ♦ get a passport

Reisepaß benötigen
- ♦ require a passport

Reisepaß erhalten
- ♦ obtain a passport
- ♦ receive a passport

Reisepaßinhaber, m
- Paßinhaber, m
- ♦ holder of a passport
- ♦ passport holder
- ♦ bearer of a passport

Reisepaß ist fünf Jahre gültig
- Paß ist fünf Jahre gültig
- ♦ passport is valid for five years

Reisepaß läuft aus
- Paß läuft aus
- ♦ passport expires

Reisepaß prüfen
- Paß prüfen
- ♦ check a passport

Reisepaß verlieren
- Paß verlieren
- ♦ lose one's passport

Reisepaßvorschrift, f
- Paßvorschrift, f
- ♦ passport requirement

Reisepauschale, f
- ♦ tour package

Reisepersonal, n
- ♦ travel staff
- ♦ travel personnel

Reisephilosophie, f
- ♦ travel philosophy

Reisepille, f
- ♦ travel pill
- ♦ pill for travel sickness

Reiseplakat, n
- Reiseposter, m/n
- ♦ travel poster

Reiseplan, m
- ♦ travel plan
- ♦ plans for a journey *pl*
- ♦ plans for a tour *pl*
- ♦ plans for a trip *pl*

Reiseplan ändern
- ♦ change travel plans
- ♦ change one's travel plans

Reise planen
- ♦ plan a journey
- ♦ plan a tour
- ♦ plan a trip

Reiseplaner, m
- ♦ travel planner
- ♦ journey planner

Reisepläne schmieden
- ♦ make plans for a trip
- ♦ make plans for a tour
- ♦ make plans for a journey

Reiseplanung, f
- ♦ tour planning
- ♦ trip planning
- ♦ planning (of) a tour
- ♦ planning (of) a trip
- ♦ planning (of) a journey

Reiseplatz, m (Camping)
- Durchreiseplatz, m
- ♦ touring site

Reisepolice, f
- (Versicherung)
- ♦ travel policy

Reisepreis, m (Auszeichnung)
- Reiseauszeichnung, f
- ♦ travel award
- ♦ travel prize

Reisepreis, m (Rechnung)
- ♦ tour price
- ♦ price of a tour

Reisepreis beträgt DM 1234
- ♦ tour price is DM 1234

Reisepreiserstattung, f
- ♦ refund of the tour price
- ♦ tour price refund

Reisepreisindex, m
- ♦ travel price index

Reisepreis pro Person, m
- ♦ tour price per person

Reiseproblem, n
- ♦ travel problem

Reiseprodukt, n
- ♦ travel product

Reiseprofi, m (erfahrener Tourist) *coll*
- ♦ experienced traveler *AE*
- ♦ experienced traveller *BE*
- ♦ seasoned traveler *AE*
- ♦ seasoned traveller *BE*

Reiseprofi, m (im Reisegewerbe) *coll*
- Reisefachmann, m
- ♦ travel professional

Reiseprogramm, n (generell)
- ♦ travel program *AE*
- ♦ travel programme *BE*

Reiseprogramm, n (Tour)
- ♦ tour program *AE*
- ♦ tour(ing) programme *BE*
- ♦ tours program(me)
- ♦ program of the tour *AE*
- ♦ programme of the tour *BE*

Reiseprogramm beinhaltet etw
- ♦ tour program includes s.th. *AE*
- ♦ tour programme includes s.th. *BE*

Reiseprogrammpunkt, m
- ♦ item on the tour program *AE*
- ♦ item on the tour programme *BE*

Reiseprospekt, m
- Reisebroschüre, f
- ♦ travel brochure
- ♦ tour brochure

Reiseprospekt entwerfen
- Reiseprospekt gestalten
- ♦ design a travel brochure
- ♦ design a tour brochure

Reiseproviant

Reiseproviant, m
♦ traveling provisions *AE pl*
♦ travelling provisions *BE pl*
♦ provisions *pl*
Reisepublikum, n
♦ traveling public *AE*
♦ travelling public *BE*
Reise quer durch den Kontinent, f
♦ journey across the continent
Reise quer durch die Vereinigten Staaten, f
♦ journey across the United States
♦ trip across the United States
Reisequiz, n
♦ travel quiz
Reiserabatt, m
Reiseermäßigung, f
♦ travel discount
Reiseradius, m
Reiseumkreis, m
♦ travel radius
Reiserat, m (Gremium)
♦ travel council
Reiserat, m (Ratschlag)
Reiseratschlag, m
♦ travel advice
Reiseratgeber, m
Reiseberater, m
♦ travel counselor *AE*
♦ travel counsellor *BE*
Reiserechnung, f
♦ travel bill
Reiserecht, n
Reisegesetz, n
♦ travel law
Reisereglementierung, f
♦ regimentation of travel
♦ travel regimentation
Reiserekord, m
♦ travel record
♦ tourist record
Reiserepräsentant, m
♦ travel representative
Reiserepräsentant am Ort, m
Reiserepräsentant vor Ort, m
♦ local travel representative
♦ local travel rep *coll*
Reisereservierung, f
♦ travel reservation
Reisereservierung machen nach X
♦ make a reservation for a trip to X
Reisereservierungssystem, n
♦ travel reservation system
Reiserichtung, f
Fahrtrichtung, f
♦ travel direction
♦ direction of travel
Reiserisiko, n
♦ travel risk
Reiseroman, m
♦ travel novel
Reiseroute, f
Reisestrecke, f
Anreiseroute, f
Anreisestrecke, f
♦ travel route
♦ route
♦ itinerary
♦ tour route
Reiseroute festlegen
♦ fix the route of a journey
♦ fix the route of a tour

♦ fix the route of a trip
♦ fix the itinerary
Reiserücktritt, m
→ Reisestornierung
Reiserücktrittsgebühr, f
♦ travel cancellation fee
♦ travel cancellation charge
♦ travel cancelation fee *AE*
♦ travel cancelation charge *AE*
Reiserücktrittskosten, pl
♦ travel cancellation costs *pl*
♦ travel cancellation cost
♦ travel cancelation costs *AE pl*
♦ travel cancelation cost *AE*
Reiserücktrittsversicherung, f
Reiserücktrittskostenversicherung, f
♦ travel cancellation insurance
♦ travel cancelation insurance *AE*
Reiserücktrittsversicherung abschließen
♦ take out a travel cancellation insurance (policy)
♦ take out a travel cancelation insurance (policy) *AE*
Reisesaison, f
♦ travel season
♦ touring season
♦ tourist season
Reisesaisonmonat, m
♦ travel season month
♦ month in the travel season
♦ tourist season month
♦ month in the tourist season
Reisesaisonwoche, f
♦ travel season week
♦ week in the travel season
♦ tourist season week
♦ week in the tourist season
Reiseschau, f
Reiseausstellung, f
♦ travel show
♦ travel exhibition
Reisescheck, m
♦ traveler's check *AE*
♦ traveller's cheque *BE*
Reisescheck ausstellen
♦ issue a traveler's check *AE*
♦ issue a traveller's cheque *BE*
Reisechecks in Zahlung nehmen
Reiseschecks annehmen
♦ accept traveler's checks *AE*
♦ accept traveller's cheques *BE*
Reise schließt mit etw ab
♦ journey concludes with s.th.
♦ tour concludes with s.th.
♦ trip concludes with s.th.
Reiseschreibmaschine f
♦ portable typewriter
Reiseschriftsteller, m
♦ travel writer
Reiseschriftstellerei, f
Reiseschrifttum, n
♦ travel writing
Reiseschutz, m (generell)
♦ travel protection
Reiseschutz, m (Versicherung)
♦ travel cover
Reiseseite, f
(Zeitung)
♦ travel page

Reise selbst organisieren
selbst die Reisevorkehrungen treffen
♦ make one's own travel arrangements
Reiseservice, m
→ Reisedienst
Reisesperre, f
Reiseverbot, n
♦ ban on travelling
♦ ban on traveling *AE*
♦ travel ban
Reisespesen, pl
♦ travel expenses *pl*
♦ traveling expenses *AE pl*
♦ travelling expenses *BE pl*
Reisespesenabschluß, m
Reisespesenbericht, m
♦ travel expense report
Reisespesenerstattung, f
♦ reimbursement of travel expenses
♦ repayment of travel expenses
Reisespesenzuschuß, m
♦ allowance for travel expenses
♦ allowance for travelling expenses
♦ allowance for traveling expenses *AE*
Reisespezialist, m
♦ travel specialist
Reisespiel, n
♦ travel game
Reisestatistik, f
♦ travel statistics *pl*
Reisestipendium, n
♦ travel grant
Reise stornieren
Reise absagen
von einer Reise zurücktreten
♦ cancel a tour
♦ cancel a trip
♦ cancel a journey
Reisestornierung, f
Reiserücktritt, m
Reiseabsage, f
♦ travel cancellation
♦ travel cancelation *AE*
♦ cancellation of a tour
♦ cancelation of a tour *AE*
Reisestreß, m
♦ travel stress
Reisestrom, m
♦ travel flow
Reisestudium, n
Reisestudien, pl
♦ travel studies *pl*
Reisetag, m (Abreise)
→ Abreisetag
Reisetag, m (generell)
♦ day of a journey
♦ day of a trip
♦ day of a tour
♦ travel day
♦ travelling day *BE*
Reisetagebuch, n
♦ travel diary
Reisetagebuch führen
♦ keep a travel diary
Reisetante, f *humor*
→ Weltenbummler
Reisetasche, f
♦ travel bag
♦ travelling bag
♦ traveling bag *AE*
♦ carryall *AE*

628

Reisetätigkeit, f
→ Reiseaktivität
Reiseteilnehmer, m
♦ person taking part in a tour
♦ participant in a tour
♦ tour member
♦ person participating in a tour
♦ tour participant
Reisetermin, m
Reisedatum, n
♦ date of the journey
♦ date of the tour
♦ date of the trip
Reisetermin ändern
♦ change the travel date
Reiseterminologie, f
♦ travel terminology
Reisetip, m
Reisehinweis, m
♦ travel tip
Reisetrend, m
Reisetendenz, f
♦ travel trend
Reise über 3000 Meilen, f
♦ journey over 3000 miles
♦ 3000-mile journey
Reise über den Atlantik, f (Seereise)
♦ voyage across the Atlantic
Reise überleben
♦ survive a journey
♦ survive a tour
♦ survive a voyage
Reiseuhr, f
♦ traveling clock AE
♦ travelling clock BE
Reise um die Welt, f (generell)
♦ tour (a)round the world
♦ trip (a)round the world
♦ round-the-world trip (tour)
♦ journey (a)round the world
♦ world trip
Reise um die Welt, f (Seereise)
♦ round-the-world voyage
♦ voyage (a)round the world
Reiseumfrage, f
Reiseüberblick, m
♦ travel survey
Reiseumsatz, m
♦ travel sales pl
Reiseumwelt, f
♦ travel environment
Reise- und Freizeitausstellung, f
♦ travel and leisure exhibition
♦ travel and leisure show
Reise- und Tourismusindustrie, f
♦ travel and tourism industry
♦ travel and tourist industry
Reise- und Tourismusschau, f
Reise- und Touristikschau, f
♦ travel and tourism show
Reise- und Urlaubsschau, f
Reise- und Urlaubsausstellung, f
♦ travel and vacation show AE
♦ travel and holiday show BE
reiseunfähig, adj
♦ unfit to travel, adj
♦ not fit to travel, adj
Reiseunfähigkeit, f
♦ unfitness to travel
♦ being unfit to travel

Reiseunfall, m
♦ travel accident
Reiseunfallversicherung, f
♦ travel accident insurance
♦ insurance against accidents on travel
Reiseunfallversicherung abschließen
♦ take out a travel accident insurance
Reiseunkosten, pl
→ Reisekosten
Reise unterbrechen
♦ break one's journey
♦ break a journey
♦ interrupt one's journey
♦ stop over AE
Reise unterbrechen in X
♦ break one's journey at X
♦ break one's journey in X
♦ break a journey at X
♦ break a journey in X
Reise unterbrechen zum Essen
♦ break one's journey for a meal
♦ break a journey for a meal
Reiseunterbrechung, f
Fahrtunterbrechung, f
Unterbrechung einer Reise, f
Unterbrechung einer Fahrt, f
♦ break in a journey
♦ break of (a) journey
♦ break of (a) tour
♦ interruption of a journey
♦ stopover
Reise unter der Erde, f
♦ underground journey
Reiseunterlagen, f pl
→ Reisepapier
Reiseunternehmen, n
♦ travel enterprise
♦ travel firm
♦ travel company BE
♦ travel corporation AE
Reise unternehmen (generell)
♦ take a journey
♦ take a trip
♦ take a tour
♦ undertake a journey
♦ undertake a trip
Reise unternehmen (Seereise)
Seereise unternehmen
♦ take a voyage
Reiseunternehmer, m
♦ travel operator
Reiseurlaub, m
♦ touring vacation AE
♦ touring holiday BE
Reise veranstalten
Reise veranstalten nach Kanada
♦ operate a tour
♦ operate a tour to Canada
Reiseveranstalter, m
♦ tour operator
Reiseveranstalteraktivität, f
♦ tour operating activity
♦ tour operation activity
Reiseveranstalterbestellung, f
→ Reiseveranstalterbuchung
Reiseveranstalterbuchung, f
Reiseveranstalterbestellung, f
♦ tour operator booking
Reiseveranstalterfirma, f
♦ tour operating corporation AE
♦ tour operating company BE

Reiseveranstaltergeschäft, n
♦ tour operation business
♦ tour operating business
Reiseveranstaltergewerbe, n
Reiseveranstalterbranche, f
♦ tour operation trade
Reiseveranstaltergutschein, m
♦ tour operator voucher
Reiseveranstalter hat Österreich im Programm
♦ tour operator features Austria
Reiseveranstalterindustrie, f
Reiseveranstalterbranche, f
♦ tour operating industry
Reiseveranstalterkatalog, m
♦ tour operator catalogue
♦ tour operator catalog AE
Reiseveranstalterliste, f
♦ tour operator list
Reiseveranstaltermarkt, m
♦ tour operator market
♦ tour operator's market
♦ tour operators' market
Reiseveranstalterprodukt, n
♦ tour operator product
Reiseveranstalterprospekt, m
♦ tour operator brochure
♦ tour operator's brochure
♦ tour operators' brochure
Reiseveranstalterreservierung, f
♦ tour operator reservation
Reiseveranstalterstatistik, f
♦ tour operator statistics pl
Reiseveranstalterszene, f
♦ tour operating scene
Reiseveranstaltertochter, f
Reiseveranstaltertochterunternehmen, n
♦ tour operator subsidiary
♦ tour operating subsidiary
Reiseveranstalterurlaub, m
♦ tour operator vacation AE
♦ tour operator holiday BE
Reiseveranstalterverband, m
♦ tour operators' association
Reiseveranstalterverzeichnis, n
♦ tour operator directory
♦ tour operator list
Reiseveranstaltung, f
♦ tour operation
♦ tour operating
Reiseveranstaltungskonzern, m
Reiseveranstalterkonzern, m
♦ tour operating group
♦ tour operator group
Reiseveranstaltungsmarkt, m
♦ tour operating market
Reiseverband, m
♦ travel association
Reiseverbindung, f
♦ travel link
♦ connection
Reiseverbot, n
Reisesperre, f
♦ travel ban
♦ ban on travelling
♦ ban on traveling AE
Reiseverbot aufheben
Reisesperre aufheben
♦ lift a travel ban
Reiseverbot verhängen (über jn)
♦ impose a travel ban (on s.o.)

Reise verderben
- spoil one's journey
- spoil s.o.'s journey
- spoil one's tour
- spoil s.o.'s tour

Reiseverein, m
Reiseclub, m
- travelers' club AE
- travellers' club BE
- travel club

Reisevereinbarung, f
- travel agreement

Reisevereinsmitglied, n
Reiseclubmitglied, n
- travelers' club member AE
- travellers' club member BE
- travel club member

Reisevergnügen, n
- pleasure of travelling BE
- pleasures of travelling BE pl
- pleasure of traveling AE
- pleasures of traveling AE pl

Reisevergütung, f
Reisekostenvergütung, f
- repayment of travel expenses
- reimbursement of travel expenses
- reimbursement of travelling expenses
- reimbursement of traveling expenses AE

Reiseverhalten, n
- travel behavior AE
- travel behaviour BE

Reise verkaufen jm
- sell a tour to s.o.
- sell s.o. a tour
- sell a trip to s.o.
- sell s.o. a trip

Reiseverkäufer, m
- travel salesman
- travel seller

Reiseverkehr, m
Touristenverkehr, m
- tourist traffic
- tourism
- traveling AE
- travelling BE
- travel

Reiseverkehr aus Deutschland, m
- tourist traffic from Germany

Reiseverkehr erleichtern
Reisen erleichtern
- make travel easier

Reiseverkehr fördern (nach X)
werben für Reisen (nach X)
- promote travel (to X)

Reiseverkehr innerhalb Europas, m
- tourist traffic within Europe

Reiseverkehr nach X, m
- travel to X

Reiseverkehrsaufkommen, n
Reiseverkehrsvolumen, n
- volume of tourist traffic
- tourist traffic volume

Reiseverkehrsbeschränkung, f
- restriction of vacation traffic AE
- restriction of holiday traffic BE

Reiseverkehrskauffrau, f off
- trained female travel agent

Reiseverkehrskaufmann, m off
- trained travel agent

Reiseverkehrsmittel, n
Reisemittel, n
- means of travel

Reiseverkehr steigern nach X
- increase travel to X

Reiseverkehrszunahme, f
Reiseverkehrsanstieg, m
- increase in tourist traffic
- increase in tourism

Reiseverlauf, m
- itinerary
- tour itinerary

Reiseverlauf erstellen
- draw up an itinerary

Reiseverlauf festlegen
Reiseverlauf bestimmen
- fix the itinerary
- decide the itinerary

Reiseverlaufidee, f
- itinerary idea

Reiseverlauf planen
- plan the itinerary
- plan an itinerary

Reiseverlaufsänderung, f (geringfügig)
- alteration of the itinerary
- modification of the itinerary

Reiseverlaufsänderung, f (umfassend)
- change of the itinerary

Reiseverlauf vorbereiten
- prepare an itinerary

Reiseverlauf zusammenstellen (für jn)
- arrange an itinerary (for s.o.)

Reise verlosen
- raffle a journey
- raffle a tour
- raffle a trip

Reisevermittler m
→ Reisemittler

Reisevermittlung, f
→ Reisebüro

Reise verschieben
- postpone a journey
- postpone a trip
- postpone a tour
- put off a journey
- put off a trip

Reise verschieben auf unbestimmte Zeit
- postpone a journey indefinitely
- postpone a trip indefinitely
- postpone a tour indefinitely

Reise verschieben bis September
- postpone a journey until September
- postpone a trip until September
- postpone a tour until September
- put off a journey until September
- put off a trip until September

Reise verschieben (Seereise)
- postpone a voyage

Reise verschieben um sechs Monate
- postpone a journey for six months
- postpone a trip for six months
- postpone a tour for six months
- put off a journey for six months
- put off a trip for six months

Reiseversicherer, m
- travel insurer

Reiseversicherung, f
- travel insurance

Reiseversicherung abschließen
- take out a travel insurance
- take out a travel insurance policy

Reiseversicherungsbescheinigung, f
- travel insurance certificate

Reiseversicherungspolice, f
Reisepolice, f
- travel insurance policy
- travel policy

Reiseversicherung vereinbaren
Reiseversicherung abschließen
- arrange travel insurance

Reiseverspätung, f
Reiseverzögerung, f
- travel delay

Reiseverspätung durch Verkehrsbedingungen, f
- travel delay caused by traffic conditions

Reiseverspätungsschutz, m
- travel delay cover

Reiseverspätung tritt ein
- travel delay occurs

Reisevertrag, m
- travel contract
- tour contract

Reisevertrag abschließen
- conclude a travel contract

Reisevertrag erfüllen
- fulfill a travel contract AE
- fulfil a travel contract BE

Reisevertrag kündigen
zurücktreten von einem Reisevertrag
Reisevertrag stornieren
- cancel a travel contract

Reisevertrag machen
Reisevertrag abschließen
- make a travel contract

Reisevertragsgesetzgebung, f
- travel contract legislation

Reisevertragsrecht, n
- travel contract law

Reisevertrag unterzeichnen
Reisevertrag unterschreiben
- sign a travel contract

Reisevertrieb, m
- travel distribution

Reiseverzögerung, f
→ Reiseverspätung

Reiseverzögerungsabsicherung, f
→ Reiseverspätungsschutz

Reisevideo, n
- travel video

Reisevisum, n
Visum, n
- travel visa
- visa

Reisevokabular, n
- travel vocabulary

Reisevolk, n derog
- tavelling folk derog
- traveling folk AE derog

Reisevolumen, n
Reiseaufkommen, n
- volume of travel
- travel volume

Reise von A nach B, f
- journey from A to B
- tour from A to B
- trip from A to B

Reise von A über B nach C, f
- journey from A via B to C
- tour from A via B to C
- trip from A via B to C

Reise von gleichwertiger Qualität, f
Reise von gleicher Qualität, f

- ♦ tour of equivalent quality
- ♦ journey of equivalent quality
- ♦ trip of equivalent quality

Reise von höherer Qualität, f
- ♦ tour of superior quality

Reise von Küste zu Küste, f
- ♦ journey from coast to coast
- ♦ coast to coast journey

Reise von minderer Qualität, f
Reise von geringerer Qualität, f
- ♦ tour of lower quality

Reise von vergleichbarer Qualität, f
- ♦ tour of comparable quality
- ♦ journey of comparable quality
- ♦ trip of comparable quality

Reise von zwei Jahren, f (generell)
- ♦ journey of two years
- ♦ tour of two years
- ♦ trip of two years

Reise von zwei Jahren, f (Seereise)
- ♦ voyage of two years

Reisevoraussetzung, f
- ♦ travel prerequisite

Reise vorbereiten
- ♦ prepare a journey
- ♦ prepare a trip
- ♦ prepare a tour

Reisevorbereitung, f
- ♦ travel preparation

Reisevorbereitungen, f pl
- ♦ preparations for a journey pl
- ♦ preparations for a trip pl
- ♦ preparations for a tour pl

Reisevorbereitungen treffen
- ♦ make preparations for a journey
- ♦ make preparations for a trip
- ♦ make preparations for a tour
- ♦ arrange for a journey
- ♦ arrange for a trip

Reisevorgang, m
Reiseabwicklung, f
- ♦ travel procedure

Reisevorgang beschleunigen
Reiseabwicklung beschleunigen
- ♦ expedite the travel procedure

Reisevorkehrung, f
- ♦ travel arrangement
- ♦ arrangement for a journey
- ♦ arrangement for a trip
- ♦ arrangement for a tour

Reisevorkehrungen selbst treffen
→ Reise selbst organisieren

Reisevorkehrungen treffen
- ♦ make arrangements for a journey
- ♦ make arrangements for a trip
- ♦ make arrangements for a tour

Reise vorplanen
Reise im voraus planen
- ♦ plan a journey in advance
- ♦ plan a trip in advance
- ♦ plan a tour in advance

Reisevorschlag, m
- ♦ travel suggestion

Reise vorschlagen
- ♦ suggest a tour
- ♦ suggest a trip
- ♦ suggest a journey

Reisevorschlag machen
- ♦ make a travel suggestion

Reisevorschuß, m
Reisekostenvorschuß, m
- ♦ travel advance

Reise vorstellen
- ♦ present a tour
- ♦ present a journey
- ♦ present a trip

Reisevortrag, m
→ Reisebericht

Reisewagen, m
Reiseauto, n
- ♦ touring car

Reisewahl, f
- ♦ choice of tours
- ♦ tour choice
- ♦ choosing a tour

Reisewecker, m
- ♦ travel alarm clock

Reiseweg, m
- ♦ travel itinerary
- ♦ itinerary
- ♦ route

Reisewegänderung, f
Umroutung, f
- ♦ rerouting

Reisewelle, f
- ♦ wave of tourists
- ♦ wave of vacationers AE
- ♦ wave of holidaymakers BE
- ♦ surge of tourists

Reisewelt, f
- ♦ travel world

Reiseweltmeister, m
- ♦ world travel champion

Reiseweltmeisterschaft, f
- ♦ world travel championship

Reisewerbung, f
Reisereklame, f
- ♦ travel advertising

Reise wert sein
- ♦ be (well) worth the journey
- ♦ be (well) worth a journey
- ♦ be (well) worth the tour
- ♦ be (well) worth a tour
- ♦ be (well) worth the trip

Reisewetter, n
- ♦ vacation weather AE
- ♦ holiday weather BE
- ♦ weather for traveling AE
- ♦ weather for travelling BE

Reisewetterbericht, m
- ♦ vacation weather report AE
- ♦ holiday weather report BE

Reisewetterversicherung, f
- ♦ tourist weather insurance

Reisewettervorhersage, f
- ♦ vacation weather forecast AE
- ♦ holiday weather forecast BE

Reise wieder aufnehmen
Reise fortsetzen
- ♦ renew a journey

Reise wiederholen
Reise nochmals machen
- ♦ repeat the trip
- ♦ repeat the journey
- ♦ repeat the tour

Reisewiederverkäufer, m
- ♦ tour retailer
- ♦ travel retailer

Reisewohnmobil, n
- ♦ travel motorhome AE

- ♦ touring motor home BE
- ♦ touring motor caravan BE

Reisewohnwagen, m
Reisecaravan, m
- ♦ travel trailer AE
- ♦ touring caravan BE
- ♦ tourer BE coll

Reisewohnwagenplatz, m
Reisecaravanplatz, m
- ♦ travel trailer site AE
- ♦ touring caravan site BE
- ♦ tourer site BE coll

Reisewohnwagenstellplatz, m
- ♦ touring pitch
- ♦ pitch for a touring caravan BE

Reisewohnwagenzentrum, n
Reisecaravanzentrum, n
- ♦ travel trailer center AE
- ♦ touring caravan centre BE

Reiseworkshop, m
- ♦ travel workshop

Reiseworkshop durchführen
- ♦ mount a travel workshop

Reisewörterbuch, n
- ♦ travel dictionary

Reisewunsch, m
- ♦ travel request

Reisezahlungsbilanz, f
- ♦ travel balance of payments

Reisezeit, f (Saison)
- ♦ touring season
- ♦ travel(ing) season AE
- ♦ travelling season BE
- ♦ season for travel(l)ing
- ♦ tourist season

Reisezeit, f (Zeitdauer)
- ♦ travel time
- ♦ traveling time AE
- ♦ travelling time BE
- ♦ journey time

Reisezeitpunkt, m
- ♦ time of travel

Reisezeitraum, m
Reisezeit, f
Reiseperiode, f
- ♦ travel period
- ♦ period of travel

Reisezeitung, f
- ♦ travel newspaper

Reisezeit verringern (um eine Stunde)
- ♦ reduce the journey time (by one hour)
- ♦ reduce the travel time (by one hour)
- ♦ reduce the travelling time (by one hour)

Reisezentrum, n (Gemeinde)
- ♦ touring center AE
- ♦ touring centre BE

Reisezentrum, n (Informationsstelle)
- ♦ travel center AE
- ♦ travel centre BE

Reiseziel, n
- ♦ travel destination
- ♦ touring destination
- ♦ destination

Reisezielgebiet, n
- ♦ travel destination area

Reisezielwahl, f
Wahl des Reiseziels, f
- ♦ choice of the travel destination
- ♦ choosing a travel destination

Reise zu Bekannten und Verwandten, f
 ♦ trip to friends and relatives
 ♦ VFR trip
Reise zu Ende führen
 Reise abschließen
 ♦ complete a journey
 ♦ complete a tour
 ♦ complete a trip
Reise zu Ende führen (Seereise)
 Reise abschließen
 ♦ complete a voyage
Reise zu Land, f
 ♦ journey by land
Reise zum Erfolg werden lassen oder ruinieren
 ♦ make or break a tour
Reise zunichtemachen
 ♦ ruin a journey
 ♦ ruin a tour
 ♦ ruin a trip
Reise zu Pferd, f
 ♦ journey on horseback
Reise zusammenfassen
 ♦ summarise a journey
 ♦ summarise a tour
 ♦ summarise a trip
 ♦ summarize a journey
 ♦ summarize a tour
Reise zusammenstellen
 ♦ put together a tour
Reisezuschuß, m
 Reisekostenzuschuß, m
 ♦ travel allowance
 ♦ traveling allowance AE
 ♦ travelling allowance BE
Reisezutat, f
 ♦ travel ingredient
 ♦ tour ingredient
Reisezweck, m
 Zweck der Reise, m
 ♦ travel purpose
 ♦ purpose of travel
 ♦ purpose of a trip
 ♦ purpose of a tour
 ♦ purpose of the journey
Reisfeld, n
 ♦ rice field
Reisfüllung, f
 ♦ rice stuffing
Reisgericht, n
 ♦ rice dish
Reissalat, m
 ♦ rice salad
Reissuppe, f
 ♦ rice soup
Reiswein, m
 Sake, m
 ♦ rice wine
 ♦ sake
 ♦ saké
 ♦ saki
Reitausflug, m
 Ausflug zu Pferd, m
 ♦ excursion on horseback
 ♦ outing on horseback
Reitbahn, f
 ♦ indoor riding track AE
 ♦ indoor riding ring AE
 ♦ indoor riding-track BE
 ♦ indoor riding-ring BE
 ♦ riding ring

Reitbetrieb, m
 ♦ riding establishment
Reitclub, m
 Reitverein, m
 ♦ riding club AE
 ♦ riding-club BE
reiten
 ♦ ride (on horseback)
Reiten, n
 ♦ riding
 ♦ horseback-riding
reiten gehen
 ♦ go riding
reiten lernen
 ♦ learn to ride
reiten quer durch das Land
 ♦ ride across the country
Reiter, m
 ♦ rider
 ♦ horse-rider
Reiterbar, f
 ♦ equestrian bar
Reiterferien, pl
 Reitferien, pl
 Reiterurlaub, m
 Reiturlaub, m
 ♦ vacation on horseback AE
 ♦ holiday on horseback BE
Reiterfreizeit, f
 → Reiterurlaub
Reiterurlaub, m
 Reiturlaub, m
 Reiterferien, pl
 Reitferien, pl
 ♦ riding holiday BE
 ♦ riding vacation AE
Reitexpedition, f
 ♦ riding expedition
Reitferien, pl
 → Reiterferien
Reitgebiet, n
 Reitgelände, n
 ♦ riding country
Reitgebühr f
 ♦ riding charge
 ♦ riding fee
Reitgelegenheit, f
 Reitmöglichkeit, f
 ♦ opportunity to ride
 ♦ riding facility
 ♦ riding
Reithalle, f
 ♦ manege AE
 ♦ manège BE
 ♦ indoor riding arena
Reithose, f
 Reithosen, f pl
 ♦ jodhpurs pl
Reitkunst, f
 ♦ horsemanship
Reitkurs, m
 ♦ riding course
Reitlehrer, m
 ♦ riding instructor
 ♦ riding master
Reitmöglichkeit, f (Einrichtung)
 Reiteinrichtung, f
 ♦ riding facility
Reitmöglichkeit, f (Gelegenheit)
 → Reitgelegenheit

Reitpauschalurlaub, m
 Reitpauschalferien, pl
 ♦ package riding vacation AE
 ♦ inclusive riding vacation AE
 ♦ package riding holiday BE
 ♦ inclusive riding holiday BE
Reitpfad, m
 → Reitweg
Reitpferd, n
 ♦ riding horse
 ♦ saddle horse
Reitpferd mieten
 ♦ rent a riding horse AE
 ♦ hire a riding horse BE
Reitpferd vermieten
 ♦ rent (out) a riding horse
 ♦ hire out a riding horse BE
Reitplatz, m
 Reitgelände, n
 ♦ riding ground AE
Reitpony, n
 ♦ riding pony
Reitschule, f
 ♦ riding school AE
 ♦ riding-school BE
 ♦ riding academy AE
Reitsport, m
 ♦ riding
 ♦ equestrian sport
 ♦ equestrian sports
 ♦ equitation
Reitstall, m
 ♦ riding stable
Reitstiefel, m
 ♦ riding boot AE
 ♦ riding-boot BE
Reitstunde, f
 (Unterricht)
 ♦ riding lesson
Reittreck, m
 ♦ riding tek
Reitturnier, n
 Reit- und Springturnier, n
 ♦ horse show
Reitunterricht, m
 ♦ riding lessons pl
 ♦ riding tuition
 ♦ instruction in riding
Reitunterricht nehmen
 ♦ take riding lessons
Reiturlaub, m
 Reiterurlaub, m
 Reiterferien, pl
 Reitferien, pl
 ♦ riding vacation AE
 ♦ riding holiday BE
Reitveranstaltung, f
 ♦ equestrian event
Reitverein, m
 → Reitclub
Reitweg, m
 Reitpfad, m
 ♦ bridle way AE
 ♦ bridle path AE
 ♦ bridle trail AE
 ♦ bridle-path BE
 ♦ bridle-way BE
Reitwoche, f
 ♦ riding week
Reitzentrum, n
 Pferdezentrum, n

Rennbahn

- ◆ equestrian center *AE*
- ◆ equestrian centre *BE*

reizend, adj
- ◆ delightful, adj
- ◆ charming, adj
- ◆ attractive, adj

reizende Atmosphäre, f
- ◆ delightful atmosphere

reizende Atmosphäre bieten
- ◆ provide a delightful atmosphere

reizende Umgebung, f
- ◆ delightful surroundings *pl*

Reizklima, n
- ◆ stimulating climate
- ◆ bracing climate

reizvoll gelegen, adj
- ◆ delightfully located, adj
- ◆ delightfully positioned, adj
- ◆ delightfully situated, adj

Reklamation, f
  Beschwerde, f
  Beanstandung, f
- ◆ complaint

Reklamation bearbeiten
  Beschwerde bearbeiten
  Reklamation abwickeln
- ◆ handle a complaint
- ◆ deal with a complaint

Reklamationsschreiben, n
  Reklamationsbrief, m
  Beschwerdeschreiben, n
  Beschwerdebrief, m
- ◆ letter of complaint
- ◆ letter complaining about s.th.

Reklamationsschreiben erhalten
  Beschwerdeschreiben erhalten
- ◆ receive a letter of complaint
- ◆ receive a letter complaining about (s.th.)

Reklamation wiederholen
  Beschwerde wiederholen
- ◆ renew a complaint

Reklamation zurückweisen
  Beschwerde zurückweisen
- ◆ reject a complaint

Reklame machen
  Werbung machen
  werben
- ◆ advertise

Reklame machen für ein Hotel
  Werbung machen für ein Hotel
  werben für ein Hotel
- ◆ advertise a hotel

Reklame- und Werbeprogramm, n
- ◆ advertising and promotion program *AE*
- ◆ advertising and promotion programme *BE*

reklamieren etw
  beanstanden etw
- ◆ lodge a complaint about s.th.
- ◆ make a complaint about s.th.

Rekonvaleszent, m
  Rekonvaleszentin f
- ◆ convalescent

Rekonvaleszenz, f
- ◆ convalescence

Rekord, m
- ◆ record

Rekord aufstellen
- ◆ set up a record

Rekordauslastung, f
- ◆ record load factor

Rekordauslastung erzielen
- ◆ achieve a record load factor

Rekordbelegung, f
  Rekordauslastung, f
- ◆ record occupany

Rekordbelegungsniveau, n
  Rekordauslastungsniveau, n
- ◆ record occupancy level

Rekordbesuch, m (Besuch)
- ◆ record visit

Rekordbesuch, m (Teilnahme)
  Rekordteilnahme, f
  Besucherrekord, m
- ◆ record attendance

Rekordbesucherzahl, f
  → Besucherrekord

Rekordbeteiligung, f
  (an Veranstaltung)
  → Rekordbesuch

Rekord brechen
- ◆ break a record

Rekordbrecher, m
- ◆ record breaker

Rekordbuchung f
- ◆ record booking

Rekordertrag, m
- ◆ record earning
- ◆ record income
- ◆ record yield

Rekordfrühjahr, n
- ◆ record spring

Rekordherbst, m
- ◆ record fall *AE*
- ◆ record autumn *BE*

Rekordjahr, n
- ◆ record year
- ◆ bumper year *coll*

Rekordjahr erleben
- ◆ experience a record year
- ◆ have a record year
- ◆ experience a bumper year *coll*
- ◆ have a bumper year *coll*

Rekordmonat, m
- ◆ record month

Rekordreservierung, f
- ◆ record reservation

Rekordresultat, n
- ◆ record result

Rekordsaison, f
- ◆ record season

Rekordsommer, m
- ◆ record summer

Rekordtag, m
- ◆ record day

Rekordumsatz, m
- ◆ record sales *pl*
- ◆ record turnover

Rekordwachstum, n
  Rekordzuwachs, m
- ◆ record growth

Rekordwinter, m
- ◆ record winter

Rekordwoche, f
- ◆ record week

Rekordzahl, f
- ◆ record figure

Rekordzahl erreichen von 123
- ◆ reach the record figure of 123

Rekordzeit, f
- ◆ record time

Relais, n *FR*
  Raststätte, f
- ◆ relais *FR*
- ◆ roadhouse *AE*
- ◆ road-house *BE*

relativ kurze Zeit bleiben
- ◆ stay a relatively short time

Reliefkarte, f
- ◆ relief map

religiöse Reise, f
- ◆ religious journey
- ◆ religious tour
- ◆ religious trip

religiöses Fest, n
  kirchliches Fest, n
- ◆ religious festival

Reliquie, f
- ◆ relic

Remmidemmi, n *coll*
- ◆ hullabaloo *coll*
- ◆ hell of a noise *coll*
- ◆ racket

Remmidemmi machen (wegen etw)
- ◆ make a hullabaloo (about s.th.)

Renaissance, f
- ◆ Renaissance, the

Renaissancefassade, f
- ◆ Renaissance façade
- ◆ Renaissance facade *AE*

Renaissancegarten, m
- ◆ renaissance garden

Renaissancegebäude, n
  Renaissancebau, m
- ◆ Renaissance building

Renaissancehaus, n
- ◆ Renaissance house

Renaissancekapelle, f
- ◆ Renaissance chapel

Renaissancemöbel, n pl
- ◆ Renaissance furniture *sg*

Renaissancepalast, m
- ◆ Renaissance palace

Renaissancerathaus, n
- ◆ Renaissance town hall

Renaissanceresidenz, f
- ◆ Renaissance residence

Renaissanceschloß, n
- ◆ Renaissance castle

Renaissancestil, m
- ◆ Renaissance style

Renaissanceturm, m
- ◆ Renaissance tower

Renaissancevilla, f
- ◆ Renaissance villa

Rendezvous, n
  Stelldichein, n
- ◆ rendezvous
- ◆ date *AE*

Rendite, f
- ◆ yield
- ◆ return
- ◆ profit

Rendite pro Zimmer, f
- ◆ return per room

Renke, f
  Renken, m
  Felche, f
- ◆ whitefish

Rennbahn, f
- ◆ racecourse
- ◆ racetrack *AE*

Rennbesucher

Rennbesucher, m
- racegoer *AE*
- race-goer *BE*

Rennboot, n
- racing boat

Rennen, n
- race

Rennen beginnt in A und endet in B
- race begins at A and finishes at B
- race begins in A and finishes in B

Rennfahrer, m
Autorennfahrer, m
- racing driver

Rennjacht, f
Rennyacht, f
- racing yacht

Rennkalender, m
- racing calendar

Rennrodel, m
Rodel, m
Schlitten, m
- toboggan

Rennrodler, m
- tobogganist
- tobogganer

Rennsaison, f
- racing season

Rennsport, m
Rennen, n
- racing

Rennstrecke, f
Autorennstrecke, f
- racing circuit
- motor racing track
- racetrack *AE*

Rennveranstaltung, f
- race-meeting

Rennwagen, m
- racing car

Renommee, n
Reputation, f
- renown
- reputation
- fame

renommiert, adj
- renowned, adj
- well-known, adj
- prestigious, adj
- noted, adj

renommierter Gastbetrieb, m
Renommiergastbetrieb, m
- prestigious foodservice establishment *AE*
- prestigious foodservice operation *AE*
- prestigious catering establishment
- prestigious catering operation

renommiertes Hotel n
- prestigious hotel

renov.
renoviert, adj
- rfrb.
- refurbished, adj

Renovation, f *SCHW*
→ Renovierung

renovieren etw gründlich
- refurbish s.th. thoroughly
- renovate s.th. thoroughly

renovieren etw (streichen, tapezieren)
- redecorate s.th.

renovieren etw (umfassend)
- refurbish s.th.
- renovate s.th.

renoviert, adj (gestrichen, tapeziert)
- redecorated, adj

renoviert, adj (umfassend)
- refurbished, adj
- renovated, adj

renoviertes Hotel, n (gestrichen, tapeziert)
- redecorated hotel

renoviertes Hotel, n (umfassend)
- refurbished hotel
- renovated hotel

renoviertes Zimmer, n (gestrichen, tapeziert)
→ neu hergerichtetes Zimmer

renoviertes Zimmer, n (umfassend)
- refurbished room
- renovated room

Renovierung, f (Anstrich, Tapeten)
- redecoration

Renovierung, f (umfassend)
- renovation
- refurbishment

Renovierung durchführen
- undertake a refurbishment
- undertake a renovation

Renovierungen durchführen
- carry out renovations

Renovierungsarbeit, f
- renovation work
- refurbishment work

renovierungsbedürftig, adj
- in need of refurbishment, adj
- in need in renovation, adj

Renovierungsplan, m
- renovation scheme
- refurbishment scheme
- refurbishing plan

Renovierungsprogramm, n
- renovation program *AE*
- refurbishment program *AE*
- renovation programme *BE*
- refurbishment programme *BE*

Renovierungsprojekt, n
- renovation project
- refurbishment project

Renovierungsprojekt durchführen
- undertake a renovation project
- undertake a refurbishment project

rentabel, adj
- profitable, adj

rentabel, adv
- at a profit, adv

Rentabilität, f
- profitability

Rentabilität eines Hotels f
- profitability of a hotel

Rentabilität maximieren
- maximise profitability
- maximize profitability

Rent-a-car-Unternehmen, n
→ Mietwagenfirma

Rentner, m
Pensionär, m
Pensionist, m *ÖST/SCHW*
- old-age pensioner
- O.A.P.
- pensioner

Rentnerermäßigung, f
Ermäßigung für Rentner, f
- old-age pensioner reduction
- O.A.P. reduction
- reduction for old-age pensioners
- reduction for O.A.P.s

Reparatur, f
- repair

Reparaturauftrag, m
- repair order

Reparaturaufwand, m
- repair expenditure
- repair expense *AE*

Reparaturaufwendungen, f pl
- repair expenses *pl*

reparaturbedürftig, adj
- in need of repair, adj
- in want of repair, adj

reparaturbedürftiger Stuhl, m
- dilapidated chair

reparaturbedürftiges Bett, n
- dilapidated bed

Reparaturdienst, m
- repair service

Reparaturen durchführen
- carry out repairs

Reparaturen und Instandhaltung, f pl
- repairs and maintenance *pl*

Reparaturkosten, pl
- repair costs *pl*
- repair cost
- cost of repair
- cost of repairs

reparieren etw
- repair s.th.
- fix s.th.

Repertoire, n
(Theater)
- repertoire

Repertoire reicht von A bis C
- repertoire ranges from A to C

Repräsentant, m
- representative

Repräsentationsaufgabe, f
- representational duty

Repräsentationsaufgaben übernehmen
- take over representational duties

repräsentieren jn
- represent s.o.

Reptilienteich, m
- reptile pool

Republik Irland, f
- Republic of Ireland, the

Requisit, n
- prop

Requisitenkammer, f
(im Theater)
- property room

Reschenpaß, m
- Reschen Pass, the

Reservation, f *SCHW*
→ Reservierung

Reservation gegen Anzahlung, f *SCHW*
→ Reservierung gegen Anzahlung

Reservationsbüro, n *SCHW*
→ Reservierungsbüro

Reservationssystem, n *SCHW*
→ Reservierungssystem

Reservebett, n
Gästebett, n
Fremdenbett, n
- spare bed

Reservebus, m
- reserve bus

Reservefahrer, m
- reserve driver

Reservegabel, f
 ♦ spare fork
Reserveglas, n
 ♦ spare glass
Reservemesser, n
 ♦ spare knife
Reserveteller, m
 ♦ spare plate
Reservetisch, m
 ♦ spare table
reservierbar, adj
 ♦ reservable, adj
reservierbarer Stellplatz, m
 (Camping)
 ♦ reservable pitch
reservierbarer Tisch, m
 ♦ reservable table
reservierbares Zimmer, n
 ♦ reservable room
reservieren etw
 bereithalten etw
 ♦ reserve s.th.
reservieren etw für etw
 ♦ reserve s.th. for s.th.
reservieren etw für jn
 ♦ reserve s.th. for s.o.
reservieren etw gegen Vorkasse
 ♦ reserve s.th. against prepayment
 ♦ reserve s.th. on down payment
reservieren etw im voraus
 vorausreservieren etw
 ♦ prereserve s.th.
 ♦ reserve s.th. in advance
reservieren etw nach dem Prinzip 'Wer zuerst
 kommt, mahlt zuerst'
 ♦ reserve s.th. on a first-come-first-served basis
reservieren im Namen von jm
 reservieren im Auftrag von jm
 ♦ reserve on s.o.'s behalf
 ♦ reserve on behalf of s.o.
reservieren im voraus
 vorausreservieren
 im voraus reservieren
 ♦ reserve in advance
reservieren lassen etw bei jm
 ♦ make a reservation with s.o.
reserviert, adj
 ♦ reserved, adj
reservierte Leistung, f
 reservierter Service, m
 reservierte Dienstleistung, f
 ♦ reserved service
reservierter Parkplatz, m (für 1 Auto)
 ♦ reserved parking space
 ♦ reserved parking lot AE
 ♦ reserved parking place
reservierter Parkplatz, m (für mehrere Autos)
 ♦ reserved parking lot AE
 ♦ reserved car park BE
reservierter Sitzplatz, m
 reservierter Platz, m
 reservierter Sitz, m
 ♦ reserved seat
reservierter Stellplatz, m
 (Camping)
 ♦ reserved pitch
reservierter Tisch, m
 ♦ reserved table
reserviertes Zimmer, n
 ♦ reserved room

reservierte Unterkunft, f
 ♦ reserved accommodation
Reserviert für Hotelgäste
 (Hinweisschild)
 Nur für Hotelgäste
 ♦ For hotel guests only
Reservierung, f
 (USA: Buchung ist meist auch Reservierung)
 Bereithaltung, f
 Reservation, f SCHW
 ♦ reservation
Reservierung ablehnen
 ♦ decline a reservation
 ♦ refuse a reservation
 ♦ turn down a reservation
Reservierung abwickeln
 Reservierung bearbeiten
 ♦ handle a reservation
 ♦ process a reservation
Reservierung annehmen
 Reservierung akzeptieren
 ♦ accept a reservation
Reservierung annullieren
 → Reservierung stornieren
Reservierung arrangieren
 Reservierung vermitteln
 ♦ arrange a reservation
Reservierung auf den Namen Jürgen Herber, f
 ♦ reservation in the name of Jürgen Herber
Reservierung aufheben
 Reservierung freigeben
 ♦ release a reservation
Reservierung aufrechterhalten
 ♦ hold a reservation
Reservierung bearbeiten
 ♦ deal with a reservation
 ♦ process a reservation
 ♦ handle a reservation
Reservierung bestätigen
 ♦ confirm a reservation
Reservierung eintragen in das
 Reservierungsjournal
 ♦ enter a reservation in the reservation diary
Reservierung entgegennehmen
 ♦ take a reservation
Reservierung erhalten
 ♦ receive a reservation
Reservierung freigeben für andere Gäste
 ♦ release a reservation to other guests
Reservierung gegenbestätigen
 Reservierung rückbestätigen
 ♦ reconfirm a reservation
Reservierung haben für etw
 etw reserviert haben
 ♦ have a reservation for s.th.
 ♦ hold a reservation for s.th.
Reservierung in Anspruch nehmen
 ♦ claim a reservation
 ♦ use a reservation
Reservierung in letzter Sekunde, f
 ♦ last-minute reservation
Reservierung ist gültig
 ♦ reservation is valid
Reservierung kontrollieren
 ♦ control a reservation
Reservierung machen
 Reservierung vornehmen
 reservieren
 ♦ make a reservation

Reservierung machen von etw
 reservieren etw
 ♦ make a reservation for s.th.
Reservierung nach Anzahlung, f
 ♦ reservation on deposit
Reservierung nicht notwendig
 → Keine Reservierung notwendig
Reservierung rückgängig machen
 → Reservierung stornieren
Reservierungsablehnung, f
 ♦ refusal of a reservation
 ♦ refusing a reservation
Reservierungsabteilung, f
 ♦ reservation department
 ♦ reservations department
Reservierungsabwicklung, f
 Reservierungsbearbeitung, f
 ♦ handling a reservation
 ♦ processing a reservation
 ♦ dealing with a reservation
Reservierungsänderung, f (geringfügig)
 ♦ reservation alteration
 ♦ alteration of a reservation
 ♦ modification of a reservation
Reservierungsänderung, f (umfassend)
 ♦ change of reservation
Reservierungsanfrage, f
 ♦ reservation inquiry
 ♦ reservation enquiry
Reservierungsanfrage bearbeiten
 ♦ deal with a reservation inquiry
 ♦ deal with a reservation enquiry
 ♦ process a reservation inquiry
 ♦ process a reservation enquiry
 ♦ handle a reservation inquiry
Reservierungsanfrageformular, n
 ♦ reservation inquiry form
 ♦ reservation enquiry form
Reservierungsanfragekarte, f
 ♦ reservation inquiry card
 ♦ reservation enquiry card
Reservierungsanfrage senden
 ♦ send a reservation request
Reservierungsangaben, f pl
 ♦ details of the reservation pl
 ♦ reservations details pl
Reservierungsangaben haben sich geändert
 ♦ reservation details have changed
 ♦ reservations details have changed
Reservierungsangestellter, m
 ♦ reservation clerk
 ♦ reservations clerk
Reservierungsannahme, f
 ♦ acceptance of a reservation
 ♦ accepting a reservation
Reservierungsanzahlung, f
 ♦ reservation deposit
Reservierungsanzahlung leisten
 ♦ make a reservation deposit AE
 ♦ pay a reservation deposit BE
Reservierungsanzahlung verlangen
 Reservierungsanzahlung fordern
 ♦ require a reservation deposit
Reservierungsart, f
 ♦ type of reservation
 ♦ reservation type
Reservierungsaufkommen, n
 Reservierungsvolumen, n
 ♦ reservation volume
 ♦ reservations volume

Reservierungsaufwendungen, f pl
  Reservierungsausgaben, f pl
  ♦ reservation expenses *pl*
  ♦ reservations expenses *pl*
Reservierungsausgaben, f pl
  → Reservierungsaufwendungen
Reservierungsbeschäftigter, m
  Reservierungsangestellter, m
  Reservierungskraft, f
  ♦ reservation agent
  ♦ reservations agent
Reservierungsbestätigung, f
  ♦ confirmation of (a) reservation
  ♦ reservation confirmation
  ♦ confirming a reservation
Reservierungsbuch, n
  ♦ reservations book
  ♦ reservation book
Reservierungsbüro, n
  Reservierungsstelle, f
  ♦ reservations bureau *AE*
  ♦ reservation office
  ♦ reservations office
Reservierungsbüro über einen No-show informieren
  ♦ inform the reservations office of a no-show
Reservierungscode m
  ♦ reservation code
Reservierungscoupon, m
  ♦ reservation coupon
Reservierungsdaten, pl (Angaben)
  ♦ reservation data
  ♦ reservations data
Reservierungsdaten, pl (Details)
  Reservierungsangaben, f pl
  ♦ reservation details *pl*
  ♦ reservations details *pl*
  ♦ details of the reservation *pl*
  ♦ details of the reservations *pl*
Reservierungsdatum, n
  ♦ reservation date
  ♦ date of the reservation
  ♦ date of the reservations
Reservierungsdienst, m
  Reservierungsservice, m
  ♦ reservation service
  ♦ reservations service
Reservierung sehr frühzeitig machen
  ♦ make a reservation well in advance
Reservierungseingang, m
  ♦ receipt of a reservation
  ♦ receiving a reservation
Reservierungseinrichtung, f
  ♦ reservation facility
  ♦ reservations facility
Reservierungsentgegennahme f
  ♦ taking (of) a reservation
Reservierungsfehler, m
  ♦ mistake in a reservation
  ♦ slip-up in a reservation *coll*
Reservierungsfluß, m
  ♦ flow of reservations
  ♦ stream of reservations
Reservierungsformular n
  ♦ reservation form
Reservierungsgarantie, f
  ♦ reservation guarantee
Reservierungsgebühr f
  ♦ reservation charge
  ♦ reservation fee

Reservierungsgesellschaft, f
  ♦ reservation company
  ♦ reservations company
Reservierungsgutschein, m
  ♦ reservation voucher
Reservierungshandbuch, n
  ♦ reservation manual
  ♦ reservations manual
Reservierung sichern sich
  ♦ secure a reservation
Reservierungsjournal, n
  ♦ reservation diary
Reservierungskarte, f
  ♦ reservation card
Reservierungsklasse, f
  ♦ reservation class
Reservierungskosten, pl
  ♦ reservation costs *pl*
  ♦ reservation cost
Reservierungskraft, f
  ♦ reservationist *AE*
  ♦ reservation agent
  ♦ reservations agent
Reservierungsleiter, m
  Leiter der Reservierungsabteilung, m
  ♦ reservation manager
  ♦ reservations manager
Reservierungsliste, f
  ♦ reservations list
  ♦ reservation list
  ♦ list of reservations
Reservierungsmitteilung, f
  Reservierungsbenachrichtigung, f
  ♦ reservation notification
  ♦ notification of a reservation
Reservierungsmöglichkeit, f
  ♦ reservation possibility
  ♦ possibility of reserving s.th.
Reservierungsmonopol, n
  ♦ reservation monopoly
Reservierungsnetz, n
  ♦ reservation network
  ♦ reservations network
Reservierungsnummer, f
  ♦ reservation number
  ♦ number of the reservation
Reservierungspersonal, n
  ♦ reservation personnel
  ♦ reservation staff
  ♦ reservations personnel
  ♦ reservations staff
Reservierungsplan, m
  ♦ reservation plan
  ♦ reservations plan
Reservierungsplan erstellen
  ♦ draw up a reservation plan
  ♦ draw up a reservations plan
Reservierungsproblem, n
  ♦ reservation problem
Reservierungsprognose, f
  ♦ reservation forecast
Reservierungsprogramm, n
  ♦ reservation program *AE*
  ♦ reservations program *AE*
  ♦ reservation programme *BE*
  ♦ reservations programme *BE*
Reservierungsprovision, f
  ♦ reservation commission
Reservierungsrack n
  (Rezeption)
  ♦ reservation rack

Reservierungsservice, m
  → Reservierungsdienst
Reservierungsservicebetreiber, m
  ♦ reservation service operator
  ♦ reservations service operator
Reservierungsstatistik, f
  ♦ reservation statistics *pl*
Reservierungsstatus, m
  ♦ reservation status
Reservierungsstelle, f
  Reservierungsbüro, n
  ♦ reservation office
  ♦ reservations office
Reservierungsstornierung, f
  Reservierungsabsage, f
  Reservierungsannullierung, f
  Reservierungsrücktritt, f
  ♦ cancellation of a reservation
  ♦ cancelation of a reservation *AE*
Reservierungssystem, n
  ♦ reservation system
  ♦ reservations system
Reservierungssystem benutzen
  ♦ use a reservation system
  ♦ use a reservations system
Reservierungstafel, f
  ♦ reservation chart
Reservierungsteam, n
  ♦ reservations team
Reservierungsterminal, n
  ♦ reservation terminal
Reservierung stornieren
  Reservierung annullieren
  Reservierung rückgängig machen
  von einer Reservierung zurücktreten
  ♦ cancel a reservation
Reservierungsüberhang, m
  unerledigter Reservierungsbestand, m
  ♦ backlog of reservations
Reservierungsverfahren, n
  Reservierungsprozedur, f
  ♦ reservation procedure
Reservierungsvertrag, m
  ♦ reservation contract
  ♦ contract of reservation
Reservierungsvorgang, m
  ♦ reservation process
  ♦ reservation procedure
Reservierungsvorrang, m
  Reservierungsvortritt, m
  Reservierungspriorität, f
  ♦ reservation priority
Reservierungsweg, m
  ♦ reservation channel
Reservierungswunsch, m
  ♦ reservation request
  ♦ request for reservation
Reservierungswunsch erfüllen
  ♦ meet a reservation request
Reservierungszeitpunkt, m
  Reservierungszeit, f
  ♦ time of reservation
  ♦ reservation time
Reservierungszentrale, f
  ♦ reservations center *AE*
  ♦ reservations centre *BE*
  ♦ central reservation office
  ♦ central reservations office
Reservierung telefonisch vornehmen
  ♦ make a reservation by telephone

Reservierung überprüfen
  Reservierung prüfen
  ♦ check a reservation
Reservierung verlängern
  ♦ extend a reservation
Reservierung vermitteln
  Reservierung arrangieren
  ♦ arrange a reservation
Reservierung verweigern
  Reservierung ablehnen
  ♦ refuse a reservation
  ♦ decline a reservation
  ♦ turn down a reservation *coll*
Reservierung von etw, f
  Reservierung für etw, f
  ♦ reservation for s.th.
Reservierung von zwei Zimmern, f
  ♦ reservation for two rooms
Reservierung vornehmen
  Reservierung tätigen
  ♦ effect a reservation
  ♦ make a reservation
Reservierung vornehmen über eine Agentur
  ♦ make a reservation through an agency
Reservierung wird empfohlen
  ♦ Reservations are recommended
Reservierung wird nahegelegt
  Reservierung ist angebracht
  ♦ Reservations are suggested
Reservierung wird ungültig
  ♦ reservation lapses
Reservierung wünschen
  ♦ request a reservation
Reservierung zurückweisen
  Reservierung ablehnen
  ♦ reject a reservation
  ♦ refuse a reservation
Residenz, f
  ♦ residence
residieren
  wohnen
  ♦ reside
residieren im Buckingham-Palast
  ♦ reside in Buckingham Palace
residieren in einem Hotel
  in einem Hotel wohnen
  ♦ reside in a hotel
  ♦ reside at a hotel
residieren in etw
  wohnen in etw
  ♦ reside in s.th.
  ♦ reside at s.th.
Resort, n
  → Ferienanlage
Resorteinrichtung, f
  ♦ resort facility
Rest, m (Essensrest)
  ♦ leftover
Rest, m (Gebäude etc.)
  Überreste, m pl
  Überbleibsel, n pl
  ♦ remains *pl*
Rest, m (generell)
  ♦ rest
Rest, m (Relikt)
  ♦ relic
Rest, m (zahlenmäßig)
  ♦ remainder
Restant, m
  (Gast, der Zahlung versäumt)
  ♦ defaulter

Restaurant, n
  Speiserestaurant, n
  ♦ restaurant
Restaurantabteilung, f
  Restaurationsabteilung, f
  ♦ restaurant department
Restaurantadministration, f
  Restaurantverwaltung, f
  ♦ restaurant administration
Restaurant an einer Landstraße, n
  → Landstraßenrestaurant
Restaurantangebot, n (Gegensatz zu Nachfrage)
  ♦ supply of restaurants
  ♦ availability of restaurants
Restaurantangebot, n (Palette)
  ♦ range of restaurants
Restaurantangestellter, m
  → Restaurantbeschäftigter
Restaurantarbeit, f
  ♦ restaurant work
Restaurantarbeiter, m
  ♦ restaurant worker
Restaurantart, f
  Restauranttyp, m
  ♦ type of restaurant
  ♦ restaurant type
Restaurant aufdonnern
  ♦ tart a restaurant up
Restaurantauslastung, f
  Restaurantbelegung, f
  Restaurantfrequenz, f
  ♦ restaurant occupancy
  ♦ occupancy of a restaurant
Restaurant ausprobieren
  Restaurant probieren
  ♦ sample a restaurant
  ♦ try a restaurant
Restaurantausstattung, f
  Restaurantausrüstung, f
  ♦ restaurant equipment
Restaurantausstellung, f
  ♦ restaurant show
Restaurantbank, f
  ♦ restaurant bench
Restaurantbar, f
  ♦ restaurant bar
Restaurantbedienung, f (Person)
  → Restaurantkellner
Restaurantbedienung, f (Service)
  → Restaurantservice
Restaurant benutzen
  ♦ use a restaurant
Restaurantbenutzer m
  ♦ restaurant user
Restaurantberater, m
  Restaurantconsultant, m
  ♦ restaurant consultant
Restaurantberatung, f
  ♦ restaurant consultancy
Restaurantbereich, m (abstrakt)
  Restaurantsektor, m
  ♦ restaurant field
  ♦ restaurant sector
Restaurantbereich, m (konkret)
  ♦ restaurant area
Restaurantbeschäftigter, m
  Restaurantangestellter, m
  Restaurantmitarbeiter, m
  ♦ restaurant employee
Restaurantbesitzer, m
  Restaurantinhaber, m

♦ restaurant owner
♦ owner of a restaurant
Restaurantbestellung, f
  (Essen)
  ♦ restaurant order
Restaurantbesuch, m
  ♦ restaurant visit
  ♦ visit to a restaurant
Restaurant besuchen
  ♦ visit a restaurant
Restaurantbesucher, m
  ♦ restaurant visitor
  ♦ restaurantgoer *AE*
  ♦ restaurant-goer *BE*
Restaurant betreiben
  ♦ operate a restaurant
  ♦ run a restaurant
  ♦ manage a restauarnt
Restaurantbetreiber m
  ♦ restaurant operator
Restaurant betreten
  ♦ enter a restaurant
Restaurantbetrieb, m
  Restaurationsbetrieb, m *ÖST/SCHW*
  ♦ restaurant establishment
  ♦ restaurant operation
Restaurant bietet 123 Plätze
  ♦ restaurant provides 123 seats
Restaurant bietet das Beste an englischem Essen
  ♦ restaurant offers the best in English food
Restaurant bietet eine umfangreiche Speisekarte
  ♦ restaurant offers an extensive menu
  ♦ restaurant offers a comprehensive menu
Restaurant bietet ein Selbstbedienungsbüfett
  ♦ restaurant provides a self-service buffet
Restaurant bietet für jeden Geschmack eine große Auswahl an Speisen
  ♦ restaurant provides a large choice of dishes to suit every taste
Restaurant bietet traditionelle und moderne Küche
  ♦ restaurant offers traditional and modern cuisine
  ♦ restaurant offers traditional and modern cooking
Restaurant bleibt geöffnet
  ♦ restaurant stays open
  ♦ restaurant remains open
Restaurantbon, m
  ♦ restaurant docket
  ♦ restaurant cheque
Restaurantbrigade, f
  ♦ restaurant brigade
Restaurantbuchungsjournal, n
  ♦ restaurant booking diary
  ♦ restaurant bookings diary
Restaurant-Café, n
  ♦ restaurant-cafe *AE*
  ♦ restaurant-café *BE*
  ♦ restaurant cum cafe *AE*
  ♦ restaurant cum café *BE*
Restaurantcommis, m
  Restaurantgehilfe, m
  Commis de restaurant, m *FR*
  Restaurationscommis, m *ÖST/SCHW*
  ♦ restaurant commis
  ♦ commis de restaurant *FR*
Restaurantconsultant, m
  → Restaurantberater

Restaurantdeck

Restaurantdeck, n (Schiff)
- restaurant deck

Restaurantdependance, f
Restaurantanbau, n
- restaurant annex *AE*
- restaurant annexe *BE*

Restaurant der Spitzenkategorie, n
Restaurant der Spitzenklasse, n
- top-category restaurant
- top-class restaurant

Restaurant der Spitzenklasse, n
Spitzenklasserestaurant, n
- top-class restaurant

Restaurantdienst, m
→ Restaurantservice

Restaurantdirektor, m
Directeur de restaurant, m *FR*
- restaurant director
- directeur de restaurant *FR*

Restaurant du marché, n *FR m*
- restaurant du marché *FR*

Restauranteigentümer, m
- restaurant proprietor
- proprietor of a restaurant

Restauranteigentümerin, f
- restaurant proprietress
- proprietress of a restaurant

Restauranteingang, m
- restaurant entrance

Restauranteinheit, f
(Statistik)
- restaurant unit

Restaurant einrichten
Restaurant möblieren
- furnish a restaurant

Restauranteinrichtung, f (Fazilität)
- restaurant facility

Restauranteinrichtung, f (Möbel)
→ Restaurantmöbel

Restaurantempfang, m
- restaurant reception

Restaurant empfehlen
- recommend a restaurant

Restaurantempfehlung, f
- recommendation of a restaurant
- restaurant recommendation
- recommending a restaurant

Restaurant entwerfen
Restaurant gestalten
- design a restaurant

Restauranterfahrung, f (der Gäste)
- eating-out experience
- gastronomic experience
- restaurant experience

Restauranterfahrung, f (Personal/Gäste)
- restaurant experience

Restaurantlös, m
- restaurant revenue

Restaurant eröffnen
- open a restaurant

Restauranteröffnung, f
Eröffnung eines Restaurants, f
- opening of a restaurant
- restaurant opening

Restaurant erster Klasse, n
→ erstklassiges Restaurant

Restauranterfrag, m (GuV)
(Gewinn- und Verlustrechnung)
- restaurant income

Restaurantessen, n
Restaurantmahlzeit, f

Restaurantmahl, n
- restaurant meal

Restaurantetage, f
Restaurantgeschoß, n
Restaurationsetage, f *ÖST/SCHW*
- restaurant floor

Restaurantfachfrau, f
(offizielle Bezeichnung)
- trained waitress

Restaurantfachleute, pl
- restaurantmen *pl*
- professional restaurant people *pl*
- restaurant people *pl*

Restaurantfachmann, m
(offizielle Bezeichnung)
- trained waiter

Restaurantfläche, f
- area of a restaurant
- restaurant area

Restaurantfläche vergrößern
- extend the restaurant area
- enlarge the restaurant area

Restaurant frequentieren
Restaurant häufig besuchen
- frequent a restaurant
- patronise a restaurant
- patronize a restaurant

Restaurant führen
Restaurant leiten
- run a restaurant
- keep a restaurant
- manage a restaurant

Restaurantführer, m
(Information)
Gastronomieführer, m
- restaurant guide

Restaurant für Hausgäste, n
- residents' restaurant
- restaurant for residents

Restaurantgast, m
- restaurant guest
- restaurant customer

Restaurantgastronomie, f
- restaurant catering *BE*
- restaurant foodservice *AE*

Restaurantgedeck n
Restaurantkuvert n
Restaurantcouvert n
- restaurant cover

Restaurantgeschäft, n
- restaurant business

Restaurantgeschäftsführer, m
- restaurant manager

Restaurantgesellschaft, f
Restaurantunternehmen, n
- restaurant company

Restaurantgewerbe, n
Restaurantwesen, n
Restaurantbranche, f
- restaurant trade
- restaurant industry

Restaurantgröße f
- restaurant size
- size of a restaurant

Restaurantgruppe, f
Restaurantkonzern, m
- restaurant group

Restaurantgutschein, m
Restaurantbon, m
- restaurant voucher

Restaurant hat 60 Plätze
- restaurant has 60 seats

Restaurant hat durchschnittlich 90 Gedecke pro Tag
- restaurant averages 90 covers per day

Restaurant hat einen eigenen Eingang
- restaurant has its own entrance

Restaurant hat einen neuen Besitzer
- restaurant is under new ownership

Restaurant hat Schankkonzession bis 3 Uhr nachts
- restaurant is licensed until 3 p.m.
- restaurant is licenced until 3 p.m.

Restaurant hat sich auf Fisch spezialisiert
- restaurant specialises in fish

Restauranthosteß, f
- restaurant hostess

Restaurant im Freien, n
Freiluftrestaurant, n
- alfresco restaurant
- open-air restaurant

Restaurant im Speisewagenstil, n
Zugspeisewagen, m
Zugrestaurant, n
- diner *AE*

Restaurant in der mittleren Preiskategorie, n
- restaurant in the medium price category

Restaurant in der oberen Preiskategorie, n
- restaurant is the upper price category

Restaurant in der unteren Preiskategorie, n
- restaurant in the lower price category

Restaurant in einem Betrieb, n
Betriebsrestaurant, n
- commissary

Restaurantinhaber, m
- restaurantkeeper
- restaurant owner

Restaurant ist bekannt für gutes Essen und guten Service
- restaurant is renowned for good food and good service

Restaurant ist ein kleines Juwel
Restaurant ist ein kleines Prachtstück
- restaurant is a little gem

Restaurant ist für Nichthausgäste geöffnet
- restaurant is open to nonresidents *AE*
- restaurant is open to non-residents *BE*

Restaurant ist mittags und abends geöffnet
- restaurant is open for lunch and dinner

Restaurant ist nur abends geöffnet
- restaurant is open only in the evenings

Restaurant ist nur mittags geöffnet
- restaurant is open for luncheons only

Restaurant ist vollgestopft (mit Gästen)
- restaurant is jam-packed
- restaurant is crammed (with guests)

Restaurantjargon, m
- restaurant jargon

Restaurant kann ganzjährig benutzt werden
- restaurant can be used all year round

Restaurantkapazität, f
- restaurant capacity
- capacity of a restaurant

Restaurantkassierer, m
Restaurantkassier, m *ÖST/SCHW*
- restaurant cashier

Restaurantkategorie, f
- restaurant category
- category of restaurant

Restaurantkellner, m
  Restaurationskellner, m ÖST/SCHW
  ♦ restaurant waiter
Restaurantkellnerin, f
  Restaurationskellnerin, f ÖST/SCHW
  ♦ restaurant waitress
Restaurantkette, f
  ♦ restaurant chain
  ♦ chain of restaurants
Restaurantkonzept, n
  ♦ restaurant concept
Restaurantkonzession, f
  ♦ restaurant license
  ♦ restaurant licence
  ♦ restaurant concession
Restaurant konzessionieren
  ♦ license a restaurant
  ♦ licence a restaurant
Restaurantkosten, pl
  ♦ restaurant costs pl
  ♦ restaurant cost
Restaurantkritik, f
  ♦ restaurant review
Restaurantkritiker, m
  ♦ restaurant critic
Restaurantkritik schreiben
  Restaurantkritk machen
  ♦ review a restaurant
Restaurantküche, f
  ♦ restaurant kitchen
Restaurantküchenchef, m
  ♦ restaurant chef
Restaurantkunde m
  ♦ restaurant customer
Restaurantleistung, f
  Restaurantdienstleistung, f
  ♦ restaurant service
Restaurant leiten
  Restaurant führen
  ♦ manage a restaurant
  ♦ run a restaurant
  ♦ keep a restaurant
Restaurantleiter, m
  Restaurantmanager, m
  Restaurationsleiter, m ÖST/SCHW
  ♦ manager of a restaurant
  ♦ restaurant manager
Restaurantleiterin f
  ♦ restaurant manageress
  ♦ manageress of a restaurant
Restaurantleitung, f
  Restaurantmanagement, n
  ♦ restaurant management
  ♦ management of a restaurant
  ♦ managing a restaurant
Restaurantlokal, n
  ♦ restaurant premises pl
  ♦ restaurant's premises pl
Restaurantmanagement, n
  → Restaurantleitung
Restaurantmanager m
  → Restaurantleiter
Restaurantmarke, f
  (Markenname)
  ♦ restaurant brand
Restaurantmarkt, m
  ♦ restaurant market
Restaurantmitarbeiter, m
  → Restaurantbeschäftigter
Restaurant mit (einer) Terrasse, n
  ♦ restaurant with (a) terrace

Restaurant mit französischer Küche, f
  ♦ restaurant serving French cuisine
Restaurant mit gutem Essen, n
  ♦ restaurant with good food
  ♦ restaurant serving good food
Restaurant mit Milchprodukten, n
  ♦ dairy restaurant
Restaurant mit Nationalküche, n
  ♦ ethnic restaurant
Restaurant mit Schankerlaubnis, n
  (für alkoholische Getränke)
  ♦ licenced restaurant
  ♦ licensed restaurant
Restaurant mit Schauküche, n
  ♦ restaurant with open-to-view kitchen
Restaurant mit Schwimmbadblick, n
  ♦ poolview restaurant AE
  ♦ pool-view restaurant BE
Restaurant mit Straßenverkauf, n
  Restaurant mit Verkauf über die Straße, n
  ♦ carry-out restaurant AE
  ♦ take-out restaurant AE
  ♦ take-away restaurant BE
Restaurant mit Tanzmöglichkeiten, n
  ♦ restaurant with dancing facilities
Restaurant mit Tischbedienung, n
  Restaurant mit Tischservice, n
  ♦ restaurant offering table service
  ♦ table-service restaurant
Restaurant mit Tresenbedienung, n
  Restaurant mit Tresenservice, n
  Restaurant mit Thekenbedienung, n
  Restaurant mit Thekenservice, n
  ♦ counter-service restaurant
  ♦ restaurant offering counter service
Restaurantmöbel, n pl
  Restaurantmobiliar, n
  ♦ restaurant furniture sg
Restaurant ohne Schankerlaubnis, n
  (für alkoholische Getränke)
  ♦ unlicensed restaurant
  ♦ unlicenced restaurant
Restaurant pachten (von jm)
  ♦ lease a restaurant (from s.o.)
Restaurantparkplatz, m
  ♦ restaurant car park BE
  ♦ restaurant parking lot AE
Restaurantpersonal, n
  ♦ restaurant personnel
  ♦ restaurant staff
Restaurantpersonalknappheit, f
  ♦ restaurant staff shortage
  ♦ shortage of restaurant staff
Restaurantplatz, m
  ♦ restaurant place
Restaurantpreis, m
  Restaurationspreis, m ÖST/SCHW
  ♦ restaurant price
Restaurant probieren
  ♦ try a restaurant
Restaurantraum, m
  ♦ restaurant room
Restauranträumlichkeiten, f pl
  ♦ restaurant facilities pl
Restaurantrechnung, f
  ♦ restaurant bill
  ♦ restaurant check AE
Restaurant renovieren (streichen, tapezieren)
  ♦ redecorate a restaurant

Restauranttisch reservieren lassen

Restaurant renovieren (umfassend)
  ♦ renovate a restaurant
  ♦ refurbish a restaurant
Restaurantreservierung, f
  (des ganzen Restaurants)
  Restaurantreservation, f SCHW
  ♦ restaurant reservation
  ♦ reservation of a restaurant
  ♦ reserving a restaurant
Restaurantsachverständiger, m
  Restaurantanalytiker, m
  ♦ restaurant analyst
Restaurantschild, n
  ♦ restaurant sign
Restaurant schließen
  (Geschäft aufgeben)
  ♦ close down a restaurant
Restaurantschule, f
  gastgewerbliche Schule, f
  ♦ restaurant school
  ♦ catering school
Restaurantsektor, m
  Restaurantbereich m
  ♦ restaurant sector
Restaurantservice, m
  Restaurantdienst, m
  Restaurantbedienung, f
  Restaurationsservice, m ÖST/SCHW
  ♦ restaurant service
Restaurantservierer, m off
  ♦ restaurant server
  ♦ restaurant waiter
Restaurantserviererin, f off
  ♦ female restaurant server
  ♦ restaurant waitress
Restaurants für jeden Geschmack, n pl
  ♦ restaurants (catering) for every taste pl
  ♦ restaurants to suit every taste pl
  ♦ restaurants to suit every palate pl
  ♦ restaurants to suit all tastes pl
Restaurantsitzplatz, m
  Restaurantplatz, m
  Restaurantsitz, m
  ♦ restaurant seat
Restaurantspeisekarte, f
  ♦ restaurant menu
Restaurantstandort, m
  Restaurantlage, f
  ♦ restaurant location
  ♦ restaurant site
  ♦ location of a restaurant
  ♦ site of a restaurant
Restaurantszene, f
  Gastronomieszene, f
  ♦ restaurant scene
Restaurantterrasse, f
  ♦ restaurant terrace
  ♦ restaurant patio
Restauranttisch, m
  ♦ restaurant table
  ♦ table in a restaurant
Restauranttisch bestellen
  → Restauranttisch reservieren lassen
Restauranttisch reservieren
  ♦ reserve a restaurant table
  ♦ reserve a table in a restaurant
Restauranttisch reservieren lassen
  Restauranttisch bestellen
  ♦ book a restaurant table
  ♦ book a table in a restaurant

Restauranttrakt, m
   Gaststättentrakt, m
   ♦ restaurant wing
Restaurantturm, m
   ♦ restaurant tower
Restauranttyp, m
   Restaurantart, f
   ♦ restaurant type
   ♦ type of restaurant
Restaurantumsatz, m
   ♦ restaurant sales *pl*
   ♦ restaurant turnover
Restaurantumsatz prognostizieren
   ♦ forecast restaurant sales
   ♦ forecast restaurant turnover
Restaurant- und Gaststättenführer, m
   ♦ eating-out guide
   ♦ restaurant and bar guide *AE*
   ♦ restaurant and pub guide *BE*
Restaurantverband, m
   ♦ restaurant association
Restaurant vergrößern
   ♦ enlarge a restaurant
   ♦ extend a restaurant
Restaurant verpachten (an jn)
   ♦ lease a restaurant (to s.o.)
Restaurantverpflegung, f
   Restaurantessen, n
   ♦ restaurant food
Restaurantverzeichnis, n
   ♦ list of restaurants
   ♦ restaurant list
   ♦ restaurant directory
Restaurantviertel, n
   ♦ restaurant district
Restaurantwagen, m (im Restaurant)
   ♦ restaurant cart *AE*
   ♦ restaurant trolley *BE*
Restaurantwagen, m (Zug)
   Speisewagen, m
   Zugrestaurant, n
   ♦ restaurant car
   ♦ dining car *AE*
   ♦ dining-car *BE*
   ♦ diner *AE*
Restaurantwaren, f pl
   ♦ restaurant supplies *pl*
Restaurantwäsche, f
   ♦ restaurant linen
Restaurantweinkarte, f
   ♦ restaurant wine list
Restaurantwelt, f
   ♦ restaurant world
Restaurantwerbung, f
   ♦ restaurant promotion
   ♦ promotion of a restaurant
Restaurantwesen, n
   → Restaurantgewerbe
Restaurantzentrum, n
   ♦ restaurant center *AE*
   ♦ restaurant centre *BE*
Restaurantzuweisung, f
   (von Gästen)
   ♦ restaurant allocation
   ♦ restaurant assignment *AE*
Restaurant à la carte, n
   → A-la-carte-Restaurant
Restaurateur, m (generell)
   ♦ restaurateur
   ♦ restauranteur *AE*
   ♦ caterer

Restaurateur, m (Restaurant)
   ♦ restauranteur *AE*
   ♦ restaurateur
   ♦ owner of a restaurant
   ♦ proprietor of a restaurant
   ♦ manager of a restaurant
Restaurateur des Jahres, m
   ♦ Restaurateur of the Year
Restaurateurin, f
   ♦ restauratrice
Restauration, f (Gastronomie) ÖST/SCHW
   → Gastronomie, Restaurant
Restauration, f (Restaurierung)
   → Restaurierung
Restaurationsbetrieb, m ÖST/SCHW
   → Gastronomiebetrieb, Restaurantbetrieb
Restaurator, m
   ♦ restorer
restaurieren etw
   ♦ restore s.th.
restaurieren etw vollständig
   vollständig restaurieren etw
   ♦ restore s.th. completely
Restaurierung, f
   Restauration, f
   ♦ restoration
Restaurierungsarbeit, f
   ♦ restoration work
Restaurierungsprogramm, n
   ♦ restoration program *AE*
   ♦ restoration programme *BE*
Restaurierungsprojekt, n
   ♦ restoration project
Restbetrag, m
   Restsumme, f
   ♦ balance
   ♦ remainder
Restbetrag zahlen
   ♦ pay the balance
Restbetrag zahlen bis 1. Mai
   ♦ pay the balance by 1 May
Rest der Reise, m
   ♦ rest of the journey
   ♦ rest of the trip
   ♦ rest of the tour
Rest der Reise, m
   Reiserest, m
   ♦ remainder of the journey
   ♦ remainder of the trip
   ♦ remainder of the tour
Rest der Saison, m
   Saisonrest, m
   ♦ rest of the season
   ♦ remainder of the season
Rest des Abends, m
   ♦ rest of the evening
   ♦ remainder of the evening
Rest des Nachmittags, m
   ♦ rest of the afternoon
   ♦ remainder of the afternoon
Rest des Tages, m
   ♦ remainder of the day
   ♦ rest of the day
Rest des Tages steht zur freien Verfügung
   Rest des Tages ist zur freien Verfügung
   ♦ remainder of the day is at leisure
   ♦ rest of the day is at leisure
Rest des Urlaubs, m
   Rest der Ferien, m
   Urlaubsrest, m
   Ferienrest, m

   ♦ rest of the vacation *AE*
   ♦ rest of the holiday *BE*
Reste der Stadtmauer, m pl
   ♦ remains of the town wall *pl*
   ♦ remains of the city wall *pl*
Reste einer römischen Villa, m pl
   ♦ remains of a Roman villa *pl*
Resteessen, n
   ♦ meal of leftovers
   ♦ scrap meal
restliche Gebühren, f pl
   ♦ balance of the fees
restliche Gebühren vor Kursbeginn erhalten
   ♦ receive the balance of the fees before the course begins
restlicher Urlaub, m
   Resturlaub, m
   restliche Ferien, pl
   Restferien, pl
   ♦ remaining vacation *AE*
   ♦ remaining holiday *BE*
restlos ausgebucht, adj
   ♦ booked to capacity, adj
   ♦ fully booked, adj
restlos ausverkauft, adj
   komplett ausverkauft, adj
   ♦ completely sold out, adj
   ♦ sold out, adj
   ♦ fully booked, adj
restlos ausverkauft sein
   ♦ be completely sold out
   ♦ be fully booked
Restpachtzeit, f
   noch nicht abgelaufene Pachtzeit, f
   ♦ unexpired term of (a) lease
Restsumme, f
   → Restbetrag
Restsüße, f
   Zuckerrest, m
   ♦ residual sugar
   ♦ residual sweetness
Resturlaub, m
   → restlicher Urlaub
Restwert, m
   ♦ residual value
Rest zahlbar bei Ankunft
   ♦ remainder payable on arrival
Restzahlung, f
   ♦ payment of balance
   ♦ balance payment
Restzahlung in zwei Raten leisten
   ♦ pay the balance in two installments *AE*
   ♦ pay the balance in two instalments *BE*
Restzahlung ist 8 Wochen vor der Abreise fällig
   ♦ balance payment is due 8 weeks prior to departure
   ♦ balance payment is due 8 weeks before departure
Retraite, f
   → Refugium
Retrospektive, f
   ♦ retrospective exhibition
   ♦ retrospective
Retrospektive, f (Rückblick)
   Rückblick, m
   ♦ retrospective
Retsina, m *GR*
   ♦ Retsina *GR*
   ♦ Retzina *GR*

retten jn
- ♦ rescue s.o.
- ♦ save s.o.

Retter, m
- ♦ rescuer

Rettich, m
- ♦ radish

Rettichfest, n
- ♦ radish festival

Rettichsalat, m
- ♦ radish salad

Rettungsboot, n
- ♦ lifeboat

Rettungsfahrzeug, n
- ♦ rescue vehicle

Rettungsfloß, n
Rettungsinsel, f
- ♦ life raft

Rettungshubschrauber, m
- ♦ rescue helicopter

Rettungsinsel, f
- → Rettungsfloß

Rettungsleine, f
- ♦ lifeline

Rettungsmannschaft, f
- ♦ rescue team

Rettungsring, m
(im Schwimmbad, am Strand)
- ♦ life buoy AE
- ♦ lifebuoy BE
- ♦ lifebelt BE

Revier, n (Restaurant, Hotel)
- ♦ section
- ♦ station
- ♦ area

Revierkellner, m
Stationskellner, m
Chef de rang, m FR
Rayonkellner, m
- ♦ section waiter
- ♦ station waiter
- ♦ chef de rang FR

Revieroberkellner, m
Stationsoberkellner, m
Maître d'hôtel de carré, m FR
- ♦ section headwaiter AE
- ♦ station headwaiter
- ♦ maître d'hôtel de carré FR

Reviersystem, n
- ♦ section system
- ♦ station system

Revierzuteilung, f
Stationszuteilung, f
- ♦ allocation of a section
- ♦ allocation of a station
- ♦ assignment of a section AE
- ♦ assignment of a station AE

Revitalisierungskur, f
- ♦ revitalising treatment

Revitalisierungskurzurlaub, m
- ♦ revitalising break

Revitalisierungsurlaub, m
- ♦ revitalising vacation AE
- ♦ revitalising holiday BE

Revue, f (Theater)
Theaterrevue, f
- ♦ revue

Revuebar, f
- ♦ revue bar

Revuegirl, n
- ♦ showgirl
- ♦ chorus girl

Rezept, n (Arzt)
- ♦ prescription

Rezept, n (Speisen)
Rezeptur, f
- ♦ recipe

Rezept aus dem 18. Jahrhundert, n
- ♦ recipe from the 18th century
- ♦ 18th century recipe

Rezept aus Italien, n
- ♦ recipe from Italy

Rezept ausprobieren
Rezept probieren
- ♦ try out a recipe
- ♦ try a recipe

Rezept befolgen
Rezeptur befolgen
- ♦ follow a recipe

Rezept benutzen
Rezeptur benutzen
- ♦ use a recipe

Rezeptbestandteil, m
Rezepturbestandteil, m
- ♦ recipe item

Rezeptbuch, n
- ♦ recipe book
- ♦ book of recipes

Rezept für etw, n
Rezeptur für etw, f
- ♦ recipe for s.th.

Rezept für jeden Geschmack, n
- ♦ recipe to suit all tastes

Rezeptidee, f
- ♦ recipe idea

Rezeption, f
- → Empfang

Rezeptionsarbeit, f
Empfangsarbeit, f
- ♦ reception work
- ♦ work in reception
- ♦ front-office work

Rezeptionsbereich m
- ♦ reception area

Rezeptionsblock, m
(Camping)
Empfangsblock, m
- ♦ reception block

Rezeptionserfahrung, f
Empfangserfahrung, f
- ♦ reception experience

Rezeptionsgebäude, n
- → Empfangsgebäude

Rezeptionshalle, f
- → Empfangshalle

Rezeptionsjournal n
- ♦ reception journal

Rezeptionskraft, f
Empfangskraft, f
- ♦ front-desk employee AE
- ♦ front-desk clerk AE
- ♦ reception employee
- ♦ reception clerk

Rezeptionspersonal n
- ♦ reception personnel
- ♦ reception staff

Rezeptionsschalter, m
Empfangsschalter m
- ♦ front desk AE
- ♦ reception desk

Rezeption von einer Abreise in Kenntnis setzen
Empfang von einer Abreise benachrichtigen
- ♦ notify reception of a departure

Rezept reicht für drei Einzelportionen
Rezeptur reicht für drei Einzelportionen
- ♦ recipe is enough for three servings

Rezeptsammlung, f
Rezeptursammlung, f
- ♦ collection of recipes

Rezeptur, f
- → Rezept

Rezeptvorschlag, m
Rezepturvorschlag, m
- ♦ recipe suggestion

Rezeptwettbewerb, m
- ♦ recipe competition
- ♦ recipe contest

Rezession, f
- ♦ recession

R-Gespräch, n
- ♦ collect call AE
- ♦ reversed-charge(s) call BE
- ♦ reverse charge call BE

R-Gespräch führen
- ♦ call collect AE
- ♦ reverse (the) charge(s) BE
- ♦ make a reversed-charge call BE

RH, n
- → Reihenhaus

Rhabarber, m
- ♦ rhubarb

Rhabarberchutney, n
- ♦ rhubarb chutney

Rhabarberkonfitüre, f
- ♦ rhubarb jam

Rhabarbersorbet, n
- ♦ rhubarb sorbet

Rhein, m
- ♦ Rhine River, the
- ♦ River Rhine, the
- ♦ Rhine, the

Rheinblick, m
- ♦ Rhine view
- ♦ view of the Rhine

Rheinblick-Restaurant, n
- ♦ Rhine-view restaurant

Rheindampfer, m
- ♦ Rhine steamer

Rheindampferkreuzfahrt, f
- ♦ Rhine steamer cruise

Rheindelta, n
- ♦ Rhine delta, the

Rheindorf, n
- ♦ Rhine village

Rheinebene, f
- ♦ Rhine Plain, the

Rheinfahrt, f (am Rhein entlang)
- ♦ trip along the Rhine
- ♦ journey along the Rhine
- ♦ tour along the Rhine

Rheinfahrt, f (auf dem Rhein)
Fahrt auf dem Rhein, f
- ♦ trip on the Rhine
- ♦ journey on the Rhine
- ♦ tour on the Rhine
- ♦ Rhine cruise

Rheinfall, m
(bei Schaffhausen)
- ♦ Rhine Falls, the pl

Rheinflußtal, n
- ♦ Rhine river valley

Rheingau, m
  (Region)
  ♦ Rheingau, the
  ♦ Rhinegau, the
Rheingaustadt, f
  ♦ Rheingau town
  ♦ Rhinegau town
Rheingauwein, m
  ♦ Rheingau wine
  ♦ Rhinegau wine
Rheinhafen, m
  ♦ Rhine port
Rhein-Herne-Kanal, m
  ♦ Rhine-Herne Canal, the
Rheinhessen
  (Region)
  ♦ Rhinehesse
  ♦ Rhinehessen
  ♦ Rhenish Hesse
Rheinhessen-Pfalz
  (Region)
  ♦ Rhinehesse-Palatinate
Rheinhessenwein, m
  ♦ Rhinehesse wine
rheinhessisch, adj
  ♦ Rhinehessian, adj
Rhein in Flammen, m
  (Veranstaltung)
  ♦ Rhine in Flames, the
rheinisch, adj
  ♦ Rhenish, adj
rheinische Fröhlichkeit f
  ♦ Rhenish gaiety
Rheinischer Abend, m
  ♦ Rhenisch Evening
  ♦ Rhenish Night
Rheinische Schiefergebirge, das, n
  ♦ Rhenisch Slate Hills, the pl
Rheinkreuzfahrt f
  Kreuzfahrt auf dem Rhein, f
  ♦ Rhine cruise
  ♦ cruise on the Rhine
Rheinland, n
  (Region)
  ♦ Rhineland, the
Rheinlande, n pl
  (Region)
  ♦ Rhinelands, the pl
Rheinland-Pfalz
  ♦ Rhineland-Palatinate, the
Rheinlandschaft, f
  ♦ Rhine scenery
  ♦ Rhine landscape
  ♦ Rhine countryside
Rheinland Weinland
  ♦ Rhineland Wineland
Rhein-Main-Donau-Kanal, m
  ♦ Rhine-Main-Danube Canal, the
Rhein-Marne-Kanal m
  (Wasserstraße)
  ♦ Rhine-Marne Canal
Rheinpanorama, n
  ♦ Rhine panorama
Rheinpfalz, f
  (Region)
  ♦ Rhine Palatinate, the
Rheinpromenade, f
  ♦ Rhine promenade
Rheinquelle, f
  ♦ source of the Rhine

Rheinreise, f
  ♦ Rhine tour
Rhein-Rhône-Kanal, m
  ♦ Rhine-Rhône Canal, the
Rheinstadt, f (Großstadt)
  ♦ Rhine city
Rheinstadt, f (kleine Stadt)
  ♦ Rhine town
Rheintal, n
  ♦ Rhine valley, the
Rheintalreise, f
  ♦ Rhine valley tour
Rheinufer, m
  ♦ Rhine bank
  ♦ Rhine banks pl
Rheinwein, m
  (weiß)
  ♦ Rhine wine
  ♦ hock
  ♦ Hock
Rheuma, n
  Rheumatismus, m
  ♦ rheumatism
Rheuma heilen
  Rheumatismus heilen
  ♦ cure rheumatism
rheumatische Arthritis, f
  ♦ rheumatoid arthritis
rheumatische Beschwerden, f pl
  ♦ rheumatic disorders pl
Rheumatismus behandeln
  Rheuma behandeln
  ♦ treat rheumatism
Rhodopengebirge, n
  Rhodopen, pl
  ♦ Rhodope Mountains, the pl
Rhodos
  ♦ Rhodes
Rhön, f
  ♦ Rhön, the
  ♦ Rhön Mountains, the pl
Rhone, f
  ♦ Rhône River, the
  ♦ River Rhône, the
  ♦ Rhône, the
Rhonetal, n
  ♦ Rhône valley, the
richten etw für etw
  ♦ get s.th. ready for s.th.
  ♦ prepare s.th. for s.th.
  ♦ make preparations for s.th.
  ♦ fix s.th. AE coll
richten sich für einen Kongreß
  ♦ gear for a convention
  ♦ gear for a congress
richten sich für etw
  ♦ gear for s.th.
richten sich nach js Wünschen
  auf js Wünsche eingehen
  ♦ comply with s.o.'s wishes
  ♦ comply with s.o.'s requests
Richtfest, n
  (bei Neubau)
  ♦ roofing ceremony
  ♦ topping-out ceremony BE
  ♦ topping-out BE
Richtfest feiern
  ♦ celebrate the roofing ceremony
  ♦ celebrate the topping-out ceremony
  ♦ celebrate the topping-out

richtig ausgebildetes Personal, n
  ♦ properly trained personnel
  ♦ properly trained staff
richtiger Urlaub, m
  richtige Ferien, pl
  ♦ proper vacation AE
  ♦ proper holiday BE
richtiges Ale, n
  wahres Ale, n
  ♦ real ale
richtiges Essen n
  ordentliches Essen, n
  ♦ proper meal
richtiges Frühstück, n
  ordentliches Frühstück, n
  ♦ proper breakfast
richtiges Hotel, n
  ♦ proper hotel
richtig schlafen
  ♦ sleep properly
Richtmikrofon, n
  ♦ directional microphone
Richtpreis, m
  ♦ guide price
  ♦ guiding price
  ♦ guiding rate
  ♦ guide rate
  ♦ recommended price
Richtung, f
  ♦ direction
richtungsgebundener Fahrpreis, m
  ♦ directional fare
Richtungspfeil, m
  ♦ direction arrow
riechen nach etw
  ♦ smell of s.th.
Riegel Schokolade, m
  ♦ cake of chocolate
  ♦ bar of chocolate
Riegel Seife, m
  ♦ cake of soap
  ♦ bar of soap
Riesenappetit, m
  riesiger Appetit, m
  ♦ gigantic appetite
  ♦ huge appetite
Riesenbett, n
  ♦ gigantic bed
  ♦ giant bed
Riesenfaß, n
  ♦ giant barrel
  ♦ giant vat
Riesenfernsehschirm, m
  ♦ giant television screen
  ♦ giant TV screen
Riesenfest, n (Festival)
  ♦ giant festival
Riesengarnele, f
  ♦ giant shrimp
  ♦ giant prawn
Riesengebirge, n
  ♦ Riesengebirge, the
  ♦ Giant Mountains, the pl
riesengroßes Zimmer, n
  ♦ vast room
Riesenhunger, m
  → enormer Appetit
Riesenhunger haben coll
  ♦ be famished coll
  ♦ be starving coll
  ♦ be ravenous coll

Riesenkongreß, m
♦ huge convention
♦ huge congress
Riesenmahl, n
Riesenmahlzeit, f
♦ huge meal
Riesenrad, n
(auf Jahrmarkt)
♦ Ferris wheel
♦ big wheel
Riesenrutsche, f (Park)
♦ astra slide
Riesenrutsche, f (Schwimmbad)
♦ giant chute
Riesensaal, m
♦ huge hall
♦ giant hall
♦ gigantic hall
Riesenschach, n
♦ giant chess
Riesenslalom, m
♦ giant slalom
Riesenspaß, m
♦ tremendous fun
♦ great time
♦ terrific time
Riesenspaß haben
♦ have a terrific time
♦ have a great time
Riesentanker, m
♦ giant tanker
Riesentorte, f
♦ huge cake
♦ huge gateau
Riesenveranstaltung, f
♦ huge event
♦ huge function
Riesenvideoleinwand, f
♦ giant video screen
Riesenwasserrutsche, f
Riesenwasserrutschbahn, f
♦ giant water chute
♦ giant water slide
♦ huge water chute
♦ huge water slide
♦ mammoth water slide
riesige Auswahl, f
♦ huge choice
♦ huge selection
riesigen Appetit haben
♦ have a huge appetite
♦ have a gigantic appetite
riesige Rechnung, f
♦ huge bill
riesiger Garten, m
Riesengarten, m
♦ huge garden
riesiger Parkplatz, m
♦ huge parking lot AE
♦ huge car park BE
riesiges Vergnügen, n
Riesenvergnügen, n
♦ tremendous pleasure
riesiges Zimmer, n
♦ huge room
Riesling, m
♦ Riesling
Rieslingrebe, f
Rieslingrebstock, m
♦ Riesling vine

Rieslingsoße, f
♦ Riesling sauce
Rieslingtraube, f
♦ Riesling grape
Rieslingwein, m
♦ Riesling wine
Riff, n
♦ reef
Riffhotel, n
♦ reef hotel
Rikscha, f
♦ ricksha AE
♦ rickshaw BE
♦ jinriksha AE
Rinderbraten, m
♦ roast beef
Rindfleisch, n
Ochsenfleisch, n
♦ beef
Rindfleischgericht, n
♦ beef dish
Rindsgulasch, m/n
♦ beef goulash
Rindsragout, n/m
♦ beef stew
Rindsschulter, f
♦ beef shoulder
Ringstraße, f (generell)
♦ circular road
Ringstraße, f (um eine Stadt)
Gürtel, m ÖST
♦ belt highway AE
♦ ring road BE
♦ orbital road BE
Rioja, m SPAN
Riojawein, m SPAN
♦ Rioja SPAN
♦ Rioja wine SPAN
Rippenspeer, m
♦ spareribs AE pl
♦ spare-rib(s) BE (pl)
Risiko, n
♦ risk
Risikogebiet, n
♦ risk area
Risiko tragen
♦ bear the risk
Risikoversicherung, f
♦ risk insurance
riskieren etw
♦ risk s.th.
Risotto, m/n ITAL
♦ risotto ITAL
RIT, f
Rail-Inclusive Tour, f
Bahnpauschalreise, f
♦ RIT
♦ rail-inclusive tour
Ritt, m
Ausritt, m
♦ ride
♦ horse ride
Ritter, m
♦ knight
Ritter der Landstraße, m humor
♦ knight of the road humor
Rittersaal, m hist
♦ Knights' Hall, the hist
Ritterturnier, n
♦ knights' tournament

Ritt machen
♦ go for a ride
ritueller Kriegstanz, m
♦ ritual war dance
Riviera, f
♦ Riviera, the
Rivieraferienort, m
Rivieraurlaubsort, m
Rivieraort, m
♦ Riviera resort
Rivierafischerhafen, m
♦ Riviera fishing port
Rivierahotel, n
♦ Riviera hotel
Roadshow, f
♦ roadshow
Roadster, m
offener Sportzweisitzer, m
offener Sportwagen ohne Rücksitze, m
♦ roadster
Rochen, m
♦ ray
Rock, m (Kleidung)
♦ skirt
Rock, m (Musik)
♦ rock
Rockbügler, m
(Gerät)
♦ skirt press
Rockfan, m
♦ rock fan
Rockfest, n
Rockfestival, n
♦ rock festival
Rockgruppe, f
♦ rock group
Rockkonzert, n
♦ rock concert
Rockkonzert im Freien, n
♦ outdoor rock concert
Rockmusik, f
♦ rock music
Rockmusiker, m
♦ rock musician
Rocknacht, f
♦ rock night
Rockshow, f
♦ rock show
Rockstar, m
♦ rock star
Rocky Mountains, pl
♦ Rocky Mountains, the pl
♦ Rockies, the pl coll
Rocky Mountains Nationalpark, m
♦ Rocky Mountains National Park, the
Rodelabend, m
Schlittenabend, m
♦ toboggan evening
♦ tobogganing evening
Rodelbahn, f
♦ toboggan run
♦ toboggan chute AE
♦ toboggan slide AE
Rodelhang m
♦ toboggan slope
rodeln
♦ coast
♦ toboggan
Rodeln, n
Rodelsport, m

- ◆ tobogganing
- ◆ coasting *AE*

Rodelpartie bei Mondlicht, f
Schlittenfahrt bei Mondlicht, f
- ◆ moonlight toboggan party

Rodelrennen n
- ◆ toboggan race

Rodelschlitten, m
Schlitten, m
- ◆ coaster *AE*
- ◆ toboggan

Rodelsport, m
→ Rodeln

Rodelsport, m
→ Schlittenfahren

Rodeo, m/n
- ◆ rodeo

Rodler m
- ◆ tobogganer
- ◆ tobogganist
- ◆ coaster *AE*
- ◆ sledger

Roggen, m
- ◆ rye

Roggenbrot, n
- ◆ rye bread

Roggenmehl, n
- ◆ rye flour

roh, adj
- ◆ raw, adj

Rohbau, m
- ◆ building shell
- ◆ shell

Rohbilanz, f
- ◆ trial balance
- ◆ gross balance

roher Salat, m
- ◆ raw salad

Rohertrag, m (generell)
Bruttoertrag, m
- ◆ gross earning *AE*
- ◆ gross yield
- ◆ gross profit

Rohertrag, m (GuV)
- ◆ gross income

rohes Ei, n
- ◆ raw egg

rohes Obst, n
- ◆ raw fruit

Rohgewinn, m
→ Bruttogewinn

Rohkost, f
- ◆ raw vegetables *pl*
- ◆ raw vegetables and fruit *pl*
- ◆ green vegetables *pl*
- ◆ raw food
- ◆ uncooked food

Rohkostkur, f
- ◆ vegetable cure
- ◆ vegetarian cure

Rohkostler, m
Obstesser, m
- ◆ fruitarian

Rohmaterial, n
Rohstoff, m
- ◆ raw material

Rohr, n
Leitung, f
- ◆ pipe

Rohrbruch, m
- ◆ pipe burst

Röhrchen, n (Promilletest)
- ◆ breathalyser

Rohr ist gebrochen
- ◆ pipe has burst

Rohrleitungen, f pl
(im Haus)
- ◆ plumbing

Rohrmöbel, n pl
Peddigrohrmöbel, n pl
Rattanmöbel, n pl
- ◆ cane furniture *sg*

Rohrstuhl, m
Peddigrohrstuhl, m
Rattanstuhl, m
- ◆ cane chair

Rohrzucker, m
- ◆ cane sugar

Rohstoffkosten, pl
Rohmaterialkosten, pl
- ◆ raw material costs *pl*
- ◆ raw material cost

Rokoko, n
- ◆ rococo

Rokokoaltar, m
- ◆ rococo altar

Rokokohaus, n
- ◆ rococo house

Rokokokapelle, f
- ◆ rococo chapel

Rokokokirche, f
- ◆ rococo church

Rokokomöbel, n pl
- ◆ rococo furniture *sg*

Rokokosaal, m
- ◆ rococo hall

Rokokostil, m
- ◆ rococo style

Rokokostukkatur, f
- ◆ rococo stucco work
- ◆ rococo plaster work

Rokokotheater, n
- ◆ rococo theater *AE*
- ◆ rococo theatre *BE*

Rokokozeit, f
- ◆ rococo period
- ◆ rococo era

Rokokozimmer, n
- ◆ room furnished in rococo style

Rolladen, m
- ◆ roller shutter
- ◆ shutters *pl*
- ◆ blinds *pl*

Rollbahn, f
Rollfeld, n
Piste, f
- ◆ runway

Rollband, n
→ Rollsteig

Rollbett, n (generell)
(tagsüber unter höherem Bett)
Schiebebett, n
- ◆ trundle bed *AE*
- ◆ truckle-bed *BE*

Rollbett, n (Krankenhaus)
- ◆ wheeled bed

rollendes Material, n
(Eisenbahn)
- ◆ rolling stock

Roller, n
- ◆ scooter

Rolle Toilettenpapier, f
- ◆ toilet roll

Rollfeld, n
→ Rollbahn

Rollgeld, n
Fuhrlohn, m
Fuhrgeld, n
- ◆ cartage
- ◆ wheelage

Rollhandtuch, n
Endloshandtuch, n
- ◆ roller-towel
- ◆ jack-towel

Rollhockey, n
- ◆ roller-skate hockey

Rollschuh, m
- ◆ roller skate *AE*
- ◆ roller-skate *BE*
- ◆ skate *coll*

Rollschuhbahn, f
- ◆ roller-skating rink

Rollschuh fahren
Rollschuh laufen
- ◆ roller-skate

Rollschuhfahren, n
Rollschuhlaufen, n
Rollschuhsport, m
- ◆ roller-skating

Rollschuhfahrer, m
Rollschuhläufer, m
- ◆ roller skater *AE*
- ◆ roller-skater *BE*

Rollsteig, m
Rollsteg, m
- ◆ travellator
- ◆ travelator *AE*
- ◆ moving sidewalk *AE*

Rollstuhl, m
- ◆ wheelchair
- ◆ bath chair

Rollstuhleinrichtungen, f pl
- ◆ wheelchair facilities *pl*

Rollstuhlfahrer, m
Rollstuhlfahrerin, f
- ◆ wheelchair user
- ◆ person confined to a wheelchair
- ◆ person bound to the wheelchair

Rollstuhlfahrer sein
- ◆ be confined to a wheelchair

Rollstuhlfahrerzimmer, n
- ◆ room suitable for guests in wheelchairs

rollstuhlfreundlich, adj
- ◆ wheelchair-friendly, adj

rollstuhlfreundliches Gebäude, n
- ◆ wheelchair-friendly building

rollstuhlgerecht, adj
- ◆ suitable for wheelchairs, adj

rollstuhlgerechtes Zimmer, n
- ◆ room suitable for wheelchairs

Rolltreppe, f
- ◆ escalator

Rolltreppe benutzen
- ◆ use the escalator

Rom
- ◆ Rome

romanisch, adj
- ◆ Romanesque, adj

romanische Basilika, f
- ◆ Romanesque basilica

romanische Kathedrale, f
　romanischer Dom, m
　♦ Romanesque cathedral
romanische Kirche, f
　♦ Romanesque church
romanisches Fresko, n
　♦ Romanesque fresco
romanisches Haus, n
　♦ Romanesque house
romanisch-gotische Kirche, f
　♦ Romanesque-Gothic church
romantisch, adj
　♦ romantic, adj
romantische Atmosphäre, f
　♦ romantic atmosphere
romantische Landschaft, f
　♦ romantic scenery
　♦ romantic landscape
　♦ romantic countryside
romantische Ruine, f
　♦ romantic ruin
romantisches Abendessen, n
　romantisches Diner, n
　♦ romantic dinner
romantisches Schloß, n
　romantische Burg, f
　♦ romantic castle
Romantische Straße, f
　(Ferienstraße)
　♦ Romantic Road, the
romantisches Wochenende, n
　♦ romantic weekend
romantische Umgebung, f
　♦ romantic surroundings *pl*
　♦ romantic setting
romantisch gelegen, adj
　♦ romantically situated, adj
romantisch gelegenes Hotel, n
　♦ romantically situated hotel
Römer, m (Glas)
　♦ roemer
　♦ roemer glass
Römer, m (Person)
　♦ Roman
Römerbad, n
　→ römisches Bad
Römerstraße, f
　römische Straße, f
　♦ Roman road
Römerzeit, f
　römische Zeit, f
　♦ Roman period
　♦ Roman times *pl*
römisch, adj
　♦ Roman, adj
römische Art, adv *gastr*
　♦ Roman style, adv *gastr*
römische Mauer, f
　♦ Roman wall
römischer Tempel, m
　♦ Roman temple
römisches Bad, n
　römische Badeanlagen, f pl
　♦ Roman bath
　♦ Roman baths *pl*
römisches Dampfbad, n
　♦ Roman steam bath
römische Siedlung, f
　♦ Roman settlement
Römisches Museum, n
　♦ Roman Museum, the

römische Villa, f
　♦ Roman villa
römische Zeit, f
　Römerzeit, f
　♦ Roman times *pl*
　♦ Roman period
Römisch-Germanisches Museum, n
　♦ Roman-Germanic Museum
Römisch-Germanisches Zentralmuseum, n
　♦ Roman-Germanic Central Museum
römisch-irisches Bad, n
　♦ Roman-Irish steam bath
Rommé, n
　(Kartenspiel)
　♦ rummy
Rommé spielen
　♦ play rummy
Romwallfahrt, f
　Romfahrt, f
　Wallfahrt nach Rom, f
　♦ pilgrimage to Rome
Röntgeneinrichtung, f
　♦ X-ray facility
Röntgenuntersuchung, f
　♦ X-ray examination
Room-Rack, n
　→ Zimmerrack
Rooms Division Manager, m
　→ Leiter der Empfangsabteilung
Root Beer, n
　(nichtalkoholisches Getränk)
　♦ root beer *AE*
Rose, f
　♦ rose
Rosenduft, m
　♦ rose scent
Rosenfest, n
　♦ rose festival
Rosengarten, m
　♦ rose garden
Rosenkohl, m sg
　♦ Brussels sprouts *pl*
Rosenkönigin, f
　♦ rose queen
Rosenmontag m
　♦ Shrove Monday
Rosenmontagsball m
　♦ Shrove Monday ball
Rosenmontagsumzug, m
　Rosenmontagszug, m
　♦ Shrove Monday procession
Rosenstrauß, m
　♦ bunch of roses
Rosésekt, m
　♦ rose champagne *AE*
　♦ rosé champagne *BE*
Roséwein, m
　Rosé, m *coll*
　♦ rose wine *AE*
　♦ rose *AE coll*
　♦ rosé wine *BE*
　♦ rosé *BE coll*
rosig gebraten, adj *gastr*
　rosa gebraten, adj *gastr*
　♦ medium, adj *gastr*
Rosine, f (generell)
　♦ raisin
Rosine, f (im Kuchen)
　♦ plum
Rosinenauflauf, m
　→ Plumpudding

Rosinenkuchen, m
　♦ plum cake
Rosmarin, m
　♦ rosemary
Rosmarinzweig, m
　♦ rosemary sprig
　♦ sprig of rosemary
Rosmarinzweigchen, n
　♦ rosemary sprig
Roßhaarmatratze f
　♦ hair mattress
Rostbraten, m
　Braten, m
　♦ roast
rösten (Brot)
　♦ toast (bread)
rösten (Fleisch)
　♦ roast
　♦ grill
rösten (Kartoffeln)
　♦ fry
Rotauge, n
　Plötze, f
　♦ roach
Rotbarsch, m
　♦ redfish
　♦ rosefish
　♦ ocean perch
　♦ Norway haddock
Rotbrasse, f
　♦ pandora
rote Bete, f
　♦ beetroot
Rote-Bete-Saft, m
　♦ beetroot juice
Rote-Bete-Salat, m
　♦ beetroot salad
Rote-Bete-Suppe, f
　♦ beetroot soup
rote Bohne, f
　♦ red bean
rote Grütze, f
　♦ red grits *pl*
rote Johannisbeere, f
　♦ redcurrant
Rote Kreuz, das, n
　♦ Red Cross, the
Rotel, n
　→ Hotel auf Rädern
roten Teppich ausrollen
　♦ unroll the red carpet
Roter, m (Wein) *coll*
　roter Wein, m
　Rotwein, m
　♦ red, the *coll*
　♦ a red *coll*
　♦ red wine
roter Bordeauxwein, m
　roter Bordeaux, m
　♦ claret
roter Pfeffer, m
　♦ red pepper
Roter Salon, m
　♦ Red Lounge, the
roter Teppich, m
　♦ red carpet
roter Wermut, m
　♦ red vermouth
Rotes Meer, n
　♦ Red Sea, the

rote Traube

rote Traube, f
  ♦ red grape
Rotgrantplatz, m (Tennis)
  ♦ clay court
Rotgranttennisplatz, m
  ♦ clay tennis court
rotierende Sitzordnung, f
  Sitzplatzrotation, f
  Platzrotation, f
  ♦ seat rotation
Rotisserie, f
  Grillrestauarnt, f
  Rôtisserie, f FR
  ♦ rôtisserie FR
  ♦ grill restaurant
  ♦ grill-room BE
  ♦ grillroom AE
Rotisseur, m
  Bratenkoch, m
  Rôtisseur, m FR
  ♦ rôtisseur FR
  ♦ roast cook
Rotkohl, m
  Rotkraut, n
  ♦ red cabbage
Rotkraut, n
  → Rotkohl
Rotling, m
  (Wein)
  ♦ Rotling
Rotlingwein, m
  ♦ Rotling wine
Rotsekt, m
  roter Sekt, m
  ♦ red champagne
  ♦ pink champagne
Rotwein, m
  Roter, m coll
  ♦ red wine
  ♦ a red coll
  ♦ the red coll
Rotweinbutter, f
  ♦ red-wine butter
Rotweinerzeugung, f
  ♦ red wine production
Rotweinessig, m
  ♦ red wine vinegar
Rotweinfleck, m
  ♦ red wine stain
Rotweingebiet, n
  ♦ red wine region
Rotweinglas, n
  ♦ red wine glass
Rotweinkarte, f
  ♦ red wine list
Rotweinland, n
  Rotweingebiet, n
  ♦ red wine country
Rotweinprobe, f
  ♦ red wine tasting
Rotweinsorte, f
  ♦ red wine variety
Rotweinsoße, f
  ♦ red wine sauce
Rotweintraube, f
  ♦ red wine grape
Rotwild, n
  ♦ red deer
  ♦ deer
Rotwildmuseum, n
  ♦ deer museum

Rotwildpark m
  ♦ deer park
Rotwildschutzgebiet, n
  ♦ deer sanctuary
Roulade, f
  ♦ roulade
Rouleau, n
  Rollo, n
  ♦ shade AE
  ♦ roller blind BE
  ♦ blind BE
Roulette, n
  Roulett, n
  ♦ roulette
Rouletterad, n
  Roulettrad, n
  ♦ roulette wheel
Roulette spielen
  Roulett spielen
  ♦ play roulette
Roulette spielen in einem Kasino
  Roulette spielen in einem Kasino
  ♦ play roulette at a casino
  ♦ play roulette in a casino
Roulettespieler, m
  Roulettspieler, m
  ♦ roulette player
Roulettetisch, m
  Roulettisch, m
  ♦ roulette table
Round-table-Diskussion, f
  → Diskussion am runden Tisch
Round-table-Konferenz, f
  → Konferenz am runden Tisch
Route, f
  Strecke, f
  ♦ route
Route abseits der Hauptstrecke, f
  ♦ off-beat route
Route ändern (geringfügig)
  ♦ alter the route
  ♦ alter a route
Route ändern (umfassend)
  ♦ change the route
  ♦ change a route
Route aufgeben
  Strecke aufgeben
  ♦ abandon a route
Route ausarbeiten
  Strecke ausarbeiten
  ♦ work out a route
Route auswählen
  Strecke auswählen
  ♦ select a route
Route benutzen
  ♦ use a route
Route durch X, f
  Strecke durch X, f
  ♦ route through X
Route festlegen
  Route festsetzen
  ♦ determine a route
  ♦ fix a route
Route folgen
  ♦ follow a route
Route gabelt sich in X
  Strecke gabelt sich in X
  ♦ route forks at X
  ♦ route forks in X

Routenänderung, f (geringfügig)
  Streckenänderung, f
  ♦ alteration of (the) route
Routenänderung, f (umfassend)
  Streckenänderung, f
  ♦ change of (the) route
Routenbeschreibung, f
  Streckenbeschreibung, f
  ♦ route description
  ♦ description of the route
Route nehmen
  Strecke nehmen
  ♦ take a route
Routenplanung, f
  Streckenplanung, f
  ♦ planning a route
  ♦ route planning
Routenvorschlag, m
  ♦ route suggestion
  ♦ route proposal
Route planen
  Strecke planen
  ♦ plan the route
  ♦ plan a route
Route wählen
  Strecke wählen
  Route auswählen
  Strecke auswählen
  ♦ choose a route
  ♦ select a route
Routine, f
  ♦ routine
Routineangelegenheit, f
  ♦ routine matter
Rowdy, m
  ♦ rowdy
  ♦ hooligan
Ruanda
  ♦ Ruanda
  ♦ Rwanda
Ruander, m
  ♦ Ruandan
  ♦ Rwandan
Ruanderin, f
  ♦ Ruandan girl
  ♦ Ruandan woman
  ♦ Ruandan
  ♦ Rwandan girl
  ♦ Rwandan woman
ruandisch, adj
  ♦ Ruandan, adj
  ♦ Rwandan, adj
Rubel, m
  ♦ rouble
Rubel rollt, der
  ♦ money is rolling in, the
Rückansicht, f
  ♦ rear view
Rückantwort, f
  → Antwort
Rückantwortschein, m
  → Antwortschein
rückbestätigen etw
  → gegenbestätigen etw
Rückbestätigung, f
  → Gegenbestätigung
Rückbuchung, f
  Rückreisebuchung, f
  ♦ return booking
Rücken, m (Berg)
  ♦ ridge

Rücken, m (gastronomisch)
  ♦ saddle
Rücken, m (generell)
  ♦ back
Rückenbehandlung, f med
  ♦ back treatment med
Rücken kehren jm
  ♦ turn one's back on s.o.
Rückenlehne, f
  ♦ backrest
  ♦ back
Rückenmassage, f
  ♦ back massage
Rückenschmerz, m
  ♦ back pain
Rückenschmerzen, pl
  Rückenweh, n
  ♦ backache
  ♦ back pains pl
  ♦ back pain
rückerstattbar, adj
  erstattbar, adj
  ♦ refundable, adj
  ♦ returnable, adj
rückerstattbarer Betrag, m
  ♦ refundable amount
rückerstattbarer Gutschein, m
  ♦ refundable voucher
rückerstattbar sein
  erstattbar sein
  ♦ be refundable
  ♦ be returnable
Rückerstattung, f
  Erstattung, f
  ♦ refund
  ♦ reimbursement
  ♦ repayment
Rückerstattung beanspruchen
  ♦ claim a refund
Rückerstattung beantragen
  Erstattung beantragen
  ♦ apply for a refund
Rückerstattung bekommen
  ♦ get a refund
Rückerstattung der Konferenzgebühr, f
  ♦ refund of the conference fee
  ♦ refund of the conference charge
Rückerstattung erhalten
  ♦ receive a refund
  ♦ obtain a refund
Rückerstattung für berechtigt halten
  ♦ consider a refund justified
Rückerstattung geben
  Rückerstattung leisten
  ♦ give a refund
Rückerstattung leisten
  ♦ make a refund
Rückerstattungsantrag, m
  Erstattungsantrag, m
  Antrag auf Rückerstattung, m
  Antrag auf Erstattung, m
  ♦ application for refund
Rückerstattungsbedingungen, f pl
  ♦ refund conditions pl
Rückerstattungsbedingungen anerkennen
  ♦ accept the refund conditions
Rückerstattungsbetrag, m
  Erstattungsbetrag, m
  ♦ amount of (the) refund
Rückerstattungsgebühr, f
  ♦ refund fee

Rückerstattungsgutschrift, f
  ♦ refund voucher
Rückerstattungspolitik, f
  Rückerstattungsrichtlinien, f pl
  ♦ refund policy
Rückerstattungsquittung, f
  ♦ refund receipt
Rückerstattungswunsch, m
  ♦ refund request
  ♦ request for a refund
Rückerstattung verlangen
  ♦ demand a refund
  ♦ claim a refund
Rückerstattung wünschen
  ♦ request a refund
Rückerstattung zahlen jm
  Rückerstattung zahlen an jn
  ♦ pay a refund to s.o.
Rückfahrkarte, f
  Rückflugkarte, f
  ♦ round-trip ticket AE
  ♦ return ticket BE
Rückfahrkarte erster Klasse, f
  Erste-Klasse-Rückfahrkarte, f
  Erster-Klasse-Rückfahrkarte, f
  ♦ first-class round-trip ticket AE
  ♦ first-class return ticket BE
Rückfahrkarte kaufen
  Rückfahrkarte lösen
  ♦ buy a round-trip ticket AE
  ♦ buy a return ticket BE
Rückfahrkarte zweiter Klasse, f
  Zweite-Klasse-Rückfahrkarte, f
  ♦ second-class round-trip ticket AE
  ♦ second-class return ticket BE
Rückfahrpreis, m
  ♦ return fare
Rückfahrt, f
  ♦ return trip
  ♦ return journey
Rückfahrtbus, m
  ♦ return bus
  ♦ return coach BE
Rückfahrt mit dem Bus, f
  Busrückfahrt, f
  ♦ return trip by bus
  ♦ return trip by coach BE
  ♦ bus return trip
  ♦ coach return trip BE
Rückflug, m
  ♦ return flight
Rückflugcoupon, m
  ♦ return flight coupon
  ♦ return coupon
Rückflug erfolgt über London
  ♦ return flight is via London
  ♦ return flight will be via London
Rückflugpreis, m
  ♦ return air fare
  ♦ return fare
Rückflugreiseverkehr, m
  Rückflugreisen, n
  ♦ return air travel
Rückflugschein, m
  ♦ return air ticket
  ♦ return ticket
Rückflugtermin, m
  Rückflugdatum, n
  ♦ date of the return flight
Rückfrage, f
  ♦ query

  ♦ further inquiry
  ♦ further enquiry
Rückfrage beantworten
  ♦ answer a query
Rückfrage haben
  ♦ have a query
rückführen jn
  zurückholen jn in das Heimatland
  ♦ repatriate s.o.
Rückführung, f
  Rückholung in das Heimatland, f
  Rücktransport in das Heimatland, f
  ♦ repatriation
Rückführungsdienst, m
  (ins Heimatland)
  Rückholdienst, m
  ♦ repatriation service
Rückführungskosten, pl
  Rückholkosten, pl
  ♦ repatriation costs pl
  ♦ repatriation cost
Rückgabe, f
  ♦ return
Rückgabeflasche, f
  ♦ returnable bottle
Rückgabegebühr, f
  (z.B. bei Mietauto)
  ♦ return charge
  ♦ return fee
  ♦ drop-off charge
  ♦ drop-off fee
Rückgabeort, m
  (bei beweglichen Mietsachen)
  Rückgabestation, f
  ♦ drop-off point
  ♦ return point
Rückgaberecht, n
  ♦ right of return
Rückgabeschalter, m
  ♦ return counter
Rückgabetermin, m (Kontingent)
  Rückgabedatum, n
  Freigabetermin, m
  Freigabedatum, n
  ♦ release date
Rückgabezeit, f
  → Rückgabezeitpunkt
Rückgabezeitpunkt m
  (bei beweglichen Mietsachen)
  Rückgabezeit f
  ♦ return time
  ♦ time of return
Rückgang an Touristen, m
  ♦ decrease in (the number of) tourists
  ♦ drop in (the number of) tourists
  ♦ fall in (the number of) tourists
  ♦ shortfall in tourists
Rückgang der ausländischen Besucher, m
  ♦ decrease in (the number of) foreign visitors
  ♦ fall in (the number of) foreign visitors
  ♦ drop in (the number of) foreign visitors
Rückgang der Besucherzahlen, m
  ♦ fall in the number of visitors
  ♦ drop in the number of visitors
  ♦ decrease in the number of tourists
Rückgang der Bettenauslastung, m
  ♦ decrease in bed occupancy
  ♦ fall in bed occupancy
  ♦ drop in bed occupancy
Rückgang der Buchungen, m
  ♦ fall in bookings

Rückgang der Gästezahl

- drop in bookings
- decrease in bookings

Rückgang der Gästezahl, m
 Gästerückgang, m
- drop in the number of guests
- fall in the number of guests
- decrease in the number of guests

Rückgang der Gästezahl verkraften
- cope with the decreasing number of guests

Rückgang der Gesamtgästezahl, m
- decrease in the total number of guests
- fall in the total number of guests
- drop in the total number of guests

Rückgang der Gesamtkundenzahl, m
- fall in client total
- drop in client total

Rückgang der Gesamtkundenzahl hinnehmen müssen
- have to accept a fall in client total
- have to take a fall in client total

Rückgang der Hotelauslastung, m
 Rückgang der Hotelbelegung, m
- drop in hotel occupancy
- decrease in the hotel's occupancy
- fall in hotel occupancy
- decrease in hotel occupancy

Rückgang der Kapazitätsauslastung, m
- reduction in capacity utilisation
- reduction in capacity utilization

Rückgang der Übernachtungszahlen, m
 Abnahme der Übernachtungszahlen, f
- drop in the number of nights spent
- decrease in the number of nights spent
- fall in the number of nights spent

Rückgang des Besucherstroms, m
- recession in the flow of visitors

Rückgang erleben
- experience a decline

rückgängig gemachte Buchung, f
 → stornierte Buchung

rückgängig gemachte Reservierung, f
 → stornierte Reservierung

rückgängig machen etw
 → stornieren etw

Rückgängigmachung, f
 → Stornierung

Rückgarten, m
 Garten hinter dem Haus, m
- back garden

Rückhaus, n
 → Hinterhaus

Rückholdienst, m
 (von Autos etc)
 Rückholservice, m
- recovery service

Rückkarte, f
 → Antwortkarte

Rückkehr, f
- return

Rückkehr feiern von jm
 Ankunft feiern von jm
- kill the fatted calf humor

Rückkehr von X, f
 Rückkehr aus X, f
- return from X

Rückkreuzfahrt, f
- return cruise

Rücklage, f ökon
- reserve

rückläufig, adj
 abnehmend, adj

- decreasing, adj
- declining, adj
- downward, adj
- falling (off), adj
- dropping, adj

rückläufige Aufenthaltsdauer, f
- decreasing length of stay

rückläufige Gästezahl, f
- decreasing number of guests

rückläufige Tendenz, f
- downward trend

rückpachten etw coll
 → zurückpachten etw

Rückpachtung, f
- leaseback

Rückpachtungsvertrag, m
 Rückpachtvertrag m
- leaseback contract

Rückprojektion, f
- back projection
- rear projection

Rückprojektionsleinwand, f
 Leinwand für Rückprojektion, f
- back projection screen
- rear projection screen

Rückreise, f (bes. Seereise)
- return voyage

Rückreise, f (generell)
 Rückfahrt, f
- return journey
- return trip

Rückreiseanschluß, m
- return connection

Rückreisedatum, n
 Rückreisetermin, m
- date of the return journey
- date of the return trip

Rückreise fortsetzen
- continue one's return journey

Rückreise mit dem Bus, f
 Busrückreise, f
- return journey by bus
- return journey by coach BE
- return trip by bus
- bus return journey
- coach return journey BE

Rückreisen, n
 Rückreiseverkehr, m
- return travel

Rückreiseroute, f
 Rückreisestrecke, f
- return route

Rückreisetag, m
- day of the return trip
- day of the return journey

Rückreisetermin, m
 Rückreisedatum, n
- return date
- date of the return journey
- date of the return trip

Rückreiseverkehr, m
- homeward traffic
- return travel

Rückreisewelle, f
- homebound wave of traffic

Rucksack, m
- backpack
- rucksack
- knapsack
- sack

Rucksackexpedition, f
- backpacking expedition

Rucksackgurt, m
- rucksack strap

Rucksackreise, f
- backpacking trip
- backpacking tour
- backpacking journey

Rucksackreisen, n
 Rucksacktourismus, m
- backpacking

Rucksackreisender, m
 Rucksacktourist, m
- rucksack tourist
- rucksacker coll

Rucksacktourismus, m
 → Rucksackreisen

Rucksacktourist, m
 Schlafsacktourist, m
 Rucksackwanderer, m
 Rucksackreisender, m
- backpacker
- rucksack tourist
- rucksacker coll

Rucksackurlaub, m
- backpacking vacation AE
- backpacking holiday BE

Rucksackverein, m
 Rucksackclub, m
- rucksack club

Rucksackzelt, n
- backpacking tent

Rückseite, f (Gebäude)
- back
- rear

rückseitig, adv (Gebäude)
- at the rear, adv

rücksichtsvoll, adj
- considerate, adj

rücksichtsvoll behandeln jn
- treat s.o. very considerately
- treat s.o. with consideration

rücksichtsvoller Gast,, m
- considerate guest

rücksichtsvolles Verhalten, n
- consideration

rücksichtsvoll sein gegenüber jm
 rücksichtsvoll sein gegen jn
- be considerate to s.o.

Rücksitz, m
 Rücksitzplatz, m
- back seat
- rear seat

Rückspiel, n
- return match

Rückspiel vereinbaren
 Rückspiel ausmachen
- arrange a return match

rückständige Miete, f
 Mietrückstand, m
- back rent
- arrears of rent pl
- overdue rent
- rent in arrears

Rückstellung, f ökon
- reserve
- provision

Rückstellungen bilden
 Rückstellungen vornehmen
- set up reserves
- make provisions for s.th.

Rückstellungen für Mietausfälle, f pl
 ♦ allowances for vacancies pl
Rückstellungen machen für etw
 ♦ make provisions for s.th.
Rücktransfer, m
 ♦ return transfer
 ♦ transfer back to X
Rücktritt, m
 → Stornierung
Rücktrittsversicherung, f
 ♦ cancellation insurance
 ♦ cancelation insurance AE
Rücktrittsversicherung abschließen
 ♦ take out a cancellation insurance (policy)
 ♦ take out a cancelation insurance (policy) AE
Rücktritt von einem Vertrag, m
 Stornierung eines Vertrags, f
 ♦ cancellation of a contract
 ♦ cancelation of a contract AE
 ♦ withdrawal from a contract
Rücktritt von einer Vereinbarung, m
 ♦ withdrawal from an agreement
Rückumschlag, m
 → Freiumschlag
rückvergüten etw jm
 zurückvergüten etw an jn
 erstatten jm etw
 ♦ reimburse s.th. to s.o.
Rückvergütung, f
 Rückerstattung, f
 Rückzahlung, f
 ♦ reimbursement
 ♦ refund
 ♦ rebate
Rückwand, f
 ♦ rear wall
rückwärtiger Flügel, m
 rückwärtiger Trakt, m
 ♦ rear wing
rückwärtiges Zimmer, n
 → Zimmer nach hinten, Hinterzimmer
Rückweg, m
 ♦ way back
 ♦ way home
 ♦ return route
Rückweg antreten
 ♦ set out for home
 ♦ start back
 ♦ return
rückzahlbar, adj
 ♦ repayable, adj
Rückzahlung, f
 ♦ repayment
Rückzimmer, n
 → rückwärtiges Zimmer
Ruderboot, n
 ♦ rowboat AE
 ♦ rowing-boat BE
Ruderbootfahrt, f
 ♦ trip in a rowboat AE
 ♦ trip in a rowing-boat BE
 ♦ row
Ruderboot mieten
 Ruderboot leihen
 ♦ rent a rowboat AE
 ♦ hire a rowing-boat BE
Ruderbootverleih, m
 ♦ rowboat rental AE
 ♦ rowing-boat hire BE
Ruderboot vermieten
 Ruderboot verleihen

 ♦ rent (out) a rowboat AE
 ♦ hire out a rowing-boat BE
Ruderclub, m
 Ruderverein, m
 ♦ rowing club
Ruderer, m
 ♦ rower
Rudergerät, n
 (Gymnastikgerät)
 ♦ rowing machine
rudern
 ♦ row
Rudern, n
 Rudersport, m
 ♦ rowing
Ruderregatta, f
 ♦ rowing regatta
Rudersee, m
 ♦ rowing lake
 ♦ boating lake
Ruderveranstaltung, f
 ♦ rowing event
Ruf, m
 Reputation, f
 Renommee, n
 ♦ reputation
Rufanlage, f
 Ausrufanlage, f
 Personenrufanlage, f
 Suchanlage, f
 ♦ paging system
Ruf aufbauen als etw
 ♦ build up a reputation as s.th.
Ruf aufbauen für etw
 ♦ build up a reputation for s.th.
Ruf des Hotels, m
 ♦ reputation of the hotel
Ruf des Restaurants, m
 ♦ reputation of the restaurant
Rufen Sie mir bitte ein Taxi
 ♦ Call me a taxi, please
Rufen Sie noch heute an!
 ♦ Phone today!
 ♦ Call today!
 ♦ Ring today!
Ruf erwerben als etw
 ♦ gain a reputation as s.th.
Ruf für etw, m
 ♦ reputation for s.th.
Ruf genießen für etw
 ♦ enjoy a reputation for s.th.
Ruf gewinnen für etw
 ♦ win a reputation for s.th.
Ruf haben für etw (Aktivität)
 ♦ have a reputation for doing s.th.
Ruf haben für Gastlichkeit
 ♦ have a reputation for hospitality
Ruf schädigen
 ♦ injure one's reputation
 ♦ injure s.o.'s reputation
Ruf verbessern
 ♦ improve one's reputation
 ♦ improve s.o.'s reputation
Ruf verbessern von etw
 ♦ improve the reputation of s.th.
Ruf verdienen sich als etw
 ♦ earn a reputation as s.th.
Ruf verlieren
 ♦ lose one's reputation
Ruf verschlechtert sich
 ♦ reputation deteriorates

Rugby, n
 ♦ rugby football
 ♦ rugby
Rugbymannschaft, f
 ♦ rugby team
Rugbyplatz, m
 Rugbyfeld, n
 ♦ rugby field
Rugbyspiel, n
 ♦ rugby match
 ♦ rugby game
Rugby spielen
 ♦ play rugby
Rugbyspieler, m
 ♦ rugby player
Ruhe, bitte!
 ♦ Quiet, please!
 ♦ Silence, please!
Ruhebank, f
 → Bank
ruhebedürftig, adj
 ♦ in need of (a) rest, adj
Ruhebett, n SCHW
 ♦ rest-bed
Ruhe finden
 ♦ find rest
Ruhe genießen
 ♦ enjoy a rest
Ruhekissen, n
 → Kissen
Ruhekur, f
 → Liegekur
ruhelos, adj
 ♦ restless, adj
ruhelos auf und ab wandern im Zimmer
 ♦ wander restlessly up and down the room
ruhelose Nacht, f
 ♦ restless night
ruhelose Nacht verbringen
 ♦ spend a restless night
Ruhelosigkeit, f
 ♦ restlessness
ruhen für eine Stunde
 ausruhen sich für eine Stunde
 ♦ rest for an hour
Ruhen Sie sich erst einmal aus!
 ♦ Take a rest first!
Ruhepause, f
 ♦ rest break
 ♦ rest
 ♦ pause
 ♦ break
Ruhepause benötigen
 ♦ need a rest
Ruhepause machen
 ♦ make a pause
 ♦ take a break
 ♦ have a break
Ruheplatz, m
 ♦ resting-place
 ♦ place of rest
Ruheraum, m
 Liegeraum, m
 ♦ rest lounge
 ♦ rest room
Ruhesessel, m
 Clubsessel, m
 ♦ lounge chair
 ♦ easy chair
 ♦ club chair

Ruhe sicherstellen
♦ ensure quietness
Ruhesitz, m
Altersruhesitz, m
♦ retirement residence
♦ retirement home
Ruhesitz suchen
♦ seek a retirement residence
♦ seek a retirement home
Ruhestätte, f
(Grab)
♦ resting-place
ruhestörender Lärm, m
♦ disturbing noise
Ruhestörer, m *jur*
♦ disturber of the peace *jur*
Ruhestörer, m (Krakeeler)
→ Krakeeler
Ruhestörer, m (Lärm)
♦ noisy person
♦ noisemaker
Ruhestörung, f *jur*
♦ disturbance of the peace *jur*
♦ disturbance
Ruhestörung, f (Lärm)
♦ noisemaking
Ruhestunde, f
♦ hour of rest
Ruhe suchen
♦ seek rest
Ruhesuchender, m
♦ person seeking rest
Ruhetag, m (generell)
(Tag, an dem man sich ausruht)
♦ rest day *AE*
♦ rest-day *BE*
♦ day of rest
Ruhetag, m (Lokal)
♦ closing day
Ruhetag einlegen
♦ have a day's rest
Ruhetag (Hinweisschild)
Freitags Ruhetag
♦ Closed on ...
♦ Closed on Fridays
Ruhe und Entspannung, f
♦ rest and relaxation
Ruhe und Entspannung finden
♦ find rest and relaxation
Ruhe und Entspannung suchen
♦ seek rest and relaxation
Ruhe und Erholung, f
♦ rest and recreation
Ruhe und Erholung finden
♦ find rest and recreation
Ruhe und Erholung suchen
♦ seek rest and recreation
Ruhe und Frieden
Ruhe (f) und Frieden (m)
♦ rest and peace
Ruhe und Frieden finden
♦ find rest and peace
Ruhe und Frieden genießen
♦ enjoy rest and peace
Ruhe und Frieden suchen
♦ seek rest and peace
Ruhe und Stille genießen
♦ enjoy the peace and tranquillity *BE*
♦ enjoy the peace and tranquility *AE*

ruhevoll, adj
♦ tranquil, adj
♦ peaceful, adj
ruhevolle Atmosphäre, f
♦ tranquil atmosphere
Ruhezeit, f
♦ rest period
♦ period of rest
♦ time of rest
Ruhezone, f
♦ zone of rest
ruhig, adj
♦ quiet, adj
ruhige Atmosphäre, f
♦ quiet atmosphere
ruhige Dorflage, f
♦ quiet village location
ruhige Ecke, f
♦ quiet corner
ruhige Ecke finden
♦ find a quiet corner
ruhige Jahreszeit, f
♦ slack period of the year
♦ off-season
ruhige Lage, f
♦ quiet location
ruhige Nachbarn, m pl
♦ quiet neighbors *AE pl*
♦ quiet neighbours *BE pl*
ruhige Nachbarschaft, f
♦ quiet neighborhood *AE*
♦ quiet neighbourhood *BE*
ruhigen Ort suchen
♦ look for a quiet place
♦ seek a quiet place
ruhigen Urlaub verbringen
ruhige Ferien verbringen
♦ spend a quiet vacation *AE*
♦ spend a quiet holiday *BE*
ruhiger Abend, m
♦ quiet evening
ruhiger Aufenthalt, m
♦ quiet stay
ruhiger Monat, m
♦ quiet month
ruhiger Platz, m
ruhiger Ort, m
♦ quiet place
ruhiger Urlaub, m
♦ quiet vacation *AE*
♦ quiet holiday *BE*
ruhiges Wochenende, n
♦ quiet weekend
ruhiges Wochenende genießen
♦ enjoy a quiet weekend
ruhiges Zimmer, n
ruhig gelegenes Zimmer, n
♦ quiet room
ruhiges Zimmer wünschen
♦ request a quiet room
ruhige und abgeschiedene Lage, f
♦ quiet and secluded location
♦ quiet and secluded position
ruhige Wohnlage, f
(im Ort)
♦ quiet residential area
ruhige Zeit, f
(wenig Geschäft)
♦ quiet period

ruhige Zeit zwischen Weihnachten und Neujahr, f
♦ quiet period between Christmas and New Year
ruhig gelegen, adj
♦ quietly situated, adj
♦ quietly located, adj
♦ quietly positioned, adj
♦ peacefully situated, adj
ruhig gelegenes Hotel, n
♦ quietly situated hotel
♦ quietly located hotel
ruhig liegen
(Haus)
♦ be in a quiet area
ruhig schlafen
♦ sleep quietly
ruhig wohnen
in einem ruhigen Viertel wohnen
♦ live in a quiet area
Ruhm erwerben für etw
♦ acquire fame for s.th.
Ruhr, f
♦ dysentery
Rührei, n
Rühreier, n pl
♦ scrambled egg
♦ scrambled eggs *pl*
Ruhrgebiet, n
(Region)
♦ Ruhr District, the
♦ Ruhr, the
Rührlöffel, m
♦ stirring spoon
Rührmaschine, f
→ Mixer
Rührteig, m
♦ cake mixture
♦ batter
Rührwerk, n
→ Mixer
Ruine, f (Gebäude)
♦ ruined building
Ruinenort, m
Ruinenstelle, f
Ruinenplatz, m
♦ place of ruins
Ruinenstadt, f
♦ town in ruins
♦ ruined town
Ruinenstadt, f (Großstadt)
♦ ruined city
♦ city ruins *pl*
ruinöser Wettbewerb, m
→ Verdrängungswettbewerb
Ruländer, m
(Wein)
♦ Ruländer
♦ Pinot gris *FR*
rülpsen
♦ belch
♦ burp *inform*
Rülpser, m
♦ belch
♦ burp *inform*
Rum, m
♦ rum
Rumäne, m
♦ Romanian
♦ Rumanian *AE*

Rumänien
- ♦ Romania
- ♦ Rumania *AE*

Rumänin, f
- ♦ Romanian girl
- ♦ Romanian woman
- ♦ Romanian
- ♦ Rumanian girl *AE*
- ♦ Rumanian (woman) *AE*

rumänisch, adj
- ♦ Romanian, adj
- ♦ Rumanian, adj *AE*

Rumba, f
- ♦ rumba

Rumbutter, f
- ♦ rum butter

Rumgetränk, m
- ♦ rum drink

Rumkugel, f
- ♦ rum truffle

Rummelplatz, m
Jahrmarkt, m
- ♦ fun-fair *BE*
- ♦ fair
- ♦ fairgrounds *pl = sg*

Rummelplatzatmosphäre, f
Jahrmarktatmosphäre, f
- ♦ fairground atmosphere

Rumpelkammer, f
- ♦ lumber room *AE*
- ♦ lumber-room *BE*
- ♦ boxroom *BE*

Rumpf, m (Flugzeug)
- ♦ fuselage
- ♦ body

Rumpf, m (Schiff)
- ♦ hull
- ♦ body

Rumration, f
tägliche Rumration, f
- ♦ rum ration
- ♦ daily rum ration

Rum Toddy, m
- ♦ rum toddy

rund, adj
- ♦ round, adj

Rundball, m
(Spiel)
- ♦ rounders *pl=sg*

Rundballspiel, n
- ♦ rounders match

Rundblick, m
Rundsicht, f
Panoramablick, m
Panoramaaussicht, f
- ♦ panoramic view
- ♦ panorama

Rundblick bieten auf etw
- ♦ provide a panoramic view of s.th.
- ♦ provide a panorama of s.th.
- ♦ offer a panoramic view of s.th.
- ♦ offer a panorama of s.th.

Rundbogen, m
- ♦ circular arch

Runde, f (Gesellschaft)
- ♦ circle
- ♦ group

Runde, f (Getränk)
- ♦ round

Runde, f (Rundgang)
- ♦ round

Runde, f (Spiel)
- ♦ round

runde Badewanne, f
- ♦ round bathtub
- ♦ round bath

runde Cottage, f
- ♦ round cottage

Runde drehen im Becken *coll*
- ♦ take a dip in the pool *coll*

runde flache Platte, f
(Geschirr)
- ♦ round flat platter

Runde geht auf meine Rechnung
- ♦ round is on me

Runde Golf, f
- ♦ round of golf

Runde Golf spielen
- ♦ play a round of golf
- ♦ have a round of golf

Runde machen durch das Haus
Rundgang machen durch das Haus
- ♦ do a round of the house

Runde machen durch die Lokale
- ♦ do a round of the pubs *BE*
- ♦ do a round of the bars *AE*

runde Platte, f
(Geschirr)
- ♦ round platter

runder Tisch, m
Rundtisch, m
- ♦ round table

Runde schmeißen *coll*
einen ausgeben
Runde spendieren
- ♦ buy a round of drinks
- ♦ buy a round

runde Schüssel, f
- ♦ round bowl
- ♦ round dish

Runde Tennis spielen
- ♦ play a round of tennis

runde tiefe Platte, f
(Geschirr)
- ♦ round deep platter

Rundfahrt, f (Auto)
- ♦ drive round s.th.

Rundfahrt, f (generell)
- ♦ circular trip
- ♦ circular tour
- ♦ tour
- ♦ round trip

Rundfahrt in der Stadt, f
→ Stadtrundfahrt

Rundfahrt machen durch die Stadt (Auto)
- ♦ drive round the city
- ♦ drive round the town

Rundfahrt machen durch die Stadt (generell)
- ♦ do a tour of the city
- ♦ do a tour of the town
- ♦ make a tour of the city
- ♦ make a tour of the town

Rundfenster, n
rundes Fenster, n
- ♦ round window
- ♦ circular window

Rundflug, m (Besichtigung)
- ♦ sightseeing flight
- ♦ excursion flight

Rundflug, m (Strecke)
- ♦ circuit flight
- ♦ round voyage

Rundgang, m (Führung)
- ♦ tour

Rundgang, m (Gang)
- ♦ walk (around s.th.)

Rundgang beginnen durch etw
- ♦ begin a tour of s.th.

Rundgang durch das Bergwerk, m
Bergwerksführung, f
- ♦ tour of the mine

Rundgang durch das Museum, m (Führung)
- ♦ tour of the museum

Rundgang durch das Schloß, m (Führung)
- ♦ tour round the castle
- ♦ tour of the castle
- ♦ tour through the castle

Rundgang durch das Schloß, m (Gang)
Rundgang durch die Burg, m
- ♦ walk round the castle
- ♦ walk through the castle

Rundgang durch die Sammlungen, m
- ♦ tour of the collections

Rundgang durch etw, m (Führung)
- ♦ tour round s.th.
- ♦ tour of s.th.
- ♦ tour through s.th.

Rundgang durch etw, m (Gang)
- ♦ walk round s.th.

Rundgang machen durch etw (Führung)
- ♦ make a tour of s.th.
- ♦ do a tour of s.th.
- ♦ go on a tour of s.th.

Rundgespräch, n
- ♦ round-table discusssion

Rundhütte, f (Afrika)
(meist aus Lehm)
Rundhaus, n
- ♦ rondavel

Rundhütte, f (generell)
runde Hütte, f
- ♦ round hut

Rundkapelle, f
- ♦ round chapel

Rundkirche, f
- ♦ round church

Rundkurs, m
Rundweg, m
- ♦ circuit

Rundloipe, f
(Ski)
- ♦ cross-country circuit

Rundreise, f (generell)
- ♦ circle trip
- ♦ circular tour
- ♦ circular trip
- ♦ tour
- ♦ round trip

Rundreise, f (Meer)
- ♦ round voyage

Rundreiseleiter, m
(begleitet die gesamte Reise)
- ♦ tour manager
- ♦ tour director
- ♦ tour guide
- ♦ guide

Rundreise machen durch Kanada
- ♦ make a tour of Canada
- ♦ tour Canada
- ♦ tour in Canada

Rundreise machen in Spanien
Rundreise machen durch Spanien
- ♦ tour Spain

Rundreise machen (Meer)

- ◆ tour in Spain
- ◆ make a tour of Spain

Rundreise machen (Meer)
- ◆ make a round voyage

Rundschreiben, n
- ◆ circular letter
- ◆ circular

Rundsitzgruppe, f
- (Wohnwagen)
- ◆ U-shaped dinette

Rundstrecke, f
- ◆ circular route
- ◆ circuit

Rundtanz, m
- ◆ round dance

Rundtheke, f
- runde Theke, f
- ◆ round counter

Rundtisch, m
- → runder Tisch

Rundtischbestuhlung, f
- ◆ round-table seating
- ◆ roundtable-style seating

Rundtischform, f
- (Bestuhlung)
- Rundtischstil, m
- ◆ round-table style

Rundtischworkshop, m
- Workshop am runden Tisch, m
- ◆ round-table workshop

Rundturm, m
- runder Turm, m
- ◆ round tower

Rund-um-die-Uhr-Dienst m
- Rund-um-die-Uhr-Service m
- 24-Stunden-Service m
- Tag-und-Nacht-Dienst m
- ◆ round-the-clock service

Rund-um-die-Uhr-Service, m
- → Rund-um-die-Uhr-Dienst

Rund-um-die-Uhr-Telefondienst, m
- ◆ round-the-clock telephone service
- ◆ 24-hour telephone service

Rund-um-die-Uhr-Zimmerservice, m
- ◆ round-the-clock room service

rund und voll fressen sich *vulg*
- sich vollstopfen
- ◆ stuff oneself
- ◆ gorge oneself with food

Rundwanderung, f
- ◆ circular walking tour
- ◆ circular hiking tour
- ◆ circular walk
- ◆ circular hike

Rundwanderweg, m
- ◆ circular walk
- ◆ round walk
- ◆ circular hiking trail
- ◆ circular walking trail

Rundwanderwegenetz, n
- ◆ network of circular walks
- ◆ network of round walks

Rundweg, m
- ◆ round walk
- ◆ circular walk

Rundzelt, n
- rundes Zelt, n
- ◆ round tent
- ◆ bell tent

Rüpel, m
- ◆ lout
- ◆ yob *fam*

rupfen (Geflügel)
- ◆ pluck

rupfen jn *figur coll*
- ausnehmen jn *coll*
- neppen jn
- ◆ pluck s.o. *coll*
- ◆ rip off s.o. *coll*
- ◆ fleece s.o. *coll*

Rupie, f
- ◆ rupee

Russe, m
- ◆ Russian

Russin, f
- ◆ Russian girl
- ◆ Russian woman
- ◆ Russian

russisch, adj
- ◆ Russian, adj

russische Art, adv *gastr*
- ◆ Russian style, adv *gastr*

Russischer Abend, m
- ◆ Russian Evening
- ◆ Russian Night

russischer Service, m
- Service à la russe, m FR
- ◆ Russian service
- ◆ service à la russe *FR*

russisches Bad, n
- ◆ Russian bath

russisches Menü, n
- ◆ Russian menu

russische Speisekarte, f
- ◆ Russian menu

Rußland
- ◆ Russia

Rußlandreise, f (nach Rußland)
- Reise nach Rußland, f
- ◆ tour to Russia
- ◆ journey to Russia
- ◆ trip to Russia

Rußlandurlaub, m
- ◆ Russian vacation *AE*
- ◆ Russian holiday *BE*

rüsten
- ◆ make s.th. ready
- ◆ prepare s.th.

rüsten sich für etw
- sich vorbereiten auf etw
- ◆ prepare for s.th.

rüsten sich zu einem Fest
- sich auf ein Fest vorbereiten
- ◆ prepare for a festival

rustikal, adj
- ◆ rustic, adj

rustikale Atmosphäre, f
- ◆ rustic atmosphere

rustikaler Gasthof, m
- ◆ rustic inn

rustikaler Speisesaal, m
- ◆ rustic dining room

rustikaler Stil, m
- ◆ rustic style

rustikales Dekor, n
- rustikaler Dekor, m
- ◆ rustic decor *AE*
- ◆ rustic décor *BE*

rustikales Hotel, n
- ◆ rustic hotel

rustikales Restaurant, n
- ◆ rustic restaurant

rustikales Zimmer, n
- ◆ rustic room

rustikale Umgebung, f
- ◆ rustic surroundings *pl*

Rustikalität, f
- ◆ rusticity

Rüstung, f
- ◆ armor *AE*
- ◆ armour *BE*

Rüstungssammlung, f
- ◆ collection of armor *AE*
- ◆ collection of armour *BE*

Rüstzeit, f
- ◆ setting-up time

Rutschbahn, f
- → Rutsche

Rutsche, f
- (Spielplatz)
- Rutschbahn, f
- ◆ slide
- ◆ chute

Rutte, f
- (Fisch)
- Trüsche, f
- Aalrutte, f
- Aalputte, f
- Aalquappe, f
- ◆ burbot
- ◆ eelpout

Ruwer, f
- ◆ Ruwer River, the
- ◆ River Ruwer, the
- ◆ Ruwer, the

Ruwerwein, m
- ◆ Ruwer wine

Ryokan, m
- (japanisches Hotel)
- ◆ ryokan

S

Saal, m
♦ hall
♦ large room
Saal anmieten
→ Saal mieten
Saalanmietung, f
Hallenanmietung, f
♦ renting a hall
♦ hiring a hall *BE*
Saalausschmückung, f
→ Saaldekoration
Saalbalkon, m
Hallenbalkon, m
♦ hall balcony
Saalbar, f
Hallenbar, f
♦ hall bar
Saalboy, m
Boy m
Laufbursche m
♦ hall boy *AE*
♦ boy
Saalchef, m (Kasino etc.)
♦ hall manager
Saalchef, m (Oberkellner) *SCHW*
→ Oberkellner
Saaldekoration, f
Saalausschmückung, f
Saalschmuck, m
Hallendekoration, f
Hallenschmuck, m
♦ hall decoration
Saal dekorieren
→ Saal schmücken
Saaleingang, m
Halleneingang, m
♦ hall entrance
Saal faßt 123 Personen
Halle faßt 123 Personen
♦ hall accommodates 123 persons
Saalgröße, f
Hallengröße, f
♦ hall size
♦ size of a hall
Saal hat Platz für 123 Personen
Saal bietet für 123 Personen Sitzplätze
Halle hat Platz für 123 Personen
Halle bietet für 123 Personen Sitzplätze
♦ hall seats 123 persons
Saal ist festlich geschmückt
Halle ist festlich geschmückt
♦ hall is festively decorated
Saal ist unterteilbar
Halle ist unterteilbar
♦ hall is subdivisible
Saalkapazität, f
Hallenkapazität, f

♦ capacity of a hall
♦ hall capacity
Saalkellner, m SCHW
→ Kellner
Saalkosten, pl
Hallenkosten, pl
♦ hall costs *pl*
♦ hall cost
Saal läßt sich in sechs kleinere Einheiten unterteilen
Halle läßt sich in sechs kleinere Einheiten unterteilen
♦ hall divides into six smaller units
Saalmiete, f
Hallenmiete, f
♦ hall rental *AE*
♦ hall hire *BE*
Saal mieten
Saal anmieten
Halle mieten
♦ rent a hall
♦ hire a hall *BE*
Saal mieten für eine Tagung
♦ rent a hall for a meeting
♦ rent a room for a meeting
♦ hire a hall for a meeting *BE*
♦ hire a room for a meeting *BE*
Saalmieter, m
Hallenmieter, m
♦ hall renter *AE*
♦ hall hirer *BE*
Saalmietgebühr, f
♦ hall rental charge *AE*
♦ room rental charge *AE*
♦ hall hire charge *BE*
♦ room hiring charge *BE*
♦ room hire charge *BE*
Saal mit Fackelbeleuchtung, m
♦ torchlit hall
Saal mit flachem Boden, m
♦ flat-floored hall
Saal mit guter Akustik, m
Halle mit guter Akustik, f
♦ hall with good acoustics
Saal nimmt das ganze Erdgeschoß ein
Halle nimmt das ganze Erdgeschoß ein
♦ hall occupies the entire first floor *AE*
♦ hall occupies the entire ground floor *BE*
Saalordner, m
♦ hall usher
♦ usher
♦ hall steward
♦ steward
Saalordnerdienst m
♦ usher service
Saalpacht, f
Hallenpacht, f
♦ hall lease

Saal pachten von jm
♦ lease a hall from s.o.
Saalpächter, m
Hallenpächter, m
♦ hall leaseholder
Saalplan, m
Hallenplan, m
♦ hall plan
♦ plan of the hall
Saalschmuck, m
→ Saaldekoration
Saal schmücken
Saal dekorieren
♦ decorate a hall
Saaltisch, m
Hallentisch, m
♦ hall table
Saaltochter, f SCHW
→ Kellnerin
Saalvermieter, m
Hallenvermieter, m
♦ hall renter *AE*
♦ hall lessor *iur*
♦ person renting a hall *AE*
♦ person letting a hall *BE*
Saalvermietung, f
Hallenvermietung, f
♦ renting (out) a hall
♦ hall rental *AE*
♦ hall hire *BE*
♦ hiring out a hall *BE*
♦ letting a hall *BE*
Saal verpachten an jn
♦ lease a hall to s.o.
Saal war ganz voll
Halle war ganz voll
♦ hall was packed
Saal wurde bald voll
Halle wurde bald voll
♦ hall soon filled
Saar, f
♦ Saar River, the
♦ River Saar, the
♦ Saar, the
Saarland, n
(Region)
♦ Saarland
♦ Saar, the
Saarländer, m
♦ Saarlander
saarländisch, adj
♦ Saarland, adj
Saartal, n
♦ Saar valley, the
Saarwein, m
♦ Saar wine
Saccharin, n
♦ saccharin

Sachanlagevermögen

Sachanlagevermögen, n
  Anlagevermögen, n
  ♦ tangible assets *pl*
  ♦ fixed assets *pl*
Sachbeschädigung, f
  ♦ damage to property
  ♦ property damage
Sachbezüge, m pl
  ♦ remuneration in kind
  ♦ payment in kind
Sachen packen *coll*
  ♦ pack one's things *coll*
Sachen packen *coll*
  seine Sachen packen
  ♦ pack one's bags *coll*
  ♦ pack up one's things *coll*
Sachkosten, pl
  → Materialkosten
Sachmangel, m
  ♦ defect of quality
  ♦ defect in quality
Sachschaden, m
  ♦ material damage
Sachse, m
  ♦ Saxon
Sachsen
  (Land)
  ♦ Saxony
Sachsen-Anhalt
  (Land)
  ♦ Saxony-Anhalt
Sachsenwald, m
  ♦ Saxon Forest, the
Sächsin, f
  ♦ Saxon girl
  ♦ Saxon woman
  ♦ Saxon
sächsisch, adj (historisch)
  ♦ Saxon, adj
sächsisch, adj (Land Sachsen)
  ♦ Saxonian, adj
Sächsische Schweiz, f
  (Region)
  ♦ Saxon Switzerland
  ♦ Saxonian Switzerland
sächsische Zeit, f
  ♦ Saxon times *pl*
Sachverständiger, m (Bauten)
  ♦ surveyor
Sack, m
  ♦ sack
Sackbahnhof, m
  Kopfbahnhof, m
  ♦ terminus
Sackgasse, f
  ♦ cul-de-sac
  ♦ blind alley
Sackhüpfen, n
  → Sackrennen
Sack Kartoffeln, m
  ♦ sack of potatoes
Sacklaufen, n
  → Sackrennen
Sackrennen, n
  Sackhüpfen, n
  Sacklaufen, n
  ♦ sack race *AE*
  ♦ sack-race *BE*
Safari, f
  ♦ safari

Safariausflug, m
  ♦ safari excursion
  ♦ safari trip
Safaribüro, n
  ♦ safari office
Safaribus, m
  ♦ safari bus
  ♦ safari coach *BE*
Safariclub, m
  ♦ safari club
Safaridorf, n
  ♦ safari village
Safariexperte, m
  ♦ safari expert
Safarifahrt, f
  ♦ safari trip
  ♦ safari ride
Safarifahrzeug, n
  ♦ safari vehicle
Safarifirma, f
  ♦ safari firm
  ♦ safari company
Safariflugzeug, n
  ♦ safari plane
Safariführer, m
  ♦ safari guide
Safarigesellschaft, f
  Safarifirma, f
  ♦ safari company
  ♦ safari firm
Safarijeep, m
  ♦ safari jeep
Safarilodge, f
  ♦ safari lodge
Safari machen
  auf (eine) Safari gehen
  ♦ go on (a) safari
Safari mit Wildbeobachtung, f
  ♦ game-viewing safari
Safaripark, m
  ♦ safari park
Safaripicknick, n
  ♦ safari picnic
Safaripreis, m
  ♦ safari price
Safariprogramm, n
  ♦ safari program *AE*
  ♦ safari programme *BE*
Safariritt, m
  ♦ safari ride
Safariroute, f
  Safaristrecke, f
  ♦ safari route
Safaritourismus, m
  ♦ safari tourism
Safaritourist, m
  ♦ safari tourist
Safari- und Freizeitpark, m
  ♦ safari and leisure park
Safariurlaub, m
  Safariferien, pl
  ♦ safari vacation *AE*
  ♦ safari holiday *BE*
Safariurlauber, m
  Safariferiengast, m
  ♦ safari vacationer *AE*
  ♦ safari holidaymaker *BE*
Safariveranstalter, m
  ♦ safari operator
Safarizelt, n
  ♦ safari tent

Safe, m
  Tresor, m
  Panzerschrank, m
  ♦ safe
  ♦ depository *AE*
Safefach, n
  Tresorfach, n
  ♦ safe deposit box
  ♦ safety deposit box
Safegebühr, f
  Safemietgebühr, f
  Tresorgebühr, f
  Tresormietgebühr, f
  ♦ safe rental charge
  ♦ safe rental fee
  ♦ safe hire charge *BE*
  ♦ safe hire fee *BE*
  ♦ safe keeping charge *BE*
Safemiete, f
  → Safegebühr
Safe mieten
  Tresor mieten
  ♦ rent a safe *AE*
  ♦ hire a safe *BE*
Safenummer, f
  Tresornummer, f
  ♦ safe number
Safeschlüssel, m
  Tresorschlüssel, m
  ♦ safe key
Safe vermieten
  Tresor vermieten
  ♦ rent (out) a safe
  ♦ hire out a safe *BE*
Safran, m
  ♦ saffron
Safranreis, m
  ♦ saffron rice
Saft, m
  ♦ juice
Saftbar, f
  ♦ juice bar
Saftgetränk, n
  ♦ juice drink
Saftglas, n
  ♦ juice glass
saftig, adj
  (Obst, Fleisch)
  ♦ juicy, adj
  ♦ succulent, adj
saftige Rechnung, f *coll*
  gepfefferte Rechnung, f *coll*
  gesalzene Rechnung, f *coll*
  ♦ swinging bill *coll*
saftiges Steak, n
  ♦ succulent steak
  ♦ juicy steak
Saftkur, f
  ♦ juice diet
saftlos, adj
  (Obst, Fleisch)
  ♦ not juicy, adj
  ♦ juiceless, adj
Saftpreis, m
  ♦ juice price
sagenumwoben, adj
  sagenhaft, adj
  legendär, adj
  ♦ legendary, adj
sagenumwobener Rhein, m
  ♦ legendary Rhine

Sahara, f
 ♦ Sahara, the
 ♦ Sahara Desert, the
Sahara durchqueren
 ♦ cross the Sahara
Sahne, f
 Obers, n ÖST
 ♦ cream
Sahnejoghurt, m
 ♦ cream yoghurt
 ♦ cream yogurt
 ♦ cream yoghourt
Sahnekännchen, n
 ♦ cream jug
 ♦ creamer AE
Sahnekuchen, m
 ♦ cream cake
Sahnetorte, f
 Cremetorte, f
 ♦ cream gâteau BE
 ♦ cream gateau AE
saignant, adj FR
 nicht durchgebraten, adj
 innen noch roh, adj
 ♦ saignant, adj FR
 ♦ very red, adj
Saison, f
 ♦ season
saisonabhängige Beschäftigung, f
 → Saisonbeschäftigung
saisonabhängiger Preis, m
 ♦ seasonal price
 ♦ seasonal rate
Saison abkürzen
 → Saison verkürzen
Saisonabschluß, m
 ♦ conclusion of the season
Saisonabschlußfahrt, f
 ♦ end-of-season trip
 ♦ end-of-season tour
 ♦ end-of-season journey
saisonal, adj
 saisonabhängig, adj
 jahreszeitlich, adj
 saisonbedingt, adj
 ♦ seasonal, adj
saisonale Auslastungsschwankung, f
 ♦ seasonal load factor fluctuation
 ♦ seasonal load factor variation
saisonale Belegungsschwankung, f
 saisonale Auslastungsschwankung, f
 ♦ seasonal occupancy fluctuation
 ♦ seasonal fluctuation in occupancy
 ♦ seasonal occupancy variation
 ♦ seasonal variation in occupancy
saisonale Bereinigung, f
 (Statistik)
 ♦ seasonal adjustment
saisonale Feier, f
 ♦ seasonal celebration
saisonale Nachfrage, f
 ♦ seasonal demand
saisonale Nachfrageschwankung, f
 ♦ seasonal fluctuation in demand
saisonale Nachfragespitze, f
 saisonbedingtes Nachfragehoch, n
 ♦ seasonal peak in demand
saisonaler Besucherverkehr, m
 ♦ seasonal visitor traffic

saisonaler Einfluß, m
 Saisoneinfluß, m
 ♦ seasonal influence
saisonaler Faktor, m
 ♦ seasonal factor
saisonales Angebot n
 → Saisonangebot
saisonale Schwankung, f
 ♦ seasonal fluctuation
 ♦ seasonal variation
saisonales Nachfragetief, n
 saisonbedingtes Nachfrageloch, n
 ♦ seasonal trough in demand
saisonale Unterschiede berücksichtigen
 ♦ allow for seasonal variations
saisonale Variation, f
 saisonale Schwankung, f
 ♦ seasonal variation
saisonale Verteilung, f
 (z.B. des Tourismus)
 ♦ seasonal spread
Saisonalität, f
 Saisonabhängigkeit, f
 ♦ seasonality
Saisonalitätsgrad, m
 ♦ level of seasonality
saisonal sein
 saisonbedingt sein
 ♦ be seasonal
Saisonangebot, n
 saisonales Angebot, n
 ♦ seasonal supply
 ♦ seasonal availability
 ♦ seasonal offer
Saisonarbeit, f
 saisonale Arbeit, f
 ♦ seasonal work
Saisonarbeiter m
 ♦ seasonal worker
 ♦ itinerant worker
Saisonarbeitsplatz, m
 → Saisonstelle
Saisonartikel, m
 ♦ seasonal article
Saisonaufpreis, m
 ♦ seasonal surcharge
Saisonaufschlag, m
 → Saisonzuschlag
Saisonauftakt, m
 ♦ start to the season
Saison ausdehnen
 → Saison verlängern
saisonbedingter Buchungsanstieg, m
 ♦ seasonal increase in bookings
saisonbedingter Reservierungsanstieg, m
 ♦ seasonal increase in reservations
saisonbedingte Schließung, f
 ♦ seasonal closure
Saison beenden
 ♦ end the season
 ♦ finish the season
Saisonbeginn, m
 ♦ start of the season
 ♦ beginning of the season
 ♦ commencement of the season form
Saison beginnen
 ♦ begin the season
 ♦ start the season
 ♦ commence the season form
Saisonbeginn verschieben
 ♦ postpone the beginning of the season

Saisonbeginn vorverlegen
 Beginn der Saison vorverlegen
 ♦ advance the beginning of the season
 ♦ bring forward the beginning of the season
saisonbereinigt, adj
 ♦ seasonally adjusted, adj
saisonbereinigter Überschuß, m
 ♦ seasonally adjusted surplus
saisonbereinigte Werte, m pl
 ♦ seasonally adjusted values pl
Saisonbeschäftigung, f
 saisonabhängige Beschäftigung, f
 ♦ seasonal employment
Saison beschließen
 Saison abschließen
 ♦ conclude a season
Saisonbetrieb, m (Firma)
 ♦ seasonal establishment
 ♦ seasonal operation
Saisonbetrieb, m (Service)
 ♦ seasonal service
Saisonbuchung f
 ♦ season booking AE
 ♦ seasonal booking BE
Saisoncampingplatz, m
 saisonaler Campingplatz, m
 ♦ seasonal campsite
 ♦ seasonal campground AE
 ♦ seasonal camping site BE
 ♦ seasonal camping ground BE
Saisondauer, f
 ♦ duration of the season
 ♦ length of the season
Saison dauert 123 Tage
 ♦ season lasts 123 days
Saison dauert von April bis Oktober
 ♦ season lasts from April to October
Saisondauer verlängern
 ♦ extend the length of the season
 ♦ extend the season
Saisoneinfluß, m
 → saisonaler Einfluß
Saisonende, n
 Saisonausklang, m
 ♦ end of the season
Saison endet
 ♦ season ends
 ♦ season closes
Saisonentlassung, f
 saisonbedingte Entlassung, f
 ♦ seasonal layoff AE
 ♦ seasonal lay-off BE
Saisonergebnis, n
 ♦ seasonal result
 ♦ season's result
Saisonermäßigung f
 ♦ season reduction AE
 ♦ seasonal reduction BE
Saison eröffnen (mit etw)
 Saison beginnen (mit etw)
 ♦ open the season (with s.th.)
 ♦ begin the season (with s.th.)
 ♦ commence the season (with s.th.) form
 ♦ start the season (with s.th.)
Saisoneröffnung, f
 Eröffnung der Saison, f
 ♦ opening of the season
Saisoneröffnungsfahrt, f
 ♦ opening-of-season trip

Saisoneröffnungskonzert 656

Saisoneröffnungskonzert, n
 ◆ opening-of-season concert
 ◆ opening concert of the season
Saison erstreckt sich bis Oktober
 ◆ season stretches until October
Saisonfinale, n
 → Saisonende
Saison geht dem Ende zu
 ◆ season is drawing to its close
 ◆ season is getting to its end
Saisongemüse, n
 ◆ vegetables in season *pl*
Saisongericht, n
 Gericht der Saison, n
 ◆ seasonal dish
 ◆ dish of the season
Saisongeschäft, n
 saisonales Geschäft, n
 ◆ seasonal business
 ◆ seasonal trade
Saisongewerbe, n
 saisonales Gewerbe, n
 ◆ seasonal trade
Saison haben
 (Früchte etc.)
 ◆ be in season
Saisonhöhepunkt, m
 → Höhepunkt der Saison
Saisonhotel, n
 ◆ season hotel *AE*
 ◆ seasonal hotel *BE*
Saisonhotelier, m
 ◆ keeper of a season hotel *AE*
 ◆ keeper of a seasonal hotel *BE*
Saisonhotellerie, f
 ◆ seasonal hotel trade
Saison ist auf dem Höhepunkt
 ◆ season is at its height
 ◆ season is at its peak
Saison ist eröffnet
 ◆ season has begun
Saison ist flau
 ◆ season is dull
Saison ist kurz
 ◆ season is short
Saison ist lang
 ◆ season is long
Saison ist zu Ende
 Saison ist beendet
 ◆ season is finished
 ◆ season has ended
Saisonkarte, f (Fahrkarte, Eintritt)
 ◆ seasonal ticket
Saisonkarte, f (Speisekarte)
 ◆ menu of the season
 ◆ seasonal menu
Saison klingt aus
 ◆ season is coming to an end
Saisonkonzession, f
 ◆ seasonal license
 ◆ seasonal licence
 ◆ seasonal concession
Saisonkraft, f
 → Saisonarbeiter
Saison kürzen
 → Saison verkürzen
Saisonlänge, f
 ◆ length of (a) season
 ◆ length of the season

Saison läuft schlecht
 Saison ist schlecht
 ◆ season is poor
Saisonmitte, f
 ◆ mid-season
 ◆ middle of a season
Saisonnachfrage, f
 → saisonale Nachfrage
Saison nähert sich
 Saison rückt näher
 Saison kommt näher
 ◆ season is approaching
Saison nähert sich dem Ende
 ◆ season comes to an end
Saisonnier, m *FR*
 → Saisonarbeiter
Saisonpersonal, n
 ◆ seasonal staff
 ◆ seasonal personnel
Saisonplatz, m
 (z.B. Camping)
 ◆ seasonal site
Saisonpreis, m
 ◆ season price *AE*
 ◆ season rate *AE*
 ◆ seasonal price *BE*
 ◆ seasonal rate *BE*
Saisonrabatt, m
 saisonaler Rabatt, m
 ◆ seasonal discount
Saisonreservierung, f
 ◆ season reservation *AE*
 ◆ seasonal reservation *BE*
Saisonrest, m
 Rest der Saison, m
 ◆ remainder of the season
 ◆ rest of the season
Saisonrestaurant, n
 ◆ season restaurant *AE*
 ◆ seasonal restaurant *BE*
Saison rückt näher
 ◆ season is coming up
 ◆ season is drawing near
Saisonsalat, m
 Salat der Saison, m
 ◆ salad in season
Saison schließt mit etw ab
 ◆ season concludes with s.th.
Saison schreitet voran
 ◆ season progresses
Saisonschwankung, f
 → saisonale Schwankung
Saisonspezialität, f
 saisonale Spezialität, f
 Spezialität der Saison, f
 ◆ seasonal specialty *AE*
 ◆ seasonal speciality *BE*
Saisonspitze, f
 ◆ seasonal peak
 ◆ peak of the season
 ◆ peak of a season
Saisonstart, m
 → Saisonbeginn
Saisonstelle, f
 Saisonarbeitsstelle, f
 Saisonarbeitsplatz, m
 Saisonarbeit, f
 ◆ seasonal job
Saisonstellplatz, m
 (Camping)

 ◆ seasonal pitch
 ◆ season pitch
Saisonverbrauch, m
 ◆ seasonal consumption
Saison verkürzen
 Saison kürzen
 Saison abkürzen
 ◆ curtail a season
 ◆ make a season shorter
 ◆ shorten a season
 ◆ cut a season short
 ◆ reduce the length of a season
Saisonverkürzung, f
 Verkürzung der Saison, f
 ◆ curtailment of a season
 ◆ curtailing a season
 ◆ shortening (of) a season
Saison verlängern
 ◆ extend the season
 ◆ lengthen the season
 ◆ prolong the season
Saisonverlängerung, f
 ◆ extension of the season
 ◆ extending the season
 ◆ lengthening (of) the season
Saisonverlauf, m
 Verlauf der Saison, m
 ◆ course of the season
Saisonverlauf analysieren
 ◆ analyse the season
 ◆ analyze the course of the season *AE*
Saisonvertrag, m
 ◆ seasonal contract
Saisonzeit, f
 → Saison
Saisonzuschlag m
 ◆ season supplement *AE*
 ◆ seasonal supplement *BE*
Sake, m
 Reiswein, m
 ◆ sake
 ◆ saké
 ◆ saki
 ◆ rice wine
Salami, f
 ◆ salami
Salamisandwich, n/m
 Salamibrot, n
 ◆ salami sandwich
Salat, m
 ◆ salad
Salat anmachen
 ◆ dress the salad
Salatbar, f
 ◆ salad bar
Salatbesteck, n
 ◆ salad servers *pl*
Salatbüfett, n
 ◆ salad buffet
Salat der Jahreszeit, m
 → Salat der Saison
Salat der Saison, m
 ◆ seasonal salad
 ◆ salad in season
Salatdressing, n
 Salatsauce, f
 Salatsoße, f
 ◆ salad dressing *AE*
 ◆ salad-dressing *BE*
 ◆ dressing

Salatgabel, f
- salad fork

Salat machen
- make a salad

Salatmayonnaise, f
- mayonnaise dressing

Salatöl, n
- salad oil
- salad-oil BE

Salatplatte, f (Essen)
- dish of mixed salads

Salatplatte, f (Geschirr)
- salad platter

Salatrezept, n
- salad recipe

Salatschleuder, f
- salad spinner

Salatschüssel, f
- salad bowl
- salad dish

Salatschwenker, m
- salad shaker

Salatsuppe, f
Lattichsuppe, f
- lettuce soup

Salatteller, m
- salad plate

Salattheke, f
- salad counter

Salat vom Büfett, m
- buffet salad

Salatwagen, m
- salad cart AE
- salad trolley BE

Salat zubereiten
- prepare a salad

Salbei, m
- sage

Salbeitee, m
- sage tea

Saldo, m
- balance

Saldovortrag, m
Saldoübertrag, m
- balance carried forward

Sales Guide, m
Verkaufshandbuch, n
- sales guide

Sales Mix, m
→ Umsatzzusammensetzung

Salmi, n
Wildgeflügelragout, n/m
- salmi

Salmisoße, f
- salmi sauce

Salmonellen, pl
- salmonellae pl

Salmonellenausbruch, m
- salmonella outbreak
- outbreak of salmonella

Salmonellenvergiftung, f
- salmonella poisoning

Salon, m
- parlor AE
- parlour BE
- salon
- drawing room AE
- drawing-room BE

Salonbar, f
(in der Lounge)
Loungebar f

Clubbar f
- lounge bar

Salondeck, n (Schiff)
- saloon deck

Salonservice, m
- lounge service

Salonwagen, m (Zug)
- parlor car AE
- club car AE
- lounge car BE

Saloon, m
- saloon

Saloon Bar, f
(in Pub)
Clubbar, f
- saloon bar

Salpikon, m
- salpicon

Salz, n
- salt

salzarm, adj
- low-salt, adj

salzarme Kost f
- low-salt diet

Salzbad, n
(Aktivität)
- salt bath

Salzbergwerk, n
- salt mine

Salzbrezel, f
→ Brezel

Salzburger Alpen, die, pl
- Salzburg Alps, the pl

Salzburger Festspiele, n pl
- Salzburg Festival, the

salzen (etw)
- salt (s.th.)

salzen etw zu stark
- salt s.th too highly

Salzfaß, n
(auf Tisch)
- saltcellar AE
- salt-cellar BE

salzfrei, adj
- salt-free, adj

salzfreie Kost f
- salt-free diet

Salzgebäck, n
- savory snacks AE pl
- savoury snacks BE pl

Salzgehalt, m
- salt content

salzhaltig, adj
- saline, adj

salzhaltige Quelle, f
- saline spring

Salzhering, m (generell)
- salted herring

Salzhering, m (mariniert)
- pickled herring

salzig, adj
- salty, adj

salziges Essen, n
- salty food

salziges Essen macht durstig
salzige Speisen machen durstig
- salty food makes one thirsty

Salz in der Suppe, n figur
- that extra something

Salzkammergut, n
(Region)
- Salzkammergut, the

Salzkartoffeln, f pl
- boiled potatoes BE pl

Salzkorn, n
Körnchen Salz, n
- grain of salt

Salzlake, f gastr
Salzlauge, f gastr
- brine gastr

salzlos, adj
- saltless, adj

salzlose Diät, f
- no-salt diet

Salzmandel, f
- salted almond

Salznüsse, f pl
gesalzene Nüsse, f pl
- salted nuts pl

Salzquelle, f
- salt spring
- saline spring

Salzsee, m
- salt lake

Salzsieder, m
- salt boiler

Salzsiederfest, n
- salt boilers' festival

Salzstadt, f
- salt town

Salzstange, f
- salt stick
- salt pretzel AE

Salzstraße, f hist
- salt road hist

Salzstreuer, m
- saltshaker AE
- salt-cellar BE

Salzwasser, n (Küche)
- salted water

Salzwasser, n (Sole)
Sole, f
- saltwater AE
- salt water BE

Salzwasserbad, n (Aktivität)
Solebad, f
- saltwater bath AE
- salt-water bath BE

Salzwasserbecken, n
Solebecken, n
- saltwater pool AE
- salt-water pool BE

Salzwasserfisch, m
- saltwater fish AE
- salt-water fish BE

Salzwasserhallenbad, n
→ Solehallenbad

Salzwüste, f
- salt flats pl

Samba, f ÖST m
- samba

Samba tanzen
- dance the samba

Sambia
- Zambia

Sambier, m
- Zambian

Sambierin, f
- Zambian girl

sambisch

- ◆ Zambian woman
- ◆ Zambian

sambisch, adj
- ◆ Zambian, adj

Sammelanmeldung, f
- ◆ collective registration
- ◆ group registration
- ◆ collective booking
- ◆ group booking

Sammelbuchung f
- ◆ collective booking

Sammelfahrschein, m
- ◆ collective ticket

Sammelgarage, f
  Garagenhalle, f
- ◆ open garage
- ◆ multi-car garage
- ◆ large-capacity garage

Sammelkonto, n
- ◆ ledger account
- ◆ collective account

Sammelkonto eröffnen bei einem Hotel
- ◆ open a ledger account with a hotel

Sammelkonto eröffnen für jn
- ◆ open a ledger account for s.o.

Sammellager, n (Camp)
- ◆ assembly camp

sammeln etw
- ◆ collect s.th.

Sammelpaß, m
- ◆ collective passport
- ◆ group passport

Sammelpunkt, m
- ◆ assembly point
- ◆ rallying point

Sammelrechnung, f
- ◆ collective bill

Sammelreservierung, f
- ◆ collective reservation

Sammelruf, m
  Sammeldurchsage, f
- ◆ intercom message

Sammelrufanlage, f
  Sprechanlage, f
- ◆ Tannoy
- ◆ intercom system

Sammelversicherung, f
- ◆ collective insurance

Sammelvisum, n
- ◆ group visa
- ◆ collective visa

Sammler, m
- ◆ collector

Sammlung, f
- ◆ collection

Sammlung Alter Meister, f
  (Gemälde)
- ◆ collection of Old Masters

Sammlung beherbergen
- ◆ house a collection

Sammlung ist untergebracht in etw
- ◆ collection is housed in s.th.

Sammlung von Artefakten, f
  Sammlung von (prä)historischen Werkzeugen, f
- ◆ collection of artifacts
- ◆ collection of artefacts

Sammlung von Kunstschätzen, f
- ◆ collection of art treasures

Sammlung von Kunstwerken, f
  Kunstsammlung, f
- ◆ collection of works of art

Sammlung von Meisterwerken, f
- ◆ collection of masterpieces

Samoa
- ◆ Samoa

Samowar, m
- ◆ samovar

Samstag, m
  Sonnabend, m
- ◆ Saturday

Samstagabend, m
- ◆ Saturday evening

Samstagnacht, f
  Nacht zum Sonntagmorgen, f
- ◆ Saturday night

Samstag nachts, adv
- ◆ on Saturday night, adv
- ◆ on Saturday nights, adv

samstags, adv
- ◆ on Saturdays, adv
- ◆ on Saturday, adv

Samstagseinnahmen, f pl
- ◆ Saturday takings pl

Samstags Ruhetag
  (Hinweisschild)
  Samstag Ruhetag
- ◆ Closed on Saturday
- ◆ Closed on Saturdays

Samstags Tanz
  (Hinweisschild)
- ◆ Dancing on Saturday
- ◆ Dancing on Saturdays

Samtstrand, m
  samtener Strand, m
- ◆ velvety beach

Sanatorium, n
- ◆ sanatorium
- ◆ sanatarium AE
- ◆ sanitarium AE
- ◆ sanitorium AE

Sanatoriumsaufenthalt, m
- ◆ stay at a sanatorium
- ◆ stay at a sanitorium AE
- ◆ stay at a sanatarium AE
- ◆ stay at a sanitarium AE

Sandale, f
- ◆ sandal

Sandbad, n
- ◆ sand bath

Sandbadebucht, f (groß)
- ◆ sand bathing bay AE
- ◆ sandy bathing bay BE

Sandbadebucht, f (klein)
- ◆ sand bathing cove AE
- ◆ sandy bathing cove BE

Sandbahn, f
  Aschenbahn, f
- ◆ dirt track

Sandbahnrennen, n
  Aschenbahnrennen, n
- ◆ dirt-track race

Sandbank vor dem Hafen, f
- ◆ harbor bar AE
- ◆ harbour bar BE

Sandbucht, f (groß)
- ◆ sand bay AE
- ◆ sandy bay BE

Sandbucht, f (klein)
- ◆ sand cove AE
- ◆ sandy cove BE

Sandburg, f
- ◆ sand castle

Sandburg bauen
- ◆ build a sand castle

Sandburgenbauen, n
- ◆ sand-castle building

Sandburgenwettbewerb, m
- ◆ sand-castle competition
- ◆ sand-castle contest

Sandcampingplatz, m
- ◆ sand campsite
- ◆ sand campground AE
- ◆ sand camping site BE
- ◆ sand camping ground BE
- ◆ sand site

Sanddüne, f
- ◆ sand dune

Sandkasten, m
  (für Kinder)
- ◆ sandbox AE
- ◆ sandpit BE

Sandplatz, m (Camping)
- ◆ sand site AE
- ◆ sandy site BE

Sandplatz, m (Kinder)
  → Sandkasten

Sandsack, m
- ◆ sandbag

Sandspielplatz, m
  → Sandplatz

Sandstein, m
- ◆ sandstone

Sandsteinfels, m
- ◆ sandstone rock

Sandsteingebäude, n
- ◆ sandstone building

Sandsteinhaus, n
- ◆ sandstone house

Sandsteinmauer, f
- ◆ sandstone wall

Sandsteinrelief, n
- ◆ sandstone relief

Sandstrand m
- ◆ sand beach AE
- ◆ sandy beach BE

Sandsturm, m
- ◆ sand storm

Sandtennisanlage, f
- ◆ sand tennis complex

Sandtennisplatz, m
- ◆ sand tennis court AE
- ◆ sandy tennis court BE

Sandufer, n (Meer, Binnensee)
- ◆ sand shore AE
- ◆ sandy shore BE

Sand- und Kieselstrand, m
- ◆ sand and shingle beach

Sandwich, n/m
  belegtes Brot, n
  belegtes Brötchen, n
- ◆ sandwich

Sandwichbar f
- ◆ sandwich bar

Sandwichcafé, n
- ◆ sandwich café BE
- ◆ sandwich cafe AE

Sandwich essen
  belegtes Brot essen
- ◆ have a sandwich
- ◆ eat a sandwich

Sandwichimbiß, m
- ◆ sandwich lunch

Sandwichkarte, f
 ♦ sandwich menu
Sandwichladen, m
 ♦ sandwich shop
Sandwichplatte, f
 (Geschirr)
 ♦ sandwich tray
Sandwichstand, m
 ♦ sandwich stand
 ♦ sandwich stall BE
sanft abfallender Strand, m
 flach abfallender Strand, m
 ♦ gently sloping beach
Sänfte, f
 ♦ sedan chair AE
 ♦ sedan-chair BE
 ♦ sedan
 ♦ litter
sanfter Tourismus, m
 sanftes Reisen, n
 umweltverträglicher Tourismus, m
 Ökotourismus, m
 ökologischer Tourismus, m
 ♦ discreet tourism
 ♦ soft tourism
 ♦ ecotourism
 ♦ ecological tourism
 ♦ sustainable tourism
sanfter Tourist, m
 → Ökotourist
sanftes Reisen, n
 sanfter Tourismus, m
 Ökotourismus, m
 ökologischer Tourismus, m
 umweltverträglicher Tourismus, m
 ♦ soft tourism
 ♦ ecotourism
 ♦ ecological tourism
 ♦ green tourism
 ♦ sustainable tourism
Sänger, m
 Sängerin, f
 ♦ singer
Sängerfest, n
 ♦ singing festival
 ♦ choir festival
Sangria, f
 ♦ sangria
sanieren etw
 ♦ redevelop s.th.
 ♦ reconstruct s.th.
saniert, adj
 ♦ redeveloped, adj
 ♦ reconstructed, adj
Sanierung, f
 ♦ redevelopment
 ♦ reconstruction
Sanierungskosten, pl
 ♦ redevelopment costs pl
 ♦ reconstruction costs pl
Sanierungsplan, m
 ♦ redevelopment scheme
 ♦ reconstruction scheme
Sanierungsprogramm, n
 ♦ redevelopment program AE
 ♦ redevelopment programme BE
Sanierungsprojekt, n
 ♦ redevelopment project
 ♦ reconstruction project
sanitär, adj
 ♦ sanitary, adj

Sanitärarmatur, f
 sanitäre Armatur, f
 ♦ sanitary fitting
Sanitärausstattung, f
 ♦ sanitary equipment
Sanitärblock, m
 (Camping)
 ♦ sanitary block
sanitäre Armatur, f
 → Sanitärarmatur
Sanitäreinheit, f
 (Statistik)
 ♦ sanitary unit
Sanitäreinrichtung, f
 sanitäre Einrichtung, f
 ♦ sanitary facility
 ♦ sanitation
sanitäre Verhältnisse, n pl
 ♦ sanitary conditions pl
Sanitärgebäude, n
 (Camping)
 ♦ sanitary building
Sanitärkabine, f
 ♦ sanitary cubicle
Sanitärraum m
 ♦ sanitary room
Sanitärvorschriften, f pl
 ♦ sanitary regulations pl
Sanitäter, m
 ♦ first-aid man
 ♦ ambulance man
Sanitätsdienst, m
 ♦ medical service
Sanitätskasten, m
 ♦ first-aid kit
Sanitätsraum, m
 ♦ first-aid room
Sanitätswache, f
 ♦ ambulance station
 ♦ first-aid post
Sansibar
 ♦ Zanzibar
Sardelle, f
 Anchovis, f
 Anschovis, f
 ♦ anchovy
Sardellenbutter, f
 ♦ anchovy butter
Sardellenfilet, n
 ♦ anchovy fillet
 ♦ anchovy filet
Sardine, f
 ♦ sardine
Sardinensalat, m
 ♦ sardine salad
Sardinensandwich, n/m
 Sardinenbrot, n
 ♦ sardine sandwich
Sardinien
 ♦ Sardinia
Sardinier, m
 Sarde, m
 ♦ Sardinian
Sardinierin, f
 Sardin, f
 ♦ Sardinian girl
 ♦ Sardinian woman
 ♦ Sardinian
 ♦ Sardian girl
 ♦ Sardian woman

sardinisch, adj
 sardisch, adj
 ♦ Sardinian, adj
 ♦ Sardian, adj
Sarkophag, m
 ♦ sarcophagus
Satellitenfarbfernsehen, n
 ♦ satellite color TV AE
 ♦ satellite color television AE
 ♦ satellite colour TV BE
 ♦ satellite colour television BE
Satellitenfernsehen, n
 Satelliten-TV, n
 ♦ satellite TV
 ♦ satellite television
Satellitenkonferenz f
 ♦ satellite conference
 ♦ conference via satellite
Satellitenstadt, f
 ♦ satellite town
Satellitentelefon, n
 ♦ satellite telephone
Satelliten-TV, n
 → Satellitenfernsehen
Satsuma, f
 ♦ satsuma
satt, adj
 ♦ full, adj
 ♦ full up, adj coll
Sattel, m
 ♦ saddle
satteln etw
 ♦ saddle s.th.
Satteltasche, f
 ♦ saddlebag AE
 ♦ saddle-bag BE
satter Magen m
 → voller Magen
satt essen sich (an etw)
 ♦ eat one's fill (of s.th.)
satt haben etw
 ♦ be sick of s.th.
satt sein
 ♦ have had enough
 ♦ have had sufficient
 ♦ be full
 ♦ be full up coll
Satz Bettzeug, m
 ♦ complement of bedding
satzungsgemäß, adj
 statutengemäß, adj
 gesetzlich (vorgeschrieben), adj
 gesetzlich (begründet), adj
 ♦ statutory, adj
sauber, adj
 ♦ clean, adj
saubere Luft, f
 ♦ clean air
sauberer Strand, m
 ♦ clean beach
sauberes Zimmer, n
 ♦ clean room
saubere Umwelt, f
 ♦ clean environment
saubere Wäsche, f
 → frische Wäsche
Sauberkeit, f
 ♦ cleanliness
Sauberkeit des Strandes, f
 ♦ cleanliness of the beach

Sauberkeit eines Zimmers 660

Sauberkeit eines Zimmers, f
- cleanliness of a room

Saubohne, f
- broad bean
- horse bean

Sauce, f
→ Soße

Saucenkoch, m
→ Soßenkoch

Sauce vinaigrette, f FR
- sauce vinaigrette FR
- French dressing

Saucier, m FR
Soßenkoch, m
Saucenkoch, m
- saucier FR
- sauce cook

Sauciere, f
→ Soßenschüssel

Saudiaraber, m
- Saudi Arabian
- Saudi

Saudiaraberin, f
- Saudi Arabian girl
- Saudi Arabian woman
- Saudi Arabian

Saudi-Arabien
- Saudi Arabia

saudiarabisch, adj
- Saudi Arabian, adj

sauer, adj
- sour, adj

Sauerampfer, m
- sorrel

Sauerbraten, m
- sauerbraten
- marinated beef

Sauerkirsche, f
Morelle, f
Weichsel, f ÖST
- sour cherry
- morello

Sauerkirschsorbet, n
Weichselsorbet, n ÖST
- sour cherry sorbet
- morello sorbet

Sauerkrautsuppe, f
- sauerkraut soup

Sauerland, n
- Sauerland, the

sauerländisch, adj
- Sauerland, adj

Säuerling, m
- acidulous spring water

Sauermilch, f
Dickmilch, f
- sour milk
- soured milk

Sauerrahm, m
saure Sahne, f
- sour cream

sauer schmecken
- taste sour

Sauerstoff, m
- oxygen

Sauerstoffflasche, f
- oxygen bottle

Sauerstoffmaske, f
- oxygen mask

Sauerstoffzelt, n
- oxygen tent

Sauerteig, m
- leaven
- sourdough AE

Sauerteigbrot, n
- sourdough bread AE

sauer werden
(Speise, Milch)
- turn sour
- go off

Saufabend, m
- boozing bout coll
- booze coll
- evening drinking session
- bust coll

Saufbruder, m coll
Säufer, m
- boozer coll
- tippler coll
- toper coll
- soak sl

saufen
- booze
- tope sl
- soak sl
- swill inform derog

saufen etw
- tope s.th. sl
- drink s.th.

Säufer, m
- drunkard
- alcoholic
- guzzler inform
- boozer coll
- swiller coll

Sauferei, f vulg
Saufgelage, n
Besäufnis, n
- soak sl
- drinking binge BE coll
- drinking bout BE coll

Saufgelage, n
Sauferei, f
Besäufnis, n
- drinking bout
- carousal
- booze-up BE coll
- drinking binge BE coll
- soak sl

Saufkumpan, m coll
Trinkkumpan, m
- drinking buddy coll
- drinking pal coll

Sauforgie, f
- drinking orgy

Saufparty, f coll
- boozy party coll

Saufraß, m vulg
Hundefraß, m derog
Schweinefraß, m derog
- muck vulg
- grub derog
- swill derog
- pigswill derog

Sauftour, f vulg
→ Kneipenbummel, Zechtour

Sauftour machen vulg
Zechtour machen
Bierreise machen
auf eine Sauftour gehen vulg
- go barhopping AE
- go on a pub crawl BE

Säugling, m
→ Baby

Säuglingsbetreuung, f (generell)
- baby care

Säuglingszimmer, n
- babies' room

Säulenhalle, f
- columned hall

Säulentisch, m
(mit Säulenfuß)
- pedestal table

säumig, adj
verspätet, adj
unpünktlich, adj
- tardy, adj
- late, adj
- slow, adj

säumiger Zahler, m
- slow payer
- defaulter
- tardy payer

Saumpfad, m
- mule track

Saumur, m FR
- Saumur FR

Sauna, f
(Raum und Aktivität)
- sauna
- sauna bath

Saunaanlage, f
Saunakomplex, m
- sauna complex

Saunaausstattung, f
- sauna equipment

Saunabad, n
→ Sauna

saunabaden
saunieren
- have a sauna bath
- take a sauna bath
- have a sauna
- take a sauna

Sauna benutzen
- use the sauna

Saunabenutzer m
- sauna user
- person using the sauna

Saunabenutzung, f
- use of the sauna
- using the sauna

Saunabenutzungszuschlag, m
Saunazuschlag, m
- supplement for the use of the sauna
- supplement for using the sauna

Saunabereich, m
- sauna area

Saunabesuch, m
- visit to the sauna
- sauna session

Saunabesucher, m
- sauna visitor
- visitor to the sauna

Sauna einbauen
Sauna installieren
- install a sauna
- instal a sauna AE

Saunagang, m
Saunabesuch, m
- sauna going

Saunagebühr f
- sauna charge
- sauna fee

Sauna installieren
→ Sauna einbauen

Saunakabine, f
- sauna cubicle
- sauna cabin

Saunakomplex, m
→ Saunaanlage

Saunaofen, m
- sauna heater

Saunaraum, m
- sauna room

Saunatauchbecken, n
- sauna plunge pool

Saunavergnügen, n
- sauna pleasure
- sauna enjoyment

Sauna zur kostenlosen Benutzung durch Hausgäste
- sauna for free use of resident guests

Saunazuschlag, m
- sauna supplement

saunen
saunabaden
- have a sauna
- take a sauna

saunieren
→ saunabaden

Säure, f
(Wein)
- acidity

saure Gurken, f pl
- pickled cucumbers pl
- pickles pl

Sause, f coll
Saufgelage, n
- booze-up coll

Sause machen coll
- have a booze-up coll

Saustall, m
Schweinestall, m
- pigsty

sautieren etw gastr
- sauté s.th. gastr

Sauvignon, m FR
- Sauvignon FR

Sauvignon blanc, m FR
- Sauvignon blanc FR

Savanne, f
- savannah
- savanna

Savoyen
- Savoy

Savoyer Alpen, die, pl
- Savoy Alps, the, pl

Savoyerart, adv gastr
nach Savoyerart, adv gastr
- Savoyan style, adv gastr

S-Bahn, f
- light railway BE
- rapid transit AE
- suburban railway BE

S-Bahnhof, m
S-Bahnstation, f
- rapid transit station AE
- suburban train station
- light railway station BE

S-Bahn-Zug, m
S-Bahn, f

- rapid transit AE
- suburban train

SB-Laden, m
→ Selbstbedienungsladen

SB-Restaurant, n
→ Selbstbedienungsrestaurant

Scampi, pl
- scampi pl

Schabe, f
Küchenschabe, f
Kakerlak, m
- cockroach
- roach AE

schaben etw gastr
- scrape s.th. gastr

schäbiges Hotel, n
- shabby hotel
- seedy hotel

schäbiges Zimmer n
abgewohntes Zimmer n
- shabby room

Schach, n
- chess

Schachbrett, n
- chessboard

Schachclub, m
Schachverein, m
- chess club

Schachcomputer, m
- chess computer

Schachfan, m
- chess fan

Schachfestival, n
- chess festival

Schachfigur, f
- chessman AE
- chess-man BE

Schachmeisterschaft, f
- chess championship

Schachprofi, m
- chess professional

Schachspiel, n
Schachpartie, f
- game of chess
- chess game

Schach spielen
- play chess
- have a game of chess

Schachspieler, m
- chess player

Schachtel Pralinen, f
- box of chocolates

Schachtel Zigaretten, f
Packung Zigaretten, f
- pack of cigarettes AE
- packet of cigarettes BE

Schachturnier, n
- chess tournament

Schachweltmeister, m
- world chess champion

Schachweltmeisterschaft, f
- world chess championship

Schachwettbewerb, m
- chess competition

Schachwettkampf, m
- chess contest

Schadensersatz, m
Schadenersatz, m
Entschädigung, f
- compensation
- damages pl

Schadensersatz ablehnen
Schadensersatz verweigern
- deny compensation

Schadensersatz anbieten jm für etw
- offer compensation to s.o. for s.th.

Schadensersatzanspruch, m
Regreß, m
Ersatzanspruch, m
- compensation claim
- claim for compensation

Schadensersatz erhalten für etw
Schadensersatz erhalten für etw
Schadensersatz bekommen für etw
- receive compensation for s.th.
- get compensation for s.th.

Schadensersatz fordern (für etw von jm)
- claim damages (for s.th. from s.o.)
- claim compensation (for s.th. from s.o.)

Schadensersatzforderung, f
- claim for damages
- claim for compensation
- compensation claim

Schadensersatzformular, n
- claim form

Schadensersatz geltend machen
Schadensersatz verlangen
- claim damages

Schadensersatz leisten
- pay compensation
- pay damages

Schadensersatz leisten jm
- pay compensation to s.o.
- pay s.o. compensation

Schadensersatz verlangen
Schadensersatz geltend machen
- claim compensation
- claim damages

Schadensersatzzahlung, f
- compensation payment
- payment of compensation

Schadensersatz zusprechen jm
(Gericht)
- award damages to s.o.

Schadensschätzung, f
- damage estimate

Schaden verursachen
- cause damage

schadhaft, adj
beschädigt, adj
fehlerhaft, adj
- damaged, adj
- faulty, adj
- defective, adj

Schädlingsbekämpfung, f
- pest control

Schädlingsbekämpfungsmittel, n
- pesticide

Schäferbrunnen, m
- shepherds' fountain
- shepherd fountain

Schäferfest, n
- shepherds' festival

Schäferhütte, f
- shepherd's hut

Schäferquelle, f
- shepherds' spring

Schaffner, m (Straßenbahn, Bus)
- conductor

Schaffner, m (Zug)
- conductor AE
- guard BE

Schaffnerin, f (Straßenbahn, Bus)
- conductress

Schale, f (Geschirr)
- dish

Schale, f (Muschel, Ei)
- shell

Schalen, f pl
(von Kartoffeln etc)
- peelings pl

schälen etw (Ei)
- shell s.th.

schälen etw (generell)
pellen etw
- peel s.th.
- pare s.th.

Schalentier, n
- crustacean

schales Bier, n
abgestandenes Bier, n
- flat beer
- stale beer

schalldicht, adj
lärmisoliert, adj
- soundproof, adj AE
- sound-proof, adj BE

schalldichte Diskothek, f
- soundproof discotheque AE
- sound-proof discotheque BE

schalldichtes Zimmer, n
- soundproof room AE
- sound-proof room BE

schalldichte Trennwand, f (beweglich)
schalldichte Zwischenwand, f
- soundproof partition AE
- sound-proof partition BE

schalldichte Trennwand, f (Mauer)
schalldichte Zwischenwand, f
- soundproof dividing wall AE
- sound-proof dividing wall BE

schalldicht machen etw
- make s.th. soundproof AE
- soundproof s.th. AE
- make s.th. sound-proof BE
- sound-proof s.th. BE

Schallgeschwindigkeit, f
- speed of sound

schallisoliert, adj
- sound-insulated, adj

schallisoliertes Zimmer n
- sound-insulated room

Schallisolierung, f
Schalldämpfung, f
- sound insulation

Schallmauer, f
Schallgrenze, f
- sound barrier

Schallmauer durchbrechen
- break the sound barrier

Schallplatte, f
- record

Schallplattenspieler, m
Plattenspieler, m
- record player AE
- record-player BE

Schälmesser, n
- paring knife
- peel knife

Schalotte, f
- shallot

Schalottenbutter, f
- shallot butter

Schalter, m (Büro)
Counter, m
- desk
- counter

Schalter, m (Licht)
- switch

Schalterangestellter, m
Schalterbeamter, m
- counter clerk

Schalterbeamter, m (Fahrkarten)
Fahrkartenaussteller, m
- ticket agent AE
- booking clerk BE

Schalterpersonal, n
Counterpersonal, n
- counter staff
- counter personnel

Schaltjahr, n
- leap year

Schampus, m coll
Champagner, m
Sekt, m
- bubbly coll
- fizz coll

Schankbier, n
- beer on tap

Schankerlaubnis, f
→ Schankkonzession

Schankgast, m jur
- person visiting a bar AE
- person visiting a public house BE

Schankgehilfe, m
- potboy AE
- potman AE
- pot-boy BE
- pot-man BE

Schankkellner, m
- barman

Schankkellnerin, f
→ Bardame

Schankkonzession für alkoholische Getränke, f
Schankerlaubnis für alkoholische Getränke, f
- liquor license
- liquor licence
- justices' license BE
- justices' licence BE

Schanklizenz, f
→ Schankkonzession

Schanklokal, n jur
(mit Ausschank alkoholischer Getränke)
- licensed premises pl jur
- licenced premises pl jur

Schankraum, m
Trinkstube, f
Ausschank, m
- taproom
- bar room

Schanksteuer, f
- restaurant tax

Schankstube, f
- bar room
- bar parlor AE
- bar-parlour BE
- taproom

Schanktresen, m
→ Tresen

Schankwirt, m
- licensed victualler BE jur

Schankzeit, f
(für alkoholische Getränke)
- licensed hours pl
- licenced hours pl
- licensing hours pl
- licencing hours pl
- permitted hours pl

Schankzeit verlängern
- extend the licensed hours
- extend the licenced hours
- extend the licensing hours
- extend the licencing hours
- extend the permitted hours

Schankzeitverlängerung, f
(für alkoholische Getränke)
- extension of the licensed hours
- extension of the licenced hours
- extension of the licensing hours
- extension of the licencing hours

Scharen von Touristen, f pl
- droves of tourists pl

scharf, adj gastr
scharf gewürzt, adj
- hot, adj gastr
- highly seasoned, adj

scharfe Kurve, f
- sharp bend
- sharp curve

scharfes Messer, n
- sharp knife

scharf gewürzt, adj
- highly seasoned, adj
- hot, adj

scharf gewürztes Essen, n
- hot food

scharf gewürztes Gericht, n
- hot dish
- highly seasoned dish

Schar von Gästen, f
- drove of guests

Schaschlik, m
- shashlik

schattenlos, adj
- unshaded, adj

schattenloser Campingplatz, m
- unshaded campsite
- unshaded campground AE
- unshaded camping site BE
- unshaded camping ground BE
- unshaded site

schattenloser Platz, m (Camping)
- unshaded site

schattenloser Stellplatz, m (Camping)
- unshaded pitch

schattige Ecke, f
- shady corner

schattiger Biergarten, m
- shaded beer garden

schattiger Ort, m
- shady place

schattiger Stellplatz, m
(Camping)
- shady pitch

Schatz, m
- treasure

schätzen etw
zu schätzen wissen etw
- appreciate s.th.

Schatzhaus, n
- treasure house

Schatzkammer, f
- treasure trove

Schatzsuche, f
- ♦ treasure hunt AE
- ♦ treasure-hunt BE

Schau, f
- ♦ show

Schau abhalten
- ♦ hold a show

Schau abziehen
- Schau veranstalten
- ♦ put on a show

Schau auf die Beine Stelle stellen fam
- Schau organisieren
- ♦ lay on a show fam

Schaubild, n
- graphische Darstellung, f
- Karte, f
- Diagramm, n
- Tafel, f
- ♦ chart

Schaubühne, f
- → Bühne

Schaufel, f
- ♦ shovel

Schaufelraddampfer, m
- Raddampfer, m
- ♦ paddle-wheel steamer
- ♦ paddle steamer
- ♦ side-wheel steamer AE
- ♦ side-wheeler AE

Schaufensterbummel, m
- ♦ window-shopping

Schaufensterbummel machen
- ♦ go window-shopping

Schaufensterbummler, m
- ♦ window-shopper

Schauhaus, n
- (z.B. für potentielle Käufer)
- Musterhaus, n
- ♦ show house

Schau ist spärlich besucht
- ♦ show is sparsely attended

Schaukasten m
- (Vitrine)
- ♦ showcase

Schaukel, f
- ♦ swing

Schaukelpferd, n
- ♦ rocking horse AE
- ♦ rocking-horse BE
- ♦ rocker AE

Schaukelstuhl, m
- ♦ rocking chair AE
- ♦ rocking-chair BE
- ♦ rocker

Schauküche, f
- ♦ open-to-view kitchen

Schaum, m (Bier)
- ♦ froth
- ♦ head

Schaum, m (generell)
- ♦ foam

Schaum, m (Seife)
- ♦ lather

Schaumbad, n
- ♦ bubble bath

schäumendes Bier, n
- ♦ foaming beer

schäumen vor Wut
- ♦ foam with rage

Schaumgummi, n
- ♦ foam rubber

Schaumgummimatratze, f
- ♦ foam rubber mattress
- ♦ foam mattress

schaumig, adj
- ♦ frothy, adj

Schau mit internationalen Stars, f
- ♦ show featuring international stars

Schaumkrone, f
- (z.B. auf Bierglas)
- Blume, f
- ♦ frothy head
- ♦ head

Schaumlöffel, m
- Schaumkelle, f
- ♦ skimmer

Schaumlöschgerät, n
- Schaumlöscher, m
- ♦ foam extinguisher

Schau muß weitergehen
- ♦ show must go on

Schaumwein, m
- Perlwein, m
- ♦ sparkling wine
- ♦ fizz AE coll
- ♦ bubbly BE coll

Schaumweinsteuer f
- ♦ tax on sparkling wines

Schauspieler, m
- ♦ actor

Schauspielerin, f
- ♦ actress

Schauspielfestival, n
- ♦ drama festival

Schauspielhaus, n
- ♦ playhouse

Schauspielschule, f
- ♦ drama school

Schau stehlen jm
- ♦ steal the show from s.o.

Schausteller, m
- ♦ showman

Schaustellerei, f
- ♦ showmanship

Schau veranstalten
- Ausstellung veranstalten
- ♦ organise a show
- ♦ organize a show

Schauwohnung, f
- Musterwohnung, f
- ♦ show apartment AE
- ♦ show flat BE

Scheck, m
- ♦ check AE
- ♦ cheque BE

Scheck ausfüllen
- ♦ fill out a check AE
- ♦ complete a check AE
- ♦ fill in a cheque BE
- ♦ complete a cheque BE

Scheck ausstellen
- ♦ make out a check AE
- ♦ make out a cheque BE
- ♦ write out a check AE
- ♦ write out a cheque BE

Scheck ausstellen auf jn
- ♦ make a check payable to s.o. AE
- ♦ make a cheque payable to s.o. BE

Scheck beiliegen im Wert von DM 123
- ♦ enclose a check to the value of DM 123 AE
- ♦ enclose a cheque to the value of DM 123 BE

Scheckbetrug, m
- ♦ check fraud AE
- ♦ cheque fraud BE

Scheckbuch, n
- ♦ checkbook AE
- ♦ cheque-book BE

Scheck einlösen
- ♦ cash a check AE
- ♦ cash a cheque BE

Scheckeinlösung, f
- ♦ cashing a check AE
- ♦ check cashing AE
- ♦ cashing a cheque BE
- ♦ cheque cashing BE

Scheck gegenzeichnen
- ♦ countersign a check AE
- ♦ countersign a cheque BE

Scheck girieren
- Scheck indossieren
- ♦ endorse a check AE
- ♦ endorse a cheque BE

Scheck im Wert von DM 123, m
- ♦ check to the value of DM 123 AE
- ♦ cheque to the value of DM 123 BE

Scheck ist gedeckt
- ♦ check is covered AE
- ♦ cheque is covered BE

Scheck ist nicht übertragbar
- ♦ check is not negotiable AE
- ♦ cheque is not negotiable BE

Scheck ist ungedeckt
- ♦ check is not covered AE
- ♦ cheque is not covered BE

Scheck ist zahlbar bei Vorlage
- Scheck ist zahlbar bei Sicht
- ♦ check is payable on presentation AE
- ♦ cheque is payable on presentation BE

Scheckkarte, f
- ♦ check card AE
- ♦ cheque card BE

Scheckkarteninhaber, m
- ♦ check card holder AE
- ♦ cheque card holder BE

Scheck platzt
- ♦ check bounces AE
- ♦ cheque bounces BE

Scheck senden an jn
- Scheck schicken an jn
- ♦ send a check to s.o. AE
- ♦ send a cheque to s.o. BE

Scheck senden über DM 123
- ♦ send a check for DM 123 AE
- ♦ send a cheque for DM 123 BE

Scheck über DM 123, m
- ♦ check for DM 123 AE
- ♦ cheque for DM 123 BE

Scheck vorlegen
- ♦ present a check AE
- ♦ present a cheque BE

Scheibe, f (Fenster)
- ♦ pane
- ♦ window pane

Scheibe, f (Käse etc)
- ♦ slice

Scheibe Brot, f
- ♦ slice of bread

Scheibe Fleisch, f
- ♦ slice of meat

Scheibenbrot, n
- ♦ sliced bread

Scheinwerfer

Scheinwerfer, m
- ♦ spotlight

Schellfisch, m
- ♦ haddock

Schellfischfilet, n
- ♦ haddock fillet
- ♦ haddock filet AE
- ♦ fillet of haddock
- ♦ filet of haddock AE

Schellfischsteak, n
- ♦ haddock steak

Schemel m
- ♦ stool

Schenke, f
→ Gaststätte, Kneipe, Wirtshaus

Schere, f
- ♦ scissors pl
- ♦ pair of scissors

Scheune, f
- ♦ barn

Scheurebe, f
- ♦ Scheurebe

Schi, m ÖST
→ Ski

Schicht, f (Arbeit)
- ♦ shift

Schicht, f (Lage)
Lage, f
- ♦ layer

Schichtarbeit, f
- ♦ shift work

Schichtarbeiten, n
- ♦ shift working

Schichtbetrieb m
→ Schichtarbeit

Schichtführer, m
→ Schichtleiter

Schichtleiter, m
Schichtführer, m
- ♦ shift leader
- ♦ shift boss

schick, adj
- ♦ smart, adj inform
- ♦ in style
- ♦ swish, adj inform obs
- ♦ chic, adj FR

schick ausgehen (Essen)
- ♦ dine out in style

schick ausgehen (Kleider)
- ♦ go out looking smart

schicken jn auf die Reise
- ♦ send s.o. on a journey
- ♦ send s.o. on a trip
- ♦ send s.o. on a tour

schicker Ferienort, m
schicker Urlaubsort, m
- ♦ smart resort BE inform
- ♦ swish resort BE obs

Schickeria, f
- ♦ trendies pl
- ♦ jet set
- ♦ chic set
- ♦ fun set

schickes Hotel, n
- ♦ smart hotel BE inform
- ♦ swish hotel BE obs

schickes Restaurant, n
- ♦ smart restaurant BE inform
- ♦ swish restaurant BE obs

schick essen
→ gepfegt essen

schickes Viertel, n
(Stadtviertel)
- ♦ fashionable quarter

Schickimicki, m
- ♦ trendy type

schick möbliert, adj
- ♦ smartly furnished, adj

schick möbliertes Zimmer, n
- ♦ smartly furnished room

schick speisen
→ gepflegt speisen

Schiebebett, n (Beistellbett)
→ Beistellbett

Schiebebett, n (unter höherem Bett)
→ Rollbett

Schiebedach, n
- ♦ sliding roof

Schiebefenster, n
- ♦ sash window
- ♦ sliding window
- ♦ slide window

Schiebesitz, m
- ♦ sliding seat

Schiebetür f
- ♦ sliding door

Schiebewand, f
- ♦ sliding partition
- ♦ sliding screen

Schiebung, f
- ♦ racket

schiedsgerichtlich, adv
- ♦ by arbitration, adv

Schiedsgerichtshof, m
- ♦ court of arbitration

Schiedsgerichtsklausel, f
Schlichtungsklausel, f
- ♦ arbitration clause

Schiedsrichter, m (Schiedsverfahren)
→ Schlichter

Schiedsrichter, m (Sport)
- ♦ referee

Schiedsrichter, m (Tennis)
- ♦ umpire

schiedsrichterlich entscheiden
- ♦ settle by arbitration

Schiedsverfahren, n
Schlichtungsverfahren, n
- ♦ arbitration proceedings pl

Schieferboden, m
- ♦ slate floor

Schieferdach, n
- ♦ slate roof
- ♦ slated roof

schiefergedecktes Dach, n
- ♦ slated roof

Schieferhöhle, f
- ♦ slate cavern

Schiefersteinbruch, m
- ♦ slate quarry

schiefer Turm, m
- ♦ leaning tower

Schiefer Turm von Pisa, m
- ♦ Leaning Tower of Pisa, the

Schienenbus, m
- ♦ railcar

Schießanlage, f
→ Schießstand

Schießbude, f
- ♦ shooting gallery

Schießen, n
Schießsport, m
- ♦ shooting

Schießplatz, m
- ♦ shooting arena

Schießsport, m
- ♦ shooting sports

Schießstand, m
- ♦ shooting range
- ♦ rifle range
- ♦ range

Schießübung, f
- ♦ target practice
- ♦ target practise

Schießwettbewerb, m
- ♦ shooting competition
- ♦ shooting contest

Schi fahren ÖST
→ Ski fahren

Schiff, n (Kirche)
Kirchenschiff, n
- ♦ nave

Schiff, n (Transportmittel)
- ♦ ship
- ♦ boat

Schiff abtakeln
- ♦ unrig a ship

Schiffahrt, f
- ♦ navigation

Schiffahrtsgeschichte, f
Seefahrtsgeschichte, f
- ♦ maritime history

Schiffahrtsgesellschaft, f
Schiffahrtslinie, f
- ♦ shipping line
- ♦ shipline AE
- ♦ shipping company
- ♦ liner company

Schiffahrtslinie, f
Schiffahrtsgesellschaft, f
- ♦ shipline AE
- ♦ shipping line

Schiffahrtsmuseum, n
- ♦ maritime museum
- ♦ shipping museum

Schiffahrtsverbindung, f
- ♦ shipping link

Schiffahrtsweg, m
- ♦ shipping route
- ♦ shipping lane

schiffbar, adj
mit Schiffen befahrbar, adj
- ♦ navigable, adj

schiffbarer Fluß, m
- ♦ navigable river

Schiffbau, m
Schiffsbau, m
- ♦ shipbuilding

Schiff chartern
- ♦ charter a ship
- ♦ charter a boat

Schiffchen, n (Speise)
- ♦ barquette

Schiff geht vom Hafen ab
- ♦ ship leaves from the port
- ♦ boat leaves from the port

Schiff mieten
- ♦ rent a ship
- ♦ hire a ship BE
- ♦ rent a boat
- ♦ hire a boat BE

Schiff nehmen nach X
   Boot nehmen nach X
- take a boat to X
- take the boat to X

Schiffsanlegestelle, f
- landing-place
- quay
- wharf
- jetty

Schiffsarzt, m
- ship's doctor

Schiffsausflug, m
   Bootsausflug, m
- boat trip

Schiffsbrücke, f (auf dem Schiff)
   Brücke, f
- bridge
- ship's bridge

Schiffschaukel, f
- swingboat *AE*
- swing-boat *BE*

Schiffsfahrt von Hamburg nach Kapstadt, f
- boat trip from Hamburg to Cape Town

Schiffsführung, f
- tour of the ship
- tour of the boat

Schiffsjunge, m
- ship's boy

Schiffskapitän, m
- ship's captain

Schiffskellner, m
   Steward, m
- ship's steward
- steward

Schiffskoch, m
- ship's cook

Schiffsküche, f
   Bordküche, f
- ship's galley
- galley
- ship's kitchen
- cookhouse *AE*

Schiffsmannschaft, f
   Schiffsbesatzung, f
- ship's crew
- crew

Schiffsmodell, n
- ship model

Schiffsreise, f
   Seereise, f
- sea journey
- sea voyage
- voyage

Schiffsverkehr, m
- shipping

Schiffsverzeichnis, n
- ship directory

Schiffszubehörhändler, m
   Schiffshändler, m
- ship's chandler
- chandler

Schiffszug, m
   (mit Anschluß an ein Schiff)
- boat train

Schiffszugfahrkarte, f
- boat train ticket

Schiff vermarkten
- market a ship

Schild, n
- sign

Schildkröte, f (Land)
   Landschildkröte, f
- tortoise

Schildkröte, f (Meer)
   Seeschildkröte, f
- turtle

Schildkröteninsel, f
- tortoise island

Schildkrötensuppe, f
- turtle soup

Schilfmatte, f
- rush mat

Schillerdenkmal, n
- Schiller memorial

Schillerwein, m
- Schillerwein

Schinken, m
- ham

Schinkenbrot, n
- ham sandwich

Schinkensteak, n
- ham steak

Schirm, m
- umbrella

Schirmdach, n
   (z.B. über Hoteleingang)
- marquee

Schirmherr, m
- patron

Schirmherrin, f
- patroness

Schirmherrschaft, f
- patronage
- auspices
- aegis *lit*
- egis *lit*

Schirmherrschaft übernehmen von etw
- take over the patronage of s.th.
- agree to become patron
- become patron

Schirmherr sein bei etw
- act as patron for s.th.
- act as patron of s.th.

Schirmständer, m
- umbrella stand

Schirm stehenlassen
   Schirm vergessen
- leave one's umbrella behind

Schlackendiät, f
→ ballaststoffreiche Kost

Schlaf, m
- sleep

Schlafabteil, n
   (Zug)
- sleeping compartment
- sleeper compartment *BE*

Schlafanzugshosen, f pl
- pyjama trousers *BE pl*
- pajama pants *AE pl*

Schlafbedarf, m
- sleep requirement

Schlafbehandlung, f
   Schlafmittelbehandlung, f
- soporific treatment

Schlafbereich, m
   Unterkunftsbereich, m
- sleeping area
- bedroom area

Schläfchen, n
   kurzer Schlaf, m
   Nickerchen, n
- snooze
- nap
- short sleep

Schlafcouch, f
- sleeping couch
- divan bed
- studio couch
- convertible couch

Schlafdecke, f
   (zum Übernachten auf dem Boden)
- pallet *AE*

Schlaf des Gerechten, m
- sleep of the just

Schlaf des Gerechten schlafen
- sleep the sleep of the just

Schlafeinheit, f
   (Statistik)
- sleeping unit

schlafen
- sleep
- be asleep

schlafen auf dem Boden
- sleep on the floor

schlafen auf dem Strand
   am Strand schlafen
- sleep on the beach

schlafen auf der Erde
- sleep on the ground

schlafen auf der nackten Erde
- sleep on the bare ground

schlafen auf einer Luftmatratze
- sleep on an airmattress *AE*
- sleep on an air mattress *BE*

schlafen auf einer Matratze
- sleep on a mattress

schlafen auf einer Parkbank
- sleep on a park bench

schlafen bei offenem Fenster
   schlafen mit offenem Fenster
- sleep with the window open

schlafen bis in die Puppen
- sleep till all hours

schlafend, adv
- asleep, adv

schlafen die ganze Nacht
- sleep all night

schlafend stellen sich
- pretend to be asleep

schlafen gehen
- got to sleep
- roll in *fam*

schlafen im Auto
- sleep in the car

schlafen im Stehen
- sleep on one's feet

schlafen in einem Flugzeug
- sleep on a plane

schlafen in einem fremden Bett
- sleep in a strange bed

schlafen in einem Schloß
- sleep in a castle

schlafen in einem Zimmer
- sleep in one room

schlafen in getrennten Betten
- sleep in separate beds

schlafen in Ruhe
- sleep in peace

schlafen in seinen Kleidern
- sleep in one's clothes
- sleep with one's clothes on

schlafen legen sich
→ ins Bett gehen
schlafen mit jm
(Sex)
♦ sleep with s.o.
schlafen mit offenen Augen
♦ sleep with one's eyes open
Schlafen Sie fest! coll
♦ Sleep tight! coll
Schlafen Sie gut!
♦ Sleep well!
Schlafenszeit, f
♦ bedtime
schlafen unter js Dach
♦ sleep under s.o.'s roof
schlafen wie ein Klotz coll
♦ sleep like a log coll
schlafen wie ein Murmeltier coll
♦ sleep like a dormouse coll
schlafen wie ein Sack coll
♦ sleep like a top coll
Schläfer, m
Logiergast, m
Logisgast, m
Schlafgast, m
♦ sleeper
Schlafgalerie, f
♦ sleeping gallery
Schlafgast, m
Logiergast, m
Logisgast, m
Übernachtungsgast, m
♦ sleeping room guest AE
♦ overnight guest
♦ overnight visitor
♦ sleeper
♦ lodging guest AE
Schlafgelegenheit, f
♦ sleeping facility
Schlafgemach, n hist
(am feudalen Hof)
♦ bedchamber hist
Schlafhaus, n
(z.B. für Arbeiter)
Bettenhaus, n
♦ bunkhouse
Schlaf ist ungestört
♦ sleep is undisturbed
Schlafkabine, f (generell)
♦ sleeping cabin
Schlafkabine, f (Wohnwagen)
♦ bunk compartment
Schlafkamerad, m
→ Bettgenosse
Schlafkammer, f
kleines Schlafzimmer, n
♦ small bedroom
Schlafkoje, f
Koje, f
Bett, n
♦ sleeping berth
♦ berth
♦ bunk
Schlafkrankheit, f
♦ sleeping sickness
Schlafkur, f
♦ sleeping cure
♦ hypnotherapy
Schlafliege, f
♦ convertible divan

schlaflos, adj
♦ sleepless, adj
schlaflose Nacht, f
♦ sleepless night
schlaflose Nacht bereiten jm
♦ cause s.o. a sleepless night
♦ give s.o. a sleepless night
schlaflose Nacht verbringen
♦ spend a sleepless night
♦ pass a sleepless night
Schlaflosigkeit, f
♦ sleeplessness
♦ insomnia
Schlafmittel, n
♦ soporific
Schlafmütze, f (Mütze)
♦ nightcap
Schlafmütze, f (Person)
♦ sleepyhead
Schlaf nachholen
♦ catch up on sleep
Schlafparty, f
♦ slumber party
Schlafpavillon, m
Übernachtungspavillon, m
♦ bedroom pavilion
Schlafpille, f
♦ sleeping pill AE
♦ sleeping-pill BE
Schlafplatz, m (generell)
Schlafstelle, f
♦ sleeping place
♦ place to sleep
Schlafplatz, m (Koje)
→ Schlafkoje
Schlafplatz bereitstellen für jn
♦ provide s.o. with a place to sleep
Schlafplatz brauchen
Schlafplatz benötigen
♦ need a sleeping place
♦ require a sleeping place
Schlafquartier, n (Distrikt)
♦ sleeping quarter
Schlafquartier, n (Unterkunft)
♦ sleeping quarters pl
Schlafraum, m (mit Etagenbetten)
♦ bunkroom
Schlafraum, m (Volumen, Fläche)
Schlaffläche, f
♦ sleeping space
Schlafraum, m (Zimmer)
♦ sleeping room AE
♦ bedroom
Schlafraumetage, f
Bettengeschoß, n
♦ bedroom floor
Schlafraumflügel, m
→ Schlafraumtrakt
Schlafraumflur, m
Schlafraumkorridor, m
♦ bedroom corridor
Schlafraumhöherstufung, f
Schlafraumupgrading, n
♦ bedroom upgrading
Schlafraumkapazität, f
Übernachtungskapazität, f
♦ capacity of the bedrooms
♦ bedroom capacity
Schlafraumnachfrage, f
Schlafplatznachfrage, f
♦ demand for sleeping place

Schlafraumtrakt, m
Schlafraumflügel, m
Schlaftrakt, m
Unterkunftstrakt, m
Zimmertrakt, m
♦ bedroom wing
Schlafraumzahl, f
→ Schlafzimmerzahl
schläfrig, adj
→ verschlafen
Schläfrigkeit, f
♦ sleepiness
schläfrig machen jn
♦ make s.o. sleepy
Schlafritual, n
♦ bedtime ritual
Schlafsaal m
(z.B. in Jugendherberge)
♦ dormitory
♦ dorm coll
Schlafsaal nur für ein Geschlecht, m
♦ single sex dormitory
Schlafsaalunterbringung, f
→ Schlafsaalunterkunft
Schlafsaalunterkunft, f
(z.B. in Jugendherberge)
Schlafsaalunterbringung, f
♦ dormitory accommodation
Schlafsack, m
♦ sleeping bag AE
♦ sleeping-bag BE
Schlafsackquartier, n
♦ sleeping-bag quarters pl
Schlafsacktourist, m
→ Rucksacktourist
Schlafsackunterkunft, f
♦ sleeping-bag accommodation
Schlafsessel, m (Verkehrsmittel)
♦ sleeper seat
♦ reclining seat
Schlafsessel, m (Zimmer)
♦ chair bed
Schlafsitz, m
Schlafsessel, m
♦ sleeper chair
♦ sleeper seat
Schlafsofa, n
♦ convertible sofa
♦ sofa bed
Schlafstadt, f
♦ dormitory town
Schlafstelle, f
Schlafplatz, m
Platz zum Schlafen, m
♦ place to sleep
♦ sleeping place
Schlaf stören
♦ disturb s.o's sleep
♦ disturb one's sleep
Schlafstörungen, f pl
♦ sleeping disorders pl
♦ disturbed sleep
Schlafsucht, f
♦ narcolepsy
schlafsüchtig, adj
♦ narcoleptic, adj
Schlaftablette, f
♦ sleeping tablet
Schlaftrakt, m
→ Schlafraumtrakt

Schlaftrunk, m (alkoholisch)
　Schnäpschen, n
　♦ nightcap
Schlaftrunk, m (generell)
　Schlafgetränk, n
　♦ sleeping draught BE
schlaftrunken, adj
　♦ drowsy, adj
Schlafunterkunft, f
　(Gegensatz zu Wohnunterkunft)
　♦ sleeping accommodation
Schlafverhalten, n
　♦ sleeping behavior AE
　♦ sleeping behaviour BE
Schlafwagen, m
　(Zug)
　♦ sleeping car AE
　♦ sleeper
　♦ sleeping-car BE
　♦ sleeping carriage BE
　♦ wagon-lit FR
Schlafwagenabteil, n
　♦ sleeping-car compartment
　♦ sleeper section
Schlafwagenbett, n
　Schlafwagenkoje, f
　♦ sleeping-car berth
　♦ sleeper BE
Schlafwagenfahrt, f
　♦ journey in a sleeping car AE
　♦ ride in a sleeping car AE
　♦ journey in a sleeper AE
　♦ journey in a sleeping-car BE
　♦ ride in a sleeping-car BE
Schlafwagengesellschaft, f
　♦ sleeping-car company
Schlafwagenkarte, f
　♦ sleeping-car ticket
Schlafwagenschaffner, m
　♦ sleeping-car attendant
　♦ sleeping-car porter AE
Schlafwagenunterkunft, f
　Schlafwagenunterbringung, f
　♦ sleeping-car accommodation
Schlafwagenzug, m
　♦ sleeping-car train
Schlafwagenzuschlag, m
　♦ sleeping-car supplement
　♦ sleeper supplement
　♦ sleeping-carriage supplement BE
schlafwandeln
　♦ sleepwalk AE
　♦ sleep-walk BE
　♦ walk in one's sleep
Schlafwandeln, n
　Somambulismus, m
　♦ sleepwalking AE
　♦ sleep-walking BE
　♦ somnambulism
Schlafwandler, m
　Nachtwandler, m
　Somnambulist, m
　♦ sleepwalker AE
　♦ sleep-walker BE
　♦ somnambulist
Schlafzelt, n
　♦ sleeping tent
Schlafzimmer, n
　Schlafraum m
　♦ bedroom

Schlafzimmeraugen, n pl
　Schlafzimmerblick, m
　♦ bedroom look
　♦ come-to-bed eyes pl
Schlafzimmerbalkon m
　♦ bedroom balcony
Schlafzimmerbereich m
　♦ bedroom area
Schlafzimmerblock, m
　Schlafraumblock, m
　♦ bedroom block
Schlafzimmerboden, m
　♦ bedroom floor
Schlafzimmerdesign, n
　Schlafraumgestaltung, f
　♦ bedroom design
Schlafzimmerfenster, n
　Schlafraumfenster n
　♦ bedroom window
Schlafzimmerheizung f
　♦ bedroom heating
Schlafzimmer instandhalten
　♦ service a bedroom
Schlafzimmer kann in Wohnzimmer verwandelt werden
　♦ bedroom can be converted into a living room
Schlafzimmer mit Einbauschrank, n
　♦ bedroom with fitted wardrobe
Schlafzimmer mit integriertem Badezimmer, n
　♦ bedroom with en-suite bathroom
Schlafzimmer mit integriertem Duschraum, n
　♦ bedroom with en-suite shower room
Schlafzimmer mit integrierten Sanitäreinrichtungen
　♦ en-suite bedroom
Schlafzimmer mit Zugang von der Diele, n
　♦ hall bedroom AE
　♦ hall room AE
Schlafzimmermöbel, n pl
　Schlafzimmermobiliar, n
　♦ bedroom furniture sg
Schlafzimmermobiliar, n
　→ Schlafzimmermöbel
Schlafzimmerschlüssel, m
　Zimmerschlüssel, m (Hotel)
　♦ bedroom key
Schlafzimmerschrank, m
　♦ bedroom closet AE
　♦ bedroom wardrobe BE
Schlafzimmerteppich, m
　♦ bedroom carpet
Schlafzimmertisch, m
　♦ bedroom table
Schlafzimmertür, f
　Schlafraumtür f
　♦ bedroom door
Schlafzimmerunterkunft, f
　Schlafzimmerunterbringung, f
　♦ bedroom accommodation
Schlafzimmer wurde vor kurzem renoviert
　♦ bedroom has been recently refurbished
　♦ bedroom has been recently renovated
Schlafzimmerzahl, f
　Schlafraumzahl, f
　♦ number of bedrooms
Schlägermiete, f (Sport)
　♦ racket rental AE
　♦ racket hire BE
Schlägermiete beträgt DM 12
　♦ racket rental is DM 12 AE
　♦ racket hire is DM 12 BE

Schläger mieten (Sport)
　♦ rent a racket AE
　♦ hire a racket BE
Schlagloch, m
　♦ pothole
Schlagsahne, f
　Schlagobers, n ÖST
　♦ whipped cream
Schlammpackung, f
　→ Moorpackung
schlampiger Service m
　♦ slovenly service
Schlange, f (Reihe)
　♦ queue
Schlange, f (Tier)
　♦ snake
Schlange bildet sich
　♦ queue forms
Schlangenbiß, m
　♦ snake bite
Schlange stehen
　♦ queue up BE
　♦ line up AE
Schlangestehen (für etw), n
　♦ queuing (up for s.th.)
　♦ lining (up for s.th.)
Schlankheitsbehandlung, f
　Schlankheitskur, f
　♦ slimming treatment
Schlankheitsdiät, f
　Abmagerungskur, f
　♦ slimming diet
　♦ low-calorie diet
Schlankheitsessen, n
　Schlankheitsmahlzeit, f
　♦ slimming meal
Schlankheitsmassage, f
　♦ slimming massage
Schlankheitsmassagebehandlung, f
　♦ slimming massage treatment
Schlankheitsmenü, n
　♦ slimming menu
　♦ low-calorie menu
Schlankheitsprogramm, n
　♦ slimming program AE
　♦ slimming programme BE
Schlaraffenland, n
　♦ cockaigne
　♦ cockayne
　♦ lubberland
　♦ land of milk and honey
Schlauch, m
　♦ hose
Schlauchboot, n
　♦ rubber dinghy
　♦ rubber boat
　♦ dinghy
schlecht abgedunkelter Raum, m
　♦ poorly darkened room
schlecht ausgestattet, adj (Technik)
　♦ badly equipped, adj
　♦ poorly equipped, adj
schlecht ausgestattet, adj (Unterkunft)
　schlecht eingerichtet, adj
　♦ badly appointed, adj
schlecht behandeln jn
　♦ treat s.o. badly
schlecht belegt, adj
　schlecht ausgelastet, adj
　♦ poorly occupied, adj
　♦ poorly booked, adj

schlecht belegtes Hotel, n
- poorly occupied hotel
- poorly booked hotel

schlecht beleuchtet, adj
- badly lit, adj
- poorly lit, adj

schlecht besetztes Haus, n
(Gegensatz zu volles Haus)
- small house

schlecht besucht, adj
(Veranstaltung)
- poorly attended, adj

schlecht besuchte Veranstaltung, f
- poorly attended event
- poorly attended function

schlecht besuchte Vorstellung, f
- poorly attended performance

schlecht besucht sein
(Veranstaltung)
- be poorly attended
- be ill attended

schlecht bezahlt sein
schlecht bezahlt werden
- be ill paid

schlechte Auslastung, f
- poor load factor

schlechte Belegung, f
schlechte Auslastung, f
- poor occupancy

schlechte Beleuchtung, f
- bad lighting
- poor lighting

schlechte Buchungslage, f
- poor booking situation

schlechte Diät, f
- poor diet

schlechte Lage, f
schlechter Standort, m
- poor location

schlechte Lüftung, f
- poor ventilation

schlechte Manieren, f pl
schlechte Umgangsformen, f pl
- bad manners pl

schlechte Manieren haben
schlechte Umgangsformen haben
- have bad manners
- be ill-mannered

schlechte Nacht, f
- bad night

schlechte Nacht haben
- have a bad night

schlechten Dienst erweisen jm
- do s.o. a disservice

schlechten Service erhalten
- receive poor service
- receive bad service

schlechte Qualität, f
- poor quality

schlechter Appetit, m
- poor appetite

schlechter Dienst, m
- disservice

schlechter Geschmack, m
- bad taste

schlechter Kaffee, m
- bad coffee

schlechter Magen, m
- bad stomach

schlechter Ruf, m
übler Ruf, m
- bad reputation

schlechter Saisonbeginn m
- bad start to the season

schlechter Schläfer, m
- bad sleeper

schlechter Service, m
- poor service
- bad service

schlechter Wein, m
- bad wine
- poor wine

schlechtes Abendessen, n (Dinner)
- bad dinner

schlechtes Abendessen, n (Supper)
- bad supper

schlechte Saison, f
- bad season
- poor season

schlechte Saison erleben
- experience a bad season
- experience a poor season

schlechtes Buchungsniveau, n
- poor level of bookings

schlechtes Essen, n (generell)
- poor food

schlechtes Essen, n (Mahlzeit)
- poor meal
- bad meal

schlechtes Essen haben (Mahlzeit)
- have a poor meal
- have a bad meal

schlechtes Frühstück, n
- bad breakfast

schlechtes Gefühl im Magen, n
- sick feeling in the stomach

schlechtes Hotel n
- bad hotel

schlechtes Management, n
- bad management

schlechtes Omen, n
- bad omen

schlechtes Programm n
- poor program *AE*
- poor programme *BE*

schlecht essen
- eat badly

schlechtes Weinjahr, n
schlechter Weinjahrgang, m
- bad year for wine
- bad vintage year

schlechtes Wetter, n
- bad weather

schlechtes Zimmer, n
- poor room
- bad room

schlechtes Zimmer bekommen
- get a poor room
- get a bad room

schlechte Teilnahme, f
geringe Teilnahme, f
- poor audience

schlechte Wahl, f
- bad choice

schlecht geführtes Hotel, n
- badly run hotel
- badly managed hotel

schlecht gekocht, adj
- badly cooked, adj

schlecht gekochte Speise, f
- badly cooked food

schlechtgelaunter Gast, m
- bad-tempered guest

schlecht gelegen, adj
- badly situated, adj
- badly located, adj
- badly positioned, adj

schlecht informiert, adj
- badly informed, adj

schlecht informiert sein
- be badly informed

schlecht kochen
- be a bad cook
- cook badly

schlecht markiert, adj
- badly marked, adj
- poorly marked, adj

schlecht möbliert, adj
schlecht eingerichtet, adj
- badly furnished, adj

schlecht möbliertes Zimmer n
- badly furnished room

schlecht organisiert, adj
- badly organised, adj
- badly organized, adj

schlecht organisierte Konferenz, f
- badly organised conference
- badly organized conference

schlecht proportioniert, adj
- badly proportioned, adj

schlecht schlafen
- sleep badly

schlecht schmecken
(Speise)
- taste bad

schlecht serviert, adj
- badly served, adj

schlecht serviertes Essen, n
- badly served meal

schlecht temperiert, adj
falsch temperiert, adj
- at the wrong temperature, adv

schlecht untergebracht, adj
- ill-accommodated, adj
- ill-lodged, adj

schlecht untergebracht sein
- be ill-accommodated
- be ill-lodged *AE*

Schlechtwetterbetrieb, m
- bad weather operation

Schlechtwetterperiode, f
- spell of bad weather

Schlechtwetterprogramm, n
- bad weather program *AE*
- bad weather programme *BE*
- all weather program *AE*
- all weather programme *BE*

Schlechtwettertag, m
- bad weather day

Schleie, f
Schlei, m
- tench

Schleife machen
(Fluß)
- make a loop

schlemmen
- feast (on s.th.)
- gormandise
- gormandize

Schlemmer, m
→ Gourmet, Gourmand
Schlemmerecke, f
Feinschmeckerecke, f
♦ gourmet corner
Schlemmeressen, n
→ Feinschmeckeressen
Schlemmerfest, n (Party)
♦ gourmet party
Schlemmerfrühstück, n
Feinschmeckerfrühstück, n
Gourmetfrühstück, n
♦ gourmet breakfast
schlemmerisch, adj
♦ gourmand, adj
Schlemmerkorb, m
Feinschmeckerkorb, m
♦ gourmet basket
Schlemmerküche, f (Speisen)
→ Feinschmeckerküche
Schlemmerlokal, n
→ Feinschmeckerrestaurant
Schlemmermahl, n
großes Essen, n
♦ gourmet's feast
♦ feast
Schlemmermenü, n
→ Feinschmeckermenü
Schlemmerorgie, f
♦ gourmet blow-out AE sl
♦ gourmet blow-out BE sl
Schlemmerpalast, m
Feinschmeckerpalast, m
Gourmetpalast, m
♦ gourmet palace
Schlemmerreise, f
Feinschmeckerreise, f
Gourmetreise, f
♦ gourmet tour
Schlemmertempel, m
Feinschmeckertempel, m
Gourmettempel, m
♦ gourmet's Mecca
Schlemmerurlaub, m
Feinschmeckerurlaub, m
Gourmeturlaub, m
♦ gourmet vacation AE
♦ gourmet holiday BE
Schlemmerwoche, f
Feinschmeckerwoche, f
Gourmetwoche, f
♦ gourmet week
Schlemmerwochenende, n
Feinschmeckerwochenende, n
Gourmetwochenende, n
♦ gourmet weekend
schleppen etw. (Koffer)
♦ lug s.th.
schleppen jn (Person)
♦ drag s.o.
schleppen (Kunden)
Kunden anlocken
♦ tout for s.o.
Schlepper, m (Boot)
♦ tugboat
Schlepper, m (Person)
(lockt Kunden an)
Kundenschlepper m
♦ tout
♦ lugger sl

Schlepplift, m
(Ski)
♦ drag lift
♦ T-bar lift AE
♦ T-bar AE
♦ teleskis AE
♦ téléski FR
Schleppliftanlage, f
♦ drag-lift system
♦ T-bar lift system AE
Schleppzug, m
(Schiffe)
♦ barge train
Schlesien
♦ Silesia
Schlesier, m
♦ Silesian
Schlesierin, f
♦ Silesian girl
♦ Silesian woman
♦ Silesian
schlesisch, adj
♦ Silesian, adj
Schleswig
(Region)
♦ Schleswig
Schleswig-Holstein
(Land)
♦ Schleswig-Holstein
Schleuderpreis, m
Spottpreis, m
♦ cut-rate price AE
♦ giveaway price AE
♦ giveaway rate AE
♦ give-away price BE
♦ give-away rate BE
Schleuse, f
♦ lock
schlichten etw
durch Schiedsverfahren schlichten etw
♦ settle s.th. by arbitration
Schlichter, m
♦ arbitrator
schlichte Unterkunft, f
♦ plain accommodation
Schlichtung, f
♦ arbitration
Schlichtungsausschuß, m
Schiedsausschuß, m
♦ arbitration committee
Schlichtungsstelle, f
Schiedsstelle, f
♦ board of arbitration
Schlichtungssystem, n
Schiedssystem, n
♦ arbitration system
Schlichtungssystem haben
Schiedssystem haben
♦ operate an arbitration system
Schlichtungsvereinbarung, f
Schiedsvereinbarung, f
♦ arbitration agreement
Schlichtungsverfahren, n
→ Schiedsverfahren
Schlichtungsversuch, m
Schiedsversuch, m
♦ attempt at arbitration
schließen etw
♦ close s.th.
schließen etw für den Tourismus
(Tourismus ausschließen)

sperren etw für den Tourismus
♦ close s.th. for tourism
schließen etw vorübergehend
♦ close s.th. temporarily
schließen für fünf Monate im Jahr
♦ close for five months in the year
schließen in der Nebensaison
♦ close in the off-season
schließen wegen Renovierung
♦ close for renovation
♦ close for refurbishment
schließen wegen Umbauten
♦ close for alterations
Schließfach, n
♦ locker
♦ storage locker
Schließung der Grenze, f
♦ closure of the border
♦ closure of the frontier
Schließung eines Hotels, f
♦ closure of a hotel
♦ closing a hotel
Schließungszeitpunkt, m
(Zeitpunkt, wann etw geschlossen wird)
Schließungszeit, f
♦ closing time
schlimme Zeit durchmachen
schlecht gehen
♦ have a rough time
schlingen (Essen)
Essen hinunterschlingen
♦ bolt one's food
♦ bolt down one's food
Schling' nicht so!
♦ Don't bolt your food!
Schlitten, m (für 1 Person)
Rennschlitten, m
Rodelschlitten, m
♦ luge
Schlitten, m (generell)
Rodelschlitten, m
♦ sledge
♦ sled AE
♦ coaster AE
♦ toboggan
Schlitten, m (groß, Pferd)
♦ sleigh
Schlittenabend, m
→ Rodelabend
Schlittenabfahrt, f (Strecke)
Schlittenbahn, f
Rodelbahn, f
♦ toboggan slide
♦ toboggan run
♦ coasting slide AE
♦ coasting chute AE
Schlittenbahn, f
♦ coasting slide AE
♦ toboggan run
♦ toboggan slide
♦ coasting path AE
♦ coasting chute AE
Schlitten fahren
rodeln
♦ toboggan
♦ sledge
♦ coast AE
Schlittenfahren, n
♦ coasting AE
♦ sledging
♦ tobogganing

schlittenfahren gehen
- ♦ go tobogganing
- ♦ go sledging
- ♦ go sledding *AE*
- ♦ go coasting *AE*

Schlittenfahrer, m
Rodler, m
- ♦ coaster *AE*
- ♦ tobogganer *AE*
- ♦ sledge rider

Schlittenfahrt, f (generell)
- ♦ toboggan ride
- ♦ sledge ride

Schlittenfahrt, f (mit Pferd)
- ♦ sleigh ride

Schlittenfahrt machen (generell)
- ♦ take a toboggan ride
- ♦ take a sledge ride

Schlittenfahrt machen (mit Pferd)
- ♦ take a sleigh ride

Schlittenhang, m
Hang zum Schlittenfahren, m
- ♦ slope for tobogganing

Schlittenhund, m
- ♦ sledge dog

Schlittenlift, m
- ♦ toboggan tow
- ♦ sledge tow

Schlitten mieten
- ♦ rent a toboggan *AE*
- ♦ rent a coaster *AE*
- ♦ hire a toboggan *BE*
- ♦ rent a sledge *AE*
- ♦ hire a sledge *BE*

Schlittenpartie, f
Rodelpartie, f
Schlittenfahrt, f
- ♦ toboggan party

Schlittenrennen, n
- ♦ toboggan race
- ♦ sledge race

Schlitten vermieten
- ♦ rent (out) a toboggan
- ♦ rent (out) a coaster *AE*
- ♦ rent (out) a sledge
- ♦ hire out a sledge *BE*
- ♦ hire out a toboggan *BE*

Schlittschuhbahn, f
- ♦ ice-skating rink
- ♦ skating rink

Schlittschuhe, m pl
- ♦ ice skates *AE pl*
- ♦ ice-skates *BE pl*
- ♦ skates *pl*

schlittschuhfahren gehen
- ♦ go skating

Schlittschuh laufen
Schlittschuh fahren
eislaufen
- ♦ ice-skate
- ♦ skate

Schlittschuhlaufen, n
Schlittschuhfahren, n
Schlittschuhsport, m
Eislaufen, n
Eislaufsport, m
- ♦ ice-skating
- ♦ skating

Schlittschuhläufer, m
Schlittschuhfahrer, m
Eisläufer, m

- ♦ ice skater *AE*
- ♦ ice-skater *BE*
- ♦ skater

Schlittschuhwettbewerb, m
Eislaufwettbewerb, m
- ♦ ice-skating competition
- ♦ skating competition

Schlitzbrett n
(Rezeption)
- ♦ slotted board

Schloß, n (Gebäude)
Burg, f
- ♦ castle
- ♦ palace
- ♦ château

Schloß, n (Tür)
- ♦ lock

schloßartig, adj
burgartig, adj
- ♦ castlelike, adj

schloßartiges Hotel, n
burgartiges Hotel, n
- ♦ castlelike hotel

Schloßbeleuchtung, f
- ♦ illumination of the castle
- ♦ illuminated castle

Schloßberg, m
Burgberg, m
- ♦ castle hill
- ♦ castle mound

Schloß besichtigen
- ♦ view the castle
- ♦ visit the castle

Schloß besuchen
- ♦ visit the castle

Schloßblick, m (auf das Schloß)
Blick auf das Schloß, m
Burgblick, m
Blick auf die Burg, f
- ♦ castle view
- ♦ view of the castle

Schloßblick, m (von dem Schloß)
Blick vom Schloß, m
Burgblick, m
Blick von der Burg, m
- ♦ castle view
- ♦ view from the castle

Schloßfest, n
Schloßfestspiele, n pl
Burgfest, n
Burgfestspiele, n pl
- ♦ castle festival

Schloßführer, m
Burgführer, m
- ♦ castle guide

Schloßführung, f
- ♦ guided tour of the castle
- ♦ guided tour of the palace

Schloßgarten, m
Schloßanlage, f
Burggarten, m
Burganlage, f
- ♦ castle grounds *pl*

Schloßgaststätte, f
Burggaststätte, f
- ♦ castle pub *BE*
- ♦ castle bar *AE*

Schloßhotel, n (Eigenname)
Burghotel, n
- ♦ Castle Hotel, the

Schloßhotel, n (generell)
Burghotel, n
- ♦ castle hotel

Schloßhügel, m
Schloßberg, m
Burghügel, m
Burgberg, m
- ♦ castle mound

Schloß ist von einem Wassergraben umgeben
Burg ist von einem Wassergraben umgeben
- ♦ castle is surrounded by a moat

Schloßkapelle, f
Burgkapelle, f
- ♦ castle chapel

Schloßkirche, f
Burgkirche, f
- ♦ castle church

Schloßkonzert, n
- ♦ concert in the castle
- ♦ concert in the palace

Schloß Meersburg, n
- ♦ Meersburg Castle

Schloßmuseum, n
Burgmuseum, n
- ♦ castle museum

Schloßpark, m
Burgpark, m
- ♦ castle gardens *pl*

Schloßplatz, m
Burgplatz, m
- ♦ castle square

Schloßrestaurant, n
Burgrestaurant, n
- ♦ castle restaurant

Schloßruine, f
Burgruine, f
- ♦ castle ruins *pl*
- ♦ ruined castle
- ♦ ruins of a castle *pl*

Schloßstadt, f (Großstadt)
Burgstadt, f
- ♦ castle city

Schloßstadt, f (kleine Stadt)
Burgstadt, f
- ♦ castle town

Schloßtaverne, f
Burgtaverne, f
- ♦ castle tavern

Schloßtor, n
Burgtor, n
- ♦ castle gate

Schloßturm, m
Burgturm, m
- ♦ castle tower

Schloßurlaub, m
Burgurlaub, m
Schloßferien, pl
Burgferien, pl
- ♦ castle vacation *AE*
- ♦ castle holiday *BE*

Schloß verfiel
Burg verfiel
- ♦ castle fell into decay
- ♦ castle fell into ruin

Schloß Windsor, n
- ♦ Windsor Castle

Schlucht, f
- ♦ ravine
- ♦ gorge

Schlucht hochklettern
- ♦ scramble up a ravine

Schluck, m (generell)
 ♦ gulp
 ♦ mouthful
Schluck, m (kleiner)
 → Schlückchen
Schluck, m (tüchtiger)
 (alkoholisches Getränk)
 ♦ swig
Schluckauf, m
 ♦ hiccups pl
Schluckauf bekommen
 ♦ get (the) hiccups
Schluckauf haben
 ♦ have (the) hiccups
Schluck aus der Flasche, m
 ♦ swig from the bottle coll
 ♦ swill from the bottle coll
Schluck Brandy, m
 ♦ swig of brandy
Schlückchen, n
 kleiner Schluck, m
 ♦ sip
 ♦ drop
 ♦ wee dram
schlückchenweise trinken etw
 ♦ sip s.th.
schlucken etw
 ♦ swallow s.th.
schlucken gehen einen
 trinken gehen einen
 ♦ go for a tipple
Schluckimpfung, f
 ♦ oral vaccination
Schluck Kaffee, m
 ♦ some coffee
 ♦ drop of coffee
Schluckspecht, m
 → Trinker
Schluck Wasser, m
 ♦ some water
 ♦ drop of water
Schluck Wein, m
 ♦ some wine
 ♦ drop of wine
schluckweise, adv
 schlückchenweise, adv
 ♦ in sips, adv
Schlummertrunk, m
 → Abendtrank
Schlupfwinkel, m
 ♦ haunt
schlürfen (etw)
 ♦ slurp (s.th.)
Schlußbericht, m
 Abschlußbericht, m
 abschließender Bericht, m
 ♦ final report
Schlußbestand m
 → Endbestand
Schlüssel, m
 ♦ key
Schlüssel abgeben bei der Rezeption
 ♦ leave one's key at reception
Schlüssel abgeben bei jm
 ♦ leave the key with s.o.
Schlüssel abholen
 ♦ collect a key
Schlüssel abholen bei der Rezeption
 Schlüssel abholen bei dem Empfang
 ♦ collect one's key at reception
 ♦ pick up one's key at reception

Schlüsselanlage, f
 ♦ key system
Schlüsselausgabe, f
 Schlüsselübergabe, f
 Schlüsselverteilung, f
 ♦ issue of a key
 ♦ issuing a key
 ♦ issuing keys
Schlüssel ausgeben (an jn)
 Schlüssel übergeben (an jn)
 ♦ issue a key (to s.o.)
Schlüsselbrett, n
 Schlüsselrack, n
 Schlüsselkasten, m
 ♦ key-rack
 ♦ keyboard
schlüsselfertig, adj
 ♦ turnkey, adj
 ♦ ready to move into, adj
 ♦ ready for occupancy, adj
schlüsselfertiges Appartement, n
 ♦ turnkey apartment
Schlüsselfrau, f
 ♦ key lady
Schlüssel für Zimmer und Haustür, m
 ♦ key to room and front door
Schlüssel hinterlegen bei jm
 ♦ deposit the key with s.o.
Schlüsselkarte, f
 ♦ key card
Schlüsselkarte ausfüllen
 ♦ fill out a key card AE
 ♦ fill in a key card BE
 ♦ complete a key card
Schlüsselkarte ausgeben (an einen Gast)
 ♦ issue a key card (to a guest)
Schlüsselkarte aushändigen (an einen Gast)
 ♦ hand out a key card (to a guest)
Schlüsselkarte vorzeigen
 Schlüsselkarte vorweisen
 Schlüsselkarte zeigen
 ♦ present one's key card
 ♦ produce one's key card
 ♦ show one's key card
Schlüsselkarte zeigen
 Schlüsselkarte vorweisen
 ♦ show one's key card
 ♦ present one's key card
Schlüsselposition, f
 ♦ key position
Schlüsselrückgabe, f
 ♦ return of the key
 ♦ returning the key
Schlüssel steckt im Schloß
 ♦ key is in the lock
Schlüsseltresor, m
 (Rezeption)
 ♦ key safe
Schlüsselübergabe, f
 → Schlüsselausgabe
Schlüssel übergeben (an jn)
 → Schlüssel ausgeben
Schlüssel verlangen
 (bei Rezeption)
 ♦ claim one's key
Schlußetappe, f
 ♦ final stage
 ♦ final leg
Schlußetappe der Reise, f
 ♦ final stage of the journey
 ♦ final stage of the tour

Schlußfeier, f
 → Abschlußfeier
Schlußrechnung, f (Faktur)
 → Endrechnung
Schlußrechnung, f (generell)
 Schlußabrechnung, f
 ♦ final bill
 ♦ final check AE
Schlußrechnung ausstellen
 ♦ make out the final bill
 ♦ make out the final check AE
Schlußreinigung f
 → Endreinigung
Schlußveranstaltung, f
 Abschlußveranstaltung, f
 abschließende Veranstaltung, f
 ♦ final function
 ♦ final event
Schlußwoche, f
 letzte Woche, f
 Abschlußwoche, f
 abschließende Woche, f
 ♦ final week
Schlußzahlung, f
 → Abschlußzahlung
schmackhaft, adj
 wohlschmeckend, adj
 ♦ tasty, adj
 ♦ palatable, adj
 ♦ delicate, adj
 ♦ savory, adj AE
 ♦ savoury, adj BE
schmackhaftes Essen, n (generell)
 ♦ tasty food
schmackhaftes Essen, n (Mahlzeit)
 schmackhafte Mahlzeit, f
 ♦ tasty meal
schmackhaftes Mittagessen n
 ♦ tasty lunch
Schmackhaftigkeit, f
 ♦ tastiness
schmackhaft zubereitetes Essen, n
 ♦ tastefully prepared meal
schmale Kost, f
 ♦ short commons pl
schmales Bett, n
 ♦ narrow bed
schmales Zimmer, n
 ♦ narrow room
Schmalhans ist Küchenmeister coll
 ♦ be on short commons coll
Schmalspurbahn, f
 Schmalspureisenbahn, f
 Kleinbahn, f
 ♦ narrow-gage railroad AE
 ♦ narrow-gauge railway BE
Schmalspurdampfeisenbahn, f
 ♦ narrow-gage steam railroad AE
 ♦ narrow-gauge steam railway BE
Schmankerl, n OST
 → Leckerbissen
Schmaus, m
 Festessen, n
 Festschmaus, m
 Festmahl, n
 üppiges Mahl, n
 ♦ feast
schmeckbar, adj
 ♦ tastable, adj
 ♦ tasteable, adj

schmecken lassen sich etw
- enjoy s.th.
- eat s.th. with relish
- relish s.th.

schmecken nach (dem) Korken (Getränke)
- taste of (the) cork
- be corked

schmecken nach etw
- taste of s.th.

schmecken nach Fisch
- taste of fish

schmecken nach nichts
- nach nichts schmecken
- have no taste whatsoever
- taste like nothing at all
- be quite insipid

schmecken wie etw
- taste like s.th.

Schmeckt es Ihnen?
- Do you like it?
- Are you enjoying your meal?

Schmerbauch, m
- paunch
- potbelly

Schmerztablette, f
- pain-killing tablet
- pain-killer

Schmetterlingsfarm, f
- butterfly farm

Schmetterlingshaus, n
- butterfly house

Schmetterlingspark, m
- butterfly park

Schmiede, f
- smithy

Schmiedefest, n
- blacksmiths' festival

Schmierentheater, n
- Schmiere, f
- penny gaff *BE sl*

Schminkberatung, f
- makeup consultation *AE*
- make-up consultation *BE*

Schminkkurs, m
- makeup class *AE*
- make-up class *BE*

Schminkspiegel, m
- makeup mirror *AE*
- make-up mirror *BE*

Schminkunterricht, m
- makeup lessons *AE pl*
- make-up lessons *BE pl*

schmoren (etw)
- stew (s.th.)
- braise (s.th.)

Schmuck, m
- jewelry *AE*
- jewellery *BE*

Schmuckgeschäft n
- → Juwelierladen

schmuckloses Zimmer, n
- austere room

Schmuckmuseum, n
- jewelry museum *AE*
- jewellery museum *BE*

Schmucksachen, f pl
- → Schmuck

Schmucksammlung, f
- collection of jewels

schmuddelig, adj
- schäbig, adj
- dingy, adj
- mucky, adj *fam*

schmuddeliger Saal, m
- schäbiger Saal, m
- dingy hall

schmuddeliges Zimmer, n
- schäbiges Zimmer, n
- dingy room

Schmuggel, m (bes. alkoholische Getränke)
- Alkoholschmuggel, m
- illegaler Verkauf von Alkohol, m
- bootlegging

schmuggeln etw
- smuggle s.th.

Schmuggler, m
- smuggler

Schmugglerbar, f
- smugglers' bar

Schmugglergasthof, m
- smugglers' inn

Schmugglerkneipe, f
- Schmugglertreffpunkt, m
- Schmugglertreff, m
- smugglers' haunt

Schmugglermuseum, n
- smugglers' museum

Schmutz, m
- dirt

schmutziger Strand, m
- dirty beach

schmutziger Teller, m
- dirty plate

schmutziges Zimmer n
- verschmutztes Zimmer n
- dirty room

schmutzige Wäsche f
- soiled linen
- dirty linen

Schnäppchen, n
- snip *inform*

Schnäppchenjäger, m *inform*
- bargain hunter

Schnaps, m
- schnapps
- spirits *pl*

Schnapsbrenner, m
- distiller

Schnapsbude, f
- (schlechtes Wirtshaus)
- Schnapsladen, m
- grogshop *BE*
- groggery *AE*
- boozer *BE coll*

Schnäpschen, n
- snifter
- quickie
- quick one

Schnapsfahne haben
- → Fahne haben

Schnapsglas, n
- shot glass
- measure

Schnapsladen, m
- (Geschäft)
- groggery *AE*

Schnapsnase, f coll
- grog blossom *coll*
- drinker's nose

Schnapszahl, f
- nice number

schnarchen
- snore

Schnarchen, n
- snoring

Schnarcher, m
- snorer

Schneckenbutter, f
- snail butter

Schneeanzug, m
- snowsuit

Schneeball, m
- snowball

Schneebälle werfen
- Schneeballschlacht machen
- throw snowballs
- snowball

Schneeballschlacht f
- snowball fight

schneebedeckt, adj
- snow-covered, adj
- snow-clad, adj *lit*
- snow-capped, adj *lit*

schneebedeckter Berg, m
- snow-covered mountain
- snow-clad mountain *lit*
- snow-capped mountain *lit*

schneebedeckter Gipfel, m
- snow-covered peak
- snow-clad peak *lit*
- snow-capped peak *lit*

Schneebedingungen, f pl
- → Schneeverhältnisse

Schneebericht m
- snow report

Schneebesen, m *gastr*
- Schneeschläger, m *gastr*
- whisk *gastr*
- egg-whisk *gastr*
- egg-beater *gastr*

schneeblind, adj
- snow-blind, adj
- snow-blinded, adj

Schneebrille, f
- snow goggles *pl*

Schneedecke, f
- blanket of snow

Schneefall, m
- snowfall

Schneefeld, n
- snow-field

Schneefest, n
- snow festival

Schneeflocke, f
- snowflake

Schneegarantie, f
- snow guarantee

Schneegarantie geben
- give a snow guarantee

Schneegebiet n (groß)
- snow region

Schneegebiet n (klein)
- snow area

schneegeräumt, adj
- snow-cleared, adj
- cleared of snow, adj

Schneegrenze, f
- snow line *AE*
- snow-line *BE*

Schneehang, m
♦ snow slope
Schneehütte, f
→ Iglu
Schneekanone, f
♦ snow machine
♦ snow cannon
Schneekette, f
♦ snow-chain
♦ tire chain AE
♦ tyre chain BE
Schneekettenverleih, m
♦ snow-chain rental AE
♦ snow-chain hire BE
Schneeland, n
Schneegebiet, n
♦ snow country
Schneeloch, n
♦ snow hole
Schneemangel, m (Knappheit)
♦ shortage of snow
Schneemangel, m (völliges Fehlen)
♦ lack of snow
Schneemann, m
♦ snowman
Schneepflug, m
♦ snowplow AE
♦ snow-plough BE
Schneeräumung, f
♦ snow removal
♦ snow-clearing
♦ snow clearance
Schneeregen, m
♦ sleet
Schneereifen, m
♦ snow tire AE
♦ snow tyre BE
Schneesaison, f
♦ snowy season
Schneeschläger, m gastr
Schneebesen, m gastr
♦ egg-whisk gastr
♦ whisk gastr
♦ egg-beater gastr
Schneeschuh, m
♦ snowshoe AE
♦ snow-shoe BE
Schneeschuhrennen, n
♦ snowshoe race AE
♦ snow-shoe race BE
Schneeschuhwanderung, f
♦ snowshoe walk AE
♦ snow-shoe walk BE
schneesicher, adj
♦ snow guaranteed
schneesichere Region, f
♦ region with snow guaranteed
schneesicheres Gebiet, n
♦ area with snow guaranteed
Schneesturm, m
♦ snowstorm
Schneetiefe, f
♦ snow depth
Schnee- und Wetterbedingungen, f pl
Schnee- und Wetterverhältnisse, f pl
♦ snow and weather conditions pl
Schneeurlaub, m
Schneeferien, pl
♦ snow vacation AE
♦ snow holiday BE

Schneeverhältnisse, n pl
Schneebedingungen, f pl
♦ snow conditions pl
Schneewanderung, f
♦ walk in the snow
♦ snow walk
Schneewinter, m
♦ snow winter
Schneezone, f
(Zone mit Schnee)
♦ snow range
Schneidbrett, n
♦ cutting board
Schneidemaschine, f
♦ slicer
schneiden etw
♦ cut s.th.
schneiden etw in Servierportionen
♦ cut s.th. in serving portions
schneiden (etw) in Streifen
♦ cut (s.th.) into strips
schneiden jn
übersehen jn
♦ cut s.o.
schneiden jn völlig
übersehen jn völlig
♦ cut s.o. dead
♦ snub s.o.
Schneider, m
♦ tailor
Schneiderin, f
♦ dressmaker
schneien
♦ snow
Schnellaufzug, m
Schnell-Lift, m
Expreßaufzug, m
Expreßlift, m
♦ high-speed elevator AE
♦ high-speed lift BE
Schnellboot, n
♦ speedboat
Schnellbootfahren, n
Schnellbootsport, m
♦ speedboating
Schnellbüfett, n
Schnellrestaurant, n
♦ quick-lunch restaurant
♦ quick-lunch coll
♦ fast-food restaurant
♦ convenience restaurant
Schnellbus, m
♦ express bus
♦ fast bus
♦ fast coach BE
♦ express coach BE
♦ flyer AE
Schnelldienst, m
♦ fast service
♦ quick service
♦ express service
schnelle Mahlzeit f
♦ quick meal
schneller Besuch, m
♦ quick visit
schneller Service, m
♦ quick service
♦ fast service
schnelles Mittagessen, n
♦ quick lunch

schnelles Motorboot, n
♦ powerboat AE
♦ power-boat BE
schnell essen etw
♦ eat s.th. quickly
schnelle Straße, f
♦ fast road
schnell fahren (Auto)
♦ drive fast
♦ drive quickly
Schnellfahrstuhl, m
→ Schnellaufzug
schnellfrosten etw
♦ quick-freeze s.th.
Schnellgaststätte, f
♦ quick service restaurant
♦ fast-food bar AE
♦ lunchroom AE
♦ fast-food restaurant
♦ fast-food place
Schnellgericht, n
(in Restaurant)
♦ short order
♦ quick meal
Schnellgerichtkoch, m
Schnellkoch, m
♦ short-order cook
♦ short-order chef
Schnellgerichtsverpflegung, f
Schnellverpflegung, f
♦ short-order catering
Schnellimbiß, m (Essen)
♦ quick snack
♦ quick lunch
♦ instant meal
Schnellimbiß, m (Raum)
→ Schnellimbißstube
Schnellimbißstube, f
Schnellimbiß, m
♦ quick-lunch bar
♦ quick-lunch counter
♦ quick-lunch AE
♦ luncheonette AE
♦ buffet AE
Schnellkochtopf, m
♦ pressure cooker
Schnellkurs, m
♦ crash course
Schnell-Lift, m
→ Schnellaufzug
schnell reisen
♦ travel fast
♦ go fast
Schnellrestaurant, n
♦ convenience restaurant
♦ fast-food restaurant
♦ quick-lunch restaurant
♦ quick-lunch AE
Schnellrestaurantkette, f
→ Fast-Food-Kette
Schnellservice, m
→ Expressdienst
Schnellstraße, f
♦ speedway AE
♦ expressway AE
♦ dual carriageway BE
♦ divided highway AE
♦ fast road
Schnellwäscherei, f
♦ quick laundry

Schnellwäschereidienst

Schnellwäschereidienst, m
→ Schnellwäschereiservice
Schnellwäschereiservice, m
Schnellwäschereidienst, m
♦ express laundry service
♦ quick laundry service BE
Schnellzug, m
♦ fast train
♦ express train
♦ express
Schnepfe, f
♦ woodcock
Schnepfenfüllpastete, f
♦ woodcock timbale
Schnepfensalmi, n
♦ woodcock salmi
schnetzeln etw gastr
in Streifen schneiden etw gastr
♦ shred s.th. gastr
Schnickschnack, m
→ Firlefanz
Schnittlauch, m
♦ chives pl
Schnittsalat, m
Pflücksalat, m
♦ spring salad
Schnitz, m
(z.B. Zitronenschnitz)
♦ wedge
Schnitzel, n
♦ escalope
♦ schnitzel
Schnitzeljagd, f
(Spiel)
♦ paperchase
schnitzen (etw)
♦ carve (s.th.)
Schnorchel, m
♦ snorkel
schnorcheln
♦ snorkel
Schnorcheln, n
Schnorchelsport, m
♦ snorkeling AE
♦ snorkelling BE
Schnorchelurlaub, m
Schnorchelferien, pl
♦ snorkeling vacation AE
♦ snorkelling holiday BE
schnorren etw bei jm
♦ cadge s.th. from s.o. inform
♦ sponge s.th. from s.o.
♦ mooch s.th. from/off s.o. AE sl
♦ scrounge s.th. from/off s.o. coll
Schnorrer, m
Nassauer, m
♦ cadger inform
♦ sponger inform
♦ scrounger inform
♦ mooch(er) AE coll
♦ freeloader inform
Schnuller, m
(für Babies)
♦ pacifier AE
♦ baby's dummy BE
♦ dummy BE
♦ comforter BE
Schnupperangebot, n
→ sehr günstiges Angebot
Schnupperpreis, m
→ sehr günstiger Preis

schockgefrieren etw
♦ shock-freeze s.th.
Schokolade, f
♦ chocolate
Schokoladeaufstrich, m
Schokoladenaufstrich, m
♦ chocolate spread
Schokoladecreme, f
Schokoladencreme, f
♦ chocolate cream
Schokoladecremesoße, f
Schokoladencremesoße, f
♦ chocolate cream sauce
Schokoladeei, n
Schokoladenei, n
♦ chocolate egg
Schokoladeeis, n
Schokoladeneis, n
♦ chocolate ice cream AE
♦ chocolate ice-cream BE
♦ choc-ice inform
Schokoladekuchen, m
Schokoladenkuchen, m
♦ chocolate cake
Schokolademeringe, f
Schokoladenmeringe, f
♦ chocolate meringue
Schokolademousse, f
Schokoladenmousse, f
Schokoladeschaum, m
Schokoladenschaum, m
♦ chocolate mousse
Schokoladeparfait, n
Schokoladenparfait, n
♦ chocolate parfait
Schokoladepudding, m
Schokoladenpudding, m
♦ chocolate pudding
Schokoladesoße, f
Schokoladensoße, f
♦ chocolate sauce
Schokoladesoufflé, n
Schokoladensoufflé, n
Schokoladeauflauf, m
Schokoladenauflauf, m
♦ chocolate soufflé
Schokoladetorte, f (flach)
Schokoladentorte, f
♦ chocolate tart
Schokoladetorte, f (Sahne)
Schokoladentorte, f
♦ chocolate gâteau BE
♦ chocolate gateau AE
Schokoladetrüffel, m
Schokoladentrüffel, m
♦ chocolate truffle
Scholle, f
♦ plaice
♦ plaise
Schollenfilet, n
♦ plaice fillet
♦ plaice filet AE
schön ausgestattet, adj
♦ beautifully equipped, adj
schöne Aussicht, f
♦ beautiful view
schöne Aussicht haben
♦ have a beautiful view
schöne Aussicht haben von hier oben
♦ have a beautiful view from up here

schöne Erinnerungen zurückbringen an etw
♦ bring back happy memories of s.th.
Schöne Ferien!
♦ Have a pleasant vacation! AE
♦ Have a good holiday! BE
schöne Gegend, f
schönes Gebiet, n
♦ beautiful area
♦ beautiful region
♦ beauty spot
schön eingerichtetes Zimmer, n
♦ beautifully appointed room
schöne Insel, f
♦ beautiful island
schöne Lage, f
♦ beautiful location
♦ beautiful position
♦ beautiful setting
♦ beautiful situation
schöne Lage einnehmen
♦ command a beautiful position
schöne Lage haben
♦ have a beautiful position
♦ have a beautiful location
♦ have a beautiful situation
♦ have a beautiful setting
schöne Landschaft, f
♦ beautiful scenery
♦ beautiful countryside
♦ beautiful landscape
schönen Aufenthalt jm wünschen
♦ wish s.o. an enjoyable stay
♦ hope that s.o. will have an enjoyable stay
schönen Dinge im Leben schätzen
♦ appreciate the good things in life
schönen Urlaub bereiten jm
jm schöne Ferien bereiten
♦ provide a nice vacation for s.o. AE
♦ provide a nice holiday for s.o. BE
schöner, als man sich vorstellen kann
♦ more beautiful than one can imagine
Schoner, m
♦ schooner
schöner Aufenthalt, m
♦ enjoyable stay
schön erhalten, adj
♦ beautifully preserved, adj
schöner Ort, m
Naturschönheit, f
♦ beauty spot
schöner Rahmen, m
♦ beautiful setting
schöner Strand, m
♦ beautiful beach
♦ fine beach
schöner Urlaub, m
schöne Ferien, pl
♦ fine vacation AE
♦ fine holidays BE pl
♦ fine holiday BE
schönes Hotel, n
♦ beautiful hotel
schöne Spaziergänge bieten jm
♦ provide beautiful walks for s.o.
Schönes Wochenende!
♦ Have a nice weekend!
schönes Zimmer, n
♦ beautiful room
schöne Zeit haben
gutgehen lassen es sich
schöne Zeit machen sich

- ◆ have a good time
- ◆ enjoy oneself
- ◆ have a ball *AE coll*
- schöne Zeit machen sich
  - schöne Zeit haben
  - ◆ have a ball *AE coll*
  - ◆ have a good time
- schön gedeckter Tisch, m
  - ◆ beautifully laid table
- schön gelegen, adj
  - ◆ beautifully situated, adj
  - ◆ beautifully located, adj
  - ◆ beautifully positioned, adj
- schön gelegenes Dorf, n
  - ◆ beautifully situated village
  - ◆ beautifully located village
- schön gelegenes Hotel, n
  - Hotel in schöner Lage, n
  - ◆ beautifully situated hotel
  - ◆ beautifully located hotel
  - ◆ beautifully positioned hotel
- Schönheitsabteilung, f
  - Kosmetikabteilung, f
  - ◆ beauty department
- Schönheitsbehandlung, f
  - Schönheitskur, f
  - ◆ beauty treatment
- Schönheitsbehandlungsraum, m
  - ◆ beauty treatment room
- Schönheitsclub, m
  - ◆ beauty club
- Schönheitsfarm, f
  - ◆ beauty farm
- Schönheitsklinik, f
  - ◆ beauty clinic
- Schönheitskönigin, f
  - ◆ beauty queen
- Schönheitskurzurlaub, m
  - ◆ beauty break
- schönheitsorientiert, adj
  - ◆ beauty-oriented, adj *AE*
  - ◆ beauty-orientated, adj *BE*
- Schönheitspauschale, f
  - ◆ beauty package
- Schönheitspflaster, n
  - (im Gesicht)
  - ◆ beauty spot
- Schönheitspflege, f
  - ◆ beauty care
- Schönheitspraxis, f
  - Schönheitsräume, f
  - ◆ beauty suite
- Schönheitsraum, m
  - Kosmetikraum, m
  - ◆ beauty room
- Schönheitsreparaturen, f pl
  - ◆ home improvements *pl*
- Schönheitssalon, m
  - Kosmetiksalon, m
  - ◆ beauty salon
  - ◆ beauty shop *AE*
- Schönheitsschlaf, m
  - ◆ beauty sleep
- Schönheitsschlaf machen
  - ◆ have one's beauty sleep
- Schönheitsstudio, n
  - Kosmetikstudio, n
  - ◆ beauty studio
- Schönheitsstudio mit Solarium, n
  - Kosmetikstudio mit Solarium, n
  - ◆ beauty studio with solarium

- Schönheitstag, m
  - ◆ beauty day
- Schönheitstherapeut, m
  - ◆ beauty therapist
- Schönheitstherapie, f
  - ◆ beauty therapy
- Schönheitstherapieklinik, f
  - ◆ beauty therapy clinic
- Schönheitstherapieraum, m
  - ◆ beauty therapy room
- Schönheitswettbewerb, m
  - Mißwahl, f
  - ◆ beauty competition
  - ◆ beauty contest
- Schönheitswoche, f
  - ◆ beauty week
- Schonklima, n
  - mildes Klima, n
  - ◆ mild climate
  - ◆ relaxing climate
- Schonkost, f
  - ◆ mild diet
  - ◆ bland diet
- schön möbliert, adj
  - schön eingerichtet, adj
  - ◆ beautifully furnished, adj
- schön möbliertes Zimmer n
  - ◆ beautifully furnished room
- schön proportioniert, adj
  - ◆ beautifully proportioned, adj
- schön renoviert, adj
  - ◆ beautifully refurbished, adj
  - ◆ beautifully renovated, adj
- schön renoviertes Hotel, n
  - ◆ beautifully refurbished hotel
  - ◆ beautifully renovated hotel
- schönste Ordnung, f *coll*
  - ◆ apple-pie order *coll*
- schönste Zeit im Leben haben
  - sich bestens vergnügen
  - ◆ have the time of one's life
- Schonzeit, f
  - (Jagd)
  - ◆ close season *AE*
  - ◆ closed season *BE*
  - ◆ fence month
- Schonzeitmonat, m
  - Schonzeit, f
  - ◆ fence month
- Schöpflöffel, m
  - Kelle, f
  - ◆ ladle
- Schoppenwein, m
  - → offener Wein
- Schornstein, m
  - ◆ chimney
- Schornsteinkappe, f
  - ◆ chimney cowl
- Schotte, m
  - ◆ Scotsman
  - ◆ Scot
- Schottin, f
  - ◆ Scotswoman
- schottisch, adj (Person)
  - ◆ Scottish, adj
- schottisch, adj (Produkt)
  - ◆ Scotch, adj
- schottische Art, adv *gastr*
  - nach schottischer Art, adv *gastr*
  - ◆ Scottish style, adv *gastr*

- Schottische Hochland, das, n
  - ◆ Scottish Highlands, the *pl*
  - ◆ Highlands, the *pl*
- Schottischer Abend, m
  - ◆ Scottish Evening
  - ◆ Scottish Night
- schottischer Whisky, m
  - ◆ Scotch whisky
  - ◆ Scotch
- schottisches Gericht, n
  - ◆ Scottish dish
- schottische Soße, f
  - ◆ Scottish sauce
- Schottisches Tiefland, n
  - ◆ Lowlands, the *pl*
- Schottland
  - ◆ Scotland
- Schottlandurlaub, m
  - Schottlandferien, pl
  - ◆ Scottish vacation *AE*
  - ◆ Scottish holiday *BE*
  - ◆ vacation in Scotland *AE*
  - ◆ holiday in Scotland *BE*
- Schrank, m
  - ◆ cupboard
- Schrank, m (Kleider)
  - Kleiderschrank, m
  - ◆ wardrobe *BE*
  - ◆ closet *AE*
  - ◆ clothes closet *AE*
  - ◆ clothespress *AE*
- Schrank, m (Wäsche)
  - Wäscheschrank, m
  - ◆ clothespress *AE*
  - ◆ linen closet *AE*
  - ◆ linen cupboard *BE*
- Schrankbett, n
  - ◆ wardrobe bed
  - ◆ Murphy bed
  - ◆ murphy bed
  - ◆ fold-away bed
- Schrankdoppelbett, n
  - ◆ double wardrobe bed
- Schranke, f (Zug)
  - ◆ gate
- Schrankelement, n
  - ◆ cupboard unit
- Schrankenwärter, m
  - (Zug)
  - ◆ gatekeeper
- Schrankfach, n
  - ◆ compartment
- schrankfertig, adj
  - (Wäsche)
  - ◆ washed and ironed, adj
- schrankgroßes Zimmer, n
  - ◆ cupboard-size room
- Schrankklappbett, n
  - ◆ folding wardrobe bed
  - ◆ wardrobe bed
- Schrankkoffer, m
  - ◆ wardrobe trunk
  - ◆ trunk
- Schranknische, f
  - ◆ cupboard recess
- Schrankpreis m
  - → Rackrate
- Schrankraum, m
  - Kleiderschrankraum, m
  - ◆ wardrobe space
  - ◆ closet space *AE*

Schrankwand

Schrankwand, f
- wall unit
- wall-to-wall cupboard

schreckliches Essen, n
- dreadful food

schreckliches Hotel, n
- terrible hotel

Schreibartikel, m pl
- writing supplies *pl*

Schreibauflage, f
(am Stuhl)
- writing arm

Schreibblock, m
- writing pad *AE*
- writing-pad *BE*
- writing block

Schreiben Sie noch heute!
- Write today!

Schreibmaschine f
- typewriter

Schreibmaterial, n
- writing material

Schreibpapier, n
- writing paper *AE*
- writing-paper *BE*

Schreibservice, m
→ Sekretariatsdienst

Schreibtafel, f
→ Tafel

Schreibtisch, m
- writing desk *AE*
- writing-desk *BE*
- desk

Schreibtischgarnitur, f
- desk set

Schreibtischlampe, f
- desk lamp

Schreibtischschublade, f
Schreibtischschubfach, n
- desk drawer

Schreibwaren, f pl
- stationery

Schreibwarengeschäft, n
Schreibwarenhandlung f
Papierwarengeschäft n
Papierwarenhandlung f
- stationery store *AE*
- stationer's shop *BE*
- stationer's *BE*

Schreibwarenhändler m
Papierwarenhändler m
- stationer

Schreibzimmer, n
Schreibraum, m
- writing room *AE*
- writing-room *BE*

Schreiner, m
- cabinetmaker *AE*
- cabinet-maker *BE*

schriftlich, adj
- written, adj
- in writing, adv

schriftlich, adv
- in writing, adv

schriftlich bestätigen etw
- confirm s.th. in writing
- make a confirmation in writing
- send a written confirmation

schriftlich buchen etw
- book s.th. in writing
- make a booking in writing

schriftliche Bestätigung f
- written confirmation
- confirmation in writing

schriftliche Bestätigung senden
- send a written confirmation

schriftliche Buchung, f
schriftliche Bestellung, f
- written booking
- booking in writing

schriftliche Buchungsbestätigung, f
- written confirmation of the booking

schriftliche Buchungsbestätigung senden jm
- send s.o. a written confirmation of the booking

schriftliche Buchungsstornierung, f
- cancellation of a booking in writing
- cancelation of a booking in writing *AE*
- written cancellation of a booking
- written cancelation of a booking *AE*

schriftliche Einladung, f
- written invitation

schriftlich einladen jn
schriftliche Einladung senden an jn
- send s.o. a written invitation

schriftliche Kündigung, f
Kündigungsschreiben, n
- written notice

schriftliche Preisangabe, f
- written quotation

Schriftliche Preisangaben auf Wunsch
- Written quotations on request

schriftliche Reisebestätigung, f
- written travel confirmation
- written confirmation of a tour

schriftliche Reservierung, f
- written reservation
- reservation in writing

schriftliche Reservierungsbestätigung, f
- written confirmation of the reservation

schriftlicher Mietvertrag, m
- written lease

schriftliche Rückbestätigung, f
schriftliche Gegenbestätigung, f
- written reconfirmation
- reconfirmation in writing

schriftlicher Vertrag, m
- written contract

schriftliche Stornierung, f
schriftlicher Rücktritt, m
schriftliche Absage, f
- written cancellation
- written cancelation *AE*
- cancellation in writing
- cancelation in writing *AE*

schriftliche Unterkunftsanfrage, f
- letter requesting accommodation

schriftliche Zimmerbestätigung, f
schriftliche Zimmerzusage, f
- written confirmation of the room
- written room confirmation

schriftliche Zustimmung, f
- written consent

schriftlich kündigen (etw)
- give notice in writing

schriftlich melden jm etw
- report s.th. in writing to s.o.

schriftlich reservieren etw
- reserve s.th. in writing
- make a reservation in writing

schriftlich rückbestätigen etw
schriftlich gegenbestätigen etw
- reconfirm s.th. in writing

schriftlich stornieren etw
- cancel s.th. in writing
- make a cancellation in writing
- make a cancelation in writing *AE*

Schriftwechsel, m
→ Korrespondenz

Schritt fahren (Auto)
- drive at walking speed

Schrotbrot, n
- coarse bread

Schrothkurhotel, n
- hotel offering Schroth treatment

Schublade, f
Schubfach, n
- drawer

Schuh, m
- shoe

Schuhbürste, f
- shoe brush

Schuhcreme, f
- shoe polish
- shoe cream

Schuhe putzen
- polish one's shoes
- polish s.o.'s shoes
- shine one's shoes *coll*
- shine s.o.'s shoes *coll*

Schuhlöffel, m
- shoehorn
- shoespoon *AE*

Schuhmesse, f
- shoe fair

Schuhmuseum, n
- shoe museum

Schuhpoliermaschine, f
→ Schuhputzautomat

Schuhputzapparat m
→ Schuhputzautomat

Schuhputzautomat,
Schuhputzapparat m
- shoe-cleaning machine

Schuhputzautomat benutzen
- use the shoe-cleaning machine

Schuhputzdienst, m
Schuhputzservice, m
- shoe-cleaning service
- shoeshine service *AE*

Schuhputzer, m
- shoeblack
- bootblack
- boots *BE*

Schuhputzlappen, m
Schuhputztuch, n
- shoe-shining cloth

Schuhputzmaschine, f
→ Schuhputzautomat

Schuhspanner, m
- shoe tree *AE*
- shoe-tree *BE*

Schuhwerk, n
- footwear

Schulabenteuerurlaub, m
Schulabenteuerferien, pl
- school adventure vacation *AE*
- school adventure holiday *BE*

Schulausflug, m
- school excursion
- school outing
- school treat BE

Schulaustauschfahrt, f
- school exchange trip

Schulbus, m
- school bus

Schuld bezahlen
- pay a debt

schulden jm etw
- owe s.o. s.th.
- owe s.th. to s.o.

Schule, f
- school

Schule besuchen
- attend school

schulen jn
→ ausbilden jn

Schüleraustausch, m
- exchange of pupils
- exchange of students

Schülersprachreise, f
- student language trip

Schulessen, n (generell)
- school meal

Schulessen, n (mittags)
- school lunch AE
- school dinner BE

Schulfahrt, f
- school trip

Schulfahrt machen
- go on a school trip

Schulferien, pl
- school vacation AE
- school holidays BE pl

Schulferienzeit, f
- school vacation period AE
- school holiday period BE

Schulfest, n
- school party
- school treat BE

Schulgruppe, f
- school group
- school party

Schulhaus, n
- schoolhouse

Schulhotel, n SCHW
→ Lehrhotel

Schulkantine, f
- school canteen

Schulklasse, f
- school class

Schullandheim n
- school hostel in the country

Schulmensa, f
- school refectory

Schulmittagessen, n
Schulessen, n
- school dinner BE
- school lunch AE

Schulmuseum, n
- school museum

Schulreisen, n
Schulreiseverkehr, m
- school travel

Schulsaal, m
Schulraum, m
- schoolroom

Schulspeise, f
- school food

Schulter, f
- shoulder

Schulterfilet, n
- shoulder fillet
- shoulder filet

Schultermassage, f
- shoulder massage

Schulturnhalle, f
- school gymnasium
- school gym coll

Schulung, f
- schooling
- instruction
- training

Schulungsabend, m
- evening training

Schulungskurs, m
→ Ausbildungskurs

Schulungsprogramm, n
→ Ausbildungsprogramm

Schulungsraum, m
- training room

Schulungsseminar, n
- training seminar

Schulungsveranstaltung, f
- training event

Schulungszentrum, n
Trainingszentrum, n
- training center AE
- training centre BE

Schulverpflegung, f
- school foodservice AE
- school catering BE

Schulzeit, f
(Gegensatz zu Ferien)
- term-time

schummerig beleuchtete Bar, f
- dimly lit bar

schunkeln
- sway

Schunkeln, n
- swaying

schunkeln zur Musik
- sway to the music

Schuppe, f
- scale

Schuppen, m (Lagerung)
- shed

Schuppen, m (Lokal)
billiges Lokal, n
- shack

Schürhaken, m
(für Ofen)
- poker

Schürze, f
- apron

Schuß, m (Flüssigkeit)
- stick AE

Schüttelbecher, m
(Bar)
Mixbecher, m
Mischbecher, m
Shaker, m
- shaker

schütteln etw
- shake s.th.

schütteln etw kräftig
- shake s.th. vigorously

Schutz bieten
- offer shelter
- provide shelter

Schutz bieten für Reisende
- offer shelter for travellers
- offer shelter for travelers AE
- provide shelter for travellers
- provide shelter for travelers AE

Schutz der Landschaft, m
Landschaftsschutz, m
- protection of the countryside
- conservation of the countryside

Schützenfest, n
- marksmen's festival
- shooting festival

schützen sich gegen unvorhersehbare Ereignisse
- protect oneself against unforeseen eventualities

Schutzgebiet, n
(für Tiere)
- sanctuary

Schutzgeld, n
- protection money

Schutzgeld zahlen
- pay protection money

Schutzheiliger, m
Schutzpatron, m
- patron saint

Schutzhütte, f
- refuge
- shelter
- hut

Schutzimpfung, f
- protective inoculation
- protective vaccination

Schutzzone, f
- protection zone

Schwabe, m
- Swabian

Schwaben
(Region)
- Swabia

Schwäbin, f
- Swabian girl
- Swabian woman
- Swabian

schwäbisch, adj
- Swabian, adj

Schwäbische Alb, f
(Region)
- Swabian Jura, the
- Swabian Alb, the

Schwäbische Allgäu, das, n
- Swabian Allgäu, the
- Swabian Algäu, the

Schwäbische Dichterstraße, f
(Ferienstraße)
- Swabian Route of Poets, the
- Swabian Road of Poets, the

schwäbische Küche, f
- Swabian cuisine
- Swabian cooking

Schwäbische Weinstraße, f
- Swabian Wine Road, the
- Swabian Wine Route, the

schwach alkoholisch, adj
- mildly alcoholic, adj

schwach alkoholisches Getränk, n
- mildly alcoholic drink
- mildly alcoholic beverage

schwach besucht, adj
(Lokal)
schlecht besucht, adj
- poorly frequented, adj

schwach besuchtes Seminar, n
♦ poorly attended seminar
schwache Auslastung, f
→ geringe Auslastung
schwache Auslastungszeit, f
→ Belegungsflaute
schwache Belegung, f
schwache Auslastung, f
♦ slack occupancy
♦ low occupancy
schwache Belegung haben
schwache Auslastung haben
♦ have a slack occupancy
♦ have a low occupancy
Schwäche haben für etw
♦ have a soft spot for s.th.
schwacher Esser, m
♦ poor eater
schwacher Punkt, m
♦ weak point
schwache Saison, f
♦ poor season
schwach gebucht, adj
schlecht gebucht, adj
♦ poorly booked, adj
schwach gebuchtes Hotel, n
♦ poorly booked hotel
Schwamm, m
♦ sponge
schwanken
(Zahlen)
♦ fluctuate
Schwankung, f
♦ fluctuation
schwärmen von etw
♦ rave about s.th.
Schwarzafrika
♦ Black Africa
Schwarzarbeit, f
♦ moonlighting
♦ illicit work
schwarzarbeiten
♦ moonlight
♦ do illicit work
schwarz brennen
(illegal Akohol distillieren)
♦ moonshine AE
Schwarzbrenner, m
♦ illegal distiller
♦ illicit distiller
♦ moonshiner AE
Schwarzbrennerei, f (Aktivität)
♦ illegal distilling
♦ illicit distilling
♦ moonshining AE
Schwarzbrennerei, f (Anlage)
♦ illegal distillery
♦ illicit distillery
♦ moonshining still AE
♦ illicit still
Schwarzbrot, n
♦ brown bread
♦ black bread
schwarze Brigade, f
(Kellner)
♦ black brigade
Schwarze Johannisbeere, f
♦ blackcurrant
Schwarze Johannisbeerkonfitüre, f
♦ blackcurrant jam

Schwarze Liste, f
♦ blacklist
Schwarze Liste führen
♦ keep a blacklist
Schwarze Meer, das, n
♦ Black Sea, the
schwarze Olive, f
♦ black olive
Schwarze Piste, f
(sehr schwierige Skipiste)
Schwarze Abfahrt, f
♦ black run
schwarzer Kaffee, m
→ Kaffee ohne Milch
schwarzer Pfeffer, m
♦ black pepper
Schwarzes Brett, n
Informationsbrett, n
♦ bulletin board AE
♦ notice board BE
♦ newsboard BE
Schwarzfahrer, m
♦ deadhead fam
♦ fare dodger
♦ dodger
Schwarzgastronomie, f
♦ illegal catering
♦ illicit catering
♦ illegal foodservice AE
♦ illicit foodservice AE
Schwarzhändler, m (bes. alkoholische Getränke)
Alkoholschmuggler, m
♦ bootlegger
Schwarzmarktkurs, m
♦ black market rate
Schwarzmeerferienort, m
Schwarzmeerurlaubsort, m
♦ Black Sea resort
Schwarzmeerflotte, f
♦ Black Sea fleet
Schwarzmeerhafen, f
♦ Black Sea port
Schwarzmeerheilbad, n
♦ Black Sea health resort
Schwarzmeerkreuzfahrt, f
♦ Black Sea cruise
Schwarzmeerkurort, m
♦ Black Sea spa
Schwarzmeerküste, f
♦ Black Sea coast
Schwarzmeerstadt, f
♦ Black Sea town
Schwarzriesling, m
♦ Black Riesling
Schwarztourismus, m
Schwarztouristik, f
♦ illegal tourism
♦ illegal tour operating
Schwarzwald, m
♦ Black Forest, the
Schwarzwaldabend, m
♦ Black Forest Evening
♦ Black Forest Night
Schwarzwaldbahn, f
♦ Black Forest Railroad AE
♦ Black Forest Railway BE
Schwarzwalddorf, n
♦ Black Forest village
Schwarzwälder Kirschtorte, f
♦ Black Forest cherry cake

Schwarzwaldgipfel, m
♦ Black Forest peak
Schwarzwaldhaus, n
♦ Black Forest house
Schwarzwaldkurort, m
♦ Black Forest spa
Schwarzwaldlandschaft, f
♦ Black Forest scenery
♦ Black Forest landscape
Schwarzwaldmuseum, n
♦ Black Forest museum
Schwarzwaldsammlung, f
♦ Black Forest collection
Schwarzwaldschinken, m
Schwarzwälder Schinken, m
♦ Black Forest ham
Schwarzwaldstadt, f (Großstadt)
♦ Black Forest city
Schwarzwaldstadt, f (kleine Stadt)
♦ Black Forest town
Schwarzwaldtal, n
♦ Black Forest valley
Schwarzwaldtälerstraße, f
♦ Black Forest Valley Road, the
Schwarzwaldtorte, f
Schwarzwälder Torte, f
♦ Black Forest gateau AE
♦ Black Forest gâteau BE
Schwarzwalduhr, f
♦ Black Forest clock
Schwarzwaldverein, m
♦ Black Forest Association, the
Schwarzweißfernseher m
♦ black-and-white TV
♦ black-and-white television
♦ b/w TV
Schwarzweißfilm, m
♦ black-and-white film
♦ b/w film
Schwarzweißfoto, n
♦ black-and-white photo
♦ black-and-white photograph
♦ b/w photo(graph)
Schwarzwurzel, f
♦ salsify
Schwebebahn, f
♦ suspension railroad AE
♦ suspension railway BE
♦ hovertrain
Schwede, m
♦ Swede
Schweden
♦ Sweden
Schwedenbüfett, n
→ Smorgasbord
Schwedenpunsch, m
♦ Swedish punch
Schwedin, f
♦ Swedish girl
♦ Swedish woman
♦ Swede
schwedisch, adj
♦ Swedish, adj
schwedische Art, adv gastr
nach schwedischer Art, adv gastr
♦ Swedish style, adv gastr
Schwefelquelle, f
♦ sulphur spring
♦ sulfur spring AE

Schwefelwasser, n
 ♦ sulphur water
 ♦ sulfur water AE
Schwein, n
 ♦ pig
Schweinebraten, m
 Schweinsbraten, m SCHW/ÖST
 ♦ roast pork
Schweinebratenstück, n (roh)
 (Stück zum Braten)
 ♦ joint of pork
Schweinefilet, n
 ♦ pork fillet
 ♦ pork filet
 ♦ filet of pork
 ♦ fillet of pork
Schweinefleisch, n
 ♦ pork
Schweinefleischgericht, n
 ♦ pork dish
Schweinefleischscheibe, f
 ♦ pork slice
 ♦ slice of pork
Schweinefleischwürfel, m
 ♦ pork cube
Schweinefraß, m derog
 Saufraß, m derog
 ♦ swill derog
 ♦ pigswill derog
Schweinefrikassee, n
 ♦ pork fricassee
Schweinehaschee, n
 ♦ minced pork
Schweinehaxe, f
 ♦ knuckle of pork
 ♦ pork knuckle
Schweinekebab, m
 ♦ pork kebab
Schweinekotelett, n
 ♦ pork cutlet
Schweinekotelett, n (entbeint)
 ♦ pork chop
Schweineleber, f
 ♦ pig's liver
Schweinelende, f
 ♦ tenderloin of pork
 ♦ loin of pork
 ♦ pork tenderloin
Schweinelendenbraten, m
 ♦ roast loin of pork
Schweinepastete, f
 ♦ pork pâté
 ♦ pork pie
Schweineragout, n/m
 ♦ pork stew
Schweineschmalz, n
 ♦ lard
Schweinesteak, n
 ♦ pork steak
Schweinewurst, f
 ♦ pork sausage
 ♦ pork banger BE inform
Schweiz, f
 ♦ Switzerland
schweizer, adj
 schweizerisch, adj
 ♦ Swiss, adj
Schweizer, m
 ♦ Swiss
Schweizer Alpen, die, pl
 ♦ Swiss Alps, the, pl

Schweizerart, adv gastr
 nach Schweizerart, adv gastr
 ♦ Swiss style, adj gastr
schweizer Grenze, f
 ♦ Swiss border
 ♦ Swiss frontier
Schweizer Hotelier-Verein, m
 SHV, m
 ♦ Swiss Hotel Association
 ♦ SHA
Schweizerin, f
 ♦ Swiss girl
 ♦ Swiss woman
 ♦ Swiss
Schweizer Jura m
 (Region)
 ♦ Swiss Jura
Schweizer Käse, m
 ♦ Swiss cheese
Schweizer Küche, f
 ♦ Swiss cuisine
 ♦ Swiss cooking
Schwelle, f (Eisenbahn)
 ♦ sleeper BE
 ♦ tie AE
Schwelle, f (Tür)
 ♦ threshold
Schwenker, m
 (Glas)
 ♦ balloon glass
 ♦ balloon
schwerbehindert, adj
 ♦ seriously disabled, adj
 ♦ severely handicapped, adj
Schwerbehindertenzimmer, n
 ♦ room suitable for a seriously disabled person
Schwerbehinderter, m
 Schwerbeschädigter, m
 ♦ seriously disabled person
 ♦ person who is seriously disabled
schwerbeladen, adj
 ♦ heavily laden, adj
schwerbeladenes Flugzeug, n
 ♦ heavily laden plane
Schwerbeschädigter, m
 → Schwerbehinderter
schwerer Wein, m
 ♦ heavy wine
 ♦ full-bodied wine
schweres Essen, n
 ♦ heavy meal
schweres Gepäck, n
 ♦ heavy baggage AE
 ♦ heavy luggage BE
schwer im Magen liegen
 ♦ lie heavy on the stomach
Schweriner See, m
 ♦ Lake of Schwerin, the
Schwerpunkt liegt auf dem Komfort
 Betonung liegt auf dem Komfort
 ♦ accent is on comfort
schwer verdaulich, adj
 unverdaulich, adj
 unverdaubar, adj
 ♦ indigestible, adj
 ♦ heavy, adj
schwer verdauliches Essen, n (Mahl)
 ♦ indigestible meal
schwer verdauliches Essen, n (Speisen)
 ♦ indigestible food

schwer verdauliches Schulessen, n
 ♦ stodgy school meal
schwer verdauliches Zeug, n
 Fraß, m coll
 ♦ stodge sl
schwerverdaulich sein
 ♦ be indigestible
schwer zu finden sein
 ♦ be difficult to find
Schwesterbetrieb, m
 ♦ sister establishment
 ♦ sister operation
Schwesterhotel, n
 ♦ sister hotel
Schwesterinsel, f
 ♦ sister island
Schwesternheim, n
 ♦ nurses' home
Schwesterrestaurant n
 ♦ sister restaurant
Schwesterschiff, n
 ♦ sister ship
schwierige Abfahrt, f (Ski)
 (meist schwarz gekennzeichnet)
 schwierige Piste, f
 ♦ difficult ski run
 ♦ difficult run
schwierigen Gast enttäuschen
 ♦ disappoint a difficult guest
schwieriger Esser, m
 ♦ fussy eater
schwieriger Gast, m
 ♦ difficult guest
schwieriger Kunde, m
 ♦ difficult customer
 ♦ difficult client
Schwierigkeitsgrad, m
 ♦ degree of difficulty
Schwimmanfänger, m
 ♦ novice swimmer
Schwimmanlage, f
 Schwimmkomplex, m
 ♦ swimming complex
Schwimmanzug, m
 (für Frauen)
 Badeanzug, m
 ♦ swimsuit AE
 ♦ swim-suit BE
Schwimmbad, n
 ♦ swimming pool AE
 ♦ swim pool AE
 ♦ swimming-pool BE
Schwimmbadanlage, f
 Schwimmbadkomplex, m
 ♦ swimming-pool complex
Schwimmbadannehmlichkeit, f
 ♦ poolside amenity
Schwimmbadbar, f
 ♦ swimming-pool bar
 ♦ poolside bar
 ♦ pool bar
Schwimmbad beheizen
 Schwimmbad heizen
 ♦ heat a swimming pool AE
 ♦ heat a swimming-pool BE
 ♦ heat a pool
Schwimmbadbeheizung, f
 Schwimmbadheizung, f
 ♦ heating (of) a swimming pool AE
 ♦ heating (of) a swimming-pool BE
 ♦ heating (of) a pool

Schwimmbad benutzen

Schwimmbad benutzen
Schwimmbad nutzen
♦ use the swimming pool *AE*
♦ use the swimming-pool *BE*
♦ use the pool
Schwimmbadbenutzer, m
♦ person using the swimming pool *AE*
♦ person using the swimming-pool *BE*
♦ swimming-pool user
Schwimmbadbenutzung, f
♦ use of the swimming pool *AE*
♦ using a swimming pool *AE*
♦ use of the swimming-pool *BE*
♦ using the swimming-pool *BE*
Schwimmbadbenutzung ist im Preis enthalten
Schwimmbadbenutzung ist im Preis inbegriffen
♦ use of the swimming pool is included in the price *AE*
♦ use of the swimming-pool is included in the price *BE*
Schwimmbadbereich, m
Schwimmbeckenbereich, m
♦ swimming-pool area
♦ pool area
Schwimmbadbesuch, m
♦ visit to the swimming pool *AE*
♦ visit to the swimming-pool *BE*
♦ visit to the pool
Schwimmbadbetrieb, m
♦ swimming-pool establishment
♦ swimming-pool operation
♦ operating a swimming pool
Schwimmbadblick, m
♦ poolview *AE*
♦ pool view *BE*
Schwimmbadcafé, n
♦ poolside cafe *AE*
♦ poolside café *BE*
Schwimmbadcafeteria f
♦ poolside cafeteria
Schwimmbadeinrichtung, f
♦ swimming-pool facility
Schwimmbaderöffnung, f
Eröffnung eines Schwimmbads, f
♦ opening of a swimming pool *AE*
♦ opening of a swimming-pool *BE*
♦ opening of a pool
Schwimmbadfläche, f
♦ swimming-pool area
♦ pool area
Schwimmbad für Hausgäste, n
♦ residents' swimming pool *AE*
♦ swimming pool for residents
♦ residents' swimming-pool *BE*
Schwimmbadgebühr, f
♦ swimming-pool charge
♦ swimming-pool fee
Schwimmbadgrill, m
♦ poolside barbecue
Schwimmbad hat eine Kinderecke
♦ swimming pool has a children's corner *AE*
♦ swimming-pool has a children's corner *BE*
Schwimmbad hat einen Kinderteil
Schwimmbecken hat einen Kinderteil
♦ swimming pool has a children's section *AE*
♦ swimming-pool has a children's section *BE*
Schwimmbad hat ein flaches Ende für Kinder
Schwimmbecken hat ein flaches Ende für Kinder
♦ swimming pool has a shallow end for children *AE*
♦ swimming-pool has a shallow end for children *BE*

Schwimmbadimbißstube, f
Schwimmbadimbiß, m
♦ poolside snack bar
Schwimmbad im Freien, n
→ Freibad
Schwimmbad im Garten, n
♦ swimming pool in the garden *AE*
♦ swimming-pool in the garden *BE*
♦ pool in the garden
Schwimmbad ist nachts beleuchtet
♦ swimming pool is illuminated at night *AE*
♦ swimming-pool is illuminated at night *BE*
Schwimmbadkomplex, m
→ Schwimmbadanlage
Schwimmbad liegt in einem gepflegten Rasen
♦ swimming pool is set in a well-kept lawn *AE*
♦ swimming-pool is set in a well-kept lawn *BE*
Schwimmbad mit Nichtschwimmerteil, n
♦ swimming pool with nonswimmers' section *AE*
♦ swimming-pool with non-swimmers' section *BE*
Schwimmbadpersonal, n
♦ swimming-pool personnel
♦ swimming-pool staff
Schwimmbadrestaurant, n
♦ poolside restaurant
Schwimmbadservice, m
Schwimmbaddienst, m
♦ swimming-pool service
♦ pool service
Schwimmbadstuhl, m
♦ poolside chair
Schwimmbadterrasse, f
Schwimmbeckenterrasse, f
♦ swimming-pool terrace
♦ pool terrace
Schwimmbadwartung, f
♦ swimming-pool maintenance
Schwimmbadwasser, n
Schwimmbeckenwasser, n
♦ swimming-pool water
Schwimmbassin, n
→ Schwimmbecken
Schwimmbecken, n
Schwimmbassin, n
♦ swim pool *AE*
♦ swimming pool *AE*
♦ swimming-pool *BE*
♦ lido *AE*
♦ pool
Schwimmbeckenbereich, m
→ Schwimmbadbereich
Schwimmbecken mit Olympiamaßen, n
♦ Olympic-size swimming pool *AE*
♦ Olympic-size swimming-pool *BE*
Schwimmbeckenterrasse, f
→ Schwimmbadterrasse
Schwimmbrille, f
♦ swim goggles *pl*
Schwimmeinrichtung, f
♦ swimming facility
Schwimmeister, m
(in Schwimmbad)
♦ swimming-pool attendant
♦ pool attendant
schwimmende Ferienwohnung, f
schwimmende Urlaubswohnung, f
♦ floating vacation apartment *AE*
♦ floating holiday flat *BE*
schwimmender Garten, m
♦ floating garden

schwimmender Markt, m
♦ floating market
schwimmender Wohnplatz, m
schwimmende Wohnung, f
♦ floating residence
schwimmendes Hotel, n
Hotelschiff, n
♦ floating hotel
♦ boatel *humor*
♦ botel *humor*
schwimmendes Kasino, n
♦ floating casino
schwimmendes Luxushotel, n
♦ floating deluxe hotel *AE*
♦ floating luxury hotel *BE*
schwimmendes Museum, n
♦ floating museum
schwimmendes Restaurant n
♦ floating restaurant
schwimmende Wohnung, f
♦ floating apartment *AE*
♦ floating flat *BE*
schwimmen (Gegenstand)
♦ float
schwimmen gehen
♦ go for a swim
♦ go swimming
schwimmen im See
schwimmen in dem See
♦ swim in the lake
schwimmen (Person)
♦ swim
♦ have a swim
Schwimmer, m
♦ swimmer
Schwimmerbecken, n
(Gegensatz zu Nichtschwimmerbecken)
♦ swimmers' pool
Schwimmfest, n
♦ swimming gala
Schwimmflosse, f
♦ swim fin
Schwimmgelegenheit, f
♦ opportunity for swimming
Schwimmgelegenheiten anbieten
♦ offer opportunities for swimming
Schwimmgürtel, m
♦ swimming belt
Schwimmhalle, f
→ Hallenbad
Schwimmkampf, m
♦ swimming contest
Schwimmkleidung, f
♦ swimwear
Schwimmkurs, m
♦ swimming course
♦ swim course *AE*
♦ swimming class
Schwimmkurs belegen
♦ take a swimming course
Schwimmkurs machen
♦ do a swimming course
♦ do a swim course *AE*
Schwimmkurs mit Unterkunft, m
Schwimmlehrgang mit Unterkunft, m
♦ residential swimming course
Schwimmlehrer, m
♦ swimming instructor
Schwimmlehrerin f
♦ swimming instructress

680

Schwimmparadies n
- swimmer's paradise
- swimming paradise

Schwimmsaison, f
Badesaison, f
- swimming season

Schwimmschule f
- swimming school

Schwimmspaß, m
- swimming fun

Schwimmstadion, n
- swimming stadium

Schwimmstrand, m
- swimming beach

Schwimmstunde, f
- swimming lesson

Schwimmtrikot, n
- swimming-costume BE
- bathing-costume BE

Schwimmunterricht, m
- swimming instruction
- swimming lessons pl
- swimming instruction

Schwimmunterricht geben
- give swimming lessons

Schwimmunterricht nehmen
- take swimming lessons

Schwimmverein, m
Schwimmclub, m
- swimming club

Schwimmweste, f
- life jacket AE
- life-jacket
- life vest AE

Schwimmwettbewerb, m
- swimming competition

Schwindel, m
- swindle
- swizz BE inform
- swizzle BE inform

Schwips, m
Rausch, m
- jag
- tipsiness

Schwips haben
→ beschwipst sein

Schwitzbad, n
Dampfbad, n
- vapor bath AE
- vapour bath BE
- Turkish bath
- steam bath
- Russian bath

schwul, adj coll
- queer, adj coll
- gay, adj

Schwulenbar, f
- gay bar

Schwuler, m coll
- queer derog
- gay
- pansy coll

Schwund, m
Schwundverlust, m
- shrinkage

Scilly-Inseln, f pl
- Scilly Isles, the pl
- Isles of Scilly, the pl

Scotch Broth, m
(schottische Hammelsuppe)
- Scotch broth

Sechsbettcaravan, m
Sechsbettwohnwagen, m
- six-berth caravan BE
- six-berth van BE coll
- six-berth trailer AE

Sechsbettenschlafsaal, m
Schlafsaal mit sechs Betten, m
- six-bed dormitory

sechsbettig, adj
- six-bedded, adj

sechsbettiges Zimmer, n
- six-bedded room

Sechsbettvilla, f
- six-bed villa

Sechsbettwohnwagen, m
Sechsbettcaravan, m
- six-berth trailer AE
- six-berth caravan BE
- six-berth van BE coll

Sechsbettzimmer, n
- six-bed room
- six-bedded room

sechseckig, adj
- hexagonal, adj

sechseckiger Tisch, m
- hexagonal table

Sechsertisch, m
Sechspersonentisch, m
- table for six persons
- table for six
- table to seat six persons

sechsgängig, adj (Essen)
- six-course, adj
- consisting of six courses, adj

sechsgängiges Abendessen, n (Dinner)
- six-course dinner

sechsgängiges Abendessen, n (Supper)
- six-course supper

sechsgängiges Bankett, n
- six-course banquet

sechsgängiges Essen, n
- six-course meal

sechsgängiges Menü n
- six-course menu

sechsgängiges Mittagessen, n
- six-course luncheon
- six-course lunch

Sechs-Gang-Menü, n
→ sechsgängiges Menü

Sechsgangrad, n
Rad mit sechs Gängen, n
- six-gear bike

sechsköpfige Familie, f
- family of six

Sechskornbrot, n
- six-cereal bread

Sechspersonenzelt, n
- six-person tent

Sechsraumwohnung, f
→ Sechszimmerwohnung

sechsstöckiges Gebäude, n
- six-story building AE
- six-storey building BE
- six-floor building

sechsstöckiges Hotel, n
- six-floor hotel
- six-story hotel AE
- six-storey hotel BE

sechsstündig, adj
- six-hour, adj
- lasting six hours
- of six hours' duration

sechsstündiger Marsch, m
- six hours' march

sechsstündige Veranstaltung, f
- six-hour event
- six-hour function

sechsstündige Verspätung, f
- six-hour delay

Sechstagearrangement, n
- six-day arrangement

Sechstagefahrt, f
→ sechstägige Fahrt

Sechstagekonzession, f
(für sechs Wochentage)
Sechstagelizenz, f
- six-day license
- six-day licence
- six-day concession

Sechstagepaß, m
- six-day pass

Sechstageskipaß, m
- six-day ski pass

sechstägig, adj
- six-day, adj
- six days'
- of six days' duration
- lasting six days

sechstägige Fahrt, f
Sechstagefahrt, f
- six-day trip
- six days' trip

sechster Gang, m (Menü)
- sixth course

sechster Gang, m (Motor)
- sixth gear

sechstes Stockwerk, n
sechste Etage, f
sechstes Obergeschoß, n
- seventh floor AE
- seventh story AE
- sixth floor BE
- sixth storey BE

sechswöchig, adj
- six-week, adj
- lasting six weeks
- of six weeks' duration

sechswöchige Reise, f
- six-week journey
- six-week tour
- six-week trip

sechswöchige Tournee, f
- six-week tour

Sechszimmerappartement, n
- six-room apartment

Sechszimmerferienwohnung, f
Sechszimmerurlaubswohnung, f
- six-room vacation apartment AE
- six-room holiday flat BE

sechszimmerig, adj
- six-roomed, adj

sechszimmerige Wohnung, f
- six-roomed apartment AE
- six-roomed flat BE

Sechszimmerwohnung, f
- six-room flat BE
- six-room apartment AE

Sechzig-Betten-Hotel, n
- sixty-bed hotel

Secrétaire de réception, m FR
Empfangssekretär, m

See

Empfangssekretärin, f
♦ secrétaire de réception *FR*
See, f
→ Meer
See, m
♦ lake
Seeaal, m
Meeraal, m
♦ conger eel
♦ conger
Seealge, f
♦ sea alga
Seealgenbad, n *med*
♦ seaweed bath *med*
Seealgenkörperpackung, f
♦ seaweed body wrap
Seealpen, pl
♦ Maritime Alps, the *pl*
Seeappartement, n (Binnensee)
♦ lakeside apartment
♦ lakefront apartment *AE*
♦ lake-front apartment *BE*
Seeappartement, n (Meer)
♦ seaside apartment
♦ seafront apartment *AE*
♦ sea-front apartment *BE*
Seebad, n (Binnensee)
(Ort)
♦ lakeside resort
Seebad, n (Meer)
(Ort)
♦ seaside resort
♦ seaside watering place
Seebadekur, f
♦ marinotherapy
Seebaden, n
Meerbaden, n
Baden im Meer, n
Baden in der See, n
♦ sea bathing
Seebadestrand, m (Binnensee)
♦ lakeside lido
Seebadestrand, m (Meer)
♦ seaside lido
♦ lido
Seebadhotel, n (Binnensee)
♦ lakeside resort hotel
Seebadhotel, n (Meer)
♦ seaside resort hotel
Seebahnhof, n (Binnensee)
♦ lakeside station
Seebahnhof, m (Meer)
♦ seaside station
Seebarbe, f
Meerbarbe, f
♦ red mullet
Seeblick, m (Binnensee)
Blick auf den See m
♦ lakeview *AE*
♦ lake view *BE*
♦ view of the lake
Seeblick, m (Meer)
→ Meeresblick
Seeblickrestaurant, n (Binnensee)
♦ lakeview restaurant *AE*
♦ lake-view restaurant *BE*
Seeblickrestaurant, n (Meer)
♦ seaview restaurant *AE*
♦ sea-view restaurant *BE*
Seeblickterrasse, f (Meer)
♦ seaview terrace *AE*

♦ sea-view terrace *BE*
♦ ocean-view terrace
Seeblickterrasse f (Binnensee)
♦ lakeview terrace *AE*
♦ lake-view terrace *BE*
Seeblickzimmer, n (Binnensee)
♦ lakeview room *AE*
♦ lake-view room *BE*
Seeblickzimmer, n (Meer)
♦ seaview room *AE*
♦ sea-view room *BE*
Seeblickzuschlag, m (Binnensee)
Zuschlag für Seeblick, m
♦ lakeview supplement *AE*
♦ lake-view supplement *BE*
♦ supplement for lakeview *AE*
♦ supplement for lake view *BE*
Seeblickzuschlag, m (Meer)
♦ seaview supplement *AE*
♦ supplement for seaview *AE*
♦ sea-view supplement *BE*
♦ supplement for sea-view *BE*
Seebühne, f (am Binnensee)
♦ lakeside stage
Seebühne, f (auf dem Binnensee)
♦ lake stage
Seebungalow, m (Binnensee)
♦ lakeside bungalow
♦ lakefront bungalow *AE*
♦ lake-front bungalow *BE*
Seebungalow, m (Meer)
♦ seaside bungalow
♦ seafront bungalow *AE*
♦ sea-front bungalow *BE*
Seecafé, n (Binnensee)
♦ lakeside cafe *AE*
♦ lakeside café *BE*
Seecafé, n (Meer)
♦ seaside café *BE*
♦ seaside cafe *AE*
Seecampingplatz, m (Binnensee)
♦ lakeside campsite
♦ lakeside campground *AE*
♦ lakeside camping site *BE*
♦ lakeside camping ground *BE*
♦ lakeside site
Seecampingplatz, m (Meer)
♦ seaside campsite
♦ seaside campground *AE*
♦ seaside camping site *BE*
♦ seaside camping ground *BE*
♦ seaside site
Seecaravanpark, m (Binnensee)
Seewohnwagenpark, m
♦ lakeside caravan park *BE*
♦ lakeside trailer park *AE*
Seecaravanpark, m (Meer)
Seewohnwagenpark, m
♦ seaside caravan park *BE*
♦ seaside trailer park *AE*
Seecaravanplatz, m (Binnensee)
Seewohnwagenplatz, m
♦ lakeside caravan site *BE*
♦ lakeside trailer site *AE*
Seecaravanplatz, m (Meer)
Seewohnwagenplatz, m
♦ seaside caravan site *BE*
♦ seaside trailer site *AE*
Seedampfer, m (Binnensee)
♦ lake steamer

Seedampfer, m (Ozean)
→ Ozeandampfer
Seedienst, m (Meer)
♦ sea service
Seedorf, n (Binnensee)
♦ lakeside village
Seedorf, n (Meer)
♦ seaside village
Seefähre, f (Meer)
♦ sea ferry
Seefahrer, m
Seemann, m
♦ seafarer
Seefahrtsmuseum, n
Schiffahrtsmuseum, n
♦ nautical museum
Seeferien, pl (Binnensee)
Seeurlaub, m
♦ lakeside holidays *BE pl*
♦ lakeside holiday *BE*
♦ lakeside vacation *AE*
Seeferien, pl (Meer)
Seeurlaub, m
Ferien an der See, pl
Urlaub an der See, m
♦ seaside holiday *BE*
♦ seaside vacation *AE*
Seeferiengast, m (Binnensee)
Seeurlauber, m
♦ lakeside holidaymaker *BE*
♦ lakeside vacationer *AE*
Seeferiengast, m (Meer)
Seeurlauber, m
♦ seaside holidaymaker *BE*
♦ seaside vacationer *AE*
Seeferienhotel, n (Binnensee)
Seeurlaubshotel, n
♦ lakeside holiday hotel *BE*
♦ lakeside vacation hotel *AE*
Seeferienhotel, n (Meer)
Seeurlaubshotel, n
♦ seaside holiday hotel *BE*
♦ seaside vacation hotel *AE*
Seefest, n (Binnensee)
Seefestspiele, n pl
♦ lake festival
seefest sein
nicht seekrank werden
♦ be a good sailor
Seefisch, m (Binnensee)
♦ lake fish
Seeforelle, f (Binnensee)
♦ lake trout
Seegarten, m (Binnensee)
♦ lakeside garden
Seehafen, m (Binnensee)
♦ lake port
♦ lake harbor *AE*
♦ lake harbour *BE*
Seehafen, m (Meer)
♦ seaport
Seehandel, m
♦ sea trade
♦ sea trading
Seehecht, m
♦ hake
Seeheilbad, n (Binnensee)
♦ lakeside health resort
Seeheilbad, n (Meer)
♦ seaside health resort
♦ marine spa

Seehotel, n (Binnensee)
 ♦ lakeside hotel
Seehotel, n (Meer)
 ♦ seaside hotel
 ♦ seafront hotel *AE*
 ♦ sea-front hotel *BE*
Seehotel (Eigenname, Binnensee)
 ♦ Lake Hotel, The
Seehund, m
 ♦ seal
Seehundschutzgebiet, n
 ♦ seal sanctuary
Seeklima, n
 Meeresklima, n
 maritimes Klima, n
 ♦ sea climate
 ♦ maritime climate
seekrank, adj
 ♦ seasick, adj
Seekrankheit, f
 ♦ seasickness
Seekurort, m (Binnensee)
 ♦ lakeside spa
Seekurort, m (Meer)
 → Meereskurort
Seelachs, m
 → Lachsersatz
Seelagune, f
 ♦ seafront lagoon *AE*
 ♦ sea-front lagoon *BE*
Seelandschaft, f (Binnensee)
 ♦ lake scenery
Seeluft, f (Meer)
 → Meeresluft
See-Luft-Reise, f
 ♦ sea-air voyage
Seemann, m
 Matrose, m
 ♦ seaman
 ♦ sailor
Seemannsheim, n
 ♦ sailor's home
 ♦ sailor's rest
Seemannskneipe, f
 → Matrosenkneipe
seenah, adv (Binnensee)
 ♦ close to the lake, adv
seenah, adv (Meer)
 ♦ close to the sea, adv
Seenähe, f (Binnensee)
 ♦ closeness to the lake
Seenähe, f (Meer)
 ♦ closeness to the sea
Seengebiet, n
 Seenplatte, f
 ♦ lake district
 ♦ lakeland
 ♦ lake country
Seeort, m (Binnensee)
 ♦ lakeside place
Seeort, m (Meer)
 ♦ seaside place
Seepalast, m (Binnensee)
 Seeschloß, n
 ♦ lakeside palace
Seepalast, m (Meer)
 Seeschloß, n
 ♦ seaside palace
Seepanorama, n (Binnensee)
 ♦ lakeside panorama

Seepanorama, n (Meer)
 ♦ seaside panorama
Seepark, m (Binnensee)
 ♦ lakeside park
Seepark, m (Meer)
 ♦ seaside park
Seepassage, f
 ♦ passage (on a ship)
Seepension, f (Binnensee)
 ♦ lakeside boardinghouse *AE*
 ♦ lakeside boarding-house *BE*
 ♦ lakeside guesthouse *AE*
 ♦ lakeside guest-house *BE*
 ♦ private hotel at the lakeside
Seepension, f (Meer)
 ♦ seaside boardinghouse *AE*
 ♦ seaside boarding-house *BE*
 ♦ seaside guesthouse *AE*
 ♦ seaside guest-house *BE*
 ♦ private hotel at the seaside
Seeplatz, m (Binnensee)
 (z.B. Campingplatz)
 ♦ lakeside site
Seeplatz, m (Meer)
 (z.B. Campingplatz)
 ♦ seaside site
Seepromenade, f (Binnensee)
 ♦ lakeside promenade *AE*
 ♦ lakefront *AE*
 ♦ lake front *BE*
Seepromenade, f (Meer)
 ♦ seaside promenade
 ♦ seafront *AE*
 ♦ sea front *BE*
 ♦ seafront promenade *AE*
 ♦ sea-front promenade *BE*
Seereise, f
 Schiffsreise, f
 ♦ sea voyage
 ♦ voyage
 ♦ sea passage
 ♦ journey by sea
 ♦ sea journey
Seereise arrangieren
 ♦ arrange a voyage
Seereise machen
 ♦ make a voyage
Seereise machen
 ♦ make a sea journey
 ♦ go on a sea journey
Seereisemarkt, m
 ♦ sea voyage market
 ♦ sea journey market
Seereisen, n
 Seereiseverkehr, m
 ♦ sea travel
Seereisender, m
 Reisender, m
 ♦ voyager
Seereise um die Welt, f
 ♦ voyage around the world
Seerestaurant n (Binnensee)
 ♦ lakeside restaurant
Seerestaurant n (Meer)
 ♦ seaside restaurant
Seesack, m
 ♦ kitbag
Seeschenke, f (Binnensee)
 Seebar, f
 ♦ lakeside bar *AE*

 ♦ lakeside pub *BE*
 ♦ lakeside public house *BE*
Seeschenke, f (Meer)
 ♦ seaside bar *AE*
 ♦ seaside pub *BE*
 ♦ seaside public house *BE*
Seeseite, f (Binnensee)
 (Gegensatz zur Landseite)
 ♦ lakefront *AE*
 ♦ lake front *BE*
Seeseite, f (Meer)
 (Gegensatz zur Landseite)
 Meerseite, f
 Seepromenade, f
 ♦ seafront *AE*
 ♦ sea front *BE*
seeseitig, adj (Binnensee)
 ♦ lakefront, adj *AE*
 ♦ lake-front, adj *BE*
seeseitig, adj (Meer)
 ♦ seafront, adj *AE*
 ♦ sea-front, adj *BE*
Seesicht, f
 → Seeblick
Seespaß, m (Binnensee)
 ♦ lakeside fun
Seespaß, m (Meer)
 ♦ seaside fun
Seespazierweg, m (Binnensee)
 Seewanderweg, m
 ♦ lakeside walk
Seespazierweg, m (Meer)
 Seewanderweg, m
 ♦ seaside walk
Seestadt, f (Binnensee, Großstadt)
 ♦ lakeside city
Seestadt, f (Binnensee, kleine Stadt)
 ♦ lakeside town
Seestadt, f (Meer, Großstadt)
 ♦ seaside city
Seestadt, f (Meer, kleine Stadt)
 ♦ seaside town
Seestraße, f (Binnensee)
 ♦ lakeside road
 ♦ lakeside street
Seestraße, f (Meer)
 ♦ seaside road
Seesuite, f (Binnensee)
 ♦ lakeside suite
 ♦ lakefront suite *AE*
 ♦ lake-front suite *BE*
Seesuite, f (Meer)
 ♦ seaside suite
 ♦ seafront suit *AE*
 ♦ sea-front suite *BE*
Seetaverne, f (Binnensee)
 ♦ lakeside tavern
Seetaverne, f (Meer)
 ♦ seaside tavern
Seetemperatur, f (Binnensee)
 ♦ lake temperature
Seeterrasse, f (Meer)
 ♦ seafront terrace *AE*
 ♦ sea-front terrace *BE*
Seeterrasse f (Binnensee)
 ♦ lakeside terrace
Seetourismus, m
 ♦ sea tourism
 ♦ maritime tourism

Seetourist

Seetourist, m
- sea tourist
- maritime tourist

Seetransportgesellschaft, f
- sea carrier

Seeufer, n (Binnensee)
- lakeshore AE
- lake-shore BE

Seeufer, n (Meer)
Meerufer, n
Meeresufer, n
- seashore AE
- sea-shore BE

Seeufercottage, f (Binnensee)
- lakeshore cottage AE
- lake-shore cottage BE

Seeufercottage, f (Meer)
- seashore cottage AE
- sea-shore cottage BE

Seeuferstraße, f (Binnensee)
- lakeshore road AE
- lake-shore road BE

Seeuferstraße, f (Meer)
- seashore road AE
- sea-shore road BE

See und Sand
See (f) und Sand (m)
- sea and sand

seeuntüchtig, adj (Schiff)
- unseaworthy, adj

Seeuntüchtigkeit, f
- unseaworthiness

seeuntüchtig werden
- become unseaworthy

Seeurlaub, m (Binnensee)
- lakeside vacation AE
- lakeside holiday BE

Seeurlaub, m (Meer)
- seaside vacation AE
- seaside holiday BE

Seeurlauber, m (Binnensee)
- lakeside vacationer AE
- lakeside holidaymaker BE

Seeurlauber, m (Meer)
- seaside vacationer AE
- seaside holidaymaker BE

Seeurlaubshotel, n (Binnensee)
- lakeside vacation hotel AE
- lakeside holiday hotel BE

Seeurlaubshotel, n (Meer)
- seaside vacation hotel AE
- seaside holiday hotel BE

Seeverkehr, m (Meer)
- sea traffic

See versorgt das Dorf mit Wasser
- lake provides the village with water

Seevilla, f (Binnensee)
- lakeside villa
- lakefront villa AE
- lake-front villa BE

Seevilla, f (Meer)
- seaside villa
- seafront villa AE
- sea-front villa BE

Seewohnung, f (Binnensee)
- lakeside flat BE
- lake-front flat BE
- lakeside apartment AE
- lakefront apartment AE

Seewohnung, f (Meer)
- seaside flat BE
- sea-front flat BE
- seaside apartment AE
- seafront apartment AE

Seewohnwagenpark, m (Binnensee)
Seewohnwagenpark, m
- lakeside trailer park AE
- lakeside caravan park BE

Seewohnwagenpark, m (Meer)
Seecaravanpark, m
- seaside trailer park AE
- seaside caravan park BE

Seewohnwagenplatz, m (Binnensee)
Seecaravanplatz, m
- lakeside trailer site AE
- lakeside caravan site BE

Seewohnwagenplatz, m (Meer)
Seecaravanplatz, m
- seaside trailer site AE
- seaside caravan site BE

Seewolf, m
- seawolf

Seezimmer, n (Binnensee)
- lakeside room
- lakefront room AE
- lake-front room BE

Seezimmer, n (Meer)
- seaside room
- seafront room AE
- sea-front room BE

Seezunge f
- sole

Seezungenfüllpastete, f
- sole timbale

Sefa, n
→ Servicefach

Segel, n
- sail

Segelausflug, m
- sailing excursion

Segelbegeisterter, m
- sailing enthusiast

Segelboot, n
- sailboat AE
- sailing-boat BE
- sailing-dinghy BE

Segelboot mieten
- rent a sailboat AE
- hire a sailing-boat BE
- hire a sailing-dinghy BE

Segelbootrennen, n
- sailboat race AE
- sailing-boat race BE

Segelbootverleih, m
- sailboat rental AE
- sailing-boat hire BE
- sailing-dinghy hire BE

Segelboot vermieten
- rent (out) a sailboat AE
- hire out a sailing-boat BE
- hire out a sailing-dinghy BE

Segelclub, m
Segelverein, m
- sailing club

Segelfahrt machen
- go for a sail

Segelfan, n
- sailing fanatic
- sailing fan

segelfliegen
- glide
- sailplane AE

Segelfliegen, n
Segelflugsport, m
- gliding
- sailplaning AE

Segelflieger, m
- glider pilot
- glider
- sailplane pilot AE

Segelfliegerclub, m
Segelfliegerverein, m
- gliding club
- sailplaning club AE

Segelfliegerferienkurs, m
- gliding vacation course AE
- gliding holiday course BE

Segelfliegerkurs, m
Segelfliegerlehrgang, m
- gliding course

Segelfliegerschule, f
- gliding school
- glider school

Segelflugplatz, m
- gliding field

Segelflugschein, m
- gliding certificate
- gliding license AE
- gliding licence BE

Segelflugsport, m
→ Segelfliegen

Segelflugurlaub, m
- gliding holiday BE
- sailplaning vacation AE

Segelflugverein, m
Segelfliegerclub, m
- sailplaning club AE
- gliding club

Segelflugwettbewerb, m
- gliding competition
- gliding contest
- sailplaning competition AE
- sailplaning contest AE

Segelflugzeug, n
- glider
- sailplane AE

Segelgebiet, n (groß)
- sailing region

Segelgebiet, n (klein)
- sailing area

Segelgelegenheit, f
- sailing opportunity

Segelgewässer, pl
- sailing waters pl

Segelhafen, m
- sailing harbor AE
- sailing harbour BE

Segel hissen
Segel setzen
- hoist a sail
- hoist the sails
- hoist some sail

Segeljacht, f
Segelyacht, f
- sailing yacht

Segelkreuzfahrt, f
- sailing cruise

Segelkurs, m
Segellehrgang, m
- sailing course

Segelmöglichkeiten anbieten
- offer opportunities for sailing

segeln
- sail

Segeln, n
→ Segelsport

segeln auf einer Jacht
auf einer Yacht segeln
auf einer Jacht fahren
auf einer Yacht fahren
segeln
- yacht

segeln gehen
segeln
- go sailing

segeln gehen mit jm
zum Segeln mitnehmen jn
- take s.o. for a sail

segeln hart am Wind
hart am Wind segeln
- sail close to the wind

Segeln mit dem Fallschirm, n
Fallschirmsegeln, n
- parasailing
- parachute sailing

segeln über den Atlantik
- sail (across) the Atlantic

segeln um die Welt
Welt umsegeln
um die Welt segeln
- sail around the world
- sail round the world

segeln von A nach B
- sail from A to B

Segelpartie, f
Segelausflug, m
- sailing trip

Segelregatta, f
- sailing regatta

Segelregatta abhalten
- hold a sailing regatta

Segelreise, f
- sailing journey
- sailing tour
- sailing trip

Segelreise, f
- sail
- sailing tour

Segelrevier, n
- cruising ground

Segelsaison, f
- sailing season
- yachting season

Segelschiff, n
- sailing ship
- sailship AE
- sailing vessel

Segelschiffexkursion, f
- sailing ship excursion
- sailship excursion AE

Segelschiff-Fahrt, f
- sailing ship trip
- sailship trip AE

Segelschule, f
- sailing school
- yachting school

Segelschulschiff, n
- sailing schoolship
- sail training ship

Segelsee, m
- sailing lake

Segel setzen
- set the sails

- hoist a sail
- hoist some sail

Segelsport, m
Segeln, n
- sailing

Segeltörn, n
- sailing turn

Segeltour, f
- sailing tour

Segeltuch, n
- canvas
- sailcloth

Segeltuchliegestuhl, m
- canvas deck-chair

Segeltuchplane, f
→ Zeltbahn

Segeltuchzelt, n
- canvas tent

Segelunterricht, m
- sailing tuition
- sailing lessons pl

Segelurlaub, m
Segelferien, pl
- sailing vacation AE
- sailing holiday BE

Segelurlaub machen
- take a sailing vacation AE
- take a sailing holiday BE

Segelurlaubsort, m
Segelferienort, m
Segelort, m
- sailing resort

Segelurlaubsveranstalter, m
- sailing vacation operator AE
- sailing holiday operator BE

Segelwoche, f
- sailing week
- week's sailing

Segelwochenende, n
- sailing weekend

Segelzentrum, n
- sailing center AE
- sailing centre BE

Segler, m (Sport)
→ Sportsegler

Segment, n
- segment

Segment ansprechen
- appeal to a segment

Sehen Sie sich um, bevor Sie buchen!
(Preisvergleich)
- Look before you book!
- Shop around before you book!

sehenswert, adj
sehenswürdig, adj
- worth seeing, adj
- well worth seeing, adj

sehenswerter Ort, m
- place worth seeing
- place of interest

sehenswerte Sache, f
- thing worth seeing

sehenswert sein
- be worth seeing
- be well worth seeing

Sehenswürdigkeit, f
- sight
- tourist attraction
- place of interest
- place to visit
- point of interest

Sehenswürdigkeiten
(Kapitelüberschrift)
- What to see

Sehenswürdigkeiten besichtigen (von X)
- see the sights (of X)
- view the sights (of X)

Sehenswürdigkeiten besuchen
- visit the sights

Sehenswürdigkeiten erkunden
- explore the sights

Sehenswürdigkeiten zeigen jm
- show s.o. the sights
- show the sights to s.o.

sehnen sich nach etw
sich nach etw sehnen
- long for s.th.

sehnen sich nach Hause
sich nach Hause sehnen
- long to go home
- be longing to go home

sehr besuchenswert, adj
am besuchenswertesten, adj
- most worth visiting, adj
- most worth a visit, adj

sehr besuchenswert sein
- be most worth visiting
- be most worth a visit
- be very worth a visit coll

sehr einfache Unterkunft, f
(ohne jeden Komfort)
- basic accommodation

sehr einladend aussehen
- look very inviting

sehr empfehlenswert, adj
- highly recommended, adj
- highly recommendable, adj
- highly commendable, adj

sehr empfehlenswertes Hotel, n
- highly recommended hotel
- highly recommendable hotel
- highly commendable hotel

sehr empfehlenswertes Restaurant, n
- highly recommended restaurant
- highly recommendable restaurant
- highly commendable restaurant

Sehr empfehlenswert (Plakette)
- Highly Commended

sehr geringe Miete f
(nur der Form halber)
- nominal rent

sehr geringe Miete zahlen
- pay a nominal rent

sehr geringe Pacht, f
(nur der Form halber)
- nominal lease
- nominal rent

sehr günstiger Preis, m
Schnupperpreis, m
- very favorable price AE
- very favourable price AE
- very favorable rate AE
- very favourable rate BE
- bargain price

sehr günstiges Angebot, n
Schnupperangebot, n
- bargain offer
- snip BE inform

sehr guter Wein, m
- very good wine

sehr gut essen
- eat very well

sehr reichliches Essen, n
  ◆ generous food
sehr starker Kaffee, m
  ◆ very strong coffee
sehr unterernährt, adj
  ◆ seriously undernourished, adj
  ◆ badly undernourished, adj
Sehr verbunden
  (Höflichkeitsformel)
  ◆ Much obliged
sehr weit reisen
  ◆ travel very far
sehr wenig kosten
  ◆ cost very little
sehr wenig schlafen
  ◆ sleep very little
sehr zu meinem Bedauern
  ◆ much to my regret
sehr zu unserem Bedauern
  ◆ much to our regret
seicht, adj
  flach, adj
  ◆ shallow, adj
seichter Strand, m
  ◆ shallow beach
seichtes Programm, n
  ◆ insipid program AE
  ◆ insipid programme BE
Seidel, m
  Stein, m
  ◆ stein AE
  ◆ mug
Seidenmalerei, f
  ◆ silk painting
Seidenstraße, f
  ◆ Silk Route, the
Seien Sie mein Gast!
  ◆ Be my guest!
Seien Sie unser Gast!
  ◆ Be our guest!
Seife, f
  ◆ soap
Seifenhalter, m
  ◆ soap holder
Seifenkiste, f
  (für Kinder)
  ◆ soapbox
Seifenkistenrennen, n
  ◆ soapbox derby
Seifenschüssel, f
  Seifenschale, f
  ◆ soap tray
  ◆ soap dish
Seifenspender, m
  ◆ soap dispenser
Seife stellen
  ◆ provide soap
seihen etw gastr
  durchseihen etw
  ◆ drain s.th. gastr
Sei kein Spielverderber!
  ◆ Be a sport!
Seil, n (generell)
  ◆ rope
  ◆ cable
Seil, n (Seiltanz)
  ◆ tightrope
Seilakrobat, m
  ◆ funambulator
  ◆ funambulist

Seilakrobatik, f
  ◆ funambulation
Seilakrobatik machen
  ◆ funambulate
Seilbahn, f (Boden)
  Standseilbahn, f
  Kabinenbahn, f
  ◆ cable railway BE
  ◆ cable railroad AE
  ◆ funicular railway BE
  ◆ funicular railroad AE
  ◆ funicular
Seilbahn, f (Luft)
  ◆ cableway
  ◆ ropeway
  ◆ teleferic AE
Seilbahn, f (Luft oder Boden)
  ◆ cable car AE
  ◆ cable-car BE
Seilbahndienst, m
  Seilbahnverbindung, f
  ◆ cable-car service
Seilbahnfahrt, f
  ◆ cable-car ride
  ◆ cable-car trip
Seilbahngesellschaft, f
  ◆ cable-car company
Seilbahn nehmen (Boden)
  ◆ take the funicular
Seilbahn nehmen (Luft oder Boden)
  ◆ take the cable car AE
  ◆ take the cable-car BE
Seilbahnstation, f
  ◆ cable-car station
Seiltanz, m
  Seiltanzen, n
  ◆ ropedancing
  ◆ ropewalking
  ◆ tightrope walking
  ◆ walking the tightrope
seiltanzen
  ◆ walk the tightrope
  ◆ tightrope
Seiltänzer, m
  ◆ tightrope walker
  ◆ ropewalker
  ◆ ropedancer
Seine, f
  ◆ Seine River, the
  ◆ River Seine, the
  ◆ Seine, the
seinem Namen gerecht werden
  ◆ live up to one's name
  ◆ live up to its name
seinem Ruf gerecht werden
  ◆ live up to one's reputation
  ◆ live up to its reputation
seinen Urlaub nehmen
  ◆ take one's vacation AE
  ◆ take one's holiday BE
Seitenaltar, m
  ◆ side altar
Seitenchor, m
  → Seitenschiff
Seiteneingang, m
  → Nebeneingang
Seitenfenster, n
  ◆ side window
Seitenflügel, m
  → Nebentrakt

Seitenschiff, n (Kirche)
  Seitenchor, m
  ◆ aisle
  ◆ side aisle
Seitensitzgruppe, f
  (Wohnwagen)
  ◆ side dinette
Seitenstraße, f
  ◆ side road AE
  ◆ side street BE
  ◆ side-street BE
  ◆ side-road BE
  ◆ off X street
Seitental, n
  ◆ side valley
Seitentrakt, m
  → Nebentrakt
Seitentür, f
  Nebentür, f
  ◆ side door
Seitenwand, f
  ◆ side wall
seitlicher Meeresblick, m
  ◆ side seaview AE
  ◆ side sea view BE
seit undenklichen Zeiten
  ◆ from times immemorial
Sekretariatsdienst, m
  Sekretariatsservice, m
  Schreibdienst, m
  Schreibservice, m
  ◆ secretarial service
Sekretärin, f
  Sekretär, m
  ◆ secretary
Sekt, m
  (Sekt ist nicht identisch mit Champagner; das Wort wird jedoch im weiteren Sinn als "champagne" übersetzt)
  ◆ Sekt
  ◆ champagne
Sektabendessen, n
  Champagnerabendessen, n
  ◆ champagne dinner
Sektbar, f
  Champagnerbar, f
  ◆ champagne bar
Sektbrunch, m
  Champagnerbrunch, m
  ◆ champagne brunch
Sektcocktail, m
  Champagnercocktail, m
  ◆ champagne cocktail
Sekteimer, m
  Champagnereimer, m
  ◆ champagne bucket
Sektempfang, m
  Champagnerempfang, m
  ◆ champagne reception
Sektessen, n
  Champagneressen, n
  ◆ champagne meal
Sektfabrikant, m
  → Sekthersteller
Sektfest, n
  Champagnerfest, n
  ◆ champagne festival
Sektfirma, f
  Champagnerfirma, f
  ◆ champagne firm

Sektflasche, f
  Champagnerflasche, f
  ♦ champagne bottle
Sekt fließt in Strömen
  Champagner fließt in Strömen
  ♦ champagne flows freely
  ♦ champagne flows like water
Sektflöte, f
  Champagnerflöte, f
  ♦ champagne flute
Sektfrühstück, n
  Champagnerfrühstück, n
  ♦ champagne breakfast
Sektglas, n
  Champagnerglas, n
  ♦ champagne glass
Sekthandel, m
  Champagnerhandel, m
  ♦ champagne trade
Sekthauptstadt, f
  ♦ champagne capital
Sekt herstellen
  ♦ produce champagne
Sekthersteller, m
  Sektproduzent, m
  Sektfabrikant, m
  Champagnerhersteller, m
  ♦ champagne producer
Sektherstellung, f
  Champagnerherstellung, f
  ♦ champagne production
Sektindustrie, f
  Champagnerindustrie, f
  ♦ champagne industry
Sektionskoch, m
  Chef de partie, m *FR*
  ♦ specialty chef *AE*
  ♦ chef de partie *FR*
Sektkarte, f
  Champagnerkarte, f
  ♦ champagne list
Sektkelch, m
  Champagnerkelch, m
  ♦ champagne tulip
Sektkeller, m
  ♦ champagne cellar
Sektkellerei, f (Firma)
  Champagnerfirma, f
  ♦ champagne house
Sektkellerei, f (Keller)
  Champagnerkellerei, f
  ♦ champagne cellars *pl*
Sektkonsum, m
  Sektverbrauch, m
  Sektverzehr, m
  ♦ champagne consumption
Sektkork, m
  Sektkorken, m
  Champagnerkork, m
  Champagnerkorken, m
  ♦ champagne cork
  ♦ champagne stopper
Sektkorken knallten
  Champagnerkorken knallten
  ♦ champagne corks were popping
Sektkühler, m
  Sektkübel, m
  Champagnerkühler, m
  Champagnerkübel, m
  ♦ champagne cooler

Sektmarkt, m
  Champagnermarkt, m
  ♦ champagne market
Sektmittagessen, n
  Champagnermittagessen, n
  ♦ champagne luncheon
  ♦ champagne lunch
Sektparty, f
  Champagnerparty, f
  ♦ champagne party
Sektpicknick, n
  → Champagnerpicknick
Sektpreis, m
  Champagnerpreis, m
  ♦ champagne price
Sektprobe, f
  Champagnerprobe, f
  ♦ champagne tasting
Sektreklame, f
  ♦ champagne advertisement
Sektschale, f
  Champagnerschale, f
  ♦ champagne saucer
  ♦ champagne coupe
Sektstand, m
  Champagnerstand, m
  ♦ champagne stand
  ♦ champagne stall *BE*
Sektsteuer, f
  Champagnersteuer, f
  ♦ champagne tax
  ♦ (excise) tax on champagne
Sekttag, m
  Champagnertag, m
  ♦ champagne day
Sekt trinken
  ♦ have a glass of champagne
  ♦ drink champagne
Sektumsatz, m
  Champagnerumsatz, m
  ♦ champagne sales *pl*
Sektzelt, n
  Champagnerzelt, n
  ♦ champagne tent
selbes Vorjahrsquartal, n
  ♦ same quarter last year
  ♦ same quarter in the previous year
selbständig, adj
  ♦ self-employed, adj
selbständiger Hotelbesitzer, m
  ♦ independent hotel owner
selbständiger Reisemittler, m
  unabhängiger Reisemittler, m
  ♦ independent travel agent
selbständig geführt, adj
  ♦ independently run, adj
selbständig geführtes Hotel, n
  ♦ independently run hotel
selbständig geführtes Restaurant, n
  ♦ independently run restaurant
selbständig machen sich
  ♦ set up one's own business
selbstangebautes organisch-biologisches Produkt, n
  ♦ homegrown organic produce
selbst bedienen sich mit etw
  ♦ help oneself to s.th.
Selbstbedienung, f
  ♦ self-service
Selbstbedienungsaufzug, m
  → Selbstfahrerlift

Selbstbedienungsbar, f
  ♦ self-service bar
Selbstbedienungsbüfett, n
  ♦ self-service buffet
  ♦ help-yourself buffet
Selbstbedienungscafé, n
  ♦ self-service cafe *AE*
  ♦ self-service café *BE*
Selbstbedienungscafeteria, f
  ♦ self-service cafeteria
Selbstbedienungsfahrstuhl, m
  → Selbstfahrerlift
Selbstbedienungsfrühstück n
  ♦ self-service breakfast
  ♦ help-yourself breakfast
Selbstbedienungsfrühstücksbüfett, n
  Frühstücksbüfett mit Selbstbedienung, n
  ♦ self-service buffet breakfast
Selbstbedienungsfrühstücksraum m
  ♦ self-service breakfast room
Selbstbedienungsgeschäft, n
  Selbstbedienungsladen, m
  ♦ self-service store *AE*
  ♦ self-service shop *BE*
Selbstbedienungsgetränkeschrank, m
  Getränkeschrank für Selbstbedienung, m
  ♦ self-service drinks cabinet
Selbstbedienungshotel n
  ♦ self-service hotel
Selbstbedienungsimbiß, m (Essen)
  ♦ self-service snack
Selbstbedienungsimbiß, m (Raum)
  → Selbstbedienungsimbißstube
Selbstbedienungsimbißstube, f
  Imbißstube mit Selbstbedienung, f
  ♦ self-service snack bar *AE*
  ♦ self-service snack-bar *BE*
  ♦ self-service buttery *BE*
Selbstbedienungskantine, f
  ♦ self-service canteen
Selbstbedienungskorb, m
  ♦ help-yourself basket
  ♦ self-service basket
Selbstbedienungsladen, m
  → Selbstbedienungsgeschäft
Selbstbedienungslift, m
  → Selbstfahrerlift
Selbstbedienungsmahlzeit, f
  Selbstbedienungsessen, n
  ♦ self-service meal
Selbstbedienungsmittagessen, n
  ♦ help-yourself lunch
  ♦ help-yourself luncheon
  ♦ self-service lunch
  ♦ self-service luncheon
Selbstbedienungsmittagsbüfett, n
  Mittagsbüfett mit Selbstbedienung, n
  ♦ self-service lunch buffet
Selbstbedienungsregal, n
  ♦ self-service rack
Selbstbedienungsrestaurant, n
  SB-Restaurant, n
  ♦ self-service restaurant
Selbstbedienungsspeisesaal, m
  ♦ self-service dining room *AE*
  ♦ self-service dining-room *BE*
Selbstbedienungssystem, n
  ♦ self-service system
Selbstbedienungstankstelle, f
  SB-Tankstelle, f
  ♦ self-service gasoline station *AE*

Selbstbedienungstheke

- ♦ self-service gas station AE
- ♦ self-service petrol station BE
- ♦ self-service filling station

Selbstbedienungstheke, f
  Selbstbedienungstresen m
  Selbstbedienungsschalter m
- ♦ self-service counter

Selbstbedienungsunterkunft, f
- ♦ self-service accommodation

Selbstbedienungsversorgungseinrichtung, f
  Versorgungseinrichtung mit Selbstbedienung, f
- ♦ self-service catering facility

Selbstbedienungswäscherei, f
- ♦ self-service laundry

Selbstbedienungswaschsalon, m
  Waschsalon mit Selbstbedienung, m
- ♦ self-service launderette BE
- ♦ self-service laundrette BE
- ♦ self-service laundromat AE

selbst buchen
- ♦ make one's own bookings

Selbstfahrer, m (Eigentümer)
- ♦ owner-driver

Selbstfahrer, m (Mietauto)
- ♦ driver of a self-drive car

Selbstfahreraufzug, m
  → Selbstfahrerlift

Selbstfahrerauto, n
  → Mietwagen für Selbstfahrer

Selbstfahrerlift, m
  Selbstfahreraufzug, m
- ♦ self-service elevator AE
- ♦ self-service lift BE

Selbstfahrerpauschale, f
- ♦ self-drive package

Selbstfahrerurlaub, m
  Urlaub für Selbstfahrer, m
  Selbstfahrerferien, pl
  Ferien für Selbstfahrer, pl
- ♦ self-drive vacation AE
- ♦ self-drive holiday BE

selbstgebacken, adj
  selbstgemacht, adj
- ♦ home-baked, adj BE
- ♦ home-made, adj BE
- ♦ homemade, adj AE

selbstgebackener Kuchen, m
  zuhause gebackener Kuchen m
- ♦ homemade cake AE
- ♦ home-made cake BE

selbstgebackenes Brot, n
- ♦ home-baked bread BE
- ♦ home-made bread BE
- ♦ homemade bread

selbstgebraut, adj
- ♦ home-brewed, adj

selbstgebrautes Bier, n
- ♦ home-brewed beer

selbstgebrautes Getränk, n
- ♦ homebrew

selbstgekocht, adj
- ♦ home-cooked, adj

selbstgekochtes Essen, n
- ♦ home-cooked meal

selbstgemachter Likör, m
- ♦ homemade liqueur AE
- ♦ home-made liqueur BE

Selbstheilung, f med
- ♦ self-healing med

Selbsthilfe, f
- ♦ self-help

Selbsthypnosetraining, n
- ♦ self-hypnosis training

selbst kochen
- ♦ do one's own cooking

Selbstkocher, m
  → Selbstversorger

Selbstkosten, pl
- ♦ original cost
- ♦ flat cost

Selbstkostenpreis, m
  Selbstkosten, pl
- ♦ cost price
- ♦ prime cost

Selbstkosten pro Übernachtung, pl
- ♦ hotel's cost per person per night
- ♦ cost per person per night

selbst verkostigen sich
- → selbst verpflegen sich

Selbstverköstigung f
  → Selbstverpflegung

selbst verpflegen sich
- → verpflegen sich

Selbstverpfleger, m
  Selbstversorger, m
  Selbstverköstiger, m
- ♦ self-caterer

Selbstverpflegung, f
  Selbstversorgung, f
  Selbstverköstigung, f
- ♦ self-catering
- ♦ catering to oneself
- ♦ s/c

Selbstverpflegung anbieten
  Selbstversorgung anbieten
  Selbstverköstigung anbieten
- ♦ offer self-catering

Selbstverpflegungsangebot, n (Palette)
  (Häuser)
  Selbstversorgungsangebot, n
- ♦ range of self-catering properties

Selbstverpflegungsanlage, f
  Selbstverpflegungskomplex, m
  Selbstversorgungsanlage, f
  Selbstversorgungskomplex, m
- ♦ self-catering complex

Selbstverpflegungsappartement, n
  Selbstversorgungsappartement, n
  Selbstverköstigungsappartement, n
- ♦ self-catering apartment

Selbstverpflegungsarrangement, n
  Selbstversorgungsarrangement, n
  Selbstverköstigungsarrangement, n
- ♦ self-catering arrangement

Selbstverpflegungsbereich, m
  Selbstversorgungsbereich, m
  Selbstverpflegungssektor, m
  Selbstversorgungssektor, m
- ♦ self-catering sector

Selbstverpflegungsbetrieb, m
  Selbstversorgungsbetrieb, m
- ♦ self-catering establishment
- ♦ self-catering operation

Selbstverpflegungsbungalow, m
  Selbstversorgungsbungalow, m
- ♦ self-catering bungalow

Selbstverpflegungseinheit, f
  (Statistik)
  Selbstversorgungseinheit, f
- ♦ self-catering unit

Selbstverpflegungseinrichtung, f
  Selbstversorgungseinrichtung, f

  Selbstverköstigungseinrichtung, f
- ♦ self-catering facility

Selbstverpflegungsferien, pl
  Selbstversorgungsferien, pl
  Selbstverpflegungsurlaub, m
  Selbstversorgungsurlaub, m
- ♦ self-catering holiday BE
- ♦ self-catering vacation AE

Selbstverpflegungsferienhaus, n
  Selbstversorgungsferienhaus, n
  Ferienhaus für Selbstversorger, n
- ♦ self-catering vacation home AE
- ♦ self-catering holiday home BE

Selbstverpflegungsgast, m
  Selbstversorgungsgast, m
  Selbstverköstigungsgast, m
- ♦ self-catering guest

Selbstverpflegungsgruppe, f
  Selbstversorgungsgruppe, f
  Selbstverköstigungsgruppe, f
- ♦ self-catering group
- ♦ self-catering party

Selbstverpflegungshaus, n
  Selbstversorgungshaus, n
  Selbstverköstigungshaus, n
- ♦ self-catering house
- ♦ self-catering home

Selbstverpflegungshäuserangebot, n (Palette)
- ♦ range of self-catering houses
- ♦ range of self-catering properties

Selbstverpflegungshütte, f
  Selbstversorgungshütte, f
- ♦ self-catering hut

Selbstverpflegungsimmobilie, f
  Selbstversorgungsimmobilie, f
  Selbstverpflegungshaus, n
- ♦ self-catering property

Selbstverpflegungskategorie, f
  Selbtsversorgungskategorie, f
- ♦ self-catering category

Selbstverpflegungsküche, f (Raum)
  Selbstversorgungsküche, f
- ♦ self-catering kitchen

Selbstverpflegungslandhaus, n
  Selbstversorgungslandhaus, n
- ♦ self-catering cottage

Selbstverpflegungsoption, f
  Selbstversorgungsoption, f
- ♦ self-catering option

Selbstverpflegungspauschalreise, f
  Pauschalreise mit Selbstverpflegung, f
- ♦ self-catering package tour

Selbstverpflegungspreis, m
  Selbstversorgungspreis, m
  Selbstverköstigungspreis, m
- ♦ self-catering price
- ♦ self-catering rate

Selbstverpflegungsquartier, n
  Selbstversorgungsquartier, n
- ♦ self-catering place
- ♦ self-catering quarters pl

Selbstverpflegungsspezialist, m
  Selbstversorgungsspezialist, m
- ♦ self-catering specialist

Selbstverpflegungstag, m
  Selbstversorgungstag, m
  Selbstverköstigungstag, m
- ♦ self-catering day

Selbstverpflegungsunterkunft, f
  Selbstversorgungsunterkunft, f
  Selbstverköstigungsunterkunft, f

Unterkunft mit Selbstverpflegung, f
♦ **self-catering accommodation**
Selbstverpflegungsunternehmen, n
  Selbstversorgungsunternehmen, n
  ♦ **self-catering enterprise**
Selbstverpflegungsurlaub, m
  Selbstversorgungsurlaub, m
  Selbstverköstigungsurlaub, m
  ♦ **self-catering vacation** AE
  ♦ self-catering holiday BE
Selbstverpflegungsurlaubsanlage, f
  Selbstverpflegungsurlaubskomplex, m
  Selbstversorgungsurlaubsanlage, f
  Selbstversorgungsurlaubskomplex, m
  ♦ **self-catering vacation complex** AE
  ♦ self-catering holiday complex BE
Selbstverpflegungsveranstalter, m
  Selbstversorgungsveranstalter, m
  ♦ **self-catering operator**
Selbstverpflegungsvereinbarung, f
  Selbstversorgungsvereinbarung, f
  Selbstverköstigungsvereinbarung, f
  ♦ **self-catering agreement**
  ♦ self-catering arrangement
Selbstverpflegungsvilla, f
  Selbstversorgungsvilla, f
  Selbstverköstigungsvilla, f
  ♦ **self-catering villa**
Selbstverpflegungswoche, f
  Selbstversorgungswoche, f
  Selbstverköstigungswoche, f
  ♦ **self-catering week**
Selbstverpflegungswohnung, f
  Selbstversorgungswohnung, f
  Selbstverköstigungswohnung, f
  ♦ **self-catering flat** BE
  ♦ self-catering apartment AE
selbst versorgen sich
  → selbst verpflegen sich
Selbstversorger, m
  → Selbstverpfleger
Selbstversorgerhütte, f
  → Selbstverpflegungshütte
Selbstversorgung f
  → Selbstverpflegung
Selbstverteidigungskurs, m
  ♦ **self-defence class**
Selbstwähltelefon, n
  ♦ **self-dial telephone**
  ♦ self-dialling telephone BE
  ♦ subscriber trunk dialling telephone BE
  ♦ STD telephone BE
  ♦ s.t.d. telephone BE
Selbstzahler, m
  ♦ **self-paying guest**
  ♦ person paying his/her own bill
Sellerie, m (Knollensellerie)
  Knollensellerie, m
  ♦ **celeriac**
Sellerie, m (Staudensellerie)
  Staudensellerie, m
  ♦ **celery**
Sellerieblatt, n
  ♦ **celery leaf**
Selleriecremesuppe, f
  ♦ **cream of celery soup**
Sellerieknolle, f
  ♦ **celery root**
Selleriesalat, m
  ♦ **celery salad**

Selleriesalz, n
  ♦ **celery salt**
Selleriestange, f
  ♦ **celery stick**
Selleriestengel, m
  ♦ **celery stalk**
Selleriesuppe, f
  ♦ **celery soup**
seltene Pfanze, f
  ♦ **rare plant**
seltener Besuch, m
  ♦ **rare visit**
seltener Besucher, m
  ♦ **rare visitor**
seltener Gast, m
  ♦ **rare guest**
  ♦ infrequent guest
  ♦ rare bird idiom
  ♦ rara avis LAT
Selterswasser, n
  → Mineralwasser
seltsamer Gast, m
  ♦ **queer guest**
Semesterferien, pl
  ♦ **vacation**
  ♦ vac coll
Semesterferienzeit, f
  ♦ **vacation period**
Semillon, m FR
  ♦ **Semillon** FR
Seminar, n
  Seminarveranstaltung, f
  ♦ **seminar**
Seminar abhalten
  Seminar halten
  ♦ **hold a seminar**
Seminar abhalten unter der Schirmherrschaft von jm
  ♦ **hold a seminar under the auspices of s.o.**
  ♦ hold a seminar under the patronage of s.o.
Seminar abschließen
  Seminar schließen
  ♦ **conclude a seminar**
Seminar anbieten
  ♦ **offer a seminar**
Seminarangebot, n (Palette)
  ♦ **range of seminars**
Seminarbedürfnis, n
  ♦ **seminar need**
Seminarbericht, m
  ♦ **seminar proceedings** pl
Seminar buchen
  ♦ **book a seminar**
Seminardokumentation, f
  ♦ **seminar documentation**
Seminar durchführen
  ♦ **run a seminar**
Seminar eröffnen
  ♦ **open a seminar**
Seminargast, m
  ♦ **seminar guest**
  ♦ seminar attendant
Seminargebühr f
  ♦ **seminar charge**
  ♦ seminar fee
Seminargeschäft, n
  ♦ **seminar business**
Seminarhotel, n
  ♦ **seminar hotel**
Seminar ist ausgebucht
  ♦ **seminar is fully booked**

Seminarist m
  → Seminarteilnehmer
Seminar leiten
  ♦ **conduct a seminar**
Seminarleiter, m (generell)
  ♦ **seminar leader**
  ♦ seminar conductor
Seminarleiter, m (Tutor)
  Tutor, m
  ♦ **tutor**
Seminarmoderator, m
  ♦ **seminar presenter** BE
Seminar moderieren
  ♦ **present a seminar**
Seminarort m
  ♦ **seminar venue**
  ♦ venue of a seminar
Seminar planen
  ♦ **plan a seminar**
Seminarprogramm, n
  ♦ **seminar program** AE
  ♦ seminar programme BE
  ♦ program of seminars AE
  ♦ programme of seminars BE
Seminarraum, m
  Seminarzimmer n
  ♦ **seminar room**
Seminarräumlichkeiten, f pl
  ♦ **seminar facilities** pl
Seminarreihe, f
  Seminarserie, f
  ♦ **seminar series**
  ♦ series of seminars
  ♦ course of seminars
Seminarserie, f
  → Seminarreihe
Seminarsitzung, f
  ♦ **seminar session**
  ♦ seminar meeting
Seminartechnik, f
  ♦ **seminar equipment**
Seminarteilnehmer, m (aktiv)
  ♦ **participant in a seminar**
  ♦ seminar participant
  ♦ person participating in a seminar
  ♦ person taking part in a seminar
Seminarteilnehmer, m (passiv)
  ♦ **seminar attendant**
  ♦ person attending a seminar
Seminartermin, m
  Seminardatum, n
  ♦ **seminar date**
  ♦ date of the seminar
Seminartreffen, n
  Seminarveranstaltung, f
  ♦ **seminar meeting**
Seminarunterlagen, f pl
  ♦ **seminar documents** pl
Seminar veranstalten
  Seminar organisieren
  ♦ **organise a seminar**
  ♦ organize a seminar
  ♦ put on a seminar
Seminarveranstalter, m
  ♦ **seminar organiser**
  ♦ seminar organizer
  ♦ organiser of a seminar
  ♦ organizer of a seminar
Seminarveranstaltung, f
  → Seminar

Seminar vorsitzen

Seminar vorsitzen
  einem Seminar vorsitzen
  Seminar leiten
  ♦ chair a seminar
Seminar wiederholen
  ♦ repeat a seminar
Seminarzentrum, n
  ♦ seminar center AE
  ♦ seminar centre BE
Seminarziel, n
  ♦ seminar objective
  ♦ aim of the seminar
Seminarzimmer n
  → Seminarraum
Seminar zu etw, n
  Seminar über etw, n
  ♦ seminar on s.th.
Semmel, f
  → Brötchen
Semmeringpaß, m
  ♦ Semmering Pass, the
senden etw
  ♦ send s.th.
Senegal, m
  ♦ Senegal
Senegaler, m
  Senegalese, m
  ♦ Senegalese
Senegalerin, f
  Senegalesin, f
  ♦ Senegalese girl
  ♦ Senegalese woman
  ♦ Senegalese
senegalisch, adj
  senegalesisch, adj
  ♦ Senegalese, adj
Senf, m
  Mostrich, m
  ♦ mustard
Senfbutter, f
  ♦ mustard butter
Senfdressing, n
  ♦ mustard dressing
Senflöffel, m
  ♦ mustard spoon
Senfsoße, f
  ♦ mustard sauce
Senior, m
  ♦ senior citizen
Seniorenappartement, n
  ♦ retirement apartment
Seniorenausflug, m
  ♦ senior-citizen excursion
  ♦ senior-citizen outing
Seniorenclub, m
  ♦ senior-citizen club
  ♦ old people's club
Seniorenermäßigung, f
  ♦ senior-citizen reduction
  ♦ reduction for senior citizens
Seniorenfahrt, f
  ♦ senior-citizen trip
Seniorengruppe, f
  ♦ senior-citizen group
  ♦ senior citizens' group
  ♦ group of senior citizens
Seniorenheim, n
  Seniorenresidenz, f
  Heim für Pensionäre, n
  ♦ retirement home

Seniorennachmittag m
  ♦ afternoon for senior citizens
Seniorenpaß, m
  (Eisenbahn)
  ♦ senior citizen's railcard
Seniorenprogramm, n
  ♦ senior citizens' program AE
  ♦ senior citizens' programme BE
  ♦ program for senior citizens AE
  ♦ programme for senior citizens BE
Seniorenreise, f
  ♦ senior-citizen tour
  ♦ tour for senior citizens
Seniorenresidenz, f
  ♦ residence for senior citizens
Seniorensegment, n
  ♦ senior-citizen segment
Seniorentourismus, m
  ♦ senior-citizen tourism
Seniorentreff, m
  (Lokal)
  Seniorentreffpunkt, m
  ♦ senior-citizen haunt
Seniorenwoche, f
  ♦ senior-citizen week
Seniorenwochenende, n
  ♦ senior-citizen weekend
  ♦ weekend for senior citizens
Seniorenwohnheim, n
  ♦ home for senior citizens
Seniorenzentrum, n
  ♦ senior-citizen center AE
  ♦ senior-citizen centre BE
Senkgrube, f
  ♦ cesspool
  ♦ cesspit
Senkrechtstarter, m (Flugzeug)
  ♦ jump-jet
Sennhütte, f
  Berghütte, f
  ♦ mountain bothy
  ♦ bothy
  ♦ bothie
Sensationssüchtiger, m
  ♦ thrill seeker
separat, adj
  getrennt, adj
  eigen, adj
  ♦ separate, adj
separate Dusche f
  ♦ separate shower
separate Küche, f
  ♦ separate kitchen
separater Eingang, m
  ♦ separate entrance
separater Eßbereich m
  ♦ separate dining area
separater Platzteil für Spätankünfte, m
  (Camping)
  separates Feld für spät Ankommende, n
  ♦ separate enclosure for late arrivals
separater Zähler, m
  (für Strom, Gas etc.)
  ♦ separate meter
separates Bad, n
  ♦ separate bath
separates Badezimmer, n
  ♦ separate bathroom
separates Bett n
  getrenntes Bett n

einzelnes Bett n
  ♦ separate bed
separates Haus, n
  ♦ separate house
separates Schlafzimmer, n
  → getrenntes Schlafzimmer
separates Schwimmbecken für Kinder, n
  ♦ separate swimming pool for children AE
  ♦ separate swimming-pool for children BE
separates Zimmer, n
  ♦ separate room
separate Wohnung, f
  (abgeschlossene Wohnung)
  ♦ separate apartment AE
  ♦ separate flat BE
separat wohnen
  (permanent)
  ♦ live on one's own
Séparée, f
  ♦ snug BE
  ♦ booth AE
September, m
  ♦ September
Septemberauslastung, f
  Auslastung im September, f
  ♦ September load factor
  ♦ load factor in September
Septemberbelegung, f
  Septemberauslastung, f
  ♦ September occupancy
  ♦ occupancy in September
Septemberfeier, f
  ♦ September celebration
Septembertagung, f
  Septembertreffen, n
  ♦ September meeting
Septemberurlaub, m
  Septemberferien, pl
  ♦ September vacation AE
  ♦ September holiday BE
Septemberwoche, f
  ♦ September week
Septimerpaß, m
  ♦ Septimer Pass, the
Serbe, m
  ♦ Serb
  ♦ Serbian
Serbien
  ♦ Serbia
Serbin, f
  ♦ Serb girl
  ♦ Serb woman
  ♦ Serb
  ♦ Serbian girl
  ♦ Serbian woman
serbisch, adj
  ♦ Serbian, adj
  ♦ Serb, adj
Serenade, f
  ♦ serenade
Serenadenkonzert, n
  ♦ serenade concert
Serpentine, f (Straßenkehre)
  ♦ double bend
Serpentine, f (Strecke)
  ♦ switchback BE
Serpentinenstraße, f
  ♦ serpentine road
  ♦ switchback road BE
  ♦ winding road

Service, m
  Dienst, m
  Dienstleistung, f
  Leistung, f
  ♦ service
Service, n (Geschirr)
  ♦ service
  ♦ set
Service 130, m
  (gebührenfreier Telefonanruf)
  ♦ toll-free telephone call
Service anbieten jm
  → Leistung anbieten jm
Service an Bord, m
  ♦ service on board
Service an Einzeltischen, m
  → A-part-Service
Serviceanforderung, f
  → Leistungsanforderung
Serviceangebot, n (Gegensatz zu Nachfrage)
  ♦ supply of services
Serviceangebot, n (Palette)
  → Leistungsangebot
Serviceangebotsausweitung, f
  Leistungsangebotssteigerung, f
  ♦ increase in the range of services offered
  ♦ increase in the range of services
Serviceangestellter, m
  Serviceangestellte, f
  Servicemitarbeiter, m
  Servicemitarbeiterin, f
  ♦ service employee
Service an Ort und Stelle, m
  ♦ on-the-spot service
Serviceanspruch, m
  Serviceanforderung, f
  ♦ service requirement
Service arrangieren für jn
  Service vermitteln für jn
  ♦ arrange a service for s.o.
Serviceart, f
  (z.B. à la carte, Büfettservice)
  ♦ service mode
  ♦ mode of service
Serviceaufzug, m
  Servicefahrstuhl, m
  Servicelift, m
  ♦ service lift BE
  ♦ service elevator AE
Serviceaushilfe, f
  → Hilfskellner
Servicebar, f
  → Bar mit Bedienung
Service beibehalten
  ♦ retain a service
Service benötigen
  → Leistung benötigen
Servicebereich, m (abstrakt)
  Servicesektor, m
  ♦ service sector
Servicebereich, m (konkret)
  ♦ service area
Service bieten
  Leistung bieten
  ♦ provide a service
Service bieten jm
  ♦ provide s.o. with a service
Servicebrigade, f
  ♦ service brigade
Service buchen
  Serviceleistung buchen

Dienstleistung buchen
  Leistung buchen
  Service bestellen
  ♦ book a service
Servicebüro, n
  → Serviceoffice
Service compris FR
  Service inbegriffen
  ♦ service compris FR
  ♦ service included
Service d'étage, m FR
  Etagenservice, m
  ♦ service d'étage FR
  ♦ floor service
Service einführen
  ♦ introduce a service
Serviceeinrichtung f
  ♦ service facility
Service einschränken
  Leistung einschränken
  Service reduzieren
  Leistung reduzieren
  ♦ curtail a service
  ♦ cut a service
  ♦ reduce a service
Serviceeinschränkung, f
  Leistungseinschränkung, f
  ♦ curtailment of service
  ♦ cut in service
  ♦ cut in services
Service einstellen
  Service aufgeben
  Dienst einstellen
  Verkehr einstellen
  ♦ discontinue a service
Service erhalten
  Leistung erhalten
  ♦ be given a service
  ♦ be given service
Serviceerweiterung, f
  ♦ service expansion
  ♦ expansion of service
Service-Etage f
  Servicestockwerk n
  Servicegeschoß n
  ♦ service floor
Servicefachlehrling, m SCHW
  → Kellnerlehrling
Servicefachleute, pl
  ♦ trained waiters pl
  ♦ trained waitresses pl
Servicefahrstuhl, m
  Servicelift, m
  Serviceaufzug, m
  ♦ service elevator AE
  ♦ service lift BE
Serviceform, f
  ♦ form of service
  ♦ service form
Servicefunktion, f
  ♦ service function
Servicegehilfe, m
  Serviergehilfe, m
  Kellnergehilfe, m
  Kellnercommis, m
  ♦ commis waiter
  ♦ assistant waiter
Service geht über alles
  → Service wird großgeschrieben
Service genießen
  ♦ enjoy a service

Servicegestaltung, f
  ♦ organisation of a service
  ♦ organization of a service
  ♦ developing a service
Serviceglocke, f
  ♦ service bell
Servicegutschein, m
  → Leistungsgutschein
Servicehilfe, f
  → Hilfskellner
Service im Stundentakt, m
  ♦ hourly service
Service in Anspruch nehmen
  → Leistung in Anspruch nehmen
serviceintensiv, adj
  ♦ service-intensive, adj
Service ist angemessen
  Service ist ausreichend
  ♦ service is adequate
Service ist angenehm und freundlich
  ♦ service is pleasant and cheerful
Service ist aufmerksam
  ♦ service is attentive
Service ist diskret
  ♦ service is discreet
Service ist eingeschränkt
  Service ist begrenzt
  ♦ service is limited
  ♦ service is restricted
Service ist erstklassig
  ♦ service is first class
  ♦ service is first rate coll
Service ist fehlerlos
  Service istt fehlerfrei
  ♦ service is faultless
Service ist freundlich
  ♦ service is cheerful
Service ist gepflegt
  Service ist kultiviert
  ♦ service is sophisticated
Service ist geschwind
  ♦ service is brisk
Service ist gut
  ♦ service is good
Service ist gut organisiert
  ♦ service is well organised
Service ist 1a
  ♦ service is A1
Service ist kostenlos
  ♦ service is free
  ♦ service is free of charge
Service ist kühl
  ♦ service is cool
Service ist langsam
  ♦ service is slow
Service ist mürrisch
  ♦ service is surly
Service ist ordentlich
  ♦ service is orderly
Service ist persönlich
  ♦ service is personal
Service ist reibungslos
  ♦ service is smooth
Service ist schlecht
  ♦ service is bad
  ♦ service is poor
Service ist schlechter geworden
  ♦ service has deteriorated
Service ist schnell
  ♦ service is fast
  ♦ service is rapid

Service ist Spitze
♦ service is top class
Service ist tadellos
♦ service is impeccable
Service ist überdurchschnittlich
♦ service is above average
Service ist unaufdringlich
♦ service is unobtrusive
Service ist uneffizient
♦ service is inefficient
Service ist unpersönlich
♦ service is impersonal
Service ist verbindlich
♦ service is suave
Service ist vorzüglich
♦ service is superb
Service ist ziemlich gut
♦ service is fair
Service ist zuverlässig
♦ service is reliable
Servicekapazität, f
Bedienungskapazität, f
♦ service capacity
♦ capacity of service
Serviceklasse f
(Preisklasse)
♦ service class
♦ class of service
Servicekonzept, n
→ Dienstleistungskonzept
Servicekraft, f
→ Servicemitarbeiter
Serviceküche, f
♦ service kitchen
Service kürzen
Leistung kürzen
♦ curtail a service
♦ cut a service
Servicelehrling, m
→ Kellnerlehrling
Serviceleistung, f
♦ service
♦ rendering a service
Serviceleistung buchen
→ Service buchen
Serviceleistungen kürzen
Service einschränken
♦ curtail services
Serviceleistung erbringen
→ Dienstleistung erbringen
Serviceleiter, m
Serviceführer, m
Chef de service, m FR
♦ service manager
♦ chef de service FR
Serviceleiterin, f
Serviceführerin, f
♦ service manageress
♦ female service manager
Serviceliste, f
Serviceverzeichnis, n
Leistungsverzeichnis, n
♦ list of services
♦ service list
Servicemanagement, n
♦ service management
Servicemitarbeiter, m
→ Serviceangestellter
Service mit Rückgabe am selben Tag, m
♦ same-day service

Servicemix, m
♦ service mix
♦ mix of services
Servicemöglichkeit, f
♦ service possibility
♦ service facility
Service nach dem Flug, m
♦ afterflight service AE
♦ after-flight service BE
Servicenebenkosten, pl
♦ incidental service costs pl
♦ incidental service cost
Serviceniveau, n
Leistungsniveau, n
♦ level of service
♦ service level
Serviceniveau verbessern
Leistungsniveau steigern
♦ improve the level of service
♦ improve the service level
Serviceoffice, n
Servicebüro, n
♦ service office
♦ office
♦ pantry
♦ stillroom
♦ service room
Serviceorganisation, f
♦ service organisation
♦ service organization
servicepaket, n
→ Dienstleistungspaket
Servicepalette, f
→ Serviceangebot
Servicepersonal n
Bedienungspersonal n
♦ service personnel
♦ service staff
Servicepraktikant, m
♦ service trainee
Serviceproblem, n
♦ service problem
Serviceprogramm, n
→ Leistungsprogramm
Servicequalität f
♦ service quality
♦ quality of (the) service(s)
Serviceraum, m
(z.B. für Zimmerservice)
Anrichteraum, m
♦ service room
Service rund um die Uhr, m
→ Rund-um-die-Uhr-Dienst
Service schätzen
Service zu schätzen wissen
♦ appreciate a service
Servicestandard, m
♦ service standard
♦ standard of service
Servicestandard halten
♦ maintain the service standard
Service steht zur Verfügung
♦ service is available
Servicestil, m
♦ style of service
♦ service style
Service streichen
Leistung entfallen lassen
♦ cancel a service
Servicestruktur, f
♦ service structure

Serviceteam n
♦ service team
Servicetechnik, f
♦ service technique
Servicetechnologie, f
♦ service technology
Servicetisch, m
♦ service table
Servicetuch, n
♦ service cloth
Servicetür, f
♦ service door
Servicetyp, n
Serviceart, f
♦ service type
♦ type of service
Service übertrifft etw
♦ service exceeds s.th.
Serviceumfang, m
Leistungsumfang, m
♦ service extent
♦ extent of (the) service(s)
♦ service range
♦ range of service(s)
♦ range of service(s) offered
Service verbessern
♦ improve (a) service
Service verkaufen
Dienstleistung verkaufen
Leistung verkaufen
♦ sell a service
Service vermarkten
→ Dienstleistung vermarkten
Service vermitteln jm
→ Service arrangieren für jn
Serviceverspätung, f
♦ service hold-up
Serviceverspätung beheben
♦ remedy a service hold-up
Serviceverzeichnis, n
Serviceliste, f
♦ service list
♦ list of (the) services
Service vor dem Flug, m
♦ preflight service AE
♦ pre-flight service BE
Servicewagen, m
Servierwagen, m
♦ service wagon AE
♦ service cart AE
♦ service trolley BE
Service wieder einführen
Dienst wieder aufnehmen
♦ reintroduce a service
Service wird großgeschrieben
Service geht über alles
♦ service is paramount
♦ service is foremost
Servicewunsch, m
♦ service request
Service zeichnet das Hotel aus
♦ service distinguishes the hotel
Servicezeit, f
Bedienungszeit f
♦ service time
♦ hours of service pl
Servicezentrum, n
Servicecenter, n
♦ service center AE
♦ service centre BE

Servicezimmer, n
→ Serviceraum
Service zu allen Tag- und Nachtzeiten, m
Rund-um-die-Uhr-Service, m
24-Stunden-Service, m
♦ service round the clock
♦ 24-hour service
♦ round-the-clock service
Servicezuschlag m
♦ service supplement
Service à la carte, m
offener Service, m
Bedienung à la carte, f
♦ service à la carte BE
♦ service a la carte AE
Service à la française, m FR
französischer Service, m
♦ service à la française FR
♦ French Service
Service à l'américaine, m FR
amerikanischer Service, m
♦ service à l'américaine FR
♦ American service
Service à l'anglaise, m FR
englischer Service, m
♦ service à l'anglaise FR
♦ English service
♦ silver service
Service à l'anglaise avec guéridon, m FR
englischer Service mit Guéridon, m
♦ service à l'anglaise avec guéridon FR
♦ English service with guéridon
Service à la russe, m FR
russischer Service, m
♦ service à la russe FR
♦ Russian service
Service à part, m FR
Einzelservice, m
Service an Einzeltischen, m
♦ service à part FR
Servierbrett, n
Serviertablett, n
♦ salver
♦ tray
♦ server
servieren
bedienen
♦ wait at a table
servieren als Hauptgericht
♦ serve as the main dish
servieren etw
reichen etw
♦ serve s.th.
servieren etw als Nachtisch
♦ serve s.th. as dessert
♦ serve s.th. for dessert
servieren etw am Tisch
♦ serve s.th. at the table
servieren etw auf einem Teller
♦ serve s.th. on a plate
servieren etw direkt nach etw
♦ serve s.th. directly after s.th.
servieren etw garniert mit etw
♦ serve s.th. garnished with s.th.
servieren etw lauwarm
♦ serve s.th. lukewarm
servieren etw mit der richtigen Temperatur
♦ serve s.th. at the correct temperature
servieren etw sehr kalt
♦ serve s.th. very cold

servieren etw sofort
♦ serve s.th. immediately
servieren etw warm oder kalt
♦ serve s.th. warm or cold
servieren etw zum Frühstück
♦ serve s.th. for breakfast
servieren etw à la carte
♦ serve s.th. à la carte BE
♦ serve s.th. a la carte AE
servieren jm etw
♦ serve s.o. s.th
♦ serve s.th. to s.o.
servieren lernen
♦ learn to serve
Servierer, m off
Kellner, m
♦ server
♦ male server
♦ waiter
Serviererfahrung, f
♦ experience as a waiter
♦ experience as a waitress
♦ waiting experience
Serviererin, f off
Kellnerin, f
♦ female server
♦ waitress
servierfähig, adj
→ servierfertig
servierfertig, adj
♦ ready-to-serve, adj
servierfertiges Gericht, n
♦ ready-to-serve dish
Serviergehilfe, m
→ Servicegehilfe
Servierhelfer, m
→ Hilfskellner
Servierkännchen, n
♦ serving jug
Servierkunst f
♦ art of serving
Servierlöffel, m
Vorlegelöffel, m
♦ service spoon
♦ serving spoon
Serviermädchen, n
→ Serviererin
Serviermeister, m
(offizielle Bezeichnung)
♦ headwaiter
Servierpersonal, n
♦ serving staff
♦ serving personnel
♦ waiting staff
♦ waiting personnel
Servierplatte, f
♦ serving platter
♦ platter
Servierportion, f
♦ serving portion
Servierschürze f
♦ waiter's apron
♦ waitress's apron
Servierschüssel, f
♦ serving dish
♦ serving bowl
Serviertablett n
→ Servierbrett
Serviertasche, f
Serviceportemonnaie, n
♦ waiter's purse

Serviertasse f
→ Servierbrett
Servierteller, m
♦ serving tray
♦ serving plate
♦ waiter
Serviertemperatur, f
♦ serving temperature
Serviertheke, f
Serviertresen, m
♦ service counter
Serviertisch, m (beweglich)
Servierwagen, m
♦ coaster
♦ cart AE
♦ trolley BE
Serviertisch, m (feststehend)
Anrichtetisch, m
♦ serving table
♦ service table
♦ sideboard table
♦ sideboard
Serviertochter, f SCHW
→ Kellnerin
Serviertuch, n
♦ waiter's napkin
♦ waiter's cloth
♦ waitress's napkin
♦ waitress's cloth
Serviervorschlag, m
♦ serving suggestion
Servierwagen, m
♦ serving cart AE
♦ serving trolley BE
Servierzeit, f (Dauer)
Servierdauer, f
♦ serving period
♦ service period
Servierzeit, f (Zeitpunkt)
Servierzeitpunkt, m
♦ serving time
♦ service time
Serviette, f
♦ napkin
♦ serviette
Serviette falten
♦ fold a napkin
♦ fold a serviette
Serviettenring, m
♦ napkin ring
♦ serviette ring
Serviettentasche f
♦ napkin case
♦ serviette case
Servobremse, f
♦ power brake
Servolenkung, f
♦ power steering
Sesam, öffne Dich!
♦ Open Sesame!
Sessel, m
♦ armchair
Sessellift, m
♦ chair lift AE
♦ chair-lift BE
Sesselliftanlage, f
♦ chair-lift system
Sesselliftkarte, f
♦ chair-lift ticket
Sesselliftstation, f
♦ chair-lift station

Set

Set, n
- ◆ table mat
- ◆ place mat *AE*
- ◆ place-mat *BE*

setzen etw auf den Speiseplan
→ setzen etw auf die Speisekarte

setzen etw auf die Rechnung jm
- ◆ charge s.th. to s.o.

setzen etw auf die Zimmerrechnung
- ◆ charge s.th. to the room bill

setzen jn auf die Schwarze Liste
auf die Schwarze Liste jn setzen
- ◆ put s.o. on the blacklist
- ◆ blacklist s.o.

setzen jn auf die Straße
- ◆ chuck s.o. into the street *coll*

setzen jn auf die Vormerkliste
→ setzen jn auf die Warteliste

setzen jn auf die Warteliste
jn auf die Vormerkliste setzen
- ◆ put s.o. on the waiting list *AE*
- ◆ put s.o. on the wait list *AE*
- ◆ put s.o. on the waiting-list *BE*

Setzen Sie es auf die Rechnung von Zimmer 123
- ◆ Charge it to room 123

Setzen Sie es bitte auf meine Rechnung
- ◆ Put it on my bill, please

Setzen Sie sich zu uns!
- ◆ Come and sit with us!
- ◆ Join us!

Sèvres-Porzellan, n
- ◆ Sèvres porcelain
- ◆ Sèvres china

Sexclub, m
- ◆ sex club

Sextourismus, m
- ◆ sex tourism

Sextourist, m
- ◆ sex tourist

Sexwochenende verbringen in X
- ◆ spend a dirty weekend at X
- ◆ spend a dirty weekend in X

Seychellen, die, pl
- ◆ Seychelles, the *pl*

Shampoo, n
- ◆ shampoo

Sherpa, m
- ◆ sherpa

Sherpaexpedition, f
- ◆ sherpa expedition

Sherry, m
- ◆ sherry

Sherryempfang m
- ◆ sherry reception

Sherryglas, n
- ◆ sherry glass

Sherrypunsch, m
- ◆ sherry punch

Sherrysorbet, n
- ◆ sherry sorbet

Shetland
- ◆ Shetland
- ◆ Shetlands, the *pl*

Shetländer, m
Shetländerin, f
- ◆ Shetlander

Shetlandinseln, die, f pl
- ◆ Shetland Islands, the *pl*
- ◆ Shetlands, the *pl*

shetländisch, adj
- ◆ Shetland, adj

Shetlandpony, n
- ◆ Shetland pony

Shopping, n
→ Einkaufen

Shortdrink, m
(bis 5 cl)
- ◆ short drink

Show, f
→ Schau

Showabend, m
Schauabend, m
- ◆ show evening

Show auf die Bühne bringen
- ◆ stage a show

Showband, f
- ◆ show band

Show feiern
- ◆ celebrate a show

Showgeschäft, n
- ◆ show business
- ◆ showbiz *inform*

Show inszenieren
- ◆ mount a show
- ◆ stage a show

Show machen
- ◆ make a show

Showmaster, m
- ◆ emcee
- ◆ MC
- ◆ host
- ◆ master of ceremonies

Showprogramm, n
- ◆ show program *AE*
- ◆ show programme *BE*

Sibirer, m
- ◆ Siberian

Sibirerin, f
- ◆ Siberian girl
- ◆ Siberian woman
- ◆ Siberian

Sibirien
- ◆ Siberia

sibirisch, adj
- ◆ Siberian, adj

sichere Fahrt, f
- ◆ safe trip
- ◆ safe ride

sicherer Badestrand, m
- ◆ safe bathing beach

sichere Reise, f (generell)
- ◆ safe journey
- ◆ safe tour
- ◆ safe trip

sichere Reise, f (Seereise)
- ◆ safe voyage

sicherer Ort, m
- ◆ safe place

sicherer Strand m
- ◆ safe beach

sicheres Baden, n
- ◆ safe bathing

sicheres Parken, n
- ◆ secure parking
- ◆ safe parking

sicher fühlen sich
- ◆ feel safe

Sicherheitsabfertigung, f
- ◆ security clearance

Sicherheitsanweisung, f
- ◆ safety instruction

Sicherheitsbeauftragter, m
Sicherheitsbeamter, m
- ◆ security officer
- ◆ safety officer

Sicherheitsbeleuchtung, f
- ◆ security lighting

Sicherheitsbindung, f
(Ski)
- ◆ safety binding

Sicherheitsdienst, m
- ◆ security service

Sicherheitsgebühr, f
- ◆ security charge
- ◆ security fee

Sicherheitsglas, n
- ◆ safety glass

Sicherheitsgurt, m
- ◆ safety strap

Sicherheitsgürtel durchbrechen
- ◆ breach the security cordon

Sicherheitsgürtel (um etw), m
- ◆ security cordon (round s.th.)

Sicherheitskonferenz, f
(Politik)
- ◆ security conference

Sicherheitskontrolle, f
- ◆ safety check

Sicherheitsmaßnahme, f
- ◆ security measure
- ◆ safety measure

Sicherheitsmaßnahmen ergreifen
- ◆ take security measures

Sicherheitsnadel, f
- ◆ safety pin

Sicherheitspersonal, n
Wachpersonal, n
- ◆ security staff
- ◆ security personnel

Sicherheitsproblem, n
- ◆ safety problem
- ◆ security problem

Sicherheitsprüfung, f
- ◆ security check

Sicherheitsrisiko, n
- ◆ security risk

Sicherheitsschloß, n
- ◆ safety lock

Sicherheitsstandard, m
- ◆ safety standard

Sicherheitsstandard überwachen
- ◆ monitor the safety standard

Sicherheitssystem, n
- ◆ security system

Sicherheitstür, f
- ◆ security door

Sicherheitsvorkehrung, f
- ◆ safety precaution arrangement
- ◆ security arrangement
- ◆ security precaution

Sicherheitsvorkehrungen treffen
Sicherheitsvorkehrungen ergreifen
- ◆ take safety precautions
- ◆ take security precautions

Sicherheitsvorschriften, f pl
- ◆ security regulations *pl*
- ◆ safety regulations *pl*

sichern sich etw
- ◆ secure s.th.

Sicherung, f
(Strom)
- ◆ fuse

Sicherung ist durchgebrannt
♦ fuse is blown
Sicherungskasten, m
(Strom)
♦ fuse box
sichtbar, adj
♦ visible, adj
sichtbar sein
♦ be visible
Sichtvermerk, m
→ Visum
Sicht versperren
Ausblick versperren
Aussicht versperren
♦ block one's view
♦ block s.o.'s view
♦ obstruct one's view
♦ obstruct s.o.'s view
Sichtweite, f
Sicht, f
♦ sight
Sideboard, n
♦ sideboard
Sieb, n
♦ sieve
♦ strainer
siebenbettig, adj
♦ seven-bedded, adj
siebenbettiges Zimmer, n
♦ seven-bedded room
Siebenbettzimmer, n
♦ seven-bed room
♦ seven-bedded room
Siebenbürgen
Transsilvanien
♦ Transylvania
♦ Transilvania
sieben (etw)
durch ein Sieb geben (etw)
♦ sift (s.th.)
♦ sieve (s.th.)
♦ pass s.th. through a sieve
siebengängig, adj (Essen)
♦ seven-course, adj
♦ consisting of seven courses, adj
siebengängiges Essen, n
♦ seven-course meal
siebengängiges Menü, n
♦ seven-course menu
Siebengebirge, n
(Region)
♦ Siebengebirge, the
♦ Seven Mountains, the pl
siebensitzig, adj
♦ seven-seater, adj
siebenstündig, adj
♦ seven-hour, adj
♦ lasting seven hours
♦ of seven hours' duration
siebenstündige Reise, f
♦ seven-hour journey
♦ seven-hour tour
♦ seven-hour trip
siebenstündiger Marsch, m
♦ seven hours' march
siebenstündiges Programm, n
♦ seven-hour program AE
♦ seven-hour programme BE
siebenstündige Verspätung, f
♦ seven-hour delay

Siebentagefahrt, f
→ siebentägige Fahrt
Siebentagepaß, m
♦ seven-day pass
Siebentagepauschale, f
♦ seven-day package
Siebentagerechnung, f
♦ seven-day bill
♦ seven-day check AE
Siebentageskipaß, m
♦ seven-day ski pass
♦ one-week ski pass
Siebentagezeitraum, m
♦ seven-day period
siebentägig, adj
♦ seven-day, adj
♦ seven days'
♦ of seven days' duration
♦ lasting seven days
siebentägige Fahrt, f
Siebentagefahrt, f
♦ seven-day trip
♦ seven days' trip
siebentägige Kündigungsfrist, f
♦ seven days' notice
Sieben Weltwunder, die, n pl
♦ Seven Wonders of the World, the pl
Sieben Weltwunder der Antike, die, n pl
♦ Seven Wonders of the Ancient World, the, pl
siebenwöchig, adj
♦ seven-week, adj
♦ lasting seven weeks
♦ of seven weeks' duration
siebenwöchige Reise, f
♦ seven-week journey
♦ seven-week tour
♦ seven-week trip
siebenwöchige Tournee, f
♦ seven-week tour
siebenzimmerig, adj
♦ seven-roomed, adj
siebenzimmeriges Haus, n
♦ seven-roomed house
Sieben-Zimmer-Villa, f
♦ seven-room villa
Siebschüssel, f
Durchschlag, m
Seiher, m
♦ colander
siebter Gang, m (Essen)
♦ seventh course
siebtes Stockwerk, n
siebte Etage, f
siebtes Obergeschoß, n
♦ eighth floor AE
♦ eighth story AE
♦ seventh floor BE
♦ seventh storey BE
siedendheiß, adj
siedend heiß, adj
♦ boiling hot, adj
sieden etw
kochen etw
♦ boil s.th.
Siedlung, f (historisch)
♦ settlement
Siedlung, f (Wohnsiedlung)
♦ development AE
♦ housing estate BE
♦ housing development BE

Siedlung aus römischer Zeit, f
♦ settlement from the Roman period
Siedlungshaus, n
♦ house on a development AE
♦ house on an housing estate BE
Siegel, n
♦ seal
Siegerehrung, f
♦ prize-giving ceremony
Sie haben die Wahl
♦ choice is yours
♦ the choice is yours
siehe Preisliste
s. Preisliste
♦ see price list
♦ see tariff
Sie können den Wagen auf dem Parkplatz abstellen
Sie können das Auto auf dem Parkplatz parken
♦ You can leave the car in the parking lot AE
♦ You can park the car in the parking lot AE
♦ You can leave the car in the car park BE
♦ You can park the car in the car park BE
Sie können hier bleiben
♦ You can stay here
Sie können nach Belieben kommen und gehen
♦ You can come and go at pleasure
Sie möchten Ihr Zimmer behalten?
♦ You would like to keep your room?
Sierra Leone
♦ Sierra Leone
Sierraleoner, m
♦ Sierra Leonean
Sierraleonerin, f
♦ Sierra Leonean girl
♦ Sierra Leonean woman
♦ Sierra Leonean
sierraleonisch, adj
♦ Sierra Leonean, adj
Sie sind eingeladen, daran teilzunehmen (aktiv)
♦ You are welcome to participate
Sie sind eingeladen, daran teilzunehmen (passiv)
♦ You are welcome to attend
Sie sind immer willkommen
Sie sind jederzeit willkommen
♦ You are always welcome
Sie sind jederzeit willkommen
Sie sind zu jeder Zeit willkommen
♦ You are welcome any time
♦ You are welcome at all times
Sie Sind nicht satt zu bekommen!
♦ You are insatiable!
Siesta, f
♦ siesta
Siesta machen
♦ have a siesta
♦ take a siesta
Sie werden hiermit eingeladen
♦ You are hereby invited
Sie werden wahrscheinlich nicht enttäuscht
♦ You are not likely to be disappointed
Sightseeing, n
→ Besichtigung
Silber, n
♦ silver
Silberbergwerk, n
♦ silver mine
Silberbesteck, n
♦ silver cutlery

Silberfisch

Silberfisch, m
- silverfish *AE*
- silver-fish *BE*

Silbergabel, f
  silberne Gabel, f
- silver fork

Silbergeschirr, n
- silverware
- silver dishes *pl*
- silver plate
- silver

Silberlachs, m
  (Jugendstadium der Meerforelle)
- whitling

Silberlöffel, m
  silberner Löffel, m
- silver spoon

Silbermedaille, f
- silver medal

Silbermesser, n
- silver knife

silberne Hochzeit, f
  Silberhochzeit, f
- silver wedding

silberne Hochzeit feiern
- celebrate one's silver wedding

silberner Jahrestag, m
- silver anniversary

silbernes Hochzeitsjubiläum, n
- silver wedding anniversary

silbernes Jubiläum, n
- silver jubilee

Silberputzer, m
- silver polisher

Silberschüssel, f
  silberne Schüssel, f
- silver dish
- silver bowl

Silberspüle, f (Raum)
  → Silberspülraum

Silberspülraum, m
  Silberspüle, f
- silver room

Silberstrand, m
- silvery beach

Silbertablett, n
- silver salver

Silberteller, m
  silberner Teller, m
- silver plate

Silvaner, m
  (Wein)
  Sylvaner, m
- Silvaner
- Sylvaner

Silvanerrebe, f
- Silvaner vine

Silvanertraube, f
- Silvaner grape

Silvanerwein, m
- Silvaner wine

Silver putzen
- polish the silver

Silvester, m
  Sylvester, m/n
  Silvesterabend, m
- New Year's Eve
- Hogmanay *SCOT*

Silvesterabend, m
  → Silvester

Silvesterball m
- New Year's Eve ball

Silvesterbankett n
- New Year's Eve banquet
- banquet on New Year's Eve

Silvesterbüfett, n
- New Year's Eve buffet

Silvesterdiner, n
  Silvesteressen, n
- New Year's Eve dinner

Silvesteressen, n
- New Year's Eve meal
- New Year's Eve dinner

Silvesterfeier f
- New Year's Eve celebration
- New Year's Eve party

Silvester feiern
- celebrate New Year's Eve

Silvesterfestessen, n
  → Silvestergaladiner

Silvesterfete, f
- New Year's Eve fete *AE*
- New Year's Eve fête *BE*

Silvesterfeuerwerk, n
- New Year's Eve fireworks *pl*
- New Year's Eve fireworks display

Silvestergaladiner, n
  Silvesterfestessen, n
- New Year's Eve gala dinner

Silvestergalamenü, n
- New Year's Eve gala menu

Silvestergast, m
- New Year's Eve guest
- guest on New Year's Eve

Silvestermenü, n
- New Year's Eve menu

Silvesternacht f
- night of New Year's Eve

Silvesterparty, f
- New Year's Eve party

Silvesterprogramm, n
- New Year's Eve program *AE*
- New Year's Eve programme *BE*

Silvesterpunsch, m
- New Year's Eve punch

Silvestertanzdiner, n
- New Year's Eve dinner dance

Silvesterzeit, f
  → Silvester

Simbabwe
- Zimbabwe

Simbabwer, m
- Zimbabwean

Simbabwerin, f
- Zimbabwean girl
- Zimbabwean woman
- Zimbabwean

simbabwisch, adj
- Zimbabwean, adj

Simplonpaß, m
- Simplon Pass, the

Simultananlage, f
  → Simultandolmetschanlage

Simultandolmetschanlage f
  Simultandolmetscheranlage f
- simultaneous interpretation system

Simultandolmetschdienst m
  Simultandolmetscherdienst m
  Simultandolmetschservice m
- simultaneous interpretation service

Simultandolmetschen, n
- simultaneous interpreting

Simultandolmetscher, m
- simultaneous interpreter

Simultandolmetschkanal, m
- simultaneous interpretation channel

Simultanübersetzungsdienst m
  Simultanübersetzungsservice m
  Simultanübersetzer m
- simultaneous translation service

Sinai, m
- Sinai, the

Sinaigebirge, n
- Mount Sinai

Sinaihalbinsel, f
- Sinai Peninsula, the

Sind die Sitzplätze numeriert?
  Sind die Plätze numeriert?
- Are the seats numbered?

Sind Sie müde?
- Are you tired?

Sind Sie zufrieden mit der Wohnung?
- Are you pleased with the apartment? *AE*
- Are you pleased with the flat? *BE*

Sind Sie zum ersten Mal in X?
- Is this your first time in X?

Sind wir quitt?
- Are we quits?
- Are we square?

Sinfonie, f
- symphony

Sinfoniekonzert, n
- symphony concert

Sinfonieorchester, n
- symphony orchestra

Sinfoniesaal, m
- symphony hall

Singapur
- Singapore

singen und tanzen die ganze Nacht
- sing and dance all night

Singfest, n
- singing meet *AE*

Singkneipe, f *coll*
  Gaststätte, in der gesungen wird, f
- singing pub *BE*

Single, m
- single
- single person

Singlebar, f
- singles' bar

Singleprogramm, n
- singles' program *AE*
- singles' programme *BE*

Singleurlaub, m
  Singleferien, pl
- singles' vacation *AE*
- singles' holiday *BE*

Singlewochenende, n
- singles' weekend

Siphon, m (Bar)
- soda siphon

Siphon, m (Sanitär)
- siphon

Sirup, m
- syrup

Sitz, m (Sitzplatz)
  → Sitzplatz

Sitzabstand, m
  (Abstand der Sitze hintereinander)
- seat pitch

Sitzanordnung, f
　Anordnung der Sitze, f
　♦ arrangement of (the) seats
　♦ seating arrangement
Sitzanordnung im Cocktailstil, f
　♦ cocktail-style seating
Sitzanzahl, f
　→ Sitzzahl
Sitzauslastung, f
　Sitzplatzauslastung, f
　Platzauslastung, f
　Sitzbelegung, f
　♦ seat occupancy
Sitzbad, n (Vorgang)
　♦ hip bath
　♦ sitz bath
Sitzbad, n (Wanne)
　→ Sitzbadewanne
Sitzbadewanne, f
　♦ sitz bath
　♦ sit-down bath
Sitzbank, f
　♦ bench seat
　♦ settee
　♦ bench
Sitzbelegung, f
　→ Sitzauslastung
Sitzbereich, m
　♦ sitting area
Sitzbezug, m
　♦ seat cover
Sitzcouch f
　→ Couch
Sitzecke, f
　♦ corner seating unit
sitzen auf einem Stuhl
　♦ sit on a chair
sitzen beim Ofen
　♦ sit by the stove
　♦ sit near the stove
sitzen gegenüber von jm
　♦ sit opposite s.o.
sitzen in einem Flugzeug
　in einem Flugzeug sitzen
　♦ sit in a plane
sitzen neben jm
　♦ sit next to s.o.
Sitzen Sie bequem?
　♦ Are you sitting comfortably?
　♦ Are you comfortable?
sitzen vor dem Ofen
　♦ sit in front of the stove
sitzen zwischen A und B
　♦ sit between A and B
Sitzfleisch haben
　♦ be in no hurry to go
Sitzgarnitur, f
　Sitzgruppe, f
　♦ living-room suite
　♦ three-piece suite
Sitzgelegenheit, f
　Sitz, m
　♦ place to sit down
　♦ seat
Sitzgruppe, f (Garnitur)
　→ Sitzgarnitur
Sitzgruppe, f (Wohnwagen)
　♦ dinette
Sitzgruppentisch, m
　(Wohnwagen)
　♦ dinette table

Sitzgurt, m
　Sicherheitsgurt, m
　♦ seat belt AE
　♦ seat-belt BE
　♦ safety-belt BE
Sitzgurt tragen
　♦ wear a seat belt
Sitz in der ersten Reihe, m
　♦ front-row seat
　♦ seat in the front row
Sitzkapazität, f
　→ Sitzplatzkapazität
Sitz-Kilometer, m
　♦ seat kilometer AE
　♦ seat kilometre Be
Sitzkissen, n
　♦ seat cushion
　♦ cushion
Sitzladefaktor, m
　Sitzauslastung, f
　♦ seat load factor
Sitz mit verstellbarer Rückenlehne, m
　→ Liegesitz
Sitzmöbel, n pl
　♦ seating furniture sg
　♦ chairs pl
　♦ seating
Sitznische, f (Restaurant)
　Sitzgruppe, f
　♦ booth
Sitzplan, m
　Bestuhlungsplan, m
　♦ plan of the seating arrangement
　♦ seating plan
Sitzplan ändern (geringfügig)
　♦ alter the seating plan
Sitzplan ändern ((umfassend)
　♦ change the seating plan
Sitzplan ist auf dem Buchungsformular
　abgedruckt
　♦ seating plan is shown on the booking form
Sitzplatz, m
　Platz, m
　Sitz, m
　♦ seat
Sitzplatz am Fenster, m
　Platz am Fenster, m
　Fenstersitzplatz, m
　Fensterplatz, m
　♦ seat by the window
　♦ seat at the window
　♦ window seat
Sitzplatz an Bord, m
　Platz an Bord, m
　♦ seat on board
Sitzplatzanordnung, f
　♦ layout of seating
　♦ seating arrangement
Sitzplatz auf flachem Boden, m
　Sitz auf flachem Boden, m
　♦ flat-floored seat
Sitzplatzauslastung, f
　→ Sitzauslastung
Sitzplatz aussuchen
　Sitz wählen
　Platz auswählen
　♦ choose a seat
　♦ select a seat
Sitzplatzauswahl, f
　Platzwahl, f
　Sitzwahl, f

Sitzplatzwahl, f
　♦ seat selection
　♦ selection of a seat
　♦ selection of seats
　♦ selecting a seat/seats
　♦ choosing a seat/seats
Sitzplatz auswählen
　Platz auswählen
　Sitz auswählen
　♦ select a seat
Sitzplatz auswählen im voraus
　Platz auswählen im voraus
　Sitz auswählen im voraus
　♦ select a seat in advance
Sitzplatz bekommen
　Platz bekommen
　Sitz bekommen
　♦ get a seat
Sitzplatz belegen
　Sitz belegen
　Platz belegen
　Sitzplatz einnehmen
　Platz einnehmen
　♦ occupy a seat
Sitzplatzbelegung, f
　→ Sitzplatzauslastung
Sitzplatzbereich, m
　Sitzbereich, m
　♦ seating area
Sitzplatz bestellen
　Platz bestellen
　♦ bespeak a seat
Sitzplatz bleibt unverkauft
　♦ seat remains unsold
Sitzplatz buchen
　Platz buchen
　Sitzplatz bestellen
　Platz bestellen
　♦ book a seat
Sitzplatz entfernen
　Sitz entfernen
　♦ remove a seat
Sitzplatzentfernung, f
　Sitzentfernung, f
　♦ removal of a seat
　♦ seat removal
Sitzplatz erhalten links von jm
　♦ be seated to the left of s.o.
Sitzplatz erhalten neben jm
　♦ be seated next to s.o.
Sitzplatz erhalten rechts von jm
　♦ be seated to the right of s.o.
Sitzplatz füllen
　Sitzplätze füllen
　♦ fill a seat
　♦ fill seats
Sitzplatz garantieren jm
　Platz garantieren jm
　Sitz garantieren jm
　♦ guarantee a seat to s.o.
　♦ guarantee s.o. a seat
Sitzplatz ist besetzt
　♦ seat is taken
Sitzplatz ist verfügbar
　♦ seat is available
Sitzplatzkapazität f
　♦ seating capacity
Sitzplatzkosten, pl
　Sitzkosten, pl
　Platzkosten, pl
　♦ seat costs pl

Sitzplatz kostet zwischen DM 12 und DM 123

- ♦ seat cost
- ♦ costs per seat *pl*
- ♦ cost per seat

Sitzplatz kostet zwischen DM 12 und DM 123
- Sitz kostet zwischen DM 12 und DM 123
- Platz kostet zwischen DM 12 und DM 123
- ♦ **seat costs between DM 12 and DM 123**

Sitzplatz numerieren
- Sitz numerieren
- Platz numerieren
- ♦ **number a seat**

Sitzplatzpreis, m
- Platzpreis, m
- Sitzpreis, m
- ♦ **seat price**

Sitzplatz reservieren
- Platz reservieren
- Sitz reservieren
- ♦ **reserve a seat**

Sitzplatzreservierung, f
- Platzreservierung, f
- ♦ **seat reservation**
- ♦ reservation of a seat
- ♦ reserving a seat

Sitzplatzreservierungswunsch, m
- Platzreservierungswunsch, m
- ♦ **request for seat reservation**

Sitzplatzrotation, f
- → rotierende Sitzordnung

Sitzplatz sichern sich
- Platz sich sichern
- Sitz sich sichern
- ♦ **secure a seat**

Sitzplatzsystem, n
- ♦ **seating system**

Sitzplatzverfügbarkeit, f
- Platzverfügbarkeit, f
- ♦ **seat availability**

Sitzplatzverfügbarkeit feststellen
- Platzverfügbarkeit feststellen
- ♦ **ascertain seat availability**

Sitzplatzvergabe, f
- Sitzplatzzuweisung, f
- Platzvergabe, f
- Platzzuweisung, f
- ♦ **allocation of a seat**
- ♦ seat allocation
- ♦ seat assignment *AE*
- ♦ assignment of a seat *AE*

Sitzplatz vergeben an jn
- Platz vergeben an jn
- Sitzplatz zuweisen jm
- Platz zuweisen jm
- ♦ **allocate a seat to s.o.**
- ♦ assign a seat to s.o. *AE*

Sitzplatz verkaufen
- Platz verkaufen
- Sitz verkaufen
- ♦ **sell a seat**

Sitzplatz verweigern
- Platz verweigern
- Sitz verweigern
- ♦ **refuse a seat**

Sitzplatzwahl, f
- → Sitzplatzwahl

Sitzplatzwechsel, m
- Platzwechsel, m
- Sitzwechsel, m
- ♦ **change of seats**
- ♦ changing seats
- ♦ seat swap

- ♦ swapping seats
- ♦ swopping seats

Sitzplatz wechseln
- Platz wechseln
- Sitz wechseln
- ♦ **change seats**
- ♦ swap seats
- ♦ swop seats

Sitzplatzwunsch, m
- Sitzwunsch, m
- Platzwunsch, m
- ♦ **seat request**
- ♦ request for a seat

Sitzplatzwunsch äußern
- Sitzwunsch äußern
- Platzwunsch äußern
- ♦ **make a seat request**

Sitzplatz wurde zweimal vergeben
- ♦ **seat was double booked**

Sitzplatzzahl, f
- → Sitzzahl

Sitzplatz zuteilen jm
- Platz zuteilen jm
- Sitzplatz zuweisen jm
- Platz zuweisen jm
- ♦ **assign a seat to s.o.** *AE*
- ♦ allocate a seat to s.o. *BE*

Sitzplatz zuweisen
- Sitzplatz zuteilen
- ♦ **allocate a seat**

Sitzplatzzuweisung, f
- Platzzuweisung, f
- Sitzplatzvergabe, f
- Platzvergabe, f
- ♦ **seat assignment** *AE*
- ♦ seat allocation *BE*

Sitzreihe f
- ♦ **row of seats**

Sitzrestaurant n
- (Gegensatz zu Stehrestaurant)
- ♦ **sit-down restaurant**

Sitzt hier jemand?
- ♦ **Is anyone sitting here?**

Sitztoilette, f
- ♦ **British-style toilet**

Sitzung, f
- ♦ **session**
- ♦ meeting

Sitzung abhalten (Konferenz)
- ♦ **hold a session**

Sitzung absagen
- Sitzung streichen
- Treffen absagen
- ♦ **cancel a meeting**

Sitzung beiwohnen
- → teilnehmen an einer Sitzung

Sitzung dauert 20 Minuten
- ♦ **meeting lasts 20 minutes**

Sitzung einberufen
- ♦ **call a meeting**
- ♦ convene a meeting

Sitzungen finden gleichzeitig statt
- Sitzungen laufen parallel
- ♦ **sessions run concurrently**

Sitzung festlegen auf Montag
- ♦ **fix a meeting for Monday**

Sitzung geht von 14 bis 18 Uhr
- ♦ **meeting runs from 2 until 6 p.m.**
- ♦ meeting runs from 2 to 6 p.m.

Sitzung leiten
- ♦ **conduct a meeting**

Sitzung leiten (als Vorsitzender)
- Sitzung vorsitzen
- ♦ **chair a meeting**
- ♦ chair a session

Sitzung leiten (generell)
- ♦ **run a meeting**
- ♦ run a session

Sitzungsbericht, m
- ♦ **minutes of the meeting** *pl*

Sitzungskellner, m
- ♦ **meeting room waiter**

Sitzungskellnerin, f
- ♦ **meeting room waitress**

Sitzungsraum, m (generell)
- ♦ **meeting room**

Sitzungsraum, m (klein)
- ♦ **syndicate room**

Sitzungssaal, m
- (wie in Firmen)
- Sitzungsraum, m
- ♦ **boardroom**

Sitzung verlegen von Raum 1 in Raum 2
- ♦ **shift a meeting from room 1 to room 2**

Sitzverteilung, f
- ♦ **distribution of seats**
- ♦ allocation of seats

Sitzzahl, f
- Sitzanzahl, f
- Sitzplatzzahl, f
- Platzzahl, f
- ♦ **number of seats**

Sizilianer, m
- ♦ **Sicilian**

Sizilianerin, f
- ♦ **Sicilian girl**
- ♦ Sicilian woman
- ♦ Sicilian

sizilianisch, adj
- ♦ **Sicilian, adj**

sizilianische Art, adv *gastr*
- nach sizilianischer Art, adv *gastr*
- ♦ **Sicilian style, adv** *gastr*

Sizilien
- ♦ **Sicily**

Skandal machen
- ♦ **kick up a fuss**

skandalöser Preis, m
- ♦ **scandalous price**
- ♦ scandalous rate

Skandinavien
- ♦ **Scandinavia**

Skandinavienfest, n
- Skandinavienfestival, n
- ♦ **Scandinavian festival**

Skandinavier, m
- ♦ **Scandinavian**

Skandinavierin, f
- ♦ **Scandinavian girl**
- ♦ Scandinavian woman
- ♦ Scandinavian

skandinavisch, adj
- ♦ **Scandinavian, adj**

Skat, m
- (Kartenspiel)
- ♦ **skat**

Skatabend, m
- ♦ **skat evening**
- ♦ evening of skat
- ♦ skat night

Skatbruder, m
♦ skat enthusiast
♦ skat mate
Skatclub, m
Skatverein, m
♦ skat club
Skateboard, n
♦ skateboard
Skateboarder, m
Skateboardfahrer, m
♦ skateboarder
Skateboard fahren
♦ skateboard
♦ ride a skateboard
Skateboardfahren, n
♦ skateboarding
Skatrunde, f
Skatpartie, f
♦ round of skat
♦ game of skat
Skat spielen
♦ play skat
Skatturnier n
♦ skat tournament
Skatveranstaltung, f
♦ skat event
Skeetschießanlage, f
♦ skeet shooting range
Skeetschießen, n
♦ skeet shooting
♦ skeet
Skeet- und Trapstand, m
♦ skeet and trap stand
Ski, m
Schi, m ÖST
♦ ski
Skiabfahrt, f
Abfahrtsstrecke, f
Abfahrt, f
Piste, f
♦ ski run
♦ run
Ski Alpin, m
→ Alpinski
Skialpinschule, f
Alpinskischule, f
♦ down-hill ski school
♦ Alpine ski school
Skianfänger, m
♦ ski novice
♦ beginner
♦ novice skier
♦ novice at skiing
Skianzug, m
♦ ski suit
♦ skiing suit
Skiarena, f
♦ ski arena
♦ skiing arena
Skias, n
♦ skiing ace
♦ ace skier
Skiausflug, m
♦ ski excursion
♦ skiing excursion
♦ ski trip
♦ skiing trip
Skiausrüstung, f (generell)
♦ ski equipment
♦ skiing equipment

♦ skiing gear
♦ skiing things pl
Skiausrüstung, f (Kleidung)
Skikleidung, f
♦ ski outfit
Skiausrüstung mieten
Skiausrüstung leihen
♦ rent ski equipment AE
♦ hire ski equipment BE
♦ hire skiing equipment BE
Skiausrüstung vermieten
Skiausrüstung verleihen
♦ rent (out) ski equipment
♦ hire (out) ski equipment BE
♦ hire (out) skiing equipment BE
Skiball, m
♦ ski ball
Skibedingungen, f pl
♦ ski conditions pl
♦ skiing conditions pl
Skibeförderung, f
Skitransport, m
♦ transport of skis BE
♦ transportation of skis AE
♦ carriage of skis
Skibegeisterter, m
♦ ski enthusiast
♦ skiing enthusiast
Skibergsteiger, m
♦ skiing mountaineer
Skibindung, f
♦ ski binding
Skibob, m
♦ ski bob AE
♦ ski-bob BE
Skibobfahren, n
Skibobsport, m
♦ ski bobbing AE
♦ ski-bobbing BE
Skibobfahrer, m
♦ ski bobber AE
♦ ski-bobber BE
Skibobschule, f
♦ ski-bob school
Skibrille, f
♦ ski goggles pl
♦ skiing goggles pl
Skibus, m
♦ ski bus
Skibusdienst m
Skibusverbindung f
Skibusverkehr m
♦ ski bus service
Skibushaltestelle f
♦ ski bus stop
Skibusservice, m
→ Skibusdienst
Skibusverbindung, f
♦ ski bus connection
♦ ski bus service
Skichalet n
♦ ski chalet
Skiclub, m
Skiverein, m
♦ ski club
♦ skiing club
Skicoupon, m
♦ ski coupon
Skidorado, n
→ Skiparadies

Skidorf, n
♦ ski village
♦ skiing village
Skieinrichtung, f
♦ ski facility
♦ skiing facility
Skiexpedition, f
♦ ski expedition
Ski fahren
Ski laufen
♦ ski
♦ go skiing
Skifahren, n
→ Skilauf
skifahren gehen
♦ go skiing
Skifahrer, m
→ Skiläufer
Skifahrerhotel, n
♦ skier's hotel
Skifahrerparadies n
Skiparadies n
♦ skier's paradise
♦ skiing paradise
Skifan, m
Brettlfan, m coll
♦ ski fan
♦ ski buff coll
Skiferien, pl
Skiurlaub, m
♦ ski holiday BE
♦ skiing holiday BE
♦ ski vacation AE
Skiferienhütte, f
♦ ski vacation hut AE
♦ ski vacation lodge AE
♦ ski holiday hut BE
♦ ski holiday lodge BE
Skiferienort, m
Skiurlaubsort, m
Skiort, m
♦ ski holiday resort BE
♦ ski vacation resort AE
Skifreizeit, f
→ Skiurlaub
Skifreizeitort, m
→ Skiurlaubsort
Skiführer, m
(Person oder Buch)
♦ ski guide
♦ skiing guide
Skigebiet, n (groß)
♦ ski region
♦ skiing region
♦ skiing country
Skigebiet n (klein)
♦ ski area
♦ skiing area
Skigelände, n (Abfahrten)
♦ ski slopes pl
Skigelände, n (Gebiet)
→ Skigebiet
Skigelände, n (generell)
♦ ski terrain
♦ skiing terrain
Skigelegenheit f
♦ ski opportunity
♦ skiing opportunity
Skigepäckträger, m
(z.B. auf Auto)

Skigeschäft

Skiträger, m
- ski rack

Skigeschäft, n (Laden)
Skiladen, m
- ski store *AE*
- ski shop *BE*

Skigeschäft n (allgemein)
- ski business

Skigruppe, f
- ski group

Skigymnastik, f
- ski exercises *pl*
- skiing exercises *pl*

Skihandschuhe, m pl
- ski gloves *pl*

Skihang, m
Abfahrtshang, m
- ski slope

Skihaserl, n *fam*
- ski bunny *fam*
- snow bunny *fam*

Skihose, f
- ski pants *AE pl*
- ski trousers *BE pl*
- skiing trousers *BE pl*

Skihotel n
- ski hotel

Skihütte, f
- ski hut
- ski lodge *AE*

Skijöring, n
(von Pferd oder Motor gezogen)
- skijoring
- skiöring *AE*

Skikarte f
(Landkarte)
- ski map

Skikindergarten, m
- ski kindergarten

Skikleider, n pl
- ski clothes *pl*
- skiing clothes *pl*

Skikleidung, f
- ski clothing
- skiwear
- ski outfit

Skikurs, m (Gruppe)
Skiklasse, f
- ski class

Skikurs, m (Lehrgang)
Skilehrgang, m
- ski course
- skiing course

Skikurs machen
- do a ski course

Skilager, n
- ski camp
- skiing camp

Skilanglauf, m
Skilanglaufen, n
Langlauf, m
- cross-country skiing

Skilangläufer, m
Langläufer, m
- cross-country skier

Skilanglaufort, m
Langlaufort, m
- cross-country ski resort
- cross-country resort

Skilanglaufschule, f
- cross-country ski school

Skilauf, m
Skilaufen, n
Skifahren, m
Skisport, m
- skiing

Ski laufen
→ Ski fahren

Skiläufer, m
Skifahrer, m
- skier
- skiier *AE rare*

Skilehrer, m
- ski instructor
- skiing instructor

Skilehrerin f
- ski instructress
- skiing instructress

Ski leihen
Ski mieten
- rent skis *AE*
- hire skis *BE*

Skileihgebühr, f
Skimietgebühr, f
- ski rental charge
- ski rental fee
- ski rental
- ski-hire charge *BE*
- ski-hire fee *BE*

Skilift, m
- ski lift *AE*
- ski-lift *BE*

Skiliftbetreiber, m
- ski-lift operator

Skilift ist in Betrieb
- ski lift is in operation *AE*
- ski-lift is in operation *BE*

Skiliftkarte, f (Landkarte)
- ski-lift map

Skiliftkarte, f (Ticket)
- ski-lift ticket

Skiliftpaß, m
- ski-lift pass

Skilifttageskarte, f
- ski-lift day ticket

Skiliftticket, n
→ Skiliftkarte

Skiliftzeitkarte, f
- ski-lift season ticket

Skilodge, f
- ski lodge
- skiing lodge

Skimarathon, m/n
- ski marathon
- skiing marathon

Skimeisterschaft f
- ski championship

Ski mieten
→ Ski leihen

Skimöglichkeiten, f pl
- ski possibilities *pl*
- skiing possibilities *pl*

Skimuseum, n
- ski museum

Skimütze, f
- ski hat
- skiing hat
- ski cap
- skiing cap

Skiort, m
Schiort, m ÖST
- ski resort
- skiing resort
- ski village
- ski town

Skiortführer m
(Buch)
- ski resort guide

Skipaket, n
- ski pack

Skiparadies, n
Skidorado, n
- skiing paradise
- skier's paradise

Skiparka, m
- ski parka

Skipaß, m
- ski pass

Skipaß für eine Woche m
- one-week ski pass

Skipaß ist 7 Tage gültig
- ski pass is valid for 7 days

Skipauschale, f
- ski package

Skipauschalurlaub, m
Skipauschalferien, pl
- ski package vacation *AE*
- ski package holiday *BE*

Skipendelbus, m
- ski shuttle bus

Skipendelbusdienst m
Skipendelbusverbindung f
Skipendelbusverkehr m
- ski shuttle-bus service

Skipendeldienst m
- ski shuttle service

Skipiste, f
- ski piste
- ski trail
- ski run

Skipiste sperren
Skipiste schließen
- close a ski run
- close a ski run
- close a ski trail

Skiprospekt, m
- ski brochure

Skiraum, m
- ski room
- ski storage room

Skiregion, f
→ Skigebiet

Skireise, f
- ski trip
- skiing trip

Skirennen, n
- ski race

Skirennen gewinnen
- win a ski race

Skirevier, n
→ Skigebiet

Skirowdy, m
- ski hooligan
- ski rowdy

Skisachen, f pl
- ski things *pl*
- skiing things *pl*

Skisafari, f
- ski safari

Skisaison f
- ski season
- skiing season

Skischanze, f
→ Skisprungschanze
Skischau, f
♦ ski show
Skischaukel, f
♦ interconnecting lifts pl
♦ interconnecting ski lifts pl
Skischein, m
→ Skipaß
Skischlepplift, m
♦ ski tow AE
♦ ski drag lift BE
Skischuhe, m pl
♦ ski shoes pl
Skischule, f
♦ ski school
Skischule leiten
♦ run a ski school
Skischulleiter, m
♦ head of the ski school
Skiseilbahn f
♦ ski cable lift
Skisocken, f pl
♦ ski socks pl
Skispaß, m
♦ ski fun
♦ skiing fun
Skispind, m
♦ ski locker
Skisport, m
→ Skilauf
Skispringen n
♦ ski jumping
Skispringer, m
♦ ski jumper
Skisprungschanze, f
Skischanze, f
♦ ski jump AE
♦ ski-jump BE
♦ jumping hill
Skispur, f
Loipe, f
♦ ski track
♦ track
Skistation f
♦ ski station
Skistiefel, m
♦ ski boot
♦ skiing boot
Skistock, m
♦ ski pole
♦ ski stick BE
Skistunde f
♦ ski lesson
Skiszene, f
♦ ski scene
Skital, n
♦ ski valley
♦ skiing valley
Skiterrain, n
Skigelände, n
♦ skiing terrain
♦ ski terrain
Skitour, f
♦ ski tour
Skitourismus, m
♦ ski tourism
Skitourist m
♦ ski tourist

Skiunfall, m
♦ ski accident
♦ skiing accident
Skiunterricht, m
♦ ski lessons pl
♦ skiing lessons pl
♦ ski instruction
♦ skiing instruction
Skiunterricht geben
♦ teach skiing
Skiunterricht nehmen
♦ take ski lessons
♦ take skiing lessons
Skiurlaub, m
Skiferien, pl
♦ ski vacation AE
♦ skiing vacation AE
♦ ski holiday BE
♦ skiing holiday BE
Skiurlauber, m
♦ ski vacationer AE
♦ person taking a ski vacation AE
♦ ski holidaymaker BE
♦ person taking a skiing holiday BE
Skiurlaub machen
♦ take a ski vacation AE
♦ take a skiing vacation AE
♦ take a ski holiday BE
♦ take a skiing holiday BE
Skiurlaubsort, m
Skiferienort, m
Skifreizeitort, m
♦ ski vacation resort AE
♦ ski holiday resort BE
♦ ski resort
Skiurlaubsreise, f
♦ ski vacation trip AE
♦ ski holiday trip BE
Skiverband, m
♦ ski association
Skiverein, m
Skiclub, m
♦ skiing club
♦ ski club
Skiverleih, m
♦ ski rental AE
♦ ski hire BE
♦ ski hire shop BE
Ski verleihen
♦ rent (out) skis
♦ hire out skis BE
Skiwachs, n
♦ ski wax
♦ skiing wax
Skiwacht, f
Skiaufsicht, f
♦ ski patrol
Skiwandergebiet, n
Tourenskigebiet, n
♦ ski touring area
Skiwandern, n
♦ ski rambling
♦ ski touring
♦ ski hiking
Skiwanderung, f
♦ ski ramble
♦ ski tour
♦ hike on skis
Skiwanderweg, m
♦ ski hiking trail
♦ ski trail

Skiweltmeister, m
♦ world ski champion
♦ world champion skier
Skiwettbewerb, m
♦ ski contest
♦ skiing contest
♦ ski competition
♦ skiing competition
Skiwoche, f
♦ week's skiing
♦ one week's skiing
Skiwochenende n
♦ ski weekend
♦ skiing weekend
Skiwochenendkurs, m
♦ weekend course in skiing
Skizentrum n
♦ ski center AE
♦ ski centre BE
♦ skiing centre BE
Skizirkus, m
♦ ski circus
♦ ski circuit
Skizug, m
(Eisenbahn)
Wintersportzug, m
♦ snow train AE
Skonto, m/n
Barzahlungsrabatt, m
♦ cash discount
♦ discount
Skonto von 3% geben
♦ give 3% cash discount
♦ give a cash discount of 3%
♦ allow 3% cash discount
♦ allow a cash discount of 3%
Skulpturenausstellung, f
♦ exhibition of sculpture
S-Kurve, f
♦ S-bend
S-Kurve machen
♦ make an S-bend
Slalomskifahren, n
Slalomskilauf, m
♦ slalom skiing
Slalomstrecke f
(Ski)
♦ slalom course
Slalomturnier, n
♦ slalom tournament
Slawe, m
♦ Slav
Slawin, f
♦ Slav girl
♦ Slav woman
♦ Slav
slawisch, adj
♦ Slav, adj
Slawonien
♦ Slavonia
Slibowitz, m
Sliwowitz, m
♦ Slivovitz
Slot, m
♦ slot
Slowake, m
♦ Slovak
♦ Slovac
♦ Slovakian
Slowakei, f
♦ Slovakia

Slowakin

Slowakin, f
- ♦ Slovak girl
- ♦ Slovak woman
- ♦ Slovac girl
- ♦ Slovac woman

slowakisch, adj
- ♦ Slovak, adj
- ♦ Slovac, adj
- ♦ Slovakian, adj

Slowene, m
- ♦ Slovene
- ♦ Slovenian

Slowenien
- ♦ Slovenia

Slowenin, f
- ♦ Slovene girl
- ♦ Slovene woman
- ♦ Slovene
- ♦ Slovenian girl
- ♦ Slovenian woman

slowenisch, adj
- ♦ Slovene, adj
- ♦ Slovenian, adj

Slum, m
- ♦ slum

Slumbewohner, m
- ♦ slum-dweller

Slumsiedlung, f
- ♦ slum development AE
- ♦ slum housing estate BE

Smoking, m
- ♦ tuxedo AE
- ♦ dinner jacket

Smorgasbord, n
- ♦ smorgasbord

Smorgasbordessen, n
- ♦ smorgasbord lunch

Snack, m
- → Imbiß

Snackbar, f
- → Imbißstube

Snackservice, m
- → Imbißservice

Snob, m
- ♦ snob

Snooker, m
- ♦ snooker

Snookerclub, m
- ♦ snooker club

Snookerraum, m
  Snookerzimmer, n
- ♦ snooker room

Snookerspiel, n
- ♦ snooker match

Snooker spielen
- ♦ play snooker

Snookerspieler, m
- ♦ snooker player

Snookertisch, m
- ♦ snooker table

Snookerturnier, n
- ♦ snooker tournament

Snowboard, n
- ♦ snowboard

snowboarden
  snowboardfahren
- ♦ snowboard

Snowboarder, m
  Snowboardfahrer, m
- ♦ snowboarder

Snowboarding, n
  Snowboardfahren, n
- ♦ snowboarding

Snowdonia Nationalpark, m
- ♦ Snowdonia National Park, the

sobald die Saison beginnt
- ♦ as soon as the season begins

so bald wie möglich
  baldmöglichst
- ♦ as soon as possible
- ♦ a.s.a.p.

Soda, n
- ♦ soda

Sodawasser n
- ♦ soda water

Sodbrennen, n
- ♦ heartburn

Sofa, n
- ♦ sofa
- ♦ davenport

Sofabett, n
  Bettsofa, n
- ♦ settee-bed BE
- ♦ bed-settee BE
- ♦ put-you-up BE
- ♦ put-u-up BE coll
- ♦ duplex bed AE

Sofadoppelbett, n
- ♦ duplex sofa AE
- ♦ double sofa-bed

sofort abreisen
- ♦ leave immediately
- ♦ depart immediately

Sofortbelegung, f
  sofortige Belegung, f
  Sofortbezug, m
- ♦ immediate occupancy
- ♦ immediate occupation

sofort bestätigen etw
- ♦ confirm s.th. instantly
- ♦ confirm s.th. immediately

Sofortbestätigung f
  sofortige Bestätigung f
- ♦ instant confirmation

Sofortbestätigungsdienst, m
  Sofortbestätigungsservice, m
  Sofortbestätigung, f
- ♦ instant confirmation service

sofort beziehbar, adj
- ♦ available for immediate occupancy, adj

Sofortbezug, m
  (Unterkunft)
  sofortiger Bezug, m
- ♦ immediate occupation
- ♦ immediate occupancy

sofort buchen
  an Ort und Stelle buchen
- ♦ book straightaway AE
- ♦ book straight away BE

sofort buchen etw
- ♦ book s.th. instantly
- ♦ book s.th. immediately
- ♦ book s.th. straightaway AE
- ♦ book s.th. straight away BE

Sofortbuchung, f
  sofortige Buchung, f
- ♦ instant booking

Sofortbuchungsdienst, m
  Sofortbuchungsservice, m
- ♦ instant booking service

Sofortbuchungsservice, m
- → Sofortbuchungsdienst

Sofortbuchungssystem, n
- ♦ instant booking system

sofortig, adj
  unverzüglich, adj
- ♦ instant, adj
- ♦ immediate, adj
- ♦ prompt, adj

sofortige Bestätigung, f
  unverzügliche Bestätigung, f
- ♦ immediate confirmation
- ♦ instant confirmation

sofortige Bestätigung einer Buchung, f
- ♦ instant confirmation of a booking

sofortige Bestätigung einer Reservierung, f
- ♦ instant confirmation of a reservation

sofortige Entlassung, f
  fristlose Entlassung f
- ♦ instant dismissal

sofortige On-line-Bestätigung, f
- ♦ instant on-line confirmation

sofortiges warmes Wasser, n
- ♦ instant hot water

sofort reservieren etw
- ♦ reserve s.th. instantly
- ♦ reserve s.th. immediately

Sofortreservierung, f
  sofortige Reservierung, f
- ♦ instant reservation

Sofortreservierungsdienst, m
  Sofortreservierungsservice, m
- ♦ instant reservation service

Sofortreservierungssystem, n
- ♦ instant reservation system

sofort stornieren etw
- ♦ cancel s.th. instantly
- ♦ cancel s.th. immediately

sofort verfügbar, adj
- ♦ instantly available, adj
- ♦ immediately available, adj

Sofort zu vermieten
  (Hinweisschild)
- ♦ For immediate rent AE
- ♦ To let immediately BE

Softball, m
- ♦ softball

Softballplatz, m
- ♦ softball court

Softdrink, m
  Erfrischungsgetränk, n
- ♦ soft drink

Softdrinkautomat, m
- ♦ soft drink machine

Softdrinkfirma, f
- ♦ soft drink company

Softdrinkhersteller, m
- ♦ soft drink manufacturer

Softdrinkindustrie, f
- ♦ soft drink industry
- ♦ soft drinks industry

Softdrinkmarkt, m
- ♦ soft drink market

Softdrinkproduktion, f
- ♦ soft drink production

Soft Opening, n
- ♦ soft opening

Software, f
- ♦ software

Softwareprogramm, n
- software program *AE*
- software programme *BE*

Soiree, f
Abendgesellschaft, f
- soiree *AE*
- soirée *BE*
- evening party

Soiree besuchen
Abendgesellschaft besuchen
- attend a soiree *AE*
- attend a soirée *BE*
- attend an evening party

Soiree geben
Abendgesellschaft geben
- give a soiree *AE*
- give a soirée *BE*
- give an evening party

Sojasoße, f
- soy sauce

So jung kommen wir nicht mehr zusammen
- We won't be so young when we meet again

solange der Vorrat reicht
- subject to availability
- while stocks last

solarbeheizt, adj
- solar-heated, adj

solarbeheiztes Schwimmbad, n
- solar-heated swimming pool *AE*
- solar-heated swimming-pool *BE*
- solar-heated pool

Solarheizung, f
- solar heating

Solarium, n
- solarium

Solarium benutzen
- use the solarium
- use a solarium

Solariumbenutzung, f
- use of the solarium
- using the solarium

Solariumbenutzungsgebühr, f
Solariumgebühr, f
- charge for the use of the solarium
- fee for the use of the solarium
- charge for using the solarium
- fee for using the solarium

Sole, f
- brine
- saltwater *AE*
- salt water *BE*

Solebad, n (Aktivität)
Solbad, n
- brine bath
- saltwater bath *AE*
- salt-water bath *BE*

Solebad, n (Ort)
Soleheilbad, n
Solbad, n
- saltwater resort *AE*
- salt-water resort *AE*
- brine spa

Solebecken, n
- brine pool

Solebewegungsbad, n
- saltwater wave pool *AE*
- salt-water wave-pool *BE*

Solefreibad, n
Solefreibecken, n
- outdoor saltwater pool *AE*
- outdoor salt-water pool *BE*

Solehallenbad, n
- indoor saltwater pool *AE*
- indoor salt-water pool *BE*

Solehallenschwimmbad, n
Solehallenbad, n
- indoor saltwater swimming pool *AE*
- indoor salt-water swimming-pool *BE*
- indoor saltwater pool *AE*
- indoor salt-water pool *BE*

Solehallenschwimmbad, n
→ Solehallenbad

Soleheilbad, n (Aktivität)
Soletherapiebad, n
- therapeutic brine bath

Soleheilbad, n (Ort)
→ Solebad

Solekur, f
- brine treatment

Solekurort m
- brine spa

Solequelle, f
Solquelle, f
- brine spring
- salt spring

Solethermalbad, n
Solethermalbecken, n
Thermalsolebad, n
Thermalsolebecken, n
- saltwater thermal swimming pool *AE*
- salt-water thermal swimming-pool *BE*
- saltwater thermal pool *AE*
- salt-water thermal pool *BE*

Solethermalfreibad, n
- outdoor saltwater thermal swimming pool *AE*
- outdoor salt-water thermal swimming-pool *BE*
- outdoor saltwater thermal pool *AE*
- outdoor salt-water thermal pool *BE*

Solethermalhallenbad, n
- indoor saltwater thermal swimming pool *AE*
- indoor salt-water thermal swimming-pool *BE*
- indoor saltwater thermal pool *AE*
- indoor salt-water thermal pool *BE*

solide Möbel, n pl
- solid furniture *sg*

Solist, m
- soloist

Soll-Auslastung, f
angestrebte Auslastung, f
- target load factor

Soll-Auslastung erreichen
- reach the target load factor
- achieve the target load factor

Soll-Belegung, f
Soll-Auslastung, f
- target occupancy

Soll-Belegung erreichen
Soll-Auslastung erreichen
- reach the target occupancy
- achieve the target occupancy

Soll erfüllen
- achieve one's target

Soll-Gedeckzahl, f
- target number of covers

Soll-Gewinn, m
- target profit

Soll ich die Suppe servieren oder möchten Sie sich
selbst bedienen?
- Shall I serve out the soup or would you like to
- help yourself?

Soll ich Ihnen ein Zweibettzimmer reservieren
lassen?
- Shall I reserve you a twin-bed room? *AE*
- Shall I book you a twin-bedded room? *BE*

Soll ich Sie am Bahnhof abholen?
- Shall I meet you at the station?

Soll-Kosten, pl
- target costs *pl*
- target cost

Soll-Lagerbestand, m
- target stock

Soll-Miete, f
- target rent

Soll-Umsatz, m
- target sales *pl*
- target turnover

Soll- und Ist-Vergleich, m
- comparison of target and actual figures

Soll-Verbrauch, m
- target consumption

Sollzahl, f
→ Soll-Zahl

Soll-Zahl, f
- target figure

Somalia
- Somalia

Somalier, m
- Somali

Somalierin, f
- Somali girl
- Somali woman
- Somali

somalisch, adj
- Somali, adj

Sommelier, m *FR*
Weinkellner, m
- sommelier *FR*
- wine waiter
- wine steward *AE*
- wine butler

Sommelier des Jahres, m
Weinkellner des Jahres, m
- Sommelier of the Year
- Wine waiter of the Year

Sommer, m
- summer

Sommerabend, m
- summer evening

Sommerakademie, f
- summer academy

Sommerangebot, n
Sommerofferte, f
- summer offer

Sommerarbeitsplatz, m
- summer job

Sommerarrangement, n
- summer arrangement

Sommeraufenthalt, m
- summer stay
- stay during the summer

Sommerausflug, m
- summer excursion
- summer outing

Sommerauslastung, f
- summer load factor

Sommerausstellung, f
- summer exhibition
- summer exhibit *AE*
- summer show

Sommerball, m
- summer ball

Sommerbelegung

Sommerbelegung, f
　Sommerauslastung, f
　♦ summer occupancy
　♦ occupancy in (the) summer
Sommerbesuch, m
　♦ summer visit
Sommerbesucher, m
　Sommerfrischler, m *obs*
　♦ summer visitor
　♦ summer guest
Sommerbett, n
　♦ summer bed
Sommerbowle, f
　♦ summer cup
　♦ summer bowl
Sommerbuchung, f
　♦ summer booking
　♦ summer reservation *AE*
Sommercamper, m
　♦ summer camper
Sommercamping, n
　♦ summer camping
Sommercampingplatz, m
　♦ summer campsite
　♦ summer campground *AE*
　♦ summer camping site *BE*
　♦ summer camping ground *BE*
　♦ summer site
Sommercurlingbahn, f
　♦ summer curling rink
Sommererholungsort, m
　→ Sommerurlaubsort
Sommerfahrplan, m
　Sommerflugplan, mm
　♦ summer schedule *AE*
　♦ summer timetable
Sommerfahrt, f
　♦ summer trip
Sommerferien, pl
　Sommerurlaub, m
　♦ summer holidays *BE pl*
　♦ summer holiday *BE*
　♦ summer vacation *AE*
Sommerferiendorf, n
　Sommerurlaubsdorf, n
　♦ summer vacation village *AE*
　♦ summer holiday village *BE*
Sommerferiengast, m
　Sommerurlaubsgast, m
　Sommerfrischler, m *obs*
　♦ summer holidaymaker *BE*
　♦ summer vacationer *AE*
Sommerferienkursprogramm, n
　♦ summer vacation course program *AE*
　♦ summer holiday course programme *BE*
Sommerferienort, m
　→ Sommerurlaubsort
Sommerferienort, m
　Sommererholungsort, m
　Sommerurlaubsort, m
　Sommerort, m
　♦ summer resort
Sommerferiensaison, f
　Sommerurlaubssaison, f
　♦ summer vacation season *AE*
　♦ summer holiday season *BE*
Sommerfest, n (Festival)
　Sommerfestival, m
　Sommerfestspiele, n pl
　♦ summer festival

Sommerfest, n (Party)
　→ Sommerparty
Sommerfestlichkeit, f
　Sommerfest, n
　♦ summer festivity
Sommerfestspiele, n pl
　→ Sommerfestival
Sommerflaute, f
　→ Sommerloch
Sommerflug
　♦ summer flight
Sommerflugplan, m
　Sommerfahrplan, m
　♦ summer timetable
　♦ summer schedule *AE*
Sommerfreizeit, f
　→ Sommerurlaub
Sommerfrische, f
　→ Sommerurlaub
Sommerfrische, f (Ort) *obs*
　Sommerurlaubsort, m
　Sommerferienort, m
　♦ summer holiday resort *BE*
　♦ summer vacation resort *AE*
　♦ summer resort
Sommerfrischler, m *hist*
　→ Sommerbesucher
Sommergast, m
　♦ summer guest
　♦ summer visitor
Sommergäste ins Quartier nehmen
　♦ take summer guests
　♦ take summer visitors
Sommergeschäft, n
　♦ summer business
Sommergetränk, n
　♦ summer drink
　♦ summer beverage
Sommerhalbjahr, n
　♦ summer half year
Sommerhaus, n
　Ferienhaus, n
　♦ summer house
　♦ summer home
　♦ summer cottage
　♦ holiday house *BE*
Sommerhochsaison, f
　♦ summer high season
Sommerhotel n
　♦ summer hotel
Sommerinvasion, f
　♦ summer invasion
Sommerkatalog, m
　♦ summer catalogue
　♦ summer catalog *AE*
Sommerkonferenz, f
　♦ summer conference
Sommerkonzert, n (Veranstaltung)
　♦ summer concert
Sommerkreuzfahrt, f
　♦ summer cruise
Sommerkur, f
　♦ summer treatment
　♦ summer cure
Sommerkurort, m
　♦ summer health resort
Sommerkurs, m
　Sommerlehrgang, m
　♦ summer course
Sommerkurs besuchen
　♦ attend a summer course

Sommerkurse anbieten
　Sommerlehrgänge anbieten
　♦ offer summer courses
Sommerkurzurlaub, m
　♦ summer break
Sommerlager, n
　→ Ferienkolonie
Sommerlager betreiben
　Ferienlager betreiben
　♦ operate a summer camp
Sommerlandhaus, n
　Sommerferienhaus, n
　♦ summer cottage
sommerlich, adj
　♦ summery, adj
Sommerloch, n
　Sommerflaute, f
　♦ summer trough
Sommermenü, n
　♦ summer menu
　♦ set summer meal
Sommermesse f
　♦ summer fair
　♦ summer trade fair
Sommermieter, m (Immobilien)
　♦ summer tenant
　♦ summer renter
Sommermittagessen, n
　Sommeressen, n
　♦ summer lunch
　♦ summer luncheon
Sommermonat, m
　♦ summer month
Sommermusikkurs, m
　Sommermusiklehrgang, m
　♦ summer music course
Sommernachmittag, m
　♦ summer afternoon
Sommeröffnungszeit, f
　♦ summer opening
Sommerpalast, m
　♦ summer palace
Sommerparadies, n
　♦ summer paradise
Sommerparty, f
　Sommerfest, n
　♦ summer party
Sommerpauschale, f
　♦ summer package
Sommerpause, f (generell)
　♦ summer break
Sommerpause, f (Institution)
　Sommerferien, pl
　♦ summer recess
Sommerpicknick, n
　♦ summer picnic
Sommerplatz, m
　(z.B. Camping)
　♦ summer site
Sommerpreis, m
　♦ summer price
　♦ summer rate
Sommerpreisliste, f
　♦ summer tariff
Sommerprogramm n
　♦ summer program *AE*
　♦ summer programme *BE*
Sommerprospekt m
　♦ summer brochure
Sommerquartier, n
　♦ summer quarters *pl*

Sommerrabatt, m
- summer discount

Sommerrefugium, n
- summer retreat

Sommerreise, f
- summer journey
- summer tour
- summer trip

Sommerreisender, m
- summer traveler *AE*
- summer traveller *BE*
- summer tourist

Sommerreiseverkehr, m
- summer tourist traffic

Sommerreservierung, f
- summer reservation

Sommerresidenz, f
- → Sommersitz

Sommerrodelbahn, f
- summer toboggan run
- summer toboggan slide *AE*
- summer toboggan chute *AE*
- artificial toboggan run

Sommersaison, f
- summer season

Sommersaisonaufschlag, m
- summer-season surcharge

Sommersaisonauslastung f
- summer-season load factor

Sommersaisonbelegung, f
- Sommersaisonauslastung, f
- summer-season occupancy

Sommersaisonbuchung, f
- summer-season booking

Sommersaisonermäßigung f
- summer-season reduction

Sommersaisoneröffnung, f
- summer-season opening
- opening of the summer season

Sommersaison geht von Anfang April bis Ende Oktober
- summer season runs from the beginning of April
- until the end of October

Sommersaisonmonat, m
- summer-season month
- month in the summer season

Sommersaisonpersonal, n
- summer-season staff
- summer-season personnel

Sommersaisonpreis, m
- summer-season price
- summer-season rate

Sommersaisonprogramm, m
- summer-season program *AE*
- summer-season programme *BE*

Sommersaisonreservierung, f
- summer-season reservation

Sommersaisonspitze, f
- summer-season peak

Sommersaisontag, m
- summer-season day
- day in the summer season

Sommersaisontarif, m
- summer-season tariff
- summer-season rates *pl*
- summer-season rate
- summer-season terms *pl*

Sommersaisonwoche, f
- summer-season week
- week in the summer season

Sommersaisonzeit f
- summer-season period

Sommersaisonzuschlag m
- summer-season supplement

Sommersalat, m
- summer salad

Sommerschau, f
- Sommerausstellung, f
- summer show

Sommerschlittenfahren, n
- Sommerrodeln, n
- Sommerrodelsport, m
- summer tobogganing

Sommerschule, f
- summer school

Sommerschulferien, pl
- summer school vacation *AE*
- summer school holidays *BE pl*

Sommerschulferienzeit, f
- summer school vacation period *AE*
- summer school holiday period *BE*

Sommersemesterferien, pl
- summer vacation *BE*

Sommerseminar, n
- summer seminar

Sommersitz, m
- Sommerresidenz, f
- summer residence

Sommersitzung, f
- summer meeting

Sommerski, m
- Sommerskilauf, m
- summer ski
- summer skiing

Sommerskigebiet, n (groß)
- summer ski region

Sommerskigebiet, n (klein)
- summer ski area

Sommerskilauf m
- summer skiing

Sommerskischule, f
- summer ski school

Sommerskisprungschanze, f
- summer ski jump *AE*
- summer ski-jump *BE*

Sommersonderangebot, n
- special summer offer

Sommersonne, f
- summer sun

Sommerspaß, m
- summer fun

Sommerspeisekarte f
- summer menu

Sommerspiele, n pl (Olympiade)
- summer games *pl*

Sommerspitzenzeit, f
- peak summer period

Sommersprachschule, f
- summer language school

Sommerstellplatz, m
- *(Camping)*
- summer pitch

Sommersuppe, f
- summer soup

Sommersymposion, n
- summer symposium

Sommertag, m
- summer day

Sommertagung, f
- Sommertreffen, n
- summer meeting

Sommertarif, m
- summer rates *pl*
- summer rate
- summer terms *pl*
- summer tariff

Sommerterrasse, f
- summer terrace

Sommertheater, n
- summer theater *AE*
- summer theatre *BE*

Sommertourismus, m
- Sommerfremdenverkehr, m
- summer tourism

Sommertourist m
- summer tourist

Sommertournee, f
- summer tour

Sommerurlaub, m
- Sommerfrische, f *obs*
- Sommerferien, pl
- summer vacation *AE*
- summer holiday *BE*

Sommerurlauber, m
- Sommerurlaubsgast, m
- Sommerferiengast, m
- summer vacationer *AE*
- summer holidaymaker *BE*

Sommerurlaubaufenthalt, m
- Sommerferienaufenthalt, m
- summer vacation stay *AE*
- summer holiday stay *BE*

Sommerurlaubsgast, m
- Sommerferiengast, m
- summer vacation guest *AE*
- summer holiday guest *BE*

Sommerurlaubsgebiet, n (groß)
- Sommerferiengebiet, n
- summer vacation region *AE*
- summer holiday region *BE*

Sommerurlaubsgebiet, n (klein)
- Sommerferiengebiet, n
- summer vacation area *AE*
- summer holiday area *BE*

Sommerurlaubsmarkt, m
- Sommerferienmarkt, m
- summer vacation market *AE*
- summer holiday market *BE*

Sommerurlaubsort, m
- Sommerferienort, m
- summer vacation resort *AE*
- summer holiday resort *BE*
- summer resort

Sommerurlaubsprogramm, n
- Sommerferienprogramm, n
- summer vacation program *AE*
- summer holiday programme *BE*

Sommerurlaubssaison, f
- Sommerferiensaison, f
- summer holiday season *BE*
- summer vacation season *AE*

Sommerurlaubsspitze, f
- Sommerferienspitze, f
- summer vacation peak *AE*
- summer holiday peak *BE*

Sommerurlaubsstadt, f (Großstadt)
- Sommerferienstadt, f
- summer vacation city *AE*
- summer holiday city *BE*

Sommerurlaubsstadt, f (kleine Stadt)
- Sommerferienstadt, f

Sommerurlaubsumsatz

♦ summer vacation town *AE*
♦ summer holiday town *BE*
Sommerurlaubsumsatz, m
♦ summer vacation sales *AE pl*
♦ summer holiday sales *BE pl*
Sommerurlaubsveranstaltung, f
Sommerferienveranstaltung, f
♦ summer vacation event *AE*
♦ summer holiday event *BE*
Sommerurlaubszentrum, n
Sommerferienzentrum, n
♦ summer vacation center *AE*
♦ summer holiday centre *BE*
Sommerveranstaltung, f
♦ summer event
♦ summer function
Sommer verbringen in X
♦ spend the summer at X
♦ spend the summer in X
♦ summer at X
♦ summer in X
Sommerwanderer, m
♦ summer walker
♦ summer hiker
Sommerwandern, n
♦ summer walking
♦ summer hiking
Sommerwanderung, f
♦ summer walk
♦ summer hike
Sommerwanderung machen
♦ go on a summer walk
♦ go on a summer hike
Sommerweide, f
♦ summer pasture
Sommerwoche, f
♦ summer week
Sommerwochenende, n
♦ summer weekend
Sommerzeit, f (Jahreszeit)
♦ summertime
Sommerzeit, f (Uhrenumstellung)
♦ summer time
♦ daylight saving time
♦ daylight time *AE*
♦ fast time *AE*
Sommerzeit, f (Zeitraum)
Sommerzeitraum, m
♦ summer period
Sommerzeitvertreib, m
♦ summer pastime
Sommerziel, n
Sommerzielort, m
♦ summer destination
Somnambulismus, m
Schlafwandeln, n
♦ somnambulism
♦ sleepwalking *AE*
♦ sleep-walking *BE*
Somnambulist, m
Schlafwandler, m
♦ somnambulist
♦ sleepwalker *AE*
♦ sleep-walker *BE*
Sonderabfertigung, f
♦ special handling
Sonderabfertigung erhalten
♦ receive special handling
Sonderaktion, f
♦ special action

Sonderangebot, n
Sonderofferte, f
Spezialofferte, f
♦ **special offer**
♦ bargain
Sonderangebot gilt bis zum 30. November
♦ **special offer runs until 30 November**
Sonderangebotspreis, m
sehr günstiger Preis, m
♦ **bargain price**
♦ bargain rate
Sonderangebotsurlaub, m
Sonderangebotsferien, pl
♦ **special offer holiday** *BE*
♦ special offer vacation *AE*
Sonderangebotswochenendpreis, m
♦ **bargain weekend price**
♦ bargain weekend rate
Sonderarrangement, n
→ spezielles Arrangement
Sonderausstellung, f
Spezialausstellung, f
♦ **special exhibition**
♦ special show
♦ special exhibit *AE*
Sonderbehandlung, f
Sonderbetreuung, f
♦ **special treatment**
Sonderbetreuung, f
♦ **special attention**
Sonderbetreuung erhalten
♦ **receive special attention**
Sonderbus, m (Spezialbus)
Spezialbus, m
spezieller Bus, m
♦ **special bus**
♦ special coach *BE*
Sonderbus, m (zusätzlich)
♦ **extra bus**
♦ extra coach *BE*
♦ additional bus
♦ additional coach *BE*
Sonderdekoration, f
spezielle Dekoration, f
♦ **special decoration**
Sonderdiät, f
→ spezielle Diät
Sonderdienst, m
→ Sonderleistung
Sondereinrichtung, f (Fazilität)
Spezialeinrichtung, f
spezielle Einrichtung, f
♦ **special facility**
Sondereinrichtung, f (Mobiliar)
♦ **special furniture** *sg*
♦ special furnishings *pl*
Sonderermäßigung f
besondere Ermäßigung f
spezielle Ermäßigung f
♦ **special reduction**
Sonderessen, n
(z.B. koscheres Essen)
♦ **special food**
♦ special diet
Sonderfahrpreis, m
♦ **special fare**
Sonderfahrt, f
♦ **special trip**
♦ special journey
♦ extra tour
♦ special tour

Sonderfaltblatt, n
spezielles Faltblatt, n
♦ **special leaflet**
Sonderflug, m
♦ **special flight**
♦ extra flight
Sonderflugzeug, n
♦ **special plane**
♦ extra plane
Sondergutschein, m
♦ **special voucher**
Sonderkatalog, m
→ Spezialkatalog
Sonderkomfort, m
spezieller Komfort, m
♦ **special comfort**
♦ extra comfort
Sonderkonditionen, f pl
♦ **special terms** *pl*
♦ special conditions *pl*
Sonderkongreß, m
♦ **special convention**
♦ special congress
♦ extra convention
♦ extra congress
Sonderkontingent, n
♦ **special allotment**
♦ special quota
♦ special allocation
♦ special contingent *mil*
Sonderkosten, pl
→ Extrakosten
Sonderkreuzfahrt, f
♦ **special cruise**
Sonderleistung, f
spezielle Leistung, f
spezieller Service, m
Sonderdienst, m
♦ **special service**
♦ extra service
Sondermenü, n
spezielles Menü, n
♦ **special menu**
Sonderofferte, f
→ Sonderangebot
Sonderpauschalangebot, n
♦ **special inclusive offer**
Sonderpauschalarrangement n
Sonderpauschalvereinbarung f
♦ **special package arrangement**
Sonderpauschale, f
Spezialpauschale, f
♦ **special package**
Sonderpauschalpreis, m
→ Sonderpauschale
Sonderpauschalpreis, m
Spezialpauschalpreis, m
♦ **special package price**
♦ special package rate
♦ special inclusive price
♦ special inclusive rate
Sonderpreis, m
spezieller Preis, m
Spezialrate, f
♦ **special price**
♦ special rate
Sonderpreise aushandeln
♦ **negotiate special prices**
♦ negotiate special rates
Sonderpreis erhalten
speziellen Preis erhalten

- ♦ receive a special rate
- ♦ receive a special price

Sonderpreis für Großabnehmer, m
- ♦ special price for bulk buyers
- ♦ special bulk price
- ♦ special bulk rate

Sonderpreis für Gruppen, m
- ♦ special price for groups
- ♦ special price for parties
- ♦ special rate for groups
- ♦ special rate for parties

Sonderprogramm, n
Spezialprogramm, n
spezielles Programm, n
- ♦ special program AE
- ♦ special programme BE
- ♦ extra program AE
- ♦ extra programme BE

Sonderprospekt, m
Spezialprospekt, m
spezieller Prospekt, m
- ♦ special brochure

Sonderprospekt anfordern bei jm (schriftlich)
- ♦ write for (the) special brochure to s.o.

Sonderrabatt, m
- ♦ special discount

Sonderrabatt auf etw, m
- ♦ special discount on s.th.

Sonderrabatt gewähren
- ♦ grant a special discount

Sonderrate, f
→ Sonderpreis

Sonderreise, f
- ♦ special tour
- ♦ special journey
- ♦ special trip

Sonderschau, f
Sonderausstellung, f
- ♦ special show

Sonderschicht, f
- ♦ extra shift

Sonderservicezuschlag m
- ♦ special-service supplement

Sonderstand, m
Spezialstand, m
- ♦ special stand
- ♦ special stall

Sondertarif, m
Spezialtarif m
- ♦ special tariff
- ♦ special terms pl
- ♦ special rates pl
- ♦ special rate

Sondertisch, m
spezieller Tisch, m
- ♦ special table
- ♦ extra table

Sonderurlaub, m (Arbeitnehmer)
- ♦ special leave (of absence)

Sonderurlaub, m (Militär)
- ♦ emergency leave

Sonderurlaubsarrangement, n
spezielles Urlaubsarrangement, n
- ♦ special vacation deal AE
- ♦ special holiday deal BE

Sonderveranstaltung, f
- ♦ special function
- ♦ special event

Sonderveranstaltungspreis m
(Preis bei einer Sonderveranstaltung)

- ♦ special event rate
- ♦ special event price

Sondervereinbarung f
spezielle Vereinbarung f
- ♦ special arrangement

Sondervergütung, f
→ Gratifikation

sonderverpflegungsvereinbarung, f
Sonderverpflegungsarrangement n
spezielle Verpflegungsvereinbarung f
- ♦ special meal arrangement
- ♦ special catering arrangement
- ♦ special board arrangement

Sondervisum, n
- ♦ special visa

Sondervorstellung, f (Theater)
- ♦ special performance

Sonderwoche, f
- ♦ special week

Sonderwunsch, m
spezieller Wunsch, m
- ♦ special request

Sonderwunsch angeben
Sonderwunsch äußern
Sonderwunsch anmelden
- ♦ make a special request

Sonderwunsch bearbeiten
- ♦ deal with a special request

Sonderwunsch erfüllen
- ♦ meet a special request
- ♦ fulfill a special request AE
- ♦ fulfil a special request BE

Sonderwunsch haben
- ♦ have a special request

Sonderzimmerpreis, m
spezieller Zimmerpreis, m
- ♦ special room rate
- ♦ special room price

Sonderzug, m (Ausflügler)
- ♦ excursion train

Sonderzug, m (generell)
- ♦ special train

Sonderzug einsetzen
- ♦ run an extra train

Sonderzuschlag m
besonderer Zuschlag m
spezieller Zuschlag m
- ♦ special supplement

Son et Lumière FR
- ♦ son et lumière FR
- ♦ sound and light show
- ♦ sound and slide show

Sonnabend, m
→ Samstag

sonnabends, adv
→ samstags

Sonne, Sand und See
- ♦ sun, sand and sea

Sonne hereinlassen
(in das Zimmer)
- ♦ let in the sun

Sonnenanbeter, m humor
- ♦ sun worshipper humor

Sonnenaufgang, m
- ♦ sunrise

Sonnenbad, n
- ♦ sunbath

sonnenbaden
sich sonnen
- ♦ sunbathe

- ♦ bask in the sun
- ♦ bathe in the sun

Sonnenbadender, m
- ♦ sunbather
- ♦ person basking in the sun
- ♦ person bathing in the sun

Sonnenbad nehmen
- ♦ take a sunbath

Sonnenbalkon m
- ♦ sun balcony

Sonnenbank, f
Sonnenliege, f
Bräunungsliege, f
- ♦ sunbed

Sonnenbankbehandlung, f
- ♦ sunbed treatment

Sonnenbanksitzung, f
- ♦ sunbed session

Sonnenbrand, m
- ♦ sunburn

Sonnenbrand bekommen
- ♦ get sunburnt
- ♦ get sunburned

Sonnenbrand haben
- ♦ have sunburn

Sonnenbräune, f
Bräune, f
- ♦ suntan AE
- ♦ sun-tan BE

Sonnenbrille, f
- ♦ sunglasses AE pl
- ♦ sun-glasses BE pl

Sonnencreme, f
- ♦ suntan lotion AE
- ♦ sun-tan lotion BE

Sonnendach, n (Auto)
- ♦ sunroof

Sonnendach, n (Gebäudeteil)
- ♦ sun deck AE
- ♦ sun-deck BE

Sonnendachterrasse, f
→ Dachterrasse zum Sonnen, Sonnendeck

Sonnendeck, n (Schiff)
- ♦ sun deck AE
- ♦ sun-deck BE

sonnengebräunt, adj
gebräunt, adj
- ♦ suntanned, adj AE
- ♦ sun-tanned, adj BE
- ♦ tanned, adj

Sonnenhang, m
sonniger Hang, m
- ♦ sunny slope

Sonnenhof, m
Sonnenterrasse, f
- ♦ sun patio

sonnenhungrig, adj
- ♦ sun-seeking, adj
- ♦ longing for sunshine, adj

Sonnenhungriger, m
- ♦ sun-seeker

sonnenhungriger Tourist, m
- ♦ sun-seeking tourist

Sonnenhut, m
- ♦ sun hat AE
- ♦ sun-hat BE

Sonnenkur, f
- ♦ sun treatment
- ♦ heliotherapy

Sonnenlage, f
- ♦ sunny position

Sonnenlicht

- ♦ sunny location
- ♦ sunny situation

Sonnenlicht, n
- ♦ sunlight

Sonnenliegeterrasse, f
→ Sonnenterrasse

Sonnenloggia f
- ♦ sun loggia

sonnenlos, adj
- ♦ sunless, adj

sonnenloser Tag, m
- ♦ sunless day

Sonnenöl, n
- ♦ sun oil

Sonnenschein, m
- ♦ sunshine

Sonnenscheindauer, f
- ♦ duration of sunshine

Sonnenscheingarantie f
- ♦ sunshine guarantee

Sonnenscheinrekord, m
- ♦ sunshine record

Sonnenscheinstunden, f pl
- ♦ sunshine hours pl

Sonnenschirm, m
- ♦ parasol
- ♦ sun umbrella
- ♦ umbrella
- ♦ sunshade

Sonnenschutz, m
(z.B. am Strand)
- ♦ sun shelter

sonnen sich
- ♦ sun oneself
- ♦ bask in the sun

Sonnenstich, m
- ♦ sunstroke

Sonnenstich bekommen
- ♦ get sunstroke

Sonnenstich haben
- ♦ have sunstroke

Sonnenstudio, n
- ♦ tanning salon AE
- ♦ solarium

Sonnentag, m
→ sonniger Tag

Sonnenterrasse, f
Terrasse zum Sonnen, f
- ♦ sun terrace
- ♦ sun deck AE
- ♦ sun-deck BE

Sonnenuhr, f
- ♦ sundial

Sonnenuntergang, m
- ♦ sunset
- ♦ sundown AE

Sonnenurlaub, m
Sonnenferien, pl
- ♦ sunshine vacation AE
- ♦ sunshine holiday BE
- ♦ vacation in the sun AE
- ♦ holiday in the sun BE

Sonnenveranda, f
- ♦ sun veranda
- ♦ sun verandah
- ♦ sun parlor AE
- ♦ sun porch AE
- ♦ sun lounge BE

sonnenverbrannt, adj
- ♦ sunburnt, adj
- ♦ sunburned, adj

Sonnenziel, n
- ♦ sun destination
- ♦ sunshine destination

Sonnenzimmer, n
- ♦ sun-room AE

Sonne-Sand-und-See-Ziel, n
Sonne-Sand-und-See-Destination, f
- ♦ sun, sand and sea destination
- ♦ sun-sand-sea destination

sonnig, adj
- ♦ sunny, adj

sonnige Lage, f
- ♦ sunny location
- ♦ sunny position
- ♦ sunny situation
- ♦ sunny setting

sonnige Loggia f
- ♦ sunny loggia

sonniger Balkon m
- ♦ sunny balcony

sonniger Monat, m
Sonnenmonat, m
- ♦ sunny month

sonniger Platz, m
sonniger Ort, m
sonnige Stelle, f
- ♦ sunny spot
- ♦ sun-trap

sonniger Stellplatz, m
(Camping)
- ♦ sunny pitch

sonniger Tag, m
Sonnentag, m
- ♦ sunny day

sonniges Appartement, n
- ♦ sunny apartment

sonniges Zimmer, n
- ♦ sunny room

sonnige Veranda, f
Glasveranda, f
- ♦ sun parlor AE
- ♦ sun porch AE

Sonntag, m
- ♦ Sunday

Sonntagabend, m
- ♦ Sunday evening

Sonntagnacht, f
- ♦ Sunday night

Sonntag nachts
- ♦ on Sunday night
- ♦ on Sunday nights

sonntags, adv
- ♦ on Sundays, adv
- ♦ on Sunday, adv

Sonntagsarbeit, f
- ♦ Sunday work
- ♦ Sunday working

sonntagsausflug, m (Auto)
→ Sonntagsfahrt

Sonntagsausflug, m (generell)
- ♦ Sunday excursion
- ♦ Sunday trip
- ♦ Sunday outing

Sonntagsausflügler, m
Wochenendausflügler, m
- ♦ weekend tripper

Sonntagsbesuch, m
- ♦ Sunday visit

Sonntagsbraten, m
- ♦ Sunday roast

Sonntagsbrunch, m
- ♦ Sunday brunch

Sonntagsbüfett, n
- ♦ Sunday buffet

Sonntagsfahrer, m derog
- ♦ Sunday driver derog

Sonntagsfahrkarte,
- ♦ Sunday excursion ticket

Sonntagsfahrt, f (Auto)
Sonntagsausflug, m
- ♦ Sunday drive

Sonntagsfahrt, f (generell)
- ♦ Sunday trip

Sonntagsfrühstück, n
- ♦ Sunday breakfast

Sonntagslunch, m
→ Sonntagsmittagessen

Sonntagsmaler, m
- ♦ Sunday painter
- ♦ amateur painter

Sonntagsmarkt, m
- ♦ Sunday market

Sonntagsmatinee, f
(in USA und GB meist nachmittags)
- ♦ Sunday matinée BE
- ♦ Sunday matinee AE

Sonntagsmittagessen, n
- ♦ Sunday lunch
- ♦ Sunday luncheon

Sonntagsrede, f
- ♦ weekend speech

Sonntagsrückfahrkarte, f
Sonntagsfahrkarte, f
- ♦ weekend return ticket BE
- ♦ weekend ticket

Sonntags Ruhetag
(Schild)
Sonntag Ruhetag
- ♦ Closed on Sundays
- ♦ Closed on Sunday

Sonntagsspaziergang, m
- ♦ Sunday walk

Sonntags Tanz
(Hinweisschild)
- ♦ Dancing on Sunday
- ♦ Dancing on Sundays

sonntags und feiertags, adv
- ♦ on Sundays and holidays

Sonntags und montags Ruhetag
(Hinweisschild)
- ♦ Closed on Sunday and Monday
- ♦ Closed on Sundays and Mondays

Sonntagszeitung, f
- ♦ Sunday newspaper
- ♦ Sunday paper

Sonn- und Feiertags Geschlossen
(Hinweisschild)
An Sonn- und Feiertagen Geschlossen
- ♦ Closed on Sundays and Public Holidays
- ♦ Closed on Sundays and Bank Holidays BE

Sonn- und Feiertagsvergütung, f
- ♦ extra pay for Sunday and holiday work

Sonnwende feiern
- ♦ celebrate the solstice

Sonnwendfeier, f
- ♦ solstice celebration

sonstig, adj
verschieden, adj
divers, adj
- ♦ sundry, adj

- miscellaneous, adj
- other, adj

sonstige Aufwendungen, f pl
- other expenses pl

sonstige betriebliche Aufwendungen, f pl
 sonstige Betriebsaufwendungen f pl
- other operating expenses pl

sonstige Betriebskosten, pl
→ sonstige betriebliche Aufwendungen

sonstige Einnahmen, f pl
- other income
 other takings pl
 other revenues pl
 other receipts pl
- other revenue

sonstige Erlöse, m pl
- other revenues pl
 other revenue

sonstige Erträge, m pl (GuV)
 (Gewinn- und Verlustrechnung)
- other income

sonstige Gebühren, f pl
- miscellaneous charges pl
- miscellaneous fees pl

sonstiger Reiseverkehr, m
- other travel

sonstiges Personal, n
- other staff
- other personnel

sonstige Umsätze, m pl
- other sales pl

Sorbet, n
 Sorbett, n
 Scherbett, m/n
- sorbet

sorgen dafür, daß
- ensure s.th.
- make sure that

sorgenfrei, adj
 sorgenlos, adj
- carefree, adj

sorgenfreien Aufenthalt genießen
- enjoy a carefree stay

sorgenfreier Aufenthalt, m
- carefree stay

sorgenfreier Urlaub, m
 sorgenloser Urlaub, m
 unbeschwerter Urlaub, m
 sorgenfreie Ferien, pl
- carefree vacation AE
- carefree holiday BE

sorgen für das leibliche Wohl
→ Essen und Trinken bieten

sorgen für die Getränke
- look after the drinks
- see to the drinks

sorgen für die Verköstigung
- provide food

sorgen für eine bestimmte Atmosphäre
- ensure a certain atmosphere

sorgen für etw
 sich kümmern um etw
- take care of s.th.

sorgen für Ruhe
 für Ruhe sorgen
- make sure that everything is quiet

sorgen für Stimmung bei etw
- liven s.th. up

sorgen für Unterhaltung
- arrange entertainment

sorgen für viel Urlaubsspaß
 viel Ferienspaß bieten
- provide plenty of vacation fun AE
- provide plenty of holiday fun BE

Sorgen machen sich wegen etw
 sorgen sich wegen etw
- worry about s.th.

Sorgfalt, f
- care

sorgfältig ausgearbeitete Route, f
- carefully worked out route

sorgfältig ausgewählt, adj
- carefully selected, adj
- carefully chosen, adj

sorgfältig ausgewähltes Hotel, n
- carefully selected hotel
- carefully chosen hotel

sorgfältig ausgewählte Unterkunft, f
- carefully selected accommodation
- carefully chosen accommodation

sorgfältiger Planung bedürfen
- need careful planning

sorgfältig gedeckter Tisch, m
- meticulously laid out table

sorgfältig markiert, adj
- carefully marked, adj

sorgfältig restauriert, adj
- carefully restored, adj

sorgfältig zubereitet, adj
- carefully prepared, adj

sorgfältig zubereitetes Essen, n
→ mit Sorgfalt zubereitetes Essen

Sorte von Gast, f
- sort of guest

Soße, f (Bratensoße)
→ Bratensoße

Soße, f (generell)
 Sauce, f
- sauce

Soße machen
- make the sauce
- make a sauce

Soßenkoch, m
 Saucenkoch m
 Saucier, m FR
- sauce cook
- saucier FR

Soßenlöffel, m
 Saucenlöffel, m
- sauce spoon
- gravy spoon

Soßenrezept, n
- sauce recipe

Soßenschüssel, f
 Sauciere, f
- sauceboat
- gravy boat

Soufflé, n
 Auflauf, m
- soufflé

Souffléschüssel, f
 Auflaufschüssel, f
- soufflé dish
- soufflé bowl

Souffleur, m
 Souffleuse, f
- prompter

Souffleurkasten, m
- prompt box

soufflieren
- prompt
- act as prompter

Souk, m
- suq
- souk
- suk

Souschef, m FR
 Stellvertreter des Küchenchefs, m
- sous-chef FR
- assistant chef

Souterrain, n
 Kellergeschoß, n
 Untergeschoß, n
- basement

Souterrainappartement n
- basement apartment

Souterrainarbeitszimmer, n
- basement study

Souterrainbad, n
 Souterrainbecken, n
- basement pool

Souterrainbar, f
- basement bar

Souterrainbecken, n
→ Souterrainbad

Souterrainfenster, n
- basement window

Souterraingarage, f
 Kellergarage, f
 Tiefgarage, f
- basement garage

Souterraingaststätte, f
 Kellergaststätte, f
- basement pub BE
- basement bar AE

Souterraingeschoß, n
→ Souterrain

Souterrainküche, f
- basement kitchen

Souterrainraum, m
 Souterrainzimmer, n
- basement room

Souterrainsauna, f
- basement sauna

Souterrainschlafzimmer, n
- basement bedroom

Souterrainschwimmbad, n
 Souterrainschwimmbecken, n
- basement swimming pool AE
- basement swimming-pool BE
- basement pool

Souterrainschwimmbecken, n
→ Souterrainschwimmbad

Souterrainwohnung, f
 Kellerwohnung, f
- basement flat BE
- basement apartment AE

Souvenir, n
→ Andenken

Souvenirgeschäft, n
→ Andenkengeschäft

Souvenirjäger, n
→ Andenkenjäger

Souvenirstand, m
→ Andenkenstand

Soviel-man-essen-kann-Frühstück, n
- all-you-can-eat breakfast

Sozialabgaben, f pl
- social security contributions pl

Sozialbeiträge

Sozialbeiträge, m pl
 ◆ social welfare contributions *pl*
Sozialgeschichte, f
 ◆ social history
Sozialleistungen, f pl
 (Einzahlungen)
 ◆ social security payments *pl*
Sozialraum, m
 → Aufenthaltsraum
Sozialtourismus m
 ◆ social tourism
Sozialtourist m
 ◆ social tourist
Sozialversicherung, f
 ◆ social security
 ◆ social insurance
Sozialversicherungsbeitrag, m
 ◆ social security contribution
Sozius, m
 (Motorrad)
 ◆ pillion
Soziusfahrer, m
 ◆ pillion passenger
 ◆ pillion rider
Soziussitz, m
 ◆ pillion seat
spachteln
 → tüchtig zulangen
Spaghetti, pl
 ◆ spaghetti *sg*
Spaghettiabendessen, n
 ◆ spaghetti dinner
Spaghettiplatte, f
 ◆ spaghetti platter
Spanferkel, n
 ◆ sucking pig
Spanferkel am Spieß, n
 ◆ sucking pig on the spit
Spanferkel am Spieß braten
 ◆ roast a sucking pig on the spit
Spanien
 ◆ Spain
Spanienreise, f (in Spanien)
 Spanienrundreise, f
 ◆ tour of Spain
 ◆ tour through Spain
 ◆ Spanish tour
Spanienurlaub, m
 Spanienferien, pl
 ◆ Spanish vacation *AE*
 ◆ Spanish holiday *BE*
Spanienurlaub machen
 Urlaub in Spanien machen
 ◆ take a vacation in Spain *AE*
 ◆ take a holiday in Spain *BE*
Spanier, m
 ◆ Spaniard
Spanierin, f
 ◆ Spanish girl
 ◆ Spanish woman
 ◆ Spaniard
spanisch, adj
 ◆ Spanish, adj
spanische Art, adv *gastr*
 nach spanischer Art, adv *gastr*
 ◆ Spanish style, adv *gastr*
Spanische Reitschule, f
 ◆ Spanish Riding School, the
spanischer Wein, m
 ◆ Spanish wine

Spanische Treppe, die, f
 (in Rom)
 ◆ Spanish Steps, the *pl*
spanische Wand, f
 → Faltwand
Spannbettuch, n
 Spannlaken, n
 ◆ fitted sheet
 ◆ contour sheet *AE*
Spanne, f
 Marge, f
 ◆ margin
Spannlaken, n
 → Spannbettuch
Spannteppich m
 ◆ fitted carpet
Spannung, f (Volt)
 → Voltspannung
Spannung abbauen
 ◆ reduce tension
Spargel, m
 ◆ asparagus
Spargelanbau, m
 ◆ cultivation of asparagus
 ◆ growing of asparagus
Spargelbeet, n
 ◆ asparagus bed
Spargelcremesuppe, f
 ◆ asparagus cream soup
Spargelessen, n
 ◆ meal of asparagus
Spargelfeld, n
 ◆ asparagus field
Spargelfest, n
 ◆ asparagus festival
Spargelgericht, n
 ◆ asparagus dish
Spargelsalat, m
 ◆ asparagus salad
Spargelspitzen, f pl
 ◆ asparagus tips *pl*
Spargelspitzensalat, m
 ◆ salad of asparagus tips
Spargelsproß, m
 Spargelstange, f
 ◆ asparagus spear
Spargelstange, f
 ◆ asparagus stalk
 ◆ stalk of asparagus
Spargel stechen
 ◆ cut asparagus
Spargelsuppe, f
 ◆ asparagus soup
Spargelzeit, f
 Spargelsaison, f
 ◆ asparagus season
spärlich besucht, adj
 ◆ sparsely attended, adj
spärlich besuchte Veranstaltung, f
 ◆ sparsely attended event
spärlich möbliert, adj
 ◆ sparsely furnished, adj
spärlich möbliertes Zimmer, n
 ◆ sparsely furnished room
Sparpreis, m
 → Niedrigpreis
Sparsaison, f
 ◆ budget season
sparsam, adj
 ◆ economical, adj

sparsames Auto, n
 ◆ economical car
sparsame Verpflegung, f
 (nicht teure Verpflegung)
 ◆ economical catering
spartanisch, adj
 ◆ spartan, adj
spartanisches Essen, n
 (Mahlzeit)
 ◆ spartan meal
spartanisches Hotel, n
 ◆ spartan hotel
spartanisches Leben führen
 → spartanisch leben
spartanisches Zimmer, n
 ◆ spartan room
spartanische Unterkunft, f
 ◆ spartan accommodation
 ◆ spartan lodging *AE*
spartanisch leben
 spartanisches Leben führen
 ◆ lead a spartan life
Spartarif, m
 Billigtarif, m
 ◆ economy tariff
 ◆ economy terms *pl*
 ◆ economy rates *pl*
 ◆ economy rate
Spaßabend, m
 ◆ fun evening
Spaßbad, n
 Spaßschwimmbad, n
 ◆ fun swimming pool *AE*
 ◆ fun swimming-pool *BE*
 ◆ fun pool
Spaßbaden, n
 ◆ fun-bathing
Spaßbecken, n
 Gaudibecken, n *coll*
 Spaßbad, n
 ◆ fun pool
Spaß bieten
 ◆ provide fun
Spaßfahrt, f
 ◆ fun ride
 ◆ fun trip
Spaßfest, n
 ◆ fun festival
Spaß haben
 ◆ have fun
 ◆ have a good time
Spaß haben an etw
 Vergnügen haben an etw
 Freude haben an etw
 ◆ take pleasure in s.th.
 ◆ take pleasure at s.th.
Spaß in der Sonne, m
 ◆ fun in the sun
spaßliebend, adj
 ◆ fun-loving, adj
Spaß machen
 ◆ be fun
Spaßpaket, n
 ◆ fun pack
Spaßpark, m
 ◆ funpark
Spaßpotential, n
 ◆ fun potential
Spaß suchen
 Vergnügen suchen
 ◆ seek fun

Spaßtag, m
 ◆ fun day
 ◆ day of fun
Spaß verderben jm
 Vergnügen verderben jm
 ◆ spoil s.o.'s pleasure
 ◆ spoil s.o.'s fun
Spaßverderber, m
 ◆ spoilsport
 ◆ wet blanket fam
Spaßwettbewerb, m
 Gaudiwettbewerb, m coll
 ◆ fun competition
spät, adj
 ◆ late, adj
spät abends, adv
 am späten Abend, adv
 ◆ late in the evening, adv
spät ankommender Gast, m
 Spätankunft, f
 spät anreisender Gast, m
 ◆ guest arriving late
 ◆ late arrival
Spätankömmling m
 → Spätankunft
Spätankunft f
 (Gasttyp, nach 18.00 Uhr)
 ◆ late arrival
 ◆ guest arriving late
Spätanmeldung, f
 → späte Anmeldung
spät anreisender Gast, m
 → spät ankommender Gast
Spätaufführung, f
 → Spätvorstellung
spät aufstehen
 ◆ rise late
 ◆ get up late
 ◆ be a late riser
spät aufstehen und spät schlafengehen
 ◆ keep late hours
Spätaufsteher m
 ◆ late riser
spät buchen
 ◆ book late
Spätbucher m
 ◆ late booker
Spätbuchung, f
 späte Buchung, f
 späte Bestellung, f
 ◆ late booking
 ◆ late reservation AE
Spätbuchungsanfrage f
 ◆ late-booking inquiry
 ◆ late-booking enquiry
Spätbuchungsangebot, n
 Spätbuchungsschnäppchen, n
 Spätbuchungssonderangebot, n
 ◆ late-booking bargain
Spätbuchungsdienst, m
 Spätbuchungsservice, m
 ◆ late-booking service
Spätbuchungsfahrpreis, m
 ◆ late-booking fare
Spätbuchungskunde, m
 ◆ late-booking customer
 ◆ late-booking client
Spätbuchungsrabatt m
 ◆ late-booking discount
Spätbuchungsservice, m
 → Spätbuchungsdienst

Spätbüfett, n
 ◆ late supper buffet
Spätburgunder, m
 ◆ Late Burgundy
 ◆ Pinot noir FR
Spät-Check-out, m
 → später Check-out
späte Abreise, f (Hotel)
 ◆ late check-out
späte Anmeldung, f
 Spätanmeldung, f
 ◆ late registration
spätelisabethanisch, adj
 ◆ late Elizabethan, adj
spätelisabethanisches Haus, n
 ◆ late Elizabethan house
später Abend, m
 ◆ late evening
später Nachmittag, m
 → Spätnachmittag
spätes Abendessen, n
 → Abendessen
spätes Frühstück n
 ◆ late breakfast
spätes Gastmahl, n
 spätes Essen, n
 ◆ late evening dinner party
spätestens, adv
 ◆ at the latest, adv
 ◆ not later than, adv
spätestens um ein Uhr
 ◆ no later than one o'clock
Spätgotik, f (Stil, generell)
 ◆ late Gothic style
 ◆ late Gothic
Spätgotik, f (Stil, im UK)
 ◆ Perpendicular style
 ◆ Perpendicular
Spätgotik, f (Zeit)
 ◆ late Gothic period
spätgotisch, adj (generell)
 ◆ late Gothic, adj
spätgotisch, adj (im UK)
 ◆ Perpendicular, adj
spätgotisches Haus, n
 ◆ late Gothic house
Spätherbst m
 ◆ late fall AE
 ◆ late autumn BE
Spätherbsturlaub m
 ◆ late-fall vacation AE
 ◆ late-autumn holiday BE
spät in der Nacht, adv
 spätabends, adv
 ◆ late at night, adv
spät in der Saison, adv
 ◆ late in the season, adv
Spätlese, f (Ernte)
 ◆ late gathering
Spätlese, f (Wein)
 ◆ late vintage wine
 ◆ spaetlese
Spätlese, f (Weinlese)
 ◆ late vintage
 ◆ late harvest
Spätnachmittag, m
 später Nachmittag, m
 ◆ late afternoon
Spätnachmittagsessen, n
 Spätnachmittagsmahlzeit, f
 ◆ late-afternoon meal

Spätprogramm, n
 ◆ late program AE
 ◆ late programme BE
Spätreservierung, f
 späte Reservierung, f
 ◆ late reservation
Spätrevue, f
 ◆ late-night revue
Spätsaison, f
 ◆ late season
Spätsaisonbesucher m
 ◆ late-season visitor
 ◆ late-season guest
Spätsaisonbuchung f
 ◆ late-season booking
Spätsaisonermäßigung f
 ◆ late-season reduction
Spätsaisongast m
 ◆ late-season guest
 ◆ late-season visitor
Spätsaisonmonat, m
 ◆ late-season month
 ◆ month in the late season
Spätsaisonpreis, m
 ◆ late-season price
 ◆ late-season rate
Spätsaisonrabatt m
 ◆ late-season discount
Spätsaisonreservierung, f
 ◆ late-season reservation
Spätsaisontag, m
 ◆ late-season day
 ◆ day in the late season
Spätsaisontarif, m
 ◆ late-season tariff
 ◆ late-season terms pl
 ◆ late-season rates pl
 ◆ late-season rate
Spätsaisonwoche, f
 ◆ late-season week
 ◆ week in the late season
Spätsaisonzeit f
 ◆ late-season period
Spätsaisonzuschlag m
 ◆ late-season supplement
Spätschicht f
 ◆ late shift
Spätschicht haben
 Spätschicht arbeiten
 ◆ work a late shift
Spätservice, m
 Spätdienst, m
 ◆ late-night service
Spätsommer, m
 ◆ late summer
Spätsommerurlaub m
 ◆ late-summer vacation AE
 ◆ late-summer holiday BE
Späturlaub, m
 später Urlaub, m
 ◆ late vacation AE
 ◆ late holiday BE
Spätvorstellung, f
 Spätaufführung, f
 ◆ late-night performance
spät zu Bett gehen
 ◆ go to bed late
Spätzug, m
 ◆ late train
spät zuhause ankommen
 ◆ arrive home late

spät zurückkehren
spät zurückkommen
- return late

spazierenfahren
Fahrt machen
- go for a run *inform*
- go for a drive
- go for a ride
- go for a spin *inform*

spazierenführen jn (in einem Wald)
spazierengehen mit jm (in einem Wald)
- take s.o. for a walk (in a wood)

spazierengehen
Spaziergang machen
Wanderung machen
- walk
- have a walk

spazierengehen am Fluß entlang
- walk along the riverside

spazierengehen am Strand
Spaziergang machen am Strand
- walk on the beach
- go for a walk on the beach

Spazierfahrt, f (Autofahrer)
Vergnügungsfahrt, f
- pleasure drive

Spazierfahrt, f (generell)
Vergnügungsfahrt, f
- pleasure ride
- pleasure trip

Spaziergang, m
Wanderung, f
- walk
- stroll

Spaziergang am Meer, m
- walk along the seaside
- seaside walk

Spaziergang am See, m
- walk along the lakeside
- lakeside walk

Spaziergang am Seeufer, m (Binnensee)
Spaziergang entlang des Seeufers, m
- walk on the lakeshore *AE*
- walk along the lakeshore *AE*
- walk on the lake-shore *BE*
- walk along the lake-shore *BE*

Spaziergang am Seeufer, m (Meer)
Spaziergang entlang des Seeufers, m
- walk on the seashore *AE*
- walk along the seashore *AE*
- walk on the sea-shore *BE*
- walk along the sea-shore *BE*

Spaziergang durch Wälder und Felder, m
Wanderung durch Wälder und Felder, f
- walk through forests and fields

Spaziergänge machen
- go for walks

Spaziergänger, m
- walker
- stroller

Spaziergang in das Land, m
Wanderung in das Land, f
- walk into the countryside

Spaziergang machen
- go for a walk

Spaziergang machen am Strand
spazierengehen am Strand
- go for a walk on the beach
- walk on the beach

Spaziergang machen im Wald
- go for a walk in the woods

Spaziergang unternehmen
- take a walk

Spaziergang unternehmen im Park
- take a walk in the park

Spazierstock, m
- walking stick *AE*
- walking-stick *BE*

Spazierweg, m
- walk
- footpath
- path

Spazierweg ist ausgeschildert
- walk is signposted

Spazierwegnetz, n
Wegenetz, n
- footpath network

Special-Interest-Gruppe, f
Gruppe mit einem speziellen Interessengebiet, f
- special interest group

Special-Interest-Kurzurlaub, m
- special interest break

Special-Interest-Pauschale, f
- special interest package

Special-Interest-Pauschalreise, f
- special interest package tour

Special-Interest-Programm, n
- special interest program *AE*
- special interest programme *BE*

Special-Interest-Reise, f
- special interest journey
- special interest tour
- special interest trip

Special-Interest-Sitzung, f
(bei einer Konferenz)
- special interest session

Special-Interest-Tour, f
- special interest tour

Special-Interest-Tourismus, m
- special interest tourism

Special-Interest-Tourist, m
- special interest tourist

Special-Interest-Urlaub, m
Special-Interest-Ferien, pl
- special interest vacation *AE*
- special interest holiday *BE*

Special-Interest-Wochenende, n
- special interest weekend

Spécialité de la maison, f FR
Hausspezialität, f
- spécialité de la maison *FR*
- house specialty *AE*
- house speciality *AE*

Speck, m
- bacon

Speckbohnen, f pl
- beans and bacon *pl*

Speckbrot, n
- bacon sandwich

Speckdressing, n
- bacon dressing

Speckkartoffeln, f pl
- bacon potatoes *pl*

Specklinsen, f pl
- lentils with bacon *pl*

Speckscheibe, f (gebraten/gebacken)
- rasher of bacon
- bacon rasher

Speckscheibe, f (generell)
- slice of bacon
- bacon slice

Speckschwarte, f
- bacon rind

Speckseite, f
(unterer Teil)
- gammon

Speckstreifen, m
- strip of bacon

Speck und Eier
Speck (m) und Eier (n pl)
- bacon and eggs

Spediteur, m (Güterverkehr)
Transportunternehmer, m
- haulage contractor
- hauler *AE*
- haulier *BE*
- carrier

Spediteur, m (Möbel)
- mover *AE*
- remover *BE*

Speichellecker, m
Kriecher, m
- lickspittle *AE*
- lick-spittle *BE*
- toady
- sycophant

Speicherofen, m
- storage heater

Speiseabfälle, m pl
- scraps *pl*

Speiseartikel, m
- food item
- menu item

Speiseautomat, m
(in Automatenrestaurant)
- automatic food vendor *AE*
- automatic snack vendor *AE*
- food vending machine
- snack vending machine
- food slot-machine *BE*

Speise bestellen
Speisen bestellen
- order food

Speisebetrieb, m
- food establishment
- food operation

Speiseclub, m
- restaurant club
- lunch club
- luncheon club

Speisecoupon, m
Speisemarke, f
- dining coupon

Speiseeinrichtung, f
- dining facility

Speiseeis, n
→ Eiskrem

Speiseerlebnis, n
- dining experience
- gastronomic experience

Speisefett, n
Kochfett, n
- edible fat
- cooking fat

Speisegast, m
→ Essensgast

Speisegaststätte, f
- food bar *AE*
- restaurant

Speise hat einen europäischen Geschmack
- food has a European flavor *AE*
- food has a European flavour *BE*

Speisehaus, n
  ◆ eating house
  ◆ eating establishment
  ◆ restaurant
  ◆ eaterie *humor*
  ◆ ordinary *obs*
Speise ist nicht eßbar
  ◆ food is inedible
Speisekabine, f
  ◆ dining cabin
Speise kalt halten
  Speisen kalt halten
  ◆ keep food cold
Speisekammer f
  ◆ larder
  ◆ pantry
  ◆ buttery *BE*
Speisekarte, f
  Speisenkarte, f
  ◆ menu
  ◆ bill of fare *BE*
  ◆ menu card *AE*
Speisekarte ansehen
  ◆ look at the menu
Speisekarte aufschlüsseln
  ◆ break down the menu
Speisekarte aushängen
  ◆ display the menu
Speisekarte ausprobieren
  ◆ try the menu
Speisekarte bietet eine reichhaltige Auswahl
  ◆ menu offers plenty of choice
Speisekarte bringen
  ◆ bring the menu
Speisekarte drucken
  ◆ print the menu
Speisekarte durchblättern
  ◆ browse through the menu
Speisekarte enthält etw
  ◆ menu includes s.th.
Speisekarte entwerfen
  ◆ draft a menu
Speisekarte erstellen
  ◆ draw up a menu
  ◆ compile a menu
Speisekarte erweitern
  ◆ expand the menu
Speisekarte für Kinder, f
  Kinderspeisekarte, f
  ◆ kids' menu *coll*
  ◆ children's menu
Speisekarte ist abwechslungsreich
  ◆ menu is varied
Speisekarte ist ausgewogen
  ◆ menu is well balanced
Speisekarte ist groß
  ◆ menu is large
Speisekarte ist handgeschrieben
  ◆ menu is handwritten
Speisekarte ist mittags und abends gleich
  ◆ menu is the same at lunch and dinner
Speisekarte ist traditionell
  Speisekarte ist herkömmlich
  ◆ menu is traditional
Speisekarte ist umfangreich
  ◆ menu is extensive
Speisekarte ist ziemlich begrenzt
  ◆ menu is fairly restricted
Speisekarte lesen
  ◆ read the menu

Speisekarte liegt auf
  ◆ menu is on display
Speisekarte mit internationalem Niveau anbieten
  ◆ offer a menu of international standard
Speisekarte mit italienischem Einschlag, f
  ◆ menu with Italian influence
Speisekartenänderung, f
  Speisekartenwechsel, m
  ◆ menu change
Speisekartenänderung vornehmen
  ◆ make a menu change
Speisekartenartikel, m
  ◆ menu item
Speisekartenausdruck, m
  Speisekartenbegriff, m
  ◆ menu term
  piece of menu jargon
Speisekartenaushang, m
  ◆ menu display
  display of the menu
Speisekartenbegriff, m
  → Speisekartenausdruck
Speisekartengestaltung f (formal)
  ◆ menu design
  design of a menu
Speisekartengestaltung f (inhaltlich)
  → Speisekartenplanung
Speisekartenjargon, m
  ◆ menu jargon
Speisekartenkasten, m
  ◆ menu box
Speisekartenplanung, f
  Planung der Speisekarte, f
  ◆ menu planning
  planning the menu
Speisekartenpreis, m
  (auf Speisekarte angegeben)
  ◆ menu price
Speisekartenpreise ohne Mwst. und Trinkgeld
  ◆ menu prices exclude VAT and gratuities
Speisekartensprache, f
  ◆ menu language
Speisekartentafel, f
  (Tafel, auf der Speisen annonciert werden)
  ◆ menu board
Speisekartenterminologie, f
  ◆ menu terminology
Speisekartenwechsel, m
  → Speisekartenänderung
Speisekarte planen
  ◆ plan the menu
Speisekarte präsentiert etw
  ◆ menu features s.th.
Speisekarte stehlen
  ◆ steal the menu
Speisekarte studieren
  ◆ study the menu
Speisekarte testen
  ◆ test a menu
Speisekarte tippen
  ◆ type a menu
Speisekarte überarbeiten
  ◆ revise a menu
Speisekarte variieren
  ◆ vary the menu
Speisekarte vorausplanen
  Speisekarte im voraus planen
  ◆ plan the menu in advance
Speisekarte vorlegen
  ◆ present the menu

Speisekarte wechselt alle zwei Wochen
  ◆ menu changes every two weeks
  ◆ menu is changed every two weeks
  ◆ menu changes fortnightly *BE*
  ◆ menu is changed fortnightly *BE*
Speisekarte wechselt häufig
  ◆ menu is changed frequently
Speisekarte wechselt regelmäßig
  ◆ menu changes regularly
Speisekarte wechselt täglich
  ◆ menu changes every day
Speisekarte wird der Jahreszeit angepaßt
  ◆ menu is varied with the season
Speisekarte zeigt eine Fülle von feinen Gerichten
  ◆ menu abounds in fine dishes
Speisekarte zusammenstellen
  ◆ compile the menu
  ◆ compile a menu
Speiselokal, n
  ◆ dinner house *AE*
  ◆ eating place
  ◆ eating spot *BE coll*
  ◆ foodservice establishment *AE*
  ◆ restaurant
Speiselokalkette, f
  ◆ dinner-house chain *AE*
Speisemöglichkeit, f
  ◆ dining possibility
  ◆ dining facility
speisen
  dinieren *form*
  ◆ dine
  ◆ eat
  ◆ sup *iron*
speisen am Strand
  ◆ dine on the beach
Speisenangebot, n (Gegensatz zu Nachfrage)
  ◆ supply of food
Speisenangebot, n (Palette)
  ◆ range of food offered
  ◆ range of food
speisen auf dem Zimmer
  ◆ dine in one's room
speisen auf der Terrasse
  ◆ dine on the terrace
Speisen auftragen
  Essen servieren
  ◆ serve the meal
Speisenaufzug, m (generell)
  ◆ food elevator *AE*
  ◆ food (service) lift *BE*
  ◆ food hoist
  ◆ service lift *BE*
  ◆ plate carrier
Speisenaufzug, m (klein)
  Küchenaufzug, m
  ◆ dumbwaiter
Speisen ausgeben
  ◆ dispense food
speisen außer Haus
  ◆ dine away from home
  ◆ dine out
Speisen austeilen
  ◆ dish out
Speisenauswahl, f
  Auswahl an Speisen, f
  ◆ choice of dishes
  ◆ selection of dishes
  ◆ choice of food
  ◆ selection of food
  ◆ food selection

speisen bei Kerzenlicht
- dine by candlelight

Speisenbereich, m
- food sector

Speisenbüfett, n
- food buffet

Speiseneinnahmen, f pl
- food takings pl

Speisenerlös, m
- food revenue
- food proceeds pl

Speisenfolge, f
Gangfolge, f
- order of courses
- order of dishes
- sequence of courses
- menu

speisen im Freien
- dine alfresco
- dine in the open air
- dine in the open
- dine outdoors

speisen im Garten
- dine in the garden

speisen in einem Restaurant
im Restaurant speisen
- dine in a restaurant
- dine at a restaurant

speisen jn
→ nähren jn

speisen jn (Gäste)
- dine s.o.
- feed s.o.

Speisenkalkulation, f
- food calculation

Speisenkarte f
→ Speisekarte

Speisenkellner, m
- food waiter

Speisenkontrolle, f
- food control

Speisenkosten, pl
(Wareneinsatzkosten Speisen durch Speisenumsatz)
- food cost
- food costs pl

Speisenmanagement, n
- food management

speisen mit dem Kapitän
- dine with the captain

speisen mit jm
dinieren mit jm form
- dine with s.o.

speisenorientiertes Hotel, n
- food-oriented hotel AE
- food-orientated hotel BE

Speisenpreis, m
- food price

Speisenproduktion, f
Speisenherstellung, f
- food production

Speisenrechnung, f
- food check AE
- food bill

Speisenreste, m pl
Speisereste, m pl
Reste, m pl
- leftovers AE pl
- left-overs BE pl
- scraps pl

Speisenservice, m
Speisendienst, m
- dining service
- food service

Speisen servieren
Speise servieren
- serve food

Speisenumsatz, m
- food sales pl
- food turnover

Speisen und Getränke, pl
- food and beverages pl
- food and drink
- meals and beverages pl

Speisen und Getränke abgeben an das Personal
- furnish food and beverages to the employees

Speisen und Getränke anbieten
- offer food and drink
- offer food and drinks
- offer food and beverages

Speisen- und Getränkeangebot, n (Gegensatz zu Nachfrage)
- supply of food and beverages

Speisen- und Getränkeangebot, n (Offerte)
- food and beverages offered pl

Speisen- und Getränkeangebot, n (Palette)
- range of food and beverages
- range of meals and beverages

Speisen- und Getränkebetrieb, m
- food and drink establishment
- food and drink operation

Speisen- und Getränkeherstellung, f
- food and drink manufacture
- food and drink production

Speisen- und Getränkekammer, f
- buttery BE
- pantry

Speisen und Getränke liefern
- cater

Speisen und Getränke servieren
- serve food and drink
- serve food and beverages

Speisen und Getränke verkaufen
- sell food and beverages
- sell food and drink

Speisenverkauf, m
- food sale
- sale of food
- selling food

Speisenverzehr außerhalb des Lokals, m
- off-premise dining

Speisen vorlegen
→ Speisen servieren

Speisenwahl, f
(Gast kann Speisen auswählen)
Menüwahl, f
- choice of menu
- menu choice
- menu selection

Speisenzubereitung, f
- food preparation
- preparing food

Speisen zum Mitnehmen, f pl
(Verkauf über die Straße)
- take-away food
- take-away

speisen à la carte
→ à la carte speisen

Speiseöl, n
Kochöl, n
- cooking oil

Speiseordnung, f
→ Speisefolge

Speisepatio, m
Speiseterrasse, f
- dining patio
- dining terrace

Speiseplan, m (generell)
- meal plan
- menu plan
- catering plan

Speiseplan, m (speziell)
- this week's menu
- menu

Speiseplan ausarbeiten
- work out a meal plan
- work out a menu plan
- work out a catering plan

Speiseplan erstellen
- draw up a meal plan
- draw up a menu plan
- draw up a catering plan

Speiseplangestaltung, f
- meal planning
- menu planning

Speiseraum, m (generell)
→ Speisesaal

Speiseraum, m (Militär, Schiff)
(für Personal)
- messroom
- mess

Speiseraum, m (Schiff)
(für Passagiere)
- dining saloon

Speiseräumlichkeiten, f pl
- dining facilities pl

Speiserechnung, f (vom Gast abzuzeichnen)
Rechnung, f
- chit

Speiserechnung abzeichnen
Rechnung abzeichnen
- sign a chit

Speiserestaurant, n
→ Restaurant

Speisereste, m pl
→ Speisenreste

Speiseritual, n
Eßritual, n
- dining ritual

Speisesaal, m (generell)
- dining room

Speisesaal, m (in Schloß etc.)
- dining hall AE
- dining-hall BE

Speisesaalbetrieb, m
- dining-room operation

Speisesaaleinrichtung, f (Fazilität)
- dining-room facility

Speisesaaleinrichtung, f (Mobiliar)
Speisesaalmobiliar, n
Speisesaalmöbel, n pl
- dining-room furniture sg
- dining-room furnishings pl

Speisesaalerfahrung, f
- dining-room experience

Speisesaal faßt 123 Personen
- dining room accommodates 123 persons

Speisesaalhosteß, f
- dining-room hostess

Speisesaal im Freien, m
Freiluftspeisesaal, m
- open-air dining room

Speisesaalkapazität, f
 ♦ dining-room capacity
Speisesaalkellner, m
 Speisesaalservierer, m
 ♦ dining-room waiter
Speisesaalkellnerin, f
 Speisesaalserviererin, f
 ♦ dining-room waitress
Speisesaalkraft f
 ♦ dining-room employee
Speisesaal leiten
 ♦ manage a dining room
Speisesaalleiter, m
 Speisesaalmanager, m
 ♦ dining-room manager
 ♦ manager of a dining room
Speisesaalleitung, f
 ♦ dining-room management
Speisesaalmanager m
 → Speisesaalleiter
Speisesaal mit Schankerlaubnis, m
 (für alkoholische Getränke)
 ♦ licensed dining room
 ♦ licenced dining room
Speisesaalpersonal, n
 ♦ dining-room staff
 ♦ dining-room personnel
Speisesaalräumlichkeiten, f pl
 ♦ dining-room facilities pl
Speisesaalservice m
 ♦ dining-room service
Speisesaalserviererin, f
 → Speisesaalkellnerin
Speisesaalsteward, m
 ♦ dining-room steward
Speisesaaltischzeit, f
 ♦ dining-room sitting
Speisesaal überprüfen
 ♦ check the dining room
Speisesaalwäsche f
 ♦ dining-room linen
Speiseschrank, m
 ♦ food cupboard
 ♦ larder
Speiseservice, m
 → Speisenservice
Speiseservice, n (Geschirr)
 → Tafelgeschirr, Eßgeschirr
Speiseterrasse, f
 ♦ dining terrace
 ♦ dining patio
 ♦ terrace for dining
Speisetisch m
 ♦ dinner table
Speise- und Weinkarte, f
 ♦ menu and wine list
Speiseunternehmen, n
 ♦ foodservice enterprise AE
 ♦ catering enterprise BE
Speiseveranstaltung, f
 ♦ dinner function
 ♦ dinner event
Speisewagen, m
 Zugspeisewagen, m
 Zugrestaurant, n
 ♦ dining car AE
 ♦ dining-car BE
 ♦ restaurant car
 ♦ diner AE
Speisewagenschaffner, m
 ♦ dining-car attendant

Speise warm halten
 Speisen warm halten
 ♦ keep food hot
Speisezettel, m
 → Speisekarte
Speisezimmer, n
 → Speisesaal, Eßzimmer
Speis' und Trank arch
 ♦ meat and drink arch
 ♦ food and drink
Speisung, f
 ♦ feeding
Spelunke, f
 ♦ barrelhouse AE sl
 ♦ gin mill AE coll
 ♦ jerry BE sl
 ♦ low dive BE
 ♦ honky-tonk AE sl
spendabel, adj
 ♦ open-handed, adj
 ♦ generous, adj
Spende, f
 ♦ donation
Spendenaufruf, m
 ♦ appeal for donations
Spendenaufruf machen
 ♦ launch an appeal for donations
spenden etw
 Geld spenden
 ♦ donate money
 ♦ make a donation
Spendenteller, m
 ♦ collecting plate
 ♦ plate
Spendenteller umherreichen (für etw)
 ♦ pass round the plate (for s.th.)
Spender, m
 ♦ donor
spendieren jm ein Getränk
 ♦ stand s.o. a drink
spendieren jm etw
 ♦ buy s.o. s.th.
 ♦ stand s.o. s.th.
 ♦ treat s.o. to s.th.
Spendierhosen, f pl humor
 ♦ spending mood
Spendierhosen anhaben
 ♦ be in a spending mood
Sperrgebiet, n
 ♦ prohibited area
 ♦ prohibited zone
 ♦ restricted area
Sperrgebiet sein für Soldaten (Bar, Kneipe)
 ♦ be out of bounds to soldiers BE
 ♦ be off limits to soldiers AE
Sperrholzmöbel, n pl
 ♦ plywood furniture sg
Sperrsitz, m (Theater)
 Parkett, n
 ♦ orchestra AE
 ♦ stalls BE pl
Sperrsitzplatz, m (Theater)
 Parkettplatz, m
 Sperrsitz, m
 ♦ orchestra seat AE
 ♦ seat in the orchestra AE
 ♦ seat in the stalls BE
Sperrstunde, f (Lokal)
 Polizeistunde, f
 ♦ closing hour
 ♦ closing time

Sperrstunde, f (Militär)
 Beginn des Ausgangsverbots, m mil
 Ausgangssperre, f mil
 Sperrzeit, f mil
 ♦ curfew mil
Sperrzone, f
 ♦ prohibited area
 ♦ off limits area
 ♦ restricted area
Spesen, pl
 ♦ expenses pl
Spesenabendessen, n (Dinner)
 ♦ expense-account dinner
Spesenabendessen, n (Supper)
 ♦ expense-account supper
Spesenessen, n
 ♦ expense-account meal
spesenfrei, adj
 ♦ expenses paid, adj
spesenfreie Fahrt, f
 ♦ expenses-paid trip
Spesenfrühstück, n
 ♦ expense-account breakfast
Spesenkonto n
 ♦ expense account
Spesenkontrolle, f
 ♦ control of expenses
 ♦ expense control
Spesenmittagessen, n
 ♦ expense-account lunch
 ♦ expense-account luncheon
Spesenrechnung, f
 ♦ expense check AE
 ♦ expense bill BE
Spesenreisender m
 ♦ expense-account traveler AE
 ♦ expense-account traveller BE
Spesenritter, m humor
 → Spesenreisender
Spessart, der, m
 (Region)
 ♦ Spessart, the
 ♦ Spessart Mountains, the pl
Spezialausstellung, f
 → Sonderausstellung
Spezialbehandlung, f
 → Sonderbehandlung
Spezialbier, n
 ♦ special beer
Spezialbrot, n
 ♦ special bread
Spezialdressing, n
 spezielles Dressing, n
 ♦ special dressing
Spezialeinrichtung, f
 → Sondereinrichtung
Spezialessen, n
 → besonderes Essen
Spezialfrühstück n
 spezielles Frühstück n
 ♦ special breakfast
spezialisieren sich auf etw
 ♦ specialise in s.th.
 ♦ specialize in s.th.
spezialisieren sich auf Tagungen
 ♦ specialise in meetings
 ♦ specialize in meetings
Spezialist, m
 Fachmann, m
 Experte, m

Spezialist für Österreich

- specialist
- expert

Spezialist für Österreich, m
Österreichspezialist, m
- specialist in Austria
- tour operator specialising in Austria
- firm specializing in Austria

Spezialität, f
- specialty AE
- speciality BE

Spezialität des Hauses, f
(Essen)
Hausspezialität f
- specialty of the house AE
- speciality of the house BE
- spécialité de la maison FR
- house specialty AE
- house speciality BE

Spezialität des Monats, f
Monatsspezialität, f
- specialty of the month AE
- speciality of the month BE

Spezialitätenbetrieb, m
- specialty establishment AE
- specialty operation AE
- speciality establishment BE
- speciality operation BE

Spezialitätenbüfett, n
- specialty buffet AE
- speciality buffet BE

Spezialitätengericht, n
- specialty dish AE
- speciality dish BE

Spezialitätengeschäft, n
- specialty store AE
- speciality shop BE

Spezialitätenkarte, f
(Speisekarte)
- specialty menu AE
- speciality menu BE

Spezialitätenküche, f
- specialty cooking AE
- speciality cooking BE

Spezialitätenlokal, n
- specialty place AE
- eating place with its own specialities BE

Spezialitätenrestaurant n
- specialty restaurant AE
- speciality restaurant BE

Spezialitätenschau f
- specialty show AE
- speciality show BE

Spezialitätenwoche, f
- specialty week AE
- speciality week BE

Spezialitätenwochenende, n
- specialty weekend AE
- speciality weekend BE

Spezialkatalog, m
Sonderkatalog, m
- special catalogue
- special catalog AE

Spezialkost, f
→ spezielle Diät

Spezialkurs, m
spezieller Kurs, m
Sonderkurs, m
- special course
- extra course

Spezialkurzurlaub, m
- special break

Spezialmesse, f
(Gegensatz zu Publikumsmesse)
- special fair
- special trade fair
- specialized fair
- specialized trade fair

Spezialofferte, f
→ Sonderangebot

Spezialprogramm, n
→ Sonderprogramm

Spezialprospekt, m
→ Sonderprospekt

Spezialrate, f
→ Sonderpreis

Spezialreise, f
- specialist tour
- specialist trip
- specialist journey

Spezialreisebüro, n
- specialist travel agency
- specialist travel agent

Spezialreiseveranstalter, m
Spezialveranstalter m
- specialist tour operator
- specialist operator

Spezialrezeptur, f
Spezialrezept, n
- special recipe

Spezialtarif, m
→ Sondertarif

Spezialtoilette, f
- special toilet

Spezialveranstalter, m
(Reiseveranstalter)
- special operator
- specialist operator

Spezialzimmer, n
spezielles Zimmer, n
besonderes Zimmer, n
- special room

spezielle Anforderung, f
Sonderanforderung, f
Spezialanforderung, f
- special requirement

spezielle Annehmlichkeiten, f pl
→ besondere Annehmlichkeiten

spezielle Außer-Saison-Preise, m pl
- special out-of-season prices pl
- special out-of-season rates pl
- special out-of-season terms pl

spezielle Diät, f
Spezialdiät, f
Sonderkost, f
- special diet

spezielle Diätanforderung, f
- special dietary requirement

spezielle Diätbedürfnisse erfüllen
- cater for special dietary needs

spezielle Diät verordnen
- prescribe a special diet

Spezielle Diätwünsche müssen 6 Stunden vorher angegeben werden
- Special dietary requests need 6 hours' notice

spezielle Konferenzpauschale, f
- special conference package

spezielle Pauschalvereinbarung, f
Sonderpauschalarrangement, n
- special package deal
- special package arrangement

spezieller Diätwunsch, m
Sonderdiätwunsch, m
besonderer Diätwunsch, m
- special dietary request

spezieller Gast, m
→ besonderer Gast

spezieller Kindertarif, m
- special tariff for children
- special terms for children pl
- special rates for children pl

spezieller Konferenztarif, m
- special conference tariff
- special conference terms pl
- special conference rates pl
- special conference rate

spezieller Service, m
→ Sonderleistung

spezielles Arrangement, n
spezielle Vereinbarung, f
Sonderarrangement, n
Spezialarrangement, n
- special arrangement

spezielles Arrangement benötigen
- require a special arrangement

spezielles Arrangement wünschen
- request a special arrangement

spezielles Kinderessen, n
- special children's meal

spezielles Sonderangebot, n
- special bargain offer

spezielle Unterkunft, f
- special accommodation

spezielle Verpflegungsanforderung f
- special catering requirement

spezielle Verpflegungsvereinbarung f
spezielles Verpflegungsarrangement n
- special catering arrangement
- special meal arrangement
- special board arrangement

spezielle Zubereitung, f
(Speisen)
- special preparation

speziell markierte Strecke, f
- specially marked route

spezifische Bedürfnisse erfüllen von jm
- meet the specific needs of s.o.

spezifische Behandlung, f
- specific treatment

spezifischer Service, m
spezifische Leistung, f
- specific service

spezifizieren etw
(Rechnung)
- itemize s.th.
- itemise s.th.

spezifizierte Rechnung, f
detaillierte Rechnung f
- itemized bill
- itemized check AE
- itemized account

Sphinx, f
- Sphinx, the
- sphinx

spicken etw
- lard s.th.

Spicknadel, f
- larding needle

Spiegel, m
- mirror

Spiegelbad, n
- mirrored bath**

Spielbadezimmer, n
 ♦ mirrored bathroom
Spiegelei n
 ♦ fried egg
Spiegel polieren
 ♦ polish a mirror
Spiegelsaal, m
 ♦ hall of mirrors
Spiegelschrank, m
 ♦ mirrored cabinet
 ♦ mirrored wardrobe
 ♦ wardrobe fitted with a mirror
Spiegelwand, f
 ♦ mirror wall
Spiegelzimmer, n
 ♦ room of mirrors
 ♦ mirrored room
Spielautomat, m
 ♦ slot machine
 ♦ one-armed bandit AE
 ♦ fruit machine BE
 ♦ gambling machine
 ♦ gaming machine
Spielbank, f
 → Spielkasino
Spielbankbesucher, m
 ♦ gambling casino visitor
 ♦ visitor to a gambling casino
 ♦ visitor to a gaming casino
 ♦ casino visitor
Spielbecken, n
 ♦ play pool
Spielbude, f
 (z.B. auf einem Jahrmarkt)
 Spielstand, m
 ♦ game booth
Spielclub, m (generell)
 Spielverein, m
 ♦ games club
Spielclub, m (Glücksspiel)
 ♦ gambling club
 ♦ gaming club
Spielecke, f
 ♦ play-corner
Spieleinrichtung, f (Glücksspiel)
 ♦ gaming facility
 ♦ gambling facility
Spielen, n (Glücksspiel)
 ♦ gambling
 ♦ gaming
Spielen, n (Vergnügen)
 ♦ playing
spielen (Glücksspiel)
 ♦ gamble
spielen ohne Gage
 ♦ play without salary
spielen vor einem ausverkauften Haus
 ♦ play to a packed house
spielen vor einem vollen Haus
 ♦ play to a full house
spielen vor leeren Bänken
 ♦ play to empty benches
Spieler, m (Glücksspiel)
 ♦ gambler
Spieler, m (Vergnügen)
 ♦ player
Spielfeld, n
 ♦ pitch
 ♦ playing field
Spielfest, n
 ♦ games festival

Spielfilm, m
 ♦ feature film
Spielgarten, m
 ♦ play garden
Spielgelände n
 (für Kinder)
 ♦ play area
 ♦ playing area
Spielhalle, f (Glücksspiele)
 ♦ amusement arcade
 ♦ game parlor AE
Spielhalle, f (Unterhaltungsspiele)
 ♦ large game room AE
 ♦ large games room BE
Spielhallenbesitzer, m (Glücksspiele)
 ♦ owner of an amusement arcade
 ♦ owner of a game parlor AE
Spielhaus, n (Glücksspiele)
 ♦ gambling house
 ♦ gaming house
Spielhölle, f
 ♦ gambling den
 ♦ gaming den
Spielinsel, f
 (z.B. im Schwimmbad)
 ♦ play island
Spielkamerad, m
 ♦ playmate
Spielkarte, f
 ♦ playing card
 ♦ card
Spiel Karten, n
 ♦ pack of cards
Spielkasino, n
 Spielbank, f
 ♦ gambling casino
 ♦ gaming casino
 ♦ casino
Spielkasinobesuch, m
 ♦ visit to the gambling casino
 ♦ visit to the casino
 ♦ casino visit
Spielkasino betreiben
 ♦ operate a gambling casino
Spielkasinoerlös, m
 Kasinoerlös, m
 ♦ casino revenue
Spielkasinogeschäft, n
 Kasinogeschäft, n
 ♦ gambling casino business
 ♦ casino business
Spielkasinokassierer, m
 Kasinokassierer, m
 ♦ casino cashier
Spielkasinokunde, m
 Kasinokunde, m
 ♦ casino customer
Spielkasinostammkunde, m
 Kasinostammkunde, m
 ♦ casino patron
Spielland, n
 ♦ playland
Spielmarke, f
 → Chip
Spielmöglichkeit, f
 ♦ possibility of play
Spielort, m (Glücksspiel)
 (z.B. Las Vegas)
 ♦ gambling resort
 ♦ gaming resort

Spielpaket, n
 ♦ games pack BE
Spielpalast, m (Glücksspiel)
 ♦ gambling palace
 ♦ gaming palace
Spielplan, m (Theater)
 ♦ program (of events) AE
 ♦ programme (of events) BE
Spielplatz, m (für Erwachsene und Kinder)
 Spielfeld n
 ♦ recreation ground
 ♦ rec ground
Spielplatz, m (generell)
 ♦ playground
Spielplatz, m (Glücksspiel)
 Spielort, m
 ♦ gambling place
 ♦ gaming place
Spielplatz, m (Sport)
 ♦ playing field
Spielplatz für die Reichen, m
 ♦ playground for the rich
Spielrasen, m
 ♦ playing lawn
 ♦ play lawn
Spielsaal m (Glücksspiel)
 ♦ gambling hall
 ♦ gaming hall
Spielsalon, m (Glücksspiel)
 ♦ gambling salon
 ♦ gaming salon
 ♦ penny arcade BE
Spielschuld, f (Glücksspiel)
 ♦ gambling debt
 ♦ gaming debt
Spielstraße, f
 ♦ playstreet
Spieltisch, m (generell)
 ♦ games table
Spieltisch, m (Glücksspiel)
 ♦ gambling table
 ♦ gaming table
Spieltisch, m (Kartenspiel)
 ♦ card table
Spielverein, m
 → Spielclub
Spielwarengeschäft, n
 ♦ toy store AE
 ♦ toy shop BE
Spielwarenmesse, f
 ♦ toy fair
Spielwiese, f
 (für Rasenspiele)
 ♦ playing field
Spielzeug, n
 Spielsache, f
 ♦ toy
Spielzeugfahrzeug, n
 ♦ toy vehicle
Spielzeugmuseum, n
 ♦ toy museum
Spielzeugsammlung, f
 ♦ toy collection
 ♦ collection of toys
Spielzimmer, n (für Unterhaltung)
 ♦ game room AE
 ♦ games room BE
Spielzimmer, n (Glücksspiel)
 Spielraum, m
 ♦ gambling room
 ♦ gaming room

Spielzimmer

Spielzimmer, n (Kinder)
♦ playroom
Spieß, m (Fleisch)
Fleischspießchen, n
Fleischspieß, m
♦ skewer
♦ meat skewer
spießen etw *gastr*
aufspießen etw *gastr*
♦ skewer s.th. *gastr*
Spinat, m
♦ spinach
Spinatauflauf, m
Spinatsoufflé, n
♦ spinach soufflé
Spinatblatt, n
♦ spinach leaf
Spinatbutter, f
♦ spinach butter
Spinatsoufflé, n
→ Spinatauflauf
Spinatsuppe, f
♦ spinach soup
Spinatterrine, f
♦ spinach terrine
Spindraum, m
♦ locker room
Spion, m
Guckloch, n
♦ spyhole *AE*
♦ spy-hole *BE*
♦ peephole *AE*
♦ peep-hole *BE*
Spirituose, f
(besonders Brandy und Whisky)
alkoholisches Getränk, n
Alkohol, m
♦ liquor
Spirituosen, f pl
geistige Getränke, n pl
♦ spirits *pl*
♦ liquor
♦ alcoholic beverages *pl*
♦ alcoholic drinks *pl*
Spirituosenausschank, m (Verkauf)
♦ sale of liquor *AE*
♦ selling liquor *AE*
♦ sale of spirits
♦ selling spirits
Spirituoseneinnahmen, f pl
Einnahmen aus alkoholischen Getränken, f pl
♦ liquor takings *AE pl*
♦ liquor revenue *AE*
♦ liquor income *AE*
♦ liquor receipts *AE pl*
Spirituosengeschäft, n
Spirituosenladen, m
♦ liquor store *AE*
♦ liquor shop *BE*
♦ off-licence liquor store *AE*
♦ off-license shop *BE*
♦ off-licence
Spirituosenhandel, m
♦ liquor trade
Spirituosenhändler, m
♦ liquor dealer
Spirituosenpreis, m
♦ liquor price
Spirituosenumsatz, m
♦ spirits sales *pl*

Spirituosenumsatz, m
Umsatz alkoholischer Getränke, m
♦ liquor sales *pl*
♦ liquor turnover
Spirituosen- und Weingeschäft, n
Wein- und Spirituosenladen, m
♦ off-licence *BE*
♦ package store *AE*
Spirituosenwagen, m
(im Restaurant)
♦ liquor cart *AE*
♦ liquor trolley *BE*
Spiritus, m
♦ spirit
Spirituskocher, m
♦ spirit cooker
♦ spirit stove
Spirituslampe, f
♦ spirit lamp
Spitzbergen
♦ Spitsbergen
Spitze, f
♦ peak
♦ top
Spitze der Belegung, f
Belegungsspitze, f
Auslastungsspitze, f
♦ peak of occupancy
Spitze der Touristensaison, f
Spitze der Reisezeit, f
♦ peak of the tourist season
Spitzenauslastung, f
♦ peak load factor
Spitzenauslastung erreichen
Spitzenauslastung erzielen
♦ achieve (the) peak load factor
Spitzenausstattung, f
♦ top-class equipment
Spitzenbelegung, f
Spitzenauslastung, f
Spitzenfrequenz, f
♦ peak occupancy
Spitzenbelegung erreichen
Spitzenauslastung erreichen
Spitzenfrequenz erreichen
♦ achieve peak occupancy
Spitzenbesuchstag, m
♦ peak visiting day
Spitzenbuchungszeit f
♦ peak booking period
Spitzenchef, m
Spitzenkoch, m
♦ top chef
Spitzendestination, f
→ Spitzenzielort
Spitzeneinrichtung, f
♦ top-class facility
♦ top facility
Spitzenferienzeit, f
Spitzenurlaubszeit, f
♦ peak holiday period *BE*
♦ peak holiday season *BE*
♦ peak vacation period *AE*
♦ peak vacation season *AE*
Spitzenfrequenz, f
→ Spitzenauslastung
Spitzengastronomie, f
♦ top-class foodservice *AE*
♦ top-class catering *BE*
Spitzengeschwindigkeit, f
♦ top speed

Spitzenhotel, n
♦ top hotel
♦ top-class hotel
Spitzenhotels haben französische und chinesische Küche
♦ top hotels have French and Chinese kitchens
Spitzenjahr n
♦ peak year
Spitzenkapazität, f
♦ peak capacity
Spitzenkapelle, f
Spitzenband, f
♦ top band
Spitzenkategorie, f
Spitzenklasse, f
♦ top category
Spitzenklassebetrieb, m
Betrieb der Spitzenklasse, m
♦ top-class establishment
♦ top-class operation
Spitzenklassehotel, n
Hotel der Spitzenklasse
Spitzenkoch m
♦ top cook
Spitzenküche, f (Speisen)
♦ top-class cuisine
♦ top-rate cuisine *coll*
♦ top-class cooking
♦ top-rate cooking *coll*
Spitzenlage, f
♦ top location
♦ prime location
Spitzenmonat m
♦ peak month
Spitzennachfrage, f
♦ peak demand
Spitzennachfrage erfüllen
♦ meet the peak demand
Spitzenorchester, n
♦ top-class orchestra
♦ top orchestra
Spitzenort, m
Spitzenferienort, m
Spitzenurlaubsort, m
♦ top resort
Spitzenpreis, m
♦ peak price
♦ peak rate
♦ top price
♦ top rate
Spitzenprogramm, n
♦ top program *AE*
♦ top-class program *AE*
♦ top programme *BE*
♦ top-class programme *BE*
Spitzenqualität, f
♦ top quality
Spitzenqualitätswein, m
♦ top quality wine
Spitzenreisetag, m
♦ peak travel day
Spitzenreisewoche, f
♦ peak travel week
Spitzenreisezeit, f
♦ peak travel season
Spitzenrestaurant, n
♦ top restaurant
♦ top-class restaurant

Spitzensaison, f
♦ peak season
♦ top season
Spitzensaisonaufpreis, m
♦ peak-season surcharge
Spitzensaisonauslastung, f
♦ peak-season load factor
Spitzensaisonbelegung, f
Spitzensaisonauslastung, f
♦ peak-season occupancy
Spitzensaisonbuchung f
♦ peak-season booking
Spitzensaisonermäßigung f
♦ peak-season reduction
Spitzensaisonmonat, m
♦ peak-season month
month in the peak season
Spitzensaisonpreis, m
♦ peak-season price
peak-season rate
♦ top-season price
♦ top-season rate
Spitzensaisonreservierung, f
♦ peak-season reservation
Spitzensaison sich nähern
♦ approach the peak season
Spitzensaisontag, m
♦ peak-season day
day in the peak season
Spitzensaisonurlaub, m
Spitzensaisonferien, pl
♦ peak-season vacation AE
♦ peak-season holiday BE
Spitzensaisonwoche, f
♦ peak-season week
week in the peak season
Spitzensaisonzeit f
♦ peak-season period
Spitzensaisonzuschlag m
♦ peak-season supplement
Spitzenservice, m
♦ top service
♦ top-class service
Spitzenstunde f
♦ peak hour
Spitzentag, m
Hochbetriebstag, m
♦ peak day
Spitzenunterhalter, m
♦ top-class entertainer
♦ top entertainer
Spitzenunterhaltung f
erstklassige Unterhaltung f
♦ top-class entertainment
Spitzenurlaubsort, m
♦ top vacation resort AE
♦ top holiday resort Be
Spitzenurlaubszeit, f
Spitzenferienzeit, f
♦ peak vacation period AE
♦ peak vacation season AE
♦ peak holiday period BE
♦ peak holiday season BE
Spitzenurlaubsziel, n
Spitzenurlaubsdestination, f
beste Urlaubsdestination, f
Spitzenferienziel, n
♦ prime vacation destination AE
♦ prime holiday destination BE
Spitzenwein, m
♦ top-class wine

♦ top wine
♦ vintage wine
Spitzenwoche f
♦ peak week
Spitzenzeit, f
♦ peak period
♦ peak time
Spitzenzeitnachfrage, f
Spitzennachfrage, f
♦ peak period demand
Spitzenzielort, m
Spitzenziel, n
Spitzendestination, f
♦ top destination
Spitze verteilen
♦ spread the peak
Splitcharter, m
♦ split charter
Splügenpaß, der, m
♦ Splügen Pass, the
sponsern etw.
♦ sponsor s.th.
Sponsor, m (Firma)
♦ sponsoring company
♦ sponsoring firm
Sponsor, m (generell)
♦ sponsor
Sponsorengruppe, f
♦ sponsoring group
Sponsoring, n
♦ sponsoring
♦ sponsorship
Sponsor von etw, m
♦ sponsor of s.th.
spontane Abreise, f
unüberlegte Abreise, f
♦ impulsive departure
Spontanreise, f
spontane Reise, f
♦ impulse trip
♦ impulse tour
♦ impulse journey
Spontantourismus, m
♦ impulse tourism
Spontantourist, m
♦ impulse tourist
Spontanurlaub, m
♦ impulse vacation AE
♦ impulse holiday BE
Spontanurlauber, m
♦ impulse vacationer AE
♦ impulse holidaymaker BE
sporadischer Besuch, m
seltener Besuch, m
♦ infrequent visit
sporadischer Besucher, m
♦ infrequent visitor
Sport, Spaß und Unterhaltung anbieten
♦ offer sport, fun and entertainment
Sportabteilung, f
♦ sports department
Sportaktivität, f
sportliche Betätigung, f
♦ sports activity
Sportangebot, n (Palette)
♦ range of sports facilities
♦ range of sports activities
Sportanlage, f
Sportkomplex, m
♦ sports complex

Sportannehmlichkeit, f
♦ sports amenity
Sportarrangement, n
♦ sports arrangement
Sportart, f
♦ type of sport
♦ sport type
Sportausrüstung, f
Sportausstattung, f
♦ sports equipment
Sportausrüstung mieten
♦ rent sports equipment AE
♦ hire sports equipment BE
Sportausstattung, f
→ Sportausrüstung
Sportbad n
→ Sportschwimmbad
Sportbar, f
♦ sports bar
Sportbegeisterter, m
♦ sports enthusiast
♦ sports fan
Sportboot, n
♦ sports boat
Sportbüro, n
♦ sports office
Sportclub, m
→ Sportverein
Sportcoupé, n
♦ sports coupe AE
♦ sports coupé BE
Sportdirektor, m
♦ sports director
Sportdorf, n
♦ sports village
Sporteinrichtung, f
♦ sports facility
Sporteinrichtung buchen
♦ book a sports facility
Sportfan, m coll
♦ sports fan coll
Sportfeld, n
♦ sports field
Sportferienort, m
Sporturlaubsort, m
Sportort, m
♦ sports resort
Sportfest, n (generell)
♦ sports meet
Sportfest, n (Schule)
♦ sports day
Sportfischen, n
♦ sport fishing
Sportflugzeug, n
♦ sports plane
♦ light plane
Sportfreund, m
♦ sporting man
♦ sports enthusiast
♦ sports fan
Sportgelegenheit, f
♦ sports opportunity
sportgerät, n
♦ apparatus
Sportgeschäft, n
♦ sports store AE
♦ sports shop BE
Sporthalle, f
♦ sports hall
♦ gymnasium

Sporthotel

Sporthotel, n
- ♦ sports hotel

Sport Ihrer Wahl, m
- ♦ sport of your choice

Sport im Freien, m
- ♦ outdoor sports

Sportindustrie, f
- ♦ sports industry

Sportinteressierte, m/f pl
- ♦ sports-minded, the, pl

Sportkleidung, f
- ♦ sportswear
- ♦ sports clothes *pl*

Sportkomplex, m
→ Sportanlage

Sportkurzurlaub, m
- ♦ sports break

Sportlehrer, m
- ♦ sports instructor
- ♦ sports teacher

Sportlehrerin, f
- ♦ sports instructress

Sportler, m
- ♦ sportsman

Sportler des Jahres, m
- ♦ Sportsman of the Year

Sportlerin, f
- ♦ sportswoman

Sportlerin des Jahres, f
- ♦ Sportswoman of the Year

Sportliebhaber, m
- ♦ sports lover

Sportmassage, f
- ♦ sports massage

Sportmeisterschaft, f
- ♦ sports championship

Sportmöglichkeit, f
- ♦ sports possibility
- ♦ sports facility

sportorientiertes Hotel, n
- ♦ sports-oriented hotel *AE*
- ♦ sports-orientated hotel *BE*

Sportparadies, n
Sportlerparadies, n
- ♦ sports paradise
- ♦ sportsman's paradise

Sportpaß, m
- ♦ sports pass

Sportplatz, m
- ♦ sports grounds

Sportprogramm, n
- ♦ sports program *AE*
- ♦ sports programme *BE*

Sportraum, m
→ Gymnastikraum

Sportreise, f
- ♦ sports tour
- ♦ sports trip
- ♦ sports journey

Sportreisen, n
Sportreiseverkehr, m
- ♦ sports travel

Sportreiseveranstalter, m
- ♦ sports tour operator

Sportsaison, f
- ♦ sports season
- ♦ sporting season *BE form*

Sportschuh, m
- ♦ sports shoe

Sportschwimmbad, n
- ♦ watersports pool *AE*
- ♦ water-sports pool *BE*

Sportsegler, m
Segler, m
- ♦ yachtsman

Sportstadion, n
- ♦ sports stadium
- ♦ athletics stadium *BE*

Sportstar, m
- ♦ sports star

Sportszene, f
- ♦ sports scene

Sporttag, m
- ♦ sports day
- ♦ sport day

sporttauchen
(ohne Atemgerät)
- ♦ skin dive *AE*
- ♦ skin-dive *BE*

Sporttauchen, n
- ♦ skin diving *AE*
- ♦ skin-diving *BE*

Sporttaucher, m
- ♦ skin diver *AE*
- ♦ skin-diver *BE*

Sporttourismus, m
- ♦ sports tourism

Sporttourist, m
- ♦ sports tourist

Sporttrainer, m
- ♦ sports coach

Sporttraining, n
- ♦ sports coaching

Sport treiben
- ♦ do sports
- ♦ do sport

Sportturnier, n
- ♦ sports tournament

Sport- und Fitneßzentrum, n
- ♦ sports and fitness center *AE*
- ♦ sports and fitness centre *BE*

Sport- und Freizeiteinrichtung, f
- ♦ sports and leisure facility

Sport- und Freizeitzentrum, n
- ♦ sports and leisure center *AE*
- ♦ sports and leisure centre *BE*

Sportunterricht, m
- ♦ sports lessons *pl*
- ♦ sports tuition
- ♦ sports instruction

Sporturlaub, m
Sportferien, pl
- ♦ sports vacation *AE*
- ♦ sports holiday *BE*

Sporturlauber, m
- ♦ sports vacationer *AE*
- ♦ sports holidaymaker *BE*

Sporturlaubskurs, m
Sportferienkurs, m
- ♦ sports vacation course *AE*
- ♦ sports holiday course *BE*

Sportveranstaltung, f
- ♦ sports event
- ♦ sports activity

Sportverein, m
Sportclub, m
- ♦ sports club

Sportverletzung, f
- ♦ sports injury

Sportwagen, m
- ♦ sports car
- ♦ sport car *AE*

Sportwagencamper, m
- ♦ sports car camper
- ♦ sport car camper *AE*

Sportwettkampf, m
- ♦ sports competition
- ♦ sports contest

Sportwoche, f
- ♦ sports week

Sportwochenende, n
- ♦ sports weekend

Sportzentrum, n
- ♦ sports center *AE*
- ♦ sports centre *BE*

spottbillig, adj
- ♦ dirt cheap, adj
- ♦ at bargain rates

spottbillig sein
- ♦ be dirt cheap

Spottpreis, m
Schleuderpreis, m
- ♦ giveaway price *AE*
- ♦ giveaway rate *AE*
- ♦ give-away price *BE*
- ♦ give-away rate *BE*
- ♦ ridiculously low price

Sprachausbildung, f
- ♦ language training

Sprachendienst, m
Übersetzungs- und Dolmetscherdienst, m
- ♦ translating and interpreting service

sprachenkundig, adj
- ♦ proficient in languages, adj
- ♦ polyglot, adj
- ♦ well versed in a language, adj

Sprachenproblem, n
Sprachproblem, n
- ♦ language problem

Sprachenzuschlag m
Sprachzuschlag m
- ♦ language supplement

Sprachferien, pl
→ Sprachurlaub

Sprachführer, m
(Buch)
- ♦ phrase book

Sprachkenntnisse, f pl
- ♦ language skills *pl*
- ♦ knowledge of languages
- ♦ command of languages

sprachkundiger Reiseleiter, m
- ♦ linguist-courier

sprachkundig sein
- ♦ have a knowledge of languages

Sprachkurs, m
Sprachlehrgang, m
- ♦ language course

Sprachkurs machen
Sprachlehrgang machen
- ♦ do a language course
- ♦ take a language course

Sprachlehrer, m
- ♦ language teacher

Sprachlehrgang, m
→ Sprachkurs

Sprachreise, f
- ♦ language trip
- ♦ language tour

Sprachreise machen
♦ make a language trip
♦ make a language tour
Sprachreisemarkt, m
♦ language tour market
Sprachreiseveranstalter, m
♦ language tour operator
Sprachschule, f
♦ language school
Sprachunterricht, m
♦ language lessons pl
♦ language instruction
Sprachurlaub, m
♦ language vacation AE
♦ language holiday BE
♦ vacation to learn a language AE
♦ holiday to learn a language BE
Sprachurlauber, m
♦ person on a language trip
♦ person on a language tour
♦ language student
Sprachzentrum, n
Sprachenzentrum, n
♦ language center AE
♦ language centre BE
Sprechanlage, f
(an Haustür)
♦ entryphone
Sprecher, m
♦ spokesman
Sprecherin, f
♦ spokeswoman
Spreewald, der, m
(Region)
♦ Spree Forest, the
sprichwörtlich, adj
♦ proverbial, adj
sprichwörtliche Gastfreundschaft, f
sprichwörtliche Gastlichkeit, f
♦ proverbial hospitality
sprichwörtlicher Geiz, m
sprichwörtliche Knausrigkeit, f
♦ proverbial meanness
Springbrunnen, m
→ Brunnen
Springform, f gastr
♦ springform gastr
Sprinkleranlage, f
→ Feuerlöschanlage
Sprit, m
→ Benzin
Spritzer, m
(Bar: 0,1 cl)
♦ dash
Spritzflasche, f
(in der Bar)
♦ dash bottle
Spritztour, f (generell)
kurze Vergnügungsfahrt, f
♦ spin inform
♦ jaunt
Spritztour, f (oft in gestohlenem Auto)
♦ joy ride
Spritztour machen
kurze Vergnügungsfahrt machen
♦ go for a spin inform
♦ go on a spin
♦ go for a jaunt
♦ go on a jaunt

Sproßenwand, f
(Gymnastik)
♦ wall bars pl
Sprudel, m
♦ sparkling water
♦ sparkling mineral water
Sprudelbad, n
→ Whirlpool
Sprudelbassin, n
→ Whirlpool
Sprudelbecken, n
→ Whirlpool
Sprudelgetränk, n
sprudelndes Getränk, n
♦ fizzy drink
sprudelnd, adj
♦ fizzy, adj
Sprudelwasser, n
♦ fizzy water
Sprung, m (Geschirr)
♦ crack
Sprungbecken n
(im Schwimmbad)
♦ plunge pool
♦ diving pool
Sprungbrett, n
♦ springboard
♦ diving board
Sprungfedermatratze, f
♦ interior-sprung mattress
♦ spring mattress
sprungfixe Kosten, pl
Sprungkosten, pl
Mischkosten, pl
♦ semivariable costs pl
sprunghafter Anstieg der Spätbuchungen, m
♦ boost to late bookings
Sprungschanze, f
→ Skisprungschanze
Sprungturm m
(Schwimmbad)
♦ diving tower
♦ diving platform
Spucknapf, m
♦ spittoon
♦ cuspidor AE
Spukhaus, n
♦ haunted house
Spukhotel, n
♦ haunted hotel
Spukschloß, n
♦ haunted castle
Spukzimmer, n
♦ haunted room
Spülabteilung, f
♦ stewarding department
Spülautomat, m
→ Spülmaschine
Spülbecken, n
Spülstein, m obs
♦ sink
♦ dishwashing sink
Spüle, f
♦ sink unit
Spüleinrichtung, f
Spülgelegenheit, f
♦ dishwashing facility
♦ washing-up facility BE
spülen (abwaschen)
abwaschen
♦ wash up BE

♦ do the dishes AE
♦ wash the dishes BE
♦ do the washing-up BE
spülen etw (Glas etc)
ausspülen etw
nachspülen etw
klarspülen etw
♦ rinse s.th.
spülen etw (Toilette)
♦ flush s.th.
Spüler, m
Spülkraft, f
Geschirrspüler, m
♦ dishwasher
♦ washer-up BE coll
♦ steward
♦ scullion obs
Spülklosett, n
→ Wasserklosett
Spülkraft, f
→ Spüler
Spülküche, f
Abspülküche, f
Abwaschküche, f
♦ scullery
Spülküchenleiter, m
(in Hotel)
♦ steward
Spülmädchen, n
♦ scullery maid
Spülmannschaft, f
♦ dishroom crew AE
♦ dishwashing crew BE
Spülmaschine, f
Spülautomat, m
♦ dishwasher
♦ washing-up machine BE
spülmaschinenfest, adj
♦ dishwasher-safe, adj
Spülmittel, n
♦ dishwashing liquid
♦ dishwashing powder
♦ detergent
♦ washing-up liquid BE
Spülpersonal, n
♦ dishwashing staff
♦ dishwashing personnel
♦ stewarding staff
♦ stewarding personnel
Spülraum, m
♦ dishroom AE
♦ dishwashing room BE
♦ washing-up room BE
Spülstein, m
→ Spülbecken
Spültoilette, f
Spül-WC, n
♦ flush toilet
Spültuch, n
♦ dish towel AE
♦ tea-towel BE
Spülwasser, n (Geschirr)
♦ dishwater
♦ washing-up water BE
♦ swill inform
Spülwasser, n (Gläser)
♦ rinsing water
Spül-WC, n
→ Spültoilette

Spund

Spund, m
(eines Fasses)
- spigot

Spundloch, n
- bung-hole

Spundzapfen, m
Spund, m
- bung

Square Dance, m
- square dance

Squash, m
- squash

Squashanlage, f
- squash complex

Squashball, m
- squash ball

Squashcenter, n
- squash center *AE*
- squash courts *pl*
- squash centre *BE*

Squashhalle, f
- indoor squash court

Squashmeisterschaft, f
- squash championship

Squashplatz, m
- squash court

Squashraum, m
- squash room

Squashschläger, m
- squash racket

Squashspiel, n
- game of squash
- squash game

Squash spielen
- play squash

Squashspieler, m
- squash player

Squashwettbewerb, m
- squash competition

Squashzelle, f
Squashbox, f
- squash box

Sri Lanka
- Sri Lanka

Srilanker, m
- Sri Lankan

Srilankerin, f
- Sri Lankan girl
- Sri Lankan woman
- Sri Lankan

srilankisch, adj
- Sri Lankan, adj

staatlich anerkannt, adj
- state-approved, adj
- state-acknowledged, adj
- officially approved, adj

staatlich anerkannter Kurort, m
- state-approved spa
- state-acknowledged spa
- officially approved spa

staatlich anerkannter Luftkurort, m
- state-approved climatic health resort

staatlich anerkanntes Erholungsgebiet, n
- state-approved recreation(al) area
- officially approved recreation(al) area

staatliche Kunstgalerie, f
- state art gallery

staatlicher Campingplatz, m
- state(-owned) campsite
- state(-owned) campground *AE*
- state(-owned) camping site *BE*
- state(-owned) camping ground *BE*
- state(-owned) site

staatliches Hotel, n
- state-owned hotel

staatliches Kongreßbüro, n
- national convention bureau

staatliche Spielbank, f
- state-owned gambling casino
- state-owned gaming casino
- state-owned casino

Staatsangehöriger, m
- national
- citizen
- subject *BE jur*

Staatsangehörigkeit, f
- nationality
- citizenship

Staatsbad, n
- state-owned spa

Staatsbadhotel n
- hotel in a state-owned spa
- state-owned spa hotel

Staatsbankett n
- state banquet
- official banquet

Staatsbegräbnis, n
- state funeral

Staatsbesuch, m
- state visit

Staatsbesuch abstatten
- pay a state visit

Staatsbesucher, m
- state visitor

Staatscampingplatz, m
staatlicher Campingplatz, m
- state campsite
- state campground *AE*
- state-owned camping site *BE*
- state-owned camping ground *BE*
- state site

Staatsdiner, n
- state dinner

Staatsdomäne, f
- state domain

staatseigen, adj
staatlich, adj
- state-owned, adj

Staatseisenbahn, f
staatliche Eisenbahn, f
- state railroad *AE*
- state railway *BE*

Staatsempfang m
- state reception
- official reception

Staatsfeiertag, m
→ Nationalfeiertag

Staatsfest, n
staatliches Fest, n
- state festival

Staatsflagge, f
→ Nationalfahne

Staatsgast, m
- state guest
- official guest

Staatsgästehaus, n
- state guesthouse *AE*
- state guest-house *BE*

Staatsgrenze, f
- national frontier
- frontier

- national border
- border

Staatshotel, n
- state hotel
- state-owned hotel

Staatshotelkette, f
- state-owned hotel chain

Staatsmuseum, n
- state museum

Staatsoberhaupt, n
- head of state

Staatsoper, f
- state opera house

Staatsorchester, n
- state orchestra

Staatspark, m
- state park

Staatsplatz, m
(z.B. Camping)
- state site
- state-owned site

Staatstaxe, f
- government tax

Staatstheater, n
- state theater *AE*
- state theatre *BE*

Staatswald, m
- state-owned forest
- state forest
- state-owned wood
- state wood

Staatsweingut, n
- state wine estate
- state winery

stabiler Preis, m
- stable price
- stable rate

Stabkirche, f
- stave church

Stabsstelle, f
- staff position

Stachelbeere, f
- gooseberry

Stachelbeerkonfitüre, f
- gooseberry jam

Stachelbeerpüree, n
- gooseberry purée *BE*
- gooseberry puree *AE*

Stachelbeersoße, f
- gooseberry sauce

Stadion, n
- stadium
- bowl *AE*

Stadionkonzert, n
- stadium concert

Stadt am Rhein, f (Großstadt)
- city on the Rhine

Stadt am Rhein, f (kleine Stadt)
- town on the Rhine

Stadtausflug, m (Großstadt)
- city excursion

Stadtausflug, m (kleine Stadt)
- town excursion

Stadtautobahn, f
- urban expressway *AE*
- urban motorway *BE*

Stadtbad, n (Großstadt)
- city baths *pl*

Stadtbad, n (kleine Stadt)
- town baths *pl*

Stadtbauernhof, m (Großstadt)
♦ city farm
Stadtbauernhof, m (kleine Stadt)
♦ town farm
Stadtbefestigung, f (Großstadt)
♦ city fortification
Stadtbefestigung, f (kleine Stadt)
♦ town fortification
Stadtbesichtigung, f
♦ city sightseeing
♦ city sightseeing tour
♦ city tour
Stadt besuchen (Großstadt)
♦ visit a city
Stadt besuchen (kleine Stadt)
♦ visit a town
Stadtbesucher, m (Großstadt)
♦ visitor to the city
Stadtbesucher, m (kleine Stadt)
♦ visitor to the town
Stadtblick, m (Großstadt)
♦ city view
♦ view of the city
Stadtblick, m (kleine Stadt)
♦ town view
♦ view of the town
Stadtbummel, m (Großstadt)
♦ stroll through the city
♦ walk through the city
Stadtbummel, m (kleine Stadt)
♦ stroll through the town
♦ walk through the town
Stadtbüro, n (Fluggesellschaft, Großstadt)
♦ city terminal
Stadtbüro, n (Fluggesellschaft, kleine Stadt)
♦ town terminal
Stadtbüro, n (Großstadt)
♦ city office
Stadtbüro, n (kleine Stadt)
♦ town office
Stadtbus, m (Großstadt)
♦ city bus
Stadtbus, m (kleine Stadt)
♦ town bus
Stadtcampingplatz, m (Großstadt)
♦ city campsite
♦ city campground *AE*
♦ city camping site *BE*
♦ city camping ground *BE*
♦ city site
Stadtcampingplatz, m (kleine Stadt)
♦ town campsite
♦ town campground *AE*
♦ town camping site *BE*
♦ town camping ground *BE*
♦ town site
Stadt des Weins und der Kongresse, f
♦ town of wine and congresses
♦ town of wine and conventions
Städtekurzurlaub, m
♦ city break
Städtekurzurlaubswochenende, n
♦ city break weekend
Städtepartnerschaft, f
♦ town twinning
♦ twin towns *pl*
Städtepartnerschaft haben mit X
♦ be twinned with X
♦ X and Y are twin towns

Städtereise, f
♦ city tour
♦ city trip
Städtereisenprogramm, n
♦ city tour program *AE*
♦ city tour programme *BE*
Städtereiseveranstalter, m
♦ city tour operator
Stadt erkunden (Großstadt)
♦ explore a city
Stadt erkunden (kleine Stadt)
♦ explore a town
Stadt erstreckt sich von A bis B
♦ town extends from A to B
Städtetourismus, m
♦ city tourism
Städtetourist, m
Städtereisender, m
♦ city tourist
Stadtfahrt, f (Großstadt)
Fahrt um die Stadt, f
♦ ride around the city
♦ trip around the city
Stadtfahrt, f (kleine Stadt)
Fahrt um die Stadt, f
♦ ride around the town
♦ trip around the town
Stadtfest, n (Großstadt)
Stadtfestspiele, n pl
♦ city festival
Stadtfest, n (kleine Stadt)
Stadtfestspiele, n pl
♦ town festival
Stadtführer, m (Großstadt)
♦ city guide
Stadtführer, m (kleine Stadt)
♦ town guide
Stadtführung f (Großstadt)
♦ guided city tour
♦ guided tour of the city
Stadtführung f (kleine Stadt)
♦ guided town tour
♦ guided tour of the town
Stadtgalerie, f (Großstadt)
♦ city gallery
Stadtgalerie, f (Kleinstadt)
♦ town gallery
Stadtgarten, m
♦ town garden
Stadtgaststätte, f (Großstadt)
Stadtbar, f
♦ city bar *AE*
♦ city pub *BE*
Stadtgaststätte, f (kleine Stadt)
Stadtbar, f
♦ town bar *AE*
♦ town pub *BE*
Stadtgefängnis, n
♦ town jail
♦ town gaol *BE*
Stadtgrenze, f (Großstadt)
♦ city boundary
Stadtgrenze, f (kleine Stadt)
♦ town boundary
Stadthalle, f
städtische Halle, f
♦ municipal hall
♦ civic centre *BE*
♦ community center *AE*
♦ community centre *BE*

Stadthaus, n
♦ town house
Stadthotel, n (Großstadt)
→ Großstadthotel
Stadthotel, n (kleine Stadt)
♦ town hotel
Stadthotellerie, f (Großstadt)
♦ city hotel trade
Stadthotellerie, f (kleine Stadt)
♦ town hotel trade
städtisch, adj
stadteigen, adj
in städtischem Besitz
kommunal, adj
♦ municipal, adj
städtische Bibliothek, f
städtische Bücherei, f
♦ municipal library
städtische Galerie, f
♦ municipal gallery
städtische Kunstgalerie, f
♦ municipal art gallery
städtische Musikschule, f
♦ municipal school of music
städtischer Campingplatz, m
♦ municipal campsite
♦ municipal campground *AE*
♦ municipal camping site *BE*
♦ municipal camping ground *BE*
♦ municipal site
städtischer Park, m
Stadtpark, m
♦ municipal park
städtischer Parkplatz, m (für mehrere Autos)
Parkplatz in städtischem Besitz, m
♦ municipal parking lot *AE*
♦ municipal car park *BE*
städtischer Verkehrsverein, m
♦ municipal tourist association
städtisches Bad, n
♦ municipal pool
städtisches Hotel, n
♦ municipal hotel
städtisches Kultur- und Fremdenverkehrsamt, n
♦ municipal office of culture and tourism
städtisches Museum, n
♦ municipal museum
städtisches Schwimmbad, n
♦ municipal swimming pool *AE*
♦ municipal swimming-pool *BE*
♦ municipal pool
städtisches Theater, n
Stadttheater, n
♦ municipal theater *AE*
♦ municipal theatre *BE*
städtisches Verkehrsamt, n
städtisches Fremdenverkehrsamt, n
♦ municipal tourist office
städtische Veranstaltung, f
Bürgerveranstaltung, f
♦ civic function
Stadt ist in 5 Minuten zu erreichen
♦ town can be reached in 5 minutes
Stadt ist Partnerstadt von X
♦ town is twinned with X
Stadtkarte, f (Großstadt)
♦ city map
♦ map of the city
Stadtkarte, f (kleine Stadt)
♦ town map
♦ map of a town

Stadtkern

Stadtkern, m (Großstadt)
♦ city core
Stadtkern, m (kleine Stadt)
♦ town core
Stadtkirche, f (Großstadt)
♦ city church
Stadtkirche, f (kleine Stadt)
♦ town church
Stadtlage, f (Lage der Stadt)
♦ situation of the city
♦ situation of the town
Stadtlage, f (Nähe)
in Stadtnähe gelegen, adj
♦ situated near the town
♦ situated close to the town
♦ convenient situation to the town
Stadtmauer, f (Großstadt)
♦ city wall
Stadtmauer, f (kleine Stadt)
♦ town wall
Stadt mit vielen Gesichtern, f
♦ town of many faces
Stadtmuseum, n (Großstadt)
♦ city museum
Stadtmuseum, n (kleine Stadt)
♦ town museum
stadtnah, adv
♦ close to (the) town, adv
♦ close to the city, adv
Stadtpark, m (Großstadt)
♦ city park
Stadtpark, m (kleine Stadt)
♦ town park
Stadtparkplatz, m (Großstadt)
(für mehrere Autos)
Parkplatz in der Stadt, m
♦ city parking lot AE
♦ city car park BE
Stadtparkplatz, m (kleine Stadt)
(für mehrere Autos)
Parkplatz in der Stadt, m
♦ town parking lot AE
♦ town car park BE
Stadtplan, m (Großstadt)
♦ city plan
♦ plan of the city
Stadtplan, m (kleine Stadt)
♦ town plan
♦ plan of the town
Stadtplatz, m (Großstadt)
♦ city square
Stadtplatz, m (kleine Stadt)
♦ town square
Stadtprospekt, m (Großstadt)
♦ city brochure
Stadtprospekt, m (kleine Stadt)
♦ town brochure
Stadtrand, m (Großstadt)
♦ outskirts of a city pl
♦ edge of a city
Stadtrand, m (kleine Stadt)
♦ outskirts of a town pl
♦ edge of a town
Stadtrandlage, f (Großstadt)
am Stadtrand gelegen, adj
♦ situated on the outskirts of a city
Stadtrandlage, f (kleine Stadt)
am Stadtrand gelegen, adj
♦ situated on the outskirts of a town
Stadtrat, m (Gremium, Großstadt)
♦ city council

Stadtrat, m (Gremium, kleine Stadt)
♦ town council
Stadtrat, m (Person, Großstadt)
♦ city councillor
♦ city councillor AE
Stadtrat, m (Person, kleine Stadt)
♦ town councillor
♦ town councilor AE
Stadtrecht, n
♦ town status
Stadtrecht erhalten
♦ be granted town status
Stadtrestaurant, n (Großstadt)
♦ city restaurant
Stadtrestaurant, n (kleine Stadt)
♦ town restaurant
Stadtrundfahrt, f (Autofahrer, Großstadt)
Rundfahrt in der Stadt, f
♦ drive round the city
Stadtrundfahrt, f (Autofahrer, kleine Stadt)
Rundfahrt in der Stadt, f
♦ drive round the town
Stadtrundfahrt, f (Bus)
♦ city sightseeing tour
♦ sightseeing tour of a city
♦ city tour
♦ tour of the city
Stadtrundfahrt arrangieren
♦ arrange a city sightseeing tour
♦ arrange a city tour
Stadtrundgang, m (kleine Stadt)
Rundgang in der Stadt, m
Rundgang durch eine Stadt, m
♦ walk through a town
♦ walk around the town
♦ stroll through a town
♦ stroll around the town
Stadt seiner Träume, f
♦ town of one's dreams
Stadtstaat, m
♦ city state
Stadtstrand, m
♦ town beach
Stadtstreicherin, f
♦ bag lady
Stadttheater, n
♦ civic theatre BE
♦ city theater AE
♦ city theatre BE
Stadttor, n (Großstadt)
♦ city gate
Stadttor, n (kleine Stadt)
♦ town gate
Stadttourismus, m
♦ urban tourism
Stadt umfahren (Großstadt)
♦ bypass a city
Stadt umfahren (kleine Stadt)
♦ bypass a town
Stadtveranstaltung, f (Großstadt)
♦ city event
♦ city function
Stadtveranstaltung, f (kleine Stadt)
♦ town event
♦ town function
Stadt vermarkten (Großstadt)
♦ market a city
Stadt vermarkten (kleine Stadt)
♦ market a town

Stadt verschönern
♦ embellish the town
♦ embellish the city
Stadtwohnung, f (Großstadt)
♦ apartment in the city AE
♦ flat in the city BE
Stadtwohnung, f (kleine Stadt)
♦ apartment in town AE
♦ flat in town BE
Stadtzentrum, n
→ Innenstadt
Stadtzoo, m (Großstadt)
♦ city zoo
Stadtzoo, m (kleine Stadt)
♦ town zoo
Staffellauf, m
♦ relay race
Staffelpreis, m
♦ graduated price
♦ graduated rate
♦ tiered price
♦ tiered rate
Staffelpreisbildung, f
Staffelpreis, m
♦ tiered pricing
Staffelprovision, f
gestaffelte Provision, f
♦ graduated commission
♦ staggered commission
Staffelsitzanordnung, f
♦ tiered seating
Staffelsitzplatz, m
Staffelsitz, m
Staffelplatz, m
♦ tiered seat
Staffeltarif, m
♦ graduated tariff
♦ graduated rates pl
♦ sliding scale
Staffeltarifpreis, m
♦ sliding price
Stagiaire, m/f FR/SCHW
→ Praktikant
Stagnation, f
♦ stagnation
Stagnation der Übernachtungszahlen, f
♦ little movement in the number of nights spent
♦ little movement in the number of overnights stays
stagnieren
♦ stagnate
♦ be stagnant
♦ remain stagnant
stagnierend, adj
♦ stagnant, adj
Stahlrohrmöbel, n pl
♦ tubular steel furniture sg
♦ tubular furniture sg
Stahlrohrstuhl, m
♦ tubular steel chair
Stahlrohrtisch, m
♦ tubular steel table
Stahltank, m
♦ steel tank
Stall, m
♦ stable
Stallrestaurant, n
♦ stable restaurant
Stallungen umwandeln in Zimmer
♦ convert mews to rooms

Stallungshaus, n
(war früher Stallung)
♦ mews house
Stammcafé, n
♦ one's usual café BE
♦ one's usual cafe AE
Stammdatei, f
Hauptkartei, f
♦ master file
stammen aus dem letzten Jahrhundert
aus dem letzten Jahrhundert stammen
♦ date back to the last century
Stammessen, n
Table d'hôte-Essen, n
♦ table d'hôte meal
♦ meal with fixed menu
♦ residents' menu
Stammgast, m
♦ regular guest
♦ regular client
♦ regular coll
♦ patron
♦ habitué FR m
Stammgästeanteil m
♦ ratio of regular guests
♦ proportion of regular guests
Stammgästedatei f
♦ card index of regular guests
Stammgast sein in einem Hotel
♦ patronise a hotel
♦ patronize a hotel
Stammgericht n
♦ regular dish
♦ standard dish
Stammhaus, n (Hotel)
→ Stammhotel
Stammhotel n
♦ one's usual hotel
Stammkarte, f (Speisekarte)
→ Stammspeisekarte
Stammkneipe, f
Stammlokal, n
♦ one's usual bar AE
♦ local (pub) BE
♦ one's usual pub BE
♦ hangout AE sl
♦ hang-out BE sl
Stammkunde, m
♦ regular customer
♦ regular client
♦ regular coll
♦ patron
♦ habitué FR m
Stammkundenpreis, m
♦ regular customers' price
♦ regular customers' rate
♦ regular clients' price
♦ regular clients' rate
Stammkundenrabatt, m
♦ discount for regular customers
♦ regular clients' discount
Stammkundschaft, f
Stammklientel, f
Gästestamm, m
Kundenstamm, m
♦ regular clientele
♦ regular customers pl
♦ regular guests pl
Stammkundschaft aufbauen
→ Kundenstamm aufbauen

Stammlokal, n (Kneipe)
Stammkneipe, f
♦ local pub BE
♦ local BE coll
♦ hangout AE sl
♦ hang-out BE sl
Stammlokal, n (Restaurant)
♦ one's usual restaurant
Stammpersonal, n
♦ basic staff
♦ basic personnel
♦ permanent staff
♦ permanent personnel
Stammplatz, m (Sitzplatz)
♦ one's usual seat
♦ one's usual place
♦ one's habitual seat
♦ one's habitual place
Stammplatz am Tisch, m
♦ habitual place at the table
Stammpublikum, n
→ Stammkundschaft
Stammtisch, m (Personen)
♦ round of regulars
♦ regulars pl
Stammtisch, m (Tisch)
♦ regulars' table
♦ table reserved for regulars
♦ table for regular guests
Stammtischbruder, m
Zechkumpan, m
♦ drinking mate fam
♦ drinking companion
Stammtischrunde, f
♦ group of regular guests
♦ group of regulars coll
♦ round of regulars
Stammtischveranstaltung, f
♦ regular guests' function
Stammwirtschaft, f
Stammkneipe, f
♦ hangout AE sl
♦ hang-out BE sl
Stampe, f sl
(schlechtes Restaurant)
♦ beanery AE sl
Stand, m (Messe)
♦ stand
Stand, m (Taxi)
♦ stand
Stand, m (Verkauf)
Verkaufsstand, m
♦ stand
♦ stall BE
♦ booth AE
Standabbau, m
♦ dismantling a stand
Stand abbauen (Messe)
♦ dismantle a stand
Stand abbauen (Verkauf)
♦ dismantle a stall
♦ dismantle a stand
♦ dismantle a booth
Standangaben, f pl
♦ stand details pl
Standard, m
♦ standard
Standard anheben
Standard heben
♦ raise the standard

Standardanzahlung, f
Standardkaution, f
♦ standard deposit
Standardappartement n
♦ standard apartment
Standardarrangement n
Standardvereinbarung f
♦ standard arrangement
Standardausrüstung, f
(Sport)
♦ standard gear
Standardausstattung, f
Standardausrüstung, f
♦ standard facilities pl
♦ standard equipment
Standardbadezimmer, n
♦ standard bathroom
Standardbett n
♦ standard bed
Standardchalet, n
♦ standard chalet
Standarddekoration, f
♦ standard decoration
Standarddoppelzimmer n
♦ standard double room
Standard einhalten
♦ adhere to a standard
Standardeinrichtung, f
♦ standard facility
Standardeinzelzimmer n
♦ standard single room
Standard erfüllen
♦ meet a standard
Standardermäßigung f
♦ standard reduction
Standardessen, n (generell)
♦ standard food
Standardessen, n (Mahlzeit)
Standardmahlzeit, f
♦ standard meal
Standardfahrpreis, m
♦ standard fare
Standard festsetzen
Standard festlegen
♦ set a standard
♦ set (the) standards
♦ set down standards
Standardfestzelt, n
♦ standard marquee
Standardfreizeiteinrichtung, f
♦ standard leisure facility
Standardfrühstück, n
Einheitsfrühstück, n
♦ standard breakfast
Standardgarage, f
♦ standard garage
Standardgästezimmer, n
Standardgastzimmer, n
♦ standard guest room AE
♦ standard guest-room BE
Standardgebühr f
♦ standard charge
♦ standard fee
Standardgericht, n
Einheitsgericht, n
♦ standard dish
Standardgutschein, m
♦ standard voucher
Standardhotel, n
♦ standard hotel

Standardhotelarrangement

Standardhotelarrangement, n
  Standardhotelvereinbarung, f
  ♦ standard hotel arrangement
Standardhoteltarif, m
  ♦ standard hotel tariff
  ♦ standard hotel rates *pl*
  ♦ standard hotel rate
  ♦ standard hotel terms *pl*
standardisieren etw
  ♦ standardise s.th.
  ♦ standardize s.th.
standardisiert, adj
  ♦ standardised, adj
  ♦ standardized, adj
standardisierte Möbel, n pl
  ♦ standardised furniture *sg*
  ♦ standardized furniture *sg*
standardisierter Speiseartikel, m
  ♦ standardised food item
  ♦ standardized menu item
standardisiertes Rezept, n
  standardisierte Rezeptur, f
  ♦ standardised recipe
  ♦ standardized recipe
Standardisierung, f
  ♦ standardisation
  ♦ standardization
Standardkarte, f (Speisekarte)
  → Standardspeisekarte
Standardklasse, f
  ♦ standard class
Standardkost, f
  ♦ standard fare
  ♦ standard food
Standardküche, f (Speisen)
  ♦ standard cooking
  ♦ standard cuisine
Standardleistung, f
  → Standardservice
Standardmenü, n
  Einheitsmenü, n
  ♦ standard menu
Standardmodell, n
  ♦ standard model
Standardmotel, n
  ♦ standard motel
Standardportion, f
  ♦ standard portion
Standardportionsgröße, f
  ♦ standard portion size
Standardportionsgröße festlegen
  ♦ establish a standard portion size
Standardportionswert, m
  ♦ standard portion value
Standardpreis, m
  Normalpreis, m
  ♦ standard price
  ♦ standard rate
Standardpreise berechnen
  Normaltarif berechnen
  ♦ charge standard prices
  ♦ charge standard rates
Standardprovision, f
  ♦ standard commission
Standardqualität, f
  ♦ standard quality
Standardreise, f
  ♦ standard tour
  ♦ standard trip
  ♦ standard journey

Standardreiseverlauf, m
  ♦ standard itinerary
Standardrestaurant, n
  ♦ standard restaurant
Standardrezept, n
  Standardrezeptur f
  ♦ standard recipe
Standardrückfahrpreis, m
  ♦ standard return fare
Standardsaison f
  ♦ standard season
Standardschlafzimmer, n
  ♦ standard bedroom
Standardschlafzimmergröße, f
  ♦ standard bedroom size
Standard senken
  Standard absenken
  ♦ lower the standard
Standardservice m
  Standardleistung f
  ♦ standard service
Standardspeisekarte f
  Standardkarte f
  ♦ standard menu
Standardsuite, f
  ♦ standard suite
Standardtageskarte, f (Speisekarte)
  ♦ standard daily menu
Standardtarif, m
  ♦ standard tariff
  ♦ standard rates *pl*
  ♦ standard rate
  ♦ standard terms *pl*
Standardtyp, m
  ♦ standard type
  ♦ standard model
Standardunterbringung, f
  → Standardunterkunft
Standardunterkunft, f
  Standardunterbringung, f
  ♦ standard accommodation
  ♦ standard lodging *AE*
Standardurlaub, m
  Standardferien, pl
  ♦ standard vacation *AE*
  ♦ standard holiday *BE*
Standardurlaubsprogramm, n
  Standardferienprogramm, n
  ♦ standard vacation program *AE*
  ♦ standard holiday programme *BE*
Standardvilla, f
  ♦ standard villa
Standardvoltzahl f
  ♦ standard voltage
Standardwerbebroschüre, f
  Standardwerbeprospekt, m
  ♦ standard advertising brochure
Standardwohnung, f
  ♦ standard flat *BE*
  ♦ standard apartment *AE*
Standardwohnzimmer, n
  ♦ standard living room *AE*
  ♦ standard living-room *BE*
  ♦ standard sitting room *AE*
  ♦ standard sitting-room *BE*
Standardzimmer, n
  Normalzimmer, n
  ♦ standard room
Standardzimmergröße, f
  ♦ standard room size

Standardzimmerpreis, m
  Rackrate, f
  Tarifpreis, m
  ♦ standard room rate
  ♦ rack rate
Standardzubereitungszeit, f
  ♦ standard preparation time
Standardzuschlag m
  ♦ standard supplement
Standardzweibettzimmer, n (generell)
  ♦ standard two-bedded room
Standardzweibettzimmer, n (zwei Einzelbetten)
  ♦ standard twin-bedded room
  ♦ standard twin room
Standascher, m
  ♦ pedestal ashtray
Standaufbau, m
  Standbau, m
  ♦ stand erection
  ♦ erection of a stand
  ♦ erecting a stand
  ♦ stand construction
  ♦ construction of a stand
Stand auf einer Ausstellung, m
  ♦ stand at an exhibition
  ♦ stand at an exhibit *AE*
Stand auf einer Messe, m
  ♦ stand at a trade fair
  ♦ stand at a fair
Stand aufschlagen
  ♦ put up a stand
  ♦ put up a stall
  ♦ set up a booth
  ♦ set up a stall
Stand belegen
  ♦ occupy a stand
  ♦ occupy a stall
Stand besuchen
  ♦ visit a stand
  ♦ visit a stall
Stand betreiben (Messe)
  ♦ operate a stand
  ♦ run a stand
Stand betreiben (Verkauf)
  ♦ operate a stall
  ♦ operate a stand
  ♦ run a stand
  ♦ run a stall
Stand bezahlen
  Stand zahlen
  ♦ pay for a stand
  ♦ pay for a stall
Standbezug, m
  ♦ occupation of the stand
  ♦ occupation of a stall
  ♦ occupying a stand
  ♦ occupying a stall
Stand buchen
  Stand bestellen
  ♦ book a stand
  ♦ book a stall
Stand-by, n
  ♦ standby *AE*
  ♦ stand-by *BE*
Stand-by-Flug, m
  ♦ standby flight *AE*
  ♦ stand-by flight *BE*
Stand-by-Passagier, m
  Stand-by-Fluggast, m
  ♦ standby passenger *AE*
  ♦ stand-by passenger *BE*

Stand-by-Preis, m
Stand-by-Fahrpreis, m
♦ **standby fare** AE
♦ **stand-by fare** BE
Stand-by reisen
♦ **travel standby** AE
♦ travel stand-by BE
♦ travel on a standby basis AE
♦ travel on a stand-by basis BE
Stand-by-Ticket, n
♦ **standby ticket** AE
♦ stand-by ticket BE
Standcaravan, m
stationärer Caravan, m
Standwohnwagen, m
stationärer Wohnwagen, m
Standwagen, m
♦ **sited caravan** BE
♦ static caravan BE
♦ sited trailer AE
♦ static trailer AE
Standeinheit, f
♦ **stand unit**
Stand entfernen (Messe)
♦ **remove a stand**
Ständer, m
Stativ, n
♦ **stand**
Stand errichten
Stand aufbauen
♦ **erect a stand**
♦ put up a stand
♦ erect a stall
♦ put up a stall
Standfläche, f
♦ **stand area**
♦ area of a stand
♦ stand space
♦ stallage BE
Standfläche mieten
♦ **rent stand space**
♦ hire stand space BE
Standflächenkosten, pl
♦ **stand space cost**
Standfläche vermieten
♦ **rent (out) stand space**
♦ hire out stand space BE
♦ let stand space BE
Stand frequentieren
♦ **frequent a stand**
♦ frequent a stall
Stand führen
Stand leiten
♦ **run a stand**
♦ run a stall
Stand für drei Taxis, m
♦ **stand for three taxis**
Standgebühr, f
(für einen Stand)
Standmiete, f
♦ **pickage**
♦ piccage
Standgeld, n
Marktgeld, n
♦ **stallage** BE
Stand gestalten
♦ **design a stand**
♦ design a stall
Standgestalter, m
♦ **stand designer**

Standgestaltung, f
Standdesign, n
♦ **stand design**
♦ design of a stand
♦ designing a stand
♦ stall design
Standgröße, f
♦ **stand size**
♦ size of the stand
♦ stall size
♦ size of a stall
Standgrundmietgebühr, f
♦ **basic stand rental fee** AE
♦ basic stand rental charge AE
♦ basic stand rental AE
♦ basic stand hire charge BE
♦ basic stand hiring charge BE
Standgrundriß, m
Standplan, m
Standanordnung, f
♦ **stand layout**
♦ stall layout
Stand haben
♦ **have a stand**
♦ have a stall
Standhelfer, m
♦ **stand assistant**
ständiger Besucher, m
♦ **regular visitor**
ständiger Gast, m
Stammgast, m
♦ **patron**
♦ regular patron
♦ habitué FR
♦ regular guest
♦ regular
ständiger Reisender, m
♦ **perpetual traveller**
♦ perpetual traveler AE
ständiger Wohnsitz, m
♦ **permanent address**
ständig gebucht, adj
ständig belegt, adj
♦ **continuously booked, adj**
ständig geöffnet, adj
→ durchgehend geöffnet
ständig steigende Besucherzahl, f
♦ **continuously rising number of visitors**
ständig wechselnde Ausstellungen, f pl
♦ **continually changing exhibitions** pl
ständig wechselnde Speisekarte, f
♦ **constantly changing menu**
Stand in einer Fachausstellung, m
♦ **stand in a trade exhibition**
Standinhaber, m
♦ **stand-holder**
♦ stall-holder
♦ holder of a stand
♦ holder of a stall
Stand ist besetzt mit zwei Personen
♦ **stand is manned by two persons**
♦ stall is manned by two persons
Stand ist schlecht plaziert
♦ **stand is badly positioned**
♦ stand is badly sited
♦ stand is badly situated
♦ stall is badly positioned
♦ stall is badly sited
Standmaße, n pl
Maße eines Stands, n pl

♦ **stand dimensions** pl
♦ dimensions of a stand pl
Standmiete, f
♦ **stand rental** AE
♦ stand hire BE
♦ pickage
♦ piccage
Stand mieten
♦ **rent a stand**
♦ hire a stand BE
♦ hire a stall BE
Standmietgebühr pro Quadratmeter, f
Standmietgebühr pro qm, f
♦ **stand rental fee per square meter** AE
♦ stand rental charge per square meter AE
♦ stand rental per square meter AE
♦ stand hire charge per square metre BE
♦ stand hiring charge per square metre BE
Stand nehmen
♦ **take a stand**
♦ take a stall
Standort, m
♦ **location**
Standortanforderung, f
Anforderung an den Standort, f
♦ **locational requirement**
Standort auswählen
Standort wählen
♦ **select a location**
♦ choose a location
Standort ist außergewöhnlich
♦ **location is exceptional**
Standort ist schlecht
♦ **location is poor**
Standortnachteil m
♦ **locational disadvantage**
Standortplanung, f
♦ **location planning**
Standortproblem n
♦ **locational problem**
♦ problem concerning the location
Standortreiseleiter, m
Reiseleiter am Aufenthaltsort, m
♦ **local tour guide**
♦ local guide
Standortuntersuchung, f
♦ **location study**
Standortverlegung, f
Umzug, m
♦ **relocation**
Standortvorteil, m
♦ **locational advantage**
♦ location advantage AE
Standortwahl, f
Wahl des Standorts, f
♦ **choice of (a) location**
♦ selection of (a) location
Standort wählen
Standort auswählen
♦ **choose a location**
♦ select a location
Standort wechseln
♦ **change locations**
Standpersonal, n
♦ **stand staff**
♦ stand personnel
Standpersonalkosten, pl
♦ **stand staff costs** pl
♦ stand personnel costs pl
Standplan, m
Standgrundriß, m

Standplatz

- ◆ layout of a stand
- ◆ stand layout
- ◆ layout of a stall
- ◆ stall layout

Standplatz, m (Messe)
Standplazierung, f
- ◆ **stand location**
- ◆ location of a stand

Standplatz, m (Stellplatz)
→ Stellplatz

Standquartier, n
→ Quartierort

Standreinigung, f
- ◆ **stand cleaning**
- ◆ cleaning (of) a stand

Stand reservieren
- ◆ **reserve a stand**
- ◆ reserve a stall

Standseilbahn, f
- ◆ **funicular railway** BE
- ◆ funicular
- ◆ cable railway BE

Stand stornieren
- ◆ **cancel a stand**
- ◆ cancel a stall

Standsystem, n (Messe)
- ◆ **stand system**

Standtyp, m
Standart, f
- ◆ **stand type**
- ◆ type of stand
- ◆ stall type
- ◆ type of stall

Standvergabe, f
Standzuteilung, f
- ◆ **stand allocation**
- ◆ allocation of a stand
- ◆ allocation of stands
- ◆ stall allocation
- ◆ allocating a stand

Stand vergeben an jn
Stand zuteilen jm
- ◆ **allocate a stand to s.o.**
- ◆ allocate a stall to s.o.

Stand vermieten
- ◆ **rent (out) a stand**
- ◆ hire out a stand BE
- ◆ let a stand BE
- ◆ hire out a stall BE

Stand von 3 x 3 m, m
- ◆ **stand of 3 x 3 m**
- ◆ 3 x 3 m stand
- ◆ stall of 3 x 3 m
- ◆ 3 x 3 m stall

Standwagen, m
→ Standwohnwagen

Standwand, f
- ◆ **stand partition**

Standzahl, f
Zahl der Stände, f
- ◆ **number of stands**
- ◆ number of stalls BE

Stangenbohne, f
- ◆ **runner bean**

Stangenzelt, n
- ◆ **pole tent**

Stangenzimt, m
- ◆ **cinnamon stick**

stapelbar, adj
- ◆ **stackable, adj**

stapelbarer Stuhl, m
- ◆ **stackable chair**

Star, m
- ◆ **star**

Starattraktion, f
- ◆ **star attraction**

Starbesetzung, f
- ◆ **star cast**
- ◆ all-star cast

Stargast, m
→ Gaststar

stark alkoholisch, adj
- ◆ **strongly alcoholic, adj**

stark alkoholisches Getränk, n
- ◆ **strongly alcoholic drink**
- ◆ strongly alcoholic beverage

stark befahren, adj (Straße)
- ◆ **heavily travelled, adj**
- ◆ heavily traveled, adj AE

stark befahrene Strecke, f
- ◆ **heavily travelled route**
- ◆ heavily traveled route AE

stark bereist, adj (Gebiet)
- ◆ **heavily travelled, adj**
- ◆ heavily traveled, adj AE

stark bereistes Gebiet, n
- ◆ **heavily travelled area**
- ◆ heavily traveled area AE

stark besucht, adj
stark frequentiert, adj
- ◆ **much-frequented, adj**
- ◆ having a lot of visitors

stark besuchter Ferienort, m
- ◆ **much-frequented resort**

stark besuchtes Hotel, n
- ◆ **much-frequented hotel**

stark betrunken, adj
- ◆ **very drunk, adj**

Starkbier, n (Ale)
- ◆ **strong ale**

Starkbier, n (generell)
- ◆ **stout**
- ◆ strong beer

starke Auslastung, f
→ hohe Auslastung

starke Beteiligung, f
große Beteiligung, f
- ◆ **large attendance**
- ◆ large number of persons attending

starke Ermäßigung, f
- ◆ **great reduction**
- ◆ big cut coll

Stärkemehl, n
(bes. aus Mais oder Reis)
- ◆ **cornflour** AE
- ◆ cornstarch AE

starke Nachfrage, f
- ◆ **heavy demand**
- ◆ great demand

stärken sich mit etw
(Essen, Trinken)
- ◆ **fortify oneself with s.th.**

starker Appetit, m
- ◆ **keen appetite**

starker Esser, m
- ◆ **big eater**
- ◆ gourmand

starker Kaffee, m
- ◆ **strong coffee**

starker Kaffeetrinker, m
- ◆ **coffee addict**

stark ermäßigt, adj
stark reduziert, adj
- ◆ **greatly reduced, adj**
- ◆ much reduced, adj

stark ermäßigter Preis, m
stark herabgesetzter Preis, m
stark reduzierter Preis, m
- ◆ **greatly reduced price**
- ◆ much reduced price
- ◆ greatly reduced rate
- ◆ much reduced rate

starker Raucher, m
- ◆ **heavy smoker**

starker Trinker, m
- ◆ **hard drinker** AE
- ◆ heavy drinker

starker Trinker sein
- ◆ **be a heavy drinker**
- ◆ be a hard drinker AE
- ◆ drink deep

starker Verkehr, m
- ◆ **heavy traffic**

Stärke sein
- ◆ **be a strong point**

starkes Getränk, n
- ◆ **hard drink** AE
- ◆ strong drink

stark frequentiert, adj
→ stark besucht

stark gebucht, adj
- ◆ **heavily booked, adj**

stark gebuchter Zeitraum, m
stark gebuchte Zeit, f
- ◆ **heavily booked period**

stark gebuchtes Hotel, n
- ◆ **heavily booked hotel**

stark gebucht sein
- ◆ **be heavily booked**

stark gesalzen, adj
- ◆ **very salty, adj**

stark gewürzt, adj
- ◆ **strongly seasoned, adj**
- ◆ highly seasoned, adj

Starkoch, m
Starküchenchef, m
- ◆ **star chef**
- ◆ star cook

stark reduziert, adj
→ stark ermäßigt

stark unterbeansprucht, adj
(Kapazität)
- ◆ **greatly underutilised, adj**
- ◆ greatly underutilized, adj
- ◆ greatly underused, adj

stark unterbeansprucht sein
(Kapazität)
- ◆ **be greatly underutilised**
- ◆ be greatly underutilized
- ◆ be greatly underused

stark verbesserte Unterkunft, f
- ◆ **much improved accommodation**

Starnberger See m
- ◆ **Starnbergersee**

Starnummer, f
Starauftritt, m
- ◆ **star turn**

Starprogramm, n
- ◆ **program featuring stars** AE
- ◆ programme featuring stars BE

Start, m (Flugzeug)
Abflug, m

♦ takeoff *AE*
♦ take-off *BE*
Start, m (generell, Sport)
♦ start
Start abbrechen (Flugzeug)
♦ abort the takeoff *AE*
♦ abort the take-off *BE*
Startbahn, f (Flughafen)
♦ takeoff runway *AE*
♦ take-off runway *BE*
startbereit, adj (Flugzeug)
startklar, adj
♦ ready to take off, adj
♦ ready for takeoff, adj *AE*
♦ ready for take-off, adj *BE*
startbereit, adj (generell)
♦ ready to go, adj
START-Buchung f
(mit dem START-System)
♦ START booking
♦ booking by START
START-Computer, m
♦ START computer
starten in den Urlaub
→ aufbrechen in den Urlaub
starten von X (Flugzeug)
♦ take off from X
Starterlaubnis, f (Flugzeug)
♦ takeoff permission *AE*
♦ take-off permission *BE*
Startgebühr, f (Flugzeug)
♦ takeoff fee *AE*
♦ takeoff charge *AE*
♦ take-off fee *BE*
♦ take-off charge *BE*
startklar, adj (Flugzeug)
♦ ready for takeoff, adj *AE*
♦ ready for take-off, adj *BE*
Startslot, m
♦ takeoff slot *AE*
♦ take-off slot *BE*
Start und Ziel (Sport)
Start (m) und Ziel (n)
♦ start and finish
Startzeit, f (Flugzeug)
♦ take-off time
Station, f (Restaurant, Hotel)
Revier, n
♦ station
♦ section
Station, f (Zug)
Bahnhof, m
♦ station
stationär, adj
♦ static, adj
♦ sited, adj
stationär behandelter Patient, m
♦ in-patient
stationäre Behandlung, f
♦ in-patient treatment
stationärer Caravan, m
stationärer Wohnwagen, m
Standcaravan, m
Standwohnwagen, m
♦ sited trailer *AE*
♦ sited caravan *BE*
♦ static trailer *AE*
♦ static caravan *BE*
stationärer Wohnwagen, m
stationärer Caravan, m
Standwohnwagen, m

Standcaravan, m
♦ static trailer *AE*
♦ static caravan *BE*
stationäres Zelt, n
Standzelt, n
♦ static tent
stationiert sein *mil*
♦ be stationed *mil*
Station machen
Reise unterbrechen
♦ make a halt
♦ take up station
♦ break one's journey
♦ stop over
Station machen für die Nacht
♦ stop for the night
Station machen in einem Hotel
→ absteigen in einem Hotel
Station machen in X
Reise unterbrechen in X
♦ make a halt at/in X
♦ break one's journey at/in X
♦ stop over at/in X
Stationskellner, m
Revierkellner, m
Chef de rang, m *FR*
♦ station waiter
♦ section waiter
♦ chef de rang *FR*
Stationsoberkellner, m
Revieroberkellner, m
Maître d'hôtel de carré, m *FR*
♦ station headwaiter
♦ section headwaiter
♦ maître d'hôtel de carré *FR*
Statistik, f
♦ statistics *pl*
Statistik auswerten
♦ interpret statistics
statistische Angabe, f
♦ statistical information
♦ statistic
statistische Angaben zu etw, f pl
♦ statistical information on s.th.
♦ statistical data on s.th.
Stativ, n (dreibeinig)
dreibeiniges Stativ, n
♦ tripod
Stativ, n (generell)
Staffelei, f
♦ easel
Stativkamera, f
Atelierkamera, f
♦ stand camera
Stätte, f
Ort, m
Platz, m
♦ site
stattfinden
♦ take place
♦ be
stattfinden gleichzeitig mit etw
stattfinden parallel zu etw
♦ run concurrently with s.th.
stattfinden unter der Schirmherrschaft von jm
♦ take place under the auspices of s.o.
stattfinden vom 1. bis 5. Oktober
♦ take place from 1 to 5 October
♦ take place from 1 until 5 October
Statue, f
♦ statue

Statue enthüllen
♦ unveil a statue
Statue errichten (für jn)
♦ erect a statue (to s.o.)
status, m
♦ status
Statusanfrage, f
♦ status inquiry
♦ status enquiry
Statusanfrage beantworten
♦ answer a status inquiry
♦ answer a status enquiry
Status melden
(eines Zimmers)
♦ notify the status
Statussymbol, n
♦ status symbol
Stau, m
Verstopfung, f
Stauung, f *ÖST*
♦ jam
♦ congestion
Staub, m
♦ dust
Stauballergie, f
♦ dust allergy
staubiges Zimmer, n
♦ dusty room
Staubmilbe, f
♦ dust mite
staubsaugen (etw)
♦ vacuum (s.th.) *AE*
♦ vacuum-clean (s.th.) *AE*
♦ hoover *BE*
Staubsauger, m
♦ vacuum cleaner
♦ hoover *BE*
Staubtuch, n
♦ duster
♦ dustcloth
Staubwedel, m
♦ feather duster
♦ duster
Staubzucker, m
♦ powder sugar *AE*
♦ icing sugar *BE*
Staudamm, m
♦ dam
♦ barrage
Stauferdynastie, f
♦ Staufer dynasty
Stauferkaiser, m
♦ Staufer emperor
Stauferkönig, m
♦ Staufer king
Stauferzeit, f
♦ Staufer times *pl*
♦ Staufer period
Stauraum, m
→ Lagerraum
Stausee, m
♦ reservoir
♦ artificial lake
♦ dam
Steak, n
♦ steak
Steakbar, f
♦ steak bar
Steakgericht, n
♦ steak dish

Steakhaus

Steakhaus, n
- steak house

Steakrestaurant n
- steak restaurant

Steak vom Holzkohlengrill, n
- charcoal-grilled steak

Steakwürfel, m
- steak cube

Steckdose, f
- outlet AE
- socket BE
- point BE

Steckdose für Elektrorasierer, f
- electric shaver point
- shaver point
- shaving outlet AE
- razor point
- electric razor point

steckenbleiben im Hals
- stick in one's throat

steckenbleiben in einem Verkehrsstau
festsitzen in einem Verkehrsstau
- get stuck in a traffic jam coll
- be stuck in a traffic jam
- be stuck in a traffic congestion

steckenbleiben mit dem Fahrstuhl
- be stuck in an elevator AE
- be stuck in a lift BE

Steckenpferd, n
- hobbyhorse AE
- hobby-horse BE

Stecker, m
- plug

Steckschloß, n
- mortice lock

Steelband, f
- steel band

Steeplechase, f (Pferdesport)
(ursprünglich von Kirchturm zu Kirchturm)
Hindernisrennen, n
Jagdrennen, n
- steeplechase

Steeplechase-Veranstaltung, f (Pferdesport)
- steeplechase meeting

Stegreifrede, f
- impromptu speech

Stegreifrede halten
- give an impromptu speech

Stehausschank, m
→ Stehbar

Stehbar, f
Stehausschank, m
- stand-up bar

Stehbierhalle f
- stand-up beer hall

Stehbüfett, n
- stand-up buffet
- fork buffet

Stehcafé, n
- stand-up cafe AE
- stand-up café BE

Stehcafeteria, f
- stand-up cafeteria

Stehempfang, m
- stand-up reception
- standing reception
- cocktail reception

stehen auf dem Speiseplan
- be included in the menu
- be on the menu

stehen auf dem Speisezettel
→ stehen auf dem Speiseplan

stehen auf der Speisekarte
- be on the menu

stehenbleiben (Essen)
- be left untouched
- be left

stehend applaudieren jm
- give s.o. a standing ovation

stehend Applaus erhalten
stehend Applaus bekommen
- be given a standing ovation
- get a standing ovation

stehenlassen etw
zurücklassen etw
vergessen etw
liegenlassen etw
- leave s.th. behind

Stehessen, n (generell)
Essen im Stehen, n
- stand-up meal

Stehessen, n (mittags)
Mittagessen im Stehen, n
- stand-up lunch
- stand-up luncheon
- fork lunch

Stehimbiß, m (Essen)
- stand-up snack

Stehimbiß, m (Lokal)
- stand-up snack bar AE
- stand-up snack-bar BE

Stehkneipe, f coll
Stehbar, f
- stand-up pub BE coll
- stand-up bar AE

Stehkonvent, m humor
- standing conference
- standing meeting

Stehlampe, f
- floor lamp AE
- standard lamp BE

Stehleiter, f
- step-ladder

stehlen etw jm
- steal s.th. from s.o.
- pilfer s.th. from s.o.

Stehplatz, m (Bus)
- space to stand

Stehplatz, m (Theater)
- standing room

Stehplatz für 123 Personen
- standing room for 123 persons

Stehplatzkarte, f (Theater)
Stehkarte, f
- standing-room ticket
- standing ticket

Stehpult, n
- standing desk
- high desk

Stehservice, m
Bedienung im Stehen, f
- stand-up service

Stehtheke, f
Stehtresen, m
- stand-up counter

Stehtisch, m
- stand-up table

Stehtoilette, f
französische Toilette, f
sitzlose Toilette, f
- seatless toilet
- French-style toilet
- squatter BE coll

Steiermark f
(Region)
- Styria

steife Atmosphäre, f
formelle Atmosphäre f
- formal atmosphere

steigende Besucherzahl, f
zunehmende Besucherzahl, f
- increasing number of visitors

steigende Betriebskosten, pl
- increasing operating costs pl
- rising operating costs pl

steigende Kosten, pl
- increasing costs pl
- rising costs pl

Steigerung der Gesamtauslastungszahl, f
Steigerung der Gesamtbelegungszahl, f
- increase in the total occupancy figure

Steigerung des allgemeinen Wohlbefindens, f
- improvement in one's general well-being

Steigerwald, m
(Region)
- Steigerwald, the

steil abfallend, adj
- steeply sloping, adj
- steeply shelving, adj

steil abfallender Strand, m
- steeply sloping beach
- steeply shelving beach

steiler Fels, m
- steep rock

steiler Pfad, m
- steep path

Steilhang, m
steiler Hang, m
- steep slope

Steiltal, n
steiles Tal, n
- steep valley

Steilufer, n (Fluß)
steiles Ufer, n (Fluß)
- steep bank

Steilwandzelt, n
- high-wall tent
- wall tent
- frame tent

Steinbeißer, m
- groundling

Stein Bier, m
Krug Bier, m
Seidel Bier, m
- stein of beer AE
- mug of beer

Steinboden, m
- stone floor

Steinbrücke, f
- stone bridge

Steinbutt, m
- turbot

Steindenkmal, n
- stone monument

Steindorf, n
- stone village

Stein entfernen gastr
entsteinen gastr
- remove the stone gastr

Steinfigur, f
- stone figure

Steingarten, m
♦ rock garden
Steingebäude, n
  Steinbau, m
♦ stone building
Steingut, n (gelbfarbig)
♦ queenware
Steingut, n (generell)
♦ stoneware
♦ earthenware
Steinhäger, m regist
♦ Steinhaeger regist
Steinhaus, n
♦ stone house
steiniger Strand, m
  Steinstrand, m
♦ stony beach AE
♦ stoney beach AE rare
Steinkreis, m
♦ stone circle
Steinkrug, m
♦ stone pitcher
Steinlandhaus, n
♦ stone cottage
Steinofen, m
♦ stone oven
Steinpilz, m
♦ cepe
♦ cep
♦ boletus scient
Steinsarg, m
♦ stone coffin
Steinsitz, m
  Steinsitzplatz, m
  Steinplatz, m
♦ stone seat
Steinstatue, f
♦ stone statue
Steinstrand, m
  steiniger Strand, m
♦ stone beach AE
♦ stony beach BE
♦ stoney beach AE rare
Steintisch, m
♦ stone table
Steinwand, f
  Steinmauer, f
♦ stone wall
Steinzeit, f
♦ Stone Age, the
Steinzeitsiedlung, f
♦ Stone Age settlement
Steirer, m
♦ Styrian
Steirerin, f
♦ Styrian girl
♦ Styrian woman
♦ Styrian
steirisch, adj
♦ Styrian, adj
Stelldichein, n
→ Rendezvous
stellen etw
  zur Verfügung stellen etw
  abgeben etw
♦ furnish s.th.
♦ provide s.th.
Stellplatz, m (Camping)
  (Stellfläche für ein Fahrzeug, ein Zelt etc.)
  Stellfläche, f
  Parzelle, f

♦ pitch
♦ site AE
Stellplatz, m (Parkplatz)
→ Parkplatz
Stellplatzart, f
  (Camping)
  Stellplatztyp, m
♦ pitch type
♦ type of pitch
Stellplatz auswählen
  (Camping)
  Stellplatz wählen
♦ select a pitch
♦ choose a pitch
Stellplatz buchen
  (Camping)
♦ book a pitch
Stellplatzbuchung, f
  (Camping)
♦ pitch booking
♦ booking (of) a pitch
Stellplatzbuchungsgebühr, f
  (Camping)
♦ pitch booking fee
♦ pitch booking charge
Stellplätze nehmen Fläche von einem Hektar ein
  (Camping)
♦ pitches cover one hectare
Stellplätze sind eben
  (Camping)
♦ pitches are level
Stellplätze sind markiert durch Steine
  (Camping)
♦ pitches are marked by stones
Stellplätze sind markiert und numeriert
  (Camping)
♦ pitches are marked and numbered
Stellplätze sind numeriert
  (Camping)
♦ pitches are numbered
Stellplatzfläche, f
  (Camping)
♦ pitch area
♦ pitch space
Stellplatz freihalten für jn (Camping)
♦ keep a pitch for s.o.
Stellplatz für einen Reisewohnwagen, m
♦ pitch for a travel trailer AE
♦ pitch for a touring caravan BE
♦ touring pitch
Stellplatz für einen Wohnwagen, m
♦ pitch for a trailer AE
♦ pitch for a caravan BE
Stellplatz für ein Mobilheim, m
  Stellplatz für ein großes Wohnmobil, m
♦ pitch for a mobile home
Stellplatz für ein Reisemobil, m
  Stellplatz für ein Wohnmobil, m
♦ pitch for a motorhome AE
♦ pitch for a motor home BE
♦ pitch for a motor caravan BE
Stellplatz für ein Zelt, m
♦ pitch for a tent
Stellplatzgebühr, f (Camping)
♦ pitch fee
♦ pitch charge
Stellplatzgebühr beträgt DM 12 pro Person pro Tag
♦ pitch fee is DM 12 per person per day
Stellplatzgebühr erheben von DM 12 pro Einheit
♦ charge a pitch fee of DM 12 per unit

Stellplatzreservierung vornehmen

Stellplatzgröße, f
  (Camping)
♦ pitch size
♦ size of a pitch
Stellplatz ist belegt von jm
  (Camping)
♦ pitch is occupied by s.o.
Stellplatz ist frei
  (Camping)
♦ pitch is free
♦ pitch is vacant
Stellplatz ist unbesetzt
  (Camping)
♦ pitch is unoccupied
Stellplatz kann nicht im voraus gebucht werden
  (Camping)
  Stellplatz kann nicht vorgebucht werden
♦ pitch cannot be booked in advance
Stellplatzmiete, f (Camping)
♦ pitch rental
♦ pitch hire BE
♦ site rental AE
Stellplatzmiete, f (Parken)
  Parkplatzmiete, f
♦ parking lot rental AE
♦ car park hire BE
Stellplatz mieten (Camping)
♦ rent a pitch
♦ hire a pitch BE
Stellplatz mieten (für 1 Auto)
  Parkplatz mieten (für 1 Auto)
♦ hire a parking place BE
♦ rent a parking space
♦ rent a parking lot AE
♦ rent a parking place
♦ hire a parking space BE
Stellplatz mit Blick auf etw, m
  (Camping)
♦ pitch with a view of s.th.
Stellplatz mit Drainage, m
  (Camping)
♦ drained pitch
Stellplatzpreis, m
  (Camping)
  Preis pro Stellplatz, m
♦ price per pitch
♦ rate per pitch
Stellplatzpreis pro Übernachtung, m
  (Camping)
  Stellplatzpreis pro Nacht, m
♦ price per pitch per night
♦ rate per pitch per night
Stellplatz räumen
  (Camping)
  Stellplatz frei machen
♦ vacate a pitch
Stellplatz reservieren (Camping)
♦ reserve a pitch
Stellplatzreservierung, f (Camping)
♦ pitch reservation
♦ reservation of a pitch
♦ reserving a pitch
Stellplatzreservierungsgebühr, f
  (Camping)
♦ pitch reservation charge
♦ pitch reservation fee
Stellplatzreservierung vornehmen
  (Camping)
♦ make a pitch reservation

Stellplatz sichern sich

Stellplatz sichern sich
(Camping)
♦ secure a pitch
Stellplatz stornieren
(Camping)
Stellplatz abbestellen
♦ cancel a pitch
Stellplatzstornierung, f
(Camping)
Stellplatzabsage, f
♦ pitch cancellation
♦ pitch cancelation AE
♦ cancellation of a pitch
♦ cancelation of a pitch AE
Stellplatz von durchschnittlicher Größe, m
(Camping)
♦ pitch of average size
Stellplatz vorbuchen
(Camping)
♦ book a pitch in advance
♦ prebook a pitch
Stellplatz wählen
(Camping)
Stellplatz auswählen
♦ choose a pitch
♦ select a pitch
Stellplatzzahl, f
(Camping)
Zahl der Stellplätze, f
♦ number of pitches
Stellplatz zugeteilt bekommen
(Camping)
Stellplatz zugeteilt erhalten
♦ have a pitch allocated
Stellplatz zur Verfügung stellen (für 1 Auto)
Parkplatz zur Verfügung stellen (für 1 Auto)
♦ provide a parking space
♦ provide a parking place
Stellplatz zuteilen jm
(Camping)
Stellplatz zuweisen jm
♦ allocate a pitch to s.o. BE
♦ allocate a site to s.o. AE
stellvertretende Empfangsdame, f
stellvertretende Rezeptionistin, f
♦ deputy female receptionist
stellvertretende Generalgouvernante, f SCHW
stellvertretende Erste Hausdame, f
♦ deputy head housekeeper
♦ deputy executive housekeeper
stellvertretender Direktor, m
♦ deputy director
♦ deputy manager
♦ submanager
stellvertretender Empfangschef, m
stellvertretender Chef de réception, m SCHW
♦ deputy chief receptionist AE
♦ deputy head receptionist
♦ deputy reception manager
♦ deputy front-office manager AE
stellvertretender Empfangsherr, m
stellvertretender Rezeptionist, m
♦ deputy receptionist
stellvertretender Generaldirektor, m
♦ deputy general director
♦ deputy general manager
♦ deputy GM
stellvertretender geschäftsführender Direktor, m
♦ deputy managing director
stellvertretender Geschäftsführer, m
♦ deputy manager

stellvertretender Rezeptionist, m
→ stellvertretender Empfangsherr
stellvertretender Vorsitzender, m
♦ deputy chairman
stellvertretender Wirtschaftsdirektor, m
♦ deputy food and beverage manager
♦ deputy food & beverage manager
♦ deputy f&b manager
Stellvertreter, m
Stellvertreterin, f
♦ deputy
Stellvertreter des Küchenchefs, m
Souschef, m
♦ deputy chef
♦ sous-chef
Stellwand, f
bewegliche Stellwand, f
♦ display screen
Stempel, m
♦ stamp
Stempelkissen, n
♦ stamp pad
stempeln etw
abstempeln etw
♦ stamp s.th.
Stempelsteuer, f
(auf Urkunden)
Stempelgebühr, f
Stempelabgabe, f
♦ stamp duty
stempelsteuerfrei, adj
♦ exempt from stamp duty, adj
stempelsteuerpflichtig, adj
♦ liable to stamp duty, adj
♦ subject to stamp duty, adj
Stengel, m (Stiel)
♦ stalk
Stengel, m (Zweigchen)
→ Zweigchen
Stenograf, m
♦ stenographer AE
♦ shorthand typist BE
Stephansdom, der, m
♦ St. Stephen's (Cathedral) AE
♦ St Stephen's (Cathedral) BE
Steppdecke, f
♦ quilt
♦ comforter AE
Stepptanz, m
♦ tap dance AE
♦ tap dancing AE
♦ tap-dance BE
♦ tap-dancing BE
Stepptänzer, m
♦ tap dancer AE
♦ tap-dancer BE
sterben im Urlaub
im Urlaub sterben
♦ die on vacation AE
♦ die while on vacation AE
♦ die on holiday BE
♦ die while on holiday BE
sterbenslangweilig, adj
♦ deadly dull, adj
sterben vor Durst
→ verdursten
Sterbeurkunde, f
♦ death certificate
Stereoanlage, f
♦ stereo system

Stereoschallplatte, f
♦ stereo record
Stereoverstärkeranlage, f
♦ stereo amplifier system
Stern, m
♦ star
Stern bekommen
♦ get a star
Sternebewertung, f
Bewertung mit Sternen, f
♦ star rating
Sternebewertungssystem, n
♦ star-rating system
Sternekategorie, f
♦ star category
Sternekoch, m
♦ star-winning chef
♦ star-winning cook
Stern erhalten
♦ be awarded a star
Sternfahrt, f
Rallye, f
Autosternfahrt, f
♦ motor rally
♦ rallye AE
♦ rally
♦ car rally
sternhagelvoll, adj sl
♦ blind drunk, adj sl
sternhagelvoll sein sl
Vollrausch haben
♦ be blind drunk sl
Stern verdienen
♦ deserve a star
Stern vergeben an ein Hotel
♦ award a star to a hotel
Sternwarte, f
♦ observatory
stets zu Ihren Diensten
♦ at your service at all times
Steuer, f
♦ tax
Steuer auf alkoholische Getränke, f
Branntweinsteuer, f
♦ liquor excise AE
♦ liquor tax
♦ tax on liquors
Steuerbefreiung, f
♦ tax exemption
Steuerberater, m
♦ tax consultant
♦ tax adviser
Steuerberatungskosten, pl
♦ tax consultant's fee
Steuerbord, n
♦ starboard side
♦ starboard
Steuer erheben auf Weine und Spirituosen
♦ impose a tax on wines and spirits
steuerfrei, adj
♦ tax-free, adj
Steuerjahr, n
♦ fiscal year
Steuern zahlen
♦ pay tax
Steuerrad, n
♦ steering wheel AE
♦ steering-wheel BE
Steuersatz, m
♦ tax rate

Steuerzahler, m
 ♦ taxpayer
Steward, m
 ♦ steward
Steward, m (Flugzeug)
 Flugbegleiter, m
 ♦ air steward
Stewardeß, f (Flugzeug)
 ♦ air hostess
 ♦ hostess
 ♦ air stewardess
 ♦ stewardess
Stewardeß, f (Schiff und Flugzeug)
 ♦ stewardess
Stewarding n
 (Arbeitsbereich)
 ♦ stewarding
Stewardservice, m
 ♦ steward service
Stichprobe, f
 ♦ spot check
Stichprobe machen
 ♦ make a spot check
 ♦ spot-check
Stichtag, m
 → Frist
stickiges Zimmer, n
 muffiges Zimmer, n
 ♦ stuffy room
 ♦ musty room
Stiefeljunge, m
 Stiefelputzer, m
 ♦ bootboy
Stiefellecker, m
 ♦ bootlicker
Stiel, m (Glas)
 ♦ stem
Stierkampf, m
 ♦ bullfight
Stierkampfarena, f
 ♦ bullring
Stierkämpfer, m
 ♦ bullfighter
Stierkampffestival, n
 ♦ bullfight festival
Stierreiten, n
 ♦ bull riding
Stift, n
 ♦ protestant college
Stiftskirche, f
 ♦ Collegiate Church, the
Stil, m
 ♦ style
Stil der Zeit, m
 Zeitstil, m
 ♦ style of the period
Stileinrichtung, f
 ♦ period furnishings pl
Stilgebäude, n
 Gebäude im Stil der Zeit, n
 ♦ period building
Stilhaus, n
 → Haus im Stil der Zeit
Stilhotel, n
 → Hotel im Stil der Zeit
stille Jahreszeit, f
 ♦ quiet season
stiller Ort, m
 ♦ quiet spot
 ♦ quiet place

stiller Winkel, m
 ♦ quiet nook
stille Saison, f
 ♦ slack season
 ♦ quiet season
 ♦ slack period
stilles Mineralwasser, n
 ♦ still mineral water
stilles Örtchen, n humor
 Toilette, f
 ♦ smallest room humor
 ♦ lavatory euph
 ♦ john AE coll
 ♦ loo BE coll
Stillraum m
 (für stillende Mütter)
 ♦ nursing room
stillschweigende Verlängerung, f
 ♦ tacit extension
 ♦ tacit prolongation
Stilmöbel, n pl (echt)
 ♦ period furniture sg
 ♦ period furnishings pl
Stilmöbel, n pl (imitiert)
 ♦ reproduction furniture sg
 ♦ reproduction furnishings pl
Stilschlafzimmer, n
 ♦ period bedroom
Stilstuhl, m
 ♦ period chair
Stilsuite, f
 ♦ period suite
Stiltisch, m
 ♦ period table
Stiltonkäse, m
 Stilton, m
 ♦ Stilton cheese
 ♦ Stilton
stilvoll, adv
 gepflegt, adv
 ♦ in style, adv
stilvoll eingerichtet, adj
 ♦ furnished in style, adj
stilvoll möbliert, adj
 modisch möbliert, adj
 ♦ stylishly furnished, adj
stilvoll möbliertes Zimmer, n
 modisch möbliertes Zimmer, n
 ♦ stylishly furnished room
Stilzimmer, n
 ♦ period room
Stimmgabel, f
 ♦ tuning fork AE
 ♦ tuning-fork BE
Stimmung, f
 ♦ spirits pl
 ♦ mood
 ♦ atmosphere
Stimmung ist glänzend
 ♦ spirits are high
Stimmungsmusik, f
 ♦ mood music
stimmungsvoll, adj
 ♦ full of atmosphere, adj
 ♦ evocative, adj
stimmungsvolle Atmosphäre, f
 ♦ evocative atmosphere
stinkfein, adj sl
 ♦ dead posh, adj sl
 ♦ super-posh, adj sl

stinkfeines Hotel, n sl
 ♦ dead posh hotel sl
 ♦ super-posh hotel sl
Stipendium, n
 Zuschuß, m
 ♦ grant
Stipendium beantragen
 ♦ apply for a grant
Stippvisite, f
 Kurzbesuch, m
 ♦ flying visit
 ♦ short visit
 ♦ short call
Stippvisite machen
 ♦ make a flying visit
 ♦ make a short visit
 ♦ make a short call
Stippvisite machen bei jm
 Stippvisite abstatten jm
 ♦ pay s.o. a flying visit
 ♦ pop in on s.o.
 ♦ drop in on s.o.
 ♦ call in on s.o.
 ♦ pay a short call on s.o.
Stippvisite machen nach X
 ♦ go on a flying visit to X
Stocherkahn, m
 ♦ punt
Stocherkahnfahren, n
 ♦ punting
Stocherkahnfahrer, m
 ♦ punter
Stocherkahn mieten
 ♦ rent a punt AE
 ♦ hire a punt BE
stochern in den Zähnen
 in den Zähnen stochern
 ♦ pick at one's teeth
stochern in seinem Essen
 in seinem Essen herumstochern coll
 etw mit langen Zähnen essen
 ♦ pick at one's food
stockbesoffen, adj coll
 stockbetrunken, adj
 ♦ dead drunk, adj
 ♦ tight, adj sl
 ♦ sozzled, adj
 ♦ sloshed, adj BE sl
stockbetrunken, adj
 stockbesoffen, adj coll
 ♦ sozzled, adj
 ♦ dead drunk, adj
 ♦ sloshed, adj BE sl
 ♦ tight, adj sl
stockbetrunken sein
 stockbesoffen sein coll
 ♦ be dead drunk
 ♦ be tight sl
 ♦ be sloshed BE sl
Stockbett n
 → Etagenbett
Stock-Car, m
 ♦ stock car
Stock-Car-Rennen, n
 ♦ stock car race
 ♦ stock car racing
Stockfisch, m
 ♦ dried cod
stocknüchtern, adj
 ♦ stone-cold sober, adj
 ♦ cold sober, adj

stocknüchtern sein

stocknüchtern sein
- be stone-cold sober
- be cold sober
- be sober as a judge

Stockwerk, n
Geschoß, n
Etage, f
- story *AE*
- storey *BE*
- floor

Stockwerksbad, n
→ Etagenbad

Stoffhandtuch, n
Textilhandtuch, n
textiles Handtuch, n
- cloth towel

Stoffserviette, f
- linen napkin
- cloth napkin
- linen serviette

Stoffwechsel, m
- metabolism

Stoffwechselkrankheit, f
- metabolic disease

Stoffwechselkrankheiten behandeln
- treat metabolic diseases

stolz sein auf etw
- pride oneself on s.th.
- take pride in s.th.
- be proud of s.th.

stolz sein auf seinen ausgezeichneten Gästeservice
- be proud of one's excellent guest service

Stopover, m
→ Zwischenaufenthalt

Stopoverhotel, n
→ Zwischenaufenthaltshotel

Stopoverpunkt, m
→ Flugunterbrechungspunkt

Stopp empfehlen
(z.B. in Gasthaus)
Halt empfehlen
- recommend a stop

Stopp für ein Essen, m
Halt für ein Essen, m
- stop for a meal

Stopp unterwegs, m
Halt unterwegs, m
Rast unterwegs, f
- en route stop
- stop en route

Stöpsel, m
(z.B. für Badewanne)
- plug

Store, m
- net curtain

stören jn
- disturb s.o.

stornierbar, adj
annullierbar, adj
absagbar, adj
- cancellable, adj
- cancelable, adj *AE*

Stornieren, n
Zurücktreten, n
Annullieren, n
- cancelling
- canceling *AE*

stornieren etw
rückgängig machen etw
absagen etw

zurücktreten von etw
annullieren etw
- cancel s.th.

stornieren etw aus bestimmten Gründen
- cancel s.th. for certain reasons

stornieren etw automatisch
- cancel s.th. automatically

stornieren etw infolge von etw
- cancel s.th. as a result of s.th.

stornieren etw vor dem Reisetermin
- cancel s.th. prior to the date of travel
- cancel s.th. before the date of travel

stornieren etw vorher
im voraus zurücktreten von etw
vorher absagen etw
- cancel s.th. in advance
- precancel s.th.

stornieren etw vorsorglich
vorsorglich absagen etw
- cancel s.th. as a precaution

stornieren etw wegen eines Arbeitskampfes
- cancel s.th. due to industrial action
- cancel s.th. due to industrial disputes

stornieren etw wegen mangelnder Buchungen
- cancel s.th. through insufficient bookings

stornieren etw wegen Streik
- cancel s.th. due to strike

stornieren wegen anderweitiger Verpflichtungen
absagen wegen anderweitiger Verpflichtungen
- cancel due to other commitments

stornieren wegen einem unvorhersehbaren Ereignis
absagen wegen eines unvorhersehbaren Ereignisses
- cancel due to an unforeseen event

stornieren wegen einer (plötzlichen) Erkrankung
absagen wegen einer (plötzlichen) Erkrankung
- cancel due to (sudden) illness

stornieren wegen eines Unfalls
absagen wegen eines Unfalls
- cancel due to an accident

stornieren wegen familiärer Gründe
absagen aus familiären Gründen
- cancel due to family reasons

Stornierer, m
- canceller
- canceler *AE*

storniert, adj
abgesagt, adj
annulliert, adj
abbestellt, adj
rückgängig gemacht, adj
- cancelled, adj
- canceled, adj *AE*

stornierte Buchung, f
rückgängig gemachte Buchung, f
- cancelled booking
- canceled booking *AE*
- canceled reservation *AE*

stornierte Reservierung, f
rückgängig gemachte Reservierung, f
- cancelled reservation
- canceled reservation *AE*

stornierter Urlaub, m
stornierte Ferien, pl
abgesagter Urlaub, m
abgesagte Ferien, pl
- canceled vacation *AE*
- cancelled holiday *BE*

Stornierung, f
Absage, f

Rücktritt, m
Abbestellung, f
Annullierung, f
- cancellation
- cancelation *AE*

Stornierung ablehnen
Rücktritt ablehnen
Stornierung zurückweisen
- reject a cancellation
- reject a cancelation *AE*

Stornierung bearbeiten
Absage bearbeiten
Rücktritt bearbeiten
- process a cancellation
- deal with a cancellation
- handle a cancellation
- process a cancelation *AE*
- deal with a cancelation *AE*

Stornierung bestätigen
Rücktritt bestätigen
Annullierung bestätigen
Abbestellung bestätigen
Absage bestätigen
- confirm a cancellation
- confirm a cancelation *AE*

Stornierungen müssen schriftlich mitgeteilt werden
- Cancellations must be notified in writing
- Cancelations must be notified in writing *AE*

Stornierungen werden nur schriftlich akzeptiert
- Cancellations are only accepted in writing
- Cancelations are only accepted in writing *AE*

Stornierung erhalten
Stornierungserklärung erhalten
Rücktrittserklärung erhalten
Annullierungserklärung erhalten
- receive a cancellation
- receive a cancelation *AE*

Stornierung gegenbestätigen
Rücktritt gegenbestätigen
Absage gegenbestätigen
- reconfirm a cancellation
- reconfirm a cancelation *AE*

Stornierung geht ein
Absage geht ein
- cancellation is received
- cancelation is received *AE*

Stornierung in letzter Minute, f
Absage in letzter Minute, f
- last-minute cancellation
- last-minute cancelation *AE*

Stornierung ist gültig
Rücktritt ist gültig
Absage ist gültig
Annullierung ist gültig
- cancellation is effective
- cancelation is effective *AE*

Stornierungsablehnung, f
Rücktrittsablehnung, f
- refusal of a cancellation
- refusal of a cancelation *AE*
- refusing a cancellation
- refusing a cancelation *AE*

Stornierungsbedingungen, f pl
Rücktrittsbedingungen, f pl
Annullierungsbedingungen, f pl
Stornobedingungen, f pl
- cancellation conditions *pl*
- cancelation conditions *AE pl*
- conditions of cancellation *pl*
- conditions of cancelation *AE pl*

Stornierungsbedingungen anerkennen
Rücktrittsbedingungen anerkennen
- accept the cancellation conditions
- accept the cancelation conditions *AE*

Stornierungsbestätigung, f
Rücktrittsbestätigung, f
Annullierungsbestätigung, f
Absagebestätigung, f
- confirmation of (a) cancellation
- confirmation of (a) cancelation *AE*
- confirming a cancellation

Stornierung schriftlich machen
Abbestellung schriftlich machen
- make a cancellation in writing
- make a cancelation in writing *AE*

Stornierung schriftlich mitteilen
Rücktritt schriftlich mitteilen
Annullierung schriftlich mitteilen
Abbestellung schriftlich mitteilen
- notify a cancellation in writing
- notify a cancelation in writing *AE*

Stornierungsdatum, n
Stornierungstermin, m
Rücktrittsdatum, n
Rücktrittstermin, m
Annullierungsdatum, n
- cancellation date
- date of cancellation
- cancelation date *AE*
- date of cancelation *AE*

Stornierungserklärung, f
Rücktrittserklärung, f
- notification of cancellation
- notification of cancelation *AE*
- cancellation
- cancelation *AE*

Stornierungserklärung erhalten
→ Stornierung erhalten

Stornierungsfall, m
Rücktrittsfall, m
- case of cancellation
- case of cancelation *AE*
- event of cancellation
- event of cancelation *AE*

Stornierungsformular, n
Rücktrittsformular, n
Annullierungsformular, n
- cancellation form
- cancelation form *AE*

Stornierungsfrist, f (Zeitpunkt)
Rücktrittsfrist, f
Annullierungsfrist, f
- cancellation deadline
- cancelation deadline *AE*
- deadline for cancellation
- deadline for cancelation *AE*

Stornierungsfrist, f (Zeitraum)
Rücktrittsfrist, f
Annullierungsfrist, f
- notice of cancellation
- notice of cancelation *AE*

Stornierungsfrist einhalten
Rücktrittsfrist einhalten
Annullierungsfrist einhalten
- meet the cancellation deadline
- meet the cancelation deadline *AE*

Stornierungsfrist überschreiten
Rücktrittsfrist überschreiten
Annullierungsfrist überschreiten
- miss the cancellation deadline
- miss the cancelation deadline *AE*

Stornierungsgebühr, f
Rücktrittsgebühr, f
Annullierungsgebühr, f
Stornogebühr, f
- cancellation charge
- cancellation fee
- cancelation charge *AE*
- cancelation fee *AE*

Stornierungsgebühr ausrechnen
Rücktrittsgebühr ausrechnen
Annullierungsgebühr ausrechnen
- calculate the cancellation charge
- calculate the cancellation fee
- calculate the cancelation charge *AE*
- calculate the cancelation fee *AE*

Stornierungsgebühr erheben
Rücktrittsgebühr erheben
Annullierungsgebühr erheben
Stornogebühr erheben
- charge a cancellation fee
- levy a cancellation charge
- levy a cancellation fee
- charge a cancelation fee *AE*
- levy a cancelation charge *AE*

Stornierungsgebühr von DM 123 berechnen jm
Rücktrittsgebühr von DM 123 berechnen jm
Annullierungsgebühr von DM 123 berechnen jm
- charge s.o. a cancellation fee of DM 123
- charge s.o. a cancelation fee of DM 123 *AE*

Stornierungsgebühr zahlen
Rücktrittsgebühr zahlen
Annullierungsgebühr zahlen
- pay a cancellation charge
- pay a cancellation fee
- pay a cancelation charge *AE*
- pay a cancelation fee *AE*

Stornierungsgebühr zurückerhalten
Rücktrittsgebühr zurückerhalten
Annullierungsgebühr zurückerhalten
- recover a cancellation charge
- recover a cancellation fee
- recover a cancelation charge *AE*
- recover a cancelation fee *AE*

Stornierungsgesuch, m
→ Stornierungswunsch

Stornierungsklausel, f
Rücktrittsklausel, f
- cancellation clause
- cancelation clause *AE*

Stornierungskosten, pl
Rücktrittskosten, pl
Annullierungskosten, pl
Stornokosten, pl
- cancellation costs *pl*
- cancelation costs *AE pl*
- cost of cancellation
- cost of cancelation *AE*

Stornierungsmöglichkeit, f
Rücktrittsmöglichkeit, f
Abbestellungsmöglichkeit, f
Stornomöglichkeit, f
- possibility of cancellation
- possibility of cancelation *AE*

Stornierungsnummer, f
Rücktrittsnummer, f
- cancellation number
- cancelation number *AE*

Stornierungspolitik, f
Rücktrittspolitik, f
Annullierungspolitik, f
Stornierungsrichtlinien, f pl
- cancellation policy
- cancelation policy *AE*

Stornierungsquote, f
Stornierungsrate, f
- cancellation rate
- cancelation rate *AE*

Stornierungsrechnung, f
Rücktrittsrechnung, f
Stornorechnung, f
- cancellation invoice
- cancelation invoice *AE*

Stornierungsrecht, n
Recht zur Stornierung, n
Rücktrittsrecht, n
Annullierungsrecht, n
- right of cancellation
- right of cancelation *AE*
- right to cancel (s.th.)

Stornierungsrecht vorbehalten sich
Rücktrittsrecht sich vorbehalten
- reserve the right to cancel (s.th.)

Stornierungsrisiko, n
Rücktrittsrisiko, n
Annullierungsrisiko, n
Stornorisiko, n
- risk of cancellation
- risk of cancelation *AE*

Stornierungsrückzahlung, f
- cancellation refund
- cancelation refund *AE*

Stornierungsschutz, m
Rücktrittsschutz, m
Annullierungsschutz, m
Stornoschutz, m
- cancellation cover
- cancelation cover *AE*

Stornierungsstrafgeld, n
Stornierungsstrafe, f
Rücktrittsstrafgeld, n
Annullierungsstrafgeld, n
Stornostrafgeld, n
- cancellation penalty
- cancelation penalty *AE*

Stornierungstermin, m
→ Stornierungsdatum

Stornierungsvorgang, m
Annullierungsvorgang, m
Rücktrittsvorgang, m
- cancellation procedure
- cancelation procedure *AE*

Stornierungswelle, f
- wave of cancellations
- wave of cancelations *AE*

Stornierungswunsch, m
Rücktrittswunsch, m
Annullierungswunsch, m
Stornowunsch, m
Stornierungsgesuch, m
- cancellation request
- request for cancellation
- cancelation request *AE*
- request for cancelation *AE*

Stornierungszeitpunkt, m
Rücktrittszeitpunkt, m
Annullierungszeitpunkt, m
Stornozeitpunkt, m
- time of cancellation
- time of cancelation *AE*

Stornierung verweigern
Stornierung ablehnen
Rücktritt verweigern

Stornierung vornehmen

Rücktritt ablehnen
- refuse a cancellation
- refuse a cancelation *AE*

Stornierung vornehmen
Abbestellung vornehmen
Annullierung vornehmen
Rücktritt vornehmen
- make a cancellation
- make a cancelation *AE*
- cancel s.th.

Stornobedingungen, f pl
→ Stornierungsbedingungen

Stößel, m
- pestle

stoßen auf ein Hotel
auf ein Hotel stoßen
- come across a hotel

Stoßverkehr, m
- rush-hour traffic
- peak-hour traffic

Stoßzeit, f (Hochbetrieb)
→ Hochbetrieb

Stoßzeit, f (Verkehr)
- rush hour *AE*
- rush-hour *BE*

Strafzettel für falsches Parken, m
- parking ticket
- parking-ticket *BE*

Strand, m
- beach

Strandanlagen, f pl
- beach facilities *pl*

Strandanzug, m
- beach suit

Strandappartement, n (in Strandnähe)
- beachside apartment
- beachfront apartment *AE*
- beach-front apartment *BE*

Strandarbeiter, m
- beachman

Strandaufzug, m
→ Strandfahrstuhl

Strandbad, n
- beach with bathing facilities
- lido *BE*

Strandbadeort, m
- beach resort

Strandbar, f
- beach bar

Strandbenutzung, f
- use of the beach
- using the beach

Strandbenutzungsgebühr, f
Strandgebühr, f
- charge for the use of the beach
- fee for the use of the beach
- charge for using the beach
- fee for using the beach

Strandbenutzungszuschlag, m
Strandzuschlag, m
- supplement for the use of the beach
- supplement for using the beach

Strand besteht aus grobem Sand und Kiesel
- beach is composed of coarse sand and shingle

Strandbetrieb, m
(z.B. Hotel am Strand)
- beach establishment
- beach operation

Strandblick, m
Blick auf den Strand, m

- beach view
- view of the beach

Strandbüfett, n
- beach buffet

Strandbuggy, m
- beach buggy

Strandbungalow, m
- beach bungalow
- beachside bungalow
- beachfront bungalow *AE*
- beach-front bungalow *BE*

Strandcafé, n (auf dem Strand)
- beach café
- beach cafe *AE*

Strandcafé, n (in Strandnähe)
- beachside café
- beachside cafe *AE*
- beachfront cafe *AE*
- beach-front café *BE*

Strandclub m
- beach club

Stranddiskothek f
- beach discotheque
- beach disco

Strandfahrstuhl, m
Strandlift, m
Strandaufzug, m
Fahrstuhl zum Strand, m
Lift zum Strand, m
- beach elevator *AE*
- beach lift *BE*
- elevator to the beach *AE*
- lift to the beach *BE*

Strand fällt sanft ab
- beach slopes gently

Strand fällt steil ab
- beach slopes steeply

Strandferienwohnung, f (in Strandnähe)
Strandurlaubswohnung, f
- beachside vacation apartment *AE*
- beachfront vacation apartment *AE*
- beachside holiday flat *BE*
- beach-front holiday flat *BE*

Strandfest, n
Strandparty, f
- beach party

Strandfläche, f
- beach space
- beach area

Strandgebiet, n
- beach area

Strandgebühr, f
- beach fee

Strandgebühr, f
Strandbenutzungsgebühr f
- fee for the use of the beach
- charge for the use of the beach
- fee for using the beach
- charge for using the beach

Strandgetränk, n
- beach drink

Strandgrillfest, n
- beach barbecue
- beachfront barbecue

Strandgutjäger, m
Herumtreiber, m
Nichtstuer, m
- beachcomber

Strandhaus, n (auf dem Strand)
- beach cottage
- beach house

Strandhaus, n (in Strandnähe)
Strandcottage, f
- beachside cottage
- beachfront cottage *AE*
- beach-front cottage *BE*
- beachside house

Strandhotel, n (auf dem Strand)
- beach hotel

Strandhotel, n (in Strandnähe)
- beachside hotel
- beachfront hotel *AE*
- beach-front hotel *BE*

Strandhotelanlage, f
Strandhotelkomplex m
- beach hotel complex

Strandhütte, f
(zum Umkleiden)
- beach hut

Strand ist eine Meile lang
- beach is one mile long

Strand ist in fünf Minuten zu Fuß erreichbar
- beach is within a five-minute walk

Strand ist leer
- beach is empty

Strand ist (nur) einen Katzensprung entfernt
- beach is a stone's throw away

Strand ist überlaufen
Strand ist überfüllt
- beach is overcrowded

Strand ist unberührt
- beach is unspoiled
- beach is unspoilt *BE*

Strandkasino, n
- beach casino

Strandkindergarten, m
- beach kindergarten

Strandkleidung, f
- beachwear

Strandkneipe, f coll
Strandgaststätte, f
Strandbar, f
- beach pub *BE*
- beach bar *AE*

Strandkonzert, n
- beach concert

Strandkorb, m
- beach chair
- wicker beach chair

Strandkorb mieten
- rent a beach chair *AE*
- hire a beach chair *BE*

Strandkorb vermieten
- rent (out) a beach chair
- hire out a beach chair *BE*

Strandlage, f (Lage des Strands)
- situation of the beach

Strandlage, f (Nähe)
in Strandnähe gelegen, adj
- situated near the beach
- situated close to the beach
- convenient situation for the beach

Strandliege, f
- beach lounge *AE*
- beach lounger *BE*
- beach sunbed

Strandlift, m
→ Strandfahrstuhl

Strandlokal, n
→ Strandrestaurant

strandlos, adj
- beachless, adj

Strandmotel, n (auf dem Strand)
- beach motel

Strandmotel, n (in Strandnähe)
- beachside motel
- beachfront motel *AE*
- beach-front motel *BE*

strandnah, adj
→ nahe am Strand

Strandnähe, f
- nearness to the beach
- closeness to the beach
- proximity to the beach

strandnahe Lage, f
→ Strandlage

Strandolympiade, f
- beach olympics *pl*

Strandparadies, n
- beach paradise

Strandparty, f
→ Strandfest

Strandpavillon, m (in Strandnähe)
Strandclubhaus, n
- beachside pavilion
- beachfront pavilion *AE*
- beach-front pavilion *BE*

Strandpenner, m
- beach bum *AE sl*

Strandpicknick, n
- beach picnic

Strandprogramm, n
- beach program *AE*
- beach programme *BE*

Strandpromenade, f
- beachfront *AE*
- beach front *BE*
- promenade (along the beach)

Strand reinigen
- clean the beach

Strandrestaurant, n (auf dem Strand)
- beach restaurant

Strandrestaurant, n (in Strandnähe)
- beachside restaurant
- beachfront restaurant *AE*
- beach-front restaurant *BE*

Strandschirm, m
- beach umbrella

Strand schließen
- close a beach

Strandschuh, m
- beach shoe

Strandsegeln, n
Strandsegelsport, m
- sand yachting

Strandsegler, m
- sand yacht

Strandspiel n
- beach game

Strandsport, m
Strandsportarten, f pl
- beach sport
- beach sports *pl*

Strandsuite, f (in Strandnähe)
- beachside suite
- beachfront suite *AE*
- beach-front suite *BE*

Strandtasche f
- beach bag

Strandtaverne, f
- beach tavern

Strandterrasse, f (in Strandnähe)
- beachside terrace

- beachfront terrace *AE*
- beach-front terrace *BE*
- beachside patio
- beachfront patio *AE*

Strandtourismus, m
Badetourismus, m
- beach tourism

Strandtourist, m
Badetourist, m
- beach tourist

Strandtuch, n
großes Badetuch, n
- beach towel

Strand überprüfen
- check the beach

Strandurlaub, m
Badeurlaub, m
Strandferien, pl
Badeferien, pl
- beach vacation *AE*
- beach holiday *BE*

Strandurlaubsort, m (Ferienort)
Strandferienort, m
Badeurlaubsort, m
Badeferienort, m
- beach vacation resort *AE*
- beach holiday resort *BE*
- beach resort

Strandurlaubsort, m (wo man Ferien macht)
Strandferienort, m
Badeurlaubsort, m
Badeferienort, m
- beach vacation place *AE*
- beach holiday place *BE*

Strandurlaubssegment, n
Strandferiensegment, n
Badeurlaubssegment, n
Badeferiensegment, n
- beach vacation segment *AE*
- beach holiday segment *BE*

Strandurlaubswohnung, f
→ Strandferienwohnung

Strandverkäufer, m
- beach vendor

Strandverschmutzung, f
- pollution of the beach
- beach pollution

Strandvilla, f (in Strandnähe)
- beachside villa
- beachfront villa *AE*
- beach-front villa *BE*
- beach villa

Strand vor der Haustür haben
- have the beach on one's doorstep

Strandwärter, m
- beach attendant
- lifeguard

Strand wartet auf Ihren Besuch
- beach awaits your pleasure

Strandzimmer, n (in Strandnähe)
- beachside room
- beachfront room *AE*
- beach-front room *BE*

Strandzuschlag, m
- beach supplement

Strandzustand m
- state of the beach
- condition of the beach

strapaziös, adj
- gruelling, adj
- grueling, adj *AE*

Straßburger Münster, das, n
- Strasbourg Minster

Straße, f (Geschäftsstraße)
- street

Straße, f (nicht Geschäftsstraße)
- road

Straße blockieren
- block a road
- block a street

Straße der Staufer, f
(Ferienstraße)
- Staufer Road, the
- Staufer Route, the

Straße entlang der Küste, f
- road along the coast
- route along the coast

Straße folgen nach X
- follow the road to X

Straße führt zum Gipfel
- road leads to the summit

Straße geht weiter nach X
- road continues to X

Straße ist für den Verkehr gesperrt
- road is closed to traffic
- street is closed to traffic

Straße ist gut ausgeschildert
- road is well signposted

Straße ist im Winter geschlossen
- road is closed in (the) winter

Straße ist überschwemmt
- road is flooded
- street is flooded

Straße ist unpassierbar
- road is impassable
- street is impassable

Straßenatlas, m
- road atlas

Straßenbahn, f
- streetcar *AE*
- tram *BE*

Straßenbahnendstation, f
Straßenbahnendhaltestelle, f
- streetcar terminus *AE*
- tram terminus *BE*

Straßenbahnfahrt, f
- streetcar ride *AE*
- tram ride *BE*

Straßenbahnhaltestelle, f
- streetcar stop *AE*
- tram stop *BE*

Straßenbahnlinie, f
- tramline *BE*
- streetcar line *AE*

Straßenbahnschiene, f
- tram track *BE*
- streetcar track *AE*

Straßenbahnstrecke, f
- tram route *BE*
- streetcar route *AE*

Straßenbahnwagen, m
- tramcar *BE*
- streetcar *AE*

Straßenbau, m
- road building
- building roads
- building a road
- road construction

Straßenbauprogramm, n
- road building program *AE*
- road building programme *BE*

Straßenbenutzer

Straßenbenutzer, m
♦ road user
Straßenbrücke, f
♦ road bridge
Straßencafé, n (im Ort)
♦ sidewalk cafe *AE*
♦ pavement café *BE*
♦ street café
♦ street cafe *AE*
Straßencafé, n (Landstraße)
→ Landstraßencafé
Straße nehmen nach X
♦ take the road to X
Straßenfahrrad, m
stabiles Tourenrad, n
♦ roadster
Straßenfest, n (Festival)
♦ street festival
Straßenfest, n (Party)
♦ street party
Straßengebühr, f
Straßenbenutzungsgebühr, f
Maut, f
♦ road toll
♦ toll
Straßenhändler, m
♦ street trader
Straßenjahrmarkt, m
♦ street fair
Straßenkarte, f
♦ road map
♦ street map
Straßenkiosk, m
♦ street kiosk
Straßenkreuzung, f
♦ road junction
♦ street junction
♦ road intersection
♦ junction
Straßenlärm, m
♦ noise of the street
♦ road noise
Straßenlobby, f
♦ road lobby
Straßenmarkt, m
♦ street market
Straßenname, m
♦ street name
♦ road name
Straßennetz, n
♦ road network
Straßennummer, f
♦ road number
Straßenplan, m
♦ street plan
♦ road plan
Straßenraub, m
Straßenräuberei, f
♦ mugging
Straßenräuber, m
♦ mugger
Straßenreise, f
♦ road journey
♦ road trip
Straßenreiseverkehr, m
♦ road travel
Straßenrestaurant, n
♦ sidewalk restaurant *AE*
♦ pavement restaurant *BE*
♦ street restaurant

Straßenschild, n
♦ street sign
♦ road sign
Straßenstand, m
♦ street stall
♦ street stand
♦ roadside stall
♦ roadside stand
Straßensteuer, f
Straßenabgabe, f
♦ road tax
Straßentheater, n
♦ street theater *AE*
♦ street theatre *BE*
Straßentunnel, m
♦ road tunnel
Straßenunterhalter, m
♦ street entertainer
Straßenunterhaltung, f
♦ street entertainment
Straßenverbindung, f
♦ road connection
♦ road link
Straßenverkäufer, m
♦ street vendor
♦ street seller
Straßenverkaufsstelle, f
♦ take-away store *AE*
♦ take-away shop *BE*
♦ take-away
Straßenverkehr, m
♦ road traffic
Straßenzimmer, n
Zimmer zur Straße, n
♦ room looking onto the street
♦ room looking onto the road
Straßenzustand, m
♦ road conditions *pl*
Straßenzustandsbericht, m
♦ road report
Straße sperren
♦ close a road
♦ close a street
Straße zweigt ab
♦ road branches
strategische Lage, f
♦ strategic position
Strauß, m (Pflanze)
Bund, m
♦ bunch
Straußwirtschaft, f
♦ improvised winegrower's bar *AE*
♦ improvised winegrower's pub *BE*
Strebebogen, m *archit*
♦ flying buttress *archit*
Strecke abkürzen
Route abkürzen
♦ cut the route short
Strecke bedienen
Route bedienen
♦ operate a route
Strecke befliegen
Strecke bedienen
♦ fly a route
Strecke beginnt in A und endet in B
Route beginnt in A und endet in B
♦ route starts at X and finishes in B
♦ route begins in X and ends at B
♦ route commences at X and finishes at B *form*

Strecke beschreiben
Route beschreiben
♦ describe a route
Strecke der Reise, f
Abschnitt der Reise, m
Reisestrecke, f
Reiseabschnitt, m
♦ stretch of the journey
Strecke ist gut markiert
Route ist gut markiert
♦ route is well marked
Streckendetail, n
Routendetail, n
♦ route detail
Streckenfreigabe, f
Streckenderegulierung, f
♦ route deregulation
Streckenkarte, f
Routenkarte, f
♦ route map
Streckenmanagement, n
♦ route management
Streckenmanager, m
♦ route manager
Streckennetz, n
♦ route network
Streckenplanung, f
Routenplanung, f
♦ route planning
♦ planning a route
Strecke sichern
Route sichern
♦ secure a route
Strecke von A nach B, f
Route von A nach B, f
♦ route from A to B
streichen, falls unzutreffend
(Formular)
♦ delete if inapplicable
streichen etw (Formular)
ausstreichen etw
♦ delete s.th.
streichen etw (stornieren)
→ stornieren
streichen etw von der Speisekarte
♦ remove s.th. from the menu
♦ take s.th. off the menu
streichen etw von einem Programm
♦ drop s.th. from a program *AE*
♦ drop s.th. from a programme *BE*
♦ delete s.th. from a program *AE*
♦ delete s.th. from a programme *BE*
Streichholz, n
Zündholz, n
♦ match
Streichholzheft, n
Zündholzheft, n
♦ matchbook
Streichholzschachtel, f
Zündholzschachtel, f
♦ matchbox
Streichkäse, m
♦ cheese spread
Streichorchester, n
♦ string orchestra
Streichung einer Leistung f
♦ withdrawal of a service
Streik, m
♦ strike

streiken
　im Streik sein
　◆ be on strike
Streik geht weiter
　◆ strike continues
Streitfall gütlich beilegen
　◆ settle a dispute amicably
strenge Diät, f
　◆ strict diet
strenge Fastenkur, f
　◆ hunger cure
Streß, m
　◆ stress
Streßabbau, m
　Streßminderung, f
　◆ stress release
Streß abbauen
　◆ relieve stress
Streßbewältigung, f
　◆ stress management
streßfrei, adj
　◆ stress-free, adj
streßfreier Urlaub, m
　streßfreie Ferien, pl
　◆ stress-free vacation AE
　◆ stress-free holiday BE
streßfreie Umgebung, f
　◆ stress-free environment
stressig, adj
　anstrengend, adj
　◆ stressful, adj
Streßkontrolle, f
　◆ stress control
Streßkrankheit, f
　Managerkrankheit, f
　◆ stress disease
Streßlinderungsbehandlung, f
　◆ stress relief treatment
streuen etw auf etw
　◆ sprinkle s.th. on s.th.
streuen etw über etw
　◆ sprinkle s.th. over s.th.
Streuselkuchen, n
　◆ streusel cake
Strichjunge, m
　◆ rent boy
Strichkneipe, f
　(mit Prostituierten)
　◆ pick-up joint sl
Strichliste, f
　Kerbholz, n hist
　◆ tally
Strichliste führen von etw
　◆ keep a tally of s.th.
Strichlokal, n
　◆ pick-up place
Strichmädchen, n
　◆ streetwalker AE
　◆ hooker AE
　◆ street-walker BE
　◆ tart BE
Strickleiter, f
　◆ rope ladder
Strip machen
　strippen
　◆ do a strip
strippen
　◆ strip
Stripperin, f
　Stripper, m
　◆ stripper

Striptease, m
　◆ striptease AE
　◆ strip-tease BE
Stripteasebar, f
　Stripteaseclub, m
　Stripteaselokal, n
　◆ striptease bar AE
　◆ girlie bar AE sl
　◆ strip-tease club BE
　◆ strip club
Stripteaselokal, n
　→ Stripteasebar
Stripteaseschuppen, m sl
　◆ striptease joint AE sl
　◆ strip-tease joint BE sl
　◆ strip joint AE sl
Stripteaseshow, f
　◆ striptease show AE
　◆ strip-tease show BE
Stripteasetänzerin, f
　Stripteasetänzer, m
　◆ striptease dancer AE
　◆ strip-tease dancer BE
Strohbett, n
　◆ straw bed
Strohdach, n
　◆ thatched roof
　◆ straw roof
Strohdachhütte, f
　strohgedeckte Hütte, f
　◆ thatched hut
Strohflechten, n
　◆ straw-plaiting
strohgedeckte Rundhütte, f
　(in Afrika, meist aus Lehm)
　strohgedecktes Rundhaus, n
　◆ thatched rondavel
strohgedecktes Haus, n
　◆ thatched house
Strohhalm, m
　Trinkhalm, m
　◆ straw
Strohhut, m
　◆ straw hat
Strohlager, n
　Lager aus Stroh, n
　◆ bed of straw
　◆ straw bed
　◆ pallet
Strohmatratze, f
　◆ straw mattress
　◆ mattress filled with straw
Strohmatte, f
　◆ straw mat
Strohsack, m
　◆ pallet
　◆ paillasse
　◆ palliasse
　◆ straw bed
　◆ straw mattress
Strohschirm m
　(Strand)
　◆ straw umbrella
Strohwitwe, f
　◆ grass widow
Strohwitwer, m
　◆ grass widower
Strom, m (Elektrizizät)
　◆ electricity

Strom, m (Fluß)
　◆ large river
　◆ river
Strom abstellen
　◆ cut off electricity
Stromanschluß, m
　(Camping)
　Netzstrom, m
　◆ mains electricity
　◆ electric hook-up
stromaufwärts, adv
　gegen den Strom, adv
　stromaufwärts gelegen, adv
　◆ upstream, adv
stromaufwärts fahren
　gegen den Strom fahren
　◆ go upstream
stromaufwärts rudern
　gegen den Strom rudern
　◆ row upstream
stromaufwärts schwimmen
　gegen den Strom schwimmen
　◆ swim upstream
Stromausfall, m
　◆ power failure
Strom der Gästeankünfte, m
　◆ flow of guest arrivals
Stromgenerator, m
　◆ electric generator
　◆ power generator
Stromkabel, n
　◆ electricity cable
Stromkosten, pl
　◆ electricity costs pl
　◆ electricity cost
Stromkosten sind in der Miete enthalten
　Strom ist in der Miete enthalten
　◆ electricity is included in the rent
Strompreis m
　◆ electricity price
　◆ electricity rate
Stromrechnung f
　◆ electricity bill
Stromsperre, f
　◆ power cut
Stromtarif, m
　◆ electricity tariff
Stromverbrauch, m
　◆ electricity consumption
Strom verbrauchen
　◆ consume electricity
Stromversorgung, f
　◆ electricity supply
Strom von Touristen, m
　Touristenstrom, m
　◆ stream of tourists
Stromzähler, m
　◆ electricity meter
Strudel, m
　◆ strudel
Stubaier Alpen, die, pl
　◆ Stubai Alps, the, pl
Stubenhocker, m
　Ofenhocker, m
　◆ homebody
　◆ stay-at-home
Stuck, m
　◆ stucco
Stück, n
　◆ piece

Stuckdecke

Stuckdecke, f
- ◆ stucco ceiling
- ◆ stuccoed ceiling

Stuckfassade, f
- ◆ stucco façade
- ◆ stucco facade AE

Stück Kuchen, n
- ◆ piece of cake

Stück Seife, n
- ◆ bar of soap
- ◆ cake of soap
- ◆ tablet of soap

Stück vom Fremdenverkehrskuchen, n
- Stück vom Tourismuskuchen, n
- ◆ slice of the tourism cake

Stuckzimmer, n
- ◆ stucco room
- ◆ stuccoed room

Stück Zucker, n
- Zuckerstück, n
- ◆ lump of sugar

Student, m
- ◆ student

Studentenaustausch, m
- ◆ student exchange
- ◆ exchange of students

Studentenaustauschprogramm, n
- ◆ student exchange program AE
- ◆ student exchange programme BE

Studentenausweis, m
- ◆ student identity card
- ◆ student card

Studentenbesuch, m
- ◆ student visit

Studentenbude, f
- Studentenzimmer, n
- ◆ student's digs BE pl coll

Studentencharterflug, m
- ◆ student charter flight

Studentenermäßigung, f
- ◆ student reduction
- ◆ students' reduction

Studentenfahrkarte, f
- Studentenkarte, f
- ◆ student ticket

Studentenfahrpreis, m
- ◆ student fare

Studentengruppe, f
- ◆ student group
- ◆ group of students

Studentenheim, n
- ◆ student hostel
- ◆ students' hostel

Studentenkantine, f
- ◆ student canteen

Studentenkneipe, f
- ◆ student bar AE
- ◆ student pub BE

Studentenrabatt, m
- ◆ student discount

Studentenreise, f
- ◆ student tour
- ◆ student trip

Studentenreisebüro, n
- ◆ student travel agency

Studentenreisen, n
- Studentenreiseverkehr, m
- ◆ student travel

Studententarif, m
- ◆ student tariff
- ◆ student rates pl

- ◆ student rate
- ◆ student terms pl

Studententreff, m
- Studententreffpunkt, m
- Studentenkneipe, f
- ◆ student haunt

Studentenunterkunft, f
- ◆ student accommodation

Studentenunterkunftsvermittlung, f (Büro)
- ◆ student accommodation agency
- ◆ student acommodation bureau

Studentenunterkunftsvermittlung, f (Service)
- ◆ student accommodation service

Studentenviertel, n
- (einer Stadt)
- ◆ student quarter

Studentenvisum, n
- ◆ student visa

Studentenwohnheim, n
- (bes. auf Campusgelände)
- ◆ hall of residence
- ◆ hall
- ◆ dormitory AE

studentischer Mieter, m
- ◆ student tenant

Studie in Auftrag geben
- ◆ commission a study

Studienausflug, m
- → Studienfahrt

Studienausflug machen
- ◆ make a study trip
- ◆ go on a study trip

Studienbesuch m
- ◆ study visit

Studienfahrt, f
- ◆ study trip

Studiengruppe, f
- ◆ study group

Studienkreis für Tourismus, m hist
- ◆ Tourism Study Group hist

Studienmaterial, n
- ◆ study material

Studienprogramm, n
- ◆ study program AE
- ◆ study programme BE

Studienreise, f
- ◆ study tour

Studienreisegruppe, f
- ◆ study tour group
- ◆ study group

Studienreiseleiter, m
- ◆ study tour guide

Studienreise machen
- ◆ make a study tour
- ◆ go on a study tour

Studienreisemarkt, m
- ◆ study tour market

Studienreisender m
- ◆ person on a study tour
- ◆ person taking part in a study tour

Studienreiseveranstalter, m
- ◆ study tour operator

Studienreiseveranstaltung, f
- ◆ study tour operation

Studientag, m
- ◆ study day

Studienurlaub, m
- ◆ study vacation AE
- ◆ study holiday BE

Studienzentrum, n
- ◆ study center AE
- ◆ study centre BE

Studio, n
- ◆ studio

Studioappartement, n
- ◆ studio apartment

studioartiges Zimmer, n
- ◆ studio-style room

studioartige Wohnung, f
- ◆ studio-style apartment AE
- ◆ studio-style flat BE

Studioausstellung, f
- Atelierausstellung, f
- ◆ studio exhibition
- ◆ studio exhibit AE

Studiobett, n
- ◆ studio bed

Studio haben
- ◆ have a studio

Studio mit Kochgelegenheit, n
- ◆ studio efficiency AE
- ◆ studio with cooking facilities

Studiopreis, m
- ◆ studio price
- ◆ studio rate

Studioschlafzimmer, n
- ◆ studio bedroom

Studiostil, m
- ◆ studio style

Studiosuite, f
- ◆ studio suite

Studiowohnung, f
- ◆ studio flat BE
- ◆ studio apartment AE

Studiozimmer, n
- ◆ studio room

Stufengiebel, m
- ◆ stepped gable

Stuhl, m
- ◆ chair

Stuhlbein, n
- ◆ leg of a chair
- ◆ chair leg

Stuhlgang, m
- ◆ bowel movement

Stuhl ist gepolstert
- ◆ chair is upholstered

Stuhllehne, f
- ◆ chair back

stuhllos, adj
- ◆ chairless, adj

Stuhl mit geneigter Lehne, m
- Stuhl mit nach hinten geneigter Lehne, m
- ◆ raked chair

Stuhlreihe, f
- ◆ row of chairs

Stuhlsitz, m
- ◆ chair bottom

Stuhl tauschen
- Sitz wechseln
- ◆ change chairs
- ◆ swap chairs
- ◆ swop chairs

Stuhl vor die Tür setzen jm
- ◆ turn s.o. out

Stuhl wackelt
- ◆ chair wobbles

Stukkatur, f
- ◆ stucco work
- ◆ stucco

◆ plaster work
◆ plastering
Stulle, f
→ Sandwich
stumpfes Messer, n
◆ blunt knife
Stunde, f
◆ hour
Stunde Mittagspause haben
◆ have an hour's break for lunch
Stunde Mittagspause machen
◆ take an hour's break for lunch
Stunde nehmen
Unterricht nehmen
◆ take a lesson
Stundenhotel, n
Absteige, f
◆ short-time hotel
◆ sleazy hotel
stunden jm etw
(Zahlung)
◆ give s.o. time to pay s.th.
stundenlangen Spaß bieten
◆ provide hours of fun
Stundenlohn, m
◆ hourly wage rate
Stundenplan, m (Schule)
◆ timetable
Stundentakt, m
◆ hourly interval
stundenweise, adv
◆ by the hour, adv
◆ on an hourly basis, adv
stundenweise mieten etw
◆ rent s.th. by the hour
◆ hire s.th. by the hour BE
Stunde schlafen
◆ sleep for an hour
stündlich, adj
◆ hourly, adj
stündlich, adv
◆ every hour, adv
◆ hourly, adv
Stundung, f
◆ deferment (of payment)
◆ extension (of time)
Stundung erhalten
◆ get an extension (of time)
Stunk machen
◆ make a hell of a fuss
Stürme der Jahrhunderte überdauern
◆ stand the test of centuries
stürmen in ein Zimmer
◆ storm into a room
◆ rush into a room
sturmfreie Bude haben
◆ be able to have female visitors
◆ be able to have male visitors
stürmisch begrüßen jn
◆ give s.o. a tumultuous welcome
stürmisch begrüßt werden
◆ be given a rapturous welcome
stürmische Begrüßung, f
◆ rapturous welcome
stürmischen Empfang bereiten jm
◆ give s.o. a rapturous reception
◆ give s.o. a rapturous welcome
stürmischer Applaus, m
◆ tumultuous applause
stürmischer Empfang, m
◆ rapturous reception

stürmische Überfahrt, f
◆ rough crossing
Sturmlaterne, f
◆ storm lantern
stürzen auf den Tisch sich
sich auf den Tisch stürzen
losstürmen zum Essen
◆ make a dash for the table
stürzen auf etw
sich stürzen auf etw
losstürmen auf etw
◆ make a dash for s.th.
stürzen in ein Zimmer
◆ burst into a room
stürzen sich auf die Bar
sich auf die Bar stürzen
◆ make for the bar
stürzen sich auf etw
sich auf etw stürzen
◆ make for s.th.
Sturzhelm, m
◆ crash helmet
Styropor, n
◆ polysterene
◆ styrofoam
Styroporbuchstabe, m
(z.B. an einem Messestand)
◆ polysterene letter
◆ styrofoam letter
subtropisch, adj
◆ subtropical, adj
subtropisches Klima, n
◆ subtropical climate
subtropische Vegetation, f
◆ subtropical vegetation
Subunternehmer, m
◆ subcontractor
Subvention, f
◆ subsidy
subventionieren etw
◆ subsidize s.th.
◆ subsidise s.th.
Suchanlage, f
→ Rufanlage
suchen etw
◆ look for s.th.
◆ seek s.th.
Südafrika
◆ South Africa
◆ Southern Africa
Südafrikaner, m
◆ South African
Südafrikanerin, f
◆ South African girl
◆ South African woman
◆ South African
südafrikanisch, adj
◆ South African, adj
Südalpen, die, pl
◆ Southern Alps, the, pl
Südamerika
◆ South America
Südamerikaner, m
◆ South American
Südamerikanerin, f
◆ South American girl
◆ South American woman
◆ South American
südamerikanisch, adj
◆ South American, adj
◆ south American, adj

Sudan, m
◆ Sudan, the
Sudaner, m
Sudanese, m
◆ Sudanese
◆ Soudanese
Sudanerin, f
Sudanesin, f
◆ Sudanese girl
◆ Sudanese woman
◆ Sudanese
◆ Soudanese girl
◆ Soudanese woman
sudanisch, adj
◆ Sudanese, adj
◆ Soudanese, adj
Südappartement, n
◆ south-facing apartment
◆ apartment facing south
Südatlantik, m
◆ South Atlantic, the
Südatlantikinsel, f
◆ South Atlantic island
Südbaden
(Region)
◆ South Baden
◆ southern Baden
Südbalkon m
◆ south-facing balcony
◆ balcony facing south
Südbalkonzimmer, n
Zimmer mit (einem) Südbalkon, n
◆ room with (a) south-facing balcony
süddeutsch, adj
◆ South German, adj
◆ Southern German, adj
Süddeutscher, m
◆ South German
◆ Southern German
◆ southern German
Süddeutschland
◆ South Germany
◆ Southern Germany
Südeingang, m
◆ south entrance
Südengland
◆ Southern England
◆ southern England
Sudeten, die, pl
◆ Sudetic Mountains, the, pl
◆ Sudeten Mountains, the, pl
◆ Sudetes, the, pl
Südeuropa
◆ South Europe
◆ Southern Europe
◆ southern Europe
Südeuropäer, m
◆ South European
Südeuropäerin, f
◆ South European girl
◆ South European woman
◆ South European
südeuropäisch, adj
◆ South European, adj
◆ Southern European, adj
◆ southern European, adj
Südfassade, f
◆ south façade
◆ south facade AE
◆ south front

Südfenster

Südfenster, n
- ♦ south-facing window
- window facing south
- window to the south

Südflügel, m
Südtrakt, m
- ♦ south wing

Südfrankreich
- ♦ South of France
- south of France
- Southern France
- southern France

südfranzösisch, adj
- ♦ Southern French, adj
- ♦ southern French, adj

Südgarten, m
nach Süden liegender Garten, m
- ♦ south-facing garden
- ♦ s/f garden

Südgebäude, n
- ♦ south building

Südgrenze, f
- ♦ south border
- southern border

Südhang, m
- ♦ south-facing slope
- ♦ south-facing hillside

Südhessen
- ♦ Southern Hesse

Südindien
- ♦ South India
- Southern India
- southern India

Süditalien
- ♦ South Italy
- Southern Italy
- southern Italy

Süditaliener, m
- ♦ South Italian
- Southern Italian

Süditalienerin, f
- ♦ South Italian girl
- South Italian woman
- ♦ South Italian
- Southern Italian girl
- Southern Italian woman

süditalienisch, adj
- ♦ South Italian, adj
- ♦ Southern Italian, adj

Südkorea
- ♦ South Korea

Südkoreaner, m
- ♦ South Korean

Südkoreanerin, f
- ♦ South Korean girl
- South Korean woman
- ♦ South Korean

südkoreanisch, adj
- ♦ South Korean, adj

Südküste, f
- ♦ south coast
- southern coast

Südlage f
- ♦ south-facing position

Südlichen Kalkalpen, die, pl
- ♦ Southern Limestone Alps, the, pl

südliche Route, f
- ♦ southerly route

südliches Africa, n
- ♦ southern Africa
- Southern Africa

südliches Ambiente, n
- ♦ southern ambience
- southern atmosphere

südliches Mittelmeer, n
- ♦ southern Mediterranean, the

südliches Querhaus, n (Kirche)
südliches Querschiff, n
Südtransept, m/n
- ♦ south transept
- southern transept

südlich liegen von etw
- ♦ lie south of s.th.
- be situated to the south of s.th.

südlichst, adj
- ♦ southernmost, adj
- most southerly, adj

südlichster Punkt, m
- ♦ most southerly point

südlichste Spitze, f
- ♦ southernmost tip

südlich von etw
- ♦ south of s.th.

Südloggia f
- ♦ south-facing loggia
- loggia facing south

Süd-Nord-Verbindung, f
- ♦ south-north link
- south-north connection

Südostafrika
- ♦ Southeast Africa AE
- ♦ South-East Africa BE

Südostasien
- ♦ Southeast Asia AE
- ♦ South-East Asia BE

Südosten, m
- ♦ southeast AE
- south-east BE
- South-East BE

Südostküste, f
- ♦ southeast coast AE
- south-east coast BE

südöstliche Richtung, f
- ♦ southeasterly direction AE
- south-easterly direction BE

Südpazifik, m
- ♦ South Pacific, the
- Southern Pacific, the

Südpazifikinsel, f
- ♦ South Pacific island

Südpol, m
- ♦ South Pole, the

Südpolarkreis, m
- ♦ Antarctic Circle, the

Südportal, n (Kirche)
- ♦ south porch

Südschwarzwald, m
- ♦ Southern Black Forest, the

Südschweiz, f
- ♦ Southern Switzerland
- South Switzerland

Südsee, die, f
- ♦ South Seas, the pl

Südseite, f
- ♦ south side
- southern side

Südspanien
- ♦ South Spain
- Southern Spain
- southern Spain

Südstrand, m
- ♦ south beach

Südterrasse, f
- ♦ south-facing terrace
- south-facing patio
- terrace facing south
- patio facing south

Südtirol
(Region)
- ♦ South Tirol, the
- South Tyrol, the

Südtiroler, m
- ♦ South Tirolean
- South Tyrolean
- South Tyrolese
- South Tirolese

südtirolisch, adj
- ♦ South Tirolean, adj
- South Tyrolean, adj
- South Tirolese, adj
- South Tyrolese, adj

Südtor, n
- ♦ south gate
- southern gate

Südtribüne, f
- ♦ south stand
- south stands pl

Südturm, m
- ♦ south tower
- southern tower

Südufer, n (Fluß)
- ♦ south bank

Südufer, n (Meer, Binnensee)
- ♦ south shore
- southern shore

Südveranda, f
- ♦ south-facing veranda
- south-facing verandah
- veranda facing south
- verandah facing south

Südverkehr, m
Verkehr nach Süden, m
- ♦ southbound traffic

Südvogesen, die, pl
- ♦ Southern Vosges, the, pl

Südwales
- ♦ South Wales

südwärts, adv
- ♦ southwards, adv
- southward, adv
- to the south, adv
- south, adv

südwärts reisen
- ♦ travel southward(s)

südwärts wandern
- ♦ walk southward(s)

südwärts ziehen
südwärts wandern
- ♦ migrate southward(s)

Südwein, m
- ♦ fortified wine

Südwestdeutschland
- ♦ Southwest Germany AE
- South-West Germany BE

Südwesten, m
- ♦ southwest AE
- south-west BE
- South-West BE

Südwestküste, f
- ♦ southwest coast AE
- south-west coast BE

südwestliche Richtung, f
- ♦ southwesterly direction AE
- ♦ south-westerly direction BE

Südwürttemberg-Hohenzollern
- ♦ South Württemberg-Hohenzollern

Südzimmer n
Zimmer nach Süden n
nach Süden gelegenes Zimmer n
- ♦ south-facing room
- ♦ room facing south

Suezkanal, m
- ♦ Suez Canal, the

süffeln
- ♦ have a bit of a tipple
- ♦ have a tipple
- ♦ tipple

Suite, f
Zimmerflucht, f
- ♦ suite

Suite auf zwei Geschossen, f
- ♦ bi-level suite

Suite besteht aus drei Räumen
- ♦ suite consists of three rooms

Suite besteht aus Schlafzimmer und Salon
- ♦ suite consists of bedroom and parlor AE
- ♦ suite consists of bedroom and parlour BE

Suite besteht aus Wohn- und Schlafzimmer
- ♦ suite consists of living and bedroom

Suite buchen
- ♦ book a suite

Suite erhalten
- ♦ obtain a suite
- ♦ get a suite
- ♦ be given a suite
- ♦ be provided with a suite

Suite für Hochzeitsreisende, f
Flitterwochensuite, f
- ♦ honeymoon suite

Suite haben
- ♦ have a suite

Suite-Haus, n
→ Suitenhotel

Suite im dritten Obergeschoß, f
Suite auf der dritten Etage, f
Suite im dritten Stockwerk, f
- ♦ suite on the fourth floor AE
- ♦ suite on the third floor BE
- ♦ fourth-floor suite AE
- ♦ third-floor suite BE

Suite im traditionellen Stil, f
Suite im herkömmlichen Stil, f
- ♦ traditional-style suite

Suite ist benannt nach jm
- ♦ suite is named after s.o.

Suite mit Bedienung, f
- ♦ service suite
- ♦ serviced suite

Suite mit einem Schlafzimmer, f
- ♦ one-bedroom suite
- ♦ one-bedroomed suite
- ♦ suite with one bedroom

Suite mit Hauptschlafzimmer, f
Suite mit besonders großem Schlafzimmer, f
- ♦ master bedroom suite

Suite mit Kochgelegenheit f
- ♦ housekeeping suite

Suite mit Küche, f
Suite mit einer Küche, f
- ♦ suite with kitchen
- ♦ suite with a kitchen

Suite mit vier Schlafzimmern, f
- ♦ four-bedroom suite
- ♦ four-bedroomed suite
- ♦ suite with four bedrooms

Suitenbeschreibung, f
- ♦ suite description
- ♦ description of a suite

Suitenhotel, n
Suitehotel, n
- ♦ suite hotel

Suitennummer, f
- ♦ suite number

Suitenunterkunft, f
Suitenunterbringung, f
- ♦ suite accommodation

Suite ohne Kochgelegenheit f
- ♦ sleeping suite AE

Suite reservieren
- ♦ reserve a suite

Suite verfügt über ein Klavier
- ♦ suite has a piano

Suitezimmer, n
Zimmer einer Suite, n
- ♦ suite room

Sultanine, f
- ♦ sultana

Sumatra
- ♦ Sumatra

sündhaft teuer sein coll
- ♦ cost an arm and a leg coll

Superabend, m
- ♦ super evening inform

Superessen, n
- ♦ super meal inform

Superfähre, f
- ♦ super ferry inform

Superferienort, m
Superurlaubsort, m
Superort, m
- ♦ super resort inform

Super-Flieg-und-Spar-Tarif, m
APEX-Tarif, m
- ♦ APEX tariff

Superhotel, n
- ♦ super hotel inform

Superkoch, m
Superküchenchef, m
- ♦ super chef inform

Superkongreß, m
- ♦ super congress inform
- ♦ super convention inform

Supermarkt, m
- ♦ supermarket

Supermarkt ist nur 250 m entfernt
- ♦ supermarket is only 250 m away
- ♦ supermarket is only 250 m distant

Superpreis, m
- ♦ super price inform

Superprovision, f
- ♦ super commission inform

Supersaison, f
- ♦ super season inform

superschneller Service, m
- ♦ superquick service

Superstar, m
- ♦ superstar

Superstrand, m
- ♦ super beach inform

Supersuite, f
- ♦ super suite inform

Superzielort, m
Superziel, n
- ♦ super destination inform

Superzimmer, n
- ♦ super room inform

Superzug, m
- ♦ super train inform

Suppe, f
- ♦ soup

Suppe auslöffeln müssen
- ♦ have to face the music

Suppe braucht mehr Salz
- ♦ soup needs more salt

Suppe ist eiskalt
- ♦ soup is stone-cold

Suppe ist zu salzig
- ♦ soup is too salty

Suppe kalt werden lassen
- ♦ let the soup get cold
- ♦ let the soup cool off

Suppe kommt
- ♦ soup arrives

Suppengang m
- ♦ soup course
- ♦ soups course

Suppenkelle, f
Suppenschöpflöffel, m
- ♦ soup ladle

Suppenkoch, m
Potagier, m FR
- ♦ soup cook
- ♦ potagier FR

Suppenküche, f
(für Arme etc.)
- ♦ soup kitchen
- ♦ soup-kitchen BE

Suppenlöffel m
- ♦ soup spoon
- ♦ soup-spoon BE

Suppenrezept, n
Suppenrezeptur, f
- ♦ soup recipe

Suppenschüssel, f
Suppenterrine, f
- ♦ soup bowl
- ♦ soup tureen AE
- ♦ soup-tureen BE
- ♦ tureen

Suppensektion, f
Suppenabteilung, f
Suppenstation, f
- ♦ soup section

Suppenstation, f
Suppentheke, f
- ♦ soup counter

Suppentasse, f
- ♦ soup cup AE
- ♦ soup-cup BE

Suppenteller, m
- ♦ soup plate
- ♦ soup-plate BE

Suppenterrine, f
Suppenschüssel, f
- ♦ soup tureen AE
- ♦ soup-tureen BE
- ♦ soup bowl

Suppentopf, m
→ Suppenschüssel

Suppe schlürfen
- ♦ slurp one's soup

Suppe servieren
♦ serve the soup
Suppe versalzen
♦ oversalt the soup
Suppe verschütten
♦ spill (the) soup
Surfbrett, n
♦ surfboard
Surfbrett, n (Windsurfen)
♦ sailboard
Surfbrettverleih, m
♦ surfboard rental AE
♦ surfboard hire BE
surfen
wellenreiten
♦ surf
♦ go surfing
Surfen, n
Wellenreiten, n
Surfsport, m
♦ surfing
surfen gehen
♦ go surfing
Surfer, m
Wellenreiter, m
♦ surfer
Surflehrer, m
♦ surfing instructor
Surfparadies, n
♦ surfer's paradise
♦ surfing paradise
Surfschule, f
♦ surfing school
Surfstrand, m
♦ surfing beach
Surfstunde, f
♦ surfing lesson
Surfunterricht, m
♦ surfing instruction
♦ surfing tuition
♦ surfing lessons pl
Surfzentrum, n
♦ surfing center AE
♦ surfing centre BE
Surinam
♦ Suriname
Surinamer, m
♦ Surinamese
Surinamerin, f
♦ Surinamese girl
♦ Surinamese woman
♦ Surinamese
surinamisch, adj
♦ Surinamese, adj
süß, adj
♦ sweet, adj
süße Dickmilch, f
♦ junket gastr
süßen (etw)
♦ sweeten (s.th.)
süßen etw mit Zucker
♦ sweeten s.th. with sugar
Süßkartoffel, f
♦ sweet potato
Süßkirsche, f
♦ sweet cherry
Süßmost, m
♦ unfermented juice
♦ unfermented fruit juice
Süßrahmbutter, f
♦ creamery butter

süß-sauer, adj
♦ sweet and sour, adj
süß-saure Soße, f
♦ sweet and sour sauce
süß schmecken
♦ taste sweet
Süßspeise, f
Mehlspeise, f ÖST
♦ sweet dish
♦ sweet BE
♦ dessert
Süßspeisenkoch, m
→ Küchenkonditor
Süßspeisenteller, m
♦ sweet plate
Süßwarengeschäft, n
♦ confectioner's shop
♦ candy store AE
♦ sweetshop BE
♦ tuck-shop BE
Süßwasser, n
♦ freshwater AE
♦ fresh water BE
Süßwasserbad, n
Süßwasserbecken, n
♦ freshwater pool
Süßwasserbecken, n
→ Süßwasserbad
Süßwasserdusche, f
♦ freshwater shower
Süßwasserfisch, m (außer Lachs und Forelle)
♦ coarse fish BE
Süßwasserfisch, m (generell)
♦ freshwater fish
Süßwasserfischfang, m (außer Lachs und Forelle)
Süßwasserfische fangen
Süßwasserfische angeln
♦ coarse fishing BE
Süßwasserfreibad, n
♦ outdoor freshwater swimming pool AE
♦ outdoor freshwater swimming-pool BE
♦ outdoor freshwater pool
Süßwasserhallenbad, n
Süßwasserhallenschwimmbad, n
Süßwasserhallenschwimmbecken, n
♦ indoor freshwater swimming pool AE
♦ indoor freshwater swimming-pool BE
♦ indoor freshwater pool
Süßwasserhallenschwimmbad, n
→ Süßwasserhallenbad
Süßwasserplanschbecken, n
♦ freshwater wading pool AE
♦ freshwater paddling pool BE
Süßwasserschwimmbad, n
Süßwasserschwimmbecken, n
♦ freshwater swimming pool AE
♦ freshwater swimming-pool BE
♦ freshwater pool
Süßwassersee, m
♦ freshwater lake
Süßwassserteich, m
♦ freshwater pond
Süßwein, m (generell)
süßer Wein, m
♦ sweet wine
♦ dessert wine
Süßwein, m (hell)
♦ sack
Sustenpaß, der, m
♦ Susten Pass, the

Swasi, m
Swasi, f
♦ Swazi
Swasiland
♦ Swaziland
swasiländisch, adj
♦ Swazi, adj
♦ Swaziland, adj
Swimmingpool, m
→ Schwimmbad
Sylt
(Insel)
♦ Sylt
Symbol, n
♦ symbol
Symbolerklärung, f
Symbolschlüssel, m
♦ symbol key
symbolische Gebühr f
♦ token charge
♦ token fee
Symposion, n
♦ symposium
Symposion abhalten
Symposion veranstalten
♦ hold a symposium
Symposionanordnung, f (Bestuhlung)
(Reihenbestuhlung mit mehreren Podiumsitzen)
♦ symposium arrangement
Symposion planen
♦ plan a symposium
Synode, f
♦ synod
Syrer, m
Syrier, m
♦ Syrian
Syrerin, f
Syrierin, f
♦ Syrian girl
♦ Syrian woman
♦ Syrian
Syrien
♦ Syria
syrisch, adj
♦ Syrian, adj
Szenenwechsel, m (Ortsveränderung)
→ Ortsveränderung
Szenenwechsel machen figur
♦ get a change of scene figur
♦ have a change of scene figur

T

Tabak, m
- tobacco

Tabakdose, f
- tobacco box

Tabakhändler m
- tobacconist

Tabakkosten, pl
- tobacco costs *pl*
- tobacco cost

Tabakladen, m
- Tabakgeschäft, n
- tobacco store *AE*
- cigar store *AE*
- tobacconist's (store) *AE*
- tobacconist's (shop) *BE*
- tobacco shop

Tabaksteuer, f
- tobacco tax

Tabakumsatz, m
- Rauchwarenumsatz, m
- tobacco turnover
- tobacco sales *pl*

Tabakverkauf m
- Tabakwarenverkauf m
- tobacco sale
- sale of tobacco
- selling (of) tobacco

Tabakwaren, f pl
- tobacco products *pl*

Tabakwarenerlös, m
- tobacco revenue

Tabakwarenertrag, m
- (Gewinn- und Verlustrechnung)
- Tabakertrag m
- tobacco income

Tabakwarenkosten, pl
- cost of tobacco sales

Tabakwarenumsatz, m
- → Tabakumsatz

Tabasco, m
- (Warenzeichen)
- Tabasco

Tabascosoße, f
- (Warenzeichen)
- Tabasco sauce

tabellarischer Lebenslauf, m
- personal data sheet

Tabelle, f
- table
- chart

Tabellenpreis, m
- price listed in the table
- rate listed in the table
- advertised price
- advertised rate

Taberna, f
- taberna
- taverna

Tabernakel, n/m
- tabernacle

Table d'hôte, f *FR*
- gemeinsames Menü zum festen Preis, f
- gemeinsame Tafel zum festen Preis, f
- Gästetafel, f
- table d'hôte *FR*
- set meal (taken together) at a fixed price
- set meal (taken together) at a set price
- fixed-price meal (taken together)

Table d'hôte-Abendessen, n (Dinner)
- table d'hôte dinner

Table d'hôte-Abendessen, n (Supper)
- table d'hôte supper

Table d'hôte-Essen, n
- → Stammessen

Table d'hôte-Gericht, n
- table d'hôte dish

Table d'hôte-Menü, n
- table d'hôte menu

Table d'hôte-Mittagessen, n
- → gemeinsames Mittagessen

Table d'hôte-Service, m
- table d'hôte service

Table d'hôte-Speisekarte, f
- table d'hôte menu

Tablett, n
- tray
- salver
- platter

Tachometer, m
- speedometer
- speedo *coll*

Taco, m *MEX*
- (gefüllte Tortilla)
- taco *MEX*

tadellos, adj
- fehlerlos, adj
- impeccable, adj
- faultless, adj

tadellose Manieren, pl
- impeccable manners *pl*

tadelloser Service m
- impeccable service

tadelloses Benehmen, n
- impeccable behavior *AE*
- impeccable behaviour *BE*

tadellos sauber, adj
- blitzsauber, adj
- immaculately clean, adj
- spotslessly clean, adj

Tadschike, m
- Tajik
- Tadzhik
- Tadjik

Tadschikin, f
- Tajik girl
- Tajik woman
- Tajik

tadschikisch, adj
- Tajik, adj
- Tadzhik, adj
- Tadjik, adj

Tadschikistan
- Tajikistan
- Tadzhikistan

Tadsch Mahal, der, m
- Taj Mahal, the

Tafel, f (Information)
- board

Tafel, f (Schokolade)
- Tafel Schokolade, f
- bar
- bar of chocolate

Tafel, f (Schultafel)
- blackboard
- chalkboard *AE*

Tafel, f (Tisch)
- → Tisch

Tafelberg, m
- Table Mountain, the

Tafelbesteck, n
- best cutlery *coll*
- best silver *coll*

Tafelbestuhlung, f
- → Tischbestuhlung

Tafel decken
- → Tisch decken

Tafeldekor, n
- → Tischdekor

Tafelfreuden, f pl
- Gaumenfreuden, f pl
- kulinarische Genüsse, m pl
- pleasures of the table *pl*
- culinary delights *pl*

Tafelgeschirr, n
- Eßgeschirr, n
- Speiseservice, n
- dinner set
- dinner service

Tafelkarte, f
- → Bankettspeisekarte

Tafelmesser, n
- → Tischmesser

Tafelmusik, f
- → Tischmusik

tafeln
- feast
- dine
- banquet

tafeln wie Lukull
- have a Lucullan feast

Tafelobst, n
- dessert fruit

Tafelplan

Tafelplan, m
→ Tischplan
Tafelrunde, f (von König Artus)
♦ Round Table, the
Tafelsalz, n
♦ table salt
Tafel Schokolade, f
♦ bar of chocolate
Tafelsilber, n
♦ table silver
Täfelung, f
♦ panelling
♦ paneling AE
Tafelwasser, n
♦ table water
Tag, an dem man abreist
♦ day on which one leaves
Tag, m
♦ day
Tag abrunden mit etw
♦ round off the day with s.th.
Tag abschließen
♦ conclude the day
Tag am Meer, m
♦ day at the seaside
Tag am Meer verbringen
Tag an der See verbringen
♦ spend a day at the seaside
Tag beenden mit etw
♦ end the day with s.th.
♦ finish the day with s.th.
Tag beginnen mit etw
♦ start the day with s.th.
♦ start the day with/by doing s.th.
♦ commence the day with s.th. *form*
Tag der Arbeit, m
♦ Labor Day AE
♦ Labour Day BE
Tag der offenen Tür, m
♦ open day
Tag des Gastes, m
♦ day of the guest
Tagdienst, m
(Personal)
Tagesdienst, m
♦ daytime duty
tagen
♦ meet
♦ sit
♦ have a meeting
tagen bis zum Morgen
♦ sit until morning
tagen unter Ausschluß der Öffentlichkeit
tagen hinter geschlossenen Türen
♦ meet behind closed doors
♦ meet in camera *jur*
Tagesabrechnung, f
→ Tagesrechnung
Tagesaufenthalt, m (eintägig)
Eintagesaufenthalt, m
eintägiger Aufenthalt, m
♦ day's stay
♦ one-day stay
Tagesaufenthalt, m (während des Tages)
♦ stay during the day
Tagesausflug, m
Tagestour, f
♦ day trip AE
♦ day-trip BE
♦ day excursion

♦ day('s) outing
♦ full-day excursion
Tagesausflugentfernung, f
♦ day-trip distance
Tagesausflügler, m
Tagestourist, m
♦ day tripper AE
♦ day-tripper BE
♦ day excursionist
Tagesausflug machen
♦ make a day excursion
♦ go on a day excursion
♦ go on a day trip
Tagesausflug machen in die Berge
Tagesausflug in das Gebirge machen
♦ make a day excursion to the mountains
♦ go on a day excursion to the mountains
♦ go on a day trip to the mountains
Tagesausflugsdienst, m
♦ day-trip service
♦ day-excursion service
Tagesausflugsmarkt, m
♦ day-trip market
Tagesausflugsverkehr, m
♦ day-trip traffic
Tagesausflugsziel, n
♦ day-trip destination
Tagesausgabe, f
(z.B. durch Touristen)
♦ daily expenditure
♦ expenditure per day
Tagesauslastung, f
tägliche Auslastung, f
Tagesbelegung, f
tägliche Belegung, f
♦ daily occupancy
♦ occupancy per day
Tagesausstellung, f
eintägige Ausstellung, f
♦ one-day exhibition
♦ one-day exhibit AE
Tagesbar f
♦ day bar
Tagesbelegung, f
→ Tagesauslastung
Tagesbericht, m
♦ daily report
Tagesbericht erstellen
♦ draw up the daily report
Tagesbesuch, m (eintägig)
eintägiger Besuch, m
♦ one-day visit
♦ full-day visit
♦ whole-day visit
♦ one-day trip
♦ full-day trip
Tagesbesuch, m (tagsüber)
♦ day visit
♦ daytime visit
Tagesbesuch eines Ortes organisieren (eintägig)
eintägigen Besuch in einem Ort organisieren
♦ organise a one-day visit to a place
♦ organize a one-day visit to a place
Tagesbesuch eines Orts organisieren (tagsüber)
♦ organise a day visit to a place
♦ organize a day visit to a place
Tagesbesucher m
♦ day visitor
Tagesbesuch in X, m (tagsüber)
♦ day visit to X
♦ daytime visit to X

Tagesbett, n
♦ day-bed
Tagesbettdecke, f
(gesteppt)
Tagesdecke, f
♦ comforter AE
♦ bedspread
Tagesbrigade, f
(Gegensatz zu Nachtbrigade)
♦ day brigade
Tagesbüfett, n
♦ today's buffet
♦ daily buffet
Tagescafé, n
♦ day cafe AE
♦ day café BE
Tagesdecke, f
Bettdecke, f
♦ bedspread
♦ counterpane BE
♦ comforter AE
Tagesdienst, m
Tagesservice m
♦ day service
Tagesdurchschnitt, m
♦ daily average
Tagesdurchschnittspreis, m
→ durchschnittlicher Tagespreis
Tageseinnahmen, f pl
(Kassa)
♦ day's takings pl
♦ daily takings pl
♦ day's receipts pl
♦ daily receipts pl
♦ daily earnings pl
Tagesempfangsdame, f
Tagesrezeptionistin, f
♦ female day receptionist
Tagesempfangsherr, m
Tagesrezeptionist m
♦ day receptionist
Tageserlös, m
♦ daily revenue
♦ revenue per day
Tagesetappe, f
♦ daily stage
♦ daily lap
Tagesfahrpreis, m
♦ day fare
Tagesfahrt, f (Auto)
♦ day's drive
♦ day drive
Tagesfahrt, f (eintägig)
eintägige Fahrt, f
♦ one-day trip
♦ one-day ride
♦ whole-day tour
♦ whole-day trip
♦ day-trip
Tagesfahrt, f (während des Tags)
♦ daytime tour
♦ day tour
Tagesfahrt bringt Sie nach X (Auto)
♦ day's drive takes you to X
♦ day's drive will take you to X
Tagesfest, n (Festival, eintägig)
eintägiges Fest, n
eintägige Festspiele, n pl
♦ one-day festival
Tagesfest, n (Festival, tagsüber)
♦ day festival

Tagesfest, n (Party, eintägig)
  eintägiges Fest, n
  eintägige Party, f
  ♦ one-day party
Tagesfest, n (Party, tagsüber)
  ♦ day party
Tagesflug, m (während des Tags)
  Tagflug, m
  ♦ day flight
  ♦ daytime flight
Tagesfrau, f
  ♦ daily woman
Tagesgast, m
  ♦ day guest
Tagesgastanzahl, f
  Tagesgästezahl, f
  ♦ number of day guests
Tagesgästeliste f
  ♦ list of day guests
Tagesgästepauschale, f
  ♦ day guest package
Tagesgebühr, f
  → Gebühr pro Tag
Tagesgedeck, n
  → Tagesplatte
Tagesgericht, n
  Plat du jour, f FR m
  ♦ dish of the day
  ♦ special dish of the day
  ♦ today's specialty AE
  ♦ today's speciality BE
  ♦ today's special
Tagesgrundpreis, m
  Grundpreis pro Tag, m
  ♦ basic rate per day
  ♦ basic price per day
Tagesgrundpreis pro Person, m
  ♦ basic rate per day per person
  ♦ basic price per day per person
Tageshotel, n
  ♦ day hotel
Tagesinklusivpreis, m
  ♦ inclusive price per day
  ♦ inclusive rate per day
  ♦ daily inclusive price
  ♦ daily inclusive rate
Tagesjournal, n
  → Journal
Tageskabine, f
  ♦ day cabin
Tageskapazität f
  ♦ daily capacity
Tageskarte, f (Fahrkarte)
  ♦ one-day ticket
  ♦ whole-day ticket
  ♦ full-day ticket
  ♦ day ticket
Tageskarte, f (Speisekarte)
  Carte du jour, f FR
  ♦ menu of the day
  ♦ today's menu
  ♦ carte du jour FR
  ♦ daily menu
  ♦ today's bill of fare
Tageskasse, f
  Kasse, f
  ♦ ticket office
Tageskassenbericht, m
  ♦ daily cash report
Tageskellnerin, f
  ♦ day waitress

Tageskellner m
  ♦ day waiter
Tageskinderbetreuungspersonal, n
  ♦ daytime child-care staff
  ♦ daytime child-care personnel
Tageskreuzfahrt, f (eintägig)
  eintägige Kreuzfahrt, f
  ♦ one-day cruise
  ♦ whole-day cruise
  ♦ full-day cruise
Tageskreuzfahrt, f (während des Tages)
  ♦ day cruise
  ♦ daytime cruise
Tageskurs, m (Lehrgang)
  Tageslehrgang, m
  ♦ one-day course
  ♦ full-day course
  ♦ whole-day course
  ♦ day course
Tageskurs, m (Satz)
  → aktueller Kurs
Tageskurtaxe, f
  Kurtaxe pro Tag, f
  ♦ spa tax per day
Tageslehrgang, m
  Tageskurs, m
  ♦ day course
Tageslicht, n
  ♦ daylight
Tageslichtfolie, f
  Overheadfolie, f
  ♦ overhead transparency
  ♦ OHP transparency
Tageslichtprojektion, f
  Overheadprojektion, f
  ♦ overhead projection
Tageslichtprojektionsleinwand, f
  Leinwand für Tageslichtprojektion, f
  ♦ overhead projection screen
Tageslichtprojektor, m
  Overheadprojektor, m
  OH-Projektor, m
  ♦ overhead projector
  ♦ OH projector
Tagesmarsch, m
  ♦ day's march
  ♦ day's trek
Tagesmenü, n (abends)
  Abendmenü, n
  ♦ set dinner
  ♦ dinner menu
Tagesmenü, n (generell)
  Plat du jour, f FR m
  ♦ today's menu
  ♦ plat du jour FR m
  ♦ day's menu
  ♦ daily menu
Tagesmenü, n (mittags)
  Mittagsmenü, n
  ♦ set lunch
  ♦ set luncheon
Tagesmenükarte, f
  ♦ daily menu card
  ♦ today's menu card
Tagesmiete, f
  → Miete pro Tag
Tagesmiete pro Person, f
  → Miete pro Person pro Tag
Tagesnachfrage, f
  tägliche Nachfrage, f
  ♦ daily demand

Tagesnetzkarte, f
  ♦ one-day runabout ticket BE
Tagesniveau, n
  ♦ daily level
Tagesordnung, f
  ♦ agenda
Tagesordnungspunkt, m
  ♦ agenda item
  ♦ item on the agenda
Tagespauschale, f
  ♦ day package
  ♦ daily package
Tagespauschalpreis, m
  ♦ daily inclusive price
  ♦ daily inclusive rate
  ♦ daily package price
  ♦ daily package rate
  ♦ inclusive price per day
Tagespersonal, n
  ♦ day staff
  ♦ day personnel
Tagesplatte, f
  Plat du jour, m FR
  Tagesgericht, n
  Tagesgedeck, n
  ♦ today's special
  ♦ today's specialty AE
  ♦ today's speciality BE
  ♦ plat du jour FR
Tagesportier, m
  ♦ day porter
Tagesportierdienst, m
  Tagesportierservice, m
  ♦ daytime porterage
Tagespreis, m (aktuell)
  → aktueller Preis
Tagespreis, m (generell)
  (für Zimmerbenutzung bis 18 Uhr)
  ♦ day rate
  ♦ day price
  ♦ use rate AE
Tagespreisgast, m
  ♦ day-rate guest
Tagesprogramm, n
  ♦ day's program AE
  ♦ day's programme BE
  ♦ daily program(me)
  ♦ day program(me)
  ♦ today's program(me)
Tagesration, f
  → Tagesverpflegung
Tagesraum, m
  (in Heim, Krankenhaus)
  Aufenthaltsraum, m
  ♦ dayroom
  ♦ day-room
Tagesrechnung, f
  Tagesabrechnung, f
  ♦ daily bill
  ♦ daily check AE
  ♦ daily account
Tagesrechnung vorlegen
  ♦ present the daily bill
  ♦ present the daily check AE
  ♦ present the daily account
Tagesreise, f (am Tag)
  Tagestour, f
  ♦ day's journey
  ♦ day's tour
  ♦ day tour
  ♦ day's travel

Tagesreise

Tagesreise, f (eintägig)
  eintägige Reise, f
  ◆ one-day tour
  ◆ whole-day tour
  ◆ full-day tour
  ◆ one-day journey
  ◆ one-day trip
Tagesrestaurant n
  ◆ day restaurant
Tagesrezeptionist, m
  → Tagesempfangsherr
Tagesroute, f
  Tagesstrecke, f
  tägliche Route, f
  tägliche Strecke, f
  ◆ daily route
Tagesrückfahrkarte, f
  ◆ day-return ticket
  ◆ day-return
Tagessatz, m
  Tagespreis, m
  ◆ per diem rate
  ◆ per diem price
  ◆ per diem
  ◆ daily rate
Tagesschule, f
  ◆ day school
Tagesseminar, n (eintägig)
  eintägiges Seminar, n
  ◆ one-day seminar
  ◆ whole-day seminar
  ◆ full-day seminar
Tagesservice, m
  → Tagesdienst
Tagesskikurs, m
  eintägiger Skikurs, m
  ◆ one-day ski course
  ◆ one-day skiing course
Tagesspesen, pl
  ◆ daily expenses pl
  ◆ per diem expenses pl
  ◆ per diem
Tagesspesensatz, m
  ◆ per diem allowance
Tagesspezialität, f
  ◆ today's specialty AE
  ◆ today's speciality BE
  ◆ today's special dish
Tagesspiegel, m
  (bei Zimmerbelegung)
  → Tagesstatistik
Tagesstatistik f
  ◆ daily statistics pl
Tagessuppe, f
  Potage du jour, f FR
  ◆ soup of the day
  ◆ potage du jour FR m
  ◆ day's soup
Tagestarif, m
  ◆ daily tariff
  ◆ daily rates pl
  ◆ daily rate
  ◆ daily terms pl
Tagestarif pro Person, m
  ◆ daily terms per person pl
  ◆ daily rates per person pl
  ◆ daily rate per person
Tagestelefonist, m
  Tagestelefonistin, f
  ◆ day telephonist

Tagestemperatur, f
  ◆ daytime temperature
Tagestour, f
  → Tagesreise, Tagesausflug
Tagestourismus, m
  ◆ day tourism
  ◆ day tripping AE
  ◆ day-tripping BE
Tagestourist, m
  ◆ day tourist
  ◆ day tripper AE
  ◆ day-tripper BE
  ◆ excursionist
Tagesumsatz, m
  ◆ daily sales pl
  ◆ sales per day pl
  ◆ daily turnover
  ◆ turnover per day
  ◆ day's turnover
Tagesumsatzbericht, m
  ◆ daily sales report
Tagesunterhaltungsprogramm, n
  ◆ day entertainment program AE
  ◆ day entertainment programme BE
Tagesurlauber, m
  → Tagesausflügler, Tagesbesucher
Tagesveranstaltung, f (eintägig)
  eintägige Veranstaltung, f
  ◆ one-day function
  ◆ one-day event
Tagesveranstaltung, f (während des Tages)
  ◆ day function
  ◆ daytime function
  ◆ day event
  ◆ daytime event
Tagesverpflegung, f
  Tagesration, f
  ◆ daily rations pl
  ◆ daily ration
Tageswanderung, f
  ◆ day's walking
  ◆ day's hiking
  ◆ day's rambling
Tageszeit, f
  ◆ time of day
Tageszentrum, n
  (z.B. für Obdachlose)
  ◆ day center AE
  ◆ day centre BE
Tagesziel, n
  ◆ day's destination
Tageszimmer, n (Hotel, zur Vermietung tagsüber)
  ◆ day-let BE
  ◆ day room
Tageszimmermädchen n
  ◆ day chambermaid
Tageszug, m
  ◆ day train
  ◆ daytime train
tageweise, adv
  ◆ by the day, adv
  ◆ on a day-to-day basis, adv
tageweise mieten etw (Immobilien)
  ◆ rent s.th. by the day
tageweise mieten etw (Mobilien)
  ◆ rent s.th. by the day
  ◆ hire s.th. by the day BE
tageweise vermieten etw (Immobilie)
  ◆ rent (out) s.th. by the day
  ◆ let s.th. by the day BE
  ◆ hire out s.th. by the day BE

tageweise vermieten etw (Mobilie)
  ◆ hire out s.th. by the day BE
  ◆ rent (out) s.th. by the day
Tag festlich begehen
  Tag feiern
  ◆ celebrate a day
täglich, adj
  ◆ daily, adj
täglich, adv
  ◆ on a daily basis, adv
  ◆ by the day, adv
täglich buchen etw
  tageweise buchen etw
  ◆ book s.th. on a daily basis
tägliche Gästezahl f
  ◆ daily number of guests
  ◆ number of guests per day
tägliche Gebühr, f
  Tagesgebühr, f
  ◆ daily charge
  ◆ daily fee
tägliche Hausarbeit, f
  ◆ chores pl
  ◆ household chores pl
  ◆ domestic chores pl
tägliche Mahlzeit, f
  tägliches Mahl, n
  tägliches Essen, n
  ◆ daily meal
tägliche Massage, f
  ◆ daily massage
tägliche Ration, f
  ◆ daily ration
tägliche Ration Bier, f
  tägliches Quantum Bier, n
  ◆ daily ration of beer
täglicher Bettwäschewechsel, m
  ◆ daily change of bed linen
tägliche Rechnungsstellung f
  ◆ daily billing
tägliche Rechnungstellung wünschen
  ◆ request (a) daily billing
tägliche Reinigung f
  ◆ daily cleaning
täglicher Handtuchwechsel, m
  ◆ daily change of towels
täglicher Kurs, m
  täglicher Lehrgang, m
  ◆ daily class
tägliche Routine, f
  ◆ daily routine
täglicher Preis, m
  Tagespreis, m
  ◆ daily price
  ◆ daily rate
täglicher Reinigungsdienst m
  ◆ daily cleaning service
täglicher Service, m
  täglicher Dienst, m
  tägliche Betreuung, f
  ◆ daily service
täglicher Tischwäschewechsel, m
  ◆ daily change of table linen
täglicher Toilettenwäschewechsel, m
  ◆ daily change of toilet linen
täglicher Wäschewechsel m
  ◆ daily change of linen
täglicher Zimmermädchenservice, m
  täglicher Zimmermädchendienst, m
  ◆ daily chambermaid service
  ◆ daily maid service

täglicher Zimmerpreis, m
- daily room rate
- daily room price
- daily room charge

tägliches Brot, n
- one's daily bread

tägliches Leben, n
- daily life

tägliche Speisekarte, f
- daily menu

tägliches Programm, n
Tagesprogramm, n
- daily program AE
- daily programme BE

tägliche Wanderung, f
- daily walk
- daily hike
- daily ramble

tägliche Zimmerreinigung, f
- daily room cleaning

Täglich ganzjährig geöffnet
- Open daily throughout the year

täglich verkehren
(Verkehrsmittel)
- operate daily

täglich wechselnde Speisekarte, f
- menu that changes daily
- daily changing menu

Tag ohne Programm, m
programmfreier Tag, m
freier Tag, m
- day at one's disposal
- day at leisure
- free day

Tag ohne Unterkunft, m
- nonresidential day AE
- non-residential day BE

Tagschicht, f
Tagesschicht, f
- day shift

Tagschicht haben
- be on day shift

tagsüber, adv
während des Tages, adv
- during the day, adv

Tag-und-Nacht-Dienst, m
Tag-und-Nacht-Service, m
- day and night service
- round-the-clock service
- 24-hour service

Tag und Nacht geöffnet
- Open day and night

Tagung, f
- meeting

Tagung abhalten
- hold a meeting

Tagung absagen
- cancel a meeting

Tagung abschließen
- close a meeting
- conclude a meeting

Tagung abwickeln
- handle a meeting

Tagung arrangieren
Treffen arrangieren
- arrange a meeting

Tagung ausrichten (als Gastgeber)
- host a meeting
- host a conference

Tagung beenden
- end a meeting
- finish a meeting

Tagung dauert zwei Tage (lang)
- meeting lasts (for) two days

Tagung einberufen
- convene a meeting

Tagung eröffnen
- open a meeting

Tagung findet vom 1. bis 5. Oktober statt
- meeting will take place from 1 - 5 October

Tagung inszenieren
Tagung ausrichten
- stage a meeting

Tagung ist gut besucht
- meeting is well attended

Tagung koordinieren
- coordinate a meeting

Tagung läuft perfekt
- meeting runs perfectly

Tagung läuft reibungslos
- meeting runs smoothly

Tagung leiten
- lead a meeting
- run a meeting

Tagung ohne Unterkunft, f
- nonresidential meeting AE
- non-residential meeting BE

Tagung organisieren
- organise a meeting
- organize a meeting
- organise a conference
- organize a conference

Tagung planen
- plan a meeting

Tagungsabteilung, f
- meetings department
- meeting department

Tagungsanfrage, f
- meeting inquiry
- meeting enquiry
- inquiry about a meeting
- enquiry about a meeting

Tagungsangebot, n (Palette)
- range of meetings

Tagungsanschlußprogramm, n
- post-meeting program AE
- post-meeting programme BE

Tagungsarrangement, n
Tagungsvereinbarung, f
- meeting arrangement

Tagungsaufwand, m
- meeting expenditure
- meetings expenditure

Tagungsausgaben, f pl
Tagungsspesen, pl
- meeting expenses pl

Tagungsausrichter, m (Gastgeber)
- host of a meeting

Tagungsausschuß, m
- meeting committee
- meetings committee

Tagungsausstatter, m
- meeting contractor
- meetings contractor

Tagungsausweis, m
- meeting ticket
- meeting card

Tagungsbankett, n
- meeting banquet

Tagungsbereich, m (abstrakt)
- meetings field
- meeting field

Tagungsbereich, m (konkret)
- meetings area
- meeting area

Tagungsbereich, m (Sektor)
- meeting sector
- meetings sector
- conference sector

Tagungsbericht, m (Sitzungsbericht)
- meeting proceedings pl
- proceedings of a meeting pl

Tagungsbericht, m (über die Tagung)
- report of a meeting
- meeting report

Tagungsbesucher, m
- meeting visitor
- meetings visitor

Tagungsbetrieb, m
- meetings establishment
- meeting establishment
- meetings operation
- meeting operation

Tagungsbranche, f
→ Tagungsindustrie

Tagungsbroschüre, f
Tagungsprospekt, m
- meeting's brochure

Tagungsbuchung, f
- booking (of) a meeting

Tagungsbudget, n
- meeting budget

Tagungsbüro, n
- meeting office
- meetings office

Tagungsdauer, f
- duration of a meeting
- length of a meeting
- duration of a conference
- length of a conference

Tagungsdienst, m
Tagungsservice, m
Tagungsdienstleistung, f
- meeting service
- meetings service

Tagungsdokumentation, f
- meeting documentation

Tagungseinrichtung, f
Tagungsfazilität, f
Tagungsstätte, f
- meeting facility

Tagungseröffnung, f
Eröffnung einer Tagung, f
- opening of a meeting

Tagungsetage, f
- meeting floor
- meetings floor

Tagungsfachmann, m
Tagungsprofi, m
- meetings professional
- meeting professional

Tagungsfazilität, f
→ Tagungseinrichtung

Tagungsfläche, f
- meeting area
- meetings area
- meeting space
- meetings space

Tagungsgast

Tagungsgast, m
♦ meeting guest
♦ meeting customer
Tagungsgebäude, n
Tagungsstätte, f
♦ meetings building
♦ meeting building
Tagungsgebühr, f
♦ meeting charge
♦ meeting fee
Tagungsgeschäft, n
♦ meetings business
♦ meeting business
Tagungsgewerbe, n
♦ meetings trade
♦ meetings industry
Tagungshalle, f
Tagungssaal, m
♦ meetings hall
♦ meeting hall
Tagungshotel, n
♦ meetings hotel
♦ meeting hotel
Tagungsindustrie, f
Tagungswesen, n
Tagungsbranche, f
♦ meeting industry
♦ meetings industry
Tagungsinformation, f
♦ meeting information
♦ meetings information
Tagungskapazität, f
♦ meetings capacity
♦ meeting capacity
Tagungsklientel, f
♦ meetings clientele
♦ meeting clientele
Tagungskonzept, n
♦ meeting concept
Tagungskoordination, f
♦ meeting coordination
♦ meetings coordination
Tagungskoordinator, m
♦ meetings coordinator
♦ meeting coordinator
Tagungskunde, m
♦ meetings customer
♦ meeting customer
♦ meeting client
Tagungsland, n
♦ meetings country
♦ meeting country
Tagungsleiter, m
♦ meeting leader
♦ meetings leader
Tagungsleitung, f (Person)
→ Tagungsleiter
Tagungsmanagement, n
Tagungsleitung, f
♦ meetings management
♦ meeting management
Tagungsmappe, f
♦ meeting folder
♦ meeting kit *AE*
Tagungsmarketing, n
♦ meetings marketing
♦ meeting marketing
Tagungsmarkt, m
♦ meetings market
♦ meeting market

Tagungsorganisator, m
Organisator einer Tagung, m
Tagungsveranstalter, m
♦ organiser of a meeting
♦ organizer of a meeting
♦ meeting organiser
♦ meeting organizer
tagungsorientiertes Hotel, n
♦ meeting-oriented hotel *AE*
♦ meeting-orientated hotel *BE*
Tagungsort, m
Tagungsstätte, f
♦ meeting venue
♦ meeting place
♦ venue
Tagungsort aussuchen
♦ choose a meeting venue
♦ choose a venue
Tagungsortauswahl, f
♦ venue selection
♦ selecting a venue
Tagungsort bestimmen
Tagungsort festlegen
♦ decide the meeting venue
♦ decide the venue
Tagungsort buchen
♦ book a venue
Tagungsort empfehlen jm
♦ recommend a meeting venue to s.o.
♦ recommend a conference venue to s.o.
♦ recommend a venue to s.o.
Tagungsort für eine Konferenz, m
♦ venue for a conference
♦ venue of a conference
Tagungsortleiter, m
Ortsleiter, m
♦ venue manager
Tagungsortleitung, f
Ortsleitung, f
♦ venue management
Tagungsort vorschlagen
♦ suggest a meeting venue
♦ suggest a venue
Tagungsortwahl, f
♦ selection of a meeting venue
♦ choice of the conference venue
♦ selecting a meeting venue
♦ selection of the conference site
♦ choice of the conference site
Tagungsort wählen
Tagungsort auswählen
♦ select a meeting venue
♦ select a venue
Tagungspaket, n
(Informationen)
♦ meeting pack
Tagungspauschale, f
♦ meeting package
♦ meetings package
Tagungspauschalpreis, m
♦ meeting package price
♦ meeting package rate
Tagungspause, f
♦ meeting break
Tagungspavillon, m
♦ meeting pavilion
♦ meetings pavilion
Tagungsplaner, m
(Person)
♦ meeting planner

Tagungsplanung, f
♦ meetings planning
♦ planning (of) a meeting
Tagungspotential, n
♦ meeting potential
Tagungspreis, m
♦ meeting price
♦ meeting rate
Tagungsprodukt, n
♦ meeting product
♦ meetings product
Tagungsprofi, m
♦ meeting professional
Tagungsprogramm, n
♦ meeting program *AE*
♦ meeting programme *BE*
Tagungsprospekt, m
♦ meetings brochure
♦ meeting brochure
Tagungsraum, m (Volumen, Fläche)
Tagungsfläche, f
♦ meeting space
Tagungsraum, m (Zimmer)
Tagungszimmer, n
♦ meeting room
♦ meetings room
Tagungsraumgeschäft, n
♦ meeting room business
Tagungsräumlichkeiten, f pl
♦ meeting facilities *pl*
♦ meetings facilities *pl*
♦ conference facilities *pl*
Tagungsraum mieten
♦ rent a meeting room
♦ hire a meeting room *BE*
Tagungsraumservice, m
Tagungsraumdienst, m
♦ meeting room service
Tagungsraumumsatz, m
♦ meeting space sales *pl*
♦ meeting space turnover
Tagungsraum vermieten
♦ rent (out) a meeting room
♦ hire out a meeting room *BE*
♦ let a meeting room *BE*
Tagungsreihe, f
♦ series of meetings
Tagungsreisender, m
♦ person traveling to a meeting *AE*
♦ person travelling to a meeting *BE*
♦ conference tourist
Tagungssaal, m
♦ large meeting room
♦ meetings hall
♦ meeting hall
Tagungssaison, f
♦ meeting season
♦ meetings season
Tagungssektor, m
→ Tagungsbereich
Tagungsservice, m
→ Tagungsdienst
Tagungsservicepersonal, n
Tagungsdienstpersonal, n
♦ meeting service staff
♦ meeting service personnel
Tagungsspezialist, m
♦ meetings specialist
Tagungsstadt, f (Großstadt)
♦ meetings city
♦ meeting city

Tagungsstadt, f (kleine Stadt)
♦ meetings town
♦ meeting town
Tagungsstätte, f (Einrichtung)
→ Tagungseinrichtung
Tagungsstätte, f (Gebäude)
→ Tagungsgebäude
Tagungsstätte, f (Stadt)
→ Tagungsstadt
Tagungssuite, f
♦ meetings suite
♦ meeting suite
Tagungsszene, f
♦ meetings scene
Tagungstechnik, f
♦ meeting equipment
♦ meetings equipment
Tagungsteilnehmer, m (aktiv)
♦ meeting participant
♦ participant in a meeting
♦ person participating in a meeting
♦ person taking part in a meeting
Tagungsteilnehmer, m (passiv)
♦ meeting delegate
♦ person attending a meeting
Tagungstermin, m
♦ meeting date
♦ date of a meeting
Tagungstitel, m
♦ title of the meeting
Tagungstourismus, m
♦ meetings tourism
♦ meeting tourism
Tagungstourist, m
♦ meetings tourist
♦ meeting tourist
Tagungstrakt, m
Tagungsflügel, m
♦ meetings wing
♦ meeting wing
Tagung subventionieren
♦ subsidize a meeting
♦ subsidise a meeting
Tagungsumsatz, m
♦ meetings sales pl
♦ meetings turnover
Tagungs- und Ausstellungsindustrie, f
♦ meetings and exhibition industry
♦ meeting and exhibition industry
Tagungs- und Konferenzdienst, m
Tagungs- und Konferenzservice, m
♦ meeting and conference service
Tagungsunterlagen, f pl
♦ meeting documents pl
Tagungsveranstalter, m
Tagungsorganisator, m
♦ meeting organiser
♦ meetings organizer
Tagungsverkehr, m
♦ meetings traffic
♦ meeting traffic
Tagungsvermarkter, m
♦ meetings marketer
♦ meeting marketer
Tagungsvorbereitung, f
♦ preparation of a meeting
Tagungsvorprogramm, n
♦ pre-meeting program AE
♦ pre-meeting programme BE
Tagungsvorsprechung, f
♦ pre-meeting discussion

Tagungswerbung, f
Tagungsförderung, f
♦ meetings promotion
Tagungswesen, n
→ Tagungsindustrie
Tagungszentrum, n
♦ meeting center AE
♦ meetings center AE
♦ meeting centre BE
♦ meetings centre BE
Tagungszentrum leiten
♦ manage a meeting center AE
♦ manage a meetings center AE
♦ manage a meeting centre BE
♦ manage a meetings centre BE
♦ be the manager of a meeting center AE
Tagungszentrumleiter, m
♦ meeting center manager AE
♦ meetings center manager AE
♦ meeting centre manager BE
♦ meetings centre manager BE
Tagungszentrumleitung, f
♦ meeting center management AE
♦ meetings center management AE
♦ meeting centre management BE
♦ meetings centre management BE
Tagungszielort, m
Tagungsdestination, f
♦ meeting destination
Tagungszimmer, n
→ Tagungsraum
Tagung vermarkten
♦ market a meeting
Tagung vorbereiten
♦ prepare a meeting
Tag verbringen am Strand
♦ spend a day on the beach
♦ laze away a day on the beach
Tag verbringen in der Sonne
♦ spend a day in the sun
♦ spend the day in the sun
Tag verbringen in seiner Unterkunft
♦ spend a day in one's accommodation
Tag verbringen in X
♦ spend a day at X
♦ spend a day in X
Tag verbummeln
Tag mit Nichtstun verbringen
♦ laze away a day
Tag war vertan
♦ day was ruined
Tag zur freien Verfügung
(Prospekthinweis)
♦ day at leisure
Tag zur freien Verfügung haben
♦ have the day at leisure
Tahiter, m
♦ Tahitian
Tahiterin, f
♦ Tahitian girl
♦ Tahitian woman
♦ Tahitian
Tahiti
♦ Tahiti
tahitisch, adj
♦ Tahitian, adj
Taiga, f
♦ taiga
Taiwan
♦ Taiwan

Taiwaner, m
♦ Taiwanese
Taiwanerin, f
♦ Taiwanese girl
♦ Taiwanese woman
♦ Taiwanese
taiwanisch, adj
♦ Taiwanese, adj
Takelung, f
Takelage, f
Takelzeug, n
♦ rig
♦ rigging
Takt, m
♦ tact
♦ tactfulness
taktlos, adj
♦ tactless, adj
Taktlosigkeit, f
♦ tactlessness
♦ want of tact
♦ indiscretion
Taktlosigkeit, f (grob)
♦ gaffe
Taktlosigkeit begehen (grob)
♦ make a gaffe
taktvoll, adj
♦ tactful, adj
Tal, n
♦ valley
♦ dale rare
Talblick, m
Blick auf das Tal m
♦ valley view
♦ view of the valley
Talboden, m
♦ valley floor
Tal der Könige, n
(in Ägypten)
♦ Valley of the Kings, the
Talfahrt, f (Auto)
♦ downhill drive
Talfahrt, f (Reise)
♦ downward journey
♦ downward ride
Talfahrt, f (Rückgang)
Rückgang, m
Abnahme, f
♦ decline
Talfahrt, f (Ski)
→ Abfahrtslauf
Talkmaster, m
♦ talk-show host AE
♦ chat-show host BE
Talkshow, f
♦ talk show AE
♦ chat show BE
Talon, m FR
Kontrollabschnitt, m
♦ counterfoil
♦ talon FR
Talsperre, f
Staudamm, m
Damm, m
♦ dam
Talstation f
(Lift)
♦ valley station
♦ bottom station
Talstraße, f
♦ valley road

Talverkehr

Talverkehr, m (Schiff)
- ♦ downstream traffic

Tamile, m
- ♦ Tamil

Tamilin, f
- ♦ Tamil girl
- ♦ Tamil woman
- ♦ Tamil

tamilisch, adj
- ♦ Tamil, adj

Tandem, n
- ♦ tandem

Tango, m
- ♦ tango

Tango tanzen
- ♦ dance the tango
- ♦ do the tango
- ♦ tango

Tank, m
- ♦ tank

tanken (Auto)
- ♦ fuel
- ♦ refuel
- ♦ fill up with petrol BE
- ♦ fill up with gasoline AE

tanken (Flugzeug)
- auftanken
- ♦ refuel

tanken (trinken)
- ♦ tank up

Tankgutschein, m
- → Benzingutschein

Tankstelle, f
- ♦ gasoline station AE
- ♦ gas station AE
- ♦ petrol station BE
- ♦ filling station
- ♦ service station

Tankwart, m
- ♦ gasoline station attendant AE
- ♦ petrol station attendant BE
- ♦ filling station attendant
- ♦ garage hand
- ♦ garage attendant

Tanne, f
- Tannenbaum, m
- ♦ fir
- ♦ fir tree

Tannenbaum, m (generell)
- Tanne, f
- Weißtanne, f
- ♦ fir tree
- ♦ fir

Tannenbaum, m (Weihnacht)
- → Weihnachtsbaum

Tannenwald, m
- ♦ fir wood

Tansania
- ♦ Tanzania

Tansanier, m
- ♦ Tanzanian

Tansanierin, f
- ♦ Tanzanian girl
- ♦ Tanzanian woman
- ♦ Tanzanian

tansanisch, adj
- ♦ Tanzanian, adj

Tante-Emma-Laden, m
- ♦ corner shop
- ♦ mom-and-pop store AE

Tantieme, f (Autor)
- ♦ royalty

Tantieme, f (Gewinnbeteiligung)
- ♦ share of profits
- ♦ share in profits

Tantiemegebühr, f
- Erlaubnisgebühr, f
- ♦ royalty fee

Tanz, m
- Tanzveranstaltung, f
- ♦ dance
- ♦ dancing

Tanzabend, m (privat)
- ♦ dancing in the evening
- ♦ dance
- ♦ dance night
- ♦ evening dancing

Tanzabend, m (Vorstellung)
- ♦ evening of dancing
- ♦ evening of dance
- ♦ dance show

Tanzabend abhalten
- Tanzabend veranstalten
- ♦ hold a dance evening
- ♦ hold a dance night

Tanzband, f
- → Tanzkapelle

Tanzbar, f
- ♦ bar with dancing
- ♦ bar with a dance band
- ♦ dancing bar

Tanzbär, m
- ♦ dancing bear

Tanzbegeisterter, m
- ♦ dance enthusiast
- ♦ dancing enthusiast

Tanzbein schwingen humor
- ♦ shake a leg humor

Tanzboden, m
- → Tanzfläche

Tanzcafé, n
- ♦ cafe with dancing AE
- ♦ café with dancing BE

Tanzclub, m
- Tanzverein, m
- ♦ dancing club
- ♦ dance club AE

Tanzdiele, f
- → Tanzsaal

Tanzdiner, n
- → Abendessen mit Tanz

tanzen
- ♦ dance

Tanzen, n
- ♦ dancing

Tanzen am Abend, n
- ♦ evening dancing
- ♦ dancing in the evening

tanzen bis in den frühen Morgen
- ♦ dance until the early hours

tanzen bis in die frühen Morgenstunden
- ♦ dance into the small hours

tanzend, adj
- ♦ dancing, adj

tanzendes Paar, n
- ♦ dancing couple

tanzen gehen
- ♦ go dancing

tanzen mit jm
- ♦ dance with s.o.

tanzen zu einem Orchester
- ♦ dance to an orchestra

tanzen zu einer Kapelle
- ♦ dance to a band

tanzen zur Klaviermusik
- ♦ dance to piano music

Tänzer, m
- ♦ dancer

Tänzerin, f
- ♦ female dancer
- ♦ dancer

Tanzfest, n (Festival)
- ♦ dance festival
- ♦ dancing festival

Tanzfest, n (Party)
- Tanzparty, f
- ♦ dancing party

Tanzfestival, n
- → Tanzfest

Tanzfläche, f
- Tanzboden, m
- ♦ dance floor AE
- ♦ dance-floor BE
- ♦ dancing area

Tanzgruppe, f
- ♦ dance group
- ♦ dancing group

Tanzgymnastik, f
- ♦ dance exercise

Tanzgymnastikkurs, m
- ♦ dance exercise class

Tanzhalle, f
- → Tanzsaal

Tanz im Freien, m
- Tanzen im Freien, n
- ♦ open-air dance
- ♦ open-air dancing

Tanzkapelle, f
- ♦ dance band AE
- ♦ dance-band BE

Tanzkapelle spielt jeden Abend
- ♦ dance band plays every evening AE
- ♦ dance-band plays every evening BE

Tanzkasino, n
- ♦ casino with dancing

Tanzkeller, m
- ♦ basement dance floor AE
- ♦ basement with dance floor AE
- ♦ basement dance-floor BE
- ♦ basement with dance-floor BE

Tanzkonzession, f
- ♦ dancing license
- ♦ dancing licence
- ♦ dance license
- ♦ dance licence

Tanzkurs, m
- ♦ dancing course

Tanzlehrer, m
- ♦ dancing instructor

Tanzlehrerin, f
- ♦ dancing instructress

Tanzlokal, n
- ♦ dancing spot coll
- ♦ dance room AE
- ♦ dance-room BE
- ♦ dancing saloon AE

tanzlustig, adj
- ♦ fond of dancing, adj

Tanzmeister, m
- ♦ dancing master

Tanz mit Kapelle, m
♦ dancing to a band
Tanz mit Live-Band, m
♦ dancing to live band
Tanzmöglichkeiten, f pl
(Einrichtungen)
♦ dancing facilities pl
Tanzmusik, f
♦ dance music
♦ music for dancing
Tanzorchester, n
♦ dance orchestra
Tanzpalast, m
♦ dance palace AE
♦ palais de dance FR
♦ dance hall AE
♦ dance-hall BE
Tanzpartner, m
♦ dancing partner
♦ partner
Tanzparty, f
→ Tanzfest
Tanzprogramm n
♦ dance program AE
♦ dance programme BE
Tanzraum, m
♦ dance room AE
♦ dance-room BE
Tanzrestaurant, n
♦ restaurant with dancing
Tanzsaal, m
Tanzdiele, f
♦ dance hall AE
♦ dance-hall BE
♦ large dance room AE
♦ large dance-room BE
♦ ballroom
Tanzsalon, m
♦ dancing saloon
Tanzschuh, m
♦ dancing shoe
Tanzschule, f
♦ dance school
♦ school of dancing BE
Tanzschüler, m (Erwachsener)
♦ dance student
Tanzschüler, m (Kind)
♦ dancing pupil
Tanzsouper, n
Abendessen mit Tanz, n
♦ supper with dance
Tanzsport, m
♦ competition dancing
Tanzstar, m
♦ dancing star
Tanzstätte, f
♦ dance venue
Tanzstudio, n
♦ dance studio
Tanzstunde, f
♦ dancing lesson
♦ dancing class
Tanztaverne, f
♦ tavern with dancing
Tanztee, m
♦ tea dance
♦ afternoon-tea dance
♦ afternoon dance
♦ thé dansant FR
Tanztee abhalten
♦ hold a tea dance

Tanzterrasse, f
♦ open-air dance floor (on the terrace) AE
♦ open-air dance-floor (on the terrace) BE
Tanztheater, n
♦ dance theater AE
♦ dance theatre BE
Tanztruppe, f
♦ dance troupe
Tanzturnier, n
♦ dancing tournament
Tanzunterhaltung, f
→ Tanz
Tanzunterricht, m
♦ dancing lessons pl
Tanzveranstaltung, f
Tanz, m
♦ dance event
♦ dance
Tanzveranstaltung abhalten
Tanz abhalten
♦ hold a dance
Tanzveranstaltungen mehrmals in der Woche
♦ Dancing several nights a week
Tanzvorführung, f
Tanzshow, f
♦ dance show
Tanzwagen, m
(Zug)
♦ dancing car
Tanzwettbewerb, m
♦ dancing contest
♦ dance contest
♦ dancing competition
♦ dance competition
Tanz zu Live-Musik, m
♦ dancing to live music
Tanz zu Schallplatten, m
♦ dancing to records
Tanz zu Schallplattenmusik, m
♦ dancing to recorded music
Tapete, f
♦ wallpaper
♦ paper
Tapete für das Zimmer, f
♦ wallpaper for the room
♦ paper for the room
Tapetentür, f
versteckte Tür, f
Geheimtür, f
♦ concealed door
tapezieren etw
♦ paper s.th.
♦ wallpaper s.th.
Tapezierer, m
♦ paperhanger
♦ paperer
♦ decorator
tapeziert, adj
♦ wallpapered, adj
♦ decorated, adj
Tara, f
♦ tare
Taragewicht, n
♦ tare weight
Tarif, m
♦ tariff
♦ rates pl
♦ rate
♦ terms pl
Tarif ändern (geringfügig)
♦ alter the tariff

♦ alter the rates
♦ alter the rate
♦ alter the terms
Tarif ändern (umfassend)
♦ change the tariff
♦ change the rates
♦ change the rate
Tarif ändert sich mit der Saison
♦ tariff varies with the season
Tarif anheben
♦ raise the tariff
♦ increase the tariff
♦ raise the rate(s)
♦ increase the rate(s)
Tarifanhebung, f
♦ tariff raising
♦ raising of the tariff
♦ tariff increase
♦ increase in the tariff
♦ increase in the rate(s)
Tarif anpassen an etw
♦ adjust the tariff to s.th.
♦ adjust the terms to s.th.
♦ adjust the rates to s.th.
Tarifanpassung, f
♦ tariff adjustment
♦ adjustment of the tariff
♦ adjustment of rates
Tarifausschuß, m
♦ tariff committee
Tarif bleibt unverändert
♦ tariff remains unchanged
♦ rates remain unchanged pl
♦ rate remains unchanged
♦ terms remain unchanged pl
Tarifbreite, f
Tarifspanne, f
♦ tariff range
Tarifbroschüre, f
♦ tariff brochure
Tarif einführen für etw
♦ introduce a tariff for s.th.
Tariferhöhung, f
♦ tariff increase
Tarifermäßigung, f
Tarifsenkung, f
♦ tariff reduction
♦ reduction of the tariff
♦ tariff cut
♦ reduction of the rates
♦ reduction of the rate
Tarif festsetzen
Tarif festlegen
♦ fix the tariff
Tariffestsetzung, f
♦ tariff making AE
Tarif findet Anwendung
♦ tariff is in operation
♦ tariff is applicable
Tarif für Übernachtung mit Frühstück, m
Garnitarif, m
♦ bed-and-breakfast tariff
♦ bed-and-breakfast rates pl
♦ bed-and-breakfast terms pl
♦ b&b tariff
♦ b&b terms pl
Tarifgefüge, n
→ Tarifstruktur
Tarif gilt vom 1. Januar bis 31. März
♦ tariff is effective from 1 January to 31 March

Tarifgruppe 754

Tarifgruppe, f
  ♦ tariff group
Tarifkampf, m
  → Tarifkrieg
Tarifklasse, f
  ♦ tariff class
Tarifkrieg, m
  Tarifkampf, m
  ♦ tariff war
Tariflohn, m
  ♦ standard wages pl
  ♦ standard wage
Tarifpreis, m
  ♦ tariff price
  ♦ tariff rate
Tarifsatz, m
  ♦ tariff rate
Tarifschranke, f
  Tarifbarriere, f
  ♦ tariff barrier
Tarif senken
  ♦ lower the tariff
  ♦ reduce the tariff
  ♦ cut the tariff
Tarifstruktur, f
  Tarifgefüge, n
  ♦ tariff structure
Tarifsystem, n
  ♦ tariff system
Tarifurlaub, m
  (Arbeitnehmer)
  ♦ collectively agreed vacation AE
  ♦ collectively agreed holiday BE
Tarifvorschrift, f
  ♦ tariff provision
Tarifzugeständnis, n
  ♦ tariff concession
Tasche, f
  Tragetasche, f
  ♦ bag
Tasche, f gastr
  (z.B. Apfeltasche)
  ♦ turnover, gastr
Taschendieb, m
  ♦ pickpocket
Taschendiebstahl, m
  ♦ pickpocketing
Taschenfahrplan, m
  ♦ pocket timetable
  ♦ pocket schedule AE
Taschenführer, m
  ♦ pocket guide
  ♦ pocket guide book
Taschengeld, n
  ♦ pocket money AE
  ♦ pocket-money BE
  ♦ spending money
Taschenlampe, f
  ♦ flashlight AE
  ♦ torch BE
Taschenmesser, n
  ♦ penknife
Taschenrechner, m
  ♦ pocket calculator
Taschentuch, n
  ♦ handkerchief
Taschenüberprüfung, f
  Taschenkontrolle, f
  ♦ bag check
Tasmanien
  ♦ Tasmania

Tasmanier, m
  ♦ Tasmanian
Tasmanierin, f
  ♦ Tasmanian girl
  ♦ Tasmanian woman
  ♦ Tasmanian
tasmanisch, adj
  ♦ Tasmanian, adj
Tässchen, n
  (für Mokka)
  ♦ after-dinner cup AE
  ♦ demitasse AE
  ♦ demi-tasse BE
Tasse, f
  ♦ cup
Tasse Kaffee, f
  ♦ cup of coffee
Tasse Kaffee, f (hohe Tasse)
  ♦ mug of coffee
Tasse Kaffee einschenken jm
  ♦ pour s.o. a cup of coffee
Tasse Kaffee sich machen
  ♦ make oneself a cup of coffee
Tasse Kaffee trinken
  ♦ have a cup of coffee
  ♦ drink a cup of coffee
tassenfertig, adj gastr
  ♦ instant, adj gastr
tassenfertiges Getränk, n
  ♦ instant drink
Tasse starken Kaffees, f
  ♦ cup of strong coffee
Tasse Tee, f (generell)
  ♦ cup of tea
  ♦ cuppa BE coll
Tasse Tee, f (hohe Tasse)
  ♦ mug of tea
Tasse Tee einschenken jm
  ♦ pour s.o. a cup of tea
Tasse Tee sich machen
  ♦ make oneself a cup of tea
Tasse Tee trinken
  ♦ have a cup of tea
  ♦ drink a cup of tea
Tasse und Untertasse, f
  ♦ cup and saucer
Tasse zerbrechen
  ♦ break a cup
Tastatur, f
  ♦ keyboard
Taste, f
  ♦ key
Tatar, m (Person)
  ♦ Tartar
Tatar, m (Speise)
  ♦ steak tartare
  ♦ raw minced beef
Tatarei, f
  ♦ Tartary
Tatarenart, adv gastr
  ♦ Tatar style, adv gastr
Tatarensoße, f
  ♦ Tatar sauce
tatarisch, adj
  ♦ Tartar, adj
tätig sein im Gaststättengewerbe
  ♦ be employed in the catering trade
tätig sein in der Gastronomie
  ♦ be employed in the catering industry
Tatra, f
  ♦ Tatra Mountains, the pl

tatsächlich belegtes Bett n
  ♦ occupied bed
tatsächliche Abflugzeit, f
  ♦ actual time of departure
  ♦ ATD
tatsächliche Abreisezeit, f
  ♦ actual departure time
  ♦ actual time of departure
  ♦ ATD
tatsächliche Ankunftszeit, f
  ♦ actual time of arrival
  ♦ ATA
tatsächliche Auslastung, f
  → Ist-Auslastung, Ist-Belegung
tatsächliche Belegung, f
  → tatsächliche Auslastung
tatsächlicher Preis, m
  Ist-Preis, m
  ♦ actual price
  ♦ actual rate
tatsächliche Verbrauch, m
  → Ist-Verbrauch
tatsächlich erzielter Zimmerpreis, m
  ♦ actual room rate achieved
tatsächliche Saisonlänge f
  effektive Saisonlänge f
  ♦ effective length of (a) season
tatsächlich zur Verfügung stehende Zimmer, n pl
  ♦ rooms available pl
Taube, f
  ♦ pigeon
Taubenbrust, f
  ♦ pigeon breast
Taubenfüllpastete, f
  ♦ pigeon timbale
Taubenpastete, f
  ♦ pigeon pie
Taubenschlag, m
  ♦ pigeon house AE
  ♦ pigeon-house BE
Tauchabenteuer, n
  ♦ diving adventure
Tauchanzug, m
  Taucheranzug, m
  ♦ diving suit
  ♦ wetsuit
Tauchausrüstung, f
  ♦ diving equipment
  ♦ diver's gear
Tauchausrüstung, f (mit Atemgerät)
  ♦ scuba-diving equipment
  ♦ scuba-diving gear
Tauchbad n
  (Vorgang)
  ♦ plunge bath
  ♦ immersion bath
Tauchbecken n
  (im Schwimmbad)
  ♦ diving pool
  ♦ plunge pool
Tauchbegeisterter, m
  ♦ diving enthusiast
Tauchclub, m
  Tauchverein, m
  Taucherclub, m
  Taucherverein, m
  ♦ diving club
Tauchen, n
  Tauchsport, m
  ♦ diving

tauchen gehen
   tauchen
   ♦ go diving
tauchen (generell)
   tauchen gehen
   ♦ dive
   ♦ go diving
tauchen (mit Atemgerät)
   ♦ scuba-dive
tauchen (ohne Atemgerät)
   → sporttauchen
Taucher, m
   ♦ diver
Taucherbrille, f
   ♦ diving goggles *pl*
   ♦ diver's goggles *pl*
Taucherin, f
   ♦ female diver
   ♦ woman diver
Taucherurlaub, m
   → Tauchurlaub, m
Tauchfan, m
   ♦ diving fan
Tauchferien, pl
   Tauchurlaub, m
   ♦ diving holiday *BE*
   ♦ diving vacation *AE*
Tauchführer, m
   ♦ diving guide
   ♦ dive leader *AE*
Tauchgang, m
   Tauchfahrt, f
   ♦ dive
Tauchgerät, n
   ♦ diving apparatus
Tauchkreuzfahrt, f
   ♦ diving cruise
Tauchkurs, m
   Tauchlehrgang, m
   ♦ diving course
   ♦ diving class
Tauchlehrer, m
   ♦ diving instructor
   ♦ dive instructor *AE*
Tauchlehrerin, f
   ♦ diving instructress
Tauchleine, f
   Signalleine, f
   ♦ diving line
   ♦ lifeline
Tauchmuseum, n
   Tauchermuseum, n
   ♦ diving museum
Tauchreise, f
   ♦ diving tour
Tauchsaison, f
   ♦ diving season
Tauchschiff, n
   ♦ diving vessel
Tauchschule f
   ♦ diving school
Tauchsieder m
   ♦ immersion heater
Tauchsport, m
   → Tauchen
Tauchurlaub, m
   Tauchferien, pl
   ♦ diving vacation *AE*
   ♦ diving holiday *BE*

Tauchurlaubsspezialist, m
   ♦ diving vacation specialist *AE*
   ♦ diving holiday specialist *BE*
Tauchutensilien, f pl
   ♦ diving utensils *pl*
Tauchverbot, n
   ♦ diving ban
   ♦ ban on diving
Tauchwochenende, n
   ♦ diving weekend
Tauchzentrum, n
   ♦ diving center *AE*
   ♦ diving centre *BE*
Taufbecken, n
   Taufstein, m
   ♦ font
Taufschein, m
   ♦ baptismal certificate
Taunus, m
   (Region)
   ♦ Taunus, the
   ♦ Taunus Mountains, the *pl*
Tausch, m
   ♦ swap
   ♦ swop
   ♦ exchange
tauschen etw gegen etw
   ♦ exchange s.th. for s.th.
   ♦ swap s.th. for s.th.
   ♦ swop s.th. for s.th.
tauschen etw gegen etw mit jm
   ♦ exchange s.th. for s.th. with s.o.
   ♦ swap s.th. for s.th. with s.o.
   ♦ swop s.th. for s.th. with s.o.
täuschen jn wissentlich
   ♦ mislead s.o. knowingly
Tausch machen
   ♦ do a swap
   ♦ do a swop
Tausendjahrfest, n
   ♦ millennium festival
   ♦ millenium
tausend Möglichkeiten, f pl
   ♦ a thousand possibilities *pl*
Tauziehen, n
   ♦ tug-of-war *AE*
   ♦ tug of war *BE*
Taverne, f
   ♦ tavern
Tavernenprügelei, f
   ♦ tavern brawl
Tawny-Portwein, m
   ♦ tawny port wine
Taxe, f (Abgabe)
   → Abgabe
Taxe, f (Taxi)
   → Taxi
Taxe berechnen
   ♦ charge a tax
Taxe einziehen
   → Abgabe einziehen
Taxi, n
   Taxe, f *dial*
   ♦ taxi
   ♦ taxicab
   ♦ cab
   ♦ hack *AE*
Taxibeförderung, f
   Taxistransfer, m
   ♦ cab transfer
   ♦ taxi transfer

Taxi benutzen
   ♦ use a taxi
   ♦ use a cab
Taxibesitzer, m
   ♦ taxi owner
   ♦ owner of a taxi
Taxi bestellen
   ♦ order a taxi
   ♦ order a cab
Taxichauffeur, m
   Taxifahrer, m
   ♦ cab driver
   ♦ taxi driver
Taxidienst, m
   Taxiservice, m
   Taxiverkehr, m
   Taxiverbindung, f
   ♦ taxi service
   ♦ cab service
Taxi erreichen
   Taxi nehmen
   ♦ catch a taxi
   ♦ catch a cab
Taxi fahren (Fahrer)
   ♦ drive a taxi
   ♦ drive a cab
   ♦ hack *AE inform*
Taxi fahren (Fahrgast)
   mit dem Taxi fahren
   ♦ go by taxi
   ♦ go by cab
Taxifahrer, m
   ♦ taxi driver
   ♦ cab driver
Taxifahrpreis, m
   ♦ taxi fare
   ♦ cab fare
Taxifahrt, f
   ♦ taxi ride
   ♦ cab ride
Taxigebühr, f
   ♦ taxi charge
   ♦ cab charge
Taxigewerbe, n
   ♦ taxi trade
   ♦ cab trade
Taxi herbeirufen
   ♦ summon a taxi
   ♦ summon a cab
Taxi herbeiwinken
   ♦ hail a taxi
   ♦ hail a cab
Taxi ist besetzt
   ♦ taxi is taken
   ♦ cab is taken
Taxi ist frei
   Taxi ist leer
   ♦ taxi is empty
   ♦ cab is empty
Taxi ist kostenlos
   ♦ taxi is free
   ♦ taxi is free of charge
   ♦ cab is free
   ♦ cab is free of charge
Taxikonzession, f
   ♦ taxi license
   ♦ taxi licence
   ♦ hack license *AE*
   ♦ cab license
Taxi mieten
   ♦ rent a taxi

Taxi nehmen (nach X) 756

Taxi nehmen (nach X)
- ◆ rent a cab
- ◆ hire a taxi BE

Taxi nehmen (nach X)
- ◆ take a taxi (to X)
- ◆ take a cab (to X)

Taxi nehmen zum Flughafen
- ◆ take a taxi to the airport
- ◆ take a cab to the airport

Taxi nehmen zum Hotel
- ◆ take a taxi to the hotel
- ◆ take a cab to the hotel

Taxipendeldienst, m
Taxipendelservice, m
- ◆ taxi shuttle service
- ◆ cab shuttle service

Taxi rufen
- ◆ call a taxi
- ◆ call a cab

Taxischalter, m
(z.B. in einem Hotel)
- ◆ taxi desk
- ◆ cab desk

Taxiservice, m
→ Taxidienst

Taxistand, m
- ◆ taxi stand
- ◆ cabstand AE
- ◆ cab-rank BE
- ◆ taxi-rank BE

Taxitransfer, m
- ◆ taxi transfer
- ◆ transfer by taxi
- ◆ cab transfer
- ◆ transfer by cab

Taxiverbindung, f
Taxiverkehr, m
- ◆ cab service
- ◆ taxi service

Teakmöbel, n pl
- ◆ teak furniture sg

Team, n
Mannschaft, f
- ◆ team

Tea Room, m
→ Teestube

Techniker, m
- ◆ technician

Technikmuseum, n
technisches Museum, n
- ◆ technical museum

technische Abteilung f
- ◆ engineering department

technische Anschlüsse, m pl
(z.B. für Strom)
- ◆ connections pl

technische Ausstattung, f
technisches Gerät, n
- ◆ technical equipment

technischer Betriebsleiter, m
- ◆ technical manager

technischer Direktor, m
technischer Leiter, m
- ◆ technical director
- ◆ technical manager

technisches Gerät, n
→ technische Ausstattung

technisches Personal, n
- ◆ engineering staff
- ◆ engineering personnel

Technologieausstellung, f
- ◆ technology exhibition

Technologiemuseum, n
Museum für Technologie, n
- ◆ technology museum
- ◆ museum of technology

Teddybärmuseum, n
- ◆ teddy bear museum

Tee, m
- ◆ tea

TEE, m (Zug)
Trans-Europ-Express, m
- ◆ TEE
- ◆ Trans-Europ-Express

Tee anbieten
- ◆ offer tea

Tee auf Bestellung
- ◆ tea to order

Tee aufgießen
- ◆ brew tea

Teebar, f
- ◆ tea bar

Tee bestellen
- ◆ order tea

Teebestellung, f
- ◆ tea order
- ◆ ordering tea

Teebeutel, m
- ◆ tea bag AE
- ◆ tea-bag BE

Tee bezahlen
- ◆ pay for the tea

Teeblatt, n
- ◆ tea leaf AE
- ◆ tea-leaf BE

Teebrett, n
(Tablett)
- ◆ teaboard AE
- ◆ tea tray AE
- ◆ tea-tray BE

Teebüchse, f
Teedose, f
- ◆ tea caddy AE
- ◆ tea-caddy BE
- ◆ caddy

Teedose, f
→ Teebüchse

Tee-Ei, n
- ◆ tea ball AE
- ◆ infuser

Teefilter, m
(löffelartig)
- ◆ tea maker AE
- ◆ teaette AE

Teegarten, m
(öffentl. Garten, wo Tee serviert wird)
- ◆ tea garden
- ◆ tea-garden BE

Teegebäck, n
- ◆ cookies AE pl
- ◆ biscuits pl
- ◆ tea biscuits pl
- ◆ scones pl

Teegeschirr, n
- ◆ tea things AE pl
- ◆ tea-things BE pl

Teegesellschaft, f
Teeparty, f
- ◆ tea party AE
- ◆ tea-party BE

Teehändler, m
- ◆ tea merchant

Teehaube, f
→ Teewärmer

Teehaus, n
- ◆ teahouse

Tee im Bett, m
- ◆ tea in bed

Teeimbiß, m
- ◆ tea

Tee-Kaffeetablett, n
- ◆ tea/coffee tray

Teekanne f
- ◆ teapot

Teekarte, f
→ Nachmittagskarte

Teekessel, m
- ◆ teakettle

Tee kochen
Tee machen
- ◆ make tea
- ◆ make the tea

Tee konsumieren
- ◆ consume tea

Teeküche, f
- ◆ tea pantry
- ◆ tea kitchen
- ◆ stillroom BE obs

Teelicht, n
- ◆ tea warmer
- ◆ tea warmer candle

Teelöffel, m
- ◆ teaspoon

Teelöffelvoll, m
- ◆ teaspoonful
- ◆ tsp

Teelokal, n
- ◆ tea place

Tee machen
→ Tee kochen

Teemarke, f
(wie eine Münze)
Teechip, m
- ◆ tea token

Teemaschine, f
(groß, z.B. in Café)
- ◆ tea urn AE
- ◆ tea-urn BE

Teemischung, f
- ◆ blend of tea

Tee mit einem Schuß Rum, m
- ◆ tea with a dash of rum
- ◆ tea with a stick of rum AE

Tee mit Milch m
- ◆ tea with milk

Tee mit Sahne, m
(in GB zusätzlich Teegebäck mit Konfitüre)
- ◆ cream tea

Tee mit Zitrone m
- ◆ tea with lemon

Teenager, m
- ◆ teenager

Teeparty, f
→ Teegesellschaft

Teeparty abhalten
- ◆ hold a tea party

Teepause, f
- ◆ tea break AE
- ◆ tea-break BE

Teepause machen
- ◆ have a tea break AE
- ◆ take a tea break AE

♦ have a tea-break BE
♦ take a tea-break BE
Teepavillon, m
♦ tea pavilion
Teeplantage, f
♦ tea plantation
Teepunsch, m
♦ tea punch
Teerestaurant, n
→ Teestube
Teerose, f
♦ tea rose
Teerstraße, f
geteerte Straße, f
♦ tarred road
♦ tarred street
Teerunde, f
♦ tea round
Teesalon, m
♦ tea lounge
♦ tea-room BE
♦ tearoom AE
♦ tea parlour BE
♦ tea salon
Teeschale, f
♦ teabowl AE
Teeservice, m (Dienstleistung)
♦ tea service
Teeservice, n (Geschirr)
♦ tea set AE
♦ tea-set BE
♦ tea service AE
♦ tea-service BE
Tee servieren
♦ serve (the) tea
Teesieb, n
♦ tea strainer AE
♦ tea-strainer BE
Teestand, m
♦ tea stand
♦ tea stall BE
Teestube, f
♦ tearoom AE
♦ tea-room BE
♦ tea-shop BE
Teestunde, f
Teezeit, f
♦ teatime AE
♦ tea-time BE
Teetablett, n
♦ tea tray AE
♦ tea-tray BE
♦ tray of tea
Teetasse, f
♦ teacup
Teetisch, m
♦ tea table AE
♦ tea-table BE
Tee trinken
♦ have tea
♦ drink tea
♦ have a cup of tea
Teetrinken, n
♦ tea drinking
Tee trinken mit jm
♦ take tea with s.o.
Teetrinker, m
♦ tea drinker
Tee- und Kaffeemaschine, f
(auf dem Zimmer)

Tee- und Kaffeezubereitung, f
♦ tea and coffee-making facility
Teeverbrauch, m
Teekonsum, m
♦ tea consumption
♦ consumption of tea
Teeverkoster, m
Teeprüfer, m
♦ tea taster
Teewagen, m
♦ tea cart AE
♦ tea wagon AE
♦ tea-trolley BE
♦ tea-wagon BE
Teewärmer, m
(zum Warmhalten)
Teehaube, f
♦ tea cozy AE
♦ tea-cosy BE
Teezeit, f
→ Teestunde
Teezeremonie, f
(in Japan)
♦ tea ceremony
Tee zubereiten
♦ prepare tea
Teich, m
♦ pond
Teig, m
♦ dough
♦ paste
Teigwaren, f pl
Nudeln, f pl
♦ pasta sg
♦ pastas pl
Teigwarengericht, n
♦ pasta dish
Teigwarenrestaurant, n
Nudelrestaurant, n
♦ pasta restaurant
Teiländerung, f
teilweise Änderung, f
♦ partial change
Teiländerung bei einer Reservierung, f
♦ partial change in a reservation
Teilaussicht auf etw, f
♦ partial view of s.th.
Teilbad, n
♦ partial bath
Teilbeschäftigung, f
→ Teilzeitbeschäftigung
Teil der Reise, m
Bestandteil der Reise, m
♦ part of the journey
♦ part of the trip
♦ part of the tour
Teil der Saison, m
♦ part of the season
Teil des Essens, m
♦ part of the meal
Teil des Vertrages bilden
♦ form part of the contract
Teilhaber, m
♦ joint owner
Teilkreuzfahrt, f
♦ part cruise
Teilleistung, f
→ Teilservice
Teilmassage, f
♦ partial massage

Teilmeeresblick, m
→ teilweiser Meeresblick
teilmöbliert, adj
teilweise möbliert, adj
♦ partly furnished, adj
teilmöbliertes Appartement n
♦ partly furnished apartment
teilmöblierte Wohnung, f
♦ partly furnished flat BE
♦ partly furnished apartment AE
Teilnahme an der Sitzung ist Pflicht (aktiv)
♦ participation in the meeting is mandatory
♦ participation in the meeting is obligatory
Teilnahme an der Sitzung ist Pflicht (passiv)
♦ attendance at the meeting is mandatory
♦ attendance at the meeting is obligatory
Teilnahme an einer Ausstellung, f (aktiv)
Ausstellungsteilnahme, f
♦ participation in an exhibition
♦ participation in an exhibit AE
Teilnahme an einer Ausstellung, f (passiv)
♦ attendance at an exhibition
♦ attendance at an exhibit AE
Teilnahme an einer Konferenz, f (aktiv)
♦ participation in a conference
Teilnahme an einer Konferenz, f (passiv)
♦ attendance at a conference
Teilnahme an einer Messe, f
→ Messebeteiligung
Teilnahme an einer Sitzung, f (aktiv)
♦ participation in a meeting
Teilnahme an einer Sitzung, f (passiv)
Teilnahme an einem Treffen, f
Teilnahme an einer Tagung, f
♦ attendance at a meeting
Teilnahme an einer Veranstaltung, f (aktiv)
Veranstaltungsteilnahme, f
♦ participation in an event
Teilnahme an einer Veranstaltung, f (passiv)
♦ attendance at an event
♦ attendance at a function
Teilnahme an etw, f (aktiv)
♦ participation in s.th.
Teilnahme an etw, f (passiv)
♦ attendance at s.th.
Teilnahme anmelden
→ anmelden
Teilnahmeanmeldung, f
→ Teilnehmeranmeldung
Teilnahmebedingungen, f pl
♦ entry conditions pl
♦ conditions of participation pl
Teilnahme bestätigen
♦ confirm s.o.'s participation
♦ confirm s.o.'s attendance
Teilnahmegebühr, f
♦ participation fee
♦ registration fee
♦ registration charge
♦ participation fee
♦ charge (fee) for participating in s.th.
Teilnahme ist fakultativ (aktiv)
♦ participation is optional
Teilnahme ist fakultativ (passiv)
♦ attendance is optional
Teilnahme ist nicht Pflicht (aktiv)
♦ participation ist not compulsory
♦ participation is not obligatory
♦ participation is not mandatory
Teilnahme ist nicht Pflicht (passiv)
♦ attendance is not compulsory

Teilnahme ist obligatorisch (aktiv)

- ♦ attendance is not obligatory
- ♦ attendance is not mandatory

Teilnahme ist obligatorisch (aktiv)
- ♦ participation is obligatory
- ♦ participation is mandatory

Teilnahme ist obligatorisch (passiv)
Teilnahme ist Pflicht
- ♦ attendance is obligatory
- ♦ attendance is mandatory

Teilnahme ist Pflicht (aktiv)
Teilnahme ist obligatorisch
- ♦ participation is mandatory
- ♦ participation is obligatory

Teilnahme ist Plicht (passiv)
Teilnahme ist obligatorisch
- ♦ attendance is mandatory
- ♦ attendance is obligatory

Teilnahmemöglichkeit an etw, f (aktiv)
- ♦ opportunity to take part in s.th.
- ♦ opportunity to participate in s.th.

Teilnahmemöglichkeit an etw, f (passiv)
- ♦ opportunity to attend s.th.

Teilnahme nur nach vorheriger Vereinbarung (aktiv)
- ♦ participation by prior arrangement only

Teilnahme nur nach vorheriger Vereinbarung(passiv)
- ♦ attendance by prior arrangement only

Teilnahmerekord brechen
alle früheren Teilnahmerekorde brechen
Teilnehmerrekord brechen
- ♦ break the attendance record
- ♦ break all previous attendance records

Teilnahmetag, m
- ♦ day of attendance

Teilnahme verhindern von jm an etw
js Teilnahme an etw verhindern
- ♦ prevent s.o. from attending s.th.

teilnehmen an der Eröffnung (aktiv)
- ♦ participate in the opening
- ♦ take part in the opening

teilnehmen an der Eröffnung (passiv)
- ♦ attend the opening

teilnehmen an der Zweihundertjahrfeier (aktiv)
- ♦ participate in the bicentennial celebration
- ♦ take part in the bicentennial celebration

teilnehmen an der Zweihundertjahrfeier (passiv)
- ♦ attend the bicentennial celebration

teilnehmen an einem Abendessen (als Gast)
- ♦ attend a dinner

teilnehmen an einem Ball
- ♦ attend a ball

teilnehmen an einem Bankett
teilnehmen an einem Festessen
- ♦ attend a banquet

teilnehmen an einem Diner (als Gast)
teilnehmen an einem Essen
- ♦ attend a dinner

teilnehmen an einem Empfang (aktiv)
- ♦ take part in a reception
- ♦ participate in a reception

teilnehmen an einem Empfang (passiv)
- ♦ attend a reception

teilnehmen an einem Essen (mitessen)
mitessen
- ♦ partake in a meal

teilnehmen an einem Festival (aktiv)
teilnehmen an einem Fest
- ♦ take part in a festival

teilnehmen an einem Fest (passiv)
teilnehmen an einem Festival
- ♦ attend a festival

teilnehmen an einem Festschmaus
- ♦ take part in a feast

teilnehmen an einem Frühstück
- ♦ attend a breakfast

teilnehmen an einem Kongreß (aktiv)
- ♦ participate in a convention
- ♦ participate in a congress
- ♦ take part in a convention
- ♦ take part in a congress

teilnehmen an einem Kongreß (passiv)
- ♦ attend a convention
- ♦ attend a congress

teilnehmen an einem Lager
- ♦ go to a camp

teilnehmen an einem Landausflug (aktiv)
(bei Kreuzfahrt)
- ♦ participate in a shore excursion
- ♦ take part in a shore excursion
- ♦ go on a shore excursion

teilnehmen an einem Mittagessen (als Gast)
- ♦ attend a luncheon
- ♦ attend a lunch

teilnehmen an einem Quiz
- ♦ take part in a quiz

teilnehmen an einem Seminar
- ♦ attend a seminar

teilnehmen an einem Staatsdiner (als Gast)
- ♦ attend a state dinner

teilnehmen an einem Treffen (aktiv)
- ♦ participate in a meeting
- ♦ take part in a meeting

teilnehmen an einem Treffen (passiv)
teilnehmen an einer Tagung
teilnehmen an einer Sitzung
- ♦ attend a meeting

teilnehmen an einem Wettbewerb (aktiv)
- ♦ take part in a competition
- ♦ participate in a competition
- ♦ take part in a contest

teilnehmen an einer Aktivität (aktiv)
- ♦ take part in an activity
- ♦ participate in an activity

teilnehmen an einer Ausstellung (aktiv)
- ♦ take part in an exhibition
- ♦ participate in an exhibition

teilnehmen an einer Ausstellung (passiv)
- ♦ attend an exhibition
- ♦ attend an exhibit AE

teilnehmen an einer Eröffnungsfeier (passiv)
- ♦ attend an opening ceremony

teilnehmen an einer Expedition
- ♦ take part in an expedition

teilnehmen an einer Feier (aktiv)
- ♦ take part in a celebration
- ♦ participate in a celebration

teilnehmen an einer Feier (passiv)
- ♦ attend a celebration

teilnehmen an einer Festlichkeit (aktiv)
- ♦ take part in a festivity
- ♦ participate in a festivity

teilnehmen an einer Hochzeit (als Gast)
- ♦ attend a wedding

teilnehmen an einer Konferenz (aktiv)
- ♦ take part in a conference
- ♦ participate in a conference

teilnehmen an einer Konferenz (passiv)
- ♦ attend a conference

teilnehmen an einer Messe (aktiv)
- ♦ participate in a fair
- ♦ participate in a trade fair
- ♦ take part in a fair
- ♦ take part in a trade fair

teilnehmen an einer Messe (passiv)
- ♦ attend a fair
- ♦ attend a trade fair

teilnehmen an einer Opernaufführung (passiv)
- ♦ attend an opera performance

teilnehmen an einer Party
- ♦ take part in a party

teilnehmen an einer Sitzung (aktiv)
- ♦ participate in a session
- ♦ participate in a meeting
- ♦ take part in a session
- ♦ take part in a meeting

teilnehmen an einer Sitzung (passiv)
Sitzung beiwohnen
- ♦ attend a session
- ♦ attend a meeting

teilnehmen an einer Sportveranstaltung (aktiv)
- ♦ take part in a sports event
- ♦ take part in a sport event
- ♦ take part in a sporting event

teilnehmen an einer Sportveranstaltung (passiv)
- ♦ attend a sports event
- ♦ attend a sport event
- ♦ attend a sporting event

teilnehmen an einer Veranstaltung (aktiv)
- ♦ participate in an event
- ♦ participate in a function
- ♦ take part in an event
- ♦ take part in a function
- ♦ participate in an activity

teilnehmen an einer Veranstaltung (passiv)
- ♦ attend an event
- ♦ attend a function

teilnehmen an einer Veranstaltung (Wettbewerb)
- ♦ compete in an event

teilnehmen an etw als Beobachter
- ♦ attend s.th. as an observer

teilnehmen an etw (passiv)
teilnehmen
- ♦ attend s.th.
- ♦ attend

teilnehmen an Gesprächen (passiv)
- ♦ attend talks

teilnehmen an Veranstaltungen
mitmachen bei Veranstaltungen
- ♦ take part in activities

teilnehmend, adj (aktiv)
- ♦ participating, adj

teilnehmend, adj (passiv)
- ♦ attending, adj

Teilnehmer, m (aktiv)
- ♦ participant

Teilnehmer, m (einer Gruppe)
- ♦ person in the party

Teilnehmer, m (passiv)
- ♦ attendant
- ♦ attendee AE
- ♦ attender

Teilnehmer, m (Wettkampf)
Wettkampfteilnehmer, m
- ♦ contestant
- ♦ entrant
- ♦ competitor

Teilnehmer an Abendkursen, m
- ♦ attender at evening classes
- ♦ evening-class student

Teilnehmer anmelden
- register an attendant
- register a participant

Teilnehmeranmeldung, f
   Teilnahmeanmeldung, f
- registration of participants
- registration of a participant
- delegate registration

Teilnehmergruppe, f (aktiv)
- group of participants
- participating group

Teilnehmergruppe, f (Konferenz)
- group of delegates

Teilnehmerkarte, f
- participant's card

Teilnehmerland, n (aktiv)
   teilnehmendes Land, n
- participating country

Teilnehmerliste, f (aktive Teilnehmer)
→ Teilnehmerverzeichnis

Teilnehmerliste, f (Anwesenheit)
→ Anwesenheitsliste

Teilnehmerliste, f (Konferenz)
   Teilnehmerverzeichnis, n
- list of delegates
- delegate list

Teilnehmerliste, f (Sportkampf)
   Teilnehmerverzeichnis, n
- list of entrants
- list of participants

Teilnehmerliste, f (Wettkampf)
- list of contestants
- list of competitors
- list of entrants

Teilnehmer registrieren
   (Tagung)
- register a delegate

Teilnehmerrekord, m
- attendance record

Teilnehmerrekord brechen
- break an attendance record

Teilnehmerrekorde schlagen
- beat attendance records

Teilnehmerverzeichnis, n (aktive Teilnehmer)
   Teilnehmerliste, f
- list of participants

Teilnehmerverzeichnis, n (passive Teilnehmer)
- list of attendants

Teilnehmerzahl, f (aktive Teilnehmer)
- number of participants

Teilnehmerzahl, f (Aufzählung/Liste)
- Numbers attending: ...

Teilnehmerzahl, f (Konferenz)
- number of delegates

Teilnehmerzahl, f (Sportkampf)
- number of entrants
- number of participants

Teilnehmerzahl, f (Wettkampf)
- number of contestants
- number of competitors
- number of entrants

Teilnehmerzahl, f (Zahl der Anwesenden)
- attendance figure
- number of attendants

Teilnehmerzahl erhöhen
- increase attendance

Teilnehmerzahl ist begrenzt (aktiv)
- participation is limited

Teilnehmerzahl ist begrenzt (passiv)
- attendance is limited

Teilpacht, f (Bauernhof)
- share tenancy
- time-share tenancy
- share leasing
- time-share leasing

Teilpacht, f (ökon)
- partial lease
- partial rent

Teilpächter, m
- share tenant
- share renter

Teilpauschale, f
- part package

Teilpension, f
   Teilverpflegung, f
   TP, f
- part board
- partial board
- p/b

Teilpension anbieten
   Teilverpflegung anbieten
- offer part board
- offer partial board

Teilpension benötigen
- require part board
- require partial board
- need part board
- need partial board

Teilpension bieten
   Teilverpflegung bieten
- provide part board
- provide partial board

Teilpension buchen
   Teilverpflegung buchen
- book part board
- book partial board

Teilpensionbuchung, f
   Teilverpflegungsbuchung, f
- part-board booking
- partial board booking

Teilpensiongast, m
   Teilpensionsgast, m
   Gast mit Teilpension, m
   Teilverpflegungsgast, m
- part-board guest
- partial board guest
- part-board client
- partial board client
- guest on part board

Teilpension nehmen
- take part board
- take partial board

Teilpensionpauschale, f
- part-board package
- partial board package

Teilpensionpreis, m
   Teilverpflegungspreis, m
- part-board price
- part-board rate
- partial board price
- partial board rate

Teilpension reservieren
- reserve part board
- reserve partial board

Teilpensionreservierung, f
   Teilverpflegungsreservierung, f
- part-board reservation
- partial board reservation

Teilpensiontarif, m
   Teilverpflegungstarif, m
- part-board tariff

- part-board rates pl
- part-board rate
- part-board terms pl

Teilpensionunterkunft, f
   Teilpensionsunterkunft, f
   Teilpensionunterbringung, f
   Teilverpflegungsunterkunft, f
- part-board accommodation
- partial board accommodation

Teilpensionvereinbarung, f
   Teilpensionsvereinbarung, f
   Teilpensionarrangement, n
   Teilpensionsarrangement, n
- part-board arrangement
- partial board arrangement

Teilpension wünschen
- request part board
- request partial board

Teilpensionzuschlag, m
   Teilpensionszuschlag, m
   Teilverpflegungszuschlag, m
- part-board supplement
- partial board supplement
- supplement for part board
- supplement for partial board

Teilrückerstattung, f
   Teilerstattung, f
- partial refund

Teilrücktritt, m
→ Teilstornierung

Teilrückvergütung, f
- partial reimbursement

Teilrückzahlung, f
- partial repayment

teils ebener, teils abfallender Platz, m
   (Camping)
- partly level, partly sloping site

Teilservice, m
   teilweiser Service, m
   Teildienst, m
   Teilleistung, f
- partial service

Teilstornierung, f
   Teilrücktritt, m
   Teilannullierung, f
- partial cancellation
- partial cancelation AE

Teilstrecke, f
   Etappe, f
- lap
- stage

Teilunterbringung, f
→ Teilunterkunft

Teilunterkunft, f
   Teilunterbringung, f
- part accommodation
- partial accommodation

Teilurlaub, m
   Teilferien, pl
- partial vacation AE
- part vacation AE
- partial holiday BE
- part holiday BE

Teilverpflegung, f
→ Teilpension

teilweise, adj
- partial, adj

teilweise erhalten, adj
- partially preserved, adj

teilweise erhalten sein
- have been partially preserved

teilweise in A

teilweise in A, teilweise in B wohnen
♦ live partly in A, partly in B
teilweise möbliert, adj
→ teilmöbliert
teilweiser Blick auf das Meer, m
teilweiser Meeresblick, m
♦ **partial view of the sea**
♦ partial seaview AE
♦ partial sea view BE
teilweise renoviert, adj
teilrenoviert, adj
♦ **partially renovated, adj**
♦ partially refurbished, adj
teilweiser Meeresblick, m
teilweiser Blick auf das Meer m
♦ **partial seaview** AE
♦ partial view of the sea
♦ partial sea view BE
Teilzahlung, f (generell)
Abschlagszahlung, f
♦ **part payment**
♦ partial payment
Teilzahlung, f (Ratenzahlung)
♦ **payment by installments** AE
♦ payment by instalments BE
Teilzeitarbeit, f
♦ **part-time work**
♦ part-time job
Teilzeit arbeiten
♦ **be on a part-time basis**
Teilzeitarbeiter, m
♦ **part-time worker**
♦ part-timer
Teilzeitbeschäftigter, m
Teilzeitbeschäftigte, f
Teilzeitmitarbeiter, m
Teilzeitmitarbeiterin, f
♦ **part-time employee**
teilzeitbeschäftigter Fremdenführer, m
♦ **part-time tourist guide**
Teilzeitbeschäftigung, f
♦ **part-time employment**
Teilzeitkellner, m
♦ **part-time waiter**
Teilzeitkellnerin f
♦ **part-time waitress**
Teilzeitkräfte, f pl
→ Teilzeitpersonal
Teilzeitmitarbeiter, m
→ Teilzeitbeschäftigter
Teilzeitpersonal, n
Teilzeitkräfte, f pl
♦ **part-time staff**
♦ part-time personnel
Telefax, n
Fax, n
♦ **telefax**
♦ fax
Telefaxanschluß, m
Faxanschluß m
♦ **telefax connection**
♦ fax connection
Telefaxeinrichtung, f
Telefaxmöglichkeit, f
Faxeinrichtung, f
Faxmöglichkeit, f
♦ **telefax facility**
♦ fax facility
Telefaxgerät, n
Faxgerät, n

♦ **telefax machine**
♦ fax machine
Telefaxnummer, f
Faxnummer, f
♦ **telefax number**
♦ fax number
Telefax senden jm
Telefax senden an jn
♦ **send a telefax to s.o.**
♦ send s.o. a telefax
Telefaxservice, m
Faxservice, m
Telefaxdienst, m
Faxdienst, m
♦ **telefax service**
♦ fax service
Telefon, n
Telefonapparat, m
♦ **phone**
♦ telephone
Telefon abstellen
♦ **cut the telephone off**
♦ cut the phone off
Telefonabteilung f
→ Telefonzentrale
Telefonanlage, f
♦ **telephone system**
Telefonanruf, m
♦ **telephone call**
♦ phone call
Telefonanrufbeantworter, m
→ Anrufbeantworter
Telefonanruf machen
Anruf machen
♦ **make a telephone call**
♦ make a phone call coll
Telefonanschluß m
♦ **telephone connection**
Telefonapparat, m
Telefon, n
♦ **telephone**
♦ phone
Telefonat bestätigen
Telefongespräch bestätigen
♦ **confirm a telephone conversation**
Telefonaufwand, m
♦ **telephone expense** AE
♦ telephone expenditure BE
Telefonaufwendungen, f pl
♦ **telephone expenses** AE pl
♦ telephone expenditures pl
Telefonbeleg, m
(Buchhaltung)
♦ **telephone voucher**
Telefon benutzen
♦ **use the telephone**
♦ use the phone
Telefonbenutzung, f
♦ **use of the telephone**
♦ using the telephone
Telefonbuch, n (der Post)
♦ **telephone directory**
♦ telephone book
♦ phone book
Telefonbuch, n (mit Gästetelefonaten)
♦ **telephone book**
Telefondienst, m
Telefonservice, m
♦ **telephone service**
♦ phone service

760

Telefondienstgebühr, f
Telefonservicegebühr, f
♦ **telephone service charge**
♦ telephone service fee
Telefonerlös, m
♦ **telephone revenue**
Telefonertrag, m
(Gewinn- und Verlustrechnung)
♦ **telephone income**
Telefon funktioniert
♦ **telephone works**
Telefongebühr, f
♦ **telephone charge**
♦ telephone fee
Telefongebührenzähler, m
(bei Fernsprechteilnehmer)
♦ **subscriber's meter**
Telefongesellschaft, f
♦ **telephone company**
Telefongutschein, m
♦ **telephone voucher**
Telefonhörer, m
♦ **telephone receiver**
telefonieren mit jm
anrufen jn
♦ **telephone s.o.**
♦ phone s.o.
Telefon in allen Zimmern
♦ **All rooms with telephone**
telefonisch bestätigen etw
telefonisch zusagen etw
♦ **confirm s.th. by telephone**
♦ confirm s.th. by phone
telefonisch buchen etw
telefonisch bestellen etw
♦ **make a telephone booking**
♦ book s.th. by telephone
♦ book s.th. by phone
telefonische Anfrage, f
♦ **telephone inquiry**
♦ telephone enquiry
♦ inquiry by telephone
♦ enquiry by telephone
telefonische Bestätigung, f
telefonische Zusage, f
♦ **telephone confirmation**
♦ confirmation by telephone
telefonische Bestellung, f
♦ **telephone order**
telefonische Buchung, f
♦ **telephone booking**
♦ booking by telephone
telefonischer Auskunftsdienst, m
telefonischer Informationsdienst, m
♦ **telephone information service**
telefonische Reservierung, f
Telefonreservierung, f
♦ **telephone reservation**
♦ reservation per telephone
♦ reservation by telephone
telefonische Stornierung, f
telefonischer Rücktritt, m
telefonische Absage, f
♦ **telephone cancellation**
♦ telephone cancelation AE
♦ cancellation by telephone
♦ cancelation by telephone AE
telefonische Vorbestellung, f
♦ **advance booking by telephone**
telefonisch stornieren etw
telefonisch absagen etw

- ♦ cancel s.th. by telephone
- ♦ make a cancellation by telephone
- ♦ make a cancelation by telephone *AE*

Telefonist, m
Telefonistin, f
- ♦ telephonist

Telefon ist außer Betrieb
- ♦ telephone is out of order

Telefonistin, f
- ♦ female telephonist
- ♦ telephonist

Telefonitis, f *humor*
- ♦ telephonitis *humor*

Telefonkosten, pl
- ♦ telephone costs *pl*
- ♦ telephone cost

Telefonleitung, f
Leitung, f
- ♦ telephone line
- ♦ phone line
- ♦ line

Telefonmarketing, n
- ♦ telephone marketing
- ♦ telemarketing *AE*

Telefonmietgebühr, f
- ♦ telephone rental charge
- ♦ telephone rental
- ♦ telephone hire charge *BE*
- ♦ telephone hiring charge *BE*

Telefonmitteilung, f
telefonische Mitteilung, f
telefonische Nachricht, f
- ♦ telephone message

Telefonnummer, f
- ♦ telephone number
- ♦ phone number

Telefonpersonal, n
- ♦ telephone staff
- ♦ telephone personnel

Telefonraum, m
Telefonzimmer, n
Fernsprechraum, m
Fernsprechzimmer, n
- ♦ telephone room
- ♦ phone room

Telefonrechnung, f
- ♦ telephone bill
- ♦ phone bill

Telefonreservierung, f
→ telephonische Reservierung

Telefonumsatz, m
- ♦ telephone sales *pl*
- ♦ telephone turnover

Telefonvermittlung, f (in einer Firma)
→ Fernsprechvermittlungsdienst

Telefonvermittlung, f (Postamt)
- ♦ telephone operator
- ♦ operator

Telefonzelle, f
- ♦ telephone-box *BE*
- ♦ phone-box *BE*
- ♦ call-box *BE*
- ♦ telephone booth *AE*
- ♦ phone booth *AE*

Telefonzentrale, f (in einer Firma)
Fernsprechvermittlung, f
- ♦ switchboard

Telefonzentrale, f (Postamt)
→ Fernsprechamt

Telefonzentrale bedienen (Hotel)
- ♦ operate the switchboard

Telefonzimmer, n
→ Telefonraum

Telegrafenamt, n
- ♦ telegraph office

telegrafieren (etw)
- ♦ cable (s.th.)
- ♦ wire (s.th.)

telegrafische Anweisung, f
- ♦ telegraphic money-order

telegrafische Bestätigung, f
- ♦ telegram confirmation
- ♦ confirmation by telegram

Telegramm, n
- ♦ telegram
- ♦ cable

Telegrammanschrift, f
Telegrammadresse, f
- ♦ telegraphic address

Telegrammbuchung, f
- ♦ telegram booking
- ♦ booking by telegram

Telegrammformular, n
- ♦ telegram form

Telegrammgebühr, f
- ♦ telegram charge
- ♦ telegram fee

Telekommunikation, f
- ♦ telecommunications *pl/sg*

Telekonferenz, f
- ♦ teleconference

Telekonferenzeinrichtung f
- ♦ teleconference facility

Telex, n
- ♦ telex

Telexanschluß, m
- ♦ telex connection

Telexbuchung, f
- ♦ telex booking
- ♦ booking by telex

Telexdienst m
Fernschreibdienst m
Telexservice m
Fernschreibservice m
- ♦ telex service

Telexeinrichtung, f
- ♦ telex facility

Telexgebühr, f
- ♦ telex charge
- ♦ telex fee

Telexgerät, n
- ♦ telex
- ♦ ticker *coll*

Telexnummer, f
- ♦ telex number

Telexraum, m
Telexzimmer, n
Fernschreibraum, m
Fernschreibzimmer, n
- ♦ telex room

Telexreservierung, f
- ♦ telex reservation
- ♦ reservation by telex

Telexzimmer, n
→ Telexraum

Teller, m
- ♦ plate

Teller abräumen
- ♦ clear away a plate
- ♦ clear away the plates

Teller abtragen
- ♦ remove the plate

Tellerbrett, n
(an der Wand)
Tellerhalter, m
- ♦ plate rail

Tellercloche, f
- ♦ plate cover

Tellergericht, n
Schmorgericht, n
Eintopfgericht, n
- ♦ casserole
- ♦ stew

Tellerkorb, m
Besteckkorb, m
- ♦ plate basket

Teller leeren
- ♦ empty one's plate

Teller leer essen
Teller leeren
- ♦ clear one's plate
- ♦ eat it all up
- ♦ clean one's plate

Teller nachspülen
Teller klarspülen
- ♦ rinse a plate
- ♦ rinse plates

Tellerschrank, m
- ♦ plate cupboard

Tellerservice, m
Tellerbedienung, f
- ♦ plate service

Tellerspüler, m
→ Tellerwäscher

Tellerstapel, m
- ♦ pile of plates
- ♦ stack of plates

Teller Suppe, m
- ♦ plate of soup

Tellervoll, m
- ♦ plateful

Tellerwärmer, m
- ♦ plate-warmer

Tellerwäscher, m
Tellerspüler, m
- ♦ plate-washer
- ♦ dishwasher

Teller wegnehmen
- ♦ take the plate away

Tempel des Himmlischen Friedens, m
(in Beijing)
- ♦ Temple of Heavenly Peace, the

Tempelhof, m
- ♦ temple courtyard

Temperatur, f
- ♦ temperature

Temperaturanstieg, m
- ♦ rise in temperature
- ♦ rise of temperature

Temperatur fällt unter 10°
- ♦ temperature drops below 10°

Temperaturregler, m
→ Thermostat

Temperaturrückgang, m
- ♦ fall in temperature
- ♦ drop in temperature

temperieren etw
- ♦ keep s.th. at the right temperature

temperiert, adj
- ♦ temperature-controlled, adj

temperiertes Schwimmbad, n
- ♦ temperature-controlled swimming pool *AE*
- ♦ temperature-controlled swimming-pool *BE*

Tempo

Tempo, n
- ♦ speed
- ♦ tempo
- ♦ pace

Tempo bestimmen
- ♦ set the pace

Tempolimit, n
- → Geschwindigkeitsbegrenzung

Teneriffa
- ♦ Tenerife

Tennis, n
- ♦ tennis

Tennisanlage, f
  Tenniskomplex, m
- ♦ tennis complex

Tennisarm, m
  (Schmerz)
- ♦ tennis elbow

Tennisas, n
- ♦ tennis ace

Tennisausrüstung, f
- ♦ tennis equipment

Tennisball, m
- ♦ tennis ball

Tennisbar, f
- ♦ tennis bar

Tennisbegeisterter, m
- ♦ tennis enthusiast

Tennisclub, m
  Tennisverein, m
- ♦ tennis club

Tennisclubhaus, n
- ♦ tennis pavilion

Tennisfan, m
- ♦ tennis fan

Tennisferien, pl
- → Tennisurlaub

Tennisferienort, m
  Tennisurlaubsort, m
  Tennisort, m
- ♦ tennis resort

Tennisfreiplatz, m
- → Außentennisplatz

Tennisfreund, m
- ♦ tennis lover

Tennisgebühr, f
- → Tennisplatzgebühr

Tennisgeschäft, n
  Tennisladen, m
- ♦ tennis shop

Tennishalle, f
- ♦ indoor tennis court

Tennishartplatz, m
- → Harttennisplatz

Tennishotel n
- ♦ tennis hotel

Tennis im Freien, n
- ♦ open-air tennis

Tenniskenntnisse, f pl
- ♦ tennis skills pl

Tennislager, n
- ♦ tennis camp

Tennislehrer, m
- ♦ tennis instructor

Tennislehrerin, f
- ♦ tennis instructress

Tennismeister, m
- ♦ tennis champion

Tennismeisterschaft, f
- ♦ tennis championship

Tennismeisterschaft gewinnen
- ♦ win the tennis championship

Tennismuseum, n
- ♦ tennis museum

Tennisnetz, n
- ♦ tennis net

Tennispauschale, f
- ♦ tennis package

Tennispauschalurlaub, m
- ♦ tennis package vacation AE
- ♦ tennis package holiday BE

Tennisplatz, m
- ♦ tennis court

Tennisplatzanlage, f
  Tennisplatzkomplex, m
- ♦ tennis court complex

Tennisplatzbenutzung, f
- ♦ use of the tennis court
- ♦ using the tennis court

Tennisplatzbenutzungsgebühr, f
  Tennisplatzgebühr, f
- ♦ charge for the use of the tennis court
- ♦ charge for using the tennis court
- ♦ fee for the use of the tennis court
- ♦ fee for using the tennis court

Tennisplatzbenutzungszuschlag, m
  Tennisplatzzuschlag, m
- ♦ supplement for the use of the tennis court
- ♦ supplement for using the tennis court

Tennisplatz buchen
  (den ganzen Platz)
- ♦ book a tennis court

Tennisplatzbuchung, f
- ♦ tennis court booking
- ♦ booking (of) a tennis court

Tennisplatzgebühr, f
  Tennisgebühr, f
- ♦ tennis court charge
- ♦ tennis court fee

Tennisplatz ist nachts beleuchtet
- ♦ tennis court is floodlit at night

Tennisplatz mit Flutlicht, m
- → Flutlichttennisplatz

Tennisplatzzuschlag, m
  Tennisplatzbenutzungszuschlag m
- ♦ tennis court supplement
- ♦ supplement for the use of the tennis court

Tennisprofi, m
- ♦ tennis professional
- ♦ tennis pro coll

Tennissandplatz, m
- → Sandtennisplatz

Tennisschläger, m
- ♦ tennis racket
- ♦ racket

Tennisschläger können gemietet werden
- ♦ Tennis rackets can be rented AE
- ♦ Tennis rackets can be hired BE

Tennisschläger mieten
- ♦ rent a tennis racket AE
- ♦ hire a tennis racket BE

Tennisschläger vermieten
- ♦ rent (out) a tennis racket
- ♦ hire out a tennis racket BE

Tennisschuhe, m pl
- ♦ tennis shoes pl

Tennisschule, f
- ♦ tennis school

Tennisspiel, n
- ♦ game of tennis

- ♦ tennis match
- ♦ tennis

Tennis spielen
- ♦ play tennis
- ♦ have a game of tennis

Tennisspieler, m
- ♦ tennis player

Tennisstunde, f
- ♦ tennis lesson

Tennisstunde nehmen
- ♦ take a tennis lesson

Tennistrainer, m
- ♦ tennis coach

Tennistraining, n
- ♦ tennis training
- ♦ tennis coaching

Tennistrainingswand, f
- ♦ tennis training wall

Tennisturnier n
- ♦ tennis tournament

Tennisunterricht, m
- ♦ tennis lessons pl
- ♦ tennis instruction

Tennisurlaub, m
  Tennisferien, pl
- ♦ tennis vacation AE
- ♦ tennis holiday BE

Tennisurlaubszentrum, n
- ♦ tennis vacation center AE
- ♦ tennis holiday centre BE

Tennisverband, m
- ♦ tennis federation

Tennisverein, m
- → Tennisclub

Tenniswand, f
- ♦ tennis wall

Tennisweltmeister, m
- ♦ world tennis champion

Tennisweltmeisterschaft, f
- ♦ world tennis championship

Tenniswettbewerb, m
- ♦ tennis competition

Tenniswettbewerb veranstalten
- ♦ organise a tennis competition
- ♦ organize a tennis competition
- ♦ organise a tennis contest
- ♦ organize a tennis contest

Tenniswettkampf, m
- ♦ tennis contest

Tenniswoche, f
- ♦ tennis week
- ♦ week's tennis

Tenniswochenende, n
- ♦ tennis weekend

Tenniswochenpauschale, f
- ♦ inclusive price for one week's tennis
- ♦ inclusive rate for one week's tennis

Tenniszentrum, n
- ♦ tennis center AE
- ♦ tennis centre BE

Tenniszuschlag, m
- ♦ tennis supplement

Tenniszuschlag erheben
- ♦ charge a tennis supplement

Teppich, m
- ♦ carpet

Teppichboden, m
- ♦ wall-to-wall carpet
- ♦ wall-to-wall carpeting
- ♦ fitted carpet

Teppichkehrmaschine, f
- carpet sweeper

Teppichleger, m
- carpet layer

Teppichmuseum, n
- carpet museum

Teppich reinigen
- clean a carpet

Teppichreinigung, f
- carpet cleaning
- cleaning (of) a carpet

Teppich staubsaugen
- hoover a carpet *BE*
- vacuum a carpet *AE*
- vacuum-clean a carpet *AE*

Tequila, m
- tequila

Termin, m (Frist)
→ Frist

Termin, m (Tag)
- date

Termin, m (Verabredung)
- appointment

Terminal, m/n
- terminal

Terminalhotel, n (beim Flughafen)
- terminal hotel

Termin bei jm, m
Verabredung mit jm, f
- appointment with s.o.

Termin bestimmen
Termin festlegen
- determine a date

Termine abstimmen
Termine aufeinander abstimmen
- correlate dates

Termin einhalten (Frist)
→ Frist einhalten

Termin festlegen für das Treffen
- appoint a date for the meeting
- fix a date for the meeting

Termin festlegen für etw
Termin vereinbaren für etw
Termin festsetzen für etw
- **fix a date for s.th.**
- appoint a date for s.th.
- assign a date for s.th.

Termin festsetzen
Termin festlegen
- **set a date**
- appoint a date
- fix a date
- assign a date

termingerecht, adv
pünktlich, adv
- **on schedule, adv**
- on time, adv
- punctually, adv

termingerechte Ankunft, f
fristgerechte Ankunft f
Ankunft zum festgesetzten Termin, f
- arrival on the appointed date
- arrival at the appointed time

terminieren etw für den 08. November
ansetzen etw für den 08. November
- schedule s.th. for 8 November

Terminierung, f
- timing

Terminkalender, m
- appointments schedule *AE*
- appointments book *BE*

- tickler *coll*
- schedule

Termin vereinbaren
- **schedule an appointment**
- agree on a date

Termin verlegen
→ Termin verschieben

Terminverlegung, f
→ Terminverschiebung

Termin verschieben (Datum)
- **postpone a date**
- postpone the date

Termin verschieben (Verabredung)
Termin verlegen
- **postpone an appointment**

Termin verschieben vom 1. April auf den 2. Mai (Verabredung)
- **postpone an appointment from 1 April to 2 May**
- put off an appointment from 1 April to 2 May

Terminverschiebung, f
- postponement of an appointment

Termin verwechseln
- mistake the date

Termin wählen, der am besten paßt
- choose the date that suits one best

Terracottavase, f
- terracotta vase

Terrain, n
- terrain

Terrainkur, f
Geländekur, f
- terrain treatment
- terrain cure

Terrainweg, m
Terrainkurweg, m
Geländeweg, m
- terrain path

Terrarium, n
- terrarium

Terrasse, f
(in südlichen Ländern auch Patio)
- terrace
- patio

Terrasse liegt nach Norden
Terrasse geht nach Norden
- terrace faces north

Terrasse liegt nach Osten
Terrasse geht nach Osten
- terrace faces east

Terrasse liegt nach Süden
Terrasse geht nach Süden
- terrace faces south

Terrasse liegt nach Westen
Terrasse geht nach Westen
- terrace faces west

Terrasse mit Blick auf das Meer, f
Terrasse mit Blick auf die See, f
- terrace overlooking the sea
- terrace with a view of the sea

Terrasse mit Blick auf den See, f
- terrace overlooking the lake
- terrace with a view of the lake

Terrasse mit Blick über den See, f
- terrace with a view over the lake
- terrace with a view across the lake

Terrasse mit Blumen, f
- terrace with flowers
- patio with flowers

Terrassenbad, n
Terrassenbecken, n
- terrace pool

Terrassenbar, f
- terrace bar
- patio bar

Terrassencafé, n
- terrace cafe *AE*
- terrace café *BE*
- patio cafe *AE*
- patio café *BE*

Terrassendach, n
- terrace roof

Terrassenfläche, f
- terrace area
- patio area

Terrassenfreibad, n
- outdoor swimming pool on the terrace *AE*
- outdoor swimming-pool on the terrace *BE*
- open-air terrace swimming pool *AE*
- open-air terrace swimming-pool *BE*
- open-air terrace pool

Terrassengarten, m
- terrace garden
- terraced garden

Terrassenhang, m
- terraced slope

Terrassenhotel, n
- terrace hotel

Terrassenliege, f
- terrace lounge *AE*
- patio lounge *AE*

Terrassenlokal, n
- terrace place

Terrassenmöbel, n pl
Terrassenmobiliar, n
- terrace furniture *sg*
- patio furniture *sg*

Terrassenmobiliar, n
→ Terrassenmöbel

Terrassenrestaurant n
- terrace restaurant

Terrassenschwimmbad, n
- terrace swimming pool *AE*
- terrace swimming-pool *BE*
- terrace pool

Terrassenservice m
Terrassenbedienung f
- terrace service

Terrassensitzplatz, m
Terrassenplatz, m
Terrassensitz, m
- terrace seat

Terrassenspeisesaal, m
- terrace dining room

Terrassenstuhl m
- terrace chair

Terrassentisch, m
- terrace table
- patio table

Terrassenzimmer, n
- terrace room
- room with (a) terrace

Terrassenzuschlag m
- terrace supplement
- supplement for (a) terrace

Terrasse zum Sonnen, f
→ Sonnenterrasse

Terrasse zum Sonnenbaden, f
→ Liegeterrasse

Terrazzofußboden

Terrazzofußboden, m
   Terrazzoboden, m
   ♦ terrazzo floor
Terrine, f
   ♦ tureen
   ♦ terrine
tertiäre Bereich, m
   tertiäre Sektor, m
   ♦ tertiary sector
Tessin, das, n
   (Region)
   ♦ Ticino
Tessiner, m
   ♦ Ticinese
Tessinerin, f
   ♦ Ticinese girl
   ♦ Ticinese woman
   ♦ Ticinese
tessinisch, adj
   ♦ Ticinese, adj
Test, m
   ♦ test
Testbuchung, f
   Probebuchung, f
   ♦ trial booking
Testessen, n
   Testmahlzeit, f
   Probeessen, n
   ♦ trial meal
Testhotel, n
   ♦ test hotel
Testmenü, n
   ♦ trial menu
Testpilot, m
   ♦ test pilot
Testrestaurant, n
   ♦ test restaurant
Tetanus, m
   Wundstarrkrampf, m
   Starrkrampf, m
   ♦ tetanus
Tetanusimpfung, f
   ♦ tetanus vaccination
tête-à-tête, adv *FR*
   ♦ tête-à-tête, adv *FR*
Tête-à-tête, n *FR*
   ♦ tête-à-tête *FR*
Tête-à-tête-Abendessen, n
   ♦ tête-à-tête dinner
tête-à-tête speisen mit jm
   ♦ dine tête-à-tête with s.o.
teuer, adj
   ♦ expensive, adj
   ♦ dear, adj
   ♦ pricy, adj *coll*
   ♦ pricey, adj *coll*
teuer möbliert, adj
   ♦ expensively furnished, adj
teuer möbliertes Zimmer, n
   ♦ expensively furnished room
teuerstes Hotel am Ort, n
   ♦ most expensive hotel in the place
Teufelsmoor, n
   ♦ Devil's Moor, the
teure Reise, f
   ♦ expensive tour
   ♦ expensive journey
   ♦ expensive trip
teures Hotel, n
   ♦ expensive hotel

   ♦ pricy hotel *coll*
   ♦ pricey hotel *coll*
teures Hotelzimmer, n
   ♦ expensive hotel room
   ♦ pricy hotel room *coll*
   ♦ pricey hotel room *coll*
teures Restaurant, n
   ♦ expensive restaurant
   ♦ pricy restaurant *coll*
   ♦ pricey restaurant *coll*
teures Zimmer, n
   ♦ expensive room
   ♦ pricy room *coll*
   ♦ pricey room *coll*
Teutoburger Wald, m
   ♦ Teutoburg Forest, the
Textblock, m
   ♦ text block
Textilhandtuch, n
   → Stoffhandtuch
Textilhotel, n
   (im Gegensatz zu FKK-Hotel)
   ♦ nonnudist hotel *AE*
   ♦ non-nudist hotel *BE*
Textilmuseum, n
   ♦ textile museum
Textilserviette, f
   ♦ cloth napkin
Textilstrand, m
   (Gegensatz zu Naturistenstrand)
   ♦ nonnudist beach *AE*
   ♦ non-nudist beach
Textinformation, f
   ♦ text information
Texttafel, f
   ♦ text panel
T-förmig, adj
   ♦ T-shaped, adj
TGV, m *FR*
   Train à grande vitesse, m *FR m*
   ♦ TGV *FR*
   ♦ train à grande vitesse m *FR*
Thai, m
   Thailänder, m
   ♦ Thai
Thailand
   ♦ Thailand
Thailänderin, f
   ♦ Thai girl
   ♦ Thai woman
   ♦ Thai
thailändisch, adj
   ♦ Thai, adj
Thalassotherapie, f
   ♦ thalassotherapy
   ♦ saltwater cure *AE*
   ♦ salt-water cure *BE*
Thalassotherapiebehandlung, f
   ♦ thalassotherapy treatment
Thalassotherapiepraxis, f
   Thalassotherapieräume, m pl
   ♦ thalassotherapy suite
Theater, n
   ♦ theater *AE*
   ♦ theatre *BE*
Theaterabend, m
   ♦ theater evening *AE*
   ♦ theatre evening *BE*
Theateraufführung, f
   ♦ theater performance *AE*

   ♦ theatre performance *BE*
   ♦ theatrical performance
Theaterbestuhlung, f
   → Reihenbestuhlung
Theaterbesuch, m
   ♦ theater visit *AE*
   ♦ theatre visit *BE*
   ♦ visit to the theater *AE*
   ♦ visit to the theatre *BE*
   ♦ theatergoing *AE*
Theaterbesucher, m
   ♦ playgoer
   ♦ theatergoer *AE*
   ♦ theatre-goer *BE*
Theaterbühne, f
   ♦ theatrical stage
Theaterdarbietung, f
   ♦ theatrical presentation
Theaterfestspiele, n pl
   Theaterfestival, n
   ♦ theater festival *AE*
   ♦ theatre festival *BE*
Theaterform, f (Bestuhlung)
   → Vortragsform
Theaterführer, m
   (Information)
   ♦ theater guide *AE*
   ♦ theatre guide *BE*
Theater ist ausverkauft
   ♦ theater is sold out *AE*
   ♦ theatre is sold out *BE*
Theaterkarte, f
   ♦ theater ticket *AE*
   ♦ theatre ticket *BE*
Theaterkarte bestellen
   ♦ order a theater ticket *AE*
   ♦ book a theater ticket *AE*
   ♦ order a theatre ticket *BE*
   ♦ book a theatre ticket *BE*
Theaterkarte kaufen
   ♦ buy a theater ticket *AE*
   ♦ buy a theatre ticket *BE*
Theaterkartenschalter, m
   (z.B. im Hotel)
   ♦ theater ticket desk *AE*
   ♦ theatre ticket desk *BE*
Theaterkartensofortvermittlung, f
   ♦ instant theater booking service *AE*
   ♦ instant theatre booking service *BE*
Theaterkartenverkauf, m (Verkauf)
   ♦ sale of theater tickets *AE*
   ♦ sale of theatre tickets *BE*
Theaterkartenverkauf, m (Verkaufsstelle)
   Theaterkartenverkaufsstelle, f
   ♦ theater ticket office *AE*
   ♦ theatre ticket office *BE*
Theaterkartenvermittlung, f (Büro)
   ♦ theater (ticket) agency *AE*
   ♦ theatre (ticket) agency *BE*
   ♦ theater (ticket) bureau *AE*
   ♦ theatre (ticket) bureau *BE*
   ♦ theatre booking agency *BE*
Theaterkartenvermittlung, f (Service)
   ♦ theater ticket service *AE*
   ♦ theatre ticket service *BE*
   ♦ theater booking service *AE*
   ♦ theatre booking service *BE*
Theaterkartenvorverkauf, m
   ♦ advance booking of theater tickets *AE*
   ♦ advance booking of theatre tickets *BE*

Theaterkarte vorbestellen
- ◆ prebook a theatre ticket *AE*
- ◆ prebook a theatre ticket *BE*

Theaterkasse, f
- ◆ theater box office *AE*
- ◆ theatre box-office *BE*
- ◆ box office *AE*
- ◆ box-office *BE*

Theaterleben, n
- ◆ theatrical life

Theaterliebhaber, m
- ◆ theater lover *AE*
- ◆ theatre lover *BE*

Theater mit 123 Plätzen, n
- ◆ theater with 123 seats *AE*
- ◆ 123-seat theater *AE*
- ◆ theatre with 123 seats *BE*
- ◆ 123-seat theatre *BE*

Theaternarr, m
- ◆ theater buff *AE*
- ◆ theatre buff *BE*

Theaterpause, f
- ◆ theater interval *AE*
- ◆ theatre interval *BE*

Theaterplatz, m
Theatersitzplatz, m
- ◆ theater seat *AE*
- ◆ theatre seat *BE*

Theaterpremiere, f
- ◆ theater premiere *AE*
- ◆ theatre première *BE*

Theaterprogramm, n
- ◆ theater program *AE*
- ◆ theatre programme *BE*

Theaterreise, f
- ◆ theater trip *AE*
- ◆ theater tour *AE*
- ◆ theatre trip *BE*
- ◆ theatre tour *BE*

Theaterrestaurant n
- ◆ theater restaurant *AE*
- ◆ theatre restaurant *BE*

Theatersaison, f
- ◆ theater season *AE*
- ◆ theatre season *BE*
- ◆ theatrical season

Theaterstück, n
- ◆ play

Theaterveranstaltung, f
- ◆ theatrical event

Theaterverein, m
- ◆ theater club *AE*
- ◆ theatre club *BE*

Theatervermittlungsdienst, m
Theaterkartenvermittlung, f
- ◆ theater booking service *AE*
- ◆ theatre booking service *BE*

Theatervorhang, m
- ◆ theatrical curtain

Theaterwerkstatt, f
- ◆ theater workshop *AE*
- ◆ theatre workshop *BE*

Theaterwochenende, n
- ◆ theater weekend *AE*
- ◆ theatre weekend *BE*

Theke, f
Tresen, m
- ◆ counter

Thekenpersonal, n
Tresenpersonal, n
Counterpersonal, n

- ◆ counter personnel
- ◆ counter staff

Thekenservice, m
Thekenbedienung f
Tresenservice m
Tresenbedienung f
- ◆ counter service

Thema der Konferenz, n
- ◆ theme of the conference

Thema der Konferenz ist ...
- ◆ theme of the conference is ...

Thema der Tagung, n
- ◆ theme of the meeting

Thema des Kongresses, n
- ◆ theme of the convention
- ◆ theme of the congress

Themenpark, m
→ Erlebnispark

Thementourismus, m
→ Erlebnistourismus

Themse, f
- ◆ Thames River, the
- ◆ River Thames, the
- ◆ Thames, the

Themsetal, n
- ◆ Thames valley, the

Therapeut, m
- ◆ therapist

therapeutisch, adj
heilend, adj
- ◆ therapeutic, adj

Therapie, f
- ◆ therapy

Therapieabteilung, f
- ◆ therapy department

Therapiebad, n
- ◆ therapeutic bath

Therapiebecken n
- ◆ therapy pool
- ◆ therapeutic pool

Therapiegymnastik, f
Heilgymnastik, f
- ◆ therapeutic exercise

Therapieklinik, f
- ◆ therapy clinic

Therapiekombination, f
- ◆ combination of therapies

Therapiereise, f
- ◆ therapeutic tour

Therapietag, m
- ◆ therapy day

Therapiewoche, f
- ◆ therapy week

Therapiewochenende, f
- ◆ therapy weekend

Therapiezentrum, n
- ◆ therapy center *AE*
- ◆ therapy centre *BE*

Thermalbad, n (Aktivität)
- ◆ thermal bath
- ◆ hot-water bath

Thermalbad, n (Ort)
→ Thermalkurort

Thermalbad, n (Schwimmbad)
→ Thermalschwimmbad

Thermalbadanlage, f
Thermalbadkomplex, m
- ◆ thermal pool complex

Thermalbaden, n
- ◆ thermal bathing

Thermalbadeort, m
→ Thermalkurort

Thermalbecken, n
- ◆ thermal pool

Thermalbewegungsbad, n
- ◆ thermal wave pool

Thermalfreibad, n
- ◆ outdoor thermal swimming pool *AE*
- ◆ outdoor thermal swimming-pool *BE*
- ◆ outdoor thermal pool

Thermalfreibecken, n
Thermalfreibad, n
- ◆ outdoor thermal pool

Thermalgrotte, f
- ◆ thermal grotto

Thermalhallenbad, n
Thermalhallenschwimmbad, n
Thermalschwimmhalle, f
- ◆ indoor thermal swimming pool *AE*
- ◆ indoor thermal swimming-pool *BE*
- ◆ indoor thermal pool

Thermalhallenschwimmbad, n
→ Thermalhallenbad

Thermalhotel, n
- ◆ thermal hotel

Thermalkörperwickel, m
- ◆ thermal body wrap

Thermalkur, f
- ◆ thermal treatment

Thermalkurort, m
Thermalbad, n
- ◆ thermal spa

Thermalort, m
Thermalferienort, m
- ◆ thermal resort
- ◆ hot-spring resort

Thermalquelle, f
- ◆ thermal spring
- ◆ hot spring

Thermalquellwasser, n
- ◆ thermal springwater *AE*
- ◆ thermal spring water *BE*

Thermalschwimmbad, n
Thermalschwimmbecken, n
Thermalbad, n
- ◆ thermal swimming pool *AE*
- ◆ thermal swimming-pool *BE*
- ◆ thermal pool

Thermalschwimmbecken, n
→ Thermalschwimmbad

Thermalschwimmhalle, f
→ Thermalhallenbad

Thermalsolebad, n
→ Solethermalbad

Thermalsole-Bewegungsbad, n
- ◆ saltwater thermal wave pool *AE*
- ◆ salt-water thermal wave pool *BE*

Thermalstadt, f (Großstadt)
- ◆ thermal city

Thermalstadt, f (kleine Stadt)
- ◆ thermal town

Thermaltourismus, m
- ◆ thermal tourism

Thermaltourist, m
- ◆ thermal tourist

Thermalwasser, n
- ◆ thermal water

Thermalwasserbecken, n
- ◆ thermal-water pool
- ◆ thermal pool

Thermalwickel

Thermalwickel, m
- thermal wrap

Thermalzentrum, n
- thermal center *AE*
- thermal centre *BE*

Thermometer, n
- thermometer

Thermosflasche, f
- thermos flask
- Thermos bottle *AE*
- Thermos *AE*

Thermostat, m
Temperaturregler, m
- thermostat

thesaurierter Gewinn, m
zurückbehaltener Gewinn, m
- retained profit
- retained earnings *AE pl*

Thessalien
- Thessaly

Thousand-Island-Dressing, n
- thousand-island dressing

Thronsaal, m
(im Schloß)
- throne room

Thuner See, m
- Lake Thun
- Lake of Thun

Thunfisch, m
Thun, m
- tuna fish
- tuna

Thunfischcocktail, m
- tuna cocktail

Thüringen
(Land)
- Thuringia

Thüringer, m
- Thuringian

Thüringer Becken, n
- Thuringian Basin, the

Thüringerin, f
- Thuringian girl
- Thuringian woman
- Thuringian

Thüringer Wald, m
(Region)
- Thuringian Forest, the

thüringisch, adj
- Thuringian, adj

Thymian, m
- thyme

Thymianzweigchen, n
Thymianzweig, m
- thyme sprig

Tibet
- Tibet

Tibeter, m
Tibetaner, m
- Tibetan

Tibeterin, f
Tibetanerin, f
- Tibetan girl
- Tibetan woman
- Tibetan

tibetisch, adj
tibetanisch, adj
- Tibetan, adj

tibetischer Tee, m
- Tibetan tea

Ticket, n
→ Karte, Fahrkarte

Ticketing, n
→ Fahrkartenausstellung

Tidebecken, n
- tidal basin

tiefen Schlaf haben
- be a heavy sleeper
- be a sound sleeper

tiefen Schluck nehmen
- take a deep draft *AE*
- take a deep draught *BE*

tiefe Platte, f
(Geschirr)
- deep platter

tiefer Schlaf, m
- deep sleep

tiefer Schläfer, m
- heavy sleeper
- sound sleeper

tiefer Schluck, m
(z.B. Bier)
- deep draft *AE*
- deep draught *BE*

tieferstufen etw
niedriger einstufen etw
runterstufen etw *coll*
- downgrade s.th.

Tieferstufung, f
Herabstufung, f
niedrigere Einstufung, f
- downgrading

tiefer Teil, m
(Schwimmbad)
- deep end

tiefer Teller, m
- deep plate

tiefes Geschirr, n
- hollowware

tiefes Tal, n
- deep valley

Tiefgarage, f (generell)
- underground garage

Tiefgarage, f (im Souterrain)
→ Souterraingarage

Tiefgarage, f (mehrere Autos)
- underground parking lot *AE*
- underground car park *BE*

Tiefgaragenfläche, f
- underground parking area

Tiefgaragenparkplatz, m (für 1 Auto)
Tiefgaragenstellplatz, m
- underground parking place
- underground parking space
- underground parking lot *AE*

tiefgefroren, adj
- deep-frozen, adj

tiefgekühlt, adj (Getränk)
→ gekühlt

tiefgekühlt, adj (Speisen)
- deep-frozen, adj
- frozen, adj

tiefgekühlte Lebensmittel, pl
- frozen food

tiefgekühltes Gemüse, n
- frozen vegetable

tiefkühlen etw
tiefgefrieren etw
- deep-freeze s.th.

Tiefkühlfach, n
- deep-freeze compartment
- freezing compartment
- freezer compartment
- freezer

Tiefkühlkost, f
- frozen foods *pl*
- frozen food

Tiefkühlschrank, m
- deep-freeze cabinet

Tiefkühltruhe, f
- deep-freeze
- chest freezer
- freezer

Tiefland, n
→ Flachland

Tiefpreisspezialist, m
- low-price specialist

tief schlafen
- be fast asleep
- sleep soundly

Tiefschnee, m
tiefer Schnee, m
- deep snow

Tiefschneeabfahrt, f
- deep-snow downhill run
- deep-snow run

Tiefschneefahrer, m
Tiefschneeläufer, m
- deep-snow skier

Tiefschneesafari, f
- deep-snow safari

Tiefseetaucher, m
- deep-sea diver

tiefste Provinz, f
hinterste Provinz, f
jwd
- back of beyond, the

Tiefstpreis, m
tiefster Preis, m
allerniedrigster Preis, m
- rock-bottom price *inform*
- rock-bottom rate *inform*
- lowest price
- lowest rate

Tiefststand, m
tiefster Stand, m
- rock-bottom level

Tiefsttemperatur, f
- minimum temperature
- lowest temperature

Tiegel, m
Kasserolle, f
- skillet *BE*

Tier, n (generell)
- animal

Tier, n (Haustier)
→ Haustier

Tierarzt, m
- veterinarian *AE*
- veterinary surgeon *BE*
- veterinary *BE*
- vet *coll*

Tiere in freier Wildbahn, n pl
- wildlife

Tierfreund, m
Tierliebhaber, m
- animal lover

tierfreundlich, adj
haustierfreundlich, adj
- suitable for pets, adj
- welcoming pets, adj

tierfreundliches Hotel, n
  (Haustiere)
  ♦ hotel welcoming pets
  ♦ hotel which accepts pets
  ♦ hotel which is suitable for pets
Tiergarten, m
  → Zoo
Tiergehege, n
  Wildgehege, n
  ♦ game enclosure
  ♦ game preserve
Tierhalter, m
  (Haustiere)
  ♦ pet owner
Tierpark, m
  (Tiere in freier Natur)
  ♦ wildlife park
Tiersafari, f
  Safari zu den Tieren in freier Wildbahn, f
  ♦ wildlife safari
Tierschutzgebiet, n
  ♦ wildlife sanctuary
Tier- und Pflanzenwelt, f
  ♦ wildlife
Tierzentrum, n
  ♦ wildlife center AE
  ♦ wildlife centre BE
Tierzoo, m
  ♦ animal zoo
Tigergehege, n
  ♦ tiger enclosure
tilgen etw
  zurückzahlen etw
  Schulden tilgen
  ♦ amortise s.th.
  ♦ amortize s.th.
  ♦ pay off s.th.
Timbale, f
  → Füllpastete, f
Timelag, m
  Zeitverschiebung, f
  zeitliche Verzögerung, f
  ♦ time lag AE
  ♦ time-lag BE
Timeshare-Appartement, n
  Appartement in Zeiteigentum, n
  ♦ timeshare apartment
Timeshare-Bereich, m
  Timeshare-Sektor, m
  ♦ timeshare sector
  ♦ timesharing sector
Timeshare-Besitzer, m
  ♦ timeshare owner
Timeshare-Dorf, n
  ♦ timeshare village
Timeshare-Ferienanlage, f
  Timeshare-Ferienort, m
  Timeshare-Urlaubsort, m
  ♦ timeshare resort
Timeshare-Gesellschaft, f
  ♦ timeshare company
Timeshare-Immobilie, f
  ♦ timeshare property
Timeshare-Industrie, f
  ♦ timeshare industry
Timeshare-Käufer, m
  ♦ timeshare buyer
Timeshare-Konzept, n
  ♦ timeshare concept
Timeshare-Pauschale, f
  Timeshare-Pauschalpreis, m

  ♦ timesharing package AE
  ♦ time-sharing package BE
Timeshare-Unterkunft, f
  Unterkunft in Zeiteigentum, f
  ♦ timeshare accommodation
Timeshare-Vereinbarung, f
  Timeshare-Arrangement, n
  ♦ timesharing arrangement AE
  ♦ time-sharing arrangement BE
Timesharing, n
  Zeitmiteigentum, n
  zeitliches begrenztes Eigentum, n
  ♦ timesharing AE
  ♦ time-sharing BE
Timor
  ♦ Timor
Tingeltangellokal, n
  Tingeltangel, m/n
  ♦ honky-tonk AE
  ♦ dive
Tintenfisch, m (Gemeiner Tintenfisch)
  ♦ cuttle fish
Tintenfisch, m (zehnarmig)
  zehnarmiger Tintenfisch, m
  ♦ squid
Tip, m
  Hinweis, m
  ♦ tip
Tip für Reisende, m
  Hinweis für Reisende, m
  ♦ tip for travelers AE
  ♦ tip for travellers BE
Tipgeben, n
  → Trinkgeldgeben
Tipi, n
  (kegelförmiges Indianerzelt)
  ♦ tepee
Tippelbruder, m sl
  Pennbruder, m sl
  Penner, m sl
  ♦ dosser BE sl
  ♦ hobo AE sl
  ♦ bum AE sl
  ♦ vagrant
  ♦ tramp
tippeln
  ♦ tramp
tipptopp, adj
  ♦ tip-top, adj
  ♦ spotless, adj
Tirol
  (Region)
  ♦ Tyrol (the)
  ♦ Tirol (the)
Tiroler, m
  ♦ Tyrolean
  ♦ Tirolean
  ♦ Tyrolese
  ♦ Tirolese
Tiroler Abend, m
  ♦ Tyrolean Evening
  ♦ Tirolean Evening
  ♦ Tyrolean Night
  ♦ Tirolean Night
Tiroler Alpen, pl
  ♦ Tyrolean Alps, the pl
  ♦ Tirolean Alps, the pl
Tirolerart, adv gastr
  ♦ Tyrolean style gastr
Tirolerin, f
  ♦ Tyrolean girl

  ♦ Tyrolean woman
  ♦ Tyrolese girl
  ♦ Tirolese woman
  ♦ Tirolean
Tiroler Stube, f
  ♦ room furnished in Tyrolean style
  ♦ room furnished in Tirolean style
  ♦ room furnished in Tyrolese style
  ♦ room furnished in Tirolese style
tirolisch, adj
  tirolerisch, adj ÖST
  ♦ Tyrolean, adj
  ♦ Tirolean, adj
  ♦ Tyrolese, adj
  ♦ Tirolese, adj
Tisch, m
  Tafel, f
  ♦ table
Tisch abbestellen
  ♦ cancel a table
Tisch abräumen
  Tisch abdecken
  Geschirr abräumen vom Tisch
  ♦ clear the table
  ♦ bus a table AE
Tisch abwischen
  ♦ wipe the table
Tisch am Fenster, m
  Fenstertisch, m
  ♦ table at the window
  ♦ table by the window
  ♦ window table
Tischanordnung, f
  Tischarrangement, n
  Anordnung der Tische, f
  ♦ table arrangement
  ♦ arrangement of (the) tables
Tischarrangement, n
  Tischanordnung, f
  Anordnung der Tische, f
  ♦ arrangement of (the) tables
  ♦ table arrangement
Tisch aufstellen
  ♦ set up a table
Tischaufsteller, m (Karte)
  → Tischreiter
Tischausstellung, f
  (auf dem Tisch)
  ♦ tabletop display
Tisch bedienen
  ♦ serve a table
Tischbedienung, f
  Tischservice, m
  ♦ table service
Tischbein, n
  ♦ table leg AE
  ♦ table-leg BE
Tisch bekommen (zum Abendessen)
  ♦ get a table (for dinner)
Tisch belegen
  Tisch besetzen
  ♦ occupy a table
Tischbesen, m
  ♦ crumb brush
Tischbesteck n (einzelnes)
  ♦ set of knife, fork and spoon
  ♦ knife, fork and spoon
Tischbesteck, n (mehrere Personen)
  ♦ set of cutlery
  ♦ cutlery

Tisch bestellen für 20 Uhr

Tisch bestellen für 20 Uhr
- ♦ book a table for 8 p.m.

Tisch bestellen (für jn)
- Tische reservieren lassen (für jn)
- ♦ book a table (for s.o.)
- ♦ reserve a table (for s.o.)

Tisch bestellen im voraus
- Tisch im voraus buchen
- ♦ book a table in advance
- ♦ prebook a table

Tisch bestellen in einem Restaurant
- ♦ reserve a table at a restaurant AE
- ♦ reserve a table in a restaurant AE
- ♦ book a table at a restaurant BE
- ♦ book a table in a restaurant BE

Tischbestellung f
- ♦ booking (of) a table

Tischbestuhlung, f
- Tafelbestuhlung; f
- ♦ classroom-style seating
- ♦ classroom seating

Tischbezug, m
- ♦ table cover

Tischbock, m
- ♦ trestle

Tisch buchen
- → Tisch bestellen

Tischchen, n
- ♦ small table

Tischdame f
- ♦ dinner partner
- ♦ lady partner at table

Tischdecke, f
- → Tischtuch

Tisch decken
- Tisch eindecken
- ♦ lay the table
- ♦ set the table
- ♦ lay the cloth

Tisch decken für zwei Personen
- ♦ lay the table for two persons
- ♦ set the table for two (persons)
- ♦ lay covers for two (persons)

Tischdekoration, f
- Tischschmuck, m
- ♦ table decoration

Tisch eindecken
- Tisch decken
- ♦ set the table
- ♦ lay the table
- ♦ lay the cloth

Tischeindeckung, f
- ♦ table laying
- ♦ laying the table
- ♦ laying (the) tables
- ♦ setting the table
- ♦ table setting

Tischende, n (gegenüber Kopfende)
- → unteres Tischende

Tischende, n (generell)
- ♦ end of the table

Tischende, n (Kopfende)
- ♦ head of the table

Tischerücken, n
- (Séance)
- ♦ table-turning

Tische werden mit Kerzen beleuchtet
- ♦ tables are lit by candle

tischfertig, adj
- ♦ table-ready, adj
- ♦ ready-to-serve, adj

tischfertiges Gericht, n
- ♦ ready-to-serve dish

Tisch fest zusagen
- ♦ guarantee a table

Tischfeuerzeug, n
- ♦ table cigarette lighter
- ♦ table cigaret lighter AE
- ♦ table lighter

Tischform, f (Bestuhlung)
- Klassenzimmerform, f
- ♦ schoolroom style
- ♦ classroom style

Tisch freimachen für jn
- (abräumen)
- ♦ clear the table for s.o.

Tischfußball, m
- ♦ table football BE
- ♦ table soccer AE

Tischgabel, f
- Tafelgabel, f
- ♦ table fork

Tischgarnitur, f
- ♦ table set

Tischgast, m
- ♦ dinner guest
- ♦ diner
- ♦ table guest

Tisch geben jm
- ♦ give s.o. a table

Tischgebet, n
- ♦ grace
- ♦ table grace

Tischgebühr f
- ♦ table charge
- ♦ table fee

Tischgenosse, m (Abendessen)
- ♦ dinner companion

Tischgenosse, m (generell)
- ♦ table companion

Tischgenosse, m (Mittagessen)
- Tischgenosse beim Mittagessen, m
- ♦ lunch companion
- ♦ lunching companion BE

Tischgerät, n
- (Fernseher, Radio)
- ♦ table set

Tischgeschirr, n
- Tafelgeschirr, n
- ♦ tableware
- ♦ dishes pl

Tischgesellschaft, f (Dinner)
- → Abendgesellschaft

Tischgesellschaft, f (Lunch)
- → Mittagsgesellschaft

Tischgesellschaft, f (Unterhaltung)
- ♦ company at table

Tischgespräch, n
- ♦ table talk AE
- ♦ conversation at table
- ♦ table-talk BE

Tischgetränk, n
- Tafelgetränk, n
- ♦ table drink
- ♦ table beverage

Tischglocke, f
- ♦ dinner bell

Tischgröße, f
- ♦ table size
- ♦ size of a table

Tischgruppe, f
- ♦ group of tables

Tischherr m
- ♦ dinner partner
- ♦ partner at table

Tisch im Freien, m
- ♦ outdoor table

Tisch im voraus reservieren
- ♦ reserve a table in advance

Tisch ist besetzt
- ♦ table is occupied
- ♦ table is taken

Tisch ist frei
- ♦ table is vacant
- ♦ table is free

Tisch ist für eine Person gedeckt
- ♦ table is set for one person

Tisch ist gedeckt
- Tisch ist eingedeckt
- ♦ table is laid

Tisch ist leer
- ♦ table is empty

Tischkante, f
- ♦ edge of the table

Tischkarte, f
- (auf Tisch, mit Namen)
- ♦ place card
- ♦ name card
- ♦ dinner card
- ♦ guest card

Tischkellner, m
- ♦ table waiter

Tischkellnerin, f
- ♦ table waitress

Tischlampe, f
- ♦ table lamp

Tischläufer, m
- ♦ runner

Tischleindeckdich, n
- ♦ easy street AE sl
- ♦ cushy set-up BE
- ♦ (be on a) cushy number BE

Tischler, m
- Schreiner, m
- ♦ joiner
- ♦ carpenter

Tischmanieren, f pl
- Tischsitten, f pl
- ♦ table manners pl

Tischmesser, n
- Tafelmesser, n
- ♦ table knife AE
- ♦ table-knife BE

Tischmikrofon, n
- ♦ table microphone
- ♦ desk microphone

Tischmusik, f
- Tafelmusik, f
- ♦ table music

Tischnachbar, m
- Tischnachbarin, f
- ♦ neighbor at table AE
- ♦ neighbour at table BE
- ♦ person sitting next to one

Tisch neben der Tür, m
- ♦ table next to the door
- ♦ table beside the door

Tisch nehmen bei dem Fenster
- ♦ take a table by the window

Tisch neu eindecken
- Tisch neu decken
- ♦ relay the table
- ♦ reset the table AE

Tisch numerieren
♦ number a table
Tischnumerierung f
♦ numbering (of) tables
Tischnummer, f
♦ table number
♦ number of a table
Tischordnung, f
♦ seating plan at table
♦ seating plan
♦ seating order at table
♦ seating order
Tischplan, m
Betischungsplan, m
Tafelplan, m
♦ table plan
Tischplatte, f
♦ tabletop
Tischplatz m
(Platz an einem Tisch)
♦ seat at a table
♦ place at a table
Tischpult, n
Rednerpult, n
♦ speaker's desk
♦ lectern
Tischrechaud, n/m
♦ table rechaud
♦ table réchaud FR
♦ hot-plate
♦ chafing-dish obs
Tischrede, f
♦ after-dinner speech
♦ speech made at table
♦ dinner speech AE
Tischrede halten
♦ make a speech at table
Tischredner m
♦ speaker at table
♦ speaker
Tischreihe f
♦ row of tables
Tischreiter, m
(Karte mit Informationen)
Tischaufsteller, m
Zeltaufsteller, m
♦ table tent
Tischreservation, f SCHW
→ Tischreservierung
Tisch reservieren für einen Gast
♦ reserve a table for a guest
Tisch reservieren (für jn)
♦ reserve a table (for s.o.)
Tisch reservieren für zwei Personen
♦ reserve a table for two persons
♦ reserve a table for two
Tisch reservieren in einem Restaurant
♦ reserve a table in a restaurant
Tisch reservieren lassen
♦ make a table reservation
♦ reserve a table
♦ book a table
Tischreservierung, f
Tischreservation, f SCHW
♦ table reservation
♦ reservation of a table
Tischreservierung empfohlen
♦ Table reservation recommended
Tischreservierungen erbeten
♦ Table reservation required

Tischreservierung ist angebracht
Tischreservierung ist ratsam
♦ table reservation is advisable
Tischreservierung ratsam
♦ Table reservation advisable
Tischreservierungsformular n
♦ table reservation form
Tischreservierungswunsch, m
♦ table reservation request
♦ request for table reservation
Tischreservierung wird empfohlen
♦ Table reservations are recommended
Tisch richten für das Essen
♦ get the table ready for the meal
♦ arrange the table for the meal
♦ lay the table for the meal
♦ set the table for the meal
Tischschmuck, m
→ Tischdekoration
Tisch schmückt den Rasen
♦ table decorates the lawn
Tischschoner, m
♦ table protector
Tischservice, m
→ Tischbedienung
Tischservicebetrieb, m
♦ table-service establishment
♦ table-service operation
Tischservicepersonal, n
Tischbedienungspersonal, n
♦ table-service staff
♦ table-service personnel
Tischservicerestaurant, n
Restaurant mit Tischbedienung, n
♦ table-service restaurant
Tischserviette, f
♦ table napkin
Tischset, n
Platzdeckchen, n
Set, n
♦ place mat AE
♦ place-mat BE
♦ table mat AE
♦ table-mat BE
Tischsitten, f pl
→ Tischmanieren
Tischspiel, n
♦ table game
Tischsteward, m
♦ table steward
Tischsystem, n
♦ table system
Tisch teilen mit Fremden
♦ share a table with strangers
Tisch teilen mit jm
♦ share a table with s.o.
Tischtelefon n
♦ table telephone
♦ desk telephone
Tischtennis, n
♦ table tennis
♦ ping-pong
Tischtennisball, m
♦ table-tennis ball
Tischtennishalle, f
♦ table-tennis hall
Tischtennisraum, m
Tischtenniszimmer, n
♦ table-tennis room

Tischtennisschläger, m
♦ table-tennis paddle AE
♦ table-tennis bat BE
Tischtennisspiel, n
♦ table-tennis match
♦ game of table tennis
Tischtennis spielen
♦ play table tennis
♦ play ping-pong
Tischtennisspieler, m
♦ table-tennis player
Tischtennistisch, m
♦ table-tennis table
♦ ping-pong table
Tischtennisturnier, n
♦ table-tennis tournament
Tischtennisturnier abhalten
♦ hold a table tennis tournament
Tischtenniswettbewerb, m
Tischtenniswettkampf, m
♦ table-tennis competition
♦ table-tennis contest
Tischterminal, n
(Computer)
♦ desk-top terminal
Tischtuch, n
Tischdecke, f
♦ tablecloth AE
♦ table-cloth BE
Tisch und Bett
Tisch (m) und Bett (n)
Kost (f) und Logis (n)
♦ bed and board
♦ board and lodging
Tisch und Bett anbieten
♦ offer bed and board
Tisch und Bett verlassen
(Scheidung von Eheleuten)
♦ abandon the conjugal bed
Tischvitrine, f
♦ table showcase
Tisch vorbestellen
Tisch im voraus bestellen
♦ prebook a table
♦ book a table in advance
Tisch wackelt
♦ table wobbles
Tischwäsche, f
♦ table linen AE
♦ table-linen BE
♦ napery AE
Tischwäschewechsel, m
Wechsel der Tischwäsche, m
♦ change of table linen AE
♦ change of table-linen BE
Tischwäsche wechseln
♦ change the table linen AE
♦ change the table-linen BE
Tisch wechseln
(anderen Tisch benutzen)
♦ change tables
♦ swap tables
♦ swop tables
Tischwein, m
♦ table wine
♦ ordinary wine
♦ dinner wine
Tischzeit, f
Essenszeit für eine Gruppe, f
♦ sitting

Tisch zuteilen jm

Tisch zuteilen jm
  Tisch zuweisen jm
  ♦ **assign a table to s.o.** *AE*
  ♦ allocate a table to s.o. *BE*
Tischzuteilung, f
  Tischzuweisung, f
  Tischvergabe, f
  ♦ **table assignment** *AE*
  ♦ assignment of a table *AE*
  ♦ assigning a table *AE*
  ♦ table allocation *BE*
Tisch zuweisen einem Gast
  ♦ **allocate a table to a guest**
  ♦ assign a table to a guest *AE*
Tischzuweisung, f
  Tischzuteilung, f
  Tischvergabe, f
  ♦ **table allocation**
  ♦ allocation of a table
  ♦ allocating a table
  ♦ allocating tables
  ♦ table assignment *AE*
Titisee, m
  ♦ **Lake Titisee**
Tivoli, m
  ♦ **tivoli**
Tivolipark, m
  ♦ **tivoli gardens** *pl*
Toast, m (Speise)
  Toastscheibe, f
  ♦ **toast**
Toast, m (Trinkspruch)
  → Trinkspruch
Toast auf Bestellung
  ♦ **toast to order**
Toastbrot, n
  ♦ **toasted bread**
Toasten, n
  ♦ **toasting**
toasten etw
  rösten etw
  ♦ **toast s.th.**
Toaster, m
  (Gerät)
  ♦ **toaster**
Toastgabel, f
  Röstgabel, f
  ♦ **toasting fork** *AE*
  ♦ toasting-fork *BE*
Toast machen zum Frühstück
  ♦ **make some toast for breakfast**
Toastmeister, m
  Toastmaster, m
  ♦ **toastmaster** *AE*
  ♦ toast-master *BE*
Toastmeisterin, f
  ♦ **toastmistress** *AE*
  ♦ toast mistress *BE*
Toastsandwich, n
  ♦ **toasted sandwich**
Toastscheibe, f
  ♦ **slice of toast**
  ♦ piece of toast
  ♦ toast
Toastständer, m
  ♦ **toast rack** *AE*
  ♦ toast-rack *BE*
Toastteller, m
  ♦ **toast plate**
Tochter, f (Kellnerin) *SCHW*
  → Kellnerin

Tochtergesellschaft, f
  ♦ **subsidiary company**
  ♦ subsidiary
Tochterhotel, n
  ♦ **subsidiary hotel**
  ♦ daughter hotel
Toddy, m
  Grog, m
  ♦ **toddy**
todlangweilig, adj
  ♦ **deadly boring, adj**
Togo
  ♦ **Togo**
Togoer, m
  Togolese, m
  ♦ **Togolese**
Togoerin, f
  Togolesin, f
  ♦ **Togolese girl**
  ♦ Togolese woman
  ♦ Togolese
togoisch, adj
  ♦ **Togolese, adj**
Tohuwabohu, n
  ♦ **complete chaos**
Toi, toi, toi!
  ♦ **Touch wood!**
Toilette, f (öffentlich)
  ♦ **rest room** *AE euph*
  ♦ washroom *AE euph*
  ♦ toilet
  ♦ public conveniences *BE pl*
  ♦ cloakroom *BE euph*
Toilette, f (privat)
  ♦ **toilet**
  ♦ rest room *AE euph*
  ♦ lavatory
  ♦ WC
  ♦ bathroom *AE euph*
Toilette benutzen
  ♦ **use a toilet**
Toilette ist beheizt
  ♦ **toilet is heated**
Toilette ist verstopft
  ♦ **toilet is blocked**
Toilette mit Leitungswasser, f
  (Camping)
  ♦ **mains water toilet**
Toilettenanlagen, f pl
  ♦ **toilet facilities** *pl*
Toilettenartikel, m
  ♦ **toilet item**
Toilettenartikel, m pl
  ♦ **toiletry**
Toilettenbenutzung, f
  ♦ **use of the toilet**
  ♦ using the toilet
Toilettenbereich, m
  ♦ **toilet area**
  ♦ lavatory area
Toilettenblock m
  (z.B. Campingplatz)
  ♦ **toilet block**
  ♦ loo block *BE coll*
Toilettenbrille, f
  → Toiletttensitz
Toilettenbürste, f
  ♦ **toilet brush**
  ♦ lavatory brush

Toilettendeckel, m
  ♦ **toilet lid**
  ♦ lavatory lid
Toiletteneinrichtung, f
  ♦ **toilet facility**
  ♦ rest-room facility *AE euph*
Toiletteneinrichtung benutzen
  ♦ **use a toilet facility**
  ♦ use a rest-room facility *AE euph*
Toilettenfrau, f
  ♦ **toilet attendant**
  ♦ lavatory attendant
  ♦ rest room attendant *AE euph*
  ♦ cloakroom attendant *BE euph*
Toilettengarnitur, f
  ♦ **toilet set**
  ♦ toilet service
Toilettenhaus n
  ♦ **toilet house**
Toilettenkabine, f (generell)
  ♦ **toilet cabin**
Toilettenpapier, n
  ♦ **toilet paper** *AE*
  ♦ toilet-paper *BE*
  ♦ toilet tissue *AE*
  ♦ lavatory paper
Toilettenpapierhalter, m
  ♦ **toilet-paper holder**
Toilettenpersonal, n
  ♦ **toilet personnel**
  ♦ toilet staff
  ♦ washroom personnel *AE euph*
  ♦ rest-room personnel *AE euph*
  ♦ cloakroom staff *BE euph*
Toilettenraum, m
  ♦ **toilet room**
Toilettenschüssel f
  ♦ **toilet bowl**
Toilettenseife, f
  ♦ **toilet soap**
Toiletten sind die ganze Nacht beleuchtet
  ♦ **toilets are lit all night**
Toilettensitz, m
  Toilettenbrille, f
  ♦ **toilet seat**
  ♦ lavatory seat
Toilettenspülung, f
  ♦ **toilet flushing**
Toilettentisch, m
  Frisiertisch, m
  ♦ **vanity table** *AE*
  ♦ vanity *AE*
  ♦ dressing table *AE*
  ♦ dressing-table *BE*
  ♦ dresser *coll*
Toilettenwagen, m
  fahrbare Toilette, f
  ♦ **mobile toilet**
Toilettenwäsche, f
  ♦ **toilet linen**
Toilettenwäschewechsel, m
  Wechsel der Toilettenwäsche, m
  ♦ **change of toilet linen**
Toilettenwäsche wechseln
  ♦ **change the toilet linen**
Toilettenzelle, f
  (im Wohnwagen)
  Toilettenkabine, f
  ♦ **toilet compartment**
Toilettenzelt n
  ♦ **toilet tent**

770

Toilette spülen
♦ flush the toilet
Toilette wird von vier Personen benutzt
♦ toilet is shared by four persons
Tokaier, m
Tokajer, m
Tokaierwein, m
Tokajerwein, m
♦ Tokay
tolle Party, f
♦ rave-up sl
tolle Zeit, f coll
♦ smashing time coll
tolle Zeit haben coll
♦ have a smashing time coll
♦ have a whale of a time obs
Tollwut, f
♦ rabies
Tollwutimpfbescheinigung, f
♦ rabies inoculation certificate
Tollwutimpfung, f
♦ anti-rabies vaccination
♦ rabies inoculation
Tollwutimpfzeugnis, n
♦ certificate of anti-rabies vaccination
Tomate, f
Paradeiser, m ÖST
♦ tomato
Tomatenauflauf, m
Tomatensoufflé, n
♦ tomato souffle AE
♦ tomato soufflé BE
Tomatenbutter, f
♦ tomato butter
Tomatenchutney, n
♦ tomato chutney
Tomatencocktail, m
♦ tomato cocktail
Tomatencremesuppe, f
♦ tomato cream soup
Tomatendressing, n
♦ tomato dressing
Tomatenfondue, n
♦ tomato fondue
♦ tomato fondu AE
Tomatenhälfte, f
♦ tomato half
Tomatenketchup, n/m
♦ tomato ketchup
Tomatenpüree, n
Tomatenmark, n
♦ tomato puree AE
♦ tomato purée BE
Tomatenreis, m
♦ tomato rice
Tomatensaft m
♦ tomato juice
Tomatensalat, m
♦ tomato salad
Tomatenscheibe, f
♦ tomato slice
♦ slice of tomato
Tomatenschnitz, m
♦ tomato wedge
Tomatensoße, f
♦ tomato sauce
Tomatensuppe, f
♦ tomato soup
Tomatentoast, m
♦ tomato toast

Tombola, f
♦ raffle
♦ tombola BE
Tombola abhalten
♦ hold a raffle
Tombola durchführen
♦ run a raffle
Tombolaerlös, m
→ Erlös einer Tombola
Tombolagewinn, m
♦ raffle prize
Tombolalos, n
Los, n
♦ raffle ticket
Tombolalos kaufen
Los kaufen
♦ buy a raffle ticket
Tombolastand, m
♦ raffle stand
♦ raffle stall
♦ tombola stand
♦ tombola stall
Tombola veranstalten
♦ organise a raffle
♦ organize a raffle
Ton angeben (bei etw)
♦ set the tone (of s.th.)
Tonanlage, f
♦ sound system
Tonaufnahme, f
♦ sound recording
Tonband, n
♦ tape
Tonbandaufnahme, f
♦ tape recording AE
♦ tape-recording BE
Tonbandgerät, n
Tonbandmaschine, f
♦ tape recorder AE
♦ tape-recorder BE
Tonbandmaschine, f
→ Tonbandgerät
Tonbildschau, f
♦ tape/slide show
♦ Son et Lumière FR
♦ Sound and Light performance
Toneffekt, m
♦ sound effect
Tonfilm, m
♦ sound film
Tonga
♦ Tonga
Tongaer, m
♦ Tongan
Tongaerin, f
♦ Tongan girl
♦ Tongan woman
♦ Tongan
tongaisch, adj
♦ Tongan, adj
Tongefäß, n
♦ earthenware vessel
Tongeschirr, n
♦ earthenware
Tonic, n
♦ tonic
Tonicwasser, n
Tonic Water, n
♦ tonic water
Tonmeister, m
♦ sound mixer

Tonnengewölbe, n
♦ barrel vault
Tonnenkilometer, m
♦ ton-kilometre BE
Tonprojektion, f
♦ sound projection
Tonprojektor, m
♦ sound projector
Tontaube, f
♦ clay pigeon
Tontaubenschießen, n
♦ clay-pigeon shooting
Tontaubenschießplatz, m
♦ clay-pigeon shooting arena
Tontaubenschießstand, m
♦ clay-pigeon shooting range
Tontechnik, f (Aktivität)
♦ sound engineering
Tontechnik, f (Ausrüstung)
♦ sound equipment
Tontechniker, m
♦ sound engineer
Tontopf, m
♦ earthenware pot
Tonverstärkeranlage, f
♦ sound amplifier system
Tonvorrichtung, f
Tonausrüstung, f
♦ sound rig
Topf, m (generell)
♦ pot
Topf, m (Kochtopf)
♦ saucepan
Topf, m (Nachttopf) coll
♦ jerry coll
Töpfer, m
♦ potter
Töpferei, f
Töpferwerkstatt, f
♦ potter's shop
♦ pottery
Töpfereimuseum, n
♦ pottery museum
Töpferkurs, m
♦ pottery course
Töpferkurs machen
♦ do a pottery course
Töpferurlaub, m
Töpferferien, pl
♦ pottery vacation AE
♦ pottery holiday BE
Töpferwaren, f pl
♦ pottery
♦ earthenware
Topflappen, m
♦ oven cloth
Topfspüle, f
→ Topfspülraum
Topfspülen, n
♦ potwashing
Topfspüler, m
Plongeur, m FR
♦ potwasher
♦ plongeur FR
Topfspülraum, m
→ Plonge
Topgastronomie, f
→ Spitzengastronomie
Tophotel, n
→ Spitzenhotel

Topographie

Topographie, f
♦ topography
topographisch, adj
♦ topographical, adj
Topprogramm, n
→ Spitzenprogramm
Toprestaurant, n
→ Spitzenrestaurant
Topservice, m
→ Spitzenservice
Toque de cuisinier, f *FR*
Kochmütze, f
♦ toque de cuisinier *FR*
♦ chef's hat
Tor, n
♦ gate
Torf, m
♦ peat
Torffeuer, n
♦ peat fire
Torfmoorbad, n
(Aktivität)
♦ moor peat bath
Törggelekeller, m
→ Weinprobenkeller
törggelen
→ neuen Wein trinken
Törggelen, n *ÖST*
(Weinprobe mit Imbiß)
→ Weinprobe
Törggeletour, f *ÖST*
→ Weinprobentour
Törn, m
(Segelreise)
♦ turn
Tornisterrolle, f
(bei Soldaten, Wanderern etc)
Nachtpack m
♦ blanket roll *AE*
Törtchen, n
♦ tartlet
Torte, f (flach)
♦ tart
Torte, f (mit Sahne)
♦ gâteau *BE*
♦ gateau *AE*
Tortenheber, m
♦ cake server
Tortenplatte, f
♦ flat cake plate
♦ cake plate
Tortilla, f
♦ tortilla
Tortonibecher, m
(Eisbecher)
♦ Tortoni cup
Torturm, m
♦ gate tower
♦ gateway tower
Torweg, m
Tor, n
Zugang, m
Einfahrt, f
♦ gateway
Tor zur Welt, n
♦ gateway to the world
Toskana, die, f
♦ Tuscany
Toskaner, m
♦ Tuscan

Toskanerin, f
♦ Tuscan girl
♦ Tuscan woman
♦ Tuscan
toskanisch, adj
♦ Tuscan, adj
Totalauslastung, f
Gesamtauslastung, f
Gesamtbelegung, f
♦ total occupancy
total ausverkauft, adj
völlig ausverkauft, adj
♦ totally sold out, adj
total renoviert, adj
völlig renoviert, adj
♦ totally refurbished, adj
♦ totally renovated, adj
Totalrenovierung, f
vollständige Renovierung, f
♦ complete refurbishment
♦ complete renovation
♦ total refurbishment
♦ total renovation
Totalrenovierung erfordern
♦ require complete refurbishment
♦ require complete renovation
♦ require total refurbishment
♦ require total renovation
Totalverdunkelung, f
totale Verdunkelung, f
♦ dead black-out
♦ DBO
tote Jahreszeit, f
geschäftslose Zeit, f
♦ dead season
Tote Meer, das, n
♦ Dead Sea, the
Totenkopfbar, f
Seeräuberbar, f
Piratenbar, f
♦ Jolly Roger bar
Tour, f
→ Reise, Ausflug
Tour abschließen
→ Reise abschließen
Tour ausarbeiten
♦ work out a tour
Tour beginnt bei der Kathedrale
Rundgang beginnt am Dom
♦ tour starts at the cathedral
♦ tour begins at the cathedral
♦ tour commences at the cathedral *form*
Tour de France, f
♦ Tour de France, the
Tour d'horizon, f *FR*
♦ tour d'horizon *FR*
Tourenangebot, n
→ Reiseangebot
Tourengespann, n
→ Reisegespann
Tourenhotel, n
→ Reisehotel
Tourenkarte, f
♦ touring map
Tourenlänge, f
→ Ausflugsdauer
Tourenmöglichkeiten, f pl
→ Ausflugsmöglichkeiten
Tourenrad, n
Tourenfahrrad, n
♦ touring bicycle

♦ touring bike *coll*
♦ touring cycle
Tourenroute, f
Tourroute, f
Reiseroute, f
♦ tour route
♦ touring route
Tourenski, m
♦ touring ski
Tourenskifahren, n
♦ ski touring
Tourenvorschlag, m
→ Reisevorschlag, Ausflugsvorschlag
Tourenwagen, m
♦ touring car
Touring-Club, m
♦ touring club *AE*
♦ touring-club *BE*
Tourismus, m
Fremdenverkehr, m
Fremdenverkehrswesen, n
Touristik, f
♦ tourism
Tourismusabteilung, f (eines Unternehmens)
Fremdenverkehrsabteilung, f
♦ tourism division
♦ tourist division
Tourismusagentur, f
Fremdenverkehrsagentur, f
♦ tourism agency
♦ tourist agency
Tourismusamt, n
→ Verkehrsamt
Tourismusanbieter, m
touristischer Anbieter, m
Fremdenverkehrsanbieter, m
♦ tourism supplier
♦ tourist supplier
Tourismusangebot, n (Gegensatz zu Nachfrage)
touristisches Angebot, n
Fremdenverkehrsangebot, n
♦ tourism supply
♦ tourist supply
Tourismusangelegenheit, f
Fremdenverkehrsangelegenheit, f
♦ tourism matter
♦ tourist matter
♦ matter of tourism
Tourismus anheizen
Fremdenverkehr anheizen
♦ boost tourism
Tourismusankunft, f
♦ tourism arrival
Tourismusannehmlichkeit, f
touristische Annehmlichkeit, f
Fremdenverkehrsannehmlichkeit, f
♦ tourism amenity
♦ tourist amenity
Tourismus anregen
Tourismus stimulieren
Fremdenverkehr anregen
Fremdenverkehr stimulieren
♦ stimulate tourism
Tourismusanreiz, m
Fremdenverkehrsanreiz, m
♦ tourism incentive
Tourismusart, f
Tourismustyp, m
Fremdenverkehrsart, f
Fremdenverkehrstyp, m
♦ type of tourism

Tourismus auf dem Land, m
→ ländlicher Tourismus
Tourismusaufkommen, n
Tourismusvolumen, n
Fremdenverkehrsaufkommen, n
Fremdenverkehrsvolumen, n
♦ volume of tourism
♦ tourism volume
♦ tourist volume
Tourismus ausbauen
→ Tourismus entwickeln
Tourismusausbildung, f
→ Touristikausbildung
Tourismusausschuß, m
Fremdenverkehrsausschuß, m
♦ tourism committee
♦ tourist committee
♦ committee for tourism
Tourismusausstellung, f
Fremdenverkehrsausstellung, f
♦ tourism exhibition
♦ tourism exhibit AE
♦ tourism show
Tourismus ausweiten
Fremdenverkehr ausweiten
♦ expand tourism
Tourismusausweitung, f
Ausweitung des Tourismus, f
Fremdenverkehrsausweitung, f
Ausweitung des Fremdenverkehrs, f
♦ expansion of tourism
♦ tourism expansion
♦ tourist expansion
Tourismus behindern
Fremdenverkehr behindern
♦ impede tourism
♦ hinder tourism
Tourismusbehörde, f
Fremdenverkehrsbehörde, f
♦ tourism authority
♦ tourist authority
Tourismusbeirat, m
Fremdenverkehrsbeirat, m
♦ tourism advisory board
Tourismusberater, m
Fremdenverkehrsberater, m
♦ tourism consultant
♦ tourism adviser
Tourismusbereich, m (Sektor)
Tourismussektor, m
Fremdenverkehrsbereich, m
Fremdenverkehrssektor, m
♦ tourism sector
♦ tourist sector
Tourismusberuf, m
touristischer Beruf, m
Fremdenverkehrsberuf, m
♦ tourism profession
♦ tourist profession
tourismus beschäftigt 2 Millionen Menschen
Fremdenverkehr beschäftigt 2 Millionen Menschen
♦ tourism employs 2 million people
Tourismusbetrieb, m
touristischer Betrieb, m
Fremdenverkehrsbetrieb, m
♦ tourism establishment
♦ tourist establishment
♦ tourism operation
♦ tourist operation
tourismusbezogen, adj
fremdenverkehrsbezogen, adj

♦ tourism-related, adj
♦ tourist-related, adj
♦ related to tourism, adj
tourismusbezogene Industrie, f
tourismusbezogene Branche, f
fremdenverkehrsbezogene Industrie, f
fremdenverkehrsbezogene Branche, f
♦ tourism-related industry
tourismusbezogene Infrastruktur, f
fremdenverkehrsbezogene Infrastruktur, f
♦ tourism-related infrastructure
Tourismusbilanz, f
Fremdenverkehrsbilanz, f
♦ tourism balance
♦ tourist balance
Tourismusboom, m
Fremdenverkehrsboom, m
♦ tourism boom
♦ tourist boom
Tourismus boomt
Fremdenverkehr boomt
♦ tourism is booming
♦ tourism booms
Tourismusbörse, f
♦ tourism exchange
♦ tourist exchange
Tourismusboykott, m
Fremdenverkehrsboykott, m
♦ tourism boycott
Tourismus boykottieren
Fremdenverkehr boykottieren
♦ boycott tourism
Tourismusbranche, f
→ Tourismusindustrie, Tourismusgeschäft
Tourismus bringt wirtschaftliche Vorteile
Fremdenverkehr bringt wirtschaftliche Vorteile
♦ tourism brings economic benefits
Tourismusbüro, n
Fremdenverkehrsbüro, n
♦ tourism office
♦ tourist office
♦ tourist bureau AE
Tourismusdollar, m
Fremdenverkehrsdollar, m
♦ tourism dollar
♦ tourist dollar
Tourismuseinfluß (auf etw), m
Tourismusauswirkung (auf etw), f
Fremdenverkehrseinfluß (auf etw), m
Fremdenverkehrsauswirkung (auf etw), f
♦ tourism impact (on s.th.)
♦ impact of tourism (on s.th.)
Tourismuseinnahme, f
Fremdenverkehrseinnahme, f
♦ tourism revenue
♦ tourist revenue
♦ tourism income
♦ tourist income
♦ revenue from tourism
Tourismuseinnahmen, f pl
Fremdenverkehrseinnahmen, f pl
♦ tourism receipts pl
♦ tourism revenues pl
♦ tourism income
♦ tourism takings pl
♦ earnings from tourism pl
Tourismuseinrichtung, f
touristische Einrichtung, f
Fremdenverkehrseinrichtung, f
♦ tourism facility
♦ tourist facility

Tourismus entwickeln
Fremdenverkehr entwickeln
Tourismus ausbauen
Fremdenverkehr ausbauen
♦ develop tourism
Tourismusentwicklung, f (generell)
Ausbau des Tourismus, m
Fremdenverkehrsentwicklung, f
Ausbau des Fremdenverkehrs, m
♦ development of tourism
♦ tourism development
Tourismusentwicklung, f (historisch)
Fremdenverkehrsentwicklung, f
♦ tourism evolution
♦ evolution of tourism
Tourismus erzeugen
Fremdenverkehr erzeugen
♦ generate tourism
Tourismusexperte, m
Fremdenverkehrsexperte, m
♦ tourism expert
♦ tourist expert
♦ expert in tourism
♦ specialist in tourism
Tourismusfachkenntnisse, f pl
Tourismuskenntnisse, f pl
Fremdenverkehrsfachkenntnisse, f pl
Fremdenverkehrskenntnisse, f pl
♦ tourism expertise sg
Tourismusfirma, f
Fremdenverkehrsfirma, f
♦ tourism firm
♦ tourist firm
♦ tourism company
♦ tourist company
Tourismusflaute, f
Fremdenverkehrsflaute, f
♦ tourism trough
♦ tourist trough
♦ lull in tourism
Tourismus floriert
Tourismus blüht
Fremdenverkehr floriert
Fremdenverkehr blüht
♦ tourism is thriving
♦ tourism thrives
Tourismus fördern
Fremdenverkehr fördern
♦ promote tourism
Tourismusförderung, f
Fremdenverkehrsförderung, f
♦ tourism promotion
♦ tourist promotion
♦ promotion of tourism
♦ promotion of the tourism industry
♦ promotion of the tourism trade
Tourismusform, f
Fremdenverkehrsform, f
♦ form of tourism
♦ tourism form
Tourismusforschung, f
Fremdenverkehrsforschung, f
♦ tourism research
♦ tourist research
♦ research in the field of tourism
Tourismusforum, n
Fremdenverkehrsforum, n
♦ tourism forum
Tourismusführer, m
(Information)
Fremdenverkehrsführer, m

Tourismusfunktionär 774

- ◆ tourism guide
- ◆ tourist guide

Tourismusfunktionär, m
Fremdenverkehrsfunktionär, m
- ◆ tourism official
- ◆ tourist official
- ◆ tourism officer
- ◆ tourist officer
- ◆ tourism functionary

Tourismusgebiet, n (groß)
Tourismusregion, f
Fremdenverkehrsgebiet, n
Fremdenverkehrsregion, f
- ◆ tourism region
- ◆ tourist region

Tourismusgebiet, n (klein)
Fremdenverkehrsgebiet, n
- ◆ tourism area
- ◆ tourist area

Tourismusgeschäft, n
Fremdenverkehrsgeschäft, n
Tourismusbranche, f
Fremdenverkehrsbranche, f
- ◆ tourism business
- ◆ tourist business

Tourismusgesetzgebung, f
Fremdenverkehrsgesetzgebung, f
- ◆ tourism legislation
- ◆ tourist legislation
- ◆ legislation regarding tourism

Tourismusgewerbe, n
Fremdenverkehrsgewerbe, f
Tourismusbranche, f
Fremdenverkehrsbranche, f
- ◆ tourism trade
- ◆ tourist trade

Tourismusgremium, n
Fremdenverkehrsgremium, n
- ◆ tourism body
- ◆ tourist body

Tourismusimage, n
touristische Image, n
Fremdenverkehrsimage, n
- ◆ tourism image
- ◆ tourist image

Tourismus im großen Umfang, m
Fremdenverkehr im großen Umfang, m
- ◆ large-scale tourism

Tourismus im kleinen Umfang, m
Fremdenverkehr im kleinen Umfang, m
- ◆ small-scale tourism

Tourismusindustrie, f
Fremdenverkehrsindustrie, f
Tourismusbranche, f
Fremdenverkehrsbranche, f
- ◆ tourism industry
- ◆ tourist industry

Tourismusindustrie ankurbeln
Fremdenverkehrsindustrie ankurbeln
- ◆ boost the tourism industry

Tourismusindustrie ist gut entwickelt
Fremdenverkehrsindustrie ist gut entwickelt
- ◆ tourism industry is well developed
- ◆ tourist industry is well developed

Tourismusinfrastruktur, f
Fremdenverkehrsinfrastruktur, f
- ◆ tourism infrastructure
- ◆ tourist infrastructure

Tourismus in Kanada, m
Kanadatourismus, m

Fremdenverkehr in Kanada, m
- ◆ tourism in Canada

Tourismusinstitut, n
Fremdenverkehrsinstitut, n
Touristikinstitut, n
- ◆ tourism institute
- ◆ tourist institute

Tourismusinstitution, f
Fremdenverkehrsinstitution, f
- ◆ tourism institution
- ◆ tourist institution

Tourismusintensität, f
Fremdenverkehrsintensität, f
- ◆ tourism intensity

Tourismus ist im Aufwind
Fremdenverkehr ist im Aufwind
Tourismus steigt stark an
Fremdenverkehr steigt stark an
- ◆ tourism is surging

Tourismusjahr, n
Fremdenverkehrsjahr, n
- ◆ tourism year
- ◆ tourist year

Tourismuskampagne, f
Fremdenverkehrskampagne, f
- ◆ tourism campaign

Tourismuskampagne durchführen
Fremdenverkehrskampagne durchführen
- ◆ undertake a tourism campaign

Tourismuskapazität, f
Fremdenverkehrskapazität, f
- ◆ tourism capacity
- ◆ tourist capacity

Tourismuskonferenz, f
Fremdenverkehrskonferenz, f
- ◆ tourism conference

Tourismuskongreß, m
Fremdenverkehrskongreß, m
- ◆ tourism congress
- ◆ tourism convention

Tourismuskonsument, m
Fremdenverkehrskonsument, m
- ◆ tourism consumer

Tourismuskonzept, n
Fremdenverkehrskonzept, n
- ◆ tourism concept
- ◆ tourism plan

Tourismuskonzern, m
Fremdenverkehrskonzern, m
- ◆ tourism group
- ◆ tourism concern

Tourismuskooperation, f
Fremdenverkehrskooperation, f
- ◆ cooperation in tourism
- ◆ tourism cooperation

Tourismuskuchen, m *figur*
Fremdenverkehrskuchen, m *figur*
- ◆ tourism cake *figur*

Tourismusland, n
Fremdenverkehrsland, n
- ◆ tourism country
- ◆ tourist country

Tourismusliteratur, f
touristische Literatur, f
Fremdenverkehrsliteratur, f
- ◆ tourism literature
- ◆ tourist literature

Tourismusmanagement, n
Fremdenverkehrsmanagement, n
Fremdenverkehrsleitung, f

- ◆ tourism management
- ◆ tourist management

Tourismusmanager, m
Fremdenverkehrsmanager, m
- ◆ tourism manager
- ◆ tourist manager
- ◆ tourism executive
- ◆ tourist executive

Tourismusmark, f
Fremdenverkehrsmark, f
- ◆ tourism mark
- ◆ tourist mark

Tourismusmarketing, n
Fremdenverkehrsmarketing, n
- ◆ tourism marketing
- ◆ tourist marketing
- ◆ marketing of tourism

Tourismusmarketingberater, m
Fremdenverkehrsmarketingberater, m
- ◆ tourism marketing consultant

Tourismusmarkt, m
Fremdenverkehrsmarkt, m
- ◆ tourism market
- ◆ tourist market

Tourismusmesse, f
Touristikmesse, f
Fremdenverkehrsmesse, f
- ◆ tourism fair
- ◆ tourist fair

Tourismus minderer Qualität, m
Fremdenverkehr minderer Qualität, m
- ◆ low-quality tourism

Tourismusminister, m
- ◆ Minister of Tourism
- ◆ tourism minister

Tourismusministerium, n
- ◆ tourism ministry
- ◆ tourist ministry
- ◆ Ministry of Tourism

Tourismus mit Einsicht, m
- ◆ tourism with insight

Tourismusnachfrage, f
touristische Nachfrage, f
Fremdenverkehrsnachfrage, f
- ◆ tourism demand
- ◆ tourist demand
- ◆ demand for tourism

Tourismus nach Kanada, m
Kanadatourismus, m
Fremdenverkehr nach Kanada, m
- ◆ tourism to Canada

Tourismusorganisation, f
touristische Organisation, f
Fremdenverkehrsorganisation, f
- ◆ tourism organisation
- ◆ tourism organization
- ◆ tourist organisation
- ◆ tourist organization
- ◆ organisation of tourism

Tourismus organisieren
Fremdenverkehr organisieren
- ◆ organise tourism
- ◆ organize tourism

Tourismusort, m
Fremdenverkehrsort, m
- ◆ tourism resort
- ◆ tourist resort

Tourismusperspektive, f
Fremdenverkehrsperspektive, f
- ◆ tourism perspective
- ◆ tourist perspective

Tourismusplakat, n
  Fremdenverkehrsplakat, n
  ◆ tourism poster
  ◆ tourist poster
Tourismusplaner, m
  Fremdenverkehrsplaner, m
  ◆ tourism planner
Tourismusplanung, f
  Fremdenverkehrsplanung, f
  ◆ tourism planning
  ◆ tourist planning
  ◆ planning (of) tourism
Tourismuspolitik, f
  Fremdenverkehrspolitik, f
  ◆ tourism policy
  ◆ tourist policy
Tourismuspotential, n
  Fremdenverkehrspotential, n
  ◆ tourism potential
  ◆ tourist potential
Tourismuspraktiker, m
  Fremdenverkehrspraktiker, m
  ◆ tourism practitioner
Tourismuspraxis, f
  Fremdenverkehrspraxis, f
  ◆ tourism practice
Tourismuspreis, m (Auszeichnung)
  Fremdenverkehrspreis, m
  ◆ tourism award
  ◆ tourism prize
Tourismuspreis, m (Kosten)
  Fremdenverkehrspreis, m
  ◆ tourism price
  ◆ tourist price
  ◆ tourism rate
  ◆ tourist rate
Tourismusprodukt, n
  touristisches Produkt, n
  Fremdenverkehrsprodukt, n
  ◆ tourism product
  ◆ tourist product
Tourismusprodukt vermarkten
  touristisches Produkt vermarkten
  Fremdenverkehrsprodukt vermarkten
  ◆ market a tourism product
  ◆ market a tourist product
Tourismusprogramm, n
  Fremdenverkehrsprogramm, n
  ◆ tourism program *AE*
  ◆ tourist program *AE*
  ◆ tourism programme *BE*
  ◆ tourist programme *BE*
Tourismusprojekt, n
  Fremdenverkehrsprojekt, n
  ◆ tourism project
  ◆ tourist project
Tourismusprospekt, m
  Fremdenverkehrsprospekt, m
  ◆ tourism brochure
  ◆ tourist brochure
Tourismusquelle, f
  Quelle des Tourismus, f
  ◆ source of tourism
Tourismusrahmen, m
  Fremdenverkehrsrahmen, m
  ◆ tourism framework
Tourismusrat, m (Gremium)
  Fremdenverkehrsrat, m
  ◆ tourism council
  ◆ tourist council

Tourismusratgeber, m
  Tourismusberater, m
  Fremdenverkehrsratgeber, m
  Fremdenverkehrsberater, m
  ◆ tourist counsellor
  ◆ tourist counselor *BE*
Tourismus reduzieren
  Fremdenverkehr vermindern
  ◆ reduce tourism
Tourismusreferent, m
  (z.B. in einer Gemeinde)
  Fremdenverkehrsreferent, m
  ◆ tourism officer
  ◆ tourist officer
  ◆ tourism official
  ◆ tourist official
Tourismusregion, f
  → Tourismusgebiet
Tourismusreise, f
  → Touristenreise
tourismusrelevant, adj
  fremdenverkehrsrelevant, adj
  ◆ tourism-relevant, adj
Tourismusressource, f
  Fremdenverkehrsressource, f
  ◆ tourism resource
Tourismus revolutionieren
  Fremdenverkehr revolutionieren
  ◆ revolutionise tourism
  ◆ revolutionize tourism
Tourismusrückgang, m
  Fremdenverkehrsrückgang, m
  ◆ decrease in tourism
  ◆ decline in tourism
  ◆ drop in tourism
Tourismussachbearbeiter, m
  Fremdenverkehrssachbearbeiter, m
  ◆ tourism clerk
  ◆ tourist clerk
Tourismussaison verlängern
  Fremdenverkehrssaison verlängern
  ◆ lengthen the tourist season
  ◆ extend the tourist season
Tourismus schädigen
  Fremdenverkehr schädigen
  ◆ hurt tourism
  ◆ damage tourism
Tourismussektor, m
  → Tourismusbereich
Tourismusseminar, n
  Touristikseminar, n
  Fremdenverkehrsseminar, n
  ◆ tourism seminar
  ◆ seminar on tourism
Tourismus setzt DM 1234 Millionen um
  Fremdenverkehr setzt DM 1234 Millionen um
  ◆ tourism turns over DM 1234m
Tourismusspezialist, m
  Fremdenverkehrsspezialist, m
  ◆ tourism specialist
Tourismussphäre, f
  Fremdenverkehrssphäre, f
  ◆ tourism sphere
Tourismusstaatssekretär, m
  ◆ tourism state secretary
Tourismus stagniert
  Fremdenverkehr stagniert
  ◆ tourism is stagnating
  ◆ tourism stagnates
Tourismusstatistik, f
  Fremdenverkehrsstatistik, f

  ◆ tourism statistics *pl*
  ◆ tourist statistics *pl*
Tourismus steckt noch in den Kinderschuhen
  Fremdenverkehr steckt noch in den Kinderschuhen
  ◆ tourism still is in its infancy
Tourismus steigern
  Fremdenverkehr steigern
  ◆ increase tourism
Tourismusstrategie, f
  Fremdenverkehrstrategie, f
  ◆ tourism strategy
  ◆ tourist strategy
Tourismusstrom, m
  Fremdenverkehrsstrom, m
  ◆ tourism flow
  ◆ flow of tourism
Tourismusstruktur, f
  Fremdenverkehrsstruktur, f
  ◆ tourism structure
  ◆ tourist structure
Tourismussystem, n
  Fremdenverkehrssystem, n
  ◆ tourism system
Tourismusszene, f
  Fremdenverkehrsszene, f
  ◆ tourism scene
  ◆ tourist scene
Tourismustheorie, f
  Fremdenverkehrstheorie, f
  ◆ tourism theory
Tourismustrend, m
  Fremdenverkehrstrend, m
  ◆ tourism trend
  ◆ tourist trend
  ◆ trend in tourism
Tourismusüberblick, m
  Tourismusumfrage, f
  Fremdenverkehrsüberblick, m
  Fremdenverkehrsumfrage, f
  ◆ tourism survey
  ◆ tourist survey
Tourismusumwelt, f
  Fremdenverkehrsumwelt, f
  ◆ tourism environment
Tourismus- und Freizeitindustrie, f
  Fremdenverkehrs- und Freizeitindustrie, f
  ◆ tourism and leisure industry
  ◆ tourist and leisure industry
Tourismusunternehmen, n
  Fremdenverkehrsunternehmen, n
  ◆ tourism enterprise
  ◆ tourist enterprise
Tourismusunternehmer, m
  Fremdenverkehrsunternehmer, m
  ◆ tourism entrepreneur
Tourismusverband, m
  Fremdenverkehrsverband, m
  ◆ tourism association
  ◆ tourist association
Tourismusverbindung, f
  Fremdenverkehrsverbindung, f
  ◆ tourist link
  ◆ tourist connection
Tourismusverkäufer, m
  Fremdenverkehrsverkäufer, m
  ◆ tourism salesman
  ◆ tourism seller
Tourismusverkehr, m
  Reiseverkehr, m
  ◆ tourism traffic
  ◆ tourist traffic

Tourismus vermarkten 776

Tourismus vermarkten
  Fremdenverkehr vermarkten
  ♦ market tourism
Tourismuswachstum, n
  Fremdenverkehrswachstum, n
  ♦ tourism growth
  ♦ tourist growth
  ♦ growth of tourism
  ♦ increase in tourism
Tourismuswerbung, f
  Fremdenverkehrswerbung, f
  ♦ tourism advertising
  ♦ tourist advertising
Tourismuswesen, n
  → Tourismus
Tourismuswirtschaft, f
  Fremdenverkehrswirtschaft, f
  ♦ tourism economy
  ♦ tourist economy
  ♦ economics of tourism
Tourismuswoche, f
  Fremdenverkehrswoche, f
  ♦ tourism week
Tourismuszeitschrift, f
  Fremdenverkehrszeitschrift, f
  ♦ tourism journal
  ♦ tourist journal
  ♦ journal of tourism
Tourismuszentrum, n
  touristisches Zentrum, n
  Fremdenverkehrszentrum, n
  ♦ tourism center *AE*
  ♦ tourist center *AE*
  ♦ tourism centre *BE*
  ♦ tourist centre *BE*
Tourismusziel, n
  Fremdenverkehrsziel, n
  ♦ tourism objective
  ♦ tourist objective
Tourismuszirkus, m
  → Tourismusrummel
Tourismuszuwachs, m
  Tourismusanstieg, m
  Fremdenverkehrszuwachs, m
  Fremdenverkehrsanstieg, m
  ♦ increase in tourism
  ♦ tourism increase
Tourist, m
  ♦ tourist
Tourist aus Spanien, m
  ♦ tourist from Spain
Touristenabgabe, f
  Touristensteuer, f
  ♦ tourist tax
  ♦ visitors' tax
Touristenabreise, f
  ♦ tourist departure
Touristenandrang, m
  Touristenansturm m
  ♦ influx of tourists
  ♦ inrush of tourists
  ♦ crowd of tourists
  ♦ throng of tourists
Touristenankunft, f
  Fremdenankunft, f
  ♦ tourist arrival
Touristenankunftsstatistik, f
  ♦ tourist arrival statistics *pl*
Touristenanlage, f
  Touristenkomplex, m
  Fremdenverkehrsanlage, f

Fremdenverkehrskomplex, m
  ♦ tourist complex
Touristenappartement, n
  ♦ tourist apartment
  ♦ economy apartment
Touristenattraktion, f
  touristische Attraktion, f
  Fremdenverkehrsattraktion, f
  ♦ tourist attraction
Touristenattraktion vermarkten
  ♦ market a tourist attraction
Touristenaufnahmegebiet, n
  ♦ tourist receiving area
Touristenausgaben, f pl
  Ausgaben durch Touristen, f pl
  ♦ tourist spending
  ♦ tourism spending
  ♦ tourist expenditures *pl*
  ♦ expenditure by tourists
Touristen ausrauben
  Touristen berauben
  ♦ rob a tourist
  ♦ rob tourists
Touristenausweis, m
  Touristenkarte, f
  ♦ tourist card
Touristenauto, n
  ♦ tourist car
  ♦ tourist's car
Touristenbaisse, f
  → Tourismusflaute
Touristenbungalow m
  ♦ tourist bungalow
Touristenbus, m
  ♦ tourist bus
  ♦ tourist coach *BE*
Touristendollar, m
  ♦ tourist dollar
Touristen durch die Stadt führen
  Touristen die Stadt zeigen
  ♦ show tourists round the town
  ♦ show tourists round the city
Touristeneinnahme steigern
  ♦ increase tourist revenue
  ♦ increase tourism revenue
Touristen einsammeln *coll*
  ♦ gather tourists together
Touristenessen, n
  ♦ tourist meal
  ♦ economy meal
Touristenfahrkarte, f
  ♦ tourist ticket
Touristenfahrpreis, m
  ♦ tourist fare
Touristenfahrt, f
  ♦ tourist trip
Touristenfalle, f
  → Touristennepp
Touristenflug, m
  ♦ tourist flight
  ♦ economy flight
Touristenflugpreis, m
  ♦ tourist air fare
Touristenflugzeug, n
  ♦ tourist plane
  ♦ tourist aircraft
  ♦ tourist airplane *AE*
  ♦ tourist aeroplane *BE*
Touristenflut, f
  Touristenschwemme, f

♦ flood of tourists
♦ floodtide of tourists
Touristenführer, m
  → Fremdenführer
Touristengasthaus, n
  ♦ tourist bar *AE*
  ♦ tourist pub *BE*
Touristengebiet, n
  → Fremdenverkehrsgebiet
Touristengeschäft, n (Fremdenverkehr)
  → Fremdenverkehrsgeschäft
Touristengeschäft, n (Laden)
  Touristenladen, m
  ♦ tourist shop *BE*
  ♦ tourist store *AE*
Touristengetto, n
  Touristenghetto, n
  ♦ tourist ghetto
Touristengruppe f
  ♦ tourist group
  ♦ group of tourists
Touristenhaus, n
  Touristenheim, n
  ♦ tourist house
  ♦ tourist hostel
Touristenheim, n
  Fremdenheim, n
  ♦ tourist hostel
Touristenherberge, f
  ♦ tourist hostel
  ♦ tourist accommodation
Touristenhochburg, f *humor*
  Fremdenverkehrszentrum, n
  ♦ tourist center *AE*
  ♦ tourist centre *BE*
Touristenhorde, f
  ♦ tourist horde
  ♦ horde of tourists
Touristenhotel, n
  ♦ tourist hotel
  ♦ economy hotel
  ♦ hotel for tourists
Touristeninformation, f
  ♦ tourist information
Touristeninformationszentrale, f
  ♦ tourist information center *AE*
  ♦ tourist information centre *BE*
  ♦ TIC
Touristeninformationszentrale aufsuchen
  ♦ consult a tourist information center *AE*
  ♦ consult a tourist information centre *BE*
  ♦ consult a TIC
Touristeninsel, f
  ♦ tourist island
Touristeninvasion, f
  ♦ tourist invasion
  ♦ invasion of tourists
Touristenkabine, f
  ♦ tourist cabin
  ♦ economy cabin
  ♦ deck cabin
Touristenkarte, f (Eintritt)
  ♦ tourist ticket
Touristenkarte, f (Landkarte)
  ♦ tourist map
Touristenkategorie, f
  ♦ tourist category
Touristenklasse, f
  ♦ tourist class
  ♦ economy class

Touristklassehotel, n
  Hotel der Touristklasse, n
  ♦ **tourist-class hotel**
  ♦ economy-class hotel
Touristenklassetarif, m
  ♦ **tourist-class tariff**
  ♦ tourist-class rates *pl*
  ♦ tourist-class rate
  ♦ tourist-class terms *pl*
Touristen kommen in Scharen hierher
  ♦ **tourists flock here**
Touristenkundschaft, f
  touristische Kundschaft, f
  ♦ **tourist clientele**
Touristenkurs, m
  (Geldwechsel)
  Touristenwechselkurs m
  ♦ **tourist rate**
  ♦ tourist exchange rate
Touristenladen m
  Touristengeschäft n
  ♦ **tourist store** *AE*
  ♦ tourist shop *BE*
Touristenlodge, f
  ♦ **tourist lodge**
Touristenmahlzeit, f
  Touristenessen, n
  ♦ **economy meal**
  ♦ tourist meal
Touristenmark, f
  ♦ **tourist mark**
Touristenmekka, n
  Mekka für Touristen, n
  ♦ **tourist mecca**
  ♦ mecca for tourists
Touristenmenü, n
  ♦ **economy menu**
  ♦ tourist menu
Touristenmetropole, f
  ♦ **tourist metropolis**
Touristennepp, m
  Touristennepplokal, n
  Touristenfalle, f
  ♦ **tourist trap**
touristenorientiert, adj
  fremdenverkehrsorientiert, adj
  ♦ **tourist-oriented, adj** *AE*
  ♦ tourist-orientated, adj *BE*
Touristenort, m
  Fremdenverkehrsort, m
  ♦ **tourist place**
  ♦ tourist town
  ♦ tourist spot *coll*
  ♦ tourist resort
Touristenparadies, n
  Fremdenverkehrsparadies, n
  ♦ **tourist paradise**
  ♦ tourist's paradise
  ♦ tourists' paradise
Touristenpark, m
  ♦ **tourist park**
Touristenpfad, m *humor*
  ♦ **tourist trail**
  ♦ tourist track
  ♦ beaten track of tourism
Touristenplatz, m (Campingstellplatz)
  → Touristenstellplatz
Touristenprogramm, n
  touristisches Programm, n
  Programm für Touristen, n
  ♦ **program for tourists** *AE*

  ♦ programme for tourists *BE*
  ♦ tourist program *AE*
  ♦ tourist programme *BE*
Touristenreise, f
  touristische Reise, f
  ♦ **tourist journey**
  ♦ tourist trip
Touristenreise machen
  ♦ **make a tourist trip**
Touristenrekord, m
  touristischer Rekord, m
  Fremdenverkehrsrekord, m
  ♦ **tourist record**
  ♦ tourism record
Touristenrekord melden
  ♦ **report a tourist record**
Touristenrestaurant, n
  ♦ **tourist restaurant**
Touristenrummel, m
  Touristentrubel, m
  ♦ **tourist bustle**
Touristenrundgang, m
  ♦ **tourist circuit**
Touristenschwemme, f
  Touristenflut, f
  ♦ **floodtide of tourists**
  ♦ flood of tourists
Touristensiedlung, f
  ♦ **tourist development**
Touristensilo, m/n *derog*
  ♦ **skyscraper tourist hotel**
  ♦ tourist tower block
Touristensitzplatz, m
  Touristenplatz, m
  ♦ **tourist seat**
  ♦ economy seat
Touristenstadt, f (Großstadt)
  ♦ **tourist city**
Touristenstadt, f (kleine Stadt)
  ♦ **tourist town**
Touristenstellplatz, m
  (Camping)
  Touristenplatz, m
  ♦ **tourist pitch**
Touristensteuer, f
  → Touristenabgabe
Touristenstrand m
  ♦ **tourist beach**
Touristenstrecke, f
  Touristenroute, f
  ♦ **tourist route**
Touristenstrom, m
  ♦ **tourist flow**
  ♦ flow of tourists
  ♦ stream of tourists
Touristenstrom ausgleichen
  Touristenstrom gleich verteilen
  ♦ **even out tourist flows**
Touristentauchboot, n
  ♦ **tourist submarine**
Touristenteller, m (Speisen)
  Touristenessen, n
  ♦ **tourist menu**
  ♦ tourist dish
  ♦ menu touristique *FR*
Touristentod, m
  ♦ **tourist death**
  ♦ death of a tourist
Touristentum, n
  ♦ **touristhood**

Touristentyp, m
  ♦ **type of tourist**
  ♦ tourist type
Touristentypologie, f
  ♦ **typology of tourists**
touristenüberlaufen, adj *derog*
  ♦ **touristy, adj** *derog*
  ♦ overrun with tourists, adj
touristenüberlaufene Stadt, f *derog*
  ♦ **touristy town** *derog*
Touristenübernachtung, f (Statistik)
  → Fremdenübernachtung
Touristenunfall, m
  ♦ **tourist accident**
Touristenunterkunft, f
  Fremdenunterkunft, f
  ♦ **tourist accommodation**
  ♦ accommodation for tourists
Touristenveranstaltung, f
  touristische Veranstaltung, f
  ♦ **tourist event**
  ♦ tourist function
Touristenverhalten, n
  ♦ **tourist behavior** *AE*
  ♦ tourist behaviour *BE*
Touristenverkehr, m
  → Reiseverkehr
Touristenvermittlung, f
  Touristenagentur, f
  Fremdenverkehrsagentur, f
  ♦ **tourist agency**
  ♦ tourism agency
Touristen verscheuchen
  ♦ **scare off tourists**
Touristenvisum, n
  ♦ **tourist visa**
Touristenwechselkurs, m
  (Geldwechsel)
  Touristenkurs m
  ♦ **tourist exchange rate**
  ♦ tourist rate
Touristenweg, m
  übliche Touristenstrecke, f
  ♦ **beaten track of tourism**
  ♦ beaten track
Touristenwelle, f
  Tourismuswelle, f
  Fremdenverkehrswelle, f
  ♦ **tourist wave**
Touristenwohnung, f
  Fremdenwohnung, f
  ♦ **tourist flat** *BE*
  ♦ tourist apartment *AE*
Touristenzahl, f
  Zahl der Touristen, f
  ♦ **number of tourists**
Touristenziel, n
  touristischer Zielort, m
  ♦ **tourist destination**
  ♦ tourism destination
Touristenzielgebiet, n
  touristisches Zielgebiet, n
  ♦ **tourist destination area**
Touristenzimmer, n
  ♦ **tourist room**
  ♦ economy room
Touristenzug, m
  ♦ **tourist train**
Touristenzuwachs, m
  → Zunahme der Touristen

Touristik

Touristik, f
→ Tourismus
Touristikamt, n
→ Fremdenverkehrsamt
Touristikausbilder, m (akademisch)
Tourismusausbilder, m
Touristikdozent, m
♦ tourism educator
Touristikausbilder, m (nicht akademisch)
Tourismusausbilder, m
♦ tourism trainer
Touristikausbildung, f (akademisch)
Tourismusausbildung, f
♦ tourism education
Touristikausbildung, f (nicht akademisch)
Tourismusausbildung, f
♦ tourism training
Touristikausbildungsprogramm, n (akademisch)
Tourismusausbildungsprogramm, n
♦ tourism education program AE
♦ tourism education programme BE
Touristikausbildungsprogramm, n (nicht akademisch)
Tourismusausbildungsprogramm, n
♦ tourism training program AE
♦ tourism training programme BE
Touristikberater, m
→ Tourismusberater
Touristikbereich, m (einer Firma)
→ Tourismusbereich
Touristikbetriebswirtschaft, f
♦ business administration in tourism
Touristiker, m
♦ tourism professional
♦ tourism expert
Touristikfachwirt, m
♦ trained tourist expert
Touristikkurs, m
Touristiklehrgang, m
♦ tourism course
♦ course in tourism
Touristikkurs anbieten
♦ offer a tourism course
Touristikkurs einführen
♦ establish a tourism course
Touristikschule, f
♦ tourism school
Touristikstudiengang, m
Touristikkurs, m
♦ tourism program AE
♦ tourism programme BE
Touristikunternehmen, n
→ Tourismusunternehmen
Touristin, f
♦ female tourist
♦ woman tourist
♦ lady tourist
touristisch, adj
♦ tourist, adj
♦ touristic, adj AE
♦ touristical, adj AE rare
touristisch, adv
♦ touristically, adv
touristische Aktivität, f
♦ tourist activity
touristische Attraktivität, f
♦ tourist attractiveness
♦ tourist appeal
touristische Dienstleistung, f
touristische Leistung, f
♦ tourist service

touristische Einrichtung, f
→ Tourismuseinrichtung
touristische Erfahrung, f
♦ tourist experience
touristische Infrastruktur, f
♦ tourist infrastructure
touristische Nutzung, f
♦ tourist use
touristischer Anbieter, m
♦ tourist provider
♦ tourist supplier
touristischer Auftraggeber, m
♦ tourist principal
♦ tourism principal
touristischer Besucher, m
♦ tourist visitor
touristischer Markt, m
Touristenmarkt, m
Fremdenverkehrsmarkt, m
♦ tourist market
touristischer Reisender, m
♦ tourist traveller
♦ tourist traveler AE
touristisches Angebot, n (Offerte)
Tourismusangebot, n
♦ tourist offer
♦ tourism offer
touristische Sehenswürdigkeit, f
♦ tourist sight
touristisches Kleinod, n
♦ tourist jewel
touristische Sogwirkung, f
♦ tourist pull
touristisches Produkt, n
→ Fremdenverkehrsprodukt
touristisches Quell-Land, n
♦ tourist source country
Tournant, m FR
Fliegender, m sl
♦ tournant FR
♦ relief cook
Tournee, f
Gastspielreise, f
♦ tour
Tournee abbrechen
♦ cut short a tour
Tournee absolvieren
♦ do a tour
Tourneebuchhalter, m
Reisebuchhalter, m
♦ tour accountant
Tourneediskothek, f
♦ touring discotheque
♦ touring disco
Tournee durch das ganze Land, f
♦ nationwide tour
Tournee durch Spanien, f
Spanientournee, f
♦ tour of Spain
♦ tour through Spain
Tourneegebiet, n
♦ touring region
Tournee machen durch etw
Gastspielreise machen durch etw
♦ tour s.th.
Tourneerunde, f
♦ touring circuit
Tourpreis, m
→ Reisepreis
Tour unternehmen
♦ undertake a tour

Tourziel, n
→ Reiseziel
Tour zu Fuß, f
♦ tour on foot
Tower, m
(in London)
♦ Tower, the
TP, f
Teilpension, f
Teilverpflegung, f
♦ p/b
♦ part board
♦ partial board
Trabrennen, n
♦ trotting race
Tracht, f
→ Landestracht
Trachtenfest n
♦ festival of traditional costumes
♦ festival of national costumes
Trachtengruppe, f
♦ group in national costumes
Trachtenkleid, n
♦ traditional dress
♦ traditional costume
Trachtenmuseum, n
Kleidermuseum, n
♦ museum of costume
Trachtensammlung, f
♦ collection of costumes
♦ costume collection
Trachtenumzug, m
♦ procession in national costumes
Trachtenvorführung, f
♦ show of national costumes
traditionelle Atmosphäre, f
♦ traditional atmosphere
traditionelle Gastfreundlichkeit, f
♦ traditional hospitality
traditionelle Kost, f
herkömmliche Kost, f
♦ traditional fare
traditionelle Landatmosphäre erhalten
♦ maintain the traditional country atmosphere
traditionelle englisches Frühstück, n
♦ traditional English breakfast
traditionelles Gericht, n
herkömmliches Gericht, n
♦ traditional dish
traditionelles Getränk, n
herkömmliches Getränk, n
♦ traditional drink
♦ traditional beverage
traditionelle Speisekarte, f
herkömmliche Speisekarte, f
♦ traditional menu
traditionelles Rezept, n
traditionelle Rezeptur, f
♦ traditional recipe
traditionelle Werte, m pl
♦ traditional values pl
traditionell möbliert, adj
herkömmlich möbliert, adj
♦ traditionally furnished, adj
traditionell möbliertes Zimmer, n
herkömmlich möbliertes Zimmer, n
♦ traditionally furnished room
Tradition fortsetzen
♦ continue the tradition
Tradition geht zurück bis 1905
♦ tradition goes back to 1905

Traditionscafé, n
- ♦ old-established cafe AE
- ♦ old-established café BE

Traditionsfest, n
- ♦ old-established festival
- ♦ traditional festival

Traditionsgaststätte, f
- Traditionsgasthaus n
- Traditionsgastwirtschaft f
- ♦ old-established bar AE
- ♦ old-established public house BE
- ♦ old-established pub BE

Traditionshaus, n
- → Traditionshotel

Traditionshotel, n
- Traditionshaus, n
- traditionsreiches Hotel, n
- Hotel mit Tradition, n
- ♦ old-established hotel

Traditionsküche, f (Speisen)
- traditionelle Küche, f
- ♦ traditional cuisine
- ♦ traditional cooking

traditionsreich, adj
- ♦ steeped in tradition, adj
- ♦ old-established, adj

traditionsreicher Ferienort, m
- traditionsreicher Urlaubsort, m
- ♦ old-established resort

traditionsreiches Hotel, n
- → Traditionshotel

traditionsreiche Vergangenheit, f
- ♦ past rich in tradition

Traditionszielort, m
- traditioneller Zielort, m
- traditionelles Ziel, n
- ♦ traditional destination

Trafik, f ÖST
- → Tabakladen

Tragbahre, f
- ♦ stretcher

tragbar, adj
- ♦ portable, adj

tragbarer Herd, m
- ♦ portable stove
- ♦ portable cooker

tragbares Bett, n
- Tragbett, n
- ♦ portable bed

tragbares Telefon, n
- ♦ portable telephone

tragbare Toilette, f
- ♦ portable toilet
- ♦ portaloo BE coll

Tragbett n
- → tragbares Bett

Trage, f
- Sänfte, f
- ♦ litter

Tragegurt, m
- ♦ carrying strap

tragen etw (Gewicht)
- ♦ carry s.th.

tragen etw (Kleidung)
- ♦ wear s.th.

Tragen Sie hier bitte Ihren Namen ein
- ♦ Please enter your name here

Träger, m
- → Gepäckträger, Leistungsträger

Tragetasche, f
- ♦ carrier bag
- ♦ carry-on bag AE

Tragflächenboot n
- → Tragflügelboot

Tragflügelboot, n
- Tragflächenboot, n
- ♦ hydrofoil

Tragflügelbootdienst, m
- Tragflächenbootdienst, m
- ♦ hydrofoil service

Traglufthalle, f
- ♦ airhouse

Trailbike, n
- → geländegängiges Motorrad

Trainer, m
- ♦ coach

trainieren jn
- ♦ coach s.o.

Training, n (Sport)
- ♦ coaching
- ♦ training

Trainingsanzug, m
- ♦ track suit

Trainingsflug, m
- Übungsflug, m
- ♦ training flight

Trainingshotel, n
- → Ausbildungshotel

Trainingskurs, m
- Trainingslehrgang, m
- ♦ coaching course

Trainingslager, n
- → Übungslager

Trainingsraum, m
- → Gymnastikraum

Trainingsschuh, m
- ♦ training shoe
- ♦ trainer

Trainingssitzung, f
- Trainingsstunde, f
- Schulungssitzung, f
- Schulungsstunde, f
- ♦ training session

Trainingswand, f
- ♦ training wall

Train à grande vitesse, m FR
- TGV, m FR
- ♦ train à grande vitesse FR
- ♦ TGV FR

Trakt, m
- → Flügel

Traktor, m
- ♦ tractor

Traktorfahrt, f
- ♦ tractor ride
- ♦ tractor trip

Tram, f
- → Straßenbahn

Traminer, m
- Traminerwein, m
- ♦ Traminer
- ♦ Traminer wine

Traminerrebe, f
- ♦ Traminer vine

Traminertraube, f
- ♦ Traminer grape

Tramp, m
- Tippelbruder, m
- ♦ tramp

- ♦ hobo AE sl
- ♦ bum AE sl

Trampelpfad, m
- ♦ beaten path
- ♦ beaten track

trampen
- per Anhalter fahren
- per Anhalter reisen
- ♦ hitchhike AE
- ♦ hitch-hike BE
- ♦ hitch

Trampen, n
- Autostopp, m
- ♦ hitchhiking AE
- ♦ hitch-hiking BE
- ♦ hitching

trampen durch Europa
- ♦ hitchhike through Europe AE
- ♦ hitch-hike (a)round Europe BE
- ♦ hitch-hike through Europe BE
- ♦ hitch through Europe
- ♦ hitch (a)round Europe

trampen nach X
- ♦ hitchhike to X AE
- ♦ hitch-hike to X BE
- ♦ hitch to X

Tramper, m
- → Anhalter

Trampolin, n
- ♦ trampoline

Trampolin springen
- ♦ trampoline

Trampolinspringen, n
- ♦ trampolining

Trancheur, m FR
- Tranchierer, m
- ♦ trancheur FR
- ♦ carver

Tranchierbesteck, n
- ♦ carving set

Tranchierbrett, n
- ♦ carving board

tranchieren etw gastr
- vorschneiden etw gastr
- zerlegen etw gast
- ♦ carve s.th. gastr

Tranchierer, m
- Trancheur, m FR
- ♦ carver
- ♦ trancheur FR

Tranchiermesser, n
- ♦ carving knife

Tranchiertisch, m
- ♦ carving table

Tranchierwagen, m
- ♦ carving trolley BE
- ♦ carving cart AE

Tränke, f
- ♦ drinking trough
- ♦ watering place

Transatlantikflug, m
- ♦ transatlantic flight

Transatlantikflugpreis, m
- ♦ transatlantic air fare

Transatlantikflugreiseverkehr, m
- ♦ transatlantic air travel

Transatlantikkreuzfahrt, f
- ♦ transatlantic cruise

Transatlantikliniendienst, m
- Transatlantiklinienverkehr, m
- ♦ scheduled transatlantic service

Transatlantikpassagier

Transatlantikpassagier, m
  Transatlantikfahrgast, m
  ♦ transatlantic passenger
Transatlantikreise, f (generell)
  ♦ transatlantic journey
  ♦ transatlantic tour
  ♦ transatlantic trip
Transatlantikreise, f (Schiff)
  ♦ transatlantic voyage
Transatlantikreisemarkt, m
  ♦ transatlantic travel market
Transatlantikreiseverkehr, m
  Transatlantikreisen, n
  ♦ transatlantic travel
Transatlantikroute, f
  Transatlantikstrecke, f
  ♦ transatlantic route
Transfer, m
  ♦ transfer
Transferarrangement, n
  Transfervereinbarung, f
  ♦ transfer arrangement
Transfer arrangieren für jn
  Transfer vermitteln für jn
  Transfer besorgen für jn
  ♦ arrange (a) transfer for s.o.
Transferbus m
  ♦ transfer bus
  ♦ transfer coach BE
Transfer des Gepäcks, m
  ♦ transfer of baggage AE
  ♦ transfer of luggage BE
Transferdienst, m
  → Transferservice
Transfergebühr, f
  ♦ transfer charge
  ♦ transfer fee
transferieren etw
  ♦ transfer s.th.
Transferkosten, pl
  ♦ transfer costs pl
  ♦ transfer cost
Transferliste, f
  ♦ transfer list
Transfer mit Limousine, m
  ♦ transfer by limousine
  ♦ limousine transfer
Transferreisender, m
  ♦ transfer passenger
Transferschalter, m
  ♦ transfer desk
Transferservice, m
  Transferdienst, m
  ♦ transfer service
Transfertheke, f
  Transferschalter, m
  ♦ transfer counter
Transfer vom Flughafen zum Hotel, m
  ♦ transfer from the airport to the hotel
Transferzeit f
  ♦ transfer time
Transfer zum Hotel, m
  ♦ transfer to the hotel
Transfer zu und von dem Hotel, m
  Transfer zum und vom Hotel, m
  ♦ transfer to and from the hotel
Transfer zwischen A und B, m
  ♦ transfer between A and B
Transformator, m
  ♦ transformer

Transit, m
  ♦ transit
Transitabfertigung, f
  ♦ transit clearance
Transitabkommen, n
  ♦ transit convention
Transitbesucher, m
  ♦ transit visitor
  ♦ in-transit visitor AE
  ♦ visitor in transit
Transitfluggast, m
  Transitflugreisender, m
  ♦ transit air passenger
  ♦ air passenger in transit
Transitflughafen, m
  ♦ transit airport
Transitgast, m
  ♦ transit guest
  ♦ nonstaying guest AE
  ♦ non-staying guest BE
Transithafen, m
  ♦ transit port
Transithalle, f
  (Flughafen)
  ♦ transit hall
  ♦ hall for transit passengers
  ♦ transit lounge
  ♦ lounge for transit passengers
Transithotel n
  ♦ transit hotel
Transitlager, n
  → Durchgangslager
Transitland, n
  → Durchgangsland
Transitpassagier, m
  ♦ transit passenger
Transitraum, m
  (Flughafen)
  ♦ transit passengers' waiting room
  ♦ waiting room for transit passengers
Transitreise, f
  ♦ transit journey
  ♦ transit tour
Transitreisender, m
  ♦ transit passenger
  ♦ passenger in transit
Transitstrecke, f
  Transitroute, f
  ♦ transit route
Transitvereinbarung, f
  ♦ transit agreement
Transitverkehr, m
  ♦ transit traffic
Transitvisum, n
  Durchgangsvisum, n
  ♦ transit visa
Transitvorschriften, f pl
  Transitbestimmungen, f pl
  ♦ transit regulations pl
Transkaukasien
  ♦ Transcaucasia
transkontinental, adj
  ♦ transcontinental, adj
Transkontinentaleisenbahn, f
  ♦ transcontinental railroad AE
  ♦ transcontinental railway BE
Transkontinentalflug, m
  ♦ transcontinental flight
Transkontinentalreise, f
  ♦ transcontinental journey

♦ transcontinental trip
♦ transcontinental tour
Transkontinentalzug, m
  ♦ transcontinental train
Transport, m
  Beförderung, f
  ♦ transportation AE
  ♦ transport BE
  ♦ conveyance
  ♦ carriage
Transportabteilung, f
  ♦ transportation department AE
  ♦ transport department BE
Transportanbieter, m
  ♦ supplier of transportation AE
  ♦ supplier of transport BE
  ♦ transportation supplier AE
  ♦ transport supplier BE
  ♦ transport provider BE
Transportangebot, n
  ♦ supply of transportation AE
  ♦ supply of transport BE
  ♦ transportation supply AE
  ♦ transport supply BE
Transportarbeiter, m
  ♦ transportation worker AE
  ♦ transport worker BE
Transportarrangement, n
  Beförderungsarrangement, n
  ♦ transportation arrangement AE
  ♦ transport arrangement BE
Transportart, f
  Beförderungsart, f
  ♦ mode of transportation AE
  ♦ mode of transport BE
  ♦ transportation mode AE
  ♦ transport mode BE
Transportbedingungen, f pl
  ♦ transportation conditions AE pl
  ♦ transport conditions BE pl
Transportbereich, m
  Transportsektor, m
  ♦ transportation sector AE
  ♦ transport sector BE
Transportbetrieb, m
  Transportunternehmen, n
  ♦ transportation operation AE
  ♦ transport operation BE
Transportdienstleistung, f
  Transportleistung, f
  Transportservice, m
  ♦ transportation service AE
  ♦ transport service BE
Transporteinrichtung, f
  ♦ transportation facility AE
  ♦ transport facility BE
Transportflugzeug, n
  ♦ transport aircraft
  ♦ transport airplane AE
  ♦ transport aeroplane BE
  ♦ transport plane
Transportform, f
  Beförderungsform, f
  Form des Transports, f
  Form der Beförderung, f
  ♦ form of transportation AE
  ♦ form of transport BE
Transportgesellschaft, f
  ♦ transportation company AE
  ♦ transport company BE

transportierbar, adj
  beförderbar, adj
  ◆ transportable, adj
transportieren etw
  ◆ transport s.th.
transportieren etw mit der Bahn
  ◆ transport s.th. by rail
transportieren etw von A nach B
  ◆ transport s.th. from A to B
transportieren jn
  ◆ transport s.o.
Transportindustrie, f
  ◆ transportation industry AE
  ◆ transport industry BE
Transportkapazität, f
  ◆ transportation capacity AE
  ◆ transport capacity BE
Transportkosten, pl
  ◆ transportation costs AE pl
  ◆ transportation cost AE
  ◆ transport costs BE pl
  ◆ transport cost BE
Transportleistung, f
  Verkehrsleistung, f
  ◆ transportation service AE
  ◆ transport service BE
Transportmethode, f
  Transportart, f
  Beförderungsmethode, f
  Beförderungsart, f
  ◆ method of transportation AE
  ◆ method of transport BE
Transportminister, m
  → Verkehrsminister
Transportmittel, n
  Beförderungsmittel, n
  Verkehrsmittel, n
  ◆ means of transportation AE sg
  ◆ means of transport BE sg
Transportmuseum, n
  Verkehrsmuseum, n
  ◆ transport museum BE
  ◆ transportation museum AE
  ◆ museum of transport BE
  ◆ museum of transportation AE
Transportproblem, n
  ◆ transportation problem AE
  ◆ transport problem BE
Transportproblem lösen
  ◆ solve a transportation problem AE
  ◆ solve a transport problem BE
Transportprojekt, n
  ◆ transportation project AE
  ◆ transport project BE
Transportschiff, n
  Frachtschiff, n
  ◆ transport ship
  ◆ transport vessel
Transportsystem, n
  ◆ transportation system AE
  ◆ transport system BE
Transportunternehmer, m
  ◆ transport contractor
  ◆ transport carrier
  ◆ transport operator BE
Transportverbindung, f
  ◆ transportation connection AE
  ◆ transport connection BE
Transportversicherung, f
  ◆ transportation insurance AE
  ◆ transport insurance BE

Transportvertrag, m
  ◆ transportation contract AE
  ◆ transport contract BE
Transportwesen, n
  → Transport
transsibirisch, adj
  ◆ trans-Siberian, adj
Transsibirische Eisenbahn, n
  ◆ Trans-Siberian Railroad AE
  ◆ Trans-Siberian Railway BE
Transvestit, m
  ◆ transvestite
Transvestitenrevue, f
  ◆ transvestite floor show
Trapper, m
  ◆ trapper
Trapschießen, n
  → Wurftaubenschießen
Trasimenischer See, m
  ◆ Lake Trasimene
Trattoria, f ITAL
  ◆ trattoria ITAL
  ◆ trat BE coll
Traube, f
  ◆ grape
Traubenblatt, n
  ◆ grape leaf
Traubenernte, f
  → Traubenlese
Trauben ernten
  ◆ harvest (the) grapes
Traubengelee, n
  ◆ grape jelly
Traubenkern, m
  ◆ grapestone
Traubenkonfitüre, f
  ◆ grape jam
Traubenkur, f
  ◆ grape cure
Traubenkurort m
  ◆ grape cure resort
Traubenlese, f
  Weinlese, f
  Lese, f
  Weinernte, f
  Traubenernte, f
  ◆ grape harvest
  ◆ vintage
Trauben lesen
  Trauben pflücken
  ◆ pick (the) grapes
Traubenmost, m
  ◆ grape must
  ◆ must
Trauben pflücken
  ◆ pick grapes
Traubensaft, m
  ◆ grape juice
Traubensorte, f
  ◆ grape variety
  ◆ type of grape
  ◆ grape
Traubenzucker, m
  ◆ grape sugar AE
  ◆ grape-sugar BE
  ◆ dextrose
Trauerfeier, f
  ◆ funeral ceremony
Trauerfeierlichkeiten, f pl
  ◆ obsequies pl

Trauergast, m
  ◆ mourner
Traumappartement, n
  ◆ dream apartment
Traumauto, n
  Traumwagen, m
  ◆ dream car
Traumberuf, m
  ◆ dream job
Träumer, m
  Traumtänzer, m
  ◆ dreamer
Traumfabrik, f
  ◆ dream factory
Traumferien, pl
  Traumurlaub, m
  ◆ dream holiday BE
  ◆ dream vacation AE
Traumfrau, f
  ◆ woman of one's dreams
traumhafte Lage, f
  Traumlage, f
  ◆ marvelous situation AE
  ◆ marvellous situation BE
traumhafter Blick, m
  traumhafter Ausblick, m
  traumhafte Aussicht, f
  ◆ marvelous view AE
  ◆ marvellous view BE
traumhaft gelegen, adj
  ◆ marvelously situated, adj AE
  ◆ marvellously situated, adj BE
  ◆ marvelously sited, adj AE
  ◆ marvellously sited, adj BE
traumhaft gelegenes Hotel, n
  ◆ marvelously situated hotel AE
  ◆ marvellously situated hotel BE
  ◆ marvelously sited hotel AE
  ◆ marvellously sited hotel BE
traumhaft schön, adj
  ◆ absolutely beautiful, adj
Traumhaus, n
  ◆ dream house
  ◆ dream home
Traumhochzeit, f
  ◆ fairy-tale wedding
Traumhotel n
  ◆ dream hotel
Trauminsel, f
  ◆ island of one's dreams
Traumkneipe, f
  ◆ dream bar AE
  ◆ dream pub BE coll
Traumlage f
  → traumhafte Lage
Traumland, n
  ◆ dream country
  ◆ country of one's dreams
  ◆ dreamland
Traumlandhaus, n
  ◆ dream cottage
Traumlandschaft, f
  ◆ dream landscape
  ◆ landscape of one's dreams
  ◆ dream scenery
  ◆ dream countryside
traumlos, adj
  ◆ dreamless, adj
traumlos schlafen
  ◆ have a dreamless sleep
  ◆ sleep a dreamless sleep

Traummann

Traummann, m
♦ man of one's dreams
Traumpiste, f
♦ dream piste
♦ dream ski run
Traumreise, f
♦ dream journey
♦ dream tour
Traumreise gewinnen
♦ win a dream journey
♦ win a dream tour
Traumschloß, n
♦ dream castle
♦ castle of dreams
Traumstrand m
♦ dream beach
Traumurlaub, m
♦ dream vacation AE
♦ dream holiday BE
Traumvilla f
♦ dream villa
♦ dream of a villa
♦ dream mansion
Traum von einem Hotel sein
Traumhotel sein
♦ be the dream of a hotel
Traumwelt, f
♦ dream world
♦ world of fantasy
Traumwohnung, f
♦ dream flat BE
♦ dream apartment AE
Traunsee m
♦ Lake Traun
trauriger Abschied, m
♦ sad farewell
Trautes Heim, Glück allein
♦ My home is my happiness
Travellerscheck, m
→ Reisescheck
Travel Mart, m
(in London)
♦ Travel Mart, the
Travestieshow, f
♦ drag show
Treck, m
♦ trek
Treff, m (Lokal)
Treffpunkt, m
♦ haunt
Treff, m (Veranstaltung)
♦ meet
Treffen, n
Zusammentreffen, n
Zusammenkunft, f
♦ meeting
Treffen in der Wochenmitte, n
♦ midweek meeting
treffen jm in einem Restaurant
♦ meet s.o. at a restaurant
♦ meet s.o. in a restaurant
treffen jn auf halbem Weg
♦ meet s.o. halfway AE
♦ meet s.o. half-way BE
treffen jn in einem Hotel
abholen jm im Hotel
♦ meet s.o. at a hotel
treffen jn zum Mittagessen in einem Gasthof
♦ meet s.o. at an inn for lunch

treffen sich zum Abendessen (Dinner)
zum Abendessen zusammenkommen
♦ meet for dinner
treffen sich zum Abendessen (Supper)
zum Abendessen zusammenkommen
♦ meet for supper
treffen sich zum Mittagessen
zum Mittagessen zusammenkommen
♦ meet for lunch
♦ meet for luncheon
Treffen vereinbaren
♦ arrange a meeting
♦ fix (up) a meeting
Treffen verschieben
Sitzung verschieben
Tagung verschieben
♦ postpone a meeting
Treffen war gut besucht
Tagung war gut besucht
♦ meeting was well attended
Treffen zwischen Herrn A und Frau B, n
♦ meeting between Mr. A and Mrs. B AE
♦ meeting between Mr A and Mrs B BE
Treffpunkt, m (Austragungsort)
→ Austragungsort
Treffpunkt, m (Stadt)
♦ meeting place
Treffpunkt der Künstler, m
Künstlertreff, m
Künstlertreffpunkt, m
♦ haunt of artists
♦ artists' haunt
Treffpunkt m (Punkt)
♦ meeting point
Treibhauseffekt, m
♦ greenhouse effect
Treibjagd, f
♦ battue
♦ drive
Treibstoff, m
♦ fuel
Treibstoffaufpreis, m
♦ fuel surcharge
Treibstoff einsparen
Treibstoff sparen
♦ save fuel
Treibstoffeinsparung, f
Brennstoffeinsparung, f
♦ fuel saving
♦ saving (of) fuel
♦ saving (in) fuel
Treibstoffgutschein, m
♦ fuel voucher
Treibstoffkosten, pl
♦ fuel costs pl
♦ fuel cost
♦ costs of fuel pl
♦ cost of fuel
Treibstoffkosten senken
♦ cut fuel costs
Treibstoffpreis, m
♦ fuel price
♦ price of fuel
Treibstoffproblem, n
♦ fuel problem
Treibstofftank, m
♦ fuel tank
Treibstoffverbrauch, m
♦ fuel consumption
♦ consumption of fuel

Treibstoffverteuerung, f
♦ fuel-price increase
Treibstoffzuschlag m
♦ fuel supplement
Treidelboot, n
♦ horse-drawn boat
Treidelkahn, m
♦ horse-drawn barge
Treidelpfad, m
Leinpfad, m
Treidelweg, m
♦ towpath AE
♦ towing path
♦ tow-path BE
trekken (im Himalaja)
♦ go trekking (in the Himalayas)
♦ trek (in the Himalayas)
Trekker, m
♦ trekker
Trekking, n
♦ trekking
Trekkingerfahrung, f
♦ trekking experience
Trekkingerlaubnis, f
♦ trekking permit
Trekkingexpedition, f
♦ tekking expedition
Trekkingfahrrad, n
♦ trekking bicycle
♦ trekking cycle
♦ trekking bike coll
Trekkinggesellschaft, f
Trekkingfirma, f
♦ trekking company
Trekkinggruppe, f
♦ trekking party
♦ trekking group
Trekkingreise, f
Trekkingtour, f
♦ trekking tour
♦ trek
Trekkingreiseveranstalter, m
♦ trekking tour operator
Trekkingspezialist, m
♦ trekking specialist
Trekkingveranstalter, m
♦ trekking operator
Trekkingweg, m
♦ trekking trail
Trekkingzentrum, n
♦ trekking center AE
♦ trekking centre BE
Trend, m
♦ trend
Trend entsprechen
♦ conform to a trend
Trend folgen
♦ follow a trend
Trend von X zu Y, m
♦ trend from X towards Y
Trend zu etw, m
♦ trend towards s.th.
Trend zu kürzeren Aufenthalten, m
♦ trend towards shorter stays
Trend zu Kurzurlauben, m
♦ trend towards short vacations AE
♦ trend towards short holidays BE
Trennkost, f
(Diät)
♦ Hay diet, the

- ♦ compatible eating
- ♦ food combining

Trenntür, f
Zwischentür, f
- ♦ dividing door

Trennvorhang, m
- ♦ dividing curtain

Trennwand, f
→ Zwischenwand

Treppe hinaufgehen
→ nach oben gehen

Treppenabsatz, m
→ Treppenhausabsatz

Treppengeländer, n
- ♦ banisters pl

Treppenhaus, n
- ♦ staircase
- ♦ stairwell AE

Treppenhausabsatz, m
Treppenabsatz, m
Podest, m
- ♦ landing

Treppenläufer, m
- ♦ stair carpet

Treppenlift, m
(für Behinderte)
- ♦ stair lift

Treppenschacht, m
- ♦ stairwell

Treppen steigen
Treppen hinaufsteigen
- ♦ climb stairs

Treppenstufe, f
- ♦ stair
- ♦ step

Treppenturm, m
- ♦ staircase tower

Tresen, m
Theke, f
Schanktresen, m
- ♦ bar
- ♦ counter

Tresenbedienung, f
→ Thekenbedienung

Tresencafé, n
Thekencafé, n
- ♦ counter cafe AE
- ♦ counter café BE

Tresenpersonal, n
→ Thekenpersonal, Schalterpersonal

Tresor, m
→ Safe

Tretauto, n
- ♦ pedal car

Tretboot, n
Wasservelo, n SCHW
- ♦ pedal boat
- ♦ pedalo

Tretboot fahren
- ♦ go pedal-boating

Tretbootfahren, n
Wasservelofahren, n SCHW
- ♦ pedal-boating

Tretboot mieten
Wasservelo mieten SCHW
- ♦ rent a pedal boat
- ♦ rent a pedalo
- ♦ hire a pedal boat BE
- ♦ hire a pedalo BE

Tretbootverleih, m
Wasserveloverleih, m SCHW

- ♦ pedal boat rental AE
- ♦ pedalo rental AE
- ♦ pedal boat hire BE
- ♦ pedalo hire BE

Tretboot vermieten
Wasservelo vermieten SCHW
- ♦ rent (out) a pedal boat
- ♦ rent (out) a pedalo
- ♦ hire out a pedal boat BE
- ♦ hire out a pedalo BE

Treteimer, m
- ♦ pedal bin

Treueprämie, f
- ♦ loyalty bonus

Treuerabatt, m
- ♦ patronage discount
- ♦ loyalty discount

treuer Kunde, m
- ♦ faithful customer
- ♦ loyal client

Tribüne, f
- ♦ stands pl
- ♦ stand

Tribüne aufbauen
Tribüne bauen
- ♦ build a stand

Tribünenplatz, m
- ♦ stand seat
- ♦ seat in the stand

Trichter, m
- ♦ funnel

Trickbetrüger, m
- ♦ confidence trickster

Trickskilauf, m
- ♦ freestyle skiing
- ♦ hot-dogging coll

Trimaran, m
- ♦ trimaran

Trimm-dich-Anlage, f
Fitneßanlage, f
Trimmanlage, f
- ♦ keep-fit complex
- ♦ fitness complex

Trimm-dich-Bahn, f
Trimm-dich-Pfad, m
Trimmpfad, m
Trimmbahn, f
Trimm-dich-Parcours, m
- ♦ keep-fit track
- ♦ keep-fit-trail
- ♦ fitness track
- ♦ fitness trail

Trimm-dich-Parcours, m
→ Trimm-dich-Pfad

Trimm-dich-Pfad, m
Trimm-dich-Bahn, f
Trimmpfad, m
Trimmbahn, f
Fitneßbahn, f
- ♦ keep-fit trail
- ♦ fitness trail
- ♦ keep-fit track

Trimm-dich-Raum, m
→ Trimmraum

Trimm-dich-Strecke, f
→ Trimm-dich-Bahn

Trimm-dich-Stunde, f
Fitneßstunde, f
Trimmstunde, f
- ♦ keep-fit hour
- ♦ fitness hour

Trimm-dich-Waldweg, m
Fitneßwaldweg, m
Trimmwaldweg, m
- ♦ keep-fit forest trail
- ♦ fitness forest trail

Trimmeinrichtung, f
→ Fitneßeinrichtung

trimmen sich
sich in Form halten
fit bleiben
- ♦ get into shape
- ♦ get oneself into shape
- ♦ keep fit

Trimmprogramm, n
Trimm-dich-Programm, n
Fitneßprogramm, n
- ♦ keep-fit program AE
- ♦ keep-fit programme BE
- ♦ fitness program AE
- ♦ fitness programme BE

Trimmraum, m
Trimm-dich-Raum, m
Fitneßraum, m
- ♦ keep-fit room
- ♦ fitness room
- ♦ exercise room

Trimmstation, f
Fitneßstation, f
Trimm-dich-Station, f
- ♦ keep-fit station
- ♦ fitness station

Trimmübung, f
Fitneßübung, f
Trimm-dich-Übung, f
- ♦ keep-fit exercise
- ♦ fitness exercise

Trimmurlaub, m
Fitneßurlaub, m
Trimm-dich-Urlaub, m
Trimmferien, pl
Fitneßferien, pl
- ♦ keep-fit vacation AE
- ♦ fitness vacation AE
- ♦ keep-fit holiday BE
- ♦ fitness holiday BE

Trimmwelle, f
Fitneßwelle, f
Trimm-dich-Welle, f
- ♦ keep-fit vogue
- ♦ fitness vogue

Trinidad
- ♦ Trinidad

trinkbar, adj
- ♦ drinkable, adj
- ♦ potable, adj form

Trinkbar, f
→ Getränkebar

Trinkbruder, m coll
Trinkkumpan, m
- ♦ drinking crony coll
- ♦ drinking pal coll

Trinkbrunnen, m
- ♦ drinking fountain

Trinkclub, m
- ♦ drinking club

Trinkdiele, f
Trinksalon, f
- ♦ drinking parlor AE

trinken
(gewohnheitsmäßig)

Trinken

- ◆ drink
- ◆ tipple *coll*

Trinken, n
Trinkerei, f
- ◆ drinking

trinken auf etw
anstoßen auf etw
prosten auf etw
- ◆ drink to s.th.
- ◆ toast s.th.

trinken auf jn
anstoßen auf jn
prosten auf jn
- ◆ drink to s.o.
- ◆ toast s.o.

trinken auf js Gesundheit
- ◆ drink to s.o.'s health
- ◆ drink s.o.'s health
- ◆ drink a health to s.o.

trinken auf js Glück
- ◆ drink to s.o.'s happiness

trinken etw
- ◆ drink s.th.
- ◆ have a drink

trinken etw auf nüchternen Magen
- ◆ drink s.th. on an empty stomach

trinken etw aus der Flasche
aus der Flasche etw trinken
- ◆ drink s.th. from the bottle

trinken etw fässerweise
fässerweise etw trinken
- ◆ drink s.th. by the barrel

trinken etw gekühlt
- ◆ drink s.th. chilled

trinken etw in einem Schluck
trinken etw mit einem Schluck
- ◆ drink s.th. at one draft *AE*
- ◆ drink s.th. at one draught *BE*

trinken etw mit jm
- ◆ take a drink with s.o.
- ◆ have a drink with s.o.

trinken etw sofort
- ◆ drink s.th. immediately

trinken etw zu etw
(Speise)
- ◆ drink s.th. with s.th.

trinken gehen etw
einen trinken gehen *coll*
- ◆ go for a drink

trinken in regelmäßigen Zügen
- ◆ drink in regular drafts *AE*
- ◆ drink in regular draughts *BE*

trinken jn unter den Tisch
unter den Tisch jn trinken
- ◆ drink s.o. under the table

Trinken Sie etwas mit uns?
- ◆ Will you have a drink with us?
- ◆ Will you join us in a drink?

Trinken Sie noch eins!
- ◆ Have one more drink!
- ◆ Have one more!

Trinken Sie noch ein Schlückchen?
- ◆ Will you have another drop?

trinken wie ein Loch *coll*
saufen wie ein Loch *coll*
saufen wie ein Bürstenbinder *coll*
- ◆ drink like a fish *coll*

Trinker, m (Alkoholiker)
- ◆ heavy drinker
- ◆ drunkard
- ◆ (hard) drinker

- ◆ alcoholic
- ◆ tippler *BE inform*

Trinker, m (genereII)
- ◆ drinker

Trinkerei, f
→ Trinken

Trinkerheilanstalt, f
- ◆ alcohol treatment unit
- ◆ A.T.U
- ◆ drying-out unit *BE coll*

Trinkerleber, f
- ◆ hobnail liver

trinkfertig, adj
- ◆ ready-to-drink, adj

trinkfertiges Getränk, n
- ◆ ready-to-drink beverage

trinkfest, adj
- ◆ able to drink a lot, adj
- ◆ holding one's drink, adj
- ◆ holding one's liquor, adj

Trinkfestigkeit, f
- ◆ ability to hold one's drink
- ◆ ability to hold one's liquor

trinkfest sein
- ◆ hold one's drink well
- ◆ hold one's liquor well
- ◆ be able to take a lot

trinkfreudig sein
- ◆ like one's drink
- ◆ be fond of one's drink

Trinkgarten, m
- ◆ drinking garden

Trinkgaststätte, f
(Gegensatz zu Speisegaststätte)
- ◆ drinking bar *AE*
- ◆ drinking pub *BE*

Trinkgefäß, n
- ◆ drinking vessel

Trinkgelage, n
- ◆ drinking spree
- ◆ drinking bout
- ◆ booze-up *BE coll*

Trinkgelage machen
Sauferei veranstalten *vulg*
Trinkgelage veranstalten
- ◆ have a drinking-bout
- ◆ have a booze-up *BE coll*

Trinkgeld, n
- ◆ tip
- ◆ gratuity

Trinkgeldablöse, f
→ Bedienungsgeld

Trinkgeld bekommen
- ◆ get a tip

Trinkgeld bleibt dem Ermessen überlassen
- ◆ tipping is discretionary

Trinkgeld eingeschlossen
Trinkgeld inbegriffen
- ◆ tip included
- ◆ tipping included

Trinkgelder austeilen nach allen Seiten
- ◆ hand out tips left, right and center *AE*
- ◆ hand out tips left, right and centre *BE*

Trinkgeld erhalten
- ◆ receive a tip
- ◆ get a tip

Trinkgeld erwarten
- ◆ expect a tip

Trinkgelder zusammenlegen
- ◆ pool tips

Trinkgeld für jn, n
- ◆ tip for s.o.

Trinkgeldgeben, n
- ◆ tipping

Trinkgeldgeben bleibt dem Ermessen überlassen
- ◆ tipping is left to discretion

Trinkgeldgeben ist nicht üblich
- ◆ tipping is not customary

Trinkgeldgeben ist üblich
- ◆ tipping is customary

Trinkgeld geben jm
- ◆ tip s.o.
- ◆ give s.o. a tip

Trinkgeldgutschein, m
- ◆ tipping voucher

Trinkgeld inbegriffen
- ◆ Gratuity included
- ◆ Tips included

Trinkgeld jm aufnötigen
- ◆ force a tip into s.o.'s hands

Trinkgeld nehmen
Trinkgeld annehmen
- ◆ take a tip
- ◆ accept a tip

Trinkgeld von 1 Dollar geben jm
- ◆ tip s.o. with 1 dollar
- ◆ tip s.o. 1 dollar

Trinkgeld zurücklassen
- ◆ leave a tip

Trinkgeld zustecken jm
- ◆ slip s.o. a tip

Trinkgewohnheit f
- ◆ drinking habit

Trinkglas, n
- ◆ drinking glass *AE*
- ◆ drinking-glass *BE*

Trinkhalle, f (Kiosk)
- ◆ refreshment kiosk
- ◆ refreshment stand
- ◆ refreshment stall *BE*

Trinkhalle, f (Kurort)
Wandelhalle, f
- ◆ pump room *AE*
- ◆ pump-room *BE*

Trinkhalle betreiben
- ◆ operate a refreshment kiosk
- ◆ operate a refreshment stand
- ◆ operate a refreshment stall *BE*
- ◆ run a refreshment kiosk
- ◆ run a refreshment stand

Trinkhallenkonzession, f
- ◆ refreshment kiosk licence
- ◆ refreshment kiosk license
- ◆ refreshment stand license
- ◆ refreshment stall licence *BE*

Trinkhallenmuseum, n (Kurort)
- ◆ pump-room museum

Trinkhalm, m
- ◆ drinking straw
- ◆ straw

Trinkkumpan, m
Trinkbruder, m
- ◆ drinking pal *coll*
- ◆ drinking companion
- ◆ drinking partner

Trinkkur, f
- ◆ hydrotherapeutic cure
- ◆ pump-room cure
- ◆ taking the waters

Trinkkur machen
 ◆ take the waters
 ◆ drink the waters
Trinkkurmachen, n
 ◆ taking the waters
Trinklied, n
 ◆ drinking song
Trinklokal, n
 ◆ drinking establishment
 ◆ drinking place
 ◆ drinking spot *coll*
Trinkmilch, f
 ◆ certified milk
Trinkplatz, m
 Trinklokal, n
 ◆ drinking place
Trinkritual, n
 ◆ drinking ritual
Trinkschokolade, f
 ◆ drinking chocolate
Trinkspruch, m
 Prosit, n
 ◆ toast
Trinkspruch ausbringen auf jn
 ◆ propose a toast to s.o.
 ◆ give a toast to s.o.
 ◆ drink a toast to s.o.
Trinkspruch erwidern
 ◆ reply to the toast
 ◆ respond to the toast
Trinkstube, f (Haus)
 ◆ drinking house
Trinkstube, f (Lokal, Raum)
 → Schankraum
Trinkstube, f (Zimmer)
 → Trinkzimmer
Trinktemperatur, f
 ◆ drinking temperature
Trinkterrasse, f
 ◆ drinking terrace
 ◆ drinking patio
Trinkverhalten, n
 ◆ drinking pattern
Trinkwasser, n
 ◆ drinking water
 ◆ potable water *form*
Trinkwasseraufbereitungsanlage, f
 ◆ water purification plant
Trinkwasser aus der Leitung, n
 ◆ piped drinking water
Trinkwasserversorgung, f
 ◆ drinking water supply
 ◆ supply of drinking water
Trinkzeit, f
 Schankzeit, f
 ◆ drinking hours *pl*
Trinkzimmer, n
 Trinkstube, f
 ◆ drinking room
Trinkzwang, m
 ◆ obligation to order beverages
 ◆ obligation to order drinks
Trinkzweck, m
 ◆ drinking purpose
Trio, n
 ◆ trio
Trip, m
 → Fahrt, Reise
Triptychon, n
 dreiteiliges Altarbild, n

dreiteiliges Bild, n
 ◆ triptych
Triptyk, n
 Triptik, n
 ◆ triptyque
 ◆ tryptique
 ◆ tryptyque
Trittbrettfahrer, m
 Schnorrer, m
 ◆ freeloader
trocken, adj
 ◆ dry, adj
trocken, adj (keinen Alkohol trinken) *inform*
 ◆ on the wagon *inform*
Trockenautomat, m
 → Wäschetrockner
Trockenblume, f
 Strohblume, f
 ◆ everlasting flower
Trockenblumenstrauß, m
 Stohblumenstrauß, m
 ◆ bunch of everlasting flowers
Trockendock, n
 ◆ dry dock
Trockeneinrichtung, f
 Trockengelegenheit, f
 ◆ drying facility
Trockeneis, n
 ◆ dry ice
trockener Monat, m
 ◆ dry month
trockener Rotwein, m
 ◆ dry red wine
trockener Stellplatz, m
 (Camping)
 ◆ dry pitch
trockener Wein, m
 ◆ dry wine
trockener Weißwein, m
 ◆ dry white wine
trockenes Klima, n
 ◆ dry climate
Trockengelegenheit, f
 → Trockeneinrichtung
Trockengemüse, n
 ◆ dried vegetables *pl*
Trockengestell, n (Geschirr)
 ◆ drying rack
Trockengestell, n (Wäsche)
 → Wäschespinne
Trockengewicht, n
 ◆ dry weight
Trockenklosett, n
 → chemische Toilette
Trockenkost, f
 ◆ dry diet
Trockenmilch, f
 ◆ dried milk
 ◆ powdered milk
Trockenmöglichkeiten, f pl
 ◆ drying facilities *pl*
Trockenplatz, m
 (Wäsche)
 ◆ place for drying laundry
trocken rasieren sich
 ◆ dry-shave
Trockenraum, m
 Wäschetrockenraum, m
 Kleidertrockenraum, m
 ◆ drying room

Trockenschleuder, f
 → Wäscheschleuder
trocken sein
 keinen Alkohol mehr trinken
 trocken werden
 ◆ be on the wagon *inform*
 ◆ go on the wagon *inform*
Trockenskihang, m
 ◆ dry-ski slope
Trockenskikurs, m
 ◆ dry-ski course
 ◆ dry-skiing course
 ◆ dry-ski class
 ◆ dry-skiing class
Trockenskilauf, m
 Trockenskilaufen, n
 ◆ dry skiing
Trockenskischule, f
 ◆ dry-ski school
 ◆ dry-skiing school
Trockentoilette, f
 Plumpsklo, n *coll*
 Latrine, f
 ◆ dry toilet
 ◆ latrine
Trockenzeit f
 (Klima)
 ◆ dry season
trocknen etw
 ◆ dry s.th.
Trockner, m
 → Wäschetrockner
Trödel, m
 Kram, m
 Plunder, m
 ◆ junk
Trödeljahrmarkt, m
 Trödelmarkt, m
 ◆ rag fair
Trödelladen, m
 ◆ junk shop
Trödelmarkt, m
 ◆ junk market
 ◆ flea market
Trolleybus, m
 → Obus
Trollinger, m
 (Wein)
 ◆ Trollinger
Trollingerrebe, f
 ◆ Trollinger vine
Trollingerwein, m
 ◆ Trollinger wine
Trommel schlagen für etw
 (Werbung)
 ◆ bang the drum for s.th.
Tronc, m
 (gemeinsame Kasse für Trinkgelder)
 Trinkgeldschüssel, f
 ◆ tronc
 ◆ pooled tip
Troncsystem, n
 ◆ tronc system
Troncsystem anwenden
 ◆ operate a tronc system
Tropen, pl
 ◆ tropics, the *pl*
Tropenanzug, m
 ◆ tropical suit
Tropenaquarium, n
 ◆ tropical aquarium

Tropenbecken

Tropenbecken, n
♦ tropical pool
Tropenblume, f
♦ tropical flower
Tropenferienort, m
Tropenurlaubsort, m
Tropenort, m
♦ tropical resort
tropenfest, adj
♦ tropic-proof, adj
♦ tropics-proof, adj
Tropenfieber, n
♦ tropical fever
Tropenfrucht, f
♦ tropical fruit
Tropengarten, m
tropischer Garten, m
♦ tropical garden
Tropengebiet, n (groß)
Tropenregion, f
♦ tropical region
Tropengebiet, n (klein)
♦ tropical area
Tropengetränk, n
♦ tropical drink
♦ tropical beverage
Tropenhaus, n
♦ tropical house
Tropenhelm, m
♦ pith helmet
♦ topee
Tropenhimmel, m
♦ tropical sky
Tropenhitze, f
tropische Hitze, f
♦ tropical heat
Tropenhotel n
♦ tropical hotel
Tropenhut, m
♦ pith hat
Tropeninsel, f
♦ tropical island
Tropenklima, n
♦ tropical climate
Tropenkoller, m
♦ tropical frenzy
Tropenkrankheit, f
♦ tropical disease
Tropenland, n
♦ tropical country
♦ tropical land
Tropenlandschaft, f
♦ tropical scenery
♦ tropical landscape
♦ tropical countryside
Tropenmedizin, f
♦ tropical medicine
Tropennacht, f
♦ tropical night
Tropenort, m
♦ tropical place
Tropenparadies, n
tropisches Paradies, n
♦ tropical paradise
Tropenpflanze, f
♦ tropical plant
Tropenreise, f
♦ journey to the tropics
♦ tour to the tropics
♦ tropical journey

Tropenreisender, m
♦ traveler in the tropics AE
♦ traveller in the tropics BE
♦ tropical traveler AE
♦ tropical traveller BE
Tropenschwimmbad, n
♦ tropical swimming pool AE
♦ tropical swimming-pool BE
Tropensonne, f
♦ tropical sun
Tropenstadt, f (Großstadt)
♦ tropical city
Tropenstadt, f (kleine Stadt)
♦ tropical town
Tropenstrand, m
♦ tropical beach
Tropensturm, m
♦ tropical storm
tropentauglich, adj
♦ fit for the tropics, adj
Tropenwald, m
♦ tropical forest
Tropfen, m
♦ drop
Tropfen Whisky, m
♦ drop of whisky
Tropfsteinhöhle, f
♦ stalactite cave
Trophäe, f
♦ trophy
tropisch, adj
♦ tropical, adj
tropischer Regenwald, m
♦ tropical rainforest
tropische Vegetation, f
♦ tropical vegetation
Trostgeschenk, n
♦ consolation gift
trostlos, adj
♦ comfortless, adj
trostlose Nacht verbringen
unbehagliche Nacht verbringen
♦ spend a comfortless night
Trostpflaster, n
♦ consolation
Trostpreis, m
♦ consolation prize
♦ consolation award
Trubel, m
♦ bustle
Trüffel, f
♦ truffle
Trüffelbutter, f
♦ truffle butter
Trüffelfüllpastete, f
♦ truffle timbale
Trüffelsalat, m
♦ truffle salad
Trüffelsoße, f
♦ truffle sauce
Truhenbett, n
→ Kastenbett
Trunk, m humor
♦ potation humor
Trunkenheit, f
♦ drunkenness
Trunkenheit am Steuer, f
♦ drink-driving
♦ drunken driving
Trunkenheitsdelikt, n
♦ drinking offense

♦ drinking offence
♦ alcohol offense
♦ alcohol offence
Trunkenheitsfahrt, f
Trunkenheit am Steuer, f
♦ drunk driving
Trunksucht, f
♦ dipsomania
Trunksüchtiger, m
→ Alkoholiker
Trunksüchtiger, m
Alkoholiker, m
♦ dipsomaniac
♦ dipso coll
♦ alcoholic
trunksüchtig sein
Alkoholiker sein
♦ be an alcoholic
Truthahn, m
Puter, m
Pute, f
♦ turkey
♦ turkey cock
Truthahnbraten, m
Putenbraten, m
♦ roast turkey
Truthahnbrust, f
Putenbrust, f
♦ turkey breast
Truthahnfleisch, n
Putenfleisch, n
♦ turkey meat
Truthahnleber, f
Putenleber, f
♦ turkey liver
Truthahnschnitzel, n
Putenschnitzel, n
♦ turkey escalope
Truthenne, f
Pute, f
♦ turkey hen
Tschad, m
♦ Chad
Tschader, m
♦ Chadian
Tschaderin, f
♦ Chadian girl
♦ Chadian woman
♦ Chadian
tschadisch, adj
♦ Chadian, adj
Tscheche, m
♦ Czech
Tschechin, f
♦ Czech girl
♦ Czech woman
♦ Czech
tschechisch, adj
♦ Czech, adj
Tschechische Republik, f
♦ Czech Republic, the
Tschechoslowake, m
♦ Czechoslovak
♦ Czechoslovakian
Tschechoslowakei, f
♦ Czechoslovakia
Tschechoslowakin, f
♦ Czechoslovak girl
♦ Czechoslovak woman
♦ Czechoslovak

- ♦ Czechoslovakian girl
- ♦ Czechoslovakian woman

tschechoslowakisch, adj
- ♦ Czechoslovak, adj
- ♦ Czechoslovakian, adj

Tschüs! coll
  Wiedersehen! coll
- ♦ By! AE coll
- ♦ Bye! BE coll
- ♦ See you! coll
- ♦ By-by! AE coll
- ♦ Bye-bye! BE coll

Tube Zahnpasta, f
- ♦ tube of toothpaste

Tuch, n
- ♦ cloth

Tuchhalle, f
- ♦ cloth hall

tüchtigen Appetit haben
  richtig hungrig sein
- ♦ be really hungry
- ♦ have a healthy appetite

tüchtiger Esser, m
- ♦ good eater

tüchtiger Schluck, m
  kräftiger Schluck, m
- ♦ good swig

tüchtig zulangen
  tüchtig zugreifen
  tüchtig essen
  reinhauen fam
  spachteln fam
- ♦ dig in inform
- ♦ tuck in inform

Tudorgebäude, n
  Tudorbau, m
- ♦ Tudor building

Tudorhaus, n
- ♦ Tudor house

Tudorstil, m
- ♦ Tudor style

Tudorzeit, f
- ♦ Tudor times pl

Tülle, f
- ♦ spout

Tulpe, f (Blume)
- ♦ tulip

Tulpe, f (Glas)
- ♦ tulip-shaped glass
- ♦ tulip glass

Tulpenfest, n
  Tulpenfestival, n
- ♦ tulip festival

Tummelplatz, m
- ♦ stamping ground

tünchen etw
  weißen etw
- ♦ whitewash s.th.
- ♦ paint s.th.

Tunesien
- ♦ Tunisia

Tunesier, m
- ♦ Tunisian

Tunesierin, f
- ♦ Tunisian girl
- ♦ Tunisian woman
- ♦ Tunisian

tunesisch, adj
- ♦ Tunisian, adj

Tunke, f
- ♦ dip

Tunnel, m
- ♦ tunnel

Tunnelbetreiber, m
- ♦ tunnel operator

Tunte, f sl
- ♦ pansy sl
- ♦ fairy sl
- ♦ queen sl
- ♦ nancy boy sl

Tüpfelchen auf dem i, n
- ♦ icing on the cake

Tür, f
- ♦ door

Tür abschließen
  Tür zusperren
- ♦ lock a door

Tür an Tür wohnen (dauernd)
  nebeneinander wohnen
- ♦ live next door to each other

Tür an Tür wohnen (vorübergehend)
  nebeneinander wohnen
- ♦ stay next door to each other

Türbehang, m
- ♦ door hanging

Turbine, f
- ♦ turbine

Turbinenantrieb, m
- ♦ turboprop engine AE
- ♦ turbo-prop engine BE

Turbinendampfer, m
- ♦ turbine steamer

Turbinenflugzeug, n
- ♦ turbine aircraft

Turbinenmotor, m
- ♦ turbine engine

Turbo-Prop-Flugzeug, n
  Turbinen-Propeller-Flugzeug, n
- ♦ turboprop aircraft AE
- ♦ turbo-prop aircraft BE
- ♦ turboprop AE
- ♦ turbo-prop BE

Turbostrahltriebwerk, n
- ♦ turbojet engine
- ♦ turbojet

Türboy, m
  Boy, m
- ♦ bellboy AE
- ♦ bellhop AE sl
- ♦ page

Türbreite, f
- ♦ door width
- ♦ width of the door

turbulente Begrüßung, f
- ♦ tumultuous welcome

Türfüllung, f
- ♦ door panel

Tür geht in den Garten
  Tür führt zum Garten
- ♦ door opens into the garden

Tür geht nach innen auf
- ♦ door opens inwards
- ♦ door opens inward

Türgriff, m
  → Türklinke

Türgröße, f
- ♦ door size
- ♦ size of the door

Türhöhe, f
- ♦ door height
- ♦ height of the door

Türhüter, m
- ♦ doorkeeper

Tür ist sperrangelweit offen
- ♦ door is wide open

Türke, m (Lokal)
- ♦ Turkish place
- ♦ Turkish restaurant

Türke, m (Person)
- ♦ Turk

Türkei, f
- ♦ Turkey

Türkeibesucher, m
- ♦ visitor to Turkey

Türkeireiseverkehr, m
  Reisen in die Türkei, n
- ♦ travel to Turkey

Türkeispezialist, m
- ♦ Turkey specialist

Türkin, f
- ♦ Turkish girl
- ♦ Turkish woman
- ♦ Turk

türkisch, adj
- ♦ Turkish, adj

türkische Art, adv gastr
- ♦ Turkish style gastr

türkischer Honig, m
- ♦ Turkish delight

türkischer Kaffee, m
- ♦ Turkish coffee

türkisches Bad, n
  Dampfbad, n
  Schwitzbad, n
- ♦ Turkish bath

Tür klemmt
- ♦ door sticks

Türklinke, f
  Türgriff, m
- ♦ door handle AE
- ♦ door-handle BE

Türklopfer, m
  (statt Klingel)
- ♦ knocker
- ♦ door-knocker

Turkmene, m
- ♦ Turkman
- ♦ Turkoman
- ♦ Turcoman

turkmenisch, adj
- ♦ Turkmenian, adj
- ♦ Turkoman, adj
- ♦ Turcoman, adj
- ♦ Turkmen, adj

Turkmenistan
  Turkmenien
- ♦ Turkmenistan

Türknopf, m
- ♦ doorknob

türlos, adj
- ♦ doorless, adj

Turm, m
- ♦ tower

türmen sl
  abhauen sl
  verduften sl
- ♦ skip off coll
- ♦ lam AE sl
- ♦ vamoose AE sl
- ♦ bolt sl
- ♦ do a bunk sl

Turmhotel

Turmhotel, n
- tower hotel

Turmrestaurant, n
- tower restaurant

Turmruine, f
- ruined tower
- tower ruins *pl*

Turmsuite f
- tower suite

Turm von Pisa, m
- Tower of Pisa, the

Turmzimmer n
- tower room

Turn-down-Service, m
→ Aufwartungsdienst

turnen
- do gymnastics

Turner, m
Kunstturner, m
- gymnast

Turnfest, n
- gymnastic festival
- gymnastic display

Turnhalle, f
Turnsaal, m
Gymnastikhalle, f
Gymnastiksaal, m
- gym *coll*
- gymnasium

Turnhallenübungsgeräte, n pl
- gymnasium exercise equipment

Turnhose, f
- gym shorts *pl*

Turnier, n (Ritter) *hist*
- joust *hist*

Turnier, n (Wettkampfserie)
- tournament

Turnier abhalten
- hold a tournament

Turnier durchführen
- run a tournament

Turnierpferd, n
- show horse

Turnierplatz, m
- show jumping arena
- arena

Turnierreiter, m
- show jumper

Turniersieger, m
- winner of the tournament

Turnierspiel, n
- tournament match

Turnierspieler, m
- tournament player

Turniertanz, m
- ballroom dancing

Turniertänzer, m
- ballroom dancer

Turnlehrer, m
- gym instructor

Turnlehrerin, f
- gym instructress

Turnraum, m
- gym room

Turnschuhe, m pl
- sneakers *AE pl*
- plimsolls *BE pl*

Turnstunde, f
- gym lesson
- gym session
- gymnasium session

Turnübung, f
- gymnastic exercise
- exercise

Turnus, m
- rota

turnusmäßig, adj
- rotational, adj
- alternating, adj

turnusmäßig, adv
- by turns, adv
- in rotation, adv

turnusmäßige Veranstaltung, f
(zwischen zwei Orten)
- alternating function

turnusmäßig wechseln
- rotate
- alternate

Tür offenhalten für jn
- hold the door open for s.o.

Tür offenlassen
- leave the door open

Tür öffnen
- open the door

Türöffner, m
(Gerät)
- door opener

Türpfosten, m
- doorpost
- door jamb

Türrahmen, m
- doorframe *AE*
- door-frame *BE*

Türschild, n
- doorplate

Tür schließen von innen
- lock the door from the inside
- lock the door on the inside

Türschloß, n
- door lock

Tür sichern mit einer Kette
- secure a door with a chain

Türsprechanlage, f
- entryphone system
- entryphone

Türsteher, m
Portier, m
- doorman *AE*
- doorkeeper
- porter
- bellman *AE*

Türvorhang, m
Portiere, f
- door curtain *AE*
- door-curtain *BE*
- portiere *AE*
- portière *BE*

Tür zeigen jm
- show s.o. the door

Tusch, m
- flourish

Tuskulum, n *LAT*
→ Landrefugium

TV, n
Fernsehen, n
- TV
- television

TV-Anschluß, m
Fernsehanschluß, m
- TV socket *BE*
- TV connection
- television socket *BE*
- television connection

Twin, n
→ Zweibettzimmer

Twin-Size-Bett n
- twin-size bed

Typ, m
Art, f
Sorte, f
- type

Typ des Reisenden, m
Art des Reisenden, f
- type of traveller
- type of traveler *AE*

Typhus, m
- typhoid
- typhoid fever
- camp fever

Typhusimpfung, f
- typhoid vaccination
- inoculation against typhoid fever

typisch, adj
- typical, adj

typisch, adv
- typically, adv

typisch englisches Gericht, n
- typically English dish

typischer britischer Pub, m
- typical British pub *BE*

typisches englisches Gericht, n
- typical English dish

typisch italienische Gastlichkeit, f
typisch italienische Gastfreundschaft, f
- typically Italian hospitality

Typologie der Reisenden, f
- typology of travellers
- typology of travelers *AE*

Tyrrhenische Meer, das, n
- Tyrrhenian Sea, the

U

Ü, f
  Übernachtung, f
  ♦ nt
  ♦ night
U-Bahn, f
  Untergrundbahn, f
  ♦ **underground railroad** *AE*
  ♦ **subway** *AE*
  ♦ underground railway *BE*
  ♦ underground *BE*
  ♦ tube *BE coll*
U-Bahnbediensteter, m
  ♦ **subway official** *AE*
  ♦ underground official *BE*
  ♦ tube official *BE*
U-Bahn fahren
  mit der U-Bahn fahren
  ♦ **go by subway** *AE*
  ♦ go by underground *BE*
  ♦ go by tube *BE*
U-Bahnfahrgast, m
  ♦ **subway passenger** *AE*
  ♦ underground passenger *BE*
  ♦ tube passenger *BE*
U-Bahnfahrpreis, m
  ♦ **subway fare** *AE*
  ♦ underground fare *BE*
  ♦ tube fare *BE*
U-Bahnfahrschein, m
  ♦ **subway ticket** *AE*
  ♦ underground ticket *BE*
  ♦ tube ticket *BE*
U-Bahnfahrt, f
  ♦ **subway ride** *AE*
  ♦ underground ride *BE*
  ♦ underground trip *BE*
  ♦ tube trip *BE*
  ♦ tube ride *BE*
U-Bahnhaltestelle, f
  ♦ **subway stop** *AE*
  ♦ underground stop *BE*
  ♦ tube stop *BE*
U-Bahnkarte, f (Fahrschein)
  → U-Bahnfahrschein
U-Bahnkarte, f (Verzeichnis)
  ♦ **subway map** *AE*
  ♦ underground map *BE*
  ♦ tube map *BE*
U-Bahnlinie, f
  ♦ **subway line** *AE*
  ♦ underground line *BE*
  ♦ tube line *BE*
U-Bahn nehmen
  ♦ **take the subway** *AE*
  ♦ take the underground *BE*
  ♦ take the tube *BE*
U-Bahnnetz, n
  ♦ **subway system** *AE*

  ♦ underground railway system *BE*
  ♦ underground system *BE*
  ♦ tube system *BE*
U-Bahnstation, f
  U-Bahnhof, m
  U-Bahnhaltestelle, f
  ♦ **subway station** *AE*
  ♦ underground station
  ♦ underground railroad station *BE*
  ♦ underground railway station *BE*
  ♦ tube station *BE*
U-Bahnunfall, m
  ♦ **subway crash** *AE*
  ♦ underground crash *BE*
  ♦ tube crash *BE*
U-Bahnwagen, m
  ♦ **subway car** *AE*
  ♦ underground carriage *BE*
  ♦ tube carriage *BE*
U-Bahnzug, m
  ♦ **subway train** *AE*
  ♦ underground train *BE*
  ♦ tube train *BE*
übel, adj
  (Brechreiz)
  unwohl, adj
  zur Übelkeit neigend, adj
  ♦ **sick, adj**
  ♦ queasy, adj
übel fühlen sich
  (Brechreiz)
  unwohl fühlen sich
  ♦ **feel sick**
  ♦ feel queasy
Übelkeit, f
  Unwohlsein, n
  Empfindlichkeit, f
  ♦ **queasiness**
Übelkeit, f (Brechreiz)
  → Brechreiz
üben (etw)
  ♦ **practice (s.th.)**
  ♦ practise (s.th.)
überall herrscht Ferienstimmung
  ♦ **there is a vacation atmosphere everywhere** *AE*
  ♦ there is a holiday atmosphere everywhere *BE*
überall hinreisen
  überall reisen
  ♦ **travel everywhere**
überall in dem Hotel ist eine gemütliche
  Atmosphäre zu spüren
  ♦ **cosy atmosphere permeates the hotel**
  ♦ cosy atmosphere prevails in the hotel
überalteten Hotelbestand ersetzen
  ♦ **replace the obsolete hotel stock**
überalteter Hotelbestand, m
  ♦ **obsolete hotel stock**

Überangebot, n
  ♦ **oversupply**
  ♦ surplus
Überangebot an Betten, n
  Überangebot von Betten, n
  Bettenüberangebot, n
  ♦ **oversupply of beds**
  ♦ surplus of beds
Überangebot an Gästebetten, n
  Überangebot von Gästebetten, n
  Gästebettenüberangebot, n
  ♦ **oversupply of guest beds**
  ♦ surplus of guest beds
Überangebot an Hotels, n
  Überangebot von Hotels, n
  Hotelüberangebot, n
  ♦ **oversupply of hotels**
  ♦ surplus of hotels
Überangebot an Luxushotels, n
  Überangebot von Luxushotels, n
  Luxushotelüberangebot, n
  ♦ **oversupply of deluxe hotels** *AE*
  ♦ surplus of deluxe hotels *AE*
  ♦ oversupply of luxury hotels
  ♦ surplus of luxury hotels
Überangebot an Zimmern, n
  Überangebot von Zimmern, n
  Zimmerüberangebot, n
  ♦ **oversupply of rooms**
  ♦ surplus of rooms
überarbeiten etw
  revidieren etw
  ♦ **revise s.th.**
  ♦ go over s.th. (again)
  ♦ redraft s.th.
  ♦ rework s.th.
überarbeitete Zimmerpreisstruktur, f
  ♦ **revised room rate structure**
überbackene Käseschnitte, f
  ♦ **Welsh rarebit**
  ♦ Welsh rabbit
überbacken etw in der Muschelschale
  ♦ **scallop s.th.**
  ♦ scollop s.th.
überbeansprucht, adj
  (Kapazität)
  ♦ **overutilised, adj**
  ♦ overutilized, adj
  ♦ overused, adj
überbeansprucht sein
  (Kapazität)
  ♦ **be overutilised**
  ♦ be overutilized
  ♦ be overused
Überbeanspruchung, f
  ♦ **overutilisation**
  ♦ overutilization

Überbeanspruchung

Überbeanspruchung von Kapazität, f
- overutilisation of capacity
- overutilization of capacity

überbelegen etw
- overcrowd s.th.
- overbook s.th.
- fill s.th. beyond capacity

überbelegt, adj
- filled beyond capacity, adj
- overbooked, adj
- overutilised, adj
- overcrowded, adj

überbelegtes Haus, n
- overcrowded house

überbelegtes Hotel n
- overcrowded hotel

überbelegtes Zimmer, n
- overcrowded room

überbelegte Wohnung, f
- overcrowded apartment AE
- overcrowded flat BE

überbelegt sein
- be filled beyond capacity
- be overbooked
- be booked beyond capacity
- be overcrowded
- be overutilised

Überbelegung, f (generell)
- overcrowding

Überbelegung, f (Überbuchung)
→ Überbuchung

überbelegungspolitik, f
→ Überbuchungspolitik

Überbelegungsproblem, n
→ Überbuchungsproblem

Überbelegungsquote, f
→ Überbuchungsquote

überbesetzt, adj
- overstaffed, adj

überbesetzt sein
- be overstaffed

überbesucht, adj
- overvisited, adj

überbesuchtes Gebiet, n
- overvisited area
- overvisited region

überbesucht sein
- be overvisited

überbevölkert, adj
- overpopulated, adj

überbevölkertes Gebiet, n
- overpopulated area

überbewerten etw
- overrate s.th.

überbewertet sein
- be overrated

Überbewertung, f
- overrating

überbezahlen etw
zuviel bezahlen für etw
- overpay s.th.

Überblick, m
Umfrage, f
- survey

Überblick über die Hotelauslastung, m
→ Übersicht über die Hotelauslastung

über Bord werfen (etw)
- jettison (s.th.)

überbreites Bett, n
- extra-wide bed

überbuchen etw
- overbook s.th.

überbucht, adj
- overbooked, adj

überbucht sein
überbelegt sein
- be overbooked

Überbuchung, f
- overbooking

Überbuchung einer Wohnung, f
Wohnungsüberbuchung, f
- overbooking of an apartment AE
- overbooking an apartment AE
- overbooking of a flat BE
- overbooking a flat BE

Überbuchung eines Zimmers, f
Zimmerüberbuchung, f
- overbooking of a room
- overbooking a room

Überbuchungspolitik, f
- overbooking policy

Überbuchungsproblem, n
- overbooking problem
- problem of overbooking

Überbuchungsquote, f
Überbuchungsrate, f
- overbooking rate

Überbuchungsstrategie, f
- overbooking strategy

Überbuchungstechnik, f
- overbooking technique

Überbuchung verhindern
- prevent overbooking

Überbuchung vermeiden
- avoid overbooking

überdacht, adj
- covered, adj

überdachte Ausstellungsfläche, f
- covered exhibition space

überdachte Eisbahn, f
- covered ice rink AE
- covered ice-rink BE

überdachte Frühstücksterrasse f
- covered breakfast terrace

überdachte Garage, f
- covered garage

überdachter Außenflur, m
- covered exterior corridor

überdachter Balkon, m
- covered balcony

überdachter Eingang m
- covered entrance

überdachter Garagenplatz m
- covered garage space

überdachter Gehweg, m
- covered walkway

überdachter Innenhof, m
- covered patio
- covered interior courtyard
- covered interior court
- covered inner courtyard
- covered inner court

überdachter Parkplatz, m (für 1 Auto)
- covered parking place
- covered parking space
- covered parking lot AE

überdachter Parkplatz, m (für mehrere Autos)
- covered parking lot AE
- covered car park BE

überdachter Tennisplatz, m
- covered tennis court

überdachtes Bad, n
überdachtes Becken, n
- covered pool

überdachte Speiseterrasse, f
- covered dining terrace
- covered dining patio

überdachtes Schwimmbad, n
überdachtes Schwimmbecken, n
- covered swimming pool AE
- covered swimming-pool BE

überdachte Terrasse, f
- covered terrace
- covered patio

über das Wochenende
- over the weekend

über das Wochenende bleiben
- stay over the weekend

über dem Meeresspiegel
- above sea level AE
- above sea-level BE

Über den Geschmack läßt sich streiten
- There's no accounting for taste

über die Bühne gehen
- be put on stage
- be staged

überdimensioniert, adj fam
→ übergroß

überdurchschnittlich, adj
- above average, adj
- higher than average, adj

überdurchschnittliche Auslastung, f
- higher than average load factor

überdurchschnittliche Belegung, f
überdurchschnittliche Auslastung, f
- higher than average occupancy

überdurchschnittliche Verweildauer f
- higher than average length of stay

übereilen sich
- rush things

übereilt, adj
- overhasty, adj
- hasty, adj
- precipitate, adj
- rash, adj

übereilte Abreise, f
- overhasty departure
- hurried departure
- hasty departure

Übereilung, f
- haste
- rashness

überernährt, adj
- overnourished, adj
- overfed, adj

überernährt sein
- be overnourished
- be overfed

Überernährung, f
- overnourishment
- overfeeding

überessen sich
- overeat

Überfahrt, f (Meer)
- crossing
- sea crossing
- passage

Überfahrt buchen
- book a crossing

Überfahrt mit dem Luftkissenboot, f
- crossing by hovercraft

Überfahrt mit dem Schiff, f
- crossing by ship
- crossing by boat

Überfahrtszeit, f
- crossing time

Überfall, m
- holdup AE
- hold-up BE
- raid

überfliegen etw
- fly over s.th.
- fly across s.th.

Überflug, m
- overflight

Überflug eines Landes, m
- overflight of a country

überflüssiges Zimmer, n
- superfluous room

Überführung, f (Bauwerk)
Hochstraße, f
Viadukt, n
- flyover BE
- overpass AE
- viaduct

Überführung, f (Beförderung)
→ Beförderung

überfüllt, adj
überlaufen, adj
überbelegt, adj
- overcrowded, adj
- crowded, adj

überfüllter Saal, m
überfüllte Halle, f
- overcrowded hall
- crowded hall

überfüllter Strand, m
überlaufener Strand, m
- crowded beach

überfülltes Zimmer, n
überfüllter Raum, m
- crowded room

überfüllt sein
- be overcrowded
- be crowded

Überfüllung, f
- overcrowding

Übergangsquartier, n
→ vorübergehendes Quartier

Übergangsunterkunft, f
→ vorübergehende Unterkunft

Übergangszeit, f (Epoche)
- transition period

Übergangszeit, f (Umsteigen)
- connecting time
- wait between trains

übergar, adj
übertrieben, adj
- overdone, adj

übergeben sich
- be sick
- vomit

Übergepäck, n
- excess baggage AE
- excess luggage BE

Übergepäckbeförderungspreis, m
- excess baggage fare AE
- excess luggage fare BE

Übergepäckgebühr, f
- excess-baggage charge AE
- excess-baggage fee AE

- excess-luggage charge BE
- excess-luggage fee BE

Übergepäckpreis, m
- excess baggage rate AE
- excess luggage rate BE

Übergepäckstückpreis, m
- excess baggage rate per piece AE
- excess luggage rate per piece BE

Übergepäckzuschlag, m
- excess baggage supplement AE
- excess luggage supplement BE

Übergewicht, n
- excess weight

übergewichtig, adj
- overweight, adj

übergewichtiges Gepäck, n
Gepäck mit Übergewicht, n
- overweight baggage AE
- overweight luggage BE

übergroß, adj
- oversized, adj
- outsize, adj
- outsized, adj

übergroße Portion, f
- oversized portion
- outsize portion
- overgenerous portion

übergroßes Bad, n
- outsized bath
- outsize bath
- oversized bath

übergroßes Badezimmer, n
- oversized bathroom
- outsize bathroom

übergroßes Bett, n
- oversized bed

übergroßes Zimmer, n
- oversized room
- outsize room

überheizen (etw)
- overheat (s.th.)

überheizt, adj
- overheated, adj

überheiztes Zimmer, n
- overheated room

überhöhte Gebühr f
- excessive charge
- excessive fee

überhöhte Miete f
- overcharge of rent

überhöhter Preis, m
- excessive price
- excessive rate

Überholbucht, f
(an einer Straße)
- passing bay

überholen etw
- overtake s.th.

überholen jn
- overtake s.o.

Überholverbot
(Schild)
- No overtaking

Überholverbotschild, n
- No overtaking sign

Überkapazität, f
- overcapacity
- surplus capacity

Überkapazität schaffen
- create overcapacity
- create surplus capacity

überkochen
- boil over

überladen, adj
- overloaded, adj

überladene Fähre, f
- overloaded ferry

überladenes Boot, n
überladenes Schiff, n
- overloaded boat

überladen (etw)
- overload (s.th.)

Überlandbus m
- overland bus
- overland coach BE

Überlandfahrt, f
- overland trip

Überlandreise, f
- overland journey
- overland trip
- overland tour

Überlandreisen, n
Überlandreiseverkehr, m
- overland travel

Überlandroute, f
Überlandstrecke, f
- overland route

überlanges Bett, n
- extra-long bed
- long-boy bed AE
- long boy AE

überlassen jm etw
- let s.o. have s.th.

Überlassung, f
- loan

überlastet sein (Personal)
- be overburdened

überlaufen, adj
- overrun, adj
- overcrowded, adj
- crowded, adj

überlaufener Ort, m
- crowded resort
- overcrowded resort

überlaufenes Gebiet, n (groß)
- overcrowded region
- crowded region

überlaufenes Gebiet, n (klein)
- overcrowded area
- crowded area

überlaufen sein
- be crowded
- be overcrowded

überlaufen sein von Touristen
- be overrun with tourists
- be crowded with tourists
- be overcrowded with tourists
- be touristy

überlaufen von Touristen
- crowded with tourists
- overcrowded with tourists
- overrun with tourists
- touristy prd

Überlebender, m
- survivor

überleben (etw)
- survive (s.th.)

Überlebensexperte, m
- survival expert

Überlebenstrainingslager, n
- survival camp

Überlebenstrainingslager

übermäßige Vorratshaltung, f
♦ overstocking
übermüdet, adj
♦ overtired, adj
Übermüdung, f
♦ overtiredness
Übernachfrage f
♦ excess demand
über Nacht, adv
♦ overnight, adv
über Nacht bleiben
  übernachten
  ♦ stay the night
  ♦ stay for (the) night
  ♦ overnight AE
  ♦ spend the night
übernachten
  über Nacht bleiben
  ♦ stay overnight
  ♦ stay (for) the night
  ♦ overnight AE
  ♦ spend the night
Übernachten, n
  ♦ staying overnight
  ♦ spending the night
  ♦ overnighting AE
übernachten auf einer Holzbank
  ♦ spend the night on a wooden bench
übernachten bei einem Freund
  ♦ stay overnight at a friend's house
übernachten bei Freunden
  ♦ stay the night with friends
  ♦ stay overnight with friends
übernachten bei jm (privat)
  ♦ spend the night at s.o.'s place
  ♦ spend the night at s.o.'s house
  ♦ stay overnight at s.o.'s place
Übernachtender, m
  ♦ person staying overnight
übernachten im Auto
  ♦ spend the night in the car
übernachten im Freien
  übernachten unter freiem Himmel
  ♦ spend the night outdoors
  ♦ spend the night in the open air
  ♦ sleep in the open air
  ♦ sleep in the open
  ♦ sleep outdoors
übernachten in einem Hotel
  ♦ spend the night at a hotel
  ♦ spend the night in a hotel
  ♦ stay the night at a hotel
  ♦ stay the night in a hotel
  ♦ overnight in a hotel AE
übernachten in einer Jugendherberge
  ♦ spend the night at a youth hostel
  ♦ spend the night in a youth hostel
  ♦ overnight in a youth hostel AE
übernachten in X
  ♦ spend the night at X
  ♦ spend the night in X
  ♦ make an overnight stay in X
  ♦ stay the night at X
  ♦ stay the night in X
übernachten unter einem falschen Namen
  ♦ overnight under a false name AE
  ♦ spend the night under a false name
  ♦ stay the night under a false name
übernachten unter einem fremden Namen
  ♦ overnight under an assumed name AE

♦ spend the night under an assumed name
♦ stay the night under an assumed name
übernachten zweimal in einem Hotel
  ♦ stay two nights at a hotel
Übernachter, m
  → Übernachtungsgast
über Nacht heimlich ausziehen
  (ohne zu zahlen)
  ♦ do a moonlight flit BE inform
Übernachtung, f (Aufenthalt)
Ü, f
  ♦ overnight stay
  ♦ one-night stay
  ♦ overnight stop
  ♦ night's stay
  ♦ nt
Übernachtung, f (mit Verpflegungsangabe)
  ♦ bed
  ♦ night
Übernachtung, Frühstück und Abendessen
  ♦ bed, breakfast and dinner
Übernachtung, f (Statistik)
  ♦ night spent
Übernachtung, f (Unterkunft)
  → Übernachtungsunterkunft
Übernachtung arrangieren
  Übernachtung vermitteln
  ♦ arrange an overnight stay
Übernachtung buchen
  ♦ book overnight accommodation
  ♦ reserve overnight accommodation AE
Übernachtungen, f pl
  ♦ nights accommodation pl
  ♦ nights pl
Übernachtungen mit Frühstück, f pl
  ♦ nights with breakfast pl
  ♦ nights breakfast pl
Übernachtungen mit Halbpension, f pl
  ♦ nights on half board pl
  ♦ nights half board pl
Übernachtungen mit Teilpension, f pl
  Übernachtungen mit Teilverpflegung, f pl
  ♦ nights on partial board pl
  ♦ nights on part board pl
  ♦ nights' partial board pl
  ♦ nights' part board pl
Übernachtungen mit Vollpension, f pl
  ♦ nights on full board pl
  ♦ nights full board pl
Übernachtungen sind gestiegen
  ♦ number of nights spent (has) increased
Übernachtungen sind gesunken
  ♦ number of nights spent (has) decreased
Übernachtung in einem Hotel, f
  Hotelübernachtung, f
  ♦ overnight stay in a hotel
  ♦ overnight stay at a hotel
Übernachtung in einem Hotel kostet DM 123
  ♦ one-night stay at a hotel costs DM 123
  ♦ one-night stay in a hotel costs DM 123
Übernachtung in Privatzimmern, f
  ♦ overnight stay in private rooms
  ♦ overnight stay in private houses
Übernachtung kostenlos
  ♦ night free
Übernachtung mit Frühstück, f
  Zimmer mit Frühstück, n
  ♦ b and b
  ♦ b&b
  ♦ B&B

♦ B and B
♦ bed and breakfast
Übernachtung mit Frühstück bieten
  ♦ provide bed and breakfast
Übernachtung mit Frühstück kostet ab DM 123
  ♦ bed and breakfast costs from DM 123
Übernachtung mit Halbpension, f
  ♦ bed and half board
  ♦ bed and demipension AE
  ♦ night's half board
  ♦ night's demipension AE
Übernachtung mit Teilpension, f
  ♦ bed and partial board
  ♦ bed and part board
  ♦ night's partial board
  ♦ night's part board
Übernachtung mit Vollpension, f
  ♦ bed and full board
  ♦ bed and full pension AE
  ♦ night's full board
  ♦ night's full pension AE
Übernachtungsangebot, n (Gegensatz zu Nachfrage)
  ♦ supply of overnight accommodation
  ♦ supply of overnight accommodations AE
  ♦ availability of overnight accommodation
  ♦ availability of overnight accommodations AE
Übernachtungsangebot, n (Palette)
  ♦ range of overnight accommodation
  ♦ range of overnight accommodations AE
  ♦ available overnight accommodation
  ♦ available overnight accommodations AE pl
Übernachtungsanstieg, m
  Übernachtungszunahme, f
  ♦ increase in the number of nights spent
Übernachtungsart, f
  ♦ type of overnight accommodation
Übernachtungsaufenthalt, m (generell)
  Übernachtung, f
  ♦ night's stay
  ♦ one-night stay
  ♦ overnight stay
Übernachtungsaufenthalt, m (Verkehrsmittel)
  ♦ overnight stop
  ♦ overnight halt
Übernachtungsaufenthalt unterwegs, m
  ♦ overnight stop en route
  ♦ overnight halt en route
Übernachtungsaufkommen, n
  Übernachtungsvolumen, n
  ♦ volume of overnight stays
  ♦ volume of nights spent
  ♦ overnight volume
Übernachtungsaufpreis, m
  ♦ overnight surcharge
Übernachtungsbereich, m (abstrakt)
  Übernachtungssektor, m
  ♦ overnight sector
Übernachtungsbereich, m (konkret)
  → Schlafraumbereich
Übernachtungsbesuch, m
  → Logierbesuch
Übernachtungsbetrieb, m
  → Beherbergungsbetrieb
Übernachtungsbuchung, f
  ♦ overnight booking
  ♦ one-night booking
  ♦ booking (of) overnight accommodation
Übernachtungsbuchung annehmen
  Übernachtungsbuchung akzeptieren

- ♦ accept an overnight booking
- ♦ accept a one-night booking

Übernachtungscampingplatz, m
- ♦ overnight campsite
- ♦ overnight campground AE
- ♦ overnight camping site BE
- ♦ overnight camping ground BE
- ♦ overnight site

Übernachtungsform, f
- ♦ form of overnight accommodation

Übernachtungsgast, m (generell)
  Logisgast, m
  Logiergast, m
- ♦ overnight guest
- ♦ overnighter sl
- ♦ one-nighter sl
- ♦ sleeper

Übernachtungsgast, m (Passant)
  → Passant

Übernachtungsgebühr, f
- ♦ overnight charge
- ♦ overnight fee
- ♦ charge per night
- ♦ fee per night

Übernachtungsgebühr für ein Gespann, f
  (Pkw und Wohnwagen)
- ♦ overnight charge for an outfit

Übernachtungsgutschein, m
- ♦ overnight voucher

Übernachtungsheim, n
  → Obdachlosenheim

Übernachtungshotel, n (generell)
- ♦ overnight hotel

Übernachtungshotel, n (Passanten)
  → Passantenhotel

Übernachtungshotel erreichen
- ♦ reach the overnight hotel

Übernachtungskapazität, f
  Schlafraumkapazität, f
- ♦ bedroom capacity
- ♦ capacity of the bedrooms

Übernachtungskosten, pl
  Übernachtungsspesen, pl
- ♦ overnight expenses pl

Übernachtungsmöglichkeit, f
- ♦ overnight facility
- ♦ overnight accommodation

Übernachtungsmöglichkeiten reservieren (lassen)
- ♦ reserve overnight facilities

Übernachtungsort, m
  (bei Benutzung von Verkehrsmitteln)
  Übernachtungsstelle, f
  Übernachtungspunkt, m
  Übernachtungsstation, f
- ♦ overnight stopping point

Übernachtungspauschale, f
- ♦ overnight package

Übernachtungspauschalpreis, m
- ♦ inclusive rate per night
- ♦ inclusive price per night
- ♦ inclusive charge per night

Übernachtungsplatz, m
  (Camping)
- ♦ overnight site

Übernachtungsplus n
  → Übernachtungsanstieg

Übernachtungspreis, m
  Preis pro Übernachtung, m
- ♦ rate per night
- ♦ price per night
- ♦ overnight price
- ♦ overnight (accommodation) rate
- ♦ overnight charge

Übernachtungspreis beträgt DM 123
- ♦ rate per night is DM 123
- ♦ price per night is DM 123
- ♦ nightly rate is DM 123
- ♦ charge per night is DM 123
- ♦ overnight rate is DM 123

Übernachtungspreis pro Teilnehmer, m
  (Konferenz)
- ♦ rate per night per delegate
- ♦ price per night per delegate
- ♦ overnight rate per delegate
- ♦ overnight charge per delegate

Übernachtungspreis schließt etw ein
  Übernachtungspreis beinhaltet etw
- ♦ overnight rate covers s.th.
- ♦ overnight charge covers s.th.
- ♦ overnight price covers s.th.
- ♦ overnight price includes s.th.
- ♦ overnight rate includes s.th.

Übernachtungsrate, f
  → Übernachtungspreis

Übernachtungsreservierung, f
- ♦ overnight reservation

Übernachtungsrückgang, m
  Rückgang der Übernachtungen, m
- ♦ decrease in the number of nights spent

Übernachtungsrückgang verzeichnen
- ♦ record a decrease in the number of nights spent

Übernachtungssachen, f pl
  (Ersatz für nicht angekommenes Gepäck)
  Overnight Kit, m
- ♦ overnight kit

Übernachtungsscheck, m
  → Übernachtungsgutschein

Übernachtungsstadt, f (Großstadt)
- ♦ overnight city
- ♦ city where one spends the night

Übernachtungsstadt, f (kleine Stadt)
- ♦ overnight town
- ♦ town where one spends the night

Übernachtungsstation, f
  → Übernachtungsort

Übernachtungsstatistik, f
- ♦ statistics of nights spent pl

Übernachtungsstelle, f (Heim)
  → Übernachtungsheim

Übernachtungsunterkunft, f
  eine Übernachtungsunterkunft, f
  zwei Übernachtungsunterkünfte, f pl
- ♦ overnight accommodation
- ♦ night's lodging AE
- ♦ lodging for the night AE
- ♦ one night's accommodation
- ♦ two nights' accommodation

Übernachtungsunterkunft anbieten
- ♦ offer overnigt accommodation

Übernachtungsunterkunft reservieren (lassen)
- ♦ reserve overnight accommodation

Übernachtungsverkauf, m
- ♦ bedroom sale
- ♦ sale of a bedroom
- ♦ selling a bedroom

Übernachtungsvertrag, m
  → Beherbergungsvertrag

Übernachtungszahl, f
  Zahl der Übernachtungen, f
- ♦ number of overnight stays
- ♦ number of nights

Übernachtungszahlen steigern
- ♦ increase the number of nights spent

Übernachtungszahl sinkt
- ♦ number of nights spent decreases

Übernachtungszahl steigt an
- ♦ number of nights spent increases

Übernachtungszahl verdoppeln
- ♦ double the number of nights spent

Übernachtungszimmergebühr, f
- ♦ charge per room per night
- ♦ charge for a room per night

Übernachtungszunahme, f
  → Übernachtungsanstieg

Übernachtungszuschlag, m
- ♦ overnight supplement

überportionieren (etw)
- ♦ overportion (s.th.)
- ♦ overdo the portion

überportioniert, adj
- ♦ overportioned, adj
- ♦ overdone, adj

Überportionierung, f
- ♦ overportioning
- ♦ overdoing

Überpreis m
- ♦ exorbitant price
- ♦ exorbitant rate
- ♦ excessive price
- ♦ excessive rate
- ♦ overcharge

Überproduktion, f
- ♦ overproduction

Überprovision, f
  zusätzliche Provision, f
- ♦ overriding commission
- ♦ override AE

überprüfen etw
  prüfen etw
- ♦ check s.th.
- ♦ review s.th.
- ♦ verify s.th.

überprüfen etw anhand von etw
  vergleichen etw mit etw
- ♦ check s.th. against s.th.

Überprüfung, f
- ♦ checking
- ♦ inspection

überpünktlich, adj
- ♦ overpunctual, adj

überpünktlich sein
- ♦ be overpunctual

überqueren etw
- ♦ cross s.th.

überqueren etw zu Fuß
- ♦ cross s.th. on foot

Überquerung der Antarktis, f
  Antarktisüberquerung, f
- ♦ crossing of the Antarctic
- ♦ crossing the Antarctic

überraschender Besuch, m
  Überraschungsbesuch, m
- ♦ surprise visit

überraschen jn
- ♦ surprise s.o.

überrascht werden
- ♦ be surprised
- ♦ come as a surprise to s.o.

Überraschung, f (generell)
- ♦ surprise

Überraschung, f (Geschenk)
→ kleine Überraschung
Überraschungsabend, m
♦ surprise evening
Überraschungsbesuch, m
→ überraschender Besuch
Überraschungsbesucher, m
überraschender Besucher, m
♦ surprise visitor
Überraschungsfest, n
♦ surprise party
Überraschungsfest machen für jn
♦ give s.o. a surprise party
Überraschungsgast m
überraschender Gast m
♦ surprise guest
♦ surprise visitor
Überraschungsgetränk, n
♦ surprise drink
♦ surprise beverage
Überraschungsgrapefruit, f
Überraschungspampelmuse, f
♦ grapefruit surprise
Überraschungsmenü, n
♦ surprise menu
Überraschungsschau, f
Überraschungsshow, f
♦ surprise show
Überraschungsurlaub, m
Überraschungsferien, pl
♦ surprise vacation AE
♦ surprise holiday BE
überregional, adj
♦ supraregional, adj
überregionale Konferenz, f
♦ supraregional conference
überreif, adj
♦ overripe, adj
überreife Traube, f
♦ overripe grape
Überschalldüsenflugzeug, n
Überschalljet, m
♦ supersonic jet
Überschallflug, m
♦ supersonic flight
Überschallflugzeug, n
♦ supersonic aircraft
Überschallgeschwindigkeit, f
♦ supersonic speed
überschätzen etw
♦ overestimate s.th.
Überschätzung, f
♦ overestimation
überschlafen etw
♦ sleep on s.th.
überschlagen sich
(Fahrzeug)
♦ overturn
Überschuß, m
♦ surplus
Überschuß an Unterkünften, m
Überschuß von Unterkünften, m
♦ surplus of accommodations AE
♦ surplus accommodations AE pl
♦ surplus of accommodation BE
♦ surplus accommodation
Überschuß haben
♦ have a surplus
überschüssige Kapazität, f
♦ excess capacity

♦ excess of capacity
♦ surplus capacity
überschüssige Kapazität haben
♦ have some excess capacity
überschüssige Unterkunft, f
♦ surplus accommodation
überschüssige Zimmer, n pl
überzählige Zimmer, n pl
Zimmerüberhang, m
♦ surplus rooms pl
überschütten jn mit Geschenken
♦ shower s.o. with gifts
überschütten jn mit Komplimenten
♦ shower s.o. with compliments
überschwappen
♦ slop over
überschwemmte Straße, f
♦ flooded road
♦ flooded street
Überseeankünfte, f pl
Ankünfte aus Übersee, f pl
♦ overseas arrivals pl
♦ arrivals from overseas pl
Überseeaufenthalt, m
♦ overseas stay
Überseeaussteller, m
Aussteller aus Übersee, m
♦ overseas exhibitor
♦ overseas exhibiter AE
Überseebesuch, m
♦ overseas visit
Überseebesucher, m
Besucher aus Übersee, m
♦ overseas visitor
♦ visitor from overseas
Überseebesucherübernachtung, f
(Statistik)
♦ overseas visitor night
Überseebuchung, f
♦ overseas booking
Überseebüro, n
♦ overseas office
♦ office overseas
Übersee-Erfahrung, f
♦ overseas experience
♦ experience gained overseas
Überseefahrt, f
♦ overseas trip
Überseeferien, pl
Ferien in Übersee, pl
Überseeurlaub, m
Urlaub in Übersee, m
♦ overseas holiday BE
♦ holiday overseas BE
♦ overseas vacation AE
♦ vacation overseas AE
Überseefremdenverkehrsausgaben, f pl
♦ overseas tourist expenditure
Überseegast, m
Gast aus Übersee, m
♦ overseas guest
♦ guest from overseas
Überseehotel, n
♦ overseas hotel
♦ hotel overseas
überseeisch, adj
♦ overseas, adj
Überseekoffer, m
♦ steamer trunk
♦ trunk

Überseeland, n
♦ overseas country
Überseemarketing, n
♦ overseas marketing
Überseemarkt, m
♦ overseas market
Überseenachfrage, f
♦ overseas demand
♦ demand overseas
Überseepauschalreise, f
♦ overseas package tour
♦ overseas inclusive tour
Überseereise, f (generell)
♦ overseas journey
♦ overseas tour
♦ overseas trip
Überseereise, f (Schiff)
♦ overseas voyage
♦ transoceanic voyage
Überseereiseintensität, f
♦ overseas travel intensity
Überseereisemarkt, m
♦ overseas travel market
Überseereisen, n
Überseereiseverkehr, m
♦ overseas travel
♦ traveling overseas AE
♦ travelling overseas BE
Überseereisender, m
♦ tourist traveling overseas AE
♦ tourist travelling overseas BE
Überseerepräsentant, m
Überseevertreter, m
♦ overseas representative
♦ representative overseas
Überseestrecke, f
Überseeroute, f
♦ overseas route
Überseestudent, m
Student aus Übersee, m
♦ overseas student
♦ student from overseas
Überseetelefongespräch, n
♦ overseas telephone call
♦ overseas phone call
Überseetourismus, m
Tourismus aus Übersee, m
♦ overseas tourism
♦ tourism from overseas
Überseetourist, m
Tourist aus Übersee, m
♦ overseas tourist
♦ tourist from overseas
Überseeurlaub, m
Urlaub in Übersee, m
Überseeferien, pl
Ferien in Übersee, pl
♦ overseas vacation AE
♦ vacation overseas AE
♦ overseas holiday BE
♦ holiday overseas BE
Überseeveranstaltung, f
Veranstaltung in Übersee, f
♦ overseas event
♦ event overseas
♦ overseas function
♦ function overseas
♦ overseas activity
Überseeverbindung, f
♦ overseas connection
♦ overseas link

Überseeverkehr, m
  ♦ overseas traffic
Überseezielort, m
  Überseeziel, n
  Überseedestination, f
  ♦ overseas destination
übersehen jn
  ignorieren jn
  ♦ overlook s.o.
  ♦ ignore s.o.
  ♦ disregard s.o.
übersetzen etw
  ♦ translate s.th.
übersetzen jn über einen Fluß
  ♦ ferry s.o. across a river
  ♦ ferry s.o. over a river
Übersetzer m
  ♦ translator
Übersetzung, f
  ♦ translation
Übersetzungskosten, pl
  ♦ translation costs pl
  ♦ translation cost
Übersetzungsanlage, f
  ♦ translation system
Übersetzungsausstattung, f
  Übersetzungstechnik, f
  ♦ translation equipment
Übersetzungsdienst m
  Übersetzungsservice m
  ♦ translation service
Übersetzungseinrichtungen, f pl
  ♦ translation facilities pl
Übersetzungsfirma, f
  ♦ translation company
  ♦ translation firm
Übersetzungsgebühr, f
  ♦ translation charge
  ♦ translation fee
Übersetzungsservice, m
  → Übersetzungsdienst
Übersichtskarte, f
  ♦ large-scale map
  ♦ general map
Übersichtsplan, m
  ♦ general plan
Übersicht über die Hotelauslastung, f
  Überblick über die Hotelauslastung, f
  ♦ survey of hotel occupancy
  ♦ hotel occupancy survey
übers Ohr gehauen werden
  geneppt werden
  ♦ be fleeced
  ♦ be riiped off BE coll
  ♦ be rooked
übers Ohr hauen jn
  neppen jn
  ♦ pull a fast one on s.o.
  ♦ rip s.o. off
  ♦ rook s.o.
  ♦ diddle s.o. fam
übersteigen etw
  überschreiten etw
  ♦ exceed s.th.
Überstunden, f pl
  ♦ overtime
Überstundenbezahlung, f
  ♦ overtime pay
Überstunden machen
  ♦ work overtime
  ♦ do overtime

Überstundenvergütung, f
  ♦ remuneration for overtime
Überstundenzuschlag, m
  ♦ overtime premium
überstürzt, adj
  hastig, adj
  eilig, adj
  ♦ hurried, adj
  ♦ hasty, adj
überstürzt abreisen
  ♦ leave hurriedly
  ♦ depart hurriedly
überstürzte Abreise, f
  überstürzte Abfahrt f
  ♦ hurried departure
  ♦ precipitate departure
  ♦ hasty departure
überstürzten Besuch machen bei etw
  ♦ make a hurried visit to s.th.
überstürzter Besuch, m
  ♦ hurried visit
überteuert, adj
  ♦ overpriced, adj
überteuertes Bier, n
  ♦ overpriced beer
Übertrag, m
  (Buchhaltung)
  ♦ amount carried forward
übertragbar, adj
  ♦ transferable, adj
  ♦ negotiable, adj
übertragbare Fahrtkarte, f
  übertragbare Karte, f
  ♦ transferable ticket
übertragbarer Gutschein, m
  ♦ transferable voucher
Übertragbarkeit, f
  ♦ transferability
übertragbar sein
  ♦ be transferable
Übertragungseinrichtung, f
  ♦ broadcast facility
  ♦ broadcasting facility
überversichert, adj
  ♦ overinsured, adj
überversichert sein
  ♦ be overinsured
überversorgt, adj
  ♦ oversupplied, adj
überversorgt sein mit etw
  ♦ be oversupplied with s.th.
Überversorgung, f
  → Überangebot
überwacht, adj
  bewacht, adj
  ♦ supervised, adj
überwachte Kinderkrippe, f
  ♦ supervised crèche
überwachter Kinderspielplatz, m
  ♦ supervised children's playground
überwachter Parkplatz, m
  → bewachter Parkplatz
überwachtes Bad, n
  überwachtes Becken, n
  ♦ supervised pool
überwachtes Planschbecken, n
  ♦ supervised wading pool AE
  ♦ supervised paddling pool BE
überwachtes Schwimmbad, n
  ♦ supervised swimming pool AE
  ♦ supervised swimming-pool BE

Überwachung des Tourismus, f
  Überwachung des Fremdenverkehrs, f
  Kontrolle des Tourismus, f
  Kontrolle des Fremdenverkehrs, f
  ♦ control of tourism
Überwasserschiff, n
  ♦ surface ship
überweisen etw
  ♦ transfer s.th.
  ♦ remit s.th.
Überweisung, f
  ♦ transfer
  ♦ remittance
  ♦ payment
überwiegend ebener Platz, m
  (Camping)
  ♦ mainly level site
überwintern in X (Person)
  ♦ spend the winter in X
  ♦ spend the winter at X
überwintern (Tier)
  Winterschlaf halten
  ♦ hibernate
überwintern (Winter überstehen)
  ♦ overwinter
über X (Route)
  ♦ via X
  ♦ by way of X
übler Ruf, m
  → schlechter Ruf
übles Gesöff, n fam
  ♦ wicked stuff fam
  ♦ wicked brew fam
üble Spelunke, f
  ♦ low dive
übliche Ausreden auftischen
  ♦ serve up the usual excuses
übliche Gebühr, f
  ♦ usual charge
  ♦ usual fee
übliche Kost, f
  ♦ usual diet
  ♦ usual fare
üblicher Fahrpreis, m
  ♦ usual fare
übrigen Reisenden, die, pl
  ♦ remaining travellers, the pl
  ♦ remaining travelers, the AE pl
übriglassen etw von seiner Portion
  ♦ leave part of one's helping
Übungsfahrt, f
  Trainingsfahrt, f
  Probefahrt, f
  ♦ practice run
Übungsfahrt durchführen
  ♦ carry out a practice run
  ♦ make a practice run
Übungsflug, m
  Trainingsflug, m
  ♦ practice flight
  ♦ training flight
Übungsgelände, n
  ♦ training ground
Übungshang m
  (Ski)
  ♦ practice slope
Übungshotel, n
  → Ausbildungshotel
Übungslager, n
  Trainingslager, n
  ♦ training camp

Übungspiste

Übungspiste, f
(Ski)
♦ practice course
♦ practice run
Übungssegelflugzeug, n
♦ training glider
♦ training sailplane AE
ÜF, f
→ Übernachtung mit Frühstück
Ufer, n (Fluß)
♦ bank
Ufer, n (Meer, Binnensee)
♦ shore
Ufer des Flusses, n
♦ bank of the river
Ufer des Sees, n
Seeufer, n
♦ shore of the lake
Uferpromenade, f (Binnensee)
♦ promenade (along the lake)
♦ lakefront AE
♦ lake front BE
Uferpromenade, f (Fluß)
♦ promenade (along the river)
♦ riverfront AE
♦ river front BE
Uferpromenade, f (Meer)
♦ promenade (along the beach)
♦ seafront AE
♦ sea front BE
Uferseite, f
(bei Ort)
♦ river front
U-Form, f
(Bestuhlung)
♦ U-form style
U-Form-Bestuhlung, f
U-förmige Bestuhlung, f
♦ U-form seating
♦ U-form-style seating
♦ seating arranged in a horseshoe
U-förmig, adj
♦ U-shaped, adj
♦ horseshoe-shaped, adj
U-förmiger Tisch, m
♦ U-shaped table
♦ horseshoe-shaped table
UG, n
→ Untergeschoß
Uganda
♦ Uganda
Ugander, m
♦ Ugandan
Uganderin, f
♦ Ugandan girl
♦ Ugandan woman
♦ Ugandan
ugandisch, adj
♦ Ugandan, adj
Uhr, f
♦ clock
Uhrenindustrie, f
♦ clock industry
♦ watch and clock industry
Uhrenmuseum, n
♦ clock museum
Uhrensammlung, f
♦ collection of clocks
♦ clock collection
Uhrenträger, m *hist*
♦ clock carrier *hist*

Uhrenturm, m
Uhrturm, m
♦ clock tower
Uhrmacher, m
♦ clockmaker
♦ watchmaker
Uhrmacherzentrum, n
♦ clock-making center AE
♦ clock-making centre BE
Ukraine, f
♦ Ukraine, the
Ukrainer, m
♦ Ukrainian
Ukrainerin, f
♦ Ukrainian girl
♦ Ukrainian woman
♦ Ukrainian
ukrainisch, adj
♦ Ukrainian, adj
UK-Reise, f
UK-Tournee, f
♦ UK tour
Ultraleichtflugzeug, n
♦ microlight plane
♦ microlight aircraft
♦ microlight
Ultraleichtzelt, n
♦ ultra-light tent
ultramodern, adj
→ hypermodern
Ultraviolettstrahlung, f
UV-Strahlung, f
UV-Strahlen, m pl
♦ ultraviolet rays *pl*
Umbau, m (andere Nutzung)
♦ conversion
Umbau, m (Gebäudeteil)
umgebauter Teil, m
♦ altered section
Umbau, m (generell)
♦ rebuilding
♦ structural alteration(s)
♦ alteration(s)
♦ reconstruction
♦ structural change
umbauen etw (teilweise)
♦ alter s.th.
umbauen etw (vollständig)
♦ rebuild s.th.
umbauen etw zu einem Hotel
♦ convert s.th. into a hotel
♦ turn s.th. into a hotel
umbauen etw zu einer Wohnung
♦ convert s.th. into an apartment AE
♦ convert s.th. into a flat BE
umbauen etw zu etw
umbauen etw in etw
♦ convert s.th. (in)to s.th.
♦ turn s.th. (in)to s.th.
umbauen zu Wohnungen
♦ convert into apartments AE
♦ convert into flats BE
Umbauprogramm, n
♦ rebuilding program AE
♦ rebuilding programme BE
umbauter Raum, m
♦ enclosed space
umbenennen etw
neu benennen etw
neuen Namen geben etw
♦ rename s.th.

umbetten jn
(Krankenhaus)
♦ move to another bed
Umbrien
♦ Umbria
umbrisch, adj
♦ Umbrian, adj
umbuchbar, adj
♦ rebookable, adj
umbuchen
♦ rebook
♦ change one's booking
♦ change s.o.'s booking
♦ change one's reservation
♦ change reservations
umbuchen auf den 20. Mai
♦ rebook on 20 May
umbuchen auf ein Datum
♦ rebook on a date
umbuchen auf eine andere Reise
♦ transfer to another tour
umbuchen auf eine bessere Serviceklasse
♦ rebook to a better class of service
♦ change to a better class of service
umbuchen auf Samstag
♦ rebook on Saturday
♦ change one's reservation to Saturday
umbuchen in eine höhere Klasse
♦ rebook to a higher category
umbuchen nach einem Ort
♦ rebook to a place
umbuchen nach München
♦ rebook to Munich AE
♦ change one's booking to Munich
umbuchen nach X
♦ rebook to X
Umbuchung, f
♦ rebooking
♦ change of booking
♦ change in booking
♦ change in reservation
♦ change of reservation(s)
Umbuchungsentgelt n
♦ rebooking fee
♦ rebooking charge
Umbuchungserklärung, f
♦ rebooking notification
♦ rebooking statement
Umbuchungsgebühr, f
♦ rebooking charge
♦ rebooking fee
♦ change of booking fee
♦ change of reservation fee
Umbuchungsgrund, m
♦ reason for rebooking
Umbuchung vornehmen
♦ make a rebooking
♦ make a change in reservation AE
um das Mittelmeer
♦ around the Mediterranean
♦ round the Mediterranean
um den Schlaf gebrachter Bewohner, m
♦ sleep-starved resident
um die Welt
♦ around the world
♦ round the world
um die Welt fahren (Auto)
♦ motor around the world
♦ motor round the world
um die Welt fahren (generell)
→ reisen um die Welt

Umkleide

um die Welt fliegen
 ♦ fly around the world
 ♦ fly round the world
um die Welt kreuzen
 ♦ cruise around the world
 ♦ cruise round the world
um die Welt trampen
 ♦ hitchhike around the world *AE*
 ♦ hitchhike round the world *AE*
 ♦ hitch-hike around the world *BE*
 ♦ hitch-hike round the world *BE*
 ♦ hitch (a)round the world
umdisponieren
 ♦ make new arrangements
 ♦ change one's plans
 ♦ redispose
Umdisponierung, f
 ♦ change in arrangements
 ♦ change of arrangements
 ♦ redisposition
umfahren etw
 umgehen etw
 vorbeifahren an etw
 ♦ bypass s.th.
Umfang, m (Ausmaß)
 ♦ extent
Umfang, m (Maßangabe)
 ♦ circumference
Umfang der Dienstleistung, m
 Dienstleistungsumfang, m
 ♦ extent of the service
 ♦ extent of (the) services
Umfang haben von 12 Meilen
 ♦ be 12 miles in circumference
umfangreiche Renovierung, f
 umfassende Renovierung, f
 ♦ extensive renovation
 ♦ extensive refurbishment
umfangreiche Renovierungsarbeit, f
 ♦ extensive renovation work
 ♦ extensive renovation
 ♦ extensive refurbishment work
 ♦ extensive refurbishment
umfangreiche Restaurierung, f
 ♦ extensive restoration
umfangreiche Restaurierung erhalten
 ♦ undergo extensive restoration
umfangreiches Frühstück, n
 ♦ extensive breakfast
umfangreiche Speisekarte, f
 ♦ extensive menu
 ♦ wide-ranging menu *AE*
umfangreiche Speisekarte anbieten
 ♦ offer a comprehensive menu
 ♦ offer an extensive menu
umfangreiches Programm, n
 ♦ extensive program *AE*
 ♦ extensive programme *BE*
umfangreiches Programm bewältigen
 ♦ manage an extensive program *AE*
 ♦ manage an extensive programme *BE*
umfangreiches Programm haben
 ♦ have an extensive program *AE*
 ♦ have an extensive programme *BE*
umfangreiches Renovierungsprogramm, n
 ♦ extensive renovation program *AE*
 ♦ extensive refurbishment program *AE*
 ♦ extensive renovation programme *BE*
 ♦ extensive refurbishment programme *BE*

umfangreiche Umbau- und Renovierungsarbeiten, f pl
 ♦ extensive rebuilding and renovation works *pl*
umfangreiche Weinkarte, f
 ♦ extensive wine list
 ♦ comprehensive wine list
umfassende Ausstellung, f
 ♦ comprehensive exhibition
 ♦ comprehensive exhibit *AE*
 ♦ comprehensive show
umfassender Service, m
 umfassender Dienst, m
 umfassende Dienstleistung, f
 ♦ comprehensive service
umfassende Sanierung, f
 ♦ comprehensive redevelopment
umfassendes Leistungspaket, n
 ♦ comprehensive package of services
umfassende Verpflegung, f
 ♦ comprehensive foodservice *AE*
 ♦ comprehensive catering *BE*
umfassende Werbung, f
 ♦ extensive promotion
Umfrage, f
 ♦ inquiry
 ♦ enquiry
 ♦ survey
Umfrage durchführen
 ♦ carry out a survey
Umfrageergebnis, n
 ♦ survey result
 ♦ result of the survey
Umfrage machen über etw
 Umfrage machen zu etw
 ♦ make an inquiry about s.th.
 ♦ make an enquiry about s.th.
Umgang mit Gästen, m
 Gästeumgang, m
 ♦ dealing with guests
 ♦ relations with guests *pl*
 ♦ guest relations *pl*
Umgang mit Kunden, m
 Kundenumgang, m
 Kundenbeziehung, f
 ♦ dealing with customers
 ♦ customer relations *pl*
Umgangsformen, f pl
 → Manieren
umgebaut, adj (andere Nutzung)
 ♦ converted, adj
umgebaut, adj (renoviert)
 ♦ rebuilt, adj
umgebauter Lieferwagen, m
 (z.B. für Camping)
 ♦ converted van
umgebauter Stall, m (andere Nutzung)
 ♦ converted stable
umgebaute Scheune, f
 ♦ converted barn
umgebautes Gebäude, n (andere Nutzung)
 ♦ converted building
umgebaute Wohnung, f (andere Nutzung)
 ♦ converted apartment *AE*
 ♦ converted flat *BE*
umgeben sein von etw
 ♦ be surrounded by s.th.
umgeben von Luxus
 ♦ surrounded by luxury
 ♦ lapped in luxury
Umgebung, f
 Umland, n

 ♦ surrounding area
 ♦ surroundings *pl*
 ♦ surrounding countryside
 ♦ environs *pl*
Umgebung erkunden
 ♦ explore the surrounding area
 ♦ explore the surroundings
Umgebung ist ideal für etw
 ♦ surrounding area is ideal for s.th.
 ♦ surroundings are ideal for s.th.
Umgebungskarte, f
 ♦ map of the environs
umgehend, adv, (generell)
 ♦ immediately, adv
 ♦ without delay, adv
 ♦ promptly, adv
 ♦ instantly, adv
umgehend, adv (Post)
 ♦ by return (of) mail, adv *AE*
 ♦ by return (of) post, adv *BE*
 ♦ by return, adv
umgehend antworten
 postwendend antworten
 ♦ reply by return (of) mail *AE*
 ♦ reply by return (of) post *BE*
 ♦ reply by return
umgehend beziehbar, adj
 → zum Sofortbezug
Umgehung, f
 Umgehungsstraße, f
 ♦ beltway *AE*
 ♦ bypass
Umgehungsstraße, f
 Umgehung, f
 ♦ bypass
 ♦ beltway *AE*
 ♦ belt *AE*
Umgehungsstraße nehmen
 Umgehung nehmen
 ♦ take the bypass
 ♦ take the beltway *AE*
umgekehrte Reihenfolge, f
 ♦ reverse order
umgeleitet, adj
 ♦ diverted, adj
umgeleiteter Flug, m
 ♦ diverted flight
umgerechnet in Dollar
 ♦ in dollars
umherreisen
 ♦ travel about
 ♦ tour (a)round
umherreisen in Europa
 ♦ travel about Europe
 ♦ tour (a)round Europe
umherstreifen
 wandern
 ♦ roam about
 ♦ rove
 ♦ wander
umherstreifen ziellos
 ♦ roam about aimlessly
umkehren
 ♦ turn back
 ♦ turn round
 ♦ go back
Umkehrpunkt, m (Flug)
 ♦ point of turnaround
Umkleide, f
 → Umkleidekabine

Umkleidebereich

Umkleidebereich, m
♦ changing area
Umkleideeinrichtung, f
Unkleidemöglichkeit, f
♦ changing facility
Umkleidekabine, f
(Schwimmbad etc.)
Umkleide, f
♦ changing cabin
♦ changing cubicle
umkleiden sich
♦ change
umkleiden sich zum Abendessen
♦ change for dinner
♦ dress for dinner
Umkleideraum, m (Garderobe)
→ Garderobe
Umkleideraum, m (generell)
Umkleidezimmer, n
♦ changing room
♦ changeroom AE
Umkleideraum, m (Sport)
♦ locker room
♦ changing room BE
Umkleideräumlichkeiten, f pl
♦ changing facilities pl
Umkleidezimmer, n
→ Umkleideraum
umladen etw (Schiff)
♦ transship s.th.
♦ tranship s.th.
Umladung, f (Schiff)
♦ transshipment
♦ transhipment
Umland, n
♦ surrounding country
Umlaufvermögen, n
♦ current assets pl
umlegen etw auf etw (Kosten)
♦ apportion s.th. to s.th.
Umlegung, f (Kosten)
♦ apportionment
Umlegung, f (Unterkunftswechsel)
→ Changement, Zimmerwechsel
Umlegung der Kosten auf etw, f
Aufteilung der Kosten auf etw, f
♦ apportionment of costs to s.th.
Umlegung der Kosten auf jn, f
Aufteilung der Kosten auf jn, f
♦ apportionment of costs to s.o.
umleiten etw
♦ divert s.th.
Umleitung, f (Aktivität)
♦ rerouting
♦ diversion
Umleitung, f (Strecke)
♦ detour AE
♦ diversion BE
Umleitung benutzen
Umgehung benutzen
♦ use a detour AE
♦ use a diversion BE
Umleitung (Hinweisschild)
♦ Detour (sign) AE
♦ Diversion BE
Umleitungsstrecke, f
→ Umleitung
Umluftheizofen, m
(im Zimmer)
♦ convector heater

Umluftofen, m
(für Speisenbereitung)
♦ convection oven
♦ convector oven
ummauerte Stadt, f (Großstadt)
Stadt mit einer Stadtmauer, f
♦ walled city
ummauerte Stadt, f (kleine Stadt)
Stadt mit einer Stadtmauer, f
♦ walled town
um Mitternacht
♦ at midnight
um nur einige zu nennen
♦ to name but a few
umorganisieren etw
neu organisieren etw
♦ reorganise s.th.
♦ reorganize s.th.
umquartieren jn
verlegen jn
♦ move s.o. to another accommodation
♦ move s.o. to another room
♦ move s.o. to another hotel
umrahmen etw
dienen als Rahmen für etw
♦ serve as a setting for s.th.
Umrahmung, f
(einer Veranstaltung)
♦ frame work
♦ setting
umräumen etw
(Z.B. Zimmer, Möbel)
♦ rearrange s.th.
umrechnen etw
♦ convert s.th.
umrechnen in Dollar
♦ convert into dollars
Umrechnung, f
♦ conversion
Umrechnung in Dollars, f
♦ conversion into dollars
Umrechnungstabelle, f
♦ conversion table
umrühren (etw)
♦ stir (s.th.)
Umsatz, m
♦ sales pl
♦ turnover
Umsatzanstieg, m
♦ sales rise
♦ sales increase
♦ increase in sales
♦ rise in sales
Umsatzbereich, m
(in einem Betrieb)
♦ operated department
Umsatzbereich Getränke, m
♦ operated beverage department
Umsatzbereich Speisen, m
♦ operated food department
Umsatzbereichsrechnung, f
♦ schedule AE
Umsatzerlös, m
♦ gross profit on sales proceeds
♦ gross profit on turnover proceeds
♦ income from sales
♦ income from turnover
Umsatzerlöse, m pl
(Bilanz)
♦ sales pl

Umsatzerlöse Keller, m pl
♦ gross profit on beverage sales
♦ income from beverage sales
Umsatzerlöse Küche, m pl
♦ gross profit on kitchen sales
♦ income from kitchen sales
Umsatzerträge, m pl
♦ sales revenue
Umsatz erzielen von DM 1234
♦ achieve sales of DM 1234
♦ achieve turnover of DM 1234
Umsatzgewinn, m
♦ gross profit on sales
♦ sales gain
Umsatz haben von $ 123
♦ have sales of $ 123
♦ have a turnover of $ 123
Umsatz hochtreiben
Umsatz in die Höhe treiben
♦ boost turnover
♦ boost sales
Umsatzhöhe, f
♦ sales revenue
Umsatz ist abgesackt
♦ sales have slumped
Umsatz kräftig steigern
♦ boost sales
♦ boost turnover
Umsatzmix, m
→ Umsatzzusammensetzung
Umsatz optimieren
♦ maximise sales
♦ maximize turnover
Umsatzpotential, n
♦ sales potential
Umsatz pro Beschäftigter, m
♦ sales per employee pl
♦ turnover per employee
Umsatzprognose, f
♦ sales forecast
Umsatz prognostizieren
♦ forecast sales
♦ forecast turnover
Umsatz pro Jahr, m
♦ sales per year pl
♦ turnover per year
Umsatz pro Monat, m
♦ sales per month pl
♦ turnover per month
Umsatz pro Tag, m
♦ sales per day pl
♦ turnover per day
Umsatz pro Urlaub, m
♦ turnover per vacation AE
♦ sales per vacation AE pl
♦ turnover per holiday BE
♦ sales per holiday BE pl
Umsatz pro Urlauber, m
♦ turnover per vacationer AE
♦ sales per vacationer AE pl
♦ turnover per holidaymaker BE
♦ sales per holidaymaker BE pl
Umsatzprovision, f
♦ sales commission
Umsatz pro Woche, m
♦ sales per week pl
♦ turnover per week
Umsatzrückgang, m
♦ drop in sales
♦ drop in turnover

Umsatz stagniert
♦ turnover stagnates
♦ sales stagnate
Umsatz steigern
♦ increase sales
♦ increase turnover
Umsatzsteigerung, f
♦ sales increase
♦ increase in sales
♦ increase in turnover
Umsatzsteuer, f
♦ sales tax
♦ turnover tax
♦ tax on sales
♦ tax on turnover
♦ receipts tax AE rare
Umsatzstruktur, f
♦ sales structure
♦ structure of sales
♦ turnover structure
♦ structure of turnover
Umsatztantieme, f
(z.B. für Geschäftsführer)
♦ bonus
Umsatzvolumen, n
♦ sales volume
♦ volume of sales
♦ turnover volume
♦ volume of turnover
Umsatzzahl, f
♦ sales figure
♦ turnover figure
Umsatzziel, n
♦ sales goal
♦ target sales pl
Umsatzziel erreichen
♦ meet the sales goal
♦ reach the target sales
Umsatzzusammensetzung, f
Umsatzmix, m
♦ sales mix
Umsatzzusammensetzung untersuchen
♦ analyse the sales mix
♦ analyze the sales mix AE
Umschlag, m ökon
Umsatz, m
♦ turnover
♦ sales pl
Umschulungskurs, m
Umschulungslehrgang, m
♦ retraining course
umsehen sich
♦ browse around
um seinen Urlaub kommen (Ferien)
♦ miss one's vacation AE
♦ miss one's holiday BE
umseitig, adv
♦ overleaf, adv
umsetzen
Umsatz haben
♦ turn over
umsetzen etw
ausführen etw
durchführen etw
♦ implement s.th.
umsonst wohnen (als Gast der Geschäftsleitung)
♦ be a guest of the management
♦ have free quarters
Umsteigebahnhof, m
♦ connecting station

Umsteigekarte, f
♦ transfer ticket
Umsteigen, n
♦ change (of trains etc)
♦ changing (trains etc)
umsteigen (Bus)
♦ change buses
♦ change busses AE
♦ change
umsteigen (Flugzeug)
♦ change planes
♦ change
umsteigen in einen Bus
♦ change to a bus
♦ transfer to a bus
umsteigen in X
♦ change at X
♦ change in X
umsteigen in X in einen anderen Zug
♦ change at X for another train
♦ change in X for another train
umsteigen nach X
♦ change to X
♦ change for X
umsteigen von einem Flug auf einen anderen
♦ change from one flight to another (flight)
umsteigen (Zug)
♦ change trains
♦ change
Umsteigeort, m
Umsteigepunkt, m
♦ connecting point
Umsteigepunkt, m
→ Umsteigeort
Umsteigeverbindung, f
♦ transfer connection
Umtauschkurs, m
→ Wechselkurs
Umtrunk, m
♦ drink
Umtrunk veranstalten
♦ get (s.o.) together for a drink
U-Musik, f
→ Unterhaltungsmusik
Umverteilung f
→ Neuverteilung
Umweg, m
Umwegstrecke, f
♦ detour
Umweg machen
Abstecher machen
♦ make a detour
Umwegstrecke, f
→ Umweg
Umwelt, f
♦ environment, the
Umweltaktion, f
♦ environmental action
Umweltaktionsplan, m
♦ environmental action plan
Umweltaktionsplan erstellen
♦ draw up an environmental action plan
Umweltänderung, f
Umweltveränderung, f
♦ environmental change
Umweltangelegenheit, f
Umweltfrage, f
♦ environmental issue
Umweltaspekt, m
♦ environmental aspect

Umweltausstellung, f
♦ environmental exhibition
♦ environmental exhibit AE
Umweltbeauftragter, m
♦ environmental health officer
Umweltbedeutung, f
Umweltrelevanz, f
♦ environmental relevance
♦ environmental importance
Umweltbedingungen, f pl
♦ environmental conditions pl
umweltbelastend, adj
♦ polluting, adj
♦ harmful to the environment, adj
Umweltbelastung, f
♦ environmental strain
Umweltbelastung mildern
♦ relieve environmental strain
Umweltbereich, m
♦ environmental field
Umweltbewertung, f
♦ environmental evaluation
umweltbewußt, adj
♦ environment-conscious, adj
♦ environmentally aware, adj
umweltbewußter Urlauber, m
♦ environment-conscious vacationer AE
♦ environment-conscious holidaymaker BE
umweltbewußt sein
♦ be aware of the environment
Umweltbewußtsein, n
♦ environmental awareness
Umweltbewußtsein fördern
♦ promote environmental awareness
umweltbewußt werden
♦ become aware of the environment
♦ become environmentally aware
Umwelteinfluß, m
Umweltauswirkung, f
Umweltbelastung, f
♦ environmental impact
Umwelteinstellung, f
Einstellung zur Umwelt, f
♦ attitude towards the environment
umweltempfindlich, adj
umweltsensibel, adj
♦ environmentally sensitive, adj
umweltempfindliches Gebiet, n
♦ environmentally sensitive area
Umweltengagement, n
♦ environmental commmitment
Umwelterhaltung, f
Erhaltung der Umwelt, f
♦ preservation of the environment
♦ conservation of the environment
Umweltfaktor, m
♦ environmental factor
Umweltfolgen, f pl
♦ environmental consequences pl
Umweltfrage, f
Umweltangelegenheit, f
♦ environmental question
♦ environmental issue
umweltfreundlich, adj
♦ environmentally friendly, adj
♦ environment-friendly, adj
umweltfreundlicher Tourismus, m
♦ environment-friendly tourism
♦ environmentally-friendly tourism

umweltfreundliches Hotel

umweltfreundliches Hotel, n
- **environment-friendly hotel**
- **environmentally-friendly hotel**

umweltfreundliches Produkt, n
- **environmentally-friendly product**
- **environment-fiendly product**

umweltfreundliches Transportmittel, n
  umweltfreundliches Verkehrsmittel, n
- **environment-friendly means of transportation** *AE*
- **environment-friendly means of transport** *BE*

Umweltfreundlichkeit, f
- **environmental friendliness**

Umweltgesetz, n
- **environmental law**

Umweltgesetzgebung, f
- **environmental legislation**

Umweltinformation, f
- **environmental information**

Umweltinitiative, f
- **environmental initiative**

Umweltinteresse, n
  Interesse an der Umwelt, n
- **concern for the environment**

umweltinteressiert, adj
- **interested in the environment, adj**
- **environmentally minded, adj**

Umweltkatastrophe, f
- **environmental disaster**

Umweltkontrolle, f
- **environmental control**

Umweltleistungskraft, f
  Umweltleistung, f
- **environmental performance**

Umweltlobby, f
- **environmental lobby**

Umweltmanagement, n
- **environmental management**

Umweltmanager, m
- **environmental manager**
- **environment manager**

Umweltmaßnahme, f
- **environmental measure**

Umweltmerkmal, n
- **environmental feature**

Umweltmesse, f
- **environmental fair**

Umweltminister, m
- **minister of the environment**
- **environment minister**
- **Secretary (of State) for the Environment** *BE*
- **Environment Secretary** *BE*
- **minister for the environment**

Umweltministerium, n
- **ministry of the environment**
- **environment ministry**
- **Environmental Protection Agency** *AE*
- **Department of the Environment** *BE*

Umweltorganisation, f
- **environmental organisation**
- **environmental organization**

umweltorientiert, adj
  umweltbegeistert, adj
- **environmentally minded, adj**

umweltorientierter Kunde, m
- **environmentally-minded customer**

Umweltplanung, f
- **environmental planning**

Umweltpolitik, f
- **environmental policy**

Umweltproblem, n
- **environmental problem**

Umweltproblem lösen
- **solve an environmental problem**

Umweltprogramm, n
- **environmental program** *AE*
- **environment program** *AE*
- **environmental programme** *BE*
- **environment programme** *BE*

Umweltprojekt, n
- **environmental project**

Umweltqualität, f
- **environmental quality**

Umweltressource, f
- **environmental resource**

Umweltschaden, m
  Umweltschädigung, f
- **environmental damage**
- **damage to the environment**

Umweltschaden verursachen
- **cause environmental damage**

Umwelt schädigen
- **damage the environment**

umweltschädlich, adj
- **damaging to the environment, adj**
- **harmful to the environment, adj**
- **ecologically harmful, adj**

Umwelt schonen
  Umwelt verschonen
- **spare the environment**

Umweltschutz, m
  Schutz der Umwelt, m
- **environmental protection**
- **protection of the environment**

Umwelt schützen
- **protect the environment**

Umweltschützer, m
- **environmentalist**
- **conservationist**

Umweltschutzgesetz, n
- **Environmental Protection Act** *BE*

Umweltsektor, m
  Umweltbereich, m
- **environmental sector**

Umweltsensibilität, f
- **environmental sensitivity**

Umweltsünder, m
- **environmental polluter**
- **polluter**

Umwelttechnologie, f
- **environmental technology**

Umwelttourismus, m
- **environmental tourism**

Umwelttourist, m
- **environmental tourist**

umweltverantwortlich, adj
- **environmentally responsible, adj**

umweltverantwortlicher Tourismus, m
- **environmentally responsible tourism**

Umweltverantwortung, f
  Verantwortung gegenüber der Umwelt, f
- **environmental responsibility**
- **responsibility towards the environment**

Umwelt verbessern
- **improve the environment**

Umweltverbesserung, f
  Verbesserung der Umwelt, f
- **environmental improvement**
- **improvement of the environment**

Umweltverbrechen, n
- **environmental crime**

Umweltvergehen, n
- **environmental misdeed**

Umweltverhältnisse, n pl
  Umweltbedingungen, f pl
- **environmental conditions** *pl*

Umweltverhältnisse verbessern
  Umweltbedingungen verbessern
- **improve environmental conditions**

Umwelt verschmutzen
- **pollute the environment**

Umweltverschmutzung, f
- **pollution of the environment**
- **environmental pollution**

umweltverträglich, adj
- **environmentally compatible, adj**

umweltverträglicher Tourismus, m
  nachhaltiger Tourismus, m
  Ökotourismus, m
  ökologischer Tourismus, m
  sanfter Tourismus, m
- **sustainable tourism**
- **ecotourism**
- **ecological tourism**
- **green tourism**
- **soft tourism**

Umweltverträglichkeit, f
- **environmental compatibility**

Umweltverträglichkeitsprüfung, f
- **environmental impact assessment**

Umweltvorschriften, f pl
- **environmental regulations** *pl*

Umweltzerstörung, f
- **destruction of the environment**
- **environmental destruction**

Umweltziel, n
- **environmental objective**

Um wieviel Uhr ist das Abendessen? (Dinner)
  Wann ist das Abendessen?
- **At what time is dinner?**
- **What time is dinner?**

Um wieviel Uhr ist das Abendessen? (Supper)
- **At what time is supper?**
- **What time is supper?**

Um wieviel Uhr ist das Frühstück?
  Wann ist das Frühstück?
- **At what time is breakfast?**
- **What time is breakfast?**

Um wieviel Uhr ist das Mittagessen?
  Wann ist das Mittagessen?
- **At what time is lunch?**
- **What time is lunch?**

Um wieviel Uhr möchten Sie es gern?
- **At what time would you like it?**
- **What time would you like it?**

Um wieviel Uhr reisen Sie ab?
- **At what time are you leaving?**
- **What time are you leaving?**

Um wieviel Uhr soll ich Sie anrufen?
- **At what time would you like me to call you?**
- **What time would you like me to call you?**

Um wieviel Uhr soll ich Sie wecken?
- **At what time shall I wake you?**
- **What time shall I wake you?**

Um wieviel Uhr werden Sie ankommen?
- **What time will you be arriving, Sir?**
- **What time will you be arriving, Madam?**

umziehen auf das Land
- **move to the country**
- **remove (in)to the country**

umziehen (Haus)
- ◆ move house
- ◆ move home

umziehen in ein anderes Hotel
- ◆ move to another hotel

umziehen in ein anderes Zimmer
- ◆ move (in)to another room
- ◆ move from one room to another

umziehen in einen anderen Stadtteil
- ◆ move to another part of the town

umziehen nach Kanada
- ◆ move to Canada

umziehen nach London
move house to London
- ◆ move to London

umziehen sich
Kleider wechseln
- ◆ change one's clothes
- ◆ change

umziehen sich zum Mittagessen
- ◆ change for lunch

umziehen von A nach B
- ◆ move from A to B
- ◆ remove from A to B
- ◆ relocate from A to B

umziehen von einem Hotel in ein anderes
- ◆ move from one hotel to another

umziehen (Wohnung)
- ◆ change apartments AE
- ◆ move flats BE
- ◆ relocate

umziehen (Zimmer)
Quartier wechseln
- ◆ change one's lodgings
- ◆ change one's quarters
- ◆ change

Umzug, m (Festzug)
→ Festzug

Umzug, m (historisch)
→ Festzug

Umzug, m (Möbel)
- ◆ removal
- ◆ relocation

Umzug der Möbel, m
- ◆ removal of furniture

Umzug in ein Zimmer, m
- ◆ removal to a room

Umzugsausgaben, f pl
- ◆ relocation expenses pl
- ◆ removing expenses pl

Umzugsfirma, f
Möbelspeditionsfirma, f
Speditionsfirma, f
- ◆ removal firm BE

Umzugsgeschäft, n
- ◆ removal business

Umzugskosten, pl
- ◆ removal costs pl
costs of moving pl
cost of moving

Umzugskostenzuschuß, m
Umzugszuschuß, m
Umzugsbeihilfe, f
- ◆ relocation allowance
- ◆ removal allowance

Umzugsspezialist, m
- ◆ removal specialist

Umzugswagen, m
Möbelwagen, m
- ◆ removal van BE
- ◆ removing van BE

unabhängig, adj
selbständig, adj
- ◆ independent, adj

unabhängiger Betrieb, m
selbständiger Betrieb, m
Eigentumsbetrieb, m
- ◆ independent operation
- ◆ independent establishment

unangekündigt, adj
unangemeldet, adj
- ◆ unannounced, adj

unangekündigter Besuch, m
unangemeldeter Besuch, m
- ◆ unannounced visit

unangekündigter Besucher, m
unangemeldeter Besucher, m
- ◆ unannounced visitor

unangekündigt kommen
- ◆ arrive unannounced

unangemeldet, adj
ungemeldet, adj
nicht gemeldet, adj
nicht registriert, adj
- ◆ unregistered, adj
- ◆ not registered, adj

unangemeldeter Besucher, m
- ◆ unregistered visitor

unangemeldeter Gast, m
→ ungemeldeter Gast; Passant

unangemeldeter Platz, m
→ ungemeldeter Platz

unangemeldetes Hotel n
nicht angemeldetes Hotel
- ◆ unregistered hotel

unangenehme Arbeit, f
- ◆ unpleasant job

unangenehmen Nachgeschmack hinterlassen
- ◆ leave an unpleasant aftertaste

unangenehme Pflicht, f
- ◆ unpleasant duty

unangenehmer Gast, m
- ◆ unpleasant guest
- ◆ disagreeable guest
- ◆ tiresome guest

Unannehmlichkeit, f
- ◆ inconvenience

Unannehmlichkeiten bereiten jm
- ◆ cause s.o. trouble

unappetitlich, adj
- ◆ unappetising, adj
- ◆ unappetizing, adj

unappetitliche Bar, f
- ◆ unappetising bar
- ◆ unappetizing bar

Unappetitlichkeit f
- ◆ unsavoriness AE
- ◆ unsavouriness BE

unaufdringlich, adj
nicht aufdringlich, adj
- ◆ unobtrusive, adj

unaufdringlicher Service, m
- ◆ unobtrusive service

unaufgeräumtes Zimmer, n
unordentliches Zimmer, n
nicht aufgeräumtes Zimmer, n
- ◆ untidy room

unaufmerksam, adj
- ◆ unattentive, adj

unaufmerksamer Service m
- ◆ unattentive service

unausgezeichnetes Gepäck, n
nicht mit einem Gepäckanhänger versehenes Gepäck, n
- ◆ unlabelled lugagge BE
- ◆ unlabeled baggage AE

unbeantworteter Brief, m
- ◆ unanswered letter

unbebautes Grundstück, n
- ◆ undeveloped plot of land

unbedingt notwendig, adj
- ◆ essential, adj

unbedingt notwendig sein
- ◆ be essential

unbedingt notwendig vorzubuchen
- ◆ essential to book in advance

unbefahrbar, adv (Gewässer)
unschiffbar, adv
- ◆ unnavigable, adj

unbefahrene Straße, f
- ◆ untravelled road
- ◆ untraveled road AE

unbefestigte Straße, f
- ◆ dirt road AE
- ◆ dirt track
- ◆ dirt lane

unbefriedigende Auslastung, f
unbefriedigende Belegung, f
- ◆ unsatisfactory occupancy

unbegleitet, adj
- ◆ unescorted, adj
- ◆ unaccompanied, adj

unbegleitete Person, f
Person ohne Begleitung, f
- ◆ unaccompanied person

unbegleitete Reise, f
Reise ohne Begleitung, f
- ◆ unescorted tour

unbegleitetes Kind, n
Kind ohne Begleitung, f
- ◆ unescorted child
- ◆ unaccompanied child

unbegrenzte Kilometerzahl, f
unbegrenzte Kilometerleistung, f
- ◆ unlimited milage
- ◆ unlimited mileage

unbegrenztes Reisen, n
unbegrenzter Reiseverkehr, m
- ◆ unlimited travel

unbegrenztes Urlaubsvergnügen, n
unbegrenztes Ferienvergnügen, n
- ◆ unlimited vacation pleasure AE
- ◆ unlimited holiday pleasure BE

unbeheizt, adj
→ ungeheizt

unbeheiztes Schwimmbad, n
- ◆ unheated swimming pool AE
- ◆ unheated swimming-pool BE
- ◆ unheated pool

unbeheiztes Zimmer, n
→ ungeheiztes Zimmer

unbehinderte Sicht, f
unbehinderter Blick, m
unbehinderter Ausblick, m
unbehinderte Aussicht, f
- ◆ unrestricted view
- ◆ unobstructed view

unbekannt, adj
- ◆ unknown, adj

unbekannter Gast, m
- ◆ unknown guest

unbekanntes Land, n
♦ unknown country
unbelegt, adj
♦ unoccupied, adj
♦ not occupied, adj
unbelegtes Bett n
♦ unoccupied bed
♦ bed not occupied
unbelegtes Zimmer, n
♦ room not occupied
♦ unoccupied room
unbemanntes Schiff, n
♦ unmanned ship
♦ unmanned boat
unbenutzbar, adj
♦ unusable, adj
Unbenutzbarkeit, f
♦ unusableness
Unbenutzbarkeit der Einrichtungen, f
♦ unusableness of the facilities
unbenutzt, adj
ungenutzt, adj
♦ unused, adj
♦ not used
unbenutztes Appartement, n
♦ unused apartment
unbenutzte Suite, f
♦ unused suite
unbenutztes Zimmer, n
♦ unused room
Unbequemlichkeit, f
♦ discomfort
Unbequemlichkeit und Unannehmlichkeiten ertragen
♦ endure discomfort and inconvenience
unberechtigte Reklamation f
♦ unjustified complaint
unberechtigte Reklamation zurückweisen
♦ reject an unjustified complaint
unbereist, adj
unbefahren, adj
♦ untravelled, adj
♦ untraveled, adj AE
unbereistes Gebiet, n
♦ untravelled area
♦ untraveled area AE
unbereiste Welt, f
♦ untravelled world
♦ untraveled world AE
unberührt, adj
(Natur)
♦ unspoiled, adj
♦ unspoilt, adj BE
♦ untouched, adj
unberührte Küste, f
♦ untouched coast
unberührte Landschaft, f
♦ unspoiled countryside
♦ unspoilt countryside BE
♦ unspoiled landscape
♦ unspoilt landscape BE
♦ unspoiled scenery
unberührte Natur, f
♦ unspoilt Nature
♦ unspoilt Nature BE
unberührter Strand, m
♦ unspoiled beach
♦ unspoilt beach BE
unberührtes Gebiet, n (groß)
♦ unspoiled region
♦ unspoilt region BE

unberührtes Gebiet, n (klein)
♦ unspoiled area
♦ unspoilt area BE
unberührt lassen etw
(Essen)
♦ leave s.th. untouched
unberührt vom 20. Jahrhundert
♦ untouched by the 20th century
unberührt von etw
♦ untouched by s.th.
unbeschädigt, adj
♦ undamaged, adj
unbeschränkte Benutzung von etw, f
unbegrenzte Benutzung von etw, f
♦ unlimited use of s.th.
♦ unrestricted use of s.th.
unbeschränkter Urlaub, m (Arbeitnehmer)
unbegrenzter Urlaub, m
♦ indefinite leave
unbeschränkter Zugang, m
♦ free access
unbeschwerter Urlaub, m
→ sorgenfreier Urlaub
unbesetzt, adj (Personal)
♦ unstaffed, adj
♦ unmanned, adj
unbesetzt, adj (Raum, Platz)
♦ unoccupied, adj
unbesetzten Tisch finden
♦ find an unoccupied table
unbesetzter Tisch, m
unbelegter Tisch, m
♦ unoccupied table
unbestätigt, adj
nicht bestätigt, adj
♦ unconfirmed, adj
unbestätigte Buchung f
♦ unconfirmed booking
unbestätigte Reservierung, f
♦ unconfirmed reservation
unbestätigte Stornierung, f
unbestätigter Rücktritt, m
unbestätigte Absage, f
unbestätigte Annullierung, f
♦ unconfirmed cancellation
♦ unconfirmed cancelation AE
unbewacht, adj
♦ unsupervised, adj
♦ unattended, adj
♦ unguarded, adj
♦ unwatched, adj
unbewachter Parkplatz, m
♦ unsupervised parking lot AE
♦ unsupervised car park BE
♦ unattended parking lot AE
♦ unattended car park BE
unbewachter Platz, m (Camping)
♦ unguarded site
unbewohnbar, adj
♦ uninhabitable, adj
unbewohnt, adj (Gebäude)
♦ unoccupied, adj
♦ vacant, adj
unbewohnt, adj (Gebiet)
♦ uninhabited, adj
unbewohnte Insel, f (bes. in den Tropen)
♦ desert island
unbewohnte Insel, f (generell)
♦ uninhabited island
unbewohntes Haus, n
unbelegtes Haus, n

♦ unoccupied house
♦ vacant house
unbezahlbar, adj (Leistung)
♦ unaffordable, adj
♦ far too expensive
unbezahlbar, adj (Preis)
unerschwinglich, adj
♦ prohibitive, adj
unbezahlte Miete, f
♦ unpaid rent
unbezahlten Urlaub nehmen
♦ take unpaid leave
unbezahlte Rechnung, f (Faktur)
♦ unpaid invoice
unbezahlte Rechnung, f (Lokal)
♦ unpaid bill
♦ unpaid check AE
unbezahlter Urlaub, m (Arbeitnehmer)
♦ unpaid leave
♦ leave without pay
♦ payless vacation AE
unbezahlter Urlaub, m (Beamter)
♦ unpaid furlough
♦ unpaid leave
unbezahlter Urlaub, m (generell)
♦ unpaid vacation AE
♦ unpaid holiday BE
undankbar, adj
♦ ungrateful, adj
undankbarer Gast, m
♦ ungrateful guest
undankbar sein
♦ be ungrateful
Und danach?
(Frage des Kellner)
♦ And to follow, Sir?
♦ And to follow, Madam?
♦ Then to follow?
und vieles, vieles mehr
♦ and much, much more
und vieles andere mehr
♦ and lots more
uneffizienter Service, m
♦ inefficient service
uneinbringliche Außenstände, m pl
♦ bad debts pl
uneingeladen, adj
ungeladen, adj
nicht eingeladen, adj
♦ uninvited, adj
♦ unasked, adj
♦ without invitation
uneingeladener Gast, m
ungeladener Gast, m
♦ uninvited guest
uneingelöster Gutschein, m
unbenutzter Gutschein, m
♦ unused voucher
uneinnehmbar, adj
♦ impregnable, adj
uneinnehmbare Festung, f
♦ impregnable fortress
uneinnehmbar machen etw
♦ make s.th. impregnable
uneinnehmbar sein
♦ be impregnable
unelegant, adj
♦ inelegant, adj
♦ unelegant, adj AE
unentdeckt, adj
♦ undiscovered, adj

unentdeckte Italien, das, n
- undiscovered Italy

unentgeltlich, adj
 kostenlos, adj
- courtesy, adj AE
- free of charge, adj
- free, adj
- complimentary, adj

unerfahren, adj
- inexperienced, adj
- unseasoned, adj

unerfahrener Camper, m
- inexperienced camper

unerfahrener Reisender, m
- inexperienced traveler AE
- unseasoned traveler AE
- inexperienced traveller BE
- unseasoned traveller BE

unerfreuliches Urlaubserlebnis, n
 unangenehmes Ferienerlebnis, n
- unpleasant vacation experience AE
- unpleasant holiday experience BE

Unerkunftszuschuß, m
 Unterkunftsbeihilfe, f
- accommodation allowance

unerledigte Korrespondenz, f
- unanswered letters pl
- unanswered correspondence
- backlog in correspondence

unerschwinglicher Preis, m
- prohibitive price
- prohibitive rate

unerwartet, adj
- unexpected, adj

unerwartet, adv
- unexpectedly, adv

unerwartet ankommen
- arrive unexpectedly

unerwartete Abreise, f
- unexpected departure

unerwartete Ankunft, f
- unexpected arrival

unerwarteter Besuch, m
- unexpected visit

unerwarteter Besucher, m
- unexpected visitor

unerwarteter Gast, m
- unexpected guest

unerwartetes Vergnügen, n
- unexpected pleasure

unerwartete Umstände, m pl
- unexpected circumstances pl

unerwartete Umstände treten ein
- unexpected circumstances arise

unerwünscht, adj
 ungewünscht, adj
- unwanted, adj
- undesirable, adj

unerwünschten Gast abweisen
- reject an unwanted guest
- reject an undesirable guest

unerwünschte Person, f
- unwanted person
- persona non grata
- undesirable person
- undesirable

unerwünschter Ausländer, m
 lästiger Ausländer, m
- undesirable foreigner
- undesirable alien jur
- unwanted foreigner

unerwünschter Dauergast, m humor
 (Person)
- unwanted fixture humor

unerwünschter Gast m
- unwanted guest
- undesirable guest
- undesirable

UNESCO-Weltkulturgut, n (Gebäude)
- UNESCO listed building

unetikettiert, adj
 unausgezeichnet, adj
 ohne Etikett
 ohne Aufschrift
- unlabelled, adj
- unlabeled, adj AE

Unfall, m
- accident

Unfallarzt, m
- casualty doctor

Unfallbeteiligter, m
- person involved in an accident

Unfallflucht, f
- hit-and-run offence
- hit-and-run offense
- hit-and-run driving

Unfall haben
- have an accident

Unfallklinik, f
 Unfallkrankenhaus, n
- casualty hospital

Unfallort, m
- crash site

Unfallstation, f (Erste Hilfe)
- first-aid station

Unfallstation, f (Krankenhaus)
- casualty ward

Unfallstelle, f
 Unfallort, m
- scene of the accident

Unfallverhütung, f
- accident prevention

Unfallversicherung, f
- accident insurance

Unfallversicherung abschließen
- take out an accident insurance policy
- take out an accident insurance

Unfall verursachen
- cause an accident

unfreiwillige Zuhörerschaft, f
- captive audience

unfrequentiert, adj
 unbesucht, adj
- unfrequented, adj

unfreundlich, adj
- unfriendly, adj
- unkind, adj
- unobliging, adj

unfreundlich behandeln jn
- treat s.o. unkindly

unfreundliche Bedienung, f
→ unfreundliche Kellnerin

unfreundliche Kellnerin, f
- disagreeable waitress

unfreundlichen Empfang jm bereiten
- give s.o. a rough welcome sl

unfreundlicher Kellner, m
- unhelpful waiter
- unobliging waiter

unfreundlicher Service, m
- unhelpful service
- unobliging service

unfreundliches Klima, n
 rauhes Klima, n
- inclement climate

unfreundliches Personal, n
- unhelpful staff
- unhelpful personnel
- unobliging staff
- unobliging personnel

unfreundliches Wetter, n
 rauhes Wetter, n
- inclement weather

unfreundliches Zimmer, n
- cheerless room

Ungar, m
- Hungarian

Ungarin, f
- Hungarian girl
- Hungarian woman
- Hungarian

ungarisch, adj
- Hungarian, adj

ungarische Art, adv gastr
 nach ungarischer Art, adv gastr
- Hungarian style, adv gastr

ungarischer Wein, m
 Ungarwein, m
- Hungarian wine

Ungarn
- Hungary

Ungarnreise, f (in Ungarn)
 Ungarnrundreise, f
- tour of Hungary
- tour through Hungary
- Hungarian tour

Ungarnreise, f (nach Ungarn)
 Ungarnfahrt, f
- trip to Hungary
- journey to Hungary
- tour to Hungary

ungastlich, adj
 unwirtlich, adj
- inhospitable, adj

Ungastlichkeit, f
 Unwirtlichkeit, f
- inhospitality
- inhospitableness

ungastlich sein
- be inhospitable

ungebetener Besucher, m
 ungeladener Gast, m
 ungeladener Teilnehmer, m
- gatecrasher

ungebetener Gast, m
- unbidden guest
- uninvited guest

ungebeten erscheinen
- come unasked
- come without being asked
- come without invitation

ungebeten kommen
 ungebeten erscheinen
- gatecrash
- come unasked
- come without being asked
- come without being invited

ungebucht, adj
- unbooked, adj

ungebuchter Flug, m
- unbooked flight

ungedeckter Scheck, m
- uncovered check AE

ungedeckter Tisch

- ◆ dud check *AE*
- ◆ uncovered cheque *BE*
- ◆ dud cheque *BE*
- ◆ rubber check *AE sl*

ungedeckter Tisch, m
- ◆ unlaid table

ungeeignet, adj
- unpassend, adj
- ◆ unsuitable, adj

ungeeignetes Zimmer, n
- ◆ unsuitable room

ungeeignet für Kinder unter acht Jahren
- ◆ unsuitable for children under eight years (of age)

ungefähr, adv
- ◆ approximately, adv
- ◆ about, adv

ungefähre Abreisezeit, f
- ◆ approximate departure time
- ◆ approximate time of departure

ungefähre Abreisezeit angeben
- ◆ give the approximate time of departure
- ◆ give the approximate departure time

ungefähre Abreisezeit mitteilen
- ◆ indicate the approximate time of departure
- ◆ indicate the approximate departure time

ungefähre Ankunftszeit, f
- ◆ approximate arrival time
- ◆ approximate time of arrival

ungefähre Ankunftszeit angeben
- ◆ give the approximate time of arrival
- ◆ give the approximate arrival time

ungefähre Ankunftszeit mitteilen
- ◆ indicate the approximate time of arrival
- ◆ indicate the approximate arrival time

ungefälliges Personal, n
- unfreundliches Personal, n
- ◆ unobliging staff
- ◆ unobliging personnel

ungeführt, adj
- ohne Führer
- ohne Führung
- ◆ unguided, adj

ungeführter Rundgang, m
- ◆ unguided tour

ungegessen, adj
- nicht konsumiert, adj
- ◆ uneaten, adj

ungegessene Mahlzeit, f
- nicht konsumiertes Essen, n
- ◆ uneaten meal

ungegoren, adj
- unvergoren, adj
- ◆ unfermented, adj

ungeheizt, adj
- unbeheizt, adj
- ◆ unheated, adj

ungeheiztes Zimmer, n
- unbeheiztes Zimmer, n
- ◆ unheated room

ungehindert reisen
- frei reisen
- ◆ travel freely

ungekocht, adj (Speise)
- roh, adj
- ◆ uncooked, adj
- ◆ raw, adj

ungekocht, adj (Wasser)
- ◆ unboiled, adj

ungekochte Lebensmittel, n pl
- ◆ uncooked food

ungekochtes Frühstück, n
- ◆ uncooked breakfast

ungekürzter Tarif, m
- ◆ unreduced tariff
- ◆ unreduced rates *pl*
- ◆ unreduced rate
- ◆ unreduced terms *pl*

ungeladen, adj
- → uneingeladen

ungelernte Arbeitskräfte, f pl
- ◆ unskilled labor *AE*
- ◆ unskilled labour *BE*

ungelüftet, adj
- ◆ unaired, adj
- ◆ unventilated, adj

ungelüftetes Zimmer, n
- ◆ unaired room
- ◆ unventilated room

ungemeldeter Campingplatz, m
- nicht angemeldeter Campingplatz, m
- ◆ unregistered campsite
- ◆ unregistered campground
- ◆ unregistered camping site *BE*
- ◆ unregistered camping ground *BE*
- ◆ unregistered site

ungemeldeter Gast, m
- *(nicht im Fremdenbuch eingetragen)*
- ◆ unregistered guest
- ◆ unregistered visitor

ungemeldeter Platz, m (Camping)
- nicht angemeldeter Platz, m
- ◆ unregistered site

ungemütlich, adj
- ◆ uncomfortable, adj

ungemütlicher Schlafsaal, m
- ◆ uncomfortable dormitory

ungemütliches Zimmer, n
- ◆ uncomfortable room

Ungemütlichkeit, f
- ◆ uncomfortableness

Ungemütlichkeit eines Zimmers, f
- Unfreundlichkeit eines Zimmers, f
- ◆ cheerlessness of a room

ungenehmigt, adj
- ohne Genehmigung, adj
- wild, adj
- ◆ unauthorised, adj
- ◆ unauthorized, adj
- ◆ without permission
- ◆ without leave

ungenehmigter Urlaub, m (Arbeitnehmer)
- ◆ absence without leave

ungenießbar, adj (nicht schmackhaft)
- ◆ unpalatable, adj

ungenießbar, adj (unverzehrbar)
- unverzehrbar, adj
- ◆ uneatable, adj
- ◆ inedible, adj
- ◆ undrinkable, adj

ungenießbares Essen, n
- ◆ unpalatable food

Ungenießbarkeit, f (nicht eßbar)
- ◆ inedibility

Ungenießbarkeit, f (nicht schmackhaft)
- ◆ unpalatability
- ◆ distastefulness

ungenügende Buchungen, f pl
- ◆ insufficient bookings *pl*

ungenügende Reservierungen, f pl
- ◆ insufficient reservations *pl*

ungenügend gekocht, adj
- ◆ insufficiently cooked, adj

ungenügend gekochte Kartoffeln, f pl
- ◆ insufficiently cooked potatoes *pl*

ungenutzt, adj
- unbenutzt, adj
- unbeansprucht, adj
- ◆ unutilised, adj
- ◆ unutilized, adj
- ◆ unused, adj

ungenutzte Kapazität, f
- ◆ unutilised capacity
- ◆ unutilized capacity
- ◆ unused capacity

ungeöffnet, adj
- ◆ unopened, adj

ungeöffnete Flasche, f
- ◆ unopened bottle

ungepanscht, adj
- ◆ unadulterated, adj

ungepanschter Wein, m
- ◆ unadulterated wine

ungepflegt adj (Person)
- ◆ untidy, adj
- ◆ scruffy, adj *inform*
- ◆ unkempt, adj

ungeplant, adj
- ◆ unplanned, adj

ungeplante Veranstaltung, f
- ◆ unplanned event
- ◆ unplanned function

ungeräuchert, adj
- ◆ unsmoked, adj
- ◆ uncured, adj

ungern ziehen lassen jn
- ◆ be sorry to see s.o. go

ungesalzen, adj
- ◆ unsalted, adj

ungesalzene Butter, f
- ◆ unsalted butter

ungesäuert, adj (Brot)
- ◆ unleavened, adj

ungeschält, adj
- ◆ unpeeled, adj

ungeschälter Apfel, m
- ◆ unpeeled apple

ungeschmückter Raum, m
- ungeschmücktes Zimmer, n
- ◆ unadorned room

ungestört, adj
- ◆ undisturbed, adj

ungestörte Lage, f
- ◆ undisturbed location
- ◆ undisturbed position
- ◆ undisturbed situation
- ◆ undisturbed setting

ungestörter Blick, m
- ungestörte Aussicht, f
- ◆ uninhibited view
- ◆ uninterrupted view

ungestörter Schlaf, m
- ◆ undisturbed sleep

ungestörtes Alleinsein, n
- ◆ undisturbed privacy

ungesund, adj
- ◆ unhealthy, adj
- ◆ unwholesome, adj
- ◆ bad for your health
- ◆ bad for you

ungesunde Mahlzeit, f
- ◆ unhealthy meal

ungesundes Essen, n
- unhealthy food

ungesüßt, adj
- unsweetened, adj

ungewöhnlichen Ort suchen
- look for an unusual place

ungewöhnliches Glück, n
- bread buttered on both sides
- stroke of luck

ungewöhnliches Hotel, n
- unusual hotel

ungewöhnlich langer Urlaub, m
ungewöhnlich lange Ferien, pl
- unusually long vacation AE
- unusually long holiday BE

ungewohntes Essen, n
- unfamiliar food

Ungeziefer, n
- vermin pl
- bugs pl

Ungeziefer ausrotten
- exterminate vermin

Ungezieferbekämpfung, f
- vermin control
- pest control

ungezwungene Atmosphäre, f
→ entspannte Atmosphäre

ungleichmäßige Auslastung, f
ungleichmäßige Belegung, f
- uneven occupancy

ungültig, adj (Geld)
- uncurrent, adj
- not current, adj

ungültig, adj (generell)
- invalid, adj
- not valid, adj
- null and void, adj
- void, adj

ungültiger Reisepaß, m
abgelaufener Reisepaß, m
- invalid passport

ungültiger Vertrag, m
- invalid contract
- void contract

Ungültigkeit, f
- invalidity
- voidness

ungünstige Lage, f
- unfavorable location AE
- unfavourable location BE
- inconvenient situation
- inconvenient position
- inconvenient location

ungünstigen Eindruck gewinnen
- gain an unfavorable impression AE
- gain an unfavourable impression BE

ungünstiger Eindruck, m
- unfavorable impression AE
- unfavourable impression BE

ungünstiger Wechselkurs, m
- unfavorable exchange rate AE
- unfavourable exchange rate BE

ungünstiges Wetter, n
- adverse weather
- unfavorable weather AE
- unfavourable weather BE

ungünstig gelegen, adj
- inconveniently situated, adj
- inconveniently located, adj
- inconveniently positioned, adj

unharmonisch, adj
- inharmonious, adj

unheilbarer Trinker, m
unheilbarer Säufer, m
- incurable drunkard

unhöflich, adj
- impolite, adj

Unhöflichkeit, f
- impoliteness

unhygienisch, adj
- unhygienic, adj

Uniform, f
- uniform

uniformiert, adj
- uniformed, adj

uniformiertes Hotelpersonal, n
Uniform tragendes Hotelpersonal, n
- uniformed hotel staff
- uniformed hotel personnel

uniformiertes Personal, n
Uniform tragendes Personal, n
- uniformed staff
- uniformed personnel

Universalhotelgutschein, m
- universal hotel voucher

Universalkreditkarte, f
- universal credit card

Universalreisegutschein, m
- universal travel voucher

Universitätsbibliothek, f
- university library

Universitätsferien, pl
- university holidays pl
- vacation

Universitätsgelände, n
Universitätscampus, m
- university campus

Universitätsplatz, m
- university square

Universitätsstadt, f (Großstadt)
- university city

Universitätsstadt, f (kleine Stadt)
- university town

Universitätszimmer, n
Universitätsraum, m
- university room

unklassifizierbares Essen, n
- nondescript food

unkomfortabel, adj
→ ungemütlich

unkontrollierter Tourismus, m
- uncontrolled tourism

unkonventionell, adj
- unconventional, adj

unkonventionelles Getränk, n
- unconventional beverage
- unconventional drink

unkonventionelles Hotel, n
- unconventional hotel

Unkosten, pl
→ Kosten

unlauteren Wettbewerb verhindern zwischen A und B
- prevent unfair competition between A and B

unlauterer Wettbewerb, m
- unfair competition

unlizenziertes Reisebüro, n
(ohne IATA-Lizenz etc.)
- unappointed travel company AE
- travel promoter AE

unmarkiert, adj (Weg)
- unmarked, adj (path)

unmarkierter Stellplatz, m (Camping)
→ unparzellierter Stellplatz

unmarkierter Stellplatz, m (Parken)
- unmarked parking space
- unmarked parking place
- unmarked parking lot AE

Unmassen von Touristen, pl
Schwärme von Touristen, m pl
- shoals of tourists pl

unmäßiger Alkoholgenuß, m
Unmäßigkeit, f
- crapulence

Unmäßigkeit, f
Zügellosigkeit, f
unmäßiger Alkoholgenuß, m
Trunksucht, f
- intemperance

Unmenge von Besuchern, f
Masse von Besuchern, f
Besuchermasse, f
- host of visitors

unmittelbare Arbeitskosten, pl
- direct labor costs AE pl
- direct labour costs BE pl

unmittelbare Nähe von etw, f
- immediate vicinity of s.th.
- immediate proximity of s.th.

unmittelbarer Materialaufwand, m
- direct materials costs pl
- direct materials cost

unmittelbare Umgebung, f
nähere Umgebung, f
- immediate surroundings, the pl
- immediate vicinity

unmittelbar vor der Ankunft
- immediately before the arrival
- immediately prior to the arrival

unmöbliert, adj
- unfurnished, adj

unmöbliertes Appartement n
- unfurnished apartment

unmöbliertes Haus, n
- unfurnished house
- unfurnished home

unmöbliertes Quartier, n
- unfurnished lodging
- unfurnished quarters pl

unmöbliertes Zimmer, n
- unfurnished room

unmöblierte Wohnung, f
- unfurnished flat BE
- unfurnished apartment AE

Unmögliches fertigbringen
- manage the impossible

unordentliches Zimmer, n
- disorderly room
- untidy room

Unordentlichkeit, f
- untidiness
- disorderliness

unparzelliert, adj (Camping)
- unmarked, adj (camping)

unparzellierter Stellplatz, m (Camping)
- unmarked pitch

unpassierbar, adj
- impassable, adj

unpassierbare Straße, f
- impassable road
- impassable street

unpassierbar sein

unpassierbar sein
(Straße)
♦ be impassable
unpersönlich, adj
♦ impersonal, adj
unpersönliche Atmosphäre, f
neutrale Atmosphäre f
♦ impersonal atmosphere
unpersönlicher Service m
♦ impersonal service
unpersönliche Umgebung, f
♦ impersonal surroundings pl
unpersönlich möbliert, adj
♦ impersonally furnished, adj
unpersönlich möbliertes Zimmer, n
♦ impersonally furnished room
unpfändbar, adj jur
♦ unseizable, adj jur
unprofessionell, adj
nicht professionell, adj
♦ unprofessional, adj
unprofessioneller Service, m
nicht professioneller Service, m
♦ unprofessional service
unpünktlich, adj (generell)
♦ unpunctual, adj
unpünktlich, adj (verspätet)
→ verspätet
unpünktliche Abfahrt, f
verspätete Abfahrt, f
unpünktliche Abreise, f
verspätete Abreise, f
♦ tardy departure
unpünktliche Abreise, f
→ unpünktliche Abfahrt
unpünktliche Ankunft, f
verspätete Ankunft, f
♦ tardy arrival
Unpünktlichkeit, f
♦ unpunctuality
unpünktlich sein (generell)
♦ be unpunctual
unpünktlich sein (verspätet)
→ verspätet sein
unrentabel, adj
♦ unprofitable, adj
Unrentabilität, f
♦ unprofitableness
unrentable Nebenstrecke stillegen
(Eisenbahn)
♦ close an uneconomic branch line
unrentables Hotel, n
♦ unprofitable hotel
unrentable Strecke, f
unrentable Route, f
♦ unprofitable route
unsachgemäße Lagerung, f
♦ careless storage
unsauber, adj
schmutzig, adj
♦ messy, adj
♦ dirty, adj
Unsauberkeit, f
♦ uncleanliness
Unsauberkeit eines Zimmers, f
♦ uncleanliness of a room
unschlagbar, adj
♦ unbeatable, adj
unschlagbare Auswahl, f
♦ unbeatable choice

unschlagbare Auswahl anbieten an etw
♦ offer an unbeatable choice of s.th.
♦ offer an unbeatable selection of s.th.
unschlagbarer Preis, m
♦ unbeatable price
♦ unbeatable rate
unschlagbares Preis-/Leistungsverhältnis, n
♦ unbeatable value for money
unschlagbares Preis-/Leistungsverhältnis anbieten
♦ offer unbeatable value for money
unschmackhaft, adj
unappetitlich, adj
♦ unsavory, adj AE
♦ unsavoury, adj BE
Unser Küchenchef empfiehlt
♦ Our chef suggests
unsichtbare Erträge, m pl
passive Erträge, m pl
♦ invisible earnings pl
unsichtbare Exporte, m pl
→ passive Dienstleitungen
unsichtbare Importe, m pl
unsichtbare Einfuhren, f pl
♦ invisible imports pl
unsinkbar, adj
♦ unsinkable, adj
unstetes Leben, n
♦ unsettled life
♦ nomadic life
unstillbar, adj (Durst)
♦ unquenchable, adj
unstillbar, adj (Hunger)
♦ insatiable, adj
unstillbarer Appetit, m
♦ insatiable appetite
unstillbarer Durst, adj
♦ unquenchable thirst
unstillbarer Hunger, m
♦ insatiable hunger
unstillbar sein (Durst)
♦ be unquenchable
unstillbar sein (Hunger)
♦ be insatiable
untadeliger Service, m
♦ flawless service
untenerwähnt, adj
unten erwähnt, adj
♦ below-mentioned, adj
♦ mentioned below, adj
unter ... Jahren
♦ under the age of ... years
unter 12 Jahren
unter zwölf Jahren
♦ under 12 years (of age)
♦ under twelve years (of age)
♦ under the age of twelve years
Unterägypten
♦ Lower Egypt
unter Alkoholeinfluß
unter dem Einfluß von Alkohol
♦ under the influence of alcohol
♦ under the influence coll
Unterauslastung f
→ Unterbeanspruchung
unter Ausschluß der Öffentlichkeit
hinter verschlossenen Türen
hinter geschlossenen Türen
♦ in camera jur
♦ behind closed doors

Unteraussteller, m
♦ subexhibitor
♦ subexhibiter AE
unterbeanspruchen etw
♦ underutilse s.th.
♦ underutilize s.th.
♦ underuse s.th.
unterbeansprucht, adj
♦ underutilised, adj
♦ underutilized, adj
♦ underused, adj
♦ not used to capacity, adj
unterbeanspruchte Kapazität, f
♦ underutilised capacity
♦ underutilized capacity
♦ underused capacity
unterbeanspruchte Zeit, f
♦ underutilised period
♦ underutilized period
♦ underused period
unterbeansprucht sein
♦ be underused
♦ be underutilized
♦ be underutilised
♦ not be used to capacity
♦ not be used to the full
Unterbeanspruchung, f
(von Kapazität)
Unterbelegung, f
♦ underutilisation
♦ underutilization
unterbelegen etw
♦ underbook s.th.
unterbelegt, adj (Kapazität)
♦ underused, adj
♦ underutilisaed, adj
♦ not fully occupied (utilised), adj
♦ not full, adj
♦ not filled to capacity, adj
unterbelegt, adj (Kurs)
♦ undersubscribed, adj
unterbelegtes Hotel, n
♦ underutilised hotel
♦ underbooked hotel
unterbelegt sein
♦ be booked below capacity
♦ be underbooked
♦ be underutilised
♦ be not fully occupied
♦ be underused
Unterbelegung, f (Beanspruchung)
→ Unterbeanspruchung
Unterbelegung, f (Unterbuchung)
→ Unterbuchung
Unterbelegungsquote, f
→ Unterbuchungsquote
unterbesetzt, adj
♦ understaffed, adj
unterbesetzt sein
♦ be understaffed
unterbesucht, adj
♦ undervisited, adj
unterbesuchtes Gebiet, n
♦ undervisited area
♦ undervisited region
unterbesucht sein
♦ be undervisited
Unterbett n
→ unteres Bett

unterbewerten etw
♦ underrate s.th.
♦ undervalue s.th.
unterbewertet sein
♦ be underrated
♦ be undervalued
unterbezahlt, adj
♦ underpaid, adj
unterbieten etw
♦ undercut s.th.
unterbieten sich gegenseitig
♦ undercut one another
♦ undercut each other
unterbrechen (eine Fahrt)
♦ break (a journey)
unterbrechen etw (generell)
♦ interrupt s.th.
♦ disrupt s.th.
Unterbrechung, f (Fahrt)
♦ break
Unterbrechung, f (generell)
♦ interruption
Unterbrechung der Fahrt, f
Fahrtunterbrechung, f
♦ break of (the) trip
Unterbrechung der Reise, f
Reiseunterbrechung, f
♦ break of (the) journey
♦ break of (the) tour
♦ interruption of the journey
♦ stopover
unterbringen jm in einem Zelt
♦ accommodate s.o. in a tent
♦ put s.o. up in a tent
unterbringen jn
beherbergen jn
♦ fix s.o. (up) AE coll
♦ lodge s.o.
♦ put s.o. up BE coll
♦ accommodate s.o.
unterbringen jn bei jm
♦ accommodate s.o. with s.o.
♦ put s.o. up with s.o.
♦ put s.o. up at s.o.'s place
unterbringen jn billig
♦ lodge s.o. cheaply
♦ accommodate s.o. cheaply
♦ put s.o. up cheaply
unterbringen jn für eine Nacht
Nachtquartier jm geben
♦ accommodate s.o. for a night
♦ put s.o. up for a night BE coll
♦ fix s.o.up for the night AE coll
unterbringen jn in Baracken
♦ accommodate s.o. in barracks
unterbringen jn in einem Doppelzimmer
♦ put s.o. up in a double room
♦ accommodate s.o. in a double room
unterbringen jn in einem Einzelzimmer
♦ put s.o. up in a single room
♦ accommodate s.o. in a single room
unterbringen jn in einem Heim
♦ put s.o. into a home
unterbringen jn in einem Hotel
einquartieren jn in einem Hotel
♦ book s.o. into a hotel
♦ put s.o. up in a hotel
♦ put s.o. up at a hotel
unterbringen jn in einem Krankenhaus
♦ put s.o. into a hospital

unterbringen jn in einem Zimmer
♦ put s.o. up in a room
♦ accommodate s.o. in a room
unterbringen jn in einem Zweibettzimmer
♦ put s.o. up in a twin-bed room
♦ accommodate s.o. in a twin-bed room
unterbringen jn in einer Baracke
♦ put s.o. up in a barrack
unterbringen jn in etw (generell)
♦ accommodate s.o. in s.th.
♦ put s.o. up in s.th.
unterbringen jn in etw (Krankenhaus, Heim)
♦ put s.o. into s.th.
unterbringen jn kostenlos
♦ accommodate s.o. free of charge
♦ accommodate s.o. free
unterbringen jn privat
♦ put s.o. up in a private house
♦ accommodate s.o. in a private house
unterbringen jn vorläufig
♦ accommodate s.o. provisionally
♦ put s.o. up provisionally
unterbringen jn vorübergehend
♦ accommodate s.o. temporarily
♦ put s.o. up temporarily
Unterbringung erfolgt bei einer Familie
♦ accommodation is with a family
♦ accommodation will be with a family
Unterbringung erfolgt in Doppelzimmern
♦ accommodation is in double rooms
♦ accommodation will be in double rooms
Unterbringung erfolgt in einem sehr guten Hotel
♦ accommodation is in a very good hotel
♦ accommodation will be in a very good hotel
Unterbringung erfolgt in Einzelzimmern
♦ accommodation is in single rooms
♦ accommodation will be in single rooms
Unterbringung erfolgt in Privathäusern
♦ accommodation is in private houses
♦ accommodation will be in private houses
Unterbringung erfolgt in X
♦ accommodation is in X
♦ accommodation will be in X
Unterbringung erfolgt in Zelten
♦ accommodation is in tents
♦ accommodation will be in tents
Unterbringung erfolgt in Zweibettzimmern
♦ accommodation is in twin-bed rooms
♦ accommodation will be in twin-bed rooms
Unterbringung im Hotel, f
Unterkunft im Hotel, f
♦ accomodation in the hotel
♦ accommodation at the hotel
♦ hotel accommodation
Unterbringungsart, f
→ Unterkunftsart
Unterbringungsgebühr, f
Unterkunftsgebühr, f
Logisgebühr, f
♦ accommodation charge
♦ accommodation fee
Unterbringungsgebühr erheben
♦ levy an accommodation charge
♦ levy an accommodation fee
Unterbringungskategorie, f
Unterkunftskategorie, f
♦ category of accommodation
♦ accommodation category
Unterbringungsvorschlag, m
♦ accommodation suggestion

Unterbringungsvorschlag machen
♦ make an accommodation suggestion
unterbrochene Reise, f (Seereise, lange Reise)
♦ broken voyage
unterbucht, adj
unterbelegt, adj
♦ underbooked, adj
unterbucht sein
unterbelegt sein
nicht ausgelastet sein
♦ be underbooked
Unterbuchung, f
Unterbelegung, f
♦ underbooking
Unterbuchungsquote, f
Unterbelegungsquote, f
Unterbelegungsrate, f
Unterbuchungsrate, f
♦ underbooking rate
Unterdeck, n
unteres Deck, n
♦ lower deck
Unterdeckkabine, f
♦ lower deck cabin
unter dem Meeresspiegel
♦ below sea level AE
♦ below sea-level BE
unter dem Motto
mit dem Motto
♦ under the motto
♦ with the motto
unter dem Motto stehen
♦ have as a motto
unter dem Namen von X
♦ under the name of X
unter dem Tisch
♦ under the table
unter Denkmalschutz stehen
denkmalgeschützt sein
♦ be listed
unter der Dusche
♦ in the shower
unter der gemeinsamen Schirmherrschaft von jm
♦ under the joint auspices of s.o.
unter der Leitung von Herrn A
♦ under the management of Mr A
unter der Regie von jm
♦ directed by s.o.
unter der Schirmherrschaft von jm
♦ under the patronage of s.o.
♦ under s.o.'s patronage
♦ under the auspices of s.o.
♦ under s.o.'s auspices
unterdurchschnittlich, adj
♦ below average, adj
♦ lower than average, adj
♦ subaverage, adj
unterdurchschnittliche Verweildauer f
♦ lower than average length of stay
unter einem falschen Namen
♦ under a false name
unter einem fremden Namen
unter einem angenommenen Namen
♦ under an assumed name
unter einem Tropenhimmel
♦ under a tropical sky
untere Kategorie, f
♦ lower category
untere Koje, f
untere Schlafkoje, f
♦ lower berth

Unterelsaß

Unterelsaß, n
  (Region)
  ♦ Lower Alsace
Unterengadin n
  (Region)
  ♦ Lower Engadine
unter englischer Leitung
  ♦ under English management
unterentwickelt, adj
  ♦ underdeveloped, adj
untere Preiskategorie, f
  untere Preisklasse, f
  ♦ lower price category
  ♦ bottom price range
untere Preisklasse, f
  untere Preiskategorie, f
  ♦ bottom price range
  ♦ bottom price bracket
  ♦ lower price category
unterernährt, adj
  ♦ undernourished, adj
unterernährt sein
  ♦ be undernourished
Unterernährung, f
  ♦ undernourishment
unterer Stock, m
  → unteres Stockwerk
unteres Bett, n (Etagenbett)
  Unterbett, n
  ♦ lower bed
  ♦ lower bunk
unteres Bett, n (Schlafkoje)
  → untere Koje
unteres Preissegment, n
  ♦ lower price segment
  ♦ lower rate segment
unteres Stockwerk, n
  untere Etage, f
  unteres Geschoß, n
  ♦ lower floor
unteres Tischende, n
  Tischende, n
  ♦ foot of the table
  ♦ end of the table
Unterfranken
  (Region)
  ♦ Lower Franconia
unter freiem Himmel übernachten
  ♦ sleep under the open sky
  ♦ sleep in the open
  ♦ sleep outdoors
Unterführung, f (Fußgänger)
  Fußgängerunterführung, f
  ♦ pedestrian underpass AE
  ♦ underpass
  ♦ pedestrian subway BE
  ♦ subway BE
Unterführung, f (generell)
  ♦ underpass
untergärig, adj
  ♦ bottom-fermented, adj
untergäriges Bier, n
  ♦ bottom-fermented beer
Untergärung, f
  ♦ bottom fermentation
untergebracht sein in einem Zimmer mit drei Betten
  ♦ be accommodated in a room with three beds
  ♦ be put up in a room with three beds

untergebracht sein (Person)
  ♦ be accommodated
  ♦ be put up
untergebracht sein (Sache)
  ♦ be housed
Untergeschoß, n
  → Souterrain
Untergrundbahn, f
  → U-Bahn
Unterhaardt, f
  (Region)
  ♦ Lower Haardt, the
Unterhalt, m
  (einer Person)
  ♦ keep
Unterhalt bezahlen
  (einer Person)
  ♦ pay for one's keep
unterhaltend, adj
  → unterhaltsam
unterhaltendes Programm, n
  ♦ entertaining program AE
  ♦ entertaining programme BE
unterhalten (jn)
  ♦ entertain (s.o.)
unterhalten jn vom Nachmittag bis in die Nacht
  ♦ entertain s.o. from the afternoon into the night
unterhaltsam, adj
  unterhaltend, adj
  ♦ entertaining, adj
unterhaltsamer Ausflug, m
  ♦ entertaining outing
Unterhaltung
  (Kapitelüberschrift)
  ♦ Where to go
Unterhaltung, f (Vergnügen)
  ♦ entertainment
  ♦ amusement
Unterhaltung, f (Wartung)
  → Wartung, Instandhaltung
Unterhaltung anbieten
  ♦ offer entertainment
Unterhaltung bieten
  für Unterhaltung sorgen
  ♦ provide entertainment
Unterhaltung bringen
  ♦ put on entertainment
Unterhaltung für Familien, f
  ♦ family entertainment
Unterhaltung für jeden Geschmack, f
  ♦ entertainment for every taste
Unterhaltung im Freien, f
  ♦ outdoor entertainment
Unterhaltung ist dürftig
  ♦ entertainment is poor
Unterhaltung ist knapp
  ♦ entertainment is scarce
Unterhaltung organisieren
  ♦ lay on entertainment fam
Unterhaltung organisieren für jn
  ♦ organise entertainment for s.o.
Unterhaltung reicht von X bis Y
  ♦ entertainment ranges from X to Y
Unterhaltungsabend, m
  ♦ evening of entertainment
Unterhaltungsabteilung, f
  ♦ entertainments department
  ♦ entertainments division

Unterhaltungsagentur, f
  Unterhaltungsvermittlung, f
  ♦ entertainment agency
Unterhaltungsangebot, n (Offerte)
  ♦ entertainment offered
Unterhaltungsangebot, n (Palette)
  ♦ range of entertainment
Unterhaltungsarchitektur, f
  ♦ entertainment architecture
Unterhaltungsbedürfnis, n
  ♦ need of entertainment
  ♦ entertainment need
Unterhaltungsbedürfnisse befriedigen
  ♦ fulfill the entertainment needs AE
  ♦ fulfil the entertainment needs BE
Unterhaltungsbetrieb, m
  ♦ entertainments establishment
  ♦ entertainments operation
Unterhaltungsclub, m
  ♦ entertainment club
Unterhaltungsdirektor, m
  Unterhaltungschef, m
  ♦ entertainments director
Unterhaltungseinrichtung, f
  ♦ entertainment facility
Unterhaltungsform, f
  Form der Unterhaltung, f
  ♦ form of entertainment
Unterhaltungsführer m
  (Buch)
  ♦ entertainment guide
Unterhaltungsgeschäft, n
  ♦ entertainment business
Unterhaltungsgewerbe, n
  ♦ entertainments trade
Unterhaltungshauptstadt, f
  ♦ entertainment capital
Unterhaltungsindustrie, f
  ♦ entertainments industry
Unterhaltungskonzern, m
  ♦ entertainments group
Unterhaltungskonzert, n
  ♦ entertainment concert
Unterhaltungskonzession, f
  ♦ entertainment license
  ♦ entertainment licence
Unterhaltungskosten, pl (Amüsement)
  ♦ entertainment costs pl
  ♦ entertainment cost
Unterhaltungskosten, pl (Instandhaltung)
  → Instandhaltungskosten
Unterhaltungsleistung, f
  → Unterhaltungsservice
Unterhaltungslokal, n
  Vergnügungsstätte, f
  ♦ place of entertainment
  ♦ entertainment spot coll
Unterhaltungsmarkt, m
  ♦ entertainment market
Unterhaltungsmöglichkeit, f
  ♦ entertainment possibility
  ♦ entertainment facility
Unterhaltungsmusik, f
  U-Musik, f
  ♦ popular music
  ♦ light music
Unterhaltungsort, m
  ♦ entertainment venue
Unterhaltungspersonal, n
  ♦ entertainment staff
  ♦ entertainment personnel

Unterhaltungsprogramm, n
- entertainment program *AE*
- entertainment programme *BE*
- program of entertainments *AE*
- programme of entertainments *BE*

Unterhaltungsprogramm bieten
- provide an entertainment program *AE*
- provide an entertainment programme *BE*

Unterhaltungsprogramm erweitern
- increase the entertainment program *AE*
- increase the entertainment programme *BE*

Unterhaltungspromoter, m
- entertainment promoter

Unterhaltungsraum, m
Unterhaltungszimmer, n
- entertainment room

Unterhaltungssaal, m
- entertainment hall
- entertainments hall

Unterhaltungsschau, f
Unterhaltungsshow, f
- entertainment show

Unterhaltungsservice, m
Unterhaltungsdienst, m
Unterhaltungsdienstleistung, f
Unterhaltungsleistung, f
- entertainment service

Unterhaltungsspezialist, m
- entertainments specialist

Unterhaltungsszene, f
- entertainment scene

Unterhaltungsteam, n
- entertainment team

Unterhaltung suchen
- seek entertainment
- look for entertainment

Unterhaltungsveranstalter, m
- entertainment organiser

Unterhaltungsveranstaltung, f
- entertainment activity
- entertainment show
- entertainment

Unterhaltungswert, m
- entertainment value

Unterhaltungszentrum, n
- entertainment center *AE*
- entertainment centre *BE*

Unterhaltungszimmer, n
→ Unterhaltungsraum

unter Hausarrest stellen jn
- place s.o. under house arrest

unterirdisch, adj
- underground, adj

unterirdische Garage, f
→ Tiefgarage

unterirdische Ladenpassage, f
- underground shopping mall
- underground shopping arcade

unterirdische Reise, f
Reise unter der Erde, f
- underground trip
- underground journey

unterirdischer Raum, m
- subterranean room

unterirdischer See, m
- underground lake

unterirdischer Tunnel, m
- underground tunnel

unterirdisches Parkhaus, n
→ Tiefgarage

unterirdische Stadt, f (groß)
- underground city

unterirdische Stadt, f (klein)
- underground town

unterirdisches Zimmer, n
unterirdischer Raum, m
- underground room

Unteritalien
- Lower Italy

Unterkapazität, f
- undercapacity

Unterkühlung, f
Untertemperatur, f *med*
Hypothermie, f *med*
- hypothermia *med*

Unterkunft, f (generell)
Unterkünfte, f pl
- accommodation
- lodging *AE*
- accommodations *AE pl*

Unterkunft, f (Obdach)
→ Obdach

Unterkunft, Frühstück und Abendessen benötigen
- require accommodation, breakfast and dinner

Unterkunft anbieten
- offer accommodation

Unterkunft arrangieren
→ Unterkunft beschaffen

Unterkunft aussuchen
Unterbringung aussuchen
- choose accommodation

Unterkunft auswählen
Unterbringung auswählen
- select accommodation

Unterkunft belegen
- occupy accommodation

Unterkunft benötigen
- require accommodation

Unterkunft benutzen
- use the accommodation
- use accommodation

Unterkunft bereitstellen
Unterkunft stellen
- provide accommodation

Unterkunft bereitstellen für die Reisenden
Unterkunft den Reisenden bieten
- provide accommodation for the travellers *BE*
- provide accommodations for the travelers *AE*

Unterkunft bereitstellen für jn
- provide s.o. with accommodation
- provide accommodation for s.o.
- provide s.o. with lodgings

Unterkunft beschaffen
- arrange accommodation

Unterkunft besichtigen
- view the accommodation

Unterkunft besorgen
Unterkunft beschaffen
Unterkunft vermitteln
- arrange for accommodation

Unterkunft besorgen für jn
Unterkunft vermitteln an jn
Quartier besorgen für jn
- arrange accommodation for s.o.

Unterkunft besteht aus zwei Zimmern
- accommodation consists of two rooms

Unterkunft bezahlen
Unterbringung bezahlen
- pay for accommodation
- pay for one's accommodation

Unterkunft bieten für Familien
Unterkünfte bieten für Familien
- provide accommodation for families
- provide accommodations for families *AE*

Unterkunft buchen
Unterkünfte buchen
- book accommodation
- book accommodations *AE*
- book accommodation *BE*

Unterkünfte für 123 Gäste haben
- have accommodations for 123 guests *AE*
- have accommodation for 123 guests *BE*

Unterkünfte für jeden Geschmack und Geldbeutel
- accommodations for every taste and budget *AE pl*
- accommodation for every taste and budget *BE*

Unterkünfte gibt es in Hülle und Fülle
- accommodation is plentiful

Unterkunft erfolgt in Doppelzimmern
→ Unterbringung erfolgt in Doppelzimmern

Unterkunft erfolgt in Privathäusern
→ Unterbringung erfolgt in Privathäusern

Unterkunft erfolgt in X
→ Unterbringung erfolgt in X

Unterkunft erfolgt in Zweibettzimmern (generell)
(mit Doppelbett oder zwei Einzelbetten)
- accommodation is in two-bedded rooms
- accommodation is in two-bed rooms

Unterkunft erfüllt die Ansprüche
Unterkunft erfüllt die Anforderungen
- accommodation meets one's requirements

Unterkunft erfüllt nicht die Erwartungen
- accommodation does not meet one's expectations

Unterkunft erhalten (durch die Unterkunftsvermittlung)
- obtain accommodation (through the accommodation
- service)

Unterkünfte sind knapp
- accommodations are scarce *AE pl*
- accommodation is scarce *BE*

Unterkünfte sind primitiv
- accommodations are rough and ready *AE*
- accommodation is rough and ready *BE*

Unterkünfte sind sehr einfach
- accommodations are basic *AE*
- accommodation is basic *BE*

Unterkunft finden (für jn)
- find accommodation (for s.o.)

Unterkunft freigeben an jn
Unterkunft zurückgeben an jn
- release accommodation to s.o.

Unterkunft füllen
- fill accommodation

Unterkunft für die nächste Nacht, f
- accommodation for the following night

Unterkunft für die Nacht, f
- lodging for the night
- accommodation for the night
- night's lodging

Unterkunft für die Nacht finden
- find accommodation for the night
- find a lodging for the night

Unterkunft für jn, f
Unterbringung für jn, f
- accommodation for s.o.

Unterkunft für Verheiratete, f
(Militär)
Unterbringung für Verheiratete, f
- married accommodation *AE*

Unterkunft geben jm

Unterkunft geben jm
♦ give s.o. accommodation
♦ provide s.o. with accommodation
♦ fix accommodation for s.o. *AE inform*
♦ fix s.o. up with a place to stay *AE inform*
Unterkunft im Freien f
♦ outdoor accommodation
Unterkunft im Haus, f
(für das Personal)
♦ live-in accommodation
Unterkunft im Hotel Ihrer Wahl, f
Unterbringung im Hotel Ihrer Wahl, f
♦ accommodation at the hotel of your choice
♦ accommodation in the hotel of your choice
Unterkunft im Privatbesitz, f
Unterkunft in Privatbesitz, f
♦ accommodation in private ownership
♦ privately owned accommodation
Unterkunft im voraus reservieren
♦ reserve accommodation in advance
♦ make an advance reservation of accommodation
Unterkunft in Anspruch nehmen
Unterkunft beziehen
♦ take up accommodation
Unterkunft in ausgewählten Hotels, f
Unterbringung in ausgewählten Hotels, f
♦ accommodation at selected hotels
♦ accommodation in selected hotels
Unterkunft in der unteren Preislage f
♦ low-priced accommodation
Unterkunft in Doppelzimmern, f
Unterbringung in Doppelzimmern, f
♦ accommodation in double rooms
Unterkunft in einem Bauernhaus, f
Unterbringung in einem Bauernhof, f
Bauernhausunterkunft, f
Bauernhofunterbringung, f
♦ farmhouse accommodation
♦ farmhouse lodging *AE*
Unterkunft in einem Doppelzimmer, f
Unterbringung in einem Doppelzimmer, f
♦ accommodation in a double room
Unterkunft in einem Einzelzimmer, f
Unterbringung in einem Einzelzimmer, f
♦ accommodation in a single room
Unterkunft in einem Hotel, f
Unterbringung in einem Hotel, f
♦ accommodation at a hotel
♦ accommodation in a hotel
Unterkunft in einem Zweibettzimmer, f (2 Betten)
♦ accommodation in a twin-bed room
♦ accommodation in a twin-bedded room
Unterkunft in einem Zweibettzimmer, f (generell)
(mit Doppelbett oder zwei Einzelbetten)
Unterbringung in einem Zweibettzimmer, f
♦ accommodation in a two-bedded room
♦ accommodation in a two-bed room
Unterkunft in Einzelzimmern, f
Unterbringung in Einzelzimmern, f
♦ accommodation in single rooms
Unterkunft in mittlerer Preislage f
♦ medium-priced accommodation
Unterkunft in Zweibettzimmern, f
(mit zwei einzelnen Betten)
Unterbringung in Zweibettzimmern, f
♦ accommodation in twin-bed rooms
♦ accommodation in twin-bedded rooms
Unterkunft in Zweibettzimmern, f (generell)
(mit Doppelbett oder zwei Einzelbetten)
Unterbringung in Zweibettzimmern, f

♦ accommodation in two-bedded rooms
♦ accommodation in two-bed rooms
Unterkunft irgendwo finden
♦ fix up somewhere *AE coll*
Unterkunft ist behelfsmäßig
Unterkunft ist mehr schlecht als recht
♦ accommodation is rough and ready
Unterkunft ist einfach
♦ accommodation is plain
Unterkunft ist mehr schlecht als recht
→ Unterkunft ist behelfsmäßig
Unterkunft ist primitiv
♦ accommodation is rough
Unterkunft ist sehr einfach
Unterkunft ist ohne jeden Komfort
♦ accommodation is basic
Unterkunft ist spartanisch
♦ accommodation is spartan
Unterkunft ist ungenutzt
Unterkunft is unbenutzt
♦ accommodation is unused
Unterkunft ist unterbeansprucht
♦ accommodation is underutilised
♦ accommodation is underutilized
Unterkunft kaufen
♦ buy accommodation
Unterkunft mit Bedienung, f
Unterkunft mit Service, f
♦ serviced lodging *AE*
♦ serviced accommodation
♦ service accommodation
Unterkunft mit Frühstück benötigen
♦ require accommodation and breakfast
♦ require bed and breakfast
Unterkunft mit Halbpension f
♦ accommodation with half board
♦ accommodation with demi-pension
Unterkunft mit hohem Standard, f
hochwertige Unterkunft, f
♦ high-standard accommodation
Unterkunft mit hohem Standard benutzen
hochwertige Unterkunft benutzen
♦ use high-standard accommodation
Unterkunft mit integrierten Sanitäreinrichtungen,f
♦ en-suite accommodation
Unterkunft mit Selbstversorgung, f
→ Selbstverpflegungsunterkunft
Unterkunft mit Service, f
Unterkunft mit Bedienung, f
♦ serviced accommodation
♦ service accommodation
♦ serviced lodging *AE*
Unterkunft mit unverwechselbarem Charakter, f
♦ character accommodation
Unterkunft mit Verpflegung, f
→ Unterkunft und Verpflegung
Unterkunft mit vier Schlafzimmern, f
♦ four-bedroom accommodation
Unterkunft mit Vollpension f
♦ accommodation with full board
♦ accommodation with full pension
Unterkunft ohne Service, f
Unterkunft ohne Bedienung, f
♦ nonserviced accommodation *AE*
♦ non-serviced accommodation *BE*
Unterkunft ohne Verpflegung
nur Unterkunft
nur Übernachtung
nur Zimmer
♦ accommodation only
♦ AO

♦ room only
♦ European Plan
♦ EP
Unterkunft organisieren
♦ fix (up) accommodation
unterkunftorientiertes Hotel n
♦ accommodation-oriented hotel *AE*
♦ accommodation-orientated hotel *BE*
Unterkunft reservieren
♦ reserve accommodation
♦ reserve one's accommodation
Unterkunft reservieren in einem Hotel
♦ reserve accommodation at a hotel
Unterkunftsanbieter, m
Unterkunftsgeber, m
♦ accommodation supplier
♦ accommodation provider
♦ supplier of accommodation
♦ provider of accommodation
Unterkunftsanforderung, f
Unterkunftserfordernis, n
♦ accommodation requirement
Unterkunftsanfrage, f
♦ accommodation inquiry
♦ accommodation enquiry
♦ letter inquiring about accommodation
♦ letter enquiring about accommodation
♦ letter requesting accommodation
Unterkunftsangebot, n (Gegensatz zu Nachfrage)
♦ accommodation supply
♦ supply of accommodations *AE*
♦ supply of accommodation *BE*
♦ supply of lodging *AE*
♦ supply of lodgings *AE*
Unterkunftsangebot, n (offeriert)
angebotene Unterkunft, f
offerierte Unterkunft, f
♦ accommodation on offer
Unterkunftsangebot, n (Offerte)
♦ offer of accommodation
Unterkunftsangebot, n (Palette)
♦ range of accommodations (offered) *AE*
♦ range of accommodation (offered) *BE*
♦ variety of lodging *AE*
♦ variety of lodgings *AE*
Unterkunftsangebot erhalten
Unterkunftsofferte erhalten
♦ receive an offer of accommodation
Unterkunftsangebot erweitern (Palette)
♦ increase the range of accommodations *AE*
♦ increase the range of accommodation *BE*
Unterkunftsangebot verbessern
♦ improve the supply of accommodations *AE*
♦ improve the supply of accommodation *BE*
Unterkunftsangebot verstärken
♦ enhance the accommodation supply
♦ enhance the supply of accommodation
Unterkunftsanzahlung, f
♦ accommodation deposit
Unterkunftsarrangement, n
Unterbringungsarrangement, n
Unterbringungsvorkehrungen, f pl
♦ accommodation arrangement
♦ accommodation arrangements *pl*
Unterkunftsart, f
Unterbringungsart, f
Beherbergungsart, f
♦ accommodation type
♦ type of accommodation
♦ type of lodging *AE*

Unterkunftsnachweis

Unterkunftsausgaben, f pl
 → Unterkunftsspesen
Unterkunftsauslastung, f
 Unterkunftsbelegung, f
 ♦ accommodation occupancy
Unterkunftsbeispiel, n
 ♦ accommodation example
Unterkunftsberatung, f
 ♦ accommodation advice
 ♦ advice on accommodation
Unterkunftsbereich, m (abstrakt)
 Unterkunftssektor, m
 ♦ accommodation field
 ♦ accommodation sector
Unterkunftsbereich, m (konkret)
 → Schlafbereich
Unterkunftsbereitsteller, m
 → Unterkunftsgeber
Unterkunftsbereitstellung, f
 Bereitstellung von Unterkunft, f
 ♦ provision of accommodation
 ♦ providing accommodation
Unterkunftsbeschreibung, f
 ♦ description of the accommodation
 ♦ accommodation description
Unterkunftsbestand, m
 ♦ accommodation stock
 ♦ stock of accommodation
Unterkunftsbestandteil, m
 ♦ accommodation component
Unterkunftsbestellung, f
 Unterkunftsbuchung, f
 ♦ booking (of) accommodation
 ♦ booking (of) a room
Unterkunftsbetreiber, m
 → Beherbergungsunternehmer
Unterkunftsbetrieb, m
 Beherbergungsbetrieb, m
 ♦ accommodation establishment
 ♦ accommodation operation
 ♦ lodging establishment AE
 ♦ lodging operation AE
 ♦ establishment of the hotel trade
Unterkunftsbezahlung, f
 ♦ payment for accommodation
Unterkunftsblock, m
 ♦ accommodation block
Unterkunftsbon, m
 → Unterkunftsgutschein
Unterkunftsbuchung, f
 Unterkunftsbestellung, f
 ♦ accommodation booking
 ♦ booking (of) accommodation
 ♦ reservation of accommodation AE
Unterkunftsbüro, n
 → Unterkunftsvermittlung
Unterkunftseinheit f
 (Statistik)
 ♦ accommodation unit
Unterkunftseinnahmen, f pl
 ♦ accommodation takings pl
 ♦ accommodation income
 ♦ accommodation receipts pl
 ♦ accommodation revenue
Unterkunftseinrichtung, f (Stätte)
 Unterkunftsstätte, f
 ♦ accommodation facility
 ♦ lodging facility AE
Unterkunftseinteilung, f
 Unterkunftsklassifizierung, f
 ♦ classification of accommodation

Unterkunftseintrag, m
 (z.B. in einem Verzeichnis)
 ♦ accommodation entry
Unterkunftseinzelheiten, f pl
 ♦ accommodation details pl
Unterkunft selbst besorgen sich
 ♦ arrange one's own accommodation
Unterkunftsengpaß m
 ♦ accommodation bottleneck
Unterkunftsengpaß vermeiden
 ♦ avoid an accommodation bottleneck
Unterkunftserfassung, f
 Unterkunftsanmeldung, f
 ♦ accommodation registration
 ♦ registration of accommodation
 ♦ registration of accommodations AE
Unterkunftsform, f
 Form der Unterkunft, f
 Form der Unterbringung, f
 ♦ form of accommodation
Unterkunftsführer, m
 (Buch)
 ♦ accommodation guide
 ♦ accommodation guidebook
Unterkunftsgeber, m
 Unterkunftsbereitsteller, m
 Unterkunftsanbieter, m
 ♦ accommodation provider
 ♦ provider of accommodation
 ♦ accommodation supplier
 ♦ supplier of accommodation
Unterkunftsgebühr, f
 Logisgebühr, f
 Unterbringungsgebühr, f
 ♦ accommodation fee
 ♦ accommodation charge
Unterkunftsgebühr erheben
 ♦ levy an accommodation fee
 ♦ levy an accommodation charge
Unterkunftsgeschäft, n
 → Beherbergungsgeschäft
Unterkunftsgutschein, m
 Unterkunftsbon, m
 Quartiergutschein, m
 ♦ accommodation voucher
Unterkunftshaus, m
 (offizielle Bezeichnung)
 ♦ lodging house BE
Unterkunftshinweis, m
 ♦ tip on where to stay
Unterkunftshinweise (Überschrift)
 (in Publikationen)
 Hotelliste
 ♦ Where to stay
Unterkunft sich selbst besorgen
 ♦ make one's own arrangements for
  accommodation
 ♦ make one's own accommodation arrangements
Unterkunftsimmobilie, f
 ♦ accommodation property
Unterkunftsinformation, f
 ♦ accommodation information
Unterkunftsinformationsführer, m
 ♦ accommodation information guide
Unterkunftskapazität, f
 ♦ accommodation capacity
 ♦ capacity of accommodation
Unterkunftskartei f
 ♦ accommodation index
Unterkunftskategorie, f
 Beherbergungskategorie, f

 ♦ accommodation category
 ♦ category of accommodation
Unterkunftskategorie Ihrer Wahl, f
 Unterbringungskategorie Ihrer Wahl, f
 ♦ accommodation category of your choice
Unterkunftskette, f
 ♦ accommodation chain
Unterkunftsklassifizierung, f
 ♦ accommodation classification
 ♦ classification of accommodation
Unterkunftsklassifizierungsplan, m
 Unterkunftsklassifizierungsprojekt, n
 ♦ accommodation classification scheme
Unterkunftsklassifizierungssystem, n
 ♦ accommodation classification system
Unterkunftsknappheit, f
 ♦ accommodation shortage
 ♦ shortage of accommodations AE
 ♦ shortage of accommodation BE
Unterkunftskonsortium, n
 ♦ provision of accommodation consortium
Unterkunftskontingent, n
 ♦ allocation of accommodation
 ♦ allotment of accommodation
Unterkunftskosten, pl
 Unterbringungskosten, pl
 Beherbergungskosten, pl
 ♦ costs of accommodation pl
 ♦ cost of accommodation
 ♦ accommodation costs pl
 ♦ accommodation cost
Unterkunftsleistung, f
 → Beherbergungsleistung
Unterkunftsliste, f
 Unterkunftsverzeichnis, n
 Gastgeberverzeichnis, n
 ♦ accommodation list
 ♦ list of accommodations AE
 ♦ list of accommodation BE
Unterkunftsmangel, m (Knappheit)
 ♦ shortage of accommodation
 ♦ shortage of accommodations AE
 ♦ accommodation shortage
Unterkunftsmangel, m (völliges Fehlen)
 ♦ lack of accommodations AE
 ♦ lack of accommodation BE
Unterkunftsmarketing, n
 ♦ accommodation marketing
 ♦ marketing (of) accommodation
Unterkunftsmarkt, m
 Beherbergungsmarkt, m
 ♦ accommodation market
 ♦ lodging market AE
Unterkunftsmöglichkeit, f
 Unterbringungsmöglichkeit, f
 ♦ possibility of accommodation
 ♦ accommodation possibility
 ♦ accommodation facility
Unterkunftsnachfrage, f
 ♦ accommodation demand
 ♦ demand for accommodation
 ♦ lodging demand AE
 ♦ demand for lodging AE
Unterkunftsnachweis, m jur
 ♦ accommodation certificate jur
Unterkunftsnachweis, m
 Unterkunftsvermittlung, f
 Zimmernachweis, m
 Zimmervermittlung, f
 ♦ accommodation agency
 ♦ accommodation bureau

Unterkunftsniveau

- ♦ room agency
- ♦ accommodations office *AE*

Unterkunftsniveau, n
- ♦ level of accommodation

Unterkunftspräferenz, f
- → Unterkunftsvorliebe

Unterkunftspreis, m
- Unterbringungspreis, m
- Logispreis, m
- ♦ accommodation rate
- ♦ accommodation price
- ♦ accommodation charge
- ♦ lodging rate *AE*
- ♦ lodging price *AE*

Unterkunftspreis festsetzen
- ♦ price accommodation

Unterkunftspreis ist in dem Gesamtpreis enthalten
- ♦ accommodation charge is included in the total
- ♦ price

Unterkunftsproblem, n
- Unterbringungsproblem, n
- ♦ accommodation problem

Unterkunftsproblem haben
- Unterbringungsproblem haben
- ♦ have an accommodation problem

Unterkunftsproblem lösen
- Unterbringungsproblem lösen
- ♦ solve an accommodation problem

Unterkunftsprodukt, n
- → Beherbergungsprodukt

Unterkunftsprogramm, n
- ♦ accommodation scheme

Unterkunftsprospekt, m
- ♦ accommodation brochure

Unterkunftsquartier, n
- → Quartier

Unterkunftsraum, m
- (Gegensatz zu Büroraum)
- ♦ accommodation room
- ♦ lodging room *AE*

Unterkunftsrechnung, f
- ♦ accommodation bill
- ♦ bill for accommodation

Unterkunftsregister, n
- (z.B. bei Verkehrsamt)
- Unterkunftsverzeichnis, n
- ♦ accommodation register

Unterkunftsregistrierung, f
- → Unterkunftserfassung

Unterkunftsreklame, f
- ♦ accommodation advertisement

Unterkunftsreservierung, f
- Unterkunftsbereithaltung, f
- ♦ reservation of accommodation
- ♦ accommodation reservation
- ♦ reserving accommodation

Unterkunftsreservierung vornehmen
- ♦ make a reservation of accommodation

Unterkunftssektor, m
- ♦ accommodation sector

Unterkunftsspesen, pl
- Unterkunftsausgaben, f pl
- ♦ accommodation expenses *pl*

Unterkunftsstandard, m
- ♦ accommodation standard
- ♦ standard of accommodation

Unterkunftsstätte, f
- → Unterkunftseinrichtung

Unterkunftssteuer f
- ♦ accommodation tax

Unterkunftsstornierung, f
- Unterkunftsabsage, f
- Unterkunftsrückritt, m
- ♦ cancellation of accommodation
- ♦ cancelation of accommodation *AE*
- ♦ cancelling accommodation
- ♦ canceling accommodation *AE*

Unterkunftsstruktur, f
- ♦ accommodation structure
- ♦ structure of accommodation

Unterkunftssuchdienst, m
- ♦ accommodation-finding service

Unterkunftssuche, f
- ♦ accommodation search
- ♦ search for accommodation
- ♦ looking for accommodation

unterkunftssuchend, adj
- ♦ accommodation-seeking, adj

Unterkunftstabelle, f
- Unterkunftsdiagramm, n
- ♦ accommodation chart

Unterkunftstarif, m
- ♦ accommodation tariff
- ♦ accommodation rates *pl*
- ♦ accommodation rate
- ♦ accommodation terms *pl*

Unterkunft steht kurzfristig zur Verfügung
- ♦ accommodation is available at short notice

Unterkunft steht zur Verfügung
- ♦ accommodation is available

Unterkunft stornieren
- Unterkunft absagen
- Unterkunft rückgängig machen
- ♦ cancel accommodation

Unterkunftstrakt, m
- → Schlafraumtrakt

Unterkunftstyp, m
- Unterkunftsart, f
- ♦ type of accommodation
- ♦ accommodation type
- ♦ type of lodging *AE*

Unterkunftsüberschuß m
- Beherbergungsüberschuß m
- ♦ excess of accommodations *AE*
- ♦ excess of accommodation *BE*

Unterkunftsuche, f
- ♦ search for accommodation
- ♦ looking for accommodation
- ♦ seeking accommodation

Unterkunftsuche einstellen
- ♦ give up looking for accommodation
- ♦ give up seeking accommodation

Unterkunft suchen
- eine Unterkunft suchen
- ♦ look for accommodation
- ♦ be looking for accommodation
- ♦ seek accommodation

Unterkunftsuchender, m
- ♦ person looking for accommodation
- ♦ person seeking accommodation
- ♦ accommodation seeker

Unterkunftsumsatz, m
- → Beherbergungsumsatz

Unterkunftsvereinbarung, f
- Unterbringungsvereinbarung, f
- ♦ accommodation arrangement

Unterkunftsverkauf, m
- ♦ sale of accommodation
- ♦ selling (of) accommodation

Unterkunftsvermittlung, f
- Unterkunftsnachweis, m
- Zimmervermittlung, f
- ♦ accommodation service
- ♦ accommodation bureau
- ♦ accommodation office
- ♦ accommodation agency

Unterkunftsvermittlungsdienst, m
- → Unterkunftsvermittlung

Unterkunftsverzeichnis, n
- ♦ accommodation directory

Unterkunftsvorliebe, f
- Unterkunftspräferenz, f
- ♦ accommodation preference

Unterkunftswahl, f
- ♦ choice of accommodation
- ♦ choice of lodging *AE*
- ♦ choosing accommodation

Unterkunftswesen, n
- ♦ lodging industry *AE*
- ♦ accommodation industry

Unterkunftswunsch, m
- ♦ accommodation request
- ♦ request for accommodation

Unterkunftszuschlag m
- ♦ accommodation supplement

Unterkunftszuschuß, m
- Unterbringungszuschuß, m
- ♦ accommodation subsidy
- ♦ accommodation allowance

Unterkunft teilen mit jm
- ♦ share accommodation with s.o.

Unterkunft überwachen
- ♦ monitor accommodation

Unterkunft umfaßt vier Zimmer
- ♦ accommodation comprises four rooms

Unterkunft und Verpflegung, f
- Kost (f) und Logis (n)
- Pension, f
- ♦ accommodation and catering *BE*
- ♦ accommodation and board
- ♦ board and lodging
- ♦ bed and board

Unterkunft und Verpflegung bereitstellen für jn
- Unterkunft und Verpflegung jm bieten
- ♦ provide accommodation and catering for s.o. *BE*

Unterkunft und Verpflegung bieten
- → Kost und Logis bieten

Unterkunft verbessern
- ♦ improve accommodation

Unterkunft verkaufen
- ♦ sell accommodation

Unterkunft verlangen
- um eine Unterkunft bitten
- Unterbringung verlangen
- um Unterbringung bitten
- ♦ ask for accommodation

Unterkunft vermarkten
- ♦ market accommodation

Unterkunft vermitteln an jn
- → Unterkunft besorgen für jn

Unterkunft verschaffen jm für die Nacht
- unterbringen jn über Nacht
- ♦ fix s.o. up for the night *AE coll*
- ♦ put s.o. up for the night *BE coll*
- ♦ accommodate s.o. for the night

Unterkunft verweigern (jm)
- Unterbringung verweigern (jm)
- ♦ refuse accommodation (to s.o.)
- ♦ refuse (s.o.) accommodation

Unterkunft vorbuchen
  Unterkunft im voraus bestellen
  ♦ **prebook accommodation**
  ♦ book accommodation in advance
  ♦ book accommodation ahead
Unterkunft weitervermieten
  Unterkunft wieder vermieten
  ♦ **rerent accommodation** *AE*
  ♦ **relet accommodation** *BE*
Unterkunft wieder vermieten
  Unterkunft erneut vermieten
  Unterkunft weitervermieten
  ♦ **relet accommodation** *BE*
  ♦ **rerent accommodation** *AE*
Unterkunft wünschen
  ♦ **request accommodation**
Unterkunft zur Verfügung stellen
  Unterkunft stellen
  ♦ **supply accommodation**
  ♦ **provide accommodation**
Unterkunft zu vermieten
  ♦ **Accommodation to let** *BE*
  ♦ **Accommodation for rent** *AE*
Unterlizenz, f
  Unterkonzession, f
  ♦ **sublicence**
  ♦ **sublicense**
Unterlizenzgeber, m
  Unterkonzessionsgeber, m
  ♦ **sublicenser**
  ♦ **sublicensor**
Unterlizenznehmer, m
  Unterkonzessionsnehmer, m
  ♦ **sublicencee**
  ♦ **sublicensee**
Untermatratze, f
  (zum Schutz der eigentlichen Matratze)
  ♦ **palliasse** *AE*
Untermiete, f
  ♦ **subtenancy**
  ♦ **sublease**
  ♦ **underlease**
  ♦ **undertenancy**
Untermieter, m
  ♦ **lodger**
  ♦ **roomer** *AE*
  ♦ **subtenant**
  ♦ **undertenant**
  ♦ **sublessee** *jur*
Untermieter nehmen
  ♦ **take in roomers** *AE*
  ♦ **take in lodgers**
Untermieter sein
  ♦ **be a subtenant**
  ♦ **be a lodger**
  ♦ **be an undertenant** *AE*
  ♦ **be a roomer** *AE*
Untermietverhältnis n
  ♦ **subtenancy**
  ♦ **undertenancy**
Unternehmen, n
  ♦ **enterprise**
  ♦ **company**
  ♦ **corporation** *AE*
  ♦ **business**
Unternehmenserscheinungsbild, n
  → Corporate Design
Unternehmensidentität, f
  → Corporate Identity
Unternehmer, m (generell)
  ♦ **entrepreneur**

Unternehmer, m (Werkvertrag)
  ♦ **contractor**
unternehmerisch, adj
  ♦ **entrepreneurial, adj**
Unternehmung, f
  ♦ **venture**
unternehmungslustig, adj
  ♦ **enterprising, adj**
Unternehmungslustigeren, die, m/f pl
  ♦ **more active, the** *pl*
  ♦ **more energetic, the** *pl*
unternehmungslustiger Reisender, m
  ♦ **enterprising traveller**
  ♦ **enterprising traveler** *AE*
unternehmungslustig sein
  ♦ **be active**
  ♦ **be energetic**
  ♦ **be enterprising**
  ♦ **be adventurous**
unter neuer Leitung
  unter neuer Führung
  ♦ **under new management**
unter neuer Leitung sein
  ♦ **be under new management**
Unterpacht, f
  ♦ **sublease**
  ♦ **subtenancy**
  ♦ **underlease**
  ♦ **undertenancy**
Unterpächter, m
  Untermieter, m
  ♦ **subtenant**
  ♦ **undertenant**
  ♦ **sublessee** *jur*
  ♦ **underlessee** *AE jur*
unter persönlicher Leitung des Besitzers
  unter der persönlichen Leitung des Besitzers
  ♦ **personally managed by the owner**
  ♦ **personally supervised by the owner**
unter persönlicher Leitung des im Haus wohnenden Besitzers
  ♦ **personally managed by the resident owner**
  ♦ **personally supervised by the resident owner**
unterportionieren (etw)
  ♦ **underportion (s.th.)**
unterportioniert, adj
  ♦ **underportioned, adj**
Unterportionierung, f
  ♦ **underportioning**
unter Quarantäne
  ♦ **in quarantine**
Unterricht, m
  ♦ **tuition**
  ♦ **lessons** *pl*
Unterricht bieten
  ♦ **provide tuition**
  ♦ **provide lessons**
Unterricht geben (in etw)
  ♦ **give lessons (in s.th.)**
  ♦ **give tuition (in s.th.)**
Unterricht nehmen
  ♦ **take lessons**
Unterrichtsgebühr f
  ♦ **tuition charge**
  ♦ **tuition fee**
Unterrichtsraum, m
  Klassenzimmer, n
  ♦ **classroom**
unterschätzen etw
  ♦ **underestimate s.th.**

unterschlagen etw
  ♦ **embezzle s.th.**
Unterschlagung, f
  ♦ **embezzlement**
Unterschlupf, m (Obdach)
  → Obdach
Unterschlupf, m (Versteck)
  → Versteck
unterschlüpfen
  Schutz finden
  ♦ **take shelter**
Unterschlupf finden in X
  ♦ **find a place in X**
Unterschlüssel, m
  Bereichsschlüssel, m
  ♦ **sub master key**
  ♦ **sub master**
unterschreiben (etw)
  unterzeichnen (etw)
  signieren (etw)
  abzeichnen (etw)
  ♦ **sign (s.th.)**
Unterschreiben Sie bitte hier
  ♦ **Sign here, please**
unterschrieben, adj
  unterzeichnet, adj
  ♦ **signed, adj**
unterschriebene Buchung, f
  ♦ **signed booking**
Unterschrift, f
  ♦ **signature**
Unterschrift des Vormunds, f
  ♦ **signature of the guardian**
Unterseeboot, n
  U-Boot, n
  ♦ **submarine**
Unterstadt, f
  ♦ **lower town**
  ♦ **Low Town, the**
Unterstand, m
  (z.B. im Park)
  ♦ **shelter**
Unterstellplatz, m
  → Stellplatz
Untersuchung der Urlaubsgewohnheiten, f
  Untersuchung der Feriengewohnheiten, f
  ♦ **study on the vacation habits** *AE*
  ♦ **study on the holiday habits** *BE*
Untersuchung leiten
  ♦ **conduct an investigation**
Unter-Tage-Führung, f
  → Führung unter Tage
Untertasse, f
  ♦ **saucer**
unterteilbar, adj
  abteilbar, adj
  ♦ **subdivisible, adj**
  ♦ **can be partitioned (off)**
unterteilbarer Raum, m
  ♦ **subdivisible room**
unterteilbarer Saal, m
  ♦ **subdivisible hall**
unterteilen einen Raum
  ♦ **partition a room**
  ♦ **subdivide a room**
unterteilen etw
  (durch Wände etc.)
  ♦ **partition s.th.**
  ♦ **subdivide s.th.**
Unterteller, m
  ♦ **underplate**

untervermieten etw (an jn)
  weitervermieten etw (an jn)
  ♦ **sublet s.th. (to s.o.)**
  ♦ **sublease s.th. (to s.o.)**
  ♦ **underlet s.th. (to s.o.)**
  ♦ **underlease s.th. (to s.o.)**
  ♦ **underrent s.th. (to s.o.)** AE
Untervermieter, m
  ♦ **sublessor** iur
  ♦ subletter
  ♦ underlessor
untervermietet, adj
  ♦ **sublet, adj**
untervermietetes Zimmer, n
  ♦ **sublet room**
Untervermietung, f
  Weitervermietung, f
  ♦ **subletting**
  ♦ sublease
Untervermietung ist nicht gestattet
  ♦ **sublease is not allowed**
  ♦ sublease is not permitted
  ♦ subletting is not allowed
  ♦ subletting is not permitted
Untervermietungsplan, m
  ♦ **subletting scheme**
Untervermietungsrecht, n
  ♦ **right of sublease**
unterverpachten etw (an jn)
  weiterverpachten etw (an jn)
  ♦ **sublease s.th. (to s.o.)**
  ♦ underlease s.th. (to s.o.)
  ♦ underlet s.th. (to s.o.)
  ♦ sublet s.th. (to s.o.)
Unterverpachtung, f
  Untervermietung, f
  ♦ **sublease**
  ♦ subletting
unter verschiedener Leitung
  unter getrennter Leitung
  ♦ **under separate management**
unterversichern (etw)
  unter dem Wert versichern (etw)
  ♦ **underinsure (s.th.)**
unterversichert, adj
  ♦ **underinsured, adj**
unterversichert sein
  ♦ **be underinsured**
Unterversicherung, f
  ♦ **underinsurance**
unterversorgt, adj
  ♦ **undersupplied, adj**
unterversorgt sein mit etw
  ♦ **be undersupplied with s.th.**
unterversorgt sein mit Hotelzimmern
  ♦ **be undersupplied with hotel rooms**
unter Vertrag, adv
  ♦ **under contract, adv**
Untervertrag, m
  Nebenvertrag, m
  ♦ **subcontract**
unter Vertrag genommenes Bett, n
  ♦ **contracted bed**
unter Vertrag nehmen etw
  ♦ **contract s.th.**
  ♦ contract for s.th.
unter Vertrag nehmen jn
  ♦ **sign s.o. on**
Unterwasserausrüstung, f
  ♦ **underwater equipment**

Unterwasserexkursion, f
  ♦ **underwater excursion**
Unterwasserfahrzeug, n
  ♦ **underwater craft**
Unterwasserfischen, n
  ♦ **underwater fishing**
Unterwassergymnastik, f
  ♦ **underwater exercises** pl
Unterwasserhöhle, f
  ♦ **underwater cave**
Unterwasserjagd, f
  ♦ **underwater hunting**
Unterwasserkamera, f
  ♦ **underwater camera**
Unterwassermassage, f
  ♦ **underwater massage**
Unterwassermassageeinrichtung, f
  ♦ **underwater massage facility**
Unterwassertherapie, f
  ♦ **underwater therapy**
Unterwasserwelt, f
  Welt unter Wasser, f
  ♦ **underwater world**
unterwegs, adv
  auf dem Weg, adv
  ♦ **on the way, adv**
  ♦ en route, adv
unterwegs anhalten
  ♦ **stop on the way**
  ♦ stop en route
unterwegs nach X
  ♦ **en route to X**
  ♦ en route for X
  ♦ on the way to X
  ♦ bound for X
unterwegs sein
  auf der Straße sein
  ♦ **be on the road**
  ♦ be out and about
unterwegs sein in Nordengland
  ♦ **tour the north of England**
Unterwelt, f
  ♦ **underworld**
Unterzeichneter, m
  Unterzeichner, m
  ♦ **undersigned**
untrinkbar, adj
  ♦ **undrinkable, adj**
untrinkbares Wasser, n
  ♦ **undrinkable water**
unübertroffen, adj
  ♦ **unsurpassed, adj**
  ♦ matchless, adj
unübertroffen sein
  ♦ **be unsurpassed**
unverändert bleiben
  ♦ **remain unchanged**
unverbesserlicher Optimist, m
  ♦ **confirmed optimist**
unverbindlich, adj (Angebot)
  ♦ **nonbinding, adj** AE
  ♦ non-binding, adj BE
  ♦ without commitment
  ♦ without obligation
  ♦ subject to alteration
unverbindlich, adj (Person)
  ♦ **noncommittal, adj** AE
  ♦ non-committal, adj BE
unverbindlich, adv (Information)
  ♦ **without guarantee, adv**

unverbindlicher Preis, m
  ♦ **price subject to alteration**
  ♦ rate subject to alteration
unverbindlicher Zimmervorschlag, m
  ♦ **room suggestion without obligation**
unverbindliches Preisangebot, n
  unverbindliche Preisangabe, f
  ♦ **quotation without obligation**
unverdaubar, adj
  → schwer verdaulich
unverdauliches Essen, n
  → unverträgliches Essen
unverdünnt, adj (generell)
  ♦ **undiluted, adj**
unverdünnt, adj (Whisky, Wodka)
  pur, adj
  ♦ **neat, adj** BE
  ♦ straight, adj AE
unverdünnter Wein, m
  purer Wein, m
  ♦ **undiluted wine**
unverdünnter Whisky, m
  Whisky pur, m
  ♦ **straight whisky** AE
  ♦ straight whiskey AE
  ♦ neat whisky BE
  ♦ neat whiskey BE
unverdünnter Wodka, m
  Wodka pur, m
  ♦ **straight vodka** AE
  ♦ neat vodka BE
unvergeßlich, adj
  ♦ **unforgettable, adj**
unvergeßlicher Aufenthalt, m
  ♦ **unforgettable stay**
unvergeßlicher Blick, m
  unvergeßliche Aussicht, f
  unvergeßlicher Ausblick, m
  ♦ **unforgettable view**
unvergeßlicher Urlaub, m
  ♦ **unforgettable vacation** AE
  ♦ unforgettable holiday BE
unvergeßliches Erlebnis, n
  unvergeßliches Erlebnis für jn
  ♦ **unforgettable experience**
  ♦ unforgettable experience for s.o.
unvergeßliche Stunden, f pl
  ♦ **unforgettable hours** pl
unvergleichlich, adj
  einzigartig, adj
  ♦ **incomparable, adj**
  ♦ unrivaled, adj AE
  ♦ unrivalled, adj BE
unvergleichliche Atmosphäre, f
  ♦ **incomparable atmosphere**
unvergleichliche Gastfreundschaft, f
  unvergleichliche Gastlichkeit, f
  ♦ **incomparable hospitality**
unvergleichlichen Komfort anbieten
  ♦ **offer unrivalled comfort**
unvergleichlicher Komfort, m
  ♦ **unrivalled comfort**
  ♦ unrivaled comfort AE
unvergleichlicher Service, m
  ♦ **incomparable service**
unvergleichliche Saison, f
  ♦ **unrivalled season**
  ♦ unrivaled season AE
  ♦ incomparable season

unvergleichliches Essen, n (Mahl)
  einzigartiges Essen n
  ♦ incomparable meal
unvergleichliches Hotel, n
  ♦ incomparable hotel
unvergleichliche Speisen, f pl
  einzigartige Speisen f pl
  ♦ incomparable food
unverheiratet, adj
  ledig, adj
  alleinstehend, adj
  ♦ unmarried, adj
  ♦ single, adj
Unverheirateter, m
  Unverheiratete, f
  ♦ single person
  ♦ single
unverhoffter Gast, m
  ♦ unanticipated guest
unverkauft, adj
  nicht verkauft, adj
  ♦ unsold, adj
unverkaufte Kapazität, f
  ♦ unsold capacity
unverkaufter Sitzplatz, m
  unverkaufter Sitz, m
  unverkaufter Platz, m
  ♦ unsold seat
unverkaufter Urlaub, m
  ♦ unsold vacation AE
  ♦ unsold holiday BE
unverkauftes Zimmer, n
  nicht verkauftes Zimmer, n
  ♦ unsold room
  ♦ room not sold
unverletzt, adj
  ♦ unhurt, adj
unverletzt sein
  ♦ be unhurt
unvermietbar, adj
  ♦ unrentable, adj
  ♦ not rentable, adj
  ♦ cannot be rented AE
  ♦ cannot be let BE
unvermietbares Zimmer, n
  nicht vermietbares Zimmer, n
  ♦ OOO room
  ♦ out-of-order room
unvermietet, adj
  ♦ unrented, adj AE
  ♦ unlet, adj BE
unverschämt, adj
  ♦ impertinent, adj
  ♦ insolent, adj
  ♦ rude, adj
unverschämter Gast, m
  ♦ impertinent guest
  ♦ insolent guest
  ♦ rude guest
unverschämter Preis, m
  ♦ outrageous price
  ♦ outrageous rate
Unverschämtheit, f
  ♦ impertinence
  ♦ insolence
  ♦ rudeness
unverträgliches Essen, n
  → schwer verdauliches Essen
unverwechselbare Atmosphäre, f
  einzigartige Atmosphäre, f
  ♦ unique atmosphere

unverzüglich, adj
  sofortig, adj
  ♦ immediate, adj
  ♦ prompt, adj
unverzüglich, adv
  ♦ without delay, adv
  ♦ immediately, adv
  ♦ promptly, adv
  ♦ straightaway, adv
unverzüglich buchen
  ♦ book without delay
  ♦ book without any delay
unvollständig, adj
  ♦ incomplete, adj
unvorhergesehene Verspätung f
  unvorhersehbare Verspätung f
  ♦ unforeseen delay
unvorhersehbares Ereignis, n
  ♦ unforeseen event
  ♦ unanticipated event
unvorhersehbare Umstände, m pl
  ♦ unforeseen circumstances pl
unwillkommen, adj
  nicht willkommen, adj
  ♦ unwelcome, adj
  ♦ not welcome, adj
unwillkommene Gäste abschieben zu Verwandten
  ♦ palm unwelcome guests off on (the) relatives
unwillkommener Gast m
  ♦ unwelcome guest
unwillkommen sein
  nicht willkommen sein
  ♦ be unwelcome
unwirsches Personal, n
  schroffes Personal, n
  ♦ uncivil personnel
  ♦ uncivil staff
unwirtlich, adj
  → ungastlich
Unwirtlichkeit, f
  → Ungastlichkeit
unwirtschaftlich, adj
  ♦ uneconomical, adj
  ♦ unproductive, adj
  ♦ inefficient, adj
  ♦ unviable, adj
unwohl, adj
  ♦ unwell, adj
unwohler Magen, m
  (Brechreiz)
  ♦ queasy stomach
unwohl sein
  ♦ be unwell
unzeitiges Essen, n
  unzeitige Mahlzeit, f
  ♦ unseasonable meal
unzufriedener Gast, m
  ♦ dissatisfied guest
unzufriedener Kunde, m
  ♦ dissatisfied customer
  ♦ dissatisfied client
Unzufriedenheit, f
  ♦ dissatisfaction
  ♦ discontentment
Unzufriedenheit ausdrücken mit etw
  ♦ express dissatisfaction with s.th.
Unzufriedenheit ausdrücken mit seinem Zimmer
  ♦ express dissatisfaction with one's room
Unzufriedenheit mit etw, f
  ♦ dissatisfaction with s.th.
  ♦ dissatisfaction at doing s.th.

Unzufriedenheit mit jm, f
  ♦ dissatisfaction with s.o.
unzufrieden sein mit seinem Zimmer
  ♦ be dissatisfied with one's room
  ♦ be unhappy with one's room
unzugänglich, adj
  ♦ inaccessible, adj
Unzugänglichkeit, f
  ♦ inaccessibility
unzureichend, adj
  unzulänglich, adj
  ♦ inadequate, adj
  ♦ insufficient, adj
unzureichende Hotelkapazität, f
  ♦ insufficient hotel capacity
unzureichende Nahrungsmittelvorräte, m pl
  ♦ insufficient food supplies pl
unzureichender Service, m
  mangelhafter Service, m
  ♦ inadequate service
unzureichender Zimmerservice, m
  ♦ inadequate room service
unzuverlässig, adj
  ♦ unreliable, adj
Unzuverlässigkeit, f
  ♦ unreliability
Upgrade, m (Höherstufung)
  → Höherstufung
Upgrade, m (Verbesserung)
  → Verbesserung
üppig beschenken jn
  ♦ shower s.o. with presents
üppiges Frühstück, n
  ♦ sumptuous breakfast
üppiges Mahl, n
  luxuriöses Essen, n
  ♦ luxurious meal
üppig speisen
  ♦ dine sumptuously
Ural, m
  ♦ Ural Mountains, the pl
  ♦ Urals, the pl
uralte Kultur, f
  ♦ age-old culture
Uraufführung, f
  → Premiere
urbanes Hotel, n
  Stadthotel, n
  ♦ urban hotel
urgemütlich, adj
  ♦ really cosy, adj
  ♦ really cozy, adj AE
urgemütliche Atmosphäre, f
  ♦ really cosy atmosphere
  ♦ really cozy atmosphere AE
urig, adj (Gebäude)
  → rustikal
urig, adj (Person)
  ♦ earthy, adj
  ♦ unsophisticated, adj
urige Atmosphäre, f
  ♦ earthy atmosphere
  ♦ rustic atmosphere
urige Gaststätte, f
  → rustikale Gaststätte
uriges Hotel, n
  → rustikales Hotel
Urin, m
  ♦ urine

Urinalbecken

Urinalbecken, n
Urinal, n
♦ urinal
urinieren
♦ urinate
Urlaub, m (Arbeitnehmer)
Beurlaubung, f
♦ leave
Urlaub, m (Beamter)
♦ furlough
Urlaub, m (Ferien)
♦ vacation AE
♦ holiday BE
Urlaub abbrechen
Ferien abbrechen
♦ cut short a vacation AE
♦ cut short a holiday BE
Urlaub abkürzen
Ferien abkürzen
♦ shorten one's vacation AE
♦ curtail one's vacation AE
♦ shorten one's holiday BE
♦ curtail one's holiday BE
Urlaub absagen
→ Urlaub stornieren
Urlaub am Bauernhof, m ÖST
→ Urlaub auf dem Bauernhof
Urlaub am Meer, m
Urlaub an der See, m
Ferien am Meer, pl
Ferien an der See, pl
Seeurlaub, m
♦ vacation by the sea AE
♦ vacation at the sea Ae
♦ seaside vacation AE
♦ holiday by the sea BE
♦ seaside holiday BE
Urlaub an einem Ort, m
Ferien an einem Ort, pl
♦ vacation in a place AE
♦ holiday in a place BE
Urlaub annullieren
→ Urlaub stornieren
Urlaub antreten (Arbeitnehmer)
→ in Urlaub gehen
Urlaub antreten (Ferien)
aufbrechen in den Urlaub
Ferien antreten
aufbrechen in die Ferien
♦ set out on one's vacation AE
♦ set out on one's holiday BE
Urlaub auf dem Bauernhof, m
Bauernhofurlaub, m
Urlaub am Bauernhof, m ÖST
Ferien auf dem Bauernhof, pl
♦ farmhouse vacation AE
♦ farm vacation AE
♦ farmhouse holiday BE
♦ farm holiday BE
Urlaub auf dem Bauernhof machen
Ferien auf dem Bauernhof machen
♦ take a farmhouse vacation AE
♦ take a farm vacation AE
♦ take a farmhouse holiday BE
♦ take a farm holiday BE
Urlaub auf dem Campingplatz verbringen
Ferien auf dem Campingplatz verleben
♦ spend a vacation on a campsite AE
♦ spend one's vacation on a campground AE
♦ spend a holiday on a campsite BE
♦ spend one's holiday on a camping site BE

Urlaub auf dem Land, m
Ferien auf dem Land, pl
Landurlaub, m
Landferien, pl
♦ country vacation AE
♦ country holiday BE
♦ rural vacation AE
♦ rural holiday BE
Urlaub auf Ehrenwort, m
♦ leave on parole
Urlaub auf einem Bauernhof, m
Ferien auf einem Bauernhof, pl
♦ vacation on a farm AE
♦ holiday on a farm BE
Urlaub aufteilen
Ferien aufteilen
♦ split vacations AE
♦ split holidays BE
Urlaub aus familiären Gründen, m (Arbeitnehmer)
♦ compassionate leave
Urlaub ausprobieren
Ferien ausprobieren
♦ sample a vacation AE
♦ sample a holiday BE
Urlaub auswählen
Urlaub auswählen
Ferien auswählen
Ferien wählen
♦ select a vacation AE
♦ select a holiday BE
♦ choose a vacation AE
♦ choose a holiday BE
Urlaub beantragen (Arbeitnehmer)
♦ apply for leave
♦ ask for leave
Urlaub beenden
Ferien beenden
♦ finish one's vacation AE
♦ finish one's holiday BE
♦ end a vacation AE
♦ end a holiday BE
Urlaub beginnen
Urlaub antreten
Ferien beginnen
Ferien antreten
♦ start one's vacation AE
♦ begin one's vacation AE
♦ start one's holiday BE
♦ begin one's holiday BE
♦ commence one's vacation form
Urlaub benötigen
Urlaub brauchen
Urlaub nötig haben coll
Ferien benötigen
Ferien brauchen
♦ be in need of a vacation AE
♦ be in need of a holiday BE
Urlaub bestätigen
Urlaub zusagen
Ferien bestätigen
Ferien zusagen
♦ confirm a vacation AE
♦ confirm a holiday BE
Urlaub bezahlen
Ferien bezahlen
♦ pay for a vacation AE
♦ pay for a holiday BE
Urlaub bis zum Wecken, m (Militär)
♦ night leave
Urlaub brauchen
Ferien brauchen

♦ need a vacation AE
♦ need a holiday BE
Urlaub buchen
Ferien buchen
♦ book a vacation AE
♦ book a holiday BE
Urlaub buchen in X
Urlaub nach X buchen
Ferien in X buchen
♦ book a vacation to X AE
♦ book a holiday to X BE
Urlaub des Lebens, m
Ferien des Lebens, pl
♦ vacation of a lifetime AE
♦ vacation of one's lifetime AE
♦ holiday of a lifetime BE
♦ holiday of one's lifetime BE
Urlaub dringend benötigen
Ferien dringend benötigen
♦ badly need a vacation AE
♦ want a vacation AE
♦ badly need a holiday BE
♦ want a holiday BE
Urlaub durchführen
Ferien durchführen
♦ run a vacation AE
♦ run a holiday BE
Urlaub empfehlen jm
Ferien empfehlen jm
♦ recommend a vacation to s.o. AE
♦ recommend a holiday to s.o. BE
urlauben coll
Urlaub machen
Ferien machen
♦ vacation AE
♦ be vacationing AE
♦ holiday BE
♦ be holidaying BE
Urlauber, m
Feriengast, m
♦ vacationer AE
♦ holidaymaker BE
♦ vacationist AE
Urlauber aus dem Ausland, m
Feriengast aus dem Ausland, m
ausländischer Urlauber, m
ausländischer Feriengast, m
♦ vacationer from abroad AE
♦ holidaymaker from abroad BE
♦ foreign vacationer AE
♦ foreign holidaymaker BE
Urlaubergruppe, f
Feriengruppe, f
♦ group of vacationers AE
♦ vacationer group AE
♦ group of holidaymakers BE
Urlaub erhalten für etw (Arbeitnehmer)
♦ be given leave to do s.th.
Urlauberhorden, f pl
Ferienhorden, f pl
♦ tribes of vacationers AE pl
♦ tribes of holidaymakers BE pl
Urlauberparadies, n
Ferienparadies, n
♦ vacationer's paradise AE
♦ holidaymaker's paradise BE
Urlauberprofil, n
Feriengastprofil, n
♦ profile of vacationers AE
♦ profile of holidaymakers BE

Urlauberstrom, m
  Ferienstrom, m
  ◆ stream of vacationers *AE*
  ◆ stream of holidaymakers *BE*

Urlauberstrom bleibt aus
  Ferienstrom bleibt aus
  ◆ vacationers stay away *AE*
  ◆ holidaymakers stay away *BE*

Urlauberstrom setzt ein
  Ferienstrom setzt ein
  ◆ stream of vacationers starts *AE*
  ◆ stream of holidaymakers starts *BE*

Urlauber terrorisieren
  ◆ terrorise a vacationer *AE*
  ◆ terrorize a holidaymaker *BE*

Urlaubertyp, m
  ◆ type of vacationer *AE*
  ◆ type of holidaymaker *BE*

Urlaubertypologie; f
  ◆ typology of vacationers *AE*
  ◆ typology of holidaymakers *BE*

Urlauberzahl, f
  Zahl der Urlauber, f
  ◆ number of vacationers *AE*
  ◆ number of holidaymakers *BE*

Urlauberzug, m (Militär)
  ◆ leave train

Urlaub festmachen
  Urlaub festlegen
  Ferien festmachen
  Ferien festlegen
  ◆ fix up a vacation *AE coll*
  ◆ fix up a holiday *BE coll*

Urlaub fortsetzen
  Ferien fortsetzen
  ◆ continue one's vacation *AE*
  ◆ continue one's holiday *BE*

Urlaub für anspruchsvolle Gäste, m
  Ferien für anspruchsvolle Gäste, pl
  ◆ vacation for discerning guests *AE*
  ◆ holiday for discerning guests *BE*

Urlaub geben jm (Arbeitgeber)
  ◆ give s.o. leave

Urlaub geben jm (Beamter)
  → beurlauben jn

Urlaub genießen
  Ferien genießen
  ◆ enjoy a vacation *AE*
  ◆ enjoy one's vacation *AE*
  ◆ enjoy a holiday *BE*
  ◆ enjoy one's holiday *BE*

Urlaub gestalten
  Ferien gestalten
  ◆ organise a vacation *AE*
  ◆ organize a vacation *AE*
  ◆ use a vacation *AE*
  ◆ organise a holiday *BE*
  ◆ organize a holiday *BE*

Urlaub gewähren jm (Beamter)
  ◆ grant furlough to s.o.

Urlaub gewinnen (für zwei Personen)
  Ferien gewinnen (für zwei Personen)
  ◆ win a vacation (for two persons) *AE*
  ◆ win a holiday (for two persons) *BE*

Urlaub guthaben (Arbeitnehmer)
  Urlaub zugut haben
  noch 10 Tage Urlaub guthaben
  ◆ be due some days' holiday *BE*
  ◆ be still due 10 days' holiday *BE*

Urlaub haben
  Ferien haben
  ◆ have a vacation *AE*
  ◆ have a holiday *BE*
  ◆ have holidays *BE*

Urlaub Ihrer Wahl, m
  Ferien Ihrer Wahl, pl
  ◆ vacation of your choice *AE*
  ◆ holiday of your choice *BE*

Urlaub im Ausland machen
  Ferien im Ausland machen
  ◆ take one's vacation abroad *AE*
  ◆ take one's holiday abroad *BE*

Urlaub im Ausland verbringen
  Ferien im Ausland verbringen
  ◆ spend one's vacation abroad *AE*
  ◆ spend a vacation abroad *AE*
  ◆ spend one's holiday abroad *BE*
  ◆ spend a holiday abroad *BE*

Urlaub im Freien, m
  Ferien im Freien, pl
  Urlaub in freier Natur, m
  Ferien in freier Natur, pl
  ◆ outdoor vacation *AE*
  ◆ outdoor holiday *BE*

Urlaub im Freien verbringen
  Ferien im Freien verbringen
  ◆ spend a vacation outdoors *AE*
  ◆ spend a holiday outdoors *BE*

Urlaub in den Alpen, m
  Ferien in den Alpen, pl
  ◆ vacation in the Alps *AE*
  ◆ holiday in the Alps *BE*

Urlaub in den Bergen, m
  Ferien in den Bergen, pl
  ◆ vacation in the mountains *AE*
  ◆ holiday in the mountains *BE*

Urlaub in der Ferienwohnung, m
  Ferien in der Ferienwohnung, pl
  ◆ vacation in the vacation apartment *AE*
  ◆ holiday in the holiday flat *BE*

Urlaub in der Karibik, m
  Ferien in der Karibik, pl
  Karibikurlaub, m
  Karibikferien, pl
  ◆ vacation in the Caribbean *AE*
  ◆ holiday in the Caribbean *BE*

Urlaub in der Sonne, m
  Ferien in der Sonne, pl
  ◆ vacation in the sun *AE*
  ◆ holiday in the sun *BE*

Urlaub in Deutschland, m
  Deutschlandurlaub, m
  Ferien in Deutschland, pl
  Deutschlandferien, pl
  ◆ vacation in Germany *AE*
  ◆ German vacation *AE*
  ◆ holiday in Germany *BE*
  ◆ German holiday *BE*

Urlaub in Deutschland machen
  Deutschlandurlaub machen
  Ferien in Deutschland machen
  Deutschlandferien machen
  ◆ take a holiday in Germany *BE*
  ◆ take a vacation in Germany *AE*

Urlaub in einem Hotel verbringen
  Ferien in einem Hotel verbringen
  ◆ spend a vacation in a hotel *AE*
  ◆ spend a vacation at a hotel *AE*
  ◆ spend a holiday in a hotel *BE*
  ◆ spend a holiday at a hotel *BE*

Urlaub in letzter Sekunde, m
  Ferien in letzter Sekunde, pl
  ◆ last-minute vacation *AE*
  ◆ last-minute holiday *BE*

Urlaub in schöner Landschaft, m
  Ferien in schöner Landschaft, pl
  ◆ vacation in beautiful countryside *AE*
  ◆ vacation in beautiful scenery *AE*
  ◆ holiday in beautiful countryside *BE*
  ◆ holiday in beautiful scenery *BE*

Urlaub in vollen Zügen genießen
  Ferien in vollen Zügen genießen
  ◆ enjoy one's vacation to the full *AE*
  ◆ enjoy one's holiday to the full *BE*

Urlaub kaufen
  einen Urlaub kaufen
  Ferien kaufen
  ◆ buy a vacation *AE*
  ◆ buy a holiday *BE*

Urlaub kürzen
  → Urlaub abkürzen

Urlaub leisten sich
  Urlaub sich leisten können
  Ferien sich leisten
  Ferien sich leisten können
  ◆ afford a vacation *AE*
  ◆ can afford a vacation *AE*
  ◆ afford a holiday *BE*
  ◆ can afford a holiday *BE*

Urlaub machen
  Ferien machen
  ◆ take a vacation *AE*
  ◆ vacation *AE*
  ◆ take a holiday *BE*
  ◆ holiday *BE*
  ◆ go vacationing *AE*

Urlaubmachen, n
  Ferienmachen, n
  ◆ taking a vacation *AE*
  ◆ taking a holiday *BE*

Urlaub machen an der Costa Brava
  Ferien machen an der Costa Brava
  ◆ vacation on the Costa Brava *AE*
  ◆ take a vacation on the Costa Brava *AE*
  ◆ holiday on the Costa Brava *BE*
  ◆ take a holiday on the Costa Brava *BE*

Urlaub machen im Ausland
  Ferien im Ausland machen
  ◆ take a vacation in a foreign country *AE*
  ◆ take a holiday in a foreign country *BE*

Urlaub machen im eigenen Land
  Ferien machen im eigenen Land
  ◆ vacation in one's own country *AE*
  ◆ take a vacation in one's own country *AE*
  ◆ holiday in one's own country *BE*
  ◆ take a holiday in one's own country *BE*

Urlaub machen in Übersee
  Überseeurlaub machen
  Ferien in Übersee machen
  Überseeferien machen
  ◆ take a vacation overseas *AE*
  ◆ take a holiday overseas *BE*

Urlaub machen in X
  Ferien machen in X
  ◆ vacation in X *AE*
  ◆ take a vacation in X *AE*
  ◆ holiday in X *BE*
  ◆ take a holiday in X *BE*

Urlaub machen mit jm
  jn in den Urlaub mitnehmen
  Ferien machen mit jm
  jn in die Ferien mitnehmen

Urlaub mit Bezahlung 818

♦ take s.o. on a vacation *AE*
♦ take s.o. on a holiday *BE*
Urlaub mit Bezahlung, m
Ferien mit Bezahlung, pl
♦ **vacation with pay** *AE*
♦ **holiday with pay** *BE*
Urlaub mit dem Auto, m
Urlaub mit dem Pkw, m
Ferien mit dem Auto, pl
Ferien mit dem Pkw, pl
♦ **vacation by car** *AE*
♦ **holiday by car** *BE*
Urlaub mit dem Bus, m
Ferien mit dem Bus, pl
♦ **vacation by bus** *AE*
♦ **holiday by bus** *BE*
♦ **holiday by coach** *BE*
Urlaub mit dem Flugzeug, m
Flugurlaub, m
Ferien mit dem Flugzeug, pl
Flugferien, pl
♦ **vacation by air** *AE*
♦ **air vacation** *AE*
♦ **holiday by air** *BE*
♦ **air holiday** *BE*
Urlaub mit der Bahn, m
Ferien mit der Bahn, pl
♦ **vacation by rail** *AE*
♦ **holiday by rail** *BE*
Urlaub mit Komfort, m
Ferien mit Komfort, pl
♦ **vacation with all amenities** *AE*
♦ **holiday with all amenities** *BE*
Urlaub nehmen (Arbeitnehmer)
♦ **take leave**
Urlaub nehmen von sechs Wochen (Ferien)
sechswöchigen Urlaub nehmen
Ferien nehmen von sechs Wochen
sechswöchige Ferien nehmen
♦ **take six weeks' vacation** *AE*
♦ **take six weeks' holiday** *BE*
Urlaub ohne Bezahlung, m
Ferien ohne Bezahlung, pl
♦ **leave without pay**
♦ **vacation without pay** *AE*
♦ **holiday without pay** *BE*
Urlaub ohne Komfort, m
Ferien ohne Komfort, pl
♦ **vacation without any amenities** *AE*
♦ **holiday without any amenities** *BE*
Urlaub planen
Ferien planen
♦ **plan a vacation** *AE*
♦ **plan a holiday** *BE*
Urlaub riskieren
Ferien riskieren
♦ **risk a vacation** *AE*
♦ **risk a holiday** *BE*
Urlaub rückgängig machen
→ Urlaub stornieren
Urlaubsabenteuer, n
Ferienabenteuer, n
♦ **vacation adventure** *AE*
♦ **holiday adventure** *BE*
Urlaubsabsage, f
→ Urlaubsstornierung
Urlaubsabsicht, f
Ferienabsicht, f
♦ **vacation intention** *AE*
♦ intention to take a vacation *AE*

♦ holiday intention *BE*
♦ intention to take a holiday *BE*
Urlaubsaccessoire, n
Ferienaccessoire, n
♦ **vacation accessory** *AE*
♦ **holiday accessory** *BE*
Urlaubsadresse, f
Urlaubsanschrift, f
Ferienadresse, f
Ferienanschrift, f
♦ **vacation address** *AE*
♦ **holiday address** *BE*
Urlaubsadresse hinterlassen
Urlaubsanschrift hinterlassen
Ferienadresse hinterlassen
Ferienanschrift hinterlassen
♦ **leave one's vacation address** *AE*
♦ **leave one's holiday address** *BE*
Urlaubsagentur, f
Ferienagentur, f
Urlaubsvermittlung, f
Ferienvermittlung, f
♦ **vacation agency** *AE*
♦ **holiday agency** *BE*
urlaubsähnlich, adj
ferienähnlich, adj
♦ **vacation-like, adj** *AE*
♦ **holiday-like, adj** *BE*
urlaubsähnliche Atmosphäre, f
ferienähnliche Atmosphäre, f
♦ **vacation-like atmosphere** *AE*
♦ **holiday-like atmosphere** *BE*
Urlaubsaktivität, f
Urlaubsbeschäftigung, f
Ferienaktivität, f
Ferienbeschäftigung, f
♦ **vacation activity** *AE*
♦ **holiday activity** *BE*
Urlaubsanbieter, m
Ferienanbieter, m
♦ **vacation provider** *AE*
♦ provider of a vacation *AE*
♦ **holiday provider** *BE*
♦ provider of a holiday *BE*
Urlaubsandenken, n
Urlaubssouvenir, n
Ferienandenken, n
Feriensouvenir, n
Souvenir, n
♦ **vacation souvenir** *AE*
♦ **holiday souvenir** *BE*
♦ souvenir
Urlaubsanfang, m (Ferien)
Urlaubsbeginn, n
Urlaubsantritt, m
Ferienanfang, m
Ferienbeginn, m
♦ **start of the vacation** *AE*
♦ beginning of the vacation *AE*
♦ commencement of the vacation *AE form*
♦ **start of the holiday** *BE*
♦ beginning of the holiday *BE*
Urlaubsangebot, n (Gegensatz zu Nachfrage)
Ferienangebot, n
♦ **vacations available** *AE pl*
♦ vacations offered *AE pl*
♦ **holidays available** *BE pl*
♦ holidays offered *BE pl*
Urlaubsangebot, n (Offerte)
Urlaubsofferte, f
Ferienangebot, n

Ferienofferte, f
♦ **vacation offer** *AE*
♦ **holiday offer** *BE*
Urlaubsangebot, n (Palette)
Ferienangebot, n
♦ **range of vacations** *AE*
♦ **range of holidays** *BE*
Urlaubsangebot sichern sich
sich ein Ferienangebot sichern
♦ **secure a vacation offer** *AE*
♦ **secure a holiday offer** *BE*
Urlaubsanlage, f
Urlaubskomplex, m
Ferienanlage, f
Ferienkomplex, m
♦ **vacation complex** *AE*
♦ **holiday complex** *BE*
♦ resort *AE*
♦ resort complex
Urlaubsannehmlichkeit, f
Ferienannehmlichkeit, f
♦ **vacation amenity** *AE*
♦ **holiday amenity** *BE*
Urlaubsannonce, f
Urlaubsreklame, f
Ferienannonce, f
Ferienreklame, f
♦ **vacation advertisement** *AE*
♦ **holiday advertisement** *BE*
Urlaubsanregung, f
→ Urlaubsvorschlag
Urlaubsanschrift, f
→ Urlaubsadresse
Urlaubsanspruch, m (Arbeitnehmer)
Urlaubsberechtigung, f
♦ **leave entitlement**
♦ vacation privilege *AE*
♦ vacation right *AE*
♦ **holiday entitlement** *BE*
♦ claim to holiday entitlement *BE*
Urlaubsanspruch haben (Arbeitnehmer)
urlaubsberechtigt sein
♦ **be eligible for leave**
Urlaubsantrag, m (Arbeitnehmer)
♦ **application for leave (of absence)**
♦ application for vacation *AE*
♦ application for holiday *BE*
Urlaubsantritt, m
→ Urlaubsbeginn
Urlaubsappartement n
→ Ferienappartement
Urlaubsarrangement n
Ferienarrangement n
♦ **vacation arrangement** *AE*
♦ **holiday arrangement** *BE*
Urlaubsart, f
Ferienart, f
♦ **vacation type** *AE*
♦ type of vacation *AE*
♦ **holiday type** *BE*
♦ type of holiday *BE*
Urlaubsarzt, m
Ferienarzt, m
♦ **vacation doctor** *AE*
♦ **holiday doctor** *BE*
Urlaubsatmosphäre, f
Ferienatmosphäre f
Urlaubsstimmung f
Ferienstimmung f
♦ **vacation atmosphere** *AE*
♦ **holiday atmosphere** *BE*

Urlaubsaufenthalt, m
 Ferienaufenthalt m
 ♦ vacation stay AE
 ♦ holiday stay BE
Urlaubsaufwand, m
 Ferienaufwand, m
 ♦ vacation expenditure AE
 ♦ holiday expenditure BE
Urlaubsausflug, m
 Ferienausflug, m
 ♦ vacation excursion AE
 ♦ vacation outing AE
 ♦ holiday excursion BE
 ♦ holiday outing BE
Urlaubsausgaben, f pl
 Ferienausgaben, f pl
 ♦ vacation expenses AE pl
 ♦ vacation spending AE
 ♦ holiday expenses BE pl
 ♦ holiday spending BE
Urlaubsausgaben im Ausland, f pl
 Ferienausgaben im Ausland, f pl
 ♦ spending by vacationers abroad AE
 ♦ spending by holidaymakers abroad BE
Urlaubsauto, n
 Urlaubswagen, m
 Urlaubs-Pkw, m
 Ferienauto, n
 Ferienwagen, m
 ♦ vacation car AE
 ♦ holiday car BE
Urlaubsbauernhof, m
 Ferienbauernhof, m
 ♦ vacation farm AE
 ♦ holiday farm BE
Urlaubsbedingungen, f pl (Arbeitnehmer)
 ♦ leave conditions pl
Urlaubsbedingungen, f pl (Ferien)
 Ferienbedingungen, f pl
 ♦ vacation conditions AE pl
 ♦ holiday conditions BE pl
urlaubsbedürftig, adj
 urlaubsreif, adj
 ferienbedürftig, adj
 ferienreif, adj
 ♦ in need of a vacation AE
 ♦ in need of a holiday BE
Urlaubsbedürftiger, m
 Ferienbedürftiger, m
 Erholungsbedürftiger, m
 ♦ person in need of a vacation AE
 ♦ person in need of a holiday BE
Urlaubsbeginn, m (Arbeitnehmer)
 ♦ start of the leave
 ♦ beginning of the leave
 ♦ commencement of the leave form
Urlaubsbeginn, m (Ferien)
 Urlaubsanfang, m
 Urlaubsantritt, m
 Ferienbeginn, m
 Ferienanfang, m
 ♦ beginning of the vacation AE
 ♦ start of the vacation AE
 ♦ commencement of the vacation AE form
 ♦ beginning of the holiday BE
 ♦ start of the holiday BE
Urlaubsbegleiter, m
 Urlaubsbegleitung, f
 Ferienbegleiter, m
 Ferienbegleitung, f

 ♦ vacation companion AE
 ♦ holiday companion BE
Urlaubsbekanntschaft, f
 Ferienbekanntschaft, f
 ♦ vacation acquaintance AE
 ♦ holiday acquaintance BE
Urlaubsbenutzung, f
 Urlaubsgebrauch, m
 ♦ vacation use AE
 ♦ holiday use BE
urlaubsberechtigt, adj (Arbeitnehmer)
 ♦ eligible for leave, adj
 ♦ eligible for vacation, adj AE
urlaubsberechtigt sein
 ♦ be eligible for vacation AE
 ♦ be eligible for leave
Urlaubsbestätigung, f
 Ferienbestätigung, f
 Urlaubszusage, f
 Ferienzusage, f
 ♦ confirmation of a vacation AE
 ♦ vacation confirmation AE
 ♦ confirmation of a holiday BE
 ♦ holiday confirmation BE
Urlaubsbestimmungen, f pl (Arbeitnehmer)
 ♦ leave regulations pl
 ♦ vacation regulations pl
Urlaubsbesuch, m
 Ferienbesuch, m
 ♦ vacation visit AE
 ♦ holiday visit BE
Urlaubsbesucher, m
 Ferienbesucher, m
 ♦ vacation visitor AE
 ♦ holiday visitor BE
Urlaubsbesuch in England, m
 Ferienbesuch in England, m
 ♦ vacation visit to England AE
 ♦ holiday visit to England BE
Urlaubsbetreuungsdienst, m
 (z.B. für Behinderte)
 Ferienbetreuungsdienst, m
 ♦ vacation care service AE
 ♦ holiday care service BE
Urlaubsboom, m
 Ferienboom, m
 ♦ vacation boom AE
 ♦ holiday boom BE
Urlaubsbroschüre, f
 → Urlaubsprospekt
Urlaubsbuch, n (Ferienlektüre)
 Ferienbuch, n
 ♦ vacation book AE
 ♦ holiday book BE
Urlaubsbuch, n (Unternehmen)
 ♦ leave book
 ♦ leave roster
Urlaubsbuchung, f
 Ferienbuchung, f
 ♦ vacation booking AE
 ♦ holiday booking BE
 ♦ booking (of) a vacation AE
 ♦ booking (of) a holiday BE
 ♦ vacation reservation AE
Urlaubsbuchungsanfrage, f
 Ferienbuchungsanfrage, f
 ♦ vacation reservation inquiry AE
 ♦ vacation reservation enquiry AE
 ♦ holiday booking inquiry BE
 ♦ holiday booking enquiry BE

Urlaubsbuchungsdienst, m
 Urlaubsbuchungsservice, m
 Ferienbuchungsdienst, m
 Ferienbuchungsservice, m
 ♦ vacation reservation service AE
 ♦ holiday booking service BE
Urlaubsbudget, n
 Urlaubskasse, f
 Ferienbudget, n
 Ferienkasse, f
 ♦ vacation budget AE
 ♦ holiday budget BE
Urlaubsbudget belasten
 Urlaubskasse belasten
 Ferienbudget belasten
 Ferienkasse belasten
 ♦ strain the vacation budget AE
 ♦ strain the holiday budget BE
Urlaubsbungalow, m
 Ferienbungalow, m
 ♦ vacation bungalow AE
 ♦ holiday bungalow BE
Urlaubscamper, m
 Feriencamper, m
 ♦ vacation camper AE
 ♦ holiday camper BE
Urlaubscamping, n
 Feriencamping, n
 ♦ vacation camping AE
 ♦ holiday camping BE
Urlaubscampingplatz, m
 Feriencampingplatz, m
 ♦ vacation campsite AE
 ♦ vacation campground AE
 ♦ holiday campsite BE
 ♦ holiday camping site BE
 ♦ holiday camping ground BE
Urlaubschalet, n
 Ferienchalet, n
 ♦ vacation chalet AE
 ♦ holiday chalet BE
Urlaubsclub, m
 Ferienclub, m
 ♦ vacation club AE
 ♦ holiday club BE
Urlaubsclubdorf, n
 Ferienclubdorf, n
 ♦ vacation club village AE
 ♦ holiday club village BE
Urlaubsclubgast, m
 Ferienclubgast, m
 ♦ vacation club guest AE
 ♦ holiday club guest BE
Urlaubsclubmitglied, n
 Ferienclubmitglied, n
 ♦ vacation club member AE
 ♦ holiday club member BE
Urlaubsclubmitgliedschaft, f
 Ferienclubmitgliedschaft, f
 ♦ vacation club membership AE
 ♦ holiday club membership BE
Urlaubscomputer, m
 Feriencomputer, m
 ♦ vacation computer AE
 ♦ holiday computer BE
Urlaubsdarlehen, n
 Urlaubskredit, m
 Feriendarlehen, n
 Ferienkredit, m
 ♦ vacation loan AE
 ♦ holiday loan BE

Urlaubsdatum 820

Urlaubsdatum, n
  Urlaubstermin, m
  Feriendatum, n
  Ferientermin, m
  ♦ date of (the) vacation AE
  ♦ vacation date AE
  ♦ holiday date BE
  ♦ date of (the) holiday BE
Urlaubsdauer, f
  Dauer des Urlaubs, f
  Feriendauer, f
  Dauer der Ferien, f
  ♦ duration of a vacation AE
  ♦ vacation duration AE
  ♦ duration of a holiday BE
  ♦ holiday duration BE
Urlaubsdevisen, pl
  Feriendevisen, pl
  ♦ vacation currency AE
  ♦ holiday currency BE
Urlaubsdevisenabfluß, m
  Feriendevisenabfluß, m
  ♦ vacation currency outflow AE
  ♦ holiday currency outflow BE
Urlaubsdia, n
  Feriendia, n
  ♦ vacation slide AE
  ♦ holiday slide BE
Urlaubsdiarrhö, f
  Feriendiarrhö, f
  ♦ vacation diarrhoea AE
  ♦ holiday diarrhoea BE
Urlaubsdienst, m
  → Urlaubsservice
Urlaubsdollar, m
  Feriendollar, m
  ♦ vacation dollar AE
  ♦ holiday dollar BE
Urlaubsdomizil, n
  Feriendomizil, n
  ♦ vacation domicile AE
  ♦ vacation residence AE
  ♦ holiday domicile BE
  ♦ holiday residence BE
Urlaubsdorado, n
  → Urlaubsparadies
Urlaubsdorf, n
  Feriendorf, n
  ♦ vacation village AE
  ♦ holiday village BE
  ♦ resort village
  ♦ resort
Urlaubsdorfanlage, f
  Urlaubsdorfkomplex, m
  Feriendorfanlage, f
  Feriendorfkomplex, m
  ♦ vacation village complex AE
  ♦ resort village complex AE
  ♦ resort complex
  ♦ holiday village complex BE
Urlaubseigentumswohnung, f
  Ferieneigentumswohnung, f
  ♦ freehold vacation apartment AE
  ♦ freehold holiday flat BE
Urlaubseinrichtung, f
  Ferieneinrichtung, f
  ♦ vacation facility AE
  ♦ holiday facility BE
Urlaub selbst organisieren
  Ferien selbst organisieren

  ♦ organise one's own vacation AE
  ♦ organise one's own holiday BE
Urlaubsende, n (Arbeitnehmer)
  ♦ end of the leave
  ♦ end of one's leave
Urlaubsende, n (Ferien)
  Ferienende, n
  ♦ end of the vacation AE
  ♦ end of one's vacation AE
  ♦ end of the holiday BE
  ♦ end of one's holiday BE
Urlaubsenergie, f
  Ferienenergie, f
  ♦ vacation energy AE
  ♦ holiday energy BE
Urlaubsentschädigung, f
  Ferienentschädigung, f
  ♦ vacation compensation AE
  ♦ holiday compensation BE
Urlaubsentscheidung, f
  Ferienentscheidung, f
  ♦ vacation decision AE
  ♦ holiday decision BE
urlaubserfahren, adj
  ferienerfahren, adj
  ♦ experienced in taking vacations, adj AE
  ♦ experienced in taking holidays, adj BE
Urlaubserfahrung, f
  Ferienerfahrung f
  ♦ vacation experience AE
  ♦ holiday experience BE
Urlaubserfahrung haben
  Urlaubserfahrung besitzen
  Ferienerfahrung haben
  Ferienerfahrung besitzen
  ♦ have vacation experience AE
  ♦ have holiday experience BE
Urlaubserinnerungen, f pl
  Ferienerinnerungen, f pl
  ♦ vacation memories AE pl
  ♦ memories of one's vacation AE pl
  ♦ holiday memories BE pl
  ♦ memories of one's holiday BE pl
Urlaubserlebnis, n
  Ferienerlebnis, n
  ♦ vacation experience AE
  ♦ holiday experience BE
Urlaubserlebnis schmälern
  Ferienerlebnis schmälern
  ♦ diminish the vacation experience AE
  ♦ diminish the holiday experience BE
Urlaubsersparnisse, f pl
  für den Urlaub Erspartes, n
  Ferienersparnisse, f pl
  für die Ferien Erspartes, n
  ♦ vacation savings AE pl
  ♦ holiday savings BE pl
Urlaubserwartung, f
  Ferienerwartung, f
  ♦ vacation expectation AE
  ♦ holiday expectation BE
Urlaubserwartungen erfüllen von jm
  js Urlaubserwartungen erfüllen
  js Ferienerwartungen erfüllen
  ♦ meet s.o.'s vacation expectations AE
  ♦ meet s.o.'s holiday expectations BE
Urlaubsessen, n
  Ferienessen, n
  ♦ vacation meal AE
  ♦ holiday meal BE

Urlaubsetat, m
  → Urlaubsbudget
Urlaubsexodus, m
  Ferienexodus, m
  ♦ vacation exodus AE
  ♦ holiday exodus BE
Urlaubsexperte, m
  Ferienexperte, m
  ♦ vacation expert AE
  ♦ holiday expert BE
Urlaubsextra, n
  Ferienextra, n
  ♦ vacation extra AE
  ♦ holiday extra BE
urlaubsfähig, adj
  ferienfähig, adj
  ♦ fit for a vacation, adj AE
  ♦ fit for a holiday, adj BE
Urlaubsfahrpreis, m
  Ferienfahrpreis, m
  ♦ vacation fare AE
  ♦ holiday fare BE
Urlaubsfahrt, f
  Ferienfahrt, f
  ♦ vacation trip AE
  ♦ holiday trip BE
Urlaubsfahrzeug, n
  Ferienfahrzeug, n
  ♦ vacation vehicle AE
  ♦ holiday vehicle BE
Urlaubsfarm, f
  → Urlaubsbauernhof
Urlaubsfavorit, m
  Ferienfavorit, m
  ♦ vacation favorite AE
  ♦ holiday favourite BE
Urlaubsfieber, n
  Ferienfieber, n
  Reisefieber, n
  ♦ vacation fever AE
  ♦ holiday fever BE
  ♦ travel nerves pl
Urlaubsfilm, m
  Ferienfilm, m
  ♦ vacation film AE
  ♦ holiday film BE
Urlaubsfirma, f
  Ferienfirma, f
  ♦ vacation firm AE
  ♦ vacation company AE
  ♦ holiday firm BE
  ♦ holiday company BE
Urlaubsflug, m
  Ferienflug, m
  ♦ vacation flight AE
  ♦ holiday flight BE
Urlaubsform, f
  Ferienform, f
  ♦ form of (the) vacation AE
  ♦ form of (the) holiday BE
Urlaubsfoto, n
  Urlaubsschnappschuß, m
  Ferienfoto, n
  Ferienschnappschuß, m
  ♦ vacation snap AE
  ♦ holiday snap BE
Urlaubsfrage, f
  Ferienfrage, f
  ♦ vacation question AE
  ♦ holiday question BE

Urlaubsfragebogen, m
　Ferienfragebogen, m
　◆ vacation questionnaire *AE*
　◆ vacation questionaire *AE*
　◆ vacation questionary *AE*
　◆ holiday questionnaire *BE*
Urlaubsfreude, f
　Ferienfreude, f
　◆ vacation amusement *AE*
　◆ holiday amusement *BE*
Urlaubsführer, m
　Ferienführer, m
　◆ vacation guide *AE*
　◆ holiday guide *BE*
Urlaubsgag, m
　Urlaubsmätzchen, n
　Feriengag, m
　Ferienmätzchen, n
　◆ vacation gag *AE*
　◆ vacation gimmick *AE*
　◆ holiday gag *BE*
　◆ holiday gimmick *BE*
Urlaubsgarderobe, f
　Feriengarderobe, f
　◆ vacation wardrobe *AE*
　◆ holiday wardrobe *BE*
Urlaubsgast, m
　Feriengast, m
　◆ vacation guest *AE*
　◆ holiday guest *BE*
Urlaubsgebiet, n (groß)
　Feriengebiet, n
　Urlaubsregion, f
　Ferienregion, f
　◆ vacation region *AE*
　◆ holiday region *BE*
Urlaubsgebiet, n (klein)
　Feriengebiet, n
　◆ vacation area *AE*
　◆ holiday area *BE*
　◆ holiday district *BE*
Urlaubsgebiet erschließen
　Feriengebiet erschließen
　◆ develop a vacation area *AE*
　◆ develop a vacation region *AE*
　◆ develop a holiday area *BE*
　◆ develop a holiday region *BE*
Urlaubsgeld, n (Arbeitnehmer)
　◆ leave pay *AE*
　◆ vacation pay *AE*
　◆ holiday pay *BE*
Urlaubsgeld, n (im Urlaub)
　Feriengeld, n
　◆ vacation money *AE*
　◆ holiday money *BE*
Urlaubsgelegenheit, f
　Feriengelegenheit, f
　◆ vacation opportunity *AE*
　◆ holiday opportunity *BE*
Urlaubsgelegenheit bieten jm
　Urlaubsgelegenheit geben jm
　Feriengelegenheit bieten jm
　Feriengelegenheit geben jm
　◆ provide s.o. with a vacation opportunity *AE*
　◆ provide s.o. with a holiday opportunity *BE*
Urlaubsgenuß, m
　Urlaubsvergnügen, n
　Feriengenuß, m
　Ferienvergnügen, n
　◆ vacation enjoyment *AE*
　◆ holiday enjoyment *BE*

Urlaubsgenuß beeinträchtigen
　Urlaubsvergnügen beeinträchtigen
　Feriengenuß beeinträchtigen
　Ferienvergnügen beeinträchtigen
　◆ impair one's vacation enjoyment *AE*
　◆ impair s.o.'s vacation enjoyment *AE*
　◆ impair one's holiday enjoyment *BE*
　◆ impair s.o.'s holiday enjoyment *BE*
Urlaubsgenuß erhöhen
　Urlaubsvergnügen erhöhen
　Feriengenuß erhöhen
　Ferienvergnügen erhöhen
　◆ increase one's vacation enjoyment *AE*
　◆ increase s.o.'s vacation enjoyment *AE*
　◆ increase one's holiday enjoyment *BE*
　◆ increase s.o's holiday enjoyment *BE*
Urlaubsgepäck, n
　Feriengepäck, n
　◆ vacation baggage *AE*
　◆ holiday luggage *BE*
Urlaubsgeschäft, n
　Feriengeschäft, n
　◆ vacation business *AE*
　◆ holiday business *BE*
Urlaubs-/Geschäftsreise, f
　Ferien-/Geschäftsreise, f
　◆ vacation and business trip *AE*
　◆ holiday and business trip *Be*
Urlaubsgeschenk, n
　Feriengeschenk, n
　◆ vacation present *AE*
　◆ vacation gift *AE*
　◆ holiday present *BE*
　◆ holiday gift *BE*
Urlaubsgesellschaft, f (Firma)
　Urlaubsfirma, f
　Feriengesellschaft, f
　Ferienfirma, f
　◆ vacation company *AE*
　◆ holiday company *BE*
Urlaubsgestaltung, f
　Feriengestaltung, f
　◆ organisation of a vacation *AE*
　◆ vacation organisation *AE*
　◆ organisation of a holiday *BE*
　◆ holiday organisation *BE*
　◆ use of one's vacation *AE*
Urlaubsgesuch, n (Arbeitnehmer)
　◆ request for vacation *AE*
　◆ vacation request *AE*
　◆ request for holiday *BE*
　◆ holiday request *BE*
Urlaubsgesundheitsführer, m
　Feriengesundheitsführer, m
　◆ vacation healthcare guide *AE*
　◆ holiday healthcare guide *BE*
Urlaubsgesundheitsprüfliste, f
　Gesundheitsprüfliste für die Ferien, f
　◆ vacation healthcare checklist *AE*
　◆ holiday healthcare checklist *BE*
Urlaubsgewerbe, n
　Feriengewerbe, n
　◆ vacation trade *AE*
　◆ holiday trade *BE*
Urlaubsgewohnheit, f
　Feriengewohnheit, f
　◆ vacation habit *AE*
　◆ holiday habit *BE*
Urlaubsgewohnheiten untersuchen
　Feriengewohnheiten untersuchen

　◆ study the vacation habits *AE*
　◆ study the holiday habits *BE*
Urlaubsgratifikation, f
　◆ vacation bonus *AE*
　◆ holiday bonus *BE*
Urlaubsgrüße, m pl
　Feriengrüße, m pl
　◆ vacation greetings *AE pl*
　◆ holiday greetings *BE pl*
Urlaubsgutschein, m
　Feriengutschein, m
　◆ vacation voucher *AE*
　◆ holiday voucher *BE*
Urlaubshaus, n
　Ferienhaus, n
　◆ vacation home *AE*
　◆ holiday home *BE*
Urlaubshausanbieter, m
　Ferienhausanbieter, m
　◆ vacation home supplier *AE*
　◆ supplier of vacation homes *AE*
　◆ holiday home supplier *BE*
　◆ supplier of holiday homes *BE*
Urlaubshausanlage, f
　Urlaubshauskomplex, m
　Ferienhausanlage, f
　Ferienhauskomplex, m
　◆ vacation home complex *AE*
　◆ summer house complex *AE*
　◆ holiday home complex *BE*
Urlaubshaus buchen
　Ferienhaus buchen
　◆ book a vacation home *AE*
　◆ reserve a vacation home *AE*
　◆ book a holiday home *BE*
Urlaubshausgebiet, n
　Ferienhausgebiet, n
　◆ vacation home area *AE*
　◆ summer house area *AE*
　◆ holiday home area *BE*
Urlaubshauskatalog, m
　Ferienhauskatalog, m
　◆ vacation home catalogue *AE*
　◆ vacation home catalog *AE*
　◆ holiday home catalogue *BE*
Urlaubshausmarkt, m
　Ferienhausmarkt, m
　◆ vacation-home market *AE*
　◆ holiday-home market *BE*
Urlaubshaus mieten
　Ferienhaus mieten
　◆ rent a vacation home *AE*
　◆ hire a holiday home *BE*
　◆ rent a holiday home *BE*
Urlaubshausprospekt, m
　Ferienhausprospekt, m
　◆ vacation home brochure *AE*
　◆ holiday home brochure *BE*
Urlaubshaus reservieren
　Ferienhaus reservieren
　◆ reserve a vacation home *AE*
　◆ reserve a holiday home *BE*
Urlaubshaustausch, m
　Ferienhaustausch, m
　◆ vacation home exchange *AE*
　◆ holiday home exchange *BE*
Urlaubshaus vermieten
　Ferienhaus vermieten
　◆ rent a vacation home *AE*
　◆ let a holiday home *BE*
　◆ hire out a holiday home *BE*

Urlaubshausvermietung

Urlaubshausvermietung, f
Ferienhausvermietung, f
♦ vacation home rental *AE*
♦ renting a vacation home *AE*
♦ letting a holiday home *BE*
Urlaubshausvermittlung, f (Agentur)
Ferienhausvermittlung, f
♦ vacation home agency *AE*
♦ holiday home agency *BE*
Urlaubshausvermittlung, f (Tätigkeit)
Ferienhausvermittlung, f
♦ vacation home reservation service *AE*
♦ holiday home booking service *BE*
Urlaubshausvermittler, m
Ferienhausvermittler, m
♦ vacation home agent *AE*
♦ holiday home agent *BE*
Urlaubshochburg, f *humor*
Ferienhochburg, f *humor*
♦ popular vacation resort *AE*
♦ popular holiday resort *BE*
Urlaubshotel, n
Ferienhotel, n
♦ vacation hotel *AE*
♦ holiday hotel *BE*
Urlaubshotel an der See, n
→ Seeurlaubshotel
Urlaubshotelbesitzer, m
Ferienhotelbesitzer, m
♦ vacation hotel owner *AE*
♦ holiday hotel owner *BE*
Urlaubshütte, f (Lodge)
Urlaubslodge, f
Ferienhütte, f
Ferienlodge, f
♦ vacation lodge *AE*
♦ holiday lodge *BE*
Urlaubsidee, f
Ferienidee, f
♦ vacation idea *AE*
♦ holiday idea *BE*
♦ idea about/for/of a vacation *AE*
♦ idea about/for/of a holiday *BE*
Urlaubsimmobilie, f
Ferienimmobilie, f
♦ vacation property *AE*
♦ holiday property *BE*
Urlaubsindividualist, m
Ferienindividualist, m
♦ vacation individualist *AE*
♦ holiday individualist *BE*
Urlaubsindustrie, f
Ferienindustrie, f
♦ vacation industry *AE*
♦ holiday industry *BE*
Urlaubsinformation, f
Ferieninformation, f
♦ vacation information *AE*
♦ holiday information *BE*
Urlaubsinformationspaket, n
Ferieninformationspaket, n
♦ vacation information pack *AE*
♦ vacation information kit *AE*
♦ holiday information pack *BE*
Urlaubsinsel, f
Ferieninsel, f
♦ vacation island *AE*
♦ holiday island *BE*
Urlaubsinteresse, n
(Statistik)
Urlaubsneigung, f
Urlaubsgeneigheit, f
Ferieninteresse, n
♦ vacation propensity *AE*
♦ holiday propensity *BE*
Urlaubsinteressent, m
Ferieninteressent, m
♦ prospective vacationer *AE*
♦ prospective holidaymaker *BE*
♦ potential vacationer *AE*
♦ potential holidaymaker *BE*
Urlaubsinvestition, f
Ferieninvestition, f
♦ vacation investment *AE*
♦ holiday investment *BE*
Urlaubsjahr, n (Ferien)
Ferienjahr, n
♦ vacation year *AE*
♦ holiday year *BE*
Urlaubsjahr, n (Hochschule)
Ferienjahr, n
♦ sabbatical year
Urlaubsjet, m
Ferienjet, m
♦ vacation jet *AE*
♦ holiday jet *BE*
Urlaubsjob, m
Urlaubsarbeit, f
Ferienjob, m
Ferienarbeit, f
♦ vacation job *AE*
♦ holiday job *BE*
Urlaubskalender, m
Ferienkalender, m
♦ vacation calendar *AE*
♦ holiday calendar *BE*
Urlaubskapazität, f
Ferienkapazität, f
♦ vacation capacity *AE*
♦ holiday capacity *BE*
Urlaubskasse, f
→ Urlaubsbudget
Urlaubskatalog, m
Ferienkatalog, m
♦ vacation catalogue *AE*
♦ vacation catalog *AE*
♦ holiday catalogue *BE*
Urlaubskater, m *figur*
Ferienkater, m *figur*
♦ vacation hangover *AE*
♦ holiday hangover *BE*
Urlaubskatzenjammer, m
Urlaubsdepression, f
Ferienkatzenjammer, m
Feriendepression, f
♦ vacation blues *AE pl*
♦ holiday blues *BE pl*
Urlaubskleinod, n
Ferienkleinod, n
♦ vacation gem *AE*
♦ holiday gem *BE*
Urlaubskleinwohnung f
kleine Urlaubswohnung, f
Ferienkleinwohnung, f
kleine Ferienwohnung, f
♦ small vacation apartment *AE*
♦ small holiday flat *BE*
♦ holiday flatlet *BE*
Urlaubskoffer, m
Urlaubsreisekoffer, m
Ferienkoffer, m
Ferienreisekoffer, m
♦ vacation suitcase *AE*
♦ holiday suitcase *BE*
Urlaubskombination, f
Ferienkombination, f
♦ vacation combination *AE*
♦ holiday combination *BE*
Urlaubskomfort, m
Urlaubsannehmlichkeiten, f pl
Ferienkomfort, m
Ferienannehmlichkeiten, f pl
♦ vacation amenities *AE pl*
♦ holiday amenities *BE pl*
Urlaubskoordinator, m
Ferienkoordinator, m
♦ vacation coordinator *AE*
♦ holiday coordinator *BE*
Urlaubskosten, pl
Ferienkosten, pl
Kosten eines Urlaubs, pl
Kosten der Ferien, pl
♦ vacation costs *AE pl*
♦ costs of a vacation *AE pl*
♦ cost of a vacation *AE*
♦ holiday costs *BE pl*
♦ cost(s) of a holiday *BE (pl)*
Urlaubskostensteigerung, f
Ferienkostensteigerung, f
♦ increase in vacation costs *AE*
♦ increase in holiday costs *BE*
Urlaubskosten zurückerstatten
Urlaubskosten erstatten
Ferienkosten zurückerstatten
Ferienkosten erstatten
♦ refund the cost of a vacation *AE*
♦ refund the cost of a holiday *BE*
Urlaubskredit, m
Urlaubsdarlehen, n
Ferienkredit, m
Feriendarlehen, n
♦ vacation credit *AE*
♦ vacation loan *AE*
♦ holiday credit *BE*
♦ holiday loan *BE*
Urlaubskredit aufnehmen
Urlaubsdarlehen aufnehmen
Ferienkredit aufnehmen
Feriendarlehen aufnehmen
♦ take out a vacation loan *AE*
♦ take out a holiday loan *BE*
Urlaubskreuzfahrt, f
Ferienkreuzfahrt, f
♦ vacation cruise *AE*
♦ holiday cruise *BE*
Urlaubskriminalität, f
Urlaubsverbrechen, n pl
Ferienkriminalität, f
Ferienverbrechen, n pl
♦ vacation crimes *AE pl*
♦ holiday crimes *BE pl*
Urlaubskunde, m
Ferienkunde, m
♦ vacation customer *AE*
♦ vacation client *AE*
♦ holiday customer *BE*
Urlaubskurs, m
Urlaubslehrgang, m
Ferienkurs, m
Ferienlehrgang, m
♦ vacation course *AE*
♦ holiday course *BE*

Urlaubsküste, f
  Ferienküste, f
  ♦ vacation coast *AE*
  ♦ holiday coast *BE*
Urlaubsladen, m
  Urlaubsgeschäft, n
  Ferienladen, m
  Feriengeschäft, n
  ♦ vacation store *AE*
  ♦ holiday shop *BE*
Urlaubslager, n
  Ferienlager, n
  ♦ vacation camp *AE*
  ♦ holiday camp *BE*
  ♦ summer camp
Urlaubslager betreiben
  Ferienlager betreiben
  ♦ operate a vacation camp *AE*
  ♦ operate a holiday camp *BE*
  ♦ operate a summer camp
Urlaubslagerbetreiber, m
  Ferienlagerbetreiber, m
  ♦ vacation camp operator *AE*
  ♦ summer camp operator *AE*
  ♦ holiday camp operator *BE*
Urlaubslagerleiter, m
  Ferienlagerleiter, m
  ♦ vacation camp director *AE*
  ♦ summer camp director *AE*
  ♦ holiday camp manager *BE*
Urlaubslager organisieren
  Urlaubslager veranstalten
  Ferienlager organisieren
  Ferienlager veranstalten
  ♦ organise a vacation camp *AE*
  ♦ organise a summer camp *AE*
  ♦ organise a holiday camp *BE*
Urlaubsland, n
  Ferienland, n
  ♦ vacation country *AE*
  ♦ holiday country *BE*
Urlaubslandschaft, f
  Ferienlandschaft, f
  ♦ vacation scenery *AE*
  ♦ vacation landscape *AE*
  ♦ holiday scenery *BE*
  ♦ holiday landscape *BE*
  ♦ holiday countryside *BE*
Urlaubslänge, f
  Ferienlänge, f
  ♦ length of the vacation *AE*
  ♦ vacation length *AE*
  ♦ length of a holiday *BE*
  ♦ holiday length *BE*
Urlaubsleben, n
  Ferienleben, n
  ♦ vacation life *AE*
  ♦ holiday life *BE*
Urlaubslebensstil, m
  Ferienlebensstil, m
  ♦ vacation lifestyle *AE*
  ♦ holiday lifestyle *BE*
Urlaubsleistung, f
  → Urlaubsservice
Urlaubslektüre, f
  Ferienlektüre, f
  ♦ vacation reading *AE*
  ♦ holiday reading *BE*
Urlaubsliste, f (Unternehmen)
  ♦ leave roster

Urlaubsmarke, f
  Ferienmarke, f
  ♦ vacation brand *AE*
  ♦ holiday brand *BE*
Urlaubsmarkt, m
  Ferienmarkt, m
  ♦ vacation market *AE*
  ♦ holiday market *BE*
Urlaubsmarktanteil, m
  Ferienmarktanteil m
  ♦ vacation market share *AE*
  ♦ holiday market share *BE*
Urlaubsmätzchen, n
  Ferienmätzchen, n
  ♦ vacation gimmick *AE*
  ♦ holiday gimmick *BE*
Urlaubsmiete, f
  Ferienmiete, f
  ♦ vacation rent *AE*
  ♦ holiday rent *BE*
Urlaubsmißgeschick, n
  Ferienmißgeschick, n
  ♦ vacation misadventure *AE*
  ♦ holiday misadventure *BE*
Urlaubsmöglichkeit, f
  Ferienmöglichkeit, f
  ♦ vacation possibility *AE*
  ♦ holiday possibility *BE*
  ♦ possibility of taking a vacation *AE*
  ♦ possibility of taking a holiday *BE*
Urlaubsmonat, m
  Ferienmonat, m
  ♦ vacation month *AE*
  ♦ holiday month *BE*
Urlaubsmotel, n
  Ferienmotel, n
  ♦ vacation motel *AE*
  ♦ holiday motel *BE*
Urlaubsmotiv, n
  Ferienmotiv, n
  ♦ motive for taking a vacation *AE*
  ♦ motive for taking a holiday *BE*
  ♦ vacation motivation *AE*
  ♦ holiday motivation *BE*
Urlaubsmotivation, f
  Urlaubsmotiv, n
  Ferienmotivation, f
  Ferienmotiv, n
  ♦ vacation motivation *AE*
  ♦ holiday motivation *BE*
  ♦ motivation for taking a vacation *AE*
  ♦ motive for taking a holiday *BE*
Urlaubsnachfrage, f
  Feriennachfrage, f
  ♦ vacation demand *AE*
  ♦ demand for vacations *AE*
  ♦ holiday demand *BE*
  ♦ demand for holidays *BE*
Urlaubsnachrichten, f pl
  Feriennachrichten, f pl
  ♦ vacation news *AE pl = sg*
  ♦ holiday news *BE pl = sg*
Urlaubsoase, f
  Ferienoase, f
  ♦ vacation oasis *AE*
  ♦ holiday oasis *BE*
Urlaubsofferte, f
  → Urlaubsangebot
Urlaubsoption, f
  Ferienoption, f

  ♦ vacation option *AE*
  ♦ holiday option *BE*
Urlaubsorganisation, f
  Ferienorganisation, f
  ♦ vacation organisation *AE*
  ♦ holiday organisation *BE*
Urlaubsort, m
  Ferienort, m
  ♦ vacation resort *AE*
  ♦ holiday resort *BE*
Urlaubsortatmosphäre, f
  Ferienortatmosphäre, f
  ♦ vacation resort atmosphere *AE*
  ♦ holiday resort atmosphere *BE*
  ♦ resort atmosphere
Urlaubsorthotel, n
  → Ferienorthotel
Urlaubsort mit gutem Nachtleben, m
  Ferienort mit gutem Nachtleben, m
  ♦ vacation resort with good night life *AE*
  ♦ holiday resort with good night-life *BE*
Urlaubspaket, n
  (Information)
  Ferienpaket, n
  ♦ vacation pack *AE*
  ♦ holiday pack *BE*
Urlaubsparadies, n
  Ferienparadies, n
  ♦ vacation paradise *AE*
  ♦ holiday paradise *BE*
Urlaubspark, m
  Ferienpark, m
  ♦ vacation park *AE*
  ♦ holiday park *BE*
Urlaubspartner, m
  Ferienpartner, m
  ♦ vacation partner *AE*
  ♦ holiday partner *BE*
Urlaubspauschalarrangement, n
  Ferienpauschalarrangement, n
  ♦ vacation package deal *AE*
  ♦ holiday package deal *BE*
Urlaubspauschale, f
  Ferienpauschale, f
  ♦ vacation package *AE*
  ♦ holiday package *BE*
Urlaubspauschalpreis, m
  Ferienpauschalpreis, m
  ♦ inclusive vacation price *AE*
  ♦ inclusive holiday price *BE*
Urlaubspension, f
  Ferienpension, f
  ♦ vacation guesthouse *AE*
  ♦ private vacation hotel *AE*
  ♦ holiday guest-house *BE*
  ♦ private holiday hotel *BE*
Urlaubsphilosophie, f
  Ferienphilosophie, f
  ♦ vacation philosophy *AE*
  ♦ holiday philosophy *BE*
Urlaubsplan, m (Privatperson)
  Ferienplan, m
  ♦ vacation plan *AE*
  ♦ holiday plan *BE*
Urlaubsplan, m (Unternehmen)
  Urlaubsordnung, f
  ♦ leave schedule
  ♦ vacation schedule *AE*
  ♦ holiday schedule *BE*
Urlaubspläne besprechen
  Ferienpläne besprechen

Urlaubspläne diskutieren

- talk about one's vacation plans *AE*
- talk about one's holiday plans *BE*

Urlaubspläne diskutieren
Ferienpläne diskutieren
- discuss one's vacation plans *AE*
- discuss one's holiday plans *BE*

Urlaubsplaner, m
Ferienplaner, m
- vacation planner *AE*
- holiday planner *BE*

Urlaubspläne zurückschrauben
Ferienpläne zurückschrauben
- cut back one's vacation plans *AE*
- cut back one's holiday plans *BE*

Urlaubsplanung, f
Ferienplanung, f
- vacation planning *AE*
- planning (of) a vacation *AE*
- holiday planning *BE*
- planning (of) a holiday *BE*

Urlaubsplatz, m (Camping)
Ferienplatz, m
- vacation site *AE*
- holiday site *BE*

Urlaubsplatz, m (generell)
Ferienplatz, m
- vacation place *AE*
- vacation spot *AE*
- holiday place *BE*
- holiday spot *BE*

Urlaubsplatz, m (Ort)
Urlaubsort, m
Ferienplatz, m
Ferienort, m
- vacation spot *AE*
- vacation place *AE*
- holiday spot *BE*
- holiday place *BE*

Urlaubsplatz sichern sich
Ferienplatz sich sichern
- secure a vacation place *AE*
- secure a holiday place *BE*

Urlaubspost, f
Ferienpost, f
- vacation mail *AE*
- holiday mail *BE*

Urlaubspostkarte, f
Urlaubskarte, f
Ferienpostkarte, f
Ferienkarte, f
- vacation postcard *AE*
- postcard from s.o. on vacation *AE*
- holiday postcard *BE*
- postcard from s.o. on holiday *BE*

Urlaubspräferenz, f
→ Urlaubsvorliebe

Urlaubspreis, m (Gewinn)
Urlaubsauszeichnung, f
Ferienpreis, m
Ferienauszeichnung, f
- vacation prize *AE*
- holiday prize *BE*

Urlaubspreis, m (Kosten)
Ferienpreis, m
- vacation price *AE*
- vacation rate *AE*
- holiday price *BE*
- holiday rate *BE*
- price of a vacation *AE*

Urlaubspreis ist exklusive Unterkunft
Ferienpreis ist exklusive Unterbringung

- vacation price is exclusive of accommodation *AE*
- holiday price is exclusive of accommodation *BE*

Urlaubspreis ist inklusive Unterkunft
Ferienpreis ist inklusive Unterbringung
- vacation price inludes accommodation *AE*
- vacation price is inclusive of accommodation *AE*
- holiday price includes accommodation *BE*
- holiday price is inclusive of accommodation *BE*

Urlaubspreiskrieg, m
Ferienpreiskrieg, m
- vacation price war *AE*
- holiday price war *BE*

Urlaubspreiskrieg beginnen
Ferienpreiskrieg beginnen
- start a vacation price war *AE*
- start a holiday price war *BE*
- begin a vacation price war *AE*
- begin a holiday price war *BE*

Urlaubspreiskrieg bricht aus
- vacation price war breaks out *AE*
- holiday price war breaks out *BE*

Urlaubspriorität, f
Ferienpriorität, f
- vacation priority *AE*
- holiday priority *BE*

Urlaubsproblem, n
Ferienproblem, n
- vacation problem *AE*
- holiday problem *BE*

Urlaubsprodukt, n
Ferienprodukt, n
- vacation product *AE*
- holiday product *BE*

Urlaubsprogramm, n
Ferienprogramm, n
- vacation program *AE*
- holiday programme *BE*
- programme of holidays *BE*

Urlaubsprojekt, n
Ferienprojekt, n
- vacation project *AE*
- holiday project *BE*

Urlaubsprospekt, m
Ferienprospekt, m
- vacation brochure *AE*
- holiday brochure *BE*

Urlaubsprüfliste, f
Ferienprüfliste, f
- vacation checklist *AE*
- holiday checklist *BE*

Urlaubsquartier, n
Urlaubsunterkunft, f
Ferienquartier, n
- vacation quarters *AE pl*
- holiday quarters *BE pl*

Urlaubsrabatt, m
Ferienrabatt, m
- vacation discount *AE*
- holiday discount *BE*

Urlaubsrechnung, f
Ferienrechnung, f
- vacation bill *AE*
- holiday bill *BE*

Urlaubsrecht, n
Ferienrecht, n
- vacation law *AE*
- holiday law *BE*

Urlaubsregion f
Ferienregion f

- vacation area *AE*
- holiday region *BE*

urlaubsreif, adj
→ urlaubsbedürftig

Urlaubsreise, f
Ferienreise, f
- vacation tour *AE*
- vacation trip *AE*
- holiday trip *BE*
- holiday tour *BE*

Urlaubsreiseaufkommen, n
Ferienreiseaufkommen, n
Urlaubsreisevolumen, n
Ferienreisevolumen, n
- vacation travel volume *AE*
- volume of vacation travel *AE*
- holiday travel volume *BE*
- volume of holiday travel *BE*

Urlaubsreisebereich, m
Urlaubsreisesektor, m
Ferienreisebereich, m
Ferienreisesektor, m
- vacation travel sector *AE*
- holiday travel sector *BE*

Urlaubsreise buchen
Ferienreise buchen
- book a vacation trip *AE*
- book a vacation tour *AE*
- book a holiday trip *BE*
- book a holiday tour *BE*

Urlaubsreise machen
Urlaubsreise unternehmen
Ferienreise machen
Ferienreise unternehmen
- make a vacation trip *AE*
- go on a vacation trip *AE*
- make a holiday trip *BE*
- go on a holiday trip *BE*

Urlaubsreisemarkt, m
Ferienreisemarkt, m
- vacation travel market *AE*
- holiday travel market *BE*

Urlaubsreisemesse, f
Ferienreisemesse, f
- vacation travel fair *AE*
- holiday travel fair *BE*

Urlaubsreisen, n
Urlaubsreiseverkehr, m
Ferienreisen, n
Ferienreiseverkehr, m
- vacation travel *AE*
- holiday travel *BE*

Urlaubsreisender, m
Ferienreisender, m
- vacation traveler *AE*
- holiday traveller *BE*

Urlaubsreisen machen 40 % aller Besuche aus
Ferienreisen machen 40 % aller Besuche aus
- vacation trips account for 40 % of all visits *AE*
- holiday trips account for 40 % of all visits *BE*

Urlaubsreise stornieren
Urlaubsreise absagen
Urlaubsreise streichen
Ferienreise stornieren
Ferienreise absagen
- cancel a vacation trip *AE*
- cancel a holiday trip *BE*

Urlaubsreise unternehmen
Ferienreise unternehmen
- take a vacation trip *AE*

824

- ◆ take a vacation tour *AE*
- ◆ take a holiday trip *BE*
- ◆ take a holiday tour *BE*

Urlaubsreiseverkehrsmittel, n
Ferienreiseverkehrsmittel, n
- ◆ means of vacation transportation *AE*
- ◆ means of holiday transport *BE*

Urlaubsreservierung, f
Ferienreservierung, f
- ◆ reservation of a vacation *AE*
- ◆ vacation reservation *AE*
- ◆ reservation of a holiday *BE*
- ◆ holiday reservation *BE*
- ◆ reserving a vacation *AE*

Urlaubsresidenz, f
Ferienresidenz, f
- ◆ vacation residence *AE*
- ◆ holiday residence *BE*

Urlaubsrest, m
Ferienrest, m
Rest des Urlaubs, m
Rest der Ferien, m
- ◆ remainder of one's vacation *AE*
- ◆ remainder of one's holiday *BE*
- ◆ rest of the vacation *AE*
- ◆ rest of the holiday *BE*

Urlaubsrest in X verbringen
Ferienrest in X verbringen
- ◆ spend the remainder of one's vacation in X *AE*
- ◆ spend the remainder of one's vacation at X *AE*
- ◆ spend the remainder of one's holiday in X *BE*
- ◆ spend the remainder of one's holiday at X *BE*

Urlaubsritual, n
Ferienritual, n
- ◆ vacation ritual *AE*
- ◆ holiday ritual *BE*

Urlaubsromanze, f
Ferienromanze, f
- ◆ vacation romance *AE*
- ◆ holiday romance *BE*

Urlaubsroute, f
→ Urlaubsstrecke

Urlaubsroutine, f
Ferienroutine, f
- ◆ vacation routine *AE*
- ◆ holiday routine *BE*

Urlaubsrücktritt, m
→ Urlaubsstornierung

Urlaubsrummel, m
Urlaubstrubel, m
Ferienrummel, m
Ferientrubel, m
- ◆ hustle and bustle of a vacation resort *AE*
- ◆ hustle and bustle of a holiday resort *BE*

Urlaubssaison, f
Feriensaison, f
- ◆ vacation season *AE*
- ◆ holiday season *BE*

Urlaubssaison rückt näher
Feriensaison rückt näher
- ◆ vacation season is drawing near *AE*
- ◆ holiday season is drawing near *BE*

Urlaubssaison verlängern
Feriensaison verlängern
- ◆ lengthen the vacation season *AE*
- ◆ lengthen the holiday season *BE*

Urlaubsschau, f
Urlaubsausstellung, f
Ferienschau, f
Ferienausstellung, f

- ◆ vacation show *AE*
- ◆ holiday show *BE*

Urlaubsschiff, n
Ferienschiff, n
- ◆ vacation liner *AE*
- ◆ holiday liner *BE*

Urlaubsschlafraum, m
Ferienschlafraum, m
- ◆ vacation bedroom *AE*
- ◆ holiday bedroom *BE*

Urlaubsschlager, m
Ferienschlager, m
- ◆ vacation hit *AE*
- ◆ holiday hit *BE*

Urlaubsschnäppchen, n
Ferienschnäppchen, n
- ◆ vacation bargain *AE*
- ◆ vacation snip *AE coll*
- ◆ holiday bargain *BE*
- ◆ holiday snip *BE coll*

Urlaubsschnappschuß, m
Ferienschnappschuß, m
- ◆ vacation snapshot *AE*
- ◆ holiday snapshot *BE*

Urlaubssegment, n
Feriensegment, n
- ◆ vacation segment *AE*
- ◆ holiday segment *BE*

Urlaubssektor, m
Urlaubsbereich, m
Feriensektor, m
Ferienbereich, m
- ◆ vacation sector *AE*
- ◆ holiday sector *BE*

Urlaubsservice, m
Urlaubsdienst, m
Urlaubsdienstleistung, f
Urlaubsleistung, f
Ferienservice, m
- ◆ vacation service *AE*
- ◆ holiday service *BE*

Urlaubssex, m
Feriensex, m
- ◆ vacation sex *AE*
- ◆ holiday sex *BE*

Urlaubssicherheit, f
Feriensicherheit, f
- ◆ vacation security *AE*
- ◆ holiday security *BE*

Urlaubssommer, m
Feriensommer, m
- ◆ vacation summer *AE*
- ◆ holiday summer *BE*

Urlaubssonderzug, m
Feriensonderzug, m
- ◆ special vacation train *AE*
- ◆ special holiday train *BE*

Urlaubssonnenschein, m
Feriensonnenschein, m
- ◆ vacation sunshine *AE*
- ◆ holiday sunshine *BE*

Urlaubsspaß, m
Ferienspaß, m
- ◆ vacation fun *AE*
- ◆ holiday fun *BE*

Urlaubssperre, f (Arbeitnehmer)
- ◆ ban on leave
- ◆ ban on vacation *AE*

Urlaubssperre, f (Ferien)
Feriensperre, f
- ◆ ban on vacation *AE*

- ◆ vacation ban *AE*
- ◆ ban on holidays *BE*
- ◆ holiday ban *BE*

Urlaubsspezialist, m
Ferienspezialist, m
- ◆ vacation specialist *AE*
- ◆ holiday specialist *BE*

Urlaubsstadt, f (Großstadt)
Ferienstadt, f
- ◆ vacation city *AE*
- ◆ holiday city *BE*

Urlaubsstadt, f (kleine Stadt)
Ferienstadt, f
- ◆ vacation town *AE*
- ◆ holiday town *BE*

Urlaubsstaffelung, f
Ferienstaffelung, f
- ◆ staggering of vacations *AE*
- ◆ staggering vacations *AE*
- ◆ staggering of holidays *BE*
- ◆ staggering holidays *BE*

Urlaubsstandort, m
Urlaubsort, m
Ferienstandort, m
Ferienort, m
- ◆ vacation location *AE*
- ◆ holiday location *BE*

Urlaubsstätte, f
Ferienstätte, f
- ◆ vacation venue *AE*
- ◆ holiday venue *BE*

Urlaubsstellplatz, m
(Camping)
Ferienstellplatz, m
- ◆ vacation pitch *AE*
- ◆ vacation site *AE*
- ◆ holiday pitch *BE*

Urlaubsstimmung, f (Atmosphäre)
→ Urlaubsatmosphäre

Urlaubsstimmung, f (einer Person)
Ferienstimmung, f
- ◆ vacation mood *AE*
- ◆ holiday mood *BE*

Urlaubsstimmung, f (Gefühl)
Urlaubsgeist, m
Ferienstimmung, f
Feriengeist, m
- ◆ vacation spirit *AE*
- ◆ holiday spirit *BE*

Urlaubsstornierung, f
Urlaubsabsage, f
Urlaubsrücktritt, m
Urlaubsannullierung, f
Ferienstornierung, f
- ◆ cancelation of a vacation *AE*
- ◆ cancellation of a holiday *BE*

Urlaubsstrand, m
Ferienstrand, m
- ◆ vacation beach *AE*
- ◆ holiday beach *BE*

Urlaubsstraße, f
Ferienstraße, f
- ◆ vacation road *AE*
- ◆ vacation route *AE*
- ◆ holiday road *BE*
- ◆ holiday route *BE*

Urlaubsstrecke, f
Urlaubsroute, f
Ferienstrecke, f
Ferienroute, f

Urlaubsstudie

♦ vacation route AE
♦ holiday route BE
Urlaubsstudie, f
Ferienstudie, f
♦ vacation study AE
♦ holiday study BE
Urlaubsstudienzentrum, n
Ferienstudienzentrum, n
♦ vacation study center AE
♦ holiday study centre BE
Urlaubsstunde, f
Ferienstunde, f
♦ vacation hour AE
♦ holiday hour BE
Urlaubssüchtiger, m
Feriensüchtiger, m
♦ vacation addict AE
♦ holiday addict BE
Urlaubsszene, f
Ferienszene, f
♦ vacation scene AE
♦ holiday scene BE
Urlaub staffeln
Ferien staffeln
♦ stagger vacation AE
♦ stagger holidays BE
Urlaubstag, m (Arbeitnehmer)
freier Tag, m
♦ day of one's leave
♦ day off
Urlaubstag, m (Ferien)
Ferientag, m
♦ vacation day AE
♦ day of one's vacation AE
♦ day of one's holiday BE
♦ holiday BE
Urlaubstarif, m
Ferientarif, m
♦ vacation tariff AE
♦ vacation rates AE pl
♦ vacation rate AE
♦ vacation terms AE pl
♦ holiday tariff AE
Urlaubstermin, m
Ferientermin, m
♦ vacation date AE
♦ date of vacation AE
♦ holiday date BE
♦ date of holiday BE
Urlaubstermine besprechen
Ferientermine besprechen
♦ discuss the vacation dates AE
♦ discuss the holiday dates BE
Urlaubstip, m
Ferientip, m
♦ vacation tip AE
♦ holiday tip BE
Urlaub stornieren
Urlaub rückgängig machen
Urlaub absagen
Urlaub annullieren
Ferien stornieren
♦ cancel a vacation AE
♦ cancel a holiday BE
Urlaubstourismus, m
Ferientourismus, m
♦ vacation tourism AE
♦ holiday tourism BE
Urlaubstourist, m
Ferientourist, m

♦ vacation tourist AE
♦ holiday tourist BE
Urlaubstransport, m
Urlaubsbeförderung, f
Ferientransport, m
Ferienbeförderung, f
♦ vacation transportation AE
♦ holiday transport BE
Urlaubstransportart, f
Ferientransportart, f
♦ mode of vacation transport AE
♦ mode of holiday transport BE
Urlaubstraum, m
Ferientraum, m
♦ vacation dream AE
♦ holiday dream BE
Urlaubstraum wird wahr
Ferientraum wird wahr
♦ vacation dream comes true AE
♦ holiday dream comes true BE
Urlaubstreff, m
Urlaubstreffpunkt, m
Urlaubslokal, m
Ferientreff, m
Ferientreffpunkt, m
♦ vacation haunt AE
♦ holiday haunt BE
Urlaubstrubel, m
→ Urlaubsrummel
Urlaubsübernachtung, f (generell)
Ferienübernachtung, f
♦ vacation night AE
♦ holiday night BE
Urlaubsübernachtung, f (Statistik)
Ferienübernachtung, f
♦ vacation night spent AE
♦ holiday night spent BE
Urlaubsumgebung, f
Ferienumgebung, f
♦ vacation environment AE
♦ vacation setting AE
♦ holiday environment BE
♦ holiday setting BE
Urlaubs- und Reiseversicherung, f
Ferien- und Reiseversicherung, f
♦ vacation and travel insurance AE
♦ holiday and travel insurance BE
Urlaubsunterhaltung, f
Ferienunterhaltung, f
♦ vacation entertainment AE
♦ holiday entertainment BE
Urlaubsunterkunft, f
Ferienunterkunft, f
♦ vacation accommodation AE
♦ vacation lodging AE
♦ holiday accommodation BE
Urlaubsunterkunft buchen
Ferienunterkunft buchen
♦ book vacation accommodation AE
♦ book holiday accommodation BE
Urlaubsunterkunft festmachen
Ferienunterkunft festmachen
Urlaubsunterkunft organisieren
Ferienunterkunft organisieren
♦ fix up one's vacation accommodation AE
♦ fix up one's holiday accommodation BE
Urlaubsunterkunft für Selbstversorger, f
Urlaubsunterkunft für Selbstverpfleger, f
Ferienunterkunft für Selbstversorger, f
Ferienunterkunft für Selbstverpfleger, f

♦ self-service vacation accommodation AE
♦ self-service holiday accommodation BE
Urlaubsunterkunftsvermittlung, f
Urlaubsunterkunftsnachweis, m
Ferienunterkunftsvermittlung, f
Ferienunterkunftsnachweis, m
♦ vacation accommodation agency AE
♦ holiday accommodation agency BE
Urlaubsvariablen, f pl
Ferienvariablen, f pl
♦ vacation variables AE pl
♦ holiday variables BE pl
Urlaubsveranstalter, m
Ferienveranstalter, m
♦ vacation operator AE
♦ holiday operator BE
Urlaubsvergnügen, n
Ferienvergnügen, n
♦ vacation pleasure AE
♦ vacation enjoyment AE
♦ holiday pleasure BE
♦ holiday enjoyment BE
Urlaubsvergütung, f (Arbeitnehmer)
Ferienvergütung, f
♦ vacation remuneration AE
♦ holiday remuneration BE
Urlaubsverhalten, n (Person)
Ferienverhalten, n
♦ vacation behavior AE
♦ holiday behaviour BE
Urlaubsverhalten, n (Statistik)
Ferienverhalten, n
♦ vacation pattern AE
♦ holiday pattern BE
Urlaubsverhalten beeinflussen (Person)
Ferienverhalten beeinflussen
♦ affect the vacation behavior AE
♦ affect the holiday behaviour BE
Urlaubsverkehr, m
Ferienverkehr, m
♦ vacation traffic AE
♦ holiday traffic BE
Urlaubsverkehrsbereich, m
Ferienverkehrsbereich, m
♦ vacation traffic sector AE
♦ holiday traffic sector BE
Urlaubsverkehrsstau, m
Ferienverkehrsstau, m
♦ vacation traffic congestion AE
♦ holiday traffic congestion BE
Urlaubsverkürzung, f (Arbeitnehmer)
♦ curtailment of one's leave
Urlaubsverkürzung, f (Beamter)
♦ curtailment of one's furlough
Urlaubsverkürzung, f (Ferien)
Urlaubsabkürzung, f
Ferienverkürzung, f
Ferienabkürzung, f
♦ curtailment of one's vacation AE
♦ curtailment of one's holiday BE
Urlaubsverlängerung, f (Arbeitnehmer)
♦ extension of one's leave
♦ extension of one's vacation AE
♦ prolongation of one's leave
♦ prolongation of one's vacation AE
Urlaubsverlängerung, f (Beamter)
♦ extension of one's furlough
Urlaubsverlängerung, f (Ferien)
Ferienverlängerung, f
♦ extension of one's vacation AE
♦ vacation extension AE

- ♦ extension of one's holiday BE
- ♦ holiday extension BE
- ♦ prolongation of one's vacation AE

Urlaubsvermietung, f
Ferienvermietung, f
- ♦ vacation rental AE
- ♦ holiday letting BE

Urlaubsvermittlung, f (Agentur)
→ Urlaubsagentur

Urlaubsversicherung, f
Ferienversicherung, f
- ♦ vacation insurance AE
- ♦ holiday insurance BE

Urlaubsversicherung abschließen
Ferienversicherung abschließen
- ♦ take out a vacation insurance AE
- ♦ take out a holiday insurance BE

Urlaubsversicherungspolice, f
Ferienversicherungspolice, f
- ♦ vacation insurance policy AE
- ♦ holiday insurance policy BE

Urlaubsverspätungsversicherung, f
Ferienverspätungsversicherung, f
- ♦ vacation delay insurance AE
- ♦ holiday delay insurance BE

Urlaubsvertrag, m (Ferien)
Ferienvertrag, m
- ♦ vacation contract AE
- ♦ contract for a vacation AE
- ♦ holiday contract BE
- ♦ contract for a holiday BE

Urlaubsvertrag machen
Ferienvertrag machen
- ♦ make a vacation contract AE
- ♦ make a holiday contract BE

Urlaubsvertretung, f (Firma)
Ferienvertretung, f
- ♦ vacation replacement AE
- ♦ holiday replacement BE

Urlaubsvertretungsplan, m (Firma)
Ferienvertretungsplan, m
- ♦ vacation stand-in scheme AE
- ♦ holiday stand-in scheme BE

Urlaubsverweildauer, f
Dauer des Urlaubsaufenthalts, f
Ferienverweildauer, f
Dauer des Ferienaufenthalts, f
- ♦ duration of the vacation (stay) AE
- ♦ length of the vacation (stay) AE
- ♦ duration of the holiday (stay) BE
- ♦ length of the holiday (stay) BE

Urlaubsvideo, n
Ferienvideo, n
- ♦ vacation video AE
- ♦ holiday video BE

Urlaubsvilla, f
Ferienvilla, f
- ♦ vacation villa AE
- ♦ holiday villa BE

Urlaubsvorliebe, f
Urlaubspräferenz, f
Ferienvorliebe, f
Ferienpräferenz, f
- ♦ vacation preference AE
- ♦ holiday preference BE

Urlaubsvorschlag, m
Ferienvorschlag, m
- ♦ vacation suggestion AE
- ♦ holiday suggestion BE

Urlaubsvorschlag machen
Ferienvorschlag machen

- ♦ make a vacation suggestion AE
- ♦ make a holiday suggestion BE

Urlaubswahl, f
Ferienwahl, f
- ♦ vacation choice AE
- ♦ choice of a vacation AE
- ♦ selection of a vacation AE
- ♦ holiday choice BE
- ♦ choice of a holiday BE

Urlaubswanderung, f
Ferienwanderung, f
- ♦ vacation hike AE
- ♦ vacation walk AE
- ♦ holiday hike BE
- ♦ holiday walk BE

Urlaubswelt, f
Ferienwelt, f
- ♦ vacation world AE
- ♦ holiday world BE

Urlaubswerbung, f
Ferienwerbung, f
- ♦ vacation advertising AE
- ♦ holiday advertising BE

Urlaubswert, m
Ferienwert, m
- ♦ vacation value AE
- ♦ value of a vacation AE
- ♦ holiday value BE
- ♦ value of a holiday BE

Urlaubswesen, n
Ferienwesen, n
- ♦ vacation system AE
- ♦ vacation industry AE
- ♦ holiday system BE
- ♦ holiday industry BE
- ♦ holiday business BE

Urlaubswinter, m
Ferienwinter, m
- ♦ vacation winter AE
- ♦ holiday winter BE

Urlaubswoche, f
Ferienwoche, f
- ♦ vacation week AE
- ♦ week of one's vacation AE
- ♦ holiday week BE
- ♦ week of one's holiday BE

Urlaubswochenende, n
Ferienwochenende, n
- ♦ vacation weekend AE
- ♦ holiday weekend BE

Urlaubswohnung, f
Ferienwohnung, f
Fewo, f
- ♦ vacation apartment AE
- ♦ holiday flat BE

Urlaubswohnung mit allem Komfort, f
Ferienwohnung mit allem modernen Komfort, f
Fewo mit allem modernen Komfort, f
- ♦ vacation apartment with all modern conveniences AE
- ♦ holiday flat with all modern conveniences BE

Urlaubswohnung mit Selbstversorgung, f
Ferienwohnung mit Selbstversorgung, f
Fewo mit Selbstversorgung, f
- ♦ self-catering vacation apartment AE
- ♦ self-catering holiday flat BE

Urlaubswohnungsanbieter, m
Ferienwohnungsanbieter, m
Fewo-Anbieter, m
- ♦ vacation apartment supplier AE
- ♦ supplier of vacation apartments AE

- ♦ holiday flat supplier BE
- ♦ supplier of holiday flats BE

Urlaubswohnungsbereich, m (konkret)
Urlaubswohnungsgebiet, n
Ferienwohnungsgebiet, n
- ♦ vacation apartment area AE
- ♦ holiday flat area BE

Urlaubswohnungsbereich, m (Sektor)
Urlaubswohnungssektor, m
Ferienwohnungsbereich, m
Ferienwohnungssektor, m
- ♦ vacation apartment sector AE
- ♦ holiday flat sector BE

Urlaubswohnungskatalog, m
Ferienwohnungskatalog, m
Fewo-Katalog, m
- ♦ vacation apartment catalogue AE
- ♦ vacation apartment catalog AE
- ♦ holiday flat catalogue BE

Urlaubswohnungsprospekt, m
Ferienwohnungsprospekt, m
Fewo-Prospekt, m
- ♦ vacation apartment brochure AE
- ♦ holiday flat brochure BE

Urlaubswohnwagen, m
Urlaubscaravan, m
Ferienwohnwagen, m
Feriencaravan, m
- ♦ vacation trailer AE
- ♦ holiday caravan BE

Urlaubswohnwagenpark, m
Urlaubscaravanpark, m
Ferienwohnwagenpark, m
Feriencaravanpark, m
- ♦ vacation trailer park AE
- ♦ holiday caravan park BE

Urlaubswunsch, m
Ferienwunsch, m
- ♦ vacation request AE
- ♦ request for a vacation AE
- ♦ holiday request BE
- ♦ request for a holiday BE

Urlaubswunschliste, f
Ferienwunschliste, f
- ♦ list of vacation requests AE
- ♦ list of holiday requests BE

Urlaubszeit, f
Ferienzeit, f
- ♦ vacation time AE
- ♦ vacation period AE
- ♦ vacation season AE
- ♦ holiday time BE
- ♦ holiday period BE

Urlaubszeitraum, m
Ferienzeitraum, m
- ♦ vacation period AE
- ♦ holiday period BE

Urlaubszentrale, f
- ♦ vacation headquarters AE pl + sg
- ♦ holiday headquarters BE pl + sg

Urlaubszentrum, n
Ferienzentrum, n
- ♦ vacation center AE
- ♦ holiday centre BE

Urlaubszentrum betreiben
Ferienzentrum betreiben
- ♦ operate a vacation center AE
- ♦ operate a holiday centre BE

Urlaubszentrumbetreiber, m
Ferienzentrumbetreiber, m

Urlaubsziel

- ♦ vacation center operator *AE*
- ♦ holiday centre operator *BE*

Urlaubsziel, n
  Urlaubszielort, m
  Ferienziel, n
  Ferienzielort, m
- ♦ vacation destination *AE*
- ♦ holiday destination *BE*

Urlaubsziel wählen
  Ferienziel wählen
- ♦ choose a vacation destination *AE*
- ♦ choose a holiday destination *BE*

Urlaubszimmer, n
  Ferienzimmer, n
- ♦ vacation room *AE*
- ♦ holiday room *BE*

Urlaubszug, m
  Ferienzug, m
- ♦ vacation train *AE*
- ♦ holiday train *BE*

Urlaubszulage, f
  Ferienzulage, f
- ♦ vacation time allotment *AE*
- ♦ holiday allowance *BE*

Urlaubszusage, f
  → Urlaubsbestätigung

Urlaubszutat, f
  Ferienzutat, f
- ♦ vacation ingredient *AE*
- ♦ ingredient of a vacation *AE*
- ♦ holiday ingredient *BE*
- ♦ ingredient of a holiday *BE*

Urlaubszweck, m
  Ferienzweck, m
- ♦ vacation purpose *AE*
- ♦ holiday purpose *BE*

Urlaub überschreiten (Arbeitnehmer)
- ♦ overstay one's leave

Urlaub übertragen in das nächste Jahr
- ♦ carry over the vacation to the following year *AE*
- ♦ carry over the holiday to the following year *BE*

Urlaub unterbrechen
  Ferien unterbrechen
- ♦ interrupt one's vacation *AE*
- ♦ break one's vacation *AE*
- ♦ interrupt one's holiday *BE*
- ♦ break one's holiday *BE*

Urlaub unter der Woche, m
  Ferien unter der Woche, pl
- ♦ midweek vacation *AE*
- ♦ midweek holiday *BE*

Urlaub unternehmen
  → Urlaub machen

Urlaub verbinden mit dem Erlernen von Englisch
  Ferien verbinden mit dem Erlernen von Englisch
- ♦ combine a vacation with learning English *AE*
- ♦ combine a holiday with learning English *BE*

Urlaub verbinden mit etw
  Ferien verbinden mit etw
- ♦ combine a vacation with s.th. *AE*
- ♦ combine a holiday with s.th. *BE*

Urlaub verbringen
  Ferien verbringen
- ♦ spend a vacation *AE*
- ♦ spend a holiday *BE*

Urlaub verbringen am Meer
  Urlaub an der See verbringen
  Ferien am Meer verbringen
  Ferien an der See verbringen
- ♦ spend one's vacation at the seaside *AE*
- ♦ spend one's vacation by the sea *AE*
- ♦ spend one's holiday at the seaside *BE*
- ♦ spend one's holiday by the sea *BE*

Urlaub verbringen in einem Hotel
  Ferien in einem Hotel verbringen
- ♦ spend a vacation at a hotel *AE*
- ♦ spend a vacation in a hotel *AE*
- ♦ spend a holiday at a hotel *BE*
- ♦ spend a holiday in a hotel *BE*

Urlaub verbringen in X
  Ferien in X verbringen
- ♦ spend a vacation at X *AE*
- ♦ spend a vacation in X *AE*
- ♦ spend a holiday at X *BE*
- ♦ spend a holiday in X *BE*
- ♦ spend one's vacation in/at X *AE*

Urlaub verderben
  Ferien verderben
- ♦ spoil a vacation *AE*
- ♦ spoil a holiday *BE*

Urlaub verderben jm
  js Urlaub verderben
  Ferien verderben jm
  js Ferien verderben
- ♦ spoil s.o.'s vacation *AE*
- ♦ spoil s.o.'s holiday *BE*

Urlaub verkaufen
  Ferien verkaufen
- ♦ sell a vacation *AE*
- ♦ sell a holiday *BE*

Urlaub verkürzen
  → Urlaub abkürzen

Urlaub verlängern (Arbeitnehmer)
- ♦ extend a leave

Urlaub verlängern (Ferien)
  Ferien verlängern
- ♦ extend a vacation *AE*
- ♦ prolong a vacation *AE*
- ♦ extend a holiday *BE*
- ♦ prolong a holiday *BE*

Urlaub verleben
  → Urlaub verbringen

Urlaub vermarkten
  Ferien vermarkten
- ♦ market a vacation *AE*
- ♦ market a holiday *BE*

Urlaub von drei oder mehr Übernachtungen, m
  Ferien von drei oder mehr Übernachtungen, pl
- ♦ vacation of three or more nights *AE*
- ♦ holiday of three or more nights *BE*

Urlaub von etw, m
  Ferien von etw, pl
- ♦ vacation from s.th. *AE*
- ♦ holiday from s.th. *BE*

Urlaub vorzeitig abbrechen
  Ferien vorzeitig abbrechen
- ♦ break off one's vacation prematurely *AE*
- ♦ break off one's holiday prematurely *BE*

Urlaub vorzeitig beenden
  Urlaub abkürzen
  Ferien vorzeitig beenden
  Ferien abkürzen
- ♦ curtail one's vacation *AE*
- ♦ curtail one's holiday *BE*

Urlaub wählen
  Ferien wählen
  Urlaub auswählen
  Ferien auswählen
- ♦ choose a vacation *AE*
- ♦ choose a holiday *BE*

- ♦ select a vacation *AE*
- ♦ select a holiday *BE*

Urlaub wurde durch schlechtes Wetter verdorben
  Ferien wurden durch schlechtes Wetter verdorben
- ♦ vacation was spoiled by bad weather *AE*
- ♦ holiday was spoilt by bad weather *BE*

Urlaub zu Hause, m
  Urlaub zuhause, m
  Ferien zu Hause, pl
  Ferien zuhause, pl
- ♦ vacation at home *AE*
- ♦ holiday at home *BE*

Urlaub zu Hause verbringen
  seinen Urlaub zuhause verbringen
  Ferien zu Hause verbringen
  seine Ferien zuhause verbringen
- ♦ spend a vacation at home *AE*
- ♦ spend one's vacation at home *AE*
- ♦ spend a holiday at home *BE*
- ♦ spend one's holiday at home *BE*

Urlaub zunichtemachen
  Ferien zunichtemachen
- ♦ ruin a vacation *AE*
- ♦ ruin a holiday *BE*

Urlaub zunichtemachen jm
  js Urlaub zunichtemachen
  js Ferien zunichtemachen
- ♦ ruin s.o.'s vacation *AE*
- ♦ ruin s.o.'s holiday *BE*

Urlaub zusammenstellen
  Ferien zusammenstellen
- ♦ make a vacation *AE*
- ♦ make a holiday *BE*

Urne, f
- ♦ urn

Ursache einer Reklamation, f
  Ursache einer Beschwerde, f
  Beschwerdesache, f
- ♦ cause of a complaint

Ursache einer Reklamation beseitigen
  Beschwerdesache beseitigen
- ♦ eliminate the cause of a complaint

ursprünglich angegebene Abreisezeit, f
- ♦ originally stated departure time

ursprüngliche Buchung, f
  ursprüngliche Bestellung, f
- ♦ original booking

ursprünglicher Abreisetermin, m
  ursprüngliches Abreisedatum n
  ursprünglicher Abfahrtstermin m
  ursprüngliches Abfahrtsdatum n
- ♦ original departure date
- ♦ original date of departure

ursprüngliche Reservierung, f
- ♦ original reservation

ursprüngliches Gebäude, n
  Originalgebäude, n
- ♦ original building

ursprüngliches Hotel, n
- ♦ original hotel

ursprüngliche Stornierung, f
  ursprünglicher Rücktritt, m
  ursprüngliche Absage, f
  ursprüngliche Anullierung, f
- ♦ original cancellation
- ♦ original cancelation *AE*

Ursprungsland, n
  → Herkunftsland

Urteil, n
- ♦ judgement
- ♦ judgment

urtümliches Zimmer, n
  altes Zimmer, n
  ♦ **pristine room**
Uruguay
  ♦ **Uruguay**
Uruguayer, m
  ♦ **Uruguayan**
Uruguayerin, f
  ♦ **Uruguayan girl**
  ♦ Uruguayan woman
  ♦ Uruguayan
uruguayisch, adj
  ♦ **Uruguayan, adj**
Urwald, m (generell)
  ♦ **primeval forest**
  ♦ virgin forest
Urwald, m (Tropen)
  ♦ **jungle**
USA, die, pl
  ♦ **US, the** *pl=sg*
  ♦ **USA, the** *pl=sg*
Usbeke, m
  ♦ **Uzbeg**
  ♦ Uzbeg
  ♦ Usbek
  ♦ Usbeg
Usbekin, f
  ♦ **Uzbek girl**
  ♦ Uzbek woman
  ♦ Uzbek
  ♦ Usbeg girl
  ♦ Usbeg woman
usbekisch, adj
  ♦ **Uzbek, adj**
  ♦ Uzbeg, adj
  ♦ Usbek, adj
  ♦ Usbeg, adj
Usbekistan
  ♦ **Uzbekistan**
Utahsee, m
  ♦ **Lake Utah**
UV-Strahlung, f
  → Ultraviolettstrahlung

Vagabund, m
  Tramp, m
  Penner, m
  Tippelbruder, m
  ♦ vagabond
  ♦ tramp
  ♦ hobo *AE sl*
  ♦ bum *AE sl*
Vagabundenleben, n
  ♦ vagabond life
  ♦ life of a vagabond
Vagabundenleben führen
  ♦ live the life of a vagabond
vagabundieren
  Vagabundenleben führen
  ♦ drift from place to place
  ♦ live the life of a vagabond
vakant, adj
  → leerstehend
vakantes Zimmer, n
  → freies Zimmer
Vakanz, f
  ♦ vacancy
Vakanzanzeige, f
  ♦ notice of vacancy
Vakanzliste, f (Appartements)
  ♦ list of vacant apartments
Vakanzliste, f (Wohnungen)
  ♦ list of vacant flats *BE*
  ♦ list of vacant apartments *AE*
Vakanzliste, f (Zimmer)
  ♦ list of vacant rooms
Vakanzmitteilung, f
  ♦ notification of a vacancy
  ♦ notification of vacancies
vakuumverpackt, adj
  ♦ vacuum-packed, adj
Valentinstag, m
  (14. Februar)
  ♦ Valentine's Day
  ♦ St Valentine's Day
Valentinstagsfest, n
  ♦ Valentine's Day party
validieren etw
  gültig machen etw
  ♦ validate s.th.
  ♦ make s.th. valid
validierte Fahrkarte, f
  validierter Flugschein, m
  ♦ validated ticket
Valpolicella, m
  ♦ Valpolicella
Vandalismus, m
  ♦ vandalism
Vanille, f
  ♦ vanilla
Vanilleauflauf, m
  ♦ vanilla soufflé

Vanillemilchmixgetränk, n
  ♦ vanilla milk shake
Vanilleparfait, n
  ♦ vanilla parfait
variable Aufwendungen, f pl
  ♦ variable expenses *pl*
variable Betriebskosten, pl
  ♦ variable costs of operation *pl*
  ♦ variable costs of operating *pl*
variable Kosten, pl
  ♦ variable costs *pl*
  ♦ variable cost
variable Kosten pro Zimmer, pl
  ♦ variable costs per room *pl*
  ♦ variable cost per room
variable Kosten steigen mit der Auslastung
  ♦ variable costs rise with occupancy
variabler Erlös, m
  ♦ variable revenue
Variantenfahrer, m
  (Ski)
  ♦ off-piste skier
Variantenskifahren, n
  Variantenskilaufen, n
  Variantenskilauf, m
  ♦ off-piste skiing
Varietéakt, m
  Varieténummer, f
  ♦ variety act
Varieténummer, f
  ♦ variety turn
Varietétheater, n
  ♦ variety theater *AE*
  ♦ variety theatre *BE*
  ♦ music-hall *BE*
Varietévorstellung, f
  ♦ variety show
Vase f
  ♦ vase
Veganer, m
  (100%iger Vegetarier)
  ♦ vegan
veganische Diät, f
  ♦ vegan diet
veganischer Obstkuchen, m
  ♦ vegan fruit cake
  ♦ vegan fruit pie
veganisches Restaurant, n
  ♦ vegan restaurant
Vegetarier, m
  ♦ vegetarian
Vegetarierrestaurant, n
  → vegetarisches Restaurant
vegetarisch, adj
  ♦ vegetarian, adj
vegetarische Kochvorführung, f
  ♦ vegetarian cookery demonstration *BE*

vegetarische Kost, f
  ♦ vegetarian diet
  ♦ vegetarian fare
vegetarische Küche, f (Speisen)
  ♦ vegetarian cooking
  ♦ vegetarian cuisine
vegetarische Nahrung, f
  vegetarisches Essen, n
  vegetarische Kost, f
  ♦ vegetarian food
vegetarischer Gast, m
  ♦ vegetarian guest
vegetarisches Essen, n
  vegetarische Mahlzeit, f
  ♦ vegetarian meal
vegetarisches Gericht, n
  ♦ vegetarian dish
vegetarisches Lokal, n
  Vegetarierlokal, n
  ♦ vegetarian place
vegetarisches Menü, n
  ♦ vegetarian menu
vegetarische Spezialität, f
  ♦ vegetarian specialty *AE*
  ♦ vegetarian speciality *BE*
vegetarisches Restaurant n
  Vegetarierrestaurant n
  ♦ vegetarian restaurant
vegetarisch essen
  ♦ eat vegetarian food
vegetarische Vollwertküche, f (Speisen)
  ♦ vegetarian wholefood cuisine
  ♦ vegetarian wholefood cooking
vegetarische Wahlmöglichkeit, f
  ♦ vegetarian option
  ♦ vegetarian choice
vegetarisch leben
  Vegetarier sein
  ♦ be a vegetarian
Veltliner, m
  ♦ Veltliner
Veltlinertraube, f
  ♦ Veltliner grape
Venedig
  ♦ Venice
Venedig des Nordens, n
  ♦ Venice of the North, the
venezianisch, adj
  ♦ Venetian, adj
venezianische Art, adv *gastr*
  ♦ Venetian style, adv *gastr*
Venezolaner, m
  Venezueler, m
  ♦ Venezuelan
Venezolanerin, f
  Venezuelerin, f
  ♦ Venezuelan girl

venezolanisch

- venezolanisch
  - ◆ Venezuelan woman
  - ◆ Venezuelan
- venezolanisch, adj
  - venezuelisch, adj
  - ◆ Venezuelan, adj
- Venezuela
  - ◆ Venezuela
- Ventilator m
  - ◆ ventilator
  - ◆ fan
- verabreden sich mit jm
  - ◆ arrange to meet s.o.
- verabredete Zeit, f
  - ◆ appointed time
- verabschieden jn
  - ◆ say good-bye to s.o. *AE*
  - ◆ say goodbye to s.o. *BE*
  - ◆ bid s.o. good-bye *AE*
  - ◆ bid s.o. goodby *BE*
  - ◆ bid s.o. farewell *lit*
- verabschieden sich
  - ◆ say good-bye to each other *AE*
  - ◆ say goodbye to each other *BE*
  - ◆ say good-bye *AE*
  - ◆ say goodbye *BE*
- verabschieden sich auf französisch
  - sich (auf) französisch empfehlen
  - Abschied nehmen auf französisch
  - ◆ take French leave
  - ◆ filer à l'anglaise *FR*
- verabschieden sich von etw
  - ◆ say good-bye to s.th. *AE*
  - ◆ say goodbye to s.th. *BE*
  - ◆ bid farewell to s.th. *lit*
- verabschieden sich von jm
  - ◆ take (one's) leave of s.o. *AE*
  - ◆ say goodbye to s.o. *BE*
  - ◆ bid farewell to s.o. *lit*
  - ◆ say good-bye to s.o. *AE*
- Verabschiedung, f
  - ◆ saying good-bye *AE*
  - ◆ saying goodbye *BE*
  - ◆ farewell
  - ◆ send-off
- veraltetes Hotel, n
  - ◆ dated hotel
- Veranda, f
  - ◆ veranda
  - ◆ verandah
  - ◆ porch *AE*
- Verandabar f
  - ◆ veranda bar
  - ◆ verandah bar
- Verandarestaurant, n
  - ◆ veranda restaurant
  - ◆ verandah restaurant
- Verandatür, f
  - Fenstertür, f
  - ◆ French window
  - ◆ French door
- veranstalten etw
  - ◆ organise s.th.
  - ◆ organize s.th.
  - ◆ put s.o. on *coll*
- Veranstalten von Reisen, n
  - Reiseveranstaltung, f
  - ◆ tour operating
  - ◆ tour operation
- Veranstalter, m (Organisator)
  - → Organisator

- Veranstalter, m (Reiseveranstalter)
  - ◆ operator
- Veranstalter, m (Sport)
  - Promoter, m
  - ◆ promoter
- Veranstalterbüro, n
  - ◆ organiser's office
  - ◆ organizer's office
- Veranstalterkatalog, m (Reiseveranstalter)
  - → Reiseveranstalterkatalog
- Veranstalterpreis, m (Reiseveranstalter)
  - ◆ operator's price
  - ◆ operator's rate
- Veranstalterprogramm, n
  - → Reiseveranstalterprogramm
- Veranstalter von Reisen nach England, m
  - ◆ operator of tours to England
- Veranstalter vor Ort, m (Reiseveranstalter)
  - örtlicher Veranstalter, m
  - ◆ local operator
- Veranstaltung, f (private Festlichkeit)
  - ◆ function
- Veranstaltung, f (Sport etc.)
  - ◆ event
  - ◆ activity
- Veranstaltung abhalten
  - ◆ hold a function
  - ◆ hold an event
- Veranstaltung absagen
  - ◆ cancel a function
  - ◆ cancel an event
- Veranstaltung abwickeln
  - ◆ handle a function
  - ◆ handle an event
- Veranstaltung arrangieren
  - ◆ arrange an event
  - ◆ arrange a function
- Veranstaltung aufzeichnen
  - ◆ record an event
  - ◆ record a function
- Veranstaltung ausrichten (als Gastgeber)
  - ◆ host an event
  - ◆ host a function
- Veranstaltung beginnt mit etw
  - ◆ event starts with s.th.
  - ◆ event begins with s.th.
  - ◆ event commences with s.th. *form*
  - ◆ function starts with s.th.
  - ◆ function begins with s.th.
- Veranstaltung buchen
  - ◆ book a function
- Veranstaltung durchführen
  - ◆ run an event
  - ◆ run a function
- Veranstaltungen aller Art, f pl
  - ◆ functions of all kinds *pl*
  - ◆ events of all kinds *pl*
  - ◆ functions of all types *pl*
  - ◆ events of all types *pl*
- Veranstaltungen laufen parallel
  - ◆ events run simultaneously
- Veranstaltung fällt aus
  - Veranstaltung ist abgesagt
  - ◆ function has been cancelled
  - ◆ function has been canceled *AE*
  - ◆ event has been cancelled
  - ◆ event has been canceled *AE*
  - ◆ function does not take place
- Veranstaltung findet mit Unterstützung von X statt
  - Veranstaltung wird gesponsert von X

- ◆ event is sponsored by X
- ◆ function is sponsored by X
- Veranstaltung findet nicht statt
  - ◆ function does not take place
  - ◆ function has been cancelled
  - ◆ event does not take place
  - ◆ event has been cancelled
  - ◆ event has been canceled *AE*
- Veranstaltung im Freien, f
  - ◆ outdoor event
  - ◆ outdoor function
- Veranstaltung inszenieren
  - Veranstaltung ausrichten
  - ◆ stage an event
  - ◆ stage a function
- Veranstaltung ist professionell organisiert
  - ◆ function is professionally organised
  - ◆ event is professionally organised
- Veranstaltung kaufen
  - ◆ buy a function
- Veranstaltung koordinieren
  - ◆ coordinate an event
  - ◆ coordinate a function
- Veranstaltung mit Bewirtung, f
  - ◆ function with catering *BE*
  - ◆ function with foodservice *AE*
  - ◆ event with catering *BE*
  - ◆ event with foodservice *BE*
  - ◆ hospitality function
- Veranstaltung mit Eintrittskarte, f
  - ◆ ticket event
  - ◆ admission by ticket only
  - ◆ ticket activity
- Veranstaltung mit Essen, f
  - Essensveranstaltung, f
  - ◆ meal function
  - ◆ meal event
  - ◆ food function
  - ◆ food event
- Veranstaltung mit Unterkunft, f
  - ◆ residential function
  - ◆ residential event
- Veranstaltung mit Verpflegung, f
  - Gastronomieveranstaltung, f
  - gastronomische Veranstaltung, f
  - ◆ catering function *BE*
  - ◆ catering event *BE*
  - ◆ foodservice function *AE*
  - ◆ foodservice event *AE*
- Veranstaltung ohne Bewirtung, f
  - Veranstaltung ohne Verpflegung, f
  - ◆ function without catering
  - ◆ event without catering
  - ◆ function without foodservice *AE*
  - ◆ event without foodservice *AE*
- Veranstaltung ohne Eintritt, f
  - ◆ nonticket function *AE*
  - ◆ nonticket event *AE*
  - ◆ non-ticket event *BE*
  - ◆ non-ticket function *BE*
- Veranstaltung ohne Eintrittskarte, f
  - ◆ nonticket event *AE*
  - ◆ non-ticket event *BE*
  - ◆ nonticket activity *AE*
  - ◆ non-ticket activity *BE*
- Veranstaltung organisieren
  - ◆ organise an event
  - ◆ organize an event
  - ◆ organise a function
  - ◆ organize a function
  - ◆ organise an activity

Veranstaltung planen
 ♦ plan a function
 ♦ plan an event
Veranstaltungsabteilung, f
 ♦ events department
Veranstaltungsangebot, n (Palette)
 ♦ range of events
 ♦ range of functions
Veranstaltungsart, f
 Veranstaltungstyp, m
 ♦ function type
 ♦ type of function
Veranstaltungsauslastung, f
 Veranstaltungsbelegung, f
 ♦ function occupancy
Veranstaltungsausrichter, m (Gastgeber)
 ♦ host of a function
Veranstaltungsbeginn, m
 ♦ beginning of a function
 ♦ start of a function
 ♦ commencement of a function *form*
Veranstaltungsbestellformular, n
 ♦ function order form
Veranstaltungsbewertung, f
 ♦ evaluation of an event
Veranstaltungsbewirtung, f
 Veranstaltungsgastronomie, f
 Veranstaltungscatering, n
 Veranstaltungsverpflegung, f
 ♦ function catering
 ♦ function foodservice *AE*
Veranstaltungsblatt, n
 ♦ events pamphlet
Veranstaltungsbuch, n
 (Hotel)
 ♦ function book
Veranstaltungsbuchung, f
 ♦ function booking
 ♦ booking (of) a function
Veranstaltungsbüfett, n
 ♦ function buffet
Veranstaltungsbüro, n
 ♦ function office
Veranstaltungsdatum, n
 Veranstaltungstermin, m
 ♦ date of the event
 ♦ event date
 ♦ date of the function
 ♦ function date
Veranstaltungsdauer, f
 ♦ duration of an event
 ♦ length of an event
 ♦ duration of a function
 ♦ length of a function
Veranstaltungsdauer kürzen (um zwei Tage)
 ♦ cut the length of the event (by two days)
Veranstaltungsdienst, m
 Veranstaltungsservice, m
 ♦ event service
 ♦ events service
 ♦ function service
Veranstaltungsdirektor, m
 ♦ events director
 ♦ event director
Veranstaltungsende, n
 ♦ end of a function
 ♦ end of an event
Veranstaltungserfolg, m
 ♦ success of the event
 ♦ event success

 ♦ success of the function
 ♦ function success
Veranstaltungserfolg bewerten
 ♦ evaluate the success of a function
 ♦ gauge the success of a function
 ♦ evaluate the success of an event
 ♦ gauge the success of an event
Veranstaltungserfolg sicherstellen
 ♦ ensure the success of the event
Veranstaltungsfläche, f
 ♦ function area
 ♦ function space
Veranstaltungsfolge, f
 ♦ sequence of events
 ♦ order of events
Veranstaltungsführer, m
 (Information)
 ♦ events guide
 ♦ What's on
Veranstaltungsgast, m
 ♦ function guest
Veranstaltungsgastronomie, f
 Veranstaltungsbewirtung, f
 Veranstaltungscatering, n
 Veranstaltungsverpflegung, f
 ♦ function foodservice *AE*
 ♦ function catering
Veranstaltungsgeschäft, n
 ♦ function business
 ♦ event business
Veranstaltungsgrundplan, m
 ♦ event outline
Veranstaltungshalle, f
 Veranstaltungssaal, m
 ♦ events hall
 ♦ function hall
Veranstaltungsimage, n
 ♦ event image
 ♦ image of the event
Veranstaltungsjournal, n
 ♦ function diary
Veranstaltungskalender, m
 ♦ calendar of events
 ♦ events calendar
 ♦ timetable of events
Veranstaltungskostenberechnung, f
 ♦ function costing
Veranstaltungskostenblatt, n
 ♦ function cost sheet
Veranstaltungsleiter, m (generell)
 Veranstaltungsmanager, m
 ♦ events manager
 ♦ event manager
Veranstaltungsleiter, m (im Hotel)
 ♦ functions manager
Veranstaltungsleitung, f
 Veranstaltungsmanagement, n
 ♦ events management
 ♦ event management
Veranstaltungsliste, f
 ♦ function list
 ♦ list of functions
Veranstaltungsliste aufstellen
 ♦ prepare a function list
Veranstaltungsmanagement, n
 → Veranstaltungsleitung, f
Veranstaltungsmannschaft, f
 ♦ events team
Veranstaltungsmarkt m
 ♦ function market

Veranstaltungsmenü, n
 ♦ function menu
Veranstaltungsmitte, f
 ♦ middle of a function
 ♦ middle of an event
Veranstaltungsnachfrage, f
 Nachfrage nach Veranstaltungen, f
 ♦ demand for events
 ♦ demand for functions
Veranstaltungsoberkellner, m
 ♦ function headwaiter
Veranstaltungsorganisation, f
 Organisation einer Veranstaltung, f
 ♦ organisation of a function
 ♦ organization of a function
 ♦ organisation of an event
 ♦ organization of an event
 ♦ organising a function
Veranstaltungsorganisator, m
 Organisator einer Veranstaltung, m
 ♦ function organiser
 ♦ organiser of a function
 ♦ event organiser
 ♦ organiser of an event
Veranstaltungsort, m
 ♦ function site
 ♦ site of a function
 ♦ site of an event
 ♦ event venue
 ♦ venue
Veranstaltungsplan, m
 (im Hotel)
 ♦ function plan
Veranstaltungsplaner, m
 ♦ event planner
Veranstaltung sponsern
 ♦ sponsor an event
 ♦ sponsor a function
Veranstaltungsprogramm, n
 Programm der Veranstaltungen, n
 ♦ program of events *AE*
 ♦ programme of events *BE*
 ♦ events' program *AE*
 ♦ events' programme *BE*
Veranstaltungspromoter, m
 Veranstalter einer Veranstaltung, m
 ♦ event promoter
Veranstaltungsprospekt, m
 (Verkaufsmaterial)
 ♦ function prospectus
Veranstaltungsrahmen, m
 Rahmen einer Veranstaltung, m·
 ♦ setting of a function
 ♦ setting of an event
Veranstaltungsraum, m (Volumen, Fläche)
 Veranstaltungsfläche, f
 ♦ function space
 ♦ function area
Veranstaltungsraum, m (Zimmer)
 Veranstaltungszimmer, n
 Nebenzimmer, n
 Nebenraum, m
 ♦ function room
Veranstaltungsraumbar, f
 ♦ function room bar
Veranstaltungsraum buchen
 ♦ book a function room
Veranstaltungsräumlichkeiten, f pl
 ♦ function facilities *pl*
Veranstaltungsräumlichkeiten können 50 bis 100 Personen aufnehmen

Veranstaltungsräumlichkeiten können von 10 bis 100 Personen aufnehmen

- function facilities can accommodate 50 to
- 100 persons

Veranstaltungsräumlichkeiten können von 10 bis 100
Personen aufnehmen
- function facilities can accommodate from 10 to 100
- persons

Veranstaltungsraum reservieren
- reserve a function room

Veranstaltungsrechnung f
- function bill

Veranstaltungsreigen, m
Reigen der Veranstaltungen, m
- round of events
- sequence of events

Veranstaltungsreihe, f
Reihe von Veranstaltungen, f
- series of events

Veranstaltungssaal, m
Veranstaltungshalle, f
- function hall
- large function room
- events hall
- large events room

Veranstaltungssektor, m
Veranstaltungsbereich, m
- event sector
- function sector

Veranstaltungsservice, m
Veranstaltungsdienst, m
- function service
- event service
- events service

Veranstaltungsspeisekarte, f
- function menu

Veranstaltungssponsoring, n
- event sponsorhip

Veranstaltungssuite, f
- function suite

Veranstaltungstag, m
- function day
- day of the function
- event day
- day of the event

Veranstaltungstagebuch, n
- diary of events

Veranstaltungstermin, m
Veranstaltungsdatum, n
- function date
- date of a function
- event date
- date of an event

Veranstaltung stornieren
Veranstaltung absagen
- cancel an event
- cancel a function

Veranstaltungstourismus, m
- event tourism

Veranstaltungstourist, m
- event tourist

Veranstaltungsverkausfleiter, m
- events sales manager

Veranstaltungsverpflegung, f
- event catering BE
- function catering BE
- event foodservice AE
- function foodservice AE

Veranstaltungsverzeichnis, n
- list of events
- events list

Veranstaltungsverzeichnis veröffentlichen
- publish a list of events

Veranstaltungszahl, f
- number of events
- number of functions

Veranstaltungszahl reduzieren
Veranstaltungszahl kürzen
Veranstaltungszahl senken
- reduce the number of events
- reduce the number of functions

Veranstaltungszeit, f
Veranstaltungszeitpunkt, m
- time of the function

Veranstaltungszentrum, n (generell)
- events center AE
- events centre BE

Veranstaltungszentrum, n (private Veranstaltungen)
- function center AE
- function centre BE

Veranstaltung unter dem Motto "XYZ", f
- event with the motto "XYZ"

Veranstaltung unterstützen
- back an event
- support an event
- back a function
- support a function

Veranstaltung verkaufen
- sell a function

Veranstaltung verläuft nach Plan
- event runs according to plan
- function runs according to plan

Veranstaltung vorbereiten
- prepare an event
- prepare a function

Veranstaltung zu einem Erfolg werden lassen
- make the event a success

verantwortungsbewußter Tourismus, m
- responsible tourism

Verband, m
- association

Verband der Britischen Ausstellungsausstatter, m
- Association of British Exhibition Contractors

Verband der Firmenreisestellenleiter, m
- Association of Corporate Travel Executives AE

Verband gründen
Vereinigung gründen
- form an association

Verbandskonferenz, f
- association conference

Verbandskongreß, m
- association congress
- association convention

Verbandsmarkt, m
- association market

Verbandstagung, f
Verbandstag, m
Verbandstreffen, n
- association meeting

Verbandsveranstaltung, f
- association event
- association function

verbessern etw
- improve s.th.

verbesserter Service, m
- improved service

verbesserte Unterkunft, f
- improved accommodation

Verbesserung, f
- improvement
- upgrade
- upgrading

Verbesserung der Umwelt, f
Umweltverbesserung, f
- improvement of the environment
- environmental improvement

Verbesserungen vornehmen
- make improvements

verbesserungsfähig, adj
- open to improvement, adj

Verbesserungsprogramm, n
Verschönerungsprogramm, n
- improvement program AE
- improvement programme BE

verbilligt, adj
herabgesetzt, adj
reduziert, adj
billig, adj
- cut-price, adj
- cut-rate, adj

verbilligtes Mittagessen, n
subventioniertes Mittagessen, n
- subsidised lunch
- subsidized lunch
- subsidised luncheon
- subsidized luncheon

verbindlicher Service, m
- suave service

Verbindung, f
- connection
- link

Verbindungsbahn, f (Zug)
Nebenbahn, f
- junction line

Verbindungsflugschein, m
- conjunction ticket

Verbindungsgang, m
Gang, m
Durchgang, m
- gangway

Verbindungskorridor, m
- interconnecting corridor

Verbindungsstraße, f
- secondary road BE
- connection road

Verbindungstür, f
Durchgangstür f
- connecting door

Verbindungsweg, m
- passageway

Verbindung von Geschäft mit Vergnügen, f
- combination of business and pleasure

Verbot, n
- ban

Verbot aufheben
- lift a ban

Verbotene Stadt, f
(in Peking)
- Forbidden City, the

Verbot tritt in Kraft
Verbot von etw tritt in Kraft
- ban comes into effect
- ban on s.th. comes into effect

Verbot von etw, n
- ban on s.th.

Verbot von Verkehrsflügen, n
- ban on commercial flights

Verbraucher, m
　Konsument, m
　♦ consumer
Verbraucherausstellung, f
　♦ consumer exhibition
　♦ exhibition for consumers
verbraucherfreundlich, adj
　♦ consumer-friendly, adj
Verbrauchergeschmack, m
　♦ consumer taste
Verbrauchergewohnheit, f
　♦ consumer habit
Verbrauchermesse, f
　♦ consumer fair
Verbraucherschau, f
　♦ consumer show
Verbrauchersegment, n
　♦ consumer segment
Verbraucherurlaubsschau, f
　♦ consumer vacation show AE
　♦ consumer holiday show BE
Verbrauchssteuer, f
　♦ excise duty
Verbrauchssteuer erheben (auf etw)
　♦ levy excise duty (on s.th.)
Verbrauchszahl, f
　♦ consumption figure
verbrennen
　(Person)
　♦ burn to death
verbrühen etw
　♦ scald s.th.
verbuchen etw
　(Buchhaltung)
　♦ enter s.th. (in the books)
verbuchen etw auf einem Konto
　♦ enter s.th. on an account
Verbundglas, n
　♦ laminated glass
verbürgen sich für etw
　bürgen für etw
　♦ vouch for s.th.
　♦ guarantee s.th.
verchartern etw an jn
　♦ charter s.th. to s.o.
verdauen (etw)
　♦ digest (s.th.)
Verdauung, f
　♦ digestion
Verdauungsbeschwerden, f pl
　♦ digestive disorders pl
Verdauungsproblem, n
　♦ digestive problem
Verdauungsspaziergang, m
　♦ constitutional humor
Verdauungsspaziergang machen
　Verdauungsspaziergang unternehmen
　♦ go for a constitutional humor
　♦ take a constitutional humor
Verdauungsstörung, f
　♦ dyspepsia
　♦ dyspepsy
Verderb, m
　(z.B. von Obst)
　Verlust, m
　♦ spoilage
verderbliches Produkt, n
　♦ perishable product
Verderb und Schwund, m
　(Lagervorräte)
　♦ spoilage and shrinkage

verdorbener Magen, m
　verstimmter Magen, m
　♦ upset stomach
verdorbener Urlaub, m
　♦ spoilt vacation AE
　♦ spoiled vacation AE
　♦ spoilt holiday BE
verdorbene Speise, f
　♦ spoilt food
Verdrängungswettbewerb, m
　Konkurrenzkampf bis aufs Messer, m
　ruinöser Wettbewerb, m
　♦ cut-throat competition
verdunkelbar, adj (teilweise)
　♦ can be darkened
verdunkelbar, adj (völlig)
　♦ can be blacked out
verdunkelbarer Raum, m
　(völlig verdunkelbar)
　♦ room that can be blacked out
verdunkelbar (mit einem Helligkeitsregler), adj
　♦ dimmable, adj
verdunkeln etw (teilweise)
　(z.B. Raum)
　♦ darken s.th.
verdunkeln etw (völlig)
　(z.B. Raum)
　♦ black out s.th.
Verdunkelungseinrichtung, f
　♦ blackout facility AE
　♦ black-out facility BE
Verdunkelungsmöglichkeiten, f pl
　Verdunkelungsvorrichtungen, f pl
　♦ blackout facilities AE pl
　♦ black-out facilities BE pl
Verdunkelungsvorhang, m
　♦ blackout curtain AE
　♦ black-out curtain BE
Verdunkelungsvorrichtung, f
　♦ blackout equipment AE
　♦ black-out equipment BE
Verdunster, m
　♦ humidifier
verdursten
　sterben vor Durst
　♦ die of thirst
Verein, m
　→ Club
vereinbart, adj
　♦ agreed, adj
vereinbarte Miete, f
　♦ agreed rent
vereinbarte Mietzeit, f (kurz, meist Mobilien)
　(z.B. Wohnwagen)
　♦ agreed rental period
　♦ agreed hire period BE
vereinbarte Mietzeit, f (lang, meist Immobilien)
　♦ agreed term of lease
　♦ agreed duration of a lease
　♦ agreed length of lease
　♦ agreed lease period
　♦ agreed term of tenancy
vereinbarte Provision, f
　♦ agreed commission
vereinbarter Abreisetermin, m
　♦ agreed date of departure
vereinbarter Ankunftstermin, m
　♦ agreed date of arrival
vereinbarter Aufenthaltsbeginn, m
　♦ agreed beginning of stay
　♦ date agreed for beginning of stay

vereinbarter Fahrpreis, m
　♦ agreed fare
vereinbarter Festpreis, m
　♦ agreed fixed price
vereinbarter Preis, m
　♦ agreed price
　♦ agreed rate
vereinbartes Menü, n
　♦ agreed menu
Vereinbarung, f (Abkommen)
　♦ agreement
Vereinbarung, f (Arrangement)
　→ Arrangement
Vereinbarung eingehen mit jm
　♦ enter into an agreement with s.o.
Vereinbarung einhalten
　♦ honor the agreement AE
　♦ honour the agreement BE
Vereinbarungen bestätigen
　♦ confirm the arrangements
Vereinbarungen rückgängig machen
　♦ cancel the arrangements
Vereinbarung kündigen
　♦ cancel an agreement
Vereinbarungsentwurf, m
　♦ draft agreement
Vereinbarung treffen für etw
　♦ make an arrangement for s.th.
Vereinbarung überarbeiten
　♦ redraft an agreement
Verein beitreten
　→ Club beitreten
Vereinigte Königreich, das, n
　♦ United Kingdom, the
　♦ UK, the
Vereinigten Arabischen Emirate, die, n pl
　♦ United Arab Emirates, the pl
Vereinigten Staaten von Amerika, die, m pl
　♦ United States of America, the pl
Verein mit Schankkonzession, m
　→ Club mit Schankkonzession
Vereinsabend, m
　→ Clubabend
Vereinsmeier, m
　♦ clubman
　♦ clubber coll
　♦ joiner fam
Vereinsschriftführer, m
　♦ club secretary
vereister Hang, m
　Eishang, m
　♦ icy slope
vereiste Straße, f
　♦ icy road
　♦ icy street
verfallen, adj
　→ baufällig
verfallen (ablaufen)
　→ ablaufen
verfallenes Hotel, n
　♦ decayed hotel
verfallen (Gebäude)
　♦ fall into decay
　♦ fall into ruin
verfallen (Haus)
　♦ go into disrepair
　♦ go to ruin
verfallen lassen etw
　(Gebäude)
　♦ dilapidate s.th.

Verfallsdatum

Verfallsdatum, n (Abmachung, Gutschein)
  Verfallstermin, m
  ♦ expiry date
Verfallsdatum, n (Lebensmittel)
  ♦ best-before date
  ♦ best-by date
  ♦ pull date *AE*
verfressen, adj *vulg*
  ♦ greedy, adj
Verfressenheit, f *vulg*
  ♦ greed
  ♦ voraciousness
  ♦ voracity
verfressen sein *vulg*
  ♦ be a glutton
  ♦ be a greedy pig *vulg*
verfrühte Abreise, f
  → vorzeitige Abreise
verfrühte Ankunft; f
  → vorzeitige Ankunft
verfügbar, adj
  ♦ available, adj
  ♦ at one's disposal
verfügbare Bettenkapazität, f
  ♦ available bed capacity
verfügbare Kapazität, f
  ♦ available capacity
verfügbares Zimmer, n
  ♦ available room
verfügbar für jn
  ♦ available for s.o.
  ♦ available to s.o.
Verfügbarkeit, f
  ♦ availability
Verfügbarkeit eines Service, f
  Verfügbarkeit einer Leistung, f
  ♦ availability of a service
Verfügbarkeit eines Zimmers, f
  ♦ availability of a room
Verfügbarkeitsstatus, m
  ♦ availability status
Verfügbarkeit von Hotelzimmern, f
  ♦ hotel room availability
  ♦ availability of hotel rooms
verfügbar werden
  ♦ become available
verfügen über etw
  etw haben
  ♦ have s.th.
Vergabe, f
  → Zuweisung
Vergabe von Ausstellungsfläche, f
  Zuteilung von Ausstellungsfläche, f
  ♦ allocation of exhibition space
  ♦ allocating exhibition space
  ♦ assignment of exhibition space *AE*
  ♦ assigning exhibit(ion) space *AE*
vergangener Besuch, m
  ♦ past visit
vergangene Saison, f
  ♦ past season
vergangene Sommersaison, f
  ♦ past summer season
vergangene Tage, m pl
  ♦ bygone days *pl*
  ♦ days gone by *pl*
vergangene Zeiten, f pl
  ♦ bygone times *pl*
  ♦ times gone by *pl*
Vergangenheit, f
  ♦ past

Vergangenheit lebendig werden lassen
  ♦ bring the past alive
vergattern jn
  ♦ brief s.o.
  ♦ instruct s.o.
Vergatterung, f
  → Instruktion
vergeben etw an jn
  → zuweisen etw an jn
vergessen etw im Hotel
  liegenlassen etw im Hotel
  ♦ leave s.th. behind in the hotel
vergessen etw (zurücklassen)
  → stehenlassen etw
Vergessen Sie nicht, mich morgen wecken zu lassen
  ♦ Don't forget to have me called tomorrow
verglast, adj
  ♦ glassed-in, adj
  ♦ glazed, adj
verglaster Balkon, m
  Erker, m
  ♦ gazebo
verglastes Fenster, n
  ♦ glazed window
verglaste Veranda, f
  ♦ glassed-in veranda
  ♦ glassed-in verandah
vergleichbare Qualität, f
  ♦ comparable quality
vergleichbarer Betrieb, m
  ♦ comparable establishment
  ♦ establishment of similar standard
vergleichbares Hotel, n
  ♦ comparable hotel
  ♦ hotel of similar standard
vergleichbares Zimmer n
  ♦ comparable room
vergleichbare Unterkunft, f
  ♦ comparable accommodation
  ♦ accommodation of a comparable standard
vergleichbare Zimmerart, f
  vergleichbarer Zimmertyp, m
  ♦ comparable room type
Vergleichsjahr n
  (Statistik)
  ♦ corresponding year
Vergleichsmiete, f
  ♦ comparable rent
Vergleichsmonat, m
  entsprechender Monat, m
  ♦ corresponding month
Vergleichszahl, f
  Vergleichsziffer, f
  ♦ comparative figure
Vergnügen, n
  ♦ pleasure
  ♦ enjoyment
  ♦ fun
Vergnügen bereiten jm
  ♦ give s.o. pleasure
Vergnügen finden an etw
  ♦ find pleasure in s.th.
  ♦ enjoy s.th.
Vergnügen haben, jn begrüßen zu können in X
  ♦ have the pleasure of welcoming s.o. to X
vergnügen sich
  ♦ take one's pleasure
  ♦ enjoy oneself

Vergnügen steigern
  ♦ add to s.o.'s pleasure
  ♦ add to s.o.'s enjoyment
Vergnügen suchen
  ♦ seek pleasure
  ♦ seek fun
vergnüglicher Teil des Urlaubs, m
  ♦ enjoyable part of the vacation *AE*
  ♦ enjoyable part of the holiday *BE*
Vergnügung, f
  Amüsement, n
  ♦ amusement
  ♦ pleasure
  ♦ entertainment
Vergnügungsanlage, f
  Vergnügungskomplex, m
  ♦ amusement complex
Vergnügungsaufenthalt, m
  ♦ pleasure stay
Vergnügungsbad, n
  ♦ pleasure baths *pl*
Vergnügungsbar, f
  ♦ amusement bar
Vergnügungsboot, n
  Vergnügungsschiff, n
  ♦ pleasure boat
  ♦ pleasure craft
Vergnügungsdampfer, m
  ♦ pleasure steamer
Vergnügungsfahrt, f (Auto)
  → Spazierfahrt
Vergnügungsfahrt, f (Erlebnispark)
  ♦ amusement ride
Vergnügungsfahrt, f (generell)
  ♦ pleasure trip
  ♦ pleasure ride
Vergnügungsfahrzeug, n
  ♦ pleasure vehicle
Vergnügungsflug, m
  ♦ pleasure flight
Vergnügungsführer, m
  ♦ amusement guide
Vergnügungsgebiet, n
  Vergnügungsgegend, f
  ♦ amusement area
Vergnügungsgelände, n
  ♦ pleasure grounds *pl*
Vergnügungsindustrie, f
  ♦ entertainment industry
Vergnügungskreuzer, m
  Vergnügungskreuzfahrtschiff, n
  ♦ pleasure cruiser
Vergnügungskreuzfahrt, f
  ♦ pleasure cruise
Vergnügungslokal, n (Kabarett)
  → Kabarett
Vergnügungslokal, n (Nachtbar)
  → Nachtbar
vergnügungsorientiert, adj
  ♦ pleasure-oriented, adj
  ♦ pleasure-orientated, adj
Vergnügungsort, m (generell)
  ♦ pleasure place
Vergnügungsort, m (Resort)
  ♦ pleasure resort
Vergnügungspalast, m
  ♦ pleasure dome
Vergnügungsparadies, n
  ♦ pleasure paradise
Vergnügungspark, m
  ♦ amusement park

- fun park
- pleasure park

Vergnügungsplatz, m
- pleasure ground

Vergnügungsprogramm, n
→ Unterhaltungsprogramm

Vergnügungsreise, f
- pleasure tour
- pleasure trip
- junket *AE coll iron*

Vergnügungsreise, f (oft auf Kosten anderer)
Vergnügungsfahrt, f (oft auf Kosten anderer)
angebliche Dienstreise, f
- junket *AE*

Vergnügungsreise machen
- go on a pleasure trip
- take a pleasure trip

Vergnügungsreisemarkt, m
- pleasure-travel market

Vergnügungsreisen, n
Vergnügungsreiseverkehr, m
- pleasure travel
- traveling for pleasure *AE*
- travelling for pleasure *BE*

Vergnügungsreisender, m
- pleasure traveler *AE*
- pleasure traveller *BE*
- person traveling for pleasure *AE*
- person travelling for pleasure *BE*

Vergnügungssegeln, n
Vergnügungssegelsport, m
- pleasure sailing

Vergnügungsspiel, n
- amusement game

Vergnügungsstadt, f
- pleasure town

Vergnügungsstätte, f
Unterhaltungslokal, n
- place of amusement
- place of entertainment

Vergnügungssteuer, f
- entertainment tax
- amusement tax

Vergnügungsstrand, m
- pleasure beach

Vergnügungssucht, f
- hunt for pleasure
- craving for pleasure
- hedonism

vergnügungssüchtig, adj
- pleasure-seeking, adj
- pleasure-hunting, adj
- pleasure-loving, adj
- hedonistic, adj

Vergnügungssüchtiger, m
- pleasure-seeker
- pleasure-hunter

Vergnügungsviertel, n (Bordelle)
→ Bordellviertel

Vergnügungsviertel, n (generell)
- entertainments district

Vergnügungswart, m
(im Verein)
- entertainment steward

Vergnügungszentrum, n
- amusement center *AE*
- amusement centre *BE*
- entertainment center *AE*
- entertainment centre *BE*

vergriffen sein
- be out of stock

vergrößern etw
ausweiten etw
- extend s.th.
- enlarge s.th.

Vergrößerung, f
- enlargement

Vergrößerung der Garage, f
- enlargement of the garage

Vergrößerung des Restaurants, f
- enlargement of the restaurant

Vergrößerung eines Fotos, f
- enlargement of a photograph

vergünstigter Zimmerpreis, m
→ ermäßigter Zimmerpreis

Vergütung, f
Entlohnung, f
Bezahlung, f
- remuneration

Verhalten, n
- behavior *AE*
- behaviour *BE*

Verhalten im Falle eines Brandes, n
- procedure in the event of fire

Verhandlung, f
- negotiations *pl*

Verhandlungen abbrechen
- break off negotiations

Verhandlungen aufnehmen
- start negotiations
- enter into negotiations

Verhandlungen führen (mit jm über etw)
- conduct negotiations (with s.o. on s.th.)

Verhandlung mit jm, f
- negotiations with s.o. *pl*

Verhandlungsforum, n
- negotiating forum

Verhandlungssache, f
VHS
Rabatt Verhandlungssache
Rabatt VHS
- by negotiation, adv
- discount by negotiation

Verhandlungstisch m
- negotiating table
- bargaining table

verhätscheln jn
verwöhnen jn
- cosset s.o.
- pamper s.o.

verhätschelt werden
verwöhnt werden
- be pampered
- be cosseted

verhören jn
- question s.o.

verhungern
- die of hunger
- starve (to death)
- die of starvation

verirren sich
verlaufen sich
- get lost
- lose one's way

Verjüngung, f *med*
- rejuvenation *med*

Verjüngungskur, f
Verjüngungsbehandlung, f
- rejuvenation treatment

Verjüngungskurzurlaub, m
- rejuvenation break

Verjüngungsurlaub, m
- rejuvenation vacation *AE*
- rejuvenation holiday *BE*

Verjüngungswoche, f
- rejuvenation week

verkatert, adj
(von übermäßigem Trinken oder Essen)
- crapulent, adj
- crapulous, adj *AE*

verkaterter Magen, m
(von übermäßigem Trinken oder Essen)
verstimmter Magen, m
- crapulous stomach *AE*

verkatert fühlen sich
- feel hung-over *BE inform*

verkatert sein
an einem Kater leiden
- suffer from a hangover

Verkauf, m
- sale
- selling

Verkauf einer Dienstleistung, m
Verkauf einer Leistung, m
- sale of a service
- selling a service

Verkauf eines Franchisebetriebs, m
- sale of a franchise establishment
- sale of a franchise operation
- sale of a franchise

Verkauf eines Gästezimmers, m
- sale of a guest room
- selling a guest room

Verkauf eines Hotels, m
- sale of a hotel
- selling a hotel

Verkauf eines Zimmers, m
- sale of a room
- selling a room

verkaufen etw
- sell s.th.

verkaufen etw gegen Provision
- sell s.th. on commission

verkaufen etw kistenweise
- sell s.th. by the crate

verkaufen etw über die Theke
- sell s.th. over the counter

Verkäufer, m (generell)
- seller
- vendor

Verkäufer, m (Verkaufskraft)
Verkaufskraft, f
- salesman
- shop assistant
- sales-clerk *AE*

Verkäufermarkt, m
- seller's market

Verkauf in letzter Sekunde, m
- last-minute sale

Verkauf mit anschließender Rückpachtung m
- sale-leaseback deal

Verkaufsabteilung f
- sales department

Verkaufsagent, m
- sales agent
- selling agent

Verkaufsagentur, f
- sales agency

Verkaufsaktivität, f
- sales activity

Verkaufsausstellung, f
- sales exhibition

Verkaufsautomat

- sales exhibit *AE*
- sales show

Verkaufsautomat, m
- automatic vending machine
- vending machine
- slot machine
- vendomat *AE*

Verkaufsbroschüre, f
  Verkaufsprospekt, m
- sales brochure

Verkaufsbüro, n
  Verkaufsstelle, f
- sales office

Verkaufsdatum, n
  Verkaufstermin, m
- date of sale

Verkaufsdirektor, m
- sales director
- director of sales *form*

Verkaufserlös, m
- sales proceeds *pl*
- sales revenue

Verkaufsfläche, f
  Verkaufsgebiet, n
- sales area

Verkaufsförderung, f
- sales promotion

Verkaufsförderungsmaßnahme, f
- sales promotion measure

Verkaufsförderungsprogramm, n
- sales promotion program *AE*
- sales promotion programme *BE*

Verkaufsförderungsseminar, n
- sales promotion seminar

Verkaufsförderungstagung, f
  Verkaufsförderungskonferenz, f
- sales promotion conference

Verkaufsförderungsveranstaltung, f
- sales promotion event
- sales promotion function

Verkaufsforum, n
- sales forum

Verkaufshandbuch, n
- sales manual
- sales guide

Verkaufskonferenz, f
  Verkaufsbesprechung, f
- sales conference

Verkaufsleiter, m
- sales manager

Verkaufsliteratur, f
- sales literature

Verkaufsmesse, f
- sales fair
- sales trade fair

Verkaufsmix, m
  → Umsatzmix

Verkaufsnetz, n
- sales network

Verkaufspersonal, n
- sales staff
- sales personnel

Verkaufspreis, m
  VKP, m
- selling price
- sale price

Verkaufsprogramm, n
- sales program *AE*
- sales programme *BE*

Verkaufspunkt, m
  Verkaufsstelle, f

- point of sale
- POS

Verkaufsrepräsentant m
- sales representative

Verkaufsschau, f
  Verkaufsausstellung, f
- sales show

Verkaufsseminar, n
- sales seminar

Verkaufsstand, m
  → Stand

Verkaufsstelle, f
- sales outlet
- outlet

Verkaufstagung, f
  Verkaufsbesprechung, f
- sales meeting

Verkaufstraining, n
- sales training

Verkaufstrainingssitzung, f
- sales training session

Verkaufs- und Marketingdirektor, m
- sales and marketing director
- director of sales and marketing *form*

Verkaufsvertrag, m
- contract of sale
- sales contract

Verkaufsvitrine, f
  → Vitrine

Verkaufsvorführung, f
  Verkaufspräsentation, f
- sales presentation

verkaufte Bettnacht, f
- sold bed-night

verkauftes Essen, n
- sold meal
- meal sold

verkauftes Zimmer, n
- sold room

verkaufte Zimmernacht, f
- sold room-night

Verkauf über die Straße, m (Essen)
  Lokal mit Verkauf über die Straße, n
- take-away
- take-away (food)
- take-away (restaurant)

Verkauf über die Straße, m (Laden)
- take-away shop
- take-away

Verkauf von Gästezimmern, m
- sale of guest rooms
- selling guest rooms

Verkauf von Getränken, m
  Getränkeausschank, m
- sale of beverages
- sale of drinks
- selling beverages
- selling drinks

Verkauf von Reisen, m
- sale of tours
- selling tours

Verkauf von Speisen, m
- sale of food
- selling food

Verkauf von Speisen und Getränken, m
- sale of food and beverages
- selling food and beverages

Verkauf von Wein, m
  Weinverkauf, m
  Weinausschank, m

- sale of wine
- selling wine

Verkauf von Zimmern, m
- sale of rooms
- selling rooms

Verkauf von Zimmernächten, m
- sale of room-nights
- selling room-nights

verkehren (Fahrzeug)
- run

verkehren mit jm
- mix with s.o.

verkehren zwischen A und B (Fahrzeug)
- run between A and B
- operate between A and B

verkehren zwischen A und B (Schiff, Boot)
- ply between A and B

Verkehr liberalisieren
  Beförderung liberalisieren
  Transport liberalisieren
- liberalise transport
- liberalize transport

Verkehrsabteilung, f
- transport department

Verkehrsader, f
- traffic artery
- artery
- arterial road

Verkehrsamt, n
  → Fremdenverkehrsamt

Verkehrsamtprospekt, m
- tourist office brochure

Verkehrsamtsleiter, m
  Fremdenverkehrsamtsleiter, m
- head of the tourist office
- director of the tourist office

Verkehrsaufkommen, n
- traffic volume
- volume of traffic

Verkehrsausschuß, m
- traffic committee
- transport committee

Verkehrsbedingungen, f pl
- traffic conditions *pl*

Verkehrsbereich, m
  Verkehrssektor, m
- traffic sector

Verkehrsbericht, m
- traffic report

verkehrsberuhigend, adj
- traffic-calming, adj

verkehrsberuhigte Zone, f
- area with reduced traffic
- reduced-traffic area

Verkehrsberuhigung, f
- traffic reduction
- traffic abatement
- traffic calming

Verkehrsberuhigungsmaßnahme, f
  verkehrsberuhigende Maßnahme, f
- traffic-calming measure

Verkehrsbetriebswirtschaft, f
- business administration in transport

Verkehrsbüro, n
  → Verkehrsverein

Verkehrschaos, n
- traffic chaos
- chaos on the roads

Verkehrschaos verursachen
  (an einer Stelle)
- cause a traffic snarl-up

Verkehrsdichte, f
- traffic density
- density of traffic

Verkehrsengpaß, m
- traffic bottleneck

Verkehrsexperte, m
- traffic expert

Verkehrsflug, m
- commercial flight

Verkehrsflughafen, m
- commercial airport

Verkehrsflugzeug, n
- commercial aircraft
- commercial airplane AE
- commercial aeroplane BE
- commercial plane
- airliner

Verkehrsfluß, m
- traffic flow
- flow of traffic

verkehrsfrei, adj
- traffic-free, adj
- free of traffic, adj

verkehrsfreie Einkaufszone, f
- traffic-free shopping area

verkehrsfreier Fremdenort, m
verkehrsfreier Erholungsort, m
- traffic-free resort

verkehrsfreies Dorf, n
- traffic-free village

verkehrsfreies Zentrum, n
- traffic-free center AE
- traffic-free centre BE

verkehrsfreie Zone, f
- traffic-free zone
- area closed to traffic

verkehrsfrei halten etw
- keep s.th. free of traffic

verkehrsfrei sein
- be traffic-free

Verkehrsfunk, m
- information for motorists sg
- travel news pl=sg

verkehrsgünstige Lage f
verkehrsgünstiger Standort m
- convenient location
- convenient position
- convenient situation

verkehrsgünstig gelegen, adj
- conveniently located, adj
- conveniently situated, adj

verkehrsgünstig gelegenes Hotel n
- conveniently located hotel
- conveniently situated hotel

verkehrsgünstig liegen
günstig liegen
günstig gelegen sein
- be conveniently situated
- be conveniently located

Verkehrsinformation, f
- traffic information

Verkehrsinformationsdienst, m
Verkehrsinformationsservice, m
- traffic information service

Verkehrsinfrastruktur, f
- transport infrastructure

Verkehrskonferenz, f
- traffic conference

Verkehrskontrolle, f
- traffic control

Verkehrskreisel, m
- traffic circle AE
- rotary AE
- traffic roundabout BE
- roundabout BE

Verkehrslärm, m
- traffic noise
- noise of traffic

Verkehrsliberalisierung, f
Beförderungsliberalisierung, f
Transportliberalisierung, f
- transport liberalisation
- transport liberalization
- liberalisation of transport
- liberalization of transport

Verkehrsluftfahrt, f
- commercial aviation

Verkehrsmeldung, f
(Radio, Fernsehen)
- traffic news pl = sg

Verkehrsminister, m
- minister of transportation AE
- minister of transport BE
- Secretary of Transportation AE
- Secretary (of State) for Transport BE
- transport(ation) secretary

Verkehrsministerium, n
- ministry of transportation AE
- ministry of transport BE
- Department of Transportation AE
- Department of Transport BE
- transport(ation) ministry

Verkehrsmittel, n
- transportation
- means of transportation AE sg
- means of transport BE sg

Verkehrsmittelbenutzer, m
- transport user BE

Verkehrsmuseum, n
Transportmuseum, n
- transportation museum AE
- transport museum BE
- museum of transportation AE
- museum of transport BE

Verkehrsnetz, n
- traffic system
- road and rail networks pl

Verkehrsniveau, n
- traffic level

Verkehrsordnung, f
- traffic regulations pl

Verkehrsplanung, f
- traffic planning

Verkehrspolitesse, f
Politesse, f
- traffic warden BE
- meter maid AE

Verkehrspolitik, f
- traffic policy

Verkehrsproblem, n
- traffic problem

Verkehrsprognose, f
- traffic forecast

verkehrsreich, adj
geschäftig, adj
lebhaft, adj
- busy, adj

verkehrsreiche Straße, f
- busy road
- busy street

Verkehrsschild, n
- signboard
- road sign

verkehrsschwach, adj
flau, adj
- slack, adj

verkehrssicher, adj (Fahrzeug)
- roadworthy, adj

Verkehrssicherheit, f (Fahrzeug)
- roadworthiness

Verkehrssicherheit, f (Straßen)
- road safety

Verkehrsstatistik, f
- traffic statistics pl

Verkehrsstau, m
Verkehrsstauung, f ÖST
- traffic jam
- traffic congestion
- traffic holdup
- holdup

Verkehrsstockung, f
Stockung, f
- holdup AE
- hold-up BE

Verkehrsstrecke, f
- traffic route

Verkehrssünder, m
- traffic offender

Verkehrsträger, m
(insbes. Luftfahrtgesellschaft)
- carrier

Verkehrsumleitung, f
Umleitung, f
- diversion BE
- detour AE

Verkehrsverbindung, f
- transportation link AE
- transport link BE
- traffic link
- traffic connection

Verkehrsverein, m
→ Fremdenverkehrsverein

Verkehrswachstum, n
- traffic growth
- growth of traffic

Verkehrswarnfunk, m
→ Verkehrsfunk

Verkehrszeichen, n
- road sign

Verkehrszunahme, f
- increase in traffic

Verkehrszusammenbruch, m
- breakdown in traffic flow

Verkehr unterbrechen
- disrupt traffic

Verkehr verdoppelt sich
- traffic doubles

Verkehr verdreifacht sich
- traffic trebles

verklagen jn wegen etw
verklagen jn auf etw
- sue s.o. for s.th.
- take s.o. to court for s.th.

verklagen jn wegen Vertragsbruch vor einem Gericht
- sue s.o. for breach of contract in a court

verkleiden sich
- disguise oneself

verkleiden sich als Clown
- disguise oneself as clown

verkochen etw (generell)
♦ boil away s.th.
verkochen etw (stark)
♦ overboil s.th.
verkohlen etw
verkohlen lassen etw
♦ char s.th.
verkohlt, adj
♦ charred, adj
verkohltes Fleisch, n
♦ charred meat
verkommen, adj
versifft, adj *sl*
♦ sleazy, adj
verkommener Club, m
versiffter Club, m *sl*
♦ sleazy club
verkommenes Hotel, n
versifftes Hotel, n *sl*
♦ sleazy hotel
verkorken etw
♦ cork up s.th.
♦ cork s.th.
verkosten etw
→ kosten etw
Verkoster, m
Koster, m
♦ taster
verköstigen jn
♦ board s.o.
♦ feed s.o.
verköstigen sich selbst
→ verpflegen sich
Verköstigung, f
Kost, f
Verpflegung, f
♦ board
♦ food
♦ feeding
verkürzen etw
→ abkürzen etw
verkürzt, adj
♦ shortened, adj
♦ curtailed, adj
♦ reduced, adj
verkürzter Aufenthalt, m
♦ shortened stay
♦ curtailed stay
♦ understay *AE*
Verkürzung der Aufenthaltsdauer f
♦ reduction of the length of stay
Verladebahnhof, m
♦ loading station
verlangen $ 1 für eine Tasse Kaffee
♦ charge $ 1 for a cup of coffee
verlangen etw von jm für etw
(Geld fordern)
♦ charge s.o. sth. for s.th.
Verlangen sie Eintritt?
Verlangen sie eine Eintrittsgebühr?
♦ Do they charge for admission?
verlängerbar, adj (Vertrag)
♦ renewable, adj
verlängerbare Pacht, f
♦ renewable lease
♦ extendable lease
verlängerbarer Vertrag, m
♦ renewable contract
Verlängerer, m
Bleibe, f *sl*
♦ stay-on

♦ guest who stays on
♦ overstay *sl*
verlängern etw
♦ extend s.th.
♦ renew s.th.
verlängert, adj
♦ extended, adj
verlängerte Öffnungszeit, f
♦ extended opening hours *pl*
verlängerter Aufenthalt, m
♦ extended stay
Verlängerung, f (generell)
♦ lengthening
♦ extension
♦ prolongation
Verlängerung, f (Vertrag)
♦ renewal
Verlängerung bekommen
♦ get an extension
Verlängerung der Aufenthaltsdauer, f
♦ extension of the length of stay
♦ extending the length of stay
Verlängerung der Fremdenverkehrssaison, f
♦ extension of the tourist season
Verlängerung der Reise, f
Verlängerung der Reise nach X, f
♦ extension of the tour
♦ extension of the tour to X
Verlängerung der Saison, f
♦ lengthening (of) the season
♦ extension of the season
♦ extending the season
Verlängerung der Sommersaison, f
♦ extension of the summer season
Verlängerung des Aufenthalts, f
Aufenthaltsverlängerung, f
♦ prolongation of (one's) stay
♦ prolonging one's stay
♦ extension of (one's) stay
♦ lenghtening one's stay
Verlängerung des Besuchs, f
♦ prolongation of a visit
♦ prolongation of one's visit
♦ extension of a visit
♦ extension of one's visit
Verlängerung des Mietverhältnisses, f
♦ extension of tenancy
Verlängerung des Mietvertrags, f
Verlängerung des Pachtvertrags, f
♦ renewal of a lease
♦ lease renewal
Verlängerungsaufenthalt, m
Anschlußaufenthalt, m
Zusatzaufenthalt, m
♦ extra stay
♦ additional stay
Verlängerungsgebühr f
(bei Mitgliedschaften)
♦ renewal fee
♦ renewal charge
Verlängerungsmonat m
Zusatzmonat m
zusätzlicher Monat m
♦ extra month
♦ additional month
Verlängerungsnacht, f
Zusatznacht, f
zusätzliche Nacht, f
zusätzliche Übernachtung, f
♦ extra night
♦ additional night

Verlängerungsprogramm, n (Konferenz)
→ Anschlußprogramm
Verlängerungsstunde f
Zusatzstunde f
zusätzliche Stunde f
♦ extra hour
♦ additional hour
Verlängerungstag, m
weiterer Tag m
zusätzlicher Tag m
Zusatztag m
♦ extra day
♦ additional day
Verlängerungstermin, m
Verlängerungsdatum, n
♦ renewal date
Verlängerungswoche f
Zusatzwoche f
zusätzliche Woche f
♦ extra week
♦ additional week
Verlängerungszeit f
♦ extension period
♦ period of extension
Verlängerungszeitraum, m
verlängerte Zeit, f
♦ extended period
verlassen, adj
♦ deserted, adj
♦ abandoned, adj
verlassener Strand, m
♦ deserted beach
verlassenes Auto, n
♦ abandoned car
verlassenes Dorf, n
♦ abandoned village
verlassenes Haus, n
♦ abandoned house
verlassene Stadt, f
♦ deserted town
♦ abandoned town
verlassen etw
aufgeben etw
♦ abandon s.th.
Verlassen Sie das Lokal!
♦ Leave the premises!
Verlauf des Abends, m
♦ course of the evening
Verlauf des Aufenthalts, m
♦ course of the stay
verlaust, adj
♦ infested with lice, adj
♦ full of lice, adj
verlegen jn (in eine andere Unterkunft)
♦ board s.o. out
verlegte Karte, f
verlegte Fahrkarte, f
♦ misplaced ticket
verlegt werden in ein anderes Hotel
♦ be moved to another hotel
♦ be switched to another hotel *coll*
♦ be transferred to another hotel
verlegt werden in ein anderes Zimmer
♦ be moved to another room
♦ be switched to another room *coll*
♦ be transferred to another room
verlieben sich in ein Hotel
♦ fall in love with a hotel
verlieren etw von seiner Beliebtheit
♦ lose some of its popularity
♦ lose some of one's popularity

Verlobung feiern
- celebrate one's engagement
- celebrate s.o.'s engagement

Verlobung feiern von A mit B
- celebrate the engagement of A to B

Verlobungsfeier, f
Verlobungsfest, n
- engagement celebration
- engagement party

Verlobungsfeier mit Geschenken, f
- engagement shower *AE*

Verlobungsfest, n
Verlobungsfeier, f
- engagement party
- engagement celebration

verlockend, adj
- tempting, adj

verlockende Bar, f
- tempting bar

verlorene Karte, f
verlorene Fahrkarte, f
- lost ticket

verlorene Karte ersetzen
verlorene Fahrkarte ersetzen
- replace a lost ticket

verlorenen Marktanteil zurückgewinnen
- reclaim the lost market share

verlorener Marktanteil, m
- lost market share

verlorenes Ei, n
→ pochiertes Ei

verlorene Zeit ersetzen
- compensate for lost time

verlorengegangenes Gepäck, n
abhandengekommenes Gepäck, n
- lost baggage *AE*
- lost luggage *BE*

verlosen etw (Tombola)
- raffle s.th.
- raffle off s.th.

Verlosung, f
- draw
- lottery
- ballot
- raffle

Verlosung veranstalten
- organise a draw
- organize a draw

Verlust, m
- loss

Verlust abwenden
- mitigate a loss

Verlust der Anzahlung, f
- forfeiture of the deposit

Verlust des Gepäcks, m
→ Gepäckverlust

Verlust des Reisepasses, m
- loss of a passport
- loss of one's passport

Verlust des Reisepasses melden jm
- report the loss of a passport to s.o.
- report the loss of one's passport to s.o.

Verlust hinnehmen müssen
- have to accept a loss
- have to take a loss

verlustig gehen (einer Sache)
verlieren etw
einbüßen etw
- forfeit s.th.

Verlust machen
- make a loss

Verlust minimieren
- minimise a loss
- minimize a loss

Verlust seines Urlaubs, m
(vertaner Urlaub)
- waste of one's vacation *AE*
- waste of one's holiday *BE*

vermarktbar, adj
- marketable, adj

vermarkten etw an jn
- market s.th. to s.o.

Vermarkter, m
- marketer

vermietbar, adj
- rentable, adj

Vermietbarkeit, f
- rentability

vermietbar sein
- be rentable

vermieten etw an jn (Immobilien)
- rent (out) s.th. to s.o.
- let (out) s.th. to s.o. *BE*

vermieten etw an jn (Mobilien)
- hire (out) s.th. to s.o. *BE*
- rent (out) s.th. to s.o.

vermieten etw für DM 123
- rent s.th. for DM 123 *AE*
- let s.th. for DM 123 *BE*

vermieten etw zu einer Miete von $ 123
- rent s.th. at a rent of $ 123 *AE*
- let s.th. at a rent of $ 123 *BE*
- hire s.th. out at a rent of $ 123 *BE*

vermieten etw zu Ferienzwecken (Immobilie)
vermieten etw zu Urlaubszwecken
- rent (out) s.th. for vacation purposes
- let s.th. for holiday purposes *BE*
- hire (out) s.th. for holiday purposes *BE*

Vermieter, m (Eigentümer)
- owner of the house
- owner of the apartment *AE*
- owner of the flat *BE*

Vermieter, m (Hauswirt)
- landlord

Vermieter, m (juristisch)
- lessor *jur*
- landlord
- person renting s.th. *AE*
- person letting s.th. *BE*

Vermieterin, f
- lady lessor *jur*
- landlady

Vermieterpfandrecht, n
Pfandrecht des Vermieters, n
- landlord's lien
- right of distress by the landlord
- right of distress by the lessor

Vermieter und Mieter
- landlord and tenant

vermietet, adj (Immobilie)
- let, adj *BE*
- rented (out), adj *AE*

vermietet, adj (Mobilie)
- hired (out), adj *BE*
- rented (out), adj *AE*

vermietet auf fünf Jahre (Immobilie)
vermietet für fünf Jahre
- rented (out) for five years
- let for five years *BE*

vermietet auf fünf Jahre (Mobilie)
vermietet für fünf Jahre
- hired (out) for five years *BE*
- rented (out) for five years

vermietete Immobilie, f
- let property *BE*
- rented property *AE*

vermieteter Raum, m
→ vermietetes Zimmer

vermietetes Zimmer, n
vermieteter Raum, m
- let room *BE*
- rented room *AE*

Vermietung, f (Immobilie)
- letting *BE*
- renting (out)
- rental

Vermietung, f (Mobilie)
- hiring (out) *BE*
- rental
- renting (out)

Vermietung beginnt um 11 Uhr (Immobilie)
- rental begins at 11 o'clock *AE*
- rental commences at 11 o'clock *AE form*
- letting begins at 11 o'clock *BE*
- letting commences at 11 o'clock *BE form*

Vermietung eines Veranstaltungsraums, f
- rental of a function room
- hiring out of a function room *BE*

Vermietungsausfall, m
→ Mietausfall

Vermietungsbedingungen, f pl (Immobilie)
- terms of letting *BE pl*
- terms of rental *pl*
- terms of lease *pl*
- rental terms *pl*

Vermietungsbedingungen, f pl (Mobilien)
- hire terms *BE pl*
- terms of rental *pl*
- rental conditions *pl*
- rental terms *pl*
- hiring terms *BE pl*

Vermietungsbüro, n (Immobilie)
Vermietungsstelle, f
- letting office *BE*
- rental office *BE*

Vermietungsbüro, n (Mobilie)
- rental office
- hiring office *BE*

Vermietungsdienst, m
Vermietungsservice, m
- letting service *BE*
- rental service *AE*

Vermietungseinheit, f
(Statistik)
- rental unit *AE*
- letting unit *BE*

vermietungsfähig, adj
- available for renting, adj *AE*
- available for letting, adj *BE*
- tenantable, adj

Vermietungsmarkt, m
- letting market *BE*
- rental market *AE*

Vermietungsservice, m
Vermietungsdienst, m
Vermietung, f
- rental service
- letting service *BE*

Vermietungsspezialist, m (Immobilien)
- letting specialist *BE*
- rental specialist *AE*

Vermietungsstand 842

Vermietungsstand, m
→ Mietstand
Vermietung von Flächen, f
♦ rental of space
♦ renting space AE
♦ letting (of) space BE
Vermietung von Veranstaltungsräumen, f
♦ rental of function rooms
♦ renting function rooms AE
♦ letting (of) function rooms BE
Vermietung zu Ferienzwecken, f (Immobilie)
Vermietung für Urlaubszwecke, f
♦ renting for vacation purposes AE
♦ letting for holiday purposes BE
vermissen etw
♦ miss s.th.
Vermißtenanzeige aufgeben
♦ report s.o. missing
vermitteln etw für jn
→ arrangieren etw für jn
vermittelt, adj
arrangiert, adj
vereinbart, adj
♦ arranged, adj
Vermittler, m (Agent)
→ Agent
Vermittler, m (Mittelsmann)
♦ intermediary
♦ agent
Vermittler, m (Schlichter)
♦ mediator
♦ arbitrator
Vermittlerklausel, f
♦ agency clause
Vermittlerprovision, f
♦ agent's commission
Vermittlungsagentur, f
→ Buchungsagentur
Vermittlungsdienst, m
→ Buchungsdienst, Reservierungsdienst
Vermittlungsgebühr, f
♦ charge for arranging s.th.
♦ fee for arranging s.th.
♦ commission
♦ commission charge
♦ agency fee
Vermittlungsprovision, f
♦ agency commission
Vermögenssteuer f
♦ property tax
♦ tax on property
Vernissage f
♦ vernissage
♦ varnishing day
veröffentlichter Zimmerpreis, m
♦ published room rate
♦ published room price
Veröffentlichung der Konferenzvorträge, f
♦ publication of the conference papers
Veröffentlichung der Kongreßvorträge, f
♦ publication of the convention papers
♦ publication of the congress papers
verordnen etw
vorschreiben etw
♦ prescribe s.th.
verordnete Behandlung, f med
♦ prescribed treatment med
Verordnung, f med
♦ medication med

verpachten etw
♦ lease out s.th.
♦ tenant s.th.
verpachten etw an jn
♦ lease s.th. to s.o.
verpachten etw zur Bewirtschaftung
♦ lease s.th. for operation
Verpächter, m jur
♦ lessor jur
Verpächter und Pächter, m pl
♦ landlord and tenant, pl
♦ lessor and lessee, pl jur
verpachtet, adj
♦ tenanted, adj
♦ leased, adj
verpachtete Gaststätte, f
♦ tenanted pub BE
verpachtetes Hotel, n
♦ leased hotel
verpachtetes Land, n
♦ leased land
Verpachtung, f
♦ leasing
verpaßt, adj
versäumt, adj
♦ missed, adj
verpaßter Anschluß, m
versäumter Anschluß, m
♦ missed connection
verpflegen sich (selbst)
verköstigen sich (selbst)
♦ cater for oneself
verpflegt werden
♦ be catered for
Verpflegung, f
♦ catering BE
♦ foodservice AE
♦ meal arrangement
Verpflegung erbringen
Verpflegung liefern
♦ do the catering
Verpflegung fremdvergeben
Verpflegung an Dritte vergeben
♦ contract out a catering service
Verpflegung ist gut
♦ foodservice is good AE
♦ catering is good BE
Verpflegung ist schlecht
♦ foodservice is poor AE
♦ catering is poor BE
Verpflegung liefern für etw
♦ do the catering for s.th.
Verpflegung liefern für jn
♦ do the catering for s.o.
Verpflegungsabteilung, f
♦ catering department BE
♦ foodservice department AE
Verpflegungsanforderung, f
♦ catering requirement BE
♦ foodservice requirement AE
Verpflegungsangebot, n (Palette)
♦ range of catering BE
Verpflegungsarrangement buchen
♦ book a board arrangement
Verpflegungsart, f
♦ meal arrangement
♦ catering arrangement
♦ catering
Verpflegungsart wählen
Verpflegungsart auswählen

♦ choose a meal arrangement
♦ select a meal arrangement
Verpflegungsaufgabe, f
♦ catering task BE
♦ foodservice task AE
Verpflegungsaufwand, m (Hotel)
Gastronomieaufwand, m
Wirtschaftsaufwand, m
Aufwand für Speisen und Getränke, m
♦ food and beverage expense AE
♦ food and beverage expenditure BE
♦ f&b expense AE
♦ f&b expenditure BE
Verpflegungsberater, m
♦ catering adviser BE
Verpflegungsbereich, m
♦ catering field BE
♦ catering sector BE
♦ foodservice field AE
♦ foodservice sector AE
Verpflegungsbereich, m (Hotel)
→ Food-and-Beverage-Bereich
Verpflegungsbetrieb, m (generell)
Gastronomiebetrieb, m
Gaststättenbetrieb, m
Restaurationsbetrieb, m
♦ catering establishment BE
♦ catering operation BE
♦ foodservice establishment AE
♦ foodservice operation AE
Verpflegungsbetrieb, m (Hotel)
Gastronomiebetrieb, m
Restaurationsbetrieb, m
♦ food and beverage operation
♦ f&b operation
♦ food and beverage establishment
♦ f&b establishment
Verpflegungsbranche, f
♦ catering industry BE
♦ foodservice industry AE
Verpflegungsdienst, m
Verpflegungsleistung, f
♦ catering service BE
♦ food service AE
♦ service of food and drinks
Verpflegungseinnahmen, f pl (Hotel)
Einnahmen aus Verpflegung, f pl
Gastronomieeinnahmen, f pl
♦ food and beverage receipts pl
♦ food and beverage takings pl
♦ food and beverage income
♦ f&b receipts pl
♦ f&b takings pl
Verpflegungseinrichtung, f
Verpflegungsstätte f
♦ foodservice facility AE
♦ catering facility BE
Verpflegungserlös, m (Hotel)
Erlös aus Verpflegung, m
Gastronomieerlös, m
Wirtschaftserlös, m
♦ food and beverage revenue
♦ f&b revenue
Verpflegungsertrag, m (Hotel, Guv)
(Gewinn- und Verlustrechnung)
Gastronomieertrag, m
Ertrag aus Verpflegung, m
♦ food and beverage income
♦ f&b income

Verpflegungsfirma, f
♦ catering firm *BE*
♦ catering company *BE*
Verpflegungsgast, m
Pensionsgast, m
Gastronomiegast, m
♦ food and beverage guest
♦ f&b guest
♦ boarder
Verpflegungsgeschäft, n
♦ catering business *BE*
♦ foodservice business *AE*
Verpflegungsgewerbe, n
Verpflegungsbranche, f
♦ catering trade *BE*
♦ foodservice trade *AE*
Verpflegungsindustrie, f
Verpflegungsbranche, f
♦ catering industry *BE*
♦ foodservice industry *AE*
Verpflegungskapazität, f
♦ catering capacity *BE*
♦ food capacity
♦ foodservice capacity *AE*
Verpflegungskonzept, n
♦ catering concept *BE*
♦ foodservice concept *AE*
Verpflegungskosten, pl
♦ foodservice costs *AE pl*
♦ foodservice cost *AE*
♦ catering costs *pl*
♦ catering cost
Verpflegungsleistung, f
♦ meal arrangement
♦ catering arrangement *BE*
Verpflegungslokal, n
→ Speiselokal
Verpflegungsmagazin, n *mil*
Verpflegungsstelle, f *mil*
♦ commissary *mil*
Verpflegungsmannschaft, f
♦ foodservice team *AE*
♦ catering team *BE*
Verpflegungsmarkt, m
♦ catering market *BE*
♦ foodservice market *AE*
Verpflegungsmöglichkeit, f
♦ catering possibility *BE*
Verpflegungsoption, f
♦ meal option
Verpflegungsorganisation, f
♦ foodservice organisation *AE*
♦ catering organisation *BE*
Verpflegungspersonal, n
♦ catering staff *BE*
♦ catering personnel *BE*
♦ foodservice staff *AE*
♦ foodservice personnel *AE*
Verpflegungsplan, m (generell)
Speiseplan, m
♦ catering plan *BE*
♦ meal plan
Verpflegungsplan, n (Heim)
♦ board plan
Verpflegungsplanschlüssel m
(z.B. MAP, AP, EP)
Verpflegungsplancode m
♦ meal plan code
Verpflegungspolitik, f
♦ catering policy *BE*

Verpflegungspreis, m
♦ catering price *BE*
Verpflegungsproblem, n
gastronomisches Problem, n
♦ foodservice problem *AE*
♦ catering problem *BE*
Verpflegungsprodukt, n
gastronomisches Produkt, n
♦ foodservice product *AE*
♦ catering product *BE*
Verpflegungsprofi, m *coll*
Verpflegungsfachmann, m
♦ catering professional *BE*
♦ foodservice professional *AE*
Verpflegungsqualität, f (generell)
♦ foodservice quality *AE*
♦ quality of foodservice
♦ catering quality *BE*
♦ quality of catering
Verpflegungsqualität, f (Hotel)
Gastronomiequalität, f
gastronomische Qualität, f
♦ food and beverage quality
♦ f&b quality
Verpflegungsqualität steigern
♦ raise the foodservice quality *AE*
♦ raise the quality of foodservice *AE*
♦ raise the catering quality
♦ raise the quality of catering
Verpflegungssektor, m
Verpflegungsbereich, m
♦ catering sector *BE*
♦ foodservice sector *AE*
♦ foodservice field *AE*
♦ catering field *BE*
Verpflegungsservice, m
Verpflegungsdienst, m
Verpflegungsleistung, f
♦ catering service *BE*
Verpflegungsstand, m
Bewirtungsstand, m
♦ catering stand *BE*
♦ catering stall *BE*
Verpflegungsstandard, m
♦ catering standard *BE*
♦ standard of catering *BE*
♦ foodservice standard *AE*
Verpflegungsstatistik, f (Hotel)
Gastronomiestatistik, f
gastronomische Statistik, f
♦ food and beverage statistics *pl*
♦ f&b statistics *pl*
Verpflegungsstätte, f
Verpflegungseinrichtung, f
♦ catering facility *BE*
♦ foodservice facility *AE*
♦ eating out facility
Verpflegungssystem, n
♦ foodservice system *AE*
♦ catering system *BE*
Verpflegung stellen (für jn)
Verpflegung bieten (jm)
♦ provide catering (for s.o.)
Verpflegungstyp, m
Verpflegungsart, f
♦ catering type *BE*
♦ type of catering *BE*
♦ foodservice type *AE*
♦ type of foodservice *AE*
Verpflegungsumsatz, m (generell)
♦ catering sales *BE pl*

♦ catering turnover *BE*
♦ foodservice sales *AE pl*
Verpflegungsumsatz, m (Hotel)
Gastronomieumsatz, m
gastronomischer Umsatz, m
♦ food and beverage sales *pl*
♦ food and beverage turnover
♦ f&b sales *pl*
♦ f&b turnover
Verpflegungsvereinbarung, f
Pensionsvereinbarung, f
Verpflegungsarrangement, n
♦ catering arrangement *BE*
♦ meal arrangement
♦ board arrangement
Verpflegungsvertrag, m
♦ catering contract *BE*
♦ foodservice contract *AE*
Verpflegungsvolumen, n
♦ foodservice volume *AE*
♦ catering volume *BE*
Verpflegungswahl f
♦ choice of board
Verpflegungswunsch m
♦ meal request
Verpflegungszentrum, n
♦ catering centre *BE*
Verpflegungszuschlag, m
♦ catering supplement *BE*
♦ meal supplement
♦ board supplement
Verpflegung und Unterkunft, f
Verköstigung und Unterbringung, f
♦ board and accommodation
♦ food and lodging *AE*
Verpflegung und Unterkunft anbieten
♦ offer board and lodging
♦ offer food and accommodation
verputzen etw *sl*
→ verschlingen etw
Verrechnungsscheck, m
♦ crossed check *AE*
♦ voucher check *AE*
♦ crossed cheque *BE*
verregneter Sommer, m
nasser Sommer, m
♦ wet summer
verregneter Tag, m
♦ wet day
verregnete Saison, f
♦ wet season
verreisen
auf eine Reise gehen
♦ go on a journey
♦ go away
verreisen aus familiären Gründen
♦ travel for family reasons
verreisen aus geschäftlichen Gründen
→ reisen aus geschäftlichen Gründen
verreisen aus gesundheitlichen Gründen
♦ travel for health reasons
verreisen der Gesundheit wegen
♦ travel for health
verreisen ins Ausland
in das Ausland verreisen
♦ go abroad
♦ travel abroad
verreisen ohne Ziel
♦ set out with no particular destination
verreisen zum Vergnügen
→ reisen zum Vergnügen

verreisen zur Erholung
wegfahren zu einem Urlaub
♦ go away for a holiday AE
♦ go away for a vacation BE
verreist, adj pred
♦ away, adj pred
verreist sein
♦ be away
♦ have gone on a journey
verrufen, adj
♦ disreputable, adj
verrufene Kneipe, f coll
♦ disreputable joint coll
♦ disreputable dive BE coll
Versammlung gewaltsam beenden
Treffen auflösen
♦ break up a meeting
Versammlung im Freien, f
♦ open-air meeting
Versammlungshalle, f
→ Versammlungssaal
Versammlungsraum, m
Versammlungszimmer, n
♦ assembly room
Versammlungssaal, m
Versammlungshalle, f
♦ assembly hall
Versammlungszimmer, n
→ Versammlungsraum
Versammlungszweck, m
♦ purpose of the meeting
versäumen etw
♦ miss s.th.
Versäumen Sie nicht einen Besuch im Schloß
♦ Do not miss a visit to the castle
♦ Don't miss a visit to the castle
verschandeln etw
♦ disfigure s.th.
Verschandelung der Landschaft, f
♦ disfigurement of the countryside
verschenken etw an jn
♦ give away s.th. to s.o.
verschiebbar, adj
verstellbar, adj
beweglich, adj
mobil, adj
fahrbar, adj
♦ movable, adj
♦ moveable, adj
verschieben etw
♦ postpone s.th.
♦ put off s.th.
verschieben etw auf einen späteren Termin
verlegen etw auf einen späteren Termin
♦ postpone s.th. to a later date
♦ put off s.th. to a later date
verschieben etw auf unbestimmte Zeit
♦ postpone s.th. indefinitely
♦ postpone s.th. for an indefinite time
♦ postpone s.th. to a later day
verschieben etw um 10 Tage
♦ postpone s.th. for 10 days
Verschiebung, f
(eines Termins)
♦ postponement
Verschiebung eines Treffens, f
♦ postponement of a meeting
Verschiebung erzwingen von etw
♦ force a postponement of s.th.

verschiedene Biere, n pl
♦ different types of beer pl
♦ different beers pl
verschiedene Biere probieren
♦ sample different beers
♦ taste different beers
verschiedene Büfetts, n pl
♦ various buffets pl
verschiedene Gerichte, n pl
♦ various dishes pl
verschiedene Kosten, pl
sonstige Kosten, pl
♦ miscellaneous costs pl
verschiedene Kulturen erleben
♦ experience different cultures
verschiedene Weine, m pl
♦ different types of wine pl
♦ different wines pl
verschlafen, adj
schläfrig, adj
♦ sleepy, adj
verschlafenes Dorf, n
♦ sleepy village
verschlafene Stadt, f
♦ sleepy town
verschlafen (sich)
♦ oversleep
verschließbare Garage, f
Autobox, f
♦ lock-up garage
♦ lock-up coll
verschließen etw mit einem Korken
verkorken etw
♦ cork s.th.
♦ cork up s.th.
verschlingen etw
hinunterschlingen etw
verputzen etw coll
♦ scoff s.th.
verschlissen, adj
abgenutzt, adj
♦ worn, adj
verschlissener Teppich, m
♦ worn carpet
verschlossene Tür, f
geschlossene Tür, f
♦ closed door
verschmutzt, adj
♦ polluted, adj
verschmutzter Fluß, m
♦ polluted river
verschmutzter Strand, m
♦ polluted beach
verschmutztes Meer, n
♦ polluted sea
Verschmutzte Straße
(Schild)
♦ Mud on Road
verschmutzte Straße, f
schmutzige Straße, f
♦ dirty road
♦ dirty street
Verschnaufpause, f
♦ breather inform
Verschnaufpause einlegen
Verschnaufpause machen
♦ have a breather inform
♦ take a breather inform
verschneiter Hang, m
♦ snowy slope

Verschnitt, m
♦ blend
verschönern etw
♦ embellish s.th.
Verschönerung, f
♦ embellishment
verschütten etw
♦ spill s.th.
verschwenderisch, adj
♦ lavish, adj
verschwenderisch ausgestattet, adj
♦ lavishly equipped, adj
♦ lavishly appointed, adj
verschwenderische Festlichkeit, f
♦ lavish festivity
verschwenderische Gastlichkeit, f
verschwenderische Gastfreundschaft, f
♦ lavish hospitality
verschwenderisch eingerichtet, adj
verschwenderisch möbliert, adj
♦ lavishly furnished, adj
♦ lavishly appointed, adj
♦ opulently furnished, adj
♦ opulently appointed, adj
verschwenderisch eingerichtetes Zimmer, n
♦ lavishly furnished room
♦ opulently furnished room
verschwenderische Party, f
♦ lavish party
verschwenderisches Fest, n (Festival)
♦ lavish festival
verschwenderisches Fest, n (Party)
→ verschwenderische Party
Versehen, n
♦ oversight
versehentliche Überbuchung, f
♦ inadvertent overbooking
versetzt werden nach X
(Personal)
♦ be transferred to X
Versicherer, m
♦ insurer
♦ underwriter
versichern etw gegen etw
♦ insure s.th. against s.th.
Versicherung, f
♦ insurance
Versicherung abschließen
♦ take out an insurance policy
♦ take out an insurance
Versicherungsarrangement, n
Versicherungsvereinbarung, f
♦ insurance arrangement
Versicherungsaufwand, m
♦ insurance expense AE
♦ insurance expenditure BE
Versicherungsaufwendungen, f pl
♦ insurance expenses pl
Versicherungsbedingungen, f pl
♦ insurance conditions pl
Versicherungsbedingungen prüfen
♦ check the insurance conditions
Versicherungsbeitrag, m
♦ insurance premium
♦ premium
Versicherungsgebühr, f
♦ insurance charge
Versicherungsschein, m
Versicherungspolice, f
♦ insurance policy

Versicherungsschutz, m
  ♦ insurance cover
  ♦ insurance protection
versifftes Hotel, n
  → verkommenes Hotel
versilbert, adj
  ♦ silver-plated, adj
versoffen, adj
  ♦ boozy, adj
versoffen aussehen
  ♦ look boozy
versoffener Gast, m
  ♦ boozy guest
Versoffenheit, f
  ♦ booziness
versorgen etw
  ♦ service s.th.
versorgen jn mit etw
  etw jm zur Verfügung stellen
  etw jm bereitstellen
  ♦ provide s.o. with s.th.
Versorgungsbasis, f
  ♦ supply basis
Versorgungsinsel, f
  ♦ supply island
Versorgungskosten, pl
  (Strom, Gas, Wasser)
  ♦ utility costs pl
  ♦ utility cost
Versorgungsraum m
  ♦ ancillary room
Versorgungsschiff, n
  ♦ supply ship
Versorgungsschwierigkeiten, f pl
  Lieferschwierigkeiten, f pl
  ♦ supply difficulties pl
verspäten sich
  ♦ be late
verspätet, adj
  spät, adj
  unpünktlich, adj
  ♦ delayed, adj
  ♦ late, adj
  ♦ tardy, adj
  ♦ belated, adj
verspätete Abfahrt, f
  (Person oder Verkehrsmittel)
  verspätete Abreise, f (Person)
  ♦ late departure
  ♦ tardy departure
verspätete Abreise, f
  → verspätete Abfahrt
verspätete Ankunft, f
  ♦ delayed arrival
  ♦ late arrival
  ♦ tardy arrival
verspätet eingegangene Stornierung, f
  verspätet eingehende Stornierung, f
  verspätete Stornierung, f
  verspäteter Rücktritt, m
  verspätete Absage, f
  ♦ belated cancellation
  ♦ belated cancelation AE
verspäteter Flug, m
  Flug mit Verspätung, m
  ♦ delayed flight
verspätete Rückgabe, f
  (z.B. von Mietauto)
  ♦ late return
verspätete Rückkehr, f
  ♦ delayed return

♦ late return
♦ tardy return
verspäteter Zug, m
  ♦ delayed train
  ♦ late train
verspätete Stornierung, f
  verspäteter Rücktritt, m
  verspätete Annullierung, f
  verspätete Abbestellung, f
  ♦ late cancellation
  ♦ late cancelation AE
verspätete Weihnachtskarte, f
  ♦ belated Christmas card
Verspätung, f
  ♦ delay
Verspätung bedauern
  ♦ regret the delay
Verspätung haben (generell)
  ♦ be delayed
  ♦ be late
Verspätung haben (Verkehrsmittel)
  ♦ be behind time
  ♦ be late
  ♦ be overdue
Verspätung haben von drei Minuten
  drei Minuten zu spät sein
  ♦ be three minutes late
Verspätung so gering wie möglich halten
  ♦ minimise a delay
  ♦ minimize a delay
Verspätung von 12 Stunden, f
  ♦ delay of 12 hours
  ♦ 12-hour delay
Verspätung wieder einholen
  ♦ make up (for) the delay
  ♦ make up for (the) lost time
verspeisen etw
  etw essen
  etw konsumieren
  ♦ eat s.th.
  ♦ eat up s.th.
  ♦ consume s.th.
verspielen etw
  ♦ gamble away s.th.
Verständnis, n
  ♦ understanding
Verstärker, m
  ♦ amplifier
Verstärkeranlage f
  ♦ amplifier system
Verstärkerausrüstung, f
  ♦ amplifier equipment
  ♦ amplifying equipment
verstauchtes Knie, n
  ♦ wrenched knee
verstauen etw
  ♦ stow s.th. (away) into s.th.
  ♦ stow s.th. (away) in s.th.
Versteck, n (eines Kriminellen)
  ♦ hideout
Versteck, n (generell)
  ♦ hiding place
versteckte Bucht, f
  ♦ hidden cove
  ♦ hidden bay
versteckte Nebenkosten, pl
  versteckte Zuschläge, m pl
  ♦ hidden extras pl
versteckter Winkel, m
  → stiller Winkel

versteckter Zuschlag m
  ♦ hidden extra
verstecktes Tal, n
  ♦ hidden valley
versteckte Zuschläge, f pl
  → versteckte Nebenkosten
versteckt liegen hinter etw
  (z.B. Haus)
  ♦ be tucked away behind s.th.
versteckt liegen in etw
  (z.B. Haus)
  ♦ be tucked away in s.th.
Versteigerer, m
  ♦ auctioneer
versteigern etw
  ♦ auction s.th.
Versteigerung, f
  Auktion, f
  ♦ auction
Versteigerung abhalten
  Auktion abhalten
  ♦ hold an auction
versteinerter Wald, m
  ♦ petrified forest
verstellbar, adj
  ♦ adjustable, adj
verstellbare Rückenlehne, f
  ♦ adjustable backrest
versteuern etw
  ♦ pay tax on s.th.
verstimmter Magen, n
  → verdorbener Magen
verstopft, adj (Leitung)
  ♦ blocked, adj
  ♦ clogged up, adj
verstopft, adj (Verkehr)
  ♦ congested, adj
  ♦ traffic-choked, adj
verstopfte Straße, f
  ♦ congested road
  ♦ congested street
  ♦ traffic-choked highway AE
versuchsweise Buchung, f
  provisorische Buchung, f
  ♦ tentative booking
versuchsweise Reservierung, f
  provisorische Reservierung, f
  ♦ tentative reservation
versuchte Brandstiftung, f
  ♦ arson attempt
Versuchung widerstehen
  ♦ resist the temptation
versunkenes Dorf, n
  ♦ sunken village
vertaner Urlaub, m
  ♦ wasted vacation AE
  ♦ wasted holiday BE
Verteidigungsturm, m
  ♦ defensive tower
verteilen etw an jn
  ♦ distribute s.th. to s.o.
verteilt sein auf das ganze Jahr
  ♦ be spread throughout the year
Verteilung der Besucher, f
  (geographisch)
  ♦ spread of visitors
Verteilung der Hotelzimmer, f
  Zuteilung der Hotelzimmer f
  Vergabe der Hotelzimmer, f
  Zuweisung der Hotelzimmer, f
  ♦ allocation of the hotel rooms

Verteilung der Zimmer

- allocating (the) hotel rooms
- assignment of the hotel rooms *AE*
- assigning (the) hotel rooms *AE*

Verteilung der Zimmer, f
→ Zimmerverteilung

Vertrag, m
- contract

Vertrag abschließen
- conclude a contract

Vertrag auflösen in gegenseitigem Einverständnis
- cancel a contract by mutual agreement

Vertrag aushandeln
- negotiate a contract

Vertrag ausstellen
Vertrag ausfertigen
- issue a contract

Vertrag beenden
- terminate a contract

Vertrag eingehen
- enter into a contract

Vertrag einhalten
Vertrag halten
- honor a contract *AE*
- honour a contract *BE*

Vertrag erfüllen
- fulfill a contract *AE*
- fulfil a contract *BE*

Vertrag haben mit einem Hotel
- have a contract with a hotel

Vertrag kündigen
- cancel a contract

vertraglich, adj
- contractual, adj
- contract, adj
- stated in the contract, adj

verträglich, adj (Essen)
leicht verdaulich, adj
- easily digestible, adj
- easy to digest, adj

verträglich, adj (Klima)
- agreeable, adj

vertragliche Leistung, f
Vertragsleistung, f
- contract service

vertragliche Leistungen in Anspruch nehmen
- use the services stated in the contract

verträgliches Essen, n
verträgliche Mahlzeit, f
- easily digestible meal

verträgliches Klima, n
- agreeable climate

vertragliche Vereinbarung f
- contractual agreement

vertragliche Verpflichtung, f
Vertragsverpflichtung, f
- contractual obligation

vertragliche Verpflichtungen erfüllen
- fulfill the contractual obligations *AE*
- fulfil the contractual obligations *BER*

vertraglich festgelegte Leistung, f
vertraglich festgelegte Dienstleistung, f
vertraglich festgelegter Service, m
- service stated in the contract

vertraglich festgelegte Miete, f
- rent stated in the lease

vertraglich festgelegtes Reiseende, n
- contractual end of the journey
- contractual end of the tour
- contractual end of the trip

Verträglichkeit, f (Essen)
- digestibility

Verträglichkeit, f (Klima)
- agreeableness

vertraglich übernehmen etw
- contract for s.th.

vertraglich vereinbarte Leistung, f
vertraglich festgelegte Leistung, f
- contracted service

vertraglich vereinbarter Preis, m
vertraglich festgelegter Preis, m
- contracted price
- contracted rate

vertraglich vereinbartes Hotelkontingent, n
vertraglich festgelegtes Hotelkontingent, n
- contracted hotel allocation

Vertrag machen
- make a contract

Vertrag neu aushandeln
- renegotiate a contract

Vertragsabschluß, m
- conclusion of a contract
- conclusion of an agreement

Vertragsbasis, f
Vertragsgrundlage, f
- contract basis
- basis of a contract

Vertragsbedingungen, f pl
- contract terms *pl*
- terms of the contract *pl*

Vertragsbeginn, m
- start of the contract
- beginning of the contract
- commencement of the contract *form*

Vertragsbestimmungen, f pl
- provisions of the contract *pl*

Vertragsbett n
- contract bed

Vertragsbruch, m
- breach of contract

vertragsbrüchig werden
- commit a breach of contract
- go back on the contract

Vertragscampingplatz, m
- contract campsite
- contract campground *AE*
- contract camping site *BE*
- contract camping ground *BE*
- contract site

Vertragscatering, n
- contract catering
- contract foodservice *AE*

Vertragsdauer, f
- duration of the contract
- term of the contract

Vertragseinzelheit, f
- contract detail

Vertragsende, n
- end of the contract

Vertragsentwurf, m
- draft contract
- draft agreement

Vertragserfüllung, f
- fulfilment of (a) contract
- fulfillment of (a) contract *AE*
- performance of contract
- contract performance

Vertragsgaststätte, f
- contract bar *AE*
- contract pub *BE*

Vertragsgaststättensystem, n
(an Brauereien gebunden)
- tied-house system *BE*

Vertragsgegenstand, m
- object of the contract
- object of the agreement

vertragsgemäß, adv
- according to the contract, adv
- according to the agreement, adv

Vertragshaus, n (Gasthaus)
→ Vertragsgaststätte

Vertragshaus, n (Hotel)
→ Vertragshotel

Vertragshotel, n (Club)
- appointed hotel

Vertragshotel, n (generell)
- contract hotel
- hotel under contract
- contracted hotel

Vertragsklausel, f
- contract clause

Vertragskunde, m
- contract customer
- contract client

Vertragsleistung, f
→ vertragliche Leistung

Vertragsmusiker, m
- contract musician

Vertragspartei, f
vertragschließende Partei, f
- contracting party
- contractor

Vertragsplatz, m
(Camping)
- contract site

Vertragspreis, m
Vertragsrate, f
- contract price
- contract rate

Vertragsrate, f
→ Vertragspreis

Vertragsreisebüro, n (Club)
- appointed travel agency

Vertragsrestaurant, n (Club)
- appointed restaurant

Vertragsverhandlung, f
- contract negotiation

Vertragszeit, f
→ Vertragsdauer

Vertragszimmer, n
- contract room

Vertrag unterliegt englischem Recht
- contract is governed by English law

Vertrag verlängern (um weitere zwei Jahre bis ...)
- renew a contract (for a further two years to ...)

vertrauliche Gespräche führen mit jm
- hold confidential talks with s.o.

vertraulicher Tarif, m
(nicht veröffentlichte Sonderpreise)
- confidential tariff
- confidential rates *pl*
- confidential rate
- confidential terms *pl*

vertreiben jn aus seinem Bett
- oust s.o. from his/her bed

Vertreter m (Handelsreisender)
→ Handelsreisender

Vertrieb, m
- distribution

Vertriebsbindung, f
- tied distribution

Vertriebskosten, pl
  ♦ distributing costs *pl*
  ♦ distribution costs *pl*
  ♦ distribution cost
Vertriebsnetz, n
  ♦ distribution network
Vertriebsstelle, f
  ♦ distribution outlet
Vertriebsweg, m
  ♦ distribution channel
  ♦ channel of distribution
vertrinken (Geld)
  ♦ spend (money) on drink
vervierfachen sich
  ♦ quadruple
Verwalter, m (Gut)
  ♦ steward
Verwalter, m (Haus)
  ♦ managing agent
Verwaltung, f
  Administration, f
  ♦ administration
Verwaltungsabteilung, f
  ♦ management department
Verwaltungsaufwand, m
  Verwaltungsaufwendung, f
  Verwaltungsausgabe, f
  ♦ administrative expense
  ♦ administration expense
Verwaltungsausgaben, f pl
  ♦ administrative expenses *pl*
Verwaltungsdienst, m (Haus)
  → Hausverwaltungsdienst
Verwaltungsgebäude, n
  ♦ administration building
  ♦ administrative building
Verwaltungsgebühr, f
  ♦ administration fee
  ♦ administration charge
  ♦ administrative fee
  ♦ administrative charge
Verwaltungsgebühr, f
  Hausverwaltungsgebühr, f
  ♦ management charge
Verwaltungsgesellschaft, f
  (für Immobilien)
  Betriebsgesellschaft, f
  ♦ management company
  ♦ managing company
Verwaltungskosten, pl
  ♦ administrative costs *pl*
  ♦ administrative cost
  ♦ administration costs *pl*
  ♦ administration cost
Verwaltungspersonal, n
  ♦ administrative staff
  ♦ administrative personnel
Verwaltungsviertel, n
  Behördenviertel, n
  ♦ civic centre *BE*
Verwaltungszentrale, f
  ♦ administrative headquarters *sg=pl*
Verwaltungszentrum, n
  ♦ administrative center *AE*
  ♦ administrative centre *BE*
verwandeln etw in ein Blütenmeer
  ♦ turn s.th. into a sea of blossoms
verwandeln in ein Bett
  ♦ convert into a bed
Verwandlungsbett n
  ♦ convertible bed

Verwandlungscouch, f
  Schlafcouch, f
  ♦ convertible couch
Verwandte besuchen
  ♦ visit relatives
Verwandter, m
  Verwandte, f
  ♦ relative
verweigern etw
  ablehnen etw
  zurückweisen etw
  ausschlagen etw
  versagen etw
  ♦ refuse s.th.
Verweildauer, f
  → Aufenthaltsdauer
verweilen bei jm
  ♦ vorübergehend aufhalten sich bei jm
Verweilender, m
  Gast, m
  Besucher, m
  ♦ sojourner *form*
verwohnen etw
  ♦ let an apartment go down *AE*
  ♦ let a flat go down *BE*
verwöhnen jn
  ♦ pamper s.o.
  ♦ spoil s.o.
  ♦ give s.o. a treat
  ♦ cosset s.o.
verwöhnen lassen sich
  ♦ let oneself be spoilt
  ♦ let oneself be spoiled
verwöhnen sich
  ♦ pamper oneself
  ♦ spoil oneself
  ♦ indulge oneself (with s.th.)
  ♦ treat oneself for s.th. *AE*
  ♦ treat oneself to s.th. *BE*
Verwöhnkurzurlaub, m
  ♦ pampering break
verwöhnt, adj
  verhätschelt, adj
  ♦ spoilt, adj
  ♦ spoiled, adj
  ♦ pampered, adj
  ♦ cosseted, adj
verwohnt, adv
  (Unterkunft)
  ♦ in a bad state of repair, adv
verwöhnter Fahrgast, m
  verwöhnter Passagier, m
  ♦ pampered passenger
verwöhnter Gast, m
  ♦ pampered guest
verwöhntesten Gast entzücken
  ♦ delight the most discerning guest
verwöhntester Gaumen, m
  ♦ most discriminating palate
verwohntes Zimmer, n
  ♦ room in a bad state of repair
verwöhnt mit Komfort, adj
  ♦ cossetted in comfort, adj
verwöhnt werden
  ♦ be cosseted
  ♦ be spoilt
  ♦ be spoiled
  ♦ be pampered
Verwöhnwochenende, n
  ♦ pampering weekend

verzapfen
  ♦ have on draft *AE*
  ♦ have on draught *BE*
verzehnfachen sich
  ♦ increase tenfold
Verzehr, m
  Konsum, m
  Verbrauch, m
  ♦ consumption
Verzehr am Tisch, m
  ♦ consumption at table
Verzehr an Ort und Stelle, m
  Konsum im Lokal, m
  ♦ consumption on the premises
  ♦ consumption on the spot
  ♦ on-premises consumption
Verzehr außerhalb des Lokals, m
  ♦ consumption off the premises
  ♦ off-premises consumption
Verzehrbon, m
  → Verzehrgutschein
verzehren etw
  → verspeisen, konsumieren
Verzehrgewohnheit, f
  Verbrauchsgewohnheit, f
  Konsumgewohnheit, f
  ♦ consumption habit
Verzehrgutschein, m
  Verpflegungsgutschein, m
  Essengutschein, m
  Essenkarte, f
  Essenbon, m
  ♦ meal voucher
  ♦ meal ticket *AE*
  ♦ luncheon voucher *BE*
  ♦ lunch voucher *BE*
  ♦ LV *BE*
Verzehrzwang, m
  Konsumationszwang, m
  Gedeckzwang, m
  ♦ obligation to order
  ♦ obligation to consume s.th.
  ♦ obligatory consumption
Verzeichnis erstellen
  Liste erstellen
  ♦ compile a list
  ♦ draw up a list
  ♦ make out a list
Verzeichnis führen von etw
  ♦ keep a record of s.th.
Verzicht, m *jur*
  Verzichtserklärung, f *jur*
  Verzichtsleistung, f *jur*
  ♦ waiver *jur*
verzichten auf Annehmlichkeiten
  ♦ do without luxuries
  ♦ rough it *coll*
verzichten auf etw
  ♦ dispense with s.th.
  ♦ do without s.th.
  ♦ forgo s.th.
verzichten auf Komfort und Bequemlichkeit
  ♦ forgo comfort and convenience
Verzierung, f *gastr*
  alles, was dazu gehört
  Garnierung, f
  ♦ trimmings *pl gastr*
verzollbar, adj
  zollpflichtig, adj
  ♦ dutiable, adj
  ♦ subject to duty, adj

verzollbar sein

- ♦ liable to duty, adj
- ♦ liable to customs, adj

verzollbar sein
- ♦ be dutiable

Vesperkarte, f
→ Nachmittagskarte

vespern
Vesper zu sich nehmen
jausen ÖST
- ♦ snack *inform*
- ♦ have a snack
- ♦ take a snack

Vesperpause, f
Imbißpause, f
Pause für einen Imbiß, f
- ♦ snack break

Vesperstube, f
→ Imbißstube

Vestibül, n
- ♦ vestibule

Vesuv, m
- ♦ Vesuvius

V-förmig, adj
- ♦ V-shaped, adj

V-förmiger Tisch, m
- ♦ V-shaped table

VFR
Reisen zu Verwandten und Bekannten, n
- ♦ VFR
- ♦ visiting friends and relatives

VFR-Markt, m
Markt für Reisen zu Verwandten und Bekannten, m
- ♦ VFR market

VFR-Reise, f
Reise zu Bekannten und Verwandten, f
- ♦ VFR tour

Viadukt, m
- ♦ viaduct

Videoanlage, f
Videosystem, n
- ♦ video system

Videoaufnahmedienst, m
→ Videoaufzeichnungsdienst

Videoaufzeichnung, f
Videoaufnahme, f
- ♦ video recording

Videoaufzeichnungsdienst m
Videoaufzeichnungsservice m
Videoaufzeichnung f
- ♦ video-recording service

Videoausrüstung, f
Videotechnik, f
- ♦ video equipment

Videoband, n
- ♦ video tape

Videobänder vorführen
Videobänder zeigen
- ♦ show video tapes

Videobibliothek, f
- ♦ video library

Videocheckout, m
- ♦ video checkout

Videofernsehen, n
- ♦ video television
- ♦ video TV

Videofilm, m
- ♦ video film

Videofilm zeigen
- ♦ show a video film

Videogästecheckout, m
- ♦ video guest check-out

Videogerät, n
- ♦ video set
- ♦ video machine

Video herstellen
- ♦ produce a video

Videoherstellung, f
- ♦ video production

Videokamera f
- ♦ video camera

Videokassette f
- ♦ video cassette

Videokassettenrecorder m
- ♦ video cassette recorder

Videokonferenz, f
Bildkonferenz, f
Bildschirmkonferenz, f
- ♦ videoconference *AE*
- ♦ video conference *BE*

Videoleinwand, f
Videowand, f
- ♦ video screen

Videolounge f
- ♦ video lounge

Videomonitor, m
- ♦ video monitor

Videopräsentation, f
- ♦ video presentation

Videoprogramm, n
- ♦ video program *AE*
- ♦ video programme *BE*

Videoprojektion, f
- ♦ video projection

Videoprojektor, m
- ♦ video projector

Videoraum, m
Videozimmer, n
- ♦ video room

Videorecorder m
- ♦ video recorder

Videospiel, n
- ♦ video game

Videospiele spielen
- ♦ play video games

Videospielzimmer, n
- ♦ video game room *AE*
- ♦ video games room *BE*

Videosprechanlage, f
Videotürsprechanlage, f
- ♦ video entryphone
- ♦ video entryphone system

Videosystem, n
→ Videoanlage

Videotext, m
- ♦ teletext

Videothek, f
- ♦ videotheque

Videotürsprechanlage, f
→ Videosprechanlage

Videounterhaltung f
- ♦ video entertainment

Videoverleih, m
- ♦ video rental *AE*
- ♦ video hire *BE*

Videoverleihfirma, f
- ♦ video rental company *AE*
- ♦ video hire company *BE*

Videovorführraum, m
Videoraum, m
- ♦ video presentation room

Videovorführung, f
- ♦ video show

Videowand, f
- ♦ video wall

Videowettbewerb, m
- ♦ video competition

Videozimmer, n
→ Videoraum

Viehhirt, m
- ♦ wrangler *AE*

Viehmarkt, m
- ♦ cattle market

Viehtreiber, m
- ♦ drover

Viehwagen, m (Eisenbahn)
- ♦ cattle car
- ♦ cattle truck

Viehweg, m
Viehtreiberweg, m
- ♦ drove road
- ♦ drovers' road

viel Abwechslung bieten
- ♦ provide plenty of diversions

viel Atmosphäre haben
- ♦ have plenty of atmosphere

viel auf Reisen sein
viel auf Reisen gehen
- ♦ do a lot of traveling *AE*
- ♦ do a lot of travelling *BE*

viel Beinfreiheit haben
- ♦ have plenty of legroom

vielbesucht, adj
- ♦ much-visited, adj
- ♦ much-frequented, adj

vielbesuchter Ort, m
- ♦ much-frequented place

vielbesucht sein
- ♦ be much frequented
- ♦ be much visited

Vielbucher, m
- ♦ frequent booker

viele Besucher anziehen
- ♦ attract many visitors

viele Fahrten machen
viele Reisen machen
- ♦ make a lot of trips

Viele Köche verderben den Brei
- ♦ Too many cooks spoil the broth

Vielen Dank für Ihre Gastfreundschaft
- ♦ Thank you for your kind hospitality

Vielen Dank für Ihr Schreiben vom 7. März
Ich danke Ihnen für Ihr Schreiben vom 7. März
- ♦ Thank you for your letter of 7 March
- ♦ I thank you for your letter dated 7 March

viel essen
- ♦ eat much
- ♦ eat a lot

viel essen zum Frühstück
- ♦ eat much for breakfast

Vielesser, m
Schlemmer, m
Gourmand, m
- ♦ gourmandizer
- ♦ gormandizer *BE*
- ♦ gourmand
- ♦ glutton

viele Zimmer haben einen Balkon
- ♦ many rooms have balconies

vielfältige Unterhaltung anbieten
- ♦ offer a wide range of entertainment
- ♦ offer a wide variety of entertainment

Vielflieger, m
♦ frequent flier
♦ frequent flyer
Vielfliegerprogramm, n
♦ frequent flier program *AE*
♦ frequent flyer program *AE*
♦ frequent flier programme *BE*
♦ frequent flyer programme *BE*
Vielfraß, m *vulg*
(Person)
Gourmand, m
Fresser, m *vulg*
♦ glutton
♦ gourmand
viel Geld ausgeben
♦ be a high spender
viel Geld sparen
♦ save a lot of money
vielgereist, adj
weitgereist, adj
♦ much-travelled, adj
♦ much-traveled, adj *AE*
♦ widely-travelled, adj
♦ widely-traveled, adj *AE*
vielgereister Gast, m
♦ much-travelled guest
♦ much-traveled guest *AE*
♦ widely-travelled guest
♦ widely-traveled guest *AE*
viel gereist sein
♦ have travelled a lot
♦ have traveled a lot *AE*
♦ be much travelled
♦ be much traveled *AE*
viel reisen
♦ travel a lot
♦ travel a great deal
♦ travel widely
♦ travel much
Vielreisender, m
♦ frequent traveller
♦ frequent traveler *AE*
vielreisender Geschäftsmann, m
vielreisende Geschäftsfrau, f
♦ frequent business traveller
♦ frequent business traveler *AE*
vielseitige Küche, f
→ abwechslungsreiche Küche
vielseitige Unterhaltung, f
→ abwechslungsreiche Unterhaltung
vielseitig verwendbare Halle, f
♦ versatile hall
Viel Spaß!
♦ Enjoy yourself!
♦ Enjoy yourselves!
♦ Have fun!
Viel Spaß bei der Party!
♦ Have a nice time at the party!
Viel Spaß dabei!
♦ Enjoy it!
viel Sport treiben
♦ do a lot of sports
♦ do a lot of sport
vielstündiges Programm, n
♦ program of several hours *AE*
♦ programme of several hours *BE*
viel trinken
♦ drink a lot
♦ drink much

Viel Vergnügen!
♦ Have a nice time!
♦ Have fun!
Vielzahl von Hotels haben
unzählige Hotels haben
♦ have an abundance of hotels
Vielzahl von Unterhaltung, f
♦ wide variety of amusement
Vielzahl von Vergnügungen bieten jm
♦ offer a wide variety of amusement to s.o.
viel zu bieten haben
♦ have much to offer
viel zunehmen
(Gewicht)
stark zunehmen
♦ put on a lot of weight
viel zu wünschen übriglassen
♦ leave much to be desired
♦ leave a lot to be desired
vierbeiniger Tisch, m
♦ four-legged table
Vierbettappartement, n
♦ four-bed apartment
Vierbettcaravan, m
Vierbettwohnwagen, m
♦ four-berth caravan *BE*
♦ four-berth van *BE coll*
♦ four-berth trailer *AE*
vierbettig, adj
♦ four-bedded, adj
vierbettiges Zimmer, n
♦ four-bedded room
Vierbettkabine, f (Betten)
♦ four-bed cabin
Vierbettkabine, f (Kojen)
♦ four-berth cabin
Vierbettvilla, f
♦ four-bed villa
Vierbettwohnung, f
♦ four-bed flat *BE*
♦ four-bed apartment *AE*
Vierbettwohnwagen, m
Vierbettcaravan, m
♦ four-berth trailer *AE*
♦ four-berth caravan *BE*
♦ four-berth van *BE coll*
Vierbettzimmer, n
♦ four-bed room
♦ four-bedded room
♦ quadruple room
♦ quadruple
Vierbettzimmerunterkunft, f
Unterkunft in einem Vierbettzimmer, f
Unterbringung in einem Vierbettzimmer, f
♦ accommodation in a four-bed room
viereckig, adj
vierseitig, adj
♦ quadrangular, adj
Viererappartement, n
→ Vierbettappartement
Viererbob, m
♦ four-seater bob
Vierersessellift, m
♦ four-seat chair lift *AE*
♦ four-seater chair lift *AE*
♦ four-seat chair-lift *BE*
♦ four-seater chair-lift *BE*
Vierertisch, m
Vierpersonentisch, m
♦ table for four persons

♦ table for four
♦ table to seat four persons
Viererzimmer, n
Vierbettzimmer, n
♦ quadruple room
♦ quadruple
♦ four-bed room
♦ four-bedded room
vierflammiger Gasherd, m
♦ four-burner gas cooker
vierflammiger Gaskocher, m
vierflammiger Gasherd, m
♦ four-burner gas cooker
Vierfruchtmarmelade, f
♦ four-fruit jam
Viergangfahrrad, n
♦ four-speed bicycle
viergängig, adj (Essen)
♦ four-course, adj
♦ consisting of four courses
viergängig, adj (Fahrrad)
♦ four-speed, adj
viergängiges Abendessen, n (Dinner)
♦ four-course dinner
viergängiges Abendessen, n (generell)
Abendessen mit vier Gängen, n
♦ four-course evening meal
viergängiges Abendessen, n (Supper)
♦ four-course supper
viergängiges Menü, n
Vier-Gang-Menü, n
♦ four-course menu
viergängiges Mittagessen, n
Mittagessen mit vier Gängen, n
♦ four-course luncheon
♦ four-course lunch
Vier-Gang-Menü, n
→ viergängiges Menü
Vier-Gipfel-Wanderung, f
♦ four peaks walk
Vierhundertjahrjubiläum, n
♦ quatercentenary
Vierhundertjahrjubiläum feiern (von etw)
♦ celebrate the quatercentenary (of s.th.)
vier Jahreszeiten, f pl
♦ four seasons of the year *pl*
♦ four seasons *pl*
vierköpfige Familie, f
♦ family of four
Vierkornbrot, n
♦ four-cereal bread
Vierländerreise, f
Reise durch vier Länder, f
♦ four-country tour
♦ tour of four countries
♦ tour through four countries
Vierliterflasche, f
♦ four-liter bottle *AE*
♦ four-litre bottle *BE*
Viermannorchester, n
♦ four-man orchestra
Viermannzelt, n
♦ four-man tent
viermastig, adj
♦ four-masted, adj
♦ four-mast, adj
Viermastschoner, m
♦ four-masted schooner
viermonatig, adj
♦ four-month, adj

viermonatige Fahrt, f
- four-month trip

viermonatige Reise, f
- four-month tour
- four-month trip
- four-month journey

viermotorig, adj
- four-engine(d), adj

viermotoriges Flugzeug, n
- four-engine(d) airplane AE
- four-engine(d) aeroplane BE
- four-engine(d) plane

Vierpersonenkabine, f
- four-person cabin

Vierpersonenkuppelzelt, n
- four-person dome tent

Vierpersonentisch, m
- four-person table
- table for four persons

Vierpersonenzelt, n
- four-person tent

Vierradantrieb, m
- four-wheel drive

Vierradfahrzeug, n
- four-wheel vehicle

vierrädrig, adj
vierräderig, adj
- four-wheel, adj
- four-wheeled

vierrädriges Motorrad, m
- quad bike

Vierraumwohnung, f
→ Vierzimmerwohnung

Vierschanzentournee, f
- Four Hills Tournament

Viersitzer, m
- four-seater

viersitzig, adj
- four-seater, adj

viersprachig, adj (Person)
- quadrilingual, adj

viersprachig, adv (Sache)
- in four languages, adv

vierspurige Straße, f
- four-lane road

Vier-Sterne-Anlage, f
Vier-Sterne-Komplex m
- four-star complex

Vier-Sterne-Anwesen, n
Vier-Sterne-Objekt, n
- four-star property

Vier-Sterne-Appartement, n
- four-star apartment

Vier-Sterne-Appartementanlage, f
Vier-Sterne-Appartementkomplex, m
- four-star apartment complex

Vier-Sterne-Attraktion, f
- four-star attraction

Vier-Sterne-Bereich, m
Vier-Sterne-Sektor, m
- four-star sector

Vier-Sterne-Betrieb, m
- four-star establishment
- four-star operation

Vier-Sterne-Bewertung, f
- four-star rating

Vier-Sterne-Campingplatz, m
- four-star campsite
- four-star campground AE
- four-star camping site BE
- four-star camping ground BE

Vier-Sterne-Caravanplatz, m
Vier-Sterne-Wohnwagenplatz, m
- four-star caravan site BE
- four-star trailer site AE

Vier-Sterne-Club, m
- four-star club

Vier-Sterne-Einrichtung, f
- four-star facility

Vier-Sterne-Einstufung, f
- four-star grading

Vier-Sterne-Einstufung einem Hotel geben
- award a four-star grading to a hotel

Vier-Sterne-Ferienwohnung, f
Vier-Sterne-Fewo, f sl
vier-Sterne-Urlaubswohnung, f
- four-star vacation apartment AE
- four-star holiday flat BE

Vier-Sterne-Hotelanlage, f
Vier-Sterne-Hotelkomplex m
- four-star hotel complex

Vier-Sterne-Hotelservice, m
- four-star hotel service

Viersternekategorie, f
→ Vier-Sterne-Kategorie

Vier-Sterne-Kategorie f
- four-star category

Vier-Sterne-Koch, m
- four-star cook

Vier-Sterne-Komfort, m
- four-star comfort
- four-star amenities pl

Vier-Sterne-Komplex, m
→ Vier-Sterne-Anlage

Vier-Sterne-Kreuzfahrtschiff, n
- four-star cruise ship
- four-star cruise liner

Vier-Sterne-Küchenchef, m
- four-star chef

Vier-Sterne-Luxus, m
- four-star luxury

Vier-Sterne-Luxushaus, n
→ Vier-Sterne-Luxushotel

Vier-Sterne-Luxushotel, n
- four-star deluxe hotel AE
- four-star luxury hotel

Vier-Sterne-Niveau, n
- four-star level

Vier-Sterne-Platz, m (Camping)
- four-star site

Vier-Sterne-Preis, m
- four-star price
- four-star rate

Vier-Sterne-Qualität, f
- four-star quality

Vier-Sterne-Residenz, f
- four-star residence

Vier-Sterne-Restaurant n
- four-star restaurant

Vier-Sterne-Segment, n
- four-star segment

Vier-Sterne-Sektor, m
→ Vier-Sterne-Bereich

Vier-Sterne-Service, m
- four-star service

Vier-Sterne-Service anbieten
- offer four-star service

Vier-Sterne-Stadthotel, n (Großstadt)
- four-star city hotel

Vier-Sterne-Stadthotel, n (kleine Stadt)
- four-star town hotel

Vier-Sterne-Standard m
- four-star standard

Vier-Sterne-System, n
- four-star system

Vier-Sterne-Tagungsort, m
Vier-Sterne-Austragungsort, m
- four-star venue

Vier-Sterne-Unterkunft, f
Vier-Sterne-Unterbringung, f
- four-star accommodation
- four-star lodging AE

Vier-Sterne-Wohnwagenplatz, m
- four-star trailer site AE
- four-star caravan site BE

Vier-Sterne-Zimmer, n
- four-star room

vierstöckig, adj attr (Gebäude)
- four-floor, adj attr
- four-story, adj attr AE
- four-storey, adj attr BE

vierstöckig, adj (Bett, Kuchen)
- four-tier, adj
- four-tiered, adj

vierstöckig, adj prd (Gebäude)
- four-storied, adj prd AE
- four-storeyed, adj prd BE

vierstöckiges Bett, n
- four-tier bed
- four-tiered bed

vierstöckige Torte, f
- four-tiered cake

vierstündig, adj
- four-hour, adj
- lasting four hours
- of four hours' duration
- four hours', adj

vierstündiger Marsch, m
- four hours' march

vierstündiges Programm, n
Vierstundenprogramm, n
- four-hour program AE
- four-hour programme BE

vierstündige Verspätung, f
- four-hour delay

Viertagearrangement, n
- four-day arrangement

Viertageaufenthalt, m
viertägiger Aufenthalt, m
- four-day stay
- four days' stay

Viertagepaß, m
- four-day pass

Viertagepauschale, f
- four-day package

Viertagepauschalpreis, m
- four-day-inclusive price
- four-day inclusive rate
- four-day package price
- four-day package rate

Viertagepreis, m
Preis für vier Tage, m
- four-day rate
- four-day price
- rate for four days
- price for four days

Viertagereise, f
viertägige Reise, f
- four-day tour
- four-day trip
- four-day journey

Viertagerennen, n
♦ four-day race
Vier-Tage-Skipaß, m
♦ four-day ski pass
viertägig, adj
♦ four-day, adj
♦ lasting four days
♦ of four days' duration
♦ four days', adj
viertägiger Besuch, m
♦ four-day visit
viertägiger Urlaub, m
viertägige Ferien, pl
Viertageurlaub, m
♦ four-day vacation AE
♦ four-day holiday BE
viertägige Veranstaltung, f
Viertageveranstaltung, f
♦ four-day event
♦ four-day function
vierte Etage, f
→ viertes Stockwerk
Vierteldollar, m
♦ quarter
Viertelfinale, n
♦ quarterfinal AE
♦ quarter-final BE
Viertelfinale gewinnen
♦ win the quarterfinal AE
♦ win the quarter-final BE
Vierteljahr, n
→ Quartal
Vierteljahresfahrkarte, f
♦ quarterly ticket
Vierteljahresmiete, f
→ Quartalsmiete
Vierteljahresstatistik, f
♦ quarterly statistics pl
vierteljährlich, adv
quartalsweise, adv
♦ by the quarter, adv
♦ on a quarterly basis, adv
vierteljährliche Kündigung, f
♦ three months' notice
vierteljährliche Rechnungsstellung f
♦ quarterly billing
vierteljährliche Rechnungstellung wünschen
♦ request (a) quarterly billing
Viertelliter, m
♦ quarter of a liter AE
♦ quarter of a litre BE
Viertelliterflasche, f
♦ quarter bottle
vierteln etw
in vier Teile schneiden etw
♦ cut s.th. into quarters
Viertelpfund, n
♦ quarter of a pound
♦ quarter
Viertelstunde, f
♦ quarter of an hour
viertelstündige Pause, f
♦ fifteen-minute break
viertelstündige Rast, f
♦ quarter of an hour's rest
♦ quarter-hour's rest
♦ fifteen minutes' rest
viertelstündiger Spaziergang, m
♦ quarter of an hour's walk
♦ quarter-hour's walk
♦ fifteen minutes' walk

viertelstündlich, adj
♦ quarter-hourly, adj
♦ every fifteen minutes, adv
vierter Gang, m (Menü)
♦ fourth course
vierter Gang, m (Motor)
♦ fourth gear
viertes Quartal, n
→ viertes Vierteljahr
viertes Stockwerk, n
vierte Etage, f
viertes Obergeschoß, n
♦ fifth floor AE
♦ fifth story AE
♦ fourth floor BE
♦ fourth storey BE
viertes Vierteljahr, n
viertes Quartal, n
♦ fourth quarter
viertüriges Auto, n
♦ four-door car
Vierundzwanzig-Stunden-Informationsdienst, m
♦ twenty-four-hour information service
♦ 24-hour information service
Vierundzwanzig-Stunden-Restaurant, n
24-Stunden-Restaurant n
♦ twenty-four-hour restaurant
♦ 24-hour restaurant
Vierundzwanzig-Stunden-Service, m
24-Stunden-Service m
Rund-um-die-Uhr-Dienst m
Tag-und-Nacht-Dienst m
♦ twenty-four-hour service
♦ 24-hour service
♦ round-the-clock service
Vierundzwanzig-Stunden-Wachpatrouille, f
Tag-und-Nacht-Wachpatrouille, f
Rund-um-die-Uhr-Wachpatrouille, f
♦ twenty-four-hour security patrol
Vierundzwanzig-Stunden-Zimmerservice, m
Tag-und-Nacht-Zimmerservice, m
Rund-um-die-Uhr-Zimmerservice, m
♦ twenty-four-hour room service
♦ 24-hour room service
Vierung, f archit
(Kirchenbau)
Querung, f
♦ crossing archit
Vierwaldstätter See, m
♦ Lake Lucerne
♦ Lake of Lucerne, the
Vierwochenpauschale, f
♦ four-week package
Vierwochenpauschalpreis, m
♦ four-week inclusive price
♦ four-week inclusive rate
♦ four-week package price
♦ four-week package rate
vierwöchig, adj
♦ four-week, adj
♦ lasting four weeks
♦ of four weeks' duration
♦ four weeks', adj
vierwöchige Reise, f
♦ four-week journey
♦ four-week tour
♦ four-week trip
vierwöchiger Kurs, m
vierwöchiger Lehrgang, m
♦ four-week course

vierwöchige Tournee, f
♦ four-week tour
vierzehntägige Reise, f
♦ fourteen-day tour
♦ fourteen-day trip
♦ fourteen-day journey
♦ fortnight's tour BE
♦ fortnight's trip BE
vierzehntägiger Urlaub, m
vierzehntägige Ferien, pl
♦ fourteen-day vacation AE
♦ fourteen-day holiday BE
♦ fortnight's holiday BE
Vierzigjähriger, m
Vierzigjährige, f
♦ quadragenarian
Vierzimmerappartement, n
♦ four-room apartment
Vierzimmerferienwohnung, f
Vierzimmerurlaubswohnung, f
Vierzimmerfewo, f sl
♦ four-room vacation apartment AE
♦ four-room holiday flat BE
vierzimmerig, adj
♦ four-roomed, adj
Vierzimmerwohnung, f
♦ four-room flat BE
♦ four-room apartment AE
Vietnam
♦ Vietnam
Vietnamese, m
♦ Vietnamese
Vietnamesin, f
♦ Vietnamese girl
♦ Vietnamese woman
♦ Vietnamese
vietnamesisch, adj
♦ Vietnamese, adj
Villa, f
♦ villa
♦ mansion
Villa am Meer, f
♦ villa by the seaside
Villa aus dem 18. Jahrhundert, f
♦ eighteenth-century villa
Villa besitzen
♦ own a villa
Villa für Selbstversorger, f
→ Selbstverpflegungsvilla
Villa im Privatbesitz, f
♦ privately owned villa
Villamiete, f
♦ villa rent
♦ villa hire BE
Villenappartement, n
♦ villa apartment
Villenbesitzer, m
♦ owner of a villa
♦ villa owner
♦ proprietor of a villa
Villengröße, f
♦ villa size
♦ size of the villa
Villenhotel, n
♦ villa hotel
Villenmiete, f
♦ villa rental AE
♦ villa hire BE
Villensuite, f
♦ villa suite

Villenunterkunft

Villenunterkunft, f
  Villenunterbringung, f
  ♦ villa accommodation
Villenurlaub, m
  ♦ villa vacation *AE*
  ♦ villa holiday *BE*
Vinaigrette, f
  ♦ vinaigrette dressing
  ♦ vinaigrette sauce
  ♦ vinaigrette
Violinspieler, m
  ♦ violinist
VIP, m
  Very Important Person, f
  wichtige Persönlichkeit, f
  ♦ VIP
  ♦ Very Important Person
VIP-Behandlung f
  ♦ VIP treatment
VIP-Behandlung zukommen lassen jm
  ♦ give s.o. VIP treatment
VIP-Bereich, m
  ♦ VIP area
VIP-Bungalow, m
  ♦ VIP bungalow
VIP-Bungalowsuite, f
  ♦ VIP bungalow suite
VIP-Etagenservice, m
  (Etage ist reserviert für VIP-Gäste)
  ♦ masterfloor service
VIP-Gast, m
  ♦ VIP guest
VIP-Karte, f
  ♦ VIP card
VIP-Liste, f
  ♦ VIP list
VIP-Lounge, f
  ♦ VIP lounge
  ♦ executive lounge
VIP-Service, m
  VIP-Dienst m
  VIP-Betreuung f
  ♦ VIP service
VIP-Suite f
  ♦ VIP suite
VIP-Zimmer, n
  ♦ VIP room
Visaformalitäten, f pl
  ♦ visa formalities *pl*
Visitenkarte, f
  Karte, f
  ♦ business card
  ♦ visiting card
  ♦ calling card *AE*
Visitenkarten tauschen
  Visitenkarten austauschen
  ♦ exchange business cards
  ♦ exchange visiting cards
  ♦ exchange calling cards *AE*
visuelle Präsentation, f
  ♦ visual presentation
visuelles Hilfsmittel, n
  ♦ visual aid
Visum, n
  ♦ visa
Visum abschaffen
  ♦ abolish visas
Visumagentur, f
  Visumvermittlung, f
  ♦ visa agency

Visumantrag, m
  ♦ visa application
  ♦ application for a visa
Visumantrag ablehnen
  ♦ reject a visa application
Visumantragsformular, n
  ♦ visa application form
Visumart, f
  ♦ visa type
  ♦ type of visa
Visum aufheben
  ♦ cancel a visa
Visum ausstellen (jm)
  Visum erteilen (jm)
  ♦ issue a visa (to s.o.)
  ♦ issue (s.o.) a visa
Visumausstellung, f
  ♦ issue of a visa
  ♦ visa issue
  ♦ issuing a visa
Visum beantragen
  ♦ apply for a visa
Visum bekommen
  ♦ get a visa
Visum benötigen
  ♦ require a visa
Visumbestimmungen, f pl
  → Visumvorschriften
Visum brauchen (für Argentinien)
  ♦ need a visa (for Argentina)
Visumdienst, m
  Visumvermittlung, f
  Visumservice, m
  ♦ visa service
Visum einführen (für jn)
  ♦ introduce visas (for s.o.)
Visum erhalten
  ♦ receive a visa
  ♦ obtain a visa
Visum erneuern lassen
  ♦ have a visa revalidated
Visum erteilen
  → Visum ausstellen
visumfrei, adj
  ♦ visa-free, adj
  ♦ visa-exempt, adj
Visum für (eine) einmalige Einreise, n
  ♦ single-entry visa
Visum für ein Land, n
  ♦ visa for a country
Visum für mehrmalige Einreisen, n
  ♦ multiple-entry visa
Visum für Mexiko, n
  ♦ visa to Mexico
Visumgebühr, f
  ♦ visa fee
Visum haben
  ♦ have a visa
Visumkategorie, f
  ♦ visa category
Visumkontrolle, f
  ♦ visa control
Visum kontrollieren
  Visum prüfen
  ♦ check a visa
Visum läuft ab
  ♦ visa expires
Visumpflicht, f
  → Visumzwang
Visumschwierigkeit, f
  ♦ visa difficulty

Visum verlängern
  ♦ extend a visa
Visumverlängerung, f
  ♦ visa extension
Visumverlängerungsgebühr, f
  ♦ visa extension fee
  ♦ visa extension charge
Visum verweigern jm
  ♦ refuse s.o. a visa
  ♦ refuse a visa to s.o.
Visumverweigerung, f
  ♦ visa refusal
Visumvorschrift, f
  ♦ visa requirement
Visumvorschriften, f pl
  ♦ visa regulations *pl*
Visumzwang, m
  Visumpflicht, f
  ♦ obligation to obtain a visa
  ♦ obligatory visa
Vitalität, f
  ♦ vitality
Vitalität gewinnen
  an Vitalität gewinnen
  ♦ gain vitality
Vitalität wiederherstellen
  ♦ restore vitality
Vitaminmangel, m
  ♦ vitamin deficiency
vitaminreich, adj
  ♦ rich in vitamins, adj
vitaminreiches Essen, n
  ♦ food rich in vitamins
Vitrine f
  ♦ showcase
VKP, f
  → Verkaufspreis
Vögel beobachten
  ♦ watch birds
Vogelbeobachter, m
  ♦ bird watcher *AE*
  ♦ bird-watcher *BE*
  ♦ birder *AE*
Vogelbeobachtung, f
  ♦ bird watching *AE*
  ♦ bird-watching *BE*
Vogelgarten, m
  ♦ bird garden
Vogelhaus, n
  Voliere, f
  ♦ aviary
Vogelliebhaber, m
  Vogelfreund, m
  ♦ bird lover
Vogelpark, m
  ♦ bird park
Vogelsammlung, f
  ♦ bird collection
  ♦ collection of birds
Vogelschutz, m
  ♦ bird protection
  ♦ protection of birds
Vogelschutzgebiet, n
  ♦ bird sanctuary
Vogesen, pl
  (Region)
  ♦ Vosges Mountains, the *pl*
  ♦ Vosges, the *pl*
Voiture, f *FR*
  (im Restaurant)
  Wagen, m

Wagon, m FR
- voiture FR
- cart AE
- trolley BE
- wagon FR

Völkerkundemuseum, n
- ethnological museum
- museum of ethnology

Volksbräuche, m pl
- folk customs pl

Volksbräuche erhalten
Volksbräuche am Leben halten
- keep alive folk customs

Volksfest, n
- folk festival
- public festival
- carnival

Volksskilauf, m
Volkskunst, f
- folk art

Volkskunstmuseum, n
- folk art museum

Volkskunstsammlung, f
- folk art collection
- collection of folk art

Volksliederabend, m
- folksong evening

Volksliedersingen, n
- folk singing

Volksmuseum, n
- folk museum

Volksmusik, f
- folk music

Volkssport, m
- popular sports
- popular sport

Volkstanz, m
- folk dance
- folk dancing

Volkstänzer, m
- folk dancer

Volkstanzgruppe, f
- folk dance group
- folk dancing group

Volkstracht, f
- folk costume

Voll
(Hinweisschild)
Belegt
- Full up
- No vacancy

voll, adj (betrunken) coll
- tight, adj sl
- plastered, adj sl

Vollagentur, f
- full-service agency

vollaufen lassen sich vulg
- get tanked up vulg
- get liquored up vulg

voll ausgelastet, adj
- used to capacity
- used to the full

Vollauslastung, f
volle Auslastung, f
- full load factor
- 100% load factor

Vollauslastung anstreben
Vollbelegung anstreben
- aim at full occupancy

vollautomatisch, adj
- fully automatic, adj

vollautomatische Anmeldung, f
vollautomatisierte Anmeldung, f
- fully automated check-in

vollautomatische Kegelbahn, f
- fully automatic bowling alley

vollautomatischer Fahrstuhl m
- fully automatic elevator AE
- fully automatic lift BE

vollautomatischer Lift, m
→ vollautomatischer Fahrstuhl

Vollbad, n (Aktivität)
- full bath

Vollbad, n (Wanne)
- full-size bath
- full-sized bath
- full-length bath

vollbeladen, adj
- fully loaded, adj

vollbeladenes Flugzeug, n
- full loaded plane

Vollbelegstag, m
→ Vollbelegungstag

vollbelegt, adj
ausgebucht, adj
- booked up, adj
- booked to capacity, adj
- packed to capacity, adj
- 100 % occupied, adj
- fully booked, adj

vollbelegter Tag, m
→ Vollbelegungstag

vollbelegt sein
→ ausgebucht sein

Vollbelegung, f
volle Belegung, f
Vollauslastung, f
volle Auslastung, f
- full occupancy
- 100 % occupancy

Vollbelegung anstreben
→ Vollauslastung anstreben

Vollbelegungstag, m
vollbelegter Tag, m
Vollbelegstag, m
- fully booked day
- day when a hotel is full
- day when a hotel is filled to capacity

vollbeschäftigt sein
- be employed full-time

vollbesetzt, adj
→ vollbelegt

vollbesetzt sein
→ vollbelegt sein

Vollbesetzung, f SCHW
→ Vollauslastung, Vollbelegung

vollbestückt, adj
- fully stocked, adj

vollbestückte Bar, f
- fully stocked bar

Vollbetrieb, m
- full-service establishment
- full-service operation
- establishment offering full service
- operation offering full service

Vollbett, n (belegt)
→ volles Bett

Vollbett, n (Bettart)
- full-size bed
- full-sized bed

vollbezahlter Urlaub, m
(Arbeitnehmer)

- full-pay leave
- leave on full pay

vollcomputerisiertes Buchungssystem, n
- fully computerised booking system

voll des Lobes
- full of praise

voll des Lobes sein
- be full of praise

volle Auslastung, f
→ Vollauslastung

volle Belegung, f
→ Vollauslastung

volle Besatzung, f
volle Schiffsbesatzung, f
- full complement

volle Erstattung, f
vollständige Rückerstattung, f
- full refund

voll eingerichtet, adj
vollständig eingerichtet, adj
- fully fitted, adj
- fully equipped, adj

voll eingerichtete Küche, f
komplett eingerichtete Küche, f
- fully fitted kitchen
- f/f kitchen

volle Kost und Logis
volle Kost (f) und Logis (n)
- full board and lodging

vollelektronisch, adj
- fully electronic, adj

vollen Betrag zahlen
- pay the full amount

vollen Fahrpreis zahlen
- pay the full fare
- pay full fare

vollen Preis berechnen
- charge the full price
- charge the full rate

vollen Preis zahlen
- pay the full price
- pay the full rate

vollen Schrankpreis zahlen
- pay the full rack rate

vollen Service bieten
Vollservice bieten
- provide full service

vollen Zimmerpreis zahlen
- pay the full room rate
- pay the full room price

volle Portion, f
ganze Portion, f
- full portion

volle Provision, f
- full commission

voller Betrag, m
- full amount

voller Blick auf das Meer, m
voller Meeresblick, m
- full view of the sea
- full seaview AE
- full sea view BE

voller Campingplatzservice, m
- full campsite service
- full campground service AE
- full camping site service BE
- full camping ground service BE

Völlerei hingeben sich
- indulge in gluttony

voller Fahrpreis, m
- full fare

voller Hotelservice, m
♦ full hotel service
voller Leben, adj
♦ bustling with life, adj
♦ busy, adj
voller Leben sein
♦ be bustling with life
voller Magen, m
satter Magen, m
♦ full stomach
voller Meeresblick, m
voller Blick auf das Meer m
♦ full seaview AE
♦ full sea view BE
♦ full view of the sea
voller Preis, m
Vollpreis, m
♦ full price
♦ full rate
voller Reiseverlauf, m
♦ crowded itinerary
voller Restaurantservice m
♦ full restaurant service
voller Schrankpreis, m
♦ full rack rate
voller Service, m
→ Vollservice
voller Tarif, m
→ Volltarif
voller Zimmerpreis, m
♦ full room rate
♦ full room price
volles Abendessen, n
vollständiges Abendessen, n
♦ full dinner
♦ full-blown dinner coll
♦ full evening meal
volles Bett n
Vollbett n
♦ full bed
♦ occupied bed
volle Schankerlaubnis, f
(in und außerhalb Verkaufsstelle)
♦ full-on license BE
♦ full-on licence BE
volles englisches Frühstück, n
komplettes englisches Frühstück, n
♦ full English breakfast
volles Frühstück n
Vollfrühstück n
♦ full breakfast
volles Haus, n
♦ full house
♦ packed house
volles Haus haben
♦ have a full house
volles Hotel, n
♦ full hotel
volles Programm, n
♦ full schedule
♦ packed programme BE
volles Vortragsprogramm, n
vollständiges Vortragsprogramm, n
♦ full program of lectures AE
♦ full programme of lectures BE
volle Verpflegung, f
Vollverpflegung, f
Vollpension, f
♦ full catering
♦ full board
♦ full pension AE

♦ American Plan
♦ AP
Volleyball, m
♦ volleyball AE
♦ volley-ball BE
Volleyballplatz, m
♦ volleyball court AE
♦ volley-ball court BE
Volleyball spielen
♦ play volleyball AE
♦ play volley-ball BE
vollfett, adj
♦ full-fat, adj
vollfetter Käse, m
Vollfettkäse, m
♦ full-fat cheese
vollfressen sich
→ vollstopfen sich
Vollfrühstück, n
→ volles Frühstück
vollgefedertes Bett, n
♦ fully sprung bed
vollgefliest, adj
vollgekachelt, adj
♦ fully tiled, adj
vollgefliestes Badezimmer, n
vollgefliestes Bad, n
♦ fully tiled bathroom
♦ fully tiled bath
voll genutzt sein
♦ be used to the full
vollgepackt, adj
vollgestopft, adj
♦ jam-packed, adj coll
♦ packed, adj
vollgepacktes Programm, n
volles Programm, n
♦ packed program AE
♦ packed programme BE
♦ full program AE
♦ full programme BE
vollgestopft, adj
vollgepackt, adj
♦ packed to capacity, adj
♦ cramped, adj
♦ crowded, adj
♦ jam-packed, adj coll
vollgestopftes Restaurant, n coll
vollgepacktes Restaurant, n coll
♦ jam-packed restaurant coll
vollgestopftes Zimmer, n
(mit Sachen/Personen)
♦ cramped room
vollgestopft mit Besuchern
♦ jam-packed with visitors
vollgestopft mit etw
vollgepackt mit etw
♦ jam-packed with s.th. coll
vollgestopft mit jm
♦ jam-packed with s.o. coll
vollgestopft mit Möbeln, adj
♦ crammed with furniture, adj
vollgestopft mit Zuschauern
♦ jam-packed with spectators
vollgestopft sein
eng sein
beengt sein
♦ be cramped
♦ be packed to capacity
♦ be jam-packed coll
♦ be crowded

vollgestopft sein mit etw coll
♦ be jam-packed with s.th. coll
vollgestopft sein mit Leuten coll
♦ be jam-packed with people coll
Vollhotel, n
Hotel mit vollem Serviceangebot, n
♦ full-service hotel
♦ hotel offering full service
♦ fully serviced hotel BE
völlig ebener Stellplatz, m
(Camping)
♦ completely level pitch
völlige Enthaltsamkeit, f
völlige Abstinzenz, f
♦ total abstinence
völlige Entspannung, f
♦ total relaxation
völlig neues Reisegefühl, n
♦ totally new travel sensation
völlig renoviert, adj
→ total renoviert
völlig restauriert, adj
(Gebäude)
♦ totally restored, adj
völlig umgebaut, adj
♦ entirely reconstructed, adj
♦ completely reconstructed, adj
voll im Gang
♦ in full swing
voll im Gang sein
♦ be in full swing
voll insolvenzabgesichert, adj
♦ fully bonded, adj BE
voll insolvenzabgesicherter Reiseveranstalter, m
♦ fully bonded tour operator BE
Vollinvalide, m
♦ fully disabled person
♦ total invalid
volljährig, adj
mündig, adj
♦ of age pred
Volljähriger, m
Volljährige, f
♦ major
Vollkaskoschutz, m
♦ comprehensive cover
vollkaskoversichert, adj
♦ with comprehensive insurance
vollkaskoversichert sein
♦ have comprehensive insurance
Vollkaskoversicherung, f
♦ comprehensive insurance
vollklimatisiert, adj
♦ fully air-conditioned, adj
vollklimatisiertes Zimmer, n
♦ fully air-conditioned room
vollklimatisiert sein
♦ be fully air-conditioned
vollkonzessioniert, adj
voll-lizenziert, adj
♦ fully licenced, adj
♦ fully licensed, adj
vollkonzessioniertes Reisebüro, n
voll-lizenziertes Reisebüro, n
♦ fully licenced travel agency
♦ full licensed travel agency
Vollkornbrot, n
♦ wholemeal bread
♦ granary bread
Vollkornmehl, n
♦ wholemeal flour

Vollkornnahrung, f
♦ wholemeal food
♦ whole-grain food
Vollkornnudeln, f pl
♦ whole-wheat pasta *sg*
Vollküche, f (Raum)
♦ full kitchen
voll-lizenziert, adj
→ vollkonzessioniert
Vollmassage, f
♦ full body massage
Vollmilch, f
♦ whole milk
Vollmitglied, n
♦ full member
vollmöbliert, adj
→ vollständig möbliert
vollmöbliertes Zimmer, n
vollständig möbliertes Zimmer, n
♦ fully furnished room
vollmöblierte Wohnung, f
vollständig möblierte Wohnung, f
♦ fully furnished flat *BE*
♦ fully furnished apartment *AE*
vollmundig, adj
(Wein)
♦ full-bodied, adj
♦ full, adj
vollmundiger Wein, m
schwerer Wein, m
♦ full-bodied wine
Vollpauschale, f
♦ full package
Vollpauschalpreis, m
♦ fully-inclusive price
♦ fully-inclusive rate
Vollpauschalreise, f
(Gegensatz zu Teilpauschalreise)
♦ fully inclusive tour
♦ all-inclusive tour
Vollpension, f
Vollverpflegung f
volle Verpflegung f
VP, f
♦ full board
♦ full pension *AE*
♦ full board and lodging
♦ American Plan
♦ AP
Vollpension ab DM 321
♦ full board from DM 321
♦ full pension from DM 321 *AE*
♦ full board starting at DM 321
♦ full pension starting at DM 321 *AE*
♦ American Plan starting at DM 321
Vollpension anbieten
♦ offer full board
♦ offer full pension *AE*
Vollpensionär, m
♦ full boarder
♦ full pensioner *AE*
Vollpension bei einer Familie, f
♦ full board with a family
♦ full pension with a family *AE*
Vollpension besteht aus drei Mahlzeiten pro Tag
♦ full board consists of three meals a day
♦ full pension consists of three meals a day *AE*
Vollpensionbettnacht, f
(Statistik)
♦ full-board bed-night
♦ full-board sleeper-night

Vollpension bieten
Vollverpflegung bieten
volle Verpflegung bieten
♦ provide full board
♦ provide full pension *AE*
Vollpension buchen
Vollverpflegung buchen
volle Verpflegung buchen
♦ book full board
♦ book full pension *AE*
Vollpensionbuchung, f
♦ full-board booking
♦ full-pension booking *AE*
Vollpensioneinnahmen, f pl
♦ full-board income
♦ full-board revenues *pl*
♦ full-board receipts *pl*
♦ full-board takings *pl*
Vollpensiongast, m
Vollpensionsgast, m
Gast mit Vollpension, m
Vollverpflegungsgast, m
♦ full-board guest
♦ full-board client
♦ guest on full board
♦ guest on full pension *AE*
Vollpensiongutschein, m
Vollverpflegungsgutschein, m
♦ full-board voucher
♦ full-pension voucher *AE*
♦ AP voucher *AE*
♦ American Plan voucher *AE*
Vollpension haben
Vollverpflegung haben
♦ stay on full board
♦ stay on full pension *AE*
♦ be on full board
♦ be on full pension *AE*
Vollpensionhotelunterkunft, f
Vollpensionhotelunterbringung, f
♦ full-board hotel accommodation
♦ full-pension hotel accommodation *AE*
Vollpension nehmen
Vollverpflegung nehmen
volle Verpflegung nehmen
♦ take full board
♦ take full pension *AE*
Vollpension nicht erhältlich
Vollverpflegung nicht erhältlich
♦ full board not available
♦ full pension not available *AE*
♦ American Plan not available
Vollpensionpauschale, f
♦ full-board package
♦ full-pension package *AE*
Vollpensionpreis, m
Vollverpflegungspreis, m
♦ full-board rate
♦ full-board price
♦ full-pension rate *AE*
♦ full-pension price *AE*
♦ American Plan rate
Vollpensionpreis pro Monat, m
Vollverpflegungspreis pro Monat, m
♦ full-board price per month
♦ full-board rate per month
♦ full-pension price per month *AE*
♦ full-pension rate per month *AE*
♦ AP rate per month
Vollpensionpreis pro Tag, m
Vollverpflegungspreis pro Tag, m

♦ full-board price per day
♦ full-board rate per day
♦ full-pension price per day *AE*
♦ full-pension rate per day *AE*
♦ AP rate per day
Vollpensionpreis pro Woche, m
Vollverpflegungspreis pro Woche, m
♦ full-board price per week
♦ full-board rate per week
♦ full-pension price per week *AE*
♦ full-pension rate per week *AE*
♦ AP rate per week
Vollpensionservice, m
Vollverpflegungsservice, m
voller Verpflegungsservice, m
♦ full-board service
♦ full-pension service *AE*
♦ full catering service
Vollpensiontarif, m
♦ full-board tariff
♦ full-board rates *pl*
♦ full-board rate
♦ full-board terms *pl*
♦ en pension terms *pl*
Vollpensionumsatz, m
Vollverpflegungsumsatz, m
♦ full-board sales *pl*
♦ full-pension sales *AE pl*
♦ full-board turnover
♦ full-pension turnover *AE*
Vollpensionunterkunft, f
Vollverpflegungsunterkunft, f
Vollpensionunterbringung, f
Vollverpflegungsunterbringung, f
♦ full-board accommodation
♦ full-pension accommodation *AE*
Vollpensionurlaub, m
Vollpensionsurlaub, m
Vollpension(s)ferien, pl
♦ full-board vacation *AE*
♦ full-pension vacation *AE*
♦ full-board holiday *BE*
Vollpensionvereinbarung, f
Vollverpflegungsvereinbarung, f
Vollpensionsarrangement, n
Vollverpflegungsarrangement, n
♦ full-board arrangement
♦ en pension arrangement
♦ full-pension arrangement *AE*
♦ AP arrangement *AE*
♦ American Plan arrangement *AE*
Vollpensionwochenpreis, m
Wochenpreis für Vollpension, m
♦ weekly full-board rate
♦ weekly full-board price
♦ weekly full-pension rate *AE*
♦ weekly full-pension price *AE*
♦ full-board rate per week
Vollpensionzuschlag, m
VP-Zuschlag, m
Vollverpflegungszuschlag, m
♦ full-board supplement
♦ full-pension supplement *AE*
♦ supplement for full board
♦ supplement for full pension *AE*
Vollpreis, m
→ voller Preis
Vollrausch, m
♦ drunken stupor
Vollrausch antrinken sich
♦ drink oneself silly

Vollrausch haben

Vollrausch haben
→ sternhagelvoll sein
vollreife Traube, f
♦ fully ripe grape
♦ fully ripened grape
Vollreisebüro, n (generell)
♦ full-service travel agency
♦ travel agency offering full service
♦ travel agency providing a full range of services
Vollreisebüro, n (mit allen Lizenzen)
♦ fully appointed travel agency AE
Vollrestaurant, n
♦ full-service restaurant
♦ restaurant offering full service
Vollservice, m
voller Service m
vollständiger Service, m
kompletter Service, m
♦ full service
♦ complete service
Vollservice bieten
→ vollen Service bieten
Vollsitzung, f
→ Vollversammlung
vollständig ausgegraben, adj
vollständig freigelegt, adj
♦ completely excavated, adj
♦ fully excavated, adj
vollständig ausgestattetes Zelt, n
♦ fully equipped tent
vollständige Adresse, f
♦ full address
vollständige Bezahlung, f
volle Zahlung, f
♦ full payment
vollständige Liste, f
♦ complete list
♦ exhaustive list
vollständige Mahlzeit, f
volle Mahlzeit, f
vollständiges Essen, n
komplettes Essen, n
♦ full meal
♦ complete meal
vollständig erhalten, adj
♦ fully preserved, adj
vollständig erhaltene Mauer, f
♦ fully preserved wall
vollständiger Name, m
♦ full name
vollständiger Satz Bettzeug, m
♦ full complement of bedding
vollständiges Programm, n
volles Programm, n
♦ full program AE
♦ full programme BE
vollständige Vorauszahlung, f
volle Vorauszahlung, f
♦ full payment in advance
vollständig möbliert, adj
vollständig eingerichtet, adj
komplett möbliert, adj
komplett eingerichtet, adj
vollmöbliert, adj
♦ fully furnished, adj
♦ completely furnished, adj
vollständig möbliertes Appartement, n
komplett eingerichtetes Appartement, n
♦ fully furnished apartment
♦ completely furnished apartment

vollständig modernisiert, adj
komplett modernisiert, adj
♦ fully modernised, adj
♦ fully modernized, adj
♦ completely modernised, adj
♦ completely modernized, adj
vollständig renoviert, adj
♦ fully renovated, adj
♦ fully refurbished, adj
vollständig renoviertes Hotel, n
♦ fully renovated hotel
♦ fully refurbished hotel
vollständig restauriert, adj
komplett restauriert, adj
♦ completely restored, adj
vollstopfen etw
♦ cram s.th.
vollstopfen mit Gästen
♦ cram with guests
vollstopfen sich (mit Essen)
vollfressen sich
♦ gorge oneself with food
♦ stuff oneself (up with food)
♦ stuff one's face
Vollsuite, f
♦ full suite
Volltarif, m
voller Tarif, m
♦ full tariff
♦ full terms pl
♦ full rates pl
♦ full rate
voll Touristen
voll von Touristen
♦ filled with tourists
♦ crowded with tourists
volltrunken, adj
♦ drunk and incapable, adj
Vollunterbringung, f
→ Vollunterkunft
Vollunterkunft, f
volle Unterkunft, f
Vollunterbringung, f
volle Unterbringung, f
♦ full accommodation
Vollverpflegung, f
→ Vollpension
Vollversammlung, f
♦ plenary session
♦ plenary assembly
Vollweizenbrot, n
♦ wholewheat bread
Vollwerternährung, f
vollwertige Ernährung, f
♦ wholefood nutrition
Vollwertgericht, n
♦ wholefood dish
Vollwertkochkurs, m
♦ wholefood cooking course AE
♦ wholefood cookery course BE
♦ wholefood cookery class BE
Vollwertkost, f
♦ wholefood diet
♦ whole foods pl
Vollwertkostrestaurant, n
→ Vollwertrestaurant
Vollwertküche, f (Kost)
→ Vollwertkost
Vollwertküche, f (Speisen)
♦ wholefood cooking
♦ wholefood cuisine

Vollwertmenü, n
♦ wholefood menu
Vollwertnahrung, f
♦ whole foods pl
Vollwertrestaurant, n
♦ wholefood restaurant
♦ restaurant serving whole foods
voll wie eine Strandhaubitze
♦ drunk as a lord
♦ drunk as a fiddler
♦ tight coll
vollzahlender Erwachsener, m
♦ full-paying adult
vollzahlender Passagier, m
Vollzahler, m
♦ passenger paying the full fare
♦ full-paying passenger
Vollzahler, m (Gast)
vollzahlender Gast, m
♦ full-paying guest
♦ guest paying the full rate
♦ guest paying the full price
Vollzahler, m (Passagier)
vollzahlender Passagier, m
♦ full-paying passenger
♦ passenger paying the full fare
Vollzahlertarif, m
♦ full-fare tariff
♦ full-fare rates pl
♦ full-fare rate
Vollzeitbeschäftigter, m
♦ full-time employee
vollzeitbeschäftigter Fremdenführer, m
♦ full-time tourist guide
Vollzeitkraft, f
→ Vollzeitbeschäftigter
Vollzeitpersonal n
♦ full-time personnel
♦ full-time staff
voll zum Platzen
zum Platzen voll
♦ full to bursting
Volontär, m
♦ unpaid trainee
♦ trainee
♦ improver BE
♦ unsalaried clerk
Voltspannung, f
Spannung, f
♦ voltage
vom 10. Mai bis zum Morgen des 15. Mai
♦ from 10 May until the morning of 15 May
♦ from 10 May to the morning of 15 May
vom 3. bis 5. Juli
♦ from 3 to 5 July
♦ from 3rd to 5th July
♦ from 3 until 5 July
vom 5. bis einschließlich 23. Januar
♦ from 5 through 23 January AE
♦ from 5 to 23 January inclusive
♦ from 5 until 23 January inclusive
vom Abend der Abreise
♦ from the evening of departure
vom Abend der Ankunft
♦ from the evening of arrival
vom ADAC empfohlener Platz, m
(Camping)
♦ ADAC recommended site
♦ site recommended by the ADAC
vom Feinsten sein
♦ be of the best

vom Grill, adv
　gegrillt, adj
　♦ barbecued, adj
　♦ grilled, adj
vom Regen in die Traufe kommen
　♦ jump out of the frying pan into the fire AE
　♦ jump out of the frying-pan into the fire BE
vom Tisch aufstehen
　aufstehen vom Tisch
　♦ get up from the table
　♦ leave the table
vom Tisch nehmen etw
　♦ take s.th. off the table
　♦ remove s.th. from the table
von 9.00 Uhr bis 10.00 Uhr vormittags
　♦ from 9 a.m. to 10 a.m.
　♦ from 9 a.m. until 10 a.m.
von allen Gegenden des Globus
　♦ from around the globe
von Bord gehen
　ausschiffen
　♦ disembark
von Dienstag abend bis Donnerstag morgen
　♦ from Tuesday evening to Thursday morning
　♦ from Tuesday evening until Thursday morning
von einer Kette geführtes Hotel, n
　♦ chain-managed hotel
von gleichwertiger Qualität
　von gleicher Qualität
　♦ of equivalent quality
von höherer Qualität
　♦ of superior quality
von hoher Qualität
　♦ of high standard
von internationalem Renommee
　♦ of international renown
von internationalem Ruf
　♦ of international reputation
von Luxus umgeben
　♦ lapped in luxury
　♦ in the lap of luxury
von Mai bis September
　♦ from May until September
　♦ from May to September
von minderem Wert
　♦ of inferior value
von minderer Qualität
　von geringerer Qualität
　♦ of lower quality
von mittags bis abends
　♦ from midday until evening
von Mittag zu Mittag
　♦ from midday to midday
von mittlerer Größe
　♦ of medium size
von Montag bis einschließlich Freitag
　♦ from Monday through Friday AE
　♦ from Monday until Friday inclusive BE
von Ort zu Ort
　♦ from place to place
von seinem Namen leben
　von seinem Namen zehren
　♦ live on one's name
　♦ live on one's reputation
von vergleichbarer Qualität
　♦ of comparable quality
von weit und breit
　♦ from far and wide
von Weltruf, adv
　♦ of world repute, adv
　♦ of world renown, adv

von Westen nach Osten
　♦ from west to east
Vorabend, m
　vorhergehender Abend, m
　voriger Abend, m
　♦ eve
　♦ previous evening
　♦ evening before
　♦ previous night
vor Anker gehen in X
　♦ moor in X
voranmelden (sich)
　♦ preregister
　♦ register before arrival
Voranmeldung, f (Buchung)
　→ Vorausbuchung
Voranmeldung, f (generell)
　♦ preregistration AE
　♦ pre-registration BE
　♦ advance registration
Voranmeldungsgebühr, f
　Voranmeldegebühr, f
　♦ advance registration charge
　♦ advance registration fee
Voranmeldungspreis, m
　♦ preregistration price
Voranmeldung wird empfohlen
　♦ preregistration is recommended
　♦ advance registration is recommended
Voranzahlung, f
　♦ advance deposit
Voranzahlung verlangen
　Anzahlung fordern
　♦ require an advance deposit
Vorarlberg
　(Region)
　♦ Vorarlberg
Vorausanzahlung, f
　→ Voranzahlung
Vorausbestellung, f
　Vorbestellung, f
　Vorausbuchung, f
　Vorbuchung, f
　Voranmeldung, f
　♦ prebooking
　♦ booking (s.th.) in advance
　♦ advance booking
　♦ booking (s.th.) ahead
vorausbezahlte bestätigte Reservierung, f
　♦ prepaid confirmed reservation
vorausbezahlte Miete, f
　Mietvorauszahlung, f
　vorausbezahlte Pacht, f
　Pachtvorauszahlung, f
　♦ prepaid rent
　♦ rent paid in advance
　♦ rent in advance
vorausbezahlte Pacht, f
　Pachtvorauszahlung, f
　vorausbezahlte Miete, f
　Mietvorauszahlung, f
　♦ rent paid in advance
　♦ rent in advance
　♦ prepaid rent
vorausbezahlter Betrag, m
　♦ prepaid amount
vorausbezahlte Zusatzübernachtung, f
　(bei Pauschalreise)
　♦ prepaid extra night

vorausbuchbar, adj
　♦ prebookable, adj
　♦ bookable in advance, adj
vorausbuchbar sein
　vorbestellbar sein
　♦ be bookable in advance
　♦ be prebookable
　♦ can be booked in advanced
Vorausbucher, m
　♦ advance booker
　♦ person booking in advance
Vorausbuchung, f
　Voranmeldung, f
　Vorbestellung, f
　Vorbuchung, f
　♦ advance booking
　♦ booking (s.th.) in advance
　♦ booking (s.th.) ahead
　♦ prebooking
Vorausbuchung ist erforderlich
　♦ advance booking is required
Vorausbuchung ist notwendig
　♦ advance booking is necessary
Vorausbuchungsdienst, m
　→ Vorausbuchungsservice
Vorausbuchungsgebühr, f
　♦ advance booking charge
　♦ advance booking fee
Vorausbuchungsservice, m
　Vorausbuchungsdienst, m
　♦ advance booking service
Vorausbuchungssystem, n
　♦ advance booking system
Vorausbuchung stornieren
　Vorbuchung stornieren
　♦ cancel an advance booking
Vorausinformation, f
　→ Vorinformation
Vorausinformation erhalten
　Vorinformation erhalten
　♦ receive advance information
Vorauskasse, f
　♦ cash in advance
vorausplanen etw
　im voraus planen etw
　♦ plan s.th. in advance
Vorausplanung, f
　Vorplanung, f
　♦ advance planning
　♦ planning in advance
vorausreservieren etw
　♦ reserve s.th. in advance
Vorausreservierung, f
　Vorreservierung, f
　♦ advance reservation
　♦ reservation in advance
Vorausreservierungsabteilung, f
　♦ advance reservation department
　♦ advance reservations department
Vorausreservierungsbüro, n
　Vorausreservierungsstelle, f
　♦ advance reservation office
　♦ advance reservations office
Vorausreservierungsdienst, m
　→ Vorausreservierungsservice
Vorausreservierungsgebühr, f
　♦ advance reservation charge
　♦ advance reservation fee
Vorausreservierungsgebühr berechnen von DM 12
　♦ levy an advance reservation charge of DM 12

Vorausreservierungskraft

Vorausreservierungskraft
- make an advance reservation charge of DM 12
- charge an advance reservation fee of DM 12

Vorausreservierungskraft, f
- **advance reservation clerk**
- advance reservations clerk

Vorausreservierungsservice, m
Vorausreservierungsdienst, m
- **advance reservation service**

Vorausreservierungsstelle, f
→ Vorausreservierungsbüro

Vorausreservierungssystem, n
- **advance reservation system**

Voraussetzungen erfüllen für eine Ermäßigung
Bedingungen erfüllen für eine Ermäßigung
- **qualify for a reduction**
- be eligible for a reduction

Voraussetzung für die Mitgliedschaft, f
- **qualification for membership**

voraussichtliche Abreisezeit, f
voraussichtliche Abfahrtszeit, f
- **expected time of departure**
- expected departure time
- ETD
- estimated time of departure
- estimated departure time

voraussichtliche Abreisezeit angeben
- **state the expected time of departure**
- state the expected departure time

voraussichtliche Abreisezeit mitteilen
- **indicate the expected time of departure**
- indicate the expected departure time

voraussichtliche Ankunftszeit, f
- **expected time of arrival**
- expected arrival time
- ETA
- estimated time of arrival
- estimated arrival time

voraussichtliche Ankunftszeit angeben
- **indicate the estimated time of arrival**
- state the estimated time of arrival

voraussichtliche Ankunftszeit mitteilen
- **indicate the expected time of arrival**
- indicate the expected arrival time

voraussichtliche Ankunftszeit mitteilen
- **state the expected time of arrival**
- indicate the expected arrival time

voraussichtlich morgen eintreffen
- **be expected to arrive tomorrow**

Vorausverteilung f
Vorauszuteilung f
Vorauszuweisung f
- **pre-allocation**
- preassignment *AE*

vorauszahlbar, adj
im voraus zahlbar, adj
- **prepayable, adj**

vorauszahlen etw
im voraus zahlen etw
- **prepay s.th.**

Vorauszahlung, f
- **prepayment**

Vorauszuteilung eines Zimmers, f
Vorauszuweisung eines Zimmers, f
- **pre-allocation of a room**
- preassignment of a room *AE*

Vorauszuweisung, f
Vorauszuteilung, f
Vorverteilung, f
- **preassignment** *AE*
- **pre-allocation** *BE*

vorbeifahren an einem Gebäude
- **pass a building**

vorbeifahren an einer Stadt (Großstadt)
- **pass a city**
- drive past a city

vorbeifahren an einer Stadt (kleine Stadt)
- **pass a town**
- drive past a town

vorbeifahren an etw (Auto)
- **drive past etw**

vorbeifahren an etw (generell)
- **pass s.th.**

vorbeifahrende Schiffe beobachten
- **watch the passing ships**
- watch the passing boats

vorbeifahrendes Schiff, n
- **passing ship**
- passing boat

vorbeigehen an etw
- **walk past s.th.**
- go past s.th.
- pass s.th.

vorbeikommen in einer Bar
vorbeischauen in einer Bar
- **pop in at a bar** *coll*

vorbeikommen zum Kaffee
vorbeischauen zum Kaffee
- **pop in for coffee** *coll*
- drop in for coffee *coll*

vorbeischauen zum Kaffee und Kuchen
vorbeikommen zum Kaffee und Kuchen
- **pop in for coffee and cake** *coll*

vorbeisegeln an etw
- **sail past s.th.**

vorbereiten sich auf einen Auslandsurlaub
- **prepare for a vacation abroad** *AE*
- prepare for a holiday abroad *BE*

vorbereiten sich auf eine Reise
- **prepare for a journey**
- prepare for a trip
- prepare for a tour

vorbereiten sich (auf etw)
- **prepare oneself (for s.th.)**
- get ready (for s.th.)
- gear up (for s.th.) *coll*

Vorbereitung einer Konferenz, f
→ Konferenzvorbereitung

Vorbereitungen für eine Konferenz, f pl
Konferenzvorbereitungen, f pl
- **preparations for a conference** *pl*

Vorbereitungen treffen (für etw)
- **make preparations (for s.th.)**
- make arrangements (for s.th.)

Vorbereitungskurs, m
Vorbereitungslehrgang, m
- **preparatory course**
- preparation course

vorbestellen (buchen)
→ im voraus buchen

vorbestellen etw
- **preorder s.th.**
- order s.th. in advance

Vorbestellkarte, f
- **preorder card**

Vorbestellung, f (Buchung)
→ Vorausbuchung

Vorbestellung, f (generell)
- **advance order**

Vorbestellungsgebühr, f
→ Vorausbuchungsgebühr

Vorbestellungsservice, m
→ Vorausbuchungsservice

Vorbetriebskosten, pl
- **preoperating costs** *pl*
- preoperating cost

vorbezahlt, adj
im voraus bezahlt, adj
- **prepaid, adj**

vorbezahlter Fahrschein, m
im voraus bezahlter Fahrschein, m
vorbezahlte Karte, f
- **prepaid ticket**

vorbezahlter Flug, m
im voraus bezahlter Flug, m
- **prepaid flight**

vorbezahlter Flugschein, m
im voraus bezahlter Flugschein, m
- **prepaid air ticket**

vorbezahlter Gutschein, m
im voraus bezahlter Gutschein m
- **prepaid voucher**

vorbezahlter Reisegutschein, m
im voraus bezahlter Reisegutschein, m
- **prepaid travel voucher**

vorbuchen
→ im voraus buchen

vorbuchen etw
vorbestellen etw
im voraus bestellen etw
- **prebook s.th.**
- book s.th. in advance
- book s.th. ahead

Vorbuchung, f
→ Vorausbuchung

Vorbuchungsfrist, f (Zeitpunkt)
- **advance booking deadline**

Vorbuchungsfrist, f (Zeitraum)
Vorausbuchungsfrist, f
- **advance booking period**

Vorbuchungsgebühr, f
→ Vorausbuchungsgebühr

Vorbühne, f
Proszenium, n
- **forestage**
- proscenium

vor dem Abendessen (Dinner)
- **before dinner**

vor dem Abendessen (Supper)
- **before supper**

vor dem Ankunftsdatum
vor dem Ankunftstermin
- **before the arrival date**
- prior to the arrival date

vor dem Bezugstermin
vor der Ankunft
- **prior to arrival**
- before arrival

vor dem Frühstück
- **before breakfast**

vor dem Hotel
- **in front of the hotel**
- before the hotel

vor dem Mittagessen
- **before lunch**

vor dem Servieren
- **before serving**

vor dem Zubettgehen
- **before going to bed**

vor der Abreise
- **before departure**
- prior to departure

vor der Ankunft
    vor dem Eintreffen
    ♦ before arrival
    ♦ prior to arrival
Vorderbar, f
    ♦ front bar
Vorderdeck, n
    Back, f
    ♦ foredeck
    ♦ forecastle
    ♦ fo'c's'le BE
Vordereingang, m
    ♦ front entrance
vorderes Parkett, n (Theater)
    ♦ parquet AE
    ♦ front orchestra AE
    ♦ front stalls BE pl
Vorderfenster, n
    ♦ front window
Vorderhaus, n
    ♦ front building
vor der Haustür, adv
    direkt vor der Haustür, adv
    ♦ on the doorstep, adv
    ♦ on one's doorstep, adv
    ♦ close at hand, adv
vor der Haustür haben etw
    ♦ have s.th. on one's doorstep
vor der Haustür liegen (von etw)
    ♦ lie on the doorstep (of s.th.)
    ♦ lie on one's doorstep
    ♦ be on one's doorstep
vor der Küste
    ♦ off the coast
    ♦ off-shore
vor der Küste liegen
    ♦ lie off the coast
Vorderrad, n
    ♦ front wheel
Vorderradantrieb, m
    ♦ front-wheel drive
Vorderrhein, m
    ♦ Vorder Rhine, the
vor der Saison
    ♦ before the season
    ♦ in advance of the season
Vorderseite des Hotels, f
    ♦ front of the hotel
Vordersitz, m
    ♦ front seat
Vordersitzgurt, m
    ♦ front seat belt
vor der Tür stehen (figurativ)
    ♦ be just round the corner
vor der Tür stehen (konkret)
    ♦ be right outside
Vorderwand, f
    ♦ front wall
Vorderzimmer, n
    nach vorn gelegenes Zimmer, n
    ♦ front room
Vordruck, m
    Formular n
    ♦ printed form
Vordruck benutzen
    ♦ use a printed form
vor einer Reise
    ♦ before a journey
    ♦ before a trip
    ♦ before a tour

Voreröffnungsbüro, n
    ♦ preopening office
Voreröffnungskosten, pl
    ♦ preopening costs pl
    ♦ preopening cost
    ♦ preopening expenses pl
Voreröffnungsphase, f
    ♦ preopening phase
Voreröffnungsreise, f
    ♦ preopening tour
    ♦ preopening journey
    ♦ preopening trip
Voressen, n SCHW
    → Ragout
vorfahren (Auto)
    ♦ drive up
vorfahren bei einem Hotel (Auto)
    ♦ drive up to a hotel
Vorfastenzeit, f
    ♦ pre-Lenten season
Vorfeier, f
    ♦ precelebration
Vorfilm, m
    ♦ supporting film
vorfinanzieren
    vorfinanzieren etw
    ♦ finance in advance
    ♦ finance s.th. in advance
Vorfreude, f
    Vorfreude auf etw, f
    ♦ anticipation
    ♦ anticipatition of s.th.
    ♦ anticipation of doing s.th.
Vorfreude auf etw genießen
    ♦ enjoy the anticipation of s.th.
    ♦ enjoy the anticipation of doing s.th.
Vorführer, m
    (Person)
    ♦ projectionist
Vorführkabine, f
    (für Filme etc.)
    Projektionskabine, f
    ♦ projection booth
    ♦ projection box
Vorführpersonal, n
    ♦ projection staff
    ♦ projection personnel
Vorführraum, m (Demonstration)
    ♦ demonstration room
Vorführraum, m (Film)
    ♦ projection room
Vorführung, f (generell)
    ♦ presentation
    ♦ demonstration
    ♦ display
    ♦ show(ing)
    ♦ performance
Vorführung, f (Projektion)
    → Projektion
Vorgarten, m
    ♦ front garden
Vorgebirge, n
    Ausläufer, m pl
    ♦ foothills pl
vorgebucht, adj
    ♦ prebooked, adj
    ♦ booked in advance, adj
    ♦ booked ahead, adj
vorgefertigte Speise, f
    → vorgekochte Speisen

vorgeheizter Backofen, m
    ♦ preheated oven
vorgekocht, adj
    ♦ precooked, adj
vorgekochtes Essen, n
    vorgekochte Mahlzeit, f
    ♦ precooked meal
vorgekochte Speisen, f pl
    ♦ precooked food
Vorgericht, n
    → Vorspeise
vorgeschichtliche Funde, m pl
    ♦ prehistoric remains pl
vorgeschichtliche Reste, m pl
    ♦ prehistoric relics pl
vorgeschichtliches Museum, n
    prähistorisches Museum, n
    ♦ prehistoric museum
vorgeschichtliche Zeit, f
    prähistorische Zeit, f
    ♦ prehistoric times pl
vorgeschlagene Route, f
    ♦ suggested route
vorgeschlagener Preis, m
    ♦ suggested price
    ♦ suggested rate
vorgeschlagenes Programm, n
    Vorschlagsprogramm, n
    ♦ suggested program AE
    ♦ suggested programme BE
Vorgeschmack, m
    ♦ foretaste
Vorgeschmack auf etw, m
    ♦ foretaste of s.th.
Vorgeschmack bekommen von etw
    ♦ get a foretaste of s.th.
Vorgeschmack geben jm von etw
    ♦ give s.o. a foretaste of s.th.
vorgesehen, adj
    ♦ scheduled, adj
vorgesehene Auslastung, f
    ♦ projected load factor
vorgesehene Belegung, f
    vorgesehene Auslastung, f
    ♦ projected occupancy
vorgesehenen Besuch absagen
    ♦ cancel the projected visit
vorgesehener Besuch, m
    ins Auge gefaßter Besuch, m
    ♦ projected visit
vorgesehene Übernachtungen in A und B, f pl
    (bei Benutzung von Verkehrsmitteln)
    ♦ suggested overnight stops at A and B pl
    ♦ suggested overnight stops in A and B pl
    ♦ suggested overnight halts at A and B pl
    ♦ suggested overnight halts in A and B pl
vorgesehene Veranstaltung, f
    → Programmveranstaltung
vorgesetztes Menü, n
    ♦ menu served
    ♦ served menu
Vorhalle, f
    → Eingangshalle, Foyer
vorhandene Kapazität, f
    ♦ existing capacity
Vorhang, m
    ♦ curtain
    ♦ drape AE
Vorhang auf!
    ♦ Curtain up!

Vorhängeschloß

Vorhängeschloß, n
  ♦ padlock
Vorhangreinigung, f
  ♦ curtain cleaning
  ♦ cleaning (of) a curtain
  ♦ cleaning (of) curtains
Vorhang zuziehen
  ♦ draw the curtain
vorhergehende Saison, f
  → vorherige Saison
vorherig, adj
  vorhergehend, adj
  vorig, adj
  ♦ previous, adj
vorherige Saison, f
  vorhergehende Saison, f
  Vorsaison, f
  vorige Saison, f
  ♦ previous season
  ♦ season before
vorherige Sitzplatzauswahl, f
  vorherige Platzauswahl, f
  ♦ advance seat selection
vorherige Zahlung, f
  ♦ previous payment
Vorhof, m
  ♦ forecourt
Vorhofparkplatz, m (für 1 Auto)
  ♦ forecourt parking place
  ♦ forecourt parking space
  ♦ forecourt parking lot AE
Vorhofparkplatz, m (für mehrere Autos)
  ♦ forecourt parking lot AE
  ♦ forecourt car park BE
Vorinformation f
  ♦ advance information
Vorjahr, n
  vorhergehendes Jahr, n
  voriges Jahr, n
  ♦ previous year
  ♦ year before
  ♦ year ago
  ♦ last year
Vorjahresmonat, m
  ♦ month of the previous year
  ♦ month in the previous year
Vorjahresniveau, n
  ♦ previous year's level
Vorjahrespreis, m
  ♦ price in the previous year
  ♦ rate in the previous year
Vorjahressaison, f
  ♦ season in the previous year
  ♦ season the year before
Vorjahrestag, m
  ♦ day of the previous year
  ♦ day in the previous year
Vorjahreswoche, f
  ♦ week of the previous year
  ♦ week in the previous year
Vorjahreszahlen, f pl
  ♦ previous year's figures pl
  ♦ figures in the previous year pl
Vorjahrszeitraum, m
  Vorjahreszeitraum, m
  ♦ period of the previous year
  ♦ period in the previous year
Vorkasse, f
  Vorauszahlung, f
  ♦ advance payment

  ♦ payment in advance
  ♦ prepayment
vorkassieren
  Vorauszahlung erhalten
  ♦ receive an advance payment
Vorkaufsrecht, n
  ♦ right of first refusal
  ♦ first refusal
Vorkaufsrecht einräumen jm (an etw)
  ♦ give s.o. first refusal (on s.th.)
Vorkehrungen, f pl
  ♦ arrangements pl
Vorkehrungen selbst treffen
  ♦ make arrangements oneself
  ♦ make one's own arrangements
Vorkehrungen treffen
  Vorbereitungen treffen
  ♦ make arrangements
Vorkenntnisse, n pl
  ♦ previous knowledge sg
  ♦ previous experience sg
vorkochen etw
  ♦ precook s.th.
Vorkonferenzreise, f
  ♦ pre-conference tour
  ♦ pre-conference trip
  ♦ pre-conference journey
Vorkonferenzveranstaltung, f
  ♦ pre-conference activity
Vorkongreßreise, f
  ♦ pre-convention tour
  ♦ pre-convention journey
  ♦ pre-congress tour
  ♦ pre-congress journey
  ♦ pre-convention trip
vor Kursbeginn
  ♦ before the commencement of the course form
  ♦ before the course commences form
  ♦ before the course begins
  ♦ before the course starts
vor kurzem angekommener Gast, m
  ♦ recently arrived guest
vor kurzem wiedereröffnetes Hotel, n
  ♦ recently reopened hotel
  ♦ newly reopened hotel
vorläufig, adj
  provisorisch, adj
  ♦ preliminary, adj
  ♦ provisional, adj
vorläufige Buchung, f
  provisorische Buchung, f
  ♦ provisional booking
vorläufige Quittung, f
  provisorische Quittung, f
  ♦ provisional receipt
vorläufige Reservierung, f
  provisorische Reservierung, f
  ♦ provisional reservation
vorläufige Reservierung aufheben
  provisorische Reservierung aufheben
  ♦ release a provisional reservation
vorläufige Reservierung vornehmen
  provisorische Reservierung vornehmen
  ♦ make a provisional reservation
vorläufige Reiseverlauf, m
  ♦ preliminary itinerary
vorläufiger Termin m
  ♦ preliminary date
vorläufiges Programm, n
  ♦ preliminary program AE
  ♦ preliminary programme BE

vorläufige Unterkunft, f
  → provisorische Unterkunft
vorläufige Zahl, f
  ♦ provisional figure
vorläufig reservieren etw
  provisorisch reservieren etw
  ♦ reserve s.th. provisionally
Vorlegebesteck, n
  Servierbesteck, n
  ♦ serving spoon and fork
  ♦ service spoon and fork
  ♦ pair of servers
  ♦ servers pl
Vorlegebesteck für Fisch, n
  ♦ fish servers pl
Vorlegegabel, f
  ♦ serving fork
  ♦ service fork
Vorlegelöffel, m
  Servierlöffel, m
  ♦ serving spoon
  ♦ service spoon
vorlegen etw (Dokument)
  → vorzeigen etw
vorlegen etw (Speise)
  → servieren etw
Vorleger, m
  Brücke, f
  ♦ rug
Vorlesung, f
  ♦ lecture
Vorlesungssaal, m
  ♦ lecture hall
Vormerkliste, f
  → Warteliste
Vormerkung, f
  → Option
Vormerkung in eine feste Buchung umwandeln
  → Option in eine feste Buchung umwandeln
Vormieter, m
  vorheriger Mieter, m
  ♦ previous tenant
Vormittag frei
  (Programmhinweis)
  ♦ morning free
  ♦ morning at leisure
Vormittag ist frei für Besichtigungen
  ♦ morning is free for sightseeing
Vormittag ist frei zum Einkaufen
  ♦ morning is free for shopping
vormittags, adv
  → morgens
Vormittagsausflug, m
  ♦ morning excursion
  ♦ morning trip
Vormittagsbesuch, m
  Morgenbesuch, m
  ♦ morning visit
  ♦ morning call
Vormittagsessen, n
  → Morgenessen
Vormittagsfähre, f
  ♦ morning ferry
Vormittagsfahrt, f
  Morgenfahrt, f
  morgendliche Fahrt, f form
  vormittägliche Fahrt, f form
  ♦ morning trip
  ♦ morning ride
Vormittagsflug, m
  ♦ morning flight

860

Vormittagsimbiß, m
  Vormittagsvesper, f
  ♦ **elevenses** *BE coll*
  ♦ midmorning snack *AE*
  ♦ mid-morning snack *BE*
Vormittagskaffee, m
  ♦ **midmorning coffee** *AE*
  ♦ mid-morning coffee *BE*
Vormittagskaffeepause, f
  ♦ **midmorning coffee break** *AE*
  ♦ mid-morning coffee break *BE*
Vormittagskonzert, n
  ♦ **morning concert**
Vormittagspause, f
  ♦ **morning break**
Vormittagsprogramm, n
  Morgenprogramm, n
  ♦ **morning program** *AE*
  ♦ morning programme *BE*
Vormittagsschau, f
  Vormittagsveranstaltung, f
  ♦ **morning show**
Vormittagssitzung, f
  Morgensitzung, f
  Vormittagsrunde, f
  Morgenrunde, f
  ♦ **morning session**
Vormittagstour, f
  ♦ **morning tour**
Vormittags und nachmittags geschlossen
  (Hinweisschild)
  ♦ **Closed mornings and afternoons**
  ♦ Closed in the mornings and in the afternoons
Vormittagsunterhaltung f
  ♦ **morning entertainment**
Vormittagsveranstaltung, f
  ♦ **morning function**
  ♦ morning event
  ♦ matinee *AE*
  ♦ matinée *BE*
Vormittag zur freien Verfügung
  Morgen zur freien Verfügung
  ♦ **morning at leisure**
  ♦ free morning
  ♦ morning at one's disposal
Vormittag zur freien Verfügung haben
  Morgen zur freien Verfügung haben
  ♦ **have the morning at leisure**
vor Mitternacht nach Hause kommen
  ♦ **get home before midnight**
vor Mitternacht zu Hause sein
  vor Mitternacht zuhause sein
  ♦ **be at home before midnight** *BE*
  ♦ be home before midnight *AE*
Vormonat, m
  vorhergehender Monat, m
  voriger Monat, m
  ♦ **previous month**
  ♦ month before
  ♦ month ago
  ♦ last month
Vormund, m
  ♦ **guardian**
Vornacht, f
  vorhergehende Nacht, f
  vorherige Nacht, f
  ♦ **previous night**
  ♦ night before
  ♦ night ago
  ♦ last night

Vorname, m
  ♦ **first name**
  ♦ Christian name
vornehme Gesellschaft, f
  ♦ **people of quality** *pl*
vornehmes Hotel, n
  ♦ **distinguished hotel**
  ♦ posh hotel *coll*
Vorort, f
  → Vorstadt
Vorortzug, m
  S-Bahn-Zug, m
  ♦ **suburban train**
Vorpächter, m
  ♦ **previous leaseholder**
  ♦ previous tenant
Vorpommern
  (Region)
  ♦ **Western Pomerania**
vorportionieren etw
  ♦ **preportion s.th.**
vorportioniert, adj
  ♦ **preportioned, adj**
vorportioniertes Gericht, n
  ♦ **preportioned dish**
Vorprogramm, n
  Beiprogramm, n
  ♦ **supporting program** *AE*
  ♦ supporting programme *BE*
vorprogrammieren etw
  ♦ **preprogram s.th.** *AE*
  ♦ preprogramme s.th. *BE*
vorprogrammiert, adj
  ♦ **preprogramed, adj** *AE*
  ♦ preprogrammed, adj *BE*
Vorräte, m pl
  ♦ **stocks** *pl*
  ♦ provisions *pl*
  ♦ supplies *pl*
  ♦ reserves *pl*
  ♦ store
vorrätig, adj
  ♦ **in stock, adv**
  ♦ available, adj
Vorratskammer, f
  ♦ **larder**
  ♦ pantry
Vorratslager, n
  → Vorratsraum
Vorratsraum, m
  Vorratslager, n
  ♦ **storeroom** *AE*
  ♦ store-room *BE*
  ♦ storage room
Vorratsschrank, m (generell)
  ♦ **store cupboard**
Vorratsschrank, m (Lebensmittel)
  → Speisekammer
Vorraum, m
  → Vorzimmer
vor Reiseantritt
  ♦ **prior to the commencement of the journey**
  ♦ before the commencement of the journey
vor Reisebeginn
  ♦ **before the start of the journey**
  ♦ before the beginning of the journey
  ♦ before departure
Vorreiter, m *hist*
  berittener Begleiter, m *hist*
  ♦ **outrider**

Vorreservierung f
  → Vorausreservierung
vorrömische Zeit, f
  ♦ **pre-Roman times** *pl*
Vorsaison, f (Gegensatz zu Nachsaison)
  ♦ **pre-season**
Vorsaison, f (vorherige Saison)
  → vorherige Saison
Vorsaisonauslastung, f
  ♦ **pre-season load factor**
vor Saisonbeginn
  ♦ **before the start of the season**
  ♦ before the beginning of the season
  ♦ before the commencement of the season *form*
Vorsaisonbelegung, f
  Vorsaisonauslastung, f
  ♦ **pre-season occupancy**
Vorsaisonbesucher m
  ♦ **pre-season visitor**
  ♦ pre-season guest
Vorsaisonbuchung f
  ♦ **pre-season booking**
Vorsaisoncamper, m
  ♦ **pre-season camper**
Vorsaisoncamping, n
  ♦ **pre-season camping**
Vorsaisonermäßigung, f
  ♦ **pre-season reduction**
Vorsaisongast m
  ♦ **pre-season guest**
Vorsaisonmonat, m
  ♦ **pre-season month**
  ♦ month in the pre-season
Vorsaisonnachfrage, f
  ♦ **pre-season demand**
Vorsaisonpreis, m
  ♦ **pre-season price**
  ♦ pre-season rate
Vorsaisonreise, f
  ♦ **pre-season tour**
  ♦ pre-season trip
  ♦ pre-season journey
Vorsaisonreiseverkehr, m
  Vorsaisonreisen, n
  ♦ **pre-season travel**
Vorsaisonreservierung, f
  ♦ **pre-season reservation**
Vorsaisontag, m
  ♦ **pre-season day**
  ♦ day in the pre-season
Vorsaisonunterkunft, f
  ♦ **pre-season accommodation**
Vorsaisonvorzugspreis, m
  ♦ **special pre-season price**
  ♦ special pre-season rate
Vorsaisonwoche, f
  ♦ **pre-season week**
  ♦ week in the pre-season
Vorsaisonzeit, f
  Vorsaisonzeitraum, m
  ♦ **pre-season period**
Vorschau, f
  (Film, Veranstaltung etc.)
  ♦ **preview**
Vorschau auf das kommende Programm, f
  Programmvorschau, f
  ♦ **preview of the forthcoming programs** *AE*
  ♦ preview of the forthcoming programmes *BE*
  ♦ program preview *AE*
  ♦ programme preview *BE*

Vorschautag

Vorschautag, m
 ♦ preview day
vorschlagen als Tagungsort für etw
 ♦ suggest as a venue for s.th.
vorschlagen jm etw
 ♦ suggest s.th. to s.o.
 ♦ propose s.th. to s.o.
vorschneiden etw
 → tranchieren etw
Vorschneider, m
 → Tranchierer
Vorschrift, f
 ♦ regulation
vorsetzen jm etw
 ♦ serve s.o. a meal
 ♦ dish up s.th. to s.o.
Vorsicht, frisch gestrichen!
 (Hinweisschild)
 ♦ Wet paint
 ♦ Fresh paint AE
vorsichtige Buchungen, f pl
 ♦ cautious bookings pl
Vorsichtsmaßnahme, f
 vorsorgliche Maßnahme, f
 ♦ precaution
 ♦ precautionary measure
Vorsichtsmaßnahmen treffen
 Vorsichtsmaßnahmen ergreifen
 ♦ take precautions
Vorsitzende, f
 ♦ chairwoman
 ♦ chairlady
 ♦ chairperson
 ♦ chair
Vorsitzender, m
 ♦ chairman
 ♦ chairperson
 ♦ chair
Vorsitzender des Konferenzausschusses, m
 ♦ chairman of the conference committee
Vorsitzender des Kongreßausschusses, m
 ♦ chairman of the convention committee
 ♦ chairman of the congress committee
Vorsitzender des Organisationskomitees, m
 Vorsitzender des Organisationsausschusses, m
 ♦ chairman of the organising committee
 ♦ chairman of the organizing committee
Vorsitz führen bei etw
 ♦ chair s.th.
Vorsitz haben
 (bei Besprechung etc.)
 ♦ be in the chair
Vorsitz übernehmen
 (bei Besprechung etc.)
 ♦ take the chair
vorsorglich buchen
 ♦ make a precautionary booking
vorsorglich buchen etw
 ♦ book s.th. as a precaution
vorsorgliche Buchung, f
 ♦ precautionary booking
vorsorgliche Reservierung, f
 ♦ precautionary reservation
vorsorgliche Stornierung, f
 vorsorglicher Rücktritt, m
 vorsorgliche Absage, f
 vorsorgliche Annullierung, f
 ♦ precautionary cancellation
 ♦ precautionary cancelation AE
vorsorglich reservieren
 ♦ make a precautionary reservation

vorsorglich reservieren etw
 ♦ reserve s.th. as a precaution
vorsorglich stornieren
 ♦ make a precautionary cancellation
 ♦ make a precautionary cancelation AE
Vorspeise, f
 Hors d'oeuvre, n FR m
 Vorgericht, n
 ♦ starter
 ♦ hors d'oeuvre FR m
Vorspeisenbesteck, n (ein Satz)
 ♦ hors d'oeuvre knife and fork
 ♦ entree knife and fork AE
 ♦ entrée knife and fork BE
Vorspeisenbüfett, n
 ♦ hors d'oeuvre buffet
Vorspeisengabel, f
 ♦ hors d'oeuvre fork
 ♦ entree fork AE
 ♦ entrée fork BE
Vorspeisengang, m
 ♦ hors d'oeuvre course
 ♦ starter course
 ♦ appetiser course
 ♦ appetizer course
Vorspeisengericht, n
 → Vorspeise
Vorspeisenkoch, m
 Chef hors d'oeuvrier, m FR
 ♦ hors d'oeuvrier FR
 ♦ chef hors d'oeuvrier FR
Vorspeisenmesser, n
 ♦ hors d'oeuvre knife
 ♦ entree knife AE
 ♦ entrée knife BE
Vorspeisenteller, m
 ♦ hors d'oeuvre plate
 ♦ entree plate AE
 ♦ entrée plate BE
Vorspeisentheke, f
 ♦ hors d'oeuvre counter
Vorspeisenwagen, m
 Hors-d'oeuvre-Wagen, m
 ♦ hors d'oeuvre trolley BE
 ♦ hors d'oeuvre cart AE
Vorstadt, f
 Vorort, m
 ♦ suburb
Vorstadtgaststätte, f
 Vorstadtbar, f
 Vorortgaststätte, f
 Vorortbar, f
 ♦ suburban bar AE
 ♦ suburban pub BE
Vorstadthaus, n
 ♦ suburban house
Vorstadthotel, n
 Vororthotel, n
 ♦ suburban hotel
Vorstadtmotel, n
 Vorortmotel, n
 ♦ suburban motel
Vorstadtrestaurant, n
 Vorortrestaurant, n
 ♦ suburban restaurant
Vorstandsessen, n
 ♦ board of directors' meal
Vorstandssitzung, f
 (Vorstand und Aufsichtsrat)
 ♦ board meeting

Vorstandsvorsitzender, m
 ♦ chief executive AE
 ♦ chairman of the board (of directors)
Vorstandszimmer, n
 (wie in Unternehmen)
 ♦ boardroom
Vorstand und Aufsichtsrat, m
 ♦ board
vorstellen etw (Produkt)
 ♦ launch s.th.
Vorstellung, f (Produkt)
 ♦ launch
 ♦ product launch
Vorstellung geben
 (Theater)
 ♦ give a performance
Vortag, m
 vorhergehender Tag, m
 voriger Tag, m
 ♦ previous day
 ♦ day before
 ♦ day ago
Vorteile des Tourismus, m pl
 Wohltaten des Fremdenverkehrs, f pl
 ♦ benefits of tourism pl
vor Tisch
 ♦ before the meal
vortouristisch, adj
 ♦ pre-tourist, adj
Vortrag, m
 Vortragsveranstaltung, f form
 ♦ talk
 ♦ lecture
Vortrag halten (über etw)
 ♦ give a talk (on s.th.)
 ♦ give a talk (about s.th.)
 ♦ give a lecture (on s.th.)
 ♦ give a lecture (about s.th.)
 ♦ hold a lecture (about s.th.)
Vortragsabend, m (Solomusik)
 ♦ recital (in the evening)
Vortragsabend, m (Vortrag)
 ♦ evening lecture
Vortragsbestuhlung, f
 Reihenbestuhlung, f
 Theaterbestuhlung, f
 ♦ theater-style seating AE
 ♦ theater seating AE
 ♦ theatre-style seating BE
 ♦ theatre seating BE
Vortragsform, f
 (Bestuhlung)
 Theaterform, f
 ♦ theater style AE
 ♦ theatre style BE
Vortragspult, n
 → Lesepult
Vortragsraum, m
 Vortragszimmer, n
 ♦ lecture room
Vortragsräumlichkeiten, f pl
 ♦ lecture facilities pl
Vortragsreihe, f
 ♦ series of lectures
 ♦ lecture series
Vortragsreise, f
 Vortragstournee, f
 ♦ lecture tour
 ♦ reading tour
Vortragssaal m
 ♦ lecture hall

Vortragssitzung, f
(bei Konferenz)
♦ paper session
Vortragstournee, f
(eines Autors)
♦ reading tour
Vortragszimmer, n
→ Vortragsraum
Vortrag über etw, m
Vortrag zu etw, m
♦ talk on s.th.
♦ talk about s.th.
♦ lecture on s.th.
Vortrag veranstalten
♦ put on a lecture
Vortrag vor jm, m
♦ talk to s.o.
♦ talk before s.o.
vorübergehend aufhalten sich
verweilen
♦ sojourn form
♦ stay
vorübergehend aufhalten sich bei jm
verweilen bei jm
verweilen mit jm
♦ sojourn with s.o. form
♦ stay with s.o.
vorübergehend aufhalten sich bei jm in A für drei Wochen
verweilen bei jm in A für drei Wochen
♦ sojourn with s.o. in A for three weeks form
♦ stay with s.o. in A for three weeks
vorübergehend aufhalten sich in A
verweilen in A
♦ sojourn in A form
♦ stay in A
♦ stay at A
vorübergehend aufhalten sich unter jm
verweilen unter jm
♦ sojourn among people form
♦ stay among people
vorübergehend beschäftigtes Personal, n
Aushilfspersonal, n
♦ temporary staff
♦ temporary personnel
vorübergehender Aufenthalt, m
kurzes Verweilen, n
Verweilen, n
♦ sojourn form
♦ stay
vorübergehender Aufenthalt von einem Jahr, m
♦ sojourn of one year form
♦ stay of one year
vorübergehender Besuch, m
zeitweiliger Besuch, m
♦ temporary visit
vorübergehender Besucher, m
zeitweiliger Besucher, m
♦ temporary visitor
vorübergehender Mangel, m (Knappheit)
vorübergehende Knappheit, f
♦ temporary shortage
vorübergehender Mangel, m (völliges Fehlen)
zeitweiliger Mangel, m
♦ temporary lack
vorübergehender Wohnsitz, m
♦ temporary domicile
♦ temporary residence
vorübergehende Schließung, f
zeitweilige Schließung, f
♦ temporary closure

vorübergehendes Quartier, n
Übergangsquartier, n
♦ temporary quarters pl
♦ interim quarters pl
vorübergehendes Zuhause, f
vorübergehende Heimat, f
♦ temporary home
vorübergehende Unterkunft, f
Passantenunterkunft, f
♦ transient lodging AE
♦ transient accommodation AE
♦ temporary accommodation
Vorübergehend geschlossen
(Hinweisschild)
♦ Closed temporarily
vorübergehend niederlassen sich in X
♦ become a temporary resident of X
vorübergehend unterbringen jn
→ in Logis nehmen jn
Vor- und Nachsaison, f
♦ low season
♦ off-season
Vorurlaubszeit, f
Vorferienzeit, f
♦ pre-vacation period AE
♦ pre-holiday period BE
Vorurteil, n
♦ prejudice
Vorverkauf, m
(z.B. von Eintrittskarten)
♦ presale
♦ advance booking
♦ advance sales pl
Vorverkaufspreis, m
♦ presale price
Vorverkaufsstelle, f
♦ advance booking office
♦ booking office
Vorverkauf von Karten, m
Kartenvorverkauf, m
♦ presale of tickets
♦ advance ticket sale
vorverlegen etw (Termin)
♦ advance s.th.
♦ bring forward s.th.
♦ move up s.th.
vorverlegen etw von Mai auf März
♦ advance s.th. from May to March
Vorverlegung, f
♦ advancement
♦ earlier scheduling
Vorverlegung der Saison, f
♦ advancement of the season
vorvermieten etw
♦ prerent s.th. AE
♦ pre-let s.th. BE
Vorverstärker, m
♦ preamplifier
Vorvertrag, m
vorläufige Vereinbarung, f
♦ provisional agreement
Vorvertragsinformation, f
♦ precontract information
Vorwahl, f
(Telefon)
Vorwahlnummer, f
♦ dialling code
♦ dialing code AE
♦ area code
♦ prefix AE

Vorwahlnummernbuch, n
♦ area code book
♦ dialling code book
Vorwahl von London, f
♦ dialling code of London
♦ dialing code of London AE
♦ area code of London
♦ prefix for London AE
vorweihnachtlich, adj
♦ pre-Christmas, adj
♦ pre-Xmas, adj
Vorweihnachtsprogramm, n
vorweihnachtliches Programm, n
♦ pre-Christmas program AE
♦ pre-Xmas program AE
♦ pre-Christmas programme BE
♦ pre-Xmas programme BE
Vorweihnachtszeit, f
♦ pre-Christmas period
vorzeigen etw
♦ present s.th.
♦ show s.th.
♦ produce s.th.
Vorzeigezimmer, n
(Modellzimmer, Testzimmer)
♦ mockup room AE
♦ mock-up room BE
vorzeitig, adj
♦ premature, adj
♦ early, adj
vorzeitig abreisen
♦ leave earlier than expected
♦ leave early
♦ depart early
vorzeitig ankommen
vorzeitig eintreffen
vorzeitig anreisen
zu früh ankommen
zu früh eintreffen
♦ arrive early
♦ arrive earlier than expected
vorzeitige Abreise, f
verfrühte Abreise, f
♦ premature departure
♦ departing too early
♦ leaving too early
vorzeitige Ankunft, f
verfrühte Ankunft f
♦ premature arrival
♦ arriving too early
♦ early arrival
♦ too early arrival
vorzeitige Kündigung, f
♦ premature notice
vorzeitiges Frühstück, n
(ca. 5 Uhr morgens)
zeitiges Frühstück, n
frühes Frühstück, n
♦ early breakfast
vorzeitig zurückkehren
vorzeitig zurückfahren
♦ return early
♦ return earlier than expected
Vorzelt, n
♦ awning
Vorzimmer, n
Vorraum, m
♦ anteroom
vorzügliche Küche, f (Speisen)
♦ exquisite cooking
♦ exquisite cuisine

vorzügliche Mahlzeit

vorzügliche Mahlzeit, f
- ♦ enjoyable meal

vorzüglicher Service, m
- ♦ superb service

Vorzugsbehandlung, f
- ♦ preferential treatment

Vorzugsbehandlung erhalten
Vorzugsbehandlung bekommen
- ♦ receive preferential treatment
- ♦ get preferential treatment

Vorzugsbehandlung zukommen lassen jm
- ♦ give s.o. preferential treatment

Vorzugslage, f
→ bevorzugte Lage

Vorzugspreis, m
- ♦ preferential price
- ♦ preferential rate

Voucher, m
→ Gutschein, Beleg

Voyeur, m
- ♦ voyeur
- ♦ peeping Tom

VP, f
Vollpension, f
Vollverpflegung, f
volle Verpflegung, f
- ♦ FP *AE*
- ♦ full pension *AE*
- ♦ FB
- ♦ full board

vulgär, adj
- ♦ vulgar, adj

vulgäres Benehmen, n
ordinäres Benehmen, n
- ♦ vulgar behavior *AE*
- ♦ vulgar behaviour *BE*

Vulkan, m
- ♦ volcano

Vulkanberg, m
- ♦ volcanic mountain

Vulkanhügel, m
- ♦ volcanic hill

Vulkaninsel, f
- ♦ volcanic island

Vulkan ist aktiv
- ♦ volcano is active

Vulkankrater, m
- ♦ volcanic crater

Vulkansee, m
- ♦ volcanic lake

Vulkanstrand, m
- ♦ volcanic beach

VVIP
Very Very Important Person
- ♦ VVIP
- ♦ Very Very Important Person

W

Waadtland n
(Region)
♦ Vaud
Waage, f
♦ scale AE
♦ scales BE pl
Wachdienst m
Bewachungsdienst m
♦ guard service
Wachmann, m
♦ watchman
♦ guard
Wacholder, m
♦ juniper
Wacholderbeere, f
♦ juniper berry
Wacholderheide, f
♦ juniper heath
Wacholdersoße, f
♦ juniper sauce
Wachpersonal, n
Sicherheitspersonal, n
♦ security personnel
♦ security staff
♦ security officers pl
Wachs, n
♦ wax
Wachsbad, n
♦ wax bath
Wachsbehandlung, f
♦ wax treatment
♦ waxing treatment
wachsende Freizeit, f
♦ increased leisure time
Wachsfigur, f
♦ wax figure
♦ waxwork
Wachsfigurenausstellung, f
♦ waxwork show
Wachsfigurenkabinett, n
♦ waxworks pl
Wachsfigurenmuseum, n
♦ waxwork museum
♦ wax museum
Wachsmuseum, n
♦ wax museum
Wachstum, n
♦ growth
Wachstumsbereich, m
♦ growth area
Wachstumsindustrie, f
♦ growth industry
Wachstumsmarkt, m
♦ growth market
Wachstumspotential, n
♦ growth potential
Wachtel, f
♦ quail

Wachtelbrust, f
♦ quail breast
Wachteleier, n pl
♦ quail's eggs pl
♦ quail eggs pl
Wachtelfüllpastete, f
♦ quail timbale
Wachtturm, m
Wachtturm, m
♦ watchtower AE
♦ watch-tower BE
wackelig stehen
wackeln
♦ be wobbly
♦ wobble
wackligen Tisch stützen
♦ prop up a wobbly table
♦ prop up a wonky table BE inform
wackliger Stuhl, m
♦ wobbly chair
♦ rickety chair
♦ wonky chair BE inform
wackliger Tisch, m
♦ wobbly table
♦ rickety table
♦ wonky table BE inform
Waffel, f (Eiskrem)
♦ wafer
Waffel, f (generell)
♦ waffle
Waffeleisen, n
♦ waffle iron AE
♦ waffle-iron BE
Waffensammlung, f
♦ collections of arms
♦ collection of weapons
♦ weapons collection
Wagen, m (Restaurant)
Voiture, f FR
Wagon, m FR
♦ cart AE
♦ guéridon
♦ trolley
♦ wagon AE
♦ voiture FR
Wagen, m (Zug)
♦ car (train) AE
♦ carriage BE
♦ coach BE
Wagen abstellen
→ Auto parken
Wagen aus der Garage holen
Auto aus der Garage holen
♦ fetch one's car from the garage
♦ fetch a car from the garage
Wagencommis, m
Commis de wagon, m FR
Wagengehilfe, m

♦ assistant cart waiter AE
♦ assistant trolley waiter BE
♦ commis de wagon FR
Wagendienst, m
Wagenpflege f
Pkw-Service m
Pkw-Dienst m
♦ automobile service AE
♦ auto service AE
♦ car service
Wagen dritter Klasse, m
(Zug)
♦ third-class car AE
♦ third-class carriage BE
Wagen erster Klasse, m
(Zug)
Erste-Klasse-Wagen, m
Erster-Klasse-Wagen, m
Erstklaßwagen, m SCHW
♦ first-class car AE
♦ first-class carriage BE
Wagenheber, m
♦ jack
Wagenmeister, m
♦ carriage attendant BE *valet*
♦ doorman
♦ linkman hist
Wagenpark, m
Autopark, m
♦ fleet of cars
Wagen parken
→ Auto parken
Wagenpflege, f
Wageninstandhaltung, f
♦ car maintenance
Wagenschuppen, m
Autoschuppen, m
♦ car shed
Wagenservice, m (Speisen)
♦ cart service AE
♦ guéridon service
♦ trolley service BE
♦ wagon service
Wagenstandanzeiger, m (Zug)
♦ car position indicator AE
♦ carriage position indicator BE
Wagen zweiter Klasse, m (Zug)
Zweite-Klasse-Wagen, m
♦ second-class car (train) AE
♦ second-class carriage BE
Waggon (für Güter), m (Zug)
Güterwaggon, m
Güterwagen, m
♦ wagon BE
♦ waggon BE
♦ goods wagon BE
♦ goods waggon BE
♦ freight car AE

Waggon (für Personen), m (Zug)
   Wagen, m
   Personenwagen, m
   ♦ **carriage** BE
   ♦ **coach** BE
   ♦ **car** AE
   ♦ **passenger carriage** BE
   ♦ **passenger coach** BE
waggonweise, adv
   ♦ **by the carload,** adv AE
   ♦ **by the wagonload,** adv BE
   ♦ **by the waggonload,** adv BE
Wagon-lit, m FR m
   Schlafwagen, m
   Schlafwagen, m pl
   ♦ **wagon-lit** FR m
   ♦ **sleeping car** AE
   ♦ **sleeping-car** BE
   ♦ **wagons-lits** pl
Wahl der Verpflegungsvereinbarung, f
   Wahl des Verpflegungsarrangements, f
   ♦ **choice of a catering arrangement**
   ♦ **choice of a board arrangement**
   ♦ **selection of a catering arrangement**
   ♦ **selection of a board arrangement**
Wahl des Standorts, f
   Standortwahl, f
   ♦ **choice of location**
   ♦ **selection of location**
Wahl des Urlaubsziels, f
   ♦ **choice of the vacation destination** AE
   ♦ **choice of the holiday destination** BE
Wahl eines Hotels, f
   ♦ **choice of a hotel**
   ♦ **selection of a hotel**
   ♦ **choosing a hotel**
   ♦ **selecting a hotel**
wählen aus einer Speisekarte
   ♦ **choose from a menu**
wählen etw nach der Karte
   wählen etw von der Speisekarte
   ♦ **choose s.th. from the menu**
wählen zwischen Halb- oder Vollpension
   ♦ **choose between half board or full board**
wählerischer Esser, m
   ♦ **choosy eater** coll
   ♦ **choosey eater** coll
wählerisch sein
   ♦ **be choosy** coll
Wahlfach, n
   ♦ **optional subject**
Wahlheimat, f
   ♦ **adoptive country**
   ♦ **country of adoption**
Wahlkampfveranstaltung, f
   ♦ **campaign meeting**
Wahlmenü, n
   Auswahlmenü, n
Wahlpflichtfach, n
   ♦ **compulsory option**
Wahl zur Qual werden lassen
   ♦ **make the choice difficult**
während der Essenszeit
   ♦ **during (the) meals hours**
während der ganzen Nacht
   ♦ **throughout the night**
   ♦ **all night long**
während der ganzen Saison
   ♦ **throughout the season**
während der Hochsaison
   ♦ **during the high season**

während der Nebensaison
   ♦ **during the off-season**
während der Reise
   ♦ **during the journey**
   ♦ **during the tour**
   ♦ **during the trip**
während der Saison
   ♦ **during the season**
während der Spitzensaison
   ♦ **during the peak season**
während der Spitzenzeit
   ♦ **during the peak period**
während des ganzen Abends
   ♦ **throughout the evening**
während des ganzen Jahres
   ♦ **throughout the year**
während des ganzen Tags
   ♦ **throughout the day**
während des gesamten Aufenthaltes
   während des ganzen Aufenthalts
   ♦ **throughout the stay**
   ♦ **throughout one's stay**
während des Mittagessens
   ♦ **during luncheon**
   ♦ **during lunch**
während des Mittelalters
   ♦ **during the Middle Ages**
während eines Urlaubs in Amerika
   ♦ **during a vacation in America** AE
   ♦ **during a holiday in America** BE
wahrer Hochgenuß m
   ♦ **real treat**
wahrer Kenner, m
   echter Liebhaber, m
   ♦ **real connoisseur**
Wahrsager, m
   Wahrsagerin, f
   ♦ **fortune-teller**
wahrscheinliche Abreisezeit, f
   wahrscheinliche Abfahrtszeit, f
   wahrscheinliche Abflugzeit, f
   ♦ **probable time of departure**
wahrscheinliche Ankunftszeit, f
   ♦ **probable time of arrival**
Währung, f
   ♦ **currency**
Währung am Ort, f
   örtliche Währung, f
   ♦ **local currency**
Währungsabwertung, f
   ♦ **currency devaluation**
Währungsaufpreis, m
   ♦ **currency surcharge**
Währungsbeschränkung, f
   ♦ **currency restriction**
Währungsbestimmungen, f pl
   ♦ **currency regulations** pl
Währungscode, m
   ♦ **currency code**
Währungsschwankung f
   ♦ **currency fluctuation**
Währungsumtausch, m
   ♦ **currency exchange**
Währungszuschlag m
   ♦ **currency supplement**
Wahrzeichen n
   ♦ **landmark**
Walache, m
   ♦ **Wallachian**
Walachei, f
   ♦ **Wallachia**

walachisch, adj
   ♦ **Wallachian,** adj
Walbeobachtung, f
   ♦ **whale watching** AE
   ♦ **whale-watching** BE
Wald, m (groß)
   ♦ **forest**
Wald, m (klein)
   ♦ **wood**
   ♦ **woods** pl
Waldbad, n
   ♦ **forest pool**
Waldbrand, m
   ♦ **forest fire**
Waldbrombeere, f
   ♦ **wild blackberry**
Waldcamping, n
   ♦ **forest camping**
Waldcampingplatz, m
   ♦ **forest campsite**
   ♦ **forest campground** AE
   ♦ **forest camping site** BE
   ♦ **forest camping ground** BE
Waldcaravanplatz, m
   Waldwohnwagenplatz, m
   ♦ **forest caravan site** BE
   ♦ **forest trailer site** AE
Wäldchen, n
   Hain, m
   ♦ **small wood**
   ♦ **grove**
Waldeisenbahn, f
   ♦ **forest railroad** AE
   ♦ **forest railway** BE
Walderdbeere, f
   wilde Erdbeere, f
   ♦ **wood strawberry**
   ♦ **wild strawberry**
Waldferien, pl
   Waldurlaub, m
   ♦ **forest holiday** BE
   ♦ **woodland holiday** BE
   ♦ **forest vacation** AE
   ♦ **woodland vacation** AE
Waldferiendorf, n
   Waldurlaubsdorf, n
   ♦ **forest holiday village** BE
   ♦ **forest vacation village** AE
   ♦ **woodland holiday village** BE
   ♦ **woodland vacation village** AE
Waldfest, n (Festival)
   ♦ **festival in a forest**
   ♦ **festival in a wood**
Waldfest, n (Party)
   ♦ **party in a forest**
   ♦ **party in a wood**
Waldfläche, f
   ♦ **wooded area**
   ♦ **woodland**
   ♦ **forest area**
Waldführung, f
   ♦ **guided tour of the forest**
   ♦ **guided tour through the forest**
   ♦ **guided tour of the wood**
   ♦ **guided tour through the wood**
Waldgaststätte, f
   ♦ **forest bar** AE
   ♦ **bar in a forest** AE
   ♦ **bar in a wood** AE
   ♦ **forest pub** BE
   ♦ **pub in a forest** BE

Waldgebiet, n
  Waldgegend, f
  ♦ wooded region
  ♦ wooded area
  ♦ woodland
Waldgegend, f
  → Waldgebiet
Waldgehege, n
  ♦ forest enclosure
Waldhang, m
  ♦ wooded slope
Waldhotel n
  ♦ forest hotel
  ♦ hotel in a forest
  ♦ hotel in a wood
Waldlage, f
  (z.B. eines Hotels)
  ♦ woodland location
  ♦ woodland situation
  ♦ woodland setting
Waldland, n (generell)
  Waldgebiet, n
  ♦ woodland
Waldland, n (Holznutzung)
  ♦ timberland
Waldlandschaft, f
  ♦ wooded scenery
  ♦ wooded landscape
  ♦ wooded countryside
  ♦ forest scenery
Waldlauf, m
  → Querfeldeinlauf
Waldlehrpfad, m
  ♦ woodland nature trail
  ♦ forest nature trail
Waldlichtung, f
  ♦ forest glade
  ♦ clearing
Waldmeister, m
  ♦ woodruff
Waldmeisterbowle, f
  ♦ woodruff cup
  ♦ woodruff bowl
Waldmühle, f
  ♦ forest mill
Waldorfsalat, m
  ♦ Waldorf salad
Waldpark, m (bewaldet)
  ♦ wooded park
Waldpark, m (im Wald)
  ♦ forest park
Waldparkplatz, m
  ♦ forest parking lot *AE*
  ♦ forest car park *BE*
Waldpension, f
  ♦ forest guesthouse *AE*
  ♦ forest guest-house *BE*
Waldpfad, m
  Waldweg, m
  ♦ forest path
  ♦ forest trail
Waldpilz, m
  ♦ wild mushroom
Waldplatz, m
  (z.B. Campingplatz)
  ♦ forest site
Waldrand, m
  ♦ edge of the forest
  ♦ edge of the wood
  ♦ forest's edge
  ♦ forest edge

Waldrandlage, f
  am Waldrand gelegen, adj
  ♦ situated near the forest
  ♦ situated close to the forest
  ♦ convenient situation for the forest
  ♦ convenient situation for the wood
  ♦ situated close to the wood
Waldrasthaus, n
  ♦ forest rest house
Waldrastplatz, m
  ♦ forest resting place
Waldreitweg, m
  ♦ forest bridle way *AE*
  ♦ forest bridle path *AE*
  ♦ forest bridle-way *BE*
  ♦ forest bridle-path *BE*
Waldrestaurant n
  ♦ forest restaurant
  ♦ restaurant in a forest
  ♦ restaurant in a wood
Waldschloß, n
  Waldburg, f
  ♦ forest castle
Waldschlucht, f
  ♦ wooded gorge
  ♦ wooded ravine
Waldschwimmbad, n
  ♦ forest swimming pool *AE*
  ♦ forest swimming-pool *BE*
Waldsee, m
  ♦ forest lake
Waldspaziergang, m
  Waldwanderung, f
  ♦ walk in the wood(s)
  ♦ forest walk
  ♦ walk in the forest
  ♦ woodland walk
  ♦ woodland walking
Waldspazierweg, m
  Waldwanderweg, m
  Waldweg, m
  ♦ forest walk
  ♦ woodland walk
Waldsportpfad, m
Waldsterben, n
  ♦ dying of forests
  ♦ forest deaths *pl*
Waldstraße, f
  ♦ forest road
Waldtal, n
  bewaldetes Tal, n
  ♦ wooded valley
Waldung, f
  → Waldgebiet
Waldurlaub, m
  Waldferien, pl
  ♦ forest vacation *AE*
  ♦ woodland vacation *AE*
  ♦ forest holiday *BE*
  ♦ woodland holiday *AE*
Wald von Fontainebleau, m
  ♦ forest of Fontainebleau
Waldwanderung, f
  ♦ forest walk
Waldwanderweg, m
  ♦ woodland trail
  ♦ forest trail
Waldweg, m
  Waldpfad, m
  ♦ forest trail
  ♦ forest path

Waldwohnwagenplatz, m
  Waldcaravanplatz, m
  ♦ forest trailer site *AE*
  ♦ forest caravan site *BE*
Walensee, m
  ♦ Lake of Wallenstadt, the
  ♦ Lake Walen
Wales
  ♦ Wales
Walesbesucher, m
  ♦ visitor to Wales
Waliser, m
  ♦ Welshman
Waliserin, f
  ♦ Welshwoman
walisisch, adj
  ♦ Welsh, adj
Walk-in, m
  unangemeldeter Übernachtungsgast, m
  Passant, m
  ♦ walk-in guest
  ♦ walk-in *sl*
Walk-out, m
  → Zechpreller
Wallach, m
  ♦ gelding
  ♦ cut horse
Waller, m
  Wels, m
  ♦ catfish
  ♦ sheatfish
  ♦ sheathfish
wallfahren zu einem Ort
  → pilgern zu einem Ort
Wallfahrer, m
  → Pilger
Wallfahrt machen
  → Pilgerfahrt machen
Wallfahrtskapelle, f
  ♦ pilgrimage chapel
Wallfahrtskirche, f
  ♦ pilgrimage church
Wallfahrtsort, m
  Pilgerort, m
  ♦ place of pilgrimage
Wallfahrtsplatz, m
  Wallfahrtsstelle, f
  ♦ pilgrimage site
Wallis, n
  (Region in der Schweiz)
  ♦ Valais
Walliser, m
  (Schweiz)
  ♦ Valaisan
Walliser Alpen, pl
  ♦ Valais Alps, the *pl*
Walliserin, f
  (Schweiz)
  ♦ Valaisan girl
  ♦ Valaisan woman
  ♦ Valaisan
walliserisch, adj
  (Schweiz)
  ♦ Valaisan, adj
Wallone, m
  ♦ Walloon
Wallonien
  ♦ Wallonia
wallonisch, adj
  ♦ Wallon, adj

Walmdach

Walmdach, n
  ♦ hip roof
Walnuß, f
  ♦ walnut
Walnußbaum, m
  ♦ walnut tree
Walnußfüllung, f
  Nußfüllung, f
  ♦ walnut filling
Walnußkuchen, m
  Nußkuchen, m
  ♦ walnut cake
Walnußsoße, f
  Nußsoße, f
  ♦ walnut sauce
Walschutzgebiet, n
  ♦ whale sanctuary
Waltourismus, m
  ♦ whale tourism
Waltourist, m
  ♦ whale tourist
Walzer, m
  ♦ waltz
Walzermusik, f
  ♦ waltz music
Walzer tanzen
  ♦ dance a waltz
  ♦ waltz
Wandbehang, m
  ♦ wall hanging
Wandbett, n
  ♦ wall bed *AE*
  ♦ bunk
Wandbrause, f
  Wanddusche, f
  ♦ wall shower
Wände haben Ohren
  ♦ walls have ears
Wandelgang, m
  ♦ covered walk
Wandelhalle, f (Kurort)
  → Trinkhalle
Wandelhalle, f (Lobby)
  → Lobby
Wanderabendessen, n
  ♦ rambler's dinner
  ♦ walker's dinner
  ♦ hiker's dinner
Wanderarbeiter, m
  ♦ migrant worker
Wanderarrangement, n
  Wandervereinbarung, f
  ♦ hiking arrangement
  ♦ walking arrangement
Wanderaufenthalt, m (Rast)
  → Wanderrast
Wanderausflug, m (leger)
  ♦ walking trip
  ♦ walking tour
  ♦ walking excursion
  ♦ walk
Wanderausflug, m (profihaft)
  ♦ hiking trip
  ♦ hiking tour
  ♦ hiking excursion
  ♦ hike
Wanderausrüstung, f
  Wanderausstattung, f
  ♦ walking equipment
  ♦ hiking equipment

Wanderausstellung, f
  ♦ traveling exhibition *AE*
  ♦ travelling exhibition *BE*
  ♦ travel(l)ing show
  ♦ touring exhibition
  ♦ mobile exhibition
Wanderbedingungen, f pl
  Wanderverhältnisse, n pl
  ♦ walking conditions *pl*
Wanderbrief, m *hist*
  (für Wandergesellen)
  Reisebrief, m *hist*
  ♦ waybill *BE hist*
Wanderbühne, f
  ♦ touring company
Wanderbursche, m *hist*
  Wandergeselle, m *hist*
  ♦ traveling journeyman *AE hist*
  ♦ travelling journeyman *BE hist*
Wandercamper, m
  ♦ walker-camper
Wanderdüne, f
  ♦ shifting sand dune
Wanderer, m
  ♦ hiker
  ♦ walker
  ♦ rambler
Wanderetappe, f
  Etappe einer Wanderung, f
  ♦ stage of a walking tour
  ♦ leg of a hiking tour
Wanderexpedition, f
  ♦ walking expedition
  ♦ hiking expedition
Wanderfaltblatt, n
  ♦ walking leaflet
  ♦ hiking leaflet
Wanderferien, pl
  Wanderurlaub, m
  ♦ hiking holidays *BE pl*
  ♦ walking holidays *BE pl*
  ♦ hiking vacation *AE*
  ♦ walking vacation *AE*
Wanderfreund m
  ♦ walking enthusiast
  ♦ hiking enthusiast
Wanderfrühstück, n
  ♦ rambler's breakfast
  ♦ walker's breakfast
  ♦ hiker's breakfast
Wanderführer, m
  (Person oder Information)
  ♦ hiking guide
  ♦ walking guide
Wanderführung, f
  → geführte Wanderung
Wandergebiet, n
  Wandergelände, n
  Wandergegend, f
  ♦ walking country
  ♦ hiking area
  ♦ hiking country
  ♦ walking area
Wandergelegenheit, f
  Wandermöglichkeit, f
  ♦ walking opportunity
  ♦ hiking opportunity
Wandergeschwindigkeit, f
  ♦ walking speed
  ♦ hiking speed

Wandergewerbe, n
  (Hausierer etc)
  ♦ itinerant trade
  ♦ ambulant trade
Wandergruppe, f
  ♦ rambling group
  ♦ walking group
Wanderheim, n
  ♦ ramblers' hostel
Wanderherberge, f
  ♦ hostel for hikers
  ♦ ramblers' hostel
Wanderjacke, f
  ♦ walking jacket
Wanderjahre, n pl (generell)
  ♦ years of travel *pl*
Wanderjahre, n pl (Geselle)
  ♦ journeyman's years of travel *pl*
Wanderjause, f ÖST
  → Wanderimbiß
Wanderkarte, f (Landkarte)
  ♦ walkers' map
  ♦ walking map
  ♦ hikers' map
  ♦ hiking map
Wanderkleidung, f
  ♦ hiking gear
  ♦ walking clothing
  ♦ hiking outfit
  ♦ walking outfit
Wanderkluft, f
  → Wanderkleidung
Wanderkniebundhosen, f pl
  ♦ walking breeches *pl*
  ♦ hiking breeches *pl*
Wanderkurzurlaub, m
  ♦ hiking break
  ♦ walking break
  ♦ rambling break
  ♦ short walking holiday *BE*
  ♦ short walking vacation *AE*
Wanderland, n
  Wandergegend, f
  Wandergebiet, n
  Wanderlandschaft, f
  ♦ hiking country
  ♦ country for hiking
  ♦ country for walking
  ♦ walking country
Wanderleben, n
  ♦ vagrant life
  ♦ gypsy life *fam*
  ♦ gipsy life *fam*
Wanderlust, f
  ♦ wanderlust
Wandermesse, f
  ♦ traveling fair *AE*
  ♦ travelling fair *BE*
Wandermittagessen, n
  ♦ rambler's lunch
  ♦ walker's lunch
  ♦ hiker's lunch
Wandermöglichkeit, f
  ♦ walking possibility
  ♦ hiking possibility
Wandermöglichkeiten, f pl
  ♦ hiking possibilities *pl*
  ♦ walking possibilities *pl*
Wandermusiker, m
  Wandermusikant, m
  ♦ itinerant musician

Wandern, n
Wandersport, m
- ♦ hiking
- ♦ walking
- ♦ rambling

Wandernachmittag, m
- ♦ afternoon's walking
- ♦ afternoon's hiking
- ♦ afternoon's rambling
- ♦ afternoon of walking
- ♦ afternoon of hiking

wandern bergab
bergab wandern
- ♦ walk downhill

wandern bergauf
bergauf wandern
- ♦ walk uphill

wandern im Gebirge
- ♦ walking in the mountains
- ♦ hiking in the mountains

Wandern in den Alpen, n
- ♦ hiking in the Alps
- ♦ walking in the Alps

wandern mit leichtem Gepäck
- ♦ hike light
- ♦ walk light

wandern ohne Gepäck
- ♦ hike without baggage AE
- ♦ walk without baggage AE
- ♦ hike without luggage BE
- ♦ walk without luggage BE

Wandern ohne Gepäck, n
- ♦ walking without baggage AE
- ♦ hiking without baggage AE
- ♦ walking without luggage BE
- ♦ hiking without luggage BE
- ♦ rambling without luggage BE

wandern (profihaft)
- ♦ hike
- ♦ go on a hike
- ♦ go hiking

wandern (spazierengehen)
- ♦ go walking
- ♦ do a walk

wandern (umherstreifen)
→ umherstreifen

Wandern und Radfahren, n
- ♦ hiking and biking coll

wandern von Ort zu Ort
- ♦ wander from place to place

wandern (zum Vergnügen)
(mit oder ohne Ziel)
- ♦ ramble
- ♦ go on a ramble
- ♦ go rambling

Wanderparadies, n
- ♦ hiker's paradise
- ♦ walker's paradise

Wanderpauschalangebot, n
- ♦ inclusive hiking deal

Wanderpauschalprogramm, n
- ♦ hiking package program AE
- ♦ hiking package programme BE

Wanderpauschalurlaub, m
- ♦ inclusive hiking vacation AE
- ♦ inclusive walking vacation AE
- ♦ inclusive walking holiday BE
- ♦ inclusive hiking holiday BE

Wanderpfad, m
→ Wanderweg

Wanderpokal, m (Sport)
- ♦ challenge cup

Wanderprediger, m
- ♦ itinerant preacher
- ♦ wandering preacher

Wanderpreis, m (Sport)
- ♦ challenge trophy

Wanderprogramm, n
- ♦ walking program AE
- ♦ walking programme BE
- ♦ hiking program AE
- ♦ hiking programme BE

Wanderrast, f
- ♦ stop for hikers
- ♦ stop for walkers

Wanderreise, f
→ Wandertour

Wanderroute, f
Wanderstrecke, f
- ♦ hiking route
- ♦ hikers' route
- ♦ walking route
- ♦ walkers' route

Wanderroutenbeschreibung, f
Wanderstreckenbeschreibung, f
Beschreibung der Wanderroute, f
Beschreibung der Wanderstrecke, f
- ♦ hiking route description
- ♦ walking route description
- ♦ desciption of the hiking route
- ♦ description of the walking route

Wandersafari, f
Fußsafari, f
- ♦ walking safari

Wanderschaft, f
- ♦ travels pl

Wanderschau, f
- ♦ traveling show AE
- ♦ travelling show BE

Wanderschuh, m
- ♦ walking shoe

Wandersmann, m obs
Wanderer, m
- ♦ wanderer
- ♦ wayfarer obs

Wanderspaß, m
- ♦ hiking fun
- ♦ walking fun

Wanderstab, m
- ♦ walking staff
- ♦ staff

Wanderstiefel, m
Wanderschuh, m
- ♦ hiking boot
- ♦ walking boot

Wanderstrecke, f
Wanderroute, f
- ♦ hiker's route
- ♦ hiking route
- ♦ walker's route
- ♦ walking route

Wanderszene, f
- ♦ walking scene
- ♦ hiking scene

Wandertag, m (Schule)
- ♦ school hike
- ♦ class hike

Wandertempo, n
- ♦ walking pace
- ♦ hiking pace

Wandertheater, n
- ♦ traveling theater AE
- ♦ travelling theatre BE

Wandertip, m
- ♦ hiking tip
- ♦ walking tip

Wandertour, f
Wanderreise, f
- ♦ walking tour
- ♦ hiking tour

Wandertourismus, m
- ♦ walk-about tourism

Wandertour machen
- ♦ go on a hiking tour
- ♦ go on a walking tour
- ♦ make a walking tour
- ♦ make a hiking tour

Wanderübernachtung, f
- ♦ overnight stay for hikers
- ♦ overnight stay for walkers
- ♦ overnight stop for hikers
- ♦ overnight stop for walkers

Wanderung, f (profihaft)
- ♦ hike

Wanderung, f (Spaziergang)
→ Spaziergang

Wanderung, f (zum Vergnügen)
(mit oder ohne Ziel)
Vergnügungswanderung, f
- ♦ ramble

Wanderung aufgeben
- ♦ abandon a hike
- ♦ abandon a walk
- ♦ abandon a ramble

Wanderung beenden
- ♦ complete the walk
- ♦ complete the hike

Wanderung durch die Alpen, f
- ♦ hike through the Alps
- ♦ walk through the Alps

Wanderung durch etw, f
- ♦ hike through s.th.
- ♦ walk through s.th.

Wanderung durchführen
- ♦ run a walk
- ♦ hold a walk
- ♦ hold a ramble

Wanderung führt uns nach X
- ♦ hike takes us to X
- ♦ walk takes us to X

Wanderung machen
auf eine Wanderung gehen
- ♦ go on a hike
- ♦ go for a hike
- ♦ go on a ramble
- ♦ go for a ramble
- ♦ go on a walk

Wanderung machen
- ♦ do a walk
- ♦ do a hike
- ♦ do a ramble
- ♦ go walking
- ♦ go hiking (rambling)

Wanderung organisieren
Wanderung veranstalten
- ♦ organise a walk
- ♦ organize a walk

Wanderung über felsiges Moorland, f
- ♦ fell walk
- ♦ fell walking

Wanderung unternehmen
   Wanderung machen
   ♦ undertake a ramble
Wanderung veranstalten
   Wanderung abhalten
   ♦ hold a walk
   ♦ organise a walk
   ♦ organize a walk
Wanderunterhalter, m
   ♦ itinerant entertainer
Wanderurlaub, m
   Wanderferien, pl
   ♦ walking vacation *AE*
   ♦ hiking vacation *AE*
   ♦ walking holiday(s) *BE (pl)*
   ♦ hiking holiday(s) *BE (pl)*
   ♦ rambling holiday(s) *BE (pl)*
Wanderurlauber, m
   ♦ hiking vacationer *AE*
   ♦ hiking holidaymaker *BE*
Wanderurlaub machen
   ♦ take a walking vacation *AE*
   ♦ take a hiking vacation *AE*
   ♦ take a rambling holiday *BE*
   ♦ take a walking holiday *BE*
   ♦ take a hiking holiday *AE*
Wanderverband, m
   ♦ ramblers' association
   ♦ walking association
Wanderverein, m
   ♦ rambling club
   ♦ walking club
Wandervesper, f
   Wanderimbiß, m
   ♦ rambler's snack
   ♦ walker's snack
   ♦ hiker's snack
Wandervogel, m (historisch)
   ♦ member of the Wandervogel
Wandervogel, m (Person)
   ♦ rambler
Wandervogel, m (Vogel)
   ♦ migrating bird
   ♦ migratory bird
Wandervorschlag, m
   ♦ hiking suggestion
   ♦ walking suggestion
Wandervorschlag machen
   ♦ make a hiking suggestion
   ♦ make a walking suggestion
Wanderwald, m
   ♦ hiking forest
   ♦ walking forest
Wanderweg, m
   ♦ walking trail
   ♦ hiking path
   ♦ hiking trail
   ♦ footpath *BE*
   ♦ trail
Wanderwegenetz, n
   ♦ network of hiking trails
   ♦ network of walking trails
   ♦ network of footpaths
Wanderwegenetz, n
   ♦ walking-trail network
   ♦ hiking-trail network
Wanderwegführer, m
   (Buch)
   ♦ walking-trail guide
   ♦ hiking-trail guide
   ♦ footpath guide *BE*

Wanderwelt, f
   ♦ rambling world
Wanderwetter, n
   ♦ ideal weather for hiking
   ♦ ideal weather for rambling
Wanderwoche, f
   ♦ hiking week
   ♦ rambling week
   ♦ walking week
   ♦ week's hiking
   ♦ week's walking
Wanderwochenende, n
   ♦ walking weekend
   ♦ hiking weekend
Wanderwochenpauschale, f
   ♦ hiking week package
   ♦ walking week package
Wanderziel, n
   Ziel der Wanderung, n
   ♦ destination of a hike
   ♦ destination of a hiking tour
   ♦ destination of the walk
   ♦ destination of the walking tour
Wanderzirkus, m
   ♦ traveling circus *AE*
   ♦ travelling circus *BE*
Wände wackeln lassen
   ♦ bring the roof down
Wandgemälde, n
   Wandmalerei, f
   ♦ mural
   ♦ wall painting
Wandkarte, f
   ♦ wall map
Wandklappbett, n
   ♦ folding bunk
Wandlampe, f
   ♦ wall lamp
Wandmalerei, f
   ♦ wall painting
Wand mit Teppichbehang, f
   ♦ tapestried wall
Wandregal n
   ♦ wall shelf
Wandsafe, m
   Wandtresor, m
   ♦ wall safe
Wandschirm, m
   ♦ wall screen
Wand schmücken
   ♦ decorate the wall
Wandschrank, m
   ♦ wall cabinet
Wandspiegel m
   ♦ wall mirror
Wandsteckdose, f
   ♦ wall socket *BE*
   ♦ wall outlet *AE*
Wandtäfelung, f
   ♦ wainscot
   ♦ paneling *AE*
   ♦ panelling
Wandteller, m
   ♦ decorative plate
Wandteppich, m
   ♦ tapestry
   ♦ wall hanging
   ♦ hanging
   ♦ arras *obs*
Wandtresor, m
   → Wandsafe

Wanduhr, f
   ♦ wall clock
Wand verzieren
   Wand zieren
   ♦ adorn the wall
Wandvitrine, f
   ♦ wall showcase
Wann brauchen Sie das?
   ♦ At what time will you need that?
   ♦ What time will you need that?
Wann frühstücken Sie?
   ♦ At what time do you have breakfast?
   ♦ What time do you have breakfast?
   ♦ When do you have breakfast?
Wann geht der nächste Zug nach X?
   ♦ When is the next train to X?
Wann gibt es Tee?
   ♦ When is tea?
Wann macht die Bar auf?
   ♦ At what time does the bar open?
   ♦ What time does the bar open?
Wann reisen Sie ab?
   ♦ When are you leaving?
Wann reisen Sie nach X ab?
   ♦ When are you leaving for X?
Wann schließt das Hotel?
   Wann macht das Hotel zu?
   ♦ At what time does the hotel close?
   ♦ What time does the hotel close?
Wanze, f (illegales Abhörgerät)
   ♦ bug
Wanze, f (Insekt)
   Bettwanze, f
   ♦ bedbug
Warenaufwendungen, f pl
   → Wareneinsatzkosten
Warenaufwendungen Getränke, f pl
   ♦ cost of goods sold, beverages
   ♦ cost of goods sold, drinks
Warenaufwendungen Keller, f pl
   ♦ cost of goods sold, cellar
Warenaufwendungen Küche, f pl
   ♦ cost of goods sold, kitchen
Warenaufzug, m
   Lastenaufzug, m
   ♦ freight elevator *AE*
   ♦ goods lift *BE*
Waren ausstellen auf einer Messe
   ♦ exhibit goods at a fair
Warenautomat, m
   → Verkaufsautomat
Warenbestand, m
   → Lagerbestand
Waren einführen
   ♦ bring in goods
Wareneingangsabteilung, f
   Warenannahmeabteilung, f
   ♦ goods receiving department
   ♦ receiving department
Wareneingangsbogen, m
   ♦ goods received sheet
Wareneingangsbuch, n
   ♦ goods received book
Wareneingangsbuch führen
   ♦ keep a goods received book
Wareneingangspersonal, n
   ♦ goods receiving personnel
   ♦ goods receiving staff
   ♦ receiving personnel
   ♦ receiving staff

Wareneinsatzkontrolle, f (Hotel)
- food and beverage control
- f&b control

Wareneinsatzkontrolleur, m (Hotel)
- food and beverage controler AE
- f&b controler AE
- food and beverage controller BE
- f&b controller BE

Wareneinsatzkontrollsystem, n (Hotel)
- food and beverage control system
- f&b control system

Wareneinsatzkosten, pl
Warenaufwendungen, f pl
- cost of goods sold
- COGS

Wareneinsatzkosten alkoholische Getränke, pl
Warenkosten alkoholische Getränke, pl
- cost of liquor sales

Wareneinsatzkosten Getränke, pl
Wareneinsatzkosten für Getränke, pl
- cost of beverages sold
- cost of drinks sold
- cost of beverage sales
- cost of drinks sales

Wareneinsatzkosten pro Gericht, pl
- cost of goods sold per dish

Wareneinsatzkosten Speisen, pl
- cost of food sold

Warenersatzverwaltung, f (Hotel)
Wirtschaftsverwaltung, f
Gastronomieverwaltung, f
Verpflegungsverwaltung, f
- food and beverage administration
- f&b administration

Warenexponate, n pl
- goods and articles exhibited pl

Warenhaus, n
- department store

Warenhausrestaurant, n
- department store restaurant

Warenkontrolleur, m
- stock controller

Warenkosten, pl
- cost of sales
- cost of commodities sold
- cost of goods sold

Warenkosten für Getränke pl
Wareneinsatzkosten Getränke, pl
- cost of beverage sales
- cost of beverages sold
- cost of drinks sales
- cost of drinks sold

Warenkosten für Handelswaren, pl
- cost of commodity sales
- cost of goods sales

Warenkosten für Personalverpflegung, pl
- cost of employee meals

Warenkosten für Speisen pl
- cost of food sales
- cost of food sold

Warenkosten für Speisen und Getränke, pl
- cost of food and beverage sales

Wären Sie so freundlich und würden das tun?
- Would you oblige me to do this?

Warenumsatz, m
- sales turnover
- goods turnover
- commodity sales pl

Warenverbrauch, m
- stock consumption

- consumption of stock
- commodity consumption

warm aus dem Ofen
- hot from the oven
- warm from the oven

Warmbad, n (Bad)
→ warmes Bad

Warmbad, n (Ort)
→ Thermalbad

Warmdusche, f
warme Dusche, f
- hot shower

warm duschen (sich)
- have a hot shower
- take a hot shower

warme Atmosphäre, f
- warm atmosphere

warme Atmosphäre bieten
- provide a warm atmosphere

Wärmebehandlung, f med
- heat treatment med

warme Dusche, f
→ Warmdusche

warme Jahreszeit f
- hot season

warme Mahlzeit, f
→ warmes Essen

warme Mahlzeit erhalten pro Tag
eine warme Mahlzeit erhalten pro Tag
- receice a hot meal per day

Wärmeplatte, f
Warmhalteplatte, f
- food warmer
- hot plate AE
- hotplate BE
- warming plate

Wärmepumpe, f
- heat pump

warmer Empfang, m
- warm reception

warmer Imbiß, m
- hot snack

warmes Bad, n
- hot bath

warmes Bad nehmen
- have a hot bath

warmes Büfett, n
- hot buffet

warmes Essen, n
warme Mahlzeit, f
warmes Mahl, n
- hot meal

warmes Gericht, n
heißes Gericht, n
- hot dish

warmes Getränk, n
Warmgetränk, n
heißes Getränk, n
Heißgetränk, n
- hot beverage
- hot drink

warmes Klima, n
- warm climate

warmes Mittagessen, n
- hot lunch
- hot luncheon

warme Speisen, f pl
- hot meals pl

warm essen
- have a hot meal

warmes und kaltes Wasser, n
Warm- und Kaltwasser, n
- hot and cold water
- h & c water

warmes Würstchen, n
→ heißes Würstchen

warmes Zimmer, n
- warm room

Wärmeteller, m
- water plate

warme und kalte Speisen, f pl
- hot and cold dishes pl

warme Vorspeise, f
Petite entrée, f FR
- hot starter
- petite entrée FR

Wärmflasche f
→ Bettflasche

Warmfreibad, n (beheizt)
beheiztes Freibad, n
- heated outdoor pool
- heated outdoor swimming pool AE
- heated outdoor swimming-pool BE

Warmfreibad, n (thermal)
→ Thermalfreibad

warm halten etw
- keep s.th. hot
- keep s.th. warm

Warmluftbehandlung, f
→ Heißluftbehandlung

Warmluftheizung, f
- hot-air heating

Warmmiete, f
warme Miete f
- rent inclusive of heating
- rent including heating

warm servieren etw
- serve s.th. warm

warm serviert, adj
- served warm, adj

Warm- und Kaltwasserdusche, f
Warm- und Kaltdusche, f
- hot and cold shower
- h & c shower

Warmwasser, n
warmes Wasser n
- hot water
- warm water

Warmwasserbad, n
Warmwasserbecken, n
- hot-water pool

Warmwasserbereiter, m
Heißwasserbereiter, m
Durchlauferhitzer, m
- water heater
- geyser BE

Warmwasserdusche f
- hot-water shower

Warmwasserhahn, m
- hot-water faucet AE
- hot-water tap BE

Warmwasserheizung, f
Heißwasserheizung, f
- hot-water heating

Warmwasserheizungsanlage, f
- hot-water heating system

Warmwasserschwimmbad, n
Warmwasserschwimmbecken, n
- hot-water swimming pool AE
- hot-water swimming-pool BE

Warmwasserspeicher, m
  Warmwassertank, m
  ♦ hot-water tank
Warmwasserversorgung, f
  ♦ hot-water supply
Warndreieck, n
  (Auto)
  ♦ warning triangle
Warnschild, n
  Warntafel, f
  ♦ danger sign
Warnstreik, m
  ♦ warning strike
  ♦ token strike
Warnstreik abhalten
  ♦ hold a warning strike
  ♦ hold a token strike
Warntafel, f
  → Warnschild
Warschauer Vertrag, m
  ♦ Warsaw Convention, the
Wart, m
  Aufseher, m
  ♦ warden
Wartebereich, m
  ♦ waiting area
Wartehalle, f
  ♦ waiting lounge
Warteliste, f
  Vormerkliste, f
  ♦ waiting list *AE*
  ♦ wait list *AE*
  ♦ waiting-list *BE*
warten
  ♦ wait
warten, daß jm kommt
  ♦ wait for s.o. to come
warten auf den Besuch von jm
  (z.B. Schwimmbad)
  ♦ await s.o.'s pleasure
warten auf den nächsten Linienflug
  ♦ wait for the next scheduled flight
warten auf die Bedienung
  ♦ wait for service
warten auf die Speisekarte
  ♦ wait for the menu
warten auf eine Bestätigung
  ♦ wait for confirmation
warten auf einen Flug (ohne Reservierung)
  ♦ stand by for a flight
warten auf einen Tisch
  ♦ wait for a table
warten auf ein Essen
  warten auf eine Mahlzeit
  ♦ wait for a meal
warten auf jn
  ♦ wait for s.o.
wartender Bus, m
  ♦ waiting bus
  ♦ waiting coach *BE*
warten etw.
  ♦ service s.th.
warten in einer Schlange
  ♦ wait in a queue
warten lassen jn
  ♦ keep s.o. waiting
warten mit dem Essen auf jn
  ♦ keep dinner waiting for s.o.
Warten satthaben
  ♦ be sick of waiting

warten stundenlang
  ♦ wait for hours
Warteraum, m
  → Wartesaal
Wartesaal, m
  Warteraum, m
  Wartehalle, f
  Wartezimmer, n
  ♦ waiting room *AE*
  ♦ waiting-room *BE*
Wartezeit, f
  ♦ waiting time
  ♦ waiting period
  ♦ wait
Wartezeit so gering wie möglich halten
  ♦ minimize the waiting time
Wartezeit verringern
  ♦ reduce the waiting time
Wartezimmer, n
  → Wartesaal
Wartung, f
  Pflege, f
  ♦ servicing
  ♦ maintenance
Wartung eines Zimmers, f
  ♦ maintenance of a room
  ♦ servicing (of) a room
Wartungsdienst, m
  Wartungsservice, m
  ♦ maintenance service
wartungsfrei, adj
  ♦ maintenance-free, adj
  ♦ service-free, adj
Wartungsgang, m
  (in Gebäude)
  Wartungspassage, f
  ♦ utilidor
Wartungspersonal, n
  Instandhaltungspersonal, n
  ♦ maintenance personnel
  ♦ maintenance staff
Wartungstechniker, m
  ♦ service engineer
Was auf den Tisch kommt, wird gegessen
  ♦ You have to eat what's on the table
  ♦ You have to eat what's put on the table
Waschautomat m
  ♦ automatic washer *AE*
  ♦ automatic washing machine *BE*
Waschbecken, n
  ♦ washbowl *AE*
  ♦ washbasin *AE*
  ♦ wash-basin *BE*
  ♦ hand-wash-basin *BE*
  ♦ basin
Waschbecken ist übergelaufen
  ♦ washbase has overflowed *AE*
  ♦ wash-basin has overflowed *BE*
Waschbeutel, m
  ♦ wash bag
  ♦ toilet bag
  ♦ sponge bag
Waschblock, m
  (Campingplatz)
  ♦ washing block
Waschbrett, n
  ♦ washboard *AE*
  ♦ wash-board *BE*
Wäsche, f (generell)
  ♦ linen

Wäsche, f (zum Waschen)
  ♦ washing
  ♦ laundry
Wäsche aufbewahren
  ♦ store linen
Wäscheaufbewahrung, f
  Wäschelagerung, f
  ♦ linen storage
Wäscheaufbewahrungsraum, m
  Wäscheraum, m
  ♦ linen storage room
Wäsche aufhängen
  ♦ hang out the clothes
  ♦ hang up the clothes
Wäscheausgabe f
  ♦ linen issue
  ♦ issue of linen
Wäsche ausgeben
  ♦ issue linen
Wäsche benutzen
  ♦ use linen
Wäschebeschließerin, f
  Lingeriegouvernante, f *SCHW*
  ♦ linen room keeper
  ♦ linen keeper
  ♦ linen maid
Wäschebestand, m
  ♦ linen stock
  ♦ stock of linen
  ♦ linen inventory *AE*
Wäschebeutel, m
  → Wäschesack
Wäschebuch, n
  ♦ linen book
Wäschedienst, m
  Wäscheservice, m
  Wäschereidienst, m
  Wäschereiservice, m
  ♦ laundry service
Wäsche erledigen
  waschen
  ♦ do the laundry
Wäscheersatz m
  Ersetzung von Wäsche f
  ♦ replacement of linen
Wäschefrau, f
  Lingerieangestellte, f *SCHW*
  ♦ linen keeper
  ♦ linen maid
Wäschegarnitur, f
  ♦ set of linen
Wäsche in die Wäscherei bringen
  Wäsche zum Waschen geben
  ♦ bring the washing to the laundry
Wäsche in Ordnung bringen
  ♦ look after the linen
Wäschejunge, m
  ♦ linen boy
Wäschekammer, f
  ♦ linen store
Wäscheklammer, f
  ♦ clothespin *AE*
  ♦ clothes-peg *BE*
Wäschekorb m
  ♦ linen basket
  ♦ laundry basket
Wäschekosten, pl (Wäsche)
  ♦ linen costs *pl*
  ♦ linen cost
Wäschekosten, pl (Wäscherei)
  → Wäschereikosten

Wäscheleasing n
 ♦ leasing of linen
Wäscheleine, f
 Wäscheseil, n
 ♦ clothesline AE
 ♦ clothes-line BE
Wäscheliste f
 Wäschezettel m
 ♦ laundry list
 ♦ washing list
Wäschemädchen, n
 Lingeriemädchen, n SCHW
 Lingerieangestellte, f SCHW
 ♦ linen maid
waschen (etw)
 ♦ wash (s.th.)
waschen sich
 ♦ wash oneself
 ♦ have a wash
waschen und bügeln (etw)
 ♦ launder (s.th.)
Wäschepflege f
 ♦ linen maintenance
 ♦ maintenance of linen
Wäscheraum, m
 ♦ linen room
Wäscheraumgehilfe, m
 ♦ linen room assistant
Wäscherei, f
 ♦ laundry
Wäschereiangestellte f
 Wäschereiarbeiterin f
 Wäschereifrau f
 ♦ laundrywoman
Wäschereiangestellter m
 Wäschereiarbeiter m
 ♦ laundryman
Wäschereiaufsicht, f
 ♦ laundry supervision
Wäschereiaufwendungen, f pl
 Wäschereiausgaben, f pl
 ♦ laundry expenses pl
Wäschereiausstattung f
 ♦ laundry equipment
Wäschereibedarf, m
 ♦ laundry supplies pl
Wäschereibereich, m (konkret)
 ♦ laundry area
Wäscherei betreiben
 ♦ operate a laundry
Wäschereidienst, m
 → Wäschedienst
Wäschereihilfe, f
 Wäschereiassistent, m
 ♦ laundry assistant
Wäschereijunge m
 ♦ laundry boy
Wäschereikapazität f
 ♦ laundry capacity
 ♦ capacity of a laundry
Wäschereikosten, pl
 ♦ laundry costs pl
 ♦ laundry cost
Wäschereileiter, f
 Wäschereileiterin, f
 ♦ laundry supervisor AE
Wäschereimädchen n
 Wäscherin f
 ♦ laundry maid

Wäschereipersonal n
 ♦ laundry personnel
 ♦ laundry staff
Wäschereiraum m
 ♦ laundry room
Wäschereirechnung, f
 ♦ laundry bill
Wäscherei unterhalten
 ♦ maintain a laundry
Wäscherin, f
 Waschfrau f
 ♦ laundress
Wäschesack, m
 Wäschebeutel, m
 ♦ laundry bag
 ♦ linen bag
Wäscheschacht m
 ♦ laundry chute
Wäscheschleuder, f
 Trockenschleuder, f
 ♦ spin-drier
 ♦ spin-dryer
Wäscheschrank, m
 ♦ linen closet AE
 ♦ linen cupboard BE
 ♦ clothespress AE
Wäscheseil, n
 Wäscheleine, f
 ♦ washing line
Wäscheservice, m
 → Wäschedienst
Wäschespinne, f
 (zum Trocknen von Wäsche)
 Trockengestell, n
 ♦ clotheshorse AE
 ♦ clothes-horse BE
 ♦ drier AE
 ♦ dryer AE
Wäschestapel m
 ♦ pile of linen
Wäsche steht zur Verfügung
 ♦ linen is available
Wäschetrockenraum, m
 → Trockenraum
Wäschetrockenschrank, m
 (oft über Warmwasserboiler)
 ♦ hot press
Wäsche trocknen
 ♦ dry linen
Wäschetrockner, m (Gestell)
 ♦ drier
 ♦ dryer
 ♦ clotheshorse AE
 ♦ clothes-horse BE
Wäschetrockner, m (Maschine)
 Trockenautomat, m
 Trockner, m
 ♦ tumble-drier
 ♦ tumble-dryer
Wäscheversorgung, f
 ♦ linen supply
 ♦ supply of linen
Wäschewagen, m
 ♦ laundry cart AE
 ♦ laundry trolley BE
Wäschewaschbecken, n
 ♦ laundry washbasin AE
 ♦ laundry wash-basin BE
Wäsche waschen
 ♦ do the washing

 ♦ wash the clothes
 ♦ do the laundry
Wäschewechsel, m
 Wechsel der Wäsche, m
 ♦ change of linen
 ♦ changing (of) linen
 ♦ linen change
Wäsche wechseln
 ♦ change the linen
Wäsche wird gestellt
 ♦ linen is provided
 ♦ linen will be provided
Wäsche wird kostenlos zur Verfügung gestellt
 ♦ linen is provided free of charge
 ♦ linen will be provided free of charge
Wäschezentrale f
 ♦ central linen room
Wäsche zum Trocknen aufhängen
 ♦ put linen out to dry
Wäsche zurückgeben
 ♦ return linen
Waschfrau, f
 ♦ washerwoman
Waschgelegenheit f (für Personen)
 ♦ washing facility
Waschhaus, n
 ♦ laundry house
Waschküche, f
 ♦ laundry room
Waschküchenleiter, m
 → Wäschereileiter
Waschlappen, m
 ♦ washcloth AE
 ♦ washrag AE coll
 ♦ face-flannel BE
 ♦ face-cloth BE
 ♦ flannel BE
Waschmaschine, f
 ♦ washer AE
 ♦ washing machine BE
Waschmaschinenbenutzung, f
 ♦ use of a washer AE
 ♦ use of a washing machine BE
 ♦ using a washer AE
 ♦ using a washing machine BE
Waschmaschinenraum, m
 ♦ washer room AE
 ♦ washing-machine room BE
Waschpulver, n
 ♦ washing powder
 ♦ detergent
Waschraum, m (Personen)
 ♦ lavatory
 ♦ washroom
Waschraum, m (Wäschewaschen)
 → Wäschereiraum
Waschsalon, m
 ♦ laundromat AE
 ♦ launderette BE
 ♦ laundrette BE
Waschsalondienst, m
 → Waschsalonservice
Waschsalonservice, m
 Waschsalondienst, m
 ♦ laundromat service AE
 ♦ launderette service BE
 ♦ laundrette service BE
Waschschüssel, f
 ♦ washing bowl
Waschservice m (Wäschedienst)
 → Wäschedienst

Waschständer

Waschständer, m
(ohne Leitungsanschluß)
- washstand *AE*
- wash-stand *BE*

Waschvollautomat m
- fully automatic washer *AE*
- fully automatic washing machine *BE*

Waschzuber m
- washtub

Was darf es sein?
(z.B. im Restaurant)
- What would you like?

Was darf ich Ihnen anbieten?
- What may I offer you?

was das leibliche Wohl angeht
- as for wining and dining

Was für ein Nepp!
- What a rip-off!

Was gibt es heute zu essen? (abends)
Was gibt es heute zu Abend?
- What are we having for dinner?
- What's for dinner?

Was gibt es heute zu essen? (mittags)
Was gibt es heute zu Mittag?
- What are we having for lunch?
- What's for lunch?

Was gibt es heute zu Mittag?
→ Was gibt es heute zu essen?

Was gibt's auf der Karte?
(Speisekarte)
- What's on the menu?

Was hat Ihnen am besten gefallen?
- What did you enjoy most?
- What have you enjoyed most?

Was hätten Sie gern zum Frühstück?
- What would you like for breakfast?

Was hatten Sie zu Mittag?
Was haben Sie zu Mittag gegessen?
- What did you have for lunch?

Was ist der Zweck Ihres Besuchs?
- What is the purpose of your visit?

Was ist Ihr nächstes Reiseziel?
- Where is your next destination?

Was kann ich für Sie tun?
- What can I do for you?

Was können Sie empfehlen?
- What do you recommend?

Was kostet die Fahrt?
Was kostet der Flug?
- What's the fare?

Was kostet ein Einzelzimmer pro Nacht?
- What does a single room cost per night?

Was möchten Sie bestellen?
- What would you like to order?

Was möchten Sie zum Abendessen? (Dinner)
- What do you want for (your) dinner?

Was möchten Sie zum Nachtisch?
- What would you like for dessert?

Was möchten Sie zu trinken?
Was möchten Sie trinken?
Was trinken Sie?
- What would you like to drink?

Wasser, n
- water

Wasser abstellen
- cut off water

Wasseranschluß, m
Leitungswasser, n
- mains water

Wasseranwendung, f *med*
- water application *med*
- application of water *med*

Wasseraufbereitungsanlage, f
- water treatment plant

Wasserball, m (Ball)
- water-polo ball

Wasserball, m (Spiel)
Wasserballspiel, n
- water polo

Wasserball spielen
- play water polo

Wasserballspieler, m
- water polo player

Wasserbecher, m
- water tumbler

Wasserbehälter, m
- water container

Wasserbett, n (generell)
- water bed

Wasserbett, n (mit getrennten Kammern)
- flotation bed

Wasserbus, m
- waterbus

Wasserbusfahrt, f
- waterbus ride
- waterbus trip

wasserdicht, adj
- waterproof, adj
- watertight, adj

wasserdichtes Zelt, f
- watertight tent
- waterproof tent

Wassereinrichtung, f
- water facility

Wasserfahrt, f
- water ride
- water trip

Wasserfahrzeug, n
- watercraft
- waterborne vehicle *AE*
- water vehicle
- water-borne craft *BE*

Wasserfall, m
- waterfall

Wasserflasche, f
- water bottle *AE*
- water-bottle *BE*

Wasserflugzeug, n
- water plane
- seaplane

Wassergarten, m
- water garden

Wassergeld, n
- water rate

Wasserglas n
- water glass

Wassergymnastik, f
- water gymnastics *pl*
- water exercises *pl*

Wassergymnastikkurs, m
- water exercise class

Wasserhahn, m
- water faucet *AE*
- water tap *BE*

Wasserhahn aufdrehen
Hahn aufdrehen
- turn on the tap *BE*
- turn on the faucet *AE*

Wasserhahn im Badezimmer läßt sich nicht zudrehen
Wasserhahn im Bad läßt sich nicht ganz zudrehen
- bathroom tap can't be turned off *BE*
- bathroom faucet can't be turned off fully *AE*

Wasserhahn im Bad tropft
- bathroom tap drips *BE*
- bathroom faucet drips *AE*

Wasserhahn zudrehen
Hahn abdrehen
- turn off the tap *BE*
- turn off the faucet *AE*

Wasserheilbad, n (Aktivität)
- hydrotherapy bath

Wasserheilbad, n (Ort)
Wasserkurort, m
- hydropathic spa

Wasserheilmassage, f
- hydrotherapy massage

Wasser im Mund zusammenlaufen lassen
Mund wässerig machen
- make one's mouth water
- make s.o.'s mouth water

Wasser in die Wanne lassen
- run water into the bath
- run water into the tub

Wasser ist lauwarm
- water is lukewarm
- water is tepid

Wasserkanne, f
(z.B. für Körperwäsche)
- ewer

Wasserkelch, m
- water goblet

Wasserknappheit, f
- water shortage

Wasserkosten, pl
- water costs *pl*
- water cost

Wasserkrug, m
- water jug
- water pitcher

Wasserkur, f
- water cure

Wasserlandschaft, f
- waterscape

Wasserlilienteich, m
- waterlily pond

Wasserloch, n *fig*
Kneipe, f
- water hole *BE sl*
- watering hole *BE sl*

Wassermassage, f
- water massage

Wassermassagebad, n
(Aktivität)
- hydrotherapy massage bath

Wassermelone, f
- watermelon *AE*
- water-melon *BE*

Wassermonoski, m
- aquaplane

Wassermonoskilauf, m
- aquaplaning

Wassermonoski laufen
- aquaplane

Wasserpark, m
- water park
- aquatic park

Wasserpfeife, f
- water pipe

Wasserproblem, n
♦ water problem
Wasserqualität, f
♦ water quality
♦ quality of (the) water
Wasserratte, f
begeisterter Schwimmer, m
♦ enthusiastic swimmer
♦ keen swimmer
Wasserratte sein
♦ love the water
Wasserrechnung, f
♦ water bill
Wasserreisen, n
Reisen zu Wasser, n
Wasserreiseverkehr, m
♦ water travel
Wasserrohr, n
♦ water pipe
Wasserrohr ist geplatzt
♦ water pipe has burst
Wasserrutschbahn, f
Wasserrutsche, f
♦ water chute
♦ water slide
Wasserrutsche, f
Wasserrutschbahn, f
♦ water slide
♦ water chute
Wasserschaden, m
♦ water damage
Wasserschlauch, m
♦ water hose
Wasserschloß, n
Wasserburg, f
♦ moated castle
♦ moated palace
Wasserseite, f
(Gegensatz zu Landseite)
♦ waterfront
wasserseitig, adj
(nicht landseitig)
am Wasser, adv
♦ waterfront, adj
Wasserski, m
♦ water ski AE
♦ water-ski BE
Wasserskiboot, n
♦ water-ski boat
♦ water-skiing boat
Wasserskiclub, m
Wasserskiverein, m
♦ water-ski club
Wasserski fahren
Wasserski laufen
♦ water-ski
Wasserskifahren, n
→ Wasserskilaufen
Wasserskifahrer, m
Wasserskisportler, m
♦ water-skier
Wasserskifahrer ziehen
Wasserskiläufer ziehen
♦ tow a water-skier
Wasserskifahrt, f
♦ water-ski ride
Wasserskikurs, m
♦ water-ski course
♦ course in water-skiing
Wasserskilaufen, n
Wasserskifahren, n

Wasserskisport, m
♦ water-skiing
Wasserskirennen, n
♦ water-ski race
♦ water-ski racing
Wasserskischau, f
♦ water-ski show
♦ water-skiing show
Wasserskischule, f
♦ water-ski school
♦ water-skiing school
Wasserskisee, m
♦ water-ski lake
♦ water-skiing lake
Wasserskistrecke, f
♦ water-ski route
Wasserskiunterricht, m
♦ water-skiing tuition
♦ water-skiing lessons pl
Wasser sparen
Wasser einsparen
♦ save water
Wasserspiel, n
♦ water game
Wassersport, m
♦ water sports pl
♦ aquatic sports pl (= sg)
Wassersportangebot, n (Palette)
♦ range of water sports
♦ range of aquatic sports
Wassersportbedingungen, f pl
♦ water sports conditions pl
Wassersportbegeisterter, m
♦ water sports enthusiast
Wassersportclub, m
→ Wassersportverein
Wassersportdorado, n
→ Wassersportparadies
Wassersporteinrichtung, f
♦ water sports facility
Wassersportfan, m
♦ water sports fan
Wassersportfreund, m
→ Wassersportliebhaber
Wassersporthotel, n
♦ water sports hotel
Wassersportliebhaber, m
Wassersportfreund, m
♦ water sports lover
Wassersportmöglichkeit, f
♦ water sports possibility
Wassersportparadies, n
Wassersportdorado, n
♦ water sports paradise
Wassersportprogramm, n
♦ water sports program AE
♦ water sports programme BE
Wassersportsaison, f
♦ water sports season
Wassersportunterricht, m
♦ water sports tuition
♦ water sports lessons pl
Wassersporturlaub, m
♦ water sports vacation AE
♦ water sports holiday BE
Wassersportverein, m
Wassersportclub, m
♦ water sports club
Wassersportzentrum, n
♦ water sports center AE
♦ water sports centre BE

Wasserstelle, f
(auch figurativ)
Tränke, f
Trinkstelle, f
♦ watering place
Wasserstraße, f
♦ waterway
♦ canal
Wasserstraßentourismus, m
♦ waterway tourism
Wassertank, m
♦ water tank
Wassertarif, m
♦ water tariff
Wassertaxi, n
♦ water taxi
Wassertemperatur f
♦ water temperature
Wassertiefe, f
♦ depth of water
Wasserturm, m
♦ water tower
Wasser und Brot, n
♦ bread and water
Wasservelo, n SCHW
Tretboot, n
♦ pedalo
♦ pedal-boat
Wasserveranstaltung, f
♦ aquatic event
Wasserverbindung, f
♦ water link
Wasserverbrauch, m
♦ water consumption
♦ consumption of water
Wasser verbrauchen
♦ consume water
Wasserverkehr, m
♦ water traffic
Wasserverschmutzung, f
♦ water pollution
Wasserversorgung, f
♦ water supply
Wasserzähler, m
♦ water meter
Was steht heute auf dem Programm?
♦ What's the program for today? AE
♦ What's the programme for today? BE
Was trinken Sie?
→ Was möchten Sie zu trinken?
Was würden Sie als Hauptgang empfehlen?
♦ What would you recommend for the main course?
Was würden Sie gerne tun?
Worauf hätten Sie Lust?
♦ What would you care to do?
Watt, n
Wattenmeer, n
♦ tideland
♦ mud flats pl
Wattenmeer, n
Watt, n
♦ mud flats pl
♦ tideland
Wattgebiet, n
♦ tidal flats pl
♦ tideland
♦ mud flats pl
Wattwanderung, f
♦ walk across the mud flats (at low tide)

WC, n
♦ WC
♦ water closet
WC-Becken, n
♦ lavatory bowl
♦ water-closet bowl
WC-Deckel, m
♦ lavatory lid
WC mit Leitungswasser, n
(Camping)
♦ mains WC
WC-Sitz, m
♦ lavatory seat
WC wird von drei Personen benutzt
♦ WC is shared by three persons
WE, f
Wohneinheit, f
♦ d.u.
♦ dwelling unit
Wechsel, m (Bank)
♦ bill of exchange
♦ bill
♦ draft
Wechsel ausstellen
♦ draw a bill
♦ issue a bill
Wechselausstellung, f (Museum)
wechselnde Ausstellung, f
♦ changing exhibition
♦ changing exhibit AE
Wechselautomat, m
Münzwechsel, m
♦ change dispenser
♦ change machine
Wechselbad, n
♦ hot and cold baths pl
Wechsel der Bettwäsche, m
→ Bettwäschewechsel
Wechsel der Tischwäsche, m
→ Tischwäschewechsel
Wechseleinrichtung, f
♦ exchange facility
Wechseleinrichtungen, f pl
Wechselmöglichkeiten, f pl
♦ bureau de change facilities pl
♦ exchange facilities pl
♦ money changing facilities pl
Wechselgeld, n
♦ change
♦ float
Wechselgeld behalten
Rest behalten
♦ keep the change
Wechselgeld geben
♦ give change
Wechselgeld nachzählen
♦ check one's change
Wechselgeldteller, m
♦ change plate
Wechselkurs, m
Kurs, m
♦ exchange rate
♦ rate of exchange
♦ ROE
Wechselkurs ist günstig
♦ exchange rate is favorable AE
♦ exchange rate is favourable BE
Wechselkurs ist ungünstig
♦ exchange rate is unfavorable AE
♦ exchange rate is unfavourable BE

Wechselkursschwankung, f
♦ exchange rate fluctuation
♦ fluctuation in exchange rates
wechselnde Menüs, n pl
♦ changing menus pl
wechseln etw
♦ change s.th.
Wechselsprechanlage, f
→ Gegensprechanlage
Wechselstelle, f
(für Geld)
♦ exchange point
♦ exchange facility
Wechselstube, f
Wechselbüro, n
♦ bureau de change FR
♦ exchange bureau
♦ exchange office
♦ money changing facility
♦ exchange booth
Weckanlage, f
♦ early-call system
Weckauftrag m
♦ wake-up order
Weckbuch, n
♦ early-call book
Weckdienst, m
Weckservice, m
♦ wake-up service
♦ early-call service
♦ call service coll
Weckeinrichtung, f
♦ early-call unit
♦ morning call unit
wecken jn
♦ wake s.o.
♦ call s.o.
wecken jn morgens
♦ wake s.o. in the morning
♦ call s.o. in the morning
Wecker, m
♦ alarm clock
Wecker stellen auf 7 Uhr
♦ set the alarm for 7 o'clock
Weckliste, f
♦ early-call list
Weckliste führen
♦ keep an early-call list
Weckruf, m
♦ wake-up call
♦ early-morning call
♦ morning call
♦ early call
Weckrufanlage, f
♦ early-morning call system
Weckruf erhalten
Weckruf bekommen
♦ get a wake-up call
♦ get an early-morning call
♦ get a morning call
Weckrufliste, f
♦ call sheet BE
Weckruf vergessen
♦ forget a morning call
wedeln
(Ski)
♦ wedel
weder Fisch noch Fleisch
♦ neither fish nor flesh
♦ neither fish nor fowl

Weekend, n
→ Wochenende
Weekendpauschale, f
→ Wochenendpauschale
Weg, m
Pfad, m
♦ trail
♦ path
Weg abkürzen
→ Abkürzung nehmen
Wegbeschreibung, f
Streckenbeschreibung, f
Beschreibung des Wegs, f
Beschreibung der Strecke, f
♦ description of the route
wegbleiben von etw
draußenbleiben
♦ stay out of s.th.
Wegblume, f
Blume am Weg, f
♦ wayside flower
Weg bringt uns vorbei an etw
♦ way takes us past s.th.
Wegelagerer, m
♦ highwayman
♦ waylayer
wegelos, adj
weglos, adj
♦ trackless, adj
wegeloses Gebiet, n
♦ trackless area
wegen anderweitiger geschäftlicher Verpflichtungen
♦ due to other business commitments
Wegen Betriebsferien geschlossen
(Hinweisschild)
♦ Closed for holidays
♦ Closed for vacation
wegen einer plötzlichen Erkrankung
♦ due to sudden illness
wegen eines Unfalls
♦ due to an accident
Wegen Generalreinigung geschlossen
(Hinweisschild)
♦ Closed for general cleaning
Wegen Renovierung geschlossen
(Hinweisschild)
♦ Closed for refurbishment
♦ Closed for renovation
♦ Closed for renovations
wegen Terminschwierigkeiten
♦ due to prior commitments
Weg entlangwandern
Weg abwandern
♦ walk a trail
Wegen Umbaus geschlossen
(Hinweisschild)
♦ Closed for alterations
wegen unvorhersehbarer Ereignisse
♦ due to an unforeseen event
wegen unvorhersehbarer Umstände
♦ due to unforeseen circumstances
Wegerecht, n jur
♦ wayleave BE jur
wegessen etw jm
wegessen etw
♦ eat up s.o.'s (cake etc.)
♦ eat up s.th.
Wegetappe, f
♦ leg of the trail

Wegezeit, f
→ Fahrzeit
wegfahren (Auto)
abfahren
losfahren
♦ drive off
wegfahren in (den) Urlaub
♦ go away on vacation AE
♦ go away on holiday BE
wegfahren über das Wochenende
♦ go away for the weekend
wegfahren zu einem Urlaub
zur Erholung verreisen
♦ go away for a vacation AE
♦ go away for a holiday BE
Weg fällt 123 Fuß
Weg fällt 123 Fuß ab
♦ trail drops 123 feet
Weg folgen
Pfad folgen
♦ follow a trail
♦ follow a path
Wegführer, m
♦ trail guide
weggehen wie warme Semmeln
♦ sell like hot cakes
♦ go like hot cakes
Weg ist ausgeschildert
♦ path is signposted
Wegkarte, f
♦ trail map
wegklappbares Bett, n
→ Klappbett
Wegkreuz, n
Marterl, n dial
♦ roadside cross
weglassen etw von der Rechnung
♦ leave s.th. off the bill
weglassen etw von der Speisekarte
♦ omit s.th. from the menu
weglos, adj
unwegsam, adj
pfadlos, adj
♦ wayless, adj
Weg markieren
♦ mark a path
♦ mark a footpath
Wegmarkierung, f
♦ wayside marking
♦ waymarking
♦ waymark
Weg mit Trimmstationen, m
♦ path with fitness stations
♦ path with keep-fit stations
Wegprospekt, m
♦ trail brochure
Weg verlieren
sich verirrren
sich verlaufen
♦ lose one's way
♦ get lost
weg von dem Jubel und Trubel des Alltagslebens
♦ away from the hustle and bustle of everyday life
Weg wählen
♦ choose one's way
♦ pick one's way
Wegwerfflasche, f
Einwegflasche, f
♦ throw-away bottle
♦ nonreturnable bottle AE
♦ non-returnable bottle BE
Wegwerftasse, f
♦ throw-away cup
Wegwerfteller, m
♦ throw-away plate
Wegzeichen, n
Wegmarkierung, f
♦ waymark
Weg zum Gipfel, m
Gipfelweg, m
♦ trail to the summit
♦ path to the summit
Wehrkirche, f
befestigte Kirche, f
♦ fortified church
Weiberfastnacht, f
Weiberkarneval, m
♦ women's carnival
weiblich, adj
♦ female, adj
weiblicher Besucher, m
♦ female visitor
weiblicher Gast, m
♦ female guest
weiblicher Kellnerlehrling, m
♦ apprentice waitress
weiches Ei, n
→ weichgekochtes Ei
weichgekocht, adj
♦ soft-cooked, adj AE
♦ soft-boiled, adj BE
weichgekochtes Ei, n
weiches Ei, n
♦ soft-cooked egg AE
♦ soft-boiled egg BE
Weichsel, f
♦ Vistula River, the
♦ River Vistula, the
♦ Vistula, the
Weideland, n
♦ pastureland
♦ pasture
Weihnacht, f
Weihnachten, n
Weihnachtsfest, n
♦ Christmas
♦ Xmas coll
Weihnachten feiern
Weihnacht feiern
♦ celebrate Christmas
♦ celebrate Xmas
Weihnachten und Neujahr
♦ Christmas and New Year
Weihnachtsabend, m
→ Heiligabend
Weihnachtsangebot, n
Weihnachtsofferte, f
♦ Christmas offer
♦ Xmas offer
Weihnachtsarrangement, n
Weihnachtsvereinbarung, f
♦ Christmas arrangement
♦ Xmas arrangement
Weihnachtsausflug, m
♦ Christmas excursion
♦ Xmas excursion
Weihnachtsausflügler, m
♦ Christmas excursionist
♦ Xmas excursionist
Weihnachtsausstellung, f
♦ Christmas exhibition
♦ Christmas exhibit AE
♦ Xmas exhibition
♦ Xmas exhibit AE
Weihnachtsbankett, n
Weihnachtsfestessen, n
♦ Christmas banquet
♦ Xmas banquet
Weihnachtsbasar, m
♦ Christmas bazar
♦ Christmas bazaar
♦ Xmas bazar
♦ Xmas bazaar
Weihnachtsbaum, m
♦ Christmas tree
♦ Xmas tree
Weihnachtsbraten, m
♦ Christmas roast
♦ Xmas roast
Weihnachtsbrunch, m
♦ Christmas brunch
♦ Xmas brunch
Weihnachtsbüfett, n
♦ Christmas buffet
♦ Xmas buffet
Weihnachtsdekoration, f
→ Weihnachtsschmuck
Weihnachtsdomizil, n
♦ Christmas domicile
♦ Christmas house
♦ Xmas domicile
♦ Xmas house
Weihnachtseinkauf, m
Weihnachtseinkäufe, m pl
♦ Christmas shopping
♦ Xmas shopping
Weihnachtsessen, n
Weihnachtsmittagessen, n
♦ Xmas lunch
♦ Xmas luncheon
♦ Christmas lunch
♦ Christmas luncheon
Weihnachtsessen, n (Dinner)
♦ Christmas dinner
♦ Xmas dinner
Weihnachtsfahrt, f
♦ Christmas trip
♦ Xmas trip
Weihnachtsfeier, f
♦ Christmas celebration
♦ Xmas celebration
♦ Christmas do coll
♦ Xmas do coll
♦ Christmas party
Weihnachtsfeier, f (Party)
♦ Christmas party
♦ Xmas party
Weihnachtsferien, pl
Weihnachtsurlaub, m
♦ Christmas holiday BE
♦ Xmas holiday BE
♦ Christmas holidays BE pl
♦ Xmas holidays BE pl
♦ Christmas vacation AE
Weihnachtsferiengast, m
Weihnachtsurlauber, m
♦ Christmas holidaymaker BE
♦ Xmas holidaymaker BE
♦ Christmas vacationer AE
♦ Xmas vacationer AE

Weihnachtsfest

Weihnachtsfest, n
→ Weihnacht
Weihnachtsgans, f
♦ Christmas goose
♦ Xmas goose
Weihnachtsgänsebraten, m
♦ Christmas roast goose
♦ Xmas roast goose
Weihnachtsgast, m
♦ Christmas guest
♦ Xmas guest
Weihnachtsgebäck, n
♦ Christmas biscuits *pl*
♦ Christmas cookies *AE pl*
♦ Xmas biscuits *pl*
♦ Xmas cookies *AE pl*
Weihnachtsgeschenk, n
♦ Christmas present
♦ Xmas present
♦ Christmas gift
♦ Xmas gift
Weihnachtsgratifikation, f
♦ Christmas bonus
♦ Xmas bonus
Weihnachtskarte, f
♦ Christmas card
♦ Xmas card
Weihnachtskartenlandschaft, f
♦ Christmas-card scenery
♦ Christmas-card landscape
♦ Christmas-card countryside
Weihnachtskonzert, n
♦ Christmas concert
♦ Xmas concert
Weihnachtskreuzfahrt, f
♦ Christmas cruise
♦ Xmas cruise
Weihnachtskuchen, m
♦ Christmas cake
♦ Xmas cake
Weihnachtskurzurlaub, m
♦ Christmas break
♦ Xmas break
Weihnachtslied, n
♦ Christmas carol
♦ Xmas carol
Weihnachtsmarkt, m
Christkindlmarkt, m *dial*
♦ Christmas fair
♦ Xmas fair
♦ Christmas market
♦ Xmas fair
Weihnachtsmenü n
♦ Christmas menu
♦ Xmas menu
Weihnachtsmittagessen, n
♦ Christmas luncheon
♦ Christmas lunch
♦ Xmas luncheon
♦ Xmas lunch
Weihnachtsprogramm, n
♦ Christmas program *AE*
♦ Xmas program *AE*
♦ Christmas programme *BE*
♦ Xmas programme *BE*
Weihnachtsreise, f
♦ Christmas tour
♦ Christmas trip
♦ Christmas journey
♦ Xmas tour
♦ Xmas trip

Weihnachtssaison, f
♦ Christmas season
♦ Xmas season
Weihnachtsschau, f
Weihnachtsvorstellung, f
Weihnachtsausstellung, f
♦ Christmas show
♦ Xmas show
Weihnachtsschmuck, m
Weihnachtsdekoration, f
♦ Christmas decoration
♦ Xmas decoration
Weihnachtssonderangebot, n
♦ special Christmas offer
Weihnachtsstimmung, f (Atmosphäre)
♦ Christmas atmosphere
♦ Xmas atmosphere
Weihnachtsstimmung, f (Person)
♦ Christmas mood
♦ Xmas mood
Weihnachtstafel, f
Weihnachtstisch, m
♦ Christmas table
♦ Xmas table
Weihnachtstag, erster, m
(25. Dezember)
♦ Christmas Day
♦ Xmas Day
Weihnachtstag, zweiter, m
(26. Dezember)
♦ Boxing Day
♦ day after Christmas
Weihnachtstarif, m
♦ Christmas tariff
♦ Christmas rates *pl*
♦ Christmas rate
♦ Christmas terms *pl*
♦ Xmas tariff
Weihnachtstournee, f
♦ Christmas tour
♦ Xmas tour
Weihnachtstrubel, m
♦ Christmas rush
♦ Xmas rush
Weihnachtsurlaub, m
Weihnachtsferien, pl
♦ Christmas vacation *AE*
♦ Xmas vacation *AE*
♦ Christmas holiday *BE*
♦ Xmas holiday *BE*
♦ Christmas holidays *BE pl*
Weihnachtsurlauber, m
Weihnachtsferiengast, m
♦ Christmas vacationer *AE*
♦ Xmas vacationer *AE*
♦ Christmas holidaymaker *BE*
♦ Xmas holidaymaker *BE*
Weihnachtsveranstaltung, f
Weihnachtsfeier, f
Weihnachtsfete, f
♦ Christmas do *coll*
♦ Xmas do *coll*
Weihnachtsverkehr, m
♦ Christmas traffic
♦ Xmas traffic
Weihnachtswoche, f
♦ Christmas week
♦ Xmas week
Weihnachtswochenende, n
♦ Christmas weekend
♦ Xmas weekend

Weihnachtszeit, f
♦ Christmas time
♦ Xmas time
♦ Christmas season
♦ Xmas season
♦ Christmas
Weihnachtszuschlag, m
♦ Christmas supplement
♦ Xmas supplement
Weihwasserbecken, n
♦ stoup
Weile ausruhen (sich)
♦ rest for a while
Weiler, m
♦ hamlet
Wein, m
♦ wine
Wein, Weib und Gesang
♦ wine, woman and song
Weinabend m
♦ wine evening
Weinakademie, f
♦ wine academy
Wein altert
♦ wine ages
Weinangebot, n (Gegensatz zu Nachfrage)
♦ wine supply
Weinangebot, n (Palette)
♦ range of wines
♦ choice of wines
Wein anreichern
(Zucker)
♦ chaptalise a wine
Weinansprache, f
♦ wine language
♦ wine appreciation language
Weinart, f
♦ wine type
♦ type of wine
♦ kind of wine
Weinatlas, m
♦ wine atlas
Wein auf Bier, das rat' ich dir; Bier auf Wein, das laß sein
♦ Wine on beer gives good cheer; beer on wine you'll repine
Wein auf Flaschen ziehen
Wein abfüllen (in Flaschen)
♦ bottle wine
Weinauktion, f
→ Weinversteigerung
Weinausgabe, f
(im Hotel)
♦ wine dispense
Weinausschank, m (Verkauf)
→ Verkauf von Wein
Wein austrinken
♦ finish off the wine
Weinauswahl, f
Auswahl an Wein, f
♦ selection of wine
♦ selection of wines
♦ choice of wine(s)
♦ wine choice
♦ wine selection
Wein auswählen
♦ select (a) wine
Weinbar
♦ wine bar

Weinbau, m
♦ wine growing
♦ viticulture
Weinbaudorf, n
♦ wine-growing village
Weinbau einführen in Britannien
♦ introduce viticulture to Britain
Weinbauer, m
→ Winzer
Weinbauforschung, f
♦ viticultural research
Weinbaugebiet, n (groß)
♦ wine-growing region
Weinbaugebiet, n (klein)
♦ wine-growing area
Weinbaugemeinde, f
♦ wine-growing community
Weinbauland, n
Weinbaugegend, f
♦ wine-growing country
Weinbaumethode, f
♦ method of viticulture
Weinbaumuseum, n
♦ museum of viticulture
♦ museum of wine-growing
Weinbautradition, f
♦ wine-growing tradition
Weinbauverband, m
♦ winegrowers' association
Weinbecher, m
♦ wine cup
Weinbegeisterter, m
♦ wine enthusiast
Weinberatung, f
♦ advice on wines
Weinberg, m
♦ vineyard
Weinberg anlegen
♦ plant a vineyard
Weinbergatlas, m
♦ vineyard atlas
Weinbergbesuch, m
♦ visit to a vineyard
Weinberge säumen die Ufer
(Fluß)
♦ vineyards line the banks
Weinbergfläche, f
♦ vineyard area
Weinberglage, f
♦ vineyard site
Weinbergname, m
♦ vineyard name
Weinbergrolle, f
♦ vineyard register
Weinbergterrassen, f pl
♦ terraced vineyards *pl*
Weinbestand, m
Weinvorrat, m
Weinlager, n
♦ stock of wine
♦ wine stock
Weinbestellung f
♦ wine order
♦ order of wine
♦ ordering (of) wine
Wein besteuern
♦ tax wine
Weinbetrieb, m
♦ wine establishment
♦ wine operation

Weinbibliothek, f
♦ wine library
Weinblatt, n
♦ vine leaf
Weinbrand, m
Branntwein, m
Kognac, m
♦ brandy
Weinbuch, n
(Informationen über Wein)
♦ wine book
Weinclub, m
♦ wine club
Weincommis, m
Commis de vin, m FR
♦ assistant wine waiter
♦ commis wine waiter
♦ commis de vin *FR*
Wein dekantieren
♦ decant wine
Weindepot, n
♦ wine depot
Wein der Woche, m
♦ wine of the week
Weindomäne, f
♦ wine domain
Weindorf, m
♦ wine village
Weine der Gegend genießen
♦ enjoy the local wines
Weine der Region, m pl
♦ wines of the region *pl*
Weineinkäufer, m
♦ wine purchasing agent
Wein einkellern
Wein lagern
♦ cellar wine
Weineinzelhändler, m
♦ wine retailer
Wein empfehlen jm
♦ recommend a wine to s.o.
Weinempfehlung, f
♦ wine suggestion
Weinernte, f
Weinlese, f
Traubenernte, f
Traubenlese, f
♦ vintage
♦ grape harvest
Wein erzeugen
♦ produce wine
Weinerzeuger, m
Weinproduzent, m
♦ wine producer
Weinerzeugerdorf, n
♦ wine-producing village
Weinerzeugergebiet, n
♦ wine-producing region
Weinerzeugergemeinde, f
♦ wine-producing community
Weinerzeugerland, n
Weinerzeugergegend, f
♦ wine-producing country
Weinerzeugernation, f
♦ wine-producing nation
Weinerzeugerstaat, m
♦ wine-producing state
Weinerzeugung, f
♦ wine production
Weinessig, m
♦ wine vinegar

Weinetikett, n
♦ wine label
Weine und Spirituosen, pl
♦ wines and spirits *pl*
Weinexport, m
♦ wine export
Weinexporteur, m
♦ wine exporter
Weinfan, m
♦ wine fan
Weinfaß, n
♦ wine cask
♦ wine barrel
Weinfest, n
♦ wine festival
Weinfest abhalten
♦ hold a wine festival
Weinfestbesuch, m
♦ visit to a wine festival
Weinfest besuchen
♦ visit a wine festival
Weinfestbesucher, m
♦ visitor to a wine festival
♦ person visiting a wine festival
Weinfirma, f
♦ wine company
Weinflasche, f
♦ wine bottle
Weinflasche etikettieren
♦ label a wine bottle
Weinfliege, f
♦ wine fly
Weinfolge, f
♦ sequence of wines
♦ order of wines
Weinförderung, f
→ Weinwerbung
Weinforum, n
♦ wine forum
Weinfreund, m
→ Weinliebhaber
Weinführer, m
(Buch)
♦ wine guide
Weingala, f
♦ wine gala
Weingarten, m
→ Weinberg
Weingebiet, n
♦ wine area
♦ wine region
Wein gekühlt servieren
♦ serve the wine chilled
Weingelee, n
♦ wine jelly
Weingelehrter, m
♦ wine pundit
Weingemeinde, f
♦ wine community
Weingenossenschaft, f
♦ wine cooperative
Weingeographie, f
♦ wine geography
Weingeschäft, n (Handel)
♦ wine business
Weingeschäft, n (Laden)
→ Weinladen
Weingeschenk, n
Weinpräsent, n
♦ wine gift
♦ wine present

Weingesellschaft

Weingesellschaft, f
   Weinverband, m
   ♦ wine association
Weingesetz, n
   ♦ wine law
Weingewölbekeller, m
   Weinkeller, m
   ♦ wine-vaults *BE pl*
Weinglas n
   ♦ wineglass
Weingott, m
   Gott des Weins, m
   ♦ wine god
   ♦ god of wine
Weinguru, m
   ♦ wine guru
Wein gustieren
   → Wein probieren
Weingut, n
   ♦ winery
   ♦ wine-growing estate
   ♦ wine estate
Weingutsbesitzer, m
   ♦ wine estate owner
Weinguteigentümer, m
   ♦ wine estate proprietor
Weinhafen, m
   ♦ wine port
   ♦ wine harbor *AE*
   ♦ wine harbour *BE*
Weinhandel m
   ♦ wine trade
Weinhändler m
   ♦ wine merchant
   ♦ wine dealer
Weinhandlung, f
   Weinladen, m
   Weingeschäft, n
   ♦ wine store *AE*
   ♦ wine shop *BE*
Wein hat ein feines Bukett
   ♦ wine has a fine bouquet
Wein hat Qualität
   ♦ wine has quality
Weinhauptstadt, f
   ♦ wine capital
Weinhaus, n
   ♦ winehouse
Weinhefe, f
   ♦ wine yeast
Weinhersteller, m
   ♦ wine-maker
Weinherstellung, f
   ♦ wine-making
Wein herumreichen
   ♦ pass around the wine
Weinimport, m
   ♦ wine import
Weinimporteur, m
   ♦ wine importer
Weinindustrie, f
   Weinbranche, f
   ♦ wine industry
Weininstitut, n
   ♦ wine institute
Wein ist fruchtig
   ♦ wine is fruity
Wein ist herzhaft
   ♦ wine is hearty
Wein ist rassig
   ♦ wine is racy

Wein ist typisch für die Region
   ♦ wine is typical of the region
Weinjahrgang, m
   Weinjahr, n
   ♦ vintage year
   ♦ vintage
Weinjournalist, m
   ♦ wine journalist
Weinkanne, f
   ♦ wine jar *AE*
   ♦ wine-jar *BE*
Weinkaraffe, f
   ♦ wine carafe
   ♦ decanter
Weinkarte, f
   ♦ wine list
   ♦ wine card *AE*
Weinkarte erweitern
   ♦ expand the wine list
Weinkarte ist erlesen
   ♦ wine list is exquisite
Weinkarte ist erstklassig
   ♦ wine list is first class
Weinkarte ist kurz
   ♦ wine list is short
Weinkarte ist lang
   ♦ wine list is long
Weinkarte ist respektabel
   ♦ wine list is respectable
Weinkarte präsentiert 123 Weine
   ♦ wine list features 123 wines
Weinkarte vorlegen
   ♦ present the wine list
Weinkarte zusammenstellen
   ♦ compile a wine list
   ♦ draw up a wine list
Weinkäufer, m
   ♦ wine buyer
Weinkelch, m
   ♦ wine goblet
Weinkeller, der den Kenner erfreut, m
   ♦ wine cellar which delights the connoisseur *AE*
   ♦ wine cellar to delight the connoisseur *AE*
   ♦ wine-cellar which delights the connoisseur *BE*
   ♦ wine-cellar to delight the connoisseur *BE*
Weinkeller, m
   ♦ wine cellar *AE*
   ♦ wine-cellar *BE*
   ♦ cellar
Weinkellerei, f
   ♦ wine cellars *pl*
   ♦ winery
Weinkellner, m
   Sommelier m FR
   ♦ wine waiter
   ♦ wine butler *rare*
   ♦ sommelier *FR*
Weinkellner des Jahres, m
   ♦ Wine Waiter of the Year
Weinkellnerin, f
   ♦ wine waitress
   ♦ female sommelier
Weinkelter, f
   ♦ winepress
Weinkenner, m
   ♦ wine connoisseur
   ♦ connoisseur of wines
   ♦ vinologist
Weinkiste, f
   ♦ wine crate

Weinkönigin, f
   ♦ wine queen
Weinkonsum, m
   Weinverbrauch, m
   Weinverzehr, m
   ♦ consumption of wine
   ♦ wine consumption
Wein konsumieren
   ♦ consume wine
Weinkorb, m
   ♦ wine cradle
Weinkosten, pl
   ♦ wine costs *pl*
   ♦ wine cost
Weinkrug m
   ♦ wine jug
   ♦ wine pitcher
   ♦ wine jar
Wein kühlen
   ♦ cool wine
   ♦ cool a wine
   ♦ chill wine
   ♦ chill a wine
Weinkühler m
   ♦ wine cooler
Weinkultur, f
   ♦ wine culture
Weinkunde, f
   Önologie, f
   ♦ enology
   ♦ oenology
   ♦ vinology
Weinladen, m
   Weingeschäft, n
   Weinhandlung, f
   ♦ wine shop *BE*
   ♦ wine store *AE*
Weinlager, n (Bestand)
   → Weinbestand
Weinlager, n (Lagerraum)
   ♦ wine storeroom *AE*
   ♦ wine store-room *BE*
Weinlager, n (Volumen, Fläche)
   Weinlagerfläche, f
   ♦ wine storage space
Wein lagern
   ♦ store wine
   ♦ keep wine in cellar
Weinlagerung, f
   ♦ wine storage
   ♦ storage of wine
   ♦ storing wine
Weinland, n
   Weingegend, f
   ♦ wine country
   ♦ wine-producing country
Weinlehrpfad, m
   ♦ vineyard nature trail
   ♦ wine trail
Weinlese, f
   → Traubenlese
Weinlesefest, n
   ♦ grape harvest festival
Weinlesezeit, f
   ♦ vintage season
   ♦ vintage time
Weinliebhaber m
   Weinfreund m
   ♦ wine lover

Weinlieferant, m
  Weinlieferer, m
  ♦ wine supplier
Weinlokal, n
  ♦ wine place
  ♦ wine tavern
  ♦ wine bar
  ♦ wine restaurant
  ♦ wineshop *AE*
weinlos, adj
  ♦ wineless, adj
weinlose Party, f
  ♦ wineless party
weinloses Bankett, n
  ♦ wineless banquet
Wein machen
  Wein herstellen
  ♦ make wine
Weinmarkt m
  ♦ wine market
Weinmesse, f
  ♦ wine fair
Wein mit Korkgeschmack, m
  ♦ corky wine
Weinmuseum, n
  ♦ wine museum
Weinnarr, m
  ♦ wine buff
Weinoberkellner, m
  ♦ head sommelier
  ♦ head wine waiter
Weinorganisation, f
  ♦ wine organisation
  ♦ wine organization
Wein panschen
  ♦ adulterate wine
Weinpanscher, m
  ♦ adulterator of wine
Weinparadies, n
  ♦ wine paradise
Weinpauschale, f
  ♦ wine package
Wein prämiieren
  ♦ award a prize to a wine
Weinpräsent, n
  Weingeschenk, n
  ♦ wine present
  ♦ wine gift
Weinpreis, m
  ♦ wine price
  ♦ price of wine
Weinpreisliste, f
  ♦ wine price list
Weinprinzessin, f
  ♦ wine princess
Weinprobe, f
  ♦ wine tasting
  ♦ wine-tasting session
Weinprobe abhalten
  ♦ hold a wine tasting
Weinprobe arrangieren
  ♦ arrange a wine-tasting
  ♦ arrange a wine-tasting session
Weinprobe machen
  → Weinprobe veranstalten
Weinprobenabend, m
  Abend mit Weinprobe, m
  Törggeleabend, m *ÖST*
  ♦ wine-tasting evening

Weinprobenwoche, f
  Törggelewoche, f *ÖST*
  ♦ wine-tasting week
Weinprobe organisieren
  Weinprobe veranstalten
  ♦ organise a wine tasting
  ♦ organize a wine tasting
Weinprobe veranstalten
  Weinprobe machen
  ♦ have a wine tasting
  ♦ have a wine-tasting session
Weinprobierbude, f
  ♦ wine-tasting booth
Wein probieren (generell)
  ♦ taste the wine
  ♦ taste wines
Wein probieren (testen)
  (z.B. testen, ob er trinkbar ist)
  Wein gustieren
  ♦ sample the wine
Weinprobierstand, m
  ♦ wine-tasting stand *AE*
  ♦ wine-tasting stall *BE*
Weinprobierstube, f
  ♦ wine-tasting room
Weinproduzent, m
  → Weinerzeuger
Weinqualität, f
  ♦ wine quality
Weinrebe, f
  ♦ grapevine *AE*
  ♦ grape-vine *BE*
  ♦ vine
Weinregal, n
  ♦ wine rack *AE*
  ♦ wine-rack *BE*
  ♦ wine shelf
Weinregion, f
  Weingebiet, n
  ♦ wine region
Wein reift
  ♦ wine matures
Weinreise, f
  ♦ wine tour
  ♦ wine trip
Weinreise machen
  ♦ go on a wine tour
  ♦ go on a wine trip
Weinreklame, f
  ♦ wine advertisement
Weinrestaurant, n
  ♦ wine restaurant
  ♦ restaurant known for its wine cellar
weinrot, adj
  ♦ wine red, adj
Weinroute, f
  Weinstraße, f
  ♦ wine route
Weinsäufer m *coll*
  ♦ wine tippler *sl*
  ♦ winebibber *sl*
Weinschenke, f
  Weintaverne, f
  ♦ wine tavern
  ♦ wine bar
  ♦ wineshop *AE*
Weinschlauch, m
  ♦ wineskin
Wein schmeckt fad
  ♦ wine tastes flat
  ♦ wine has a flat taste

Wein schmeckt mir immer
  ♦ wine always tastes good to me
  ♦ I always enjoy wine
Wein schmeckt nach dem Faß
  ♦ wine tastes of the wood
Weinschriftsteller, m
  ♦ wine writer
weinselig, adj
  ♦ happy from wine, adj
  ♦ merry from wine, adj
  ♦ tipsy with wine, adj
  ♦ merry with wine, adj
  ♦ vinous, adj *iron*
Weinseminar, n
  ♦ wine seminar
  ♦ seminar on wine
  ♦ seminar about wine
Weinservice m
  ♦ wine service
Weinservicepersonal, n
  ♦ wine service staff
  ♦ wine service personnel
Wein servieren
  Wein ausschenken
  ♦ serve wine
Wein servieren zum Essen
  ♦ serve wine with a meal
  ♦ serve wine with the meal
Weinservierpersonal, n
  ♦ wine waiting staff
  ♦ wine waiting personnel
Weinsieb n
  ♦ wine strainer
Weinsiegel, n
  ♦ wine seal
Weinsnob, m
  ♦ wine snob
Weinsorte, f
  ♦ sort of wine
  ♦ type of wine
  ♦ wine type
  ♦ kind of wine
Weinsortiment, n
  ♦ assortment of wines
  ♦ selection of wines
Weinsoße, f
  ♦ wine sauce
Wein spendieren
  (für ein Fest)
  ♦ buy the wine
  ♦ supply the wine
Weinspezialität, f
  ♦ wine speciality
  ♦ wine specialty *AE*
Weinstadt, f (Großstadt)
  ♦ wine city
Weinstadt, f (kleine Stadt)
  ♦ wine town
Weinstand, m
  ♦ wine stand *AE*
  ♦ wine stall *BE*
Weinstein, m
  ♦ tartar
Weinsteuer f
  ♦ wine tax
  ♦ tax on wine
Weinsteward, m
  ♦ wine steward
Weinstraße, f
  Weinstraße, die, f (Eigenname)
  ♦ wine road

Weinstraße beginnt in X 882

- wine route
- Wine Road, the
- Wine Route, the

Weinstraße beginnt in X
- Wine Road begins in X
- Wine Road starts at X
- Wine Road starts at X *form*

Weinstube, f
- wineshop *AE*
- wine tavern
- tavern
- wine bar

Weinstubenlokal, n
- wine bar premises *pl*

Weintaverne, f
→ Weinschenke

Weintor, n
(an der Deutschen Weinstraße)
- Wine Gate, the

Weintourismus, m
- wine tourism

Weintourist, m
- wine tourist

Weintradition, f
- wine tradition

Weintraube, f
- wine grape

Wein trinken
- drink wine
- have a glass of wine

Weintrinken, n
- wine drinking

Weintrinken und Wandern, n
- wining and hiking

Wein trinken zum Essen
- have wine with one's meal

Weintrinker, m
- wine drinker

Weinumsatz, m
- wine sales *pl*
- wine turnover

Wein- und Spirituosengeschäft, n
- package store *AE*
- off-licence *BE*

Wein- und Spirituosenkette, f
- package store chain *AE*
- off-licence chain *BE*

Weinverbrauch, m
Weinkonsum, m
Weinverzehr, m
- wine consumption
- consumption of wine

Weinverbraucher, m
Weinkonsument, m
- wine consumer

Weinverkauf, m
Weinausschank, m
- wine sale
- sale of wine
- selling wine

Weinverkäufer, m
- wine seller
- wine salesman

Wein verkosten
Wein probieren
- sample wines
- taste wines

Weinverkoster, m
- wine taster

Weinverkostungspersonal, n
- wine-tasting staff
- wine-tasting personnel

Wein verschneiden
- blend wines

Wein versteigern
- auction wine

Weinversteigerung, f
Weinauktion, f
- wine auction

Weinverzehr m
→ Weinverbrauch

Wein vom Faß, m
Wein aus dem Faß, m
- wine from the cask
- wine from the wood

Weinvorrat, m
- wine stock
- stock of wine
- supply of wine
- cellar
- wine supply

Weinvorrat haben
- have a stock of wine

Weinvorschlag, m
- wine suggestion
- suggestion about wine

Wein vorschlagen
- suggest a wine

Weinwagen, m
(im Restaurant)
- wine cart *AE*
- wine trolley *BE*

Weinwanderung, f
- wine ramble
- wine walk

Weinwelt, f
- wine world
- world of wine

Weinwerbung, f
- wine promotion

Weinwettbewerb, m
- wine competition

Wein wird aus Trauben gemacht
- wine is made from grapes

Weinwoche, f
- wine week

Weinwörterbuch, n
- wine dictionary

Weinzecher, m
- wine piddler

Weinzentrum, n
- wine center *AE*
- wine centre *BE*

Wein zusprechen
- do justice to the wine

Weinzwang, m
- obligation to order wine

Weinzwang herrschen
- be obliged to order wine

Weißbrot, n
- white bread
- wheat bread

Weißbrotscheibe, f
- slice of white bread

Weißburgunder, m
Weißer Burgunder, m
- White Burgundy
- Pinot blanc *FR*

weiße Bohne, f
- white bean
- haricot bean
- haricot

weiße Brigade, f
- white brigade

weiße Flotte, f
- white fleet

weiße Industrie, f
(Tourismus)
- white industry

weiße Johannisbeere, f
- white currant

Weiße Meer, das, n
- White Sea, the

weiße Ostern, n
- white Easter

weiße Pracht voll genießen
(Schnee)
- enjoy the white beauty to the fullest

Weißer, m (Wein) *coll*
weißer Wein, m
Weißwein, m
- white, the *coll*
- a white *coll*
- white wine

Weißer Burgunder, m
→ Weißburgunder

weißer Fleck auf der Landkarte, m
- white spot on the map

weißer Pfeffer, m
- white pepper

weißer Rum, m
- white rum

Weißer Sonntag, m
- Low Sunday

weißer Strand, m
- white beach

weiße Rübe, f
Rübe, f
- turnip

weißer Wermut, m
- white vermouth

weiße Soße, f
- white sauce

weiße Wandtafel, f
- white board

weiße Weihnacht, f
(mit Schnee)
- white Christmas

Weißherbst, m
(Wein)
- Weissherbst

Weißkohl, m
Weißkraut, n
- white cabbage

Weißkohlsalat, m
Weißkrautsalat, m
- white-cabbage salad

Weißkraut, n
→ Weißkohl

Weißling, m
→ Merlan

Weißsekt, m
weißer Sekt, m
- white champagne

Weißwein, m
Weißer, m *coll*
- white wine
- the white *coll*
- a white *coll*

Weißwein bestellen
- order (a) white wine

Weißweinerzeugung, f
 ♦ white wine production
Weißweinessig, m
 ♦ white wine vinegar
Weißweingebiet, n
 ♦ white wine region
Weißweinglas, n
 ♦ white-wine glass
Weißweinkarte, f
 ♦ white-wine list
Weißweinkelch, m
 ♦ white-wine goblet
Weißweinland, n
 Weißweingebiet, n
 ♦ white wine country
Weißweinprobe, f
 ♦ white wine tasting
Weißweinsorte, f
 ♦ white wine variety
Weißweinsoße, f
 ♦ white wine sauce
Weißweintraube, f
 ♦ white-wine grape
Weiterbildung, f
 ♦ further education
Weiterbildungskurs, m
 Weiterbildungslehrgang, m
 ♦ further education course
Weiterbildungsprogramm, n
 ♦ further education program *AE*
 ♦ further education programme *BE*
Weiterbildungsseminar, n
 ♦ further-education seminar
 ♦ educational seminar
Weiterbildungszentrum, n
 ♦ continuing education center *AE*
 ♦ center for continuing education *AE*
 ♦ continuing education centre *BE*
 ♦ centre for continuing education *BE*
weiterbleiben (für drei Tage)
 weiterwohnen (für drei Tage)
 ♦ stay on (for three more days)
weiterbleiben in einem Hotel
 weiterwohnen in einem Hotel
 ♦ stay on at a hotel
Weiterbuchung, f
 ♦ onward booking
weitere Aufenthaltsnacht, f
 zusätzliche Aufenthaltsnacht f
 ♦ extra night of stay
 ♦ additional night of stay
weitere Aufenthaltswoche, f
 zusätzliche Aufenthaltswoche f
 ♦ extra week of stay
 ♦ additonal week of stay
Weitere Auskünfte durch ...
 ♦ Further information from ...
Weitere Auskünfte sind erhältlich bei ...
 ♦ Further information can be obtained from ...
Weitere Einzelheiten auf Anfrage
 ♦ Further details on application
Weitere Einzelheiten sind erhältlich durch ...
 ♦ Further particulars can be obtained through ...
weitere Einzelheiten zusenden jm auf Anfrage
 ♦ send s.o. further details on application
weitere Informationen anfordern bei jm
 ♦ write for more information to s.o.
weitere Nacht, f
 → zusätzliche Nacht

weitere Nacht bleiben
 Nacht länger bleiben
 ♦ stay on a night
 ♦ stay one more night
weiteren Tag bleiben
 Tag länger bleiben
 ♦ stay one more day
 ♦ stay on a day
weiterer Aufenthaltsmonat, m
 zusätzlicher Aufenthaltsmonat m
 ♦ extra month of stay
 ♦ additional month of stay
weiterer Aufenthaltstag, m
 zusätzlicher Aufenthaltstag m
 ♦ extra day of stay
 ♦ additional day of stay
weitere Reisen machen
 ♦ make further journeys
 ♦ make further trips
 ♦ make further tours
weiterer Tag, m
 → zusätzlicher Tag
weiterer Verlauf des Abends, m
 ♦ further course of the evening
weiteres Bett, n
 ♦ another bed
weiteres Bett, n (extra)
 zusätzliches Bett n
 Zusatzbett, n
 ♦ extra bed
 ♦ additional bed
weiteres Bettchen, n
 zusätzliches Bettchen, n
 Zusatzbettchen, n
 ♦ extra bedlet
 ♦ additional bedlet
weitere Woche, f
 → zusätzliche Woche
weitere zwei Wochen bleiben
 zwei weitere Wochen bleiben
 ♦ stay for another two weeks
weiterfahren (Auto)
 ♦ drive on
weiterfahren in die falsche Richtung (Auto)
 weiterfahren in der falschen Richtung
 ♦ drive on in the wrong direction
weiterfahren nach X (Auto)
 ♦ drive on to X
weiterfahren nach X (generell)
 ♦ go on to X
 ♦ travel on ticket
 ♦ proceed to X
 ♦ continue one's journey to X
weiterfliegen (nach X)
 ♦ fly on (to X)
 ♦ continue one's flight (to X)
Weiterflugschein, m
 ♦ onward air ticket
 ♦ onward ticket
weitergehen zu Fuß
 ♦ continue on foot
Weitermarsch, m
 ♦ onward march
weitermarschieren (nach X)
 ♦ march on (to X)
Weiterreise, f
 ♦ onward journey
 ♦ continuation of the journey
 ♦ second (third etc.) leg of the journey
Weiterreise mit dem Zug, f
 ♦ onward journey by train

weiterreisen
 Reise fortsetzen
 ♦ travel on(wards)
 ♦ continue one's journey
 ♦ continue one's trip
 ♦ proceed on one's journey *lit*
 ♦ go on
Weiterreisen, n
 Weiterreiseverkehr, m
 ♦ onward travel
weiterreisen auf dem Luftweg
 weiterreisen mit dem Flugzeug
 ♦ continue by air
weiter reisen (größere Distanz)
 ♦ travel farther
 ♦ travel further
weiterreisen nach C über B
 ♦ continue one's journey to C via B
 ♦ continue to C via B
weiterreisen nach Frankreich
 ♦ travel on into France
 ♦ continue (one's journey) to France
weiterreisen nach X
 ♦ travel on to X
 ♦ continue (one's journey) to X
 ♦ continue (one's tour) to X
 ♦ proceed (on one's journey) to X
weiterreisen von X
 ♦ travel on from X
Weiterreservierung, f
 ♦ onward reservation
 ♦ continuing reservation
weiterschlafen
 ♦ sleep on
weiterstapfen
 ♦ trudge on
weiter umherreisen
 ♦ travel farther afield
weiterverkaufen etw (an jn)
 wieder verkaufen etw (an jn)
 ♦ resell s.th. (to s.o.)
weitervermieten etw
 → untervermieten, wieder vermieten
Weitervermietung, f
 → Untervermietung
weiterverpachten etw
 → unterverpachten etw
Weiterverpachtung, f
 → Unterverpachtung
weiterwandern
 ♦ walk on
weiterziehen
 ♦ move on
weite Strecke, f
 lange Strecke, f
 ♦ long distance
 ♦ long route
weitgereist, adj
 ♦ widely travelled, adj
 ♦ widely traveled, adj *AE*
 ♦ well-travelled, adj
 ♦ well-traveled, adj *AE*
weitgereister Gast, m
 ♦ widely traveled guest *AE*
 ♦ widely travelled guest *BE*
 ♦ well-traveled guest *AE*
 ♦ well-travelled guest *BE*
weitsichtige Planung, f
 ♦ farsighted planning *AE*
 ♦ far-sighted planning *BE*

Weitsprung

Weitsprung, m
 ♦ long jump
 ♦ broad jump AE
Weizen, m
 ♦ wheat
Weizenbier, n
 ♦ wheat beer
Weizenbrot, n
 ♦ wheat bread
Weizengrieß, m
 ♦ farina AE
 ♦ semolina BE
Weizenkeimöl, n
 ♦ wheatgerm oil
Weizenkleie, f
 ♦ wheat bran
Weizenmehl, n
 ♦ wheat flour
Welcher Jahrgang ist dieser Wein?
 ♦ What vintage is this wine?
Welche Zimmernummer haben Sie?
 ♦ What is your room number, please?
Wellblechsiedlung, f
 Slumsiedlung, f
 ♦ shanty town
Wellenbad, n
 Wellenbecken, n
 ♦ wave pool
Wellenbaden, n
 ♦ surf bathing
Wellenbrecher, m
 ♦ breakwater
Wellenfreibad, n
 ♦ outdoor wave pool
Wellenhallenbad, n
 Hallenwellenbad, n
 ♦ indoor wave pool
Wellenmaschine f
 (im Schwimmbad)
 ♦ wave machine
Wellenreiten, n
 → Surfen
Wellenreiter, m
 → Surfer
Welle von Reisenden, f
 Reisewelle, f
 ♦ surge of travellers
 ♦ surge of travelers AE
Welle von Reisenden bringen nach X
 Reisewelle nach X bringen
 ♦ bring a surge of travellers to X
 ♦ bring a surge of travelers to X AE
Wellnesshotel, n
 ♦ wellness hotel
Wels, m
 Waller, m
 ♦ sheatfish
 ♦ sheathfish
 ♦ catfish
Weltatlas, m
 ♦ world atlas
Weltausstellung, f
 ♦ world expo
 ♦ world exposition
 ♦ world exhibition
 ♦ world fair
Weltbad, n
 Kurort von Weltruf, m
 ♦ spa of world renown

weltbekannt, adj
 ♦ world-renowned, adj
 ♦ known all over the world, adj
weltbekannt, adv
 von Weltruf, adv
 ♦ of world renown, adv
Welt bereisen
 durch die Welt reisen
 ♦ travel the world
 ♦ tour the world
weltberühmt, adj
 ♦ world-famous, adj
 ♦ famous all over the world, adj
 ♦ famous the world over, adj
weltberühmte Küche, f (Speisen)
 ♦ world-famous cuisine
 ♦ world-famous cooking
Welt der Abenteuer, f
 ♦ world of adventures
Weltenbummler, m
 Globetrotter, m
 Reiseonkel, m humor
 Reisetante, f humor
 ♦ globetrotter
Welt für sich, f
 ♦ world of its own
Welt für sich sein
 ♦ be a world of its own
Welthafen, m
 ♦ world port
Welthandelsmesse, f
 ♦ World Trade Fair
Welt hinter sich lassen
 Trubel hinter sich lassen
 ♦ leave the world behind
Weltjugendtag, m
 ♦ World Youth Day, the
Weltklassehotel, n
 ♦ world-class hotel
Weltklasseorchester, n
 ♦ world-class orchestra
Weltkonferenz f
 ♦ world conference
Weltkongreß m
 ♦ world convention
 ♦ world congress
Weltkreuzfahrt, f
 Kreuzfahrt um die Welt, f
 ♦ world cruise
 ♦ round-the-world cruise
 ♦ cruise (a)round the world
Weltkulturerbe, n
 ♦ world's cultural heritage
Weltkulturerbe erklären etw
 zum Weltkulturerbe erklären etw
 ♦ declare s.th. part of the world's cultural heri-
 ♦ tage
weltlicher Besucher, m
 (Gegensatz zu geistlichem Besucher)
 ♦ secular visitor
Weltmeister, m
 ♦ world champion
Weltmeisterschaft, f
 ♦ world championship
Weltmesse, f
 ♦ world fair
Weltpremière, f
 ♦ world premiere
 ♦ world première BE

Weltpremière haben
 ♦ have its world premiere AE
 ♦ have its world première BE
Weltpublikum, n
 ♦ world audience
Weltraumtourismus, m
 ♦ space tourism
Weltraumtourist, m
 ♦ space tourist
Weltreise, f (generell)
 ♦ world tour
 ♦ world trip
 ♦ tour (a)round the world
 ♦ trip (a)round the world
 ♦ journey (a)round the world
Weltreise, f (Seereise)
 ♦ world voyage
 ♦ voyage round the world
 ♦ round-the-world voyage
Weltreise machen
 ♦ go on a world tour
 ♦ go on a world trip
Weltreisen, n
 Weltreiseverkehr, m
 ♦ world travel
Weltreisender, m
 ♦ world traveller
 ♦ world traveler AE
 ♦ globetrotter
Weltruf, m
 ♦ world repute
Weltstadt, f
 ♦ cosmopolitan city
 ♦ metropolis
Weltstadthotel, n
 weltstädtisches Hotel, n
 ♦ metropolitan hotel
weltstädtisch, adj
 ♦ metropolitan, adj
weltstädtische Atmosphäre, f
 Weltstadtatmosphäre, f
 ♦ metropolitan atmosphere
 ♦ cosmopolitan atmosphere
weltstädtisches Hotel, n
 → Weltstadthotel
Welttourismus, m
 ♦ world tourism
Welttourismusmarkt, m
 ♦ world tourism market
 ♦ world tourist market
Welt-Tourismus-Organisation, f
 WTO, f
 ♦ World Tourism Organisation
 ♦ World Tourism Organization
 ♦ WTO
Welttournee, f
 ♦ world tour
Welt umsegeln
 ♦ circumnavigate the world
Weltumsegelung, f
 ♦ circumnavigation of the world
Weltumsegler, m
 ♦ round-the-world sailor
weltweit, adj
 ♦ worldwide, adj AE
 ♦ world-wide, adj BE
weltweit beachtete Fachmesse, f
 ♦ trade fair of global scope
weltweite Buchung, f
 ♦ worldwide booking AE
 ♦ world-wide booking BE

884

weltweites Buchungssystem, n
♦ worldwide booking system AE
♦ world-wide booking system BE
weltweites Hotelreservierungssystem, n
♦ worldwide hotel reservation system AE
♦ world-wide hotel reservation system BE
weltweites Reservierungssystem, n
♦ worldwide reservation system AE
♦ world-wide reservation system BE
Wem gehört dieses Haus?
♦ Who is the owner of this house?
Wendekreis des Krebses, m
♦ tropic of Cancer
Wendekreis des Krebses überqueren
♦ cross the tropic of Cancer
Wendekreis des Steinbocks, m
♦ tropic of Capricorn
Wendekreis des Steinbocks überqueren
♦ cross the tropic of Capricorn
Wendeltreppe, f
♦ spiral staircase
♦ winding staircase
wenden
→ umkehren
wenden sich an jn
♦ contact s.o.
♦ get in touch with s.o.
♦ apply to s.o.
Wendepunkt, m
♦ turning point
wenig bekannt, adj
♦ little known, adj
wenig bekannter Ferienort, m
♦ little known resort
wenig bekannter Ort, m
♦ little known place
wenig besucht, adj
♦ little visited, adj
wenig besuchte Insel, f
♦ little visited island
wenige Gäste, m pl
♦ few guests
wenige Gäste haben
♦ have few guests
weniger Aktiven, die, pl
♦ less active, the pl
♦ less energetic, the pl
♦ not-so-active, the pl
weniger aktiver Gast, m
♦ less active guest
♦ less energetic guest
weniger als 24 Stunden bleiben
♦ stay less than 24 hours
weniger als normalgroß, adj
klein, adj
♦ undersized, adj
weniger bekannt, adj
♦ less well-known, adj
♦ lesser known, adj
weniger bekannter Ort, m
♦ less well-known resort
♦ lesser known place
weniger besucht, adj
♦ less visited, adj
♦ less frequented, adj
weniger besuchtes Gebiet, n
♦ less frequented area
weniger frequentiert, adj
♦ less frequented, adj
wenig essen
♦ eat little

wenig Geld ausgeben
♦ be a low spender
wenig kosten
♦ cost little
wenig Platz haben
zu wenig Platz haben
♦ be cramped for space
wenigstens eine Nacht bleiben
♦ stay at least one night
Wenn die Katze aus dem Haus ist, tanzen die Mäuse
♦ When the cat is away, the mice will play
Wenn es am besten schmeckt, soll man aufhören
♦ One should leave off with an appetite
wenn Wände reden könnten
♦ If walls could speak
Werbeabend, m
♦ promotional evening
Werbeabend durchführen
♦ run a promotional evening
Werbeagentur f
♦ advertising agency
Werbeagenturmitarbeiter, m
♦ advertising agent
Werbeaktion, f
♦ publicity campaign
♦ promotional action
♦ advertising campaign
Werbeaktivität, f
♦ promotion activity AE
♦ promotional activity BE
Werbeangebot, n
♦ promotional offer
Werbearbeit, f
♦ promotion work AE
♦ promotional work BE
Werbeaufwand, m
♦ advertising expenditure
Werbeaufwendungen, f pl
♦ promotion expenses pl
♦ advertising expenses pl
Werbeausgaben, f pl
♦ advertising expenses pl
Werbeausstellung f
♦ promotional exhibition
♦ promotional show
Werbebotschaft, f
♦ advertising message
Werbebroschüre, f
Werbeprospekt, m
♦ promotional brochure
♦ advertising brochure
Werbebudget n
♦ advertising budget
♦ publicity budget
Werbeexperte, m
♦ advertising expert
Werbefaltblatt, n
Werbeblatt, n
♦ advertising leaflet
Werbefilm, m
♦ promotion film AE
♦ promotion movie AE
♦ promotional film BE
Werbefläche, f
♦ advertising space
Werbefoto, n
♦ promotional photograph
♦ promotional photo
Werbefotograf, m
♦ commercial photographer

Werbefotografie, f
♦ promotional photography
Werbegebühr, f
♦ advertising charge
Werbegemeinschaft, f
♦ advertising cooperative
Werbegeschenk, n
♦ giveaway AE
♦ give-away BE
♦ promotional gift
Werbeidee, f
♦ promotion idea
♦ promotional idea
Werbekampagne, f
♦ advertising campaign
♦ promotional campaign
♦ promotion campaign
♦ publicity campaign
Werbekampagne starten
♦ launch a promotion campaign
♦ launch a promotional campaign
♦ launch an advertising campaign
Werbekonzept, n
♦ advertising concept
Werbekosten, pl
♦ advertising costs pl
♦ advertising cost
♦ promotion costs pl
♦ promotion cost
♦ public relations costs pl
Werbeliteratur, f
Werbematerial, n
♦ promotion literature AE
♦ promotional literature BE
Werbemaßnahme, f
Werbeaktivität, f
♦ promotional activity BE
♦ promotion activity AE
Werbematerial, n
♦ advertising material
♦ promotion material AE
♦ promotional material BE
♦ advertising aids
♦ promotion matter package
Werbemethode, f
♦ promotional method
Werbemöglichkeit, f
♦ promotional opportunity
werben für eine Fahrt
♦ advertise a trip
werben für einen Ferienort
♦ promote a resort
werben für eine Reise
♦ advertise a journey
♦ advertise a tour
♦ advertise a trip
werben für ein Hotel
Werbung machen für ein Hotel
♦ promote a hotel
werben für etw
fördern etw
♦ promote s.th.
werben für X als Tagungszielort
werben für X als Tagungsdestination
♦ promote X as a meeting destination
Werbepauschale, f
♦ advertising package
♦ promotional package
Werbepersonal, n
♦ advertising personnel
♦ advertising staff

Werbeplakat

Werbeplakat, n
♦ advertising poster
Werbeplan, m
♦ advertising plan
Werbepreis, m
♦ promotional price
♦ promotional rate
Werbeprospekt, m
Werbebroschüre, f
♦ advertising brochure
♦ promotional brochure
Werbereise, f
♦ promotional tour
♦ promotional trip
♦ promotional journey
♦ promotion tour
♦ promotion trip
Werbeschau, f
♦ promotional show
Werbestrategie, f
♦ advertising strategy
Werbeträger, m
♦ advertising media
Werbeveranstaltung f
♦ promotional event
Werbevideo, n
♦ promotional video
Wer bezahlt, bestimmt
Wer zahlt, bestimmt
♦ He who pays the piper calls the tune
♦ He who calls the piper calls the tune
Werbung machen für ein Hotel
→ werben für ein Hotel
Werbungskosten, pl
(Steuer)
Werbungsaufwand, m
♦ professional outlay
♦ professional expenditure
Werbung und Verkaufsförderung, f
♦ advertising and sales promotion
Wer die Wahl hat, hat die Qual
♦ The wider the choice, the greater the trouble
Werft, f (Hangar)
♦ hangar
Werft, f (Schiff, Boot)
♦ shipyard
♦ boatyard
Werk ausstellen
♦ display a work
Werksausflug, m
Betriebsausflug m
♦ works outing
Werksbesuch, m
Fabrikbesuch, m
Werkbesuch, m
♦ visit to a factory
♦ factory visit
Werksführung, f
Werksbesichtigung, f
Rundgang durch das Werk, m
Rundgang durch die Fabrik, m
♦ tour of the plant
♦ tour of the factory
Werkskantine, f
Fabrikkantine, f
♦ works canteen
♦ factory canteen
Werkstatt, f
♦ workshop

Werktag, m
♦ working day
♦ workday
werktags, adv
wochentags, adv
♦ during the week, adv
♦ on weekdays, adv
Wermut, m (Getränk)
Wermutwein, m
♦ vermouth
Wermut, m (Pflanze)
♦ wormwood
Wermutbruder, m *coll*
Säufer, m
♦ wino *coll*
Wer rastet, der rostet
♦ rolling stone gathers no moss
♦ A rolling stone gathers no moss
Wer schläft, sündigt nicht
♦ He who sleeps does not sin
Wer sich entschuldigt, klagt sich an
♦ He who excuses himself, accuses himself
Wert legen auf etw
♦ put the accent on s.th.
♦ place the emphasis on s.th.
♦ attach great importance to s.th.
♦ be important for s.o.
Wert legen auf Komfort und Service
♦ attach great importance to comfort and service
♦ put the accent on comfort and service
♦ place the emphasis on comfort and service
♦ appreciate comfort and service
Wertminderung, f
♦ reduction in value
♦ loss in value
♦ depreciation in value
Wertpaket, n
♦ insured package *AE*
♦ insured parcel *BE*
Wertsachen deponieren (im Hotelsafe)
♦ deposit valuables (in the hotel safe)
Wertschöpfung, f
♦ value added
Wertsteigerung, f
♦ increase in value
wertvoll, adj
♦ valuable, adj
wertvolle Hilfe geben
♦ give valuable help
wertvolle Information, f
wertvolle Informationen, f pl
♦ valuable information *sg*
wertvolle Möbel, n pl
♦ valuable furniture *sg*
Wer zahlt die Rechnung?
♦ Who will be paying the check? *AE*
♦ Who will be paying the bill?
Wer zuerst kommt, mahlt zuerst
♦ The early bird gets the worm
♦ First come, first served
Wer zuerst kommt, wird zuerst bedient
♦ First come, first served
Weserbergland, n
(Region)
♦ Weser Mountains, the *pl*
♦ Weser Hills, the *pl*
Weshalb reisen Sie vorzeitig ab?
♦ Why are you leaving earlier than expected?

Westafrika
♦ West Africa
♦ Western Africa
Westafrikaner, m
♦ West African
westafrikanisch, adj
♦ West African, adj
Westalpen, pl
♦ Western Alps, the *pl*
Westappartement, n
♦ west-facing apartment
♦ apartment facing west
Westapsis, f
♦ west apsis
Westbalkon, m
♦ west-facing balcony
♦ balcony facing west
West-Berlin
♦ West Berlin
westdeutsch, adj
♦ West German, adj
Westdeutscher, m
♦ West German
Westdeutschland
♦ West Germany
Westeingang, m
♦ west entrance
Westengland
♦ Western England
♦ West England
Westerwald, m
(Region)
♦ Westerwald, the
♦ Westerwald Forest, the
Westeuropa
♦ West Europe
♦ Western Europe
Westeuropäer, m
♦ West European
♦ Western European
westeuropäisch, adj
♦ West European, adj
♦ Western European, adj
Westfale, m
♦ Westphalian
Westfalen
(Land)
♦ Westphalia
Westfälin, f
♦ Westphalian girl
♦ Westphalian woman
♦ Westphalian
westfälisch, adj
♦ Westphalian, adj
westfälische Art, adv *gastr*
♦ Westphalian style, adv *gastr*
Westfälische Pforte, f
(Region)
Porta Westfalica, f
♦ Westphalian Gate, the
♦ Westphalian Gap, the
♦ Porta Westfalica
westfälischer Schinken, m
♦ Westphalian ham
Westfassade, f
♦ west façade
♦ west facade *AE*
♦ west front
Westfenster, n
♦ west-facing window

- ◆ window facing west
- ◆ window to the west

Westflügel, m
- Westtrakt, m
- ◆ west wing

Westflügelanbau, m
- ◆ west wing annex *AE*
- ◆ west wing annexe *BE*

Westfranke, m (historisch)
- ◆ West Frank

Westfriesischen Inseln, die, f pl
- ◆ West Frisians, the *pl*

Westfriesland
- (Region)
- ◆ West Friesland

Westgebäude, n
- ◆ west building

Westgrenze, f
- ◆ west border
- ◆ western border

Westhang, m
- ◆ west-facing slope
- ◆ west-facing hillside

Westinder, m
- ◆ West Indian

Westinderin, f
- ◆ West Indian girl
- ◆ West Indian woman
- ◆ West Indian

Westindien
- ◆ West Indies, the *pl*

westindisch, adj
- ◆ West Indian, adj

Westküste, f
- ◆ west coast
- ◆ western coast

Westlage, f
- ◆ west-facing position

westliche Route, f
- → Westroute

westliches Mittelmeer, n
- ◆ Western Mediterranean, the

westlich liegen von etw
- ◆ lie west of s.th.
- ◆ be situated to the west of s.th.

westlichst, adj
- ◆ westernmost, adj
- ◆ most westerly, adj

westlichster Punkt, m
- ◆ most westerly point

westlichste Spitze, f
- ◆ westernmost tip

westlich von etw
- ◆ west of s.th.
- ◆ to the west of s.th.

Westloggia, f
- ◆ west-facing loggia
- ◆ loggia facing west

West-Ost-Flug, m
- ◆ west-east flight

West-Ost-Straße, f
- ◆ west-east road

West-Ost-Verbindung, f
- ◆ west-east link
- ◆ west-east connection

Westpreußen
- ◆ West Prussia

Westroute, f
- Weststrecke, f
- westliche Route, f

westliche Strecke, f
- ◆ western route

Westsamoa
- ◆ Western Samoa

westsamoanisch, adj
- ◆ Western Samoan, adj

Westschweiz, f
- ◆ Western Switzerland
- ◆ West Switzerland

Westseite, f
- ◆ west side
- ◆ western side

Weststrand, m
- ◆ west beach

Westtor, n
- ◆ west gate
- ◆ western gate

Westtribüne, f
- ◆ west stand
- ◆ west stands *pl*

Westturm, m
- ◆ west tower
- ◆ western tower

Westufer, n (Fluß)
- ◆ west bank

Westufer, n (Meer, Binnensee)
- ◆ west shore
- ◆ western shore

Westverkehr, m
- Verkehr nach Westen, m
- ◆ westbound traffic

Westwales
- ◆ West Wales

westwärts reisen
- ◆ travel westwards
- ◆ travel westward

westwärts wandern
- ◆ walk westwards

westwärts ziehen
- westwärts wandern
- ◆ migrate westwards

Westzimmer, n
- Zimmer nach Westen, n
- nach Westen gelegenes Zimmer, n
- ◆ west-facing room
- ◆ room facing west

Wettangeln, n
- Angelwettbewerb, m
- ◆ angling contest

Wettannahmestelle, f
- Wettannahme, f
- Wettbüro, n
- ◆ betting office
- ◆ betting shop

Wettbewerb, m
- Konkurrenz, f
- ◆ competition
- ◆ rivalry

Wettbewerb abhalten
- ◆ hold a competition

Wettbewerbe aller Art, m pl
- ◆ competitions of all kinds *pl*

Wettbewerb gewinnen
- ◆ win a competition

Wettbewerb ins Leben rufen
- Wettbewerb zum ersten Mal durchführen
- ◆ launch a competition

Wettbewerb machen
- ◆ have a competition
- ◆ have competitions
- ◆ hold a competition

Wettbewerbsgewinner, m
- ◆ competition winner
- ◆ winner of the competition

Wettbewerb sponsern
- ◆ sponsor a competition
- ◆ sponsor a contest

Wettbewerbssituation, f
- ◆ competitive situation

Wettbewerbsvorteil, m
- ◆ competitive advantage
- ◆ competitive edge

Wettbewerbsvorteil haben
- ◆ have a competitive advantage

Wettbewerbsvorteil halten
- ◆ keep one's competitive edge

Wettbewerb um Touristen, m
- ◆ competition for tourists

Wettbewerb veranstalten
- ◆ organise a competition
- ◆ organize a competition

Wettbewerb verstärken
- Wettbewerb intensivieren
- ◆ intensify competition

Wette eingehen
- ◆ make a bet

wetten
- ◆ bet

Wetteramt, n
- ◆ meteorological office

Wetterbedingungen, f pl
- ◆ weather conditions *pl*

Wetterbericht, m
- ◆ weather report

Wetterbericht hören
- ◆ listen to the weather report

Wetterlage, f
- ◆ weather situation

Wettersteingebirge, n
- (Region)
- ◆ Wetterstein Mountains, the *pl*

Wettervorhersage, f
- Wetterprognose, f
- ◆ weather forecast

Wettessen, n
- ◆ eating competition
- ◆ eating contest

Wettkampf, m
- ◆ contest

Wettkampf abhalten
- ◆ hold a contest

Wettkämpfe aller Art, m pl
- ◆ contests of all kinds *pl*

Wettkochen, n
- Kochwettbewerb, m
- ◆ cook-off *inform*

Wettrennen, n
- ◆ running race

Wettrinken, n
- Trinkwettstreit, m
- ◆ drinking contest

Wettschießen, n
- Preisschießen, n
- ◆ shooting match

Wettsegeln, n
- → Jachtsport

Wfl., f
- → Wohnfläche

Whg., f
- Wohnung, f
- ◆ apt. *AE*
- ◆ apartment *AE*

Whirlpool

- flt. *BE*
- flat *BE*

Whirlpool, m
Wirbelbad, n
- whirlpool

Whirlpoolanlage, f
- whirlpool system

Whirlpoolbenutzung, f
- use of a whirlpool
- using a whirlpool

Whirlpoolwanne, f
- whirlpool tub

Whiskeycocktail, m
- whiskey cocktail

Whisky, m (nicht schottisch)
- whiskey

Whisky, m (schottisch)
- whisky
- Scotch *AE*

Whiskybecher, m
- whisky tumbler

Whiskyerzeuger, m
- whisky producer

Whiskyfest, n
- whisky festival
- whiskey festival

Whiskyflasche, f
- whisky bottle
- whiskey bottle

Whiskyflasche kreisen lassen
- pass the whisky bottle round
- pass the whiskey bottle round

Whiskyglas, n
- whisky glass
- whisky tumbler

Whisky herstellen
Whisky machen
- make whisky

Whiskyherstellung, f
- whisky-making

Whisky mit Eiswürfeln, m
- whisky on the rocks
- Scotch on the rocks
- whiskey on the rocks

Whisky mit Soda, m
Whisky Soda, m
- whisky and soda
- Scotch and soda
- whiskey and soda

Whiskyprobe, f
- whisky tasting
- whisky-tasting session
- whiskey tasting
- whiskey-tasting session

Whiskyprobenabend, m
- whisky-tasting evening
- whiskey-tasting evening

Whisky probieren
- taste whisky
- taste whiskey

Whisky pur, bitte
Einen Whisky pur, bitte
- A neat whisky, please *BE*
- A neat whiskey, please *BE*
- A straight whisky, please *AE*
- A straight whiskey, please *AE*

Whisky pur, m
unverdünnter Whisky, m
- neat whisky *BE*
- neat whiskey *BE*

- straight whisky *AE*
- straight whiskey *AE*

Whisky pur mögen
- like one's whisky neat
- like one's whiskey neat
- like one's whisky straight
- like one's whiskey straight

Whisky pur trinken
- drink one's whisky straight
- drink one's whiskey straight
- drink one's whisky neat
- drink one's whiskey neat

Whiskysoße, f
- whisky sauce

Whisky Toddy, m
- whisky toddy

Whisky trinken
- drink whisky
- drink whiskey

Whiskytrinker, m
- whisky drinker
- Scotch drinker

Whiskyumsatz, m
- whisky sales *pl*

Whisky verkosten
- sample whisky
- sample whiskey

Whist, n
- whist

Whistrunde, f
- whist drive

Whist spielen
- play whist

Whistwettbewerb, m
- whist competition

Whitney-Rack n
(Rezeption)
- Whitney rack

Whitney System n
(Rezeption)
- Whitney system

wichtige Persönlichkeit, f
VIP m
- very important person
- VIP

wichtiger Gast, m
- important guest

Wickel, m *med*
- wrap *med*

Wickeleinrichtung, f
- baby changing facility

Wickelkommode, f
- changing unit

Wickelraum, m
(für Babies)
- baby changing room
- diaper changing room *AE*
- nappy changing room *BE coll*
- baby care room

Wickelstation, f
- baby station

Wickeltisch, m
- table for diaper changing *AE*
- table for nappy changing *BE coll*
- nappy changing table *BE coll*
- changing table *AE*

Widerruf, m (Stornierung)
→ Stornierung

Widerruf, m (von Erlaubnis)
- revocation

wie abgemacht
wie vereinbart
- as arranged

Wie breit ist das Zimmer?
- How wide is the room?
- What is the width of the room?

Wiederbeschaffungskosten, pl
- replacement costs *pl*
- replacement cost

wieder besuchen etw
nochmals besuchen etw
erneut besuchen etw
- revisit s.th.

wieder besucht, adj
erneut besucht, adj
- revisited, adj

wieder buchen etw
erneut buchen etw
umbuchen etw
- rebook s.th.

Wiedereinreise, f
- re-entry

Wiedereinreiseformular, n
- re-entry form

Wiedereinreisegenehmigung, f
- re-entry permit

wieder einreisen (in ein Land)
- reenter (a country) *AE*
- re-enter (a country) *BE*

wiedereröffnen (etw)
- reopen (s.th.)

wiedereröffnen nach umfangreicher Renovierung
- reopen after extensive refurbishment

wiedereröffnet nach umfangreichen Reparaturen
- reopened after extensive repairs

Wiedereröffnung f
- reopening

Wiedereröffnungskosten, pl
- reopening costs *pl*
- reopening expenses *pl*

Wiederherstellung der Gesundheit, m
- restoration of one's health
- restoration of s.o.'s health
- health restoration

Wiederholer, m
Repeater, m
- repeater

wiederholter Besuch, m
Wiederholungsbesuch, m
- repeat visit

wiederholter Urlaubsbesuch, m
- repeat vacation visit *AE*
- repeat holiday visit *BE*

Wiederholung einer Einladung, f
Einladungswiederholung, f
- renewal of an invitation

Wiederholungsbesuch, m
→ wiederholter Besuch

Wiederholungsbesucher, m
wiederholter Besucher, m
- repeat visitor

Wiederholungbucher m
- repeat booker
- repeater

Wiederholungsbuchung f
- repeat booking

Wiederholungsfahrt, f
- repeat trip

Wiederholungsgast, m
wiederkehrender Gast, m

- ♦ repeat guest
- ♦ repeater

Wiederholungsgeschäft, n
- ♦ repeat business

Wiederholungskunde, m
- ♦ repeat customer
- ♦ repeater

Wiederholungskurs, m
→ Auffrischungskurs

Wiederholungsreise, f
- ♦ repeat journey
- ♦ repeat trip
- ♦ repeat tour

Wiederholungsreisen, n
Wiederholungsreiseverkehr, m
wiederholtes Reisen, n
- ♦ repeat travel

Wiederholungsreisender, m
- ♦ repeat traveler AE
- ♦ repeat traveller BE

Wiederholungsreservierung, f
- ♦ repeat reservation

Wiederholungsurlauber, m
Wiederholungsferiengast, m
- ♦ repeat vacationer AE
- ♦ repeat holidaymaker BE
- ♦ repeater

wieder in Betrieb sein
- ♦ be running again
- ♦ be operating again

wiederkehrender Gast, m
→ Wiederholungsgast

wiederkommen
- ♦ come again
- ♦ come back
- ♦ return

wieder nach Hause zurückkehren
- ♦ return home again

Wiedersehen! coll
Tschüs! coll
- ♦ Bye! BE coll
- ♦ By! AE coll

Wiedersehen, n
- ♦ reunion

Wiedersehen (mit X), n
Wiedersehen mit London, n
- ♦ Revisited
- ♦ London Revisited

Wiedersehensfeier, f
- ♦ reunion celebration

Wiedersehensfest, n
- ♦ reunion party

Wiederverkäufer, m
- ♦ retailer

wieder vermieten etw (Immobilie)
erneut vermieten etw
weitervermieten etw
- ♦ relet s.th. BE
- ♦ rerent s.th. AE

Wiedervermietung, f (Immobilie)
- ♦ rerenting AE
- ♦ rerental AE
- ♦ reletting BE

Wiederverwertung, f
- ♦ salvage

wie die Made im Speck coll
- ♦ as snug as a bug in a rug coll
- ♦ snug as a bug in a rug coll

wie eine Suppe ohne Salz
- ♦ like ham without eggs

Wiege f
- ♦ cradle

wie gewünscht
- ♦ as requested

Wie groß ist Ihre Gruppe?
- ♦ How many are there in your party?

Wie hat Ihnen das Essen geschmeckt?
- ♦ How did you like the meal?

Wie heißen Sie?
- ♦ What is your name?

Wie hoch ist das Zimmer?
- ♦ How high is the room?
- ♦ What is the height of the room?

wie Hotels eben sind
- ♦ as hotels go

Wie ist Ihr Hotel?
- ♦ What is your hotel like?

Wie ist Ihr Name, bitte?
- ♦ What name is it, please?

Wie komme ich von hier aus zum Hotel?
- ♦ How do I get to the hotel from here?

Wie lange beabsichtigen Sie zu bleiben?
- ♦ How long do you intend to stay?
- ♦ How long do you plan to stay?

Wie lange kann ich hier parken?
- ♦ How long can I park here?

Wie lange werden Sie bleiben?
- ♦ How long will you be staying?

Wie lange werden Sie hier sein?
- ♦ How long will you be here?

Wie lang ist das Zimmer?
- ♦ How long is the room?
- ♦ What is the length of the room?

Wie man ißt, so arbeitet man
- ♦ People work as fast as they eat

Wie man sich bettet, so liegt man
- ♦ As one makes one's bed so one must lie
- ♦ As you make your bed so you must lie on it

Wie möchten Sie Ihren Kaffee?
- ♦ How do you like your coffee?

Wienerart, adv gastr
nach Wienerart, adv gastr
- ♦ Viennese style, adv gastr

Wiener Becken n
(Region)
- ♦ Vienna Basin

Wiener Schnitzel, n
- ♦ wiener schnitzel

Wiener Staatsoper, f
- ♦ Vienna State Opera

Wienerwald, m
(Region)
- ♦ Vienna Woods, the pl
- ♦ Wienerwald

Wiener Würstchen, n
Wiener, m/f
Wienerle, n coll
- ♦ vienna sausage
- ♦ vienna
- ♦ wiener

wie oben erwähnt
- ♦ as mentioned above

wie Sardinen
- ♦ like sardines

Wie schmeckt Ihnen der Wein?
- ♦ How do you like the wine?

Wiese, f
- ♦ meadow

Wiesencampingplatz, m
- ♦ meadow campsite
- ♦ meadow campground AE
- ♦ meadow camping site BE
- ♦ meadow camping ground BE
- ♦ meadow site

Wiesengelände, n
- ♦ meadowland

Wiesengolfplatz, m
Golfplatz im Wiesengelände, m
- ♦ meadowland golf course

Wiesenplatz, m
(z.B. Campingplatz)
- ♦ meadow site

Wiesenweg, m
- ♦ meadow footpath

Wie sollen wir Ihnen die Rechnung stellen?
- ♦ How shall we bill you?

wie vereinbart
laut Vereinbarung
lt. Vereinbarung
- ♦ as agreed
- ♦ as arranged

Wieviel kostet ein Doppelzimmer pro Nacht?
- ♦ How much does a double room cost per night?

Wieviel verlangen Sie für ein Zimmer?
- ♦ How much do you charge for a room?

Wie war die Italienreise?
- ♦ How was the trip to Italy?

wie zu Hause fühlen sich
- ♦ feel at home

Wigwam, m
- ♦ wigwam

Wikinger, m
- ♦ Viking

Wikingerdorf, n
- ♦ Viking village

Wikingerhaus, n
- ♦ Viking house

Wikingerschiff, n
- ♦ Viking ship
- ♦ Viking boat

Wikingerseereise, f
- ♦ Viking voyage

Wikingerstadt, f
- ♦ Viking town

Wikingerüberfall, m
- ♦ Viking raid

Wikingerzeit, f
- ♦ Viking times pl

Wildbachfahrt, f
- ♦ flume ride
- ♦ log flume ride

Wildbeobachtung, f
- ♦ game watching AE
- ♦ game-watching BE
- ♦ game viewing

Wildblume, f
- ♦ wild flower

Wildblumenwiese, f
- ♦ wild-flower meadow

Wildbraten, m (generell)
- ♦ roast game

Wildbraten, m (Hochwild)
- ♦ roast venison

Wildbratenstück, n
- ♦ roast of venison

Wildbret, n (generell)
Wild, n
- ♦ game

Wildbret, n (Hochwild)
Wild, n
- ♦ venison

wilde Erdbeere, f
   Walderdbeere, f
   ♦ wild strawberry
   ♦ wood strawberry
wilde Landschaft, f
   ♦ wild scenery
   ♦ wild countryside
wilde Nacht, f
   stürmische Nacht, f
   ♦ wild night
Wildente, f
   ♦ wild duck
Wildentensalmi, n
   ♦ wild duck salmi
wilde Orgie, f
   ♦ wild orgy
wilde Orgien feiern
   ♦ celebrate wild orgies
   ♦ indulge in wild orgies
wilde Party, f
   ♦ wild party
wilder Camper, m
   ♦ unauthorised camper
   ♦ unauthorized camper
wilder Parker, m
   ♦ unauthorised parker
   ♦ unauthorized parker
wilder Reis, m
   ♦ wild rice
wildes Campen, n
   Campen außerhalb des Campingplatzes, n
   wildes Zelten, n
   ♦ off-site camping
   ♦ wild camping
   ♦ unauthorised camping
   ♦ unauthorized camping
wildes Land, n
   wilde Gegend, f
   ♦ wild country
wildes Parken, n
   ♦ unauthorized parking
   ♦ unauthorised parking
wildes Zelten, n
   wildes Campen, n
   ♦ unauthorised camping
   ♦ unauthorized camping
Wildfahrt, f (Auto)
   Wildbeobachtungsfahrt, f
   Pirschfahrt, f
   ♦ game drive
   ♦ game-watching drive
Wildfond, m *gastr*
   ♦ game stock *gastr*
Wildfreigehege, n
   → Tiergehege
wildfremder Mensch, m
   ♦ complete stranger
Wildfütterung, f
   ♦ feeding of game
Wildgans, f
   ♦ wild goose
Wildgeflügel, n
   ♦ wildfowl
Wildgeflügelragout, n/m
   → Salmi
Wildgericht, n (generell)
   ♦ game dish
Wildgericht, n (Hochwild)
   ♦ venison dish

Wildgeschmack, m
   ♦ gamy taste
   ♦ gamey taste
Wildhüter, m
   ♦ game warden
   ♦ gamekeeper
Wildkasserolle, f (Hochwild)
   ♦ venison casserole
Wild nach Saison, n
   ♦ game in season
   ♦ game according to the season
Wildnis, f
   ♦ wilderness
Wildnisfahrt, f
   Fahrt in die Wildnis, f
   ♦ wilderness trip
Wildpark, m (generell)
   ♦ game park
Wildpark, m (Rotwild)
   → Rotwildpark
Wildpastete, f (generell)
   ♦ game pie
Wildpastete, f (Hochwild)
   ♦ venison pie
Wildragout, n/m
   ♦ game stew
Wildreservat, n
   Jagdreservat, n
   ♦ game reserve
   ♦ game preserve
wildromantische Landschaft, f
   ♦ wild, romantic scenery
   ♦ wild, romantic landscape
   ♦ wild, romantic countryside
Wildrücken, m (Hochwild)
   ♦ saddle of venison
Wildsalpikon, m
   ♦ game salpicon
Wildschutzgebiet, n
   ♦ game sanctuary
Wildschweingehege, n
   ♦ wild boar reserve
Wildsoße, f
   ♦ game sauce
Wildspezialität, f
   ♦ game specialty *AE*
   ♦ game speciality *BE*
Wildsuppe, f
   ♦ game soup
Wildtierpark, m
   ♦ wild animal park
Wildvogel, m
   ♦ game bird
Wildwasserbahn, f
   Wildwasserkanal, n
   Wildbach, m
   ♦ flume
   ♦ wild waters flume
Wildwasserfloßfahrt, f
   ♦ white-water rafting trip
   ♦ white-water raft trip
Wildwasserrafting, n
   Wildwasserfloßfahren, n
   ♦ white-water rafting
Wildwasserrennen, n
   ♦ white-water race
Wildwasserschwimmen, n
   ♦ white-water swimming
Wildwasserschwimmer, m
   ♦ white-water swimmer

Wildwassersport, m
   ♦ white-water canoeing
Wildwassertour, f
   ♦ white-water tour
Wildwoche, f
   ♦ game week
Wildzeit, f
   Wildsaison, f
   ♦ game season
Williamsbirne, f
   ♦ William pear
willkommen, adj
   ♦ welcome, adj
Willkommen, n
   → Begrüßung
willkommener Besuch, m
   ♦ welcome visit
willkommener Gast, m
   gerngesehener Gast, m
   ♦ welcome guest
willkommen fühlen sich
   ♦ feel welcome
willkommen geheißen werden in einem Hotel
   ♦ be welcomed at a hotel
willkommen heißen jn
   ♦ bid s.o. welcome *lit*
   ♦ welcome s.o.
willkommen heißen jn bei etw
   jn begrüßen zu etw
   ♦ welcome s.o. to s.th.
willkommen heißen jn herzlich
   ♦ give s.o. a warm welcome
willkommen heißen jn im Namen von jn
   ♦ welcome s.o. on behalf of s.o.
willkommen heißen jn in X
   ♦ welcome s.o. to X
willkommen heißen jn mit offenen Armen
   ♦ welcome s.o. with open arms
Willkommen im Hotel!
   ♦ Welcome to the hotel!
Willkommen in unserem Hotel!
   ♦ Welcome to our hotel!
Willkommenscocktail, m
   → Begrüßungscocktail
willkommen sein
   ♦ be welcome
willkommen sein in einem Hotel
   ♦ be welcome in a hotel
Willkommensgeschenk, n
   Begrüßungsgeschenk, n
   ♦ welcome present
   ♦ welcome gift
   ♦ welcoming gift *BE*
   ♦ welcoming present *BE*
Willkommensgruß, m
   → Willkommen
Willkommenstrunk, m
   Begrüßungsgetränk, n
   Willkommensdrink, m
   ♦ welcoming drink
   ♦ welcome drink
Willkommenszeichen n
   Zeichen des Willkommens n
   ♦ token of welcome
Willkommen zu Hause!
   ♦ Welcome home!
wimmelnd von Leuten
   ♦ lousy with people
wimmelnd von Touristen
   ♦ lousy with tourists

wimmeln von Leuten
♦ be lousy with people
wimmeln von Touristen
♦ be lousy with tourists
Wimpernbehandlung, f
Augenwimpernbehandlung, f
♦ eyelash treatment
Wimperntönung, f
Wimpernfärbung, f
♦ eylash tinting
Windel, f
♦ diaper AE
♦ nappy BE
Windfang, m
♦ porch
windgeschützt, adj
♦ sheltered from the wind, adj
♦ sheltered, adj
Windhund, m
♦ greyhound
Windhundrennbahn, f
♦ greyhound track
Windhundrennen, n
♦ greyhound race
Windhundrennsport, m
Windhundrennen, n
♦ greyhound racing
Windhundstadion, n
♦ greyhound stadium
Windmühle, f
♦ windmill
Windschutz, m
(z.B. Hecke, Tuch)
♦ windbreak
♦ wind shelter
Windschutz mieten
(z.B. am Strand)
♦ rent a windbreak AE
♦ hire a windbreak BE
Windschutzscheibe, f
♦ windscreen
Windsorsalat, m
♦ Windsor salad
Windsorsuppe, f
♦ Windsor soup
Windsurfbrett, n
♦ windsurfing board
♦ windsurfer
♦ sailboard
windsurfen
♦ windsurf
♦ sailboard
Windsurfen, n
♦ windsurfing
♦ sailboarding
windsurfen gehen
♦ go windsurfing
Windsurfer, m
♦ windsurfer
Windsurfkurs, m
Windsurflehrgang, m
♦ windsurfing course
Windsurfschule, f
♦ windsurfing school
Windsurfurlaub, m
♦ windsurfing vacation AE
♦ windsurfing holiday BE
Windsurfweltmeister, m
♦ windsurfing world champion
Windsurfweltmeisterschaft, f
♦ windsurfing world championship

Windsurfzentrum, n
♦ windsurfing center AE
♦ windsurfing centre BE
Winkel, m (Ecke)
♦ nook
Winkel, m (mathematisch)
♦ angle
Winter, m
♦ winter
Winterabend, m
♦ winter evening
Winterangebot, n
Winterofferte, f
♦ winter offer
Winterarrangement, n
♦ winter arrangement
Winteraufenthalt, m
♦ winter stay
♦ stay during the winter
Winterauslastung, f
Winterbelegung, f
♦ winter occupancy
Winterausstellung, f
♦ winter exhibition
♦ winter exhibit AE
♦ winter show
Winterball, m
♦ winter ball
Winterbelegung, f
→ Winterauslastung
Winterbesuch, m
♦ winter visit
Winterbesucher m
♦ winter visitor
♦ winter guest
Winterbuchung, f
♦ winter booking
♦ winter reservation AE
Wintercamper, m
♦ winter camper
Wintercamping, n
♦ winter camping
Wintercampingplatz, m
♦ winter campsite
♦ winter campground AE
♦ winter camping site BE
♦ winter camping ground BE
♦ winter site
Wintererholung, f
→ Winterurlaub
Wintererholungsort, m
Winterurlaubsort, m
Winterferienort, m
Winterort, m
♦ winter resort
Winterfahrplan, m
♦ winter timetable
♦ winter schedule AE
Winterfahrt, f
♦ winter trip
Winterferien, pl
♦ winter holidays BE pl
♦ winter vacation AE
Winterferiengast, m
Winterurlauber, m
♦ winter holidaymaker BE
♦ winter vacationer AE
Winterferiengebiet, n
→ Winterurlaubsgebiet

Winterferienprogramm, n
♦ winter holiday programme BE
♦ winter vacation program AE
Winterferiensaison, f
♦ winter holiday season BE
♦ winter vacation season AE
Winterfestlichkeit, f
Winterfest, n
♦ winter festivity
Winterflaute, f
(ökonomisch)
♦ winter trough
Winterflug, m
♦ winter flight
Winterflug, m
♦ winter flight
Winterflugplan, m
♦ winter schedule AE
♦ winter timetable
Winterfreizeit, f
→ Winterurlaub
Wintergarten, m
♦ winter garden
♦ conservatory
Wintergartenraum, m
Wintergartenzimmer, n
♦ conservatory room
Wintergartenrestaurant, n
♦ conservatory restaurant
Wintergartensalon, m
♦ conservatory lounge
Wintergast, m
♦ winter guest
♦ winter visitor
Wintergeschäft, n
♦ winter business
Winterhalbjahr, n
♦ winter half year
Winterhotel n
♦ winter hotel
Winterkatalog, m
♦ winter catalogue
♦ winter catalog AE
Winterkonferenz, f
♦ winter conference
Winterkonzert, n (Musikstück)
♦ winter concerto
Winterkonzert, n (Veranstaltung)
♦ winter concert
Winterkreuzfahrt, f
♦ winter cruise
Winterkur, f
♦ winter treatment
♦ winter cure
Winterkurort, m
♦ winter health resort
Winterkurzurlaub, m
♦ winter break
♦ winter short break
Winterlager, n
Wintercamp, n
♦ winter camp
Winterlandschaft, f
♦ winter scenery
♦ winter landscape
♦ winter countryside
Winterluft, f
♦ wintery air
♦ wintry air
Wintermantel, m
♦ winter coat

Wintermesse

Wintermesse, f
♦ winter fair
♦ winter trade fair
Wintermieter m (Immobilien)
♦ winter tenant
Wintermonat m
♦ winter month
Wintereröffnungszeit, f
♦ winter opening
Winterolympiade, f
♦ Winter Olympics, the *pl*
Winterort, m
♦ winter place
♦ winter spot
Winterpalast, m
♦ winter palace
Winterparadies, n
♦ winter paradise
Winterparty, f
Winterfest, n
♦ winter party
Winterpauschale, f
♦ winter package
Winterpauschalpreis, m
♦ winter package price
♦ winter package rate
Winterpauschalreise, f
♦ winter package tour
Winterpause, f (generell)
♦ winter break
Winterpause, f (Hochschule, Institution)
Winterferien, pl
♦ winter recess
Winterplatz, m
(z.B. Camping)
♦ winter site
Winterpreis, m
♦ winter price
♦ winter rate
Winterpreisermäßigung, f
Preisermäßigung während der Wintersaison, f
♦ price reduction during the winter season
Winterpreisliste, f
♦ winter price list
♦ winter tariff
Winterprogramm n
♦ winter program *AE*
♦ winter programme *BE*
Winterprospekt m
♦ winter brochure
Winterquartier, n
♦ winter quarters *pl*
Winterrabatt, m
♦ winter discount
Winterreifen, m
♦ winter tire *AE*
♦ winter tyre *BE*
♦ snow tire *AE*
♦ snow tyre *BE*
Winterreise, f
♦ winter tour
♦ winter journey
♦ winter trip
Winterreisen, n
Winterreiseverkehr, m
♦ winter travel
Winterreisender, m
♦ winter traveller
♦ winter traveler *AE*
♦ winter tourist

Winterreiseziel, n
Winterziel, n
♦ winter travel destination
♦ winter destination
Winterreservierung, f
♦ winter reservation
Wintersaison, f
♦ winter season
Wintersaisonbuchung, f
♦ winter-season booking
Wintersaisonermäßigung, f
♦ winter-season reduction
Wintersaisoneröffnung, f
♦ winter-season opening
♦ opening of the winter season
Wintersaisonmonat, m
♦ winter-season month
♦ month in the winter season
Wintersaisonpreis, m
♦ winter-season price
♦ winter-season rate
Wintersaisonprogramm, n
♦ winter-season program *AE*
♦ winter-season programme *BE*
Wintersaisonrabatt, m
♦ winter-season discount
Wintersaisonreservierung, f
♦ winter-season reservation
Wintersaisontag, m
♦ winter-season day
♦ day in the winter season
Wintersaisonwoche, f
♦ winter-season week
♦ week in the winter season
Wintersaisonzeit, f
♦ winter-season period
Wintersaisonzuschlag, m
♦ winter-season supplement
Winterschau, f
Winterausstellung, f
♦ winter show
Winterseminar, n
♦ winter seminar
Wintersitz, m
Winterresidenz, f
♦ winter residence
Wintersitzung, f
♦ winter meeting
Winterskilauf, m
Winterskifahren, n
♦ winter skiing
Winterskiläufer, m
Winterskifahrer, m
♦ winter skier
Wintersonderangebot, n
♦ special winter offer
Winterspaß, m
♦ winter fun
Winterspeisekarte f
♦ winter menu
Winterspiele, n pl (Olympiade)
♦ winter games *pl*
Wintersport, m
♦ winter sports
♦ winter sport
Wintersportanlagen, f pl
♦ winter sports facilities *pl*
Wintersportart, f
♦ winter sports type
Wintersporteinrichtung, f
♦ winter sports facility

Wintersportfan, m
♦ winter sports fan
Wintersportfreund, m
Wintersportbegeisterter, m
♦ winter sports enthusiast
Wintersportgebiet, n (groß)
♦ winter sports region
Wintersportgebiet, n (klein)
♦ winter sports area
Wintersportgerät, n
♦ winter sports equipment
Wintersporthauptstadt, f
♦ winter sports capital
Wintersporthotel, n
♦ winter sports hotel
Wintersportinfrastuktur, f
♦ winter sports infrastructure
Wintersportkleidung, f
♦ winter sportswear
Wintersportkomplex, m
Wintersportanlage, f
♦ winter sports complex
Wintersportler, m
♦ winter sportsman
Wintersportmarkt, m
♦ winter sports market
Wintersportmöglichkeiten, f pl
♦ winter sports possibilities *pl*
♦ winter sports facilities *pl*
Wintersportort, m
♦ winter sports resort
♦ ski resort
Wintersportparadies, n
♦ winter sports paradise
Wintersportplatz, m
→ Wintersportort
Wintersportsaison, f
♦ winter sports season
Wintersportspaß, m
♦ winter sports fun
Wintersporttourismus, m
♦ winter sports tourism
♦ ski tourism
♦ skiing tourism
Wintersporttourist, m
♦ winter sports tourist
♦ ski tourist
♦ skiing tourist
Wintersporturlaub, m
♦ winter sports vacation *AE*
♦ winter sports holiday *BE*
Wintersportverkehr, m
♦ winter sports traffic
Wintersportzentrum, n
♦ winter sports center *AE*
♦ winter sports centre *BE*
Winterstellplatz, m
(Camping)
♦ winter pitch
Wintersuppe, f
♦ winter soup
Wintersymposion, n
♦ winter symposium
Wintertag, m
♦ winter day
Wintertagung, f
Wintertreffen, n
♦ winter meeting
Wintertarif, m
♦ winter tariff
♦ winter rates *pl*

◆ winter rate
◆ winter terms *pl*
Wintertemperatur, f
  ◆ winter temperature
Wintertourismus, m
  Winterfremdenverkehr, m
  ◆ winter tourism
Wintertourist, m
  ◆ winter tourist
Wintertournee, f
  ◆ winter tour
Wintertreffpunkt, m
  ◆ winter haunt
Winterurlaub, m
  ◆ winter vacation *AE*
  ◆ winter holiday *BE*
Winterurlauber m
  ◆ winter vacationer *AE*
  ◆ winter holidaymaker *BE*
Winterurlaub machen
  ◆ take a winter vacation *AE*
  ◆ take a winter holiday *BE*
Winterurlaubsgast, m
  ◆ winter vacation guest *AE*
  ◆ winter holiday guest *BE*
Winterurlaubsgebiet, n (groß)
  Winterferiengebiet, n
  ◆ winter vacation region *AE*
  ◆ winter holiday region *BE*
Winterurlaubsgebiet, n (klein)
  Winterferiengebiet, n
  ◆ winter vacation area *AE*
  ◆ winter holiday area *BE*
Winterurlaubsort m
  ◆ winter vacation resort *AE*
  ◆ winter holiday resort *BE*
  ◆ winter resort
Winterurlaubsparadies n
  ◆ winter vacation paradise *AE*
  ◆ winter holiday paradise *BE*
Winterurlaubsprogramm, n
  ◆ winter vacation program *AE*
  ◆ winter holiday programme *BE*
Winterurlaubsreise, f
  ◆ winter vacation trip *AE*
  ◆ winter holiday trip *BE*
Winterurlaubssaison, f
  ◆ winter vacation season *AE*
  ◆ winter holiday season *BE*
Winterurlaubsstadt, f (Großstadt)
  Winterferienstadt, f
  ◆ winter vacation city *AE*
  ◆ winter holiday city *BE*
Winterurlaubsstadt, f (kleine Stadt)
  Winterferienstadt, f
  ◆ winter vacation town *AE*
  ◆ winter holiday town *BE*
Winterurlaubsumsatz, m
  Winterferienumsatz, m
  ◆ winter vacation sales *AE pl*
  ◆ winter holiday sales *BE pl*
Winterurlaubszentrum, n
  ◆ winter vacation center *AE*
  ◆ winter holiday centre *BE*
Winterveranstaltung, f
  ◆ winter event
  ◆ winter function
Winter verbringen in einem wärmeren Klima
  ◆ spend the winter in a warmer climate

Winter verbringen in X
  ◆ spend the winter at X
  ◆ spend the winter in X
Wintervergnügen, n
  ◆ winter pleasure
Winterwanderer, m
  ◆ winter walker
  ◆ winter hiker
Winterwandern, n
  ◆ winter walking
  ◆ winter hiking
Winterwanderung, f
  ◆ winter walk
  ◆ winter hike
Winterwanderung machen
  ◆ go on a winter walk
  ◆ go on a winter hike
Winterwoche, f
  ◆ winter week
Winterwochenende, n
  ◆ winter weekend
Winterzeit, f (Jahreszeit)
  ◆ wintertime
Winterzeit, f (Uhrzeit)
  ◆ winter time
Winterzeit, f (Zeitraum)
  Winterzeitraum, m
  ◆ winter period
Winterziel, n
  Winterdestination, f
  ◆ winter destination
Winzer, m
  ◆ winegrower
  ◆ wine-maker
  ◆ vintner
  ◆ grower
Winzerart, adv *gastr*
  ◆ winegrower's style, adv *gastr*
Winzerfamilie, f
  ◆ winegrower's family
Winzerfest, n
  ◆ winegrowers' festival
  ◆ wine festival
Winzerfrühstück, n
  ◆ winegrower's breakfast
Winzergenossenschaft, f
  Winzerverein, m
  ◆ winegrowers' cooperative
  ◆ growers' cooperative
Winzerhof, m
  → Weingut
Winzerverein, m
  → Winzergenossenschaft
winzige Bucht, f
  ◆ tiny cove
winziger Garten, m
  ◆ tiny garden
winziger Strand, m
  ◆ tiny beach
winziges Badezimmer, n
  winziges Bad, n
  ◆ tiny bathroom
  ◆ tiny bath
winziges Hotel, n
  ◆ tiny hotel
winziges Restaurant, n
  ◆ tiny restaurant
winziges Zimmer, n
  ◆ tiny room
  ◆ slip of a room *coll*

winzige Wohnung, f
  ◆ tiny apartment *AE*
  ◆ tiny flat *BE*
Wippe, f
  (für Kinder)
  ◆ seesaw *AE*
  ◆ teeter-totter *AE*
  ◆ see-saw *BE*
wippen
  schaukeln
  ◆ seesaw *AE*
  ◆ see-saw *BE*
Wir behalten uns die Berechnung einer Stornierungsgebühr vor
  ◆ We reserve the right to charge a cancellation fee
Wirbelbad, n
  → Whirlpool
Wird erledigt!
  ◆ It will be attended to!
Wir freuen uns, Sie in unserem Hotel begrüßen können
  ◆ We look forward to welcoming you to our hotel
Wir freuen uns auf Ihren Besuch
  ◆ We look forward to your visit
Wir haben am Montag geöffnet
  ◆ We are open on Monday
Wir haben bis Mitternacht geöffnet
  ◆ We are open until midnight
Wir haben keinen Kaffee. Möchten Sie stattdessen Tee?
  ◆ We have no coffee. Would you like tea instead?
Wir können Ihnen ein bequemes Zimmer zusichern
  ◆ We can assure you of a comfortable room
Wir nehmen keine Kinder auf
  ◆ We do not cater for children
Wir reisen morgen ab
  ◆ We are leaving tomorrow
Wirrwarr des modernen Lebens, m
  ◆ hurly-burly of modern life
Wir schließen um Mitternacht
  ◆ We close at midnight
Wir sind fünf Personen
  ◆ There are five of us
Wirsing, m
  ◆ savoy
Wirsingkohl, m
  Wirsing, m
  ◆ savoy cabbage
Wir stehen Ihnen gerne zu Diensten
  ◆ We look forward to being of service to you
Wirt, m
  Gastwirt, m
  ◆ publican
  ◆ landlord
  ◆ alehouse-keeper *obs*
Wirtfamilie, f (Gastgeber)
  → Gastfamilie
Wirtin, f
  Gastwirtin, f
  ◆ female publican *BE*
  ◆ female innkeeper
  ◆ lady inkeeper
  ◆ landlady
Wirtschaft, f (Gaststätte)
  → Gaststätte

Wirtschaft

Wirtschaft, f (Ökonomie)
→ Ökonomie
Wirtschaftsabteilung, f (Hotel)
→ Food-and-Beverage-Abteilung
Wirtschaftsbereich, m (Hotel)
Wirtschaftsbereich, m
Gastronomieabteilung, f
Gastronomiebereich, m
Verpflegungsbereich, m
♦ food and beverage department
♦ f&b department
Wirtschaftsbereich, m (Hotel)
Gastronomiebereich, m
Verpflegungsbereich, m
♦ food and beverage division
♦ f&b division
Wirtschaftsbüro, n (Hotel)
♦ food and beverage office
♦ f&b office
Wirtschaftsdirektion, f (Hotel)
♦ food and beverage management
♦ f&b management
Wirtschaftsdirektor, m (Hotel)
♦ food and beverage manager
♦ f&b manager
Wirtschaftsfaktor, m
♦ economic factor
Wirtschaftsflüchtling, m
♦ economic migrant
Wirtschaftsgeld, n
→ Haushaltsgeld
Wirtschaftsgeographie, f
♦ economic geography
Wirtschaftsgipfel, m
♦ economic summit
Wirtschaftskonferenz, f
♦ economic conference
Wirtschaftskongreß, m
♦ economic convention
♦ economic congress
Wirtschaftsmetropole, f
♦ economic metropolis
Wirtschaftsprüfer, m
♦ auditor
Wirtschaftsraum, m (Hausarbeit)
→ Hausarbeitsraum
Wirtschaftstagung, f
♦ economic meeting
Wirtschaftstourismus, m
♦ economic tourism
Wirtschaftstourist, m
♦ economic tourist
Wirtsfamilie, f (Gaststätte)
♦ familiy running the bar AE
♦ family running the public house BE
♦ family running the pub BE
Wirtshaus, n
♦ alehouse
♦ hostelry obs
♦ bar AE
♦ public house BE
♦ pub BE
Wirtshausbesucher, m
→ Gaststättenbesucher
Wirtshauskeller, m
Gaststättenkeller, m
Gasthauskeller, m
Barkeller, m
♦ **bar cellar** AE
♦ **bar's cellar** AE

♦ pub cellar BE
♦ pub's cellar BE
Wirtshaus mit bunter Dekoration, n
♦ gin palace
Wirtshausschild, n
Gasthausschild, n
♦ pub sign BE
Wirtsleute, pl
♦ landlord and landlady
Wirt und seine Gäste
Wirt (m) und seine Gäste (m, pl)
♦ landlord and his guests
Wir wünschen Ihnen einen angenehmen Aufenthalt
♦ We wish you a pleasant stay
Wir wünschen Ihnen einen schönen Aufenthalt und
eine gute Heimreise
♦ We wish you an enjoyable stay and a safe journey
♦ home
wissen, wo Bartel den Most holt
♦ know which side one's bread is buttered
wissenschaftliche Exkursion, f
♦ scientific excursion
wissenschaftliche Fahrt, f
♦ scientific trip
wissenschaftliche Reise, f
♦ scientific journey
♦ scientific trip
♦ scientific tour
wissenschaftliche Tagung, f
♦ scientific meeting
Wissenschaftsmuseum, n
Naturwissenschaftsmuseum, n
♦ science museum
Wo., f
Woche, f
♦ wk.
♦ week
Woche, f
Wo., f
♦ week
♦ wk.
Woche abrunden mit etw
♦ round off the week with s.th.
Woche am Meer, f
♦ week at the seaside
Woche früher nach Hause fahren
♦ return home one week earlier
Woche Halbpension, f
♦ week's half board
♦ week's demipension AE
♦ week's half pension AE
Woche Halbpension kostet DM 1234
♦ week's half board costs DM 1234
♦ week's demipension costs DM 1234 AE
♦ week's half pension costs DM 1234 AE
Woche in einem Hotel verbringen
♦ spend a week in a hotel
♦ spend a week at a hotel
Wochenanfang, m
♦ start of the week
Wochenaufenthalt, m
♦ week's stay
♦ stay during the week
Wochenausflug, m
einwöchiger Ausflug, m
♦ one-week excursion
Wochenauslastung, f
wöchentliche Auslastung, f

♦ weekly load factor
♦ load factor per week
Wochenbeginn, m
♦ beginning of the week
Wochenbelegung, f
wöchentliche Belegung, f
Wochenauslastung, f
wöchentliche Auslastung, f
♦ week's occupancy
♦ weekly occupancy
♦ occupancy per week
Wochenendangebot, n
Wochenendofferte, f
♦ weekend offer
Wochenendanreise, f
Wochenendreise, f
♦ journey on the weekend AE
♦ journey at the weekend BE
♦ weekend journey
Wochenendarrangement n
♦ weekend arrangement
Wochenendaufenthalt, m
♦ weekend stay
Wochenendaufpreis, m
♦ weekend surcharge
Wochenendausflug, m
♦ weekend excursion
♦ weekend trip
♦ weekend outing
Wochenendausflügler, m
♦ weekender
♦ weekend tripper
Wochenendauslastung f
Wochenendbelegung, f
♦ weekend occupancy
Wochenendbehandlungspauschale, f
♦ weekend treatments package
♦ weekend treatment package
Wochenendbesuch, m
♦ weekend visit
Wochenendbesucher m
♦ weekend visitor
♦ weekend guest
Wochenendbesuch machen
♦ make a weekend visit
Wochenendbuchung f
♦ weekend booking
Wochenendcamper, m
Wochenendzelter, m
♦ weekend camper
Wochenenddienst, m
Wochenendservice, m
♦ weekend service
Wochenende, n
♦ weekend
Wochenende am Meer, n
♦ weekend at the seaside
Wochenende auf dem Land, n
♦ weekend in the country
Wochenende bleiben
♦ stay (for) the weekend
Wochenende einmal anders
(Werbeslogan)
♦ weekend with a difference
Wochenende geschlossen
(Hinweisschild)
Am Wochenende geschlossen
♦ **Closed on weekends** AE
♦ Closed at weekends BE
♦ Closed at the weekend BE
♦ Closed on the weekend AE

Wochenende mit Sex und Alkohol, n
♦ dirty weekend
Wochenendentspannung, f
♦ weekend relaxation
Wochenenderholer, m
→ Wochenendausflügler
Wochenenderholung, f
♦ weekend recreation
Wochenendermäßigung, f
♦ weekend reduction
Wochenende verbringen bei jm
Wochenende verbringen mit jm
♦ spend the weekend with s.o.
Wochenende verbringen in X
♦ spend the weekend in X
♦ spend a weekend in X
♦ spend the weekend at X
♦ spend a weekend at X
♦ weekend in/at X
Wochenende zuhause verbringen
♦ spend the weekend at home
Wochenendfahrkarte, f
Wochenendfahrschein, m
♦ weekend ticket
Wochenendfahrpreis, m
♦ weekend fare
Wochenendfahrt, f
♦ weekend trip
♦ weekend ride
Wochenendferienhaus, n
♦ weekend cottage AE
Wochenendflug, m
♦ weekend flight
Wochenendfreizeitkurzurlaub, m
♦ weekend leisure break
Wochenendgast m
♦ weekend guest
Wochenendgeschäft, n
♦ weekend business
Wochenendhaus, n
♦ weekend house
♦ weekend cottage
Wochenendkonferenz, f
♦ weekend conference
Wochenendkonferenzpauschale, f
♦ weekend conference package
Wochenendkongreß, m
♦ weekend convention
♦ weekend congress
Wochenendkongreßpauschale, f
♦ weekend convention package
♦ weekend congress package
Wochenendkreuzfahrt, f
♦ weekend cruise
Wochenendkurs, m
Wochenendlehrgang, m
♦ weekend course
♦ weekend class
Wochenendkurzreise, f
kurze Wochenendreise, f
♦ short weekend trip
Wochenendkurzurlaub, m
♦ weekend short break
♦ weekend break
Wochenendkurzurlaub machen
♦ take a weekend break
Wochenendkurzurlaub mit zwei Übernachtungen, m
♦ two-night weekend break

Wochenendkurzurlaubsmarkt, m
♦ weekend short break market
♦ weekend break market
Wochenendkurzurlaubspauschale, f
♦ weekend break package
Wochenendlehrgang, m
Wochenendkurs, m
♦ weekend class
♦ weekend course
Wochenendmiete, f (Immobilie)
♦ weekend rent
Wochenendmiete, f (Mobilie)
♦ weekend rental AE
♦ weekend hire BE
Wochenendnetzkarte, f
♦ weekend runabout ticket BE
Wochenendort, m
♦ weekend resort
Wochenendpaß, m
Wochenendkarte, f
♦ weekend pass
Wochenendpauschale, f
♦ weekend package
Wochenendpauschale mit organisierten Wanderungen, f
♦ weekend package with organised hiking tours
♦ weekend package with organised walking tours
Wochenendpauschalpreis, m
Wochenendpauschale, f
♦ weekend inclusive price
♦ weekend inclusive rate
♦ weekend package rate
♦ weekend package price
♦ weekend package
Wochenendpauschalreise, f
♦ weekend package tour
Wochenendpauschalurlaub, m
♦ weekend package vacation AE
♦ weekend inclusive vacation AE
♦ weekend package holiday BE
♦ weekend inclusive holiday BE
Wochenendpreis, m
♦ weekend price
♦ weekend rate
Wochenendprogramm, n
♦ weekend program AE
♦ weekend programme BE
Wochenendrabatt, m
♦ weekend discount
Wochenendrate, f
→ Wochenendpreis
Wochenendrefugium, n
♦ weekend retreat
Wochenendreise, f
♦ weekend tour
♦ weekend trip
♦ weekend journey
Wochenendreisender, m
♦ weekend traveller
♦ weekend traveler AE
Wochenendreservierung, f
♦ weekend reservation
Wochenendseminar n
♦ weekend seminar
Wochenendservice, m
→ Wochenenddienst
Wochenendspartarif, m
♦ weekend economy tariff
♦ weekend economy terms pl
Wochenendstau, m
♦ weekend congestion

Wochenendtagesausflug, m
♦ one-day excursion on the weekend AE
♦ one-day excursion at the weekend BE
Wochenendtagung, f
♦ weekend meeting
Wochenendtarif, m
♦ weekend tariff
♦ weekend rates pl
♦ weekend rate
♦ weekend terms pl
Wochenendtemperatur, f
♦ weekend temperature
Wochenendtour, f
→ Wochenendausflug, Wochenendreise
Wochenendtourismus, m
♦ weekend tourism
Wochenendtourist, m
♦ weekend tourist
Wochenendtrip, m
→ Wochenendfahrt
Wochenendumsatz, m
♦ weekend sales pl
♦ weekend turnover
Wochenendunterhaltung, f
♦ weekend entertainment
Wochenendurlaub, m
♦ weekend vacation AE
♦ weekend holiday BE
♦ weekend break
Wochenendurlauber, m
♦ weekend vacationer AE
♦ weekend holidaymaker BE
♦ weekender
Wochenendurlaub machen
♦ take a weekend vacation AE
♦ take a weekend holiday BE
♦ take a weekend break
Wochenendurlaubskurs, m
♦ weekend vacation course AE
♦ weekend holiday course BE
Wochenendveranstaltung, f
♦ weekend event
♦ weekend function
♦ weekend activity
Wochenendvergnügen, n
♦ weekend pleasure
Wochenendverkehr, m
Ausflugsverkehr am Wochenende, m
♦ weekend traffic
Wochenendwandern, n
♦ weekend rambling
♦ weekend walking
♦ weekend hiking
Wochenendwanderung, f
♦ weekend ramble
♦ weekend walk
♦ weekend hike
Wochenendwetter, n
♦ weekend weather
Wochenendzuschlag, m
♦ weekend supplement
Wochenfahrkarte, f
♦ weekly ticket
Wochenfahrt, f
♦ week's trip
♦ one-week trip
Wochenfischschein, m
Wochenfischerlaubnis, f
♦ weekly fishing permit
Wochengebühr, f
Gebühr pro Woche, f

Wochengrundpreis

- ◆ weekly charge
- ◆ weekly fee
- ◆ charge per week
- ◆ fee per week

Wochengrundpreis, m
  Grundpreis pro Woche, m
- ◆ basic rate per week
- ◆ basic price per week

Wochenkapazität f
- ◆ weekly capacity

Wochenkarte, f (Fahrkarte)
- ◆ weekly season ticket

Wochenkarte, f (generell)
- ◆ weekly ticket

Wochenkarte, f (Speisekarte)
- ◆ menu of the week
- ◆ weekly menu

Wochenkarte für den Golfplatz, f
- ◆ weekly ticket for the golf course

Wochenkurs, m
  Wochenlehrgang, m
  einwöchigewr Kurs, m
  einwöchiger Lehrgang, m
- ◆ one-week course
- ◆ course lasting one week

wochenlang, adv
- ◆ for weeks, adv

Wochenmarkt, m
- ◆ weekly market

Wochenmiete, f (meist Immobilien)
  Miete pro Woche, f
  wöchentliche Miete, f
- ◆ week's rent
- ◆ rent per week
- ◆ weekly rent

Wochenmiete, f (meist Mobilien)
- ◆ weekly rental AE
- ◆ rental per week AE
- ◆ weekly hire BE
- ◆ hire per week BE

Wochenmiete pro Person, f
  → Miete pro Person pro Woche

Wochenmietpreis, m
- ◆ weekly rental rate AE

Wochenmitte, f
- ◆ midweek

Wochenmitte ist eine gute Reisezeit
- ◆ midweek is a good time to travel

Wochenmittetarif, m
  Tarif für die Wochenmitte, m
- ◆ midweek tariff

Wochennachfrage, f
  wöchentliche Nachfrage, f
- ◆ weekly demand

Wochenpaß, m
- ◆ one-week pass

Wochenpauschale, f
- ◆ week's package
- ◆ one-week package

Wochenpauschalpreis, m
  Pauschalpreis pro Woche, m
  Wochenpauschale, f
- ◆ package price per week
- ◆ package rate per week
- ◆ inclusive price per week
- ◆ inclusive rate per week

Wochenpreis, m
  Preis pro Woche, m
- ◆ weekly price
- ◆ weekly rate

- ◆ rate per week
- ◆ price per week

Wochenpreis für Halbpension, m
- ◆ weekly price for half board
- ◆ weekly rate for half board
- ◆ weekly price for demipension AE
- ◆ weekly rate for half pension AE

Wochenpreis für Teilverpflegung, m
  Wochenpreis für Teilpension, m
- ◆ weekly price for partial board
- ◆ weekly rate for partial board
- ◆ weekly price for part board
- ◆ weekly rate for part board

Wochenpreis für Vollpension, m
  Wochenpreis für Vollverpflegung, m
- ◆ weekly price for full board
- ◆ weekly rate for full board
- ◆ weekly price for full pension AE
- ◆ weekly rate for full pension AE

Wochenprogramm, n (einwöchig)
  einwöchiges Programm, n
- ◆ one-week program AE
- ◆ one-week programme BE

Wochenprogramm, n (wöchentlich)
- ◆ weekly program AE
- ◆ weekly programme BE
- ◆ week's program AE
- ◆ week's programme BE

Wochenrechnung f
- ◆ weekly bill

Wochenreise, f
  einwöchige Reise, f
- ◆ one-week tour
- ◆ week's tour
- ◆ weekly tour

Wochenskipaß, m
- ◆ weekly ski pass

Wochenspezialität, f
- ◆ week's specialty AE
- ◆ week's speciality BE
- ◆ week's special dish

Wochenstatistik, f
- ◆ weekly statistics pl

Wochentag m
- ◆ weekday

wochentags, adv
  → werktags

Wochentagspauschale, f
  Pauschale für Tage unter der Woche, f
- ◆ workday package

Wochentagspreis, m
- ◆ weekday price
- ◆ weekday rate

Wochentagsveranstaltung, f
- ◆ weekday event
- ◆ weekday function

Wochentarif, m
- ◆ weekly tariff
- ◆ weekly rates pl
- ◆ weekly rate
- ◆ weekly terms pl

wöchentlich, adj
- ◆ weekly, adj

wöchentlich, adv
  wochenweise, adv
- ◆ by the week, adv
- ◆ on a weekly basis, adv

wöchentlich buchen etw
  wochenweise buchen etw
- ◆ book s.th. on a weekly basis

wöchentliche Belegung, f
  wöchentliche Auslastung, f
  Wochenauslastung, f
  Wochenbelegung, f
- ◆ weekly occupancy
- ◆ occupancy per week
- ◆ week's occupancy

wöchentliche Kündigung, f
- ◆ weekly notice
- ◆ week's notice
- ◆ one week's notice

wöchentliche Miete, f
  Wochenmiete, f
- ◆ weekly rent

wöchentlicher Bettwäschewechsel m
- ◆ weekly change of bed linen

wöchentliche Rechnungsstellung f
- ◆ weekly billing

wöchentliche Rechnungstellung wünschen
- ◆ request (a) weekly billing

wöchentliche Reinigung, f
- ◆ weekly cleaning

wöchentlicher Halbpensionspreis, m
  → Halbpensionwochenpreis

wöchentlicher Handtuchwechsel, m
- ◆ weekly change of towels

wöchentlicher Kurs, m
  Wochenkurs, m
- ◆ weekly course

wöchentlicher Tischwäschewechsel, m
- ◆ weekly change of table linen

wöchentlicher Toilettenwäschewechsel, m
- ◆ weekly change of toilet linen

wöchentlicher Wäschewechsel, m
- ◆ weekly change of linen

wöchentliche Verweildauer, f
- ◆ weekly length of stay

wöchentliche Zimmerreinigung, f
- ◆ weekly room cleaning

wöchentlich mieten etw (meist Immobilien)
  wochenweise mieten etw
- ◆ rent s.th. by the week
- ◆ rent s.th. on a weekly basis

wöchentlich mieten etw (Mobilien)
- ◆ hire s.th. by the week BE
- ◆ hire s.th. on a weekly basis BE
- ◆ rent s.th. by the week AE
- ◆ rent s.th. on a weekly basis AE

wöchentlich vermieten etw (Immobilie)
  wochenweise vermieten etw
- ◆ rent (out) s.th. by the week
- ◆ rent (out) s.th. on a weekly basis
- ◆ let s.th. by the week BE
- ◆ let s.th. on a weekly basis BE

wöchentlich vermieten etw (Mobilien)
- ◆ hire (out) s.th. by the week BE
- ◆ hire (out) s.th. on a weekly basis BE
- ◆ rent (out) s.th. by the week
- ◆ rent (out) s.th. on a weekly basis

wöchentlich vermietetes Zimmer, n
- ◆ room rented on a weekly basis AE
- ◆ room let on a weekly basis BE

wöchentlich wechselnde Speisekarte f
- ◆ weekly changing menu
- ◆ menu that changes every week

Wochentreffen, n
- ◆ weekly meeting

Wochenübersicht, f
- ◆ weekly survey

Wochenurlaub, m
♦ week's vacation *AE*
♦ week's holiday *BE*
Wochenwanderung, f (Woche lang)
♦ week's walk
♦ week's hike
♦ week's ramble
Wochenwanderung, f (wöchentlich)
wöchentliche Wanderung, f
♦ weekly walk
♦ weekly hike
♦ weekly ramble
wochenweise, adv
→ wöchentlich
wochenweise mieten etw
→ wöchentlich mieten etw
wochenweise vermieten etw
→ wöchentlich vermieten etw
Woche ohne Unterkunft, f
♦ nonresidential week *AE*
♦ non-residential week *BE*
Woche Urlaub nehmen
♦ take a week's vacation *AE*
♦ take a week's holiday *BE*
Woche Urlaub sich genehmigen
Woche Ferien sich genehmigen
Woche Urlaub sich gönnen
Woche Ferien sich gönnen
♦ allow oneself a week's vacation *AE*
♦ allow oneself a week's holiday *BE*
Woche verbringen am Meer
♦ spend a week at the seaside
♦ spend a week by the seaside
Woche verbringen in einem Hotel
♦ spend a week at a hotel
♦ spend a week in a hotel
Woche verbringen in London
♦ spend a week in London
♦ have a week in London
Woche Vollpension, f
♦ week's full board
♦ week's full pension *AE*
Woche vom 7. bis 14. April, f
♦ week of 7 to 14 April
♦ week beginning on 7 and ending on 14 April
Wodka, m
♦ vodka
Wodkacocktail, m
♦ vodka cocktail
Wodkagetränk, n
♦ vodka drink
Wodka pur, m
unverdünnter Wodka, m
♦ neat vodka *BE*
♦ straight vodka *AE*
Wodkatrinker, m
♦ vodka drinker
Wo gehobelt wird, fallen Späne
♦ You cannot make an omelette without breaking eggs
Wohin geht die Reise?
♦ Where are you off to?
Wohin reisen Sie?
♦ Where are you bound for? *form*
Wohlbefinden, n
Wohlergehen, n
♦ well-being
Wohlbefinden eines Gasts fördern
♦ promote the well-being of a guest
Wohlbefinden seiner Gäste, n
♦ well-being of one's guests

Wohlbefinden unserer Gäste, n
♦ well-being of our guests
Wohlbefinden wiederherstellen
♦ restore well-being
Wohlbehagen, n
→ Wohlbefinden
wohlbehalten ankommen
♦ arrive safe and sound
♦ arrive safely
Wohlergehen, n
→ Wohlbefinden
Wohlfahrtsverpflegung, f
♦ welfare catering *BE*
♦ welfare foodservice *AE*
wohl fühlen sich (gesund)
gesund fühlen sich
♦ feel well
wohl fühlen sich (zufrieden)
zufrieden fühlen sich
♦ feel comfortable
♦ feel at ease
Wohlgeschmack, m
angenehmer Geschmack, m
♦ pleasant taste
wohlhabend, adj
♦ wealthy, adj
♦ well-to-do, adj
♦ well-off, adj
wohlhabender Besucher, m
♦ wealthy visitor
Wohlleben, n
♦ high living
wohlschmeckend, adj
schmackhaft, adj
♦ palatable, adj
♦ tasty, adj
♦ delicate, f
wohlschmeckendes Essen, n
♦ palatable food
Wohlstand bringen einer Stadt
♦ bring prosperity to a town
♦ bring prosperity to a city
Wohlstand erlangen
zu Wohlstand kommen
♦ achieve prosperity
Wohltätigkeitsabend m
♦ charity evening
Wohltätigkeitsaufführung, f
Wohltätigkeitsvorstellung, f
♦ charity performance
Wohltätigkeitsball, m
♦ charity ball
Wohltätigkeitsbasar, m
♦ charity bazar
♦ charity bazaar
♦ fancy fair
Wohltätigkeitsdiner, n
♦ charity dinner
Wohltätigkeitsgala, f
♦ charity gala
Wohltätigkeitsgalaball, m
♦ charity gala ball
Wohltätigkeitskonzert, n
Benefizkonzert, n
♦ charity concert
Wohltätigkeitskonzert geben
♦ give a charity concert
Wohltätigkeitsritt, m
Wohltätigkeitsfahrt, f
♦ charity ride

Wohltätigkeitsveranstaltung, f (generell)
♦ charity event
♦ charity function
Wohltätigkeitsveranstaltung, f (Sport)
♦ charity fixture
Wohltätigkeitsverkauf, m
Wohltätigkeitsbasar, m
♦ jumble sale *BE*
♦ rummage sale *AE*
Wohltätigkeitsverkaufsveranstaltung, f
Wohltätigkeitsbasar, m
♦ rummage sale *AE*
♦ jumble sale *BE*
wohlverdient, adj
♦ well-earned, adj
♦ well-deserved, adj
wohlverdiente Ruhepause, f
♦ well-deserved rest
♦ well-earned rest
wohlverdienter Urlaub, m
♦ well-earned vacation *AE*
♦ well-earned holiday *BE*
Wohnadresse, f
♦ residential address
Wohnanhänger, m
♦ trailer caravan *BE*
♦ trailer van *BE*
♦ trailer *AE*
♦ camper *AE*
Wohnanlage, f
(mit mehreren Häusern)
Wohnsiedlung, f
♦ housing estate *BE*
♦ residential complex
♦ residential development *AE*
♦ housing development *AE*
Wohnanlagenverwaltung, f
♦ housing estate management *BE*
Wohnaufenthalt, m
♦ residential stay
Wohnausstellung, f
Ausstellung zum Wohnen, f
♦ housing exhibition
Wohnbeihilfe, f
Mietzuschuß, m
♦ lodging allowance
♦ housing benefit *BE*
Wohnbereich, m
♦ living area
Wohnbetrieb, m
♦ residential establishment
Wohnbezirk, m
♦ uptown *AE*
♦ residential district
Wohnblock, m
♦ residential block
Wohnboot, n
→ Hausboot
Wohncontainer, m
(Behelfsunterkunft)
♦ container dwelling
Wohneigentumsanlage, f
Anlage mit Eigentumswohnungen, f
Komplex mit Eigentumswohnungen, m
♦ condominium complex *AE*
♦ condominium *AE*
Wohneinheit, f
(Statistik)
WE, f
♦ dwelling unit

wohnen auf dem oberen Stockwerk

- d.u.
- ♦ residential unit

wohnen auf dem oberen Stockwerk
  wohnen in dem Obergeschoß
- ♦ live on the upper floor

wohnen auf einer Insel (dauernd)
  leben auf einer Insel
- ♦ live on an island

wohnen auf einer Insel (vorübergehend)
- ♦ stay on an island

wohnen bei jm aus Gefälligkeit (vorübergehend)
- ♦ stay with s.o. by courtesy

wohnen bei jm (dauernd)
- ♦ live with s.o.

wohnen bei jm (vorübergehend)
  logieren bei jm
- ♦ stay with s.o.
- ♦ lodge with s.o.

wohnen im Ausland *off*
  im Ausland wohnen
- ♦ reside abroad *off*

wohnen im Obergeschoß
  → wohnen auf dem oberen Stockwerk

wohnen im Südosten (dauernd)
- ♦ live in the southeast *AE*
- ♦ live in the south-east *BE*
- ♦ live in the South-East *BE*

wohnen in einem Appartement (vorübergehend)
- ♦ stay in an apartment
- ♦ stay at an apartment

wohnen in einem eleganten Viertel
- ♦ live in a fashionable area
- ♦ live in a posh area *coll*

wohnen in einem engen Zimmer (dauernd)
  in einem engen Zimmer wohnen
- ♦ live in a cramped room

wohnen in einem Hotel (dauernd)
  → in einem Hotel leben

wohnen in einem Hotel (vorübergehend)
  logieren in einem Hotel
- ♦ stay in a hotel
- ♦ stay at a hotel

wohnen in einem Zelt (dauernd)
  in einem Zelt wohnen
- ♦ live in a tent

wohnen in einem Zelt (vorübergehend)
- ♦ stay in a tent

wohnen in einer angenehmen Umgebung (dauernd)
- ♦ live in pleasant surroundings

wohnen in einer Frühstückspension
- ♦ stay bed and breakfast
- ♦ stay B&B

wohnen in einer Großstadt (dauernd)
- ♦ live in a city

wohnen in einer Großstadt (vorübergehend)
- ♦ stay in a city

wohnen in einer Höhle
- ♦ dwell in a cave

wohnen in einer Kaserne
  in einer Kaserne wohnen
- ♦ live in barracks
- ♦ be in barracks

wohnen in einer Stadt (dauernd)
- ♦ live in a town

wohnen in einer Stadt (vorübergehend)
- ♦ stay in a town

wohnen in js Haus (dauernd)
  wohnen bei jm
- ♦ stay at s.o.'s house

wohnen in js Wohnung (langzeitig)
- ♦ live in s.o.'s apartment *AE*
- ♦ live in s.o.'s flat *BE*

wohnen in verschiedenen Unterkünften (vorübergehend)
- ♦ stay in separate accommodations *AE*
- ♦ stay in separate accommodation *BE*

wohnen in X (amtlich)
- ♦ reside at X
- ♦ reside in X

wohnen in X (dauernd)
- ♦ live at X
- ♦ live in X

wohnen um die Ecke herum
- ♦ live close at hand
- ♦ live round the corner

wohnen zum halben Preis
  logieren zum halben Preis
- ♦ stay at half (the) price
- ♦ stay at half (the) rate

Wohn-Eßraum, m
  → Wohn-Eßzimmer

Wohn-Eßzimmer, n
- ♦ living-cum-dining room
- ♦ living-dining room

Wohnetage, f (Hotel)
  → Zimmeretage

Wohnfahrzeug, n
- ♦ residential vehicle

Wohnfläche, f
  Wfl., f

Wohnraum, m
- ♦ living space
- ♦ habitable space

Wohngebäude, n
- ♦ residential building

Wohngebiet, n
  Wohngegend, f
  Wohnbezirk, m
- ♦ residential district
- ♦ residential area
- ♦ uptown *AE*

Wohngeld, n
- ♦ housing subsidy *BE*

Wohngeldzuschuß, m
  Wohngeld, n
- ♦ housing allowance

Wohngemeinschaft, f
- ♦ apartment-sharing community *AE*
- ♦ flat-sharing community *BE*

wohnhaft, adj
  in dem gleichen Haus wohnend, adj
- ♦ resident, adj

Wohnhaus, n
- ♦ dwelling house

Wohnheim, n
  (z.B. für Pensionäre)
- ♦ residential home
- ♦ residence hall *AE*
- ♦ hostel

Wohnhochhaus, n
- ♦ tower block

Wohnhöhle, f *coll*
  Bude, f
- ♦ den *coll*

Wohnhotel, n
  (für Langzeitgäste)
- ♦ residential hotel

Wohnimmobilie, f
- ♦ residential property

Wohnklo, n *coll*
- ♦ shoebox apartment *AE coll*
- ♦ broom cupboard *BE coll*
- ♦ rabbit-hutch *BE coll*

Wohnkomplex, m
  Wohnanlage, f
- ♦ residential complex

Wohnkosten, pl
  → Mietkosten

Wohnküche, f
- ♦ kitchen-cum-living room
- ♦ kitchen-living room

Wohnlage, f (Gebiet)
  Wohngebiet, n
- ♦ residential area

Wohnlage, f (Ort)
- ♦ residential location

Wohnlage, f (Situation)
  Wohnsituation, f
- ♦ residential situation

Wohnland, n
- ♦ country of residence

Wohnlandschaft, f
- ♦ landscaped interior

wohnliche Atmosphäre, f
- ♦ homey atmosphere *AE*
- ♦ homely atmosphere

wohnliche Atmosphäre schaffen
- ♦ create a homely atmosphere

Wohnmaschine, f
  → Wohnsilo

Wohnmobil, n (Mobilheim)
  → Mobilheim

Wohnmobil, n (Reisemobil)
  Reisemobil, n
- ♦ motorhome *AE*
- ♦ motor home *BE*
- ♦ motor caravan *BE*
- ♦ camper *AE*

Wohnmobilbegeisterter, m
  Reisemobilbegeisterter, m
- ♦ motorhome fan *AE*
- ♦ motor-home fan *BE*
- ♦ motor-caravan fan *BE*

Wohnmobilbesitzer, m
  Reisemobilbesitzer, m
- ♦ motorhome owner *AE*
- ♦ motor-home owner *BE*
- ♦ motor-caravan owner *BE*

Wohnmobilbuchung, f
  Reisemobilbuchung, f
- ♦ motorhome booking *AE*
- ♦ motorhome reservation *AE*
- ♦ motor-home booking *BE*
- ♦ reservation of a motorhome *AE*
- ♦ booking (of) a motor home *BE*

Wohnmobil mieten (von jm)
  Reisemobil mieten (von jm)
- ♦ rent a motorhome (from s.o.) *AE*
- ♦ hire a motor home (from s.o.) *BE*
- ♦ hire a motor caravan (from s.o.) *BE*

Wohnmobilpark, m
  Reisemobilpark, m
- ♦ motorhome park *AE*
- ♦ motor-home park *BE*
- ♦ motor-caravan park *BE*

Wohnmobilplatz, m
  Reisemobilplatz, m
- ♦ motorhome site *AE*
- ♦ motor-home site *BE*
- ♦ motor-caravan site *BE*

Wohnmobil pro Nacht, n
Reisemobil pro Nacht, n
- ♦ motorhome per night *AE*
- ♦ motor home per night *BE*
- ♦ motor caravan per night *BE*

Wohnmobilreservierung, f
Reisemobilreservierung, f
- ♦ motorhome reservation *AE*
- ♦ motor-home reservation *BE*
- ♦ reservation of a motorhome *AE*
- ♦ reservation of a motor home *BE*
- ♦ reserving a motorhome *AE*

Wohnmobilstellplatz, m
Reisemobilstellplatz, m
- ♦ motorhome pitch *AE*
- ♦ motorhome site *AE*
- ♦ motor-home pitch *BE*
- ♦ motor-caravan pitch *BE*

Wohnmobilurlaub, m
Wohnmobilferien, pl
Reisemobilurlaub, m
Reisemobilferien, pl
- ♦ motorhome vacation *AE*
- ♦ motor-home holiday *BE*
- ♦ motor-caravan holiday *BE*

Wohnmobil vermieten (an jn)
Reisemobil vermieten (an jn)
- ♦ rent a motorhome (to s.o.) *AE*
- ♦ hire out a motor home (to s.o.) *BE*
- ♦ let a motor home (to s.o.) *BE*
- ♦ hire out a motor caravan (to s.o.) *BE*

Wohnnutzung, f
Nutzung zu Wohnzwecken, f
- ♦ residential use

Wohnort, m
- ♦ place of residence

Wohnpark, m
- ♦ residential park

Wohnparkbesitzer, m
- ♦ residential park owner

Wohnpark betreiben
- ♦ operate a residential park

Wohnpauschale, f
- ♦ residential package

Wohnplattform, f
(z.B. auf Ölbohrturm)
- ♦ residence platform

Wohnpreis, m (Hotel)
- ♦ residential price
- ♦ residential rate

Wohnquartier, n
Wohnraum, m
- ♦ living quarters *pl*

Wohnquartier bereitstellen
Wohnraum bereitstellen
- ♦ provide living quarters

Wohnquartierbeschaffung wird von Firma übernommen
Wohnraumbeschaffung wird von Firma übernommen
- ♦ firm undertakes to find living quarters

Wohnquartier finden
Wohnraum finden
- ♦ find living quarters

Wohnquartier stellen
Wohnraum stellen
- ♦ supply living quarters

Wohnraum, m (Fläche)
bewohnbare Fläche, f
Wohnfläche, f
- ♦ habitable area
- ♦ habitable space

Wohnraum, m (nicht Büroraum)
- ♦ dwelling room

Wohnschiff, n
- ♦ large houseboat

Wohn-Schlafbereich m
- ♦ living/sleeping area

Wohn-Schlafzimmer, n
- ♦ bedroom-cum-living room *AE*
- ♦ bedsitting-room *BE*
- ♦ bed-sitter *BE inform*
- ♦ bed-sit *BE coll*
- ♦ bedroom-cum-sitting room *BE*

Wohnsilo, n
Wohnturm, m
- ♦ high-rise flats *BE pl*
- ♦ tower block
- ♦ concrete block

Wohnsitz, m
- ♦ domicile

Wohnsitz aufschlagen in X
sich niederlassen in X
- ♦ make one's home in X
- ♦ take up one's dwelling in X

wohnsitzlos, adj
→ obdachlos

Wohnsitzloser, m
Obdachloser, m
- ♦ person without permanent residence
- ♦ homeless person
- ♦ person of no fixed abode *jur*

Wohnsitz nehmen in Heidelberg
- ♦ settle in Heidelberg

Wohnstatt, f
- ♦ dwelling

Wohnstraße, f
- ♦ residential street
- ♦ residential road

Wohnstruktur, f
- ♦ residential structure

Wohntrakt, m
- ♦ accommodation wing

Wohn- und Schlafzimmer, n
- ♦ bedsitting-room *BE*
- ♦ bed-sitter *BE inform*
- ♦ bedsit *BE coll*
- ♦ bedroom-cum-sitting room *BE*

Wohnung am Wasser, f
- ♦ waterside apartment *AE*
- ♦ waterfront apartment *AE*
- ♦ waterside flat *BE*
- ♦ waterfront flat *BE*

Wohnung ansehen
- ♦ look at an apartment *AE*
- ♦ look at a flat *BE*
- ♦ view a flat *BE*
- ♦ view an apartment *AE*

Wohnung ausrauben
Wohnung ausplündern
- ♦ ransack an apartment *AE*
- ♦ ransack a flat *BE*

Wohnung besichtigen
- ♦ view a flat *BE*
- ♦ view an apartment *AE*

Wohnung beziehen
einziehen in eine Wohnung
- ♦ move into an apartment *AE*
- ♦ move into a flat *BE*

Wohnung bietet sechs Personen Unterkunft
Wohnung bietet sechs Personen Platz
- ♦ flat sleeps six persons *BE*
- ♦ apartment sleeps six persons *AE*

Wohnung brennt
- ♦ apartment is on fire *AE*
- ♦ flat is on fire *BE*

Wohnung einrichten
Wohnung möblieren
- ♦ furnish an apartment *AE*
- ♦ furnish a flat *BE*

Wohnung finden
- ♦ find an apartment *AE*
- ♦ find a flat *BE*

Wohnung frei haben
- ♦ have a flat free *BE*
- ♦ have an apartment vacant *AE*
- ♦ have an apartment free *AE*
- ♦ have a flat vacant *BE*
- ♦ have a vacancy

Wohnung frei machen
Wohnung räumen
- ♦ vacate an apartment *AE*
- ♦ vacate a flat *BE*

Wohnung für Alleinstehende, f
→ Junggesellenwohnung

Wohnung für gehobene Ansprüche, f
- ♦ executive apartment *AE*
- ♦ executive flat *BE*

Wohnung haben
- ♦ have a flat *BE*
- ♦ have an apartment *AE*

Wohnung im dritten Stockwerk, f
- ♦ fourth-floor apartment *AE*
- ♦ third-floor flat *BE*

Wohnung im obersten Stockwerk, f
- ♦ top-floor flat *BE*
- ♦ top-floor apartment *AE*

Wohnung in einer früheren Stallung, f
- ♦ mews flat *BE*
- ♦ mews apartment *AE*

Wohnung ist eigengenutzt
- ♦ flat is owner-occupied *BE*
- ♦ apartment is owner-occupied *AE*

Wohnung ist hell
- ♦ apartment is bright *AE*
- ♦ flat is bright *BE*

Wohnung ist leer
- ♦ apartment is empty *AE*
- ♦ flat is empty *BE*

Wohnung ist mit allem Komfort ausgestattet
- ♦ apartment is equipped with all modern conveniences *AE*
- ♦ apartment is equipped with all modern amenities *AE*
- ♦ flat is equipped with all modern conveniences *BE*
- ♦ flat is equipped with all modern amenities *BE*

Wohnung kaufen
- ♦ buy an apartment *AE*
- ♦ buy a flat *BE*

Wohnung kündigen
- ♦ give notice that one is leaving the apartment *AE*
- ♦ give notice that one is leaving the flat *BE*
- ♦ give notice

Wohnung läßt sich gut vermieten
- ♦ flat lets well *BE*
- ♦ apartment rents well *AE*

Wohnung liegt direkt nach Süden
- ♦ apartment faces directly (to the) south *AE*
- ♦ flat faces directly (to the) south *BE*

Wohnung machen lassen sich
(tapezieren, streichen)

Wohnung mieten

- ◆ have one's apartment done over AE
- ◆ have one's flat done over BE

Wohnung mieten
- ◆ rent a flat BE
- ◆ rent an apartment AE

Wohnung mit allem modernen Komfort, f
- ◆ apartment with all modern conveniences AE
- ◆ apartment with all mod. cons. AE
- ◆ flat with all modern conveniences BE
- ◆ flat with all mod. cons. BE

Wohnung mit Balkon, f
- ◆ flat with balcony BE
- ◆ apartment with balcony AE

Wohnung mit Bedienung, f
Wohnung mit Service, f
- ◆ service flat BE
- ◆ service apartment AE
- ◆ serviced flat BE
- ◆ serviced apartment AE

Wohnung mitbenutzen
- ◆ share a flat BE
- ◆ share an apartment AE

Wohnung mit eigenem Eingang, f
→ abgeschlossene Wohnung

Wohnung mit einem Schlafzimmer, f
- ◆ one-bedroom flat BE
- ◆ one-bedroom apartment AE

Wohnung mit Küche und Bad, f
- ◆ flat with kitchen and bath BE
- ◆ apartment with kitchen and bath AE

Wohnung mit Service, f
→ Wohnung mit Bedienung

Wohnung mit Vollservice, f
- ◆ fully serviced flat BE
- ◆ fully serviced apartment AE

Wohnung mit zwei Badezimmern, f
- ◆ two-bathroom apartment AE
- ◆ two-bathroom flat BE

Wohnung mit zwei Schlafzimmern, f
- ◆ two-bedroom flat BE
- ◆ two-bedroom apartment AE

Wohnung möblieren
→ Wohnung einrichten

Wohnung nebenan, f
- ◆ flat next door BE
- ◆ apartment next door AE
- ◆ next-door apartment AE
- ◆ next-door flat BE

Wohnung ohne Gastgeberservice, f
Wohnung ohne Gastgeber, f
- ◆ unhosted apartment AE

Wohnung putzen
Wohnung reinigen
- ◆ clean a flat BE
- ◆ clean an apartment AE

Wohnungsamt, n
- ◆ housing office

Wohnungsangebot, n (Gegensatz zu Nachfrage)
- ◆ supply of apartments AE
- ◆ apartments available AE pl
- ◆ supply of flats BE
- ◆ flats available BE pl

Wohnungsangebot, n (Palette)
- ◆ range of apartments AE
- ◆ range of flats BE

Wohnungsanzeiger, m
→ Wohnungsliste

Wohnungsbau, m
- ◆ house building

Wohnungsbauprogramm, n
- ◆ housing scheme

Wohnungsbesetzer, m
→ Hausbesetzer

Wohnungsbesitzer, m
- ◆ flat owner BE
- ◆ owner of an apartment AE
- ◆ apartment owner AE
- ◆ owner of a flat BE

Wohnungsbrand, m
- ◆ apartment on fire AE
- ◆ flat on fire BE

Wohnungseingang, m
- ◆ apartment entrance AE
- ◆ flat entrance BE

Wohnungseinweihung, f
→ Einzugsfest

Wohnungsgeldzuschuß m
Wohngeld n
- ◆ rental allowance
- ◆ housing allowance BE

Wohnungsgenosse, m
- ◆ flat-mate BE

Wohnungsgröße, f
- ◆ size of the apartment AE
- ◆ apartment size AE
- ◆ size of the flat BE
- ◆ flat size BE

Wohnungsgrundriß, m
- ◆ layout of the apartment AE
- ◆ layout of the flat BE

Wohnungsinhaber, m
- ◆ occupant of a flat BE
- ◆ occupant of an apartment AE
- ◆ tenant
- ◆ renter AE

Wohnungsinventar, n
- ◆ apartment inventory AE
- ◆ flat inventory BE

Wohnungsknappheit, f
Wohnungsnot, f
- ◆ shortage of flats BE
- ◆ shortage of apartments AE
- ◆ housing shortage

Wohnungsliste, f
Wohnungsverzeichnis, n
Wohnungsanzeiger, m
- ◆ list of apartments AE
- ◆ list of flats BE

wohnungslos, adv (amtlich)
- ◆ without fixed abode, adv
- ◆ of no fixed abode, adv

Wohnungsmakler, m
- ◆ rental agent AE
- ◆ renting agent AE

Wohnungsmangel, m (Knappheit)
→ Wohnungsknappheit

Wohnungsmangel, m (völliges Fehlen)
- ◆ lack of apartments AE
- ◆ lack of flats BE

Wohnungsmarkt, m
- ◆ housing market

Wohnungsmietvertrag, m
- ◆ apartment lease AE
- ◆ flat lease BE
- ◆ flat letting contract BE

Wohnungsnachbar m
- ◆ person living next door

Wohnungsnot, f
Wohnungsknappheit, f
- ◆ housing shortage
- ◆ shortage of flats BE
- ◆ shortage of apartments AE

Wohnungspolitik, f
- ◆ housing policy

Wohnungspreis, m
- ◆ flat price BE
- ◆ price of a flat BE
- ◆ apartment price AE
- ◆ price of an apartment AE

Wohnungsproblem, n
- ◆ housing problem

Wohnungsschlüssel, m
- ◆ flat key BE
- ◆ apartment key AE

Wohnungssektor, m
Wohnungsbereich, m
- ◆ flat sector BE
- ◆ apartment sector AE

Wohnungssuche, f
- ◆ apartment-hunting AE
- ◆ flat-hunting
- ◆ house-hunting
- ◆ search for accommodation

wohnungssuchend, adj
- ◆ apartment-hunting, adj AE
- ◆ flat-hunting, adj BE
- ◆ accommodation-seeking, adj

Wohnungssuchender, m
- ◆ apartment-hunter AE
- ◆ flat-hunter BE
- ◆ accommodation seeker
- ◆ person looking for an apartment AE
- ◆ person looking for a flat BE

Wohnungstausch, m
- ◆ apartment-swap AE
- ◆ apartment-swapping AE
- ◆ flat-swap BE
- ◆ flat-swapping BE
- ◆ flat-swop BE

Wohnung steht leer
- ◆ flat is vacant BE
- ◆ apartment is vacant AE

Wohnung steht zum Verkauf
- ◆ flat is for sale BE
- ◆ apartment is for sale AE

Wohnungstyp, m
Wohnungsart, f
- ◆ type of apartment AE
- ◆ type of flat BE
- ◆ type of dwelling

Wohnung suchen
- ◆ look for an apartment AE
- ◆ seek an apartment AE
- ◆ look for a flat BE
- ◆ seek a flat BE

Wohnungsvermieter, m
- ◆ apartment lessor AE jur
- ◆ flat lessor BE jur
- ◆ landlord

Wohnungsvermietung, f
- ◆ renting an apartment AE
- ◆ renting apartments AE
- ◆ letting a flat BE
- ◆ letting flats BE
- ◆ flat-letting business BE

Wohnungsvermittlung, f
- ◆ rental agency
- ◆ house agency

Wohnungsverwaltung, f
- ◆ housing management

Wohnungswechsel, m
- ◆ moving house
- ◆ moving apartments AE

♦ moving flats *BE*
♦ move
Wohnung tauschen
♦ **swap apartments** *AE*
♦ swop apartments *AE*
♦ swap flats *BE*
♦ swop flats *BE*
Wohnung teilen mit jm
♦ **share an apartment with s.o.** *AE*
♦ share a flat with s.o. *BE*
Wohnung unterbewerten
♦ **underrate an apartment** *AE*
♦ undervalue an apartment *AE*
♦ underrate a flat *BE*
♦ undervalue a flat *BE*
Wohnung vermarkten
♦ **market an apartment** *AE*
♦ market a flat *BE*
Wohnung vermieten
♦ **rent an apartment** *AE*
♦ let a flat *BE*
♦ rent out a flat *BE*
Wohnung verwalten
♦ **manage an apartment** *AE*
♦ manage a flat *BE*
Wohnung wechseln
umziehen in ein anderes Haus
umziehen
♦ **move to another house**
♦ move house
♦ move
Wohnung wird für DM 12345 pro Jahr vermietet
♦ **apartment rents for DM 12345 per year** *AE*
♦ flat rents for DM 12345 per year *BE*
Wohnung zu vermieten
(Hinweisschild)
♦ **Flat to let** *BE*
♦ Apartment for rent *AE*
Wohnunterkunft, f
(Gegensatz zu Schlafunterkunft)
♦ **lodging accommodation** *AE*
♦ residential accommodation
♦ living accommodation
♦ lodging accommodation *AE*
♦ dwelling accommodation
Wohnviertel, n
(einer Stadt)
♦ **residential quarter**
Wohnwagen, m
Caravan, m
♦ **trailer** *AE*
♦ camper *AE*
♦ caravan *BE*
Wohnwagenabholstelle, f
Caravanabholstelle, f
♦ **trailer pick-up point** *AE*
♦ caravan pick-up point *BE*
Wohnwagenausstattung, f
Wohnwagenausrüstung, f
Caravanausstattung, f
Caravanausrüstung, f
♦ **trailer equipment** *AE*
♦ caravan equipment *BE*
Wohnwagenausstellung, f
Caravanausstellung, f
♦ **trailer exhibition** *AE*
♦ trailer exhibit *AE*
♦ trailer show *AE*
♦ caravan exhibition *BE*
♦ caravan show *BE*

Wohnwagenbenutzer, m
Caravanbenutzer, m
♦ **trailer user** *AE*
♦ person using a trailer *AE*
♦ caravan user *BE*
♦ person using a caravan *BE*
♦ trailerite *AE*
Wohnwagenbereich, m (konkret)
Caravanbereich, m
♦ **trailer area** *AE*
♦ caravan area *BE*
Wohnwagenbereich, m (Sektor)
→ Wohnwagensektor
Wohnwagenbesitzer, m
Caravanbesitzer, m
♦ **trailer owner** *AE*
♦ owner of a trailer *AE*
♦ caravan owner *BE*
♦ owner of a caravan *BE*
Wohnwagen bietet drei Personen Schlafmöglichkeiten
Caravan bietet drei Personen Schlafmöglichkeiten
♦ **trailer sleeps three persons** *AE*
♦ caravan sleeps three persons *BE*
Wohnwagencamper, m
Caravancamper, m
♦ **trailer camper** *AE*
♦ caravan camper *BE*
Wohnwagendorf, n
Caravandorf, n
♦ **trailer village** *AE*
♦ caravan village *BE*
Wohnwageneigentümer, m
Caravaneigentümer, m
♦ **trailer proprietor** *AE*
♦ proprietor of a trailer *AE*
♦ caravan proprietor *BE*
♦ proprietor of a caravan *BE*
Wohnwageneinheit, f
(Statistik)
Caravaneinheit, f
♦ **trailer unit** *AE*
♦ caravan unit *BE*
Wohnwagenerfahrung, f
Caravanerfahrung, f
♦ **trailer experience** *AE*
♦ caravanning experience *BE*
Wohnwagenfahrer, m
Caravanfahrer, m
♦ **trailerite** *AE*
♦ caravanner *BE*
Wohnwagengespann, n
Caravangespann, n
Anhängergespann, n
♦ **trailer outfit** *AE*
♦ caravan outfit *BE*
♦ outfit
Wohnwagengröße, f
Caravangröße, f
♦ **trailer size** *AE*
♦ size of a trailer *AE*
♦ caravan size *BE*
♦ size of a caravan *BE*
Wohnwagenindustrie, f
Caravanindustrie, f
♦ **trailer industry** *AE*
♦ caravan industry *BE*
♦ caravanning industry *BE*
Wohnwagen kann auf dem Platz untergebracht werden
Caravan kann auf dem Platz abgestellt werden

♦ **trailer can be accommodated on the site** *AE*
♦ caravan can be accommodated on the site *BE*
Wohnwagen kann bis zu sieben Personen aufnehmen
Caravan kann bis zu sieben Personen aufnehmen
♦ **trailer can accommodate up to seven persons** *AE*
♦ caravan can accommodate up to seven persons *BE*
Wohnwagenkurzurlaub, m
Caravankurzurlaub, m
♦ **trailer break** *AE*
♦ caravan break *BE*
♦ caravanning break *BE*
Wohnwagenmarke, f
Caravanmarke, f
♦ **trailer make** *AE*
♦ caravan make *BE*
Wohnwagenmiete, f
Caravanmiete, f
♦ **trailer rental** *AE*
♦ caravan hire *BE*
Wohnwagen mieten
Caravan mieten
♦ **rent a trailer** *AE*
♦ hire a caravan *BE*
Wohnwagenmietgebühr, f
Caravanmietgebühr, f
♦ **trailer rental charge** *AE*
♦ caravan hire charge *BE*
Wohnwagen mit Tandemachse, m
Caravan mit Tandemachse, m
♦ **tandem-axle trailer** *AE*
♦ tandem-axle caravan *BE*
Wohnwagenmodell, n
Caravanmodell, n
♦ **trailer model** *AE*
♦ caravan model *BE*
Wohnwagenpark, m
Caravanpark m
♦ **trailer park** *AE*
♦ caravan park *BE*
Wohnwagenparkbetreiber, m
Caravanparkbetreiber, m
♦ **trailer park operator** *AE*
♦ caravan park operator *BE*
Wohnwagenparkleiter, m
Caravanparkleiter, m
♦ **trailer park manager** *AE*
♦ caravan park manager *BE*
Wohnwagenpauschale, f
Caravanpauschale, f
♦ **trailer package** *AE*
♦ caravan package *BE*
Wohnwagenpauschalurlaub, m
Caravanpauschalurlaub, m
♦ **inclusive trailer vacation** *AE*
♦ inclusive caravan holiday *BE*
♦ inclusive caravanning holiday *BE*
Wohnwagenplatz, m
Caravanplatz, m
♦ **trailer site** *AE*
♦ caravan site *BE*
♦ trailer camp *AE*
Wohnwagenplatzbetreiber, m
Caravanplatzbetreiber, m
♦ **trailer site operator** *AE*
♦ trailer camp operator *AE*
♦ caravan site operator *BE*
Wohnwagenplatzverzeichnis, n
Caravanplatzverzeichnis, n

Wohnwagen pro Nacht

- trailer site directory *AE*
- caravan site directory *BE*

Wohnwagen pro Nacht, m
Caravan pro Nacht, m
- trailer per night *AE*
- caravan per night *BE*

Wohnwagenreise, f
Caravanreise, f
- trailer tour *AE*
- caravanning tour *BE*

Wohnwagenreise machen
Caravanreise machen
- go on a trailer tour *AE*
- go on a caravanning tour *BE*

Wohnwagenrückgabestelle, f
Caravanrückgabestelle, f
- trailer drop-off point *AE*
- caravan drop-off point *BE*

Wohnwagenschau, f
Wohnwagenausstellung, f
Caravanschau, f
Caravanausstellung, f
- trailer show *AE*
- caravan show *BE*

Wohnwagensektor, m
Wohnwagenbereich, m
Caravansektor, m
Caravanbereich, m
- trailer sector *AE*
- caravan sector *BE*

Wohnwagenstandort, m
Caravanstandort, m
- location of the trailer *AE*
- location of the caravan *BE*

Wohnwagenstellplatz, m
Caravanstellplatz, m
- trailer site *AE*
- caravan pitch *BE*

Wohnwagentarif, m
Caravantarif, m
- trailer tariff *AE*
- trailer rates *AE pl*
- trailer rate *AE*
- caravan tariff *BE*
- caravan rates *BE pl*

Wohnwagentyp, m
Caravantyp, m
- trailer type *AE*
- type of trailer *AE*
- caravan type *BE*
- type of caravan *BE*

Wohnwagenunterkunft, f
Wohnwagenunterbringung, f
Caravanunterkunft, f
Caravanunterbringung, f
- trailer accommodation *AE*
- trailer lodging *AE*
- caravan accommodation *BE*

Wohnwagen untervermieten
Caravan untervermieten
- sublease a trailer *AE*
- sublet a trailer *AE*
- sublet a caravan *BE*
- sublease a caravan *BE*

Wohnwagenurlaub, m
Wohnwagenferien, pl
Caravanurlaub, m
Caravanferien, pl
- trailer vacation *AE*
- caravan holiday *BE*
- caravanning holiday *BE*

Wohnwagenurlaub für Selbstfahrer, m
Caravanurlaub für Selbstfahrer, m
- self-driving caravanning holiday *BE*
- self-drive trailer vacation *AE*

Wohnwagenurlaub machen
- go on a trailer vacation *AE*
- go on a caravanning holiday *BE*
- take a trailer vacation *AE*
- take a caravanning holiday *BE*
- go caravanning *BE*

Wohnwagen vermieten
Caravan vermieten
- rent (out) a trailer
- let a caravan *BE*
- hire out a caravan *BE*

Wohnwagenvermietung, f
Caravanvermietung, f
- trailer rental *AE*
- renting a trailer *AE*
- caravan hire *BE*
- hiring out a caravan *BE*
- letting a caravan *BE*

Wohnwagenvorzelt, n
Caravanvorzelt, n
- trailer awning *AE*
- caravan awning *BE*

Wohnwagen ziehen
Caravan ziehen
- tow a trailer *AE*
- tow a caravan *BE*

Wohnwagen zum Urlaubsgebrauch, m
Caravan zum Urlaubsgebrauch, m
- trailer for vacation use *AE*
- caravan for holiday use *BE*

Wohnwagen zu vermieten
(Hinweisschild; ein Wohnwagen)
- Trailer for rent *AE*
- Caravan to let *BE*
- Caravan for hire *BE*

Wohnwagen zu vermieten
(Hinweisschild; mehrere Wohnwagen)
Caravans zu vermieten
- Trailers for rent *AE pl*
- Caravans to let *BE pl*

Wohnwand, f
- wall-to-wall cupboard

Wohnzelt, n
- dwelling tent
- residential tent

Wohnzimmer, n
- sitting-room *BE*
- sitting room *AE*
- living room *AE*
- living-room *BE*

Wohnzimmerbalkon, m
- living-room balcony
- sitting-room balcony

Wohnzimmersofa, n
- sitting-room sofa
- living-room sofa

Wohnzimmertür, f
- living-room door
- sitting-room door

Wohnzimmervorhang, m
- living-room curtain
- sitting-room curtain

Wohnzweck, m
- residential purpose

Wo ist der Speisesaal?
- Where is the dining room?

Wo ist die Damentoilette?
- Where is the Ladies?

Wo ist die Herrentoilette?
- Where is the Gents?

Wo kann ich das Auto parken?
- Where can I park the car?

Wo kann ich den Wagen abstellen?
Wo kann ich das Auto abstellen?
- Where can I leave the car?

Wolfgangsee m
- Wolfgangsee

Wolfsbarsch, m
- bass

Wolga, f
- Volga River, the
- River Volga, the
- Volga, the

Wo liegt das Hotel?
- Where is the hotel situated?

Wolkenkratzer, m
- skyscraper

Wolkenkuckucksland, n
- cloud-cuckoo land

Wolle, f
- wool

Wollen Sie eine Anzahlung machen oder den Betrag
ganz zahlen?
- Do you wish to make a deposit or to pay in full?

Wollen Sie ein Zimmer?
- Do you want a room?

Wollen Sie heute abend unser Gast sein?
- Will you be our guest tonight?
- Will you dine with us tonight?

Wollen Sie sich unserer Gruppe anschließen?
- Will you join our party?

Wollhandel, m
- wool trade

Wollhändler, m
- wool merchant

Wollindustrie, f
- wool industry

Wollstadt, f
- wool town

Wo möchten Sie sitzen? Am Fenster oder weiter hinten?
- Where would you like to sit? By the window or
- further back?

Worauf haben Sie Appetit?
- What do you fancy?

Worcestershire
- Worcestershire

Worcestersoße, f
- Worcestershire sauce

Workshop, m
- workshop

Workshop abhalten
- hold a workshop

Workshop durchführen
- run a workshop

Workshopeinführung, f
- workshop introduction

Workshop leiten (als Vorsitzender)
Workshop vorsitzen
- chair a workshop

Workshop leiten (generell)
- conduct a workshop
- lead a workshop

Workshopsitzung, f
 ♦ workshop session
Workshop zu etw, m
 ♦ workshop on s.th.
World Travel Market, m
 ♦ World Travel Market, the
Worte der Begrüßung, n pl
 ♦ words of welcome pl
Worte der Begrüßung an jn richten
 ♦ address a few words of welcome to s.o.
Wo wird das Frühstück serviert?
 ♦ Where is breakfast served?
Wo wohnen Sie? (dauernd)
 ♦ Where do you live?
Wo wohnen Sie? (vorübergehend)
 Wo sind Sie untergebracht?
 ♦ Where are you staying?
WTO, f
 Welt-Tourismus-Organisation, f
 ♦ WTO
 ♦ World Tourism Organisation
 ♦ World Tourism Organization
Wuchergebühr, f
 ♦ cutthroat charge
 ♦ cutthroat fee
 ♦ extortionate charge
 ♦ extortionate fee
wucherischer Vermieter, m
 ♦ rack-renter
Wuchermiete, f
 ♦ rack rent AE
 ♦ rack-rent BE
 ♦ extortionate rent
Wuchermiete verlangen
 ♦ rack-rent
Wucherpreis, m
 ♦ cutthroat rate
 ♦ cutthroat price
 ♦ extortionate price
 ♦ extortionate rate
Wuchervermieter, m
 → wucherischer Vermieter
wunderbare Lage, f
 ♦ wonderful location
 ♦ wonderful position
 ♦ wonderful situation
 ♦ wonderful setting
wunderbare Lage einnehmen
 ♦ occupy a wonderful location
 ♦ occupy a wonderful position
 ♦ occupy a wonderful situation
 ♦ occupy a wonderful setting
wunderbare Möglichkeiten für Wintersport, f pl
 ♦ wonderful facilities for wintersports pl
wunderbaren Blick auf etw bieten
 ♦ offer a wonderful view of s.th.
wunderbarer Blick, m
 wunderbarer Ausblick, m
 wunderbare Aussicht, f
 ♦ wonderful view
 ♦ splendid view
wunderbar gelegen, adj
 ♦ wonderfully positioned, adj
 ♦ wonderfully located, adj
 ♦ wonderfully situated, adj
wunderbar gelegenes Hotel, n
 ♦ wonderfully positioned hotel
 ♦ wonderfully located hotel
 ♦ wonderfully situated hotel
Wunder der Baukunst, n
 ♦ architectural wonder

Wunderheilung, f
 ♦ miracle cure
Wunderland, n
 ♦ wonderland
wunderschöne Zeit verbringen
 ♦ have a wonderful time
Wunder von Ägypten, die, n pl
 ♦ wonders of Egypt, the, pl
Wunsch, m
 ♦ request
Wunsch ablehnen
 ♦ reject a request
 ♦ turn down a request
Wunsch ablehnen jm
 Wunsch jm versagen
 ♦ deny s.o. a wish
Wunsch angeben
 ♦ state a request
 ♦ indicate a request
 ♦ state a requirement
 ♦ indicate a requirement
Wunsch äußern
 ♦ express a wish
Wunsch bearbeiten
 ♦ process a request
Wünsche erfüllen von jm
 js Wünsche erfüllen
 ♦ meet s.o.'s wishes
wünschen etw
 nachsuchen um etw
 bitten um etw
 ♦ request s.th.
Wünschen Sie morgen früh geweckt zu werden?
 ♦ Do you wish to be called in the morning?
Wünschen Sie noch etwas?
 ♦ Would you like anything else?
Wunsch erfüllen jm
 ♦ fulfill s.o.'s wish AE
 ♦ fulfil s.o.'s wish
Wunsch geht in Erfüllung
 ♦ wish comes true
 ♦ wish is fulfilled
Wunsch jm von den Augen ablesen
 ♦ anticipate s.o.'s wish
Wunschkonzert, n
 ♦ request program AE
 ♦ request programme BE
Wunsch offenlassen
 ♦ leave a wish unsatisfied
Wunschtarif, m
 ♦ whichever-is-cheaper tariff
Wunsch wiederholen
 ♦ renew a request
Wunsch zustimmen
 ♦ agree to a request
Würden Sie bitte die Anmeldung unterschreiben?
 ♦ Would you mind signing the register?
Würden Sie bitte dieses Formular ausfüllen?
 ♦ Would you mind filling out this form? AE
 ♦ Would you mind filling in this form? BE
 ♦ Would you mind completing this form?
Würden Sie bitte hier entlang kommen?
 ♦ Would you please come this way?
 ♦ Would you come this way, please?
Würden Sie bitte hier unterschreiben?
 ♦ Would you sign here, please?
Würden Sie mir bitte folgen?
 ♦ Will you please follow me, Sir?
 ♦ Will you please follow me, Madam?
Würdenträger, m
 ♦ dignitary

würdige Atmosphäre, f
 ♦ dignified atmosphere
würdige Atmosphäre verleihen etw
 ♦ lend s.th. a dignified atmosphere
Würfel, m
 ♦ cube
würfeln etw gastr
 in Würfel schneiden etw gastr
 ♦ dice s.th. gastr
Würfelzucker, m
 ♦ cube sugar
 ♦ cut sugar
Wurftaubenschießen, n
 Trapschießen, n
 ♦ trap shooting
Wurst, f
 Würstchen, n
 ♦ sausage
 ♦ banger BE inform
Wurstaufschnitt, m
 ♦ assorted sausages pl
Würstchen, n
 ♦ small sausage
Würstchenbude, f
 Wurststand, m
 ♦ sausage stand
 ♦ sausage stall
 ♦ hot-dog stand
Würstchenstand, m
 Wurststand, m
 ♦ hot-dog stand AE
 ♦ sausage stand
 ♦ sausage stall BE
 ♦ hot-dog stall BE
Wurstfüllung, f
 Wurstfüllsel, n
 Wurstmasse, f
 ♦ sausage meat
Wurst grillen
 Würstchen grillen
 ♦ grill a sausage
Wursthaut, f
 ♦ sausage skin
Wurstmarkt m
 (Fest)
 ♦ Sausage Fair
Wurstplatte, f
 ♦ sausage platter
 ♦ platter of cold cuts
Wurstsandwich, n
 ♦ sausage sandwich
Wurststand, m
 → Würstchenstand
Württemberg
 (Region)
 ♦ Wuerttemberg
Württemberger Wein, m
 ♦ Wuerttemberg wine
Würzbutter, f
 ♦ spicy butter
Würze, f (das Würzen)
 ♦ seasoning
Würze, f (Gewürz)
 ♦ condiment
 ♦ spice
 ♦ relish
Wurzelgemüse, n
 ♦ root vegetable
 ♦ root vegetables pl
würzen etw
 abschmecken etw

würzen etw mit Salz

- season s.th.
- flavor s.th. *AE*
- flavour s.th. *BE*

würzen etw mit Salz
- season s.th. with salt

würzen etw nach Geschmack
- season s.th. to taste

Wurzenpaß, m
- Wurzen Pass, the

würzig, adj
- spicy, adj

Wüste, f
- desert

Wüstenferienort, m
- desert resort

Wüstengebiet, f
- desert area

Wüstenlandschaft, f
- desert landscape
- barren landscape

Wüstenregion, f
- desert region

Wüstenreise, f
- desert tour
- tour through the desert

Wüstensafari, f
- desert safari

Wüstenschiff, n
(Kamel)
- ship of the desert

Wüste Sahara, f
- Sahara Desert, the

Wüstling, m
- rake
- debauchee

WW, n
Warmwasser, n
- HW
- hot water

X Y Z

x-beliebig, adj
- ♦ any ... you like

x-beliebiges Hotel, n
- ♦ any hotel you like

xenophob, adj
- fremdenfeindlich, adj
- ♦ xenophobic, adj
- ♦ hostile to strangers, adj
- ♦ hostile to foreigners, adj

Xenophobie, f
- Fremdenfeindlichkeit, f
- ♦ xenophobia

X-fache, n
- ♦ umpteen times

x-förmig, adj
- ♦ x-shaped, adj

X für ein U vormachen jm
- ♦ pull the wool over s.o.'s eyes
- ♦ try to pull the wool over s.o.'s eyes

x-tes Mal, n
- ♦ umpteenth time

Xylophon, n
- ♦ xylophone

Yacht, f
- → Jacht

Yankee, m
- ♦ Yankee
- ♦ Yank

Yen, m
- ♦ yen

Y-förmig, adj
- ♦ Y-shaped, adj

Yield Management, n
- ♦ yield management

Yoga, n
- ♦ yoga

Yogakurs, m
- ♦ yoga class
- ♦ yoga course

Yogastunde, f
- Yogasitzung, f
- ♦ yoga session

Yogaübung, f
- ♦ yoga exercise

Yogaunterricht, m
- ♦ yoga lessons *pl*

Yogi, m
- ♦ yogi

Yorkshire
- ♦ Yorkshire

Yorkshire Dales, pl
- ♦ Yorkshire Dales, the *pl*

Yosemite Nationalpark, m
- ♦ Yosemite National Park, the

Yukatan
- ♦ Yucatan

Yukatan-Halbinsel, f
- ♦ Yucatan peninsula, the

Yuppie, m
- ♦ yuppie

zähes Fleisch, n
- ♦ tough meat

Zahl, f
- ♦ figure
- ♦ number

zahlbar, adj (fällig)
- → fällig

zahlbar, adj (generell)
- ♦ payable, adj

zahlbar an Ort und Stelle
- ♦ payable on the spot

zahlbar auf Anforderung
- ♦ payable on demand

zahlbar bei Vorlage
- ♦ payable on presentation
- ♦ payable at sight

zahlbar sein
- ♦ be payable

Zahl der angebotenen Zimmer, f
- ♦ number of rooms offered
- ♦ number of rooms on offer

Zahl der angebotenen Zimmer erhöhen
- ♦ increase the number of rooms on offer

Zahl der angebotenen Zimmer senken
- ♦ lower the number of rooms on offer
- ♦ reduce the number of rooms on offer

Zahl der Ankünfte f
- ♦ number of arrivals

Zahl der Auslandsreisen, f
- ♦ number of trips abroad
- ♦ number of journeys abroad
- ♦ number of tours abroad

Zahl der belegten Zimmer, f
- ♦ number of occupied rooms

Zahl der Besuche, f
- Besuchszahl, f
- ♦ number of visits

Zahl der Besucher, f
- Besucherzahl

Zahl der Betten, f
- ♦ number of beds

Zahl der Betten hat sich verdoppelt
- ♦ number of beds (has) doubled

Zahl der Betten hat sich verdreifacht
- ♦ number of beds (has) trebled
- ♦ number of beds (has) tripled

Zahl der Betten hat sich vervierfacht
- ♦ number of beds (has) quadrupled

Zahl der Bettnächte f
- Bettnächtezahl f
- ♦ number of bed-nights

Zahl der erwarteten Gäste, f
- ♦ number of expected guests

Zahl der Essen, f
- ♦ number of meals

Zahl der Fremdenübernachtungen, f (generell)
- ♦ number of tourist nights

Zahl der Fremdenübernachtungen, f (Statistik)
- ♦ number of tourist bed-nights spent
- ♦ number of tourist bed-nights

Zahl der Gästeankünfte, f
- ♦ number of guest arrivals

Zahl der Gäste pro Zimmer, f
- ♦ number of guests per room

Zahl der Hotelgästezimmer, f
- ♦ number of hotel bedrooms

Zahl der Hotelneubauten, f (fertiggestellt)
- ♦ number of newly built hotels
- ♦ number of newly constructed hotels

Zahl der Hotelneubauten, f (gerade im Bau)
- ♦ number of hotels under construction

Zahl der Hotels, f
- ♦ number of hotels

Zahl der Reisen, f
- ♦ number of trips
- ♦ number of journeys
- ♦ number of tours

Zahl der Stellplätze, f
- → Stellplatzzahl

Zahl der Übernachtungen, f (generell)
- Anzahl der Übernachtungen, f
- ♦ number of nights

Zahl der Übernachtungen, f (Statistik)
- ♦ number of nights spent

Zahl der verfügbaren Zimmer, f
- ♦ number of available rooms

Zahl der verkauften Essen, f
- ♦ number of meals sold

Zahl der verkauften Zimmer, f
- ♦ number of rooms sold

Zahl der vermieteten Zimmer, f
- ♦ number of rooms rented *AE*
- ♦ number of rooms let *BE*

Zahl der Zimmernächte f
- Zimmernächtezahl f
- ♦ number of room-nights

Zahl der zum Verkauf angebotenen Zimmer, f
- ♦ number of rooms on sale

zahlen
- ♦ pay

zählen auf js Diskretion
- ♦ count on s.o.'s discretion

zahlende Gäste aufnehmen
- ♦ take in paying guests

zahlender Besucher, m
- ♦ paying visitor

zahlender Gast, m
- ♦ paying guest
- ♦ P.G.

zahlender Passagier, m
  ♦ revenue passenger
zahlender Zuschauer, m
  ♦ paying spectator
zahlendes Mitglied, n
  ♦ paying member
zahlen etw innerhalb einer Woche
  ♦ pay s.th. within a week
zahlen für Komfort und Bequemlichkeit
  ♦ pay for comfort and convenience
zahlen für Luxus
  ♦ pay for luxury
zahlen im voraus
  im voraus zahlen
  ♦ pay in advance
zahlen in klingender Münze
  ♦ pay in hard cash
zahlen mit Kreditkarte
  zahlen per Kreditkarte
  ♦ pay by credit card
  ♦ pay with a credit card
zahlen per Kreditkarte
  → zahlen mit Kreditkarte
zahlen per Scheck
  zahlen mit Scheck
  ♦ pay by check *AE*
  ♦ pay by cheque *BE*
Zahlen Sie bar oder mit Scheck?
  ♦ Are you paying in cash or by check? *AE*
  ♦ Are you paying in cash or by cheque? *BE*
zahlen unter Vorbehalt
  zahlen mit Vorbehalt
  ♦ pay with reservation
  ♦ pay with proviso
  ♦ pay on condition
Zahlenverhältnis, n
  Verhältnis, n
  ♦ ratio
Zahlenverhältnis des Personals zu den Gästen, n
  ♦ ratio of staff to guests
zählen zu den Gästen
  ♦ count amongst the guests
zählen zu den Spezialitäten
  (Speisekarte)
  ♦ rate among the specialties *AE*
  ♦ rate among the specialities *BE*
Zähler, m
  (für Strom, Gas, Wasser etc.)
  ♦ meter
Zähler ablesen
  ♦ read a meter
Zählermiete, f
  ♦ meter rental
Zählerstand, m
  ♦ meter reading
Zahlkarte, f
  ♦ money order
  ♦ postal money order
Zahlkellner, m
  → Oberkellner
zahllose Möglichkeiten, f pl
  ♦ countless possibilities *pl*
zahllose Möglichkeiten bieten für etw
  ♦ provide countless possibilities for s.th.
Zahlmeister, m (Schiff)
  ♦ purser
Zahlmeisterbüro, n
  ♦ purser's office
zahlreiche Besucher, m pl
  ♦ numerous visitors *pl*

Zahlung, f
  ♦ payment
Zahlungen müssen bar in DM erfolgen
  ♦ payments must be made in DM in cash
Zahlungen müssen durch Kreditkarte erfolgen
  ♦ payments must be made by credit card
Zahlungen müssen per Scheck erfolgen
  ♦ payments must be made by check *AE*
  ♦ payments must be made by cheque *BE*
Zahlung garantieren
  ♦ guarantee payment
Zahlung leisten
  ♦ make payment
  ♦ effect payment
Zahlungsart, f
  Art der Bezahlung, f
  Zahlungsweise, f
  ♦ mode of payment
  ♦ method of payment
Zahlungsart angeben
  ♦ indicate the method of payment
  ♦ state the method of payment
Zahlungsaufforderung, f
  ♦ invitation to pay
  ♦ request for payment
Zahlungsbedingungen, f pl
  ♦ terms of payment *pl*
  ♦ terms *pl*
  ♦ conditions of payment *pl*
  ♦ payment conditions *pl*
Zahlungsbestätigung, f
  ♦ confirmation of payment
Zahlungsbilanz, f
  ♦ balance of payments
Zahlungsbilanzdefizit, n
  ♦ balance of payments deficit
Zahlungsbilanzüberschuß, m
  ♦ balance of payments surplus
Zahlungsfähigkeit, f
  Bonität, f
  ♦ solvency
Zahlungsform, f
  ♦ form of payment
zahlungskräftig, adj
  zahlungsfähig, adj
  solvent, adj
  ♦ solvent, adj
zahlungskräftiger Gast m
  ♦ solvent guest
zahlungskräftiger Kunde, m
  ♦ solvent customer
  ♦ solvent client
Zahlungsmodus, m
  → Zahlungsweise, Zahlungsart
Zahlungsort, m
  ♦ place of payment
zahlungsunfähig, adj
  insolvent, adj
  ♦ insolvent, adj
zahlungsunfähiger Gast, m
  ♦ insolvent guest
Zahlungsunfähigkeit, f
  Insolvenz, f
  ♦ insolvency
zahlungsunfähig werden
  ♦ become insolvent
Zahlungsverweigerung, f
  ♦ refusal to pay
Zahlungsverzug, m
  ♦ default in payment

  ♦ default
  ♦ delay in payment
Zahlungsweise, f
  ♦ method of payment
  ♦ mode of payment
Zahnarzt, m
  ♦ dentist
Zahnärztekongreß m
  ♦ dentists' convention
Zahnarztpraxis, f
  ♦ dental suite
  ♦ dentist's practice
Zahnbürste, f
  ♦ toothbrush
Zähne putzen (sich)
  ♦ brush one's teeth
Zahnpasta, f
  Zahncreme, f
  ♦ toothpaste
Zahnradbahn, f
  ♦ rack railroad *AE*
  ♦ rack-railway *BE*
  ♦ cog-railway *AE*
  ♦ cogwheel-railway *BE*
Zahnradbergbahn, f
  ♦ rack mountain railroad *AE*
  ♦ rack mountain railway *BE*
Zahnstocher m
  ♦ toothpick
zäh wie Leder
  (Fleisch etc.)
  ♦ tough as leather
Zaire
  ♦ Zaire
Zairer, m
  ♦ Zairean
Zairerin, f
  ♦ Zairean girl
  ♦ Zairean woman
  ♦ Zairean
zairisch, adj
  ♦ Zairean, adj
Zander, m
  ♦ pike perch
  ♦ zander
Zanderfilet, n
  ♦ pike-perch fillet
  ♦ pike-perch filet
Zange, f
  ♦ tongs *pl*
  ♦ pair of tongs
Zänker, m
  Streiter, m
  ♦ wrangler
Zapfanlage, f
  ♦ tapping mechanism
zapfen etw
  ♦ tap s.th.
  ♦ draw s.th.
Zapfenstreich, m *mil*
  ♦ last post *BE mil*
  ♦ curfew *mil*
  ♦ tattoo
  ♦ taps *AE pl*
Zapfer, m
  ♦ tapster
  ♦ barman
Zapfhahn, m
  Hahn, m
  ♦ faucet *AE*
  ♦ tap

Zahnpflege- und Rasierset = Dental care and razor set

zart, adj *gastr*
 ♦ tender, adj *gastr*
zartes Fleisch, n
 ♦ tender meat
Zauberbrunnen, m
 ♦ wishing well
Zauberer, m
 ♦ conjuror
zauberhafte Landschaft, f
 ♦ enchanting scenery
 ♦ enchanting countryside
 ♦ enchanting landscape
Zauberinsel, f
 ♦ magic island
Zaubertrick, m
 ♦ conjuring trick
Zauber vergangener Zeiten, m
 ♦ charm of bygone days
Zauber verlieren
 Charme verlieren
 ♦ lose one's charm
 ♦ lose its charm
Zaungast, m
 ♦ onlooker
 ♦ railbird *sl*
Zebrastreifen, m
 ♦ zebra crossing
 ♦ pelican crossing *BE*
Zeche, f
 ♦ bill
 ♦ check *AE*
Zeche bezahlen
 Zeche zahlen
 ♦ pay the bill
 ♦ pay one's bill
 ♦ foot the bill *coll*
 ♦ stand the shot *BE coll*
Zeche bezahlen müssen
 ♦ have to foot the bill
 ♦ have to pay the bill
zechen
 ♦ carouse
 ♦ booze *coll*
 ♦ tipple
 ♦ quaff *obs*
Zechen, n
 ♦ boozing
 ♦ carousing
 ♦ quaffing *obs*
zechen bis in die frühen Morgenstunden
 ♦ carouse until the small hours
 ♦ carouse until the early hours
zechen bis in die Puppen *coll*
 zechen bis in die frühen Morgenstunden
 ♦ revel into the small hours
Zeche prellen
 Zeche nicht zahlen
 Rechnung nicht zahlen
 ♦ bilk
 ♦ dodge paying the bill
 ♦ duck paying the bill *AE coll*
 ♦ duck out *AE sl*
 ♦ not pay the bill
Zecher, m (generell)
 ♦ carouser
 ♦ reveler *AE*
 ♦ reveller *BE*
 ♦ boozer *coll*
 ♦ tippler
Zecher, m (gewohnheitsmäßig)
 Säufer, m

 ♦ toper
 ♦ heavy drinker
 ♦ tippler
 ♦ boozer *coll*
Zeche zahlen (für etw)
 ♦ foot the bill (for s.th.)
 ♦ pay the bill (for s.th.)
Zeche zahlen lassen jn
 ♦ make s.o. pay one's bill
Zechkumpan, m
 ♦ drinking companion
Zechpreller, m
 ♦ walk-out guest
 ♦ walk-out *sl*
 ♦ bilker
 ♦ defrauder
 ♦ skip *AE sl*
Zechprellerei, f
 ♦ bilking
 ♦ hotel fraud
 ♦ bill dodging
Zechprellerei begehen (Hotel)
 → Hotelbetrug begehen
Zechschuld, f
 ♦ drinking debt
Zechschulden haben
 ♦ have drinking debts
Zechtour, f
 Kneipenbummel, m
 Sauftour, f *vulg*
 ♦ pub crawl *BE*
 ♦ barhop *AE*
Zechtour machen
 auf eine Zechtour gehen
 Bierreise machen
 Sauftour machen *vulg*
 ♦ go on a pub crawl *BE*
 ♦ barhop *AE*
 ♦ go barhopping *AE*
Zecke, f
 ♦ tick
Zehe Knoblauch, f
 ♦ clove of garlic
zehnbettig, adj
 ♦ ten-bedded, adj
zehnbettiger Schlafsaal, m
 ♦ ten-bedded dormitory
zehngängig, adj (Essen)
 ♦ ten-course, adj
 ♦ consisting of ten courses
zehnminütig, adj
 ♦ ten-minute, adj
 ♦ lasting ten minutes
 ♦ of ten minutes' duration
zehnminütiger Spaziergang, m
 ♦ ten-minute walk
zehnstöckig, adj attr
 ♦ ten-floor, adj attr
 ♦ ten-story, adj attr *AE*
 ♦ ten-storey, adj attr *AE*
zehnstöckig, adj prd
 ♦ ten-storied, adj prd *AE*
 ♦ ten-storeyed, adj prd *BE*
zehnstöckiges Hotel, n
 ♦ ten-floor hotel
 ♦ ten-story hotel *AE*
 ♦ ten-storey hotel *BE*
zehnstündig, adj
 ♦ ten-hour, adj
 ♦ ten hours', adj

 ♦ of ten hours' duration
 ♦ lasting ten hours
zehnstündiger Marsch, m
 ♦ ten hours' march
zehnstündige Verspätung, f
 ♦ ten-hour delay
Zehntagepaß, m
 ♦ ten-day pass
Zehntagepreis, m
 ♦ ten-day price
 ♦ ten-day rate
zehntägig, adj
 ♦ ten-day, adj
 ♦ ten days', adj
 ♦ of ten days' duration
 ♦ lasting ten days
zehnter Gang, m (Menü)
 ♦ tenth course
Zehnthaus, n
 ♦ tithe house
Zehntscheuer, f
 Zehntscheune, f
 ♦ tithe barn
Zehntwein, m
 ♦ tithe wine
zehnwöchig, adj
 ♦ ten-week, adj
 ♦ lasting ten weeks
 ♦ of ten weeks' duration
zehnwöchige Reise, f
 ♦ ten-week journey
 ♦ ten-week tour
 ♦ ten-week trip
zehnwöchige Tournee, f
 ♦ ten-week tour
Zehnzimmerhotel, n
 ♦ ten-room hotel
 ♦ ten-roomed hotel
zehnzimmerig, adj
 ♦ ten-roomed, adj
zehnzimmeriges Hotel, n
 ♦ ten-roomed hotel
Zehnzimmervilla, f
 ♦ ten-room villa
Zeichenblock, m
 ♦ drawing pad
Zeichensprache, f
 ♦ sign language
zeigen, was man kann
 ♦ give a taste of one's quality
zeigen etw in einer Ausstellung
 ♦ show s.th. in an exhibition
 ♦ display s.th. in an exhibition
zeigen etw jm
 ♦ show s.o. s.th.
 ♦ show s.th. to s.o.
Zeigestock, m
 (bei Tagungen)
 Zeigestab m
 ♦ pointer
Zeit, ins Bett zu gehen
 ♦ time to go to bed
Zeitablauf, m
 (Programm)
 ♦ timetable
Zeit aufbringen für etw
 ♦ afford time for s.th.
Zeit der Anmeldung, f
 → Zeitpunkt der Anmeldung

Zeit der Spitzennachfrage

Zeit der Spitzennachfrage, f
   Zeit des Spitzenbedarfs f
   ♦ period of peak demand
Zeit des Zwischenstopps, f
   Zeitpunkt des Zwischenstopps, m
   ♦ time of the intermediate stop
Zeiteigentum, n
   (von Immobilien)
   Zeitmiteigentum, n
   Timeshare-Eigentum, n
   ♦ timeshare ownership
   ♦ ownership of the timeshare
Zeiteigentümer, m
   (von Immobilien)
   Zeitmiteigentümer, m
   Timeshare-Eigentümer, m
   ♦ timeshare holder
   ♦ timeshare owner
Zeitfahrkarte, f
   → Zeitkarte
Zeit für das Reisen, f
   ♦ time for travel
Zeit für den Kaffee, f
   ♦ time for coffee
Zeit für einen Urlaub, f
   ♦ time for a vacation AE
   ♦ time for a holiday BE
zeitgenössische Möbel, n pl
   ♦ contemporary furniture sg
zeitig ankommen
   → rechtzeitig ankommen
zeitiges Frühstück, n
   → vorzeitiges Frühstück
Zeitkarte, f
   (z.B. Zug, Tram)
   Zeitfahrkarte, f
   ♦ season ticket
   ♦ commutation ticket AE
Zeitkarteninhaber, m
   ♦ season ticket holder
   ♦ commutation ticket holder AE
zeitlich begrenztes Timesharing, n
   (ohne Grundstücksübertragungsurkunde)
   ♦ right-to-use timesharing AE
Zeitlosigkeit, f
   ♦ timelessness
Zeitmiteigentum kaufen
   ♦ buy timeshare
Zeitplan, m
   ♦ time schedule
   ♦ schedule
Zeitpunkt der Anmeldung, m
   Zeitpunkt der Registrierung, m
   Zeit der Anmeldung, f
   Zeit der Registrierung, f
   ♦ time of registration
Zeitpunkt des Check-in, m
   Zeit des Check-in, f
   ♦ time of check-in
Zeitpunkt des Einpassierens, m
   → Eintreffenszeit
zeitraubend, adj
   ♦ time-consuming, adj
Zeitraum, m
   Zeitspanne, f
   Frist, f
   ♦ period of time
   ♦ period
Zeitraum mit schwacher Belegung, m
   Zeitraum mit schwacher Auslastung, m

   ♦ period of slack occupancy
   ♦ period of low occupancy
Zeitreisender, m
   (Science Fiction)
   Reisender durch die Zeiten, m
   ♦ time traveller
   ♦ time traveler AE
Zeitschriftenlesesaal, m
   ♦ periodicals room
   ♦ newsroom BE
Zeit totschlagen
   ♦ kill time
   ♦ laze the hours away
   ♦ while away (the) time
   ♦ while away one's time
Zeitüberschreitung, f
   (z.B. bei Vermietung)
   ♦ expiry of the fixed time limit
Zeit übrig haben
   ♦ have time to spare
Zeit und Geld sparen
   ♦ save time and money
Zeitung, f
   ♦ newspaper
   ♦ paper
Zeitung lesen
   ♦ read a newspaper
   ♦ read a paper
Zeitungsannonce, f
   ♦ newspaper advertisement
   ♦ advertisement
Zeitungsbeilage, f
   ♦ insert
   ♦ supplement
Zeitungsgeschäft, n
   ♦ newspaper store AE
   ♦ newspaper shop BE
Zeitungshändler, m
   Zeitungsverkäufer, m
   ♦ newsagent
   ♦ news dealer AE
Zeitungsjunge, m
   ♦ paper boy
Zeitungskiosk, m
   ♦ newspaper kiosk
Zeitungsstand, m
   Zeitungskiosk m
   ♦ newsstand AE
   ♦ news stall BE
Zeitungsverkäufer, m
   ♦ news vendor
Zeitungswerbung, f
   Zeitungsreklame, f
   ♦ newspaper advertising
Zeitunterschied, m
   ♦ time difference
Zeit verbummeln
   ♦ idle away one's time
   ♦ waste (one's) time
Zeit verkürzen sich
   (die) Zeit verbringen
   ♦ while away (the) time
   ♦ while away one's time
Zeit verträumen
   Stunden verträumen
   ♦ dream the hours away
Zeitvertreib, m
   ♦ pastime
zeitweilig, adj
   vorübergehend, adj
   ♦ temporary, adj

zeitweiliger Auslandsaufenthalt, m
   vorübergehender Auslandsaufenthalt, m
   ♦ temporary stay abroad
zeitweilige Schließung, f
   → vorübergehende Schließung
zeitweise, adv
   ♦ at times, adv
   ♦ occasionally, adv
   ♦ from time to time, adv
Zeitwert, m
   ♦ current value
Zeitzone, f
   ♦ time zone
Zeit zum Aufbrechen, f
   ♦ time to set off
Zeit zum Einkaufen, f
   ♦ time for shopping
Zeit zur freien Verfügung
   (in Programm)
   ♦ time at leisure
Zellophan, n
   ♦ cellophane
Zelltherapie, f
   ♦ cellular therapy
Zelt, n (für Feste)
   → Festzelt
Zelt, n (generell)
   ♦ tent
Zelt abbauen
   ♦ dismantle a tent
Zelt abschlagen
   Zelt abbrechen
   Zelte abbrechen
   ♦ strike a tent
   ♦ strike the tent
   ♦ strike tents
Zelt aufbauen
   ♦ set up a tent
   ♦ put up a tent
Zelt auf Rädern, n
   ♦ tent on wheels
Zelt aufschlagen
   Zelt aufbauen
   ♦ pitch a tent
   ♦ put up a tent
Zelt aufschlagen für die Nacht
   ♦ pitch a tent for the night
Zelt aufstellen
   ♦ put up a tent
   ♦ fix up a tent AE
   ♦ set up a tent
Zeltausrüstung, f
   Zeltausstattung, f
   ♦ tent equipment
Zeltbahn, f
   Zeltplane, f
   Segeltuchplane, f
   ♦ tarpaulin
Zeltbau, m
   ♦ tented structure
Zeltbenutzer, m
   ♦ tent user
   ♦ person using a tent
Zeltbesitzer, m
   ♦ tent owner
   ♦ owner of a tent
Zeltbewohner, m
   ♦ occupier of a tent
   ♦ camper

Zeltboden, m
♦ tent floor
♦ ground sheet
Zeltbodenplane, f
♦ ground sheet
Zeltcamp, n
→ Zeltlager
Zeltcamper, m
♦ tent camper
Zeltcamping, n
♦ tent camping
Zeltcampingplatz, m
♦ tent campsite
♦ tent campground *AE*
♦ tent camping site *BE*
♦ tent camping ground *BE*
♦ tent site
Zeltcaravan, m
Zeltwohnwagen, m
♦ trailer tent *BE*
♦ camper trailer *AE*
♦ tent trailer *AE*
Zeltdach, n
zeltförmiges Dach, n
♦ tent roof
♦ tented roof
Zeltdiebstahl, m
Diebstahl eines Zeltes, m
♦ tent theft
Zeltdorf, n
♦ tent village
Zelte abbrechen in X (abstrakt)
♦ strike one's tent in X
Zelte abbrechen (konkret)
Lager räumen
♦ decamp
Zelte aufschlagen in X *figur*
seine Zelte aufschlagen in X
sich niederlassen in X
♦ pitch one's tents in X *figur*
zelten
♦ tent
♦ camp out
♦ camp
Zelten, n
→ Camping
zelten gehen
campen gehen
♦ go camping
zelten im Garten
♦ camp out in the garden
Zelten ist verboten
→ Camping ist verboten
zelten über Nacht
über Nacht zelten
♦ camp overnight
Zelten verboten
(Hinweisschild)
♦ No camping
Zelt errichten
♦ erect a tent
♦ erect the tent
Zeltexpedition, f
Campingexpedition, f
♦ camping expedition
Zeltfahrt, f
→ Campingfahrt
zeltförmig, adj
♦ tent-shaped, adj
♦ tented, adj

zeltförmiges Dach, n
Zeltdach, n
♦ tent-shaped roof
♦ tented roof
Zeltfreizeit, f
→ Zeltferien
Zelt für sechs Personen, n
♦ tent for six persons
Zeltgebühr, f
(auf Campingplatz)
♦ tent charge
♦ tent fee
Zelthering, m
♦ tent peg *AE*
♦ tent-peg *BE*
Zeltkarte, f
♦ tent card
Zeltlager, n
♦ tent camp
♦ tented camp
♦ camp
Zeltlageraufenthalt, m
♦ tent camp stay
♦ stay at a tent camp
♦ stay in a tent camp
Zeltlagersafari, f
♦ tent camp safari
Zeltlagerurlaub, m
♦ tent camp vacation *AE*
♦ tent camp holiday *BE*
Zelt leihen (gegen Gebühr)
♦ hire a tent *BE*
♦ rent a tent *AE*
Zelt leihen (unentgeltich)
Zelt borgen
♦ borrow a tent
Zeltleine, f
♦ tent rope
Zeltleinwand, f
Segeltuch, n
♦ tent canvas
♦ tent canvass *AE*
♦ canvas
♦ canvass *AE*
Zeltler, m *off*
Zelter, m
♦ tenter
Zeltmast, m
♦ tent mast
Zelt mieten
♦ rent a tent *AE*
♦ hire a tent *BE*
Zeltparzelle, f
♦ tent site
Zeltplane, f
→ Zeltbahn
Zeltplatz, m
Campingplatz, m
♦ campground *AE*
♦ camping ground *BE*
♦ campsite
♦ camping site *BE*
♦ tent site
Zeltplatzgebühr, f
♦ campground fee *AE*
♦ campground charge *AE*
♦ camping fee
♦ camping charge
Zelt pro Nacht, n
♦ tent per night

Zeltreise, f
Zelttour, f
♦ tent tour
♦ tenting tour *BE*
Zeltreise machen
Zelttour machen
♦ go on a tent tour
♦ go on a tenting tour *BE*
Zeltsafari, f
Campingsafari, f
♦ camping safari
Zeltsiedlung, f
♦ tent settlement
Zeltstadt, f (groß)
♦ tent city
♦ city of tents
Zeltstadt, f (klein)
♦ tent town
♦ town of tents
Zeltstange, f
♦ tent pole
Zeltstellplatz, m
♦ tent pitch
Zeltstoff, m
♦ tent fabric
Zelttour, f
→ Zeltreise
Zelttreck, m
♦ camping trek
Zelttür, f
♦ tent door
Zeltunterkunft, f
Zeltunterbringung, f
♦ tent accommodation
♦ tented accommodation
Zelturlauber, m
→ Camper
Zeltverleih, m
♦ tent rental *AE*
♦ tent hire *BE*
Zelt vermieten
♦ rent (out) a tent
♦ hire out a tent *BE*
Zeltvordach, n
♦ tent awning
Zeltwohnwagen, m
Zeltcaravan, m
♦ camper trailer *AE*
♦ tent trailer *AE*
♦ trailer tent *BE*
Zelt zurückgeben
Zelt zurückbringen
♦ return a tent
Zelt zusammenpacken
♦ pack up a tent
Zeltzuweisung, f
Zeltzuteilung, f
♦ allocation of a tent
♦ assignment of a tent *AE*
Zentralafrika
♦ Central Africa
Zentralafrikanische Republik, f
♦ Central African Republic, the
Zentralalpen, pl
♦ Central Alps, the *pl*
Zentralbahnhof, m
♦ central station
zentralbeheiztes Zimmer, n
→ zentralgeheiztes Zimmer
Zentralbuchung, f
→ zentrale Buchung

Zentralbühne

Zentralbühne, f
♦ central stage
Zentralcomputer, m
♦ central computer
Zentrale, f
Hauptsitz, m
Hauptgeschäftsstelle, f
♦ headquarters *pl + sg*
♦ head office
zentrale Bettenvermittlung, f
→ zentrale Zimmervermittlung
zentrale Buchung, f
Zentralbuchung, f
♦ central booking
zentrale Hotelvermittlung, f
zentraler Hotelvermittlungsdienst, m
♦ central hotel accommodation service
Zentraleinkauf, m
♦ central buying
zentrale Klimaanlage, f
♦ central air conditioning *AE*
♦ central air-conditioning *BE*
♦ central air-conditioner
zentrale Lage f
Zentrallage, f
♦ central situation
♦ central location
♦ central position
zentrale Reservierungsabteilung, f
♦ central reservations department
♦ central reservation department
zentraler Reservierungsdienst, m
zentraler Reservierungsservice, m
♦ central reservation service
♦ central reservations service
zentraler Wohnsitz, m
♦ central residence
zentrales Reservierungsbüro, n
zentrale Reservierungsstelle, f
♦ central reservation office
♦ central reservations office
♦ CRO
zentrales Reservierungssystem, n
♦ central reservations system
♦ central reservation system
zentrale Stadtlage, f (Großstadt)
♦ central city location
zentrale Stadtlage, f (kleine Stadt)
♦ central town location
zentrale Telexreservierung, f
♦ central telex reservation
zentrale Zimmervermittlung, f (Agentur)
♦ central accommodation agency
♦ central accommodation bureau
zentrale Zimmervermittlung, f (Tätigkeit)
♦ central accommodation service
♦ central accommodation booking service
Zentralgebäude, n
→ Mittelgebäude
zentralgeheizt, adj
zentralbeheizt, adj
♦ centrally heated, adj
zentralgeheiztes Zimmer, n
zentralbeheiztes Zimmer, n
♦ centrally heated room
zentral gelegen, adj
im Zentrum gelegen, adj
♦ centrally located, adj
♦ centrally situated, adj
♦ centrally sited, adj
♦ centrally placed, adj

zentral gelegener Stellplatz, m
(Camping)
♦ centrally located pitch
♦ centrally situated pitch
zentral gelegenes Hotel, n
♦ centrally located hotel
♦ centrally situated hotel
♦ centrally placed hotel
♦ centrally sited hotel
Zentralheizung, f
ZH, f
♦ central heating
♦ CH
zentralisiertes Reservierungssystem, n
♦ centralised reservations system
♦ centralized reservation system
Zentralküche, f
♦ central kitchen
Zentrallage f
zentrale Lage f
♦ central location
♦ central position
♦ central situation
Zentrallobby, f
♦ central lobby
Zentralplatz, m
zentraler Platz, m
♦ central square
Zentralrestaurant, n
♦ central restaurant
Zentralschlüssel, m
♦ master key
Zentralschlüsselanlage, f
♦ master key system
Zentralwäscherei f
zentrale Wäscherei f
♦ central laundry
Zentrum, n
Center, n
Mitte, f
♦ center *AE*
♦ centre *BE*
Zentrum für moderne Sprachen, n
♦ center for modern languages *AE*
♦ centre for modern languages *BE*
Zeppelin, m
♦ Zeppelin airship
zerbrechen etw
brechen etw
unterbrechen etw
♦ break s.th.
Zeremonie, f
Feierstunde, f
Festakt, m
♦ ceremony
Zeremonie abhalten
♦ hold a ceremony
Zeremonie beiwohnen
anwesend sein bei einer Zeremonie
Festakt beiwohnen
anwesend sein bei einem Festakt
♦ be present at a ceremony
zeremoniell, adj
förmlich, adj
feierlich, adj
♦ ceremonial, adj
♦ formal, adj
Zeremonienmeister, m
♦ master of ceremonies
♦ MC
♦ emcee *coll*

zerfressen von Motten, adj
von Motten zerfressen, adj
♦ moth-eaten, adj
zergehen auf der Zunge
♦ melt in one's mouth
zergehen lassen etw *gastr*
♦ melt s.th. *gastr*
zerklüftet, adj
unwegsam, adj
♦ rugged, adj
zerklüfteter Berg, m
unwegsamer Berg, m
♦ rugged mountain
zerkochen etw
♦ overcook s.th.
zerkocht, adj
♦ overcooked, adj
zerkochtes Essen, n
♦ overcooked food
zerlassene Butter, f
♦ melted butter
zerlegbare Möbel, n pl
♦ knockdown furniture *AE sg*
♦ knock-down furniture *BE sg*
zerlegbares Möbelstück, n
♦ collapsible piece of furniture
♦ knock-down *AE coll*
zerrissene Wäsche f
♦ torn linen
zerstampfen etw
→ zerstoßen etw
Zerstörung entgehen
der Zerstörung entgehen
♦ escape destruction
zerstoßen etw *gastr*
(im Mörser)
zerstampfen etw *gastr*
♦ pound s.th. *gastr*
Zerstreuung, f
Unterhaltung, f
♦ diversion
Zeugen der Vergangenheit, m pl
♦ relics of the past
Zeughaus, n
♦ arsenal
Zeugnis ablegen von etw
♦ bear witness to s.th.
ZH, f
Zentralheizung, f
♦ CH
♦ central heating
Zi., n
Zimmer, n
♦ rm.
♦ room
Zickzackkurs, m
♦ zigzag course
Zickzackroute, f
Zickzackstrecke, f
♦ zigzag route
Zickzackweg, m
♦ zigzag trail
Ziegeldach, n
♦ tiled roof
Ziegenkäse, m
♦ goat's cheese
Ziehbrunnen, m
♦ draw well
ziehen von Ort zu Ort
von Ort zu Ort ziehen

umherziehen
- ♦ move from place to place

Zieht es Ihnen?
(Luftzug)
- ♦ Are you in a draft? AE
- ♦ Are you in a draught? BE

Ziel, n (Sport)
- ♦ finish

Zielauslastung, f
- → Sollauslastung

Ziel auswählen
Zielort auswählen
- ♦ select a destination
- ♦ choose a destination
- ♦ pick a destination

Zielbahnhof, m
Bestimmungsbahnhof, m
- ♦ destination station
- ♦ station of destination

Ziel der Veranstaltung ist es …
- ♦ aim of the event is to …

Zielflughafen m
- ♦ destination airport

Zielgast m
- ♦ target guest

Zielgebiet, n (groß)
Zielregion, f
- ♦ destination region

Zielgebiet, n (klein)
- ♦ destination area

Zielgebietsagentur, f
- ♦ destination agency

Zielgruppe angehen
- ♦ tap a target group

Zielgruppe f
- ♦ target group

Zielkunde, m
- ♦ target customer

Zielland, n
- ♦ destination country
- ♦ country of destination

Ziellinie, f
- ♦ finish line

Zielmarkt m
- ♦ target market

Zielmarktsegment, n
- ♦ target market segment

Zielortangebot, n (Palette)
- ♦ range of destinations

Zielort auswählen
- → Ziel auswählen

Zielortbericht, m
- ♦ destination report

Zielort erreichen
Ziel erreichen
Bestimmungsort erreichen
- ♦ reach a destination
- ♦ reach the destination
- ♦ reach one's destination

Zielortmanagement, n
Fremdenverkehrsortmanagement, n
- ♦ destination management

Zielortmanagementgesellschaft, f
Fremdenverkehrsortmanagementgesellschaft, f
- ♦ destination management company
- ♦ DMC

Zielortmarketing, n
Fremdenverkehrsortmarketing, n
- ♦ destination marketing

zielortorientiert, adj
- ♦ destination-oriented, adj AE
- ♦ destination-orientated, adj BE

Zielort vermarkten
Fremdenverkehrsort vermarkten
- ♦ market a destination

Zielortwahl, f
Zielwahl, f
- ♦ choice of (the) destination
- ♦ destination choice

Zielpreis, m
- ♦ target price
- ♦ target rate

Zielpublikum, n
- ♦ target audience

Zielpunkt, m
(z.B. bei einer Wanderung)
Ziel, n
- ♦ finishing point

Zielsegment, n
- ♦ target segment

Zierbecken n
(im Garten)
- ♦ ornamental pool

Zierdeckchen, n
- → Deckchen

Ziergarten, m
- ♦ ornamental garden

Zierquittengelee, n
- ♦ japonica jelly

Ziersee, m
- ♦ ornamental lake

Zierstrauch, m
- ♦ ornamental shrub

Zigarette, f
- ♦ cigarette
- ♦ cigaret AE

Zigarettenanzünder, m
- ♦ cigarette lighter
- ♦ cigaret lighter AE
- ♦ lighter

Zigarettenasche, f
- ♦ cigarette ash
- ♦ cigaret ash AE

Zigarettenautomat, m
- ♦ cigarette machine
- ♦ cigaret machine AE
- ♦ cigarette slot machine BE

Zigarettenetui, n
- ♦ cigarette case
- ♦ cigaret case AE

Zigarettenpause, f
- ♦ break for a smoke
- ♦ smoke
- ♦ smoke break AE
- ♦ smoking break BE

Zigarettenpause machen
- ♦ stop for a smoke
- ♦ take a break for a cigarette
- ♦ take a break for a cigaret AE

Zigarettenrauch, m
- ♦ cigarette smoke
- ♦ cigaret smoke AE

Zigarettenraucher, m
- ♦ cigarette smoker
- ♦ cigaret smoker AE

Zigarettenschachtel, f
- ♦ cigarette pack AE
- ♦ cigaret pack AE
- ♦ cigarette packet BE

Zigarettenstummel, m
- ♦ cigarette end
- ♦ cigarette butt
- ♦ cigarette stub
- ♦ fag end sl
- ♦ butt

Zigarettenumsatz, m
- ♦ cigarette sales pl
- ♦ cigaret sales AE pl
- ♦ cigarette turnover
- ♦ cigaret turnover AE

Zigarettenverkäuferin, f
(im Lokal)
- ♦ cigarette girl
- ♦ cigaret girl AE

Zigarette rauchen
- ♦ smoke a cigarette
- ♦ smoke a cigaret AE

Zigarillo, m/n
- ♦ cigarillo
- ♦ cigarito AE
- ♦ minicigar BE

Zigarre, f
- ♦ cigar

Zigarre anzünden
- ♦ light a cigar

Zigarrenabschneider, m
- ♦ cigar cutter

Zigarrenanzünder, m
- ♦ cigar lighter

Zigarrenetui, n
- ♦ cigar case

Zigarrenkiste, f
- ♦ cigar box

Zigarrenraucher, m
- ♦ cigar smoker

Zigarrenservice, m
- ♦ tobacco service

Zigarrenstummel, m
- ♦ cigar end
- ♦ cigar butt
- ♦ cigar stub
- ♦ butt
- ♦ stub

Zigarrenumsatz, m
- ♦ cigar sales pl
- ♦ cigar turnover

Zigarrenwagen, m
- ♦ tobacco cart AE
- ♦ tobacco trolley BE

Zigarre rauchen
- ♦ smoke a cigar

Zigeuner, m
- ♦ gypsy
- ♦ gipsy

Zigeunerfest, n
- ♦ gypsy festival
- ♦ gipsy festival

zigeunerhaft, adj
- ♦ gypsylike, adj
- ♦ gipsylike, adj

Zigeunerin, f
- ♦ gypsy woman
- ♦ gipsy woman
- ♦ gypsy girl
- ♦ gipsy girl

Zigeunerkapelle, f
- ♦ gypsy band
- ♦ gipsy band
- ♦ group of gypsy musicians
- ♦ group of gipsy musicians

Zigeunerlager

Zigeunerlager, n
- gypsy camp
- gipsy camp

Zigeunerleben, n
- gypsy life
- gipsy life

Zigeunerleben führen
- live a gypsy life
- live a gipsy life
- lead a gypsy life
- lead a gipsy life

Zigeunermädchen, n
- gypsy girl
- gipsy girl

Zigeunermusik, f
- gypsy music
- gipsy music

zigeunern
wie ein Zigeuner umherziehen
- roam around like a gypsy
- roam around like gypsies
- lead a gypsy life
- lead a gipsy life

zigeunern durch die Welt
- roam the world

Zigeunerprimas, m
- primas

Zigeunerwagen, m
- gypsy caravan
- gipsy caravan
- horse-drawn caravan

Zigeunerwagenurlaub, m
- gypsy caravan vacation *AE*
- gipsy caravan vacation *AE*
- gypsy caravan holiday *BE*
- gipsy caravan holiday *BE*

Zigeunerwohnwagenplatz, m
- gypsy caravan site *BE*
- gipsy caravan site *BE*

Zillertaler Alpen, pl
(Region)
- Zillertal Alps, the *pl*

Zimmer, das mit einem Teppich ausgelegt ist
- carpeted room

Zimmer, das mit Trödelkram vollgestopft ist
- room lumbered up with junk

Zimmer, Frühstück und Abendessen
- room, breakfast and dinner

Zimmer, n (Gemach)
→ Gemach

Zimmer, n (generell)
- room

Zimmer, n (Untermiete)
- lodgings *pl*
- room
- digs *BE coll pl*

Zimmer abbestellen
→ Zimmer stornieren

Zimmer ab DM 123, n
- room from DM 123

Zimmerabgabe, f
→ Zimmersteuer

Zimmer abrufen auf dem Computer
- call up a room on the computer
- retrieve a room on the computer

Zimmer abschließen
Zimmer absperren
- lock a room

Zimmer abstauben
- dust a room

Zimmer abteilen
Zimmer unterteilen
- partition off a room
- screen off a room

Zimmer abteilen durch eine Mauer
Zwischenwand einziehen
- wall off part of a room

Zimmer abteilen durch einen Vorhang
- curtain off part of a room

Zimmer am Ende des Flurs, n
- room at the end of the corridor

Zimmer anbauen
- add a room
- add rooms

Zimmer anbieten jm
Zimmer offerieren jm
Zimmer andienen jm *form*
- offer a room to s.o.
- offer s.o. a room

Zimmer anbieten zu einem bestimmten Preis
- offer a room at a certain rate
- offer a room at a certain price

Zimmer anbieten zum halben Preis
- offer a room at half price
- offer a room at half rate

Zimmer andienen jm
→ Zimmer anbieten jm

Zimmeranforderung, f
Anforderung an ein Zimmer, f
- room requirement

Zimmeranfrage, f
- inquiry about a room
- enquiry about a room

Zimmerangaben, f pl
(z.B. auf Buchungsformular)
Zimmerdetails, n pl
Zimmereinzelheiten, f pl
- room details *pl*

Zimmerangebot, n (Gegensatz zu Nachfrage)
- room supply
- supply of rooms

Zimmerangebot, n (generell)
- available rooms *pl*
- rooms available *pl*

Zimmerangebot, n (Palette)
- range of rooms

Zimmerangebot erhöhen
- increase the number of rooms

Zimmer an jn anderen vergeben
Zimmer an jn anderen geben
- give a room to s.o. else

Zimmerannahme, f *jur*
- acceptance of a room *jur*

Zimmeranordnung, f
(in einem Gebäude)
Zimmerdisposition, f
Zimmeraufteilung, f
- disposition of rooms

Zimmerantenne, f
- indoor antenna *AE*
- indoor aerial *BE*

Zimmer anweisen jm
→ Zimmer zuteilen jm

Zimmeranzahl, f
→ Zimmerzahl

Zimmerart, f
Zimmertyp, m
- room type
- type of room

Zimmer auf dem dritten Stockwerk, n
→ Zimmer im dritten Stockwerk

Zimmer auf der Rückseite, n
- room on the rear side
- room at the back

Zimmer auf einem unteren Stockwerk, n
- low-floor room

Zimmer aufgeben
- give up one's room

Zimmeraufpreis, m
- room surcharge

Zimmer aufräumen
- tidy a room

Zimmer aufschließen
Zimmer aufsperren, coll
- unlock a room

Zimmer aufteilen
→ unterteilen einen Raum

Zimmeraufwendungen, f pl
Beherbergungsaufwendungen, f pl
- room expenses *pl*
- rooms expenses *pl*

Zimmer ausfegen
Zimmer fegen
- sweep a room

Zimmerauslastung, f
Zimmerbelegung, f
- room occupancy
- occupancy of a room
- occupancy of (the) rooms

Zimmerauslastungskrise, f
Zimmerbelegungskrise, f
- room occupancy crisis

Zimmerauslastungsniveau, n
- room occupancy level

Zimmerauslastungsprozentsatz, m
- percentage room occupancy

Zimmerauslastungsquote, f
Zimmerauslastungsquote, f
Zimmerbelegungsquote, f
Zimmerbelegungsrate, f
- room occupancy rate

Zimmerauslastungsrate, f
→ Zimmerauslastungsquote

Zimmerauslastungstendenz, f
Zimmerbelegungstendenz, f
- room occupancy tendency

Zimmerauslastungstrend, m
Zimmerbelegungstrend, m
- room occupancy trend

Zimmerauslastungszahl, f
Zimmerbelegungszahl, f
- room occupancy figure

Zimmer auslegen mit einem Teppich
- carpet a room

Zimmerausmaße, n pl
Zimmermaße, n pl
- measurements of a room *pl*

Zimmer ausmessen
- take the dimensions of a room

Zimmer ausrauben
Zimmer ausplündern
- ransack a room

Zimmer ausräuchern
Zimmer begasen
Zimmer desinfizieren
- fumigate a room

Zimmer ausräumen
(Möbel entfernen)
- clear out a room
- clear a room of furniture

Zimmerausstattung, f
- room equipment
- equipment of a room

Zimmer auswählen aus dem Zimmerlageplan
- select a room from the floor plan

Zimmerausweis, m
→ Zimmerpaß

Zimmerbad, n
→ Privatbad

Zimmerbar, f
- room bar
- private bar in room
- bell captain *BE*

Zimmer bauen
- build a room
- construct a room

Zimmerbedienung f
→ Zimmerservice

Zimmer befindet sich im Erdgeschoß
- room is on the first floor *AE*
- room is on the ground floor *BE*

Zimmer behalten
- keep one's room

Zimmer behelfsmäßig herrichten
- rig up a room

Zimmer bekommen
- get a room

Zimmer belegen
Zimmer bewohnen
- occupy a room

Zimmer belegen für zehn Tage
- occupy a room for ten days

Zimmer belegen für zwei Nächte
- occupy a room for two nights

Zimmerbeleger, m
Zimmerinhaber, m
Zimmerbewohner, m
- occupant of a room
- room occupant

Zimmerbelegung, f (Benutzung)
- room occupation
- occupation of a room

Zimmerbelegung, f (Statistik)
→ Zimmerauslastung

Zimmerbelegungskontrolle, f
- room occupancy control

Zimmerbelegungsplan, m
- room occupancy plan

Zimmerbelegungsplan erstellen
- draw up a room occupancy plan

Zimmerbelegungsrate, f
→ Zimmerauslastungsquote

Zimmerbelegungssteuer f
- room occupancy tax

Zimmerbelegungszahl, f
→ Zimmerauslastungszahl

Zimmerbeleuchtung, f
- room lighting
- light in a room

Zimmer benennen nach jm
- name a room after s.o.

Zimmer benötigen
- require a room
- need a room

Zimmer benutzen
Zimmer nutzen
- use a room
- utilise a room
- utilize a room

Zimmerbenutzung, f
- use of a room
- using a room

Zimmerbereich, m
→ Beherbergungsbereich

Zimmer bereithalten
- hold a room

Zimmer bereithalten bis 18 Uhr
- hold a room until 6 p.m.

Zimmer bereithalten für jn
- hold a room (in readiness) for s.o.

Zimmer bereithalten für jn für die Zeit vom..bis..
- hold a room for s.o. for the period from..to..

Zimmer bereithalten für jn (reservieren)
→ Zimmer reservieren für jn

Zimmer bereitstellen
Zimmer zur Verfügung stellen
- provide a room

Zimmer bereitstellen für jn (geben)
Zimmer jm zur Verfügung stellen
- provide s.o. with a room

Zimmerbericht m
- room report

Zimmer beschreiben
- describe a room

Zimmerbeschreibung, f
- room description
- description of a room
- describing a room

Zimmerbesetzung, f SCHW
→ Zimmerauslastung

Zimmer besichtigen
Raum besichtigen
- view a room

Zimmer besorgen jm
- find s.o. a room
- get s.o. a room *coll*

Zimmerbestand, m
Bestand an Zimmern, m
- room stock
- stock of rooms

Zimmerbestand erhöhen
- increase the room stock

Zimmer bestätigen
Zimmer zusagen
- confirm a room

Zimmerbestätigung, f
Zimmerzusage, f
- room confirmation
- confirmation of a room
- confirming a room

Zimmer bestellen
→ Zimmer buchen

Zimmerbesteller, m
- person booking a room

Zimmerbestellkarte, f
Zimmerreservierungskarte, f
- room reservation card *AE*

Zimmerbestellung, f
→ Zimmerbuchung

Zimmer besteuern
- tax a room

Zimmer betreten
- enter a room

Zimmerbetriebskosten, pl
- room operating costs *pl*

Zimmer bevorzugen
- prefer a room

Zimmer bewohnen
- inhabit a room *AE*
- occupy a room

Zimmer bezahlen
für ein Zimmer zahlen
- pay for a room

Zimmer beziehen
einziehen in ein Zimmer
- move into a room
- claim a room

Zimmerbezug, m
- moving into a room
- claiming a room

Zimmer bietet Blick auf den Garten
- room looks onto the garden

Zimmer bietet einen atemberaubenden Blick
- room affords a breathtaking view

Zimmer bietet Panoramaaussicht
Zimmer bietet Rundblick
Zimmer bietet Panoramablick
- room affords a panoramic view

Zimmer bietet Schlafmöglichkeiten für 3 Personen
- room sleeps 3 persons

Zimmer bleibt frei
- room remains empty

Zimmerboom, m
- room boom

Zimmerbrand, m
- room fire

Zimmer brauchen
- need a room

Zimmer brennt
Zimmer steht in Brand
- room is on fire

Zimmer brieflich buchen
- book a room by letter

Zimmer buchen
- book a room

Zimmer buchen für drei Nächte ab dem 1. August
- book a room for three nights from 1 August

Zimmer buchen für mindestens eine Nacht
- book a room for a minimum of one night
- book a room for at least one night

Zimmer buchen für zwei Wochen
- book a room for two weeks

Zimmer buchen in einem Hotel
- book a room at a hotel
- book a room in a hotel
- reserve a room at a hotel *AE*
- reserve a room in a hotel *AE*

Zimmer buchen über den Hotelbuchungsdienst
→ Zimmer buchen über die Hotelvermittlung

Zimmer buchen über die Hotelvermittlung
- book a room through the hotel booking service

Zimmer buchen über eine Buchungszentrale
- book a room through a central booking office

Zimmer buchen über ein Reisebüro
- book a room through a travel agency

Zimmer buchen über jn
Zimmer buchen lassen durch jn
- book a room through s.o.
- reserve a room through s.o. *AE*

Zimmer buchen unter dem Namen Y buchen
- book a room under the name Y

Zimmer buchen vom 7. bis einschließlich 10. März
- book a room from 7 to 10 March inclusive
- book a room from 7 through 10 March *AE*

Zimmer buchen von Montag bis inklusive Freitag
Zimmer buchen von Montag bis einschließlich Freitag

Zimmer buchen zu $ 100 pro Nacht

- book a room from Monday until Friday inclusive
- book a room from Monday through Friday AE

Zimmer buchen zu $ 100 pro Nacht
- book a room at $ 100 per night

Zimmerbuchung, f
Zimmerbestellung, f
- room booking
- booking (of) a room
- reservation of a room AE
- reservation of rooms AE

Zimmerdatei, f
(z.B. in Rezeption)
Zimmerverzeichnis, n
- room register

Zimmerdecke, f
Decke, f
- room ceiling
- ceiling

Zimmerdekor, m/n
- room decor AE
- room décor BE

Zimmer desinfizieren (durch Dämpfe)
→ Zimmer ausräuchern

Zimmer desinfizieren (generell)
- disinfect a room

Zimmer dient als Wohn- und Eßzimmer
Zimmer ist zugleich Wohn- und Eßzimmer
- room serves as living and dining room

Zimmerdisposition, f
→ Zimmeraufteilung

Zimmer doppelt vergeben
→ Zimmer zweimal vergeben

Zimmer dringend benötigen
- require a room urgently
- urgently require a room
- require rooms urgently
- urgently require rooms

Zimmerdurchschnittspreis, m
→ durchschnittlicher Zimmerpreis

Zimmer durchsuchen
- search a room

Zimmerdurchsuchung, f
- room search
- searching a room

Zimmerecke, f
- corner of a room

Zimmer eignet sich für etw
→ Zimmer ist geeignet für etw

Zimmer eines Gast aufräumen
- tidy a guest's room

Zimmer eines Gasts betreten
- enter the room of a guest
- enter a guest's room

Zimmer eines Gasts reinigen
Zimmer eines Gastes putzen
- clean a guest's room

Zimmereinheit, f
Schlafraumeinheit, f
- bedroom unit

Zimmereinrichtung, f (Aktivität)
- furnishing a room

Zimmereinrichtung, f (Einrichtung)
- furnishings of a room pl

Zimmerendreinigung, f
- cleaning a room on departure
- end-of-contract cleaning
- end-of-let cleaning BE

Zimmerendreinigungsgebühr, f
- charge for cleaning a room on departure
- fee for cleaning a room on departure

- end-of-contract cleaning charge
- end-of-let cleaning charge BE

Zimmer erhalten
- obtain a room
- get a room
- be given a room
- be provided with a room

Zimmererlös, m
Beherbergungserlös, m
- room revenue
- rooms revenue

Zimmererlös entstehen lassen
- generate room revenue
- generate rooms revenue

Zimmerertrag, m
Beherbergungsertrag, m
- income from rooms
- rooms income
- room income

Zimmer erzielt einen hohen Preis
- room commands a high price
- room commands a high rate

Zimmeretage, f
Wohnetage, f
- bedroom floor

Zimmer fernschriftlich buchen
Zimmer über Telex buchen
- book a room per telex

Zimmer fernschriftlich reservieren lassen
- have a room reserved by telex

Zimmerfernsehen, n
- room television
- room TV

Zimmer fest zusagen
- guarantee a room

Zimmer fest zusagen jm für den 8. November
Zimmer garantieren jm für den 8. November
- guarantee s.o. a room for 8 November
- guarantee s.o. a room for the 8th November

Zimmer finden
- find a room

Zimmer finden für jn
- find a room for s.o.
- find s.o. a room

Zimmerflucht, f
Zimmerreihe, f
- suite of rooms
- suite
- rooms en suite pl

Zimmerflucht bewohnen
Zimmerflucht belegen
- occupy a suite of rooms

Zimmerfolge, f
- series of rooms
- suite

Zimmer frei (ein Zimmer)
(Hinweisschild)
- Vacancy

Zimmer freigeben
Zimmer zurückgeben
- release a room

Zimmer freigeben zum Verkauf
Zimmer zurückgeben zum Verkauf
- release a room for sale

Zimmer frei haben
- have a room free
- have room vacant
- have a vacancy

Zimmer frei halten
→ Zimmer bereithalten

Zimmer frei halten für jn
- keep a room free for s.o.
- keep a room for s.o.

Zimmer frei (mehrere Zimmer)
(Hinweisschild)
- Vacancies

Zimmer freundlich machen
(durch Farben etc)
- brighten up a room

Zimmerfrühstück, n
- breakfast served in the room

Zimmer füllen
- fill a room
- fill (the) rooms

Zimmer für DM 123, n
- room for DM 123
- DM 123 room

Zimmer für drei Personen, n
- room for three persons

Zimmer für Empfänge, n
- room for receptions

Zimmer für Tagesaufenthalt, n
→ Tageszimmer

Zimmer ganz oben, n
- room at the top
- top room

Zimmergarantie, f
- room guarantee

Zimmergarantie geben
- give a room guarantee
- guarantee a room

Zimmer garantieren
→ Zimmer fest zusagen

Zimmer geben an jn
- give s.o. a room
- give a room to s.o.

Zimmergebühr, f
Zimmerpreis, m
- room charge
- room rate
- room price

Zimmer gefällt jm
- room pleases s.o.
- room pleases one

Zimmer geht nach der Straße
- room faces the road

Zimmer geht nach Norden
→ Zimmer liegt nach Norden

Zimmer geht nach Westen
→ Zimmer liegt nach Westen

Zimmergenosse, m
- roommate AE
- room-mate BE

Zimmergeschäft, n
Beherbergungsgeschäft, n
Logisgeschäft, n
- room business
- rooms business

Zimmergestaltung, f
Raumgestaltung, f
- room design

Zimmer gewährt einen schönen Blick auf das Meer
- room commands a fine view of the sea

Zimmergewinn, m
Beherbergungsgewinn, m
- room profit
- rooms profit

Zimmergröße, f
- room size
- size of a room

Zimmergrundpreis, m
Grundpreis pro Zimmer, m
♦ **basic room rate**
♦ basic room price
♦ basic rate per room
♦ basic price per room
Zimmergrundriß, m
♦ **room layout**
♦ layout of the room
Zimmergrundtarif, m
♦ **basic room tariff**
♦ basic room rates *pl*
♦ basic room rate
Zimmergüte f
→ Zimmerqualität
Zimmergutschein, m
♦ **room voucher**
Zimmer haben
♦ **have a room**
♦ have rooms
Zimmer haben eine Verbindungstür
♦ **rooms are interconnected**
Zimmer haben im fünften Stockwerk
Zimmer auf der fünften Etage haben
Zimmer im fünften Obergeschoß haben
♦ **have a room on the sixth floor** *AE*
♦ have a room on the fifth floor *BE*
Zimmer haben integrierte Sanitäreinrichtungen
♦ **rooms have en-suite facilities**
Zimmer hat Blick auf das Meer
♦ **room overlooks the sea**
Zimmer hat Blick auf das Tal
♦ **room overlooks the valley**
Zimmer hat Blick auf den Fluß
♦ **room overlooks the river**
Zimmer hat Blick auf den Hof
♦ **room overlooks the courtyard**
Zimmer hat Blick auf den Park
♦ **room overlooks the park**
Zimmer hat Blick auf die Stadt (Großstadt)
♦ **room overlooks the city**
Zimmer hat Blick auf die Stadt (kleine Stadt)
♦ **room overlooks the town**
Zimmer hat Blick über den See
♦ **room overlooks the lake**
Zimmer hat drei Betten
♦ **room has three beds**
Zimmer hat eine Breite von 5 m, eine Länge von 7 m, und eine Höhe von 3 m
♦ **room has a width of 5 m, a length of 7 m, and a height of 3 m**
Zimmer hat einen Aufpreis
♦ **room carries a supplement**
Zimmer hat einen Blick auf etw
♦ **room has a view of s.th.**
♦ room overlooks s.th.
Zimmer hat einen Blick über den Park
♦ **room looks over the park**
♦ room has a view over the park
Zimmer hat einen guten Grundriß
♦ **room is well laid out**
Zimmer hat eine Tür zur Terrasse
♦ **room opens onto the terrace**
♦ room opens to the terrace
Zimmer hat immer die Sonne
♦ **room always gets the sun**
Zimmer hat zwei Betten
♦ **room has two beds**
Zimmer heizen
Zimmer beheizen
♦ **heat a room**

Zimmerherr, m
(Untermieter)
Zimmer herrichten
Zimmer richten
♦ **set a room straight**
♦ clean a room
Zimmer herrichten für eine Feier
♦ **arrange a room for a party**
Zimmer hüten
auf dem Zimmer bleiben
♦ **keep to one's room**
♦ stay in one's room
♦ stay indoors
zimmerig, adj
♦ **roomed, adj**
Zimmer Ihrer Wahl, n
♦ **room of your choice**
Zimmer im Anbau, n
♦ **room in the extension**
Zimmer im Chaletstil, n
♦ **chalet-style room**
Zimmer im Dachgeschoß, n
→ Zimmer im obersten Stockwerk
Zimmer im dritten Stock, n
→ Zimmer im dritten Stockwerk
Zimmer im dritten Stockwerk, n
Zimmer auf der dritten Etage, n
Zimmer im dritten Obergeschoß, n
♦ **room on the fourth floor** *AE*
♦ fourth-floor room *AE*
♦ room on the third floor *BE*
♦ third-floor room *BE*
Zimmer im Erdgeschoß, n
Zimmer auf dem Erdgeschoß, n
♦ **room on the first floor** *AE*
♦ room on the ground floor *BE*
♦ downstairs room
Zimmer im fünften Stockwerk, n
Zimmer auf der fünften Etage, n
Zimmer im fünften Obergeschoß, n
♦ **room on the sixth floor** *AE*
♦ six-floor room *AE*
♦ room on the fifth floor *BE*
♦ fifth-floor room *BE*
Zimmer im Haupthotel, n
Zimmer im Haupthaus, n
♦ **room in the main hotel**
Zimmer im letzten Obergeschoß, n
→ Zimmer im obersten Stockwerk
Zimmer im Nordflügel, n
♦ **room in the north wing**
Zimmer im oberen Stockwerk, n
Zimmer im oberen Geschoß, n
oben gelegenes Zimmer, n
oberes Zimmer, n
♦ **upstairs room**
Zimmer im obersten Stockwerk, n
Zimmer im letzten Obergeschoß, n
♦ **room on the top floor**
Zimmer im Ostflügel, n
♦ **room in the east wing**
Zimmer im Parterre, n
Zimmer im Erdgeschoß, n
♦ **downstairs room**
♦ first-floor room *AE*
♦ ground-floor room *BE*
Zimmer im Südflügel, n
♦ **room in the south wing**
Zimmer im vierten Stockwerk, n
Zimmer auf der vierten Etage, n
Zimmer im vierten Obergeschoß, n

♦ room on the fifth floor *AE*
♦ fifth-floor room *AE*
♦ room on the fourth floor *BE*
♦ fourth-floor room *BE*
Zimmer im voraus bestellen
→ Zimmer vorbestellen
Zimmer im voraus zuteilen
Zimmer im voraus verteilen
Zimmer im voraus zuweisen
♦ **pre-allocate a room**
♦ preassign a room *AE*
Zimmer im voraus zuweisen
Zimmer im voraus zuteilen
♦ **preassign a room** *AE*
♦ pre-allocate a room *BE*
Zimmer im Westflügel, n
♦ **room in the west wing**
Zimmer im zweiten Stockwerk, n
Zimmer auf der zweiten Etage, n
Zimmer im zweiten Obergeschoß, n
♦ **room on the third floor** *AE*
♦ third-floor room *AE*
♦ room on the second floor *BE*
♦ second-floor room *BE*
Zimmer im Zwischengeschoß, n
♦ **room on the mezzanine floor**
♦ room on the mezzanine
Zimmer in allen Formen und Größen, n pl
♦ **rooms in all shapes and sizes** *pl*
Zimmer in allen Größen, n pl
♦ **rooms of all sizes** *pl*
Zimmeranspruchnahme, f
♦ **claiming a room**
♦ using a room
♦ utilisation of a room
♦ utilising a room
♦ use of a room
Zimmer in Anspruch nehmen
Zimmer beanspruchen
♦ **claim a room**
Zimmer in Brand setzen
Zimmer in Brand stecken
♦ **set fire to a room**
Zimmer in der Dependance, n
Zimmer im Nebengebäude, n
♦ **room in the annex** *AE*
♦ room in the annexe *BE*
Zimmer in der Nachbarschaft, n
♦ **nearby room**
Zimmerinhaber, m
Zimmerbeleger, m
Zimmerbewohner, m
♦ **room occupant**
♦ occupant of a room
Zimmer in Ordnung bringen
Zimmer aufräumen
Zimmer herrichten
♦ **put a room in order**
♦ tidy (up) a room
♦ set a room straight
Zimmerinspektion, f
Zimmerüberprüfung, f
♦ **inspection of a room**
Zimmer inspizieren
Zimmer überprüfen
♦ **inspect a room**
Zimmerinstandhaltung, f
♦ **room maintenance**
Zimmerinventar, n
♦ **room inventory**

Zimmerinventarkontrolle

Zimmerinventarkontrolle, f
   Zimmerinventarüberprüfung, f
   ♦ room inventory control
Zimmerinventarüberprüfung, f
   → Zimmerinventarkontrolle
Zimmer ist 10 Fuß auf 15 Fuß groß
   ♦ room is 10 feet by 15 feet
   ♦ room is 10 foot by 15 foot *inform*
Zimmer ist 12 x 16 Fuß groß
   ♦ room is 12 x 16 ft.
Zimmer ist 3 m hoch
   ♦ room is 3 m high
Zimmer ist 4 m breit
   ♦ room is 4 m wide
Zimmer ist 6 m lang
   ♦ room is 6 m long
Zimmer ist ab 14 Uhr frei
   ♦ room is available from 2 p.m.
Zimmer ist ab 18 Uhr gebucht
   ♦ room is booked from 6 p.m.
Zimmer ist ab 28. August gebucht
   ♦ room is booked from 28 August
Zimmer ist achteckig
   ♦ room is octagonal
Zimmer ist angemessen möbliert
   Zimmer ist ausreichend möbliert
   ♦ room is adequately furnished
Zimmer ist angenehm
   ♦ room is pleasant
Zimmer ist angenehm möbliert
   ♦ room is pleasantly furnished
Zimmer ist ansprechend
   Zimmer ist sympathisch
   ♦ room is agreeable
Zimmer ist attraktiv
   ♦ room is attractive
Zimmer ist attraktiv möbliert
   ♦ room is attractively furnished
Zimmer ist auf der Rückseite
   ♦ room is at the back
Zimmer ist aufwendig möbliert
   ♦ room is sumptuously furnished
Zimmer ist ausgezeichnet möbliert
   ♦ room is excellently furnished
Zimmer ist belegt
   ♦ room is occupied
   ♦ room is taken
Zimmer ist bereits belegt
   ♦ room is already occupied
Zimmer ist bereits besetzt
   ♦ room is already taken
Zimmer ist bereits gebucht
   ♦ room is already booked
Zimmer ist besetzt
   ♦ room is taken
Zimmer ist bezaubernd möbliert
   ♦ room is charmingly furnished
Zimmer ist dezent möbliert
   ♦ room is discreetly furnished
Zimmer ist eigengenutzt
   ♦ room is owner-occupied
Zimmer ist ein bißchen klein
   ♦ room is smallish
Zimmer ist einfach
   ♦ room is plain
   ♦ room is simple
Zimmer ist einladend
   ♦ room is inviting
   ♦ room is welcoming
Zimmer ist eng
   ♦ room is cramped

Zimmer ist farbenprächtig möbliert
   Zimmer ist auffallend möbliert
   ♦ room is flamboyantly furnished
Zimmer ist freundlich
   ♦ room is cheerful
Zimmer ist ganz mit Teppich ausgelegt
   ♦ room is fully carpeted
Zimmer ist geeignet für 2 Erwachsene und 2 Kinder
   ♦ room is suitable for 2 adults and 2 children
Zimmer ist geeignet für etw
   Zimmer eignet sich für etw
   ♦ room is suitable for s.th.
Zimmer ist geeignet für jn
   Zimmer eignet sich für jn
   ♦ room is suitable for s.o.
Zimmer ist gefällig
   Zimmer ist ansprechend
   ♦ room is pleasing
Zimmer ist geheizt
   Zimmer ist beheizt
   ♦ room is heated
Zimmer ist gemütlich
   ♦ room is cosy
   ♦ room is cozy *AE*
   ♦ room is comfortable
Zimmer ist gepflegt
   ♦ room is well maintained
   ♦ room is well looked after
Zimmer ist geräumig
   ♦ room is spacious
Zimmer ist geschmackvoll möbliert
   ♦ room is tastefully furnished
Zimmer ist getäfelt
   ♦ room is panelled
   ♦ room is paneled *AE*
Zimmer ist gigantisch
   ♦ room is gigantic
Zimmer ist groß
   ♦ room is large
   ♦ room is big
Zimmer ist großartig
   ♦ room is grand
   ♦ room is great
   ♦ room is manificent
Zimmer ist großartig möbliert
   ♦ room is magnificently furnished
Zimmer ist großzügig bemessen
   ♦ room is ample in size
Zimmer ist großzügig proportioniert
   ♦ room is amply proportioned
Zimmer ist gut ausgestattet
   ♦ room is well equipped
Zimmer ist gut eingerichtet
   ♦ room is well appointed
Zimmer ist gut geplant
   ♦ room is well planned
Zimmer ist gut gestaltet
   ♦ room is well designed
Zimmer ist gut möbliert
   ♦ room is well furnished
Zimmer ist gut proportioniert
   ♦ room is well proportioned
Zimmer ist gut und komfortabel
   ♦ room is good and comfortable
Zimmer ist hell
   ♦ room is bright
Zimmer ist hellhörig
   ♦ room is poorly soundproofed
   ♦ room is not soundproof

Zimmer ist hoch
   ♦ room is high-ceilinged
Zimmer ist hübsch
   ♦ room is handsome
Zimmer ist hübsch möbliert
   ♦ room is handsomely furnished
Zimmer ist im Bau
   ♦ room is being built
   ♦ room is being constructed
   ♦ room is under construction
Zimmer ist im Landhausstil möbliert
   ♦ room is furnished in country-house style
Zimmer ist im Stil der Zeit gehalten
   ♦ room is decorated in the style of the period
Zimmer ist im Stil der Zeit möbliert
   ♦ room is furnished in the style of the period
   ♦ room is furnished in period
Zimmer ist intelligent möbliert
   ♦ room is intelligently furnished
Zimmer ist klein
   ♦ room is small
Zimmer ist kühl
   ♦ room is cool
Zimmer ist leer
   ♦ room is empty
Zimmer ist liebevoll möbliert
   ♦ room is lovingly furnished
Zimmer ist luftig
   ♦ room is airy
Zimmer ist luxuriös
   ♦ room is luxurious
Zimmer ist makellos sauber
   ♦ room is meticulously clean
   ♦ room is spotlessly clean
Zimmer ist mit antiken Möbeln möbliert
   ♦ room is furnished with antique furniture
Zimmer ist mit Antiquitäten eingerichtet
   ♦ room is furnished with antiques
Zimmer ist mit Geschmack möbliert
   ♦ room is furnished with taste
Zimmer ist mit Herrn X belegt
   ♦ room is occupied by Mr X
   ♦ room is taken by Mr X
Zimmer ist mit Teppich ausgelegt
   ♦ room is carpeted
Zimmer ist modern
   ♦ room is modern
Zimmer ist neben meinem
   ♦ room is next to mine
Zimmer ist nett möbliert
   ♦ room is nicely furnished
Zimmer ist neu
   ♦ room is new
Zimmer ist neu möbliert
   ♦ room is newly furnished
   ♦ room has been refurnished
Zimmer ist nicht abschließbar
   ♦ room cannot be locked
Zimmer ist nicht belegbar
   ♦ room is 'off'
   ♦ room is not available for occupation
Zimmer ist nicht verfügbar
   ♦ room is not available
Zimmer ist palastartig
   ♦ room is palatial
Zimmer ist perfekt möbliert
   ♦ room is perfectly furnished
Zimmer ist renoviert (worden)
   ♦ room has been refurbished
   ♦ room has been renovated

Zimmer ist riesengroß
♦ room is vast
Zimmer ist riesig
♦ room is huge
Zimmer ist ruhig
♦ room is quiet
Zimmer ist rustikal
♦ room is rustic
Zimmer ist sauber
♦ room is clean
Zimmer ist schlecht
♦ room is poor
♦ room is bad
Zimmer ist schlecht eingerichtet
♦ room is badly appointed
Zimmer ist schön ausgestattet
♦ room is beautifully equipped
Zimmer ist schön eingerichtet
♦ room is beautifully appointed
Zimmer ist schön möbliert
♦ room is beautifully furnished
Zimmer ist schön tapeziert
♦ room is beautifully wallpapered
♦ room is beautifully decorated
Zimmer ist sehr groß
♦ room is very large
♦ room is very big
Zimmer ist seit Jahren nicht bewohnt
♦ room has not been occupied for years
♦ room has not been lived in for years
Zimmer ist spartanisch
♦ room is spartan
Zimmer ist überbelegt
♦ room is overcrowded
Zimmer ist übergroß
♦ room is overlarge
Zimmer ist unbelegt
♦ room is unoccupied
♦ room is vacant
Zimmer ist unbenutzt
♦ room is unused
Zimmer ist ungewöhnlich geräumig
♦ room is unusually spacious
Zimmer ist ungewöhnlich groß
♦ room is unusually large
♦ room is unusually big
Zimmer ist unpersönlich möbliert
♦ room is impersonally furnished
Zimmer ist uns zugewiesen worden
♦ room has been assigned to us AE
♦ room has been allocated to us
Zimmer ist unterteilbar
♦ room is divisible
♦ room can be partitioned (off)
Zimmer ist vermietbar
♦ room is rentable
Zimmer ist vollgestopft mit etw
♦ room is crammed with s.th.
Zimmer ist wie ein Eiskeller
♦ room is like an icebox
Zimmer ist zeitlos
♦ room is timeless
Zimmer ist zentralbeheizt
♦ room is centrally heated
Zimmer ist ziemlich groß
♦ room is quite large
♦ room is quite big
♦ room is fairly large
♦ room is fairly big
♦ room is sizable

Zimmer ist (ziemlich) groß
♦ room is sizable
♦ room is sizeable
Zimmer ist zugig
♦ room is drafty AE
♦ room is draughty BE
Zimmer ist zu laut
♦ room is too noisy
Zimmer ist zweckmäßig
♦ room is functional
Zimmerjournal, n
♦ room diary
Zimmerjunge, m
♦ room boy
Zimmerkaffeeservice, n (Geschirr)
Kaffeeservice auf dem Zimmer, n
♦ in-room coffee service
Zimmer kann bis zu fünf Personen aufnehmen
♦ room can accommodate up to five persons
Zimmer kann leicht bis zu vier Personen aufnehmen
♦ room can easily accommodate up to four persons
Zimmer kann unterteilt werden
Raum kann abgeteilt werden
♦ room can be partitioned (off)
Zimmer kann zwei Personen aufnehmen
♦ room accommodates two persons
Zimmerkapazität, f
Raumkapazität, f
♦ room capacity
♦ capacity of a room
♦ capacity of the rooms
Zimmerkarte, f
♦ room card
♦ bedroom card
Zimmerkarte erhalten
♦ receive a room card
♦ receive a bedroom card
Zimmerkartei, f
♦ room index
Zimmerkartei führen
♦ keep a room index
Zimmerkarteikarte, f
♦ room index card
Zimmerkarteikarte ausfüllen
♦ fill in a room index card BE
♦ fill out a room index card AE
♦ complete a room index card
Zimmerkarte zeigen
Zimmerkarte vorweisen
♦ show one's room card
♦ show one's bedroom card
♦ present one's room card
♦ present one's bedroom card
Zimmerkategorie, f
Zimmerklasse f
♦ room category
Zimmer kaufen
♦ buy a room
Zimmerkäufer, m
♦ room buyer
Zimmerkellner, m
♦ room waiter
Zimmerklasse f
→ Zimmerkategorie
Zimmer klassifizieren gemäß etw
♦ classify a room according to s.th.
Zimmerknappheit, f
♦ room shortage
♦ shortage of rooms

Zimmerknappheit mildern
Zimmerknappheit lindern
♦ alleviate a shortage of rooms
Zimmerkontingent, n
♦ allotment of rooms
♦ quota of rooms
♦ allocation of rooms
♦ room allocation
Zimmerkontingent buchen
♦ book an allotment of rooms
♦ book a quota of rooms
♦ book an allocation of rooms
Zimmerkontingente nehmen
♦ take allotments of rooms
♦ take allocations of rooms
Zimmerkontingente vermitteln
♦ arrange room allocations
Zimmerkontingent geben an jn
→ Zimmerkontingent vergeben an jn
Zimmerkontingent haben
♦ have an allocation of rooms
♦ have an allotment of rooms
Zimmerkontingent kaufen
♦ buy an allotment of rooms
♦ buy an allocation of rooms
♦ buy a quota of rooms
Zimmerkontingent nehmen
♦ take an allotment of rooms
♦ take an allocation of rooms
♦ take a quota of rooms
Zimmerkontingent reservieren
♦ reserve an allotment of rooms
♦ reserve an allocation of rooms
♦ reserve a quota of rooms
Zimmerkontingent vergeben an jn
Zimmerkontingent geben an jn
♦ make an allotment of rooms to s.o.
♦ make an allocation of rooms to s.o.
♦ give a quota of rooms to s.o.
Zimmerkonto, n
(wird bei Leistungen belastet)
♦ room account
Zimmerkontrollbuch, n
♦ room-inspection book
Zimmerkontrolle, f (generell)
♦ room control
♦ rooms control
♦ control of a room
♦ control of rooms
♦ controling a room AE
Zimmerkontrolle, f (Inspektion)
♦ room inspection
♦ inspection of a room
♦ inspecting a room
Zimmer kostenlos haben
♦ have a room free of charge
♦ have a room free
Zimmer kostet $ 123
♦ room costs $ 123
Zimmer kostet $ 123 inklusive Frühstück
♦ room costs $ 123 including breakfast
Zimmerkühlschrank, m
♦ room refrigerator
♦ room fridge coll
Zimmerlage, f
♦ position of a room
♦ situation of a room
♦ location of a room
♦ room position
♦ room location (situation)

Zimmerlageplan

Zimmerlageplan, m
  Lageplan, m
  Zimmerspiegel, m
  ♦ floor plan
Zimmer läßt sich gut vermieten
  ♦ room rents well *AE*
  ♦ room lets well *BE*
Zimmerlautstärke, f
  (von Radio etc.)
  ♦ moderate volume
  ♦ domestic listening level
Zimmer liegen nach allen Seiten
  Zimmer gehen nach allen Seiten
  ♦ rooms face all sides
Zimmer liegen nach allen (vier) Richtungen
  ♦ rooms face all (four) directions
Zimmer liegt auf zwei Ebenen
  ♦ room is split-level
Zimmer liegt gut
  Zimmer ist gut gelegen
  ♦ room is well located
Zimmer liegt im Erdgeschoß
  ♦ room is situated on the first floor *AE*
  ♦ room is situated on the ground floor *BE*
Zimmer liegt im zweiten Stockwerk
  Zimmer liegt auf der zweiten Etage
  Zimmer liegt im zweiten Obergeschoß
  ♦ room is located on the third floor *AE*
  ♦ room is located on the second floor *BE*
Zimmer liegt nach dem Inland
  ♦ room faces inland
Zimmer liegt nach hinten
  ♦ room faces the back
Zimmer liegt nach Norden
  Zimmer ist nach Norden gelegen
  Zimmer geht nach Norden
  ♦ room faces north
Zimmer liegt nach Nordosten
  ♦ room faces northeast *AE*
  ♦ room faces north-east *BE*
Zimmer liegt nach Nordwesten
  ♦ room faces northwest *AE*
  ♦ room faces north-west *BE*
Zimmer liegt nach Osten
  Zimmer ist nach Osten gelegen
  Zimmer geht nach Osten
  ♦ room faces east
Zimmer liegt nach Osten zum Gebirge
  ♦ room faces east to the mountains
Zimmer liegt nach Süden
  Zimmer ist nach Süden gelegen
  Zimmer geht nach Süden
  ♦ room faces south
Zimmer liegt nach Süden zum Meer
  ♦ room faces south to the sea
Zimmer liegt nach Südosten
  ♦ room faces southeast *AE*
  ♦ room faces south-east *BE*
Zimmer liegt nach Südwesten
  ♦ room faces southwest *AE*
  ♦ room faces south-west *BE*
Zimmer liegt nach vorn
  Zimmer ist nach vorn gelegen
  ♦ room faces the front
Zimmer liegt nach Westen
  Zimmer ist nach Westen gelegen
  Zimmer geht nach Westen
  ♦ room faces west
Zimmer liegt neben meinem
  Zimmer grenzt an meines an
  ♦ room adjoins mine

Zimmer liegt zu dem Ozean
  ♦ room faces the ocean
Zimmer liegt zum Fluß
  ♦ room faces the river
Zimmer liegt zum Garten
  ♦ room faces the garden
Zimmer liegt zum Hafen
  ♦ room faces the harbor *AE*
  ♦ room faces the harbour *BE*
Zimmer liegt zum Kanal
  ♦ room faces the canal
Zimmer liegt zum Meer hin
  ♦ room faces the sea
Zimmer liegt zum Park
  ♦ room faces the park
Zimmer liegt zum Wald
  ♦ room faces the forest
  ♦ room faces the wood
Zimmer liegt zur Altstadt
  ♦ room faces the Old Town
Zimmer liegt zur Bergseite
  Zimmer liegt zu den Bergen hin
  ♦ room faces the mountains
Zimmer liegt zur Einkaufsstraße
  ♦ room faces the shopping street
Zimmer liegt zur Gracht
  ♦ room faces the canal
Zimmer liegt zur Lagune
  ♦ room faces the lagoon
Zimmer liegt zur Seeseite (Binnensee)
  ♦ room faces the lake
Zimmer liegt zur Seeseite (Meer)
  → Zimmer liegt zum Meer hin
Zimmer liegt zur Straße
  ♦ room faces the street
  ♦ room faces the road
Zimmerliste, f
  Zimmerverteilungsliste, f
  ♦ room list
  ♦ rooming list
Zimmerliste zusammenstellen
  ♦ compile a room list
  ♦ compile a rooming list
Zimmer lüften
  ♦ air a room
  ♦ ventilate a room
Zimmer machen
  Zimmer aufräumen
  ♦ do a room
  ♦ tidy a room
Zimmermädchen, n
  ♦ chambermaid
  ♦ maid
Zimmermädchendienst, m
  Zimmermädchenservice, m
  Aufwartungsdienst, m
  ♦ chambermaid service
  ♦ maid service
Zimmermädchen einsetzen auf einer Station
  ♦ appoint a chambermaid to a station *AE*
  ♦ appoint a chambermaid to a section *BE*
Zimmermädchenrevier, n
  Zimmermädchenstation, f
  ♦ chambermaid's station *AE*
  ♦ maid's station *AE*
  ♦ chambermaid's section *BE*
  ♦ maid's section *BE*
Zimmermädchenservice, m
  → Zimmermädchendienst
Zimmermädchenstation, f
  → Zimmermädchenrevier

Zimmermädchenwagen, m
  ♦ chambermaid's cart *AE*
  ♦ maid's cart *AE*
  ♦ chambermaid's trolley *BE*
  ♦ maid's trolley *BE*
Zimmermangel, m (Knappheit)
  Zimmerknappheit, f
  ♦ shortage of rooms
  ♦ room shortage
Zimmermangel, m (völliges Fehlen)
  Raumnot, f
  ♦ lack of rooms
Zimmermaße, n pl
  ♦ room dimensions *pl*
Zimmermiete, f
  Miete für ein Zimmer, f
  ♦ room rent
  ♦ rent for a room
  ♦ room hire *BE*
Zimmer mieten
  ♦ rent a room
  ♦ hire a room *BE*
Zimmermieter, m
  ♦ room tenant
  ♦ tenant lodger
  ♦ tenant
  ♦ lodger
Zimmer mietfrei bewohnen
  ♦ occupy a room rent-free
Zimmermietgebühr, f
  Raummietgebühr, f
  ♦ room rental charge *AE*
  ♦ room rental fee *AE*
  ♦ room hire charge *BE*
  ♦ room hire fee *BE*
Zimmer mit Alleinbenutzung, n
  → Zimmer mit Einbettbelegung
Zimmer mit allem modernen Komfort, n
  ♦ room with all modern amenities
  ♦ room with all modern facilities
  ♦ room with all mod. cons. *BE coll*
  ♦ room with all modern conveniences
  ♦ room with all modern comforts
Zimmer mit Amtstelefon, n
  ♦ room with post office telephone
  ♦ room with G.P.O. telephone *BE*
Zimmer mit Amtstelefonanschluß, n
  ♦ room with post office telephone connection
  ♦ room with GPO telephone connection *BE*
Zimmer mit Aussicht, n
  ♦ room with a view
  ♦ room with view
Zimmer mit automatischer Nachrichtenübermittlung, n
  ♦ room with automatic message system
Zimmer mit Babyüberwachungsanlage, n
  ♦ room with baby-listening unit
  ♦ room with baby-listening device
Zimmer mit Bad, n
  ♦ room with bath
Zimmer mit Badbenutzung, n
  ♦ room with use of a bathroom
Zimmer mit Bad/Dusche, n
  ♦ room with bath/shower
Zimmer mit Bad oder Dusche, n
  ♦ room with bath or shower
Zimmer mit Bad und Balkon, n
  ♦ room with bath and balcony
Zimmer mit Balkon, n
  ♦ room with balcony

Zimmer mitbenutzen
♦ share a room
Zimmer mit Bergblick, n
  Zimmer mit Blick auf die Berge, n
♦ room with mountain view
♦ room with (a) view of the mountains
Zimmer mit Bidet, n
♦ room with bidet
Zimmer mit Blick auf das Land, n
  Zimmer mit Landblick, n
♦ room with land view
Zimmer mit Blick auf das Meer, n
♦ room with a view of the sea
Zimmer mit Blick auf den See, n
♦ room with a view of the lake
Zimmer mit Blick auf die Bucht, n
♦ room with a view of the bay
♦ room with bay view *BE*
Zimmer mit Blick auf etw, n
♦ room with a view of s.th.
Zimmer mit Blick über den Garten, n
♦ room overlooking the garden
Zimmer mit Blick über den See, n
♦ room overlooking the lake
Zimmer mit Blick über den Strand, n
♦ room overlooking the beach
Zimmer mit Blick über etw, n
♦ room overlooking s.th.
♦ room with a view over s.th.
♦ room with a view across s.th.
Zimmer mit Dachschräge, n
  Zimmer mit schrägem Dach, n
♦ room with sloping roof
Zimmer mit danebenliegendem Bad, n
  Zimmer mit angrenzendem Bad, n
♦ room with adjoining bath
Zimmer mit direktem Meeresblick, n
  Zimmer mit vollem Meeresblick, n
♦ room with full seaview *AE*
♦ room with full sea-view *BE*
Zimmer mit Doppelbelegung, n
♦ double-occupancy room
Zimmer mit Doppelbett, n
♦ double-bedded room
♦ double-bed room
♦ double room
Zimmer mit Doppelscheiben, n
♦ room with double-glazed windows
Zimmer mit Doppelverglasung, n
  Zimmer mit Doppelscheiben, n
♦ room with double-glazing
♦ room with double-glazed windows
Zimmer mit drei Betten, n
♦ room with three beds
Zimmer mit Durchwahltelefon, n
♦ room with direct-dial telephone
♦ room with s.t.d telephone
♦ room with subscriber trunk dialling
Zimmer mit Duschbenutzung, n
♦ room with use of the shower
Zimmer mit Dusche, n
♦ room with shower
Zimmer mit Dusche und WC, n
♦ room with shower and WC
Zimmer mit Eichentäfelung, n
♦ room with oak panelling
♦ room with oak paneling *AE*
Zimmer mit eigenem Bad, n
♦ room with private bath
Zimmer mit eigenem Badezimmer, n
♦ room with private bathroom

Zimmer mit eigenem Bad und Dusche, n
♦ room with private bath and shower
Zimmer mit eigenem Bad und Toilette, n
♦ room with private bath and toilet
Zimmer mit eigenem Bad und WC, n
♦ room with private bath and WC
Zimmer mit eigenem Balkon, n
  Zimmer mit Privatbalkon, n
♦ room with private balcony
Zimmer mit eigenem Eingang, n
♦ room with private entrance
Zimmer mit eigenem Safe, n
  Zimmer mit eigenem Tresor, n
  Zimmer mit Privattresor, n
♦ room with private safe
Zimmer mit eigenem WC, n
♦ room with private WC
Zimmer mit eigenen Sanitäreinrichtungen, n
♦ room with private facilities
Zimmer mit eigener Sonnenterasse, n
♦ room with private sun terrace
Zimmer mit eigener Terrasse, n
♦ room with private terrace
♦ room with private patio
Zimmer mit eigener Toilette, n
♦ room with private toilet
Zimmer mit eigener Veranda, n
♦ room with private veranda
♦ room with private verandah
Zimmer mit eigener Zimmerbar, n
  → Zimmer mit Privatbar
Zimmer mit Einbettbelegung, n
  Zimmer mit einbettiger Belegung, n
  Zimmer mit Alleinbenutzung, n
♦ single-occupancy room
Zimmer mit (einem) Babybett, n
♦ room with (a) crib *AE*
♦ room with (a) cot *BE*
Zimmer mit einem Bett, n
♦ room with one bed
Zimmer mit einem Waschbecken, n
♦ room with a washbasin
Zimmer mit (einem) Zusatzbett, n
♦ room with (an) extra bed
♦ room with (an) additional bed
Zimmer mit einem zusätzlichen Bett, n
♦ room with an additional bed
Zimmer mit einer besonderen Aussicht, n
♦ room with a special view
Zimmer mit Etagenbad, n
♦ room with bathroom on floor
Zimmer mit Etagendusche, n
♦ room with shower on floor
Zimmer mit Farbfernseher, n
♦ room with color T.V. *AE*
♦ room with color television *AE*
♦ room with colour T.V. *BE*
♦ room with colour television *BE*
Zimmer mit Fax, n
♦ room with fax
Zimmer mit Fernsehanschluß, n
  Zimmer mit TV-Anschluß, n
♦ room with TV connection
♦ room with TV socket *BE*
Zimmer mit fließendem warmen und kaltem Wasser, n
♦ room with hot and cold running water
Zimmer mit fließendem Wasser, n
♦ room with running water
Zimmer mit Fließwasser, n *ÖST*
  → Zimmer mit fließendem Wasser

Zimmer mit Flußblick, n
♦ room with river view
Zimmer mit Frigobar, n
  → Zimmer mit Kühlbar
Zimmer mit Frühstück, n
♦ bed and breakfast
♦ room and breakfast
♦ B&B
♦ CP
♦ Continental Plan
Zimmer mit Gartenblick, n
♦ room with garden view
Zimmer mit Gelegenheit zum Kochen, n
  Zimmer mit Kochgelegenheit, n
♦ efficiency room *AE*
♦ efficiency *AE*
♦ room with cooking facility
Zimmer mit Gepäckablage, n
♦ room with baggage stand *AE*
♦ room with luggage stand *BE*
Zimmer mit Halbpension, n
  Zimmer mit Halbverpflegung, n
♦ room with half board
♦ room with demipension *AE*
♦ room with half pension *AE*
● Modified American Plan
● MAP
Zimmer mit Hausmusik, n
♦ room with piped-in music
Zimmer mit Hausradio, n
♦ room with piped music
Zimmer mit Haustelefon, n
♦ room with internal telephone
♦ room with house telephone
Zimmer mit hoher Decke, n
  → hohes Zimmer
Zimmer mit integriertem Bad, n
♦ room with bath en suite
♦ room with en-suite bath
Zimmer mit integriertem Badezimmer, n
♦ room with bathroom en suite
♦ room with en-suite bathroom
Zimmer mit integriertem Duschraum, n
♦ room with shower room en suite
Zimmer mit integriertem WC, n
♦ room with WC en suite
♦ room with private WC en suite
Zimmer mit integrierten Sanitäreinrichtungen, n
♦ room with en suite facilities
♦ en-suite room
Zimmer mit integrierter Dusche, n
♦ room with shower en suite
♦ room with private shower en suite
Zimmer mit integrierter Toilette, n
♦ room with toilet en suite
♦ room with private toilet en suite
Zimmer mit Kabelfarbfernsehen, n
♦ room with cable color TV *AE*
♦ room with cable colour TV *BE*
Zimmer mit Kinderbett, n
♦ room with a child's bed
♦ room with a cot *AE*
Zimmer mit Klimaanlage, n
♦ room with air conditioning *AE*
♦ room with air-conditioning *BE*
Zimmer mit Kochgelegenheit, n
♦ room with cooking facility
♦ efficiency room
♦ efficiency *AE*
Zimmer mit Kochnische, n
♦ room with kitchenette

Zimmer mit Küchenbenutzung

Zimmer mit Küchenbenutzung
♦ room with use of kitchen
♦ room with kitchen privileges
Zimmer mit Kühlbar, n
Zimmer mit Frigobar, n
♦ room with refrigerated bar
Zimmer mit Kühlschrank, n
♦ room with refrigerator
♦ room with fridge *coll*
Zimmer mit Lage nach Norden, n
→ Zimmer nach Norden
Zimmer mit Landblick, n
♦ landview room *AE*
♦ land-view room *BE*
Zimmer mit Lichtrufanlage, n
♦ room with luminous calling system
♦ room with light indicator
Zimmer mit Loggia, n
♦ room with loggia
Zimmer mit Meeresblick, n
Zimmer mit Blick auf das Meer, n
Zimmer mit Meerblick, n
Zimmer mit Seeblick, n
♦ room with seaview *AE*
♦ room with sea view *BE*
♦ room with a view of the sea
♦ room with ocean view
Zimmer mit Meeresblickbalkon, n
♦ room with sea-view balcony
Zimmer mit Meeresblickfenster, n
Zimmer mit Meerblickfenster, n
♦ room with sea-view window
Zimmer mit Meeresblickterrasse, n
♦ room with sea-view terrace
Zimmer mit Minibar, n
♦ room with minibar
Zimmer mit Möbeln ausstatten
♦ equip a room with furniture
♦ furnish a room
Zimmer mit Musikanlage, n
→ Zimmer mit Hausradio
Zimmer mit Naßzelle, n
♦ room with shower cubicle
Zimmer mit niedriger Decke, n
→ niedriges Zimmer
Zimmer mit Ofenheizung, n
♦ room with stove heating
Zimmer mit offenem Kamin, n
♦ room with open fireplace
Zimmer mit Panoramablick, n
♦ room with panoramic view
Zimmer mit Parkblick, n
♦ room with park view
Zimmer mit Privatbar, n
Zimmer mit eigener Bar, n
♦ room with private bar
Zimmer mit Privattresor, n
→ Zimmer mit eigenem Safe
Zimmer mit Radio, n
♦ room with radio
Zimmer mit Radioanschluß, n
♦ room with radio connection
Zimmer mit Radio/Sprechanlage, n
♦ room with radio/intercom
Zimmer mit Rasiersteckdose, n
♦ room with electric shaver point
♦ room with electric razor point
Zimmer mit Rückansicht, n
Zimmer mit Blick nach hinten, n
♦ room with rear view

Zimmer mit Schwarzweißfernsehen, n
♦ room with black and white T.V.
♦ room with b/w T.V.
Zimmer mit Seeblick, n (Binnensee)
♦ room with lakeview *AE*
♦ room with lake view *BE*
Zimmer mit Seeblick, n (Meer)
→ Zimmer mit Meeresblick
Zimmer mit Selbstwähltelefon, n
♦ room with self-dial telephone
♦ room with self-dialling telephone
Zimmer mit separatem Ankleideraum, n
♦ room with separate dressing room
Zimmer mit separatem Eingang, n
♦ room with separate entrance
Zimmer mit Service, n
Zimmer mit Bedienung, n
♦ serviced room
Zimmer mit Sitzecke, n
♦ room with corner seating
Zimmer mit Sonnenbalkon, n
♦ room with sun balcony
Zimmer mit Sprechanlage, n
♦ room with intercom
Zimmer mit Talblick, n
♦ room with valley view
Zimmer mit Teilpension, n
♦ room with part board
♦ room with partial board
Zimmer mit teilweisem Meeresblick, n
♦ room with partial seaview *AE*
♦ room with partial sea view *BE*
Zimmer mit Telefax, n
♦ room with telefax
Zimmer mit Telefon, n
♦ room with telephone
Zimmer mit Telefonanschluß, n
♦ room with telephone connection
♦ room with phone connection
Zimmer mit Telexanschluß, n
♦ room with telex connection
Zimmer mit Terrasse, n
Zimmer mit einer Terrasse, n
♦ room with terrace
♦ room with a terrace
Zimmer mit Toilette, n
♦ room with toilet
Zimmer mit Veranda, n
♦ room with veranda
♦ room with verandah
Zimmer mit Verbindungstür, n
♦ communicating room
Zimmer mit Vollbad, n
♦ room with full bath
Zimmer mit Vollpension, n
Zimmer mit Vollverpflegung, n
Zimmer mit voller Verpflegung, n
♦ room with full board
♦ room with full pension *AE*
♦ American Plan
♦ AP
Zimmer mit Waschgelegenheit, n
♦ room with washing facilities
Zimmer mit WC, n
♦ room with WC
♦ room with toilet
Zimmer mit Weckanlage, n
♦ room with early-call system
Zimmer mit Zentralheizung, n
♦ room with central heating

Zimmer mit Zimmertelefon, n
♦ room with room telephone
Zimmer mit zwei Betten, n
♦ room with two beds
Zimmer mit zwei Doppelbetten, n
♦ room with two double beds
Zimmer möblieren
♦ furnish a room
Zimmer modernisieren
♦ modernise a room
♦ modernize a room
♦ update a room
Zimmernachbar, m
♦ person in the next room
♦ next-door neighbor *AE*
♦ next-door neighbour *BE*
Zimmernachbarn, m pl
♦ people in the next room *pl*
Zimmernachfrage, f
Nachfrage nach Zimmern, f
♦ rooms demand
♦ room demand
♦ demand for rooms
♦ demand for a room
Zimmernachfrage quantifizieren
♦ quantify the rooms demand
♦ quantify the demand for rooms
Zimmer nach hinten, n
rückwärtiges Zimmer, n
♦ room at the back
♦ back room
Zimmer nach Norden, n
♦ room facing north
♦ north-facing room
Zimmer nach Osten, n
♦ room facing east
♦ east-facing room
Zimmer nach Süden, n
♦ room facing south
Zimmernacht, f
(Statistik)
♦ room-night
Zimmernachtkapazität, f
♦ room-night capacity
Zimmernachtnachfrage, f
♦ room-night demand
Zimmernachtumsatz, m
♦ room-night sales *pl*
♦ room-night turnover
Zimmernachtzahl, f
♦ room-night figure
Zimmer nach vorn, n
♦ room at the front
♦ front room
Zimmernachweis, m
→ Zimmervermittlung
Zimmernachweisgebühr f
♦ accommodation service charge
♦ accommodation service fee
Zimmer nach Westen, n
♦ room facing west
♦ west-facing room
Zimmername, m
Name des Zimmers, m
♦ room name
♦ name of the room
Zimmer nebenan, n
Nachbarzimmer, n
♦ next room
Zimmer nehmen
Zimmer sich nehmen

- ◆ take a room
- ◆ book in

Zimmer neu möblieren
- ◆ refurnish a room

Zimmer neu tapezieren
  Zimmer neu streichen
  Zimmer renovieren
- ◆ redecorate a room

Zimmer neu vermieten
  Zimmer wieder vermieten
  Zimmer erneut vermieten
- ◆ rerent a room AE
- ◆ relet a room BE

Zimmer nicht in Anspruch nehmen
- ◆ not use a room
- ◆ not claim a room

Zimmer nimmt bis zu drei Personen auf
- ◆ room takes up to three persons

Zimmer nimmt zwei Personen auf
- ◆ room takes two persons

Zimmerniveau, n
  (Lage)
- ◆ room level

Zimmernummer, f
- ◆ room number
- ◆ number of a room

Zimmernummerkarte, f
- ◆ room number card

Zimmer nur teilweise benutzen
- ◆ occupy a room only part of the time

Zimmer offerieren jm
  → Zimmer anbieten jm

Zimmer ohne Berechnung, n
  kostenloses Zimmer, n
  Gratiszimmer, n
  Freizimmer, n
- ◆ room free of charge
- ◆ free room
- ◆ courtesy room AE
- ◆ complimentary room

Zimmer ohne etw, n
- ◆ room without s.th.

Zimmer ohne fließendes Wasser, n
  Zimmer ohne Fließwasser, n ÖST
- ◆ room without running water

Zimmer ohne Frühstück, n
- ◆ room without breakfast

Zimmer ohne Service, n
  Zimmer ohne Bedienung, n
- ◆ nonserviced room AE
- ◆ non-serviced room BE
- ◆ room without service

Zimmer ohne Verpflegung, n
  nur Zimmer
- ◆ room without board
- ◆ room only
- ◆ EP
- ◆ European Plan

Zimmer ordentlich machen
  Zimmer in Ordnung bringen
- ◆ settle a room

Zimmerpaar, n
  Paar Zimmer, n
- ◆ pair of rooms

Zimmerpartner, m
- ◆ person sharing a room
- ◆ roommate AE
- ◆ room-mate BE

Zimmerpaß, m
  Zimmerausweis, m
- ◆ room pass

Zimmerpaß erhalten
- ◆ receive a room pass
- ◆ receive the room pass

Zimmerpauschale, f
  Zimmerpauschalpreis, m
  Zimmerpreispauschale, f
- ◆ inclusive room rate
- ◆ inclusive room price

Zimmerpauschalpreis, m
  → Zimmerpauschale

Zimmerpersonal, n
- ◆ room staff
- ◆ room personnel
- ◆ chamber staff AE rare

Zimmer persönlich buchen
- ◆ book a room in person

Zimmerpflanze, f
- ◆ indoor plant

Zimmerpflege, f (generell)
- ◆ servicing a room

Zimmerpflege, f (Reinigung)
  → Zimmerreinigung

Zimmer pflegen
- ◆ service a room

Zimmerplan, m (generell)
- ◆ room plan

Zimmerplan, m (Lageplan)
  → Zimmerlageplan

Zimmer plündern
  Zimmer ausplündern
- ◆ loot a room

Zimmerpräferenz f
  Vorliebe für ein Zimmer f
  Zimmerwunsch m
- ◆ room preference

Zimmerpreis, m
  Zimmerrate, f
- ◆ room rate
- ◆ room price
- ◆ room charge

Zimmerpreisänderung, f (geringfügig)
- ◆ room rate alteration
- ◆ alteration of the room rates

Zimmerpreisänderung, f (umfassend)
- ◆ room rate change
- ◆ change in the room rates

Zimmerpreisanstieg, m
- ◆ room rate increase
- ◆ increase in (the) room rates

Zimmerpreisaufschlüsselung, f
  Aufschlüsselung der Zimmerpreise, f
- ◆ breakdown of the room rates
- ◆ breakdown of the room prices

Zimmerpreise anpassen
- ◆ adjust room rates
- ◆ adjust room prices

Zimmerpreise aufschlüsseln
- ◆ break down the room rates
- ◆ break down the room prices

Zimmerpreise festsetzen
- ◆ determine the room rates
- ◆ determine the room prices

Zimmerpreise garantieren
- ◆ guarantee the room rates
- ◆ guarantee the room prices

Zimmerpreise liegen zwischen DM 123 und DM 321 pro Nacht
- ◆ room rates range from DM 123 to DM 321 per night
- ◆ room prices range from DM 123 to DM 321 per night

Zimmerpreise nennen
- ◆ quote the room rates
- ◆ quote the room prices

Zimmerpreisermäßigung, f
- ◆ room rate reduction
- ◆ room price reduction
- ◆ reduction of room rates
- ◆ reduction of room prices
- ◆ reduction in room rates

Zimmerpreisermäßigung geben jm
- ◆ give s.o. a room rate reduction
- ◆ give s.o. a reduction on the room rate

Zimmerpreisermäßigung von 20 % anbieten
- ◆ offer a 20 % reduction on the room rate

Zimmerpreisgruppe, f
- ◆ room rate group
- ◆ room price group

Zimmerpreiskalkulation, f
  Zimmerpreisberechnung, f
- ◆ room rate calculation
- ◆ calculation of room rates

Zimmerpreis kalkulieren
  Zimmerpreis berechnen
- ◆ calculate the room rate
- ◆ calculate the room price

Zimmerpreiskarte f
- ◆ room rate card

Zimmerpreisliste, f
- ◆ room tariff

Zimmerpreis mit Frühstück, m
- ◆ charge for bed and breakfast

zimmerpreispauschale, f
  → Zimmerpauschale

Zimmerpreis pro Übernachtung, m
- ◆ room rate per night
- ◆ room price per night
- ◆ room charge per night

Zimmerpreisstruktur f
- ◆ room rate structure

Zimmerpreisstruktur überprüfen
- ◆ review the room rate structure

Zimmerpreisuntersuchung, f
  Zimmerpreisstudie, f
- ◆ room rate study

Zimmerpreisverzeichnis n
- ◆ room rate list
- ◆ list of room rates

Zimmer putzen
  Zimmer saubermachen
  Zimmer säubern
- ◆ dress a room
- ◆ clean a room

Zimmerqualität f
  Zimmergüte f
- ◆ room quality
- ◆ quality of a room

Zimmerrack n
- ◆ room rack

Zimmerrate, f
  → Zimmerpreis

Zimmer räumen
  Zimmer frei machen
- ◆ vacate a room

Zimmer räumen bis 11 Uhr
  Zimmer frei machen bis 11 Uhr
- ◆ vacate a room by 11 o'clock

Zimmerräumung

Zimmerräumung, f
- vacation of a room
- vacation of rooms
- vacating a room
- vacating rooms

Zimmerrechnung, f
- room bill

Zimmer rechtzeitig abbestellen
  Zimmer rechtzeitig stornieren
  Zimmer rechtzeitig absagen
- cancel a room in time

Zimmerreihe, f
→ Zimmerflucht

Zimmer reinigen
  Zimmer putzen
- clean a room

Zimmer reinigen und instandhalten
- clean and service a room

Zimmerreinigung, f
- room cleaning
- rooms cleaning
- cleaning of a room
- cleaning of rooms

Zimmerreinigungsdienst m
  Zimmerreinigungsservice m
  Zimmerreinigung f
- room-cleaning service

Zimmerreinigungsgebühr f
- room-cleaning charge
- room-cleaning fee

Zimmerreinigungsservice, m
→ Zimmerreinigungsdienst

Zimmerreservation, f SCHW
→ Zimmerreservierung

Zimmer reservieren
- reserve a room
- reserve rooms

Zimmer reservieren auf den Namen Miller
- reserve a room in the name of Miller

Zimmer reservieren für einen bestimmten Termin
- reserve a room for a certain date

Zimmer reservieren für einen Gast
- reserve a room for a guest

Zimmer reservieren für jn
  Zimmer bereithalten für jn
- reserve a room for s.o.

Zimmer reservieren lassen
- make a room reservation

Zimmer reservieren lassen über Computer
- have a room reserved by computer

Zimmer reservieren lassen über ein Reisebüro
- reserve a room through a travel agency

Zimmer reservieren lassen über jn
  Zimmer reservieren lassen durch jn
- reserve a room through s.o.

Zimmer reservieren über einen Reservierungsdienst
- reserve a room through a reservation service
- reserve a room through a reservations service

Zimmer reserviert halten
→ Zimmer bereithalten

Zimmer reserviert halten bis 18 Uhr
→ Zimmer bereithalten bis 18 Uhr

Zimmerreservierung, f
  Reservierung eines Zimmers, f
  Zimmerreservation, f SCHW
- room reservation
- reservation of a room
- reserving a room

Zimmerreservierung annehmen
  Zimmerreservierung akzeptieren
- accept a room reservation

Zimmerreservierung bestätigen
- confirm a room reservation

Zimmerreservierung entgegennehmen
- take a room reservation

Zimmerreservierungsliste, f
- room reservation list
- rooms reservations list

Zimmerreservierungssystem, n
  ZRS, n
- room reservation system
- room reservations system
- RRS

Zimmerreservierungswunsch, m
- room reservation request
- request for room reservation

Zimmerreservierung tätigen
→ Zimmer reservieren lassen

Zimmer richten
  Zimmer herrichten
- make up a room AE
- set a room straight
- tidy a room up

Zimmerruf, m
- room call
- radio room call

Zimmersafe, m
  Zimmertresor, m
- room safe

Zimmer säubern
→ Zimmer putzen

Zimmerschlüssel, m
- room key
- key to a room
- key of a room

Zimmerschlüssel abgeben am Empfangsschalter
- hand in the room key at the reception desk

Zimmerschlüssel abholen
- collect the room key
- collect one's room key
- pick up the room key
- pick up one's room key

Zimmerschlüssel abholen bei der Rezeption
- collect the room key from the receptionist
- collect one's room key from the receptionist
- pick up the room key from the receptionist
- pick up one's room key from the receptionist

Zimmerschlüssel aushändigen (an einen Gast)
  Zimmerschlüssel aushändigen (einem Gast)
- hand out a room key (to a guest)

Zimmerschlüssel bekommen
- get a room key
- get one's room key

Zimmerschlüssel erhalten
  Zimmerschlüssel empfangen
- receive the room key
- receive one's room key

Zimmerschlüssel übergeben an einen Gast
- issue a room key to a guest

Zimmerschlüssel verlieren
- lose one's room key

Zimmerschlüssel zurückgeben jm
- return the room key to s.o.

Zimmer schriftlich buchen
- book a room in writing

Zimmerservice, m
  Zimmerbedienung f
- room service

Zimmerservice anrufen
- telephone room service
- phone room service
- ring room service BE
- call room service

Zimmerserviceaufzug, m
- room service lift BE
- room service elevator AE

Zimmerservicebestellung, f
- room service order

Zimmerservice bieten
- provide room service

Zimmerservicefahrstuhl m
- room service elevator AE
- room service lift BE

Zimmerservicefrühstück n
- room service breakfast

Zimmerservicegebühr f
- room service charge

Zimmerservicekarte, f
  Zimmerservicespeisekarte, f
- room service menu

Zimmerservicekellner, m
- room service waiter

Zimmerservicekellnerin, f
- room service waitress

Zimmerserviceküche, f
- room service kitchen

Zimmerserviceleute, pl
  Zimmerservice, m
- room service people pl

Zimmerservice nutzen
- use the room service
- make use of the room service

Zimmerserviceoberkellner, m
- room service headwaiter

Zimmerserviceoffice n
- room service office

Zimmerservicepersonal n
- room service staff
- room service personnel

Zimmerservicerechnung f
- room service bill

Zimmerserviceumsatz, m
- room service sales pl
- room service turnover

Zimmerserviceverzeichnis, n
  Verzeichnis der Zimmerserviceleistungen, n
- room service directory

Zimmer sichern sich
- secure a room

Zimmer sieht aus wie ein Schlachtfeld
- room looks like a battlefield

Zimmer sieht aus wie ein Schweinestall
- room looks like a pigsty

Zimmer sind ganz verschieden
  Zimmer sind alle verschieden
- rooms are all different

Zimmer sind großzügig bemessen
- rooms are ample in size

Zimmer sind identisch möbliert
  Zimmer sind gleich möbliert
- rooms are identically furnished

Zimmer sind knapp
- rooms are in short supply

Zimmer sind rar
- rooms are scarce

Zimmer sind verschieden
- rooms are different

Zimmer sind verschieden groß
- rooms vary in size

922

Zimmer sind verschieden in der Qualität
- ♦ rooms vary in quality

Zimmer sollte sofort bei Ankunft bezogen werden
- ♦ room should be claimed immediately on arrival

Zimmer sperren
- *(Rezeption)*
- Zimmer blocken
- Zimmer nicht freigeben
- ♦ block a room

Zimmerspiegel, m
- → Zimmerlageplan

Zimmerstatistik, f
- ♦ room statistics *pl*

Zimmerstatistik anfertigen
- ♦ compile room statistics

Zimmerstatistik führen
- ♦ keep room statistics

Zimmerstatus, m
- Zimmerzustand, m
- ♦ room status
- ♦ room state

Zimmerstatusanlage f
- ♦ room status system

Zimmerstatusbericht m
- ♦ room status report

Zimmerstatusrack n
- Zimmerrack n
- ♦ room status rack
- ♦ room rack

Zimmerstatustafel, f
- Zimmerstatusbrett, n
- Zimmerzustandstafel, f
- Zimmerzustandstableau, n
- ♦ room status board
- ♦ room board

Zimmerstatustafel auf dem laufenden halten
- ♦ keep the room status board up-to-date
- ♦ up-date the room status board

Zimmer steht in Brand
- → Zimmer brennt

Zimmer steht leer
- ♦ room is vacant

Zimmer steht zur Verfügung
- Zimmer ist frei
- Zimmer ist verfügbar
- ♦ room is available

Zimmer steht zur Verfügung vom 8. bis 10. November
- ♦ room will be available from 8 to 10 November

Zimmersteuer, f
- Zimmertaxe, f
- Zimmerabgabe, f
- ♦ room tax

Zimmersteward, m
- ♦ room steward

Zimmer stornieren
- Zimmer abbestellen
- Zimmer absagen
- ♦ cancel a room

Zimmerstornierung, f
- Zimmerabbestellung, f
- ♦ room cancellation
- ♦ room cancelation *AE*
- ♦ cancellation of a room
- ♦ cancelation of a room *AE*
- ♦ cancel(l)ing a room

Zimmer streichen
- Zimmer anstreichen
- ♦ paint a room
- ♦ decorate a room

Zimmerstrichliste, f
- ♦ room checklist

Zimmer stundenweise vermieten
- ♦ rent (out) a room by the hour
- ♦ hire out a room by the hour *BE*
- ♦ let a room by the hour *BE*

Zimmersuchdienst, m
- ♦ room-finding service

Zimmersuche, f
- ♦ room hunting
- ♦ looking for a room
- ♦ looking for rooms

Zimmersuche einstellen
- ♦ give up hunting for a room

Zimmer suchen (generell)
- Zimmer (sich) suchen
- ♦ look for a room
- ♦ seek a room

Zimmer suchen (Untermieter)
- Zimmer (sich) suchen
- ♦ look for lodgings

Zimmer tapezieren
- ♦ paper a room
- ♦ wallpaper a room

Zimmertarif, m
- ♦ room tariff
- ♦ room rates *pl*
- ♦ room rate

Zimmertausch, m
- ♦ room exchange
- ♦ room-swap
- ♦ room-swop
- ♦ room-swapping
- ♦ room-swopping

Zimmer tauschen
- ♦ exchange rooms
- ♦ swap rooms
- ♦ swop rooms

Zimmer tauschen mit jm
- ♦ exchange one's room with s.o.
- ♦ swap one's room with s.o.
- ♦ swop one's room with s.o.

Zimmertaxe, f
- → Zimmersteuer

Zimmer teilen mit jm
- ♦ share a room with s.o.

Zimmer teilweise mit ...
- ♦ some rooms with ...
- ♦ some rooms have ...

Zimmer teilweise mit Meerblick
- ♦ some rooms with sea views

Zimmer telefonisch buchen
- ♦ book a room by telephone

Zimmer telefonisch reservieren
- ♦ reserve a room by telephone

Zimmer telefonisch reservieren lassen
- ♦ have a room reserved by telephone

Zimmertelefon n
- ♦ room telephone
- ♦ room phone

Zimmertemperatur, f
- Raumtemperatur, f
- ♦ room temperature
- ♦ ambient temperature

Zimmertheater, n
- ♦ little theater *AE*
- ♦ little theatre *BE*
- ♦ cellar theater *AE*
- ♦ cellar theatre *BE*

Zimmerthermometer, n
- ♦ indoor thermometer

Zimmerthermostat, m
- ♦ room thermostat

Zimmertrakt, m
- → Schlafraumtrakt

Zimmertresor, m
- → Zimmersafe

Zimmertür läßt sich nicht abschließen
- ♦ door of the room cannot be locked

Zimmer-TV, n
- ♦ room TV

Zimmertyp, m
- Zimmerart, f
- ♦ type of room
- ♦ room type

Zimmerüberangebot, n
- Überangebot an Zimmern, n
- Zimmerüberhang, m
- ♦ surplus of rooms
- ♦ oversupply of rooms

Zimmer überprüfen
- ♦ check a room

Zimmerumfang, m
- Zimmerrauminhalt, m
- Raumvolumen, n
- ♦ contents of a room *pl*

Zimmer umräumen
- ♦ rearrange a room

Zimmerumsatz, m
- ♦ room sales *pl*
- ♦ rooms sales *pl*
- ♦ room turnover
- ♦ rooms turnover

Zimmer umwandeln in etw
- Zimmer verwandeln in etw
- ♦ convert a room into s.th.
- ♦ turn a room into s.th.

Zimmer und Frühstück getrennt berechnen
- ♦ charge room and breakfast separately

Zimmer und Verpflegung
- Zimmer (n) und Verpflegung (f)
- ♦ room and board

Zimmer und Verpflegung bekommen
- ♦ get room and board

Zimmer untervermieten
- ♦ sublet a room

Zimmer unter Vertrag nehmen
- ♦ contract a room
- ♦ contract rooms

Zimmervakanz f
- ♦ room vacancy

Zimmer verbessern
- Zimmer verschönern
- ♦ improve a room

Zimmervereinbarung, f
- Zimmerarrangement, n
- ♦ room arrangement

Zimmerverfügbarkeit, f
- ♦ room availability

Zimmerverfügbarkeitsstatus, m
- ♦ room availability status

Zimmer verfügt über einen Balkon
- ♦ room has a balcony

Zimmervergabe, f
- Zimmerverteilung, f
- Zimmerzuteilung, f
- Zimmerzuweisung, f
- ♦ room assignment *AE*
- ♦ assignment of a room *AE*
- ♦ assignment of rooms *AE*
- ♦ room allocation
- ♦ allocation of a room

Zimmer vergeben an einen Gast

Zimmer vergeben an einen Gast
   Zimmer einem Gast zuteilen
   Zimmer einem Gast zuweisen
  ◆ **assign a room to a guest** *AE*
  ◆ allocate a room to a guest
Zimmerverkauf, m
  ◆ **room sale**
  ◆ sale of a room
  ◆ sale of rooms
  ◆ selling a room
  ◆ selling rooms
Zimmer verkaufen
  ◆ **sell a room**
Zimmer verkaufen zu einem bestimmten Preis
  ◆ **sell a room at a certain price**
  ◆ sell a room at a certain rate
Zimmer verlangen
  ◆ **demand a room**
  ◆ require a room
  ◆ request a room
Zimmer verlassen
  ◆ **leave the room**
Zimmer verlassen heimlich
  ◆ **leave a room stealthily**
Zimmer vermarkten
  ◆ **market a room**
Zimmer vermieten als Einzelzimmer
  ◆ **rent (out) a room as single room**
  ◆ let a room as single room *BE*
Zimmer vermieten an einen Studenten
  ◆ **rent (out) a room to a student**
  ◆ let a room to a student *BE*
Zimmer vermieten an jn
  ◆ **rent (out) a room to s.o.**
  ◆ let a room to s.o. *BE*
Zimmer vermieten (generell)
  ◆ **rent (out) a room**
  ◆ let a room *BE*
Zimmer vermieten (Privathaus)
  untervermieten
  ◆ **take in lodgers**
  ◆ let lodgings *BE*
Zimmervermieter, m (in Privathaus)
  ◆ **landlord**
Zimmervermieterin, f (in Privathaus)
  ◆ **landlady**
Zimmervermietung, f
  ◆ **room rental** *AE*
  ◆ renting (of) rooms *AE*
  ◆ renting (of) a room *AE*
  ◆ letting (of) rooms *BE*
  ◆ letting (of) a room *BE*
Zimmer vermitteln an jn
  ◆ **arrange a room for s.o.**
Zimmervermittlung, f (Agentur)
  ◆ **room agency**
  ◆ accommodation agency
  ◆ accommodation bureau
  ◆ tourist accommodations office *AE*
  ◆ accommodations office *AE*
Zimmervermittlung, f (Tätigkeit)
  ◆ **accommodation service**
  ◆ accommodation booking service *BE*
Zimmer verschlossen halten
  ◆ **keep a room locked**
  ◆ keep the room locked
  ◆ keep one's room locked
Zimmer verschönern
  ◆ **embellish a room**
Zimmer verteilen
  Zimmer vergeben

Zimmer zuteilen
  Zimmer zuweisen
  ◆ **allocate a room**
  ◆ allocate (the) rooms
Zimmer verteilen auf die Gäste
  ◆ **allocate the rooms amongst the guests**
Zimmerverteilung, f
  Zimmervergabe, f
  Zimmerzuteilung, f
  Zimmerzuweisung, f
  ◆ **allocation of a room**
  ◆ room allocation
  ◆ allocation of rooms
  ◆ allocating rooms
  ◆ room assignment *AE*
Zimmerverteilung ändern (geringfügig)
  ◆ **alter the allocation of rooms**
Zimmerverteilung erledigen
  ◆ **deal with the allocation of rooms**
Zimmerverteilung findet um 18 Uhr statt
  ◆ **room allocation takes place at 6 p.m.**
  ◆ room assignment takes place at 6 p.m. *AE*
Zimmerverteilungsliste, f
  Zimmerliste, f
  ◆ **rooming list**
  ◆ room list
Zimmervertrag, m
  ◆ **contract for a room**
  ◆ contract for rooms
Zimmerverwaltung, f
  Zimmermanagement, n
  ◆ **room management**
Zimmer verwandeln in etw
  ◆ **transform a room into s.th.**
  ◆ convert a room into s.th.
Zimmer verweigern
  ◆ **refuse a room**
Zimmerverzeichnis, n
  → Zimmerdatei
Zimmervoll, n
  ◆ **roomful**
Zimmer voller Leute
  ◆ **roomful of people**
Zimmer voller Ungeziefer, n
  Zimmer voll Ungeziefer, n
  ◆ **room alive with vermin**
  ◆ room crawling with vermin
Zimmer vollstellen mit Möbeln
  ◆ **clutter a room with furniture**
Zimmer vollstopfen mit Möbeln
  ◆ **lumber a room with furniture**
Zimmer von ausreichender Größe, n
  ausreichend großes Zimmer, n
  ◆ **room of adequate size**
Zimmer von durchschnittlicher Größe, n
  ◆ **room of average size**
Zimmer von erster Qualität, n
  ◆ **superior room**
Zimmer von verschiedener Größe, n pl
  Zimmer von unterschiedlicher Größe, n pl
  ◆ **rooms of varying size** *pl*
Zimmervorausverteilung, f
  Zimmervorauszuteilung, f
  Zimmervorauszuweisung, f
  Zimmervorausvergabe, f
  ◆ **room pre-allocation**
  ◆ pre-allocation of a room
  ◆ pre-allocation of rooms
  ◆ preassignment of a room *AE*
Zimmer vorbereiten
  ◆ **prepare a room**

Zimmer vorbestellen
  Zimmer im voraus bestellen
  Zimmer vormerken lassen
  ◆ **book a room in advance**
Zimmervorbestellung, f
  Zimmervorausbestellung, f
  ◆ **advance booking of a room**
  ◆ booking a room in advance
  ◆ prebooking a room
Zimmervorschlag, m
  ◆ **room suggestion**
Zimmervorschlag machen
  ◆ **make a room suggestion**
  ◆ suggest a room
Zimmerwäsche f
  ◆ **room linen**
Zimmerwechsel, m
  ◆ **room change**
  ◆ change of room
  ◆ change of rooms
  ◆ changing rooms
Zimmerwechselbeleg, m
  ◆ **move notification slip**
  ◆ room-change notice
Zimmerwechselbenachrichtigung f
  (Rezeption)
  ◆ **move notification**
  ◆ notification of a move
  ◆ notification of moves
Zimmerwechselbenachrichtigungsformular, n
  ◆ **move notification form**
Zimmer wechseln
  (umziehen in ein anderes Zimmer)
  ◆ **change rooms**
  ◆ change one's room
  ◆ move to another room
Zimmerwechsel wünschen
  ◆ **request a room change**
  ◆ request a change of rooms
Zimmer weiter behalten
  (Gast)
  ◆ **keep a room on**
Zimmer weitervermieten
  → Zimmer untervermieten, Zimmer wieder vermieten
Zimmer werden dringend benötigt
  Zimmer werden dringend gesucht
  ◆ **rooms are urgently required**
Zimmer werden stark nachgefragt
  für Zimmer besteht eine große Nachfrage
  ◆ **rooms are in great demand**
  ◆ rooms are much in demand
Zimmer werden täglich gereinigt
  ◆ **rooms are cleaned daily**
Zimmer werden wöchentlich gereinigt
  ◆ **rooms are cleaned weekly**
Zimmer wieder vermieten
  Zimmer erneut vermieten
  Zimmer weitervermieten
  ◆ **relet a room** *BE*
  ◆ rerent a room *AE*
Zimmer wird frei
  ◆ **room becomes vacant**
Zimmer wird geräumt
  (durch Gast)
  Zimmer wird frei
  ◆ **room is vacated**
Zimmer wird im voraus bezahlt
  ◆ **room is paid for in advance**

Zimmer wird renoviert (gestrichen, tapeziert)
Zimmer wird gerade renoviert
♦ **room is being redecorated**
Zimmer wird renoviert (umfassend)
Zimmer wird gerade renoviert
♦ **room is being refurbished**
♦ room is being renovated
Zimmer wird stark genutzt
♦ **room is highly utilised**
♦ room is highly utilized
Zimmer wochenweise vermieten
♦ **rent (out) a room on a weekly basis**
♦ hire out a room on a weekly basis *BE*
♦ let a room on a weekly basis *BE*
Zimmerwunsch, m
♦ **room request**
♦ request for a room
♦ room preference
Zimmerwunsch angeben
♦ **state one's room preference**
Zimmer wünschen
♦ **request a room**
Zimmer wünschen für drei Nächte
♦ **request a room for three nights**
Zimmer wünschen im dritten Stockwerk
Zimmer auf der dritten Etage wünschen
Zimmer im dritten Obergeschoß wünschen
♦ **request a room on the fourth floor** *AE*
♦ request a room on the third floor *BE*
Zimmerwunsch haben
Vorliebe für ein Zimmer haben
♦ **have a room preference**
Zimmerwunsch mitteilen
♦ **indicate one's room preference**
Zimmerzahl, f
Zimmeranzahl, f
♦ **number of rooms**
Zimmer zahlen
→ Zimmer bezahlen
Zimmerzahl erhöhen auf 123
♦ **increase the number of rooms to 123**
Zimmer zeigen jm
♦ **show s.o. a room**
♦ show s.o. his/her room
Zimmer zeigen lassen sich
♦ **ask to be shown the room**
Zimmer zerstören
♦ **vandalise a room**
♦ vandalize a room
Zimmer zu DM 123 pro Übernachtung, n
♦ **room at DM 123 a night**
♦ room at DM 123 per night
Zimmer zugeteilt erhalten
Zimmer zugewiesen bekommen *coll*
♦ **have a room allocated**
♦ have a room assigned *AE*
Zimmer zugewiesen erhalten
Zimmer zugeteilt bekommen *coll*
♦ **have a room assigned** *AE*
♦ have a room allocated
Zimmer zum Garten, n
♦ **room facing the garden**
♦ room looking onto the garden
♦ room looking to the garden
Zimmer zum Hof, n
♦ **room facing the courtyard**
♦ room looking onto the courtyard
♦ room looking to the courtyard
Zimmer zum Innenhof, n
♦ **room facing the patio**

♦ room looking onto the patio
♦ room looking to the patio
Zimmer zum Meer, n
♦ **room facing the sea**
Zimmer zum Park, n
Zimmer zur Parkseite, n
Parkzimmer, n
♦ **room facing the park**
♦ room looking onto the park
♦ room looking to the park
Zimmer zum Schlafen, n
♦ **room for sleeping**
Zimmer zur Außenseite n
→ Außenzimmer
Zimmer zur Hausnutzung, n
Zimmer zur internen Nutzung, n
♦ **room for house use**
Zimmer zur Parkseite, n
→ Zimmer zum Park
Zimmer zur Straße, n (generell)
♦ **room facing the road**
♦ room looking onto the road
♦ room looking to the road
Zimmer zur Straße, n (Geschäftsstraße)
Zimmer zur Straßenseite, n
♦ **room facing the street**
♦ room looking onto the street
♦ room looking to the street
Zimmer zurückerhalten zur Neuvermietung
♦ **receive a room back to rerent** *AE*
♦ receive a room back to relet *BE*
Zimmer zurückhalten
♦ **hold back a room**
Zimmer zur Verfügung gestellt erhalten
♦ **be provided with a room**
Zimmer zur Verfügung haben
♦ **have a room at one's disposal**
Zimmer zur Verfügung stellen jm
→ Zimmer bereitstellen für jn
Zimmer zur Verfügung stellen jm vom 1. bis 5. März
Zimmer bereitstellen für jn vom 1. bis 5. März
♦ **provide s.o. with a room from 1 to 5 March**
♦ provide s.o. with a room from 1 until 5 March
Zimmerzusage, f
Zimmerbestätigung, f
♦ **confirmation of a room**
♦ confirmation of rooms
♦ room confirmation
♦ rooms confirmation
♦ confirming a room
Zimmer zusagen
→ Zimmer bestätigen
Zimmer zusagen für den 23. Januar
♦ **confirm a room for the 23 January**
Zimmer zusagen jm
Zimmer bestätigen jm
♦ **confirm a room to s.o.**
Zimmerzuschlag m
♦ **room supplement**
Zimmerzustand, m (generell)
♦ **condition of a room**
♦ state of a room
Zimmerzustand, m (Status)
→ Zimmerstatus
Zimmerzustandsanzeiger, m
→ Zimmerstatustafel
Zimmerzustandsanzeigetafel, f
→ Zimmerstatustafel
Zimmerzustandstableau, n
→ Zimmerstatustafel

Zimmerzustandstafel f
→ Zimmerstatustafel
Zimmerzuteilung f
→ Zimmerverteilung f
Zimmerzuteilungsfehler, m
Zimmerverteilungsfehler, m
Fehler bei der Zimmervergabe, m
♦ **room allocation error**
♦ room assignment error *AE*
Zimmer zu vermieten (ein Zimmer)
(Hinweisschild)
♦ **Room for rent** *AE*
♦ Room to let *BE*
Zimmer zu vermieten (mehrere Zimmer)
(Hinweisschild)
♦ **Rooms for rent** *AE*
♦ Rooms to let *BE*
Zimmer zuweisen einem Gast
Zimmer vergeben an einen Gast
♦ **allocate a room to a guest**
♦ assign a room to a guest *AE*
Zimmer zuweisen (jm)
Zimmer anweisen (jm)
♦ **assign a room (to s.o.)** *AE*
♦ allocate a room (to s.o.) *BE*
Zimmerzuweisung, f
Zimmerzuteilung, f
Zimmerverteilung, f
Zimmervergabe, f
♦ **room allocation**
♦ room assignment *AE*
♦ allocation of a room
♦ assignment of a room *AE*
♦ allocating a room
Zimmer zweimal vergeben
Zimmer doppelt buchen
♦ **double book a room**
Zimmerzwischenfall, m
♦ **incident in a room**
Zimt, m
♦ **cinnamon**
Zimtrinde, f
♦ **cinnamon bark**
Zimtstange, f
Stange Zimt, f
♦ **stick of cinnamon**
♦ cinnamon stick
Zinn, n (generell)
♦ **tin**
Zinn, n (legiert)
♦ **pewter**
Zinnbecher, m
♦ **pewter mug**
Zinnfigur, f
♦ **pewter figure**
Zinnfolie, f
♦ **tinfoil**
Zinngabel, f
♦ **pewter fork**
Zinngeschirr, n
♦ **pewterware**
♦ pewter
Zinnkanne, f
♦ **pewter jug**
Zinnkrug, m
(mit Deckel)
♦ **pewter tankard**
Zinnlöffel, m
♦ **pewter spoon**
Zinnplatte, f
♦ **pewter platter**

Zinnsoldat

Zinnsoldat, m
 ♦ tin soldier
Zinnteller, m
 ♦ pewter plate
Zinntopf, m
 ♦ pewter pot
Zins, m
 Zinsen, m pl
 ♦ interest sg
Zinsaufwand, m
 ♦ interest expense
 ♦ interest expenditure
 ♦ interest paid
Zinsen aus Kapitalanlagen, m pl
 Anlagenverzinsung, f
 ♦ interest on investments sg
Zinsen berechnen
 ♦ charge interest
Zinsertrag, m
 (Gewinn- und Verlustrechung)
 ♦ interest income
Zinserträge, m pl
 ♦ interest earnings pl
zinsfrei, adj
 zinslos, adj
 ♦ interest-free, adj
Zinskosten, pl
 ♦ interest cost
Zinssatz, m
 Zinsfuß, m
 ♦ interest rate
 ♦ rate of interest
Zinszahlung, f
 ♦ interest payment
zirka, adv
 → circa
Zirkus, m
 ♦ circus
Zirkusliebhaber, m
 ♦ circus lover
Zirkusmanege, f
 ♦ circus ring
Zirkusvorstellung, f
 ♦ circus show
Zirkuswagen, m
 ♦ circus caravan
Zirkuszelt, n
 ♦ circus tent
 ♦ big top
Zisterne, f
 ♦ cistern
Zisterzienser, m
 ♦ Cistercian
Zisterzienserabtei, f
 ♦ Cistercian abbey
Zisterzienserkirche, f
 ♦ Cistercian church
Zisterzienserkloster, n (Frauen)
 ♦ Cistercian convent
 ♦ Cistercian nunnery
Zisterzienserkloster, n (Männer)
 ♦ Cistercian monastery
Zisterziensermönch, m
 ♦ Cistercian monk
Zisterzienserorden, m
 ♦ Cistercian order
zisterziensisch, adj
 ♦ Cistercian, adj
Zitadelle, f
 ♦ citadel

Zither, f
 ♦ zither
Zitherabend, m
 ♦ zither recital
Zitherspieler, m
 ♦ zitherist
Zitrone, f
 ♦ lemon
Zitronenchutney, n
 ♦ lemon chutney
Zitroneneis, n
 ♦ lemon ice cream AE
 ♦ lemon ice-cream BE
Zitronengelee, n
 ♦ lemon jelly
Zitronenhain, m
 ♦ lemon grove
Zitronenlikör, m
 ♦ lemon liqueur
Zitronenlimonade, f (generell)
 ♦ lemonade
Zitronenlimonade, f (Konzentrat)
 ♦ lemon squash
Zitronenparfait, n
 ♦ lemon parfait
Zitronenpresse, f
 ♦ lemon squeezer
Zitronensaft, m
 ♦ lemon juice
Zitronenschale, f
 ♦ lemon peel
 ♦ lemon rind
Zitronenscheibe, f
 ♦ lemon slice
 ♦ slice of lemon
Zitronenschnitz, m
 ♦ lemon wedge
Zitronensorbet, n
 ♦ lemon sorbet
Zitronensoße, f
 ♦ lemon sauce
Zitronensuppe, f
 ♦ lemon soup
Zitronentee, m
 ♦ lemon tea
Zitrusfrucht, f
 ♦ citrus fruit
zivile Preise verlangen
 ♦ charge moderate prices
 ♦ charge moderate rates
ziviler Preis, m
 mäßiger Preis, m
 ♦ moderate rate
 ♦ reasonable rate
 ♦ moderate price
 ♦ reasonable price
Zivilflugzeug, n
 ♦ civil aircraft
 ♦ civil airplane AE
 ♦ civil aeroplane BE
 ♦ civil plane
 ♦ private aircraft
Zivillinienflugzeug, n
 ♦ civil airliner
Zivilluftfahrt, f
 ♦ civil aviation
Zofe, f (bei Hof)
 Hofdame, f
 ♦ lady-in-waiting

Zofe, f (generell)
 Kammerzofe, f
 ♦ lady's maid
Zoll, m (Abgabe)
 → Zollabgabe
Zoll, m (Behörde)
 Zollbehörde, f
 ♦ customs pl + sg
Zollabfertigung, f
 Grenzabfertigung, f
 ♦ customs clearance
 ♦ customs procedure
Zollabfertigungsgebühr, f
 ♦ clearance charge
Zollabgabe, f
 Zoll, m
 Zollabgaben, f pl
 ♦ customs duty
 ♦ duty
 ♦ customs duties pl
Zollamt, n
 Zollstelle, f
 ♦ customs office
 ♦ customhouse
 ♦ customs house BE
Zollbeamter, m
 ♦ customs officer
 ♦ customs official
Zollbehörde, f
 ♦ customs authorities pl
 ♦ customs pl + sg
Zollbestimmungen, f pl
 → Zollvorschriften
Zollbezirk, m
 ♦ customs district
Zollcarnet, n
 ♦ customs carnet
Zolldokumente, n pl
 ♦ customs documents pl
Zoll erheben (auf etw)
 ♦ charge customs duty (on s.th.)
Zollerklärung, f
 ♦ customs declaration
Zollerklärung abgeben
 ♦ make a customs declaration
Zollformalitäten, f pl
 ♦ customs formalities pl
zollfrei, adj
 ♦ duty-free, adj
Zollfreibetrag, m
 ♦ customs allowance
zollfreie Einkaufsware, f
 ♦ duty-free purchase
zollfreier Artikel, m
 ♦ duty-free item
zollfreier Einkauf, m
 ♦ duty-free shopping
zollfreier Preis, m
 ♦ duty-free price
zollfreie Spirituosen, f pl
 ♦ duty-free liquor
zollfreie Zigarette, f
 ♦ duty-free cigarette
 ♦ duty-free cigaret AE
Zollgebiet, n
 ♦ customs area
Zollhalle, f
 ♦ customs hall
Zollinspektion, f
 ♦ customs inspection

Zollkontrolle, f
- customs control
- customs check
- customs examination

Zoll passieren
- pass through customs

zollpflichtig, adj
- subject to duty, adj
- liable to duty, adj
- liable to customs, adj
- dutiable, adj

Zollposten, m
- customs post

Zollschuppen, m
- customs shed

Zolltarif, m
- customs tariff
- tariff

Zoll- und Paßabfertigung, f
- passport and customs clearance

Zollvorschriften, f pl
- customs regulations pl

Zoll zahlen für etw
- pay duty on s.th.

Zoo, m
- zoo

Zoobesuch, m
- visit to the zoo
- zoo visit

Zoologischer Garten, m
- zoological garden AE
- zoological gardens BE pl

zoologisches Museum, n
Zoologiemuseum, n
- zoological museum

Zoopark, m
- zoo park

zu Abend essen (Dinner)
zu Abend speisen
- have dinner
- dine
- eat dinner

zu Abend essen mit jm (Dinner)
- have dinner with s.o.

zu Abend essen mit jm (Supper)
- have supper with s.o.

zu Abend essen (Supper)
zu Abend speisen
- have supper
- eat supper

zu Abend speisen (Dinner)
→ zu Abend essen

zu Anschaffungskosten
- at cost

zu Beginn von etw
am Anfang von etw
- at the start of s.th.
- at the beginning of s.th.
- at the commencement of s.th. form

Zubehörgeschäft, n
- accessory store AE
- accessory shop BE

Zuber, m
Wanne, f
- tub

zubereiten etw
- prepare s.th.

zubereiten etw appetitlich
- prepare s.th. appetizingly
- prepare s.th. appetisingly

zubereiten etw auf Bestellung
- prepare s.th. to order
- cook s.th. to order

zubereitet am Tisch
- prepared at table
- prepared at the table
- cooked before your eyes

zubereitet auf Bestellung
auf Bestellung zubereitet
- cooked to order
- prepared to order

zubereitet nach alten englischen Rezepten
- cooked to traditional English recipes

Zubereitung, f
(z.B. von Speisen)
- preparation

Zubereitung eines Getränks, f
- preparation of a drink
- preparation of a beverage

Zubereitungsart, f
(von Speisen)
Zubereitungsweise, f
- method of preparation
- mode of preparation

Zubereitungszeit, f
Vorbereitungszeit, f
- preparation time

zu Besuch kommen
→ auf Besuch kommen

zu Bett begeben sich
- retire to bed
- go to bed

zu Bett gehen
in die Falle gehen coll
- turn in BE coll
- go to bed

Zubettgehen, n
- going to bed

Zubringerbus, m (am/zum Flughafen)
→ Flughafenbus

Zubringerbus, m (generell)
- feeder bus
- feeder coach BE

Zubringerdienst m
- feeder service

Zubringerlinie, f
- feeder line

Zubringerstraße, f
- feeder road

zubuchen etw
zusätzlich buchen etw
- book s.th. in addition to s.th.

Zubuchung, f
zusätzliche Buchung, f
- additional booking
- additional reservation AE

Zucchini, pl
- zucchini AE pl
- courgettes pl

Zucchinisuppe, f
- courgette soup

Zuchtforelle, f
- farm trout

Zucker, m
- sugar

zuckerarm, adj
- low-sugar, adj

zuckerarme Diät, f
- low-sugar diet
- diet containing little sugar

Zuckerbäcker, m ÖST
→ Konditor

Zuckerbäckerei, f
→ Konditorei

Zuckerdiät, f
→ Diabetesdiät

Zuckerdose, f
- sugar bowl

Zuckerersatz, m
- sugar substitute

Zuckergebackenes, n
Konditoreiwaren, f pl
- confectionery
- confectionary AE

Zuckergehalt, m
- sugar content

Zuckergeschmack, m
- sugary taste

Zuckerglasur, f
Zuckerguß, m
- sugarcoating AE
- sugar-coating BE
- icing
- frosting

Zuckerguß, m
Zuckerglasur, f
- icing
- frosting
- sugarcoating AE
- sugar-coating BE

Zucker haben coll
Diabetiker sein
- be a diabetic
- be diabetic

zuckerhaltig, adj
- containing sugar, adj

zuckerig, adj
- sugary, adj

zuckerkrank, adj
- diabetic, adj

Zuckerkranker, m
→ Diabetiker

Zuckerlöffel, m
- sugar spoon

zuckerlos, adj
- sugarless, adj
- without sugar

Zuckermais, m
- sweetcorn

zuckern etw
- sugar s.th.

Zuckerrohr, n
- sugar cane

Zuckerschale, f
- sugar basin

Zuckersirup, m
- sugar syrup

Zuckerstreuer, m
- sugar caster

Zuckerstück, n
- sugar lump

Zuckerung, f
- sugaring

Zuckerwasser, n
- sugared water
- sugar water

Zuckerwatte, f
- candy floss BE
- cotton candy AE

Zuckerwürfel, m
- sugar cube

Zuckerzange

Zuckerzange, f
- ♦ sugar tongs *AE pl*
- ♦ sugar-tongs *BE pl*

zu den gewünschten Terminen
- ♦ on the desired dates

zu den obengenannten Bedingungen
- ♦ on the above terms
- on the terms mentioned above

zu Diensten sein
zu Diensten stehen
- ♦ be of service

zu Diensten stehen jm
zu Diensten sein jm
- ♦ be at s.o.'s service

zu Ehren von jm
- ♦ in honor of s.o. *AE*
- ♦ in honour of s.o. *BE*

zu einem erschwinglichen Preis
- ♦ at a reasonable price
- ♦ at a reasonable rate

zu einer Festgebühr von DM 12 pro Tag
- ♦ at a fixed charge of DM 12 per day

zu einer Miete von DM 10.000 pro Jahr
- ♦ at a rent of DM 10,000 per year
- ♦ at a rent of DM 10,000 per annum
- ♦ at a rent of DM 10,000 p.a.

zu einer nominellen Miete
zu einer symbolischen Miete
- ♦ at a peppercorn rent

zu einer ungünstigen Zeit
zur unpassenden Zeit
- ♦ at an inconvenient time

zu einer Weinprobe gehen
- ♦ go to a wine tasting

zu Ende gehen
- ♦ come to an end

zuerkennen jm etw
vergeben etw an jm
zusprechen etw jm
- ♦ award s.th. to s.o.

zu ermäßigten Preisen
- ♦ at reduced prices
- ♦ at reduced rates

zu erschwinglichen Preisen
- ♦ at reasonable prices
- ♦ at reasonable rates

zuerst hätte ich gerne ein Glas Sherry
- ♦ I'd like to start with a glass of sherry

zu essen besorgen sich etw
sich etw zu essen besorgen
- ♦ get oneself s.th. to eat
- ♦ buy oneself s.th. to eat

Zufahrtsstraße, f
Zufahrt, f
- ♦ access road

Zufahrt zu dem Hotel ist gut ausgeschildert
- ♦ access to the hotel is well signposted

zufällig auf ein Hotel stoßen
- ♦ come across a hotel by accident

zufällige Reise, f
- ♦ chance trip

zufälliges Treffen, n
zufälliges Zusammentreffen, n
- ♦ chance meeting

Zufallsgast, m
→ Passant

zu Ferienzwecken
→ zu Urlaubszwecken

Zuflucht finden
Schutz finden
- ♦ find shelter

Zufluchtsort, m
- ♦ place of refuge
- ♦ refuge
- ♦ retreat
- ♦ asylum

Zufluchtsort für jn, m
- ♦ retreat for s.o.
- ♦ refuge for s.o.

Zufluchtstätte, f
Zufluchtsort, m
Zuflucht, f
- ♦ refuge
- ♦ retreat

Zuflucht suchen
Zuflucht nehmen
- ♦ take refuge

zufrieden, adj
- ♦ satisfied, adj
- ♦ content, adj

zufriedener Gast, m
- ♦ satisfied guest

zufriedener Kunde, m
- ♦ satisfied customer
- ♦ satisfied client

zufriedengeben sich mit etw
- ♦ content oneself with s.th.
- ♦ put up with s.th.

zufriedengestellter Kunde, m
zufriedener Kunde, m
- ♦ contented customer

Zufriedenheit, f
- ♦ satisfaction

Zufriedenheitsgrad, m
- ♦ level of satisfaction
- ♦ satisfaction level

zufrieden sein mit dem Buchungsniveau
- ♦ be satisfied with the booking level

zufrieden sein mit dem Service
- ♦ be satisfied with service

zufrieden sein mit der Teilnahme
zufrieden sein mit der Teilnehmerzahl
- ♦ be pleased with the attendance

zufrieden sein mit seinem Zimmer
- ♦ be satisfied with one's room
- ♦ be happy with one's room

zufrieden sein mit wenigem
- ♦ be content with little

zufriedenstellende Auslastung, f
- ♦ satisfactory load factor

zufriedenstellende Auslastungsraten erreichen
- ♦ achieve satisfactory occupancy rates

zufriedenstellender Service, m
befriedigender Service, m
- ♦ satisfactory service

zufriedenstellen jn
- ♦ please s.o.
- ♦ satisfy s.o.

zu früh abreisen
- ♦ leave early
- ♦ leave too early
- ♦ depart early
- ♦ depart too early

zu früh ankommen (für etw)
zu früh eintreffen (für etw)
- ♦ arrive too early (for s.th.)

zu früh eintreffen zu einer Versammlung
- ♦ arrive early for a meeting

zu Fuß
- ♦ on foot

zu Fuß erreichbar sein
- ♦ be within walking distance

zu Fuß gehen
- ♦ go on foot
- ♦ walk

zu Fuß kommen
- ♦ come on foot

zu Fuß nach Hause gehen
- ♦ walk home

zu Fuß nicht erreichbar sein
- ♦ be beyond walking distance

zu Fuß wandern
zu Fuß reisen
- ♦ wayfare *obs*

Zug, m (Luftzug)
Zugluft, f
Luftzug, m
- ♦ draught *BE*
- ♦ draft *AE*

Zug, m (Verkehrsmittel)
- ♦ train

Zugabe!
(z.B. bei Konzert)
- ♦ Encore!
- ♦ Again!
- ♦ Repeat!

Zugabestück, n (Konzert etc.)
Zugabe, f
- ♦ encore piece
- ♦ encore

Zugabe verlangen
- ♦ call for an encore

Zugabteil, n
Zugsabteil, n *ÖST*
- ♦ train compartment

Zugang, m
Zutritt, m
- ♦ access

Zugang bieten zu etw
- ♦ afford access to s.th.

Zugangsstraße, f
Zufahrtsstraße, f
- ♦ approach road
- ♦ access road

Zugangstür, f
- ♦ access door

Zuganreise, f
- ♦ outward train journey
- ♦ outward journey by train

Zuganreise möglich
- ♦ outward journey possible by train

Zug auf der Fahrt nach Paris, m
Zug nach Paris, m
- ♦ train bound for Paris
- ♦ train for Paris

Zugbegeisterter, m
- ♦ train enthusiast

Zugbegleiter, m
- ♦ railway guard *BE*
- ♦ guard *BE*
- ♦ conductor *AE*

Zug besteigen
einsteigen in einen Zug
- ♦ board a train
- ♦ get on a train

Zugbrücke, f
- ♦ drawbridge

Zugdieb, m
- ♦ train thief

Zugdiebstahl, m
- ♦ train theft

Zugdienst, m
Zugverbindung, f

Zugverkehr, m
- ◆ train service

Züge enden in X
- ◆ trains terminate at X
- ◆ trains terminate in X
- ◆ trains end at/in X

zu gegebener Zeit, adv
- ◆ in due time, adv

Zugehfrau, f
- Putzfrau, f
- ◆ charlady BE
- ◆ cleaning woman
- ◆ cleaner
- ◆ charwoman BE
- ◆ char BE coll

zügelloser Tourismus, m
- überhandnehmender Tourismus, m
- ◆ rampant tourism

Zugereister, m
- Neuling, m
- ◆ newcomer
- ◆ incomer

Zug erreichen
- ◆ catch the train
- ◆ catch a train

Zuger See, m
- ◆ Lake of Zug, the

Zugeständnis an den Komfort, n
- ◆ concession to comfort

zugeteilter Stand, m
- zugewiesener Stand, m
- ◆ allocated stand
- ◆ assigned stand AE
- ◆ allocated stall

zugeteiltes Zimmer n
- zugewiesenes Zimmer n
- ◆ allocated room
- ◆ assigned room AE

zugeteilte Unterkunft, f
- zugewiesene Unterkunft, f
- ◆ allocated accommodation
- ◆ assigned accommodation AE

zugewiesene Fläche, f
- zugeteilte Fläche, f
- ◆ allocated area
- ◆ allocated space

zugewiesener Tisch, m
- zugeteilter Tisch, m
- ◆ assigned table AE
- ◆ allocated table

zugewiesenes Quartier, n
- → zugeteiltes Quartier

zugewiesenes Zimmer n
- → zugeteiltes Zimmer

Zugfähre, f
- ◆ train ferry

Zugfahrer, m (Führer)
- ◆ train driver

Zugfahrkarte, f
- Zugfahrschein, m
- Zugkarte, f
- ◆ train ticket

Zugfahrplan, m
- ◆ train schedule AE
- ◆ train timetable BE

Zugfahrt, f
- ◆ train ride
- train journey
- train trip

Zug fährt fahrplanmäßig um 20 Uhr ab
- ◆ train is scheduled to leave at 8 p.m.

Zugfahrt machen
- ◆ take a ride on a train

Zugfahrt mit Führung, f
- ◆ conducted train tour

Zug fährt um 21 Uhr ab
- ◆ train leaves at 9 p.m.

Zugfahrzeug, n
- (z.B. für Wohnwagen)
- ◆ towing vehicle

Zugführer, m
- Zugsführer, m ÖST
- ◆ chief guard BE
- ◆ conductor AE

Zuggesellschaft, f
- ◆ train company

Zuggleis, n
- ◆ train track

Zug hält in X an
- ◆ train calls at X
- ◆ train stops at X
- ◆ train stops in X

Zug hat wieder Verspätung
- ◆ train is late again

zugig, adj
- ◆ drafty, adj AE
- ◆ draughty, adj BE

zugiges Zimmer n
- ◆ drafty room AE
- ◆ draughty room BE

Zug ist gestrichen
- ◆ train is cancelled
- ◆ train is canceled AE

Zugjunge, m
- (verkauft Erfrischungen etc.)
- Zugverkäufer, m
- ◆ trainboy AE

Zugkatastrophe, f
- Zugunglück, n
- ◆ train disaster
- ◆ train crash

Zug kommt fahrplanmäßig um 10.00 Uhr an
- ◆ train is due at 10 o'clock

Zug kommt um 7.10 an
- ◆ train arrives at 7.10

Zugladung, f
- ◆ trainload

Zuglinie, f
- ◆ train line

Zug nehmen (von A nach B)
- ◆ take the train (from A to B)
- ◆ take a train (from A to B)

Zugnummer, f (Eisenbahn)
- ◆ train number

Zugnummer, f (Theater etc.)
- ◆ crowd-puller
- ◆ big attraction
- ◆ box-office draw
- ◆ draw

Zugpersonal, n
- ◆ train staff
- ◆ train personnel

Zugreise, f
- ◆ train journey
- train trip
- train tour

Zugreisen, n
- Zugreiseverkehr, m
- ◆ train travel

Zugreisender, m
- ◆ train traveler AE
- ◆ train traveller BE

Zugrestaurant, n
- → Restaurantwagen

Zug rollt in einen Bahnhof
- ◆ train rolls into a station

zu großes Lager führen
- ◆ be overstocked

Zugschaffner, m
- ◆ guard BE
- ◆ conductor AE

Zugstrecke, f
- Zugroute, f
- ◆ train route

Zugstreik, m
- ◆ train strike

Zugtelefon, n
- ◆ train telephone

Zugtür, f
- ◆ train door

Zugunglück, n
- ◆ train accident
- ◆ train crash

zugunsten von jm
- (Veranstaltung)
- ◆ in aid of s.o.

Zugunternehmer, m
- Zugbetreiber, m
- ◆ train operator

Zugverbindung, f
- ◆ train connection
- ◆ train link

Zugverbindung nach X, f
- ◆ train connection to X
- ◆ train link with X

Zugverbindung über X, f
- ◆ train connection via X
- ◆ train link via X

Zugverkehr, m
- Zugsverkehr, m ÖST
- ◆ train traffic
- ◆ train service
- ◆ train services pl

Zug verpassen
- → Zug versäumen

Zug versäumen
- Zug verpassen
- ◆ miss the train

Zugverspätung, f
- ◆ delay of a train
- ◆ train delay
- ◆ delay

Zugvogel, m
- ◆ bird of passage
- ◆ passage bird

Zugvogel, m (Person)
- ◆ rolling stone

Zugzusammenstoß, m
- Zugunglück, n
- ◆ train crash

Zuhälter, m
- ◆ pimp
- ◆ pander
- ◆ procurer

Zuhälterei, f
- ◆ pimping
- ◆ pandering
- ◆ procuring s.o.

Zuhause, n
- ◆ home

zuhause ankommen
- ◆ arrive home
- ◆ get home

Zuhause auf Zeit

Zuhause auf Zeit, n
zweites Zuhause, n
  ♦ home away from home
  ♦ home from home
zuhause bleiben
  ♦ stay home AE
  ♦ stay at home BE
  ♦ stop in
zuhause bleiben im Urlaub
zuhause bleiben in den Ferien
  ♦ stay at home for one's vacation AE
  ♦ stay at home for one's holiday BE
zuhause essen
  ♦ eat at home
  ♦ eat in
Zuhause ist es am besten
  ♦ There's no place like home
zuhause sein
  ♦ be home AE
  ♦ be at home BE
zuhause Urlaub machen
  ♦ vacation at home AE
  ♦ holiday at home BE
zuhause wohnen (dauernd)
  ♦ live at home
zu Ihren Diensten
  ♦ at your service
zu Ihrer Information
  ♦ for your information
zu Ihrer Linken, adv
links, adv
  ♦ to your left, adv
zu Ihrer Orientierung
  ♦ for your guidance
zu Ihrer Rechten, adv
rechts, adv
  ♦ to your right, adv
zu jeder Jahreszeit
  ♦ at any time of the year
  ♦ in all seasons
zu jeder Tages- oder Nachtzeit
  ♦ at any time of the day or night
zu kleines Lager führen
  ♦ be understocked
Zukunft haben im Tourismus
  ♦ have a future in tourism
zukünftige Buchung, f
  ♦ future booking
zukünftige Nachfrage, f
  ♦ future demand
zukünftiger Erlös, m
  ♦ future revenue
zukünftige Reservierung, f
  ♦ future reservation
zukünftiger Kunde, m
voraussichtlicher Kunde, m
möglicher Kunde, m
  ♦ prospective customer
  ♦ prospective client
zukünftiger Urlaub, m
zukünftige Ferien, pl
  ♦ future vacation AE
  ♦ future holiday BE
zu Lasten des Teilnehmers gehen
  (Kosten)
  ♦ be at the participant's own expenses
zu Lasten gehen von jm
  (Kosten)
  ♦ be s.o.'s charge
  ♦ be payable by s.o.
  ♦ be debited to s.o.

  ♦ be at the expense of s.o.
  ♦ be at s.o.'s expense
zum Abendessen kommen (Dinner)
  ♦ come for dinner
  ♦ come to dinner
zum Abendessen kommen (Supper)
  ♦ come for supper
  ♦ come to supper
zum Abendessen zu Gast sein bei jm
  ♦ be entertained at dinner by s.o.
zum Abholen schicken jn
  ♦ send s.o. to meet s.o.
zum Auftakt
  ♦ to start with
  ♦ as a curtain-raiser
zum Auftakt des Fests (Festival)
zum Auftakt der Festspiele
zum Auftakt des Festival
  ♦ to start the festival (off)
  ♦ to launch the festival
zum Auftakt von etw
  ♦ to start s.th. (off)
  ♦ to launch s.th.
  ♦ to get s.th. under way
zum Ausklang der Festlichkeiten
  ♦ to finish off the festivities
  ♦ to end the festivities
zum Ausklang des Abends
  ♦ to finish off the evening
  ♦ to end the evening
zum Ausklang des Fests (Festival)
zum Ausklang der Festspiele
zum Ausklang des Festivals
  ♦ to finish off the festival
  ♦ to end the festival
zum Ausklang von etw
  ♦ to finish off s.th.
  ♦ to end s.th.
zum Bahnhof bringen jn (Abschied)
zum Zug bringen jn
  ♦ see s.o. off to the station
  ♦ see s.o. off at the station
zum Bahnhof bringen jn (generell)
  ♦ transfer s.o. to the station
  ♦ take s.o. to the station
zum Bestätigungszeitpunkt
zum Zeitpunkt der Bestätigung
  ♦ at the time of confirmation
zum Buchungszeitpunkt
zum Zeitpunkt der Buchung
  ♦ at the time of booking
zum Einkaufspreis
  ♦ at cost price
zum Empfang von jm erscheinen
zu js Empfang kommen
  ♦ come to receive s.o.
zum ermäßigten Preis
  ♦ at a reduced price
  ♦ at a reduced rate
zum Essen kommen (Mittagessen)
  → zum Mittagessen kommen
zum Flughafen bringen jn (Abschied)
  ♦ see s.o. off at the airport
  ♦ see s.o. off on a plane
zum Flughafen bringen jn (generell)
  ♦ transfer s.o. to the airport
  ♦ take s.o. to the airport
zum Frühstück
  ♦ for breakfast

zum Frühstück essen etw
  ♦ eat s.th. for breakfast
  ♦ have s.th. for breakfast
zum halben Preis
zum halben Tarif
  ♦ at half (the) price
  ♦ at half (the) rate
  ♦ for half the price
  ♦ for half the rate
  ♦ half-price
zum halben Tarif
  → zum halben Preis
zum Hals heraushängen
Essen nicht mehr ertragen können
  ♦ be sick to death of eating s.th.
zum herabgesetzten Preis
  ♦ at a discounted price
  ♦ at a discounted rate
zum Hotel bringen jn
  ♦ transfer s.o. to the hotel
zum Inventar gehören humor
  (Personen)
  ♦ be one of the fixtures humor
zu Mittag essen
zu Mittag speisen
  ♦ have lunch
  ♦ have luncheon
  ♦ lunch
  ♦ eat lunch
zu Mittag essen an Bord
  ♦ have lunch on board
  ♦ lunch on board
zu Mittag essen auf der Terrasse
  ♦ have lunch on the terrace
  ♦ lunch on the terrace
zu Mittag essen etw
  ♦ have s.th. for lunch
  ♦ eat s.th. for lunch
zu Mittag essen in einem Restaurant
  ♦ have lunch at a restaurant
  ♦ lunch at a restaurant
zu Mittag essen mit jm
  ♦ have lunch with s.o.
  ♦ lunch with s.o.
zu Mittag speisen
  → zu Mittag essen
zum Kochen bringen etw
  ♦ bring s.th. to the boil
zum Komfort beitragen
  ♦ contribute to the comfort
  ♦ contribute to the general comfort
  ♦ add to the comfort
zum Langzeittarif
  ♦ at long-term rates
zum Mietzeitpunkt (Immobilie)
  ♦ at the time of renting
  ♦ at the time of rental AE
  ♦ at the time of letting BE
zum Mietzeitpunkt (Mobilie)
  ♦ at the time of rental AE
  ♦ at the time of hire BE
  ♦ at the time of hiring BE
zum Mittagessen kommen
  ♦ come for lunch
  ♦ come for luncheon
  ♦ come to lunch
  ♦ come to luncheon
zum Nachtisch
  ♦ as dessert
  ♦ for afters BE fam

zum Normaltarif
♦ at standard rates
♦ at standard prices
zum Nulltarif
→ gratis
zum Pauschalpreis von $ 123
♦ at the inclusive price of $ 123
♦ at the inclusive rate of $ 123
zum Preis von DM 123
♦ at the price of DM 123
♦ at the rate of DM 123
zum Programm gehören
Teil des Programms sein
♦ be part of the program AE
♦ be part of the programme BE
zum Reservierungszeitpunkt
zum Zeitpunkt der Reservierung
♦ at the time of reservation
zum Saisonauftakt
♦ to open the season
♦ to kick off the season
zum Saisonbeginn
am Saisonbeginn
bei Saisonbeginn
♦ at the beginning of the season
♦ at the start of the season
♦ at the commencement of the season form
zum Sofortbezug
(Unterkunft)
zur sofortigen Belegung
♦ for immediate occupancy
zum Stornierungszeitpunkt
zum Rücktrittszeitpunkt
zum Zeitpunkt der Stornierung
zum Zeitpunkt des Rücktritts
♦ at the time of cancellation
♦ at the time of cancelation AE
zum Tanz aufspielen
♦ play for dancing
♦ play music for dancing
♦ play dances
♦ play dance-music
zum Tanz gehen
♦ go to a dance
zum Tee kommen
♦ come for tea
zum Teil, adv
teilweise, adv
♦ partly, adv
♦ in parts, adv
♦ part, adv
zum vereinbarten Preis
♦ at the agreed price
♦ at the agreed rate
zum Vergnügen
♦ for fun
zum Vergnügen von jm
zu js Vergnügen
♦ for s.o.'s amusement
zum Vergnügen werden lassen etw
♦ make s.th. a pleasure
zum Verkauf stehen für DM 123
♦ be for sale at DM 123
zum Verzehr geeignet, adj
♦ fit to eat, adj
♦ edible, adj
zum vollen Preis
♦ at full price
♦ at full rate

zum Vorzugspreis
♦ at a privileged price
♦ at a privileged rate
zum Wallen bringen etw
♦ bring s.th. to the simmer
zum Willkommen Blumenstrauß überreichen
♦ present s.o. with a welcome bouquet
♦ present s.o. with a welcoming bouquet BE
♦ present s.o. with a bouquet as a token of welcome
Zum Wohl!
♦ Cheers!
zum Wohlbefinden von jm
♦ for the well-being of s.o.
zum Wohlfühlen
zum allgemeinen Wohlbefinden
♦ for the well-being
♦ for the general well-being
zum Zeitpunkt meines Besuchs
♦ at the time of my visit
zum Zeitvertreib
♦ to pass the time
Zunahme der Gesamtkundenzahl, f
♦ increase in the total number of customers
♦ increase in the customers totals
♦ increase in the client totals
Zunahme der Touristen, f
Zuwachs an Touristen, m
♦ increase in tourists
Zuname, m
Nachname, m
♦ last name
♦ second name
♦ surname
Zündholz, n
→ Streichholz
zunehmen
(Gewicht)
♦ put on weight
zunehmend beliebter werden
♦ become increasingly popular
zunehmende Reiseintensität, f
♦ increasing travel intensity
zünftig zugehen
♦ have a good time (of it)
Zunge verbrennen sich
♦ burn one's tongue
♦ scald one's tongue
zu Ostern
→ an Ostern
zu Pauschalpreisen
♦ on inclusive terms
zu Pferd, adv
♦ on horseback, adv
zuprosten jm
♦ raise one's glass to s.o.
zur Abendessenszeit (Dinner)
♦ at dinnertime AE
♦ at dinner-time BE
zur Abendessenszeit (Supper)
♦ at suppertime AE
♦ at supper-time BE
zur Abwechslung
♦ for a change
zur Erfrischung
als Erfrischung
♦ for refreshment
♦ as refreshment
zur Erholung
♦ for recreation
♦ as a recreation

zur Erholung fahren nach X
♦ go to X for a rest
♦ go to X to relax
zur Erinnerung an jn
♦ to the memory of s.o.
zur Essenszeit
♦ at meal time
zur Feier des Tages
♦ in honor of the day AE
♦ in honour of the day BE
♦ to celebrate the day
♦ to celebrate the occasion
zur Feier von etw
♦ in celebration of s.th.
zur festgesetzten Zeit
zur verabredeten Zeit
♦ at the appointed time
zur Frühstückszeit
♦ at breakfast time
zur Gästebenutzung
♦ for guest use AE
♦ for guests' use
♦ for the use of guests
Züricher See m
Zürichsee m
♦ Lake Zürich
zur Kaffeestunde
♦ at coffeetime AE
♦ at coffee-time BE
zur Kur gehen
→ in Kur gehen
zur Landseite, adv
♦ facing inland, adv
zur Miete haben etw
♦ tenant s.th.
zur Miete wohnen bei jm (Untermieter)
→ zur Untermiete wohnen bei jm
zur Miete wohnen (generell)
♦ live in a rented apartment AE
♦ live in a rented flat BE
♦ live in a rented house
zur Miete wohnen (Untermieter)
→ zur Untermiete wohnen
zur Mittagszeit
♦ at lunchtime AE
♦ at lunch-time BE
zur Ordnung rufen jn
(Sitzung)
♦ call s.o. to order
zur Parkseite, adv
♦ facing the park, adv
♦ facing the gardens, adv
zur Räumung zwingen jn jur
(im Weg der Zwangsvollstreckung)
♦ evict s.o. jur
zur Reinigung schicken etw
♦ send s.th. to the cleaners
zur Schau stellen etw
ausstellen etw
♦ display s.th.
Zurschaustellung, f
Ausstellung, f
Display, n
♦ display
zur See gehen (Matrose)
♦ go to sea
zur sofortigen Belegung
→ zum Sofortbezug
zur Standardausrüstung gehören
♦ standard equipment includes

zur Teestunde

zur Teestunde
- at teatime *AE*
- at tea-time *BE*

zur Toilette gehen
- go to the toilet
- spend a penny *coll*

zurückbehaltener Gewinn, m
→ thesaurierter Gewinn

Zurückbehaltungsrecht, n
→ Pfandrecht

zurückbleiben in London
in London bleiben
- stay in London
- remain in London

zurückblicken auf eine neunhundertjährige Geschichte
- look back on 900 years of history

zurückbringen etw in sein Heimatland
- take s.th. back to one's home country
- bring s.th. back to one's home country

zurückbringen jn nach X
- take s.o. back to X
- bring s.o. back to X

zurückbringen jn zum Hotel
- return s.o. to the hotel
- bring s.o. back to the hotel

zurückerstatten etw
- refund s.th.
- reimburse s.th.

zurückerstatten etw vollständig
- refund s.th. in full

zurückerwarten jn
- expect s.o. back

zurückerwartet werden (am Donnerstag)
- be due to return (on Thursday)

zurückfahren am selben Tag (Auto)
- drive back on the same day

zurückfahren am selben Tag (generell)
- return on the same day
- go back on the same day

zurückfahren (Auto)
- drive back

zurückfahren (generell)
- go back
- return

zurückfahren nach X (Auto)
- drive back to X
- go back to X

zurückfahren nach X (generell)
- go back to X
- return to X

zurückfahren nach X mit dem Bus
- return to X by bus
- return to X by coach *BE*
- go back to X by bus
- go back to X by coach *BE*

zurückfliegen jn nach X
- fly s.o. back to X

zurückfliegen (nach X)
- fly back (to X)

zurückfordern etw
- claim s.th. back

zurückgehen ins Bett
- return to bed

zurückgehen nach X
- walk back to X
- go back to X

zurückkehren
- return

zurückkehren aus X
aus X zurückkommen
- return from X

zurückkehren in das Hotel
- return to the hotel

zurückkehren in sein Quartier
- return to one's quarters

zurückkehren nach Hause
- return home

zurückkehren nach Hause auf dem Luftweg
- return home by air

zurückkehren nach X
- return to X

zurückkehren nach X über Y
- return to X via Y

zurückkehren nach X zum Abendessen
- return to X for dinner

zurückkehren von einem Besuch
- return from a visit

zurückkehren von einem Urlaub
aus den Ferien zurückkommen
- return from a vacation *AE*
- return from a holiday *BE*

zurückkehren von einer Reise (generell)
- return from a journey
- return from a trip
- return from a tour

zurückkehren von einer Reise (Seereise)
- return from a voyage

zurückkehren zum Ausgangspunkt seiner Wanderung
- return to the starting point of one's walk
- return to the starting point of one's hike

zurückkommen
- come back
- return

zurückkommen jedes Jahr
- return year after year
- return every year

zurückkommen nach X auf Urlaub
zurückkommen nach X im Urlaub
- return to X on vacation *AE*
- return to X on holiday *BE*

zurückkommen voll des Lobes
voller Lob zurückkehren
- return full of praise

zurückkommen von einer Wanderung
- return from a walk

zurücklegen 123 Meilen pro Tag
zurücklegen 123 Meilen am Tag
- cover 123 miles per day
- cover 123 miles a day

zurücklegen eine lange Strecke
- cover a long distance

zurückpachten etw
rückpachten etw *coll*
- lease s.th. back

zurückreisen
- travel back

zurückreisen ein Jahrhundert
- travel back a century

zurückreisen in unsere Quartiere
- travel back to our quarters

zurückreisen nach X
- travel back to X

zurücksein von den Reisen
- be back from one's travels

zurücktreten von einem Hotelvertrag
→ Hotelvertrag stornieren

zurücktreten von einem Reisevertrag
→ Reisevertrag stornieren

zurücktreten von einem Vertrag
- withdraw from a contract

zurücktreten von einer Buchung
→ Buchung stornieren

zurücktreten von einer Reise
→ Reise stornieren

zurücktreten von einer Reservierung
→ Reservierung stornieren

zurücktreten von etw
→ stornieren etw

zurückvergüten etw an jn
→ rückvergüten etw an jn

zurückvermieten etw an jn
rückvermieten etw an jn
- rent s.th. back to s.o. *AE*
- let s.o. back to s.o. *BE*

zurückversetzen etw in den ursprünglichen Zustand
- return s.th. to its original state

zurückversetzt sein von etw (Gebäude)
- be set back from s.th.

Zurückweisung, f
Ablehnung, f
Verweigerung, f
- rejection

zurückzahlen (etw)
- repay (s.th.)
- refund (s.th.)

zurückziehen sich in sein Zimmer
zurückziehen sich auf sein Zimmer
- withdraw to one's room
- retire to one's room

zurückzuerstattende Gebühr f
- returnable fee
- returnable charge

zurück zur Natur
- back to nature

zur unerwünschten Person erklären jn
- declare s.o. persona non grata

zur Unterhaltung von jm
zu js Unterhaltung
- for s.o.'s entertainment

zur Untermiete wohnen
in Untermiete wohnen
- live in lodgings
- be a subtenant
- be an undertenant *AE*
- be a roomer *AE*
- be a lodger *BE*

zur Untermiete wohnen bei jm
- room with s.o. *AE*
- lodge with s.o.
- lodge at s.o.'s (place)

zur Urlaubsbenutzung
zum Urlaubsgebrauch
- for vacation use *AE*
- for holiday use *BE*

zur verabredeten Zeit
→ zur festgesetzten Zeit

zur Verfügung haben etw
- have s.th. at one's disposal

zur Verfügung stehen
- be available

zur Verfügung stehen für Beratungen
- be available for consultation

zur Verfügung stehen jm
- be at s.o.'s disposal
- be available to s.o.
- be available for s.o. *AE*
- be at the disposal of s.o.

zur Verfügung stellen etw jm
 ♦ place s.th. at s.o.'s disposal
 ♦ put s.th. at s.o.'s disposal
Zusage, f (bei Einladung)
 Einladungszusage, f
 Einladungsannahme, f
 ♦ acceptance of an invitation
 ♦ acceptance of the invitation
Zusage, f (Bestätigung)
 → Bestätigung
Zusage machen (Bestätigung)
 → Bestätigung vornehmen
Zusage machen (generell)
 ♦ promise to do s.th.
 ♦ undertake to do s.th.
zusagen (Einladung)
 → Einladung annehmen
zusagen etw
 → bestätigen etw
zusagen jm (Umgebung etc)
 ♦ appeal to s.o.
 ♦ agree with s.o.
 ♦ like s.th.
zusammen abreisen
 ♦ leave together
zusammen ankommen
 ♦ arrive together
Zusammenarbeit, f
 Mitarbeit, f
 ♦ cooperation
zusammenarbeiten mit einem Buchungssystem
 ♦ cooperate with a booking system
zusammenarbeiten mit einem Reservierungssystem
 ♦ cooperate with a reservations system
 ♦ cooperate with a reservation system
Zusammenbruch der Hotelpreise, m
 ♦ collapse of the hotel prices
 ♦ collapse of the hotel rates
zusammendrängen sich
 ♦ throng together
zusammen essen
 ♦ eat together
zusammen essen in einem Restaurant
 ♦ eat together in a restaurant
 ♦ eat together at a restaurant
zusammenfaltbar, adj
 zusammenlegbar, adj
 klappbar, adj
 ♦ foldaway, adj
 ♦ folding, adj
 ♦ collapsible, adj
Zusammenfluß, m
 ♦ confluence
Zusammenfluß des Rheins und der Mosel, m
 ♦ confluence of the Rhine and the Mosel
zusammen frühstücken
 ♦ have breakfast together
 ♦ breakfast together
zusammengepfercht sein wie Sardinen
 ♦ be packed (together) like sardines
zusammengepfercht wie in einer Sardinenbüchse
 ♦ packed (together) like sardines coll
 ♦ like sardines in a can AE coll
 ♦ like sardines in a tin BE coll
zusammengepfercht wie Ölsardinen
 ♦ packed like sardines
 ♦ squashed (together) like sardines
zusammengerolltes Bettzeug, n
 (zum Tragen)
 ♦ bedroll

zusammenhängende Doppelzimmer, n pl
 ♦ connecting double rooms pl
zusammenhängende Einzelzimmer, n pl
 ♦ connecting single rooms pl
zusammenhängender Urlaub, m
 zusammenhängende Ferien, pl
 ♦ continuous vacation AE
 ♦ continuous holiday BE
zusammenhängende Zimmer, n pl
 (durch Tür verbunden)
 miteinander verbundene Zimmer, n pl
 ♦ connecting rooms pl
 ♦ rooms en suite pl
zusammenhängende Zweibettzimmer, n pl
 (Einzelbett)
 ♦ connecting twin-bedded rooms pl
 ♦ connecting twin rooms pl
zusammenhängende Zweibettzimmer, n pl
 (generell)
 ♦ connecting two-bedded rooms pl
zusammen in den Urlaub fahren
 zusammen in die Ferien verreisen
 ♦ travel together on vacation AE
 ♦ travel together on holiday BE
zusammenklappbar, adj
 klappbar, adj
 ♦ collapsible, adj
 ♦ folding, adj
zusammenkommen
 ♦ come together
 ♦ meet
 ♦ get together
zusammenkommen in einem schönen Rahmen
 ♦ gather in a beautiful setting
zusammenkommen zu einem Treffen
 ♦ gather for a meeting
zusammenkommen zu einer Konferenz
 ♦ gather for a conference
Zusammenkunft, f (Treffen)
 → Treffen
Zusammenkunft, f (Versammlung)
 Versammlung, f
 ♦ gathering
Zusammenkunft, f (zwanglos)
 → Beisammensein
zusammen mit etw
 ♦ together with s.th.
 ♦ accompanied by s.th.
zusammenpacken
 ♦ pack up
zusammen reisen
 zusammen verreisen
 zusammen fahren
 ♦ travel together
zusammenrücken
 ♦ move closer together
zusammen schlafen
 (Sex)
 ♦ sleep together
Zusammenschluß von Hotels, m
 → Hotelzusammenschluß
zusammenschnüren (etw) gastr
 ♦ truss (s.th.) gastr
Zusammensein, n
 → Beisammensein
zusammenstellen etw
 erstellen etw
 ♦ compile s.th.
 ♦ put together s.th.
Zusammentreffen, n
 → Treffen

zusammentreffen mit jm
 ♦ meet with s.o.
 ♦ meet s.o.
zusammentreten zu einer Konferenz
 ♦ have a conference
Zusammentritt einer Konferenz, m
 ♦ meeting of a conference
Zusammenwohnen, n (dauernd)
 ♦ living together
Zusammenwohnen, n (Unverheiratete)
 ♦ cohabitation
zusammen wohnen (dauernd)
 ♦ live together
zusammen wohnen mit jm (dauernd)
 ♦ live together with s.o.
zusammen wohnen mit jm (Unverheiratete)
 ♦ cohabit with s.o.
 ♦ live (together) with s.o.
zusammen wohnen (Untermieter)
 ♦ room together AE
 ♦ lodge together
zusammen wohnen (Unverheiratete)
 ♦ cohabit
 ♦ live together
zusammen zu Mittag essen
 ♦ have lunch together
 ♦ lunch together
Zusatzaufenthalt, m
 Verlängerungsaufenthalt, m
 ♦ additional stay
 ♦ extra stay
Zusatzbehandlung, f
 zusätzliche Behandlung, f
 ♦ extra treatment
Zusatzbestellung, f (Buchung)
 → Zusatzbuchung
Zusatzbestellung, f (generell)
 ♦ additional order
Zusatzbett, n
 → zusätzliches Bett
Zusatzbettpreis m
 ♦ extra bed rate
Zusatzbuchung, f
 zusätzliche Buchung f
 Zusatzbestellung f
 zusätzliche Bestellung f
 ♦ additional booking
 ♦ extra booking
Zusatzcouch, f
 zusätzliche Couch, f
 Zustellcouch, f
 ♦ additional couch
 ♦ extra couch
Zusatzgast, m
 zusätzlicher Gast, m
 weiterer Gast, m
 ♦ extra guest
 ♦ additional guest
Zusatzgebühr f
 zusätzliche Gebühr f
 ♦ additional charge
 ♦ additional fee
 ♦ extra charge
 ♦ extra fee
Zusatzkopfkissen, n
 ♦ extra pillow
Zusatzkosten, pl
 → zusätzliche Kosten
Zusatzleistung, f (Lohnnebenleistung)
 Lohnnebenleistung, f
 Gehaltsnebenleistung, f

Zusatzleistung

zusätzliche Sozialleistung, f
♦ fringe benefit
♦ fringe benefits pl
Zusatzleistung, f (Service)
zusätzliche Leistung, f
♦ **service available at extra cost**
♦ extra service
♦ other service
♦ additional service
zusätzlich, adj
♦ **additional, adj**
♦ **extra, adj**
zusätzliche Aufenthaltsnacht, f
weitere Aufenthaltsnacht f
♦ **additional night of stay**
♦ additional night
♦ extra night of stay
♦ extra night
zusätzliche Aufenthaltswoche, f
weitere Aufenthaltswoche f
♦ **additional week of stay**
♦ extra week of stay
zusätzliche Behandlung, f
♦ **additional treatment**
zusätzliche Bettcouch, f
♦ **extra couch bed**
♦ extra bed-settee BE
♦ extra sofa bed
zusätzliche Buchung, f
Zusatzbuchung, f
♦ **extra booking**
♦ additional booking
zusätzliche Dienstleistung, f
→ zusätzliche Leistung
zusätzliche Gäste unterbringen
zusätzliche Gäste aufnehmen
♦ **accommodate additional guests**
♦ accommodate extra guests
zusätzliche Hilfskraft, f
♦ **extra help**
zusätzliche Hilfskräfte engagieren
♦ **engage extra help**
zusätzliche Kapazität f
♦ **additional capacity**
♦ extra capacity
zusätzliche Kapazität schaffen
♦ **create additional capacity**
♦ create extra capacity
zusätzliche Kosten, pl
Zusatzkosten, pl
♦ **additional costs** pl
♦ additional cost
♦ extra costs pl
♦ extra cost
zusätzliche Liege, f
Zusatzliege, f
♦ **additional divan**
♦ extra divan
zusätzliche Nacht, f
weitere Nacht, f
Verlängerungsnacht, f
Zusatznacht, f
zusätzliche Übernachtung, f
♦ **additional night**
♦ extra night
zusätzliche Person, f
Zusatzperson, f
♦ **additional person**
♦ extra person
zusätzlicher Aufenthaltsmonat, m
weiterer Aufenthaltsmonat m

♦ **additional month of stay**
♦ extra month of stay
zusätzlicher Aufenthaltstag, m
weiterer Aufenthaltstag m
♦ **additional day of stay**
♦ extra day of stay
zusätzliche Reinigung, f
♦ **extra cleaning**
zusätzlicher Ferientag, m
zusätzlicher Urlaubstag, m
♦ **extra day's holiday** BE
♦ extra day's vacation AE
zusätzlicher Flug, m
♦ **additional flight**
zusätzlicher Gast, m
♦ **additional guest**
♦ extra guest
zusätzlicher Kunde, m
♦ **additional customer**
♦ extra customer
♦ additional client
♦ extra client
zusätzlicher Monat m
Zusatzmonat, m
Verlängerungsmonat m
♦ **additional month**
♦ extra month
zusätzlicher Service, m
→ Zusatzservice
zusätzlicher Sitzplatz, m
zusätzlicher Platz, m
♦ **extra seat**
♦ additional seat
zusätzlicher Stuhl, m
Zusatzstuhl, m
♦ **extra chair**
♦ additional chair
zusätzlicher Tag, m
Zusatztag m
Verlängerungstag m
weiterer Tag m
♦ **additional day**
♦ extra day
zusätzlicher Urlaub, m
zusätzliche Ferien, pl
♦ **additional vacation** AE
♦ additional holiday BE
zusätzlicher Zug, m
Zusatzzug, m
♦ **additional train**
zusätzliches Bett, n
Zusatzbett, n
weiteres Bett, n
♦ **additional bed**
♦ extra bed
zusätzliches Bett bereitstellen
♦ **provide an additional bed**
♦ provide an extra bed
zusätzliches Bettchen, n
Zusatzbettchen, n
weiteres Bettchen, n
♦ **additional bedlet**
♦ extra bedlet
zusätzliches Bett in ein Zimmer stellen
♦ **put an extra bed in a room**
♦ place an extra bed in a room
zusätzliches Personal, n
♦ **extra staff**
♦ additional staff
♦ extra personnel
♦ additonal personnel

zusätzliches Personal einstellen
♦ **employ extra staff**
♦ employ additional staff
zusätzliche Stühle benötigen
♦ **need extra chairs**
♦ need additional chairs
zusätzliche Stunde f
Zusatzstunde f
Verlängerungsstunde f
♦ **additional hour**
♦ extra hour
zusätzliches Urlaubsgepäck, n
♦ **extra vacation baggage** AE
♦ extra holiday luggage BE
zusätzliche Übernachtung, f
→ zusätzliche Nacht
zusätzliche Unterkunft f
♦ **additional accommodation**
♦ extra accommodation
zusätzliche Woche, f
Zusatzwoche f
Verlängerungswoche f
weitere Woche f
♦ **additional week**
♦ extra week
Zusatzliege, f
zusätzliche Liege, f
♦ **extra divan**
♦ additional divan
Zusatzmonat, m
→ Verlängerungsmonat
Zusatznacht, f
→ Verlängerungsnacht
Zusatzperson, f
zusätzliche Person, f
♦ **extra person**
♦ additional person
Zusatzprämie, f
zusätzliche Prämie, f
♦ **additional premium**
Zusatzprogramm, n
zusätzliches Programm, n
♦ **additional program** AE
♦ additional programme BE
Zusatzprospekt m
♦ **additional brochure**
♦ extra brochure
Zusatzprovision, f
zusätzliche Provision, f
Extraprovision, f
♦ **additional commission**
♦ extra commission
Zusatzservice, m
Zusatzdienst, m
Zusatzdienstleistung, f
Zusatzleistung, f
zusätzliche Leistung, f
♦ **additional service**
♦ extra service
Zusatztag, m
→ Verlängerungstag
Zusatztherapie, f
♦ **extra therapy**
♦ additonal therapy
Zusatzversicherung, f
zusätzliche Versicherung, f
♦ **additional insurance**
Zusatzvisum, n
♦ **additional visa**
Zusatzwoche, f
→ Verlängerungswoche

Zuschauer von den Sitzen reißen
  ♦ sweep the audience off their feet
Zuschlag, m (generell)
  ♦ supplement
  ♦ extra charge
Zuschlag, m (Verkehrsmittel)
  ♦ supplementary fare
  ♦ supplement
Zuschlag bei lediglich einer Übernachtung, m
  ♦ one-night supplement
Zuschlag berechnen jm für etw
  ♦ charge s.o. a supplement for s.th.
Zuschlag erheben
  Zuschlag berechnen
  ♦ charge a supplement
Zuschlag für Alleinbenutzung, m
  (z.B. bei Doppelzimmer)
  Alleinbenutzungszuschlag, m
  ♦ supplement for single occupancy
  ♦ single-occupancy supplement
Zuschlag für Bergblick, m
  ♦ supplement for mountain view
Zuschlag für besondere Aussicht, m
  ♦ special-view supplement
  ♦ supplement for special view
Zuschlag für die Belegung mit drei Personen, m
  ♦ supplement for occupancy by three persons
Zuschlag für die Benutzung von etw, m
  → Benutzungszuschlag für etw
Zuschlag für Doppelzimmer, m
  ♦ supplement for double room
Zuschlag für (eine) besondere Aussicht, m
  ♦ supplement for (a) special view
  ♦ special-view supplement
Zuschlag für ein Einzelzimmer, m
  ♦ supplement for a single room
Zuschlag für ein Einzelzimmer beträgt DM 123
  ♦ supplement for a single room is DM 123
Zuschlag für (einen) Sonderservice, m
  Zuschlag für (eine) Sonderleistung, m
  ♦ supplement for (a) special service
Zuschlag für (ein) Zimmer mit Bad, m
  ♦ supplement for (a) room with bath
Zuschlag für (ein) Zimmer mit Balkon, m
  ♦ supplement for (a) room with balcony
Zuschlag für (ein) Zimmer mit Dusche, m
  ♦ supplement for (a) room with shower
Zuschlag für etw beträgt DM 123
  ♦ supplement for s.th. is DM 123
Zuschlag für Halbpension, m
  Halbpensionszuschlag, m
  ♦ supplement for half board
  ♦ supplement for demipension AE
Zuschlag für Teilpension, m
  ♦ supplement for part-board
  ♦ supplement for partial board
Zuschlag für Vollpension, m
  Vollpensionszuschlag, m
  ♦ supplement for full board
  ♦ supplement for full pension AE
Zuschlag in der Saisonmitte, m
  ♦ mid-season supplement
Zuschlagsart f
  ♦ supplement type
  ♦ type of supplement
Zuschlagsgebühr, f
  ♦ supplementary charge
zuschlagspflichtig, adj
  ♦ subject to a supplement, adj
Zuschlagspreis, m
  ♦ supplement price

Zuschlag verlangen
  Zuschlag fordern
  ♦ require a supplement
Zuschlag von $ 12 pro Person pro Monat, m
  ♦ supplement of $ 12 per person per month
Zuschlag von $ 12 pro Person pro Tag, m
  ♦ supplement of $ 12 per person per day
Zuschlag von $ 12 pro Person pro Woche, m
  ♦ supplement of $ 12 per person per week
Zuschlag von DM 10 erheben für etw
  Zuschlag von DM 10 berechnen für etw
  ♦ charge a supplement of DM 10 for s.th.
Zuschlag zahlen
  ♦ pay a supplement
zuschließen etw
  (Tür)
  absperren etw
  ♦ lock s.th.
zu sein s/
  betrunken sein
  ♦ be tight s/
zu seinem Zimmer geführt werden
  ♦ be shown to one's room
zu sich nehmen etw
  → essen etw
zu spät ankommen für das Mittagessen
  ♦ arrive late for lunch
zu spät kommen
  mit Verspätung kommen
  ♦ come late
  ♦ be late
Zuspätkommender, m
  → Nachzügler
zu spät kommen zum Essen (Dinner)
  ♦ be late for dinner
zu spät kommen zum Essen (Lunch)
  ♦ be late for lunch
zu spät kommen zum Frühstück
  ♦ be late for breakfast
Zustand eines Zimmers, m
  → Zimmerzustand
Zusteigestelle, f
  (z.B. bei Busfahrt)
  Zusteigemöglichkeit, f
  ♦ joining point
Zustellbett, n
  → Beistellbett
Zustellcouch, f
  zusätzliche Couch, f
  ♦ extra couch
  ♦ additional couch
Zustimmung finden von jm
  js Zustimmung finden
  ♦ meet with s.o. approval
Zustrom, m
  Andrang, m
  ♦ stream
  ♦ influx
  ♦ rush
Zustrom von Besuchern, m
  Besucherstrom, m
  ♦ stream of visitors
  ♦ influx of visitors
  ♦ rush of visitors
Zutat, f
  ♦ ingredient
zuteilen etw an jn
  zuweisen etw an jn
  vergeben etw an jn
  ♦ allocate s.th. to s.o.

♦ assign s.th. to s.o.
♦ allot s.th. to s.o.
Zuteilung, f
  ♦ allocation
  ♦ assignment
  ♦ allotment
Zuteilungsvorgang, m
  Zuteilungsprozedur, f
  Vergabevorgang, m
  Vergabeprozedur, f
  ♦ allocation procedure
  ♦ assignment procedure AE
Zuteilung von Sitzplätzen, f
  Zuweisung von Plätzen, f
  ♦ allocation of seats
zu Tisch bitten (Dinner)
  ♦ announce that dinner is served
zu Tisch bitten (Frühstück)
  ♦ announce that breakfast is served
zu Tisch bitten (Mittagessen)
  ♦ announce that lunch is served
zu Tisch bitten (Supper)
  ♦ announce that supper is served
zu Tisch gehen
  ♦ go to table
  ♦ go in to table
zu Tisch setzen sich
  ♦ sit down at table
zu Tode frieren sich
  erfrieren
  ♦ freeze to death
zu Tode trinken sich
  ♦ drink oneself to death
zutrinken jm
  ♦ raise the glass to s.o.
Zutritt, m
  → Zugang, m
Zutritt beschränken (zu etw)
  ♦ restrict access (to s.th.)
Zutritt erhalten zu etw
  ♦ gain access to s.th.
  ♦ be admitted to s.th.
Zutritt verboten
  (Hinweisschild)
  ♦ No entry
zu Urlaubszwecken
  zu Ferienzwecken
  ♦ for vacation puposes AE
  ♦ for holiday purposes BE
Zu verkaufen
  (Hinweisschild)
  ♦ For sale
zu verkaufen sein
  zum Verkauf stehen
  ♦ be for sale
zuverlässig, adj
  ♦ reliable, adj
zuverlässiger Service, m
  ♦ reliable service
Zuverlässigkeit, f
  ♦ reliability
Zu vermieten ab 1. Juni (meist Immobilien)
  (Hinweisschild)
  ♦ For rent from 1 June AE
  ♦ To let from 1 June BE
Zu vermieten (meist Immobilien)
  (Hinweisschild)
  ♦ For rent AE
  ♦ To let BE
Zu vermieten (meist Mobilien)
  (Hinweisschild)

zuviel berechnen

- For hire *BE*
- For rent *AE*

zuviel berechnen
  zuviel verlangen
  zuviel Geld verlangen
- overcharge

zuviel berechnen für den Wein
  zuviel verlangen für den Wein
- overcharge for the wine

zuviel berechnen für einen Artikel
  zuviel verlangen für einen Artikel
- overcharge for an item
- overcharge on an item

zuviel berechnen für etw
  zuviel verlangen für etw
  zuviel berechnen bei etw
  zuviel verlangen bei etw
- overcharge for s.th.
- overcharge on s.th.

zuviel berechnen jm für etw
  zuviel verlangen von jm für etw
- overcharge s.o. for s.th.

zuviel Bier trinken
- drink too much beer
- have too much beer

zuviel essen
- eat too much
- overeat
- stuff oneself *coll*

zuviel in Rechnung stellen jm
  zuviel fordern von jm
- overcharge s.o.

zuviel Raum einnehmen
- take up too much space

zuviel trinken
- drink too much

zuviel verlangen
→ zuviel berechnen

zuviel verlangen für etw
→ zuviel berechnen für etw

zuviel zahlen
- overpay

zu vorgerückter Stunde
- at a late hour

zuvorkommend, adj
  entgegenkommend, adj
- obliging, adj
- helpful, adj

zuvorkommende Betreuung, f
- obliging attention
- kind attention

zuvorkommender Service, m
  zuvorkommende Bedienung, f
- obliging service

zuvorkommendes Personal, n
- obliging staff
- obliging personnel

Zuwachs, m
  Anstieg, m
  Steigerung, f
  Erhöhung, f
- increase

Zuwachs der Besucherzahlen, m
- growth in visitor numbers

Zuwachs der Gästeübernachtungen verzeichnen
- record an increase in overnight guests
- register an increase in overnight guests

Zuwachs der Gesamtgästezahl, f
- increase in the guest count

Zuwachs der Übernachtungsgäste, m
- increase in overnight guests

Zuwachs gegenüber dem Vorjahr, m
  Steigerung gegenüber dem Vorjahr, f
  Anstieg gegenüber dem Vorjahr, m
- increase on the previous year

Zuwachsrate, f
- growth rate
- rate of growth
- rate of increase

zuweisen etw an jn
  zuteilen etw an jn
  vergeben etw an jn
- assign s.th. to s.o. *AE*
- allocate s.th. to s.o.

Zuweisung, f
  Zuteilung, f
  Vergabe, f
  Verteilung, f
- assignment *AE*
- allocation

Zuweisung einer Unterkunft, f
  Unterkunftszuweisung, f
- allocation of accommodation
- assignment of accommodation *AE*

Zuweisung vornehmen
  Zuteilung vornehmen
- make an allocation

Zu welcher Tageszeit möchten Sie fahren?
- At what time of day would you like to go?
- What time of day would you like to go?

zuwenig berechnen
  zuwenig verlangen
  zuwenig Geld verlangen
- undercharge

zuwenig verlangen für einen Artikel
  zuwenig berechnen für einen Artikel
- undercharge for an item

zuwenig verlangen für etw
  zuwenig berechnen für etw
- undercharge for s.th.

zu wünschen übriglassen etw
- leave s.th. to be desired

zuzahlen
- pay (s.th.) extra

Zuzahlung, f
  zusätzliche Zahlung, f
- extra payment
- additional payment

zuzüglich, adv
- plus, adv

zuzüglich Getränke und Bedienung
- drinks and service charge extra

zuzüglich Mehrwertsteuer
  zuzüglich Mwst
- plus value added tax
- plus VAT

zuzüglich Mwst
  zuzüglich Mehrwertsteuer
- plus VAT
- plus value added tax

zuzüglich Nebenkosten
- plus extras

zuzüglich Porto
- plus postage

Zu zweit ist es besser als zu dritt
- Two is company, three is a crowd

zu zweit reisen
- travel with a partner

zwanglose Atmosphäre, f
  ungezwungene Atmosphäre f
  informelle Atmosphäre f

- informal atmosphere
- casual atmosphere

zwanglose Atmosphäre bieten
- provide an informal atmosphere

zwanglose Kleidung, f
  legere Kleidung, f
- informal dress

zwanglose Mahlzeit, f
  zwangloses Essen, n
- casual meal
- informal meal

zwanglosen Rahmen bieten für etw
- provide an informal setting for s.th.

zwangloser Anlaß, m
  zwanglose Gelegenheit f
- informal occasion

zwangloser Besuch, m
- informal visit

zwangloser Rahmen, m
- informal setting

zwangloses Beisammensein, n
  zwangloses Zusammensein, n
- casual get-together
- informal get-together

zwangloses Essen, n
  zwanglose Mahlzeit, f
- informal meal

zwangloses Gespräch, n
- informal talk

zwangloses Treffen, n
  zwangloses Zusammenkunft f
- informal gathering
- informal meeting

zwangloses Zusammensein, n
  zwangloses Beisammensein, n
- informal get-together
- casual get-together

zwanglose Unterhaltung, f
- informal conversation

zwanglose Vereinbarung, f
  zwangloses Arrangement n
- informal arrangement

zwanglose Weinprobe, f
- informal wine tasting

zwanglose Zusammenkunft, f
  zwangloses Treffen, n
  informelles Treffen, n
- informal meeting

Zwangsernährung, f
- forced feeding

Zwangsräumung, f (Besitzer) *jur*
  Zwangsenteignung, f
- dispossession *jur*

Zwangsräumung, f (Mieter, Pächter) *jur*
- eviction *jur*

Zwangsräumung durchführen gegen einen Mieter *jur*
  Räumungsverfahren durchführen gegen einen Mieter *jur*
- evict a tenant *jur*

Zwangsräumung wegen Mietschulden, f *jur*
- eviction for nonpayment of rent *AE jur*
- eviction for non-payment of rent *BE jur*

Zwangsurlaub, m (Beamter)
- mandatory furlough

zwangsweise Räumung, f
→ Zwangsräumung

Zwangswohnsitz, m
- necessary domicile

zwanzigstöckiges Hotel, n
  20-stöckiges Hotel, n

- ♦ twenty-floor hotel
- ♦ twenty-story hotel *AE*
- ♦ twenty-storey hotel *BE*
- ♦ 20-floor hotel

Zwanzigtausend Meilen unter dem Meer
(Roman von Jules Verne)
- ♦ Twenty Thousand Leagues Under the Sea

Zweckbau, m
- ♦ functional building

Zweck der Reise, m
Reisezweck, m
- ♦ purpose of the journey
- ♦ purpose of the trip
- ♦ purpose of the tour
- ♦ purpose of travel
- ♦ travel purpose

Zweck des Aufenthaltes, m
Aufenthaltszweck, m
- ♦ purpose of the stay

Zweck des Besuchs, m
Besuchszweck, m
- ♦ purpose of s.o.'s visit
- ♦ purpose of one's visit
- ♦ purpose of visit

zweckmäßig, adj
funktional, adj
funktionell, adj
- ♦ functional, adj

zweckmäßig eingerichtet, adj
- ♦ functionally furnished, adj

zweckmäßig eingerichtetes Zimmer n
- ♦ functionally furnished room

zweckmäßige Möbel, n pl
- ♦ functional furniture *sg*

zweckmäßiges Zimmer, n
- ♦ functional room

zweckmäßige Unterkunft, f
- ♦ functional accommodation

zweiachsiger Caravan, m
zweiachsiger Wohnwagen, m
- ♦ two-axle caravan *BE*
- ♦ two-axle trailer *AE*

zwei aufeinanderfolgende Nächte, f pl
zwei Nächte hintereinander
- ♦ two consecutive nights *pl*

Zweibettappartement, n
Appartement mit zwei Betten, n
- ♦ two-bed apartment

Zweibettaußenkabine, f (Betten)
- ♦ two-bed outside cabin

Zweibettaußenkabine, f (Kojen)
- ♦ two-berth outside cabin

Zweibettbelegung, f
- ♦ twin occupancy

Zweibettcaravan, m
Zweibettwohnwagen, m
- ♦ two-berth caravan *BE*
- ♦ two-berth van *BE coll*
- ♦ two-berth trailer *AE*

Zweibettchalet, n
- ♦ two-bed chalet

Zwei-Betten-Studio, n
→ Zweibettstudio

Zweibetthauszelt, n
- ♦ two-berth ridge tent

zweibettig, adj (generell)
- ♦ two-bedded, adj
- ♦ with two beds

zweibettig, adj (zwei Einzelbetten)
- ♦ twin-bedded, adj
- ♦ with tiwn beds

zweibettig belegbar, adj (zwei Einzelbetten)
- ♦ available for twin-bed occupancy, adj
- ♦ available for twin occupancy, adj

zweibettige Belegung, f (Doppelbett)
- ♦ double-bed occupancy
- ♦ double occupancy

zweibettige Kabine, f (zwei Einzelbetten)
- ♦ twin-bedded cabin

zweibettiges Zimmer, n (generell)
- ♦ two-bedded room

zweibettiges Zimmer, n (zwei Einzelbetten)
- ♦ twin-bedded room

Zweibettinnenkabine, f (Betten)
- ♦ two-bed inside cabin

Zweibettinnenkabine, f (Kojen)
- ♦ two-berth inside cabin

Zweibettkabine, f (Kojen, generell)
- ♦ two-berth cabin

Zweibettkabine, f (zwei Einzelbetten)
- ♦ twin-bed cabin
- ♦ twin cabin

Zweibettkabine, f (zwei Einzelkojen)
- ♦ twin-berth cabin
- ♦ twin cabin

Zweibettschlafzimmer, n
(mit zwei einzelnen Betten)
- ♦ twin bedroom

Zweibettstudio, n
- ♦ two-bed studio

Zweibettunterkunft, f (generell)
- ♦ two-bedded accommodation

Zweibettunterkunft, f (zwei Einzelbetten)
- ♦ twin-bedded accommodation

Zweibettvilla, f
- ♦ two-bed villa

Zweibettwohnung, f
Wohnung mit zwei Betten, f
- ♦ two-bed flat *BE*
- ♦ two-bed apartment *AE*

Zweibettwohnwagen, m
Zweibettcaravan, m
- ♦ two-berth trailer *AE*
- ♦ two-berth caravan *BE*
- ♦ two-berth van *BE coll*

Zweibettzelt, n
- ♦ two-berth tent

Zweibettzimmer, n (generell)
(mit Doppelbett oder zwei Einzelbetten)
- ♦ two-bed room

Zweibettzimmer, n (zwei Einzelbetten)
(mit zwei einzelnen Betten)
- ♦ twin-bed room
- ♦ twin-bedded room
- ♦ twin (room)
- ♦ room with twin beds
- ♦ twn. rm.

Zweibettzimmerbelegung, f (zwei Einzelbetten)
- ♦ twin room occupancy
- ♦ twin occupancy

Zweibettzimmerbuchung, f (zwei Einzelbetten)
- ♦ twin-room booking
- ♦ booking of a twin room

Zweibettzimmerpreis, m (zwei Einzelbetten)
- ♦ twin-room price
- ♦ twin-room rate
- ♦ price for a twin-bedded room
- ♦ rate for a twin-bedded room
- ♦ price for a room with twin beds

zwei Bier
- ♦ two beers *pl*
- ♦ two glasses of beer *pl*

zwei Einzelbetten, n pl (Betten)
- ♦ twin beds *pl*
- ♦ two separate beds *pl*

zwei Einzelbetten, n pl (Kojen)
- ♦ twin bunks *pl*
- ♦ twin berths *pl*

zwei Einzelkojen, f pl
zwei Einzelbetten, n pl
- ♦ twin berths *pl*

Zweierapartement, n
→ Zweibettappartement

Zweierbelegung, f
→ Doppelbelegung

Zweiertisch, m
Zweipersonentisch, m
- ♦ table for two persons
- ♦ table for two
- ♦ table to seat two persons
- ♦ deuce *AE*

zweifache Ausfertigung, f
- ♦ duplicate

Zweifamiliencottage, f
- ♦ two-family cottage
- ♦ duplex cottage *AE*
- ♦ cottage for two families

Zweifamilienhaus, n
- ♦ two-family house
- ♦ duplex house *AE*
- ♦ house for two families

zweiflammig, adj
- ♦ two-burner, adj

zweiflammiger Gaskocher, m
zweiflammiger Gasherd, m
- ♦ two-burner gas cooker

zweiflammiger Herd, m
zweiflammiger Ofen, m
- ♦ two-burner stove

zwei Frühstücke, n pl
- ♦ two breakfasts *pl*

zweigängig, adj (Essen)
- ♦ two-course, adj
- ♦ consisting of two courses

zweigängiges Abendessen, n (Dinner)
- ♦ two-course dinner

zweigängiges Abendessen, n (Supper)
- ♦ two-course supper

zweigängiges Menü, n
- ♦ two-course menu

zweigängiges Mittagessen, n
- ♦ two-course lunch
- ♦ two-course luncheon

zwei Garagenplätze, m pl
→ zwei Garagenstellplätze

zwei Garagenstellplätze, m pl
zwei Garagenplätze m pl
zwei Stellplätze in der Garage m pl
zwei Einstellplätze in der Garage m pl
- ♦ garage space for two cars
- ♦ garaging space for two cars

zwei Garagenstellplätze buchen
- ♦ book garage space for two cars
- ♦ book garaging space for two cars

Zweig Brunnenkresse, m
Zweigchen Brunnenkresse, n
- ♦ sprig of watercress
- ♦ watercress sprig

Zweigchen, n
Zweig, m
- ♦ sprig

zweigeschossig, adj attr
zweistöckig, adj attr

zweigeschossig

- ♦ two-story, adj attr *AE*
- ♦ two-storey, adj attr *BE*
- ♦ two-floor, adj attr

zweigeschossig, adj prd
zweistöckig, adj prd
- ♦ two-storied, adj prd *AE*
- ♦ two-storeyed, adj prd *BE*

zweigeschossiger Pavillon, m
zweistöckiger Pavillon, m
- ♦ two-floor pavilion
- ♦ two-story pavilion *AE*
- ♦ two-storey pavilion *BE*

zweigeschossiges Haus, n
zweistöckiges Haus, n
- ♦ two-story house *AE*
- ♦ two-storey house *BE*
- ♦ two-floor house

zweigeschossiges Hotel, n
zweistöckiges Hotel, n
- ♦ two-story hotel *AE*
- ♦ two-storey hotel *BE*
- ♦ two-floor hotel

zwei getrennte Betten, n pl
- ♦ two separate beds *pl*
- ♦ twin beds *pl*

Zweigipfelwanderung, f
- ♦ two peaks walk

zwei Glas Wein
zwei Gläser Wein, n pl
- ♦ two glasses of wine *pl*

Zweig Petersilie, m
Zweigchen Petersilie, n
- ♦ sprig of parsley
- ♦ parsley sprig

zwei Herren dienen
- ♦ serve two masters

Zweihundertjahrfeier, f
- ♦ bicentennial celebration

Zweijahreskonferenz, f
alle zwei Jahre stattfindende Konferenz, f
- ♦ biennial conference

Zweijahreskongreß, m
alle zwei Jahre stattfindender Kongreß, m
- ♦ biennial convention
- ♦ biennial congress

Zweijahrestagung, f
alle zwei Jahre stattfindende Tagung, f
- ♦ biennial meeting

Zweiklassenservice, m
- ♦ two-class service

zweiköpfige Familie, f
- ♦ family of two

Zweiländerreise, f
- ♦ two-country tour
- ♦ tour of two countries
- ♦ tour through two countries

Zweiliterflasche, f
- ♦ two-liter bottle *AE*
- ♦ two-litre bottle *BE*

zwei Löffel Zucker, m pl
- ♦ two spoonfuls of sugar *pl*

zweimalige Hotelübernachtung, f
- ♦ two-night hotel stay

zweimalige Übernachtung, f
- ♦ two-night stay

zweimal wöchentlich, adv
- ♦ twice a week, adv
- ♦ twice weekly, adv

Zweimannorchester, n
- ♦ two-man orchestra

Zweimannzelt, n
- ♦ two-man tent

zweimotorig, adj
- ♦ two-engine(d), adj
- ♦ twin-engine(d), adj

zweimotoriges Flugzeug, n
- ♦ two-engine(d) plane
- ♦ two-engine(d) aeroplane *BE*
- ♦ two-engine(d) airplane *BE*
- ♦ twin-engine(d) plane

zwei Nächte bleiben
zweimal übernachten
- ♦ stay for two nights
- ♦ stay two nights

Zweinächtepreis, m
- ♦ two-night price
- ♦ two-night rate

Zweipersonenlandhaus, n
- ♦ two-person cottage

Zweipersonenpreis, m
- ♦ two-person price
- ♦ two-person rate
- ♦ price for two persons
- ♦ rate for two persons

Zweipersonenwohnung, f
- ♦ two-person apartment *AE*
- ♦ two-person flat *BE*

Zweipersonenzelt, n
- ♦ two-person tent

zwei Pkw-Stellplätze benötigen
zwei Parkplätze benötigen
- ♦ require parking space for two cars

Zweiradfahrzeug, n
- ♦ two-wheel vehicle

zweirädrig, adj
- ♦ two-wheel, adj
- ♦ two-wheeled, adj

Zweiraumwohnung, f
→ Zweizimmerwohnung

zwei Reisen machen (generell)
- ♦ make two journeys
- ♦ make two trips
- ♦ make two tours

zwei Reisen machen (Seereisen)
- ♦ make two voyages

Zweisaisonbetrieb, m
- ♦ two-season establishment
- ♦ two-season operation

Zweisaisonferienort, m
Zweisaisonurlaubsort, m
- ♦ two-season resort

Zweisaisonhaus, n (Hotel)
→ Zweisaisonhotel

Zweisaisonhotel, n
- ♦ two-season hotel

zweischiffig, adj
- ♦ two-nave, adj
- ♦ two-naved, adj

zweischiffige Kirche, f
- ♦ two-nave church
- ♦ two-naved church

zweischläfriges Bett, n
Bett für zwei Personen, n
- ♦ bed for two persons
- ♦ double bed
- ♦ twin bed

Zweisitzer, m
- ♦ two-seater

zweisitzig, adj (generell)
- ♦ two-seated, adj
- ♦ two-seater, adj

zweisitzig, adj (hintereinander)
- ♦ tandem-seated, adj

zweisitzige Couch, f
- ♦ two-seater settee

zweispännig, adj
- ♦ two-horse, adj

zweispurige Straße, f
- ♦ two-lane road

zweistellig, adj
- ♦ two-digit, adj
- ♦ double-digit, adj

zweistelliger Umsatzanstieg, m
- ♦ double-digit increase in turnover

zweistelliges Wachstum, n
zweistelliger Zuwachs, m
- ♦ double-digit growth

zweistellige Wachstumsrate, f
zweistellige Zuwachsrate, f
- ♦ double-digit growth rate

Zwei-Sterne-Anlage, f
Zwei-Sterne-Komplex m
- ♦ two-star complex

Zwei-Sterne-Anwesen, n
Zwei-Sterne-Objekt, n
- ♦ two-star property

Zwei-Sterne-Appartement, n
- ♦ two-star apartment

Zwei-Sterne-Appartementanlage, f
Zwei-Sterne-Appartementkomplex, m
- ♦ two-star apartment complex

Zwei-Sterne-Attraktion, f
- ♦ two-star attraction

Zwei-Sterne-Bereich, m
Zwei-Sterne-Sektor, m
- ♦ two-star sector

Zwei-Sterne-Betrieb, m
- ♦ two-star establishment
- ♦ two-star operation

Zwei-Sterne-Bewertung, f
- ♦ two-star rating

Zwei-Sterne-Campingplatz, m
- ♦ two-star campsite
- ♦ two-star campground *AE*
- ♦ two-star camping site *BE*
- ♦ two-star camping ground *BE*
- ♦ two-star site

Zwei-Sterne-Caravanplatz, m
Zwei-Sterne-Wohnwagenplatz, m
- ♦ two-star caravan site *BE*
- ♦ two-star trailer site *AE*

Zwei-Sterne-Club, m
- ♦ two-star club

Zwei-Sterne-Einrichtung, f
- ♦ two-star facility

Zwei-Sterne-Einstufung, f
- ♦ two-star grading

Zwei-Sterne-Ferienwohnung, f
Zwei-Sterne-Fewo f
- ♦ two-star vacation apartment *AE*
- ♦ two-star holiday flat *BE*

Zwei-Sterne-Haus, n
→ Zwei-Sterne-Hotel

Zwei-Sterne-Hotel, n
- ♦ two-star hotel

Zwei-Sterne-Hotelanlage, f
Zwei-Sterne-Hotelkomplex m
- ♦ two-star hotel complex

Zwei-Sterne-Hotelservice, m
- ♦ two-star hotel service

Zweisternekategorie, f
→ Zwei-Sterne-Kategorie

Zwei-Sterne-Kategorie f
  ♦ two-star category
Zwei-Sterne-Koch, m
  ♦ two-star cook
Zwei-Sterne-Komfort, m
  ♦ two-star comfort
  ♦ two-star amenities *pl*
Zwei-Sterne-Komplex, m
  → Zwei-Sterne-Anlage
Zwei-Sterne-Kreuzfahrtschiff, n
  ♦ two-star cruise ship
  ♦ two-star cruise liner
Zwei-Sterne-Küchenchef, m
  ♦ two-star chef
Zwei-Sterne-Luxus, m
  ♦ two-star luxury
Zwei-Sterne-Luxushaus, n
  → Zwei-Sterne-Luxushotel
Zwei-Sterne-Luxushotel, n
  ♦ two-star deluxe hotel *AE*
  ♦ two-star luxury hotel
Zwei-Sterne-Niveau, n
  ♦ two-star level
Zwei-Sterne-Platz, m (Camping)
  ♦ two-star site
Zwei-Sterne-Platz, m (Tennis)
  ♦ two-star court
Zwei-Sterne-Preis, m
  ♦ two-star price
  ♦ two-star rate
Zwei-Sterne-Qualität, f
  ♦ two-star quality
Zwei-Sterne-Residenz, f
  ♦ two-star residence
Zwei-Sterne-Restaurant n
  ♦ two-star restaurant
Zwei-Sterne-Segment, n
  ♦ two-star segment
Zwei-Sterne-Sektor, m
  → Zwei-Sterne-Bereich
Zwei-Sterne-Service, m
  ♦ two-star service
Zwei-Sterne-Service anbieten
  ♦ offer two-star service
Zwei-Sterne-Stadthotel, n (Großstadt)
  ♦ two-star city hotel
Zwei-Sterne-Stadthotel, n (kleine Stadt)
  ♦ two-star town hotel
Zwei-Sterne-Standard m
  ♦ two-star standard
Zwei-Sterne-System, n
  ♦ two-star system
Zwei-Sterne-Tagungsort, m
  Zwei-Sterne-Austragungsort, m
  ♦ two-star venue
Zwei-Sterne-Unterkunft, f
  Zwei-Sterne-Unterbringung, f
  ♦ two-star accommodation
  ♦ two-star lodging *AE*
Zwei-Sterne-Wohnwagenplatz, m
  Zwei-Sterne-Caravanplatz, m
  ♦ two-star trailer site *AE*
  ♦ two-star caravan site *BE*
Zwei-Sterne-Zimmer, n
  ♦ two-star room
zweistöckig, adj attr (Gebäude)
  doppelstöckig, adj attr
  zweigeschossig, adj attr
  ♦ two-floor, adj attr
  ♦ two-story, adj attr *AE*
  ♦ two-storey, adj attr *BE*

zweistöckig, adj (Bett, Kuchen)
  ♦ two-tier, adj
  ♦ two-tiered, adj
zweistöckiges Bett n
  ♦ two-tier bed
  ♦ two-tiered bed
zweistöckiges Etagenbett n
  ♦ two-tier bunk bed
  ♦ two-tiered bunk bed
zweistöckiges Gebäude, n
  zweigeschossiges Gebäude, n
  ♦ two-floor building
  ♦ two-story building *AE*
  ♦ two-storey building *BE*
zweistündig, adj
  ♦ two-hour, adj
  ♦ two hours', adj
  ♦ of two hours' duration
  ♦ lasting two hours
zweistündige Fahrt, f (Auto)
  ♦ two-hour drive
zweistündige Fahrt, f (generell)
  ♦ two-hour trip
  ♦ two-hour journey
zweistündiger Marsch, m
  ♦ two hours' march
zweistündiges Programm, n
  ♦ two-hour program *AE*
  ♦ two-hour programme *BE*
zweistündige Verspätung, f
  ♦ two-hour delay
Zweitagearrangement, n
  ♦ two-day arrangement
Zweitageaufenthalt, m
  zweitägiger Aufenthalt m
  ♦ two-day stay
  ♦ two days' stay
  ♦ stay of two days
Zweitagehotelaufenthalt, m
  → zweitägiger Hotelaufenthalt
Zweitagepaß, m
  ♦ two-day pass
Zweitagepauschale, f
  ♦ two-day package
Zweitagepauschalpreis, m
  ♦ two-day inclusive price
  ♦ two-day inclusive rate
  ♦ two-day package price
  ♦ two-day package rate
Zweitagepreis, m
  ♦ two-day price
  ♦ two-day rate
  ♦ price for two days
  ♦ rate for two days
Zweitagerennen, n
  ♦ two-day race
Zweitageskipaß, m
  ♦ two-day ski pass
Zweitagetour, f
  zweitägige Tour, f
  ♦ two-day tour
zweitägig, adj
  ♦ two-day, adj
  ♦ two days', adj
  ♦ of two days' duration
  ♦ lasting two days
zweitägige Konferenz, f
  ♦ two-day conference
zweitägiger Aufenthalt, m
  Zweitageaufenthalt m

  ♦ two-day stay
  ♦ stay of two days
zweitägiger Hotelaufenthalt, m
  Zweitagehotelaufenthalt m
  ♦ two-day hotel stay
  ♦ two-day stay at a hotel
  ♦ two-day stay in a hotel
  ♦ stay of two days at a hotel
  ♦ stay of two days in a hotel
zweitägiger Kongreß, m
  ♦ two-day convention
  ♦ two-day congress
zweitägiger Urlaub, m
  ♦ two-day vacation *AE*
  ♦ two-day holiday *BE*
zweitägiger Zwischenaufenthalt, m
  ♦ two-day stopover
zweitägige Tagung, f
  ♦ two-day meeting
Zweitauto, n
  zweites Auto, n
  ♦ second car
Zweite Bardame, f
  ♦ second barmaid
Zwei Tee, bitte
  ♦ Two teas, please
Zweite Etagenhausdame, f
  Zweite Etagengouvernante, f *SCHW*
  ♦ second floor housekeeper
Zweite Hausdame, f
  ♦ second housekeeper
zweite Heimat, f
  → zweites Zuhause, Zweithaus
zweite Klasse, f
  ♦ second class
Zweite-Klasse-Abteil, n
  (Zug)
  Zweiter-Klasse-Abteil, n
  Abteil zweiter Klasse, n
  ♦ second-class compartment
Zweite-Klasse-Fahrpreis, m
  ♦ second-class fare
Zweite-Klasse-Kabine, f
  Zweiter-Klasse-Kabine, f
  Kabine zweiter Klasse, f
  Kabine in der zweiten Klasse, f
  Zweitklaßkabine, f *SCHW*
  ♦ second-class cabin
Zweite-Klasse-Rückfahrkarte, f
  Rückfahrkarte zweiter Klasse, f
  ♦ second-class return ticket *BE*
  ♦ second-class round-trip ticket *AE*
Zweite-Klasse-Sitzplatz, m
  Zweite-Klasse-Sitz, m
  Zweite-Klasse-Platz, m
  ♦ second-class seat
Zweite-Klasse-Tarif, m
  ♦ second-class tariff
  ♦ second-class rates *pl*
  ♦ second-class rate
  ♦ second-class terms *pl*
zweiten Gang beenden
  ♦ finish the second course
zweiten Gang bilden
  (Menü)
  ♦ form the second course
Zweiter Barman, m
  Zweiter Barmann, m
  ♦ second barman
Zweiter Chef de réception, m
  ♦ second chef de réception

Zweiter Chef de service, m
♦ second chef de service
Zweiter Commis, m
♦ second commis
Zweiter Concierge, m
Zweite Concierge, f
♦ second concierge
Zweiter Empfangssekretär, m
Zweite Empfangssekretärin, f
♦ second receptionist
Zweite Rezeptionssekretärin, f
→ Zweite Empfangssekretärin
zweiter Gang, m (Menü)
♦ second course
zweiter Gang, m (Motor)
♦ second gear
zweiter Klasse fliegen
♦ fly second class
zweiter Klasse logieren
zweiter Klasse wohnen
♦ stay second class
zweiter Klasse reisen
zweiter Klasse fahren
♦ travel second class
Zweiter Küchenchef, m
♦ second chef
Zweiter Maître d'hôtel, m
Deuxième maître d'hôtel, m FR
♦ junior maître d'hôtel
♦ deuxième maître d'hôtel FR
♦ junior headwaiter
♦ second headwaiter
Zweiter Oberkellner, m
♦ second headwaiter
zweiter Rang, m (Theater)
♦ amphiteater AE
♦ upper circle BE
Zweiter Souschef, m
♦ second sous-chef
Zweite Saaltochter, f SCHW
Zweite Serviererin, f
♦ second waitress
zweites Frühstück, n
Gabelfrühstück, n
Déjeuner à la fourchette, n FR
♦ second breakfast
♦ mid-morning snack
♦ elevenses BE coll
♦ déjeuner à la fourchette FR
zweite Sitzung, f
(im Speisesaal)
zweite Tischzeit, f
♦ second sitting
zweites Quartal, n
→ zweites Vierteljahr
zweites Stockwerk, n
zweite Etage, f
zweites Obergeschoß, n
♦ third floor AE
♦ third story AE
♦ second floor BE
♦ second storey BE
zweites Vierteljahr, n
zweites Quartal, n
♦ second quarter
zweites Zuhause, n
♦ home from home
♦ home away from home
zweites Zuhause anbieten jm
♦ offer s.o. a home from home
♦ offer s.o. a home away from home

zweites Zuhause finden
♦ find a home from home
♦ find a home away from home
zweite Tischzeit, f
→ zweite Sitzung
zweite Wahl, f (Qualität)
minderwertige Qualität, f
mittlere Qualität, f
♦ inferior quality
♦ medium quality
Zweithaus, n
zweites Haus, n
♦ second home
zweitklassig, adj
♦ second-class, adj
♦ second-rate, adj coll
zweitklassiges Hotel, n
Hotel zweiter Klasse, n
♦ second-class hotel
♦ second-rate hotel coll
Zweitklaßwagen, m
→ Wagen zweiter Klasse
zweitrangig, adj
zweitklassig, adj
♦ second-rate, adj coll
♦ second-class, adj
Zweitreise, f
zweite Reise, f
♦ second trip
♦ second tour
♦ second journey
zweitürig, adj
♦ two-door, adj
zweitüriges Auto, n
♦ two-door car
Zweiturlaub, m
zweiter Urlaub, m
♦ second vacation AE
♦ second holiday BE
Zweiturlaub machen
♦ take a second vacation AE
♦ take a second holiday BE
Zweitwohnsitz, m
zweiter Wohnsitz, m
♦ second domicile
♦ secondary residence
Zweitwohnung, f
zweite Wohnung, f
♦ second apartment AE
♦ second flat BE
♦ second home
zwei Übernachtungen in einem Hotel, f pl
♦ two nights at a hotel pl
♦ two nights in a hotel pl
Zwei Whisky, bitte
♦ Two whiskies, please
zwei Wochen bleiben
♦ stay for two weeks
♦ stay two weeks
zwei Wochen Halbpension
♦ two weeks' half board
♦ two weeks' demipension AE
Zweiwochenpauschale, f
♦ two-week package
Zweiwochenpauschalpreis, m
Zweiwochenpauschale, f
♦ two-week inclusive price
♦ two-week inclusive rate
♦ two-week package price
♦ two-week package rate

Zweiwochenpreis, m
♦ two-week price
♦ two-week rate
♦ price for two weeks
♦ rate for two weeks
Zweiwochenprogramm, n
♦ two-week program AE
♦ two-week programme BE
♦ program of two weeks AE
♦ programme of two weeks BE
♦ two weeks' program AE
zweiwöchentlich, adv
♦ every two weeks, adv
♦ biweekly, adv
♦ fortnightly, adv BE
♦ two-weekly, adv
zweiwöchentliche Kündigung, f
♦ two weeks' notice
♦ fortnight's notice BE
Zweiwochenurlaub, m
zweiwöchiger Urlaub, m
♦ fortnight's holiday BE
♦ two-week holiday BE
♦ two-week break
♦ two-week vacation AE
zwei Wochen zum Preis von einer
♦ two weeks for the price of one
zwei Wochen zum Preis von einer anbieten
♦ offer two weeks for the price of one
zweiwöchig, adj
♦ two-week, adj
♦ two weeks', adj
♦ of two weeks' duration
♦ fortnight's, adj BE
♦ lasting two weeks
zweiwöchigen Urlaub machen
zwei Wochen Urlaub machen
♦ take a two-week vacation AE
♦ take a two-week holiday BE
♦ take a two-week break
zweiwöchige Reise, f
♦ two-week tour
♦ two-week journey
♦ two-week trip
zweiwöchiger Urlaub, m
Zweiwochenurlaub, m
♦ two-week vacation AE
♦ two-week holiday BE
♦ fortnight's holiday BE
♦ two-week break
zweiwöchige Tournee, f
♦ two-week tour
Zweizimmerappartement, n
♦ two-room apartment
Zweizimmerferienwohnung, f
♦ two-room vacation apartment AE
♦ two-room holiday flat BE
zweizimmerig, adj
♦ two-roomed, adj
zweizimmerige Cottage, f
♦ two-roomed cottage
zweizimmerige Suite, f
♦ two-roomed suite
♦ two-room suite
zweizimmerige Wohnung, f
♦ two-roomed apartment AE
♦ two-roomed flat BE
zwei Zimmer mit dazwischenliegendem Bad, n pl
♦ two rooms with connecting bathroom pl
♦ two rooms with connecting bath pl

Zweizimmer-Suite, f
→ Zweizimmersuite
Zweizimmersuite f
♦ two-room suite
Zweizimmerwohnung, f
♦ two-room flat *BE*
♦ two-room apartment *AE*
Zwetschge, f
→ Pflaume
Zwieback, m
♦ rusk
Zwiebel, f
♦ onion
Zwiebelfest, n
♦ onion festival
Zwiebelkuchen, m
♦ onion cake
Zwiebelpastete, f
♦ onion pie
Zwiebelreis, m
♦ onion rice
Zwiebelring, m
♦ onion ring
Zwiebelsalat, m
♦ onion salad
Zwiebelscheibe, f
♦ onion slice
♦ slice of onion
Zwiebelsoße, f
♦ onion sauce
Zwiebelsuppe, f
♦ onion soup
Zwillinge, m pl
♦ twins *pl*
Zwillingshotel, n
♦ twin hotel
Zwillingstürme, m pl
♦ twin towers *pl*
Zwinger, m
(für Tiere)
♦ kennel
Zwinger für Haustiere, m
♦ kennel for pets
zwischen 10 und 50 Personen fassen
(Saal)
♦ hold from 10 to 50 persons
Zwischenakt, m
(Theater)
♦ interval
♦ intermission *AE*
Zwischenarrangement, n
Interimsvereinbarung, f
♦ interim arrangement
Zwischenaufenthalt, m
♦ stopover
Zwischenaufenthalt in Rom machen
♦ make a stopover in Rome
Zwischenaufenthaltsbesucher, m
♦ stopover visitor
♦ stopover guest
Zwischenaufenthaltsgast, m
♦ stopover guest
♦ stopover visitor
Zwischenaufenthaltshotel n
♦ stopover hotel
Zwischenaufenthaltsort, m
Zwischenaufenthaltsplatz, m
Zwischenstation, f
♦ stopover place
♦ stopover

Zwischenbuchung, f
♦ interim booking
Zwischenfall, m
♦ incident
Zwischengang, m *gastr*
Zwischengericht, n *gastr*
Nebengericht, n *gastr*
♦ side dish *AE*
♦ side-dish *BE*
♦ side order
Zwischengericht, n (Entrée)
→ Entrée
Zwischengericht n (Entremets)
→ Entremets
Zwischengeschoß, n
Zwischenstockwerk n
Zwischenstock m
Zwischenetage f
Mezzaningeschoß n
♦ mezzanine floor
♦ mezzanine story *AE*
♦ mezzanine storey *BE*
♦ entresol
♦ intermediate story *AE*
Zwischengeschoßsalon, m
Zwischengeschoßlounge, f
♦ mezzanine lounge
zwischenlanden
♦ stop over
♦ make a stopover
Zwischenlandung, f
♦ stopover
♦ intermediate stop
♦ intermediate landing
Zwischenlandung machen (generell)
♦ make a stopover
♦ stop over
Zwischenlandung machen (Notlandung)
♦ make an emergency stopover
Zwischenlandung zum Auftanken, f
♦ refuelling stop
♦ refueling stop *AE*
♦ stop for refuelling
♦ stop for refueling *AE*
Zwischenmahlzeit, f
♦ snack between meals
♦ snack
Zwischenmieter, m
♦ interim tenant
Zwischenmonat m
(Zwischensaison)
♦ shoulder month
Zwischenpause, f
→ Pause
Zwischenquartier, n
vorübergehende Unterkunft, f
Interimsquartier, n
♦ temporary lodgings *pl*
♦ temporary quarters *pl*
♦ interim quarters *pl*
♦ temporary accommodation
Zwischenquittung, f
♦ interim receipt
Zwischenrechnung, f
♦ interim bill
Zwischenreinigung f
♦ interim cleaning
Zwischenreinigungsgebühr, f
♦ charge for interim cleaning
♦ fee for interim cleaning

Zwischenrippensteak, n
♦ entrecôte *BE*
♦ entrecote *AE*
Zwischensaison, f
♦ shoulder season
♦ in-between season
Zwischensaisonauslastung, f
♦ shoulder-season load factor
Zwischensaisonbelegung, f
Zwischensaisonauslastung, f
♦ shoulder-season occupancy
Zwischensaisonbuchung, f
♦ shoulder-season booking
Zwischensaisonermäßigung f
♦ shoulder-season reduction
Zwischensaison geschlossen
(Hinweisschild)
In der Zwischensaison geschlossen
♦ Closed between seasons
Zwischensaisonpreis, m
♦ shoulder-season price
♦ shoulder-season rate
Zwischensaisonreservierung, f
♦ shoulder-season reservation
Zwischensaisonzuschlag m
♦ shoulder-season supplement
Zwischenspeise, f
→ Zwischengericht
Zwischenspeisenkoch, m
→ Entremetier
Zwischenstation, f (Aufenthalt)
→ Zwischenaufenthalt
Zwischenstation, f (Zug)
♦ way station *AE*
Zwischenstation machen in X
kurz haltmachen in X
♦ stop over in X
♦ stop over at X
♦ stop off in/at X
♦ make a stop in X
♦ make a stop at X
Zwischenstecker, m
(für Elektrogeräte)
♦ adaptor
♦ adapter *AE*
Zwischenstecker leihen (unentgeltlich)
Zwischenstecker borgen
♦ borrow an adaptor
♦ borrow an adapter *AE*
Zwischenstockwerk, n
→ Zwischengeschoß
Zwischenstopp, m
Zwischenlandung, f
♦ intermediate stop
Zwischenstopp auf der Hochzeitsreise, m
♦ honeymoon stopover
Zwischentür, f
♦ interconnecting door
♦ connecting door
Zwischenübernachtung, f
♦ overnight stay en route
♦ overnight stop
Zwischenvermietung, f
♦ temporary renting *AE*
♦ temporary rental
♦ temporary letting *BE*
Zwischenverpflegung, f
♦ meal in between
Zwischenwand, f (beweglich)
Trennwand, f
♦ partition

Zwischenwand, f (Mauer)
   Trennwand, f
    ♦ **dividing wall**
Zwischenwand einziehen
   → Zimmer abteilen durch eine Mauer
Zwischenwand entfernen (beweglich)
   Trennwand entfernen
    ♦ **remove a partition**
Zwischenwand entfernen (Mauer)
   Trennwand entfernen
    ♦ **remove a dividing wall**
Zwischenwirt, m
   (Biologie)
    ♦ **intermediate host**
Zwischenzeit, f
    ♦ **interim period**
    ♦ **interim**
zwitschern einen *sl*
   einen zwitschern *sl*
   einen heben *coll*
    ♦ **have a quick one** *coll*
    ♦ **wet one's whistle** *coll*
    ♦ **go for a quick one** *coll*
zwölftägiger Treck, m
    ♦ **twelve-day trek**
Zypern
    ♦ **Cyprus**
Zypriote, m
   Zyprer, m
    ♦ **Cypriot**
    ♦ Cypriote *AE*
Zypriotin, f
   Zyprerin, f
    ♦ **Cypriot girl**
    ♦ Cypriot woman
    ♦ Cypriot *AE*
    ♦ Cypriote girl *AE*
    ♦ Cypriote woman *AE*
zypriotisch, adj
   zyprisch, adj
    ♦ **Cypriot, adj**
    ♦ Cypriote, adj *AE*